PRICEWATERHOUSECOOPERS

Manual of Accounting – UK GAAP

The definitive guide to UK accounting law and practice – 2008

UK Accounting Consulting Services
PricewaterhouseCoopers LLP, Chartered Accountants

Published by

CCH
a Wolters Kluwer business

145 London Road
Kingston-upon-Thames
Surrey
KT2 6SR
Tel: +44 (0) 844 561 8166
Fax: +44 (0) 208 247 1184
E-mail: customerservices@cch.co.uk
Web site: www.cch.co.uk

This book has been prepared for general guidance on matters of interest only, and does not constitut professional advice. You should not act upon the information contained in this book withou obtaining specific professional advice. Accordingly, to the extent permitted by law, Pricewaterhou seCoopers LLP (and its members, employees and agents) and publisher accept no liability, an disclaim all responsibility, for the consequences of you or anyone else acting, or refraining from acting in reliance on the information contained in this document or for any decision based on it, or for an consequential, special or similar damages even if advised of the possibility of such damages.

ISBN 978-1-84140-978-8

Printed and bound in Italy by LegoPrint.

British Library Cataloguing-in-Publication Data.

A catalogue record for this book is available from the British Library.

P002

Authors

PricewaterhouseCoopers' Manual of Accounting is written by the UK Accounting Consulting Services of PricewaterhouseCoopers LLP.

Writing team led by

Barry Johnson
Peter Holgate

Project managers and editors

Zoe Anderson
Anjani Shah
Julie Thomas
Sarah Troughton

UK Accounting Consulting Services team members and other contributors

Zoe Anderson
Gary Berckowitz
Nicola Bruyns
Dasa Brynjolffssen
Karen Burrows
Lucy Crofts
Clare de Arostegui
Nigel Dealy
Margaret Cassidy
Fredré Ferreira
Michael Gaull
Jyoti Ghosh (principal author)
Marek Grabowski
Margaret Heneghan
Eddie Hodgson (principal author)
Peter Hogarth (principal author)
Mary Holden
Barry Johnson (principal author)
Hannah King
Sabine Koch
Janice Lingwood
Stephen Lomax
Elizabeth Lynn
Joanna Malvern
Helen McCann (principal author)
Susannah McKay
Janet Milligan
Tina Patel
Tatiana Psaraki
David Quest
Marian Scott
Iain Selfridge
Anjani Shah
Anne Simpson
Laura Taylor
Julie Thomas
Sandra Thompson
Sarah Troughton
Gail Tucker
Stanislav Varkalov
Andrew Walker
Dave Walters
Katie Woods

Authors

PricewaterhouseCoopers' Manual of Accounting is written by the UK Accounting Consulting Services of PricewaterhouseCoopers LLP.

Writing team led by

Barry Johnson
Peter Holgate

Project managers and editors

Zoe Anderson
Anjana Shah
Julie Thomas
Sarah Troughton

UK Accounting Consulting Services team members and other contributors

Zoe Anderson
Gary Berkowitz
Nicola Bruyns
Dasa Brynjolfsson
Karen Burrows
Lucy Crotty
Claire de Arostegui
Nigel Dealy
Margaret Cassidy
Frédéric Ferreira
Michael Gaull
Jyoti Ghosh (principal author)
Marek Grabowski
Margaret Heneghan
Eddie Hodgson (principal author)
Peter Hogarth (principal author)
Mary Honan
Barry Johnson (principal author)
Hannah King
Sabine Koch
Janice Lakwood
Stephen Lomas
Elizabeth Lynn
Joanna Malvern
Helen McCann (principal author)
Susannah McKay
Janet Milligan
Tina Patel
Tatiana Pasnak
David Quest
Marian Scott
Iain Selfridge
Anjana Shah
Anne Simpson
Laura Taylor
Julie Thomas
Sandra Thompson
Sarah Troughton
Gail Tucker
Stanislav Varkalov
Andrew Walker
Dave Walters
Katie Woods

Foreword

By Sir David Tweedie
Chairman
International Accounting Standards Board

Much of the work of practising accountants and standard-setters today is concerned with the global harmonisation of accounting – an endeavour in which the International Accounting Standards Board and various national standard-setters including the UK Accounting Standards Board have a large and important role. We all look forward to the time when national differences in accounting have been eliminated and, hence, financial statements from anywhere in the world can be read and understood in the same way by the global business and financial communities. In such a world the cost of capital will have been cut by the removal of a major investment risk – and concerns over different accounting practices – leading to lower costs and higher employment and growth.

In the meantime, the day-to-day reality is that national GAAP continues to be used. However, many countries, including the UK, are making the transition to IFRSs. Both UK GAAP and IFRSs are based partly on application rules and partly on principles and judgement. Judgement is, of course, most likely to be sound when it is based on experience. In today's rapidly changing environment, I commend this Manual of Accounting and its sister edition, Manual of Accounting – IFRS for the UK, which give preparers and practitioners the benefits of the extensive experience and professional judgement of PricewaterhouseCoopers.

November 2007

Foreword

By Sir David Tweedie
Chairman
International Accounting Standards Board

Much of the work of practising accountants and standard setters today is concerned with the global harmonisation of accounting – an endeavour in which the International Accounting Standards Board and various national standard setters, including the UK Accounting Standards Board, have a large and important role. We all look forward to the time when national differences in accounting have been eliminated and, hence, financial statements from anywhere in the world can be read and understood in the same way by the global business and financial communities. In such a world, the cost of capital will have been cut by the removal of a major investment risk – and concerns over different accounting practices – leading to lower costs and higher employment and growth.

In the meantime, the day-to-day reality is that national GAAP continues to be used. However, many countries, including the UK, are making the transition to IFRSs. Both UK GAAP and IFRSs are based partly on application rules and partly on principles and judgement. Judgement is, of course, most likely to be sound when it is based on experience. In today's rapidly changing environment, I commend this Manual of Accounting and its sister edition, Manual of Accounting – IFRS for the UK, which give preparers and practitioners the benefits of the extensive experience and professional judgement of PricewaterhouseCoopers.

November 2007

Preface

PricewaterhouseCoopers' Manual of Accounting – UK GAAP is a practical guide to UK accounting law and practice. It encompasses: the accounting provisions of the Companies Acts 1985 and 2006; the requirements of accounting standards; Urgent Issues Task Force Abstracts; and other Generally Accepted Accounting Principles. The Manual includes practical advice based on our work in PricewaterhouseCoopers LLP's UK Accounting Consulting Services team in advising the firm's clients, partners and staff.

The Manual deals with accounting principles and rules and company reporting. It covers diverse areas of accounting, from disclosure of financial instruments to accounting for deferred taxation. It explains in detail the rules that apply to preparing consolidated financial statements and considers other statements that appear in annual reports, such as cash flow statements. The Manual also considers a number of concessions given to smaller companies and oversea companies. The text now includes reference to the Companies Act 2006 throughout, which becomes active progressively through 2007 and 2008.

This Manual is accompanied by a supplement, 'Manual of Accounting – Management reports and governance', which includes aspects of financial reporting that remain the same for entities reporting under either IFRS or UK GAAP. These areas are often referred to as the 'front half' of financial statements and cover the operating and financial review, directors' report and the remuneration report and corporate governance, together with other legal matters.

Even in a work of this size it is not possible to cover every aspect of company reporting. For example, the manual does not cover the specific accounting requirements in Schedule 9 and 9A of the Act that apply to banking and insurance companies, although much of the advice given in the text will assist them.

Furthermore, as international accounting has become increasingly important, we have also written a sister publication, Manual of Accounting – IFRS for the UK, which follows a similar format to this Manual and explains the rules that apply to UK listed companies and to other UK companies that choose to apply IFRS.

We hope that finance directors, accountants, auditors, analysts and other users of financial statements will find this Manual useful.

On behalf of the whole writing team we thank Barbara Willis for her work in editing the text and for Barbara, Gemma Barratt and Hagen Selinger's significant contribution in processing the text.

Barry Johnson, Peter Holgate
PricewaterhouseCoopers LLP
London
November 2007

Contents

		Page
Abbreviations and terms used		P0011
Accounting rules and principles		
1	Introduction	1001
2	Accounting principles and rules	2001
3	Reporting the substance of transactions	3001
4	Format of financial statements	4001
5	Other profit and loss account items	5001
6	Financial instruments including derivatives	6001
7	Foreign currencies	7001
8	Reporting financial performance	8001
Profit and loss account and related notes		
9	Revenue recognition	9001
10	Segmental reporting	10001
11	Retirement benefits	11001
12	Share-based payment	12001
13	Taxation	13001
14	Earnings per share	14001
Balance sheet and related notes		
15	Intangible fixed assets	15001
16	Tangible fixed assets	16001
17	Investment property	17001
18	Impairment of fixed assets and goodwill	18001
19	Leases and HP contracts	19001
20	Stocks and long-term contracts	20001
21	Provisions, contingencies and commitments	21001
22	Post balance sheet events	22001
23	Share capital and reserves	23001

Consolidated financial statements

24 Consolidated financial statements 24001
25 Acquisition accounting 25001
26 Disposals of subsidiaries 26001
27 Associates, joint ventures and joint undertakings 27001
28 Merger accounting 28001

Other reports and statements

29 Related party disclosures 29001
30 Cash flow statements 30001
31 Small and medium-sized companies 31001
32 Oversea companies 32001

Index I001

Abbreviations and terms used

AAPA	Association of Authorised Public Accountants
ABI	Association of British Insurers
AC	Appeal Cases, law reports
accounts	financial statements
ADR	American depositary receipts
AESOP	all employee share ownership plan
the Act/the 1985 Act/the Companies Act	the Companies Act 1985 (as amended by the Companies Act 1989)
the 1989 Act	the Companies Act 1989
ACCA	Association of Chartered Certified Accountants
ACT	advance corporation tax
AFS	available-for-sale
AG	Application Guidance
AGM	Annual General Meeting
AIM	Alternative Investment Market
AIMR	Alternative Investment Market Rules
AITC	Association of Investment Trust Companies
All ER	All England Law Reports
AMPS	auction market preferred shares
APB	Auditing Practices Board
APC	Auditing Practices Committee
App	Application note of a Financial Reporting Standard
app	appendix
ARC	Accounting Regulatory Committee
ASB	Accounting Standards Board
ASC	Accounting Standards Committee
BBA	British Bankers' Association
BC	Basis for Conclusions (to an accounting standard)
BCLC	Butterworths Company Law Cases
BERR	Department for Business, Enterprise and Regulatory Reform (formerly the Department of Trade and Industry (DTI))
BES	business expansion scheme
BNA 1985	Business Names Act 1985
CCA	current cost accounting
CCAB	Consultative Committee of Accountancy Bodies Limited
CC	The Combined Code – Principles of good governance and code of best practice
CC(CP)	Companies Consolidation (Consequential Provisions) Act 1985
CEO	chief executive officer
CESR	Committee of European Securities Regulators
CGAA	Co-ordinating Group on Audit and Accounting Issues
CGU	cash-generating unit
CA85	the Companies Act 1985

CA06	the Companies Act 2006
Ch	Chancery Division, law reports
chp	chapter
chapter (1)	'PricewaterhouseCoopers' Manual of accounting' – chapter (1)
CIF	cost, insurance, freight
CIMA	Chartered Institute of Management Accountants
CIPFA	Chartered Institute of Public Finance and Accountancy
CISCO	The City Group for Smaller Companies
Cmnd	Command Paper
CBO	collateralised bond obligation
CDO	collateralised debt obligation
CLO	collateralised loan obligation
CMO	collateralised mortgage obligation
COSO	Committee of Sponsoring Organisations of the Treadway Commission
CPP	current purchasing power
CR	Report of the committee on The Financial Aspects of Corporate Governance (the 'Cadbury Report')
CSR	corporate social responsibility
CTD	cumulative translation difference
CUV	continuing use value
DG XV	Directorate General XV
the 7th Directive	EC 7th Directive on Company Law
DP	discussion paper
DRC	depreciated replacement cost
DTI	Department of Trade and Industry
DTR	double taxation relief
EASDAQ	European Association of Securities Dealers Automated Quotation
EBIT	earnings before interest and tax
EBITDA	earnings before interest, tax, depreciation and amortisation
EC	European Community
ECU	european currency unit
ED	exposure draft
EFRAG	European Financial Reporting Advisory Group
EGM	extraordinary general meeting
EITF	Emerging Issues Task Force (US)
EPS	earnings per share
ESOP	employee share ownership plan
ESOT	employee share ownership trust
EU	European Union
EU 2005 Regulation	Regulation (EC) No 1606/2002 on the application of International Accounting Standards
EUV	existing use value
FASB	Financial Accounting Standards Board (US)
FEE	The European Federation of Accountants
FIFO	first-in, first-out
financial statements	accounts
FLA	Finance and Leasing Association
FM	facilities management

FOB	free on board
FPI	foreign private investors (US-listed)
FRAG	Financial Reporting and Auditing Group of the ICAEW
Framework	Framework for the preparation and presentation of financial statements
FRED	Financial Reporting Exposure Draft
FRA	forward rate agreement
FRC	Financial Reporting Council
FRN	floating rate note
FRRP	Financial Reporting Review Panel
FRS	Financial Reporting Standard
FRSSE	Financial Reporting Standard for Smaller Entities
FSA	Financial Services Authority
FVTPL	at fair value through profit or loss
GAAP	generally accepted accounting principles (and practices)
GAAS	generally accepted auditing standards
GB	Great Britain
GCFR	Going Concern and Financial Reporting - published by the joint working group of the Hundred Group of finance directors, ICAEW and ICAS
GRI guidelines	Global Reporting Initiative guidelines
HMSO	Her Majesty's Stationery Office
HP	hire purchase
HMRC	HM Revenue & Customs
IAASB	International Auditing and Assurance Standards Board
IAS	International Accounting Standard (see also IFRS)
IASB	International Accounting Standards Board
IASC	International Accounting Standards Committee
IBF	Irish Bankers' Federation
IBNR	incurred but not reported
ICAEW	Institute of Chartered Accountants in England and Wales
ICAI	Institute of Chartered Accountants in Ireland
ICAS	Institute of Chartered Accountants of Scotland
ICFR	Internal Control and Financial Reporting - published by the joint working group of the Hundred Group of finance directors, ICAEW and ICAS
ICR	Industrial Cases Reports
ICSA	Institute of Chartered Secretaries and Administrators
IFAC	International Federation of Accountants
IFRIC	International Financial Reporting Interpretations Committee
IFRS	International Financial Reporting Standard (see also IAS)
IG	Implementation Guidance (to an accounting standard)
IGU	income-generating unit
IIMR	Institute of Investment Management and Research (see SIP)
IoD	Institute of Directors
IOSCO	International Organisation of Securities Commissions
IPO	initial public offering
IPR&D	in-process research and development
IR	Statement on interim reporting issued by ASB
ISA	International Standard on Auditing

ISA (UK & Ire)	International Standard on Auditing (UK and Ireland)
ISDA	International Swap Dealers Association
ISP	internet service provider
IVSC	International Valuation Standards Committee
JANE	joint arrangement that is not an entity
JWG	Joint Working Group
LIBID	London inter-bank bid rate
LIBOR	London inter-bank offered rate
LIFFE	the London International Financial Futures and Options Exchange
LIFO	last-in, first-out
LR	UK Listing Authority's Listing Rules
MBO	management buy-out
MD&A	management's discussion and analysis
MR	Master of the Rolls
NASDAQ	National Association of Securities Dealers Automated Quotations
NCU	national currency unit
NIC	national insurance contributions
NPAEs	non-publicly accountable entities
OFR	operating and financial review
OEICs	open-ended investment companies
OIAC	Oil Industry Accounting Committee
OTC	over-the-counter market
PA	preliminary announcement
para(s)	paragraph(s) of Schedules to the Companies Acts, or IFRSs or IASs or FRSs, or SSAPs, or FREDs, or EDs, or DPs, or text
PCAOB	Public Company Accounting Oversight Board (US)
PE	price-earnings
PFI	Private Finance Initiative
PPE	property, plant and equipment
PPERA	Political Parties, Elections and Referendums Act 2000
PPF	Pension Protection Fund
PRAG	Pensions Research Accountants Group
PS	Practice Statements
QC	Queen's Counsel
QUEST	qualifying employee share ownership trust
R&D	research and development
RDG	regional development grant
Reg	regulation of a statutory instrument (for example, SI 1995/2092 Reg 5 = regulation 5 of The Companies (Summary Financial Statements) Regulations 1995)
RICS	Royal Institution of Chartered Surveyors
RS	Reporting Standard
SAC	the Standards Advisory Council
SAS	Statement of Auditing Standards
SC	Session Cases

Sch	Schedule to the Companies Act 1985 (eg 4A Sch 85 = Schedule 4A, paragraph 85)
SDC	Standards Development Committee
SEC	Securities and Exchange Commission (US)
Sec(s)	Section(s) of the 1985 Act/sections of the 2006 Act
SEE	social, environmental and ethical
SERPS	State earnings related pension scheme
SFAC	Statement of Financial Accounting Concepts issued in the US
SFAS	Statement of Financial Accounting Standards issued in the US
SI	Statutory Instrument
SIC	Standing Interpretation Committee of the IASC (see IFRIC)
SIP	Society of Investment Professionals (formerly IIMR)
SIPs	share incentive plans
SMEs	small and medium-sized entities
SOI	Statement of Intent
SoP	Statement of principles
SORIE	statement of recognised income and expense
SORP	Statement of Recommended Practice
SPE	special purpose entity
SPV	special purpose vehicle
SSAP	Statement of Standard Accounting Practice
Stock Exchange (or LSE)	the London Stock Exchange
STRGL	statement of total recognised gains and losses
TR	Technical Release of the ICAEW
TUPE	Transfer of Undertakings (Protection of Employment) Regulations
UITF	Urgent Issues Task Force
UK	United Kingdom
US	United States of America
VAT	value added tax
VIE	variable interest entity
WACC	weighted average cost of capital
WLR	Weekly Law Reports

Chapter 1

Introduction

	Page
UK GAAP today.	1001
The approach in this Manual.	1003

Chapter 1

Introduction

UK GAAP today

1.1 In the listed company arena, and in the press, there is now so much emphasis on international financial reporting standards (IFRS) that it is easy to forget that there is, in the UK, another type of accounting commonly practiced – and that is UK GAAP. UK GAAP is still used by most unlisted companies and groups and by most individual entities – parent entities and UK subsidiaries – in listed groups. Hence, by number at least, the vast majority of entities in the UK use UK GAAP. This Manual is addressed to their needs.

1.2 UK GAAP has developed over many years and includes both company law and UK accounting standards – SSAPs and FRSs. But the nature of UK GAAP has changed considerably in the past few years. Until about year 2000, UK GAAP was, albeit internationally influenced to some degree, essentially home-grown. The last conventional UK accounting standard was FRS 19 on deferred tax, which was published in December 2000. But nearly all the standards since then are almost exact copies of IFRSs. Hence the role of the UK Accounting Standards Board has changed fundamentally from one of developing and improving UK GAAP to one of implementing IFRS into UK GAAP.

1.3 The development of IFRS for global application and its partial implementation into the UK are major trends. Three major factors underlie them. First, the case for harmonisation is compelling. Global businesses and international investors need to have accounting information that they can understand when running businesses and making investment decisions. Despite the different histories and cultural backgrounds that have led to the many national GAAPs found today, there is an overwhelming need for accounting principles to be harmonised worldwide.

1.4 Secondly, the International Accounting Standards Board (IASB), launched in April 2001 with a full-time board, chaired by Sir David Tweedie, who headed the UK ASB during the 1990s, has been a major player in the quest for global convergence and harmonisation. While the Enron débâcle rocked the profession and the business world, it is fair to say that the IASB benefited from it, insofar that US accounting was seen to be not as good as previously advertised. This made the IASB's (relatively) principles-based approach more attractive and led to the otherwise unlikely October 2002 'Norwalk Agreement' between the IASB and the US standard-setter, the Financial Accounting Standards Board (FASB), to work towards eliminating differences.

1.5 Thirdly, the factor that most directly affects accounting in the UK is the June 2002 European Commission Regulation that required all EU listed companies from 2005 to prepare their consolidated financial statements using IFRS, rather than national GAAP. This is good news for harmonisation, but with an important proviso. The EU needs to bring IFRSs into EU law and it cannot do so without a formal process of adopting them. To achieve this, it has developed a complex 'endorsement mechanism'. This comprises the Commission; an official Accounting Regulatory Committee (ARC); and a private sector body – the European Financial Reporting Advisory Group (EFRAG) – which works with the IASB to ensure full understanding of the European viewpoint and advises the Commission and the ARC. The process has been made even more elaborate by introducing a role for the European Parliament, and creating a new body, the Standards Advice Review Group, whose role it is to advise the Commission, before it takes a decision on endorsement of an IFRS or an IFRIC, whether EFRAG's opinion on endorsement is well balanced and objective.

1.6 Whilst UK and other EU listed companies have now had their first taste of IFRS following first time adoption in the financial statements for year ends from December 2005 to November 2006, this applies to the consolidated financial statements only. The EU Regulation introduces a permissive regime for other entities. Some entities adopted IFRS for 2005, but more remained on UK GAAP. Concerns about the effect of IFRS on distributable profits have been the main factor behind this retention of UK GAAP.

1.7 The UK is currently at something of a watershed in terms of how UK GAAP should progress and the ASB currently has important policy choices to make. One approach would be to join the global harmonisation train: as IFRS is being adopted so widely, it seems obvious, from one perspective at least, for UK GAAP to continue the recent trend and pick up the remaining IFRSs that have not already been implemented into UK GAAP. It seemed reasonably obvious about two years ago that this is what should be done.

1.8 However, attitudes on this point have changed. Many people are now concerned about the way in which IFRS is progressing. The programme of convergence with the US standard setters (the FASB) seems a good idea in principle. But the concern is that it is making IFRS too much like US GAAP in the process. This has two aspects. First, the actual rules of US GAAP are coming into IFRS; this is not a one-way street, but it does appear that the majority of convergence is towards the US rule. Secondly, the approach in US GAAP of being very detailed and prescriptive may be suitable for the litigious and complex US environment, but does not lend itself well to export, via IFRS, to many countries where the economy, business environment and profession are very different.

1.9 As a result, it is unclear how the UK ASB should progress. Some clarity, though, is starting to emerge as a result of the IASB's work on a version of IFRS for small and medium-sized entities (IFRS for SMEs). The IASB published an exposure draft of this during 2007. Prior to this, there had been concerns that adoption of full IFRS into UK GAAP would introduce too much complexity into a UK GAAP that by now applies to privately-owned companies. The proposals on IFRS for SMEs help in that regard. Although there are arguments at the margin as to whether this or that requirement is sufficiently simplified, nonetheless the overall approach looks helpful and seems to be gathering significant support. Certainly, as the years pass, the case for having a separate set of rules called UK GAAP for UK companies that are outside the listed sector looks less and less tenable. A simplified version of IFRS, on the other hand, has substantial appeal, not only in the UK but in many other countries where full IFRS would introduce too much complexity, too many disclosures and would generally not be fit for purpose.

The approach in this Manual

1.10 Questions about how UK GAAP develops and to what extent IFRS affects it are important, but are for the future. For the moment, there are many aspects of UK GAAP that demand analysis and interpretation and the remainder of this work seeks to provide helpful guidance in that regard. We discuss the requirements of company law, accounting standards, UITF abstracts and the Listing Rules. We also give our views on what is good accounting in the many areas in which there are no rules or guidance. As part of that approach, this Manual contains hundreds of examples and extracts from financial statements. This Manual also has a strong company law bias: we are aware from practical experience that many of the questions that arise in practice cannot be answered based solely on accounting principles, but that many of them have to be answered at the interface of accounting and company law. Many of the chapters that follow reflect this. This work is also available in electronic form on pwcinform.com, where it is hypertext linked to the originating source regulations such as the Companies Act and accounting standards.

1.11 The 'PricewaterhouseCoopers' Manual of Accounting – Management reports and governance', which supports this Manual, provides UK companies with guidance on the legal and other regulatory requirements that impact elements of financial statements that are common to users of both IFRS and UK GAAP, often referred to as the 'front half' of the financial statements. The sister edition of this book, 'PricewaterhouseCoopers' Manual of Accounting – IFRS for the UK', sets out detailed guidance on how IFRS now affects UK listed groups and other UK entities that opt into IFRS.

Chapter 2

Accounting principles and rules

	Page
Introduction	2001
UK GAAP	2001
The meaning and composition of UK GAAP	2001
The development of UK GAAP	2003
The Companies Act 1985 and 2006	2007
The requirement to prepare financial statements	2007
The true and fair requirement	2011
Compliance with accounting standards and UITF abstracts	2013
True and fair override disclosures	2014
The UK financial reporting structure	2015
The Dearing Report proposals	2015
The Companies Act 1989 requirements	2016
The Financial Reporting Council	2017
The Accounting Standards Board	2020
FRSs and SSAPs	2024
SORPs	2026
Counsel's opinion on true and fair view and role of accounting standards	2027
The Urgent Issues Task Force	2028
The Financial Reporting Review Panel	2029
Companies Act and FRS 18 — accounting principles	2032
Introduction	2032
Going concern	2033
Disclosures	2035
Accruals	2037
Prudence and realisation	2038
Separate valuation	2039
Accounting policies	2040
Selecting most appropriate accounting policies	2042
Disclosing accounting policies	2043
Reviewing and changing accounting policies	2044
Consistency — issues for groups	2045
Estimation techniques	2046
Accounting conventions	2048
Capital maintenance concepts	2048
Valuation bases	2049
Units of measurement	2050
Conventions	2050
Historical cost convention	2050
Modified historical cost convention	2050

Fair value convention 2051
Current purchasing power 2051
Current cost accounting 2052
Frameworks for setting accounting standards 2052
Background to the frameworks 2052
The ASB's Statement of principles 2054
Objective 2055
The reporting entity 2055
Qualitative characteristics 2055
Materiality 2056
Elements 2057
Recognition 2058
Measurement 2058
Presentation 2059
Accounting for interests in other entities 2059

Chapter 2

Accounting principles and rules

Introduction

2.1 As discussed in chapter 1, the accounting framework in the UK is subject to a greater number of increasingly complicated rules. The sources of accounting principles and rules in the UK range from legislation and accounting standards to customs practised by professionals over many years. In addition, accounting under UK standards is increasingly influenced by practice overseas, for example, in the US and the IASB. International developments in particular are now a crucial source of UK GAAP: the UK ASB has accelerated its agenda of convergence with IFRS and is now focusing on bringing international standards into UK GAAP.

2.2 This chapter explores the framework and sources of authority for the generally accepted accounting principles in the UK and how the Companies Act and accounting standards impact on the overriding requirement for financial statements to give a true and fair view.

[The next paragraph is 2.4.]

2.4 The ASB's convergence policy was prompted by the requirement for many companies to adopt IFRS in 2005. The EU approved a Regulation in June 2002 that requires all listed companies in the EU (including banks and insurance companies) to prepare their consolidated financial statements under EU-adopted IFRS ('IFRS') for financial years beginning on or after 1 January 2005. Member States had the option to extend this requirement to unlisted companies and to individual company financial statements. From 2005, any UK company (with the exception of charities) is permitted to prepare its financial statements using IFRS. It is, however, required that a consistent framework should be adopted within UK groups in most circumstances (see further para 2.22.5). Companies that do not choose to use IFRS will continue to prepare their financial statements under UK GAAP.

UK GAAP

The meaning and composition of UK GAAP

2.5 Generally Accepted Accounting Principles in the United Kingdom (UK GAAP) is a much-used, but undefined term. The components of UK GAAP vary according to the type of company or entity in question. However, in general terms, UK GAAP can be described as follows. The components are divided into elements that are mandatory (in law or in practice) and elements that are not mandatory. The core *mandatory* elements are:

- The Companies Act 1985 and the Companies Act 2006 when implemented.
- Accounting standards. That is:
  - Statements of Standard Accounting Practice (SSAPs) developed originally by the Accounting Standards Committee (ASC) and adopted in 1990 by the Accounting Standards Board (ASB).
  - Financial Reporting Standards (FRSs) issued by the ASB since 1990.
- Abstracts issued by the ASB's Urgent Issues Task Force (UITF).
- For listed companies, the Listing Rules.

2.6 Other elements of UK GAAP are authoritative to varying degrees but non-mandatory. These include:

- The ASB's Statement of principles for financial reporting. The Statement does not have the status of an accounting standard. Nevertheless, it is authoritative in two senses. First, the main purpose of the Statement of principles is to provide a frame of reference to guide the ASB in its development of standards. Therefore, it should be helpful in guiding companies and auditors as to the meaning and intention of individual accounting standards, if they are not clear. Secondly, the Statement is intended to provide a valuable source of reference in connection with the accounting treatment of transactions for which there is no specific GAAP.
- Other statements issued by the ASB. These include:
  - 'Half-yearly financial reports' – this was published as a non-mandatory document, but compliance with it was encouraged. Interim reports are discussed in detail in chapter 31.
  - 'Preliminary announcements' – the ASB's guidance on preliminary announcements has been issued as a non-mandatory statement (see chapter 31).
  - 'Operating and financial review' – in January 2006, the ASB published a best practice reporting statement on the operating and financial review (OFR), which builds on the ASB's previous 2003 statement of best practice on the OFR. See further chapter 2 in the Manual of Accounting – IFRS and UK Supplement.
- Statements and recommendations from the professional bodies. Examples are ICAEW Technical Releases (previously called 'FRAGs') such as Tech 02/07, 'Distributable profits: implications of recent accounting changes', and ICAEW accounting recommendations such as the members' handbook statements on materiality and 'Accounting for goods sold subject to reservation of title'.

- Established practice. Quite literally, practices that are generally accepted, even though not codified in official literature, can be regarded as part of UK GAAP. Much of this practice is set out in the guidance from leading accounting firms, such as in this Manual.

2.7 A key question is whether the output of the Financial Reporting Review Panel (FRRP) constitutes part of UK GAAP. The practical answer to the question is that it does. As discussed from paragraph 2.85, the FRRP does not issue rules, but announces its findings in relation to individual companies. In general, the companies in question have changed their accounting practices or given additional disclosure, following discussion with the Panel. The Panel generally issues formal statements only where it has concluded that companies have deviated from existing requirements of the Act or accounting standards. However, in some cases, the Panel's views have added to, or modified, the previous understanding of UK GAAP. For example, the Review Panel's press release on the financial statements of Trafalgar House led to the UITF issuing an Abstract on accounting for transfers from current assets to fixed assets. Consequently, companies and auditors should pay particular heed to the announcements from the Panel.

2.8 In addition, there are elements of UK GAAP that relate to specific sectors. Examples are the accounting requirements contained in legislation for banks, housing associations, and charities. Some sector-specific guidance is non-mandatory, and much of this appears in the form of Statements of recommended practice (SORPs), which are discussed from paragraph 2.74.

2.9 The Companies Act 1985 does not define the term 'generally accepted accounting principles', but references are included in section 262(3) (definition of realised profits and realised losses), in Schedule 4A paragraph 2(1) (consolidation adjustments) and paragraph 10(d) (adoption of the merger method of accounting). Similarly, the Companies Act 2006 does not define the term 'generally accepted accounting principles', but similarly makes reference in section 853(4) (definition of realised profits and realised losses). In addition, the Companies Act 1989 introduced a requirement for companies to state whether the financial statements have been prepared in accordance with applicable Accounting standards and to give particulars of any departures and the reasons for it (see also from para 2.41). [CA85 4 Sch 36A].

The development of UK GAAP

2.10 In recent years, the financial statements of UK companies have changed considerably, reflecting the development of UK GAAP.

2.11 Prior to 1970, the regulatory framework was modest. The Companies Acts 1948 and 1967 contained general requirements relating to the need to prepare, distribute and file financial statements for companies and groups. However, there was very little detail in the Act — the detail was left to the practices of accountants. This began to change in 1970 with the formation of the ASC. The

SSAPs issued by the ASC between 1970 and 1990 gradually changed practice — mostly for the better — and the standards were in general complied with even though the six Institutes that comprise the CCAB and which sponsored the ASC had no authority over companies as such. Their authority, such as it was, was over their members, both as prepares and auditors of financial statements. This authority was undermined around 1980 as a result of widespread objections to, and eventually non-acceptance of, the ASC's standard SSAP 16 on current cost accounting. Following the withdrawal of SSAP 16, the ASC continued to issue standards until 1990, but its authority had been injured by the SSAP 16 débâcle.

2.12 During the late 1980s the inadequacy in the ASC's authority was recognised and this led to the appointment of the Dearing Committee in 1987. The Dearing report, 'The making of accounting standards' was published in 1988. It recommended that the ASC be replaced by a structure headed by an independent Financial Reporting Council (FRC). The structure that was put in place with effect from 1990 is very closely based on the Dearing proposals. Indeed, Sir Ron Dearing was appointed the first chairman of the FRC, a post he held until 1993. The FRC structure is discussed in more detail from paragraph 2.51.

2.13 The ASC's programme of accounting standards added to the regulatory framework gradually during the 1970s and 1980s, but a major impact was also made by new legislation. The Companies Act 1981 introduced major reforms to UK accounting. Its main function was to implement in the UK the provisions of the EC 4th Company Law Directive.

2.14 The 4th Directive is a major element of the EC's harmonisation programme. It sought to harmonise the accounting practice of companies within the EC and did so by making rules about:

- Format of accounts.
- Accounting principles.
- Valuation rules.
- Disclosures.

2.15 In doing so, the directive achieved a degree of harmonisation. However, the process can only be regarded as a partial success. The directive did not deal with all accounting issues. For example, it is silent on foreign currency translation, pension costs and leasing. In addition, there is flexibility in the directive. There are choices in the formats and choices as to measurement basis. The benchmark treatment is historical cost, but valuations can be introduced on a voluntary basis. Furthermore, Member States have not in all cases interpreted the directive in the same way.

2.16 The implementation of the 4th Directive through the 1981 Act was a major upheaval at the time. Following its introduction, changes were necessary to some standards. For example, SSAP 9's provisions at that time relating to work in progress were incompatible with the 1981 Act's requirement that stock should be stated at purchase price or production cost (that is, it was not permissible to include a profit element in the figure for stock and work in progress). Also, SSAP 4's treatment of capital grants had to be changed, as the Act does not allow a grant to the deducted from the cost of an asset.

2.17 More generally, the 1981 Act restricted considerably the possible treatments that could be adopted. The formats were regarded as something of a straitjacket, and the very fact that many accounting issues were set out in legislation resulted in the ASC and the ASB having less scope than perhaps they would like to develop accounting rules. One example was the ASB's ability to introduce 'marking to market' as a method of accounting for current asset investments being restricted by the Act's rules. This restriction has, however, changed as a result of the Fair Value Directive (see para 2.20.2).

2.18 The EC 7th Directive has a similar role to the 4th, but in connection with consolidated financial statements. Its objective again was to harmonise practice within the Community, but its effect on the UK was less dramatic than had been the case with the 4th Directive. This is because the basis of the 7th Directive was, to a large extent, the Anglo-Saxon model of consolidation, whereas the 4th Directive had been based more on continental practices.

2.19 Nevertheless, the 7th Directive, which was implemented in the UK through the Companies Act 1989, had the following effects:

- Compared with the previous position, there were more rules regarding consolidations enshrined in legislation. For example, most of Schedule 4A to the 1985 Act (the 1989 Act introduced changes to the 1985 Act) is derived from the 7th Directive.
- Although the overall model of consolidation is broadly in line with previous practice, there were major changes affecting the composition of groups for the purposes of consolidated financial statements. These changes rendered SSAP 14 inconsistent with the Act and so led to the replacement of SSAP 14 on group accounts with a new standard, FRS 2.
- The 7th Directive was aimed at larger groups, whereas previous UK legislation had required all groups, however small, to prepare group accounts. The 1989 Act introduced exemptions for small and medium-sized groups, as explained in detail in chapter 32.

2.20 There is now considerable overlap between the accounting requirements of the Act and the requirements of accounting standards. This applies to both the accounting principles and the disclosure requirements.

2.20.1 More recently, EU accounting legislation has been influenced by moves towards international convergence. Two Directives, the Fair value Directive and the Modernisation Directive, were issued, respectively, in September 2001 and May 2003. These were introduced into companies legislation by The Companies Act 1985 (International Accounting Standards and Other Accounting

Amendments) Regulations 2004 (SI 2004/2947), applicable for accounting periods commencing on or after 1 January 2005.

2.20.2 The Regulations implement the Fair Value Directive by permitting (rather than requiring) all companies to use fair value accounting for certain financial instruments (including derivative financial instruments and certain commodity contracts) in both their individual and consolidated financial statements. Companies that do not use fair value accounting are required to disclose the fair value of any derivative financial instruments that they hold. See further chapter 6.

2.20.3 The Modernisation Directive amended the existing Accounting Directives: the 4th Directive and 7th Directive on entity and consolidated financial statements and the Directives on the financial statements of banking and other financial institutions and insurance undertakings. In the main the Accounting Directives will no longer apply to companies adopting IFRS from 2005, as they will be overridden by the EU Regulation that requires listed companies in their consolidated financial statements to comply with IFRS. However, the EU has recognised that there will still be up to five million companies in Europe to which IFRS does not apply and that the Directives need to be modernised to reflect updated thinking in financial reporting. This is intended to create a 'level playing field' between companies applying IFRS and those that do not, by removing any inconsistencies between the Accounting Directives and IFRS.

2.20.4 The Regulations implement parts of the Modernisation Directive by requiring that the presentation of items within the balance sheet and profit and loss account must have regard to the substance of the reported transaction or arrangement. Also, all companies are permitted under the law to account for investment properties and biological assets at fair value (with fair value changes reported in the profit and loss account), in both their individual and consolidated financial statements. The requirement for a participating interest in the definition of a subsidiary undertaking has been removed and the definition extended to include *"the power to exercise dominant influence or control"*. The changes resulting from the implementation of the Modernisation Directive are dealt with in the relevant chapters in this Manual.

2.20.5 On 8 November 2006, the Companies Act 2006 ('the Act') received Royal Assent. The Act, the largest piece of legislation ever to be passed by Parliament, consists of approximately 1,300 sections and 16 schedules and is a thorough modernisation and a substantial, but not complete, consolidation of existing company legislation, following an extensive review and consultation process. Company law is redrafted in the Act to meet better the needs of small business by adopting a 'think small first' approach. The Act extends GB company law to Northern Ireland, where previously it had required separate Northern Ireland legislation. Implementation will be phased, with the intention of full implementation by October 2008. At the time of writing many of the Schedules to the Companies Act 2006 have still to be published.

The Companies Act 1985 and 2006

2.21 Although many detailed accounting rules have been added to companies legislation in recent years, its most important accounting requirements are, perhaps unsurprisingly, those that have been there longest (although not in exactly the same words), namely the requirement for companies to prepare financial statements and the true and fair requirement.

The requirement to prepare financial statements

2.22 The directors are required to prepare financial statements for the company for each financial year that are either in compliance with section 226A ('Companies Act individual financial statements') or in accordance with EU-adopted IFRS ('IFRS individual financial statements'). [CA85 Sec 226(1)(2) amended by SI 2004/2947; CA06 Sec 394, 395(1)]. Companies Act individual financial statements must comprise a balance sheet as at the last day of the financial year and a profit and loss account for the financial year. [CA85 Sec 226A inserted by SI 2004/2947; CA06 Sec 396]. The balance sheet must give a true and fair view of the company's state of affairs as at the end of the financial year; and the profit and loss account must give a true and fair view of the company's profit or loss for the financial year. In addition, the financial statements must comply with Schedule 4 to the Act, or provision made by the Secretary of State by regulations. [CA06 Sec 396(3)(4)]. as to form and content and additional information required. [CA85 Sec 226A(3)(4) inserted by SI 2004/2947; CA06 Sec 396(3)(4)]

2.22.1 Companies preparing IFRS individual financial statements are simply required to prepare financial statements in accordance with international accounting standards (and to state that they have done so in the note to the financial statements). [CA85 Sec 226B inserted by SI 2004/2947; CA06 Sec 397]. 'International accounting standards' means IFRS as endorsed by the EU. [CA85 Sec 262 amended by SI 2004/2947; CA06 Sec 474]. Schedule 4 does not apply to IFRS financial statements. Financial statements prepared under EU-adopted IFRS are dealt with in the Manual of Accounting – IFRS for the UK.

2.22.2 In addition, if, at the end of the financial year, the company is a parent company within the meaning of the Companies Act 1985, the directors must also prepare consolidated financial statements for the group for the year. [CA85 Sec 227(1) amended by SI 2004/2947; CA06 Sec 399(2) unless exempt].

2.22.3 Companies required to prepare consolidated financial statements under the Act that have any security listed on a regulated market within the EU are required to prepare those consolidated financial statements under EU-adopted IFRS (see para 2.4). These financial statements will be 'IFRS consolidated financial statements'. Companies that are not required to prepare consolidated IFRS financial statements may choose to do so. These financial statements will also be prepared in accordance with EU-adopted IFRS. Where the directors of a parent company prepare IFRS consolidated financial statements, they must state in the notes that the financial statements have been prepared in accordance with international accounting standards. [CA85 Sec 227B amended by SI 2004/2947; CA06 Sec 406].

2.22.4 Companies that are parent companies and that do not prepare IFRS consolidated financial statements are required to prepare 'Companies Act consolidated financial statements'. Such financial statements must give a true and fair view of the state of affairs at the end of the financial year and of the profit or loss for the financial year of the undertakings included in the consolidation as a whole, so far as concerns the parent company's members and should consist of a consolidated balance sheet dealing with the state of affairs of the parent company and its subsidiaries as at the last date of the financial year and a profit and loss account for the financial year. In addition, the financial statements must comply with Schedule 4A to the Act or provision made by the Secretary of State by regulations as to form and content and additional information required. [CA85 Sec 227A(1) to (3) inserted by SI 2004/2947; CA06 Sec 404(3)]. The exemptions from the requirement to prepare consolidated financial statements provided in the Act are discussed in chapter 24.

2.22.5 In most cases, companies have a free choice for financial years beginning on or after 1 January 2005 as to whether they prepare their *individual* financial statements under EU-adopted IFRS or under UK GAAP. Similarly, UK companies whose securities are not traded on a regulated market may prepare their *consolidated* financial statements under EU-adopted IFRS or under UK GAAP. However, the government has implemented some restrictions and conditions:

- Once a company has prepared its financial statements under EU-adopted IFRS, it cannot revert to UK GAAP in a later financial year, unless there is a *"relevant change in circumstance"*. A relevant change in circumstance occurs if the company becomes a subsidiary of an undertaking that is not preparing its individual financial statements under EU-adopted IFRS or if the company (or its parent) ceases to have its securities traded on a regulated market. [CA85 Sec 226(4)(5) amended by SI 2004/2947; CA06 Sec 395(3)(5)].

- A parent company may elect to prepare its individual financial statements under UK GAAP even if it elects to use EU-adopted IFRS in its consolidated financial statements.

- Where the parent company prepares group accounts, companies in the same group must adopt the same accounting framework as each other, unless there are *"good reasons"* not do so. That is, the parent must ensure that all UK companies in the group use either EU-adopted IFRS or UK GAAP. There is an exception to this requirement: where a parent adopts EU-adopted IFRS in both its consolidated financial statements and its individual financial statements, it will not be required to ensure that all its subsidiaries use EU-adopted IFRS too. [CA85 Sec 227C inserted by SI 2004/2947; CA06 Sec 407]. The DTI has issued guidance notes on these rules, including an explanation of when there might be 'good reasons' (see para 2.22.6 below).

- Building societies are subject to the same requirements as companies in that they have the option of adopting IFRS in their individual and consolidated financial statements.
- Charitable companies may not prepare financial statements under IFRS. IFRS does not specifically address charity sector transactions and the government believes that the direct application of IFRS without modification through a SORP might create 'interpretational issues'. In addition, there are no plans to permit unincorporated charities to use IFRS; adoption of IFRS by charitable corporations would, therefore, lead to inconsistency within the charity sector.

2.22.6 The DTI has issued guidance notes to help companies to apply the new rules and these include an explanation of where there might be 'good reasons' for the directors not to prepare all the individual financial statements within a group by using the same accounting framework. The provision is intended to allow a degree of flexibility where there are genuine, including cost/benefit, grounds for not using the same framework. Such reasons would include:

- An IFRS group acquires a subsidiary that does not use IFRS. In the year of acquisition, it might not be practicable for the newly-acquired subsidiary to switch to IFRS straight away.
- A group might include subsidiaries that are themselves publicly traded, in which case market pressures or regulatory requirements to use IFRS might come into play, without necessarily justifying a switch to IFRS by the non-publicly traded subsidiaries.
- Where a subsidiary or a parent is planning to list and so might wish to convert to IFRS in advance, but the rest of the group is not intending to list.
- The group might include small subsidiaries where the cost of switching the accounting framework might outweigh the benefits from doing so.

It is essential that if the parent's directors decide to adopt a different framework for any entities within the group that they are able to justify any inconsistency to shareholders, regulators or other interested parties. [DTI Guidance para 4.16].

2.22.7 The DTI guidance notes do not make any specific mention of tax as a 'good reason' for adopting a different framework for one subsidiary within a group. In commercial terms tax is a business cost like any other. Hence, it may seem reasonable to take the view that if a group's existing tax position would be significantly adversely affected by a company in the group using EU-adopted IFRS, that this might be a 'good reason' for the parent company's directors to decide that that particular UK subsidiary should continue to use UK GAAP. However, we consider that continuing to use UK GAAP for a subsidiary in order to enter into future tax arrangements that rely on the differences between UK

GAAP and EU-adopted IFRS, would not be a good reason for inconsistent accounting frameworks.

2.22.7.1 Whether tax issues are a 'good reason' will depend on the individual facts and circumstances. The following scenarios provide some additional guidance. In all cases it is assumed that the rest of the group's UK subsidiaries will be adopting EU-adopted IFRS and that the proposed accounting of the company that would not use EU-adopted IFRS will be fully in accordance with UK GAAP.

- In the case of existing arrangements or structures, where a transition to EU-adopted IFRS would result in a significant increase or potential volatility in taxable profits, or a significant acceleration of tax cash outflows, or introduce a significant new tax exposure, compared with the company continuing to use UK GAAP, then the tax consequences may well be a 'good reason' to keep one subsidiary on UK GAAP. For example, a company's revenue recognition might be accelerated under IFRS and thus tax payments might also be accelerated. In this context, 'significant' might be in absolute terms or relative to the size of the company affected. However, a trivial tax effect should not be used as an excuse to keep a company on UK GAAP.

- The conclusion above regarding pre-existing arrangements or structures should not be altered by the fact that they represented a tax planning strategy based on a proper interpretation of tax law, even if HM Revenue & Customs may be expected to challenge it and try to defeat it through litigation or through a change of law. If, as a result of a company using EU-adopted IFRS, the group could no longer claim the benefits of existing tax planning (or the benefits would be significantly reduced or new tax risks would arise under EU-adopted IFRS such that the planning would not have been entered into with companies using EU-adopted IFRS) the tax effect of using EU-adopted IFRS may be a good reason to remain on UK GAAP.

- If a company has not changed to EU-adopted IFRS because it would adversely affect a tax planning strategy and that strategy has come to an end, it should change to EU-adopted IFRS from the start of the accounting period following that in which the tax planning strategy had ended, unless there was another 'good reason' not to do so.

- Similarly, it is likely that setting up a new company (or activating an existing dormant company) that uses UK GAAP solely for tax planning purposes would not constitute a 'good reason' for an inconsistent adoption of the appropriate GAAP in the individual accounts within a group.

2.22.8 Further guidance on which companies are required to use IFRS and which companies may optionally use it is given in chapter 2 of the Manual of Accounting – IFRS for the UK.

The true and fair requirement

2.23 In relation to Companies Act individual accounts, in addition to requiring companies to prepare accounts, the Companies Act 1985 section 226A and the Companies Act 2006 section 394 require that:

- *"The balance sheet must give a true and fair view of the state of affairs of the company as at the end of the financial year; and the profit and loss account must give a true and fair view of the profit or loss of the company for the financial year."* [CA85 Sec 226A(2) inserted by SI 2004/2947; CA06 Sec 396(2)].

- *"Companies Act individual accounts must comply with the provisions of Schedule 4 as to the form and content of the balance sheet and profit and loss account and additional information to be provided by way of notes to the accounts."* [CA85 Sec 226A(3) inserted by SI 2004/2947]. *"Companies Act individual accounts must comply with provision made by the Secretary of State by regulations as to the form and content of the balance sheet and profit and loss account and additional information to be provided by way of notes to the accounts."* [CA06 Sec 396(3)].

2.24 In most cases, companies are able to comply with both of these sub-sections at the same time. That is, compliance with the detailed rules of Schedule 4 or provisions made by the Secretary of State is consistent with the requirement to give a true and fair view.

2.25 However, this will not always be the case. The Act makes clear that the true and fair requirement is overriding, and sets this out in the following way:

- The Companies Act 1985 section 226A(4) (CA06 Sec 396(4)) provides that:

  "Where compliance with the provisions of [Schedule 4] and the other provisions..." [CA85] or "Where compliance with the regulation and any other provision..." the [CA06] "of this Act as to the matters to be included in a company's individual accounts or in notes to those accounts, would not be sufficient to give a true and fair view, the necessary additional information must be given in the accounts or in a note to them."

- The Companies Act 1985 section 226A(5) (CA06 Sec 396(5)) adds that:

  "If in special circumstances compliance with any of those provisions is inconsistent with the requirement to give a true and fair view, the directors must depart from that provision to the extent necessary to give a true and fair view."

- The Companies Act 1985 section 226A(6) (CA06 Sec 396(5)) notes that:

  "Particulars of any such departure, the reasons for it and its effect must be given in a note to the accounts."

2.26 The true and fair requirement, as set out in these sub-sections, is a very important element of the Act and of UK GAAP. Questions are sometimes asked about the interplay between sections 226A(4) and 226A(5) of the Companies Act 1985 and sections 396(4) and 396(5) of the Companies Act 2006 . In a previous version of the Companies Act 1985 (when the true and fair override was dealt with in section 226), it was more explicit that they were sequential. That is, if following Schedule 4 did not result in a true and fair view, the first requirement was to add more information. If the financial statements then gave a true and fair view, compliance with the Act was achieved and resort to section 226(5) did not arise. Only if a true and fair view was still not obtained, even after the addition of more information, was a company required to resort to section 226(5).

2.27 The wording is now not so explicitly sequential. However, the practical effect is much the same as before, in that additional information satisfies the requirement in some cases, but not others. The Companies Act 1985 Section 226A(4) (CA06 Sec 396(4)) can be seen as saying merely that the specific requirements of Schedule 4 or regulation and other parts of the Act are the minimum requirement. There may be a number of situations in which additional information has to be given, for example, to explain a somewhat unusual transaction. Without that explanation, the financial statements could not be said to give a true and fair view; but with the explanation added they do. Adding the information is the obvious solution and there is no need to consider departing from the specific rules. An example might be that, in order to give a true and fair view, it might be necessary to give information about a transaction with a related party.

2.28 The Companies Act 1985 section 226A(5) (CA06 Sec 396(5)), on the other hand, comes into operation when, owing to 'special circumstances', the accounting treatment otherwise required by the Act does not give a true and fair view, that is, if the treatment otherwise required by the Act is inconsistent with a true and fair view. Such treatment cannot become true and fair even if extensive additional information is given.

2.29 The Companies Act 1985 sub-sections 226A(4) and 226A(5) (CA06 Sec 396(4)(5)) can, therefore, be seen not so much as sequential provisions, but as alternative provisions to assist in achieving a true and fair view. Each has a role in its own circumstances: sub-section 226A(4) of the Companies Act 1985 (CA06 Sec 396(4)) comes into play where there is *insufficient* information; sub-section 226A(5) of the Companies Act 1985 (CA06 Sec 396(5)) comes into play where there is the *wrong kind* of accounting treatment.

2.30 Although the notion of departing from the otherwise specific rules in order to give a true and fair view is a powerful and important one, that does not mean it is something that should be done frequently or cavalierly. Indeed, it is a treatment to be adopted sparingly. As sub-section 226A(5) of the Companies Act 1985 (CA06 Sec 396(5)) makes clear, it is only to be used 'in special circumstances'. This means that it is not intended to be used as a route through which all companies can disregard a specific rule of the Act.

2.31 With few exceptions, such as SSAP19 (where companies are required to value investment properties rather then depreciate them, which is what the Act requires), the general understanding is that the override should only be used in the special circumstances of an individual company that has a different situation from most other companies. In practice, this can be extended to a class of companies, for example, in a particular industry, which have considerations that differ from the generality of companies. An example here is that in the past it has been regarded as acceptable for companies in the securities industry to use the override to 'mark to market' their current asset investments and take the resultant gains to the profit and loss account rather than, as the Act required, to the revaluation reserve. The reason it was acceptable for these types of companies is that, because of the nature of their businesses, this treatment gave a true and fair view of their performance, whereas the Act's treatment did not generally do so. However, other types of companies that adopted that practice had to demonstrate that they have special circumstances of their own. (The Act's rules have now been changed to permit fair value accounting for certain financial instruments – see further chapter 6.)

2.32 The majority of departures from the Act's accounting provisions in practice derive from requirements of accounting standards where the applicable accounting standard is inconsistent with the Act — for example, non-amortisation of goodwill with indefinite life (FRS 10).

2.33 The Companies Act 1985 sub-section 226A(6) (CA06 Sec 396(5)) requires certain disclosures to be given when the override is used. These disclosures are detailed in paragraph 2.42.

2.34 As discussed above, Companies Act consolidated financial statements are also required to give a true and fair view. [CA85 Sec 227A(2) inserted by SI 2004/2947; CA06 Sec 404(2)]. The Companies Act 1985 sub-sections 227A(4) to 227A(6) (CA06 Secs 404(4)(5)) contain identical provisions with respect to consolidated financial statements as sub-sections 226A(4) to 226(6) (CA06 Secs 396(4)(5)) respectively. Therefore, the discussion above applies equally to Companies Act consolidated financial statements.

Compliance with accounting standards and UITF abstracts

2.35 FRS 18, 'Accounting policies' recognises that the Act's requirement to give a true and fair view is paramount:

> "*An entity should adopt accounting policies that enable its financial statements to give a true and fair view. Those accounting policies should be consistent with the requirements of accounting standards, Urgent Issues Task Force (UITF) Abstracts and companies legislation.*" [FRS 18 para 14].

2.36 There is a general presumption that compliance with accounting standards is required to meet the true and fair requirement. The legal opinion supporting this presumption is discussed from paragraph 2.78. In addition, paragraph 36A of Schedule 4 to the Companies Act 1985 requires companies to state in their financial statements whether they have been prepared in accordance with applicable accounting standards and to give the particulars and reasons for any material departures from those standards. Table 2.1 contains an example of a paragraph 36A statement.

Table 2.1 — Eleco plc — Annual report and financial statements — 30 June 2006

1 Accounting policies (extract)

The financial statements have been prepared in accordance with applicable accounting standards in the United Kingdom.

A summary of the more important Group accounting policies, which have been applied consistently, is set out below.

[The next paragraph is 2.38.]

2.38 While compliance with accounting standards and UITF Abstracts is usually required in order for financial statements to give a true and fair view, in exceptional circumstances a departure from an accounting standard or UITF Abstract may be necessary to meet the true and fair requirement. Where compliance with the requirements of an accounting standard or UITF Abstract is inconsistent with the requirement to give a true and fair view, FRS 18 requires a departure to the extent necessary to give a true and fair view. [FRS 18 para 15].

2.39 FRS 18's true and fair override in respect of accounting standards and UITF Abstracts is similar to the Act's true and fair override in respect of the Act's accounting provisions and applies to all types of entities whose financial statements are intended to give a true and fair view. Departures from accounting standards are, however, very rare indeed and should be handled with great care. The ASB's Foreword to Accounting Standards emphasises that compliance with accounting standards will normally be necessary to give a true and fair view because they are formulated with the objective of ensuring that the resulting financial information faithfully represents the underlying commercial activity.

2.40 FRS 18 explicitly provides a sequential approach to the true and fair override. First, entities need to consider what can be achieved by additional disclosure. A departure from an accounting standard is a last resort when a true and fair view cannot be achieved by additional disclosure. [FRS 18 para 16].

True and fair override disclosures

2.41 Where a company departs from any of the Act's accounting provisions in order to give a true and fair view, the Act requires that *"...particulars of any such departure, the reasons for it and its effect shall be given in a note to the accounts"*. [CA85 Sec 226A(6) inserted by SI 2004/2947; CA06 Sec 396(5)].

2.42 The true and fair override disclosures required by FRS 18 give a more precise meaning to particulars, reasons and effect and bring together equivalent disclosures in respect of departures from the accounting provisions of the Companies Act or other relevant legislation, accounting standards and UITF Abstracts. FRS 18 adopted the previous requirements set out in UITF Abstract 7, which dealt specifically with departures from the Act. The disclosures should include:

- A clear and unambiguous statement that there has been a departure from the requirements of an accounting standard, a UITF Abstract or companies legislation and that the departure is necessary to give a true and fair view.
- A statement of the treatment that would normally be required in the circumstances and a description of the treatment actually adopted.
- A statement as to why the treatment prescribed would not give a true and fair view.
- A description of how the position shown in the financial statements is different as a result of the departure, normally with quantification of the difference (except where quantification is self-evident or cannot reasonably be made, in which latter case the circumstances should be explained).

[FRS 18 para 62].

2.43 The disclosures referred to in the previous paragraph should be given considerable prominence. They should either be included in the note that discloses compliance with applicable accounting standards under paragraph 36A of Schedule 4 to the Companies Act 1985, or that note should include a cross reference to where such disclosures can be found. [FRS 18 para 64]. As explained earlier, the most common uses of the 'true and fair override' are overrides of company law that are required by accounting standards. In these cases, the applicable accounting standards have of course been complied with.

2.44 It should be noted that the fact that quantification of the effect may be regarded as misleading or meaningless is not, under FRS 18 or the Act, an acceptable reason for omitting it. To give an example of an override that cannot reasonably be quantified, it is not normally possible to quantify the effect of departing from the Companies Act where goodwill on an acquisition is not amortised — by ascribing an indefinite life (as permitted by FRS 10 in special circumstances), there is no benchmark for calculating an amortisation charge required by the Act.

The UK financial reporting structure

The Dearing Report proposals

2.45 In November 1987, the Consultative Committee of Accountancy Bodies (the CCAB) appointed a Review Committee under the chairmanship of Sir Ron

Dearing to review and make recommendations on the standard-setting process. The terms of reference were to consider, *inter alia*, the status of accounting standards in relation to company law and the procedures for monitoring compliance with standards and their enforcement.

2.46 In discharge of that remit, the Review Committee in their report (the Dearing Report) submitted to the CCAB in September 1988 stated that accounting standards should remain, as far as possible, the responsibility of auditors, preparers and users of financial statements and there should not be a general move towards incorporating them into law. But the report recommended the government should introduce legislation along the following lines:

- For all large companies, directors should be required to state in the notes to the financial statements whether they are drawn up in accordance with applicable accounting standards and to draw attention to any material departures, explaining the reasons for the departures.
- There should be a new statutory power under civil law for certain authorised bodies or the Secretary of State to apply to the courts for an order requiring the revision of financial statements that do not give a true and fair view.
- A small levy should be added to the fees paid by all companies to the Companies Registration Office to assist meeting the cost of setting and monitoring standards.

2.47 In addition, the Committee recommended that the task of devising accounting standards should be discharged by a newly constituted, expert Accounting Standards Board (ASB) that would issue standards on its own authority. A Financial Reporting Council (FRC) should be created that would provide guidance to the ASB on priorities for its work programme and on issues of public interest and would act as an instrument for promoting good practice in relation to accounting standards. In securing compliance with accounting standards in support of the 'true and fair' requirement, the Committee recommended establishing a Review Panel to examine contentious departures from accounting standards by large companies.

The Companies Act 1989 requirements

2.48 The legislative changes necessary to bring the above recommendations of the Review Committee into effect were implemented by the Companies Act 1989. Paragraph 36A of Schedule 4 to the Companies Act 1985 (as amended by the Companies Act 1989) requires all companies to state whether the financial statements have been prepared in accordance with applicable accounting standards as discussed in paragraph 2.36 above.

2.49 In providing a framework for the implementation of the Dearing Committee proposals for an independent Accounting Standards Board overseen by a Financial Reporting Council and backed up by a Review Panel, the Act gave the Secretary of State power to make grants to such bodies concerning:

- Issuing accounting standards.
- Overseeing and directing the issue of such standards.
- Investigating departures from such standards or from the Act's accounting requirements and taking steps to secure compliance with them.

[CA85 Sec 256(3) subsequently repealed and replaced by CA04 Sec 16(2); CA06 Sec 1274(2)].

2.50 In addition, the Companies Act 1989 introduced procedures enabling directors voluntarily to revise financial statements that are discovered to be defective. [CA85 Sec 245; CA06 Sec 454]. Further enabling provisions permit the Secretary of State to improve the enforcement of accounting provisions by requiring an explanation from directors of apparent failures to prepare financial statements that comply with the Act. [CA85 Sec 245A(1); CA06 Sec 455(1)(2)]. If a satisfactory explanation is not received, the Secretary of State may apply to the court for a declaration that a company's financial statements do not comply with the Act and to order them to be revised. [CA85 Sec 245A(3); CA06 Sec 455(4)]. The Act's provisions relating to the revision of defective financial statements are dealt with in chapter 8 of the Manual of Accounting – IFRS and UK supplement.

The Financial Reporting Council

2.51 The Financial Reporting Council Limited (FRC) was established in 1990 along with two subsidiaries, the Accounting Standards Board Limited and the Financial Reporting Review Panel Limited, all as companies limited by guarantee. The purpose of these bodies is to provide an institutional framework to underpin financial reporting in the UK and to implement the proposals of the Dearing Report. The accountancy profession, the City and the government share equally in the funding of these bodies.

2.52 Following the collapse of Enron and the concerns raised over financial reporting and the role of auditors, the government decided to review the UK's arrangements for audit and accountancy regulation. In January 2003, the Secretary of State for Trade and Industry and the Chancellor of the Exchequer announced reforms drawn from the recommendations in the final report of the Co-ordinating Group on Audit and Accounting Issues (CGAA) and the report on the Review of the Regulatory Regime of the Accountancy Profession ('the Regulatory Review').

2.53 The Regulatory Review was instructed to review the workings of the recently formed Accountancy Foundation. This body had been set up in 2000 to provide independent regulation of the accountancy profession. Regulation had previously been directly under the control of the six professional accountancy bodies. The Accountancy Foundation was formed following proposals made by the CCAB and a consultation document issued by the DTI. The Foundation was set up with the *"overriding objective...to maintain and enhance the standards of work and of conduct of accountants working in the United Kingdom and the Republic of Ireland"*. ['Independent regulation of the accountancy profession', The

Accountancy Foundation]. The Foundation was set up with four legal subsidiaries, each constitutionally independent of the Foundation: the Ethics Standards Board; the Auditing Practices Board; the Investigation and Discipline Board; and the Review Board.

2.53.1 Under the new regulatory structure the FRC has assumed the role of the Accountancy Foundation and is the single independent accountancy regulator. It comprises a Board, the Council and six operating bodies. The organisation of the FRC is represented in the following diagram:

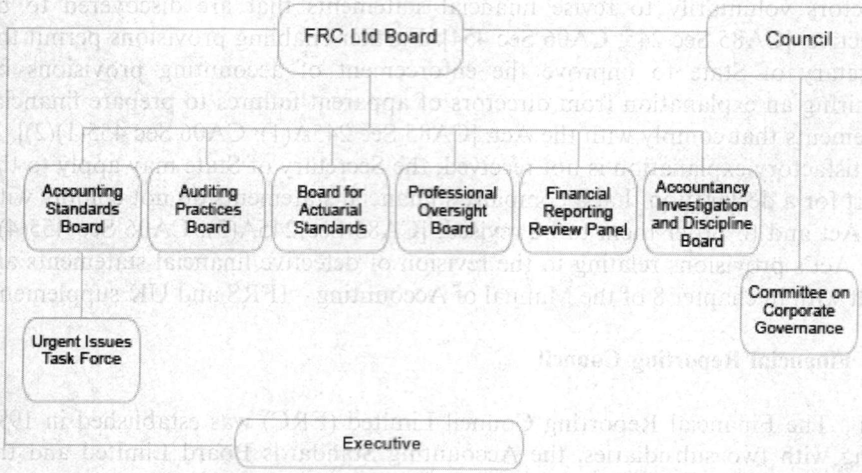

2.53.2 The directors of the FRC Board are appointed by the Secretary of State for Trade and Industry. The Board:

- Determines the FRC's strategy and priorities.
- Sets the FRC's budget, secures the necessary funding and monitors expenditure.
- Oversees the delivery by each operating body of their functions.
- Oversees the performance of the Executive
- Makes appointments to the Council, the operating bodies and senior management.
- Approves any significant structural changes to the FRC.
- Ensures that the FRC and its operating bodies achieve high levels of accountability and transparency.
- Undertakes an annual assessment of the risks to the FRC's overall success and oversees risk mitigation.
- Undertakes annual evaluation of the FRC's performance and that of its committees.

[FRC web site 2007].

2.53.3 The FRC Council has up to 30 members (including the six directors of the Board, the chairs of the operating bodies) representing business, investors, professional and other communities with an interest in corporate reporting and governance. In addition, there are a number of observers from other bodies with an interest in the FRC's work. The Council:

- Monitors the Combined Code on Corporate Governance and approves any changes to the Code and related guidance.
- Provides advice on the FRC's strategy and priorities.
- Gives advice on the FRC's budget and funding.
- Gives advice on structural and any other relevant issues.
- Monitors and gives advice on the FRC's activities on the basis of regular reports from all parts of the FRC.

[FRC web site 2007].

2.53.4 The FRC now has six subsidiary operating boards:

- The Accounting Standards Board, which itself oversees the work of the Urgent Issues Task Force (see further para 2.54).
- The Financial Reporting Review Panel (see further para 2.85).
- The Professional Oversight Board. This body has delegated to it the Secretary for Trade and Industry's functions for authorising the professional accountancy bodies to act as supervisory bodies and to give professional qualifications. It oversees an Audit Inspection Unit, which monitors the audit of significant listed companies and other public interest entities (including both the audit process and significant audit judgements). It also oversees the regulatory activities of the professional accountancy bodies.
- The Auditing Practices Board (APB). The APB's responsibilities have increased and now encompass setting ethical standards for auditors as well as setting auditing standards.
- The Accountancy Investigation and Discipline Board. This body is responsible for investigating significant public interest disciplinary cases, including sanctioning those found guilty of misconduct.
- The Board for Actuarial Standards (BAS). This body has the objective of promoting competence and transparency of actuarial practice and will do this by establishing and improving actuarial standards and ensuring that they are coherent, consistent and comprehensive.

In addition, the Committee on Corporate Governance, whose members are drawn from the FRC, assists it in its work on corporate governance.

2.53.5 The operating bodies:

- Make the regulatory decisions for which they are responsible.
- Keep under review any emerging risks or other matters that could affect those aspects of confidence in corporate reporting and governance that fall within their remit.
- Make appointments to working groups and committees, in consultation, where appropriate, with the Chair of the FRC.
- Undertake annual evaluations of their own performance and that of their sub-committees.

[FRC web site 2007].

2.53.6 The FRC's regulatory philosophy is:

- Working on the basis that a well-informed market is the best regulator.
- Targeting the use of its powers, taking a proactive, risk-based and proportionate approach, making effective use of Regulatory Impact Assessments.
- Emphasising principles and clarity in its standard-setting and rule-making.
- Being consultative – involving preparers, auditors, users of corporate reports and other regulatory organisations in its decision-making and allowing adequate time for consultation, without compromising its independence or confidentiality.
- Recognising the importance of professional judgement in the way in which standards and rules are applied and enforced.
- Where discharging a judicial or quasi-judicial function, to do so in accordance with the FRC's formal powers and the rules of natural justice.
- Being transparent, accountable and efficient in its work, and ensuring that it receives appropriate publicity.

[FRC web site 2007].

2.53.7 The FRC notes that it does not regard regulation as an end in itself and that it will use its influence and powers to promote a regulatory regime in which high standards of corporate reporting and governance are seen to contribute to competitiveness, wealth creation and general prosperity.

The Accounting Standards Board

2.54 The Accounting Standards Board (ASB) is the authority that has been prescribed by statutory instrument as the standard making body for the purposes of section 256(1) of the Companies Act 1985. [CA06 Sec 464(1)]. The accounting standards (designated FRSs) that it issues, amends and withdraws are 'accounting standards' for the purpose of the Act's accounting requirements. This is in contrast to the accounting standards that were set by the ASC that were designated as SSAPs. Previously neither the ASC nor its SSAPs were given statutory recognition. At its inception, the ASB adopted the SSAPs extant at that time so that, until they are withdrawn by the ASB, they now have the same authority and statutory backing as FRSs.

2.55 Unlike the ASC, the ASB is totally independent and needs no outside approval for its actions either from the Council, from government, or from any other source. The ASC had been criticised as being slow in setting standards since agreement for a new standard was required from all its sponsoring bodies. These sponsoring bodies were the six accountancy bodies making up the CCAB. The ASB has a full-time chairman and full-time technical director and is supported by greater staff resources than the ASC. However, the Board has fewer members than the ASC. In addition, other part-time Board members are drawn from industry and commerce, investor institutions and others with an interest in financial reporting as well as the accountancy profession. Membership of the ASB is limited to ten and since a majority of seven is needed for any decision to adopt, revise or withdraw an accounting standard, the standard setting process is designed be more streamlined.

2.56 However, the ASB has stated that it wishes to ensure wide consultation and to be as open as possible in its dealings. As well as issuing exposure drafts of proposed FRSs (FREDs), it publishes discussion papers on topics as they reach an appropriate stage of development and, in exceptional circumstances, it may hold public hearings about a particular problem. The ASB held the first such public hearings, on accounting for goodwill, in September and October 1995.

2.57 The ASB has published a 'Statement of aims' which sets out its approach to the task of setting standards and lists the guidelines it will follow in conducting its affairs. The ASB intends to achieve its aims by:

- Developing principles to guide it in establishing standards and providing a framework within which others can exercise judgement in resolving accounting issues.
- Issuing new accounting standards, or amending existing ones, in response to evolving business practices, new economic developments and deficiencies being identified in current practice.
- Addressing urgent issues promptly.

[Statement of aims].

2.58 In 1990, alongside its other projects, the ASB began developing a conceptual framework of financial reporting principles. The first complete exposure draft of the Statement of principles was issued late in 1995. That draft met with resistance and was subsequently re-written. A revised draft was issued in 1999, quickly followed by the final Statement later in that year. The development of the Statement of principles and its contents are discussed from paragraph 2.191.

2.59 In order to improve the timeliness of its response to issues, a committee of the ASB, the Urgent Issues Task Force, was set up to assist the Board in areas where an accounting standard or Companies Act provision exists, but where unsatisfactory or conflicting interpretations have developed or seem likely to develop. The UITF is considered further from paragraph 2.81.

2.60 When the ASB first took responsibility for accounting standards in 1990, it set about fundamentally reforming those aspects of financial reporting practices where there were significant perceived shortcomings. A significant part of the ASB's early work programme consisted of projects where the ASC had issued exposure drafts. In its first four years, the ASB issued seven new FRSs. This completed its first major phase of reforms. In the process, it changed the appearance of the profit and loss account and balance sheet and introduced new primary statements: a cash flow statement and a statement of total recognised gains and losses.

2.61 The next major reform phase occurred in late 1997 to early 1999, when the ASB issued seven new standards. These standards were intended to further tighten up the rules to prevent abuse and increase accountability.

2.62 The continuing project to put in place a Statement of principles on which new standards, and revisions of existing standards, can be based was another important aspect of the ASB's work during the whole of the 1990s. The effort to create such a framework placed much more emphasis on the underlying concepts. The Statement of principles also supports the ASB's expectation that the spirit and reasoning of accounting standards should be followed, not merely the rules contained within them.

2.63 The ASB has had a strategy of convergence with international developments for some time. Indeed, one of its aims (issued in July 1991) is *"To ensure that through a process of regular communication, accounting standards are produced with due regard to international developments"*. [Statement of aims]. Accounting standards published since 1994 have had an appendix detailing compliance with international accounting standards and many standards since FRS 11, 'Impairment of fixed assets and goodwill', have been broadly in line with international developments. This process has, however, been accelerated and more formally set out in recent years, primarily because of the EU 2005 Regulation (see para 2.4).

2.63.1 The ASB responded to the 2005 Regulation by accelerating its aim of convergence with IFRS. It has stated that it will not generally independently issue new UK standards, but instead will work with the IASB on its international projects and will bring IFRS into the UK as accounting standards where appropriate. This has the effect that, in due course, IFRS will in substance apply to all companies in the UK and not just to those companies that are the subject of the EU 2005 Regulation or who elect to adopt IFRS voluntarily. The ASB has noted, however, that it will consider retaining a UK standard or changing an IFRS if it believes that the cost of introducing an IFRS would be greater than the benefit. One example of this is FRS 26 (IAS 39), 'Financial instruments: Measurement'. This standard introduces many of the requirements of IAS 39, 'Financial instruments: Recognition and measurement', but it initially only applies to listed entities and those applying the fair value accounting rules set out in the Companies Act 1985. The extension of the standard's scope to all companies is subject to further consultation.

2.63.2 In terms of the speed of convergence, the ASB stated that it wishes to adopt a 'gradual' approach to conversion. It was envisaged that this would be relatively straight forward, with many new standards replacing the UK ones without too many differences. To achieve this aim, the ASB initially proposed introducing various standards that were either very similar to existing UK ones or that were not subject to change. However, the IASB's subsequent announcement of a plan to converge with US GAAP made this original ASB plan difficult to implement. Fewer than half of the exposure drafts published by the ASB in summer 2002 have been turned into accounting standards.

2.63.3 In March 2004, the ASB then issued a discussion paper, 'UK accounting standards: a strategy for convergence with IFRS'. The paper proposed a phased approach to convergence, including new standards in 2005 and 2006 and, thereafter, a series of 'step changes' replacing one or more existing UK standards. Under this approach the ASB has issued standards on, *inter alia*, financial instruments, foreign currency and earnings per share. These come on top of standards dealing with share-based payment (FRS 20) and post-balance sheet events (FRS 21).

2.63.4 In March 2005, the ASB issued an exposure draft, 'Accounting standard-setting in a changing environment: the role of the Accounting Standards Board'. This confirmed the proposal in the March 2004 discussion paper that the ASB planned to converge UK GAAP to IFRS, over the four years to 2009. In addition, the exposure draft set out the ASB's views on how it sees its role – namely as contributing to international standard-setting, influencing European policy on IFRS endorsement, continuing to issue entity-specific and sector-specific guidance and issuing guidance on company communication.

2.63.5 The convergence of UK GAAP with IFRS is proving controversial, not least because of the IASB's own plans to converge with US GAAP. In May 2006, the ASB issued a further consultation in a press notice, 'ASB seeks view on future application of reporting requirements for UK companies'. This confirmed that the ASB was moving to finalise its plans for convergence with IFRS and requested views on the future application of IFRS for UK companies. The ASB is considering a number of options, depending on the type of company. These include the use of full IFRS; the use of full IFRS for measurement and recognition, but with reduced disclosure requirements; the use of full UK GAAP; and the use of the ASB's FRSSE for an expanded category of companies. The press release set out the ASB's thinking on the application of IFRS to (i) UK quoted and other publicly accountable companies; (ii) small and medium-sized companies; (iii) UK subsidiaries of group that apply full IFRS; and (iv) other companies.

2.63.6 In October 2006, the ASB posted onto its web site feedback on the tentative proposals outlined in the above press notice. The responses to the press notice broadly support a two-tier approach, with the lower level potentially (and ideally) being based on the IASB's SME project. However, the feedback statement made clear that the ASB would not come to a firm view on the convergence of UK standards with IFRS until there was a much clearer understanding on the IASB's proposals on accounting for SMEs.

2.63.7 In February 2007, the ASB issued a press notice, 'ASB welcomes IASB's international financial reporting standard exposure draft for small and medium-sized entities' and noted that the ASB would be issuing its own consultation. In April 2007, the ASB issued its consultation in a press notice, 'ASB consults on proposed IFRS for SMEs'.

2.64 In addition to issuing accounting and reporting standards, the ASB may, from time to time, issue other forms of guidance on best practice. The ASB is attempting to create a virtuous circle where companies are encouraged to provide more informative financial statements. For instance, non-mandatory statements of best practice have been issued on the contents of half-yearly reports and preliminary announcements of full year results.

FRSs and SSAPs

2.65 For entities operating under the Companies Act and standards issued by the ASB, (that is, those entities not adopting IFRS), FRSs and SSAPs are applicable to all financial statements of an entity that are intended to give a true and fair view. These accounting standards also apply to consolidated financial statements, including amounts relating to overseas entities that are included in the consolidation.

2.66 However, accounting standards need not be applied to immaterial items. Accounting standards also do not override exemptions from disclosure given by law to certain types of entity. For example, groups that are exempt by virtue of their size from the Companies Act requirements to prepare consolidated financial statements, are not expected to comply with accounting standards dealing with consolidated financial statements.

2.67 In addition, accounting standards themselves may exclude certain entities from their scope. For example, the requirements of SSAP 25, 'Segmental reporting', that are additional to the statutory segmental disclosure requirements and certain disclosure requirements of SSAP 13, 'Accounting for research and development', do not apply to private limited companies unless they exceed the criteria, multiplied in each case by 10, for defining a medium-sized company under section 247 of the Companies Act 1985 (CA06 Sec 465).

2.68 The application of accounting standards to smaller entities has been a controversial issue for a number of years. Various studies were carried out and recommendations made. In the mid 1990's a new approach emerged, that small companies should comply with a single simplified accounting standard designed specifically for them. The ASB issued the 'Financial reporting standard for smaller entities' (FRSSE) in November 1997 and has revised and updated it periodically (see chapter 32).

2.69 The Foreword to accounting standards states that the prescription of accounting requirements for the public sector in the UK is a matter for government. The government's requirements with regard to public sector bodies that prepare financial statements may or may not refer to accounting standards. Therefore public sector bodies are not specifically required to comply with accounting standards although there is an expectation that they should do so if their financial statements are required to give a true and fair view, unless the government considers it inappropriate.

2.70 The ASB has stated that, in general, when a new accounting standard is issued, it should be applied to all material transactions regardless of the date they were entered into. This would prevent similar transactions being accounted for in different ways in the same financial statements depending on when they occurred. It would also aid comparability between the financial statements of different entities.

2.71 However, the ASB accepts that in a few instances the application of a new accounting standard to past transactions would involve considerable work and may result in information that would be difficult for users to interpret. In these instances, the ASB may exclude transactions that took place before the standard came into force from its scope. FRS 6 and FRS 7, for example, applied in respect of business combinations first accounted for in financial statements relating to accounting periods commencing on or after 23 December 1994. Therefore, the accounting treatment of acquisitions and mergers that were first accounted for before these standards came into effect was not changed.

2.72 The ASB states in the Foreword that until an exposure draft (or discussion paper) is converted into a standard, the requirements of any existing standard that would be affected by the proposals remain in force. FRS 18 reiterates the position that entities should not adopt new proposals if they conflict with existing accounting standards or UITF Abstracts. Exposure drafts are subject to amendment and even more amendment can be expected to proposals contained in discussion papers. Companies wishing to incorporate new proposals into their financial statements may do so as long as the new proposal does not conflict with an existing accounting standard. Alternatively, additional information could be provided in a supplementary form such as in *pro forma* financial statements. [Foreword paras 31, 32; FRS 18 para 47]

2.73 Accounting standards are kept under review and are revised from time to time to reflect changes in the business environment and in accounting thinking.

However, it has been the ASB's practice to ensure that standards are given an appropriate period to become established before they are subject to review.

SORPs

2.74 Specific industry groups are recognised by the ASB to develop Statements of Recommended Practice (SORPs) under a code of practice. SORPs give guidance on the application of accounting standards to specialised industries and non-profit-making sectors. Whilst the ASB does not approve or frank SORPs, it monitors their development and, if satisfied, provides a negative assurance statement confirming that the SORP does not appear to contain any fundamental points of principle that are unacceptable in the context of current accounting practice or conflict with existing accounting standards.

2.75 The sectors for which SORPs are presently in issue, or under development, are:

- Authorised funds.
- Banking (see para 2.77.1 below).
- Charities.
- Further and higher education institutions.
- Insurance.
- Investment trusts.
- Local authorities.
- Oil and gas.
- Pension schemes.
- Registered social landlords.
- Unit trusts.
- Leasing.
- Open-ended investment companies (OEICs).
- Limited liability partnerships.

2.76 Although SORPs are themselves non-mandatory, their status in UK GAAP was enhanced by the publication of FRS 18. FRS 18 indicates that if accounting practices set out in a SORP are generally followed in an industry, they will be particularly persuasive in the selection of the most appropriate accounting policies by entities in the industry. FRS 18 also introduced a requirement for entities that fall within the scope of a SORP to provide a compliance statement in their financial statements. Such entities should:

- State the title of the SORP and whether the financial statements have been prepared in accordance with the SORP's provisions currently in effect.
- If the financial statements do not comply with the SORP, give a brief description of the departure, including:
  - the reasons why any treatment that is not in accordance with the SORP is judged more appropriate to the entity's particular circumstance; and
  - details of any disclosures recommended by the SORP that have been omitted and reasons for the omission.

[FRS 18 para 58].

2.77 Other relevant authorities may also encourage compliance with SORPs. For example, the Occupational Pension Schemes (Requirement to obtain Audited Accounts and a Statement from the Auditor) Regulations 1996 require pension schemes to which the regulations apply to state whether the financial statements have been prepared in accordance with the relevant SORP and to disclose any material departures.

2.77.1 In January 2006, the British Bankers' Association (BBA) announced that its four SORPs on financial instruments (covering advances, commitments and contingencies, derivatives and securities) are superseded on adoption of FRS 26, 'Financial instruments: Measurement'. Wording has been added to the four SORPs such that on adopting FRS 26, the non-compliance statement required by FRS 18 (see para 2.76) no longer applies. The BBA's SORP on segmental reporting remains in place for companies reporting under UK GAAP, until UK and international standards converge.

Counsel's opinion on true and fair view and role of accounting standards

2.78 As discussed from paragraph 2.23 above, the Act's overriding requirement is that 'Companies Act' financial statements must give a true and fair view of the entity's state of affairs at the balance sheet date and its profit and loss for the financial period ending on that date. The question then arises as to what is meant by a 'true and fair view'. In particular, there is the question of whether the requirement that all financial statements should give a true and fair view includes compliance with the relevant accounting standards. True and fair is a legal concept that can only be interpreted by the courts.

2.79 In light of the changes to the Companies Act detailed in paragraph 2.48 above, the ASB obtained a revised opinion from Mary Arden QC on the relationship between compliance with accounting standards and the requirement that all financial statements should give a true and fair view.

2.80 To obtain a full understanding of Counsel's arguments, the opinion should be read in its entirety. However, the opinion makes the following important points.

- Although the question of whether financial statements satisfy the true and fair requirement is a matter of law, the court cannot interpret the requirement without evidence as to the practices and views of accountants. The more authoritative these practices and views are, the more ready the court will be to follow them.

- Accounting standards initially identify proper accounting practice for the benefit of preparers and auditors of financial statements. However, because financial statements commonly comply with accounting standards, the effect of the standards is to create a common understanding between users and preparers about how particular items are dealt with and to create an expectation that financial statements will comply with applicable accounting standards, unless there is a good reason not to comply.

- The Companies Act 1989 gives statutory recognition to the existence of accounting standards. The court will infer from the Companies (Audit, Investigations and Community Enterprise) Act 2004 section 16(2) (CA06 Sec 1274(2)) that statutory policy favours both the issue of accounting standards (by a body prescribed by regulation) and compliance with them. The court will also infer from paragraph 36A of Schedule 4 to the Companies Act 1985 that, since there is a requirement to disclose particulars of non-compliance, financial statements that meet the true and fair requirement will generally follow rather than depart from accounting standards. Therefore, the likelihood is increased that the courts will hold that, in general, compliance with applicable accounting standards is necessary to meet the true and fair requirement.
- As a result of implementing the Dearing Report recommendations, the court is bound to give even further weight to the opinions of the ASB than to ASC. If a standard was not generally accepted in practice, it does not follow that the court would conclude that compliance with the standard was not necessary to meet the true and fair requirement.

- Paragraph 36A of Schedule 4 to the Companies Act 1985 envisages the possibility of a departure from applicable accounting standards, provided that particulars of the departure and the reasons for it are disclosed in the financial statements. However, the departure must be appropriate in the particular circumstances of the company. If the court is satisfied that an accounting standard should have been followed to meet the true and fair requirement, then non-compliance, even with the necessary disclosure, will result in a breach of the true and fair requirement.

The Urgent Issues Task Force

2.81 Although not envisaged by the revisions to the Act, the ASB also issues UITF Abstracts that set out the consensus reached by its committee, the Urgent Issues Task Force. The main role of the UITF is not to write new accounting standards, but to assist in areas where an accounting standard or Companies Act provision exists, but where unsatisfactory or conflicting interpretations have developed or seem likely to develop. In addition, the ASB may seek the UITF's view on significant accounting developments in areas where there is no extant legal provision or accounting standard.

2.82 The UITF seeks to reach a consensus among its fifteen voting members who are drawn from the accounting profession and the wider business community. Eleven voting members constitute a quorum at meetings and a consensus is achieved if not more than two of the voting members present at a meeting dissent. Although the UITF exposes draft Abstracts, the time for comment is generally much shorter than for accounting standards. Therefore, the UITF should be able to respond more quickly to emerging issues than the ASB. However, since the consultation time is reduced, the ASB ensures that matters on the UITF's agenda and other information about its activities are published.

2.83 The ASB regards UITF Abstracts as generally accepted accounting practice in the areas they address and as part of the body of accounting pronouncements that must be followed in order for financial statements to give a true and fair view. The ASB expects to adopt a UITF consensus, unless it conflicts with law, accounting standards or the ASB's policy or future plans. To date, the ASB has not rejected any Abstracts prepared by the UITF. However, one Abstract, UITF 10, 'Disclosure of directors' share options', was issued in non-mandatory form since the ASB received legal advice that disclosures proposed by the Abstract went beyond what is required by the Companies Act, and so did not fall within the powers delegated to the UITF. However, the subsequent adoption of this UITF by the Greenbury committee, and later by the Hampel Committee in the Combined Code, effectively made it mandatory, although it was withdrawn with effect for accounting periods ending on or after 31 December 2002.

2.84 The status of UITF Abstracts is considered in the ASB's legal opinion (see para 2.79). This opinion sets out the process of creating UITF Abstracts and their consideration and publishing by the ASB. It then argues that since the CCAB, the ASB and the profession expect UITF Abstracts to be followed and this expectation has been borne out in practice, there will be a readiness on the part of the court to accept that compliance with UITF Abstracts is also necessary to meet the true and fair requirement.

The Financial Reporting Review Panel

2.85 The role of the Financial Reporting Review Panel (FRRP) is to examine material departures from the Act's accounting requirements, including departures from the requirements of applicable accounting standards. The Secretary of State for Trade and Industry authorised the FRRP to discuss such departures with the company's directors and, if necessary, seek an order from the court to remedy them under section 245B of the Act as discussed in paragraph 2.50 above. By agreement with the DTI, the FRRP considers the financial statements of public and large private companies, with the DTI dealing with all other companies. Therefore, the following types of companies fall within the FRRP's authority:

- Public limited companies, unless they are subsidiaries in small or medium-sized groups.
- Companies within a group headed by a public limited company.
- Any private company that does not qualify as small or medium-sized as defined by section 247 of the Companies Act 1985.
- Any private company within a group that does not qualify as small or medium-sized.

[FRRP operating procedures para 1].

2.86 The FRRP does not routinely examine all the financial statements of the companies falling within its authority. Rather, it has from 1990 to 2003 acted on matters drawn to its attention either directly or indirectly. In January 2003 the Co-ordinating Group on Audit and Accounting Issues (the CGAA) reported to the government. The CGAA had been set up to take a wide ranging look at the accounting profession following Enron and similar scandals in the USA. The CGAA had proposed in its interim report that the FRRP become more proactive. The FRRP responded positively to this proposal and it was reiterated in the CGAA's final January 2003 report, also recommending that the FSA, which regulates companies listed on the London Stock Exchange, also plays a role. The FRRP's response to the CGAA's initial recommendations was to develop a proactive, risk-based approach to the selection of published accounts for review.

2.86.1 The FRRP now, in addition to responding to complaints, selects financial statements on the basis of risk. It will select reports, *"by methods which take into account the Panel's assessment of the risk of non-compliance and the consequence of non-compliance"*. [FRRP operating procedures para 3]. In December 2004 the panel announced that it would focus its activities on the financial statements in specific industries, following its risk-based assessment and after discussions with the FSA and the panel's Standing Advisory Group. The panel also announced that it would conduct targeted reviews to check compliance with specific accounting requirements and that it would focus on those companies expected to have significant changes on adoption of IFRS. [FRRP PN 81].

2.86.2 In addition to changing the way that financial statements are selected, the panel is now authorised to issue an order regarding compliance with the Act in respect of the directors' report of large and medium-sized companies. The panel is also now empowered to examine all financial information published by listed companies, including interim reports and preliminary announcements. The FRRP will liaise with the FSA in this respect and has signed a memorandum of understanding with the FSA in order to facilitate co-operation and sharing of information.

2.86.3 In a further, related, change to FRRP's activities, the Companies (Audit, Investigations and Community Enterprise) Act 2004 amended the Companies Act 1985 allowing HM Revenue & Customs (HMRC) to disclose information to the panel that will assist the panel in its investigations. [CA85 Sec 245D; CA06 Sec

458]. Following this, the panel agreed a memorandum of understanding (MoU) with HMRC. This MoU is more restrictive than the one agreed with the FSA, in line with the provisions of the Act. HMRC may only disclose information to the panel that relates to issues of apparent non-compliance with the Act and accounting standards and it will discuss its concerns with the company concerned and will tell the company that it is contacting the panel. There are no provisions for the panel to disclose any information to HMRC with regard to accounting, tax or any other issues.

2.86.4 Although the FRRP now has an MoU setting out how it will work with the FSA, the FSA itself has traditionally not been involved with enforcement of accounting standards in the UK, since that responsibility has been undertaken by the FRRP. The FSA is part of the Committee of European Securities Regulators (CESR) and since the EU 2005 Regulation applies to listed entities in the EU, CESR has decided to set standards on enforcement of IFRS. CESR issued its first standard on financial information, 'Enforcement of standards on financial information in Europe', in April 2003. The standard sets out 21 high level principles. The main points are that:

- Member States should set up competent independent authorities to take responsibility for enforcement.
- The competent authority should comply with standards on enforcement issued by CESR.
- Enforcers cannot use a purely rotational or reactive approach to selection of information for review: it should at least include a risk-based approach, preferably with sampling or rotation as well.
- Ex-post enforcement is the normal procedure, but this does not preclude pre-clearance. However, *"CESR recognises that it is important that pre-clearance should not result in enforcers becoming standard setters"*.
- Enforcers should be able to take appropriate corrective action, normally by asking for public restatement of errors.
- Co-ordination of decisions taken by the independent authorities will take place.

The principles allow for a body such as the UK FRRP to continue to exist, as the competent independent authority, in the more proactive, risk-based role that it takes. However, the principles apply only to those companies whose securities are admitted (or who are applying for admission) to trading on a regulated market. The FRRP, as the UK's competent independent authority also enforces accounting standards for those entities that are currently within the FRRP's constituency, but are not listed, that is, large private companies.

2.86.5 The formal procedures that the FRRP follows in considering financial statements have twice been revised (in 1993 and 2000) in order to deal with cases more speedily. A further revision took place in 2005 to deal with the changes to the Act and the FRRP's new procedures for selecting financial statements. No outside approval, either from the FRC or from the company's directors, is required for the FRRP's actions. Members of the FRRP are selected by the appointments committee of the FRC, which attempts to ensure that its membership is drawn from the wider business community. Generally, a group of five or more members, drawn from its membership of approximately 20, is assembled to investigate individual cases.

2.87 The FRRP normally attempt to seek a voluntary agreement with the company's directors about any necessary revisions to the financial statements in question. This allows the directors to follow the rules regarding the voluntary revision of defective financial statements rather than those for revision by court order (see chapter 46). However, if the FRRP cannot reach an agreement with the company's directors, it has authority from the Secretary of State for Trade and Industry to use the Act's powers to compel the revision of financial statements if the court finds that they are defective. It also has funds available to it to fund any legal proceedings. To date, all cases examined by the FRRP have been resolved without involving adjudication by the courts.

Companies Act and FRS 18 — accounting principles

Introduction

2.88 Certain basic accounting principles and concepts have been contained in accounting standards since 1971 and in the Act since 1981. SSAP 2, the applicable accounting standard from 1971 to 2000 that dealt with fundamental accounting concepts, was replaced by FRS 18, 'Accounting policies', in December 2000. Changes to SSAP 2 were necessary to reflect updated thinking in the ASB's 'Statement of principles for financial reporting', which was issued in December 1999.

2.89 Many of the accounting principles and rules that are included in accounting standards overlap with those in Part II of Schedule 4 and Schedule 4A to the Companies Act 1985.

2.90 Part II of Schedule 4 to the Companies Act 1985 is divided into four sections:

- Accounting principles. This section sets out some basic principles, which have to some extent been refined in FRS 18:
  - Going concern.
  - Consistency.
  - Prudence and realisation.
  - Accruals basis.
  - Separate valuation of assets and liabilities.

- Historical cost accounting rules. This section covers accounting bases, specific accounting rules, depreciation and amounts necessary to write down cost to a lower net realisable value.

- Alternative accounting rules. This section deals with the accounting treatment of items where the accounting rules applied are designed to take account, in some way, of either inflation or other fluctuations in value (such as, the change in a property's value).

- Fair value accounting rules. This section permits companies to use fair value accounting for certain financial instruments (including derivative financial instruments and certain commodity contracts) in both their individual and consolidated financial statements. Companies that do not use fair value accounting are required to disclose the fair value of any derivative financial instruments that they hold. See further chapter 6.

2.91 Schedule 4A to the Companies Act 1985 deals exclusively with the provisions concerning consolidated financial statements. The Schedule covers, *inter alia*: the elimination of intra-group transactions; acquisition and merger accounting; the treatment of minority interests; interests of subsidiary undertakings excluded from consolidation; and the consolidation of joint ventures and associated companies.

2.92 SSAP 2 featured four fundamental accounting concepts: the going concern concept; the consistency concept; the prudence concept; and the accruals concept. These mirrored the first four accounting principles in the Act. FRS 18 replaced these with a framework that requires accounting policies to be selected against the objectives of relevance, reliability, comparability and understandability (these are the core qualities of financial information set out in the Statement of principles). FRS 18 nevertheless regards the going concern and accruals concepts as distinct concepts that play a pervasive role in financial statements. Prudence and consistency, however, are treated as qualities that contribute to the reliability and comparability, respectively, of financial information.

2.93 The Act permits a company's directors to depart from any of the five accounting principles (that is, going concern, consistency, prudence, accruals and separate valuation) where there are special reasons to do so. If they do so, however, the notes to the financial statements must give particulars of the departure, the directors' reasons for it, and its effect. [CA85 4 Sch 15]. FRS 18 requires disclosures about the particulars, reasons and effect that are equivalent to the 'true and fair override' disclosures in respect of a departure from the requirements of an accounting standard, UITF Abstract or companies legislation (see para 2.41 above). [FRS 18 para 65].

Going concern

2.94 One of the accounting principles contained in the Act is that *"the company shall be presumed to be carrying on business as a going concern"*. [CA85 4 Sch 10]. The presumption can be rebutted if there are special reasons for doing so. The Act does not explain the circumstances that might give rise to special reasons for departing from the going concern principle, but requires the particulars, reasons and effect to be disclosed in the notes.

2.95 FRS 18 is more explicit. An entity should prepare its financial statements on a going concern basis, unless:

- the entity is being liquidated or has ceased trading; or
- the directors either intend to liquidate the entity or to cease trading, or have no realistic alternative but to do so.

[FRS 18 para 21 as amended by FRS 21].

2.96 The going concern concept is reflected in the principles used to determine the amounts recognised in financial statements. Both assets and liabilities are usually recorded on the basis that their carrying amounts will be recovered or discharged in the normal course of business. For example, the carrying values of fixed assets (such as depreciated cost or recoverable amount) reflect costs or values that the business expects to recover from future cash flows relating to their continued use and ultimate disposal. If, however, the business is not a going concern, the fixed assets should be valued at their 'break-up' value.

2.97 The following example illustrates this:

Example

A company that manufactures a particular children's toy has the following fixed assets:

	Cost C'000	Depreciation C'000	Net book value C'000	Break-up value C'000
Factory buildings	500	25	475	350
Plant and machinery	150	75	75	10
	650	100	550	360

The net book value of the fixed assets is C550,000 whereas their break-up value is C360,000. This difference results from two facts. First, in order to adapt the factory from its present use to a different use, it would need to be altered considerably. Secondly, the plant and machinery would have only a scrap value if the company ceased to manufacture the toy.

So long as the company is a going concern, the financial statements will properly reflect the fixed assets at their net book value of C550,000 (assuming their recoverable amount exceeds this figure). If, however, the company ran into severe financial difficulty (so that it could no longer be regarded as a going concern), the fixed assets would have to be written down to their break-up value of C360,000.

2.98 In the circumstances described in paragraph 2.95, FRS 18 states *"the entity should prepare its financial statements on a basis other than that of a going concern"*. [FRS 18 para 21 as amended by FRS 21]. Any financial statements prepared in such circumstances should reflect the amounts recoverable from a quick sale or scrap, that is the current 'break-up' values of assets. Provisions may be necessary for closure costs and losses to the date of termination, including redundancies and penalties for early termination of contracts. In addition, fixed assets and long-term liabilities would need to be reclassified as current assets and liabilities.

2.99 It should be noted that FRS 18 takes an 'entity' view of the going concern basis. A subsidiary that is no longer a going concern may be part of a group that continues to be a going concern. In such circumstances, whereas the subsidiary's financial statements would be prepared on a 'break-up' basis, the consolidated financial statements would be prepared on a going concern basis.

2.100 For all entities, FRS 18 requires the directors to assess the entity's ability to continue as a going concern at the time the financial statements are prepared. [FRS 18 para 23]. If there are significant doubts about the entity's ability to continue as a going concern, details of the uncertainties should be disclosed (see para 2.102). It should be noted, however, that if the directors believe there are significant doubts about the entity's ability to continue as a going concern, the FRS nevertheless requires the financial statements to be prepared on a going concern basis, unless a cessation is intended, occurring or cannot realistically be avoided.

2.101 Events that occur after the balance sheet date may indicate that the entity is no longer a going concern — for example, a deterioration in performance or a breach of loan covenants. In a situation where the directors might have believed at the year end that a company was a going concern, but their post-year end assessment leads them to decide that there is no realistic alternative but to liquidate the entity or to cease trading, rebuttal of the going concern assumption in any financial statements that are prepared after that assessment (including the financial statements in respect of which the directors are making the assessment) is consistent with FRS 21 (IAS 10), 'Events after the balance sheet date'. FRS 21 brings in almost all the requirements of the international standard IAS 10 to UK GAAP, though it retains the disclosures required by FRS 18, 'Accounting policies', in respect of going concern (see para 2.102). FRS 21 does not state which adjustments need to be made where financial statements are not prepared on a going concern basis; it states that if the going concern basis is not appropriate then this requires a fundamental change in the basis of accounting.

Disclosures

2.102 Clearly, apart from the accounting implications, the directors' assessment of the risks of a business becoming insolvent is relevant information for investors. FRS 18 requires disclosure of:

- Any material uncertainties, of which the directors are aware in making their assessment, related to events or conditions that may cast significant doubt upon the entity's ability to continue as a going concern.
- Where the foreseeable future considered by the directors has been limited to a period of less than one year from the date of approval of the financial statements, that fact.
- Where the financial statements are not prepared on a going concern basis, that fact, and the basis on which they are prepared and the reason why the entity is not regarded as a going concern.

[FRS 18 para 61; FRS 21 para 16].

2.103 More detailed guidance on going concern reporting for listed companies is found in the Combined Code and, for auditors, in the auditing standards ISA (UK and Ireland) 570, 'Going concern', and ISA (UK and Ireland) 700, 'The auditor's report on financial statements'. According to ISA (UK and Ireland) 700, where there is a fundamental uncertainty for instance about the validity of the going concern basis, auditors are required to draw attention, by means of an explanatory note, to the note to the financial statements that explains the uncertainty. ISA (UK and Ireland) 570, a more specific auditing standard dealing with going concern, contains a list of factors that may need to be disclosed in relation to such an uncertainty.

2.104 It is generally understood that the going concern concept embodies the assumption that an entity will *"continue in operational existence for the foreseeable future"*. FRS 18 and SSAP 2 both use these words, but neither define what is meant by the 'foreseeable future'. ISA (UK and Ireland) 570 acknowledges that it would be impossible to specify a minimum length for the future period the directors should consider particularly in assessing going concern. The appropriate period of time that the directors should consider will depend on many factors such as the company's reporting and budgeting systems and the nature of the business and industry in which it operates.

2.105 However, the auditing standard considers that, where the directors have paid particular attention to a period less than one year from the date of approval of the financial statements in assessing going concern, they will need to ask management to extend the period covered by their review to 12 months from the balance sheet date. Disclosure in the financial statements is now an explicit requirement of FRS 18.

2.106 The requirement in the Combined Code for directors to confirm that the going concern basis is appropriate has, in effect, changed it from a presumption to an explicit statement for listed companies. Code provision C.1.2 says that *"the directors should report that the business is a going concern, with supporting assumptions or qualifications as necessary"*. This requirement is also contained in the Listing Rules. [LR 9.8.6 R(3)]. The guidance that directors should use to interpret this requirement, 'Going concern and financial reporting: Guidance for directors of listed companies' was issued in November 1994. This guidance recommends that directors should include their statement on going concern in the OFR. However, it also notes that if there are doubts as to the appropriateness of the going concern presumption, then the financial statements may need to reflect any relevant factors in greater detail if they are to show a true and fair view. [Going concern and financial reporting: Guidance for directors of listed companies, para 45]. The Combined Code requirements are discussed in detail in chapter 4 of the Manual of Accounting – IFRS and UK Supplement. As far as unlisted companies and other entities are concerned, FRS 18 does not require disclosure of a positive going concern opinion.

2.107 In some situations, the effect on the balance sheet of ceasing to regard the business as a going concern may be negligible. Nevertheless FRS 18 requires the financial statements to disclose that the entity is no longer regarded as a going concern. Unless there is a statement to the contrary, the FRS allows a reader to *presume* that an entity is carrying on business as a going concern. Consequently, where necessary, the company should state that it has prepared its financial statements on a break-up basis, even if the effect of doing so has not been significant.

Accruals

2.108 The accruals basis of accounting has been a longstanding fundamental accounting concept in SSAP 2 and a basic accounting principle in the Act. FRS 18 introduces an explicit black letter requirement for all entities whose financial statements are intended to give a true and fair view to adopt the accruals basis. [FRS 18 para 26]. This introduction of a black letter requirement is unlikely to have much practical effect as, previously, compliance with the accruals concept has been de facto a true and fair requirement.

2.109 More significantly, however, the FRS has subtly modified the description of the (now mandatory) accruals basis from the definition in SSAP 2 to reflect the 'asset and liability' approach advocated in the ASB's Statement of Principles. SSAP 2 defined the accruals concept as follows: *"revenue and costs are accrued (that is, recognised as they are earned or incurred, not as money is received or paid), matched with one another so far as their relationship can be established or justifiably assumed, and dealt with in the profit and loss account of the period to which they relate... Revenue and profits dealt with in the profit and loss account are matched with associated costs and expenses by including in the same account the costs incurred in earning them..."*.

2.110 FRS 18's description of the accruals basis excludes any reference to matching revenues and costs, because the ASB believes that is an inappropriate accounting principle: *"The accrual basis of accounting requires the non-cash effects of transactions and other events to be reflected, as far as is possible, in the financial statements for the accounting period in which they occur..."*.

The Statement of principles explains that revenue/expenditure matching should be restricted so that only items that meet the definitions of assets and liabilities, and satisfy their respective recognition criteria, should be recognised in the balance sheet. This in turn affects how revenues and costs are recognised in the profit and loss account. Revenue recognition issues are discussed in detail in chapter 7.

2.111 One effect of FRS 18's repositioning of the accruals concept is that the former matching aspect of the accruals concept can no longer be used to justify deferring costs that are not assets. Examples of the purging of revenue/ expenditure matching appear in recent accounting pronouncements: UITF Abstract 24 prevents start-up costs from being deferred and matched with future revenues; FRS 12 prevents gains on the expected disposal of assets from being taken into account in measuring a restructuring provision, even if the sale of assets is part of the restructuring.

Prudence and realisation

2.112 The Act requires a company to use a prudent basis in determining the amount of any item that it includes in its financial statements. [CA85 4 Sch 12]. The Act specifies two particular rules in relation to this. The first is that the profit and loss account may include only those profits that have been realised at the balance sheet date. [CA85 4 Sch 12(a)]. This principle acts as a constraint on the selection of accounting policies in areas such as revenue recognition. The directors can depart from this principle only if it appears to them that there are special reasons. For this purpose, realised profits are defined as:

> *"Such profits ... of the company as fall to be treated as realised in accordance with principles generally accepted, at the time when the accounts are prepared, with respect to the determination for accounting purposes of realised profits..."* [CA85 Sec 262(3); CA06 Sec 853(4)].

2.113 Realisation is, therefore, an accounting rather than a legal concept. In the present legal and accounting framework, companies (and auditors) need guidance on determining realised profits because:

- Directors need to know what profits recognised in the financial statements are realised so that they can determine the amount of profits available for lawful distribution.
- Companies need to comply with paragraph 15 of Schedule 4 if there is a departure from the accounting principle of including in the profit and loss account only those profits that are realised – this requires the effect of the departure to be quantified.
- The law assumes that accountants will be in a position to determine what is meant by realised.

2.114 Before FRS 18, realisation was embedded in the fundamental concept of prudence in SSAP 2. Under SSAP 2, 'realised' effectively meant realised in the form either of cash or of other assets, whose ultimate cash realisation can be assessed with reasonable certainty. Under FRS 18, prudence is no longer a fundamental concept in its own right (see para 2.131), and realisation no longer features as a pre-requisite for the recognition of assets and gains when they are uncertain. Instead, the focus is on whether assets and gains can be evidenced with sufficient reliability. Nevertheless, FRS 18 preserves the status quo with regard to SSAP 2 by stating (albeit as an explanatory note) the underlying principle of what is 'generally accepted' by the accounting profession to be realised, that is *"when realised in the form either of cash or of other assets the ultimate cash realisation of which can be assessed with reasonable certainty"*. [FRS 18 para 28]. The ICAEW and ICAS have developed detailed guidance (Tech 02/07) on determining realised profits in the context of distributions under the Companies Act 1985. This is *de facto* GAAP on what constitutes a realised profit (see chapter 9). The concepts of 'realised' and 'distributable' profits are considered further in chapters 9 and 23.

2.114.1 Furthermore, where a company uses the fair value accounting rules in Section D of Part II of Schedule 4 to the Companies Act 1985, the Act requires that, despite the rule in paragraph 12 of Schedule 4 (whereby only realised profits can be taken to the profit and loss account), changes in the fair value of financial instruments or other assets must be included in the profit and loss account, except in certain specified circumstances (see further chapter 6).

2.115 The second rule that the Companies Act 1985 specifies in connection with the prudence concept relates to liabilities. A company must take account of all liabilities that have arisen in respect of either the financial year in question or a previous financial year. Moreover, they must be included even when they become apparent only in the period between the balance sheet date and the date on which the directors sign the financial statements. [CA85 4 Sch 12(b) as amended by SI 2004/2947]. However, this requirement deals with liabilities relating to the financial year in question, or a previous financial year and does not extend to anticipating liabilities relating to future years. Accounting standards, in particular FRS 3, FRS 7 and FRS 12, contain more specific rules in this area.

Separate valuation

2.116 When a company is determining the aggregate amount of any item, it must determine separately the amount of each individual asset or liability that makes up that item. [CA85 4 Sch 14].

2.117 The treatment of investments in subsidiaries is a good example of the separate valuation principle, although the general principle applies equally to other items, such as stocks. In the parent's own financial statements, investments in subsidiaries will normally be accounted for at cost, less write-downs for any permanent diminution in value. Before the implementation of the separate valuation rules in the Companies Act 1981, investments (and particularly parents' investments in subsidiaries) were sometimes considered as a whole. If one investment had a market value that was less than book value, and all the other investments had an excess of market value over book value that more than compensated, it was argued that the investments as a whole were not overstated at book value and, therefore, no provision against the one overstated investment was necessary.

2.118 However, under the 1985 Act, investments have to be considered individually. By law, a provision must be made against an investment if there is a permanent diminution in value below cost. This applies irrespective of the value and the quality of the other investments.

2.119 The only statutory exception to the separate valuation rule is that tangible assets and raw materials and consumables may, in certain circumstances, be included in the financial statements at a fixed quantity and value. [CA85 4 Sch 25(1)].

2.120 Where there is a legal right of set-off, assets and liabilities should, in some circumstances, be netted because they do not constitute separate assets and liabilities. The rules concerning the set off of assets and liabilities have been reinforced by FRS 5. This is considered in detail in chapter 3.

Accounting policies

2.121 FRS 18's stated objectives are to ensure

- Accounting policies are adopted that are judged by the entity to be the most appropriate for giving a true and fair view. This is a black letter requirement.
- Accounting policies are reviewed regularly and changed when a new policy becomes more appropriate.
- Disclosures are given that enable users to understand the accounting policies adopted and how they have been applied.

[FRS 18 para 1].

2.122 FRS 18 defines accounting policies as the principles, bases, conventions, rules and practices for recognising, selecting measurement bases for, and presenting assets, liabilities, gains, losses and changes to shareholders' funds. [FRS 18 para 4]. Accounting policies are distinguished from estimation techniques (see para 2.139). The FRS aims to clarify the distinction between a change of accounting policy (requiring a prior year adjustment) and a change of estimate (requiring the effects to be dealt with wholly in the current year).

2.123 Examples of accounting policies involving different recognition practices are:

- Capitalising or writing-off interest relating to the construction of fixed assets.
- Capitalising or writing-off development expenditure.

2.124 Measurement bases are defined as monetary attributes such as historical cost, net realisable value or current replacement cost, or a combination of such attributes such as the lower of cost and net realisable value, or recoverable amount (the higher of value in use and net realisable value.) [FRS 18 para 4]. Examples of accounting policies involving different measurement bases are:

- Measuring fixed assets at depreciated historical cost or at current value.
- Measuring deferred tax liabilities on a discounted or undiscounted basis.
- Measuring the cost of fungible stocks on a weighted average or FIFO basis. (FRS 18 explicitly describes these as different measurement bases and, hence, different accounting policies. For non-fungible stocks, they would be different estimation techniques rather than different accounting policies).

2.125 Examples of different presentation policies are:

- Classifying depreciation charges within cost of sales or administrative expenses.
- Reclassifying fixed assets to be disposed of as current assets or retaining them within fixed assets until disposal.

2.126 The Companies Act 1985 requires disclosure of the accounting policies the company has adopted in determining the amounts to be included in the financial statements. [CA85 4 Sch 36]. Legal advice obtained by the FRRP confirmed that this requirement is separate from, and in addition to, the requirement in paragraph 36A of Schedule 4 of the Companies Act 1985 to state in the financial statements whether they have been prepared in accordance with applicable accounting standards and to give the particulars and reasons for any material departures from these standards (see para 2.36). Therefore, in addition to the paragraph 36A of Schedule 4 to the Companies Act 1985 requirement, there must be stated in the financial statements both the accounting policies adopted as the result of applying accounting standards and those, not covered by standards, that a company chooses to adopt.

2.127 FRS 18 requires a description of each of the accounting policies that is material in the context of an entity's financial statements and is more explicit in respect of the level of disclosure required where a particular accounting policy is or is not prescribed in an accounting standard. The level of disclosure should be sufficiently informative to enable users to understand the accounting policies adopted. A 'succinct description' of the policy is sufficient where the policy is prescribed by, and fully described in, an accounting standard, a UITF Abstract or companies legislation. A fuller description is required where no policy is prescribed or where alternative policies are allowed, so that users can make proper comparisons of the financial statements of different entities. [FRS 18 paras 55, 56].

Selecting most appropriate accounting policies

2.128 Where an accounting standard allows more than one accounting policy or where a policy is not specified in an accounting standard, an entity should select the policy that is judged to be *"most appropriate to its particular circumstances for the purpose of giving a true and fair view"*. [FRS 18 para 17]. The most appropriate accounting policies should be selected against the objectives of relevance, reliability, comparability and understandability. [FRS 18 para 30]. These are the core qualities of financial information set out in Chapter 3 of the ASB's Statement of principles (see para 2.195). In addition, when selecting from alternative policies, entities should take into account how the cost of providing information compares with the likely benefit of such information to users. [FRS 18 para 31].

2.129 The first objective is relevance. Relevant information helps users make economic decisions and is provided in time to influence those decisions. It has predictive value (that is, it helps users to evaluate future prospects), confirmatory value (that is, it helps users to confirm or correct their previous evaluations and assessments), or both. The priority given to relevance when selecting accounting policies could be construed as steering entities towards policies that use current values. However, the ASB clarified this issue by stating that FRS 18 does not restrict legitimate options to report assets at historical cost, as provided in FRS 15. [FRS 18 App IV para 34].

2.130 The second objective is reliability. Reliable information has the following qualities:

- Faithful representation of what it purports to represent or could reasonably be expected to represent (that is, accounting policies should make the financial statements reflect the substance of transactions or events).
- Freedom from deliberate or systematic bias.
- Freedom from material error.
- Completeness within the bounds of materiality.
- Prudence under conditions of uncertainty.

[FRS 18 para 35].

2.131 FRS 18 reflects the repositioning of the role of prudence in the Statement of principles. Rather than being a fundamental accounting concept in its own right, prudence is now a quality that contributes to the reliability of financial information where risks and uncertainties are involved. Appropriate accounting policies require more confirmatory evidence about the existence of an asset or a gain than of a liability or loss. Similarly, greater reliability of measurement is expected for assets and gains than for liabilities and losses. For liabilities and losses, prudent estimates should be made but deliberate overstatement should be avoided. This philosophy is applied in more detail in FRS 12. Similarly, deliberate understatement of assets and gains should be avoided. [FRS 18 paras 37, 38].

2.132 The third objective is comparability. FRS 18 places considerable weight on comparability in the selection of accounting policies and, in effect, obliges directors to consider whether particular policies are widely accepted in the industry and how the entity's policies compare. If the entity's policies deviate from accepted industry practices, the directors may need to be able to demonstrate why the entity's policies are judged more appropriate to its particular circumstances than the accepted industry practices. The FRS notes that industry practices will be particularly persuasive if they are set out in a SORP that has been generally accepted by an industry or sector (see also para 2.74). [FRS 18 para 40].

2.133 The fourth objective is understandability. Understandability is achieved if information is presented in a way that enables its significance to be perceived by users that have a reasonable knowledge of business and economic activities and accounting and are willing to study the information with reasonable diligence. [FRS 18 para 41].

2.134 The discussion in FRS 18 of how the objectives of relevance, reliability, comparability and understandability interrelate shows that much judgement is involved, for example as regards assessing the entity's particular circumstances. But there is an implied requirement for boards to be able to demonstrate that they have evaluated the appropriateness of alternative policies where more than one policy could give a true and fair view. Different entities will have different views as to where they are positioned with regard to matters such as trading off relevance and reliability, costs and benefits. The discussion of this aspect of the FRS in the development section (paras 28 to 34 of Appendix IV) attempts to allay some commentators' fears about these requirements by indicating that judgements ought to be valid if they are arrived at in good faith, even if it later becomes clear that a different judgement would have been more appropriate.

Disclosing accounting policies

2.134.1 FRS 18 requires disclosure in the notes to the financial statements of *"a description of each of the accounting policies that is material in the context of the entity's financial statements"*. [FRS 18 para 55(a)].

2.134.2 The purpose of this disclosure is to enable users to understand the accounting policies applied in the preparation of financial statements. It is assumed that users have a reasonable knowledge of business and accounting issues. Consequently, where an entity is applying an accounting policy that is prescribed by an accounting standard, the description need not be detailed. However, where a particular accounting treatment is not prescribed by accounting standards, a more detailed description will be needed. [FRS 18 para 56].

2.134.3 Certain accounting standards permit a choice of accounting policies. For example, FRS 15, 'Tangible fixed assets', permits certain finance costs to be either included in the cost of the asset or recognised as an expense immediately. Here, adequate disclosure is required to make it clear which of the two available options has been chosen.

2.134.4 Where accounting policies are not prescribed by accounting standards, or are specific to the reporting entity (for example, a revenue accounting policy) the disclosure of the policy will need to be detailed.

2.134.5 For some accounting policies, extensive disclosure will be required in order to enable users to understand financial statements. For example, it is expected that an entity's revenue recognition accounting policy would address as a minimum, for each principal source of revenue:

- The timing of the recognition of revenue.
- The measurement of revenue.
- The treatment of discounts offered to customers.
- The method of allocation of revenue between different components of the same transaction (where different recognition policies are applied to the components).

Reviewing and changing accounting policies

2.135 Accounting policies should be reviewed regularly to ensure that they remain the most appropriate. [FRS 18 para 45]. It follows from the general requirement to adopt the most appropriate accounting policies that an accounting policy should not be changed unless the new policy is judged to be more appropriate to the entity's particular circumstances than the old policy. The disclosures required when an accounting policy is changed are covered in chapter 8.

2.136 FRS 18 does not, however, encourage frequent changes to accounting policies, because users would find it more difficult to compare the financial statements from one year to another. Therefore, the impact on comparability is a factor that should be taken into account when considering whether or not a policy should be changed. For example, a change to an accounting policy is probably best avoided if it is likely that a further change will be required in the near future. But consistency is not an end in itself. [FRS 18 para 49].

2.137 FRS 18 makes it clear that the 'most appropriate' test does not require new accounting standards to be adopted ahead of their effective dates. However, it is unlikely that a change to (or adoption of) a new policy could be justified if it conflicts with a new FRS that has not yet become mandatory. [FRS 18 para 46].

2.138 Entities cannot adopt new proposals in exposure drafts or discussion papers if they conflict with existing accounting standards or UITF abstracts, because compliance with existing standards is an overriding requirement. But an entity would need to consider adopting a policy proposed in an exposure draft (that does not conflict with any existing standards) if, say, that policy was already widely adopted in the industry.

Consistency — issues for groups

2.138.1 Where both the consolidated financial statements and the individual financial statements of the parent and subsidiaries are being prepared under UK accounting standards, questions may arise as to whether FRS 18 makes it necessary for consistent accounting policies to be adopted in the different sets of financial statements.

2.138.2 For consolidated financial statements, the Companies Act 1985 and FRS 2 require that, other than in exceptional circumstances, uniform group accounting policies should be used. Where any subsidiaries have adopted different accounting policies in their individual financial statements, appropriate consolidation adjustments should be made to achieve uniformity. But the Act (CA85 4A Sch 3(2)) and FRS 2 paragraph 41 envisage that there may be special reasons for departing from this basic principle and retaining different accounting policies adopted by different entities in the group. In those circumstances, the Act requires that particulars of the departure, the reasons for it and its effect should be disclosed in the notes to the consolidated financial statements. Given the objectives of relevance, reliability, comparability and understandability set out in FRS 18, it is hard to envisage situations where different policies are retained in the consolidated financial statements and could both be considered to be most appropriate, or where the cost of providing information on a consistent basis in the consolidated financial statements would outweigh the benefits to users of consistency. In practice, therefore, it is most unlikely that circumstances will arise that will justify a departure from the principle of adopting uniform accounting policies in consolidated financial statements.

2.138.3 Concerning the individual financial statements of the parent and its subsidiaries, neither the Act nor FRS 2 requires the accounting policies of the parent, the subsidiaries and the group to be the same. Indeed, paragraph 4 of Schedule 4A to the Companies Act 1985 requires any differences between the accounting policies used in the parent's own financial statements and the group financial statements to be disclosed and the reasons given.

2.138.4 Overseas subsidiaries that do not prepare individual financial statements under UK GAAP are beyond the jurisdiction of FRS 18 and so the issue does not arise, unless there are equivalent local requirements for determining the most appropriate accounting policies. Even then, local GAAP (or IFRS) may permit the use of accounting policies that are not permitted by UK GAAP (or vice versa). For example, in UK GAAP, LIFO stock valuations are considered in SSAP 9 to be likely to be incompatible with the requirement to give a true and fair view. Such valuations are, however, allowed by GAAP in some other countries (for example, the US). So there may be good reasons for subsidiaries in different jurisdictions having different policies.

2.138.5 For each entity that reports individually under UK GAAP, the FRS requires the directors to go through the same accounting policy selection process as for the consolidated financial statements. Each entity should select accounting policies that enable its financial statements to give a true and fair view. If more than one policy can give a true and fair view (for example, where the law or accounting standards allow choices), each entity should select the policies that are judged to be most appropriate to their particular circumstances. In so doing, they should balance the objectives of relevance, reliability, comparability and understandability. They should also balance the cost of providing information with its likely benefit to the financial statement users. Since the factors that the parent entity's directors would take into account in determining the most appropriate accounting policies for the group's consolidated financial statements would generally also apply to the individual entities, in most cases it would be reasonable to expect that the same accounting policies would be selected for the group, the parent and the subsidiaries reporting under UK GAAP.

2.138.6 There may be special reasons, however, for adopting different policies. The particular circumstances of different reporting entities, or the cost-benefit equations between different reporting entities and their users, may differ significantly. As an example, comparability with other GAAPs might score highly in the selection of accounting policies for the consolidated financial statements, but might be less of an issue, however, for the users of the individual entities' financial statements and so other factors, such as the effect of different accounting policies on subsidiaries' distributable profits, may weigh more heavily in the selection of the most appropriate accounting policies for them.

2.138.7 Deciding to adopt consistent or different policies to some extent involves the judgements of different boards of directors. If different policies are adopted, an entity should be able to justify this with sound business or commercial reasons.

2.138.8 The issue of whether companies within a group should have consistent accounting policies when they are all reporting under UK GAAP may be distinguished from a situation (as in the UK) where legislation permits entities to use UK GAAP for the parent and subsidiary individual financial statements, with IFRS being used only for the consolidated financial statements (see para 2.22 onwards). In such situations, the use of UK GAAP for the parent and subsidiaries will clearly mean that the policies will not be consistent in many cases with the IFRS policies used in the consolidated financial statements.

Estimation techniques

2.139 FRS 18 defines estimation techniques as: *"The methods adopted by an entity to arrive at estimated monetary amounts, corresponding to the measurement bases selected, for assets, liabilities, gains, losses and changes to shareholders' funds"*. [FRS 18 para 4].

2.140 Estimation techniques are used as a proxy for making best estimates where the values of items being measured are unknown. They might be used to measure the following items:

- Depreciation of fixed assets (methods such as straight-line or reducing balance).
- Provisions (statistical methods such as 'expected value' used to measure large populations).
- After-tax revenue recognition methods for finance leases (such as actuarial-after-tax and investment period methods).
- Cost of stocks or work-in-progress (measurement methods such as FIFO or weighted average cost for non-fungible stocks). Note that for *non-fungible* stocks the change in measurement method is a change of estimate, but for *fungible* stocks the change in measurement method is a change in accounting policy as noted in example 5 in Appendix I to FRS 18.
- Cost of stocks or work-in-progress (methods of attributing overheads).
- Long-term contracts (methods of estimating turnover and profits attributable to the stage of completion).
- Fair values (market value-based or discounted cash flow methods).
- Asset provisions (methods used to calculate provisions for slow-moving stocks or bad debts).
- Sales returns provisions.
- Impairment of fixed assets and goodwill (methods of grouping assets under income generating units for the purpose of impairment reviews).

2.141 The selection of estimation techniques is given almost the same importance as the selection of accounting policies. The selected estimation techniques should enable the financial statements to give a true and fair view and they should be consistent with the requirements of accounting standards, UITF Abstracts and companies legislation. Where a number of estimation techniques are available, an entity should select those estimation techniques that are judged to be most appropriate to its particular circumstances for the purpose of giving a true and fair view. [FRS 18 paras 50, 51]. Cost-benefit considerations also come into play — techniques can be refined to achieve greater accuracy, but unless there is a material improvement in accuracy, the additional cost may not be justified.

2.142 FRS 18 requires a description of significant estimation techniques. Significance should be assessed by considering if the range of reasonable amounts at which an item could be measured is so large that a different amount from within that range could materially affect the view shown by the financial statements. [FRS 18 para 57]. Entities need to consider whether the range of possible estimates is large and how sensitive the numbers are to different assumptions underlying the techniques. The thrust of the emphasis in paragraph 57 appears to be on disclosure where an estimate is sensitive to the underlying assumptions. It also indicates that the description of any significant estimation technique will include disclosure of underlying assumptions to which the measurement of the relevant item is particularly sensitive. For example, where estimates involve present value measurements, the discount rate is likely to be a key assumption.

2.143 Many accounting standards specifically require such disclosures, for example:

- FRS 15, 'Tangible fixed assets', requires depreciation methods (estimation techniques) and the useful economic lives or depreciation rates (underlying assumptions) to be disclosed.
- FRS 10, 'Goodwill and intangible assets', requires methods (estimation techniques) and periods (underlying assumptions) of amortisation of goodwill and intangible assets to be disclosed.
- FRS 11, 'Impairment of fixed assets and goodwill', requires the discount rate underlying an impairment loss measured by reference to value in use (estimation technique) to be disclosed.
- FRS 17, 'Retirement benefits', requires the main financial assumptions used in the measurement of pension scheme liabilities to be disclosed. On 7 December 2006, the ASB published an amendment to FRS 17, 'Retirement benefits', which requires additional disclosure of the principal actuarial assumptions used as at the balance sheet date.
- FRS 12, 'Provisions, contingent liabilities and contingent assets', requires the major assumptions made concerning future events in the measurement of provisions to be disclosed.

Accounting conventions

2.144 All accounting systems depend on the capital maintenance concept adopted, the basis used to value assets and the unit of measurement used. The different options available for each of these components are considered briefly in this section.

Capital maintenance concepts

2.145 Capital maintenance is linked with the measurement of total accounting profit. Disregarding additions to capital or repayments of capital and distributions, accounting profit is the difference between a company's capital at the start of the period and at the end of the period. A company can only be considered to have made a profit if it has increased its net assets, which are represented by its capital, over and above that necessary to maintain its opening capital. Thus total accounting profit can be measured only once a definition has been established as to what capital is to be maintained.

2.146 There are at least two different concepts of capital maintenance: operating capital maintenance and financial capital maintenance. Operating capital maintenance, although it can be measured in a variety of different ways, generally seeks to ensure that the business' physical operating capacity is preserved. Financial capital maintenance attempts to conserve the value of the funds that shareholders have invested in the business. Financial capital maintained can either be the monetary value of capital attributable to shareholders or a value adjusted by a general purchasing power index to maintain capital as a fund of real purchasing power. Consider the following example.

Example

A sole trader starts a business buying and selling second-hand cars. In his first year of trading he buys one car for C1,000 and sells it for C2,000. At the time he sells the car, the cost of buying an equivalent car is C1,200 and general inflation between the dates of buying and selling is 10%. Under monetary capital maintenance, maintenance of the general purchasing power of financial capital and operating capital maintenance the trader's profit and loss account would be as follows:

Capital maintenance concepts	**Financial capital maintenance**		**Operating capital maintenance**
	Monetary capital	**General purchasing power**	
	C	**C**	**C**
Sales	2,000	2,000	2,000
Cost of sales	(1,000)	(1,000)	(1,200)
Operating profit	1,000	1,000	800
Inflation adjustment to opening capital	—	(100)	—
Total gain	1,000	900	800

Monetary financial capital maintenance, which is the basis most commonly used in accounting, takes no account of the effects of inflation. The profit of C1,000 is the amount in excess of the original capital of the business. In the second column the inflation adjustment shows the effect of the general increase in prices on the opening financial capital of C1,000 and seeks to ensure that profit is only measured after preserving the opening capital in the business in terms of its general purchasing power. The profit of C900 leaves capital of C1,100 in the business to maintain its purchasing power. Operating capital maintenance, on the other hand, is concerned with preserving the productive capacity of the business. In this example, this is the trader's ability to replace the item of stock sold. Under operating capital maintenance, the trader has a profit of C800 and capital in the business of C1,200 which is sufficient to purchase a car to begin the next period's trade.

Valuation bases

2.147 The measurement of profit is also affected by the valuation basis chosen. There are a variety of valuation bases, including historical cost, current cost and market value. Valuation bases are considered further in chapter 16.

Units of measurement

2.148 The unit of measurement chosen affects how profit is determined. Reporting can be in nominal currency or in units of constant purchasing power. Financial statements for two different years may be denominated in nominal currency, but because of inflation, the purchasing power of this nominal currency is not the same. The use of a unit of constant purchasing power eliminates these difficulties in comparability. One method is the unit of *current* purchasing power. All non-monetary assets and liabilities relating to dates prior to the reporting date are restated by reference to movements in a general price index, such as the retail price index, into the value of the currency at the reporting date.

Conventions

2.149 Capital maintenance concepts, asset valuation bases, and the units of measurement used can be combined in different ways to create different accounting conventions. Theoretically the options outlined above would result in many different accounting conventions, but not all the combinations are sensible. The more common conventions are summarised below.

Historical cost convention

2.150 The most common accounting convention is the historical cost convention. This convention values assets at their historical cost, operates financial capital maintenance and uses the nominal currency as its unit of measurement. Although this convention is familiar to all accountants, when prices are rising, historical cost accounting may distort reported profits and balance sheet values. Historical cost accounting, being simple and relatively well understood, is useful for preparing stewardship accounts. It is perhaps less useful for making investment decisions or decisions about amounts to distribute. In the example in paragraph 2.146 above, if the trader had taken the profit of C1,000 for his own use, there would not be sufficient funds in the business for it to continue to trade at the same level.

Modified historical cost convention

2.151 Sometimes the historical cost convention is modified by the revaluation of certain fixed assets. Modified historical cost accounting operates financial capital maintenance and uses the nominal currency as its unit of measurement, but certain fixed assets, usually land and buildings, are included at a valuation above historical cost. This gives some indication of the value to the business of some of the assets employed. The unrealised gains as a result of revaluing assets are generally not recognised in the profit and loss account. This suggests that the gain is an element of the capital of the business that must be retained in order to maintain the business' operating capacity, although no formalised attempt is made to employ operating capital maintenance. In addition, not all companies revalue their assets and, in the past, not all companies that revalued their assets did so on a regular basis. Therefore, comparability between different companies is reduced and, if valuations are allowed to become out of date, their usefulness as an indication of the value of the assets to the business diminishes. The ASB has considered these problems when it developed FRS 15, which is discussed in chapter 16.

Fair value convention

2.151.1 Recent years have seen accounting move towards something that might be termed the 'fair value convention'. Although it has never been explicitly stated in any framework it is clear from recent standards that the basis of accounting is changing. The fair value convention may be said to have the following features: it is balance sheet based, focusing on performance being the result of changes in the carrying values of assets and liabilities rather than a matching between income and expenditure. It focuses on the fair values of assets and liabilities. Fair value is defined in FRS 25 (IAS 32), 'Financial instruments: Disclosure and presentation', as *"the amount for which an asset could be exchanged, or a liability settled, between knowledgeable, willing parties in an arm's length transaction"*. [FRS 25 para 11].

2.151.2 Fair values are 'current' values at any balance sheet date. They are, in essence, based on discounted future cash flows. Proponents of fair values argue that their use gives users of financial statements more useful information, as it is more up to date and reflective of the real value and cost of an entity's assets and liabilities at any point in time. There are difficulties, however, in the practical application of this apparently simple concept, both in terms of its definition and its measurement.

2.151.3 Another feature of the fair value model is that changes in fair value are recorded through the profit and loss account. A full fair value model, in which all assets and liabilities would be fair valued, perhaps including internally generated intangible assets, is some way off. Not least this is because the convention is already at the edge of the sophistication of markets and of most financial statement users and preparers. The convention has, however, come closer to being achieved in the past ten years and the IASB has been a particular advocate. Standards that incorporate the use of fair values include IAS 19 on post-retirement benefits, IAS 39 on financial instruments, IAS 41 on biological assets and IFRS 2, which deals with share-based payment.

2.151.4 In terms of the fair value convention becoming part of UK GAAP, IFRS 2 has been introduced as FRS 20 and much of IAS 39 has been introduced as FRS 26 (although it is not yet compulsory for all companies). To allow this to take place the legal framework of accounting has had to change, with permission to fair value being implemented by the Fair Value Directive (see para 2.20.2).

Current purchasing power

2.152 The current purchasing power (CPP) convention also values assets at their historical cost and operates financial capital maintenance. CPP, however, uses a unit of constant purchasing power rather than the nominal currency for measurement. Therefore, all non-monetary items in the financial statements, including capital, are restated by reference to a general price index. While this maintains capital in terms of what shareholders can do with their funds in the economy as a whole, the general price index used may not move the same way as the input prices specific to the company. Therefore, the resulting asset values may bear no relationship to their current value to the business; moreover, the capital maintained may be either too much or too little to maintain the operating capacity of the business. In the example in paragraph 2.146 above, the increase in the general price index was less than the increase specific to second hand cars. As a result, if the trader had taken all the CPP profit out of the business, he would not have had sufficient capital to replace his stock.

2.153 The principal current example of the use of CPP accounting is in the countries that experience hyper-inflation. UITF Abstract 9, 'Accounting for operations in hyper-inflationary economies', and FRS 24 (IAS 29), 'Financial reporting in hyper-inflationary economies', give guidance in this area (see also chapter 7).

Current cost accounting

2.154 Current cost accounting conventions value assets at their current value to the business. Although this is often combined with operating capital maintenance and measurement in nominal currency it can also be combined with financial capital maintenance and units of constant purchasing power. Since combining current costs with nominal currency usually results in useful information, the additional complexity introduced by using units of constant purchasing power is often not warranted except in trend information. Current cost operating profit shows the current trading margin achieved by the business since it charges the costs incurred at the prices applying when the sales were made. Put another way, it takes inflationary 'holding gains' out of the measurement of income. It gives an indication of the companies' ability to generate profits from its current operations and also maintains its current operating capacity. In the operating capital maintenance example in paragraph 2.146, the operating profit is lower than under financial capital maintenance. This allows sufficient capital to be retained to replace stock and continue trading and may also give a more forward-looking perspective on future profits.

Frameworks for setting accounting standards

Background to the frameworks

2.155 The tradition in many countries, such as most of continental Europe, is that accounting rules should be made by parliaments or committees under government control. Given that accounting is closely related to the collection of tax, the distribution of profits and the protection of creditors, there are clear arguments for this control of accounting by the state in the public interest. This tradition can be seen at work in the EU, which uses governmental processes which lead to harmonising laws on accounting, such as the Companies Acts 1981 and 1989.

2.156 By contrast, the tradition in the English-speaking world is to see accounting as a technical tool designed to be commercially useful. If the capital market needs extensive audited accounting information, it will be in the interests of the relevant companies to provide it. Consequently, such rules as are necessary should be created to enable, rather than to control, accounting.

2.157 Of course, even in this tradition, governments may feel obliged to intervene in accounting, in order to protect the public interest, such as creditors or the customers of banks. The intervention usually follows a crisis. For example, compulsory audit of banks was introduced in Britain soon after the collapse of the City of Glasgow Bank in 1878. Most spectacularly, the Securities and Exchange Commission in the US was created in order to protect investors after the Wall Street crash of 1929.

2.158 Despite many such interventions, the creation of accounting rules (though not necessarily the enforcement of them) is still largely in the hands of accountants rather than governments throughout the English-speaking world. At first, the 'rules' were unpromulgated 'best practice', but gradually the accountancy profession wrote the rules down; for example, as 'Accounting research bulletins' from the 1930s in the US or as 'Recommendations' from the 1940s in the UK.

2.159 However, this system gradually came to be criticised on the grounds that the interests of the professional rule makers (mostly representatives of large audit firms and large companies) are different from the public interest, in particular the preparers and users of financial statements. The criticisms reached a crescendo in the US in the early 1970s. This led to two investigations set up by the profession: the Wheat Committee and the Trueblood Committee.

2.160 Wheat recommended that standard setting should be taken away from the profession and given to an independent body. Trueblood recommended that a vital philosophical support for an independent standard setter should be a 'conceptual framework'. It was argued that, in the absence of democratic election, the authority of standard setters needs to rest on independence backed up by due process, openness of procedure and an overt statement of objectives and fundamental principles.

2.161 These recommendations led to the setting up of the Financial Accounting Standards Board (FASB) in 1973 and to its major project which led to the 'Statements of financial accounting concepts'. Parts of a conceptual framework had been published by the FASB's predecessor, the Accounting Principles Board, in the 1960s, but a full framework was not published until the 1980s.

2.162 Meanwhile, in the UK, the ASC had been established in 1969, with no overt conceptual framework. The ASC was often criticised for standards that were not coherent or consistent. As the authority of the ASC came increasingly into question in the 1980s, some attention was given to conceptual frameworks. Indeed, in 1989, the ASC acknowledged the existence of the IASC's 'Framework for the preparation and presentation of financial statements' which had been published in that year and which clearly derives from the FASB's framework, to some extent *via* the Australian version. The IASC's framework, which has been subsequently adopted by the IASB, is covered in chapter 2 of the Manual of Accounting – IFRS for the UK.

2.163 The criticisms of standard-setting in the UK in the late 1980s were similar to those in the US in the early 1970s, and the solutions were similar also. Consequently, when the ASB was set up in the UK in 1990, it was no surprise that it immediately began to work on a 'Statement of principles' which is very close to the documents mentioned above.

[The next paragraph is 2.191.]

The ASB's Statement of principles

2.191 The ASB's Statement of principles for financial reporting is based on the IASB's framework. The statement sets out the ground rules that the ASB will follow when developing new standards. It is also intended to help preparers and auditors resolve issues that are not covered by specific rules.

2.192 There were originally seven chapters in the ASB's statement. These were issued in draft from 1991 onwards. A complete exposure draft of the statement was issued in November 1995. Some parts of the exposure draft presented a fairly radical agenda for the future direction of financial reporting. However, the ASB promised that changes will be evolutionary rather than revolutionary. In 1999 the ASB issued a revised draft of the Statement of principles, which was largely a re-write rather than a re-think. That exposure draft was accepted more quietly than the previous one and the final version was published in December 1999. The Statement of principles is not an accounting standard and does not override the requirements of any accounting standard or the law. In fact, there are some significant conflicts between the principles as set out in the statement and companies legislation in the UK. The eight chapters in the final Statement, which are discussed in the following paragraphs, are:

- Objective of financial statements.
- The reporting entity.
- Qualitative characteristics of financial information.
- Elements of financial statements.
- Recognition in financial statements.
- Measurement in financial statements.
- Presentation of financial information.

- Accounting for interests in other entities.

Objective

2.193 The ASB identifies present and potential investors as the target (or the proxy for other targets) of financial statements. The ASB has included in the objective the role of financial statements for assessing the stewardship of management as well as their usefulness for making economic decisions. The ASB specifically identifies information on 'financial adaptability' as being useful for economic decisions. Financial adaptability is described as the ability of an enterprise to alter its cash flows so that it can respond to unexpected needs or opportunities.

The reporting entity

2.194 The focus of this chapter is on determining the boundary of the reporting entity, particularly in the case of group accounts. This boundary is determined by the extent of the entity's direct and indirect control.

- Control is stated to have two aspects: the ability to deploy economic resources and the ability to benefit or suffer from their deployment.
- Direct control is said to determine the boundary of single entity accounts, while direct plus indirect control determines the boundary of the group accounts.
- The principles and discussion in this chapter is expanded upon in chapter 8 of the Statement, which deals with interests in other entities.

Qualitative characteristics

2.195 The ASB identifies relevance and reliability as the primary characteristics relating to the content of financial information. Relevance has predictive and confirmatory aspects and requires information to be provided in time to influence decisions. Reliability requires faithful representation (which requires an emphasis on substance), neutrality (that is, freedom from bias), prudence, freedom from material error and completeness.

2.196 Primary characteristics relating to how information is presented in financial statements, which follow from the above two, are comparability (which includes consistency and disclosure of policies and changes in them) and understandability.

2.197 The ASB recognises the need to trade relevance off against reliability, partly by considering timeliness and the most appropriate measurement base. Nevertheless, the importance of relevance seems to imply a move towards current values rather than historical costs.

Materiality

2.198 Materiality sets the threshold for determining whether an item is relevant. The Statement of principles explains materiality as follows: *"An item of information is material to the financial statements if its misstatement or omission might reasonably be expected to influence the economic decisions of users of those financial statements, including their assessments of management's stewardship. Whether information is material will depend on the size and nature of the item in question judged in the particular circumstances of the case"*. [SoP para 3.30 and 3.31].

2.199 An item that is not material is not relevant, it cannot influence the decisions of a user and need not be reported in financial statements. Indeed, if immaterial items are reported in financial statements, they can interfere with decision making because they may obscure the relevant information amid excessive detail. However, determining what is material is a matter of professional judgement and it would be inappropriate to set fixed monetary limits or rules.

2.200 In view of the increasing emphasis on materiality due to the Statement of principles and the public interest in materiality as a result of certain FRRP decisions, the Financial Reporting Committee of the ICAEW issued a statement in December 1996 which replaced the existing guidance on materiality in the ICAEW Members' Handbook. The statement, TECH 32/96, contains guidance to help those preparing financial statements decide what information is material, in the context of the principle that an item is material if it could influence users' economic decisions.

2.201 The statement stresses that any guidelines on determining what is material cannot substitute for careful consideration by preparers of how information could influence users' economic decisions such as whether to hold or sell investments or whether to reappoint or replace management. Judgements should be based on the needs of knowledgeable and diligent investors who are reasonable in their use of financial information.

2.202 The statement considers that there are three aspects to consider when deciding whether an item is material and then discusses each aspect in turn. These aspects are:

- Size. Whilst the monetary value of items needs to be taken into account, materiality can never be judged purely on the basis of absolute size, and no specific rule of thumb tests are recommended. In some cases size may in fact be irrelevant, for example, where the quality of management stewardship or corporate governance are at issue.

- Nature. Consideration needs to be given to the events or transactions giving rise to the item as well as their legality, sensitivity, normality and potential consequences. In addition, the identity of the parties involved in the events or transactions and the accounts captions and disclosure affected may also impact on users' decisions.

- Circumstances. When preparers consider the potential impact of information on users, they should not take a narrow view of the financial statements for a single period. They will often need to modify their views on the materiality of an item in the light of comparative figures, expected future trends, the financial statements of comparable entities and other information relating to the economic and industry background.

2.203 The statement emphasises management's responsibility by encouraging companies to develop internal guidelines on assessing materiality. These would provide relatively objective rebuttable presumptions against which subsequent judgements about particular situations can be gauged. The statement suggests guidelines can be developed by addressing the following questions:

- Who are the relevant users?
- What are their decision-making needs?
- For a given item, what is the appropriate context for assessing its materiality?
- In what range of values do items become critical in terms of materiality?
- How should particular items in these critical ranges be decided and reported?

2.204 Some practical examples are given of situations where preparers should be particularly sensitive in their judgements because critical thresholds are reached. These are where trends reverse, profits become losses, technical insolvency occurs, compliance with debt covenants is in doubt or where it is known that individuals are deciding whether or not to buy or sell shares.

Elements

2.205 The ASB identifies seven elements: assets; liabilities; ownership interest; gains; losses; contributions from owners; and distributions to owners. All the other definitions depend on those of asset and liability which are:

> *"Assets are rights or other access to future economic benefits controlled by an entity as a result of past transactions or events."*

> *"Liabilities are obligations of an entity to transfer economic benefits as a result of past transactions or events."*

2.206 These definitions are also repeated in FRS 5, which is considered in chapter 3. Ownership interest is the residual net assets.

2.207 The language used by the ASB is some what unusual. 'Gains', for this purpose includes revenues and other income, while 'losses' includes expenses write-downs and other losses.

2.208 Leaving aside transfers to and from owners in their capacity as owners (for example, dividends), gains and losses can be defined as increases or decreases in ownership interest.

2.209 The definitions still leave room for interpretation and may in due course lead to changes in specific accounting standards. For example, it is not altogether clear what sort of element is the deferred income which is shown as a credit balance as a result of a government grant.

Recognition

2.210 An element (as defined above) should be recognised when there is sufficient evidence (for example, as a result of a transaction or a contract) that there has been a change in assets or liabilities which can be measured with sufficient reliability. As with the previous chapters of the statement of principles, there are implicit challenges to existing practices. For example, are SSAP 21's operating leases recognisable assets and liabilities? They appear to fit the definitions of the elements and to meet the 'evidence' threshold for recognition. Yet the discussion of unperformed contracts in the Statement indicates that such rights and obligations result in a net position that will not require recognition until an imbalance between these rights and obligations arises. The appropriate treatment of unperformed contracts is the subject of much debate internationally and has yet to be resolved.

2.211 Chapter 5 of the Statement of principles also deals with de-recognition, (which should occur when the asset or liability has been eliminated or when the criteria for recognition is no longer met) and revenue recognition in the case of a transaction involving the provision of services or goods for a net gain, (which requires the occurrence of the critical event in the operating cycle involved). The discussion of revenue recognition is confusing and appears to be an attempt to fit existing long-standing accounting practices, where revenue recognition is linked to the concepts of matching and realisation, into the accounting framework adopted by the Statement, where revenue recognition is linked to the recognition and measurement of assets and liabilities.

Measurement

2.212 Chapter 6 of the Statement of principles describes the pros and cons of historical cost versus current value accounting. The ASB, in the original draft Statement, declared its hand by stating that practice should develop by evolving in the direction of greater use of current values, which it believes are more relevant than historical costs for depicting a company's resources, subject to reliability and cost-benefit considerations. Criticism of this by respondents to the first draft Statement clearly had an impact on the ASB, as their preference for current values is much more veiled in the final Statement. Indeed, according to this Statement, the ASB now apparently supports the mixed measurement system currently used in practice, whilst noting the potential for evolution towards greater use of current values as markets develop and current values become more relevant and reliable.

Presentation

2.213 Chapter 7 of the Statement of principles examines considerations that should guide the presentation of financial statements: communication, structure, aggregation and classification.

2.214 The chapter discusses each of the primary financial statements. For example, in the statement of financial performance (such as the profit and loss account or the statement of recognised gains and losses) components should be classified by reference to a combination of function and the nature of the item, amounts that are affected in different ways by changes in economic conditions or business activity should be distinguished, as should items that are unusual in amount or incidence or that have special characteristics. In the balance sheet, for example, the entity's resource structure and its financial structure should be delineated.

Accounting for interests in other entities

2.215 The last chapter expands the discussion in chapter 2 on the reporting entity to briefly cover consolidated accounts, equity accounting and accounting for investments where there is little or no control. Essentially, this chapter contains an overview of how to apply the principles set out in chapter 2, based upon present accounting practice.

Presentation

2.213 Chapter 7 of the Statement of principles examines considerations that should guide the presentation of financial statements–communication, structure, aggregation and classification.

2.214 The chapter discusses each of the primary financial statements. For example, in the statement of financial performance (such as the profit and loss account or the statement of recognised gains and losses) components should be classified by reference to a combination of function and the nature of the item; amounts that are affected in different ways by changes in economic conditions or business activity should be distinguished, as should items that are unusual in amount or incidence or that have special characteristics. In the balance sheet, for example, the entity's resource structure and its financial structure should be delineated.

Accounting for interests in other entities

2.215 The last chapter expands the discussion in chapter 2 on the reporting entity to briefly cover consolidated accounts, equity accounting and accounting for investments where there is little or no control. Essentially, this chapter contains an overview of how to apply the principles set out in chapter 2, based upon present accounting practice.

Chapter 3

Reporting the substance of transactions

	Page
Scope and basic principles	3001
Scope	3001
Interaction with the Act and accounting standards	3003
Principles of FRS 5	3005
Objective	3005
Identifying and recognising assets and liabilities	3006
Analysing complex transactions	3007
Severance of legal title	3007
Linkage with other transactions	3007
Options and conditions	3008
Identifying assets and liabilities	3009
Assets	3009
Liabilities	3010
Recognition of assets and liabilities	3010
Transactions in previously recognised assets	3010
Continued recognition	3012
Full derecognition	3012
Partial derecognition	3013
Insurance	3016
Linked presentation	3017
General rules	3017
Conditions in detail	3019
Linking part of the finance	3021
Profit recognition	3022
Offset rules	3023
Accounting for quasi-subsidiaries	3024
Conflict with the law?	3025
Accounting treatment	3025
Linked presentation of quasi-subsidiaries	3027
Subordinated debt and credit enhancement	3028
Securitising in a legal subsidiary	3028
Accounting treatment in the parent's financial statements	3028
Disclosure	3029
Application notes	3031
Consignment stock	3032
Sale and repurchase agreements	3032
Principal sources of benefits and risks	3032
Accounting treatment	3035
Examples of required analysis	3037
Debt factoring	3040

Main benefits and risks. 3041
Accounting treatment 3042
Derecognition. 3042
Linked presentation. 3043
Separate presentation 3044
Examples of required analysis 3044
Securitised assets 3046
Originator's financial statements 3048
Disclosure requirements 3049
Group's financial statements 3050
Disclosure requirements 3051
Interest rate swaps. 3054
Revolving assets. 3055
Reinvestment period 3056
Repayment period 3057
Multi-originator programmes. 3059
Example of required analysis. 3059
Loan transfers 3061
Disclosure requirements 3064
Private Finance Initiative and Public Private Partnership 3065
Contract separability. 3066
How to apply FRS 5. 3068
Property factors to be considered 3070
Demand risk. 3070
Third party revenues. 3071
Who determines the nature of the property. 3071
Penalties for under-performance or non-availability. 3072
Changes in relevant costs 3072
Obsolescence and changes in technology 3073
Contract termination and residual value risk. 3073
Summary of risks to consider. 3074
Accounting treatment 3076
Assets recognised by the operator — accounting by the operator 3076
Assets recognised by the operator — accounting by the purchaser 3076
Assets recognised by the purchaser — accounting by the operator 3076
Assets recognised by the purchaser — accounting by the purchaser 3078
Use of SSAP 9 3080
Pre-contract costs. 3080
Contributions — accounting by the operator 3083
Contributions — accounting by the purchaser 3084
Accounting for residuals — asset on the operator's balance sheet 3085
Accounting for residuals — asset on the purchaser's balance sheet 3086
Methods of amortising the financial asset 3086
Example of quantitative analysis. 3087
Practical issues 3090
Partial derecognition 3091
Insubstance debt defeasance. 3092
Repurchase agreements — Repos 3093

Contract purchase arrangements 3095
Stock lending 3096
Bed and breakfast transactions 3099
Purchase commitments 3100
Linked presentation and the cash flow statement 3101
Take-or-pay contracts 3101

Chapter 3

Reporting the substance of transactions

Scope and basic principles

Scope

3.1 This chapter deals with the requirements of FRS 5, 'Reporting the substance of transactions'. FRS 5 applies to all transactions of a company, subject only to the exclusion of certain specific transactions given in FRS 5 paragraph 12 (see further para 3.2) and transactions to which the recognition and derecognition of financial assets and financial liabilities within the scope of FRS 26 apply (see further para 3.6) FRS 5 also applies to transactions undertaken by other unincorporated entities, such as partnerships, where their financial statements are required to give a true and fair view. However, by 'transaction' the FRS means both single transactions and also arrangements that cover a series of transactions that are designed to have an overall commercial effect. [FRS 5 para 11].

3.2 No exemptions for particular types of undertaking are given in the FRS, although subsequent to its issue both insurance brokers and insurance companies have been exempted from FRS 5's requirements in relation to specific transactions. The FRS does, however, exclude certain specific transactions from its scope, which are:

- Forward contracts.
- Futures contracts.
- Foreign exchange.
- Interest rate swaps.
- Expenditure commitments.
- Orders.
- Contracts for differences.
- Employment contracts.

[FRS 5 para 12].

3.3 All of the transactions listed above are contracts for future performance and have been removed by the ASB from the scope of FRS 5 except in situations where they form part of a transaction (or series of transactions) that falls within the standard's scope. The standard cites as an example an interest rate swap forming part of a securitisation. In this case the swap is an integral component of the overall securitisation transaction which needs to be considered under the standard's rules (see further para 3.156), whereas a swap that is merely part of a company's treasury management does not come within the standard's scope.

3.4 Expenditure commitments and orders fall outside the scope until they are either delivered or paid for, whichever happens first. Contracts for differences, which are contracts where a net amount will be paid or received based on the movement in a price or an index, also fall outside the standard's scope.

3.5 Employment contracts are sometimes termed 'executory contracts' and generally involve agreements where performance by both parties lies in the future. Unless a person's salary is paid in advance, no asset is recognised in the employer's balance sheet in respect of the future benefit of the employee's service. Similarly, no liability is recognised in respect of the future payment that the employer has contracted to make. There is a remote contingent liability in relation to the person's employment, but this will only crystallise into a liability, for example, when the decision is taken to make the person redundant and would only be provided for where necessary in accordance with the requirements of FRS 12, 'Provisions, contingent liabilities and contingent assets'.

3.6 On 25 April 2006 the ASB published an amendment to FRS 26, 'Financial instruments: Measurement – Recognition and derecognition'. This amendment brings the recognition and derecognition requirements of IAS 39, 'Financial instruments: Recognition and measurement' into FRS 26 and changes the title of FRS 26 to 'Financial instruments: Recognition and measurement'. The amendment is effective for accounting periods commencing on or after 1 January 2007, with earlier adoption permitted. Upon implementation of the amendment, entities within FRS 26's scope should apply the derecognition requirements in FRS 26 to financial assets and liabilities (see further chapter 6) and the derecognition principles of FRS 5 to non-financial assets and liabilities. [FRS 5 para 13B]. Entities that are not within the scope of FRS 26 should continue to apply FRS 5 to the recognition and derecognition of both *financial and non-financial* assets and liabilities.

3.7 Upon implementation of the amendment, the following transactions dealt with in FRS 5 fall within FRS 26's scope:

- Debt factoring.
- Securitisation of assets.
- Loan transfers.
- Sale and repurchase agreements, where the transaction falls within the scope of paragraphs 14 to 42 of FRS 26.

[The next paragraph is 3.42.1]

Interaction with the Act and accounting standards

3.42.1 The Companies Act requirement that a company's and a group's financial statements must give a 'true and fair view' is fundamental. It overrides the detailed rules on the form and content of company, and group, financial statements and the Act's other requirements concerning matters to be included in the financial statements. The Act requires that, if necessary, either additional disclosure should be made or, in special circumstances, the financial statements should depart from the detailed rules

3.42.2 Where the 'true and fair override' is used to depart from the Act's other provisions, the financial statements must disclose, in accordance with sections 226A of the Companies Act 1985 (section 396 of the Companies Act 2006) and 227A of the Companies Act 1985 (section 404 of the Companies Act 2006), particulars of the departure, the reasons for it, and its effect. FRS 5, does not require the transaction's legal form to be disclosed in the notes to the financial statements (where that is different from its substance), although there is a general disclosure requirement which requires the financial statements to disclose enough information for users to understand the transaction's commercial effect.

3.43 Where transactions fall within FRS 5's scope and also directly within the scope of other accounting standards or legislation (for example, leasing) the FRS states that the standard or legislation that contains the more specific provisions should be applied. [FRS 5 para 13]. But there is a subtle implication here because the provisions of that more specific standard or legislation have to be applied to the *transaction's substance* and not to its legal form and for that purpose the general provisions of FRS 5 apply. [FRS 5 para 3].

3.44 There are two areas where these provisions become particularly important. The first is with pension schemes where clearly FRS 17 has specific provisions that deal with how companies should account for pension obligations. Although FRS 17 does not deal specifically with the consolidation of pension schemes into the employing company's financial statements, the ASB contends that such schemes should not be consolidated as quasi-subsidiaries (see further para 3.100). [FRS 5 para 3]. FRS 5 does, however, apply to certain pension scheme transactions, for example, where a scheme enters into a sale and leaseback arrangement for the employing company's properties.

3.45 The second area where there is considerable interaction is leasing. Generally for stand-alone leases the more specific provisions will be contained in SSAP 21. But it is now even clearer that the classification of such leases as either finance or operating should be made according to their substance. This should have been the case under SSAP 21, but in practice there has tended to be undue reliance on arithmetical analysis and insufficient attention to the substance. That is, FRS 5 confirms that it is not acceptable to look only to the 90 per cent test, but that all other aspects of the transaction must also be considered to determine the transaction's substance. The term 'stand-alone' refers to simple leasing arrangements, which are not complicated by options and buy-back clauses. However, for some leases, an example being sale and leaseback arrangements where there is also an option for the lessee to repurchase the asset, FRS 5's provisions are more specific. Generally, more complex leasing arrangements where there are a number of elements will fall within FRS 5's scope. [FRS 5 para 3]. Indeed this was confirmed by an FRRP ruling issued in February 1997 in respect of the accounting treatment of a sale and leaseback transaction undertaken by Associated Nursing Services plc (see further para 3.128.1). Table 3.1 below illustrates a situation where a group has brought leasing transactions back on balance sheet where the group retains the risks and rewards of ownership.

Table 3.1 — Inchcape plc — Annual Report & Accounts — 31 December 1994 accounting policies (extract)

b Basis of Group accounts (extract)

Following the adoption of Financial Reporting Standard 5 (FRS 5) Reporting the Substance of Transactions comparative figures in the balance sheet, cash flow statement and relevant notes to the financial statements have been adjusted but there was no material effect on reported profit.

notes to the accounts (extract)	Freehold and leasehold land and buildings	Plant, machinery and equipment	Total
14 Fixed assets-tangible assets (extract)	**£m**	**£m**	**£m**
Cost or valuation at 1st January 1994	422.0	451.1	873.1
FRS 5 adjustment	–	40.3	40.3
Cost or valuation at 1st January 1994 — restated	422.0	491.4	913.4
Exchange adjustments	(2.6)	0.8	(1.8)
Assets of subsidiaries acquired	22.1	32.1	54.2
Assets of subsidiaries sold	(26.8)	(43.0)	(69.8)
Additions	18.1	81.0	99.1
Disposals	(9.1)	(72.4)	(81.5)
Transfers (including assets held for resale)	(10.4)	8.8	(1.6)
Cost or valuation at 31st December1994	413.3	498.7	912.0

The book value of plant, machinery and equipment includes £36.5m (1993 — £22.8m) in respect of assets held under finance leases, and £Nil (1993 — £27.2m) of assets relating to contract hire operations. The FRS 5 adjustment relates to motor vehicles leased to customers where the Group retains the risk and rewards of ownership, and includes £34.0m in respect of KCVR UK which was sold in December 1994.

3.46 This means that, for the time being, straightforward operating leases will remain off the lessee's balance sheet. There is, however, a conflict between the partial derecognition rules included in the standard (see further para 3.67) and SSAP 21. For example, if the partial derecognition rules were applied to operating leases, the effect would be that the lessor would derecognise the whole asset, but would recognise new assets representing the entitlement to a stream of receivables and a residual asset. This conflict will remain unless SSAP 21 is revised to fall in line with FRS 5. In the meantime, the provisions of SSAP 21 are generally more specific for a straightforward lease. For an example of how the interaction between FRS 5 and SSAP 21 applies see examples 1 and 2 in paragraph 3.78.

Principles of FRS 5

Objective

3.47 The standard's overriding objective is to ensure that the substance of an entity's transactions is reported in its financial statements. That means that the commercial effect of the undertaking's transactions and any resulting assets, liabilities, gains or losses should be faithfully represented in its financial statements. [FRS 5 para 1].

3.48 The objective is simply stated and the standard's provisions are simple to apply where the transaction is itself simple in nature. However, determining how to account in practice for more complex transactions in accordance with their substance is fraught with difficulties. The nature of the accounting decisions made will inevitably be subjective and the resulting accounting treatment will differ depending upon the perception of the transaction's substance and its effect in practice. The answer to whether an item is on or off balance sheet under the standard will not necessarily be clear even after analysing the transaction in detail following the standard's guidance. The standard places particular emphasis on the transaction's *commercial effect in practice*. It is not adequate to review the transaction from a theoretical standpoint; it is what is likely to happen in practice and what actually happens in practice that is important.

3.49 The commercial effect in practice of a complex transaction might change from year to year as the actual or likely economic outcome becomes clearer. At the outset, the transaction has to be analysed and the likely outcome in practice determined in accordance with the facts and best estimates where future factors of the transaction are uncertain. After the transaction is initially recorded in accordance with its substance, the actual or likely outcome will have to be monitored in future accounting periods to determine whether the transaction's substance changes in practice. Where there is a subsequent change in the transaction's substance, that change will have to be accounted for when it becomes apparent.

3.50 The basic principles concerning reporting the substance of transactions can be summarised under five heads:

- Identifying and recognising assets and liabilities.
- Transactions in previously recognised assets.
- Linked presentation for non-recourse transactions.
- Offset rules.
- Accounting for quasi-subsidiaries.

Each of these is explained in the paragraphs below.

Identifying and recognising assets and liabilities

3.51 FRS 5's identification and recognition principles can be illustrated in a flow diagram (see diagram 1). As can be seen from the diagram, the steps to recognise an asset or liability are relatively straightforward in principle. It is simply a matter of analysing the relevant transactions to ascertain whether they give rise to new assets or liabilities that need to be recognised on the balance sheet or give rise to changes in existing assets and liabilities. Once an asset or liability has been identified and there is sufficient evidence that it exists *and* it can be measured sufficiently reliably, it should be recognised in the financial statements. [FRS 5 para 20]. These steps are considered in more detail below.

Diagram 1 — Recognising the substance of transactions

The numbers in square brackets refer to paragraphs of the standard.

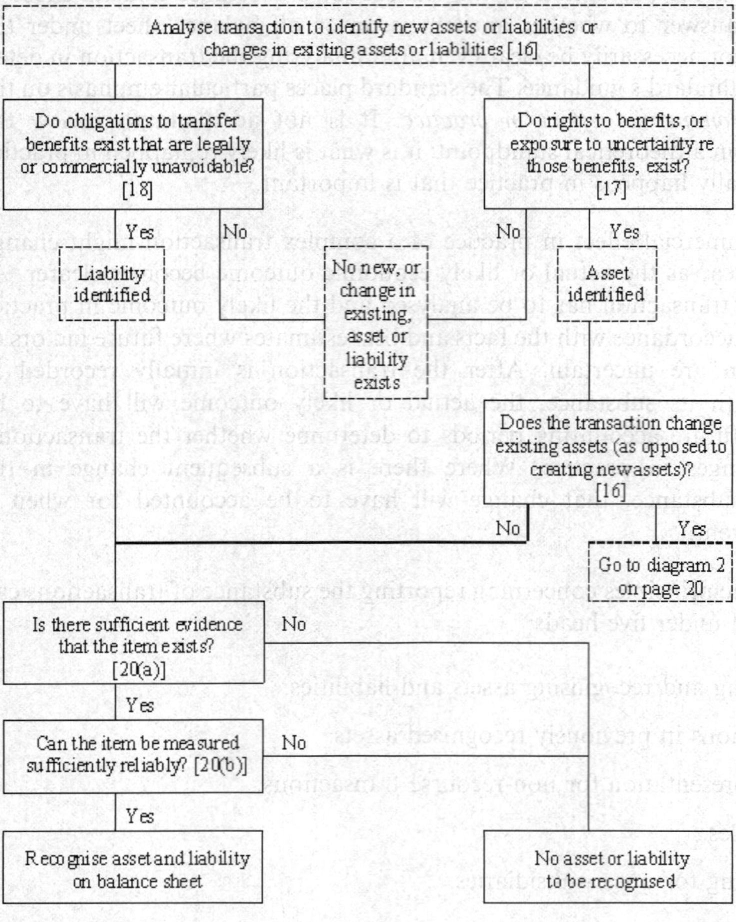

Analysing complex transactions

3.52 The first step in the process outlined above is to analyse the transaction. The most important aspect of analysing complex transactions is to consider carefully the reasons why each of the parties has entered into the transaction. What is the true commercial effect of the transaction? Is the transaction being entered into for tax reasons? Is one of the parties intending to acquire or dispose of an asset or is it intending to raise finance? What is the role of the other party? Once the commercial reason for the arrangement has been ascertained it may become obvious whether one of the parties to the transaction is merely receiving a lender's return. If this is so, then the transaction will almost certainly be a financing arrangement. More complex transactions often include the severance of legal title from the transaction's benefits and risks, some form of linkage with other transactions and put or call options.

Severance of legal title

3.53 Although the legal title to an asset may pass from a company because it enters into a particular transaction, the benefits and obligations associated with the asset often remain with the company. An example of such a transaction is a sale and repurchase of stock, where the seller agrees to repurchase stock at a price based on the original sales price. The title to the stocks passes, but the mark up in the buy-back price in substance represents a finance charge. Therefore, to accord with the standard's principles, such a transaction should remain on the seller's balance sheet with the receipt recorded as a liability. The mark up would be charged to the profit and loss account as a finance cost over the term of the transaction. Similarly, goods sold under reservation of title enable the selling company to have a lien on the goods until the purchaser has paid for them, although the benefits and risks in the goods have been transferred to the purchaser. It is common practice for the purchaser to account for the arrangement's substance and recognise such stocks in its balance sheet, although the supplier retains legal title to the goods. The supplier will treat the transaction as a sale. Conversely, with a finance lease, the lessor retains the legal title, but the transaction's substance is such that the asset and related obligation are recorded in the lessee's books.

Linkage with other transactions

3.54 A transaction is often linked with other transactions so that the commercial effect cannot be understood without considering the transactions as a whole. A simple example would be a transaction where a company sells an asset, but enters into a separate agreement to repurchase the asset at some time in the future. The commitment to repurchase is clearly linked to the sale and, therefore, the commercial outcome of the transaction should be considered as if they were a single transaction. This might, depending on the repurchase conditions, result in the transactions being accounted for as a financing arrangement rather than a sale of the asset with a separate repurchase.

Options and conditions

3.55 Simple options, such as an option to purchase shares, generally represent assets in their own right. A share option of this nature represents the right to purchase the shares at a future date and does not represent the actual shares that will be acquired on exercising the option. But with more complex transactions, options are often used in conjunction with the transaction's other aspects to give one party access to the future benefits associated with an asset, although that party might not have legal ownership of the asset.

3.56 Often options or conditions are included in the terms of a transaction which, by their nature, are almost certain to be fulfilled. In such transactions it is common for the company entering into the agreement to suffer an economic penalty if the option or condition is not fulfilled (or to receive an economic benefit if it is fulfilled). This economic penalty or benefit may be so great that the option or condition will inevitably be taken up by the entity. In determining the outcome of options in practice, greater weight should be given to those aspects and implications that are *more likely to have a commercial effect in practice*. The option's likely outcome has to be considered carefully, for example:

- Where there is no genuine commercial possibility that the option *will* be exercised, it should be ignored.
- Where there is no genuine commercial possibility that the option *will not* be exercised, its future exercise should be assumed.

[FRS 5 para 61].

3.57 In between these two extremes it will be a matter of judgement and the overall transaction's true commercial effect, including the option's likely impact, will have to be considered very carefully. As a consequence, the standard states that where a transaction incorporates one or more options, guarantees or conditional provisions, their commercial effect should be assessed in the context of all aspects and implications of the transaction in practice in order to determine what assets and liabilities exist. [FRS 5 para 19]. This does not mean, however, that the effect of an option should be judged on its probable outcome. In certain situations it might be assessed that the party's obligations and access to benefits are genuinely optional or conditional, in which case the option can be ignored. [FRS 5 para 61]. In other circumstances, the operation of options might indicate that one party has obligations (liabilities) or access to benefits (assets) that require to be recognised in its financial statements. The standard also points out that it should be assumed in the transaction's analysis that each of the parties will act in accordance with its economic interests. [FRS 5 para 62].

3.58 The following examples illustrate the application of these rules:

- Where the cost of exercising an option is expected to be lower than the benefits obtained by its exercise, it will generally be exercised and so in analysing the transaction the option's exercise should be assumed.

- If the cost of exercising an option is expected to be higher than the benefits obtained then generally it can be assumed that it will not be exercised and it can be ignored when analysing the transaction.

- Where the seller of an asset retains a call option over the asset and the buyer retains a put option, then it is almost certain that either the seller will call back the asset or the buyer will put it back to the seller. If for example, the asset is sold for £100,000 and the options are both priced at £110,000, then if the value of the asset decreases to (say) £90,000, the buyer will put it back to the seller at £110,000. Conversely, if the value moves up to £115,000, the seller will call back the asset for £110,000. In this case the asset should remain on the seller's balance sheet as a financing arrangement as the seller continues to bear the risks and rewards of ownership.

- Where the seller of an asset retains a call option over the asset and the buyer does not have an option to put the asset back to the seller the intentions of the seller and the rationale for including the option will have to be considered very carefully. As in the first two examples, the price of the option might indicate whether or not it will be exercised.

Identifying assets and liabilities

3.59 Once the transaction's commercial purpose has been ascertained it is then necessary to determine whether the transaction gives rise to new assets or liabilities or changes the entity's existing assets or liabilities.

Assets

3.60 Assets are defined in the standard as:

> *"Rights or other access to future economic benefits controlled by an entity as a result of past transactions or events."* [FRS 5 para 2].

3.61 Control over the rights to economic benefits means the ability to obtain the future economic benefits relating to an asset and the ability to restrict the access of others to those benefits. [FRS 5 para 3]. Control can be contrasted with management, which is the ability to direct the use of the item that generates the benefits. An example is a unit trust manager, who has day-to-day management of the trust's portfolio of investments, but it is the unit holders who gain the economic benefits from those assets, not the manager.

3.62 There will often be uncertainty regarding the amount of benefit flowing from an asset and this is the risk associated with the benefit. [FRS 5 para 5]. The standard uses the word 'benefit' to encompass also the risks that the benefit will be greater or smaller than expected and to cover the risks associated with the timing of the benefit's receipt. Risk is also defined in terms of the uncertainty of the amount of the benefits, including both the potential for gain and the exposure to loss. [FRS 5 para 5]. However, generally people understand and refer to benefits and risks (or risks and rewards) rather than using the term benefits to cover both.

The party who has access to the benefits of an asset will also generally be subject to the risk that they will turn out to be different from expected. Therefore, evidence of whether an entity is exposed to risks associated with an asset (that is, whether it is exposed to a loss) is evidence that the entity has access to the asset's future economic benefits.

Liabilities

3.63 Liabilities are defined as:

> *"An entity's obligations to transfer economic benefits as a result of past transactions or events."* [FRS 5 para 3].

An entity, therefore, has a liability if it has an obligation which will result in an outflow of funds. Such an obligation will exist if the entity is unable to avoid either legally or commercially an outflow of benefits. [FRS 5 para 18].

3.64 Where an entity's obligation is contingent on the outcome of one or more future events which are uncertain, a liability should not necessarily be recognised. Such an obligation should be accounted for in accordance with FRS 12 and will only give rise to a liability where it is probable that a future event will confirm a loss which can be estimated with reasonable accuracy at the date the financial statements are approved for publication. [FRS 5 para 58]. As a consequence, generally guarantees will not give rise to liabilities that require to be recognised in the financial statements unless a loss is foreseen (but they may prevent derecognition of previously recognised assets — see further para 3.67 onwards). But the commercial effects of guarantees do need to be considered very carefully as part of the overall transaction. Furthermore, some guarantees might operate in a similar way to options. Where this is so, they will need to be considered in the context of the overall transaction (see para 3.55).

Recognition of assets and liabilities

3.65 Once an asset or liability has been identified it should be recognised in the entity's balance sheet if both of the following conditions are satisfied:

- There is sufficient evidence of the item's existence.
- The item can be measured at a monetary amount with sufficient reliability.

3.66 Recognition is defined in the standard as the *"process of incorporating an item into the primary financial statements under the appropriate heading. It involves depiction of the item in words and by a monetary amount and inclusion of that amount in the statement totals"*. [FRS 5 para 6].

Transactions in previously recognised assets

3.67 FRS 5 includes rules concerning when a previously recognised asset can be taken off balance sheet (discontinued recognition, or derecognition). Before a previously recognised asset can be derecognised there must be an effective sale or disposal of the particular asset. That is, *all significant* benefits and risks relating to the asset must be transferred to another party. On the other hand, if after a transaction has been entered into by the company there has been no significant change in the entity's benefits or risks associated with a previously recognised asset, there has been no sale and the relevant asset should remain on the balance sheet.

3.68 In between these two extremes, FRS 5 contains rules to deal with the middle ground. These new rules (called in this chapter 'partial derecognition') deal with situations where:

- Part of an asset has been transferred to another party.
- All of the asset has been transferred, but for only part of its life.
- All of the asset has been transferred for all of its life, but where some significant benefits and risks are retained.

3.69 These rules mean that where there is a significant change in the entity's rights to benefits *and* exposure to risks, but the entity has not got rid of all significant rights and/or significant exposure to risks, then the original asset should be derecognised. But in its place there should be shown a new asset and corresponding liability reflecting the benefits and risks retained by the entity after the transaction. This can be contrasted with the use of the linked presentation (see para 3.83); the linked presentation typically applies in situations where significant benefits and risks are retained which are associated with the performance of the *gross* asset in question (see further para 3.84). The situations that can arise are shown in diagram 2 and are explained in more detail below.

Diagram 2 — Transactions in previously recognised assets

The numbers in square brackets refer to paragraphs of the standard.

Continued recognition of the asset on balance sheet [18]	
Rewards retained	**Risks retained**
All significant	All significant
All significant	Some or none
Some or none	All significant
Ceasing to recognise the asset in its entirety — derecognition [22]	
Rewards retained	**Risks retained**
No significant	No significant
Special cases — partial derecognition [23]	
Rewards retained	**Risks retained**
Some	Some

No significant	Some
Some	No significant

3.70 The term 'significant' is not included in the list of the standard's definitions, but in respect of these rules it should be judged in relation to the benefits and risks that are likely to occur in practice and not in relation to the total possible benefits and risks. [FRS 5 para 25]. This again emphasises the importance of the transaction's commercial effect in practice. The problem in practice will be deciding what benefits and risks are significant and this will be a matter of judgement. The standard illustrates the principle using an example: an entity sells debts of £100 million and bad debts are expected to be £2 million. There is recourse to the seller for the first £5 million of bad debts. In this case, the seller has retained all significant risks of non-payment.

Continued recognition

3.71 As can be seen from diagram 2, an asset should remain on balance sheet where there is no significant change to the entity's rights or benefits relating to the asset. Similarly, unless there is also a significant change in the risks associated with the asset, the entity's asset still has to be retained on balance sheet. [FRS 5 para 21]. Therefore, if the entity retains all significant benefits *or* all significant risks (or both) the asset should remain on balance sheet.

3.72 For those entities not applying FRS 26 the standard cites a debt factoring arrangement where the entity selling the debts retains the bad debt risk and slow payment risk as an example of a transaction where the debts clearly cannot be derecognised. In that example, the entity retains the significant risks associated with the transaction and the factor is merely supplying finance and receiving a lender's return, even though the legal title to the debts may have passed. Furthermore, the example illustrates that derecognition is not allowed where the transaction finances the entity's existing assets, even where the finance is non-recourse. With such an arrangement the entity is left with the same benefits and risks relating to the asset that existed before the financing, but in addition the transaction creates an obligation (a liability) to repay the finance, which must be recognised on the balance sheet. The only exception to this rule is where the transaction is a financing arrangement and the conditions for the linked presentation are met (see further para 3.83). [FRS 5 para 67].

Full derecognition

3.73 A previously recognised asset can only be derecognised in its entirety (without being replaced by another asset — see para 3.74) where all significant benefits *and* all significant risks relating to the asset have been transferred. For those entities not applying FRS 26, this situation will arise where an asset is sold for a single non-returnable cash payment where there is no recourse by the buyer to the entity's other assets and no further entitlements to rights on the part of the seller (for example, in a sale of a subsidiary where part of the consideration is deferred). [FRS 5 para 69].

Partial derecognition

3.74 The standard indicates that partial derecognition only applies where there is a significant change in the entity's rights to benefits *and* exposure to risks. It should be borne in mind that the type of situations where partial derecognition applies are few in number; generally previously recognised assets will either have to be retained on the balance sheet or, if they meet the criteria, derecognised in their entirety. Partial derecognition might arise where the transaction takes the form of a transfer of:

- Part of the asset.
- All of the asset for part of its life.
- All of the asset for all its life, but where the entity retains significant benefits or risks.

3.75 The principles can be illustrated as follows:

- Transfer of part of the asset — proportionate share

  For those entities not applying FRS 26, a loan transfer might involve the transfer of a proportionate share of a loan (including rights to interest and principal) such that cash flows and profits and losses are shared by the transferee and transferor in fixed proportions. In this case, the proportionate share transferred should be derecognised.

- Transfer of part of the asset — splitting benefit streams.

  For those entities not applying FRS 26, the interest benefit stream is stripped from a loan being held as an asset such that one party has the benefits and risks associated with the interest stream and the other has the benefits and risks associated with the principal. In this case, the party retaining the investment in the principal should derecognise the original asset and in its place recognise a new asset namely an investment in the non-interest bearing principal. The original carrying amount would have to be allocated to the principal and the interest stream. If the element of cost allocated to the interest stream equals the proceeds, then no profit or loss arises and the remainder is allocated to the principal. However, in principle the principal is recognised at a different amount than its original carrying value. The amount at which the principal is recorded would then earn interest, which would be added to the principal each year and credited to the profit and loss account, until the loan is redeemed at its full amount. For example, if an interest strip is made on a loan, and the amount received is £50,000, the amount of the original carrying value of the principal allocated to the interest may also be £50,000 (and would probably be arrived at by discounting the interest receivable). Therefore, no gain or loss arises on the transaction. The discount of £50,000 would be deducted from the balance of the loan and credited to the profit and loss account over the remaining term of the loan, thereby building up the loan to its redemption amount at the end of its term.

- Transfer of asset for part of its life.

  An entity sells a car, but agrees to repurchase it towards the end of its life at a value that fairly reflects the usage and depreciation over the period to repurchase. The entity now only has an interest in the residual, and also has a liability, which is its obligation to repurchase the item. Any profit or loss on sale will be the difference between the proceeds and the old book value. Whether accounting for a residual asset and liability is actually appropriate depends on the likely commercial outcome. If repurchase is intended or likely, the residual asset and liability should be recognised; and if a loss is likely on repurchase, that would be accounted for at the start by recording a residual liability in excess of a residual asset (that is, by making a provision against the asset to reduce it to its recoverable amount). But if, as for example with some manufacturer's buy-back guarantees, the manufacturer agrees to buy back an asset after say five years, but does so only at a low price such that it is much more likely that the customer will retain the asset or sell it to a third party, it would not be appropriate to record a residual asset or liability. All that is necessary in such situations is for the manufacturer to make provision for any loss that might arise on the (relatively few) units that are expected to be returned.

- Transfer of asset for all of its life where some benefit or risk is retained.

  A subsidiary might be sold with an earn-out (that is, an amount of deferred performance-related consideration), in which case the original asset (the subsidiary) would be derecognised and something else would appear in its place, namely a debtor, being a prudent estimate of the amount of further proceeds under the earn-out, discounted if appropriate.

  Another example is where an asset has been sold subject to a warranty agreement. The party selling the asset has disposed of the benefits and risks associated with the asset and can derecognise it, but has retained a liability which is the obligation under the warranty agreement. Whether this liability will be recognised will depend on the circumstances and where necessary an adequate provision should be made in accordance with the requirements of FRS 12. If a provision is necessary, a corresponding loss is recognised in the profit and loss account.

3.76 Under the partial derecognition rules, where there is a significant change in the entity's rights to benefits and exposure to risks, the original asset should be derecognised in its entirety and a different asset recognised in its place, together with a liability representing any obligations assumed. If there is no new asset, then it is necessary to provide for any liability for loss if an obligation is likely to arise.

3.77 In this type of situation, where an asset has been derecognised in its entirety a profit or loss will arise and this should be recognised on a prudent basis. For example, where the resulting profit or loss is uncertain, the standard requires that full provision should be made for any probable loss and, to the extent that any gain is in doubt, it should be deferred. [FRS 5 para 24].

3.78 The examples that follow illustrate situations where the partial derecognition rules apply and also show how the standard's provisions interact with those of SSAP 21.

Example 1

A vehicle contract hire company buys cars and enters into three-year operating leases with lessees. Economically, what was a single asset (a car) has become two assets: (a) a stream of receivables over three years; and (b) a risk on the residual value at year three. The lessor then sells the stream of rentals to a bank (with the bank taking the bad debt risk); the lessor is left with the residual position.

Following FRS 5's partial derecognition rules, the asset would be split in two (as above), the receivables would be regarded as having been sold and there would remain a different asset, namely a three-year residual, on the balance sheet. This assumes that the lessor would hold the asset at that time or would buy it back at a pre-agreed price. In these circumstances there would be an equivalent liability for the funding of the residual or the repurchase obligation.

Example 2

A slightly different example to that above is where a lessor enters into arrangements with a third party such that the lessor does not buy back the car, but merely guarantees to make good a shortfall if the market value at year three was not as great as the expected amount and, similarly, benefits from any increase in the market value above the guaranteed amount. In this circumstance, the asset would be the extent (if any) to which the market value might exceed the guaranteed amount (this would probably be booked as nil initially on prudence grounds). The obligation would be the provision (if any) that the lessor needs to make in respect of the loss that is likely to occur, which would be recognised and taken to the profit and loss account in accordance with the requirements of FRS 12.

3.79 Thus there seems to be a difference, under the partial de-recognition approach, between cases where the lessor actually holds the asset or will (or may) buy it back (that is, a new asset, the residual, is shown on the balance sheet) and cases where the lessor merely guarantees the residual value (that is, no asset is likely to arise on the balance sheet, but a provision will be required for any expected loss).

3.80 Where there is an overlap with the provisions of FRS 5 and SSAP 21, the standard states that the statement that contains the more specific provisions should be applied. In the examples above, the provisions of FRS 5 are more specific than those of SSAP 21 and hence should be applied in the way indicated.

3.81 In Table 3.2, J Bibby & Sons PLC has brought back on balance sheet following the introduction of FRS 5, repurchase obligations to re-acquire certain equipment at the end of its primary lease period.

Table 3.2 — J. Bibby & Sons PLC — Annual Report and Accounts 24 September 1994

Financial Review (extract)

FRS 5

The implementation of FRS 5 (Reporting the Substance of Transactions), which applies to accounting periods ending after 22nd September 1994, has resulted in bills and leases discounted with recourse and repurchase obligations for equipment sold being included on the balance sheet. All the transactions which gave rise to these items were entered into entirely within the normal course of business and have been included in debtors or stocks on the one hand and creditors on the other hand. The amounts are as follows:

	1994			1993		
	Total £000's	Recourse commitments £000's	Repurchase obligations £000's	Total £000's	Recourse commitments £000's	Repurchase obligations £000's
Under one year	25,477	21,241	4,236	27,195	25,296	1,899
Over one year	12,593	508	12,085	6,989	1,253	5,736
	38,070	21,749	16,321	34,184	26,549	7,635

The repurchase obligations enable our Capital Equipment and Materials Handling Divisions to re-acquire equipment, which has usually been maintained by themselves, at the end of primary periods thus providing opportunities in the used equipment market.

Insurance

3.82 It is often wrongly thought that insuring against the risks associated with a particular transaction might enable the company concerned to derecognise the related assets on the basis that it has transferred significant risks associated with the asset. This is a misconception because the risks associated with the asset (for example, bad debt risk) remain with the company and the company has a counter claim against its insurer should that risk arise (for example, when a debt is bad). In practice, this counter claim may or may not be met by the insurance company depending on whether the company has complied with its insurance conditions. It is only possible to derecognise an asset if the significant risks and benefits have been sold to another party and the risks and rewards have been transferred to that same party. However, if that other party itself insures against the same risks that the company would have insured against, then it may be possible for the transaction to be derecognised, because the company has successfully transferred its significant risks.

Linked presentation

General rules

3.83 Following representations made to the ASB by the banking industry and others, the ASB developed the 'linked presentation' for certain specialised transactions such as securitisations where non-recourse finance is involved. The only recourse allowed to the provider of the finance in such a transaction is to the specific assets being financed and not to the entity's other assets. The specific assets are, therefore, 'ring-fenced'. There must be *no recourse whatsoever* to other assets of the entity. The linked presentation represents a compromise which allows certain assets and their related finance to be 'linked' on the face of the balance sheet, whereby the finance is deducted from the asset. The presentation is said not to offend the Act's offset rules because, under the standard's principles, the asset that is being recognised on the face of the balance sheet is the net item and not the gross amount. Furthermore, as the amount of finance received is non-refundable, it does not meet the standard's definition of a liability. The gross asset and liability are being disclosed on the face of the balance sheet merely as additional information to enable the user to appreciate the full extent of the transaction.

3.84 An important condition of using this presentation is that the provider of the finance must only be repaid from the benefits generated by the assets or from the realisation of the assets themselves. The entity can retain rights to any surplus benefits that remain after repayment of the finance, but it must not have any right or obligation to keep the assets or to repay the finance from its own resources. Often in such transactions, the entity will be exposed to certain benefits and risks that will have a commercial effect in practice. This might arise, for example, because the future outcome measured in both terms of profits and cash flows will often be dependent on the performance of the gross assets transferred to the other party (for example, in the case of receivables, the performance will be affected by the amount of bad debts and the timing of payment). The ASB contends that it is the retention of these *significant* benefits or risks associated with the gross asset that distinguish this type of non-recourse financing from transactions that can be partially derecognised; where there is a transfer of the whole asset for part of its life or a transfer of part of the asset for all of its life (see para 3.74). This is an important distinction, as without it all transactions eligible for linked presentation might alternatively be partially derecognised. Where significant benefits or risks are retained and the transaction is in the nature of a financing arrangement it is still only eligible for the linked presentation if the strict conditions set out in paragraph 3.89 below can be satisfied.

3.85 The following example illustrates these points for those entities not applying FRS 26.

Example

If a company has debtors of £10m it might factor these and in return receive non-returnable proceeds of £9m. As the debtors are collected it will recover the balance of £1m less the factor's fees, but it is still subject to credit risk (that is, bad debt risk) up to a maximum of £1m on the full amount of the debt of £10m. If the bad debt risk is expected to be £0.5m it is likely to receive only a further £0.5m from the factor. In addition, the factor will charge a financing fee for providing the £9m of funds to the company which varies depending on the speed of collection (late payment risk). Consequently, the company still retains the significant risks associated with the debts (the bad debt risk and the late payment risk), albeit it has transferred the risk of catastrophe (which is negligible) to the factor. The factor's risk of loss would arise only if the bad debts exceeded £1m, which is highly unlikely. Therefore, the company has retained significant risks relating to the whole of the assets and, as a consequence, they cannot be partially derecognised, but (because the £9m is non-returnable and assuming the other criteria are met) the assets are eligible for the linked presentation. The transaction is precluded from being partially derecognised, because the company still bears the risk associated with the *gross* amount of the portfolio of debts and in practice bears the same bad debt risk before and after the transaction (albeit after the sale, it has transferred the risk of catastrophe). If, for example, the company had sold 90% of *each* debt then its risks have changed significantly and its bad debt risk on the portfolio will be very different before and after the sale. In this latter circumstance, the transaction might be eligible for the partial derecognition rules and if so it could be appropriate to derecognise the part of the debt that has been sold (that is, 90% of each debt) and retain on balance sheet the balance (that is, 10% of each debt).

If the transaction complies with the conditions for the linked presentation it would be disclosed on the face of the balance sheet in the following way:

Balance sheet (extract)	£m	£m
Current assets		
Debtors		
Trade debtors		50.0
Trade debtors subject to financing arrangements	9.5	
Less: non-returnable amounts received	9.0	0.5
Total trade debtors		50.5

The trade debtors of £9.5m is made up of the total debtors of £10m less the expected bad debt provision of £0.5m. The required disclosure clearly shows the asset of £0.5m to which the entity is exposed separately from other debtors, there being no other recourse from the providers of the finance to other assets of the entity.

If subsequently, one of the debtors that owes £3m goes into liquidation and the debt is bad, it will be necessary to reduce the gross trade debtors by this amount. However, because part of this debt is covered by non-returnable funds received from the factor it is possible to reduce the liability to the factor by £2m. Of the difference of £1m, £0.5m would be charged to the profit and loss account and the balance of £0.5m used to reduce the provision. In effect, the net presentation is carried through to the profit and loss account, the loss that falls to the company is only £0.5m: of the remainder of the loss, £2m is borne by the factor as a result of the £9m being non-returnable and £0.5m has already been provided for. Therefore, at this stage, the company has provided in full for the risks relating to the debtors of £1m that are not covered by non-recourse finance (that is, £0.5m initial bad debt provision and an additional provision of £0.5m). The linked presentation would then show gross debtors of £7m (£10m less £3m) less a gross liability of the same amount (£9m less £2m) coming to a net balance of nil. Even though the net balance is nil, the linked presentation disclosing the gross figures still has to be shown on the face of the balance sheet.

3.86 The amount of funding received may not always equate exactly to the non-returnable amount as happened in the example above. This is illustrated in the example in paragraph 3.91.

3.87 Another important restriction is that the linked presentation cannot be used where the finance relates to a business unit or to assets that are used in conjunction with other assets of the entity to generate the funds to repay the finance. Therefore, for example, a company cannot use the linked presentation for the debt it might raise to finance the company's operating properties. However, it will be a matter of judgement as to how far this rule should be taken. For example, can a property investment company use the linked presentation for an investment property that it has financed ring-fenced? The answer is probably no, because even if the company is funding the repayment of the finance from the asset's rental income, if it has the right to retain the asset at the end of its life it falls foul of one of the linked presentation conditions mentioned below.

Conditions in detail

3.88 Under the rules in the standard the linked presentation can only be used where a transaction involving a previously recognised asset is in substance a financing, but the company 'ring-fences' the asset such that:

- The finance will be repaid only from proceeds generated by the specific item it finances (or by transfer of the item itself) and there is *no possibility whatsoever* of a claim on the entity being established other than against funds generated by that item (or against the item itself).

- There is *no* provision whereby the entity may either keep the item on repayment of the finance or re-acquire it at any time.

[FRS 5 para 26].

3.89 Following these initial requirements the standard then sets down detailed conditions that must be met before the linked presentation can be used:

- The finance must relate to a specific item (or portfolio of similar items) and, in the case of a loan, must be secured on that item, but not on any other assets of the entity. [FRS 5 para 27(a)].

  The linked presentation cannot be used where the finance relates to two or more assets that are not part of a portfolio or to a portfolio covering assets that would otherwise be shown under different balance sheet captions.

- The provider of the finance must have no recourse whatsoever, either explicit or implicit, to the other assets of the entity for losses and the entity must have no obligation whatsoever to repay the provider of the finance. [FRS 5 para 27(b)].

This means that there must be no obligation whatsoever (not even a moral one) to fund losses on the assets being financed. For example, a moral obligation on an originator in a mortgage securitisation might arise if the originator were to fund a mortgage interest rate increase which could not be borne by the mortgagors (the borrowers).

- The entity's directors must state explicitly in each set of financial statements where a linked presentation is used that the entity is not obliged to support any losses, nor does it intend to do so (see for example Table 3.3). [FRS 5 para 27(c)].

- The provider of the finance must agree in writing (in the finance documentation or otherwise) that it will seek repayment of the finance, as to both principal and interest, only to the extent that sufficient funds are generated by the specific item it has financed and that it will not seek recourse in any other form, and such agreement is noted in each set of financial statements where a linked presentation is used (see also Table 3.3). [FRS 5 para 27(d)].

- If the funds generated by the item are insufficient to pay off the provider of the finance, this must not constitute an event of default for the entity. [FRS 5 para 27(e)].

  This means, for example, that where an originator in a securitisation transaction has other funds lent to it by the provider of the finance, if there are insufficient funds from the securitisation transaction to repay the finance for that deal, the provider of the finance should not be able to regard that as constituting a default on the other funds lent to the originator and, as a consequence, require their repayment. The provision would also extend to a different lender where there is a cross-default clause linked to all the company's borrowings including the securitisation.

- There must be no provision whatsoever, either in the financing arrangement or otherwise, whereby the entity has a right or an obligation either to keep the item upon repayment of the finance or (where title to the item has been transferred) to re-acquire it at any time. Accordingly:

  - where the item is one (such as a monetary receivable) that directly generates cash, the provider of the finance must be repaid out of the resulting cash receipts (to the extent these are sufficient); or

  - where the item is one (such as a physical asset) that does not directly generate cash, there is a definite point at which either the item must be sold to a third party and the provider of the finance repaid from the proceeds (to the extent these are sufficient) or the item must be transferred to the provider of the finance in full and final settlement.

  [FRS 5 para 27(f)].

  Even where there is merely an understanding between the parties that the seller will re-acquire the asset at some time in the future, this fact is enough for this condition to be breached. This clearly illustrates that all of the aspects of the transaction need to be considered including the intentions of the parties even where these are not evidenced in writing. Put and call options are commonly used to effect a repurchase and where these exist in a transaction, the linked presentation should not be used.

3.90 It is necessary to analyse a transaction very carefully to establish whether there are any recourse provisions, because recourse can come in different forms, such as:

- Substitution clauses whereby good debts are substituted for non-performing debts (see further para 3.162).
- Guarantees for performance, proceeds or other support.
- Put options to transfer assets back to the originating entity.
- Swap arrangements (see para 3.156).
- Penalty arrangements.

Warranties in relation to the condition of the assets when the arrangement is being entered into (for example, the seller has good title or has delivered the asset or warrants that the assets are in good condition) do not preclude use of the linked presentation, but warranties relating to the future condition or performance (for example, payment or speed of payment) of the assets do preclude use of the linked presentation. [FRS 5 para 83].

Linking part of the finance

3.91 If the conditions hold for only part of the finance, then the linked presentation is still used by those entities not applying FRS 26 for that part of the finance for which all the conditions are met.

Example

A company sells its debtors of £10m to a third party and receives in return an amount of £9m. Of the £9m, £7.5m is non-returnable, but £1.5m of the finance is returnable depending on the performance of the debtors. The bad debts are expected on past experience to be £0.5m. In effect, the company retains the risks associated with the first £2.5m of losses and as £1.5m is potentially returnable it cannot be included in the linked presentation and must be shown as a liability. The transaction would be disclosed in the balance sheet in the following way.

Balance sheet (extract)	£m	£m
Current assets		
Debtors		
Trade debtors		50.0
Trade debtors subject to financing arrangements	9.5	
Less: non-returnable amounts received	7.5	2.0
Total trade debtors		52.0
Creditors		
Financing of trade debtors		1.5

It would be necessary for the notes to the financial statements to explain fully the implications of the transaction and in particular to indicate that certain of the finance related to it is returnable and is included in creditors.

3.92 An example of a company that has non-recourse finance for part of its debts is given in Table 3.3.

Table 3.3 — WPP Group plc — Annual Report and Accounts — 31 December 2000

Consolidated balance sheet (extract)

		As at 31 December 2000	
		2000	**1999**
	Notes	**£m**	**£m**
Current assets			
Stocks and work in progress	16	**241.1**	**113.5**
Debtors	17	**2,181.0**	**1,068.4**
Debtors within working capital facility:	18		
Gross debts		**464.9**	**345.7**
Non-returnable proceeds		**(231.6)**	**(214.1)**
		233.3	**131.6**

Notes to the consolidated balance sheet

Debtors within working capital facility

The following are included in debtors within the Group's working capital facilities:	**2000**	**1999**
	£m	**£m**
Gross debts	**464.9**	**345.7**
Non-returnable proceeds	**(231.6)**	**(214.1)**
	233.3	**131.6**

Within the Group's overall working capital facilities, certain trade debts have been assigned as security against the advance of cash. This security is represented by the assignment of a pool of trade debts, held by one of the Group's subsidiaries, to a trust for the benefit of the providers of this working capital facility. The financing provided against this pool takes into account, inter alia, the risks that may be attached to individual debtors and the expected collection period.

The Group is not obliged (and does not intend) to support any credit-related losses arising from the assigned debts against which cash has been advanced. The providers of the finance have confirmed in writing that, in the event of default in payment by a debtor, they will only seek repayment of cash advanced from the remainder of the pool of debts in which they hold an interest, and that repayment will not be sought from the Group in any other way.

Profit recognition

3.93 Much of FRS 5 is aimed at the balance sheet and how assets and liabilities should be recognised there, but for linked presentations there is also some guidance on when profits and losses should be recognised. At the inception of the transaction a gain will only arise to the extent that the non-returnable proceeds received exceed the asset's previous carrying value. [FRS 5 para 28]. During the transaction's life, a profit or loss will arise to the extent that the income from the asset is different from the amount due to the financier. Finally, if the transaction is such that the asset is eventually sold at the end of the transaction a further profit or loss may arise, but this amount can only be recognised in the period that the onward sale takes place. Furthermore, where for example the asset generates income and there is a cost of finance in a period, it will be the net amount of profit or loss that is generally recognised in the profit and loss account (as these amounts should also be linked in a similar way to the balance sheet items from which they are generated). The gross components should be given in a note to the financial statements, unless in order to give a true and fair view it is necessary to show the gross amounts linked on the face of the profit and loss account. This latter situation might arise where the transaction is of such significance to the company's trading results that the net presentation alone does not give the transaction sufficient prominence.

3.94 What the standard does not discuss is where to show such profits and losses in the profit and loss account. On the inception of the transaction, although it is a financing arrangement, there will be a one off gain or loss that arises in effect on the transfer of benefits and risks to the other party, which is akin to a sale of an asset. For example, if debtors of £10,000 are sold for £9,000, which is non-returnable and further amounts receivable are prudently estimated at nil, a loss of £1,000 should be charged to the profit and loss account and included in the format item 'interest payable and similar charges', because it is in substance a finance charge.

3.95 During the life of a simple financing arrangement, it would seem sensible to show any net losses in an accounting period as part of the company's cost of finance and record it in the profit and loss account as interest payable and similar charges. Where the transaction generates a net profit this is similarly a finance item and should also be included within 'other interest receivable and similar income' in the profit and loss account.

3.96 If on the eventual outcome of the transaction there is a sale of the linked assets then the profit or loss arising on this part of the transaction should be accounted for in accordance with the normal rules for such profits or losses on the sale of fixed or current assets (see further chapter 8).

Offset rules

3.97 Following the publication in 2004 of FRS 25, 'Financial instruments: Disclosure and presentation', the detailed rules in FRS 5 relating to the offset of financial assets and liabilities have been replaced by those in FRS 25, which are considered in detail in chapter 6. For non-financial assets and liabilities, no offset it permitted: debit and credit balances may only be aggregated into a single net item where they do not constitute separate assets and liabilities. [FRS 5 para 29].

[The next paragraph is 3.100.]

Accounting for quasi-subsidiaries

3.100 Over time several revisions to the Companies Act have widened the definition of subsidiary, such that it is likely that many entities that were considered to be quasi-subsidiaries in past will today meet the definition of full legal subsidiaries. The Companies Act and FRS 2 definitions of subsidiary are considered in chapter 24.

3.101 However, the ASB has retained the notion of quasi-subsidiaries to close any remaining loopholes. For example, it is not clear under the Act whether trusts come within the definition of subsidiary, although it can be argued that they do. However, it is quite clear that even if they did fall outside the scope of the Act's definition, they are covered by FRS 5's definition of quasi-subsidiary.

3.102 A quasi-subsidiary is defined in FRS 5 as:

> *"... a company, trust, partnership or other vehicle that, though not fulfilling the definition of a subsidiary, is directly or indirectly controlled by the reporting entity and gives rise to benefits for that entity that are in substance no different from those that would arise were the vehicle a subsidiary ."* [FRS 5 para 7].

3.103 In determining whether a company controls another entity, regard should be had to who in practice directs the entity's financial and operating policies. [FRS 5 para 8]. The rules here are the same as those in FRS 2 where control is defined in terms of the ability of a company to direct, or have the power to direct, the entity's financial and operating policies. The ability to prevent others from enjoying the benefits arising from the vehicle's net assets is also evidence of control. However, a company will not control another entity where there is another party that has the ability to determine all major issues of policy. Consequently, if it is obvious that another party controls the entity, then it cannot be a quasi-subsidiary.

3.104 The quasi-subsidiary definition focuses on the control over the entity where that control is direct or indirect and this definition has not been changed following the amendments to FRS 2 and the Act. Now that the definition in FRS 2 and the Companies Act includes 'power to control', it will be necessary to consider the control relationship carefully, because whether the control is direct or indirect, it might arise because of a power to control. If this is the case the entity will be a full legal subsidiary rather than a quasi-subsidiary. But there might still be situations where the entity fails the revised definition of subsidiary in FRS 2 and the Act. In such a case, the entity may still be a quasi-subsidiary where the benefits the investor receives are no different from those that would arise if the entity were a subsidiary. The benefits that are of concern are those that arise from the vehicle's net assets, as with any normal subsidiary, and similarly any exposure to risks will relate again to the benefits associated with the vehicle's net assets.

3.105 Because of the inclusion of 'power to control' in the revised definitions in FRS 2 and the Companies Act, it might be argued that all entities that were treated as quasi-subsidiaries prior to the change in definition of subsidiary should now be treated as full legal subsidiaries. However, one of the reasons that the provisions in FRS 5 were introduced was to deal with arrangements where the operating and financial provisions were pre-determined (contractually or otherwise). In this type of circumstance, neither party to the contract might seem to have day-to-day control of the vehicle's financial and operating policies, but the contract might specify and determine who gains the benefits and who is exposed to the risks related to the entity. This is typically the case with special purpose vehicles (SPV) used in securitisation schemes. In these situations after the SPV has been established none of the parties to the arrangement can change the operating and financial policies and the arrangement unwinds like clockwork.

3.106 It can be argued in these circumstances that none of the parties to the arrangement control the operating and financial policies on a day to day basis (that is, they cannot be changed). Hence, FRS 5 makes reference to these types of arrangements as 'indirect control', because none of the parties to the arrangement have control or have the power to control the operating and financial policies once the arrangement has been established. Under FRS 5 the party that gains the majority of the benefits from the net assets of the entity should consolidate it as a quasi-subsidiary. If this argument is pursued, if the entity is judged to be a quasi-subsidiary and it complies with the conditions in FRS 5 for linked presentation (see para 3.113), this basis of accounting can still be used. Hence, it will be necessary to look at the detail of an arrangement very carefully to determine where the SPV is subject to control, power to control or indirect control.

Conflict with the law?

3.107 If an entity is a quasi-subsidiary it cannot be a legal subsidiary (and *vice versa*). As the Act only requires subsidiaries to be consolidated the question arises as to whether consolidation of a quasi-subsidiary as required by FRS 5 is a departure from the Act. The ASB contends that consolidation of quasi-subsidiaries represents the provision of additional information in accordance with section 227A(4) of the Act (section 404(4) of the Companies Act 2006), without which the consolidated financial statements would not give a true and fair view. Therefore, accepting ASB's reasoning, consolidation of a quasi-subsidiary is not regarded as a departure from the Act's provisions in order to give a true and fair view (section 227A(5); section 404(5) of the Companies Act 2006). As a consequence, consolidation of quasi-subsidiaries does not constitute a true and fair override and, therefore, the resulting disclosures required by the Act and FRS 18 do not have to be made.

Accounting treatment

3.108 Quasi-subsidiaries should be consolidated into the group's financial statements in the same way as for other subsidiaries and the same types of consolidation adjustments should be made (for example, the elimination of intragroup trading and profits). Therefore, the consolidated financial statements should include the quasi-subsidiary's assets, liabilities, profits, losses and cash flows in the same way as if it was a subsidiary. [FRS 5 para 35].

3.109 If a company does not have any legal subsidiaries and, therefore, does not prepare consolidated financial statements, it should provide, along with its individual financial statements, consolidated financial statements including the quasi-subsidiary. Those consolidated financial statements should be presented with equal prominence to the company's individual financial statements. [FRS 5 para 35]

3.110 An intermediate holding company does not have to prepare consolidated financial statements in certain situations where, for example, it is wholly-owned by another company that prepares its financial statements in accordance with the 7th Directive (see chapter 24). It might be inferred from the wording in paragraph 36 of the standard that, because such an intermediate holding company does not need to deal in its individual financial statements with its subsidiaries (other than by giving the normal disclosures concerning such investments) that it would similarly not need to deal with its quasi-subsidiaries in those financial statements. This, however, does not appear to be so, because as explained in the application note on securitisation (Application Note D), such an intermediate holding company will have to determine whether it has assets and liabilities, including those in the quasi-subsidiary, that need to be recognised in its own financial statements. There are three possible ways of dealing with the assets and liabilities of the quasi-subsidiary:

- The individual company need not recognise any of the quasi-subsidiary's assets and liabilities in its financial statements, because they can be regarded as completely derecognised by the company.
- The individual company should adopt the linked presentation in its financial statements, where the conditions for its use are met (see para 3.113).
- The individual company should record its interest in the assets and liabilities of the quasi-subsidiary gross.

3.111 The accounting treatment of a quasi-subsidiary's transactions in the individual company's financial statements, the group's financial statement and in the quasi-subsidiary's financial statements is considered in more detail from paragraph 3.143.

3.112 The rules concerning exclusions of a quasi-subsidiary from consolidation work in the same way as for normal subsidiaries. Quasi-subsidiaries need not be consolidated if they are immaterial or where the quasi-subsidiary is held exclusively with a view to subsequent resale and has not been previously consolidated. Where there are severe long-term restrictions that substantially hinder the exercise of the company's rights over the assets or the management of the other entity, this indicates that the company does not have the requisite control over that other entity for it to be a quasi-subsidiary. The other exceptions from consolidation given in the Companies Act, that is disproportionate expense and undue delay and where there are significant differences between the activities of the quasi-subsidiary and the rest of the group, cannot be used under the standard to justify the non-consolidation of a quasi-subsidiary, just as they cannot be used under FRS 2 (see further chapter 24).

Linked presentation of quasi-subsidiaries

3.113 In certain circumstances, a quasi-subsidiary's assets and liabilities can be consolidated into the group's consolidated financial statements using the linked presentation. The circumstances where the linked presentation can be used are where a company (the originator) puts some of its assets into a vehicle to be financed and where the vehicle is a quasi-subsidiary and effectively 'ring-fences' the transaction. If there is no recourse whatsoever to the group's other assets and the other conditions for linked presentation (set out in para 3.89 above) are met from the group's point of view, the group may account for the quasi-subsidiary in its consolidated financial statements using the linked presentation. The noteholders in the quasi-subsidiary may well have recourse to the quasi-subsidiary's other assets and this will often preclude the use of the linked presentation in its financial statements. However, the important issue from the group's point of view is that, for it to be eligible to use the linked presentation in its consolidated financial statements, there must be no recourse to the group's assets other than those within the securitised vehicle itself.

3.114 This presentation has been designed specifically for securitisation schemes, but may also apply to other schemes. In a securitisation, assets such as mortgages or credit card receivables are in effect sold to a thinly capitalised vehicle. The vehicle raises debt finance to pay for the mortgages or receivables. This debt may come in more than one form. For example, the majority may be raised from third parties on a non-recourse basis (that is, debt is secured solely on the vehicle's assets). In addition, to provide greater security to the third parties and thereby to reduce the cost of that third party debt, the originator may lend to the vehicle, for example investing in a zero coupon bond issued by the vehicle. In this situation the originator's loan will typically be subordinated to the third party debt; thus the originator will bear the first tranche of losses. Moreover, the originator will participate in any residual profits earned by the vehicle. That is, the originator will still have the benefits and risks associated with the vehicle and as a result the vehicle will be a quasi-subsidiary of the originator. Despite its being a quasi-subsidiary, where the conditions for the linked presentation can be met by the group (that is, the quasi-subsidiary is ring-fenced from the group's point of view), it does not have an asset equal to the gross amount of the vehicle's assets, nor does it have a liability for the full amount of the finance. The vehicle is a quasi-subsidiary and, in accordance with FRS 5, additional information concerning the quasi-subsidiary has to be given in the consolidated financial statements in order to give a true and fair view. In this case, the additional information is that required by the linked presentation and not that required by full consolidation.

Subordinated debt and credit enhancement

3.115 The originator may enhance the credit rating of quasi-subsidiaries (and hence the debt that the quasi-subsidiary issues to the public) by using a number of techniques varying from participation via subordinated debt or zero coupon loans to insurance against bad debts. If the originator participates via subordinated debt or a zero coupon loan, such debt will be eliminated in the group's consolidated financial statements. This will have the effect that, where the linked presentation is used, the group will recognise in its consolidated financial statements an amount of securitised assets greater than the amount of linked finance. The resulting asset is in effect financed by the company's subordinated debt or zero coupon loan and is the amount on which the group is at risk. A participation by an originator of this nature does not preclude the use of the linked presentation in the group's consolidated financial statements.

3.116 Another form of credit enhancement that is often used is 'over-collateralisation', which basically means financing a pool of assets by a smaller amount of external debt. For example, the pool of securitised assets might be worth £1 million, but loan notes of only £900,000 are issued to finance the assets. The difference of £100,000 provides a cushion against bad debts and also may cover the costs of the SPV.

Securitising in a legal subsidiary

3.117 If a similar securitisation scheme to that using a SPV is entered into, but using a legal subsidiary instead of a quasi-subsidiary, the same rationale and treatment as described above does *not* necessarily apply. This is because the entity is a legal subsidiary and is required to be consolidated in full by the Act. It will also not generally be possible in a subsidiary to link the finance with the securitised assets in a way that satisfies the standard's conditions, because the providers of the finance will often have recourse to other assets of the subsidiary (see further para 3.143). The only situation where the same result would be achieved is where the subsidiary meets the conditions for linked presentation in its own financial statements. Then on consolidation the linked presentation used by the subsidiary will be retained in the group's financial statements.

Accounting treatment in the parent's financial statements

3.118 Where a company has put some of its assets into a quasi-subsidiary under a securitisation and a linked presentation applies on consolidation, the accounting treatment adopted in that company's individual financial statements will have to be considered carefully. In contrast to a subsidiary where the parent's financial statements merely record the investment in the subsidiary, with a quasi-subsidiary three different presentations might apply (as explained in para 3.110) and it will be necessary to determine which presentation should be adopted. These presentations are considered in more detail in paragraph 3.143 onwards.

Disclosure

3.119 Where one or more quasi-subsidiaries are included in the consolidated financial statements it is necessary to disclose that fact in the financial statements and to give a summary of the financial statements of each quasi-subsidiary in the notes (quasi-subsidiaries of a similar nature may be combined). The summarised financial statements must show separately each main heading in the balance sheet, profit and loss account, statement of total recognised gains and losses and cash flow statement for which there is a material item, together with comparative figures. An example of the type of disclosure required is shown in Table 3.5. This example is unusual in that it consolidates fixed assets and non-recourse finance held in a quasi-subsidiary using the linked presentation, whereas the linked presentation is more generally used for debt factoring arrangements or securitisations (see Table 3.9 and Table 3.10).

Table 3.5 — NFC plc — ANNUAL REPORT & ACCOUNTS — 1 October 1994

Accounting Policies (extract)

a **Accounting Convention (extract)**
Under FRS 5 "Reporting the Substance of Transactions" the accounts of two companies, previously accounted for as associated undertakings, are now consolidated as quasi-subsidiaries using the linked presentation provided for in FRS 5.

Group Balance Sheet (extract)
at 1 October 1994

	Note	**1.10.94**		2.10.93	
				As restated	
		£m	**£m**	£m	£m
Fixed assets					
Tangible assets	*12*		**587.6**		542.0
Tangible assets subject to financing arrangements	*13*	**43.5**		27.6	
Non-recourse debt		**(36.5)**		(26.6)	
			7.0		1.0
Investments	*14*		**28.5**		26.5
			623.1		569.5

Notes to the Accounts (extract)

13 Tangible fixed assets subject to financing arrangements

As noted under accounting policy *a*, under FRS 5 two companies previously accounted for as associated companies become quasi-subsidiaries. They are consolidated using a linked presentation and the comparative figures have been restated accordingly, with no effects on the prior year's profit or shareholders' funds.

The tangible assets subject to financing arrangements are revenue earning vehicles on hire to third parties. The principal quasi-subsidiary is NFC Finance 1991 (S) Limited, the shares in which are owned equally by NFC plc and Ebbgate Investments Limited, a subsidiary of Barclays PLC. The other quasi-subsidiary is NFC Contracts Limited which is a wholly-owned subsidiary of NFC Finance 1991 (S) Limited. The group has entered into interest rate cap agreements on normal commercial terms to limit the interest rate exposure of these companies.

The directors confirm that there is no obligation on any part of the group to support any losses that may be incurred, in respect of the assets being financed, in excess of the net amount shown in the balance sheet and they do not intend to support any such losses in the unlikely event that they were to be incurred. The providers of the finance have agreed in writing that they will seek repayment of principal and interest only to the extent that sufficient funds are generated by the assets being financed and they will not seek recourse in any other form.

The summarised combined accounts of the quasi-subsidiaries are as follows:

Profit and loss account		
	1994	1993
	£m	£m
Turnover	**23.2**	9.8
Operating profit after management charges	**3.8**	1.2
Interest	**(3.8)**	(1.2)
Profit on ordinary activities before taxation	—	—
Taxation	—	—
Profit for the financial year	—	—

There are no recognised gains and losses other than the profit for the financial year.

	1994		1993	
Cash flow statement	**£m**	**£m**	£m	£m
Net cash inflow from operating activities		**16.7**		3.9
Interest paid		**(3.8)**		(1.2)
Net cash inflow before investing and financing		**12.9**		2.7
Investing activities				
Purchases of tangible fixed assets	**(39.5)**		(37.0)	
Disposals of tangible fixed assets	**7.5**		3.5	
Net cash outflow from investing activities	—	**(32.0)**	—	(33.5)
Net cash outflow before financing		**(19.1)**		(30.8)
Financing				
Allotment of shares	**0.5**		—	
New loans	**40.5**		37.0	
Repayment of loans	**(14.5)**		(3.0)	
Net cash inflow from financing		**26.5**		34.0
Increase in cash and cash equivalents		**7.4**		3.2

Balance sheet		**1.10.94**	2.10.93
		£m	£m
Tangible fixed assets		**43.5**	27.6
Cash at bank and in hand		**10.6**	3.2
Debtors:	Amounts due from NFC group companies	**6.8**	3.5
Creditors:	Amounts falling due within one year	**(22.4)**	(12.3)
	Amounts due to NFC group companies	**(6.5)**	(1.0)
	Other amounts falling due after more than one year	**(31.5)**	(21.0)
		0.5	—
Share capital		**0**	—
Reserves		—	—
Shareholders' funds		**0.5**	—

Note: This example pre-dates the changes made to the definition of subsidiary in both the Act and FRS 2, which have effect for accounting periods beginning on 1 January 2005. Hence, it is possible that these entities may no longer be quasi-subsidiaries.

Application notes

3.120 FRS 5's principles have to be applied to the recognition and presentation in financial statements of all transactions although, as noted earlier, FRS 5 will tend to make a difference only to the accounting for complex transactions, including those where the substance and form differ. This section considers the transactions covered by the application notes in FRS 5. Brief descriptions are given below and in chapter 9, but reference should be made to the application notes themselves for a full appreciation of the analysis. The application notes are included within FRS 5 and cover:

A Consignment stock.

B Sale and repurchase agreements.

C Debt factoring.

D Securitised assets.

E Loan transfers.

F Private finance initiative and similar contracts.

G Revenue recognition (see chapter 9).

3.121 Application notes A to F each includes a table that summarises how the FRS's principles should be applied in the analysis of the transactions. These tables are reproduced below or in chapter 20 for consignment stock in each of the sections that deal with the particular application notes.

Consignment stock

3.122 Arrangements where goods are supplied from a manufacturer to a dealer on a consignment basis are common in certain industries, particularly in the motor vehicle trade. Application Note A to FRS 5 shows how the principles of recognising assets and liabilities should be applied to these arrangements and these matters are fully considered in chapter 20.

Sale and repurchase agreements

3.123 For those entities applying FRS 26 and where the transaction falls within the scope of paragraphs 14 to 42 of FRS 26, FRS 5 Application Note B is not relevant, and the recognition and derecognition principles in FRS 26 should be applied (see further chapter 6). For those entities not within the scope of FRS 26, FRS 5's provisions should be applied to sale and repurchase agreements and the guidance in FRS 5 Application Note B is relevant. Sale and repurchase agreements are arrangements where one party sells assets to another on terms that permit, or commit, it to repurchase those assets at some future date, for example, through the use of put and/or call options. Although in some sale and repurchase agreements, the initial transaction should be accounted for as a sale, equally such agreements have been developed quite widely as methods of raising finance for assets such as properties and development land banks. Sale and repurchase arrangements also cover bed and breakfast deals (see further para 3.243). The seller often remains in control of the use or disposal of the asset, because it may continue to be used in the seller's business during the period of the agreement.

Principal sources of benefits and risks

3.124 The principles involved in analysing these transactions are relatively straightforward. The objective is to determine whether the transaction's commercial effect is that of a sale or that of a secured loan. Under the standard's provisions the main features of such transactions need to be analysed and greater weight given to those aspects that are more likely to have a commercial effect in practice. The application note identifies the main features that need to be considered in this type of transaction as:

- The sale price.
- The nature of the repurchase provision.
- The repurchase price.
- Other relevant provisions (for example, the seller's continued use of the asset).

[FRS 5 App B para B2].

3.125 The principal sources of benefits and risks arising from the main features listed above are considered in detail in the application note and the principles stemming from that discussion are then summarised in a table. The summary table is reproduced below, but with the principal features added as headings; also references are included to the paragraphs of the application note that give the narrative explanation:

Indicates sale of original asset (seller may retain a different asset)	**Indicates no sale of original asset (secured loan)**
Sale price [App B para B].	Sale price does not equal market value at date of sale.
Nature of repurchase provision	
No commitment for seller to repurchase asset, for example: — call option where there is a real possibility the option will fail to be exercised. [App B para B12].	Commitment for seller to repurchase asset, for example: — put and call option with the same exercise price [App B para B12]; — either a put or a call option with no genuine commercial possibility that the option will fail to be exercised [App B para B12]; or — seller requires asset back to use in its business, or asset is in effect the only source of seller's future sales. [App B para B11].
Repurchase price [App B para B13].	
Risk of changes in asset value borne by buyer such that buyer does not receive solely a lender's return, for example:	Risk of changes in asset value borne by seller such that buyer receives solely a lender's return, for example:
— both sale and repurchase price equal market value at date of sale/repurchase.	— repurchase price equals sale price plus costs plus interest; — original purchase price adjusted retrospectively to pass variations in the value of the asset to the seller; — seller provides residual value guarantee to buyer or subordinated debt to protect buyer from falls in the value of the asset.
Other relevant provisions	
Nature of the asset is such that it will be used over the life of the agreement, and seller has no rights to determine its use. Seller has no rights to determine asset's development or future sale. [App B Para B15].	Seller retains right to determine asset's use, development or sale, or rights to profits therefrom. [App B paras B15, B17].

3.126 Important points of guidance drawn from the application note are summarised as follows:

- It is necessary to consider all the features of the agreement (particularly the terms of options and any guarantees) that are likely to have a commercial effect in practice, in order to understand them individually and how they interact.

- Determining which party is exposed to, or protected from, a fall in the value of the assets transferred is normally central to the analysis of whether there is really a sale of an asset or whether it is in substance a refinancing.
- A transaction structured so that in practice the purchaser secures just a lender's return on the purchase price without genuine exposure to, or benefit from, changes in value of the underlying assets should be treated as a financing arrangement.

3.127 Following the analysis summarised above, the true commercial effect of a transaction is a sale if the seller genuinely relinquishes control of significant benefits and transfers the exposure to significant risks associated with the asset to the buyer. In a sale, the exposure to changes in the market value of the underlying asset will in practice be passed to the buyer.

3.128 If the repurchase price in an option to repurchase is the market value at the date of exercise, it is probable that the buyer acquires both the opportunity to benefit from any increase in the value of the asset and the risk of loss due to an adverse change in its value. In terms of FRS 5's asset recognition tests, the asset has been transferred to the buyer. If, however, the repurchase price is predetermined so that, however it is formulated, it assures the buyer of a return of the original price together with the cost of holding and financing the asset, the agreement is likely to be in substance a secured borrowing. That is because the principal benefits and risks associated with holding the asset remain with the seller. The buyer (probably a financial institution) is not taking any significantly greater risk than if it made a loan secured on the asset concerned.

3.128.1 An FRRP ruling issued in February 1997 concerned a sale and leaseback undertaken by Associated Nursing Services plc. The complex sale and leaseback arrangement involved a 25-year lease, renewable for a further 25 years, with a call option held by Associated Nursing Services plc. The FRRP's view was that the nature of the transaction was such that not all the significant rights and not all the significant exposure to the risk relating to the asset had been transferred to the purchaser. Therefore, in accordance with FRS 5, an asset should have remained on the balance sheet and the sale proceeds should have been included in borrowings. As outlined above, indicators that a substance of a sale and leaseback is a financing arrangement include an initial sale not at market value and/or an option to repurchase based on a pre-determined price (rather than market price at the date of repurchase).

3.129 The application note recognises that, in more complex situations, it may be determined that a sale and repurchase agreement is not in substance a financing transaction and that the seller only retains access to some of the benefits of the original asset. In this circumstance, the partial derecognition rules in paragraph 23 of the standard might apply (see para 3.74). [FRS 5 App B para B14]. If, for example, the buyer receives more than merely a lender's return, as other benefits and risks associated with the asset have been transferred to the buyer, the seller will not have retained the original asset. In this situation, the original asset should be derecognised and the analysis should determine whether another asset should be recognised in its place. For example, the seller might have an interest in the asset's residual value at the end of its life, in which case this asset and/or liability should be recognised in the seller's balance sheet.

Accounting treatment

3.130 Where the analysis of the particular sale and repurchase transaction shows that it is in substance a secured loan, the original asset should continue to be recognised and the proceeds received from the buyer should be shown as a liability (often under a separate heading), but if the amount were considered material separate disclosure might be appropriate. No profit or loss should be recognised on the transaction's sale as, in substance, no sale has been made. Interest on the liability should be accrued and the finance cost of the liability might, for example, represent the difference between the proceeds received and the repurchase price of the asset. Therefore, the liability would be built up over its life to equal the amount at which the liability will be repaid (which is, in legal form, the repurchase of the asset). The asset's value should be reviewed for diminution in value in the normal way and, if it is a depreciable asset, it should be depreciated. Sale and finance leasebacks would also be accounted for in this manner as explained in paragraphs 153 to 155 of the guidance notes to SSAP 21 (see Tables 3.6 and 3.7).

Table 3.6 — Ladbroke Group PLC — Report and Accounts — 31 December 1994

Financial review (extract)

Financial Reporting Standard 5

Under Financial Reporting Standard 5 (FRS 5), a change is required in the reporting of certain sale and leaseback transactions entered into by the group in prior years. The leases of five hotels and one property, previously accounted for as operating leases, are now included in the accounts with the properties shown as assets and the sale proceeds as borrowings in the balance sheet; rental charges are now shown as interest in the profit and loss account, calculated at the effective rate over the period of the leases. The effect of these presentational changes on the balance sheet is the recognition of £233 million of future lease rental obligations as liabilities at 31st December 1994 and an increase of £172 million in assets, with appropriate changes to the revaluation reserve and retained earnings. In the profit and loss account, operating profits for the year have been increased by £11.8 million (1993: £12.2 million), representing the amount of lease payments, and the interest charge has increased by £23.1 million (1993: £22.9 million). Comparative figures have been restated accordingly and the financial commentary in these financial statements is based upon the restated figures.

Table 3.7 — Arjo Wiggins Appleton p.l.c. — Directors' Report and Financial Statements — 31 December 1994

Notes to the financial statements (extract)

1. Change in presentation of the financial statements

Hitherto, obligations under finance leases have been included in 'Other creditors' in the balance sheet. Following the sale and lease-back arrangement explained in notes 13 and 17, the directors consider that it is more appropriate to treat all finance lease obligations as a form of borrowing and, consequently, these liabilities are now included within 'Short-term borrowings' and 'Medium-term and long-term borrowings', as appropriate, in the balance sheet, with a corresponding change in the presentation of prior year comparative figures. The related security deposit is deducted in arriving at the Group's net debt figure shown in note 26.

13. Security desposit

In December, 1994, the Group entered into a sale and lease-back arrangement in relation to the No. 7 paper machine situated at Locks mill and operated by Appleton Papers. This has been accounted for as a finance lease in accordance with Statement of Standard Accounting Practice (SSAP) 21. The lease has a primary period of 28 years, but can be terminated at any time by the Group. The lease obligation recorded at 31 December, 1994 resulting from this transaction amounted to £65.8 million.

The Group was able to secure lower lease-financing costs by providing a deposit as security for the lease obligations. This deposit, which bears interest at LIBOR minus 3/16% must be maintained at a minimum of 92.5% of the obligations under the lease in order to retain the benefit of the lower finance charges. These obligations have, in addition, been guaranteed by the Company as set out in note 28.

17 Borrowings (extract)

The finance lease obligations include an amount of £65.8 million (1993: nil) in respect of the lease of the No. 7 paper machine situated at Locks mill and operated by Appleton Papers. A deposit of £62.5 million (1993:nil) by a subsidiary and a guarantee by the Company have been provided as security (see notes 13 and 28).

3.131 The notes to the financial statements should include the following information concerning all sale and repurchase transactions:

- The transaction's principal features. [FRS 5 App B para B19].
- The asset's status. [FRS 5 App B para B19].

  For example, this requirement presumably means disclosure that an asset has been legally sold to another party, but has been retained on balance sheet.

- The relationship between the asset and the liability. [FRS 5 App B para B19].

  Again, where an asset has been legally sold, but has been retained on balance sheet because the transaction is considered to be a financing arrangement, the notes should explain how the finance is connected with the asset (for example, whether it is non-recourse).

3.132 In some cases a sale and repurchase transaction might entitle the seller to repurchase certain rights associated with the asset rather than the entire asset. In this type of situation, where the seller has derecognised an asset, but has in its place recognised another asset or liability, because it has retained some benefits or risks, it should deal with the liability, following the provisions of FRS 12. This means, for example, that where there is some remaining obligation it should be determined whether it should be provided for in accordance with FRS 12. In addition, where there are any doubts about the amount of profit or loss that might arise from derecognising the original asset, adequate provision should be made for any expected loss. If there is an entitlement to a residual profit, that should be recognised as an asset, but in practice, it is very likely that it should be recognised at a value of nil on prudence grounds. Also, the notes to the financial statements should give the similar information to that outlined in paragraph 3.130, noting also the terms of any provisions for repurchase or any guarantees. [FRS 5 App B para B21].

Examples of required analysis

3.133 The application note provides examples of arrangements where a property developer finances its land bank by a straightforward sale and repurchase arrangement and by a similar arrangement that makes use of a special purpose vehicle.

3.134 The following example, which is not one included in the application note, illustrates the type of analysis under FRS 5 that needs to be applied.

Example

A scheme was set up two years ago, whereby a newly incorporated company (company A) acquired a number of properties from a property development company and raised £20m of finance to make the purchase. The property company sold sufficient properties (at a discount of 10% to their market value at the time of the sale) to company A to utilise the amount raised from shareholders. The properties were let by company A on assured tenancies. An independent firm of property managers was appointed to be responsible for the day to day letting and management of the properties.

After four years company A will start to sell the properties with a view to selling them all by shortly after the end of the fifth year. company A will then be put into members' voluntary liquidation and the net assets distributed in cash to investors to provide a guaranteed return. Any surpluses over the guaranteed return will also be distributed to investors. If the properties have not been sold by the distribution date at a price sufficient to provide the guaranteed return, company A will put the properties back to the property development company at a price that guarantees the required return to the investors in company A

The principal benefits and risks of the transaction can be analysed as follows from the point of view of the property company:

	Off B/sheet	On B/sheet
Sale price		
Sold to company A at 10% below market price.		✓
Nature of repurchase provision		
The company must re-acquire the properties should their value be below the amount necessary to provide the guaranteed return to the investors.		✓
Repurchase price		
Risk of fall in the asset's value is borne by the seller as it provides a residual value guarantee.		✓
Benefit in increase in asset's value accrues to investors.	✓	
Other relevant provisions		
Properties are not managed and are not occupied by the property development company.	✓	

In determining the presentation it is not merely a matter of looking at how many ticks are in the left-hand column and how many are in the right-hand column. It is necessary to consider which of the parties bears the benefits and risks of ownership. In this example, the property development company has retained risks in the form of the residual guarantee. Whether it will be called upon to fulfil its obligation under the guarantee will depend on how the property market performs over the five years and how optimistically the guarantee price is set. Certainly over the past few years it has been difficult to determine how property prices will move and, hence, it cannot be assumed in the present market that such a guarantee will not be called.

It seems relatively clear from the analysis that the transaction's substance is that of a deferred sale (that is, the property should remain on the property development company's balance sheet until there is no further obligation under the guarantee). This is because there has been no significant change in the property development company's exposure to risks because of the existence of the guarantee. Therefore, partial derecognition cannot be justified in this case.

Furthermore, if the properties cost £80m and they were sold to company A at £90m being 10% less than their market value of £100m at the date of sale, then the potential profit on sale to the property company would be £10m. However, this profit cannot be recognised, because in substance no sale has taken place. Therefore, the entries in the property development company's books would be as follows:

	£m	£m
Dr Cash	90	
Cr Liabilities		90
To record the financing of the properties.		

The properties would be retained at their cost of £80m. If the guaranteed repurchase price is £120m, then the difference between the £90m and the £120m would represent a finance cost on the obligation of £90m. Hence, this finance cost should be charged as interest to the profit and loss account at a constant rate on the outstanding amount of the obligation (as required by FRS 4 and FRS 26) and credited to increase the obligation to £120m over the term of the scheme. If this line or argument is followed, then, if the guarantee is called, the obligation will be fully provided for and be settled at £120m and the properties retained at a cost of £80m until they are sold. If the guarantee is not called, the sale of the properties is in substance complete and a profit of £40m can be recognised, which is the difference between the outstanding obligation of £120m and the cost of the properties of £80m. This might seem a curious result, because in the latter situation, the finance cost is being charged to the profit and loss account over the five years and a substantial profit on sale is recognised at the end of year five. However, it can be rationalised as follows. The property company did not sell the properties in substance until year five. It received cash in advance at year one. Economically, such an advance payment earns interest, which matches the finance cost on the obligation. Moreover, the value of the properties at year five was clearly at least £120m, so it is right that a profit based on selling at that value should be recognised given that the sale occurred in substance at year five.

3.135 An illustration of the accounting treatment of a BES scheme (similar to the scheme described above) is given in Table 3.8.

Table 3.8 — Persimmon plc — Report & Accounts — 31 December 1997

NOTES TO THE FINANCIAL STATEMENTS
for the year ended 31 December 1997 (extract)

26 Contingent liabilities (extract)
The company has guaranteed the return to investors in the companies formed under the Business Expansion Scheme and has indemnified the company's bankers who have provided guarantees of up to £40,500,000 in support of these obligations.

27 Properties in Business Expansion Scheme (BES) companies
The group sold properties into BES companies set up under BES assured tenancy schemes from 1989 to 1993.

Persimmon plc has guaranteed the return to investors in the companies formed under the BES (see note 26). Because the company has guaranteed that the BES companies will have sufficient cash resources at scheme maturity to pay the guaranteed return to investors, the proceeds received for the properties are treated as loans under BES advances on the balance sheet. The finance cost implicit in the BES arrangements, calculated by reference to the difference between the sales proceeds received and the guaranteed distribution to investors, is being charged in the profit and loss account over the appropriate term. In addition, the net rental income arising in the BES companies is recognised in the profit and loss account in the appropriate period.

Turnover does not include properties sold to BES companies until the schemes mature, the properties being held at cost on the balance sheet as BES assets until the sale is recognised.

At 31 December 1997 only two schemes now remain, all obligations under the previous schemes having been fulfilled. The maturity dates of the two remaining schemes are 5 March 1998 and 24 January 1999. The company acts on behalf of the BES companies in the sale of the properties prior to the scheme maturity date in accordance with the original scheme rules. The company has the right to exercise its option to repurchase any properties that remain unsold at maturity date in fulfilling its obligations under the guarantees.

Debt factoring

3.136 For those entities applying FRS 26, FRS 5 Application Note C is not relevant, and the recognition and derecognition principles in FRS 26 should be applied (see further chapter 6). For those entities not within the scope of FRS 26, FRS 5's provisions should be applied to debt factoring arrangements and the guidance in FRS 5 Application Note C is relevant.

3.136.1 Factoring is a transaction which is capable of different accounting treatments. It involves raising money from the sale of a company's debtor balances before the debt is collected. Debt factoring is considered in Application Note C of FRS 5 and also encompasses invoice discounting. Factoring arrangements come with many different features; at their simplest they might, for example, feature a clean sale of debts at a fixed price without recourse. More complex arrangements might feature a sale of debts on terms where there is both recourse to the seller in respect of non-payment (bad debt or credit risk) and the price received for the debts varies according to the actual period the debts remain unpaid (slow payment risk).

3.136.2 In the former case, the seller has no further interest in the debts so they can be removed from the balance sheet by crediting them with the proceeds from the factor. In the latter case, the seller clearly retains a significant economic interest in the underlying debts and the arrangement should be accounted for as a financing with the debts remaining on balance sheet. In addition, there is now a middle ground where significant, but not all, benefits and risks have been transferred to the factor. In such a transaction, the company might be eligible to use the linked presentation where the conditions in paragraph 27 of FRS 5 are met. Partial derecognition is not an option for such transactions, because they are financing arrangements.

3.136.3 Some of the arguments contained in the application note for and against asset recognition are finely balanced and there are likely to be grey areas in practice. Therefore, individual arrangements will need to be carefully reviewed. The three accounting treatments that might apply are:

- Derecognition — where no significant benefits or risks are retained.
- Linked presentation — where the company retains significant benefits and/or risks associated with the factored debts, but the downside exposure to loss is limited to a fixed amount and the other conditions for use of the linked presentation are met.
- Separate presentation — showing the factored debts and the related finance separately (not linked) on the balance sheet, where the company retains significant benefits and/or risks relating to the assets and the conditions for the linked presentation cannot be met.

3.136.4 The application note lists the main benefits and risks of factoring arrangements as:

- The benefit arising from the future cash flows due to the payment of the debts.
- The risk of slow payment.
- The risk of non payment — credit risk.

[FRS 5 App C para C5].

Main benefits and risks

3.136.5 The main benefits and risks set out above are considered in detail in the application note and the principles stemming from that discussion are then summarised in a table. The summary table is reproduced below, but with the main benefits and risks added as headings; also included are references to the paragraphs of the application note that give the narrative explanation:

Indicates derecognition	Indicates linked presentation	Indicates separate presentation
Cash flow benefit and slow payment risk		
Transfer is for a single, non-returnable fixed sum. [App C para C6].	Some non-returnable proceeds received, but seller has rights to further sums from the factor (or *vice versa*) whose amount depends on whether or when debtors pay. [App C para C15].	Finance cost varies with speed of collection of debts, for example: – by adjustment to consideration for original transfer [App C para C8]; or – subsequent transfers priced to recover costs of earlier transfers. [App C para C8].
Credit risk		
There is no recourse to the seller for losses. [App C para C9].	There is no recourse for losses, or such recourse has a fixed monetary ceiling. [App C para C15].	There is full recourse to the seller for losses. [App C para C9].
Other indicators		
Factor is paid all amounts received from the factored debts (and no more). Seller has no rights to further sums from the factor. [App C para C12].	Factor is paid only out of amounts collected from the factored debts, and seller has no right or obligation to repurchase debts. [App C para C15].	Seller is required to repay amounts received from the factor on or before a set date, regardless of timing or amounts of collections from debtors. [App C para C6].

3.136.6 Debt factoring, as opposed to just invoice discounting, not only involves the discounting of invoices, but often includes the factor administering the sales ledger and collecting the debts on behalf of the company. Generally, for debt factoring the administration arrangements will not affect the analysis of the transaction significantly for accounting purposes provided they are at arm's length. However, with arrangements where the factor is only administering the sales ledger (that is, service-only factoring), the seller will retain access to the benefits and risks associated with the debts and hence they should remain on balance sheet.

3.136.7 In order for factored debts to be derecognised (that is, completely taken off the balance sheet), the seller cannot retain any significant benefits or risks associated with those debts. Derecognition is, therefore, only appropriate where all of the following apply:

- The transaction takes place at an arm's length price for an outright sale.
- The transaction is for a fixed amount of consideration and there is no recourse either implicit or explicit.

  Warranties given in respect of the conditions of the debts (for example, to their existence) at the time of transfer are allowed, but warranties concerning the condition of the debts in the future or their future performance (for example, payment or speed of payment) are not allowed.
- The seller will not benefit or suffer if the debts perform better or worse than expected.

[FRS 5 App C para C12].

3.136.8 Derecognition cannot be used where the seller retains significant benefits or risks, but in such a situation it might be possible to use the linked presentation. The linked presentation would normally be appropriate where the downside exposure to risk is limited to a fixed monetary amount and where the conditions for the linked presentation are met. However, the linked presentation should not be used where the factored debts cannot be separately identified.

3.136.9 It is possible in factoring arrangements where the linked presentation is used, for old debts to be replaced by new debts as long as the conditions in FRS 5, paragraph 27(b) (no recourse to other assets) and 27(f) (finance to be repaid out of the cash receipt from debt) are satisfied. The practical problems associated with achieving the linked presentation in this situation are explained in relation to credit card receivable securitisations from paragraph 3.159.

Accounting treatment

Derecognition

3.136.10 If, after analysing the transaction, it is determined that the assets can be derecognised, a loss (and in certain circumstances a profit) will arise which will simply be the difference between the carrying value of the debts and the net proceeds received from the factor. [FRS 5 App C para C18]. This amount will generally represent a finance cost and should be included within interest in the profit and loss account.

Linked presentation

3.136.11 Where the conditions for linked presentation are met, the finance should be deducted from the related debts on the face of the balance sheet, after providing for any bad debts. The interest element of the factor's charge should be accrued as it is incurred. In addition, the notes to the financial statements should include the following information:

- The main terms of the arrangement. [FRS 5 App C para C19].
- The gross amount of the outstanding factored debts at the balance sheet date. [FRS 5 App C para C19].

  Although not stated explicitly in the FRS, the amount to be disclosed is presumably before deducting bad debt provisions as otherwise this additional disclosure would appear unnecessary, because the amount of the debts factored (after deducting bad debt provisions) will be disclosed anyway in the balance sheet linked presentation, although at some point a bad debt must be written off and, therefore, eliminated from both sides.

- The factoring charges recognised in the period, analysed between interest and other charges. [FRS 5 App C para C19].
- A statement by the directors that the company is not obliged and does not intend to support any losses beyond the recourse to the specific debts linked under the scheme. [FRS 5 para 27(c)].
- A note that the factor has agreed in writing that it will seek recourse to both principal and interest only to the extent that sufficient funds are generated by the specific debts it has financed. [FRS 5 para 27(d)].

3.136.12 An example of disclosure of the statements in the last two bullet points above is seen in Table 3.8.1 in relation to hire purchase trade debtors discounted with banks, subject to strictly limited recourse.

Table 3.8.1 — Inchcape plc — Annual Report & Accounts — 31 December 1994

Consolidated balance sheet (extract)

		1994		1993 restated
	£m	**£m**	£m	£m
Current assets:				
Stocks		**1,112.1**		876.8
Debtors		**1,379.1**		1,220.5
Trade debtors subject to limited recourse financing	**34.8**		36.3	
less: non-returnable amounts received	**(24.8)**		(26.1)	
		10.0		10.2
Cash at bank and in hand		**427.3**		354.9
		2,928.5		2,462.4

17 Debtors (extract)

Trade debtors subject to limited recourse financing represent hire purchase debtors discounted with banks in the ordinary course of business, subject to strictly limited recourse so that the majority of cash received by the Group on discounting is not returnable, and which carry interest at variable rates. The returnable element of the proceeds is recorded as bank loans and overdrafts due within one year and after one year as appropriate. The Group will not make good any losses over and above the agreed recourse limit and the relevant banks have confirmed their acceptance of this position in writing.

The Group figures also include the effects of implementing FRS5 in respect of bills of exchange, trade debtors and hire purchase debtors discounted with recourse, at variable rates of interest, to banks and finance houses in the ordinary course of business. These balances have been included within trade debtors due within one year £6.0m (1993 — £32.2m) and net investment in finance leases and hire purchase contracts £0.4m due within one year and £4.0m due after one year respectively (1993 — £0.4m and £3.7m).

Separate presentation

3.136.13 Where the analysis indicates that separate presentation should be used for the transaction, the amount of the debts factored should remain in debtors on the balance sheet (net of any provisions for bad debts). The proceeds received from the factor should be recorded as a liability under the heading of, for example, 'amounts due in respect of factored receivables'. In addition, the interest element of the factor's charges should be accrued and shown as interest in the profit and loss account. Also the notes to the financial statements should show the amount of the factored debts outstanding at the balance sheet date. [FRS 5 App C para C20].

3.136.14 An example of disclosure of trade debtors and hire purchase debtors discounted with recourse is seen in Table 3.8.1 above.

Examples of required analysis

3.136.15 The application note provides two examples of factoring arrangements: one where the factor has recourse and continued recognition is required; and another where the factor has limited recourse and the linked presentation is used.

3.136.16 The following example, which is not one of those included in the application note, also illustrates the FRS 5 principles as they apply to factoring arrangements:

Example

A company has a number of large trade debtors totalling £1m, which are very unlikely to default, but are long-dated. The company decides to sell these debtors to a factoring company. Because the debtors are sound companies, there are unlikely to be any bad debts and the risk of slow payment is minimal. Even so, the seller has given the factor a guarantee up to a total of 10% of the debtors' balance in respect of credit and slow payment risk. In past experience, over the last ten years, the company has never had to provide against any balances with these customers.

Some might try to argue that such a transaction should be accounted for as a sale of assets and recognition of a new asset or liability (partial derecognition). In this case, the recognition would be of an obligation to repay the factor if the debtors go bad (which is extremely unlikely). This argument appears to be supported by paragraph 73 of FRS 5 which illustrates a similar situation; *"...an entity may sell equipment subject to a warranty in respect of the condition of the equipment at the time of sale, or subject to a guarantee of its residual value. This would normally transfer all significant rights to benefits and some significant exposure to risks to the buyer..., but leave the seller with some significant risk in the form of obligations relating to the equipment's future performance or residual value. The seller would therefore cease to recognise the equipment as an asset, but would recognise a liability for its warranty obligation or guarantee (with the liability being accounted for in accordance with the provisions of FRS 12)".* This paragraph would seem to support the argument that the obligation in the example is so remote that it does not need to be recognised and, as a consequence, the transaction can be treated as an outright sale. However, there is one primary objection to this argument, which is that partial derecognition is not available for financing transactions and this transaction is clearly a financing arrangement. In any case, paragraphs 12 and 13 of Application Note C only allow three possible accounting treatments for debt factoring: full derecognition where the transaction is an outright sale and there is no recourse; linked presentation where there is recourse and the conditions for that presentation are met; and separate presentation. *Partial derecognition is not an option.*

Therefore, using the principles of Application Note C, the benefits and risks of the transaction can be analysed as follows:

	Off B/sheet	Linked	On B/sheet
Cash flow benefit and slow payment risk			
The transfer is for a fixed sum, but part may have to be repaid if the guarantee is called.		✓	
Credit risk			
The factor has recourse via the guarantee to the company for losses, which has a fixed monetary ceiling, but is unlikely to be called.		✓	
Other indicators			
The factor is only paid out of the amounts collected from the debtors and the seller has no right or obligation to repurchase the debtors.		✓	

The company has retained significant risks associated with the debtors, because it is still liable to fund bad debts up to a limit of 10%. The company might contend, in practice, that its risk of bad debts is nil (because of past experience). This is true, but it still has retained the same significant risk that it had prior to undertaking the transaction, because it is exposed to the risk of bad debts on the gross amount of the debtors it has transferred. It has merely transferred to the factor the risk of catastrophe (the risk of bad debts exceeding the 10% limit). Consequently, the analysis above indicates that the linked presentation is the appropriate accounting treatment for this transaction, but it can only be used where the conditions for its use are met. If those conditions cannot be met, then separate presentation must be used.

The accounting treatment using the linked presentation would be as follows:

Balance sheet (extract)	£'m	£'m
Current assets		
Debtors		
Trade debtors (say)		10.0
Trade debtors subject to financing arrangements	1.0	
Less: non-returnable amounts received	0.9	
		0.1
Total trade debtors		10.1
Creditors		
Financing of trade debtors		0.1
(comprising the amount of finance with recourse)		

Securitised assets

3.137 For those entities applying FRS 26, FRS 5 Application Note D is not relevant, and the recognition and derecognition principles in FRS 26 should be applied (see further chapter 6). For those entities not within the scope of FRS 26, FRS 5's provisions should be applied to the securitisation of assets and the guidance in FRS 5 Application Note D is relevant. Securitisation of assets is a method, first used by originators of mortgage loans, to package assets together to sell as a block or pool to a thinly capitalised vehicle (known as a special purpose vehicle (SPV)). The SPV finances its purchase by issuing loan notes or other marketable debt instruments to outside investors that are secured solely on the assets securitised. Also other pools of debts, such as credit card receivables, hire purchase loans and trade debtors, are securitised in a similar way to mortgages (for example see the example concerning debt factoring in chapter 6).

3.138 The originator of the securitised assets may or may not hold an equity investment in the issuing vehicle. The loan notes issued by the SPV are attractive to investors because, by covering any risks associated with the scheme with some form of credit enhancement, the asset-backed debt provides a very high level of security. The credit enhancement used (covering most risks associated with the assets apart from catastrophe), varies in form from insurance for bad debts to the originator investing in a deep discounted bond or in subordinated debt, whose repayment at the end of the scheme depends on the liquidity of the SPV (see further para 3.115). Many of these schemes hinge on Standard & Poors (a US rating entity) giving the loan notes AAA rating, a higher credit rating than would be available for a debt issued by the originator. Consequently, the note holders' instrument can be given a lower rate of interest because of the debt's high security.

3.139 The SPVs are often companies that are owned by a charitable trust. The charitable purpose of the trust is normally 'obscure', as it is not generally the intention of such schemes that the charitable trust would benefit greatly from the business of its subsidiary. It is merely a convenient way of structuring the scheme. The trust exists to own legally the SPV in order to assist in 'ring-fencing' the transaction.

3.140 The commercial reasons for companies securitising their assets are varied. Securitisation is a means of both tapping alternative markets for funds at very competitive funding rates and permitting the institutions to take on more business by removing their risk exposure for regulatory purposes on substantial tranches of long-term receivables. The sums of money involved in securitisation schemes (particularly mortgage securitisations) are substantial. Consequently, the commercial impact of the accounting treatment is very significant.

3.141 Developing an acceptable accounting treatment was difficult, because the original lender normally retains some economic interest in the gross assets transferred and also in the issuing vehicle. For example, the originator in a mortgage securitisation may continue to administer the mortgages and take the majority of the vehicle's profit, although the vehicle may be structured so that the originator does not control it.

3.142 The ASB developed the linked presentation specifically to apply to securitisation schemes where the originator retains significant benefits and risks associated with the assets securitised, but where the downside exposure to risk is capped. The linked presentation also lends itself to other complex transactions, such as factoring (see chapter 6).

3.143 If consolidation of the SPV as a full legal subsidiary is not appropriate (see para 3.100 onwards) and the SPV has been assessed to be a quasi-subsidiary then the securitisation should be accounted for in accordance with FRS 5. Because securitisations make use of SPVs it is necessary to consider the accounting treatment in three sets of financial statements: the originator's individual financial statements; the SPV's financial statements; and the originator group's consolidated financial statements. The SPV's financial statements are probably the simplest to deal with as separate presentation of the transaction is normally appropriate. This is because the SPV often has access to all of the future benefits and risks related to the securitised assets and the noteholders usually have recourse to all of the vehicle's assets (which would include assets other than the pool of assets being securitised, such as cash balances). In the originator's individual financial statements and its group's financial statements there are three possible accounting treatments:

- Derecognition — where *no* significant benefits *or* risks are retained.
- Linked presentation — where significant benefits and/or risks are retained, but the downside exposure to loss is limited to a fixed amount and the other conditions for use of the linked presentation are met.

- Separate presentation — where significant benefits and/or risks are retained and the conditions for the linked presentation cannot be met.

Originator's financial statements

3.144 The benefits and risks associated with securitisations are considered in detail in the application note and the principles stemming from that discussion are then summarised in a table. The summary table is reproduced below, but split in two. The first section of the table below considers the analysis necessary to determine the accounting treatment in the originator's financial statements and includes references to the paragraphs of the application note that give the narrative explanation:

Indicates derecognition	Indicates linked presentation	Indicates separate presentation
Transaction price is arm's length price for an outright sale. [App D para D8].	Transaction price is not arm's length price for an outright sale.	Transaction price is not arm's length price for an outright sale.
Transfer is for a single, non-returnable fixed sum. [App D para D8].	Some non-returnable proceeds received, but originator has rights to further sums from the issuer, the amount of which depends on the performance of the securitised assets. [App D para D9].	Proceeds received are returnable, or there is a provision whereby the originator may keep the securitised asset on repayment of the loan notes or re-acquire them. [App D para D 14].
There is no recourse to the originator for losses. [App D para D8].	There is either no recourse for losses, or such recourse has a fixed monetary ceiling. [App D para D 10].	There is or may be full recourse to the originator for losses, for example: — originator's directors are unable or unwilling to state that it is not obliged to fund any losses; — noteholders have not agreed in writing that they will seek repayment only from funds generated by the securitised assets. [App D para D 14].

3.145 In order for securitised assets to be derecognised in the originator's individual financial statements, the originator must not retain any significant benefits or risks associated with those assets. Derecognition is, therefore, only appropriate where all of the following apply:

- The transaction takes place at an arm's length price for an outright sale.
- The transaction is for a fixed amount of consideration and there is no recourse (other than to the securitised assets) either implicit or explicit.

  Warranties given in respect of the asset's condition (for example, to good title or to the completeness/correctness of the documentation relating to the asset) at the time of transfer are allowed, but warranties concerning the condition of the assets in the future, or their future performance (for example, payment or speed of payment), are not allowed.

- The originator will not benefit or suffer if the assets perform better or worse than expected.

[FRS 5 App D para D8].

3.146 Derecognition cannot be used in the originator's financial statements where the originator retains significant benefits or risks, but in such a situation the linked presentation might apply. Again, as with factoring, 'significant' is judged in relation to those benefits and risks that are likely to occur in practice and not in relation to the total possible benefits and risks. It is common in securitisation schemes for the originator to retain some benefits related to the securitised assets, for example, *via* involvement in management of the securitised assets or *via* a residual interest in the SPV. Furthermore, as explained in paragraph 3.115, the linked presentation can still be used where the originator has an interest in the SPV by way of a subordinated loan or a zero coupon loan. The important point is that the linked presentation is only appropriate where the downside exposure to risk is limited to a fixed monetary amount and where the conditions for the linked presentation are met (see para 3.88).

3.147 The linked presentation should not, however, be used where the assets that have been securitised cannot be separately identified. There must generally be no provision for the originator to repurchase the securitised assets. Where there is such a provision, but for only part of the securitised assets, the maximum payment that could result should be excluded from the amount of finance deducted from the securitised assets on the face of the balance sheet and this amount should be shown separately as a liability.

Disclosure requirements

3.148 Where the originator derecognises the securitised assets, they will no longer be recognised in the balance sheet and a profit or loss will arise on their sale, which will equal the difference between their carrying amount and the proceeds of sale. Where separate gross presentation is deemed to be necessary, no profit or loss should be recognised when the securitisation transaction is entered into, unless there is a need to reassess the carrying value of the assets securitised. The notes to the financial statements should disclose the gross amount of the assets securitised at the balance sheet date.

3.149 Where the conditions for the linked presentation are satisfied, the proceeds of the note issue should be deducted from the securitised assets on the face of the balance sheet. In addition, the following disclosures should be given:

- A description of the asset securitised. [FRS 5 App D para D22(a)].

- The amount of any income or expense recognised in the period, analysed as appropriate. [FRS 5 App D para D22(b)].

- The terms of any options for the originator to repurchase assets or to transfer additional assets to the issuer. [FRS 5 App D para D22(c)].

  Where the originator can repurchase the assets, this would invalidate the use of the linked presentation and, therefore, this would seem to make the first disclosure of this requirement redundant, because the linked presentation would be precluded.

- The terms of any interest rate swap or interest rate cap agreements between the issuer and the originator that meet the conditions set out in paragraph 3.157 below. [FRS 5 App D para D22(d)].
- A description of the priority and amount of claims on the proceeds generated by the assets, including any rights of the originator to proceeds from the assets in addition to the non-recourse amounts already received. [FRS 5 App D para D22(e)].
- The ownership of the issuer. [FRS 5 App D para D22(f)].
- A statement by the directors that the company is not obliged and does not intend to support any losses beyond the recourse to the specific assets linked under the scheme. [FRS 5 para 27(c)].
- A note explaining that the noteholders have subscribed to a prospectus or offering circular that clearly stated that the originator will not support any losses of either the issuer or the noteholders. [FRS 5 App D para D10].

3.150 The standard only allows aggregation on the face of the balance sheet and in the notes where a company enters into more than one securitisation which relates to a single type of asset. Where securitisation schemes relate to different types of asset, the balance sheet disclosures and those outlined above should not be aggregated.

Group's financial statements

3.151 The table below is taken from the table given in the application note and considers the analysis necessary to determine the accounting treatment in the group's financial statements and includes references to the paragraphs of the application note that give the narrative explanation:

Indicates derecognition	**Indicates linked presentation**	**Indicates separate presentation**
Issuer is owned by an independent third party that made a substantial capital investment, has control of the issuer, and has the benefits and risks of its net assets. [App D para D19].	Issuer is a quasi-subsidiary of the originator, but the conditions for a linked presentation are met from the point of view of the group. [App D para D20].	Issuer is a subsidiary of the originator. [App D para D17].

3.152 Where the special purpose vehicle meets the definition of a subsidiary under the Act and FRS 2, it should be consolidated in the group's financial statements in the normal way (that is, separate presentation, unless the linked presentation is possible in the subsidiary – see para 3.117). Often, SPVs used in securitisation schemes may fall within the definition of a quasi-subsidiary (see from para 3.100). This is likely to be so where the vehicle's financial and operating policies are predetermined as explained in paragraph 3.105.

3.153 Furthermore, it should be presumed that a vehicle, which is not a legal subsidiary, is a quasi-subsidiary where either of the following apply:

- The originator has rights to the benefits generated by the securitised assets that remain after meeting the claims of noteholders and other expenses of the issue.
- The originator has the risks inherent in those benefits. That is, where the benefits are greater or less than expected, the originator gains or suffers.

[FRS 5 App D para D18].

Disclosure requirements

3.154 Where the undertaking is a quasi-subsidiary and the conditions for the linked presentation (see para 3.88) are met at the group level, that presentation should be used in the consolidated financial statements. Where the linked presentation is used in the consolidated financial statements, then the same disclosures as outlined in paragraph 3.149 should be given. Where the conditions are not met at the group level, then the quasi-subsidiary should be accounted for in the same way as a legal subsidiary, that is, by full consolidation (see para 3.108).

3.155 An illustration of a company that has used the linked presentation for a mortgage securitisation scheme is given below in Table 3.9 and an example of a group using the linked presentation for securitising rent receivables is given in Table 3.10.

Table 3.9 — Legal & General Group plc — Annual Reports & Accounts — 31 December 1994

Consolidated Balance Sheet (extract)
on 31 December 1994

	1994 £m	1993 £m	Notes
ASSETS			
Investments	29,204	29,110	11a
Mortgage lending and related assets	416	338	11b
other assets	982	951	11c
	30,602	30,400	
Securitised mortgages and related assets	149	228	20
Non-recourse borrowings	(149)	(228)	20

Notes to Financial Statements (extract)

20. SECURITISED MORTGAGES AND RELATED ASSETS

During 1989 and 1991 Legal & General Mortgage Services Limited (LGMSL) sold £298m of mortgages, via Temple Court Originations Limited (TCO) to Temple Court Mortgages (No. 1) Plc and Temple Court Mortgages (No. 2) Plc (TCM 1&2). TCM2 redeemed all of its securities during 1994. These companies issued debt to purchase the mortgages, the written terms of which provide no recourse to LGMSL. Neither LGMSL nor any other member of the Group is obliged, or intends, to support any losses in respect of the sold mortgages. Mortgage payments (interest and principal) in respect of the portfolio are used to pay the capital and interest due on borrowings and other administration expenses. Any residue is payable as deferred consideration to LGMSL. During 1994 this amounted to £3.9m (1993, £5.3m) and is reported within the mortgage lending result under Other Operations. TCO and TCM 1&2 are quasi subsidiaries of the Group and their summarised financial statements at 31 December, which form the basis of the linked presentation in the consolidated balance sheet are:

	Assets	Liabilities	Assets	Liabilities
	1994	**1994**	**1993**	**1993**
	£m	**£m**	**£m**	**£m**
Securitised mortgages	152	—	234	—
Other related assets	7	—	10	—
Non-recourse borrowings	—	(159)	—	(244)
Share capital and reserves	—	0	—	0
Amount reported by quasi subsidiaries	159	(159)	244	(244)
Mortgage backed securities purchased by LGMSL*	(10)	—	16	—
Borrowings for mortgage lending*	—	10	—	16
Amounts shown in linked presentation	149	(149)	228	(228)

The quasi subsidiaries had gross financial income and expenses of approximately £16m (1993, £22.3m). At 31 December 1994 LGMSL held as investments £10m of notes issued by TCM1.

*These investments have been included as mortgage lending and related assets and the related borrowings have been included in borrowings for financing mortgage lending.

Note: This example pre-dates the changes made to the definition of subsidiary in both the Act and FRS 2. Hence, it is possible that these entities may no longer be quasi-subsidiaries.

Table 3.10 — Zeneca Group PLC — Annual Report and Accounts — 31 December 1994

Notes relating to the accounts (extract)

2 BASIS OF PRESENTATION OF FINANCIAL INFORMATION (extract)

In accordance with the provisions of FRS 5 "Reporting the Substance of Transactions", the financial statements include the securitisation of rent receivables from a property which had been effected by Stauffer Chemical Company in 1984, prior to its acquisition by the Group in 1987 (see Note 15). The net effect of these transactions was recorded in the accounts as part of the acquisition accounting in 1987. The adoption of FRS 5 also resulted in recognition of an insurance liability and its related reinsurance recovery, with separate recording in debtors and creditors.

Balance sheets (extract)

			Group			Company	
As at 31 December			*1994*		**1993*	*1994*	*1993*
	Notes		*£m*		*£m*	*£m*	*£m*
Current assets							
Stocks	14		776		776	—	—
Debtors	15		1,396		1,483	1,765	1,483
Securitised rent receivables	15	56		58		—	—
Less: Non-recourse Secured Notes	15	(54)	2	(57)	1	—	—
Short-term investments	16		594		925	—	401
Cash	16		141		124	—	—
			2,909		3,309	1,765	1,884

15 DEBTORS (extract)

Included in debtors are amounts totalling £177m (1993 £145m) in respect of the Group's insurance subsidiaries relating to reinsurance contracts.

Rent receivables in respect of a property were securitised under an arrangement established by Stauffer Chemical Company (SCC) in 1984. The receivables were securitised under a Trust Indenture in connection with the issue of $245m of non-recourse Zero Coupon Secured Notes due 1994-2018 on behalf of SCC. SCC's interest in the receivables and its obligations under the Trust Indenture were vested in Zeneca Holdings Inc. (ZHI) by way of an assignment and assumption agreement. Neither SCC as the issuer of the notes nor ZHI as assignee of SCC's interest is obliged to support any losses of the assets pledged under the trust indenture, nor does either intend to do so. Repayment of the finance is solely secured by rent receivables from the property, payment of which is further secured by an irrecoverable letter of credit drawn on a first class bank. The net present value of these arrangements amounts to a net asset of £6m — this asset was recorded in the accounts as part of the acquisition accounting of Stauffer since 1987. Under FRS 5 this is now reported as an asset of £56m and a liability of £54m, using a linked presentation, with £4m included in cash and short-term investments. The net income recorded in the Group accounts amounted to £1m (1993 £1m). A summary of the financial statements of Stauffer Chemical Company Trust is set out below.

Stauffer Chemical Company Trust	***1994*** ***£m***	***1993*** ***£m***
Income and Expenditure account		
Surplus for the financial year	1	1
Trust distributions	(1)	—
Surplus retained for the year	—	1
Balance sheet		
Debtors	56	58
Cash and short-term investments	4	5
Total assets	60	63
Creditors	(54)	(57)
Net assets	6	6
Cash flow		
Increase in cash and cash equivalents	—	—

Note: This example pre-dates the changes made to the definition of subsidiary in both the Act and FRS 2. Hence, it is possible that these entities may no longer be quasi-subsidiaries.

Interest rate swaps

3.156 Often securitisation schemes originated by banks make use of interest rate swaps between the originator and the issuer. The British Bankers Association (BBA) made representations to the ASB to deal specifically with interest rate swaps in the standard, because it was concerned that under the proposals in FRED 4 the linked presentation could not be used for many securitisations undertaken by banks. Swaps have a number of benefits in securitisation schemes as, from the point of view of the issuer, they provide a way in which noteholders can receive an interest stream in a form that accommodates their needs (for example, payment at a rate based on LIBOR, rather than a bank's mortgage rate). In addition, a swap can help the originator to manage its own interest rate position. For example, a bank might have a portfolio of mortgages on which it is receiving a fixed rate. A bank would normally hedge this interest rate exposure.

Hence, when it sells the mortgages to the securitisation vehicle, without further action the bank's interest rate position becomes unmatched. If the bank arranges a swap with the issuer, such that it receives a fixed rate and pays a rate based on LIBOR, the bank's interest rate position is restored. The issuer will then receive fixed rate interest on the mortgages which it will pay to the bank and receive in return a rate based on LIBOR, which will cover its liability to its noteholders. This type of arrangement provides a cost-effective way of protecting a bank's position. Therefore, in such circumstances, it can be argued that the interest rate swap does not expose the bank to additional risk.

3.157 As a result of its discussions with the BBA and others, the ASB confirmed that the conditions for the linked presentation can be regarded as being met notwithstanding the existence of an interest rate swap, provided all of the following conditions are met:

- The swap is on arm's length market-related terms and the obligations of the issuer under the swap are not subordinated to any of its obligations under the loan notes.

  The words 'arm's length market-related terms' have been used rather than just merely 'arm's length' to allow originator banks to provide the interest rate swap instrument for their own securitisation schemes. If this wording was not included, originator banks would have to look to outside third parties to provide swap instruments.

- The variable interest rates that are swapped are determined by reference to publicly quoted rates that are not under the originator's control.

  Again, this condition has been made to ensure that if an originator bank provides the interest swap it does so at arm's length prices.

- At the time of transfer of the assets to the issuer, the originator had hedged exposures relating to these assets (either individually or as part of a larger portfolio) and entering into the swap effectively restores the hedge position left open by their transfer. Thereafter, where the hedging of the originator's exposure under the swap requires continuing management, any necessary adjustments to the hedging position are made on an ongoing basis.

[FRS 5 App D para D11].

[The next paragraph is 3.159.]

Revolving assets

3.159 There are many examples of credit card securitisations in the US. Because of the fluctuating nature of credit card balances, a special structure is used in the US to effect the securitisation. A trust is set up which acquires the rights to the credit card balances from the originator (usually a bank). The balances are then split in two: the first element is a fixed amount; and the second element is the balance of the credit card receivables, which fluctuates. A SPV issues loan notes to investors and finances the fixed amount of the credit card receivables, the fluctuating balance is financed by the originator as illustrated in the graph below. Some form of credit enhancement will also be used. The originator's staff normally administer the receivables.

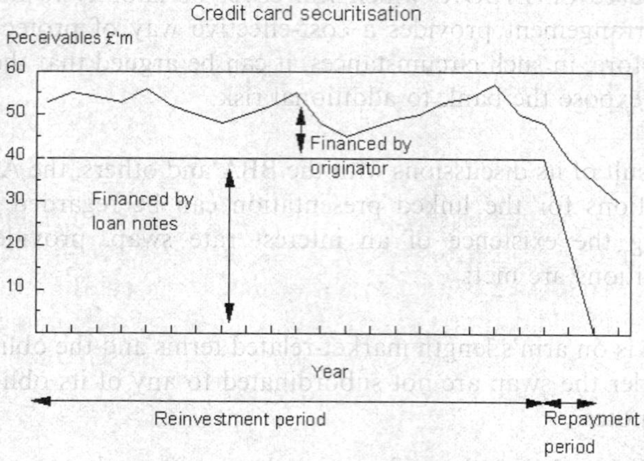

3.160 Generally, in the US, the monies collected, being the repayment of principal and interest, are applied in proportion to the outstanding fixed and fluctuating balances. The proportion of interest collected allocated to the fixed amount is used by the SPV to pay interest on its loan notes. The interest differential between that charged on the receivables and that paid on the loan notes is considerable and the excess is used to finance expenses of the SPV and its bad debts. The amount of principal collected is initially, during the reinvestment period, invested in new receivables such that the balance securitised remains constant. After a set period (typically five years) the amount of principal received stops being used to reinvest in new receivables and is instead used to repay the loan notes during the repayment period.

3.161 In the UK the requirements of FRS 5, have precluded the use of the linked presentation for US-style credit card securitisations, because it has proved difficult for companies to satisfy two of the linked presentation conditions. The two problematical conditions are: condition (b) in paragraph 27, which requires the provider of the finance to have no recourse (implicit or explicit) and the originator no obligation to repay the finance; and condition (f) in paragraph 27, which seeks to ensure that the originator has no obligation or right to re-acquire the securitised assets. These conditions need to be considered carefully.

Reinvestment period

3.162 During the reinvestment period the proceeds from old balances are reinvested in new credit card receivables to maintain the fixed amount finance by the SPV. It is important, during this period, that there is no recourse to the originator (which is the condition in paragraph 27(b) of the standard); this can happen if poorly performing debts are replaced in the SPV by good ones. Consider the following diagram:

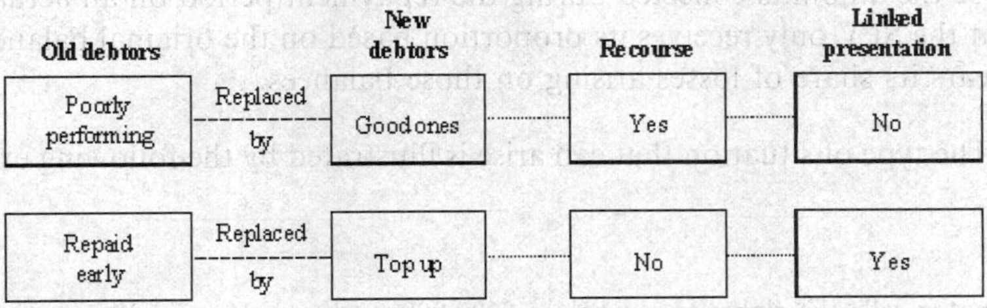

Where, in the pool of debtors securitised, old poorly performing debtors are replaced by sound ones, there is recourse as the originator in effect re-acquires some of the old debts. As a consequence, the linked presentation cannot be used. However, where the old debtors are repaid early then it is acceptable to top up the pool of debtors with new debtors and the linked presentation can be used provided the other conditions for its use are met. [FRS 5 App D para D13]. It is important, therefore, in a credit card securitisation that the SPV is allocated its share of bad debts and that these do not fall solely to the originator.

Repayment period

3.163 As mentioned above, in a credit card securitisation the loan notes are usually repaid from proceeds received during the repayment period. The monies collected during that period arise from balances existing at the beginning of the repayment period and new balances arising subsequently that continue to be financed by the originator. In the US schemes, the proceeds from the repayment of principal relating both to old and to new balances are allocated in proportion to the fixed amount and to the fluctuating balance of the receivables that arises at the beginning of the repayment period. However, in practice, this proportion will change significantly during the repayment period as the old balances financed by the SPV are repaid. For example, if the proportion of fixed to fluctuating debt is 80:20 at the beginning of the repayment period, it can soon become (say) 40:60. If the SPV is still being allocated 80 per cent (and in some US schemes they allocate an arbitrary 99 per cent) of the cash balances received, when it should only be receiving 40 per cent, the effect is that the noteholders are being repaid out of proceeds of the new balances as well as the old ones that existed at the beginning of the repayment period. Therefore, because of this apportionment, the noteholders are being repaid partly out of assets belonging to the originator and only partly out of the assets they were financing at the beginning of the repayment period. As a consequence, the condition in paragraph 27(f) is not met, because the noteholders are not being repaid solely out of the cash receipts generated by the balances that existed at the start of the repayment period.

3.164 In order for conditions (b) and (f) to be satisfied, only the cash collected from the old balances can be used to repay the loan notes during the repayment period. This is necessary to ensure that the issuer is allocated its proper share of losses on those old balances so they do not fall to the originator. [FRS 5 App D para D12]. Therefore, in order for such a scheme to work in the UK it is necessary to analyse the amounts collected during the repayment period on an actual basis such that the SPV only receives its proportion based on the original balances and hence bears its share of losses arising on those balances.

3.165 The type of situation that can arise is illustrated by the following example:

Example

An originator sells the rights to a pool of £600,000 credit card receivables to a SPV, of which £400,000 is funded by noteholders and the balance £200,000 by a loan from the originator. The rights to all new receivables generated during a reinvestment period will be offered for sale to and purchased by the SPV. Increases in the balances of rights to receivables bought by the SPV are to be funded by the originator. The funding by noteholders remains constant. Initially the securitisation covers the rights to a portfolio of 400 debtors and soon after the initial securitisation a number of the card holders have increased their balances as follows:

Pool debtors	**On securitisation**	**Shortly thereafter**
	£	£
1	100	450
2	500	500
3	1,200	1,200
4	750	750
5	240	280
6 — 400	597,210	696,820
	600,000	700,000
Funded by:		
Originator	200,000	300,000
Noteholders	400,000	400,000
	600,000	700,000
Originator's interest in debtor 3 (for example)		
On securitisation		
$1,200 \times \dfrac{200,000}{600,000}$	400	
Shortly thereafter		
$1,200 \times \dfrac{300,000}{700,000}$		514

If the debtor of £1,200 went bad, then the originator would bear £400 of the loss initially, but after the increase in the pool would bear a loss of £514. The example shows that the originator is exposed to a bigger loss on the original asset, which breaches paragraphs 27(f) as it seems that in effect it has re-acquired part of its interest in the debtor of £1,200. This outcome might seem to indicate that it would not be possible under that standard to securitise credit card receivables in this way. However, it can be argued in this case, that this is purely an arithmetic result rather than a matter of principle and in reality the originator's participation will move up and down over the life of the credit card scheme and so fluctuations of this nature can be ignored. This is a pragmatic argument and one that would probably be accepted in practice. What is important is that new credit card balances introduced to the scheme in this period are only used to top up the scheme and not to replace bad debts. Furthermore, in the repayment period, where there is a desire to unwind the scheme and repay the loan notes as fast as possible, it is necessary to ensure that sufficient cash is generated from those balances that existed at the beginning of the repayment period, to make the relevant repayments to the noteholders; or that, if there is not, the relevant part of any loss falls to the noteholders.

Multi-originator programmes

3.166 In certain securitisation schemes, the SPV might serve a number of originators. Such arrangements are often structured so that the originator's benefits and risks are based on the performance of a defined pool of assets (that is, those that it has transferred to the SPV). Where this is so, and the originator is shielded from the benefits and risks on the other assets held by the SPV, the originator should include as an asset in its financial statements the pool of mortgages from which its benefits and risks arise. The related finance can be linked on the face of the balance sheet provided the conditions for that presentation are met, otherwise it should be recorded separately as a liability. [FRS 5 App D para D15].

Example of required analysis

3.167 Application note D unfortunately provides no examples of securitisation transactions to illustrate its provision. The example below illustrates the principles as they apply to a credit card securitisation:

Example

Company A owns credit card receivables that it wishes to securitise. A third party company, company B, acquires the rights from company A to the credit card receivables. Company C is a SPV owned by a charitable trust. The rights sold to company B entitle it to all present and future credit card receivables on those accounts. The legal ownership remains with company A. The transaction is illustrated in the diagram below.

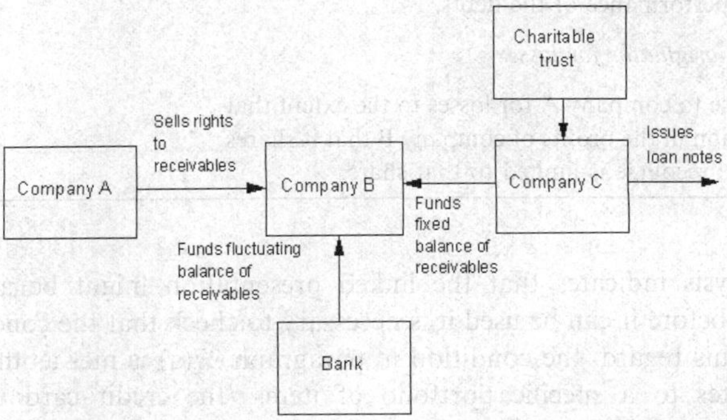

Company A services the accounts and charges company B a fee for doing so and is also entitled to a share of the profits of company B during the first five years of the scheme. The acquisition of the rights to the credit card balances by company B is funded partly by company B issuing loan notes to company C and partly by company B raising money from a third party bank. The total amount funded equals the book value of the debts whose rights are transferred. Company B's loan notes held by company C entitle company C to a share of the cash flows generated by the receivables. Company C's share is a fixed amount which does not fluctuate with the change of the amounts due on the credit card receivables. Company C funds its acquisition of the loan notes in company B by issuing loan notes to third party investors. The amount of the bank's share of the receivables varies and is the difference between company C's share and the total of the receivables.

During the scheme's first five years, repayments in respect of principal are reinvested in new credit card receivables. The level of funding provided by company C remains constant, any variations being funded by the bank. After year five the repayment period starts and company C's loan to company B is repaid from its proportionate share of the principal of the receivables collected. The bank's funding will reduce, but at a slower rate than that of company A, so that eventually the bank will fund whatever receivables are left in company B, which will continue to fall.

In analysing the transaction it is necessary to consider how the transaction should be accounted for in company A's financial statements and in company A's group consolidated financial statements. In company A's financial statements, there are three possible treatments: derecognition of the credit card receivables in their entirety; linked presentation where the conditions for its use are satisfied; and full gross presentation on the balance sheet. Using the principles of Application Note D, the benefits and risks of the transaction can be analysed as follows:

	Off B/ sheet	Linked	On B/ sheet
Transaction price			
The transaction price is arm's length, because company B's acquisition of the rights is based on the receivable's book value.	✓		
Amount of non-returnable proceeds			
Company A receives non-returnable proceeds for the disposal of its rights to the credit card receivables to company B, but retains a right to further sums, which will depend on the performance of the debts.		✓	
Recourse to the originator for losses			
There is recourse to company A for losses to the extent that there is a variation in the profits of company B that it shares in, however, the recourse is limited to that share.		✓	

The initial analysis indicates that the linked presentation might be available for this transaction, but before it can be used it is necessary to check that the conditions for its use can be met. In this regard, the condition in paragraph 27(a) is met as the finance for the transaction relates to a specific portfolio of items (the credit card receivables). The condition in paragraph 27(c) can be easily met, because this merely requires the directors of company A to confirm that they have no obligation to support losses of company B and company C in their financial statements. The provider of the finance, company B, is required in the condition in paragraph 27(d) to agree in writing (and for that agreement to be noted in the financial statements) that it will seek repayment of the finance only to the extent that sufficient funds are generated by the assets it has financed and that it will not seek recourse in any other form. The condition in paragraph 27(e) is met as long as the bank cannot regard company A as being in default on any other loans it might have from the bank if there are insufficient funds generated in company B to repay the bank's finance.

The problematical conditions with regard to credit card securitisations are those in paragraphs 27(b) and 27(f) as explained in paragraph 3.161. In typical credit card securitisations in the US, there is recourse to the originator, and the originator in effect reacquires a proportion of bad balances, because the allocation of proceeds from the repayment of the principal might include a share of the losses on the balances that are outstanding at the beginning of the repayment period. This is because the originator generally finances the fluctuating balance of the receivables. However, in this example, the bank takes that risk and, as a consequence, there is no recourse to the originator. In conclusion, therefore, it appears that company A can present this securitisation using the linked presentation in its individual financial statements. It would show the finance provided by company B deducted from the credit card receivables on the face of its balance sheet (that is, all of it, not just that from company C's loan notes).

With regard to the presentation in the group's consolidated financial statements, it seems that company B and company C may be quasi-subsidiaries of company A as long as it has been ascertained that company B and company C are not controlled by company A and, hence, are not full legal subsidiaries. Then, following the arguments above, the conditions for the linked presentation can also be justified at the group level. In the consolidated financial statements, the same presentation would be given as in company A's individual financial statements, except that the description of the finance would change and the loan from company B would be replaced by a loan from the bank and the loan notes issued to third parties.

Loan transfers

3.168 For those entities applying FRS 26, FRS 5 Application Note E is not relevant, and the recognition and derecognition principles in FRS 26 should be applied (see further chapter 6). For those entities not within the scope of FRS 26, FRS 5's provisions should be applied to loan transfers and the guidance in FRS 5 Application Note E is relevant. Application Note E deals with other types of loan transfers that do not involve the use of SPVs. The principles involved in analysing these transactions closely follow those applicable to securitisation schemes and factoring. The application note refers to three methods under which the benefits and risks associated with loans can be transferred to a third party:

- Novation — where with the consent of the parties a new contract is substituted for an existing one, generally, in this context, having the effect of changing the party who is the lender.
- Assignment — where rights to interest and repayment of principal (but not obligations) are transferred to a third party (assignee—sub-participant). There are two types of assignment. First, a statutory assignment which must relate to the whole loan and comply with certain conditions before it will be

a valid statutory assignment. For instance, the assignment must take the form of an out and out transfer which deprives the assignor of all further interest in the loan. In addition, notice in writing must be given to the borrower and guarantors. Secondly, an equitable assignment (which may only relate to part of the loan and does not require all the legal formalities of a statutory assignment). No particular form is required to constitute a valid equitable assignment.

- Sub-participation — where the lender enters into an agreement with a third party (sub-participant) for that party to deposit an amount equal to the whole or part of the loan with the lender on a non-recourse basis. The sub-participant receives an interest in the cash flows arising on the loan, but the loan itself is not transferred. The sub-participant, therefore, assumes a risk exposure to the original borrower, because it only receives its share of the interest and principal if the borrower performs on the loan. The sub-participant is also exposed to the original lender, because the cash flows are often routed through the lender.

3.169 As with securitisation schemes, there are three possible treatments in the lender's financial statements:

- Derecognition — where the loan or part of it is removed from the balance sheet and no liability is shown in respect of the amounts received from the transferee.
- Linked presentation — where the liability in respect of the amounts received from the transferee is deducted from the amount of the loan on the face of the balance sheet.
- Separate presentation — where the loan continues to be shown as an asset and the amount received from the transferee is shown as a liability.

3.170 The benefits to the lender associated with such loan transfers remain the cash flows of interest and principal received from the borrower, although these will eventually be paid to the transferee. The risks associated with such transactions are:

- Credit risk — risk of bad debts.
- Slow payment risk.
- Interest rate risk — risk that the interest rate received from the borrower will not match the rate paid to the transferee.
- Reinvestment/early redemption risk — risk that interest earned on amounts received and reinvested by the lender, before repayment to the transferee, are lower than those payable to the transferee.
- Moral risk — risk that the lender is morally obliged to fund any losses on the loans, because of its association with them.

[FRS 5 App E para E6].

3.171 These main benefits and risks are considered in detail in the application note and the principles stemming from that discussion are then summarised in a table. The summary table is reproduced below; also included are references to the paragraphs of the application note that give the narrative explanation:

Indicates derecognition	**Indicates linked presentation**	**Indicates separate presentation**
[App E para E15].	[App E para E17].	[App E para E18].
Transfer is for a single, non-returnable fixed sum.	Some non-returnable proceeds received, but lender has rights to further sums whose amount depends on whether or when the borrowers pay.	The proceeds received are returnable in the event of losses occurring on the loans.
There is no recourse to the lender for losses from any cause.	There is either no recourse for losses, or such recourse has a fixed monetary ceiling.	There is full recourse to the lender for losses.
Transferee is paid all amounts received from the loans (and no more), as and when received. Lender has no rights to further sums from the loans or the transferee.	Transferee is paid only out of amounts received from the loans, and lender has no right or obligation to repurchase them.	Lender is required to repay amounts received from the transferee on or before a set date, regardless of the timing or amount of payments by the borrowers.

3.172 In order for loans to be derecognised in the lender's financial statements, the lender must not retain any significant benefits *or* risks associated with the loan. Derecognition is, therefore, only appropriate where all of the following apply:

- The transaction takes place at an arm's length price for an outright sale.
- The transaction is for a fixed amount of consideration and there is no recourse (other than to the loan itself) either implicit or explicit.

  Warranties given in respect of the loan's condition (for example, that the loan is not in arrears) at the time of transfer are allowed, but warranties concerning the loan's condition in the future or its future performance (for example, the loan will not move into arrears) are not allowed.
- The lender will not benefit or suffer if the loans perform better or worse than expected.

[FRS 5 App E para E15].

3.173 Generally, whether or not the lender continues to administer the loans will be of no consequence unless, for example, its servicing fee is not priced at arm's length. This might indicate that the lender has retained significant benefits and risks.

3.174 Normally, in novation agreements all the significant benefits and risks are transferred and the loan can be derecognised (subject to any side agreements). Also in assignments, all significant benefits and risks might be transferred as long as there are no outstanding obligations (for example, to supply additional funds if the loan is restructured), no side agreements and doubts concerning intervening equitable rights can be satisfied. [FRS 5 App E para E14].

3.175 With sub-participations, derecognition might be appropriate, but only where the lender's obligation to pay amounts to the transferee eliminates its access to benefits from the loans, but extends only to those benefits. There must be no possibility that the lender could be required to pay amounts to the sub-participant, where it has not received equivalent amounts from the borrower. If the lender has an obligation to agree to rescheduling the loan without a similar undertaking by the sub-participant, derecognition is not appropriate. [FRS App E para E14].

3.176 Where derecognition is inappropriate the linked presentation may be used, but only if there is absolutely no doubt that the lender's downside exposure to loss is limited to a fixed monetary amount and the linked presentation conditions can be met. If these conditions are not met then the lender will have to adopt separate presentation.

3.177 In some loan transfers only part of the loan is transferred to the sub-participant. In this circumstance, part of the loan might be able to be derecognised or linked with the related finance, but only where the principles of the standard apply. Such arrangements are considered in detail in paragraphs E19 and E20 of Application Note D.

Disclosure requirements

3.178 Where the conditions for the linked presentation are met and that presentation is given on the face of the balance sheet, the notes to the financial statements should also disclose:

- The arrangement's main terms. [FRS 5 App E para E23].
- The gross amount of the loans transferred and outstanding at the balance sheet date. [FRS 5 App E para E23].

  This information will normally already be given on the face of the balance sheet as part of the linked presentation, unless there are any provisions against the loan to cover irrecoverability.

- Any profit or loss recognised in the period, analysed as appropriate. [FRS 5 App E para E23].
- A statement by the directors that the company is not obliged and does not intend to support any losses beyond the recourse to the specific loans linked under the scheme. [FRS 5 para 27(c)].
- A note that the sub-participant has agreed in writing that it will seek recourse to both principal and interest only to the extent that sufficient funds are generated by the specific loans it has financed. [FRS 5 para 27(d)].

3.179 Where the conditions for the linked presentation cannot be met and derecognition is not appropriate, separate presentation should be adopted and the gross loans should be shown on the face of the balance sheet (but not linked). The notes to the financial statements should also disclose the amount of the loans subject to transfer agreements that are outstanding at the balance sheet date. [FRS 5 App E para E24].

Private Finance Initiative and Public Private Partnership

3.179.1 The Private Finance Initiative (PFI) and Public Private Partnerships (PPP) were developed to allow the public sector to procure the provision of services from the private sector. The objective of PFI and PPP is to give the public sector a value for money service. Therefore, value for money is intended to be the key determinant of whether a project should go ahead, not the accounting treatment. In particular, the public sector has been directed to focus on how the procurement of services can achieve the transfer of risk in a way that optimises value for money, so they should not transfer risks to the operator at the expense of value for money. The accounting issue is determining whether or not the risks and rewards relating to the assets included within the contract are retained by the service provider or have been transferred to the public sector purchaser. The most specific accounting standard that applies to PFI and similar transactions is FRS 5, but SSAP 21 is also relevant.

3.179.2 In 1998, the ASB published a further application note 'F' to FRS 5 entitled 'Private finance initiative and similar contracts'. Whilst the application note was written with PFI contracts in mind, its principles can be applied to PPP and other similar contracts. In addition, the Treasury Taskforce published new guidance in Technical Note No. 1 (Revised): How to Account for PFI Transaction [TT TN 1 (revised)] that provides additional guidance for public sector entities when applying the FRS 5 application note principles.

3.179.3 FRS 5's objective is to ensure that the substance of an entity's transactions is reported in its financial statements. This is done by considering the risks and rewards associated with a transaction to determine whether assets and liabilities arise which need to be reflected in the entity's financial statements. Typically, the public sector is provided with a service for which it pays a unitary amount (that is, the single payment made for both the use of the asset and any facilities management (FM) services). In PFI contracts, the unitary payment covers both the cost of the asset and the cost of the other ancillary services being provided.

3.179.4 As mentioned above, the key question in accounting for PFI is who should include on their balance sheet the assets used to fulfil the contract. In essence, the application note requires that, unless the contract contains a stand-alone lease (in which case SSAP 21 should apply), this question should be answered by looking at the extent to which each party bears variations in profits and losses. The problem is which payments and variations should be taken into account and whether the contract should be separated into different elements or regarded as a whole.

[The next paragraph is 3.179.6.]

3.179.6 It is also important to note that the ASB's application note applies also to contracts that are similar to PFI transactions, such as, capital intensive outsourcing/franchising arrangements.

3.179.7 There are a number of stages that have to be considered in establishing on whose balance sheet the PFI assets will reside and these are considered in the paragraphs that follow.

Contract separability

3.179.8 In many schemes it is possible to see clearly how the unitary payment is made up because, for example, the asset element is indexed by a different factor to the ancillary service element. Where such an analysis can be made, the rules in SSAP 21 are easily applied to the asset element and an evaluation of these payments will often result in the conclusion that the transaction is a full pay-out finance lease, which should be on the public sector's balance sheet.

3.179.9 Where it is possible to see through the unitary payment and identify the element that relates to the property and the element that relates to the provision of the facilities management (FM) service, the property element should be analysed using SSAP 21 principles (as it represents a stand-alone lease) and the service element should be ignored. [FRS 5 App F paras F11, F12]. The discount rate to be applied in the SSAP 21 net present value test should not be the return from the entire PFI contract, but should be estimated by reference to the rate that would be expected on a similar lease. [FRS 5 App F para F16]. The minimum lease payments to be taken into account include the expected PFI payments for the property, less any amounts for which there is a genuine possibility of non-payment. [FRS 5 App F para F17]. (See chapter 19 for further explanation concerning lease evaluation under SSAP 21.) The application note lists three examples of situations where a contract may be separable as explained in the paragraphs that follow.

3.179.10 The standard says the contract will be separable where an element of the payment stream varies according to the availability of the property and another element varies according to the usage or performance of services. [FRS 5 App F para F10(a)]. However, as explained above, the underlying intention in most PFI schemes is that individual elements of the unitary payment should not be related to the delivery of specific inputs and should not contain an element designed to cover the debt service costs of the operator with no variation for performance.

3.179.11 The Treasury guidance categorises the more common payment mechanisms used in PFI transactions into three broad models. Model A is where the unitary payment is based on the number of available places, for example, prisoner places. For a 'place' to be available, not only must there be a physical space available, there must also be associated core services, such as heating and food. There are no separate payment streams for any non-core services, but deductions from the unitary payment will be made for substandard performance of these services. This payment model is regarded as non-separable. [TT TN 1 (revised) para 3.4].

3.179.12 Under model B, which is also considered to be non-separable, the unitary payment is based on the full provision of an overall accommodation requirement, which is divided into different units. Availability is defined in terms of being usable and accessible and, in common with model A, will include some associated core services such as heating. There will be no separate payments for any non-core services but, as with model A, substandard performance leads to payment deductions. [TT TN 1 (revised) para 3.5].

3.179.13 In contrast to models A and B, model C is considered to be separable. Under this model, unitary payment is a combination of an availability payment stream and a separate performance related facilities management payment stream. The availability payment stream relates to areas, divided into units, that are attributed a different deduction percentage for unavailability according to their importance. Availability is defined in terms of being usable accessible and may include some associated core services. The facilities management payment stream is made up of the combination of a performance payment for each required service, with deductions for failure to meet the required performance levels. [TT TN 1 (revised) para 3.6].

3.179.14 Another example of separability is where different parts of the contract run for different periods or can be terminated separately, which might arise where a particular service element can be terminated independently. [FRS 5 App F para F10(b)]. An example is where an accommodation contract running for 25 years includes provision of IT services, but this element of the service may be renegotiated at the end of 10 years and/or may be terminated at any time for persistent poor performance without affecting the continuation of the rest of the contract. [TT TN 1 (revised) para 3.7]. However, changes to the service requirements during the contract term that result in the entire unitary payment being renegotiated would not indicate separability.

3.179.15 A further example of separability is where different parts of the contract can be renegotiated separately. This covers market testing and would apply where a service element is market tested and *some or all* of the cost increases or reductions are passed on to the purchaser in such a way that the part of the unitary payment that relates specifically to that service can be identified. [FRS 5 App F para F10(c)]. This applies regardless of whether the market testing is undertaken by the purchaser or the operator. If the purchaser market tests what it pays for an element of an individual service, with an adjustment made to that payment, then there will be a separately identifiable payment stream for that service and hence the contract will be separable. Another situation is where the operator market tests what it pays to subcontractors for an element of an individual service and passes on some or all of the cost increases or decreases to the purchaser, by means of an adjustment made to the unitary payment rather than a separately identifiable payment stream. In this situation, although the part of the payment by the purchaser for that service element may not be separately identified from the contract itself, the substance is that the purchaser has effectively renegotiated what it is paying for an individual service element and hence the contract is separable. However, the fact that the purchaser or operator, at their own volition, conduct market testing of some aspects of the service and, as a result, the parties voluntarily renegotiate the contract does not, in itself, render the contract separable. [TT TN 1 (revised) paras 3.8 to 3.11].

3.179.16 For other contracts where there are some non-separable service elements, the provisions of FRS 5 and application note F should be applied.

How to apply FRS 5

3.179.17 PFI contracts involve the delivery of outputs to a definable standard for the payment of a unitary amount. Generally, the unitary payment varies depending on a number of measurable deliverables. For example, if the demand for the service (demand risk) is greater or less than predicted or expected, this is likely to impact on the unitary payment. If the service is not being performed to a high enough standard (performance risk) then this will probably also have an impact on the unitary payment. Similarly, if the service is not available (availability risk) this would normally reduce the amount paid by the public sector purchaser. Contracts often have performance and availability criteria that are not related purely to services. Criteria set at such a high level that they never affect the amount paid by the public sector purchaser should not be taken into account in the analysis. If the contract is truly the provision of an integrated service then it is reasonable that it should not be paid for, or there should be a reduction in the payment, if that integrated service is not provided or it is not up to the specified standard. So, under PFI a service provider could provide, for example, heat and light to definable standards or provide serviced office accommodation, with demand, availability and performance criteria set realistically.

3.179.18 From an accounting view point, FRS 5 is concerned with what actually happens in practice. The accounting treatment not only takes into account whether the performance and availability criteria have been set at realistic levels of performance and availability, it also considers whether those targets are measurable and whether this measurement actually takes place in practice. There is growing expertise in this area and very sophisticated measurement techniques are now being applied effectively.

3.179.19 The party that should recognise the asset on its balance sheet is the one that has access to the asset's benefits and exposure to its risks. In this analysis it is necessary to look at the potential variations in property profits (or losses) that each party bears. Any profit variations that relate purely to service should be ignored. For example, penalties arising from the inadequacy in the training of prison security staff or from the standard of food used in catering facilities should not be taken into account even if those penalties affect the whole of the unitary payment. [FRS 5 App F para F20].

3.179.20 After excluding variations related to service, there may still be a significant number of property factors that need to be considered. In this analysis, greater weight should be given to those factors that are more likely to have a commercial effect in practice. [FRS 5 App F para F21]. It is not appropriate to focus on one feature in isolation, rather the combined effect of all relevant factors should be considered for a range of reasonable possible scenarios. [FRS 5 App F para F49]. It is necessary to consider both the probability of any future profit variation arising from a property factor and its likely financial effect. For example, if it is cheaper to correct a problem rather than to incur a much larger penalty, the relevant variation to consider is the rectification cost. [FRS 5 App F para F21].

3.179.21 Furthermore, a financing transaction will be indicated where, in the event that the contract is terminated early, the bank financing will be paid in full by the purchaser under all events of default. [FRS 5 App F para F50].

3.179.22 Hence it is clear from the above that to establish on whose balance sheet the assets associated with the PFI contract should lie, the analysis should focus on the variations in property profits and losses that each of the parties to the contract bear. While the application note gives no guidance on how this should be done in practice, the Treasury guidance does, by providing a methodology for undertaking a quantitative risk analysis. This involves identifying the key commercial risks borne by each party, evaluating the net present value of the potential variations in property profits of each party and then comparing the two. This gives a quantitative indicator of which party has an asset of the property. The guidance contains two simplified examples of how this is done. These examples are set out in paragraph 3.179.56. However, the Treasury guidance warns that care must be taken to ensure that the quantitative risk analysis model is not applied in a mechanistic way. The validity of the results depends on the accuracy, certainty and completeness of the inputs and assumptions made regarding those inputs. Therefore, the results of the quantitative risk analysis must be assessed together with those risks that are not quantifiable, that is, the qualitative indicators and those risks that may not be capable of meaningful quantification, because of the high level of uncertainty surrounding them. [TT TN 1 (revised) paras 4.1 to 4.58].

3.179.23 In general, where the majority (that is, more than 50 per cent) of these risks and rewards remain with the operator, then the assets should remain as fixed assets on the operator's balance sheet. The purchaser would in this case merely record the unitary payment. Where in contrast the majority of the risks and rewards associated with the property lie with the purchaser, the purchaser would record the assets in its balance sheet (based on the fair value of the asset) and an equivalent obligation. The operator in this situation would record a receivable (similar to a finance lease receivable) representing the present value of the property element of the minimum unitary payments it would receive over the term of the contract, which should equate to the market value of the property. Any additional amounts (that is, in addition to the property-related element of the unitary payments) should be treated as revenue by the operator and expenses by the purchaser.

3.179.24 The analysis, therefore, will concentrate on the variation in profits and losses that arise from the property related risks and rewards. These risks and rewards are considered in the paragraphs that follow.

Property factors to be considered

Demand risk

3.179.25 Demand risk is the risk that the demand for the property will be greater or less than predicted or expected. [FRS 5 App F para F24]. Where demand risk is insignificant little weight should be given to it in the analysis. Longer term contracts create greater demand risk, because of the uncertainties concerning demand in the future. Demand risk might be insignificant even, where there is uncertainty over demand for a particular type of property in the long-term, if the purchaser would fill the PFI property in preference to non-PFI properties. [FRS 5 App F para F27].

3.179.26 Demand risk is significant and borne by the *operator*, for example, where the payments between the operator and the purchaser vary proportionately to reflect usage of the property over all reasonably likely levels of demand — the purchaser will not have to pay the operator for the property to the extent it is not used. Another indication would be where the operator gains if future demand is greater than expected. [FRS 5 App F para F28].

3.179.27 It should be relatively obvious who bears the demand risk from the contract terms and how this impacts on the analysis. For example, where the operator bears the demand risk the unitary payment will vary with demand, but the operator's cost base may stay substantially the same or vary in a non-proportionate way, such that operator bears these variations in profits and losses. Where the purchaser bears demand risk, the operator's revenue is protected and the operator can pass on variations in its costs to the purchaser.

3.179.28 Certain types of PFI transaction have significantly less demand risk, for example with a prison contract or a contract for a hospital the variation in demand may not be very great. In these circumstances, the assets associated with such contracts might be judged to be on the public sector's balance sheet, unless there are significant variations in the profits and losses stemming from the property which arise from the other risks associated with the transaction, which are considered below.

Third party revenues

3.179.29 An indication that a property is an asset of the operator is if there are extensive third party revenues, which are necessary for the operator to cover its costs. Significant restrictions on third party usage might on the other hand indicate that the asset is the property of the purchaser. In addition, where there is a guarantee of the operator's property income this indicates that the asset should be on the purchaser's balance sheet. [FRS 5 App F para F32-F34].

3.179.30 Third party revenues that can be taken into the analysis are those that are expected to cover the operator's property costs and flow from features of the property. This might include, for example, income from a car park provided for hospital patients.

Who determines the nature of the property

3.179.31 If the purchaser determines the key features of how the property is to be built and how it will be operated, then this is an indication that it should be on the purchaser's balance sheet as it bears the design risk [FRS 5 App F para 35]. However, the fact that the key features of the property are recorded in the PFI contract, which is agreed by the purchaser, does not necessarily mean that the purchaser has determined those key features. [TT TN 1 (revised) para 4.11].

3.179.32 The purchaser may implicitly determine the key features of the property. For example, a road contract might specify that the road should revert to the purchaser in a predefined state after a short operating period. This might indicate that the operator has no discretion over the standard of road built and how it will be maintained. [FRS 5 App F para F35]

3.179.33 Conversely, where the operator has significant and ongoing discretion over how to fulfil the PFI contract and makes the key decisions on what property is built and how it is operated, bearing the consequent costs and risks, this is an indication that the property is the operator's asset. For example, in a PFI contract to design and build a road and operate it for a long period, the operator may have complete discretion over the balance between the quality of the original road built and the consequent level of maintenance costs. [FRS 5 App para F36].

3.179.34 Although design risk is a key indicator, it is the costs flowing from the design that will impact the analysis. For example, even where the property is designed by the purchaser, if the design is faulty then this will have an impact on running costs. It will then be the party that bears these cost variations which will have an impact on the analysis. If the costs incurred through faulty design can be passed straight onto the purchaser, then the purchaser clearly has this risk. However, if no matter who specifies the design, costs associated with faulty design are borne by the operator, then this indicates that the assets should remain on the operator's balance sheet.

3.179.35 Construction risk refers to who bears the financial implications of cost and time overruns during the construction period and is generally not relevant in the analysis, because such risk has no impact during the property's operational life. But where the purchaser bears construction risk and the property is claimed to be that of the operator it is necessary to consider carefully whether the property is actually the purchaser's asset. [FRS 5 App F para F37].

3.179.36 Where, however, a delay in completing the property means that the unitary payment will not start on the expected date, this variation in the operator's revenue should be taken into account in the analysis.

3.179.37 Also, while construction risk is generally not relevant to the analysis, some risks during construction phase will relate to design risk rather than construction risk. For example the operator may have the freedom to make the design changes during the construction period that, whilst not being necessary to meet the contract requirements, are made in the expectation of reducing expected operating and life cycle costs. Where the financial implications of such changes cannot be quantified, this should be considered as one of the qualitative factors. [TT TN 1 (revised) para 4.40].

Penalties for under-performance or non-availability

3.179.38 Only those penalties for under-performance or non-availability that are significant and have a reasonable possibility of occurring should be taken into the analysis. For example, significant penalties on the operator arising from lane closures for more than a minimal period in a road contract should be taken into account and are an indication that the property is an asset of the operator. [FRS 5 App F para F38, F39].

3.179.39 Clearly, where it is more cost effective for the operator to rectify a problem rather than incur a significant penalty, the cost of the rectification should come into the analysis rather than the penalty. [FRS 5 App F para F21]. This in based on the FRS 5 principle that only those matters that are likely to have an impact in practice should be taken into account.

3.179.40 It is also necessary to distinguish service related penalties, which are irrelevant, from property related penalties, which are relevant. For example, in a PFI contract for a catering service, deductions caused by a leaking kitchen roof are relevant, but deductions due to meals being too small are not. [TT TN 1 (revised) para 4.42].

Changes in relevant costs

3.179.41 Where *significant* increases in future costs are passed onto the purchaser this is an indication that the asset should be on its balance sheet. For example, this would be the case where the PFI payments vary with specific indices to reflect the operator's increased costs, but this would not be so where the payments vary with a general price index, such as the RPI. [FRS 5 App F paras F40,F41].

3.179.42 It is also necessary to determine which costs should be taken into the analysis. Clearly, the costs should be those that relate to the property, but the distinction between the costs associated with the asset and those related to the service might not be obvious. The costs will include capital expenditure to be incurred in replacing the asset over the term of the contract, which would include those costs associated with the buildings, equipment and furniture and fittings. Furthermore, operating costs associated with repairing the fixed assets would also be included. As explained in paragraph 3.179.33 above, the costs associated with rectifying design faults will need to be taken into account, but other costs associated with design might also be relevant. For example, if the design of serviced accommodation specified single-glazed windows, then variations in heating costs and who bears those variations are relevant to the analysis as they stem from a feature of the property.

3.179.43 Other costs that are totally independent of the property, for example, the costs of the raw materials and consumables in a catering facility which is part of a hospital contract, should be excluded from the analysis where they relate purely to services.

Obsolescence and changes in technology

3.179.44 Where the potential for obsolescence or changes in technology are significant who bears the costs and gains any associated benefits will be an indication of who should recognise the asset. [FRS 5 App F para F42]. Although separately identified in the standard, this is just another cost variation that needs to be taken into account in the analysis together with the other cost variations mentioned above.

Contract termination and residual value risk

3.179.45 PFI contracts are generally for the long term, primary terms of 25 to 30 years are typical. Such long periods might indicate that the arrangement is a full payout one for the asset. There is also a problem with what happens to the asset at the end of the term. Often the asset reverts back to the public sector for nil or a nominal sum. Some argue that the residual should not matter over such a long term, because its discounted value will be minimal. However, reversion back to the public sector for a nominal amount could equally be viewed as further evidence that the public sector is buying an asset over the contract term.

3.179.46 Residual value risk is explained in the standard as the risk that the actual residual value of the property at the end of the contract will be different from that expected. The risk is obviously more significant the shorter the contract term. Where residual value risk is significant the purchaser will bear it if it has agreed to purchase the property for a substantially fixed or nominal amount; or if the asset is transferred to a new operator selected by the purchaser for a substantially fixed or nominal amount; or if payments over the contract term are sufficiently large for the operator not to rely on an uncertain residual value. The practical effect of options for the purchaser to acquire the asset or for the operator to 'walk' from the contract need to be considered carefully. [FRS 5 para F44-F48]. Where the purchaser has an option to purchase or walk away and there is no genuine possibility that the purchase option will be exercised, this indicates that the residual value risk is borne by the operator. Alternatively, where there is no genuine possibility that the walk option will be exercised, this indicates that the residual value risk with the purchaser. [TT TN 1 (revised) para 4.52].

3.179.47 However, residual value risk will not have a significant impact on the analysis if, the public sector is to acquire the asset during the term of the contract or at the end of the contract, based on a market value payment for the asset. Alternatively, there could be arrangements whereby the public sector body can re-negotiate an extension of the service term. Sometimes, there are clauses that allow other service providers to re-compete for a subsequent term of the contract. If any transfer of assets to the new service provider is made at market value then the risks associated with assets do not reside with the public sector.

3.179.48 When evaluating residual value risk, a distinction needs to be made between specialised properties, for which there are no practical alternative uses (for example, hospitals and prisons) and alternative use properties, for which there is an alternative use, whether or not such use involves the provision of the same service (for example, office accommodation in areas where there is demand from other users). In the case of specialised properties, in most cases it is unlikely that the operator will accept residual value risk at an acceptable price and, therefore, this risk is usually borne by the purchaser. [TT TN 1 (revised) paras 4.54 to 4.58].

Summary of risks to consider

3.179.49 The principles stemming from the above discussion are summarised in application note F in a table. The summary table is reproduced below; also included are references to the paragraphs of the application note that include the narrative explanation.

<table>
<tr><td colspan="2">Variations in profits/losses for the property, in transactions falling directly within FRS 5 rather than SSAP 21

Three principles govern the assessment of the indications set out below:

• Only variations in property profits/losses are relevant.
• The overall effect of all of the factors taken together must be considered.
• Greater weight should be given to those factors that are more likely to have a commercial effect in practice.</td></tr>
<tr><td>Indications that the property is an asset of the purchaser</td><td>Indications that the property is an asset of the operator</td></tr>
<tr><td>Demand risk is significant and borne by the purchaser, for example:</td><td>Demand risk is significant and borne by the operator, for example:</td></tr>
</table>

• The payments between the operator and the purchaser will not reflect usage of the property so that the purchaser, will have to pay the operator for the property whether or not it is used. [App F para F28(a)]. • The purchaser gains where future demand is greater than expected. [App F para F28(b)].	• The payments between the operator and the purchaser will vary proportionately to reflect usage of the property over all reasonably likely levels of demand so that the purchaser will not have to pay the operator for the property to the extent it is not used. [App F para F28(a)]. • The operator gains where future demand is greater than expected. [App F para F28(b)].
There is genuine scope for significant third-party use of the property but the purchaser significantly restricts such use. [App F para F33].	The property can be used, and paid for, to a significant extent by third parties and such revenues are necessary for the operator to cover its costs. [App F para F32]. The purchaser does not guarantee the operator's property income. [App F para F33].
The purchaser determines the key features of the property and how it will be operated. [App F para F35].	The operator has significant ongoing discretion over what property is to be built and how it will be replaced. [App F para F36].
Potential penalties for under-performance or non-availability of the property are either not significant or are unlikely to occur. [App F para F38].	Potential penalties for under-performance or non-availability of the property are significant and have a reasonable possibility of occurring. [App F para F39].
Relevant costs are both significant and highly uncertain and all potential material cost variations will be passed on to the purchaser. [App F para F40].	Relevant costs are both significant and highly uncertain and all potential material cost variations will be borne by the operator. [App F para F41].
Obsolescence or changes in technology are significant and the purchaser will bear the costs and any associated benefits. [App F para F43].	Obsolescence or changes in technology are significant and the operator will bear the costs and any associated benefits. [App F para F43].
Residual value risk is significant (the term of the PFI contract is materially less than the useful economic life of the property) and borne by the purchaser. [App F para F44-48].	Residual value risk is significant (the term of the PFI contract is materially less than the useful economic life of the property) and borne by the operator. [App F para F44-48].
The position of the parties to the transaction is consistent with the property being an asset of the purchaser, for example: • The operator's debt funding is such that it implies the contract is in effect a financing arrangement. [App F para F50]. The bank financing would be fully paid out by the purchaser if the contract is terminated under all events of default including operator default. [App F para F50].	The position of the parties to the transaction is consistent with the property being an asset of the operator, for example: • The operator's funding includes a significant amount of equity. [App F para F50]. • The bank financing would be fully paid out by the purchaser only in the event of purchaser default or limited force majeure circumstances. [App F para F50].

Accounting treatment

Assets recognised by the operator — accounting by the operator

3.179.50 Where the analysis indicates that the asset should be recognised by the operator, then the property will be capitalised as a fixed asset. The normal capitalisation rules of FRS 15 will apply. Depending upon the operator's accounting policy, qualifying interest costs may be capitalised during the asset's construction.

3.179.51 Depreciation will be charged on the asset so that the asset is depreciated to its residual value over its useful economic life which, depending upon the circumstances, may be a different period to the contract term.

3.179.52 It is sometimes argued that the annuity method of depreciation could be used in PFI and PPP type contracts. The annuity method of depreciation involves calculating the annual depreciation charge by taking into account the cost of financing the asset. In the early years of the asset's life the notional capital invested is high, which gives high interest charges. This method provides that such interest and depreciation combined remain approximately the same over the period and, hence, depreciation in the early years is low.

3.179.53 The annuity method may be appropriate where an entity's rate of consumption of the economic benefits of an asset increases over its life. This may be the case where there is a separable operating lease and the operator is acting as a lessor. However, in general, the annuity method of depreciation should not be used.

Assets recognised by the operator — accounting by the purchaser

3.179.54 Where it is concluded that the purchaser does not have an asset of the property, then the purchaser will simply record the unitary payments as an expense as they are incurred by the purchaser. However, there may be other assets and liabilities for example residuals and contributions that need to be accounted for. These are considered further below in paragraphs 3.179.55.15 and 3.179.55.18.

Assets recognised by the purchaser — accounting by the operator

3.179.55 Where it is concluded that the operator does not have a physical asset of the property, it will, instead have a financial asset. This financial asset is a debt due from the purchaser for the fair value of the property. The asset is recorded at the outset and is reduced in subsequent years as payments are received from the purchaser. In addition, finance income on the financial asset is recognised using a property specific rate. Guidance on determining the property specific rate is given in paragraph F16 to the application note in FRS 5. A rate based upon the return for the entire PFI contract may not be an appropriate rate to use as it will include an allowance for risk on the service element of the contract. Where sufficient information is not available to derive a property specific rate from the PFI contract, the rate can be estimated by reference to the rates that would be expected on a similar lease.

3.179.55.1 Application note F does not provide detailed guidance on how the financial asset should be recognised. Three methods of recognising the asset have been suggested.

- Debit costs directly to the financial asset.

  All costs incurred in constructing assets under the PFI contract are debited directly to a financial asset balance. This is consistent with the idea that the operator is building a property on behalf of the purchaser and will recover the costs it incurs over time. In principle, the operator's asset is an interest yielding financial receivable.

  It may be possible to recognise interest income on the financial asset from day one. However, the operator will have to review the contract to ensure that there is sufficient certainty over recovery of this income. It seems unlikely that the operator should recognise interest income in excess of the interest costs it has incurred in the construction period.

  This approach to recognising the financial asset will in most cases be the most appropriate as it reflects the fact that the operator does not have the benefits and risks associated with the property.

- Initial recognition as work in progress.

  Under this approach all costs incurred are debited directly to work in progress. On completion of the asset the work in progress balance is transferred to financial assets. This could be achieved in one of two ways either:

- A direct balance sheet transfer from work in progress to financial assets.

  - Dr Financial assets
    Cr Work in progress

  Or

  - A transfer *via* the profit and loss account. That is:

    Dr Profit and loss account (cost of sales)
    Cr Work in progress
    Dr Finance receivable
    Cr Profit and loss account (sales)

  The second method is the correct method as it recognises that the asset has been sold by the operator to a third party in return for a finance receivable.

  In certain limited cases, where it is possible to determine the fair value of the property constructed, it may be possible to recognise a manufacturer's profit on completion of the property. Also, in certain limited situations, it may be possible to recognise turnover, costs and profits during the construction phase using principles similar to those used in long-term contract accounting under SSAP 9. However, whenever it is proposed to recognise a profit, it is necessary to consider the recoverability of the resulting finance receivable and to ensure that any profit recognised does not result in an artificially low return on the service element of the contract.

Initial recognition of the property as work in progress may be appropriate where the operator has significant property risks during the construction phase of the contract that reduce once construction has been completed.

- Initial recognition as a fixed asset

  Under this approach all costs incurred are debited directly to fixed assets. On completion of the asset, the fixed asset is transferred to financial assets.

  This is not an acceptable way to recognise the financial asset. Fixed assets are defined as assets intended for continuing use within a business. It is difficult to see how an asset whose benefits and risks rest with another party (the purchaser) could be described as being intended for continuing use within the operator's business.

3.179.55.2 Once the financial asset has been recognised, the question arises as to how the balance should be amortised. In a PFI type contract, the operator will receive a single unitary payment. This payment is intended both to reward the operator for the services it provides and to allow it to collect the receivable in respect of the property it has constructed. The unitary payment must, therefore, be split between earning a return on the financial asset, collection of the financial asset and turnover in respect of the service element of the arrangement. This is illustrated below with an example.

Example

Company A is a PFI operator. The asset constructed by company A is being accounted for as a financial asset. In year 5, a unitary payment of £100 is received of which £10 is interest on the financial asset, £60 is collection of the financial asset and £30 is in respect of services provided. The correct way to account for this receipt is as follows:

Dr Cash	100	
Cr Financial asset		60
Cr Interest income		10
Cr Turnover		30

The receipt in respect of the financial asset is a collection of a debtor, so it would not be appropriate to show the £60 flowing through the profit and loss account.

Assets recognised by the purchaser — accounting by the purchaser

3.179.55.3 Where it is concluded that the purchaser has an asset of the property and a liability to pay for it, these should be initially recorded on the purchaser's balance sheet at the fair value of the property. The asset will be depreciated over its useful economic life in accordance with FRS 15. The liability will be reduced as payments for the property are made. In addition, an imputed finance charge on the liability will be recorded in the purchaser's profit and loss account. The charge will be calculated using a property specific rate. The remainder of the PFI payments (that is, the full payments, less the capital repayment and the imputed finance charge) should be recorded as an operating cost in respect of the service element of the arrangement. Again an example will help to illustrate.

Example

Company B is a PFI purchaser. The asset constructed by the operator will be recorded on company B's balance sheet. In year 5, company B makes a unitary payment of £100 of which £10 is interest payable on the outstanding liability, £60 is repayment of that liability and £30 is in respect of services provided by the operator to Company B. In addition, depreciation of £15 is charged on the property. The double entry is as follows:

Dr Interest payable (profit and loss account)	10	
Dr Operating costs	30	
Dr Creditors	60	
Cr Cash		100

To recognise the payment of the unitary charge.

Dr Operating costs	15	
Cr Accumulated depreciation		15

To recognise depreciation on the property.

3.179.55.4 There may be practical problems with this treatment where, for instance, there is a significant variation in the unitary payment due to a service related issue.

Example

Under a small PFI contract, where the purchaser has recognised the asset and the operator has recognised a finance receivable, the normal monthly unitary payment is £1,000, which is, split between a finance cost of £100, a repayment of capital of £700 and the balance attributable to the provision of the integrated service of £200. During a particular month there is a complete breakdown in the service provision, which has a significant impact on the unitary payment. Instead of £1,000, only £600 is payable for the month. The question then arises as to how to allocate the reduced payment. If £700 is treated as a capital repayment and £100 the finance cost, a credit of £200 would have to be recorded in the purchaser's profit and loss account for the service element. This might be the appropriate treatment over the term of the contract if the credit represents a claw-back of the element of the unitary payment that relates to service. It will, however, in practice be necessary to determine whether or not the reduced payment has an impact on the value of the asset. It might indicate, for example, that there is an impairment and that it is necessary for the purchaser to provide against the asset's carrying value. If the impairment is likely to impact further unitary payments, it might be appropriate to reduce both the asset and the corresponding liability.

3.179.55.5 The point at which the purchaser recognises the asset will usually be when it comes into use, unless the purchaser bears significant construction risk in which case it should recognise the property as it is constructed.

Use of SSAP 9

3.179.55.6 Some operators in PFI type transactions have sought to argue that the principles of SSAP 9 for long-term contract accounting could be applied to the PFI or PPP contract as a whole (rather than just the construction phase as described above in paragraph 3.179.55.1.

3.179.55.7 SSAP 9 defines a long-term contract as *"a contract entered into for the design, manufacture or construction of a single substantial asset or the provision of a service (or of a combination of assets or services which together constitute a single project) where the time taken substantially to complete the contract is such that the contract activity falls into different accounting periods"*. [SSAP 9 para 22].

3.179.55.8 It is difficult to support the use of SSAP 9 when the asset would be on the operator's balance sheet under FRS 5. SSAP 9 is designed to account for assets or services that are sold to another party. If the substance of the transaction is such that the risks and rewards of ownership of the asset are with the operator then the asset has not been sold and should be treated as a fixed asset.

3.179.55.9 It can be argued that there is more scope for applying SSAP 9 when the constructed asset is off the operator's balance sheet as clearly a sale of some description has taken place. However, paragraph F60 of the application note to FRS 5 states that where the operator does not have an asset of the property, the operator should recognise a financial asset, being a debt due from the purchaser for the fair value of the property. This statement appears to preclude the use of SSAP 9 for the contract as a whole.

[The next paragraph is 3.179.55.12.]

Pre-contract costs

3.179.55.12 Entities involved in PFI and PPP type arrangements often incur significant costs in bidding for and securing contracts. UITF Abstract 34 requires that directly attributable pre-contract costs are recognised as an asset only when it is virtually certain that a contract will be obtained and the contract is expected to result in future net cash inflows with a present value not less than all amounts recognised as an asset. All other pre-contract costs should be expensed as incurred. [UITF 34 para 15(a)]. The reinstatement of costs incurred before the virtual certainty condition is met is not permitted by the abstract. [UITF 34 para 15(b)].

3.179.55.13 It should be noted that 'virtual certainty' is a very high test to meet. For the recovery of the pre-contract costs to be virtually certain, it is essential that the entity has been awarded sole preferred bidder status. However, preferred bidder status on its own is not sufficient. The abstract notes that *"virtual certainty is not achieved if the award of the contract is subject to uncertain future events not wholly within the control of the entity or the purchaser (such as the need for regulatory approval or the likelihood of legal challenge)"*. PFI projects can often be subject to some form of legal challenge. However, we believe that the wording in the abstract should be interpreted as meaning a substantive legal challenge, that is, a challenge that could affect either the viability of the contract as a whole or one that could lead to the contract not being finally awarded to the bidder in question.

3.179.55.14 The abstract also requires that the recovery by consortium members of pre-contract costs from a SPV should reflect the same principles as those used by the SPV itself. This is probably best illustrated with an example:

Example

In each of the following scenarios, assume the following:

- Costs incurred before the virtual certainty test is met £60,000
- Costs incurred after the virtual certainty test is met £40,000
- Company A has a 25% stake in the contracting SPV and equity accounts for its investment
- The SPV is entirely debt funded

Scenario 1 – SPV incurs the costs directly

SPV entity financial statements

The SPV will expense the costs incurred before the virtual certainty test has been met (£60,000) and record the remaining £40,000 of costs as an asset.

Company A's financial statements

In its consolidated financial statements, company A will account for its share of the SPV's loss (25% of £60,000 = £15,000) and its share of the SPV's net liabilities (£15,000).

Scenario 2 – Company A incurs the costs and recharges at cost to the SPV once the virtual certainty test has been met

SPV entity financial statements

The costs incurred by the SPV can be viewed in one of two ways:

- It could be argued that, as the SPV is so closely related to company A, it should reflect the accounting that would have been required had the SPV incurred the costs itself. That is, record an asset of £40,000 and an expense of £60,000.

- Alternatively, as far as the SPV is concerned, all the costs have been incurred after the virtual certainty test has been met. Therefore, the SPV will capitalise the full amount as an asset (£100,000).

Whilst both approaches are probably acceptable, the first approach is the preferred method as it simplifies the treatment in the consolidated financial statements (see below).

Company A's entity financial statements

Before recharging the costs to the SPV, company A in its entity financial statements will have:

- expensed £60,000 for costs incurred before the virtual certainty test had been met; and

- recorded an asset of £40,000.

The treatment of the reimbursement from the SPV will depend upon the substance of the payment. If the receipt from the SPV is in any way repayable or gives rise to any continuing obligations in company A, then the full amount of the receipt (£100,000) should be treated as a financing and held as deferred income. £60,000 of this amount would be amortised to the profit and loss account over the contract term and £40,000 would be amortised to match the depreciation of the asset. It should be noted that if company A guarantees the debt of the SPV, then the reimbursement is in substance repayable.

If, however, the receipt is not repayable and does not give rise to any continuing obligations in company A, then company A will credit the amount received from the SPV (£100,000) to recovery of the asset (£40,000) and then to its profit and loss account (£60,000) – offsetting the previously recognised expense.

Company A's consolidated financial statements (assuming the receipt from the SPV has not been treated as deferred income)

The treatment in A's consolidated financial statements will depend upon the treatment that has been adopted in the SPV's entity financial statements.

Where the SPV has expensed pre-virtual certainty costs, company A will simply account for its share of the loss of the SPV (25% of £60,000 = £15,000) and its share of the SPV's net liabilities (£15,000). It should be noted that this approach would also result in the other SPV members recognising as an expense an appropriate share of the pre-virtual certainty costs in their consolidated financial statements.

Where the SPV has recognised the full amount recharged by company A as an asset, paragraph 13 of UITF 34 requires an additional consolidation adjustment to be made.

In accordance with FRS 9, in its consolidated financial statements company A will equity account for its share of the SPV's results (£nil) and its share of the SPV's net assets (£nil — that is 25% of £100,000 asset less cash outflow £100,000). On consolidation, company A will make a consolidation adjustment to ensure that the group's share of the pre-contract costs (that is, 25% of £60,000 = £15,000) is debited to the profit and loss account in accordance with the UITF abstract and credit deferred income. The deferred income being released to the profit and loss account over the term on the contract.

Whichever approach is adopted, the net loss for the group is £15,000, which is the same as in scenario 1 above.

Company A's consolidated financial statements (assuming the receipt from the SPV has been treated as deferred income)

Where the SPV has recognised the full amount recharged by company A as an asset, no consolidation adjustments would be required, because company A's individual financial statements will already show pre-contract costs as an expense, which will flow through to the consolidated financial statements.

Scenario 3 – Company A incurs the costs and recharges £120,000 to the SPV once the virtual certainty test has been met

We believe that any profit recharged by company A is in substance an advance on the profits of contract as a whole and should be deferred and recognised over the contract term in both the entity and the consolidated financial statements of company A.

Contributions — accounting by the operator

3.179.55.15 A public sector organisation may sometimes contribute land and/or other assets to a PFI operator. Where the land is simply leased to the operator and it is required for the operator to carry out his obligations under the contract, then the full value of the land should remain on the balance sheet of the purchaser. However, where the land is transferred to the operator and/or the land is not required under the contract, the accounting is more complex. The effect of these types of contributions is illustrated in the following examples:

Example 1

Terms

A purchaser wishes to make an upfront payment to an operator. This may be done directly or through a third party. The purchaser will often require that the funds injected are used to meet the costs of construction to demonstrate that it is receiving full value from the contribution. In the event of default by the operator, the asset and any amounts remaining from the upfront payment will be returned to the purchaser.

Accounting treatment

Under FRS 5, the accounting treatment would follow the substance of the transaction. It is assumed initially that the new asset being constructed under the PFI contract is on the balance sheet of the operator. Thus the total capital costs of the project would be debited to the fixed asset account in the operator's balance sheet. The accounting standard on government grants (SSAP 4) and paragraph 17 of Schedule 4 to the Companies Act requires that a fixed asset should be recorded at its 'purchase price or production cost' — meaning that (apart from depreciation) the cost cannot be reduced by other adjustments such as grants received or other similar contributions. Hence it requires that a grant received should not be netted against the cost of the asset, but should instead be shown separately as a deferred income; this deferred income is then released into income over a period. A contribution in a PFI scheme is treated in the same way.

As a result of the above, the accounting treatment to be followed by the operator is as follows. The total capital costs are recorded as fixed assets and depreciated in the normal way. The contribution is recorded separately as deferred income, which is released into income over a period. Often (for example, with a grant) the deferred income is released into income over the life of the related asset.

Where the physical asset is off the operator's balance sheet and hence the operator instead has a financial receivable, the requirements of paragraph 17 of Schedule 4 to the Companies Act do not apply (as they apply only to fixed assets and to stock). Hence, the operator initially sets up a receivable for the total amount of its investment and any contribution received will be credited to this receivable. Where the amount of the contribution exceeds the financial receivable, the excess should be recognised as a liability in the balance sheet. This liability will be reduced by subsequent investment in the property by the operator. This treatment reflects the substance of the contribution, which is effectively an upfront loan to fund the construction of the property.

Example 2

Terms

A purchaser wishes to contribute land to a PFI project involving say, the construction of a property on a new site (site A). The purchaser agrees that once the building on the new site can be occupied the old site (site B) will be vacated and title will pass to the operator. The operator takes title to site B at the end of the construction phase and sells it at some later date. The calculation of the unitary charge assumes a sale of site B for £5m.

Accounting treatment

The accounting treatment would be similar to that set out in example 1 above in the situation where a cash contribution has been received upfront. The total costs of the new development would be shown gross in the operator's financial statements. When site B is contributed, it will be recorded by debiting land and crediting deferred income with the fair value of the land at the time of its transfer to the operator. As in example 1, the deferred income would be released into income usually over the contract term.

An additional point is that the operator will have to monitor the carrying value of site B for possible impairment, under FRS 11, 'Impairment of fixed assets'. Under FRS 11, any loss on an asset is required to be recorded when the loss is known. Recoveries of value are also recorded. Hence, the carrying value of the site may fluctuate until the time its value is established by sale.

Alternatively, where the operator carries a financial asset rather than a physical asset, as with example 1, the value attributed to site B would be taken to reduce the carrying value of the financial receivable, that is, debit land and credit financial receivable.

Contributions — accounting by the purchaser

3.179.55.16 The required accounting by the purchaser for contributions is described in paragraph F54 to application note F of FRS 5. Where the contributions give rise to reduced service payments going forward, the carrying value of the property will be reclassified as a prepayment. The prepayment will be amortised to the profit and loss account over the period of reduced PFI payments.

3.179.55.17 Where no future benefit accrues to the purchaser, the carrying value of the contributed asset will be charged to the profit and loss account when the contribution is made.

Accounting for residuals — asset on the operator's balance sheet

3.179.55.18 In some PFI transactions, all or part of the property will pass to the purchaser at the end of the contract. If the contract requires the transfer to take place at market value at the date of the transfer then no accounting is required until the date of transfer.

3.179.55.19 If the contract specifies the amount at which the transfer is to take place then any difference between the price specified by the contract and the expected fair value of the residual must be accounted for over the life of the contract in the financial statements of both the operator and the purchaser. This is illustrated in the following example:

Example

Contract term	30 years
Expected residual value at year 30	£20m
Contract specified price	£30m

The operator will recognise income over the contract term and build up an asset, that is:

Dr Long-term receivable	10	
Cr P&L		10

At the end of the contract the operator will have a fixed asset with a carrying value of £20m and a long-term receivable balance of £10m. On sale of the asset to the purchaser, the operator will make the following entries:

Dr Cash	30	
Cr Fixed assets		20
Cr Long-term receivable		10

It might appear that an alternative is to depreciate the fixed asset down to its expected proceeds of 30, as opposed to the open market residual of 20. However, this only works if there will be one asset throughout the whole contract term, for example, a single property. It will not work if there is a series of shorter life assets, as the final asset in the series (but not the others) would be depreciated at a different rate. Therefore, the method set out above is preferred as it spreads the effect over the whole contract term rather than the life of the final asset in the series.

Accounting by the purchaser is as follows:

Over the contract term:

Dr P&L	10	
Cr Provisions		10

On purchase of the asset:

Dr Fixed assets	20	
Dr Provisions	10	
Cr Cash		30

This accounting ensures that the correct charge is recognised in the profit and loss account of the purchaser and the correct income is recognised in the accounts of the operator.

3.179.55.20 In cases where the expected residual value is greater than the price specified by the contract the accounting will be reversed. That is, the operator will build up a provision whilst the purchaser will build up an asset over the contract term.

Accounting for residuals — asset on the purchaser's balance sheet

3.179.55.21 Where the transfer is to take place at market value, the operator will amortise the finance receivable down to the expected residual value of the asset over the life of the contract. The purchaser will amortise the creditor it recognises in a similar way. The payment made by the purchaser for the residual will, therefore, be used to pay off the outstanding balance on the creditor.

3.179.55.22 Any difference between the residual payment required by the contract and the expected fair value of the residual will be built up in the similar way to that illustrated in 3.179.55.19 above.

Methods of amortising the financial asset

3.179.55.23 In general, a financial asset will be amortised using principles similar to those used by lessors under SSAP 21. However, in some situations the substance of the contract may require different methods of amortising the financial asset to be considered. For example, it may be clear from the profile of cash receipts that payments for the asset element of the contract are being accelerated or deferred. In which case, it may be necessary to consider increasing or decreasing the amount allocated to repayment of the financial asset in any given year.

[The next paragraph is 3.179.56.]

Example of quantitative analysis

3.179.56 The following examples are reproduced from the Treasury Taskforce Technical Note 1 (revised) Annex A.

Example 1

Stage 1 — Identify the key commercial risks borne by each party

For illustration purposes assume that the key risks in the PFI contract can be allocated as follows:

Risk/Principal factor	Borne by purchaser	Borne by operator
Demand risk	✓	
Third party revenues		✓
Design risk		✓
Penalties for under performance		✓
Penalties for non-availability		✓
Potential changes in relevant costs		✓
Obsolescence		✓
Residual value	✓	

Stage 2 — Evaluate the NPV of the potential variations in property profits/losses for the operator

A range of modelling techniques can be used to perform the risk analysis depending on the size and complexity of the project. These techniques include sensitivity analyses, scenario analyses or a Monte Carlo simulation. For this example a Monte Carlo simulation has been performed which automatically gives greatest weight to those factors which are likely to have the greatest commercial effect in practice. One of the key features which needs to be borne in mind when assigning probability distributions to the different risks/principal factors, is the requirement to identify whether there are any interdependencies between the probability distributions or whether the risks are independent of others.

Risk/principal factor	Min (cost)/ revenue NPV £m	Most probable (cost)/revenue NPV £m	Max (cost)/ revenue NPV £m	Probability Distribution
Third party revenues	0	20	40	Normal: SD = 10 mean = 20
Design risk	(30)	(25)	(10)	Triangular: most likely = (25), min = (30), max = (10)
Penalties for under-performance	(30)	(10)	0	Triangular most likely = (10), min = (30), max = 0
Penalties for non-availability	(60)	(40)	0	Triangular: most likely = (40), min = (60), max = 0
Relevant costs	(30)	(20)	(10)	Normal: SD = 5, mean = (20)
Obsolescence	(30)	(25)	(20)	Triangular: most likely = (25), min = (30), max = (20)

The Monte Carlo simulation gives the following results, where the lower and upper limits are at the 5%/95% ends of the distribution.

Lower limit	£(123)m
Mean	£(93)m
Upper limit	£(62)m

Stage 3 — Evaluate the NPV of the potential variations in property profits/losses for the purchaser

Risk/principal factor	Min (cost)/ revenue	Most probable (cost)/revenue	Max (cost)/ revenue	Probability Distribution
	NPV £m	NPV £m	NPV £m	
Demand risk	(20)	(10)	0	Normal: SD = 5, mean = (10)
Residual value	0	10	20	Triangular: most likely = 10, min = 0, max = 20

The Monte Carlo simulation gives the following results:

Lower limit	£(10)m
Mean	£nil
Upper limit	£11m

Stage 4 — Compare the potential variations in property profits/losses for both the operator and the purchaser to determine which party has an asset of the property

The end product of the detailed risk analysis can be summarised as follows:

Operator	– Expected NPV of property profits/losses £(93)m
	– 95% lower limit £(123)m
	– 95% upper limit £(63)m
	– Range (95% confidence interval) £61m
Purchaser	– Expected NPV of property profits/losses £nil
	– 95% lower limit £(10)m
	– 95% upper limit £11m
	– Range (95% confidence interval) £21m

The total potential variation in property profits/losses is therefore £82m, of which the purchaser bears £21m (26%) and the operator £61m (74%). The results of the quantitative risk analysis would therefore indicate that the operator has an asset of the property. However, as noted *in* paragraphs 3.179.22, the results of the quantitative risk analysis should always be assessed in the context of the qualitative indicators and those risks which may not be capable of meaningful quantification for inclusion in the quantitative risk analysis.

Example 2

Stage 1 – Identify the key commercial risks borne by each party

For illustration purposes assume that the key risks in the PFI contract can be allocated as follows:

Risk/principal factor	Borne by purchaser	Borne by operator
Demand risk	✓	
Third party revenues		✓
Design risk	✓	✓
Penalties for under performance		✓
Penalties for non-availability		✓
Potential changes in relevant costs		✓
Obsolescence	✓	✓
Residual value	✓	

Stage 2 – Evaluate the NPV of the potential variations in property profit/losses for the operator

Risk/principal factor	Min (cost)/ revenue NPV £m	Most probable (cost)/revenue NPV £m	Max (cost)/ revenue NPV £m	Profitability Distribution
Third party revenues	10	20	30	Normal: SD = 5, mean = 20
Design risk	(15)	(10)	(5)	Triangular: most likely = (10), min = (15), max = (5)
Penalties for under-performance	(30)	(20)	0	Triangular: most likely = (10), min = (30), max = 0
Penalties for non-availability	(30)	(20)	(5)	Triangular: most likely (20), min = (30), max = (5)
Relevant costs	(30)	(20)	(10)	Normal: SD = 5, mean = 20
Obsolescence	0	0	0	

The Monte Carlo simulation gives the following results, where the lower and upper limits are at the 5%/95% ends of the distribution:

Lower limit	£(59)m
Mean	£(42)m
Upper limit	£(24)m

Stage 3 – Evaluate the NPV of the potential variations in property profits/losses for the purchaser

Risk/principal factor	Min (cost)/ revenue NPV £m	Most probable (cost)/revenue NPV £m	Max (cost)/ revenue NPV £m	Profitability Distribution
Demand risk	(60)	(30)	—	Normal: SD = 15, mean = (30)
Design risk	(15)	(10)	(5)	Triangular: most likely = (10), min = (15), max = (5)
Residual value	0	20	40	Triangular: most likely 20, min = (30), max = 0

The Monte Carlo simulation gives the following results:

Lower limit	£(47)m
Mean	£(20)m
Upper limit	£8m

Stage 4 – Compare the potential variations in property profits/losses for both the operator and the purchaser to determine which party has an asset of the property.

The end product of the detailed risk analysis can be summarised as follows:

Operator	–	Expected NPV of property profits/losses £(42)m
	–	95% lower limit £(59)m
	–	95% upper limit £(24)m
	–	Range (95% confidence interval) £35m
Purchaser	–	Expected NPV of property profits/losses £(20)m
	–	95% lower limit £(47)m
	–	95% upper limit £8m
	–	Range (95% confidence interval) £55m

The total potential variation in property profits/losses is therefore £90m, of which the purchases bears £55m (61%) and the operator £35 (39%). The results of the quantitative risk analysis would therefore indicate that the purchaser has an asset of the property. Moreover, the results of the quantitative risk analysis should always be assessed in the context of the qualitative indicators and those risks which may not be capable of meaningful quantification for inclusion in the quantitative risk analysis.

[The next paragraph is 3.180.]

Practical issues

3.180 The implications of FRS 5's provisions are very wide; potentially they can have an effect on *any* transaction. A considerable amount of thought and work was undertaken by the ASB and others in developing the guidance concerning six complex transactions included in the application notes, that is: consignment stock; sale and repurchase agreements; debt factoring; securitised assets; loan transfers and transactions arising from PFI. These transactions are considered from paragraph 3.120. As accountants have considered the standard's implications it has become clearer what other transactions are affected by it. A number of these types of transactions are considered in the paragraphs that follow and might cause some surprises; for example, few would have thought that discounted bills of exchange would come back on balance sheet under the standard's requirements. This section also considers the implications of the standard for a number of particular industries.

Partial derecognition

3.181 One of the main differences between FRS 5's provisions and those of FRED 4 is that, in certain special situations, an asset can be derecognised and in its place another asset recorded. A simple example is where a company sells an asset, but retains an interest in its residual. This might mean that the asset is derecognised and in its place is recognised another asset — its interest in the residual. This aspect of the standard allows certain transactions that would have been on balance sheet under FRED 4's provisions to be removed from the balance sheet. These rules are explained in more detail in paragraph 3.67 onwards and the example that follows illustrates how the standard's rules might apply in practice:

Example

Company A has a property that cost £75m whose market value is £90m. It is sold at £90m to a joint venture company which is party financed by company A and partly by company B. Company B, as a consequence, acquires some significant benefits and risks associated with the asset. The idea is that the joint venture will sell the asset in five years and that there is a sharing of risks and rewards. The likely range of outcomes as to the value in year five is (say) £70m to £120m (that is, any reduction in value below £70m is considered remote).

The agreement is that if the value in year five:

- Is above £90m, company A benefits from 60% of the excess and company B from 40%.
- Falls between £80m to £90m, company A and company B share the loss.
- Is worth less than £80m, company B will bear the loss.

Company A's position is that it gains 60% of any excess above £90m and suffers 50% of the loss in the range £80m to £90m. Company B gains 40% of the excess above £90m, bears 50% of the loss in the range £80m to £90m and bears 100% of the loss below £80m (but a value below £70m is considered remote).

In analysing the above transaction it has to be established whether the investee is a quasi-subsidiary of company A, but if company A does not have the requisite control over the investee then it will be a joint venture under FRS 9 (assuming there is shared control). In the transaction some, but not all, significant benefits and risks have been transferred from company A to company B. Therefore, it appears that it is acceptable under FRS 5's rules for company A to derecognise the asset and to recognise another one in its place. However, the question then arises as to what type of asset and liability should be recognised on the balance sheet in its place. If partial derecognition is considered in isolation, then because there is sufficient uncertainty concerning the risks and rewards to company A, it can be argued that the new asset is a contingent one and that it should be prudently measured at nil. Therefore, only when profits arise in the joint venture should they be taken into account by company A. Furthermore, if subsequently the directors of company A believe that the property is worth only (say) £80m, they should make a provision for the 50% of the loss, that is £5m. But the partial derecognition rules cannot be considered in isolation in this circumstance, because the properties are held by a joint venture which should be equity accounted in company A's consolidated financial statements. In that case, company A will recognise, through equity accounting, its share of any subsequent profits or losses of the joint venture. Consequently, where in this type or arrangement the entity holding the assets and related finance is a joint venture of the group, its treatment under equity accounting arrives at the same result as required under the partial derecognition rules.

With regard to the profit to be recognised on the disposal of the properties to the joint venture, if initially the property is worth £90m on transfer, the company would recognise a profit on the disposal which represents the proportion acquired by the other party to the joint venture, that is, 50% of the total profit of £15, but less if it is thought it likely to be worth say £80m.

In conclusion, the result under FRS 5 is that, albeit certain risks and rewards are retained, the asset and liability will be taken off balance sheet, except to the extent that there is a need to make provision for subsequent diminution in value. If, however, it were company A's intention to re-acquire the asset, then the answer would be different and the standard's Application Note B (on sale and repurchase transactions) would apply. Also another factor that might have an impact on the accounting treatment would be if company A continued to occupy the property. In that situation, it would be harder to justify removing the property from the balance sheet.

3.182 It is also important to remember that partial derecognition cannot be used where the transaction is of a financing nature. For example, it cannot be used for securitisation transactions or factoring arrangements (see para 3.137 and 3.136). This is why the tables at the end of Application Notes C and D do not include columns for partial derecognition.

[The next paragraph 3.184.]

Insubstance debt defeasance

3.184 Where a company irrevocably places cash or other essentially risk-free monetary assets in a trust solely for satisfying a debt, is known in the US as 'insubstance defeasance of debt'. The essence of insubstance debt defeasance is that the assets put into trust are ring-fenced such that they can only be used to repay the loan in due course, further recourse to the company is remote. Typically the creditor is not aware of the arrangement.

3.185 Under FRS 5 it is not possible to derecognise such debt, because these arrangements do not meet FRS 25's offset rules as the company cannot insist on net settlement. In addition, it is not possible to use the linked presentation for such arrangements unless the conditions for the linked presentation are met, which is unlikely because, for one reason, the creditor will usually have recourse to the company's other assets.

Example

A company has a fixed interest sterling Eurobond in issue and has invested in fixed interest gilts to match exactly the repayment of interest and principal on the Eurobond. The company wishes to offset these two balances and considers that this should be acceptable because as the asset is a gilt, and a sterling one, there is no settlement risk attached to the transaction. In addition, there is no interest rate risk because both interest rates are fixed and matched.

Although these transactions appear to be perfectly matched, it is not possible to offset the balances under FRS 25 because the company cannot insist on net settlement. In addition, the Eurobond holders on liquidation of the company would have recourse to the company's other assets. Therefore, also the linked presentation is denied in such an arrangement. In fact it is unlikely that it would ever be possible to link a Eurobond with an asset it finances, because it would be difficult to get the Eurobond holders' consent in writing that they would seek repayment of the finance only to the extent that sufficient funds are generated by the specific assets it has financed.

[The next paragraph is 3.219.]

Repurchase agreements — Repos

3.219 Repo agreements are transactions involving the sale of a security with a simultaneous agreement to repurchase the same or a substantially identical security at a specified future date. The main accounting issue, therefore, is whether the repo should be accounted for as a sale or a financing transaction. Whilst a repo transfers legal title to the securities from the seller to the buyer, the accounting treatment depends on whether the risks and rewards of ownership have in substance been transferred.

3.220 Such transactions clearly fall within the scope of FRS 5's Application Note B (see para 3.123). For those entities applying FRS 26 and where the transaction falls within the scope of paragraphs 14 to 42 of FRS 26, FRS 5 Application Note B is not relevant and the recognition and derecognition principles in FRS 26 should be applied (see further chapter 6). For those entities not within the scope of FRS 26, FRS 5's provision should be applied to sales and repurchase agreement and the guidance in FRS 5 Application Note B is relevant. They are also dealt with in the BBA SORP, 'Securities' and the treatment required by the SORP is consistent with the requirements of FRS 5, which in effect has superseded the SORP in this respect. The standard's application note states that in a straightforward situation, the substance of a sale and repurchase agreement will be that of a secured loan. It goes on to say that the seller in such a transaction should account for the arrangement by showing the original asset on its balance sheet together with a liability for the amounts received from the buyer. Some repo transactions are complex and the guidance in the application note is useful in determining whether the instrument's buyer is merely receiving a lender's return. If it is, then, in substance, no sale has been made and the asset and related finance should be retained on the seller's balance sheet.

3.221 Even in repo transactions where different securities are returned to the seller, if they are substantially similar, such that the risks and rewards are unchanged, the substance of the transaction will still be that of a financing. Therefore, generally the securities subject to a repo should be retained on the seller's balance sheet and valued in accordance with the company's normal accounting policy for its legally owned securities (which would normally be market value). The cash advanced by the buyer would be recorded as a liability and termed, for example, 'securities sold under agreements to repurchase'. Where material the liability should be disclosed separately on the face of the balance sheet. The interest expense (in whatever legal form) should then be charged to the profit and loss account over the life of the agreement.

3.222 From the buyer's point of view, in substance it has not bought an asset, therefore, it will not record the security in its balance sheet or recognise any profits or losses arising from changes in its market value. The cash it has advanced to the seller should be shown as an asset and termed, for example, 'securities purchased under agreements to resell'. The interest income (in whatever legal form) should be accrued over the life of the instrument. The notes to the financial statements and accounting policies of both the seller and the buyer would have to explain the treatment they have adopted.

3.223 It is also necessary to consider the accounting treatment of any additional collateral that passes between the seller and the buyer as a result of changes in the market value of the securities underlying the repo. Collateral takes one of two forms: cash or securities. To the extent that cash collateral is used, this should be treated as a separate asset or liability unless the relevant conditions for offset can be met (see para 3.97) in which case it should be offset against the amount of the repo. If additional securities are used, then these should be treated consistently with those of the original repo.

3.224 For some more complex repo arrangements it is possible that the criteria for derecognition could be met, that is where the seller transfers all significant benefits and all significant risks of ownership to the buyer. This might arise, for example, if the agreement incorporates terms whereby the buyer assumes price risk or in the case of repos to maturity where the repo's maturity date coincides with that of the underlying securities. In such circumstances, the transaction should be treated as a sale. However, if material the nature of the repurchase commitment should still be disclosed in the financial statements.

[The next paragraph is 3.228.]

Contract purchase arrangements

3.228 In a typical hire purchase contract, the substance of the transaction is a sale of an asset where the price is paid over a period of time, with interest charged on the outstanding balance. However, the legal form is that of a hire of the asset to the purchaser with the rentals being equivalent to the purchase price plus interest on the outstanding balance. The title to the goods remains with the vendor and the purchaser is given an option to acquire the asset for a nominal amount (normally for £1) at the end of the hire term and it is at this stage that the title to the asset passes. It is clear, however, in a hire purchase agreement that the risks and rewards of ownership rest with the purchaser and the asset is consequently reflected in its financial statements, with its obligation to the vendor shown as a liability.

3.229 In a contract *hire* arrangement, the hirer does not take title to the goods at the end of the contract term, but the goods are returned to the lessor and are either relet by him or more commonly sold to another party. Such arrangements are clearly operating leases under SSAP 21 as the residual risk remains with the lessor. The hired assets will, therefore, remain on the lessor's balance sheet. In a contract *purchase* transaction there is generally a balloon rental at the end of the lease term (as illustrated in the graph below) and a nominal sum is paid to acquire the title to the asset (in a similar way to a hire purchase agreement). In addition, the lessee has a put option to sell the vehicle on to another party for a pre-agreed price, which is often a subsidiary of the lessor. Therefore, the transaction is a full pay-out lease, but it can be argued that as the option mechanism puts the residual risk back to the lessor the asset should not be recognised on the hirer's balance sheet.

3.230 If the lessee exercises his put option, and puts the asset back to the subsidiary of the lessor, the commercial effect of the balloon payment and the option taken together is similar in cash flow terms to a contract hire arrangement, in that the residual risks are in practice being taken by the lessor's group. However, the lessee's liability to the lessor is for the full amount of the asset purchased and the related finance costs — often the contract will be non-cancellable — and the title will pass at the end of the lease term. The right to sell the asset to a subsidiary of the lessor in the future does not remove or limit the obligation in any way. Therefore, a liability exits in FRS 5 terms and should be recognised in the lessee's financial statements.

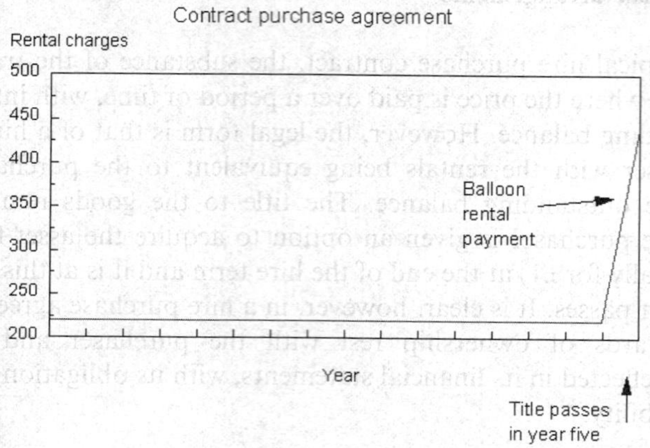

3.231 Consequently, also in accordance with SSAP 21, the asset and liability should appear on the lessee's balance sheet and the transaction should be treated as a finance lease. The partial derecognition rules of FRS 5 may also be relevant to such transactions. These rules state that, in special cases, an asset can be derecognised and another recognised in its place where significant risks and rewards relating to the original asset have been transferred to another party. It could be argued that because of the option's existence, the lessee has in substance transferred significant risks and rewards with regard to the residual to the other party. However, generally in such transactions this will not be so, because the sale will be contingent until it takes place. Normally there are important conditions that the lessee will have to comply with before the option can be exercised and these will often affect the price. Therefore, it is unlikely that the partial derecognition rules can be applied to contract purchase arrangements, because the risks and rewards of ownership reside with the lessee until the conditions to exercise the option have been complied with.

Stock lending

3.232 Another type of arrangement that can be affected by FRS 5 is stock lending. Stock lending is a growing activity within the investment management industry, affecting the assets of insurance companies, investment and unit trusts and the pension fund sector. Stock lending involves three parties: the lender (such as pension funds, insurance companies or building societies); a money broker (who acts as an intermediary); and a market maker (the borrower). Stock lending is a method used to help the liquidity of the stock market, by allowing a market maker who is short of a particular stock to borrow that stock from another party (the lender). Such arrangements are, therefore, generally only entered into for a short period of time. The borrowing is made through a money broker in order to ensure that the identity of the borrower and lender remain confidential. On receipt of the stock the market maker provides collateral to the money broker for the loan. If dividends are paid during the lending period on the stock transferred, the holder of the stock receives the dividends and the market maker pays an equivalent amount to the lender with relevant tax deducted and accounted for by the market maker as manufactured dividends. Although the process is called stock lending, the title to the stock actually passes to the market maker. Most of the business risks associated with stock lending can be managed by the provision of a legally binding agreement. There are basically three types of arrangement that can arise as outlined below.

3.233 In the first example, the market maker gives cash collateral for the loan to the money broker who in turn passes it on to the lender as illustrated in the diagram below:

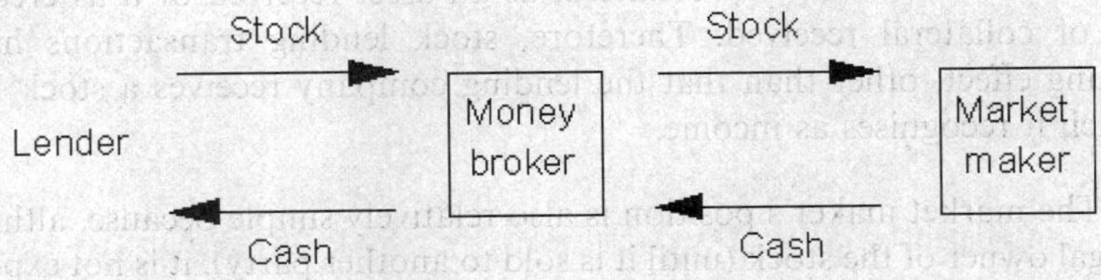

Although this is the simplest example of stock lending it is not the most frequent method used. In the situation described, the market maker deposits the cash collateral with the money broker and the money broker passes it on to the stock lender. Interest earned on the cash is passed to the market maker, but after the money broker and lender have deducted their fee.

3.234 In the next example illustrated below, the market maker borrows back the cash given to the money broker as collateral and deposits gilts with the money broker, who in turn passes these on to the lender.

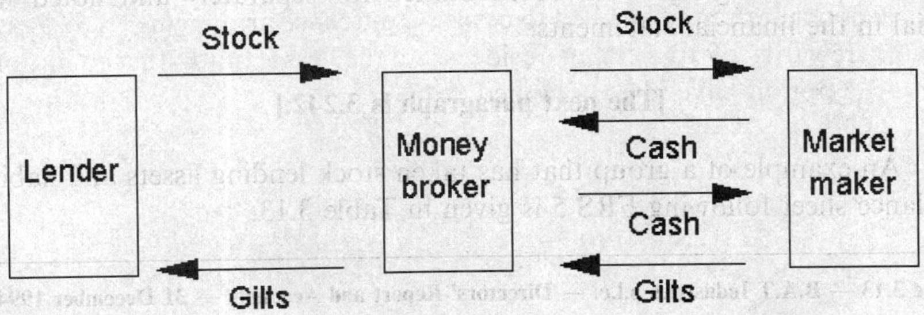

The market maker will pay a higher rate of interest on the cash it borrows back from the money broker than the rate it receives on the initial cash deposit. The difference is partly kept by the money broker and partly paid to the lender as his fee under the arrangement. If an interest payment is due on the gilts during the term of the loan, the market maker has to take the gilts back (and receive the income), but also has to substitute equivalent collateral for the gilts returned. This is the most common form of stock lending.

3.235 In some situations, the market maker will not borrow back the cash and the money broker will invest it in short-term paper (for example, certificates of deposit) and this investment is then passed to the lender as collateral. The interest earned on the collateral is passed to the market maker after deducting the lender and money broker's fees.

3.236 The position of the entity lending the stock is relatively simple in that it is exposed to normal market risks on the price of the stock and receives the equivalent of dividends on the stocks lent. Therefore, under FRS 5 the lender should retain the investment on its balance sheet and this was the practice adopted prior to FRS 5. In the event of default there is a legal right of offset of the amounts owed to and by the lender and the borrower. The practical effect of this for the lender is that he should show on his balance sheet the original securities lent, but should not show the collateral as an asset received or a as creditor in respect of collateral received. Therefore, stock lending transactions have no accounting effect, other than that the lending company receives a stock lending fee, which it recognises as income.

3.237 The market maker's position is also relatively simple because, although it is the legal owner of the stock (until it is sold to another party), it is not exposed to the risk of changes in the stock's market value. In addition, any dividends received on the stock are paid to the lender. Therefore, under FRS 5 the market maker does not retain any of the risks or rewards of ownership and hence should not recognise the stock on its balance sheet, but will reflect any cash collateral deposited with the money broker as a debtor in its balance sheet.

3.238 Both the lender and the market maker should disclose the arrangements and any contingencies or commitments in their financial statements. This might include the aggregate value of the securities on loan (or borrowed) at the balance sheet date, together with the value of collateral held (or given) in respect of those securities. The 'margin' should be accounted for separately and noted where material in the financial statements.

[The next paragraph is 3.242.]

3.242 An example of a group that has taken stock lending assets and liabilities off balance sheet following FRS 5 is given in Table 3.13.

Table 3.13 — B.A.T Industries p.l.c. — Directors' Report and Accounts — 31 December 1994

Directors' Report (extract)

Accounting policies (extract)

The group has adopted three new accounting standards. FRS 5 'Reporting the Substance of Transactions', FRS 6 'Mergers and Acquisitions' and FRS 7 'Fair Values in Acquisition Accounting'.

FRS5 has required reclassification of certain comparative figures, although there is no effect on the Group's equity or profit. . .

. . .Thirdly, stock lending arrangements with financial institutions, previously shown as separate assets and liabilities on the balance sheet, are now deemed not to result in the creation of an additional asset or liability. As a result, the comparative figures for life business 'other assets' and 'other liabilities' have each been reduced by £113 million.

3.242.1 Entities within the scope of FRS 26 should apply the derecognition requirements in FRS 26 to financial assets and liabilities (see further chapter 6) and the derecognition principles of FRS 5 to non-financial assets and liabilities. [FRS 5 para 13B]. Entities that are not within the scope of FRS 26 should continue to apply FRS 5 to the recognition and derecognition of both *financial and non-financial* assets and liabilities.

Bed and breakfast transactions

3.243 Bed and breakfast transactions are examples of sale and repurchase transactions to which the provisions of Application Note B apply. In such transactions, a company agrees to sell certain assets (such as securities) to a third party (normally a broker) and arranges to repurchase them, or identical assets, shortly thereafter, usually over night, for the same price. The essence of the agreement is that the entity takes no risk of loss, other than the extremely remote risk that the counterparty will default and similarly has no reward apart from any tax effect and potentially an effect on realised profits. Transactions of this nature are sometimes used in an attempt to turn unrealised revaluation gains on investments into realised gains so that they can be used for distribution by way of dividends to shareholders.

3.244 Under FRS 5, it is necessary to determine whether an actual sale has taken place in a bed and breakfast transaction. Although the legal title to the asset may have passed, generally the benefits and risks associated with it will not have. Normally, a transaction of this nature should be treated as a financing arrangement rather than a sale, leaving the asset and a corresponding liability on the balance sheet of the original owner. Furthermore, any profit or loss would not be reflected in the company's financial statements. The information required by Application Note B would also have to be given in the notes to the financial statements (see para 3.131).

3.245 There may be a few situations in practice where the substance of the transaction is a disposal of the asset and a reacquisition, which should be accounted for as such. In such transactions a realised gain may arise. In general in order to recognise a realised gain on such a transaction it is necessary to show that the risks and rewards of ownership have passed to the party buying the asset and the proceeds of the disposal are in the form of qualifying consideration (see further chapter 9).

[The next paragraph is 3.248.]

3.248 In practice, a bed and breakfast transaction involves contracting to sell to a broker with no express contract to buy back the following day. However, it is clearly understood that the shares will be repurchased at an agreed price. If the seller does not repurchase, the broker will be unlikely to deal for him again. Thus there is a moral contract. Consequently, it can be strongly argued that the sale and repurchase are linked and that the transaction is not 'arm's length', because there is an obligation, moral if not legal, for the sale to be reversed the next day. It seems reasonable to conclude that if the substance is not to dispose of the asset, but merely to change the tax base then no sale has occurred in substance and, in addition, no gain should be recognised. This conclusion is further reinforced by the probability that, because the sale and repurchase are generally between the same parties, no cash will actually pass.

3.249 For those entities applying FRS 26 and where the transaction falls within the scope of paragraphs 14 to 42 of FRS 26, FRS 5 Application Note B is not relevant, and the recognition and derecognition principles in FRS 26 should be applied (see further chapter 6). For those entities not within the scope of FRS 26, FRS 5's provisions should be applied to sale and repurchase agreements and the guidance in FRS 5 Application Note B is relevant.

Purchase commitments

3.250 One of the types of transaction that falls outside the scope of FRS 5 is a purchase commitment. In certain transactions it might not be as straightforward as it seems to spot a purchase commitment, for example:

Example

A vehicle manufacturer sells a vehicle to a dealer (an outright sale). At the same time a subsidiary of the manufacturer grants the dealer an option to sell the vehicle to the subsidiary after three years for 40% of the original sales price charged by the manufacturer (40% is the estimated residual value). In the subsidiary's financial statements the residual value and corresponding liability would not be recorded unless and until the dealer exercises his option and delivery takes place. This is because, even if the subsidiary were committed from day one to purchase the residual, it would not record the asset and liability until delivery takes place. In the manufacturer's consolidated financial statements, it would be necessary to determine whether or not it was likely that the option would be exercised. If it was likely then the sale of the vehicle would still be recognised, but the residual value and corresponding liability might need to be recorded in the consolidated financial statements under the partial derecognition provisions of FRS 5 (see further para 3.74). This would mean that any probable loss if the residual value is expected to be less than 40% should be provided for and a similar provision would be required in the subsidiary company.

Linked presentation and the cash flow statement

3.251 There is no guidance in FRS 5 concerning how to account for transactions in the cash flow statement where the linked presentation is used for the balance sheet and profit and loss account. For example, where a company uses the linked presentation for a factoring arrangement where the conditions in FRS 5 are met, there are two possible ways that the arrangement can be reflected in the cash flow statement: either treat the movement in the net debtors as an operating cash flow; or treat the proceeds from factoring as a source of finance under 'financing'. FRS 5 states that a scheme that qualifies for the linked presentation is in substance a financing, but the non-returnable proceeds are not a liability, nor is the original gross amount of the debtor an asset. These two statements may seem contradictory, but since the net amount is regarded as the asset, it is logical to show the non-returnable proceeds in the cash flow statement as an operating cash flow, that is, to treat the non-returnable proceeds as a partial collection of the debtors.

Take-or-pay contracts

3.252 In 'take-or-pay' contracts an entity enters into a long-term contract with a supplier at a pre-determined price for the supply of either goods or services and undertakes to pay for a minimum quantity whether or not the quantity is actually required. The advantage for the purchaser is that he is guaranteed delivery of a certain quantity of goods and will be able to negotiate a competitive price. Throughput contracts are very similar in nature to take-or-pay contracts. They are common in the oil industry, where more than one company might share, for example, an oil pipe line. The parties to the contract enter into an agreement to share the use of the facility and each party will pay a certain amount that will not necessarily depend on the amount of their oil that they transport through the pipe line.

3.253 Take-or-pay contracts and throughput contracts have not been specifically dealt with in FRS 5, but an argument can be made that they fall under the heading of expenditure commitments and as such are exempted from the standard's provisions. Essentially under such a contract the purchaser has a contractual commitment to pay a minimum amount to the supplier. The purchaser may or may not receive goods or services to the value of the amount committed, but he has the right to.

3.254 The guidance notes on SSAP 21 refer to take or pay contracts in a discussion of whether certain arrangements should, in exceptional cases, be treated as being in substance leases, although different terms might be used to describe them. They give the example of a company (company A) that builds a plant on the basis that company B is obliged to buy sufficient of the plant's output in order to give company A a full payout on the cost of the assets involved, together with a normal profit margin. They state that such arrangements will in many cases be in substance more in the nature of long-term purchase and supply contracts than contracts which are in substance leases of assets.

3.255 Therefore, if such a contract is a lease it will have to be accounted for in accordance with the requirements of SSAP 21 and, if it is a finance lease, recorded on the lessee's balance sheet. Alternatively, such an arrangement might purely be a long-term purchase or supply contract that is exempted form the requirements of FRS 5 because its is an expenditure commitment, in which case the purchaser has a contingent obligation which should be treated in accordance with the provisions of FRS 12. [FRS 5 para 58]. If it is necessary to make a provision for the purchase commitment in accordance with FRS 12, then this should be charged to the profit and loss account rather than recognised as an asset. Where it is determined that no provision should be made for the contract after considering FRS 12, the notes to the financial statements still have to give particulars of the financial commitment to comply with the Act.

3.256 Table 4.14 below illustrates the treatment and disclosure of a typical take-or-pay contract.

Table 3.14 — Imperial Chemical Industries PLC — Annual report and accounts — 31 December 1997

Notes relating to the accounts

41 Commitments and contingent liabilities (extract)

Significant take-or-pay contracts entered into by subsidiaries are as follows:

(i) the purchase of electric power which commenced April 1993 for 15 years. The present value of the remaining commitment is estimated at £688m.

(ii) the purchase of electric power, which will commence in the second quarter of 1998, for 15 years. The present value of this commitment is estimated at £141m.

3.256.1 For entities reporting in accordance with FRS 26, 'Financial instruments: Measurement', take-or-pay contracts will need assessing as to whether they contain an embedded derivative. This is because the price per unit paid varies in response to changes in the volume purchased. Embedded derivatives are considered in detail in chapter 6.

Chapter 4

Format of financial statements

	Page
Introduction	4001
General rules	4003
Choice of formats	4003
Headings and sub-headings	4004
Corresponding amounts	4008
Offsetting	4010
The balance sheet	4010
Individual company formats	4010
Format 1	4010
Format 2	4014
Rules concerning particular items	4016
Transfers from current assets to fixed assets	4016
Participating interests	4019
Own shares	4019
Payments on account	4020
Presentation of debtors	4020
Pre-payments and accrued income	4020
Cash at bank and in hand	4024
Definition of cash	4024
Right of set-off of bank balances	4024
Restricted cash balances	4025
Net current assets and liabilities	4026
Liabilities	4026
Disclosure	4026
Classification as short-term or long-term	4027
Debentures	4028
Amounts received on account	4029
Trade creditors	4029
Obligations in respect of trade loans	4029
Other creditors including taxation and social security	4032
Accruals and deferred income	4032
Other liabilities	4033
Consolidated formats	4033
Rules concerning particular items in consolidated formats	4035
Interests in and amounts due to and from group undertakings	4038
The profit and loss account	4039
Individual company formats	4039
Classification of expenses by function	4039
Classification of expenses by type	4040
Consolidated formats	4041

Rules concerning particular items 4042
The effect of FRS 3 on the profit and loss account formats 4043
Parent's profit and loss account 4046
The notes to the balance sheet and the profit and loss account 4047
General requirements of the Act 4047
Additional statements required by FRS 3 4048
Compliance with accounting standards 4049
True and fair override disclosures 4049
Accounting policies 4049
Financial instruments 4050
Reserves and dividends 4050
Summary financial statements 4050
Format for small companies 4051
Listed companies' historical summaries 4051
Pro forma financial statements 4053

Chapter 4

Format of financial statements

Introduction

4.1 The general provisions that relate to the format and content of company financial statements prepared in accordance with UK GAAP are detailed in Schedule 4 to the Companies Act 1985 ('the Act' or 'the 1985 Act'). Schedule 4A deals with the format of consolidated financial statements prepared in accordance with UK GAAP. These provisions are supplemented by specific requirements of accounting standards. The formats set out in the Act apply both to the financial statements of those companies that are limited by either shares or guarantee and to the UK GAAP financial statements of unlimited companies. Special accounting and disclosure provisions apply to the UK GAAP financial statements of banks and insurance companies and are included in Schedule 9 and 9A respectively to the Act. These special provisions are not considered in this chapter.

4.1.1 The Companies Act 2006 ('the 2006 Act') received Royal Assent in November 2006 and is being implemented in stages. Parts 15 and 16 of the 2006 Act, 'Accounts and Reports' and 'Audit' respectively, will replace Part VII of the 1985 Act, 'Accounts and Audit', with effect from financial years beginning on or after 6 April 2008. The 2006 Act, including Part 15, gives the Secretary of State the power to make regulations in specified areas. At the time of writing, these regulations have not been finalised. In particular, the schedules that will replace Schedules 4, 4A, 9 and 9A have yet to be finalised, but will be provided through secondary legislation in time for the commencement of Part 15 of the 2006 Act.

4.2 Four primary statements are included within a company's financial statements:

- Balance sheet. [CA85 Sec 226A(1)(a); CA06 Sec 396(1)(2)]
- Profit and loss account. [CA85 Sec 226A(1)(b); CA06 Sec 396(1)(2)].
- Statement of total recognised gains and losses. [FRS 3 para 27].
- Cash flow statement. [FRS 1 para 4].

4.3 Schedule 4 sets out two alternative formats for the balance sheet and four alternative formats for the profit and loss account. It also lays down certain general guidelines to be followed. In addition, the Schedule requires companies to disclose considerable detail both in the notes to the balance sheet and in the notes to the profit and loss account. These formats, guidelines and notes are discussed in this chapter.

4.4 The Act does not require companies to include in their financial statements a statement of total recognised gains and losses or a cash flow statement. These primary statements are required by FRS 3, 'Reporting financial performance', and FRS 1, 'Cash flow statements (revised 1996)', respectively, for all reporting entities' financial statements that are intended to give a true and fair view. The only exceptions to these requirements are that a cash flow statement is not required for most small companies and for subsidiaries, 90 per cent or more of whose voting rights are controlled within the group, provided the consolidated financial statements in which the subsidiary undertaking is included are publicly available.

4.5 The formats of UK GAAP consolidated financial statements are substantially similar to those of financial statements prepared by individual companies. Consolidated financial statements have to comply as far as practicable with the provisions of Schedule 4 to the Act as if the undertakings included in the consolidation were a single company. [4A Sch 1(1)]. In addition, the consolidated financial statements have to comply with the provisions of Schedule 4A as to their form and content. [CA85 Sec 227A(3); CA06 Sec 404(3)]. A group's consolidated financial statements will include the following primary statements and related notes:

- The consolidated balance sheet and related notes of the parent company and its subsidiary undertakings. [CA85 Sec 227A(1)(a), (3); CA06 Sec 404(1)(a)].
- The consolidated profit and loss account and related notes of the parent company and its subsidiary undertakings. [Sec 227A(1)(b),(3); CA06 Sec 404(1)(b)].
- The group's cash flow statement and related notes. [FRS 1 para 4].
- The group's statement of total recognised gains and losses. [FRS 3 para 27].
- The parent company's individual balance sheet and related notes. [CA85 Sec 226A(1)(a); CA06 Sec 396(1)(a)].

The parent company's individual profit and loss account should be published, unless advantage is taken of the exemption given by section 230 of the Act (section 408 of the 2006 Act) (see para 4.122 below). In practice, the exemption is usually taken and the parent's own profit and loss account is omitted from the published financial statements.

4.5.1 In addition to the required primary statements, FRS 3 also requires the reporting entity (that is, the company or, for consolidated financial statements, the group) to produce:

- A note of historical cost profits and losses, appearing immediately after the profit and loss account or the statement of total recognised gains and losses. [FRS 3 para 26].
- A reconciliation of the movement in shareholders' funds. [FRS 3 para 28].

[The next paragraph is 4.6.]

4.6 The contents of the financial statements required by FRS 1 (cash flow) and FRS 3 (financial performance) are considered in chapter 30 and 8 respectively. The other statements mentioned above — balance sheet, profit and loss account and related notes — whose form and content is governed by the Act, are considered in this chapter, together with a summary of the rules that apply to the formats.

General rules

Choice of formats

4.7 Schedule 4 leaves the choice of particular formats to the company's directors. Once the directors have selected the particular formats that they are going to adopt for the balance sheet and the profit and loss account, they should not subsequently change them without good reason. [4 Sch 2(1)]. An example of such a reason might occur if a company changes both its operations and its accounting methods significantly and considers that, following the changes, its financial statements fit more naturally into a different format.

4.8 In most situations, however, few companies will have good reason to change their formats, and so they must select carefully the formats that they wish to adopt when they prepare their first set of financial statements after incorporation. If a company does eventually change its formats, it may incur a considerable amount of extra work, because it will have to restate the corresponding amounts for the previous year in accordance with the new formats. In addition, where the formats are changed, the notes to the financial statements must disclose:

- The fact that the company has adopted a different format.
- The directors' reasons for the change.

[4 Sch 2(2)].

4.9 Table 4.1 illustrates the disclosure relating to a change of profit and loss account format.

Table 4.1 — British Gas plc — Annual Report and Accounts — 31 December 1993

Notes to the accounts (extract)

2 Operating costs — continuing operations

The Group profit and loss account in the 1992 Annual Report and Accounts was prepared on the basis of Format 1 of the Companies Act 1985, under which non-exceptional operating costs were divided into cost of sales, distribution costs and administrative expenses. In the opinion of the Directors such a division has become increasingly less appropriate for the Group for the reasons set out below.

There has always been a substantial degree of subjectivity and discretion in the allocation and apportionment of costs over these categories. More recently the Group has diversified and grown in areas outside the traditional gas business, for which the cost structures are different and the division of operating costs under Format 1 is less appropriate. Further, the major restructuring of the UK Gas Business into five units will result in an organisation where, for the Transportation and Storage Unit, Format 1 would be inappropriate. Finally FRS 3 requires exceptional charges before operating profit to be allocated over the statutory format headings to which they relate. The allocation of such charges over cost of sales, distribution costs and administrative expenses (Format 1) would be subject to the same reservations as for the allocation and apportionment of operating costs for non-exceptional charges.

Accordingly, at the same time as implementing the changes to the Group profit and loss account required by FRS 3, the Directors have decided that the Company should adopt for the Group profit and loss account another format, referred to in the Companies Act 1985 as Format 2, under which the operating costs are allocated according to type of expense. They consider that this will enable the operating costs, including the exceptional charges, to be divided in a less subjective and more helpful way and will enable readers of the Group's accounts to more easily compare and follow trends in particular operating costs.

Headings and sub-headings

4.10 The formats give a list of items either as main headings or as sub-headings. In the balance sheet, main headings are designated either by letters or by Roman numerals, and sub-headings are designated by Arabic numerals. The object of this notation is for identification purposes only, so that the Act can refer to items by their prefix. There is no requirement for financial statements, when they are prepared, actually to show these letters or numbers. [4 Sch 1(2)]. In the profit and loss account Formats 1 and 2, all items are designated by Arabic numerals.

4.11 Whichever of the balance sheet formats and profit and loss account formats a company chooses, the company must show the items in the fixed order and under the headings and the sub-headings set out in the formats it has adopted. [4 Sch 1(1)]. There are, however, certain exceptions to this rule, which are explained in paragraphs 4.12 to 4.17 below.

4.12 An item may be shown in greater detail than the prescribed formats require. [4 Sch 3(1)]. For example, most companies include motor vehicles under the sub-heading 'Fixtures, fittings, tools and equipment'. But where such motor vehicles are significant in value, additional details may be disclosed as follows:

Fixtures, fittings, tools and equipment:		
Motor vehicles	X	
Other	X	X

4.13 An item representing an asset or a liability, or an item of income or expenditure that is not covered in any of the prescribed formats may be shown separately. [4 Sch 3(2)]. An example is where a company holds stocks that do not fall easily within the sub-headings of raw materials and consumables, work in progress, finished goods and goods for resale, and payments on account. Tables 4.2 and 4.3 give two examples where companies have provided additional headings: Bellway p.l.c included showhomes and part exchange properties as a separate category of stocks; Carlton Communications Plc included programme and film rights as a separate category of current assets.

Table 4.2 — Bellway p.l.c. — Annual Report — 31 July 1997

NOTES TO THE ACCOUNTS (extract)

10 Stocks	**1997**	1996
	£000	£000
Group		
Work in progress and stocks	**317,440**	281,793
Grants	**(13,061)**	(13,231)
Payments on account	**(4,986)**	(3,129)
	299,393	265,433
Showhomes	**14,560**	14,926
Part exchange properties	**5,760**	7,569
	319,713	287,928

Table 4.3 — Carlton Communications Plc — Annual Report and Accounts — 30 September 2001

Consolidated balance sheet (extract)

		2001	2000 (as restated)
	Notes	£m	£m
Current assets			
Stocks	15	**7.1**	47.7
Programme and film rights	16	**187.4**	171.6
Debtors	17	**216.6**	670.5
Investments		**214.8**	8.4
Cash and other liquid funds	19	**458.5**	341.8
		1,084.4	1,240.0

4.14 Items that are preceded by Arabic numerals in the Act may be combined in the company's financial statements where either of the following circumstances apply:

- Their individual amounts are not material in assessing the company's state of affairs or profit or loss. [4 Sch 3(4)(a)].

- The combination facilitates the assessment of the company's state of affairs or profit or loss (that is, it results in greater clarity). Where this applies, however, the detailed breakdown of the combined items must be given in the notes to the financial statements. [4 Sch 3(4)(b)].

4.15 A heading or a sub-heading need not be shown where there is no amount to be included for both the financial year in question and the immediately preceding financial year. [4 Sch 3(5), 4(3)].

4.16 The arrangement, the headings and the sub-headings of items set out in the formats and preceded by Arabic numerals must be adapted if the special nature of the company's business requires this. [4 Sch 3(3)]. Table 4.4 shows an example where a company has adapted the format prescribed by the Act.

Table 4.4 — British Telecommunications plc — Report and Accounts — 31 March 1994

Notes to the financial statements (extract)

2 Operating costs	**1994 £m**	1993 £m
Staff costs		
Wages and salaries	**3,486**	3,625
Social Security costs	**294**	276
Pension costs (note 23)	**272**	161
Total staff costs	**4,052**	4,062
Own work capitalised	**(465)**	(473)
Depreciation (note 12)	**2,156**	2,116
Payments to telecommunication operators	**1,174**	1,020
Redundancy charges (a)	**517**	1,034
Other operating costs	**3,279**	3,120
Other operating income	**(53)**	(73)
Total operating costs	**10,660**	10,806
Operating costs included the following:		
Research and development	**265**	233
Rental costs relating to operating leases, including plant and equipment hire £21m (1993 — £27m)	**277**	234
Costs relating to HM Government sale of BT shares under combined offers	**3**	–

(a) Redundancy charges for the year ended 31 March 1994 included £305m (1993 — £550m) being the cost of providing incremental pension benefits for employees taking early retirement in the year.

In prior years' accounts, the group's share of results of associated undertakings, which have been immaterial, was included within operating costs. In this year's accounts, these results are shown on the face of the group profit and loss account. Prior year comparative figures have been restated for this reclassification.

> The directors believe that the nature of the group's business is such that the analysis of operating costs required by the Companies Act 1985 is not appropriate. As required by the Act, the directors have therefore adapted the prescribed format so that operating costs are disclosed in a manner appropriate to the group's principal activity.

4.17 The Act requires that companies should use the headings and sub-headings detailed in the formats [4 Sch 1(1)] and this was certainly the intention of the 4th Directive. Nevertheless, some companies in practice depart from this requirement, for example, describing 'land and buildings' as 'property', or 'stocks' as 'inventories' or 'turnover' as 'sales'. This practice is considered allowable, provided that the revised wording is not likely to mislead readers of the financial statements and provided that the item remains the same.

4.18 A company should consider the presentation of its financial statements in three stages.

- First, it should consider which of the formats are most suitable for its purposes.
- Secondly, if the special nature of its business requires it, it must adapt the arrangement and headings and sub-headings of any items designated by Arabic numerals in the selected formats as set out in Schedule 4.
- Thirdly, it should consider whether it needs to show any item listed in the formats in greater detail, and, if so, it may do so. (Unlike the adaptation of the formats, which is compulsory if the special nature of a company's business requires it, the Companies Act gives the reporting company the option to include greater detail under any heading if it wishes to do so. However, FRS 3 may require such additional disclosure – see further chapter 8.)

4.19 After having considered the presentation of the financial statements, the company must next consider whether compliance with the requirements of Schedule 4 as regards the format of the financial statements, and compliance with other statutory requirements as to the information to be included in the notes to the financial statements, enable the financial statements to give a true and fair view of the state of the company's affairs as at the end of the financial year and of its profit or loss for the year. If the company decides that compliance with Schedule 4 would not give a true and fair view, it should examine whether the solution to this problem might be to provide additional information in the financial statements. If in special circumstances, compliance with the Act would be inconsistent with the requirement to give a true and fair view, the directors must depart from the Act's provisions. In such a situation, particulars of the departure, the reasons for it, and its effect must be given in the notes to the financial statements (see further chapter 2).

Corresponding amounts

4.19.1 FRS 28, 'Corresponding amounts', sets out the requirements for the disclosure of corresponding amounts for amounts shown in an entity's primary statements and notes to the financial statements. 'Corresponding amounts' are sometimes described as 'comparative figures' or 'comparative information' in other accounting standards. FRS 28 is applicable for financial years that start on or after 1 January 2005 *and* end on or after 1 October 2005.

4.20 Corresponding amounts for the year immediately preceding the year in question must be shown in respect of every item in each of the reporting entity's primary statements. [FRS 28 para 5]. This applies even when no such item exists to be disclosed in respect of the current financial year. [FRS 28 para 7].

4.20.1 For the purpose of this requirement, the primary statements specifically mentioned in FRS 28 that require comparatives are:

- Statements of financial performance (for example, a profit and loss account or a STRGL).
- A statement of financial position (for example, a balance sheet).
- A cash flow statement.
- A reconciliation of movements in shareholders' funds (if presented as a primary statement, as permitted by FRS 3).

[FRS 28 para 6].

4.20.2 Although FRS 28 does not specifically require the inclusion of corresponding amounts in respect of a statement of historical cost profits and losses, where one is required by FRS 3, we consider the requirement general enough that this falls within the scope of 'Statements of performance' and corresponding amounts are required.

[The next paragraph is 4.21.]

4.21 In general, the corresponding amounts for the previous financial year must be given in respect of each item shown in the notes to the financial statements. [FRS 28 para 9(a)]. The only exceptions to this relate to:

- Information relating to acquisitions taking place in the financial year (required by paragraph 11 of Schedule 4A).
- Details of shareholdings in subsidiaries held by the reporting entity (required by paragraphs 2 and 16 of Schedule 5).
- Details concerning the identity and class of shares held in undertakings (and the proportion of nominal value represented by those shares) where the investment is 20 per cent or more of any class of shares (required by paragraphs 8(3), 24(3)(4) and 27(3)(4) of Schedule 5).

- The proportion of the capital of joint ventures held by the reporting entity (required by paragraph 21(1)(d) of Schedule 5).
- The identity and proportion of each class of shares held in associated undertakings (required by paragraph 22(4)(5) of Schedule 5).
- Movements on fixed assets (required by paragraph 42 of Schedule 4).
- Movements on reserves and provisions (required by paragraph 46 of Schedule 4).

[FRS 28 para 10].

4.21.1 Prior to the revision of the Companies Act 1985 and the application of FRS 28, there was also an exemption from the requirement to present corresponding amounts in respect of the information required to be disclosed in the notes to the financial statements in respect of loans and other dealings in favour of directors under Parts II and III of Schedule 6 to the Companies Act 1985. However, no such exemption is included in FRS 28. This is considered further in chapter 6 of the Manual of Accounting – IFRS and UK Supplement.

[The next paragraph is 4.22.]

4.22 Where the amount for the previous year is not comparable with the amount to be shown in respect of the current year, the previous year's amount must be adjusted. Where this applies, particulars of the adjustment and the reasons for it must be disclosed in the notes to the financial statements. This requirement applies in respect of every item in a reporting entity's primary statements and in respect of each item shown in the notes to the financial statements. [FRS 28 paras 8, 9(a)]. An example is shown in Table 4.5.

Table 4.5 — Royal Doulton plc — Annual Report — 31 December 1994

Notes to the financial statements (extract)

2 COMPARATIVE FIGURES

The comparative figures for the cost of sales, distribution costs and administrative expenses have been adjusted to reflect a reclassification between the administrative and distribution activities of the group. The effect is as follows:

	As previously reported *£000*	*Transfer* *£000*	*1993 (as restated)* *£000*
Cost of sales	129,218	(1,370)	127,848
Distribution costs	8,060	51,967	60,027
Administrative expenses — ordinary	73,315	(50,597)	22,718
	210,593	–	210,593

4.23 This provision accords with the treatment required by FRS 3 in respect of prior period adjustments. A prior period adjustment (that has arisen, for example, because there has been a change of accounting policy during the year) is accounted for by restating the previous year's figures in the primary statements and notes and, where it is affected, by adjusting the opening balance of reserves accordingly. Where practicable, the effect of the change on the results for the previous year should be disclosed. [FRS 3 para 29].

4.24 In addition, the Companies Act 1985 requires that accounting policies should be applied consistently within the same financial statements and from one financial year to the next. [CA85 4 Sch 11]. It allows the directors to depart from this principle (that is, to change an accounting policy) if there are special reasons for doing so, but the particulars, reasons and effect of the departure from the principle of consistency should be disclosed. [CA85 4 Sch 15]. The accounting and disclosure implications of changes in accounting policies are considered in chapter 8.

Offsetting

4.25 Asset and liability items may not be set off against each other. Similarly, income and expenditure items may not be set off against each other. [4 Sch 5]. Consequently, companies cannot, for example, show hire-purchase liabilities as a deduction from the related asset. (They may, however, deduct from stock the payments they have received on account of orders.) [4 Sch Balance sheet formats note 8]. It should be noted that the offset rules do not preclude netting, for example, depreciation of fixed assets against their cost or provisions for bad debts against debtors — they are simply adjustments to asset values.

4.26 The rule against offsetting assets and liabilities is also covered in FRS 25, 'Financial instruments: Disclosure and presentation'. FRS 25 sets out conditions that must be met before debit and credit balances can be aggregated into a single net asset or liability, that is, where they do not constitute separate assets and liabilities. This is discussed in chapter 6.

The balance sheet

Individual company formats

4.27 The Act sets out two alternative balance sheet formats.

Format 1

4.28 In Format 1, net assets can be shown as equal in total to the aggregate of share capital and reserves. This method of presentation probably represents UK companies' most common practice. The Act does not, however, prescribe the place where the totals should be struck. Consequently, in this format a company can, unless it has a defined benefit pension asset (see below), equate total assets less current liabilities, on the one hand, with the aggregate of creditors falling due after more than one year, provisions for liabilities, and capital and reserves, on the other hand. Format 1 is set out below and is also illustrated in Table 4.6 (where the company's balance sheet total is struck at the earlier position of total assets less current liabilities).

4.28.1 However, FRS 17,'Retirement benefits', requires that companies show the defined benefit asset or defined benefit liability on the face of the balance sheet and is specific as to the position of the pension balance in the Schedule 4 formats. FRS 17 states:

> "*Any unpaid contributions to the scheme should be presented in the balance sheet as a creditor due within one year. The defined benefit asset or liability should be presented separately on the face of the balance sheet:*
>
> *(a) in balance sheets of the type prescribed for companies in Great Britain by the Companies Act 1985, Schedule 4, format 1: after item J Accruals and deferred income but before item K Capital and reserves; and*
>
> *(b) in balance sheets of the type prescribed for companies in Great Britain by the Companies Act 1985, Schedule 4, format 2: any asset after ASSETS item D Prepayments and accrued income and any liability after LIABILITIES item D Accruals and deferred income."*

[FRS 17 para 47].

4.28.2 For Format 1 presentations, FRS 17 prescribes the same positioning in the balance sheet for the pension balance, regardless of whether it is a pension asset or pension liability. As discussed above, companies are permitted to strike their balance sheet totals to equate total assets less current liabilities with the sum of non-current liabilities, provisions, capital and reserves. However, where a company has a defined benefit asset, the requirements of FRS 17 and Schedule 4 Format 1 taken together would mean that this pension asset would be included in the 'non-current liabilities/provisions/capital and reserves section' of the balance sheet. Therefore, where there is a pension asset, companies should not strike their balance sheet totals in this way, but should instead strike a total at net assets before and after the pension asset, as illustrated in Appendix 1 of FRS 17. Under this approach, total assets less current liabilities will be reported excluding the pension asset which, at first glance, would seem an inappropriate presentation but, as described in paragraph 6 of Appendix II to FRS 17, the ASB received legal advice that the FRS 17 requirements do not contravene the Companies Act 1985. Where the company has a pension deficit, it will be acceptable to strike the total to equate total assets less current liabilities with the sum of non-current liabilities, provisions, capital and reserves, because the pension liability will appear in the 'non-current liabilities/provisions/capital and reserves section' of the balance sheet.

Balance sheet — Format 1

A Called up share capital not paid

B Fixed assets

I Intangible assets
1 Development costs
2 Concessions, patents, licences, trade marks and similar rights and assets
3 Goodwill
4 Payments on account

II Tangible assets
1 Land and buildings
2 Plant and machinery
3 Fixtures, fittings, tools and equipment
4 Payments on account and assets in course of construction

III Investments
1 Shares in group undertakings
2 Loans to group undertakings
3 Participating interests
4 Loans to undertakings in which the company has a participating interest
5 Other investments other than loans
6 Other loans
7 Own shares

C Current assets

I Stocks
1 Raw materials and consumables
2 Work in progress
3 Finished goods and goods for resale
4 Payments on account

II Debtors
1 Trade debtors
2 Amounts owed by group undertakings
3 Amounts owed by undertakings in which the company has a participating interest
4 Other debtors
5 Called-up share capital not paid
6 Prepayments and accrued income

III Investments
1 Shares in group undertakings
2 Own shares
3 Other investments

IV Cash at bank and in hand

D Prepayments and accrued income

E Creditors: amounts falling due within one year
1 Debenture loans
2 Bank loans and overdrafts
3 Payments received on account
4 Trade creditors
5 Bills of exchange payable
6 Amounts owed to group undertakings
7 Amounts owed to undertakings in which the company has a participating interest
8 Other creditors including taxation and social security
9 Accruals and deferred income

F Net current assets (liabilities)

G Total assets less current liabilities

H Creditors: amounts falling due after more than one year
- 1 Debenture loans
- 2 Bank loans and overdrafts
- 3 Payments received on account
- 4 Trade creditors
- 5 Bills of exchange payable
- 6 Amounts owed to group undertakings
- 7 Amounts owed to undertakings in which the company has a participating interest
- 8 Other creditors including taxation and social security
- 9 Accruals and deferred income

I Provisions for liabilities
- 1 Pensions and similar obligations
- 2 Taxation, including deferred taxation
- 3 Other provisions

J Accruals and deferred income

K Capital and reserves
- I Called up share capital
- II Share premium account
- III Revaluation reserve
- IV Other reserves
  - 1 Capital redemption reserve
  - 2 Reserve for own shares
  - 3 Reserves provided for by the articles of association
  - 4 Other reserves
- V Profit and loss account

Table 4.6 — British Telecommunications plc — Report and Accounts — 31 March 1994

Balance sheet of the company

	Notes	1994 £m	1993 £m
Fixed assets			
Tangible assets	12	**13,603**	13,710
Investments	13	**3,518**	2,822
Total fixed assets		**17,121**	16,532
Current assets			
Stocks		**118**	139
Debtors	14	**2,908**	2,702
Investments	15	**2,311**	1,327
Cash at bank and in hand		**2**	1
Total current assets		**5,339**	4,169
Creditors: amounts falling due within one year			
Loans and other borrowings	16	**1,269**	637
Other creditors	17	**5,472**	4,335
Total creditors: amounts falling due within one year		**6,741**	4,972
Net current liabilities		**(1,402)**	(803)
Total assets less current liabilities		**15,719**	15,729
Creditors: amounts falling due after more than one year			
Loans and other borrowings	16	**3,173**	3,323
Provisions for liabilities and charges*	18	**506**	929
Capital and reserves			
Called up share capital	19	**1,553**	1,546
Share premium account	20	**364**	314
Capital redemption reserve	20	**750**	750
Profit and loss account	20	**9,373**	8,867
Total capital and reserves	21	**12,040**	11,477
		15,719	15,729

Debtors include amounts receivable after more than one year of £297m (1993 — £354m).

* Note that for years beginning on or after 1 January 2005, SI 2004/2947, 'The Companies Act 1985 (International Accounting Standards and Other Amendments) Regulations 2004' amended the Schedule 4 format to replace 'provisions for liabilities and charges' with 'provisions for liabilities'.

Format 2

4.29 In Format 2, assets are shown as equal in total to liabilities (which include capital and reserves). Because the information disclosed in Format 2 is identical in all respects (apart from one) to the information disclosed in Format 1, Format 2 has not been reproduced here, but an example is given in Table 4.7. The only difference between Format 1 and Format 2 is that Format 2 aggregates, on the face of the balance sheet, creditors due within one year and those due after more than one year. However, in respect of each item included in creditors the split between the amount due within one year and the amount due after more than one year, together with the aggregate, must still be disclosed either on the face of the balance sheet or in the notes. [4 Sch Balance sheet formats note 13]. This method of presentation is more common in some other EU countries (for example, France and Germany) than in the UK.

Table 4.7 — The Peninsular and Oriental Steam Navigation Company — Annual Report and Accounts — 31 December 1998

Company balance sheet

		Company	
	Note	1998 £m	1997 £m
Assets			
Fixed assets			
Intangible assets: Goodwill	9	—	—
Tangible assets			
Ships	10	393.2	486.8
Properties	11	12.8	6.3
Other fixed assets	12	13.1	8.6
Investments			
Subsidiaries	13	3,286.3	3,213.7
Joint ventures		812.4	535.6
Associates		—	1.2
Other investments		0.2	0.2
	14	812.6	537.0
		4,518.0	4,252.4
Current assets			
Development and dealing properties	15	—	—
Stocks	16	4.6	4.9
Debtors	17	237.1	297.0
Investments		—	—
Cash at bank and in hand		10.7	4.9
		252.4	306.8
		4,770.4	4,559.2
Liabilities			
Capital and reserves			
Called up share capital	18	769.3	751.3
Share premium account	19	595.8	562.7
Revaluation reserve	19	1.5	0.9
Other reserves	19	—	—
Profit and loss account	19	410.8	352.3
Equity stockholders' funds		1,627.6	1,516.9
Non-equity stockholders' funds	19	149.8	150.3
Stockholders' funds		1,777.7	1,667.2

Other liabilities			
Provisions for liabilities and charges*	21	30.8	44.8
Loans: convertible	22	164.8	189.8
non-convertible	22	983.7	1,093.5
Other creditors	23	1,813.7	1,563.9
		2,993.0	2,892.0
		4,770.4	4,559.2

* Note that for years beginning on or after 1 January 2005, SI 2004/2947, 'The Companies Act 1985 (International Accounting Standards and Other Amendments) Regulations 2004' amended the Schedule 4 format to replace 'provisions for liabilities and charges' with 'provisions for liabilities'.

Rules concerning particular items

Transfers from current assets to fixed assets

4.30 The Act defines a fixed asset as one intended for use on a continuing basis in the company's activities and any which are not intended for such use are current assets. [CA85 Sec 262(1)]. Where, at a date subsequent to its original acquisition, a current asset is retained for use on a continuing basis in the company's activities, it becomes a fixed asset and the question arises as to the appropriate transfer value. An example is a property that is reclassified from trading properties to investment properties.

4.31 A problem arises as a result of the different rules for valuing fixed and current assets. Fixed assets are carried at depreciated cost less any provision for permanent diminution in value whereas current assets are carried at the lower of cost and net realisable value (that is, after writing down for both temporary and permanent diminutions in value). The different rules gave rise to concerns that companies could avoid charging the profit and loss account with write downs to net realisable value arising on unsold trading assets. This could be done by transferring the relevant assets from current assets to fixed assets at above their net realisable value, as a result of which any later downward revaluation might be debited to the revaluation reserve.

4.32 One company that decided to retain its development properties rather than sell at unattractive prices was Trafalgar House. In its financial statements for the year ended 30 September 1991 the properties were transferred from current assets to fixed assets. The write down was taken to the revaluation reserve rather than to the profit and loss account as a result of which the company faced criticism from the financial press and analysts. However, arguably, at the time this was legally acceptable.

4.33 This criticism attracted the attention of the FRRP, which in February 1992 notified the company that it was considering certain matters in connection to the 1991 financial statements, including the reclassification of properties. The company argued against the FRRP's view, but the FRRP evidently held its ground and eventually the directors of Trafalgar House agreed to make the changes in order to avoid litigation. The FRRP issued a strongly worded Press Notice that stated:

> "*On the basis of independent legal and accounting advice the directors of Trafalgar House have hitherto not accepted the Review Panel's view on the two principal matters in contention. The Review Panel has therefore been minded to make an application to the court under section 245B of the Companies Act 1985 for an order requiring the directors of the company to prepare revised accounts. However the directors of the company have now undertaken to make appropriate changes and adjustments in the accounts of the company for the year ended 30 September 1992 to meet the Review Panel's concerns, and on this undertaking the Review Panel will not be proceeding with the section 245B court application.*"

4.34 As a result of this case, the UITF was requested to produce rules dealing with such reclassification. In July 1992, UITF Abstract 5, 'Transfers from current assets to fixed assets', was issued. This states that where assets are transferred from current to fixed, the current asset accounting rules should be applied up to the effective date of transfer, which is the date of management's change of intent. Consequently, the transfer should be made at the lower of cost and net realisable value and, accordingly, an assessment should be made of the net realisable value at the date of transfer and if this is less than its previous carrying value the diminution should be charged in the profit and loss account, reflecting the loss to the company while the asset was held as a current asset. [UITF 5 para 5].

4.35 The timing of the transfer of current assets to fixed assets should reflect the timing of management's change of intent and should not be backdated (for example, to the start of the financial year). This change of intent will need to be evidenced, for instance in board minutes. Since the date of the management's decision is unlikely to correspond with the balance sheet date, at which a full review of carrying values would be made, consideration must be given to the appropriate amounts at which such assets should be transferred at the time of transfer.

4.36 Whether assets are transferred at cost or at net realisable value in accordance with UITF 5, the fixed asset accounting rules will apply to the assets subsequent to the date of transfer. In cases where the transfer is at net realisable value, the asset should be accounted for as a fixed asset at a valuation (under the Act's alternative accounting rules) as at the date of the transfer. At subsequent balance sheet dates it may or may not be revalued depending on the company's policy under FRS 15, but in either event the disclosure requirements appropriate to a valuation should be given. These disclosure requirements are discussed in chapter 16.

4.37 The abstract deals only with situations where current assets are included in the balance sheet at the lower of cost and net realisable value under paragraphs 22 and 23 of Schedule 4 to the Act. Therefore, it does not apply to current assets that are accounted for under the alternative accounting rules, for example, investments.

4.38 As a result of the challenge by the FRRP, the prior year figures in the 1992 financial statements of Trafalgar House were restated. Property write downs previously charged to the revaluation reserve were reflected in the profit and loss account for the year. This is shown in Table 4.7.1.

Table 4.7.1 – Trafalgar House Public Limited Company – Report and Accounts – 30 September 1992

CHAIRMAN'S AND GROUP CHIEF EXECUTIVE'S REPORT (extract)

Financial Reporting (extract)

In February 1992 the Financial Reporting Review Panel notified the company that it was considering certain matters in connection with the company's accounts for the year ended 30th September 1991. The Panel's principal concerns related to the reclassification of certain properties from current assets to fixed assets and the amount of ACT carried forward in the balance sheet.

On the basis of independent legal and accounting advice, your Board was of the view that the treatment of those matters in the 1991 accounts was in accordance with accounting standards and complied with the Companies Acts. However, the Panel continued to express concern and, after due consideration, and in order to avoid the delays and uncertainties which would have resulted from prolonged litigation, your Board agreed to make certain changes and adjustments in the 1992 accounts and to the comparative figures for 1991 in these accounts. The Panel did not require the 1991 accounts to be reissued.

We agreed to adopt, early, the requirements of Urgent Issues Task Force Abstract 5, issued on 22nd July 1992, in our 1992 accounts. Consequently, the 1991 comparative figures show deficits on revaluations of property of £102.7m as a charge to the profit and loss account rather than to reserves. We also agreed to write off £20.0m of ACT to the prior period.

NOTES TO THE ACCOUNTS

1 Basis of preparation

The accounts and notes are prepared in accordance with applicable accounting standards.

The particular accounting policies adopted are described in Note 2.

In particular, in these accounts:

* FRS 3 (Reporting financial performance) has been adopted;

* UITF 3 (Treatment of goodwill on disposal of a business) has been adopted; and

* In accordance with the agreement reached with the Financial Reporting Review Panel, UITF 5 (Transfer from current assets to fixed assets) has been adopted early and ACT amounting to £20m has been written off to the prior period.

Comparative figures have been restated to reflect these changes in the basis of preparation of the accounts. This can be summarised as follows:

	Shareholders' Funds at 30th September 1991 £million
September 1991 published accounts	704.6
ACT write off as described above	(20.0)
September 1992 accounts-comparatives	684.6

	Year ended 30th September 1991 Profit/(loss) for the financial year £million
September 1991 published accounts (before dividends)	44.9
Property write downs previously charged to revaluation reserve, now reflected in the profit and loss account in accordance with UITF 5	(102.7)
ACT write off as described above	(20.0)
Goodwill reflected in loss on disposal of discontinued operations in accordance with UITF 3	(21.6)
September 1992 accounts – comparatives	(99.4)

Participating interests

4.39 'Participating interest' means an interest held by an undertaking in the shares of another undertaking that it holds on a long-term basis for the purpose of securing a contribution to its activities by the exercise of control or influence arising from or related to that interest. [CA85 Sec 260(1)]. A holding of 20 per cent or more of the shares of an undertaking is presumed to be a participating interest unless the contrary is shown. [CA85 Sec 260(2)]. In this context, a participating interest does not include an interest in a subsidiary undertaking. [CA85 Sec 260(6)]. It will however include associated companies as defined in FRS 9, 'Associates and joint ventures'. (see further chapter 27).

Own shares

4.40 The Schedule 4 balance sheet formats include a line item within investments (fixed and current) for 'Own shares'. However, in October 2003, the UITF issued Abstract 37, 'Purchases and sales of own shares', which requires a company's holdings of its own shares to be accounted for as a deduction in arriving at shareholders' funds, rather than as an asset. This was superseded by FRS 25 (issued in December 2004 and applicable for years beginning on or after 1 January 2005) but the requirement to recognise treasury shares as a deduction in arriving at shareholders' funds remains. The accounting treatment of 'own shares' is dealt with in chapter 24 for treasury shares and in chapter 12 for shares held by an ESOP trust.

Payments on account

4.41 'Payments on account' relate, as appropriate, to payments that a company makes in advance in respect of the acquisition of intangible assets, tangible assets or stocks (see further chapters 15, 16 and 20).

Presentation of debtors

4.42 The amount of each item to be shown under the heading 'Debtors' must be split between those receivable within one year of the balance sheet date and those receivable later than that. [Schedule 4 note 5 to the balance sheet formats]. For this purpose, a debtor is considered to be receivable on the earliest date on which payment is due, rather than on the earliest date on which payment is expected.

4.43 The Act does not require this disclosure to be given on the face of the balance sheet. However, this means that there is an imbalance between the treatment of long-term debtors and long-term creditors where the latter are disclosed as long-term on the face of the balance sheet and not included in net current assets. There will be some instances where the absence of disclosure of long-term debtors on the face of the balance sheet may mean that users misinterpret the financial statements.

4.44 As a result of this imbalance, UITF Abstract 4, 'Presentation of long-term debtors in current assets', requires disclosure of debtors due after more than one year on the face of the balance sheet if the amount is material in the context of net current assets. [UITF 4 para 3]. The Abstract gives long-term trade debtors of lessors and deferred consideration on the sale of assets as examples where this additional disclosure may be appropriate. The debtor will still be included in current assets, but will be shown separately on the face of the balance sheet, normally as an additional line item 'Debtors: amounts falling due after more than one year' in the current assets section of the balance sheet.

4.45 Prior to the issue of UITF 4, some companies chose to show long-term debtors of this type as a separate category between fixed and current assets on the grounds that compliance with the Schedule 4 formats, that is, including the long-term debtors within current assets, did not give a true and fair view. We consider that, following UITF 4, the inclusion of such an additional asset category on the balance sheet could only be achieved by using the true and fair override and that in most situations a true and fair view will be given by following the disclosure requirements of UITF 4. Therefore, long-term debtors should not normally be shown in a separate category between fixed and current assets. If a company wished to depart from the Act's formats it would have to justify this and give the disclosures required by FRS 18 (see chapter 2).

Pre-payments and accrued income

4.46 Pre-payments and accrued income may be disclosed in one of two alternative positions. [Note 6 on the balance sheet formats]. They may be disclosed either as a category of debtors (within current assets) or as a separate category in their own right. Where pre-payments and accrued income are disclosed within debtors, the Act requires disclosure of the amount due in more than one year. If, however, they are included as a separate category, then strictly under the Act no such analysis is required. However, UITF Abstract 4, requires separate disclosure of debtors due after more than one year where the amount is material in the context of the total net current assets. We consider that this applies to pre-payments and accrued income regardless of whether the total is included in debtors or shown as a separate category.

4.47 An example of disclosure of long-term pre-payments within debtors can be seen in the accounts of Seton Healthcare Group plc (see Table 4.7.2).

Table 4.7.2 — Seton Healthcare Group plc — Annual Report — 28 February 1994

NOTES TO THE FINANCIAL STATEMENTS

16 DEBTORS: AMOUNTS FALLING DUE AFTER MORE THAN ONE YEAR

	Group		Company	
	1994	1993	**1994**	1993
	£'000	£'000	**£'000**	£'000
Other debtors	**1,779**	1,913	**–**	–
Prepayment	**453**	753	**453**	753
	2,232	2,666	**453**	753

Included within other debtors are £153,000 of deferred tax recoverable on the exceptional losses in 1992 and a £1,626,000 debt arising from the disposal of the USA businesses repayable over 5 years.

The prepayment of £453,000 is an advance payment relating to products to be supplied under a 5 year manufacturing agreement ending September 1996.

4.48 Pre-payments are not defined in the Act, the Statement of Principles or any accounting standard. However, simply put, a pre-payment is expenditure incurred before the balance sheet that relates to activities and benefits arising after the balance sheet date. In addition, where costs are deferred as a pre-payment, the resultant asset must meet the definition of an asset in FRS 5. Therefore, the pre-payment should give rise to rights or other access to future economic benefits that are controlled by the entity, where control is the ability to obtain the future economic benefits relating to that asset and to restrict the access of others to those benefits. [FRS 5 paras 2, 3].

4.49 Pre-payments do not include expenditure that meets the criteria for recognition as a different category of asset under another accounting standard, such as FRS 10, 'Goodwill and intangible assets', SSAP 13, 'Accounting for research and development', FRS 15, 'Tangible fixed assets', or SSAP 9, 'Stocks and long-term contracts'.

4.50 Furthermore, applying the recognition criteria in FRS 5, a pre-payment should only be recognised in the balance sheet if:

- There is sufficient evidence of the existence of the item, including evidence that a future inflow of benefit will occur.

- The item can be measured at a monetary amount with sufficient reliability.

[FRS 5 para 20].

4.51 In order to determine whether costs relating to activities of future periods can be deferred as pre-payments therefore, the key issues are:

- Whether the entity *controls* those future benefits (that is, has the ability to obtain future economic benefits and can restrict others rights to those benefits).

- Whether there is sufficient evidence as to the *certainty* of those future economic benefits.

4.52 This is consistent with the approach adopted by the UITF in Abstract 24, 'Start up costs', (see chapter 16) and Abstract 34, 'Pre-contract costs', (see chapter 3), which both require a high level of certainty before the recognition of such costs as assets. There would generally need to be a strong connection between the cost and the expected future benefit.

4.53 In addition, consideration needs to be given as to the period in which the deferred cost should be recognised in the profit and loss account. This would generally be a defined period over which the expected benefits are to be received. However, if there is uncertainty over the amount of the expected benefits and timing of such a period, then the circumstances are more likely to lead to earlier recognition of the cost.

4.54 The following examples illustrate the principles described above.

Example 1

A company with a December year end makes a payment in December 20X1 to a film production crew to make a television advertisement in 20X2.

This is a 'traditional' pre-payment and under the accruals basis in most cases it will appropriate to defer such expenditure as a pre-payment. The benefit is the future services to be received, which the company controls by means of its contract and payment to the film production crew. Unless there are indications to the contrary, such as the film production crew being insolvent, there is certainty that the future benefit will be received.

Example 2

The same company has paid a different production crew for another television advertisement that has been produced before the year end, but it is not to be aired on television until after the year end.

This is similar to the treatment of 'stock', but in respect of non-stock items. Again, in such a case in most instances it would be appropriate to defer the production cost as an asset at the balance sheet date, rather than expense it as soon as the production of the advertisement has finished. The supplier has carried out its contractual duties, so that the entity has received the goods or services, but the entity has not yet made use of them.

To defer such costs, however, it is necessary to demonstrate that the entity still controls the benefits. In this example, the entity owns the rights to the advertisement and can control when and where it is aired on television. There would also need to be evidence to support the certainty that the entity will benefit from those rights and some assurance that the amount is 'recoverable', that is that future inflows are reasonably expected. Clearly, there may be evidence after the year end of such inflows and past experience of similar events will also help to support such a case.

Example 3

By March 20X2, both of the advertisements described above have been aired.

In this scenario it is more difficult to make a case supporting continued deferral of the costs in a balance sheet produced at the end of March 20X2. Once the advertisement has been aired, the company no longer has direct control over the benefits it may receive as a result. Increased sales may be expected but the absolute amount and the period over which these sales are generated would generally be uncertain.

However, in some cases there may be a strong direct link between the future benefit (that is, new sales) and the asset on the balance sheet. For example, where a holiday company can clearly track specific sales generated from a brochure that has been sent to targeted potential customers, it may be appropriate to defer the costs of that brochure and release them to the profit and loss account over the period expected to benefit, that is the period in which those sales are recognised in the profit and loss account. Factors to consider in such circumstances would include whether:

- There is sufficient and strong evidence of a direct link between the expenditure being deferred and the future income or other benefit generated from that specific item. Where sales could be generated by more than one source, is there a way of tracking sales primarily to that source.
- There is a high expectation of sales or contracts for future services or goods that have not been generated by the time the financial statements are signed, but are expected from the item being deferred, for example by reference to past experience and current circumstances, market share etc.
- Deferring such costs is in line with industry practice.
- There is a defined period to which those costs relate.
- The costs to be deferred are limited to incremental external costs.
- The deferred cost is recoverable.

Cash at bank and in hand

Definition of cash

4.55 Schedule 4 to the Act requires cash at bank and in hand to be included as a separate line item within current assets. The Act does not define cash and this has resulted in inconsistencies in practice.

4.56 FRS 1, 'Cash flow statements' revised in October 1996, defines cash as *"Cash in hand and deposits repayable on demand with any qualifying financial institution, less overdrafts from any qualifying financial institution repayable on demand. Deposits are repayable on demand if they can be withdrawn at any time without notice and without penalty or if a maturity or period of notice of not more than 24 hours or one working day has been agreed. Cash includes cash in hand and deposits denominated in foreign currencies*".

4.57 Therefore, the FRS 1 definition of cash includes deposits repayable on demand with any bank or other financial institution and so would include, for example, accounts with Building Societies. The definition excludes any term deposits with banks or other financial institutions.

[The next paragraph is 4.62.]

Right of set-off of bank balances

4.62 Assets and liabilities are only allowed to be offset against one another in financial statements where there is a legally enforceable right of set-off between the balances. This stems from the requirement in paragraph 5 of Schedule 4 to the Act, which states that amounts in respect of items that represent assets or income may not be offset against amounts in respect of items that represent liabilities or expenditure, or *vice versa*.

4.63 FRS 25, 'Financial instruments: Disclosure and presentation', expands upon this and sets out conditions that have to be met in order for offset to apply. The standard's rules require offset where, and only where, both the following conditions are met:

- The company has a legally enforceable right to set off the recognised amounts.
- The company intends either to settle on a net basis, or to realise the asset and settle the liability simultaneously.

[FRS 25 para 42].

4.64 These conditions are more restrictive than those contained in FRS 5 (which were withdrawn on the issuance of FRS 25), which did not require any intention to net settle, focussing entirely on an ability to do so.

4.65 Extreme care needs to be taken in consolidated financial statements, where it may be difficult to arrange for an amount that one group company owes to another party (such as a bank) to be offset against the amount of a deposit that another member of the group has lodged with that party. However, where a bank funds members of a group of companies this situation would be different if all of the following conditions applied:

- Each individual depositing company in the group has a joint and several liability to pay the same debts as the borrowing companies (that is, each is deemed to be a principal debtor for the same debts).
- The bank has a liability to each individual depositing company in respect of its deposit.
- The group has a demonstrable intention to net settle these balances.

4.66 In these circumstances such assets and liabilities may be offset against each other if all the criteria are met, although the restrictions imposed by FRS 25 make this rare. Tesco PLC has bank deposits at subsidiary undertakings which have been offset against borrowings in the parent company under a legal right of set-off (see Table 4.7.5). It is not made clear whether Tesco PLC has an intention to net settle, but the example demonstrates the disclosure where the conditions are met.

Table 4.7.5 — Tesco PLC — Annual Report and Accounts — 22 February 2003

Note 17 Creditors falling due within one year (extract)

	Group		Company	
	2003 £m	2002 £m	**2003 £m**	2002 £m
Bank loans and overdrafts (a)	**1,286**	1,474	**1,162**	1,890

(a) Bank deposits in subsidiary undertakings of £299m (2002 – £1,636m) have been offset against borrowings in the parent company under a legal right of set-off.

Restricted cash balances

4.71 Cash at bank and in hand will sometimes include balances that can only be used for a specific purpose or where access is restricted. If these amounts are material then they should be disclosed, normally in the notes to the financial statements. Examples of such disclosure are found in the accounts of John Mowlem & Company PLC (cash balances subject to legal charges, see Table 4.7.6), Cable and Wireless plc (cash balances subject to exchange regulation, see Table 4.7.7) and Imperial Chemical Industries PLC (short-term deposits and cash held by insurance subsidiaries, see Table 4.7.8).

Table 4.7.6 — John Mowlem & Company PLC — Annual Report and Accounts — 31 December 1994

NOTES TO THE ACCOUNTS

18 Cash

At 31 December 1994, cash balances with banks include £6.4 million (1993 £4.4 million) of cash deposits which are subject to either a legal assignment or a charge in favour of a third party. It is expected that they will be released in 1995.

Table 4.7.7 — Cable and Wireless plc — Annual report and Accounts — 31 March 2003

Notes to the Accounts

20. SHORT-TERM DEPOSITS AND CASH AT BANK AND IN HAND (extract)

Of the total amounts shown, £49 million (2002–£45 million) is held in countries subject to exchange regulations which may delay repatriation.

Table 4.7.8 — Imperial Chemical Industries PLC — Annual Report and Accounts and Form 20-F — 31 December 2001

Notes relating to the accounts

18 Current asset investments and short-term deposits (extract)

Included in unlisted investments and short-term deposits and cash are amounts totalling £104m (2000 £224m) held by the Group's insurance subsidiaries. In 2001 £38m (2000 £24m) was readily available for the general purposes of the Group.

Net current assets and liabilities

4.72 In determining the amount to be shown under 'Net current assets (liabilities)' in Format 1, a company must take into account any amount that is shown separately under the heading 'Prepayments and accrued income'. [4 Sch Balance sheet formats note 11]. This applies whether the amount in question is shown as a sub-heading of debtors (C.II.6) or as a main heading (D). But as the alternative positions of this heading within Format 1 both automatically fall within net current assets (liabilities), this seems to be a self-evident requirement. In practice, it is fairly rare for prepayments to be disclosed as a main heading.

Liabilities

Disclosure

4.73 All items included under creditors must be analysed between amounts that will fall due within one year of the balance sheet date and amounts that will fall due after more than one year. [Schedule 4 balance sheet formats]. The Act requires that creditors should be analysed into the following categories:

- Debenture loans.
- Bank loans and overdrafts.
- Payments received on account.
- Trade creditors.
- Bills of exchange payable.
- Amounts owed to group undertakings.
- Amounts owed to undertakings in which the company has a participating interest.
- Other creditors including taxation and social security.
- Accruals and deferred income.

[4 Sch formats].

4.74 An item representing a liability that is not covered by the prescribed format may be shown separately. [4 Sch 3(2)]. Examples of creditors that are sometimes shown as separate categories within total creditors are amounts due in respect of factored debts or bills of exchange discounted with recourse, finance lease payables and deferred consideration in respect of acquisitions.

4.75 Both the Act and FRS 25 specify a considerable amount of detail that a company should disclose in its financial statements in respect of its indebtedness. These disclosure requirements are considered in detail in chapter 6.

4.76 Where any item that is shown under the heading 'Creditors' includes liabilities for which the company has given security, these liabilities must be disclosed in aggregate. Also, the notes must give an indication of the nature of the securities given. [4 Sch 48(4)]. For this requirement to be meaningful, the financial statements should show some disaggregation of the relevant liabilities. This is because it could be misleading merely to disclose the aggregate of securities compared with the aggregate of liabilities.

Classification as short-term or long-term

4.77 For the purpose of the Act, a loan falls due for repayment (or an instalment falls due for payment) on the earliest date on which the lender could require repayment (or payment) if the lender were to exercise all options and rights available to him. [4 Sch 85].

4.78 FRS 25 clarifies that liabilities should be regarded (and classified) as falling due within one year even if:

- The original term was for a period longer than a year.

- An agreement to refinance, or to reschedule payments, on a long-term basis is completed after the balance sheet date and before the financial statements are authorised for issue.

[FRS 25 para 50A].

4.79 If, however, the company has the right, at the balance sheet date, to defer payments for more than one year, a liability should be classified as falling due in more than one year. [FRS 25 para 50B].

Example

A company entered into a loan agreement with a bank on 15 January 20X5. The loan is due for repayment in five equal instalments payable at the end of each quarter until 31 March 20X6. The company's directors intend to keep to this payment schedule and cash flow forecasts indicate that the company will be able to do so. The loan agreement contains a clause permitting the company to defer all payments until 31 March 20X6 (the disadvantage of doing so being a higher total interest cost). The full amount of the debt should be classified as falling due in more than one year, because the company has the right to defer payments until after 31 December 20X5.

4.80 Where a covenant in a loan agreement is breached before the year end and this results in the loan becoming repayable on demand (or within 12 months of the balance sheet date), the full amount of the loan should be classified as falling due within one year, even if the lender agrees after the year end not to demand repayment as a consequence of the breach, or agrees to a period of grace during which the breach can be rectified. [FRS 25 para 50C, 50E].

Debentures

4.81 There is no precise definition of a debenture, either in law or in practice. In legal terms it is generally construed as formal acknowledgment of a debt. However, section 744 of the Act (section 738 of the Companies Act 2006) refers to debentures as including *"debenture stock, bonds and any other securities of a company, whether constituting a charge on the assets of the company or not"*. This definition is very wide. It does not distinguish clearly between a debenture loan and any other loan. Whether a particular loan is a debenture or not will depend on the documentation. A formal loan agreement, whether containing security or not, will often constitute a debenture. Although a bank loan may be a debenture loan, the balance sheet formats distinguish between bank loans and other debenture loans.

4.82 For accounting measurement and disclosure purposes, there is no difference between debentures, loans and other debt instruments. They are all capital instruments issued for raising finance and are dealt with in detail in chapter 6.

Amounts received on account

4.83 Unless a company shows the payments it has received on account of orders as a deduction from stocks, it must show them under creditors. [4 Sch Balance sheet formats note 8].

Trade creditors

4.84 Trade creditors normally represents amounts owed to suppliers of goods and services. It could comprise either all items included in the creditors ledger or simply those items that relate to the cost of sales. If companies classify all creditors ledger items as trade creditors, such treatment could distort the cost of sales/trade creditors ratio. A company should ensure that, whatever treatment it adopts, it is consistent from year to year.

Obligations in respect of trade loans

4.85 Trade loans are common in a number of industries, a typical example being the brewing industry. Trade loans are often given by brewers to their tied houses and in consideration for the loan the tied house will agree to take a certain quantity of beer from the brewer. Such arrangements can be financed in a variety of ways, for example, by advances from the brewer, or from a bank. FRS 5 requires the substance of the arrangement to be accounted for and so, depending on the circumstances of the particular agreement, the obligation in respect of the trade loans may have to be shown on the brewer's balance sheet.

4.86 From the 1994 financial statements of Bass PLC, it can be seen that the trade loans and related obligations have been brought on balance sheet following the introduction of FRS 5 (see Table 4.7.9). The liability has been included within the total for 'other borrowings'.

Table 4.7.9 — Bass PLC — Annual Report — 30 September 1994

Accounting Policies (extract)

iii) Investments

Fixed asset investments are stated individually at cost less any provision for permanent diminution in value. Fixed asset investments comprise trade loans and advances, trade investments in the equity of other undertakings, quoted securities and debentures. Trade loans are principally advances made to operators of UK on-licensed outlets by the Brewing division, either directly or through an arrangement with a bank. They are advanced in order to obtain a beer supply agreement and are generally cancellable at three months' notice.

Notes to the Financial Statements

13 Fixed asset investments (extract)

To comply with FRS 5 arrangements entered into by the Group with a number of banks to advance loans to third party outlets are now incorporated within both fixed asset investments and borrowings (see note 20). Trade loans and advances cost at 30 September 1993 has been restated accordingly by £80m.

4.87 An example of a company in a different industry recognising obligations in respect of trade loans to third parties, as a result of FRS 5, is Burmah Castrol plc (see Table 4.7.10). Obligations to banks in respect of the provision of financial assistance to customers in the group's fuel and marketing operations have been brought on balance sheet.

Table 4.7.10 — Burmah Castrol plc — Annual Report — 31 December 1994

FINANCIAL REVIEW (extract)

Accounting policies (extract)

The group's lubricants and fuels marketing operations sometimes entail entering into agreements whereby customers receive financial assistance from banks. The group has an obligation to banks in respect of such loans, which are normally serviced and repaid by the withholding of sales rebates. At 31 December 1994, the total amount outstanding under such obligations was £76 million (1993, £60 million). In accordance with FRS5, which came into effect in 1994, these amounts have been incorporated into the group's consolidated balance sheet, both as an asset under trade advances and similar arrangements, and as a liability under obligations to banks in respect of trade advances. The costs and benefits to the group of these arrangements continue to be included in operating profit.

NOTES TO THE ACCOUNTS

2 Changes to corresponding figures (extract)

(b) In compliance with FRS5, certain obligations relating to the provision of financial assistance to third parties have been included in the group's consolidated balance sheet. Corresponding figures for 1993 have been adjusted, increasing fixed asset investments by £60.3 million, creditors falling due within one year by £16.1 million and creditors falling due after one year by £44.2 million. Also, retained on balance sheet are bills discounted with recourse, which at 31 December 1993 amounted to £6.9 million. Current assets and creditors falling due within one year have been adjusted by this amount.

4.88 As mentioned above, there are various forms that trade loans can take and some will clearly be on balance sheet and some clearly off balance sheet. However, there are a number of grey areas where the risks and rewards will have to be considered very carefully to determine whether such loans are on or off balance sheet. Consider the following situations using brewers as an example:

Example 1

A bank makes a loan to a brewer and the brewer makes a loan to its tied house at a lower interest rate than that charged by the bank.

In such circumstances, it is clear that both loans should be on the brewer's balance sheet, one as an asset and the other as a liability.

Example 2

A bank makes a loan to the tied house which is guaranteed by the brewer. In consideration for the guarantee, the tied house agrees to take a certain quantity of beer from the brewer on normal commercial terms.

This type of transaction is likely to be off the brewer's balance sheet, because the fact that it has guaranteed the loan would not of itself result in a liability that needs to be recorded on its balance sheet. The guarantee would be disclosed as a contingent liability in accordance with FRS 12.

Example 3

The facts are the same as the example above, but the brewer subsidises part of the interest cost on the loan to the tied house. This is done either by making payments direct to the bank or by making payments to the tied house.

It can be argued that the substance of this arrangement is a subsidised loan made from the brewer to the tied house. Consequently, the brewer's position is no different from the situation where the bank makes a loan to the brewer and the brewer then lends those funds to the tied house at a subsidised rate (example 1). The risks and rewards to the brewer are identical. If the tied house defaults on the loan then the bank has full recourse *via* the guarantee to the brewer. The brewer also bears the interest differential. Alternatively, it can be argued that this transaction is similar to example 2 above and its substance is that of a contingent liability arising from the guarantee and the interest subsidy is a way of giving the tied house a trade discount. These are finely balanced arguments and strictly in accordance with FRS 5 this type of arrangement should probably be accounted for as a financing transaction.

Example 4

The bank makes a loan to the tied house which is guaranteed by the brewer. The brewer does not subsidise the interest payments, but the tied house agrees to take a certain quantity of beer from the brewer and is given a trade discount (which is not normally available).

Again, the substance of such a transaction would have to be considered very carefully. If the substance is similar to that in example 3 above, because there is a strong correlation between the amount of the loan and the amount of business (such that the amount of the trade discount is similar to the amount which would have been paid as interest subsidy), then there seems to be an argument for saying that the substance is a financing and the full amount of the loan should be recorded as a liability on the brewer's balance sheet. If, however, there is little or no correlation between the amount of business and the loan, such that the discount given differs from the amount that would have been paid as interest subsidy, then there is an argument for saying that the substance has changed and the loan should not be recognised on the brewer's balance sheet.

4.89 Alternatively, there may be ways whereby the trade loans can be structured so that the risks to the brewer are capped. If, for example, the brewer's portfolio of trade loans was £100 million and the bank advances (say) £80 million of non-recourse finance, the bank would be protected if the bad debts on the portfolio are expected to be only £5 million. The brewer is still exposed to the bad debt risk, but its downside risk is capped at £20 million and the bank is exposed merely to the unlikely risk of catastrophe. In this circumstance, it might be possible to use the linked presentation. The non-recourse finance could then be deducted from the trade loans it finances on the face of the balance sheet; the difference (£20 million in the example) less a provision for bad debts (say £5 million) is the asset included in the balance sheet totals. The presentation would be as follows:

	£m	£m
Trade loans	95	
Less: Non-recourse finance	80	
		15

4.90 This presentation could only be justified, however, if the finance is to be repaid from the specific item it finances and there is no possibility whatsoever of a claim on the brewer being established other than against funds generated by the trade loans. Furthermore, the strict linked presentation conditions in paragraph 27 of FRS 5 would also have to be met before this approach could be used (see chapter 3).

Other creditors including taxation and social security

4.91 The line 'other creditors including taxation and social security' must be analysed between other creditors, and taxation and social security. [4 Sch Balance sheet formats note 9]. The 'taxation and social security' headings should include the following items:

- Corporation tax.
- VAT.
- ACT payable on dividends.
- Social security and other amounts (such as PAYE owed in respect of wages and salaries).
- Excise duty.

The heading 'Other creditors' should include items that cannot be appropriately analysed elsewhere.

4.92 'Other creditors including taxation and social security' contrasts with the line under provisions for 'taxation, including deferred taxation'. The latter item will comprise all deferred tax liabilities.

Accruals and deferred income

4.93 In the same way that 'prepayments and accrued income' may be shown in either of two positions in the formats, the item 'accruals and deferred income' may be disclosed either as a category of creditors or as a separate category in its own right. [4 Sch Balance sheet formats note 10]. Where 'accruals and deferred income' is disclosed under creditors, it must be analysed between those amounts that will fall due within one year and those amounts that will fall due after more than one year. [4 Sch Balance sheet formats note 13]. No such analysis is required if 'accruals and deferred income' is included as a separate category.

4.94 'Accruals and deferred income' could include government grants of a capital or revenue nature that are accounted for as deferred credits. These are discussed in chapters 9 and 16.

Other liabilities

4.95 The Act requires the amount of any convertible loans included in the caption of debenture loans to be shown separately. [4 Sch Balance sheet formats note 7]. FRS 25, 'Financial instruments: Disclosure and presentation' requires the debt component of convertible debt (which is treated as a compound financial instrument) to be reported withing liabilities. We consider that, in order to comply with the Act's requirements, the liability element of convertible loans should be separately disclosed as part of debentures. FRS 25 is considered in detail in chapter 6.

4.96 The following items may be shown in alternative positions in the balance sheet (references given are for Format 1):

- Called up share capital not paid (A and C.II.5).
- Prepayments and accrued income (C.II.6 and D).
- Accruals and deferred income (E.9, H.9 and J).

Consolidated formats

4.97 The Act requires consolidated financial statements to comply as far as practicable with the provisions of Schedule 4 to the Act as if the undertakings included in the consolidation were a single company. [4A Sch 1(1)]. In addition, the consolidated financial statements have to comply with the provisions of Schedule 4A as to their form and content. [CA85 Sec 227A(3); CA06 Sec 404(3)].

4.98 Schedule 4A to the Act includes provisions that modify the formats detailed in Schedule 4, to include certain additional items that require disclosure in the consolidated balance sheet. [4A Sch 17(2), 21(2)]. The Format 1 balance sheet set out below includes the requirements of both Schedules 4 and 4A (the additional requirements of Schedule 4A are shown in bold and modifications to the numbering and lettering have been made for illustrative purposes). The Format 2 balance sheet is not given as it is identical in all respects (apart from one) to the information disclosed in Format 1 (see para 4.29).

4.99 The format chosen by the group's parent for its individual balance sheet would normally also be used to present the consolidated balance sheet. However, there is nothing in the legislation to prevent the parent from adopting a different format for its consolidated balance sheet, although this is unlikely to happen in practice, unless the group has banking or insurance activities and the parent does not.

Consolidated balance sheet — Format 1

A Called up share capital not paid

B Fixed assets

I Intangible assets
1 Development costs
2 Concessions, patents, licences, trade marks and similar rights and assets
3 Goodwill
4 Payments on account

II Tangible assets
1 Land and buildings
2 Plant and machinery
3 Fixtures, fittings, tools and equipment
4 Payments on account and assets in course of construction

III Investments
1 Shares in group undertakings
2 Loans to group undertakings
3 Interests in associated undertakings
4 Other participating interests
5 Loans to undertakings in which the company has a participating interest
6 Other investments other than loans
7 Other loans
8 Own shares

C Current assets

I Stocks
1 Raw materials and consumables
2 Work in progress
3 Finished goods and goods for resale
4 Payments on account

II Debtors
1 Trade debtors
2 Amounts owed by group undertakings
3 Amounts owed by undertakings in which the company has a participating interest
4 Other debtors
5 Called-up share capital not paid
6 Prepayments and accrued income

III Investments
1 Shares in group undertakings
2 Own shares
3 Other investments

IV Cash at bank and in hand

D Prepayments and accrued income

E Creditors: amounts falling due within one year
1 Debenture loans
2 Bank loans and overdrafts
3 Payments received on account
4 Trade creditors
5 Bills of exchange payable
6 Amounts owed to group undertakings
7 Amounts owed to undertakings in which the company has a participating interest
8 Other creditors including taxation and social security
9 Accruals and deferred income

F Net current assets (liabilities)

G Total assets less current liabilities

H Creditors: amounts falling due after more than one year
1 Debenture loans
2 Bank loans and overdrafts
3 Payments received on account
4 Trade creditors
5 Bills of exchange payable
6 Amounts owed to group undertakings
7 Amounts owed to undertakings in which the company has a participating interest
8 Other creditors including taxation and social security
9 Accruals and deferred income

I Provisions for liabilities
1 Pensions and similar obligations
2 Taxation, including deferred taxation
3 Other provisions

J Accruals and deferred income

K Minority interests (alternative position M)

L Capital and reserves
I Called up share capital
II Share premium account
III Revaluation reserve
IV Other reserves
1 Capital redemption reserve
2 Reserve for own shares
3 Reserves provided for by the articles of association
4 Other reserves
V Profit and loss account

M Minority interests (alternative position K)

Rules concerning particular items in consolidated formats

4.100 The following items may be shown in alternative positions in the balance sheet (references given are for Format 1):

- Called up share capital not paid (A and C.II.5).
- Pre-payments and accrued income (C.II.6 and D).
- Accruals and deferred income (E.9, H.9 and J).
- Minority interests (K and M).

4.101 An example of a Format 1 consolidated balance sheet is given in Table 4.8.

Table 4.8 – Glaxo Holdings p.l.c. – Annual Report and Accounts – 30 June 1994

Consolidated Balance Sheet

At 30th June	Notes	**1994 £m**	1993 £m
FIXED ASSETS			
Tangible assets	11	**3,184**	2,959
Investments	12	**55**	61
		3,239	3,020
CURRENT ASSETS			
Stocks	13	**575**	595
Debtors	14	**1,310**	1,346
Investments	15/17	**2,708**	2,434
Cash at bank	17	**55**	63
		4,648	4,438
CREDITORS: Amounts falling due within one year	16	**2,130**	2,200
NET CURRENT ASSETS		**2,518**	2,238
TOTAL ASSETS LESS CURRENT LIABILITIES		**5,757**	5,258
CREDITORS: Amounts falling due after more than one year	16	**169**	120
CONVERTIBLE BONDS	18	**129**	123
PROVISIONS FOR LIABILITIES AND CHARGES	19	**293**	358
NET ASSETS	4	**5,166**	4,657
CAPITAL AND RESERVES			
Called up share capital	22	**762**	758
Share premium account	23	**229**	151
Other reserves	23	**4,052**	3,637
EQUITY SHAREHOLDERS' FUNDS	24	**5,043**	4,546
MINORITY INTERESTS		**123**	111
CAPITAL EMPLOYED		**5,166**	4,657

4.102 As explained in paragraph 4.29, in Format 2 assets are shown as equal in total to liabilities. An example is given in Table 4.9. In Format 2 there is only one position for minority interests, between 'capital and reserves' and 'provisions for liabilities'. [4A Sch 17(2)].

Table 4.9 – The Peninsular and Oriental Steam Navigation Company – Annual Report and Accounts – 31 December 1998

Group balance sheet
at 31 December 1998

	Note	Group 1998 £m	1997 £m
Assets			
Fixed assets			
Intangible assets: Goodwill	9	6.8	–
Tangible assets			
Ships	10	1,877.8	1,885.4
Properties	11	1,351.7	1,396.6
Other fixed assets	12	567.7	567.4
Investments			
Subsidiaries	13	–	–
Joint ventures:			
Share of gross assets		1,731.3	1,315.4
Share of gross liabilities		(971.4)	(763.9)
Share of net assets		759.9	551.5
Associates		109.1	61.4
Other investments		31.5	17.0
	14	900.5	629.9
		4,704.5	4,479.3
Current assets			
Development and dealing properties	15	359.9	330.9
Stocks	16	125.0	124.0
Debtors	17	1,106.4	1,368.0
Investments		12.7	11.3
Cash at bank and in hand		134.1	122.6
		1,738.1	1,956.8
		6,442.6	6,436.1
Liabilities			
Capital and reserves			
Called up share capital	18	769.3	751.3
Share premium account	19	595.8	562.7
Revaluation reserve	19	46.6	8.6
Other reserves	19	527.5	522.8
Profit and loss account	19	1,048.5	972.9
Equity stockholders' funds	19	2,837.9	2,668.0
Non-equity stockholders' funds		149.8	150.3
Stockholders' funds		2,987.7	2,818.3

Other liabilities			
Equity minority interests	20	39.7	32.9
Provisions for liabilities and charges*	21	103.0	138.9
Loans: convertible	22	164.8	189.8
non-convertible	22	1,309.0	1,618.6
Other creditors	23	1,838.4	1,637.6
		3,454.9	3,617.8
		6,442.6	6,436.1

* Note that for years beginning on or after 1 January 2005, the statutory line item required by the Companies Act 1985 (as amended by SI 2004/2947), 'The Companies Act 1985 (International Accounting Standards and Other Amendments) Regulations 2004', is 'provisions and liabilities'.

Interests in and amounts due to and from group undertakings

4.103 The Format 1 balance sheet specifies the place where the aggregate amounts should be shown of any amounts owed to and from, and any interests in, group undertakings. These items can be summarised as follows:

B	Fixed assets
III	Investments 1 Shares in group undertakings 2 Loans to group undertakings
C	Current assets
II	Debtors 2 Amounts owed by group undertakings
III	Investments 1 Shares in group undertakings
E	Creditors: amounts falling due within one year 6 Amounts owed to group undertakings
H	Creditors: amounts falling due after more than one year 6 Amounts owed to group undertakings

4.104 Because amounts owed by and to group undertakings have to be shown in specific positions in the formats, these balances should not be netted off into a single balance disclosed in the balance sheet as 'Investment in subsidiaries'. This applies even where a note to the financial statements gives additional information that explains the net balance. Although shares in and loans to subsidiaries may, if they qualify as fixed asset investments and 4 Sch 3(4) applies, be aggregated on the face of the balance sheet, the disclosure that follows is not permitted (because it is outside 4 Sch 3(4)).

Investment in subsidiaries — presentation *not* permitted

Shares in subsidiaries	X
Amounts owed by subsidiaries	X
Amounts owed to subsidiaries	(X)
	X

4.105 Moreover, the amounts owed and owing have to be ascertained on an undertaking by undertaking basis. [4 Sch 5]. Consequently, for accounting disclosure purposes in the parent's financial statements, amounts that one subsidiary owes to the parent cannot be offset against amounts the parent owes to another subsidiary. Set-off can be allowed only in circumstances where there is a legal right of set-off and the company has an intention to net settle (see further chapter 6).

4.106 Undertakings have to analyse 'amounts owed by (and to) group undertakings' between amounts that will fall due within one year and amounts that will fall due after more than one year. [4 Sch Balance sheet formats notes 13 and 15]. The results of this analysis will largely depend both on the way in which group undertakings are financed and on the terms of any formal or informal agreements between the undertakings.

The profit and loss account

Individual company formats

4.107 The Act permits companies to use any one of the four alternative formats of the profit and loss account and it leaves the choice between these formats to the company's directors.

4.108 Unlike the choice between the balance sheet formats, the choice between the profit and loss account formats is significant. A company can choose not only between a vertical presentation (Formats 1 and 2) and a presentation in which it shows charges separately from income (Formats 3 and 4), but also between classifying expenses by function or by type. Thus, depending on which format a company chooses, its financial statements will contain certain additional information, for example, own work capitalised, as well as certain different information.

Classification of expenses by function

4.109 In Formats 1 and 3, expenses are classified by function (for example, cost of sales, distribution costs, administrative expenses). These formats, both of which require identical information, have much in common with the management accounts that many UK companies prepare on a regular basis. It should be noted that there is no line item for 'operating profit' in the statutory profit and loss account formats — the disclosure of operating profit derives from FRS 3 (see para 4.65). Format 1, which is the vertical presentation, is set out below, and illustrated in Table 4.10.

Profit and loss account — Format 1

1	Turnover
2	Cost of sales
3	Gross profit or loss
4	Distribution costs
5	Administrative expenses
6	Other operating income
7	Income from shares in group undertakings
8	Income from participating interests
9	Income from other fixed asset investments
10	Other interest receivable and similar income
11	Amounts written off investments
12	Interest payable and similar charges
13	Tax on profit or loss on ordinary activities
14	Profit or loss on ordinary activities after taxation
15	Extraordinary income
16	Extraordinary charges
17	Extraordinary profit or loss
18	Tax on extraordinary profit or loss
19	Other taxes not shown under the above items
20	Profit or loss for the financial year

Classification of expenses by type

4.110 In Formats 2 and 4, expenses are classified by type (for example, raw materials and consumables, staff costs, and depreciation). Format 2, which is the vertical presentation, is set out below, and also illustrated in Table 4.11.

Profit and loss account — Format 2

1	Turnover
2	Change in stocks of finished goods and in work in progress
3	Own work capitalised
4	Other operating income
5	(a) Raw materials and consumables
	(b) Other external charges
6	Staff costs:
	(a) Wages and salaries
	(b) Social security costs
	(c) Other pension costs
7	(a) Depreciation and other amounts written off tangible and intangible fixed assets
	(b) Exceptional amounts written off current assets
8	Other operating charges
9	Income from shares in group undertakings
10	Income from participating interests
11	Income from other fixed asset investments
12	Other interest receivable and similar income
13	Amounts written off investments

14	Interest payable and similar charges
15	Tax on profit or loss on ordinary activities
16	Profit or loss on ordinary activities after taxation
17	Extraordinary income
18	Extraordinary charges
19	Extraordinary profit or loss
20	Tax on extraordinary profit or loss
21	Other taxes not shown under the above items
22	Profit or loss for the financial year

Consolidated formats

4.111 For a consolidated profit and loss account, Schedule 4A to the Act details the items that should be added to the formats prescribed in Schedule 4. [4A Sch 17(3)(4), 21(3)]. The formats illustrated below include the requirements of both Schedule 4 and 4A (the additional requirements of Schedule 4A are shown in bold and modifications to the numbering have also been made for illustrative purposes). Formats 3 and 4 are not given as they are rarely used and they replicate the information in Formats 1 and 2.

Consolidated profit and loss account — Format 1

1	Turnover
2	Cost of sales
3	Gross profit or loss
4	Distribution costs
5	Administrative expenses
6	Other operating income
7	Income from shares in group undertakings
8	**Income from interests in associated undertakings**
9	**Income from other participating interests**
10	Income from other fixed asset investments
11	Other interest receivable and similar income
12	Amounts written off investments
13	Interest payable and similar charges
14	Tax on profit or loss on ordinary activities
15	Profit or loss on ordinary activities after taxation
16	**Minority interests**
17	Extraordinary income
18	Extraordinary charges
19	Extraordinary profit or loss
20	Tax on extraordinary profit or loss
21	**Minority interests** (in extraordinary items)
22	Other taxes not shown under the above items
23	Profit or loss for the financial year

Consolidated profit and loss account — Format 2	
1	Turnover
2	Change in stocks of finished goods and in work in progress
3	Own work capitalised
4	Other operating income
5	(a) Raw materials and consumables
	(b) Other external charges
6	Staff costs:
	(a) Wages and salaries
	(b) Social security costs
	(c) Other pension costs
7	(a) Depreciation and other amounts written off tangible and intangible fixed assets
	(b) Exceptional amounts written off current assets
8	Other operating charges
9	Income from shares in group undertakings
10	**Income from interests in associated undertakings**
11	**Income from other participating interests**
12	Income from other fixed asset investments
13	Other interest receivable and similar income
14	Amounts written off investments
15	Interest payable and similar charges
16	Tax on profit or loss on ordinary activities
17	Profit or loss on ordinary activities after taxation
18	**Minority interests**
19	Extraordinary income
20	Extraordinary charges
21	Extraordinary profit or loss
22	Tax on extraordinary profit or loss
23	**Minority interests** (in extraordinary items)
24	Other taxes not shown under the above items
25	Profit or loss for the financial year

Rules concerning particular items

4.112 All items in the profit and loss account are preceded by an Arabic numeral and so they may be combined on the face of the profit and loss account and disclosed individually in the notes, if that treatment is considered to make a company's results more understandable. [4 Sch 3(4)]. However, FRS 3 requires that certain items (including turnover and operating profit) are shown on the face of the profit and loss account (see para 4.65). Also, whichever format of profit and loss account a company adopts, the account must, however, show separately on its face the amount of the company's or group's profit or loss on ordinary activities before taxation. [4 Sch 3(6)].

[The next paragraph is 4.115.]

4.115 The Act attaches to the formats certain notes and comments on specific profit and loss account items.

4.116 Where expenses are classified by function (Formats 1 and 3), the amounts to be shown under cost of sales, distribution costs and administrative expenses are to be stated after taking into account any necessary provisions for depreciation and for diminution in the value of assets. [4 Sch Profit and loss account formats note 14]. The amounts of the provisions for depreciation, or for the diminution in the value of tangible and intangible fixed assets, must be disclosed separately in the notes to the financial statements. [4 Sch Profit and loss account formats note 17].

4.117 Income or interest derived from group undertakings must be shown separately from income and interest derived from other sources. [4 Sch Profit and loss account formats note 15]. Similarly, any interest or similar charges payable to group undertakings must be shown separately. [4 Sch Profit and loss account formats note 16].

4.118 In the light of present practice in the UK, it is unlikely that any amount would fall to be disclosed under the heading 'Other taxes not shown under the above items'.

4.119 The two items for 'minority interests' in each of the consolidated formats are not alternatives, as the item on line 21 of Format 1 and on line 23 of Format 2 relate to the minority's share of extraordinary items. [4A Sch 17(4)].

The effect of FRS 3 on the profit and loss account formats

4.120 FRS 3 contains supplementary provisions relating to the format of the profit and loss account. These do not alter the requirements of the Act, but include standards for minimum disclosure that should be given on the face of the profit and loss account, together with certain additional disclosures. The detailed requirements of FRS 3 are considered in chapter 8. The following requirements are relevant to the formats.

- The face of the profit and loss account should include, as a minimum, an analysis of turnover and operating profit showing separately amounts attributable to continuing operations, acquisitions as a component of continuing operations, and discontinued operations. (There is no format heading for 'operating profit' in the Act; FRS 3 defines it as being normally, for non-financial entities, the profit before 'income from shares in group undertakings'.) [FRS 3 para 14].

- Exceptional items (apart from those items listed below) should be included under the statutory format headings to which they relate and should be disclosed on the face of the profit and loss account if that is necessary to give a true and fair view. [FRS 3 para 19].

- The following items, including provisions in respect of such items, should be disclosed separately on the face of the profit and loss account after operating profit and before interest, classified under continuing or discontinued operations as appropriate:

  - Profits or losses on the sale or termination of an operation.

- Costs of a fundamental reorganisation or restructuring having a material effect on the nature and focus of the reporting entity's operations.
- Profits or losses on the disposal of fixed assets.

[FRS 3 para 20].

- A company's ordinary activities have been defined so broadly that extraordinary items have all but disappeared from the profit and loss accounts of UK companies. Consequently, the line items in the Act's formats for extraordinary income and charges, tax on and minority interests in extraordinary items, are practically redundant.

4.121 Tables 4.10 and 4.11 are examples of published profit and loss accounts that follow Formats 1 and 2 respectively.

Table 4.10 — BPB plc — annual report — 31 March 1999

Group profit and loss account

Year to 31 March	Note	**1999** **£m**	1998 £m
Turnover			
Group and share of joint ventures and associates		**1,417.4**	1,401.1
Less: share of joint ventures' turnover		**(24.6)**	(24.3)
share of associates' turnover		**(77.5)**	(76.6)
Group turnover	3	**1,315.3**	1,300.2
Cost of sales		**(837.0)**	(838.5)
Gross profit		**478.3**	461.7
Net operating expenses	4	**(304.4)**	(298.1)
Operating profit	3	**173.9**	163.6
Share of operating profit in:			
Joint ventures		**0.8**	(0.8)
Associates		**12.2**	12.4
Exceptional items: continuing operations			
Disposals of fixed assets	7	**2.3**	2.7
Sale and termination of operations	7	**(20.1)**	(26.3)
Profit on ordinary activities before interest		**169.1**	151.6
Exceptional interest charge on bond buy-back	8	**(2.1)**	(14.9)
Other net interest payable	8	**(4.7)**	(2.1)
Profit on ordinary activities before tax		**162.3**	134.6
Tax on profit on ordinary activities	9	**(59.1)**	(50.1)
Profit on ordinary activities after tax		**103.2**	84.5
Minority interests		**0.5**	(0.8)
Profit attributable to BPB plc		**103.7**	83.7
Dividends	10	**(56.8)**	(56.9)
Retained profit for the year		**46.9**	26.8
Basic earnings per share	11	**20.5p**	16.3p
Diluted earnings per share	11	**20.4p**	16.1p

Underlying results			
Before net exceptional charge of £19.9 million *(1998 £38.5 million)*:			
Profit on ordinary activities before tax (£m)		**182.2**	173.1
Earnings per share	11	**23.9p**	22.3p
4 Net operating expenses			
Distribution costs		**187.6**	179.7
Administrative expenses		**125.6**	132.2
Other operating expenses		**(8.8)**	(13.8)
		304.4	298.1
The following are included within operating expenses:			
Redundancy costs			
— Building materials		**6.8**	5.7
— Paperboard		—	2.1
		6.8	7.8
Research and development costs		**4.4**	6.4

Table 4.11 — English China Clays plc 1994 — Annual Report and Accounts — 31 December 1994

Group Profit and Loss Account (extract)
for the year ended 31st December 1994

	Note		1994 £M	1993 £M (Re-stated-see Accounting policies)
Turnover				
Continuing operations			**877.6**	766.0
Discontinued operations			**163.2**	364.7
	1(a)		**1,040.8**	1,130.7
Operating costs	2(a)		**(927.5)**	(1,025.5)
Operating profit				
Continuing operations		**109.6**		89.7
Discontinued operations		**3.7**		15.5
			113.3	105.2
Non operating items				
Continuing operations				
Profit on sale of properties			–	0.8
(Loss)/Profit on disposal of operations			**(1.6)**	0.1
Discontinued operations				
Profit on sale of properties			–	0.9
Costs of fundamental restructuring			**(4.4)**	(1.7)
Profit on ordinary activities before interest and taxation			**107.3**	105.3
Net interest expense	2(b)		**(14.3)**	(17.4)
Profit on ordinary activities before taxation	1(b)		**93.0**	87.9
Tax on profit on ordinary activities	3(a)		**(31.6)**	(27.3)
Profit on ordinary activities after taxation			**61.4**	60.6
Minority interests			**(0.4)**	(0.3)

Profit for the year		**61.0**	60.3
Dividends paid and proposed*	4		
Equity shareholders			
— ordinary shares		**(49.7)**	(60.5)
— demerger		**(224.0)**	–
Non-equity shareholders		–	(1.6)
Retained deficit		**(212.7)**	(1.8)

Movements in reserves are set out in Note 16.

Notes to the Accounts (extract)

2 PROFIT AND LOSS ACCOUNT (extract)

	Continuing £M	**Dis-continued £M**	**1994 Total £M**	Continuing £M	Dis-continued £M	1993 Total £M
(a) Operating costs						
Change in stocks of finished goods and work in progress	**17.6**	**5.8**	**23.4**	24.5	1.0	25.5
Own work capitalised	**(1.8)**	**(0.2)**	**(2.0)**	(1.6)	(0.8)	(2.4)
Other operating income	**(10.3)**	**(0.7)**	**(11.0)**	(5.1)	(1.6)	(6.7)
Raw materials and consumables	**163.0**	**54.7**	**217.7**	139.9	116.6	256.5
Other external charges	**317.1**	**42.1**	**359.2**	275.8	100.5	376.3
Employment costs (Note 6(b))	**210.3**	**41.6**	**251.9**	175.1	95.1	270.2
Depreciation of tangible fixed assets	**50.0**	**6.3**	**56.3**	46.5	16.3	62.8
Net income from interests in associated undertakings	**(0.7)**	**(0.4)**	**(1.1)**	(0.6)	(0.5)	(1.1)
Income from loan to unlisted undertakings	**–**	**–**	**–**	–	(0.1)	(0.1)
Operating lease rentals —						
property	**3.6**	**0.6**	**4.2**	4.2	1.2	5.4
plant and machinery	**8.4**	**3.4**	**11.8**	7.5	8.2	15.7
Hire of plant and machinery	**10.1**	**6.3**	**16.4**	9.3	13.1	22.4
Auditors' remuneration	**0.7**	**–**	**0.7**	0.8	0.2	1.0
	768.0	**159.5**	**927.5**	676.3	349.2	1,025.5

* Note that for years beginning on or after 1 January 2005, FRS 21 prohibits the recognition of proposed final dividends until they have been approved by shareholders at an AGM.

Parent's profit and loss account

4.122 When a parent company prepares consolidated financial statements in accordance with the Act, it is not required to include its own profit and loss account and related notes if the financial statements satisfy the following requirements:

- The notes to the parent company's individual balance sheet show the company's profit or loss for the financial year determined in accordance with the provisions of the Act. [CA85 Sec 230(1)(b); CA06 Sec 408(1)(b)].
- The parent company's board of directors must approve the company's individual profit and loss account in accordance with the rules concerning

approval of the company's financial statements. [CA85 Sec 230(3); CA06 Sec 408(3)].

- The notes to the financial statements disclose the fact that the parent company has taken advantage of this exemption. [CA85 Sec 230(4); CA06 Sec 408(4)].

4.123 Where the consolidated financial statements do not include the company's profit and loss account, it need not include certain supplementary information when presented to the Board for their approval. [CA85 Sec 230(2); CA06 Sec 408(2)]. The information that can be excluded is specified in paragraphs 52 to 57 of Schedule 4 to the Act, which includes the following:

- Interest and similar charges. [4 Sch 53].
- Detailed particulars concerning tax. [4 Sch 54].
- Disaggregated information concerning turnover. [4 Sch 55].
- Certain miscellaneous matters including:
  - The effect of including any preceding year items in the current year's profit and loss account.
  - Particulars of extraordinary income or extraordinary charges.
  - The effect of any exceptional items.

[4 Sch 57].

4.124 Suitable wording for a note to be included in the consolidated financial statements when the parent's profit and loss account is not reproduced would be:

Example

As permitted by section 230(3) of the Companies Act 1985, the parent company's profit and loss account has not been included in these financial statements. The parent company's profit for the financial year was £x (20XX: £y).

The notes to the balance sheet and the profit and loss account

General requirements of the Act

4.125 Schedule 4 to the Act requires companies to disclose considerable detail in the notes to their financial statements. The objects of the requirements are:

- To supplement the information given in the financial statements in respect of any particular items that are shown in either the balance sheet or the profit and loss account.
- To give details of anything else that is relevant, in the light of the information so given, to the assessment of the state of the company's affairs.

- To explain any particular circumstances that affect items shown in the profit and loss account.

[4 Sch 37, 52].

4.126 Any information that the Act requires to be shown by way of a note to the financial statements may, alternatively, be shown in the company's profit or loss account or balance sheet. [4 Sch 35]. However, the Act does not permit a company to use the directors' report as an alternative method of disclosure.

4.127 Schedule 5 to the Act requires companies to disclose considerable detail about their investments in subsidiaries and other related undertakings. The disclosures are grouped in the following categories:

- Subsidiaries included in consolidated financial statements (considered in chapter 24).
- Subsidiaries that are excluded from consolidation (considered in chapter 24).
- Disclosures about subsidiaries where the parent does not prepare consolidated financial statements (considered in chapter 24).
- Joint ventures, associated undertakings and other significant holdings (considered in chapter 27).

4.128 Schedule 5 also requires a subsidiary to name its ultimate holding company and indicate where that company was incorporated (or registered if incorporated in Great Britain). This is considered in chapter 24.

4.129 Schedule 6 to the Act sets out the disclosure requirements concerning directors' emoluments and transactions and other arrangements involving directors. In addition, Schedule 7A sets out the disclosure requirements for a directors' remuneration report by quoted companies. These disclosures are considered in chapters 5 and 6 of the Manual of Accounting – IFRS and UK supplement.

4.130 The Act's disclosure requirements are supplemented by the requirements contained in individual accounting standards considered in the paragraphs that follow.

Additional statements required by FRS 3

4.131 FRS 3 requires two statements of a memorandum nature:

- A note of historical profits and losses should appear immediately after the profit and loss account or the statement of total recognised gains and losses. This note is required where assets have been revalued in the financial statements and there is a material difference between the results as disclosed in the profit and loss account and the results as they would have been reported on a pure historical cost basis. [FRS 3 para 26].

- A reconciliation of movements in shareholders' funds, providing a statement of all changes in shareholders' funds in the period, should be disclosed in a note or as a primary statement. This statement brings together the gains and losses for the period as reported in the primary financial statements, with other changes including dividends, new share capital issued and share capital redeemed. [FRS 3 para 28].

Where consolidated financial statements are presented, the note of historical profits and losses and the reconciliation of movements in shareholders' funds need only deal with the consolidated results, and not those of the parent company. These statements are considered in greater detail in chapter 8.

Compliance with accounting standards

4.132 The Act requires companies to state whether the financial statements have been prepared in accordance with applicable accounting standards. In addition, if there are any material departures from these standards, the particulars and the reasons for the departure must be given. [4 Sch 36A]. These requirements are dealt with in chapter 2.

True and fair override disclosures

4.133 Where a company departs from any of the accounting provisions of the Act in order to give a true and fair view, the Act requires that *"particulars of any such departure, the reasons for it and its effect shall be given in a note to the accounts."* [CA85 Sec 226A(6), 227A(6); CA06 Sec 396(5), 404(5)]. These requirements are dealt with in chapter 2.

Accounting policies

4.134 The notes to the financial statements must set out the accounting policies the company has adopted in determining the amounts to be included in the financial statements. [4 Sch 36]. In particular, they must include:

- The method of determining the provision both for depreciation and for diminution in the value of assets. [4 Sch 36].

- The method of translating foreign currency amounts into sterling. [4 Sch 58(1)].

The disclosure of accounting policies is considered in chapter 2.

4.135 Many companies disclose their accounting policies as a separate statement that they locate before the remainder of the notes. This is generally accepted accounting practice and it has the advantage that the accounting policies are given more prominence and are not lost within the individual notes to the financial statements. Where this treatment is adopted, to ensure that the accounting policies are shown in compliance with the Act, the page numbers that identify the financial statements for the purpose of the directors' adoption of the financial statements, and for the purpose of the auditors' opinion, should include the statement of accounting policies.

4.136 Where a company's financial statements have been drawn up under the alternative accounting rules the accounting convention used should be stated in those financial statements. The company should usually also refer to the specific policy for each item that it has accounted for under the alternative rules and this disclosure would normally be made as part of the company's accounting policies.

Financial instruments

4.137 The Act imposes additional disclosure requirements in respect of financial instruments. The nature of the disclosure requirements varies depending on whether the company has adopted fair value accounting; these disclosure requirements are considered in detail in chapter 6.

[The next paragraph is 4.139.]

Reserves and dividends

4.139 Disclosure is required in the notes to the financial statements of:

- Any amount set aside or proposed to be set aside to, or withdrawn or proposed to be withdrawn from, reserves.
- The aggregate amount of dividends paid in the financial year (other than those for which a liability existed at the immediately preceding balance sheet date).
- The aggregate amount of dividends that the company is liable to pay at the balance sheet date.
- The aggregate amount of dividends that are proposed before the date of approval of the accounts, and not otherwise required to be disclosed.

[4 Sch 35A].

Summary financial statements

4.140 The Act permits, in certain circumstances, summary financial statements to be sent to members of listed companies instead of the company's full financial statements. The conditions that must be complied with, together with the form and content of the statements, are considered in chapter 8 of the Manual of Accounting – UK and IFRS supplement.

Format for small companies

4.141 The Act exempts small companies from certain disclosure requirements of Schedule 4 that relate to the annual accounts and directors' report that are prepared for shareholders. The Act also permits abbreviated financial statements to be filed with the Registrar for small and medium-sized companies and exempts certain small and medium-sized groups from preparing group accounts. The form and content of small and medium-sized company financial statements are considered in chapter 32.

[The next paragraph is 4.143.]

Listed companies' historical summaries

4.143 Although the Act does not require a company to include a historical summary of information in its financial statements, many companies do so. This practice arose because the chairman of the Stock Exchange wrote to all listed companies in 1964 recommending that they should include a ten-year historical summary in their annual financial statements. Disclosure of a historical summary has never become a requirement, but it has become well established practice, although most companies give a historical summary for a shorter period such as five years.

4.144 There is no set format for historical summaries, but the type of information that listed companies normally give in them is as follows:

Balance sheet

- Tangible assets.
- Other assets.
- Net borrowings.
- Capital and reserves.
- Minority interests.

Profit and loss account

- Turnover.
- Operating profit.
- Interest.
- Profit on ordinary activities before taxation.
- Taxation.
- Profit after taxation.

- Minority interests and preference dividends.
- Ordinary dividends and retained earnings.

Statistical information

- Earnings per share.
- Dividends per ordinary share.
- Dividend cover.
- Return on capital employed.

4.145 The historical summary will normally show the actual figures that were reported for each year. However, in certain situations, the reported figures for earlier years may need to be adjusted. The circumstances where adjustments may be necessary are as follows:

- Where there is a change in accounting policy, FRS 3 requires the comparative figures for the preceding period to be restated if this is necessary to ensure that the reported figures for each year are stated on a consistent basis. In historical summaries, the figures for each year would usually be restated if it is practical to do so; it should also be made clear which figures have been restated. If the figures have not been restated, then this fact should be disclosed.
- Where the results of operations are shown separately as discontinued in a financial year, FRS 3 requires the comparative profit and loss account figures to be adjusted to show those discontinued operations separately. In historical summaries, the figures for each previous year would usually also be adjusted where it is practical to do so; thus the results attributable to continuing operations would relate to operations that are currently continuing.
- Where fundamental errors have been corrected by a prior year adjustment, then the historical summary should be changed and again it should be made clear which figures have been restated.
- Earnings per share figures that are reported should be amended to reflect any:
    - New equity shares that have been issued by capitalising reserves.
    - Equity shares that have been split into shares of a lower nominal value.
    - New equity shares that have been issued by way of rights issues.

  The earnings per share figures should be adjusted in the ways explained in chapter 14.

- Dividends per share should also be adjusted where there have been changes in the number of equity shares in issue due to capitalisation of reserves, a rights issue, or a split in the nominal value of shares in issue.

4.146 Because an historical summary is not a requirement of law or of accounting standards, and it is not required in order for the financial statements to show a true and fair view, the auditors do not need to report on it. They should, however, read such information and, if they identify any apparent misstatements or inconsistencies with the audited financial statements, should take appropriate action. [ISA (UK & Ire) 720].

Pro forma financial statements

4.147 Some companies include, as additional information, *pro forma* balance sheet or profit and loss information where this assists disclosure about the financial effect of certain significant post balance sheet events. Such events would be classified as non-adjusting events under FRS 21, 'Events after the balance sheet date', that is, they do not result in changes to the amounts recognised in financial statements but they are so significant to the company that disclosure of their financial effect may be required. Examples include:

- Material business disposals occurring after the year end.
- Material acquisitions and mergers.
- Rights issues or other financings and financial reconstructions.
- Redemptions or purchases of own shares.

4.148 Formats vary where proformas are used. They are sometimes presented as additional columns (sometimes headed as unaudited *pro forma*) on the face of the balance sheet or profit and loss account; in other cases *pro forma* summarised balance sheets or profit and loss accounts are presented as part of the note to the financial statements disclosing the effect of a post balance sheet event.

4.149 Table 4.12 is an example of a proforma statement on the face of the balance sheet; Table 4.13 is an example of a proforma balance sheet included in a post balance sheet event note.

Table 4.12 — Babcock International Group PLC — Annual Report & Financial Statements — 31 March 1994

GROUP BALANCE SHEET

	Notes	Pro forma 1994 £'000	**1994 £'000**	1993 £'000
Fixed Assets				
Tangible assets	12	58,354	**58,354**	99,021
Investments	14	4,434	**4,434**	5,715
		62,788	**62,788**	104,736
Current Assets				
Stocks	15	27,968	**27,968**	36,054
Debtors – due within one year	16	185,343	**185,343**	158,324
– due after more than one year	16	39,248	**39,248**	54,114
Cash and bank balances	17	125,342	**88,047**	64,507
		377,901	**340,606**	312,999
Creditors: Amounts due within one year	18	(279,778)	**(321,083)**	(279,399)
Net current assets		98,123	**19,523**	33,600
Total assets less current liabilities		160,911	**82,311**	138,336
Creditors: Amounts due after more than one year	19	(10,292)	**(10,292)**	(14,018)
Provisions for liabilities and charges*	21	(24,674)	**(24,674)**	(31,437)
Net assets	1	125,945	47,345	92,881
Capital and reserves				
Called up share capital	24	84,572	53,819	53,764
Share premium account	25	67,054	19,207	19,262
Profit and loss account	26	9,234	9,234	55,939
Goodwill	26	(38,446)	(38,446)	(38,204)
Shareholders' funds		122,414	43,814	90,761
Minority interests		3,531	3,531	2,120
		125,945	47,345	92,881

The pro forma balance sheet shows the effect on the 31 March 1994 group balance sheet of the rights issue announced on 21 April 1994 as if the net proceeds of the rights issue had been received on 31 March 1994. Of the proceeds, £41.3 million has been set off against borrowings and £37.3 million has been added to cash and bank balances.

* Note that for years beginning on or after 1 January 2005, the statutory line item required by the Companies Act 1985 (as amended by SI 2004/2947, 'The Companies Act 1985 (International Accounting Standards and Other Amendments) Regulations 2004' is 'provisions for liabilities'.

Table 4.13 — Kingfisher plc — Annual Report & Accounts — 30 January 1993

Notes to the accounts (extract)

28 Post balance sheet event

Proposed merger with Darty and rights issue

On 18 February 1993 Kingfisher announced agreement on the terms of a merger with Financière Darty. Kingfisher has agreed to purchase up to the whole of the issued share capital of Financière Darty, which owns 95.3% of the share capital of Darty. The merger agreement has been entered into with shareholders representing over 95% of Financière Darty's issued share capital and Kingfisher has agreed to acquire the balance on the same terms upon the remaining shareholders agreeing to dispose of the shares. If 100% of Financière Darty is acquired the total consideration will comprise 68m Kingfisher shares and cash of FF 1,650m. After taking account of Financière Darty's term borrowings the total consideration for the whole of Financière Darty is approximately £1,139m. Following the merger and the related rights issue the vendors will hold approximately 11% of the Kingfisher's enlarged share capital.

The merger has been partly financed by a rights issue which will raise £313m net of expenses. The Company is issuing 71,286,966 stock units by way of rights. Qualifying holders are being offered the right to subscribe for stock units on the basis of one stock unit for every seven Kingfisher shares. The stock units are being issued at the price of 450p each payable in two instalments of 225p each. The first instalment, which is payable irrespective of whether the merger is completed, is due not later than 15 March 1993. The obligation to pay the second instalment is conditional on the merger being completed. If the merger is not completed every two partly paid stock units will automatically convert into one new Kingfisher share and the aggregate amount received net of expenses, totalling approximately £155m will be used to reduce Group borrowings. If the merger is completed each fully paid stock unit will convert into one new Kingfisher share. The new Kingfisher shares arising on conversion of the stock will be credited issued as fully paid and will rank pari passu in all respects with the Kingfisher shares currently in issue including the right to receive the final dividend in respect of the year ended 30 January 1993.

Proforma Statement of net assets of the enlarged Group

An illustrative proforma statement of the combined net assets of the enlarged Group taking into account the merger and the rights issue is set out below. This is based on the net assets of Kingfisher at 30 January 1993, extracted from the audited consolidated balance sheet, and of the Financière Darty Group at 31 August 1992, extracted from the accountant's report issued by Price Waterhouse dated 18 February 1993 and translated at an exchange rate of FF7.96 = £1. This proforma statement is prepared on the basis set out in the notes below.

£millions	Kingfisher	Financière Darty	Adjustments	Proforma statement of combined net assets
Fixed assets				
Tangible assets	992.4	271.7	–	1,264.1
Investments	37.2	5.8	–	43.0
	1,029.6	277.5	–	1,307.1
Current assets				
Development work in progress	59.3	–	–	59.3
Stocks	571.7	131.0	–	702.7
Debtors	254.7	64.6	–	319.3
Investments	153.9	109.4	–	263.3
Cash at bank and in hand	161.7	19.4	49.7	230.8
	1,201.3	324.4	49.7	1,575.4
Creditors				
Amounts falling due within one year	(940.2)	(256.0)	–	(1,196.2)
Net current assets	261.1	68.4	49.7	379.2
Total assets less current liabilities	1,290.7	345.9	49.7	1,686.3
Creditors				
Amounts falling due after more than one year	(132.3)	(652.0)	–	(784.3)
Provisions for liabilities and charges*	(0.6)	1.0	–	0.4
Net assets/(liabilities)	1,157.8	(305.1)	49.7	902.4

Notes

1 The adjustments comprise the net effect of:

Net cash proceeds of the 1 for 7 rights issue
Cash element of the consideration payable to the vendors of Financière Darty
Purchase of the 4.7% minority shareholding in Darty

2 No adjustment has been made for the fair value of the assets to be acquired
3 No adjustment has been made to take account of trading since the respective balance sheet dates

* Note that for years beginning on or after 1 January 2005, the statutory line item required by the Companies Act 1985 (as amended by SI 2004/2947, 'The Companies Act 1985 (International Accounting Standards and Other Amendments) Regulations 2004', is 'provisions for liabilities'.

4.150 *Pro forma* financial statements are not used exclusively in connection with post balance sheet events. Other reasons may include: presenting a continuous track record where a group reorganisation has occurred; presenting annualised figures where a company has changed its accounting reference period; and presenting financial statements that show the effect of eliminating from comparative figures the results and balance sheets of operations that have been demerged during the period. Table 4.14 shows extracts from the financial statements of Charter plc where the existing parent company was acquired by a newly incorporated parent company in a group reorganisation. Whilst the statutory consolidated financial statements only included the results of the group from the date of transfer to the new parent company, extensive use was made of *pro forma* information to present results, balance sheets and cash flows of the group as if it had always been a single reporting entity.

Table 4.14 — Charter plc — Annual Report — 31 March 1994

Consolidated profit and loss account
Year ended 31 March 1994

Note		Proforma 1994 £m	Proforma 1993 £m	Statutory Period £m
2 & 3	**Turnover**			
	Continuing operations	**545.8**	537.7	301.7
	Discontinued operations	–	667.1	–
		545.8	1,204.8	301.7
2 & 3	**Operating profit**			
	Continuing operations	**33.8**	35.2	18.7
	Discontinued operations	–	24.9	–
		33.8	60.1	18.7
4	**Non-operating exceptional items**			
	Profit on sale of fixed assets in continuing operations	**2.4**	0.3	–
	Profits on losses on sale or termination of discontinued operations	–	217.2	–
		2.4	217.5	–
	Profit on ordinary activities before interest	**36.2**	277.6	18.7
5	Net interest	**13.9**	11.6	5.3
2	**Profit on ordinary activities before taxation**	**50.1**	289.2	24.0
	Tax on ordinary activities	**(16.3)**	(27.4)	(7.1)
	Profit on ordinary activities after taxation	**33.8**	261.8	16.9
	Minority interests — equity	**(3.5)**	(4.3)	(2.2)
	Profit for the financial year	**30.3**	257.5	14.7
10	Dividends — equity	**(15.4)**	(23.3)	(15.4)
	Prior year dividend waived by Minorco	**5.7**	–	–
25	Retained profit/(loss) for the financial year	**20.6**	234.2	(0.7)
11	**Earnings per share**	**36.4p**	242.9p	21.5p

The first statutory accounting reference period for Charter plc was from incorporation on 1 March 1993 to 31 March 1994. The company commenced operations on 23 August 1993.

OPERATING AND FINANCIAL REVIEW (extract)

Scheme of Arrangement and presentation of results

Charter plc acquired Charter Consolidated P.L.C. on 23 August 1993 through a Scheme of Arrangement. The figures for the year are presented on a proforma basis to provide an annual record of the group's operations, unbroken by the consequences of the Scheme of Arrangement. The proforma accounts have been prepared on the same basis as that adopted for the statutory accounts. The consolidated statutory accounts of Charter plc include only the results of the operations of the group from 23 August 1993 to 31 March 1994.

The proforma accounts are presented to provide all the disclosures that would have been given had they been a normal set of statutory accounts. In so doing these proforma accounts also provide, particularly in respect of the balance sheet, a significant number of the disclosures necessary for this year's actual statutory accounts. The remaining statutory disclosures are provided on a shaded background, either on the face of the relevant primary statements or in the separate section of the notes headed 'Additional notes to the accounts for statutory purposes'. The additional notes on pages 39 to 43 must be read in conjunction with the notes to the accounts on pages 22 to 38, as common disclosures have not been repeated in the additional notes.

The comparative figures have been taken from the accounts of Charter Consolidated P.L.C. for the year to 31 March 1993 as amended by the prior year adjustment detailed in note 14.

Chapter 5

Other profit and loss account items

	Page
Introduction	5001
Cost of sales, distribution costs and administrative expenses	5001
Gross profit	5004
Own work capitalised	5004
Staff costs and numbers	5004
Employee costs	5004
Average number of employees	5006
Directors	5006
Disclosures by groups	5007
Practical problems relating to employee costs	5007
Depreciation (including other amounts written off assets)	5009
Other operating charges (including other external charges)	5010
Income from investments	5011
Interest payable and similar charges	5012
Auditors' remuneration	5013
Audit work	5014
Individual financial statements	5014
Consolidated financial statements	5015
Audit-assist	5017
Disclosure in which year	5018
Other services	5018
Format of disclosure	5018
Sub-totals	5020
Categories of 'Other services'	5020
Category 1 — Audit of the company's 'associates' pursuant to legislation	5020
Category 2 — Fees for other services supplied pursuant to such legislation	5021
Category 3 — Other services relating to taxation	5022
Category 9 — Services relating to corporate finance transactions	5022
Category 10 — All other services	5022
Practical applications	5023
Sarbanes-Oxley section 404	5023
Form 20-F filings	5024
The auditors' associates	5024
The company's associates	5026
The company's associated pension schemes	5027
How to determine whether a pension scheme is associated with a company	5028
Obtaining the information to be disclosed	5029

Exemptions from disclosure 5029
Audit fees 5029
Fees for 'Other services' 5030
Single audit fees for the group 5032
Fees receivable from third parties 5032
More than one auditor 5034
Joint auditors 5034
Change of auditor 5034
Appointment after the year end 5034
Practical issues 5034
Discontinued operations 5034
Overseas branches 5035
Shared service centres 5035
Annex — Example of disclosure of services provided by the company's auditor and its associates 5037

Chapter 5

Other profit and loss account items

Introduction

5.1 The profit and loss account is one of the primary statements that a company must include in its financial statements. The Companies Act 1985 requires the profit and loss account to comply with one of four alternative formats set out in Schedule 4 to the Act: Formats 1 and 3 are vertical presentations; and Formats 2 and 4 show charges separately from income. These formats are set out and discussed in chapter 3. The format a company chooses can be significant because, depending on the format, some of the information the company discloses in its profit and loss account will be different. Some of the items that are discussed below may relate only to one pair of formats. At the time of writing, the equivalent schedules to the Companies Act 2006 have still to be published.

5.2 Chapter 9 deals with the measurement and disclosure of items included under the main revenue headings in the profit and loss account. This chapter considers other categories of income and expenditure that are recognised in the profit and loss account, insofar as they are not dealt with separately in other chapters, together with supplementary disclosure requirements.

5.3 Of the items included in the Act's formats, only 'turnover' (see chapter 9) and 'staff costs' (see para 5.15 below) are actually defined in the Act. The allocation to statutory captions of certain other items of income and expenditure included in companies' charts of accounts requires companies to reach internal definitions and interpretations in order to achieve reasonable and consistent classifications.

Cost of sales, distribution costs and administrative expenses

5.4 These headings from Formats 1 and 3, which require the classification of expenditure by its function, give rise to many questions concerning the allocation of costs and overheads. The following lists are intended to provide guidance as to the items that may be included under each heading.

5.5 *Cost of sales* will normally include:

- Opening (less closing) stocks.
- Direct materials.
- Other external charges (such as the hire of plant and machinery or the cost of casual labour used in the productive process).
- Direct labour.

- All direct production overheads, including depreciation, and indirect overheads that can reasonably be allocated to the production function.
- Product development expenditure.
- Cash discounts received on 'cost of sales' expenditure (this is not a set-off, but an effective reduction in the purchase price of an item).
- Stock provisions.

5.6 *Distribution costs* are generally interpreted more widely than the name suggests and often include selling and marketing costs. Items normally included in this caption comprise:

- Payroll costs of the sales, marketing and distribution functions.
- Advertising.
- Salesperson's travel and entertaining.
- Warehouse costs for finished goods.
- Transport costs concerning the distribution of finished goods.
- All costs of maintaining sales outlets.
- Agents' commission payable.

5.7 *Administrative expenses* will normally include:

- The costs of general management.
- All costs of maintaining the administration buildings.
- Bad debts.
- Professional costs.
- Cash discounts on sales.
- Research and development expenditure that is not allocated to cost of sales (sometimes this is shown as a separate item).

5.8 If Format 1 or 3 is adopted, charges for depreciation or the diminution in value of assets have to be analysed under the above headings. [Profit and loss account sheet formats 4 Sch note 14]. The type of analysis will depend on the function of the related assets (see also para 5.29).

5.9 In some specific instances, the allocation of costs between the headings proposed above may not be appropriate. For example, in the context of a mail-order company, agents' commission payable may be regarded as a cost of sale rather than as a distribution cost.

5.10 The way in which a company analyses its costs will depend very much on the nature of its business. Where a company incurs significant operating expenses that it considers do not fall under any one of the headings 'cost of sales', 'distribution costs' and 'administrative expenses', there is nothing to prevent the company including an additional item for these expenses in Formats 1 or 3. The overriding consideration is that a company should analyse its operating expenses consistently from year to year. Exceptional items included in operating profit should be included within the statutory line item to which they relate. [FRS 3 para 19].

5.11 Some companies have adapted the statutory line items or shown additional items. However, these companies are in a minority. This is probably because the items are general enough to apply to most companies' expenditure. Examples of adaptations and additional items that companies have used in their financial statements are shown below.

Examples of adaptation of items:

- Selling and distribution costs.
- Marketing, selling and distribution costs.
- Distribution costs, including marketing.
- Administrative and selling expenses.
- Selling and general administration expenses.

Examples of additional items:

- Sales commission (shown in addition to distribution costs).
- Research and development.

5.12 Table 5.1 shows an extract from the profit and loss account of Rolls-Royce plc, where the analysis of operating expenses has been adapted.

Table 5.1 — Rolls-Royce plc — Annual Report — 31 December 1994

Group Profit and Loss Account (extract)
for the year ended December 31, 1994

	Notes	1994 £m	1993 £m
Turnover	2	3,163	3,518
Cost of sales	3	(2,646)	(2,995)
Gross profit		517	523
Commercial, marketing and product support costs		(117)	(105)
General and administrative costs		(91)	(89)
Research and development (net)		(218)	(253)
Operating profit		91	76

Gross profit

5.13 The gross profit or loss has to be shown as a separate item in Format 1, and it can be readily ascertained from the items that are disclosed in Format 3. Formats 2 and 4 analyse expenditure in a different manner, that is, by its nature rather than its function and, as a result, gross profit is not disclosed.

Own work capitalised

5.14 Where a company has constructed some of its own tangible fixed assets, and it adopts either Format 2 or Format 4 for its profit and loss account, it should include the costs of direct materials, direct labour and overheads it has capitalised as a credit under the heading 'own work capitalised'. The costs of direct materials, direct labour and overheads are charged in the profit and loss account, by including these amounts under the relevant expenditure headings. The amount capitalised is then credited in the profit and loss account as own work capitalised and it is debited to tangible fixed assets. Thus, items such as raw material costs in the profit and loss account will include the costs connected with such work.

Staff costs and numbers

Employee costs

5.15 Disclosure is required in the financial statements of the costs a company incurs in respect of the persons it employs under contracts of service. A contract *of service* (or a contract of employment as it is also called) is an agreement under which the employer agrees to employ the employee for a wage or a salary in return for the employee's labour. This agreement must be made in writing. However, self-employed persons are not employed by the company, but merely have contracts to perform specific services for that company. The costs of self-employed people should normally be excluded from staff costs, because their contracts will be contracts *for services*. Examples of such persons are consultants and contractors. Their costs should normally be included under 'other external charges' in Formats 2 and 4, and under an appropriate functional expense heading in Formats 1 and 3.

5.16 The item 'staff costs' does not appear in the profit and loss account Formats 1 and 3. This is because expenses are classified in these formats by function, rather than by type. However, where a company prepares its profit and loss account in the style of either Format 1 or Format 3, it has to disclose, in the notes to the profit and loss account, the equivalent information to that given when Formats 2 and 4 are used.

5.17 In summary, either the profit and loss account format or the notes must disclose, in aggregate, each of the following amounts:

- The wages and salaries that were either paid to employees or are payable to them, in respect of the financial year in question.
- Social security costs that the company has incurred on behalf of its employees. For this purpose, social security costs are any contributions the company makes to any social security or pension scheme, or fund or arrangement that the State runs. These costs will include the employer's national insurance contributions.
- Other pension costs the company has incurred on behalf of employees. For this purpose, pension costs include:
  - Any costs incurred by the company in respect of any non-State occupational pension scheme that is established to provide pensions for employees or past employees.
  - Any sums the company has set aside for the future payment of pensions directly to current or former employees.
  - Any amounts the company has paid in respect of pensions, without those amounts having first been so set aside.

  Pension costs will, therefore, include the cost in respect of the company's participation in any pension scheme other than the State scheme. [CA85 Sec 231A, 4 Sch 94; CA06 Sec 411].

5.18 An illustration of these disclosure requirements is given in Table 5.2.

Table 5.2 — Scottish & Newcastle plc — Annual Report and Accounts — 2 May 1999

Notes to the Accounts (extract)

5 EMPLOYEE COSTS AND NUMBERS

(i) Employee costs	**1999 £m**	**1998 £m**
Wages and salaries	**463.4**	463.3
Social security costs	**47.3**	44.9
Other pension costs	**31.3**	30.0
Employee profit sharing scheme	**–**	8.5
	542.0	546.7

(ii) Number of employees	**1999**	**1998**
The average numbers of employees during the year were:		
Retail	**27,290**	26,851
Beer	**7,080**	7,103
Leisure	**12,468**	11,964
Group central functions	**283**	281
	47,121	46,199

[The next paragraph is 5.21.]

Average number of employees

5.21 In addition to requiring that the notes to the profit and loss account should disclose employee costs, the Act requires that those notes should include information in respect of the number of employees.

5.22 The two disclosures that the notes must contain in connection with the number of employees are:

- The average number of employees in the financial year. The number must be calculated by:
  - Ascertaining the number of persons employed under contract of service, whether full-time or part-time, for each month in the year.
  - Adding together all the monthly numbers.
  - Dividing the resulting total by the number of months in the financial year.

  The average number of employees includes persons who work wholly or mainly overseas, as well as persons who work in the UK.

- The average number of employees by category. This number must be calculated by applying the same method of calculation as outlined above to each category of employees. For this purpose, the categories of persons employed are to be such categories as the directors select, having regard to the way in which the company's activities are organised.

[CA85 Sec 231A; CA06 Sec 411].

5.23 Because the guidance on how to select categories is rather vague, directors of companies have chosen a variety of different categories. Methods have included splitting between part-time employees and full-time employees; between hourly-paid, weekly-paid and salaried staff; between production, sales and administration staff; and between staff employed in different geographical areas. If the company presents segmental information in accordance with SSAP 25, 'Segmental reporting', it may be appropriate to give the employee numbers on the basis of the segments presented.

These disclosure requirements are illustrated in Table 5.2.

5.24 There is no exemption from disclosure where the number of employees is small, or (for example) where a company is a wholly-owned subsidiary.

Directors

5.25 Directors who have a contract of service with the company are to be regarded as employees. Therefore, their salaries, their social security costs and their other pension costs must be included in the required analysis under staff costs, even if a note is included stating that directors' emoluments are shown elsewhere. In addition, directors' emoluments have also to be disclosed separately in accordance with the requirements of Part I of Schedule 6 to the Companies Act 1985. In that disclosure, their emoluments will exclude those social security costs that the company bears, because such amounts are neither paid to the director nor paid in respect of a pension scheme. The disclosure of directors' aggregate emoluments, will, however, include the estimated money value of any benefits in kind.

5.26 In contrast to payments under a contract *of service* (where the director is employed), amounts paid to directors under contracts *for services* (equivalent to the director being self-employed) should not be disclosed under staff costs. But, under Part I of Schedule 6 to the Companies Act 1985, they must be disclosed as directors' emoluments in the notes to the financial statements. Whether a director's contract with the company is a *contract of service* or a contract *for services* is a question of fact in each circumstance. Usually, however, executive directors will have contracts *of service*, whereas non-executive directors will have contracts *for services*. Contracts *for services* might include, for example, consultancy arrangements.

5.26.1 Directors' emoluments are dealt with further in chapter 5 of the Manual of Accounting – Management reports and governance.

Disclosures by groups

5.26.2 Where a parent company prepares group financial statements, the disclosure of staff costs and numbers is required to be presented for the consolidated group. Under the Companies Act 1985, there is no exemption for a parent company (whether it prepares group financial statements or not) from the requirement to present details of staff numbers or staff costs. Consequently, the notes to a company's consolidated financial statements will need to include disclosures both for the group and for the parent company. This is the case regardless of whether the parent company takes the exemption from presenting its own profit and loss account as permitted by section 230 of the Companies Act 1985.

5.26.3 When Part 15 of the Companies Act 2006 is implemented, there will be no requirement for the parent company to present particulars of staff for the company (employee numbers and costs). This will be the case regardless of whether the parent company takes the exemption from presenting its own profit and loss account. [CA06 Sec 408]. The current expectation is that Part 15 of the Companies Act 2006 will be implemented for years commencing on or after 6 April 2008.

Practical problems relating to employee costs

5.27 In practice, there may be problems in deciding on the employees to include in staff costs and in identifying the average number of employees. One of the most frequent problems arises where employees clearly work for one company, but their contracts of service are with another company (for example, the holding company). Also, further complications arise when that other company pays the wages and salaries of these employees. If section 231A of the Companies Act 1985 (section 411 of the Companies Act 2006) was strictly interpreted in these situations, it could lead to the disclosure of misleading information in the financial statements. Accordingly, as well as giving the statutory disclosures, a company may need to give additional information to enable its financial statements to give a true and fair view.

5.28 Some of the more common problems that arise in this respect are considered in the examples that follow:

Example 1

Employees work full time for, and are paid by, a subsidiary company, but their contracts of service are with the parent company.

It would be misleading if there were no disclosure of staff costs or numbers in the subsidiary company's financial statements. Consequently, the wages and salaries the subsidiary company pays to those employees should be disclosed as 'staff costs' in its financial statements and those employees should be included in the calculation of the average number of staff employed.

The notes to the subsidiary company's financial statements should explain that those staff have contracts of service with another group company. They should also explain why their remuneration and average number are disclosed in the financial statements.

The parent company's consolidated financial statements normally will not be affected (unless the subsidiary is not included in the consolidated financial statements), because they will show the average number of employees and staff costs of the group as a whole, as well as those of the parent company separately. Consequently, no explanatory note should be necessary in the parent company's financial statements.

(However, if the contracts of service are with a fellow subsidiary company, then that fellow subsidiary company's financial statements should include those employees in the calculation of staff costs and average number of employees and explain that certain employees having service contracts with the company work for and are paid for wholly by a fellow subsidiary company.)

Example 2

Employees work full time for the subsidiary company, but they are not paid by the subsidiary company and they do not have service contracts with it. However, the subsidiary company bears a management charge for their services from the company that pays the employees and it can ascertain the proportion of the management charge that relates to staff costs.

Again, in this situation it could be misleading if the subsidiary company's financial statements disclosed no information about staff costs or numbers. Accordingly, the proportion of the management charge that relates to staff costs should be disclosed in the subsidiary company's financial statements as 'staff costs'. The employees concerned should be included in the calculation of the average number of employees. The notes to the financial statements should explain that the employees do not have contracts of service with the company, and they should also explain why their costs and average number are disclosed in the financial statements.

(If the contracts of service are with, and the employees are paid by, a fellow subsidiary company then that fellow subsidiary's financial statements should disclose the staff costs and average number in respect of all its employees and give details regarding the staff costs that are recharged to the fellow subsidiary.)

Example 3

The facts are the same as in example 2 except that the subsidiary company is unable to break down the management charge and ascertain the part of it that relates to staff costs.

The notes to the subsidiary company's financial statements should explain that the employees' contracts of service are with the parent company and that their remuneration is included in the parent company's financial statements. The notes should also explain that the management charge that the parent company makes includes the cost of these employees, but that it is impossible to ascertain separately the element of the management charge that relates to staff costs.

(If the employees' contracts of service are with a fellow subsidiary, rather than with the parent company, and that fellow subsidiary also pays the employees, the fellow subsidiary's financial statements should disclose the employees' remuneration in its staff costs and should also include the employees in the calculation of average number employed. The notes should explain that these employees work for a fellow subsidiary company and that the company recharges the cost of their employment to that fellow subsidiary as part of a management charge.)

Example 4

The facts are the same as in example 2 above, except that no management charge is made for the employees' services. This will often apply where staff work either full-time or part-time for small companies.

In this situation, the notes to the subsidiary company's financial statements should explain that the company is not charged for the services provided by the employees that work for it. If appropriate, the notes should also indicate that the cost of these employees and their average number are included in the parent company's consolidated financial statements.

(Once again, if it is a fellow subsidiary that employs and pays the employees, its financial statements should include the cost of these employees in its staff costs and should include these employees in the average number employed. If appropriate, the notes to the financial statements should explain that these employees work for a fellow subsidiary company, but that no management charge is made for their services to that company.)

Depreciation (including other amounts written off assets)

5.29 Where the company prepares its profit and loss account in accordance with either Format 1 or Format 3, expenses are classified by function. Consequently, any provisions for either depreciation or the diminution in value of tangible and intangible fixed assets will not be disclosed in the profit and loss account format. Accordingly, the Act requires that this information must be disclosed separately in the notes to the financial statements. [Note 17 on the profit and loss account formats].

5.30 In addition, the Act requires separate disclosure of the aggregate amount of:

- Any provision against a fixed asset investment for diminution in value.
- Any provision against a fixed asset for permanent diminution in value.
- Any write back of such provisions which are no longer necessary.

[CA85 4 Sch 19(1)-(3)].

5.31 Accounting for depreciation and diminutions in value of fixed assets (under both the historical cost and alternative accounting rules) is considered fully in chapters 16 and 18.

Other operating charges (including other external charges)

5.32 The relevant formats (Formats 2 and 4) place 'other external charges' next to 'raw materials and consumables' under a single item number. Therefore, such charges are likely to include any production costs from external sources that are not included under other headings (for example, equipment rentals and the costs of subcontractors).

5.33 'Other operating charges' is a separate line item which tends to be a residual class of all charges relating to the trading activities of a business that do not fall into any other category. Losses on exchange may also be included under this heading (except for losses that are required by SSAP 20, 'Foreign currency translation', or FRS 23, 'The effects of changes in foreign exchange rates', to be taken directly to reserves).

5.34 In practice, the distinction between 'other external charges' and 'other operating charges' is blurred. Some companies do not attempt to make a distinction, and include only one heading to cover all residual operating costs. Table 5.3 gives an example in which a company discloses no 'other external charges', but analyses residual operating expenses under the heading 'other operating charges'.

Table 5.3 — British Gas plc — Annual Report and Accounts — 31 December 1994

Notes to the accounts (extract)

4 Operating costs (extract)

	1994			
	Continuing operations £m	Other Discontinued operations £m	Exceptional charges £m	Total £m
Other operating charges:				
Other exploration expenditure	88	–	–	88
Monetary working capital adjustment	24	–	–	24
Lease rentals:				
Plant, machinery and equipment	24	–	–	24
Other assets	38	–	–	38
Research and development	74	1	–	75
Environmental costs	–	–	90	90
Other expenses	1,550	31	105	1,686

Income from investments

5.35 Each of the four profit and loss account formats for individual companies contain the same four investment income captions.

- Income from shares in group undertakings.
- Income from participating interests.
- Income from other fixed asset investments.
- Other interest receivable and similar income.

5.36 The Act also requires the last two items referred to above, that is income from other fixed asset investments and other interest, to be split between that derived from group undertakings and that derived from other sources. [Note 15 on the profit and loss account formats].

5.37 FRS 16, 'Current tax', requires that incoming dividends, interest or other income should be included in the profit and loss account at an amount that includes any withholding taxes, but excludes any other taxes, such as attributable tax credits, not payable wholly on behalf of the recipient. Thus the amounts included in the profit and loss account for incoming dividends that are subject to withholding taxes will be the gross dividend, that is an amount greater than the cash received. As withholding taxes do not arise in the UK, dividends received from UK resident companies would be included at the amount of cash received or receivable.

[The next paragraph is 5.39.]

5.39 Dividends received and receivable from both subsidiary and fellow subsidiary companies will be included in 'income from shares in group undertakings'. In a group's consolidated financial statements, this line will appear only if dividends are received or receivable from subsidiaries that have not been consolidated. The accounting for dividend income is dealt with in chapter 9.

5.40 In an investing company's individual profit and loss account 'Income from participating interests' will include, for example, income from the following undertakings in which the investing company holds on a long-term basis 20 per cent or more of the shares in that undertaking.

- Income from bodies corporate (including dividends received from associated undertakings).
- Share of profits from partnerships.
- Share of profits from unincorporated associations carrying on a trade or business, with or without a profit.

5.41 Chapter 27 explains the meaning of participating interests and associated undertakings and describes the accounting treatment of income from interests in associated undertakings in consolidated financial statements.

Interest payable and similar charges

5.42 'Interest payable and similar charges' appears as a separate item in all the profit and loss account formats. Apart from interest, the caption may include other finance costs such as:

- Accrued discounts in respect of zero coupon and deep discount bonds.
- Accrual of the premium payable on the redemption of debt.
- Gains or losses arising on the repurchase or early settlement of debt.

5.43 The Act requires certain additional disclosures in respect of interest. Note 16 to the profit and loss account formats requires that interest payable to group undertakings must be disclosed separately. In addition, Schedule 4 requires the disclosure of the amount of the interest on or any similar charges in respect of:

- Bank loans and overdrafts.
- Loans of any other kind made to the company.

[CA85 4 Sch 53(2)].

5.44 The requirement to give the above analyses does not apply to either interest or charges on loans from group undertakings. But it does apply to interest or charges on all other loans, whether or not these are made on the security of a debenture. [CA85 4 Sch 53(2)].

[The next paragraph is 5.52.]

Auditors' remuneration

5.52 The Companies Act 1985 (and the Companies Act 2006) requires separate disclosure of the amounts of remuneration receivable by a company's auditors, in their capacity as auditors and also in respect of services other than audit. The current legal requirements are set out in the Companies (Disclosure of Auditor Remuneration) Regulations 2005 ('the Regulations'). These are expected to be replaced by new, but virtually identical, regulations (The Companies (Disclosure of Auditor Remuneration and Liability Limitation Agreements) Regulations 2007 ('the 2007 Regulations')) that will come into effect for accounting periods commencing on or after 6 April 2008. The amount to be disclosed for audit fees and within each of the 'Other services' (see para 5.59) fee categories includes any expenses and the estimated money value of any benefits in kind. [CA85 Sec 390B, SI 2005/2417 Regs 3, 4; CA06 Sec 494(1), 501(1)(2)].

5.53 The disclosures required by the Regulations apply irrespective of the accounting framework used in preparing the individual and/or group financial statements. However, these requirements apply only to companies incorporated in Great Britain and do not yet extend to companies incorporated in Northern Ireland. [Tech 6/06 (revised) para 3.2]. It is expected that the 2007 Regulations will have effect in Northern Ireland as they are made under the Companies Act 2006, which applies to the whole of the UK.

5.54 On 12 October 2006, the ICAEW issued Tech 6/06, 'Disclosure of auditor remuneration', to provide guidance on applying the Regulations' disclosure requirements in the form of frequently asked questions. The Regulations applied for the first time to companies with accounting periods commencing on or after 1 October 2005. To reflect practical experience from the first full cycle of operating with the legislation, the ICAEW revised the technical release in July 2007. Tech 6/06 (revised) expands the guidance in the original technical release to address some additional areas and to clarify the recommended approach to the disclosure of auditor remuneration in others. The paragraphs that follow deal with some of the more common issues surrounding the requirement's application. Tech 06/06 (revised) contains a considerable amount of additional guidance and should be used to supplement this Manual.

5.54.1 The Regulations specify that the principal purpose of the disclosures is to address "*concerns that an auditor whose income from any one audit client derives mainly from non-audit services might face a conflict of interest which could result in a less robust appraisal of the company's accounts than would otherwise be the case.*" [SI 2005/2417, Explanatory Memorandum, para 7.2].

5.54.2 Consequently, the disclosures required by the Regulations are aimed principally at providing information on the amount of fees that the auditor and its associates have obtained from a company, its subsidiaries and associated pension schemes. In effect, companies are required to disclose:

- Fees payable to the company's auditor for the statutory audit of the company's annual financial statements. See paragraphs 5.55 to 5.58.
- Fees payable to the company's auditor and its associates for the statutory audits of the company's associates and for other services provided to the company and its associates (analysed between types of service). See paragraphs 5.59 to 5.68.8.
- Fees payable to the company's auditor and its associates for audit and other services (analysed by type of services) supplied to the company's associated pension schemes. In respect of other services, this is irrespective of whether or not the company's auditor or any of its associates are the auditors of the pension schemes. See paragraphs 5.71 to 5.73.

5.54.3 Associates of the company and of the auditor for the purposes of this disclosure are not defined consistently with accounting literature. The definitions relevant to these disclosures as specified in the legislation are considered in paragraphs 5.70 and 5.69 respectively.

5.54.4 The emphasis of the disclosure is on the fees receivable by the auditors and their associates. The fees should be shown net of VAT as the auditors are not the beneficiaries of the VAT paid and, therefore, it would not be appropriate to show the VAT as a benefit to them. This is the case regardless of whether the VAT is recoverable or irrecoverable by the company. [Tech 6/06 (revised) para 49.1].

5.54.5 The directors of a company are responsible for ensuring the company's compliance with the Regulations. Where the information is not available within the accounting records of the company or its subsidiaries, the company's auditor is required to "*supply the directors of the company with such information as is necessary to enable the disclosure required [by the Regulations] to be made*". [SI 2005/2417 Reg 6].

5.54.6 Many of the principles of the disclosure requirement are illustrated in a worked example included in the annex to this chapter.

Audit work

Individual financial statements

5.55 Every company is required to disclose, in the notes to its financial statements, remuneration receivable by its auditor for the statutory audit of its financial statements (which includes material presented together with the financial statements on which work is required to be performed by the auditors, such as the directors' remuneration report of a quoted company), with comparative information.

Consolidated financial statements

5.56 Where the company is required to prepare consolidated financial statements, the audit fee disclosed (with comparative information) is the aggregate fee payable to the company's auditor in respect of:

- the statutory audit of the company's individual financial statements;
- the consolidation itself (for instance, review of consolidation returns, audit of consolidation adjustments and work on the consolidated financial statements); and
- work performed on material presented together with the financial statements that the auditor is required to perform to satisfy their responsibilities under the law and auditing standards (for instance, auditing parts of a quoted company's remuneration report and reviewing the non-auditable parts of that report and other information presented in the annual report).

5.56.1 The fee disclosed as the audit fee does not include amounts payable to associates of the company's auditor (for example, other members of its network of firms) for any work performed in connection with the group audit. In addition, the fee disclosed as audit fee does not include any fees payable to the parent company's auditor for any work performed in respect of the statutory audit of a subsidiary of the company. [Tech 06/06 (revised) paras 18.3, 23.1, 23.3, 37.2 and 37.3].

5.56.2 In many cases, work will be performed on a subsidiary that is common to both the audit of the local statutory financial statements and the consolidation pack that is used for the purposes of the group audit. Under company law, an auditor is appointed to perform the audit of a company regardless of who may own that company. As such, the stance taken by the legislators is that such work performed on a subsidiary is, in the first instance, performed for the purposes of executing the auditors' contract to carry out the subsidiary company's statutory audit. The treatment of these fees is, therefore, determined on this basis.

5.56.3 Where a subsidiary has been invoiced separately (that is, where the parent has not been invoiced with a single fee for the entire group), the fee will generally relate to all the work performed at that subsidiary (including work common to both the consolidation pack and the local statutory financial statements, work relating solely to the local statutory financial statements and work relating solely to the audit of the consolidation pack). It will generally be reasonable to show the combined amount as being the subsidiary's audit fee for the purposes of disclosure in the subsidiary's own financial statements and to be included in 'Other services' Category 1 (statutory audit of the company's associates) (see para 5.59) in the group's disclosures. [Tech 6/06 (revised) para 18.4]. However, this treatment may not be reasonable if there is a clearly identifiable element of the subsidiary's fee that relates to work solely necessary for the audit of the consolidation pack. See further paragraph 5.56.4 below.

Example

B plc is audited by X&Co (UK). B plc has two subsidiaries: C Limited, a GB company, which is also audited by X&Co (UK) and D SA, a French company that is audited by a French audit firm, X&Co (Fr), an associate of the UK firm X&Co (UK).

C Limited pays X&Co (UK) £200,000 for its audit and D SA pays X&Co (Fr) €100,000 for its audit. There is no clearly identifiable element of either of the subsidiary fees that relates to work solely for the purpose of auditing the consolidation pack.

The audit fee disclosed in B plc's consolidated financial statements includes the fees receivable by X&Co (UK) for the audit of B plc's parent company individual financial statements and the audit of its consolidation.

The following fees are excluded from the audit fee disclosed in the consolidated financial statements of B plc:

- The fees payable to X&Co in respect of the statutory audit of C Limited. These fees are excluded from the audit fee of B plc, regardless of the fact they are paid to X&Co (UK), as they are associated in the first instance with the statutory requirement to perform an audit of C Limited under the Companies Act 1985.
- The fees payable by D SA to X&Co (Fr) in respect of the statutory audit of D SA's financial statements. These fees are excluded from the audit fee of B plc as they are paid to X&Co (Fr), which is not the parent company auditor, X&Co (UK).

The fees for both C Limited and D SA will be disclosed by B plc in its consolidated auditor remuneration disclosure as fees received in respect of 'Other services', within Category 1 (statutory audits of the company's associates) (see para 5.65).

C Limited will disclose its audit fee for the year of £200,000, this being the fees receivable by X&Co (UK) in respect of the statutory audit of the financial statements of C Limited.

5.56.4 In those cases where the fee for work relating solely to the audit of the subsidiary's consolidation pack is clearly identifiable, its classification should be considered separately from that of the remaining subsidiary audit fee in both the subsidiary's disclosures and those in its parent's consolidated financial statements. The treatment of this amount will depend on the company to which the services for this 'consolidation pack' fee have been rendered (parent or subsidiary).

5.56.5 For example, consider a GB limited company that is a subsidiary of a listed GB parent. UK GAAP is applied at the subsidiary level. The listed parent produces consolidated financial statements under IFRS. The subsidiary auditor may provide services that do not relate to the subsidiary's statutory audit, but are necessary for the listed parent's consolidated financial statements. For example, they might relate to the audit of a consolidation return under IFRS. In this case, whether the services have been supplied to the parent or to the subsidiary depends on the facts. If the services have been rendered to the subsidiary, disclosure is given on the basis discussed in paragraphs 5.56.6 onwards below. In some cases, however, it is clear that the services were supplied to the parent although the work may physically have been carried out at the subsidiary's premises. Where this is the case, the fees for these services are not disclosed at all by the subsidiary, as they are not part of its audit fee nor are they included in the amounts disclosed by the subsidiary for 'Other services'. The service has been rendered to the parent (which is not an 'associate' of the subsidiary as defined by the Regulations – see further para 5.70 below). The parent has to include these fees in its disclosure. Factors to consider when determining to which company the services have been supplied include the addressee of the engagement letter and any reports. The identity of the company that paid the fees may be a relevant factor where the other evidence is unclear or conflicting about the identity of the company to which the services were supplied. But payment of fees is not itself the basis for disclosure where the services have clearly been supplied to another company. [Tech 6/06 (revised) para 29.7].

5.56.6 If the services in respect of the 'consolidation pack' fee have been rendered to the subsidiary and the 'consolidation pack' fee is clearly identifiable, this amount will be disclosed within Category 2 (other statutory services) (see para 5.59) in the subsidiary's financial statements. This is because the services are supplied pursuant to legislation (that is, the legislation that requires the parent company to prepare consolidated financial statements). They cannot be included in Category 1 because the parent company is not an associate (as defined in the Regulations) of its subsidiary. In practice however, the subsidiary will often be exempt from making disclosures about 'Other services'. [Tech 6/06 (revised) para 18.4C].

5.56.7 For the purposes of disclosure in the listed parent's consolidated financial statements, further consideration is still necessary. The amount is disclosed differently in the consolidated financial statements depending on whether the subsidiary's auditor is the parent company auditor or an associate of the parent company auditor. [Tech 6/06 (revised) para 18.4A].

5.56.8 In the parent's consolidated financial statements, if the subsidiary is audited by the parent company auditor, any clearly identifiable element of the subsidiary's fee relating solely to the audit of the subsidiary's consolidation pack would be disclosed within the group audit fee, because it relates to the audit of the parent company's financial statements. If the subsidiary is audited by an associate of the parent company auditor, the element of the subsidiary fee relating solely to the consolidation pack cannot be included in the audit fee in the consolidated financial statements because the services have not been supplied by the parent company auditor. It will, therefore, be included in Category 1 of 'Other services' (statutory audit of the company's associates) (see para 5.59) in the consolidated auditor remuneration disclosure in the parent's consolidated financial statements. [Tech 6/06 (revised) para 18.4B].

Audit-assist

5.57 Where fees for services performed by other parts of the audit firm that assist in the audit (that is, 'audit-assist fees') are invoiced either as part of, or separately from, the audit fee, then those fees are included within the audit fees disclosed. Examples include work performed by the tax department on the audit of tax balances or by a valuations department on the audit of valuations performed by other third parties that are included in the financial statements.

Disclosure in which year

5.58 The fees disclosed should be the fees relating to the statutory audit of the financial statements in which the disclosure is made. [SI 2005/2417 Reg 4(1)(a); Tech 06/06 (revised) para 18.5]. The amount disclosed in any particular year will be management's best estimate of the fee at the time that the financial statements are prepared and this estimate may require subsequent revision. Assuming that an under-accrual or over-accrual of audit fees does not result from an error, the prior period disclosure is not restated for a revision to an estimate, so any revision to an under-accrual or over-accrual of a previous year's audit fee should be included in the current year disclosure. However, as the amount does not relate to the statutory audit of the current year's financial statements, to the extent that the amount of the revision is material, it may be helpful if it is separately identified and disclosed.

Example

B Limited is a company that is incorporated under the Companies Act 1985. It prepares and files financial statements that are audited by C LLP. B Limited is preparing its financial statements for the year ended 31 March 20X7. The fees payable to C LLP will be disclosed in accordance with the requirements in the Regulations for the disclosure of auditors' remuneration.

In respect of the 31 March 20X6 audit, additional fees arose due to late issues. These additional fees had not been accrued for in the financial statements for the year ended 31 March 20X6. The additional fees have subsequently been agreed and C LLP has invoiced these in the year ended 31 March 20X7.

How should the additional fees for the 31 March 20X6 audit be reflected in the auditors' remuneration disclosure in B Limited's financial statements for the year ended 31 March 20X7?

Assuming that the under-accrual of audit fees does not result from an error, the prior period disclosure is not restated for a revision to an estimate of an audit fee. Therefore, the amount of additional fees subsequently invoiced in excess of the original estimate in respect of the 20X6 audit of B Limited's financial statements should be included in the 31 March 20X7 audit fee disclosure. To the extent that the amount relating to the revision of the estimate is material, it should be separately disclosed.

Other services

Format of disclosure

5.59 Every company (apart from those specifically exempt – see further from para 5.74) is required to disclose, in the notes to its annual financial statements, fees receivable by the company's auditors and its 'associates' (see para 5.69) from the company and its 'associates' (see from para 5.70) in respect of the following hierarchy of categories:

- Category 1 – The auditing of financial statements of the company's associates pursuant to legislation (including that of countries and territories outside Great Britain) (see further from para 5.65).
- Category 2 – Other services supplied pursuant to such legislation (see further from para 5.66).
- Category 3 – Other services relating to taxation (see further from para 5.67).
- Category 4 – Services relating to information technology.
- Category 5 – Internal audit services.
- Category 6 – Valuation and actuarial services.
- Category 7 – Services relating to litigation.
- Category 8 – Services relating to recruitment and remuneration.
- Category 9 – Services relating to corporate finance transactions entered into or proposed to be entered into by or on behalf of the company or any of its associates.
- Category 10 – All other services (see further from para 5.68).

[SI 2005/2417 2 Sch 1 to 10].

Sub-analysis of the individual categories is not required, although this may be helpful in some instances. [Tech 6/06 (revised) para 34.1].

5.59.1 As explained above in paragraph 5.58, the fee disclosed for the audit of the financial statements is conventionally the fee for the year on which the auditor is reporting. The same approach should be used for any fees for auditing the financial statements of the company's associates (which will be included in Category 1 of 'Other services') and for regulatory filings that relate to the signing of an audit opinion (which will be included in Category 2 of 'Other services'). Other fees that are unrelated to the audit for a particular year should be calculated on an accruals basis (that is, for work carried out in the period). [Tech 06/06 (revised) para 29.5].

5.60 For some services, it may be obvious in which category they should be included. For others, however, judgement may be required to determine the most appropriate disclosure. The Regulations require that where a service could fall into more than one category, it should be disclosed in whichever category is earlier in the list (see hierarchy in para 5.59). [SI 2005/2417 2 Sch].

5.61 It is common for several services provided by an auditor to be included in one 'bundled' fee negotiation. For example, the audit fee may include the fee for the review of the interim report, or a single tax fee quoted may be for both tax compliance work and the audit of tax. Where this is the case, the auditor should provide a suitable breakdown of the total fee into the different services to enable the company to make the required disclosure. [Tech 06/06 (revised) para 30.1].

5.62 Where there are no fees to be disclosed within any category, that category need not be listed in the disclosure. However, comparative information is required to be disclosed for each category, so where, say, services relating to taxation were provided by the audit firm in the prior year but not the current year, disclosure of this category is required. It should be noted that there is no exemption from the disclosure of immaterial fees.

5.62.1 There is no requirement to disclose the aggregated total of fees for 'Other services'. [Tech 6/06 (revised) para 36.1].

Sub-totals

5.63 Provided that the required disclosures are given, there are no restrictions on the provision of additional information and/or sub-totals. However, care should be taken that no undue prominence is given to any non-statutory disclosures. For example, in a set of consolidated financial statements, companies may choose to sub-total the group audit fee with the fees in 'Other services' Category 1 (statutory audits of the company's associates) in order to show the remuneration receivable by the parent company auditor and its associates for auditing companies within the group. [Tech 06/06 (revised) paras 19.1, 36.1].

Categories of 'Other services'

5.64 The following paragraphs consider the classification of fees for particular services in some of the more common and complex scenarios.

Category 1 — Audit of the company's 'associates' pursuant to legislation

5.65 The intention of the category, 'The auditing of financial statements of the company's associates pursuant to legislation (including that of countries and territories outside Great Britain)', is to include all fees for any statutory audit of the company's subsidiaries by the company's auditor or its associates that is required by any legislation in any part of the world. This will include 'audit-assist' fees (see para 5.57). The example in paragraph 5.56.3 illustrates these principles.

5.65.1 The disclosure for Category 1 should exclude:

- Fees paid by any part of the reporting entity (that is, company or group) to any service provider that is not an associate of the reporting entity's auditor.
- Any fees disclosed as part of the audit fee (see para 5.56).

Example

A large company, Z Limited has a US subsidiary, Y Inc that is not required by US law to prepare financial statements. Y Inc. prepares a consolidation return that Z Limited uses in the preparation of its consolidated financial statements The consolidation return is audited by a US audit firm, which is an associate of the auditors of Z Limited.

In Z Limited's consolidated financial statements, the fees receivable by the US audit firm in respect of the audit of the consolidation return are not included in the disclosure of the group audit fee. This is because the audit fees disclosed by Z Limited are those payable to its auditor only (and not to an associate of its auditor – see para 5.56.1).

Instead, they will be included within Category 1 under 'Other services' in the disclosure in Z Limited's consolidated financial statements. This is because the audit of Y Inc's consolidation return can be viewed as the audit of Y Inc's 'accounts'. Whilst Y Inc is not required by law to have financial statements audited, Z Limited is required by UK law to have its consolidated financial statements audited. Thus, to the extent that the audit of the Y Inc 'accounts' is required for the purposes of the audit of Z Limited's consolidated financial statements, the fees associated will be disclosed in Category 1 in the Z Limited consolidated financial statements. [Tech 6/06 (revised) para 37.1].

Category 2 — Fees for other services supplied pursuant to such legislation

5.66 This category includes all fees for services (other than statutory audit) performed by the company's auditors (and its associates) that the company or its subsidiaries are required by legislation (including overseas legislation) to incur. Such services include:

- Regulatory reporting under the Listing Rules of the UK Listings Authority.
- Statutory or regulatory reporting on internal controls.
- Reports relating to government grants, where the requirement for such a report to be made is set out in statute.
- Elements of reports under section 404 of the US Public Company Accounting Reform and Investor Protection Act of 2002 (Sarbanes-Oxley). See also paragraph 5.68.1 below.
- Elements of reports on forms 20-F for SEC registrants. See also paragraph 5.68.7 below.
- A review of interim financial information by the auditor of a listed company, where one is performed in accordance with APB Bulletin 1999/4, 'Review of interim financial information' or ISRE (UK & I) 2410, 'Review of interim financial information performed by the independent auditor of the entity', which the Listing Rules and the Disclosure and Transparency Rules of the UK Listings Authority refers to as a 'review by auditors', and the auditors' report is published.

[Tech 06/06 (revised) paras 38.1, 39.1].

5.66.1 The Listing Rules and the Disclosure and Transparency Rules of the UK Listings Authority form part of UK legislation, as they are established under the Financial Services and Markets Act 2000 (FSMA).

5.66.2 If a review of interim financial information is not performed in accordance with APB Bulletin 1999/4 or ISRE (UK&I) 2410 or the auditors' report is not published, then there is no requirement for the review to be performed by the company's auditors and, hence, fees for this work are excluded from Category 1. Instead, such fees will be included under Category 10 of 'Other services'. Similarly, where the auditor performs a review of interim financial information for an unlisted or AIM traded company, the fees receivable by the auditor are included within Category 10 of 'Other services'. [Tech 06/06 (revised) para 39.2].

5.66.3 The services included in Category 2 are not restricted to those that are required by legislation to be performed by the company's auditors. It is sufficient that the services themselves are required to be performed by legislation without specifying who should perform them. [Tech 6/06 (revised) para 38.2].

Category 3 — Other services relating to taxation

5.67 Fees receivable by the company's auditors and its associates for both tax compliance services and tax advisory services are disclosed under this category. They do not need to be disclosed separately, but companies may wish to do so. Fees for the audit of tax balances will be included in the audit fee disclosure (see para 5.57).

Category 9 — Services relating to corporate finance transactions

5.67.1 This category will include fees relating to work such as acquisition due diligence and long-form reports, irrespective of whether the company is the vendor or the purchaser. However, if the work is required by legislation (for example, by the UK Listing Authority's Listing or Disclosure and Transparency Rules), it will be included within Category 2 since that category is higher on the list of 'Other services'. [Tech 6/06 (revised) para 43.1].

Category 10 — All other services

5.68 Fees included in 'All other services' are all those that do not fall within any other category and will include fees for (but are not restricted to):

- Accounting advice (where this is unrelated to the audit).
- Provision of accounting services to a listed company in an emergency (as permitted by paragraph 121 of APB Ethical Standard 5).
- Non-regulatory reporting on internal controls or corporate governance matters.
- Environmental audits, corporate responsibility reports and similar services.
- Secondments of the auditors' staff to the audit client (as permitted by paragraph 33 of APB Ethical Standard 2 'Financial, business, employment and personal relationships').

- Services provided by a company of which a partner in the audit firm is a director (see further para 5.69.1).
- The audit of a subsidiary other than for consolidation purposes that was not required by local legislative requirements.
- A review of interim financial information not required by legislation (see further para 5.66.2).

[Tech 06/06 (revised) para 44.1].

Practical applications

Sarbanes-Oxley section 404

5.68.1 Tech 6/06 (revised) states that elements of fees associated with reports under section 404 should be disclosed within 'Other services' in Category 2, 'Other services supplied pursuant to legislation'. This is because the basis of the audit fee disclosure relates to what is payable to the parent company auditor for executing the work necessary for the audit required under the Companies Act 1985 or Companies Act 2006. Any fees for work that is not required for the UK audit, but is required solely to comply with foreign legislation such as Sarbanes-Oxley section 404, are not part of the audit fee.

5.68.2 However, an approach may be taken whereby work performed on internal controls will form an integral part of the overall audit procedures for the UK statutory audit and is also sufficient for the signing of the section 404 report. Consequently, in this case, the fees for work on internal controls will all be included in the audit fee disclosure. However, to the extent that there is additional cost in preparing the section 404 report itself, that cost falls to 'Other services' Category 2. [Tech 6/06 (revised) paras 38.3, 38.4].

5.68.3 On the other hand, if there is additional work to be performed on internal controls to give the section 404 report that would not be required for the UK statutory audit (for example, controls are tested that are not relied upon for the purpose of the UK statutory audit), any additional fee relating to this work falls to 'Other services' Category 2. [Tech 6/06 (revised) para 38.3].

5.68.4 Accordingly, the overall structure of the engagement should be reviewed. If work performed on internal controls for the purposes of section 404 is subject to a separate contract of engagement it will not be possible to argue that the work forms part of the statutory audit of a set of financial statements. Even if the section 404 work is subject to the same contract of engagement as the audit, the wording of the contract should be reviewed carefully. If reference is made to additional work to be performed for the purposes of section 404 or if the services to be rendered and fees to be billed for section 404 work are differentiated from those associated with the audit in any way, this may preclude companies from including fees associated with section 404 work on internal controls with the fees for the UK statutory audit.

5.68.5 In the group financial statements, only the fees relating to work performed on internal controls within the parent company and internal controls associated with the consolidation process should be included in the group audit fee. To the extent that work is performed on a subsidiary's internal controls, these fees form part of the fee for the auditing of that subsidiary. As such, from a group perspective, these fees may fall to be included within 'Other services' Category 1. However, if the work on the subsidiary's internal controls is only carried out for the purposes of the section 404 report, the fees would fall to be disclosed within 'Other services' Category 2 in the group financial statements. [Tech 6/06 (revised) para 38.4].

5.68.6 Companies should consider the classification of fees generated as a result of advisory work performed by the auditors during the scoping, implementation and testing phases of section 404. To the extent that these services were not specifically relied upon for audit purposes disclosure within Category 2 would be appropriate.

Form 20-F filings

5.68.7 Foreign registrants on US stock exchanges may be required to file forms 20-F with the SEC. In such situations, work may be performed by the auditor (or its associates) that is common to the audit of a set of UK financial statements as required for UK statutory purposes and the audit of the form 20-F for the same entity. Consistent with the principles discussed in paragraph 5.56.2 above, any fees for such 'common' work would be treated as being fees for the UK statutory audit in the first instance.

5.68.8 To the extent that additional work is required to report on the form 20-F that is over and above the work required for the statutory audit of the associated local financial statements, the fees for this additional work should be classified in Category 2 of 'Other services'. This may include, for example, fees for additional work to comply with US GAAS or fees for work on US GAAP adjustments to the statutory numbers. [Tech 6/06 (revised) para 38.1].

The auditors' associates

5.69 The definition of the auditors' associates is wide and includes:

- Any entity controlled by the auditor.
- Any entity that controls the auditor.
- Any entity whose operating and financial policies the auditor is able to influence materially.
- Any entity under common control with the auditor.
- Any director (if the auditor is a corporate) or partner (if the auditor is a partnership) of the auditor.

- Any partnership in which a director (if the auditor is a corporate) or a partner (if the auditor is a partnership) of the auditor is a partner.
- Any body corporate in which a director (if the auditor is a corporate) or a partner (if the auditor is a partnership) of the auditor is a director
- Any entity trading under, or using, the same name as the auditor, if the intention is to create the impression of a connection between that entity and the auditor.
- Any entity who is party to an arrangement with the auditor under which costs, profits, business strategy or significant professional resources are shared.

[SI 2005/2417 1 Sch 1 to 4].

5.69.1 For a global network of firms, or a number of independent firms that work together as a network, the definition of the 'associates' of the auditor clearly includes all members of that network, whether they are known by the same name as the company's auditor or not. However, there are a number of less obvious entities that may or may not be included in the definition.

Example 1

A partner in an audit firm is also a director of her husband's company, A Limited. He is an architect, working for A Limited, which is controlled by him and his wife.

A Limited is an associate of the audit firm, because a partner in that audit firm is a director of A Limited. If the architect performs services for B Limited, a GB incorporated company that is an audit client of the firm, the remuneration payable to A Limited by the audit client must be included in Category 10 of 'Other services' in B Limited's disclosure of amounts payable to the audit firm and its associates.

Although not required, it may be pragmatic for the audit client, B Limited, to disclose the nature of the services received from A Limited.

Example 2

A partner in an audit firm, auditor A, sits on the board of directors of a property management company. The partner is one of ten directors of the property management company and does not have significant influence over the company.

The property management company is an associate of the audit firm, auditor A. Even though the company and audit firm are not subject to common control or influence, the existence of one common partner/director is sufficient for the relationship to be established.

The property management company receives fees from P Limited, a GB company, which is an audit client of auditor A. The fees paid to the property management company by P Limited should be included in its auditors' remuneration disclosure in its financial statements under Category 10 of 'Other services' in the same way as in example 1 above.

Example 3

A local business awards ceremony is sponsored by five companies, one of which is an audit firm. The cost of the awards ceremony is shared equally between all five sponsors.

Despite the existence of an arrangement under which costs are shared, the audit firm's co-sponsors are not 'associates' of the audit firm, for the purposes of the auditors' remuneration disclosure requirement. The intention of this element of the definition is not to include within the definition entities (that are not part of the auditors' network) that share costs or profits with the auditor on a specific engagement only.

Example 4

An audit firm is engaged by a non-audit client to perform a review of the non-audit client's employment costs and to identify cost savings that can be made. The audit firm is working together with the non-audit client's Human Resources (HR) consultants. The audit firm and the HR consultants receive equal shares of half the first year's cost savings in consideration for their services. Does this mean the HR consultants are an associate of the audit firm, if the HR consultants provide services to audit clients of the audit firm?

No. An arrangement whereby profits from a specific engagement are shared with the audit firm would not, by itself, cause the HR consultants to be an associate of the auditor. [Tech 06/06 (revised) para 8.3].

The company's associates

5.70 For the purposes of this disclosure, the company's associates are:

- Any subsidiary of the company, other than a subsidiary in respect of which severe long-term restrictions substantially hinder the exercise of the parent company's rights over the assets or management of the subsidiary.

[SI 2005/2417 Reg 2(2)(b)(i)].

- Pension schemes, for the provision of benefits to employees and directors (or former employees and directors) of the company or any subsidiary, where the company (or a subsidiary or a person acting on behalf of either the company or subsidiary) appoints the majority of the trustees or has a dominant influence over the appointment of the scheme's auditor. For the purposes of the definition, benefits consist of or include any pension, lump sum, gratuity or other like benefit given or to be given on retirement or on death or in anticipation of retirement or, in connection with past service, after retirement or death.

[SI 2005/2417 Regs 2(2)(b)(ii), 2(1)(a)(b)].

5.70.1 A company's associates for the purposes of this disclosure are only its subsidiaries and not its associates as defined in FRS 9, 'Associates and joint ventures'. Consequently, the fees for auditing an FRS 9 associate's or joint venture's financial statements are excluded entirely from the investor's auditors' remuneration disclosure.

5.70.2 However, where the auditor of an associate or joint venture (both as defined in FRS 9) is also the auditor of the investor and an element of that audit firm's work on the associate's or joint venture's financial statements contributes to the audit of its investor's consolidated financial statements, the fees receivable by the auditor in respect of that part of its work is included in the audit fee disclosed in the investor's consolidated financial statements. [Tech 06/06 (revised) para 13.1].

5.70.3 Tech 06/06 (revised), paragraph 13.1 suggests (but does not require) that, where a company's interest in an associate or joint venture (both as defined in FRS 9) is particularly material and the auditor of that associate or joint venture is also the investor company's auditor, separate disclosure may be desirable, as good practice, in the investor company's financial statements of the audit fee of the joint venture or associate.

The company's associated pension schemes

5.71 Disclosure is required of the fees payable by a company's associated pension schemes to the company's auditor or any of its associates for any type of 'Other services' described in Categories 2 to 10. This disclosure is required whether the company's auditor is also the auditor of the pension scheme or not.

5.71.1 Separate disclosure is required in respect of services to the company and its subsidiaries and to the company's associated pension schemes. [SI 2005/2417 Reg 4(4)].

5.71.2 The disclosure will follow a similar format to the company's disclosure of fees for 'Other services' supplied by the company's auditor and its associates (see para 5.59). For the purposes of this disclosure, the provision of an audit is considered to be one of these 'other' services. Hence, if the pension scheme is audited by the same firm as audits the company (or one of its associates) fees payable by the pension scheme to the company's auditor or any of its associates for the audit are included in Category 1, if the audit of the pension scheme's financial statements is required by local legislation, or in Category 10, if the audit is not necessary for local legislative requirements.

5.71.3 Amounts payable by a company's associated pension scheme to the company's auditors (or one of its associates) for work done in connection with any regulatory returns that are required by local legislation are included in Category 2 'Other services pursuant to such legislation'.

5.71.4 The requirements in respect of pension schemes apply equally to UK pension schemes and overseas pension schemes and include both defined contribution and defined benefit schemes.

How to determine whether a pension scheme is associated with a company

5.72 A pension scheme is associated with a company if either:

- a majority of the trustees are appointed by (or by a person acting on behalf of) the company or a subsidiary of the company, or
- the company, or a subsidiary of the company, exercises a dominant influence over the appointment of the auditor (if any) of the scheme.

[Tech 06/06 (revised) para 15.1].

5.72.1 Association with a company depends entirely on the *facts* surrounding the ability of the company (or a subsidiary) to appoint scheme trustees or to influence the appointment of the scheme auditor. The test on the appointment of the scheme trustees is purely factual at the date of appointment and the relationship between the company (or its subsidiary) and the scheme or its trustees thereafter is irrelevant. [Tech 06/06 (revised) para 15.2].

5.72.2 In respect of the appointment of a scheme auditor, the company's directors will need to assess whether the company (or any of its subsidiaries) had a dominant influence over the process by which the scheme trustees appoint the scheme auditor. The fact that the company and the scheme may appoint the same auditors as the scheme auditor is not, in itself, evidence that the company has dominant influence over the appointment process. Conversely, where the company and the scheme appoint auditors who are not associated with one another, this is not conclusive evidence that the company did not actually exercise dominant influence over the appointment process.

5.72.3 Where a pension scheme is operated for a number of unconnected employers (for example, an industry-wide scheme) it is unlikely that the pension scheme will be an associate of one or more participants in the scheme. Each scheme must, however, be evaluated individually. This presumption does not apply where a pension scheme is operated on behalf of members in the same group.

Example

B plc is a GB registered company that is the immediate parent of two GB subsidiaries, C Limited and D Limited. C Limited is an intermediate parent of a UK subgroup, being the 100 per cent parent of X Limited and Y Limited. In accordance with GB company law, B plc produces audited consolidated financial statements and all companies in the group produce audited individual financial statements. In addition, the C Limited sub-group produces voluntary consolidated financial statements for bank covenant purposes.

The *group runs a defined* benefit pension scheme that is open to employees from all five group companies. B Plc is the sponsoring company of the scheme and appoints a majority of the scheme's trustees. All the group companies and the pension scheme are audited by E LLP.

How should management determine whether fees the pension scheme has paid to E LLP (and its associates) are disclosable in the financial statements of the various group companies?

X Limited, Y Limited and D Limited may take an exemption from disclosing fees for 'Other services' as discussed in paragraph 5.75. If the available exemptions are taken, management will only need to give disclosure for 'Other services' in the B plc consolidated financial statements and in the C Limited consolidated financial statements.

In this case, B plc is the sponsoring company of the pension scheme and appoints a majority of the scheme's trustees. Therefore, the pension scheme is an associate of B plc and the fees payable to E LLP (and its associates) by the pension scheme will be disclosable in B plc's financial statements.

As C Limited neither appoints a majority of trustees nor exercises dominant influence over the appointment of the scheme's auditor, the scheme will not be treated as its associate and no disclosure of the fees payable to E LLP (and its associates) by the pension scheme will be required in C Limited's financial statements.

If C Limited had appointed a majority of the scheme's trustees or exercised dominant influence over the appointment of the scheme's auditor, disclosure of fees payable by the scheme to E LLP (and its associates) would have been required not only in C Limited's consolidated financial statements, but also in the consolidated financial statements of B plc. This is because B plc would exercise dominant influence over the appointment of the scheme's auditor *via* its control of C Limited and, as such, the scheme would be an associate of both C Limited and B plc.

Obtaining the information to be disclosed

5.73 The company's management will usually need to contact the trustees of the associated pension schemes in order to obtain the information for disclosure. If the trustees refuse to provide the company with the information, then the company's auditor is obliged by law to provide the company with "*such information as is necessary to enable the disclosure required by regulation 4(1)(b) or 5(1) to be made*". [SI 2005/2417 Reg 6]. The Department for Business, Enterprise and Regulatory Reform (BERR) (formerly the DTI) has advised that the auditors' statutory obligation under Regulation 6 to provide such information to the company must be complied with, regardless of any legal or contractual duty of confidentiality owed by the auditor (or any member of its network) to the pension scheme client. [Tech 06/06 (revised) paras 7.3 and 17.1].

Exemptions from disclosure

Audit fees

5.74 All companies must disclose their individual audit fee with only one exception — where a parent company is required to (and does) prepare consolidated financial statements, there is no requirement to disclose, in addition to the group audit fee, the audit fee for the company. This is because disclosure is required of the fees for auditing the 'annual accounts', which is a term defined in, section 262(1) of the Companies Act 1985 (section 471 of the Companies Act 2006) and includes the company's individual and, where required, its consolidated financial statements. [SI 2005/2417 Reg 4; Tech 06/06 (revised) para 18.2].

Fees for 'Other services'

5.75 The disclosures in respect of fees for 'Other services' are not required to be given by:

- A small or medium-sized company.
- A small or medium-sized group.
- A subsidiary company in its individual financial statements, whose parent is required to, and does, prepare consolidated financial statements in accordance with the Companies Act 1985 or the Companies Act 2006 and the subsidiary company is included in the consolidation.
- A parent company in its individual financial statements, where the company is required to, and does, prepare consolidated financial statements in accordance with the Companies Act 1985 or the the Companies Act 2006 (see further paras 5.78 and 5.79).

[SI 2005/2417 Regs 3, 4, 5].

5.75.1 Qualification as a small or a medium-sized company or group is considered in chapter 32.

5.75.2 The exemption for a subsidiary company is available where the parent's consolidated financial statements are required to be, and are, prepared in accordance with the relevant GB (1985) or UK (2006) Companies Act and the subsidiary is included in the consolidation. This means that the exemption is only available to a subsidiary of a GB parent and not to a subsidiary of a foreign parent. This is because the foreign parent's consolidated financial statements, although they may be prepared in accordance with EU-adopted IFRS or UK GAAP, will not comply in full in other respects with that Companies Act. For example, where a GB company's parent is incorporated in, say, Germany and although that parent company prepares its consolidated financial statements in accordance with EU-adopted IFRS, it will not comply in full in other respects with the Companies Act 1985 or the Companies Act 2006 (complying instead with German law). Hence, the subsidiary of the German company is not able to take advantage of the exemption. This is illustrated in the example in paragraph 5.75.6. Once parts 15 and 16 of the Companies Act 2006 are fully implemented and thus apply in Northern Ireland together with the 2007 Regulations, references to GB companies, parents and subsidiaries should be read as UK companies, parents and subsidiaries.

5.75.3 The exemption from disclosure of the fees payable for 'Other services' to a company's auditor and its associates by a parent company in its individual financial statements is only available when it is required by the Companies Act 1985 or Companies Act 2006 to, and does, prepare consolidated financial statements. If a company has subsidiaries (say it is an intermediate parent), but does not prepare consolidated financial statements as a result of an exemption available in the Companies Act (for example, the consolidation exemption available for intermediate parent companies with non-UK EEA parents in section 228A of the Companies Act 1985 (section 401 of the Companies Act 2006)), then the exemption from disclosure of fees for 'Other services' will not be available. The disclosure of fees for 'Other services' would have to be given in the individual financial statements of the intermediate parent and, notably, these disclosures would have to include fees in respect of the entity's (unconsolidated) subsidiaries.

5.75.4 In order to obtain the disclosure exemption, the individual financial statements of the relevant parent company and subsidiaries must state that the disclosure of fees payable to the auditor and its associates for other (non-audit) services has not been made because, either "*the company's consolidated accounts are required to disclose such fees on a consolidated basis*" or "*the consolidated accounts of the company's parent are required to disclose other (non-audit) services on a consolidated basis*" as appropriate. [SI 2005/2417 Reg 5(2)].

5.75.5 For a subsidiary company, the exemption from disclosure is available regardless of whether or not the subsidiary is audited by the parent company's auditors or a member of that audit firm's network.

5.75.6 These principles are illustrated in the following example.

Example

A Limited is a subsidiary of a German parent that prepares its consolidated financial statements in accordance with EU-adopted IFRS and German law. A Limited has two subsidiaries, B Limited and C Limited. A Limited and B Limited have the same auditor, XCo but C Limited is audited by an unrelated audit firm, QCo.

A Limited is eligible for the exemption in section 228 of the Companies Act 1985 (section 400 of the Companies Act 2006) from the requirement to prepare consolidated financial statements. However, in order to be entitled to take that exemption, it must state in its financial statements that it is taking the exemption. [CA85 Sec 228(2)(c); CA06 Sec 400(2)].

If A Limited makes that statement, it is not required to prepare consolidated financial statements. As its parent is a German company and does not prepare consolidated financial statements under the GB (1985) or UK (2006) company law, A Limited must, however, in its individual financial statements, make the disclosure of fees paid both by A Limited and by B Limited for other services to its auditor, XCo (and its associates).

B Limited is also required to make disclosure in its financial statements of the amounts for other services it pays to XCo.

C Limited must disclose the amounts payable to QCo, its auditor.

5.75.7 If a subsidiary's financial statements are approved before those of its GB parent, there can be no absolute certainty that the parent will prepare consolidated financial statements and make the disclosures required by the Regulations. It may be reasonable, in some cases, for the subsidiary to assume that the parent will meet its obligations in due course and so the exemption from the Regulations should be available. This might be so, for example, where the parent is a listed GB company. However, the subsidiary's directors should in all cases make such enquiries as they consider necessary to establish that the exemption will be available. If they are in any doubt, the exemption should not be used. The GB parent company may be entitled to an exemption from preparing consolidated financial statements under company law. Where this is the case, the subsidiary should establish whether or not the parent intends to use this exemption and consider the risk that any such decision might subsequently be reversed before utilising the exemption from disclosing fees for 'Other services'. [Tech 6/06 (revised) para 26.5].

5.75.8 The exemptions are for the individual financial statements of a parent and its subsidiaries only. There is no exemption in relation to any group financial statements. [Tech 6/06 (revised) para 26.6].

Single audit fees for the group

5.76 It is common, in the audit of a group, for the audit fee for more than one company to be negotiated as a single fee and invoiced to one company, often the parent company. This may be the case either where the audit of more than one company is performed by the same auditors or where the aggregate fee for a global audit is negotiated between the parent company and its auditors.

5.76.1 Where the fee is not recharged to other companies but is borne by the parent company, for the purposes of disclosure, an allocation must be made to each subsidiary that is producing financial statements under local legislation (as these fees will be classified in 'Other services' Category 1, rather than audit fee). [Tech 6/06 (revised) para 25.2].

5.76.2 Where the fee is recharged to other companies, this will often form an appropriate basis for disclosure.

Fees receivable from third parties

5.77 Paragraph 45.1 of Tech 6/06 (revised) considers the disclosure of third party fees. It states that fees payable by a third party to a company's auditor for work carried out on the audit client, but in an engagement separate to the audit, may be disclosable by the audit client. Fees paid to a company's auditors by third parties may be captured by the disclosure requirements because companies are required to disclose 'remuneration receivable' by the company's auditors and its associates for the supply of 'Other services'. The fact that the payment is not made by the audit client is not the key to the disclosure requirements, rather it is necessary to consider the services to which the fees relate and whom these services benefit. If the benefit of the services is to the audit client, the fees will be disclosable by the audit client regardless of who has made the payment.

Example

Bank A proposes to lend money to its customer B Limited. Bank A engages audit firm X&Co, who are B Limited's auditors, to report to the Bank A on B Limited's indebtedness.

Although X&Co is engaged by and reports to Bank A, the report is prepared for the benefit of B Limited. In the disclosure of B Limited's fees payable to its auditor for 'Other services', the fees receivable by X&Co in respect of this work are included within Category 10 of 'Other services' (see further para 5.68). This is the case irrespective of whether the auditors' fees for this work are paid by the bank or directly by B Limited.

5.78 Another example is litigation support, where the auditor is appointed by and reports directly to the company's solicitors. The auditors' fees may be payable by the solicitors, but the service is provided in relation to the audit client. In this case, the fees would fall into Category 7 'Services relating to litigation' in the audit client's disclosure of fees for 'Other services'.

5.78.1 In many cases, the party commissioning the type of work referred to above from the auditor may itself be an audit client of the auditor. However, the subject of the work may be either another audit client of the firm or it may be a non-audit client. The fees may be paid by either the party commissioning the work or the subject of the work. If the party commissioning the work is an audit client, the question arises as to which audit client should disclose the fees paid to the auditor for this type of engagement within its auditors' remuneration disclosures.

Example

Bank B is an audit client of auditor Z. Company C, which obtains financing from bank B, is in financial difficulty and engages with auditor Z to provide pre-insolvency services. The report produced by auditor Z will be made available to both company C and bank B. Company C will pay the fees for this work.

To understand whether bank B is required to include in its auditor remuneration disclosure the fees paid to auditor Z by company C, the services being rendered must be considered in more detail. In particular, the primary beneficiary of the services must be identified. Consideration should be made as to whether company C requires the report for its own internal purposes or whether it has been required to obtain the report by bank B solely for bank B's purposes.

The bank may write into its conditions of lending that, should the company fall into financial difficulties, the company will be required to engage a professional firm to obtain pre-insolvency services. This implies that the bank has had some influence over a firm's appointment (maybe even to the extent that it specifies which firm is appointed). However, this is not, in itself, grounds to make the bank disclose fees that one of its clients has paid to the bank's auditor. If the associated services are to the benefit of the bank's client, it is the bank's client who should disclose the fees.

If company C has engaged with auditor Z but the report produced is allowed to be circulated to bank B, to the extent that the company is the primary beneficiary of the services provided, the fees would not be disclosable as auditor remuneration in bank B's financial statements.

For joint engagements (where both company C and bank B are bound by the terms of engagement), it will be necessary to consider why bank B is included on the engagement letter. Again, the arrangement's overall substance should help identify who is the primary beneficiary of the services being rendered by the auditors and disclosure should be made accordingly.

More than one auditor

Joint auditors

5.79 Where a company has joint auditors, remuneration receivable by each joint auditor should be disclosed separately. [Tech 6/06 (revised) para 22.1].

5.79.1 However, where more than one firm of auditors is involved in the audit of a group, this does not mean that they are joint auditors. An auditor that is not an associate of the parent company's auditor may perform the audit of a subsidiary. The disclosure of fees receivable by that subsidiary's auditors is not required although voluntary disclosure may be given.

Change of auditor

5.80 Where more that one person or firm has been appointed as a company's auditor during the period to which the financial statements relate, separate disclosure is required in respect of the remuneration of each auditor (and its associates). [SI 2005/2417 Regs 3(3) and 4(5)].

Appointment after the year end

5.81 The Regulations refer to a person being appointed as a company's auditor 'during' the period. However, it is not uncommon for a new auditor to be appointed after the year end to conduct the audit for the year that has now passed. As noted in paragraph 5.58, the financial statements on which the auditor is reporting must disclose the fees for auditing those financial statements and, thus, the timing of the audit appointment is not relevant. The fees payable to the new auditor must be disclosed separately from any fees received or receivable in respect of the year by the previous auditor who served during that year.

Practical issues

Discontinued operations

5.82 The Regulations make no distinction between continuing and discontinued operations. Disclosures must be given for all remuneration receivable by the parent company auditor and its associates for audit services and 'Other services' rendered to the company and the company's associates. This is regardless of the status of the company's associates as either continuing or discontinued. If the amounts relating to discontinued operations are material, companies may consider including additional disclosure to highlight the amounts included in the totals that relate to those operations.

Overseas branches

5.83 The Regulations are unclear about the treatment of fees paid to an associate of the auditor for the audit of a branch of the company. This might arise in the case of an overseas branch. It appears to conflict with the Regulations to include amounts paid to an associate of the auditor in the company's audit fee, as that is for fees paid to the company's auditor and not the auditor's associates. However, putting the fees into Category 1 of 'Other services' does not appear to be appropriate either, because the fees relate to the audit of the company and not to its associates. A literal interpretation of the Regulations suggests that such fees should be included in Category 2, because the services are supplied pursuant to legislation. However, the associate may be acting as the company's auditors' agent and, where this is the case, inclusion in the company audit fee would be appropriate. [Tech 6/06 (revised) para 18.8].

Shared service centres

5.84 Many groups operate shared service centres (SSCs) to obtain synergies by centralising certain processes and systems. An SSC may be either a branch of a legal entity within a group or a legal entity in its own right. There may be numerous entities within a group where the processes carried out by the SSC are critical and audit teams of those entities may obtain comfort from audit work performed at the shared service centre for the purposes of signing off on a statutory audit.

5.85 As noted in paragraph 5.56.2 above, where audit work is performed that is used for the purposes of two (or more) separate audits, this work is seen to have been carried out, in the first instance, for the purposes of the company's statutory audit. That includes the SSC where the relevant processes and transactions occurred. On this basis, to the extent that audit work performed at the SSC is necessary for the auditor to sign a statutory audit opinion on the company's financial statements that includes the SSC, the fees for the work performed should be included in the audit fee of that company. No disclosure of the fee (or proportion of the fee) for the SSC audit would be included within the audit fee for any of the other entities that benefit from the processes of the SSC.

5.86 Where additional work is performed at the SSC that is not necessary for the auditor to discharge its statutory responsibilities in relation to the company that includes the SSC, this implies that the additional work relates to services provided to other group companies. In this scenario, the fees associated with this additional work should be allocated between those group companies for which the processes carried out at the SSC are critical as part of their audit fees.

5.87 If a recharge arrangement is in place, this may form a basis for the allocation of this element of the fee. If no recharge arrangement is in place, this amount must still be allocated between the relevant companies on a reasonable basis for the purposes of this disclosure by the relevant group companies.

5.88 In some cases, the analysis in paragraph 5.85 may be appropriate to a group's particular facts and circumstances, (that is, the fees are entirely for the SSC company) but, nevertheless, group companies are recharged an allocation of the SSC's audit fee. In such a case, following the guidance above, the amount of the recharge does not form part of the group company's audit fee. Management may consider it appropriate to disclose any amount paid in respect of such a recharge as a footnote to the auditor remuneration disclosure.

Annex

Example of disclosure of services provided by the company's auditor and its associates

Background

X plc is a large trading company that has two smaller trading subsidiaries: Y Limited, a company incorporated under the UK Companies Act and Z SA, a company incorporated in France. X plc also has a material associate, A Limited and a pension scheme, the X plc pension scheme, which is operated for the benefit of staff employed by X plc and Y Limited.

Each entity referred to above pays fees to X plc's auditor (D&Co) and its associates as follows:

X plc pays D&Co:

- £1 million to the audit practice for the year end audit, of which £200,000 is in respect of the audit of the consolidation and group financial statements and £800,000 is in respect of the audit of the company's financial statements.
- £400,000 to the audit practice for their review of the consolidated interim report.
- £500,000 to the tax practice, of which £200,000 is in respect of work performed by the tax department to assist the auditor in their audit of the tax numbers in the consolidated financial statements and £300,000 is for tax compliance work for the company.

Y Limited pays D&Co:

- £67,000 to the audit practice, of which £60,000 is in respect of the year end audit, including both work on the statutory financial statements of Y Limited and work on the group consolidation pack and £7,000 is in respect of work performed contributing to D&Co's review of the interim financial statements.
- £10,000 to the tax practice for tax compliance work.

Z SA pays the French firm of D&Co (an associate of the UK firm):

- £25,000 to the audit practice for the year end audit, including both work on the statutory financial statements of Z SA and work on the group consolidation pack.
- £7,000 to the tax practice for tax compliance work.

A Limited pays D&Co:

- £7,500 to the audit practice for the audit of the statutory financial statements of A Limited. No additional fees are paid by A Limited for the audit of information to be included in the X plc consolidated financial statements: instead, this is included in the audit fee paid by X plc.
- £5,000 to the tax practice for tax compliance work.

The X plc pension scheme pays D&Co:

Other profit and loss account items

- £4,000 to the assurance practice for the audit of the pension scheme.
- £2,000 to the assurance practice for the audit of a return submitted to the pension regulator.

Disclosure in notes to financial statements

The disclosure of auditor remuneration in X plc's group and individual financial statements and Y Limited's individual financial statements will be as shown below. Comparative information has not been included in this example but is required for disclosure in financial statements. The information has been given in tabular format but this is not required by the legislation and a narrative format for some or all of the information (for example, that relating to associated pension schemes) would be acceptable.

X plc	£'000s	
Fees payable to the company's auditor for the audit of the company's annual financial statements	1,200	
Fees payable to the company's auditor and its associates for other services:		
The audit of the company's subsidiaries[1], pursuant to legislation	85	*Category 1*
Other services pursuant to legislation	407	*Category 2*
Tax services	317	*Category 3*
Fees in respect of the X plc pension scheme:		
Audit	4	*Category 1*
Other services pursuant to legislation	2	*Category 2*

Fees paid to D&Co and its associates for non-audit services to the company itself are not disclosed in the individual financial statements of X plc because the company's consolidated financial statements are required to disclose such fees on a consolidated basis.

[1] Additional voluntary disclosure of fees paid by X plc's associate may be desirable, as good practice, if the associate is particularly material (see paragraph 13.1 of Tech 06/06 (revised)).

Y Limited	£'000s
Fees for the audit of the company	60

Fees paid to the company's auditor, D&Co, and its associates for services other than the statutory audit of the company are not disclosed in Y Limited's financial statements since the consolidated financial statements of Y Limited's parent, X plc, are required to disclose non-audit fees on a consolidated basis.

Analysis of fees – working schedules

The following table has been prepared to aid understanding of the disclosures shown above. There is no requirement to publish such an analysis.

The table analyses the fees paid by companies in the group to D&Co and its associates and shows how the fees feed into the categories in the disclosure above. The audit fee disclosable in X plc's group and individual financial statements is one and the same number. [Tech 06/06 (revised) para 18.2]. Although Y Limited has taken the exemption from presenting information about fees (other than the statutory audit fee) paid to D&Co

and its associates, this table analyses them to show how they would fall to be disclosed if the exemption was not available or Y Limited elected not to apply it.

	X plc group	Y Limited
Fees paid by X plc		
Audit of group financial statements – £200,000	Audit fee	
Audit of individual financial statements – £800,000	Audit fee	
Interim review fee – £400,000	Category 2	
Tax audit fee – £200,000	Audit fee	
Tax compliance fee – £300,000	Category 3	
Fees paid by Y Limited		
Year end audit of Y Limited – £60,000	Category 1	Audit fee
Work contributing to the interim review by D&Co of the consolidated financial statements – £7,000	Category 2	Category 2
Tax compliance fee – £10,000	Category 3	Category 3
Fees paid by Z SA		
Year end audit of Z SA — £25,000	Category 1	
Tax compliance fee – £7,000	Category 3	

Chapter 6

Financial instruments including derivatives

	Page
Introduction	6001
How to use this chapter	6003
What is a financial instrument?	6004
Contracts and contractual rights	6006
FRS 13 exclusions and scope	6006
How the standards apply under UK GAAP	6007
Introduction	6007
Companies Act requirements	6008
FRS 4 — Capital instruments	6009
FRS 13 — Derivatives and other financial instruments	6009
FRS 25 — Financial instruments: Disclosure and presentation	6009
FRS 26 — Financial instruments: Recognition and measurement	6010
FRS 29 — Financial instruments: Disclosures	6010
Listed companies	6011
New fair value accounting rules	6012
Banks and insurance companies	6012
Practical examples	6013
Requirements that apply to all entities	6014
Introduction	6014
Definition of investments	6015
Classification	6016
Measurement rules	6017
Fixed asset investments	6018
Historical cost accounting rules	6018
Alternative accounting rules	6018
Current asset investments	6020
Historical cost accounting rules	6020
Alternative accounting rules	6020
Fair value accounting rules	6020
Measuring financial instruments at fair value	6021
Changes in fair value	6023
Marking to market	6023
Presentation	6024
Disclosure requirements	6024
Introduction	6024
All investments	6025
Companies Act disclosure requirements	6029
Companies adopting fair value accounting	6029
Companies not adopting fair value accounting	6030
Directors' report	6033

Comparatives 6033
Significant holdings greater than 20 per cent. 6033
Exemptions from disclosure 6035
Participating interests 6036
Associates, joint ventures and other joint arrangements 6037
Subsidiary undertakings 6040
Parent company information 6042
Membership of a qualifying undertaking 6042
Own shares and shares in own parent 6043
Loans for acquisition of own shares 6045
Other investments 6045
Requirements for entities not applying FRS 26 6046
Introduction 6046
FRS 13 6046
Scope of FRS 13 6046
Excluded financial instruments. 6049
Short-term debtors and creditors. 6050
Identification of on balance sheet financial instruments. 6051
Derivative financial instruments. 6052
Cash-settled commodity contracts. 6053
Non-equity shares and non-equity minority interests. 6055
FRS 13 disclosures 6056
Disclosure of objectives, policies and strategies. 6057
Disclosure of accounting policies. 6062
Detailed numerical disclosures. 6066
Interest rate risk and currency profiles of financial liabilities 6067
Maturity analysis of financial liabilities 6071
Maturity analysis of undrawn committed borrowing facilities . . . 6073
Details of financial assets 6074
Currency risk disclosures 6075
Fair value disclosures 6080
Determination of fair values 6080
Disclosure by category 6081
Book value versus fair value 6083
Disclosure on financial assets and liabilities held for trading 6086
Disclosures about hedges 6087
Hedging table. 6087
Disclosure related to item being hedged. 6089
Hedging using instruments other than derivatives. 6090
Disclosures gross or net 6092
Gains and losses included in fixed assets 6093
Hedging a current asset, liability or non-equity share 6093
Hedging a forward purchase of stock. 6094
Hedging the purchase of a fixed asset using an option. 6095
Hedging a net investment using a cross-currency swap 6096
Market price risk. 6098
FRS 4 — Capital instruments 6103
Background 6103

FRS 4's objectives 6103
Scope 6104
Definition of capital instrument 6104
Finance costs 6105
Elements making up finance cost 6106
Dividends or interest 6106
Issue and redemption premiums 6106
Issue costs 6106
Facility fees 6110
Term of capital instruments 6110
Definition of term 6111
Implications of options 6111
Term extended 6115
Term shortened 6116
Indeterminate term 6117
Measurement 6117
Initial recognition 6117
Treatment of finance costs 6117
Subsequent recognition and measurement 6120
Contingent payments 6121
Repurchase of debt 6122
Renegotiation of debt 6124
Disclosure 6128
Companies Act requirements 6129
Requirements for entities applying FRS 25 and FRS 26 6130
Introduction 6130
Differences between the UK standards and their international equivalents 6131
FRS 25 scope exclusion 6131
Recognition and derecognition 6131
EU carve-out of IAS 39 6132
The fair value option 6133
Other differences 6134
Transitional guidance 6134
Comparative information 6135
Hedge accounting 6137
Transition 6137
Documentation 6138
Amendments to FRS 26 6138
FRS 29 6140
Annex 1 — Example FRS 13 disclosures 6141
Example 1 6141
Example 2 6144
Example 3 6147
Example 4 6151
Annex 2 — FRS 25 and FRS 26 flow charts 6157
Annex 3 — Financial instruments 6159

Chapter 6

Financial instruments including derivatives

Introduction

6.1 Over the past ten years or so, the use of financial instruments by companies and the complexity of those instruments have increased remarkably. Many large companies now actively manage their risk using swaps, forward contracts and other such derivatives, but until recently the financial statements of such companies often gave very limited disclosure of the use of these techniques.

6.2 There have been a number of examples of what were perceived to be conservatively-managed organisations incurring substantial losses because they failed to appreciate, monitor and control the risks created by the use of financial instruments. Such problems gave financial instruments, and in particular derivatives, a reputation for increasing risk when in fact many are designed specifically to reduce or eliminate exposure to risk and achieve this when used properly.

6.3 At the heart of these well-publicised losses were internal control failures. One of the responses of this has been a call for tighter accounting rules to be set for financial instruments.

6.4 Under UK GAAP there has been, until recently, no recognition and measurement standard for financial instruments, contrasting with both US GAAP and IFRS. IAS 39, 'Financial instruments: Recognition and measurement', introduced a partial fair value measurement model under IFRS for accounting periods beginning on or after 1 January 2001. IAS 39 permits hedge accounting in certain circumstances. FAS 133, the US equivalent, includes similar rules to IAS 39.

6.5 In the UK, in February 1996, the British Bankers' Association (BBA) and the Irish Bankers' Federation (IBF) jointly issued a SORP setting out recommendations for the accounting treatment and disclosure of derivatives in the financial statements of banks, but until recently there was no UK equivalent to IAS 39 or FAS 133.

6.6 FRS 13, 'Derivatives and other financial instruments: disclosures', was published in September 1998 and applied primarily to listed companies and banks.

6.7 FRS 13 requires entities within its scope to provide both narrative and numerical disclosures. The narrative disclosures describe the role that financial instruments (including derivatives and certain commodity contracts) have in creating or changing the risks faced by an entity, including its objectives and policies in using financial instruments to manage those risks. The numerical disclosures are intended to show how those objectives and policies were implemented in the period and provide supplementary information for evaluating significant or potentially significant exposures. Together these disclosures should provide a broad overview of the entity's financial instruments and of the risk positions created by them, focussing on the risks and instruments that are of greatest significance.

6.8 Additional guidance is available to the issuer of capital instruments (a sub-set of financial instruments) in FRS 4, 'Capital instruments', which regulates how capital instruments should be classified and presented in the financial statements of the issuing entity.

6.9 In December 2004 the ASB published, as part of a suite of new accounting standards, FRS 25, 'Financial instruments: Disclosure and presentation', and FRS 26, 'Financial instruments: Measurement'. These standards brought most of the requirements of IAS 32 and IAS 39, respectively, into UK GAAP. FRS 4 was also amended. The new standards represented the most significant development in the UK accounting for financial instruments for a number of years. FRS 26 was amended in October 2005 to reflect a series of amendments to IAS 39 and was amended again in April 2006 to include IAS 39's recognition and derecognition requirements. At that time the title of the standard changed to FRS 26, 'Financial Instruments: Recognition and Measurement'.

6.9.1 The ASB published FRS 29, 'Financial Instruments: Disclosures', in December 2005 (see para 6.406.5). The standard largely replicates the requirements of the equivalent international standard, IFRS 7, and locates in one place all of the disclosures relating to financial instruments. Once applied, the standard replaces the disclosure requirements of FRS 25 and also FRS 13.

6.10 The required application date of the new standards will depend on the type of entity and, to some extent, the nature of its business and the way it accounts for that business. The rules are complex and are explained in detail in this chapter. The question of which entities should be applying which standards and when, is further complicated by the decision that some entities will need to take of whether or not to transition to IFRS. Reporting under IFRS will be a requirement for the group financial statements of listed entities, but the individual entities within those groups will have the choice of UK GAAP or IFRS for their own financial statements. See chapter 2 for guidance on this issue.

6.11 As FRS 26 is based on IAS 39, it similarly introduces a partial fair value measurement model for financial instruments. Until recently, measuring financial instruments at fair value had not been permitted by the Companies Act. For companies other than those preparing financial statements under Schedules 9 or 9A to the Companies Act 1985 (that is, banks and insurance companies), a true and fair override has been required where it was felt that only by fair valuing certain financial instruments was it possible to present a true and fair view of a company's performance and financial position (for example, when energy companies entered into speculative energy derivative contracts for trading purposes).

6.12 Hence, for UK companies to be able to apply the requirements of FRS 26, changes to the Companies Act were required. SI 2004/2947, 'The Companies Act 1985 (International Accounting Standards and Other Accounting Amendments) Regulations 2004', came into effect for accounting periods commencing on or after 1 January 2005. Amongst other changes, the amendment permits companies to apply fair value accounting to some of their financial instruments, provided that fair value can be determined reliably. This legislative change will reduce the need for a true and fair override when entities apply the fair value rules of FRS 26. However, an override may still be required in certain circumstances, as described in paragraph 6.83.

6.13 There have also been recent changes to the law regarding the ability of an entity to acquire its own shares. The Companies Act was amended in 2003 to permit entities with *'qualifying shares'* to purchase such shares out of distributable profits and hold them in treasury for resale, transfer or cancellation at a later date. The accounting for treasury shares is considered in chapter 23.

6.13.1 This chapter deals with the provisions of FRS 13, FRS 4 and the requirements under the Companies Act that apply to all companies in respect of financial instruments and investments. The chapter also covers FRS 25, FRS 26 and FRS 29. However, as these standards are replicas of the international standards on financial instruments (IAS 32, IAS 39 and IFRS 7), the guidance is primarily dealt with in Annex 3 to this chapter. Annex 1 includes examples of the disclosures required by FRS 13 and Annex 2 includes two flow charts that summarise the scope and effective dates relating to FRS 25 and FRS 26.

How to use this chapter

6.14 Due to the extent of the recent changes to UK GAAP in the area of financial instruments and the complexity of the transition rules it is difficult to prepare a coherent, cohesive guidance document that addresses all the issues. There is the old world of FRS 4 and FRS 13 and the new world of FRS 25, FRS 26 and FRS 29. The guidance will be different depending on when an entity transitions from the old to the new.

6.15 In order to ensure that the appropriate guidance in this chapter is being followed, the following steps should be taken:

Step 1 – Identify whether or not the entity transacts in financial instruments

Refer to paragraph 6.18 for the FRS 13 definition of a financial instrument and Annex 3 for the FRS 25 (IAS 32) equivalent. It is important to determine whether or not any financial instruments identified are specifically excluded from the standards.

Step 2 – Determine which standards need to be applied by the entity

Use the section entitled 'How the standards apply under UK GAAP', (see from para 6.26) to determine whether or not, in any particular period, the entity will be applying FRS 4 and FRS 13, or FRS 25, FRS 26 and FRS 29. Note that this section does not specifically address the standards' scope themselves. It simply provides guidance in determining which standards may apply.

Step 3 – Apply the guidance that is applicable to all entities

The section entitled 'Requirements that apply to all entities', (see from para 6.55) provides an explanation of the presentation requirements of FRS 25 and the Companies Act requirements that will apply to all UK GAAP reporting entities for accounting periods beginning on or after 1 January 2005.

Step 4 – Apply the relevant guidance depending on the result of step 2

The section entitled 'Requirements for entities not applying FRS 26', (see from para 6.154) describes the requirements of FRS 4 and FRS 13 whilst Annex 3 to the chapter describes the requirements of FRS 25, FRS 26 and FRS 29 by reference to the equivalent paragraphs of IAS 32, IAS 39 and IFRS 7. It is important to pay particular attention to the scope sections of this guidance to determine whether or not the entity is specifically excluded from the standards.

Step 5 – Review the transitional guidance for any standards that are being applied for the first time

Guidance on the exemptions that are available when the standards are applied for the first time is provided in the section entitled 'Transitional guidance', (see from para 6.391).

Step 6 – Read the chapter on financial instruments from the Manual of Accounting – IFRS for the UK

FRS 25, FRS 26 and FRS 29 replicate most of the requirements of IAS 32, IAS 39 and IFRS 7. Those standards are considered in detail in the Manual of Accounting – IFRS for the UK and chapter 6 of that book is attached as Annex 3 to this chapter.

Step 7 – Review the proposed future amendments

The section entitled 'Future developments', (see from para 6.407) explains the proposed changes to the new standards and hence may impact the entity when it does apply the standards.

What is a financial instrument?

6.16 As highlighted in the introduction to this chapter there are now a number of UK standards covering the accounting for financial instruments. This presents a problem, as each of the standards has its own scope, definitions and exclusions. Fortunately, the basic definition of a financial instrument is similar in FRS 13 and FRS 25.

6.17 The FRS 25 definition of a financial instrument is identical to the IAS 32 definition, which is explained in full in Annex 3 to this chapter. The FRS 13 definition of a financial instrument is explained below.

6.18 FRS 13 defines a financial instrument as *"... any contract that gives rise to both a financial asset of one entity and a financial liability or equity instrument of another entity "*. [FRS 13 para 2]. Definitions are also given for a financial asset, financial liability and an equity instrument:

- A financial asset is cash, or any asset that is a contractual right to receive cash or another financial asset from another entity, or a contractual right to exchange financial instruments with another entity under conditions that are potentially favourable, or an equity instrument of another entity.
- A financial liability is any liability that is a contractual obligation to deliver cash or another financial asset to another entity, or to exchange financial instruments with another entity under conditions that are potentially unfavourable.
- An equity instrument is an instrument that evidences an ownership interest in an entity after deducting all of its liabilities. This has a wider meaning than equity shares, because it includes some non-equity shares, as well as warrants and options to subscribe for or purchase equity shares in the issuing entity.

[FRS 13 para 2].

6.19 Examples of financial instruments, financial assets and financial liabilities include:

- Cash, including foreign currency.
- Deposits, debtors, creditors, notes, loans, bonds and debentures.
- Finance lease obligations.
- Shares, options and warrants.
- Derivatives that are to be settled in cash or by another financial instrument (that is, commodity contracts are generally excluded, but see para 6.176).
- Contingent liabilities that arise from contracts and, if they crystallise, are to be settled in cash (for example, a financial guarantee).
- Certain provisions, for example, for onerous leasehold commitments or warranties that involve a contractual obligation to pay compensation. [FRS 13, App II para 15].

6.20 Non-equity minority interests should be treated as financial liabilities for the purposes of FRS 13's disclosures (see para 6.184).

Contracts and contractual rights

6.21 The references to 'contract', 'contractual right' and 'contractual obligation' are fundamental to the definition of a financial instrument, financial asset and financial liability. Consequently, assets and liabilities that are not contractual in nature are not financial assets or financial liabilities. Hence, tax liabilities that arise from statutory requirements imposed by governments, and not from contracts, are not financial liabilities. Although a contract must have clear economic consequences that the parties have little, if any, discretion to avoid and is usually enforceable in law, it does not necessarily need to be in writing and may take a variety of forms. Thus financial assets and financial liabilities may take a variety of forms.

6.22 It is important to consider the different rights and obligations that arise under contracts and how these may change, or be added to, as the contract is performed, because some of these rights and obligations may fall within the definition of a financial instrument. For example, a purchase order for a piece of plant and machinery is not a financial instrument as the right and obligations are for the exchange of a financial asset (cash) for a physical asset (the piece of plant and machinery). However, under the same contract, once the physical asset has been delivered, the purchaser will owe the vendor the purchase price. This creditor will be a financial liability.

6.23 'Contractual rights' and 'contractual obligations' encompass rights and obligations that are contingent upon future events. An example of contingent rights and obligations are those arising under a financial guarantee since the guarantor has a liability (the contractual obligation to pay the lender if the borrower defaults) and the lender has an asset (the contractual right to receive cash from the guarantor if the borrower defaults).

6.24 Trade debtors and creditors and bonds and debentures held or issued are common examples of financial assets representing a contractual right to receive cash in the future and corresponding financial liabilities representing a contractual obligation to deliver cash in the future. Each of the examples is a financial instrument, because one party's contractual right to receive (or obligation to pay) cash is matched by the other party's equal and opposite obligation to pay (or right to receive) cash.

FRS 13 exclusions and scope

6.25 FRS 13 includes a number of exclusions for particular items that appear to fit the definition of a financial instrument but are outside the scope of the standard. In addition, the standard does not apply to all UK GAAP reporting entities. These exclusions are explained in detail in from paragraph 6.155.

How the standards apply under UK GAAP

Introduction

6.26 This section provides guidance on determining which elements of UK GAAP should be applied to which type of entity and from when. In order to eliminate some of the practical difficulties of transition to the new standards, a phased approach has been designed. There is little doubt that this phased transition will reduce some of the immediate hardship for those affected, but the downside is that the scope and application guidance has itself become complex.

6.27 There are currently six principal elements of UK GAAP for financial instruments:

- The Companies Act 1985, in particular the amendments to the Act introduced by SI 2004/2947, 'The Companies Act (International Accounting Standards and Other Accounting Amendments) Regulations 2004'.
- FRS 4, 'Capital instruments'.
- FRS 13, 'Derivatives and other financial instruments: disclosures'.
- FRS 25, 'Financial instruments: Disclosure and presentation'.
- FRS 26, 'Financial instruments: Measurement'.
- FRS 29, 'Financial instruments: Disclosure'.

6.28 For accounting periods beginning on or after 1 January 2005, all entities must apply the Companies Act disclosure requirements and FRS 25's presentation requirements. Companies must then determine whether they should apply FRS 25 in full combined with FRS 26, or FRS 4 combined with FRS 13 (where applicable). Those entities that apply FRS 26 must also apply FRS 29 in accounting periods beginning on or after 1 January 2007.

6.29 The standards that apply depend on the entity's status, in particular whether it is:

- listed;
- listed on a non-regulated market (see para 6.42);
- unlisted; or
- unlisted, but applying the Companies Act fair value accounting rules.

6.30 Listed companies must apply FRS 25 and the measurement requirements of FRS 26 for all accounting periods beginning on or after 1 January 2005. Companies listed on non-regulated markets, for example, AIM, must apply FRS 4, FRS 13 and the presentation requirements of FRS 25 (provided they do not apply Companies Act fair value accounting rules). Unlisted companies must apply FRS 4 and the presentation requirements of FRS 25 (see also para 6.40).

Unlisted companies that are applying the Companies Act fair value accounting rules have to apply FRS 25 and the measurement requirements of FRS 26 for accounting periods beginning on or after 1 January 2006. In accounting periods beginning on or after 1 January 2007, those entities that apply FRS 26 must apply that standard in full (that is, including the recognition and derecognition requirements) as well as FRS 29. At this time FRS 13 and the disclosure requirements of FRS 25 are superseded. Early application of FRS 29 is encouraged and entities that are not applying FRS 26 are encouraged to comply with the disclosure requirements in the standard, adapting them in line with the entity's accounting policies. These application dates are summarised in the table below.

	Accounting periods beginning on or after 1 January		
	2006	**2007**	**2008**
Listed and applying UK GAAP	FRS 25 and 263	FRS 25, 26 and 29	FRS 25, 26 and 29
Listed on a non-regulated market	FRS 41, 131 and 252	Will depend4	Will depend4
Unlisted (or listed on a non-regulated market) and applying fair value accounting rules	FRS 25 and 263	FRS 25 and 26 and 29	FRS 25, 26 and 29
Other unlisted (See also para 6.40)	FRS 4 and 252	FRS 4 and 252	FRS 4 and 252

1 Early application of FRS 25 and FRS 26 is encouraged for entities within the standards' scope, in which case FRS 4 and FRS 13 will not apply. Similarly early application of FRS 29 is encouraged for all entities in which case FRS 25 disclosures do not apply.
2 Only the presentation requirements in FRS 25 apply.
3 Only the measurement requirements in FRS 26 apply.
4 It will depend on the market on which the entity is listed. For example, entities listed on AIM have to apply IFRS to their consolidated financial statements from the 1 January 2007. Their separate financial statements can be prepared under IFRS or UK GAAP If they are prepared under UK GAAP then they do not meet the definition of a listed entity in FRS 26 and therefore do not mandatorily apply it. If they do not apply Companies Act fair value accounting rules then they can continue to apply FRS 4 and FRS 13.

6.30.1 Two detailed scope and application flow charts to FRS 25 and FRS 26 are included in the appendix to this chapter. The charts are reference guides that present all the key scope and application criteria for the two standards and represent a graphical illustration of the information provided below.

[The next paragraph is 6.31.]

Companies Act requirements

6.31 SI 2004/2947, 'The Companies Act 1985 (International Accounting Standards and other Accounting Amendments) Regulations 2004', amends UK company law in a number of ways, primarily to facilitate the transition to IFRS for UK companies. Of the amendments in the Statutory Instrument, the changes that are relevant to accounting for financial instruments are as follows:

- It permits companies to fair value some of their financial instruments, investment property and living plants and animals. Companies that have derivatives that are not included at fair value will be required to disclose the nature and fair value of those derivatives (see paras 6.79 and 6.101.1).
- It requires companies to classify as liabilities any preference shares that are obligations (see from para 6.89).
- It inserts additional disclosure requirements into the directors' report in relation to the use of financial instruments (see from para 6.151).

6.32 These amendments came into effect for all UK GAAP reporters for accounting periods beginning on or after 1 January 2005.

6.32.1 The above requirements will be replaced by the Companies Act 2006 and the new rules for fair value accounting, presentation and disclosure of financial instruments will be effective from the 6 April 2008. Although the requirements for disclosure and classification will not change significantly, the new Act will permit more items to be fair valued than is currently permitted.

FRS 4 — Capital instruments

6.33 For accounting periods beginning on or after 1 January 2005, FRS 25 substantially amends FRS 4 to remove the concept of non-equity shares, as all capital instruments must now be classified as either equity or liabilities.

6.34 The amended version of FRS 4 will only be applied by companies that are not applying FRS 26. FRS 4 will not apply at all to entities that are applying FRS 26. Refer to paragraph 6.288 for more detailed guidance.

FRS 13 — Derivatives and other financial instruments

6.35 FRS 13 is the existing UK disclosure standard for financial instruments. It will apply to all entities within its scope until they apply the disclosure requirements of FRS 25 or FRS 29 for the first time, when it will cease to apply. Refer to paragraph 6.155 for more detailed guidance.

FRS 25 — Financial instruments: Disclosure and presentation

6.36 The publication of FRS 25 brings the requirements of IAS 32 into UK GAAP. It is important to note that the provisions of FRS 25 are split between presentation and disclosure requirements, with different implementation criteria for each.

6.37 The *presentation* requirements of FRS 25 apply to all entities in accounting periods beginning on or after 1 January 2005.

6.38 The *disclosure* requirements apply no later than the accounting period in which the entity first applies FRS 26 (see para 6.40). Earlier adoption is encouraged, but only permitted for accounting periods beginning on or after 1 January 2005.

6.38.1 FRS 29 will replace FRS 25's disclosure requirements for accounting periods commencing on or after 1 January 2007.

[The next paragraph is 6.39.]

FRS 26 — Financial instruments: Recognition and measurement

6.39 The ASB issued FRS 26 in December 2004 and is applicable to all listed entities (not using IFRS in their individual accounts) for accounting periods beginning on or after 1 January 2005. Originally the standard only dealt with the measurement requirements of IAS 39 so that the guidance on recognition and derecognition in FRS 5, 'Reporting the substance of transactions', remained in UK GAAP. The standard was amended in April 2006 to bring IAS 39's recognition and derecognition requirements into FRS 26 with effect from 1 January 2007 (see para 6.386 onwards). These recognition and derecogntion rules only apply to entities that have adopted FRS 26. For entities not applying FRS 26, FRS 5's guidance on recognition and derecognition continues to apply.

6.40 FRS 26 does not apply to unlisted entities, unless they are applying the Companies Act fair value accounting rules (see para 6.79), in which case FRS 26 applies for accounting periods beginning on or after 1 January 2006 (also see example 3 in paragraph 6.54). Entities that are not within the scope (that is, those that are unlisted and do not apply the fair value accounting rules), may voluntarily adopt FRS 26 (and the other related standards, including FRS 23), as indicated in the ASB's preface to FRS 26. However, such a policy to voluntarily adopt FRS 26 and its related standards would need to be the most appropriate to an entity's particular circumstances for the purpose of giving a true and fair view. [FRS 18 para 17]. Further guidance on selection of accounting policies is given in chapter 2.

6.41 Unlisted entities that fair value assets without the use of the new fair value accounting rules (for example, banks that mark-to-market their transferable securities under the Schedule 9 historical cost accounting rules (see para 6.52)) need not apply FRS 26.

FRS 29 — Financial instruments: Disclosures

6.41.1 FRS 29 was published in December 2005. It largely replicates the requirements of the equivalent international standard, IFRS 7, and locates in one place all of the disclosures relating to financial instruments.

6.41.2 All entities applying FRS 26 must apply FRS 29 in accounting periods commencing on or after 1 January 2007. Exemptions are given and these are detailed in paragraph 6.406.3. Early adoption is encouraged. Once applied, the standard supersedes FRS 13 and also the disclosure requirements of FRS 25.

Listed companies

6.42 A listed entity is defined in paragraph 9A of FRS 26 as an entity that has in issue debt, shares, or other financial or similar instruments that are traded on a regulated market of any EU Member State. A regulated market is defined in Article 1(13) of Council Directive 93/22/EEC of 10 May 1993 on investment services in the securities field. Primarily, listed entities include entities listed on the London Stock Exchange (LSE), but not those that are quoted on the Alternative Investment Market (AIM).

6.43 The FRS 26 definition of listed is similar to that which determines whether or not an entity falls within FRS 13's scope, with two crucial differences.

6.44 When FRS 26 refers to a listed entity it is by reference to the status of the individual entity that has any of its securities traded on a regulated market of a EU Member State. FRS 26 does not refer to a reporting entity. Consequently, FRS 26 only applies to the single entity financial statements of the listed entity and to that entity's consolidated financial statements. The listed status of other constituent parts of an entity's group is irrelevant in determining whether the entity's consolidated financial statements have to comply with FRS 26.

Example

Company A is an unlisted parent of a group of companies and is registered in the UK. Company A does not apply the Companies Act fair value accounting rules. Company A has a UK subsidiary B, which has issued debt on the London Stock Exchange. The consolidated financial statements of company A do not fall within FRS 26's scope (and neither do company A's individual financial statements) as company A is not listed and does not apply the fair value accounting rules. However, subsidiary B is required to apply FRS 26 within its own financial statements as it has listed debt in issue.

6.45 The principle described in the previous paragraph are in contrast to FRS 13, which refers to a listed entity as *"a reporting entity that has any of its capital instruments listed or publicly traded on a stock exchange or market"* and is thus a much broader definition. Hence, in a set of consolidated financial statements, it is the group which is the reporting entity and, therefore, those financial statements have to comply with FRS 13 if any constituent part of the group has listed or traded capital instruments.

6.46 A further difference arises from the fact that the Alternative Investment Market (AIM) ceased to be a regulated market in November 2004. Hence, AIM companies are not caught by FRS 26, but remain within the scope of FRS 13 with its broader application rules.

6.47 Note that it is an entity's status at the balance sheet date that is critical for determining which standards will apply. Hence, a company that de-lists during an accounting period will be treated as unlisted for the purpose of determining whether or not FRS 26 will apply.

New fair value accounting rules

6.48 As explained above, unlisted entities that apply the Companies Act fair value accounting rules must apply FRS 26 for accounting periods beginning on or after 1 January 2006. The ASB has given these companies an additional year to prepare for the application of the new standards, in recognition of the fact that generally they have less advanced and sophisticated accounting functions than their listed counterparts.

6.49 The fair value accounting rules are those introduced by SI 2004/2947. An entity prepares its financial statements in accordance with the fair value accounting rules if it applies an accounting policy (whether written or not) that measures financial instruments at fair value through profit and loss account and this policy is not explicitly permitted by the historical cost accounting rules or the alternative accounting rules set out in Schedule 4 to the Act (or equivalents in other schedules as appropriate). [FRS 26 para 1B].

6.50 It can be difficult to determine whether or not a company prepares its financial statements in accordance with the fair value accounting rules, particularly if the company is a bank or insurance company that prepares its financial statements under Schedule 9 or Schedule 9A. These difficulties are considered from paragraph 6.52.

6.51 A Schedule 4 company that has in the past used a true and fair override in order to 'mark-to-market' and thus recognise resulting gains and losses through the profit and loss account will fall within FRS 26's scope for accounting periods beginning on or after 1 January 2006, as that policy is not explicitly permitted by either the historical cost accounting rules or the alternative accounting rules. From 1 January 2005 a true and fair override is no longer required in these circumstances as the treatment is now permitted.

Banks and insurance companies

6.52 There may be circumstances where an unlisted UK bank or insurance company is using a form of fair value accounting, but does not fall within FRS 26's scope. Schedule 9 to the Companies Act permits banks to measure transferable securities at market value and similarly Schedule 9A permits insurance companies to record their debt securities at current value as part of a historical cost accounting model. An entity applying these provisions within the Act does not, therefore, need to apply the new fair value accounting rules to continue to fair value these instruments.

6.53 It has been argued that Schedules 9 and 9A implicitly also allow derivatives to be fair valued and so in the past, it has not been necessary for banks and insurance companies to invoke a true and fair override to fair value their derivatives. However, implicit permission is insufficient to meet FRS 26's requirement for an explicit permission to be stated in law. [FRS 26 para 1B]. Hence, entities that fair value derivatives fall within FRS 26's scope.

Practical examples

6.54 The following examples illustrate some the issues that can arise when determining whether or when an entity will need to apply the new accounting standards.

Example 1

Entity E is a parent of a listed group that is preparing its consolidated financial statements in accordance with IFRS under the EU Regulations. The parent company wishes to continue to use UK GAAP in its individual accounts. Although the parent can continue to use UK GAAP, this does not mean that the parent can avoid applying both FRS 25 and FRS 26. This is because the parent entity itself is listed and hence both of these standards apply. Note that FRS 26's recognition and derecognition requirements do not apply until accounting periods commencing on or after 1 January 2007. Note also that the entity is exempt from applying FRS 29 in accounting periods beginning on or after 1 January 2007 as the consolidated financial statements should be prepared in accordance with IFRS 7 and, hence, will provide disclosures that comply with FRS 29.

Example 2

Entity A is an investment management company with no subsidiaries that is listed on the London Stock Exchange. Entity A has a 31 December year end and as a stand-alone entity is not caught by the requirement to report under IFRS. Although adopting IFRS is still an option, management wishes to avoid the complexities of IAS 32 and IAS 39 and has decided to continue reporting under UK GAAP.

As a listed entity, entity A will be within the scope of both FRS 25 and FRS 26 for the year ending 31 December 2005 and 31 December 2006.

In the year ending 31 December 2007, entity A must apply FRS 29 and once applied the disclosure requirements of FRS 25 are superseded.

Example 3

Entity B, with a December year end, de-listed from the London Stock Exchange in July 2005. Entity B trades in equity investments, both for clients and on a proprietary basis, and in the past has revalued any investments held at the balance sheet date, with movements in value being taken to the profit and loss account. This policy required a true and fair override of the Companies Act.

For the purposes of determining when the new standards should apply, it is the status of the entity at the end of the accounting period that matters. Hence, for the December 2005 accounting period, entity B is deemed to be unlisted for this purpose. However, entity B will be using the Companies Act fair value accounting rules if it maintains its current accounting policy for trading investments and will no longer need a true and fair override. It will need to comply with both FRS 25 and FRS 26's measurement requirements for the first time in the year ending December 2006 and will need to apply the presentation requirements of FRS 25 for its December 2005 accounting period. FRS 26's recognition and derecognition requirements will apply in the year ending 31 December 2007. In terms of disclosures it will need to apply FRS 25 requirements for the year ending December 2006 which will then be superceded by FRS 29 requirements in the year ending 31 December 2007. (Exemptions are given for FRS 29 disclosures and are detailed in paragraph 6.406.6).

Example 4

Entity C is a medium-sized unlisted manufacturing company with a December year end. The majority of business is transacted with UK suppliers and customers. However, there are a small number of overseas suppliers with which entity C trades. On occasion, entity C enters into forward foreign exchange contracts to reduce the risk of adverse movements in exchange rates on future purchases. Entity C has no fair value accounting policies and the forward exchange contracts are 'off-balance sheet'.

The presentation requirements of FRS 25 will need to be applied for the December 2005 year end. The finance director believes that the company can apply FRS 26 at the same time. The company can voluntarily adopt FRS 26 if it is deemed the most appropriate standard (see para 6.40). However, if it chooses to do so it will have to account for the forward contracts in accordance with FRS 26 and they will be recognised on the balance sheet. In addition the disclosure requirements of FRS 25 have to be applied from the date FRS 26 is applied , that is for the December 2005 year end and December 2006 year end. These will then be superceded by disclosure requirements in FRS 29 for the year ending 31 December 2007. (Exemptions are given for FRS 29 disclosures and are detailed in paragraph 6.406.6).

The company could also consider changing its accounting policy for the forward foreign exchange contracts to one of fair value accounting. This would require the use of the Companies Act fair value accounting rules and would automatically bring the entity within FRS 26's scope. Early application of the standard would then be permitted in the December 2005 year end. As a result, in the year ending 31 December 2007 the entity would be required to apply FRS 29.

Example 5

Entity D is a bank that applies Schedule 9 to the Companies Act. Entity D trades in equity securities on behalf of itself and its clients and has always applied a mark-to-market accounting policy for these investments. Management wishes to avoid the difficulties of the new UK accounting standards.

Entity D is permitted to fair value these particular transferable securities by the provisions of Schedule 9 and, hence, does not need to apply the Companies Act fair value accounting rules. As a result, although the FRS 25 presentation requirements will be mandatory from 2005, entity D does not need to apply either FRS 25's disclosure requirements, FRS 26 or FRS 29.

Requirements that apply to all entities

Introduction

6.55 There are two sources of UK GAAP relating to financial instruments that are relevant to all entities, whether they are applying FRS 4 and FRS 13 or FRS 25 and FRS 26. The requirements of the Companies Act are explained below. In addition, the presentation requirements of FRS 25 are applicable to all

UK reporting entities for accounting periods commencing on or after 1 January 2005. The presentation requirements of FRS 25 are the same as those of IAS 32 and are explained in Annex 3 to this chapter.

6.56 There are extensive requirements relating to the accounting for investments in the Companies Act. In particular, a significant amount of disclosure is required. Not all financial instruments are investments and not all investments are within the financial instruments standards' scope, but there is a significant overlap of items that are both financial instruments and investments. These items are within the scope of the financial instruments guidance, and also have to comply with the Companies Act requirements for investments.

Definition of investments

6.57 The Act does not provide a formal definition of investments although the model formats for the balance sheet include a heading for 'investments' under the general heading of both 'fixed assets' and 'current assets'. Moreover, there are separate sub-headings for investments under both the fixed and the current categories:

- The sub-headings identified for fixed asset investments are:
  - Shares in group undertakings.
  - Loans to group undertakings.
  - Participating interests.
  - Loans to undertakings in which the company has a participating interest.
  - Other investments other than loans.
  - Other loans.
  - Own shares.
- The sub-headings identified for current asset investments are:
  - Shares in group undertakings.
  - Own shares.
  - Other investments.

6.58 While there is no specific UK accounting standard in place dealing with the subject of investments, ED 55, 'Accounting for investments', issued by the ASC in 1990 defined an investment in general terms as "*...an asset that is characterised by its ability to generate economic benefits in the form of distributions and/or appreciation in value*". This definition is relatively broad and should cover all types of investments, such as:

- Shares.
- Debentures.
- Interest-bearing securities.
- Loan stock.
- Bonds and other debt instruments.
- Warrants and options.
- Commodities (other than those to be used in the enterprise's activities).
- Futures contracts.
- Rights to subscribe for any of these.

6.59 ED 55 also provided a negative definition as well as a positive definition of an investment. It stated that an investment is not an asset that the enterprise holds with a view to realising future benefits through its use, such as plant and equipment, land or buildings, or intangible assets, such as, patents or brands. However, where such assets are held solely with a view to profit through appreciation, that is, they are not used to generate profit through the activities of the enterprise, then they may also be deemed to be investments. Although stock held in connection with the business activities of an enterprise is not generally considered to be an investment, those enterprises that hold investments of the type listed in paragraph 6.58 as part of their businesses would generally be expected to account for them using the normal rules for investments and this was also envisaged in ED 55. ED 55 did, however, specifically exclude investment properties from its scope since these were already governed by SSAP 19. The accounting for such properties is considered in chapter 17.

6.60 There are a number of items that whilst appearing to satisfy the definition of a financial instrument are specifically excluded from the scope of FRS 13, FRS 25, FRS 26 and FRS 29. For example, interests in subsidiaries, associates and joint ventures are outside of the scope of the financial instruments standards. Much of the Companies Act guidance covered in this section is applicable to all investments including those that are scoped out of the financial instruments standards.

Classification

6.61 Under the Act, a company can treat investments in its balance sheet as either fixed asset investments or current asset investments depending on how it intends to use them. A company's investments that are "*...intended for use on a continuing basis in the company's activities*" should be classified as fixed assets in the company's financial statements. Generally, investments should be classified as fixed where the company intends to hold them for the long-term and this intention can clearly be demonstrated. Furthermore, such a situation might arise where the company's ability to dispose of an investment is restricted for a particular reason. If a company's investments do not fall within the category described above and are, therefore, not considered to be fixed asset investments, they will fall to be classified as current asset investments.

6.62 Whether a company intends to use an investment on a continuing basis (that is, hold it for the long-term) will often be obvious from the nature of the investment. Treatment as a fixed asset might also arise where there are practical restrictions on an investor's ability to dispose of the investment. Fixed asset investments will, therefore, comprise:

- Equity shareholdings in, or loan to, subsidiaries and associates.
- Investments arising from other trading relationships.
- Investments that either cannot be disposed of or cannot be disposed of without a significant effect on the operations of the investing company.
- Investments that are intended to be held for use on a continuing basis by investing companies whose objective is to hold a portfolio of investments to provide income and/or capital growth for their members.

[ED 55 para 24].

6.63 It should be remembered, however, that the mere fact that an investment has been held for a long time does not necessarily make it a long-term asset, unless it also falls within one of the categories indicated in paragraph 6.62.

Measurement rules

6.64 The paragraphs below consider the Act's measurement rules that apply to investments and, hence, apply to financial instruments that meet the definition of investments. Historically, such investments could either be recorded in the financial statements in accordance with the Act's historical cost accounting rules or its alternative accounting rules, which allow such assets to be recognised in the financial statements at a valuation. SI 2004/2947 added a third possibility measuring financial instruments in order to permit the fair value accounting required by both IAS 39 and FRS 26.

6.65 How these rules apply to all assets (including investments) is considered in detail in chapter 16 and is summarised in the paragraphs that follow. When determining the amount at which an investment should be recognised in the financial statements, each individual investment should be considered separately. [CA85 4 Sch 14]. This means that a 'portfolio' basis of valuation (that is, treating a number of investments as a single asset) cannot be used for an investment portfolio; each investment has to be considered separately.

Fixed asset investments

Historical cost accounting rules

6.66 Under the Act's historical cost accounting rules, fixed asset investments, like other fixed assets, are required to be recognised in the financial statements at their purchase price or production cost. [CA85 4 Sch 18]. Clearly, production cost is not relevant for fixed asset investments and hence they should be recorded at their purchase price. Where a fixed asset investment has diminished in value the diminution may be provided for in the profit and loss account, thereby reducing the investment to its recoverable amount. [CA85 4 Sch 19(1)]. Where the diminution in value is expected to be permanent, it must be recognised. [CA85 4 Sch 19(2)]. Therefore, in a similar way for other fixed assets, permanent diminutions in value must be taken to the profit and loss account, but also temporary diminutions in value of fixed asset investments (which would include market value fluctuations) can also be charged to the profit and loss account.

6.67 Where a diminution in value of a fixed asset investment has been charged to the profit and loss account, but the circumstances giving rise to the diminution have reversed to any extent (for example, the investment's market value has increased) the provision should be written back to the extent that it is no longer necessary. Any amounts of this nature written back should be shown in the profit and loss account or disclosed, either separately or in aggregate, in the notes. [CA85 4 Sch 19(3)].

6.68 FRS 11, 'Impairment of fixed assets and goodwill', scopes out investments that fall within FRS 13's scope. [FRS 11 para 6]. Investments other than subsidiaries, associates and joint ventures are within FRS 13's scope and so FRS 11's impairment provisions do not apply to these. [FRS 13 para 5]. However, FRS 11 does apply to investments in subsidiaries, associates and joint ventures. FRS 11's requirements are considered in chapter 18.

Alternative accounting rules

6.69 Under the Act's alternative accounting rules, fixed asset investments can be included in the balance sheet at either:

- their market value determined as at the date of their last valuation; or
- at a value determined on any basis that appears to the directors to be appropriate in the company's circumstances.

[CA85 4 Sch 31(3)].

Where a directors' valuation is used, the particulars of the method of valuation adopted and the reasons for adopting it must be disclosed in the notes to the financial statements.

6.70 Where the alternative accounting rules have been applied, the amount of any profit (or loss) arising on the revaluation must be credited to (or debited to) the revaluation reserve. Then the normal rules regarding the use of that reserve apply. Slightly different rules apply to investment companies (as defined in section 266 of the Act) who are allowed to take revaluation gains and losses to another reserve other than the revaluation reserve. In addition, they are allowed to take permanent diminutions in the value of fixed asset investments to that same reserve, whereas other companies have to take such losses to the profit and loss account.

6.71 The market value to be used where there is a quoted price for the investment would normally be the middle market price (that is the average of the bid and offer prices). But, where a company holds marketable securities of another company and the size and nature of the holding is such that the market is not capable of absorbing a sale of the investment without a material effect on its quoted price, the current market price may not be indicative of the true market value of the investment. In this type of situation, the market price should generally be adjusted to reflect the proceeds that the enterprise could realistically expect to raise by disposing of the holding in the ordinary course of business.

6.72 In certain situations, a holding of a size sufficient to affect market price, if sold, may not always be indicated by a large percentage ownership of shares. For example, where only a portion of the total is actively traded, a much smaller percentage holding could affect the market price significantly. Where this is so, the investment should normally be valued at the amount that could be raised if it was disposed of in smaller tranches, taking into account, for example, the higher transaction costs.

6.73 There may, however, be situations where an investor controls, say, five per cent of a very large enterprise. In this situation, the market price may be higher than the quoted price, because the quoted price usually reflects the trading of much smaller tranches of shares. Indeed, there may be a premium attached to such an influential stake. In this case, the quoted price would be lower than 'market' and should normally be used for valuation purposes. This would be required because any 'premium' price would not be attainable on short notice.

6.74 Where an investment is not quoted, the directors may still wish to record the investment at a value in the financial statements. As mentioned above, it is acceptable under the Act for them to carry out their own valuation as long as the disclosures set out in paragraph 6.69 are complied with. There are a number of valuation techniques that can be applied in these circumstances. One of the common approaches is to find a similar listed company to the unquoted company to be valued and apply the listed company's PE ratio to the unquoted company's earnings to arrive at a price. The valuation of unquoted investment is of great importance to certain industries, particularly the investment trust industry. Some investment trusts specialise in making high risk venture capital investments (often in management buyouts) and the British Venture Capital Association issued some guidelines in November 1993 of the valuation and disclosure of venture capital portfolios.

6.75 The rules and techniques for valuing investments that apply under the Act's alternative accounting rules are the same as those that apply when an investment is acquired as part of the acquisition of a subsidiary. The rules for fair valuing investments on such an acquisition are considered in chapter 25.

Current asset investments

Historical cost accounting rules

6.76 Current asset investments are required under the Act to be recorded at the lower of cost and net realisable value. [CA85 4 Sch 22, 23]. Therefore, where a current asset investment's net realisable value is lower that its cost an amount should be provided in the profit and loss account for the diminution in value. Where the reason for making the provision has ceased to apply to any extent, the provision should be written back through the profit and loss account to that extent. [CA85 4 Sch 23].

Alternative accounting rules

6.77 Under the Act's alternative accounting rules, current asset investments may be included in the balance sheet at their current cost. Current cost is, in effect, the value to the business of the asset and for current asset investments will often be the investment's market value, unless the investment is unquoted, when the directors can determine its value. In a same way as the rule applies for fixed asset investments, any profit or loss arising from the valuation of current asset investments must be credited or debited to the revaluation reserve. [CA85 4 Sch 34].

6.78 The rules concerning the market value to be attributed to current asset investments are the same as the rules discussed for fixed asset investments in paragraphs 6.59 and 6.60 above.

Fair value accounting rules

6.79 Schedule 4 to the Companies Act has not previously permitted the 'marking to market' or fair valuing of investments with any resulting gains or losses being recognised in the profit and loss account. Entities that report under IFRS for accounting periods beginning on or after 1 January 2005 need to apply IAS 39 and one of the fundamental requirements of that standard is that certain financial instruments are measured at fair value with movements being taken to the income statement. In addition, UK GAAP reporters that are within FRS 26's scope will need to apply the same guidance to certain financial instruments. Hence there was an urgent requirement to amend the Companies Act to permit the fair valuing of certain specific financial instruments. This need was addressed in November 2004 with the publication of The Companies Act 1985 (International

Accounting Standards and Other Accounting Amendments) Regulations 2004 (SI 2004/2947).

6.80 SI 2004/2947 amends UK company law in a number of ways, primarily to facilitate the transition to IFRS for UK companies. The Regulations insert a new paragraph into Schedule 4 to deal with the fair value option for companies preparing 'Companies Act financial statements'. The accounting standards (in particular FRS 26) determine whether, and to what extent, fair valuing should or can be used. Under the Regulations:

- *All sizes and types* of company are permitted (but not required) to apply fair value accounting to some of their financial instruments.
- Fair value accounting may be adopted in both *individual and consolidated* financial statements.
- Additional disclosure requirements are introduced, regardless of whether fair value accounting is adopted.

Measuring financial instruments at fair value

6.81 The Act now permits certain financial instruments, including derivative financial instruments, to be included at fair value, provided that fair value can be determined reliably. [CA85 4 Sch 34A]. 'Fair value' is determined as follows:

- If a reliable market can readily be identified for the financial instrument, its fair value is determined by reference to its market value.
- If a reliable market cannot readily be identified for the financial instrument but can be identified for its components or for a similar instrument, its fair value is determined by reference to the market value of its components or of the similar instrument.
- If neither of the above apply, the financial instrument's fair value is a value resulting from generally accepted valuation models and techniques. Any valuation models and techniques used must ensure a reasonable approximation to the market value.

[CA85 4 Sch 34B].

6.82 The following financial instruments may not be fair valued:

- Liabilities (except those held as part of a trading portfolio and derivatives).
- Non-derivative financial instruments held to maturity.
- Loans and receivables originated by the company and not held for trading purposes.
- Interests in subsidiary undertakings, associated undertakings and joint ventures.

- Equity instruments issued by the company.
- Contracts for contingent consideration in a business combination.
- Other financial instruments with such special characteristics that the instruments, according to generally accepted accounting principles or practice, should be accounted for differently from other financial instruments.

[CA85 4 Sch 34A(2),(3)].

6.83 Although financial liabilities should not be fair valued under the Act (except as stated above), it is envisaged that there may be circumstances in which an entity's financial statements will not present a true and fair view if certain financial liabilities are not fair valued, for example where artificial volatility could be created in the financial statements. The ASB considered this issue and in the notes accompanying FRS 26 concluded that, in such circumstances, the entity should use the true and fair override in order to measure these liabilities at fair value. The use of a true and fair override must always be justified by the particular circumstances of the entity in question, but the ASB envisages that:

- If the override is to be applied there would need to be potential for substantial artificial volatility to arise otherwise. 'Artificial volatility', in this context means that the financial statements show volatility that would not be present were the financial liabilities concerned measured at fair value through profit or loss like the financial assets they are managed with. The ASB believes that the *potential* for volatility, rather than the existence of actual volatility, is important in order to ensure that consistency in accounting practice from year to year is achieved.
- It would not generally be appropriate to apply the override if the result would be the recognition in the profit and loss account of a substantial gain arising from a fall in the fair value of financial liabilities caused by a deterioration in the entity's own credit standing.

[FRS 26 para N19].

6.84 'Hedge accounting' is permitted in-so-far as, *"a company may include any assets and liabilities that qualify as hedged items under a fair value hedge accounting system, or identified portions of such assets and liabilities, at the amount required under that system"*. [CA85 4 Sch 34C]. However, neither 'financial instruments' nor 'hedge accounting' are defined by the Act. This is deliberate as these terms are defined in accounting standards where the definitions can be kept up to date. However, 'derivative financial instruments' are stated to include *"commodity-based contracts that give either contracting party the right to settle in cash or some other financial instrument, except when such contracts —*

(a) were entered into for the purpose of, and continue to meet, the company's expected purchase, sale or usage requirements;

(b) were designated for such purpose at their inception; and

(c) are expected to be settled by delivery of the commodity."

[CA85 4 Sch 76A].

Changes in fair value

6.85 Where fair value accounting is adopted, changes in fair value must be included in the profit and loss account. [CA85 4 Sch 34E(2)]. This is subject to the following exceptions:

- Any change in value *must* be included in a separate fair value reserve:
  - where the financial instrument accounted for is a hedging instrument under a hedge accounting system that allows some or all of the change in value not to be shown in the profit and loss account; or
  - where the change in value relates to an exchange difference arising on a monetary item that forms part of the company's net investment in a foreign entity.
- Any change in value *may* be included in a separate fair value reserve where the financial instrument accounted for is an available-for-sale financial asset and is not a derivative.

[CA85 4 Sch 34E(3),(4)].

Marking to market

6.86 Historically, businesses in a number of segments, have applied a policy of 'marking to market' their current asset investments. This approach, commonly used by market makers and other dealers in investments and commodities, results in such investments being carried at market value with changes in that market value being included in the profit or loss for the period.

6.87 Whilst the alternative accounting rules do permit this balance sheet treatment, they would require any movement in the market value to be treated as a revaluation surplus or deficit and taken to the revaluation reserve, rather than being dealt with in the profit and loss account. Hence, in the past, marking to market has involved a departure from the Companies Act requirements and so it was necessary to invoke a true and fair override under section 226(5) in order to take movements in market value to the profit and loss account.

6.88 With the change to the Companies Act now permitting certain financial instruments to be measured at fair value with movements being taken to the profit and loss account, many of these entities will no longer need to invoke a true and fair override under section 226(5). However, care will be required to ensure that those instruments subject to fair value accounting are not specifically excluded from the permissions in SI 2004/2947 (see para 6.81).

Presentation

6.89 A further change to the Companies Act was required to enable entities to comply with FRS 25's presentation requirements. SI 2004/2947 inserted the following provision into Schedule 4:

> *"The directors of the company must, in determining how amounts are presented within items in the profit and loss account and balance sheet shall have regard to the substance of the reported transaction or arrangement in accordance with generally accepted accounting principles or practice."*

[CA85 4 Sch 5A].

6.90 This is intended to enable convergence of UK accounting standards with EU-adopted IFRS. IAS 32 and FRS 25 require that certain preference shares are shown as liabilities and related preference dividends are shown as interest. Similarly, the debt and equity components of financial instruments must be separated and each element shown as liabilities or equity, as appropriate. Without this change in company law, such a presentation would not be legal in the UK. Determining whether preference shares should be treated as equity or as a liability in accordance with FRS 25 and IAS 32 is considered further in Annex 3 to this chapter.

Disclosure requirements

Introduction

6.91 The Act contains extensive disclosure requirements for financial instruments. Any entity that has investments that are caught by the definition of a financial instrument will need to make these disclosures.

6.92 As noted in paragraph 6.31, SI 2004/2947 introduced additional financial instrument disclosure requirements, applicable to all companies along side the disclosures required by FRS 13 or FRS 25 (if appropriate). The extent of the disclosures differs depending on whether or not the entity is applying fair value accounting to any of its financial instruments. Where fair value accounting is applied, it is important that the reader understands, at a high level, how the fair values are determined. Hence there is a requirement to disclose, for example, the assumptions underlying the valuation models. Where no financial instruments are fair valued (typically for an entity that is yet to apply FRS 26), there are requirements for certain fair values to be disclosed.

6.93 Set out below are the disclosure requirements for all investments under the Companies Act for entities not required to prepare group accounts. The disclosure requirements for entities preparing group accounts are given in chapter 24. The disclosures required by SI 2004/2947 in relation to financial instruments are described from paragraph 6.101.1.

All investments

6.94 As mentioned above, a company can treat its investments in its balance sheet as either fixed asset investments or current asset investments depending on how it intends to use them. The model formats for the balance sheet include a heading for 'Investments' under the general heading of both 'Fixed assets' and 'Current assets'. Moreover, there are separate sub-headings for investments under both the fixed and the current categories.

6.95 For each of the sub-headings of fixed asset investments, a company has to disclose the information required for other fixed assets under Schedule 4 paragraphs 42(1)(2). These include disclosure of the aggregate amount of that item at both the beginning and the end of the financial year and certain other information about the purchase and sale of those investments.

6.96 In addition, Schedule 4 paragraph 42(3) requires details to be disclosed about any provisions made in respect of each fixed asset investment category.

6.97 Furthermore, the Act requires the notes to the financial statements to include certain information about any listed investments a company holds (irrespective of whether these are shown as fixed assets or as current assets). In particular, the notes must disclose:

- The total amount that relates to all listed investments.
- The aggregate market value of listed investments where it differs from the amount at which they are stated in the balance sheet.
- Both the market value and the stock exchange value of any listed investments must be disclosed, where the former value is taken as being higher than their stock exchange value. This disclosure is required because the market value and the stock exchange value may differ according to the size of the investment and its marketability. For example, a controlling stake could be worth proportionately more than a minority interest in a company, because stock exchange prices traditionally reflect the values of small parcels of shares.

[CA85 4 Sch 45(1)(2)].

6.98 For this purpose, a 'listed investment' means any investment that is listed either on a 'recognised investment exchange' other than an overseas investment exchange within the meaning of the Financial Services and Markets Act 2000 or on any stock exchange of repute outside Great Britain. [CA85 4 Sch 84]. All other investments are to be regarded as unlisted and no additional information is required to be disclosed for these investments. A 'recognised investment exchange' is defined in section 285 of the Financial Services and Markets Act 2000 as an investment exchange in relation to which a recognition order is in force. Currently, the only bodies designated in Great Britain as recognised investment exchanges are:

- London Stock Exchange (the Stock Exchange).
- London International Financial Futures and Options Exchange (LIFFE)
- ICE Futures.
- EDX London.
- London Metal Exchange (LME).
- PLUS Markets Plc
- VIRT-X Exchange.

6.99 There is no definition of 'stock exchange of repute' in the Act. In practice, whether a stock exchange outside Great Britain is reputable or not will depend both on its status in its own country and on the circumstances surrounding its operation.

6.100 The disclosure requirements for *listed* investments outlined above are best illustrated by an example:

Example

Details of investments held:

	Co	Balance sheet value £'000	Market value £'000	Stock exchange value £'000
Listed on the London Stock Exchange (a recognised investment exchange)	A	100	250	300
	B	150	110	110
	C	130	150	125
	D	75	25	20
		455	535	555
Listed on the New York Stock Exchange (a stock exchange of repute outside Great Britain)	E	190	200	225
	F	65	110	100
	G	15	25	25
		270	335	350
Traded on AIM		30	70	75
Total of investments		755	940	980

This disclosure may be summarised in the notes to the financial statements as follows:

Listed investments	**£'000**
Balance sheet value	725
Market value	870

The amounts shown above include certain investments for which the market value is considered to be higher than the stock exchange value. The market value of these investments is £285,000 and their stock exchange value is £245,000.

Listed investments include certain investments for which the market value is considered to be higher than the stock exchange value. The market value of these investments is £285,000 (that is £150,000 + £25,000 + £110,000) and their stock exchange value is £245,000 (that is £215,000 + £20,000 + £100,000). The investment in the company traded on AIM has been excluded from this disclosure as companies traded in this way are not listed investments.

6.101 In Table 6.1, Lonrho Plc provides an analysis for 'other' fixed asset investments.

Table 6.1 — Lonrho Plc — Annual Report and Accounts — 30 September 1994

Notes to the Accounts (extract)

20. Other investments - fixed assets

Group	**Investments**	**Loans**	**Provisions**	**Total**
	£m	**£m**	**£m**	**£m**
At 30 September 1993	26	3	(12)	17
Additions/advances	1	2		3
Disposals/repayments	(1)	(1)		(2)
Provisions			(3)	(3)
Transfers		(1)		(1)
At 30 September 1994	**26**	**3**	**(15)**	**14**

Net book value of investments shown above:-

	1994	**1993**
	£m	**£m**
Listed — on the London Stock Exchange	1	1
— on overseas stock exchanges	2	2
Unlisted	8	11
	11	14
Value at 30 September:		
Listed (market value)	11	8
Unlisted (Directors' valuation)	28	28

Company	**Investments**	**Provisions**	**Total**
	£m	**£m**	**£m**
Cost:			
At 30 September 1993 and 1994	10	(8)	2

Net book value of investments shown above:-

	1994	**1993**
	£m	**£m**
Listed — on the London Stock Exchange	1	1
Unlisted	1	1
	2	2
Value at 30 September:		
Listed (market value)	1	1
Unlisted (Directors' valuation)	1	1

6.101.1 In accounting periods beginning on or after 1 January 2005, companies have the option to adopt the fair value accounting rules in the Companies Act. Companies adopting fair value accounting must disclose:

- The significant assumptions underlying the valuation models and techniques used.
- For each category of financial instrument, the fair value of the instruments in that category and the amounts:
  - included in the profit and loss account; or
  - credited to or debited from the fair value reserve,

  in respect of instruments in that category.
- For each class of derivative financial instruments, the extent and nature of the instruments, including significant terms and conditions that may affect the amount, timing and certainty of future cash flows.
- Where any amount is transferred to or from the fair value reserve during the financial year, there shall be stated in tabular form:
  - the amount of the reserve as at the beginning of the financial year and as at the balance sheet date;
  - the amount transferred to or from the reserve during that year; and
  - the source and application respectively of the amounts so transferred.

[CA85 4 Sch 45A].

6.101.2 Companies that elect not to adopt fair value accounting for certain financial instruments must give additional disclosures relating to their derivative financial instruments. The following disclosure is required for each class of derivative financial instrument:

- the fair value of the derivatives in that class, if such a value can be determined as described in paragraph 6.81; and
- the extent and nature of the derivatives.

[CA85 4 Sch 45B].

6.101.3 These disclosures were introduced for financial years beginning on or after 1 January 2005 and must be given by all companies that apply Schedule 4, 9 or 9A of the Companies Act 1985 irrespective of whether the company applies FRS 26 or the fair value accounting rules. Schedule 8 of the Companies Act does not have similar requirements and so small companies are exempted from these disclosures.

6.101.4 In addition, where:

- a company has financial fixed assets that could be included at fair value;
- the amount at which those assets are included in the financial statements is in excess of their fair value; and

- the company has not made provision for diminution in value of those assets.

the following disclosure must be made:

- The amount at which either the individual assets or appropriate groupings of those individual assets is stated in the company's financial statements.
- The fair value of those assets or groupings.
- The reasons for not making a provision for diminution in value of those assets, including the nature of the evidence that provides the basis for the belief that the amount at which they are stated in the financial statements will be recovered.

[CA85 4 Sch 45C].

6.101.5 Regardless of whether a company adopts fair value accounting, it must give the following information in the directors' report (unless such information is not material):

- The financial risk management objectives and policies of the company and its consolidated subsidiaries, including the policy for hedging each major type of forecasted transaction for which hedge accounting is used.
- The exposure of the company and its consolidated subsidiaries to price risk, credit risk, liquidity risk and cash flow risk.

[CA85 7 Sch 5A].

6.101.6 It is likely that there will be some degree of duplication between the required Companies Act financial instrument disclosures and those required by either FRS 13 or FRS 25. Management will need to consider how the information is to be presented clearly, while ensuring that all the required disclosures are made.

6.101.7 The Act is silent on the subject of comparatives for the fair value disclosures. The normal rules should therefore be applied, so companies will be required to give comparative information for all items. [FRS 28 para 10(a)].

Companies Act disclosure requirements

Companies adopting fair value accounting

6.101.8 From accounting periods beginning on or after 1 January 2005, companies have the option to adopt the fair value accounting rules in the Companies Act. Companies adopting fair value accounting must disclose:

- The significant assumptions underlying the valuation models and techniques used.

Financial instruments including derivatives

- For each category of financial instrument, the fair value of the instruments in that category and the amounts:
  - included in the profit and loss account; or
  - credited to or debited from the fair value reserve,

  in respect of instruments in that category.
- For each class of derivative financial instruments, the extent and nature of the instruments, including significant terms and conditions that may affect the amount, timing and certainty of future cash flows.
- Where any amount is transferred to or from the fair value reserve during the financial year, there shall be stated in tabular form:
  - the amount of the reserve as at the beginning of the financial year and as at the balance sheet date;
  - the amount transferred to or from the reserve during that year; and
  - the source and application respectively of the amounts so transferred.

[CA85 4 Sch 45A].

Companies not adopting fair value accounting

6.101.9 Companies that elect not to adopt fair value accounting for certain financial instruments must give additional disclosures relating to their derivative financial instruments. The following disclosure is required for each class of derivative financial instrument:

- the fair value of the derivatives in that class, if such a value can be determined as described in paragraph 6.81; and
- the extent and nature of the derivatives.

[CA85 4 Sch 45B].

6.101.10 These disclosures were introduced for financial years beginning on or after 1 January 2005 and must be given by all companies that apply Schedule 4, 9 or 9A of the Companies Act 1985 irrespective of whether the company applies FRS 26 or the fair value accounting rules. Schedule 8 of the Companies Act does not have similar requirements and so small companies are exempted from these disclosures.

6.101.11 An example of the Companies Act disclosures under the fair value accounting rules is given below.

Example

XYZ is a limited company incorporated in the UK with a year end of 31 December 2006. The company sells computers in the UK and overseas and generates some of its revenue in

US dollars. It hedges its exposure to foreign currency fluctuations by entering into forward contracts to buy sterling and sell dollars at a future date.

What disclosures does the company need to make in the financial statements if:

(a) the company does not adopt fair value accounting for these forward contracts; and

(b) the company adopts fair value accounting as permitted by the Companies Act 1985?

(The company for the purposes of part (b) also has an available for sale (AFS) investment of 5% in G plc which was bought in December 2000 for £500,000.)

Note that the Companies Act also requires the directors' report to include;

- financial risk management objectives and policies of the company and its consolidated subsidiaries including the policy for hedging each major type of forecasted transaction for which hedge accounting is used; and
- the exposure of the company and its consolidated subsidiaries to price risk, credit risk, liquidity risk and cash flow risk.

These disclosures have been discussed further in the 'Manual of Accounting – Management reports and governance', and have not been included here.

Additionally any disclosures relating to FRS 25 and FRS 26 have not been considered here.

Company does not adopt fair value accounting

Notes to the accounts

The company's local currency is pounds sterling but approximately one quarter of its sales are to customers in the United States. These sales are denominated in US dollars. As a result, the company is subject to foreign currency exchange risk due to exchange rate movements between pounds sterling and US dollars. The company seeks to reduce this risk by entering into forward contracts.

The company has forward contracts with the following fair values at the end of the year.

	2006	2005
	£'000	£'000
Fair value of forward contracts	5,000	6,000

B Company adopts fair value accounting

Notes to the financial statements

Fair value gains and losses

The company's local currency is pounds sterling but approximately one quarter of its sales are to customers in the United States. These sales are denominated in US dollars. As a result, the company is subject to foreign currency exchange risk due to exchange rate movements between pounds sterling and US dollars. The company seeks to reduce this risk by entering into forward contracts which are fair valued with gains and losses recorded in the income statement.

Included in profit for the year are the following gains/ (losses) relating to changes in fair values of the forward contracts

	2006	2005
	£'000	£'000
Forward contracts	100	(250)

Debtors

	2006	2005
	£'000	£'000
Trade debtors	1,500	1,400
Other debtors	600	900
Derivatives – forward contracts	50	–

Available for sale investments

	2006	2005
	£'000	£'000
Investment in G plc	1,000	1,200

Fair value reserve

	2006	2005
	£'000	£'000
At 1 January	700	1,000
Fair value loss in the period	(200)	(300)
At 31 December	500	700

6.101.12 In addition, where:

- a company has financial fixed assets that could be included at fair value;
- the amount at which those assets are included in the financial statements is in excess of their fair value; and
- the company has not made provision for diminution in value of those assets.

the following disclosure must be made:

- The amount at which either the individual assets or appropriate groupings of those individual assets is stated in the company's financial statements.
- The fair value of those assets or groupings.
- The reasons for not making a provision for diminution in value of those assets, including the nature of the evidence that provides the basis for the belief that the amount at which they are stated in the financial statements will be recovered.

[CA85 4 Sch 45C].

Directors' report

6.101.13 Regardless of whether a company adopts fair value accounting, it must give the following information in the directors' report (unless such information is not material):

- The financial risk management objectives and policies of the company and its consolidated subsidiaries, including the policy for hedging each major type of forecasted transaction for which hedge accounting is used.

- The exposure of the company and its consolidated subsidiaries to price risk, credit risk, liquidity risk and cash flow risk.

[CA85 7 Sch 5A].

6.101.14 It is likely that there will be some degree of duplication between the required Companies Act financial instrument disclosures and those required by either FRS 13 or FRS 25. Management will need to consider how the information is to be presented clearly, while ensuring that all the required disclosures are made.

Comparatives

6.101.15 The Act is silent on the subject of comparatives for the fair value disclosures. The normal rules should therefore be applied, so companies will be required to give comparative information for all items. [FRS 28 para 10(a)].

Significant holdings greater than 20 per cent

6.102 Where a company at the end of its financial year has a 'significant holding' of shares of any class in another undertaking, other than a subsidiary undertaking, the Act requires the company to disclose certain information. [CA85 5 Sch 7].

6.103 For this purpose, a significant holding is a holding of 20 per cent or more of the nominal value of any class of shares in an undertaking, or a holding the carrying amount of which exceeds one fifth of the company's assets as stated in its balance sheet. [CA85 5 Sch 7(2)]. Reference to 'shares' means:

- The allotted shares in relation to an undertaking that has a share capital.

- The rights to share in the capital of an undertaking which has capital, but has no share capital. This would apply to partnerships.

- Interests that confer any right to share in the profits, or liability to contribute to the losses, of the undertaking, or that give rise to an obligation to contribute to the debts or expenses of the undertaking in the event of it being wound up. This includes most other undertakings that are not bodies corporate or partnerships.

[CA85 Sec 259(2), CA06 Sec 1161(2)].

6.104 In interpreting the Act's disclosure requirements, shares held on behalf of the company by any other person should be attributed to the company and shares held by the company on behalf of another person should not be attributed to the company. Furthermore, shares held by a company (company A) by way of security should be treated as held by the company providing them as security (company B), where both of the following conditions apply:

- The rights attached to the shares (other than the right to exercise them for the purpose of preserving the security or of realising it) are exercisable only in accordance with the instructions of company B.
- Where the shares are held in connection with the granting of loans as part of normal business activities, those rights (other than the right to exercise them for the purpose of preserving the security or of realising it) are exercisable only in the interests of company B.

[CA85 5 Sch 13(3)(4)].

6.105 Where a company has significant holdings, the notes to the financial statements must disclose in respect of each such undertaking:

- Its name.
- Its country of incorporation, where it is incorporated outside Great Britain.
- If it is unincorporated, the address of its principal place of business.
- The identity of each class of shares the investing company holds.
- The proportion of the nominal value of the shares of each class that the investing company holds.

[CA85 5 Sch 8].

6.106 In addition, the following information should be given:

- The aggregate amount of the capital and reserves of the undertaking at the end of its relevant financial year.
- The profit or the loss of that undertaking as disclosed by those financial statements.

[CA85 5 Sch 9(1)].

The 'relevant financial year' is the financial year ending on or before the investing company's balance sheet date. [CA85 5 Sch 9(5)].

6.107 British Aerospace Public Limited Company included more than the minimum information about the results of its investment in Hutchison Telecommunications (UK) Limited (see Table 6.2).

Table 6.2 — British Aerospace Public Limited Company — Annual Report — 31 December 1994
Notes to the accounts (extract)

13 Fixed Assets — Investments (extract)
Included within investments of the Group and Company is a 30% interest in the ordinary share capital of Hutchison Telecommunications (UK) Limited, a company registered in England and Wales; the remaining shares are controlled by Hutchison Whampoa Limited (65%) and Barclays Bank PLC (5%). In view of this shareholding structure the investment is not accounted for as an associated undertaking. The latest published consolidated accounts available for Hutchison Telecommunications (UK) Limited are for the year ended 31st December, 1993 and show an aggregate deficit on capital and reserves of £325 million and a retained loss for the year of £240 million. This loss is stated after charging exceptional costs of £182 million relating to withdrawal of the public telepoint service, write down of goodwill relating to the cellular services division, provision for mobile data development costs and provision for other restructuring costs. During 1994, the Company replaced guarantees with interest bearing shareholder loans of £247 million to Hutchison Telecommunications (UK) Limited. These loans are included within the above addition to loans.

Exemptions from disclosure

6.108 Except as described below, where any of the information required by Schedule 5 relates to either an undertaking that is established under the law of a country outside the UK or an undertaking that carries on its business outside the UK, and the directors believe that disclosure would be seriously prejudicial to the business of that undertaking or to the business of the company or any of its subsidiary undertakings, and the company has obtained the Secretary of State's agreement, that information need not be disclosed. [CA85 Sec 231(3), CA06 Sec 409(3) and (4)]. Where advantage is taken of this exemption, this must be stated in the notes to the financial statements. [CA85 Sec 231(4), CA06 Sec 409(5)]. Exemption is not available in respect of disclosures regarding shares in a company held by its subsidiary undertakings (see para 6.142) or membership of a qualifying undertaking (see from para 6.132).

6.109 Where a company has a significant number of investments such that, in the directors' opinion, compliance with the requirements of Schedule 5 would result in disclosure of excessive length, information need only be given in respect of those undertakings whose results or financial position principally affect the figures shown in the company's financial statements. [CA85 Sec 231(5), CA06 Sec 410(1) and (2)]]. Where advantage is taken of this exemption, this must be stated in the notes to the financial statements. [CA85 Sec 231(6)(a), CA06 Sec 410(3)]. In addition, the full information (including both the information that is disclosed in the notes to the financial statements and the information that is not) must be annexed to the company's next annual return. [CA85 Sec 231(6)(b), CA06 Sec 410(3)]. Failure to do so will result in the company and any officer of it who is in default being liable to a fine. [CA85 Sec 231(7), CA06 Sec 410(4) and (5)].

6.110 The section 231(4) statement that the 'seriously prejudicial' exemption has been taken is required to be given irrespective of whether the group has taken advantage of the exemption in section 231(5) described above. Under section 231(5) the full information for all subsidiaries must be annexed to the company's next annual return, but where the secretary of state has granted exemption under section 231(3), this need not include the information regarding the subsidiary excluded on seriously prejudicial grounds.

6.111 The information described in paragraph 6.106 need not be given if it is immaterial. Furthermore, it need not be given in either of the following two situations where:

- The company is exempt by virtue of section 228 from the requirement to prepare consolidated financial statements (see chapter 24). But for this exemption to apply, the company's investment in all such undertakings must be shown, in aggregate, in the notes to the company's financial statements by way of the equity method of valuation (that is, by stating the company's share of the undertaking's net assets).

- The company's investment is in an undertaking that is not required by any of the Act's provisions to deliver a copy of its balance sheet to the Registrar of Companies and it does not otherwise publish that balance sheet in Great Britain or elsewhere. Where this situation exists, the information need not be given, provided the company's holding is less than 50 per cent of the nominal value of the shares in the undertaking.

[CA85 5 Sch 9(2)(3)].

Participating interests

6.112 'Participating interest' is defined in section 260(1) of the Act as "...*an interest held by an undertaking in the shares of another undertaking which it holds on a long-term basis for the purpose of securing a contribution to its activities by the exercise of control or influence arising from or related to that interest*". The term was introduced by the Companies Act 1989 and derives from a category of investments that the Companies Act 1981 introduced as 'shares in related companies'. The term 'related companies' was removed by the Companies Act 1989. In its place the Act now refers to 'undertakings in which the company has a participating interest'.

6.113 A holding of 20 per cent or more of the shares of an undertaking is presumed to be a participating interest, unless the contrary is shown. With regard to the presentation specified in paragraph 6.115 below, a participating interest does not include an interest in a subsidiary undertaking. It will, however, include associates and joint ventures as defined in both the Act and FRS 9.

6.114 The term 'associated undertaking' is defined in the Act for consolidated financial statements purposes. Consequently, this term does not appear in any of the balance sheet formats of an individual company. Therefore, where an investing company that is not required to prepare consolidated financial statements holds 20 per cent or more of the shares, whether voting or non-voting, in another undertaking, that investment will generally be shown as a 'participating interest' in the company's balance sheet. Participating interests will include associates and joint ventures as defined in FRS 9. If, however, the company is included in the consolidated financial statements of a larger group, in the group's consolidated balance sheet, any holding of 20 per cent or more of the voting shares in an undertaking (that is, in an associate or a joint venture) will be shown under the sub-headings 'interests in associated undertakings' or 'interests in joint ventures' as appropriate, and any holding of 20 per cent or more of the non-voting shares in an undertaking will be shown under the sub-heading 'other participating interests'.

6.115 'Participating interests' and 'loans to undertakings in which the company has a participating interest' appear as separate sub-headings under the fixed asset main heading of 'investments' in both balance sheet formats. Also, both balance sheet formats require the presentation of 'amounts owed by undertakings in which the company has a participating interest' under 'debtors' and the 'amounts owed to undertakings in which the company has a participating interest' under 'creditors'. In addition, 'amounts owed by and to undertakings in which the company has a participating interest' that are due for payment within one year must be shown separately from amounts due after one year. [Notes 5 and 13 to the balance sheet formats]. Paragraph 55 of FRS 9 additionally requires that these balances are analysed into amounts relating to loans and amounts relating to trading balances. These format requirements effectively prohibit companies from showing participating interests and investments in associates and joint ventures as a single net figure including the cost of the shares in the undertakings, loans to them and after deducting loans from them.

Associates, joint ventures and other joint arrangements

6.116 As stated in paragraph 6.113 above, participating interests include investments in associates and joint ventures. Investments in associates and joint ventures should be shown in the investing company's own financial statements as follows:

- Income from associates and joint ventures should be shown as dividends received and receivable.
- Unless it is shown at a valuation, the amount at which the investing company's interests in associates and joint ventures should be shown is the cost of the investment less any amounts written off. [FRS 9 paras 20, 26].

The treatment of an investing group's interests in associates and joint ventures is covered in chapter 27.

6.117 If the investing company does not prepare consolidated financial statements then it will only report its own profit and loss account and balance sheet. The only income that can properly be included in that profit and loss account will be dividends received from the associate or joint venture. Inclusion of dividends rather than share of earnings is necessary because of the Act's requirement that only realised profits can be included in a company's profit and loss account. For this reason FRS 9 requires that a company should show its share of its associate's or joint venture's results and net assets by presenting a separate proforma profit and loss account in addition to its own profit and loss account. Alternatively, the company could add the information in supplementary form to its own profit and loss account in such a way that its share of the associate's or joint venture's profits is not treated as realised for the purposes of the Act, as illustrated below. [FRS 9 para 48].

Example

The supplementary information could be included on the face of the profit and loss account or in the notes to the company's financial statements.

Company profit and loss account			
		Proforma information	
(All figures relate to continuing activities)	**Company**	**Joint ventures & Associates**	**Total**
	£'000	**£'000**	**£'000**
Turnover	200	120	320
Cost of sales	120		
Gross profit	80		
Administrative expenses	40		
Operating profit	40	54	94
Interest	(20)	(22)	(42)
Profit on ordinary activities before tax	20	32	52
Tax on profit on ordinary activities	5	7	12
Profit for the financial year	15	25	30
Equity dividends	4		4
Retained profit for the year	11		26

6.118 Similarly, as the company's balance sheet will carry the investment at cost less amounts written off, FRS 9 requires that a separate proforma balance sheet should be given in which the associate or joint venture is presented on the equity method of accounting. Alternatively, the information could be added in supplementary form to the company's own balance sheet as illustrated below. [FRS 9 para 48].

Example

Company balance sheet		*Proforma information*
	Company	**Company including associates & joint ventures**
	£'000	**£'000**
Fixed assets		
Tangible assets	898	898
Investments:		
Company	238	
Joint ventures:		
Share or gross assets		2,359
Share of gross liabilities		1,448
		911
Associates		67
Other investments		82
		1,060
	1,136	1,958
Current assets		
Stocks	321	321
Debtors: amounts falling due after one year	10	10
Debtors: amounts falling due within one year	229	229
Cash at bank and in hand	43	43
	603	603
Creditors: amounts falling due within one year	520	520
Net current assets	83	83
Total assets less current liabilities	1,219	2,041
Creditors: amounts falling due after more than one year	647	647
Borrowings and other creditors	35	35
Provisions for liabilities and charges	204	204
	886	886
Net assets	333	1,155
Capital and reserves		
Called up share capital	200	
Share premium account	500	
Profit and loss account	(367)	
Total shareholders' funds—all equity	333	

6.119 In order to comply with FRS 9, it would also be necessary for the proforma information concerning joint ventures and associates to be further analysed in the notes between amounts relating to joint ventures and amounts relating to associates. It is also necessary to give additional information concerning the company's share of items appearing in the joint venture's or associate's statement of total recognised gains and losses and cash flow statement. Furthermore, FRS 9 requires more detailed information to be given for associates and joint ventures in aggregate and individually where they are particularly material to the company. These issues are considered further in chapter 27.

6.120 The disclosures described in paragraphs 6.117 to 6.119 above need not be given where the investing company is exempt from preparing consolidated financial statements, or would be exempt, if it had subsidiaries. [FRS 9 para 48]. However, the information described in paragraph 6.106 must still be given, unless advantage is taken of the exemptions described from paragraph 6.108.

6.121 FRS 9 also deals with the accounting requirements that apply to joint arrangements that are not entities and to structures with the form, but not the substance of, a joint venture. For both of these types of joint arrangements, the standard requires that the investing company should account in its individual financial statements for its share or part of the assets, liabilities and cash flows stemming from the arrangement. [FRS 9 paras 18, 24]. The accounting requirements explained above for associates and joint ventures do not apply to these types of joint arrangements. Such joint arrangements and their accounting requirements are considered in detail in chapter 27.

Subsidiary undertakings

6.122 Where, at the end of a financial year, a company does not prepare consolidated financial statements, but has subsidiary undertakings, the investing company's financial statements have to disclose the information outlined in paragraph 6.105 above for each of its subsidiary undertakings. [CA85 5 Sch 1, 2(1)].

6.123 In presenting this information, interests include not only those held by the company itself, but also those held by its subsidiaries. Consequently, the identity and proportion of the shares in each class that the investing company and its subsidiaries hold in a subsidiary undertaking has to be shown, distinguishing between those held by the company itself and those held by any of its subsidiaries. [CA85 5 Sch 2(2)].

6.124 The Act also requires the company to state the reasons for not preparing consolidated financial statements. [CA85 5 Sch 1(4)]. If the reason why the company is not required to prepare consolidated financial statements is that its subsidiary undertakings fall within the exclusions from consolidation provided for in section 229, the reason for exclusion should be stated for each subsidiary undertaking. [CA85 5 Sch 1(5)]. Section 229 exclusions are covered in detail in chapter 24.

6.125 Except where one of the conditions below is satisfied, the information outlined in paragraph 6.106 above must also be given for each subsidiary. [CA85 5 Sch 3(1)].

- The company is exempt by virtue of section 228 from the requirement to prepare consolidated financial statements (see chapter 24). [CA85

5 Sch 3(2)]. Section 228A extended the exemption from the requirement to prepare consolidated accounts to companies with a parent outside the EEA but Schedule 5 has not been amended to take account of this extension, therefore, companies claiming the section 228A exemption are required to give the information outlined in paragraph 6.106 above.

- The company's investment is included in its financial statements using the equity method of valuation. [CA85 5 Sch 3(2A) inserted by SI 1996/189].
- The company's investment is in a subsidiary undertaking that is not required by any of the Act's provisions to deliver a copy of its balance sheet to the Registrar of Companies and it does not otherwise publish that balance sheet in Great Britain or elsewhere. Where this situation exists, the information need not be given, provided the company's holding is less than 50 per cent of the nominal value of the shares in the undertaking. [CA85 5 Sch 3(3)].
- The information to be disclosed is not material. [CA85 5 Sch 3(4)].

6.126 Directors are under an obligation to ensure that the financial years of the group's subsidiaries coincide with that of the parent, unless there are good reasons for a subsidiary's year end to be different. But where the financial year of a subsidiary undertaking does not coincide with that of the company and the company is not exempt from the giving the information set out in paragraph 6.106 above the notes to the company's financial statements must disclose the date on which the subsidiary's last financial year ended. [CA85 5 Sch 4].

6.127 The company need not give any of the above information required by Schedule 5 where either of the exemptions described in paragraphs 6.108 and 6.109 are taken. The exemption described in paragraph 6.111 is not available as it is replaced in the case of investments in subsidiaries by the exemption described in paragraph 6.125.

6.128 The balance sheet formats specify locations for amounts owed by and to and interests in group undertakings. Hence, it is not acceptable for companies to net these balances off and to disclose the net balance, together with the cost of the investments, in the balance sheet as 'Investments in subsidiaries'. Such offset is also precluded by FRS 5 paragraph 29 and FRS 25 paragraph 42. This applies even where a note to the financial statements gives additional information that explains the net balance.

6.129 Moreover, the amounts owed and owing have to be ascertained on an undertaking by undertaking basis. [CA85 4 Sch 5]. Consequently, for accounting presentation purposes, amounts that one subsidiary owes to the parent cannot be offset against amounts the parent owes to another subsidiary. Set-off can be allowed only where the offset criteria in FRS 5 and FRS 25 are met (see further chapter 3).

6.130 Furthermore, undertakings have to analyse 'amounts owed by (and to) group undertakings' between amounts that will fall due within one year and amounts that will fall due after more than one year. [Notes 5 and 13 on the balance sheet formats]. The results of this analysis will largely depend both on the way in which group undertakings are financed and on the terms of any agreements between the undertakings.

Parent company information

6.131 Where, at the end of a financial year, a company is a subsidiary of another undertaking, certain information concerning the name and country of incorporation, etc, should be disclosed with respect to the company (if any) regarded by the directors as the company's ultimate parent company. In addition, similar information relating to potentially two further parent undertakings in the same group may have to be disclosed where the ultimate parent company does not prepare consolidated financial statements. The rules concerning these disclosures are complex and are considered in detail in chapter 24 in relation to companies that are required to prepare consolidated financial statements (that is, those covered by Part II of Schedule 5 to the Act). Furthermore, these rules apply in the same way to companies that are not required to prepare consolidated financial statements (that is, those covered by Part I of Schedule 5 to the Act) as the legislation is duplicated in paragraphs 11 and 12 of Schedule 5.

Membership of a qualifying undertaking

6.132 For the purpose of these rules, 'qualifying undertakings', can either be companies or partnerships. A qualifying company (or qualifying partnership) is an unlimited company (or partnership) incorporated in (or governed by the laws of any part of) Great Britain if each of its members is:

- a limited company; or
- another unlimited company, or a Scottish firm, each of whose members is a limited company.

The references to limited company, another unlimited company and Scottish firm also encompasses any comparable undertakings incorporated in, or formed under the law of, any country or territory outside Great Britain. [SI 1993/1820 Reg 3, 9].

6.133 Where at the year end the company is a member of a qualifying undertaking, it has to give the following information in its financial statements if material:

- The name and legal form of the undertaking.
- The address of the undertaking's registered office or, if it does not have such an office, its head office.

[CA85 5 Sch 9A(1)(2)].

6.134 In addition, where the qualifying undertaking is a qualifying partnership one of the following must also be stated:

- That a copy of the latest financial statements of the undertaking has been, or is to be, appended to the copy of the company's financial statements sent to the Registrar under section 242 of the Act.
- The name of at least one body corporate (which may be the company) in whose consolidated financial statements the undertaking has been, or is to be, dealt with by the method of full consolidation, proportional consolidation or the equity method of accounting.

[CA85 5 Sch 9A(3)].

6.135 The information required to be disclosed in the second bullet point of the previous paragraph need not be given if the partnership is dealt with either by consolidation, proportional consolidation or equity accounting in the consolidated financial statements prepared by:

- a member of the partnership that is established under the law of a member State; or
- a parent undertaking of such a member established in the same way.

[SI 1993/1820 Reg 7(1)].

6.136 The exemption can only be taken, however, where the following two conditions are complied with:

- The consolidated financial statements are prepared and audited under the law of the Member State in accordance with the provisions of the 7th Directive.
- The notes to those consolidated financial statements disclose that advantage has been taken of the exemption.

[SI 1993/1820 Reg 7(2)].

Own shares and shares in own parent

6.137 Generally, prior to 1 December 2003, when a company purchased its own shares, it had to cancel them at the time it purchased them. However, 'The Companies (Acquisition of Own Shares) (Treasury Shares) Regulations 2003' (SI 2003/1116), which came into force on 1 December 2003, amend the Companies Act 1985 to permit companies with *'qualifying shares'* to purchase such shares out of distributable profits and hold them in treasury for resale, transfer or cancellation at a later date. 'Qualifying shares' are defined as shares that:

- are included in the official list (that is, listed on the London Stock Exchange);
- are traded on AIM;
- are officially listed in another EEA State; or

- are traded on a market established in an EEA State, which is a regulated securities market.

[CA85 Sec 162(4) as inserted by SI 2003/1116, CA06 Sec 724(2)].

6.138 The Schedule 4 balance sheet format has a sub-heading 'own shares'. However, shares held in treasury are not classified as investments, but are instead deducted in arriving at shareholders' funds. UITF Abstract 37, 'Purchases and sales of own shares', states that an entity's purchase of its own shares gives rise to a reduction in the entity's ownership interest, not an asset and it requires that the consideration paid for an entity's own shares should be deducted in arriving at shareholders' funds. [UITF 37 paras 5, 7]. The rules relating to treasury shares, including disclosures, are dealt with in more detail in chapter 23.

6.139 A subsidiary company cannot normally hold own shares in its parent company. [CA85 Sec 23(1), CA06 Sec 136(1)]. However, this prohibition does not apply where the subsidiary is acting as a personal representative for a third party, or as trustee and the holding company or a subsidiary of it has no beneficial interest under the trust. [CA85 Sec 23(2), CA06 Sec 138(1) and (2)]. This provision also does not extend to market makers. [CA85 Sec 23(3), CA06 Sec 141(1) and (2)]. However, the prohibition does include those shares that might be held on behalf of the subsidiary by another person as its nominee. [CA85 Sec 23(7), CA06 Sec 144].

6.140 Where a body corporate becomes a subsidiary company because of the changes in the definition of subsidiaries included in section 736 of the Act, it may retain any shares that it already held in its parent. However, where shares are held in this way, they will carry no right to vote at company meetings. [CA85 Sec 23(4), CA06 Sec 137(1) and (2)].

6.141 In certain situations, a subsidiary may find that it does hold shares in its parent. This may arise, for example, where the parent has recently acquired the subsidiary which owned shares in the parent before it became a group member. Before the introduction of the Companies Act 1989, such holdings may have been in breach of section 23(1) of the Act. Now, however, where a company acquires shares in its parent after the commencement of the new section 23(1), but before it becomes a subsidiary of the parent, it may retain those shares. Also in this circumstance, those shares will carry no right to vote at company meetings. [CA85 Sec 23(5), CA06 Sec 137(1) and (2)].

6.142 In the past, such shares have been classified as an asset, 'own shares', in the parent's consolidated financial statements. However, UITF Abstract 37, 'Purchases and sales of own shares', effective for accounting periods ending on or after 23 December 2003, requires that where shares in a holding company are purchased or held by a subsidiary, the consideration paid should be deducted in arriving at shareholders' funds in the holding company's consolidated financial statements. [UITF 37 paras 7, 8]. This applies to all such shareholdings, including those held by subsidiaries that carry on a business of dealing in securities. However, in the individual financial statements of a subsidiary that holds shares in its parent, such shares are treated as an asset, rather than deducted in arriving at shareholders' funds, as these are not 'own shares' for the subsidiary itself.

6.143 The notes to the parent's financial statements must disclose the number, description and the amount of the shares that subsidiaries or their nominees hold. [CA85 5 Sch 6(1)]. This information is not required, however, where the subsidiary holds the shares as personal representative or as trustee. [CA85 5 Sch 6(2) as amended by SI 1996/189]. However, the exemption for a subsidiary acting as a trustee will not be available if the company or any of its subsidiaries is beneficially interested under the trust, unless the beneficial interest is by way of security for the purpose of a transaction entered into by it in the ordinary course of business, which includes the lending of money. [CA85 5 Sch 6(3)]. Additionally, in the consolidated financial statements, UITF Abstract 37 requires separate disclosure of the amounts of reductions to shareholders' funds for a parent's shares held by subsidiaries and the number of such shares held. [UITF 37 paras 8, 7(d)].

6.144 In recent years, many companies have established employee share ownership plans (ESOP), because of the tax advantages that they afford employees. The accounting treatment of shares held by an ESOP trust is considered in more detail in chapter 12.

Loans for acquisition of own shares

6.145 Where any outstanding loans made in respect of the acquisition of the company's shares under either section 153(4)(b) [(bb)] or (c) or section 55 of the Act (various situations of financial assistance by a company for purchase of its own shares) are included under any item in the balance sheet, these must be disclosed in aggregate for each item. [CA85 4 Sch 51(2)]. The acquisition by a company of its own shares is considered in chapter 7 of the Manual of Accounting – IFRS and UK supplement.

Other investments

6.146 The category 'other investments' will normally include the following items (other than investments in subsidiaries and companies in which the investing company has a participating interest):

- Listed and unlisted securities.
- Life assurance policies.
- Joint ventures and partnerships, if they are not subsidiaries or participating interests.

6.147 Building society deposits and bank deposits could be included either as 'other investments' (either under fixed assets or under current assets – depending on the nature of the deposits) or as 'cash at bank and in hand'. If the amount is material, the accounting policies should disclose where such items are included. This is considered in more detail in chapter 4.

[The next paragraph is 6.154.]

Requirements for entities not applying FRS 26

Introduction

6.154 As explained above, those entities that do not yet apply FRS 26 will still potentially be within the scope of the disclosure standard, FRS 13, and will need to apply FRS 4 for any capital instrument they issue. Such entities are encouraged to apply FRS 29, although if the standard is applied early, that fact must be stated in the financial statements. This section covers the FRS 13 disclosure requirements and explains the amended requirements of FRS 4. FRS 29 is discussed from paragraph 6.406.2 onwards.

FRS 13

Scope of FRS 13

6.155 IAS 32 and IAS 39 apply under the EU Regulations to listed entities' consolidated financial statements. FRS 13 applies to all other entities that have any of their capital instruments (generally shares and debt, including minority interests) listed or publicly traded on a stock exchange or market (domestic or foreign). [FRS 13 paras 2, 119]. Hence FRS 13 continues to apply to some listed entities that do not have subsidiaries and are not required to prepare consolidated financial statements and to those entities that are not listed on a regulated market. (Companies registered on the Alternative Investment Market (AIM) have to prepare consolidated financial statements under EU adopted IFRS from 1 January 2007. However for the parent entity financial statements they have a choice of adopting IFRS or continue to use UK GAAP.) Other companies that are also caught by FRS 13's requirements are those companies whose only listed capital instrument is a Eurobond quoted on, for example, the Luxembourg Stock Exchange and those companies whose shares are traded on OFEX or similar markets.

6.156 In addition, all banks and similar financial institutions (for example, building societies), whether quoted or not, must make the required disclosures unless they fall within the requirements of the EU directive to prepare IFRS financial statements. [FRS 13 para 82].

6.156.1 The rules in FRS 13 continue to apply to these types of entities and groups until the disclosure requirements of FRS 25 or FRS 29 come into effect (see paras 6.38 and 6.38.1).

[The next paragraph is 6.157.]

6.157 The FRS sets different rules for non-financial entities, for banks and for other financial institutions that are not banks. The last category includes leasing companies, investment and unit trusts, money brokers and 'in-store' credit card companies. [FRS 13 para 119]. Although the required narrative disclosures are common to all entities the reporting entity's classification determines the type of numerical disclosures that should be given. Accordingly, the standard is split into three parts:

- Part A deals with disclosures for quoted reporting entities other than banks and other financial institutions.
- Part B deals with disclosures for all banks and similar institutions.
- Part C deals with disclosures for quoted non-bank financial institutions.

6.158 As the Manual of Accounting – UK GAAP does not deal with banks and similar institutions or non-bank financial institutions, this chapter considers only the disclosures required for other reporting entities as set out in Part A of the standard.

6.159 The FRS does not apply to insurance companies or groups. Entities to which the standard does not apply are encouraged, but not required, to comply with it. An entity seeking a listing of their equity or debt is required to prepare financial information as if it already was listed. This means it must provide the full FRS 13 narrative and numerical disclosures in the listing particulars.

6.160 Reporting entities and subsidiaries that themselves have no listed or traded capital instruments, unless they are banks or similar institutions, need not comply. Moreover, a quoted parent company is not required to give the disclosures in its own financial statements if they are given on a group basis in its accompanying consolidated financial statements. [FRS 13 para 3(b)].

6.161 In the context of FRS 13, group refers solely to the parent entity and its subsidiaries and quasi-subsidiaries. Hence, details of an associate's or joint venture's own financial instruments should not be included in the FRS 13 disclosures for the investing group as the individual amounts are not included in the consolidation. However, if an associate's or joint venture's use of financial instruments is material to an understanding of the effect of the investments on the investing group, separate disclosures about their financial instruments would need to be considered in the light of the requirement in FRS 9 to make disclosure of such material matters. [FRS 9 para 53].

6.162 The exemption from giving entity-own disclosures needs to be considered carefully as illustrated in the following group structures as either the group or some subsidiaries will have to provide FRS 13 disclosures in circumstances where the fact that the FRS requires disclosure may not be readily apparent.

Example 1

An unquoted non-financial institution UK holding company H has an unquoted non-financial institution UK subsidiary S and another non-financial institution UK subsidiary L, which has a eurobond quoted on the Luxembourg Stock Exchange. Which reporting entities must comply with FRS 13?

Subsidiary L has a quoted capital instrument, its eurobond, and thus must comply with FRS 13 and give the required disclosures in respect of all of its financial instruments, including inter-company balances (unless they fall within short-term 'trade' debtors and creditors (see para 6.166 below)).

As H group has quoted debt, namely subsidiary L's eurobond, its group financial statements must comply with FRS 13 and deal with all of H group's financial instruments including those in subsidiary S. In its individual financial statements, H group will be entitled to the 'entity-own' exemption from providing separate disclosures about its financial instruments, because they are given on a group basis in its accompanying consolidated financial statements.

Subsidiary S does not have to comply itself with FRS 13 since it is an unquoted non-financial institution. However, as noted it will, nevertheless, have to provide H with information on all its financial instruments.

Example 2

TreasCo plc, a wholly-owned subsidiary of XYZ plc, is also an intermediate parent company and provides treasury operations for the entire XYZ group. TreasCo has a series of eurobonds, quoted on the Luxembourg Stock Exchange. To what extent does TreasCo have to comply with FRS 13?

Although TreasCo is a wholly-owned subsidiary of XYZ plc it is required to prepare group financial statements as it cannot claim the 'intermediate parent' exemption under section 228(3) of the Companies Act 1985 because it has debt quoted on the Luxembourg Stock Exchange. Consequently, TreasCo's group financial statements will have to give all of FRS 13's narrative and numerical disclosures about its sub-group's financial instruments that have not eliminated on consolidation. By virtue of paragraph 3(b) of the FRS, separate disclosures are not required in respect of solely TreasCo's financial instruments and, thus, the full picture of its treasury operations may be somewhat obscured.

XYZ plc will have to give the FRS 13 disclosures in respect of its group.

Example 3

Using the same facts as in example 2 except that TreasCo has no subsidiaries. What is the effect on TreasCo's FRS 13 disclosures?

TreasCo must give in its individual financial statements the FRS 13 disclosures about its own financial instruments, including inter-company items (unless they fall within short-term 'trade' debtors and creditors (see para 6.166 below)). This is because it is not entitled to the shelter of the 'entity-own' exemption under paragraph 3(b) of FRS 13, since it has no subsidiaries and does not prepare consolidated financial statements. Hence a full picture of its treasury operations should be disclosed.

Again, as in example 2, XYZ plc will have to give the FRS 13 disclosures for its group.

Excluded financial instruments

6.163 The FRS 13 definition of a financial instrument (see para 6.18) is deliberately wide in order to capture instruments that may be devised in the future without the need for continual updating of the accounting standard. However, the following items, which appear to satisfy the definition, are specifically excluded:

- Interests in subsidiaries, quasi-subsidiaries, associates, partnerships and joint ventures, other than those held exclusively with a view to resale. This exclusion does not cover loans to or from subsidiaries, quasi-subsidiaries, associates and joint ventures and they should be dealt with in the disclosures.
- Equity minority interests. [FRS 13 para 5(a) footnote].
- Employer's obligations under employee option and share schemes and any shares held in order to fulfil such obligations (for example, shares held in an ESOP trust).
- Pensions and other post-retirement benefits.
- Obligations under operating leases (unless they become onerous and provision has to be made under FRS 12).
- Equity shares issued by the reporting entity and warrants or options on them, other than those held exclusively with a view to resale. But all non-equity shares (for example, preference shares) fall to be dealt with in the disclosures as a separate category of financial liabilities. [FRS 13 para 8].
- Financial assets, financial liabilities and cash-settled commodity contracts of an insurance company or group.

[FRS 13 para 5].

6.164 There is no exclusion for 'intra-group financial instruments' in FRS 13. This is important because in some situations, although intra-group financial instruments in FRS 13 eliminate on consolidation they will still feature in some of FRS 13's disclosures (see para 6.236). In addition, it is also relevant in situations where perhaps an intermediate parent has listed securities and thus has to prepare consolidated financial statements that have to comply with FRS 13. Inter-company balances with its parent and fellow subsidiaries will not eliminate on consolidation and thus have to be dealt with in the FRS 13 disclosures (see examples in para 6.162 above).

6.165 Appendix II to the standard makes clear that the following are not financial instruments:

- Physical assets, such as stock, property, plant and equipment.
- Intangible assets, such as patents and trademarks.

- Prepayments for goods or services, since these will not be settled in cash or another financial instrument, similarly deferred costs and expenses.
- Obligations to be settled by the delivery of goods or rendering of services, such as most executory contracts or most warranty obligations.
- Forwards, swaps and options to be settled by the delivery of goods or the rendering of services.
- Income taxes (including deferred tax), since these are statutory rather than contractual obligations, although this seems a very fine distinction.
- Contingent items that do not arise from contracts, for example, a contingent liability for a tort judgement.
- Equity minority interests that arise on consolidating a subsidiary that is not wholly-owned.

[FRS 13 App II para 4].

Short-term debtors and creditors

6.166 Although debtors and creditors fall within the definition of a financial instrument an entity can opt either to exclude certain short-term debtors and creditors from all the disclosures (other than the currency disclosures (see para 6.230)) required by the standard or to include them. Whatever it does, the reporting entity must state how such items have been dealt with. [FRS 13 para 6].

6.167 Short-term debtors and creditors that may be excluded are those financial assets and liabilities that meet all of the following criteria.

- They would be included under one of the following balance sheet headings if the entity was preparing its financial statements in accordance with Schedule 4 to the Companies Act 1985.
  - Debtors.
  - Pre-payments and accrued income.
  - Creditors: amounts falling due within one year, other than items that would be included under the 'debenture loans' and 'bank loans and overdrafts' sub-headings.
  - Provisions for liabilities and charges.
  - Accruals and deferred income.
- They mature or become payable within 12 months of the balance sheet date.
- They are not a derivative financial instrument.

[FRS 13 para 2].

6.168 Items that fall within the criteria are trade debtors and creditors, 'trade' balances due from or to associates and joint ventures, bills of exchange payable and payments received on account, perhaps in respect of a short-term contract, that have a maturity of less than 12 months. Short-term bank loans and overdrafts do not meet the criteria and cannot be excluded.

6.169 The Schedule 4 balance sheet headings and sub-headings, however, do not specifically include a home for 'obligations under finance leases'. Indeed, SSAP 21 paragraph 51 states that such amounts "*should be disclosed separately from other obligations and liabilities, either on the face of the balance sheet or in the notes to the accounts*". This is interpreted as creating new sub-headings within the two creditors captions (under one year and over one year) rather than totally different headings. For the purposes of FRS 13, any finance lease obligations falling within creditors under one year should not be excluded from the disclosures under the provision of paragraph 6 of the standard because they are of a financing nature. Similarly, short-term finance lease receivables should also be dealt with in the disclosures.

Identification of on balance sheet financial instruments

6.170 The first step when preparing FRS 13 disclosures is to identify all on balance sheet financial instruments. It is important, when performing this exercise, to drill down through each balance sheet caption in some detail to determine whether there is a financial instrument. When a list of all on balance sheet financial instruments has been compiled it is then necessary to go through the list and establish whether the instruments identified should be excluded from disclosure, either because they are specifically excluded by FRS 13 or because they fall under the short-term debtors and creditors exclusion, as discussed above.

6.171 The list below is an *aide-mémoire* to help the identification of on balance sheet financial instruments.

FRS 13 – Financial instruments

The following is a non-exhaustive list of common balance sheet items

	Financial instrument	Excluded from disclosure (1)	Can be excluded (2)
Tangible fixed assets	X		
Intangible fixed assets	X		
Investment in subsidiary – not held for resale	✓	✓	–
Investment in subsidiary – held for resale	✓	–	–
Investment in associate/joint venture – not held for resale	✓	✓	–
Other investments	✓	–	–
Stocks	X		
Trade debtors (short-term)	✓	–	✓
Trade debtors (long-term)	✓	–	–
Prepayments – goods and services	X		
Accrued income (short-term)	✓	–	✓
Dividends receivable (short-term)	✓	–	✓
Cash	✓	–	–

	Financial instrument	Excluded from disclosure (1)	Can be excluded (2)
Bank loans and overdrafts (short-term)	✓	–	–
Bank loans and overdrafts (long-term)	✓	–	–
Convertible debt	✓	–	–
Debentures – current portion	✓	–	–
Debentures – long term portion	✓	–	–
Trade creditors (short-term)	✓	–	✓
Trade creditors (long-term)	✓	–	–
Accruals – goods and services	✓	–	✓
Deferred income	X		
Pensions and similar obligations	✓	✓	–
Provisions under 1 year (contractual obligation for cash or other financial asset)	✓	–	✓
Provisions over 1 year (contractual obligation for cash or other financial asset)	✓	–	–
Warranty obligations (settled by delivery of goods)	X		
Warranty obligations (settled by delivery of cash or other financial asset)	✓	–	–
Finance lease obligations	✓	–	–
Operating lease creditor	✓	✓	–
Taxation and social security	X		
Equity shares	✓	✓	–
Non-equity shares	✓	–	–
Investment in own shares	✓	✓	–
Equity minority interests	X		
Non-equity minority interests	✓	–	–
Final dividends proposed	X		
Interim dividend payable	✓	–	✓

1 Financial assets and liabilities that are excluded from the disclosures (other than the currency disclosures) by FRS 13 paragraph 5.

2 Financial assets and liabilities that may be excluded from all disclosures (other than the currency disclosure) by the short-term debtors and creditors exclusion per FRS 13 paragraphs 6-7.

Note also that inter-company balances and balances with associates and joint ventures are financial instruments. Short-term trade type balances may be excluded from disclosures by the short-term debtors and creditors exclusion noted in footnote 2 above.

Derivative financial instruments

6.172 A derivative is specifically defined in FRS 13 as: *"A financial instrument that derives its value from the price or rate of some underlying item"*. [FRS 13 para 2]. Such underlying items could include equities, bonds, commodities, interest rates, stock market and other indices. Hence, the term 'derivative' would apply to the following instruments, although the range and complexity of other derivatives, which are effectively hybrids of these, are not only substantial but increasing:

- Forward contracts — contracts for the purchase or sale of a specified amount of a commodity or financial instrument (such as foreign currency) at a fixed price with delivery and settlement at a specified future date.

- Futures contracts — similar to forward contracts except that the purchase or sale is of standardised amounts that are traded on an exchange.
- Options and warrants — give the purchaser the right, but not the obligation, to purchase (call) or sell (put) a fixed amount of a commodity or financial instrument at a fixed price with delivery and settlement at either a specified future date or over a fixed future period.
- Swaps — parties to the contract exchange cash flows in order to access a particular market as if they had entered it directly. For example, interest paid at a fixed rate may be exchanged for interest paid at a floating rate (an interest rate swap) or borrowings denominated in different currencies may be exchanged (a cross-currency swap).
- Caps — an interest rate cap is an agreement whereby the seller reimburses the purchaser with the excess of interest costs over and above a specified rate. Hence, interest costs for the purchaser are capped.
- Collars — an interest rate collar is a combination of a cap and its natural opposite, referred to as a floor. Hence, the purchaser locks into a specified range of interest rates.

6.173 Although worded differently to the FRS 26/IAS 39 definition of a financial instrument (see Annex 3), the meaning is essentially the same. An FRS 13 derivative would in most cases be an FRS 26/IAS 39 derivative, and *vice versa.*

6.174 On inception, derivative financial instruments give one party a contractual right to exchange financial assets with another party under conditions that are potentially favourable, or conversely a contractual obligation to make such an exchange under potentially unfavourable conditions. Some instruments include both a right and an obligation to make an exchange (for example, a forward foreign exchange contract). It is important to monitor the instrument, since the terms that were set at inception may become either favourable or unfavourable as prices in financial markets change.

6.175 But not all derivatives are financial instruments. Any derivative whose terms do not include the receipt or delivery of financial assets or exchange of financial instruments is not a financial instrument. For example, an option to buy or sell land is not a financial instrument. Similarly, commodity contracts that require settlement by physical delivery are not financial instruments.

Cash-settled commodity contracts

6.176 Cash-settled commodity contracts, such as commodities futures contracts, are to be treated as if they are financial assets and liabilities for the purposes of the following disclosures:

- Objectives, policies and strategies (see from para 6.189).
- Fair values (see from para 6.241).

- Financial assets and liabilities issued for trading purposes (see from para 6.257).
- Hedges (see from para 6.260).

[FRS 13 para 64].

6.177 They are not included in the interest rate risk and currency profile disclosures of financial liabilities and financial assets (see from paras 6.209 and 6.230 respectively), as this is not required by paragraph 64 of the standard. Cash and government securities should not be treated as commodities, but for this purpose commodity contracts include hard commodities (such as metals including gold) and soft commodities (such as oils, grains, cocoa, cotton, soya beans and sugar). But contracts for the purchase of commodities for actual delivery and use by an entity in its business, such as raw materials in the manufacture of its products, are not cash-settled commodity contracts and so are outside the scope of the standard. [FRS 13 para 2].

6.178 An example of a company, other than a commodity trader, providing information of this nature is British Airways plc.

Table 6.3 – Cash-settled comodity contract

British Airways Plc – Report & Accounts – 31 March 2000

Operating and financial review (extract)

Derivative financial instruments (extract)

British Airways uses derivative financial instruments (derivatives) with off-balance sheet risk selectively for treasury and fuel risk management purposes.

The risk management strategy for both treasury and fuel operations is implemented by the respective departments within the guidelines and parameters laid down by the board of Directors, and reflects a risk averse policy. The company's policy is not to trade in derivatives but to use these instruments to hedge anticipated expenses.

The company's fuel risk management strategy aims to provide the airline with protection against sudden and significant increases in oil prices while ensuring that the airline is not competitively disadvantaged in a serious way in the event of a substantial fall in the price of fuel. The strategy operates within limits set by the Board and agreed in detail by the Fuel Hedging Committee, which is made up of representatives from fuel, finance, treasury and strategy.

In meeting these objectives, the fuel risk management programme allows for the judicious use of a number of derivatives traded on regulated exchanges in London (the Institute of Petroleum Exchange) and New York (the New York Mercantile Exchange) as well as on the Over The Counter (OTC) markets with approved counterparties and within approved limits. The instruments used include futures and forward contracts, options, collars, caps and swaps. The hedging committee reviews the use of these instruments on a regular basis.

Notes to the accounts (extract)

43 Fair values of financial instruments (extract)

b Derivative financial instruments held to manage the interest rate and currency profile

£ million	2000 Fair value	*1999 Fair value*
Interest rate swaps	(4)	*(15)*
Forward currency transactions	10	*14*
Fuel derivatives	55	*10*

Included within forward currency transactions are derivative financial instruments held to hedge the currency exposure on expected future sales.

c Hedges

The instruments used to hedge future exposures are interest rate swaps, forward currency contracts and fuel derivatives.

At March 31, 2000 there were unrecognised gains of £65 million and unrecognised losses of £4 million relating to hedges of future exposures. Of the unrecognised gains, £63 million are expected to occur within one year and £2 million after one year, and of the unrecognised losses, £1 million are expected to occur within one year and £3 million after one year.

At March 31, 1999 there were unrecognised gains of £26 million and unrecognised losses of £17 million. Of the unrecognised gains £24 million related to the period to 31 March, 2000 and £2 million related to periods over one year and of the unrecognised losses, £9 million related to the year to March 31, 2000 and £8 million related to periods in excess of one year.

6.179 A reporting entity might participate in an illiquid commodity market dominated by very few participants. Where this is the case, disclosure of some of the information on fair values and financial assets and liabilities held or issued for trading or hedging purposes required by the FRS in respect of its commodity positions could move the market significantly and prejudice the entity's interests. In order to avoid this happening, the standard allows disclosures that would be prejudicial in these circumstances to be omitted. [FRS 13 para 65]. The fact that the information has not been disclosed and the reasons for the omission must be stated.

6.180 References in this chapter to financial instruments include commodity contracts with similar characteristics as defined above, notwithstanding the commercial confidentiality exemption discussed in the previous paragraph.

Non-equity shares and non-equity minority interests

6.181 FRS 13 defines non-equity shares as those shares that have any of the following characteristics:

- Any of the rights of the shares to receive payments (whether in respect of dividends, in respect of redemption or otherwise) are for a limited amount that is not calculated by reference to the company's assets or profits or the dividends on any class of equity share.

- Any of their rights to participate in a surplus in a winding up are limited to a specific amount that is not calculated by reference to the company's assets or profits and such limitation had a commercial effect in practice at the time the shares were issued or, if later, at the time the limitation was introduced.

- The shares are redeemable either according to their terms, or because the holder, or any party other than the issuer, can require their redemption.

[FRS 13 para 2].

6.182 This definition is identical to the definition previously contained within FRS 4. The concept of non-equity shares has been removed from FRS 4 following the introduction of FRS 25 and all shares are now categorised and accounted for as either a financial liability or as equity. However, it is interesting to note that FRS 13 has not been amended. For clarity an entity could provide details alongside the FRS 13 disclosures of how the non-equity shares have been classified within the financial statements.

6.183 Under FRS 13, all non-equity shares issued by the reporting entity should be dealt with in the disclosures, both narrative and numerical, as if they are financial liabilities. However, they should be distinguished separately from financial liabilities in the disclosures. [FRS 13 para 8]. This is described as a pragmatic solution by the ASB to avoid introducing a complexity into the standard. A strict interpretation of the definitions would otherwise require all shares to be categorised as either equity or liabilities.

6.184 By extension, non-equity minority interests should be dealt with as financial liabilities and should be separately disclosed.

FRS 13 disclosures

6.185 For conventional instruments, such as shares and loans, other disclosure requirements give some indication of the risks to which a reporting entity is exposed. For example, the following disclosures are required by the Companies Act:

- Details of redeemable shares including the period for redemption and whether any premium is payable. [CA85 4 Sch 38(2)].

- Details of any options to subscribe for shares in the company including the number in issue, the period during which they may be exercised and the price to be paid. [CA85 4 Sch 40].

- Repayment terms and interest rates applicable to long-term liabilities. [CA85 4 Sch 48(2)].

- Market values of listed investments if different to the book value. [CA85 4 Sch 45(2) — see para 6.97].

6.186 Until FRS 13, neither company law nor accounting standards included detailed disclosure requirements in respect of derivatives. The Act does, however, require disclosure of financial commitments to the extent that they are relevant to a proper understanding of the company's state of affairs. [CA85 4 Sch 50(5)]. Therefore, where a company has outstanding forward contracts, the amounts outstanding under the forward contracts have had to be disclosed under this requirement. An example where a company discloses outstanding forward contracts, is given in Table 6.4 below.

Table 6.4 – Disclosure of outstanding forward contracts

British Airways Plc – Report & Accounts – 31 March 1999

Notes to the accounts (extract)

35 Forward Transactions

The Group had outstanding forward transactions to hedge foreign currencies and fuel purchases as follows:

	in currency		Sterling equivalents	
	1999	*1998*	**1999**	*1998*
Maturing within one year:				
– to cover future capital commitments in US Dollars	**US$774m**	*US$485m*	**£473m**	*£289m*
– to hedge future currency revenues in US Dollars	**US$27m**	*US$127m*		
– to hedge future currency revenues against sterling			**£62m**	*£65m*
– to hedge future operating payments against US Dollars	**US$66m**	*US$130m*		*£78m*
– to hedge future fuel costs in US Dollars	**US$319m**	*US$415*	**£194m**	*£247m*
– to hedge future operating payments against sterling				*£82m*
– to hedge debt in a foreign currency	**US$225m**	*US$150m*	**£138m**	*£90m*
Maturing after one year:				
– to cover future capital commitments in US Dollars	**US$90m**	*US$170m*	**£54m**	*£101m*
– to hedge future currency revenues against sterling			**£2m**	*£1m*
– to hedge future operating payments against US Dollars				*£16m*

6.187 FRS 13 requires a range of disclosures that are, in most areas, consistent with those required by FRS 25. Broadly, these disclosures may be divided into narrative and numerical information. The former is intended as an explanation of why the entity uses financial instruments, what it hopes to achieve and whether this is demonstrated by the latter period-end numerical disclosures. [FRS 13 paras 13, 20]. All of the required disclosures are outlined below, as are other disclosures that are made by certain companies, but that are not specifically required by the FRS.

6.188 Annex 1 to this chapter contains examples of narrative and numerical disclosures for some typical financial instruments (provided on an individual basis) and which comply with the disclosure requirements explained below and the numerical disclosures that are explained from paragraph 6.207.

Disclosure of objectives, policies and strategies

6.189 FRS 13 requires that an entity should provide an explanation of the role that financial instruments have had during the period in creating or changing the risks it faces in its activities. This should include an explanation of the objectives and policies for holding or issuing financial instruments (including derivatives) and similar contracts, such as cash-settled commodity contracts, and the strategies that have been followed in the period for achieving those objectives as agreed by the directors. [FRS 13 para 13]. For example, a company might have an objective of having 70 per cent of its borrowings at fixed rates. Its strategy to achieve this might be to borrow directly in this ratio or alternatively to use derivatives such as swaps, caps and collars to convert floating rate borrowings to fixed in the desired ratio.

6.190 The narrative should involve describing management's attitude to risk, in particular whether it is averse to cash flow risk or market price risk (steps taken to mitigate one often increases exposure to the other). For example, where an entity holds ten per cent gilts, changes in interest rates will cause their value to fluctuate (market price risk), but such changes do not alter future income (that is, no cash flow risk). If management is market price risk adverse, it will act to protect the gilts' value by, say, swapping the fixed rate interest for floating rate; but in doing so it creates cash flow risk, because net income from the gilts and the swap will fluctuate with changes in interest rates. The disclosure of its accounting (including hedging), treasury and risk management policies should be clear and concise.

6.191 The nature and extent of the discussion will vary depending on the circumstances of the organisation, but the ASB expects it to be at a high level and not commercially sensitive. Basically, it should set the scene for the numerical disclosures and should contain sufficient information to enable a reader to understand the reporting entity's objectives and policies and the strategies for achieving those objectives.

6.192 The discussion should focus only on the major financial risks faced during the period. Typically the major financial risks faced by entities include interest rate risk, liquidity risk and currency risk. Any other significant risks the entity might face should also be considered when considering the financial risks of the entity as a whole. The narrative on each of the financial risks faced by the entity should be structured to cover the requirements described below.

6.193 An explanation should be given of the role that financial instruments have had during the period in creating or changing the risks faced by the reporting entity. This should include an explanation of its objectives and policies for holding or issuing financial instruments and similar contracts and its strategies for achieving those objectives. [FRS 13 para 13].

- This disclosure would usually include a discussion of the nature of and purposes for which the main types of financial instruments and similar contracts are held or issued. This should cover separately instruments used for financing, risk management or hedging and for trading or speculation. [FRS 13 para 14].

- This disclosure would also typically include a discussion of the reporting entity's main risk management and treasury policies, quantified where appropriate, on:
  - The fixed/floating split, maturity profile and currency profile of financial liabilities (including borrowings) and financial assets.
  - The extent to which foreign currency financial assets and financial liabilities are hedged to the functional currency of the business unit concerned.
  - The extent to which foreign currency borrowings and other financial instruments (that is, derivatives) are used to hedge foreign currency net investments.
  - Any other hedging.

[FRS 13 para 15].

6.194 If the explanations given above reflect a significant change from the explanations given in the previous accounting period this should be explained and the reasons for the change given. [FRS 13 para 16].

6.195 If the directors have agreed before the date of approval of the financial statements to change significantly the role that financial instruments will have in the next accounting period, this should be explained. [FRS 13 para 18].

6.196 An explanation of how the period-end figures shown in the financial statements represent the objectives, policies and strategies of the reporting entity, or, if the period-end position shown by the financial statements is considered to be materially unrepresentative of the entity's use of financial instruments and thus its exposure to risks, an explanation of the extent to which it is considered unrepresentative. [FRS 13 para 20].

6.197 Where a reporting entity uses financial instruments as hedges it should describe:

- The transactions and risks that are hedged, including the time until they are expected to occur.
- The instruments used for hedging, disclosing those that have been accounted for using hedge accounting and those that have not. [FRS 13 para 21].

Note that the term 'hedge' here is with reference to original UK GAAP hedge accounting (see para 6.403) and is not the same as the hedge accounting that may be permitted under the provisions of FRS 26/IAS 39.

6.198 The reference to the period end figures in paragraph 6.196 above relates to the interest rate risk disclosures for financial assets and liabilities, the currency risk disclosures for the net amount of monetary assets and liabilities and the maturity profile of financial liabilities. The narrative disclosures should be consistent with each of these balance sheet orientated numerical disclosures. The narrative disclosures should be specific to the reporting entity concerned, explaining its year end position and any material movements from the previous year end position. An example of a company clearly explaining its year end position relative to its objectives, policies and strategies for assessing interest rate risk is given in Table 6.5 below.

Table 6.5 – Interest rate risk

South African Breweries Plc – Annual Report and Accounts – 31 March 2000

Notes to the Consolidated Financial Statements (extract)

Interest rate risk

The group finances its operations through a mixture of retained reserves and bank borrowings. The group borrows principally in rand, and increasingly in US dollars at both fixed and floating rates of interest. The interest rate characteristics of new borrowings and the refinancing of existing borrowings are positioned according to expected movements in interest rates. In order to hedge specific exposures in the interest rate repricing profile of existing borrowings and anticipated peak additional borrowings the group makes use of interest rate swaps and forward rate agreements to generate the desired interest profile and to manage the group's exposure to interest rate fluctuations. The group's policy is to keep between 25%, and 75%, of its borrowings (measured on a rolling basis) at a fixed rate of interest — intended to limit the impact, of a 1% change in interest rates, to 1% of group operating profit excluding exceptional items. As at 31 March 2000 – 8% (31 March 1999 – 29%) of the group's borrowings were at fixed rates after taking account of any interest rate swaps and forward rate agreements. The relatively low fixed rate percentage at 31 March 2000 is analysed further (in this note) under the interest rate risk profile of financial liabilities and financial assets.

6.199 The disclosures referred to above should be included within the financial statements, the directors' report or the non-mandatory OFR. If the disclosures are included in the directors' report or the OFR they should be incorporated within the financial statements by a clear reference in the notes to the statement in which they are located. (It should also be remembered that these disclosures, as they form part of the financial statements, are required to be audited.) In any event it will aid users of financial statements to include in one place the structured discussion on the financial risks faced by the entity as required by the standard

6.200 Carlton Communications plc, provides an example (Table 6.6 below) of the type of narrative disclosure required by the standard.

Table 6.6 – Disclosure of objectives, policies and strategies
Carlton Communications Plc – Annual report and accounts – 30 September 2001

Finance Director's review (extract)

FINANCING
Carlton 's policy is to finance itself long-term using debt instruments with a range of maturities. Carlton has traditionally raised fixed rate debt from the US and European Capital Markets, as well as obtaining bank facilities from the UK Syndicated Market.

In March 2001 Carlton established a £1,000m Euro Medium Term Note programme which provides standard documentation for both public bond issues and private placement loan notes. By the year end Carlton had issued loan notes under the programme in a variety of currencies (swapped back to sterling) totalling about £168m. In April 2001 Carlton arranged a £300m 5 year Syndicated bank facility which has not been drawn at the date of writing. The purpose of the facility is to provide financial flexibility through short-term liquidity pending longer-term refinancing.

In November 2001 Carlton announced the issue of €638.6m (£397.6m) exchangeable bonds which will mature in 2007, will carry a coupon of 2.25 per cent per annum, and have a fixed exchange price of €41.2. The bonds will be exchangeable into 15.5m ordinary shares in Thomson representing Carlton 's underlying total equity interest in the company. Carlton also announced that it has reached agreement in principle for the sale of US$175m nominal amount of loan notes issued by Thomson which are unguaranteed. Both transactions are expected to complete early in the New Year.

OBJECTIVES, POLICIES AND STRATEGIES
The most significant treasury exposures faced by Carlton are raising finance, managing interest rate and currency positions and investing surplus cash in high quality assets. Clear parameters have been established, including levels of authority, on the type and use of financial instruments to manage these exposures. Transactions are only undertaken if they relate to underlying exposures. Regular reports are provided to senior management and treasury operations are subject to periodic independent reviews and internal audit.

INTEREST RATE MANAGEMENT
Carlton uses interest rate swaps, options and forward rate agreements to manage its interest rate exposures on its debt and cash positions with the objective of minimising its net interest cost.

The interest rate profile of Carlton 's interest bearing assets and liabilities at the year end are detailed in notes 18, 19, 21 and 25(a) respectively.

Net interest payable was £35.6m (2000 – £28.4m). A 1 per cent decrease in short-term sterling and dollar interest rates based on the year-end position would increase profits before tax by about £2.0m.

Borrowings are denominated in currencies that match Carlton 's net assets as described below. The fair values of borrowings and cash at the year-end are compared to their book values in Note 25(b).

CURRENCY MANAGEMENT
Carlton faces currency exposure on trading transactions undertaken by its subsidiaries in foreign currencies. In addition, Carlton is also subject to currency exposures resulting from the Technicolor sale consideration.

Carlton hedges a proportion of its transactional exposures by taking out forward foreign exchange contracts of up to four years forward against its anticipated and known sales and purchases. The decision to hedge is influenced by the size of exposure, the certainty of it arising, the trading and market position of the company in which the exposure arises and the current exchange rate.

At the year-end Carlton estimated that its net purchases of foreign currency in 2002 relating to trading transactions would total less than £50m after taking into account foreign currency hedging in place. The year-end fair value of hedging maturing in 2002 was £3.1m below book value, due to forward purchases of Swiss Francs to match Champion's League payments undertaken in previous years when sterling was weaker.

Carlton 's balance sheet translation exposure is managed by partially matching currency assets with a combination of currency borrowings and forward foreign exchange contracts. Post completion of the sale of Technicolor, exposure to the economic interest in 15.5m shares of Thomson has been Carlton 's largest single currency exposure. In November 2001 Carlton entered into a foreign exchange option contract to protect up to half of the anticipated currency translation exposure. A one per cent movement in the Sterling/Euro exchange rate should not impact the value of this investment by more than £3m.

INVESTMENT OF CASH

Carlton operates strict investment guidelines with respect to surplus cash and the emphasis is on preservation of capital. Consequently, discretionary investments with maturity greater than one year must be rated AA or better and discretionary investments of less than one year must be rated A1 or P1 by the major credit rating agencies. There are also conservative limits for individual counter-parties. The maturity profile of investments is managed according to the forecast cash needs of the Group.

Disclosure of accounting policies

6.201 FRS 18 requires financial statements to include a clear, fair and concise explanation of all material or critical accounting policies. Clearly, the disclosure of accounting policies for financial instruments and hedging will be necessary for all companies that are required to comply with FRS 13 as financial instruments and hedging practices are likely to be material for all listed companies. Furthermore, for other companies that use financial instruments, it will be necessary to explain material accounting policies to accord with FRS 18. FRS 18, reinforced by FRS 13, requires that such disclosure should include:

- The methods used to account for derivatives, the types of derivatives accounted for under each method and the criteria that determine the method used.
- The basis for recognising, measuring (both on initial recognition and subsequently) and ceasing to recognise financial instruments.
- How income and expenses (and other gains and losses) are recognised and measured.
- The treatment of financial instruments not recognised, including an explanation of how provisions for losses are recognised on financial instruments that have not been recognised.
- Policies on offsetting.

[FRS 13 para 74].

6.202 Where a company carries its financial instruments at historical cost, the accounting policies would typically cover the treatment of:

- Premiums and discounts on financial assets.
- Changes in the estimated amount of determinable future cash flows associated with a financial instrument, such as a debenture indexed to a commodity price.
- A fall in the fair value of a financial asset to below the asset's carrying value.
- Restructured financial liabilities.

[FRS 13 para 75].

6.203 Where a company accounts for its hedges using hedge accounting, the accounting policies should include a description of:

- The circumstances when a financial instrument is accounted for as a hedge.
- The recognition and measurement principles applied to a hedge instrument.
- The method used to account for an instrument that ceases to be accounted for as a hedge.
- The method used to account for a hedge when the underlying item or position matures, is sold, extinguished, or terminated.
- The method used to account for a hedge of a future transaction when that transaction is no longer likely to occur.

[FRS 13 para 76].

6.204 Again, note that the term 'hedge' here is with reference to original UK GAAP hedge accounting (see para 6.403) and is not the same as the hedge accounting that may be permitted under the provisions of FRS 26/IAS 39.

6.205 It might be expected that these requirements would mean companies producing at least one common disclosure in respect of the use of forward currency and similar contracts. This disclosure would explain whether the company follows the predominant practice as permitted by SSAP 20 paragraph 46 and translates its foreign currency assets and liabilities that it is hedging using, say, forward currency contracts, at the contracted rate. Alternatively, a company's accounting policy might be to amortise the forward premium in the forward currency contract to profit and loss account over the life of the contract and the hedged item would be recorded at the spot rate at inception of the forward contract. Whatever policy a company adopts, it will have an impact on the numerical disclosures on hedging (see from para 6.260).

6.206 Examples of accounting policies from the financial statements of BAE SYSTEMS plc, BP p.l.c. and BG plc are shown in Tables 6.7 to 6.9 below.

Table 6.7 – Accounting policies

BAE SYSTEMS plc – Annual Report – 31 December 2002

Notes to the accounts (extract)

Accounting policies (extract)

Foreign currencies

Transactions in overseas currencies are translated at the exchange rate ruling at the date of the transaction or, where forward cover contracts have been arranged, at the contracted rates. Monetary assets and liabilities denominated in foreign currencies are retranslated at the exchange rates ruling at the balance sheet date or at a contracted rate if applicable and any exchange differences arising are taken to the profit and loss account.

For consolidation purposes the assets and liabilities of overseas subsidiary undertakings and joint ventures are translated at the closing exchange rates. Profit and loss accounts of such undertakings are consolidated at the average rates of exchange during the year. Exchange differences arising on foreign currency net investments are taken to reserves.

Financial instruments

The Group uses derivative financial instruments to hedge its exposures to fluctuations in interest and foreign exchange rates. Instruments accounted for as hedges are designated as a hedge at the inception of contracts. Receipts and payments on interest rate instruments are recognised on an accruals basis, over the life of the instrument. Gains and losses on foreign currency hedges are recognised on maturity of the underlying transaction, other than translational hedges of foreign currency investments which are taken to reserves. Gains and losses arising from retiming of foreign exchange transactional cover are deferred to match the maturity of the underlying exposure. Gains or losses arising on hedging instruments which are cancelled due to the termination of underlying exposure are taken to the profit and loss account immediately. Finance costs associated with debt issuances are charged to the profit and loss account over the life of the instruments.

Table 6.8 – Accounting policies

BP p.l.c. – Annual accounts 31 December 2001

Accounting policies (extract)

Derivative financial instruments

The group uses derivative financial instruments (derivatives) to manage certain exposures to fluctuations in foreign currency exchange rates and interest rates, and to manage some of its margin exposure from changes in oil and natural gas prices. Derivatives are also traded in conjunction with these risk management activities.

The purpose for which a derivative contract is used is identified at inception. To qualify as a derivative for risk management, the contract must be in accordance with established guidelines which ensure that it is effective in achieving its objective. All contracts not identified at inception as being for the purpose of risk management are designated as being held for trading purposes, as are all oil price derivatives, and accounted for using the fair value method, as are all oil price derivatives.

The group accounts for derivatives using the following methods:

Fair value method : derivatives are carried on the balance sheet at fair value ('marked to market') with changes in that value recognized in earnings of the period. This method is used for all derivatives which are held for trading purposes. Interest rate contracts traded by the group include futures, swaps, options and swaptions. Foreign exchange contracts traded include forwards and options. Oil and natural gas price contracts traded include swaps, options and futures.

Accrual method : amounts payable or receivable in respect of derivatives are recognized ratably in earnings over the period of the contracts. This method is used for derivatives held to manage interest rate risk. These are principally swap agreements used to manage the balance between fixed and floating interest rates on long-term finance debt. Other derivatives held for this purpose may include swaptions and futures contracts. Amounts payable or receivable in respect of these derivatives are recognized as adjustments to interest expense over the period of the contracts. Changes in the derivative's fair value are not recognized.

Deferral method : gains and losses from derivatives are deferred and recognized in earnings or as adjustments to carrying amounts, as appropriate, when the underlying debt matures or the hedged transaction occurs. This method is used for derivatives used to convert non-US dollar borrowings into US dollars, to hedge significant non-US dollar firm commitments or anticipated transactions, and to manage some of the group's exposure to natural gas price fluctuations. Derivatives used to convert non-US dollar borrowings into US dollars include foreign currency swap agreements and forward contracts. Gains and losses on these derivatives are deferred and recognized on maturity of the underlying debt, together with the matching loss or gain on the debt. Derivatives used to hedge significant non-US dollar transactions include foreign currency forward contracts and options and to hedge natural gas price exposures include swaps, futures and options. Gains and losses on these contracts and option premia paid are also deferred and recognized in the income statement or as adjustments to carrying amounts, as appropriate, when the hedged transaction occurs.

Where derivatives used to manage interest rate risk or to convert non-US dollar debt or to hedge other anticipated cash flows are terminated before the underlying debt matures or the hedged transaction occurs, the resulting gain or loss is recognized on a basis that matches the timing and accounting treatment of the underlying debt or hedged transaction. When an anticipated transaction is no longer likely to occur or finance debt is terminated before maturity, any deferred gain or loss that has arisen on the related derivative is recognized in the income statement together with any gain or loss on the terminated item.

Table 6.9 – Accounting policies

BG plc – Annual Report and Accounts – 31 December 1999

Principal accounting policies (extract)

Financial instruments
Derivative instruments utilised by the Group are interest rate swaps, foreign currency swaps, forward rate agreements, interest rate swaptions, tax equalisation swaps and forward exchange contracts.

A derivative instrument is considered to be used for hedging purposes when it alters the risk profile of an existing underlying exposure of the Group in line with the Group's risk management policies. Derivatives used for hedging are accounted for on an accruals basis. During the year there were no derivatives used for trading purposes.

Termination payments made or received in respect of derivatives are spread over the shorter of the life of the original instrument or the life of the underlying exposure in cases where the underlying exposure continues to exist. Where the underlying exposure ceases to exist, any termination payments are taken to the profit and loss account.

Interest differentials on derivative instruments are recognised by adjusting the net interest charge. Premiums or discounts on derivative instruments are amortised over the shorter of the life of the instrument or the underlying exposure.

Currency swap agreements and forward exchange contracts are retranslated at the rates ruling in the agreements and contracts. Resulting gains or losses are offset against foreign exchange gains or losses on the related borrowings or, where the instrument is used to hedge a committed future transaction, are deferred until the transaction occurs.

Detailed numerical disclosures

6.207 The aim of the numerical disclosures required in FRS 13 is to show how the entity's objectives and policies were implemented under its strategies in the period and provide supplementary information for evaluating significant or potentially significant exposures. For example, the disclosures include information relevant to an assessment of interest rate and currency risk together with an analysis of fair values and information on the impact of using hedge accounting.

6.208 The disclosures required by the FRS are intended to be highly summarised and the FRS prescribes in some detail the offsetting and aggregation to be used for particular disclosures. However, this does not mean that the offsetting permitted in the disclosures is appropriate for recognition and measurement purposes in the primary financial statements. [FRS 13 para 24]. One effect of the high degree of aggregation and offsetting required, or encouraged, by the FRS is that it may not be possible to trace components of the disclosures back to their respective balance sheet captions. Where this is the case, the FRS encourages additional detail to be provided to facilitate such a reconciliation, unless it would unduly complicate the disclosure. [FRS 13 para 25].

Interest rate risk and currency profiles of financial liabilities

6.209 The standard requires extensive disclosure in respect of interest rate risks by currency related to the company's financial liabilities and where material, its financial assets (see para 6.224 below). An entity's financial liabilities are its contractual obligations to deliver cash or other financial assets to another entity or to exchange financial instruments with another entity under conditions that are potentially unfavourable. [FRS 13 para 2]. Consequently, this disclosure will embrace an entity's borrowings, finance lease obligations, trade creditors, certain provisions (such as those for onerous leasehold commitments) and, for the reasons explained in paragraphs 6.182 and 6.183, its non-equity shares and non-equity minority interests. A company may exclude from these disclosures those items that fall within the definition of short-term 'trade' creditors. [FRS 13 para 6].

6.210 For each major currency, financial liabilities should be analysed to show those at fixed rates, those at floating rates and those on which no interest is paid. Finance lease obligations, deep discounted bonds and other liabilities where the finance cost is allocated in accordance with FRS 4 or SSAP 21 are interest-bearing liabilities and should not be included as 'financial liabilities on which no interest is paid'. [FRS 13 para 27]. Non-interest bearing financial liabilities would include long-term trade creditors or qualifying provisions that are not discounted. Floating rate financial liabilities are defined as those that have their interest rate reset at least once a year. [FRS 13 para 2]. Those that reset less frequently are to be treated as fixed rate financial liabilities. However, the standard is silent on items such as deferred consideration or long-term monetary provisions where these are discounted. It can be argued that such discounted items are floating rate financial liabilities as the discount rate will have to be re-appraised, and changed if necessary, at least once a year to ensure that the financial liability reflects current market assessments of the time value of money and the risks specific to the liability, as required by FRS 12 'Provisions, contingent liabilities and contingent assets'.

6.211 The standard requires the interest rate risk disclosures to be shown on a gross basis, that is without netting off cash, other liquid resources or similar items. [FRS 13 para 31]. Where a company wishes to show the interest rate risk disclosures on a net basis, for example where it manages its interest rate risk on a net basis, it can do so by giving additional information showing the net position as long as the gross position is also disclosed.

6.212 For each of the major currencies, the following details of interest rates should be disclosed:

- The weighted average interest rate for fixed rate financial liabilities.
- The weighted average period for which interest rates are fixed.
- The weighted average period until maturity of non-interest bearing financial liabilities.

- The benchmark rate for determining interest rate payments for floating rate financial instruments. This could, for example, result in disclosure that floating rate borrowings bear interest based on LIBOR. Although the standard has no requirement for disclosure of the interest differential this may well be caught by the disclosure requirement in the Companies Act (see para 6.185), as suggested by the footnote to the illustrative disclosures in appendix III to the standard.

[FRS 13 para 30].

6.213 The analysis should take account of instruments such as swaps and other derivatives, the effect of which is to alter the interest basis or currency of the financial liability (described as 'non-optional derivatives'). For example, if the company has a floating rate borrowing and has taken out an interest rate swap to swap its interest obligation to fixed rate, the borrowing would be disclosed in the table as a fixed rate borrowing. Other instruments, such as caps and collars, that are associated with these financial liabilities and which convert those liabilities over only a limited range of interest rates (described as 'optional derivatives') and cannot be adequately reflected in the analysis should be excluded and explained separately, as should any financial liabilities and non-optional derivatives with unusual terms. [FRS 13 para 26]. Convertible debt is an example of a financial liability that may be more appropriately dealt with separately outside the analysis.

6.214 For those instruments excluded from the analysis, there should be disclosure of the main terms and conditions sufficient to enable the reader to understand their significance. This could include a summary of the following:

- Notional principal amounts involved.
- Rates of interest.
- Periods for which contracts are operative.
- Terms of any options contained within the instrument.

[FRS 13 para 29].

6.215 Examples of the disclosures outlined above are shown in Tables 6.10 and 6.11 below by companies that have included FRS 13 disclosures in their financial statements. Table 6.10 illustrates an occasion when provisions that meet the definition of a financial liability are included in the disclosure.

Table 6.10 – Interest rate risk and currency profiles of financial liabilities

BG plc – Annual Report and Accounts – 31 December 1999

Notes to the accounts (extract)

19 Currency and Interest Rate Composition of The Group's Financial Liabilities and Borrowings (extract)

The following table analyses the currency and interest rate composition of the Group's financial liabilities after the effect of swaps.

	Fixed rate weighted average period years	Fixed rate weighted average interest rate %	Fixed borrowings £m	Floating borrowings £m	Gross borrowings £m	Other financial liabilities (a) £m	**1999 Total £m**	1998 Total £m
Currency:								
Sterling	6.7	6.2	3 246	3 407	6 653	217	**6 870**	4 120
US dollars	3.7	8.4	311	378	689	–	**689**	683
Brazilian reals	1.9	11.4	46	12	58	–	**58**	–
Indian rupees	4.1	14.0	24	–	24	–	**24**	26
			3 627	3 797	7 424	217	**7 641**	4 829

For the purposes of the above tables, debt with a maturity within one year, such as commercial paper, bills of exchange and other money market borrowings, has been treated as fixed. Index-inked bonds have been treated as floating. Borrowings falling due after more than one year of £5 333m (1998 £3 199m) (after currency and interest rate swaps) can be analysed as fixed interest rate 33% (1998 68%) and floating interest rate 67% (1998 32%).

(a) The weighted average period of other financial liabilities, which relate to provisions for long-term gas sales contracts (see Note 23), was 7 years as at 31 December 1999. These provisions have been discounted at around 10%.

Table 6.11 – Interest rate risk profile of financial liabilities and financial assets

South African Breweries Plc – Annual Report – 31 March 1999

Notes to the Consolidated Financial Statements (extract)

30 Financial instruments

Interest rate risk profile of financial liabilities and financial assets

After taking into account the Group's interest rate and currency swaps and forward rate agreements the currency and interest rate exposures of the gross borrowings of the Group for the year ended 31 March 1999 were:

	Total	Floating rate financial liabilities	Fixed rate financial liabilities	Financial liabilities where no interest is paid
Currency	**US$m**	**US$m**	**US$m**	**US$m**
Rand	488	325	163	
US dollars	186	88	98	114
Central European currencies	41	41	–	–
EU currencies	86	83	3	
Other currencies	152	141	11	–
At 31 March 1999	**953**	**678**	**275**	**114**
Rand	640	439	201	–
US dollars	341	257	84	139
Central European currencies	50	49	1	–
EU currencies	11	11	–	–
Other currencies	10	10	–	–
At 31 March 1998	1,052	766	286	139

Based on the above floating rate borrowings at 31 March 1999, a 1 per cent change in interest rates would impact Group pre-tax profits, over a twelve month period, by approximately US$7 million (R41 million)

	Fixed rate financial liabilities		Financial liabilities on which no interest is paid
Currency	**Weighted average interest rate %**	**Weighted average period for which rate is fixed (years)**	**Weighted average term to maturity years**
Rand	15	2	–
US dollars	8	2	1
EU currencies	5	4	–
Other currencies	6	4	–
At 31 March 1999	**12**	**2**	**1**
Rand	15	2	–
US dollars	9	3	2
Other currencies	16	2	–
At 31 March 1998	13	3	2

Floating rate borrowings are mainly bank sourced and bear interest at various money market rates which include overnight call, 90 day bankers' acceptance, and up to the 12 month term rates in respect of SA rand activities. US dollar floating rate borrowings are fixed in advance for periods ranging from 90 to 180 days and are mainly priced by references to LIBOR. Central European borrowing rates vary significantly between the various functional currency areas comprising this region, but are priced by reference to a combination of local market rates or LIBOR depending on the sophistication of the various markets.

The Group held the following financial assets, as part of the financing arrangements of the Group, during the year ended 31 March 1999.

	1999	1998	**1999**	1998
	US$m	US$m	**Rm**	£m
US dollar listed equity investments	–	177	–	891
Rand short-term deposits	–	–	**3**	–
US dollar short-term deposits	**587**	–	**3,638**	–
Other short-term deposits	**25**	10	**152**	49
Rand cash	**28**	327	**168**	1,650
US dollar cash	**57**	13	**357**	64
Other cash	**52**	75	**322**	377
	749	602	**4,640**	3,031

The above financial assets are all priced at floating rates with interest rates reset and/or maturity dates within one year. Rand assets attract interest rates at the overnight money market call rate, and US dollar assets attract LIBOR related interest rates at various margins. Other currencies include those of central European countries, the African continent and Australasia. No other currency represents a significant amount.

Rand cash and short-term deposits are subject to South African exchange control regulations. South Africa's exchange control regulations provide for restrictions on exporting capital from South Africa.

Maturity analysis of financial liabilities

6.216 A maturity profile of the carrying amount of financial liabilities (that is, those recognised on the balance sheet) is also required. This would show the total amounts falling due within the following time bands:

- In one year or less, or on demand.
- In more than one year, but not more than two years.
- In more than two years, but not more than five years.
- In more than five years.

[FRS 13 para 38].

6.217 This profile, which is, to a large extent, an aggregation of the analyses of debt and finance leases already required by the original FRS 4 and SSAP 21, is based on the carrying amounts determined by reference to the earliest date on which payment can be required or on which the liability falls due. The standard requires the maturity analysis to include all financial liabilities, other than short-term 'trade' creditors (if the exemption is utilised), and thus embraces the same liabilities that are analysed in the interest risk disclosure. Financial liabilities will also include, for example, swaps and non-optional derivatives, if they are recognised on balance sheet.

6.218 An amount that is due exactly five years after the balance sheet date falls within the third band 'in more than two years, but not more than five years', rather than the fourth one 'in more than five years'. Similarly an amount due exactly two years after the balance sheet date falls within the second band, 'in more than one year, but not more than two years'.

6.219 Where the original FRS 4 analysis of debt and the SSAP 21 analysis of finance lease obligations are disclosed in the same table as the FRS 13 maturity analysis, the analysis of debt and finance lease obligations will need to be based on the carrying amounts. They should not, for example, be based on the amounts to be paid on maturity or, in the case of finance lease obligations, on the gross obligations before deducting finance charges. Also the maturity analysis specified in SSAP 21 for finance leases only requires disclosure of the amounts payable in the second to fifth years inclusive, hence, this amount would have to be further analysed to satisfy FRS 13's requirements into amounts that are payable in more than one year, but not more than two years and those that are payable in more than two years, but not more than five years. [FRS 13 para 39]. In addition, an analysis of other financial liabilities would need to be given. An illustration of a combined disclosure using a columnar approach is given below.

Illustration of the maturity analysis

The maturity profile of the carrying amount of the group's financial liabilities, other than short-term trade creditors and accruals and the non-redeemable non-equity minority interests, at 31 December was as follows:

	Debt	Finance leases	Other financial liabilities	20X1 Total	Debt	Other financial liabilities	20X0 Total
	£m	£m	£m	£m	£m	£m	£m
In one year or less, or on demand	88.9	3.5	51.7	144.1	41.7	4.1	45.8
In more than one year but not more than two years	0.5	3.5	16.8	20.8	0.9	1.0	1.9
In more than two years but not more than five years	284.1	6.1	13.8	304.0	-	1.0	1.0
In more than five years	4.1	-	29.4	33.5	3.0	3.8	6.8
	377.6	13.1	111.7	502.4	45.6	9.9	55.5

Debt due after five years includes £2.0m (20X0: £2.0m) in respect of the company's preference shares. Other financial liabilities include the provisions for vacant leasehold properties £68.4m (20X0: £6.3m).

The company's £224.7m bank loan (gross of unamortised issue costs of £4.2m) is repayable within twelve months of the balance sheet date, but as the amount is drawn under a five year committed multi-option facility it is classified in the table above as repayable between two and five years on the basis of the expiry date of the facility in May 20X5.

6.220 Table 6.12 illustrates another method of disclosure by presenting a maturity analysis of total financial liabilities (including relevant provisions), gross borrowings and net borrowings. The latter is not required by the standard, but is an interesting interpretation of the suggestion in paragraph 43 of the standard that it might be helpful to provide a maturity analysis of financial assets in order to put the maturity analysis of financial liabilities and borrowing facilities in their proper context.

Table 6.12 – Maturity analysis of financial liabilities

BG plc — Annual Report and Accounts — 31 December 1999

Notes to the Accounts (extract)

18 Borrowings and financial instruments (extract)

Maturity profile of the Group's financial liabilities
The following table analyses the Group's financial liabilities comprising gross borrowings plus any long-term contractual obligations to deliver cash or other financial assets to another entity, after taking account of currency and interest rate swaps. These are repayable as follows:

	Total financial liabilities		Gross borrowings		Net borrowings (i)	
	1999	1998	**1999**	1998	**1999**	1998
	£m	£m	**£m**	£m	**£m**	£m
Within one year	**2 082**	1 403	**2 091**	1 394	**1 539**	850
Between one and two years	**613**	357	**613**	357	**613**	357
Between two and three years	**357**	755	**354**	755	**354**	755
Between three and four years	**778**	152	**762**	149	**762**	149
Between four and five years	**486**	759	**464**	743	**464**	743
After five years	**3 325**	1 403	**3 140**	1 195	**3 140**	1 195
	7 641	4 829	**7 424**	4 593	**6 872**	4 049

Further information on total financial liabilities is given in Note 19.
Net borrowings comprise gross borrowings less current asset investments and cash at bank and in hand.

Maturity analysis of undrawn committed borrowing facilities

6.221 FRS 13 also requires an analysis to be given of the maturity of material undrawn committed borrowing facilities, showing separately amounts expiring:

- In one year or less.
- In more than one year, but not more than two years.
- In more than two years.

[FRS 13 para 40].

If there are conditions that attach to a particular facility, then it should only be included in the above analysis if all the conditions are satisfied at the balance sheet date.

6.222 The maturity analysis of financial liabilities outlined in paragraph 6.216 above will include the drawn element of certain committed borrowing facilities. For example, a company might have an overdraft facility of £50 million, and by the year end it might have drawn on this facility and have an overdraft balance of £20 million, which would be included in the financial liabilities maturity analysis as an amount falling due for repayment 'in one year or less, or on demand'. To avoid double-counting, any amounts drawn down under borrowing facilities should not also be disclosed in the maturity analysis of undrawn committed borrowing facilities. [FRS 13 para 41]. Consequently, in this example only £30 million, which is the undrawn element of the committed facility, would be included in the undrawn committed facilities table. Furthermore, its inclusion in a particular banding in the analysis would depend on the date on which the facility expires. For example, if it were to expire in 18 months time, then the £30 million would appear in the line for amounts expiring 'in more than one year but not more than two years' even though the overdraft balance itself is categorised in the financial liabilities maturity analysis as 'in one year or less, or on demand'.

6.223 In order to enable the reader to assess the significance of these facilities, the FRS recommends that disclosure is given of the purpose and the period for which these facilities are committed and the extent to which they are subject to annual review by the provider of finance. This additional information is not mandatory. [FRS 13 para 42]. In any case, listed companies that continue to prepare an OFR should, and when preparing a business review may, already include a comment on liquidity and this may include details such as those suggested in the FRS (see further chapter 2 of the Manual of Accounting – IFRS for the UK).

Details of financial assets

6.224 If the reporting entity has significant holdings of financial assets, interest rate risk and currency profile analyses similar to those required for financial liabilities and described from paragraph 6.209 above should be provided (see Table 6.10 in para 6.215). [FRS 13 para 32]. A maturity profile similar to that described in paragraph 6.216 is not required, but may be presented if this would show the maturity analyses of financial liabilities and borrowing facilities in their proper context. [FRS 13 para 43].

6.225 Financial assets, those on-balance sheet and any derivative or other financial assets that are off-balance sheet, will have to be dealt with in the fair value disclosures (see from para 6.241). In the case of derivative financial assets used as hedging instruments these will also feature in the hedge disclosures (see from para 6.260).

6.226 Financial assets include holdings of cash, short-term deposits with banks, buildings societies or other financial institutions, money market investments, certificates of deposit, another company's commercial paper or loan stock, gilts and any other instruments that are classified as current asset investments or cash at bank and in hand in the balance sheet. Consequently, they include those assets regarded as liquid resources for cash flow classification purposes under FRS 1. Financial assets also include trade debtors, finance lease receivables, investments in equity shares (for example, trade investments) and other instruments that neither pay interest nor have a maturity date.

6.227 In determining the necessity for making the disclosures, the following points should be borne in mind. Short-term trading receivables due from associates and joint ventures can be excluded from the interest rate analysis under the exemption in paragraph 6 of the standard (with appropriate disclosure). However, long-term trading receivables due from, and all loans to or other financing type balances with, associates and joint ventures have to be dealt with in the interest rate disclosure. Such items also feature in the fair value disclosure.

6.228 In certain situations inter-company balances with parents, subsidiaries and fellow subsidiaries have to be included in the interest rate and currency profile and fair value disclosures. A particular example is the situation where an intermediate parent company has listed securities and has to prepare consolidated financial statements that comply with FRS 13. Although inter-company balances with subsidiaries should eliminate on consolidation, those with parents and fellow subsidiaries do not and are thus caught. The disclosures of the fair value of intra-group balances of the nature discussed in paragraphs 6.227 and 6.228 go beyond those required by FRS 8, 'Related party disclosures', and they may well have implications for tax purposes, particularly where the loan or other arrangement is not on an arm's length basis.

6.229 For equity shares and similar instruments, the disclosures will be typically limited to a footnote stating that they had been excluded from the interest rate risk and currency profile, as they have no maturity date and would thus distort the weighted average period information and the provision of pertinent information about any currency exposures involved. [FRS 13 para 33]. Financial assets on which no interest is earned include undiscounted long-term trade debtors, but do not include, for example, investments in deep discounted bonds for which an interest income can be imputed or holdings of another company's preference shares. [FRS 13 para 27]. In the latter case, the coupon is regarded as interest.

Currency risk disclosures

6.230 FRS 13 requires an analysis of the net amount of monetary assets and monetary liabilities at the balance sheet date, by reference to the principal functional currency of the reporting entity's operations, showing the amount denominated in each principal currency. [FRS 13 para 34]. Functional currency is defined in an identical manner to SSAP 20's definition of local currency, namely, "*the currency of the primary economic environment in which an entity operates and* *generates net cash flows*". [FRS 13 para 2]. The purpose of this analysis is to explain the currency exposures that give rise to those exchange gains and losses that are taken to the profit and loss account. [FRS 13 para 35]. The analysis will, therefore, need to be constructed to reflect the entity's application of SSAP 20. [FRS 13 para 36].

6.231 The term 'monetary assets and liabilities' refers to money held and amounts to be received or paid in money. [SSAP 20 para 44]. Consequently, whether or not short-term 'trade' debtors and creditors have been included within the other disclosures required by FRS 13, they are required to be included in the table of currency risk exposures (see further para 6.166). [FRS 13 para 6]. The amounts disclosed should be after taking account of currency swaps, forward contracts and other derivatives that contribute to the matching of the foreign currency exposures. [FRS 13 para 34(d)]. Thus, for example, if a UK company has taken out a forward exchange contract in respect of euro debtors to effectively convert the amounts receivable into sterling, then for the purpose of this analysis these debtors should be treated as a sterling asset. Therefore, in extreme circumstances where all currency exposures are hedged with counterparties external to the reporting entity there will be nothing to report, as demonstrated in Table 6.14 below (see para 6.240). In addition, a summary of the main effect should be given of any derivative financial instruments that have not been taken into account.

6.232 Only the principal functional currencies and the principal currencies in which the monetary items are denominated need be given. Monetary assets and liabilities denominated in the same functional currency as the particular operation should be excluded from the analysis. Similarly, where a company has foreign currency borrowings that provide a hedge against foreign net investments, under SSAP 20 gains and losses arising on translation would be taken to the statement of total recognised gains and losses not to the profit and loss account; consequently, such borrowings are 'matched' and are excluded from the analysis. [FRS 13 para 34]. As the analysis is prepared at the year end, it is somewhat forward looking as an indicator of those currency exposures that might give rise to gains and losses in the following year's profit and loss account, as well as representing the currency exposures that existed throughout the year. If the period end position is regarded as materially unrepresentative of the entity's position during the period then an explanation is required. [FRS 13 para 20]. The fact that the net position for the group as a whole may be zero due to compensating exposures in different parts of the group does not remove the necessity to provide the disclosure.

6.233 To illustrate the requirement consider the following example.

Example

Group A plc consists of the parent company in the UK, two subsidiaries in North America, one in the USA and the other in Canada, a subsidiary in Japan, a subsidiary in France and a number of small subsidiaries in other countries. The principal functional currencies of group A's operations are thus sterling, US dollar, the Yen and the euro. Since the Canadian dollar is aligned with the US dollar, it is considered to have the same currency risk and is thus not separately identified. To compile the required currency risk disclosure, each of the companies' operations has to analyse its year end balance sheet to identify those monetary assets and monetary liabilities that are in currencies other than its own functional currency (excluding those that it has hedged into its functional currency). This process determines that: the UK parent has US dollar, Yen and euro exposures; the French subsidiary has sterling, US dollar and Yen exposures; the North American operations are exposed to sterling only; the Japanese subsidiary has exposures in sterling, US dollar and the euro; and the other subsidiaries, collectively, have sterling, US dollar and euro exposures as well as some smaller exposures to other currencies. Consequently, group A constructs the following grid to make the required disclosure.

Illustration of the disclosure of currency exposures

Functional currency of group operation	Net foreign currency monetary assets/(liabilities)					
	Sterling £m	**US dollar £m**	**Yen £m**	**Euro £m**	**Other £m**	**Total £m**
Sterling	–	20	10	–	–	30
US dollar	15	–	–	–	–	15
Yen	(30)	30	–	(90)	–	(90)
Euro	25	(300)	40	–	–	(235)
Other	(10)	(30)	–	40	10	10
Total	–	(280)	50	(50)	10	(270)

The amounts in the table take into account the effect of currency swaps, forward contracts and other derivatives entered into to manage currency exposures.

6.234 In this example, group A has US dollar monetary assets of £20 million in the UK and £30 million in Japan and US dollar liabilities of £300 million in France and £30 million in other countries. Hence, at the balance sheet date the group has £280 million of aggregate US dollar net liabilities, which result in gains or losses being recognised in the profit and loss account.

6.235 If the £300 million US dollar liabilities in France was a borrowing and was treated as a hedge of US dollar assets on consolidation, group A's US dollar position would be reduced to an asset of only £20 million and the total net foreign currency exposure would be only £30 million. Hence, it is easy to see how the picture portrayed by this analysis can be changed significantly. For groups with sophisticated treasury functions and diverse geographic operations the collation of the information from subsidiaries is not an easy task and the preparation and interpretation of this disclosure can be complex.

6.236 In preparing the required analysis, the interaction of foreign currency inter-company balances should not be overlooked. For example, if, in the above illustration, company A has sold goods or services to its US subsidiary and invoiced for these in sterling, the inter-company balance so created will cause a sterling exposure for the US operation. The exchange gains or losses on retranslation into US dollars at each balance sheet date until the balance is settled will go to the US profit and loss account and hence flow through into group A's consolidated profit and loss account. Although the inter company balances eliminate on consolidation, there is no elimination of the exchange differences in the profit and loss account. Consequently, in the above example, the sterling/US dollar inter-company exposure would be included in the £15 million sterling net monetary assets in the US.

6.237 Alternatively, assume that company A has made a US dollar loan to its US subsidiary to finance its activities and that, for all practical purposes, this is as permanent as equity and thus treated under SSAP 20 paragraph 20 as part of its net investment in the US. The US dollar/sterling exposure arising in company A would not feature in the required analysis since the exchange gains and losses would be taken to the statement of total recognised gains and losses under the provisions of SSAP 20.

6.238 Another feature that should not be overlooked when preparing the currency risk disclosure is the consequence of hedging transactions where the counterparty is another group company, perhaps one acting as a group treasury function. Any hedging transaction that removes the currency risk from one area of the group's operations to another merely shifts the place that the exposure is reported. Only in circumstances where the risk is on-hedged with counterparties external to the group or the internal counterparty has an existing, and opposite, currency risk, is the exposure reduced or removed and thus reported as such in the analysis required by FRS 13.

6.239 For example, a UK parent company has €10 million of creditors due for payment in three months from the balance sheet date. Its French subsidiary has £6.5 million of debtors due to be received in three months from the balance sheet date. If neither company hedges its exposures to foreign currencies, the group's currency risk disclosure would show the UK parent with a euro exposure of £6.5 million (assuming €1 = £0.65) and the French subsidiary with a sterling exposure of £6.5 million. However, if the parent company and its French subsidiary enter into a three month forward currency contract with each other at the balance date to buy euro and sell sterling, the French subsidiary removes its exposure to sterling and thus regards the sterling debtors as euro for the purposes of the currency risk analysis. For UK parent the forward contract eliminates the euro exposure on its creditors. Hence, there is nothing to show for either group operation under the currency risk disclosures. However, in the absence of the euro creditors in the UK parent company, the forward currency contract removes the reportable sterling exposure from France and creates a reportable euro exposure in the UK within the group's currency risk disclosure.

6.240 An example of the required disclosure is provided by South African Breweries Plc in Table 6.13 in its March 1999 financial statements. However, in the case where a company's policy is to hedge all currency exposures the disclosure becomes a 'nil report' as shown in example 2 of annex 1 to this chapter and by Imperial Chemical Industries PLC in Table 6.14.

Table 6.13 – Disclosure of currency exposures

South African Breweries Plc – Annual Report & Accounts – 31 March 1999

Notes to the accounts (extract)

30 Financial instruments (extract)

Currency exposures

The Group seeks to mitigate the effect of the currency exposures arising from its net investments overseas by borrowing as far as possible in the same currencies as the operating currencies of its main operating units. Gains and losses arising on net investments overseas and the financial instruments used to hedge the currency exposures are recognised in the statement of total recognised gains and losses.

The table adjacent shows the extent to which group companies have monetary assets and liabilities in currencies other than their local currency. Foreign exchange differences on translation of earnings are taken to the profit and loss account of the Group.

Net foreign currency monetary assets/(liabilities)

	Rand	US dollar	Central European currencies	EU currencies	Other African currencies	Other currencies	Total
Functional currency of Group operation	US$m	US$m	US$m	US$m	US$m	US$m	US$m
Rand	–	6	–	(2)	–	–	4
US dollars	–	–	1	–	–	–	1
Central European currencies	–	(13)	–	(8)	–	–	(21)
Other African currencies	(3)	(22)	–	(1)	–	–	(26)
Other currencies	–	–	–	5	–	–	5
31 March 1999	(3)	**(29)**	1	(6)			(37)
Rand	–	20	–	–	–	–	20
US dollars	–	–	–	–	19	(2)	17
Central European currencies	–	(4)	–	(11)	–	–	(15)
Other African currencies	(13)	(16)	–	(2)	–	–	(31)
Other currencies	–	(3)	–	–	–	–	(3)
31 March 1998	**(13)**	**(3)**	–	(13)	19	(2)	(12)

Table 6.14 – Currency exposures on monetary assets and liabilities

Imperial Chemical Industries PLC – Annual report and accounts and Form 20-F-31 December 1999

Notes relating to the accounts (extract)

40 Financial risk management (extract)

(b) Currency exposures on monetary assets and liabilities
As explained in the Operating and financial review, on page 22, the Group's policy is, where practicable, to hedge all exposures on monetary assets and liabilities.

Fair value disclosures

6.241 Disclosure is required of the fair values of all financial assets and liabilities, whether recognised (on-balance sheet) or not (off-balance sheet), compared to their book value, other than those exempted under paragraph 5 of the FRS (see para 6.163). [FRS 13 para 44]. In addition, disclosure of the fair value of short-term 'trade' debtors and creditors is not required if the exemption in paragraph 6 of the FRS is used (see para 6.166). The fair value should be given regardless of whether or not the instrument is used for hedging purposes. Such instruments are, like other instruments, to be disclosed by category and the standard suggests that it might be useful to indicate the link between the hedging instrument and the item that it is hedging and explain whether the fair value of the hedged item is also disclosed. [FRS 13 para 47].

6.242 It should be remembered that in producing the disclosure, unlike other FRS 13 disclosures, fair values should be given without taking into account related derivatives For example, a fixed rate debt that has been swapped into floating rate debt by an interest rate swap will not appear as a floating rate debt in the fair value disclosure, as it does in the interest rate risk disclosure. It will be included as fixed rate debt within the fair value disclosure and the fair value of the interest rate swap will be included within, say, a category of 'derivative financial instruments used to manage interest rate risk'. The fair value of the synthetic floating rate debt is thus shown by the separate fair values of its constituent elements.

Determination of fair values

6.243 For the purpose of the required disclosures, fair value is defined as "*. . .the amount at which an asset or liability could be exchanged in an arm's length transaction between informed and willing parties, other than in a forced or liquidation sale*". [FRS 13 para 2]. Often, quoted market prices will provide the best evidence of fair value. However, where there is little or no activity in a particular market, or there is no market at all, the FRS requires that estimation techniques are used (such as prices of similar instruments, discounted cash flows or option-pricing models) that will usually give a sufficiently reliable measure of fair value. If measurement of fair value proves particularly difficult, a range of values could be disclosed. [FRS 13 para 54(a); App IV paras 7-9]. In certain circumstances although a fair value might not be available for an individual financial instrument, it might be possible to value a portfolio of such instruments. Where this is so the standard requires the portfolio value to be used and disclosed. [FRS 13 para 54(b)]. The methods used and any significant assumptions used to determine fair value should be disclosed. [FRS 13 para 51]. Further guidance on fair valuing is given in appendix IV to the standard.

6.244 In extreme cases, where it is not practicable to estimate fair values with sufficient reliability, no fair value need be disclosed, but the following must be disclosed instead:

- A description of the financial asset or liability and its carrying amount
- The reasons why it is not practicable to estimate fair value with sufficient reliability.
- Information about the principal characteristics of the instrument that are pertinent to estimating its fair value (for example, the factors that determine or affect the instrument's cash flows and the market for such instruments). But such information need not be disclosed if in the directors' opinion its disclosure at the level of aggregation and date of disclosure would be seriously prejudicial to the company's interests. The fact that such information has not been disclosed and the reason for non-disclosure should then be given.

[FRS 13 para 53].

6.245 The ASB expects that this exemption should be used only as a last resort, after all viable alternatives have been exhausted and it suggests that the following factors should generally be present if the exemption is to be invoked:

- The instrument is unique and no comparable instruments exist.
- The future cash flows associated with the instrument are difficult to predict with any degree of reliability.
- A reliable valuation model is not available from either internal or external sources.

[FRS 13 para 55].

6.246 It might only be possible for the fair value to be ascertained for some of the financial instruments included within a category. Where this is so, the standard requires the fair value of that sub-set to be disclosed and the disclosures set out in paragraph 6.244 above to be given for the rest of that category. [FRS 13 para 54(c)].

Disclosure by category

6.247 Unless a reporting entity has very few financial instruments or the differences between book value and fair value are immaterial, a table is the best means of disclosure. For this purpose instruments should be grouped into appropriate categories. The illustrative examples given in the appendices to FRS 13 group financial instruments into the following categories:

- Primary financial instruments held or issued to finance the group's operations
- Derivative financial instruments held to manage the interest rate and currency profile.
- Derivative financial instruments held or issued to hedge the currency exposure on expected future sales.
- Financial instruments held or issued for trading.

As a result of grouping, a loan and a cross-currency swap will appear in different categories, for example, the loan in 'primary instruments' and the swap in 'derivative financial instruments used to manage interest rate and currency profile'.

6.248 In the illustrative example given in the appendices to the standard, fair values are given for each of the groups of financial instruments within the categories noted above. The standard's wording requires that for each category there should be disclosure of the aggregate fair value together with the aggregate carrying amount. Taken together with the illustration in appendix II, we interpret this to mean that each of the group's of financial instruments should be aggregated together and shown below each of the categories specified in the bullet points in paragraph 6.247.

6.249 When grouping financial instruments into categories, it is important to group like with like. Typically, the categories will follow the same structure as, but be in more detail than, that used in discussing the objectives, policies and strategies for holding or issuing financial instruments. Therefore, although financial assets and financial liabilities would not usually be included in the same category, an exception might be made to group together similar derivatives held or issued for the same purpose, regardless of whether their fair value was positive or negative. For example, interest rate and currency derivatives used for hedging would usually be grouped separately from those that are traded. However, the standard suggests that these categories should be analysed in more detail, for example, interest rate swaps shown separately from currency swaps and there should be separate disclosure of optional derivatives, such as currency options and interests caps and collars. [FRS 13 para 46].

6.250 The standard allows disclosure for a particular category of financial instrument of either the aggregate fair values (that is, a net figure) at the balance sheet date or the aggregate fair value of items with a positive fair value and the aggregate of items with a negative fair value. [FRS 13 para 44(a)(b)]. For example, some forward contracts will be in the money and have a positive fair value, whereas others will be out of the money and have a negative fair value. At any one time, an entity could have a portfolio of forward contracts, each issued for the same purposes, having both positive and negative fair values. A single forward contract could change from being a financial asset to a financial liability over time as it moves in and out of the money. Although the standard allows disclosure of either a single net fair value or the gross fair values (both negative and positive), it points out that for companies that may be developing systems to capture information for disclosure, a subsequent FRS on recognition and measurement of financial instruments might require that most or all financial assets and financial liabilities should be carried on the balance sheet at fair values. In this case, gross figures would be required.

Book value versus fair value

6.251 In preparing the fair value disclosure, it is important to remember that the standard requires the disclosure of the fair value of the separate instruments used by the reporting entity, albeit grouped together in appropriate categories as discussed above. It is less clear what should be shown alongside each of the fair values, because the standard refers only to the aggregate carrying amount in paragraph 44(a). This issue is considered further in paragraph 6.277.

6.252 All derivative financial instruments will have a fair value; whether they have a book value will depend on how much cash has been paid or received and will also depend on the accounting policy for such items. A 'book value' can arise because the accounting policy might be to mark-to-market the derivatives and recognise them on-balance sheet.

6.253 For some short-term financial instruments such as cash, and for floating rate debt, the difference between carrying amount and fair value will generally be immaterial. In such cases, the carrying amount may be used in place of fair value. However, both the carrying amount and fair value, which in this case will be the same figure, should still be disclosed; in some cases, it may be possible to state that the numbers are the same. [FRS 13 para 48]. Clearly, certain longer-term debtors, creditors and provisions if they are undisclosed might have market values that differ from their carrying values. This will be the case for long-term fixed rate debt and also for long-term debtors where the delay in settlement is not compensated by interest at current market rates.

6.254 In preparing the disclosure a practical problem arises if the book amount of a borrowing includes unamortised issue costs in accordance with FRS 4. Should the fair value of that borrowing be adjusted for an equivalent amount of unamortised issue costs? A solution would be to show the 'book value' of the borrowing gross of the unamortised issue costs as a comparison to the borrowing's 'clean' fair value. A footnote to the fair value disclosure should explain the adjustment made to the book amount of the borrowing thus providing the ability to trace the item back to its balance sheet caption. [FRS 13 para 25].

6.255 When obtaining fair values of borrowings, either internally or by asking the company's bankers or broker to do so, care should be taken to request a valuation that is clean of any interest accrual. The book amount of borrowings will not include the interest accrual, so neither should the fair value.

6.256 Examples of the fair value disclosures are shown below in Tables 6.15, South African Breweries Plc and 6.16, British Telecommunications plc. Whereas South African Breweries Plc analyses its derivatives by function, that is, their use to manage interest and currency profile or as anticipatory hedges. British Telecommunications plc shows their association with assets and liabilities.

Table 6.15 – Fair value disclosure

South African Breweries Plc – Annual Report and Accounts – 31 March 2000

Notes to the Consolidated Financial Statements (extract)

30 Financial instruments (extract)

Fair values of financial assets and financial liabilities

The following table presents the carrying amounts and the fair values of the group's financial instruments as at 31 March 2000. Fair value is the amount at which a financial instrument could be exchanged in an arm's length transaction between informed and willing parties, other than in a forced or liquidation sale and excludes accrued interest. Where available, market values have been used to determine fair values. Where market values are not available, fair values have been calculated by discounting expected cash flows at prevailing interest and exchange rates. The estimated net fair values, have been determined using available market information and appropriate valuation methodologies, as detailed below, but are not necessarily indicative of the amounts that the group could realise in the normal course of business.

	2000		1999	
	Book value US$m	**Fair value US$m**	Book value US$m	Fair value US$m
Primary financial instruments held or issued to finance the Group's operations				
Short-term borrowings and current portion of long-term borrowings	**308**	**308**	278	278
Long-term borrowings	**294**	**294**	675	682
Financial assets	**651**	**651**	1,320	1,320
Other financial liabilities	**1,085**	**1,085**	1,044	1,044
Derivative financial instruments held to manage the interest rate and currency profile				
Interest rate swaps and forward rate agreements	–	–	–	1
Forward foreign exchange contracts	–	**2**	–	1
Derivative financial instruments held or issued to hedge the currency exposure on expected future transactions				
Interest rate swaps and forward rate agreements	–	–	–	–
Forward foreign exchange contracts	–	1	–	–

Table 6.16 – Fair value disclosure

British Telecommunications plc – Annual Report and Form 20-F – 31 March 2001

Notes to the Financial Statements (extract)

33. Financial instruments and risk management (extract)

(d) Fair value of financial instruments
The following table shows the carrying amounts and fair values of the group's financial instruments at 31 March 2001 and 2000. The carrying amounts are included in the group balance sheet under the indicated headings, with the exception of derivative amounts, which are included in debtors or other creditors or as part of net debt as appropriate. The fair values of the financial instruments are the amount at which the instruments could be exchanged in a current transaction between willing parties, other than in a forced or liquidation sale.

	Carrying amount		Fair value	
	2001 £m	2000 £m	**2001 £m**	2000 £m
Non-derivatives				
Assets				
Cash at bank and in hand	**412**	253	**412**	253
Short-term investments (a)	**2,557**	2,051	**2,562**	2,052
Fixed asset investments – loans to joint ventures (b)	**737**	1,073	**737**	1,073
Liabilities				
Short-term borrowings (c)	**10,220**	5,121	**10,219**	5,121
Long-term borrowings, excluding finance leases (d)	**20,592**	5,874	**20,852**	6,085
Derivatives relating to investments and borrowings (net) (e)				
Assets	**259**	44	–	–
Liabilities	–	–	–	100

(a) The fair values of listed short-term investments were estimated based on quoted market prices for those investments. The carrying amount of the other short-term deposits and investments approximated to their fair values due to the short maturity of the instruments held.

(b) The fair value of loans to joint ventures approximated to carrying value due to loans bearing commercial rates of interest.

(c) The fair value of the short-term borrowings approximated to carrying value due to the short maturity of the instruments.

(d) The fair value of the group's bonds, debentures, notes and other long-term borrowings has been estimated on the basis of quoted market prices for the same or similar issues with the same maturities where they existed, and on calculations of the present value of future cash flows using the appropriate discount rates in effect at the balance sheet dates, where market prices of similar issues did not exist.

(e) The fair value of the group's outstanding foreign currency and interest rate swap agreements was estimated by calculating the present value, using appropriate discount rates in effect at the balance sheet dates, of affected future cash flows translated, where appropriate, into pounds sterling at the market rates in effect at the balance sheet dates.

Disclosure on financial assets and liabilities held for trading

6.257 The standard defines trading in financial assets and financial liabilities as *"buying, selling, issuing or holding financial assets and financial liabilities in order to take advantage of short-term changes in market prices or rates"*. [FRS 13 para 2]. A financial asset or liability that is classified as a trading instrument under FRS 13, will meet the definition of 'held for trading' under paragraph 9 of FRS 26. Consequently, if a reporting entity holds or issues financial instruments and meets this definition of trading the following disclosures have to be made:

- The net gain or loss from trading such instruments during the period included in the profit and loss account, analysed by type of financial instrument, business activity, risk or in such other way that is consistent with the entity's management of the activity.
- If the analysis above is given other than by type of financial instrument, a description for each line of that analysis of the types of financial instruments involved.
- The period-end fair values of financial assets and separately, of financial liabilities held or issued for trading.

[FRS 13 para 57].

6.258 An example of a company that has disclosed the required information in respect of its trading activities is BT Group plc in its 31 March 2002 financial statements.

Table 6.17 – Disclosure of financial assets and liabilities held for trading

BT Group plc – Annual report and Form 20-F – 31 March 2003

Notes to the accounts (extract)

36. Financial instruments and risk management (extract)

Fair value of financial assets held for trading	**2003** **£m**	**2002** **£m**
Net gain included in profit and loss account	**34**	**50**
Fair value of financial assets held for trading at 31 March	**2,610**	**1,510**

The net gain was derived from government bonds, commercial paper and similar debt instruments. The average fair value of financial assets held during the year ended 31 March 2003 did not differ materially from the year end position.

6.259 If the period-end position is considered to be materially unrepresentative of the reporting entity's use of financial instruments for trading purposes during the period, the average fair value of instruments held in the period should be disclosed. The average should be calculated using daily figures, or where these are not available, the most frequent interval, generated for management, regulatory or other reasons, should be used. An example of this disclosure is given in Table 6.20 (see para 6.285).

Disclosures about hedges

6.260 Companies use financial instruments for hedging purposes to reduce the risk associated with the hedged item. Depending on the accounting policy the company adopts, gains and losses on hedging instruments are often not recognised in the financial statements until the hedged transaction takes place. Companies that do recognise losses and gains on hedging instruments carry them forward in their balance sheets to match the gains and losses on the hedged items in the next or later financial year. In the past in the UK, hedge accounting has been permitted simply where it was believed that the resulting presentation in the primary statements better represented the economics of the situation. It is important to note that these FRS 13 hedging disclosure requirements apply to all such hedge relationships and not just to the hedging relationships that would qualify as FRS 26/IAS 39 hedges.

Hedging table

6.261 Where financial assets and financial liabilities are used by a company for hedging purposes, FRS 13 requires the following information about gains and losses to be disclosed.

- The cumulative aggregate gains and aggregate losses that are 'unrecognised' at the balance sheet date. Where, however, the item's fair value has not been disclosed, which is allowed for unique financial instruments where reliable estimates of fair value cannot be obtained (see para 6.243 and 6.244) or for cash-settled commodity contracts in the situation described in paragraph 6.179, any gain or loss on that item need not be dealt with in this disclosure.

- The cumulative aggregate gains and aggregate losses carried forward in the balance sheet at the balance sheet date (that is, 'deferred') pending their recognition in the profit and loss account.

- The extent to which the gains and losses disclosed in the above two points are expected to be recognised in the profit and loss account in the next accounting period.

- The amount of gains and losses included in the reporting period's profit and loss account that arose in previous years and were either unrecognised or carried forward in the balance sheet at the start of the reporting period.

[FRS 13 para 59].

6.262 It should generally be possible to tie in the figures for the fair values of derivatives disclosed in the fair value table to the figures given in the hedging table. This is also illustrated in examples 3 and 4 included in annex 1 to this chapter.

6.263 Read in isolation, the disclosure requirements set out above are, perhaps, not as clearly expressed by the standard as they might be. For example, it is not clear what is regarded as hedge accounting for this purpose (since the standard deals with disclosure and not accounting treatment). The standard avoids defining hedge accounting, because it seeks the reporting entity to explain what it means by hedging and thus set the numerical disclosures in context. An example of such an explanation is given by Imperial Chemical Industries Plc, which helpfully sets out in its accounting policies what it considers to be hedge accounting. This is reproduced in Table 6.18 below.

Table 6.18 – Definition of hedge accounting

Imperial Chemical Industries PLC – Annual Report and Accounts and Form 20-F – 31 December 1999

Notes to the accounts (extract)

Accounting policies (extract)

Financial derivatives

Hedge accounting

The Group uses various derivative financial instruments to reduce exposure to foreign exchange risks. These include currency swaps, forward currency contracts and currency options. The Group also uses interest rate swaps, forward rate agreements and interest rate caps derivatives to adjust interest rate exposures. The Group considers its derivative financial instruments to be "hedges" (i.e. an offset of foreign exchange and interest rate risks) when certain criteria are met. Under hedge accounting for currency options, the Group defers the instrument's impact on profit until it recognises the underlying hedged item in profit. Other material instruments do not involve deferral since the profit impact they offset occurs during the terms of the contracts.

Foreign currency derivative instruments:

The Group's criteria to qualify for hedge accounting are:

- The instrument must be related to a foreign currency asset or liability that is probable and whose characteristics have been identified;
- It must involve the same currency as the hedged item; and
- It must reduce the risk of foreign currency exchange movements on the Group's operations.

Interest rate derivative instruments:

The Group's criteria to qualify for hedge accounting are:

- The instrument must be related to an asset or a liability, and
- It must change the character of the interest rate by converting a variable rate to a fixed rate or vice versa.

Derivative financial instruments reported in the financial statements:

- The unamortised premium paid on purchased currency options is included in debtors in the balance sheet.

Cash flows related to foreign currency derivative transactions are reported along with related transactions in net cash inflow from operating activities or returns on investment and servicing of finance, as appropriate, in the Statement of Group cash flow.

Currency swaps
Principal amounts are revalued at exchange rates ruling at the date of the Group balance sheet and included in the sterling value of loans; exchange gains/losses are included in the Statement of Group total recognised gains and losses in accordance with SSAP 20.

Interest rate swaps and forward rate agreements
Interest payments/receipts are accrued with net interest payable. They are not revalued to fair value or shown on the Group balance sheet at period end. If they are terminated early, the gain/loss is spread over the remaining maturity of the original instrument.

Interest rate caps
The option premia are recognised on the Group balance sheet as 'other receivables'. The option premia, net of any realised gains or individual caplets, are taken to net interest payable spread evenly over the lifetime of the cap.

Forward currency contracts
Those forward currency contracts hedging transaction exposures (purchases and sales held in the books of account) are revalued to balance sheet rates with net unrealised gains/losses being shown as trade receivables/payables. Both realised gains and losses on purchases/sales and unrealised gains/losses on forward contracts are recognised in trading profit.

Those contracts used to change the currency mix of net debt are revalued to balance sheet rates with net unrealised gain/losses being shown as part of the debt they are hedging. The difference between spot and forward rate for these contracts is recognised as part of net interest payable over the period of the contract. Realised and unrealised exchange gains/losses are shown in the financial statements in the same place as the underlying borrowing/deposit.

Currency options
Option premia are recognised at their historic cost in the Group balance sheet as 'other receivables'. At maturity, the option premia net of any realised gains on exercise, are taken to the financial statements as trading profit.

Disclosure related to item being hedged

6.264 Another issue is whether the disclosures for hedging required by FRS 13 are concerned with the hedging instrument or with the underlying item which is being hedged (or with both). The UITF in its information sheet IS 33 indicated that it had confirmed with the ASB that the illustration in appendix III to FRS 13 reflects the ASB's intentions that paragraph 59 requires disclosure only of the gross gains or losses arising on the hedging instrument itself and not on the instrument being hedged. Hence, a one-sided disclosure is given that could suggest there are incremental profits to be taken or exposures exist when this is not the case. To counter such an impression, some explanation could be given adjacent to the disclosure to put it in context. The UITF added that its conclusion did not discourage disclosure also of the gain or loss on the instrument being hedged, for example, as part of the hedging strategy followed in the period.

6.265 To illustrate this point, consider the following example:

Example

Company A enters into a three year fixed rate loan of £20m at 7%. At the same time it enters into an interest rate swap for the same period to switch the loan to floating rate. Company A now has a synthetic floating rate loan of £20m and under the swap it will receive £1.4m a year and pay a variable rate on £20m. The amount received under the swap will cover its interest obligations on the original loan. Shortly afterwards the Bank of England's Monetary Policy Committee cuts Minimum Lending Rate by 0.5% and interest rates fall commensurately. Consequently Company A's interest rate swap acquires a positive value of, say £350,000. Another result of the interest rate cut is the fair value of the original 7% fixed rate loan will increase to, say, £20.35m.

The interest rate swap is hedging the interest cash flows on the fixed rate loan and, therefore, the swap is the hedging instrument. Consequently, the unrecognised gain on the swap of £350,000 will be included in the hedging disclosure required by paragraph 59. The unrecognised loss in the fair value of the hedged item, that is, the increase in the fair value of the fixed rate loan, is not included in the hedging disclosure.

6.266 As can be seen from Table 6.19, BG plc has only included the net unrecognised losses on the derivative financial instruments it has used for hedging purposes in its hedging disclosures. In addition, BG has indicated in a footnote that substantially all of the losses shown by the table will in fact be offset by corresponding gains on the hedged items; this is what would be expected where there is a proper hedging relationship.

Hedging using instruments other than derivatives

6.267 A further nuance that emerges from an analysis of FRS 13's requirements is that the disclosure is solely about gains and losses on *derivatives* that have been used as the hedging instruments. Hedging which is achieved through the use of primary financial instruments – that is, those that are on-balance sheet non-derivatives – do not produce unrecognised or deferred gains or losses that are the feature of paragraph 59's requirements. This is clearly illustrated by BG plc in Table 6.19, where the net losses on the derivative instruments shown in the fair value table are signposted to the hedging disclosure in the table below.

Table 6.19 — Hedging using instruments other than derivatives

BG plc — Annual Report and Accounts — 31 December 1999

Notes to the accounts (extract)

21 Financial instruments (extract)

Fair values of financial instruments	**1998**		1998	
	Book value £m	**Fair value £m**	Book value £m	Fair value £m
Primary financial instruments held or issued to finance the Group's operations:				
Short-term borrowings	**(2 091)**	**(2 091)**	(1 394)	(1 394)
Long-term borrowings	**(5 333)**	**(5 369)**	(3 199)	(3 477)
Current asset investments	**508**	**508**	504	504
Cash at bank and in hand	**44**	**44**	40	40
Other financial liabilities	**(217)**	**(217)**	236	236
Derivative financial instruments held to manage the interest rate and currency profile:				
Interest rate-related derivatives	–	**48**	–	3
Currency rate-related derivatives	–	**(102)**	–	(81)
Unrecognised total net losses (see Gains and losses on hedges below)	–	**(150)**	–	(78)
Other financial liabilities	**(217)**	**(217)**	236	236
Derivative financial instruments held to manage the interest rate and currency profile:				
Interest rate-related derivatives	–	**48**	–	3
Currency rate-related derivatives	–	**(102)**	–	(81)
Unrecognised total net losses (see Gains and losses on hedges below)	–	**(150)**	–	(78)

For the purpose of the above table, the fair value of short-term borrowings, related derivative instruments, current asset investments and cash at bank and in hand approximate to book value due to the short maturity of these instruments.

Hedges of future transactions

As at 31 December 1998 the value of future transactions hedged was £145m (1998 £nil).

Gains and losses on hedges

The table below shows the extent to which the Group has off-balance sheet (unrecognised) and on-balance sheet (deferred) gains and losses in respect of hedges at the beginning and end of the year.

	Unrecognised			Deferred	
	Gains £m	Losses £m	Net total £m	Gains £m	Losses £m
Gains/(losses) on hedges at 1 January 1999	131	(209)	(78)	27	(24)
Transfer from gains to losses	(62)	62	–	–	–
Transfer from losses to gains	(7)	7	–	–	–
(Gains)/losses arising in previous years that were recognised in 1999	(33)	128	95	4	(4)
Gains/(losses) not recognised in 1999					
Arising before 1 January 1999	29	(12)	17	19	(20)
Arising in 1999	107	(274)	(167)	12	(54)
Gains/(losses) on hedges as at 31 December 1999	**136**	**(286)**	**(150)**	**31**	**(74)**
Of which:					
Gains (losses) expected to be included in 2000 income	–	–	–	7	(15)
Gains (losses) expected to be included in 2001 income or later	136	(286)	(150)	24	(59)

£102m (1998 £81m), of the unrecognised total net losses above of £150m (1998 £78m), are offset by foreign exchange gains on the related foreign currency denominated borrowings.

Disclosures gross or net

6.268 In Table 6.19, BG Plc discloses the aggregate unrecognised gains and losses in line with the standard. The standard is ambiguous as to whether gains and losses should be shown net or gross. However in the illustrative example given in the appendices to the standard, the gains and losses are shown gross. Furthermore, the illustrative example presents the unrecognised gains and losses information in the form of a reconciliation of the opening to closing balances, which is not a requirement of the standard, but which we believe to be best practice (as illustrated by the hedging table given in appendix III to FRS 13). An example of how this hedging table might look is given below.

Illustration of the disclosure of unrecognised and deferred gains and losses

	Unrecognised			Deferred		
	Gains £m	**Losses £m**	**Total net gains/losses £m**	**Gains £m**	**Losses £m**	**Total net gains/losses £m**
Gains and losses on hedges at 1 January 20X0	3.2	–	3.2	2.5	–	2.5
Arising in previous years included in 20X0 income	(3.2)	–	(3.2)	(2.5)	–	(2.5)

Gains and losses not included in 20X0 income						
Arising before 1 January 20X0	–	–	–	–	–	–
Arising in 20X0	6.4	(4.3)	2.1	–	–	–
Gains and losses on hedges at 31 December 20x0	**6.4**	**(4.3)**	**2.1**	–	–	–
of which:						
Gains and losses expected to be included in 20X1 income	6.4	(2.1)	4.3	–	–	–
Gains and losses expected to be included in 20X2 income or later	–	(2.2)	(2.2)	–	–	–

£8.5m of the net gain of £7.2m on the euro currency swaps has been recognised in 20X0 in the statement of total recognised gains and losses where it offsets the loss on retranslation of the net investments in the French and Dutch subsidiaries. The balance of £1.2m is an unrecognised loss in respect of the interest differential on the cross-currency swaps and is reflected in the above table.

Gains and losses included in fixed assets

6.269 The standard includes an exemption from the disclosures required in the last three bullet points in paragraph 6.261 on pragmatic grounds in respect of gains and losses on hedges that are included in the carrying amount of a fixed asset. This is because of the problems that can arise in trying to keep records of such gains and losses over a long period of time. Such amounts need not be included in the analysis of hedging gains and losses; they are of course included in the carrying value of the fixed asset amortised to the profit and loss account. [FRS 13 paras 60, 61].

Hedging a current asset, liability or non-equity share

6.270 The exemption in paragraph 6.269, however, does not extend to situations where the hedged item is a current asset, a liability or non-equity shares and the gain or loss on the hedging instrument has been accounted for by adjusting the carrying amount of the current asset, liability or shares. Common examples include foreign currency debtors and foreign currency borrowings that are translated into sterling in accordance with the company's accounting policy at the contracted exchange rate in the forward foreign exchange contracts or cross-currency swaps that have been used to hedge them.

6.271 The effect of adopting such an accounting policy is that the carrying value of the debtors or borrowings has been initially recorded at the forward rate, and has remained recorded at the forward rate at the year end. As a result, the exchange gain or loss, that would have arisen on translating the currency carrying amount at the closing rate, and the offsetting gain or loss on the forward contract, have not been recorded at all. Consequently, under such an accounting policy, for a forward contract open over the year end there will be an unrecognised gain or loss that would fall to be disclosed in the hedging table. A reporting entity that applies such an accounting policy must have adequate accounting systems to track the movement in value of the hedging instruments and the proportion of the unrecognised gains or losses that are taken to the profit and loss account in each accounting period. The gain or loss will become recognised at the forward transaction date, where there will also be an equal and opposite gain or loss arising on the hedged item. These, in effect, net out in the profit and loss account.

6.272 An illustration of the treatment of a forward currency contract taken out in anticipation of a future purchase is given in paragraph 6.273 below.

Hedging a forward purchase of stock

6.273 The example below, which deals with the purchase of raw materials, illustrates how a forward purchase of stock would be dealt with under FRS 13, it also illustrates the extent of data collection and compilation that the hedging disclosure entails.

Example

Company B has a 31 March 20X0 year end. It decides in March 20X0 to place an order for materials with its supplier in France for €100,000. At the same time it takes out a forward foreign exchange contract to purchase €100,000 for £67,000. The materials are delivered in September, paid for, turned into finished products and sold in May 20X1. Assuming that, at 31 March 20X0 the company could take out an equivalent forward contract to purchase €100,000 for the remaining five months of the contract for £65,500, the fair value of the forward contract is (£1,500). When the goods are delivered and paid for, the euros could be bought for £69,000, what disclosures are required by FRS 13?

At 31 March 20X0

Company B has an unrecognised loss of £1,500 on the forward contract. Hence in the fair value disclosure, the forward contract will be shown under the heading 'Derivatives used to hedge anticipated transactions' with a book value of £nil and a fair value of £(1,500). The hedging disclosure will show the unrecognised loss of £1,500 arising in the year but not included in 20X0 profit and loss account and thus carried forward. This amount will also be shown as an amount expected to be included in income for the year ending 31 March 20X2.

At 31 March 20X1

Company B will have to disclose a gain of £2,000 (the difference between the spot rate price of £69,000 at date of delivery and the forward rate in the contract of £67,000) carried forward in the balance sheet (within stocks). This will pose a number of presentational issues. There will be nothing to disclose in the fair value disclosure as there is no financial instrument involved any longer; the forward contract was settled in the year and stocks are not financial instruments. In the hedging disclosure £1,500 will be shown as the opening loss under unrecognised gains and losses. However, it will be necessary to show the change in value of the contract (£3,500) and to transfer the net gain of £2,000 to the deferred gains and losses section of the disclosure to reconcile to the carried forward deferred gain of £2,000. This amount will also be shown as an amount expected to be included in income for the year ending 31 March 20X2.

At 31 March 20X2

Company B will have to disclose that a gain of £2,000 has been included in the profit and loss account for the year. The hedging disclosure will show £2,000 as a deferred gain brought forward which is reduced to £nil carried forward at 31 March 20X2 by the amount recognised in the profit and loss account for the year.

The hedging disclosure for the three years to March 20X2 may be summarised in the tabular format likely to be used by most companies:

	March 20X2		March 20X1	March 20X0
	Deferred	Unrecognised	Deferred	Unrecognised
	£	£	£	£
Gain/(loss) at 1 April	2,000	(1,500)	–	–
Change in value from 1 April to settlement	–	3,500	–	–
Arising before 1 April not included in current year income and now deferred	–	(2,000)	2,000	–
(Gain)/loss arising in previous year(s) included in current year income	(2,000)	–	–	–
Arising in current year not included in current year income	–	–	–	(1,500)
Gain/(loss) on hedges at 31 March	**-**	**-**	**2,000**	**(1,500)**
Of which:				
Loss expected to be included in 20X1 income			–	–
(Loss)/gain expected to be included in 20X2 income	–	–	2,000	(1,500)

6.274 Note that example 4 included in annex 1 to this chapter contains example narrative and numerical disclosures for a forward contract taken out to hedge a purchase of raw materials.

Hedging the purchase of a fixed asset using an option

6.275 Some companies' hedging strategies involve the use of options. The question thus arises as to how option contracts should be dealt with in the fair value and hedging table required by the standard, particularly as the option may not have to be exercised at the balance sheet date.

Example

Company C purchases a foreign currency call option for a premium of £100,000 that gives it the right, but not the obligation, to buy US$5m at a pre-determined rate if the $/£ exchange rate is below $1.63 on 28 February 20X1. This is the date that the company expects to pay $5m for the purchase of a fixed asset. If the exchange rate at the end of February 20X1 has fallen below $1.63, company C will exercise the option. Company C has a 31 December year end.

Inception

At inception, company C paid the premium of £100,000. Its accounting policy (which should be disclosed) is to defer the premium in respect of anticipated commitments until they occur and thus the premium is included in the balance sheet as 'other debtors'.

At 31 December 20X0

The exchange rate is $1.55: £1 and, consequently, the option is 'in the money'. Company C determines from its broker that the mark to market value of the option is £165,000. In its fair value disclosure, it will show a 'book value' of the option of £100,000 with a £165,000 comparable fair value. In the hedging disclosure, the gain of £65,000 (the fair value of the option contract less the unamortised premium) will be included in the 'unrecognised' gains section of the disclosure. However, as the option is a hedge of an anticipated fixed asset purchase, the gain will not feature in the disclosure of the "*extent to which the gains and losses....are expected to be recognised in the next accounting period*". This is because of the exemption in paragraph 60 of the standard relating to gains and losses that adjust the carrying value of a fixed asset. However, it would be helpful to provide an explanation of this effect in the disclosure.

At 31 December 20X1

The purchase of the fixed asset took place as expected on 28 February 20X1, when the exchange rate was $1.60:£1. At this rate company C chose to exercise the option as it was cheaper than purchasing the US$5m at the spot rate. Company C wrote off the premium of £100,000 for the option. In our view the premium is not a directly attributable cost under FRS 15, 'Tangible fixed assets', as it relates to financing the purchase. The fixed asset is recorded at the option rate of $1.63:£1. This is a synthetic rate in that it incorporates the fixed asset recorded at the spot rate of $1.60:£1 and a deferred gain on the option, being the difference between recording the fixed asset at the option rate and recording it at the spot rate. In respect of this option contract, there are no FRS 13 fair value or hedging disclosures to be made. In the former case this is because the option contract is no longer outstanding and in the latter because of the exemption in paragraph 60. In this case the 'deferred' gain included in the book value of the fixed asset is the exchange difference between recording the fixed asset at the spot rate and recording it at the option rate.

Hedging a net investment using a cross-currency swap

6.276 Further complications arise where, say, a sterling borrowing is swapped into a foreign currency and this synthetic foreign currency borrowing is used to hedge a net investment in a foreign subsidiary. For example, a £100 million borrowing is swapped into US$150 million in order to provide a hedge of the US$150 million net investment in the group's US subsidiaries. At the balance sheet date, the $/£ exchange rate is $2:£1. The forward leg of the swap (to sell US$150 million) is revalued at the spot rate at £75 million, rather than the forward rate of exchange, since the interest rate differential between the spot and forward rates is reflected in the periodic payments made between the parties. The gain of £25 million (£100 million-£75 million) is netted against the £100 million carrying value of the sterling loan to adjust it to £75 million. The other side of the entry is recognised in the statement of total recognised gains and losses where it matches with the foreign exchange loss taken on the US investment.

6.277 As already stated in paragraph 6.241, the fair value of the separate instruments should be grouped together in appropriate categories. Therefore, the loan and the cross-currency swap will appear in different categories, for example, the loan in 'primary instruments' and swap in 'derivative financial instruments used to manage interest rate and currency profile'. However, there is also the question of what are the comparable 'book values' to be shown alongside these fair values?

6.278 There are two approaches that can be adopted.

- It is possible to separate the two instruments in the 'fair value' part of the disclosure, the loan could be shown as having an aggregate carrying amount of, say, £100 million and the gain (recognised on balance sheet and in the STRGL) of, say, £25 million shown as the aggregate carrying amount of the swap. The fair value of the swap will be different from the gain already recognised since the on-balance sheet amount merely measures the currency element of the swap, whereas the fair value of the swap includes the measure of the interest differential. The difference between the two is thus 'unrecognised' as it is not reflected on-balance sheet. If this approach is adopted, there should be a footnote to explain that the book values of the loan and swap need to be recombined to trace the amount to the borrowings shown in the balance sheet.
- Alternatively, the aggregate carrying amount of the loan could be shown as £75 million and a nil amount shown as the 'book value' of the swap. In this case, it would be appropriate to recognise the fair value of the interest differential only as the equivalent amount to be recognised next to the nil book value of the swap. This value would then be treated as unrecognised in the hedging table.

6.279 The first approach has an advantage in that, by highlighting the gain already recognised, it is not forgotten when constructing the required hedging disclosure considered from paragraph 6.260.

6.280 Paragraph 59 of FRS 13 requires disclosure of the cumulative aggregate gains and aggregate losses, both 'deferred' and 'unrecognised', at the balance sheet date together with the amount of such gains and losses recognised in the reporting period's profit and loss account or expected to be recognised in the profit and loss account in the next accounting period. To construct the disclosure requires, therefore, that those hedging gains and losses that have been recognised, or are expected to be recognised, in the profit and loss account to be separately identified. Assuming the fair value of the cross-currency swap is, say, £20 million the hedging disclosure starting with the year end position would be constructed to show the following:

			Unrecognised
	Gains £m	Losses £m	Total £m
At balance sheet date	–	(5)	(5)
Of which:			
Expected to be recognised in 20X0 income	–	(1)	(1)
Expected to be recognised in 20X1 income	–	(4)	(4)

Market price risk

6.281 Disclosure of some measure of market price risk is an evolving area of financial reporting, both in the UK and internationally. Various techniques have been developed, but there is as yet no consensus as to which is the best method of providing adequate and meaningful information in a cost effective manner. Hence, the ASB encourages, rather than requires, entities other than banks to give some measure of the market price risk of all the financial instruments they hold or have issued (including cash settled commodity contracts and, if significant, all other items carrying market price risk). [FRS 13 para 66]. Banks must give market price risk information in respect of their trading book. [FRS 13 para 104]. Market price risk is the risk of loss arising from changes in market prices, such as interest rates or exchange rates. It is necessary to appreciate that any disclosures concerning market price risk can only give an estimate of the risks to a company and can never be precise or accurate.

6.282 Entities providing market price risk information should include:

- A discussion of market price risk where necessary to set the numerical information in context and to assist in its interpretation.
- Additional numerical disclosures that facilitate an assessment of the magnitude of market price risk over the period. These disclosures should include:
  - An explanation of the method used and the key parameters and assumptions underlying the data provided.
  - An explanation of the objective of the method used and of the limitations that may cause the information not to reflect fully the overall market price risk of the assets and liabilities involved.
  - The reasons for material changes in the amount of reported risk compared to the previous accounting period.

[FRS 13 paras 67, 69].

6.283 The method chosen to measure market price risk should reflect how management manages the risk. If different approaches are used to manage market price risk in different parts of a business, separate disclosure for each part of the business is encouraged. [FRS 13 para 66]. In its simplest form, the information could be presented as a sensitivity analysis showing the impact on profit of, say, a one per cent change in interest rates. However, other methods such as 'value at risk' – that is, the expected loss from an adverse market movement with a specified probability over a specified period of time – may be more appropriate. Five possible approaches for reporting market price risk are discussed in paragraph 68 of the FRS, but it is acknowledged that this list is not exhaustive and other methods may be more appropriate.

6.284 Where material changes are made to the method or key assumptions and parameters used to calculate market price risk from one period to the next, the reasons for the change should be given and the previous period's information should be restated onto the new basis. [FRS 13 para 71].

6.285 An example of disclosure of market price risk based on the sensitivity of market values is shown in Table 6.20 below, which also includes disclosure of fair values, instruments held for trading and information on credit risk.

Table 6.20 – Disclosure of market price risk

BP p.l.c. – annual accounts – 31 December 2001

Notes on accounts (extract)

28 Derivatives and other financial instruments

In the normal course of business the group is a party to derivative financial instruments (derivatives) with off balance sheet risk, primarily to manage its exposure to fluctuations in foreign currency exchange rates and interest rates, including management of the balance between floating rate and fixed rate debt. The group also manages certain of its exposures to movements in oil and natural gas prices. The underlying economic currency of the group's cash flows is mainly the US dollar. Accordingly, most of our borrowings are in US dollars, are hedged with respect to the US dollar or swapped into US dollars. Significant non-dollar cash flow exposures are hedged. Gains and losses arising on these hedges are deferred and recognized in the income statement or as adjustments to carrying amounts, as appropriate, only when the hedged item occurs. In addition, we trade derivatives in conjunction with these risk management activities. The results of trading are recognized in income in the current period.

The group co-ordinates certain key activities on a global basis in order to optimize its financial position and performance. These include the management of the currency, maturity and interest rate profile of borrowing, cash, other significant financial risks and relationships with banks and other financial institutions. International oil and natural gas trading and risk management relating to business operations are carried out by the group's oil and natural gas trading units.

BP is exposed to financial risks, including market risk, credit risk and liquidity risk, arising from the group's normal business activities. These risks and the group's approach to dealing with them are discussed below.

Market risk

Market risks include the possibility that changes in currency exchange rates, interest rates or oil and natural gas prices will adversely affect the value of the group's financial assets, liabilities or expected future cash flows. Market risks are managed using a range of financial and commodity instruments, including derivatives. We also trade derivatives in conjunction with these risk management activities.

Currency exchange rates Fluctuations in exchange rates can have significant effects on the group's reported profit. The effects of most exchange rate fluctuations are absorbed in business operating results through changing cost competitiveness, lags in market adjustment to movements in rates, and conversion differences accounted for on specific transactions. For this reason the total effect of exchange rate fluctuations is not identifiable separately in the group's reported profit.

The main underlying economic currency of the group's cash flows is the US dollar and the group's borrowings are predominantly in US dollars. Our foreign exchange management policy is to minimize economic and material transactional exposures arising from currency movements against the US dollar. The group co-ordinates the handling of foreign exchange risks centrally, by netting off naturally occurring opposite exposures wherever possible, to reduce the risks, and then dealing with any material residual foreign exchange risks. Significant residual non-dollar exposures are managed using a range of derivatives.

Interest rates The group is exposed to interest rate risk on short- and long-term floating rate instruments and as a result of the refinancing of fixed rate finance debt. Consequently, as well as managing the currency and the maturity of debt, the group manages interest expense through the balance between generally lower-cost floating rate debt, which has inherently higher risk, and generally more expensive, but lower-risk, fixed rate debt. The group is exposed redominantly to US dollar LIBOR (London Inter-Bank Offer Rate) interest rates as borrowings are mainly denominated in, or are swapped into, US dollars.

The group uses derivatives to manage the balance between fixed and floating rate debt. During 2001, the proportion of floating rate debt was in the range 32-43% of total net debt outstanding.

Oil and natural gas prices BP's trading units use financial and commodity derivatives as part of the overall optimization of the value of the group's equity oil production and as part of the associated trading of crude oil, products and related instruments. They also use financial and commodity derivatives to manage certain of the group's exposures to price fluctuations on natural gas transactions.

Market risk management and trading In market risk management and trading, conventional exchange-traded derivative instruments such as futures and options are used as well as non-exchange-traded instruments such as swaps, 'over-the-counter' options and forward contracts.

Where derivatives constitute a hedge, the group's exposure to market risk created by the derivative is offset by the opposite exposure arising from the asset, liability, cash flow or transaction being hedged. By contrast, where derivatives are held for trading purposes, changes in market risk factors give rise to realized and unrealized gains and losses, which are recognized in the current period.

All financial instrument and derivative activity, whether for risk management or trading, is carried out by specialist teams which have the appropriate skills, experience and supervision. These teams are subject to close financial and management control, meeting generally accepted industry practice and reflecting the principles of the Group of Thirty Global Derivatives Study recommendations. A Trading Risk Management Committee has oversight of the quality of internal control in the group's trading units. Independent control functions monitor compliance with BP's policies. The control framework includes prescribed trading limits that are reviewed regularly by senior management, daily monitoring of risk exposure using value-at-risk principles, marking trading exposures to market and stress testing to assess the exposure to potentially extreme market situations. As part of its approach to ensuring that control over trading is maintained to a high and consistent standard, the group's business units dealing in the oil, natural gas and financial markets were brought together within a single integrated supply and trading organization during 2001.

Credit risk
Credit risk is the potential exposure of the group to loss in the event of non-performance by a counterparty. The credit risk arising from the group's normal commercial operations is controlled by individual operating units within guidelines. In addition, as a result of its use of financial and commodity instruments, including derivatives, to manage market risk, the group has credit exposures through its dealings in the financial and specialized oil and natural gas markets. The group controls the related credit risk by entering into contracts only with highly credit-rated counterparties and through credit approvals, limits and monitoring procedures, and does not usually require collateral or other security. Counterparty credit validation, independent of the dealers, is undertaken before contractual commitment.

Liquidity risk
Liquidity risk is the risk that suitable sources of funding for the group's business activities may not be available. The group has long-term debt ratings of Aa1 and AA+ assigned respectively by Moody's and Standard and Poor's. The group has access to a wide range of funding at competitive rates through the capital markets and banks. It co-ordinates relationships with banks, borrowing requirements, foreign exchange requirements and cash management centrally. The group believes it has access to sufficient funding and also has undrawn committed borrowing facilities to meet currently foreseeable borrowing requirements. At 31 December 2001, the group had available undrawn committed facilities of $3,400 million ($3,450 million). These committed facilities, which are mainly with a number of international banks, expire in 2002. The group expects to renew the facilities on an annual basis.

Trading activities
The group maintains active trading positions in a variety of derivatives. This activity is undertaken in conjunction with risk management activities. Derivatives held for trading purposes are marked to market and any gain or loss recognized in the income statement. For traded derivatives, many positions have been neutralized, with trading initiatives being concluded by taking opposite positions to fix a gain or loss, thereby achieving a zero net market risk.

The following table shows the fair value at 31 December of derivatives and other financial instruments held for trading purposes. The fair values at the year end are not materially unrepresentative of the position throughout the year.

				$ million
		2001		2000
	Fair value asset	**Fair value liability**	Fair value asset	Fair value liability
Interest rate contracts	**–**	**–**	–	–
Foreign exchange contracts	**14**	**(17**	10	(10)
Oil price contracts	**248**	**(222**	159	(123)
Natural gas price contracts	**799**	**(787)**	1,288	(1,264)
	1,061	**(1,026)**	1,457	(1,397)

The group measures its market risk exposure, i.e. potential gain or loss in fair values, on its trading activity using value-at-risk techniques. These techniques are based on a variance/covariance model or a Monte Carlo simulation and make a statistical assessment of the market risk arising from possible future changes in market values over a 24-hour period. The calculation of the range of potential changes in fair value takes into account a snapshot of the end-of-day exposures, and the history of one-day price movements over the previous 12 months, together with the correlation of these price movements. The potential movement in fair values is expressed to three standard deviations which is equivalent to a 99.7% confidence level. This means that, in broad terms, one would expect to see an increase or a decrease in fair values greater than the value at risk on only one occasion per year if the portfolio were left unchanged.

The group calculates value at risk on all instruments that are held for trading purposes and that therefore give an exposure to market risk. The value-at-risk model takes account of derivative financial instruments such as interest rate forward and futures contracts, swap agreements, options and swaptions, foreign exchange forward and futures contracts, swap agreements and options and oil price futures, swap agreements and options. Financial assets and liabilities and physical crude oil and refined products that are treated as trading positions are also included in these calculations. The value-at-risk calculation for oil and natural gas price exposure also includes derivative commodity instruments (commodity contracts that permit settlement either by delivery of the underlying commodity or in cash) such as forward contracts.

The following table shows values at risk for trading activities.

								$ million
				2001				2000
	High	**Low**	**Average**	**Year end**	High	Low	Average	Year end
Interest rate trading	**1**	**–**	**–**	**–**	2	–	1	–
Foreign exchange trading	**3**	**–**	**1**	**–**	15	–	1	1
Oil price trading	**29**	**10**	**18**	**17**	23	4	13	13
Natural gas price trading	**21**	**4**	**10**	**9**	16	1	6	13

The presentation of trading results shown in the table below includes certain activities of BP's trading units which involve the use of derivative financial instruments in conjunction with physical and paper trading of oil and natural gas. It is considered that a more comprehensive representation of the group's oil and natural gas price trading activities is given by the classification of the gain or loss on such derivatives along with the gain or loss arising from the physical and paper trades to which they relate, representing the net result of the trading portfolio.

				$ million
			2001	2000
			Net	Net
	Oil	**Natural gas**	**gain (loss)**	gain (loss)
Derivative financial and commodity instruments	**419**	**(129)**	**290**	94
Physical trades	**265**	**405**	**670**	549
Total trading	**684**	**276**	**960**	643
Interest rate trading			**1**	1
Foreign exchange trading			**81**	52
			1,042	696

6.286 While the practice of disclosing a measure of market price risk is evolving, it should be recognised that this may not be the most significant risk faced by the reporting entity. For example, wage inflation or sales volumes may be far more significant. Clearly, therefore, any disclosed measure of market price risk should not be portrayed as comprehensive.

[The next paragraph is 6.288.]

FRS 4 — Capital instruments

Background

6.288 During the 1980s there was considerable growth in the range of capital instruments available for raising finance. The development of such instruments had a sound economic purpose and provided issuers and investors with significant benefits. However, as investors and issuers became more sophisticated, the instruments became more complex with the result that accounting failed to keep pace with their development. The central issue that required resolution was the criteria to be used to determine whether a capital instrument represents debt or equity.

6.289 In December 1993, the ASB issued FRS 4, 'Capital instruments', with the aim of bringing much needed consistency to the treatment of the many different forms of capital instrument available. The standard took a rather legalistic approach towards accounting for capital instruments by ignoring the economic substance of the instruments and merely reflecting their legal form. Many argued that FRS 4's provisions were inconsistent with FRS 5, 'Reporting the substance of transactions'. Nevertheless, the standard provided guidance on many aspects of accounting for share capital, debt and minority interests that were the subject of differing treatments and interpretations prior to its publication. The standard prescribed methods that should be used to determine the amounts to be attributed to capital instruments and their associated costs and specifies how the instruments should be disclosed.

6.290 However, FRS 4's classification and presentation requirements have been withdrawn following the introduction of the presentation requirements of FRS 25 for all entities for accounting periods beginning on or after 1 January 2005. The remaining paragraphs of FRS 4 apply to all entities not applying FRS 26 (see further para 6.26). The provisions of FRS 4 concern the allocation of the costs of capital instruments that are classified as liabilities.

FRS 4's objectives

6.291 Following its revision in December 2004, FRS 4's objective is to ensure that costs associated with capital instruments that are classified as liabilities are allocated to accounting periods on a fair basis over the period of the instrument. [FRS 4 para 1].

6.292 Ensuring appropriate classification, presentation and disclosure of capital instruments is no longer an objective of the standard, as this is now achieved by the application of those sections of FRS 25 that are mandatory for all entities for accounting periods commencing on or after 1 January 2005 (see para 6.37).

Scope

6.293 The scope of the revised standard is unchanged from the original 1993 version. FRS 4 applies to all financial statements intended to give a true and fair view of a reporting entity's financial position and profit or loss (or income and expenditure) for the period. Although the standard was written primarily for companies, its provisions apply to other entities, which should adapt the terminology used in the statement as appropriate. [FRS 4 para 18].

6.294 The standard's requirements apply to issuers of capital instruments and not to investments in capital instruments issued by other entities. [FRS 4 para 19]. Furthermore, its requirements apply to all capital instruments as defined in the standard (see para 6.296 below) apart from:

- Warrants issued to employees under employee share schemes.
- Leases, which should be accounted for in accordance with SSAP 21.
- Equity shares issued as part of a business combination that is accounted for as a merger.

[FRS 4 para 21].

6.295 Capital instruments that are issued at the same time in a composite transaction should be considered together. They should be accounted for as a single instrument, unless they can be transferred, cancelled or redeemed independently of each other. [FRS 4 para 22]. In accounting periods beginning on or after 1 January 2005 all entities are required to comply with the presentation requirements of FRS 25. These requirements deal with the accounting for capital instruments including compound instruments. For example, debt is sometimes issued with a warrant attached. Where the debt and the warrants are capable of being transferred independently, they should be accounted for separately under FRS 25.

Definition of capital instrument

6.296 FRS 4's definition of capital instruments is not as wide as the definition of financial instruments, which is discussed from paragraph 6.16, but is restricted to primary instruments like shares and debt as well as options and warrants to obtain such instruments. Consequently, derivative instruments that are issued for managing foreign exchange and interest rate risks rather than for raising finance are outside of FRS 4's scope. Capital instruments are defined in of FRS 4 to mean:

> *"All instruments that are issued by reporting entities as a means of raising finance, including shares, debentures, loans and debt instruments, options and warrants that give the holder the right to subscribe for or obtain capital instruments. In the case of consolidated financial statements the term includes capital instruments issued by subsidiaries except those that are held by another member of the group included in the consolidation."* [FRS 4 para 2].

6.297 It follows from the above definition that the instrument's principal purpose must be for raising finance. An instrument may come within the above definition whether or not the consideration given for its issue takes the form of cash. For example, the consideration may be a specified amount of commodity (commodity linked instruments) or other capital instruments. Furthermore, a capital instrument may take the form of contracts between two parties (for example, a borrower and its bank). [FRS 4 para 68].

6.298 Capital instruments that are either fully or in part classified as liabilities come in various forms. They may be: straightforward debentures and loan capital; convertible into shares; subordinated to other borrowings; perpetual in nature; or sometimes issued on terms that the lender's recourse is limited. The features of these type of instruments are examined in Annex 3 to this chapter.

Finance costs

6.299 Following its amendment in 2004, FRS 4's primary focus is to ensure that finance costs (as defined) associated with a capital instrument are charged to the profit and loss account over the instrument's term. (The term of a capital instrument is considered from para 6.326.) This basic principle applies to the finance costs of capital instruments that are classified as liabilities. Finance costs are defined in the standard as:

> *"The difference between the net proceeds of an instrument and the total amount of the payments (or other transfers of economic benefits) that the issuer may be required to make in respect of the instrument."* [FRS 4 para 8].

6.300 For shares classified as liabilities, the finance costs include issue costs, the total dividend payments to be made on the shares over the term and the difference between any premium on issue and any redemption premium (see for example Table 6.23). Similarly for debt, the finance costs include issue costs, interest payments over the term, any redemption premium and any discount on issue. The implications of FRS 4 on the calculation of minority interests is considered in chapter 24.

Table 6.23 – Shares classified as liabilities

Pearson plc – Annual Report – 31 December 1997

Notes to the Accounts (extract)

1 Accounting policies (extract)

m) Capital instruments
Capital instruments are included at cost, adjusted for discount accretion or premium amortisation where the intention is to hold them to maturity. Interest receivable thereon and the premium or discount where relevant is taken to the profit and loss account so as to produce a constant rate of return over the period to the date of expected redemption.

Forward foreign exchange contracts and other off-balance sheet instruments are valued at the market prices prevailing at the balance sheet date. Borrowing is classified according to the maturity date of the respective individual holdings.

[The next paragraph is 6.305.]

Elements making up finance cost

6.305 Finance costs can be split into three separate elements:

- Dividends or interest.
- The difference between any premium received on the issue of an instrument and any redemption premium; or the discount on issue added to any redemption premium.
- Issue costs.

Dividends or interest

6.306 Where the dividend or interest is floating rather than fixed, it will not be possible to determine it in advance. Therefore, it will not be possible to calculate the total finance cost, but that should not cause a difficulty, because the floating rate interest charge or dividend appropriation made each year will be the correct amount to be shown in the profit and loss account for that year. Contingent payments of this nature are dealt with further in paragraph 6.352.

Issue and redemption premiums

6.307 There may be circumstances where it is difficult to establish what the final redemption value of a capital instrument will be. For example, it may be linked in some way to future profits or to the market price of the company's shares, or it might be difficult to determine when the redemption might occur. These issues are considered further from paragraph 6.352.

Issue costs

6.308 The ASB considers that issue costs are incurred to provide funds over a period of time and to charge those costs in full to the profit and loss account in the year of issue is not in accordance with the matching concept. However, deferral of such costs as some form of prepayment is not appropriate because the Act does not allow these costs to be carried forward nor does the prepayment qualify as an asset as defined in the ASB's Statement of principles. Accordingly, issue costs are accounted for as a deduction from the amount of the consideration received. This will result in issue costs for non-equity shares and debt being written off over the instrument's life. If it became clear that the instrument would be redeemed early, the amortisation of the issue costs and any discount on issue would need to be accelerated. Where the instrument does not have a term, for example, perpetual debt, costs incurred in their issue would not be amortised (see paras 6.344).

6.309 Issue costs are defined in the standard as:

> *"The costs that are incurred directly in connection with the issue of a capital instrument, that is, those costs that would not have been incurred had the specific instrument in question not been issued."* [FRS 4 para 10].

6.310 Clearly this definition is intended to be restrictive and the first point to note is that it excludes indirect costs. Consequently, the costs have to be directly related to the issue of the capital instrument before they fall to be treated as issue costs. This is rather obvious, otherwise inclusion of other indirect costs incurred on the issue as part of the cost of the instrument would only serve to defer those costs to future periods by overstating the finance cost charged in each period. Therefore, care needs to be taken in determining which costs fall to be treated as part of the cost of issuing the instrument.

6.311 In particular, the standard explains that the definition of issue costs does not allow the inclusion of costs incurred in:

- Researching sources of finance.
- Negotiating sources of finance.
- Ascertaining the suitability or feasibility of particular instruments.

[FRS 4 para 96].

6.312 Furthermore, the standard does not allow a company to allocate a proportion of its internal costs that would have been incurred had the instrument not been issued. This exemption would preclude, for example, management remuneration to cover their time involved with the issue from being treated as issue costs. [FRS 4 para 96]. Prudence should be exercised to ensure that only those costs that can be demonstrated to relate directly to the issue of the financial instrument are treated as issue costs.

6.313 The rules mentioned above relating to the types of costs that should be treated as issue costs are very similar to the rules concerning the costs that can be written off to the share premium account on the issue of shares or debentures. And for all practical purposes, issue costs can be regarded as the same as the costs that can be charged to the share premium account. Use of the share premium account is governed by the Act and it can only be used for specific purposes, namely to:

- Pay up fully paid bonus shares.
- Write off preliminary expenses.
- Write off expenses of any issue of shares or debentures.
- Write off commission paid or discount allowed on any issue of shares or debentures.
- Provide for the premium payable on any redemption of debentures.

[CA85 Sec 130(2)].

6.314 There are certain direct costs of issuing shares and debt that are clearly able to be written off against share premium and should be treated under FRS 4 as issue costs. These costs include underwriting fees, registration fees and certain legal, merchant bank and accounting fees where these are incurred solely in the production of a prospectus offering shares to the public or incurred in relation to documentation drawn up to cover a debt instrument. In a straightforward issue of new shares to the public where a company already has a listing it is quite possible that all the costs incurred will be issue costs.

6.315 Lawyers fees in a complex financing (such as a management buyout) could cover general corporate finance work and tax advice, but will also inevitably include fees to cover drafting of legal documentation in relation to the issue of capital instruments. These latter costs are issue costs, but the former are less likely to be unless they are incurred directly in relation to the issue of shares or debt. Accountants' fees will also cover a wide variety of work and unless specifically related to the issue of the capital instruments will not be issue costs. However, where a company can make a reasonable allocation of such fees, as between those attributable to the issue of shares (for instance, costs of preparing and advising on a rights issue document), those attributable to the issue of the debt and those attributable to the other aspects of the financing, only the last of these will not fall to be treated as issue costs.

6.316 As to how a reasonable allocation can be made in practice, it may be possible for the company to ask its advisors to indicate on their invoices the amount of costs that are attributable to each area of the advisors' work. However, the invoices may not be definitive. If no such allocation is possible, but there is a list of the work which the professional advisors have done, then an analysis of the invoices would have to be made to segregate costs associated with the issue from other costs. If there is neither an allocation nor an analysis of professional advisors' costs, an estimate of the extent to which advisors' costs have been incurred on the issue, on some reasonable basis, would have to be made.

6.317 The fees charged by banks and other financial institutions for finance will be charged in two ways. First there is an arrangement fee, which is normally a fixed percentage of the finance raised, and secondly, the finance interest coupon. The arrangement fee, as it relates to the specific instrument, should normally be treated as an issue cost as it can be regarded as part of the overall finance cost, having the effect of increasing the coupon. Syndication fees are charged by banks and financial institutions to arrange for other banks and financial institutions to participate in funding capital instruments (sub-participation). Again, these costs seem clearly to fall within the definition of issue costs.

6.318 Where several classes of equity, non-equity shares or debt are issued at once, it would be reasonable to make an apportionment of the total issue costs to each category on the basis of gross proceeds.

6.319 With regard, however, to costs incurred in connection with a financial restructuring or renegotiation, paragraph 96 of FRS 4 states that they do not qualify as issue costs. These costs are regarded under the FRS as relating to previous sources of finance even where a new instrument is issued following the restructuring or renegotiation. So costs incurred in negotiating with a financial institution to extend the term or change the interest rate on debt would be disallowed, even where a new debt instrument is issued. This also follows from paragraph 32 of the FRS which requires that gains and losses arising on the repurchase of early settlement of debt should be recognised in the profit and loss account in the period during which the repurchase or early settlement is made. But where an offer document is issued in relation to raising new debt or shares, the relevant costs of the offer should be regarded as issue costs, even though the debt so raised might be used to pay off previous borrowings.

6.320 It is not generally possible to write off issue costs to the profit and loss account in the year an instrument is issued. The only exceptions will be:

- Where issue costs are immaterial, the provisions of FRS 4 do not apply and, therefore, they can be charged to the profit and loss account immediately.
- If the term is only one year or less.
- Where the costs associated with an issue do not fall within the strict definition of issue costs.
- Where the costs, if spread, would give rise to an excessively high finance cost on the instrument, which is out of line with that expected to be charged.

The last two points are considered in the paragraphs that follow.

6.321 FRS 4 states in paragraph 96 that costs that do not qualify as issue costs should be written off to the profit and loss account. However, this statement is made as part of the explanatory section rather than in the FRS standard section and seems to be dealing with the basic situation where a company is simply raising finance for its continuing operations or organic growth. It does not seem to be intended to preclude a company that has issued capital instruments to fund an acquisition of another company from capitalising as part of its cost of investment external costs it has incurred in connection with the acquisition, which do not fall within the strict definition of 'issue costs' (see chapter 25). FRS 25 contains requirements in relation to transaction costs that are applicable to all entities and which supports this view. Under FRS 25, transaction costs of an equity transaction are deducted from equity, unless the costs were incurred in relation to the acquisition of a business, in which case FRS 6 is applied. [FRS 25 para 35]. Transaction costs are defined in FRS 26 as *"incremental costs that are directly attributable to the acquisition, issue or disposal of a financial asset or financial liability"*. [FRS 26 para 9]. Capitalisation of such costs can be made even where merger relief is taken, but where merger accounting is used for the acquisition, FRS 6, 'Acquisitions and mergers', requires such costs to be expensed (see further chapter 28).

6.322 Finance costs might be overstated where a company is in financial difficulties and in order to raise finance to continue trading it incurs material costs related to the issue. It may be imprudent for such a company to spread these excessive issue costs forward. In this type of situation, it would be prudent for the company to recognise some or all of the issue costs an exceptional finance cost in the year that they are incurred.

Facility fees

6.323 Where a company negotiates with a bank or other financial institution for a loan facility, the institution will charge a facility fee at the time of putting the loan facility in place. For example, such an arrangement might provide for the total facility to be £20 million which can be drawn down in specified or unspecified tranches over the life of the facility. The facility gives the company financial flexibility to draw down a range of finance from the full amount of the facility to nothing at all. Facility fees are very similar in nature to issue costs. Prior to the issue of the original FRS 4, facility fees of this nature were generally written off to the profit and loss account as incurred. Now only costs that are directly incurred in connection with the issue of a capital instrument fall to be treated as issue costs and included in the calculation of finance costs. The facility fee is a cost of negotiating a source of finance, which represents the cost the company is prepared to incur in order to obtain the necessary financial flexibility. The fee is not related to any specific loan. Consequently, in accordance with paragraph 96 of the standard, facility fees do not generally qualify as issue costs and should be written off to the profit and loss account as incurred.

6.324 As mentioned, the costs do not relate to a specific loan, as no loan is necessarily issued when the facility is granted. But where, for example, a facility was granted for £20 million and £5 million of the facility was drawn down immediately, then it could be argued that a quarter of the facility fee represents an issue cost of the £5 million loan. If, however, the initial draw down does not occur shortly after the facility is put in place or occur in a different accounting period from the one in which the facility fee is paid, the full fee should be written off to the profit and loss account when it is incurred. It is not possible to carry forward (say) half of the facility fee on the basis that £10 million is anticipated to be drawn down in three years' time.

6.325 Where a facility is obtained for a specific project for which there is an agreed business plan, such that it is virtually certain that the facility will be drawn down, and it can be demonstrated that the facility fee is in substance an advance payment of interest, because the actual interest rate is below what the market rate would be for an entity in similar circumstances. In such a case it would be acceptable to regard the whole of the facility fee as an issue cost and to set it against the first tranche drawn down up to the amount of that first tranche. If for any reason at a later stage the project did not proceed and the balance of the loan was not drawn down the proportion of the facility fee relating to the amount not drawn down should be immediately written off.

Term of capital instruments

6.326 Capital instruments come with various terms, which might be fixed, varying or indeterminate. A capital instrument's term is not necessarily the same period as its life. A capital instrument might have a number of different dates during its life when it can be redeemed or converted. These rights of redemption or conversion can be at the behest of the holder or the issuer of the instrument and are often granted by the use of options. The life of the instrument might extend for (say) ten years, but the impact of the options, if they are exercised, might be to shorten or lengthen the term considerably.

6.327 Under FRS 4 it is necessary to determine the term of an instrument for two reasons. First, the calculation of finance costs may depend on the term. For example a ten year bond might have an option to redeem after (say) five years at a premium of 20 per cent, but if not redeemed until year ten, the premium might reduce to (say) ten per cent. One of these premiums should be treated as part of the finance costs of the instrument, but the question is which one and this will depend on the instrument's term. Therefore, it is important to establish whether the term is five or ten years. Secondly, once determined, the finance costs are required by FRS 4 to be amortised over the instrument's term.

Definition of term

6.328 The term of capital instruments is defined in FRS 4 in the following way:

> *"The period from the date of issue of the capital instrument to the date at which it will expire, be redeemed, or be cancelled .*
>
> *If either party has the option to require the instrument to be redeemed or cancelled and, under the terms of the instrument, it is uncertain whether such an option will be exercised, the term should be taken to end on the earliest date at which the instrument would be redeemed or cancelled on exercise of such an option .*
>
> *If either party has the right to extend the period of an instrument, the term should not include the period of the extension if there is a genuine commercial possibility that the period will not be extended."* [FRS 4 para 16].

Implications of options

6.329 In many situations it will be obvious what the instrument's term is and this will in the majority of cases be the life of the instrument. However, where there are options built into the instrument the term becomes complicated. As can be seen from the second paragraph of the definition, where there is an option to redeem or cancel, the term is taken to end on the earliest date on which the option can be exercised. Paragraph 73 of FRS 4 goes on to comment that if there is an option for early redemption, the term should be taken to end on the earliest date the option could be exercised, unless there is *no* genuine commercial possibility that the option will be exercised. This requirement might at first sight seem a little odd, but it is based on the premise that options are normally granted for a purpose, for instance to allow a borrower to repay the debt early if the borrower either no longer needs debt or finds its interest rate unattractive. Therefore, because most options will have a genuine commercial reason, instruments' terms will often be determined to end on the earliest date on which an option can be exercised.

6.330 For example, a company might have a ten year £100,000 redeemable fixed rate five per cent bond which is redeemable at a premium of ten per cent and on which its costs of issue amounted to £2,000. In addition as part of the terms of the instrument, the company might hold an option to redeem the bond after year five and incur a premium of 15 per cent if early redemption is taken. If interest rates move down sufficiently, then it might pay the company to redeem the instrument early and this is a decision that the company will take in year five. The option, therefore, does have an economic purpose and under the provisions of the amended FRS 4 it appears that the option should be taken into account when determining the instrument's term, because it cannot be said that there is *no* genuine commercial possibility that the option will not be exercised.

6.331 Companies believed that this rule was too harsh, because they argued that in this circumstance the option is merely a right of the issuer (but not the investor) to redeem the instrument early on the payment of the premium (known as an issuer call option). In the example, the company will make the decision to refinance the debt in year five and any additional costs (such as the premium) should rightly be borne in the year the decision is taken. This issue was taken up with the UITF who agreed that the amount of premium payable under an issuer call option is not a payment *"that the issuer may be required to make in respect of the instrument"* and, consequently, does not fall within the definition of 'finance costs'.

6.332 The UITF, as a consequence, issued Abstract 11, 'Capital instruments: issuer call options', in September 1994 which concluded that where an instrument includes a call option that can be exercised only by the issuer, the payment required on exercise of that option does not form part of the instrument's finance costs. [UITF 11 para 6]. UITF 11 still applies for those entities that are not yet applying FRS 26. Therefore in the example given above, the premium of 15 per cent that could be payable in year five does not form part of the instrument's finance costs although it might seem to under a strict interpretation of FRS 4. But the Abstract's consensus can only be applied to genuine options and, as a consequence, does not apply to situations where it is clear that the issuer would be commercially obliged to exercise the call option. The UITF cites an example of such a case where the instrument's terms and conditions give the issuer the option of early redemption, but it is clear from the outset that in all conceivable circumstances it would be advantageous for the issuer to exercise the option rather than to allow the debt to remain in issue. [UITF 11 para 8].

6.333 Furthermore, the UITF also commented that where an instrument has an issuer call option the exercise of which is uncertain, the instrument's term will end on the date on which the option is exercisable. [UITF 11 para 7]. This statement is somewhat anomalous, because although the Abstract allows in the example above the 15 per cent premium to be excluded from finance costs, the instrument's term is still determined as five years. This means in practice that the costs of issuing the instrument have to be written off over the period to the option date (in the example five years and not the full ten years). It has been argued that the requirement that the term should end on the date the option is exercisable implies that all of the instrument's finance costs should be written off to the profit and loss account over this period, including any premium payable on the instrument's eventual redemption (a premium of ten per cent in the example payable in year ten). We do not believe that the UITF intended this outcome as it seems totally wrong to accrue ten years' interest and the £10,000 premium in the example over the first five years of the instrument and, therefore, not to accrue any finance cost over the last five years of the instrument's term. We, therefore, consider in this type of situation that issue costs should be charged to the profit and loss account over the shorter term, but interest cost and any redemption premium payable on the instrument's eventual redemption should be accrued over its full term.

6.334 Continuing with the example in paragraph 6.330, under UITF Abstract 11's provisions and our interpretation given above, the finance costs to be allocated to the first five years would be £32,000, comprising the fixed interest cost of £25,000 plus half of the premium arising on the eventual redemption of £10,000 plus the whole of the issue costs of £2,000. The example assumes that interest is paid semi-annually in arrears. The finance cost is allocated to accounting periods at a constant rate on the outstanding balance and for the first five years this rate is calculated to be 6.3385 per cent.

Interest rate compound semi-annually. Overall finance cost 6.3385%

Year	Balance b/f	Finance cost 6 mths	Interest 6 mths	Balance	Finance cost 6 mths	Interest 6 mths	Balance c/f
1	98,000	3,106	(2,500)	98,606	3,125	(2,500)	99,231
2	99,231	3,145	(2,500)	99,876	3,165	(2,500)	100,541
3	100,541	3,180	(2,500)	101,228	3,208	(2,500)	101,936
4	101,936	3,231	(2,500)	102,666	3,254	(2,500)	103,420
5	103,420	3,278	(2,500)	104,198	3,302	(2,500)	105,000
		15,945	(12,500)		16,055	(12,500)	
					15,945	(12,500)	
Total finance and interest costs					32,000	(25,000)	

6.335 For the second five years of the term, the interest rate reduces slightly to 5.6 per cent because all of the issue costs have been amortised over the first five year term. The total finance costs over the ten years come to £62,000, which is made up of interest of £50,000, redemption premium of £10,000 and issue costs of £2,000.

Interest rate compounded semi-annually. Overall finance cost 5.6%

Year	Balance b/f	Finance cost 6 mths	Interest 6 mths	Balance	Finance cost 6 mths	Interest 6 mths	Balance c/f
6	105,000	2,940	(2,500)	105,440	2,953	(2,500)	105,893
7	105,893	2,965	(2,500)	106,358	2,978	(2,500)	106,836
8	106,836	2,992	(2,500)	107,328	3,005	(2,500)	107,833
9	107,833	3,020	(2,500)	108,353	3,034	(2,500)	108,887
10	108,887	3,049	(2,500)	109,436	3,064	(2,500)	110,000
		14,966	(12,500)		15,035	(12,500)	
					14,966	(12,500)	
Total finance and interest costs					30,000	(25,000)	

6.336 The UITF made one exception to the general rule concerning issuer call options where the effective rate of interest increases after the date on which the option is exercisable. [UITF 11 para 9]. This type of circumstance arises where the economics of the instrument are such that the premium payable on exercising the option compensates the investor for forgoing the increase in interest due after the option date. In this circumstance, the finance costs calculation must include the redemption premium payable on exercising the option; and the term would remain, in the example, five years.

6.337 Where in the example in paragraph 6.330, the option is a put option, the instrument's term should be taken to be five years. In this case, the finance cost over the first five years is £42,000 comprising the fixed interest cost of £25,000 plus the early redemption premium of £15,000 and issue costs of £2,000. The example assumes that interest is paid semi-annually in arrears. The finance cost is allocated to accounting periods at a constant rate of 7.9923 per cent on the outstanding balance.

Interest rate compounded semi-annually. Overall finance cost 7.9923%

Year	Balance b/f	Finance cost 6 mths	Interest 6 mths	Balance	Finance cost 6 mths	Interest 6 mths	Balance c/f
1	98,000	3,916	(2,500)	99,416	3,973	(2,500)	100,889
2	100,889	4,032	(2,500)	102,421	4,093	(2,500)	104,014
3	104,014	4,157	(2,500)	105,670	4,223	(2,500)	107,393
4	107,393	4,292	(2,500)	109,184	4,363	(2,500)	111,048
5	111,048	4,438	(2,500)	112,985	4,515	(2,500)	115,000
		20,834	(12,500)		21,167	(12,500)	
					20,834	(12,500)	
Total finance and interest costs					42,000	(25,000)	

6.338 If, however, the option is not taken up in year five, then depending upon the terms of the *instrument* the finance cost for the next period of five years until the instrument is ultimately redeemed will be less than for the first five years. This is because a higher redemption premium has been accrued over the first five year period. This is illustrated in the table below which shows the allocation of the finance costs of £20,000 for the latter five year term. The finance cost is made up of £25,000 of interest plus £10,000 premium payable on redemption less £15,000 of premium already accrued.

Interest rate 5% compounded semi-annually. Overall finance cost 3.5454%

Year	Balance b/f	Finance cost 6 mths	Interest 6 mths	Balance	Finance costs 6 mths	Interest 6 mths	Balance c/f
6	115,000	2,039	(2,500)	114,539	2,030	(2,500)	114,069
7	114,069	2,022	(2,500)	113,591	2,014	(2,500)	113,105
8	113,105	2,005	(2,500)	112,610	1,996	(2,500)	112,106
9	112,106	1,987	(2,500)	111,593	1,978	(2,500)	111,071
10	111,071	1,969	(2,500)	110,540	1,960	(2,500)	110,000
		10,022	(12,500)		9,978	(12,500)	
					10,022	(12,500)	
Total finance and interest costs					20,000	(25,000)	

6.339 The requirement to take the term of the instrument, where an option (apart from an issuer call option) to redeem or cancel exists, to be up to the earliest date the option can be exercised has some odd consequences in practice. For example, in a typical management buyout (MBO), options for early repayment of redeemable shares and debt will often feature in the terms of those instruments. These may well operate to allow repayment of the finance at any time after the instrument has been issued. Where this is the case, unless it can be shown that there will be *no* genuine commercial possibility that the option will be exercised, the term will be less than one year (in effect it will be the notice period required). Thus, the whole of the finance costs should be written off to the profit and loss account in the year the instrument is issued and treated as an exceptional interest cost separately disclosed where material. The finance cost so written off will include the interest cost for the period and any issue costs. Finance costs should also include the difference between any premium on issue and any redemption premium. In the next year, if the instrument continues to be outstanding, the finance costs charged to the profit and loss account will merely be the interest cost for the period.

Term extended

6.340 As indicated in the definition, the term should not include any period for which the instrument might be extended, unless at the time the instrument is issued it is virtually certain that the term will be extended. [FRS 4 para 73]. Consequently, the economic interests of the parties to the instrument are important in determining its term. The FRS cites as an example the situation where a zero coupon bond is issued. If the terms of the bond are such that on early redemption the lender receives merely the original issue price, then the lender is unlikely to require early redemption unless there is a severe deterioration in the creditworthiness of the borrower. Therefore, at the outset, the bond's term should be taken to extend to its final maturity. [FRS 4 para 74].

6.341 These principles are illustrated in the two examples that follow:

Example 1

A company issues £1m 10% preference shares that are classified as liabilities. The terms are that £500,000 is redeemable in 20X2 and the balance is redeemable at the company's option in any year up to 20X9, when the balance must be redeemed. If the £500,000 is not redeemed in 20X2 additional dividends of 5% will accrue on that amount. The company is in financial difficulties and is unlikely to be able to redeem the shares in 20X2.

If there is no genuine possibility that redemption of the £500,000 will occur in 20X2, the term should be taken to be to the year 20X9 for the whole of the £1m preference shares. This means that the finance costs should include the additional dividends on the £500,000 that will not be redeemed in 20X2. The additional dividends should be accrued for over the whole of the instrument's term.

Example 2

A company has issued a bond to raise money from a securities house pending a flotation. The bond is convertible into shares when the company is floated. It has a low coupon at first, but if the company is not floated, it is repayable at a fixed date in the future at a premium. The term of the liability component of the instrument should be taken to be up to the date that is fixed for repayment in the event that the company is not floated. The total finance costs, including the premium should be amortised over this period to give a constant periodic rate of charge.

Term shortened

6.342 During an instrument's life, it is possible that its term could be shortened, for example, if for some reason the instrument is to be redeemed early in a way that was not foreseen. In this situation, the amortisation of issue costs and any discount on issue, or premium on redemption, should be accelerated over the remaining period of the shortened term from the point where it becomes clear that the instrument will be redeemed early. [FRS 4 para 94].

Example

A company has issued £10m of debt and has written off £0.5m of issue costs against the debt. The debt is redeemable in 5 years time and carries interest at 5% per annum. An effective interest rate (EIR) of 6.19% is applied to amortise the issue costs to the profit and loss account over the 5 years. (See para 6.346 onwards for details on EIR.)

At the end of the first year, it becomes clear that the company will redeem the debt at the end of year 3. The company has amortised 1 years worth of issue costs to date. In year 2, the company should revise the EIR (now 7.29%) to record the un-amortised issue costs in the profit and loss account over the remaining term of the debt of 2 years.

6.343 The point at which it *becomes clear* that an instrument will be redeemed early is debatable. A tentative board decision alone is unlikely to be sufficient and there would need to be a clear strategic reason for the early redemption, a timescale and sufficient funds to complete the transaction.

Indeterminate term

6.344 If the life of an instrument is indeterminate (for example, a perpetual bond) then FRS 4 comments that the benefit of the issue costs is reflected in the terms of the financing indefinitely. [FRS 4 para 95]. Where, for example, a perpetual bond of £100,000 is issued by a company and it incurs £2,000 of issue costs, the issue costs should reduce the carrying amount of the debt shown in the company's balance sheet. They would only be charged to the profit and loss account if and when the instrument is repurchased from the lender and would form part of the eventual profit or loss arising on the repurchase.

Measurement

Initial recognition

6.345 FRS 4 requires that immediately after issue, debt should be stated at the amount of the net proceeds (for example, see Table 6.24). [FRS 4 para 27]. The net proceeds are defined as the fair value of the consideration received on the issue of a capital instrument after deducting issue costs. [FRS 4 para 11]. Where debt is issued at a discount, the discount cannot be treated as an asset, rather the debt should be recorded at the fair value of the consideration received net of any discounts given.

Table 6.24 – Borrowings stated at fair value

Bass PLC – Annual Report –30 September 1994

Borrowings

All borrowings are initially stated at the fair value of the consideration received after deduction of issue costs. Issue costs together with finance costs are charged to the profit and loss account over the term of the borrowings and represents a constant proportion of the balance of capital repayments outstanding. Accrued finance costs attributable to borrowings where the maturity at the date of issue is less than 12 months are included in accrued charges within current liabilities. For all other borrowings, accrued finance charges and issue costs are added to the carrying value of those borrowings.

Treatment of finance costs

6.346 Having established that debt should be recognised initially at the amount of the net proceeds, the next question to consider is the value at which the debt should be stated in balance sheets drawn up at dates between the original issue of the debt and its redemption. The answer lies essentially in how payments are accounted for between the date of issue and redemption and the recognition of finance costs.

6.347 Finance costs are considered from paragraph 6.299 and comprise the issue costs, the interest payable over the instrument's life, the difference between any premium received on issue and any premium payable on redemption and any discount allowed on the instrument's issue.

6.347.1 Finance costs should be recognised as an expense over an instrument's life. The simplest method of accounting would be to recognise finance costs on a straight line basis. However, although this method of allocation is simple, it fails to reflect the true cost of finance. This is because the amount charged each year does not necessarily bear any relationship to the outstanding obligation; that is, the method ignores the time value of money which is clearly relevant for financial decisions. For this reason, the ASB rejected the straight line method of allocation and opted instead for a more sophisticated method.

6.347.2 Under the method adopted by FRS 4, finance costs are charged to the profit and loss account at a constant rate on the carrying amount of the instrument. [FRS 4 para 28]. The constant rate is the discount rate that equates the present value of the net proceeds of the instrument with the present value of the total amount repaid on the instrument. It is better known as 'the internal rate of return' or sometimes referred to as 'the effective periodic rate' or 'the effective yield'; and it is equivalent to 'the rate implicit in the lease' under SSAP 21. It may be found by mathematical techniques involving an iterative process or by using a financial calculator or computer. Various examples are included in this chapter that illustrate the allocation of finance costs to accounting periods using this method.

6.347.3 Therefore, generally, it will not be acceptable to use the straight line method to allocate finance costs, unless this produces a similar result to a basis which achieves a constant rate. In this respect the standard adds that in certain instances the nominal interest rate on debt will not be materially different from the amount required by the FRS to achieve a constant rate and in those circumstances the nominal interest rate can be charged in the profit and loss account instead. [FRS 4 para 75]. This will often be so where the issue costs on a debt instrument are immaterial and there is no redemption premium to be accrued over its term. Consequently, for simple debt, such as straightforward bank loans and overdrafts where issue costs are immaterial or do not feature, the actual interest charged on the debt should be the amount recorded in the profit and loss account. Otherwise a basis similar to that illustrated in the example in paragraph 6.348 should be used.

6.347.4 Clearly, the finance cost is not necessarily equal to the amount of interest payable. The following example illustrates the issues that arise.

Example

A company issues 5% debentures having a nominal value £100,000 at a discount of 10% repayable in five years' time at a premium of 20%. Debt issue costs amounted to £5,000 and interest is payable annually in arrears.

	£	£
Net proceeds received:		
Nominal value		100,000
Discount on issue @ 10%		(10,000)
Issue costs		(5,000)
		85,000
Total amount payable:		
Interest @ 5% for 5 years		25,000
Redemption premium		20,000
Nominal value		100,000
		145,000
Finance cost:		
Interest	25,000	
Issue costs	5,000	
Discount on issue	10,000	
Redemption premium	20,000	
		60,000

6.348 As explained in paragraph 6.301, the finance cost should be recognised over the term of the loan, that is, five years at a constant rate on the outstanding obligation. In the example used above, the rate can be found to be 12.323 per cent. If the finance costs are allocated to accounting periods using this rate, the movements on the loan would be as follows:

Interest rate 5% compounded annually. Overall finance cost 12.323%

Year	Balance b/f	Finance cost @ 12.323%	Interest paid	Balance c/f
1	85,000	10,474	(5,000)	90,474
2	90,474	11,149	(5,000)	96,623
3	96,623	11,906	(5,000)	103,529
4	103,529	12,757	(5,000)	111,286
5	111,286	13,714	(5,000)	120,000
Total finance costs and interest		60,000	(25,000)	

6.349 The effective interest rate of 12.323 per cent is higher than the nominal interest rate of 5 per cent because of the incidence of issue costs, the discount on issue and the premium payable on redemption. As explained in paragraph 6.301, in some circumstances the nominal interest rate may not be materially different from the effective interest rate, in which case the nominal interest rate may be used.

6.349.1 Although the FRS requires that the finance cost should be charged to the profit and loss account over the instrument's term, it does not preclude capitalising those costs. Where it is appropriate to capitalise finance costs as part of the cost of an asset, the costs should still initially be written off to the profit and loss account as part of the interest cost, but should also be credited simultaneously to the profit and loss account and debited to the asset in order to record the capitalisation. [FRS 4 para 76]. As a result, the interest charge shown on the face of the profit and loss account would be the net amount and in the notes this would be expanded to show the gross amount and the amount capitalised deducted. However, for assets of the company being constructed, only the finance costs incurred during the period of construction of the asset can be capitalised (see further chapter 16).

6.350 The Act allows issue costs on debentures to be written off to the share premium account, which seems to conflict with the provisions of FRS 4. However, although FRS 4 requires issue costs on debt to be charged to the profit and loss account over the term of the debt as part of the finance costs, it does not preclude the subsequent charging of those issue costs to the share premium account. [FRS 4 para 97]. Therefore, when part of the issue costs are charged to the profit and loss account in a particular year, a reserve transfer of the same amount can be made from the profit and loss account reserve to the share premium account (see for example Table 6.25). This treatment may be adopted where issue costs are material in order to protect distributable reserves.

Table 6.25 – Debt issue costs

Cable and Wireless plc – Annual report and accounts – 31 March 2001

Statement of Accounting Policies (extract)

Debt issue costs

The costs of issue of capital instruments such as bonds and debentures are charged to the profit and loss account on an annual basis over the life of the instrument. A corresponding amount is subsequently transferred to the share premium account from the profit and loss account reserve.

Subsequent recognition and measurement

6.351 Once the effective interest rate on the debt has been calculated by reference to the initial carrying value and the future cash outflows, it is a relatively simple matter to arrive at the carrying value of debt at each period end. As evident from the table above, the carrying value at the end of each period is obtained by adding to the carrying value at the beginning of the period the finance cost in respect of the reporting period (calculated by applying the effective interest rate to the carrying value at the beginning) and deducting any payments made in respect of the debt in that period. [FRS 4 para 29]. In fact, the carrying value at each balance sheet date is the discounted amount of the future payments specified in the debt instrument using the effective interest rate inherent in the amount at which the debt was initially recognised. The requirement to record the carrying value of debt at a discounted amount in financial statements is relatively new in UK financial reporting, although discounting is widely used in investment appraisals.

Contingent payments

6.352 The effective interest rate and, hence, the carrying value of debt is relatively easy to calculate where the cash outflows specified in the instrument are known or fixed at the outset. However, where the future cash outflows are not known in advance, but are variable, an effective interest rate cannot be calculated. For example, in the case of floating rate notes where the amount of periodic payments of interest is calculated by reference to a particular formula or by reference to LIBOR, say LIBOR plus two per cent, the interest payments over the instruments' life are not known in advance. Another example is that of index linked loans, which may be redeemable at the principal amount multiplied by an index. The effect of each is that the effective interest rate of the instrument over its life is not only unknown, but also changes every time there is a change in circumstance. The most practical way of accounting for such instruments is not to try to anticipate the change in circumstance, but to take account of it in the period in which the change occurs.

6.353 Therefore, the standard requires that where the amount of payments required by a debt instrument is contingent on uncertain future events such as changes in an index, those events should be taken into account in calculating finance costs and the carrying amount once they have occurred. [FRS 4 para 31]. In other words, the initial accounting for the instrument should take no account of those events, but the carrying value of the instrument at each subsequent balance sheet date should be recalculated to take account of the changes that have occurred in the period. The resulting change in carrying amount should be accounted for as an adjustment to the finance cost for the period. The treatment specified in the standard is illustrated by reference to a floating rate instrument below.

Example

A company borrows £1m from a bank repayable in five years' time. Interest is paid annually in arrears at a rate equal to the bank's prime rate plus 1%. Due to arrangement fees and bank commission, the company receives a net amount of £980,000. The bank's prime rate in years 1 and 2 remains at 5%. At the beginning of year 3, the prime rate rises to 6%.

As an effective interest rate cannot be calculated at inception without advanced knowledge of the change in future rates, the finance cost in each period would need to be calculated by reference to the actual rate prevailing in that period. The example is slightly complicated because of the incidence of issue costs of £20,000. The amortisation of the issue costs over the five year period can either be carried out if immaterial on a straight line basis (or written off to the profit and loss account immediately), or when they are material, on a constant interest rate basis by regarding them as being similar to a discount on issue. On the latter basis, the interest rate for amortising the issue costs over the five year period is 0.4049%. The additional finance cost which is the interest element would be charged in the period at the actual rate incurred.

			Finance cost			
Year	**Balance b/f**	**Issue cost 0.4049%**	**Interest for period**	**Total charge**	**Interest paid**	**Balance c/f**
1	980,000	3,968	60,000	63,968	(60,000)	983,968
2	983,968	3.984	60.000	63.984	(60,000)	987,952
3	987,952	4,000	70.000	74,000	(70,000)	991,952
4	991,952	4.016	70,000	74,016	(70,000)	995,968
5	995,968	4,032	70,000	74,032	(70.000)	1,000,000
Total costs		20,000	330,000	350,000		

6.354 It is doubtful whether the above treatment can be applied to all situations where the amount of cash outflows on the instrument is not known in advance. Consider a situation, where a shareholder makes a non-interest bearing loan to his company which is redeemable at the end of three years at a premium determined by applying a known percentage to the aggregate profits for a three year period in excess of a benchmark amount. In this situation, the premium payable on redemption is contingent on the company achieving profits in excess of the benchmark amount and this amount will only be known at the end of the third year. If the wording of the standard is read literally, no amount of the premium payable will fall to be accrued in the first two years, but the whole amount will be charged in the profit and loss account in the third year, thus distorting the results for that year. Clearly this treatment does not accord with the spirit of FRS 4. Therefore, a 'best estimate' of the likely premium payable on redemption should be made at the outset and a proportion provided for every year. The provision would require adjustments in years two and three when the outcome becomes clearer and eventually known.

6.355 If, in the situation explained above, the company had incurred some issue costs and the loan was interest bearing, these components of finance costs should be charged to the profit and loss account at a constant rate, thus leaving the unknown element to be dealt with in the manner specified above.

Repurchase of debt

6.356 Companies sometimes have the opportunity to repurchase their own debt or settle debt early at an amount that differs from the amount at which the debt is stated in their balance sheet at the time. For example, a company may decide to take advantage of falling interest rates by repurchasing its existing long-term fixed interest debt, even though this may involve payment of a premium. The question arises as to how the difference on the repurchase or early settlement should be accounted for. Accounting for repurchase of debt was first addressed by UITF Abstract 8, which was superseded by FRS 4.

6.357 Some accountants supported the view that the difference on repurchase should be deferred on the grounds that the opportunity to repurchase the debt at a gain or loss is created principally by movements in interest rates. In effect, the economic decision to repurchase the debt is neutral, because the gain or loss is effectively counter balanced by a corresponding increase or decrease in interest costs in the future. Therefore, they argued that the accounting for the effect of the repurchase should also be neutral and, accordingly, the gain or loss should be deferred. The UITF, however, reached the conclusion that the gain or loss on repurchase should be taken to the profit and loss account in the period in which the repurchase occurs. The UITF reached this conclusion on the grounds that the finance cost reported by an entity should normally reflect only its current borrowing arrangements and should not be influenced by any arrangement that previously existed, but that had now been terminated.

6.358 FRS 4 follows the UITF's ruling, and accordingly, requires that gains or losses should be recognised in the profit and loss account in the period during which the repurchase or early settlement is made. [FRS 4 para 32].

6.359 The only time that it might be possible to argue that no profit or loss has arisen in the period is (following the principles of FRS 5) where in substance there is no repurchase and the old debt being repurchased has been replaced by new debt, which in effect gives the same economic result as the old debt. This was the argument followed in UITF Abstract 8 (see below), but it rests on the foundation that the new debt must give the same economic result as the old debt. In the majority of situations in practice this is unlikely to be the case, because there will always be a commercial reason compelling the change; otherwise why would the company repurchase? Consider the following example:

Example

A company repays £150,000 debt early and incurs a penalty of £5,000 which is specified in the agreement, but replaces it with a new loan of £150,000 from the same party. The terms of the loan and the loan covenants are very similar. The company is willing to pay this penalty, because the new loan is a variable rate loan, whereas the old loan is fixed rate. Therefore, although the loan is very similar in nature, the cash flows related to interest payments are different and because the penalty is pre-determined it does not reflect accurately the difference between the fixed rate of interest and the current and expected future variable interest rates. It seems clear in this situation that there has been a change in substance in relation to these loans and that as a result the £5,000 penalty should be charged in the profit and loss account in the year of repurchase.

6.360 UITF Abstract 8 was developed at the time that certain major utility companies were repurchasing their government debt to help reduce the government's public sector borrowing requirement. Some of these repurchases were special in nature and required different rules to normal repurchases. The Abstract was withdrawn on FRS 4's issue, but remains a good source of guidance to help determine those exceptional cases where in substance there has been no repurchase. UITF Abstract 8 made two exceptions to the requirement for immediate recognition of a gain or loss arising on the repurchase of debt. The exceptions, which are considered below are referred to in appendix III of FRS 4 which deals with the standard's development. The two exceptions are where:

- The agreement to repurchase the debt is also connected with its refinancing on substantially the same terms (other than interest costs). This would apply where the original debt is fully replaced by new debt which gives the same economic result as the original debt, that is, there has been no change of substance in the debt. For this to be the case, as a minimum the following conditions must be satisfied:

- The replacement debt and the original debt are both fixed rate.
- The replacement debt is of a comparable amount to the original debt.
- The maturity of the replacement debt is not materially different from the remaining maturity of the original debt.
- The covenants of the replacement debt are not materially different from those of the original debt.

A refinancing may fall within this exception whether or not the lender of the replacement debt is the same as the lender of the original debt.

- The agreement to repurchase the debt is not carried out on a fair value basis because the overall finance costs of the replacement debt are significantly different from market rates. This condition has been introduced to prevent recognition of an artificial profit, compensated by higher costs in the future.

6.361 Where either of the above exceptions apply, the gain or loss should be spread forward either over the remaining maturity of the original debt or, if not significantly different, over the maturity of the replacement debt. In addition, the circumstances should be disclosed, together with the method of accounting adopted and the principal terms of the original and replacement borrowing.

Renegotiation of debt

6.362 A company that is experiencing financial difficulties and is unable to meet its scheduled debt repayments may seek to renegotiate the terms of its debt obligations with its lenders. As a result of the negotiations, the lender may agree to a reduction or a deferral of the payments due to him. Since the company's obligations are significantly reduced, a gain may arise. The recognition and measurement of this gain are central to the accounting for renegotiation of debt.

6.363 The accounting for renegotiation of debt is not included in the standard, but the ASB's initial proposals, first published for public comment in a bulletin issued in July 1993 (which are also discussed in paragraphs 41 to 44 of appendix III of the FRS), are examined here.

6.364 Accounting for the effects of the renegotiation (the concession granted by the lender) involves two particular issues, namely:

- The way in which the concession should be recognised. That is, whether the finance costs should be reduced over the remaining period in which the debt is in issue or whether the gain should be recognised at the time of the renegotiation.

- If it is considered that a gain arises, the way in which the gain should be determined. That is, whether market interest rates prevailing at the time of renegotiation should be used or whether the revised payments should be discounted at the rate inherent in the original debt.

6.365 With respect to the first point above, some support deferral of the gain on the grounds that they consider it paradoxical to recognise a gain that relates primarily to a deterioration of the company's financial condition. They believe that no gain should be recognised, but the benefit of the reduction should be recognised over the term of the replacement loan by way of a reduced interest burden. Others argue that the recognition of the gain at the time of renegotiation reflects the economic consequences of the concession granted by the lender. It also ensures that both liabilities and finance costs for subsequent periods are shown at amounts that properly represent the agreement then in force. The ASB supported the latter view and proposed that in principle the gain should be recognised in the period in which the renegotiation was concluded.

6.366 The ASB argued that the renegotiation was a transaction that effectively resulted in the original loan being replaced by a new loan giving rise to revised payments and, therefore, the amount relating to the old, superseded, debt was no longer relevant. Accordingly, the ASB proposed that the debt should be stated at its market value at the time of renegotiation, because this treatment best reflected the economic circumstances prevailing at that time. As the debt would generally not be traded, its market value would often be determined by discounting the revised payments by reference to the rate of interest which the company would have expected to pay on a loan of similar characteristics to that resulting from the renegotiation. Any change in the company's credit rating since the original loan was made, as well as changes in the general level of interests rates, would be reflected in that rate. Several respondents objected to this aspect of the ASB's proposal. Their objections can best be illustrated by an example.

Example

A company took out a long-term bank loan of £1m on 1 January 20X0 at a fixed rate of 8% per annum for 10 years. Interest on the loan is paid yearly in arrears. As a result of deteriorating financial condition, the company successfully agreed with its bankers to reduce the yearly interest payments from £80,000 to £20,000 per annum with effect from 1 January 20X4, but the loan is still repayable at the original amount on 31 December 20X9. At 1 January 20X4, the company would have paid 15% per annum on a loan of similar characteristics to that resulting from the renegotiation. Had the company's credit rating not declined, the interest rate on similar borrowings would have been 10% per annum.

	Original rate	Market rate excluding decline in credit rating	Market rate including decline in credit rating
Rate (%)	8.00%	10.00%	15.00%
	£'000	£'000	£'000
Original loan	1,000	1,000	1,000
PV of revised repayments	723	652	508
Gain on renegotiation	277	348	492
Future finance costs			
31 December 20X4	57	65	76
31 December 20X5	61	70	85
31 December 20X6	64	75	94
31 December 20X7	68	80	106
31 December 20X8	71	86	118
31 December 20X9	76	92	133
Total finance costs	397	468	612
Less: interest payments	120	120	120
Gain	277	348	492
Carrying value			
31 December 20X4	761	697	564
31 December 20X5	802	747	629
31 December 20X6	846	802	703
31 December 20X7	894	862	788
31 December 20X8	944	928	887
31 December 20X9	1.000	1,000	1.000

6.367 Under the ASB's proposal, the carrying value of the loan of £1,000,000 immediately after renegotiation, calculated by discounting the revised payments by reference to the market rate for new borrowings that takes account of the decline in the company's credit standing, would be restated at £508,000 giving rise to a gain of £492,000 that would be recognised immediately. This gain would reverse as finance costs are recognised at a higher amount of £612,000 over the subsequent six years compared with the actual interest payments of £120,000 over the same period, as indicated above. However, as is evident from the table above, the gain of £492,000 under the ASB's proposals is made up of three components:

- A gain of £277,000 (that is, £1,000,000 — £723,000) which is equal to the present value of the actual reduction in financing costs from £80,000 to £20,000, that is, £60,000 per annum for six years discounted at eight per cent.
- A gain of £71,000 (that is, £723,000 — £652,000) attributable to the change in market rate of interest from eight per cent to ten per cent.
- A gain of £144,000 (that is, £652,000 — £508,000) attributable to the decline in the credit standing of the company.

6.368 Many argue that in most cases the combined effect of the above components will mean that the more distressed the company's financial condition is, the greater will be the gain on renegotiation as a consequence of using a higher discount rate as the ASB proposed. This is highly imprudent and rather anomalous. Also, the second element of the gain is not considered to be suitable under existing accounting framework. Furthermore, the ASB's own draft Statement of principles recognised this anomaly when considering how to deal with changes in the market value of liabilities that result from changes in market interest rates. A footnote to paragraph 26 of chapter 5 of the ASB's original draft Statement of principles issued in 1995 stated:

> *"Some would wish to take account only of changes in the general rates of interest rather than in the rate applicable to the entity, since otherwise an entity will report gains and losses relating to changes in its own perceived creditworthiness. It is particularly questionable whether it is appropriate to reflect a gain relating to a decrease in creditworthiness, because the compensating loss is usually a change in future earning power, or the value of assets, some of which are not reflected in the financial statements."*

6.369 Accordingly, opponents of the ASB's proposals believe that if a gain is recognised, it should be calculated by reference to the future expected cash flows as modified by the renegotiation, but discounted at the effective rate of interest inherent in the original loan.

6.370 Because of the above concerns, the ASB decided not to address the accounting for renegotiation of debt in FRS 4. With the introduction of FRS 26, it will no longer need to consider this issue. In the absence of adequate current UK guidance for those entities not yet applying FRS 26, it is regarded as preferable not to recognise the gain, but the effects of the renegotiation should be treated as an interest subsidy. It may be necessary to disclose the nature and amount of the renegotiation to give a true and fair view of the company's financing arrangements. This means that the debt would remain in the balance sheet at £1,000,000 and the new finance cost of £20,000 would be charged each year giving an effective interest rate of two per cent from the date of renegotiation to date of maturity.

6.371 Some would argue that a gain should be recognised, but based only on discounting the revised payments at the original interest rate of eight per cent (that is, the gain of £277,000 in the above example). The effect would be to restate the carrying value of the loan at £723,000 at the time of the renegotiation. In subsequent periods, the effective rate of interest charged in the profit and loss account is eight per cent on the new carrying value of the loan (which is increased in each period by the difference between the interest charged at eight per cent and the actual interest paid of £20,000). Furthermore, they argue that as a reduction in a liability is considered to be a realised profit, the gain of £277,000 should be reported in the profit and loss account. However, although this method is acceptable, it is less prudent because it leads to recognising a future gain arising from the reduction of future interest charges when the company is in financial distress.

Disclosure

6.372 Both the Act and the original standard specify a considerable amount of detail that a company's financial statements must give in respect of its borrowings. In addition, companies listed on the Stock Exchange are required to give further information.

6.373 However, one of the most significant changes to FRS 4 as a result of the publication of FRS 25 is the deletion of all the disclosure requirements. These disclosure requirements are not necessarily replaced by equivalent FRS 25 requirements, as it is only the presentation requirements of FRS 25 that are mandatory for all entities for accounting periods beginning on or after 1 January 2005.

6.374 An entity that is not required to comply with the disclosure requirements of FRS 25 should consider whether it should continue to provide the existing FRS 4 disclosures, until it falls within the scope of the FRS 25 disclosures. Existing FRS 4 disclosures include:

- Details about convertible debt. For example see Table 6.25.1 below.
- Maturity analysis of debt. For example see Table 6.25.2 below.

Table 6.25.1 — Inchcape plc — Annual Report & Accounts — 31 December 1994

consolidated balance sheet AS AT 31 st DECEMBER 1994 **(extract)**

Notes (pages 44-66)		**£m**	**1994 £m**	£m	1993 restated £m
	Net current assets		**308.9**		323.3
	Total assets *less* current liabilities		**1,121.1**		1,178.0
20(b)	**Creditors — amounts falling due after more than one year:**				
20,21	Borrowings	**(57.1)**		(54.2)	
20	6¼% Convertible Subordinated Bonds Due 2008	**(125.0)**		(125.0)	
	Other	**(80.9)**		(74.4)	
		(263.0)		(253.6)	
22	**Provisions for liabilities and charges**	**(109.5)**		(52.1)	
			(372.5)		(305.7)
	Net assets		**748.6**		872.3

Notes to the accounts
(extract)

20 Creditors (extract)

The £125m 6¼% Convertible Subordinated Bonds Due 2008 are convertible at the option of the holder, on or prior to 3rd May 2008, into folly paid ordinary shares of 25p each of Inchcape plc at 689 pence per share. Interest is payable semiannually on 10th May and 10th November. None of the bonds were converted during the year. If the conversion rights attaching to the bonds outstanding at 31 st December 1994 were exercised 18,142,235 ordinary shares of25p each of Inchcape plc would fall to be issued. Unless previously redeemed or converted, the bonds will be redeemed at par on 10th May 2008. The bonds may be redeemed at the option of the Company, in whole or in part, at par at any time after 30th May 1988 or earlier if certain conditions are met.

Table 6.25.2 — TI Group plc — Annual Report — 31 December 1995

Notes to the financial statements (extract)

21 LOANS AND OTHER BORROWINGS FALLING DUE AFTER MORE THAN ONE YEAR

Loans repayable partly or wholly after five years include debts of $105m and $100m privately placed by TI Group Inc with major US institutional investors. These debts have fixed coupons of 8.52% and 8.853% respectively, with final maturity during 1996 but where committed facilities from the same lender are in place until 2002. Similarly, £92.6m of unsecured bank and other loans repayable wholly within five years (1994 £98.8m) comprise revolving credit facilities with drawings maturing during 1996 but where committed facilities from the same lender are in place until 2000. All these drawings are therefore shown as due for repayment on maturity of the facilities, comprising £nil between one and two years (1994 £83.5m), £92.6m between two and five years (1994 £15.3m), and £22.5m after five years (1994 £nil).

Companies Act requirements

6.375 Under the Act, capital instruments in the form of debentures, loans and debt instruments fall to be included under the general heading of 'Creditors'. All items included under creditors must be analysed between amounts that will fall due within one year of the balance sheet date and amounts that will fall due after more than one year. [Note 13 on the balance sheet formats].

6.376 In distinguishing between the above two categories, a loan is regarded as falling due for repayment (or an instalment is regarded as falling due for payment) on the earliest date on which the lender could require repayment (or payment) if he were to exercise all options and rights available to him. [CA85 4 Sch 85].

6.377 For each item shown under creditors (whichever balance sheet format is adopted) there must be disclosed separately the aggregate amounts of debts falling into the two categories below:

- Debts that are payable or repayable otherwise than by instalments and falling due for payment or repayment after the end of the five year period beginning with the day after the end of the financial year.

- Debts that are payable or repayable by instalments, any of which will fall due for payment after the end of that five year period.

[CA85 4 Sch 48(1)].

6.378 The requirement is to disclose one figure showing the aggregate of the above two items, but the aggregation of instalment and non-instalment debts results in a figure that is rather meaningless. The DTI's intention seems to have been to require disclosure of the amount of debts and instalments which are payable in over five years, to bring the disclosure in line with that required by Article 43(1)(6) of the 4th Directive. In practice, it seems sensible to give the intended disclosure as this is more meaningful.

6.379 The terms of payment or repayment and the applicable rate of interest for each debt covered by the disclosure under the preceding paragraph must also be given. [CA85 4 Sch 48 (2)]. Where the number of debt instruments is such that, in the directors' opinion, this requirement would result in a statement of excessive length, this information need be given only in general terms. [CA85 4 Sch 48(3)].

6.380 Where any item that is shown under the heading 'Creditors' includes debts for which the company has given security, these debts must be disclosed in aggregate. Also, the notes must give an indication of the nature of the securities given. [4 Sch 48(4)]. For this requirement to be meaningful, the financial statements should show some disaggregation of the relevant liabilities. This is because it could be misleading merely to disclose the aggregate of a basket of securities compared with the aggregate of a basket of liabilities. However, in practice, companies often describe the charge in general terms, referring, for example, to 'mortgages on freehold land and buildings' rather than specifying the particular properties involved.

6.381 If a company has issued any debentures during the financial year, the notes to the financial statements must disclose:

- The classes of debentures issued.
- The amount issued and the consideration the company received in respect of each class of debentures issued.

[CA85 4 Sch 41(1)].

[The next paragraph is 6.383.]

Requirements for entities applying FRS 25 and FRS 26

Introduction

6.383 FRS 25 and FRS 26 are the UK equivalents of the international standards IAS 32 and IAS 39. With a small number of exceptions, the text of the UK standards is an exact replica of that of the international standards. Hence the guidance on financial instruments in the Manual of Accounting – IFRS in the UK is relevant to entities applying FRS 25 and FRS 26. The relevant extracts from that book are reproduced as Annex 3 to this chapter.

6.383.1 In accounting periods beginning on or after 1 January 2007, entities that apply FRS 26 are required to also apply FRS 29. Once FRS 29 is applied, the disclosure requirements in FRS 25 are superseded. FRS 29 largely replicates the requirements of IFRS 7 and the details are covered in Annex 3 to this chapter.

[The next paragraph is 6.384.]

Differences between the UK standards and their international equivalents

FRS 25 scope exclusion

6.384 As explained in paragraph 6.37, the application of the presentation requirements of FRS 25 should be considered separately to the application of the disclosure requirements. Note that FRS 25 scopes out entities that apply the Financial Reporting Standard for Smaller Entities (FRSSE).

6.384.1 Entities that do not apply FRS 26 are exempt from the disclosure requirements of FRS 25. In addition, the following entities are also exempt from the disclosure requirements of FRS 25 provided that they are included in publicly available consolidated financial statements that include disclosures that comply with the standard:

- Subsidiaries that are not themselves banks or insurance companies, 90 per cent or more of whose voting rights are controlled within the group.
- Parent companies in respect of their single-entity financial statements.

[FRS 25 para 3C].

[The next paragraph is 6.386.]

Recognition and derecognition

6.386 When, in 2003, the IASB were exposing proposed changes to IAS 39, they were considering a 'continuing involvement' model for the derecognition of financial assets. In the UK, the ASB did not believe that this model best addressed the accounting issues in this area and, hence, the recognition and derecognition guidance in IAS 39 was not implemented in FRS 26 when it was issued in December 2004. The ASB was satisfied that the application of the principles in FRS 5 for the recognition and derecognition of both financial and non-financial assets and liabilities provided a better solution to the proposed international approach. FRS 5's requirements and principles are considered in chapter 3.

6.387 The derecognition model that was finally adopted by the IASB in 2003 was a revised version of that originally proposed. As a result, the ASB amended

FRS 26 in April 2006 to bring the IAS 39 recognition and derecognition guidance into UK GAAP. The title of the standard changed to FRS 26, 'Financial Instruments: Recognition and measurement'. However, FRS 5 continues to apply to the recognition and derecognition of non-financial assets and liabilities.

6.387.1 Entities that apply FRS 26 are required to apply the recognition and derecognition amendment in accounting periods commencing on or after 1 January 2007. Earlier adoption is permitted. Those entities that are not within FRS 26's scope and those that choose not to early adopt the amendment must continue to apply FRS 5 to the recognition and derecognition of both financial and non-financial assets and liabilities.

6.387.2 The ASB recognised that entities may not have all of the necessary information to apply the amendment retrospectively and to obtain all of the information may not be practicable. Hence, transitional provisions have been provided for initial adoption of the requirements.

6.387.3 An entity can choose to apply the requirements to either:

- transactions entered into after the beginning of the comparative period for the accounting period the entity first applies the standard's derecognition requirements; or
- transactions entered into after an earlier date of the entity's choosing, provided information sufficient to apply the standard was obtained at the time of initial accounting for each transaction.

[FRS 26 paras 108E, F].

6.387.4 In addition, if a transaction that occurred before the transition date resulted in linked presentation under FRS 5, the derecognition of the gross asset and liability must be re-examined under the new derecognition requirements of FRS 26. [FRS 26 para 108E].

6.387.5 The details of the standard's recognition and derecognition requirements are given in Annex 3 to this chapter.

[The next paragraph is 6.388.]

EU carve-out of IAS 39

6.388 This is an area where there are no differences between IAS 32/39 and FRS 25/26. However, there is an important difference between the UK standards and the version of the international standards that is applied in the UK by entities and groups that report under IFRS.

6.389 Prior to the initial adoption of IAS 39 by the EU, the IASB had been in extensive discussion with the banking and insurance communities for over a year. These institutions (especially those from certain continential countries) and some regulators (including the European Central Bank and the Basel Committee) had objected to various aspects of IAS 39; the IASB had made certain changes, but objections remained. To overcome the impasse, the EC, together with the Accounting Regulatory Committee (ARC), decided to endorse a 'carve-out' version of IAS 39 under which certain words and paragraphs, relating solely to the use of the fair value option for financial liabilities and certain aspects of hedge accounting that troubled the banks or the regulators, were deleted. This approach was confirmed by the ARC at its meeting in October 2004 and the 'carve-out' standard was endorsed by the Commission on 19 November 2004 as Regulation EC 2086/2004. The Commission stated that its aim is full adoption of IAS 39 and that once these issues have been resolved the revised version of the standard that is issued by the IASB will be adopted for use in the EU.

6.389.1 In November 2005, the EC adopted the IASB's amendments to IAS 39 published in June 2005 in relation to the fair value option. The hedge accounting carve-out remains.

6.390 Hence, for the time being, UK entities applying IFRS are using a modified version of IAS 39. In publishing FRS 26, the ASB used the full, unamended version of IAS 39. The EU carve out, therefore, has no impact on those entities that continue to report under UK GAAP.

The fair value option

6.390.1 When FRS 26 was issued in December 2004, the standard permitted an entity to designate any financial asset or liability as at fair value through profit or loss when initially recognised, except for investments in equity instruments that do not have a quoted market price in an active market and whose fair value cannot be reliably measured. However, the standard was amended for the fair value option in October 2005. The fair value option restricts when an entity can designate a financial asset or liability as at fair value through profit or loss and is applicable for accounting periods beginning on or after 1 January 2006 with earlier application encouraged.

6.390.2 Entities that adopt the fair value option in an accounting period beginning before 1 January 2006 must designate any financial assets or liabilities as at fair value through profit or loss, before 1 December 2005, where the relevant criteria are met. IAS 39 requires such designations to be made by 1 September 2005.

6.390.3 Note that the fair value option is subject to the constraints imposed by the new fair value accounting rules of the Companies Act 1985, which specifically do not permit companies to fair value their non-trading financial liabilities. The exemption to this general rule is that entities have a further opportunity to perform this designation when they apply FRS 26 for the first time. [FRS 26 para 105].

6.390.4 When FRS 26 is first applied an entity is permitted to designate a previously recognised financial asset or financial liability as a financial asset or financial liability at fair value through profit or loss or available for sale despite the usual requirement to make such designation on initial recognition. However, companies will often only be able to adopt this treatment for financial liabilities if they use the true and fair override to the Companies Act 1985 (see para 6.83).

6.390.5 Details on the fair value option are given in paragraph 6.406.1.

Other differences

6.390.6 In addition to the differences highlighted above, there are two further distinctions that should be noted:

- Certain paragraphs of IAS 1, 'Presentation of financial statements', have been included in FRS 25 (paras 50A-50E) to provide guidance in respect of the classification of current and non-current liabilities, particularly in relation to breaches of long-term loan covenants and refinancing arrangements. Refer to chapter 4 of the Manual of Accounting – IFRS in the UK for further guidance.
- For those entities that are not applying FRS 26, FRS 25 (para 3D) encourages (not mandatory) disclosures consistent with the disclosure requirements of FRS 25, adapted in line with the entity's accounting policies for the relevant transactions. In particular the following are encouraged:
  - Interest rate disclosures should be based on the rate according to the entity's accounting policies if the rate is different from the effective interest rate in FRS 26.
  - FRS 26 disclosures for hedging should be given applied to the entity's own hedge accounting policies.
  - Instruments that are treated by the entity as insurance contracts should be treated as insurance contracts even if they meet the definition of a financial instrument under FRS 26.

[FRS 25 para 3D].

Transitional guidance

6.391 As explained in paragraph 6.26 onwards, the timing of the first time application of these new UK accounting standards will depend on whether the entity is listed or if it applies the fair value accounting rules. For a number of years from 2005, UK companies will be applying the new standards for the first time at different times. Although the standards can be applied early by those entities that fall within their scope, they cannot be applied before accounting periods commencing on or after 1 January 2005.

6.392 FRS 25 and FRS 26 represent a major shift away from existing UK GAAP and the impact on the financial statements of those entities impacted may be significant. In addition to the direct impact on the financial statements, there are other considerations such as changes to accounting systems and processes. To some extent a new mindset will be required among accounting staff and the transition may prove to be a difficult time for those involved.

6.393 Listed groups that are required to adopt IFRS face an even tougher challenge in the year of transition, having to apply a whole raft of new accounting standards. To ease the transition, the IASB issued IFRS 1, 'First-time adoption of IFRS', in June 2003. This standard sets out the basic rule of full retrospective application of all relevant standards, but then offers a number of optional exemptions and mandatory exceptions to that rule, with the aim of easing the transition. Full retrospective application of all relevant IFRS would create immense accounting difficulties, particularly in complex areas such as business combinations and financial instruments. Hence the exemptions and exceptions target a number of particularly difficult areas and provide alternatives to full retrospective adoption.

6.394 UK GAAP has no equivalent to IFRS 1, but the difficulties of having to apply FRS 25 and FRS 26 for the first time are no less apparent than those experienced by groups transitioning to IAS 32 and IAS 39. Hence the standards themselves include detailed transitional guidance for first-time adopters of FRS 25 and FRS 26 based on those contained in IFRS 1 for first-time adopters of IAS 32 and IAS 39.

6.395 As in IFRS, the basic rule is one of full retrospective adoption. [FRS 25 para 97, FRS 26 para 104]. As outlined below there are a number of specific transitional provisions that ease the burden of full retrospective adoption.

Comparative information

6.396 In the first reporting period in which FRS 25 and FRS 26 are applied, it would be usual, given the requirement for full retrospective adoption, to restate the comparative information for the impact of those standards. Hence a listed entity reporting to 31 December 2005 would need to restate the 2004 comparative information for FRS 25 and FRS 26. This could prove difficult, in particular with regard to the hedging requirements as appropriate hedge documentation must be in place before hedge accounting can be applied.

6.397 Similar to IFRS 1, FRS 25 and FRS 26 provide exemptions from the need to restate comparatives when the standards are adopted before certain dates. The table below summarises the available optional exemptions.

Optional exemption for restatement of comparative information	Available for accounting periods commencing before	Reference
FRS 25 presentation (paras 15-50)	1 January 2006	FRS 25 para 97B
FRS 25 disclosures (paras 51-95)	1 January 2007	FRS 25 para 97B
FRS 26	1 January 2007	FRS 26 para 108D

Example

Company A is a UK company that is listed on the London Stock Exchange. Company B is unlisted and applies the fair value accounting rules as set out in the Companies Act. Company C is not listed and does not apply the fair value accounting rules. Each of the companies has a December year end. How should each of the companies apply FRS 25 and FRS 26 in its comparative period?

Company A must apply both FRS 25 and FRS 26 in full in 2005. The table below summarises the comparative exemptions available:

	Year end 2005	Year end 2006	Year end 2007
FRS 25 presentation	✓	×	×
FRS 25 disclosures	✓	×	n/a[1]
FRS 26	✓	×	×

✓ = exemption is available
× = exemption is not available
[1] = FRS 29 disclosures will apply

Company B must apply the FRS 25 presentation requirements and can apply FRS 26 voluntarily in 2005. Company B must apply FRS 26 and full FRS 25 from 2006. The table below summarises the comparative exemptions available:

	Year end 2005	Year end 2006	Year end 2007
FRS 25 presentation	✓	×	×
FRS 25 disclosures	✓	✓	n/a[1]
FRS 26	n/a	✓	×

✓ = exemption is available
× = exemption is not available
[1] = FRS 29 disclosures will apply

Company C must apply the FRS 25 presentation requirements in 2005, but will not be required to apply FRS 26 or the disclosure requirements of FRS 25. Company C cannot early adopt the FRS 25 disclosures or FRS 26 until it falls within FRS 26's scope. The table below summarises the comparative exemptions available:

			Year end
	2005	**2006**	**2007**
FRS 25 presentation	✓	×	×
FRS 25 disclosures	n/a	n/a	**n/a**
FRS 26	n/a	n/a	**n/a**

✓ = exemption is available
× = exemption is not available

6.398 Where any of the above exemptions are taken, existing accounting policies should be applied to financial instruments in the comparative period. In other words, the comparative period will be presented in exactly the same way as would have been expected in the absence of the new standards. This would include, for example, all of the applicable FRS 13 disclosures if the entity was within that standards' scope. The entity must disclose the fact that it has taken the exemption and explain the basis used to prepare the comparative information that is presented.

6.399 In addition to the above, disclosure is required of the nature of the main adjustments that would make the information comply with FRS 25 and FRS 26. These adjustments do not need to be quantified, but their nature should be sufficiently well explained to enable a reader to understand their potential impact. Furthermore, the adjustments between the balance sheet at the end of the comparative period and the balance sheet at the start of the first period that includes FRS 25 or FRS 26 information should be treated as arising from a change in accounting policy and the appropriate FRS 18 disclosures should be given. [FRS 25 para 97B, FRS 26 para 108D].

6.400 It should be noted that when an entity first applies FRS 26, it is also required to adopt FRS 23, 'The effects of changes in foreign exchange rates', for the first time (see chapter 7). There is no equivalent FRS 23 exemption for comparative information. Hence all comparative information will need to be restated in accordance with FRS 23.

[The next paragraph is 6.403.]

Hedge accounting

Transition

6.403 FRS 26 contains detailed transition rules on how to measure derivatives and implement FRS 26's hedging requirements for the first time. The exemptions given in the transitional rules are identical to those in IFRS 1 for first-time adopters of IFRS. Under the rules, an entity cannot reflect in its opening balance sheet on adoption of FRS 26, any hedging relationship that would not qualify for hedge accounting under FRS 26. [FRS 26 para 108B]. It is expected that there will be many such instances for UK companies, because the existing rules in SSAP 20 for hedge accounting were limited and hence a flexible approach has been applied in the UK. The standard gives the examples of cash instruments and written options that may have qualified as hedging items under UK GAAP, but that do not qualify as hedging items under FRS 26. Entities should discontinue UK GAAP hedges that do not qualify for hedge accounting under FRS 26. [FRS 26 para 108C]. Further details on the hedging exemptions that are available on first time adoption of IFRS are given in chapter 3 of the Manual of Accounting – IFRS for the UK.

Documentation

6.404 As for entities transitioning to IFRS, hedge accounting in accordance with FRS 26 can only be applied prospectively from the date when all of the documentation is in place. That is, any new hedges that are identified by an entity under FRS 26 cannot be designated retrospectively.

6.405 Assuming an entity opts not to restate comparatives to comply with FRS 26 in its first year of adoption of the standard and assuming a hedging relationship otherwise qualifies for hedge accounting, the relevant documentation must be in place by 1 January 2005 (1 January 2004 if the comparative exemption is not taken) for a 31 December year end.

6.406 Should management fail to ensure the appropriate documentation is in place by these deadlines, then hedge accounting will not be permitted until the documentation is complete. Inadequate preparations for the application of FRS 26 may have unfortunate consequences for the hedging strategies of companies impacted by the new requirements.

Amendments to FRS 26

6.406.1 Since FRS 26 was issued in November 2004, several amendments have been made to the standard to align it with the equivalent international standard, IAS 39. The details of the amendments are discussed in the Manual of Accounting – IFRS for the UK, presented as annex 3 to this chapter. The amendments made to FRS 26 (including the transition rules) are identical to those made to IAS 39 with the following exceptions:

- Under the amendment to IAS 39 for the fair value option, an entity must take into account criteria set out in IAS 8, 'Accounting policies', when deciding whether to designate items as at fair value through profit and loss. As there is no UK standard equivalent to IAS 8, the ASB has amended the guidance to refer to the need to consider objectives against which an entity should judge the appropriateness of accounting policies as set out in FRS 18, 'Accounting policies'.
- The IASB's definition of key management personnel is contained in IAS 24, 'Related party disclosures'. In the UK key management is defined in FRS 8, 'Related party disclosures'. For the purpose of defining key management

within FRS 26 the ASB considered it appropriate to use the IASB's definition which is defined as:

"...those persons having authority and responsibility for planning, directing and controlling the activities of the entity, directly or indirectly, including any director (whether executive or otherwise) of the entity. For example, the entity's board of directors and chief executive officer".

- The ASB has reservations over the value of some of the disclosures required by the IASB's amendment to FRS 25; these include the disclosures within paragraph 94(g) relating to the credit risk of loans and receivable designated as at fair value through profits and loss. The ASB has not, therefore, implemented this disclosure requirement.

- The amendment to FRS 26 omits some of the transition requirements contained in the amendment to IAS 39 for an entity that applies the fair value option for annual periods beginning before 1 January 2006. In addition, entities that adopt the fair value option in an accounting period beginning before 1 January 2006 must designate any financial assets or liabilities as at fair value through profit or loss, before 1 December 2005, where the relevant criteria are met. IAS 39 requires such designations to be made by 1 September 2005.

- The amendment to FRS 26 for cash flow hedge accounting of intra-group forecast transactions clarifies that the gain or loss for a hedge of a forecast intragroup transaction that qualifies for hedge accounting should be recognised directly through the statement of total recognised gains and losses. These gains or losses are recognised in equity under the amendment to IAS 39.

- The IASB amended example 9 in appendix C to IAS 37, 'Provisions, contingent liabilities and contingent assets', so that it refers to accounting in accordance with IAS 39. The equivalent example is contained in FRS 12 and the ASB has made a corresponding amendment. However, as the amendment for financial guarantee contracts and credit insurance is only applicable to entities when they adopt FRS 26, the change is noted in appendix B to the standard.

6.406.2 All of the amendments mentioned above are effective for accounting periods beginning on or after 1 January 2006, but can be early adopted.

6.406.3 In IFRIC Interpretation 5, 'Rights to interests arising from decommissioning restoration and environmental rehabilitation funds', the IASB amended the scope of IAS 39 to exclude rights to payments to reimburse the entity from expenditure required to settle a liability that it recognises as a provision. The ASB has made a corresponding amendment to FRS 26.

6.406.4 The implementation of the IAS Regulation in the Republic of Ireland took advantage of the member state option to defer the effective date of the Regulation to accounting periods commenting on or after 1 January 2007 for entities with listed debt but no listed equity. The ASB has agreed to permit a deferral for one year for Irish securitisation entities, as defined in Irish tax legislation, that have listed debt but no listed equities.

FRS 29

6.406.5 In accounting periods beginning on or after 1 January 2007, entities that apply FRS 26 are required to also apply FRS 29. Once FRS 29 is applied, the disclosure requirements in FRS 25 are superseded (as is FRS 13 for entities that apply FRS 26 for the first time in 2007 and that had continued to apply FRS 13). FRS 29 largely replicates the requirements of IFRS 7 and the details are covered in annex 3 to this chapter.

6.406.6 The following entities are exempt from the standard:

- Subsidiary undertakings, other than banks and insurance companies, where 90 per cent or more of the voting rights are controlled within the group, provided the entity is included in publicly available consolidated financial statements which include disclosures that comply with FRS 29.
- Parent companies in their single entity financial statements, provided the entity is included in publicly available consolidated financial statements which include disclosures that comply with FRS 29.
- FRSSE companies.

6.406.7 As noted above, the standard applies for accounting periods beginning on or after 1 January 2007, although earlier application is encouraged. An entity that applies the standard early and that has not previously applied the disclosure requirements of FRS 25 need not present the comparative disclosures required by FRS 29 (except for those mentioned in appendix E to the standard) in the first period in which it applies the standard. Appendix E to FRS 29 contains disclosure requirements relating to capital that the IASB made as an amendment to IAS 1, 'Presentation of financial statements'.

[The next paragraph is 6.407.]

Annex 1 — Example FRS 13 disclosures

Set out in this Annex are examples of the narrative and numerical disclosures required by part A of FRS 13 for the following four instruments:

- Example 1 — Fixed rate borrowing.
- Example 2 — SSAP 20 hedge.
- Example 3 — Fixed rate borrowings with interest rate swap.
- Example 4 — Purchases covered by foreign currency contract.

The example disclosures relate only to those required for each individual instrument in isolation. The narrative disclosures have been written based on assumed group objectives, policies and strategies and would have to be tailored for each entities individual situation.

Example 1

Description

It is very common for companies to take out fixed rate loans, that is, those having specified interest rates and maturity dates.

Borrowing information

GAAP UK plc has a ten year fixed rate sterling borrowing with the following terms:

- Original principal of £110 million.
- Annual repayments of £11 million on each anniversary of the borrowing.
- Final maturity on 31 December 2010.
- Fixed rate of 7.65 per cent.
- At 31 December 2005 there are five years remaining to maturity.
- The market rate at the year end for the same maturity period was 7.4 per cent (2000 – 7.8 per cent).

The disclosures required by FRS 13, solely in relation to this liability, should look similar to the following.

Accounting policies

Fixed rate bank borrowings are initially stated at the amount of the consideration received after deduction of issue costs. Issue costs together with finance costs are charged to the profit and loss account over the term of the borrowings and represent a constant proportion of the balance of capital repayments outstanding.

Objectives, policies and strategies

The financial risks faced by the group include interest rate risk and liquidity risk. The board reviews and agrees policies for managing each of these risks.

The group's financial instruments comprise fixed rate borrowings, the main purpose of which is to raise finance for the group's operations.

The group seeks to ensure stability in its cash flows and thus interest rate risk is managed through borrowing at fixed rates. The group's policy is to maintain 100 per cent (2000 – 100 per cent) of its borrowings at fixed rates, which is consistent with the year end position.

The group seeks to minimise the risk of uncertain funding in its operations by borrowing with a spread of maturity periods and by having committed facilities available. The group's policy is for current borrowings to be repayable in broadly equal instalments over no less than three years and for projected net borrowing needs to be covered by committed facilities. At the year end the group's borrowings were repayable in instalments over the next five years (2004 – six years) and the group had sufficient undrawn committed facilities available to cover its projected net borrowing needs as at each year end.

Note: It would be good practice to state whether these objectives, policies and strategies are consistent with those in the previous year. Also it would be helpful to indicate whether the balance sheet positions at 31 December 2005 are representative of the positions throughout the year.

Interest rate risk profile of financial liabilities

The interest rate profile of the group's financial liabilities at 31 December was:

	Total	Floating rate financial liabilities	Fixed rate financial liabilities	Financial liabilities on which no interest is paid
Currency	**£m**	**£m**	**£m**	**£m**
2005				
Sterling	55	–	55	–
2004				
Sterling	66	–	66	–

	Fixed rate financial liabilities		Financial liabilities upon which no interest is paid
	Weighted average fixed interest rate	**Weighted average period for which rate is fixed***	**Weighted average period until maturity**
Currency	**%**	**Years**	**Years**
2005			
Sterling	7.65	3.0	–
2004			
Sterling	7.65	3.5	–

Note — Given the loan is a reducing balance loan the period for which the rate is fixed is calculated on a weighted average basis. Note that where there is one amortising loan the weighted average period for which the rate is fixed is calculated by treating each repayment as if it were a separate loan. (For example, the 2005 weighted average period above has been calculated treating each of the 5 repayment periods as different loans. The weighted average period is 1 + 2 + 3 + 4 + 5 = 15 years divided by 5 loans = 3.)

Currency exposures

Not applicable

Maturity of financial liabilities

The maturity profile of the group's financial liabilities at 31 December was as follows:

	2004 £m	2004 £m
In one year or less, or on demand	11	11
In more than one year but not more than two years	11	11
In more than two years but not more than five years	33	33
In more than five years	–	11
Total	55	66

Borrowing facilities

The group has an undrawn committed facility of £100 million which is negotiated on an annual basis with its bank.

Fair values of financial assets and financial liabilities

A comparison by category of fair values and book values of the group's financial liabilities at 31 December was as follows:

	Book value 2005 £m	Fair value 2005 £m	Book value 2004 £m	Fair value 2004 £m
Primary financial instruments held or issued to finance the group's operations:				
Short-term borrowings and current portion of long-term borrowings	11.0	11.0	11.0	11.0
Long-term borrowing	44.0	44.4	55.0	54;.7

The fair value of the fixed rate borrowing has been calculated by discounting cash flows at prevailing market interest rates.

Gains and losses on hedges

Not applicable

Example 2

Description

It is common for companies to hedge their exposure to foreign currency exchange fluctuations arising from their overseas investments by borrowing in the same currencies. The resulting translation gains and losses may be taken to reserves (STRGL) in accordance with SSAP 20. In the example below the group has adopted this policy.

Borrowing information

GAAP UK plc has two ten year foreign currency borrowings as follows:

■ US$ loan — original principal US$ 180 million.	■ € loan — original principal € 1,000 million.
■ Fixed rate of 5.65 per cent.	■ Floating rate
■ Bullet repayment of US$ 180 million on 31 December 2011	■ Bullet repayment of € 1,000 million on 31 July 2009
■ At 31 December 2005 there are six years remaining to maturity	■ At 31 December 2005 there are three year and seven months remaining to maturity

The year end exchange rates were as follows:

2005		2004	
£/US$	– 1.641	£/US$	– 1.500
£/€	– 10.452	£/€	– 10.00

The US$ market interest rate at year end for the 2011 maturity was 5.5 per cent (2004 – 5.8 per cent)

The disclosures required by FRS 13, solely in relation to these instruments, should look similar to the following.

Accounting policies

Assets and liabilities of subsidiaries in foreign currencies are translated into sterling at rates of exchange ruling at the end of the financial year and the results of foreign subsidiaries are translated at the average rate of exchange for the year. Differences on exchange arising from the retranslation of the opening net investment in subsidiary companies, and from the translation of the results of those companies at average rate, are taken to reserves and are reported in the statement of total recognised gains and losses. All other foreign exchange differences are taken to the profit and loss account in the year in which they arise.

Objectives, policies and strategies

The financial risks faced by the group comprise interest rate risk, liquidity risk and currency risk. The board reviews and agrees policies for managing each of these risks.

The group's financial instruments comprise fixed and floating rate borrowings, the main purposes of which are to raise finance for the group's operations.

The group seeks to minimise its exposure to an upward change in interest rates while enabling the group to benefit from a fall in interest rates by borrowing at a mix of fixed and floating rates. The group's current policy is to maintain 50 per cent to 65 per cent (2004 – 50 per cent to 65 per cent) of its borrowings at fixed rates with the remaining at floating rates. At the year end 53 per cent (2004 – 55 per cent) of the group's borrowings were at fixed rates.

The group seeks to minimise the risk of uncertain funding in its operations by borrowing within a spread of maturity periods and by having committed facilities available. The group's policy is for current borrowings to be repayable beyond at least three years and for undrawn committed facilities to be available to supplement the currency borrowings which provide a hedge against the group's net investments in its overseas subsidiaries. At the year end 53 per cent (2000 – 55 per cent) of the group's borrowings were repayable in six years (2004 – seven years) with the remaining 47 per cent (2004 – 45 per cent) repayable in four years (2004 – five years). The group had sufficient undrawn committed facilities available as at each year end.

The group seeks to minimise the currency risk arising from translation of the its net investments in its overseas subsidiaries in the United States and France by taking out borrowings in the denominated currencies. The group's policy is to operate with 80 per cent to 100 per cent (2000 – 80 per cent to 100 per cent) of its net investments to be covered by these foreign currency borrowings. At the year end 100 per cent (2000 – 100 per cent) of the total currency exposure was covered by currency borrowings.

Note: It would be good practice to state whether these objectives, policies and strategies are consistent with those in the previous year. Also it would be helpful to indicate whether the balance sheet position at 31 December 2005 are representative of the positions throughout the year.

Interest rate risk profile of financial liabilities

The interest rate profile of the group's financial liabilities at 31 December was:

Financial instruments including derivatives

Currency	Total £m	Floating rate financial liabilities £m	Fixed rate financial liabilities £m	Financial liabilities on which no interest is paid £m
2001				
US$	110	–	110	–
FFr	98	98	–	–
Total	208	98	110	–
2000				
US$	120		120	–
FFr	100	100	–	–
Total	220	100	120	–

	Fixed rate financial liabilities		Financial liabilities upon which no interest is paid
Currency	Weighted average fixed interest rate %	Weighted average period for which rate is fixed Years	Weighted average period until maturity Years
2001			
US$	5.65	6.0	–
2000			
US$	5.65	7.0	–

The floating rate financial liabilities comprise € denominated bank borrowings that bear interest rates based on 3 month Euribor (European Inter-Bank Offer Rate).

Currency exposures

Not applicable. The group uses its foreign borrowings to provide a hedge against its foreign net investments and the exchange gains or losses on its borrowings are included in the STRGL as permitted by SSAP 20. In accordance with paragraph 34c of FRS 13, these borrowings are not included in the currency analysis as the exchange gains and losses on the borrowings do not flow through the profit and loss account.

Maturity of financial liabilities

The maturity profile of the group's financial liabilities at 31 December was as follows:

	2005 £m	2004 £m
In one year or less, or on demand	–	–
In more than one year but not more than two years	–	–
In more than two years but not more than five years	98	100
In more than five years	110	120
Total	208	220

Borrowing facilities

The group has undrawn committed facilities of US$180 million and €30 million which are negotiated on an annual basis with its bank.

Fair values of financial assets and financial liabilities

A comparison by category of fair values and book values of the group's financial liabilities at 31 December was as follows:

	Book value 2005 £m	Fair value 2005 £m	Book value 2004 £m	Fair value 2004 £m
Primary financial instruments held or issued to finance the group's operations:				
Long-term borrowings	208.0	208.2	220.0	219.0

The fair value of the fixed rate borrowing has been calculated by discounting the cash flows at prevailing market interest rates.

Gains and losses on hedges

Not applicable

Example 3

Description

It is very common for companies to take out fixed rate loans, that is, having specified interest rates and maturity dates. Interest rate swaps enable a company to convert its fixed interest rate borrowings to floating rate and *vice versa* and commit a company to exchange interest cash flows on specified settlement dates. The notional principal of the swap is used to calculate the expected interest amounts.

Borrowing and interest rate swap information

GAAP UK plc has a ten year fixed rate sterling borrowing with the following terms:

- Original principal of £110 million.
- Fixed rate of 7.65 per cent.
- Two bullet payments of £55 million each on 31 December 2003 (that is, part paid) and 31 December 2008.
- At 31 December 2005 the loan had three years remaining to maturity
- The group also has the following interest rate swap:
  - Receive fixed of 7.65 per cent.
  - Pay LIBOR.
  - Notional principal of £55 million to 31 December 2008.
- The market rate for the interest rate swap at the year end was 7.4 per cent (2004 – 7.9 per cent)

The disclosures required by FRS 13, solely in relation to these instruments, should look similar to the following.

Accounting policies

Fixed rate bank borrowings are initially stated at the amount of the consideration received after deduction of issue costs. Issue costs together with finance costs are charged to the profit and loss account over the term of the borrowings and represent a constant proportion of the balance of capital repayments outstanding.

The interest differential amounts due to/from on interest rate swaps are accrued until settlement date and are recognised as an adjustment to interest expense.

Objectives, policies and strategies

The financial risks faced by the group include interest rate risk and liquidity risk. The board reviews and agrees policies for managing each of these risks.

The group's financial instruments comprise fixed rate borrowings, the main purpose of which is to raise finance for the group's operations. The group also enters into interest rate swaps, the purpose of which is to manage the interest rate risk arising from the group's borrowings.

The group seeks to minimise its exposure to an upward change in interest rates while enabling the group to benefit from a fall in interest rates by borrowing at fixed rates and, where overall borrowing costs can be reduced, by using interest rate swaps to convert such borrowings from fixed to floating rates. The group's policy is, while interest rates are declining, to maintain between 80 per cent and 100 per cent (2004 – 80 per cent and 100 per cent) of its borrowings at floating rates. At the year end all (2004 — all) of the group's fixed rate borrowings were at floating rates after taking account of interest rate swaps. The group hedges its exposure to interest rate fluctuations over five year periods.

The group seeks to minimise the risk of uncertain funding in its operations by borrowing within a spread of maturity periods and by having committed facilities available. The group's policy is for at least 80 per cent (2004 – 80 per cent) of borrowings to be repayable after two years and for projected net borrowing needs to be covered by committed facilities. At the year end the group's borrowings were repayable beyond three years (200 – four years) and the group had sufficient undrawn committed facilities available to cover its projected net borrowing needs as at each year end.

Note: It would be good practice to state whether these objectives, policies and strategies are consistent with those in the previous year. Also, it would be helpful to indicate whether the balance sheet position at 31 December 2005 are representative of the positions throughout the year.

Interest rate risk profile of financial liabilities

Paragraph 26 (a) of FRS 13 requires that this interest rate risk analysis be shown after taking into account the effect of interest rate swaps. The group's underlying borrowings are all on fixed rate terms, but these are all covered by interest rate swaps. Thus the borrowings are included in the table as floating rate borrowings.

After taking into account the interest rate swaps entered into by the group, the interest rate profile of the group's financial liabilities at 31 December was:

Currency	Total £m	Floating rate financial liabilities £m	Fixed rate financial liabilities £m	Financial liabilities on which no interest is paid £m
2005				
Sterling	55	–	55	–
2004				
Sterling	66	–	66	–

Currency	Fixed rate financial liabilities: Weighted average fixed interest rate %	Fixed rate financial liabilities: Weighted average period for which rate is fixed Years	Financial liabilities on which no interest is paid: Weighted average period until maturity Years
2005			
Sterling	–	–	–
2004			
Sterling	–	–	–

After taking into account the interest rate swaps, the floating rate financial liabilities comprise sterling denominated bank borrowings that bear interest at rates based on the six-month LIBOR.

Currency exposures

Not applicable

Maturity of financial liabilities

The maturity profile of the group's financial liabilities at 31 December was as follows:

	2005 £m	2004 £m
In one year or less, or on demand	–	–
In more than one year but not more than two years	–	–
In more than two years but not more than five years	55	55
In more than five years	–	–
Total	55	55

Borrowing facilities

The group has an undrawn committed facility of £100 million, which is negotiated on an annual basis with its bank.

Fair values of financial assets and financial liabilities

Note: The fair value of the fixed rate borrowing and that of the related interest rate swap must be shown separately in the fair value table.

A comparison by category of fair values and book values of the group's financial liabilities at 31 December was as follows:

	Book value 2005 £m	Fair value 2005 £m	Book value 2004 £m	Fair value 2004 £m
Primary financial instruments held or issued to finance the group's operations:				
Long-term borrowing	55.0	55.4	55.0	54.5
Derivative financial instruments held to manage the interest rate profile:				
Interest rate swap	–	(0.4)	–	0.5

The fair values of the fixed rate borrowing and the interest rate swap have been calculated by discounting the fixed cash flows at the prevailing interest rates at the year end.

Gains/losses on hedges

The fair value adjustments in relation to interest rate swaps represent unrecognised gains and losses that should be reported in the hedge effects table, as well as in the fair value table.

Note that a comparative table may be required but is not included in this example.

An analysis of the unrecognised gains and losses on the interest rate swap is as follows:

	Gains £m	(Losses) £m	Total net gains/(losses) £m
Unrecognised gains and losses on hedges at 1 January 2005		**(0.5)**	**(0.5)**
Gains and losses arising in previous years that were recognised in 2005		0.1*	0.1
Changes in value arising in 2005 and unrecognised during 2005		0.8	0.8
Gains and losses arising before 1 January 2005 and during 2005 that were not recognised in 2005	–	**0.4**	**0.4**
Transfer of gain position at the end of the year. †	0.4	(0.4)	–
Unrecognised gains and losses on hedges at 31 December 2005	**0.4**	–	**0.4**
Of which			
Gains and losses expected to be recognised in 2006	0.1*	–	0.1
Gains and losses expected to be recognised in 2007 or later	0.3	–	0.3

Notes:

* *These movements represent the interest rate swap differential payments that are made on a six monthly basis each year. For the purpose of this example these amounts have been estimated.*

† *As a result of the movement of £0.8 million, the balance is now a gain and hence it has been moved to the gain column.*

As the interest rate swaps are unrecognised on the balance sheet there are no deferred gains and losses shown on this table.

Example 4

Description

It is common for companies to use forward currency contracts to hedge against foreign currency exposure arising from product sales and stock purchases denominated in foreign currencies.

Financial instruments including derivatives

In this example the company uses a forward currency contract to hedge against committed purchases denominated in US dollars. The forward currency purchased under the forward contract is used to limit the group's exposure to US dollar fluctuations by fixing the purchase exchange rate at the forward currency contract rate.

Purchase commitment and forward currency contract information:

On 1 December 2004 GAAP UK plc entered into a purchase commitment with the following details:

- Purchase of 100,000 units of widgets – Price – $900,000.
- Delivery and payment date – 31 May 2005.
- On 1 December 2004 the group took out a forward currency contract to cover the purchase commitment. The terms of the contract are as follows:
  - Purchase of $900,000.
  - Forward rate – £1 = $1.50.
  - Settlement date – 31 May 2005.
- Other details:
  - Year end date – 31 December 2004, £1 = $1.47.
  - Settlement date – 31 May 2005, £1 = $1.43.
  - At 31 December 2005 GAAP UK plc had 60,000 units remaining in stock. The other 40,000 units were used in products sold in the year.

The disclosures required by FRS 13, solely in relation to these instruments, should look similar to the following.

Accounting policies

Transactions in foreign currencies are translated at the exchange rate ruling at the date of the transaction or, where forward foreign currency contracts have been taken out, at contractual rates. Monetary assets and liabilities are retranslated at the rates of exchange ruling at the balance sheet date or at a forward contractual rate if applicable. Exchange gains and losses are taken to the profit and loss account.

Forward currency contracts, entered into as hedges of committed purchases denominated in foreign currencies, are not recognised until they mature. At maturity gains and losses are included in the carrying value of the related stocks and work in progress.

Objectives, policies and strategies

The financial risks faced by the group include foreign currency risk. The board reviews and agrees policies for managing this risk.

The group's financial instruments, other than derivatives, comprise short-term monetary assets and liabilities that arise directly from the group's operations. The group also enters into forward currency contracts to manage the currency risk arising from foreign currency denominated purchase commitments, entered into by the group.

The group seeks to minimise its exposure to fluctuations in exchange rates by taking out forward currency contracts to hedge against foreign currency denominated purchase commitments. The group's policy is to enter into forward currency contracts for all such commitments immediately those purchase commitments are made. At the year end 100 per cent (2004 – 100 per cent) of purchase commitments were hedged by foreign currency contracts.

Note: It would be good practice to state whether these objectives, policies and strategies are consistent with those in the previous year. Also, it would be helpful to indicate whether the balance sheet positions at 31 December 2005 are representative of the positions throughout the year.

Interest rate risk profile of financial liabilities

Not applicable

Currency exposures

Note: The amounts disclosed in this table should be after taking account of forward contracts. [FRS 13, para 34(d)]. In this case the forward contract converts the US dollar amount payable to a sterling liability. Monetary liabilities denominated in the same currency as the functional currency of the operations, in this case sterling, are not be included in this analysis. Although the analysis is not applicable in this case a note such as the following may be appropriate:

As explained in the objectives, policies and strategies note the group's policy is, where practicable, to hedge its currency exposure to monetary liabilities fully.

Maturity of financial liabilities

Not applicable

Borrowing facilities

Not applicable

Fair values of financial assets and financial liabilities

The fair value of the forward contract must be shown separately in the fair value table throughout the period from its inception until its maturity.

Note: The accounting policy for the group is to recognise the gain and loss on its forward contracts at maturity in the carrying value of the related stocks and work in progress. Consequently, no book value for forward contracts is included in the table below. In this example the forward contract is open over the 31 December 2004 year end so its fair value at that date is included in the table. By 31 December 2005 the contract has matured so no fair value is shown.

If, for instance, the stock had been delivered prior to the year end and payment to the supplier was outstanding, then the fair value of the creditor would need to be taken into account separately from the forward contract. The creditor would be recorded at the contract rate applicable to the forward contract, giving rise to a book/fair value difference.

A comparison by category of fair values and book values of the group's financial liabilities at 31 December was as follows:

	Book value 2005 £'000	Fair value 2005 £'000	Book value 2004 £'000	Fair value 2004 £'000
Primary financial instruments held or issued to finance the group's operations:				
Short term financial liabilities	–	–	–	–
Derivative financial instruments held to manage the interest rate profile:				
Forward foreign currency contract	–	–	–	12.2

The fair value of the forward currency contract has been determined by reference to prices available from the markets on which the instrument involved is traded.

Gains/losses on hedges

Note: The fair value of the forward foreign currency contract is an unrecognised gain at 31 December 2004 that should be reported in the hedge effects table, as well as in the fair value table. As per its accounting policy, GAAP UK plc does not recognise gains and losses on its forward contracts until the contracts mature. The fair value recognised in the table above is equal to the unrecognised gain at 31 December 2004.

When the contract is settled, in May 2005, the resulting gain is recognised in the balance sheet but the gain is not recognised in the profit and loss account until the stock purchased, covered by the forward contract, is sold. In between the gain being recognised and stock being sold the gain is deferred in the balance sheet carrying value of the stock. FRS 13 paragraph 59 requires detailed disclosure of deferred gains and losses of, inter alia, this nature other than gains and losses deferred in the carrying value of fixed assets. [FRS 13 para 60].

The calculations of the amounts included are explained in the notes immediately following the table. A comparative table is required but is not included in this example.

An analysis of the unrecognised/deferred gains and losses on the forward currency contract is as follows:

				Unrecognised:				Deferred:
		Gains	**Losses**	**Total net gains/(losses)**		**Gains**	**Losses**	**Total net gains/(losses)**
		£'000	**£'000**	**£'000**		**£'000**	**£'000**	**£'000**
Gains and losses on hedges at 1 January 2005	(i)	**12.2**	–	**12.2**		–	–	–
Change in value from 1 January 2004 to settlement	(ii)	17.2	–	17.2		–	–	–
Gains and losses arising before 1 January 2005 and during the period from 1 January 2005 to settlement that were recognised in 2005 and deferred	(ii)	(29.4)	–	(29.4)		29.4	–	29.4
Deferred gains and losses that were recognised in current year income.					(iii)	(11.7)	–	(11.7)
Gains and losses on hedges at 31 December 2005		–	–	–	**(iv)**	17.6	–	**17.6**
Of which:								
Gains and losses expected to be included in 2006 income		–	–	–		17.6	–	17.6
Gains and losses expected to be included in 2007 income or later		–	–	–		–	–	–

Notes:

(i) *At 31 December 2004 the contract was outstanding and no gain or loss in respect of the contract was recognised in the balance sheet. The unrecognised gain brought forward also represents the fair value of the contract at 31 December 2004*

For this exercise it has been assumed that the fair value of the forward contract is £12,245. The most accurate method to derive the fair value of a forward contract outstanding at the balance sheet date is to obtain a forward rate at the balance sheet date for the remaining maturity of the contract. The gain or loss is then calculated by taking the difference between the foreign currency amount of the forward contract translated at the balance sheet forward rate and the contracted forward rate (or the forward rate last used to measure an earlier gain or loss on the contract). As this gain/loss strictly arises on the maturity of the contract, it should be discounted by reference to the remaining maturity of the contract. In practice, however, the effect of discounting is immaterial given the short duration periods for forwards and is normally ignored. Where a company is unable to get a forward rate at the balance sheet date, then, as proxy, the fair value can be calculated by adding the 'deemed' unamortised premium (where it has been fully written off) to the gain/loss calculated as the difference between translating the currency amount at the spot rate on inception of the contract and translating it at the year end rate.

(ii) *During 2005 the contract was settled. On settlement of the contract the gain on the contract is recognised and is calculated as the difference between translating the currency amount at the contract rate and translating it at the spot rate on the settlement date.*

($900,000/1.43) – ($900,000/1.50) = £29,371.

The gain of £29,371 is deferred until the stock is sold when the resulting gain would be included in income for the year.

The change in value between 1 January 2005 and settlement in May is £17,200 (£29,371 – £12,245).

(iii) *At 31 December 2005, 40 per cent (£11,748) of the full gain (of £29,371) arising on settlement of the contract in May was initially deferred in stock and was subsequently realised in current year income when the stock was sold.*

(iv) *The remaining 60 per cent (£17,623) of the full gain of £29,371 arising on settlement of the contract in May remained deferred in stock, which was unsold at the year end. This stock is expected to be sold next year.*

Annex 2 — FRS 25 and FRS 26 flow charts

FRS 25 – Financial instruments: Disclosure and presentation

Scope and effective date and Companies Act requirements for a UK GAAP reporter

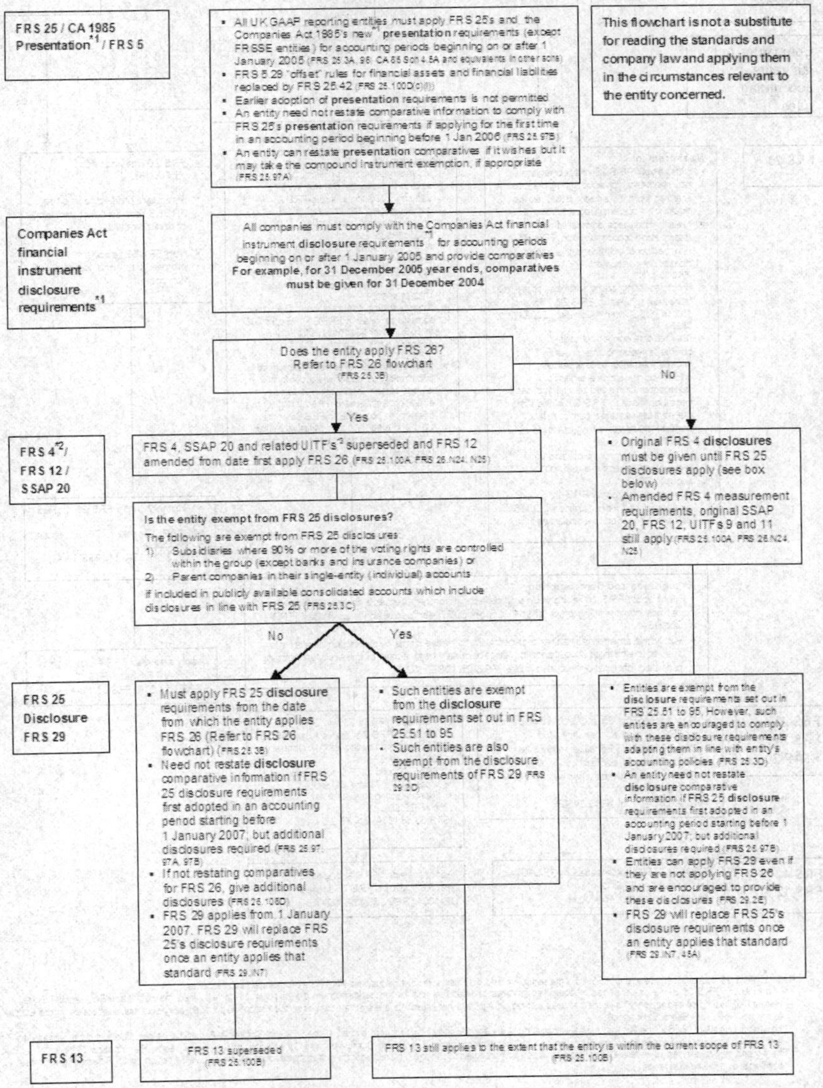

*1 Refers to the presentation and disclosures requirements inserted into the Companies Act 1985 by the Companies Act 1985 (International Accounting Standards and Other Accounting Amendments) Regulations 2004.

*2 FRS 25 substantially amends FRS 4 'Capital instruments' to remove the concept of non-equity shares as all capital instruments (or components thereof) must be presented as equity or debt for accounting periods starting from 1 January 2005.

*3 Related UITFs are as follows: FRS 26 supersedes UITF 11 Capital Instruments: issuer call options for those applying FRS 26. FRS 25 presentation requirements supersede UITF 33 Obligations in capital instruments and UITF 37 Purchases and sales of own shares for accounting periods starting from 1 January 2005. FRS 24 supersedes UITF 9 for those applying FRS 24.

FRS 26 – Financial instruments: Recognition and measurement

Scope and effective date and Companies Act requirements for a UK GAAP reporter

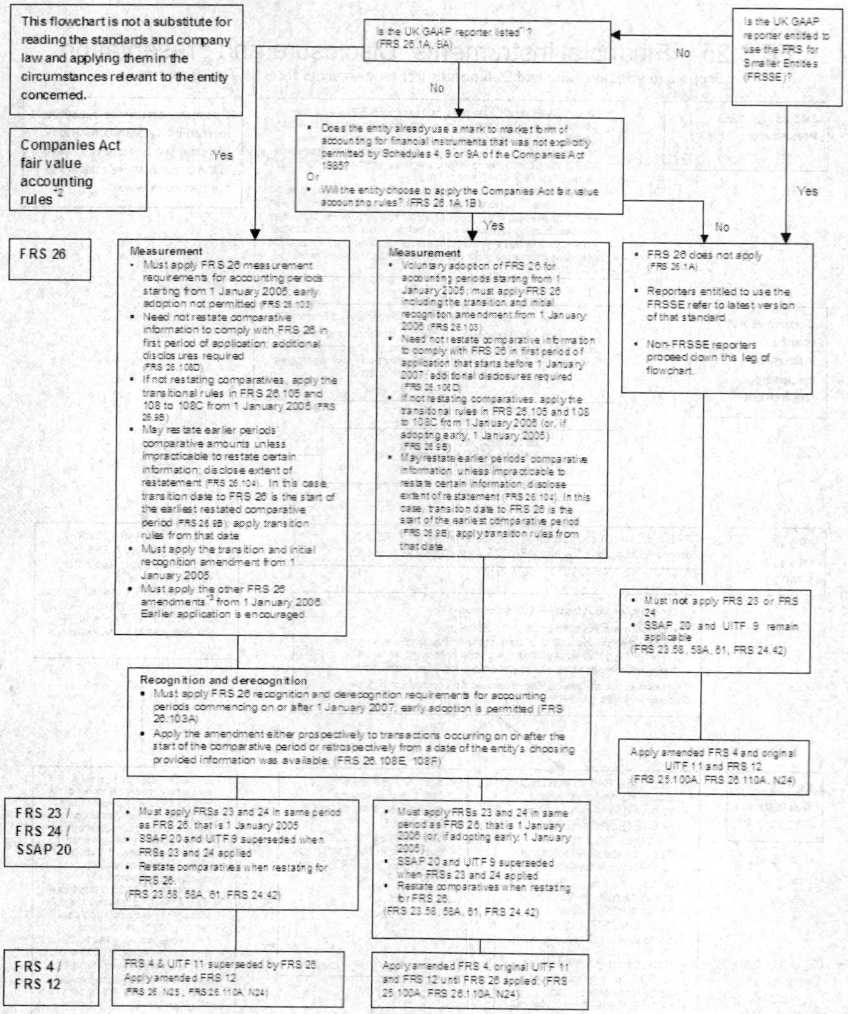

Refer to FRS 25 flowchart for details of FRS 25's presentation and disclosure requirements and FRS 29's disclosure requirements.

[1] A listed entity (FRS 26.9A) is one that has in issue debt, shares or other financial or similar instrument that is traded on a regulated market of any EU Member State. Hence, AIM companies that only have their shares quoted on AIM are not listed nor are entities that have their securities traded only on a market outside of the EU (for example, New York Stock Exchange).

[2] The Companies Act 1985's (the Act) fair value accounting rules are those set out in paragraphs 34A and 34C of Schedule 4, and their equivalents in other schedules. The Act's requirements were inserted by the Companies Act 1985 (International Accounting Standards and Other Accounting Amendments) Regulations 2004.

[3] The amendments referred to here are in relation to 'Cash flow hedge accounting of forecast intra-group transactions', 'the fair value option'; and 'Financial guarantee contracts and credit insurance'.

Annex 3 — Financial instruments

Introduction

Attached as an annex to this chapter is a copy of chapter 6 of the Manual of Accounting – IFRS for the UK. It is important to note that there are some differences that remain between the international and the UK standards and these are highlighted in paragraph 6.384.

Annex 3 — Financial instruments including derivatives

Contents

	Page
Section 01 — Overview	6169
Section 02 — Introduction	6183
Accounting for financial instruments	6183
Development of financial instruments standards	6183
EU adoption	6184
The way forward	6184
Structure of the sections	6185
Section 03 — Objectives and scope of IAS 32, IFRS 7 and IAS 39	6187
Objectives	6187
Scope	6187
Interests in subsidiaries, associates and joint ventures	6188
Employee benefit plans and share-based payments	6189
Business combinations	6189
Own equity instruments	6190
Rights and obligations under lease contracts	6190
Rights and obligations under insurance contracts	6190
Loan commitments	6196
Contracts to buy or sell non-financial assets	6197
Section 04 — Nature and characteristics of financial instruments	6201
Introduction	6201
Definitions relating to financial instruments	6201
Key features of the definitions	6202
Identification of financial instruments	6206
Derivative financial instruments	6209
Introduction	6209
Definition	6210
Key features of the definition	6210
Specific examples of derivative instruments	6216
Contracts to buy or sell non-financial items	6217
Contracts that are in substance derivatives	6217
Regular way contracts	6218
Accounting for derivatives	6218
Section 05 — Embedded derivatives in host contracts	6219
Introduction	6219
Definition and key characteristics	6219
Conditions for separation	6220
Interpretation of 'closely related'	6222
Identifying the terms of embedded derivative and host contracts	6224
Assessment of closely related criterion	6225
Application of closely related criterion to different types of hosts	6226
Embedded derivatives in debt host contracts	6227

Embedded derivatives in equity host contracts 6245
Embedded derivatives in lease host contracts 6246
Embedded derivatives in executory contracts 6252
Embedded derivatives in insurance contracts 6268
Accounting for embedded derivatives 6268
Embedded derivatives as hedging instruments 6274
Section 06 — Classification of financial instruments 6275
Introduction 6275
Classification of financial assets 6275
Financial assets at fair value through profit or loss 6275
Loans and receivables 6296
Available-for-sale financial assets 6298
Reclassification of assets between categories 6300
Classification of financial liabilities 6301
Section 07 — Financial liabilities and equity 6305
Introduction 6305
Principles for classifying financial liabilities and equity instruments 6306
Contracts that are settled in cash or another financial assets 6310
Contracts settled in cash or other financial asset that are discretionary or at the option of the issuer 6315
Contracts that will or may be settled in an entity's own equity instruments 6317
Contingent settlement provisions 6321
Compound financial instruments 6328
Preference shares with various rights 6345
Debt to equity conversions 6348
Derivatives over own equity instruments 6350
Treatment of interest, dividends, gains and losses 6362
Treasury shares 6365
Section 08 — Recognition and derecognition 6367
Introduction 6367
Initial recognition 6368
General principles 6368
Derecognition of financial assets 6376
Introduction 6376
Mixed approach for derecognition 6377
Flow chart for derecognition 6377
Practical application of the derecognition criteria 6395
Accounting treatment 6408
Derecognition of financial liabilities 6435
Extinguishment of a financial liability 6435
Exchange and modification of debt instrument 6438
Section 09 — Measurement of financial assets and liabilities 6443
Introduction 6443
Initial measurement 6443
Initial fair value 6443

Transaction costs 6447
Settlement date accounting for regular way transactions 6449
Subsequent measurement of financial assets 6449
General 6449
Financial assets at fair value through profit or loss 6450
Loans and receivables 6451
Held-to-maturity investments 6451
Available-for-sale assets 6451
Designation as hedged items 6455
Reclassifications between categories 6455
Settlement date accounting for regular way transactions 6457
Negative fair values 6458
Subsequent measurement of financial liabilities 6458
Financial liabilities at fair value through profit or loss . 6458
Arising on transfers of financial assets 6458
Financial guarantee contracts 6459
Intra-group financial guarantee contracts 6460
Commitments to provide off-market loans 6460
Designation as hedged items 6461
Amortised cost and the effective interest method 6461
General 6461
Estimation of cash flows 6462
Transaction costs and fees 6463
Amortisation period 6463
Illustrations of the effective interest rate method of amortisation 6464
Changes in estimated cash flows 6467
Issuer call option in debt instruments 6468
Floating rate instruments 6471
Perpetual debt instruments 6473
Fair value measurement considerations 6474
General 6474
Quoted prices in an active market 6476
Unquoted equity instruments and related derivatives. . . 6488
Day '1' gain or loss 6489
Demand deposit liabilities 6490
Credit risk of liabilities 6491
Impairment of financial assets 6492
Incurred versus expected losses 6492
Objective evidence of impairment 6493
Financial assets carried at amortised cost 6496
Financial assets carried at cost 6503
Available-for-sale financial assets 6504
Foreign currency financial instruments 6506
Section 10 — Hedge accounting 6513
Introduction 6513
What is hedging? 6513
What is hedge accounting? 6513

Hedge accounting under IAS 39 6514
Hedged items 6515
Definition 6515
Designation of groups of items as hedged items 6516
Designation of financial items as hedged items 6519
Designation of non-financial items as hedged items 6525
Firm commitments 6527
Forecast transactions 6527
Intra-group and intra-entity hedging transactions 6528
Items that do not qualify as hedged items 6530
Hedging instruments 6536
Definition 6536
Derivative financial instruments 6536
Non-derivative financial instruments 6563
Items that do not qualify as hedging instruments 6564
The hedge accounting models 6565
Risk reduction and hedge accounting 6565
Fair value hedges 6566
Cash flow hedges 6575
Net investment hedges 6585
Criteria for obtaining hedge accounting 6591
Documentation and designation 6592
Documentation relating to forecast transaction 6592
Hedge effectiveness 6594
Hedge ineffectiveness 6613
Portfolio (or macro) hedging 6618
Comprehensive examples 6619
Fair value hedge of fixed rate debt 6620
Cash flow hedge of a highly probable forecast purchase in foreign currency 6637
Net investment hedge in a foreign operation 6660
Section 11 — Presentation and disclosure 6679
Presentation of financial instruments 6679
Presentation as current or non-current 6679
Offsetting a financial asset and a financial liability 6685
Disclosure of financial instruments 6689
Scope of IFRS 7 6689
Objectives of IFRS 7 6690
Effective date and transition to IFRS 7 6691
General matters 6691
Classes of financial instruments 6691
Location, level of disclosure and aggregation 6692
Risks arising from financial instruments 6693
Balance sheet disclosures 6694
Financial assets or liabilities at fair value through profit or loss 6696
Other sundry balance sheet disclosure 6700
Income statement and equity disclosures 6702

Items of income, expense, gains or losses. 6702
Other disclosures 6704
Accounting policies 6704
Hedge accounting 6705
Fair value 6708
Financial instrument risk disclosures 6713
Qualitative disclosures. 6714
Quantitative disclosures 6719
Credit risk. 6721
Liquidity risk 6726
Market risk. 6733
Section 12 — Companies Act 1985 requirements 6743
Section 13 — First-time adoption of IFRS 6745

Section 1

Overview

A6.1.1 Current requirements for financial instruments are included in IAS 30, 'Disclosures in the financial statements of banks and similar financial institutions', IAS 32, 'Financial instruments: Disclosure and presentation', and IAS 39, 'Financial instruments: Recognition and measurement'. However, in August 2005 the IASB published IFRS 7, 'Financial instruments: Disclosures', which applies for annual periods beginning on or after 1 January 2007 and supersedes both IAS 30 and the disclosure requirements of IAS 32. The latter has been renamed 'Financial instruments: Presentation'. This publication focuses on the accounting and disclosure requirements applicable from 2007 and so considers IFRS 7's disclosure requirements rather than those contained within IAS 30 and IAS 32.

A6.1.2 To apply in the EU, IFRSs must be endorsed by an EU 'endorsement mechanism'. In November 2004, the European Commission adopted a 'carve-out' version of IAS 39, which deleted a limited number of words and paragraphs from IAS 39 relating to the use of the 'fair value option' for financial liabilities and certain aspects of hedge accounting. Since that time, the IASB has published an amendment to IAS 39 incorporating a revised 'fair value option' and this has been adopted for use within the EU. However, differences between the IASB's 'full IAS 39' and the EU's 'carve-out' version of the standard still remain. Further discussion of the development of the financial instruments standards and of their adoption for use within the EU is provided in section 2.

Objectives and scope of IAS 32, IAS 39 and IFRS 7

A6.1.3 IAS 32 establishes principles for presenting financial instruments as liabilities or equity and for offsetting financial assets and liabilities. It applies to classification of financial assets, financial liabilities and equity instruments from the issuer's perspective; the classification of related interest, dividends, losses and gains; and the circumstances in which financial assets and liabilities can be offset.

A6.1.4 IAS 39 is an extremely long and complex standard that establishes principles for recognising and measuring financial assets, financial liabilities and some contracts to buy or sell non-financial items. IAS 39 also deals with derecognition of financial assets and liabilities and hedge accounting.

A6.1.5 IFRS 7 requires entities to provide disclosures that enable users to evaluate:

- the significance of financial instruments for the entity's financial position and performance; and
- the nature and extent of risks arising from financial instruments to which the entity is exposed and how the entity manages them.

A6.1.6 The scope of the three standards is very wide ranging. The definition of a financial instrument under IFRS is *"any contract that gives rise to a financial asset of one entity and a financial liability or equity instrument of another entity"*. This definition encompasses cash, debt and equity investments, trade receivables and payables, debt, certain provisions, net cash-settled commodity contracts and derivatives (including embedded derivatives). However, certain financial instruments are excluded from the scope of one or all of the standards, as summarised in the table below.

Within scope of IAS 32, IAS 39 and IFRS 7	**Within scope of IAS 32 and IFRS 7 only**	**Out of scope**
Debt and equity investments		Investments in subsidiaries, associates and joint ventures Contingent consideration in a business combination
Loans and receivables	Lease receivables (Note 1)	
Own debt	Lease payables (Note 1) Own equity	Employee benefits Share-based payments
Cash and cash equivalents		
Derivatives – for example: ● Interest rate swaps ● Currency forwards/ swaps ● Purchased/written options ● Commodity contracts (Note 2) ● Collars/caps ● Credit derivatives ● Cash or net share settleable derivatives on own shares	Derivatives on own shares settled only by delivery of a fixed number of shares for a fixed amount of cash	Own use commodity contracts (Note 2)
Derivatives on subsidiaries, associates and joint ventures		
Embedded derivatives		
Loan commitments held for trading (Note 3)	Other loan commitments	
Financial guarantees (Note 4)		Insurance contracts
		Weather derivatives

> Note 1 – Lease receivables are included in IAS 39's scope for derecognition and impairment purposes only. Finance lease payables are subject to the derecognition provisions. Any derivatives embedded in lease contracts are also within IAS 39's scope.
>
> Note 2 – Contracts to buy or sell non-financial items are within IAS 32's scope, IAS 39 and IFRS 7 if they can be settled net in cash or another financial asset and they do not meet the test of being entered into and continuing to be held for the purpose of receipt or delivery of non-financial items to meet the entity's expected purchase, sale or usage requirements (known as "own use commodity contracts"). Settling net includes taking delivery of the underlying and selling it within a short period after delivery to generate a profit from short-term fluctuations in price.
>
> Note 3 – Loan commitments are outside IAS 39's scope if they cannot be settled net in cash or by some other financial instrument unless: they are held for trading or to generate assets of a class which the entity has a past practice of selling; or the entity chooses to include them with other derivatives under IAS 39.
>
> Note 4 – From the issuer's perspective, financial guarantee contracts are within IAS 39's scope, unless the issuer has previously asserted explicitly that it regards such contracts as insurance contracts and has used accounting applicable to insurance contracts, in which case either IAS 39 or IFRS 4, 'Insurance contracts' may be applied.

A6.1.7 The objectives and scope of IAS 32, IAS 39 and IFRS 7 is explained in greater detail in section 3.

Nature and characteristics of financial instruments

A6.1.8 The definition of a financial instrument is set out in paragraph A6.1.6 above. One of the key components of the definition is that all financial instruments are defined by contracts. It follows that non-contractual obligations, such as taxation, are not financial instruments.

A6.1.9 A financial asset is any asset that is:

- Cash.
- An equity instrument of another entity.
- A contractual right:
  - to receive cash or another financial asset from another entity; or
  - to exchange financial assets or financial liabilities with another entity under conditions that are potentially favourable to the entity.
- A contract that will or may be settled in the entity's own equity instruments and is:
  - a non-derivative for which the entity is or may be obliged to receive a variable number of the entity's own equity instruments; or
  - a derivative that will or may be settled other than by the exchange of a fixed amount of cash or another financial asset for a fixed number of the entity's own equity instruments. For this purpose the entity's own equity instruments do not include instruments that are themselves

contracts for the future receipt or delivery of the entity's own equity instruments.

A6.1.10 A financial liability is any liability that is:

- A contractual obligation:
  - to deliver cash or another financial asset from another entity; or
  - to exchange financial assets or financial liabilities with another entity under conditions that are potentially unfavourable to the entity.
- A contract that will or may be settled in the entity's own equity instruments and is:
  - a non-derivative for which the entity is or may be obliged to deliver a variable number of the entity's own equity instruments; or
  - a derivative that will or may be settled other than by the exchange of a fixed amount of cash or another financial asset for a fixed number of the entity's own equity instruments. For this purpose the entity's own equity instruments do not include instruments that are themselves contracts for the future receipt or delivery of the entity's own equity instruments.

A6.1.11 An equity instrument is any contract that evidences a residual interest in the assets of an entity after deducting all of its liabilities. Examples of equity instruments include non-puttable ordinary shares, some types of preference shares, share warrants or written call options that allow the holder to subscribe for or purchase a fixed number of non-puttable ordinary shares in the issuing entity in exchange for a fixed amount of cash or another financial asset.

A6.1.12 Derivatives are financial instruments that derive their value from an underlying price or index, such as an interest rate, a foreign exchange rate or commodity price. IAS 39 defines a derivative as a financial instrument or other contract with all of the following characteristics:

- Its value changes in response to the change in a specified interest rate, financial instrument price, commodity price, foreign exchange rate, index of prices or rates, credit rating or credit index, or other variable, provided in the case of a non-financial variable that the variable is not specific to a party to the contract (sometimes called the 'underlying').
- It requires no initial net investment or an initial net investment that is smaller than would be required for other types of contracts that would be expected to have a similar response to changes in market factors.
- It is settled at a future date.

A6.1.13 The nature and characteristics of financial instruments are considered further in section 4.

Embedded derivatives

A6.1.14 A derivative instrument that falls within IAS 39's scope need not be free-standing. Terms and conditions may also be embedded within another financial instrument or non-financial contract (referred to as the 'host' contract) that behave like a free standing derivative. These 'embedded derivatives' should be recognised at their fair value, separately from the non-derivative host contract, when they have economic characteristics and risks that are not closely related to those of the host contract. However, an entity may designate a contract that contains one or more embedded derivative as a financial asset or financial liability at fair value through profit or loss, unless the embedded derivative does not significantly modify the cash flows required by the contract or it is clear that separation of the embedded derivative is prohibited.

A6.1.15 Analysing non-derivative financial instruments and executory contracts for potential embedded derivatives is one of the more challenging aspects of IAS 39. This subject is considered further in section 5.

Classification of financial instruments

A6.1.16 IAS 39 is a partial rather than a full fair value model. Financial assets and liabilities are measured at fair value or amortised cost depending on which defined category they fall into under the standard.

6.1.17 IAS 39 has four clearly defined categories of financial assets:

- A financial asset is 'at fair value through profit or loss' if it is either:
  - Held-for-trading, that is:
    - it was acquired or incurred principally for the purpose of selling or repurchasing it in the near term;
    - it forms part of a portfolio of identified financial instruments that are managed together and for which there is evidence of a recent actual pattern of short-term profit-taking; or
    - it is a derivative (except for a derivative that is a designated and effective hedging instrument).
  - Designated on initial recognition as 'at fair value through profit or loss'. For annual periods beginning on or after 1 January 2006, the conditions that are required to be met in order to designate a financial asset (or a financial liability) as 'at fair value through profit or loss' are any of the following:
    - Where the designation eliminates or significantly reduces an accounting mismatch.
    - When a group of financial assets, financial liabilities or both are managed and their performance is evaluated on a fair value basis in accordance with a documented risk management or

investment strategy and information about this group is provided on that basis to the entity's key management personnel.

- When a contract contains an embedded derivative that meets particular conditions.

The designation is irrevocable.

- Loans and receivables are non-derivative financial assets with fixed or determinable payments that are not quoted in an active market, with the following exceptions:
  - Those that are to be sold immediately or in the near future (held-for-trading) and any others that are designated as 'at fair value through profit or loss' on initial recognition.
  - Those that are designated as available-for-sale on initial recognition.
  - Those where the entity may not recover substantially all of its original investment, other than because of credit deterioration. Such assets should be classified as available-for-sale.
- Held-to-maturity investments are non-derivative financial assets with fixed or determinable payments and fixed maturity (for example, debt securities, loans and mandatory redeemable preferred shares) that an entity has the positive intention and ability to hold to maturity. Exceptions are those investments that an entity designates on initial recognition as 'at fair value through profit or loss' or as 'available-for-sale' and those that meet the definition of 'loans and receivables'. Held-to-maturity instruments must have a maturity date, so investments in equity shares cannot fall into this category. There are a number of conditions set out in IAS 39 that restrict an entity's ability to categorise investments as held-to-maturity. For example, an entity may not classify any financial assets as held-to-maturity if during the current or preceding two financial years it has sold or reclassified more than an insignificant amount of held-to maturity investments, except in certain very narrowly defined circumstances.
- Available-for-sale financial assets are non-derivative financial assets that are designated as such on initial recognition or that are not classified in any other category.

A6.1.18 IAS 39 defines two categories of financial liabilities:

- A financial liability is 'at fair value through profit or loss' if it is either held-for-trading or designated at initial recognition as 'at fair value through profit or loss' (see the first major bullet point in para A6.1.17).
- All other financial liabilities fall into the other liabilities category.

A6.1.19 *The classification of financial assets and financial liabilities is considered* further in section 6.

Financial liabilities and equity

A6.1.20 The classification of a financial instrument as either a financial liability (debt) or equity is governed by its substance rather than its legal form. An instrument is debt when the issuer is or can be required to deliver either cash or another financial asset to the holder. This is the critical feature that distinguishes debt from equity. An instrument is classified as equity when it represents a residual interest in the issuer's net assets.

A6.1.21 All relevant features need to be considered when classifying a financial instrument. For example:

- If the issuer can or will be forced to redeem the instrument, classification as debt is appropriate.
- If the choice of settling a financial instrument in cash or otherwise is contingent on the outcome of circumstances beyond the control of both the issuer and the holder, the instrument is debt as the issuer does not have an unconditional right to avoid settlement.
- An instrument that includes an option for the holder to put the rights inherent in that instrument back to the issuer for cash or another financial instrument is debt.

A6.1.22 The treatment of interest, dividends, losses and gains in the income statement follows the classification of the related instrument. So, if a preference share is classified as debt, its coupon is shown as interest. But the coupon on an instrument that is treated as equity is shown as a distribution.

A6.1.23 Not all instruments are either debt or equity. Some, known as compound instruments, contain elements of both in a single contact. Such instruments, such as bonds that are convertible into equity shares either mandatorily or at the holder's option, must be split into debt and equity components. Each is then accounted for separately. The debt element is determined first by fair valuing the cash flows excluding any equity component and the residual is assigned to equity.

A6.1.24 Derivative contracts that only result in the delivery of a fixed amount of cash or other financial assets for a fixed number of an entity's own equity instruments are classified as equity instruments. All other derivatives on own equity are treated as derivatives and accounted for as such. This includes any that:

- can or must be settled on a net basis in cash (or other financial assets) or in shares;
- may be settled gross by delivery of a variable number of own shares; or
- may be settled by delivery of a fixed number of own shares for a variable amount of cash (or other financial assets).

Any derivative on own equity that gives either party a choice over how it is settled is a financial asset or liability, unless all of the settlement alternatives would result in equity classification.

A6.1.25 The classification of financial instruments as either debt or equity and the treatment of contracts that may be settled in an entity's own shares are considered further in section 7.

Recognition and derecognition

A6.1.26 A financial asset or liability is recognised on the balance sheet when an entity becomes a party to the contract. IAS 39's rules for removing or 'derecognising' a financial asset or liability are far more complex.

A6.1.27 IAS 39 includes a flow chart that summarises the criteria for derecognising a financial asset and this is reproduced below.

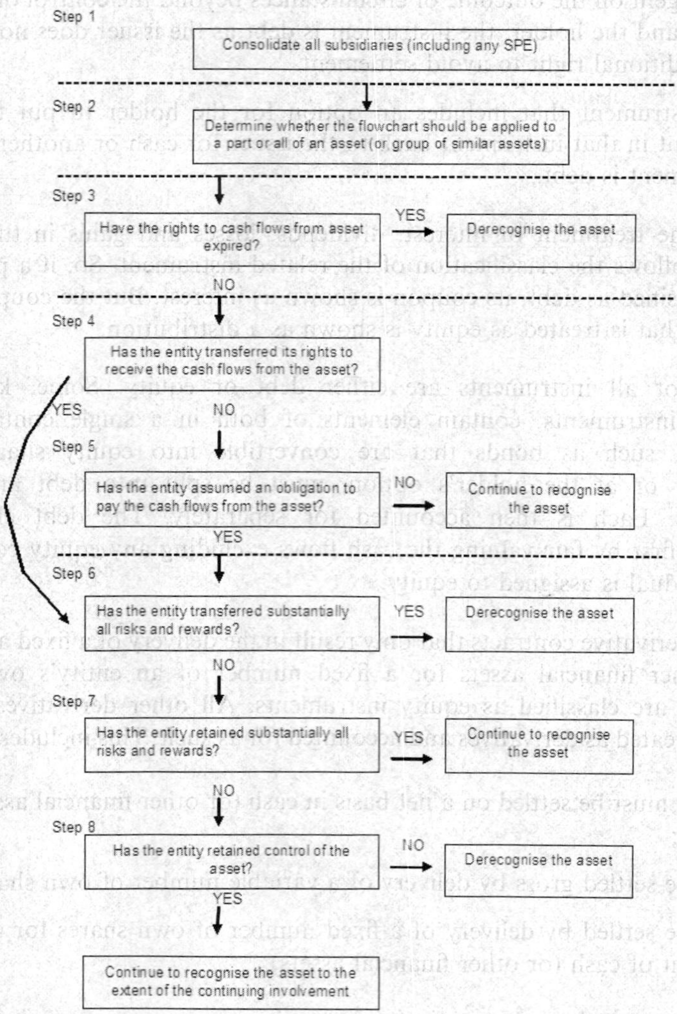

A6.1.28 A financial liability is derecognised when it is extinguished, that is when the obligation is discharged, cancelled or expired. This condition is met when the liability is settled by paying the creditor or when the debtor is released from primary responsibility for the liability, either by process of law or by the creditor.

A6.1.29 Entities frequently negotiate with bankers or bond-holders to cancel existing debt and replace it with new debt on different terms. For example, an entity may decide to cancel its exposure to high-interest fixed-rate debt, pay a fee or penalty on cancellation and replace it with variable-rate debt. IAS 39 provides guidance to distinguish between the settlement of debt that is replaced by new debt and the restructuring of existing debt. The distinction is based on whether or not the new debt has substantially different terms from the old debt.

A6.1.30 Recognition and derecognition are discussed in detail in section 8.

Measurement

A6.1.31 The categorisations of financial assets and financial liabilities have a significant impact on their subsequent measurement. The following table summarises the measurement principles for financial assets.

Measurement of assets		
	Measurement after initial recognition*	Changes in carrying amount
At fair value through profit or loss	Fair value	Income statement
Loans and receivables	Amortised cost	Income statement
Held-to-maturity	Amortised cost	Income statement
Available-for-sale	Fair value	Equity (but interest, dividends, foreign exchange differences on monetary assets and changes due to impairment are taken to income statement)
Unquoted investments for which fair value cannot be reliably measured	Cost	Yields and impairments are taken to income statement

* All categories of financial assets are initially measured at fair value plus transaction costs, except for assets 'at fair value through profit or loss' where transaction costs are not included. Fair value is normally the transaction price (that is, the fair value of the consideration given for the asset), but the transaction price may have to be adjusted to fair value where, for example, a non-interest bearing loan or receivable is acquired.

A6.1.32 An assessment should be made at each balance sheet date as to whether there is any objective evidence that a financial asset (or a group of financial assets) is impaired. IAS 39 sets out rules for accounting for impairment losses on financial assets carried at amortised cost, at cost and for available-for-sale assets.

A6.1.33 The following table summarises the measurement principles for financial liabilities.

Measurement of liabilities		
	Measurement after initial recognition*	**Changes in carrying amount**
At fair value through profit or loss	Fair value	Income statement
Other liabilities	Amortised cost	Income statement

* Liabilities 'at fair value through profit or loss' are initially measured at fair value (transaction costs are not included). Other liabilities are initially measured at fair value less transaction costs. Fair value is generally the transaction price, but the transaction price may have to be adjusted to fair value where, for example, convertible debt is issued and it is necessary to separate out the element of proceeds that relates to the conversion right, which is an equity instrument.

A6.1.34 The carrying amount of a financial instrument measured at amortised cost is computed as the amount to be paid/re-paid at maturity (usually the principal amount or par/face value), plus or minus any unamortised original premium or discount, net of any origination fees and transaction costs and less principal repayments. The amortisation is calculated using the effective interest method, which calculates the rate of interest that is necessary to discount the estimated stream of principal and interest cash flows (excluding any impact of credit losses) through the expected life of the financial instrument or, when appropriate, a shorter period to equal the amount at initial recognition. That rate is then applied to the carrying amount at each reporting date to determine the interest income (assets) or interest expense (liabilities) for the period. In this way, interest income or expense is recognised on a level yield to maturity basis.

A6.1.35 Fair value is the amount for which an asset could be exchanged, or a liability settled, between knowledgeable, willing parties in an arm's length transaction. There is a general presumption that fair value can be reliably measured for all financial instruments. In looking for a reliable measure of fair value, IAS 39 provides a hierarchy to be used in determining an instrument's fair value.

- Active market – quoted market price. The existence of published price quotations in an active market is the best evidence of fair value and they must be used to measure the financial instrument. The price can be taken from the most favourable market readily available to the entity, even if that was not the market in which the transaction actually occurred. The quoted market price cannot be adjusted for 'blockage' or 'liquidity' factors. The fair value of a portfolio of financial instruments is the product of the number of units of the instrument and its quoted market prices.

- No active market – valuation technique. If the market for a financial instrument is not active, fair value is established by using a valuation technique. Valuation techniques that are well established in financial markets include recent market transactions, reference to a transaction that is substantially the same, discounted cash flows and option pricing models. An acceptable valuation technique incorporates all factors that market participants would consider in setting a price and should be consistent with accepted economic methodologies for pricing financial instruments. Normally the amount paid or received for a financial instrument is the best estimate of fair value at inception. However, where all data inputs to a valuation model are obtained from observable market transactions, the resulting calculation of fair value can be used for initial recognition.
- No active market – equity instruments. Normally it is possible to estimate the fair value of an equity instrument that an entity has acquired from an outside party. However, if the range of reasonable fair value estimates is significant, and no reliable estimate can be made, an entity is permitted to measure the equity instrument at cost less impairment as a last resort. A similar dispensation applies to derivative financial instruments that can only be settled by physical delivery of such unquoted equity instruments.

A6.1.36 The principles for measuring financial assets and liabilities are considered further in section 9.

Hedge accounting

A6.1.37 In simple terms, 'hedge accounting' is a technique that modifies the normal basis for recognising gains and losses (or income and expenses) on associated hedging instruments and hedged items so that both are recognised in earnings in the same accounting period.

A6.1.38 A hedged item is an asset, liability, firm commitment, highly probable forecast transaction or net investment in a foreign operation that exposes the entity to risk of changes in fair value or future cash flows that could affect profit or loss. In particular, a hedged item could be:

- A single asset, liability, firm commitment or highly probable forecast transaction.
- A group of assets, liabilities, firm commitments or highly probable forecast transactions with similar risk characteristics.
- A portion of the risk or cash flows of a financial asset or liability.
- A non-financial asset or liability (such as inventory) for either foreign currency risk or the risk of changes in the fair value of the entire item.
- A held-to-maturity investment for either foreign currency risk or credit risk (but not interest rate risk).
- A net investment in a foreign operation.

A6.1.39 Generally, only assets, liabilities, firm commitments or highly probable forecast transactions that involve a party external to the entity can be designated as hedged items. However, there are exceptions to this rule for certain foreign currency intra-group transactions.

Hedging instruments

A6.1.40 Derivatives that involve an external party may be designated as hedging instruments, except for some written options. An external non-derivative financial asset or liability may not be designated as a hedging instrument, except as a hedge of foreign currency risk.

A6.1.41 A proportion of the entire hedging instrument, such as 50 per cent of the notional amount, may be designated as the hedging instrument. However, a hedging relationship may not be designated for only a portion of the time period during which a hedging instrument remains outstanding.

Hedge accounting criteria

A6.1.42 In order to qualify for hedge accounting, an entity should formally designate and document the hedging relationship. This includes identifying the hedging instrument, the hedged item or transaction, the nature of the risk being hedged and how the entity will assess hedge effectiveness, together with the entity's risk management objective and strategy for undertaking the hedge.

A6.1.43 The entity must also be able to measure and track the hedging instrument's effectiveness at the start and on an ongoing basis. IAS 39 does not require a hedge to be perfectly effective, although it is expected to be 'highly effective'. A hedge is regarded as highly effective if both of the following conditions are met:

- At the inception of the hedge and in subsequent periods, the hedge is expected to be highly effective in achieving offsetting changes in fair value or cash flows attributable to the hedged risk during the period for which the hedge is designated.
- The actual results of the hedge are within a range of 80-125 per cent.

Hedge accounting rules

A6.1.44 In order to apply hedge accounting the above criteria must be met and the hedging relationship must fall into one of three defined categories.

A6.1.45 A 'fair value hedge' is a hedge of the exposure to changes in fair value of a recognised asset, liability or unrecognised firm commitment, or identified portion thereof, that is attributable to a particular risk and could affect profit or loss. An example is an interest rate swap hedging a fixed rate borrowing. A fair value hedge is accounted for as follows:

- The hedging instrument is measured at fair value if it is a derivative. Non-derivatives may only be designated as hedging instruments for hedges of a foreign currency risk and in that case it is only the foreign currency element of the non-derivative that is remeasured in accordance with IAS 21, 'The effects of changes in foreign exchange rates'.

- The carrying value of the hedged item is adjusted for the hedged risk only. If it is normally carried at cost, the hedged item is not adjusted to its full fair value. For example, a fixed rate borrowing is still basically measured at amortised cost and is adjusted only for the hedged risk (for example, foreign currency risk).

- All gains and losses are taken to the income statement so the result is that there is no net profit and loss effect, other than any hedge ineffectiveness. Where the hedged item is an available-for-sale financial asset, the gain or loss attributable to the hedged risk is recognised in profit or loss, rather than equity, although the remainder of any fair value gain or loss is recognised in equity.

A6.1.46 A 'cash flow hedge' is a hedge of the exposure to variability in cash flows that is attributable to a particular risk associated with a recognised asset or liability or a highly probable forecast transaction and could affect profit or loss. An example is an interest rate swap hedging a variable rate borrowing. A cash flow hedge is accounted for as follows:

- The hedging instrument is measured at fair value.

- The portion of the gain or loss on the hedging instrument that is determined to be an effective hedge is recognised directly in equity. The ineffective portion of the gain or loss on the hedging instrument is recognised in profit or loss.

- The gain or loss deferred in equity is recycled to the income statement when the hedged cash flows affect income. If the hedged cash flows result in the recognition of a non-financial asset or liability on the balance sheet, the entity can choose to adjust the basis of the asset or liability by the amount deferred in equity. This choice has to be applied consistently to all such hedges.

A6.1.47 A 'hedge of a net investment' in a foreign operation is a hedge of the reporting entity's interest in the net assets of that operation. For this purpose, net investment includes any monetary items that are accounted for as part of the net investment under IAS 21. In the consolidated financial statements, the foreign operation's net assets are retranslated with gains and losses being recognised in equity. The hedging instrument (whether a derivative or a non-derivative) is accounted for similarly to a cash flow hedge with the portion of the gain or loss on the hedging instrument that is determined to be an effective hedge being recognised directly in equity. The ineffective portion is recognised in profit or loss. The gain or loss that has been recognised in equity is recycled to profit or loss on the foreign operation's disposal.

Discontinuing hedge accounting

A6.1.48 Hedge accounting is discontinued prospectively if any of the following occur:

- The hedge fails the effectiveness tests.
- The hedging instrument is sold, terminated or exercised.
- The hedged item is settled.
- The entity decides to revoke the hedge relationship.
- In a cash flow hedge, the forecast transaction that is hedged is no longer expected to occur.

A6.1.49 When a non-derivative liability has been adjusted for changes in fair value under a hedging relationship, the adjusted carrying amount becomes amortised cost. Any 'premium' or 'discount' is then amortised through the income statement over the remaining period to the liability's maturity.

A6.1.50 If a cash flow hedge relationship ceases, the amounts accumulated in equity will be maintained in equity until the hedged item affects profit or loss. However, if the hedge accounting ceases because the forecast transaction that was hedged is no longer expected to occur, gains and losses deferred in equity are recognised in profit or loss immediately. Similarly, any amounts accumulated in equity while a hedge of net investment was effective remain in equity until the disposal of the related net investment.

A6.1.51 Hedge accounting is considered in greater detail in section 10.

Presentation and disclosure

A6.1.52 A financial asset and a financial liability should be offset when, and only when, an entity currently has a legally enforceable right to offset the recognised amounts and intends either to settle on a net basis or to realise the asset and settle the liability simultaneously.

A6.1.53 For periods beginning prior to 1 January 2007, disclosure requirements for financial instruments are set out in IAS 30 and IAS 32. For periods commencing on or after 1 January 2007, the disclosure requirements have been combined in a single standard. IFRS 7 incorporates many of IAS 32's disclosures as well as additional qualitative and quantitative disclosures regarding the risks arising from financial instruments.

A6.1.54 IFRS 7's disclosure requirements and IAS 32's requirements for presenting financial instruments are described in section 11.

Section 2

Introduction

Accounting for financial instruments

A6.2.1 Financial markets have experienced, and continue to experience, significant developments since the 1980s. As foreign exchange rates, interest rates and commodity prices became increasingly volatile, a need arose to manage the commercial risks arising from the instability of these markets. Primary financial instruments, such as bonds and shares, that comprised much of the traditional financing and risk management activities, gave way to derivative products, such as futures, options, forward contracts and swaps, in managing risks. Entities were able to change substantially their financial risk profile, virtually instantaneously, by entering into interest rate or foreign exchange swaps, or by acquiring options or forward contracts to hedge or take positions on future price movements. With the globalisation of financial markets, growth in international commerce, advancement in financial risk management and information technology, the development and use of cost effective innovative derivative products and complex financial instruments for managing risk and improving return on assets became commonplace.

A6.2.2 However, it became apparent that this growth in the use of financial instruments had outstripped the development of guidance for their accounting. Traditional realisation and cost-based measurement concepts were no longer adequate to portray effectively their impact and risks, as some derivatives (for example, forward contracts and swaps) with no initial cost were simply not recognised in the financial statements until settlement. Deficiencies in current accounting practices, inconsistent treatment of economically similar transactions and the lack of visibility in the financial statements caused difficulty for both preparers and users of financial statements. This resulted in an atmosphere of uncertainty, which many people believed might discourage the legitimate use of derivative instruments. Concern about inadequate accounting for derivatives was also heightened by the publicity surrounding large derivative-instrument losses at several companies. As a result, a pervasive need to develop a single, comprehensive standard for accounting and disclosure of financial instruments and hedging activities became a necessity.

Development of financial instruments standards

A6.2.3 In 1988, the International Accounting Standards Committee (IASC), the predecessor body of the IASB, started work developing a comprehensive standard on the recognition, measurement and disclosure of financial instruments. a comprehensive standard on the recognition, measurement and disclosure of financial instruments. The first standard, IAS 32, 'Financial instruments:

Presentation and disclosure,' was issued in 1995 followed by IAS 39, 'Financial instruments: Recognition and measurement', in March 1999. However, when the IASB was formed in 2001, it undertook a project to improve international standards inherited from the IASC. As a result, revised versions of IAS 32 and IAS 39 were issued in December 2003. Since then further amendments have been made to these standards, the principal one being the issue of a new standard IFRS 7, 'Financial instruments: Disclosures', in August 2005. As IFRS 7 includes all the disclosure requirements relating to financial instruments, the title of IAS 32 was amended to 'Financial instruments – Presentation'. These three standards now form the main body of standards dealing with financial instruments.

EU adoption

A6.2.4 The EU Regulation required listed groups to prepare their consolidated financial statements using IFRS for periods commencing on or after 1 January 2005. For this to happen, IFRSs had to be brought into EU law through a complex endorsement mechanism. Although most of the IASB standards were endorsed, IAS 39 was not endorsed in full. Some aspects of IAS 39, namely the option to fair value all liabilities and certain aspects of hedge accounting that troubled banks and regulators, did not find favour with the EU and were removed. This 'carved out' version was endorsed by the EU in November 2004. The 'carve out' relating to the fair value option was removed as a result of a subsequent amendment to IAS 39 and endorsement by the EU in November 2005, but the one relating to hedge accounting remains with the result that there is still a difference between full IAS 39 and EU endorsed IAS 39.

The way forward

A6.2.5 Although significant improvements were made to IAS 39 since it was first issued, the IASB is keen to find a better accounting solution for financial instruments that will produce meaningful results without undue complexity and dependence on detailed rules. However, the IASB appreciates that an ideal solution will take several years to develop. In the meantime, the IASB believes that the provisions of IAS 32, IFRS 7 and IAS 39 are essential to provide credibility to financial statements prepared under IFRS.

A6.2.6 The IASB has also established a financial instruments working group with the objective of continuing to improve IAS 39 on an ad hoc basis while working toward an ideal solution. The working group will take a fresh look at IAS 39 by examining and questioning the fundamentals of the standard within the context of the IASB's Framework. The review will, therefore, focus on improving, simplifying and ultimately replacing IAS 39 and will examine broader questions of the application and extent of fair value accounting – a topic on which the IASB has not reached any conclusion. Although any major revision of IAS 39 may take several years to complete, it is likely that IAS 32 and IAS 39 will be further amended as part of the IASB's annual improvement process. This process is intended to eliminate inconsistencies between standards and to clarify wording.

The first batch of proposed improvements will be published in October 2007 and any changes made to these standards are expected to be effective from 1 January 2009.

Structure of the sections

A6.2.7 Detailed discussion of accounting for financial instruments is structured around the following sections:

- Objectives and scope of IAS 32, IFRS 7 and IAS 39.
- Nature and characteristics of financial instruments.
- Embedded derivatives in host contracts.
- Classification of financial instruments.
- Financial liabilities and equity.
- Recognition and derecognition of financial instruments.
- Measurement of financial instruments.
- Hedging and hedge accounting.
- Presentation and disclosure of financial instruments.

A6.2.8 The above sections address the requirements of IAS 32, IFRS 7 and IAS 39 extant as at 31 October 2007. All three standards are supplemented by application guidance that is an integral part of the standards and, where relevant, by illustrative examples that accompany them, but that are not part of the standards. In addition, IAS 39 and IFRS 7 are also supplemented by implementation guidance that is not part of the standards. Furthermore, as IAS 39 is largely based on the US standard FAS 133, 'Accounting for derivative instruments and hedging activities', the sections that follow draw on the guidance of that standard where it is considered appropriate and necessary to do so.

Section 3

Objectives and scope of IAS 32, IFRS 7 and IAS 39

Objectives

A6.3.1 IAS 32's objective is to establish principles for presenting financial instruments as financial liabilities or equity and for offsetting financial assets and financial liabilities. It applies to the classification of financial instruments into financial assets, financial liabilities and equity instruments from the perspective of the issuer. Furthermore, it deals with the classification of related interest, dividends, losses and gains; and the circumstances in which financial assets and liabilities should be offset. [IAS 32 para 2].

A6.3.2 IFRS 7's objective is to require entities to provide disclosures that enable users to evaluate:

- The significance of financial instruments for the entity's financial position and performance.
- The nature and extent of risks arising from financial instruments to which the entity is exposed during the period at the reporting date and how the entity manages these risks.

[IFRS 7 para 1].

A6.3.3 IAS 39's objective is to establish principles for recognising and measuring financial assets, financial liabilities and some contracts to buy or sell non-financial items. [IAS 39 para 1]. IAS 39 also deals with derecognition of financial assets and financial liabilities and hedge accounting. Requirements for presenting and disclosing information about financial instruments set out in IAS 32 and IFRS 7 are designed to complement those principles.

Scope

A6.3.4 Generally, IAS 32, IAS 39 and IFRS 7 have to be applied by all entities preparing their financial statements in accordance with IFRS and to all types of financial instruments, except for those specifically excluded from their scope [IAS 32 para 4; IAS 39 para 2; IFRS 7 para 3]. The definition of a financial instrument is broad and is discussed in section 4.

A6.3.5 The scope of the three standards is very wide-ranging, but not identical. While IAS 32 and IAS 39 only deal with recognised financial instruments, IFRS 7 applies to both recognised as well as unrecognised financial instruments. Recognised financial instruments include financial assets and financial liabilities that are within IAS 39's scope. Unrecognised financial instruments include some financial instruments, for example, loan commitments that, although scoped out of IAS 39, are within IFRS 7's scope. [IFRS 7 para 4]. In other words, all financial instruments that are scoped out of IFRS 7 are also scoped out of IAS 39, but IAS 39 contains additional scope exclusions that go beyond IFRS 7 and IAS 36.2. [IAS 32 para 4; IFRS 7 para 3; IAS 39 para 2]. In general, items are scoped out of all the three standards if another standard is more prescriptive.

Interests in subsidiaries, associates and joint ventures

A6.3.6 Interests in subsidiaries, associates and joint ventures that are accounted for using the cost method prescribed in IAS 27, 'Consolidated and separate financial statements', IAS 28, 'Investment in associates', and IAS 31, 'Interest in joint ventures', or that are accounted for in accordance with IFRS 5, 'Non-current assets held for sale and discontinued operations,' [IAS 27 para 37; IAS 28 para 14; IAS 31 para 2(a)] are outside the scope of IAS 32, IFRS 7 and IAS 39.

A6.3.7 However, such interests fall within the scope of the financial instrument standards in either of the following circumstances:

- The parent or the investor accounts for such interests in its separate financial statements in accordance with IAS 39 either as at fair value through profit or loss or as available for sale. [IAS 27 para 37]. In that situation, the interest in a subsidiary, associate or joint venture falls within IAS 32's and IFRS 7's scope. [IAS 32 para 4(a); IFRS 7 para 3(a)]. In addition, the disclosure requirements of IAS 27, IAS 28 and IAS 31 continue to apply.
- An interest in an associate or a joint venture that is scoped out of IAS 28 or IAS 31, because it is held by a venture capital organisation, mutual fund, unit trust and similar entity including an investment-linked insurance fund that upon initial recognition is designated as at fair value through profit or loss (so called fair value option) or categorised as held for trading. [IAS 28 para 1, IAS 31 para 1]. In that situation, the investment is accounted for in accordance with IAS 39 and the disclosure requirements of IFRS 7, as well as IAS 28 and IAS 31, apply.

[IAS 32 para 4(a), IFRS 7 para 3(a), IAS 39 para 2(a)].

A6.3.8 Derivatives linked to interests in subsidiaries, associates and joint ventures always fall within the scope of IAS 32, IFRS 7 and IAS 39, except where the derivative meets the definition of an equity instrument in IAS 32. In that situation, it is scoped out of IAS 39 and accounted for as equity in accordance with IAS 32. [IAS 32 para 4(a); IFRS 7 para 3(a); IAS 39 para 2(a)].

A6.3.9 An investor may, in addition to having a present ownership interest, hold share options in an investee (that is not presently a subsidiary) that, if exercised, give the investor voting power or reduce another party's voting power over the financial and operating policies of the investee (potential voting rights). Such potential voting rights that are currently exercisable and give access to the economic benefits would have been taken into account in establishing not only whether the investor has control, significant influence or joint control, but also in determining the share of the investment (economic interest) to be accounted for by consolidation, equity method or proportional consolidation. [IAS 27 paras 14, IG 4-5; IAS 28 para 8]. When instruments containing potential voting rights in substance currently give access to the economic benefits associated with an ownership interest and so affect the share of profits the investee accounts for when consolidating, proportionately consolidating or applying the equity method, the instrument is scoped out of IAS 39. [IAS 27 para IG 7]. This exclusion makes sense as it avoids double counting the same instrument twice, first by inclusion in the economic interest calculation and, secondly, by fair valuing the derivative through profit or loss. Therefore, in this situation, IAS 32 and IFRS 7 apply, but not IAS 39.

Employee benefit plans and share-based payments

A6.3.10 Employee rights and obligations under employee benefit plans are financial instruments, because they are contractual rights or obligations that will result in the flow of cash to the past and present employees. However, as they are specifically accounted for under IAS 19, 'Employee benefits', they are outside the scope of IAS 32, IFRS 7 and IAS 39. [IAS 32 para 4(b); IFRS 7 para 3(b); IAS 39 para 2(c)].

A6.3.11 Similarly, share-based payment transactions to which IFRS 2, 'Share-based payment', applies are outside the scope of IAS 32, IFRS 7 and IAS 39. However, IAS 32, IFRS 7 and IAS 39 apply to contracts to buy or sell non-financial items in share based payment transactions that can be settled net, unless they fall within the own use purchase and sale exception (see para A6.3.33 below). For example, if an entity enters into a contract to purchase a fixed quantity of a particular commodity in exchange for issuing a fixed number of own equity instruments that could be settled net in cash, the contract would fall within IAS 39's scope, unless it qualifies for the own use exception. [IAS 32 para 4(f)(i); IFRS 7 para 3(e); IAS 39 para 2(i)].

A6.3.12 Furthermore, IAS 32 applies to treasury shares that are purchased, sold, issued or cancelled in connection with employee share option plans, employee share purchase plans and all other share-based payment arrangements. [IAS 32 paras 4(f)(ii), 33, 34].

Business combinations

A6.3.13 Contracts for contingent consideration in a business combination are specifically dealt with under IFRS 3, 'Business combinations'. As a result, such contracts are scoped out of IAS 32, IFRS 7 and IAS 39. This exemption applies only to the acquirer. [IAS 32 para 4(c), IFRS 7 para 3(c); IAS 39 para 2(f)]. However, no guidance is provided in IAS 39 as to how the seller in a business combination should account for such contracts. The matter was considered by the IFRIC, but it decided not to pursue the issue further, because it is not pervasive in practice; and the IASB was currently looking at contingent consideration from the purchaser's perspective as part of its business combinations Phase II project. [IFRIC Update Aug 2002]. Nevertheless, the issue remains as to whether IAS 37, 'Provisions, contingent liabilities and contingent assets', or IAS 39 applies. Even though a contingent receivable meets the definition of a financial asset, IAS 39 acknowledges that such contingent assets are not always recognised in the financial statement as discussed in paragraph 4.14. Indeed, IAS 37 specifically forbids recognition of a contingent asset. [IAS 37 para 31].

A6.3.14 Contracts between an acquirer and a vendor in a business combination to buy or sell an acquiree at a future date are also scoped out of IAS 39. [IAS 39 para 2(g)].

Own equity instruments

A6.3.15 Financial instruments issued by an entity, including options and warrants that meet the definition of an equity instrument in IAS 32, are outside IAS 39's but inside IAS 32's scope. Such instruments, along with other equity accounts including retained earnings, represent the residual interest of the reporting entity and are therefore subject to different measurement considerations to those relevant to financial assets and financial liabilities. However, the holder (but not issuer) of such an instrument should apply IAS 39 unless it meets the exceptions discussed in paragraphs 6.3.6 to 6.3.9 above. [IAS 39 para 2(d)]. IFRS 7 deals with disclosures of financial instruments in general and doesn't scope out issuers own equity instruments, for example, disclosure about compound financial instruments in IFRS 7 para 17.

Rights and obligations under lease contracts

A6.3.16 Finance lease contracts that give rise to financial assets for lessors and financial liabilities for lessees are financial instruments that are specially dealt with in IAS 17, 'Leases'. Therefore, they fall within the scope of IAS 32 and IFRS 7, but outside of IAS 39's scope, except as follows:

- Lease receivables are included in IAS 39's scope for derecognition and impairment purposes only.
- Finance lease payables are subject to IAS 39's derecognition provisions.
- Any derivatives embedded in lease contracts are also within IAS 39's scope.

[IAS 39 para 2(b)].

Rights and obligations under insurance contracts

A6.3.17 An insurance contract is a contract under which one party (the insurer) *accepts significant insurance risk* from another party (the policyholder) by agreeing to compensate the policyholder if a specified uncertain future event (the insured event) adversely affects the policyholder. [IFRS 4, App A]. Principally, rights and obligations under insurance contracts are scoped out of IAS 32, IFRS 7 and IAS 39 and are accounted for under IFRS 4, because the policyholder transfers to the insurer significant insurance rather than financial risk. [IAS 32 para 4(d); IAS 39 para 2(e)]. Financial risk is the risk of a possible future change in one or more of a specified interest rate, financial instrument price, commodity price, foreign exchange rate, index of prices or rates, credit rating or credit index or other variable, provided in the case of a non-financial variable that the variable is not specific to a party to the contract. [IFRS 4, App A]. If a financial instrument takes the form of an insurance contract, but involves the transfer of financial risks, as opposed to insurance risk, the contract would fall within the financial instrument standards. The distinction between insurance risk and other risks are set out in Appendix B to IFRS 4. [IFRS 4 App B paras 8-17]. IFRS 4 contains numerous examples of insurance contracts that fall within IFRS 4's scope and those that are not insurance contracts and may fall within the scope of IAS 32, IFRS 7 and IAS 39. [IFRS 4 App B paras 18-19] IFRS 7 provides disclosure only for those rights and obligations under insurance contracts that are also in IAS 39's scope. [IFRS 7 para 3(d)].

Contracts with discretionary participating features

A6.3.18 Financial instruments that are within IFRS 4's scope, because they contain a discretionary participation feature are also scoped out of IAS 39. A discretionary participation feature is a contractual right to receive significant additional benefits, as a supplement to guaranteed benefits, whose amount and timing is at the issuer's discretion and that are contractually based on the performance of a specified pool of contracts, investment returns or profit or loss of the company, fund or other entity that issues the contract. [IFRS 4 App A]. However, these instruments are in IFRS 7's scope and subject to the requirements of IAS 32 except for those with respect to the distinction between financial liabilities and equity instruments. [IAS 32 para 4(e); IAS 39 para 2(e)].

Derivatives embedded in insurance contracts

A6.3.19 Derivatives embedded in insurance contracts or in contracts containing discretionary participating features as discussed above are within the scope of IAS 32, IFRS 7 and IAS 39 if they require separation in accordance with IAS 39. [IAS 39 para 2(e); IFRS 4 para 34(d)]. For example, separate accounting would be required in circumstances where contractual payments embedded in a host insurance contract that is indexed to the value of equity instruments are not related to the host instrument, because the risks inherent in the host and the embedded derivative are dissimilar. [IAS 39 para AG 30(d)]. However, no separation is required if the embedded derivative itself is an insurance contract. [IAS 39 para 2(e); IFRS 4 para 7].

Financial guarantee contracts

A6.3.20 Financial guarantee contracts (sometimes known as 'credit insurance') require the issuer to make specified payments to reimburse the holder for a loss it incurs if a specified debtor fails to make payment when due under a debt instrument's original or modified terms. [IAS 39 para 9]. That is, the holder is exposed to and has incurred a loss on the failure of the debtor to make payments. These contracts are often written by financial guarantee insurers in the form of insurance contracts, or they may be written by banks and entities that do not operate as insurance entities in other forms (for example, letter of credit, credit default contracts).

A6.3.21 A contract that compensates the holder for more than the loss incurred does not meet the definition of a financial guarantee contract. For the definition to be met, the amount of reimbursement must be either less than the amount of the loss incurred or equal to the amount incurred in order to reimburse some or all of the loss the holder suffered because the debtor defaulted.

A6.3.22 Contracts that provide compensation if another party fails to perform a contractual obligation, such as an obligation to construct a building, are performance guarantees. They do not transfer credit risk and, therefore, do not meet the definition of a financial guarantee contract. These type of guarantees are accounted for under IFRS 4 as insurance contracts.

A6.3.23 Prior to the publication of the amendment to IAS 39 and IFRS 4 in relation to financial guarantee contracts in August 2005, such contracts had been initially scoped into IAS 39 (IAS 39 revised, December 2003) and subsequently scoped out of IAS 39 as they met the definition of an insurance contract and the IASB wished to make the scope change after due process. The amendment has been designed to address both the needs of entities that have considered financial guarantee contracts to be another type of financial instruments as well as credit insurers who have always considered that financial guarantee contracts are another form of insurance contract. The resulting amendment introduced an accounting regime based on the business model the reporting entity adopted (that is, insurance business model or other business model).

A6.3.24 The reference to the entity's business model preserves the key principle that the accounting treatment of a financial guarantee contract should not depend on its legal form. It also brought them into IAS 39's scope, but with an option available to insurers to continue to account for these contracts under IFRS 4 if they had met two conditions (see below). Accordingly, it included a definition of financial guarantee contract as stated in paragraph A6.3.20 above, and amended IAS 39 to require that issuers of financial guarantee contracts should account for such contracts as financial liabilities The amendment does not address the accounting for financial guarantee contracts by the holder. The effect of the amendment is that, although these contracts meet the definition of an insurance contract, when the risk transferred is significant they come within the scope of IAS 39, not IFRS 4. However, if the issuer has previously *asserted* explicitly that it regards such contracts as insurance contracts and has used accounting applicable to *insurance contracts*, the issuer may elect to apply either IFRS 4 or IAS 39 to such financial guarantee contracts. The issuer can make the election on a contract by contract basis, but the election for each contract is irrevocable. [IAS 39 paras 2(e), AG4]. Assertions that the issuer regards contracts as insurance can typically be found in business documentation, contracts, accounting policies, financial statements and communication with customers and regulators. [IAS 39 para AG 4].

A6.3.25 In contrast, some credit related guarantees do not, as a precondition for payment, require that the holder is exposed to, and has incurred a loss on, the failure of the debtor to make payments on the guaranteed asset when due. Such guarantees are not financial guarantee contracts as defined in paragraph A6.3.20 above and are not insurance contracts as defined in IFRS 4. Such guarantees are derivatives that must be accounted for as such under IAS 39. [IAS 39 para AG 4(b)]. However, a contract that requires an entity to make payments when the counterparty to a derivative contract fails to make a payment when due, is considered to meet the definition of a financial guarantee contract. This is because it is not the risk inherent in the derivative that is being guaranteed; it is the counterparty's credit risk that is being guaranteed in the event the counterparty defaults.

Example 1 – Credit related guarantee

A bank issues a credit-related guarantee contract (sometimes referred to as credit derivative) that provides for payment if the credit rating of a debtor falls below a particular level.

In this situation, the credit related contract will be accounted for as a derivative financial instrument under IAS 39, because the contract holder is not required to suffer a loss on a specified debt instrument – the bank will pay for the decrease in the credit worthiness of the debtor even if the debtor does not actually default. However, if the contract provides for payment only in the event that the entity suffers loss as a result of non-payment by the debtor, the contract would be a financial guarantee contract. Holders and issuers of credit derivatives will always account for them under IAS 39.

Example 2 – Residual value guarantee

An insurer is required to make payments to the insured party based on the fair value of a non-financial asset at a future date under a residual value guarantee contract.

In this situation, the risk of changes in the fair value of the non-financial asset is not a financial risk because the fair value reflects not only changes in market prices for such assets (a financial variable), but also the condition of the specific asset held (a non-financial variable). As the change in fair value of the non-financial asset is specific to the owner, it is not a derivative instrument and, therefore, the contract will be accounted for as an insurance contract in accordance with IFRS 4. However, if the contract compensates the insured party only for changes in market prices and not for changes in the condition of the specific non-financial asset held, the contract is a derivative and within IAS 39's scope. [IFRS 4, IG example 1.15, IAS 39 para AG 12A].

A6.3.26 There is no exemption under IAS 39 for financial guarantee contracts issued between members of a group or entities under common control similar to those under US GAAP FIN 45, 'Guarantor's accounting and disclosure requirements for guarantees, including direct guarantees of indebtedness to others'. Such guarantees are inter-company transactions that are eliminated on consolidation. However, in the individual financial statements of the group member issuing the guarantee, the guarantee contract will need to be accounted for in accordance with IAS 39. This is considered further in section 9.

Example – Parent provides a comfort letter to a subsidiary

A subsidiary of a group takes out a loan with a bank. The parent provides a comfort letter to the subsidiary such that if the subsidiary fails to repay the loan to the bank when due, the parent will pay on its behalf.

The comfort letter simply constitutes an undertaking given by the parent to its subsidiary that, in the event, the subsidiary fails to repay the loan to the bank when due, the parent will step in and discharge the subsidiary's debt. This is not a financial guarantee contract as the parent has not provided any guarantee to the bank (nor would the bank be able to enforce payment under what is effectively a private arrangement between the parent and its subsidiary) to repay the loan if the subsidiary defaults.

A6.3.27 Intra-group guarantees also frequently cover other obligations, such as pension plan contributions, lease rentals and taxes. The issue is whether, in the group members' individual financial statements, such obligations are financial guarantee contracts or insurance cointracts. As noted in paragraph A6.3.17 above, if a financial instrument takes the form of an insurance contract, but involves the transfer of financial risks, as opposed to insurance risk, the contract would fall within the financial instrument standards. It is, therefore, necessary to determine whether the risk transferred represents insurance risk or financial risk. The risk transferred in a guarantee of pension plan contributions, operating lease rentals and taxes is the risk that the subsidiary (or joint venture or associate) will not make a payment when due. The reasons for non-payment could vary widely and, whilst they might include some financial risk variables, it is likely that a significant part of the risk transferred will be operational (for example, cash flow difficulties or, at the extreme, bankruptcy). Hence, it appears that the significant risk transferred in a typical guarantee of pension plan contributions, operating lease rentals and taxes will be insurance risk. It is arguable, therefore, that guarantees of pension plan contributions, operating lease rentals and taxes should be treated as insurance contracts and accounted for accordingly.

A6.3.28 Notwithstanding that guarantees of pension plan contributions, operating lease rentals and taxes are insurance contracts within IFRS 4's scope, it is still necessary to consider whether they meet the definition of financial guarantee contracts within IAS 39's scope.The definition of a financial guarantee contract refers specifically to the terms of a debt instrument. Althought the term 'debt instrument' is not specifically defined in IFRS, it is clear from the various references made in IAS 32 that a debt instrument is a type of loan, involving a borrower and a lender. It can be concluded, therefore, that pension plan contributions and tax liabilities are not debt instruments. As regards leases, paragraph 9 of IAS 32 states that *"a finance lease is regarded as primarily an entitlement of the lessor to receive, and an obligation of the lessee to pay, a stream of payments that are substantially the same as blended payments of principal and* *interest under a loan agreement. ... An operating lease, on the other hand, is regarded as primarily an uncompleted contract committing the lessor to provide the use of an asset in future periods in exchange for consideration similar to a fee for a service".* This analysis suggests that a finance lease resembles a debt instrument, while an operating lease does not. Even where leases do fall within IAS 32's scope (that is, in respect of individual payments currently due and payable), the amounts represent short-term payables, which paragraph 95 of IAS 32 suggests are something other than a debt instrument. Accordingly, guarantees of finance leases, but not operating leases, should be included within IAS 39's definition of a financial guarantee contract.

A6.3.29 Financial guarantee contracts fall within the scope of IAS 32 and IFRS 7 if they are accounted for in accordance with IAS 39. However, if the issuer elects to apply IFRS 4 to those contracts, the disclosure requirements of IFRS 4 and not IFRS 7 apply. [IAS 32 para 4(d); IFRS 7 para 3(d)]. The accounting treatment of financial guarantee contracts is considered further in section 9.

Weather derivatives

A6.3.30 Some contracts require a payment based on climatic variables (sometimes described as weather derivatives) or on geological or other physical variables. For such contracts, payments are sometimes made on the amount of loss suffered by the entity and sometimes not. Prior to IAS 39's revision, all such contracts were scoped out of IAS 39 and treated as insurance contracts. However, following IFRS 4's publication, such contracts are accounted for as follows:

- Contracts that require a payment only if a particular level of the underlying climatic, geological, or other physical variables adversely affects the contract holder.

  These are insurance contracts as payment is contingent on changes in a physical variable that is specific to a party to the contract.

- Contracts that require a payment based on a specified level of the underlying variable regardless of whether there is an adverse effect on the contract holder.

  These are derivatives and are within IAS 39's scope.

[IAS 39 para AG 1, IFRS 4 para BC 55].

Example – Weather derivatives

A farming entity in Punjab, a State in India, relies on the prospect of a good monsoon that would favourably impact its earnings for the season. A good monsoon in Punjab involves an average rainfall of about 400mm during the months of June, July and August. The entity enters into a contract with a counterparty that would pay a fixed sum of Rs1m if the entity suffers loss due to poor production caused by below average rainfall during the monsoon months. The premium paid on the contract is Rs50,000.

This is an example of a highly tailored or customised policy that provides the entity protection against an adverse impact on earnings due to poor production caused by poor monsoon in Punjab, irrespective of whether the rest of India has a good monsoon or not. Hence, the contract is an insurance contract and is scoped out of IAS 39. It should be noted that even if the farming entity's loss due to poor production is less than Rs1m, the entity would receive Rs1m as stipulated in the contract. The definition of an insurance contract does not limit the payment by the insurer to an amount equal to the financial impact of the adverse event. [IFRS 4 App para B13].

If, on the other hand the sum of Rs1m was paid if the average rain fall was below 400mm during the months of June, July and August and it would be payable irrespective of fact that the farming entity in Punjab had suffered any damage, then the contract would be accounted for as a derivative instrument. This is because payment is made following the change in average rainfall which is a non-financial variable that is not specific to the holder of the contract and hence one of the variables considered in the definition of financial risk.

Loan commitments

A6.3.31 Loan commitments are firm commitments to provide credit under pre-specified terms and conditions. [IAS 39 BC15]. They are usually entered into by financial institutions such as banks for providing loans to third parties at a specified rate of interest during a fixed period of time. Such a commitment is a derivative, since it has no initial net investment, it has an underlying variable (interest rate) and it will be settled at a future date. In effect, the lender has written an option that allows the potential borrower to obtain a loan at a specified rate.

A6.3.32 The following loan commitments are within IAS 39's scope:

- Loan commitments that the entity designates as financial liabilities at fair value through profit or loss. This may be appropriate, for example, if the entity manages risk exposures related to loan commitments on a fair value basis. [IAS 39 para 4(a)].
- An entity that has a past practice of selling the assets resulting from its loan commitments shortly after origination should apply IAS 39 to all its loan commitments in the *same class*. The term 'same class' is not explained in the standard, but we believe that a commitment to provide borrowing facilities to a corporate entity is not in the same class as a commitment to provide residential mortgage loans, because of differing risk return profiles. [IAS 39 para 4(a)].
- Loan commitments that can be settled net in cash or by delivering or issuing another financial instrument. These loan commitments are derivatives. A loan commitment is not regarded as settled net merely because the loan is paid out in instalments (for example, a mortgage construction loan that is paid out in instalments in line with the progress of construction). [IAS 39 para 4(b)].
- Commitments to provide a loan at a below-market interest rate (see section 9). [IAS 39 para 4(c)].

A6.3.33 Loan commitments that are not within IAS 39's scope should be accounted for in accordance with IAS 37. Where events make such a loan commitment an onerous contract, the contract falls within IAS 37's scope and a liability exists that should be recognised. However, all loan commitments, whether scoped in or out of IAS 39, are subject to IAS 39's derecognition provisions and to IFRS 7's disclosure requirements. [IAS 39 para 2(h); IFRS 7 para 4].

Contracts to buy or sell non-financial assets

A6.3.34 Contracts to buy or sell non-financial items are, in general, not financial instruments. Many commodity contracts are of this type. However, if such contracts can be settled net in cash or by exchanging another financial instrument, they fall within the scope of IAS 32, IFRS 7 and IAS 39 as if they were financial instruments (derivatives). This is so, unless the contracts were entered into and continue to be held for the purpose of receipt or delivery of non-financial items to meet the entity's expected purchase, sale or usage requirements (often referred to as 'own use' purchase or sale exception). [IAS 32 paras 8-10; IFRS 7 para 5; IAS 39 para 5]. In other words, if the own use exception is met, the contract must not be accounted for as a derivative (that is, the application of the own use exception is not a choice).

Contracts that can be settled net

A6.3.35 There are various ways in which a contract to buy or sell a non-financial asset can be settled net in cash, including when:

- The terms of the contract permit either party to settle net in cash or another financial instrument or by exchanging financial instruments. Net settlement means that the entity will pay or receive cash (or an equivalent value in other financial assets) to and from the counterparty, equal to the net gain or loss on the contract on exercise or settlement.
- The ability to settle the contract net is not explicitly stated in the contract, but the entity has a practice of settling similar contracts net in cash (whether with the counterparty, by entering into offsetting contracts or by selling the contract before its exercise or lapse). For example, a futures exchange permits an entity to enter into offsetting contracts that relieves the entity of its obligation to make or receive delivery of the non-financial asset.
- For similar contracts, the entity has a practice of taking delivery of the underlying and selling it within a short period after delivery to generate a profit from short-term fluctuations in price or dealer's margin. An example is an exchange that offers a ready opportunity to sell the contract.
- The non-financial asset that is the subject of the contract is readily convertible into cash.

[IAS 32 para 9; IAS 39 para 6].

A6.3.36 Where the second and third bullet points above apply, the entity's activities make it clear that the contracts cannot qualify for 'normal' purchase or sale exception. Accordingly, such contracts are within the scope of the financial instrument standards. Other contracts that can be settled net should be evaluated to determine whether they qualify for the exception. For example, to qualify for the exception, a contract's terms must be consistent with the terms of an entity's normal purchases or sales; that is, the quantity specified in the contract must be expected to be used or sold by the entity over a reasonable period in the normal course of business. Other factors that may be relevant in determining whether or not the contract qualifies for the exception may include the locations to which delivery of the items will be made, the period of time between entering into the contract and delivery and the entity's prior practices with regard to such contracts. See further paragraph 5.83.

Example – Forward contract to purchase a commodity

Entity XYZ enters into a fixed price forward contract to purchase one million kilograms of copper in accordance with its expected usage requirements. The contract permits XYZ to take physical delivery of the copper at the end of 12 months or to pay or receive a net settlement in cash, based on the change in fair value of copper.

The above contract needs to be evaluated to determine whether it falls within the scope of the financial instruments standards. The contract is a derivative instrument because there is no initial net investment, the contract is based on the price of copper and it is to be settled at a future date. However, if XYZ intends to settle the contract by taking delivery and has no history for similar contracts of settling net in cash, or of taking delivery of the copper and selling it within a short period after delivery for the purpose of generating a profit from short-term fluctuations in price or dealer's margin, the contract is not accounted for as a derivative under IAS 39. Instead, it is accounted for as an executory contract. [IAS 39, IG A1].

In the above example, it is possible for entity XYZ and the counterparty to reach different conclusions about whether the contract falls within IAS 39's scope. For example, a 'normal' sale by the counterparty may not be a 'normal' purchase by entity XYZ that would treat the contract as a derivative. This is one of the few areas of IAS 39 where a contract may be treated as a derivative by one party, but not be treated as a derivative by the counterparty.

Written options

A6.3.37 A written option to buy or sell a non-financial item that can be settled net in accordance with paragraph A6.3.34 above cannot be considered to be entered into for the purpose of the receipt or delivery of the non-financial item in accordance with the entity's expected purchase, sale or usage requirements. This is because an option written by the entity is outside its control as to whether the holder will exercise or not. Such contracts are, therefore, always within the scope of IAS 32 and IAS 39. [IAS 32 para 10; IAS 39 para 7]. See further paragraph 5.85.

Royalty agreements

A6.3.38 Although not specifically mentioned in IAS 39's scope section, the standard does not change the accounting treatment of royalty agreements which are based on the volume of sales or service revenues and that are accounted for in accordance with IAS 18, 'Revenue'. [IAS 39 para AG 2]. However, derivative contracts that are based on sales volume are not excluded from IAS 39's scope, as set out in the example in paragraph 4.30 below.

Section 4

Nature and characteristics of financial instruments

Introduction

A6.4.1 Financial instruments embrace a broad range of assets and liabilities. They include both primary financial instruments – financial assets such as cash, receivables and equity securities of another entity and financial liabilities such as debt – and derivative financial instruments such as financial options, forwards, swaps and futures. Derivative financial instruments are considered separately from paragraph A6.4.23 below.

Definitions relating to financial instruments

A6.4.2 The definitions relating to financial instruments that appear in paragraph 11 of IAS 32 are common to all the three financial instrument standards. The definitions are noted below.

A6.4.3 A financial instrument is any contract that gives rise to a financial asset of one entity and a financial liability or equity instrument of another entity. The revised version of IAS 32 has expanded the definitions of a financial asset and financial liability stated below to include some contracts that will or may be settled in the entity's own equity instruments. This is because a contract is not an equity instrument solely because it may result in the receipt or delivery of the entity's own equity instruments. The expanded definitions cover both derivative and non-derivative contracts that will or may be settled in the entity's own equity instruments.

A6.4.4 A financial asset is any asset that is:

- Cash.
- An equity instrument of another entity.
- A contractual right:
  - to receive cash or another financial asset from another entity; or
  - to exchange financial assets or financial liabilities with another entity under conditions that are potentially favourable to the entity.
- A contract that will or may be settled in the entity's own equity instruments and is:
  - a non-derivative for which the entity is or may be obliged to receive a variable number of the entity's own equity instruments; or

- a derivative that will or may be settled other than by the exchange of a fixed amount of cash or another financial asset for a fixed number of the entity's own equity instruments. For this purpose the entity's own equity instruments do not include instruments that are themselves contracts for the future receipt or delivery of the entity's own equity instruments.

A6.4.5 A financial liability is any liability that is:

- A contractual obligation:
  - to deliver cash or another financial asset from another entity; or
  - to exchange financial assets or financial liabilities with another entity under conditions that are potentially unfavourable to the entity.
- A contract that will or may be settled in the entity's own equity instruments and is:
  - a non-derivative for which the entity is or may be obliged to deliver a variable number of the entity's own equity instruments; or
  - a derivative that will or may be settled other than by the exchange of a fixed amount of cash or another financial asset for a fixed number of the entity's own equity instruments. For this purpose the entity's own equity instruments do not include instruments that are themselves contracts for the future receipt or delivery of the entity's own equity instruments.

A6.4.6 An equity instrument is any contract that evidences a residual interest in an entity's assets after deducting all of its liabilities. [IAS 32 para 11]. The term 'entity' includes individuals, partnerships, incorporated bodies and government agencies. [IAS 32 para 14]. Examples of equity instruments include non-puttable ordinary shares, some types of preference shares and share warrants or written call options that allow the holder to subscribe for or purchase a fixed number of non-puttable ordinary shares in the issuing entity in exchange for a fixed amount of cash or another financial asset.

Key features of the definitions

A6.4.7 Some of the important concepts associated with the various terms that are included in the above definitions are considered below. An understanding of these concepts is particularly important and relevant in evaluating instruments that might qualify as financial instruments including derivatives.

Contractual basis

A6.4.8 All financial instruments are defined by contracts. The rights or obligations that comprise financial assets or financial liabilities are derived from the contractual provisions that underlie them. The terms 'contract' and 'contractual' refer to an agreement between two or more parties that has clear economic consequences that the parties have little, if any, discretion to avoid, usually because the agreement is enforceable in law. Contracts defining financial instruments may take a variety of forms and need not be in writing. [IAS 32 para 13]. An example of an item that would not meet the definition of a financial instrument is an entity's tax liability, as it is not based on a contract between the entity and the tax authority, but arising through statute. Similarly, constructive obligations, as defined in IAS 37, 'Provisions, contingent liabilities and contingent assets', do not arise from contracts and are not financial liabilities. [IAS 32 para AG 12]. On the other hand, a provision for an onerous contract (for example, provision for vacant leasehold property that is being sublet) is a financial liability as it arises from the unavoidable cost of meeting the obligations under the contract. Nevertheless, such provisions are scoped out of IAS 39 and are accounted for in accordance with IAS 37. [IAS 37 para 66].

A6.4.9 A contractual right or contractual obligation to receive, deliver or exchange financial instruments is itself a financial instrument. This is evident from the definitions of financial assets and liabilities that include the terms financial assets and financial instruments within them. However, the terms are not circular. They envisage the possibility that a chain of contractual rights or contractual obligations may be established, but this chain must end ultimately with the receipt or payment of cash or to the acquisition or issue of an equity instrument. [IAS 32 para AG 7].

A6.4.10 As the IAS 32 definitions require all financial instruments to be contracts, some question whether cash can be considered to be a contract. However, this concern is overcome because the definition of a financial asset stated in paragraph A6.4.4 above specifically states that cash is a financial instrument. IAS 32 application guidance also clarifies that currency (cash) is a financial asset because it represents the medium of exchange and is, therefore, the basis on which all transactions are measured and recognised in financial statements. A deposit of cash with a bank or similar financial institution is a financial asset because it represents the contractual right of the depositor to obtain cash from the institution or to draw a cheque or similar instrument against the balance in favour of a creditor in payment of a financial liability. [IAS 32 para AG 3]. On the other hand gold bullion is not a financial instrument like cash. It is a commodity. Although the bullion market is highly liquid, there is no contractual right to receive cash or another financial instrument inherent in bullion. [IAS 39 para IG B1].

A6.4.11 Some common examples of financial instruments that give rise to financial assets representing a contractual right to receive cash in the future for the holder and corresponding financial liabilities representing a contractual obligation to deliver cash in the future for the issuer are as follows:

- Trade accounts receivable and payable.
- Notes receivable and payable.

- Loans receivable and payable.
- Bonds receivable and payable.

In each case, one party's contractual right to receive (or obligation to pay) cash is matched by the other party's corresponding obligation to pay (or right to receive). [IAS 32 para AG 4].

A6.4.12 Another type of financial instrument is one for which the economic benefit to be received or given up is a financial asset other than cash. For example, a note payable in government bonds gives the holder the contractual right to receive and the issuer the contractual obligation to deliver government bonds, not cash. The bonds are financial assets because they represent obligations of the issuing government to pay cash. The note is, therefore, a financial asset of the note holder and a financial liability of the note issuer. [IAS 32 para AG 5].

Conditional (contingent) rights and obligations

A6.4.13 The ability to exercise a contractual right or the requirement to satisfy a contractual obligation may be absolute, or it may be contingent on the occurrence of a future event. A note receivable or payable is an unconditional promise to pay, but a financial guarantee is a conditional financial instrument as it results in a contractual right of the lender to receive cash from the guarantor and a corresponding contractual obligation of the guarantor to pay the lender, if the borrower defaults. The contractual right and obligation exist because of a past transaction or event (assumption of the guarantee), even though the lender's ability to exercise its right and the requirement for the guarantor to perform under its obligation are both contingent on a future act of default by the borrower. [IAS 32 para AG 8].

A6.4.14 Even though a contingent right and obligation can meet the definition of a financial asset and a financial liability, they are not always recognised in the financial statements. Some of these contingent rights and obligations may be insurance contracts within IFRS 4's scope, whilst others may be excluded from the standards' scope. [IAS 32 para AG 8].

A6.4.15 Other contingencies that may require the payment of cash but do not as yet arise from a contract, such as a contingent receivable or payable for a tort judgment, are not financial instruments. However, when those judgments become enforceable by a government or a court of law, and are thereby contractually reduced to fixed payment schedules, the judgment would be a financial instrument. To elaborate, if and when the parties agree to payment terms and those payment terms are reduced to a contract, then a financial instrument exists. Contrast this with a fine, which is not contractual.

Exchange under potentially favourable or unfavourable terms

A6.4.16 The definitions of financial assets and financial liabilities make references to exchanges under conditions that are 'potentially favourable' or 'potentially unfavourable'. The meaning of these terms and the way they work in practice are best explained by means of an example.

Example – Exchange under potentially favourable or unfavourable terms

Entity A holds an option to purchase equity shares in a listed entity B for C5 per share at the end of a 90 day period.

The above call option gives entity A a contractual right to exchange cash of C5 for an equity share in another entity and will be exercised if the market value of the share exceeds C5 at the end of the 90 day period. This is because as the terms will be favourable to entity A at the end of term, it will exercise the call option. Since entity A stands to gain if the call option is exercised, the exchange is potentially favourable to the entity. Therefore, the option is a derivative financial asset from the time the entity becomes a party to the option contract.

On the other hand, if entity A writes an option under which the counterparty can force the entity to sell equity shares in the listed entity B for C5 per share at any time in the next 90 days, entity A has a contractual obligation to exchange equity shares in another entity for cash of C5 per share on potentially unfavourable terms if the holder exercises the option, because the market price per share exceeds the exercise price of C5 per share at the end of the 90 day period. Since entity A stands to lose if the option is exercised, the exchange is potentially unfavourable and the option is a derivative financial liability from the time the entity becomes a party to the option contract.

Comparison with non-financial assets and liabilities

A6.4.17 As discussed above, financial instruments represent contractual rights or obligations to receive or pay cash or other financial assets. Non-financial items have a more indirect, non-contractual relationship to future cash flows.

A6.4.18 The non-financial assets of a business (such as inventories, property, plant and equipment and intangibles) are inputs to some productive process. They are expected to contribute, along with other inputs, to the production and sale of goods or services. They must be used in a productive activity, and effectively transformed into goods or service, which must be sold, before there is any right to receive cash. Control of such physical and intangible assets creates an opportunity to generate an inflow of cash or another financial asset, but it does not give rise to a present right to receive cash or another financial asset. [IAS 32 para AG 10]. Even where physical assets, such as properties, are held as investments rather than as inventories, they are not financial instruments.

A6.4.19 A contract to acquire or sell a non-financial asset at a specified price at a future date is not a financial instrument, because the contractual right of one party to receive a non-financial asset and the corresponding obligation of the other party do not establish a present right or obligation of either party to receive, deliver or exchange a financial asset. For example, contracts that provide for settlement only by the receipt or delivery of a non-financial item (for example, an option or forward contract on silver) are not financial instruments. Many commodity contracts are of this type. However, as stated in paragraph A6.3.33

above, contracts to buy or sell non-financial items that can be settled net or by exchanging financial instruments, or in which the non-financial item is readily convertible to cash, are treated as if they are financial instruments. [IAS 32 para AG 20]. For the same reasons as stated above, a firm commitment that involves the receipt or delivery of a physical asset is not a financial instrument. [IAS 32 para AG 21].

A6.4.20 Another example is an operating lease to rent an office building. Under the lease, the lessor has committed to provide office space in future periods for consideration similar to a fee for a service. The contractual right of the lessee to receive the service and the corresponding obligation of the lessor do not establish a present right or obligation of either party to receive, deliver or exchange a financial asset. On the other hand, a finance lease is regarded as primarily an entitlement of the lessor to receive, and an obligation of the lessee to pay, a stream of payments that are substantially the same as a loan agreement. The lessor accounts for its investment in the amount receivable under the lease contract rather than the leased asset itself. [IAS 32 para AG 9]. Accordingly, an operating lease is not regarded as a financial instrument (except as regards individual payments currently due and payable), but a finance lease is regarded as one.

A6.4.21 Assets (such as pre-paid expenses) for which the future economic benefit is the receipt of goods or services, rather than the right to receive cash or another financial asset, are not financial assets. Similarly, items such as deferred revenue and most warranty obligations are not financial liabilities, because the outflow of economic benefits associated with them is the delivery of goods and services, rather than a contractual obligation to pay cash or another financial asset. [IAS 32 para AG 11].

Identification of financial instruments

A6.4.22 Paragraphs 6.4.8 to 6.4.21 considered some of the important concepts associated with the definitions relating to financial instruments supplemented, where necessary, with examples. For ease of understanding and as a practical aid, the table below provides a list of common balance sheet items and applies the concepts discussed above to determine whether the items meet the definition of a financial instrument. Paragraph references are included where applicable. The list is by no means exhaustive, but provides an aide-mémoire to help in identifying primary financial instruments. For the sake of completeness, the last two columns also establish whether the instruments so identified fall within or outside the scope of IAS 32, IFRS 7 or IAS 39 discussed in detail from paragraph A6.3.4 above.

Balance sheet item	Financial instrument? Yes = ✓ No = X	Included within the scope of IAS 32 and IFRS 7 Yes = ✓ No = X	Included within the scope of IAS 39 Yes = ✓ No = X
Intangible assets	X – para 6.4.18	n/a	n/a
Property, plant and equipment	X – para 6.4.18	n/a	n/a
Investment property	X – para 6.4.18	n/a	n/a
Interests in subsidiaries, associates and joint ventures – accounted for under IAS 27, IAS 28 or IAS 31 respectively	✓ – para 6.4.6	X – para 6.3.6	X – para 6.3.6
Interests in subsidiaries, associates and joint ventures held for sale under IFRS 5	✓ – para 6.4.6	X – para 6.3.6	X – para 6.3.6
Interests in subsidiaries, associates and joint ventures – accounted for under IAS 39 (in accordance with IAS 27 para 37(b))	✓ – para 6.4.6	✓ – para 6.3.7	✓ – para 6.3.7
Inter-company trading balances with subsidiaries, associates and joint ventures	✓ – para 6.4.18	✓	✓
Investments in other entities (available-for-sale and held for trading)	✓ – para 6.4.4	✓	✓
Inventories	X – para 6.4.18	n/a	n/a
Construction contract work in progress	X – para 6.4.18	n/a	n/a
Construction contract receivables	✓ – para 6.4.11	✓	✓
Finance lease receivables (recognised by a lessor)	✓ – para 6.4.20	✓ – para 6.3.16	X – para 6.3.16
Trade receivables	✓ – para 6.4.11	✓	✓

Pre-payments – goods and services	X – para 6.4.21	n/a	n/a
Cash and cash equivalents	✓ – para 6.4.4	✓	✓
Trade payables	✓ – para 6.4.11	✓	✓
Contingent consideration in a business combination (acquirer only)	✓ – para 6.4.14	X – para 6.3.13	X – para 6.3.13
Accruals – goods and services (settlement in cash)	✓ – para 6.4.11	✓	✓
Deferred income	X – para 6.4.21	n/a	n/a
Debt instruments	✓ – para 6.4.5	✓	✓
Derivative instruments	✓ – para 6.4.1	✓	✓
Net settled commodity-based contracts	✓ – para 6.3.33	✓ – para 6.3.33	✓ – para 6.3.33
Retirement benefit obligations	✓ – para 6.3.10	X – para 6.3.10	X – para 6.3.10
Provisions (as defined in IAS 37)	X – para 6.4.8	n/a	n/a
Vacant leasehold property provision	✓ – para 6.4.8	✓	X – para 6.4.8
Warranty obligations (settled by delivery of goods or service)	X – para 6.4.21	n/a	n/a
Warranty obligations (settled by delivery of cash or other financial asset)	✓ – para 6.4.5	✓	✓
Financial guarantee contracts	✓ – para 6.4.9	✓ – para 6.3.27	✓ – para 6.3.22
Operating lease	X – para 6.4.20	n/a	n/a
Finance lease obligations	✓ – para 6.4.20	✓ – para 6.3.16	X – para 6.3.16
Dividend payable	note 1	✓ – note 1	X – para 6.3.15
Current and deferred tax	X – para 6.4.8	n/a	n/a
Preference shares (debt)	✓ – para 6.4.5	✓	✓

Entity's own equity shares	✓ – para 6.4.6	✓ – para 6.3.15	X – para 6.3.15
Employee share options	✓ – para 6.4.6	X – para 6.3.10	X – para 6.3.10
Other options over own equity shares	✓ – para 6.4.6	✓ – para 6.3.15	X – para 6.3.15
Minority interests	note 2	✓ – note 2	n/a

Notes:

1 Dividend payable on the balance sheet is a financial liability when the dividend has been formally declared by the members in a general meeting and becomes a legal obligation of the entity to deliver cash to shareholders for the amount of the declared dividend. [IAS 32 para AG 13].

2 The minority interest that may arise on consolidating a subsidiary is not a financial liability or an equity instrument of the parent, but it is presented in the consolidated balance sheet within equity, separately from the parent's shareholders' equity. [IAS 27 para 33; IAS 32 para AG 29]. However, where the parent or any fellow subsidiary undertaking has an obligation to deliver cash or another financial asset in respect of a subsidiary's shares (for example, by virtue of a written put option), they are treated as financial liabilities in consolidated financial statements under IAS 32. [IAS 32 para AG 29].

Derivative financial instruments

Introduction

A6.4.23 Derivatives are financial instruments that derive their value from an underlying price or index, which could be for example, an interest rate, a foreign exchange rate or commodity price. Their primary purpose is to create rights and obligations that have the effect of transferring between the parties to the instrument one or more of the financial risks inherent in an underlying primary instrument. Consequently, they may be used for trading purposes to generate profits from risk transfers or they may be used as a hedging instrument for managing risks. Generally, there is no transfer of the underlying instrument between the parties either at inception or at maturity, but there are some exceptions.

A6.4.24 On inception, a derivative instrument gives one party a contractual right to exchange financial assets or financial liabilities with another party under conditions that are potentially favourable, or a contractual obligation to exchange financial assets or financial liabilities with another party under conditions that are potentially unfavourable. Because the terms of the exchange are determined at inception, as prices in the financial markets change, those terms may become favourable or unfavourable (see para 6.4.16 above). Derivative instruments may either be free-standing or embedded in a financial instrument or in a non-financial contract.

Definition

A6.4.25 IAS 39 defines a derivative as a financial instrument or other contract with all of the following characteristics:

- its value changes in response to the change in a specified interest rate, financial instrument price, commodity price, foreign exchange rate, index of prices or rates, credit rating or credit index, or other variable, provided in the case of a non-financial variable that the variable is not specific to a party to the contract (sometimes called the 'underlying');
- it requires no initial net investment or an initial net investment that is smaller than would be required for other types of contracts that would be expected to have a similar response to changes in market factors; and
- it is settled at a future date.

[IAS 39 para 9].

Key features of the definition

A6.4.26 The characteristics referred to above make the definition of a derivative not only complex but fairly wide. For example, many contracts such as loan commitments (see para A6.3.30 above), certain contracts to buy or sell a non-financial item (see para A6.3.33 above) and regular way trades (see para A6.4.41 below) meet the definition of a derivative, in addition to the more commonly used and typical derivative instruments such as forwards, swaps, futures and options. Therefore, an understanding of these characteristics is particularly important and relevant in evaluating instruments that might qualify as, or contain, a derivative instrument. The paragraphs that follow examine some of the important concepts associated with these characteristics.

Underlying

A6.4.27 As evident from the first characteristic stated in paragraph A6.4.25 above, an underlying is a variable, such as:

- An interest rate (for example, LIBOR).
- A security price (for example, the price of an XYZ entity equity share listed on a regulated market).
- A commodity price (for example, the price of a bushel of wheat).
- A foreign exchange rate (for example, €/$ spot rate).
- An index (for example, FTSE 100, a retail price index).
- A credit rating or a credit index (for example, Moody's credit rating).
- An insurance index or catastrophe-loss index.

- Other variable (for example, sales volume indices specifically created for settlement of derivatives).
- Non financial variable (for example, a climatic or geological condition such as temperature, rainfall, or earthquake severity).

A6.4.28 Generally, an underlying may be any variable whose changes are observable or otherwise objectively verifiable. It may be the price or rate of an asset or liability that changes in response to changes in the market factors, but it is not the asset or the liability itself in most instances. Accordingly, the underlying will generally be the referenced index that determines whether or not the derivative instrument has a positive or a negative value.

A6.4.29 If the underlying is a non-financial variable as referred to in the last bullet point in paragraph A6.4.27 above, it must not be specific to a party to the contract in order for the derivative definition to be met. In other words, the terms of the contract must be sufficiently generic in nature to qualify as a derivative. For example, such variables might include an index of earthquake losses in a particular region or an index of temperatures in a particular city. On the other hand, non-financial variables that are specific to a party to the contract can include the occurrence or non-occurrence of a fire that damages or destroys an asset of a party to the contract, or EBITDA or sales revenue. A change in the fair value of a non-financial asset is specific to the owner if the fair value reflects not only changes in market prices for such assets (a financial variable) but also the condition of the specific non-financial asset held (a non-financial variable). [IAS 39 para AG 12A]. Such contracts may fall to be treated as insurance contracts (see para A6.3.25 example 2 above).

A6.4.30 A derivative instrument may have more than one underlying or variable. A typical example is a cross-currency interest rate swap that has one underlying based on a foreign exchange rate and another underlying based on an interest rate. A complex option may have two such variables, one based on an interest rate and the other based on the price of a commodity such as oil. Another example based on IAS 39's implementation guidance is given below.

Example – Foreign currency contract based on sales volume

Entity XYZ, whose functional currency is the US dollar, sells products in France denominated in euro. XYZ enters into a contract with an investment bank to convert euro to US dollars at a fixed exchange rate. The contract requires XYZ to remit euro based on its sales volume in France in exchange for US dollars at a fixed exchange rate of 1.20.

The contract has two underlying variables (the foreign exchange rate and the volume of sales), no initial net investment or an initial net investment that is smaller than would be required for other types of contracts that would be expected to have a similar response to changes in market factors and a payment provision. If a contract has two or more underlyings, and at least one of those underlyings is not a non-financial variable specific to a party to a contract, the entire contract is accounted for as a derivative (assuming the rest of the definition of a derivative is met).

Therefore, the contact is a derivative even though one of the variables (sales volume) is a non-financial variable that is specific to a party to the contract. IAS 39 does not exclude from its scope derivatives that are based on sales volume. [IAS 39 para IG B8].

6.4.30.1 There have been various discussions at the IASB and IFRIC regarding the scope of 'non financial' and 'specific' in terms of looking at variables. The IASB confirmed at its meeting in January 2007 that it had intended that only contracts within the scope of IFRS 4 should be excluded from the definition of a derivative. Therefore, the IASB tentatively decided to propose deletion of the exclusion as part of its annual improvement process.

Notional amounts and payment provisions

A6.4.31 A derivative usually has a notional amount, which is an amount of currency, a number of shares, a number of units of weight or volume or other units specified in the contract. However, a derivative instrument does not require the holder or writer to invest or receive the notional amount at the inception of the contract. The interaction of the notional amount and the underlying determines the settlement amount under a derivative instrument. The interaction may consist of a simple multiplication (for example, price × number of shares), or it may involve a formula that has leverage factors or other constants (for example, notional amount × interest rate where interest rate = 15 per cent — 2.5 × LIBOR; the effect of any change in LIBOR is magnified by two and a half times).

A6.4.32 Alternatively, a derivative could contain a 'payment provision' specifying a fixed payment or payment of an amount that can change (but not proportionally with a change in the underlying) as a result of some future event that is unrelated to a notional amount. For example, a contract may require a fixed payment of C1,000 if six month LIBOR increases by 100 basis points. Such a contract is a derivative even though a notional amount is not specified. [IAS 39 para AG 9]. Another example is where an entity receives C10 million if the share price of another entity decreases by more than five per cent during a six month period, but pays C10 million if the share price increases by more than five per cent during the same six month period. No payment is made if the share price is less than five per cent up or down. This is a derivative contract where there is no notional amount to determine the settlement amount. Instead, there is a payment provision that is based on changes in the underlying.

Initial net investment

A6.4.33 The second characteristic of a derivative instrument is that it has no initial net investment, or one that is *smaller* than would be required for other types of contracts that would be expected to have a similar response to changes in market factors. Professional judgement is required in interpreting the term in italic as it does not necessarily mean insignificant in relation to the overall investment. It is a relative measure and needs to be interpreted with care. This reflects the inherent leverage features typical of derivative instruments compared to the underlying instruments.

A6.4.34 The following examples illustrate how initial net investment is determined in various circumstances:

Example 1 – No initial net investment of the notional amount

Forward based derivative contracts such as forward foreign exchange contracts and interest rate swaps are typical derivative instruments that do not require an initial net investment. This is because they are priced at-the-money at inception, which means that the fair value of the contracts is zero. If the fair value of the contract is not zero at inception, the contract is recognised as an asset or liability.

Under a forward foreign exchange contract the two parties agree to purchase or sell a foreign currency at a specified price, with delivery or settlement at a specified future date. Although the forward contract has a notional amount equal to the amount of the foreign currency, it does not require the holder or the writer to invest or receive the notional amount at the inception of the contract. Indeed, forward contracts do not have cash flows during the contract term. Settlement takes place at maturity of the contract.

Similarly, an interest rate swap may be viewed as a variation of a forward contract in which the two parties agree to exchange one set of interest cash flows calculated with reference to a fixed interest rate for another set of interest cash flows calculated with reference to a floating interest rate. No exchange of principal takes place. Typically, the rates are set so that the fair values of the fixed and floating legs are equal and opposite at inception with the result that the fair value of the swap on initial recognition is nil. As no money changes hands at inception, there is no initial net investment. Swap cash flows occur at regular intervals over the life of the swap contract based on a notional principal amount and fixed and floating rates specified in the swap.

Example 2 – Initial net investment less than the notional amount

Option contracts are derivative instruments that do require an initial net investment. An option is a contractual agreement that gives the buyer of the option the right, but not the obligation, to purchase (call) or sell (put) a specified security, currency or commodity (the underlying) at a specified price (exercise price) during a specified period of time (or on a specified date). For this right, the buyer pays a premium, which is the amount the seller requires to take on the risk involved in writing the option. Although this premium can be significant, it is often less than the amount that would be required to buy the underlying financial instrument to which the contract is linked. As such, the option fulfils the initial net investment criterion. [IAS 39 para AG 11].

On the other hand, if the option premium is so deep in-the-money that the premium paid is close to making an investment in the underlying, then the option contract will fail the initial net investment criterion. In that situation, the instrument would not be accounted for as a derivative under IAS 39, but rather as an investment in the underlying asset itself.

Example 3 – Exchange of currencies

Some contracts may require a mutual exchange of currencies or other assets, in which case the net investment is the difference between the fair values of the assets exchanged. An example is a currency swap that requires the exchange of currencies at both inception and at maturity. The initial exchange of currencies at fair values in those arrangements (zero net investment) is not seen as an initial net investment. Instead, it is an exchange of one kind of cash for another kind of cash. [IAS 39 para AG 11].

Example 4 – Margin accounts

Many derivative instruments, such as futures contracts and exchange traded written options, require a margin payment – an initial amount that must be deposited before trading begins and which approximately equals the daily price fluctuation permitted for the contract being traded. Such payments are not part of the initial net investment. Rather, they are a form of collateral for the counterparty or clearing house to ensure that traders will perform on their contractual obligations. The initial margin may take the form of cash, securities or other specified assets, typically liquid assets. These are separate assets that are accounted for separately. [IAS 39 para IG B10]. Any variation in margin payments would be adjusted against the asset.

Example 5 – Pre-paid interest rate swap (fixed leg pre-paid)

Entity S enters into a C100m notional amount five-year pay-fixed, receive-variable interest rate swap. The interest rate of the variable part of the swap is reset on a quarterly basis to three month LIBOR. The interest rate of the fixed leg of the swap is 10% per year. At inception of the swap, Entity S pre-pays its fixed obligation of C50m (C100m × 10% × 5 years) discounted using market interest rates, while retaining the right to receive interest payments on the C100m reset quarterly based on three-month LIBOR over the life of the swap.

As stated in example 1 above at the money interest rate swap has a zero fair value at inception. Since entity S has pre-paid the fixed leg of the swap at inception at its fair value, the amount pre-paid is also equal to the fair value of the variable leg of the swap. This amount is however significantly less than the notional amount (C100m) on which the variable payments under the variable leg will be calculated. In other words, the initial net investment (the amount pre-paid) is still smaller than investing in a similar primary instrument, such as a variable rate bond, that responds equally to changes in the underlying interest rate. Therefore, a pre-paid fixed leg swap fulfils the initial net investment criterion of IAS 39. Even though entity S has no future performance obligation, the ultimate settlement of the contract is at a future date and the value of the contract changes in response to changes in the LIBOR index. Accordingly, the contract is a derivative instrument.

On the other hand, if the fixed rate payment obligation is pre-paid subsequent to initial recognition, that is, during the term of the swap, then that would be regarded as a termination of the old swap and an origination of a new instrument that is evaluated under IAS 39. [IAS 39 para IG B4]. There is no explanation in the implementation guidance as to why this is so. Presumably this is because a significant fall in LIBOR between inception date and pre-payment date would cause the amount pre-paid (that is, the fair value of the fixed leg at the date of the pre-payment) to be significantly higher than the fair value of the fixed leg at date of inception. Therefore, the entity receiving the variable payments may not recover substantially all of its pre-paid investment under the contractual terms resulting in the termination of the old swap and the creation of a new instrument.

Example 6 – Pre-paid interest rate swap (floating leg pre-paid)

Entity S enters into a C100m notional amount five-year pay-variable, receive-fixed interest rate swap. The variable leg of the swap is reset on a quarterly basis to three-month LIBOR. The fixed interest payments under the swap are calculated as 10% times the swap's notional amount, that is, C10m per year. Entity S pre-pays its obligation under the variable leg of the swap at inception at current market rates, while retaining the right to receive fixed interest payments of 10% on C100m per year.

As stated in the previous example, the fair value of the fixed leg and the fair value of a floating leg are equal and offsetting so that the fair value of the interest rate swap at inception is zero. Since entity S has pre-paid the variable leg of the swap at inception at its fair value, the amount pre-paid, all else being equal, is also equal to the fair value of the fixed leg of the swap. That is, the initial net investment (the amount pre-paid) is equal to the present value of a fixed annuity of C10m per year over the swap's life. Thus, the initial net investment is equal to the investment required in a non-derivative contract that has a similar response to changes in market conditions. In other words, the amount pre-paid provides a return that is the same as that of an amortising fixed rate debt instrument of the amount of the pre-paid. For this reason, the instrument fails the initial net investment criterion of IAS 39. Therefore, the contract is not accounted for as a derivative. By discharging the obligation to pay variable interest rate payments, entity S in effect provides a loan to the counterparty. [IAS 39 para IG B5].

Example 7 – Pre-paid forward

Entity XYZ enters into a forward contract to purchase 1m entity T ordinary shares in one year. The current market price of entity T's shares is C50 per share; the one-year forward price of entity T's shares is C55 per share. XYZ is required to pre-pay the forward contract at inception with a C50m payment.

The initial investment in the forward contract of C50m is less than the notional amount applied to the underlying, 1m shares at the forward price of C55 per share, that is, C55m. However, the initial net investment *approximates* the investment that would be required for other types of contracts that would be expected to have a similar response to changes in market factors because entity T's shares could be purchased at inception for the same price of C50m. Accordingly, the pre-paid forward contract does not meet the initial net investment criterion of a derivative instrument. In this situation, the entity would record the investment itself as a non-derivative financial asset. [IAS 39 para IG B9].

It is not clear why the example in the implementation guidance uses the term 'approximate' when the initial net investment of C50m is equal to the amount that would be exchanged to acquire the asset relating to the underlying (market price of the share). Presumably the term is used to emphasise the point that the initial net investment test is a relative measure as indicated in paragraph A6.4.33 above and that a pre-payment amount of C42.5m (15% smaller than the original amount) may still meet the initial net investment criterion.

Settlement at a future date

A6.4.35 The final part of the definition relates to settlement at a future date. All derivatives are settled at a future date. As explained in example 1 above, forward contracts are settled at a specified date in the future, whilst for an interest rate swap settlement occurs at regular intervals over the swap's life. An option is settled upon exercise or at maturity. Therefore, even if an option is expected not to be exercised, for example, because it is out-of-the-money and no additional exchange of consideration is expected to take place, the option still meets the settlement criterion, because expiry at maturity is a form of settlement. [IAS 39 para IG B7].

A6.4.36 A derivative can be settled net in cash (that is, the entity has the right to receive or the obligation to pay a single net amount) or gross in cash/other financial asset (exchange of cash/other financial asset). Consider the following example:

Example – Interest rate swap with net or gross settlement

Entity ABC enters into an interest rate swap with a counterparty (XYZ) that requires ABC to pay a fixed rate of 8% and receive a variable amount based on three month LIBOR, reset on a quarterly basis. The fixed and variable amounts are determined based on a C100m notional amount. ABC and XYZ do not exchange the notional amount. ABC pays or receives a net cash amount each quarter based on the difference between 8% and three-month LIBOR. Alternatively, settlement may be on a gross basis.

As the swap contract is settled on a periodical basis, each interest payment can be viewed as a series of forward contracts to exchange and receive cash on potentially favourable or unfavourable terms. The contract meets the definition of a derivative regardless of whether each interest payment is settled net or gross, because its value changes in response to changes in an underlying variable (LIBOR). There is no initial net investment and settlements occur at future dates. In other words, it makes no difference whether ABC and XYZ actually make the interest payment to each other (gross settlement). [IAS 39 para IG B3].

A6.4.37 Settlement may also occur gross through physical delivery of the underlying financial item. An example is a forward contract to purchase C100 million of five per cent fixed rate bond at a specified fixed date in the future. In this situation, at settlement date the entity would exchange cash for physical delivery of the bond (the underlying financial item) whose nominal value is equal to the notional amount of the contract and the market interest rate is the underlying. [IAS 39 para AG10].

Specific examples of derivative instruments

A6.4.38 The key characteristics of a derivative contract were explained and illustrated above, where relevant, with examples. The following table provides typical examples of contracts that normally qualify as derivatives together with the relevant underlying, notional and settlement amounts.

Derivative	Underlying	Notional amount	Settlement amount
Stock options	Market price of share	Number of shares	(Market price at settlement – Strike Price) × Number of shares
Currency forward	Currency rate	Number of currency units	(Spot rate at settlement – Forward rate) × number of currency units
Commodity future	Commodity price per unit	Number of commodity units	Net settlement occurs daily and is determined by the change in the futures price and discounted to reflect the time to maturity
Interest rate swap	Interest rate index (receive 5% fixed and pay LIBOR)	Amounts in C's	Net settlement occurs periodically throughout the contract's term based on the formula: (Current interest rate index – fixed rate specified in the contract) × Amounts in C's
Fixed payment contract	6 month LIBOR increases by 100 points	Not specified	Settlement amount based on payment provision in the contract.

Contracts to buy or sell non-financial items

A6.4.39 An entity may also have a contract to buy or sell a non-financial item that can be settled net in cash or another financial instrument, or by exchanging financial instruments. Such contracts may fall within the definition of a derivative if they meet certain criteria (see further section 3 para A6.33 above). [IAS 39 para AG 10].

Contracts that are in substance derivatives

A6.4.40 Non-derivative transactions should be aggregated and treated as a derivative when, in substance, the transactions result in a derivative instrument. Indicators of this would include circumstances where the transactions:

- Are entered into at the same time and in contemplation of one another.
- Have the same counterparty.
- Relate to the same risk.

- Have no substantive business purpose or there is no apparent economic need for structuring the transactions separately that could not also have been accomplished in a single transaction.

[IAS 39 para IG B6].

Example – In substance derivatives

Entity A makes a five-year fixed rate loan to entity B, while entity B at the same time makes a five-year variable rate loan for the same amount to entity A. There are no transfers of principal at inception of the two loans, since entities A and B have a netting agreement.

The contractual effect is that the loans are, in substance, equivalent to an interest rate swap arrangement that meets the definition of a derivative – there is an underlying variable, no initial net investment and future settlement. The same answer would apply if entity A and entity B did not have a netting agreement, because the definition of a derivative instrument does not require net settlement. [IAS 39 para IG B6].

Regular way contracts

A6.4.41 A regular way purchase or sale is a purchase or sale of a financial asset under a contract whose terms require delivery of the asset within the time frame established generally by regulation or convention in the marketplace concerned. [IAS 39 para 9]. Such contracts give rise to a fixed price commitment between trade date and settlement date that meets the definition of a derivative. However, because of the commitment's short duration, it is not recognised as a derivative financial instrument. Rather, IAS 39 provides for special accounting for such regular way contracts which is dealt with in section 7. [IAS 39 para AG 12].

Accounting for derivatives

A6.4.42 The measurement requirements of IAS 39 require all derivatives to be measured at fair value on the balance sheet, with changes in fair value being accounted through profit or loss, except for derivatives that qualify as effective hedging instruments and derivatives that are linked to and must be settled by delivery of unquoted equity instruments whose fair value cannot be reliably measured. Measurement and hedging requirements are dealt with further in sections 9 and 10 respectively.

Section 5

Embedded derivatives in host contracts

Introduction

A6.5.1 A derivative instrument that falls within IAS 39's scope need not be free-standing. Terms and conditions may also be embedded in a financial instrument or in a non-financial contract (referred to as the 'host' contract) that behave like a free standing derivative. These terms and conditions are referred to as embedded derivatives. The combination of the host contract and the embedded derivative is referred to as a 'hybrid instrument'.

A6.5.2 An embedded derivative can arise from deliberate financial engineering, for example to make low interest-rate debt more attractive by including an equity-linked return. However, in other cases, they arise inadvertently through market practices and common contractual arrangements, such as leases and insurance contracts. Even purchase and sale contracts that qualify as executory contracts may contain embedded derivatives. In fact, they may occur in all sorts of contracts and instruments – the objective being to change the nature of cash flows that otherwise would be required by the host contract and effectively shift financial risks between the parties.

A6.5.3 Analysing non-derivative financial instruments and executory contracts for potential embedded derivatives is one of the more challenging aspects of IAS 39. However, the challenge does not end there. As will be apparent later, a derivative identified in a host contract needs further evaluation to determine whether it should be accounted for separately as a stand alone derivative at fair value. Not all embedded derivatives would fall to be accounted for separately from the host contract in which they reside.

Definition and key characteristics

A6.5.4 An embedded derivative is a component of a hybrid instrument that also includes a non-derivative host contract – with the effect that some of the cash flows of the hybrid instrument vary in a way similar to a stand-alone derivative (see para A6.5.1). An embedded derivative causes some or all of the cash flows that otherwise would be required by the contract to be modified according to a specified interest rate, financial instrument price, commodity price, foreign exchange rate, index of prices or rates, credit rating or credit index, or other variable, provided in the case of a non-financial variable that the variable is not specific to a party to the contract. [IAS 39 para 10]. Variation of the cash flows over the contract's term is a critical indicator of the presence of one or more embedded derivatives. An example of a hybrid instrument is a loan that pays interest based on changes in the FTSE 100 index. The component of the contract that is to repay the principal amount is the host contract – this is the 'base state' with a pre-determined term and pre-determined cash flows. The component of the contract that is to pay interest based on changes in the FTSE 100 index is the embedded derivative – this component causes some or all of the cash flows of the host contract to change. A diagrammatic representation explaining the above terms is given below:

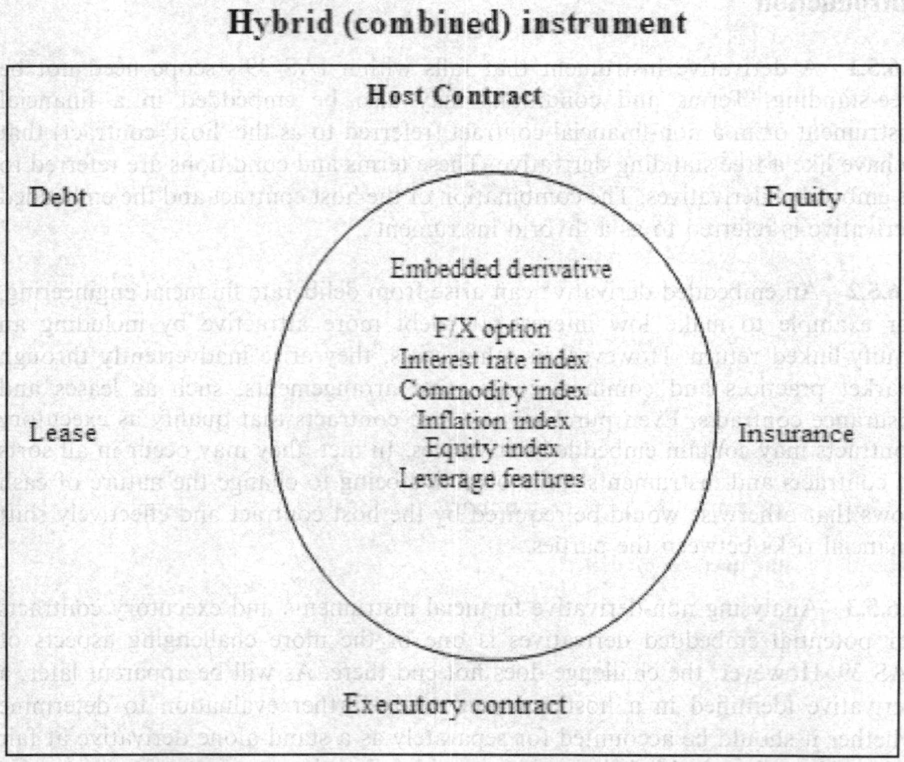

A6.5.5 A derivative that is attached to a financial instrument but is contractually transferable independently of that instrument, or has a different counterparty from that instrument, is not an embedded derivative, but a separate financial instrument [IAS 39 para 10]. An example is a bond with a detachable warrant where the owner of the bond-warrant package can exercise the warrant and buy shares for cash but keep the bond, unlike an owner of a convertible bond who has to give up the bond in order to exercise the option.

Conditions for separation

A6.5.6 IAS 39 states that an embedded derivative should be separated from the host contract and accounted for as a derivative if all of the following three conditions are met:

- the economic characteristics and risks of the embedded derivative are not closely related to the economic characteristics and risks of the host contract;
- a separate instrument with the same terms as the embedded derivative would meet the definition of a derivative; and
- the hybrid instrument is not measured at fair value with changes in fair value recognised in profit or loss.

[IAS 39 para 11].

A6.5.7 In relation to the third bullet point above, if a contract contains one or more embedded derivatives, an entity may designate the entire hybrid contract as a financial asset or financial liability at fair value through profit or loss unless:

- the embedded derivative(s) does not significantly modify the cash flows that otherwise would be required by the contract; or
- it is clear with little or no analysis when a similar hybrid instrument is first considered that separation of the embedded derivative(s) is prohibited, such as a pre-payment option embedded in a loan that permits the holder to pre-pay the loan for approximately its amortised cost.

[IAS 39 para 11A].

A6.5.8 These requirements are summarised in the diagram below.

Questions that need to be asked

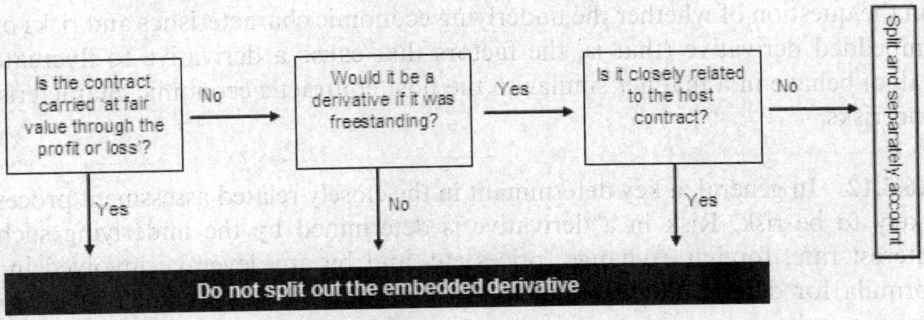

A6.5.9 The rationale for the above requirements is to ensure that all the underlying risks in an instrument are properly accounted for, which would not otherwise be apparent from the accounting. For instance, a debt host contract may contain an embedded derivative that exposes the contract to risks that are non-interest related. If there were no requirement to separate the non-interest related exposure from the host debt instrument, entities would be able to achieve an accounting result different from the accounting result that it would have achieved if it had issued two separate contracts. Therefore, separation of the embedded derivative not only ensures that the accounting faithfully represents the contract's underlying nature and its exposure to various risks, but also achieves consistency in accounting with freestanding derivatives. However, measuring an embedded derivative separately from its host contract requires judgment, and sometimes such measurements may be difficult. Therefore, as a practical expedient IAS 39 provides that an embedded derivative need not be separated if it is regarded as closely related to its host contract.

A6.5.10 Although the requirement to separate an embedded derivative from a host contract applies to both parties to a contract (that is, both the issuer and the holder of a hybrid instrument), the two parties to the contract might reach different accounting treatments when applying the decision tree in paragraph A6.5.8 above. For example, an equity conversion feature embedded in a convertible debt instrument denominated in the functional currency of the issuer is not closely related to the host debt instrument from the perspective of the holder of the instrument. However, from the issuer's perspective, the equity conversion option is an equity instrument and excluded from IAS 39's scope, provided it meets the conditions for that classification under IAS 32.

Interpretation of 'closely related'

A6.5.11 Once an embedded derivative is identified, it is necessary to consider whether its economic characteristics and risks (that is, the factors that cause the derivative to fluctuate in value) are closely related to the economic characteristics and risks of the host contract. IAS 39 does not provide a definition of 'closely related'. Instead, the application guidance to the standard provides examples of situations where the embedded derivative is, or is not, closely related to the host contract. Those examples have an underlying theme. They tend to focus attention on the question of whether the underlying economic characteristics and risks of an embedded derivative (that is, the factors that cause a derivative to fluctuate in value) behave in a manner similar to the host contract's economic characteristics and risks.

A6.5.12 In general, a key determinant in the closely related assessment process is likely to be risk. Risk in a derivative is determined by the underlying such as interest rate, foreign exchange, prices etc, and by any leverage involved in the formula for determining settlement. An embedded derivative such as a cap or floor on the interest rate (interest rate risk) that bears a close economic relationship to its host debt contract would be considered closely related. Conversely, when a derivative that is embedded in a debt instrument embodies an equity instrument's economic characteristics (for example, the derivative has a rate of return that is tied to the DAX 30 index), the economic characteristics of the derivative (equity-price risk) and host contract (interest rate risk) are different. In this situation, the embedded derivative would not be considered closely related to the host.

A6.5.12.1 The following example illustrates how quantitative as well as qualitative factors should be taken into account in determining whether the economic characteristics and risks of an embedded derivative are closely related to those of the host contract.

Example – Electricity contract linked to coal prices

Entity A, an electricity provider, has a number of electricity contracts that have prices linked to coal prices. Management believes that, from a qualitative perspective, the electricity price is linked to the price of coal, as coal is a major input to the electricity generation process. A quantitative analysis reveals that electricity prices are not directly correlated with coal prices.

A qualitative approach should be supported by quantitative analysis when determining whether the economic characteristics and risks of an embedded derivative are closely related to those of the host contract (that is in this case, when determining whether the coal price is closely related to the electricity price).

Whilst coal is an important input in the production of electricity, the price of electricity is driven by many other factors and therefore it is important to assess the extent to which the economic characteristics and risks of coal are in practice closely related to those of electricity. A quantitative assessment of correlation is relevant to this determination.

Leverage embedded features in host contracts

A6.5.13 Leverage embedded features can significantly modify some or all of the cash flows that otherwise would be required by the host contract. IAS 39 does not define the term 'leverage', although the term appears in several examples in paragraph AG33. In general, a hybrid instrument is said to contain embedded leverage features if some or all of its contractually required cash flows, determined by reference to changes in one or more underlyings, are modified in a manner that multiply or otherwise exacerbate the effect of those changes. An example of this would be a lease with payments linked to RPI multiplied by a factor of 2.5. It follows that the effect of leverage is only relevant for those embedded derivatives that are considered to be 'closely-related' to the non-derivative host contract. This is because embedded derivatives that are not 'closely-related' would have to be separated out from the host contract in any event, irrespective of whether they are considered to be leveraged.

A6.5.14 Although, in general, leverage has a multiplying effect, the standard does not quantify a numerical measure of leverage for closely related embedded derivatives. In other words, although it may be clear that any embedded feature that leverages the exposure of the host contract to more than an insignificant amount would require separation, no guidance is given as to what would constitute an acceptable threshold. An example of this would be a contract for delivery of paper where the price is linked to a pulp index, transportation index and relevant RPI where the indices are multiplied by percentages that reflect relative weighting of the cost factor in the production of paper. Such percentages would normally add up to 100 per cent. Since they represent leverage factors it has to be demonstrated that it was the normal way to price commercial contract in the market for paper at the time when the contract entered into. That could be done, for example, by reference to web sites of relevant industry associations, commodity or goods exchanges, etc. Therefore, judgement should be exercised after considering all relevant facts and circumstances that are specific to the situation.

Identifying the terms of embedded derivative and host contracts

A6.5.15 Because an assessment of whether an embedded derivative is 'closely related' to the host contract requires an understanding of the economic characteristics and risks of both the host contract and the derivative, it is necessary to consider the general principles that may be helpful in identifying the hosts and any derivatives that may be embedded in them.

A6.5.16 Determining the type of host should not cause undue difficulty in practice as its economic characteristics and risks are readily transparent. In practice, there is generally a handful of common types of host contracts that have derivatives embedded in them and these are stated below.

- Debt instruments.
- Equity instruments.
- Leases.
- Executory contracts such as purchase and sales contracts.
- Insurance contracts.

The economic characteristics and risks of each of these contracts are considered in the application section below. Other hosts may exist, but as these are likely to be rare they are not considered in this section.

A6.5.17 Difficulties begin to surface and become challenging when searching for derivatives that may be embedded in the above hosts. Because few hybrid contracts actually use the term 'derivative', a thorough evaluation a contract's terms must be performed to determine whether the contract contains an embedded derivative. Certain terms and phrases, however, may indicate the presence of an embedded derivative in a contract. Such terms and phrases may include:

- Pricing based on a formula.
- The right to purchase/sell additional units.
- Exchange/exchangeable into.
- Indexed to/adjusted by/referenced to.
- Premium/strike/limits.
- The right to cancel/extend/repurchase/return.

A6.5.18 Another method of determining whether a contract has an embedded derivative is to compare the terms of a contract (such as interest rate, maturity date(s), cancellation provisions, etc) with the corresponding terms of a similar, non-complex contract. In other words, an entity should ascertain whether there are differences between typical market terms and the terms of the contract that is being evaluated. An investigation of differences may uncover an embedded derivative.

6.5.18.1 The following list illustrates how the nature of a host contract and embedded derivative may be determined:

Instrument	Host contract	Embedded derivative
Convertible bond	Debt instrument	Purchased call option on equity securities
Debt paying interest quarterly based on an equity index	Debt instrument	Four forward contracts p.a. on equity index
A two-year fixed-quantity sales contract including maximum and minimum pricing limits	Purchase contract	Commodity price collar
A two-year fixed-quantity sale contract of mobile phones denominated in GBP between a French seller and German buyer both with Euro functional currencies	Purchase contract	Foreign currency forward contract

Assessment of closely related criterion

A6.5.19 It is clear that the assessment of the closely related criterion should be made when the contract is initially recognised, which is usually at inception of the contract. However, the standard is silent as to whether this initial assessment should be revisited during the contract's life. For example, an entity may determine, based on market conditions existing at the date of inception, that an embedded derivative in a host contract is closely related. Subsequently, market conditions change and the entity concludes that the embedded derivative is not closely related and, therefore, separate accounting may be required. The converse situation can also arise. The issue is whether in these circumstances the entity should make this reassessment, and if so, with what frequency.

A6.5.20 The above issue was considered by the IFRIC. IFRIC 9, 'Reassessment of embedded derivatives', reconfirms the treatment in the IAS 39 that an entity should assess whether an embedded derivative is required to be separated from the host contract and accounted for as a derivative when the entity first becomes a party to the contract. This initial assessment is not revised, unless the contractual terms change and the change significantly modifies the expected future cash flows associated with the embedded derivative, the host contract or both relative to the previously expected cash flows on the contract. [IFRIC 9 para 7]. It follows that if the market conditions change and the market was the principal factor in determining whether the host contract and the embedded derivative are closely related, no reassessment is required, unless the terms of the contracts are changed and the changes result in the revised expected cash flows being significantly different from the previously expected cash flows. An example is given below.

A6.5.21 Similarly, a first time adopter of IFRS should assess whether an embedded derivative is required to be separated from the host contract and accounted for as a derivative on the basis of the conditions that existed at the later of the date it first became a party to the contract and the date a reassessment is required by the above paragraph. [IFRIC 9 para 8]. It follows that as the conditions existing at the date the entity first adopts IFRS are of no relevance to the assessment of whether the embedded derivative is closely related or not, there is no difference in treatment between a continuing IFRS reporter and a first time adopter of IFRS. [IFRS 1 para IG 55].

Example – Re-assessment of embedded derivative

A UK entity entered into an 'own use' long-term electricity purchase contract in the late 1980s. At that time, there was no market for electricity. However, prices for gas and electricity were linked and, there was high correlation between the two prices. Hence, the price of the electricity contract was linked to gas prices. However, following deregulation of the energy market in the UK in the mid 1990s, the prices of gas and electricity are no longer correlated. On transition to IFRS, the contract has a remaining maturity of two years.

When considered at the date of transition to IFRS the price adjustment feature would have been regarded as closely related, reflecting market conditions prevailing at the date the contract was entered into. Given that there were no amendments to the terms of the contract, in accordance with paragraph A6.5.20 above, the initial assessment is not updated even though over time market conditions have changed and prices of gas and electricity are no longer correlated at the date of transition to IFRS.

On the other hand, if the entity entered into a similar contract after deregulation of the energy market, but before transition to IFRS, the price adjustment feature (electricity price in the contract is linked to gas prices and not market price of electricity) would not be regarded as closely related. Therefore, the embedded derivative would have to be separated and accounted for as a derivative at the date of transition to IFRS in accordance with paragraph A6.5.21 above.

Application of closely related criterion to different types of hosts

A6.5.22 As stated in paragraph A6.5.11 above, the application guidance to IAS 39 provides examples of situations where the embedded derivative is, or is not, closely related to the host contract. [IAS 39 paras AG30-AG33]. This guidance is not an exhaustive list of contract features or embedded derivatives. It contains many of the common features found in typical host contracts. Therefore, a considerable degree of judgement will be required to analyse situations that are not included in the standard's examples. However, as determining what is closely related can prove very challenging in practice, we have supplemented the standard's examples by providing additional examples where relevant. The following paragraphs deal with the application of the closely related criterion to different types of hosts and embedded derivatives.

Embedded derivatives in debt host contracts

A6.5.23 The most common host for an embedded derivative is a debt contract. However, it is first necessary to identify the host debt in the hybrid instrument. The implementation guidance states that the terms of the host debt instrument should reflect the stated or implied substantive terms of the hybrid instrument. [IAS 39 para IG C1]. For example, if the terms indicate that the host instrument has a stated or predetermined maturity and pays a fixed, floating or zero-coupon rate of interest, then its economic characteristics and risks are those of a debt instrument.

A6.5.24 In the absence of implied or stated terms, the entity makes its own judgement of the terms. However, in exercising such judgement, the entity should not endeavour to seek out a component that is not specified in the contract. Nor should it endeavour to establish terms of the host debt instrument in a manner that would result in the separation of an embedded derivative that is not already clearly present in the hybrid instrument, that is to say, it cannot create a cash flow that does not exist. For example, if a five-year debt instrument has fixed interest payments of C40,000 annually and a principal payment at maturity of C1 million multiplied by the change in an equity price index, it would be inappropriate to identify a floating rate host contract and an embedded equity swap that has an offsetting floating rate leg in lieu of identifying a fixed rate host. In that example, the host contract is a fixed rate debt instrument that pays C40,000 annually, because there are no floating interest rate cash flows in the hybrid instrument. [IAS 39 para IG C1].

A6.5.25 The value of a debt instrument is determined by the interest rate that is associated with the contract. The interest rate stipulated in the debt instrument is usually a function of the following factors:

- Risk free interest rate.
- Credit risk.
- Expected maturity.
- Liquidity risk.

Thus, embedded derivatives that affect the yield on debt instruments because of any of the above factors would be considered to be closely related (unless they are leveraged or do not change in the same direction as interest rates such as an inverse floater in example 3 of para A6.5.30 below). On the other hand, if the economic characteristics and risks of the embedded derivatives have features that are unrelated to interest rates (such as equity or commodity features), they would not be considered to be closely related to the debt host. Examples relating to the application of closely related criterion to a debt host and different types of derivatives embedded in it are considered in the paragraphs that follow.

Indexed linked interest payments

A6.5.26 It is not uncommon for debt instruments to contain embedded interest rate indices that can change the amount of interest that would otherwise be paid or received. Typical interest rate indices are LIBOR and the prime rate index. More complex ones include leveraged interest rate indices, such as levered inverse floaters, range floaters, etc.

A6.5.27 An embedded derivative in which the underlying is an interest rate or interest rate index that can change the amount of interest that would otherwise be paid or received on an interest-bearing host debt contract (or insurance contract) is closely related to the host contract unless:

- the combined instrument can be settled in such a way that the holder would not recover *substantially all* of its recognised investment; or
- the embedded derivative *could* at least double the holder's initial rate of return on the host contract *and could* result in a rate of return that is at least twice what the market return would be for a contract with the same terms as the host contract.

[IAS 39 para AG 33(a)].

Note that this assessment is made when the entity becomes party to the contract and on the basis of market conditions existing then (see para A6.5.20).

A6.5.28 An example of an instrument meeting the first condition would be a bond callable by the issuer at an amount significantly lower than its fair value. Should the issuer decide to exercise the call option (that is, repurchase the bond) the holder would be required to sell it and, therefore, not recover substantially all of its recognised investment. The first condition that *"the holder would not recover substantially all of its recognised investment"* is not satisfied if the terms of the combined instrument permit, but do not require, the investor to settle the combined instrument in a manner that causes it not to recover substantially all of its recognised investment and the issuer has no such right (for example, a puttable debt instrument). Accordingly, an interest-bearing host contract with an embedded interest rate derivative with such terms is regarded as closely related to the host contract. The condition that *"the holder would not recover substantially all of its recognised investment"* applies to situations in which the holder can be forced to accept settlement at an amount that causes the holder not to recover substantially all of its recognised investment. [IAS 39 para IG C10]. The term 'substantially all' is not defined in IAS 39 and, therefore, judgment should be exercised after considering all the relevant facts and circumstances that are specific to the situation.

A6.5.29 The second condition has two parts and, therefore, both these parts should be met for the embedded derivative not to be considered closely related. So, for example, if the embedded derivative feature results in doubling the initial return under a possible future interest rate scenario no matter how remote, but, at the same time, that interest rate scenario would not result in a rate of return that is at least twice what the then-current market return would be for a contract that has the same terms as the host, then only one part of the condition would have been met and the embedded derivative would be regarded as closely related to the host.

A6.5.30 The above provisions are intended to 'scope in' those embedded derivatives that cause the hybrid instrument to perform less like a debt instrument and more like a derivative (for example, hybrid instruments that are highly leveraged). The following examples illustrate the application of the above guidance to various interest rate index linked debt instruments.

Example 1 – Floating rate debt

Entity A takes out a floating rate loan with a bank. The contractually determined interest rate on the debt is six-month LIBOR plus two percentage points (assuming credit spread is two percentage points).

A plain vanilla floating rate instrument with a normal credit spread that is always reset to market interest rate cannot contain an embedded derivative.

Example 2 – Floating rate debt with investor payment provision

Entity A issues a floating rate debt with a face value of C50m. The contractually determined interest rate on the debt is six-month LIBOR. However, there is a provision that if six-month LIBOR increases by 200 basis points, the investor will pay C2m to the issuing company.

In this situation, the embedded derivative consists of a contingent payment provision that depends on the LIBOR increasing by 200 basis points in any year. The embedded derivative is not separated, because the investor will receive C50m and the C2m payment is not considered to reduce its initial investment substantially. Therefore, the first condition in paragraph A6.5.27 above is not met. Furthermore, there is no provision in the contract that causes the investor's yield to increase to at least twice the initial rate. Therefore, the second condition is not met. According, the embedded derivative is closely related to the debt host and no separation is necessary. The fact that LIBOR may increase by 200 basis points in a year is simply a condition that triggers the payment and is not relevant to determining whether the embedded derivative is closely related.

Example 3 – Leveraged inverse floater

Entity A takes out a loan with a bank. The contractually determined interest rate on the debt is calculated as 14.5% — 2.5 × three-month LIBOR (sometimes referred to as a leveraged inverse floater).

Three-month LIBOR at inception = 4% giving an initial yield of 4.5%.

The embedded derivative has an underlying that is highly leveraged such that there is the possibility of either a negative yield or a significantly higher than market yield. This is because, if under a future interest rate scenario three-month LIBOR increases to 6%, the yield would be negative, that is, -0.5% (14.5% — 15%) and the investor would not be able to recover substantially all of its recognised investment. Therefore, as the first condition in paragraph A6.5.27 above is satisfied, the embedded derivative is not closely related to the host contract and will be accounted for separately. In practice sometimes the yield will not be allowed to go negative. To prevent this happening, a floor is often imposed on the coupon rate.

Note that in this example there is no need to evaluate the second condition in paragraph A6.5.27 above. But if this condition were to be evaluated the result would be the same, that is, the embedded derivative would not be considered closely related to the host debt contract. This is because, for example, if under a future interest rate scenario, three-month LIBOR falls to 2%, the yield would be 9% which is twice the initial yield of 4.5%. Furthermore, the yield of 9% is also likely to be twice the then market yield for a contract with the same terms as the host.

Example 4 – Forward starting interest rate swap

Entity A issues a 8% fixed rate debt instrument that matures at the end of year 5. The entity has an option to convert the loan into a variable rate debt at LIBOR + 3% after two years. LIBOR at inception is 5%.

The embedded derivative included in the above debt host is an option on a forward starting interest rate swap that changes the fixed rate interest payments to floating rate after two years. In order to determine whether the option on the forward starting swap should be accounted for as a separate derivative, it is necessary to apply the second condition in paragraph A6.5.28 above.

Accordingly, if, under a future interest rate scenario (however remote), LIBOR increases to 14%, the increase would have the effect of more than doubling the initial return on the investment from 8% to 17% (14% + 3%). However, that interest rate scenario of 14% does not result in a market rate of interest that is twice the current market rate for a contract with the same terms as the host contract, which is only 17% assuming no change in credit rating. Therefore, as only one part of the second condition in paragraph A6.5.29 is satisfied, the embedded option on the forward starting interest rate swap is closely related to the debt host and no separation is permitted.

Inflation-linked interest and principal payments

A6.5.31 There is a very close relationship between interest rates and inflation in an economy. The nominal rate of interest is often thought of as the real interest rate (the amount earned on a sum loaned or deposited in a bank) plus the rate of inflation. The more precise version that allows for the compounding effect is given by the following relationship know as the Fisher equation:

$$1 + n = (1 + r)(1 + i)$$

where:
n = nominal interest rate

r = real rate of interest
i = expected inflation rate

A6.5.32 The above equation illustrates that the nominal interest rate reflects compensation to the lender for expected decreases, due to inflation, in the purchasing power of the principal and interest during the course of the loan. In other words, the nominal interest rate will vary directly with the expected rate of inflation, indicating that, in general, there is a strong correlation between the two.

A6.5.33 A strong correlation is particularly true for a country whose interest and inflation rates are managed together as part of the country's monetary policy decisions. For example, the Bank of England in the UK, like the Federal reserve system in the US, is responsible for setting interest rates that are aimed at accommodating economic growth in an environment of stable prices. Consider, however, countries in the Eurozone where the interest rate is set by the European Central Bank (ECB). Although the ECB sets short-term interest rates aimed at maintaining inflation rates in the Eurozone below, but close to, two per cent (measured by year-on-year increase in the Harmonised Index of Consumer Prices) over the medium term, the inflation rate in a particular country within the Eurozone may be different from overall Eurozone inflation due to, for example, differences in national rates of growth, local market regulation, etc.

A6.5.34 Therefore, where a company issues a debt instrument where the amount of interest or the principal to be repaid or both is linked to an inflation index, it would be necessary to perform both a qualitative and quantitative analysis to determine whether the underlying inflation index is closely related. This analysis should be performed on a case by case basis and would include at least the following considerations:

- Demonstration via a regression analysis to support the contention that there is a long run statistically significant relationship between the interest rate specified in the debt instrument denominated in the currency of the economy and the inflation measure defined in that debt instrument.
- The inflation index is the one that is a recognised measure of inflation in the economic environment in which the loan originates. If the inflation index relates to a different economy or is not one that is commonly used for the purpose of lending and borrowing, the underlying inflation index will not be regarded as closely related to the debt host. In the UK, inflation indices that are most commonly used are the retail price index and the consumer price index. Therefore, no other inflation indices will be appropriate where the bond is linked to UK interest rate indices.
- The inflation adjustment is related to the same period that the interest payments relate.
- The resulting real rate of return delivered by the inflation linked debt is itself a rate that would not be considered an embedded derivative under IAS 39 and is not dissimilar to market estimates of real rates at the time when the debt is issued.

- The inflation index is not leveraged in any way.
- A judgmental qualitative analysis to support the potential arguments that any short term deviations from the defined relationship are not indicative that the two measures are no longer closely related. For example, it is likely that short-term deviations between the two measures may indicate a disparity in a country whose interest and inflation rates are not managed together as part of the country's monetary policy decisions aimed at maintaining price stability.
- A quantitative analysis that the inflation index would not result in the rate of return on the debt instrument that would at least double the holder's initial rate of return on the instrument or at any point would not exceed twice what the market rate would be a contract with the same terms as the host debt instrument.

A6.5.35 An entity issuing an inflation linked bond would need to perform the above analysis at inception to determine whether the inflation index is closely related to the host debt instrument. If the above conditions are not met, the embedded derivative would have to be separated from the host contract and accounted for as a derivative.

Example – Inflation-linked bond

A UK entity issues an inflation-linked sterling bond that pays a fixed interest of 5% per annum. The return of the principal amount is linked to UK Retail Price Index (RPI), which is a recognised headline measure of inflation in the economic environment in which the entity operates.

As the coupon on the bond is 5%, and the underlying principal of the bond is £100, the bond pays £5 interest per annum. If the inflation index increases to 10%, the principal of the bond would then increase to £110 and the interest payment increases to £5.50 (5% × C110).

In this example, as the principal payment is non-leveraged and indexed to the headline measure of inflation in the economic environment in which the entity operates and, assuming all the other conditions in the above paragraph are met, the inflation index is regarded as closely related to the host debt instrument.

Equity and commodity linked interest and principal payments

A6.5.36 Equity-indexed interest or principal payments embedded in a host debt instrument or insurance contract – by which the amount of interest or principal is indexed to the value of equity instruments – are not closely related to the host instrument, because the risks inherent in the host and the embedded derivative are dissimilar. [IAS 39 para AG 30(d)]. Similarly, commodity-indexed interest or principal payments embedded in a host debt instrument or insurance contract – by which the amount of interest or principal is indexed to the price of a commodity (such as gold) – are not closely related to the host instrument, because the risks inherent in the host and the embedded derivative are dissimilar. [IAS 39 para AG 30(e)]. Therefore, where interest and principal payments in a debt instrument are indexed to an equity-index, a commodity index or any other non-financial index, the embedded derivative must be accounted for separately.

Example 1 – Cash settled put option in a convertible bond

Entity A issues convertible bonds to entity H. The term of the bonds is 3 years and the par value is C2m. Each bond pays fixed interest annually at 6% a year and is convertible at any time by entity H until maturity into entity A's ordinary shares. Entity H also has the option to put the convertible bond back to entity A for cash at par.

Entity A has determined that the market rate for a loan with comparable credit status and providing substantially the same cash flows on the same terms, but without the conversion option, is 7%.

Entity A's management should separate the convertible bond's equity and liability elements. [IAS 32 para 28]. The conversion option is an equity instrument of entity A since it can only be settled by physical delivery of a fixed number of shares for a fixed amount of cash or other financial assets. It is not accounted for as a derivative. [IAS 39 para 2(d)].

The option to put the convertible bond back to entity A for cash at par is an embedded derivative. This option is closely related to the host debt instrument, as the exercise price is approximately equal to the bond's amortised cost before separating the equity element under IAS 32. [IAS 39 para AG30(g)].

Management should, therefore, determine the present value of the bond's cash flows by discounting expected cash flows using the 7% market rate of interest for a similar bond and attribute the balance to the equity component. [IAS 32 para AG31].

Example 2 – Call option linked to an equity index

An entity issues a debt instrument at par with a term of five years. The debt is callable by the issuer 3 years after issue. If the debt is called, the holder will receive a sum that is the greater of the par value of the debt or the par value as adjusted by the percentage increase in the FTSE 100 index.

The embedded call option that is exercisable 3 years after the issue of the debt instrument is not closely related to the debt host as the payoff is indexed to an equity index. The equity linked feature provides an upside to the investor, which is linked to an index representing different risks from those of the ordinary debt instrument. Hence, the option should be separated from the host debt instrument and accounted for separately.

Example 3 – Payments linked to share price of UK plc

An entity issues a debt instrument at par with a term of five years. The debt is also redeemable at par. However, the loan agreement provides that during the term of the loan the entity will either receive or pay an amount based on the changes in the share price of an unrelated listed company A plc, the reference point being the market price of A plc at the date of issue of the debt instrument.

As the interest payments are based on the changes in the price of an equity instrument (equity risk), they are not closely related to the host debt instrument (characterised mainly by interest rate and credit risk). Therefore, the embedded equity linked amounts should be separated by both the issuer and the holder of the debt instrument and recorded on the balance sheet at fair value, with subsequent changes in fair value recognised in the income statement.

The answer would be the same if the interest or principal payments were linked to the movement in an equity index, such as S&P500 and even if they were linked to the market price of the entity's own shares as explained in paragraph A6.5.36 above.

Example 4 – Equity linked bond with repayment floor

Entity A purchases a one-year debt instrument issued by bank B for its principal amount of C1,000 on the issue date. Bank B will make no interest payments during the life of the instrument. At maturity the holder will receive the principal amount plus any increase in the S&P 500 index since the issue date. The fair value of an at-the-money European option maturing in one year is C48 at issuance date.

Entity A classifies the debt instrument as held-to-maturity.

Management should recognise the hybrid instrument as a combination of a call option and a zero-coupon debt instrument. Entity A should first determine the option contract's fair value and strike price. [IAS 39 para AG 28].

Since the holder only receives increases in the value of the index since the issue date, the embedded option is at the money at the date of issue and its fair value consists only of its time value and no intrinsic value. Consequently, its fair value at the issue date is C48 and the balance of the consideration given (C1000 – C48 = C952) is attributed to the carrying amount of the zero-coupon debt instrument.

The zero-coupon host contract should be recognised at amortised cost with interest accreted at the original effective interest rate of 5% to reach C1,000 at maturity. The option should be recognised at fair value against the benchmark of C1,000, with gains or losses recognised in the income statement.

Example 5 – Commodity linked bond

A gold mining company issues a debt instrument with a face value of C10m and contingent interest payments in addition to a guaranteed minimum interest payment of 4% per annum. The contingent payments are linked to the price of gold such that an additional interest payment of 0.5% would be paid for every US$25 increase in gold price above US$260. The price of gold at issue date was US$310 per ounce. The market rate for a fixed interest loan is 5%.

A commodity linked bond such as the one described above enables the issuer to reduce its financing cost by offering contingent payments to investors, whilst the investor is assured of a guaranteed minimum, but able to participate in any increase in the price of gold.

In this situation, the issuer would be viewed as having (a) issued a host debt instrument at a market rate of interest of 5%; and (b) purchased a swap contract to receive 1% fixed interest and pay a variable amount equal to the movement in the gold price above US$260. The swap contract is not closely related to the debt instrument as the factors that cause the swap to change in value (commodity price risk) are not the same as the factors that cause the debt host to change in value (interest rate risk).

Accordingly, the embedded swap contract should be separated from the host contract by both the issuer and the holder and recorded on the balance sheet at fair value, with subsequent changes in fair value recognised in the income statement.

6A.5.37 Example 1 in the previous paragraph dealt with call options held by the issuer. A similar treatment arises in circumstances where the holder has the right to put the debt instrument back to the issuer in exchange for an amount of cash or other financial assets that varies on the basis of the change in an equity or commodity index that may increase or decrease. These instruments are commonly referred to as 'puttable instruments'. Unless the issuer on initial recognition designates the puttable instrument as a financial liability at fair value through profit or loss, it is required to separate an embedded derivative (that is, the indexed payment). [IAS 39 paras AG30(a), AG31].

Interest rate caps, floors and collars

A6.5.38 Floating rate securities may have a maximum coupon that is paid at any reset date. The maximum coupon rate is called a cap. For example, suppose for a floating rate note with a coupon of three-month LIBOR + 50 basis points, there is a cap of eight per cent. If the three-month LIBOR at the coupon reset date is eight per cent, then the coupon rate would be eight and a half per cent. However, the cap would restrict the coupon rate to eight per cent. Therefore, a cap can be attractive to the issuing company as a protection against rises in interest rates. A cap can be thought of as an embedded option requiring no action by the issuer to take advantage of a rise in interest rates. Effectively, the bondholder has granted to the issuer the right not to pay more than the cap. For the grant of this privilege, the issuer of the bond (the cap buyer) will have to pay a premium that will increase the overall cost of funds. If the relevant/market interest rate rises above the cap strike rate, then payments are made by the seller to the buyer to compensate for the excess. This means that the cap is in-the-money whenever the strike rate is the lower than the relevant/market rate of interest. It is out-of-the-money whenever the strike rate is above the relevant/market rate of interest.

A6.5.39 In contrast, there could be a minimum coupon rate specified for a floating rate security. The minimum coupon rate is called a floor. If the coupon formula provides a coupon rate that is below the floor, the floor rate is paid instead. A floor is the mirror image of a cap. While a cap benefits the issuer if interest rates rise, a floor benefits the bondholder if interest rate falls. As with other options, the buyer must pay a premium to the issuer of the bond (the cap seller) that will reduce the issuer's overall cost of funds. If the coupon rate falls below the floor strike rate then payments are made by the seller to the buyer to compensate for the shortfall. This means that the floor is in-the-money whenever the strike rate is the above the relevant/market rate of interest. It is out-of-the-money whenever the strike rate is lower than the relevant/market rate of interest.

A6.5.40 A floating rate security can have a cap and a floor. This feature is referred to as a collar. The buyer of a collar limits the maximum rate that he will pay and sets a minimum rate that he will pay and, therefore, will be exposed to interest rate movements within a range. Hence, as long as interest rates are within this band, no payment is made or received by the buyer and the collar is said to be out-of-the-money.

A6.5.41 An embedded floor or cap on the interest rate on a debt contract is closely related to the host contract, provided when the instrument is issued:

- the floor is at or below the market rate of interest (out-of-the-money); or
- the cap is at or above the market rate of interest (out-of-the-money); and
- the cap or floor is not leveraged in relation to the host contract.

[IAS 39 para AG 33(b)].

A6.5.42 Since the assessment of whether the cap or floor is closely related to the host is made when the debt is issued and is not revised subsequently, it follows from the above that only in-the-money caps and floors at inception or leverage provision would fail the closely related test. Therefore, a derivative embedded in a variable rate debt instrument that has a floor on the interest rate would not be separated from the host and accounted for separately, even though, in a falling interest rate environment, the debt instrument may have a return to the investor that is significantly above the market return of a similar debt instrument that does not contain a floor provision. Similar considerations apply to caps.

Example – Debt subject to an interest rate collar

Company A has borrowed cash from a bank. The debt is interest-bearing at a variable rate, but within a collar. The variable rate on the date of inception of the loan was 7%, the floor was 5% and the cap was 9%.

In this situation, the embedded derivative is a collar that modifies the cash flows of variable rate debt if the variable rate moves outside the range of the collar. IAS 39 does not specifically deal with collars, although the guidance relating to caps and floors can be extended to collars. Since at the time when the variable rate debt instrument is issued, the interest rate is 7%, which is within the collar, the collar is out-of-the-money. Hence, based on the guidance in paragraph A6.5.41 above, the embedded collar is regarded as closely related and separate accounting for the embedded derivative is prohibited.

Calls, puts and pre-payment options

A6.5.43 The terms of a debt instrument may include an issuer call option (a callable bond), that is, a right of the issuer (but not the investor) to redeem the instrument early and pay a fixed price (generally at a premium over the par value). There may also be other pre-payment features that cause the whole or part of the outstanding principal to be repaid early. Adding call options and/or other pre-payment options should make it less attractive to buyers, since it reduces the potential upside on the bond. As interest rates go down and the bond price increases, the bonds are likely to be called back. Alternatively, the investor may have a put option to force early redemption of the outstanding principal. Such call option, put option and pre-payment features that are embedded in the debt host are derivatives.

A6.5.44 The application guidance explains that these embedded derivatives are not closely related to the host debt contract, unless the option's exercise price is approximately equal on each exercise date to the host debt instrument's amortised cost. [IAS 39 para AG 30(g)].

Example 1 – Calls and puts in debt instruments

An entity issues the following debt instruments:

- 5 year zero coupon debt for proceeds of C7m with a face value of C10m; issue costs are insignificant. The debt is callable by the issuer at its amortised cost calculated on the basis of the effective interest rate method in the event of a change in control.
- 5 year zero coupon debt for proceeds of C7m with a face value of C10m; issue costs are insignificant. The debt is puttable at its face value in the event the issuer has an initial public offering (IPO).

In both scenarios above, the zero coupon debt will be recorded at its fair value of C7m, which is the consideration received. The debt will accrete to its final value of C10m at maturity in year 5. Therefore, between inception and maturity the debt's amortised cost will not be the same as its face value, except in the period close to maturity.

In the first scenario, if the debt is called by the issuer at its amortised cost, the call option does not accrete the repayment of principal as the option's exercise price is the same as the debt's amortised cost (the exercise price is not fixed but variable), even though the debt was initially issued at a substantial discount. Therefore, in accordance with paragraph AG 30(g) of IAS 39, the call option is closely related to the debt host and would not be accounted for separately.

In the second scenario, if the debt is put back by the holder at its face value before maturity, the put option's exercise price of C10m (fixed at the outset) would not be the same as the debt's amortised cost at exercise date. Therefore, in accordance with paragraph AG 30(g) of IAS 39, the put option is not closely related to the debt host. This means that the put option must be bifurcated and separately accounted for.

Even though both debt instruments contain terms that allow the debts to be called or put back on the occurrence of a contingent event (change in control or IPO) and these terms (relating to factors other than interest rate risk and credit risk of the issuer) are not closely related to the debt hosts, determining whether the call or the put option is closely related is based solely on the difference between the option's exercise price and the debt's amortised cost and not on any trigger events (contingent or otherwise).

Example 2 – Pre-payment option in debt instruments

Entity A takes out a fixed rate loan with a bank for C1m. The loan is repayable in quarterly instalments. The debt contains a pre-payment option that may be exercised by entity A on the first day of each quarter. The exercise price is the remaining capital amount outstanding on the debt plus a penalty of C100,000.

At inception, entity A would record the financial liability at its fair value of C1m. As entity A makes repayments of capital to the bank, the amortised cost of the debt will change.

The exercise price of the pre-payment option at inception is C1m plus the penalty of C100,000. Whether the entity will exercise its option to pre-pay the loan early may depend on a number of reasons, but the level of interest rates is a critical variable. If there is a significant decline in interest rates, any potential gain from early pre-payment may well be more that the cost of the pre-payment (the penalty payable).

Therefore, given the penalty payable is fixed, the option's exercise price (outstanding principal + penalty) will always exceed the debt's amortised cost at each option exercise date as the loan is paid off in instalments. Hence, the pre-payment option is not closely related to the debt host and should be separately accounted for. The fair value of the option would need to be calculated and this will be a positive value to the entity as the value of the pre-payable bond = value of straight bond − value of pre-payment feature. If interest rates decline, the option's value will increase making it more attractive to the entity to repay the debt early.

Sometimes the pre-payment option's exercise price is a 'market adjusted value'. A market adjusted value is calculated by discounting the contractual guaranteed amount payable at the end of the specified term to present value using the current market rate that would be offered on a new loan having a maturity period equal to the remaining maturity period of the current loan. As a result, the market adjusted value may be positive or negative, depending upon market interest rates at each option exercise date. In that situation, the pre-payment option enables the holder simply to cash out of the instrument at fair value at the date of pre-payment. Since the holder receives only the market adjusted value, which is equal to the fair value of the loan at the date of pre-payment, the pre-payment option has a fair value of zero at all times. Infact, on a stand-alone basis, the pre-payment option with a strike price equal to market value would not meet the definition of a derivative, so it cannot be an embedded derivative.

6A.5.45 An embedded pre-payment option in an interest-only or principal-only strip (that is, an interest or principal cash flow stream that has been separated and payable at different dates) is closely related to the host contract provided the host contract:

- initially resulted from separating the right to receive contractual cash flows of a financial instrument that, in and of itself, did not contain an embedded derivative; and
- does not contain any terms not present in the original host debt contract.

[IAS 39 para AG 33(e)].

Term-extending options

A6.5.46 Sometimes clauses are included in debt instruments that allow the issuer to extend the debt's term beyond its original maturity. An option or automatic provision to extend the remaining term to maturity of a debt instrument is not closely related to the host debt instrument, unless there is a concurrent adjustment to the approximate current market rate of interest at the time of the extension. [IAS 39 para AG 30(c)]. Thus, if there is no reset of interest rates at the time of the extension, the embedded derivative is not closely related to the debt host.

Example 1 – Term-extending options not reset to market rates

An entity issues 6% fixed rate debt that has a fixed term of 3 years. The entity is able to extend the debt before its maturity for an additional 2 year period at the same 6% interest.

In this example, as the entity is able to extend the debt's term at the same interest rate and there is no reset to current market rates, the term extending option is not considered to be closely related to the debt host.

Such term-extending options could be valuable to the entity as it allows the issuer to refinance the debt at the same interest rate when market rates are rising. Similarly, if market rates are falling, the entity would not exercise its options to extend. Therefore, the option is a derivative that would need to be separated from the debt host and accounted for separately, even though its value is closely related to interest rates that also affect the value of the underlying debt host.

The above treatment regarding term-extending options is justified, because otherwise such options could be used to circumvent the requirement to bifurcate a derivative in circumstances where the investor might not recover substantially all its initial recorded investment (see further para A6.5.27 above). Term-extending options in host debt typically involve postponement of the repayment of the principal and, even though such postponement does not cause the failure to recover substantially all of its initial recorded investment, it can significantly reduce the fair value of the recovery of that investment.

Example 2 – Term-extending option reset to market rates.

An entity issues a 6% fixed rate debt that has a fixed term of 3 years. The company is able to extend the debt before its maturity for an additional 2 year period, but the rate for the period of extension is the market rate at the time of the extension.

In this example, as the option to extend the term causes the interest rate to reset to current market rates, the option is regarded as closely related to the host debt. Common sense would also suggest such an option has no real value to the entity. This is because if the market interest rate at the time of extension is 8%, the entity cannot extend the term without paying an additional 2% interest anyway. On the other hand, if the market interest rate drops to 4%, the extension is equivalent to taking out a new loan at 4%.

6A.5.47 If an entity issues a debt instrument and the holder of that debt instrument writes a call option on the debt instrument to a third party, the issuer regards the call option as extending the term to maturity of the debt instrument provided the issuer can be required to participate in or facilitate the remarketing of the debt instrument as a result of the call option being exercised. [IAS 39 para AG 30 (c)].

A6.5.48 It is interesting to note that a bond that has a put option is economically no different to one that has a term-extending option, yet IAS 39 prescribes a different treatment for the derivatives embedded in them. Consider the following example:

Example – Comparison of put and extension option

An entity purchasers two bonds A and B with the following terms:

- Bond A has a stated maturity of 10 years, but the entity can put it back to the issuer at par after 3 years.
- Bond B has a stated maturity of 3 years, but after 3 years the entity can extend the maturity to 10 years (that is, 7 more years) at the same initial rate (that is, the interest rate is not reset to the interest rate at the date of extension).

Both bonds are issued by the same issuer at par and have a coupon rate of 6%.

Assume also that the following two scenarios exist at the end of year 3:

Scenario 1: For the issuer, the interest rate for 7 year debt is at 8%.

- The holder will put bond A back to the issuer and reinvest the par amount of the bond at 8%.
- The holder will not extend the maturity of bond B and, instead, will reinvest the principal at 8%.

Scenario 2: For the issuer, the interest rate for 7 year debt is at 4%.

- The holder will not put bond A back to the issuer and, instead, will continue to receive 6% for the next 7 years.
- The holder will extend the term of bond B and continue to receive 6% for the next 7 years.

As can be seen from the above, the entity is in the same position with respect to either Bond A or Bond B. However, IAS 39 prescribes a different treatment for the put and the term extension options embedded in Bond A and Bond B respectively.

As discussed in paragraph A6.5.44 above, the embedded put option derivative in Bond A is regarded as closely related to the Bond as the bond's amortised cost based on the effective interest rate at the end of three years is the same as par, which is also the put option's exercise price. This is because the expected cash flows would take into account the possibility of the debt being pre-paid early for the purposes of calculating the effective interest rate. [IAS 39 para 9]. Therefore, the embedded put option would not be recognised separately and fair valued.

On the other hand, the embedded term extension option is not regarded as closely related to the host debt, because under Bond B's terms the interest rates are not reset when the option is exercised. Therefore, the option would be separated and fair valued.

The above example illustrates that two instruments that are economically similar, but different in form by virtue of the way in which the terms of the embedded options are expressed, can lead to different accounting treatments for the embedded options.

To be able to rationalise the apparent conflict in accounting treatment between these two economically identical situations, it is necessary to consider the issuer's expectation of the instrument's life for the purposes of the effective interest rate calculation. Thus the issuer will not follow the legal form of the terms, but the economics in determining whether the instrument has a put option or a term extending option and thus the appropriate accounting treatment.

Credit sensitive payments and credit derivatives

A6.5.49 IAS 39 does not deal specifically with payments based on the creditworthiness of the issuer of an instrument. However, as the stated in paragraph A6.5.25 above, the creditworthiness of the issuer is a key factor in setting the level of interest rate on the debt instrument. Thus, for debt instruments that provide for the interest rate to be reset in the event of a change in the issuer's published credit rating (say down from A to BBB) or a change in the issuer's creditworthiness, the embedded derivative would be closely related to the debt host, and so would not be separated from the host contract.

Example – Credit sensitive payments

Entity A issues two types of coupon step-up bonds as follows:

- Bond A requires the issuer to pay an additional coupon to bondholders in the event of deterioration in the issuer's credit rating below a specified level. The coupon payable on the bond will return to the initial fixed rate in the event that the issuer's credit rating returns to the specified level.
- Bond B requires the issuer to pay an additional coupon to bondholders in the event of deterioration in the issuer's interest cover ratio (calculated as profit before interest divided by interest expense) below a specified level. The coupon payable on the bond will return to the initial fixed rate in the event that the issuer's interest cover ratio returns to the specified level.

The coupon step-up clause in each case meets the definition of a derivative as the value fluctuates in response to an underlying (credit rating); it requires no initial net investment and it is settled at a future date.

The economic characteristics and risks of the embedded derivatives in both cases are closely related to the economic characteristics and risks of the host bond because:

- both the embedded derivative and the host contract are driven by changes in the issuer's credit rating (credit risk); and
- such clauses do not transfer the credit risk to another party external to the original contractual relationships created by the debt instrument (see para A6.5.50 below).

The two embedded derivatives are not accounted for separately from the host debt contract.

Embedded derivatives in host contracts

6A.5.50 IAS 39 does, however, deal with credit derivatives that are embedded in host debt instruments. A credit derivative is a financial instrument designed to transfer credit risk from the person exposed to that risk to a person willing to take on that risk. The derivative derives its economic value by reference to a specified debt obligation, often described as the 'reference asset'.

A6.5.51 Credit derivatives that are embedded in a host debt instrument and allow one party (the 'beneficiary') to transfer the credit risk of a particular reference asset, which it may not own, to another party (the 'guarantor') are not closely related to the host debt instrument. Such credit derivatives allow the guarantor to assume the credit risk associated with the reference asset without directly owning it. [IAS 39 para 30(h)].

Example – Credit-linked note

An investment bank issues a credit-linked note to another party (the investor) in return for a consideration equal to the par value of the note. The coupon on the note is linked to the credit risk of a portfolio of third party bonds (the reference asset). In economic terms, the credit-linked note comprises a fixed income instrument with an embedded credit derivative.

The embedded credit derivative must be accounted for separately as it is linked to credit risks of debt instruments issued by third parties and not to the credit risk of the host debt instrument issued by the investment bank. The notion of an embedded derivative in a hybrid instrument refers to provisions incorporated into a single contract and not to provisions in separate contracts between different counterparties.

Equity conversion features

A6.5.52 When an investor holds debt securities that are convertible into the issuer's equity shares at the investor's option, the equity conversion feature represents an embedded written option on the issuer's equity shares. The embedded derivative is not closely related to the host debt instrument from the investor's perspective. [IAS 39 para IG C3]. From the issuer's perspective, the written equity conversion option is an equity instrument and excluded from IAS 39's scope provided it meets the conditions for that classification under IAS 32. [IAS 39 para AG 30(f)]. If, on the other hand, the debt instrument is convertible (or exchangeable) into shares of another entity, both the issuer and the holder would have to separate the embedded derivative from the host contract.

A6.5.53 If the holder of a convertible bond is required to separate the embedded derivative, the holder is generally precluded from accounting for the debt host contract as a held-to-maturity investment. This is because classification as a held-to-maturity investment would be inconsistent with paying for the conversion feature – the right to convert into equity shares before maturity. However, the investor will be able to classify the bond as an available-for-sale financial asset provided it is not purchased for trading purposes. If the bond is classified as available-for-sale (that is, fair value changes are recognised directly in equity until the bond is sold), the equity conversion option (the embedded derivative) is separated. The accounting for the holder, which is significantly different from the issuer and considered in section 7, is as follows:

- The embedded derivative's fair value (the equity conversion option from the issuer's perspective) is calculated first and this becomes the embedded derivative's fair value. The option's fair value comprises its time value and its intrinsic value, if any. The option has value on initial recognition even when it is out of the money.

  After initial recognition, the embedded derivative is constantly remeasured at fair value at each balance sheet date and changes in the fair value are recognised in profit or loss, unless the option is part of a cash flow hedging relationship.

- The carrying value of the host contract (the liability component from the issuer's perspective) is assigned the residual amount after deducting from the fair value of the instrument as a whole (the consideration paid to acquire the hybrid instrument) the amount separately determined for the embedded derivative.

If the convertible bond is measured at fair value with changes in fair value recognised in profit or loss, separating the embedded derivative from the host bond as illustrated above is not permitted. [IAS 39 para IG C3].

A6.5.54 Another type of embedded derivative that is often found in practice relates to a type of funding provided by venture capital entities as illustrated in the example below.

Example – Equity kicker

A venture capital entity provides a subordinated loan that, in addition to interest and repayment of principal, contain terms that entitles the venture capital company to receive shares of the borrower free of charge or at a very low price (an 'equity kicker') in the event the borrower undergoes an IPO. As a result of this feature, the interest on the subordinated loan is lower than it would otherwise be.

The 'equity kicker' meets the definition of a derivative even though the right to receive shares is contingent upon the future listing of the borrower. IAS 39 paragraph AG 9 states that a derivative could require a payment as a result of some future event that is unrelated to a notional amount. An 'equity kicker' feature is similar to such a derivative except that it does not give a right to a fixed payment, but an option right, if the future event occurs. Therefore, as the economic characteristics and risks of an equity return are not closely related to the economic characteristics and risks of a host debt instrument, the embedded derivative would be accounted for separately by the venture capital entity. [IAS 39 para IG C4].

Foreign currency features

A6.5.55 An entity may issue debt in a currency other than its functional currency. Such a foreign currency loan is accounted for under IAS 21, 'The effects of changes in foreign exchange rates', which requires foreign currency gains and losses on monetary items to be recognised in profit or loss. Therefore, a foreign currency derivative that may be embedded in such a host debt instrument is considered closely related and is not separated. This also applies to an embedded foreign currency derivative that provides a stream of principal or interest payments that are denominated in a foreign currency and embedded in a host debt instrument (for example, a dual currency bond). [IAS 39 para AG 33(c)].

Example – Dual currency bond

An entity with pound sterling as a functional currency issues a £10m debt instrument that provides for the annual payment of interest in euros and the repayment of principal in pound sterling.

This dual currency bond can be viewed as containing a foreign currency swap that converts the pound sterling interest payments to euro interest payments. As discussed above, this embedded swap is not accounted for separately as under IAS 21, any exchange gains and losses arising on the annual euro interest payments due to exchange rate changes are themselves reported in profit or loss. [IAS 21 para 28].

6A.5.56 Although many embedded foreign currency derivatives will not have to be separated from a foreign currency host debt instrument, certain embedded foreign currency features may require separation. For example, an entity would be required to separate the embedded foreign currency derivative involving a loan with a foreign currency option. Consider the following examples:

Example 1 – Loan with foreign currency option

An entity issues a C10m loan at an above average market rate. The entity has the option to repay the loan at par for C10m or a fixed amount in a foreign currency, say €15m.

The debt instrument can be viewed as combining a loan at prevailing market interest rates and a foreign currency option. In effect, the issuer has purchased a foreign currency option that allows it to take advantage of changes in foreign currency exchange rates during the outstanding period of the loan. The premium for the option is paid as part of the higher interest cost. Similarly, the lender has written an option that exposes it to foreign currency risk. Because the borrower has the option of repaying the loan in its functional currency or in a foreign currency, the option is not closely related to the debt instrument (that is, it is not directly related to the currency of the loan or the interest rate that applies to that currency). Therefore, the principle discussed in paragraph A6.5.55 above does not apply since application of IAS 21 rules for revaluing of monetary items would not lead to revaluation of the foreign currency option. Accordingly, the embedded foreign currency option should be separated from the host contract and accounted for separately by both parties to the contract. In contrast, if both the principal and the interest payments were made in a foreign currency (that is, if no optionality was involved), there would be no embedded derivative.

Example 2 – Interest payments linked to foreign currency exchange rates

An entity issues a £10m debt security at par. Quarterly interest payments, which are payable in pound sterling, are computed based on a formula that is linked to the £/€ exchange rate.

In this example, the quarterly interest is not denominated in foreign currency and, therefore, the principle discussed in paragraph A6.5.55 above does not apply. Since the formula for computing the interest payable on a sterling bond is linked to the £/€ exchange rate and not based on an interest rate or an index based on interest rates, an inflation index or the creditworthiness of the debtor, it is an embedded derivative that is not closely related to the sterling bond. Hence, it should be accounted for separately. The embedded derivative is a forward foreign exchange contract.

Embedded derivatives in equity host contracts

A6.5.57 For embedded derivatives in an equity host contract, an analysis should first be performed to determine whether the host contract is an equity host. In carrying out this analysis, it is necessary to determine whether the host contract has any stated or pre-determined maturity and, if not, whether the residual interest represents a residual interest in the entity's net assets (see section 7 of this financial instruments section for more detail on the definition of equity). Generally, when a host contract encompasses a residual interest that involves the rights of ownership, it is an equity host. The value of an equity instrument is a function of the underlying equity price or index. Therefore, an embedded derivative would need to possess equity characteristics related to the same entity to be regarded as closely related. [IAS 39 para AG 27].

Calls and puts

A6.5.58 A call option embedded in an equity instrument that enables the issuer to re-acquire that equity instrument at a specified price is not closely related to the host equity instrument from the holder's perspective. From the issuer's perspective, on the other hand, the call option is an equity instrument provided it meets the conditions for that classification under IAS 32, in which case it is excluded from IAS 39's scope. [IAS 39 para AG 30(b)].

A6.5.59 A put option that requires the issuer to re-acquire an equity instrument at a specified price is similarly not closely related to the host equity instrument from the holder's perspective. From the issuer's perspective, the put option is a written option that gives the counterparty the right to sell the issuer's own equity instrument to the entity for a fixed price. Under paragraph 23 of IAS 32, the issuer recognises a financial liability equal to the present value of the redemption amount (that is, the present value of the option's exercise price). See further section 7.

A6.5.60 In the case of a puttable instrument that can be put back at any time for cash equal to a proportionate share of the entity's net asset value (such as units of an open-ended mutual fund or some unit-linked investment products), the effect of separating an embedded derivative and accounting for each component is to measure the combined instrument at the redemption amount that is payable at the balance sheet date if the holder exercised its right to put the instrument back to the issuer. [IAS 39 para AG 32]. This will apply to both the issuer and the investor in such an instrument.

A6.5.61 The treatment of call and put options embedded in preference shares require careful consideration. This is because the terms of the preference share must be analysed first to determine whether the preference shares are more akin to an equity instrument or a debt instrument. Consider the following examples:

Example 1 – Puttable preference shares

An entity issues C50m mandatorily redeemable preference shares at par with a fixed dividend of 8% per annum. The preference shares are puttable to the company for cash at par if market interest rate exceeds 12%.

The mandatorily redeemable preference shares are a financial liability of the issuer and akin to a debt instrument. Furthermore, the embedded put option's exercise price, which is par, is approximately equal to the preference's shares amortised cost. Hence, the put option is considered closely related to the debt host.

Example 2 – Convertible preference shares

An entity issues C50m of irredeemable preference shares that give the holders a preferential right to return of capital in a winding up, but which are also convertible into a fixed number of ordinary shares at the holder's option. Any dividends paid in the year are at the discretion of the issuer.

As the preference shares are irredeemable and there is no obligation on the issuer to pay dividends, the shares are equity in nature. The conversion feature represents an embedded written call option on the company's ordinary shares, which on a free-standing basis would be an equity instrument of the entity. As both the embedded call option and the host are equity instruments, the entity does not account for the embedded option separately. Similarly, the investor would not have to account for the embedded option separately.

Embedded derivatives in lease host contracts

A6.5.62 Embedded derivatives may be present in lease host contracts, whether the lease is an operating or a finance lease. The approach for determining whether an embedded derivative is closely related to a lease host is similar to the approach that is used for a debt host.

Inflation indexed rentals

A6.5.63 An embedded derivative in a host lease contract is closely related to the host contract if the embedded derivative is an inflation-related index such as an index of lease payments to a consumer price index provided:

- the lease is not leveraged; and

- the index relates to inflation in the entity's own economic environment.

[IAS 39 para AG 33(f)].

A6.5.64 The first bullet point makes it clear that an embedded inflation adjustment in the lease contract would not be closely related if it is considered to be leveraged. In determining whether inflation features embedded in lease contracts are leveraged, the guidance stated in paragraph A6.5.34 above should be followed. Generally, lease contracts often stipulate that the payments will increase in line with inflation, in which case, the indexed linked lease payments would not be considered leveraged. Where this is not the case, an inflationary adjustment of greater than one would be considered sufficiently leveraged for the inflation feature to be accounted for separately. This is because, in practice, the market would expect the prices of goods and services to move in line with inflation, all other factors being equal. Therefore, any inflationary adjustment in a lease contract that has the effect of increasing the indexed cash flows by more than the normal rate of inflation are considered to be leveraged.

A6.5.65 The second bullet point in paragraph A6.5.63 states that the index should relate to inflation in the entity's own economic environment. IAS 39 is silent as to whether the entity's own economic environment refers to the lessee's or the lessor's economic environment. It is reasonable to assume, however, that the economic environment that is most relevant to the lease contract is the one in which the leased asset is located, as the inflation index of that economic environment is the one that directly affects the lease rentals and, hence, the leased property's value. Consequently, the economic environment in which the lessee or the lessor operates is not relevant to the analysis.

Example 1 – Inflation linked rentals

A UK entity leases a property in France. The rentals are paid in euros and increase each year in line with the increase in the rate of inflation in France. The lessor is located in France.

The future cash flows (the rental payments) will change in response to changes in the inflation index of France. The embedded inflation indexed payments are not leveraged and relate to the economic environment in which the leased asset is located. Therefore, the inflation adjustment is closely related to the lease contract and separation is not required.

Note: this is a lease payable in a currency that is not the functional currency of the UK lessee. Foreign currency features in lease contracts are discussed further from paragraphs A6.5.72 below.

Example 2 – Inflation linked rentals (leveraged)

A UK entity is the tenant in a 10 year lease of a property in the UK with rental payments in pound sterling that are contractually determined for the first year, but thereafter increasing at a rate of one and a half times the change in UK RPI (Retail Price Index).

The future cash flows (the rental payments) will change in response to changes in the UK RPI. Since the cash flows changes by an amount in excess of one times the change in RPI, such cash flows are considered to be leveraged as discussed in paragraph A6.5.64 above. Therefore, the embedded inflation indexed payments would be accounted for separately.

A question arises as to whether the embedded derivative should be measured by reference to one times UK RPI or one and a half times UK RPI.

Some would favour the former treatment on the grounds that as the leverage portion of the embedded derivative is the amount over and above the change in the UK inflation index, this portion (half times RPI) should be accounted for separately as a derivative. On this basis, the host contract would contain the non-leveraged portion (one times RPI) that is considered to be closely related.

However, we consider that splitting the change in the fair value of an indexed linked derivative between a leveraged amount and a non-leveraged amount is not appropriate for the following reasons:

- A derivative has a single value and splitting a portion out in the above manner is not permitted under IAS 39.
- The leveraged and non-leveraged portions relate to the same risk and, since the inflation is leveraged overall, the entire link to RPI is no longer considered closely related.
- The separation creates cash flow patterns that are not evident in the lease contract because, in practice, the actual cash flows would consist of the minimum rentals plus amounts relating to the entire change in the inflation adjustment.

Therefore, the leveraged portion of the embedded derivative should be based on the total change in the UK inflation index, that is, one and a half times RPI, whilst the host would consist of a non-inflation linked lease rental contract.

Example 3 – Inflation linked rentals not related to the entity's economic environment

Facts are the same as in example 1 except that the inflation adjustment relates to a specified US annual inflation rate (for example, Retail Price Index, Consumer Price Index etc). The landlord is a US entity.

The future cash flows (the rental payments) will change in response to changes in the US inflation index. The embedded inflation indexed payments, although not leveraged, relate to a different economic environment to that in which the leased asset is located and the UK entity operates. Therefore, the inflation indexed payment is not closely related to the lease host contract and would be accounted for separately.

Example 4 – Upward only inflation-linked rentals

Entity A is a tenant in a 10 year UK property lease agreement. The rent for the first year is contractually determined at C100,000. The rental payments will change in line with an index of UK prices so if, at the end of year 1, the index had increased by 3%, the rent for year 2 would be C103,000. However, the lease provides that the rent may not be decreased. So if, during year 2, the index fell by 1%, the rent for year 3 would remain at C103,000. The index shows that UK prices are generally increasing at the inception of the lease (that is, there is UK inflation).

The rental payments are linked to an index. They follow that index while it is increasing, but do not follow it if it decreases. This feature is often known as 'upward only'. However, this lease contains a floor in the rental payments because of the upward-only feature, so it is necessary to identify whether the floor is in or out-of-the-money at the inception of the lease. Because the upward-only feature of the rent reviews means that the rentals can never fall below the floor, the floor is always out-of-the-money (not influencing the cash flows) both at inception and subsequently. Therefore, its presence does not alter the expected cash flows and so the derivative is closely related.

Contingent rentals based on related sales

A6.5.66 Lease contracts may include contingent rentals that are based on certain sales of the lessee. Such a contingent rental-related embedded derivative is considered to be closely related to the lease host contract and would not be accounted for separately. [IAS 39 para AG 33(f)].

Example – Lease rentals related to sales

A UK entity leases a property located in the UK. The rentals consist of a base rental of C10,000 plus 5% of the lessee's sales each month.

The rental payments will vary, depending on an underlying, being the entity's sales.

However, as stated above, the portion of the contingent rentals based on related sales is considered to be closely related to the host lease contract. Therefore, the sales related payments should not be separated.

Contingent rentals based on a variable interest rate

A6.5.67 Where lease contracts include contingent rentals that are based on variable interest rates, the contingent rental-related embedded derivative is considered to be closely related to the lease host contract and would not be accounted for separately. [IAS 39 para AG 33(f)]. This is because a lease contract is akin to a debt instrument and, therefore, the obligation to make future payments for the use of the asset and the adjustment of those payments to reflect changes in a variable interest rate index such as the LIBOR are considered to be closely related.

Example – Lease rentals indexed to LIBOR

A UK entity leases a property located in the UK. The lease rentals are indexed to the UK LIBOR rate. The contract does not contain any leverage feature.

The embedded derivative does not need to be separated as the rentals are based on a variable interest rate index of the UK economy.

On the other hand, if the rentals were indexed to a variable interest rate of an economic environment that is different from the economic environment in which the leased asset is located, the related embedded derivative would not be regarded as closely related in the same way that a similarly indexed inflation payment would not be regarded as closely related (see para A6.5.63 above).

Purchase options in lease agreements

A6.5.68 Often lease contracts may include an option that allows the lessee to purchase the asset at the end of the lease term. Such a purchase option would not qualify as an embedded derivative for a number of reasons. First, the purchase option is based on a non-financial variable (the underlying price of the leased asset) that is specific to a party to the contract and, hence, fails the definition of a derivative. [IAS 39 para AG12A]. Secondly, in order to exercise the option, the lessee must pay the purchase price in cash and the lessor must physically deliver the leased asset (a non-financial asset). This constitutes a gross settlement and, therefore, the option is not a financial instrument. However, if the terms in the contract allow the lessee to settle net in cash (considered unlikely) or the leased asset is readily convertible into cash (because an active trading market exists for the asset in question and, therefore, it is not specific to a party to the contract), the purchase option could qualify as a derivative (see further para 3.34 above).

Term extension or renewal options

A6.5.69 A finance lease is viewed as being equivalent to debt for accounting and disclosure purposes. However, the right to extend the lease term is different from the right to extend the term of a debt instrument. The right to extend the lease is not a right to borrow funds for a further period as would be the case with a debt instrument; rather, the right to extend the lease is a right to use a non-financial asset for an additional period. Furthermore, under IAS 17 the extension term would either be included in the calculation of the minimum lease term if it is reasonably certain that, at the inception of the lease, the lessee will exercise the option; or the renewal would constitute a new lease because the leased asset and the corresponding liability (if either exists) would have been amortised to nil by the end of the original lease term. In either case, the renewal or the extension option would not meet the definition of a derivative, for it does not contain a net settlement provision.

Residual value guarantee in lease agreements

A6.5.70 Where a lease includes a residual value guarantee, the lessee undertakes to make a payment if the residual value of the asset at the end of the lease falls below a pre-determined amount. A residual value guarantee does not meet the definition of a derivative because it has an underlying (price of the leased asset) that is specific to a party to the contract. Furthermore, under IAS 17, the gross amount of any residual guarantee is treated as part of the minimum lease payments and is accounted for as such. Therefore, it is not accounted for under IAS 39.

Termination clause in lease agreements

A6.5.71 Lease agreements are generally irrevocable, that is, the lessee is obliged to lease the asset during the non-cancellable period of the lease. However, the lease may contain an early termination clause that allows the lessee to terminate the contract, but only on the payment of a penalty. This penalty payment (sometimes referred to as the 'stipulated loss value') ensures that the lessor will be able to recover its remaining investment in the lease. This situation is similar in substance to a pre-payment option in a debt instrument, which is considered closely related in circumstances where the option's exercise price is approximately equal to the amortised cost of the debt instrument. See example 2 in paragraph A6.5.44 above where the penalty payment clause resulted in a fair value of zero, until the option was actually exercised.

Lease payments in foreign currencies

A6.5.72 Finance lease contracts that give rise to financial assets in lessors and financial liabilities in lessees are financial instruments. Therefore, as a finance lease denominated in a foreign currency is similar in nature to a foreign currency loan, no separation of the embedded foreign currency derivative is required, because the foreign currency lease receivable and payable are monetary items that are accounted for in accordance with IAS 21. The guidance that applies to foreign currency loans is also applicable to foreign currency finance leases (see para A6.5.55), that is, the embedded derivative is not separated.

A6.5.73 On the other hand, an operating lease is not regarded as a financial instrument. Therefore, an operating lease agreement that provides for payments in foreign currency may contain foreign currency embedded derivatives that may require separation. Paragraph AG33(d) of IAS 39 contains provisions that deal with embedded foreign currency derivatives in a host contract that is not a financial instrument. These are considered in paragraph A6.5.84 below. That guidance has been applied to the examples given below.

Example 1 – Operating lease rentals denominated in foreign currency

A UK company enters into an operating lease with a European lessor that is denominated in euros. The functional currency of the lessee and the lessor are the pound sterling and the euro respectively.

Paragraph AG33(d) of IAS 39 provides that contracts, other than financial instruments, that specify payments denominated in the functional currency of any substantial party to the contract are closely related to the host contract.

In this example, the lease payments are denominated in the functional currency of the lessor – a substantial party to the contract. Therefore, the embedded derivative is closely related to the host contract and not separated. It is not appropriate to argue that because the payments are in a foreign currency and the UK lessee is exposed to currency risk that there is an embedded foreign currency forward converting sterling payments to euros.

On the other hand, if the lease payments are denominated in a currency that is unrelated to each party's functional currency (for example, US dollars), the embedded foreign currency forward should be separated from the host contract and accounted for as a derivative. This applies to both parties to the contract.

Example 2 – Operating lease rentals denominated in foreign currency

On 1 June 20X2 entity A, a Russian oil refinery, entered into an arrangement with entity S to lease a building in Moscow for a 10-year period. The lease is classified as an operating lease. Entity A's management has determined its functional currency to be the US dollar.

Entity S is a property management and development entity located in Russia. Its management has determined its functional currency to be the Russian Rouble.

Entity S set the monthly lease repayments in Swiss Francs to avoid exposure to any devaluation in the Russian Rouble and to obtain a natural hedge for the repayment of its Swiss Franc denominated bonds.

As the Swiss Franc is neither the functional currency of one of the substantial parties to the lease contract, nor a currency commonly used in Russia, nor the currency in which leases are routinely denominated in the world, the lease contract contains an embedded derivative that is not closely related to the host contract.

From entity S's perspective, the lease contract contains a series of embedded forward contracts to buy Swiss Francs against Russian Roubles. These embedded derivatives are not closely related to the host contract (lease contract denominated in Russian Rouble) and, therefore, should be accounted for separately.

From entity A's perspective, the lease contract contains a series of embedded forward contracts to sell Swiss Francs against US Dollars. These embedded derivatives are not closely related to the host contract (lease contract denominated in USD) and, therefore, should be accounted for separately.

Example 3 – Subsidiary's foreign currency lease payments guaranteed by parent

A major French operating subsidiary of a US parent enters into a lease with a Swiss company that requires lease payments in US dollars. The lease payments are guaranteed by the US parent. The functional currencies of the respective entities are their local currencies.

In this example, the substantial parties to the lease contract are the French lessee and the Swiss lessor. The guarantor is not a substantial party to the contract and, therefore, its functional currency is of no relevance to the analysis (see further para A6.5.85 below). Since the lease payments are made in US dollars, which is neither the functional currency of the lessee nor the lessor, the embedded foreign currency swap would need to be accounted for separately.

Embedded derivatives in executory contracts

A6.5.74 Contracts to buy or sell a non-financial asset that qualify as executory contracts, including commitments (for example, take or pay contracts) that are entered into to meet the entity's expected purchase, sale or usage requirements and are expected to be settled by physical delivery, are not financial instruments.

Accordingly, they are scoped out of IAS 39 under the own use purchase or sale exception. However, even though such contracts are not financial instruments, they may contain embedded derivatives. Embedded derivatives may also be present in some service contracts.

A6.5.75 IAS 39 contains little specific guidance relating to derivatives embedded in such contracts, except for features involving foreign currency. Therefore, it would be necessary to consider carefully the economic characteristics and risks of such contracts in assessing whether embedded derivatives are present and, if so, whether they should be separately accounted for. In doing so, it would be necessary to consider both quantitative and qualitative factors. Sometimes it may be possible to draw on the guidance discussed above for other host contracts. Indeed, it would not be unreasonable to do so, particularly for features such as pricing adjustments, inflation adjustments and caps, floors and collars on prices and quantities.

Pricing adjustments features

A6.5.76 Normal purchase and sale contracts may contain price clauses that modify the contract's cash flows. In assessing the closely related criterion for the embedded derivative, it would be necessary to establish whether the underlying in a price adjustment feature incorporated into such a contract is related or unrelated to the cost or fair value of the goods or services being sold or purchased.

Example 1 – Price adjustment feature in supply contracts

An entity enters into a contract to build a production line for a customer. Although it prepares budgets before it starts to construct the production line, it does not know with certainty what the final costs will be. Therefore, in order to build in contingency for any cost overruns and to protect its profit margin, the entity sets the contract sale price at cost plus 20%.

The cash flows under the supply contract (host contract) will vary in response to changes in a variable, the company's costs of building the production line (the embedded derivative). The derivative adjusts the price for the production line to align it with the price that would have been quoted by the entity, had the costs to manufacture been known with certainty at the inception of the contract. Therefore, the pricing clause is closely related to the supply host contract and would not be accounted for separately.

Example 2 – Price adjustment linked to market prices of goods purchased

An entity (whose functional currency is pound sterling) contracts to purchase 200 tonnes of aluminium from a UK supplier in 12 months' time. The aluminium is intended for use in the course of entity's business. The purchase price will be the market price at the contract date plus an amount determined by a specified index of aluminium prices. The contract does not contain any leverage feature.

The future cash outflows are linked to movements in the market price for aluminium. The purpose of the embedded derivative is to ensure that the price paid for the aluminium is the market price at the date of purchase/supply rather than the date the two parties entered into the supply contract. This ensures that the seller passes any price risk to the entity. As the underlying is related to the price of the aluminium purchased, the derivative is closely related to the aluminium supply contract (host) and would not be accounted for separately.

Example 3 – Coal purchase contract linked to changes in the price of electricity

An entity enters into a coal purchase contract that includes a clause that links the price of coal to a pricing formula based on the prevailing electricity price at the date of delivery. The entity purchases the coal for its own use and there are no provisions to settle the contract net.

The coal purchase contract is the host contract. The pricing formula that changes the price risk from coal price to electricity price is the embedded derivative. Although coal may be used for the production of electricity, the underlying based on electricity prices is not pertinent to both the changes in the cost and the changes in the fair value of coal. Therefore, the embedded derivative (the electricity price adjustment) is not closely related to the host contract and should be accounted for separately.

Example 4 – Supply contract subject to multiple pricing adjustments

An entity has entered into a contract with a customer to sell 10,000 wooden chairs for a period of five years. The price per chair is contractually determined at C100 per chair for the first year and thereafter increases in line with changes in certain indices. 50% of the price of each chair is linked to an index of timber prices, 30% is linked to the UK wage inflation index. So if the timber index rises by 10% and the wage inflation index increases by 5%, the price for each chair will be C106.50 (being C50 × 1.1 + C30 × 1.05 + C20). The sales contract in its entirety does not meet the definition of a derivative as it will be settled by physical delivery in the normal course of business.

There are two embedded derivatives contained in this contract, because the price of chairs over the contract term is linked to the two indices (timber and wage inflation). The purpose of these embedded derivatives is to protect the entity's profit margin over the contract term by ensuring that changes in the prices of inputs are passed on to the end customer.

Although both the indices are considered to be relevant and pertinent to the cost or fair value of the chairs being sold, they would be considered to be closely related to the host contract if, and only if, the entity can reliably demonstrate that the standard mix of direct material and direct labour for each chair produced is maintained.

If, however, the entity is unable to demonstrate reliably the clear linkage, then the embedded derivatives *may* be leveraged (because the percentage of the price linked to each index may not accurately reflect the cost structure). In other words, the magnitude of the price adjustment may cause the price of the host contract to increase by more than a significant amount (see para A6.5.14 above). In that situation, the indexed linked price adjustments would not be considered to be closely related.

6A.5.77 Where a contract to buy or sell non-financial assets does not qualify for the own use purchase or sale exception, the entire contract would fall to be treated as if it were a financial instrument (and in most cases a derivative). In that situation, as the entire derivative contract would be accounted for at fair value through profit or loss, any derivatives embedded in such contracts would no longer need to be accounted for separately.

Example – Contract not qualifying for 'normal' purchase or sale exception

An entity enters into a forward contract to purchase 10,000 tonnes of coal. The contract does not qualify for the 'normal' purchase or sale exception as there is a provision in the contract for net settlement and the entity's past practice indicates that it will settle the contract net. Settlement is based on changes in the fair value of coal during the contract's term plus a payment provision based on a formula linked to prevailing electricity prices.

Given that the own use exception does not apply, the entire forward contract to purchase coal will be accounted for as a derivative in accordance with IAS 39 with gains and losses on the entire contract reported in the profit and loss account. Therefore, there is no need to identify separately the leverage payment provision as an embedded derivative.

Volume adjustment features

A6.5.78 Many contracts for the supply of goods usually give the buyer the right to take either a minimum quantity of goods or any amount based on the buyer's requirements. A minimum annual commitment does not create a derivative as long as the entity expects to purchase all the guaranteed volume for its 'own use'. However, if it becomes likely that the entity will not take the product and, instead pay a penalty under the contract based on the market value of the product or some other variable, a derivative or an embedded derivative may well arise. In this situation, since physical delivery is no longer probable, the derivative would be recorded at the amount of the penalty payable. Changes in market price will affect the penalty's carrying value until the penalty is paid. On the other hand, if the amount of the penalty payable is fixed or pre-determined, there is no derivative as the penalty's value remains fixed irrespective of changes in the market value of the product. In other words, the entity will need to provide for the penalty payable once it becomes clear that non-performance is likely.

A6.5.79 On the other hand, if the quantity specified in the contract is more than the entity's normal usage requirement and the entity intends to net settle part of the contract that it does not need in the normal course of the business, the contract will fail the 'own use' exemption. Section 3 sets out a number of ways in which the entity can settle the contract net. For example, the entity could take all the quantities specified in the contract and sell on the excess or it could enter into an offsetting contract for the excess quantity. In such situations, the entire contract falls within IAS 39's scope and should be marked-to-market.

A6.5.80 From the supplier's perspective, however, the volume flexibility feature in the contract allowing the customer to take whatever quantity it requires constitutes a written option and may well prevent the supplier from claiming the 'own use' exemption. This is because a written option cannot be entered into for the purpose of the receipt or delivery of a non-financial item in accordance with the entity's expected purchase, sale or usage requirements. [IAS 39 para 7]. As explained in paragraph 3.36, such written options have to be accounted for in accordance with IAS 39 if it can be settled net in cash. Settled net in cash means that the item that is the subject of the contract is readily convertible into cash.

A6.5.81 Therefore, it is necessary to consider whether the contract contains a written option. A contract will not contain a true written option if the buyer intends to use all quantities purchased for its own use and did not pay any premium to receive the option. Receipt of a premium to compensate the supplier for the risk that the buyer may not take the optional quantities specified in the contract is one of the distinguishing features of a written option. [IAS 39 IG F1.3(a)(b)]. Therefore, it would be necessary to consider whether a net premium is received either at inception or over the contract's life in order to determine the accounting treatment. Any penalty payable for non-performance by the buyer may well amount to the receipt of a premium. If no premium can be identified, other terms of the contract may need to be examined to determine whether it contains a written option, in particular, whether the buyer is able to secure economic value from the option's presence. Contracts need to be considered on a case-by-case basis in order to determine whether they contain written options.

Example 1

Entity A, a car manufacturer enters into a contract to sell cars to entity B that is engaged in renting cars. The contracts provide for entity A to supply 50 cars of a specific model at a specified future date at a fixed price. Entity B has the option to take between 90% and 110% of the contract quantity. Available market information indicates that a similar contract for 50 cars but without volume flexibility would also be priced at the same fixed price specified in the contract. Entity B cannot monetise the value of the contract by selling on any excess cars in the market.

The supply contract would not be considered a written option, as the pricing of the contract is the same as that for a similar contract with no volume flexibility. There is, therefore, no premium associated with the contract. Entity B cannot exercise any value from the option's presence; the contract is, therefore, not a written option and qualifies for the own-use exemption.

Example 2

Entity A, an electricity producer, enters into a contract to sell electricity to entity B. The contracts provide for entity A to supply 100 units of electricity at a specified future date to entity B at a fixed price per unit. Entity B has the option to take between 90% and 110% of the contract quantity. The total quantity taken will be priced at 0.21 per unit. Available market information indicates that a similar contract for 100 units of electricity but without volume flexibility would be priced at 0.20 per unit. Entity B is also a supplier of electricity and can, therefore, monetise the contract's value by selling on any excess power into the market.

The pricing of the contract is not the same as that for a similar contract without volume flexibility. The price per cubic meter includes a premium for the additional risk accepted by entity A in offering volume flexibility. The contract is, therefore, a written option and entity A cannot claim the own-use exemption. In that situation, the contract will be marked-to-market in accordance with IAS 39.

Inflation related features

A6.5.82 It is not uncommon for purchase, sale or long-term service contracts to contain terms that are linked to an inflation index, particularly in periods of rising inflation. Inflation escalator clauses are included in such long-term contracts to protect the seller's margin in real terms. Although IAS 39 is silent on the treatment of inflationary adjustments in such executory contracts, there is no reason, in principle, as to why the guidance relating to inflation adjustment features in lease host contracts would not be appropriate for such contracts. That guidance states that an embedded inflation-related index is closely related to the lease host contract if the index is not leveraged and the index relates to inflation in the entity's own economic environment. [IAS 39 para AG 33(f)]. The application of this principle to lease contracts is considered from paragraphs 6.5.63 above. We believe similar considerations can be applied also to purchase, sale and service contracts.

Example – Purchase contract linked to inflation

A UK entity contracts to purchase a fixed quantity of certain raw material from a UK supplier in 12 months' time. The raw materials are intended for use in the entity's business. The purchase price will be the market price at the contract date plus an adjustment for UK RPI from the beginning of the contract. The contract does not contain any leverage feature.

The future cash flows are linked to an inflation index that is not leveraged and the index is in the local economic environment. Therefore, the embedded derivative is closely related to the host purchase contract.

If, on the other hand, the entity is unable to demonstrate that these goods are to be used in the course of its business, that is, the own use exception does not apply, the entire contract would be treated as a forward purchase contract that would fall to be settled net in accordance with paragraph 3.33 above. In that situation, the forward purchase contract meets the definition of a derivative and, is itself, accounted for at fair value through profit or loss. So there is no need to account separately for any derivatives that may be embedded in it.

Caps, floors and collars

A6.5.83 Contracts to buy or sell a non-financial asset may contain provisions that provide for payments to be made at the market price at the time of payment, but set an upper or lower limit or both on the final price to be paid or received. Such caps, floors or collars included in contracts are embedded derivatives. IAS 39 states that provisions included in a contract to purchase or sell an asset (for example, a commodity) that establish a cap and a floor on the price to be paid or received for the asset are closely related to the host contract if both the cap and floor were out-of-the-money and are not leveraged. [IAS 39 para AG 33(b)]. This guidance can be extended to a collar that would be closely related if it was out-of-the-money at inception (see para A6.5.40 above).

Example – Purchase contract with selling price subject to a cap and a floor

A manufacturer enters into a long-term contract to purchase a specified quantity of certain raw materials from a supplier. Under the contract, the supplier will provide the raw materials at the list price prevailing at the delivery date, but within a specified range. For example, the purchase price may not exceed C20 per kg or fall below C15 per kg. The current list price at inception of the contract is C18 per kg.

From the manufacturer's perspective, the embedded derivatives contained in the purchase contracts are two options; a purchased call option with a strike price of C20 per kg and a written put with a strike price of C15 per kg. These options would each meet the definition of a derivative if they were free standing, because they have a notional amount (the fixed quantity to be purchased), have an underlying (the price per kg), require no initial net investment and will be settled in the future.

The economic characteristics and risks of the two options are closely related to the purchase contract, because the options are indexed to the asset's purchase price that is the subject of the contract and both the embedded cap (cap price of C20 is greater than current list price of C18) and the floor (floor price of C15 is lower than current list price of C18) are out-of-the-money at inception of the contract. Hence, the embedded derivatives are closely related and the host contract can be considered to be a purchase contract that requires delivery of the specified quantity of raw materials at a price equal to the current list price.

Foreign currency features

A6.5.84 IAS 39 provides specific guidance for an embedded foreign currency derivative in a host contract that is not a financial instrument. An embedded foreign currency derivative in a host contract that is not a financial instrument (such as a contract for the purchase or sale of a non-financial item where the price is denominated in a foreign currency) is closely related to the host contract provided it is not leveraged, does not contain an option feature and requires payments denominated in one of the following currencies:

- The functional currency of any substantial party to that contract.
- The currency in which the price of the related goods or service that is acquired or delivered is routinely denominated in commercial transactions around the world (such as the US dollar for crude oil transactions).
- A currency that is commonly used in contracts to purchase or sell non-financial items in the economic environment in which the transaction takes place (for example, a relatively stable and liquid currency that is commonly used in local business transactions or external trade).

[IAS 39 para AG 33(d)].

A6.5.85 The term 'substantial party' to the contract referred to in the first bullet point above is not explained in IAS 39. Generally, it is taken to mean a party that is acting as principal to the contract, that is, the buyer/seller. A bank that provides a guarantee on behalf of a local importer to a foreign supplier that the buyer will meet its payment obligations in foreign currency under the contract's terms is not a substantial party to the contract. Furthermore, the guarantor's functional currency is of no relevance in determining whether the payments denominated in the foreign currency are closely related to the contract.

A6.5.86 A question also arises in practice as to the efforts one party to a contract needs to employ to determine the functional currency of its counterparty. Generally, there would be a rebuttable presumption that the local currencies of the economic environment in which the counterparties operate would be their functional currencies. In addition, the local currency is always presumed to be commonly used. Therefore, if the contract requires payment in either one of the two local currencies of the counterparties, the condition in the first bullet point above would be met. The position is less clear if payments are denominated in a third currency that is not the local currency of either party to the contract. In that situation, the contracting parties would need to determine whether that third currency is the functional currency of their counterparty. In practice, this determination should be made on the basis of all available evidence and reasonable assumptions about the counterparty. Furthermore, the guidance for determining functional currency in IAS 21 would need to be considered in determining the functional currency. An entity should not necessarily rely on a single indicator such as the currency in which the counterparty's sales are denominated. Rather, the entity should consider all relevant available information in determining the counterpary's functional currency.

Example 1 – Payments denominated in the functional currency of a party to the contract

A UK entity (whose functional currency is pound sterling) contracts to sell goods to a French purchaser whose functional currency is the euro. The contract will be fulfilled by the physical delivery of goods and payments by the French buyer would be made in euros.

In this example, the payment in euros exposes the UK entity to currency risk as the cash flows under the contract will vary with the £/€ exchange rate. The contract can be viewed as a host contract that is denominated in sterling containing an embedded foreign currency swap that converts payments in pound sterling to euros or an embedded foreign currency forward contract to sell pound sterling and buy euros. However, the embedded swap or the forward contract is not separated as the payments are denominated in the functional currency of the French buyer who is a substantial party to the contract.

Example 2 – Payments denominated in a third currency

A UK entity (whose functional currency is pound sterling) contracts to sell goods to a Swiss purchaser whose functional currency is the Swiss francs. The contract will be fulfilled by the physical delivery of goods and payments by the Swiss buyer would be made in euros. The goods are not commonly priced in euros.

In this example, the payment and the receipt in euros exposes both the substantial parties to the contract to exchange risk. Since the contract requires that payments be denominated in euros, which is not the functional currency of either party to the transaction, the embedded derivative is not closely related and should be accounted for separately at fair value by both the Swiss buyer and the UK seller. From the UK seller's point of view the embedded derivative would be to buy euros and sell sterling. In the books of the Swiss buyer the embedded derivative would be to sell euros and buy Swiss francs. The nominal amount of the embedded forwards will be equal to the amount specified under the terms of the supply contract.

A particular issue arises in connection with the nature of the foreign currency embedded derivative in a foreign currency purchase/sale contracts when the embedded derivative is required to be separated under AG 33(d). The issue is whether the embedded derivative is a forward contract that matures on the date on which goods are physically delivered, or on the date when cash settlement takes place.

Assume that the UK entity enters into the contract with the Swiss buyer to sell goods amounting to €100 on 1 March 20X6 for delivery on 30 June 20X6 and settlement on 31 July 20X6. The goods are not commonly priced in €. The UK entity's year end is 31 March 20X6. The following data is relevant.

Date	Event	Spot €/£	Forward €/£ (maturity June 20X6)	Forward €/£ (maturity July 20X6)
1 Mar 20X6	UK entity enters into a contract to sell goods for €100	0.70	0.725	0.72
31 Mar 20X6	UK entity's year end. Embedded derivative revalued	0.73	0.745	0.74
30 Jun 20X6	Goods delivered	0.75		0.77
31 Jul 20X6	Invoice amounting to €100 settled	0.78		

In this example, from the perspective of the UK seller, the firm commitment to sell goods is separated into two contracts – a host contact that is a firm commitment to sell goods in pound sterling and an embedded forward contract to buy euro and sell pound sterling with an inception date of 1 March 20X6. However, as stated above there is some debate regarding the deemed date of settlement/maturity of the embedded derivative.

Some take the view that the embedded derivative's settlement/maturity date is 30 June 20X6 when the goods are delivered. This is because the derivative that is embedded in the host firm commitment can no longer exist after that date as there is no host contract – the seller having fulfilled its commitment by delivering the goods to the customer. Following performance by the seller, the seller has an unconditional right to receive consideration from the customer. In other words, the embedded derivative is in the sales contract not in the receivable; the derivative being effectively settled by creation of a financial asset (receivable). Under this view, the accounting entries would be as follows:

Accounting for sale and embedded derivative

		Dr (Cr)				
		Sales	**Debtors**	**Cash**	**Derivative**	**Profit and loss**
Date	**Transaction**	C	C	C	C	C
1 Mar 20X6	Embedded derivative – nil fair value					
31 Mar 20X6	Change in fair value of embedded derivative – 100 @ (0.745 – 0.725) – ignoring discounting – there is a loss as €100 will cost C74.5 instead of C72.5				2.0	(2.0)
30 Jun 20X6	Change in fair value of embedded derivative – 100 @ (0.75 – 0.745)				0.5	(0.5)
30 Jun 20X6	Recording sales at forward rate – 100 @ 0.725	(72.5)	72.5			
30 Jun 20X6	Embedded derivative settled against debtors		2.5		(2.5)	
31 Jul 20X6	Debtor carried at spot rate at 30 June 20X6 settled by receipt of €100 at spot rate – 100 @ 0.78		(75.0)	78		(3.0)
	Effect on proft or loss and balance sheet	(72.5)	–	78	–	(5.5)

Others take the view that the embedded derivative being a forward foreign exchange contract matures at the date of cash settlement on the grounds that the cash leg of the firm commitment is settled at that date. Under this view, the sale and the corresponding receivable are recognised in local currency using the forward rate when the goods are delivered, that is (C72). The embedded derivative and the debtor is settled when cash is received at 30 June 20X6 with any gain or loss arising on settlement recorded in profit or loss. Under this view, the accounting treatment would be as follows:

Accounting for sale and embedded derivative

		Dr (Cr)				
		Sales	Debtors	Cash	Derivative	Proft and loss
Date	**Transaction**	C	C	C	C	C
1 Mar 20X6	Embedded derivative – nil fair value					
31 Mar 20X6	Change in fair value of embedded derivative – 100 @ (0.74 – 0.72) – ignoring discounting – there is a loss as €100 will cost C74 instead of C72				2.0	(2.0)
30 Jun 20X6	Change in fair value of embedded derivative – 100 @ (0.77 – 0.74)				3.0	(3.0)
30 Jun 20X	Recording sales at forward rate – 100 @ 0.72	(72.0)	72.0			
31 Jul 20X6	Settlement date – receipt of €100 at spot rate – 100 @ 0.78		(72.0)	78	(5.0)	(1.0)
	Effect on profit and loss and balance sheet	(72.0)	–	78	–	(6.0)

Although both views can be sustained, in practice, entities generally adopt the first treatment as they view these types of contract as hedges of future sales.

Example 3 – Payments denominated in the functional currency of a party to the contract, but the functional currency changes subsequently

A UK entity (whose functional currency is pound sterling) contracts to sell goods to a Japanese purchaser whose functional currency is the yen. The contract will be fulfilled by the physical delivery of goods and payments by the Japanese buyer would be made in yen. Subsequently, because of changes in economic circumstances, the Japanese buyer changes its functional currency to US dollars.

The UK entity is required to assess whether the embedded derivative should be separated from the host sales contract and accounted for as a derivative when it first becomes a party to the contract. At the time the UK entity entered into the contract, the functional currency of the Japanese buyer was the yen. Therefore, no separation of the embedded derivative is required as yen is the functional currency of a substantial party to the contract. The issue is whether this initial assessment should be revisited following the change in the functional currency of the Japanese buyer.

As explained in paragraph A6.5.20 above, IFRIC 9 prohibits reassessment, unless there is a change in the contract's terms that significantly modifies the cash flow that otherwise would be required under the contract, in which case reassessment is required. In this situation, the contract terms remain unchanged, that is, the UK entity will still make payments in yen irrespective of the fact that the functional currency of the Japanese supplier has subsequently changed to US dollars. Therefore, the contract continues to be accounted for in the same manner as before, irrespective of the fact that the factors that led to the initial assessment have changed. However, any yen denominated contracts entered into with the Japanese buyer after it has changed its functional currency to US dollar would fail the closely related criterion, as they would not be in the functional currency of either party to the contract.

The above treatment also applies to the Japanese buyer even though it will be exposed to Yen/dollar currency risk when it makes payments under the contract. Such exchange gains and losses will fall to be accounted for in accordance with IAS 21. In other words, as long as the contract terms remain unchanged, the Japanese buyer cannot create an embedded currency exposure that did not exist at the date it became a party to the contract.

Example 4 – Option to make payments in alternative currencies

Facts are the same as in example 1 except that the contract contains an option to make payment in either euros or in Swiss francs.

In this example, the UK seller has written an option to receive payments in a currency that is not its functional currency and, therefore, exposes it to £/€ or £/Swiss Fr currency risk. Although euro is the functional currency of the other substantial party to the contract, there is no certainty at inception of the contract that settlement will be in euros. Hence, the foreign currency option is not closely related to the host.

Similarly, the French buyer has effectively purchased an option to make payments in its own functional currency (€) or in a foreign currency (Swiss Fr) that exposes it to €/Swiss Fr currency risk. Although the French buyer has the option to settle the contract in its own currency and eliminate any exchange risk, there is no certainty at inception of the contract that it would eventually exercise that option. Since the contract could also be settled in Swiss francs, the settlement can either be potentially favourable or unfavourable and is not closely related to the purchase contract.

Accordingly, the embedded option should be separated from the host contract and accounted for separately by both parties to the contract.

A6.5.87 In relation to the second bullet point in paragraph A6.5.84 above, the currency in which the price of the related goods or services is routinely denominated in commercial transactions around the world is a currency that is used for similar transactions *all around the world*, not just in one local area. For example, if cross-border transactions in natural gas in North America are routinely denominated in US dollars and such transactions are routinely denominated in euros in Europe, neither the US dollar nor the euro is a currency in which natural gas is routinely denominated in commercial transactions around the world. [IAS 39 para IG C9]. Accordingly, apart from crude oil and some metals which are routinely denominated in US dollar in international commerce, very few items, if any, are likely to meet this requirement.

Example – Leveraged foreign currency provision

Entity A, whose functional currency is the euro, enters into a contract with entity B, whose functional currency is the Norwegian krone, to purchase oil in six months for US$10m. The host oil contract is not within IAS 39's scope, because it was entered into and continued to be for the purpose of delivery of a non-financial item in accordance with the entity's expected purchase, sale or usage requirements. The oil contract includes a leveraged foreign exchange provision that states that the parties, in addition to the provision of, and payment for, oil will exchange an amount equal to the fluctuation in the exchange rate of the US dollar and Norwegian krone applied to a notional amount of US$100,000.

In the example above, the payment provision under the host oil contract of US$10m can be viewed as a foreign currency derivative because the US dollar is neither entity A's nor entity B's functional currency. This foreign currency derivative would not be separated, however, because it follows from the second bullet point of paragraph A6.5.84 above that a crude oil contract that requires payment in US dollars is not regarded as a host contract with a foreign currency derivative.

However, the leveraged foreign exchange provision that states that the parties will exchange an amount equal to the fluctuation in the exchange rate of the US dollar and Norwegian krone applied to a notional amount of US$10m is in addition to the required payment for the oil transaction. It is unrelated to the host oil contract and, therefore, should be separated from the host oil contract, and accounted for as an embedded derivative. [IAS 39 para IG C8].

A6.5.88 The third bullet point in paragraph A6.5.84 refers to a currency that is *commonly used* in contracts to purchase or sell non-financial items in the economic environment in which the transaction takes place (for example, a relatively stable and liquid currency that is commonly used in local business transactions or external trade). This flexibility was added when IAS 39 was revised so that entities domiciled in small or developing economies may find it more convenient to denominate business contracts with entities from other small or developing economies in an internationally liquid currency (such as the US dollar or the euro) rather than the local currency of any parties to the contract.

A6.5.89 The standard uses the term 'commonly used' to mean a currency that is relatively stable or liquid and that is commonly used in local business transactions or external trade. A currency is commonly used in local business transactions when monetary amounts are viewed by the general population not in terms of the local currency, but in terms of a relatively stable foreign currency and prices may be quoted in that foreign currency. [IAS 39 para BC40]. Indeed, undertaking business transactions in a stable or hard currency is fairly common for entities operating in a hyperinflationary economy as a protection against inflation. [IAS 29 para 3(b)]. It follows that the currency must be commonly used within the country, not just commonly used within a particular industry or particular market. This is an exemption to the general rule that foreign currency embedded derivative derivatives need to be separated. The exemption's application should be supported by an appropriate analysis specific to the respective country.

A6.5.90 Many countries around the world use more than one stable or liquid currency in undertaking local business transactions or external trade. Therefore, where such countries undertake transactions in those stable or liquid currencies rather than in their local currencies, the foreign currency derivative would be viewed as closely related to the host contract and would not be accounted for separately. Examples of such countries and currencies are given in the table below.

Countries	**International stable currency commonly used**
Europe:	
Russia, Central and Eastern Europe countries, Turkey.	US$ and €
Caribbean:	
Saudi Arabia, Qatar, UAE, Bahrain Oman, Kuwait.	US$
West Indies:	
Bermuda, Turks & Caicos, Antigua & Bermuda, Cayman Islands, Jamaica.	US$
Asia:	
China (excluding Hong Kong), Vietnam, Cambodia, Indonesia, Malaysia, Laos.	US$
Africa:	
South Africa, Tanzania, Uganda.	US$
South America:	
Brazil, Peru	US$
Research has also indicated a list of countries where no other currency other than local currency is 'commonly used':	
Hong Kong.	
Singapore.	
Thailand.	
Philippines.	

Example – Contract denominated in a currency commonly used in local business transactions

An entity located in a country with a hyper-inflationary economy contracts to purchase raw materials for use in its manufacturing process. The contract is denominated in US$, a stable currency, and not in the local currency, as most local transactions and external trade are undertaken in US$.

The embedded foreign currency derivative (denominated in a currency other than the local currency) does not need to be separated as the contract is denominated in a currency that is commonly used in the local economic environment.

If, however, the contract was priced in another international stable currency say the euro rather than the US$, and euro is not a currency than is commonly used in local business transactions, the embedded derivative (euro *versus* the entity's functional currency) would have to be separated.

Flow chart for identifying embedded derivatives in executory contracts

A6.5.91 As stated previously, IAS 39 provides little or no guidance on derivatives that may be embedded in purchase, sale or service contracts. As identification of such embedded derivatives can be a complex process, a flow chart is given below to aid in the identification process. It should be noted that the flow chart has been constructed from the discussions undertaken above. In practice, such contracts may contain other terms and conditions whose interaction with the host is not obvious. Options that allow early termination of a contract by paying a penalty, options to change the quantities to be delivered and options to defer delivery are some examples of terms and condition that can be problematic and would require careful consideration.

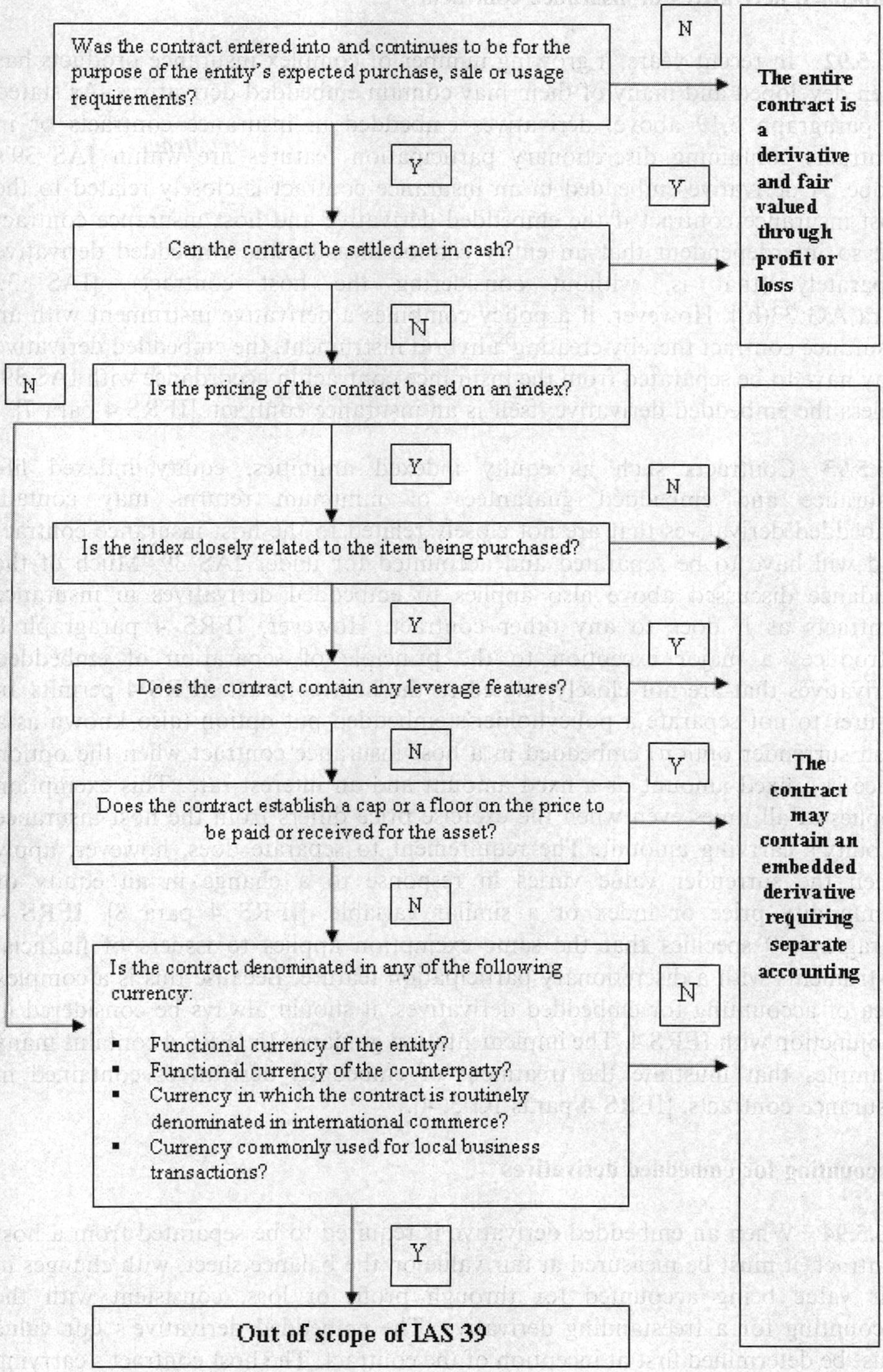
Was the contract entered into and continues to be for the purpose of the entity's expected purchase, sale or usage requirements?
N
The entire contract is a derivative and fair valued through profit or loss
Y
Can the contract be settled net in cash?
Y
N
N
Is the pricing of the contract based on an index?
Y
N
Is the index closely related to the item being purchased?
Y
Y
Does the contract contain any leverage features?
N
Y
Does the contract establish a cap or a floor on the price to be paid or received for the asset?
The contract may contain an embedded derivative requiring separate accounting
N
Is the contract denominated in any of the following currency:
▪ Functional currency of the entity?
▪ Functional currency of the counterparty?
▪ Currency in which the contract is routinely denominated in international commerce?
▪ Currency commonly used for local business transactions?
N
Y
Out of scope of IAS 39

Embedded derivatives in insurance contracts

A6.5.92 In recent years, a growing number of complex insurance products has been developed and many of them may contain embedded derivatives. As stated in paragraph 3.19 above, derivatives embedded in insurance contracts or in contracts containing discretionary participation features are within IAS 39's scope. A derivative embedded in an insurance contract is closely related to the host insurance contract if the embedded derivative and host insurance contract are so interdependent that an entity cannot measure the embedded derivative separately (that is, without considering the host contract). [IAS 39 para AG 33(h)]. However, if a policy combines a derivative instrument with an insurance contract thereby creating a hybrid instrument, the embedded derivative may have to be separated from the insurance contract in accordance with IAS 39, unless the embedded derivative itself is an insurance contract. [IFRS 4 para 7].

A6.5.93 Contracts such as equity indexed annuities, equity indexed life insurance and embedded guarantees of minimum returns may contain embedded derivatives that are not closely related to the host insurance contract and will have to be separated and accounted for under IAS 39. Much of the guidance discussed above also applies to embedded derivatives in insurance contracts as it does to any other contract. However, IFRS 4 paragraph 8 introduces a major exception to the principle of separation of embedded derivatives that are not closely related to the host contract. IFRS 4 permits an insurer to not separate a policyholder's embedded put option (also known as a cash surrender option) embedded in a host insurance contract when the option price is a fixed amount or a fixed amount and an interest rate. This exemption applies at all times even when the exercise price differs from the host insurance liability's carrying amount. The requirement to separate does, however, apply when the surrender value varies in response to a change in an equity or commodity price or index or a similar variable. [IFRS 4 para 8]. IFRS 4 paragraph 9 specifies that the same exemption applies to issuers of financial instruments with a discretionary participation feature. Because this is a complex area of accounting for embedded derivatives, it should always be considered in conjunction with IFRS 4. The implementation guidance to IFRS 4 contains many examples that illustrate the treatment of embedded derivatives contained in insurance contracts. [IFRS 4 paras IG 3, 4].

Accounting for embedded derivatives

A6.5.94 When an embedded derivative is required to be separated from a host contract, it must be measured at fair value on the balance sheet, with changes in fair value being accounted for through profit or loss, consistent with the accounting for a freestanding derivative. The embedded derivative's fair value must be determined first at inception of the contract. The host contract's carrying *value at initial* recognition is the difference between the consideration paid or received to acquire the hybrid contract and the embedded derivative's fair value. [IAS 39 para AG 28].

A6.5.95 Published price quotations in an active market are normally the best evidence of fair value. Valuation techniques are used to determine the derivative's fair value if there is no active market that matches the embedded derivative's exact terms and conditions. Valuing a derivative usually involves the exercise of judgement by management in making certain estimates such as the discount rate, extrapolation of future interest rates, foreign exchange rates and so on. The use of estimates for certain valuation parameters could be subjective, especially for long-term contracts that are common in the energy industry. Furthermore, certain embedded derivatives, in particular those arising from complex structured products, may contain several underlying variables making the valuation process extremely complex.

A6.5.96 If an entity is unable to determine reliably the fair value of an embedded derivative on the basis of its terms and conditions (for example, because the embedded derivative is based on an unquoted equity instrument), the embedded derivative's fair value is the difference between the fair value of the hybrid (combined) instrument and the host contract's fair value, if those can be determined reliably. [IAS 39 para 13]. If the entity is unable to determine the embedded derivative's fair value using this method either at acquisition or at a subsequent financial reporting date, the entity should fair value the hybrid (combined) instrument and designate it as at fair value through profit or loss. [IAS 39 paras 12, 13]. Designation of financial instruments is discussed in section 6.

Example – Debt instrument that is exchangeable into shares of an unlisted entity

An entity issues a debt instrument that is exchangeable into shares of an unlisted entity whose fair value cannot be reliably measured. The unlisted equity investment is recorded on the balance sheet at cost in accordance with paragraph 46(c) of IAS 39.

In this situation, the equity exchangeable feature is not closely related to the debt host and should be separated. However, although the equity instrument's fair value cannot be measured reliably, it would not be appropriate to measure the embedded derivative at cost. Instead, the entire combined contract is designated as a financial instrument at fair value through profit or loss. [IAS 39 para 12]. This presumes that the combined contract's fair value can be measured reliably.

However, the entity might conclude that the combined instrument's equity component may be sufficiently significant to preclude it from obtaining a reliable estimate of the entire instrument. In that case, the combined instrument is measured at cost less impairment. [IAS 39 para IG C.11].

It should be noted that as embedded derivative's fair value that is linked to, and must be settled by delivery of, the above unlisted equity instrument cannot be measured, the embedded derivative cannot be designated as a hedging instrument. [IAS 39 para AG 96].

6A.5.97 The requirement to identify an embedded derivative in a hybrid instrument, assess whether it is required to be separated from the host contract and, for those that are required to be separated, measure the derivatives at fair value at initial recognition and subsequently, can be complex or may result in less reliable measures than measuring the entire instrument at fair value through profit or loss. For that reason, the standard permits the entire instrument to be designated as at fair value through profit or loss. The option would be particularly helpful to banks and other entities that issue structured products containing several embedded derivatives.

A6.5.98 Therefore, if a contract contains one or more embedded derivatives, an entity may designate the entire hybrid (combined) contract as a financial asset or financial liability at fair value through profit or loss, unless:

- the embedded derivative(s) does not significantly modify the cash flows that otherwise would be required by the contract; or
- it is clear with little or no analysis when a similar hybrid (combined) instrument is first considered that separation of the embedded derivative(s) is prohibited, such as a pre-payment option embedded in a loan that permits the holder to pre-pay the loan for approximately its amortised cost.

[IAS 39 para 11A].

A6.5.99 If an embedded derivative is separated, the host contract should be accounted for in accordance with IAS 39 if it is a financial instrument and in accordance with other appropriate standards if it is not a financial instrument. IAS 39 does not address whether an embedded derivative should be presented separately on the face of the balance sheet. [IAS 39 para 11].

Separating a non-option-based embedded derivative

A6.5.100 When separating a non-option-based embedded derivative, such as an embedded forward or swap, the standard requires the embedded derivative to be separated from its host contract on the basis of its stated or implied substantive terms, so as to result in it having a fair value of zero at initial recognition. [IAS 39 para AG 28]. If it were permitted to separate embedded non-option derivatives on other terms, a single hybrid instrument could be decomposed into an infinite variety of combinations of host instruments and embedded derivatives. However, as already explained in paragraph A6.5.24 above, an embedded derivative that is not already clearly present should not be separated, that is a cash flow that does not exist cannot be created. If the terms of an embedded forward contract were determined so as to result in a fair value other than zero at the inception of the hybrid instrument, that amount would essentially represent a borrowing or lending. Therefore, it is inappropriate to separate an embedded non-option derivative on terms that result in a fair value other than zero at the inception of the hybrid instrument. [IAS 39 paras IG C1, C2]. This means that the forward price should generally be at market rates.

Example – Separation of a non-option-based derivative to produce zero fair value at inception

Entity X advances C900 to entity Y for one year at 6% interest rate and concurrently enters into an equity-based derivative in which it will receive any increase or pay any decrease in the current market price (C100) of entity Z's equity shares. The current forward price for one year for entity Z's equity shares is C200. These two transactions (the loan and the derivative) can be bundled into a structured note that could have almost an infinite variety of terms. Three possible contractual terms for the structured note that would be purchased by entity X for C900 are shown below.

- Entity X to receive at the end of the year C954 plus any excess (minus any shortfall) in the current market price of entity Z's equity shares over (or under) C200.
- Entity X to receive at the end of the year C1,054 plus any excess (minus any shortfall) in the current market price of entity Z's equity shares over (or under) C300.
- Entity X to receive at the end of the year C755 plus any excess (minus any shortfall) in the current market price of entity Z's equity shares over (or under) C1.

All the above terms of the structured note will provide the same cash flows, given a specified market price of entity Z's shares. If the market price of entity Z's shares remains at C200 at the end of year 1, entity A will receive C954 under all the three options. Similarly, if the market price of entity Z's shares increases to C306, entity A will receive C1,060 under all the options.

As is apparent, the difference in terms under the above three options are totally arbitrary, because those differences have no impact on the ultimate cash flows under the structured note. Thus those differences are not substantive and should have no influence on how the terms of the embedded derivatives are identified. Therefore, the hybrid instrument's separation into an embedded derivative and a host debt instrument should be the same for all the three options described above for the structured note.

That separation would generally result in the structured note being accounted for as a debt host contract with an initial carrying amount of C900 and a fixed annual interest rate of 6% and an embedded forward contract with C200 forward price, which results in an initial fair value of zero.

Separating an option-based embedded derivative

A6.5.101 An embedded option-based derivative (such as an embedded put, call, cap, floor or swaption) is separated from its host contract on the basis of the option feature's stated terms. The initial host instrument's carrying amount is the residual amount after separating the embedded derivative. [IAS 39 para AG 28].

Embedded derivatives in host contracts

A6.5.102 The implementation guidance explains that the economic behaviour of a hybrid instrument with an option-based embedded is fundamentally different from a non-option based derivative and depends critically on the strike price (or strike rate) specified for the option feature in the hybrid instrument.

A6.5.103 If an entity were required to identify the terms of an embedded option-based derivative so as to achieve a fair value of the embedded derivative of zero, the strike price (or strike rate) generally would have to be determined so as to result in the option being infinitely out-of-the-money. This would imply a zero probability of the option feature being exercised. However, since the probability of the option feature in a hybrid instrument being exercised generally is not zero, it would be inconsistent with the likely economic behaviour of the hybrid instrument to assume an initial fair value of zero. Similarly, if an entity were required to identify the terms of an embedded option-based derivative so as to achieve an intrinsic value of zero for the embedded derivative, the strike price (or strike rate) would have to be assumed to equal the price (or rate) of the underlying variable at the initial recognition of the hybrid instrument. In this case, the option's fair value would consist only of time value. However, such an assumption would not be consistent with the likely economic behaviour of the hybrid instrument, including the probability of the option feature being exercised, unless the agreed strike price was indeed equal to the price (or rate) of the underlying variable at the initial recognition of the hybrid instrument. [IAS 39 para IG C.2].

A6.5.104 Adjusting the strike price of an option-based embedded derivative, therefore, alters the nature of the hybrid instrument, whereas adjusting the strike price of a forward based embedded derivative does not necessarily alter the nature of the hybrid instrument. For example, if an option based embedded derivative is in-the-money, that intrinsic value does not represent a lending activity since the option may never be exercised (that is, it may expire out-of-the money due to a change in the underlying). Therefore, the separation of an option-based embedded derivative (including any embedded put, call, cap, floor, caption, floortion or swaption feature in a hybrid instrument) should be based on the stated terms of the option feature documented in the hybrid instrument. As a result, the embedded derivative would not necessarily have a fair value or intrinsic value equal to zero at the initial recognition of the hybrid instrument. [IAS 39 para IG C.2].

Multiple embedded derivatives

A6.5.105 A host contract may contain more than one embedded derivative. Each individual derivative must be identified and assessed to see whether they warrant separate accounting. Separate accounting is required in circumstances where the derivatives relate to different risk exposures and are readily separable and independent of each other. [IAS 39 para AG 29].

A6.5.106 Where, however, it is not possible to value each embedded derivative separately because of inter-dependencies, they should be bundled together and treated as a single compound embedded derivative. [IAS 39 para AG 29]. In that situation, the single compound derivative should be valued in accordance with the guidance discussed from paragraph A6.5.94 above. For the avoidance of doubt it should be noted that those embedded derivatives that are closely related to the host contract should not be included in the single compound embedded derivative that is separated from the host and accounted for separately.

Example 1 – Callable convertible bond

An entity issues callable 20,000 convertible bonds at a total par value of C2 million. Each bond pays fixed interest and is convertible at any time up to maturity into the entity's ordinary shares. Each bond also contains an embedded call option that gives the bond's issuer the right to call and redeem the bond at any time before maturity.

The bond has two embedded options that are held by different parties. The bond's holder has the option to convert the bond into a specified number of shares. The issuer has the option to call back the bond and pay an amount generally at a premium over par value.

From the issuer's perspective, the equity conversion option is an equity instrument of the issuer and, therefore, outside IAS 39's scope. Under IAS 32, the issuer must separate the equity and the liability elements of the compound instrument. As far as the issuer's call option (the right to call and redeem the bond) is concerned, this must be valued separately (using an option pricing model) as it is distinct in character and risk from the written equity conversion option. This value is then included in the liability component before separating the equity component under IAS 32. The call option may need to be accounted for separately unless the option exercise price is approximately equal to the amortised cost of the host debt instrument. [IAS 39 para AG 30(g); IAS 32 paras 31, IE 37].

From the holders' perspective, the purchase call option (to convert) and the written call (to redeem) are interlinked. This is because as the share price increases the issuer is likely to call the bond, thereby depriving the holder of the opportunity to make further returns on the bond. Although the optimal policy is to call the bond when its conversion price is equal to the call price, in practice, companies can establish a variety of call policies such as calling the instant the market value of the convertibles rises above the call price or waiting until the market value is well in excess of the call price. This interaction between the two options implies that they have to be valued together using an option pricing model. The single compound derivative is then accounted for separately from the host plain vanilla bond. Alternatively, the holder can designate the entire bond as at fair value through profit or loss as discussed in paragraph A6.5.98 above.

Example 2 – Bond with embedded forward and option features

An entity issues a debt instrument at par with a term of 5 years. The debt is callable 3 years after the issue. If the debt is called, the holder will receive an amount that is adjusted by the percentage change in the FTSE 100 index and that amount doubles if the FTSE 100 index exceeds a certain level.

In the above instrument, there are two embedded derivatives – a forward contract that pays double if the FTSE 100 index exceeds a certain level and an option that is linked to changes in the FTSE 100 index. It is not appropriate to separate both a forward and an option on the equity index, because those derivative features relate to the same risk exposure. Instead the forward and option elements are treated as a single compound, embedded derivative.

Embedded derivatives as hedging instruments

A6.5.107 IAS 39 does not restrict the circumstances in which a derivative may be designated as a hedging instrument provided the hedge accounting criteria are met (subject to some limitations on written options). [IAS 39 para 72]. Therefore, embedded derivatives that are accounted for separately can be designated as hedging instruments, like any free standing derivatives, as long as the hedge accounting criteria are met. Hedge accounting is considered in section 10.

Section 6

Classification of financial instruments

Introduction

A6.6.1 IAS 39 classifies all financial assets and financial liabilities into specific categories. The need to classify financial instruments into specific categories arises from the mixed measurement model in IAS 39, under which some financial instruments are carried at amortised cost whilst others are carried at fair value. Consequently, a particular financial instrument's classification that is carried out at initial recognition drives the subsequent accounting treatment. IAS 39 prescribes four categories for financial assets and two categories for financial liabilities.

Classification of financial assets

A6.6.2 IAS 39 has four clearly defined categories of financial assets, as follows:

- Financial assets 'at fair value through profit or loss' (FVTPL).
- Held-to-maturity investments (HTM).
- Loans and receivables.
- Available-for-sale financial assets (AFS).

[IAS 39 para 9].

As stated above, the classification is important as it dictates how the financial assets and liabilities are subsequently measured in the financial statements. This classification is also relevant when looking at whether embedded derivatives need to be bifurcated (split).

In the above list, the first and the last items are measured at fair value whilst the remaining two are measured at amortised cost.

Financial assets at fair value through profit or loss

Definition

A6.6.3 A financial asset can be classified as at fair value through profit or loss only if it meets either of the following conditions:

- Upon initial recognition, it is designated by the entity as at fair value through profit or loss.
- It is classified as held for trading.

[IAS 39 para 9].

A6.6.4 It should be noted that fair value through profit or loss is a new category that was introduced in the 2003 revision to IAS 39. It incorporates the previous 'held for trading' category. More significantly, it gave entities the option to classify any financial instruments at fair value with all gains and losses taken to profit and loss account with only very limited restrictions. The option was seen by many as the revised standard's best feature, because it was exactly that – an option – and did not require entities to measure more financial instruments at fair value. However, as explained in section 2, the fair value option did not find favour with regulators. They were concerned that the option might be used in circumstances when the fair value of the financial instruments is not verifiable; would lead to considerably more income statement volatility; and would result, in particular, in recognising of gains and losses associated with changes in the entity's own creditworthiness. As a result, in June 2005 the IASB amended IAS 39 to restrict the situations in which an entity may designate a financial instrument at fair value through profit or loss (see further para A6.6.80).

Designation at fair value through profit or loss on initial recognition

A6.6.5 An entity *may* designate a financial asset at fair value through profit or loss on initial recognition only in the following three circumstances:

- The designation eliminates or significantly reduces a measurement or recognition inconsistency (sometimes referred to as an 'accounting mismatch') that would otherwise arise (see para A6.6.8).
- A group of financial assets, financial liabilities or both is managed and its performance is evaluated on a fair value basis, in accordance with a documented risk management or investment strategy (see para A6.6.17).
- The item proposed to be designated at fair value through profit or loss is a hybrid contract that contains one or more embedded derivatives unless:
  - the embedded derivative(s) does not significantly modify the cash flows that otherwise would be required by the contract; or
  - it is clear with little or no analysis when a similar hybrid (combined) instrument is first considered that separation of the embedded derivative(s) is prohibited, such as a pre-payment option embedded in a loan that permits the holder to pre-pay the loan for approximately its amortised cost. [IAS 39 para 11A]. See further section 5.

[IAS 39 para 9].

A6.6.6 The decision to designate a financial asset at fair value through profit or loss in the above situations is similar to an accounting policy choice where the policy selected is one that provides more relevant information. However, unlike an accounting policy choice, the above designation need not be applied consistently to all similar transactions. [IAS 39 para AG 4C]. In other words, the designation can be applied on an asset-by-asset or a liability-by-liability basis, with the result that different holdings of the same type of asset or liability may be accounted for differently, some using the fair value option and others not. For example, assume an entity expects to issue a number of similar financial liabilities amounting to C100 and expects to acquire a number of similar financial assets amounting to C50 that will be carried at fair value. Provided the criteria are satisfied, the entity may significantly reduce the measurement inconsistency by designating at initial recognition all of the assets but only some of the liabilities (for example, individual liabilities with a combined total of C45) as at fair value through profit or loss. The remaining liabilities amounting to C55 can still be carried at amortised cost.

A6.6.7 The option can be applied only to whole instruments and not to portions, such as component of a debt instrument (that is, changes in value attributable to one risk such as interest rate risk and not credit risk); or proportions (that is, percentages). [IAS 39 para AG 4G]. This is because it may be difficult to isolate and measure the portion of a financial instrument if the portion is affected by more than one risk; the amount recognised in the balance sheet for that portion would be neither fair value nor cost; and the fair value adjustment for the portion may move the carrying amount of an instrument away from its fair value.

Accounting mismatch

A6.6.8 IAS 39 imposes a mixed measurement model under which some financial instruments are measured at fair value and others at amortised cost; some gains and losses are recognised in profit or loss and others initially in equity. This combination of measurement and recognition requirements can result in inconsistencies (sometimes referred to as an 'accounting mismatch') between the accounting for an asset (or group of assets) and a liability (or group of liabilities). An accounting mismatch occurs when assets and liabilities that are economically related (that is, share a risk) are treated inconsistently. This could occur where, in the absence of the fair value option, a financial asset is classified as available-for-sale (with most changes in fair value recognised directly in equity) while a related liability is measured at amortised cost (with changes in fair value not recognised). In such circumstances, an entity may conclude that its financial statements would provide more relevant information if both the asset and the liability were classified as at fair value through profit or loss. [IAS 39 para AG 4D].

A6.6.9 As explained above, the use of the fair value option may eliminate measurement anomalies for financial assets and liabilities that provide a natural offset of each other because they share the same risk, but where hedge accounting cannot be used because none of the instruments is a derivative. More importantly, even if some of the instruments are derivatives that could qualify for fair value hedge accounting, classification of both items at fair value through profit or loss achieves the same accounting result whilst avoiding the designation, tracking and assessing of hedge effectiveness that hedge accounting entails. It follows that the use of the fair value option as an alternative to hedge accounting can be of significant benefit to entities. However, such advantage also has a cost. Under the fair value option the entire change in fair value of the asset or liability would fall to be recognised in profit or loss, not simply the change in fair value attributable to the risk that is hedged by an offsetting derivative. As a result, the amount reported in profit or loss under the fair value option is unlikely to be the same as the change in fair value of the hedging derivative. This may lead to greater profit or loss volatility. Furthermore, hedge accounting can be revoked at any time, but the fair value option is irrevocable.

A6.6.10 The IASB has not established a percentage, or a 'bright line', for interpreting 'significant' in the context of an accounting mismatch. However, the Basis for Conclusion makes it clear that an effectiveness test similar to that used for hedge accounting is not required to demonstrate that a reduction in an accounting mismatch is significant. [IAS 39 BC para 75B]. This means judgement is required to determine when the fair value option should be applied. In this regard, management should look at the objective of the proposed designation as 'at fair value through profit or loss'. Comparing the accounting impact – that is, the measurement basis and the recognition of gains and losses — of all relevant items (including, for example, any funding that it is not proposed to be designated at fair value through profit or loss before and after the designation will give an indication of whether an accounting mismatch has been eliminated or significantly reduced.

A6.6.11 Although it is necessary to demonstrate that there is an accounting mismatch, the extent of evidence needed to identify the accounting mismatch for which the fair value option is to be used need not be extensive. It may be possible to use the same evidence for a number of similar transactions, depending on the circumstances — for example, by identifying a particular kind of accounting mismatch that arises from one of the entity's chosen risk management strategies. It is not necessary to have the extensive documentation required for hedge accounting, but the entity does need to provide evidence that the fair value option was designated at inception. Also, IFRS 7 require disclosure of the carrying amounts of assets and, separately, liabilities designated as 'at fair value through profit or loss'. The evidence must, therefore, include precise identification of the assets and liabilities to which the fair value option has been applied.

Example 1 – Fixed rate assets financed by fixed rate debentures

An entity is about to purchase a portfolio of fixed rate assets that will be financed by fixed rate debentures. Both financial assets and financial liabilities are subject to the same interest rate risk that gives rise to opposite changes in fair value that tend to offset each other.

In the absence of the fair value option, the entity may have classified the fixed rate assets as available-for-sale with gains and losses on changes in fair value recognised in equity and the fixed rate debentures at amortised cost. Reporting both the assets and the liabilities at fair value through profit and loss corrects the measurement inconsistency and produce more relevant information. [IAS 39 para AG 4E(d)(i)].

Example 2 – Fixed rate bond converted to floating rate

An entity purchases a fixed rate bond and immediately enters into an interest rate swap to convert the fixed rate to floating rate.

Instead of claiming hedge accounting, the entity could designate the bond at fair value through profit or loss. Since both the bond and the swap will be measured at fair value through profit or loss, the entity achieves a similar accounting result to if fair value hedge accounting has been applied, but without the added burden of designating, assessing and measuring hedge effectiveness that hedge accounting entails.

It should be noted that the bond is fully fair valued for all risks and not just for the hedged interest rate risk that hedge accounting would require. Furthermore, the fair value option is irrevocable. Hedge accounting is revocable (see section 9).

Example 3 – Fixed rate loan offset by derivative liabilities

An entity is about to originate a 10-year fixed rate loan that, if not designated as at fair value through profit or loss, will be measured at amortised cost. The entity also has a nine-year derivative that it regards as related to, and shares the same risk as, the loan. The entity wishes to designate the asset as at fair value through profit or loss to eliminate the measurement and recognition inconsistency with the derivative.

Although, in this example, the relationship does not completely eliminate the economic exposure, the entity can still designate the asset at fair value through profit or loss. The difference in maturities does not prevent the entity from designating the asset at fair value through profit or loss, provided there is a perceived economic relationship between the asset and the derivative. The fair value option does not require the elimination of economic volatility; it requires the elimination or significant reduction of an accounting mismatch. In the above example, the asset is measured at amortised cost and the derivative is measured at fair value, hence the accounting mismatch. Secondly, there is a perceived economic relationship between the asset and liability — for example, they share a risk that gives rise to opposite changes in fair value that tend to offset.

Example 4 – Financing a group of loans with traded bonds

An entity is about to originate a specified group of loans to be financed by issuing traded bonds whose changes in fair value tend to offset each other. The entity expects to regularly buy and sell the bonds but rarely, if ever, to buy and sell the loans.

Reporting both the loans and the bonds at fair value through profit or loss eliminates the inconsistency in the timing of recognition of gains and losses that would otherwise result from measuring them both at amortised cost and recognising a gain or loss each time a bond is repurchased. [IAS 39 para AG 4E(d)(ii)].

Example 5 – Subsidiary's debt offset by interest rate swap with parent

A subsidiary is about to issue a liability to a third party and enter into a related interest rate swap with its parent. An accounting mismatch exists in the subsidiary's stand alone financial statements, and it intends to designate the liability as at fair value through profit or loss.

Although it is appropriate for the subsidiary to designate the liability as at fair value through profit or loss in its individual financial statements, such designation is not possible in the consolidated financial statements. This is because the inter-company swap will be eliminated, and the 'mismatch' will not exist in the consolidated financial statements. However, if the parent can identify an external swap or other instrument that gives rise to an accounting mismatch on a consolidated basis, this may justify designating the liability as at fair value through profit or loss in the consolidated financial statements.

6A.6.12 An accounting mismatch need not occur only between related financial assets and financial liabilities. It could also occur between a financial asset and a related non-financial liability or between a non-financial asset and a related financial liability. In both situations, the entity may use the fair value option, provided it concludes that the changes in fair value of both items are subject to the same risk and an accounting mismatch will be eliminated or significantly reduced by the designation.

Example 1 – Financial assets offsetting non-financial liabilities

An insurer holds financial assets whose fair value exposure offsets that of non-financial liabilities under insurance contracts that are measured using techniques that incorporate current market information, but are not measured at fair values.

Reporting both the insurance liability at fair value (as permitted by para 24 of IFRS 4) and the financial asset at fair value through profit or loss eliminates the inconsistency that would otherwise result from measuring the insurance liability at cost and the financial asset at available-for-sale or at amortised cost. [IAS 39 para AG 4E(b)].

6A.6.13 Designations as at fair value through profit or loss should be made at initial recognition and once made are irrevocable. For practical purposes, the entity need not enter into all of the assets and liabilities giving rise to measurement or recognition inconsistency at exactly the same time. A reasonable delay is permitted provided that each transaction is designated as at fair value through profit or loss at its initial recognition and, at that time, any remaining transactions are expected to occur. [IAS 39 para AG 4F].

A6.6.14 Reasonable delay should be assessed on a case-by-case basis, based as to what is reasonable in the circumstances. For example, a 'reasonable delay' could be a fairly short period in the case of entering into a derivative to offset some of the risks of an asset. A longer period could be justified if the delay arises from the need to assemble a portfolio of similar assets and arrange their funding. However, all financial assets and liabilities designated as at fair value through profit or loss must be accounted for on this basis from their initial recognition (and not only from the time any offsetting position is entered into).

A6.6.15 It should be noted that if, for some reason, one of the offsetting instruments is derecognised, for instance, the fixed rate assets in example 1 or the interest rate swap in example 2 in paragraph A6.6.11 above, the other offsetting instrument – the fixed rate debentures in example 1 or the fixed rate bond in example 2 – would continue to be carried at fair value with gains and losses reported in profit or loss. This is because the designation at fair value through profit or loss at initial recognition is irrevocable, irrespective of whether the initial conditions that permitted the use of the option (to correct an accounting mismatch) still hold.

A6.6.16 IFRS 7 also requires the entity to provide disclosures about financial assets and financial liabilities it has designated as at fair value through profit or loss, including how it has satisfied those conditions. For instruments that qualify for designation as at fair value through profit or loss in accordance with paragraph A6.6.8 above, the disclosure should include a narrative description of the circumstances underlying the measurement or recognition inconsistency that would arise. [IAS 39 para 9(b); IFRS 7 para B(5)]. See further section 11.

Group of financial assets and liabilities managed on a fair value basis

A6.6.17 An entity may manage and evaluate the performance of a group of financial assets, financial liabilities or both in such a way that measuring that group at fair value through profit or loss results in more relevant information. Therefore, in order to designate financial instruments at fair value through profit or loss under the second criterion in paragraph A6.6.5 above, the designation should be based on the manner in which the entity manages and evaluates performance, rather than on the nature of those financial instruments. [IAS 39 para AG 4H]. An entity should designate all eligible financial instruments that are managed and evaluated together. [IAS 39 para AG 4J]. However, designation under this criterion must meet the following two requirements:

- The financial instruments are managed and performance evaluated on a fair value basis in accordance with a documented risk management or investment strategy.
- Information about the group is provided internally on that basis to the entity's key management as defined in IAS 24, 'Related party disclosures' (for example, the entity's board of directors and chief executive officer).

[IAS 39 para 9(b)(ii)].

A6.6.18 The requirement that a group of financial assets and liabilities should be managed and performance evaluated on a fair value basis means that management should evaluate the portfolio on a full fair value basis and not on a risk-by-risk basis. For example, an entity that originates fixed interest rate loans and manages the interest rate risk of this portfolio based on the fair value attributable only to interest rate changes will be unable to use the fair value option. This is because the fair value concept is a broader notion than hedge accounting, such that evaluating the portfolio's performance for only some risks is not sufficient. Therefore, an entity's risk management policy and the resulting management information should look at the entire change in fair value and not for only some risks to justify the fair value option's use.

A6.6.19 The required documentation of the entity's strategy need not be on an item-by-item basis, nor need it be in the level of detail required for hedge accounting. Documentation may be on a portfolio or group basis as long as it clearly identifies the items for which the fair value option is to be used. If the documentation relies on several other pre-existing documents, there needs to be an overall document that references these other documents and clearly demonstrates that the entity manages and evaluates the relevant financial assets or financial liabilities on a fair value basis. The documentation also needs to be sufficient to demonstrate that using the fair value option is consistent with the entity's risk management or investment strategy. In many cases, the entity's existing documentation, as approved by key management personnel, should be sufficient for this purpose. For example, if the performance management system for a group — as approved by the entity's key management personnel — clearly demonstrates that its performance is evaluated on a total return basis, no further documentation is required to demonstrate compliance with the above requirements. [IAS 39 para AG 4K].

A6.6.20 As stated in paragraph A6.6.16 above, IFRS 7 requires the entity to provide disclosures about financial assets and financial liabilities it has designated as at fair value through profit or loss, including how it has satisfied those conditions. For instruments that qualify for designation as at fair value through profit or loss as a group of financial assets on liablities, in accordance with paragraph A6.6.17 above, the disclosure should include a narrative description of how designation as at fair value through profit or loss is consistent with the entity's documented risk management or investment strategy. [IAS 39 para 9(b); IFRS 7 para B(5)]. See further section 11.

Example 1 – Portfolio of financial assets held by venture capital firms

A venture capital organisation invests in a portfolio of financial assets with a view to profiting from their total return in the form of interest or dividends and changes in fair value and evaluates its performance on that basis. Some investments meet the definition of associates and joint ventures, while others do not.

IAS 28, 'Investments in associates' and IAS 31, 'Interests in joint ventures' allow such investments to be measured at fair value through profit or loss rather than using equity accounting.

The fair value option allows the other investments, which are also managed and evaluated on a total return basis, but which fall outside the scope of IAS 28 and IAS 31 to be measured at fair value through profit or loss if that is consistent with the manner in which the entity manages and evaluates the performance of these investments. [IAS 39 para AG 4I(a)].

In other words, the entire portfolio can be measured at fair value through profit or loss provided the two requirements of paragraph A6.6.17 above are met.

Example 2 – Portfolio of financial assets held to back specific liabilities

An entity holds a portfolio of financial assets. The entity manages the portfolio so as to maximise its total return (that is, interest or dividends and changes in fair value) and evaluates its performance on that basis. The portfolio is held to back specific liabilities.

In this situation, the entity may designate the portfolio at fair value through profit or loss, because it is likely that the entity's strategy to maximise total return would be set by, and information about performance of the portfolio would be provided to, key management on a timely basis. This is so regardless of whether the entity also manages and evaluates the liabilities on a fair value basis. [IAS 39 para AG 4I(c)].

Exception

A6.6.21 The fair value option is not available for investments in equity instruments that do not have a quoted market price in an active market and whose fair value cannot be reliably measured. [IAS 39 para 9]. Therefore, in the absence of a quoted market price in an active market, if the fair value of an equity investment is not reliably measurable, because the range of reasonable fair value estimates is significant and the probabilities of the various estimates within the range cannot be reasonably assessed, an entity is precluded from measuring the instrument at fair value. [IAS 39 paras AG 80, AG 81].

Held for trading

A6.6.22 A financial asset is held for trading if it is:

- acquired or incurred principally for the purpose of selling or repurchasing it in the near term;
- part of a portfolio of identified financial instruments that are managed together and for which there is evidence of a recent actual pattern of short-term profit taking; or
- a derivative (except for a derivative that is a financial guarantee contract or a designated and effective hedging instrument).

[IAS 39 para 9].

A6.6.23 Financial assets held for trading include:

- Debt and equity securities that are actively traded by the entity.
- Loans and receivables acquired by the entity with the intention of making a short-term profit from price or dealer's margin.
- Securities held under repurchase agreements.

Derivatives are always categorised as held for trading, unless they are accounted for as effective hedging instruments.

A6.6.24 Trading generally reflects active and frequent buying and selling and financial instruments held for trading generally are used with the objective of generating a profit from short-term fluctuations in price or dealer's margin. [IAS 39 para AG 14]. Whether an entity holds financial assets to generate profit on short-term differences in prices must be assessed on the basis of the facts and circumstances surrounding the trading activity rather than on the individual transaction's terms. Evidence of this is based on the frequency of buying and selling, the turnover rate or average holding period of the financial assets included in the portfolio (portfolio churning). All available evidence should be considered to determine whether the entity is involved in trading activities.

A6.6.25 Financial assets that are brought and held principally in a portfolio for the purpose of selling them in the near term (thus held for only a short period of time) should be classified as trading at acquisition date. Although the term 'portfolio' is not explicitly defined in IAS 39, the context in which it is used suggests that a portfolio is a group of financial assets or financial liabilities that are managed together. Also the phrases 'selling them in the near term' and 'held for only a short period of time' are not explained in IAS 39. Therefore, in practice, an entity should adopt a suitable definition of these phrases and apply them on a consistent basis to avoid any ambiguity. For example, it is likely that if a security was acquired with the intent of selling it within a few weeks or months, the security would be classified as held for trading. After being designated as held for trading, a single instrument in a portfolio may in fact be held for a longer period of time, as long as there is evidence of a recent actual pattern of short-term profit taking on financial instruments included in such a portfolio.

Example – Shares held for trading

An entity purchased quoted equity shares from the market with the intention of profiting from short-term price fluctuations. The entity held the shares for three years due to a large unexpected downturn in the stock market after which it sold the shares in a more buoyant market.

Since management's intention at acquisition was to profit from short-term price fluctuations, the entity would have classified the shares as held-for-trading. The fact that after designation the shares were in fact held for a longer term, because the entity was unable to sell the shares at a loss in a bear market, would not frustrate the held-to-trading classification. Indeed, IAS 39 does not limit the period for which such an instrument can be held as long as the principal purpose at acquisition was to sell them in the near term. Furthermore, as there is no definition of 'near term' it is important for the entity to adopt a suitable definition and apply it consistently as explained in paragraph A6.6.24 above.

Held-to-maturity investments

Definition

A6.6.26 Held-to-maturity investments are non-derivative financial assets with fixed or determinable payments and fixed maturity that an entity has the positive intention and ability to hold to maturity other than:

- Those that the entity upon initial recognition designates as at fair value through profit or loss.
- Those that the entity designates as available-for-sale.
- Those that meet the definition of loans and receivables.

[IAS 39 para 9].

A6.6.27 For most financial assets, the standard regards fair value as a more appropriate measure than amortised cost. Classifying a security as held-to-maturity means that the enterprise is indifferent to future opportunities to profit from changes in the security's fair value and intends to accept the debt security's stipulated contractual cash flows, including the repayment of principal at maturity. The held-to-maturity category is, therefore, an exception. Consequently, its use is restricted to instruments that have specific terms and characteristics and by a number of detailed conditions, largely designed to test whether the entity has genuine intention and ability to hold those instruments to maturity. Also, significant penalties exist for entities that classify an instrument as held-to-maturity, but which is sold before maturity. These issues are considered below.

Fixed or determinable payments and fixed maturity

A6.6.28 Instruments classified as held-to-maturity must have fixed or determinable payments and fixed maturity, which means that a contractual arrangement defines the amounts and dates of payments to the holder, such as interest and principal payments. Investments in equity shares have indefinite lives and, therefore, cannot be held-to-maturity financial assets. Other equity instruments, such as share options and warrants, cannot be classified as held-to-maturity because the amounts the holder receives may vary in a manner that is not predetermined. [IAS 39 para AG 17]. It follows that since held-to-maturity financial assets must have fixed maturity, it is mainly debt instruments that fall within this category. A mandatorily redeemable preference share is also, in substance, a debt instrument that may fall within this category.

A6.6.29 The amount of determinable payment of principal or interest is normally established by reference to a source other than the financial instrument, and may involve a calculation. For example, floating rate interest on a financial instrument that is calculated from a reference interest rate such as the LIBOR or a bank's prime, and a principal amount that is linked to a price index such as the market price of a commodity like oil, are examples of determinable cash flows.

Example 1 – Floating rate note

Entity A purchases a note with variable interest rate and a fixed payment at maturity.

The floating rate note could qualify as a held-to-maturity investment since its payments are fixed (the principal) and the interest payments are specified by reference to a market or bench mark rate such as the LIBOR, which is determinable. A held-to-maturity classification for floating rate notes is, however, of little benefit, since its fair value will not change significantly in response to changes in interest rates.

Example 2 – Indexed linked principal payments

Entity A purchases a five-year equity-index-linked note with an original issue price of C10 at a market price of C12 at the time of purchase. The note requires no interest payments before maturity. At maturity, the note requires payment of the original issue price of C10 plus a supplemental redemption amount that depends on whether a specified share price index exceeds a predetermined level at the maturity date. If the share index does not exceed or is equal to the predetermined level, no supplemental redemption amount is paid. If the share index exceeds the predetermined level, the supplemental redemption amount equals the product of 1.15 and the difference between the level of the share index at maturity and the level of the share index when the note was issued divided by the level of the share index at the time of issue. Entity A has the positive intention and ability to hold the note to maturity.

The embedded equity feature is not closely related to the debt host and must be separated. Once the embedded derivative is fair valued and separated, the debt host can be classified as a held-to-maturity investment because it has a fixed payment of C10 and fixed maturity and entity A has the positive intention and ability to hold it to maturity. [IAS 39 paraIG B13].

In this example, the purchase price of C12 is allocated between the host debt instrument and the embedded derivative. If, for instance, the fair value of the embedded equity feature at acquisition is C4, the host debt instrument is measured at C8 on initial recognition. In this case, the discount of C2 that is implicit in the host bond (principal of C10 minus the original carrying amount of C8) is amortised to profit or loss over the term to maturity of the note using the effective interest method.

Example 3 – Indexed linked interest

Entity A purchases a bond with a fixed payment at maturity and a fixed maturity date. The interest payments on the bond are indexed to the price of a commodity or equity and the entity has the positive intention and ability to hold the bond to maturity.

The commodity-indexed or equity-indexed interest payments result in an embedded derivative that is not closely related to the bond. Hence, it is necessary to separate the host debt investment (the fixed payment at maturity) from the embedded derivative (the index-linked interest payments).

Once the embedded derivative has been separated, the debt host can be classified as held-to-maturity as it has a fixed payment and a fixed maturity and entity A has the positive intention and ability to hold the bond to maturity. [IAS 39 para IG B14].

Example 4 – Perpetual debt instrument

Entity A purchases two perpetual debt instruments X and Y as follows:

- Instrument X pays an interest rate of 10% per annum for an indefinite period.
- Instrument Y pays an interest rate of 16% for the first 10 years and zero per cent in subsequent periods.

Entity A cannot classify instrument X that provides for interest payments for an indefinite period as held-to-maturity, because there is no maturity date. [IAS 39 para AG 17].

As far as instrument Y is concerned, it may be possible to argue from an economic perspective, that the instrument has a fixed maturity of 10 years. This is because the initial amount is amortised to zero over the first ten years using the effective interest method, since a portion of the interest payments represents repayments of the principal amount. The amortised cost is zero after year 10, because the present value of the stream of future cash payments in subsequent periods is zero (there are no further cash payments of either principal or interest in subsequent periods). Since the only cash flows under the terms are fixed interest payments over a period of 10 years, there is a strong argument to support held-to-maturity classification on the grounds that entity A has recovered all of its initial investment and the rights in the event of a liquidation has no value, notwithstanding that the terms do not specify a maturity date.

Intent to hold to maturity

A6.6.30 A positive intent to hold financial assets to maturity is a much higher hurdle than simply having no present intention to sell. An entity does not have a positive intention to hold to maturity an investment in a financial asset with a fixed maturity if:

- The entity intends to hold the financial asset for an undefined period. In other words, as the entity has not actually defined a period, the positive intent to hold-to-maturity does not exist.
- The entity stands ready to sell the financial asset (other than if a situation arises that is non-recurring and could not have been reasonably anticipated by the entity) in response to changes in market interest rates or risks, liquidity needs, changes in the availability of and the yield on alternative investments, changes in financing sources and terms or changes in foreign currency risk. All these situations are indicative that the entity intends to profit from changes in the asset's fair value and has no intention of holding the financial asset to maturity.
- The issuer has a right to settle the financial asset at an amount significantly below its amortised cost. Where this is the case and the issuer is expected to exercise that right, the entity cannot demonstrate a positive intent to hold the financial asset to maturity. See further paragraph A6.6.32 below.

[IAS 39 para AG 16]

A6.6.31 An entity's intention to hold a financial asset to maturity is not negated by unusual and unlikely events that could not be anticipated at the time of the original classification. For example, a disaster scenario that is only remotely possible, such as a run on a bank or a similar situation affecting an insurer, is not something that is assessed by an entity in deciding whether it has the positive intention and ability to hold an investment to maturity. [IAS 39 para AG 21].

A6.6.32 A financial asset that is callable by the issuer would satisfy the criteria for classification as a held-to-maturity investment if the holder intends and is able to hold it until it is called or until maturity and the holder would recover substantially all of its carrying amount. This means that if the issuer can call the instrument at or above its carrying amount, the holder's original classification of the instrument as held-to-maturity is not invalidated because the call option, if exercised, would simply accelerates the asset's maturity. However, if the financial asset is callable on a basis that would result in the holder not recovering substantially all of its carrying amount, the financial asset cannot be classified as a held-to-maturity investment. Any premium paid and capitalised transaction costs should be considered in determining whether the carrying amount would be substantially recovered. [IAS 39 para AG 18].

A6.6.33 On the other hand, a financial asset that is puttable (that is, the holder has the right to require that the issuer repay or redeem the financial asset before maturity) cannot be classified as a held-to-maturity investment, because paying for a put feature in a financial asset is inconsistent with the positive intent to hold the financial asset until maturity. [IAS 39 para AG 19].

A6.6.34 Similarly, an investment in a convertible bond that is convertible before maturity generally cannot be classified as a held-to-maturity investment, because that would be inconsistent with paying for the conversion feature — the right to convert into equity shares before maturity. [IAS 39 para IG C3]. By paying for the conversion feature in terms of a lower interest rate, the investor hopes to benefit from appreciation in value of the option embedded in the debt security. Therefore, in general, it is unlikely that the investor will be able to assert the positive intent and ability to hold a convertible debt security to maturity and forego the opportunity to profit by exercising the conversion option. Even if the convertible debt is separated into an equity option and a host debt instrument (see section 7), it generally still would be contradictory to assert the positive intent and ability to hold the debt host contract to maturity and forego the opportunity to exercise the conversion option. On the other hand, if the conversion option can only be exercised at maturity, it may be possible for the holder to demonstrate positive intent to hold the bond to maturity.

Ability to hold to maturity

A6.6.35 It is not sufficient for the entity to demonstrate a positive intent to hold a financial asset to maturity; the entity must also demonstrate its ability to hold such an asset to maturity. An entity cannot demonstrate that ability if:

- it does not have the financial resources available to continue to finance the investment until maturity; or
- it is subject to an existing legal or other constraint that could frustrate its intention to hold the financial asset to maturity (although as noted in para A6.6.32 above, an issuer's call option does not necessarily frustrate this intention).

[IAS 39 para AG 23].

For example, it is unlikely that an open ended fund would be able to classify any financial asset as held-to maturity. Management might intend to hold the investments to maturity, but calls for redemption of shares or units could constrain the fund's ability to hold its investments to maturity.

A6.6.36 An entity's intention and ability to hold debt instruments to maturity is not necessarily constrained if those instruments have been pledged as collateral or are subject to a repurchase agreement or securities lending agreement. However, an entity does not have the positive intention and ability to hold the debt instruments until maturity if it does not expect to be able to maintain or recover access to the instruments. [IAS 39 para IG B18].

Example 1 – Pledge of held-to-maturity assets as security

Entity A requires C18 million of cash for its operating activities in 20X7. The entity's latest cash-flow forecast indicates a C2 million shortfall. The entity intends to raise the funds required by pledging its investments in bonds, which are classified as held-to-maturity, to a bank to the obtain a banking facility.

The bonds can continue to be classified as held-to-maturity provided that the entity is able to fulfil the conditions of the banking facility such that the bank will not exercise the pledge. Short-term liquidity problems do not necessarily undermine the entity's ability to hold the investments until maturity.

Assessment of held-to-maturity classification

A6.6.37 An entity should assess its intention and ability to hold its held-to-maturity investments to maturity not only when those financial assets are initially recognised, but also at each subsequent balance sheet date. [IAS 39 para AG 25]. Because an entity is expected not to change its *intent* about a held-to-maturity security, the requirement to reassess the appropriateness of a security's classification would necessarily focus on the entity's *ability* to hold a security to maturity. Facts and circumstances may change that may cause the entity to lose its ability to hold a debt security to maturity. Unless those facts and circumstances fall within one of the exceptions discussed in paragraph A6.6.41 below, the entity would be forced to reclassify its held-to-maturity investments to available-for-sale.

The tainting rules

A6.6.38 Because management must assert that the criteria for a held-to-maturity investment have been met for each investment, the sale, reclassification or exercise of a put option of certain held-to-maturity securities will call into question ('taint') management's intent to hold all securities in the held-to-maturity category. As a result, where an entity during the current financial year has sold or reclassified more than an insignificant amount of held-to-maturity investments before maturity (more than insignificant in relation to the total amount of held-to-maturity investments), it is prohibited from classifying any financial asset as held-to-maturity for a period of two years after the occurrence of this event. Furthermore, all the entity's held-to-maturity investments, not just investments of a similar type, must be reclassified into the available-for-sale category and measured at fair value (see further para A6.6.74 below). In a sense a penalty is imposed for a change in management's intention. When the prohibition ends (at the end of the second financial year following the tainting), the portfolio becomes 'cleansed' and the entity is once more able to assert that it has the intent and ability to hold debt securities to maturity. [IAS 39 paras 9, 52].

A6.6.39 The tainting rules do not apply if only an insignificant amount of held-to-maturity investments is sold or reclassified. The standard does not define what an insignificant amount means, except that it should be measured by reference to the total amount of held-to-maturity investments. Therefore, judgement is needed to assess what is insignificant in each particular situation.

Example 1 – Application of the tainting rules

An entity's held-to-maturity portfolio consists of a mixture of sterling corporate bonds, treasury bonds and Eurodollar bonds. The entity prepares its financial statements to 31 December 20X5. During September 20X5, the entity sold a certain Eurodollar bond to realise a large gain.

The fact that the entity has sold one Eurodollar investment (not considered insignificant in relation to the total held-to-maturity portfolio) does not mean that only the Eurodollar sub-category has been tainted. The tainting rule is very clear. If an entity has sold or reclassified more than an insignificant amount of held-to-maturity investments, the entire portfolio and all remaining investments must be reclassified to the available-for-sale category. [IAS 39 para IG B20]. It follows that sub-classification of securities for the purpose of limiting the impact of sales or transfers of held-to-maturity securities is not acceptable practice.

The reclassification is recorded in the reporting period in which the sales occurred (that is, the year to 31 December 20X5). Furthermore, as explained in paragraph A6.6.38 above, the entity is prohibited from reclassifying any investments in the held-to-maturity category for two full financial years after 31 December 20X5. This means that any fixed interest securities acquired during 20X6 and 20X7, which could qualify for held-to-maturity classification, cannot be classified as such in those years. The earliest date that the entity is able to classify investments as held-to-maturity is 1 January 20X8 as shown in the diagram below:

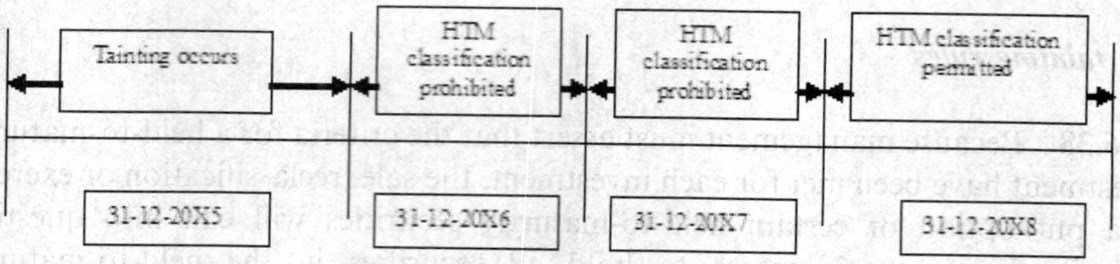

At 1 January 20X8 when the portfolio becomes cleansed, and it once again becomes appropriate to carry securities at held-to-maturity, the fair value of the affected securities on 1 January 20X8 becomes the new amortised cost. Furthermore, as tainting occurs in the year to 31 December 20X5, the held-to-maturity classification for the comparative period to 31 December 20X4 is not affected.

Example 2 – Regular disposal of small amounts of held-to-maturity securities

Entity X has a portfolio of financial investments that is classified as held-to-maturity. In the current period, it sold small amounts of investments from time to time.

Regular or systematic sales or transfers of immaterial amounts are indicative of management's intention not to hold financial assets to maturity. The tainting rules would apply and the entity should reclassify all its held-to-maturity investments as available for sale and measure them at fair value.

In addition, the entity may not create a sub-category of held-to-maturity in which to hold these investments. (The aim of this sub-categorisation would have been so that the sale of investments prior to maturity from that sub-category did not taint the entire held-to-maturity portfolio.)

Tainting in group situations

A6.6.40 The tainting rules are designed to test an entity's assertion that it has the positive intent and ability to hold each security to maturity. The rules apply to all entities within a group. Therefore, if a subsidiary operating in a different legal or economic environment sells more than an insignificant amount of held-to-maturity investments, it would preclude the entire group from using the held-to-maturity category. This means that the entity would have to reclassify all its held-to-maturity investments in its consolidated financial statements, unless the sale qualifies for one of the exceptions noted in paragraph A6.6.41 below. [IAS 39 para IG B21]. Furthermore, at least two full financial years must pass before the entity can again classify financial assets as held-to-maturity in its consolidated financial statements. Sales between group entities generally would not taint the held-to-maturity classification at the group level, but may do so at the individual entity level. As the consequences of breaching the conditions are harsh, entities should carefully consider any plans to sell, transfer or exercise put options before classifying any asset to this category.

Exceptions to the tainting rules

A6.6.41 There are a number of exceptions to the tainting rules. As already discussed in paragraph A6.6.38 above, a sale or reclassification of an insignificant amount of held-to-maturity investment would not result in tainting. Similarly, a sale or reclassification would not taint the rest of the portfolio if it was:

- so close to maturity or the financial asset's call date (for example, less than three months before maturity) that changes in the market rate of interest would not have a significant effect on the financial asset's fair value;
- made after the entity has collected substantially all of the financial asset's original principal through scheduled payments or pre-payments; or
- due to an isolated event that is beyond the entity's control, is non-recurring and could not have been reasonably anticipated by the entity.

[IAS 39 para 9].

A6.6.42 The conditions referred to in the first and second bullet points above relate to situations in which an entity can be expected to be indifferent whether to hold or sell a financial asset, because movements in interest rates after substantially all of the original principal has been collected or when the instrument is close to maturity will not have a significant impact on its fair value. Accordingly, in such situations, a sale would not affect reported net profit or loss and no price volatility would be expected during the remaining period to maturity. For example, if an entity sells a financial asset less than three months prior to maturity, that would generally qualify for use of this exception because the impact on the fair value of the instrument for a difference between the stated interest rate and the market rate generally would be small for an instrument that matures in three months relative to an instrument that matures in several years.

A6.6.43 The term 'substantially all' in the second bullet point of paragraph A6.6.41 above is not defined in IAS 39. The guidance to the previous version of IAS 39 stated that if an entity sells a financial asset after it has collected 90 per cent or more of the financial asset's original principal through scheduled payments or pre-payments, that would generally qualify for this exception. However, if the entity has collected, say, only 10 per cent of the original principal, then that condition clearly is not met. Although the previous guidance has not been carried forward in the revised version, we believe that, in practice, applying a 90 per cent threshold as a rule of thumb to test whether 'substantially all' of the original principal has been collected is acceptable. Clearly, though, it cannot be applied as a hard and fast rule.

A6.6.44 In relation to the last bullet point in paragraph A6.6.41 above, very few events would qualify as isolated events beyond the entity's control, that are non-recurring or reasonably unanticipated. A disaster scenario that is only remotely possible, such as a run on a bank or a similar situation affecting an insurer, would qualify as it is not something that would be assessed by an entity in deciding whether it has the positive intention and ability to hold an investment to maturity. [IAS 39 para AG 21]. The corollary is that if the sale or reclassification resulted from an event that is not isolated but within the entity's control or is potentially recurring or could have been anticipated at the date the held-to-maturity classification was made, this inevitably will cast doubt on the entity's intent and ability to hold a security to maturity. Consider the following example:

Example – Permitted sales

Entity X has a portfolio of financial assets that is classified as held-to-maturity. In the current period, at the direction of the board of directors, the senior management team has been replaced. The new management wishes to sell a portion of the held-to-maturity financial assets in order to carry out an expansion strategy designated and approved by the board.

A change in management is not identified under the standard as an instance where sales or transfers from held-to-maturity do not compromise the classification as held-to-maturity (see para A6.6.41 below).

Although the previous management team had been in place since the entity's inception and entity X had never before undergone a major restructuring, sales in response to a change in management would, nevertheless call into question entity X's intention to hold remaining held-to-maturity financial assets to maturity. [IAS 39 IG B16].

6A.6.45 In addition to the above, the standard identifies some specific circumstances that may not have been anticipated at the time of the initial held-to-maturity classification and, therefore, would justify the sale of a security classified as held-to-maturity without calling into question management's intent to hold other debt securities to maturity in the future. Thus a sale or transfer of a held-to-maturity security due to one of the following circumstances would not result in tainting of a held-to-maturity portfolio.

- A significant deterioration in the issuer's credit worthiness (see para A6.6.46).
- Changes in tax laws (see para A6.6.49).
- Major business combination or disposition, such as a sale of a segment (see para A6.6.50).
- Changes in statutory or regulatory requirements (see para A6.6.53).

[IAS 39 para AG 22].

A significant deterioration in the issuer's creditworthiness

A6.6.46 A sale due to a significant deterioration in the issuer's creditworthiness (evident by a downgrade in the issuer's credit rating by an external rating agency) might not raise a question about the entity's intention to hold other investments to maturity. However, the deterioration in creditworthiness must be significant judged by reference to the credit rating at initial recognition. If the rating downgrade in combination with other information provides evidence of impairment (for example, if it becomes probable that all amounts due (principal and interest) will not be collected), the deterioration in creditworthiness often would be regarded as significant. Also, the significant deterioration must not have been reasonably anticipated when the entity classified the investment as held-to-maturity in order to meet the condition in IAS 39. A credit downgrade of a notch within a class or from one rating class to the immediately lower rating class could often be regarded as reasonably anticipated. Therefore, a sale triggered by such a downgrade would result in tainting of the held-to-maturity portfolio. Similarly, a sale as a result of the issuer's bankruptcy would be regarded as a permitted sale, but not one where the bankruptcy was anticipated at the acquisition date and the investor was, therefore, able to control the outcome. [IAS 39 para IG B15].

A6.6.47 Where a credit rating is not available from an external rating agency to assess a decline in the issuer's creditworthiness, the entity is permitted to use its internal credit rating system to support the demonstration of significant deterioration in the issuer's creditworthiness. However, the internal credit rating system must be sufficiently robust to provide a reliable and objective measure of the issuer's credit rating and changes in those ratings on a consistent basis.

A6.6.48 A sale following a significant deterioration in the issuer's creditworthiness should normally take place as soon as the entity becomes aware of the credit downgrade and not left until a later date. This is because if the sale or reclassification out of held-to-maturity category is not made immediately or shortly afterwards following the credit downgrade, it provides evidence that the entity is indifferent to the loss incurred in its held-to-maturity portfolio and intends to hold those investments to maturity. If, then a sale occurs many months after the credit downgrade, it is likely to be for reasons other than a credit downgrade.

Changes in tax laws

A6.6.49 A sale following a change in tax law that eliminates or significantly reduces the tax-exempt status of interest on the held-to-maturity investment (but not a change in tax law that revises the marginal tax rates applicable to interest income) would not compromise the classification of held-to-maturity. This is because such a change was not contemplated at the time of the initial classification. On the other hand, if an entity undertakes a sale in anticipation of a change in the tax law that was not substantively enacted at the time of sale or reclassification, the entire held-to-maturity portfolio may well be tainted. Similarly, a sale as a result of change in tax law that revises the marginal tax rates for interest income will taint the entire held-to-maturity portfolio, since the change is likely to affect all debt instruments not simply the ones sold.

Major business combination or disposition

A6.6.50 Following a business combination or disposal of a business segment, it may be necessary for the entity to sell or reclassify some of its own held-to-maturity securities in order to maintain the entity's existing interest rate risk position or credit risk policy that predated the business combination or disposal. In a business combination, it may also be necessary to sell some of the acquired entity's held-to-maturity securities, even though all of the acquired securities would be classified anew following such an acquisition. Although a business combination is an event that is within the entity's control, sales or reclassifications that are necessary to maintain the entity's existing interest rate risk position or credit risk policy arises as a direct consequence of the business combination or disposition and are not anticipated. Hence, such sales or reclassifications would not taint the entity's held-to-maturity portfolio.

A6.6.51 On the other hand, sales of held-to-maturity securities to fund an acquisition that is within the entity's control would taint the portfolio. This is because such sales are not a consequence of the acquisition. Rather, as they have been made to fund the acquisition, they call into question the entity's intent and ability to hold the investment to maturity. Similarly, a sale in response to an unsolicited tender offer or a sale due to a change in the entity's business strategy would also taint the held-to-maturity portfolio. This is because such events are unlikely to fall into the category of isolated events that are beyond the entity's control, are non-recurring events and could not have been reasonably anticipated by the entity.

A6.6.52 An entity should reassess its held-to-maturity classification either concurrently or shortly after the major business combination or disposition. This is because as time passes it may be increasingly difficult for the entity to demonstrate that the sale or reclassification out of held-to-maturity was necessitated by the business combination and not other events or circumstances.

Changes in statutory or regulatory requirements

A6.6.53 IAS 39 identifies the following situations where sale or reclassification out of the held-to-maturity category necessitated by changes in statutory or regulatory requirements would not call into question the entity's intent and ability to hold other investments to maturity.

- A change in statutory or regulatory requirements significantly modifying either what constitutes a permissible investment or the maximum level of particular types of investments, thereby causing an entity to dispose of a held-to-maturity investment.
- A significant increase in the risk weights of held-to-maturity investments used for regulatory risk-based capital purposes.
- A significant increase in the industry's regulatory capital requirements that causes the entity to downsize by selling held-to-maturity investments.

[IAS 39 para AG22(d-f)].

A6.6.54 Sales of held-to-maturity securities resulting from statutory or regulatory requirements that affect the whole regulated industry as set out above are clearly isolated events beyond the entity's control, are non-recurring and could not have been reasonably anticipated by the entity.

A6.6.55 In relation to the last situation in paragraph A6.6.53 above, if an entity is forced to downsize to comply with a significant increase in the industry's capital requirements, the sale of one or more held-to-maturity securities in connection with that downsizing would not call into question the classification of other held-to-maturity securities. Sometimes downsizing may be required to comply with a significant increase in *entity-specific* capital requirements imposed by regulators. In that situation, it may be difficult for the entity to demonstrate that the regulators action could not have been reasonably anticipated at the time of the initial classification. Therefore, in this situation, the entity can avoid tainting only if it can demonstrate that the downsizing results from an increase in capital requirements, which is an isolated event that is beyond its control, is non-recurring and could not have been reasonably anticipated. [IAS 39 para IG B17].

A6.6.56 It follows that blanket sales of held-to-maturity investments made as a matter of course to comply with regulatory capital requirements are not consistent with held-to-maturity accounting. For example, a sale of a held-to-maturity investment to realise gains to replenish regulatory capital depleted by a loan loss provision would taint the entire held-to-maturity portfolio, because realising such a gain is inconsistent with the held-to-maturity classification.

Decision tree for classifying financial assets as held-to-maturity

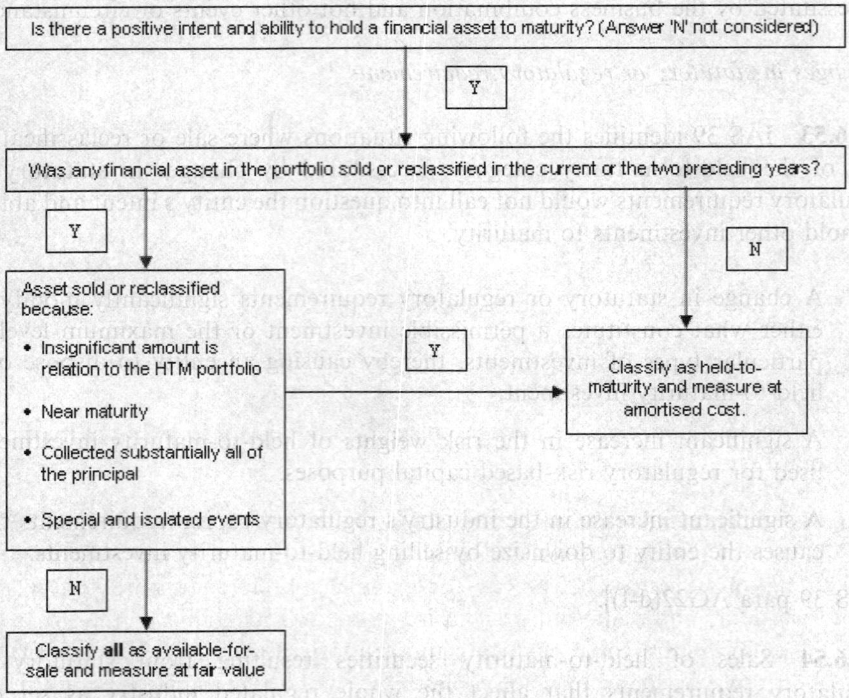

A6.6.57 A decision tree for classifying financial assets as held-to-maturity is shown below.

Loans and receivables

A6.6.58 Loans and receivables are non-derivative financial assets with fixed or determinable payments that are not quoted in an active market other than:

- Those that the entity intends to sell immediately or in the near term, which should be classified as held-for-trading, and those that the entity upon initial recognition designates as at fair value through profit or loss.
- Those that the entity upon initial recognition designates as available-for-sale.
- Those for which the holder may not recover substantially all of its initial investment, other than because of credit deterioration, which should be classified as available-for-sale.

[IAS 39 para 9].

A6.6.59 Loans and receivables typically arise when an entity provides money, goods or services directly to a debtor with no intention of trading the receivable. Examples include trade receivables, bank deposits and loan assets originated by the entity either directly or by way of syndication/participation arrangements. It also includes loans that are *purchased* in a secondary market that is not active and the loans are not quoted. Investments in debt securities that are quoted in a non-active market can also be classified as loans and receivables.

Example – Bank deposits in other banks

Banks make term deposits with a central bank or other banks. Sometimes, the proof of deposit is negotiable, sometimes not. Even if negotiable, the depositor bank may or may not intend to sell it. Such a deposit meets the definition of loans and receivables, whether or not the proof of deposit is negotiable, unless the depositor bank intends to sell the instrument immediately or in the near term, in which case the deposit is classified as a financial asset held-for-trading. [IAS 39 para IG B23].

6A.6.60 The principal difference between loans and receivables and other financial assets is that loans and receivables are not subject to the tainting provisions that apply to held-to-maturity investments. Consequently, loans and receivables that are not held-for-trading may be measured at amortised cost even if an entity does not have the positive intention and ability to hold the loan asset until maturity.

A6.6.61 Instruments that meet the definition of an equity instrument under IAS 32 cannot be classified as loans and receivables by the holder. On the other hand, if a non-derivative instrument (for example, a preference share) that has the legal form of an equity instrument, but is recorded as a liability by the issuer and it has fixed or determinable payments and is not quoted in an active market, can be classified within loans and receivables by the holder, provided the definition is otherwise met. [IAS 39 para IG B22].

A6.6.62 An interest acquired in a pool of assets that are not loans or receivables (for example, an interest in a mutual fund or a similar fund) cannot be clarrified as a loan or receivable. [IAS 39 para 9]. The corollary is that a purchase of a securitised asset that consists of a pool of loans and receivables that meets the definition of loans and receivables can be classified as loan and receivables by the holder. However, where an entity securitises its own portfolio of loans and receivables that were classified as loans and receivables before the securitisation and the derecognition provisions of IAS 39 apply, the securitisation may give rise to a new financial asset that is classified a new in accordance with the four categories of financial assets.

Purchased loans

A6.6.63 The inclusion of purchased loans that meet the definition of 'loans and receivables' classification is a change from the previous version of the standard.

The previous version used the category 'originated loans and receivables' and only allowed those loans that were originated by the entity either directly or by way of syndication to be included in the category. All purchased loans were categorised as either held-to-maturity, available-for-sale or trading as appropriate. However, in response to the exposure draft of proposed amendments to IAS 39, some commentators suggested that purchased loans should be eligible for classification as loan and receivables. They noted that some entities typically manage purchased and originated loans together and there are systems problems of segregating purchased loans from originated loans given that a distinction between them is likely to be made only for accounting purposes. The IASB was persuaded by the comments and decided to remove the requirement that loans or receivables must be originated by the entity to meet the definition of 'loans and receivables'. [IAS 39 para BC28].

A6.6.64 However, in making the above concession, the IASB was concerned that it might result in some instruments that should be measured at fair value meeting the definition of loans and receivables and thus being measured at amortised cost. In particular, the Board was concerned that this would be the case for a debt instrument in which the purchaser may not recover its investment. For example, a purchaser of a fixed rate interest-only strip created in a securitisation and subject to pre-payment risk may not recover substantially all of its investment due to pre-payment. The Board therefore decided to exclude from the definition of loans and receivables instruments for which the holder may not recover substantially all of its initial investment, other than because of credit deterioration. Such assets are accounted for as available-for-sale or at fair value through profit or loss. [IAS 39 para BC29].

Debt instruments quoted in an active market

A6.6.65 As stated in paragraph A6.6.58 above, an entity is not permitted to classify as a loan or receivable an investment in a debt instrument that is quoted in an active market. The IASB considered that the ability to measure a financial asset at amortised cost (as in the case of loans and receivables) is most appropriate when there is no liquid market for the asset. It is less appropriate to extend the category to debt instruments traded in liquid markets. Accordingly, for such investments an amortised cost basis of measurement is only permitted if the entity can demonstrate its positive intention and ability to hold the investments until maturity (see para A6.6.26 above). It is likely, therefore, that many originated investments in quoted bonds would be classified as available-for-sale.

Available-for-sale financial assets

A6.6.66 Available-for-sale (AFS) financial assets are those non-derivative financial assets that are designated as available-for-sale or are not classified as:

- Loans and receivables.
- Held-to-maturity investments.

- Financial assets at fair value through profit or loss.

[IAS 39 para 9].

A6.6.67 Under the previous version of IAS 39, available-for-sale was a residual category for all those financial assets that did not properly belong in one of the three other categories – originated loans and receivables, trading or held-to-maturity. The revision introduces a degree of choice, on initial recognition to classify any non-derivative financial asset, except those held for trading or at FVTPL, as available-for-sale and, therefore, to measure it at fair value with changes in fair value recognised directly in equity. In other words, only assets that would otherwise be classified as loans and receivables can be designated as available-for-sale at initial recognition. (An asset that is classified as held-to-maturity cannot by definition at the same time be regarded as available-for-sale.)

A6.6.68 Examples of available-for-sale financial assets that are likely to be included in this category are:

- Equity investments that are not designated on initial recognition as at fair value through profit and loss.
- Financial assets that could have been classified as loans and receivables on initial recognition, but the holder chooses to designate on initial recognition as available-for-sale.
- Financial assets where the holder is unable to recover substantially all its initial investment.
- Puttable quoted debt securities that cannot be classified either as held-to-maturity because they are puttable (see para A6.6.33 above) or any quoted debt instrument that fails the held-to-maturity criteria (because they may be sold in response to liquidity needs (see para A6.6.38) or loans and receivables because they are quoted (see para A6.6.58)).

Therefore, the main issue, in practice, is likely to focus on whether investments quoted in an active market should be classified as trading or designated as available-for-sale on initial recognition.

Example – Balancing a portfolio

Entity A has an investment portfolio of debt and equity instruments. The documented portfolio management guidelines specify that the portfolio's equity exposure should be limited to between 30 and 50% of total portfolio value. The portfolio's investment manager is authorised to balance the portfolio within the designated guidelines by buying and selling equity and debt instruments.

Whether entity A is permitted to classify the instruments as available-for-sale would depend on entity A's intentions and past practice. If the portfolio manager is authorised to buy and sell instruments to balance the risks in a portfolio, but there is no intention to trade and there is no past practice of trading for short-term profit, the instruments can be classified as available-for-sale. If the portfolio manager actively buys and sells instruments to generate short-term profits, the financial instruments in the portfolio are classified as held for trading. [IAS 39 para IG B12].

Reclassification of assets between categories

A6.6.69 Once a financial asset has been classified into a particular category on initial recognition, transfers into or out of that category from or to other categories are impossible for some categories and should be rare in other circumstances.

Transfer into and out of fair value through profit or loss

A6.6.70 As explained above, entities are permitted to designate on initial recognition any financial asset at fair value through profit and loss. However, to impose discipline on this approach, no financial asset can be transferred into or out of this category while it is held or issued. [IAS 39 para 50]. Such irrevocable designation at inception prevents 'cherry picking', because it will not be known at initial recognition whether the investment's fair value will increase or decrease.

A6.6.71 However, the prohibition of reclassifying financial assets into or out of this category does not prevent a derivative that was initially classified as trading from being designated as a hedging instrument while it is held. Nor does it prevent a derivative that was designated as a hedging instrument from being re-designated as trading following revocation of the hedge. IAS 39's hedge accounting provisions, which are considered in section 10, make it clear that these are not regarded as prohibited reclassifications.

Transfer into and out of loans and receivables

A6.6.72 Because an entity can choose to designate a financial asset that satisfies the loan and receivable definition as available-for-sale or fair value through profit or loss only on initial recognition or on date of transition to IFRS, reclassifications of financial assets into or out of this category are not permitted.

Transfer out of held-to-maturity into available-for-sale

A6.6.73 Where, as a result of a change in intention or ability, it is no longer appropriate to classify an investment as held-to-maturity, it should be reclassified as available-for-sale and remeasured at fair value. [IAS 39 para 51(b)]. As explained in paragraph A6.6.37 above, a sale or reclassification calls into question management's intent and ability to hold financial assets to maturity and 'taints' the entire portfolio. Therefore, whenever sales or reclassification of more than an insignificant amount of held-to-maturity investments that do not meet any of the conditions of permitted sales set out in paragraph A6.6.40 occurs, any remaining held-to-maturity investments should be reclassified as available-for-sale. In such circumstances, the assets are re-measured to fair value, with any difference recognised in equity. [IAS 39 para 52]. Accounting for reclassifications is dealt with in section 9.

Transfer out of available-for-sale into held-to-maturity

A6.6.74 An entity is allowed to reclassify a financial asset from available-for-sale to held-to-maturity, except in periods where the held-to-maturity category is tainted. For example, a quoted loan in an active market that was initially classified as available-for-sale may subsequently be reclassified to held-to-maturity category if the entity intends and has the ability to hold the loan to maturity. An instrument may be reclassified into the held-to-maturity category when the tainted held-to-maturity portfolio has been 'cleansed' at the end of the second financial year following the tainting (see para A6.6.38). In this case, the financial asset's carrying value, that is, its fair value at the date of reclassification, becomes the asset's new amortised cost. [IAS 39 para 54(a)]. Accounting for reclassifications is dealt with in section 9.

Classification of financial liabilities

A6.6.75 IAS 39 has two defined categories of financial liabilities, as follows:

- Financial liabilities 'at fair value through profit or loss'.
- Other financial liabilities (measured at amortised cost).

A6.6.76 Like financial assets, a financial liability can be classified as at fair value through profit or loss only if it meets either of the following conditions:

- Upon initial recognition, it is designated by the entity at fair value through profit or loss.
- It is classified as held for trading.

[IAS 39 para 9].

Designation at fair value through profit or loss on initial recognition

A6.6.77 An entity *may* designate a financial liability at fair value through profit or loss on initial recognition only in the following circumstances:

- The designation eliminates or significantly reduces a measurement or recognition inconsistency (sometimes referred to as an 'accounting mismatch') that would otherwise arise.
- A group of financial assets, financial liabilities or both is managed and its performance is evaluated on a fair value basis, in accordance with a documented risk management or investment strategy.
- The item proposed to be designated at fair value through profit or loss is a hybrid contract that contains one or more embedded derivatives unless:
  - the embedded derivative(s) does not significantly modify the cash flows that otherwise would be required by the contract; or

- it is clear with little or no analysis when a similar hybrid (combined) instrument is first considered that separation of the embedded derivative(s) is prohibited, such as a pre-payment option embedded in a loan that permits the holder to pre-pay the loan for approximately its amortised cost. [IAS 39 para 11A].

[IAS 39 para 9].

A6.6.78 As explained above, the entity's ability to designate a financial instrument at fair value through profit or loss is an option. It does not restrict an entity's ability to measure a financial liability at amortised cost. Furthermore, as the above three conditions for designating a financial liability at fair value through profit or loss on initial recognition also apply to financial assets, similar considerations that apply to financial assets and dealt with in paragraphs A6.6.6 to A6.6.20 also apply to financial liabilities.

A6.6.79 It should be noted, however, that the above situations effectively reduce the possibility of measuring an entity's own debt instruments at fair value and, thereby, recognising income as a result of deteriorating credit quality (and an expense as a result of improving credit quality) that was possible under the unrestricted fair value option in the 2003 revision of IAS 39 and that caused a significant amount of controversy. However, this does not mean that where an entity takes the fair value option and measures its own debt at fair value, because it falls within one of the first two situations mentioned in paragraph A6.6.78 above, changes in the entity's creditworthiness should not be reflected in the fair value measurement of own debt instruments. This issue is considered further in section 9.

Held for trading

A6.6.80 A financial liability is held for trading if it is:

- acquired or incurred principally for the purpose of selling or repurchasing it in the near term;
- part of a portfolio of identified financial instruments that are managed together and for which there is evidence of a recent actual pattern of short-term profit taking; or
- a derivative (except for a derivative that is a designated and effective hedging instrument).

[IAS 39 para 9].

A6.6.81 Financial liabilities held for trading include:

- Derivative liabilities that are not accounted for as hedging instruments. For example, it will include derivatives with a negative fair value.
- Obligations to deliver financial assets borrowed by a short seller. A short sale is a transaction in which an entity sells securities it does not own, with

the intention of buying securities at an agreed price on a future date to cover the sale. Securities borrowed are not recognised on the balance sheet, unless they are sold to third parties, in which case the obligation to return the securities is recorded as a trading liability and measured at fair value and any gains or losses are included in the income statement.

- Financial liabilities that are incurred with an intention to repurchase them in the near term. For example, a quoted debt instrument that the issuer may buy back in the near term depending on changes in its fair value.
- Financial liabilities that are part of a portfolio of identified financial instruments that are managed together and for which there is evidence of a recent pattern of short-term profit-taking.

The fact that a liability is incurred and used to fund trading activities does not mean that the liability is classified as held-for-trading.

[IAS 39 para AG 15].

Other financial liabilities

A6.6.82 Financial liabilities that are not classified as at fair value through profit or loss would automatically fall into this category and are measured at amortised cost. Common examples are trade payables, borrowings and customer deposits.

Reclassification between categories

A6.6.83 As with financial assets, reclassification into or out of fair value through profit or loss is prohibited. However, as explained in paragraph A6.6.71 above, the prohibition does not apply to derivative financial liabilities that are designated or re-designated as hedging instruments.

Financial guarantee contracts

A6.6.84 Financial guarantee contracts do not fit clearly into any category above if they were not initially classified as at fair value through profit or loss. They seem to form a separate category of their own. This is because subsequent measurement of these contracts, unless designated at inception as at fair value through profit or loss, is not consistent with that of the categories described above. Measurement of financial guarantee contracts is considered further in section 9.

the intention of buying securities at an agreed price on a future date to cover the sale. Securities borrowed are not recognised on the balance sheet unless they are sold to third parties, in which case the obligation to return the securities is recorded as a trading liability and measured at fair value and any gains or losses are included in the income statement.

- Financial liabilities that are incurred with an intention to repurchase them in the near term. For example, a quoted debt instrument that the issuer may buy back in the near term depending on changes in its fair value.

- Financial liabilities that are part of a portfolio of identified financial instruments that are managed together and for which there is evidence of a recent pattern of short-term profit-taking.

The fact that a liability is incurred and used to fund trading activities does not mean that the liability is classified as held-for-trading.

[IAS 39 para AG 15]

Other financial liabilities

A6.6.82 Financial liabilities that are not classified as at fair value through profit or loss would automatically fall into this category and are measured at amortised cost. Common examples are trade payables, borrowings and customer deposits.

Reclassification between categories

A6.6.83 As with financial assets, reclassification into or out of fair value through profit or loss is prohibited. However, as explained in paragraph A6.6.71 above, the prohibition does not apply to derivative financial liabilities that are designated or are designated as hedging instruments.

Financial guarantee contracts

A6.6.84 Financial guarantee contracts do not fit clearly into any category above if they were not initially classified as at fair value through profit or loss. They seem to form a separate category of their own. This is because subsequent measurement of these contracts, unless designated at inception as at fair value through profit or loss, is not consistent with that of the categories described above. Measurement of financial guarantee contracts is considered further in section 9.

Section 7

Financial liabilities and equity

Introduction

A6.7.1 Accounting for financial instruments available for raising debt finance (such as debentures and capital notes) or equity finance (such as ordinary shares, options and warrants on such shares) has historically been dictated by their legal form. As a result, the accounting was fairly uncontroversial as debt instruments were recorded in liabilities and shares and warrants in shareholders' equity.

A6.7.2 However, during the 1980s there was a considerable growth in the number of complex forms of finance, driven mostly by the fact that debt instruments and shares often have different tax consequences, both for the issuer and the holder. New features were included in some instruments (for example, redemption options in preference shares exercisable in some instances by the holder and in other instances by the issuer) that made it difficult to establish whether the instruments were, in substance, debt or equity. Others contained features that exhibited characteristics of debt and equity (for example, debt instruments that are convertible into equity). Still others were structured to achieve liability treatment for tax purposes and equity treatment for accounting purposes.

A6.7.3 Although the development of such instruments had a sound economic purpose and provided issuers and investors with significant benefits, the accounting for some of these new instruments has not always been uniform and a variety of arguments have been advanced to justify differing treatments. Some of these arguments have called into question methods of accounting based on the instrument's legal form that have been used for many years and had previously appeared uncontroversial. The central issues that required resolution were the criteria to be used to determine whether an instrument represents a liability or equity and the treatment of instruments containing both debt and equity characteristics.

A6.7.4 IAS 32, issued in 1995, establishes principles for distinguishing between liabilities and equity. The substance of the contractual arrangement of a financial instrument, rather than its legal form, governs its classification. The contractual arrangement's substance is not to be confused with 'economic substance'; they can be different and may be different from the legal form (see para A6.7.10 below). The overriding criteria are that if an entity does not have an unconditional right to avoid delivering cash or another financial asset to settle a contractual obligation and the contract does not, in substance, evidence a residual interest in the entity's assets after deducting all its liabilities, the contract is not an equity instrument.

A6.7.5 The original standard went through a series of amendments in 1998 and 2000. It was then revised in December 2003 as part of the IASB's improvements project. However, the standard's fundamental approach to the classification of financial instruments as liability or equity remained unchanged. The classification of liability and equity instruments in IAS 32 is complex. The impact that an incorrect classification can have on such issues as borrowings and other ratios (including debt covenants) and reported earnings can be highly significant to investors and other users of financial statements.

Principles for classifying financial liabilities and equity instruments

A6.7.6 Before considering IAS 32's general principles for classifying a financial instrument as a financial liability or equity, it is appropriate to set out the standard's basic definitions of a financial liability and an equity instrument.

A6.7.7 IAS 32 defines a financial liability as any liability that is:

- A contractual obligation
  - to deliver cash or another financial asset to another entity; or
  - to exchange financial assets or financial liabilities with another entity under conditions that are potentially unfavourable to the entity.
- A contract that will or may be settled in the entity's own equity instruments and is:
  - a non-derivative for which the entity is or may be obliged to deliver a variable number of the entity's own equity instruments; or
  - a derivative that will or may be settled other than by the exchange of a fixed amount of cash or another financial asset for a fixed number of the entity's own equity instruments. For this purpose the entity's own equity instruments do not include instruments that are themselves contracts for the future receipt or delivery of the entity's own equity instruments.

[IAS 32 para 11].

A6.7.8 IAS 32 defines an equity instrument as any contract that evidences a residual interest in an entity's assets after deducting all of its liabilities. [IAS 32 para 11]. A residual interest is not necessarily a proportionate interest ranking *pari passu* with all other residual interests, for example, it may be an interest in a fixed amount that may rank first in preference. However, for the purposes of determining whether a financial instrument is an equity instrument rather than a financial liability, the standard requires an issuer to apply the following expanded definition of an equity instrument that is essentially a converse of the above definition of a financial liability. Accordingly, an instrument is an equity instrument if, and only if, both of the conditions below are met:

- The instrument includes no contractual obligation:
  - to deliver cash or another financial asset to another entity; or
  - to exchange financial assets or financial liabilities with another entity under conditions that are potentially unfavourable to the entity.
- If the instrument will or may be settled in the issuer's own equity instruments, it is:
  - a non-derivative that includes no contractual obligation for the issuer to deliver a variable number of its own equity instruments; or
  - a derivative that will be settled only by the issuer exchanging a fixed amount of cash or another financial asset for a fixed number of its own equity instruments. For this purpose the issuer's own equity instruments do not include instruments that are themselves contracts for the future receipt or delivery of the issuer's own equity instruments.

A contractual obligation, including one arising from a derivative financial instrument, that will or may result in the future receipt or delivery of the issuer's own equity instruments, but does not meet both conditions above, is not an equity instrument.

[IAS 32 para 16].

A6.7.9 IAS 32 is a contract based standard. 'Contract' or 'contractual' refers to an agreement between two or more parties that has clear economic consequences that the parties have little, if any, discretion to avoid, usually because the agreement is enforceable by law. Contracts, and thus financial instruments, may take a variety of forms and need not be in writing. [IAS 32 para 13]. Liabilities or assets that are not contractual (such as income taxes) are not financial liabilities or financial assets. Similarly, constructive obligations, as defined in IAS 37, do not arise from contracts and are not financial liabilities. [IAS 32 para AG 12].

A6.7.10 IAS 32 states that an issuer of a financial instrument should classify a financial instrument, or *its component parts,* on initial recognition as a financial liability, a financial asset or an equity instrument in accordance with the contractual arrangement's substance and the definitions of a financial liability, a financial asset and an equity instrument. [IAS 32 para 15]. The role of 'substance' in the classification of financial instrument should be restricted to considering the instrument's contractual terms. Anything that falls outside the contractual terms should not be considered for the purpose of assessing whether an instrument should be classified as a liability under IAS 32. Furthermore, in assessing the substance of the terms and conditions of a financial instrument, the impact of relevant local laws, regulations and the entity's governing charter in effect at the date of classification should also be considered, but not expected future amendments to those laws, regulations and charter. [IFRIC 2 para 5].

A6.7.11 The IFRIC discussed the role of contractual and economic obligations in the classification of financial instruments under IAS 32 in March 2006. The

IFRIC agreed that a contractual financial obligation was necessary in order that a financial instrument be classified as a liability. Such a contractual obligation could be established explicitly or could be indirectly established (see para A6.7.27). However, the obligation must be established through the terms and conditions of the financial instrument. It was agreed that economic compulsion, by itself, would not result in a financial liability being classified as a liability.

Example 1 – 'Step-up' instrument

An entity issues an irredeemable callable bond where the fixed dividend of 5% can be deferred at the issuer's option. The instrument includes a 'step-up' dividend clause that would increase the dividend to 25% at a pre-determined date in the future unless the instrument had previously been called by the issuer.

The IFRIC agreed that this instrument included no contractual obligation to pay the dividends or to call the instrument. Although there is an economic compulsion for the issuer to call the instrument on the date the dividend payment 'steps-up', there is no contractual obligation to do so. Therefore, the instrument would be classified as an equity instrument.

Example 2 – Discretionary dividends that have historically been paid each year.

An entity issues a non-redeemable callable subordinated loan note with a fixed 6% coupon. The coupon can be deferred at the issuer's option. The issuer has a history of paying the coupon each year and the current bond price is predicated on the holders' expectation that the coupon will continue to be paid each year. In addition the stated policy of the issuer is that the coupon will be paid each year, which has been publicly communicated.

Although there is both an economic compulsion for the issuer to pay the coupon, to maintain the bond price, and a constructive obligation to pay the coupon, there is no contractual obligation to do so. Therefore the bond will be classified as an equity instrument.

6A.7.12 Examining a financial instrument's component parts is key to correct classification. This is because debt instruments and shares come in many forms. They may be redeemable or non-redeemable. The return on them may be mandatory or discretionary or may combine elements of both. Sometimes they may contain features (such as put and call options) that may or may not oblige the issuer to settle the instrument in cash or other financial assets. Consequently, it is necessary to examine the contractual terms of each component carefully, bearing in mind the definitions of a financial liability and an equity instrument, to determine whether they exhibit characteristics of a financial liability or equity. Once the characteristics of the individual components are determined, they can be combined to arrive at the overall assessment of whether the entire instrument is classified as a financial liability, or an equity instrument, or a compound instrument containing both liability and equity features.

A6.7.13 Where an entity issues two or more instruments at (or nearly at) the same time to the same counterparty, the indicators outlined in IAS 39 must be considered when determining whether the contracts are linked and viewed as a single arrangement or as two separate contracts. Indicators that contracts are linked include:

- they are entered into at the same time and in contemplation of one another;
- they have the same counterparty;
- they relate to the same risk;
- there is no apparent economic need or substantive business purpose for structuring the transaction separately that would not also have been accomplished in a single transaction; and
- they cannot be transferred or redeemed separately.

[IAS 39 paras AG 51(e) and IG B.6]

A6.7.14 IAS 32 should be applied by all entities to all types of financial instruments except those outside the scope of the standard. The scope exemptions to IAS 32 are discussed in section 3. In practice one of the more common and complex scope exemptions relates to contracts that fall within the scope of IFRS 2 or IAS 19. Where the holder is an employee, director or provider of service to the entity, the contract should be carefully analysed to determine whether it is within the scope of IFRS 2 or IAS 19 or IAS 32.

A6.7.15 The equity or liability classification is made by the entity at initial recognition. However, if the contractual terms and conditions are subsequently changed, it may well result in derecognition of the original instrument (equity or liability) and the recognition of a new instrument (liability or equity). The classification of a financial instrument may also change as a result of a lapse in a key term that initially resulted in the instrument's classification. For example, an irredeemable preference share with discretionary dividends was issued with a clause that allowed the holder to redeem the share for cash if the company did not IPO in the first three years. This clause would have resulted in the instrument being classified as a financial liability as there is a contractual obligation to deliver cash. If, however, the instrument was not redeemed and three years passed, this term would lapse and the instrument would become an irredeemable share with discretionary dividends, that is classified as equity.

A6.7.16 The principles described above appear to be relatively simple, but the application in practice often presents difficulties. The contractual arrangement's substance and its legal form are commonly consistent, but not always. Since the contractual arrangement's substance rather than its legal form takes precedence, there could be situations where instruments that qualify as equity for regulatory or legal purposes are, on closer examination, liabilities for financial reporting purposes. Examples of such situations are highlighted in paragraph A6.7.2 above. Others include shares with special terms and conditions, puttable instruments and perpetual instruments.

Contracts that are settled in cash or another financial assets

Contractual obligation to settle in cash or another financial asset

A6.7.17 It is apparent from the above IAS 32 definitions of liability and equity instrument that the critical feature that distinguishes a liability from an equity instrument is the existence of a contractual obligation to deliver cash or another financial asset to the holder or to exchange financial asset or financial liability with the holder under conditions that are potentially unfavourable to the issuer. In other words, if the issuer does not have an unconditional right to avoid delivering cash or another financial asset to settle a contractual obligation, the obligation meets the definition of a liability.

A6.7.18 An instrument that an issuer may be obliged to settle in cash or another financial instrument is a liability regardless of the manner in which it otherwise could be settled. For example, the obligation to deliver cash may cover the basic obligation either to repay the principal or interest/dividends or both. Also, the obligation need not be discharged in cash or another financial asset; it could be discharged by transfer of other kinds of assets in certain circumstances (for example, a property) as illustrated in paragraph A6.7.27 below. Indeed, in some circumstances it can even be settled by the issuer's own equity instruments. As long as the instrument involves a contractual unconditional obligation to deliver cash or another financial asset, it should be classified and accounted for as a liability. Some examples of instruments that contain an obligation to transfer cash are considered below:

Example 1 – 6% mandatorily redeemable preference shares with mandatory fixed dividends

Preference share is the name given to any share that has some preferential rights in relation to other classes of shares, particularly in relation to ordinary shares. These preferential rights are of great variety, but refer normally to the right to a *fixed dividend*, although they could also refer to the right on winding up to receive a fixed part of the *capital* or otherwise to participate in the distribution of the company's assets (shares with such rights are often known as participating preference shares).

As explained in paragraph A6.7.16 above, in determining whether a mandatorily redeemable preference share is a financial liability or an equity instrument, it is necessary to examine the particular contractual rights attaching to the instrument's principal and return components.

The instrument, in this example, provides for mandatory periodic fixed dividend payments (whether cumulative or non-cumulative) and mandatory redemption by the issuer for a fixed amount at a fixed future date. Since there is a contractual obligation to deliver cash (for both dividends and repayment of principal) to the shareholder that cannot be avoided, the instrument is a financial liability in its entirety.

Example 2 – Non-redeemable preference shares with mandatory fixed dividends

When preference shares are non-redeemable, the appropriate classification is determined by the other rights that attach to them. Classification is based on an assessment of the contractual arrangement's substance and the definitions of a financial liability and an equity instrument. [IAS 32 para AG 26].

It is necessary to examine the particular contractual rights attaching to the instrument's principal and return components. In this example, the shares are non-redeemable and thus the amount of the principal has equity characteristics, but the entity has a contractual obligation to pay dividends (whether fixed or cumulative) that provides the shareholders with a lender's return. This obligation is not negated if the entity is unable to pay the dividends because of lack of funds or insufficient distributable profits. Therefore, the obligation to pay the dividends meets the definition of a financial liability. The overall classification is that the shares may be a compound instrument and may need to be split accounted (see further para A6.7.65 below). It would be a compound instrument if the coupon was initially set at an off-market rate or the terms specified payment of discretionary dividends in addition to the fixed coupon. If the coupon on the preference shares was set at market rates at the date of issue and there were no provisions for the payment of discretionary dividends, the entire instrument would be classified as a financial liability.

Example 3 – Perpetual debt

'Perpetual' debt instruments (such as 'perpetual' bonds, debentures and capital notes) normally provide the holder with the contractual right to receive payments on account of interest at fixed dates extending into the indefinite future. The holder either has no right to receive a return of principal or a right to a return of principal under terms that make it very unlikely or very far in the future.

In this example, the instrument is perpetual and non-redeemable, but the entity has a contractual obligation to deliver cash in the form of interest payments to perpetuity. The obligation to pay interest meets the definition of a financial liability. For example, an entity may issue a financial instrument requiring it to make annual payments in perpetuity equal to a stated interest rate of 8% applied to a stated par or principal amount of C1m. Assuming 8% to be the market rate of interest for the instrument when issued, the instrument is classified as a liability in its entirety at the net present value of the interest payments. In this situation, the instrument's holder and issuer have a financial asset and a financial liability, respectively. [IAS 32 para AG 6].

Example 4 – Zero coupon bond

A zero coupon bond is an instrument where no interest is payable that is normally issued at a deep discount to the value at which it will be redeemed. Although there are no mandatory periodic interest payments, the instrument provides for mandatory redemption by the issuer for a determinable amount at a fixed or determinable future date. Since there is a contractual obligation to deliver cash for the value at which the bond will be redeemed, the instrument is classified as a financial liability.

Restriction on the ability to satisfy contractual obligations

A6.7.19 A restriction on the ability of an entity to satisfy a contractual obligation, such as lack of access to foreign currency or the need to obtain approval for payment from a regulatory authority, does not negate the entity's contractual obligation or the holder's contractual right under the instrument.

[IAS 32 para 19(a)]. For example, an obligation is not negated even if the instrument's terms are such that the amount payable on redemption is dependent on the company having sufficient distributable profits or reserves. A type of income bond where the bond is not redeemable by the issuer, but interest is payable only in the event that the issuer has sufficient distributable profits, is such an instrument. The bond would be classified as a liability because of the obligation to pay interest. The fact that the obligation to pay is dependent on the existence of profits makes the obligation contingent, but it does not remove the obligation (see further section 4).

Puttable instruments

A6.7.20 A financial instrument that gives the holder the right to put it back to the issuer for cash or another financial asset (a 'puttable instrument') is a financial liability. For example, an entity that issues a preference share that is puttable by the holder at some future date would recognise a financial liability. The holder has a put option that requires the issuer to redeem the instrument at a fixed amount at some future date. Since the existence of an option for the holder to put the instrument back to the issuer for cash or another financial asset means that the issuer does not have an unconditional right to avoid delivering cash or cash equivalent, the puttable instrument meets the definition of a financial liability. This is so even when the amount of cash or other financial assets to be delivered to the holder is not fixed, but is determined on the basis of an index or other item that has the potential to increase or decrease the final amount payable, or when the puttable instrument's legal form gives the holder a right to a residual interest in the issuer's assets. [IAS 32 para 18(b)]. In these situations, from the issuer's perspective, the embedded put option is a written option that may need to be separated from the host contract, unless the whole instrument is accounted for at fair value through profit or loss. Embedded derivatives are discussed in section 5.

A6.7.21 Puttable instruments that give the holder a right to redeem the instruments at any time for cash equal to their proportionate share of the asset value of the issuer are commonly issued by open-ended mutual funds, unit trusts, partnerships and some co-operative entities. Although the legal form of such financial instruments give the holders a right to the residual interest in the entity's assets, the inclusion of an option for the holder to put the instrument back to the entity for cash or another financial asset means that the instrument meets the financial liability's definition. The classification as a financial liability is independent of considerations such as when the right is exercisable, how the amount payable or receivable upon exercise of the right is determined and whether the puttable instrument has a fixed maturity. [IAS 32 para 18(b)].

A6.7.22 Classifying instruments that are puttable at a *pro rata* share of the fair value of the net assets of the issuer may have some bizarre consequences for the above entities' financial statements. Those entities in the fund management industry that report the full fair value of assets in their balance sheet and that have hitherto reported positive shareholders' equity (attributable to members or unitholders) may have to report a nil amount. This is because IAS 39 requires the liability to be measured at settlement amount (fair value) with changes in that amount recognised in profit or loss. Those entities, such as some co-operatives and partnerships, that do not report the fair value of the assets in their financial statements will always show net liabilities and those net liabilities will increase the better the entity performs; assuming that the fair value of the entity is higher than the carrying amount of its net assets (excluding the puttable instruments).

A6.7.23 The IASB acknowledged a need to address the above anomalies and has proposed an amendment to amend IAS 32. In June 2006, the IASB issued an exposure draft of proposed 'Amendments to IAS 32 and IAS 1 – Financial instruments puttable at fair value and obligations arising on liquidation'. The exposure draft proposes equity classification of financial instruments puttable at the fair value of a *pro rata* share of the entity's net assets and financial instruments that entitle the holder to a *pro rata* share of the entity's net assets on liquidation, provided that certain conditions are met. The most critical of these conditions is a requirement that the instruments are the most subordinated class of instruments with a claim to the entity's net assets, that is equivalent to ordinary shares.

A6.7.24 As a result of the above, the exposure draft proposes that the definition of a financial liability is amended to exclude an obligation to redeem or repurchase a financial instrument puttable at fair value and an obligation to deliver a *pro rata* share of the entity's net assets upon liquidation. The proposal further sets out the key features that should be present in a financial instrument puttable at fair value and that entitles the holder to a *pro rata* share of the entity's net assets. The proposals make it clear that derivatives over such instruments will not be classified as equity. The proposals also include a number of new disclosures.

Own share buy-back programmes

A6.7.25 During certain times of the year (for example, before an entity releases its results), listed companies are prohibited by certain local listing rules from buying their own shares in the market. The local listing rules may permit other arrangements to be entered into with independent third parties that result in the listed entity's shares being purchased on behalf of the listed entity, for example by a bank. The contract requires the company to buy the shares the bank has purchased immediately after the prohibition period. For further details on own share buy-back programmes see section 23 of the IFRS Manual of Accounting.

A6.7.26 Own share buy-back programmes contain an obligation for an entity to purchase its own equity instruments for cash or another financial asset from the third party. This, therefore, gives rise to a financial liability for the present value of the redemption amount (for example, the present value of the forward repurchase price, option exercise price or other redemption amount).

Absence of explicit obligations

A6.7.27 IAS 32 states that the obligation to deliver cash or another financial asset need not be explicitly stated in the instrument. It may be established indirectly. However, the indirect obligation must be established through the terms and conditions of the financial instrument. [IAS 32 para 20]. IAS 32 clarifies the notion that an instrument may establish an obligation indirectly through its terms and conditions in two specific situations that are considered below.

A6.7.28 First, a financial instrument may contain a non-financial obligation that must be settled if, and only if, the entity fails to make distributions or to redeem the instrument. If the entity can avoid a transfer of cash or another financial asset only by settling the non-financial obligation, the financial instrument is a financial liability. [IAS 32 para 20(a)].

Example – Settlement of obligation by transfer of non-cash asset

A property company raises C150m for constructing a number of properties. The loan has a maturity period of 5 years. The loan agreement stipulates that the property company must transfer to the lender one of its investment properties if it is unable to settle the loan for cash at maturity.

In this agreement, if the property company is unable to settle the loan at maturity for cash, it is obliged to settle the obligation by transferring to the lender one of its other investment properties that, at the time of the settlement, may well be in excess of C150m. Therefore, an indirect financial obligation arises as the agreement contains a non-financial obligation that can be avoided only by making a transfer of cash. Hence, it is a financial liability.

6A.7.29 The second situation is where a financial instrument is a financial liability if it provides that on settlement the entity will deliver either:

- cash or another financial asset; or
- its own shares whose value is determined to exceed substantially the value of the cash or other financial asset.

Although the entity does not have an explicit contractual obligation to deliver cash or another financial asset, the value of the share settlement alternative is such that the entity will have little choice but to redeem the obligation in cash. In any event, the holder has been guaranteed, in substance, receipt of an amount that is at least equal to the cash settlement option. Hence, the instrument is a financial liability.

[IAS 32 para 20(b)].

A6.7.30 The IFRIC clarified in March 2006 that where an instrument (the 'base' instrument) contains a clause that requires cash or other financial assets to be delivered on that base instrument if there is a contractual obligation to make payment on another (the 'linked') instrument, then the inclusion of this linker clause would establish an indirect obligation to deliver cash or another financial assets on the base instrument. As a result the IFRIC agreed that the base instrument would be classified as a financial liability.

Example – Financial instrument ('base' instrument) linked to another (the 'linked') instrument

An entity issues irredeemable callable preference shares (the 'base' instrument) with dividends that must be paid if interest is paid on another (the 'linked') instrument. The issuer must pay the interest on the 'linked' instrument that is also perpetual.

In this example, the linkage to the linked instrument, on which there is a contractual obligation to pay interest, results in an indirect contractual obligation to pay dividends on the base instrument. If the linked instrument is callable by the issuer at any time, the issuer could avoid paying the dividends on the base instrument. Therefore, until the linked instrument is called, a contractual obligation to pay dividends on the base instrument exists. If the present value of the expected dividend stream to perpetuity is equal to the whole principal of the financial instrument, the entire instrument would be classified as a liability. On the other hand, if there is a difference an amount would fall to be attributable to the equity component.

Contracts settled in cash or other financial asset that are discretionary or at the option of the issuer

A6.7.31 An equity instrument is any contract that evidences a residual interest in an entity's assets after deducting all of its liabilities. Therefore, only those instruments that do not meet the definition of a liability will fall to be classified as equity. In other words, the entity must have an unconditional right to avoid delivery of cash or another financial asset. A typical example is an entity's non-puttable ordinary shares.

Payments that are discretionary or at the option of the issuer

A6.7.32 If an instrument does not have a contractual (including contingent) obligation to deliver cash or another financial asset, it is classified as an equity instrument. Therefore, where payments of interest/dividends or the principal amount or both are discretionary in nature, equity treatment is appropriate for some or all of the instrument. For example, dividends payable on non-puttable ordinary shares depend on the entity's profitability. However, there is no compulsion on the directors to declare a dividend even though a past pattern of dividend payments may have created an expectation on the shareholders that a dividend will be declared and payable. Such discretionary payments do not create contractual obligations, because the directors cannot be required to deliver cash or another financial asset to the shareholders. Nevertheless, a liability must be recognised in respect of such non-puttable ordinary shares where the directors formally act to make a distribution and become legally obligated to the shareholders to do so. This may be the case following the declaration of a dividend, or when the entity is being wound up and any assets remaining after the satisfaction of liabilities become distributable to shareholders. [IAS 32 para AG 13]. Section 23 of the IFRS Manual of Accounting provides further guidance on the accounting for dividends.

Example – Irredeemable preference shares with dividend payments linked to ordinary shares

An entity issues an irredeemable preference shares on which dividends are payable only if the entity also pays a dividend on its ordinary shares ('dividend pusher').

In this example, the dividend payments on the preference shares are discretionary and not contractual, because no dividends can be paid if no dividends are paid on the ordinary shares, which are an equity instrument. As the perpetual preference shares contain no contractual obligation ever to pay dividends and there is no obligation to repay the principal, they should be classified as equity in their entirety.

Where the dividend payments are also cumulative, that is, if no dividends are paid on the ordinary shares, the preference dividends are deferred, the perpetual shares will be classified as equity only if the dividends are deferred indefinitely and the entity does not have any contractual obligations whatsoever to pay those dividends.

6A.7.33 The classification of a preference share as an equity instrument or a financial liability would not be impacted by, for example:

- A history of making distributions.
- An intention to make distributions in the future.
- A possible negative impact on price of the issuer's ordinary shares if distributions are not made (because of restrictions on paying dividends on the ordinary shares if dividends are not paid on the preference shares).
- The amount of the issuer's reserves.
- An issuer's expectation of a profit or loss for a period.
- An ability or inability of the issuer to influence the amount of its profit or loss for the period.

[IAS 32 para AG 26].

A6.7.34 As explained in paragraph A6.7.16 above, where the holder has a put option that requires the issuer to redeem shares at a fixed amount at some future date, the shares are treated as a liability; the issuer cannot avoid settling the principal in cash. On the other hand, if the issuer has an option to call or redeem the shares for cash at some future date, the shares do not satisfy the definition of a financial liability as the issuer can avoid settling the principal in cash. This is because the issuer does not have a present obligation to transfer financial assets to the shareholders. In this case, redemption of the shares is solely at the issuer's discretion. An obligation may arise, however, when the issuer of the shares exercises its option, usually by formally notifying the shareholders of an intention to redeem the shares. [IAS 32 para AG 25].

A6.7.35 Where a financial instrument only results in a contractual obligation for the issuer to deliver cash or other financial assets upon the occurrence of an uncertain future event, the instrument may still need to be classified as a financial liability from initial recognition if it meets the definition of a contingent settlement event. See paragraph A6.7.50 for more details.

Contracts that will or may be settled in an entity's own equity instruments

A6.7.36 A contract is not an equity instrument solely because it may result in the receipt or delivery of the entity's own equity instruments. [IAS 32 para 21]. The classification of contracts that will or may be settled in the entity's own equity instruments is dependent on whether there is variability in either the number of own equity delivered and/or variability in the amount of cash or other financial assets received, or whether both are fixed.

A6.7.37 A contract that will be settled by the entity receiving (or delivering) a fixed number of its own equity instruments in exchange for a fixed amount of cash or another financial asset is an equity instrument [IAS 32 para 22]. This is commonly referred to as the 'fixed for fixed requirement'. For example, an entity receives C100 upfront from the holder to issue 100 of the entity's own equity in three years time. This would meet the 'fixed for fixed' requirement as both the number of own equity delivered and the cash received is fixed when the financial instrument is initially recognised. The instrument would meet the definition of an equity instrument as the holder gets a residual interest in the entity. By fixing upfront the amount paid and the number of shares received the holder benefits from any upside and suffers the loss from any fall in the residual value of the entity.

6.7.38 However, an entity may have a contractual right or obligation to receive or deliver a number of its own shares or other equity instruments that varies so that the fair value of the entity's own equity instrument to be received or delivered equals the amount of the contractual right or obligation. Such a contract may be for a fixed amount or an amount that fluctuates in part or in full in response to changes in a variable. [IAS 32 para 21]. It would be inappropriate to account for such contracts as an equity instrument when an entity's own equity instruments are used 'as currency' as such a contract represents a right or obligation for a specified amount rather than a specified residual equity interest. Therefore, such a contract would be classified as a financial liability. The underlying variable can include the entity's own share price. [IAS 32 para AG 27(d)].

Example 1 – Own shares to the value of C1 million

An entity receives C1m in exchange for its promise that it will deliver its own equity shares in an amount sufficient to equal a value of C1m at a future date. If the share price at the date on delivery of the contract is C5, the entity would be required to issue 200,000 shares ie a total value of C1m.

On the day the own equity is delivered the holder would be indifferent whether it received cash of C1m or shares to the value of C1m which it could sell and receive C1m in cash. Therefore, the entity is using its own equity as currency and as such the holder does not get a full residual interest.

Example 2 – Bermudan option with fixed but different strike prices

An entity issues an option to buy or sell a fixed number of shares at a specified exercise price. The terms of the option state that the specified exercise price varies with the share price of the entity such that:

Share price	Conversion ratio
0-10C	10 shares at 1C per share
11-20C	10 shares at 1.5C per share

The variability in the exercise price, as a function of share price of the entity, results in a variable amount of cash for a fixed number of shares. The 'fixed for fixed' requirement is therefore violated. The option is, therefore, treatment as a derivative financial liability and not as an equity instrument.

Example 3 – Call options where the underlying is an exchange ratio

Entities A, B and X are all listed companies. Entity A purchases an option to buy 5% of the share capital of entity X from entity B in return for entity A delivering its own equity shares to entity B. The exchange ratio is fixed when the option is written (for example, entity A pays 0.8 of entity A's own shares for the purchase of 1 share of entity X).

This exchange ratio will violate the 'fixed for fixed' requirement. The fixed number of entity A's shares that entity A may issue is not equal to a fixed amount of cash, as the value of each share acquired in exchange can vary. Therefore, entity A must treat its purchased option as a derivative financial instrument under IAS 39.

6A.7.39 The IASB was concerned that restricting the definition of an underlying variable could lead to structuring opportunities and abuse. Therefore, the standard requires that all forms of variability in either the own shares received or delivered, or the cash or another financial asset delivered or received, would result in financial asset or financial liability classification.

A6.7.40 A contract that will be settled by an entity delivering a fixed number of its own equity instruments in exchange for a fixed amount of foreign currency (that is a currency other than the functional currency of the entity) is a financial liability. Although not specifically addressed in IAS 32, the issue was considered by the IFRIC at its meeting in April 2005. The IFRIC noted that any obligation denominated in a foreign currency represents a variable amount of cash in the entity's functional currency. This is evidenced by the fact that IAS 39 allows cash flow hedge accounting for transactions denominated in a foreign currency, because such transactions expose the entity to variability in cash flows in the entity's functional currency. Therefore, the entire contract is a financial liability made up of two components. A host bond denominated in the functional currency (whose foreign exchange risk is accounted for under IAS 21, 'The effects of changes in foreign exchange rates') and an embedded derivative which is a written option for the holder to exchange the foreign currency bond for a fixed number of functional currency denominated shares.

Example – Foreign currency convertible bonds

A UK company (with a sterling functional currency) issues a convertible bond denominated in US dollar and convertible on a number of dates into a fixed number of shares. The host contract is a US dollars bond with an embedded written option for the holder to exchange the US dollars bond for a fixed number of sterling denominated shares. The value of the embedded written option changes in response to changes in the value of the equity of the entity. Therefore, equity indexed feature embedded in a host debt instrument are not closely related to the host instrument because the risks inherent in the host and embedded derivative are dissimilar. [IAS 39 para AG 30(d)]. Therefore, the written option will require separation and measured at fair value through profit or loss. It, therefore, fails the 'fixed for fixed' requirement and precludes the conversion option being classified as equity. The whole of the convertible bond is classified as a financial liability under IAS 32 and is subject to IAS 39 for recognition and measurement. Under IAS 39 the convertible bond will be assessed as having a host debt instrument and an embedded foreign exchange equity derivative. The latter is not closely related to the debt host so will need to be separated if the debt host is carried at amortised cost.

6A.7.41 In situations where a subsidiary issues a convertible bond that (if converted) converts into shares of the parent, the currency that should be looked to in determining whether the 'fixed for fixed' requirement in IAS 32 is met depends on the specific circumstances. For the purposes of the group's consolidated financial statements, a group must look to either the functional currency of the parent (whose shares the bond is convertible into), or that of the subsidiary (whose liability will be extinguished if the bond is converted). The choice to look to the functional currency of the subsidiary or the parent is a policy choice and should be applied on a consistent basis for all similar instruments. The IFRIC considered this issue and decided to give no guidance. In the individual financial statements of the subsidiary, the convertible is classified as a financial liability in its entirety, as the conversion option relates to the shares of the parent and not the equity of the subsidiary. In the individual financial statements of the subsidiary, under IAS 39 the conversion option is an embedded derivative that must be separated as it is not closely related to the debt host.

A6.7.42 The inclusion of a cap, floor or combination of both (a collar) that limits the variability in either the own equity instruments delivered or the cash or financial assets received in some manner does not change the classification of the own share settled instrument from being a financial asset or financial liability. For example, an entity issues an instrument that is settled in a variable number of shares but is subject to a cap to prevent excessive dilution of the existing shareholders through the issue of new shares. The cap is out of the money on issuance. Although the host instrument is a financial liability (as it is settled in a variable number of shares), the cap is not an equity instrument. It is true that a similar stand-alone cap would be classified as equity, however, the 'fixed for fixed' requirement is not met for the instrument as a whole, therefore, the instrument is settled in a variable number shares and should be classified as a financial liability.

6.7.43 A single instrument should not be separated into a number of different instruments in order to satisfy the 'fixed for fixed' requirement where otherwise it would result in variability in either the own equity or cash or another financial asset, if accounted for as a single instrument. For example, variability resulting from the passage of time:

Example – Variation in the cash received due to the passage of time

Entity A (US dollar functional currency) writes an option to entity B (not an employee) that enables entity B to buy 1 share of entity A on the following terms:

- If the option is exercised in year 1 the strike price is $1.
- If the option is exercised in year 2 the strike price is $2.
- If the option is exercised in year 3 the strike price is $3.

The contract would not meet the 'fixed for fixed' requirement. The option was issued as one financial instrument and, therefore, cannot be viewed a series of separate 'fixed for fixed' options.

6A.7.44 Complexity arises in practice when applying the principles for settlement in an entity's own equity instruments. Although IAS 32 states that variability in either the entity's own equity delivered or cash or another financial asset received results in a financial liability, not all forms of variability do in fact violate the 'fixed for fixed' requirement. The simplest example is an adjustment to the conversion ratio of a convertible bond triggered by a stock split. For example the original conversion ratio is 1 share for every £1 (with a notional value of £2), however, upon a stock split each share now has a notional value of £1. It would, therefore, be necessary to adjust the conversion ratio to 2 shares for every £1 in order to maintain the relative economic rights of the shareholders and bondholders. Although the adjustment results in variability in the number of own equity delivered, the fact that this variability serves to maintain the relative economic rights of the shareholders and bondholders results in no violation of the 'fixed for fixed' requirement.

A6.7.45 Where variability is caused by the inclusion of an anti-dilution clause, such as the stock split clause outlined above, this will not result in a violation of the 'fixed for fixed' requirement provided, firstly the relative rights of the shareholders and bondholders are maintained, and secondly the instrument would otherwise meet the 'fixed for fixed' requirement. Another example of an anti-dilutive clause is an adjustment made for the payment of dividends.

A6.7.46 A common adjustment in convertible bonds is the inclusion of a change of control clause. The clause adjusts the otherwise fixed for fixed conversion ratio upon a change of control event. The adjustment aims to compensate the bondholder for the loss of optionality either through a stated compensation amount or via a formula. As this change in control adjustment is not compensation that relates to the issuance of the equity shares but rather is compensation for the loss of optionality, it does not affect the relative rights of the shareholders and bondholders and does not result in a violation of the 'fixed for fixed' requirement.

A6.7.47 The table below sets out the classification in various scenarios where a fixed or variable monetary obligation (not indexed to the entity's own share price) is settled in a fixed number or variable number of the entity's own shares. Instruments classified as financial liabilities under IAS 32, will require further analysis under IAS 39 to determine whether any embedded derivatives require to be bifurcated.

Contract settled in the equity's own shares	Monetary value of consideration*	Number of equity shares	Classification
Scenario 1	Fixed	Variable	Financial liability
Scenario 2	Variable	Variable	Financial liability
Scenario 3	Variable	Fixed	Financial liability
Scenario 4	Fixed in a currency other than the entity's functional currency	Fixed	Financial liability
Scenario 5	Fixed	Fixed	Equity

* in the functional currency of the issuer.

A6.7.48 IAS 32 does not deal with the option to exchange a fixed number of one kind of the entity's own equity for a fixed number of a different kind of equity. An example is an option for a minority shareholder to exchange its holding of shares in a subsidiary for a fixed number of equity shares in the parent. Both legs of the contract are a fixed number of shares and in both cases the shares are a residual interest in some or all of the entity, that is is equity. The contract does not violate the part of the definition of a financial liability in paragraph 11(b)(i) of IAS 32 because, although it is a non-derivative contract, it does not oblige the entity to deliver a variable number of its own equity instruments and hence the entity is not using its own equity instruments as 'currency'. From the perspective of the parent in preparing its separate financial statements, the contract is a derivative as it is over an asset (investment in its subsidiary), rather than an equity instrument.

A6.7.49 A contract that will be settled in cash or another financial asset as opposed to the delivery of shares is a financial asset or financial liability even if the amount of cash or another financial asset that will be received or delivered is based on changes in the market price of the entity's own equity. An example is a net cash-settled share option. [IAS 32 para AG 27(c)]. Derivatives on own shares are considered further from paragraph A6.7.89 below.

Contingent settlement provisions

A6.7.50 The obligation to deliver cash or financial assets need not be actual, it may be contingent on the occurrence or non-occurrence of uncertain future events (or on the outcome of uncertain circumstances) that are beyond the control of both the issuer or the holder of the instrument. Examples of such uncertain future events may include, but are not limited to:

- Changes in stock market index or consumer price index.
- Changes in interest rates or exchange rates.
- Changes in tax laws or other regulatory requirements.
- Changes in the issuer's key performance indicators such as revenue, net income or debt-to-equity ratios.

A6.7.51 The revised IAS 32 incorporates the conclusion previously in SIC 5, 'Classification of financial instruments – contingent settlement provisions', that, in the circumstances specified above, the instrument is a financial liability. This is because at the time of the initial recognition, the issuer does not have an unconditional right to avoid delivering cash or another financial asset (or otherwise to settle it in such a way that it would be a financial liability) as it does not control the final outcome. A transfer of economic benefits as a result of a past event (the issue of the instrument) cannot be avoided depending on the outcome of the future event. Such financial instruments should, therefore, be classified as a liability.

Example 1 – Change of control events

A contract between entity A and a third party contains a requirement for entity A to make payments to the third party on a change of control of entity A. For example, where entity A may be taken over by entity B and where entity B is not connected to entity A.

The change of control event is outside the control of both the entity and the third party provided that it need not be agreed by the entity at a general meeting. This will be the case if a purchaser could approach individual shareholders and buy their shares. Payments to a third party that are contingent on a change of control event are therefore financial liabilities when no agreement by a general meeting is required.

Example 2 – Shares with an obligation to pay out a percentage of profits

A bond includes an obligation to pay out a fixed 10% of profits each year and is mandatorily redeemable at par after 20 years.

The instrument has two liability components, a contractual obligation to redeem the instrument at par after 20 years and a contractual obligation to pay 10% of profits until redemption. The latter is a financial liability because, although the payment depends on the entity making profits (an uncertain future event), the future profits are outside the control of both the issuer and holder, but if profits are made the issuer cannot avoid making the payment, hence it meets the definition of a contingent settlement event. The 10% obligation does not meet the definition of an embedded derivative as the entity's profit is a non-financial variable that is specific to a party to the contract. [IAS 39 para 9]. This view may change as the IASB has tentatively agreed to delete from the definition of a derivative the exclusion for contracts that are linked to a non-financial variable that is specific to a party to the contract with the effect that only those contracts that meet the definition of insurance contracts would fail to be treated as derivatives.

Example 3 – mandatorily redeemable where an IPO does not occur

An undated cumulative convertible bond, whose interest payments are at the discretion of the entity absent an IPO, contains a clause that states that the instrument (including all unpaid cumulative interest) will become mandatorily payable if there is not an IPO by the end of three years from the instrument's issuance date. Although it may be within the entity's control to determine whether the IPO is attempted, market and regulatory forces determine whether any attempt is successful (that is, whether the market will accept an IPO and whether all regulatory approvals will be obtained). These forces are beyond the control of the entity, therefore redemption upon an IPO event not occurring meets the definition of a contingent settlement event and results in the bond being classified as a financial liability from inception.

6A.7.52 Where the event is within the control of the issuer but not the holder, it is possible for the issuer to avoid the event occurring and hence avoid settling the instrument, hence the event would not meet the definition of a contingent settlement event. For example an undated cumulative convertible bond whose interest payments are at the discretion of the entity that contains a clause that states that the instrument (including all unpaid cumulative interest) will become mandatorily payable if a successful IPO occurs. As outlined in example 3 above, it is within an entity's control to determine whether an IPO is attempted. Therefore, the clause does not meet the definition of a contingent settlement provision and results in the bond being classified as an equity instrument from inception.

A6.7.53 There are two exceptions where uncertain events outside the control of the issuer would not meet the definition of a contingent settlement event. These are where:

- the part of the contingent settlement provision that could require settlement in cash or another financial asset (or otherwise in such a way that it would be a financial liability) is not *genuine* (see para A6.7.54); or
- the issuer can be required to settle the obligation in cash or another financial asset (or otherwise to settle it in such a way that it would be a financial liability) only in the event of liquidation of the issuer (see para A6.7.56).

[IAS 32 para 25].

Settlement terms that are not genuine

A6.7.54 The standard explains that a contingent settlement provision in a contract is not genuine if it requires settlement in cash only on the occurrence of an event that is extremely rare, highly abnormal and very unlikely to occur. In that situation, the contingent settlement provisions are not taken into account in the instrument's classification. Thus, a contract that requires settlement in cash or a variable number of the entity's own shares only on the occurrence of an event that is extremely rare, highly abnormal and very unlikely to occur is an equity instrument. Similarly, if settlement in a fixed number of an entity's own shares may be contractually precluded in circumstances that are outside the control of the entity, those circumstances can be ignored if there is no genuine possibility that they will occur. In that situation, the instrument continues to be classified as an equity instrument and not as a financial liability. [IAS 32 para AG 28].

A6.7.55 In practice, terms are included in a contract for a purpose that is likely to have commercial effect. Therefore, it would be unusual to include settlement terms in a contract that are contingent on an event that is extremely rare, highly abnormal or very unlikely to occur. If such ineffective terms are included, it should be concluded that the terms are not genuine and should be ignored in determining the instrument's classification. However, 'not genuine' should not be equated to 'remote'. The IASB makes it clear in the Basis for conclusions to IAS 32 that it is not appropriate to disregard events that are merely 'remote'. The specific facts and circumstances would need to be considered.

Example 1 – Settlement terms based on increase in an index

An entity issues an instrument that is redeemable in cash if the FTSE 100 doubles within a two month period.

In general, it is not for the entity to speculate whether an index will behave in a certain manner that may or may not trigger redemption of the instrument. As the entity will be unable to avoid a settlement in cash if the index reaches that level, the instrument should be treated as a liability.

However, in this situation, the doubling of the FTSE 100 within such a short period of time is extremely rare, highly abnormal and unlikely to occur. Furthermore, in practice, an investor is highly unlikely to advance funds on such redemption terms. Clearly the terms are artificial and not genuine and should be ignored for classification purposes.

Example 2 – Settlement terms based on changes in regulation

A bank issues an instrument that is redeemable in cash if the banking regulator changes the instrument's current classification from tier 1 capital to tier 2 capital in the future.

Whether the contingency in this example is genuine would depend upon the specific facts and circumstances. In some jurisdictions, the industry regulator has a history of applying such changes always prospectively and grandfathering existing instruments under their original classification. In that situation, a regulatory change would not affect the classification of an instrument that is currently outstanding and, consequently, the contingency would be regarded as not genuine.

Settlements that arise only on liquidations

A6.7.56 Obligations to deliver cash or other financial assets that are contingent only on the issuer's liquidation should be ignored. This is rather obvious because different rights and obligations associated with the instruments come into effect at liquidation that would not otherwise be triggered during the ordinary course of business and, hence, would be inconsistent with the going concern assumption. A contingent settlement provision that provides for payment in cash or another financial asset only on the entity's liquidation is similar to an equity instrument that has priority in liquidation. Such a provision should, therefore, be ignored in classifying the instrument. However, if the instrument is redeemable on the occurrence of an event that may ultimately lead to eventual liquidation (for example, the entity becomes insolvent, goes into receivership, administration etc), the instrument should still be classified as a liability.

Example – Obligation arising on the liquidation of the issuer

A limited partnership has a finite life of 25 years. The partnership's equity will be redeemed at the end of its term.

In this situation, the partnership's equity will be presented as a liability because the amount is payable only on liquidation and liquidation is certain as the entity has a finite life.

However, as stated in paragraph A6.7.23 above, the exposure draft on 'Financial instruments puttable at fair value and obligations arising on liquidation', if issued as a standard, would result in equity classification of instruments that entitle the holder to a *pro rata* share of the entity's net assets upon liquidation that is certain to occur and outside the entity's control (as in limited life entities), provided the instruments are in the most subordinated class of instruments with a claim to the entity's net assets. When liquidation is uncertain to occur, these instruments would also be considered equity where the holder has the option to require liquidation (as in some partnership interests) and will receive a *pro rata* share of net assets.

Where a partner's equity interest is redeemable upon a partner's death, that partner's equity interest should be classified as a liability because the redemption is based on an event that is certain to occur, although the partnership itself is not being liquidated. Even, if those shares represent the only shares of the partnership, the partnership should still classify them as liabilities, even though the death of the partner may eventually lead to the partnership's dissolution. It may also be appropriate to describe them as 'redeemable shares' to distinguish them from other liabilities.

Derivative financial instruments with settlement options

A6.7.57 Sometimes a derivative contract may contain settlement options that give either party a choice over how it is settled (for example, the issuer or the holder can choose to settle the contract net in cash, or by exchanging shares for cash). IAS 32 states that when a derivative financial instrument gives one party a choice over how it is settled, it is a financial asset or a financial liability, unless all of the settlement alternatives would result in it being an equity instrument. [IAS 32 para 26].

A6.7.58 An example of a derivative financial instrument with a settlement option that is a financial liability is an option for an entity to buy its own shares from a third party that the entity can decide to settle net in cash or by exchanging its own shares for cash. Forward and option contracts to buy or sell an entity's own equity instruments that contain settlement options are discussed in paragraph A6.7.97 below. Also, some contracts to buy or sell a non-financial item (not for 'own use') in exchange for the entity's own equity instruments are financial assets or financial liabilities and not equity instruments, if they can be settled either by delivery of the non financial item or net in cash or another financial instrument. [IAS 32 para 27]. Where the settlement option is contingent on a future event occurring, it will still fall under the settlement option accounting in accordance with paragraph 26 of IAS 32 from initial recognition.

Example – Contingent settlement options

A company has issued convertible bonds whose terms include a clause giving the issuer the option to redeem in cash the bonds at their fair market value in the event of the occurrence of an uncertain future event.

The conversion option is a derivative. The terms of the convertible bond give the issuer the option to redeem the bonds for cash at their fair market value. There is a settlement alternative for the equity conversion option, as it can be settled at fair value either in shares or in cash – that is, there is a net cash settlement option. An equity conversion option for which either party has a choice of settlement in cash or shares is a financial liability. [IAS 32 para 26]. Paragraph 26 of IAS 32 overturns the usual principle that something that is in the control of an issuer is not an obligation. This right of choice of settlement is contingent upon a future event in the example above, but the equity conversion option must still be accounted for as an embedded derivative in accordance with paragraph 26 of IAS 32.

Shares issued by subsidiaries

A6.7.59 Normally equity shares issued by subsidiaries to persons outside the group are classified as minority interests in the consolidated financial statements in accordance with IAS 1, 'Presentation of financial instruments', and IAS 27, 'Consolidated and separate financial statements'. When classifying a financial instrument (or a component of it) in consolidated financial statements, an entity should consider all the terms and conditions agreed between group members and the instrument holders in determining whether the group as a whole has an obligation to deliver cash or another financial asset in respect of the instrument, or to settle it in a manner that results in liability classification.

A6.7.60 For example, a member of the group might give a guarantee to pay amounts in respect of those shares, such as dividends or amounts due on their redemption; or another group member might undertake to purchase the shares in the event that the subsidiary issuing them fails to make the expected payments. Where this is so, the outside shareholders will look to the guarantor if the subsidiary has defaulted.

A6.7.61 Consequently, in such a situation, the subsidiary may appropriately classify the instrument without regard to these additional terms in its separate financial statements. However, in the consolidated financial statements, the effect of other agreements between group members and the instrument holders means that the group as a whole is unable to avoid the transfer of economic benefits.Therefore, where such an obligation or settlement provision exists from the perspective of the group, the instrument (or the component of it that is subject to the obligation) is classified as a financial liability in consolidated financial statements. [IAS 32 para AG 29]. (See further section 24 of the Manual of Accounting – UK GAAP.)

Decision tree for classification as a liability or equity instrument

A6.7.62 A decision tree for determining whether a non-derivative financial instrument is a liability or an equity instrument is given below.

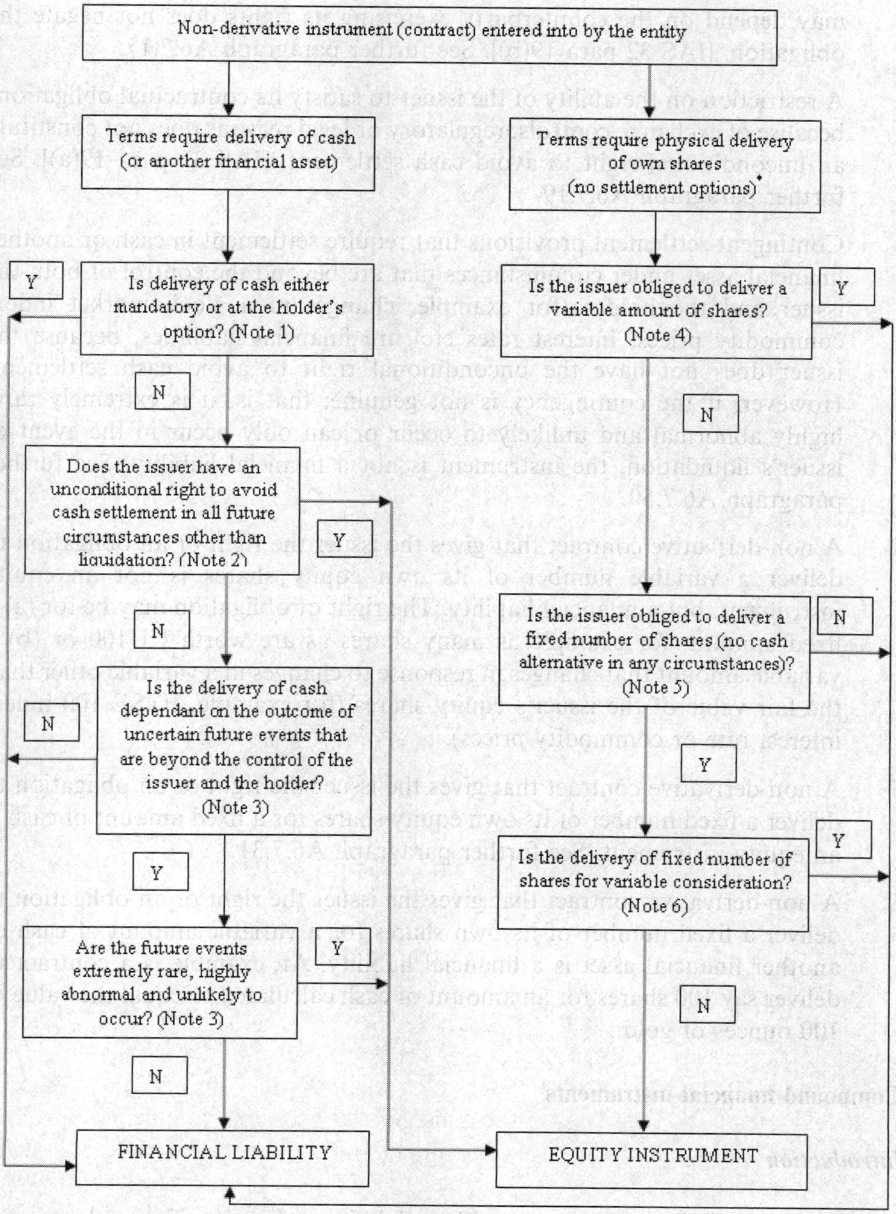

* Settlement options are dealt with in paragraph A6.7.97 below.

Notes:

1 The existence of a contractual obligation for the issuer to deliver cash (principal, interest or both) or another financial asset is an essential feature of a financial liability. [IAS 32 para 17]. The fact that any cash settlement may depend on the counterparty exercising its rights does not negate the obligation. [IAS 32 para 19(b)]. See further paragraph A6.7.17.

2 A restriction on the ability of the issuer to satisfy its contractual obligations because of exchange controls, regulatory or legal reasons does not constitute an unconditional right to avoid cash settlement. [IAS 32 para 19(a)]. See further paragraph A6.7.19.

3 Contingent settlement provisions that require settlement in cash or another financial asset under circumstances that are beyond the control of both the issuer and the holder (for example, changes in a stock market index, commodity prices, interest rates etc) are financial liabilities, because the issuer does not have the unconditional right to avoid cash settlement. However, if the contingency is not genuine; that is, it is extremely rare, highly abnormal and unlikely to occur or can only occur in the event of issuer's liquidation, the instrument is not a financial liability. See further paragraph A6.7.50.

4 A non-derivative contract that gives the issuer the right or an obligation to deliver a variable number of its own equity shares is not an equity instrument, but a financial liability. The right or obligation may be for (a) a fixed amount, for example as many shares as are worth CU100 or (b) a variable amount that changes in response to changes in a variable other than the fair value of the issuer's equity shares (for example, FTSE 100 index, interest rate or commodity prices).

5 A non-derivative contract that gives the issuer the right or an obligation to deliver a fixed number of its own equity shares for a fixed amount of cash is an equity instrument. See further paragraph A6.7.31.

6 A non-derivative contract that gives the issuer the right or an obligation to deliver a fixed number of its own shares for a variable amount of cash or another financial asset is a financial liability. An example is a contract to deliver say 100 shares for an amount of cash calculated to equal the value of 100 ounces of gold.

Compound financial instruments

Introduction

A6.7.63 Not all instruments are either liability or equity. Some, known as compound instruments, can be structured to contain elements of both in a single contact. A compound financial instrument is a non-derivative financial instrument that, from the issuer's perspective, contains both a liability and an equity component. [IAS 32 paras 28, AG 30]. Typical examples of such instruments are:

- A bond that is convertible into equity shares at the holder's option. From the issuer's perspective, such an instrument comprises two components: a financial liability (issuer's contractual obligation to deliver cash or another financial asset for payment of interest and principal, if not converted) and an equity instrument (a written call option granting the holder the right, for a specified period of time, to convert it into a fixed number of the entity's ordinary shares). The economic effect of issuing such an instrument is substantially the same as issuing simultaneously a debt instrument with an early settlement provision and warrants to purchase ordinary shares, or issuing a debt instrument with detachable share purchase warrants. [IAS 32 para 29]. If the issuer call option is contingent on a future event, it should still be for accounted for as a call option from initial recognition. For example:

Example – Provisional issuer call option to redeem at par

Entity A issues a convertible bond that, if converted, converts into a fixed number of equity shares. The bond also contains a provisional call option that gives the issuer the option to redeem the bond at par if the shares price is 130% of the conversion price for at least 20 days.

The convertible bond is a compound financial instrument with a debt host and equity conversion option. As the issuer call option is to redeem the bonds at par, it does not result in the conversion option having a cash settlement alternative. The conversion option is not, therefore, accounted for as an embedded derivative in accordance with paragraph 26 of IAS 32.

In respect of the issuer call option, the value of any derivative feature (such as a call option) embedded in a compound financial instrument, other than the equity component is included in the liability component. [IAS 32 para 31]. The call option is, therefore, considered part of the liability and not the equity component. When determining whether the embedded option is closely related, the assessment of whether the call or put option is closely related to the host debt contract from the issuer's perspective is made before separating the equity element under IAS 32. [IAS 39 para AG 30(g)].

- A mandatorily redeemable preference shares with dividend payments made at the issuer's discretion before the redemption date. Such an instrument contains a liability component (issuer's contractual obligation to deliver cash or another financial asset for payment of the redemption amount) and an equity component (the holder's right to receive dividends, if declared). [IAS 32 para AG 37].

Separation of a compound financial instrument on initial recognition

A6.7.64 The issuer of a non-derivative financial instrument should first evaluate the financial instrument's terms to determine whether it contains both a liability and an equity component. This evaluation should be done in accordance with the contractual arrangement's substance and the definition of a financial liability, financial asset and an equity component. If such components are identified, the issuer should account for the components separately as financial liabilities, financial assets or equity instruments. [IAS 32 para 28]. The liability and the equity components must be presented separately on the balance sheet. [IAS 32 para 29].

A6.7.65 The above approach is often described as 'split accounting'. Split accounting is applied by the issuer of the financial statement to measure the liability and the equity components upon initial recognition of the instrument. The method, illustrated by reference to a convertible bond that is a most common form of a compound financial instrument, but which is equally applicable to other forms of compound financial instruments, allocates the fair value of the consideration for the compound instrument into its liability and equity components, as follows:

- The fair value of the consideration in respect of the liability component is measured first, at the fair value of a similar liability (including any embedded non-equity derivative features such as an issuer's call option to redeem the bond early) that does not have any associated equity conversion option. This becomes the liability component's carrying amount at initial recognition.

  In practice, the liability component's initial carrying value is determined by discounting the contractual stream of future cash flows (interest and principal) to the present value at the current rate of interest applicable to instruments of comparable credit status and providing substantially the same cash flows on the same terms, but without the equity component (the equity conversion option).

  The value of any embedded non-equity derivative features is separately determined and included in the liability component.

- The equity component (the equity conversion option) is assigned the residual amount after deducting from the fair value of the instrument as a whole the amount separately determined for the liability component.

  The equity component is excluded from IAS 39's scope and is never remeasured after initial recognition.

Since the sum of the carrying amounts assigned to the liability and equity components on initial recognition is always equal to the consideration received, which, in most circumstances is equal to the fair value of the instrument as a whole, no gain or loss arises from initially recognising the instrument's components separately in the above manner.

[IAS 32 paras 31, AG 31].

A6.7.66 The requirement to separate the liability and the equity components of a single compound financial instrument in the above manner is consistent with the requirements for initial measurement of a financial liability in IAS 39 and the definitions in IAS 32 and the Framework of an equity instrument as a residual interest. Furthermore, the approach removes the need to estimate inputs to, and apply, complex option pricing models to measure the equity component of some compound financial instruments. [IAS 32 paras BC 29-30].

A6.7.67 Once a compound financial instrument has been separated into its liability and equity components on initial recognition, the classification of the liability and equity components is not revised as a result of a change in the likelihood that a conversion option will be exercised, even when the option's exercise may appear to have become economically advantageous to some holders. This is because the entity's contractual obligation to make future payments remains outstanding until it is extinguished through conversion, the instrument's maturity or some other transaction. [IAS 32 para 30].

Example – Separation of a convertible bond

An entity issues 600,000 convertible bonds at the start of year 1. The bonds have a 3-year term, and are issued at par with a face value of C100 per bond, resulting in total proceeds of C60m, which is also the fair value of the bonds. Interest is payable annually in arrears at a nominal annual interest rate of 6%. Each C100 nominal bond is convertible at any time up to maturity into 25 ordinary shares. When the bonds are issued, the prevailing market interest rate for similar debt without conversion options is 9%. The entity incurs issue cost of 1% on the nominal value of the bond amounting to C600,000.

As explained in paragraph A6.7.65 above, the liability component is measured first by discounting the contractually determined stream of future cash flows (interest and principal) to present value using a discount rate of 9%, the market interest rate for similar bonds having no conversion rights, as shown below.

	C
PV of interest payable at the end of year 1 – 3,600,000/1.09	3,302,752
PV of interest payable at the end of year 2 – 3,600,000/(1.09)2	3,030,048
PV of interest payable at the end of year 3 – 3,600,000/(1.09)3	2,779,861
PV of principal of C60,000,000 payable at the end of three years – 60,000,000/(1.09)3	46,331,009
Total liability component	55,443,670
Total equity component (residual)*	4,556,330
Fair value of bonds	60,000,000

* The equity component is a written call option that allows the holder to call for the shares on exercise of the conversion option at any time before maturity (American option). Since equity is a residual, application of complex option pricing models are not necessary to determine the equity component. Instead, the difference between the bond's proceeds and the liability component's fair value of the liability component as computed above – the residual – is assigned to the equity component.

In accordance with IAS 32, the issue cost of C600,000 will need to be allocated between the liability and the equity components in proportion to the allocation of the proceeds as shown below:

	Equity component	Liability component	Total
	C	C	C
Gross proceeds allocated as above	4,556,330	55,443,670	60,000,000
Issue cost	(45,563)	(554,437)	(600,000)
Net proceeds	4,510,767	54,889,233	59,400,000

The amount credited to equity of C4,510,767 is not subsequently remeasured.

The liability component of C54,889,233 will be subsequently measured in accordance with its classification under IAS 39 either as a financial liability at fair value through profit or loss or as another liability measured at amortised cost using the effective interest rate method. Under the latter classification, the liability component will accrete to its final redemption amount of C60,000,000 at the end of year 3 at an effective interest rate of 9.38837% as shown below:

Year	Opening liability	Interest @ 9.38837%	Cash paid	Closing liability
	C	C	C	C
1	54,889,233	5,153,205	(3,600,000)	56,442,438
2	56,442,438	5,299,025	(3,600,000)	58,141,464
3	58,141,464	5,458,536	(63,600,000)	–
Total finance cost		15,910,767		
Total finance cost consists of:				
Interest payments		10,800,000		
Issue cost allocated to liability component		554,437		
Discount (representing gross proceeds allocated to equity component)		4,556,330		
		15,910,767		

Separation of a compound instrument containing non-equity derivatives

A6.7.68 As explained above, a non-derivative compound financial instrument must be separated into its equity and liability components. In a convertible bond, the equity component arises from the embedded option to convert the liability into the issuer's equity. However, a convertible bond may also contain other non-equity derivative features such as a call, put or pre-payment option. The way in which a compound financial instrument with multiple derivative features is separated into its constituent parts is indicated below:

- First, the value of non-equity derivatives must be included in the liability component. [IAS 32 para 31]. This means that the liability component is established by measuring a bond's fair value with similar terms, credit status and containing similar non-equity derivative features, but without the equity conversion feature.

- Secondly, the equity component is then arrived at by deducting the fair value attributable to the bond as determined above from the compound instrument's fair value.

- Thirdly, given that the liability component contains the non-equity derivative features, it is necessary to assess whether such embedded derivative features are closely related to the host debt contract. This assessment is made before separating the equity element as determined above (see section 5). [IAS 39 para AG 30(g)]. In a convertible bond, that assessment will involve determining whether the call option's exercise price is approximately equal to the sum of the debt and the equity components, which is equal to the convertible bond's par value. If the bond is callable at par, the embedded call option is closely related to the host debt instrument. The embedded call option is not bifurcated (split out) and the liability component is determined as indicated above. If, on the other hand, the bond is callable at the carrying value of the liability component, the embedded call option is not closely related to the debt host. In that situation, the embedded call option is separated out of the liability component and accounted for separately. Separating the embedded derivative from the liability component does not affect the amount determined for the equity component as noted in bullet point two above.

Example – Convertible debt with embedded puts and calls

A company issues a convertible debt instrument that contains both an equity conversion option and embedded written puts and purchased calls. The debt component is initially measured at the fair value of a vanilla debt with the same contractual maturity plus the value of the written puts less value of the purchased calls, in accordance with paragraph 31 of IAS 32 and as illustrated in paragraphs IE 37 and IE 38 (example 10) of IAS 32.

Where the puts and calls are not required to be separated from the debt host, the debt component is measured at amortised cost using the effective interest rate method as defined in paragraph 9 of IAS 39. The puts and calls are considered in determining the expected future life of the instrument and, therefore, the expected interest rate.

- Finally, the sum of the carrying amounts assigned to the various components as indicated above on initial recognition must always be equal to the compound instrument's fair value as a whole. No gain or loss should arise from initially recognising the instrument's components separately. [IAS 32 para 31].

6A.7.69 The ability to convert the host instrument into own equity of the entity may be contingent on an uncertain future event. Where the uncertain future event meets the definition of a contingent settlement event as defined as in paragraph A6.7.50, the classification of the conversion option on initial recognition would depend on whether the conversion option meets or violates the 'fixed for fixed' requirement if the uncertain future event occurs.

Example 1 – Contingent convertible bond

Entity A issues a contingently convertible bond; the debt host becomes convertible into common shares of entity A at a fixed ratio of 1:1.25 only if the contingent event occurs. The contingent event meets the definition of a contingent settlement event in accordance with paragraph 25 of IAS 32 and is 'genuine' – for example, a change in control event. There are no adjustments to the conversion ratio upon the contingent event occurring, and there are no other put or call options.

The instrument is first separated into its component parts, namely a debt host and equity conversion option. The fact that the option is only contingently convertible will not cause liability classification of the conversion option under paragraph 25 of IAS 32 provided that, upon occurrence of the contingent event, it would be settled in such a way as to require classification as equity. If the contingent event were to occur in the example above, the conversion to own shares would still satisfy the 'fixed for fixed' requirement in paragraph 16(b)(ii) of IAS 32. The conversion option would be classified as an equity component, and the entire instrument would be a compound financial instrument.

Example 2 – Separation of a callable convertible bond

An entity issues 600,000 callable convertible bonds at the beginning of year 1. The bonds are issued at par with a face value of C100 per bond, giving total proceeds of C60m, which is also the bond's fair value. The bonds are convertible by the holder into a fixed number of shares at any time after the first anniversary of its issue. Furthermore, the bonds do not have a fixed maturity; instead the issuer can call/redeem the bond at any time at the fixed stated principal amount of the bond.

The following information is relevant:	**Cm**
Value of a straight bond without a call or equity conversion feature (plain vanilla)	57
Value of issuer call option in a similar bond without an equity conversion option based on an option pricing model (derivative asset)	2

As explained above, the value of the call option (the non-equity derivative) of C2m must be included in the liability component. In this situation, the inclusion results in the value of a callable bond without the equity conversion feature (the liability component) to be less than the value of a plain vanilla bond. This is because the issuer's right to call the bond in the event that interest rates go up and bond price increases makes the value of a callable bond less attractive to the holder than a plain vanilla bond.

Value of callable bond (the liability component)	55
Value of equity component (the conversion option) = residual	5
Fair value of bond = consideration received	60

As the liability component contains the call option, it is now necessary to assess whether the call option is closely related to the host debt instrument. In this situation, the call option's exercise price is set at C60m, the fixed stated principal of the bond. Therefore, at each exercise date, the option's exercise price of C60m is likely to be approximately equal to the amortised carrying amount of the bond plus the equity conversion option. Therefore, the call option is closely related to the host debt instrument. As a result, the call option is not separately accounted for, but remains in the liability component.

The liability component of C55m will be subsequently measured in accordance with its classification under IAS 39 either as a financial liability at fair value through profit or loss or as another liability measured at amortised cost using the effective interest rate method. Although, in this situation, the bond can be called by the issuer at any time or converted by the holder at any time after the first anniversary of its issue, the liability component of C55m is not automatically accreted to its redemption amount of C60m by the end of year 1. This is because the effective interest rate method requires the entity to discount the cash flows over the instrument's expected life, taking into account all the financial instrument's contractual terms including pre-payment, call and similar options [IAS 39 para 9]. This period may well be a period greater than one year.

On the other hand, if the call option's exercise price were set at an amount that is not approximately equal to the debt instrument's amortised carrying amount, the call option would fall to be accounted for separately. In that situation, the proceeds of the converted bond would be allocated as follows:

	Dr Cm	Cr Cm
Cash	60	
Derivative asset (issuer call option)	2	
Host debt instrument		57
Equity component (written equity call option)		5

As can be seen from the above, the separation of the call option asset affects the value of the liability and not the equity component. The derivative asset will be fair valued at each subsequent balance sheet date until the option is exercised. The liability component would be amortised over its expected life (determined without reference to the call option to avoid double counting) under the effective interest method as stated above.

Conversion at or before maturity

A6.7.70 The terms of a convertible instrument may require the instrument to be converted into the entity's ordinary shares either at or any time before maturity. IAS 32 states that on conversion of a convertible instrument at maturity, the entity derecognises the liability component and recognises it as equity. The original equity component remains in equity. There is no gain or loss on conversion at maturity. [IAS 32 para AG32].

Example 1 – Conversion at maturity

The facts are the same as the example in paragraph A6.7.67 above, except that the bond is converted at the end of its three-year term.

The amortised cost of the bond will be stated at C60m at maturity after the last payment of interest has been made. As the bond is converted, the entity will issue 15m (600,000 × 25) of C1 nominal value. The liability component will be derecognised and transferred to equity. The accounting entries would be as follows:

	Dr	Cr
	Cm	Cm
Liability	60	
Share capital		15
Reserves (a component of equity)		45

The amount that was previously recognises in equity, that is, C5 remains in equity.

Example 2 – Before maturity conversion of a convertible bond with an American conversion option

Convertible bonds with American options are regularly converted before the original maturity date of the loan. To the extent that the carrying amount at the date of conversion is not equal to the principal amount converted this should be accounted for in accordance with paragraph AG 32 of IAS 32 as the word 'maturity' means any date when the holder converts in accordance with the instrument's contractual terms. As an American option allows for conversion at any time before the expiry date, the conversion date will be the maturity date. As such, there is no gain or loss on conversion with American options. During the life of the host bond expectations about early conversion should not be taken into account when estimating the cash flows used to apply the effective interest rate. The early conversion option is a characteristic of the equity component (the conversion option) not of the host liability. The estimated cash flows used to apply the effective interest rate method are therefore the contractual cash flows based on the contractual maturity

6A.7.71 The guidance included in paragraph AG 32 of IAS 32 as discussed above deals with conversion at maturity. There is no specific guidance in IAS 32 as to what should be the accounting treatment if the holder elects to convert the bond early. However, there is no reason why a similar treatment cannot be adopted. Therefore, where a convertible debt is converted before maturity, the amount recognised in equity in respect of the shares issued should be the amount at which the liability for the debt is stated as at the date of conversion. This will ensure that no gain or loss is recognised as a result of issuing equity instruments.

Mandatorily convertible instruments

A6.7.72 A convertible bond may contain terms that *compel* the holder to convert the bond rather than being at the holder's option. Depending on the terms, the number of shares issued on conversion may be either variable or fixed. To the extent that the mandatorily convertible bond can only be settled by the issue of a variable amount of ordinary shares calculated to equal a fixed amount in the issuer's functional currency (that is, there is a repayment of principal), the instrument is a liability. To the extent that the mandatorily convertible bond can only be settled by the issue of a fixed number of ordinary shares, that part of the instrument is an equity component. Some mandatorily convertible instruments pay no interest or pay interest only if an ordinary dividend is paid (discretionary). This type of instrument has no liability component. Others pay interest until the bond is converted, in which case the issuer allocates part of the consideration received equal to the liability component. This is measured at the present value of the interest payments, discounted at the market rate of interest for a similar instrument with a similar credit status that has no conversion option. The balance of the consideration is allocated to the equity component as illustrated below.

Example – Mandatorily convertible bonds

An entity issues 600,000 convertible bonds at the start of year 1. The bonds have a 3-year term, and are issued at par with a face value of C100 per bond, resulting in total proceeds of C60m, which is also the bond's fair value. Interest is payable annually in arrears at a nominal annual interest rate of 6%. Each C100 nominal bond is mandatorily convertible at the end of the 3 year term into 25 ordinary shares. When the bonds are issued, the prevailing market interest rate for similar debt without conversion options is 9%. The entity incurs issue cost of 1% on the nominal value of the bond amounting to C600,000.

As explained in the above paragraph, the liability component is measured first by discounting the contractually determined stream of future cash flows (interest only) to present value using a discount rate of 9%, the market interest rate for similar bonds having no conversion rights, as shown below.

	C
PV of interest payable at the end of year 1 – C3,600,000/1.09	3,302,752
PV of interest payable at the end of year 2 – C3,600,000/(1.09)2	3,030,048
PV of interest payable at the end of year 3 – C3,600,000/(1.09)3	2,779,860
Total liability component	9,112,660
Total equity component (residual)*	50,887,340
Total proceeds of the bond issue	60,000,000

* The difference between the proceeds of the bond and the fair value of the liability component as computed above (the residual) is assigned to the equity component.

In accordance with IAS 32, the issue cost of C600,000 will need to be allocated between the liability and the equity components in proportion to the allocation of the proceeds as shown below:

	Equity component	Liability component	Total
	C	C	C
Gross proceeds allocated as above	50,887,340	9,112,660	60,000,000
Issue cost	(508,873)	(91,127)	(600,000)
Net proceeds	50,378,467	9,021,533	59,400,000

The amount credited to equity of C50,378,467 is not subsequently remeasured.

The liability component of C9,021,533 will be measured subsequently at amortised cost using the effective interest rate method. As the interest payments on the bonds will reduce the liability component to zero, the effective interest rate in this situation is that rate of interest which discounts the three interest payments of C3,600,000 per year to its present value of C9,021,533. This rate amounts to 9.5659% as shown below:

Year	Opening liability	Interest @ 9.5659%	Cash paid	Closing liability
	C	C	C	C
1	9,021,533	862,990	(3,600,000)	6,284,523
2	6,284,523	601,171	(3,600,000)	3,285,694
3	3,285,694	314,306	(3,600,000)	–
Total finance cost		1,778,467		

When the bond is converted, the entity issues 15 million shares of C1 each. The original equity component of C50,378,467 effectively becomes the consideration for these shares where relevant, this amount would be allocated between share capital and share premium as follows:

	C
Share capital – 15 million shares of C1 each	15,000,000
Share premium	35,378,467
Original equity component	50,378,467

In other words, a mandatorily convertible instrument issued in the functional currency of the issuer is effectively a forward contract to issue or to deliver a fixed number of shares for which the consideration has been received in advance. Contrast this with the situation of an instrument that is convertible at any time before maturity (a written call option) discussed in paragraph A6.7.67 above.

Early redemption or repurchase

A6.7.73 An entity may redeem or repurchase a convertible instrument before maturity as a result of a call option to redeem the bond at any time or through negotiations with the bondholders without affecting the conversion rights. When an entity extinguishes a convertible instrument before maturity through an early redemption or repurchase in which the original conversion privileges are unchanged, the entity should allocate the redemption consideration paid (including any transaction costs) to the instrument's liability and equity components at the date of repurchase or redemption. In making this allocation, the entity should use the same method that was used in the original allocation of proceeds received from the convertible instrument's issue between the separate components on initial recognition. [IAS 32 para AG 33].

A6.7.74 Once the allocation of the consideration has been made, any resulting gain or loss is treated in accordance with accounting principles applicable to the related component, as follows:

- The difference between the consideration allocated to the liability component and its carrying value is recognised in profit or loss.
- The amount of consideration relating to the equity component is recognised in equity.

[IAS 32 para AG 34].

Example – Early redemption of a convertible bond

The facts are the same as the example in paragraph A6.7.67 above, except that on the first day of year 2, the entity makes a tender offer to the bondholders to repurchase the bond for its fair value at that date of C63m, which the bondholders accept. At the date of repurchase, the entity could have issued a non-convertible bond with a two-year term bearing an interest rate of 7%. The transaction cost of redeeming the bonds amounted to C200,000.

The carrying value of the liability component prior to redemption at the end of year 1 as calculated previously amounts to C56,442,438. The original equity component amounts to C4,510,767.

As explained above, the repurchase price is allocated between the liability component and the equity component on the same basis used in the original allocation process. This means the fair value of the liability component is measured first by discounting the remaining stream of future cash flows (interest and principal) to present value at the beginning of year 2, using a discount rate of 7%, the market interest rate for similar bonds having no conversion rights, as shown below.

	C
PV of interest payable at the end of year 2 – C3,600,000/1.07	3,364,486
PV of interest payable at the end of year 3 – C3,600,000/(1.07)2	3,144,379
PV of principal of C60,000,000 payable at the end year 3 – C60,000,000 /(1.07)2	52,406,324
Total liability component	58,915,189
Total equity component (residual)*	4,084,811
Total consideration payable on repurchase of bonds	63,000,000

* The difference between the consideration payable and the liability component's fair value as computed above is assigned to the equity component.

In accordance with IAS 32, the issue cost of C200,000 will need to be allocated between the liability and the equity components in proportion to the allocation of the consideration as shown below:

	Equity component C	Liability component C	Total C
Consideration allocated as above	4,084,811	58,915,189	63,000,000
Redemption cost	12,968	187,032	200,000
Total	4,097,779	59,102,221	63,200,000

Difference arising on repurchase is as follows:

Consideration inclusive of costs as above	4,097,779	59,102,221	63,200,000
Carrying value prior to redemption as stated above	4,510,767	56,442,438	60,953,205
	412,988	(2,659,783)	(2,246,795)

The accounting entries in respect of the repurchase of the bond are as follows:

	Dr C	Cr C
Bond Liability	56,442,438	
Debt Settlement expense (income statement)	2,659,783	
Cash		59,102,221
To record the repurchase of the liability component and the loss arising thereon		
Equity	4,097,779	
Cash		4,097,779
To record the cash paid on the repurchase of the equity component		

The resulting balance of C412,988 relating to the equity component can be transferred to a different line item in equity, for example, retained profits.

Modification of terms to induce early conversion

A6.7.75 An entity may amend the terms of a convertible instrument to induce early conversion, for example by offering a more favourable conversion ratio or paying other additional consideration in the event of conversion before a specified date. In that situation, the entity should recognise a loss, at the date the terms are amended, calculated as the difference between:

- the fair value of the consideration the holder receives on the instrument's conversion under the revised terms; and
- the fair value of the consideration the holder would have received under the original terms.

[IAS 32 para AG 35].

Example – Early conversion of a convertible bond

The facts are the same as the example in paragraph A6.7.67 above, except that on the first day of year 2, the entity modifies the convertible instrument's terms to induce the bondholders to convert the bond within 60 days. Each C100 nominal bond is now convertible into 30 ordinary shares rather than the 25 ordinary shares under the original terms. The market value of the entity's shares at the date of the amendment is C5 per share.

As explained above, the loss arising on increasing the conversion ratio is calculated as follow:

	Cm
Fair value of consideration receivable under the new terms:	
Number of bonds (600,000) x Conversion ratio (30) x C5	90
Fair value of consideration receivable under the original terms:	
Number of bonds (600,000) x Conversion ratio (25) x C5	75
Value of additional shares issuable on conversion recognised in profit or loss	15

On the date of conversion, the entity issues 18m shares instead of 15m under the original conversion terms. Therefore, the consideration received for the 18m shares comprises the carrying value of the bond of C56,442,438 plus C15m (the market value of 3m shares @ C5 per share).

The accounting entries to record the early conversion are as follows:

	Dr	Cr
Bond liability	56,442,438	
Profit or loss (fair value of 3m shares @ C5 per share)	15,000,000	
Equity (issue of 18m shares)		71,442,438

Settlement options

A6.7.76 In some instances, a convertible instrument may contain a settlement option that allows the issuer either to deliver a fixed number of shares when the bondholders exercise their rights to convert or deliver cash equal to the fair value of those shares at the date of conversion. Consistent with paragraph A6.7.57, where a convertible instrument contains such a cash settlement option, the conversion option is not an equity instrument, even though it is indexed to the market price of the entity's shares. Rather, it is an embedded derivative (effectively a written call option issued by the entity over its own shares) that is not closely related to the debt host. This means that instead of accounting for the conversion right as an equity instrument, the entity would account for the conversion right as a financial liability (a derivative) at fair value, with changes in fair value recognised in profit or loss. The effect of fair valuing the derivative means that gains and losses based on the entity's own share price would be reported in the profit and loss account.

A6.7.77 When the holder exercises its right to convert and the entity chooses to settle its obligation by issuing a fixed number of shares, then the liability's carrying value together with the derivative's fair value would be derecognised and transferred to equity as the share issue is treated as an equity transaction. Alternatively, the entity may record the shares at fair value and the difference between the fair value of the shares and the carrying value of the liability plus the fair value of the derivative is recognised in profit or loss. The same accounting treatment is achieved if the entity chooses the cash alternative as the amount of the cash consideration that is equal to the fair value of the shares at the date of conversion will be applied to extinguish the liability and the derivative instruments with any difference taken to profit or loss. Either method is acceptable, but it is an accounting policy choice that should be disclosed and applied consistently.

Convertible bond denominated in a foreign currency

A6.7.78 It is not uncommon for an entity to issue a convertible bond that is denominated in a currency other than its functional currency. For example, an entity whose functional currency is the Swiss francs may issue a euro denominated convertible bond that can be converted into a fixed number of its own euro denominated equity instruments. In this case, the entity has written an option to exchange a fixed number of its own equity instruments for a fixed amount of cash that is denominated in a foreign currency.

A6.7.79 As discussed in paragraph A6.7.40 above, the IFRIC stated that a fixed amount of foreign currency constitutes a variable amount of cash in the entity's functional currency. Therefore, a contract that will be settled by an entity delivering a fixed number of its own equity instruments in exchange for a fixed amount of foreign currency is a financial liability. This means that the written option to deliver a fixed number of own shares for a fixed amount of foreign currency is not an equity instrument, but an embedded derivative liability that is not closely related because the risks inherent in the derivative (equity risk) and in the host are dissimilar. Therefore, the entire foreign currency convertible bond will be accounted for as a liability, comprising a host foreign currency debt instrument that will be subject to the translation rules of IAS 21 and an embedded derivative liability with equity and foreign currency characteristics that will be fair valued through profit or loss in accordance with IAS 39.

Example – Convertible debt denominated in a foreign currency

On 1 January 20X5 a company with C functional currency issued 36,000 convertible bonds at par with a face value of US$1,000 per bond, giving total proceeds of US$36m. The bonds carry a coupon rate of 4% per annum payable in arrears. Each $1,000 bond is convertible, at the holder's discretion, at any time prior to maturity on 31 December 20X9, into 100 ordinary shares of C1 nominal.

The following information is relevant:

	Spot rate	Fair value of embedded derivative*
1 January 20X5	C1 = US$1.80	C3m
31 December 20X5	C1 = US$1.75	C4m
Average rate for the year	C1 = US$1.775	

* In accordance with paragraph AG 28 of IAS 39, the embedded derivative's fair value (the written option) must be determined first at inception of the contract. In this instance, the embedded derivative is indexed to both the share price denominated in C and the C/US$ exchange rate. Generally, where the derivatives relate to different risk exposures and are readily separable and independent of each other, they should be valued and accounted for separately. [IAS 39 para AG 29]. However, in this case, the exercise price of the equity conversion option is denominated in US$, but the underlying share price is denominated in C. Therefore, it may not be possible to separate the equity price risk from the foreign currency risk and value each component separately, because the two are interdependent. In that situation, they should be bundled together and treated as a single compound derivative. [IAS 39 para AG 29]. On this basis, the fair value of the embedded derivative at initial recognition, calculated using an option pricing model, amounted to C3m and C4m respectively at 1 January 20X5 and 31 December 20X5.

As explained above, as the issuer's functional currency is C and the convertible bonds are denominated in US dollars, the conversion option is not an equity instrument, but an embedded derivative that is not closely related to the host debt instrument, because the risks inherent in the derivative (equity risk) and the host are dissimilar. Therefore, the conversion option should be separated and classified as a derivative liability.

The carrying value of the host contract at initial recognition is the difference between the consideration received of C20m ((US$36m @ 1.8) and the fair value of the embedded derivative of C3m, that is, C17m or US$30.6m (C17m @1.8).

The host foreign currency debt of US$30.6m will be retranslated at each subsequent reporting date at the closing US$/C exchange rate and measured subsequently at amortised cost using the effective interest rate method. The company will pay 4% interest per annum on US$36m, that is, US$1.44m each year for the next 4 years and a principal amount of US$36m at the end of year 4, if the debt is not converted. The effective interest rate that discounts the interest and principal payments to its present value of US$30.6m is 8.5883% as shown below:

	Opening liability	**Interest @ 8.5883%**	**Cash paid**	**Closing liability**
	$'000	$'000	$'000	$'000
Year 1	30,600	2,628	(1,440)	31,788
Year 2	31,788	2,730	(1,440)	33,078
Year 3	33,078	2,841	(1,440)	34,479
Year 4	34,479	2,961	(37,440)	0

The interest payable in US$ would be recorded in the profit and loss account at the average rate ruling during the year. The closing liability would be translated at the spot rate at the balance sheet. Any exchange difference arising is recognised in profit or loss as part of finance cost. Therefore, the amortised cost of the host foreign currency debt instrument at 31 December 20X5 would be calculated as follows:

		C'000
Opening liability	US$30,600,000 @ 1.8	17,000
Interest cost (profit or loss)	US$2,628,000 @ 1.775	1,481
Cash paid	US$1,440,000 @ 1.75	(823)
Exchange difference (profit or loss)*		507
Closing liability	US$31,788 @ 1.75	18,165

* The exchange difference comprises the exchange difference on the opening liability of C486 (US$30,600 @ [1.75-1.8] and the exchange difference on the interest cost between closing rate and average rate of C21 (US$2,628 @ [1.775-1.8].

At 31 December 20X5, the fair value of the embedded derivative liability is C4m. The increase in fair value results in a loss of C1m, which is recognised in profit or loss.

The foreign currency convertible bond would be reported and presented in the financial statements as follows:

Income statement for the year ended 31 December 20X5		**C'000**
Other gains and (losses)		
Derivative instrument		(1,000)
Finance cost		
Interest expense		(1,481)
Foreign exchange difference		(507)
		(1,988)
Balance sheet	**31 Dec 20X5**	**1 Jan 20X5**
	C'000	**C'000**
Current liabilities		
Borrowings	18,165	17,000
Derivative on convertible bond	4,000	3,000
	22,165	20,000

Alternatively, the foreign exchange difference may be presented in other gains and (losses). Similarly, the bond and the derivative can be presented as a single number on the balance sheet. The convertible bond is classified as a current liability because it can be converted at any time prior to maturity as settlement of a liability is not confined to delivery of cash or other assets.

Preference shares with various rights

A6.7.80 Preference shares come with various rights. They may be redeemable at the option of the holder or the issuer, mandatorily redeemable or non-redeemable. Dividends on such shares may be either fixed or payable at the issuer's discretion or their payments may be linked to payments on another instrument. IAS 32 requires the classification of preference shares to be based on an assessment of the contractual arrangement's substance and the definitions of a financial liability and an equity instrument. [IAS 32 paras AG 25, AG 26].

A6.7.81 Because preference shares are relatively common, we summarise below, for ease of understanding and as a practical aid, the appropriate classification of preference shares for various combinations of redemption and dividend rights.

Classification of preference shares

Terms		Classification	
Redemption of principal	Payment of dividends (assume all at market rates)	Type of Instrument	Reasons
Non-redeemable	Discretionary	Equity	There is no contractual obligation to pay cash. Any dividends paid would be recognised in equity. [See para A6.7.56].
	Non-discretionary	Liability	Liability component is equal to the present value of the dividend payments to perpetuity. As the dividends are set at market rates, the proceeds will be equivalent to the fair value (at the date of issue) of the dividends payable to perpetuity. Therefore, the entire proceeds would be classified as a liability. Any dividends paid would be presented as an interest expense.
Redeemable at the issuer's option at some future date.	Discretionary	Equity	There is no contractual obligation to pay cash. An option to redeem the shares for cash does not satisfy the definition of a financial liability. Any dividends paid would be recognised in equity (see para A6.7.33).
	Non-discretionary	Liability with an embedded call option derivative	Liability component equal to the present value of the dividend payments to perpetuity. As the dividends are set at market rates, the proceeds will be equivalent to the fair value (at the date of issue) of the dividends payable to perpetuity. Therefore, the entire proceeds would be classified as a liability. Any dividends paid would be presented as an interest expense. In addition, because the entire instrument is classified as a

Terms		Classification	
			liability, the issuer call option to redeem the shares for cash is an embedded derivative (an asset). The embedded derivative may have to be accounted for separately, unless the option's exercise price is approximately equal on each exercise date to the instrument's amortised cost (see para A6.7.65).
Mandatorily redeemable at a fixed or determinable amount at a fixed or future date	Discretionary	Compound	Liability component equal to the present value of the redemption amount. Equity component is equal to proceeds less liability component. Any dividends paid are related to the equity component and would be recognised in equity (see para A6.7.103). It should be noted, however, that if any unpaid dividends are added to the redemption amount, then the whole instrument is a financial liability. In this situation, the dividends would be presented as interest expense. [IAS 32 para AG 37].
	Non-discretionary	Liability	The entity has an obligation to pay cash in respect of both principal and dividends. Any dividends paid would be presented as an interest expense.
Redeemable at the holder's option at some future date. .	Discretionary	Compound	Liability component equal to the present value of the redemption amount. Equity component is equal to proceeds less liability component (see para A6.7.53). Any dividends paid are related to the equity component and would be recognised in equity (see para A6.7.103). It should be noted, however, that if any unpaid dividends are added to the redemption

Terms		Classification	
			amount, then the whole instrument is a financial liability. In this situation, the dividends would be presented as interest expense. [IAS 32 para AG 37].
	Non-discretionary	Liability with an embedded put option derivative	There is a contractual obligation to pay cash in respect of both the principal and dividend. Any dividends paid would be presented as an interest expense. In addition, because the entire instrument is classified as a liability, the embedded put option to redeem the shares for cash is an embedded derivative. The embedded derivative may have to be accounted for separately unless the option's exercise price is approximately equal on each exercise date to the instrument's amortised cost (see section 5).

A6.7.82 In the above table, dividend payments need not be a fixed percentage of the preference shares' nominal value. In some circumstances, the payment of dividends may be based on a fixed percentage of profits, for example, ten per cent of profits made each year. To the extent that the distribution is based on a percentage of profits are non-discretionary and cannot be avoided, such payments would give rise to a liability treatment, even though the payments are contingent on the issuer making profits (see para A6.7.50 above).

Debt to equity conversions

A6.7.83 It is not uncommon for companies to convert their existing debt instruments to equity through negotiations with their bondholders in order to reduce excessive interest burden. Indeed, such debt to equity conversions or swaps are mostly carried out by companies that are in financial distress. Bondholders often agree to swap their loans for equity in the belief that if they take an equity stake in a troubled company they will ultimately achieve a greater return.

A6.7.84 IAS 32 does not specifically deal with debt to equity conversions and so the question arises as to how such transactions should be accounted for. One argument is that the accounting treatment should be the same as when convertible debt is converted into shares. In that situation, as explained in paragraph A6.7.70 above, the carrying value of the existing debt instrument is simply transferred to equity and no gain or loss arises on the conversion. In other words, the fair value of the new shares issued is ignored. This treatment is consistent with the usual accounting for the issue of shares that are recorded at the proceeds received rather than the fair value of the shares and does not result in a gain or loss as it is a transaction with owners.

A6.7.85 Alternatively, one could argue that the replacement or exchange of an issuer's existing debt instrument with new equity instruments of the issuer is an extinguishment of the existing financial liability as the entity is legally released from its obligation to pay cash. Therefore, in accordance with paragraph 40 of IAS 39, the original debt instrument should be derecognised and new equity instruments issued should be recognised at fair value. Furthermore, paragraph 41 of IAS 39 provides that the difference between the carrying amount of the financial liability extinguished and the consideration paid (including non-cash assets transferred or liabilities assumed) should be recognised in profit or loss. Although paragraph 41 refers to cash or other non-cash assets forming part of the consideration, there is no particular reason why a gain or loss cannot be recognised when the consideration is in the form of new equity instruments. Consider the following example:

Example – Debt to equity swaps

An entity issued a debt instrument amounting to C50m repayable at par in year 10. Four years after issue it became clear that the entity was in financial difficulty and was unable to service its existing debt obligations. Accordingly, it reached an agreement whereby the debt holders agreed to accept 5m equity shares of C1 each in full and final settlement of all amounts due under the debt instrument. The fair value of the equity shares issued in exchange was C25m.

Option 1 – Treated as a conversion of existing debt

In this situation, the carrying value of the debt of C50m is transferred to equity. No gain or loss arises on conversion. The accounting entries are as follows:

	Dr	Cr
	Cm	Cm
Debt instrument	50	
Equity*		50

* In some jurisdictions, such as the UK, C50m would be split between share capital of C5m and share premium of C45m.

Option 2 – Treated as an extinguishment of existing debt and issue of new equity instrument

In this situation, the new equity instrument is recorded at its fair value of C25m and a gain is recognised on the extinguishment of the existing debt instrument. The accounting entries are as follows:

	Dr	Cr
	Cm	Cm
Debt instrument	50	
Equity*		25
Profit or loss – gain arising on extinguishment of debt		25

* In some jurisdictions, such as the UK, C25m would be split between share capital of C5m and share premium of C20m.

As the standard does not specifically deal with the above issue, we believe either approach is acceptable, provided it is used on a consistent basis.

6A.7.86 The IFRIC issued rejection wording in November 2006 that clarified the accounting treatment for transfers from equity to debt when the transfer is a result of a change in the contractual terms of an instrument. This might be achieved, for example, through changing the terms to require the coupon to be paid on the occurrence of a genuine contingent settlement event.

A6.7.87 The IFRIC clarified that a financial liability is initially recognised at the time when the contractual terms are changed, irrespective of whether the change affects the cash flows under the contract. The new liability is measured at fair value in accordance with paragraph 43 of IAS 39.

A6.7.88 The IFRIC also observed that the change in terms of the instrument gave rise to the derecognition of the original equity instrument. Paragraph 33 of IAS 32 states that no gain or loss is recognised in the profit and loss on the purchase, sale, issue or cancellation of an entity's own equity instruments. The difference between the carrying amount of the equity instrument and the fair value of the newly-recognised financial liability is recorded in equity at the time when the terms are changed. This applies even if the change has no impact on the expected cash flows of the instrument.

Derivatives over own equity instruments

A6.7.89 An entity may enter into a derivative contract for the purchase or sale of its own equity instruments. Depending upon the nature of the contract (forward based or option based) and the settlement terms (for example, gross or net in cash) in particular, such contracts may be accounted for as equity instruments, financial liabilities or as derivative assets and liabilities.

Contracts accounted for as equity instruments

A6.7.90 A derivative contract that will be settled by the entity receiving or delivering a fixed number of its own equity instruments in exchange for a fixed amount of cash or another financial asset is an equity instrument. [IAS 32 paras 22, AG 27(a)]. An example is an issued share option that gives the counterparty a right to buy a fixed number of the entity's shares for a fixed price, which is an equity instrument. The contract's fair value may change due to variation in the share price and market interest rates. However, provided that such changes in the contract's fair value do not affect the amount of cash or other financial assets to be paid or received, or the number of equity instruments to be received or delivered, on the contract's settlement, the contract is treated as an equity instrument. [IAS 32 para 22].

A6.7.91 Any consideration received (such as the premium received for a written option or warrant on the entity's own shares) is added directly to equity. Any consideration paid (such as the premium paid for a purchased option) is deducted directly from equity. Changes in an equity instrument's fair value are not recognised in the financial statements. [IAS 32 para 22].

A6.7.92 The following examples illustrate the accounting treatment discussed above where an entity enters into derivative contracts to receive or deliver a fixed amount of its own shares in exchange for a fixed amount of cash at some future date.

Example 1 – Purchased call option to receive a fixed number of own shares for a fixed sum [IAS 32 para IE 15]

On 1 February 20X5, an entity purchases a call option for C5,000 under which it has the right but not the obligation to acquire 1,000 of its own shares for cash at the option's exercise of C102 per share. The option will be gross settled in that the entity will take delivery of the shares and pay the exercise price of C102,000 (C102 × 1,000) on the fixed maturity date of 31 January 20X6.

The following information is given:

	Market price per share C	Fair value of option C
At 1 February 20X5	100	5,000
At 31 December 20X5	104	3,000
At 31 January 20X6	104	2,000

The accounting entries from inception to settlement of the contract are as follows:

At 1 February 20X5	**Dr**	**Cr**
Equity	C5,000	
Cash		C5,000

At inception of the contract, the entity would record the premium paid for the right to receive a fixed amount of its own shares in one year for a fixed price. As the contract meets the definition of an equity instrument, the premium is charged directly to equity as discussed above.

At 31 December 20X5

No entry is made on 31 December because no cash is paid or received. As the option contract meets the definition of an equity instrument, it is not subsequently re-measured as explained in paragraph A6.7.91. Therefore, the option's fair value is not relevant.

At 31 January 20X6	**Dr**	**Cr**
Equity	C102,000	
Cash		C102,000

The entity exercises the call option on the exercise date as it is in the money (exercise price of C102 per share < market price of C104 per share). As the contract is settled gross, the entity takes delivery of 1,000 of its own shares and pays a fixed amount of C102,000 to the counterparty that is recognised directly in equity. Hence, the total amount debited to equity in relation to the purchase is C107,000.

Example 2 – Written call option to deliver a fixed number of own shares for a fixed sum [IAS 32 para IE 20]

On 1 February 20X5, an entity writes a call option for C5,000 under which it has an obligation to sell 1,000 of its own shares for cash at a fixed price of C102 per share, if the counterparty exercises the option. The option will be gross settled in shares in that the entity will deliver its own shares and receive the exercise price of C102,000 (C102 × 1,000) on the fixed maturity date of 31 January 20X6.

The following information is given:

	Market price per share	**Fair value of option**
	C	**C**
At 1 February 20X5	100	5,000
At 31 December 20X5	104	3,000
At 31 January 20X6	104	2,000

The accounting entries from inception to settlement of the contract are as follows:

At 1 February 20X5	**Dr**	**Cr**
Cash	C5,000	
Equity		C5,000

At inception of the contract, the entity would record the premium received in exchange for the obligation to deliver a fixed amount of its own shares in one year for a fixed price. As the contract meets the definition of an equity instrument, the premium is credited directly to equity as discussed above.

At 31 December 20X5

No entry is made on 31 December because no cash is paid or received. As the option contract meets the definition of an equity instrument, it is not subsequently re-measured as explained in paragraph A6.7.69. Therefore, the option's fair value is not relevant.

	Dr	Cr
At 31 January 20X6		
Cash	C102,000	
Equity		C102,000

The counterparty exercises the call option on the exercise date as it is in the money (exercise price of C102 per share < market price of C104 per share). Therefore, the entity is obliged to deliver 1,000 of its own shares in exchange for C102,000 in cash. Hence, the total amount credited to equity in relation to the sale is C107,000.

Example 3 – Purchased put option to deliver a fixed number of own shares for a fixed sum [IAS 32 para IE 25]

On 1 February 20X5, an entity purchases a put option for C5,000 under which it has the right to sell 1,000 of its own shares for cash at a fixed price of C98 per share, if the entity exercises the put option. The option will be gross settled in that the entity will deliver its own shares and receive the exercise price of C98,000 (C98 × 1,000) on the fixed maturity date of 31 January 20X6.

The following information is given:

	Market price per share C	Fair value of option C
At 1 February 20X5	100	5,000
At 31 December 20X5	95	4,000
At 31 January 20X6	95	3,000

The accounting entries from inception to settlement of the contract are as follows:

	Dr	Cr
At 1 February 20X5		
Equity	C5,000	
Cash		C5,000

At inception of the contract, the entity would record the premium paid received in exchange for the obligation to deliver a fixed amount of its own shares in one year for a fixed price. As the contract meets the definition of an equity instrument, the premium is credited directly to equity as discussed above.

At 31 December 20X5

No entry is made on 31 December because no cash is paid or received. As the option contract meets the definition of an equity instrument, it is not subsequently re-measured as explained in paragraph A6.7.91. Therefore, the option's fair value is not relevant.

At 31 January 20X6	**Dr**	**Cr**
Cash	C98,000	
Equity		C98,000

The entity exercises the put option on the exercise date as it is in the money (exercise price of C98 per share > market price of C95 per share). Therefore, the counterparty is obliged to deliver C98,000 in cash to the entity in exchange for 1,000 shares. Hence, the total amount credited to equity is C93,000.

Example 4 – Forward contract to sell a fixed number of own shares for a fixed sum [IAS 32 para IE 10]

On 1 February 20X5, an entity enters into a forward sale contract under which it has an obligation to sell 1,000 of its own shares for cash at a fixed price of C104 per share on 31 January 20X6.

For simplicity, it is assumed that no dividends are paid on the underlying shares (that is the 'carry return' is zero) so that the present value of the forward price equals the spot price when the fair value of the forward contract is zero. The fair value of the forward has been computed as the difference between the market share price and the present value of the fixed forward price.

The following information is given:

	Market price per share	**Fair value of forward**
	C	**C**
At 1 February 20X5	100	Nil
At 31 December 20X5	110	(6,300)
At 31 January 20X6	106	(2,000)

The present value of the forward price on 1 February 20X5 is C100 per share.

The accounting entries from inception to settlement of the contract are as follows:

At 1 February 20X5

At inception of the contract, no entries are made as no cash is paid or received for the forward contract – it has an initial fair value of zero. As the entity enters into a forward contract to deliver a fixed number of its own shares in exchange for a fixed amount of cash or another financial asset, the forward contract meets the definition of an equity instrument because it cannot be settled otherwise than through the delivery of shares in exchange for cash.

At 31 December 20X5

No entry is made on 31 December because no cash is paid or received. As the forward contract meets the definition of an equity instrument, it is not subsequently re-measured as explained in paragraph A6.7.91. Therefore, the contract's fair value is not relevant.

At 31 January 20X6	**Dr**	**Cr**
Cash	C104,000	
Equity		C104,000

The entity settles the forward contract by delivery of 1,000 of its own shares and receives cash of C104,000 in exchange.

Contracts accounted for as financial liabilities

A6.7.93 The above circumstances deal with derivative contracts that require gross physical settlement in shares for a fixed amount of cash at some future date. These physically settled contracts are treated as equity instruments. However, a contract that contains an obligation for an entity to purchase its own equity instruments for cash or another financial asset gives rise to a financial liability for the present value of the redemption amount (for example, for the present value of the forward repurchase price, option exercise price or other redemption amount). This is the case even if the contract itself is an equity instrument. An example is an entity's obligation under a forward contract to purchase its own equity instruments for cash. When the financial liability is recognised initially under IAS 39, its fair value (the present value of the redemption amount) is reclassified from equity. Subsequently, the financial liability is measured in accordance with IAS 39. If the contract expires without delivery, the carrying amount of the financial liability is reclassified to equity.

Example 1 – Forward contract to purchase a fixed number of own shares for a fixed sum [IAS 32 IE 5]

On 1 February 20X5, an entity enters into a forward purchase contract under which it has the obligation to acquire 1,000 of its own shares for cash at a fixed price of C104 per share on 31 January 20X6.

For simplicity, it is assumed that no dividends are paid on the underlying shares (that is the 'carry return' is zero) so that the present value of the forward price equals the spot price of the entity's shares when the fair value of the forward contract is zero. The fair value of the forward has been computed as the difference between the market share price and the present value of the fixed forward price.

The following information is given:

	Market price per share C	Fair value of forward C
At 1 February 20X5	100	Nil
At 31 December 20X5	110	6,300
At 31 January 20X6	106	2,000

The present value of the forward price on 1 February 20X5 is C100 per share.

The accounting entries from inception to settlement of the contract are as follows:

At 1 February 20X5	**Dr**	**Cr**
Equity	C100,000	
Liability		C100,000

As the entity enters into a forward contract to purchase a fixed number of its own shares in exchange for a fixed amount of cash or another financial asset, the forward contract meets the definition of an equity instrument, because it cannot be settled otherwise than through the delivery of shares in exchange for cash. Furthermore, at inception of the contract the entity has an obligation to pay C104,000 in cash in one year's time. Therefore, in accordance with paragraph A6.7.93, the entity recognises a liability for the redemption amount of C104,000 payable in one year at its present value of C100,000.

At 31 December 20X5	**Dr**	**Cr**
Interest expense	C3,660	
Liability		C3,660

As the liability needs to be accreted to its final redemption amount of C104,000, the entity recognises interest expense to 31 December in accordance with the effective interest rate method.

At 31 January 20X6	**Dr**	**Cr**
Interest expense	C340	
Liability		C340

The entity recognises interest expense to 31 January with the result that the liability is stated at its redemption amount.

	Dr	**Cr**
Liability	C104,000	
Cash		C104,000

The entity settles its obligation under the forward contract to purchase its own shares for cash of C104,000.

It should be noted that whilst an entity is required to recognise a liability at inception for a forward purchase of its own shares, there is no equivalent requirement to recognise an asset for a forward sale of its own shares, even though the two contracts are economically the 'mirror image' of each other (see example 4 in para A6.7.92 above). This is because in the former situation the shares that are the subject of a forward purchase cease to be equity until acquired as the entity has an obligation to pay cash. In a forward sale, the equity shares continue to be equity until sold.

6A.7.94 An entity's contractual obligation to purchase its own equity instruments gives rise to a financial liability for the present value of the redemption amount even if the obligation to purchase is conditional on the counterparty exercising a right to redeem. An example is a written put option that gives the counterparty the right to sell an entity's own equity instruments to the entity for a fixed price. See also section 24 of the IFRS Manual of Accounting concerning obligations to acquire a minority interest.

Example 2 – Written put option to purchase a fixed number of own shares for a fixed sum [IAS 32 IE 30]

On 1 February 20X5, an entity writes a put option for C5,000 under which it has the obligation to purchase 1,000 of its own shares for cash at a fixed price of C98 per share, if the counterparty exercises the put option. The option will be gross settled in that the entity will purchase its own shares and pay the exercise price of C98,000 (C98 × 1,000) on the fixed maturity date of 31 January 20X6.

The following information is given:

	Market price per share	**Fair value of option**
	C	**C**
At 1 February 20X5	100	5,000
At 31 December 20X5	95	4,000
At 31 January 20X6	95	3,000

The present value of the option's exercise price on 1 February 20X5 is C95 per share

The accounting entries from inception to settlement of the contract are as follows:

At 1 February 20X5	**Dr**	**Cr**
Cash	C5,000	
Equity		C5,000

At inception of the contract, the entity would record the premium received in exchange for the obligation to deliver a fixed amount of its own shares in one year for a fixed price. As the contract meets the definition of an equity instrument, the premium is credited directly to equity.

	Dr	Cr
Equity	C95,000	
Liability		C95,000

Furthermore, at inception of the contract the entity has an obligation to pay C98,000 in cash in one year's time. Therefore, as stated in the above paragraph, the entity recognises the obligation's present value to pay C98,000 in one year's time, that is, C95,000 as a liability.

At 31 December 20X5	Dr	Cr
Interest expense	C2,750	
Liability		C2,750

As the liability needs to be accreted to its final redemption amount of C98,000, the entity recognises interest expense to 31 December in accordance with the effective interest rate method.

At 31 January 20X6	Dr	Cr
Interest expense	C250	
Liability		C250

The entity recognises interest expense to 31 January with the result that the liability is stated at its redemption amount of C98,000.

	Dr	Cr
Liability	C98,000	
Cash		C98,000

On the same date, the counterparty exercises the put option as it is in the money (exercise price of C98 per share > market price of C95 per share). The entity settles its obligation under the put option by taking delivery of 1,000 of its own shares and paying cash of C98,000 to the counterparty.

If, on the other hand, the contract expires unexercised, the liability of C98,000 is reclassified to equity.

Contracts accounted for as derivative assets or liabilities

A6.7.95 All other contracts on own equity that are not physically settled gross in shares for a fixed sum are treated as derivatives and accounted for as derivative assets or liabilities in accordance with IAS 39. These include contracts that are:

- Settled net in cash (or other financial assets). [IAS 32 para AG 27(c)]. Settled net in cash means that the party with a loss delivers to the party with a gain a cash payment equal to the gain and no shares are exchanged.
- Settled net in the entity's own shares. [IAS 32 para AG 27(c)]. Settled net in shares means that the party with a loss delivers to the party with a gain shares with a current fair value equal to the gain. In other words, the entity's own shares are used as a settlement currency.
- Settled net in cash or net in shares at the option of the entity or the counterparty (see para A6.7.57).

A6.7.96 The following examples illustrate the accounting treatment discussed above where an entity enters into derivative contracts on an entity's own equity instruments that require settlement either net in cash or net in shares.

Example 1 – Forward purchase contract on own shares settled net in cash or net in shares [IAS 32 IE 3, IE 4]

On 1 February 20X5, an entity enters into a forward purchase contract under which it has the obligation to acquire 1,000 of its own shares at a fixed price of C104 per share on 31 January 20X6.

In scenario 1, the contract can only be settled net in cash (no choice by either party).

In scenario 2, the contract can only be settled net in shares (no choice by either party).

For simplicity, it is assumed that no dividends are paid on the underlying shares (that is the 'carry return' is zero) so that the present value of the forward price equals the spot price of the entity's shares when the fair value of the forward contract is zero. The fair value of the forward has been computed as the difference between the market share price and the present value of the fixed forward price.

The following information is given:

	Market price per share	Fair value of forward
	C	C
At 1 February 20X5	100	Nil
At 31 December 20X5	110	6,300
At 31 January 20X6	106	2,000

The present value of the forward price on 1 February 20X5 is C100 per share.

The accounting entries from inception to settlement of the contract in the two scenarios (settled net in cash or net in shares) are as follows:

At 1 February 20X5

The price per share when the contract is agreed on 1 February 20X5 is C100, which is also the market price of the shares at that date. No entry is required, because the derivative's fair value is zero and no cash is paid or received. This applies whether the forward purchase contract is settled net in cash or net in shares.

At 31 December 20X5	**Dr**	**Cr**
Forward asset	C6,300	
Gain in profit or loss		C6,300

On 31 December 20X5, the market price per share has increased to C110 and, as a result, the forward contract's fair value has increased to C6,300. The increase in the contract's fair value is recognised in profit or loss.

At 31 January 20X6	**Dr**	**Cr**
Loss in profit or loss	C4,300	
Forward asset		C4,300

On 31 January 20X6, the market price per share has decreased to C106. The fair value of the forward contract is C2,000 [1,000 * (C106-C104)]. The decrease in the fair value on the forward contract from C6,300 to C2,000 is recognised in profit or loss.

Scenario 1 – Settled net in cash	**Dr**	**Cr**
Cash	C2,000	
Forward asset		C2,000

On the same day, the contract is settled net in cash. The entity has an obligation to deliver C104,000 in cash, being the settlement amount of the contract, to the counterparty. The counterparty has an obligation to deliver cash equal to the fair value of 1,000 shares at the date, that is C106,000 (1,000 × C106) to the entity. So the counterparty pays the net amount of C2,000 to the entity.

Scenario 2 – Settled net in shares	**Dr**	**Cr**
Equity	C2,000	
Forward asset		C2,000

If the contract is settled net in shares, the entity has an obligation to deliver C104,000 worth of its own shares to the counterparty. The counterparty has an obligation to deliver C106,000 (1,000 × C106) worth of the entity's shares to the entity. So the counterparty delivers the net amount of C2,000 worth of the entity's shares to the entity, that is, 18.9 shares (C2,000/C106). The settlement in shares is accounted for as an equity transaction.

Example 2 – Written call option on own shares settled net in cash or net in shares [IAS 32 IE 18, IE 19]

On 1 February 20X5, an entity writes a call option for C5,000 under which it has an obligation to sell 1,000 of its own shares at a fixed price of C102 per share, if the counterparty exercises the call option. The option will be settled on the fixed maturity date of 31 January 20X6.

In scenario 1, the contract can only be settled net in cash (no choice by either party).

In scenario 2, the contract can only be settled net in shares (no choice by either party).

The following information is given:

	Market price per share C	Fair value of option C
At 1 February 20X5	100	5,000
At 31 December 20X5	104	3,000
At 31 January 20X6	104	2,000

The accounting entries from inception to settlement of the contract in the two scenarios (settled net in cash or net in shares) are as follows:

At 1 February 20X5	**Dr**	**Cr**
Cash	C5,000	
Call option obligation		C5,000

At inception of the contract, the entity would record the premium received under the contract in both scenarios.

At 31 December 20X5	**Dr**	**Cr**
Call option obligation	C2,000	
Gain in profit or loss		C2,000

On 31 December 20X5, the fair value of the call option obligation has fall to C3,000. The decrease in the fair value of the obligation is recognised as a gain in profit or loss.

At 31 January 20X6	**Dr**	**Cr**
Call option obligation	C1,000	
Gain in profit or loss		C1,000

On 31 January 20X6, the fair value of the call option obligation has fallen further to C2,000. The decrease in the fair value is recognised as a gain in profit or loss.

Scenario 1 – Settled net in cash	**Dr**	**Cr**
Call option obligation	C2,000	
Cash		C2,000

If the contract is settled net in cash, the entity has an obligation to deliver C104,000 in cash, being the fair value of the 1,000 shares on 31 January 20X6, to the counterparty. The counterparty has an obligation to deliver cash equal to the option's exercise price of C102,000 to the entity. So the entity pays the net amount of C2,000 to the counterparty.

Scenario 2 – Settled net in shares	**Dr**	**Cr**
Call option obligation	C2,000	
Equity		C2,000

If, the contract is settled net in shares, the entity has an obligation to deliver C104,000 worth of its own shares to the counterparty. The counterparty has an obligation to deliver C102,000 worth of the entity's shares to the entity. So the entity delivers the net amount of C2,000 worth of its own shares to the counterparty, that is, 19.2 shares (C2,000/C104). The settlement in shares is accounted for as an equity transaction.

Issuer or holder's settlement options

A6.7.97 The examples above deal with situations where the settlement of the derivative contracts on own equity, either net in cash or net in shares, was dictated by the contractual terms (no choice). Sometimes such derivative contracts may contain settlement options that give either party a choice over how it is settled (for example, the issuer or the holder can choose to settle the contract net in cash, or net in shares or by exchanging shares for cash). As explained in paragraph A6.7.57 above, when a derivative financial instrument gives one party a choice over how it is settled, it is a financial asset or a financial liability unless all of the settlement alternatives would result in it being an equity instrument. [IAS 32 para 26].

A6.7.98 The existence of two or more settlement options (such as net in cash, net in shares or by an exchange of shares for cash) in a contract over own shares will always give rise to a derivative financial asset or a derivative financial liability. These two situations relate to forward purchase contracts (see para A6.7.93 above) and written put options (see para A6.7.94 above) that require gross physical settlement (exchange of shares for cash). In these two situations, the entity recognises a financial liability to deliver cash for the present value of the forward repurchase price or the option exercise price in exchange for receiving its own shares. [IAS 32 paras IE 6, IE 31].

Treatment of interest, dividends, gains and losses

A6.7.99 The general principle of IAS 32 is that the treatment of interest, dividends, losses and gains follows the classification of the related instrument. Therefore, where such items relate to equity instruments, they are included in equity. On the other hand, if they relate to instruments that are classified as financial liabilities, they are included in profit or loss. IAS 32, therefore, requires that:

- Interest, dividends, losses and gains relating to a financial instrument or a component that is a financial liability should be recognised as income or expense in profit or loss.
- Distributions to holders of an equity instrument should be debited by the entity directly to equity, net of any related income tax benefit.

[IAS 32 para 35].

A6.7.100 It follows from the above requirement that dividend payments on preference shares that are classified wholly as liabilities are recognised as expenses in the same way as interest on a bond. They may be presented in the income statement either with interest on other liabilities or as a separate item. The standard notes that in some circumstances, it may be desirable to disclose interest and dividends separately in the income statement, because of the differences between interest and dividends with respect to matters such as tax deductibility. Disclosure of interest and dividends is subject to the requirements of IAS 1, 'Presentation of financial statements', and IFRS 7, 'Financial instruments: Disclosures', which will supersede the disclosure requirements of IAS 32 for annual periods beginning on or after 1 January 2007. Disclosures of the tax effects should be made in accordance with IAS 12, 'Income taxes'. [IAS 32 para 40].

A6.7.101 Gains and losses associated with redemptions or refinancings of financial liabilities are recognised in profit or loss. Similarly, gains and losses related to changes in the carrying amount of a financial liability are recognised as income or expense in profit or loss. This is so even when they relate to an instrument that includes a right to the residual interest in the entity's assets in exchange for cash or another financial asset (for example, units in mutual funds that are puttable – see para A6.7.19 above). Under IAS 1, the entity presents any gain or loss arising from remeasurement of such an instrument separately on the face of the income statement when it is relevant in explaining the entity's performance. [IAS 32 para 41]. IAS 32 contains examples of income statement presentation where an entity has little or no equity. [IAS 32 paras IE 32-IE 33].

A6.7.102 Redemptions or refinancings of equity instruments are recognised in equity. Changes in the fair value of an equity instrument are not recognised in the financial statements. [IAS 32 para 36].

A6.7.103 The application of the principle in paragraph A6.7.99 above to compound financial instruments would require any payments relating to the liability component to be reported in profit or loss and any payments relating to the equity component to be reported in equity. A classic example is mandatorily redeemable preference shares with discretionary dividend payments. Such an instrument is a compound financial instrument, with the liability component being the present value of the redemption amount. The unwinding of the discount on this component is recognised in profit or loss and classified as interest expense. Any dividends paid relate to the equity component and are recognised as a distribution of profit or loss. A similar treatment would apply if the redemption was not mandatory but at the option of the holder, or if the preference shares were mandatorily convertible into a variable number of ordinary shares calculated to equal a fixed amount or an amount based on changes in an underlying variable (for example, a commodity). However, if any unpaid dividends are added to the redemption amount, the entire instrument is a liability. In such a case, any dividends are classified as interest expense that will be accounted for in accordance with the effective interest method. [IAS 32 para AG 37].

Treatment of transaction costs of equity instruments

A6.7.104 An entity typically incurs various costs in issuing or acquiring its own equity instruments. Those costs might include registration and other regulatory fees, underwriting costs and brokerage fees, amounts paid to lawyers, accountants, investment bankers and other professional advisers, fees and commissions paid to agents, brokers, and dealers, printing costs and stamp duties. Most such costs are transaction costs, that is, incremental costs that are directly attributable to the equity transaction that otherwise would have been avoided had the equity instruments not been issued. Transaction costs arising on the issue of equity instruments, however, do not include indirect costs, such as the costs of management time and administrative overheads, or allocations of internal costs that would have been incurred had the equity instruments not been issued. Nor do they include costs of researching different types of equity instruments or of ascertaining the suitability or feasibility of particular equity instruments. Generally, costs for marketing an IPO, including the 'road show', do not meet the definition of a transaction cost. Marketing costs primarily relate to the marketing of the entity itself. Therefore in most situations marketing costs for an IPO do not meet the definition of directly attributable and therefore are expensed through profit or loss.

A6.7.105 IAS 32 requires that transaction costs of an equity transaction should be accounted for as a deduction from equity, net of any related income tax benefit. [IAS 32 para 35]. This treatment is based on the view that the transaction costs incurred are a necessary part of completing the equity transaction and form an integral part of it. Linking the equity transaction and costs of the transaction reflects the net proceeds received from the transaction in equity. This approach achieves a result which is consistent with paragraph A6.7.99 above, which states that a financial instrument's classification in the balance sheet determines whether interest, dividends, losses and gains relating to that instrument are reported in the income statement. As a result, losses relating to a financial instrument classified as the issuer's equity are reported by the issuer as movements in equity.

A6.7.106 Transaction costs that relate to the issue of a compound financial instrument are allocated to the instrument's liability and equity components in proportion to the allocation of proceeds (see example in para A6.7.67).

A6.7.107 Transaction costs that relate jointly to more than one transaction (for example, costs of a concurrent offering of some shares and a stock exchange listing of other shares) are allocated to those transactions using a basis of allocation that is rational and consistent with similar transactions. [IAS 32 para 38]. This situation often arises when an entity undertakes an initial public offering (IPO) of its shares. As a result of the IPO, new shares are issued to investors to raise additional capital and, along with existing shares, subsequently become listed on a stock exchange. Costs incurred in listing existing shares on a stock exchange are not transaction costs relating to the issue of an equity instrument. This is because these costs are simply incurred to make the existing shares more marketable and are not related to the equity instrument's issue. In some situations, the existing shares may be included in a 'secondary offering'. As the cash generated from the sale of secondary shares is given to the selling shareholders, rather than the company, any costs incurred are not equity transaction costs. Therefore, these costs should be charged to the income statement. On the other hand, costs incurred in issuing new shares to raise capital ('primary offering') in an IPO are transaction costs of equity instrument and, as explained above, falls to be charged to equity. In practice, companies would need to identify the costs that are specifically attributable to the issue of new shares. All other costs of the IPO that would not have been incurred had the IPO not taken place should be allocated between the new shares and old shares on some reasonable basis, for example, in the ratio of old to new shares. It follows from the above that any costs incurred by the company in a 'secondary offering' of its own shares are not equity transaction costs. Accordingly, those costs should be charged to profit or loss.

A6.7.108 The amount of transaction costs accounted for as a deduction from equity in the period is disclosed separately under IAS 1. The related amount of income taxes recognised directly in equity is included in the aggregate amount of current and deferred income tax credited or charged to equity that is disclosed under IAS 12. [IAS 32 para 39; IAS 12 para 81(a)].

Treasury shares

A6.7.109 When an entity purchases its own shares and holds them in treasury ('treasury shares'), IAS 32 requires the following:

- The amount paid for the treasury shares is deducted from equity. This is because an entity's own equity instruments are not recognised as a financial asset regardless of the reason for which they are acquired. However, where an entity holds its own equity on behalf of others, for example, a financial institution holding its own equity on behalf of a client, there is an agency relationship and as a result those holdings are not included in the entity's balance sheet.
- No gain or loss should be recognised in profit or loss on the purchase, sale, issue or cancellation of an entity's own equity instruments. This is because the acquisition and subsequent resale of treasury shares are transactions with entity's owners rather than a gain or loss to the entity.
- Consideration paid or received for the purchase or sale of an entity's own equity instruments should be recognised directly in equity.

[IAS 32 paras 33, AG 36].

A6.7.110 IAS 32 notes that own equity instruments may be acquired and held by the entity or by other members of the consolidated group. [IAS 32 para 33]. Therefore, the above accounting applies to all interests in own equity instruments held by a company and, in consolidated financial statements, the parent's shares held by subsidiaries. In the latter case, this applies to all such shareholdings, including those held by subsidiaries that carry on a business of dealing in securities. However, in the individual financial statements of a subsidiary that holds shares in its parent, such shares are treated as an asset; that is, 'treasury shares' accounting does not apply as these are not 'own shares' for the subsidiary itself.

Example – Purchase of own shares held in treasury

Entity A (a listed company) has in issue 1,000,000 C1 ordinary shares originally issued at a premium of C9. It buys back 20,000 shares when their market value is C40 per share. The purchase is made out of retained profits and the entity holds the shares in treasury. In this situation, the entity does not reduce its issued share capital, but instead will reduce its retained profits by the consideration paid for the shares (that is, 20,000 × C40 = C800,000), as shown below.

It should be noted that this treatment only applies in the UK and the treatment in other jurisdictions may be different.

	Before purchase C'000	Purchase C'000	After purchase C'000
Net assets other than cash	20,000		20,000
Cash	5,000	(800)	4,200
	25,000	(800)	24,200
Share capital	1,000		1,000
Share premium	9,000		9,000
Capital	10,000		10,000
Retained profits	15,000	(800)	14,200
	25,000	(800)	24,200

As can be seen from the above example, the entire consideration paid for the purchase is recognised directly in equity (retained profits).

In the notes to the financial statements, entity A should explain that 20,000 C1 ordinary shares with an aggregate nominal value of C20,000 were purchased during the period and are held in treasury and that retained profits have been reduced by C800,000, being the consideration paid for these shares.

As stated in paragraph A6.7.105 above, the costs of an equity transaction should be accounted for as a deduction from equity. [IAS 32 para 35]. Therefore, expenses directly relating to the treasury share purchase should be treated as part of the overall cost of purchase and like the purchase cost itself should be recognised directly in equity (retained profits) and shown in the statement of changes in equity.

Section 8

Recognition and derecognition

Introduction

A6.8.1 Previous sections have dealt with what qualifies as financial assets and financial liabilities. The next step in the accounting is to determine when financial assets and financial liabilities should be recognised, that is, included in an entity's balance sheet. Conversely, it is also necessary to know when a financial asset or financial liability should be derecognised, that is, when a previously recognised financial asset or financial liability should be removed from an entity's balance sheet.

A6.8.2 As explained in section 3, the rights or obligations that comprise financial assets or financial liabilities are derived from the contractual provisions that underlie them. As a result, an entity only recognises a financial asset or a financial liability at the time it becomes a party to a contract. [IAS 39 para 14]. That is the point at which it has the contractual rights or contractual obligations. As the above discussion suggests, recognition issues for financial assets and financial liabilities tend to be straightforward. They are dealt with in paragraphs 6.8.5 to 6.8.23 below.

A6.8.3 Conversely, when considering whether to cease recognising (derecognise) a financial asset or a financial liability, an entity needs to consider whether it still has that asset or liability. In other words, the entity needs to determine whether the rights or obligations contained in the original asset or liability cease to be contractual rights or obligations.

A6.8.4 However, derecognition issues for financial instruments are far from straightforward, except where relatively simple financial instruments are involved. Many financial instruments comprise components – bundles of contractual rights and/or contractual obligations that are financial assets and financial liabilities in their own right. Transactions may occur that leave in place certain of the components that give rights to future benefits, while transferring the other components to one or more parties. Securitisation, debt factoring and stock lending are examples of such complex transactions. In such circumstances, the evaluation of whether or to what extent the previously recognised financial asset should be derecognised can be quite complex. IAS 39 provides a flowchart that requires the evaluation to be carried out in a strict order. Derecognition issues are discussed from paragraph A6.8.24 below.

Initial recognition

General principles

A6.8.5 Under IAS 39 an entity is required to recognise a financial asset or liability on its balance sheet when, and only when, it becomes a party to the instrument's contractual provisions. [IAS 39 para 14].

Application of the general principles

A6.8.6 Examples of situations where an entity becomes a party to the contractual provisions of a financial instrument are many and varied. Some of these situations are considered in the paragraphs that follow.

Unconditional receivables and payables

A6.8.7 Unconditional receivables and payables are recognised as assets or liabilities when the entity becomes a party to the contract and, as a consequence, has a legal right to receive or a legal obligation to pay cash. [IAS 39 para AG 35(a)].

Forwards and options

A6.8.8 When an entity becomes a party to a forward contract that falls within IAS 39's scope, it becomes exposed to risks and benefits at the contract commitment date, rather than on the date on which settlement takes place. At the commitment date, the fair values of the right and obligation are often equal, so that the net fair value of the forward contract is zero. If the net fair value of the right and obligation is not zero at inception, the contract is recognised as an asset or liability. [IAS 39 para AG 35(c)]. A forward contract that has a zero fair value at inception may become a net asset or liability in the future depending on the value of the underlying instrument or commodity that is the subject of the forward.

A6.8.9 Similarly, option contracts that fall within IAS 39's scope are recognised as assets or liabilities when the holder and the writer become a party to the contract. [IAS 39 para AG 35(d)]. Evidence that a recognisable event arises when the entities become parties to the contract lies in the fact that the option holder usually pays, and the option writer usually receives, a premium for the contract, which indicates that the rights and obligations undertaken by each party have value at that date.

Firm commitments to buy or sell non-financial assets

A6.8.10 When an entity enters into a firm commitment to purchase a non-financial asset in the future, it does not have the contractual rights that comprise the asset. This means that the entity cannot use that asset, or sell it, or pledge it as collateral until the contract matures and the underlying asset is acquired.

Therefore, assets to be acquired and liabilities to be incurred as a result of a firm commitment to purchase or sell goods or services are generally not recognised as assets or liabilities until at least one of the parties has performed under the agreement. For example, an entity that receives a firm order does not generally recognise an asset for the consideration to be paid (and the entity that places the order does not recognise a liability for the consideration to be paid) at the time of the commitment but, rather, delays recognition until the ordered goods or services have been shipped, delivered or rendered.

A6.8.11 However, as stated in section 3 above, contracts to buy or sell non-financial assets that can be settled net or by exchanging financial instruments are treated as if they are financial instruments, that is, derivatives unless they were entered into and continued to be held to meet the entity's normal purchase, sale or usage requirements. Therefore, the net fair value of the contract itself is recognised as an asset or liability at the commitment date.

A6.8.12 Also, if a previously unrecognised firm commitment is designated as a hedged item in a fair value hedge, IAS 39 requires that any change in the net fair value attributable to the hedged risk is recognised as an asset or liability after the inception of the hedge (see chapter 10). Some argue that it is conceptually incorrect to recognise an asset or liability for a firm commitment because it has been hedged. The IASB explains in the Basis of Conclusions that the only difference between a firm commitment that is not hedged and a one that is hedged is that the latter is re-measured for changes in the hedged fair value while the former is measured at its historical cost of zero. Accordingly, there is no fundamental difference in concept as far as recognition is concerned. [IAS 39 paras AG35(b), BC152].

Planned future transactions

A6.8.13 As stated in paragraph A6.8.5 above, a financial asset or a liability should not be recognised before an entity becomes a party to the contract. It follows that planned future transactions, no matter how likely, cannot give rise to assets and liabilities because the entity has not become a party to a contract. [IAS 39 para AG 35(e)]. Such future transactions are future events to be recognised in the future periods when contractual rights are acquired or obligations incurred.

Regular way transactions

A6.8.14 A regular way purchase or sale is a purchase or sale of a financial asset under a contract whose terms require delivery of the asset within the *time frame* established generally by regulation or convention in the *marketplace* concerned. [IAS 39 para 9]. Marketplace is not limited to a formal stock exchange or organised over-the-counter market. Rather, it means the environment in which the financial asset is customarily exchanged. An acceptable time frame in such a marketplace would be the period reasonably and customarily required for the parties to complete the transaction, prepare, and execute closing documents. [IAS 39 para IG B28].

A6.8.15 In many regulated financial markets, a settlement mechanism will exist under which transactions in financial instruments (particularly quoted equities and bonds) entered into on a particular date are settled a few days after this transaction date. The date on which the transaction is entered into is called the 'trade date'. It is the date on which the entity commits to purchase or sell an asset. The date on which the transaction is settled by delivery of the underlying asset is called the 'settlement date'. For example, the standard settlement periods on the London Stock Exchange for equity market securities and wholesale gilts are trade date plus 3 business days (T+3) and trade date plus 1 business day (T+1) respectively. A contract with an individual or through a broker to buy or sell a financial asset that is normally traded on a regulated financial market, but with a settlement period that differs from that established by regulation in that financial marketplace, does not qualify as a regular way transaction. [IAS 39 para IG B29, B30].

A6.8.16 A regular way purchase or sale that gives rise to a fixed price commitment between trade date and settlement date is a derivative – a forward contract. Therefore, in accordance with the principle explained in paragraph A6.8.8, a regular way purchase or sale would fall to be recognised as a forward contract at the commitment date (that is, trade date). However, because of the short duration of the commitment, such contracts are not recognised as derivative financial instruments under IAS 39. Instead, IAS 39 provides for special accounting for such regular way contracts, as discussed from paragraph A6.8.18 below. [IAS 39 para 12]. This exception is a practical expedient to prevent the recognition of derivatives for short periods where the marketplace mechanism prevents settlement at the trade or commitment date. Furthermore, the exception also removes a potential distortion that would occur by recognising changes in fair value of the asset between trade and settlement date through profit or loss, when such changes in fair value after settlement date would either not be recognised at all (where the financial asset is classified as a held-to-maturity asset), or recognised in equity (where the financial asset is classified as available-for-sale).

A6.8.17 The regular way exception requires that the transaction will be settled by physical delivery of the financial instrument within the normal market time frame. Therefore, where a contract permits net settlement in cash or other financial assets equivalent to the change in the contract's fair value, it does not qualify as a regular way transaction. Such a contract is accounted for as a derivative in the period between trade and settlement date. [IAS 39 para AG 54]. Contracts that are settled outside the normal market time frame, whether settled net in cash or gross, will always be accounted for as derivatives.

Trade date versus settlement date accounting

A6.8.18 IAS 39 provides that a regular way purchase or sale of financial assets should be recognised and derecognised, as applicable, using trade date accounting or settlement date accounting. Either method is acceptable, but it is an accounting policy choice that should be disclosed and applied consistently for all purchases and sales that belong to the same category of financial assets as set out in section 6. For this purpose assets that are held for trading form a separate category from assets designated at fair value through profit and loss. [IAS 39 para AG 53].

A6.8.19 Where an entity adopts trade date accounting (the date on which an entity commits itself to purchase or sell an asset), the accounting treatment is as follows:

- In respect of a purchase of a financial asset, the asset received and the liability to pay for it are recognised on the trade date. After initial recognition, the financial asset is subsequently measured either at amortised cost or at fair value depending on its initial classification as explained in section 9.

- In respect of a sale of a financial asset, the asset is derecognised and the receivable from the buyer for the payment together with any gain or loss on disposal are recognised on the trade date.

IAS 39 notes that, generally, interest does not start to accrue on the asset and corresponding liability until settlement date when title passes.

[IAS 39 para AG 55].

A6.8.20 Where an entity adopts settlement date accounting (the date that an asset is delivered to or by an entity), the accounting treatment is as follows:

- In respect of a purchase of a financial asset, the asset is recognised on the day it is received by the entity. Any change in the asset's fair value to be received during the period between the trade date and the settlement date is accounted for in the same way as the acquired asset. In other words:

  - for assets carried at cost or amortised cost, the change in value is not recognised;

  - for assets classified as financial assets at fair value through profit or loss, the change in value is recognised in profit or loss; and

  - for available-for-sale assets, the change in value is recognised in equity.

- In respect of a sale of a financial asset, the asset is derecognised and the receivable from the buyer for the payment together with any gain or loss on disposal are recognised on the day that it is delivered by the entity. Any change in the fair value of the asset between trade date and settlement date is not recognised, as there is an agreed upon sale price at the trade date, making subsequent changes in fair value irrelevant from the seller's perspective. In other words, the seller's right to changes in the fair value ceases on the trade date.

[IAS 39 para AG 56].

A6.8.21 The following examples illustrate the application of trade date and settlement date accounting to the various categories of financial asset identified by IAS 39. These examples are based on those included in IAS 39's implementation guidance. [IAS 39 paras IG D2.1, D2.2].

Example 1 – Regular way purchase of a financial asset

On 29 December 20X5, an entity commits to purchase a financial asset for C1,000, which is its fair value on commitment (trade) date. Transaction costs are immaterial. On 31 December 20X5 (financial year-end) and on 4 January 20X6 (settlement date) the fair value of the asset is C1,002 and C1,003, respectively.

The amounts to be recorded for the asset will depend on how it is classified and whether trade date or settlement date accounting is used, as shown in the two tables below.

Trade date accounting

Details	**Held-to-maturity investments – carried at amortised cost**	**Available- for-sale assets – remeasured to fair value with changes in equity**	**Assets at fair value through profit or loss – remeasured to fair value with changes in profit or loss**
29 December 20X5	C	C	C
Dr Financial asset	1,000	1,000	1,000
Cr Liability for payment	(1,000)	(1,000)	(1,000)
To record asset and liability for payment			
31 December 20X5			
Dr Financial asset	–	2	2
Cr Equity	–	(2)	–
Cr Income statement	–	–	(2)
To recognise change in fair value			
4 January 20X6			
Dr Financial asset	–	1	1
Cr Equity	–	(1)	–
Cr Income statement	–	–	(1)
To recognise change in fair value			
4 January 20X6			
Dr Liability for payment	1,000	1,000	1,000
Cr Cash	(1,000)	(1,000)	(1,000)
To record settlement of liability			

Asset's carrying value at 4 January 20X6	1000	1003	1003
Settlement date accounting			
29 December 20X5			
No entries are recorded at the commitment date	–	–	–
31 December 20X5			
Dr Financial asset	–	2	2
Cr Equity	–	(2)	–
Cr Income statement	–	–	(2)
To recognise change in fair value			
4 January 20X6			
Dr Financial asset	–	1	1
Cr Equity	–	(1)	–
Cr Income statement	–	–	(1)
To recognise change in fair value			
4 January 20X6			
Dr Financial asset	1,000	1,000	1,000
Cr Cash	–	(1,000)	(1,000)
To record the asset's purchase at the contracted cash amount plus changes in fair value since trade date.			
Asset's carrying value at 4 January 20X6	1000	1003	1003

Example 2 – Regular way sale of a financial asset

On 29 December 20X5 (trade date) an entity enters into a contract to sell a financial asset for its current fair value of C1,010. The asset was acquired one year earlier for C1,000 and its amortised cost is C1,000. On 31 December 20X5 (financial year-end), the fair value of the asset is C1,012. On 4 January 20X6 (settlement date), the fair value is C1,013.

The amounts to be recorded will depend on how the asset is classified and whether trade date or settlement date accounting is used as shown in the two tables below (any interest that might have accrued on the asset is disregarded).

Trade date accounting

Date	Held-to-maturity investments - carried at amortised cost	Available- for-sale assets – remeasured to fair value with changes in equity	Assets at fair value through profit or loss - remeasured to fair value with changes in profit or loss
	C	C	C
Carrying value prior to 29 December 20X5	1,000	1,010	1,010
29 December 20X5			
Dr Receivable	1,010	1,010	1,010
Cr Asset	(1,000)	(1,010)	(1,010)
Dr Equity		10	
Cr Profit or loss	(10)	(10)	

To record disposal of the asset and 'recycling' of cumulative gain from equity to profit or loss on disposal of the available-for-sale asset on trade date.

31 December 20X5
A change in the fair value of a financial asset that is sold on a regular way basis is not recorded in the financial statements between trade date and settlement date because the seller's right to changes in the fair value ceases on the trade date.

4 January 20X6			
Dr Cash	1,010	1,010	1,010
Cr Receivable	(1,010)	(1,010)	(1,010)

To record settlement of sales contract

Settlement date accounting

29 December 20X5			
Carrying value prior to 29 December 20X5	1,000	1,010	1,010

31 December 20X5
A change in the fair value of a financial asset that is sold on a regular way basis is not recorded in the financial statements between trade date and settlement date, even if the entity applies settlement date accounting, because the seller's right to changes in the fair value ceases on the trade date.

4 January 20X6			
Dr Cash	1,010	1,010	1,010
Cr Asset	(1,000)	(1,010)	(1,010)
Dr Equity		10	–
Cr Profit or loss	(10)	(10)	–

To record the disposal of the asset and 'recycling' of cumulative gain on the available-for-sale asset recognised in equity to profit or loss on settlement date.

In summary, regular way sale is accounted for as a sale on trade date if trade date accounting is used and on settlement date if settlement date accounting is used.

6A.8.22 It should be noted that the above requirements apply only to transactions in financial assets. IAS 39 does not contain any specific requirements about trade date accounting and settlement date accounting for transactions in financial instruments that are classified as financial liabilities. This means that the general recognition and derecognition requirements for financial liabilities in IAS 39 apply. [IAS 39 para IG B32]. Under IAS 39, liabilities are recognised on the date the entity 'becomes a party to the contractual provisions of the instrument' (see para A6.8.5 above). Financial liabilities are derecognised only when they are extinguished, that is, when the obligation specified in the contract is discharged or cancelled or expires (see further para A6.8.144 below).

Exchange of non-cash financial assets

A6.8.23 Sometimes an entity may enter into a regular way transaction to sell a non-cash financial asset not for cash, but in exchange for another non-cash financial asset. In this situation, a question arises as to whether any change in fair value of the financial asset to be received should be recognised between trade and settlement date in circumstances where the entity adopts settlement date accounting for the financial asset to be disposed of. The answer depends on the classification of the asset to be received in exchange and whether the entity uses trade date or settlement date accounting for purchases or sales of assets in that category. Consider the following example:

Example – Regular way sale of a financial asset for non-cash consideration

On 29 December 20X5 (trade date) entity A enters into a contract to sell note receivable A, which is carried at amortised cost, in exchange for bond B, which will be classified as held for trading and measured at fair value. Both assets have a fair value of C1,010 on 29 December, while the amortised cost of note receivable A is C1,000. Entity A uses settlement date accounting for loans and receivables and trade date accounting for assets held for trading.

On 31 December 20X5 (financial year-end), the fair value of note receivable A is C1,012 and the fair value of bond B is C1,009. On 4 January 20X6, the fair value of note receivable A is C1,013 and the fair value of bond B is C1,007.

The following entries are made:

	Dr	Cr
	C	C
29 December 20X5		
Bond B	1,010	
Liability for payment		1,010
To record the purchase of bond B on the trade date as per entity's policy of using trade date accounting for assets held for trading.		
31 December 20X5		
Profit or loss	1	
Bond B		1
To record the change in fair value of bond B from C1,010 to C1,009.		
4 January 20X6		
Liability for payment	1,010	
Note receivable A		1,000
Profit or loss		10
To record the disposal of note receivable A and the resultant gain on sale in exchange for bond B on settlement date.		
Profit or loss	2	
Bond B		2
To record the change in fair value of bond B from C1,009 to C1,007.		

Derecognition of financial assets

Introduction

A6.8.24 It is fairly common for entities to raise finance by selling financial assets, such as portfolios of trade receivables, loans, etc. No special problem arises where a transferor sells financial assets for cash or other assets, with no continuing involvement with the asset sold or with the transferee. The accounting for such transactions as sales with corresponding derecognition of the asset is well established. At the other extreme is a transfer of a financial asset where the buyer has an unconditional right and obligation to return the asset at the original price, usually with interest as in a repurchase transaction. Again, the accounting in this situation is fairly straightforward. The transaction is treated as a financing, with both the asset and the liability on balance sheet, because the risk and rewards of ownership of the asset have not been transferred.

A6.8.25 Problems begin to surface, however, when transfers are undertaken between the above two extremes in circumstances where the seller retains certain interests in the assets transferred. Examples include transfers that are subject to recourse and agreements to acquire the transferred asset or make additional payments that reflect the performance of the transferred asset. Prior to IAS 39, there was no guidance in IAS on the circumstances when financial assets subject to such arrangements should be removed from the balance sheet and whether the funding received should be regarded as a sale or secured borrowings. In the absence of specific guidance, such arrangements were often accounted for on the basis of their legal form rather than their substance, with the result that the asset transferred was removed from the balance sheet and the funding provided was not recognised on the balance sheet. Such 'off balance sheet financing' became evident during the 1980s. The exclusion of the asset being financed, as well as the finance itself, had the effect of understating the entity's resources and its financing, with a consequential flattering effect on gearing and return on assets employed. The income statement was also affected in that a profit was recognised on a 'sale' that was, in substance, a secured loan. Furthermore, along with 'off balance sheet financing' schemes, there was rapid innovation in financial markets. New arrangements for financing assets were developed, the accounting for which became inconsistent, causing confusion amongst both preparers and users of financial statements.

Mixed approach for derecognition

A6.8.26 The derecognition rules in the original version of IAS 39 were developed to address the above issues and to deal with the problems caused by the misleading effects that 'off balance sheet financing' can have on the financial statements. However, the derecognition rules in the 1998 version combined into a single mixed approach the 'risk and rewards' approach of UK FRS 5, 'Reporting the substance of transactions', and the so called 'control-components' approach of US FAS 140, 'Accounting for transfers and servicing of financial assets and extinguishment of liabilities'. This mixed approach was subject to criticism, primarily because these two different concepts governed when a financial asset should be derecognised. It was not always clear when and in what order these concepts should be applied.

[The next paragraph is 6.8.29.]

A6.8.29 The revised version of IAS 39, issued in December 2003, retains elements of both the risk and rewards and control approaches, but also introduces a new 'continuing involvement' approach, resulting in partial derecognition in a number of more complex transactions. Furthermore, the revision clarifies the requirements considerably by introducing a step-by-step approach to analysing transactions, that clearly sets out when and in what order the various approaches are to be applied.

Flow chart for derecognition

A6.8.30 The derecognition rules in IAS 39 are fairly complex. Therefore, the standard provides a flow chart to assist in evaluating whether, and to what extent, a financial asset is derecognised. [IAS 39 para AG 36]. It is important to note that the steps must be considered in the strict sequence in which they appear in the flow chart. First, it is necessary to determine whether a transfer of the financial asset has taken place. If so, the entity applies the 'risks and reward' approach before considering the 'control' approach. A detailed explanation of each step follows after the flow chart. For analysis purposes and ease of reference, each step has a number and refers to a particular step in the diagram. For example, if Step 6 =

Yes, it means that the entity has transferred substantially all the risks and rewards of ownership. Similarly, if Step 6 = No and Step 7 = No, it means that the entity has neither transferred nor retained substantially all of the risks and rewards of ownership. This notation is used throughout the remainder of the section.

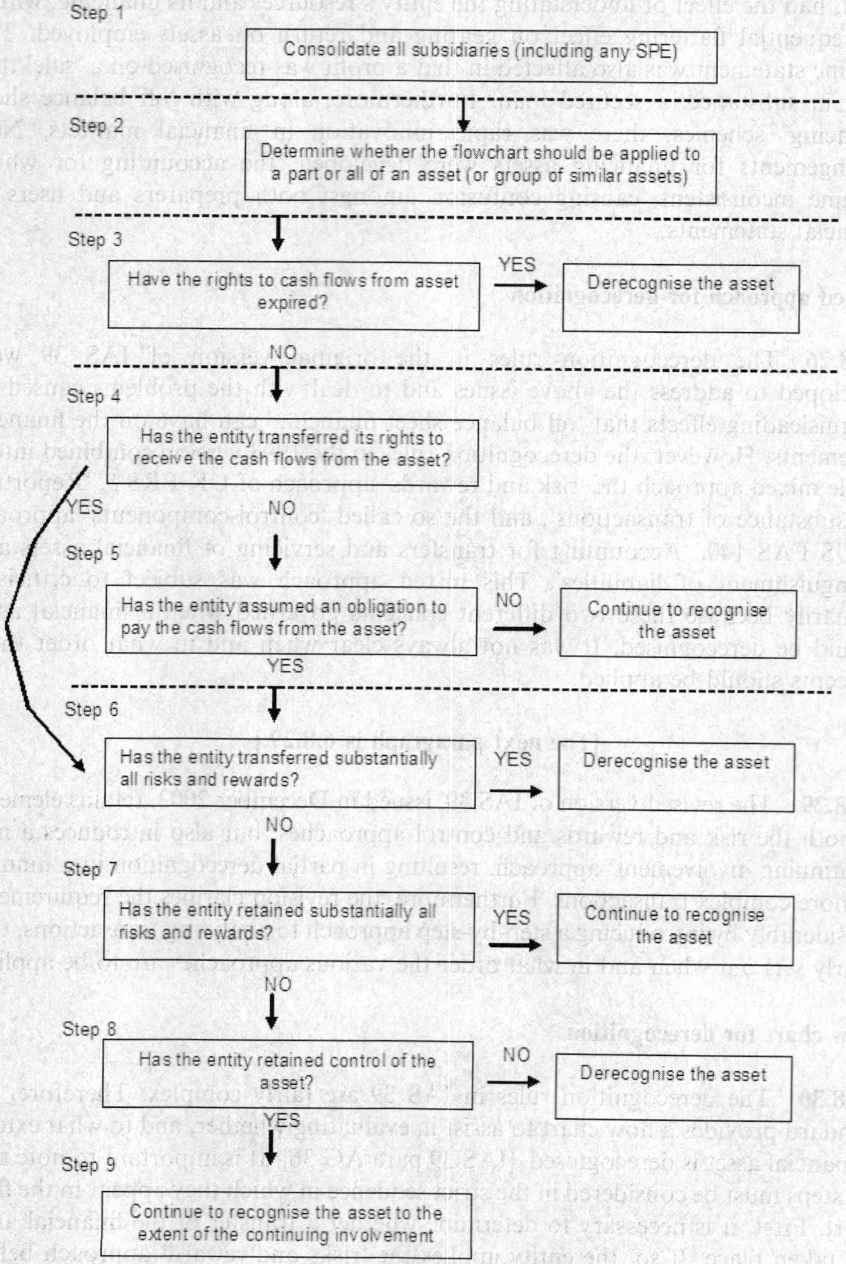

Consolidate all subsidiaries including any SPEs

A6.8.31 Many entities establish special purpose entities (SPEs), trusts, partnerships etc. for the acquisition of financial assets before these financial assets, or a portion thereof, are transferred to third party investors. The transfer of financial assets to such an entity might qualify as a legal sale. However, if the relationship between the transferor and the SPE suggests that the transferor controls the SPE, then the transferor needs to consolidate the SPE. This means that when evaluating derecognition in its group financial statements, an entity should first consolidate all subsidiaries and special purpose entities in accordance with IAS 27, 'Consolidated and separate financial statements', and SIC 12, 'Consolidation – Special purpose entities', and then apply the derecognition analysis to the resulting group (step 1 in the diagram in para A6.8.30 above). [IAS 39 para 14].

A6.8.32 Step 1, therefore, ensures that the derecognition analysis produces the same answer regardless of whether the entity transfers financial assets, or a portion thereof, directly to third party investors or through a consolidated SPE or trust that obtains the transferred assets and, in turn, transfers them directly to third party investors. [IAS 39 BC64].

Determine whether the flow chart applies to all or part of an asset

A6.8.33 The next step (step 2 in the diagram in para A6.8.30 above) is to determine whether the analysis should be applied to a part of a financial asset (or part of a group of similar financial assets) or to a financial asset in its entirety (or a group of similar assets in their entirety). The standard stipulates that the derecognition rules should be applied to a part of a financial asset (or part of a group of similar financial assets) if, and only if, the part being considered for derecognition meets one of the following three conditions:

- The part comprises only specifically identified cash flows from a financial asset (or a group of similar financial assets). For example, if an entity enters into an interest rate strip whereby the counterparty obtains the right to the interest cash flows, but not the principal cash flows, from a debt instrument the derecognition rules are applied only to the interest cash flows.

- The part comprises only a fully proportionate (*pro rata*) share of the cash flows from a financial asset (or a group of similar financial assets). For example, if an entity enters into an arrangement in which the counterparty obtains the rights to a 90 per cent share of all cash flows of a debt instrument, the derecognition rules are applied to those cash flows. If there is more than one counterparty, it is not necessary for each counterparty to have a proportionate share of the cash flows provided that the transferring entity retains a fully proportionate share.

- The part comprises only a fully proportionate (*pro rata*) share of specifically identified cash flows from a financial asset (or a group of similar financial assets). For example, if an entity enters into an arrangement in which the counterparty obtains the rights to a 90 per cent share of interest cash flows from a financial asset (the specifically identified part), the derecognition rules are applied to that 90 per cent of those interest cash flows. If there is more than one counterparty, it is not necessary for each counterparty to have a proportionate share of the specifically identified cash flows provided that the transferring entity retains a fully proportionate share.

[IAS 39 para 16(a)].

A6.8.34 The above criteria must be applied strictly to determine whether the derecognition rules should be applied either to the whole asset, or to only a part of the asset.

A6.8.35 If it is not possible to identify a part, the derecognition rules must be applied to the financial asset in its entirety (or to the group of similar financial assets in their entirety). [IAS 39 para 16(b)].

Example 1 – Transfer of the first or the last specified amount of cash flows from a financial asset

An entity enters into an arrangement to transfer the first C0.9m of cash flows receivable from a financial asset that has a fair value of C1m at the date of transfer.

In this situation, the transferor cannot apply the derecognition requirements to part of the asset, because the first C0.9m of cash flow represents neither a specifically identifiable cash flow nor a fully proportionate (*pro rata*) share of all or part of the cash flows from the asset. As a result, the derecognition rules must be applied to the whole asset. The same conclusion applies if the arrangement resulted in a transfer of the last C0.9m of cash flows.

On the other hand, if the arrangement resulted in the transfer of 90% of all cash flows from the asset, the derecognition rules would have been applied only to the proportion transferred, that is, 90%.

Example 2 – Transfer subject to a guarantee

An entity enters into an arrangement to transfer the rights to 90% of the cash flows of a group of receivables, but provides a guarantee to compensate the buyer for any credit losses up to 8% of the principal amount of the receivables.

In this situation, although the transferor has transferred 90% of all cash flows from the asset, the existence of the guarantee means that the transferor has an obligation that could involve it in repaying some of the consideration received. Therefore, the derecognition requirements must be applied to the asset in its entirety and not just to the proportion of cash flows transferred.

On the other hand, if the guarantee had not been given, the arrangement would have satisfied the condition in the second bullet point of paragraph A6.8.33 above and the derecognition rules would have been applied only to the 90% of cash flows transferred.

Example 3 – Transfer of an asset for part of its life

An entity enters into an arrangement to transfer the rights to 100% of the cash flows (interest and principal) arising in the last four years of a fixed rate loan receivable with an original maturity of 10 years. The principal is payable in a lump sum in year 10. In other words, the entity retains the right to interest cash flows for the first six years.

In this situation, it is clear that the entity has transferred the rights to the last 4 years of cash flows that represent specifically identifiable cash flows (the last 4 years of interest cash flows + principal cash flow). Therefore, in accordance with paragraph A6.8.33 above, the derecognition rules should be applied to this identifiable portion.

Example 4 – Transfer of a right to receive dividends

Entity A has a holding of shares in entity X (an available for sale financial asset). Entity A transfers to entity B the right to receive dividends paid on those shares in the next year.

In this situation, the dividends for the next year are specifically identifiable cash flows and the derecognition rules should be applied to the dividend strip.

Similarly, if entity A had transferred its holding of shares to entity B and retained the right to receive dividends for the next year, the cash flows arising on the transferred asset from the second year to perpetuity are also specifically identifiable cash flows. Therefore, the derecognition rules would be applied to only that part of the asset.

6A.8.36 Once it has been established that the derecognition rules should be applied to the whole asset (or a group of similar assets) or to the qualifying part or portion identified in step 2 above, the remaining steps of the flow chart should be applied to that whole or part identified. This is referred to as 'the financial asset' in the paragraphs that follow. [IAS 39 para 16(b)]. The meaning of 'a group of similar assets' is considered further from paragraph A6.8.52 below.

Determine whether the rights to the cash flows from the asset have expired

A6.8.37 The first two steps of the flow chart determine at what level (entity or consolidated) the derecognition rules should apply and to what identified asset (individual or group or component thereof) those rules should apply. The next step (step 3 in the diagram in para A6.8.30) is the first step in determining whether derecognition of the identified asset is appropriate or not. This step considers whether the contractual rights to the financial asset have expired. If they have, the financial asset is derecognised. [IAS 39 para 17(a)]. This would be the case, for example, when a loan is extinguished, in the normal course, by payment of the entire amount due, thereby discharging the debtor from any further obligation. Another example is where a right from a purchased financial option is extinguished as a result of the contractual terms expiring without the holder requiring the writer to deliver or purchase the underlying financial asset. Derecognition at this step is usually obvious and requires little or no analysis.

Determine whether the entity has transferred the cash flows from the asset

A6.8.38 If the contractual rights to the cash flows have not expired, an entity derecognises the financial asset when and only when it 'transfers' the cash flows from the asset. IAS 39 identifies two ways in which a transfer can be achieved. An entity 'transfers' a financial asset if, and only if, it either:

- transfers the contractual rights to receive the financial asset's cash flows. [IAS 39 para 18(a)]. See step 4 in the diagram in paragraph A6.8.30 and paragraph A6.8.39 below; or
- retains the contractual rights to receive the financial asset's cash flows, but assumes a contractual obligation to pay the cash flows to one or more recipients, in what is often referred to as a 'pass through arrangement'. [IAS 39 para 18(b)]. See step 5 in the diagram in paragraph A6.8.30 and paragraph A6.8.43 below.

A6.8.38.1 There is little guidance in IAS 39 on how to distinguish these two types of transfer. The IFRIC is currently considering whether to issue an Interpretation that would give further guidance. Our present views are set out in paragraphs 6.8.39 to 6.8.42.3 below, but may change in the light of any additional guidance issued by the IFRIC.

Transfer of contractual rights to receive cash flows

A6.8.39 IAS 39 does not explain what is meant by the phrase *"transfers the contractual rights to receive the cash flows of the financial asset"*. A literal reading of the words would suggest that the phrase would apply to an asset's legal sale, or a legal assignment of the rights to the cash flows from the asset. For example, an entity that has sold a financial asset (such as a legal sale of a bond) has transferred its rights to receive the cash flows from the asset. In this situation, the transferee has unconditional, presently exercisable rights to all the future cash flows. The transfer then has to be assessed in Step 6 in the diagram in paragraph A6.8.30 to determine whether it meets the derecognition criteria (see para A6.8.56 below).

A6.8.40 Some types of financial asset (for example, a receivable or a portfolio of receivables), cannot be 'sold' in the same way as other types (for example, a bond), but they can be transferred by means of a novation or an assignment as explained in paragraph A6.8.96 below. Both novation and assignment will generally result in the transfer of contractual rights to receive the financial asset's cash flows. However, any further conditions or obligations placed upon the transferor in an assignment need to be considered and may impact this assessment.

A6.8.41 In some instances, following the transfer of the contractual rights to receive a financial asset's cash flows, the transferor may continue to administer or provide servicing on the transferred asset. For example, a transferor may transfer all rights to cash flows, but continues to collect cash flows on behalf of the transferee in a capacity as an agent, rather than for its own benefit. This could occur where the original asset counterparties are notified that their obligation has been legally transferred to the transferee and are requested to pay the cash flows into a bank account for the transferee's benefit; in this case the transferor continues to act purely as an agent in managing the collection of the transferee's cash flows. Determining whether the contractual rights to cash flows have been transferred is not affected by the transferor retaining the role of an agent to administer collection and distribution of cash flows. Therefore, retention of servicing rights by the entity transferring the financial asset does not in itself cause the transfer to fail the requirements in paragraph 18(a) of IAS 39.

A6.8.42 Sometimes transfers of financial assets are made subject to certain conditions. Conditions attached to a transfer could include provisions relating to the existence and value of transferred cash flows at the date of transfer or conditions relating to the future performance of the asset. In our view, such conditions would not affect whether the entity has transferred the contractual rights to receive cash flows (under paragraph 18(a)). However, the existence of conditions relating to the future performance of the asset might affect the conclusion related to the transfer of risks and rewards as well as the extent of any continuing involvement by the transferor in the transferred asset.

A6.8.42.1 Where a receivable is transferred, the original debtor may have the right to offset amounts that it owes to the transferor against any receivables due from the transferor. Such two-party offset arrangements would not cause a transfer of the receivable to fail the requirements in paragraph 18(a) of IAS 39. The payment made by the transferor to the transferee if the right of offset is exercised, merely transfers to the transferee the value the transferor obtained when its liability to the original debtor was extinguished. Such rights of offset would also not impact the risks and rewards test (see further para A6.8.56 below). However, some offset arrangements involve three parties. In such an arrangement, a third party (for example, a sub-contractor who performed some of the services that gave rise to the receivable) has a right to offset amounts it is owed by the transferor against the transferred receivable. As a result, the third party has the unilateral ability to extinguish the contractual rights to receive cash flows from the original debtor. In our view, such an arrangement precludes the transfer from meeting the requirements of paragraph 18(a).

A6.8.42.2 An entity may transfer receivables in respect of which it may subsequently issue credit notes. Examples include where an entity's customer qualifies for a volume discount that is included in the general sales conditions between the entity and its customer, or credit notes issued at the entity's discretion to maintain its relationship with the customer. Such credit notes may be used against any existing or future invoice. Credit notes, both contractual or discretionary, issued by a transferor do not preclude a transfer of contractual rights to receive cash flows from an asset. Credit notes relate to the relationship between the transferor and its customer and not to the contract that is the receivable. For the same reason they should not be taken into account for the risks and rewards test (see further from para A6.8.56 below).

A6.8.42.3 Some transfers may include an option or a commitment for the transferor to repurchase the assets. These are often included for good business reasons, such as to enable the transferor to repurchase a receivable in order to maintain a good relationship with a customer, or to allow repurchase in a change of circumstances, for example, a change in tax laws. Such options do not prevent a transfer of the contractual rights to receive the cash flows from an asset, but do need to be considered when applying the risks and rewards test (see further from para A6.8.56 below).

Assumption of obligations to pay cash flows to others (pass-through arrangements)

A6.8.43 An entity that retains its contractual rights to receive the cash flows from the asset and does not have a transfer under paragraph 18(a) of IAS 39, may nevertheless assume an obligation to pass on the cash flows from the asset to another party in a 'pass-through arrangement' (see step 5 in the diagram in para A6.8.30). Such pass-through arrangements arise where the entity continues to collect cash receipts from a financial asset (or more typically a pool of financial assets), but assumes an obligation to pass on those receipts to another party that has provided finance in connection with the financial asset. They are common in securitisations and sub-participation arrangements (see further para A6.8.90 below). The entity could be the financial asset's originator, or it could be a group that includes a consolidated special purpose entity that has acquired the financial asset from the originator and passes on cash flows to unrelated third party investors.

A6.8.44 Under IAS 39, an entity (transferor) that retains the contractual rights to receive the cash flows of a financial asset (the 'original asset'), but assumes a contractual obligation to pay the cash flows to one or more recipients (the 'eventual recipients') is regarded as having transferred the original asset if, and only if, all of the following conditions are met:

- The transferor has no obligation to pay amounts to the eventual recipients, unless it collects equivalent amounts from the original asset. Short-term advances by the transferor to the eventual recipients with the right of full recovery of the amount lent plus accrued interest from the amounts eventually payable to the eventual recipients at market rates do not violate this condition.

- The transferor is prohibited by the transfer contract's terms from selling or pledging the original asset other than as security to the eventual recipients for the obligation to pay them cash flows.

- The transferor has an obligation to remit any cash flows it collects on behalf of the eventual recipients without material delay. In addition, the transferor is not entitled to reinvest such cash flows, except in cash or cash equivalents as defined in IAS 7, 'Cash flow statements', during the short settlement period from the collection date to the date of required remittance to the eventual recipients, with any interest earned on such investments being passed to the eventual recipients.

[IAS 39 paras 19(a)-(c)].

A6.8.45 The first condition ensures that the transferor is not obliged to transfer funds to the transferee that it has not collected, that is, it is not required to fund payments to the eventual recipients. This means that the transferee must bear the slow payment risk. However, short-term advances made by the transferor in periods where there are shortfalls in collection due to slow payments from the asset or differences in the dates of collection from the assets and payments to the eventual recipients will not prevent the transaction from being treated as a transfer provided:

- the short-term advances are made at market rates; and
- those advances plus any accrued interest are recoverable in full from the recipients by deduction from the amounts eventually payable to the eventual recipients.

A6.8.46 The above conditions are necessary to ensure that derecognition is not prevented simply because a short-term cash flow is provided to the transferee. This would not be the case and derecognition would be prevented if the transferor was obliged to provide short-term loans at below market rates of interest or interest free loans – in this case the transferor, and not the transferee, would bear the slow-payment risk.

A6.8.47 The second condition helps ensure that the transferee rather than the transferor has an asset. This is because if the transferor is free to sell or pledge the financial assets that are the subject of the transfer, then the transferee would not have the ability to realise the contractual rights that comprise the transferred financial asset.

A6.8.48 The third condition is designed to ensure that the transferor does not have use of, or benefit from, the cash it collects on the transferee's behalf and is required to remit them 'without material delay'. Again, this condition is necessary to ensure that the transferor has no asset. 'Without material delay' is not defined in the standard so judgment is required in making this assessment. The underlying facts and circumstances need to be reviewed carefully to assess whether the time interval between collection of the cash flows and their remittance to eventual recipients is reasonable in relation to the timing of payments on the underlying assets and market practices. For example, in some pass-through arrangements, such as securitisation of a portfolio of large number of receivables (for example, credit card balances where customers often pay off the outstanding balance on a range of days each month), it is often not practical for the entity to transfer the relatively small amount of cash collected from individual accounts as and when they arise. Instead, for administrative convenience, the contractual arrangement may provide for their remittance to be made in bulk on a weekly, monthly or quarterly basis. In such situations, a remittance period of three months or less is generally acceptable, as in most securitisations interest is paid on a quarterly basis.

A6.8.49 The third condition not only prohibits the transferor from reinvesting the cash flows received in the short settlement period between collection and remittance, but also restricts any investment made for the transferee's benefit to cash or cash equivalents as defined in IAS 7. This means that the transferor is not allowed to invest the funds in other high yielding medium-term investments for the benefit of the transferee or utilise the funds in generating further assets for securitisations (see below). Furthermore, the transferor is not permitted to retain any interest from such short-term highly liquid investments. All such interest received (but no more) must be remitted to the transferee as they arise. In practice, the funds are often paid into a trustee bank account for the transferee's benefit.

A6.8.50 It follows that these conditions are quite strict and some securitisation arrangements may well fail the pass-through tests. For example, an arrangement that is often used in practice for short-term receivables, such as credit card and trade receivables, is a 'revolving structure'. In a revolving structure an entity collects cash flows on behalf of eventual recipients and uses the amounts collected to purchase new assets instead of remitting the cash to the eventual recipients. This arrangement continues for a defined period of time. On maturity, the principal amount is remitted to the eventual recipients from the cash flows arising from the reinvested assets. Such revolving arrangements will fail the third condition stated in paragraph A6.8.44 above, because they would involve a material delay before the original collection of cash is remitted. Furthermore, the nature of the new assets typically acquired means that most revolving arrangements involve reinvestment in assets that would not qualify as cash or cash equivalents.

A6.8.51 The effect of meeting all the three pass-through conditions in paragraph A6.8.44 above is that the entity does not have an asset (second and third conditions) or a liability (first condition), as defined in the Framework. In these situations, the entity acts more as an agent of the eventual recipient than as the asset's owner. Accordingly, if the conditions are met, the arrangement is treated as a transfer and considered for derecognition (that is, subject to the risk and rewards and control tests – see below). Conversely, if the conditions are not met, the entity acts more as an asset's owner with the result that the asset should continue to be recognised.

Example – Transfer of disproportionate share of cash flows

Entity A originates a five-year interest-bearing loan of C100. Entity A then enters into an agreement with entity B in which, in exchange for a cash payment of C90, entity A agrees to pass to entity B the first C90 of all principal and interest payments collected from the loan. Entity A accepts no obligation to make any payments to entity B other than the first C90 collected. Entity A is prohibited by the agreement's terms from selling or pledging the original asset and has to remit the collected cash flows without material delay to entity B.

Entity A will have to assess the entire loan for derecognition since a disproportionate share of cash flows will be transferred (see from para A6.8.33). Although, the transfer is of a disproportionate share of cash flows, it can qualify as a pass-through arrangement. In this example, the three conditions for a pass-through arrangement are met; entity A has an obligation to pay the cash flows collected from the loan to the eventual recipients without material delay and entity A has no right to sell or pledge the transferred asset. In order to assess whether the asset can be derecognised the remaining steps in the derecognition flow chart (see para A6.8.30) will still need to be followed.

6A.8.52 In the above discussions reference was made to the cash flows from the 'original asset'. An issue that arises in practice is what may be included in the 'original asset'? For example, it is not uncommon for an entity that originates loans and receivables to enter into contracts with third parties to mitigate some of the risks of the underlying assets, such as credit insurance, interest rate swaps etc. If those loans/receivables are later transferred together with the third party contracts to a buyer, the question arises as to what should be regarded as the 'original asset'.

A6.8.53 The IFRIC is currently considering whether to issue an interpretation that will clarify this issue. Its initial view, as set out in a tentative agenda decision issued in November 2006 was that derivative assets (which are often transferred together with non-derivative financial assets) are not 'similar' to non-derivative financial assets for the purposes of determining whether, and to what extent, derecognition is appropriate. This means that contracts, such as credit insurance, transferred with the loans/receivables in a single transaction are not part of the original asset (loans/receivables). Therefore, an entity would need to apply the derecognition tests in IAS 39 to non-derivative financial assets (or groups of similar non-derivative financial assets) and derivative financial assets (or groups of similar derivative financial assets) separately, even if they are transferred at the same time. Furthermore, transferred derivatives that could be assets or liabilities (such as interest rate swaps) and that are transferred would have to meet both the financial asset and the financial liability derecognition tests. [IFRIC Update November 2006]. However, this tentative agenda decision was subsequently withdrawn in January 2007 pending completion of a project on derecognition. [IFRIC Update January 2007]. In the absence of further guidance, our present view is that the term 'original asset' can be interpreted to mean either:

- all related contracts, including purchased options, swaps and insurance contracts, transferred with the loans/receivables in a single transaction that share and mitigate some of the risks on the loans because those are the cash flows that will be paid to the eventual recipients; or
- only the transferred loans/ receivables themselves.

A6.8.54 An entity must choose one of these two approaches as its accounting policy and apply it consistently. Furthermore, when performing a risks and rewards analysis (see para A6.8.56 below), the net cash flows of the transferred asset must be determined consistently with the policy chosen for determining the original asset.

A6.8.55 Following the withdrawal in January 2007 of the tentative agenda decision dealing with the meaning of original assets and when to apply the pass-through test, further guidance in these areas is pending the completion of a project on derecognition. It is expected that this will culminate in the issuance of an IFRIC interpretation. Our present views described above may change in the light of any further guidance issued by the IFRIC.

Perform risk and rewards analysis

A6.8.56 Once an entity has established that it has transferred a financial asset, either by transferring the contractual rights to receive the cash flows or under a qualifying pass-through arrangement, it carries out the second part of the derecognition test – a risks and rewards analysis. This analysis begins in step 6 in the diagram in paragraph A6.8.30 and essentially involves an evaluation of the extent to which the entity has transferred substantially all the risks and rewards of ownership of the financial asset (see para A6.8.57 below). If it has, the transferred asset is derecognised. If the entity has not transferred substantially all the risks and rewards of ownership, a further evaluation is necessary to determine whether it has retained substantially all the risks and rewards of ownership (see para A6.8.60 below). If it has, the transferred asset will continue to be recognised. However, if the evaluation reveals that the entity has neither transferred nor retained substantially all the risks and rewards of ownership, the entity must perform a control analysis (see step 8 in the diagram in para A6.8.30 and para A6.8.66 below) to ascertain which party has control of the asset. [IAS 39 para 20].

Determine whether substantially all the risks and rewards of ownership have been transferred

A6.8.57 If the entity transfers substantially all the risks and rewards of ownership of the asset, the entity must derecognise the financial asset as shown in step 6 in the diagram in paragraph A6.8.30 above. It may also have to recognise separately as assets and liabilities any rights and obligations created or retained in the transfer (see also para A6.8.106 below). [IAS 39 para 20(a)].

A6.8.58 Determining whether the entity has transferred substantially all the risks and rewards of ownership will often be readily apparent from the terms and conditions of the transfer. Where this is not so obvious, the entity needs to undertake an evaluation. That evaluation requires the entity to compute and compare its exposure to the variability in the present value of the transferred asset's future net cash flows before and after the transfer. The computation and comparison should be made using as the discount rate an appropriate current market interest rate. All reasonably possible variability in net cash flows (as to amounts and timing) should be considered, and greater weight should be given to those outcomes that are more likely to occur, that is, the amounts and timing need to be probability weighted. [IAS 39 para 22].

A6.8.59 If, as a result of the contractual arrangements, the entity's exposure to such variability is no longer *significant in relation to the total variability* in the present value of the future net cash flows associated with the financial asset, the entity is regarded as having transferred substantially all the financial asset's risks and rewards of ownership. [IAS 39 para 21]. It should be noted that the computational comparison for derecognition is a relative and not an absolute test. That is, the extent to which the variability in the amounts and timing of the transferred asset's net cash flows is significant or not is measured in relation to the total variability. In other words, derecognition is not achieved solely if the entity's remaining exposure to the risks and rewards of an asset is small in absolute terms.

A6.8.60 IAS 39 does not provide any guidance as to what is meant by 'significant' as referred to in the above paragraph when comparing the difference between the present value of the cash flows from the financial asset before the transfer with the present value of the cash flow after the transfer. Therefore, judgement is needed to assess what is significant in each particular situation. A numerical computation is not necessarily required – often it will be obvious whether the entity has transferred substantially all risks and rewards of ownership. [IAS 39 para 22]. In other cases it will be less clear and a computation will be required. There is limited guidance in the standard as to how to perform such a computation of the entity's exposure to the variability in the present value of the future net cash flows before and after the transfer. This can be done in a number of ways, but the example below shows one way in which the calculation can be done.

Example – Variability in the amounts and timing of cash flows

An entity sells a portfolio of short term 30 day receivables with a nominal value of C1 billion to a third party. The entity guarantees first losses on the portfolio up to 1.25% of the loan volume. The average loss on similar receivables over the last 10 years amounts to 2%.

In this example, the expected losses are C20m and the entity has guaranteed C12.5m. It might, therefore, appear that, as the entity has guaranteed 62.5% of all the expected losses, it has retained substantially all the risks and rewards of ownership. This is not so as the calculation cannot be done in this manner. The test looks to who absorbs variability in the asset's cash flows, rather than who has most of the expected losses. By giving a guarantee the entity has effectively retained a subordinated interest in the receivables. If the subordinated retained interest absorbs all of the likely variability in net cash flows, the entity would retain the risks and rewards of ownership and continue to recognise the receivables in their entirety. However, this is not the case in this example. Therefore, in order to perform a risk and rewards analysis, it is necessary to determine the variability in the amounts and timing of the cash flows both before and after the transfer on a present value basis. The manner in which such a determination can be made is outlined below:

- The first step is to model different scenarios of cash flows from the C1 billion receivables portfolio that reflects the variability in the amounts and timing of cash flows before the transfer as discussed in paragraph A6.8.58 above.

- For each scenario, the present value of the cash flows is calculated by using an appropriate current market interest rate as stated in paragraph A6.8.58 above.
- Probabilities are then assigned to each scenario considering all reasonably possible variability in net cash flows, with greater probability weighting given to those outcomes that are more likely to occur.
- An expected variance is then calculated that reflects the cash flows' total variability in the amounts and timing.

The above steps are repeated for cash flows that remain after the transfer.

Finally, the expected variance after the transfer is compared with the variance before the transfer to determine whether there has been a significant change in the amounts and timing of cash flows as a result of the transfer. If the change is not significant, it can be concluded that there has been no substantial transfer of the risks and rewards of ownership. If the change is significant, it can be concluded that the risks and rewards of ownership have been substantially transferred.

An illustration of the modelling discussed above is shown below. For illustrative purposes, only six scenarios are included in this example. In practice, more scenarios may be required in order to adequately model the variability in net cash flows of the asset.

Pre-transfer Scenarios	**PV of future cash flows**	**Probability %**	**Expected PV**	**Variability in PV**	**Probability weighted**	**Expected Variability**
	1	2	3 = 1*2	4 = 1- Σ3	5=2*4	
Low loss	990,000	15.00	148,500	11,050	1,658	1,658
Normal loss and few pre-payments	985,000	20.00	197,000	6,050	1,210	1,210
Normal loss	980,000	35.00	343,000	1,050	368	368
Normal loss and many pre-payments	970,000	25.00	242,500	-8,950	-2,238	2,238
High loss	960,000	4.50	43,200	-18,950	-853	853
Very high loss	950,000	0.50	4,750	-28,950	-145	145
		100.00	978,950	-38,700	0	6,472

Post-transfer Scenarios	**PV of future cash flows**	**Probability %**	**Expected PV**	**Variability in PV**	**Probability weighted**	**Expected Variability**
	1	2	3 = 1*2	4 = 1- Σ3	5=2*4	
Low loss	10,000	15.00	1,500	-2,125	-319	319
Normal loss and few pre-payments	12,500	20.00	2,500	375	75	75
Normal loss	12,500	35.00	4,375	375	131	131
Normal loss and many pre-payments	12,500	25.00	3,125	375	94	94

High loss	12,500	4.50	563	375	17	17
Very high loss	12,500	0.50	63	375	2	2
		100.00	12,125	-250	0	638

The relative variability retained after the transfer = 638/6,470 = 9.86%. This implies that the entity has transferred substantially all of the risks and rewards of ownership of the receivables.

It should be noted that, in the above example, the cash flows' present value with their associated probabilities constitutes a discrete random variable, for which it is possible to derive an absolute value for the variability as indicated above. A better measure would be to calculate the variance. However, in this example, that would also produce the same conclusion. In practice, however, the calculation may not be so simple and specialist advice should be taken.

A6.8.61 IAS 39 provides the following examples of transactions that transfer substantially all the risks and rewards of ownership:

- An unconditional sale of a financial asset. This is the most obvious example.
- A sale of a financial asset together with an option to repurchase the financial asset at its fair value at the time of repurchase. In this situation, the entity is no longer exposed to any value risk (potential for gain and exposure to loss) on the transferred asset which is borne by the buyer. The ability for the seller to buy the asset back at its fair value at the date of repurchase is economically no different from buying a new asset.
- A sale of a financial asset together with a put or call option that is deeply out-of- the-money (that is, an option that is so far out-of-the-money it is highly unlikely to go into the money before expiry). In this situation, the seller has no substantial risks and rewards, because there is no real possibility that the call or put option will be exercised. As the option has little or no value, such a sale is economically little different from an unconditional sale.
- The sale of a fully proportionate share of the cash flows from a larger financial asset in an arrangement that meets the pass-through conditions discussed in paragraph A6.8.44 above.

[IAS 39 paras 21, AG39].

A6.8.62 If an entity determines that, as a result of the transfer, it has transferred substantially all the risks and rewards of ownership of the transferred asset, it does not recognise the transferred asset again in a future period, unless it re-acquires the transferred asset in a new transaction. [IAS 39 para AG41].

Determine whether substantially all the risks and rewards of ownership have been retained

A6.8.63 If the entity retains substantially all the risks and rewards of ownership of the asset, the entity continues to recognise the asset as shown in step 7 in the diagram in paragraph A6.8.30. [IAS 39 para 20(b)].

A6.8.64 IAS 39 provides the following examples of transactions where substantially all the risks and rewards of ownership has been retained:

- A sale and repurchase transaction where the repurchase price is a fixed price or the sale price plus a lender's return (for example, a repo or securities lending agreement).
- A sale of a financial asset together with a total return swap that transfers the market risk exposure through the swap back to the entity.
- A sale of a financial asset together with a deep in-the-money put or call option (that is an option that is so far in-the-money that it is highly unlikely to go out-of- the-money before expiry).
- A sale of short-term receivables in which the entity guarantees to compensate the transferee for all credit losses which are likely to occur.

[IAS 39 para AG 40].

A6.8.65 In the above examples it is obvious, without a numerical calculation, that the entity has retained substantially all the risks and rewards of ownership. Where it is unclear whether the entity has retained (or transferred) substantially all the risks and rewards of ownership, it must evaluate the variability of the transferred asset's cash flows before and after the transfer as discussed in paragraph A6.8.57 above. If this comparison shows that the entity's exposure to the variability in the present value of the future net cash flows (discounted at the appropriate current market interest rate) from the financial asset does not change *significantly* as a result of the transfer, the entity is regarded as having retained substantially all the risks and rewards of the asset's ownership. [IAS 39 para 21].

Perform control analysis

Determine whether control of the asset has been retained

A6.8.66 If the entity (transferor) has neither transferred nor retained substantially all the risks and rewards of ownership of the transferred financial asset – in other words it has retained some risks and rewards but not substantially all of them – it is in a middle ground in which the risks and rewards analysis does not provide a clear answer. Hence, the transferor has to determine whether it has retained control of the asset or whether the transferee has control (see step 8 in the diagram in para A6.8.30 above).

- If the transferor has not retained control, it must derecognise the financial asset and recognise separately as assets or liabilities any rights and obligations created or retained in the transfer.
- If the entity has retained control, it must continue to recognise the financial asset to the extent of its continuing involvement in the financial asset (see para A6.8.73).

[IAS 39 para 20(c)].

A6.8.67 Control, in this context does not have the same meaning as in IAS 27, 'Consolidated and separate financial statements', that is, the power to govern the financial and operating policies of an entity so as to obtain benefits from its activities. In the context of derecognition, control is based on whether the transferee has the *practical ability* to sell the transferred asset. This looks to what the transferee can do with the asset, not what the transferor can do. This is a different concept of control that tries to identify whether the transferor continues to be exposed to the variability in the cash flows of the particular asset that was the subject of the transfer as opposed to having risks of a general nature, similar to a derivative. Therefore, where the transferee has the practical ability to sell the transferred asset, it follows that the transferee has control over the asset and the entity has lost control. On the other hand, if the transferee does not have the practical ability to sell the transferred asset, then the entity has retained control of the transferred asset. [IAS 39 paras 23, AG42].

Practical ability to sell the transferred asset

A6.8.68 IAS 39 explains that the transferee has the 'practical ability' to sell the transferred asset if:

- the transferee can sell the asset in its entirety to an unrelated third party; and
- the transferee is able to exercise that ability *unilaterally* and *without imposing additional restrictions.*

The above conditions should be evaluated by considering what the transferee is able to do in practice, not what contractual rights it has with respect to the transferred asset (or indeed what contractual prohibition exists).

[IAS 39 paras 23, AG43].

A6.8.69 In the context of the first condition above, the transferee will have the practical ability to sell the transferred asset if there is an active market in that asset, because the transferee could repurchase the transferred asset in the market if it needs to return the asset to the entity. [IAS 39 para AG42]. For example, the transferor may transfer a security with an option attached that allows the entity to repurchase it from the transferee at some future date. If the security is one in which an active market exists, the transferee may well sell the security to a third party, knowing that it will be easy to obtain a replacement asset and fulfil its obligation if the transferor exercises the option. As the concern here is with what the transferee is able to do in practice, rather than what is prohibited in the contract, it is important that such an active market exists. The fact that the transferee may be unlikely to sell the transferred asset is of no relevance as long as it has the practical ability to do so. Similarly, if the transferee has a contractual right to dispose of the transferred asset, that right will have little practical effect if there is no market for the transferred asset. [IAS 39 para AG43(a)]. Consequently, such a contractual right in such circumstances does not mean that the transferee has obtained control.

A6.8.70 In the context of the second condition above, the transferee will not be able to exercise its ability 'unilaterally' if it cannot do so freely. For example, if the terms of the transfer require the transferee to obtain the transferor's consent, which consent can be withheld without reason, and that restriction is effective in practice, the transferee does not have a unilateral ability. On the other hand, if the transferor's consent is needed but it cannot reasonably be withheld, the transferee may still have the ability to transfer the asset unilaterally. Similarly, if the transferee is able to dispose of the asset independently of the actions of others, it has a unilateral ability. [IAS 39 para AG43(b)(i)].

A6.8.71 The transferee must also be able to exercise its ability to transfer the asset freely to a third party 'without having to impose additional restrictions' or 'strings' to the transfer. For example, if the transferor has a call option over the transferred asset (or component thereof) and there is a market for such an asset but it is thinly traded, the transferee is likely to be able to transfer the asset (or component) to a third party without fear of defaulting on the call option on the original transfer only by attaching a similar option to the second transfer. Similarly, if the transferor has imposed obligations on the transferee concerning the servicing of a loan asset, the transferee would need to attach a similar provision to any transfer that it makes to a third party. Such 'additional restrictions' or 'strings' impede the asset's free transfer and fail the 'practical ability' to sell test.

A6.8.72 In some situations, conditions such as a put option or a guarantee attached to the original transfer may be so valuable to the transferee that the transferee would not, in practice, sell the transferred asset to a third party without attaching a similar option, guarantee, or other restrictive conditions. In such situations, the transferee has effectively obtained two assets: the original asset that is the subject of the transfer and the put option or the guarantee. Selling the transferred asset on its own invalidates the remaining asset, since the transferee immediately loses any ability to realise its value. In the absence of an active market, the transferee will only be able to realise the asset's value by selling a similar guarantee or put option with the assets. In practice, therefore, the transferee would either sell the asset only with these additional restrictions attached, or would hold the transferred asset so as to obtain payments under the guarantee or put option. Under these circumstances, as the transferee is constrained from selling the asset without attaching additional restrictions, the 'practical ability' to sell test fails with the result that control of the transferred asset is retained by the transferor. [IAS 39 para AG44].

Continuing involvement in transferred asset

A6.8.73 Where an entity determines that it has neither retained nor transferred substantially all the risk and rewards of ownership of a financial asset, and retains control of that asset, the entity continues to recognise the asset to the extent of its continuing involvement. Continuing involvement reflects the entity's continuing exposure to the risks and rewards of the financial asset and that this exposure is not related to the entire asset, but is limited in amount. Therefore, continuing involvement will apply to those transfers of financial assets that involve a sharing, rather than a substantial transfer of the risks and rewards. Continuing involvement is discussed further from paragraph A6.8.127.

Practical application of the derecognition criteria

A6.8.74 Having discussed the criteria for derecognition, it is necessary to consider how they can be applied to various types of transfers of financial assets that are often found in practice. Such transfers include repurchase agreements and stock lending agreements, factoring arrangements, securitisation transactions, loan transfers and transfers involving derivatives. Descriptions of these common types of transfers and the consequences of applying the derecognition criteria are considered below. The accounting treatment of transfers that qualify for derecognition, those that fail derecognition and those that continue to be recognised to the extent of the continuing involvement are considered from paragraph A6.8.99 below.

Repurchase and stock lending agreements

A6.8.75 Repurchase agreements, commonly referred to as 'repos', are transactions involving the legal sale of a financial asset with a simultaneous agreement to repurchase it at a specified price at a fixed future date. In a typical repurchase agreement, an entity might sell a security such as a government bond to a third party in return for a cash consideration that is then reinvested in other assets that earn a return. At the specified date, the transferor repurchases that security. Financial institutions and other entities normally enter into these agreements because they provide liquidity and the opportunity to earn excess returns on the collateral. The main features of such agreements will usually be:

- The sale price – this may be the market value at the date of sale or another agreed price.

- The repurchase price – this may be fixed at the outset, vary with the period for which the asset is held by the buyer, or be the market price at the time of repurchase.

- The nature of the repurchase agreement – this may be an unconditional commitment for both parties, a call option exerciseable by the seller, a put option exerciseable by the buyer or a combination of put and call options.

- Other provisions – these may include, amongst others, the term of the agreement (overnight, short-term or longer), the buyer's ability to return a similar but not identical security to that which was sold; the buyer's ability to sell the security to a third party, the seller retaining access to any increase in to the asset's value (subject to the buyer receiving a lender's return) from a future sale to a third party and the seller providing any protection against loss through the operation of guarantees.

A6.8.76 Entities may also enter into stock lending (sometimes referred to as securities lending) transactions. These transactions are initiated by broker-dealers and other financial institutions to cover a short sale or a customer's failure to deliver securities sold. In a typical stock lending agreement, the transferor/lender transfers a security to the transferee/borrower for a short period of time. The borrower is generally required to provide 'collateral' to the lender, commonly cash but sometimes other securities or a standby letter of credit, with a value slightly higher than the value of the security borrowed. If the collateral is cash, the lender earns a return and if it is other than cash, the lender receives a fee. At a specified date, the borrower returns the security to the lender.

A6.8.77 Although the motivation to enter into a securities lending transaction is different from a repurchase agreement and the transactions may differ in form and sometimes risk protection, they are similar in substance. IAS 39, therefore, does not distinguish between the two types in determining whether the transferred asset qualifies for derecognition. [IAS 39 para AG 51(a)-(c)].

A6.8.78 The application of the derecognition principles to repurchase and stock lending transactions will obviously depend upon the transaction's nature and specific characteristics. However, some of the typical features that are found in such transactions and how they should be evaluated for derecognition purposes are considered below.

Requirement for a transfer

A6.8.78.1 In repurchase and stock lending agreements there is typically a legal sale of the underlying assets. Hence, the transferor has transferred the contractual rights to receive the cash flows of the financial assets and there is a transfer that meets IAS 39 paragraph 18(a) (step 4 in the diagram in 6.8.30 = yes).

Repurchase price

A6.8.79 A repurchase agreement will require the transferor to repurchase the transferred asset at a particular price. Such price may be fixed at the outset or be the market price at the time of the repurchase. Depending on the pricing arrangement, the analysis would be as follows:

- If the financial asset is loaned or sold under an agreement to repurchase the transferred asset at fair value at the date of repurchase, the transferred asset is derecognised. This is because the transferor has transferred substantially all the risk and rewards of ownership of the transferred asset (step 6 in the diagram in para A6.8.30 = Yes). [IAS 39 para AG 51(j)].

- If the financial asset is loaned or sold under an agreement to repurchase the asset at a fixed price or at a price that provides a lender's return on the sale price, the transferred asset is not derecognised. This is because the transferor retains substantially all the risk and rewards of ownership of the transferred asset (step 7 in the diagram in para A6.8.30 = Yes). [IAS 39 para AG 51(a)].

Agreement to return substantially the same asset

A6.8.80 A repurchase or stock lending agreement may require the transferor to accept back assets that are substantially the same as those initially transferred. The term 'substantially the same' is not defined in the standard. However, it is generally taken to mean that the financial assets returned or repurchased must be identical in form and type and have identical maturities and contractual interest rates, so as to provide the same rights as the asset transferred. As there is no economic difference between the asset initially transferred and the asset to be re-acquired, the analysis would be the same as indicated above.

Agreement to substitute a similar asset with equal fair value

A6.8.81 A repurchase or stock lending agreement may give the transferee the right to substitute a similar asset of equal fair value at the repurchase date. In this case, there is no economic difference in substance between returning the original asset or a similar asset of equal fair value. Depending on the repurchase price, the analysis would be identical to that discussed in the above paragraph. [IAS 39, para AG 51(c)].

Right of first refusal to repurchase at fair value

A6.8.82 If an entity sells a financial asset and retains only a right of first refusal to repurchase the transferred asset at fair value if the transferee subsequently intends to sell it, the entity derecognises the asset because it has transferred substantially all the risks and rewards of ownership (step 6 in the diagram in para A6.8.30 = Yes). [IAS 39 para AG 51(d)]. This situation is effectively no different in substance to the situation described in the first bullet point in paragraph A6.8.79 above. Although not dealt with in the standard, if the right of first refusal to repurchase the transferred asset is at a price other than the asset's fair value at the date of repurchase (for example, a price pre-determined at inception), the analysis would be similar to the transferor having a call option. This situation is described in paragraph A6.8.98.7 below.

Transferee's right to pledge

A6.8.83 A repurchase or securities lending agreement may give the transferee the right to sell or pledge the transferred asset during the term of the repurchase agreement. In this situation, if the transferor continues to recognise the asset, it should reclassify the asset on its balance sheet, for example, as a loaned asset or repurchase receivable. [IAS 39 para AG 51(a)].

A6.8.83.1 Generally, the transferee's right to sell or pledge the transferred asset effectively indicates that the transferee has control of the asset and thus if some significant risks and rewards are transferred, derecognition is appropriate. For control to pass to the transferee, the right to sell or pledge must have economic substance without any 'strings' attached, as explained in paragraphs 6.8.71 and 6.8.72 above.

Wash sales

A6.8.84 A 'wash sale' (sometimes referred to as 'bed and breakfast' transaction) is the repurchase of a financial asset shortly after it has been sold. Such a transaction involves contracting to sell the financial asset to a third party with no express contract to buy it back. Therefore, such a repurchase does not preclude derecognition provided that the original sale transaction met the derecognition requirements. In other words, the sale and the repurchase transactions are viewed as two separate transactions under IAS 39. Since the time interval between sale and repurchase can be very short, it is unlikely that the transferor would benefit or suffer from any changes in asset values. Therefore, such transactions are normally undertaken to crystallise a capital gain or capital loss for taxation purposes or to convert unrealised revaluation gains on investments into realised gains so that they can be used for distribution by way of dividends to shareholders. However, if an agreement to sell a financial asset is entered into concurrently with an agreement to repurchase the same asset at a fixed price or the sale price plus a lender's return, then the asset is not derecognised. [IAS 39 para AG 51(e)].

Security given as collateral

A6.8.85 In the sale and repurchase agreements discussed above, the sale price was assumed to be satisfied in cash. A variant often found in practice is that the sale consideration is satisfied by transfer of another security rather than in cash. For example, assume that entity A sells security X subject to a repurchase agreement to entity B. The sale consideration is met by entity B transferring security Y. Such a transaction involves two transfers and two transferors so the requirement relating to the accounting treatment relating to transfers of financial assets will need to be applied twice – transfer of security X by entity A and transfer of security Y by entity B.

A6.8.86 Each transferor will first apply the derecognition criteria discussed above to its own security – a risks and rewards approach first followed by the control approach if the risks and rewards approach is found not to be conclusive. It will then apply the derecognition criteria to the asset received as consideration from the point of view of the counterparty. If the counterparty would continue to recognise the asset under IAS 39 it is not recognised by the entity. [IAS 39 para AG50].

Factoring arrangements

A6.8.87 A factoring transaction involves a transferor transferring its rights to some or all of the cash collected from some financial asset (usually receivables) to a third party (the factor) in exchange for a cash payment. Factoring of receivables is a well established method of obtaining finance, sales ledger administration services or protection from bad debts. Factoring arrangements may take various forms, but some of the principal features are as follows:

- The cash payment – this may be fixed at the outset or vary according to the actual period the receivables remain unpaid (slow payment risk). Sometimes the factor may provide a credit facility that allows the seller to draw up to a fixed percentage of the face value of the receivables transferred.
- The nature of the agreement – may be a clean sale without recourse (the transferor has no obligations to make good any shortfall on the transferred assets) or may be more complex with various recourse provisions.
- Other provisions – these may include, amongst others, any representations or warranties provided by the transferor regarding the receivables' quality/condition at the point of transfer, servicing arrangements (whether the transferor will continue to manage the receivables or management will be taken over by the factor), or any credit protection facility (insurance cover) provided by the factor that may limit or eliminate the extent to which the factor has recourse to the seller.

Factoring without recourse

A6.8.88 In a non-recourse factoring arrangement, the transferor does not provide any guarantee about the receivables' performance. In other words, the transferor assumes no obligations whatsoever to repay any sums received from the factor regardless of the timing or the level of collections from the underlying debts. In that situation, the entity has transferred substantially all the risks and rewards of ownership of the receivables and derecognises the receivables in their entirety (step 6 in the diagram in para A6.8.30 = yes). The accounting treatment of receivables subject to non-recourse factoring is considered in the second example in paragraph A6.8.102 below. In some situations, the transferor may continue to service the receivables for which it may receive a fee. The accounting treatment for a sale of receivables with servicing retained that is not subject to recourse and when the transferor has no residual interest in the receivables is considered in paragraph A6.8.109 below.

Requirement for a transfer

A6.8.88.1 In most factoring arrangements, the factored receivables are assigned to the factor. In most cases, the transferor has transferred the contractual rights to receive the financial asset's cash flows and there is a transfer that meets IAS 39 paragraph 18(a) (step 4 in the diagram in 6.8.30 = yes). However, this may not be the case if there are three party offset rights – see paragraph A6.8.42.1 above,

Factoring with recourse

A6.8.89 In a factoring of receivables with recourse, the transferor provides the factor with full or limited recourse. The transferor is obligated under the terms of the recourse provision to make payments to the factor or to repurchase receivables sold under certain circumstances. These recourse provisions may take the form of guarantees by the seller for non-payment (bad debt credit risk) up to a certain limit or full default amount, a call option by the transferor (for example, to repurchase defaulted receivables) or a put option by the factor for any defaulted assets. In some cases, they result in the transferor retaining substantially all the risks and rewards of ownership of the receivables with the effect that the entity continues to recognise the factored receivables (step 7 in the diagram in para A6.8.30 = yes). In other cases, the recourse provisions result in the transferor retaining some, but not substantially all, risks and rewards, in which case the control test must be considered. In most factoring arrangements that are subject to recourse, the transferee is precluded from selling the receivables, which means that the transferor continues to control them (step 8 in the diagram in para A6.8.30 = yes) and continuing involvement accounting may apply. Examples dealing with the accounting treatment of receivables subject to factoring with recourse can be found under paragraphs 6.8.120 and 6.8.133 below.

Securitisations

A6.8.90 Securitisation is a method of raising finance, first used by originators of mortgage loans, through a sale of a block or pool of loans, typically to a subsidiary or a thinly capitalised vehicle specially set up for the purpose — a special purpose entity (SPE). The SPE finances the purchase by issuing loan notes or other marketable debt instruments to outside investors that are often secured on the SPE's assets. This process is known as securitisation and is also referred to as asset backed finance. Also other pools of debts, such as credit card receivables, leases, hire purchase loans and trade debtors are securitised in a similar way to mortgages. This kind of SPE structure, that isolates the assets legally from the transferor and its creditors ('ring-fence') to avoid any consequences from bankruptcy, enables the originator to raise funds at competitive rates. The following outlines a typical securitisation transaction:

- The assets to be securitised are transferred by an originator/transferor to an SPE for an immediate cash payment.
- The SPE finances the transfer by issuing loan notes to investors. The SPE's shares or residual beneficial interests, if any, are usually held by a party other than the originator (charitable trusts have often been used for this purpose). In addition, the major financial and operating policies are usually predetermined to a greater or lesser extent by the agreements that establish the securitisation (in other words, the SPE operates on so-called 'autopilot').
- Because the SPE's business activities are constrained and its ability to incur debt is limited, it faces the risk of a shortfall of cash below what it is obligated to pay investors. Arrangements are, therefore, made to protect the

investors from losses occurring on the assets by a process termed 'credit enhancement'.

A commonly used form of credit enhancement occurs *via* the issue of subordinated debt (perhaps to the transferor) and other forms of equity-like claims that have the effect of dividing the risk of loss on the underlying assets ('tranching').

Credit enhancement may take a variety of other forms, including over-collateralisation (the aggregate value of assets transferred exceeds the consideration provided by the SPE), third party guarantee of the issuer's obligations (securities backed by a letter of credit), or third party credit insurance. All the arrangements provide a cushion against losses up to some limit.

- The transferor is often granted rights to cash remaining from the transferred assets after payment of amounts due on the loan notes and other expenses of the issuer. These rights are generally intended, at least in part, to compensate the transferor for assuming some of the risk of credit or other losses. The mechanisms used to achieve this include servicing or other fees, deferred sale consideration, 'super interest' on amounts owed to the transferor (for example, subordinated debt), dividend payments and swap payments.

- Cash accumulation from the assets (for example, from mortgage redemptions) is either used to redeem the loan notes or reinvested in other more liquid assets until the loan notes are repaid. Any surplus cash usually accrues to the transferor as noted above.

- The transferor may continue to service the assets (for example, collect amounts from the borrower, set interest rates, etc) for which it may receive a 'servicing fee'. Often, the surplus cash mentioned above is extracted by an adjustment to the service fee.

A6.8.91 In many situations, the SPE will be no more than an extension of the originator rather than an economic entity in its own right and, therefore, will be consolidated under SIC 12 (step 1 in the diagram in para A6.8.30). In that situation, the right to receive the cash flows from the asset will remain with the group (step 4 in the diagram in para A6.8.30 = no). However, the group may assume an obligation to pass-through the cash flows from the transferred asset to the investors that meets all the three conditions set out in paragraph A6.8.44 above (step 5 in the diagram in para A6.8.30 = yes). Nevertheless, the group may retain substantially all the risk and rewards of ownership of the securitised assets, because of credit enhancement measures described above. The IASB recognises that many securitisations may fail to qualify for derecognition either because one or more of the three pass-through conditions are not met, as in securitisation arrangements involving 'revolving structures' (see paragraph A6.8.50 above) or because the entity has retained substantially all the risks and rewards of ownership. [IAS 39 para BC 63].

Subordinated retained interests and credit guarantees

A6.8.92 As discussed in paragraph A6.8.90 above, an entity may provide the transferee with credit enhancement by subordinating some or all of its interest retained in the transferred asset. Alternatively, an entity may provide the transferee with credit enhancement in the form of a credit guarantee that could be unlimited or limited to a specified amount. Although such credit enhancement techniques are often used in securitisation transactions, they could also be used in other forms of transfers of financial assets.

A6.8.92.1 The provision of a credit guarantee by the entity will cause the pass-through tests of IAS 39 to be failed (see step 5 in the diagram in para A6.8.30) and, therefore, will prevent derecognition for transactions in which the pass-through tests are applied. This is because any payments made by the transferor under the guarantee are not cash flows from the original asset and, therefore, the existence of a credit guarantee fails the condition in paragraph 19(a) of IAS 39 (see further para A6.8.44 above). However, the retention of a subordinated interest in the transferred asset does not, in itself, cause the pass-through tests to be failed as it does not require the entity to make payments other than out of collections on the transferred assets. However, the retention of a subordinated interest is likely to result in the transferor retaining some of the risks and rewards of the asset.

A6.8.92.2 In some securitisation structures an entity may retain an interest in the transferred assets in the form of the right to any 'excess spread'. The excess spread is generally any cash left in the SPE after paying the noteholders their interest and principal and after any costs incurred by the SPE. Again the retention of such an interest does not cause the pass-through test to be failed where the SPE is consolidated, but is likely to result in the transferor retaining at least some of the risks and rewards of the assets.

A6.8.93 If an entity has either transferred the contractual rights of the asset or assumed an obligation to pay the cash flows to others that meets the pass-through tests, but still retains substantially all the risks and rewards of ownership of the transferred asset, the asset continues to be recognised in its entirety (step 7 in the diagram in para A6.8.30 = yes). However, if the entity retains some, but not substantially all, of the risks and rewards of ownership and has retained control (step 8 in the diagram in para A6.8.30 = yes), derecognition is precluded to the extent of the amount of cash or other assets that the entity could be required to pay under the subordination or credit guarantee agreement. [IAS 39 para AG 51(n)]. The accounting treatment of continuing involvement through a guarantee is considered in paragraph A6.8.133 below. The accounting treatment of a subordinated retained interest is considered in paragraph A6.8.123 below.

Removal of accounts provisions

A6.8.94 Securitisations are sometimes carried out on terms that contain a provision that enables a transferor to call back some of the assets securitised at a subsequent date, subject to some restrictions. Such provisions are referred to as 'removal of accounts' provisions (ROAPs). Some ROAPs may allow the transferor unilaterally to specify the assets that may be removed; others may specify that the identification of assets for removal is done randomly or by the transferee. Such provisions are included for good business reasons. For example, the transferor may wish to protect the credit rating of a securitisation vehicle in the event of default of one of the securitised assets or may desire the ability to repurchase assets associated with operations to be discontinued or exited

A6.8.95 The ROAP described above is effectively a call option enabling the transferor to insist on a return of some of the transferred assets. This means that the transferor has retained control over the transferred assets, provided the transferee does not have the practical ability to sell the assets (which is usually the case in a securitisation). Therefore, if such a provision results in the entity neither retaining nor transferring substantially all the risks and rewards of ownership (step 8 in the diagram in para A6.8.30 = Yes), derecognition is precluded only to the extent of the amount subject to call/repurchase. For example, if the carrying amount and proceeds from the transfer of loan assets are C100,000 and any individual loan could be called back, but the aggregate amount of loans that could be repurchased could not exceed C10,000, C90,000 of the loans would qualify for derecognition. [IAS 39 para AG 51(l)].

Swaps

A6.8.95.1 In a securitisation involving fixed rate assets, the transferor may enter into an interest rate swap with the SPE. Under the swap's terms, the transferor may undertake to receive the fixed rate interest on the transferred assets and pay a variable rate to the SPE, such that the SPE can pay variable rate interest to noteholders. If the SPE does not fall to be consolidated, then such a swap would not prevent derecognition provided the payments on the swap are not conditional on payments being made on the transferred asset. [IAS 39 para AG48]. The swap may, however, result in the retention of some risks of the asset's rewards, for example, if the terms cause some slow payment risk to be retained.

A6.8.95.2 If, however, the SPE is consolidated and the pass-through tests apply, the swap would prevent derecognition (see step 5 in the diagram in para A6.8.30). This is because the swap results in the transferor having an obligation to pay amounts to the eventual recipients (investors in the notes) even if it does not collect equivalent amounts from the assets. The swap may require a net payment to the SPE (that is then passed to noteholders) if interest rates rise so that the interest due on the notes exceeds that due on the assets. Hence, the pass-through test in IAS 39 paragraph 19(a) is failed and derecognition is precluded.

Loan transfers

6.8.96 As explained in paragraph A6.8.40, some kinds of financial assets cannot be sold in the same way as other assets. However, they can be transferred to third parties in return for an immediate cash payment. The transfer may be of the whole of a single loan, part of a loan, or of all or part of a portfolio of similar loans. The methods by which the benefits and risks of loans can be transferred vary between jurisdictions. Common methods include those described below.

- Novation

  Under a novation, the rights and obligations of the original lender (the transferor) under the loan agreement are cancelled and replaced by new ones whose main effect is to change the lender's identity. The transferor is released from its obligations to the borrower.

  A novation, therefore, will result in the transfer of the contractual rights to receive the financial asset's cash flows. Therefore, in the absence of any side agreements, such as a guarantee or other form of recourse arrangement, a forward purchase arrangement or option, the transferor will derecognise the loan in its entirety.

- Assignment

  Under an assignment, the original lender's (the transferor's) rights to the future cash flows under the loan agreement, but not obligations (for example, warranty obligations to repair faulty goods) are transferred to the third party (the assignee). There are generally two types of assignments – assignments where the lender is required to give notice to the borrower (in some jurisdictions these are known as legal or open assignments) and assignments where no notice is required to be given to the borrower (in some jurisdictions these are known as equitable or silent assignments).

  Where the lender is required to give notice in writing to the borrower, and in the absence of any side agreements between the transferor and the transferee, the transferee normally acquires a direct legal claim on the future cash flows under the loan agreement.

  Where notice is not required to be given to the borrower, as the borrower is not aware that the lender has transferred its rights to the cash flows to another party, there is doubt as to whether the transferee has obtained the unconditional contractual rights to the cash flows of the transferred asset. In general, whether the contractual rights to the cash flows have been unconditionally transferred under such anassignment would depend on the law of the country that governs the assignment.

  Both types of assignment are subject to equitable rights arising before notice is received. For example, a right of set-off held by the borrower against the lender will be good against the assignee for any transactions undertaken before the borrower receives notice of the assignment.

  Assignments may or may not leave the transferor with continuing involvement in the loans depending on whether there are any residual interests, recourse provisions, buyback provisions, etc. The issues that arise in assignments are very similar to debt factoring and securitisations, most of which involve an assignment.

- Sub-participation

  Under a sub-participation, the lender enters into a non-recourse back-to-back arrangement with a third party (the sub-participant) and, in exchange for a cash receipt of an amount equal to the whole or fully proportionate part of the loan, passes on the cash flows (both interest and principal) collected on the loan to the sub-participant. Legally, all the contractual rights and obligations remain with the transferor.

  Like assignments, sub-participation may or may not leave the transferor with continuing involvement in the loans depending on whether there are any residual interests, recourse provisions, buyback provisions, etc. Provided the sub-participation meets all the three pass-through conditions discussed in paragraph A6.8.44 above, there is no recourse to the transferor and the transferor does not retain any significant risks and rewards of ownership of the loans, derecognition is appropriate.

Loan syndications

A6.8.97 Sometimes, a single lender may not be able to fund a large loan required by a borrower. In those situations, it is quite common for a group of lenders to fund the loan jointly. This is usually accomplished by a syndication under which several lenders share in lending to a single borrower, but each syndicate member lends a specific amount to the borrower and has the right to repayment from the borrower. Such a loan syndication is not a transfer of financial assets. Accordingly, each lender in the syndication should account for the amounts it is owed by the borrower.

A6.8.98 In some loan syndications, the lead lender may advance funds to the borrower and transfer a fully proportionate share of the loan to different lenders. The borrower makes repayments directly to a lead lender who then distributes the collections to the other syndicate lenders in proportion to the amount lent. This situation is no different in substance to a sub-participation discussed above. Derecognition of the loans transferred to the different lenders would be appropriate if the lead lender is simply functioning as an agent, all the syndicate lenders have fully proportionate shares of the total lending and all the pass-through conditions and risks and rewards conditions are met.

Transfers involving derivatives

A6.8.98.1 Transfers of financial assets often include derivatives, either explicitly or implicitly. Common derivatives that are found in transfer arrangements are call and put options, forward sale or repurchase contracts and swap agreements. Derivative instruments normally require exercise by one of the parties to the contract. In some instances, exercise of the derivative may be automatic, for example, where a transferor enters into a forward agreement to repurchase a transferred asset at a pre-determined price. In other instances, the exercise may be conditional on the occurrence of a particular event, for example, where the transferee has the right to put back to the transferor receivables that remain uncollectible.

A6.8.98.2 In some circumstances, the existence of derivatives may not prevent derecognition, for example, if the pre-determined price mentioned in the first example above is set at market price at repurchase date. In other circumstances, derivatives may well prevent a transferor from derecognising a financial asset, thereby precluding sale treatment. Derivatives may also constrain a transferee's practical ability to sell the transferred asset, even if there is no legal constraint, with the result that the transferor retains control over the transferred asset. Any derivative that serves as an impediment to the transferee from realising the economic benefits inherent in the transferred asset should be carefully analysed to determine whether or not the transferor has retained control of the transferred asset.

A6.8.98.3 Where the presence of a derivative prevents a transferor from derecognising a financial asset, the transferor's contractual rights or obligations related to the transfer are not accounted for separately as derivatives if recognising both the derivative and either the transferred asset or the liability arising from the transfer would result in recognising the same rights or obligations twice. [IAS 39 para AG 49].

A6.8.98.4 It follows that the identification and evaluation of such derivatives is crucial to the derecognition analysis. Examples of transfers involving derivatives and the implications of the presence of the derivatives as regards derecognition are considered below. The accounting for transfers including derivatives that result in continued recognition to the extent of the entity's continuing involvement in the transferred asset are considered from paragraph A6.8.134 below.

Transfers subject to deep out-of-the-money option

A6.8.98.5 A financial asset that is transferred subject only to a deep out-of-the-money put option held by the transferee or a deep out-of-the-money call option held by the transferor is derecognised. As a deep-out-of-the-money option is very unlikely to become in-the-money at the exercise date, the transferor is deemed to have transferred substantially all the risks and rewards of ownership (step 6 in the diagram in para A6.8.30 = yes). [IAS 39 para AG 51(g)].

A6.8.98.6 If, due to subsequent events or changes in market conditions, it becomes probable that a deep out-of-the-money put or call option is likely to be exercised at the exercise date, the change in the option's probability being exercised would not result in the re-recognition of the financial asset that has previously been derecognised. This is consistent with the requirements in the standard that where an entity determines that, as a result of the transfer, it has transferred substantially all the risks and rewards of ownership, the entity does not recognise the transferred asset again in a future period, unless it re-acquires the transferred asset in a new transaction. [IAS 39 para AG 41]. Instead, the option would be accounted for as a derivative at fair value with the increase in its fair value reflected in profit or loss.

Transfer of readily obtainable assets subject to at-the-money call option

A6.8.98.7 A financial asset that is readily obtainable in the market and transferred subject to the transferor holding a call option that is neither deeply in-the-money nor deeply out-of-the-money is derecognised. This is because the entity has neither retained nor transferred substantially all the risks and rewards of ownership and has not retained control (step 8 in the diagram in para A6.8.30 = no). [IAS 39 para AG 51(h)]. Although the option's existence means that the transferor has a continuing involvement in the asset, the fact that the asset is readily obtainable in the market means that the call option has no practical effect in creating any constraints on the transferee's practical ability to sell the asset. This is because if the transferred asset has been sold by the transferee and the transferor exercises the call option, the transferee will be able to fulfil its obligation by purchasing a replacement asset from the market. Therefore, the transferor retains no control over the transferred asset and derecognition of the transferred asset is appropriate. The transferor will account for the call option as a derivative at fair value with changes in fair value reflected in profit or loss.

A6.8.98.8 Although not specifically dealt with in the standard, a readily obtainable financial asset that is transferred subject to the transferee holding a put option that is neither deeply in-the-money nor deeply out-of-the-money at the date of transfer is similarly derecognised for the reasons stated above. In this situation, if the transferee decides to exercise its rights under the put, the transferee would be able to meet its obligation by purchasing the asset from the market.

Transfer of assets subject to a fair value put or call option or a forward repurchase agreement

A6.8.98.9 A transfer of a financial asset that is subject only to a put or call option or a forward repurchase agreement that has an exercise or repurchase price equal to the fair value of the financial asset at the time of repurchase results in derecognition, because of the transfer of substantially all the risks and rewards of ownership. [IAS 39 para AG 51(j)].

Transfer of assets subject to interest-rate swaps

A6.8.98.10 An entity may transfer a fixed rate financial asset to a transferee and enter into an interest rate swap with the transferee to receive a fixed interest rate and pay a variable interest rate based on a notional amount that is equal to the principal amount of the transferred financial asset. The interest rate swap does not preclude derecognition of the transferred asset provided the payments on the swap are not conditional on payments being made on the transferred asset. [IAS 39 AG51(p)].

Call and put options that are deeply in-the-money

A6.8.98.11 If a transferred financial asset can be called back by the transferor and the call option is deeply in-the-money, the transfer does not qualify for derecognition. This is because the transferor has retained substantially all the risks and rewards of the asset's ownership by virtue of the fact that the call option is so valuable that its exercise appears virtually assured at inception. As explained in paragraph A6.8.98.3, a call option retained by the transferor that prevents the transfer from being accounted for as a sale is not separately recognised as a derivative asset. The accounting treatment is similar to sale and repurchase transactions considered in paragraph A6.8.119 below. Similarly, if the financial asset can be put back by the transferee and the put option is deeply in-the-money, the transfer does not qualify for derecognition because the transferor has retained substantially all the risks and rewards of ownership. Again the put option is not recognised separately, as to do so would result in double counting the same obligation. [IAS 39 para AG 51(f].

Total return swaps

A6.8.98.12 An entity may sell a financial asset to a transferee and enter into a total return swap with the transferee, whereby all of the cash flows from the underlying asset plus any increases and less any decreases in the underlying asset's fair value are remitted to the entity in exchange for a fixed or variable rate payment. In such a case, derecognition of all of the asset is prohibited. [IAS 39 para AG 51(o)].

Accounting treatment

A6.8.99 The accounting treatment can be fairly complex, particularly in respect of transfers in which the entity (transferor) has continuing involvement in the transferred asset.

Transfers that qualify for derecognition

A6.8.100 Where an entity determines that a transfer of a financial asset qualifies as a transfer and qualifies for derecognition because either:

- the entity has transferred substantially all the risks and rewards of ownership of the asset (step 6 in the diagram in para A6.8.30 = yes); or
- the entity has neither transferred nor retained substantially all the risks and rewards of ownership of the asset, and no longer retains control of the asset (step 8 in the diagram in para A6.8.30 = no),

the transferred asset is derecognised in its entirety and any new financial assets obtained, financial liabilities assumed and any servicing obligations are recognised at fair value. [IAS 39 para 25]. It should be noted that the phrase *"in its entirety"* includes part of a financial asset (or part of a group of similar financial assets) to which the derecognition tests have been applied as explained in paragraph A6.8.33 above.

6.8.101 On derecognition of a financial asset in its entirety, the difference between the carrying amount and the sum of:

- the consideration received (including any new assets obtained less any new liabilities assumed); and
- any cumulative gain or loss that had been recognised in equity;

is recognised in profit or loss. The recycling of the cumulative gain or loss that had been recognised in equity occurs on the derecognition of an available-for-sale financial asset.

[IAS 39 para 26].

A6.8.102 There may also be instances where, following the financial asset's derecognition, a new financial asset is obtained or a new financial liability is assumed. As noted above, any new asset is part of the proceeds of sale. Any liability assumed, even if it is related to the transferred asset, is a reduction of the sales proceeds.

Example 1 – Derecognition of whole of a financial asset in its entirety

Entity A holds a small number of shares in entity B. The shares are classified as available-for-sale. On 31 March 20X6, the shares' fair value is C120 and the cumulative gain recognised in equity is C20. On the same day, entity B is acquired by entity C, a large quoted entity. As a result, entity A receives shares in entity C with a fair value of C130.

In this situation, the transfer of the shares in entity B qualifies for derecognition in their entirety as the entity no longer retains any risk and rewards of ownership. In addition, the transfer results in entity A obtaining a new financial asset, that is, shares in entity C that should be recognised at fair value as stated in paragraph A6.8.100 above. The gain on disposal, calculated in accordance with paragraph A6.8.101 above, is as follows:

	C
Proceeds received (fair value of cash or other securities received)	130
+ Fair value of any new financial asset acquired in the transfer	–
- Fair value of any new liability assumed in the transfer	–
Net proceeds	130
Carrying amount of the whole financial asset transferred	(120)
Gain or (loss) on derecognition	10
Amount recycled from equity	20
Gain or (loss) recognised in profit or loss	30

The accounting entries to record the transfer are shown below:

	Dr	Cr
	C	C
Fair value of shares in entity C acquired	130	
Carrying value of shares in entity B disposed of		120
Equity ('recycling' of cumulative gain)	20	
Gain on disposal		30

Example 2 – Factoring without recourse

Entity A (the transferor) holds a portfolio of receivables with a carrying value of C1m. It enters into a factoring arrangement with entity B (the transferee) under which it transfers the portfolio to entity B in exchange for C900,000 of cash. Entity B will service the loans after their transfer and debtors will pay amounts due directly to entity B. Entity A has no obligations whatsoever to repay any sums received from the factor and has no rights to any additional sums regardless of the timing or the level of collection from the underlying debts.

In this example, entity A has transferred its rights to receive the cash flows from the asset *via* an assignment to entity B (step 4 in the diagram in para A6.8.30 = yes). Furthermore, as entity B has no recourse to entity A for either slow payment risk or credit risk, entity A has transferred substantially all the risks and rewards of ownership of the portfolio (step 6 in the diagram in para A6.8.30 = yes). Hence, entity A derecognises the entire portfolio. The difference between the carrying value of C1m and cash received of C900,000, that is, the entire discount of C100,000 is recognised immediately as a financing cost in profit or loss.

The accounting that would apply if entity A continued to service the receivables is dealt with from paragraph A6.8.106 below.

Transferred asset is part of a larger asset

A6.8.103 Where an entity transfers an asset that is part of a larger financial asset (for example, when an entity transfers interest only cash flows that are part of a debt instrument), and the part transferred qualifies for derecognition in its entirety, the previous carrying value of the larger financial asset is allocated between the part that continues to be recognised and the part that is derecognised. The allocation is based on the relative fair values of those parts at the date of transfer. For this purpose, a retained servicing asset should be treated as part that continues to be recognised. The difference between the carrying amount allocated to the part derecognised and the sum of:

- the consideration received for the part derecognised (including any new assets obtained less any new liabilities assumed); and
- any cumulative gain or loss allocated to it that had been recognised in equity;

is recognised in profit or loss. Any cumulative gain or loss that had been recognised in equity is allocated between the part that continues to be recognised and the part that is derecognised, based on the relative fair values of those parts. The recycling of the cumulative gain or loss that had been recognised in equity arises on derecognition of an available-for-sale financial asset.

[IAS 39 para 27].

6.8.104 In making an allocation of the previous carrying amount of a larger financial asset between the part transferred and the part that continues to be recognised, it is necessary to determine the fair value of the part that continues to be recognised. When the entity has a history of selling parts similar to the part that continues to be recognised or other market transactions exist for such parts, recent prices of actual transactions provide the best estimate of its fair value. When there are no price quotes or recent market transactions to support the fair value of the part that continues to be recognised, the best estimate of the fair value is the difference between:

- the fair value of the larger financial asset as a whole; and
- the consideration received from the transferee for the part that is derecognised.

[IAS 39 para 28].

A6.8.105 In estimating the fair values of the part that continues to be recognised and the part that is derecognised, an entity should apply the fair value measurement requirements discussed in section 9. [IAS 39 para AG46].

Example – Derecognition of a part of a financial asset

On 1 April 20X2, an entity acquired corporate bonds at their face value of C5m. The bonds pay interest of 8% per annum in arrears and are redeemable at par at the end of year 10 on 31 March 20Y2.

On 31 March 20X6, when the current market rate of interest was 6%, the fair value of the bonds amounted to C5,491,732, consisting of the present value of the interest only strip of C1,966,930 and principal only strip of C3,524,802. On the same date, the entity unconditionally transferred its right to the principal only strip to a bank under a legal assignment for cash payment equal to its fair value without any recourse whatsoever. The entity retained the interest only strip (right to receive interest income on the bond at C400,000 per annum for the remaining 6 years).

In this example, the entity has transferred its rights to receive the principal cash flows to the bank *via* a legal assignment (step 4 in the diagram in para A6.8.30 = yes). Furthermore, as the entity has unconditionally sold its right to repayment when the bond matures on 31 March 20Y2 without recourse, it has transferred the risks and rewards attributable to the principal only strip that is part of a larger asset (step 6 in the diagram in para A6.8.30 = yes). Therefore, the entity can derecognise the principal only strip in its entirety.

In order to calculate the gain or loss on the principal only strip, it is necessary to allocate the carrying amount of C5m between the part sold and the part retained, based on their respective fair values as stated in paragraph A6.8.103 above. The allocation is shown below:

	Fair value	Percentage of fair value	Allocated carrying amount
	C	%	C
Principal only (PO) strip	3,524,802	64.1838	3,209,190
Interest only (IO) strip	1,966,930	35.8162	1,790,810
Total	5,491,732	100.0000	5,000,000

The accounting entries to record the part derecognised are as follows:

	Dr	Cr
	C	C
Cash received on sale of PO strip	3,524,802	
Carrying amount attributable to PO strip		3,209,190
Gain on sale of PO strip		315,612

If the bond had been classified as an available-for-sale financial asset, the bond would have been recorded at its fair value of C5,491,732 at 31 March 20X6. The amount credited to equity would have amounted to C491,732. In that situation, it would be necessary to 'recycle' that portion of the fair value gain that is attributable to the principal only strip to the income statement. As stated in paragraph A6.8.103 above, this allocation should also be based on the relative fair values of the principal only and interest only strip. Accordingly, the portion of the gain recorded in equity that is attributable to the principal only strip and fall to be recycled to the income statement amounts to C315,612 (64.1838% of C491,732).

The accounting treatment would be similar if, instead of unconditionally transferring the principal only strip at its fair value, the entity had transferred the interest only strip (the right to receive future interest income) at its fair value of C1,966,930 and retained the principal only strip. In that situation, a gain of C176,120 (C1,966,930 – C1,790,810) would have arisen on the transfer if the asset was carried at amortised cost. On the other hand, if the asset was carried at fair value as available-for-sale, the 'recycled' gain to profit or loss would have amounted to C176,120 (35.8162% of C491,732).

Servicing assets and liabilities

A6.8.106 Servicing is inherent in all loans and receivables. Servicing of mortgage loans, credit card receivables or other financial assets commonly includes, but is not limited to, collecting payments as they fall due, accounting for and remitting principal and interest payments to the transferee, monitoring non-performing loans/debtors, executing foreclosure if necessary and performing other administrative tasks. The service provider incurs the costs of servicing the assets often in return for a fee for performing the services.

A6.8.107 Servicing rights do not meet the definition of a financial instrument because they represent a commitment to supply a service and can only be settled by the service delivery. They are treated as intangible assets under IAS 38.

However, since such servicing rights are, essentially, an expected stream of cash flows that results from a contractual agreement, they are so similar to financial instruments that they are recognised and initially measured on the same basis as financial assets and liabilities. Accordingly, where an entity transfers a financial asset in a transfer that qualifies for derecognition in its entirety and retains the right to service the financial asset for a fee, IAS 39 requires the entity to recognise either a servicing asset or a servicing liability for that servicing contract as follows:

- If the fee to be received is expected to be more than adequate compensation for the servicing, the entity should recognise a servicing asset for the servicing right. This asset should be recognised at an amount of the determined on the basis of the carrying amount of the larger financial asset as discussed in paragraph A6.8.103 above.

- If the fee to be received is not expected to compensate the entity adequately for performing the servicing, the entity should recognise a servicing liability for the servicing obligations at its fair value.

[IAS 39 para 24].

A6.8.108 It follows from the above that where the benefits of servicing exactly compensates the service provider for its servicing responsibilities, there is no servicing asset or liability and the service contract's fair value is zero.

A6.8.109 In some arrangements, an entity may retain the right to a part of the interest payments on transferred assets as compensation for servicing those assets. The part of the interest payments that the entity would give up upon termination or transfer of the servicing contract is allocated to the servicing asset or servicing liability. The part of the interest payments that the entity would not give up is an interest-only strip receivable. For example, if the entity would not give up any interest upon termination or transfer of the servicing contract, the entire interest spread is an interest-only strip receivable. For the purposes of applying the requirements of paragraph A6.8.103 above in respect of a transferred asset that is part of a larger financial asset, the fair values of the servicing asset and interest-only strip receivable are used to allocate the carrying amount of the receivable between the part of the asset that is derecognised and the part that continues to be recognised. If there is no servicing fee specified or the fee to be received is not expected to compensate the entity adequately for performing the servicing, a liability for the servicing obligation is recognised at fair value. [IAS 39 para AG 45].

Example 1 – Sale of receivable with servicing retained (servicing fee not specified in the contract)

Entity A owns a portfolio of loans with a carrying amount of C5m that yield 8% interest income. The loans are accounted for as held-to-maturity investments at amortised cost.

The entity sells the entire portfolio to a bank for C5.25m without any recourse *via* a legal assignment. However, the entity agrees to service the portfolio over the remainder of its life for no additional payment and estimates that the amount that would fairly compensate it for servicing the portfolio is C200,000.

In this situation, as the entity transfers the entire portfolio including its right to receive future interest income on terms that qualify for derecognition under IAS 39, the entity would derecognise the carrying value of the portfolio of C5m. It would also recognise, in the absence of a servicing fee, a servicing liability of C200,000 in accordance with paragraph A6.8.107 above. The accounting entries to record the transfer are as follows:

	Dr	Cr
	C	C
Cash	5,250,000	
Loans		5,000,000
Servicing liability		200,000
Gain on disposal		50,000

Example 2 – Sale of receivable with servicing retained (servicing fee specified in the contract)

The facts are the same as in example 1, except that entity A transfers the entire principal amount of the portfolio plus its right to receive interest income of 6% *via* a legal assignment for a consideration of C4,900,000 without any recourse. The entity retains the right to service the portfolio for which it will be compensated through a right to receive one-half of the interest income not sold (that is, 1% of the 2% future interest income retained). The remaining 1% is considered to be an interest-only strip retained by the entity A. At the date of transfer, the fair value of the interest-only strip is C275,000 and the fair value of the servicing asset is C75,000 (calculated as the present value of servicing fee receivable less a market fee for performing the service).

In this example, it is necessary to consider whether the criteria for derecognition should be applied to the portfolio of loans in its entirety or to separate portions (step 2 in the diagram in para A6.8.30). It is assumed that 75% (6% out of the 8%) of the interest cash flows transferred represents a full proportionate share of all the interest cash flows (see third bullet point of paragraph A6.8.33). This means that the entity will consider two portions of the whole portfolio, being 100% of the principal cash flows and 75% of the interest cash flows, separately for the purposes of derecognition.

Clearly, in this example, the rights to the cash flows have not expired as the loans still exist (step 3 in the diagram in para A6.8.30 = No) and so it is necessary to consider whether the entity has transferred its rights to receive the cash flows from the asset (step 4 in the diagram in para A6.8.30). However, the entity has legally assigned its rights to all of the principal cash flows and 6% of all the interest cash flows from the bond to the bank and, even though it has retained the rights to service the portfolio, this, in itself, does not prevent a transfer under paragraph 18(a) of IAS 39. Therefore (step 4 in the diagram in para A6.8.30 = Yes). Furthermore, as the transfer was made without any recourse, entity A has transferred substantially all the risks and rewards of those portions (step 6 in the diagram in para A6.8.30 = Yes). Therefore, entity A would derecognise the transferred portions.

In order to calculate the gain or loss arising on the transfer, the carrying amount of the financial asset (the portfolio of loans) of C5m should be allocated between the part sold and the part retained based on their relative fair values. In this regard, the servicing asset is allocated to the part that continues to be recognised as indicated in paragraph A6.8.100 above.

	Fair value	Percentage of fair value	Allocated carrying amount
Interest sold/retained	C	%	C
Loan sold (principal and 6% interest)	4,900,000	93.33	4,666,500
Interest-only strip retained	275,000	5.24	262,000
Servicing asset	75,000	1.43	71,500
Total	5,250,000	100.00	5,000,000

The gain arising on sale of the portion derecognised is the difference between the sales proceeds of C4,900,000 and the allocated carrying amount of C4,666,500, that is, C233,500. The retained interest in the transferred asset amounts to C333,500 (consisting of an interest-only-strip of C262,000 + servicing asset of C71,500).

Example 3 – Sale of listed debt securities subject to a call option

On 1 January 20X6, Bank A enters into an agreement to sell a portfolio of held for trading listed debt securities to an investment fund in exchange for a cash payment of C6m. The securities are subject to a call option that allows the bank to repurchase the securities for a price of C6.7m on 31 December 20X6. The securities' fair value at the date of transfer is C6.5m. The option's fair value is C0.5m. The investment fund has the practical ability to sell the securities to a third party.

The presence of the call option means that the bank has a continuing involvement in the transferred asset. However, as the securities are listed and the investment fund has the practical ability to sell the securities to a third party unilaterally and without imposing any conditions, the bank has not retained control of the securities. According the bank will derecognise the securities (step 8 in the diagram in para A6.8.30 = No), but record its rights under the call option separately.

Given that the call option's strike price (C6.7m) is more than the fair value of the underlying securities (C6.5m), the call option is out-of-the-money. Therefore, the fair value of the call option of C0.5m wholly relates to the time value of the option, which is also the premium paid by the bank.

Therefore, at the date of transfer, the company will record the following entries:

	Dr	Cr
	C	C
Cash	6.0	
Trading portfolio		6.5
Derivative (call option)	0.5	

Bank A will recognise the call option at fair value through profit and loss.

Assume that at 31 December 20X6, the fair value of the shares increases to C7m and the bank exercises the option, Bank A will record the following entries:

	Dr	Cr
	C	C
Derivative		0.2
Profit or loss	0.2	
Trading portfolio	7.0	
Cash		6.7
Derivative		0.3

As 31 December 20X6 is the call's expiry date, its time value at that date will be zero. The decline in the time value is included in the C 0.2 loss recognised in profit or loss.

[The next paragraph is 6.8.119.]

Transfers that do not qualify for derecognition

A6.8.119 Where a transfer does not result in the transferred asset's derecognition, the entity continues to recognise the transferred asset in its entirety and recognises a financial liability for the consideration received. [IAS 39 para 29]. The asset and the associated liability cannot be offset. In subsequent periods, the entity recognises any income on the transferred asset and any expense incurred on the financial liability. Again the entity cannot offset the income and the expense. [IAS 32 para 42, IAS 39 paras 29, 36]. This reflects the transaction's substance, which is accounted for as a collateralised borrowing.

A6.8.120 It should be noted that the above treatment only applies when a financial asset is precluded from being derecognised in full (step 7 in the diagram in para A6.8.30 = yes). It does not apply in circumstances where a financial asset is not derecognised, because the entity has a continuing involvement in the financial asset (step 8 in the diagram in para A6.8.30 = yes). In those circumstances, special provisions apply and these are discussed from paragraph A6.8.127 below.

Example – Factoring with full recourse

Entity A (the transferor) holds a portfolio of receivables with a carrying value of C1m. It enters into a factoring arrangement with entity B (the transferee) under which it transfers the portfolio *via* an assignment to entity B in exchange for C900,000 of cash. All sums collected from debtors are paid by entity A to a specially nominated bank account opened by entity B (that is, entity A is only servicing the loans and has no right to the cash flows). Entity A agrees to reimburse entity B in cash for any shortfall between the amount collected from the receivable and the consideration of C900,000. Once the receivables have been repaid, any sums collected above C900,000 plus interest on the initial payment until the date debtors pay, will be paid to entity A.

In this example, entity A has transferred its rights to receive the cash flows from the asset (step 4 in the diagram in para A6.8.30 = yes).

The next step is to consider whether entity A has transferred substantially all the risks and rewards of ownership of the receivables. Under the factoring arrangement, entity A's maximum possible exposure to entity B is to repay all of the consideration of C900,000 it has received. Although this situation is unlikely, it means that entity A has given a guarantee to compensate the transferee for all credit losses that are likely to occur. In addition, entity A receives the benefit of sums collected from debtors above C900,000. Consequently, entity A has retained both the credit and late payment risk associated with the receivables. Entity A has therefore retained substantially all the risk and rewards of ownership of the receivables and continues to recognise the receivables (step 7 in the diagram in para A6.8.30 = yes).

Entity A recognises the consideration received of C900,000 as a secured borrowing. The liability is measured at amortised cost with interest expense recognised over the period to maturity of the receivables in line with the interest rate charged by the factor.

Sale and repurchase agreements

A6.8.121 The essential features of a sale and repurchase transaction are discussed from paragraphs 6.8.75 above. It is clear from the above discussions that a financial asset that is sold subject to the obligation to repurchase the same or a similar asset at a fixed price should not be derecognised. This is because the entity retains upside as well as downside exposure to gains and losses from the transferred asset. Therefore, the asset continues to be recognised in its entirety and the proceeds received are recognised as a liability. Similarly, the entity continues to recognise any income from the asset along with any expense incurred on the associated liability.

A6.8.122 In some circumstances, a repurchase agreement may contain a provision that may allow the transferor to settle net in cash. That is, instead of taking physical delivery of the asset in consideration for paying the fixed price, the transferor settles the transaction net in cash by paying or receiving the difference between the fair value of the asset at the date of repurchase and the fixed repurchase price. The fact that the transferor is able to settle the transaction net in cash does not automatically mean that the transferor has lost control of the asset. [IAS 39 para AG 51(k)]. Also the normal risks and rewards test, as well as the control test, must still be passed before the transferor can derecognise the transferred asset. Examples of sale and repurchase transactions that are gross and net settled are considered below.

Example 1 – Sale and repurchase transaction (gross settled)

An entity purchases C10m, 10%, 5 year government bonds on 1 January 20X4 with semi-annual interest payable on 30 June and 31 December for C10.8m that results in a premium of C800,000. The entity classifies the bonds as held-to-maturity investments at amortised cost. The amortisation of the bonds to maturity using the effective interest method (see section 9) is shown below.

	Cash received	Interest income @ 4.013%	Carrying amount
1 Jan 20X4			10,800,000
1 Jul 20X4	500,000	433,408	10,733,408
1 Jan 20X5	500,000	430,735	10,664,143
1 Jul 20X5	500,000	427,956	10,592,099
1 Jan 20X6	500,000	425,064	10,517,163
1 Jul 20X6	500,000	422,057	10,439,220
1 Jan 20X7	500,000	418,929	10,358,149
1 Jul 20X7	500,000	415,676	10,273,825
1 Jan 20X8	500,000	412,292	10,186,117
1 Jul 20X8	500,000	408,772	10,094,889
31 Dec 20X8	500,000	405,111	10,000,000
	5,000,000	4,200,000	

On 1 July 20X5, the entity sells the bond at its fair value of C10.6m to a third party with an agreement to repurchase the bond on 1 July 20X6 for C10.65m.

As the repurchase price is fixed at the outset, the entity is precluded from derecognising the bond as discussed in paragraph A6.8.79 above (step 7 in the diagram in para A6.8.30 = Yes). The transferee will be entitled to receive the interest due on 1 Jan 20X6 and 1 July 20X6, that is, C1m that, together with the difference between the repurchase price and sale price of C50,000, represents a lender's return of 9.8943% per annum on the sale price. Therefore, the entity will continue to recognise the bond and the interest on it, as if it still held the bonds, as noted in para A6.8.119 above.

It should be noted that although the repurchase agreement meets the definition of a derivative (it can be viewed as a forward contract), it is not separately recognised as a derivative and measured at fair value, because to do so would result in double counting of the same rights. Therefore, in this situation, the forward contract to repurchase the financial asset at a fixed price is not recorded as an asset (see further para A6.8.98.3 above).

The entity will also record a liability of C10.6m for the proceeds received. This liability will accrete to the amount payable on repurchase of C10.65m at 1 July 20X6, using the effective interest method. The entity will continue to recognise a notional interest income in the periods to 1 Jan 20X6 and 1 July 20X6 and also account for an equal amount of notional interest paid to the third party. On 1 July 20X6 following repurchase of the bond by the entity, the liability of C10.65m will be eliminated as shown below:

	Carrying value
Liability at 1 July 20X5	10,600,000
Interest payable for the half year to 31 December 20X5 @ 9.8943%	524,397
Notional cash paid to third party on 31 December 20X5*	(500,000)
Balance at 31 December 20X5	10,624,397
Interest payable for the half year to 30 June 20X6 @ 9.8943%	525,603
Notional cash paid to third party on 30 June 20X6*	(500,000)
Balance at 30 June 20X6	10,650,000
Liability repaid on 1 July 20X6 at repurchase price	(10,650,000)

* third party will receive interest directly from the bond as legal owner.

It may well be that the transferee is able to pledge or sell the bond during its period of ownership. In that situation, the transferor should reclassify the bond on its balance sheet as a loaned asset or repurchase receivable as explained in paragraph A6.8.83 above.

Example 2 – Sale and repurchase transaction (net settled in cash)

The facts are the same as in example 1 above, except that the repurchase contract is to be settled net in cash. The fair value of the asset at the date of repurchase amounts to C10.655m. This means that the entity will pay an additional C5,000 to the bank.

As explained in paragraph A6.8.98.8 above, the fact that the forward repurchase agreement requires net settlement does not automatically lead to derecognition. In this example, it is clear that the entity continues to recognise the asset as the repurchase is at a fixed price. However, as the entity will not physically get the bond back at the repurchase date, the bond will be derecognised following payment of the additional consideration of C5,000 at the repurchase date. Therefore, it would not be appropriate to continue to classify the bond as held-to-maturity at amortised cost as in example 1. Instead, the entity would need to reclassify the bond as an available-for-sale financial asset at fair value at the sale date of 1 July 20X5. (Where an entity during the current financial year has sold or reclassified more than an insignificant amount of held-to-maturity investments before maturity (more than insignificant in relation to the total amount of held-to-maturity investments), it is prohibited from classifying any financial asset as held-to-maturity for a period of two years after the occurrence of this event, see further section 6.) The reclassification results in a gain to equity as shown below:

Fair value of bond at 1 July 20X5	10,600,000
Amortised cost of bond at 1 July 20X5 as in example 1	10,592,098
Gain transferred to equity following reclassification	7,902

Therefore, the entity will record the bond at its fair value of C10,600,000 and a corresponding liability of C10,600,000. The liability will accrete to the repurchase price of C10,650,000 as shown in example 1.

At the repurchase date of 1 July 20X6, the repurchase receivable will be fair valued to C10,655,000 and a further gain of C5,000 will be recorded in equity. As the repurchase will be net settled in cash, the entity will record the following entries:

	Dr	Cr
	C	C
Liability	10,650,000	
Bond		10,655,000
Cash settlement	5,000	
Equity – recycling of cumulative gain (7,902 + 5,000)	12,902	
Gain on disposal		12,902

The above example illustrates the point that although a forward repurchase agreement that requires net settlement in cash is economically equivalent to a deferred sale, the entity cannot derecognise the asset as the risks and rewards of ownership have been retained until settlement.

Subordinated retained interests and credit guarantees

A6.8.123 An entity may provide the transferee with credit enhancement by subordinating some or all of its interest retained in the transferred asset. Alternatively, an entity may provide the transferee with credit enhancement in the form of a credit guarantee that could be unlimited or limited to a specified amount. If the entity retains substantially all the risks and rewards of ownership of the transferred asset, the asset continues to be recognised in its entirety. [IAS 39 para AG 51(n)].

Example – subordinated retained interest

Entity A originates a portfolio of 5 year interest-bearing loans of C10m. Entity A then enters into an agreement with entity B in which, in exchange for a cash payment of C9m, entity A agrees to pay to entity B the first C9m (plus interest) of cash collected from the loan portfolio. Entity A retains rights to the last C1m (plus interest). Expected collections on the loan portfolio are C9.5m and experience suggests that they are unlikely to be less than C9.3m.

Entity A's retained interest in the cash flows from the loans is effectively subordinated. This is because if entity A collects, say, only C8m of its loans of C10m because some debtors default, entity A would have to pass on to entity B all of the C8m collected and keeps nothing for itself. On the other hand, if entity A collects C9.5m, it passes C9m to entity B and retains C0.5m.

In this case, entity A retains substantially all the risks and rewards of ownership of the loans, because the subordinated retained interest absorbs all of the likely variability in net cash flows as discussed in paragraph A6.8.55. The loans continue to be recognised in their entirety even if the three pass-through conditions discussed in paragraph A6.8.44 are met, because derecognition is only achieved where, in addition, substantially all the risks and rewards of ownership are transferred. As derecognition is not achieved, the entire proceeds of C9m is recorded as a collateralised borrowing.

[The next paragraph is 6.8.127.]

Continuing involvement in transferred assets

General

A6.8.127 One of the most difficult derecognition issues relates to transfers of financial assets in which the transferor has some continuing interest in the asset. Examples include full or partial guarantees of the collectability of receivables, conditional or unconditional agreements to re-acquire the transferred assets and written or held options. The accounting treatment for some of these arrangements has been considered before in the context of failed derecognition through retention of risks and rewards. However, the accounting becomes complex when such arrangements give rise to continuing involvement accounting (that is, the transaction falls within the last box in the derecognition flowchart in para A6.8.30 above).

A6.8.128 Under the derecognition criteria discussed above, when the entity transfers some significant risks and rewards and retains others and derecognition is precluded because the entity retains control of the transferred asset, the entity continues to recognise the asset to the extent of its continuing involvement. This should be measured in such a way that ensures that any changes in value of the transferred asset that are not attributed to the entity's continuing involvement are not recognised by the entity. It follows that the extent of the entity's continuing involvement in the transferred asset is the extent to which it is exposed to changes in the transferred asset's value. [IAS 39 para 30]. Measuring a financial asset in this manner may not be in accordance with the general measurement rules for financial assets, but is necessary to ensure that the accounting properly reflects the transferor's continuing involvement in the asset. IAS 39 contains detailed guidance on how to measure the asset when the continuing involvement takes the form of a guarantee or written or purchased options (including a cash-settled option or similar provision). These issues are considered from paragraphs 6.8.133 below.

Associated liability

A6.8.129 When an entity continues to recognise an asset to the extent of its continuing involvement, the entity also recognises an associated liability. The associated liability is measured in such a way that the net carrying amount of the transferred asset and the associated liability is:

- the amortised cost of the rights and obligations retained by the entity, if the transferred asset is measured at amortised cost; or
- equal to the fair value of the rights and obligations retained by the entity when measured on a stand-alone basis, if the transferred asset is measured at fair value.

[IAS 39 para 31].

Recognition and derecognition

A6.8.130 The above measurement basis may often result in a liability amount on initial recognition that is a 'balancing figure' that will not necessarily represent the proceeds received in the transfer. This is in contrast to the treatment for transfers that do not qualify for derecognition through retention of risks and rewards where the entire proceeds are accounted for as collateralised borrowing (see para A6.8.119 above). However, as explained in paragraph A6.8.128 above, special rules are necessary to account for transfers involving continuing involvement. The standard makes this clear by providing that *"despite the other measurement requirements in this standard"*, measuring the transferred asset and the associated liability in the manner described above reflects the rights and obligations that the entity has retained. [IAS 39 para 31].

Subsequent measurement

A6.8.131 Subsequent to initial recognition, the fair value of the transferred asset and the associated liability should be accounted for consistently with each other in accordance with the general provisions of IAS 39 for measuring gains and losses. [IAS 39 para 33]. The requirement for consistent measurement means that designation of the associated liability at fair value through profit or loss is not available if the asset is measured at amortised cost. Also, the asset and the associated liability cannot be offset. [IAS 39 para 36].

A6.8.132 The entity should continue to recognise any income arising on the transferred asset to the extent of its continuing involvement. It should also recognise any expense incurred on the associated liability. [IAS 39 para 32]. This requirement is comparable to the requirements for transfers that do not qualify for derecognition through retention of risks and rewards (see para A6.8.119 above). The income and the expense cannot be offset [IAS 39 para 36].

Continuing involvement through guarantees

A6.8.133 An entity may provide a guarantee to pay for default losses on a transferred asset that prevents the transferred asset from being derecognised to the extent of the entity's continuing involvement. In that situation, the extent of the entity's continued involvement in the transferred asset, that is, the extent to which the entity continues to be exposed to the changes in the value of the transferred asset and the associated liability, is measured as follows:

- The continuing involvement asset at the date of the transfer is measured at the lower of:
  - the carrying amount of the transferred asset; and
  - the maximum amount of the consideration received in the transfer that the entity could be required to repay ('the guarantee amount').
- The associated liability is initially measured at the guarantee amount plus the fair value of the guarantee (which is normally the consideration received for the guarantee).

Subsequently, the initial fair value of the guarantee is recognised in profit or loss on a time proportion basis and the asset's carrying value is reduced by any impairment losses. If the guarantee is subsequently called, the liability is reduced by the cost of settlement. To the extent that the guarantee is not called and the entity is no longer exposed to the changes in the value of the transferred asset, that is the guarantee has lapsed unexercised, both the asset and the liability are reduced. [IAS 39 paras 30(a), AG48(a)].

Example 1 – Factoring with limited recourse (slow payment risk retained)

Entity A (the transferor) holds a portfolio of trade receivables with a carrying value of C500m. Entity A enters into a factoring arrangement with entity B (the transferee) under which it transfers the portfolio to entity B in exchange for C490m of cash. Entity A transfers the credit risk, but retains the slow payment risk up to a maximum of 180 days. After 180 days, the receivable is deemed to be in default and credit insurance takes effect. A charge is levied on the entity A for these late payments using a current rate of 6%. The fair value of the guarantee of late payment risk is C2m. Apart from slow payment risk, entity A does not retain any credit or interest rate risk and does not carry out any servicing of the portfolio. There is no active market for the receivables.

In this example, entity A has transferred some but not all the risks and rewards of ownership — it has retained slow payment risks, but has transferred credit risks (step 6 in the diagram in para A6.8.30 = No and step 7 = No). Furthermore, as there is no active market for the receivables, entity B does not have the practical ability to sell the transferred asset. Therefore, as entity B is constrained from selling the asset, the 'practical ability' test fails with the result that control of the transferred asset is retained by entity A. As a result of the above, entity A determines that it has a continuing involvement in the transferred receivables (step 8 in the diagram in para A6.8.30 = Yes).

Therefore, in accordance with paragraph A6.8.133 above, entity A measures the continuing involvement in the transferred asset at the lower of:

- the carrying amount of the transferred asset, that is, C500m; and
- the maximum amount of the consideration received in the transfer that entity A could be required to repay, that is, 6% on C500m for 180 days = 6% × 500 × 180/360 = C15m (the guaranteed amount).

Entity A will, therefore, record the continuing involvement asset at C15m.

Also in accordance with paragraph A6.8.133 above, entity A will measure the associated liability initially at the guarantee amount (C15m) + the fair value of the guarantee (C2m), a total of C17m. The associated liability is measured in such a way that the net carrying amount of the transferred asset and the associated liability is equal to the fair value of the guarantee.

Therefore, entity A would make the following entries at the date of transfer:

	Dr	Cr
Consideration received in cash	490	
Receivables transferred		500
Continued involvement in transferred asset	15	
Liability		17
Profit or loss – loss*	12	

*Consideration received of C490m – (consideration for guarantee C2m + carrying value of portfolio C500m.)

Entity A would make the following accounting entries subsequent to the date of transfer:

(i) To amortise the consideration for the guarantee over the period to which it relates (180 days):

Liability	2	
Profit or loss		2

(ii) If the guarantee lapsed unexercised, the following entries would be made over the period for which slow payment risk is retained as the maximum amount that entity A could be required to repay reduces due to timely payment on the receivables transferred:

Continued involvement in transferred asset		15
Liability	15	

(iii) When slow payment occurs, such that a charge is levied by entity B (taking an example charge of C4m), entity A would make the following entries:

Asset (to recognise the impairment of the continuing involvement asset)		4
Profit or loss	4	

(iv) The following entries would be made when a slow payment charge is actually paid by entity A (taking an example of a charge of C4m):

Liability	4	
Cash		4

Continuing involvement through options

A6.8.134 As explained in paragraph A6.8.98.2 above, derivatives included in the transfer may constrain the transferee's practical ability to sell the transferred asset, even if there is no legal constraint, with the result that the transferor retains control over the transferred asset. In those circumstances, if the entity has neither transferred nor retained substantially all the risks and rewards of ownership of the transferred asset, the entity retains a continuing involvement in the transferred asset. For example, an entity may transfer a financial asset that is not readily obtainable in the market and holds a call option or writes a put option that is neither deeply in nor deeply out-of-the money at the date of transfer. [IAS 39 paras AG51(h), AG51(i)].

A6.8.135 When the entity's continuing involvement takes the form of a written or purchased option (or both) on the transferred asset, the extent of the entity's continuing involvement is the amount of the transferred asset that the entity may repurchase. However, in case of a put option on an asset written by the transferor that is measured by the transferor at fair value, the extent of the entity's continuing involvement is limited to the lower of the fair value of the transferred asset and the option exercise price. [IAS 39 para 30(b)]. This reflects the fact that the entity will not benefit from changes in the fair value above the option's exercise price. The manner in which the options are settled (physical or cash-settled) does not affect the measurement of the continuing involvement asset. [IAS 39 para 30(c)]. Depending on whether the transferred asset is measured at amortised cost or fair value, the associated liability is measured in accordance with paragraph A6.8.129 above as explained below.

Transfer of assets measured at amortised cost

A6.8.136 Where a put option obligation written by an entity or call option right held by an entity prevents a transferred asset from being derecognised and the entity measures the transferred asset at amortised cost, the associated liability is measured at its cost (that is, the consideration received) adjusted for the amortisation of any difference between that cost and the amortised cost of the transferred asset at the option's expiration date. If the option is exercised, any difference between the associated liability's carrying amount and the exercise price is recognised in profit or loss. [IAS 39 para AG 48(b)].

Example – Asset measured at amortised cost subject to call option held by the transferor

Entity A has a portfolio of high yielding corporate bonds with an amortised carrying value of C102m. The bonds are not traded in the marketplace and are not readily obtainable. On 1 January 20X6, entity A sells the bonds to entity B for a consideration of C100m, but retains a call option to purchase the portfolio for C105m on 31 December 20X6. On that date, the amortised cost of the bonds will be C106m. The fair value of the bonds, at the date of transfer amounted to C104m.

The rights to receive cash flows from the asset have not expired (step 3 in the diagram in para A6.8.30 = no). However, entity A has transferred its right to receive cash flows (interest and principal on the bonds) to entity B (step 4 in the diagram in para A6.8.30 = yes). In this situation, the bonds are transferred, subject to a call option that is neither deeply in-the-money nor deeply out-of-the money (the option's exercise price is C105m compared to fair value of asset of C104m). The result is that the entity neither transfers nor retains substantially all the risks and rewards of ownership of the bonds (steps 6 and 7 in the diagram in para A6.8.30 = no). Furthermore, as the transferee does not have the practical ability to sell the bonds, derecognition of the bonds is precluded to the extent of the amount of the asset that is subject to the call option, because the entity has retained control of the asset (step 8 in the diagram in para A6.8.30 = yes).

As entity A has an option to buy back all of the bonds, it continues to recognise the bonds at their amortised cost, which will accrete from a carrying value of C102m to C106m at 31 December 20X6 using the effective interest rate method. The initial carrying amount of the liability is recorded at cost, that is, the consideration received of C100m. The liability is then accreted to C106m using the effective-interest rate method, which is the amortised cost of the transferred asset at the expiration date of the option (not the option's exercise price of C105m). As the asset is measured at amortised cost, the liability is also measured in a consistent manner as explained in paragraph A6.8.135 above.

Therefore, entity A would make the following entries:

	Dr	Cr
	C	C
At 1 January 20X6 (date of transfer)		
Cash	100	
Associated liability		100
For the period to 31 December 20X6		
Bonds carried at amortised cost	4	
Income from bonds (106 — 102)		4
Interest on liability (106 — 100)	6	
Liability carried at amortised cost		6

At 31 December 20X6, entity A will exercise the option if the option exercise price of C105m is less than the fair value of the bonds. In that situation, entity A would record the following entries:

	Dr	Cr
	C	C
Liability	106	
Cash (exercise price of option)		105
Gain on exercise of option		1

On the other hand, if the option lapses unexercised, both the asset and the liability are derecognised.

	Dr	Cr
	C	C
Liability	106	
Carrying value of bond		106

A similar analysis would be carried out if, instead, of purchasing a call option, entity A wrote a put option that gave entity B the right to put the bonds back at 31 December 20X6.

Transfer of assets measured at fair value

A6.8.137 Where a call option right held by the entity prevents a transferred asset from being derecognised and the entity measures the transferred asset at fair value, the transferred asset continues to be measured at fair value. This is because the call option gives the entity access to any increase in the asset's fair value. However, the measurement of the associated liability depends on whether the call option is in or at- the-money or out-of-the money, as described below.

- If the option is in or at-the-money, the associated liability is measured at the option's exercise price less the option's time value.
- If the option is out-of-the money, the associated liability is measured at the fair value of the transferred asset less the option's time value.

The effect of the above measurement basis is to ensure that the associated liability is measured in such a way that the net carrying amount of the transferred asset and the associated liability is always equal to the fair value of the call option right. [IAS 39 para AG48(c)].

Example – Asset measured at fair value subject to call option held by the transferor

Entity A has 15% equity holding in entity B that was acquired some years ago for C40m. This holding is treated as an available-for-sale financial asset and the current fair value (and carrying value) is C104m. There is no active market in entity B's shares. On 1 January 20X6, entity A sells its 15% investment in entity B to bank C for a consideration of C100m, but retains a call option to purchase the investment for C105m on 31 December 20X7.

The rights to receive cash flows from the asset have not expired (step 3 in the diagram in para A6.8.30 = no). However, entity A has transferred its right to receive cash flows (dividends on the shares) from its investment to entity B (step 4 in the diagram in para A6.8.30 = yes), subject to a call option. The result is that the entity neither transfers nor retains substantially all the risks and rewards of ownership of the transferred asset (steps 6 and 7 in the diagram in para A6.8.30 = no). This is because:

- entity A can exercise its call option so as to benefit from movements in the asset's fair value above the call option exercise price of C105m; and
- entity A is not exposed to risk from decreases in the asset's market value below the call option exercise price.

With regard to the next question, whether entity A has retained control of its investment in entity B, this will depend upon whether bank C has the practical ability to sell the asset in its entirety to an unrelated third party, unilaterally and without imposing additional restrictions on the transfer. In this situation, there is no active market in entity B's shares, so a 15% stake is not readily obtainable in the market. The call option is neither deeply in-the-money nor deeply out-of-the-money (it is slightly out-of-the-money at inception as the option exercise price of C105m is more than the market value of the shares at C104m), but it is sufficiently valuable to prevent bank C from selling the asset immediately. These facts taken together lead to the conclusion that bank C does not have the practical ability to sell its investment in entity A. Consequently, entity A has retained control and derecognition is precluded to the extent of the amount of the asset that is subject to the call option (step 8 in the diagram in para A6.8.30 = yes).

Therefore, in accordance with paragraph A6.8.137, the entity continues to recognise the investment in entity B as an available-for-sale asset at fair value. At the date of transfer, the call option is out-of-the-money (option's exercise price of C105m is greater that the fair value of the asset at C104m). The premium paid on the option (all time value) is C4m (fair value of the asset of C104m less consideration received of C100m). As the option is out-of-the-money, IAS 39 requires the associated liability to be measured at the fair value of the transferred asset less the time value of the option as explained in the above paragraph. Therefore, the associated liability is recorded at C104m – C4m = C100m, which is also equal to the consideration received. This ensures that the net amount of the transferred asset and the associated liability is equal to the fair value of the call option right. Therefore, entity A would make the following entries:

	Dr C	Cr C
At 1 January 20X6 (date of transfer)		
Cash	100	
Associated liability		100

Suppose that the asset's fair value increases to C106m at 31 December 20X6. The option is now in-the-money (exercise price of C105m < C106m) and its time value is C2m.

In accordance with paragraph AG48(c) of IAS 39, the associated liability is measured at the option's exercise price (C105m) less the time value of the option (C2m) = C103m.

This ensures that the net amount of the transferred asset (C106m) and the associated liability (C103m) is equal to the fair value of the call option right of C3m (intrinsic value of C1m + time value of C2m) as explained in paragraph A6.8.135 above.

	Dr C	Cr C
Entity A will record the following entries at 31 December 20X6		
Asset (increase in value from C104m to C106m)	2	
Liability (increase in value from C100m to C103m)		3
Equity	1	

As the associated liability should be measured in a manner consistent with the available-for-sale asset in accordance with the general provisions of IAS 39 for measuring gains and losses as explained in paragraph A6.8.131 above, the movement in the liability is also recognised in equity. The net loss of C1m recognised in equity represents the fall in the value of the option from C4m to C3m.

It should be noted that to the extent that a transfer of a financial asset does not qualify for derecognition, the transferor's contractual rights or obligations related to the transfer are not accounted for separately as derivatives, since recognising both the derivative and the transferred asset would result in recognising the same rights and = yes. Therefore, entity A does not recognise the call option separately (see para A6.8.98.3 above).

Suppose that the fair value of the asset remains unchanged at 31 December 2007. The entity will exercise the option as it is in-the-money. The accounting entries are as follows:

	Dr C	Cr C
Liability derecognised	103	
Equity	2	
Cash paid		105

The overall loss of C3m over the two year period recognised in equity represents the difference between the amount paid to re-acquire the asset for C105m and the consideration received on the transfer of C100m less the increase in the fair value of the asset of C2m (C106m – C104m) already recognised in equity.

Suppose that the fair value of the asset falls to C103m at 31 December 2007. In this situation, entity A will not exercise the option and will allow it to lapse. Both the transferred asset and the associated liability will be derecognised as shown below:

	Dr C	Cr C
Liability	103	
Asset		106
Equity (recycling of cumulative gain C104m – C40m – C1m)	63	
Gain in profit or loss		60

The gain of C60m represents the net cash received of C60m (consideration received of C100m less original cost of C40m).

6A.8.138 Where a put option written by an entity prevents a transferred asset measured at fair value from being derecognised, the transferred asset is measured at the lower of the fair value and the option exercise price. [IAS 39 para 30(b)]. This limitation is placed on the asset value because the entity has no right to the increase in the asset's fair value above the option exercise price. The associated liability is measured at the option's exercise price plus the time value of the option. This ensures that the asset's net carrying amount and the associated liability is always equal to the fair value of the put option obligation. [IAS 39 para 48(d)]. The treatment is illustrated in the example given below.

Example – Asset measured at fair value subject to put option written by the transferor

Entity A has 15% equity holding in entity B that was acquired some years ago for C40m. This holding is treated as an available-for-sale financial asset and the current fair value at 1 January 20X6 (and carrying value) is C97m. There is no active market in entity B's shares.

On 1 January 20X6, entity A sells its investment in entity B to bank C for a consideration of C102m. However, entity A has granted a put option to bank C. Under the terms of the put option, bank C has the right to sell its investment in entity B back to entity A for C96m if the market value of its investment falls below C96m at any time in the next two years.

Entity A has transferred its right to receive cash flows (dividends on the shares) from its investment to entity B (step 4 in the diagram in para A6.8.30 = yes). However, in this situation, the investment is transferred, subject to a put option. The result is that the entity neither transfers nor retains substantially all the risks and rewards of ownership of the transferred asset (steps 6 and 7 in the diagram in para A6.8.30 = no). This is because:

- entity A is still exposed to movements in fair value below C96m, because if the fair value of the investment falls below C96m, bank C will put the investment back to company A for C96m; and
- entity A has not retained any benefit from increases in the market value of entity B.

With regard to the next question, whether entity A has retained control of its investment in entity B, this will depend upon whether bank C has the practical ability to sell the asset in its entirety to an unrelated third party, unilaterally and without imposing additional restrictions on the transfer. In this situation, there is no active market in entity B's shares, so a 15% stake is not readily obtainable in the market. The put option is neither deeply in-the-money nor deeply out-of-the money (it is slightly out-of-the-money at inception as the option exercise price of C96m is less than the market value of the shares at C97m), but it is sufficiently valuable to prevent bank C from selling the asset immediately. There would need to be a significant increase in the share's value to compensate bank C for the premium they have paid for the put option. These facts taken together lead to the conclusion that bank C does not have the practical ability to sell its investment in entity A. Consequently, entity A has retained control and derecognition is precluded to the extent of the amount of the asset that is subject to the put option (step 8 in the diagram in para A6.8.30 = yes).

Therefore, in accordance with the above paragraph, the entity recognises the investment in entity B at the lower of the fair value of the asset (C97m) and the option exercise price (C96m), that is, C96m, being the option's exercise price.

The premium received by entity A for writing the put option is C5m (consideration received of C102m less fair value of the asset of C97m). As the option is out-of-the-money, the entire premium represents the time value of the option. The associated liability is measured at the option exercise price (C96m) plus the time value of the option (C5m), that is, C101m, as explained in paragraph A6.8.138 above. This ensures that the net amount of the transferred asset (C96m) and the associated liability (C101m) is equal to the fair value of the put option obligation (C5m). Therefore, entity A would make the following entries:

	Dr	Cr
	C	C
At 1 January 20X6 (date of transfer)		
Cash received	102	
Investment		1
Liability		101

Suppose that the fair value of the asset decreases to C94m at 31 December 20X6. The put option is now in-the-money (exercise price of C96m > C94m) and its time value is C2m.

In accordance with the above paragraph A6.8.138 above, the asset is measured at the lower of the asset's fair value and the option's exercise price, that is, C94m, being the fair value of the asset. The associated liability is measured at the option's exercise price (C96m) plus the time value of the option (C2m), that is, C98m.

This ensures that the net amount of the transferred asset (C94m) and the associated liability (C98m) is equal to the fair value of the put option obligation of C4m (intrinsic value of C2m + time value of C2m).

	Dr C	Cr C
Entity A will record the following entries at 31 December 20X6		
Asset (fall in value from C96m to C94m)		2
Liability (fall in value from C101m to C98m)	3	
Equity		1

As the associated liability should be measured in a manner consistent with the available-for-sale asset in accordance with the general provisions of IAS 39 for measuring gains and losses as explained in paragraph A6.8.128 above, the movement in the liability is also recognised in equity. The net gain of C1m represents the fall in the value of the put option obligation from C5m to C4m.

It should be noted that to the extent that a transfer of a financial asset does not qualify for derecognition, the transferor's contractual rights or obligations related to the transfer are not accounted for separately as derivatives, since recognising both the derivative and the transferred asset would result in recognising the same rights and = yes. Therefore, entity A does not recognise the put option separately (see para 6.8.98.3 above).

Suppose that the fair value of the asset remains unchanged at 31 December 2007. Bank C decides to exercise the option as it is in-the-money. Entity A will have to re-acquire the asset at the put option price. The accounting entries are as follows:

	Dr C	Cr C
Liability derecognised	98	
Cash paid		96
Equity		2

The overall gain of C3 recognised in equity over the two year period represents the difference of C6m (consideration received of C102m less amount paid to re-acquire the asset for C96m) less C3m (fall in asset value from C97m at inception to C94m at exercise).

Continuing involvement in a part of a financial asset

A6.8.139 An entity may have a continuing involvement in only a part of a financial asset rather than the entire asset as discussed above. This situation may arise when an entity retains an option to repurchase part of a transferred asset, or retains a residual interest that does not result in the retention of substantially all the risks and rewards of ownership and the entity retains control. Where this is so, the entity allocates the financial asset's previous carrying amount between the part it continues to recognise under continuing involvement and the part it no longer recognises on the basis of the relative fair values of those parts on the date of transfer. [IAS 39 para 34].

A6.8.140 The allocation exercise and the calculation of the gain or loss arising on the part of the asset that is no longer retained are carried out in a similar manner as described in paragraph A6.8.100 above. That is, the difference between the carrying amount allocated to the part that is no longer recognised and the sum of:

- the consideration received for the part no longer recognised; and
- any cumulative gain or loss allocated to it that had been recognised directly in equity;

is recognised in profit or loss. Any cumulative gain or loss that had been recognised in equity is allocated between the part that continues to be recognised and the part that is no longer recognised on the basis of the relative fair values of those parts. [IAS 39 para 34]. The recycling of the cumulative gain or loss that had been recognised in equity relates to the part no longer recognised of an available-for-sale financial asset. In addition to the part retained, the entity continues to recognise its continuing involvement in the asset and the associated liability. The manner in which the above guidance is applied to continuing involvement in a part of a financial asset is illustrated in paragraph AG52 of IAS 39. Although that example is not presented here, the application illustrated in that example is best understood by reference to a securitisation transaction given below.

Example – Continuing involvement in a part of a financial asset

Entity A enters into a securitisation transaction in which it transfers a pool of receivables amounting to CU1,000, but retains a subordinated interest of CU100 in that pool.

The terms of the securitisation arrangements show that the transaction is to be accounted for using the continuing involvement approach (which, *inter alia*, requires that the buyer assume significant risks and rewards).

Under the continuing involvement approach, the seller typically recognises an asset of CU200 and a liability of CU100. This gives a net asset of CU100 which might be expected as it represents the retained subordinated interest of CU100. However the gross numbers can be confusing to understand. AG52 analyses the transaction as comprising:

- a retention of a non-subordinated 10% interest in the transferred assets; and

- the subordination of that interest, that is equivalent to the seller providing a credit guarantee.

Both these elements result in continuing involvement and both need to be accounted for. The first element (the retention of a non-subordinated 10% interest) results in a continuing involvement asset of CU100. In addition, the second element (the subordination of that interest which is equivalent to the seller providing a guarantee of the first CU100 of loses) also results in a continuing involvement asset of CU100, and a liability of CU100 (being the maximum amount the entity may have to pay by losing the CU100 asset recognised for the first element). Therefore, the seller will recognised a total continuing involvement asset of CU200 and a liability of CU100.

Measuring a financial asset in the above manner may not be in accordance with the general measurement rules for financial assets, but is necessary to ensure that the accounting properly reflects the transferor's continuing involvement in the asset.

Retained servicing

A6.8.140.1 If a transaction is accounted for using continuing involvement and the transferor is required to service the assets without receiving adequate compensation for the service provided, a servicing liability should be recognised to the extent that the asset is derecognised, but no servicing liability should be recognised to the extent of the continuing involvement asset. For example, if the asset pre-transaction was C100 and the continuing involvement in the asset after the transaction was C60, the transferor would recognise a servicing liability for the C40 derecognised, but not for the C60 on the balance sheet. Servicing assets and liabilities are dealt with in detail from paragraph A6.8.106 above.

Accounting for collateral

A6.8.141 A transfer of financial assets may require the transferor to provide non-cash collateral (such as a debt or equity instruments) to the transferee. If collateral is transferred to the transferee, the custodial arrangement is commonly referred to as a pledge. Transferees sometimes are permitted to sell or repledge (or otherwise transfer) collateral held under a pledge. The accounting for the collateral by the transferor and the transferee depends on whether the transferee has the right to sell or repledge the collateral and on whether the transferor has defaulted as shown in the table below.

Circumstance	Accounting by transferor	Accounting by transferee
Transferee has the right by contract or custom to sell or repledge the collateral.	The transferor reclassifies that asset in its balance sheet (for example, as a loaned asset, pledged equity instruments or repurchase receivable) separately from other assets that are not so encumbered. [IAS 39 para 37(a)]. This is because the transferor retains all the risks and rewards of ownership of the asset pledged as collateral and, therefore, cannot derecognise it under the normal rules for derecognition.	The transferee will not recognise the collateral as an asset. In the event that the transferee sells the collateral pledged to it, it recognises the proceeds from the sale and a liability measured at fair value for its obligation to return the collateral. [IAS 39 para 37(b)].
Transferor defaults under the terms of the contract and is no longer entitled to redeem the collateral.	Transferor derecognises the collateral. [IAS 39 para 37(c)].	Transferee recognises the collateral as its asset initially measured at fair value or, if it has already sold the collateral, derecognise its obligation to return the collateral. [IAS 39 para 37(c)]. This is because the risks and rewards of ownership of the collateral have passed to the transferee.
All other situations not referred to above.	Transferor continues to recognise the collateral as its asset. [IAS 39 para 37(d)].	Transferee does not recognise the collateral as an asset. [IAS 39 para 37(d)].

Accounting by transferee

A6.8.142 Although transferees are required to follow the recognition principles discussed from paragraph A6.8.5 above, it is important to note that the accounting treatment between the transferor and the transferee is intended to be symmetrical. Therefore, to the extent that a transfer of a financial asset does not qualify for derecognition, the transferee does not recognise the transferred asset as its asset. The transferee derecognises the cash or other consideration paid and recognises a receivable from the transferor. If the transferor has both a right and an obligation to re-acquire control of the entire transferred asset for a fixed amount (such as under a repurchase agreement), the transferee may account for its receivable as a loan or receivable. [IAS 39 para AG 50]. Similarly, if a transfer of a financial asset qualifies for derecognition, the transferor will treat it as a sale and the transferee will treat it as a purchase.

Derecognition of financial liabilities

A6.8.143 The derecognition rules for financial liabilities are somewhat different from those relating to financial assets. Whereas the derecognition rules for financial assets tend to focus on risks and rewards and may not lead to derecognition even though legal transfer has occurred, the derecognition rules for financial liabilities focus solely on the legal release of the contractual obligations. Consequently, the IAS 39 provisions relating to derecognition of financial liabilities in whole or in part are relatively straight forward and less subjective than those for derecognition of financial assets. The rules in IAS 39 deal with extinguishment of financial liabilities, their modification by lenders and the recognition and measurement of any gains or losses that arise from extinguishment and modification. These issues are considered in detail below.

Extinguishment of a financial liability

General principles

A6.8.144 A financial liability (trading or other) is removed from the balance sheet when it is extinguished, that is when the obligation is discharged, cancelled or expired. [IAS 39 para 39]. This condition is met when the debtor either:

- discharges the liability (or part of it) by paying the creditor, normally with cash, other financial assets, goods or services; or
- is legally released from primary responsibility for the liability (or part of it) either by process of law or by the creditor.

[IAS 39 para AG 57].

A6.8.145 The condition for extinguishment is also met if an entity repurchases a bond that it has previously issued, even if the entity is a market maker or intends to resell it in the near term. [IAS 39 para AG 58]. This is consistent with the treatment of treasury shares re-acquired by an entity, except that in the case of extinguishing a liability, any gain or loss that may arise is recognised (see para A6.8.148 below).

Legal release by the creditor

A6.8.146 It is clear from the general conditions that a debt is extinguished only if the debtor is legally released from its obligation by the creditor. This condition is met even if a creditor releases a debtor from its present obligation to make payments, but the debtor assumes a guarantee obligation to pay if the party assuming primary responsibility defaults. In this circumstance the debtor:

- recognises a new financial liability based on the fair value of its obligation for the guarantee; and
- recognises a gain or loss based on the difference between (i) any proceeds paid and (ii) the carrying amount of the original financial liability less the fair value of the new financial liability.

[IAS 39 para AG 63].

An example illustrating the above treatment is given below. Contrast this with in-substance defeasance discussed below in paragraph A6.8.145 below.

Example – Transfer of debt obligation with legal release

Entity A transfers C100 million highly liquid government bonds into a trust that is owned by a registered charity. The trust does not fall to be consolidated by entity A. Those bonds will solely be used to repay entity A's issued C100 million fixed rate liability. The holders of the issued C100 million fixed rate liability have released entity A from its obligation to make payments. However, entity A enters into a guarantee arrangement whereby, if the trust does not make payments when due, then entity A will pay the debt holders.

In this situation, derecognition of the fixed rate debt instruments is not precluded by virtue of the guarantee. Entity A has obtained legal release, which is a necessary and sufficient condition for the debt's derecognition, notwithstanding that entity A has given a guarantee to a third party.

Entity A (the debtor) recognises a new financial liability based on the fair value of its obligation for the guarantee and recognises a gain or loss based on the difference between any proceeds paid and the carrying amount of the original financial liability less the fair value of the new financial liability. [IAS 39 para AG 63].

6A.8.147 Sometimes, instead of providing a guarantee, the debtor may pay a third party to assume the obligations under the debt and obtain legal release from its creditor. In that situation, the second condition in paragraph A6.8.144 above is met and the debt is extinguished. However, if the debtor transfers its obligations under a debt to a third party and obtains legal release from the creditor, but undertakes to make payments to the third party so as to enable it to meet its obligation, the debtor recognises a new debt obligation to the third party. [IAS 39 para AG 60].

In-substance defeasance

A6.8.148 In-substance defeasance is an arrangement whereby an entity makes a lump sum payment relating to its obligations to a third party (typically a trust). The trust then applies those funds and income thereon to discharge the entity's obligation to the lender. The entity has little or no right of access to the funds put in the trust. The trust does not assume any legal responsibility for the obligations and the lender is not a party to the in-substance arrangement. Some argue that as the entity has no right of access to those funds, it has effectively discharged its obligations to the lender. However, this view is inconsistent with the general rule in paragraph A6.8.144 above that a liability is not extinguished in the absence of a legal release. [IAS 39 para 63]. Therefore, in-substance defeasance arrangements do not result in derecognition of the liability.

Extinguishment through transfer of assets that fails derecognition

A6.8.149 Sometimes an entity may transfer financial assets (other than cash) which the lender accepts as being in full and final settlement and thereby releases the debtor from its obligations. The entity derecognises the liability as the debt has been legally discharged. However, the financial assets transferred may fail the derecognition criteria, because either the entity has retained substantially all the risks and rewards of ownership or the entity has a continuing involvement in the transferred asset by virtue of retaining control. Therefore, where the derecognition criteria are not met, the transferred assets are not derecognised and the entity recognises a new liability relating to the transferred assets. [IAS 39 para AG 61].

Gain or loss arising on extinguishment

A6.8.150 Where a financial liability (or part of a financial liability) is extinguished or transferred to another party, the entity should recognise any difference arising between the carrying amount of the financial liability (or part of the financial liability) extinguished or transferred and the consideration paid, including any non-cash assets transferred or liabilities assumed, in profit or loss. [IAS 39 para 41]. This applies even if the issuer of a debt instrument is a market maker in that instrument or intends to resell it in the near term. [IAS 39 para AG 58].

Example – Gain on extinguishment of debt in full

A bank has loaned C25m to a property investment company that invested the funds in residential properties consisting mainly of high quality appartments. However, as a result of a fall in occupancy rates, the entity is unable to meet its debt obligations. The entity successfully negotiated with the bank whereby the bank agreed to accept a property with a fair market value of C20m in full and final settlement of the C25m obligation. The property's carrying value was C21m.

As a result of the negotiation, the loan is extinguished and the entity recognises a gain on the extinguishment as follows:

	Cm
Carrying value of liability	25
Fair value of non-cash settlement	20
Gain on extinguishment of debt	5
Carrying value of property	21
Fair value of property transferred	20
Loss on disposal	(1)

The gain on extinguishment of debt would be recorded in the income statement under finance income. The loss on disposal of the property would be charged against operating profits. It would not be appropriate to show a net gain of extinguishment of C4m in finance income.

6A.8.151 If an entity repurchases only a part of a financial liability, the entity should allocate the previous carrying amount of the financial liability between the part that continues to be recognised and the part that is derecognised based on the relative fair values of those parts on the date of the repurchase. The difference between the carrying amount allocated to the part derecognised and the consideration paid, including any non-cash assets transferred or liabilities assumed, for the part derecognised is recognised in profit or loss. [IAS 39 para 42]. This means that the consideration paid for the repurchase is not simply set off against the original liability's carrying value, but a gain or loss is calculated based on the part derecognised as set out above.

Example – Derecognition of part of a liability

On 1 January 20X5, an entity issued 1 million 8% C100 nominal 10 year term bonds with interest payable each 30 June and 31 December. The bonds, which are traded in the market, were issued at par. Issue costs of C2m were incurred. Four years after the issue date, the entity repurchases 600,000 bonds at the then market value of C96 per C100 nominal. The amortised cost of the bond at 31 December 20X8 amounted to C98,655,495.

The gain arising on repurchase is calculated as follows:

	C
Carrying value allocated to amount repurchased – 60% of C98,655,495	59,193,297
Amount paid on repurchase of 600,000 @ C96	57,600,000
Gain arising on repurchase	1,593,297

Exchange and modification of debt instrument

A6.8.152 Entities frequently negotiate with lenders to restructure their existing debt obligations. There may be a variety of reasons for doing so, not necessarily when the entity is in financial difficulties. Such restructuring may result in a modification or an exchange of debt instruments with the lender that may be carried out in a number of ways. For instance, an entity may decide to take advantage of falling interest rates by cancelling its exposure to high-interest fixed-rate debt, pay a fee or penalty on cancellation and replace it with debt at a lower interest rate (exchange of old debt with new debt). Alternatively, the entity may seek to roll up the higher interest payments into a single payment that is payable on the loan's redemption or amend the amount payable on redemption (modification). Whether a modification or exchange of debt instruments represents a settlement of the original debt or merely a renegotiation of that debt determines the accounting treatment that should be applied by the borrower.

A6.8.153 IAS 39 requires an exchange between an existing borrower and lender of debt instruments with substantially different terms to be accounted for as an extinguishment of the original financial liability and the recognition of a new financial liability. Similarly, a substantial modification of the terms of an existing financial liability or a part of it (whether or not attributable to the financial difficulty of the debtor) should be accounted for as an extinguishment of the original financial liability and the recognition of a new financial liability. [IAS 39 para 40].

A6.8.154 The terms are substantially different if the discounted present value of the cash flows under the new terms, including any fees paid net of any fees received and discounted using the original effective interest rate, is at least ten per cent different from the discounted present value of the remaining cash flows of the original financial liability. [IAS 39 para AG 62].

A6.8.155 The standard does not clarify whether the quantitative analysis outlined above is an example of a term that is substantially different or whether the analysis is the definition of substantially different. There is an accounting policy choice. Although it is clear that if the discounted cash flows change by at least ten per cent, the original debt should be accounted for as an extinguishment, there is nothing in the standard to suggest that the analysis should be restricted only to cash flow changes. Indeed, in order to meet the spirit of the standard, analysis of any modification of terms that are qualitative in nature may be performed. For example, qualitative changes in risk profile of the newly modified instrument compared to the original instrument may well indicate that the changes in terms are substantially different as happens when the denomination of the original liability is changed to a different currency. In that situation, we believe it is acceptable to account for the substantial modification as an extinguishment, even though the above quantitative analysis may indicate a less than ten per cent cash flow change. Qualitative factors that should be considered include, but are not limited to the following:

- The currency that the debt instrument is denominated in.
- The interest rate (that is fixed *versus* floating rate).
- Conversion features attached to the instrument.
- Changes in covenants.

A6.8.156 Alternatively, since the standard is unclear whether the ten per cent test is the definition of substantially different, a quantitative analysis could be performed to determine whether an exchange or a modification should be accounted for as an extinguishment. Under this alternative view, if the change in discounted cash flows is less than ten per cent, the exchange or modification would not be accounted for as an extinguishment. This alternative view is also acceptable if applied consistently and properly disclosed in the notes.

Treatment of cost and fees incurred on debt restructuring

A6.8.157 If an exchange of debt instruments or modification of terms is accounted for as an extinguishment, any costs or fees incurred are recognised as part of the gain or loss on the extinguishment. If the exchange or modification is not accounted for as an extinguishment, any costs or fees incurred adjust the liability's carrying amount and are amortised over the modified liability's remaining term. [IAS 39 para AG 62].

A6.8.158 As the above paragraph refers to any cost or fees incurred, it would be appear that IAS 39 does not distinguish between costs and fees payable to third parties, such as lawyers and accountants, and those payable directly to the lender. As these costs and fees are properly incurred in connection with the modification of the instrument's terms, it is appropriate to treat them as adjustments to future interest payments rather than costs and fees in the true sense of the term. Accordingly, if the fees paid to third parties are related directly to the modification, they should be recognised as part of the gain or loss if the modification is accounted for as an extinguishment. This is true even if the modification results in the issue of a new debt instrument. Where the modification is not accounted for as an extinguishment, the fees paid to third parties are adjusted against the existing liability's carrying value.

Example – Renegotiation of debt

A company borrowed C1m on 1 January 20X0 at a fixed rate of 9% per annum for 10 years. The company incurred issue costs of C100,000. Interest on the loan is payable yearly in arrears. As a result of deteriorating financial condition during 20X5, the company approached its bondholders for a modification of the bond's terms. The following terms were agreed with effect from 1 January 20X6 (all interest paid to date):

- The interest rate is reduced to 7.5% payable yearly in arrears.
- The original amount payable on maturity is reduced to C950,000.
- The maturity of the loan is extended by two years to 31 December 20Y1.
- Renegotiation fees of C30,000 are payable on 1 January 20X6.

The loan would be recorded initially at 1 January 20X0 at net proceeds of C900,000 and would be amortised using the effective interest rate (EIR) method discussed in section 9. The EIR is 10.6749% as shown below.

	Interest	Payments	Carrying value
	10.6749%		
1 Jan 20X0			900,000
31 Dec 20X0	96,074	90,000	906,074
31 Dec 20X1	96,723	90,000	912,797
31 Dec 20X2	97,441	90,000	920,238
31 Dec 20X3	98,235	90,000	928,473
31 Dec 20X4	99,114	90,000	937,587
31 Dec 20X5	100,087	90,000	**947,674**
31 Dec 20X6	101,164	90,000	958,837
31 Dec 20X7	102,355	90,000	971,192
31 Dec 20X8	103,674	90,000	984,866
31 Dec 20X9	105,134	1,090,000	-

At 1 January 20X6, the remaining cash flows on the old debt comprise four annual interest payments of C90,000 and the C1m of principal payable at redemption. The present value of these remaining cash flows on that date amounts to C947,674 as shown above.

The present value of the cash flows under the revised terms discounted at the original EIR of 10.6749% is shown below:

		Cash Flows	Present value
1 Jan 20X6	Fees	30,000	30,000
31 Dec 20X6	Revised interest	75,000	67,766
31 Dec 20X7	Revised interest	75,000	61,230
31 Dec 20X8	Revised interest	75,000	55,324
31 Dec 20X9	Revised interest	75,000	49,988
31 Dec 20Y0	Revised interest	75,000	45,166
31 Dec 20Y1	Revised interest + principal	1,025,000	557,736
			867,210

The present value of C867,210 represents 91.5% of the present value of the old cash flows. As the difference in present values of C80,464 (947,674 – 867,210) is less than 10% of the present value of the old cash flows, the modification is not accounted for as extinguishment.

The question arises as to how to account for the present value difference of C80,464 arising from the renegotiation. One approach would be to recognise the difference immediately in profit or loss by adjusting the previous carrying value of the liability from C947,674 to C867,210. Another approach would be to recognise the difference over the remaining life of the instrument by adjusting the effective interest rate so that the previous carrying value of C947,674 accretes to the redemption amount of C950,000 by 31 December 20Y1. There is support for both approaches in IAS 39 as explained below.

The first approach is supported by paragraph AG 8 of IAS 39 that states:

> *"If the entity revises its estimates of payments or receipts, the entity shall adjust the carrying value of the financial asset or financial liability (or group of financial instruments) to reflect actual and revised estimated cash flows. The entity*

> *recalculates the carrying value by computing the present value of estimated future cash flows at the financial instrument's original effective interest rate. The adjustment is recognised as income or expense in profit or loss."* [IAS 39 para AG 8].

A renegotiation of an instrument's terms will change its contractual cash flows. This will also result in a change to the expected cash flows in most cases. Paragraph AG 8 can be read to apply to all cases in which cash flows are re-estimated, as there is nothing in that paragraph that limits it to cases when the cash flows are not renegotiated.

The second approach is supported by paragraph AG 62 as discussed in paragraph A6.8.153 above. As the change in terms is not considered to be a substantial modification and, therefore, does not result in the extinguishment of the original liability, it is a more faithful representation to recognise any net gain or loss over the modified instrument's remaining life. This is further supported by the fact that, in the previous version of IAS 39, IGC 62-1 dealt with this issue and clearly favoured this treatment. There is nothing in the revised IAS 39 that indicates that the IASB intended a change to this treatment. Indeed, the table of concordance between the old and the new standard clearly indicates that IGC 62-1 is mapped into AG 62. Furthermore, it could be argued that paragraph AG 8 is not applicable, as a renegotiation that changes the instrument's terms and, hence, the future cash flows, is not the same as the entity revising its estimates.

The effective interest rate that amortises the old carrying value, as adjusted for fees incurred of C30,000, is 8.6453 % as shown below:

	Interest@ 8.6453%	Payments	Carrying value
			947,674
Fees paid			(30,000)
01 Jan 20X0			917,674
31 Dec 20X6	79,336	75,000	922,010
31 Dec 20X7	79,710	75,000	926,720
31 Dec 20X8	80,117	75,000	931,837
31 Dec 20X9	80,560	75,000	937,397
31 Dec 20Y0	81,040	75,000	943,437
31 Dec 20Y1	81,563	1,025,000	-
	482,326	1,400,000	

As both treatments are acceptable, in practice, entities should choose the treatment that is most appropriate to the particular facts and circumstances of the transaction being accounted for. For example, if the renegotiation results in an immediate cash payment that includes a repayment of part of the principal, the first method would be more appropriate. This is because it would not be appropriate to spread forward a gain or loss that arises on a partial repayment by adjusting the EIR on the portion that continues to be recognised. Conversely, if an entity renegotiates to reduce the future interest payments on a loan in times of falling interest rates and partially compensates the lender by an immediate cash payment, the second method would be the more appropriate. This is because adjusting the EIR would best reflect the effect that the new interest rate environment has had on the remaining cash flows.

Measurement of financial assets and liabilities

Introduction

A6.9.1 An entity recognises a financial asset or a financial liability when it first becomes a party to the contractual rights and obligations in the contract. It is, therefore, necessary to measure those contractual rights and obligations on initial recognition. Under IAS 39, all financial instruments are measured initially by reference to their fair value, which is *normally* the transaction price, that is, the fair value of the consideration given or received. However, this will not always be the case.

A6.9.2 Subsequent to initial recognition, IAS 39's measurement approach is best described as a 'mixed attribute' model with certain assets and liabilities measured at cost and others at fair value. The model depends upon an instrument's classification into one of the four categories of financial assets or one of the two categories of financial liabilities discussed in section 5. For example, depending on the nature of the instrument and management's intentions, a fixed interest security intended to be held-to-maturity would be measured at amortised cost and not at fair value. Notwithstanding this, as explained in section 5, the standard gives entities the option to classify financial instruments that meet certain special criteria at fair value with all gains and losses taken to profit and loss. The ability for entities to use the fair value option simplifies the application of IAS 39 by mitigating some anomalies that result from the use of the mixed measurement model.

A6.9.3 This section deals with IAS 39's basic measurement requirements and addresses the concepts of fair value and amortised cost, including the use of the effective interest method and the standard's impairment model. However, the special form of accounting that applies when a financial asset or liability is designated by management in a hedging relationship is covered in section 10.

Initial measurement

Initial fair value

A6.9.4 When a financial asset or financial liability is recognised initially, IAS 39 requires the entity to measure it at its 'fair value' plus, in certain situations, transaction costs (see para A6.9.11 below). [IAS 39 para 43]. The standard defines fair value as the amount for which an asset could be exchanged, or a liability settled, between knowledgeable willing parties in an arm's length transaction. [IAS 39 para 9]. The concept of fair value and requirements for determining the fair value of financial instruments are discussed in detail from paragraph A6.9.72 below.

A6.9.5 Given that fair value is the price that arm's length market participants would pay or receive in a routine transaction under the market conditions at the date at which the asset or liability is to be measured for accounting purposes (the measurement date), it follows that a financial instrument's initial fair value will normally be the transaction price, that is, the fair value of the consideration given or received. [IAS 39 para AG 64].

A6.9.6 In some circumstances, however, the consideration given or received may not necessarily be the financial instrument's fair value. For example, the fair value of a long-term note receivable that carries no interest is not equal to its face amount and, therefore, part of the consideration received is something other than its fair value. As the note receivable would have to be recorded initially at its fair value, its fair value has to be estimated. The instrument's fair value may be evidenced by comparison with other observable current market transactions in the same instrument (that is, without modification or repackaging) or based on a valuation technique whose variables include only data from observable markets. [IAS 39 para AG 76]. For a long-term loan or receivable with no stated interest, the fair value is normally arrived at by using a discounted cash flow valuation method. Under this method, the fair value can be estimated as the present value of all future cash receipts discounted using the prevailing market rate of interest for a similar instrument (similar as to currency, term, type of interest rate and other factors) with a similar credit rating. Any additional amount lent is an expense or a reduction of income, unless it qualifies for recognition as some other type of asset. [IAS 39 para AG 64].

A6.9.7 However, as a pragmatic measure, the standard permits short-term receivables and payables to be measured at the original invoice amount if the effect of discounting is immaterial. [IAS 39 para AG 79]. The IFRIC also considered the accounting for extended payment terms, such as six-month's interest-free credit, and concluded that the accounting treatment under IAS 39 was clear. In such circumstances, the effect of the time value of money should be reflected when this is material. [IFRIC Update July 2004].

Example 1 – Interest free loan to a company

Entity A lends C1,000 to entity B for 5 years and classifies the asset under loans and receivables. The loan carries no interest. Instead, entity A expects other future economic benefits, such as an implicit right to receive goods or services at favourable prices.

On initial recognition, the market rate of interest for a similar 5 year loan with payment of interest at maturity is 10% per year. The loan's initial fair value is the present value of the future payment of 1,000 discounted using the market rate of interest for a similar loan of 10% for 5 years, that is, C621.

In this example, the consideration given of C1,000 is for two things – the fair value of the loan of C621 and entity A's right to obtain other future economic benefits that have a fair value of C379 (the difference between the total consideration given of C1,000 and the consideration given for the loan of C621).

Entity A recognises the loan at its initial fair value of C621 that will accrete to C1,000 over the term of the loan using the effective interest method (see further para A6.9.51 below).

The difference of C379 is not a financial asset, since it is paid to obtain expected future economic benefits other than the right to receive payment on the loan asset. Entity A recognises that amount as an expense unless it qualifies for recognition as an asset under, say, IAS 38, 'Intangible assets' or as part of the cost of investment in subsidiary, if entity B is a subsidiary of entity A.

Example 2 – Interest free loan to an employee

An entity grants an interest free loan of C1,000 to an employee for a period of two years. The market rate of interest to this individual for a two year loan with payment of interest at maturity is 10%.

The consideration given to the employee consists of two assets:

- The fair value of the loan, that is $C1{,}000/(1.10)^2 = C826$.
- The difference of C174 that is accounted for as employee compensation in accordance with IAS 19, 'Employee benefits'.

Example 3 – Interest free loan received from a government agency

An entity is located in an enterprise zone and receives an interest free loan of C500,000 from a government agency. The loan carries no interest and is repayable at the end of year three.

IAS 20, 'Accounting for government grants and disclosure of government assistance', provides guidance that loans at nil or low interest rates are a form of government assistance, but the benefit is not quantified by the imputation of interest. [IAS 20 para 37]. Therefore, the loan should be recorded at C500,000, the consideration received.

However, given that the loan meets the definition of a financial liability, the fair value of the loan is not its face amount of C500,000, the consideration received. The fair value of the loan would have to be estimated as explained above. Assuming that the fair value is estimated at C450,000, under IAS 39, the loan would be recorded initially at its fair value of C450,000.

Clearly there is a conflict between IAS 20 and IAS 39, which was acknowledged by the IASB. [IASB update July 2004]. At that time, the IASB tentatively decided in the revised version of IAS 20, to delete the reference to loans at nil or low interest rate from IAS 20 paragraph 37. However, in February 2006 the IASB decided the work on the IAS 20 project should be deferred. A revised standard is now expected in 2008.

In the interim, we believe entities have a policy choice of following either IAS 20 or IAS 39 as stated below. Whichever accounting policy is adopted, it should be applied consistently to all government loans with nil/low interest, and appropriate disclosure should be made within the accounting policy note.

- Policy choice of applying IAS 20

  The interest free loan would be recorded at C500,000, the amount received. This treatment will continue to apply until the amendments to IAS 20 are issued.

- Policy choice of applying IAS 39

  The interest free loan would be recorded at its fair value of C450,000. The difference between the consideration received and the fair value of the loan, that is, C50,000 would fall to be accounted for as a government grant in accordance with IAS 20, provided the loan from the government is income or asset related. In that situation, the grant would be recognised in income and matched to the asset/income to which it relates.

  On the other hand, if the loan is not asset or income related, it is treated as government assistance and not discounted (that is, approach 1 above).

6A.9.8 In some circumstances, instead of originating an interest free loan, an entity may originate a loan that bears an off-market interest rate (for example, a loan that carries a higher or lower rate than the prevailing current market rate for a similar loan) and pays or receives an initial fee as compensation. In that situation, the entity still recognises the loan at its initial fair value, that is, net of the fee paid or received as illustrated below. The fee paid or received is amortised to profit or loss using the effective interest method. [IAS 39 para AG 65]. A similar requirement is included in IAS 18, 'Revenue', where fees that are an integral part of a financial instrument's effective interest rate are generally treated as an adjustment to the effective interest rate. [IAS 18 para 14(a)].

Example – Off-market loan with origination fee

An entity originates a loan for C1,000 that is repayable in 5 year's time. The loan carries interest at 6%, which is less than the market rate of 8% for a similar loan. The entity receives C80 as compensation for originating a below market loan.

The entity should recognise the loan at its initial fair value of C920 (net present value of C60 of interest for 5 years and principal repayment of C1,000 discounted at 8%). This is equal to the net cash received (loan of C1,000 less origination fee of C80). The net amount of the loan of C920 accretes to C1,000 over the 5 year term using an effective interest of 8%.

In this example, the upfront fee received of C80 exactly compensates the entity for interest short fall of C20 for each of the next 5 years discounted at the market rate of 8%. Hence, no gain or loss arises on initial recognition.

6A.9.9 A further exception to the general rule that the transaction price is not necessarily the financial instrument's initial fair value is of particular relevance to banking and insurance entities. Such entities often originate structured transactions and use models to estimate their fair values. Such models may show a 'day 1' gain (that is, the fair value exceeds the transaction price). However, the IASB permits departure from the transaction price only if fair value is evidenced by observable current market transactions in the same instrument or a valuation technique whose variables include only data from observable markets. As a result, an immediate 'day 1' gain is rarely recognised on initial recognition. This issue is considered further in paragraph A6.9.107 below.

Transaction costs

A6.9.10 Transaction costs are incremental costs that are directly attributable to the acquisition or issue or disposal of a financial asset or financial liability. An incremental cost is one that would not have been incurred if the entity had not acquired, issued or disposed of the financial instrument. [IAS 39 para 9].

A6.9.11 Transaction costs include fees and commissions paid to agents (including employees acting as selling agents), advisers, brokers and dealers, levies by regulatory agencies and securities exchanges and transfer taxes and duties. Transaction costs do not include debt premiums or discounts, financing costs or internal administrative or holding costs. [IAS 39 para AG 13].

A6.9.12 It should be noted that the exposure draft preceding the revised version of IAS 39 restricted transaction costs to include only external costs. The final standard amended the definition of transaction costs to include internal costs, provided they are incremental and directly attributable to the acquisition, issue or disposal of a financial asset or financial liability. [IAS 39 para BC222(d)]. However, in practice, other than payments made to employees acting as selling agents (common in insurance contracts that fall to be accounted for under IAS 39 as financial instruments), salary costs of employees that would be incurred irrespective of whether the loan was granted are not incremental, nor are allocated indirect administrative costs or overheads.

A6.9.13 The appendix to IAS 18, 'Revenue', sets out a number of examples of financial services fees. IAS 18 distinguishes such fees between those that are an integral part of generating an involvement with the resulting financial instrument and those that are earned as services are provided. Such fees may fall into two categories: fees associated with origination of a loan (loan origination fees) and fees associated with commitment to lend (commitment fees).

A6.9.14 Loan origination fees may consist of:

- Fees that are charged to the borrower as 'pre-paid' interest or to reduce the loan's nominal interest rate (explicit yield adjustments).
- Fees to compensate the lender for origination activities such as evaluating the borrower's financial condition, evaluating and recording guarantees, collateral and other security arrangements, negotiating the instrument's terms, preparing and processing documents and closing the transaction.
- Other fees that relate directly to making the loan (for example, fees that are paid to the lender as compensation for granting a complex loan or agreeing to lend quickly).

A6.9.15 Commitment fees are fees that are charged by the lender for entering into an agreement to make or acquire a loan. Sometimes they are referred to as facility fees for making a loan facility available to a borrower. The accounting treatment depends on whether or not it is probable that the entity will enter into a specific lending arrangement and whether the loan commitment is within IAS 39's scope. If it is probable that the entity will enter into the lending agreement, the commitment fee received is regarded as compensation for an ongoing involvement with the acquisition of a financial instrument.

A6.9.16 Direct loan origination costs relate to costs incurred by the entity for undertaking activities set out in the second bullet point of paragraph A6.9.14 above. Internal costs directly related to those activities should include only that portion of employee cost directly related to time spent performing those activities (see para A6.9.14 above).

A6.9.17 It is apparent from the nature of the above fees that they are an integral part of generating an involvement with the resulting financial instrument and together with the related direct origination costs, are accounted for in a financial instrument's initial measurement as follows:

- When a financial asset or financial liability is recognised initially and not designated as at fair value through profit or loss, transaction costs (net of fees received) that are directly attributable to the acquisition or issue are included in the initial fair value. For financial assets, such costs are added to the amount originally recognised. For financial liabilities, such costs are deducted from the amount originally recognised. This applies to financial instruments carried at amortised cost and available-for-sale financial assets. [IAS 39 para 43].
- For financial instruments that are measured at fair value through profit or loss, transaction costs (net of any fees received) are not added to the initial fair value, but are immediately recognised in profit or loss on initial recognition.
- Transaction costs expected to be incurred on a financial instrument's transfer or disposal are not included in the financial instrument's measurement.

[IAS 39 para IG E1.1].

Example – Initial measurement – transaction cost

An entity acquires an available-for-sale financial asset at its fair value of C100. Purchase commission of C2 is also payable. At the end of the entity's financial year, the asset's quoted market price is C105. If the asset was to be sold, a commission of C3 would be payable.

As the asset will not be measured at fair value through profit or loss, the entity recognises the financial asset at its fair value that includes the purchase commission, that is, at C102. At the end of the entity's financial year, the asset is recorded at C105 without regard to the commission of C3 payable on sale. The change in fair value of C3 recognised in equity includes the purchase commission of C2 payable at the acquisition date.

6A.9.18 Entities may also receive fees for the provision of a service, such as loan servicing fee, or for the execution of a significant act such as placement fees for arranging a loan between two third parties and loan syndication fees. These fees are not integral to lending or borrowing and, therefore, cannot form part of the financial instrument's measurement.

A6.9.19 The treatment of transaction costs on the subsequent measurement of available-for-sale financial assets is considered in paragraph A6.9.30 below and those carried at amortised cost are considered in paragraph A6.9.59 below.

Settlement date accounting for regular way transactions

A6.9.20 When an entity uses settlement date accounting for an asset that is subsequently measured at cost or amortised cost, the asset is recognised initially at settlement date, but measured at the fair value on trade date. [IAS 39 para 44]. This is an exception to the general rule in paragraph A6.9.4 above that a financial asset should be recognised at its fair value on initial recognition. The accounting for regular way trades is considered in section 8.

Subsequent measurement of financial assets

General

A6.9.21 As set out in section 6, financial assets are classified in one of four categories. Following their initial recognition, the classification determines how the financial asset is subsequently measured, including any profit or loss recognition. The following table summarises the requirements that are considered in detail in the remainder of this section.

Classification	Financial asset	Measurement basis	Changes in carrying amount	Impairment test (if objective evidence)
At fair value through profit or loss	Debt	Fair value	Profit or loss [2,3]	No [5]
	Equity	Fair value	Profit or loss [2]	No [5]
	Derivatives not designated as effective hedging instruments	Fair value	Profit or loss [2]	-
Loans and receivables	Debt	Amortised cost	Profit or loss [3]	Yes
Held-to-maturity investments	Debt	Amortised cost	Profit or loss [3]	Yes

Available-for-sale financial assets	Debt	Fair value	Equity [2] Profit or loss [3]	Yes
	Equity	Fair value	Equity [2] Profit or loss [4]	Yes
	Equity [1]	Cost (fair value not reliably measurable)	Profit or loss [4]	Yes

1 Equity instruments that do not have any quoted market price in an active market and whose fair value cannot be reliably measured and derivative assets that are linked to and must be settled by delivery of such unquoted equity instruments.

2 Change in fair value other than those noted in note 3 or 4 below where relevant.

3 Interest calculated using the effective interest method, foreign exchange differences, impairment and reversal of impairment, where relevant, are taken to profit or loss.

4 Dividends and impairment are taken to profit or loss. Foreign exchange difference on AFS investments taken to equity and recycled to profit or loss on disposal or impairment.

5 Any impairment will be taken though profit or loss as part of the change in fair value and so separate impairment testing is not necessary.

A6.9.22 Financial assets that are designated as hedged items are subject to measurement under the hedge accounting requirements. These requirements apply in addition to, and may modify, the general accounting requirements that are discussed below. Hedge accounting is covered in section 10.

Financial assets at fair value through profit or loss

A6.9.23 After initial recognition, financial assets falling within this category (including assets held for trading and derivative assets not designated as effective hedging instruments and assets designated on initial recognition at fair value through profit or loss) are measured at fair value, without the deduction of transaction costs that the entity may incur on sale or other disposal. [IAS 39 para 46]. Such transaction costs are future costs that relate to the sale or the disposal and have no relevance to determining fair value. Therefore, they are properly included in the period in which the sale or the disposal takes place.

A6.9.24 The standard's requirements for determining the fair value of instruments that fall to be measured on this basis are considered from paragraph A6.9.72 below. Investments in equity instruments that do not have a quoted market price in an active market and whose fair value cannot be reliably measured and derivatives that are linked to and must be settled by delivery of such unquoted equity instruments, are measured at cost (see further para A6.9.104 below). [IAS 39 para 46(c)].

A6.9.25 All gains and losses arising from changes in fair value of financial assets falling within this category are recognised, not surprisingly, in profit or loss. [IAS 39 para 55(a)]. This means that assets falling within this category are not subject to review for impairment as losses due to fall in value (including impairment) would automatically be reflected in profit or loss.

Loans and receivables

A6.9.26 Loans and receivables, as defined in section 6, are measured at amortised cost using the effective interest method. [IAS 39 para 46(b)]. They are measured on this basis whether they are intended to be held-to-maturity or not. [IAS 39 para AG 68]. The amortised cost method of accounting is discussed from paragraph A6.9.51 below.

A6.9.27 Gains and losses are recognised in profit or loss when loans and receivables are derecognised or impaired and throughout the amortisation process. Special rules apply for gain or loss recognition when loans and receivables are designated as hedged items. [IAS 39 para 56].

Held-to-maturity investments

A6.9.28 Held-to-maturity investments are also measured at amortised cost using the effective interest method. Gains and losses are accounted for in the same way as loans and receivables.

Available-for-sale assets

A6.9.29 Available-for-sale financial assets are measured at fair value. As with assets designated as at fair value through profit or loss, transaction costs that will be incurred on the sale or disposal of such assets are not deducted from the measurement. However, there is an exemption from measurement at fair value of an available-for-sale asset if its fair value cannot be measured reliably (see para A6.9.24 above). This exemption only applies to unquoted equity instruments and derivative contracts based on those instruments. These instruments are measured at cost. [IAS 39 para 46(c)].

A6.9.30 As explained in paragraph A6.9.17 above, transaction costs that are directly attributable to the acquisition or issue of an available-for-sale financial asset are included in the initial fair value. For available-for-sale financial assets, transaction costs are recognised in equity as part of a change in fair value at the next remeasurement. If an available-for-sale financial asset has fixed or determinable payments and does not have an indefinite life, the transaction costs are amortised to profit or loss using the effective interest method (see para A6.9.52 below). If an available-for-sale financial asset does not have fixed or determinable payments and has an indefinite life, the transaction costs are recognised in profit or loss when the asset is derecognised or becomes impaired. [IAS 39 para AG 67].

A6.9.31 All gains and losses arising from changes in fair value of available-for-sale financial assets are recognised directly in equity, through the statement of changes in equity, except as follows:

- Interest calculated using the effective interest method is recognised in profit or loss (see further para A6.9.51 below). Dividends on an available-for-sale equity instruments are recognised in profit or loss when the entity's right to receive payment is established. [IAS 18 para 30(c)].

- Foreign exchange gains and losses on monetary financial assets are recognised in profit or loss (see further para A6.9.162 below).
- Impairment losses are recognised in profit or loss (see further para A6.9.152 below). Reversals of impairment of a debt instrument are also recognised in profit or loss, but reversals of impairment on equity instruments are not (see further para A6.9.154 below).

[IAS 39 para 55(b)].

A6.9.32 When an available-for-sale financial asset is derecognised as a result of sale or is impaired, the cumulative gain or loss previously recognised in equity is recycled and recognised in profit or loss. [IAS 39 paras 55(b), 67]. For example, assume that an entity acquires an equity security for C500 that has a fair value at the end of the year of C600. A gain of C100 is recognised in equity. In the following year, the entity sells the security for C550. In the year of sale, a profit of C50, being the difference between proceeds of C550 and original cost of C500 is recognised. This represents the difference between proceeds of C550 and previous carrying value of C600 (C50 loss) and the recycling to profit or loss of C100 gain previously recognised in equity.

A6.9.33 In the above example, a single security is used to illustrate the accounting for recycling. In practice, the entity may have acquired the same security in tranches at different dates and at different prices over a period of time. IAS 39 does not specify whether such fungible assets (or indeed any other fungible financial assets) should be considered individually or in aggregate, and, if in aggregate, which measurement basis (weighted average, first in first out (FIFO), etc) is appropriate for calculating the gain or loss on a partial disposal. This is in contrast to IAS 2, 'Inventories', which specifies the use of weighted average or FIFO in most circumstances. In practice, entities may opt, as an accounting policy choice, for any one of the methods. The method used should be applied consistently and disclosed in its accounting policy.

A6.9.34 The subsequent measurement of available-for-sale financial assets with fixed and determinable payments is complicated by the fact that fair value changes are recognised in equity, but interest income is recognised in each period in profit or loss using the effective interest method. In order to ensure that the change in fair value is correctly calculated at the measurement date, it would be necessary to compare the instrument's clean price (the fair value of the instrument less accrued interest) with its amortised cost, also excluding accrued interest, at that date. Therefore, although the instrument is measured at fair value, the amortised cost must still be calculated using the effective interest method in order to determine interest income.

Example – Debt security classified as available-for-sale investment

On 1 January 20X5, an entity purchases 10% C10 million 5 year bonds with interest payable on 1 July and 1 January each year. The bond's purchase price is C10,811,100. The premium of C811,100 is due to market yield for similar bonds being 8%. Assuming there are no transaction costs, the effective interest rate is 8% (the effective interest method is discussed further in paragraph A6.9.52 below).

The entity classifies the bond as an available-for-sale investment. The entity prepares its financial statements to 31 March each year. On 31 March 20X5, the interest on bonds with similar maturity and credit risk is 7.75%. At that date, the fair value of this bond calculated by discounting 10 semi-annual cash flows of C500,000 and principal payment of C10 million at maturity at the market rate of 7.75% amounted to C11,127,710.

Since the bond is classified as an available-for-sale, the bond will be measured at fair value with changes in fair value recognised in equity.

At 1 January 20X5, the fair value of the bond is the consideration paid of C10,811,100 and the entry to record this is as follows:

	Dr	Cr
	C	C
At 1 January 20X5		
Available-for-sale investment	10,811,100	
Cash		10,811,100

On 31 March 20X5, the entity will record interest income for the 3 months at the effective interest rate of 8%, that is, C10,811,100 × 8% × 3/12 = C216,222. Since the next coupon of C500,000 is due on 1 July 20X5, the entity will record a half-year interest accrual of C250,000. The difference of C33,778 between the interest income accrued and that recognised in the profit or loss represents the amortisation of the premium. The entry to record the interest income on 31 March 20X6 is as follows:

	Dr	Cr
	C	C
At 31 March 20X5		
Available-for-sale investment (accrued interest)	250,000	
Available-for-sale investment (premium)		33,778
Profit or loss – interest income		216,222

The bond's amortised cost at 31 March 20X5 is, therefore, C10,777,322 (10,811,100 – 33,778)

The fair value of the bond at 31 March 20X5 is C11,127,710. This includes the accrued interest of C250,000. To calculate the clean price of the bond, the accrued income is deducted from the fair value. Therefore, the clean price of the bond is C10,877,710.

A comparison of the clean price of the bond and its amortised cost at 31 March 20X5 results in a gain as follows:

	C
Fair value of bond at 31 March 20X5 – clean price	10,877,710
Amortised cost of bond at 31 March 20X5	10,777,322
Change in value – Unrealised gain	100,388

The entry to record the gain at 31 March 20X5 is as follows:

	Dr	Cr
	C	C
At 31 March 20X5		
Available-for-sale investments	100,388	
Equity		100,388

	C
The movement in available-for-sale asset is shown below:	
At 1 Jan 20X5 – Fair value (inclusive of premium)	10,811,100
Accrued income (reflected in fair value)	250,000
Amortisation of premium	(33,778)
Fair value adjustment — gain	100,388
At 31 Mar 20X5 – Fair value	11,127,710
	C
Recognised in profit or loss – income	216,222
Recognised in equity – gain	100,388
Total change in fair value	316,610

A6.9.35 As stated in paragraph A6.9.31 above, dividends on an available-for-sale equity instrument are recognised in profit or loss when the entity's right to receive payment is established. The right to receive payment is established when the equity instrument's issuer declares a dividend or in the case of quoted equity securities, at the ex-dividend date. When a share goes ex-dividend shortly before the dividend payment is actually due, the price will drop (other things being equal) by the amount of the dividend. Therefore, depending upon the ex-dividend date (when the dividend income is recognised) and the payment date (when the receivable is settled), the realisation of part of the fair value through dividend payment will affect both profit or loss and equity as illustrated below.

Example – Dividend on available-for-sale investments

An entity acquires 1,000 quoted equity shares in another entity for C20,000. The shares are classified as available-for-sale. Just prior to the entity's year end of 31 December 20X5, the security goes ex-dividend following declaration of a dividend of C1.50 per share. At 31 December 20X5, the quoted ex-dividend price of the shares amounts to C21 per share. The entity receives payment of the dividend on 6 January 20X6.

At 31 December 20X5, the entity will recognise the dividend income in profit or loss and the change in the fair value of the shares in equity as noted below:

	Dr	Cr
	C	C
Dividend receivable	1,500	
Profit or loss – dividend income – 1,000 @ 1.50		1,500
Available-for-sale financial asset	1,000	
Equity – 1,000 @ (21-20)		1,000

The shares' quoted price prior to the dividend adjustment would have been C22.50 giving a total fair value change of C2,500. However, as part of this change (C1,500) is realised as a result of the dividend income recognised in profit or loss; there is an equal and offsetting change in equity.

Designation as hedged items

A6.9.36 Financial assets that are designated as hedged items are subject to measurement under IAS 39's hedging accounting requirements. [IAS 39 para 46]. These special accounting rules generally override the normal accounting rules for financial assets. Hedge accounting is covered in section 10.

Reclassifications between categories

A6.9.37 The revised standard permits reclassification between held-to-maturity investments and available-for-sale. In practice, reclassification from held-to-maturity to available-for sale should be rare as it would 'taint' the entire portfolio, unless the reclassification meets one of the permitted exceptions (see section 6).

A6.9.38 When a held-to-maturity investment is reclassified as available-for-sale, it should be remeasured at fair value at the date of reclassification and the difference between its previous carrying amount and fair value should be recognised in equity. [IAS 39 paras 51, 52].

Example – Held-to-maturity investment reclassified as available-for-sale financial asset

On 1 January 20X0, an entity purchases 10% C10 million 10 year bonds with interest payable annually on 31 December each year. The bond's purchase price is C10,811,100, which results in a bond premium of C811,100 and an effective interest rate of 8.75%. The bonds were classified by the entity as held-to-maturity.

On 31 December 20X5, when the bonds amortised cost and fair value amounted to C10,407,192 and C10,749,395 respectively, the entity sells C1 million bonds and realises a gain as shown below:

	C
Fair value of C1 million bond (10% of C10,749,395)	1,074,940
Carrying value of C1 million bond (10% of C10,407,192)	1,040,719
Profit on disposal recognised in profit or loss	34,221

Since the entity has sold more than an insignificant amount of its held-to-maturity investments, the portfolio is tainted. As a result, the entity has to reclassify the remaining C9 million bonds as available-for-sale assets. The difference between the carrying value of C9 million bonds and their fair value is recognised in equity as shown below:

	C
Fair value of C9 million bond (90% of C10,749,395)	9,674,455
Carrying value of C9million bonds (90% of C10,407,192)	9,366,473
Gain on reclassification recognised in equity	307,982

Even though the remaining investment is classified as available-for-sale, the entity will continue to recognise the interest income and the amortisation of the premium using the effective interest method in profit or loss and fair value changes in equity as illustrated in the example in paragraph A6.9.34 above. After the tainting period is over, the entity may reinstate the bonds again to held-to-maturity. This will happen after 31 December 20X7 (two full financial years following the partial disposal).

A6.9.39 When an available-for-sale financial asset with fixed maturity is reclassified as held-to-maturity investment, the fair value carrying amount of the financial asset on that date becomes its new amortised cost. Any previous gain or loss on that asset that has been recognised directly in equity should be amortised to profit and loss over the remaining life of the held-to-maturity investment using the effective interest method. Any difference between the new amortised cost and maturity amount should also be amortised in a similar manner, akin to the amortisation of a premium or discount. If the financial asset is subsequently impaired, any gain or loss that has been recognised directly in equity is recognised in profit or loss. [IAS 39 para 54(a)].

Example – Available-for-sale debt security reclassified as held-to-maturity

The facts are the same as in the above example, except that on 1 January 20X8 after the end of the tainting period (2 full financial years following the partial disposal on 31 December 20X5), the entity reclassifies the C9 million bonds as held-to-maturity. On that date, the bonds' *fair value* carrying amount of C9,488,165 becomes the new amortised cost giving rise to a premium of C488,165 which is amortised to profit or loss during the remaining 2 years to maturity at 31 December 20X9 at a new effective rate of 7% as shown below.

In addition, the cumulative gain of C289,594 in equity as at 31 December 20X7 (fair value of C9,488,165 – amortised cost of C9,198,571) is also amortised to income during the remaining two years to maturity. The effect in profit or loss is the same as if the bond had always been classified as held-to-maturity as illustrated below:

	Cash received	Interest income @ 7%	New Amortised cost
	C	C	C
1 Jan 20X8			9,488,165
31 Dec 20X8	900,000	664,172	9,252,337
31 Dec 20X9	9,900,000	647,663	-
		1,311,835	
31 Dec 20X6		819,568	
31 Dec 20X7		812,530	
Amortisation of gain in equity in 20X8 and 20X9		289,594	
Total amount recognised in profit or loss		3,233,527	

If the C9million bonds had not been reclassified as available-for-sale, the total amount recognised in profit or loss would have been as follows:

	Cash received	Interest income @ 8.75%	Amortised cost
	C	C	C
31 Dec 20X5			9,366,473
31 Dec 20X6	900,000	819,568	9,286,041
31 Dec 20X7	900,000	812,530	9,198,571
31 Dec 20X8	900,000	804,876	9,103,447
31 Dec 20X9	9,900,000	796,553	–
Total income from date of reclassification to maturity		3,233,527	

Settlement date accounting for regular way transactions

A6.9.40 As stated in paragraph A6.9.20 above, when an entity uses settlement date accounting for an asset that is subsequently measured at cost or amortised cost, the asset is recognised initially at its fair value at trade date. Any subsequent change in fair value between trade date and settlement date is not recognised (other than impairment losses). For assets that are subsequently measured at fair value, any change in fair value between trade date and settlement date is recognised:

- In profit or loss for assets classified as at FVTPL.
- In equity for assets classified as available-for-sale.

A6.9.41 When assets measured at fair value are sold on a regular way basis, the change in fair value between trade date (the date the entity enters into the sales contract) and settlement date (the date proceeds are received) is not recorded because the seller's right to changes in fair value ceases on the trade date (see further section 6).

Negative fair values

A6.9.42 The standard clarifies that if a financial instrument that was previously recognised as a financial asset is measured at fair value and its fair value falls below zero, it becomes a financial liability that should be measured as considered below. [IAS 39 para AG 66].

Subsequent measurement of financial liabilities

A6.9.43 After initial recognition, an entity should measure financial liabilities, other than those described in paragraphs 6.9.45 to 6.9.50 below, at amortised cost using the effective interest method as discussed from paragraph A6.9.51 below. [IAS 39 para 47].

A6.9.44 Where a financial liability is carried at amortised cost, a gain or loss is recognised in profit or loss when the financial liability is derecognised or through the amortisation process. [IAS 39 para 56].

Financial liabilities at fair value through profit or loss

A6.9.45 After initial recognition, financial liabilities falling within this category (including liabilities held for trading and derivative liabilities not designated as hedging instruments) are measured at fair value. However, a derivative liability that is linked to and must be settled by delivery of an unquoted equity instrument whose fair value cannot be reliably measured should be measured at cost. [IAS 39 para 47(a)].

A6.9.46 A change in a financial liability's fair value in this category that is not part of a hedging relationship should be recognised in the profit or loss for the period. [IAS 39 para 55]. The standard's requirements for determining the fair value of instruments that fall to be measured on this basis are considered from paragraph A6.9.72 below.

Arising on transfers of financial assets

A6.9.47 Certain financial liabilities may arise when a transfer of a financial asset does not qualify for derecognition, or is accounted for using the continuing *involvement* approach. For example, a sale of an asset that is accompanied by the seller giving a guarantee of the asset's future worth may, depending on the substance, give rise to the asset's derecognition and recognition of a liability in respect of the guarantee or it may result in the asset not being derecognised and the proceeds being shown as a liability. Special rules apply for the measurement of the transferred asset and the associated liability so that these are measured on a basis that reflects the rights and obligations that the entity has retained. [IAS 39 paras 29, 31, 47(b)]. See further section 8.

Financial guarantee contracts

A6.9.48 Financial guarantee contracts are defined in section 3. Financial guarantee contracts that are accounted for as financial liabilities under IAS 39 by the issuer are initially recognised at fair value. If the financial guarantee contract was issued to an unrelated party in a stand-alone arm's length transaction, its fair value at inception would likely be to equal the premium received, unless there was evidence to the contrary. [IAS 39 para AG4(a)].

A6.9.48.1 In some circumstances, an issuer expects to receive recurring future premiums from an issued financial guarantee contract (for example, it issues a five year guarantee with annual premiums due at the start of each year). In that situation, an issue arises as to whether the issuer should recognise a receivable for the discounted value of the expected future premiums or should it recognise only the initial cash received (if any). As stated above, IAS 39 requires the financial guarantee contract to be initially recorded at fair value; that is likely to equal the premium received. By analogy with derivative contracts the fair value will take into account any future cash flows on the instrument including those relating to premiums receivable.

A6.9.48.2 IAS 39 does not explicitly prohibit the recognition of a gross receivable for future premiums not yet due. This is evidenced by the basis for conclusions, paragraph BC 23D, which states that the IAS 39 requirement for initial recognition at fair value is consistent with US GAAP as represented by FIN 45 (FIN 45 requires recognition of a gross receivable). Accordingly, entities are permitted to recognise a gross receivable (an undiscounted amount for future premiums).

A6.9.48.3 Whether an issuer should record the guarantee initially on a discounted or an undiscounted basis becomes a policy choice that should be made carefully and applied consistently to all issued financial guarantee contracts. For entities that are not banks or insurance companies, the amount of the receivable will be amortised to income using the effective interest method if discounted; or on a straight line basis where it is recorded at an undiscounted amount. The amortisation is included in other income.

A6.9.48.4 Subsequent to initial recognition, financial guarantee contracts are measured at the higher of:

- the amount determined in accordance with IAS 37, 'Provisions, contingent liabilities and contingent assets';

- the amount initially recognised (fair value) less, when appropriate, cumulative amortisation of the initial amount recognised in accordance with IAS 18, 'Revenue'.

[IAS 39 para 47(c)].

A6.9.48.5 However, the above requirements do not apply:

- if the financial guarantee contract was designated at fair value through profit or loss at inception. A contract designated at inception as at fair value through profit or loss are measured at fair value subsequently; or
- if the financial guarantee contract was entered into or retained on transferring financial assets or financial liabilities to another party and prevented derecognition of the financial asset or resulted in continuing involvement (see section 8).

[IAS 39 para 47(a)(b), AG 4].

Intra-group financial guarantee contracts

A6.9.48.6 As stated in section 3, intra-group financial guarantee contracts are not exempted from IAS 39's requirements and, on a stand-alone basis, will have to be measured in accordance with the standard. On a consolidation basis, the financial guarantee is not recognised as a separate contract, but is part of the group's liability to a third party. In the individual financial statements, the financial guarantee is recognised initially at fair value in accordance with IAS 39 (unless IFRS 4 applies).

A6.9.48.7 Establishing such a fair value may be difficult if the financial guarantee contracts between related parties were not negotiated at arm's length and there are no comparable observable transactions with third parties. Given that intra-group guarantees are unlikely to be negotiated in a 'stand-alone arm's length transaction', fair value would have to be estimated. Paragraph 6.9.103.1 provides guidance on how to measure the fair value of intra-group financial guarantees.

A6.9.48.8 As the fair value of an intra-group guarantee is unlikely to be equal to the fee charged, if any, the issuer would need to determine whether any difference should be treated as an expense or a capital contribution *via* an increase in investments in the subsidiary. This is an accounting policy choice. The method used should reflect the transaction's economic substance, be applied consistently to all similar transactions and be clearly disclosed in the financial statements. While each entity within a group can choose its own accounting policies, those policies must be aligned on consolidation.

Commitments to provide off-market loans

A6.9.49 An entity may enter into a commitment to provide a loan at a below-market rate. After initial recognition at fair value, such a commitment is subsequently measured in the same way as a financial guarantee contract stated above. [IAS 39 para 47(d)].

Designation as hedged items

A6.9.50 Financial liabilities that are designated as hedged items are subject to measurement under IAS 39's hedging accounting requirements. [IAS 39 para 47]. These special accounting rules generally override the normal accounting rules for financial liabilities. Hedge accounting is covered in section 10.

Amortised cost and the effective interest method

General

A6.9.51 The amortised cost of a financial asset or financial liability is defined as the amount at which the financial asset or financial liability is measured at initial recognition minus principal repayments, plus or minus the cumulative amortisation using the 'effective interest method' of any difference between that initial amount and the maturity amount and minus any reduction (directly or through the use of an allowance account) for impairment or uncollectibility. [IAS 39 para 9].

A6.9.52 The effective interest method is a method of calculating the amortised cost of a financial asset or a financial liability (or group of financial assets or financial liabilities) and of allocating the interest income or interest expense over the relevant period. The method's principal features are as follows:

- The effective interest rate is the rate that exactly discounts estimated future cash payments or receipts through financial instrument's the *expected life* or, when appropriate, a shorter period, to the net carrying amount of the financial asset or financial liability (see para A6.9.60 below). The effective interest rate is sometimes termed the level yield to maturity or to the next repricing date and is the internal rate of return of the financial asset or liability for that period. The internal rate of return can be calculated using a financial calculator, or the IRR function in a spreadsheet.
- When calculating the effective interest rate, an entity should estimate cash flows considering all the financial instrument's contractual terms (for example, pre-payment, call and similar options), but should not consider future credit losses.
- The calculation should include all fees and points paid or received between parties to the contract that are an integral part of the effective interest rate, transaction costs, and all other premiums or discounts.

[IAS 39 para 9].

A6.9.53 The effective interest rate method is grounded in historical transaction values, because its determination is based on the initial carrying amount of the financial asset or liability. Therefore, once determined it is not recalculated to reflect fair value changes in financial assets, for example, interest bearing available-for-sale assets due to changes in market interest rates. The effective interest method produces a periodic interest income or expense equal to a constant percentage of the carrying value of the financial asset or liability as illustrated in the example given in paragraph A6.9.62 below.

Estimation of cash flows

A6.9.54 As noted in paragraph A6.9.52 above, the effective interest method uses a set of *estimated* future cash flows through the expected life of the financial instrument using all the financial instrument's contractual terms, rather than *contractual* cash flows. However, the financial instrument's expected life cannot exceed its contracted life. This applies not only to individual financial instruments, but to groups of financial instruments as well to achieve consistency of application. As the cash flows are often outlined in a contract or linked in some other way to the financial asset or financial liability in question, there is a presumption that the future cash flows can be reliably estimated for most financial assets and financial liabilities, in particular for a group of similar financial assets and similar financial liabilities. [IAS 39 para 9]. For example, for a portfolio of pre-payable mortgage loans, banks and financial institutions often estimate pre-payment patterns based on historical data and build the cash flows arising on early settlement (including any pre-payment penalty) into the effective interest rate calculation.

A6.9.55 However, in some rare cases it might not be possible to estimate reliably the cash flows of a financial instrument (or group of financial instruments). In those rare cases, the entity should use the contractual cash flows over the full contractual term of the financial instrument (or group of financial instruments). [IAS 39 para 9].

A6.9.56 The standard requires that in estimating the future cash flows all the instrument's contractual terms, including pre-payment, call and similar options should be considered. [IAS 39 para 9]. Such pre-payment, call and put options, which are often embedded in the debt instruments, are derivatives. Therefore, as explained, in section 5, the entity must first determine whether such options need to be separately accounted for as embedded derivatives. Separate accounting for the embedded derivative will not be necessary if the option's exercise price is approximately equal to the instrument's amortised cost on each exercise date, because in that situation the embedded derivative is regarded as closely related to the debt host. [IAS 39 para AG 30(g)].

A6.9.57 Where a pre-payment, call or put option falls to be separately accounted for, its impact on estimating the future cash flows for the purposes of determining the effective interest rate should be ignored. Although this is not explained in the standard, it is rather obvious as to do otherwise would result in double counting the effects of the embedded derivative in profit or loss – first through the option's fair value movement and, secondly, through its effect on the effective interest rate. In practice, this means that if the option is regarded as closely related and not separately accounted for, the entity, in determining the instrument's expected life, needs to assess whether the option is likely to be exercised in estimating the future cash flows at inception. Furthermore, this assessment should continue in subsequent periods until the debt instrument is settled, because the likelihood of the option being exercised will affect the timing and amount of the future cash flows and will have an immediate impact in profit or loss. On the other hand, if the option is accounted for as a separate derivative, such considerations are not necessary as the likelihood of the option being exercised will be reflected in its fair value. In that situation, the effective interest rate is based on the instrument's contractual term. See further paragraph A6.9.65 below.

A6.9.58 The standard also makes it clear that expected or future credit losses (defaults) should not be included in estimates of cash flows, because this would be a departure from the incurred loss model for impairment recognition. However, in some cases, financial assets are acquired at a deep discount that reflects incurred losses (for example, purchase of impaired debt). As such losses are already reflected in the price, they should be included in the estimated cash flows when computing the effective interest rate. [IAS 39 para AG 5]. Accordingly, the effective interest rate of the acquired distressed loan would be the discount rate that equates the present value of the expected cash flows (this would be less than the contractual cash flows specified in the loan agreement because of incurred credit losses) with the purchase price of the loan. The alternative of not including such credit losses in the calculation of the effective interest rate means that the entity would recognise a higher interest income than that inherent in the price paid.

Transaction costs and fees

A6.9.59 Transaction costs and fees are discussed from paragraph A6.9.11 above. To the extent that they are integral to generating an involvement with a financial instrument, such costs and fees are included in the financial instrument's initial measurement. For financial instruments that are carried at amortised cost, such as held-to-maturity investments, loans and receivables, and financial liabilities that are not at fair value through profit or loss, transaction costs and fees are, therefore, included in calculating amortised cost using the effective interest method. This means that, in effect, they are amortised through profit or loss over the instrument's life (see para A6.9.52 above).

Amortisation period

A6.9.60 Consistent with the estimated cash flow approach outlined from paragraph A6.9.54 above, the standard requires fees, points paid or received, transaction costs and other premiums or discount that are integral to the effective interest rate to be amortised over the instrument's expected life or, when applicable, a shorter period. A shorter period is used when the variable (for example, interest rates) to which the fee, transaction costs, discount or premium relates is repriced to market rates before the instrument's expected maturity. In such a case, the appropriate amortisation period is the period to the next such repricing date. [IAS 39 AG6]. The application of this requirement in the context of a floating rate instrument is considered in paragraph A6.9.66 below.

A6.9.61 There is a presumption that the expected life of a financial instrument (or group of similar financial instruments) can be estimated reliably. However, in those rare cases when it is not possible to estimate reliably the expected life, the entity should use the full contractual term of the financial instrument (or group of financial instruments) as the amortisation period. [IAS 39 para 9]. The expected life cannot exceed the contractual term.

Illustrations of the effective interest rate method of amortisation

Fixed interest instruments

A6.9.62 The examples that follow illustrate the application of the effective interest rate method of amortisation to fixed interest loans. In example 1, the fixed rate loan asset is repayable only at maturity (a similar example is given in IAS 39 para IG B26). In example 2, the fixed rate loan asset is repayable in equal annual instalments. In example 3, the loan's predetermined rate of interest increases over the instrument's term ('stepped interest').

Example 1 – Fixed interest loan asset repayable at maturity

On 1 January 20X5, entity A originates a 10 year 7% C1 million loan. The loan carries an annual interest rate of 7% payable at the end of each year and is repayable at par at the end of year 10. Entity A charges a 1.25% (C12,500) non-refundable loan origination fee to the borrower and also incurs C25,000 in direct loan origination costs.

The contract specifies that the borrower has an option to pre-pay the instrument and that no penalty will be charged for pre-payment. At inception, the entity expects the borrower not to pre-pay.

The initial carrying amount of the loan asset is calculated as follows:

	C
Loan principal	1,000,000
Origination fees charged to borrower	(12,500)
Origination costs incurred by lender	25,000
Carrying amount of loan	1,012,500

As explained in paragraph A6.9.56 above, it is first necessary to determine whether the pre-payment option should be separately accounted for. In this example, as the loan's principal's amount is likely to be approximately equal to the loan's amortised cost at each exercise date, the borrower's option to pre-pay is closely related and not separately accounted for.

As the entity expects the borrower not to pre-pay, the amortisation period is equal to the instrument's full term. In calculating the effective interest rate that will apply over the term of the loan at a constant rate on the carrying amount, the discount rate necessary to equate 10 annual payments of C70,000 and a final payment at maturity of C1 million to the initial carrying amount of C1,012,500 is approximately 6.823%.

The carrying amount of the loan over the period to maturity will, therefore, be as follows:

	Cash in flows (coupon)	Interest income @ 6.823%	Amortisation of net fees	Carrying amount
	C	C	C	C
1 Jan 20X5				1,012,500
31 Dec 20X5	70,000	69,088	912	1,011,588
31 Dec 20X6	70,000	69,025	975	1,010,613
31 Dec 20X7	70,000	68,959	1,041	1,009,572
31 Dec 20X8	70,000	68,888	1,112	1,008,460
31 Dec 20X9	70,000	68,812	1,188	1,007,272
31 Dec 20Y0	70,000	68,731	1,269	1,006,003
31 Dec 20Y1	70,000	68,644	1,356	1,004,647
31 Dec 20Y2	70,000	68,552	1,448	1,003,199
31 Dec 20Y3	70,000	68,453	1,547	1,001,652
31 Dec 20Y4	70,000	68,348	1,652	1,000,000
	700,000	687,500	12,500	
31 Dec 20Y4		Repayment of principal		(1,000,000)
31 Dec 20Y4		Carrying value of loan		Nil

As can be seen from the above, the effective interest income for the period is calculated by applying the effective interest rate of 6.823% to the loan's amortised cost at the end of the previous reporting period. The annual interest income decreases each year to reflect the decrease in the asset's carrying value as the initial net fee is amortised. Thus the difference between the calculated effective income for a given reporting period and the loan's coupon is the amortisation of the net fees during that reporting period. The loan's amortised cost at the end of the previous period plus amortisation in the current reporting period gives the loan's amortised cost at the end of the current period. By maturity date, the net fees received are fully amortised and the loan's carrying amount is equal to the face amount, which is then repaid in full.

Example 2 – Fixed interest loan asset repayable in equal annual instalments

On 1 January 20X5, entity A originates a 10 year 7% C1 million loan. The loan is repaid in equal annual payments of C142,378 through to maturity date at 31 December 20Y4. Entity A charges a 1.25% (C12,500) non-refundable loan origination fee to the borrower and also incurs C25,000 in direct loan origination costs.

The contract specifies that the borrower has an option to pre-pay the instrument and that no penalty will be charged for pre-payment. At inception, the entity expects the borrower not to pre-pay.

The initial carrying amount of the loan is calculated as follows:

	C
Loan principal	1,000,000
Origination fees charged to borrower	(12,500)
Origination costs incurred by lender	25,000
Carrying amount of loan	1,012,500

As in the previous example, the pre-payment option will not be separately accounted for. In calculating the effective interest rate that will apply over the term of the loan at a constant rate on the carrying amount, the discount rate necessary to equate 10 annual payments of C142,378 to the initial carrying amount of C1,012,500 is approximately 6.7322%. The carrying amount of the loan over the period to maturity will, therefore, be as follows:

	Cash in flows	**Interest Income @ 6.7322%**	**Carrying amount**
	C	C	C
1 Jan 20X5			1,012,500
31 Dec 20X5	142,378	68,164	938,286
31 Dec 20X6	142,378	63,167	859,075
31 Dec 20X7	142,378	57,835	774,532
31 Dec 20X8	142,378	52,143	684,297
31 Dec 20X9	142,378	46,068	587,988
31 Dec 20Y0	142,378	39,585	485,194
31 Dec 20Y1	142,378	32,664	375,480
31 Dec 20Y2	142,378	25,278	258,381
31 Dec 20Y3	142,378	17,395	133,397
31 Dec 20Y4	142,378	8,981	–
	1,423,780	406,690	

Example 3 – Fixed interest loan asset with interest step-up

On 1 January 20X5, entity A originates a 5 year debt instrument for C1m loan that is repayable at maturity. The contract provides for 5% interest in year 1 that increases by 2% in each of the following 4 years. Entity A also receives C25,000 in loan origination fees.

The loan's initial carrying amount is calculated as follows:

	C
Loan principal	1,000,000
Origination fees charged to borrower	(25,000)
Carrying amount of loan	975,000

In calculating the effective interest rate that will apply over the term of the loan at a constant rate on the carrying amount, the discount rate necessary to equate 5 annual step-up payments and a final payment at maturity of C1m to the initial carrying amount of C925,000 is approximately 9.2934 %.

	Interest income @ 9.2934%	Cash in flows (coupon)	Carrying amount
	C	C	C
1 Jan 20X5			975,000
31 Dec 20X5	90,610	50,000	1,015,610
31 Dec 20X6	94,385	70,000	1,039,995
31 Dec 20X7	96,651	90,000	1,046,646
31 Dec 20X8	97,268	110,000	1,033,914
31 Dec 20X9	96,086	130,000	1,000,000
	475,000	450,000	

If the borrower were to repay the entire loan of C1m early, say in 20X9, when the loan asset's carrying value is C1,033,914, the excess amount of C33,914 would have to be recognised in profit or loss. This effectively represents the excess income recognised in earlier periods that is now written back as shown below:

	C
Total income recognised to 31 Dec 20X8	378,914
Amortisation of fees	(25,000)
Cash received to 31 Dec 20X8	(320,000)
Excess income recognised prior to pre-payment by borrower in 20X9	33,914

Changes in estimated cash flows

A6.9.63 As explained above, the cash flows that are discounted to arrive at the effective interest rate are estimated cash flows that are expected to occur over the instrument's expected life. However, in practice, actual cash flows rarely occur in line with expectations. There is usually variation in the amount, timing or both. Differences from the original estimates present a problem for the effective interest rate. If the variation is ignored, either the asset or liability will amortise before all of the cash flows occur, or a balance may remain after the last cash flow.

A6.9.64 The standard, therefore, requires an entity to adjust the carrying amount of the financial asset or financial liability (or group of financial instruments) to reflect actual and revised estimated cash flows whenever it revises its cash flow estimates. The entity recalculates the carrying amount by computing the present value of estimated future cash flows *at the financial instrument's original effective interest rate*. The adjustment is recognised as income or expense in profit or loss. [IAS 39 para AG 8].

Example – Changes in estimates of cash flows

The facts are the same as in example 1 in paragraph A6.9.62 above, except that on 1 January 20Y1, entity A revises its estimates of cash flows as it now expects that, because of a significant fall in interest rates during the previous period, the borrower is likely to exercise its option to pre-pay. Accordingly, entity A anticipates that 40% of the loan is likely to be repaid by the borrower in 20Y1, with the remaining 60% progressively at 20% in the following three years to maturity.

The revised cash flows are shown below. In accordance with paragraph A6.9.64 above, the opening balance at 1 January 20Y1 is adjusted. The adjusted amount is calculated by discounting the amounts the entity expects to receive in 20Y1 and subsequent years using the original effective rate of 6.823%. This results in the adjustment shown below. The adjustment is recognised in profit or loss in 20Y1.

		Carrying amount
1 Jan 20Y1	Opening amortised carrying amount before revision	1,006,003
	Adjustment for changes in estimate – profit or loss	2,563
1 Jan 20Y1	Adjusted amortised carrying amount after revision	1,003,440

	Opening amortised carrying amount	Interest income @ 6.823%	Cash in flows (coupon + repayment of principal)	Closing amortised carrying amount
	C	C	C	C
31 Dec 20Y1	1,003,440	68,465	70,000 + 400,000	601,905
31 Dec 20Y2	601,905	41,068	42,000 + 200,000	400,973
31 Dec 20Y3	400,973	27,358	28,000 + 200,000	200,331
31 Dec 20Y4	200,331	13,669	14,000 + 200,000	-

Issuer call option in debt instruments

A6.9.65 The terms of a debt instrument may include an issuer call option, that is, a right of the issuer (but not the investor) to redeem the instrument early and pay a fixed price (generally at a premium over the par value). There may also be other pre-payment features that cause the whole or part of the outstanding principal to be repaid early. Adding call options and/or other pre-payment options should make the instrument less attractive to investors, since it reduces the potential upside on the bond. As market interest rates go down and the bond price increases (reflecting its above market interest rate), the bonds are likely to be called back. As explained in paragraph A6.9.56 above, such a call option embedded in the debt host is a derivative and would fall to be separately accounted for if its exercise price is not approximately equal to the debt host's amortised cost at each exercise date. Consider the example given below.

Example – Issuer call option in debt instrument

Entity A issues a fixed rate loan for C1m and incurs issue costs of C30,000 resulting in an initial carrying value of C970,000. The loan carries an interest rate of 8% per annum and is repayable at par at the end of year 10. However, under the contract, entity A can call the loan at any time after year 4 by paying an additional premium of C50,000 to compensate the investor for loss of interest.

As explained in paragraph A6.9.56 above, it is first necessary to determine whether the call option is closely related to the host debt instrument. As the call option's exercise price is C1,050,000 (inclusive of the premium), it is unlikely to be approximately equal to the debt instrument's amortised cost in year 4, or at any time subsequently. Therefore, the call option has to be separated from the host debt contract and accounted for separately. This assumes that the expected life of the instrument is the full 10 year term. However, if the expected life is assumed to be 4 years, the 10 year loan with a call option after 4 years is economically equivalent to a 4 year loan with a 6 year extension option. Since there is no concurrent adjustment to the interest rate after 4 years, the term extension option would not be closely related and would need to be accounted for separately (see section 5).

Even though the option is out of the money at inception, because the option's exercise price is greater than the debt instrument's carrying value, it has a time value. Suppose the option's fair value is C20,000 at inception. Since the value of a callable bond is equal to the value of a straight bond less the value of the option feature, the accounting entries at inception would be as follows:

	Dr	Cr
	C	C
Embedded option (derivative asset)	20,000	
Cash	970,000	
Debt instrument (host)		990,000

Since the call option will be fair valued and accounted for separately with fair value movements taken to profit or loss, it has no impact on the entity's estimate of future cash flows as explained in paragraph A6.9.56 above and, accordingly, the amortisation period will be the debt host's period to original maturity. On this basis, the effective interest rate amounts to 8.15%. The amortisation schedule is shown below.

	Opening amortised cost	Interest expense @ 8.15%	Cash payments	Closing amortised cost
	C	C	C	C
Year 1	990,000	80,685	80,000	990,685
Year 2	990,685	80,741	80,000	991,427
Year 3	991,427	80,802	80,000	992,228
Year 4	992,228	80,867	80,000	993,095
Year 5	993,095	80,938	80,000	994,033
Year 6	994,033	81,014	80,000	995,047

Year 7	995,047	81,097	80,000	996,144
Year 8	996,144	81,186	80,000	997,330
Year 9	997,330	81,283	80,000	998,613
Year 10	998,613	81,387	1,080,000	–

The entity would recognise interest expense in profit or loss and the loan's amortised cost in the balance sheet each year in accordance with the above amortisation schedule.

In years 1 and 2, there is no change in interest rate since inception for an instrument of similar maturity and credit rating. The option's fair value (time value) at the end of year 2 is C10,000. The decrease in fair value of C10,000 since inception will be reported in profit and loss and the option will be recorded at C10,000 at the end of year 2.

At the end of year 3, interest rates have fallen and the option's fair value increases to C18,000. The increase in value of C8,000 will be recorded in profit or loss and the option will be recorded at its fair value of C18,000 at the end of year 3.

At the end of year 4, interest rates have fallen further. The option's fair value increases to £30,000 and the company decides to repay the loan at the end of year 4.

The accounting entries to reflect the change in the option's fair value and the loan's early repayment at the end of year 4 are as follows:

	Dr	**Cr**
	C	**C**
Embedded Option	12,000	
Profit or loss		12,000
Early repayment of loan		
Debt instrument (host)	993,095	
Embedded option (derivative asset)		30,000
Cash		1,050,000
Loss on derecognition of liability	86,905	

The loss of C86,905 in profit or loss reflects the fact that the fair value of the host contract has gone up in value as interest rates have fallen compared to its carrying value at amortised cost. The fair value of the host contract is actually C1,110,000, which is the option's fair value plus the fair value of the consideration given. The market rate of interest that discounts the interest payments of C80,000 for the next 6 years plus the principal repayment of C1,000,000 at maturity to the fair value of the host is 6.95%, indicating a significant fall in value compared to the instrument's stated interest rate of 8%.

Suppose that instead of an additional premium or penalty payable on early exercise, the option's exercise price is the fair value of the loan at each exercise date. In other words, the exercise price of the pre-payment option is a 'market adjusted value'. A market adjusted value is calculated by discounting the contractual guaranteed amount payable at the end of the specified term to present value using the current market rate that would be offered on a new loan with a similar credit rating and having a maturity period equal to the remaining maturity period of the current loan. As a result, the market adjusted value may be more or less than the loan principal, depending upon market interest rates at each option exercise date.

In that situation, the pre-payment option enables the issuer simply to pay off the loan at fair value at the pre-payment date. Since the holder receives only the market adjusted value, which is equal to the loan's fair value at the date of pre-payment, the pre-payment option (the embedded derivative) has a fair value of zero at all times. Since the pre-payment option, on a stand-alone basis, would not meet the definition of a derivative, it cannot be an embedded derivative, the loan is simply carried at its amortised cost as above, on the assumption that the loan is not going to be pre-paid. If, however, the entity expects to pre-pay the loan, the loan would be amortised over its expected life.

Floating rate instruments

A6.9.66 As will be apparent from the above illustrations, the application of the effective interest rate method is relatively straight forward for fixed interest instruments with fixed terms. Indeed, it appears to be specifically designed for such instruments. However, the analysis is more complicated in the case of a financial instrument that provides for future cash flows that are determinable rather than fixed. Floating rate interest on a financial instrument that is linked to a reference rate such as LIBOR and a principal amount linked to a price index are examples of determinable cash flows. The apparent complication arises because, unlike fixed interest instruments where the effective interest rate generally stays constant over the instrument's term, for floating rate instruments, the periodic re-estimation of determinable cash flows to reflect movements in market rates of interest alters the instrument's effective yield.

A6.9.67 However, although fluctuations in interest rates result in a change in the effective interest rate, there is usually no change in the instrument's fair value. Accordingly, where a floating rate instrument is acquired or issued and the amount at which it is recognised initially is equal to the principal receivable or payable at maturity, re-estimating the future interest payments normally has no significant effect on the carrying amount of the asset or liability. [IAS 39 para AG 7]. This means that the effective yield will always equal the rate under the interest rate formula (for example, LIBOR + 1%) in the instrument. The effect is that the carrying amount remains unchanged by the process, illustrated in paragraph A6.9.64 above, of re-estimating future cash flows and the effective interest rate. The result is that changes in LIBOR are reflected in the period in which the change occurs.

A6.9.68 However, if a floating rate instrument is issued or acquired at a discount or premium, or the entity receives or incurs loan origination fees or costs, the question arises as to whether the premium or discount and other transaction fees or costs should be amortised over the period to the next repricing date, or over the instrument's expected life. The answer depends upon the nature of the premium or discount and its relationship with market rates.

- An amortisation period to the next repricing date should be used if the premium or discount on a floating rate instrument reflects interest that has accrued on the instrument since interest was last paid, or changes in market interest rate since the floating interest rate was reset to market rates. This is because the premium or discount relates to the period to the next interest reset date as, at that date, the variable to which the premium or discount relates (that is interest rates) is reset to market rates. In this case, the loan's fair value at the next repricing date will be its par value. This is illustrated in example 1 below.

- The instrument's expected life should be used as the amortisation period if the premium or discount results from changes in the credit spread over the floating rate specified in the instrument, or other variables that are not reset to market rates. In this situation, the date the interest rate is next reset is not a market-based repricing date of the entire instrument, since the variable rate is not adjusted for changes in the credit spread for the specific issue. This is illustrated in example 2 below.

[IAS 39 para AG 6].

Example 1 – Amortisation of discount over the period to the next repricing date

On 15 May 20X6, an entity acquires a C100 nominal 5 year floating rate bond that pays quarterly interest at 3 month LIBOR + 50 basis points for C99.25. LIBOR at the last reset date on 30 March 20X6 was 4.50% which determines the interest that would be paid on the bond on 30 June 20X6. On the purchase date, LIBOR was 4.75%. The discount of 0.75 (5.25% − 4.50%) is amortised to the next repricing date, that is, 30 June 20X6.

Example 2 – Amortisation of discount over the expected life of the instrument

A 20 year bond is issued at C100, has a principal amount of C100, and requires quarterly interest payments equal to current 3 month LIBOR plus 1% over the instrument's life. The interest rate reflects the market-based rate of return associated with the bond issue at issuance. Subsequent to issuance, the loan's credit quality deteriorates resulting in a rating downgrade. Therefore, the bond trades at a significant discount. Entity A purchases the bond for 95 and classifies it as held-to-maturity.

In this case, the discount of C5 is amortised to net profit or loss over the period to the bond's maturity and not to the next date interest rate payments are reset, as there is no adjustment to the variable rate as a result of the credit downgrade.

6A.9.69 There is no specific guidance in the standard as to how transaction costs incurred in originating or acquiring a floating rate instrument should be amortised. Since such costs are sunk cost and are not subject to repricing, they will be amortised over the instrument's expected life. Any methodology that provides a reasonable basis of amortisation may be used. For example, entities may find it appropriate to amortise the fees and costs by reference to the interest rate at inception ignoring any subsequent changes in rates or to simply adopt a straight-line amortisation method.

Perpetual debt instruments

A6.9.70 It is not uncommon for entities to issue debt instruments on terms with no redemption date, but on which interest payments are made, usually at a fixed rate or a variable market based rate (for example, a fixed margin over LIBOR) in perpetuity. At initial recognition, assuming there are no transaction costs, the debt instrument will be recorded at its fair value, which is the amount received. The difference between this initial amount and the maturity amount, which is zero if the interest rate at inception is the market rate for that instrument, will never be amortised, as there is no repayment of principal. This means that at each reporting date the debt instrument will be recorded at its principal amount, which is also its amortised cost. This is because the amortised cost, which is the present value of the stream of future cash payments discounted at the effective interest rate (fixed for fixed rate instruments or variable for floating rate instruments) equals the principal amount in each period. [IAS 39 para IG B24]. If, on the other hand, the entity incurs transaction costs, the debt instrument will be recorded in each reporting period at its initial amount, which is the amount received less transaction costs. The result is that the transaction costs are never amortised, but reflected in the carrying amount indefinitely.

A6.9.71 Sometimes perpetual debt instruments are repackaged in such a way that the principal amount is effectively repaid. One way of achieving this is to pay a high rate of interest for a number of years (the primary period) which then falls to a negligible amount. If the interest were simply charged to profit or loss, the company would bear an artificially high interest expense during the primary period and little or no interest expense thereafter to perpetuity. Such treatment might reflect the form of the loan agreement, but not its substance. From an economic perspective, some or all of the interest payments are repayment of principal as illustrated in the example below. A similar example is included in paragraph IG B25 of IAS 39.

Example – Perpetual debt instrument with decreasing interest

An entity issues a perpetual bond for C100,000 on which interest at 14% is paid annually for the first 10 years and thereafter at a nominal rate of 0.125%.

It is clear that at the end of the ten year period, the bond has little or no value. The principal amount is repaid, in effect, over the initial 10 year primary period. Consequently, the interest payments during the primary period represent a payment for interest and repayment of capital. The effective interest rate calculated on the basis of C14,000 for 10 years followed by C125 to perpetuity is 6.84%.

	Opening amortised cost	Interest expense @ 6.84%	Cash payments	Closing amortised cost
	C	C	C	C
Year 1	100,000	6,840	14,000	92,840
Year 2	92,840	6,350	14,000	85,190
Year 3	85,190	5,827	14,000	77,017
Year 4	77,017	5,268	14,000	68,285
Year 5	68,285	4,671	14,000	58,956
Year 6	58,956	4,033	14,000	48,989
Year 7	48,989	3,351	14,000	38,340
Year 8	38,340	2,622	14,000	26,962
Year 9	26,962	1,844	14,000	14,806
Year 10	14,806	1,013	14,000	1,819
		41,819	140,000	

Although the carrying value at the end of year 10 is small, there is still an actual liability of C100,000 that may crystallise should the entity go into liquidation. In practice, however, there will usually be arrangements to enable the entity to repurchase the debt instrument for a nominal amount and, therefore, extinguish any liability on it.

Fair value measurement considerations

General

A6.9.72 The IASB believes that fair value is the most relevant measure for financial instruments and is the only relevant measure for derivative assets and liabilities. As a result, IAS 39 gives entities an option to measure all financial assets and liabilities that meet certain qualifying criteria at fair value. The importance of fair value in the measurement process arises because it is a market-based notion that is unaffected by the history of the asset or liability, the specific entity that holds the asset or the liability and the future use of the asset or the liability. Thus, it represents an unbiased measure that is consistent from year to year, within an entity and between entities. As a result, if an investor knows a financial instrument's fair value and has information about its essential terms and risks, it has all the information it needs to make decisions about that instrument.

A6.9.73 Consistent with other financial reporting standards, IAS 39 defines fair value as *"the amount for which an asset could be exchanged, or a liability settled, between knowledgeable, willing parties in an arm's length transaction"*. [IAS 39 para 9]. The price at which an asset could be exchanged is the price an entity would have received if it had sold the asset. Similarly, the price at which a liability is settled is the price an entity would have paid if it had been relieved of the liability. This implies that fair value is an estimate of the market 'exit' price that is determined by reference to a current hypothetical transaction between willing parties. Willing parties are presumed to be market-place participants representing unrelated buyers and sellers that are knowledgeable, having a common level of understanding about factors relevant to the asset or liability and the transaction and willing and able to transact in the same market(s) having the legal and financial ability to do so.

A6.9.74 Underlying the definition of fair value is a presumption that an entity is a going concern without any intention or need to liquidate, to curtail materially the scale of its operations or to undertake a transaction on adverse terms. Fair value is not, therefore, the amount that an entity would receive or pay in a forced transaction, involuntary liquidation or distress sale. However, fair value does reflect the instrument's credit quality. [IAS 39 para AG69]. This means that when a financial liability is measured at fair value, its credit quality must be reflected in the valuation process (see further para A6.9.112 below).

A6.9.75 There is a general presumption that fair value can be reliably measured for all financial instruments. Nonetheless, the measurement process can be quite complex and gives rise to numerous issues. It is not surprising, therefore, that IAS 39 provides a significant amount of guidance about how to determine fair values, in particular for financial instruments for which no quoted market prices are available. Therefore, in looking for a reliable measure of fair value, the standard provides a hierarchy for determining an instrument's fair value as shown below:

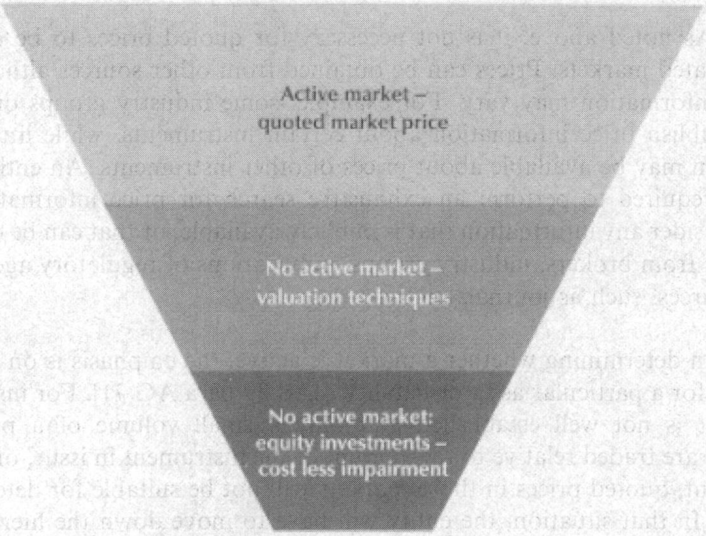

A6.9.76 As can be seen from the above, the hierarchy gives the highest priority to quoted prices in active markets. Unfortunately, for many of the financial assets for which fair values are required, there may be no active market. In the absence of an active market, fair value is established by using a valuation technique. Indeed, as financial instruments become more complex in nature, the ability to obtain a quoted market price diminishes and the requirement to derive a fair value using valuation techniques increases. Such valuation techniques include the use of recent market transactions in similar instruments between knowledgeable, willing parties in an arm's length transaction. Hence, recent market transactions and valuation techniques are given equal prominence in the hierarchy. However, as with any valuation, judgement will often be necessary. Only as a last resort, is an entity permitted to use cost and this is limited to unquoted equity instrument whose fair value cannot be measured reliably and derivatives that are linked to and must be settled in such instruments.

Quoted prices in an active market

A6.9.77 The existence of published price quotations in an active market *is* the best evidence of fair value and, where available, they *must* be used to measure the financial instrument. The phrase 'quoted in an active market' means that quoted prices are readily and regularly available from an exchange, dealer, broker, industry group, pricing service or regulatory agency and those prices represent actual and regularly occurring market transactions on an arm's length basis. [IAS 39 para AG 71]. Readily available means that the pricing information is currently accessible and regularly available means that transactions occur with sufficient frequency to provide pricing information on an ongoing basis. For example, in an active market, such as the London Stock Exchange, quoted prices that represent actual (observable) transactions that are readily and regularly available.

A6.9.78 As noted above, it is not necessary for quoted prices to be obtained from regulated markets. Prices can be obtained from other sources although the available information may vary. For example, some industry groups or pricing services publish price information about certain instruments, while little or no information may be available about prices of other instruments. An entity is not generally required to perform an exhaustive search for price information, but should consider any information that is publicly available, or that can be obtained reasonably from brokers, industry groups, publications of regulatory agencies or similar sources, such as journals and web sites.

A6.9.79 In determining whether a market is active, the emphasis is on the level of activity for a particular asset or liability. [IAS 39 para AG 71]. For instance, if the market is not well established and only a small volume of a particular instrument are traded relative to the amount of the instrument in issue, or trading is infrequent, quoted prices in those markets will not be suitable for determining fair value. In that situation, the entity will have to move down the hierarchy to determine a suitable fair value.

A6.9.80 The objective of determining fair value for a financial instrument that is traded in an active market is to arrive at the price at which a transaction would occur at the balance sheet date in that instrument (that is, without modifying or repackaging the instrument) in the *most advantageous* active market to which the entity has immediate access. [IAS 39 para AG 71]. This means that if an entity has immediate access to different markets having different prices for essentially the same financial asset, the most advantageous market is the one with the price that maximizes the net amount that would be received in a current transaction for the financial asset. For example, if a trader that originates a derivative instrument with an entity in an active 'retail' market takes out an offsetting derivative in a more advantageously priced active dealers' 'wholesale' market, the trader records the derivative with the entity at the higher value and recognises a profit on initial recognition. However, the price in the more advantageous dealers' market should be adjusted for any differences in counterparty credit risk between the derivative instrument with the entity and that with the dealers' market. [IAS 39 para BC98]. It follows that price can be taken from the most favourable market readily available to the entity, even if that was not the market in which the transaction actually occurred.

A6.9.81 For the purpose of determining the most advantageous market, costs to transact in the respective markets should be considered. If such costs are not taken into account, the entity will be unable to determine which market offers the most advantageous price. However, as explained in paragraph A6.9.17 above, the price used to estimate fair value, that is, the price in the most advantageous market, should not be adjusted for transaction costs that may be incurred on sale or disposals.

Example – Quoted prices in different markets

An entity holds financial assets that are traded in markets A and B. The entity has access to both markets. The price in market A is C25 and costs to transact in that market are C5 (the net amount that would be received for the asset in that market is C20). The price in market B is C35 and costs to transact in that market are C20 (the net amount that would be received for the asset in that market is C15). In that case, the most advantageous market is market A. The estimate of fair value would be determined using the price in market A (C25). That price would not be adjusted for costs to transact in that market.

Bid and ask prices

A6.9.82 As stated in a paragraph A6.9.77 above, financial instruments may be traded on exchanges, in dealer markets, and in brokered transactions. Closing prices of financial instruments such as stocks, bonds, options, warrants etc, are readily and regularly available on exchange markets and these are used to value instruments identical to those being traded. However, many securities and financial instruments that are not traded on the organised exchanges are traded in dealer markets, such as AIM and NASDAQ. In such markets, dealers stand ready to trade (either buy or sell for their own account), thereby providing liquidity by using their capital to hold an inventory of the securities for which they make a market. Typically, bid and ask prices are more readily and regularly available than closing prices. Similarly, in a brokered market, brokers attempt to match buyers with sellers but do not stand ready to trade for their own account. The broker knows the prices bid and asked by the respective parties, but each party is typically unaware of another party's price requirements. Prices of completed transactions are sometimes available. Brokered markets include electronic communication networks (ECNs), in which buy and sell orders are matched.

A6.9.83 In an active dealer market where bid and ask prices are more readily and regularly available than closing prices, fair value should be determined using these prices. However, the price that will normally be appropriate for valuation purposes will depend on whether the relevant financial instrument being valued is an asset or a liability, and whether it is already held or to be acquired. The standard specifies the appropriate quoted market prices that should be used as indicated in the table below. [IAS 39 para AG72].

	Instrument held	Instrument to be acquired
Financial asset	Bid	Ask
Financial liability	Ask	Bid

The bid price represents the price a dealer is willing to pay for the instrument and, therefore, the price the entity would receive if it sold the asset. The ask price represents the amount at which a dealer is willing to sell the instrument and, therefore, the price that the entity would have to pay to acquire the asset. The ask price (also known as the 'offer' price) will almost always be higher than the bid price. The difference represents the dealer's profit, which is called the 'spread'. The standard clarifies that the terms 'bid price' and 'asking (offer) price' should be used in the context of quoted market prices and the 'bid-ask' spread should be interpreted as including only transaction costs. [IAS 39 para AG70].

Example 1 – Treatment of bid-ask spread on initial recognition

An entity purchases a financial asset that it classifies as available-for-sale, paying the ask (offer) price of C102 and a brokerage commission of C3. At the balance sheet date, the entity uses the bid price to re-measure the financial asset and to recognise changes in fair value in a separate component of equity.

The following data is relevant:

Reference price	**Acquisition**	**Balance sheet date**
Bid price	C100	C110
Ask or offer price	C102	C113

Financial assets classified as available-for-sale should be initially recognised at fair value, plus transaction costs paid to acquire the asset.

As stated above, the ask price represents the amount at which a dealer is willing to sell and, therefore, the price that the entity would have to pay to acquire the asset. The difference between the bid price that represents the asset's fair value and the ask price (the bid-ask spread) is a transaction cost. The commission paid to the broker is also a transaction cost.

Given the asset is classified as available-for-sale (that is, not at fair value through profit or loss) the transaction costs are included in the initial carrying value of the asset. Therefore, the asset will be recorded at its fair value of C100 (bid price) plus the bid-ask spread (C2) plus commission (C3), a total of C105. At the balance sheet date, the asset will be valued at bid price (C110) at that date and any difference between this price and the amount recognised initially (C5) will be recorded in equity.

Therefore, the appropriate accounting entries at initial recognition and at the balance sheet date are as follows:

	Dr C	Cr C
At acquisition		
Available-for-sale asset (bid price inclusive of transaction costs)	105	
Cash		105
At balance sheet date		
Available-for-sale asset	5	
Gain in equity		5

If the asset is a debt instrument, the bid-ask spread, brokerage commission, and any premium, discount or other deferred fees and costs, are subsequently amortised and recognised as part of interest income over the asset's life using the effective interest method.

If the market price had not changed since the date of acquisition, the entity would report a loss of the difference between C105 and bid price of C100, that is a loss of C5.

Example 2 – Treatment of bid-ask spread not included in initial carrying value of a financial asset

The facts are the same as in example 1 above, except that the entity classifies the financial asset as at fair value through profit or loss.

Financial assets classified as at fair value through profit or loss should be recognised initially at fair value. As stated in paragraph A6.9.17 above, transaction costs arising on a financial asset classified as at fair value through profit or loss are immediately recognised in profit or loss and do not form part of the initial carrying value of the asset. Hence the asset is measured on initial recognition using the bid price (C100). At the balance sheet date, the asset will be valued at bid price (C110) at that date and any difference between this price and the amount recognised initially (C10) will be recorded in profit or loss.

The appropriate accounting entries at initial recognition and at the balance sheet date are as follows:

	Dr C	Cr C
At acquisition		
Available-for-sale asset (bid price)	100	
Profit or loss (bid-ask spread of C2 + commission of C3)	5	
Cash		105
At balance sheet date		
Available-for-sale asset	10	
Gain in equity		10

6A.9.84 The standard does not permit the use of mid-market price (average of bid and ask prices) for valuation purposes when quoted bid and ask prices are available. This is because applying mid-market prices to an individual instrument would result in entities recognising up-front gains and losses for the difference between the bid-ask price and the mid-market price. [IAS 39 para BC99]. This makes sense as the mid-market price cannot be relied upon to represent the price at which a market transaction would occur. However, the standard offers a concession in circumstances where an entity holds assets and liabilities with offsetting market risks. In those circumstances, the entity may use mid-market prices as a basis for establishing fair values for the offsetting risk positions and apply the bid or ask price to the net open position as appropriate. [IAS 39 para AG72]. The IASB believes that use of the mid-market price is appropriate because the entity has locked in its cash flows from the asset and liability and potentially could sell the matched position without incurring the bid-ask spread. It is presumed that such matching positions would be settled within a similar time period.

A6.9.85 The rules applicable to some investment funds require net asset values to be reported to investors on the basis of mid-market prices. The existence of regulations that require a different measurement basis for specific purposes does not justify a departure from the general requirement to use the current bid price in the absence of a matching liability position. Therefore, in its financial statements, an investment fund should measure its assets at current bid prices. In reporting its net asset value to investors, an investment fund may wish to provide a reconciliation between the fair values recognised on its balance sheet and the prices used for the net asset value calculation. [IAS 39 para IG E2.1].

Unavailability of published prices

A6.9.86 Where current prices of financial instruments are unavailable at the reporting date, the price of the most recent transaction should be used adjusted for any changes in conditions between the date of the transaction and the balance sheet date. [IAS 39 para AG 72]. This is essentially a valuation technique that is considered further from paragraph A6.9.89 below.

A6.9.87 If a published price quotation in an active market does not exist for a financial instrument in its entirety, but active markets exist for its component parts, fair value is determined on the basis of the relevant market prices for the component parts. [IAS 39 para AG 72]. This is relevant for complex financial instruments, which by their nature are illiquid and prices cannot be obtained as an instrument in their own right. An example might be a commodity-linked debt instrument whose coupon is indexed to the price of crude oil, but where the coupon can never exceed ten per cent nor be less than nil per cent. In that situation, as active markets exist for the basic components (the debt instrument and derivatives linked to that commodity), but not for the whole instrument, an overall valuation can be obtained by combining the values of the component parts.

Large blocks of instruments

A6.9.88 The fair value of a portfolio of financial instruments is the product of the number of units of the instruments and their quoted market prices. [IAS 39 paras AG71 to AG73]. This definition precludes an entity from using a 'blockage' factor (that is, a premium or discount based on the relative size of the position held, such as a large proportion of the total trading units of an instrument) in determining the fair value of a large block of financial instruments. In other words, if an entity holds a large block of a particular instrument and the only available market exit prices come from transactions involving small blocks, no adjustment should be made for the expected effect of selling the large block in a single transaction as illustrated in the following example, taken from the implementation guidance to IAS 39.

Example – Valuation of large holding

Entity A holds 15% of entity B's share capital. The shares are publicly traded in an active market. The currently quoted price is C100. Daily trading volume is 0.1% of outstanding shares. Because entity A believes that the fair value of the entity B shares it owns, if sold as a block, is greater than the quoted market price, entity A obtains several independent estimates of the price it would obtain if it sells its holding. These estimates indicate that entity A would be able to obtain a price of C105, that is, a 5% premium above the quoted price.

The published price quotation in an active market is the best estimate of fair value. Therefore, entity A should use the published price quotation (C100). Entity A cannot depart from the quoted market price solely because independent estimates indicate that entity A would obtain a higher (or lower) price by selling the holding as a block. [IAS 30 IG para E2.2].

Although the converse situation is not dealt with in the standard, it follows that if an entity holds only a small number of instruments and the available market exit prices come from transactions involving large blocks, the entity should not adjust the available price for the potential effect of selling individual instruments.

Valuation techniques in the absence of an active market

A6.9.89 The best evidence of fair value is quoted price in an active market. If the market for a financial instrument is not active, fair value should be determined using a valuation technique. The objective of using a valuation technique is to establish what the transaction price would have been on the measurement date in an arm's length exchange motivated by normal business considerations. This is by no means an easy task and involves the exercise of a significant amount of judgement. Even at the end of the most careful and detailed valuation, there will be uncertainty about the final numbers, coloured by the assumptions of risks and returns and any resulting bias introduced in the process.

A6.9.90 As the objective of the valuation process is to arrive at a reasonable estimate of a financial instrument's fair value, the technique used should reasonably reflect how the market could be expected to price the instrument. That expectation is likely to be met if the valuation technique makes maximum use of market inputs and relies as little as possible on entity-specific inputs. Also the inputs should reasonably represent market expectations and measures of the risk-return factors inherent in the financial instrument. In other words, an acceptable valuation technique should incorporate all factors that market participants would consider in setting a price, and be consistent with accepted economic methodologies for pricing financial instruments. [IAS 39 paras AG75 to AG76].

A6.9.91 Periodically, an entity should calibrate the valuation techniques it uses and test their validity using prices from any observable current market transactions in the same instrument (that is, without modification or repackaging) or based on any available observable market data. [IAS 39 para AG 76]. This process is not only important but essential, as the benchmark for comparison in most valuations remains the market price. When a value from the use of a valuation technique is significantly different from market price, there are two possibilities: one is that the valuation is correct and the market is wrong; the other is that the valuation is wrong and the market is correct. The presumption should be that the market is correct.

A6.9.92 Valuation techniques that are well established in financial markets include recent market transactions, reference to a transaction that is substantially the same and discounted cash flows and option pricing models. These techniques are considered below. If there is a valuation technique commonly used by market participants to price the instrument and that technique has been demonstrated to provide reliable estimates of prices obtained in actual market transactions, that technique should be used. [IAS 39 para AG 74]. For example, well established external proprietary software packages are available for pricing many types of financial options. An entity that holds or writes one of those options would use the model best suited for the type of option held or written.

A6.9.93 Valuation techniques used to estimate fair value should be applied on a consistent basis. A change in the valuation techniques used is appropriate only if the change results in a more reliable estimate of fair value, for example, as new markets develop or as new and improved valuation techniques become available.

Inputs to valuation techniques

A6.9.94 As explained above, an appropriate valuation technique should incorporate observable market data about the market conditions and other factors that are likely to affect the instrument's fair value. The technique would be only as robust as the inputs used. Market inputs should be determined based on information that is timely, originated from sources independent of the entity and used by market-place participants in making pricing decisions. Examples of market inputs that may be used, directly or indirectly, as a basis for determining a financial instrument's fair value include the following:

- The time value of money (that is, interest at the basic or risk-free rate).

Basic interest rates can usually be derived from observable government bond prices and are often quoted in financial publications. These rates typically vary with the expected dates of the projected cash flows along a yield curve of interest rates for different time horizons.

For practical reasons, an entity may use a well-accepted and readily observable general rate, such as LIBOR or a swap rate, as the benchmark rate. However, as benchmark is not a risk free interest rate, the credit risk adjustment appropriate to the particular financial instrument is determined on the basis of its credit risk in relation to the credit risk in this benchmark rate.

In some countries, the central government's bonds may carry a significant credit risk and may not provide a stable benchmark basic interest rate for instruments denominated in that currency. Some entities in these countries may have a better credit standing and a lower borrowing rate than the central government. In such a case, basic interest rates may be more appropriately determined by reference to interest rates for the highest rated corporate bonds issued in the currency of that jurisdiction.

- Credit risk.

  The effect on fair value of credit risk (that is, the premium over the basic interest rate for credit risk) may be derived from observable market prices for traded instruments of different credit quality or from observable interest rates charged by lenders for loans of various credit ratings.

- Foreign currency exchange prices.

  Active currency exchange markets exist for most major currencies, and prices are quoted daily in financial publications.

- Commodity prices.

  There are observable market prices for many commodities.

- Equity prices.

  Prices (and indices of prices) of traded equity instruments are readily observable in some markets. Present value based techniques may be used to estimate the current market price of equity instruments for which there are no observable prices.

- Volatility (that is, magnitude of future changes in price of the financial instrument or other item).

  Measures of the volatility of actively traded items can normally be reasonably estimated on the basis of historical market data or by using volatilities implied in current market prices

- Pre-payment risk and surrender risk.

  This is the risk that a financial instrument may be pre-paid or surrendered earlier than its maturity date. Expected pre-payment patterns for financial assets and expected surrender patterns for financial liabilities can be estimated on the basis of historical data. However, the fair value of a financial liability that can be surrendered by the counterparty cannot be less than the present value of the surrender amount (see para A6.9.110 below).

- Servicing costs for a financial asset or a financial liability.

  Costs of servicing can be estimated using comparisons with current fees charged by other market participants. If the costs of servicing a financial asset or financial liability are significant and other market participants would face comparable costs, the issuer would consider them in determining the fair value of that financial asset or financial liability. It is likely that the fair value at inception of a contractual right to future fees equals the origination costs paid for them, unless future fees and related costs are out of line with market comparables.

[IAS 39 para AG 82].

Recent transaction prices

A6.9.95 Where, current prices of financial instruments are unavailable at the reporting date, the price of the most recent transaction should be used. [IAS 39 para AG 72]. This is a fairly simple technique and provides a foundation for estimating fair value, as long as there has not been a significant change in economic circumstances since the relevant transaction occurred.

A6.9.96 If, however, conditions have changed since the relevant transaction occurred, the fair value should reflect the change in conditions by reference to current prices or rates for similar financial instruments, as appropriate. That means, the most recent market-exit transaction price would be adjusted for changes due to passage of time as long as such an adjustment is capable of producing a reasonable estimate of fair value. It would also be adjusted if changes in market conditions indicate that transactions occurring at the balance sheet date probably would not have occurred at that price. An example would be a change in the risk-free interest rate following the most recent price quote for a corporate bond. That observable price would be adjusted to reflect the interest for the period between the transaction date and the measurement date (to take into account the time value of money), the effect on fair value of the changes in rates and any cash distribution in that period. Similarly, if the entity can demonstrate that the last transaction price is not fair value (for example, because it reflected the amount that an entity would receive or pay in a forced transaction, involuntary liquidation or distress sale), that price should be adjusted. [IAS 39 para AG 72].

A6.9.97 However, it may not always be possible to make the adjustment referred to above, because not all the information may be available at each measurement date. For example, at the date that an entity makes (or acquires) a debt instrument that is not actively traded, the transaction price is also a market price. At the next measurement date, although the general level of market interest rates are available, the entity may not have information from recent transactions to determine the appropriate credit spread over the basic interest rate that market participants would consider in pricing the instrument on that date. In that situation, in the absence of evidence to the contrary, it would be reasonable to assume that no changes have taken place in the spread that existed at the date the loan was made. However, the entity would be expected to make reasonable efforts to determine whether there is evidence that there has been a change in such factors. When evidence of a change exists, the entity would consider the effects of the change in determining the financial instrument's fair value. [IAS 39 para AG 78].

Using price information about similar financial instruments

A6.9.98 Another market based valuation technique estimates a financial instrument's value by using quoted prices for similar financial instruments in active markets, adjusted as appropriate for differences, whenever that information is available. Instruments are considered to be similar if they have similar remaining maturity, cash flow pattern, currency, credit risk, collateral and interest basis. [IAS 39 para AG77]. Estimating a financial instrument's fair value based on the market price of a similar financial instrument is best explained by an example.

Example – Valuation based on market price of a similar financial instrument

On 1 January 20X5, entity A acquires a bond issued by entity B through a private placement. The consideration paid and, therefore, the bond's fair value at initial recognition is C1 million. The entity classifies the bond as at fair value through profit or loss. The bond has no observable market price. At 31 December 20X5, the entity is able to identify actively traded corporate bonds that are similar to its bond.

In carrying out the evaluation, the major elements of the two bonds that should be compared are as follows:

- The amount and timing of the contractual cash flows, including pre-payment expectations.
- The currency in which the bonds are payable.
- The credit risk rating and the factors on which changes in the credit risk rating are dependent. For example, the fair value of bonds issued by entities with different industry and geographical bases would be expected to respond differently to changes in the market factors.
- Any other term and conditions that could affect the bond's fair value.

6A.9.99 By definition, similar financial instruments are not identical and some of the differences will cause the fair value to be different. Therefore, it is necessary to ensure that the effect on fair value of any such differences is reasonably determinable. In the above example, the initial net effects of differences may be discerned by comparing the fair values of the two instruments at the acquisition date of the non-traded bond, assuming that its fair value is equal to the consideration paid. It is likely that the private placement bond's fair value will be less than that of the market-traded bond, because it is less marketable. Therefore, it may be reasonable to assume that any premium for marketability differences between the effective interest rates of the two bonds at the date the entity acquired its bond remains unchanged from period to period, except if an observable event that could be expected to affect marketability takes place.

Other valuation techniques

A6.9.100 Where it is not possible to estimate a financial instrument's fair value by reference to market prices, the entity uses other valuation techniques (pricing models and methodologies). Because they require more estimation and assumptions, they are necessarily more subjective than the market price approach. Two valuation techniques that are widely used are the discounted cash flow (present value) approach and option pricing models.

A6.9.101 Present value is a technique used to link future amounts (cash flows) to the present through a discount rate. Present value concepts are central to the development of techniques for estimating the fair value of financial instruments because the market exit price of a financial instrument represents market participant's collective estimate of the present value of its expected cash flows. Therefore, cash flows and discount rate should reflect only factors that are specific to the financial instrument being measured and should reflect assumptions that market participants would use in their estimates of fair value. Also, as the cash flows used are estimates rather than known amounts, a fair value estimate, using present value, is made under conditions of uncertainty. As market participants generally seek compensation for bearing the uncertainty inherent in cash flows (risk premium), the effect of variability (risk) in the cash flows should be reflected either in the cash flows or in the discount rate.

A6.9.102 In applying discounted cash flow analysis, an entity uses discount rates equal to the prevailing rates of return for financial instruments having substantially the same terms and characteristics, including the credit quality of the instrument, the remaining term over which the contractual interest rate is fixed, the remaining term to the principal's re-payment and the currency in which payments are to be made. Short-term receivables and payables with no stated interest rate may be measured at the original invoice amount if the effect of discounting is immaterial. [IAS 39 para AG 79].

A6.9.103 Option pricing models, first developed by Black and Scholes, can be used to value any asset (not just financial instruments) that has the characteristics of an option, with some caveats. For example, an unquoted equity instrument can be valued as a call option on the entity's assets, the exercise price of the call being equal to the value of the entity's debt. Option pricing models are based on the premise that it is possible to create a replicating portfolio using a combination of the underlying asset and risk-free borrowing and lending to create the same cash flows as the option being valued. The principles of arbitrage then apply and the option's value is then equal to the value of the replicating portfolio. Although real markets do not always follow the idealised behaviour of financial models, these portfolios constructed in line with theoretical models have been found to be robust in practice, despite their imperfections.

Application to intra-group financial guarantee contracts

A6.9.103.1 The way in which the various valuation techniques discussed above can be applied to determine the fair value of an intra-group financial guarantee contract that is not negotiated in an arm's length transaction is considered in the paragraphs that follow.

References to market prices of similar instruments

A6.9.103.2 An entity may be unable to identify a market price for financial guarantees identical to those that either it or a member of its group has issued. However, it may be possible to identify market prices for similar guarantees, credit default swaps or credit insurance products, the price of which could be adjusted. For example, parent P has guaranteed C100 million of five year debt issued by subsidiary S. It may be possible to identify credit insurance products issued by a bank relating to debt of this amount, maturity and credit quality. However, an adjustment may still be necessary, for example, to reflect liquidity aspects and differences between P's credit rating and that of the bank.

Interest rate differentials

A6.9.103.3 Under this method, the entity calculates the value of the difference between the interest charged on the guaranteed loan and what would have been charged had the loan not been guaranteed. The premise is that the interest that the bank is willing to forego represents a 'price' that it is willing to pay for the guarantee. For example, parent P has guaranteed C100 million of five year debt issued by subsidiary S. Subsidiary S pays interest of X per cent on the debt. In the absence of the guarantee, the bank would impose an interest rate of Y per cent. Hence, the fair value of the guarantee represents the difference in the present value of the interest payments over the period of the guarantee.

A6.9.103.4 This model is simple in principle, but presents practical problems when attempting to measure Y per cent. It is unlikely that the bank would provide a reliable estimate. Determining Y per cent requires an estimate of the credit spread (for example, above a base index such as LIBOR) appropriate to subsidiary S in isolation. This may prove difficult as, even without the guarantee, subsidiary S's credit rating will benefit from the company being a member of parent P's group. Nevertheless, models based on determining a stand alone credit rating for subsidiary S do exist and these should enable a reliable estimate to be made.

Discounted cash flow analysis (expected value)

A6.9.103.5 Instead of considering the 'price' that a bank would pay for a guarantee, it might be possible to consider the 'price' that the issuer would demand for accepting the guarantee obligation. This can be estimated using a probability-adjusted discounted cash flow analysis. For example, parent P has guaranteed C100 million of five year debt issued by subsidiary S. The probability of default by subsidiary S is estimated at 0.04 per cent (based on historical default rates amongst companies with the same credit rating as subsidiary S) and the loss in the event of default is estimated at 50 per cent (based on subsidiary S's asset base and other collateral available to the bank). The expected value of the liability (its fair value) would, therefore, be C20,000.

A6.9.103.6 Similar to the interest rate differential approach described above, this model is simple in principle, but presents practical problems when attempting to estimate the probability of default and the loss given default. Although data on these points is available, they rely on determining subsidiary S's credit rating as in the interest rate differential approach.

Unquoted equity instruments and related derivatives

A6.9.104 Normally it is possible to estimate an equity instrument's fair value that does not have a quoted market price in an active market, as well as derivatives that are linked to and must be settled by delivery of such unquoted equity instruments with sufficient reliability by applying valuation techniques based on reasonable assumptions. The fair values of such instruments are deemed to be reliably measurable if:

- the variability in the range of reasonable fair value estimates is not significant for that instrument; or
- the probabilities of the various estimates within the range can be reasonably assessed and used in estimating fair value.

[IAS 39 para AG 80].

A6.9.105 There are many situations in which the variability in the range of reasonable fair value estimates is likely not to be significant and, hence, the fair value is reasonably measurable. However, if the range of reasonable fair value estimates is significantly wide and the probabilities of the various estimates cannot be reasonably assessed, an entity is precluded from measuring the instrument at fair value. In that situation, such instruments are measured at cost, less impairment. [IAS 39 paras 46(c), AG81]. It is not permissible for the entity to measure the equity instrument at fair value, for instance, by judgementally picking a fair value estimate within a range.

A6.9.106 A similar dispensation applies to derivative financial instruments that can only be settled by physical delivery of such unquoted equity instruments. It does not apply to derivative instruments in any other situations as illustrated in the following example.

Example – Reliability of fair value measurement

An entity acquires a complex stand alone derivative that is based on several underlying variables, including commodity prices, interest rates and credit indices. There is no active market or other price quotation for the derivative and no active markets for some of its underlying variables. The entity contends that the derivative's fair value cannot be reliably measured.

Notwithstanding the entity's contention, there is a presumption that the fair value of derivatives can be determined reliably by reference to appropriate market prices, or prices of similar instruments, or discounted cash flow or other pricing models or by reference to prices/rates for components, with the exception only of derivatives that are linked to and must be settled by delivery of an unquoted equity instrument (see para A6.9.104 above). This is not the situation here and, therefore, the entity cannot measure the derivative at cost or amortised cost.

Day '1' gain or loss

A6.9.107 As noted in paragraph A6.9.77 above, the best evidence of the instrument's fair value on initial recognition is the transaction price. However, it is possible that the instrument's fair value may not be the transaction price. The only exception to using the transaction price is if the fair value is evidenced by comparison with other observable current market transactions in the *same* instrument, or is based on a valuation technique whose variables include *only* data from observable markets. [IAS 39 para AG 76]. In such situations, the entity is required to use this value. Consequently, the difference between the estimated fair value using a valuation technique and the transaction price results in immediate 'day 1' recognition of a gain or loss. The IASB concluded that these conditions were necessary and sufficient to provide reasonable assurance that this fair value was genuine for the purposes of recognising up-front gains or losses. In all other cases, the transaction price gives the best evidence of fair value and 'day 1' gain recognition is precluded, an approach that achieves convergence with US GAAP. [IAS 39 para BC104].

Example – Day '1' gain or loss recognition

Entity A acquires a financial asset for C110, which is not quoted in an active market. The asset's fair value based on the entity's own valuation technique amounted to C115. However, that valuation technique does not solely use observable market date, but relies on some entity-specific factors that market participants would not normally consider in setting a price.

The entity cannot recognise a 'day 1' profit of C5 and record the asset at C115. The use of unobservable entity-specific inputs to calculate a fair value that is different from transaction price on day 1 is so subjective that its reliability is called into question. Hence, recognition of a day 1 gain or loss is not appropriate. Accordingly, the entity restricts its valuation to the transaction price and the asset is recorded at C110.

6A.9.108 A question arises as to whether and how any gain or loss not recognised on 'day 1' should be recognised subsequently, or at all. The amendment to IAS 39, 'Transition and initial recognition of assets and financial liabilities', issued in December 2004, provides guidance on this issue. It clarifies that an unrecognised 'day 1' gain or loss should be recognised after initial recognition only to the extent that it arises from a change in a factor (including time) that market participants would consider in setting a price. [IAS 39 para AG

76A]. It is not clear how the phrase *"a change in a factor (including time) that market participants would consider in setting a price"* should be interpreted. One interpretation is that a gain or loss should remain unrecognised until all market inputs become observable. Another interpretation is that it permits the recognition of 'day 1' gain or loss in profit or loss on a systematic basis over time, even in the absence of any observable transaction data to support such a treatment. Indeed, some constituents asked the Board to clarify whether straight-line amortisation was an appropriate method of recognising the difference. The Board decided not to do this. It concluded that although straight-line amortisation may be an appropriate method in some cases, it will not be appropriate in others. [IAS 39 para BC222(v)(ii)]. This would appear to suggest that an unrecognised day 1 gain or loss could be amortised either on a straight line basis or on another rational basis that reflects the nature of the financial instrument (for example, a non-linear amortisation for some option-based derivatives).

A6.9.109 It should be noted that an unrecognised 'day 1' gain or loss is not separately identified in the balance sheet. However, IFRS 7 requires disclosure of the unrecognised amount, together with the change in the amount previously deferred, and the entity's accounting policy for determining when amounts deferred are recognised in profit or loss (see section 11).

Demand deposit liabilities

A6.9.110 A demand deposit represents a promise by the deposit-taking institution to deliver cash either to the depositor or to third parties designated by the depositor. It imposes a contractual obligation that is a financial liability. A typical example is a current account in a bank. The current account holder can demand settlement at any time and the bank generally has the right to return the depositor's money at any time (even though that right is seldom exercised). It is often argued that the fair value of the financial liabilities with a demand feature is less than the demand amount, because not all depositors withdraw their money at the earliest opportunity. Often there is a core of deposits (withdrawals replaced by new deposits) that is left outstanding for long periods of time.

A6.9.111 However, the IASB was not prepared to concede that demand financial liabilities could have a fair value different from face value until further work had been done, particularly, in respect of insurance contract liabilities. Consequently, IAS 39 makes it clear that the fair value of a financial liability with a demand feature is not less than the amount payable on demand, discounted from the first date that the amount could be required to be paid. [IAS 39 para 49]. This follows from the fact that the maturity date of an item with no contractual repayment terms cannot be later than the earliest date on which payment can be demanded. The Basis for Conclusion section in IAS 39 notes that recognising a financial liability with a demand feature at less than the demand amount would give rise to an immediate gain on the origination of such a deposit, which is not considered appropriate. In substance, the gain represents the benefits of future interest free or low interest use of funds expected to occur as a result of the deposit relationship. Such benefits are not considered to be directly attributable to the rights and obligations that constitute the demand deposit liabilities existing at a measurement date and accordingly should not enter into the estimation of their fair value. The future benefit of the deposit relationship may be recognised as an intangible asset in circumstances where customer relationships are acquired, together with the related portfolio of demand deposits, if the recognition criteria in IAS 38, 'Intangible assets' are met. However, the Basis for Conclusion section in IAS 39 notes that, absent such an acquisition, the market price observed for such financial liabilities is the price at which they are originated between the customer and the deposit-taker, that is, the demand amount. [IAS 39 para BC 94]. In the absence of an acquisition of a portfolio of demand deposits, this customer deposit intangible asset should not be recognised.

Credit risk of liabilities

A6.9.112 When financial liabilities are measured at fair value, changes in their credit risk should be reflected in their fair value measurement. Many question whether a liability's credit risk or changes in its credit risk should enter into the measurement of its liabilities. They argue that it is not useful to report lower liabilities when an entity is in financial difficulty precisely because its debt levels are too high and that it would be difficult to explain to users of financial statements the reasons why income would be recognised when a liability's creditworthiness deteriorates. The IASB, however, takes the view that because financial statements are prepared on a going concern basis, credit risk affects the value at which liabilities could be repurchased or settled. Accordingly, a financial liability's fair value reflects the credit risk relating to that liability. Therefore, the IASB decided to include credit risk relating to a financial liability in the fair value measurement of that liability for the following reasons:

- entities realise changes in fair value, including fair value attributable to the liability's credit risk, for example, by renegotiating or repurchasing liabilities or by using derivatives;
- changes in credit risk affect the observed market price of a financial liability and hence its fair value;
- it is difficult from a practical standpoint to exclude changes in credit risk from an observed market price; and
- a financial liability's fair value (that is, the price of that liability in an exchange between a knowledgeable, willing buyer and a knowledgeable, willing seller) on initial recognition reflects its credit risk. Therefore, it is inappropriate to include credit risk in the initial fair value measurement of financial liabilities, but not subsequently.

[IAS 39 para BC89].

A6.9.113 It should be noted that the issue relates to the financial liability's credit risk, rather than the entity's creditworthiness. Although the two are closely related, a deterioration of the entity creditworthiness may not, by itself, affect the credit risk of all the entity's liabilities in the same way. For example, the fair value of liabilities secured by valuable collateral, guaranteed by third parties or ranking ahead of virtually all other liabilities is generally unaffected by changes in the entity's creditworthiness. [IAS 39 para BC92]. If an entity designates a financial liability as at fair value through profit or loss, IFRS 7 requires it to disclose the amount of change in the fair value of the financial liability that is attributable to changes in the liability's credit risk (see further section 11).

Impairment of financial assets

A6.9.114 A financial asset measured at amortised cost is impaired when its carrying value exceeds the present value of the future cash flows discounted at the financial asset's original effective interest rate. A financial asset that is carried at fair value through profit or loss does not give rise to any impairment issues as diminution in value due to impairment is already reflected in the fair value and, hence, in profit or loss. It follows that impairment issues are only relevant to financial assets that are carried at amortised cost and available-for-sale financial assets whose fair value changes are recognised in equity.

A6.9.115 IAS 39 deals with impairment of financial assets through a two-step process. First, an entity must carry out an impairment review of its financial assets at each balance sheet date. The aim of this review is to determine whether there is objective evidence that impairment exists for a financial asset. [IAS 39 para 58]. This is considered from paragraph A6.9.120 below.

A6.9.116 Secondly, if there is objective evidence of impairment, the entity should measure and record the impairment loss in the reporting period. [IAS 39 para 58]. The measurement of impairment losses differs between financial assets carried at amortised cost (see para A6.9.126 below), financial assets carried at cost (see para A6.9.151 below) and available-for-sale financial assets (see para A6.9.152 below). There is also a difference on whether impairment losses can be reversed depending on whether the available-for-sale instrument is debt or equity (see para A6.9.154 below).

Incurred versus expected losses

A6.9.117 Under IAS 39, a financial asset or a group of financial assets is impaired and impairment losses are incurred if, and only if, there is objective evidence of impairment as a result of one or more events that occurred after the asset's initial recognition (a 'loss event'). It may not be possible to identify a single, discrete event that caused the impairment. Rather the combined effect of several events may have caused the impairment. In addition, the loss event must have a reliably measurable effect on the present value of estimated future cash flows and be supported by current observable data. [IAS 39 para 59].

A6.9.118 Losses expected as a result of future events, no matter how likely, are not recognised. Possible or expected future trends that may lead to a loss in the future (for example, an expectation that unemployment will rise or a recession will occur) are also not taken into account. The standard states that to recognise impairment on the basis of expected future transactions and events would not be consistent with an amortised cost model.

A6.9.119 As the impairment model in IAS 39 is based on the 'incurred loss' model and not on an 'expected loss' model, an impairment loss is not recognised at the time an asset is originated, that is, before a loss event can have occurred as illustrated in the following example:

Example – Recognition of an impairment loss on origination

Entity A lends C1,000 to a group of customers. Based on historical experience, entity A expects that 1% of the principal amount of loans given to the customers will not be collected.

Entity A is not permitted to reduce the carrying amount of a loan asset by C10 on initial recognition through the recognition of an immediate impairment loss.

Under the incurred loss model of IAS 39, an impairment loss is recognised only if there is objective evidence of impairment as a result of a past event that occurred after initial recognition. Furthermore, recognition of an immediate impairment loss based on future expectation would be inconsistent with the general rule that a financial asset should be initially measured at fair value. For a loan asset, the fair value is the amount of cash lent adjusted for any fees and costs (unless a portion of the amount lent is compensation for other stated or implied rights or privileges). [IAS 39 para IGE4.2]. In practice, however, the expectation of loss is built in to the credit spread for the customer.

Objective evidence of impairment

A6.9.120 IAS 39 provides examples of factors that may, either individually or taken together, provide sufficient objective evidence that an impairment loss has been incurred in a financial asset or group of financial assets. They include observable data that comes to the attention of the holder of the asset about the following loss events:

- Significant financial difficulty of the issuer or obligor.
- A breach of contract, such as a default or delinquency in interest or principal payments.
- The lender, for economic or legal reasons relating to the borrower's financial difficulty, granting to the borrower a concession that the lender would not otherwise consider.
- It becomes probable that the borrower will enter bankruptcy or other financial reorganisation.
- The disappearance of an active market for that financial asset because of financial difficulties.
- Observable data indicating that there is a measurable decrease in the estimated future cash flows from a group of financial assets since the initial

recognition of those assets, although the decrease cannot yet be identified with the individual financial assets in the group, including:

- adverse changes in the payment status of borrowers in the group (for example, an increased number of delayed payments or an increased number of credit card borrowers who have reached their credit limit and are paying the minimum monthly amount); or
- national or local economic conditions that correlate with defaults on the assets in the group (for example, an increase in the unemployment rate in the geographical area of the borrowers, a decrease in property prices for mortgages in the relevant area, a decrease in oil prices for loan assets to oil producers, or adverse changes in industry conditions that affect the borrowers in the group).

[IAS 39 para 59].

A6.9.121 A downgrade of an entity's credit rating is not, of itself, evidence of impairment, although it may be evidence of impairment when considered with other available information. Other factors that an entity considers in determining whether it has objective evidence that an impairment loss has been incurred include information about:

- The debtors' or issuers' liquidity.
- Solvency, business and financial risk exposures.
- Levels of and trends in delinquencies for similar financial assets.
- National and local economic trends and conditions.
- The fair value of collateral and guarantees.

These and other factors may, either individually or taken together, provide sufficient objective evidence that an impairment loss has been incurred in a financial asset or group of financial assets. [IAS 39 para 60, IG para E4.1].

A6.9.122 A decline in the fair value of a financial asset below its cost or amortised cost is not necessarily evidence of impairment (for example, a decline in the fair value of an investment in a debt instrument that results from an increase in the risk-free interest rate). Also, in contrast with the fifth bullet point mentioned in paragraph A6.9.120 above, the disappearance of an active market because an entity's financial instruments are no longer publicly traded is not evidence of impairment. [IAS 39 para 60].

Evidence of impairment for equity instruments

A6.9.123 The original standard did not include guidance about impairment indicators that are specific to investment in equity instruments. The IASB acknowledged that for marketable investments in equity instruments any impairment trigger other than a decline in fair value below cost is likely to be arbitrary to some extent. If markets are reasonably efficient, today's market price is the best estimate of the discounted value of the future market price. [IAS 39 para BC106]. However, questions often arise in practice about when such investments become impaired. Accordingly, the revised standard provides additional guidance about impairment indicators that are specific to investments in equity instruments. They apply in addition to the impairment indicators described above, which focus on the assessment of impairment in debt instruments.

A6.9.124 The additional impairment indicators that may indicate that the equity investment's cost may not be recovered are:

- Significant adverse changes in the technological, market, economic or legal environment in which the issuer operates. For example, such changes include but are not limited to:
  - Structural changes in the industry or industries in which the issuer operates, such as changes in production technology or the number of competitors.
  - Changes in the level of demand for the goods or services sold by the issuer resulting from factors such as changing consumer tastes or product obsolescence.
  - Changes in the political or legal environment affecting the issuer's business, such as enactment of new environment protection, tax or trade laws.
  - Changes in the issuer's financial condition evidenced by changes in factors such as its liquidity, credit rating, profitability, cash flows, debt/equity ratio and level of dividend payments.
- A 'significant' or 'prolonged' decline in the fair value of an investment in an equity instrument below its cost.

[IAS 39 para 61].

A6.9.125 The standard does not provide any quantified guidance on what is a 'significant' or 'prolonged' decline in the fair value of an equity instrument and this evaluation will require judgement. However, the IFRIC confirmed that a significant decline in fair value should be evaluated against the original cost at initial recognition and 'prolonged' should be evaluated against the period in which the fair value of the investment has been below that original cost. Furthermore, any further declines in value after an impairment loss has been recognised in profit or loss should be recognised immediately in profit or loss. [IAS 39 para IG E4.9]. IAS 39 refers to original cost on initial recognition of an equity instrument and does not permit a prior impairment to establish a new deemed cost against which subsequent declines in fair value are evaluated. [IFRIC Update April 2005].

Financial assets carried at amortised cost

General requirements

A6.9.126 Financial assets carried at amortised cost are those that are classified as either loans and receivables or held-to-maturity. If there is objective evidence that an impairment loss on such an asset has been incurred, the amount of the loss should be measured as the difference between the asset's carrying amount and the present value of estimated future cash flows. The expected cash flows should exclude future credit losses that have not been incurred and should be discounted at the financial asset's original effective interest rate (that is, the effective interest rate computed at initial recognition). [IAS 39 para 63].

A6.9.127 The standard allows the carrying amount of the asset to be reduced either directly by writing it down or through use of an allowance account such as a loan loss provision or provision for bad and doubtful debts. However, the amount of the loss should be recognised in profit or loss. [IAS 39 para 63]. The asset's carrying amount in the entity's balance sheet is stated net of any related allowance. [IAS 39 para AG 84].

A6.9.128 In some circumstances, it may not be practicable to make a reasonably reliable direct estimate of the present value of future cash flows expected from an impaired financial asset measured at amortised cost. As a practical expedient, the carrying amount of the impaired asset may be determined in these circumstances on the basis of an instrument's fair value using an observable market price. [IAS 39 para AG 84].

A6.9.129 A loan's observable market price is the loan's quoted price that can be obtained from reliable market sources. For example, loans with an active secondary market could be measured based on the observable market price. Similarly, an entity that has a viable plan to dispose of loans in a bulk sale could measure impairment by comparison to the net proceeds received on similar loan sales. However, it is likely that the use of the observable market price will be infrequent, because either there may not be a market for the loans or the market may be illiquid.

A6.9.130 The expected future cash flows that are included in the calculation are the contractual cash of the instrument itself, reduced or delayed based on the current expectations of the amount and timing of these cash flows as a result of losses incurred at the balance sheet date. In circumstances where the amount outstanding is expected to be collected in full, but the collection period is delayed, an impairment loss must still be recognised, unless the creditor receives full compensation (for example, in the form of penalty interest) for the period of the delinquency, as illustrated in the example below.

Example – Impairment arising from changes in the amount and timing of cash flows

Entity A is concerned that, because of financial difficulties, customer B will not be able to make all principal and interest payments due on a loan in a timely manner. It negotiates a restructuring of the loan. Entity A expects that customer B will be able to meet its obligations under the restructured terms in any of the 5 scenarios indicated below.

- Customer B will pay the original loan's full principal amount 5 years after the original due date, but none of the interest due under the original terms.
- Customer B will pay the original loan's full principal amount on the original due date, but none of the interest due under the original terms.
- Customer B will pay the original loan's full principal amount on the original due date with interest only at a lower interest rate than the interest rate inherent in the original loan.
- Customer B will pay the original loan's full principal amount 5 years after the original due date and all interest accrued during the original loan term, but no interest for the extended term.
- Customer B will pay the original loan's full principal amount 5 years after the original due date and all interest, including interest for both the loan's original term and the extended term.

[IAS 39 para IG E4.3].

Given that customer B is in financial difficulties, an impairment loss has been incurred, as there is objective evidence of impairment. The amount of the impairment loss for a loan measured at amortised cost is the difference between the loan's carrying amount and the present value of future principal and interest payments discounted at the loan's original effective interest rate.

In the first four scenarios above, the present value of the future principal and interest payments discounted at the loan's original effective interest rate will be lower than the loan's carrying amount. Therefore, an impairment loss is recognised in those cases.

In the final scenario, even though the timing of payments has changed, the lender will receive interest on interest, and the present value of the future principal and interest payments discounted at the loan's original effective interest rate will equal the carrying amount of the loan. Therefore, there is no impairment loss. However, this fact pattern is unlikely given customer B's financial difficulties.

6A.9.131 Where an impaired financial asset is secured by collateral, the calculation of the present value of the estimated future cash flows of the collateralised financial asset should reflect the cash flows that may result from foreclosure less costs for obtaining and selling the collateral, whether or not foreclosure is probable. [IAS 39 para AG 84]. As the measurement of the impaired financial asset reflects the collateral asset's fair value, the collateral is not recognised as an asset separately from the impaired financial asset, unless it meets the recognition criteria for an asset in another standard. [IAS 39 para IG E4.8].

Appropriate discount rate

A6.9.132 As stated above, impairment of a financial asset carried at amortised cost is measured by discounting the expected future cash flows using the financial instrument's original effective interest rate. Since impairment reflects a fall in the asset's carrying amount, which is evidenced by a decrease in the estimate of expected cash flows to be received from the financial asset, discounting at a rate of interest that reflects a current market rate of interest would impose fair value measurement on the financial asset. This would not be appropriate for assets that are measured at amortised cost. [IAS 39 para AG 84]. The historical effective rate should be used as the discount rate even where it is lower or higher than the rate on current loans originated by the entity. In other words, loan impairments are based solely on the reduction in estimated cash flows rather than on changes in interest rates. This approach ensures that a financial asset carried at amortised cost that becomes impaired continues to be carried at an amount that considers the present value of all expected future cash flows, in a manner consistent with the asset's measurement before it became impaired.

A6.9.133 Even if the terms of a loan, receivable or held-to-maturity investment are renegotiated or otherwise modified because of financial difficulties of the borrower, impairment is measured using the original effective interest rate before the terms were modified. [IAS 39 para AG 84].

A6.9.134 There are, however, two specific instances where the original discount rate is not used to measure impairment losses.

- For variable rate loans and variable rate held-to-maturity investments, the discount rate for measuring any impairment loss is the current variable rate determined under the contract. [IAS 39 para AG 84].

- For a fixed rate loan that is designated as a hedged item in a fair value hedge of interest rate risk, the loan's carrying amount is adjusted for any changes in its fair value attributable to interest rate movements. The loan's original effective interest rate before the hedge, therefore, becomes irrelevant and the effective interest rate is recalculated using the loan's adjusted carrying amount. The adjusted effective rate is used as the rate for discounting the estimated future cash flows for measuring the impairment loss on the hedged loan. [IAS 39 para IG E4.4]. Hedge accounting is considered in section 10.

Example – Impairment of fixed rate loan

The facts are the same as in example 2 in paragraph A6.9.62 above, except that at 31 December 20X9 it became clear that as a result of structural changes in the industry in which the borrower operates, the borrower was in financial difficulties and its credit rating had been downgraded. At that date, the loan's amortised carrying value, calculated at the original effective rate of 6.7322%, amounted to C587,988.

Faced with this objective evidence, the entity believes that the borrower will be unable to make all the remaining 5 annual scheduled repayments of C142,378. Accordingly, the entity restructures the loan under which the annual payment due on 31 December 20Y0 is waived followed by three annual payments of C175,000 until 31 December 20Y3. The interest on the outstanding loan under the revised payment schedule is reduced to 6.3071%.

The present value of the annual payments of C175,000 due on 31 Dec 20Y1, Y2 and Y3, discounted at the original effective interest rate of 6.7322% amounts to C432,402.

Accordingly, the entity recognises an impairment loss of C155,586 (C587,988 – C432,402) in profit or loss on 31 December 20X9. Therefore, the carrying amount is written down by the amount of the impairment loss.

6A.9.135 Consistent with the initial measurement requirements set out in paragraph A6.9.7 above, cash flows relating to short term receivables are not discounted if the effect of discounting is immaterial. [IAS 39 para AG 84].

Evaluation of impairment on a portfolio basis

A6.9.136 IAS 39 contains specific guidance for assessing and measuring the impairment losses of a group of financial assets that is carried at amortised cost. The assessment process is as follows:

- First, financial assets that are considered to be individually significant are assessed for impairment individually based on whether objective evidence of impairment exists.
- Secondly, all other assets that are not individually significant are assessed for impairment. They may be assessed either individually or collectively on a group basis as indicated below.
- Thirdly, all assets that have been individually assessed for impairment, whether significant or not, but for which there is no objective evidence of impairment, are included within a group of assets with similar credit risk characteristics and collectively assessed for impairment.
- Fourthly, assets that are individually assessed for impairment and for which an impairment loss is (or continues to be) recognised are not included in a collective assessment for impairment.

[IAS 39 para 64].

A6.9.137 It seems perhaps illogical and superfluous to subject individual loans that have been reviewed individually for impairment and found not to be impaired to be included again in a portfolio of similar loans for collective assessment. The Basis for Conclusions sets out in extensive detail the arguments for and against this requirement and concludes that impairment that cannot be identified with an individual loan may be identifiable on a portfolio basis. [IAS 39 paras BC111 to BC117].

A6.9.138 There is no guidance in the standard as to what is meant by 'individually significant'. What is significant for one entity may not be significant to another, so each entity should assess what is significant based on its own facts and circumstances.

Example – Individual versus collection assessment

An entity has a portfolio of similar receivables amounting to C100m. The entity considers that within this portfolio are C30m of loans that are individually significant. It assesses these loans for impairment on an individual basis and determines that C20m of loans are impaired. Of the remaining C70m loans that are not significant, the entity selects C15m for individual assessment and finds them all to be individually impaired. The rest of the portfolio is subject to an impairment review on a collective basis.

The result of this assessment means that loans amounting to C35m that have been assessed for impairment on an individual basis, whether significant or not, and found to be impaired will not be included for collective assessment. The remaining C65m of loans (C10m of individually significant loans that are found not to be impaired) and C55m that were not assessed for impairment on an individual basis) are included in the collective assessment.

However, loss probabilities and other loss statistics differ at a portfolio level between the C10m of individually evaluated loans that are found not to be impaired and the C55m of loans that were not individually evaluated for impairment. This means that a different amount of impairment may be required for these sub-portfolios. [IAS 39 AG87].

6A.9.139 For the purpose of a collective evaluation of impairment, financial assets should be grouped on the basis of similar credit risk characteristics that are indicative of the debtors' ability to pay all amounts due according to the contractual terms. This may be done on the basis of a credit risk evaluation or grading process that considers asset type, industry, geographical location, collateral type, past-due status and other relevant factors. If an entity does not have a group of assets with similar risk characteristics, it does not make the additional assessment. [IAS 39 para AG 87]. In that case, such assets are individually assessed for impairment.

A6.9.140 It should be noted that as soon as information is available that specifically identifies losses on individually impaired assets in a group, those assets should be removed from the group. [IAS 39 para AG 88].

A6.9.141 The Basis for Conclusions in IAS 39 provides detailed guidance on how to perform impairment assessments within groups of financial assets. Most of the detailed guidance will be highly relevant to banks and financial institutions that have large portfolios of loans and receivables. The following elements are critical to an adequate process:

- Future cash flows in a group of financial assets should be estimated on the basis of historical loss experience for assets with credit risk characteristics similar to those in the group.
- Entities that have no entity-specific loss experience or insufficient experience should use peer group experience for comparable groups of financial assets.
- Historical loss experience should be adjusted on the basis of current observable data to reflect the effects of current conditions.
- Changes in estimates of future cash flows should be directionally consistent with changes in underlying observable data (such as changes in unemployment rates, property prices, payment status, or other factors indicative of changes in the probability of losses in the group and their magnitude).

- The methodology and assumptions used for estimating future cash flows should be reviewed regularly to reduce any differences between loss estimates and actual loss experience.

[IAS 39 para BC124].

A6.9.142 Applying the above process ensures that the collective assessment of impairment for a group of financial assets is still an 'incurred' and not an 'expected' loss model that aims to reflect the loss events that have occurred with respect to individual assets in the group, but have not yet been identified on an individual asset basis. IAS 39 provides an example of an entity that determines, on the basis of historical experience, that one of the main causes of default on credit card loans is the death of the borrower. Although the death rate is unchanged from one year to the next, some of the borrowers in the group may have died in that year. This indicates that an impairment loss has occurred on those loans, even if, at the year-end, the entity is not yet aware which specific borrowers have died. It would be appropriate for an impairment loss to be recognised for these 'incurred but not reported' (IBNR) losses. However, it would not be appropriate to recognise an impairment loss for deaths that are expected to occur in a future period, because the necessary loss event (the death of the borrower) has not yet occurred. [IAS 39 para AG 90].

A6.9.143 The standard allows the use of formula-based approaches or statistical methods to determine impairment losses in a group of financial assets as long as they:

- Do not give rise to an impairment loss on a financial asset's initial recognition.
- Are consistent with the general requirements outlined above.
- Incorporate the effect of the time value of money.
- Consider the cash flows for all of the remaining life of an asset (not only the next year).
- Consider the age of the loans within the portfolio.

[IAS 39 para AG 92].

Measurement difficulties in the absence of observable data

A6.9.144 Making a reasonably reliable estimate of the amount and timing of future cash flows from an impaired financial asset is a matter of judgement. The best estimate is based on reasonable and supportable assumptions and observable data concerning the ability of a debtor to make payments in relation to circumstances existing at the impairment measurement date.

A6.9.145 However, sometimes observable data required to estimate the amount of an impairment loss on a financial asset may be limited or no longer fully relevant to current circumstances. For example, this may be the case when a borrower is in financial difficulties and there is little available historical data relating to similar borrowers. In such cases, an entity should use its judgement to estimate the amount of any impairment loss and to adjust observable data for a group of financial assets to reflect current circumstances. The use of reasonable estimates is an essential part of the financial statement's preparation and does not undermine their reliability. [IAS 39 para 62].

General provisions for bad and doubtful debts

A6.9.146 It has not been uncommon for entities under previous GAAPs to determine bad debt provisions for non-performing loans based on a provision matrix or similar formula that specifies fixed provision rates for the number of days a loan or a debt is overdue. For example, the provisioning rates could be zero per cent if less than 90 days overdue, 20 per cent if 90-180 days, 50 per cent if 181-365 days and 100 per cent if more than 365 days. Such a method of provisioning would not be acceptable under IAS 39, unless it produces a result that is sufficiently close to the one obtained by following a discounted cash flow methodology required by the standard, which is considered highly unlikely. [IAS 39 para IG E4.5].

A6.9.147 Similarly, it was fairly common for entities under previous GAAPs to make a general provision for bad and doubtful debts on the grounds of prudence and set aside sums that are not specifically related to losses in a group of assets, but intended to cover unplanned and unexpected losses. Such provisioning methods are not allowed under IAS 39 as it results in impairment or bad debt losses that are in excess of those that can be attributed to incurred losses. Accordingly, amounts that an entity might want to set aside for additional possible impairment in financial assets, such as reserves that cannot be supported by objective evidence about impairment, are not recognised as impairment or bad debt losses under IAS 39. [IAS 39 para IG E4.6]. This does not prevent an entity designating part of its reserves in equity to cover such 'prudence' or related losses.

Recognition of interest on impaired assets

A6.9.148 Once a financial asset or a group of similar financial assets has been written down as a result of an impairment loss, interest income is thereafter recognised using the rate of interest used to discount the future cash flows for the purpose of measuring the impairment loss. [IAS 39 para AG 93]. That is the discount in the carrying amount is unwound. This would be the original effective rate for fixed rate instruments and current interest rate for floating rate instruments.

A6.9.149 An entity should not stop accruing interest on loans that are non-performing. When non-performing loans are reviewed for impairment, the collection or non-collection of the future interest payments would be taken into account in the estimation of future cash flows for the purposes of the impairment calculation. Interest income would be recognised as the discount unwinds.

Example – Income recognition on impaired loans

The facts are the same as in the example in paragraph A6.9.134 above. Following recognising the impairment loss at 31 December 20X9, the amortised cost amounted to C432,402.

On the assumption that cash inflows will occur as restructured, the amortisation schedule based on the revised cash flows and the original discount rate is shown below. In accordance with paragraph A6.9.148 above, interest income is recognised at the rate of discount used to the measure the impairment.

	Cash in flows	Interest income @ 6.7322%	Carrying amount
1 Jan 20Y0			432,402
31 Dec 20Y0		29,110	461,512
31 Dec 20Y1	175,000	31,070	317,582
31 Dec 20Y2	175,000	21,380	163,962
31 Dec 20Y3	175,000	11,038	-
	525,000	92,598	

Reversal of impairment losses on assets held at amortised cost

A6.9.150 As stated in paragraph A6.9.115 above, an impairment review should be carried out at each reporting date. If, in a subsequent period, the amount of the impairment loss decreases and the decrease can be related objectively to an event occurring after the impairment was recognised (such as an improvement in the debtor's credit rating), the previously recognised impairment loss should be reversed either directly or by adjusting an allowance account. The reversal should not result in a carrying amount of the financial asset that exceeds what the amortised cost would have been had the impairment not been recognised at the date the impairment is reversed. The amount of the reversal should be recognised in profit or loss. [IAS 39 para 65]. This is in contrast with an equity instrument where an impairment loss is specifically not reversed (see para A6.9.154 below).

Financial assets carried at cost

A6.9.151 As set out in paragraph A6.9.104 above, an unquoted equity instrument that is not carried at fair value because its fair value cannot be reliably measured, or on a derivative asset that is linked to and must be settled by delivery of such an unquoted equity instrument, are measured at cost. For such instruments, if there is objective evidence that an impairment loss has been incurred, the amount of the impairment loss is measured as the difference between the carrying amount of the financial asset and the present value of estimated future cash flows discounted at the current market rate of return for a similar financial asset. Such impairment losses are not permitted to be reversed. [IAS 39 para 66].

Available-for-sale financial assets

A6.9.152 When a decline in the fair value of an available-for-sale financial asset has been recognised directly in equity and there is objective evidence that the asset is impaired, the cumulative loss that had been recognised directly in equity should be removed from equity and recognised in profit or loss even though the financial asset has not been derecognised. [IAS 39 para 67].

A6.9.153 The amount of cumulative loss that is recycled to profit or loss is the difference between the acquisition cost (net of any principal repayment and amortisation) and current fair value, less any impairment loss on that financial asset previously recognised in profit or loss. [IAS 39 para 68]. Any portion of the cumulative net loss that is attributable to foreign currency changes on that asset that had been recognised in equity is also recognised in profit or loss (see para A6.9.163 below). Any subsequent losses, including any portion attributable to foreign currency changes, are also recognised in profit or loss until the asset is derecognised. [IAS 39 para IG E4.9].

Example – Impairment of available-for-sale debt security

On 1 January 20X3, an entity purchased C10 million 5 year bond with semi-annual interest of 5% payable on 30 June and 31 December each year. The bond's purchase price was C10,811,100, which resulted in a bond premium of C811,100 and an effective interest rate of 8% (4% on a semi-annual basis). The entity classified the bond as available-for-sale.

The entity received all the interest due in 20X3 and 20X4 on a timely basis. At 31 December 20X4, the amortised cost of the loan amounted to C10,524,226. The cumulative amount recognised in equity to that date was a loss C266,322.

The entity did not receive the half-yearly interest due on 30 June 20X5 and it soon became clear that the issuer was in financial difficulties. At 31 December 20X5, the entity reviews the issuer's financial condition and prospects for repayment of the loan and determines that the bond is impaired. On the basis of the information available at the time, the entity's best estimate of future cash flows (on a yearly basis) is cash receipts of C2m on 31 December 20X6 and C7m on 31 December 20X7, the scheduled repayment date.

Although the bond is non-performing, the entity recognises the interest income for the period to 31 December 20X5 at the original effective interest rate. On this basis, the bond's amortised cost at 31 December 20X5 amounts to C11,383,002.

As the bond is classified as available-for-sale, it is necessary to determine the bond's fair value at 31 December 20X5. As there is no observable market price for the bond, the bond's fair value, can only be obtained by discounting the expected cash flows at the current market rate. As a market rate for a comparable bond may not exist, it would be necessary to derive a current market rate for the bond. One way of estimating the current rate for the bond is by reference to a benchmark rate or the risk-free rate, which is part of the bond's effective rate of interest of 8%.

Assume that when the bond was purchased on 1 January 20X3, the risk-free rate was 6% for a debt instrument with the same terms as the one purchased by the entity. Thus, the credit risk premium of the bond is 200 basis points. At 31 December 20X5, the risk-free rate for a similar type of instrument is 8%. Therefore, as the change in the bond's credit spread since acquisition would be ignored, the current interest rate for discounting the expected cash flows is 10% (8% + 200 basis point). Using this rate of 10%, the present value of the expected cash flow of C2m and C7m arising on 31 December 20X6 and 31 December 20X7 amounts to C7,603,305.

Therefore, the impairment loss recognised in profit or loss is as follows:

Amortised cost at 31 December 20X4	10,524,226
Accrual of half-yearly interest to 30 June 20X5 @ 4%	420,969
	10,945,195
Accrual of half-yearly interest to 31 December 20X5 @ 4%	437,808
Amortised cost at 31 December 20X5	11,383,003
Fair value of bond at 31 December 20X5	(7,603,305)
	3,779,698
Recycling of loss recognised in equity	266,322
Impairment recognised in profit or loss	4,046,020
Financial asset stated in the balance sheet at 31 December 20X5	7,542,843

Reversal of impairment losses

A6.9.154 It is possible that after an impairment loss has been recognised for an available-for-sale financial asset circumstances change in a subsequent period such that the fair value of the available-for-sale financial instrument increases. In those circumstances, the treatment required by the standard for reversals of impairment losses on available-for-sale debt instruments is different from those on available-for-sale equity instruments as noted below:

- For available-for-sale debt instruments (monetary assets), past impairment losses should be reversed through the profit or loss when fair value increases and the increase can be objectively related to an event occurring after the impairment loss was recognised in profit or loss. [IAS 39 para 70].

- For available-for-sale equity investments (non-monetary assets), past impairment losses recognised in profit or loss should not be reversed through profit or loss when fair value increases. [IAS 39 para 69]. This means that subsequent increases in fair value including those that have the effect of reversing earlier impairment losses are all recognised in equity. This is a significant change from the previous version of the standard.

A6.9.155 The inability to reverse impairment losses recognised in profit or loss on available-for-sale equity instruments raises a particular issue for entities that have recognised such impairment losses in their interim reports. This is because, at the subsequent reporting or balance sheet date, conditions may have changed to such an extent that a loss would not have been recognised, or a smaller loss would have been recognised, if the impairment review were first carried out at that date.

A6.9.156 The confusion arises because paragraph 28 of IAS 34, 'Interim financial reporting', requires an entity to apply the same accounting policies in its interim financial statements as are applied in its annual financial statements. This suggests that an impairment loss recognised in the interim period should not be reversed at the subsequent balance sheet date. On the other hand, the same paragraph states that 'the frequency of an entity's reporting (annual, half-yearly, or quarterly) should not affect the measurement of its annual results. To achieve this objective, measurement for interim reporting purposes should be made on a 'year-to-date' basis. This suggests that an impairment loss recognised in one interim period can be reversed at the subsequent balance sheet date.

A6.9.157 The IFRIC considered the matter and issued IFRIC 10, 'Interim report and impairment' in July 2006. The IFRIC concluded that the prohibitions on reversals of recognised impairment losses on investments in equity instruments in IAS 39 should take precedence over the more general statement in IAS 34 regarding the frequency of an entity's reporting not affecting the measurement of its annual results. Therefore, any impairment losses that are recognised in a previous interim period in respect of an investment in an equity instrument may not be reversed in a later interim periods or when preparing the annual financial statements. [IFRIC 10 para 8]. The Interpretation applies to annual periods beginning on or after 1 November 2006. Earlier application is encouraged. If an entity applies the Interpretation for a period beginning before 1 November 2006, it should disclose that fact.

Foreign currency financial instruments

General

A6.9.158 Financial instruments are often denominated in foreign currencies. The way in which changes in foreign exchange rates in foreign currency financial assets and liabilities should be dealt with is covered in IAS 21, 'The effects of changes in foreign exchange rates'. The measurement principles of IAS 39 generally do not override these rules, except in the area of hedge accounting which is considered in section 10.

A6.9.159 Under IAS 21, all transactions in foreign currencies are initially recognised at the spot exchange rate at the date of the transaction. The spot exchange rate is the exchange rate for immediate delivery. It follows that on initial recognition, all foreign currency financial instruments are translated at the spot rate into the entity's functional currency, irrespective of whether the instrument is carried at cost, amortised cost or fair value.

A6.9.160 Gains and losses associated with financial instruments, such as interest income and expense and impairment losses, are recognised at the spot exchange rate at the dates on which they arise. Dividends should be recognised in income when the shareholder's right to receive payment is established. [IAS 18 para 30(c)]. The exchange rate ruling at that date, which is normally the dividend declaration date, is used to record the income. Entities are permitted to use an average rate where it represents an approximation to the spot rate in that period.

Subsequent measurement

A6.9.161 The subsequent measurement of foreign currency financial assets and liabilities will depend on whether the assets and liabilities are monetary or non-monetary in nature. Monetary items are units of currency held and assets and liabilities to be received or paid in a fixed or determinable number of units of currency. [IAS 21 para 8]. It follows that financial assets and liabilities that are debt instruments are monetary items. Derivative financial instruments are also monetary items as they are settled at a future date, even though the underlying may be non-monetary. Non-monetary items are all items other than monetary items. In other words, the right to receive (or an obligation to deliver) a fixed or determinable number of units of currency is absent in a non-monetary item. This is the case for financial assets that are equity instruments.

Monetary financial assets

A6.9.162 IAS 21 requires that an entity should translate its foreign currency monetary items outstanding at the balance sheet date using the closing spot rate at that date. [IAS 21 para 23(a)]. Exchange differences arising on translating monetary items or on the settlement of monetary items at rates different from those at which they were translated on initial recognition during the period or in previous financial statements, are recognised in profit or loss in the period in which they arise. [IAS 21 para 28]. However, exchange differences on monetary items that are designated as hedging instruments in cash flow hedges or net investments in foreign entities are recognised in equity. [IAS 39 para AG 83].

A6.9.163 For the purpose of recognising foreign exchange gains and losses under IAS 21, a foreign currency monetary available-for-sale financial asset is treated as if it were carried at amortised cost in the foreign currency. Accordingly, for such a financial asset, exchange differences arising from changes in amortised cost, such as interest calculated using the effective interest method and impairment losses are recognised in profit or loss. All other gains and losses are recognised in equity. [IAS 39 para 55(b)]. An example illustrating the above treatment is included as example E3.2 in the Implementation Guidance to IAS 39. A similar example is given below.

Example – Available-for-sale debt security denominated in foreign currency

On 1 January 20X1, an entity whose functional currency is the local currency (LC) purchases a foreign currency (FC) denominated bond for its fair value of FC1,000. The bond has 5 years remaining to maturity and a principal amount of FC1,250 million. Interest is payable annually at 4.7% (that is, FC59) on 31 December each year. Assuming there are no transaction costs, the effective interest rate is 10%. The entity classifies the bond as available-for-sale.

The relevant foreign exchange rates are as follows:

	Average rate FC =	Closing rate FC =
1 January 20X1		LC 1.50
31 December 20X1	LC 1.75	LC 2.00
31 December 20X2	LC 2.25	LC 2.50
31 December 20X3	LC 2.35	LC 2.20
31 December 20X4	LC 2.05	LC 1.90
31 December 20X5	LC 2.10	LC 2.30

For the purpose of this illustrative example, it is assumed that the use of the average exchange rate provides a reliable approximation of the spot rates applicable to the accrual of interest income during the year.

The cumulative gain or loss that is recognised in equity is the difference between the amortised cost (adjusted for impairment, if any) and the fair value of the available-for-sale financial asset in the entity's functional currency.

At 1 January 20X1, the fair value of the bond (FC1,000) translated in the entity's functional currency is LC1.5m and the entry to record this is as follows:

At 1 January 20X5	Dr LC	Cr LC
Available-for-sale financial asset	1,500	
Cash		1,500

The amortisation schedule in foreign currency (FC) is as follows:

Date	Interest income @ 10%	Cash inflow	Amortised cost
1 Jan 20X1			1,000
31 Dec 20X1	100	59	1,041
31 Dec 20X2	104	59	1,086
31 Dec 20X3	109	59	1,136
31 Dec 20X4	113	59	1,190
31 Dec 20X5	119	59	1,250

As the entity classifies the bond as an available-for-sale investment, the asset is treated as an asset measured at amortised cost in foreign currency for the purposes of applying IAS 21. Therefore, the amortisation schedule in the entity's functional currency (LC) shown below is calculated from the above amounts at the appropriate exchange rates as follows:

	Interest income @ 10% (average rate)	Cash inflow @ 4.7% (actual rate)	Amortised cost
	LC	LC	LC
1 Jan 20X1			1,500
31 Dec 20X1	175	118	1,557
31 Dec 20X2	234	148	1,643
31 Dec 20X3	256	130	1,769
31 Dec 20X4	232	112	1,889
31 Dec 20X5	250	136	2,003
	1,147	644	

	Amortised cost as above	Amortised cost translated at year end rate	Carrying amount as determined above	Cumulative exchange difference	Exchange difference recognised in profit or loss
	FC	LC	LC	LC	LC
31 Dec 20X1	1,041	2,082	1,557	525	525
31 Dec 20X2	1,086	2,715	1,643	1,072	547
31 Dec 20X3	1,136	2,498	1,769	729	(342)
31 Dec 20X4	1,190	2,261	1,889	372	(358)
31 Dec 20X5	1,250	2,875	2,003	872	500

As the debt instrument is classified as an available-for-sale investment, it is necessary to determine the bond's fair value at each balance sheet date. The bond's fair value at each balance sheet date is given below. The difference between the amortised cost and asset's fair value is the cumulative gain or loss that is recognised in equity. This difference will include exchange differences that would not be separated out from the overall movement recognised in equity. All other changes in foreign exchange rates are recognised in profit or loss as shown above.

	Fair value	Fair value at year end rate	Amortised cost at year end rate as above	Cumulative difference	Gain or loss recognised in equity
	FC	LC	LC	LC	LC
31 Dec 20X1	1,060	2,120	2,082	38	38
31 Dec 20X2	1,070	2,675	2,715	(40)	(78)
31 Dec 20X3	1,140	2,508	2,499	9	49
31 Dec 20X4	1,200	2,280	2,261	19	10
31 Dec 20X5	1,250	2,875	2,875	0	(19)

The movements in the fair value of the bond can be summarised as follows:

	Fair value at the beginning of the period	Interest income	Cash received	Exchange difference recognised in profit or loss	Gain or loss recognised in equity	Fair value at the end of the period
	LC	LC	LC	LC	LC	LC
31 Dec 20X1	1,500	175	(118)	525	38	2,120
31 Dec 20X2	2,120	234	(148)	547	(78)	2,675
31 Dec 20X3	2,675	256	(130)	(342)	49	2,508
31 Dec 20X4	2,508	232	(112)	(358)	10	2,280
31 Dec 20X5	2,280	250	(136)	500	(19)	2,875

Non-monetary financial assets

A6.9.164 Translation of non-monetary items depends on whether they are recognised at historical cost or at fair value. Items recognised at historical cost are not retranslated at subsequent balance sheet dates. This would apply to foreign currency denominated unquoted equity instruments that are measured at cost, because their fair values cannot be reliably determined. However, most non-monetary financial instruments, such as equity instruments, are measured at fair value. Non-monetary assets that are measured at fair value in a foreign currency are translated using the exchange rates at the date when the fair value was determined. [IAS 21 para 23(c)]. When a gain or loss on a non-monetary item is recognised directly in equity, any exchange component of that gain or loss should also be recognised directly in equity. Therefore, for available-for-sale equity instruments remeasured through equity the entire change in fair value is recognised in equity. [IAS 39 para AG 83].

Impairment of foreign currency financial asset

A6.9.165 Although not specifically dealt with in IAS 39, measuring impairment losses on financial assets that are denominated in foreign currency is, in principle, no different from those that are denominated in the entity's functional currency. Thus, for a foreign currency financial asset that is carried at amortised cost, the expected future cash flows denominated in the foreign currency are discounted at the financial asset's original effective interest rate. This amount is then translated into the entity's functional currency using the foreign exchange rate at the date when the impairment is recognised. The difference between the translated present value and the carrying amount in the entity's functional currency is the impairment loss that is recognised in profit or loss. Similarly, if in a subsequent period, circumstances change that result in a reversal of the impairment loss, in whole or in part, the reversal should be measured using the foreign exchange rate at the date when the reversal is recognised.

A6.9.166 For foreign currency non-monetary assets that are held as available-for-sale with changes in fair value recognised in equity, the situation is different. In this case, the amount of the loss that is removed from equity and included in profit or loss is the difference between the asset's acquisition cost translated at the rate of exchange ruling at the acquisition's date and its current fair value translated at the rate of exchange ruling at the date of the impairment. [IAS 21 para 25]. This is because an impairment loss may be recognised in the foreign currency, but not in the entity's functional currency and *vice versa* as illustrated below.

Example – Foreign currency equity instrument designated as available-for-sale

On 1 January 20X3, an entity whose functional currency is the local currency (LC) purchases a foreign currency (FC) denominated equity instrument at its fair value of FC1,000. The entity classifies the bond as available-for-sale. The exchange rate at acquisition was FC = LC1.5. The asset's fair value at subsequent balance sheet dates in FC and the closing exchange rates are given below:

Date	Exchange rate	Fair value of asset		Change in fair value recognised in equity	
				Recognised in the period	Cumulative
		FC	LC	LC	LC
1 Jan 20X3	1.5	1,000		1,500	
31 Dec 20X3	1.7	900	1,530	30	30
31 Dec 20X4	1.6	800	1,280	-250	-220
31 Dec 20X4 Loss removed from equity and recognised in profit or loss					220
31 Dec 20X5	1.8	850	1,530	250	250

As can be seen from the above, even though the asset's fair value measured in FC at 31 December 20X3 is less than the original cost in FC, no impairment loss is recognised in that year. An impairment loss is recognised in the following year when the fair value measured in the entity's functional currency (LC1,280) is lower than the asset's acquisition price (LC1,500). The impairment loss of C220 is removed from equity and recognised in profit or loss. Even if circumstances change, as happens in 31 Dec 20X5, the loss recognised in profit or loss is never reversed. Instead, the change in fair value during the year of LC250 is recognised in equity (see further para A6.9.154 above).

6A.9.167 For foreign currency monetary assets that are held as available-for-sale, past impairment losses recognised in profit or loss can be reversed through profit or loss as explained in paragraph A6.9.154 above. Again the exchange rate at the date of the reversal should be used to measure the amount of the reversal. Since, for the purposes of recognising foreign exchange gains and losses under IAS 21, a monetary available-for-sale asset is treated as if it were carried at amortised cost in the foreign currency, all exchange differences arising on the reversal should be recognised in profit or loss.

Financial assets held in foreign operations

A6.9.168 An entity may have both financial assets that are classified as at fair value through profit or loss and available-for-sale investments. When such an entity is a foreign operation that is a subsidiary, its financial statements are consolidated with those of its parent. In that situation, IAS 39 applies to the accounting for financial instruments in the financial statements of the foreign operation and IAS 21 applies in translating the financial statements of a foreign operation for incorporation in the reporting entity's consolidated financial statements. Under IAS 21, all exchange differences resulting from translating the financial statements of a foreign operation are recognised in equity until disposal of the net investment. This would include exchange differences arising from financial instruments carried at fair value, which would include both financial assets classified as at fair value through profit or loss and financial assets that are available-for-sale as illustrated in the example below.

Example – Financial instruments held in a foreign entity – interaction of IAS 39 and IAS 21

Entity A is domiciled in the UK and its functional currency and presentation currency is pound sterling. Entity A has a foreign subsidiary, entity B, in France whose functional currency is the euro. Entity B is the owner of a debt instrument, which is held for trading and, therefore, carried at fair value under IAS 39. [IAS 39 para IE 3.3].

In entity B's financial statements for year 20X5, the fair value and carrying amount of the debt instrument is €400. In entity A's consolidated financial statements, the asset is translated into pound sterling at the spot exchange rate applicable at the balance sheet date, say €1 = £0.50. Thus, the carrying amount in the consolidated financial statements is £200.

At the end of year 20X5, the fair value of the debt instrument has increased to €440. Entity B recognises the trading asset at €440 in its balance sheet and recognises a fair value gain of €40 in its income statement. During the year, the spot exchange rate has increased from €1 = £0.50 to €1 = £0.75, resulting in an increase in the instrument's fair value from £200 to £330 (€440 @ 0.75). Therefore, entity A recognises the trading asset at £330 in its consolidated financial statements.

Since entity B is a foreign entity, entity A translates the income statement of entity B in accordance with IAS 21 *"at the exchange rates at the dates of the transactions"*. Since the fair value gain has accrued through the year, entity A uses the average rate of €1 = £0.625 as a practical approximation. Therefore, while the fair value of the trading asset has increased by £130 (£330 – £200), entity A recognises only £25 (€40 @ 0.625) of this increase in consolidated profit or loss. The resulting exchange difference, that is, the remaining increase in the debt instrument's fair value £105 (£130 – £25) is classified as equity until the disposal of the net investment in the foreign operation.

Section 10

Hedge accounting

Introduction

What is hedging?

A6.10.1 Entities face many business risks one of the most significant of which is financial risk. No two companies, however, are exposed to the same risks. Some entities may be concerned about the price of copper or oil, whilst others may be concerned about interest rates or exchange rates. Successful entities manage the types of risk described by deciding to which risk, and to what extent, they should be exposed, by monitoring the actual exposure and taking steps to reduce risks to within agreed limits, often through the use of derivatives. However, hedging one risk will undoubtedly magnify another. Management has to decide for example whether it is cash flow risk averse which will mean that it is not concerned with fair value risk.

A6.10.2 The process of entering into a derivative transaction with a counterparty in the expectation that the transaction will eliminate or reduce an entity's exposure to a particular risk is referred to as hedging. Risk reduction is obtained because the derivative's value or cash flows are expected, wholly or partly, to move inversely and, therefore, offset changes in the value or cash flows of the 'hedged position' or item. The hedged position/item can include recognised assets and liabilities, a firm commitment or a forecast transaction. Sometimes an entity can arrange its affairs so as to be naturally hedged. This would be the case, for example, if an entity's portfolio of fixed interest securities is financed by fixed rate borrowings of the same amount and duration. In this case, a rise in the general level of interest rates will decrease the value of both asset and liability positions by approximately the same amount, so that the entity has no net exposure to interest rate risk. Hedging in an economic sense, therefore, concerns the reduction or elimination of different financial risks such as price risk, interest rate risk, currency risk, etc, associated with the hedged position. It is a risk management activity that is now commonplace in many entities.

What is hedge accounting?

A6.10.3 Once an entity has entered into a hedging transaction, it will be necessary to reflect the transaction in the financial statements of the entity. Accounting for the hedged position should be consistent with the objective of entering into the hedging transaction, which is to eliminate or reduce significantly specific risks that management considers can have an adverse effect on the entity's financial position and results, whilst acknowledging that such strategies can increase other risks with which management is less concerned. This consistency can be achieved if both the hedging instrument and the hedged position are recognised and measured on symmetrical bases and offsetting gains and losses are reported in profit or loss in the same periods. Unfortunately, mismatches occur under existing recognition and measurement standards and practices. Hedge accounting practices have been developed to correct or mitigate these mismatches.

A6.10.4 In simple terms 'hedge accounting' is a technique that modifies the normal basis for recognising gains and losses (or revenues and expenses) on associated hedging instruments and hedged items so that both are recognised in earnings in the same accounting period. Hedge accounting thus affords management the opportunity to eliminate or reduce the income statement volatility that otherwise would arise if the hedged items and hedging instruments were accounted for under GAAP separately, without regard to the hedge's business purpose.

Hedge accounting under IAS 39

A6.10.5 Against a background of strong and wide-spread support for hedge accounting, standard setters began to look for ways to reflect the effects of hedge accounting in the income statement, without compromising the balance sheet. The first comprehensive recognition and measurement standard on the subject, SFAS 133, 'Accounting for derivative instruments and hedging activities', was published in the USA by the FASB in June 1998. Shortly thereafter, in December 1998, the IASC published IAS 39, which provided a framework for hedge accounting that, to a large extent, was modelled on SFAS 133, although there are important differences between the two standards.

A6.10.6 IAS 39 provides a set of strict criteria that must be met before hedge accounting can be used. These require that the hedge relationship is designated and formally documented at inception. There are also requirements to demonstrate both at inception and throughout the life of the hedge that the hedge is 'highly effective'. As a result, not all hedging activities undertaken by entities would qualify for hedge accounting. Failure to meet any of the criteria whilst the hedge is in place would result in the discontinuance of hedge accounting.

A6.10.7 The standard also specifies new methods of hedge accounting that were designed to reflect the standard's requirement to measure all derivatives at fair value. As a result, hedge accounting in IAS 39 can be applied to three types of hedging relationships as indicated below:

- Where there is a risk that the hedged item's *fair value* will change in response to some variable, such as changes in interest rates, foreign exchange rates, or market prices, gains and losses on the hedging instrument and the offsetting losses and gains on the hedged item are both recognised in profit or loss. This is referred to as a fair value hedge.

- Where there is a risk that the future hedged item's *cash flows* will change in response to such variables, the gain or loss on the hedging instrument is initially recognised in equity and subsequently recycled to profit or loss as the hedged item affects profit or loss. This is referred to as a cash flow hedge.

- Where there is a risk that the *net investment* in a foreign operation will change in response to exchange rate movements, the gain or loss on the hedging instrument is initially recognised in equity and subsequently recycled to profit or loss on disposal of that foreign operation. This is referred to as a hedge of a net investment in a foreign operation.

A6.10.8 IAS 39 does not mandate the use of hedge accounting. It is a privilege not a right. Entities intending to use hedge accounting must have proper systems and procedures to monitor each hedging relationship. Many entities may find these requirements too onerous and decide not to try to hedge account. However, this approach generally comes at a cost – income statement volatility.

Hedged items

A6.10.9 Before the hedge accounting principles and methods set out in the standard can be appreciated, it is first necessary to understand the basic definitions and concepts of hedged items and hedging instruments that underpin all hedging relationships.

Definition

A6.10.10 A hedged item is an asset, liability, firm commitment, highly probable forecast transaction or net investment in a foreign operation that:

- exposes the entity to risk of changes in fair value or future cash flows; and

- is designated as being hedged.

[IAS 39 para 9].

A6.10.11 In particular, the hedged item can be:

- a single asset, liability, firm commitment, highly probable forecast transaction or net investment in a foreign operation;

- a group of assets, liabilities, firm commitments, highly probable forecast transactions or net investments in foreign operations with similar risk characteristics; or

- in a portfolio hedge of interest rate risk only, a portion of the portfolio of financial assets or financial liabilities that share the risk being hedged.

[IAS 39 para 78].

A6.10.12 One of the key aspects of the above definition is that the hedged item must expose the entity to risk of changes in the fair value or future cash flows that could affect profit or loss. [IAS 39 para 86(a)-(b)]. This could be in the current or future periods. As a result, hedge accounting cannot apply to hedges of any items included in equity or transactions that directly affect equity (see further para A6.10.42 below).

A6.10.13 The assets or liabilities referred to above are assets and liabilities that are recognised in the entity's balance sheet. It could be a financial item or a non-financial item such as inventory. Unrecognised assets cannot qualify as a hedged item except for firm commitments. For example, internally generated core deposit intangibles (for a bank) are not recognised as intangible assets under IAS 38. Because they are not recognised, they cannot be designated as hedged items. [IAS 39 para IG F2.3].

A6.10.14 For hedge accounting purposes, only assets, liabilities, firm commitments or highly probable forecast transactions that involve a party external to the entity can be designated as hedged items. It follows that hedge accounting can be applied to transactions between entities or segments in the same group only in the individual or separate financial statements of those entities or segments and not in the consolidated financial statements of the group. [IAS 39 para 80]. However, there are exceptions to this general rule, which are considered from paragraph A6.10.36 below.

Designation of groups of items as hedged items

A6.10.15 The definition of a hedged item in paragraph in 6.10.11 above permits similar assets, or similar liabilities to be grouped together and designated as a hedged item. Designating a group/portfolio of items as a hedge requires that:

- the individual assets or individual liabilities in the group share the risk exposure that is designated as being hedged; and
- the change in the fair value attributable to the hedged risk for each individual item in the group is expected to be approximately proportional to the overall change in fair value attributable to the hedged risk of the group of items.

[IAS 39 para 83].

A6.10.16 In grouping similar assets and liabilities in a portfolio, an entity should consider various factors, including:

- The type of assets or liabilities.
- The interest rate (fixed or variable) and, in the case of fixed rate assets or liabilities, the coupon rate.
- The currency in which the assets or liabilities are denominated.
- The scheduled maturity date and, in the case of prepayable assets, the prepayment terms, past prepayment history and expected future prepayment performance.

A6.10.17 With respect to the first bullet point in paragraph A6.10.15 above, this means that the group or portfolio of items must share the same risk exposure with respect to the risk being hedged. It is not necessary that each item in the group shares all of the same risks, as long as they all share a common risk characteristic that is the subject of the hedge. For cash flow hedges, sharing the same risk exposure means not only that the forecast transactions have a common risk (for example, foreign currency risk), but also that the exposure moves in the same direction. For example, forecast foreign currency sales and purchases do not share the same risk exposure, because the risk to the entity from the purchase moves in the opposite direction to the risk exposure from the sale.

A6.10.18 With respect to the second bullet point in paragraph A6.10.15 above, the standard does not provide any guidance on the meaning of 'approximately proportional'. However, FAS 133 provides some guidance in the context of US GAAP. It considers that a movement of the fair value of the individual items within a fairly narrow range, such as from 9 per cent to 11 per cent, when the fair value of the portfolio as a whole moves 10 per cent, would be consistent with this requirement, but a move such as from 7 per cent to 13 per cent would not be consistent.

Example 1 – Designating a portfolio of bonds as the hedged item

An entity has a portfolio of fixed rate corporate bonds with different coupons. All the bonds mature within a period of 4-5 years. The entity designates an interest rate swap to hedge the entire portfolio's risk-free interest rate.

The above group of bonds may be designated as the hedged item as the risk free rate that is being hedged is common to all the bonds. However, it is also necessary to ensure that the fair value movements of each individual bond that is attributable to the hedged interest-free rate are expected to be approximately proportional to the portfolio's fair value movements that is attributable to the hedged risk. The entity's management should, therefore, model the changes of fair value of the portfolio relative to the changes in fair values of individual bonds in response to the hedged risk.

Example 2 – Designating a portfolio of shares as the hedged item

Entity A acquires a portfolio of French CAC 40 shares, in the same proportions as are used to calculate the French CAC 40 index and classifies the investments as available-for-sale. At the same time, the entity purchases a put option on the CAC 40 index to hedge changes in the fair value of the portfolio. The option constitutes a near perfect hedge of decreases in the value of the portfolio, in economic terms. Any decline in the portfolio's fair value below the options' strike price will be offset by an increase in the put option's intrinsic value.

In the scenario above, the entity cannot designate the portfolio of shares as the hedged item in a hedge of equity price risk. The hedged risk is the total change in value of each share in the portfolio. Some share prices may increase and others may decrease. The relationship will not qualify for hedge accounting, because the change in the fair value attributable to the hedged risk for each individual item in the group (individual share prices) is not expected to be approximately proportional to the overall change in fair value attributable to the hedged risk of the group.

Hedging an overall net position

A6.10.19 An entity cannot designate an overall net position as the hedged item. This is because hedging a common risk in portfolio of similar assets and liabilities would necessitate an allocation of the overall gain or loss on the hedging instrument to the individual items in the portfolio. Furthermore, if some of the items in the portfolio were producing gains and others losses, the entity would have to impute both gains and losses to the single hedging instrument to offset both the gains and the losses on the hedged items. As such an allocation would be inherently arbitrary and produce significant ineffectiveness, designating the hedged item as a net position is not permitted. [IAS 39 para 84]

A6.10.20 However, almost the same effect on profit or loss can be achieved by designating some of the underlying gross items as the hedged item equal in amount to the net position. For example, an entity (C functional currency) with a firm commitment to make a purchase in a foreign currency of FC100 and a firm commitment to make a sale in the foreign currency of FC90 can hedge the net amount of FC10 by acquiring a derivative and designating it as a hedging instrument associated with FC10 of the firm purchase commitment of FC100. Similarly, an entity with C100 of fixed rate assets and C90 of fixed rate liabilities with terms of a similar nature could hedge the net C10 exposure by designating as the hedged item C10 of those assets. [IAS 39 para AG 101].

A6.10.21 An entity's hedging strategy and risk management practices may assess cash flow risk on a net basis, but the net cash flow exposure cannot be designated as a hedged item for hedge accounting purposes. This is because, as explained above, it would not be possible to identify the net exposure arising from forecast sales and purchases as the exposure being hedged, because forecast sales and purchases are not similar items and the effectiveness test would fail. However, once again hedge accounting can be achieved by designating some of the forecast purchases or sales as the hedged item equal in amount to the net position, as illustrated in the example below.

Example 1 – Hedging a net FX position

Entity A, whose functional currency is the euro, has a global treasury centre that is responsible for collecting and assessing the group's foreign currency risks and offsetting the net position using derivative instruments with an external party. For example, it forecasts sales of US$2.5m and purchases of US$1m in June and has, therefore, entered into a forward contract to sell US$1.5m against euros in that month.

As stated in paragraph A6.10.19 above, the entity is prohibited from designating a net position as the hedged item. It is possible to achieve a similar effect by designating the hedged item as part of one of the gross positions that is equal in amount to the net position. Entity A can, therefore, designate the forward contract as a hedge of highly probable forecast sales of US$1.5m in June.

Example 2 – Hedging a net interest rate position

Entity B has a number of bank loans with different interest rates and terms. The entity also has loans receivable with different interest rates. Management proposes to hedge the net interest-rate risk position in a number of separate maturity bands through the use of interest-rate swaps for the net asset or liability in each maturity band.

Management may allocate the net exposure in each band to a specific asset or liability, so that the net position in each maturity band could qualify as a hedged item. This approach provides management with an interest-rate gap methodology to manage interest-rate risk. [IAS 39 para AG111]. Alternatively, management may choose to apply fair value hedge accounting (see paragraph A6.10.193 onwards for definition and examples of fair value hedge accounting) for a portfolio hedge of interest rate risk and designate an amount of assets or liabilities in given time buckets as hedged items. [IAS 39 para 81A].

Designation of financial items as hedged items

A6.10.22 When the hedged item is a financial instrument or a forecast transaction involving a financial instrument, the various financial risk exposures that can be hedged are described in the table below.

Financial instrument risks that can be hedged

- Market risk – the risk that a financial instrument's fair value or cash flows will fluctuate because of changes in market prices. Market risk embodies not only the potential for loss but also the potential for gain. It comprises three types of risk as follows:
    - Interest rate risk – the risk that a financial instrument's fair value or future cash flows will fluctuate because of changes in market interest rates.
    - Currency risk – the risk that a financial instrument's fair value or future cash flows will fluctuate because of changes in foreign exchange rates.
    - Other price risk – the risk that a financial instrument's fair value or future cash flows will fluctuate because of changes in market prices (other than those arising from interest rate risk or currency risk), whether those changes are caused by factors specific to the individual financial instrument or its issuer, or factors affecting all similar financial instruments traded in the market.
- Credit risk – the risk that one party to a financial instrument will cause a financial loss for the other party by failing to discharge an obligation.
- Liquidity risk – the risk that an entity will encounter difficulty in meeting obligations associated with financial liabilities.

Hedges of portions and proportions

A6.10.23 IAS 39 does not restrict hedge accounting to hedges of the entire risk of change in the fair value or all of the cash flows of a financial instrument, or the entire exposure to interest rate risk, currency risk, credit risk or other risks of changes in a financial instrument's fair value or cash flows. Provided that effectiveness can be measured, it is possible to designate a hedged financial asset or a financial liability with respect to the risks associated with only a portion of its cash flows or fair value, such as one or more selected contractual cash flows or portions of them or a percentage or a proportion of the fair value. For example, an identifiable and separately measurable portion of the interest rate exposure of an interest-bearing asset or interest-bearing liability may be designated as the hedged risk (such as a risk-free interest rate or benchmark interest rate component of the total interest rate exposure of a hedged financial instrument). [IAS 39 para 81]. It should be noted that hedges of portions apply only to financial assets and liabilities and not to non-financial assets and liabilities (see para A6.10.31 below).

Example – Hedges of portions

An entity acquires a fixed rate bond with a maturity of 5 years. The bond is classified as loans and receivables.

The entity could hedge a variety of risk exposures relating to a fixed rate debt including the following:

	Risk exposure		**Contractual cash flows**	
	All	**Specific component**	**Principal**	**Interest**
Hedge the fair value of all the cash flows for all risks (100% of fair value of the debt).	✓		✓	✓
Hedge the fair value of all the cash flows for a specific risk, for example, interest rate or credit risk (100% of fair value of the debt for a specific risk).		✓	✓	✓
Hedge a proportion of the fair value of all the cash flows for all risks (90% of fair value of the debt).	✓		90%	90%
Hedge a proportion of the fair value of all the cash flows for a specific risk, for example, interest or credit risk (90% of fair value of the debt for a specific risk).		✓	90%	90%
Hedge the fair value of a specifically identified cash flow for all risk.	✓		✓ or	✓

Hedge the fair value of a specifically identified cash flow for a specific risk (for example, interest rate or credit risk).		✓	✓ or	✓
Hedge the fair value of a portion of a specifically identified cash flow for all risk.	✓		90% or	90%
Hedge the fair value of a portion of a specifically identified cash flow for a specific risk, for example, interest rate or credit risk.		✓	90% or	90%

Hedging a risk component of a financial instrument

A6.10.24 Consistent with paragraph A6.10.23 above, financial assets or liabilities may be hedged with respect to a specific risk (a component of total risk), provided that the exposure to the specific risk component is identifiable and separately measurable, which is also a pre-requisite for measuring effectiveness. Some examples of situations where component of a risk may be hedged are given below. [IAS 39 para 81]. Other examples include: hedging the foreign currency exposure in a portfolio of foreign currency denominated equity securities, rather than hedging the full market price risk (see para A6.10.28 below) and hedging the fair value exposure to changes in credit spread in a floating rate debt instrument.

Example – Hedging a risk component of a fixed rate debt instrument

An entity issues 8% fixed rate debt instrument for C100 that is repayable at par at the end of year 2. At the time of issue the market interest rate is 6%. Therefore, the credit spread on the new issue is 2%.

In this scenario, the entity can designate an identifiable and separately measurable portion of the interest rate exposure as the hedged risk. Such a portion may be a risk-free interest rate or benchmark interest rate component of the debt instrument's total interest rate exposure, that is, the entity's own credit spread of 2% may be excluded. This is subject to the *proviso* that effectiveness can be measured.

So if the entity intends to designate the benchmark LIBOR component of 6% as the hedged risk, it may take out a receive 6% fixed pay floating LIBOR interest rate swap to hedge the changes in the debt's fair value due to changes in LIBOR. The hedge will be expected to be highly effective as the credit spread is not included in the net cash flows relating to the swap.

Note that it is not necessary for the pay leg of the swap to be the same as LIBOR (receive 6% pay LIBOR). The entity could take out a receive 8% pay floating LIBOR + 2% interest rate swap and still designate the benchmark LIBOR component as the hedged risk. This is because the fair value of the swap comprises the net of the present values of both the fixed and the floating legs. Therefore, increasing both sides of the swap by 2% (from receive 6% pay LIBOR to receive 8% pay LIBOR + 2%) will not change the fair value for a given change in interest rates. However, this is only true when the payment frequency of both legs is identical. If the fixed leg pays yearly and the variable leg pays quarterly, there would be a difference.

6A.10.25 If a portion of the cash flows of a financial asset or financial liability is designated as the hedged item, that designated portion must be less than the total cash flows of the asset or liability. As a designated portion of the cash flows cannot be greater than the whole, an entity that issues a debt instrument whose effective interest rate at issuance is below LIBOR (such an issuance of debt at below LIBOR rates may be possible by some entities with exceptionally strong credit rating), cannot designate the following components as hedges:

- a portion of the liability equal to the principal amount plus interest at LIBOR; and
- a negative residual portion.

[IAS 39 para AG 99C].

It should be noted, however, that the above prohibition does not feature in the EU carve-out version of IAS 39.

A6.10.26 However, the entity may designate all of the cash flows of the entire financial asset or financial liability as the hedged item and hedge them for only one particular risk (for example, only for changes that are attributable to changes in LIBOR) as illustrated in the example below:

Example – Designating a benchmark interest rate as the hedged risk on a fixed rate debt instrument issued at sub-LIBOR rate

An entity issues a 5% fixed rate debt instrument for C100 that is repayable at par at the end of year 2. At the time of issue, the benchmark LIBOR rate is 6%.

The entity can designate the entire financial liability as the hedged item (that is, principal + interest) and hedge the change in the fair value or cash flows of that entire liability that is attributable to changes in LIBOR. Some ineffectiveness will occur. However, the entity may choose a hedge ratio of other than one to one (a proportion of the total cash flow) in order to improve the effectiveness of the hedge. [IAS 39 para AG 99C].

6A.10.27 It is also possible to hedge the benchmark interest rate risk portion of a fixed rate financial instrument some time after its origination, by which time interest rates may have changed since the instrument's origination. This is possible if the benchmark rate is higher than the contractual rate paid on the item as illustrated in the example below. [IAS 39 para AG 99D]. It should be noted that the restriction that the hedged benchmark rate is higher than the contractual rate does not feature in the EU carve-out version of IAS 39.

Example – Designating a benchmark interest rate as the hedged risk of a fixed rate debt instrument subsequent to its origination

On 1 April 20X1, an entity issues a 6% fixed rate debt instrument for C100 that is repayable at par at the end of year 5 (31 March 20X6). Interest is payable annually in arrears. At the time of issue, the benchmark LIBOR rate is 5%. On 1 July 20X2, the entity decides to hedge the interest rate risk on the debt instrument with an interest rate swap when LIBOR has increased to 7%. At that time, the fair value of the debt instrument is C93.

The entity calculates that if it had issued the debt instrument on 1 July 20X2 when it first designates it as the hedged item for its fair value of C93, the effective yield on the instrument would have been 8.1%. Because LIBOR on 1 July 20X2 is 7% and is less than this effective yield, the entity can designate a LIBOR portion of 7% that consists partly of the contractual interest cash flows and partly of the discount that is included in the difference between the current fair value of C93 and the amount repayable on maturity of C100.

6A.10.28 Under IAS 39, when a gain or loss on a non-monetary available-for-sale equity security is recognised in equity, any exchange component of that gain or loss is also recognised directly in equity. [IAS 39 para AG 83]. Normally, items taken to equity cannot be hedged, however, foreign currency exposure in such an equity security can be hedged provided there is a clear and identifiable exposure to changes in foreign exchange rates and all the other hedge accounting criteria are met. In the case of a fair value hedge, the changes in foreign currency exposure will be recognised in profit or loss. The implementation guidance explains that this would be possible only if:

- the equity instrument is not traded on an exchange (or in another established marketplace) where trades are denominated in the same currency as the entity's functional currency (investor); and
- dividends to the investor are not denominated in the investor's functional currency.

Thus, if a share is traded in multiple currencies and one of those currencies is the reporting entity's functional currency, hedge accounting for the foreign currency component of the share price is not permitted.

[IAS 39 para IG F2.19]

Example – Hedging foreign currency risk of an available-for-sale investment

On 1 April 20X5, entity A, a Swiss company with Swiss Francs as its functional currency, buys equity shares in entity B located in the US. The shares are listed on the New York Stock Exchange and pay dividends in US$. The acquisition cost is US$1m. On that date US$ = CHF1.3 resulting in an investment of CHF1.3m. Entity A classifies the investment as available-for-sale.

At the same time, to protect itself from the exposure to changes in the foreign exchange rate associated with the shares, entity A enters into a forward contract to sell US$1m and buy

CHF. Entity A intends to roll over the forward exchange contract for as long as it retains the shares. It is assumed that the hedge is effective and the other conditions for hedge accounting are met.

Entity A could designate the currency exposure relating to the shares' fair value as the hedged risk, because it meets the two conditions set out in the above paragraph. Also, entity A could designate the forward contract as either a fair value hedge of the foreign exchange exposure of US$1m or as a cash flow hedge of a forecast sale of the shares, provided the future sale and its timing are highly probable. For the purposes of this example, it is assumed that the forward contract is designated as a fair value hedge.

At 31 March 20X6, the entity's financial year end, shares increased in value to US$2m. At that date, US$ = CHF1.20.

The change in fair value is calculated as follows:

	CHF m
Value of investment at 31 March 20X6 – US$2m @ 1.2 =	2.4
Value of investment at 1 April 20X5 – US$1m @ 1.3 =	1.3
Fair value change	1.1
Exchange component of change – US 1m (@ 1.2 – @1.3)	(0.1)
Recognised in equity – change in fair value US$1m @ 1.2	1.2

In this situation, the gain arising from the changes in the forward contract's fair value is recognised in the income statement. This includes both the spot component (which may be designated as part of the hedging relationship to improve effectiveness) and the forward points component (see further para A6.10.56 below). The entity also recognises the exchange loss of CHF100,000 in profit or loss to offset the gain on the forward contract. [IAS 39 para 89(b)]. The remaining portion of the change in fair value of CHF1.2m is deferred in equity in accordance with the subsequent measurement rules for available-for-sale investments.

Partial term hedging

A6.10.29 The ability to hedge a portion of one or more selected cash flows of a financial asset or liability means that an entity will be able to hedge exposures that have a term that is less than the hedged item's term – so called 'partial term' hedges. This is subject to the proviso that effectiveness can be measured and the other hedge accounting criteria are met. This will usually be so if the hedging derivative also has the same term, as illustrated in the example below. It should be noted that the notion of 'partial term' does not apply to a hedging instrument as stated in paragraph A6.10.61 below

Example – Partial term hedging

Entity A acquires a 10% fixed rate government bond with a remaining term to maturity of ten years. Entity A classifies the bond as available for sale. On the same date, to hedge against fair value exposure on the bond associated with the first five year interest payments, the entity acquires a 5 year pay-fixed, receive-floating swap. The swap has a fair value of zero at the inception of the hedge relationship.

The swap may be designated as hedging the fair value exposure of the interest rate payments on the government bond until year 5 and the change in value of the principal payment due at maturity to the extent affected by changes in the yield curve relating to the 5 years of the swap. [IAS 39 para IG F2.17].

The same principle applies if the hedged item had been a financial liability instead of a financial asset with the same terms. In that situation, the entity could designate the fair value exposure of the first 5 years interest payments due to changes in interest rate only and hedge that exposure using a 5 year receive-fixed, pay-floating interest rate swap.

The entity is also able to achieve effective partial term cash flow hedges. For instance, assume an entity issues a 10 year floating rate debt and wish to hedge the variability in the first three year of interest payments. This could be easily done by using a 3 year receive-floating, pay-fixed interest rate swap.

Loans and receivables

A6.10.30 Under IAS 39, loans and receivables are carried at amortised cost. An entity may decide to hold such loans and receivables to maturity. Indeed, banking institutions in many countries hold the bulk of their loans and receivables until maturity. Therefore, it would appear that as changes in the fair value of such loans and receivables that are due to changes in market interest rates will not affect profit or loss, fair value hedge accounting for loans and receivables is precluded (see para A6.10.12 above). However, it is always possible that such instruments will be disposed of or extinguished before then, in which case the change in fair values would affect profit or loss. Accordingly, fair value hedge accounting is permitted as such loans and receivables are not designated as held-to-maturity (see para A6.10.43 below). [IAS 39 para IG F2.13].

Designation of non-financial items as hedged items

A6.10.31 If the hedged item is a non-financial asset or non-financial liability, it may only be designated as a hedged item:

- for foreign currency risks; or
- in its entirety for all risks.

[IAS 39 para 82].

A6.10.32 The standard explains that changes in the price of an ingredient or component of a non-financial asset or non-financial liability generally do not have a predictable, separately measurable effect on the item's price that is comparable to the effect of, say, a change in market interest rates on a bond's price. Therefore, because of the difficulty of isolating and measuring the appropriate portion of the cash flows or fair value changes attributable to specific risks other than foreign currency risks, a non-financial asset or non-financial liability is a hedged item only in its entirety or for foreign exchange risk. [IAS 39 para AG 100]. Accordingly, when an entity chooses to hedge the fair value of inventory (a non-financial asset), the inventory cannot be separated into its commodity and other components, regardless of whether the inventory consists of a single commodity component and conversion or rework costs, or is a product comprised of multiple commodities. The standard makes no exception to this rule even though in some cases it may be possible to isolate the changes in cash flows or fair value attributable to a particular risk.

Example 1 – Separation of risks in non-financial assets

An entity manufacturers aluminium cans from sheets of aluminium. The entity intends to use aluminium futures as a fair value hedge of the exposure to changes in the aluminium cans' fair value held in inventory.

The entity cannot designate aluminium's market price as the hedged risk, even though the price of aluminium is likely to account for a significant portion of the exposure to changes in the price of aluminium cans held in inventory. Permitting an entity to designate the market price of aluminium as the hedged risk would ignore other components of the price of the cans, such as protective coating materials, labour and production overheads.

However, provided the requirement for effectiveness and other hedge accounting criteria are met (see para A6.10.136 below), the derivative instrument (aluminium futures) could be designated as a hedge of the exposure to changes in the full fair value of the inventory. See also example in paragraph A6.10.97 below

Example 2 – Forecast purchase of a non-monetary asset in foreign currency

Entity A is planning to buy a large piece of machinery from a foreign supplier. The forecast purchase will be denominated in a foreign currency, so the company enters into a forward contract to hedge the risk of movements in the relevant foreign exchange rate.

The forecast purchase can be designated as a hedged item in a cash flow hedge of foreign currency risk, provided that the forecast purchase is highly probable, the requirements for effectiveness and the other conditions for hedge accounting are met. The hedged risk (movements in exchange rates) will affect the amount paid for the machine and will, therefore, affect profit or loss as the machine is depreciated.

6A.10.33 As stated in paragraph A6.10.31 above, a non-monetary item can be hedged for foreign currency risk only if it is separately measurable. As the hedged item is remeasured in a fair value hedge (see para A6.10.93 below), a non-monetary asset that was purchased in a foreign currency and initially recorded, under IAS 21 in the purchaser's functional currency, at the exchange rate at the date of the transaction cannot be classified as a fair value hedge for foreign currency risk. This is because it is not subsequently remeasured under IAS 21 and, therefore, does not contain any separately measurable foreign currency risk. Nevertheless, if all the hedge accounting conditions are met, an entity could designate as a cash flow hedge the anticipated sale of the non-monetary asset in a foreign currency. This is because, in a cash flow hedge, the non-monetary item is not remeasured. However, in practice, it would be rare for such a hedge to meet all the hedging accounting criteria as illustrated in the example below.

Example – Foreign currency borrowings hedging a ship

A shipping entity in Denmark has a US subsidiary that has the same functional currency (the Danish Krone). In its consolidated financial statements shipping entity measures its ships at historical cost less depreciation. In accordance with IAS 21 graph 23(b), the ships are measured in Danish Krone using the historical exchange rate. To hedge, fully or partly, the potential currency risk on the ships at disposal in US dollars, the shipping entity normally finances its purchases of ships with loans denominated in US dollars.

US dollar borrowings cannot be classified as a fair value hedge of a ship, because ships do not contain any separately measurable foreign currency risk, even though the entity purchases and sells them in US dollars.

US dollar borrowing (or a portion of it) may, however, be designated as a cash flow hedge of the ship's anticipated sale proceeds in US dollars financed by the borrowing provided all the hedging criteria are met. Those conditions are likely to be met if the sale is highly probable because it is expected to occur in the immediate future, the amount of the sales proceeds designated as being hedged is equal to the amount of the foreign currency borrowing designated as the hedging instrument and the timing of the future cash flows on the debt coincides with the timing on the future cash flow from the disposal. [IAS 39 IG para F6.5].

Firm commitments

A6.10.34 A firm commitment is a binding agreement for the exchange of a specified quantity of resources at a specified price on a specified future date or dates. [IAS 39 para 9]. Therefore, the key characteristic of a firm commitment is that it must have fixed terms, namely: fixed quantity, fixed price and fixed timing of the transaction. A firm commitment must be with a party that is external to the entity (see para A6.10.14 above). As the firm commitment is a binding agreement, it is usually legally enforceable and there may well be significant penalties for non-performance. Firm commitments are discussed further in paragraph A6.10.93 below.

Forecast transactions

A6.10.35 In many cases, entities will not be hedging risk exposures arising from firm commitments but rather those arising from forecast transactions that they expect to happen, but for which there is not a binding contract. Therefore, the definition of a hedged item also includes a forecast transaction. A forecast transaction is an uncommitted but highly probable, anticipated future transaction. [IAS 39 para 9]. Concluding that an uncommitted but anticipated transaction is highly probable and will happen is more difficult than for transactions arising from firm commitments. The qualifying conditions for getting hedge accounting for forecast transactions are considered further from paragraph A6.10.108 below.

Intra-group and intra-entity hedging transactions

A6.10.36 It is fairly common for entities within a consolidated group to enter into transactions with other group members or segments. Often these transactions may expose the entities to various risks that they wish to hedge. The entity exposed to the risk can hedge it by entering into internal derivative contracts with, say, the group treasury, or through external derivative contracts. However, as stated in paragraph A6.10.14 above, only assets, liabilities, firm commitments or highly probable forecast transactions that involve a party external to the entity can be designated as hedged items. It follows that such intra group transactions can be designated as hedged items only in the individual or separate financial statements of those entities or segments and not in the consolidated financial statements of the reporting group. This is because the intra-group transactions cancel out on consolidation and, therefore, do not expose the consolidated group to any risk that affects consolidated profit or loss. There are, however, two exceptions to this general rule involving foreign currency exposures and these are considered in the paragraphs that follow.

A6.10.37 Under IAS 21, foreign exchange gains and losses on intra group monetary asset (or liability) between group entities with different functional currencies, whether short-term or long-term, do not fully eliminate in the consolidated profit or loss. This is because a foreign currency monetary item represents a commitment to convert one currency into another and exposes the reporting entity to a gain or loss through currency fluctuations. Accordingly, in the reporting entity's consolidated financial statements, such exchange differences continue to be recognised in profit or loss. For this reason, the foreign currency exposure on such an intra group monetary item can be designated as a hedged item on consolidation. [IAS 39 para 80].

Example – Hedging intra group monetary items

Subsidiary A, whose functional currency is the euro, has an intra group receivable from subsidiary B, whose functional currency is the Swiss franc. The receivable is denominated in Swiss francs and subsidiary A enters into a €/CHF forward contract with an external party to hedge the resulting foreign currency risk.

In its separate financial statements, subsidiary A translates the receivable into euros using the spot rate at the balance sheet date and recognises a foreign currency gain or loss in accordance with IAS 21. Subsidiary B, in its separate financial statements, records the payable to subsidiary A in its own functional currency and does not recognise any gain or loss. On consolidation, the gain or loss recognised by subsidiary A is translated into the group's presentation currency and is recognised in the group's income statement. There is no offsetting loss or gain arising from subsidiary B.

Subsidiary A uses the €/CHF forward contract to hedge the foreign currency exchange risk on the receivable from subsidiary B in its individual financial statements. As the receivable gives rise to an exposure to foreign currency gains or losses that is not fully eliminated on consolidation, the foreign currency exposure on the intra group receivable can be designated as the hedged item in the consolidated financial statements. The group can designate the €/CHF forward contract in subsidiary A as the hedging instrument. The hedge accounting achieved by subsidiary A is reversed on consolidation and replaced with hedge accounting achieved by the group.

For group purposes, it is not necessary for the subsidiary to take out the forward contract for the foreign exchange exposure on the intra group receivable to qualify as a hedged item on consolidation. The parent entity could have taken out the same forward contract hedging the €/CHF exchange risk instead.

Forecast intra-group transactions

A6.10.38 In April 2005, the IASB published an amendment to IAS 39 entitled, 'Cash flow hedge accounting of forecast intragroup transaction,' that is effective for accounting periods beginning on or after 1 January 2006. The amendment permits the foreign currency risk of a highly probable forecast intra group transaction to be designated as a hedged item in the consolidated financial statements, provided the following two conditions are met:

- the highly probable forecast intra group transaction is denominated in a currency other than the functional currency of the group member entering into that transaction; and
- the foreign currency risk will affect the group's consolidated profit or loss.

[IAS 39 para 80].

A6.10.39 The group member entering into the transaction can be a parent, subsidiary, associate, joint venture or branch. The first condition is necessary because, under IAS 21, a foreign currency exposure arises only when a transaction is denominated in a currency other than the functional currency of the entity entering into that transaction. The second condition is met if the forecast intra group transaction is related to an external transaction. An example is forecast sales or purchases of inventories between members of the same group if there is an onward sale of the inventory to a party external to the group (see example below). However, if there is no external related transaction, which will often be the case for royalty payments, interest payments or management charges between members of the same group, the foreign currency risk of those forecast intra group transactions would not affect consolidated profit or loss and, so, cannot qualify as hedged items. [IAS 39 para AG 99A]. Intra group foreign currency dividends can never qualify as hedged items (see para A6.10.42 below).

A6.10.40 If a hedge of a forecast intra-group transaction qualifies for hedge accounting, any gain or loss that is recognised directly in equity should be reclassified into profit or loss in the same period or periods during which the foreign currency risk of the hedged transaction affects consolidated profit or loss (see further para A6.10.118 below).

Example – Hedging the foreign currency risk of an intra group forecast transaction

Group A (pound sterling presentation currency) includes entity B with euro functional currency and entity C with US dollar functional currency in the consolidation. Entity B manufactures tyres and incurs production costs in euros. It sells most of the tyres to entity C and those transactions are denominated in US dollars. Entity C markets and sells those tyres to external customers in the US, also in US dollars.

In June 20X6 entity B forecasts that it will sell tyres to entity C in October 20X6 amounting to US$ 10m. These sales are highly probable and all the other conditions in IAS 39 for hedge accounting are met. Entity C expects to sell this inventory to external customers in early 20X7. At the same time in June 20X6, entity B enters into a euro/US$ derivative (buy €/sell US$) to hedge the foreign currency risk of the forecast sale of US$10m to entity C in October 20X6.

Group A intends to designate the forward contract as hedging the foreign currency risk of the forecast intra group sales of US$10m by entity B in a cash flow hedging relationship in the consolidated financial statements. It is able to do so because all the following conditions are met

- The intra group sales are highly probable and all the other conditions for using hedge accounting are met.
- The intra group sales are denominated in a currency (US$) other than entity B's functional currency (€).
- The existence of the expected onwards sale of the inventory in US dollars to third parties outside the group results in the hedged exposure affecting the pound sterling consolidated profit or loss. This is because the intra group profit on sale recognised in entity B is € number that is fixed according to the €/$ rate when the sale takes place in October 20X6. This profit is eliminated on consolidation against the carrying value of tyre inventory in entity C and released to consolidated profit or loss when the onward sale of inventory to third parties take place in 20X7.

Gains/losses on the €/US$ derivative are recognised initially in consolidated equity to the extent the hedge is effective. These amounts are reclassified to consolidated profit or loss in 20X7 when the external sales occur.

Items that do not qualify as hedged items

A6.10.41 There are a number of items that, for various reasons, cannot qualify as a hedged item in a hedging relationship. For such items the normal measurement and recognition rules will apply. These items are as considered below.

Own equity instruments

A6.10.42 Hedge accounting cannot be applied for hedges of any items included in equity or transactions that directly affect equity. This is because the hedged item cannot create an exposure to risk that will affect profit or loss. Therefore, hedges of risks relating to the forecast sale, purchase or redemption of an entity's *own equity shares* cannot qualify as hedged items. Similarly, distributions to holders of an equity instrument are debited by the issuer directly to equity. [IAS 32 para 25]. Therefore, such distributions cannot be designated as a hedged item. However, a dividend that has been approved in a general meeting of members and has not yet been paid and is recognised as a financial liability may qualify as a hedged item, for example, for foreign currency risk if it is denominated in a foreign currency as illustrated in the example below. [IAS 39 IG para F2.7].

Example – Inter-company dividends denominated in foreign currency

Entity A, whose functional currency is the pound sterling, has a subsidiary in the US, whose functional currency is the US dollar. On 1 January 20X6, entity A forecasts that it will receive a US$100m dividend from its US subsidiary in six months. The inter company dividend was approved in general meeting of members (or equivalent) on 30 April 20X6, at which time both entity A and its subsidiary recognised the dividend as a receivable or payable in their respective financial statements.

The foreign currency dividend receivable in entity A's balance sheet was retranslated at the reporting period end, 31 May 20X6, resulting in a foreign currency loss. The subsidiary paid the dividend on 30 June 20X6.

Entity A wanted to designate the foreign currency risk on highly probable inter-company dividend as the hedged item in its group financial statements in a cash flow hedge from 1 January 20X6 to 30 June 20X6, in order to hedge the exposure to changes in the £/US$ exchange rate. However, inter-company dividends are not foreign currency transactions that can be hedged, because they do not affect the consolidated income statement. They are distributions of earnings.

The foreign currency exposure arising from the receivable in US dollars recognised on 30 April 20X6 can be designated as a hedged item because it gives rise to foreign currency gains and losses that do not fully eliminate on consolidation and, therefore, affect the consolidated income statement (see para A6.10.37 above). Entity A can, therefore, apply hedge accounting from that date until 30 June 20X6 when the cash is received in its group financial statements.

Held-to-maturity investments

A6.10.43 Unlike loans and receivables (see para A6.10.30 above), a held-to-maturity (HTM) investment (whether it pays fixed or floating interest) cannot be hedged for interest rate risk, because designation of an investment as held-to-maturity requires the holder's positive intent and ability to hold the instrument to maturity. Held-to-maturity classification implies that the net changes in fair value stemming from changes in market interest rates from inception to maturity will not have an impact on profit or loss as the entity has committed itself to retaining the investment to maturity. Similarly, a held-to-maturity investment cannot be hedged for pre-payment risk – risk that an investment will be paid earlier or later than expected. As interest rates fall below rates on existing loans, borrowers may, and commonly do, pre-pay their existing loans and refinance at lower rates. Therefore, as pre-payment risk is primarily a function of interest rates, it is more akin to interest rate risk and, accordingly, cannot be designated as a hedged risk. However, a held-to-maturity investment can be a hedged item with respect to risks from changes in foreign currency exchange rates and credit risk. [IAS 39 para 79].

A6.10.44 Although hedge accounting is prohibited for hedging the interest rate risk of a held-to-maturity asset, the prohibition only applies to held-to-maturity assets that have already been recognised on the entity's balance sheet. The prohibition does not apply to a forecast purchase of a held-to-maturity asset as illustrated in the example in paragraph A6.10.44 below.

Example – Forecast purchase of held-to-maturity investment

An entity has a forecast transaction to purchase a financial asset that it intends to classify as held-to-maturity when the forecast transaction occurs. It enters into a derivative contract to lock in the current interest rate and designates the derivative as a hedge of the forecast purchase of the financial asset.

Provided all the hedge accounting criteria are met, the entity can apply cash flow hedge accounting to the forecast purchase of a held-to-maturity security. This is because the investment is not classified as held-to-maturity until the transaction occurs. [IAS 39 IG para F2.10].

6A.10.45 The standard also permits cash flow hedge accounting for future interest receipts from a debt instrument that originated from the re-investment of interest receipts from an held-to-maturity investment as illustrated in the example below.

Example – Hedging reinvestment risk of funds obtained from held-to-maturity investments

An entity owns a variable rate asset that it has classified as held-to-maturity. The cash from variable interest receipts is re-invested in debt instruments. The entity enters into a derivative contract to lock in the current interest rate on the reinvestment of variable rate cash flows and designates the derivative as a cash flow hedge of the forecast future interest receipts on debt instruments.

Provided all the hedge accounting criteria are met, the hedging relationship will qualify for cash flow hedge accounting even though the cash from the interest receipts that are being reinvested come from an asset that is classified as held-to-maturity. The source of the funds used to purchase the debt instrument is not relevant in determining whether the reinvestment risk can be hedged. This answer applies also if the source of the funds used to purchase the debt instrument had been a fixed rate held-to-maturity investment. [IAS 39 IF para F2.11].

Equity method investment and investment in consolidated subsidiaries

A6.10.46 An equity method investment, such as an associate, cannot be a hedged item in a fair value hedge because the equity method recognises in profit or loss the investor's share of the associate's profit or loss, rather than changes in the investment's fair value. [IAS 39 para AG 99]. Although this applies to consolidated financial statements, an entity may be able to designate an investment in an associate as a fair value hedge in its separate financial statements, provided that its fair value can be measured reliably.

A6.10.47 The ability of an entity to treat an associate as the hedged item in a cash flow hedge is considered in the following example.

Example – Forecast cash flows in associates

Entity A has a 25% investment in a foreign entity over which it has significant influence. It, therefore, accounts for the foreign entity as an associate using the equity method. The associate's functional currency, in which most of its sales and costs are denominated, differs from entity A's functional currency. In entity A's consolidated financial statements its share of the associate's net results will fluctuate with the changes in the exchange rate. The entity intends to designate a portion of the forecast cash flows in the associate as the hedged item in a hedge of foreign currency risk.

Under the functional currency concept in IAS 21, a cash flow that is denominated in an associate's functional currency does not give rise to a foreign currency (transaction) exposure for the associate in its separate financial statements. The variability in entity A's share of its associate's net results arises only in its consolidated financial statements and arises from the translation of the associate's financial statements into the group's presentation currency. This is a translation rather than a transaction exposure. IAS 39 permits an entity to apply hedge accounting to a hedge of the translation risk on its existing net investment, but this does not extend to the investee's forecast future cash flows or profits.

A6.10.48 An investment in a consolidated subsidiary cannot be a hedged item in a fair value hedge, because consolidation recognises in profit or loss the subsidiary's profit or loss, rather than changes in the investment's fair value. If a subsidiary was allowed to be designated as a hedged item, it would result in double counting, as both the income from the investment as well as changes in the fair value would be reported in profit or loss. A hedge of a net investment in a foreign operation is different because it is a hedge of the foreign currency exposure, not a fair value hedge of the change in the investment's value. [IAS 39 para AG 99]. Another example of a transaction undertaken by a foreign subsidiary that cannot be hedged at the consolidation level is considered below

Example 1 – Forecast foreign currency transaction undertaken by a foreign subsidiary

Entity A's functional currency is the euro. It has a US subsidiary, subsidiary B, whose functional currency is the US dollar. Subsidiary B has highly probable forecast sales denominated in Japanese yen.

Entity A wishes to hedge subsidiary B's forecast Japanese yen inflows back into euros (entity A's functional currency) using external foreign currency forward contracts (¥/€). Entity A's management intends to designate, in the consolidated financial statements, the forward contracts as hedging instruments in a cash flow hedge of the forecast transactions denominated in Japanese yen.

The ¥/€ forward contracts taken out by entity A do not qualify for cash flow hedge accounting on consolidation. This is because there is no ¥/€ cash flow exposure that affects consolidated profit or loss. The consolidated income statement will be exposed to ¥/US$ movements, as subsidiary B will translate its ¥ sales into its own functional currency

(US$). The exposure to movements in US/€ constitutes a translation risk rather than a cash flow exposure and, therefore, cannot be the subject of a cash flow hedge.

However, it is possible for the subsidiary B to use a ¥/US$ forward contract to designate a cash flow hedge of its ¥/US$ transaction exposure. Alternatively, entity A could use a ¥/US$ forward contract to hedge the exposure since IAS 39 does not require that the operating unit that is exposed to the risk being hedged be a party to the hedging instrument. [IAS 39 para IG F2.14].

Entity A could also hedge its net investment in subsidiary B using a €/US$ forward (see para A6.10.133 below). This would, however, not include the forecast transaction.

Example 2 – Parent hedging forecasted future revenues denominated in the functional currency of a subsidiary which is different from functional currency of the parent

Entity A, based in Germany, whose functional currency is euro, has a subsidiary in the UK, whose functional currency is GBP. The group's presentation currency is also euro. The UK subsidiary sells gas within the UK for GBP to British customers. At the group level, the group's treasury department enters into external GBP/euro forward contract to hedge against movements in GBP *versus* euro on behalf of the group.

The group cannot obtain cash flow hedge accounting for the UK subsidiary sales. The sales of the UK subsidiary are made in its functional currency so it has no foreign currency exposure. The consolidated group has a foreign currency exposure, but it will not affect the group's reported net profit or loss. At the consolidated level the foreign currency exposure will be deferred as part of cumulative translation adjustment in equity when the UK subsidiary's financial statements are translated into the group's presentation currency for consolidation [IAS 21 para 39(c)]. Group management may, therefore, consider the possibility of net investment hedge accounting under paragraph 102 of IAS 39. However, the group will not be able to obtain hedge accounting for hedges of forecasted sales – see last sentence of the example 1 above.

Example 3 – Hedging of foreign currency sales of a foreign subsidiary denominated in group's presentation currency by the parent

A European parent enity whose functional currency is euro, has a Chinese subsidiary whose functional currency is RMB. The presentation currency of the group is euro. The Chinese entity has highly probable forecast sales in euro that its management has not hedged. The parent's management enters into EUR/RMB forward contracts and designates these as cash flow hedges of the Chinese subsidiary's forecast sales.

The forecast euro sales give rise to a currency risk that will affect the subsidiary's profit or loss in its separate financial statements. This is because the EUR amount at which the sales are reported in the subsidiary's separate financial statements will be affected by the EUR/RMB exchange rate at the time the sales occur.

However, in the consolidated financial statements the sales will be translated into euro using the exchange rates at the dates of the transactions (or an average rate when this approximates the rates at the dates of the transactions) in accordance with paragraph 39(b) of IAS 21. Hence, the RMB amount at which the sales are reported in the group's consolidated financial statements will not be affected by the EUR/RMB exchange rate at the time the sales occur. Accordingly, the currency risk of these forecast sales will not affect the consolidated profit or loss when expressed in euro.

The forecast transaction meets the requirements of paragraph 88(c) of IAS 39. The reference in paragraph 88(c) of IAS 39 to 'profit or loss' refers to the subsidiary's profit or loss where the exposure is located and not to the profit or loss of the consolidated entity. This is consistent with the functional currency framework in IAS 21 under which a foreign exchange exposure arises whenever a transaction is denominated in a currency other than the functional currency of the entity entering into the transaction. Paragraph IG F.2.14 of IAS 39 also permits the hedging instrument to be entered into by the parent and states that it need not be entered into by the subsidiary that has the exposure. Hence, provided all the other criteria in paragraph 88 of IAS 39R are met, the group may obtain cash flow hedge accounting in its consolidated financial statements.

Future earnings

A6.10.49 Future earnings or future results cannot be designated as hedged items because they are the net effect of various transactions that do not share the same risk characteristic. However, future revenue or future expenditure may be separately designated as hedged items if the underlying risk exposure can be specifically identified and measured (see example in para A6.10.108 below).

Derivative instruments

A6.10.50 A derivative instrument (whether a stand-alone or separately recognised embedded derivative) cannot be designated as a hedged item, either individually or as part of a hedged group in a fair value or cash flow hedge. For instance, it is not possible to designate a pay-variable, receive-fixed forward rate agreement (FRA) as a cash flow hedge of a pay-fixed, receive-variable FRA. This is because derivative instruments are always deemed held for trading and measured at fair value with gains and losses recognised in profit or loss unless they are designated and effective hedging instruments. As an exception, IAS 39 permits the designation of a purchased option as the hedged item in a fair value hedge. [IAS 39 paras AG 94, IG F2.1]. A contract to buy or sell a non-financial asset that can be settled net in cash and that is accounted for as a derivative under IAS 39 cannot be a hedged item.

General business risk

A6.10.51 To qualify for hedge accounting, the hedge must relate to a specific identified and designated risk and not merely to the entity's general business risks and must ultimately affect the entity's profit or loss. For example, a firm commitment to acquire a business in a business combination cannot be a hedged item, except for foreign exchange risk in respect of the purchase consideration, because the other risks being hedged cannot be specifically identified and measured. These other risks are general business risks. Similarly, a hedge of the risk of obsolescence of a physical asset or the risk of expropriation of property by a government is not eligible for hedge accounting; effectiveness cannot be measured because those risks are not measurable reliably. [IAS 39 paras AG 98,

AG 110]. Similarly, the risk that a transaction will not occur such that it would result in less revenue than expected is an overall business risk that is not eligible as a hedged item. [IAS 39 para IG F2.8].

Hedging instruments

Definition

A6.10.52 A hedging instrument is a designated derivative or, for a hedge of the risk of changes in foreign currency exchange rates, only a designated non-derivative financial asset or non-derivative financial liability, whose fair value or cash flows are expected to offset changes in the fair value or cash flows of a designated hedged item. [IAS 39 para 9].

A6.10.53 For hedge accounting purposes, only instruments that involve a party external to the reporting entity (that is, external to the group, segment or individual entity that is being reported on) can be designated as hedging instruments. It follows that internal derivative contracts between members of a group (for example, a trading subsidiary entering into a derivative contract with group treasury) cannot be designated as a hedging instrument in the group's consolidated financial statements. Therefore, if an entity wishes to achieve hedge accounting in the consolidated financial statements, it must designate a hedging relationship between a qualifying external hedging instrument and a qualifying hedged item. However, internal derivative contracts may qualify for hedge accounting in the individual or separate financial statements of individual entities within the group or in segment reporting provided that they are external to the individual entity or segment that is being reported on (see para A6.10.79 below). [IAS 39 para 73].

Derivative financial instruments

A6.10.54 IAS 39 does not restrict the circumstances in which a derivative may be designated as a hedging instrument provided the hedge accounting conditions are met (see para A6.10.138 below), except for some written options. This means that derivative instruments such as forward exchange contracts, futures contracts, interest rate swaps, cross-currency and commodity swaps and purchased options can all be designated as hedging instruments. An embedded derivative that is accounted for separately from its host contract can be used as a hedging instrument. Also, those contracts for purchases or sales of non-financial assets that are accounted for as derivatives under IAS 39 (that is, can be settled net or by exchanging another financial instrument and that are not for own use) may be used as hedging instruments.

Example 1 – Hedging with a sales commitment

Entity J's functional currency is the Japanese yen. It has issued a US$ fixed rate debt instrument with semi-annual interest payments that matures in 2 years with principal due at maturity of 5 million US dollars. It has also entered into a fixed price sales commitment for

5 million US dollars that matures in two years that is not accounted for as a derivative, because it meets the exemption for normal sales. Entity J intends to designate the sales commitment as a hedge of the fair value change of the maturity amount of the debt attributable to foreign currency risk.

In this scenario, the sales commitment is accounted for as a firm commitment and not as a derivative and, therefore, cannot be designated as a hedging instrument. However, if the foreign currency component of the sales commitment is required to be separated as an embedded derivative on the grounds that US dollar is not the customer's functional currency, it could be designated as a hedging instrument in a hedge of the exposure to changes in the fair value of the debt's maturity amount attributable to foreign currency risk. [IAS 39 para IG F1.2]. However, as the exchange difference on the fixed rate debt would, in any event, be reported in profit or loss under IAS 21, a separate hedging relationship is not necessary.

Example 2 – Hedging with fixed to fixed cross currency swaps

Entity X, whose functional currency is the euro, has issued a US dollar fixed rate debt. Entity X's management intends to hedge the foreign exchange cash flow exposure on the debt's interest and principal by entering into a fixed to fixed euro/US dollar cross currency interest rate swap.

Entity X expects the cross currency interest rate swap to be a highly effective hedge of the cash flow exposure, since the critical terms of the hedging instrument and the hedged item match.

IAS 39 does not specify the methodology that should be used for effectiveness testing other than to require this to be consistent with the entity's risk management strategy. One possible method would be to apply dollar offset test comparing the following:

1 The cumulative gain or loss on the hedging instrument from inception of the hedge calculated as the difference between:

(a) the fair value of the swap at inception; and

(b) the fair value of the swap at the testing date.

2 The cumulative change in the fair value of the expected cash flows on the debt from the inception of the hedge calculated as the difference between:

(a) the present value of all fixed USD cash flows on the bond, determined using the forward USD/EUR rates for the respective maturities at inception of hedge accounting (that is, as if the USD/EUR exchange rates had been fixed at the forward USD/EUR rate on each coupon date) discounted using euro LIBOR at the testing date; and

(b) the periodic valuation of all fixed USD cash flows on the bond using the forward rate at the testing date and discounted using LIBOR at the testing date.

If all the critical terms of the swap exactly match the terms of the underlying bond, this test is likely to give rise to no ineffectiveness. If this is the case, and if all the remaining requirements of paragraph 88 of IAS 39 relating to documentation and designation are met, management could defer the entire change in the fair value of the swap in equity.

At each reporting date, the underlying bond will be re-measured through profit or loss using the spot exchange rate in accordance with IAS 21. At the same time an equivalent offsetting portion of the fair value adjustment of the swap should be recycled to profit or loss. The remaining revaluation gain or loss deferred in equity relates to the forward points, that is, the difference between the spot rate and the forward rate. These forward points deferred in equity should be recognised in profit or loss over the period of the hedging relationship (this being the period(s) in which the hedged item affects profit or loss) using the effective interest rate method.

A6.10.55 It is not necessary for an entity to enter into a new derivative contract every time it enters into a new hedging relationship. Provided the hedge accounting criteria are met, a pre-existing derivative instrument that has been held for some time and classified as held-for-trading can be designated as a hedging instrument in a new hedging relationship, as can a derivative that has been designated previously as a hedging instrument in a hedge relationship that no longer qualifies for hedge accounting. However, an existing derivative will have a non-zero fair value because of its 'off market terms'. Consequently, it cannot be assumed that the new relationship will be highly effective without performing the necessary analysis of the impact of the 'off market' nature of the derivative on the new relationship. The 'off market' nature of the derivative can be described as an 'embedded financing' within the derivative. For example, a derivative asset can be thought of as containing an 'embedded loan receivable' and a derivative liability as containing an 'embedded loan payable'. This 'embedded' financing can be a source of ineffectiveness. Changing the designation of a derivative from a trading instrument to a hedging instrument occurs at inception of the new hedging relationship.

Portions and proportions of a hedging instrument

A6.10.56 There is normally a single fair value measure for a hedging instrument in its entirety and the factors that cause changes in fair value are co-dependent. Thus, a hedging relationship is designated by an entity for a hedging instrument in its entirety. It follows that a derivative instrument cannot be split into components representing different risks with each component designated as the hedging instrument. The only exceptions permitted are:

- separating the interest element and the spot price of a forward contract; and
- separating the intrinsic value and time value of an option contract and designating as the hedging instrument only the change in intrinsic value of an option.

These exceptions are permitted because the intrinsic value of the option and the premium or discount on the forward can generally be measured separately.

[IAS 39 para 74].

Example 1 – Definition of a forward contract

For hedging purposes, entity A enters into the following derivative instruments:

- A fixed to fixed cross-currency swap.
- A floating to floating cross-currency swap.
- A floating to fixed cross-currency swap.
- A commodity contract where a series of fixed cash payments are exchanged for a series of fixed amounts of a commodity on pre-determined dates.

Entity A's management wishes to designate only the spot element of these derivatives as hedging instruments in separate hedging relationships.

Paragraph 74 of IAS 39 allows an entity to designate the spot element of a derivative as a hedging instrument provided the derivative is a forward contract. A simple forward contract is a contract to exchange a fixed amount of a financial or non-financial asset on a fixed future value date or dates beyond the spot value date. For the purposes of applying paragraph 74 of IAS 39, the term 'forward contract' should be interpreted as being any derivative instrument that is a simple forward contract or that may be constructed using only a series of simple forward contracts. Forward contracts may be settled by gross physical delivery of the financial or non-financial asset in return for cash, or on a net basis at each settlement date.

The fixed to fixed cross-currency swap entered into by entity A constitutes a forward contract under paragraph 74 of IAS 39 provided that the settlements on each leg of the swap occur on the same dates in the future (that is, there is no timing mismatch between the two legs of the swap).

Similarly, the commodity contract constitutes a forward contract under paragraph 74 of IAS 39 since it comprises a series of exchanges of fixed cash payments for fixed amounts of a commodity on pre-determined dates.

However, the other derivatives (the floating to floating cross-currency swap and the floating to fixed cross-currency swaps) are not forward contracts since they cannot be constructed using only simple forward contracts.

Example 2 – Splitting a written swaption into components

Entity A, whose functional currency is euro, issues 30-year fixed-rate debt. At the same time, entity A enters into an interest rate derivative with a third party with the following terms: entity A receives 7% fixed and pays 5% fixed for 7 years. After 7 years, the counterparty has the option to require entity A to enter into a pay fixed 5%, receive LIBOR interest rate swap with a maturity of 23 years. (Economically, entity A has sold the counterparty a swaption on a 23 year swap with 7 years until exercise date and with premium payments spread over 7 years).

Entity A proposes to split the derivative into separate components, one of which is an on-market receive fixed, pay variable interest rate swap. It would designate this component as a hedge of the first seven years of interest rate exposure under the fixed rate debt. The remaining component would be treated as a trading derivative.

Entity A must designate the entire derivative as a hedging instrument in the hedging relationship. This derivative may not be split into its components, because of the requirements of paragraph 74 of IAS 39 and paragraph IG F1.8 of IAS 39.

In addition the combined instrument is a written option and cannot be designated as a hedging instrument under paragraph AG94 of IAS 39.

6A.10.57 The fair value of a foreign exchange forward contract is affected by changes in the spot rate and by changes in the forward points. The latter derives from the interest rate differential between the currencies specified in the forward contract. Changes in the forward points may give rise to ineffectiveness if the hedged item is not similarly affected by interest rate differentials (see para A6.10.186 below).

A6.10.58 The fair value of an option can be divided into two portions: the intrinsic value, which is determined as the difference between the strike price and the current market price of the underlying; and the time value, which is the option's remaining value and depends on the volatility of the price of the underlying, interest rates and the time remaining to maturity. When the option is used to hedge a non-optional position, changes in the option's time value will not be offset by an equivalent change in the value or cash flows of the hedged item. IAS 39 does not specify how the intrinsic value of an option is determined. Intrinsic value can be defined based on the spot rate. For example, for an interest rate cap that is used to hedge exposure to interest rates on floating rate debt, the intrinsic value may be deferred by projecting all future cash flows on the cap at the current spot rate and discounting the result using the zero-coupon curve. If the current spot rate is below the market rate, the cap is 'out of the money' in all periods. Alternatively, the intrinsic value could be defined using the forward rate curve. The projected cash flows would be calculated using the forward rates. In that case the cap may be in the money in some periods, even when the current spot rate is below the strike price.

A6.10.59 Generally, it may be advantageous to exclude the forward points and the time value of an option to improve effectiveness. However, this comes at a price as it can increase the volatility in the income statement. This is because as the forward points or time value are not subject to hedge accounting, any changes in their fair value will be recognised as gains or losses in the income statement as they occur.

A6.10.60 A proportion of the entire hedging instrument, such as 50 per cent of the notional amount, may be designated as the hedging instrument. [IAS 39 para 75]. The proportion that is not acting as a hedge is either treated as held-for-trading or designated as a hedging instrument in another hedge relationship.

Example – Proportions of derivatives as hedging instruments

Entity A, whose functional currency is the euro, enters into a US$10m forward contract on 1 June 20X1 to hedge forecast future US$-denominated sales in March 20X2. At the time of entering into the forward contract, only US$8m of forecast sales are considered to be highly probable of occurring in March 20X2.

In this situation, entity A can designated 80% of the forward contract as a hedge of the highly probable future sales of US$8m in March 20X2. The remaining US$2m of the forward contract (20%) may either be designated as trading or as a hedging instrument in another hedge relationship. In other words, 20% of the total change in the fair value of the forward contract would be reported in profit or loss, or used as an offset in another hedge relationship.

6A.10.61 A hedging relationship may not be designated for only a portion of the time period during which a hedging instrument remains outstanding as illustrated in the example below. [IAS 39 para 75].

Example – Portion of the outstanding life of a derivative as a hedging instrument

An entity enters into a pay-fixed, receive-variable interest rate swap to hedge the fair value exposure of a floating rate debt instrument. Both the swap and the debt instrument are entered into on the same date. The floating rate debt instrument has a term of 5 years and the swap has a term of 7 years.

The entity cannot designate the cash flows arising in the first 5 years of the 7 year swap as a hedging instrument. The swap's fair value derives from the present value of the net settlements over the entire 7 year period, not the first 5 years. Furthermore, the fair value of the swap cannot be time apportioned using linear interpolation, as the change in the swap's fair value per unit of time is non-linear. In other words, the fair value of two separate instruments (a 5 year swap and a 5 year forward starting swap with a duration of 2 years) would not be the same as the fair value of a 7 year swap.

However, the entity can designate the entire 7 year swap as a hedge of the 5 year debt, but ineffectiveness will arise because of timing mismatches and is likely to be so large (that is, outside the 80% — 125% range, see para A6.10.146 below) as to prohibit hedge accounting.

On the other hand, if the swap's terms and the debt are reversed so that they are 5 years and 7 years respectively, the 5 year swap can be designated as a hedge of the first 5 years of the debt instrument. This is referred to as 'partial-term' hedging and is discussed in paragraph A6.10.29 above.

Hedging more than one risk with a single instrument

A6.10.62 A derivative, such as a forward contract, swap or an option, is used as a hedging instrument to hedge a single risk (foreign currency, interest rate or equity price risk). However, entities may often use a single derivative such as a cross-currency swap (combined interest rate and currency swap) to convert a variable rate position in a foreign currency to a fixed rate position in the entity's functional currency. IAS 39 permits a single hedging instrument to be designated as a hedge of more than one type of risk provided that:

- The risks hedged can be identified clearly.
- The effectiveness of the hedge can be demonstrated.
- It is possible to ensure that there is specific designation of the hedging instrument and different risk positions.

[IAS 39 para 76].

A6.10.63 If a single hedging instrument is used to hedge different risk exposures and each of these risk exposures are accounted for using different forms of hedge accounting (fair value hedge for one, cash flow hedge for the other), IFRS 7 requires separate disclosures for each type of hedge (see section 11). [IAS 39 IG para F1.12].

Example 1 – Dual foreign currency forward exchange contract to hedge currency risk

Entity A's functional currency is the Japanese yen. Entity A has a 5 year floating rate US dollar liability and a 10 year fixed rate pound sterling denominated bond (an asset). The principal amounts of the asset and liability when converted into the Japanese yen are the same. Entity A enters into a single foreign currency forward contract to hedge its foreign currency exposure on both instruments under which it receives US dollars and pays pound sterling at the end of 5 years.

Entity A designates the forward exchange contract as a hedging instrument in a cash flow hedge against the foreign currency exposure on the principal repayments of both instruments. Since entity A's functional currency is Yen, it is exposed to US$/¥ foreign currency risk on the floating rate liability and ¥/£ foreign exchange risk on the fixed rate asset.

IAS 39 permits a single hedging instrument to be designated as a hedge of multiple types of risk if three conditions stated in paragraph A6.10.62 above are met. In this example, the derivative hedging instrument satisfies all of these conditions, as follows:

- The risks hedged can be identified clearly. The risks are the exposures to changes in the exchange rates between US dollars and yen and yen and pounds, respectively.
- The effectiveness of the hedge can be demonstrated. For the pound sterling bond, the effectiveness is measured as the degree of offset between the fair value of the principal repayment in pounds sterling and the fair value of the pound sterling payment on the forward exchange contract. For the US dollar liability, the effectiveness is measured as the degree of offset between the fair value of the principal repayment in US dollars and the US dollar receipt on the forward exchange contract. Even though the receivable has a 10-year life and the forward protects it for only the first 5 years, hedge accounting is permitted for only a portion of the exposure as described in paragraph A6.10.29 above.
- It is possible to ensure that there is specific designation of the hedging instrument and different risk positions. The hedged exposures are identified as the principal amounts of the liability and the note receivable in their respective currency of denomination.

[IAS 39 para IG F1.13].

It should be noted that in respect of the second point above, the US $/£ forward is theoretically divided into two different derivatives. The Yen is imputed as the base currency for the two derivatives creating a synthetic US$/Yen (receive US dollar, pay Yen) foreign currency forward and a synthetic ¥/£ (receive Yen, pay sterling) foreign currency forward. The synthetic Yen leg is defined in such a manner that the fair value of each synthetic forward contract is nil at the hedge's inception. This can be pictorially represented as follows:

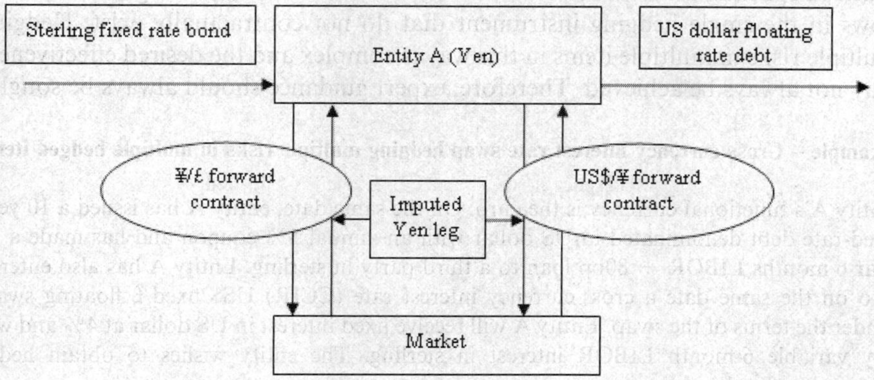

Furthermore, it should be noted that the hedge accounting criteria must be satisfied for both the designated hedged risks. For instance, if effectiveness of the hedge can be demonstrated for US$/¥ risk only and not ¥/£ risk, hedge accounting is not permitted.

Example 2 – Cross currency interest rate swap hedging multiple risks in a single hedged item

Entity A's functional currency is the euro. On 1 July 20X6, entity A issues a 10 year fixed-rate debt denominated in US dollar with an annual 5% coupon. Entity A's overall risk management policy is to borrow in its own functional currency. The entity determined, however, that its overall financing costs would be reduced if it were to issue foreign currency denominated debt and purchase a currency swap to convert the debt synthetically into a floating euro denominated debt. Accordingly, the entity hedges the transaction by entering into a cross currency interest rate swap (combined foreign currency and interest rate swap) under which it receives US$ fixed, pays euro floating. The swap's terms match those of the debt.

IAS 39 permits the cross currency swap to be designated as a hedging instrument as a hedge of more than one risk, provide the criteria described in paragraph 9.62 above are met. Therefore, the cross-currency swap can be designated either as a fair value hedge of both the interest rate risk and currency risk of the US$ debt, or as a fair value hedge of the interest rate risk and a cash flow hedge of the foreign currency risk.

If the entity had issued a US$ floating rate debt and synthetically converted it into a fixed euro debt by entering into a receive US$ floating, pay euro fixed cross-currency swap, the entity could have designated the swap as a cash flow hedge of interest rate risk and a cash flow hedge or fair value hedge of the currency risk.

In both cases, the risks being hedged are clearly identifiable, the effectiveness of the hedges can be demonstrated and it is possible to ensure that there is specific designation of the hedging instrument and different risk positions.

6A.10.64 It is also possible to use a single derivative instrument to hedge more than one risk in more than one hedged item. In order to do this, the entity should be able to identify the hedged risks in each of the hedged items and split the single derivative into its components in order to allocate those components to each hedged risk identified. As a derivative has only a single fair value, care should be taken in splitting a derivative so that it does not result in the recognition of cash flows in the single hedging instrument that do not contractually exist. Hedging multiple risks in multiple items in this way is complex and the desired effectiveness may not always be achieved. Therefore, expert guidance should always be sought.

Example – Cross currency interest rate swap hedging multiple risks in multiple hedged items

Entity A's functional currency is the euro. On the same date, entity A has issued a 10 year fixed-rate debt denominated in US dollar with an annual 5% coupon and has made a 10 year 6 months LIBOR + 80bp loan to a third party in sterling. Entity A has also entered into on the same date a cross-currency interest rate (CCIR) US$ fixed/£ floating swap. Under the terms of the swap. Entity A will receive fixed interest in US dollar at 4% and will pay variable 6-month LIBOR interest in sterling. The entity wishes to obtain hedge accounting for the swap.

With regard to the loan asset, entity A is exposed to a £/€ exchange risk, because the loan is denominated in sterling which is not entity A's functional currency. It is also exposed to cash flow interest rate risk (sterling 6 months LIBOR) because entity A will pay variable coupon on the loan. Entity A is also exposed to a credit risk (change in the credit rating of the issuer of the loan).

With regard to the liability, entity A is exposed to a risk of changes in the fair value of the debt due to €/US$ exchange risk (both the notional amount and the interest on the loan are denominated in US dollars, which is not entity A's functional currency). Entity A is also exposed to fair value interest rate risk (US$ 6 months LIBOR is defined as the benchmark risk), because it will pay fixed coupon in US$ on the debt.

Two ways in which entity A could use the CCIR swap as a hedging instrument are described below. A single swap (receive US$ 4% fixed, pay floating £) may be analysed into its separate risk components for hedging purposes by imputing a notional leg denominated in the entity's functional currency. The additional leg may be either fixed or floating, provided the chosen alternative qualifies for hedge accounting for both of the exposures hedged and effectiveness can be reliably measured for both elements. Prospective and retrospective effectiveness testing must be performed on both elements of the hedge relationship. Both elements must be highly effective in order for the hedge relationship to qualify for hedge accounting.

Therefore, the entity could separate the swap by inserting a euro floating leg (6 month LIBOR) into the CCIR swap, creating a US$ fix/€ float swap and a € float/£ float swap. entityA will end up with a fair value hedge of both the interest rate and currency risk on the US $ debt and a cash flow hedge of the foreign currency exposure on the sterling floating rate loan. This is shown in the diagram below.

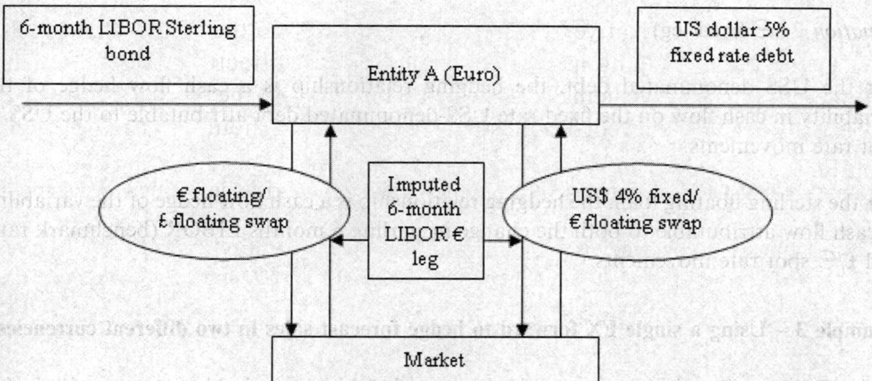

Alternatively, entity A could separate the swap by inserting a € fixed leg into the CCIR swap, creating a US $ fixed/€ fixed swap and a € fixed/£ floating swap. Entity A will end up with a cash flow hedge of the currency risk on the US$ debt and a cash flow hedge of the interest rate and foreign currency risk on the sterling floating rate loan. This is shown in the diagram below.

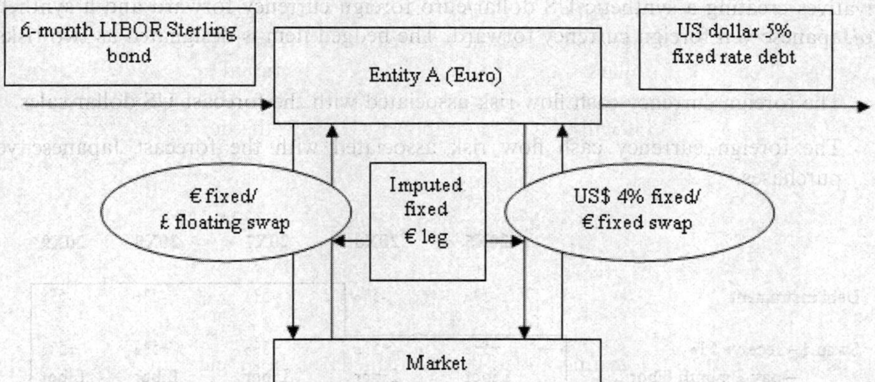

The risks hedged can be identified clearly.

Situation 1 (€ floating leg)

For the US$ denominated debt, the hedging relationship is a fair value hedge of the exposure to changes in the fair value attributable to both changes in the 6 months US LIBOR interest rate (benchmark rate) and US$/€ spot rate movements.

For the sterling floating loan, the hedging relationship is a cash flow hedge of the variability in cash flow attributable to the £/€ spot rate movements.

Situation 2 (€ fixed leg)

For the US$ denominated debt, the hedging relationship is a cash flow hedge of the variability in cash flow on the fixed rate US$-denominated debt attributable to the US$/€ spot rate movements.

For the sterling floating loan, the hedging relationship is a cash flow hedge of the variability in cash flow attributable to both the change in sterling 6 months LIBOR (benchmark rate) and £/€ spot rate movements.

Example 3 – Using a single FX forward to hedge forecast sales in two different currencies

Entity J, whose functional currency is the euro, has highly probable forecast sales in US dollars and highly probable forecast purchases in Japanese yen. Entity J enters into an external foreign currency forward contract to sell US dollars and buy Japanese yen. Entity J's management intends to designate the foreign currency forward contract as a hedge of both the US dollar/euro foreign currency risk associated with the forecast sales and the Japanese yen/euro foreign currency risk associated with the forecast purchases.

For hedge effectiveness testing the Japanese yen/US dollar forward contract is theoretically divided into two different derivatives. The euro is imputed as the base currency for the two derivatives creating a synthetic US dollar/euro foreign currency forward and a synthetic euro/Japanese yen foreign currency forward. The hedged item is designated as two risks:

- The foreign currency cash flow risk associated with the forecast US dollar sales.
- The foreign currency cash flow risk associated with the forecast Japanese yen purchases.

	20X5	20X6	20X7	20X8	20X9
Debt instrument	-5%	-5%	-5%	-5%	-5%
Swap 1 – receive 5% – pay 3 month Libor	+5% Libor	+5% Libor	+5% Libor	+5% Libor	+5% Libor
Swap 2 – receive 3 month Libor – pay 5%	Libor -5%	Libor -5%			
Net interest	-5%	-5%	Libor	Libor	Libor

Hedging instrument

The Japanese yen/US dollar forward may be designated as a cash flow hedge of both the foreign currency cash flow risks associated with the forecast sales in US dollars and the forecasted purchases in Japanese yen, provided all of the conditions in paragraph 76 of IAS 39 are met.

This solution is consistent with paragraph IG F2.18 of IAS 39, which allows a Japenese yen functional currency entity to designate a US dollar/sterling swap as a hedge of both a US dollar liability and sterling asset. However, each hedging relationship must be tested for effectiveness separately and if one of the two hedging relationships becomes ineffective (either because an effectiveness test is failed or because one of the forecast transactions is no longer highly probable to occur), hedge accounting will be discontinued prospectively for both hedge relationships.

Combination of derivative instruments

A6.10.65 A derivative may also be designated as the hedging instrument in combination with one or more other derivatives, or even, for a hedge of foreign exchange risk, in combination with groups of non-derivative assets or liabilities. Two or more derivatives or proportions of them may be viewed in combination and jointly designated as the hedging instrument, provided none of them is a written option or a net written option (see further para A6.10.70 below). For hedges of currency risk, two or more non-derivatives, or proportions of them, may be designated as the hedging instrument. [IAS 39 para 77].

A6.10.66 Derivative instruments do not have to be similar to be combined, either together or with non-derivative instruments. Even when the risks arising from some derivatives offset(s) those arising from others, the combination can still be designated as a hedging instrument. [IAS 39 para 77].

A6.10.67 Multiple derivatives need not be acquired at the same time to be designated as a hedge of the same item. They could be acquired at different times. For instance, an entity can designate two purchased options as a hedge of the same hedged item. Multiple derivatives can be used to hedge the same risk or different risks, provided that all of the other hedge criteria have been met and there is no 'duplicate' hedging of the same risk. For example, assume that two derivatives are designated as a hedge of the risk of a change in the fair value of a fixed-rate asset. One derivative hedges interest rate risk and the other hedges credit risk. In assessing an expectation of offsetting changes in fair value that are attributable to the type of risk that is being hedged, an entity would consider the two hedges separately, since the derivatives are hedging two separate risks.

Example – Combination of derivatives designated as a hedging instrument

Entity A's functional currency is pound sterling. On 1 January 20X5, the entity issues a 5 year 5% fixed-rate £100m debt with interest payable annually on 31 December. The debt is classified as other financial liabilities.

The risk management policy of entity A requires it to pay variable rate interest on debt except during the first 2 years. Accordingly, entity A enters into:

- A 5-year £100m notional receive fixed 5%, pay floating (3 month LIBOR) interest swap (swap 1).
- A 2-year £100m notional pay fixed 5%, receive floating (3 month LIBOR) interest swap (swap 2).

IAS 39 permits entity A to designate the combination of swap 1 and swap 2 as a hedge of the fair value exposure relating to interest rate movements in the debt instrument for the cash flows on the bond (principal plus interest) that will occur in period 1 January 20X7 to 31 December 20X9. This is because IAS 39 permits the designation of a portion of the fair value or cash flows of a financial instrument as a hedged item. Therefore, provided that all criteria for hedge accounting are met (in particular the hedge, as described, is expected to be highly effective and the new hedge relationship is consistent with entity A's risk management policies), fair value hedge accounting can be applied.

As a result of combining the two swaps entity A will achieve its objective of paying fixed interest in the first two years and achieve fair value hedge of the interest rate risk in the remaining 3 years as shown below:

Prospective and Retrospective Assessment

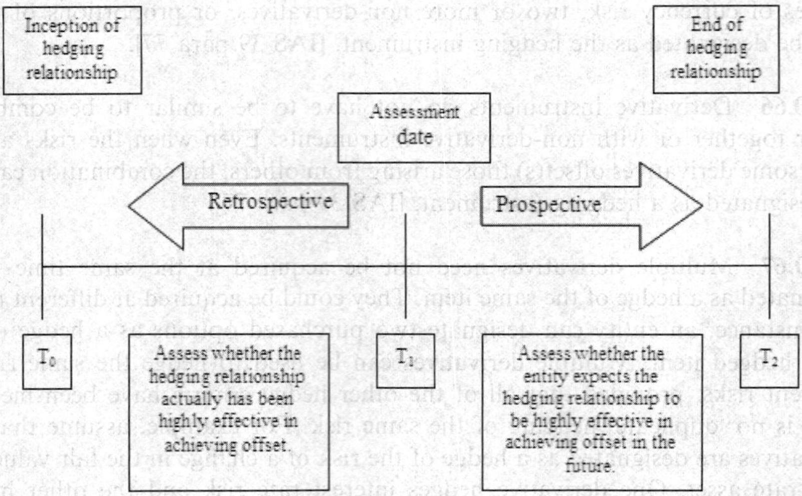

Changes in the aggregate fair value of swap 1 and swap 2 will be recognised in profit or loss. Similarly changes in the fair value of the debt attributable to interest rate movements relating to the period 1 January 20X7 to 31 December 20X9 will be recognised in profit or loss (see para A6.10.94 below). Some ineffectiveness is likely to arise because of the variable rate leg of swap 1 that is not mirrored in the hedged item. Also, the fair value of swap 2 is based on a different yield curve from the yield curve used for determining swap 1's fair value of (2 year *versus* 5 years).

A6.10.68 IAS 39 also permits derivative instruments to be combined with non-derivative instruments, or proportions of them and the combination designated as the hedging instrument, but only for hedges of foreign currency risk. For example, an entity could combine a forward currency contract (exclude forward points) and a foreign currency liability as a net investment hedge of the spot foreign exchange risk in a foreign subsidiary in its consolidated financial statements. Similarly, an entity could use a combination of foreign currency cash instrument and a derivative to hedge the foreign currency risk of a firm commitment, provided all the hedge accounting conditions are met.

Options as hedging instruments

A6.10.69 Options, in contrast to forward and swaps, give the holder the right but not the obligation to exercise the instrument and exchange the underlyings. Generally, options that have the potential to reduce risk exposure can qualify as hedging instruments. For instance, a purchased option has potential gains equal to or greater than losses and, therefore, has the potential to reduce profit or loss exposure from changes in fair values or cash flows. Therefore, it can qualify as a hedging instrument. [IAS 39 para AG 94].

Example 1 – Purchased option as a hedging instrument in cash flow hedges

Entity A operates a mail-order business. Its functional currency is the euro, but it purchases approximately 20% of its merchandise from the USA.

Entity A issues the mail-order catalogue for the coming year, incorporating its price list, before entering into a firm purchase commitment with US suppliers. Entity A, therefore, sets the prices in the catalogue based on expected exchange rates of €1 = US$1.25. It is highly probable that the entity will make purchases of at least €500,000 from the US in the first six months.

The entity's documented risk management policy requires it to hedge the risk that exchange rates will be higher than expected by purchasing a call option to buy US dollars for euros with a strike price equal to the expected exchange rate. Entity A, therefore, purchased a call option at a rate of €1 = US$1.25, for a maximum of €500,000 in six months' time at a cost of €60,000.

The spot rate at the time of entering into the option contracts was €1 = US$1.1.

Entity A can designate the purchased option as a hedge against the movements in the €/$exchange rate. The exposure being hedged is the variability in cash flows that would arise if the US dollar exchange rate exceeds the expected level of €1 = US$1.25.

Example 2 – Purchased option as a hedging instrument in fair value hedges

Entity A has issued a 5 year €100 million debt that bears interest at a fixed rate of 3%. It wishes to hedge the risk of increases in the fair value of the debt if interest rates decrease. It enters into a €100 million 5 year floor on 3 month EURIBOR with a strike rate of 3%.

The purchased option (the interest rate floor) can be designated as a hedging instrument in a hedge of changes in the fair value of the 5 year debt as a result of changes in interest rates. IAS 39 states that a financial item may be hedged with respect to the risks associated with only a portion of its cash flow or fair value, provided that effectiveness can be measured (see para A6.10.23 above). It is, therefore, possible to designate the hedge as the risk of changes in the fair value if interest rates fall below 3%. The effectiveness of the hedge will be improved if the entity designates only the intrinsic value of the floor as the hedging instrument. In this case, the floor's time value is excluded from the hedge relationship and changes in its value are recognised in the income statement as they occur.

6A.10.70 On the other hand, a *written* option exposes its writer to the possibility of unlimited loss but limits the gain to the amount of premium received. A written option serves only to reduce the potential for gain in the hedged item or hedged transaction. It leaves the potential for loss on the hedged item or hedged transaction unchanged, except for the amount of the premium received. As a result, a written option generally increase risk exposure because the potential loss on an option that an entity writes could be significantly greater than the potential gain in value of a related hedged item. In other words, a written option is not effective in reducing the profit or loss exposure of a hedged item. Therefore, a written option does not qualify as a hedging instrument, either on its own or in combination with other derivatives, unless it is designated as an offset to a purchased option. In addition, a written option can be designated as an offset to a purchase option that is embedded in another financial instrument. For example, in a callable debt, a written option can be used as a hedging instrument to hedge the callable liability where the issuer can call the debt early. [IAS 39 para AG 94].

A6.10.71 An entity may enter into a hedging strategy that involves a written put option and a purchased call option combining to form a collar. The objective of such a hedging strategy is to protect the entity from loss below a certain value (the floor/written put) and also limit the upside potential for gain above a certain value (the cap/purchased call) so as to reduce the cost of the hedging strategy. A typical example is an interest rate collar. Therefore, such an interest rate collar or other derivative instrument that combines a written option and a purchased option does not qualify as a hedging instrument if it is, in effect, a net written option (for which a net premium is received). [IAS 39 para 77].

A6.10.72 However, an interest rate collar or other derivative instrument that includes a written option may be designated as a hedging instrument, if the combination is a net purchased option or zero cost collar (that is, it is neither a net written or a net purchased option). Such a combination is not a net written option and, therefore, can be designated as a hedging instrument provided all the following conditions are met:

- No net premium is received either at inception or over the life of the combination of options. The distinguishing feature of a written option is the receipt of a premium to compensate the writer for the risk incurred.
- Except for the strike prices, the critical terms and conditions of the written option component and the purchased option component are the same (including underlying variable or variables, currency denomination and maturity date).
- The notional amount of the written option component is not greater than the notional amount of the purchased option component.

[IAS 39 para IG F1.3]

Where a collar whose fair value was zero at inception is designated as a hedging instrument some time into its life, it may have some fair value on the date of designation. If its fair value on the date of designation is negative then the first criterion above would be failed and such a collar would not be allowed for designation as a hedging instrument. If the collar's fair value is zero or positive then, subject to compliance with the criterion two and three, it would be allowed for designation as a hedging instrument.

A6.10.73 If a combination of a written option and a purchased option (such as an interest rate collar) is transacted as a single instrument with one counterparty, an entity cannot split the derivative instrument into its written option component and purchased option component and designate the purchased option component as a hedging instrument. This is because a hedging relationship is designated by an entity for a hedging instrument in its entirety. The only exceptions permitted are splitting the time value and intrinsic value of an option and splitting the interest element and spot price on a forward (see para A6.10.56 above). [IAS 39 para IG F1.8].

Example 1 – Combination of written and purchased options

Entity A purchases a call option from bank X and sells a put option to bank Y. Bank X and bank Y are not related. The contracts are entered into on the same day, with the purpose of creating a collar. The premium paid on the purchased call equals the premium received on the sold put; no net premium is, therefore, received.

The combination of these two instruments cannot be designated as a hedging instrument, as one of the options is a sold (written) option for which a premium is received. A collar can only be designated as a hedging instrument if the purchased and written option are combined in a single instrument and the collar is not a net written option (that is, no net premium is received).

If the two instruments have the same counterparty and are entered into simultaneously and in contemplation of one another with the intent of creating a collar, the two instruments should be viewed as one transaction.

Example 2 – Combination of written and purchased options

Entity A holds a variable interest rate debt and wishes to hedge the risk of the interest rate increasing above 3%. Entity A's assessment of the risk of the interest rate increasing above 4% is remote and it is prepared to bear that excess risk. It, therefore, enters into a 'cap spread' structure, which is a single instrument, consisting of:

- the purchase of an interest rate cap whose strike rate is 3% (purchased option); and
- the sale of an interest rate cap whose strike rate is 4% (written option).

The cap spread is structured as a single contract entered into with the same counterparty.

Entity A can designate the hedged risk as the risk that the interest rate rises to between 3% and 4%, provided that the cap spread does not constitute a net written option (that is, the entity does not receive a net premium for the cap spread). In this case, the entity is permitted to apply hedge accounting if the strategy is in line with the company's risk management strategy and all other conditions for hedge accounting are met.

If the entity had entered into two separate options (a purchased interest rate cap and a written interest rate cap), it could not designate both options as the hedging instrument.

This is because two or more derivatives may be jointly designated as the hedging instrument only when none of them is a written option.

Example 3 – Designating a combination of several derivatives as a hedging instrument in a fair value hedge

Entity A has issued a 7%, 5 year fixed rate bond and at the same time entered into a receive-fixed (7%), pay-floating (LIBOR) 5 year interest rate swap to hedge the bond against changes in fair values resulting from changes in interest rates. The entity has also entered into a zero cost collar (a combination of written floor at 5% and purchased cap at 10%) to limit variability in cash flows arising from the combination of the fixed rate debt and interest rate swap. There is no net premium received for the cap and floor, therefore, there is no net written option.

Entity A's management can designate the combination of the interest rate swap and the zero cost collar as a hedging instrument to hedge the changes in the bond's fair value arising from changes in the risk-free rate, provided all other hedge accounting criteria required by paragraph 88 of IAS 39 are met. Although the zero cost collar contains a written option component, this is written as a single instrument and the combination is not a net written option as no premium is received by entity A at inception or over the contract's life. The hedging documentation could specify that the hedged risk is the risk of changes in the bond's fair value arising from changes in the risk-free rate within the range from 5% to 10%. Specifying the hedge in this way would improve hedge effectiveness.

Dynamic hedging strategies

A6.10.74 IAS 39 states that a dynamic hedging strategy that assesses both an optional contract's intrinsic value and time value can qualify for hedge accounting. [IAS 39 para 74]. This allows an entity to apply hedge accounting for a 'delta neutral' hedging strategy and other dynamic hedging strategies under which the quantity of the hedging instrument is constantly adjusted in order to maintain a desired hedge ratio (for example, to achieve a delta neutral position insensitive to changes in the hedged item's fair value). For example, a portfolio insurance strategy that seeks to ensure that the hedged item's fair value item does not drop below a certain level, while allowing the fair value to increase, may qualify for hedge accounting. [IAS 39 para IG F1.9].

A6.10.75 To qualify for hedge accounting, the entity must document how it will monitor and update the hedge and measure hedge effectiveness, be able to track properly all terminations and redesignations of the hedging instrument and demonstrate that all other criteria for hedge accounting in IAS 39 are met. Also, it must be able to demonstrate an expectation that the hedge will be highly effective for a specified short period of time during which the hedge is not expected to be adjusted. [IAS 39 para IG F1.9].

Example – Dynamic hedging strategy

Entity A whose functional currency is the euro has highly probable forecast sales in US dollars. Entity A periodically re-assesses the proportion of the exposure that should be hedged in accordance with its strategy. For instance, it may reduce the level of hedge from

70% to 40% of the forecast sales. The hedging instruments are foreign currency forward contracts.

When changing the proportion of hedged exposure, entity A first:

- de-designates the existing hedge relationship;
- enters into a new foreign currency forward contract with the same maturity date to modify its position; and
- re-designates the new combination of derivative instruments (the previous hedging instrument plus the new forward) as the hedging instrument.

Entity A is permitted to periodically de-designate and re-designate the cash flow hedge relationship. However the mechanism of de-designation and re-designation must be properly documented and consistent with its risk management policy. Assuming that the other hedge accounting criteria are met, the accounting treatment at the date of de-designation and re-designation is as follows:

- Cash flow hedge accounting may be applied to the original hedge relationship until the date of its de-designation.
- Cash flow hedge accounting may be applied to the second hedge relationship starting from the date of re-designation.

The change in the fair value of the initial hedging instrument that had been reported in equity:

- Remains in equity if the forecast transaction is still expected to occur and is recycled to profit or loss when the forecast sales occur.
- Is reclassified into the income statement if the forecast transaction is no longer expected to occur.

The strategy described will require a significant amount of documentation to support the de-designation/re-designation process and a detailed monitoring of the accounting entries. Entity A will have to disclose in its financial statements the objective of this hedging strategy and the corresponding policies, together with a discussion of the associated risks and the business objectives pursued.

A6.10.76 It follows from the above that there is no prohibition in IAS 39 against terminating one hedge and initiating another with the same hedging instrument. Furthermore, there is no limitations on the frequency of such terminations/ designations and re-designations. Provided an entity can properly track all of the terminations and re-designations and demonstrate that all other qualifying criteria, such as high effectiveness, have been met, hedge accounting using the same instrument on a recurring basis is not prohibited. However, initiating new hedging relationships with existing derivatives may not qualify for hedge accounting if the ineffectiveness caused by the derivatives' 'non-zero' fair value is too great to satisfy the 80 per cent — 125 per cent range for effectiveness.

All-in-one hedges

A6.10.77 Under IAS 39, a derivative can be an instrument which is settled gross by delivery of the underlying asset and the payment of the price specified in the contract rather than by net settlement of the difference between the two legs. The implementation guidance states that such an instrument can be designated as a hedging instrument in a cash flow hedge of the variability of the consideration to be paid or received in the future transaction that will occur on gross settlement of the derivative contract itself, assuming the other cash flow hedge accounting criteria are met. Without the derivative, there would be an exposure to variability in the purchase or sale price. As the derivative eliminates the exposure, it qualifies as a hedging instrument. This applies to all fixed price contracts that are accounted for as derivatives under IAS 39.

Example – Gross settled derivative designated as an 'all-in-one hedge'

An entity enters into a forward contract to purchase a bond that will be settled by delivery. The forward contract is a derivative, because its term exceeds the regular way delivery period in the marketplace.

The entity may designate the forward as a cash flow hedge of the variability of the consideration to be paid to acquire the bond (a future transaction), even though the derivative is the contract under which the bond will be acquired. [IAS 39 para IG F2.5].

A6.10.78 Such 'all-in-one hedge' accounting strategy can be beneficial to entities. For instance, if an entity enters into a fixed price contract that falls to be accounted for as a derivative under IAS 39, the contract would be recognised at fair value with gains and losses recognised in profit or loss. By applying an all-in-one hedge accounting strategy, the entity is able to defer gains and losses on the hedging instrument in equity under cash flow hedge accounting until the hedged transaction occurs. In other words, the entity is able to keep gains and losses from being recognised in profit or loss on what is effectively a fixed price purchase or sale commitment.

Internal hedging instruments

A6.10.79 Entities with sophisticated central treasury functions often use internal hedging transactions to 'transfer' interest rate and currency risk to the treasury group. For instance, central treasury may enter into internal derivative contracts such as forward contracts and swaps with subsidiaries and various divisions of a consolidated group with the objective of 'converting' all financial assets and liabilities of those operating units to variable rate instruments in the reporting currency. Central treasury will assess its exposure to various currencies and to interest rate risk and enter into external forward contracts and swaps to manage those risks on a centralised basis, thereby generating economies of scale and pricing efficiency.

A6.10.80 Consistent with paragraph A6.10.36 above, internal derivative contracts used to transfer risk exposures between different companies within a group or divisions within a single legal entity cannot be designated as hedging instruments if the derivative contracts are *internal* to the entity being reported on. It follows that internal derivative contracts cannot be designated as hedging instruments in the consolidated financial statements. Nor can they be designated as hedging instruments in the individual or separate financial statements of a legal entity for hedging transactions between divisions in the entity. IAS 39 makes it clear that only instruments that involve a party external to the reporting entity (that is, a group, segment or an individual entity that is being reported on) can qualify as designated hedging instruments.

A6.10.81 However, if an internal contract is offset with an external party, the external contract may be regarded as the hedging instrument and the hedging relationship may qualify for hedge accounting. [IAS 39 para IG F1.4]. In such situations, the hedging relationship consists of the external instrument and the item that was the subject of the internal hedge. The internal derivative is often used as a tracking mechanism to relate the external derivative to the hedged item. Indeed, many entities take advantage of this provision in IAS 39 that allows them to net risk through a central treasury centre and thereafter hedge the net exposure by entering into external contracts with third parties. This avoids the cost of each subsidiary entering into contracts with third parties, some of which may duplicate each other. The following example illustrates the situations described above.

Example – Internal derivative contracts

The banking division of Entity A enters into an internal interest rate swap with the trading division of the same entity. The purpose is to hedge the interest rate risk exposure of a loan (or group of similar loans) in the loan portfolio. Under the swap, the banking division pays fixed interest payments to the trading division and receives variable interest rate payments in return.

If a hedging instrument is not acquired from an external party, IAS 39 does not allow hedge accounting treatment for the hedging transaction undertaken by the banking and trading divisions. This is because only derivatives that involve a party external to the entity can be designated as hedging instruments. [IAS 39 para 73]. Furthermore, any gains or losses on intra-group or intra-entity transactions are eliminated on consolidation. Therefore, transactions between different divisions within entity A do not qualify for hedge accounting treatment in entity A's financial statements. Similarly, transactions between different entities within a group do not qualify for hedge accounting treatment in entity A's consolidated financial statements.

However, if in addition to the internal swap in the above example the trading division enters into an interest rate swap or other contract with an external party that offsets the exposure hedged in the internal swap, hedge accounting is permitted under IAS 39. For the purposes of IAS 39, the hedged item is the loan (or group of similar loans) in the banking division and the hedging instrument is the external interest rate swap or other contract.

The trading division may aggregate several internal swaps or portions of them that are not offsetting each other and enter into a single third party derivative contract that offsets the aggregate exposure. Under IAS 39, such external hedging transactions may qualify for hedge accounting treatment provided that the hedged items in the banking division are identified and the other conditions for hedge accounting are met. It should be noted, however, that hedge accounting is not permitted where the hedged items are held-to-maturity investments and the hedged risk is the exposure to interest rate changes. [IAS 39 para IG F1.4].

6A.10.82 IAS 39 provides a very useful summary of its application to internal hedging transactions that is reproduced below.

- The standard does not preclude an entity from using internal derivative contracts for risk management purposes and it does not preclude internal derivatives from being accumulated at the treasury level or some other central location so that risk can be managed on an entity-wide basis or at some higher level than the separate legal entity or division.
- Internal derivative contracts between two *separate entities* within a consolidated group can qualify for hedge accounting by those entities in their individual or separate financial statements, even though the internal contracts are not offset by derivative contracts with a party external to the consolidated group.
- Internal derivative contracts between two *separate divisions* within the same legal entity can qualify for hedge accounting in that legal entity's individual or separate financial statements only if those contracts are offset by derivative contracts with a party external to the legal entity.
- Internal derivative contracts between separate divisions within the same legal entity and between separate entities within the consolidated group can qualify for hedge accounting in the consolidated financial statements only if the internal contracts are offset by derivative contracts with a party external to the consolidated group.
- If the internal derivative contracts are not offset by derivative contracts with external parties, the use of hedge accounting by group entities and divisions using internal contracts must be reversed on consolidation.

[IAS 39 para IG F1.4].

Offsetting internal hedging instruments

A6.10.83 As noted in the example in paragraph A6.10.79 above, central treasury often, before laying off the risk, first nets off internal derivative contracts against each other and then enters into a single third party derivative contract that offsets the net exposure. The circumstances in which such a single external contract can be treated as a hedging instrument on consolidation is considered below in the context of interest rate risk and foreign currency risk management.

Example 1 – Offsetting internal derivative contracts used to manage interest rate risk

Entity A has a number of subsidiaries. All treasury activities of the group are undertaken by entity A. Individual subsidiaries intending to hedge their exposure to interest rate risk are required to enter into separate derivative contracts with entity A.

Entity A then aggregates the internal derivative contracts and enters into a single external derivative contract that offsets the internal derivative contracts on a net basis. For instance, Entity A may enter into three internal receive-fixed, pay-variable interest rate swaps (total notional amount of say C100m) that lay off the exposure to variable interest cash flows on variable rate liabilities in the three subsidiaries and one internal receive-variable, pay-fixed interest rate swap (notional amount of C80m) that lays off the exposure to variable interest cash flows on variable rate assets in another subsidiary. It then enters into receive-variable, pay-fixed interest rate swap (notional amount of C20m) with an external counterparty that exactly offsets the four internal swaps. It is assumed that the hedge accounting criteria are met.

In entity A's consolidated financial statements, the single offsetting external derivative would not qualify as a hedging instrument in a hedge of an overall net position, that is, it cannot be used to hedge all of the items that the four internal derivatives are hedging, as explained in paragraph A6.10.28 above.

However, as explained in paragraph A6.10.29 above, designating a part of the underlying items as the hedged position on a gross basis is permitted, that is, the external derivative can hedge C20m of variable rate liabilities totalling C100m. Therefore, even though the purpose of entering into the external derivative was to offset internal derivative contracts on a net basis, hedge accounting is permitted if the hedging relationship is defined and documented as a hedge of a part of the underlying cash inflows or cash outflows on a gross basis. [IAS 39 Para IG F2.15].

Example 2 – Offsetting internal derivative contracts hedging foreign currency fair value risk

An entity has a number of subsidiaries. Subsidiary A has trade receivables in foreign currency (FC) of 100, due in 60 days, which it hedges using a forward contract with the treasury centre (TC) subsidiary. Subsidiary B has payables of FC50, also due in 60 days, which it hedges using a forward contact with TC. TC nets the two internal derivatives and enters into a net external forward contract to pay FC50 and receive LC in 60 days.

At the end of month 1, FC weakens against LC. Subsidiary A incurs a foreign exchange loss of LC10 on its receivables, offset by a gain of LC10 on its forward contract with TC. Subsidiary B makes a foreign exchange gain of LC5 on its payables offset by a loss of LC5 on its forward contract with TC. TC makes a loss of LC10 on its internal forward contract with subsidiary A, a gain of LC5 on its internal forward contract with subsidiary B, and a gain of LC5 on its external forward contract. At the end of month 1, the following entries are made in the individual or separate financial statements of subsidiary A, subsidiary B and TC.

Hedge accounting entries	Receivable	Dr (Cr) Payable	Derivative	P &L
Subsidiary A				
Recognition of loss on receivable	(10)			10
Recognition of gain on internal derivative			10	(10)
Subsidiary B				
Recognition of gain on payable		5		(5)
Recognition of loss on internal derivative			(5)	5
Central Treasury (TC)				
Recognition of loss on internal derivative with A			(10)	10
Recognition of gain on internal derivative with B			5	(5)
Recognition of gain on external derivative			5*	(5)
* External derivative				

The above entries are recorded in the individual financial statements of the three entities. In this case, no hedge accounting is required because gains and losses on the internal derivatives and the offsetting losses and gains on the hedged receivables and payables are recognised immediately in the income statements of entity A and entity B without hedge accounting.

In the consolidated financial statements, the internal derivative transactions are eliminated. In economic terms, the payable in B hedges FC50 of the receivables in A. The external forward contract in TC hedges the remaining FC50 of the receivable in A. Hedge accounting is not necessary in the consolidated financial statements, because monetary items are measured at spot foreign exchange rates under IAS 21 irrespective of whether hedge accounting is applied.

The net balances before and after eliminating the accounting entries relating to the internal derivatives are the same, as set out below. Accordingly, there is no need to make any further accounting entries on consolidation to meet the requirements of IAS 39.

	Receivable	Dr (Cr) Payable	Derivative	P &L
Consolidation				
Receivable in A	(10)			
Payable in B		5		
External derivative			5	

[IAS 39 para IG F1.7].

Example 3 – Offsetting internal derivative contracts hedging foreign currency cash flow risk

An entity has a number of subsidiaries. Subsidiary A has a highly probable future revenues of FC200 on which it expects to receive cash in 90 days. B has highly probable future expenses of FC500 (advertising cost), also to be paid for in 90 days. Entity A and entity B enter into separate forward contracts with TC to hedge these exposures and TC enters into an external forward contract to receive FC300 in 90 days.

FC weakens at the end of month 1.

A incurs a 'loss' of LC20 on its anticipated revenues because the LC value of these revenues decreases. This is offset by a 'gain' of LC20 on its forward contract with TC.

B incurs a 'gain' of LC50 on its anticipated advertising cost because the LC value of the expense decreases. This is offset by a 'loss' of LC50 on its transaction with TC.

TC incurs a 'gain' of LC50 on its internal transaction with B, a 'loss' of LC20 on its internal transaction with A and a loss of LC30 on its external forward contract.

Entity A and entity B complete the necessary documentation, the hedges are effective, and both entity A and entity B qualify for hedge accounting in their individual financial statements. A defers the gain of LC20 on its internal derivative transaction in a hedging reserve in equity and B defers the loss of LC50 in its hedging reserve in equity. TC does not claim hedge accounting, but measures both its internal and external derivative positions at fair value, which net to zero. At the end of month 1, the following entries are made in the individual or separate financial statements of A, B and TC.

		Dr (Cr)	
Hedge accounting entries at end of month 1	**Derivative**	**Equity**	**P&L**
Subsidiary A			
Recognition of gain on internal derivative with TC	20	(20)	
Subsidiary B			
Recognition of loss on internal derivative with TC	(50)	50	
Subsidiary TC			
Recognition of loss on internal derivative with A	(20)		20
Recognition of gain on internal derivative with B	50		(50)
Recognition of loss on external derivative	(30)*		30
* External derivative			

For the consolidated financial statements, TC's external forward contract on FC300 is designated, at the beginning of month 1, as a hedging instrument of the first FC300 of B's highly probable future expenses. IAS 39 requires that in the consolidated financial statements at the end of month 1, the accounting effects of the internal derivative transactions must be eliminated. However, the net balances before and after elimination of the accounting entries relating to the internal derivatives are the same, as set out below. Accordingly, there is no need to make any further accounting entries in order for the requirements of IAS 39 to be met.

Consolidation	Derivative	Equity	P&L
Recognition of loss on external derivative	(30)	30	

[IAS 39 para IG F1.7].

Example 4 – Offsetting internal derivative contracts hedging fair value and cash flow risks

Assume that the exposures and the internal derivative transactions are a combination of the transactions is in examples 2 and 3 above. However, instead of entering into two external derivatives to hedge separately the fair value and cash flow exposures, TC enters into a single net external derivative to receive FC250 in exchange for LC in 90 days.

TC has four internal derivatives, two maturing in 60 days and two maturing in 90 days. These are offset by a net external derivative maturing in 90 days. The interest rate differential between FC and LC is minimal and, therefore, the ineffectiveness resulting from the mismatch in maturities is expected to have a minimal effect on profit or loss in TC.

As in examples 2 and 3, subsidiary A and subsidiary B apply hedge accounting for their cash flow hedges and TC measures its derivatives at fair value. Subsidiary A defers a gain of LC20 on its internal derivative transaction in equity and subsidiary B defers a loss of LC50 on its internal derivative transaction in equity.

At the end of month 1, the following entries are made in the individual or separate financial statements of subsidiary A, subsidiary B and TC.

			Dr (Cr)		
Hedge accounting entries	**Receivable**	**Payable**	**Derivative**	**Equity**	**P&L**
Subsidiary A					
Loss on receivable	(10)				10
Gain on internal derivative with TC (FV)			10		(10)
Gain on internal derivative with TC (CF)			20	(20)	
	(10)		30	(20)	-
Subsidiary B					
Gain on payable		5			(5)
Loss on internal derivative with TC (FV)			(5)		5
Loss on internal derivative with TC (CF)			(50)	50	
		5	**(55)**	**50**	**-**

Subsidiary TC		
Loss on internal derivative with A (FV)	(10)	10
Loss on internal derivative with A (FV)	(20)	20
Gain on internal derivative with B (CF)	5	(5)
Gain on internal derivative with B (CF)	50	(50)
Loss on external contract (Net)	(25)*	25
* External derivative	-	-

The gross amounts relating to fair value of monetary assets and liabilities and the forecast transactions in subsidiary A and subsidiary B are as follows:

	Dr (Cr) Monetary items		Dr (Cr) Forecast transactions	
Subsidiary A	100			200
Subsidiary B		50	500	

For the consolidated financial statements, the following designations are made at the beginning of month 1:

- The payable of FC50 in entity B is designated as a hedge of the first FC50 of the highly probable future revenues in entity A (non-monetary item designated as a hedging instrument hedging foreign exchange risk). Therefore, at the end of month 1, the following entries are made in the consolidated financial statements: Dr Payable LC5; Cr Equity LC5.
- The receivable of FC100 in entity A is designated as a hedge of the first FC100 of the highly probable future expenses in entity B (non-monetary item designated as a hedging instrument in hedging foreign exchange risk). Therefore, at the end of month 1, the following entries are made in the consolidated financial statements: Dr Equity LC10, Cr Receivable LC10.
- The external forward contract on FC250 in TC is designated as a hedge of the next FC250 of highly probable future expenses in entity B. Therefore, at the end of month 1, the following entries are made in the consolidated financial statements: Dr Equity LC25; Cr External forward contract LC25.

In the consolidated financial statements at the end of month 1, IAS 39 requires the accounting effects of the internal derivative transactions to be eliminated. The effect of the above entries are summarised below:

Consolidation	Receivable	Payable	External derivative	Equity
Hedge accounting entries	(10)	5	(25)	30

As can be seen, the total net balances before and after elimination of the accounting entries relating to the internal derivatives are the same, as set out above. Accordingly, there is no need to make any further accounting entries to meet the requirements of IAS 39. [IAS 39 para IG F1.7].

A6.10.84 An entity's risk management objectives and strategies may require an entity to enter into a master netting agreement with a counterparty under which the entity is required to settle all external derivative contracts with that counterparty on a net basis. Although netting arrangements imply that an entity is able to set off profitable and loss making contracts against each other, this, in itself, would not preclude the external derivative contracts from being designated as hedging instruments.

Example 1 – External derivative contracts that are settled net

Entity A has a number of subsidiaries. All the group's treasury activities are undertaken by entity A. Individual subsidiaries intending to hedge their exposure to interest rate risk are required to enter into separate derivative contracts with entity A, which in turn enters into a separate offsetting matching derivative contract with a single external counterparty B. For instance, if entity A enters into an intra-group receive 5% fixed, pay LIBOR or interest rate swap, then entity A would also enter into a separate offsetting pay 5% fixed, receive LIBOR interest swap with counterparty B.

Although each of the external derivative contracts is formally documented as a separate contract, only the net of the payments on all of the external derivative contracts is settled by entity A, as there is a netting agreement with the external counterparty B.

The individual external derivative contracts, such as the pay 5% fixed, receive-LIBOR interest rate swap above, can be designated as hedging instruments of underlying gross exposures, such as the exposure to changes in variable interest payments on the pay-LIBOR borrowing above, in the group's consolidated financial statements, even though the external derivatives are settled on a net basis.

External derivative contracts that are legally separate contracts and serve a valid business purpose, such as laying off risk exposures on a gross basis, qualify as hedging instruments even if those external contracts are settled on a net basis with the same external counterparty, provided the hedge accounting criteria in IAS 39 are met. [IAS 39 para IG F2.16].

It may well be that by entering into the external offsetting contracts and including them in the centralised portfolio, entity A is no longer able to evaluate the exposures on a net basis. As a result, it may decide to manage the portfolio of offsetting external derivatives separately from the entity's other exposures. Thus, it enters into an additional, single derivative to offset the portfolio's risk.

In this situation, the individual external derivative contracts in the portfolio can still be designated as hedging instruments of underlying gross exposures. This is so even if the final external derivative is affected with the same counterparty under the same netting arrangement and, as a result, may net to zero.

The purpose of structuring the external derivative contracts in the above manner, which is consistent with the entity's risk management objectives and strategies, constitutes a substantive business purpose. Therefore, external derivative contracts that are legally separate contracts and serve a valid business purpose qualify as hedging instruments. In other words, hedge accounting is not precluded simply because the entity has entered into a swap that mirrors exactly the terms of another swap with the same counterparty if there is a substantive business purpose for structuring the transactions separately. [IAS 39 paras IG F2.16, IG F1.14].

Non-derivative financial instruments

A6.10.85 As stated in paragraph A6.10.52 above, a non-derivative financial asset or liability may not be designated as a hedging instrument, except as a hedge of foreign currency risk. Therefore, an entity can use foreign currency denominated monetary assets and liabilities as hedging instruments in hedges of foreign currency risk. This means that foreign currency cash deposits, loans and receivables, available-for-sale monetary items and held-to-maturity investments carried at amortised cost may be designated as a hedging instrument in a hedge of foreign currency risk. The following examples illustrate the type of situations in which a non-derivative financial instrument can be designated as a hedging instrument.

Example 1 – Hedging with a non-derivative the fair value exposure of an available-for-sale bond

Entity J, whose functional currency is the Japanese yen, has issued US$5m 5 year fixed rate debt. It also owns a US$5m 5 year fixed rate bond that it has classified as available-for-sale. Entity J intends to designate its US dollar liability as a hedging instrument in a fair value hedge of the entire fair value exposure of its US dollar bond.

The total change in bond's fair value is a function of interest rate risk, currency risk and credit risk. The debt instrument is a non-derivative that cannot be used to hedge the entire fair value exposure of the bond. However, the debt instrument can be designated as a hedge of the foreign currency component of the bond in either a fair value or cash flow hedge.

In this situation, hedge accounting is unnecessary since the amortised cost of the hedging instrument and the hedged item are both remeasured using closing rates with any differences arising in the period recognised in profit or loss in accordance with IAS 21. In other words, there is a natural offset regardless of whether entity J designates the relationship as a cash flow hedge or a fair value hedge. Any gain or loss on the non-derivative hedging instrument designated as a cash flow hedge is immediately recognised in profit or loss in accordance with IAS 39 paragraph 100 to correspond with the recognition of the change in spot rate on the hedged item in profit or loss. [IAS 39 para IG F1.1].

Example 2 – Hedging a firm commitment with a non-derivative financial instrument

Entity J's functional currency is the Japanese yen. It has issued a fixed rate debt instrument with semi-annual interest payments that matures in 2 years with principal due at maturity of US$5 million. It has also entered into a fixed price sales commitment for US$5 million that matures in 2 years and is not accounted for as a derivative because it meets the exemption for normal sales. Entity J intends to designate the fixed rate debt instrument as a hedge of the entire fair value change of the firm sales commitment.

The US dollar liability cannot be designated as a fair value hedge of the *entire* fair value exposure of its fixed price sales commitment and qualify for hedge accounting, because it is a non-derivative. However, as IAS 39 permits the designation of a non-derivative asset or liability as a hedging instrument in either a cash flow hedge or a fair value hedge of foreign exchange risk, entity J can designate its US dollar liability as a cash flow hedge of the foreign currency exposure associated with the future receipt of US dollars on the fixed price sales commitment.

Any gain or loss on the non-derivative hedging instrument that is recognised in equity during the period preceding the future sale is recognised in profit or loss when the sale takes place (see further para A6.10.121 below). [IAS 39 para IG F1.2].

Example 3 – Hedging a foreign currency exposure in a net investment with a hedging instrument denominated in a different currency

An entity with a Sing$ functional currency has an investment in a subsidiary in Hong Kong with a HK$ functional currency. Since the HK$ is linked to the US$, management decides to designate a US dollar borrowing as the hedging instrument in a hedge of its net investment.

Management may use a US$ borrowing to hedge a net investment denominated in HK$ if it is highly correlated to that currency, there is qualitative evidence to support the relationship and actual results are in the range of 80-125%. It is possible to designate a borrowing in one foreign currency as a hedge of a net investment in another currency with any ineffectiveness recognised in profit or loss. However, the requirements of paragraph AG105 of IAS 39 – that the hedging instrument is expected to be highly effective – is likely to prevent the use of hedge accounting for most currency pairs. A high degree of correlation between the two currencies would be achieved if one of the currencies was formally pegged to the other, as in this case, but for hedge accounting to be possible, it must be reasonable to assume that this correlation will continue. Some ineffectiveness will arise as a result of inefficiencies in the linking mechanism.

A6.10.86 Consistent with paragraph A6.10.60 above, a proportion of a non-derivative financial instrument, such as 50 per cent of the carrying amount of a foreign currency liability, may be designated as the hedging instrument. However, as stated in paragraph A6.10.61 above, an entity cannot treat the cash flows of only a proportion of the period during which a non-derivative instrument designated as a hedge against foreign currency risk remains outstanding and exclude the other cash flows from the designated hedging relationship. For example, the cash flows during the first three years of a ten – year borrowing denominated in a foreign currency cannot qualify as a hedging instrument in a cash flow hedge of the first three years of revenue in the same foreign currency.

Items that do not qualify as hedging instruments

A6.10.87 Generally, financial assets and financial liabilities whose fair value cannot be reliably measured cannot be hedging instruments. This means that an investment in an unquoted equity instrument that is not carried at fair value because its fair value cannot be reliably measured, or a derivative that is linked to and must be settled by, delivery of such an unquoted equity instrument cannot be designated as a hedging instrument. [IAS 39 para AG 96].

A6.10.88 An entity's own equity instruments are not financial assets or financial liabilities of the entity and, therefore, cannot be designated as hedging instruments. [IAS 39 para AG 97]. Similarly, minority interests in consolidated financial statements are treated as part of equity and, hence, cannot be designated as hedging instruments in the consolidated financial statements.

A6.10.88.1 Firm commitments and forecast transactions can not be designated as hedging instruments since they are not normally recognised in the financial statements. However, if the foreign currency component of the sales commitment is required to be separated as an embedded derivative under paragraph 11 of IAS 39 and paragraph AG33(d) of IAS 39, it could be designated as a hedging instrument in a hedge of the exposure to changes in the fair value of the maturity amount of the debt attributable to foreign currency risk. [IAS 39 para IG F1.2].

The hedge accounting models

A6.10.89 Hedge accounting recognises the offsetting effects on profit or loss of changes in the fair values of the hedging instrument and the hedged item. Hedge accounting may be applied to three types of hedging relationships:

- Fair value hedges (see para A6.10.91 below).
- Cash flow hedges (see para A6.10.106 below).
- Hedges of a net investment in a foreign operation (see para A6.10.124 below).

[IAS 39 para 86].

Risk reduction and hedge accounting

A6.10.90 IAS 39 does not require risk reduction on an entity-wide basis as a condition for hedge accounting. Exposure is assessed on a transaction basis. IAS 39 focuses on the risks inherent in an individual item, without requiring en entity-wide risk reduction test. For example, an entity may have a fixed rate asset and a fixed rate liability, each having the same principal amount. Under the instrument's terms, interest payments on the asset and liability occur in the same period and the net cash flow is always positive, because the interest rate on the asset exceeds the interest rate on the liability. The entity may decide to enter into an interest rate swap to receive a floating interest rate and pay a fixed interest rate on a notional amount equal to the asset's principal and designate the interest rate swap as a fair value hedge of the fixed rate asset. Although the effect of the interest rate swap on an entity-wide basis is to create an exposure to interest rate changes that did not previously exist, hedge accounting may be applied to this hedge relationship provided that the relevant hedge accounting criteria are met. [IAS 39 para IG F2.6].

Fair value hedges

Definition

A6.10.91 A 'fair value hedge' is a hedge of the exposure to changes in fair value of a recognised asset, liability or unrecognised firm commitment, or portion thereof, that is attributable to a particular risk and could affect profit or loss. [IAS 39 para 86(a)].

A6.10.92 Examples of some fair value hedges that often occur in practice are shown below:

Hedges of market price risk exposure	**Fair value exposure**
An entity fixes the value of its commodity inventory by entering into a commodity futures contract.	The entity is hedging the risk of changes in the inventory's overall fair value.
An entity purchases a put option to protect the fall in value of its quoted equity investments.	The entity is hedging the risk of fall in the fair value of the equity securities below the option's strike price.
Hedges of interest rate exposures	
An entity with fixed rate debt converts the debt into a floating rate using an interest rate swap.	The entity is hedging the risk of changes in the fair value of the debt due to changes in interest rate.
Hedges of foreign currency exposures	
An entity enters into a binding contract to purchase machinery for a fixed amount in foreign currency at a future date by entering into a forward foreign exchange contract.	The entity is hedging the risk of changes in the purchase price of machinery due to changes in foreign exchange rate.
An entity enters into a forward contract to hedge a foreign currency receivable or a payable due for settlement in six months' time.	The entity is hedging the risk of changes in the carrying amount of the receivable or payable due to changes in foreign exchange rate.

Fair value hedge accounting

A6.10.93 Under IAS 39, if a fair value hedge meets the hedge accounting conditions discussed in paragraph A6.10.137 below during the period, it should be accounted for as follows:

- the gain or loss from re-measuring the hedging instrument at fair value (for a derivative hedging instrument) or the foreign currency component of its carrying amount measured in accordance with IAS 21 (for a non-derivative hedging instrument) should be recognised in profit or loss; and

- the gain or loss on the hedged item attributable to the hedged risk adjusts the carrying amount of the hedged item and is recognised in profit or loss. This applies even if the hedged item is an available-for-sale financial asset or if it is otherwise measured at cost.

[IAS 39 para 89].

A6.10.94 As stated in the second bullet point above, where the hedged item is an available-for-sale financial asset, the gain or loss attributable to the risk being hedged is recognised in profit or loss, rather than equity, although the remainder of any fair value change is still recognised in equity (see example in para A6.10.187 below).

A6.10.95 The standard explains that if only particular risks attributable to a hedged item are hedged, recognised changes in the hedged item's fair value unrelated to the hedged risk are recognised in accordance with paragraph 55 of IAS 39 (see section 9). This means that changes in fair value of a hedged financial asset or financial liability that is not part of the hedging relationship would generally be accounted as follows:

- For instruments measured at amortised cost, such changes would not be recognised.
- For instruments measured at fair value through profit or loss, such changes would be recognised in profit or loss in any event.
- For available-for-sale financial assets, such changes would be recognised in equity as explained above. However, exceptions to this would include foreign currency gains and losses on monetary items and impairment losses, which would be recognised in profit or loss in any event.

A6.10.96 If the fair value hedge is fully effective, the gain or loss on the hedging instrument would exactly offset the loss or gain on the hedged item attributable to the risk being hedged and there would be no net effect in profit or loss. However, this would rarely be the case and often some difference would arise. The recognition of this difference in profit or loss is commonly referred to as hedge ineffectiveness. Hedge ineffectiveness is considered further from paragraph A6.10.184 below.

A6.10.97 An in-depth application of fair value hedge accounting for a hedge of interest rate risk of a fixed rate debt instrument using an interest rate swap (including full prospective and retrospective hedge effectiveness testing) is illustrated in the comprehensive examples included at the end of this section.

Example – Fair value hedge of inventory (commodity)

On 1 October 20X5, a metal refining entity has 1m troy ounces of silver in its inventory. The silver is recorded at an average historical cost of C5.00 per ounce (C5m total value). To protect the inventory from a decline in silver prices, the entity hedges its position by selling 200 silver futures contracts on a specified commodity exchange. Each contract is for 5,000 troy ounces of silver priced at C5.55 per ounce. The futures contracts mature on 31 March 20X6, which is the date that the entity has scheduled delivery of the entire silver inventory to its customer at the spot price at that date.

The entity designates the futures contract as a fair value hedge of its silver inventory (that is, it is hedging changes in the inventory's fair value). Based on historical data, the entity determines and documents that changes in the fair value of the silver futures contracts will be highly effective in offsetting all changes in the fair value of the silver inventory.

On 31 December 20X5 (the entity's financial year end) and on 31 March 20X6, the entity determines that the fair value of its silver inventory has declined cumulatively by C160,000 and C320,000 respectively. The fair value of the silver inventory has declined by more than the spot price of silver, because the fair value of the inventory is influenced by other factors such as changes in expected labour and transport costs.

On 31 March 20X6, the entity closes out its futures. On the same day it also sells the entire silver inventory at the spot price of C5.25 per ounce.

The following data is relevant:

Date	Spot price	Futures price (for delivery on 31 March 20X6)	Fair value of futures contract assuming yield curve is flat at 6% per year*
	C	C	C
1 Oct 20X5	5.40	5.55	-
31 Dec 20X5	5.30	5.40	147,830
31 Mar 20X6	5.25	5.25	300,000

*Fair value = $(1\text{m ounces} \times (5.55 - 5.40))/1.06^{1/4} = C147,830$

*Fair value = $(1\text{m ounces} \times (5.55 - 5.25)) = C300,000$

The entity assesses hedge effectiveness by comparing the entire change in the fair value of the futures contract to the entire change in the fair value of the silver inventory, based on futures prices. A summary of the hedge's effectiveness, calculated using the dollar offset method discussed in paragraph A6.10.164, is shown below.

Date	Change in full fair value of future contracts Gain (loss)	Change in full fair value of inventory Gain (loss)	Effectiveness ratio for the period
	C	C	C
31 Dec 20X5	147,830	160,000	92.39
31 Mar 20X6	152,170	160,000	95.11

Ignoring any margin payments on the futures contract, the accounting entries from inception of the hedge to its termination following closure of the future contracts (which is settled daily) and delivery of inventory are as follows:

		Dr (Cr)			
Date	**Transaction**	**Cash**	**Futures contract**	**Inventory**	**Profit or loss**
		C	**C**	**C**	**C**
31 Dec 20X5	Change in fair value of futures contract		147,830		(147,830)
31 Dec 20X5	Change in fair value of silver stock			(160,000)	160,000
31 Dec 20X5	Cumulative cash settlement for period*	147,830	(147,830)	-	-
	Entity A's year end	147,830	-	(160,000)	12,170
31 Mar 20X6	Change in fair value of futures contract		152,170		(152,170)
31 Mar 20X6	Change in fair value of silver stock			(160,000)	160,000
31 Mar 20X6	Sale of silver @ 5.25	5,250,000			(5,250,000)
31 Mar 20X6	Cost of sale			(4,680,000)	4,680,000
31 Mar 20X6	Cumulative cash settlement for period*	152,170	(152,170)	-	-
		5,550,000	-	(5,000,000)	(550,000)

* Futures contracts are settled daily. The entries summarises the daily journals for each day throughout the quarter.

The fair value hedge example illustrates that if the entity had not hedged the change in fair value of the silver stock, it would have made a gain of C250,000 (revenue of C5,250,000 less cost of sales of C5,000,000). By entering into the hedge the company has 'locked in' a net profit of C550,000, that is, gross profit of C570,000 (revenue of C5,250,000 less cost of sales of C4,680,000) less loss of C20,000 on the hedging activity. In this example, the hedge was not 100% effective, which lead to some ineffectiveness being recognised in profit or loss.

At the entity's year end, the derivative asset and the carrying value of the inventory amounted to C147,830 and C4,840,000. The carrying value of C4,840,000 is neither cost nor realisable value nor fair value. It is cost less a hedging adjustment. The gain on the derivative offsets the loss on the inventory in profit or loss, except for ineffectiveness of C12,170. This matching is achieved by accelerating the recognition in the profit or loss of part of the gain or loss on the silver inventory. In other words part of the gain or loss that would normally be recognised only on the sale of the inventory is recorded earlier. Therefore, in the case of a fair value hedge, hedge accounting accelerates income recognition on the hedged item to match the profit or loss effect of the hedging instrument.

Adjustments to hedged items

A6.10.98 The adjustment to the carrying amount of a hedged asset or liability that are made to the hedged item due to fair value changes that are attributable to a specific hedged risk, as stated in the second bullet point in paragraph A6.10.93 above, are dealt with in accordance with the normal accounting treatment for that item. The adjustment is often referred to as a 'basis adjustment', because the hedging gain or loss adjusts the carrying value of the hedged item resulting in an amount that is neither cost nor fair value. Thus, in the above example, changes in fair value of silver are adjusted against the carrying value of silver inventory and the adjusted carrying amount becomes the cost basis for the purposes of applying the lower of cost and net realisable value test under IAS 2, 'Inventories'. In other words, the basis adjustment remains part of the carrying value of inventory and enters into the determination of earnings when the inventory is sold.

A6.10.99 When the hedged item is an interest bearing financial instrument for which the effective interest rate method of accounting is used, any adjustment to the carrying amount of the hedged financial instrument should be amortised to profit or loss. The adjustment should be based on a recalculated effective interest rate at the date the amortisation begins and should be fully amortised by maturity. Amortisation may begin as soon as an adjustment exists and should begin no later than when the hedged item ceases to be adjusted for changes in its fair value attributable to the risk being hedged. However, if amortising using a re-calculated effective interest rate is not practicable, the adjustment should be amortised using a straight-line method. [IAS 39 para 92].

A6.10.100 The IASB decided to permit entities to defer amortisation of a basis adjustment until the hedged interest bearing financial instrument ceases to be basis adjusted in order to simplify the accounting and record keeping that an entity might otherwise have to undertake to track and properly account for such adjustments, as explained in the example below.

Example – Deferral of amortisation of basis adjustment

Entity A enters into an interest rate swap contract to hedge changes in the fair value of a fixed rate borrowing of C100m due for settlement in 5 years. The terms of the borrowing and the swap exactly match. Interest rates rise so that the borrowing's fair value falls to C90m and the swap's fair value changes from zero to – C10m.

Under fair value hedge accounting, the swap is carried as a liability of C10m (less any settlement paid). The carrying amount of the borrowing is reduced to C90m. Both the loss and the gain are recognised in the profit or loss. Under the amortised cost method, the C90m carrying amount of the liability would be amortised back up to C100m, giving rise to additional finance cost over the remaining period to maturity.

As explained above, the standard allows amortisation to be deferred until hedge accounting is discontinued. If the swap is in place until the borrowing's maturity date, the debt's carrying amount will be adjusted back to C100m through further hedge accounting adjustments. In other words, any fair value adjustments to the debt's carrying value would be reversed by maturity as the fair value of the liability immediately before settlement must be C100m. Therefore, no amortisation will be necessary.

However, if only the first 2 years of the debt instrument is hedged for interest rate risk and the entity chooses to defer amortisation until end of year 2 when hedge accounting ceases, a significant income statement impact could result in later periods. This is because the entity would need to 'catch up' the basis of the hedged item to its settlement amount of C100m over the remaining 3 years.

Hedges of firm commitments

A6.10.101 Hedges of firm commitments are generally treated as fair value hedges except in one situation. If a firm commitment has a price fixed in foreign currency, the standard allows the hedge of the foreign currency risk in the firm commitment to be accounted for as a cash flow hedge of the foreign currency risk. [IAS 39 para 87]. If a firm commitment has a fixed price in the functional currency of the entity rather than a price fixed in a foreign currency, there would be no cash flow variability in the entity's functional currency in the anticipated transaction and cash flow hedging would not be possible. For this reason, hedges of firm commitments, other than those denominated in a foreign currency, are accounted for as fair value hedges because the entity is exposed to changes in fair value of that commitment.

A6.10.102 When an unrecognised firm commitment to acquire an asset or assume a liability is designated as a hedged item in a fair value hedge, the accounting treatment is as follows:

- The subsequent cumulative change in the fair value of the firm commitment attributable to the hedged risk since inception of the hedge is recognised as an asset or a liability with a corresponding gain or loss recognised in profit or loss.
- The changes in the fair value of the hedging instrument are also recognised in profit or loss.
- When the firm commitment is fulfilled, the initial carrying amount of the asset or liability is adjusted to include the cumulative change in the firm commitment that was recognised in the balance sheet under point one above.

[IAS 39 paras 93, 94].

Example – Measurement of the fair value of a firm commitment

On 1 January 20X6 entity A enters into a firm commitment to purchase 100,000 widgets for C5 each in 6 month's time. On 31 March 20X6, the entity's year end, the market price of the widgets has increased to C6.

The fair value of a firm commitment represents the amount that an entity would have to pay, or the amount that it would receive, upon terminating the commitment. On 1 January 20X6, the company has an obligation to pay C500,000 in 6 month's time and a right to receive 100,000 widgets in 6 months. The initial value of the obligation and the right are generally equal, resulting in a net fair value of zero.

At 31 March 20X6 when the widget's market price increases to C6, the right's value to receive widgets increases. This is because the widget's value received in six months would be

C600,000, while the obligation to pay C500,000 in six months would remain the same, resulting in a fair value that reflects the C100,000 difference adjusted for the discount that is appropriate for the remaining three month duration of the commitment. The present value of the C100,000 represents the amount that the entity could reasonably expect to receive if the counterparty to the commitment were to terminate the commitment at 31 March 20X6.

Firm commitments represent rights and obligations that are assets and liabilities, even though they are generally not recorded. If entity A designates the firm commitment as a hedged item, it would account for the changes in the fair value of the hedged commitment due to changes in the market price of widgets in a manner similar to how that entity would account for any hedged asset or liability that it records. That is, changes in fair value (that are attributable to the risk that is being hedged) would be recognised in profit or loss and, on the balance sheet, recognised as an adjustment of the hedged item's carrying amount.

Because firm commitments normally are not recorded, accounting for the initial change in the fair value of the firm commitment would result in the entity recognising the firm commitment on the balance sheet. Therefore, in this example, the entity would record the present value of C100,000 as an asset on the balance sheet with a corresponding gain in profit or loss. A recognition of subsequent changes in fair value would adjust that recognised firm-commitment amount.

Discontinuing fair value hedge accounting

A6.10.103 Fair value hedge accounting should be discontinued prospectively if any of the following occurs:

- The hedging instrument expires or is sold, terminated or exercised. For this purpose, the replacement or rollover of a hedging instrument into another hedging instrument is not an expiration or termination if such replacement or rollover is part of the entity's documented hedging strategy.
- The hedge no longer meets the criteria for hedge accounting discussed in paragraph A6.10.137 below.
- The entity revokes the designation.

[IAS 39 para 91].

A6.10.104 When an entity ceases to apply hedge accounting because the hedge does not meet hedge effectiveness criteria, it should discontinue hedge accounting from the last date on which compliance with hedge effectiveness was demonstrated. However, if the event or change in circumstances that caused the hedging relationship to fail the effectiveness criteria can be identified and it can be demonstrated that the hedge was effective before the event or change in circumstances occurred, the entity should discontinue hedge accounting from the date of the event or change in circumstances. [IAS 39 para AG 113].

A6.10.105 The table below sets out the accounting treatment to be applied when fair value hedge accounting is discontinued.

Discontinuance of fair value hedges (including firm commitments)

Hedge termination events	**Hedging instrument**		**Hedged item**	
	Continue mark-to-market accounting	**Derecognise from the balance sheet**	**Derecognise from the balance sheet**	**Freeze basis adjustments**
	Note 1		**Note 2**	**Note 3**
Hedging instrument no longer exists (that is, sold, terminated, extinguished, exercised or expired)		✓		✓
The hedge no longer meets the criteria for hedge accounting (effectiveness)	✓			✓
The entity revokes the hedge designation	✓			✓
The hedged item is sold or extinguished	✓		✓	

Note 1 – The hedging instrument will continue to be marked to market, unless it is re-designated as a hedging instrument in a new hedge.

Note 2 – The derecognition of the hedged item occurs through profit or loss (for example, the firm commitment asset or liability or the gain or loss on sale or extinguishment of the hedged item (inclusive of fair value basis adjustments) is recognised in profit or loss).

Note 3 – The hedged item ceases to be adjusted for changes in its fair value attributable to the risk being hedged and continues to be accounted for in a manner that was applicable prior to it being hedged. Once the basis adjustment on the hedged item is frozen, it either:

- Continues as part of the carrying amount of the asset up to the date the carrying value is recovered through use or sale or the asset becomes impaired.
- Is amortised through profit or loss (for interest bearing financial instruments). Amortisation should begin no later than when the hedged item ceases to be adjusted for changes in its fair value attributable to the risk being hedged (see para A6.10.101 above).

Example 1 – Discontinuance of a fair value hedge of a bond

Two years ago, entity A issued at par a C4m, 5 year fixed interest rate bond. At the same time, it entered into a 5-year fixed-to-floating interest rate swap that it designated as a fair value hedge of the bond. After 2 years, the hedge fails a retrospective test and the entity determines it is no longer expected to be highly effective for the remaining 3 years of the hedge. At the date the hedge last passed an effectiveness test, the bond's carrying value included a cumulative adjustment of C0.2m, reflecting the change in the fair value of the hedged risk.

Entity A discontinues hedge accounting prospectively (that is, previous accounting entries are not reversed). If the reason for discontinuance is that the hedge failed an effectiveness test, hedge accounting is discontinued from the last date when the hedge was demonstrated to be effective.

The adjustments to the carrying amount of the hedged item to reflect the changes in fair value that are attributable to the hedged risk remain as part of the item's carrying value, but no further adjustments are made in future periods. When the hedged item is carried at amortised cost, these previous hedging adjustments are amortised over the item's remaining life by recalculating its effective interest rate, or on a straight-line basis if this is not practicable.

The adjusted carrying value of C4.2m will be the basis for calculating a new effective interest rate, starting from the last date the hedge passed an effectiveness test. The hedging adjustment of C0.2m is, therefore, recognised in profit or loss over the bond's remaining life.

Example 2 – Discontinuance of a fair value hedge of an available-for-sale investment

Entity A is a Swiss entity whose functional currency is the Swiss franc (CHF). Entity A buys an equity investment in entity X, which is classified as available-for-sale. Entity X's shares are listed only in the US in US dollars and it pays dividends in US dollars. The fair value at the date of purchase including transaction costs is US$10m.

Entity A does not want to be exposed to the risk of future losses if the US$ weakens against the CHF. It intends to hold the investment for 2 years and enters into a forward contract to sell US$ and receive CHF in 2 years, with a notional amount of US$9m to hedge US$9m of the fair value of the investment in entity X.

Entity A designates the forward contract as a fair value hedge of the currency risk on US$9m of its investment in entity X. This designation allows entity A to take the foreign exchange movements on US$9m of the investment to the income statement to offset the fair value changes in the derivative. The rest of the fair value movements in CHF for the instrument are retained in equity until the instrument is sold.

One year later, entity A believes that the US dollar is not likely to decline further and decides to discontinue the hedge and revoke the hedge designation. The hedge is demonstrated to have been highly effective up to the time it is discontinued.

Entity A discontinues hedge accounting prospectively (that is, previous accounting entries are not reversed). When the hedged item is an equity instrument classified as available-for-sale, all future changes in the instrument's fair value, including all changes related to exchange rate movements, are deferred in equity until the instrument is sold or impaired.

Cash flow hedges

Definition

A6.10.106 A 'cash flow hedge' is a hedge of the exposure to variability in cash flows that is attributable to a particular risk associated with a recognised asset or liability or a highly probable forecast transaction and could affect profit or loss. [IAS 39 para 86(b)].

A6.10.107 Examples of some cash flow hedges that often occur in practice are shown below:

Hedges of market price risk exposure	**Cash flow exposure**
An entity that has a highly probable sales of a commodity in the future at the then prevailing market price 'fixes' the selling price of the goods by entering into a futures contract.	The entity is hedging the risk of variability in the cash flows to be received on the sale due to changes in the good's market price.
Hedges of interest rate exposures	
An entity with floating rate debt converts the rate on the debt to a fixed rate using an interest rate swap.	The entity is hedging the risk of variability in interest payments due to changes in the interest rate specified for the debt.
An entity that has a highly probable issuance of fixed rate debt in the future at the then coupon rate enters into an interest rate swap to protect itself from the effects of changes in a specified interest rate that may occur before the debt is issued.	The entity is hedging the variability in the expected interest payments from the issuance of a debt due to changes in a specified interest rate on a debt expected to be issued within a specified period.
Hedges of foreign currency exposures	
An entity that has a highly probable sale of goods in foreign currency takes out a forward exchange contract to 'fix' the local (functional) currency price of the goods.	The entity is hedging the risk of changes in local (functional) currency amount of the sale due to changes in foreign exchange rates.
An entity enters into a forward contract to hedge a foreign currency receivable or a payable due to be settled in six months' time.	The entity is hedging the risk of changes in the amount receivable or payable on settlement in six month's time due to changes in the foreign exchange rates.

Forecast transactions

A6.10.108 A forecast transaction is an uncommitted but anticipated future transaction. [IAS 39 para 9]. To qualify for cash flow hedge accounting, the forecasted transaction should be specifically identifiable as a single transaction or a group of individual transactions. If the hedged transaction is a group of individual transactions, those individual transactions must share the same risk exposure for which they are designated as being hedged. Thus, a forecast purchase and a forecast sale cannot both be included in the same group of individual transactions that constitute the hedged transaction (see para A6.10.21 above).

A6.10.109 The key criterion for hedge accounting purposes is that the forecast transaction that is the subject of a cash flow hedge must be 'highly probable'. In IFRS terminology, probable means 'more likely than not'. Therefore, in the context of forecast transaction, the term 'highly probable' is taken to indicate a much greater likelihood of happening than the term 'more likely than not'. This is consistent with the IASB's use of highly probable in IFRS 5, 'Non-current asset held for sale and discontinued operations', where 'highly probable' is regarded as implying a significantly higher probability than 'more likely than not'. [IFRS 5 para BC81]. The other conditions are that the forecast transaction must be with a party that is external to the entity (see 6.10.14 above) and it presents an exposure to variations in cash flows for the hedged risk that could affect profit or loss (see para A6.10.12 above).

A6.10.110 IAS 39's implementation guidance explains that a transaction's probability should be supported by observable facts and the attendant circumstances and should not be based solely on management's intentions, because intentions are not verifiable. In assessing the likelihood that a transaction will occur, an entity should consider the following circumstances:

- The frequency of similar past transactions.
- The financial and operational ability of the entity to carry out the transaction.
- Substantial commitments of resources to a particular activity (for example, a manufacturing facility that can be used in the short run only to process a particular type of commodity).
- The extent of loss or disruption of operations that could result if the transaction does not occur.
- The likelihood that transactions with substantially different characteristics might be used to achieve the same business purpose (for example, an entity that intends to raise cash may have several ways of doing so, ranging from a short-term bank loan to an offering of ordinary shares).
- The entity's business plan.

[IAS 39 para IG F3.7].

A6.10.111 The length of time until a forecast transaction is projected to occur is also a factor in determining probability. Other factors being equal, the more distant a forecast transaction is, the less likely it is that the transaction would be regarded as highly probable and the stronger the evidence that would be needed to support an assertion that it is highly probable. For example, a transaction forecast to occur in five years may be less likely to occur than a transaction forecast to occur in one year. However, forecast interest payments for the next 20 years on a plain vanilla variable rate debt would typically be highly probable if supported by an existing contractual obligation and it is expected that the debt will not be paid early.

A6.10.112 In addition, other factors being equal, the greater a forecast transaction's physical quantity or future value in proportion to the entity's transactions of the same nature, the less likely it is that the transaction would be regarded as highly probable and the stronger the evidence that would be required to support an assertion that it is highly probable. For example, less evidence generally would be needed to support forecast sales of 100,000 units in the next month than 950,000 units in that month when recent sales have averaged 800,000 units per month for the past three months. [IAS 39 para IG F3.7].

A6.10.113 A history of having designated hedges of forecast transactions and then determining that the forecast transactions are no longer expected to occur would call into question both an entity's ability to predict forecast transactions accurately and the propriety of using hedge accounting in the future for similar forecast transactions. [IAS 39 para IG F3.7].

A6.10.114 The documentation that needs to be put in place before a forecast transaction can be designated as a hedged item is considered further from paragraph A6.10.139 below.

Cash flow hedge accounting

A6.10.115 Under IAS 39, if a cash flow hedge meets the hedge accounting conditions discussed in paragraph A6.10.137 below during the period, it should be accounted for as follows:

- the portion of the gain or loss on the hedging instrument that is determined to be an effective hedge should be recognised directly in equity through the statement of changes in equity; and
- the ineffective portion of the gain or loss on the hedging instrument should be recognised in profit or loss.

[IAS 39 para 95].

A6.10.116 In particular:

- the separate component of equity associated with the hedged item is adjusted to the *lesser* of the following (in absolute amounts):
  - the cumulative gain or loss on the hedging instrument from inception of the hedge; and
  - the cumulative change in fair value (present value) of the expected future cash flows on the hedged item from inception of the hedge;

- any remaining gain or loss on the hedging instrument or designated component of it (that is not an effective hedge) is recognised in profit or loss; and
- if an entity's documented risk management strategy for a particular hedging relationship excludes from the assessment of hedge effectiveness a specific component of the gain or loss or related cash flows on the hedging instrument, that excluded component of gain or loss is recognised in accordance with the instrument's normal classification. If the hedging instrument is a derivative, the excluded components can include the time value of an option or the interest element of a forward (see para A6.10.56 above) or a proportion, such as 50 per cent of a derivative (or non-derivative financial instrument for hedges of foreign currency risk) (see para A6.10.60 above). Changes in the value of those excluded components are recognised in profit or loss (unless, in the case a proportion of a derivative, the remaining portion is designated as the hedging instrument in a different cash flow hedge).

[IAS 39 para 96].

A6.10.117 The way in which an entity accounts for cash flow hedges is illustrated in the examples below. In addition, another more in-depth application of cash flow hedge accounting for a hedge of a highly probable foreign currency purchase of raw materials using a forward contract (including full prospective and retrospective hedge effectiveness testing) is given in illustration 2 at the end of this section.

Example 1 – Cash flow hedge of commodity sale

The facts are the same as in the example in paragraph A6.10.97 above, except that the entity decides to designate a silver forward contract as a cash flow hedge of the forecast sale of 1million troy ounces of silver to a customer that is expected to occur on 31 March 20X6. It is highly probable that the sale will occur based on its sales history with the customer. The entity is hedging it's exposure to change in cash flows from the highly probable sales. The futures contract entered into on 1 October 20X5 on a specified commodity exchange for 1 million troy ounces of silver at a forward price of C5.55 per ounce matures on 31 March 20X6 and will be settled net in cash. This is the date the entity expects to deliver 1 million troy ounces of silver to its customer at the forward price.

The hedging relationship qualifies for cash flow hedge accounting. The entity determines and documents the entire change in the full fair value of the forward contract will be highly effective in offsetting all the variability in cash flow from the expected sale based on the forward prices.

The entity prepares its financial statements to 31 December each year. The accounting entries from inception of the hedge to its termination following closure of the forward contract (which is settled daily) and the inventory's delivery are as follows:

Date	Transaction	Cash	Forward contract	Dr Cr Equity	Silver stock	Profit and loss
		C000	C000	C000	C000	C000
31 Dec 20X5	Change in fair value of fwd contract		147,830	(147,830)		
31 Mar 20X6	Change in fair value of fwd contract		152,170	(152,170)		
31 Mar 20X6	Sale of silver inventory	5,250,000				(5,250,000)
31 Mar 20X6	Cost of sale				(5,000,000)	5,000,000
31 Mar 20X6	Recycle of hedging gain from equity			300,000		(300,000)
31 Mar 20X6	Settlement of fwd contract	300,000	(300,000)			
		5,550,000	-	-	(5,000,000)	(550,000)

As can be seen from the above, through the hedge transaction, the entity has locked in a cash flow of C5.55 per troy ounce of silver, that is, C5,500,000. This is equivalent to the sale at spot rate plus the gain on the derivative.

Example 2 – Cash flow hedge of a variable rate debt

Entity A has a floating rate liability of C10m with 5 years remaining to maturity. It enters into a 5 year pay-fixed, receive-floating interest rate swap in the same currency and with the same principal terms as the liability to hedge the exposure to variable cash flow payments on the floating rate liability attributable to interest rate risk.

At inception, the swap's fair value is zero. Subsequently, there is an increase of C490,000 in the swap's fair value. This increase consists of a change of C500,000 resulting from an increase in market interest rates and a change of minus C10,000 resulting from an increase in the credit risk of the swap counterparty. There is no change in the fair value of the floating rate liability, but the fair value (present value) of the future cash flows needed to offset the exposure to variable interest cash flows on the liability increases by C500,000.

Entity A determines that although the hedge is not fully effective, because part of the change in the derivative's fair value is attributable to the counterparty's credit risk that is not reflected in the floating rate liability, the hedge is still highly effective. Therefore, entity A credits the effective portion of the change in fair value of the swap, that is, the net change in fair value of C490,000 to equity. There is no debit to profit or loss for the change in fair value of the swap attributable to the deterioration in the credit quality of the swap counterparty, because the cumulative change in the present value of the future cash flows needed to offset the exposure to variable interest cash flows on the hedged item, C500,000, exceeds the cumulative change in value of the hedging instrument, C490,000 (see para A6.10.117 above). If entity A concludes that the hedge is no longer highly effective, it discontinues hedge accounting prospectively as from the date the hedge ceased to be highly effective (see para A6.10.122 below).

Alternatively, if the change in the fair value of the swap increased to C510,000 of which C500,000 results from the increase in market interest rates and C10,000 from a decrease in the credit risk of the swap counterparty, there would be a credit to profit or loss of C10,000 for the change in the swap's fair value attributable to the improvement in the swap counterparty's credit quality. This is because the cumulative change in the value of the hedging instrument, C510,000 exceeds the cumulative change in the present value of the future cash flows needed to offset the exposure to variable interest cash flows on the hedged item, C500,000. The difference of C10,000 represents the ineffectiveness attributable to the derivative hedging instrument, the swap and is recognised in profit or loss. [IAS 39 para IG F5.2].

Reclassifying gains and losses from equity

A6.10.118 If a hedge of a forecast transaction subsequently results in the recognition of a financial asset or liability, the associated gains or losses that were recognised directly in equity (see para A6.10.116 above) should be reclassified into profit or loss in the same period or periods during which the asset acquired or liability assumed affects profit or loss (such as in the periods when interest expense or income is recognised). However, if an entity expects that all or a portion of a loss recognised in equity will not be recovered in one or more future periods, it should reclassify into profit or loss the amount that is not expected to be recovered. [IAS 39 para 97].

A6.10.119 If a hedge of a forecast transaction subsequently results in recognising a *non-financial* asset or liability (or a forecast transaction for a *non-financial* asset or liability becomes a firm commitment for which fair value hedge accounting is applied), then the entity should adopt either of the following approaches as its accounting policy and apply that policy consistently:

- It should reclassify the associated gains and losses that were recognised directly in equity into profit or loss in the same period or periods during which the asset acquired or liability assumed affects profit or loss (such as in the periods that depreciation or cost of sales is recognised). However, if an entity expects that all or a portion of a loss recognised directly in equity will not be recovered in one or more future periods, it should reclassify into profit or loss the amount that is not expected to be recovered.
- It should remove the associated gains and losses that were recognised directly in equity and include them in the initial cost or other carrying amount of the asset or liability (often referred to as 'basis adjustment').

[IAS 39 paras 98-99].

A6.10.120 For cash flow hedges other than those covered by paragraphs 6.10.118 and 6.10.119 above, amounts that had been recognised directly in equity should be recognised in profit or loss in the same period or periods during which the hedged forecast transaction affects profit or loss (for example, when a forecast sale occurs). [IAS 39 para 100].

Example 1 – Reclassification of derivative loss recorded in equity

Entity A regularly purchases inventory from a foreign supplier and designates a forecast purchase of particular inventory as the hedged item in a cash-flow hedge. At the date the inventory is purchased, a loss on the hedging instrument of C30 has accumulated in equity. In a subsequent period, the purchased inventory has a carrying amount of C100 (without any basis adjustment) and a fair value of C110. The entity expects to sell the inventory at a price equivalent to its fair value.

In this example, the entity determines that the combined value of the loss deferred in equity and the carrying amount of the inventory (that is, C130) exceeds the inventory's fair value of C110, such that a net loss of C20 on the hedged transaction will be recognised in a future period. Therefore, in accordance with the first bullet point in paragraph A6.10.119 above, the loss of C20 should immediately be reclassified into profit or loss since the entity determines that the loss cannot be recovered.

The same effect in profit or loss would result had the entity chosen to adjust the inventory's carrying value by the amount of the loss deferred in equity of C30 as noted in the last bullet point in paragraph A6.10.119 above. In that case, the carrying value of the inventory of C130 would be greater than fair value of C110 resulting in the recognition of an immediate loss of C20 in profit or loss in accordance with IAS 2, 'Inventory'.

Example 2 – Reclassification of derivative gain recorded in equity

Entity A regularly purchases inventory from a foreign supplier and designates a forecast future purchase of particular inventory as the hedged item in a cash-flow hedge. At the date that the inventory is purchased, a gain on the hedging instrument of C30 has accumulated in equity. In a subsequent period, the fair value of the purchased inventory, which has a carrying amount of C100 (no basis adjustment), declines to C80.

In accordance with IAS 2, the entity writes down the inventory to its net realisable value of C80 and recognises an impairment loss of C20. The entity should also reclassify from equity an equivalent amount of gain of C20 (that is, part of the total gain of C30 deferred in equity) to profit or loss. The effect of the above adjustments is that inventory is recorded at its net realisable value of C80, the gain deferred in equity is C10 and there is no net impact in profit or loss. The gain in equity of C10 would continue to be deferred until the hedged forecast transaction impacts profit or loss when the inventory is sold or there is a further reduction in fair value.

The same effect in profit or loss would result had the entity chosen to adjust the inventory's carrying value by the amount of the gain deferred in equity of C30. In that situation, the carrying value of the inventory of C70 would be less than fair value of C80 and there will be no immediate impact on profit or loss. The hedging gain of C10 included in the carrying value will affect profit or loss when the inventory is sold.

Discontinuing cash flow hedge accounting

A6.10.121 Cash flow hedge accounting should be discontinued prospectively if any of the following occurs:

- The hedging instrument expires or is sold, terminated or exercised.

For this purpose, the replacement or rollover of a hedging instrument into another hedging instrument is not an expiration or termination if such replacement or rollover is part of the entity's documented hedging strategy. In this case, the cumulative gain or loss on the hedging instrument that remains recognised directly in equity from the period when the hedge was effective should remain in equity until the forecast transaction occurs. Thereafter, it should be dealt with in accordance with paragraphs 6.10.118 to 6.10.120 above.

- The hedge no longer meets the criteria for hedge accounting discussed in paragraph A6.10.137 below.

  In this case, unless the next bullet point is also met, the cumulative gain or loss on the hedging instrument that remains recognised directly in equity from the period when the hedge was effective should remain in equity until the forecast transaction occurs. Thereafter, it should be dealt with in accordance with paragraphs 6.10.118 to 6.10.120 above.

- The forecast transaction is no longer expected to occur.

  In this case, the cumulative gain or loss on the hedging instrument that remains recognised directly in equity from the period when the hedge was effective should be recognised in profit or loss. However, a forecast transaction that is no longer highly probable (and, therefore, the hedge no longer meets the criteria for hedge accounting discussed in para A6.10.136 below) may still be expected to occur, in which case, the cumulative gain or loss is treated in the same way as set out in the first bullet point above.

- The entity revokes the designation.

  In this case, the cumulative gain or loss on the hedging instrument that remains recognised directly in equity from the period when the hedge was effective should remain in equity until the forecast transaction occurs. Thereafter, it should be dealt with in accordance with paragraphs 6.10.118 to 6.10.120 above. However, if the transaction is no longer expected to occur, the cumulative gain or loss in equity is dealt with in accordance with the third bullet point above.

[IAS 39 para 101].

A6.10.122 The above rules are summarised in the table below:

Discontinuance of cash flow hedges

	Hedging instrument		Amount accumulated in equity	
Hedge termination events	**Continue mark-to-market accounting**	**Derecognise from the balance sheet**	**Reclassify to profit or loss**	**Retain amounts in equity**
	Note 1			Note 2
Hedging instrument no longer exists (that is, sold, terminated, extinguished, exercised, or expired)		✓		✓
The hedge no longer meets the effectiveness criteria for hedge accounting	✓			✓
The entity revokes the hedge designation	✓			✓
The forecast transaction is no longer highly probable, but is still expected to occur	✓			✓
The forecast transaction is no longer expected to occur	✓		✓	
Variability of cash flow ceases (for example, the forecast transaction becomes a fixed price firm commitment)	✓			✓

Note 1 – The hedging instrument will continue to be marked to market, unless it is re-designated as a hedging instrument in a new hedge.

Note 2 – The cumulative gain or loss on the hedging instrument previously recognised directly in equity from the period when the hedge was effective remains recognised in equity and is reclassified to profit or loss when profit or loss is impacted by the hedged item.

A6.10.123 When an entity ceases to apply hedge accounting because the hedge does not meet hedge effectiveness criteria, it should discontinue hedge accounting from the last date on which compliance with hedge effectiveness was demonstrated. However, if the event or change in circumstances that caused the hedging relationship to fail the effectiveness criteria can be identified and it can be demonstrated that the hedge was effective before the event or change in circumstances occurred, the entity should discontinue hedge accounting from the date of the event or change in circumstances. [IAS 39 para AG113].

Example – Discontinuance of cash flow hedge

On 1 January 20X6, entity A has a highly probable sale that is expected to occur on 31 May 20X6. Entity A expects to collect the cash on 30 June 20X6. Entity A's functional currency is pound sterling and the sale is denominated in US dollars. At the same time on 1 January 20X6, entity A takes out a £/US$ forward contract to hedge the future sale. This forward contract matures on 30 June 20X6. Entity A has put in place all the documentation required to achieve cash flow hedge accounting.

On 1 March 20X6, the transaction is no longer considered to be highly probable, but is still expected to occur. On 1 April 20X6, the transaction is no longer expected to occur. The entity does not close out the forward contract earlier than maturity.

The fair value of the forward contract at each date is as follows:

	Fair value of forward (maturity 30 June 20X6) £'000
31 January 20X6	35,000
28 February 20X6	30,000
31 March 20X6	25,000
30 April 20X6	27,000
31 May 20X6	28,000
30 June 20X6	32,000

The accounting entries from the inception of the hedge to settlement of the forward contract, assuming perfect effectiveness (that is, the hedged risk is the forward rate and no other mismatches occur), are as follows:

		Debit (Credit)			
Date	Transaction	**Cash**	**Forward contract**	**Equity**	**Profit or loss**
		£000	**£000**	**£000**	**£000**
31 Jan 20X6	Change in fair value of forward		35	(35)	
28 Feb 20X6	Change in fair value of forward		(5)	5	
	Hedge accounting ceases prospectively from 1 March 20X6. Gain deferred in equity remains in equity but the forward is now marked to market through profit or loss				

31 Mar 20X6	Change in fair value of forward		(5)		5
30 Apr 20X6	Change in fair value of forward		2		(2)
30 Apr 20X6	Recycling of gain as hedged transaction is no longer expected to occur			30	(30)
31 May 20X6	Change in fair value of forward		1		(1)
30 Jun 20X6	Change in fair value of forward		4		(4)
30 Jun 20X6	Settlement of forward	32	(32)	-	-
		32	-	-	(32)

Had the transaction continued to be highly probable, the movements on the forward contract to the extent that the hedge was effective would continue to be taken to equity until the sale occurred in May at which date the gain would be recycled from equity to the income statement. Management would then de-designate the forward contract as a hedge and the fair value movements would be recorded through the income statement between May and June and this should offset the gain or loss on the receivable (settlement due on 30 June 20X6) caused by currency fluctuations. There would be some ineffectiveness as the interest element (forward points) included in the forward contract's fair value is not present in the undiscounted trade receivable.

Net investment hedges

A6.10.124 A net investment in a foreign operation is defined as *"the amount of the reporting entity's interest in the net assets of that operation"*. [IAS 21 para 8]. An entity may decide to hedge against the effects of changes in exchange rates in its net investment in a foreign operation. This may be done with non-derivative financial liabilities or with derivatives. Because the foreign operation's net assets are reported in the reporting entity's consolidated financial statements, hedging a net investment in a foreign operation can only be carried out at the consolidation level. Under IAS 21, 'The effect of changes in foreign currencies', the reporting entity's share of the net assets of a foreign operation is translated into the group's presentation currency at the closing exchange rate and all resulting exchange differences are recognised as a separate component in equity. It follows, therefore, that the hedge of a net investment in a foreign operation at the consolidated level is simply a hedge of the translation gains or losses that are recognised in equity.

A6.10.125 Hedges of a net investment in a foreign operation, including a hedge of a monetary item that is accounted for as part of the net investment, should be accounted for similarly to cash flow hedges. That is:

- the portion of the gain or loss on the hedging instrument that is determined to be an effective hedge should be recognised directly in equity through the statement of changes in equity; and
- the ineffective portion should be recognised in profit or loss.

[IAS 39 para 102].

A6.10.126 The gain or loss on the hedging instrument relating to the effective portion of the hedge that has been recognised directly in equity should be recognised in profit or loss on disposal of the foreign operation. [IAS 39 para 102]. This means that in a group with many foreign subsidiaries, it would be necessary to keep track of all the cumulative exchange differences relating to each subsidiary that are recognised in equity on consolidation, so that they may properly be recycled into profit or loss on the disposal of the subsidiary.

A6.10.127 The hedged item in a net investment hedge is a collection of the foreign operation's assets and liabilities. It does not matter whether some of the assets and liabilities are denominated in a currency that is different from the foreign operation's functional currency. This is because those assets and liabilities will be recorded in the foreign operation's functional currency before being included in the consolidation. Monetary items that are receivable from or payable to a foreign operation for which settlement is neither planned nor likely to occur in the foreseeable future form part of the net investment. However, unrecognised assets, such as internally generated goodwill, cannot be recognised as part of the net investment.

A6.10.128 The amount that an entity can designate as a net investment hedge may be all or a proportion of its opening net investment in the reporting period. Consequently, profits or losses arising during the period cannot be a hedged item in a net investment hedge. This is because exchange differences reported in equity on consolidation that form part of the hedging relationship, relate to the retranslation of the opening net assets. Profits or losses arising during the period will form part of the translation risk once they are included in net assets. However, changes in net assets during the year may lead to over or under hedging as illustrated in paragraph A6.10.131 below.

Criteria for hedge accounting

A6.10.129 For hedges of net investments, it is necessary to satisfy all of the hedge accounting criteria discussed in paragraph A6.10.137 below. This means that the position to be hedged (the investment in the foreign operation) should be specifically identified, the hedging instrument should be designated as a hedge of the investment in the foreign operation and the hedge should be highly effective on both a prospective and retrospective basis. Although the accounting for net investment hedges is similar to cash flow hedges, the foreign currency exposure being hedged is the translation exposure of the net investment.

Hedging with a non-derivative financial instrument

A6.10.130 As explained in paragraph A6.10.85 above, a non-derivative financial asset or a liability can only be designated as a hedging instrument for hedges of foreign currency risk. Therefore, an entity can use a non-derivative financial liability, such as a borrowing, in a hedge of a net investment in a foreign operation. In this situation, the gain or loss on the non-derivative financial liability that would otherwise be taken to profit or loss on consolidation had the borrowing not been designated as a hedging instrument would now be taken to equity to offset the retranslation loss or gain on the net investment. Indeed, such a hedge would be perfectly effective if the foreign currency borrowing is denominated in the same currency as the investment in the foreign operation and has a carrying value that is *lower* than the net investment in the foreign operation (see para A6.10.117 above). In other words, if the critical terms match at the outset, the hedge would be expected to be highly effective on a prospective basis (see para A6.10.162 below). A comprehensive example of a net investment hedge in a foreign operation using a floating rate foreign currency debt instrument is given in illustration 3 at the end of this section.

A6.10.131 A foreign currency borrowing that is denominated in a currency that is different from the functional currency of the foreign operation may be used as a hedging instrument, but only if the two currencies move in tandem. [IAS 39 para AG109]. For example, if an entity designates a foreign currency loan that is denominated in a currency other than the functional currency of the net investment that exchange rate must be expected to move in tandem with the exchange rate between the functional currency of the hedged net investment and the investor's functional currency. However, even though such a hedge may be highly effective, there will always be some ineffectiveness, which thus has to be recognised in profit or loss.

Example – Hedging a net investment

Some years ago a UK parent entity with pound sterling as its functional currency acquired a US subsidiary (functional currency US dollar) for US$10m. The acquisition was financed by a bank loan of US$10million. The carrying amounts of the subsidiary in the standalone financial statements and those used in the consolidated financial statements (after consolidation adjustments) as at 31 March 20X5 are:

	Carrying amounts of the subsidiary in the consolidated financial statements US$'000	Carrying amounts in the subsidiary's stand alone financial statements US$'000
Total assets	10,000	9,500
Goodwill on consolidation	1,200	
Liabilities		
– third parties liabilities	(200)	(200)
– trade payable to UK parent'	-	(100)
– loan from UK parent*	-	(300)
Net assets	11,000	8,900

* The US subsidiary is not contractually obliged and is not planning to settle the loan in the foreseeable future.

The foreign currency loan of US$10m was designated as a hedge of the entity's net investment in the foreign subsidiary. At 31 March 20X5, the UK parent's net investment in its foreign subsidiary amounted to:

	US$'000
Net assets (including fair value adjustments + goodwill)	11,000
Long- term loan to subsidiary regarded as part of net investment	300
Net investment in subsidiary	11,300

Accordingly, only a portion, namely, US$10m of the UK parent's net investment is designated as the hedged item at the beginning of the financial year.

During the year to 31 March 20X6, the US subsidiary, which has hitherto been profitable, incurred unexpected losses that were not foreseen by the UK parent. As a result, the net assets of subsidiary included in the consolidated financial statements at 31 March 20X6 amounted to US$8.5m.

The foreign exchange rates at 31 March 20X5 and 31 March 20X6 were £1 = US$1.88 and £1 = US$1.74 respectively.

The exchange difference on foreign currency loan was as follows:

	£'000
At 31 March 20X6 US$10m @ 1.74	5,747
At 31 March 20X5 US$10m @ 1.88	5,319
Exchange loss (that is, 88% of US$10m)	428

Because the subsidiary's net assets have declined to US$8.5m due to losses incurred during the year, the notional amount of the hedging instrument (US$10m) is no longer equal to the designated portion of the hedged item. This results in an over-hedged position at 31 March 20X6 leading to hedge ineffectiveness. The net investment at 31 March 20X6 amounts to US8,500,000 + US$300,000 = US $8,800,000. The amount of the ineffectiveness following retrospective assessment at 31 March 20X6 using dollar offset method (see para A6.10.165 below) is, therefore, 88% (8.8/10) or 114%. This ratio falls within the permitted range of 80% to 125% and, therefore, the UK parent continues to apply hedging accounting at 31 March 20X6.

However, not all of the exchange loss of £428,000 calculated above would be taken to equity. The amount of the exchange loss that can be offset in equity is limited to the exchange gain arising on the net investment of US$8.8m, which is less than the amount of US$10m designated at the beginning of the period as shown below.

	£'000
Exchange difference on net investment:	
At 31 March 20X6 US$8.800m @ 1.74	5,057
At 31 March 20X5 US$8.800m @ 1.88	4,681
Exchange gain	376

Therefore, only £376,000 of the exchange loss of £428,000 would fall to be recognised in equity. The balance of £52,000 would be recognised in profit and loss as hedge ineffectiveness.

It should be noted that had the parent been aware that the subsidiary would be expected to make losses, it could have decided to hedge a lower amount of the opening net investment balance to reduce the amount of the ineffectiveness recognised in profit or loss. Indeed, as the net investment balance will invariably change during the year, it would be appropriate for the parent to assess periodically (for example, at interim reporting dates) the original hedging relationship and decide whether it needs to remove (that is, de-designate) that original relationship and designate a new relationship for the following assessment period. For example, going forward, the entity could de-designate the original hedging relationship and re-designate a new hedging relationship prospectively as hedging 88% of the entire beginning balance of the net investment. In this way, it is possible to minimise the amount of the hedge ineffectiveness that is recognised in profit or loss due to changes in the net investment balance.

Hedging with derivatives

A6.10.132 It is also possible to hedge a net investment with derivatives. A derivative that is commonly used is a forward contract. However, in this situation, it would be necessary for the entity to designate at inception whether effectiveness would be measured by reference to changes in spot exchange rates or changes in forward exchange rates. If the spot rate method is used, only the change in the fair value of the forward contract due to changes in spot rates would be reported in equity and the balance of the fair value of the forward (due to the forward points) would be included in profit or loss. On the other hand, if the forward rate method is used, the full change in the fair value of the forward would be reported in equity. This is explained further in paragraph A6.10.186 below.

A6.10.133 It is also possible to use a currency forward as a hedge of a net investment in a foreign operation. Therefore, if the notional amount of a currency forward that swaps the functional currency of the hedged net investment into the investor's functional currency matches the portion of the net investment hedged, it is likely to be an effective hedging instrument. However, cross currency interest rate swaps having foreign exchange and interest rates as underlyings may not be effective hedging instruments since the hedged net investment is not affected by changes in interest rates. Nevertheless, cross-currency swaps could be designated as hedging instruments in a net investment hedge, provided both legs of the swap are either floating rates or fixed rates. This is because a cross-currency interest rate swap that has either two floating legs or two fixed legs has a fair value that is primarily driven by changes in foreign exchange rates rather than changes in interest rates. However, a cross-currency swap interest rate swap with one fixed-leg and one floating-rate leg is unlikely to be effective as a hedging instrument in a net investment hedge.

Hedging in individual or separate financial statements

A6.10.134 IAS 27, 'Consolidated and separate financial statements', states that in a parent's separate financial statements, investments in subsidiaries, jointly controlled entities and associates that are included in the consolidated financial statements should be carried at cost or accounted for in accordance with IAS 39. This means that the equity investment can be designated as 'available-for-sale' or 'at fair value through profit or loss' (if permitted by IAS 39). However, in some jurisdictions, entities normally record their investments in subsidiaries, associates and joint ventures at cost in their separate financial statements. A question, therefore, arises as to whether a foreign currency borrowing can be designated as a hedge of the entity's foreign equity investment in its separate financial statements where the foreign equity investment is recorded at historical cost.

A6.10.135 The answer is that it may be possible to construct a hedging relationship to achieve hedge accounting despite the apparent contradictions with IAS 21 and IAS 39. The rationale for achieving hedge accounting is set out in IG E3.4 of the implementation guidance of IAS 39. In summary, IG E3.4 states that, as an exception, if the financial asset or financial liability is designated as a hedged item in a fair value hedge of the exposure to changes in foreign currency rates under IAS 39, the hedged item is re-measured for changes in foreign currency rates even if it would otherwise have been recognised using a historical rate under IAS 21. This exception applies to non-monetary items that are carried in terms of historical cost in the foreign currency (such as equity investments in foreign subsidiaries) and are hedged against exposure to foreign currency rates. In effect, this exception allows an entity to hedge the change in the historical foreign currency cost of the foreign equity investment due to the movement in the relevant foreign currency rates. In these circumstances, the historical foreign currency cost of the foreign currency investment would be retranslated at each balance sheet date at the closing rate and the exchange difference arising on the retranslation will be recognised in profit or loss to offset the exchange difference recognised in profit or loss arising on the retranslation of the foreign currency borrowings (where these are used as the hedging instrument) or the change in the fair value of the foreign currency derivative, that is used as the hedging instrument. Although this treatment is an exception, nevertheless it is still classified as a fair value hedge. Accordingly, the hedging criteria set out in paragraph A6.10.136 below must still be met in order to achieve fair value hedge accounting in the reporting entity's separate financial statements. Whether, in practice, a parent entity would apply hedge accounting in its separate financial statements is a moot point that may well depend on the tax treatment of undertaking such hedging activities.

Example – Hedge of a foreign subsidiary in entity's separate financial statements

Entity A whose functional currency is the pound sterling acquired a subsidiary B in France for €300m in 20X0 when the £/€ exchange rate on the day of the transaction was £1 = €1.50. Entity A, therefore, measures its investment on initial recognition at £200m (€300/1.50). Entity A borrowed €300m to make the purchase and designates the euro borrowing as a hedge of the exposure to the change in £/€ spot rate.

Assuming that the hedging criteria in paragraph A6.10.136 below are met and using the exception discussed above, entity A will retranslate its investment in its French subsidiary at each balance sheet date using the closing £/€ spot rate. Therefore, if at the first balance sheet reporting date following the acquisition, the spot rate has moved to £1 = €1.75, entity A will re-measure the historical euro cost of its investment into £171.43m. The exchange difference of £28.57m is recognised as an exchange loss in profit or loss for the period. At the same time the €300m borrowing is retranslated at the closing rate and the exchange gain of £28.57m is also recognised in profit or loss. Therefore, in this case the net effect as a result of hedge accounting is £nil on profit or loss. This example ignores any tax consequences of such a strategy.

Criteria for obtaining hedge accounting

A6.10.136 Hedge accounting is an exception to the normal accounting principles for financial instruments. IAS 39, therefore, requires hedge relationships to meet certain criteria in order to qualifying for hedge accounting. The three types of hedging relationships set out in paragraph A6.10.89 above qualify for hedge accounting if and only if, all of the following conditions are met.

- At the inception of the hedge there is formal designation and documentation of the hedging relationship and the entity's risk management objective and strategy for undertaking the hedge.
- The hedge is expected to be highly effective in achieving offsetting changes in fair value or cash flows attributable to the hedged risk, consistently with the originally documented risk management strategy for that particular hedging relationship.
- A forecast transaction that is the subject of a cash flow hedge must be highly probable and must present an exposure to variations in cash flows that could ultimately affect profit or loss.
- The effectiveness of the hedge can be reliably measured, that is, the hedged item's fair value or cash flows that are attributable to the hedged risk and the hedged instrument's fair value can be reliably measured.
- The hedge is assessed on an ongoing basis and determined actually to have been highly effective throughout the financial reporting periods for which the hedge was designated.

[IAS 39 para 88(a)-(e)].

A6.10.137 The criteria for hedge accounting are onerous and have systems implications for all entities. Hedge accounting is optional and management should consider the costs and benefits when deciding whether to use it. Much of the burden and cost associated with hedge accounting arises from the effectiveness testing requirement. These requirements are considered from paragraph 6.10.145 below.

Documentation and designation

A6.10.138 Formal hedge documentation in support of the hedge must be prepared at the inception of the hedge and should include the following:

- The entity's risk management objective and strategy for undertaking the hedge.
- The nature of the risk being hedged.
- The hedged item.
- The hedging instrument.
- How the entity will assess the hedging instrument's effectiveness in offsetting the exposure to changes in the hedged item's fair value or cash flows attributable to the hedged risk.

[IAS 39 para 88(a)].

A6.10.139 Since there must be formal designation and documentation of the hedging relationship at the inception of the hedge, a hedge relationship cannot be designated retrospectively. However, IAS 39 does not require a hedging relationship to be established at the time the hedging instrument is acquired. For instance, an entity is permitted to designate and formally document a derivative contract as a hedging instrument after entering into the derivative contract. Hedge accounting will apply prospectively from the date all hedge accounting criteria in paragraph A6.10.136 above are met. [IAS 39 paras IG F3.8, F3.9].

Documentation relating to forecast transaction

A6.10.140 When the entity is hedging a forecast transaction, the hedge relationship documentation should also identify the date on, or time period in, which the forecast transaction is expected to occur. This is because to qualify for hedge accounting:

- the hedge must relate to a specific identified and designated risk;
- it must be possible to measure its effectiveness reliably; and
- the hedged forecast transaction must be highly probable.

[IAS 39 para IG F3.11].

A6.10.141 To meet the above criteria, the hedged forecast transaction must be identified and documented with sufficient specificity so that when the transaction occurs, it is clear whether the transaction is or is not the hedged transaction. Therefore, a forecast transaction may be identified as the sale of the first 15,000 units of a specific product during a specified three-month period, but it could not be identified as the last 15,000 units of that product sold during a three-month period, because the last 15,000 units cannot be identified when they are sold. For the same reason, a forecast transaction cannot be specified solely as a percentage of sales or purchases during a period. [IAS 39 para IG F3.10].

A6.10.142 An entity is not required to predict and document the exact date a forecast transaction is expected to occur. However, it is required to identify and document the time period during which the forecast transaction is expected to occur within a reasonably specific and generally narrow range, as a basis for assessing hedge effectiveness. To determine that the hedge will be highly effective, it is necessary to ensure that changes in the expected cash flow's fair value are offset by changes in the hedging instrument's fair value and this test may be met only if the cash flows occur within close proximity of each other. [IAS 39 para IG F3.11].

A6.10.143 The change in timing of the forecast transaction does not affect the validity of the designation. For instance, if, subsequent to designating a derivative as a hedging instrument in a cash flow hedge of a forecast transaction such as a commodity sale, the entity expects the forecast sale to occur in an earlier period than originally anticipated, the original designation is not invalidated. Provided the hedging relationship met all the hedge accounting conditions, including the requirement to identify and document the period in which the sale was expected to occur within a reasonably specific and narrow range of time as explained above, the entity can conclude that this transaction is the same as the one that was designated as being hedged. However, this may well affect the assessment of the effectiveness of the hedging relationship since the derivative would need to be designated as a hedging instrument for the whole remaining period of its existence, which will include a period after the forecast sale. [IAS 39 para IG F 5.4].

Example – Hedging cash flows in specific time periods

Entity A manufactures and sells ice cream. Its functional currency is the euro, but 30% of its sales are made in the UK and denominated in pounds sterling. Entity A forecasts highly probable sales in the UK for the next summer season on a monthly basis. Using these forecasts, it enters into forward contracts to sell pounds sterling in exchange for euros. Due to the nature of its business, entity A is not able to forecast or track individual sales transactions.

Although the forecast transaction should be specifically identifiable as a single transaction or a group of individual transactions in order to qualify for cash flow hedge accounting, Entity A can designate the forecast sales of ice cream as the hedged item. It should do this by designating the hedged item as the first £X million of highly probable cash flows in specific time periods (for example, in each month). To qualify for hedge accounting, the designation must be sufficiently specific to ensure that when a forecast transaction occurs, it is possible to determine objectively whether that transaction is or is not the one that is hedged. If the hedged cash flows do not occur in the designated time period, management cannot continue with hedge accounting.

Example documentation

A6.10.144 IAS 39 does not mandate any standard format for documenting the hedging relationship and, therefore, in practice, the nature and style of the documentation may vary from entity to entity. The important thing to note is that the documentation must include all of the basic contents required by IAS 39 paragraph 88 (see para A6.10.138 above) and must be in place at inception of the hedge. Examples of hedge designation and documentation are included in the three comprehensive examples illustrated from paragraph A6.10.202 below.

Hedge effectiveness

A6.10.145 The requirement to assess hedge effectiveness is critical for a hedge transaction to qualify for hedge accounting. But this requirement is also the most onerous of the hedge accounting criteria because of the time, cost and effort that it entails. Hedge effectiveness is defined as *'the degree to which changes in the fair value or cash flows of the hedged item that are attributable to a hedged risk are offset by changes in the fair value or cash flows of the hedging instrument'*. [IAS 39 para 9]. Assessing the degree or the extent to which such offset will be effective for hedge accounting purposes is by no means an easy task. The difficulty is also exacerbated by the lack of practical guidance in the standard for undertaking the effectiveness exercise. Often, it will require the use of complex statistical techniques whose output will require careful interpretations. As a result, the approach taken by entities may vary: from electing not to adopt hedge accounting and managing the resulting volatility in the income statement through communications with the market, to putting hedge accounting systems and processes in place and thereby obtaining the benefits of hedge accounting. In practice, most entities are likely to adopt a mixed approach, undertaking hedge accounting only for large material hedges and not electing to adopt hedge accounting for immaterial ones.

Requirements for assessing effectiveness

A6.10.146 To qualify for hedge accounting, IAS 39 requires a hedge to be highly effective. A hedge is regarded as highly effective if both of the following two conditions are met:

- At the inception of the hedge and in subsequent periods, the hedge is expected to be highly effective in achieving offsetting changes in fair value or cash flows attributable to the hedged risk during the period for which the hedge is designated.

- The actual results of the hedge are within a range of 80-125 per cent.

[IAS 39 para AG 105].

A6.10.147 In order to comply with the first condition above, an entity needs to perform a *prospective hedge effectiveness assessment*. This is a forward looking test that assesses whether the entity expects the hedging relationship to be highly effective in achieving offset in the future. An expectation that the hedging relationship will be highly effective can be demonstrated in various ways, including a comparison of the critical terms of the hedging instrument with those of the hedged item (see para A6.10.160 below), or a comparison of past changes in the fair value or cash flows of the hedged item that are attributable to the hedged risk with past changes in the fair value or cash flows of the hedging instrument (see para A6.10.164 below), or by demonstrating a high statistical correlation between the fair value or cash flows of the hedged item and those of the hedging instrument (see para A6.10.182 below). The entity may choose a hedge ratio of other than one to one in order to improve the effectiveness of the hedge as described in paragraph A6.10.184 below. [IAS 39 para AG 105(a)].

A6.10.148 In order to comply with the second condition above, an entity needs to perform a *retrospective hedge effectiveness assessment*. This is a backward looking test that assesses whether the hedging relationship actually has been highly effective in achieving offset. The objective is to demonstrate that the hedging relationship has been highly effective by showing that actual results of the hedge are within a range of 80-125 per cent. For example, if actual results are such that the loss on the hedging instrument is C120 and the gain on the hedged item is C100, offset can be measured by 120/100, which is 120 per cent, or by 100/120, which is 83 per cent. In this example, assuming the hedge meets the first condition above, the entity would conclude that the hedge has been highly effective. [IAS 39 para AG 105(b)].

A6.10.149 An entity is required to perform the prospective test at the inception of the hedging relationship *and* at the beginning of each assessment period to demonstrate that the hedge is expected to be highly effective in the future. If, at any point, the prospective consideration indicates that the hedging instrument is not expected to be highly effective in the future, hedge accounting must be discontinued from that point forward. An entity must also perform the retrospective test at the end of every period to demonstrate that the hedge has been highly effective through the date of the periodic assessment. If the retrospective test indicates that the hedging instrument has not been highly effective, hedge accounting must be discontinued from the point the hedging relationship ceased to be highly effective. Both tests must be met for a particular period of the hedge relationship for hedge accounting to be available. The requirements are illustrated as follows:

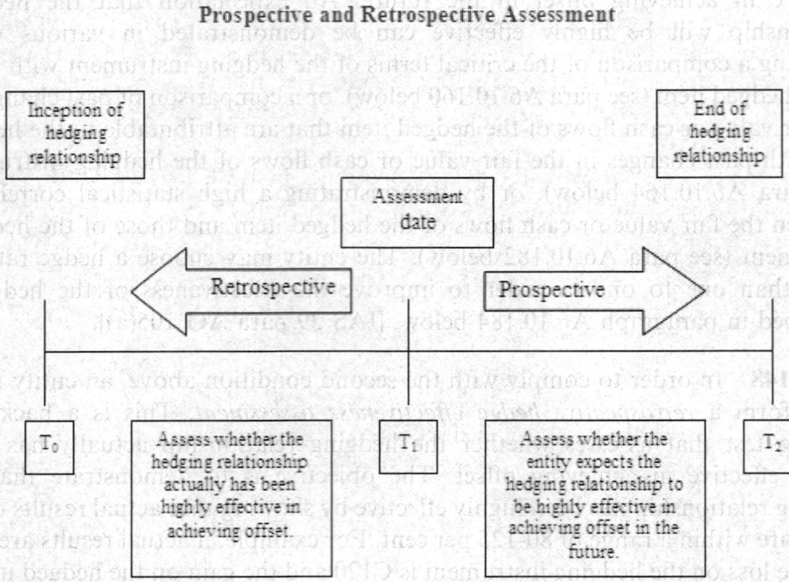

Note: The diagram refers to tests being carried out at time T, (the assessment date). It is assumed that the prospective test at inception of hedge at time T_o has been met.

A6.10.150 Given the nature of the two assessments, it is possible for an entity to pass the prospective test at the beginning of the period but fail the retrospective test at the end of the period (for example, due to unexpected market factors). In that situation, hedge accounting would be precluded for the current period in question, but could be applied in future periods, provided the prospective test continues to be met for those periods. Similarly, if the entity passes the retrospective test at the end of one period, but fails the prospective test at the beginning of the next period, hedge accounting would be permitted for the period just ended, but could not be applied in the next period. To some degree, these results will be impacted by the manner in which an entity elects to assess hedge effectiveness, because the entity is not required to use the same method for both the prospective and the retrospective assessments.

Example – Failed retrospective test with a successful prospective test

A hedge relationship designated by entity A fails the retrospective test for a given period. Accordingly, entity A ceases to apply hedge accounting from the last date on which it demonstrated effectiveness. Entity A performs a successful prospective effectiveness test with the same hedging instrument and the same hedged item at the start of the following period. It should be noted that this prospective effectiveness testing will need to take account of the fact that the derivative now has a non-zero fair value as discussed in paragraph A6.10.55 above.

In this scenario, entity A can re-designate the hedge relationship for the remaining life of the instrument following a successful prospective effectiveness test. IAS 39 does not preclude an entity from designating the same derivative as a hedge of the same item in a subsequent period, provided the hedge relationship meets the criteria for hedge accounting (including effectiveness) in that subsequent period. [IFRIC Update April 2005].

A6.10.151 Effectiveness is assessed, at a minimum, at the time an entity prepares its annual or interim financial statements. [IAS 39 para AG 106]. However, the standard does not prevent an entity from undertaking an assessment more frequently. Indeed, an entity may wish to assess effectiveness more frequently say, at the end of each month or other applicable reporting period, in order to minimise the time period during which the hedge may fail due to ineffectiveness and to better manage the hedged risk exposure.

A6.10.152 IAS 39 does not specify a single method for assessing hedge effectiveness. The method an entity adopts for assessing hedge effectiveness depends on its risk management strategy. Also the appropriateness of a given method of assessing hedge effectiveness will depend on the nature of the risk being hedged and the type of hedging instrument used. IAS 39, however, does require an entity to document at the inception of the hedge how effectiveness will be assessed. The method of assessing effectiveness must be reasonable and consistent with other similar hedges, unless different methods can be explicitly justified. The defined and documented method should be used on a consistent basis throughout the hedge's duration. [IAS 39 paras 80, IG F4.4]. There is nothing in the standard to prevent an entity from using one method for prospective testing and another different method for retrospective testing as long as the chosen methods are reasonable and properly documented upfront and used on a consistent basis throughout the hedge's duration. Methods normally used for testing hedge effectiveness are considered in paragraph A6.10.159 below.

A6.10.153 There is nothing in the standard to prevent an entity from changing its method of assessing hedge effectiveness. If an entity wishes to change its method of assessing hedge effectiveness, this will result in a new hedging relationship. Hence, the entity should de-designate the old hedging relationship and then immediately designate a new hedging relationship using the new method of assessing hedge effectiveness. As a result, new documentation would need to be prepared. It should be noted, however, that there is a danger in de-designating and re-designating the hedge relationship. This is because both the hedged item and the hedging instrument will have non-zero fair values and these may well impact the assessment of hedge ineffectiveness due to ineffectiveness caused by the non-zero fair values.

Assessment on a cumulative or a period-by-period basis

A6.10.154 IAS 39 permits an entity to assess hedge effectiveness using either a period-by-period approach or a cumulative approach, provided the chosen approach is incorporated into the hedging documentation at inception of the hedge. [IAS 39 para IG F4.2]. The period-by-period approach involves comparing the changes in the hedging instrument's fair values (or cash flows) that have occurred during the period being assessed to the changes in the hedged item's fair value (or hedged transaction's cash flows) attributable to the risk hedged that have occurred during the same period. The cumulative approach involves comparing the cumulative changes (to date from inception of the hedge) in the hedging instrument's fair values (or cash flows) to the cumulative changes in the hedged item's fair value (or hedged transaction's cash flows) attributable to the risk hedged. The two methods can produce significantly different results as illustrated below:

	Cumulative basis			Period-by-period basis		
Assessment period	Hedging instrument	Hedged item	Ratio (%)	Hedging instrument	Hedged item	Ratio (%)
Quarter 1	50	(50)	100%	50	(50)	100%
Quarter 2	105	(107)	98%	55	(57)	96%
Quarter 3	129	(120)	108%	24	(13)	184%
Quarter 4	115	(116)	99%	(14)	4	350%

A6.10.155 It is clear from the above table that the period-by-period approach of retrospective assessment results in the disqualification of hedge accounting in quarters 3 and 4. By contrast, had the cumulative method of retrospective assessment been applied, all periods would have been considered highly effective and qualified for hedge accounting. It is, therefore, important to ensure that the chosen method of assessment, in this instance, the cumulative method, is documented at the inception of the hedging relationship. Indeed, in most situations, the cumulative method would be adopted in practice as it results in less ineffectiveness. Another example of assessing expected hedge effectiveness on a cumulative basis is given below.

Example – Hedge effectiveness assessment on a cumulative basis

An entity designates a LIBOR-based interest rate swap as a hedge of a borrowing whose interest rate is a UK base rate plus a margin. The UK base rate changes, perhaps, once each quarter or less, in increments of 25-50 basis points, while LIBOR changes daily. Over a period of 1-2 years, the hedge is expected to be almost perfect. However, there will be quarters when the UK base rate does not change at all, while LIBOR has changed significantly.

Expected hedge effectiveness may be assessed on a cumulative basis if the hedge is so designated and that condition is incorporated into the appropriate hedging documentation. Therefore, even if a hedge is not expected to be highly effective in a particular period, hedge accounting is not precluded if effectiveness is expected to remain sufficiently high over the life of the hedging relationship. However, any ineffectiveness is required to be recognised in profit or loss as it occurs. [IAS 39 para IG F4.2].

Counterparty credit risk

A6.10.156 An entity must consider the likelihood of default by the counterparty to the hedging instrument in assessing hedge effectiveness. This is because an entity cannot ignore whether it will be able to collect all amounts due under the contractual provisions of the hedging instrument. When assessing hedge effectiveness, both at the inception of the hedge and on an ongoing basis, the entity should consider the risk that the counterparty to the hedging instrument will default by failing to make any contractual payments to the entity when due. For a cash flow hedge, if it becomes probable that a counterparty will default, an entity would be unable to conclude that the hedging relationship is expected to be highly effective in achieving offsetting cash flows. As a result, hedge accounting would be discontinued. For a fair value hedge, if there is a change in the counterparty's creditworthiness, the fair value of the hedging instrument will change, which affects the assessment of whether the hedge relationship is effective and whether it qualifies for continued hedge accounting. [IAS 39 para IG F4.3].

Transaction costs

A6.10.156.1 Transaction costs are never part of a fair value movement under IAS 39 and, therefore, they should be excluded from hedge effectiveness tests.

Example – transaction costs

Entity A, whose functional currency is the pound sterling, granted a US$ denominated loan to entity B. Entity A measures the loan at amortised cost, which at initial recognition is the amount lent of US$ 1 million plus transaction costs of US$ 5,000. Entity A designates the loan as a hedging instrument for the foreign exchange risk of a forecast purchase of US$ 1 million. The repayment of the loan and the forecast purchase occur on the same date and all other requirements for hedge accounting are met. Since transaction costs of US$ 5,000 would not be included in the loan's fair value if it had been carried at fair value, entity A's management should exclude transaction costs of US$ 5,000 from the effectiveness test.

Pre-payment risk

A6.10.157 Pre-payment risk will impact the effectiveness of fair value hedges of pre-payable assets, such as mortgage loans and, therefore, should be taken into account when an entity designates the hedge relationship. The hedged mortgage loans' contractual terms include the pre-payment option (for the borrower), which cannot be ignored. Furthermore, pre-payment rates are primarily a function of interest rates and, hence, IAS 39 specifies that pre-payment risk is a component of interest rate risk. Therefore, if an entity intends to hedge a portfolio of mortgage loans for interest rate risk, pre-payment risk cannot be excluded. For instance, an entity may have a portfolio of C500 million of mortgage loans that may be pre-paid at par. The entity may wish to hedge the changes in fair value of this portfolio attributable to interest rate movements by entering into a simple receive-variable, pay-fixed interest rate swap. Such a swap, however, would not be a highly effective hedging instrument, because the hedged item contains a pre-payment option that is not present in the swap. However, if the entity can demonstrate (based on historical data) that C100 million of the portfolio would not pre-pay if interest rate were to decline, it could designate a specific portion of each loan in the mortgage portfolio as the hedged item.

A6.10.158 Cash flows after the pre-payment date may be designated as the hedged item to the extent it can be demonstrated that they are 'highly probable'. For example, cash flows after the pre-payment date may qualify as highly probable if they result from a group or pool of similar assets (for example, mortgage loans) for which pre-payments can be estimated with a high degree of accuracy or if the pre-payment option is significantly out of the money. In addition, the cash flows after the pre-payment date may be designated as the hedged item if a comparable option exists in the hedging instrument. [IAS 39 para IG F2.12].

Methods used to assess hedge effectiveness

A6.10.159 IAS 39 does not specify a single method for assessing hedge effectiveness prospectively or retrospectively. The method an entity adopts for assessing hedge effectiveness depends on its risk management strategy and should be included in the documentation at the inception of the hedge. There are a number of methods that are used in practice ranging from the most simple (qualitative) to the more complex (highly quantitative). Although the particular method selected would depend on the nature and type of the hedging relationship, all of the methods attempt to gauge the relative change in value of the hedged item and the hedging instrument. The methods that are commonly used in practice to assess hedge effectiveness are described in the paragraphs that follow. It should be noted, however, that whatever method is used test the effectiveness of a hedge, a quantitative retrospective test must be performed to determine the amount of ineffectiveness that has occurred and that must be recognised in profit or loss (see para A6.10.189 below).

Critical terms comparison

A6.10.160 This method consists of comparing the principal terms of the hedging instrument with those of the hedged item. If the principal terms of the hedging instrument and of the hedged item are the same, the changes in fair value and cash flows attributable to the risk being hedged may be likely to offset each other fully, both when the hedge is entered into and afterwards. [IAS 39 para AG 108]. The principal terms of the hedging instrument and hedged items are those that are critical to the assessment of hedge effectiveness. Further, critical terms are the same if and only if the terms are exactly the same and there are no features (such as optionality) that would invalidate an assumption of perfect effectiveness. Therefore, this method may only be used in limited circumstances, but in such cases it is the simplest way to demonstrate that a hedge is expected to be highly effective on a prospective basis. This method does not require any calculation. For instance, an interest rate swap is likely to be an effective hedge if the notional and principal amounts, term, re-pricing dates, dates of interest and principal receipts and payments and basis for measuring interest rates are the *same* for the hedging instrument and the hedged item. [IAS 39 para AG 108]. A separate assessment is required for the retrospective effectiveness test, as ineffectiveness may arise even when critical terms match; for example, because of a change in the liquidity of a hedging derivative or in the creditworthiness of the derivative counterparty.

A6.10.161 Similarly, a hedge of a highly probable forecast purchase of a commodity with a forward contract is likely to be highly effective if:

- the forward contract is for the purchase of the same quantity of the same commodity at the same time and location as the hedged forecast purchase;
- the fair value of the forward contract at inception is zero; and
- either the change in the discount or premium on the forward contract is excluded from the assessment of effectiveness and recognised in profit or loss or the change in expected cash flows on the highly probable forecast transaction is based on the commodity's forward price. [IAS 39 para AG 108].

In these circumstances, the change in the derivative's fair value can be viewed as a proxy for the present value of the change in cash flows attributable to the risk being hedged. The documentation that the critical terms of the hedging instrument and hedged item match must be performed at the inception of the hedging relationship and on an ongoing basis throughout the hedging period.

A6.10.162 It should be noted that that the critical terms of the hedged item and hedging instrument listed in the above example all pertain to factors that could produce ineffectiveness in a hedging relationship. The fair value of the forward must be zero at the inception of the hedging relationship because forward contracts with a value of other than zero include a 'financing' element that is a source of ineffectiveness (see para A6.10.55 above). Accordingly, the use of this method should be restricted to situations where an entity enters into the derivative at or very close to the same time it establishes the hedging relationship.

A6.10.163 Even if all of the critical terms of a hedging relationship match, an entity *cannot assume perfect hedge effectiveness throughout the life of the hedge without further effectiveness testing*. An entity still must assess retrospectively the effectiveness of the relationship, at a minimum, at the time it prepares its annual or interim financial statements. A separate quantitative assessment is required for the retrospective effectiveness test, as ineffectiveness may arise even when critical terms match as illustrated in the following example. [IAS 39 para IG F4.7].

Example – Testing effectiveness retrospectively when critical terms match

Entity A enters into a 5 year fixed-rate borrowing. On the same date, it enters into a receive-fixed/pay-floating interest rate swap on which the floating leg is reset every 3 months. The principal terms of the swap and the debt match (start date, end date, fixed payment dates, calendar basis, principal amount, fixed interest rate) and there are no features or conditions (such as optionality) that would invalidate an assumption of perfect effectiveness.

In this section, as the principal terms of the debt and the fixed leg of the swap match and entity A is able to demonstrate and document that the change in the fair value of the floating leg of the swap will not give rise to material ineffectiveness, this is sufficient that the hedge is expected to be highly effective on a prospective basis. Thus, a numerical test is not required to demonstrate prospective effectiveness.

However, even though the critical terms of the fixed rate borrowing and the swap match, hedge effectiveness cannot be assumed throughout the life of the hedge and a retrospective test must be performed. The objective of the retrospective effectiveness test is to determine that the hedge actually has been highly effective throughout the financial reporting period for which it was designated. If the principal terms of the hedging instrument match those of the hedged item, ineffectiveness may still arise, for example if:

- in the case of a fair value hedge;
- there is a change in the swap's liquidity;
- there is a change in the swap counterparty's creditworthiness; or
- the floating rate leg is not reset on the testing date.

Dollar offset method

6.10.164 This is a quantitative method that consists of comparing the change in fair value or cash flows of the hedging instrument with the change in fair value or cash flows of the hedged item attributable to the hedged risk. If this ratio falls within the range of 80-125 per cent as explained in paragraph A6.10.150, the hedge is regarded as highly effective. Depending on the entity's risk management policies, this test can be performed either on a cumulative basis or on a period-by-period basis as explained in paragraph A6.10.155 above. The formula for assessing hedge effectiveness on cumulative basis under the dollar-offset method can be expressed as follows:

$$0.8 \leq \left| -\frac{\sum_{i=1}^{n} Xi}{\sum_{i=1}^{n} Yi} \right| \leq 1.25$$

where $\sum_{i=1}^{n} Xi$ is the cumulative sum of the periodic changes in the values of the hedging instrument and $\sum_{i=1}^{n} Yi$ is the cumulative sum of the periodic changes in the values of the hedged item and n = number of periods since inception of the hedge. Since Xi and Yi are variables that offset each other, the minus sign has been introduced to ensure that the ratio is an absolute number.

For a perfect hedge, the change in the value of the hedging instrument exactly offsets the change in the value of the hedged item. Therefore, the above ratio of the cumulative sum of the periodic changes in value of the hedging instrument and the hedged item would equal one in a perfect hedge.

Example – Dollar-offset method

Entity A has a C1,000 debt at 10% fixed rate with a 2 year term. Interest payments are made annually In order to hedge against future changes in interest rates it enters into a 2 year C1,000 notional interest rate swap requiring interest payments at one year LIBOR in exchange for the receipt of fixed interest at 10% (fair value hedge of interest rate risk).

At inception, LIBOR is expected to be 10% for the following 2 years, but at the end of year 1 LIBOR is expected to be 5% for the second year.

At the end of year 1, the retrospective test would be performed as follows:

		C
Hedged item (debt)	Fair value at inception =	1,000
	Fair value at end of year 1 = C1,000 × 1.10/1.05	1,048
	Change in fair value	(48)
Hedging instrument	Fair value at inception	0
	Fair value at end of year 1 = C50 */1.05	48
	Change in fair value	48

* Difference in anticipated swap cash flows = C1,000 × (10% – 5%)

Dollar offset test at end of year 1

$$\frac{\text{Change in fair value of hedging instrument}}{\text{Change in fair value of hedged item}} = \frac{48}{(48)} = 1$$

This hedge is, therefore, currently 100% effective.

This hedge is, therefore, currently 100% effective.

If there had been a contractual difference or delay in the timing of the cash flows either on the debt or the swap, or if effectiveness is tested at a date other than the swap re-pricing date, then some ineffectiveness would most likely result. Also no account has been taken here of the credit risk in the swap payments, which could have introduced some ineffectiveness. Note that any credit risk on the debt was not designated as part of the hedging relationship and any impact of this would be booked to the income statement anyway over time, though not on a fair value basis.

Consider the example above, but the cash flows on the debt are anticipated to slip by one month at the end of year 2. The end of year 1 retrospective test would show:

		C
Hedged item (debt)	Fair value at inception =	1,000
	Fair value at end of year 1 $= C1,000 \times 1.10/(1.05)^{13/12}$	1,043
	Change in fair value	(43)
Hedging instrument	Fair value at inception	0
	Fair value at end of year 1 = C50 */1.05	48
	Change in fair value	48

* Difference in anticipated swap cash flows = C1m × (10% – 5%)

Dollar offset test at end of year 1

$$\frac{\text{Change in fair value of hedging instrument}}{\text{Change in fair value of hedged item}} = \frac{48}{(43)} = 1.12$$

Due to the cash flow slippage on the debt ineffectiveness of C5 has been introduced. This is still within the 80-125 % range so hedge accounting is still permitted, however, the C5 will need to be recognised in profit or loss as explained further in paragraph A6.10.186 below.

6A.10.165 The above examples illustrate that the dollar-offset method has the advantage that the calculation is straightforward and does not rely on maintaining a large population of valuation data. When applied retrospectively to an assessment of actual effectiveness, the dollar-offset method can be applied either on a period-by-period basis or cumulatively from the date of the inception of the hedge as explained in paragraph A6.10.154 above. However, the example in that paragraph also indicated that even though on a cumulative basis the hedge was highly effective, two test ratios were outside the critical range on a period-by-period basis. This is an unfortunate consequence of the 80/125 rule that during periods of market stability virtually any hedge is likely to fail as small changes in the values of either the hedged item or the hedging instrument can produce extreme ratios. This is a general shortcoming of the dollar-offset method and is likely to occur when there are short testing intervals. As a result, the dollar offset method can be unreliable, causing hedges that are, by other reasonable standards, highly effective, to fail the effectiveness test. In practice, however, this short coming is often overcome by performing a cumulative dollar-offset test.

A6.10.166 Notwithstanding the above, when the dollar offset method is used for assessing retrospectively the effectiveness of a hedge, it has the advantage of determining the amount of ineffectiveness that has occurred and of generating the numbers required for the accounting entries. For instance, to the extent that the sum of the changes in the value of the hedged item and the hedging instrument is not zero, there is an element of ineffectiveness in the hedge that is included in profit or loss. Thus, even when a hedge is determined to be highly effective, there is an impact on profit or loss when there is not an exact offset of the hedged risk as illustrated in the example in paragraph A6.10.165 above.

A6.10.167 The dollar offset method can be performed using different approaches. Three approaches that are generally used in practice are:

- The hypothetical derivative method (see para A6.10.168 below).
- The benchmark rate method (see para A6.10.171 below).
- The sensitivity analysis method (see para A6.10.172 below).

Hypothetical derivative method

A6.10.168 Under the hypothetical derivative method, the hedged risk is modelled as a derivative called a 'hypothetical derivative' (as it does not exist). The hypothetical derivative approach compares the change in the fair value or cash flows of the hedging instrument with the change in the fair value or cash flows of the hypothetical derivative. The hypothetical derivative method is referred to as 'method B' in IAS 39 paragraph IGF5.5. The measurement of hedge ineffectiveness is based on a comparison of the change in fair value of the actual derivative designated as the hedging instrument and the change in fair value of a hypothetical derivative. That hypothetical derivative would have terms that identically match the critical terms of the hedged item. For example, for a cash flow hedge that involves either a variable rate asset or a liability, the hypothetical derivative would be a swap that must have the same notional amount and the same re-pricing dates. Also, the index on which the hypothetical swap's variable rate is based should match the index on which the asset or liability's variable rate is based, and must mirror any caps, floors or any other non-separated embedded derivative features of the hedged item. Thus, the hypothetical swap would be expected to perfectly offset the hedged cash flows. The change in fair value of the 'perfect' hypothetical swap is regarded as a proxy for the present value of the cumulative change in expected future cash flows on the hedged transaction.

A6.10.169 Accordingly, once an entity has determined the change in fair value of the hypothetical swap and the change in the fair value of the actual swap for particular periods, it would use this data to assess the hedging relationship's effectiveness. The actual swap would be recorded at fair value on the balance sheet and the amount reported in equity would be adjusted to a balance that reflects the lesser of either the cumulative change in the actual swap's fair value or the cumulative change in the 'perfect' hypothetical swap's fair value. Determining of the fair value of both the 'perfect' hypothetical swap and the actual swap should use discount rates based on the relevant swap curves. Thus, for the hypothetical swap the discount rates used are the spot rates implied by the current yield curve for hypothetical zero coupon bonds due on the date of each future net settlement of the swap. The amount of ineffectiveness, if any, recorded in profit or loss would then be equal to the excess of the cumulative change in the fair value of the actual swap over the cumulative change in the fair value of the 'perfect' hypothetical swap.

A6.10.170 The hypothetical derivative method often is useful in evaluating the effectiveness of cash flow hedging relationships involving other derivatives, such as cross-currency swaps, commodity swaps and forward exchange contracts.

Example – Hypothetical derivative method

Entity A hedges the foreign currency risk of highly probable forecast transactions using forward contracts. Entity A intends to measure the effectiveness of the hedge by modelling the hedged risk of the forecast transaction as a hypothetical derivative.

As explained above, this method is specifically mentioned in IAS 39. Entity A would construct a hypothetical derivative whose terms reflect the relevant terms of the hedged item. Since entity A hedges the foreign currency risk of highly probable sales, the relevant hypothetical derivative is a forward foreign currency contract for the hedged amount maturing at the date on which the cash flows are anticipated, at the relevant forward rate at inception of the hedge. The change in the fair value of the hypothetical derivative is then compared with the change in the fair value of the hedging instrument to determine effectiveness.

The benchmark rate method

A6.10.171 The benchmark rate method is an approach that is used under the dollar offset method to measure the effectiveness of cash flow hedges. Although not specifically mentioned in IAS 39, it is a variant of the hypothetical derivative method that is permitted by the standard and discussed in paragraph A6.10.170 above. Under this method, a 'target' rate is established as the benchmark rate for the hedge. For example, in an interest rate hedge of a variable rate debt instrument using an interest rate swap, the benchmark rate is usually the swap's fixed rate at the inception of the hedge. The benchmark rate method first identifies the difference between the hedging item's actual cash flows and the benchmark rate. It then compares the change in the amount or value of this difference with the change in the cash flow or fair value of the hedging instrument as illustrated in the example below.

Example – Cash flow hedge effectiveness testing – 'fixed benchmark method'

Entity A issues a variable rate bond. On the same date, it enters into an interest rate swap under which it will receive variable and pay a fixed rate of interest. An equivalent fixed rate debt instrument with the same maturity could have been issued at 8%. Entity A designates the swap as a cash flow hedge of the bond. All the criteria for hedge accounting in paragraph A6.10.136 are met.

Entity A proposes to test effectiveness both prospectively and retrospectively by comparing:

- the present value of the cumulative change in expected future cash flows on the swap; with
- the present value of the cumulative change in the expected future interest cash flows on the variable leg less the fixed rate (8%).

In this situation, entity A can use the 'fixed benchmark method' in a cash flow hedge relationship for both prospective and retrospective effectiveness testing. This method reflects the risk management objective of the hedging relationship – that is, to swap a series of future variable cash flows to a fixed rate and is consistent with the requirements in IAS 39 that the method an entity adopts for assessing hedge effectiveness depends on its risk management strategy. [IAS 39 para AG 107].

Entity A should define the hedged risk as the change in the fair value of the variable cash flows, less the change in the fair value of a fixed rate of interest that could have been achieved at the inception of the underlying debt instrument (8%). It, therefore, measures the variability against a specified fixed rate. Effectiveness testing should be performed based on the ability of the hedging instrument to deliver that specified set of cash flows and should, therefore, measure variability from that fixed rate.

Example – Hedge effectiveness testing – 'Change in variable cash flow method'

Using the facts as set out in the example 1 above, the entity's management proposes to test effectiveness both prospectively and retrospectively by comparing the present value of the cumulative change in expected future cash flows on the swap's floating rate leg and the present value of the cumulative change in the expected future interest cash flows on the floating rate liability.

This method is sometimes referred to as the 'change in variable cash flow' method. This method is an acceptable method for performing prospective effectiveness testing, but not for retrospective effectiveness testing.

The justification for using this approach for prospective effectiveness testing is that the change in variable cash flows method is consistent with the cash flow hedge objective of effectively offsetting the changes in the hedged cash flows attributable to the hedged risk and that only the floating rate leg of the swap provides the cash flow hedge protection.

The change in variable cash flow method is not permitted for retrospective effectiveness testing since only a portion of the derivative (the floating rate leg only) is used for the test. Paragraph 74 of IAS 39 states that a hedging relationship is designated by an entity for a hedging instrument in its entirety and that the only exceptions are for the split between time value and intrinsic value of an option and the spot and forward points on a foreign exchange forward. Neither of these exceptions applies when the hedging instrument is an interest rate swap. The entire fair value of the hedging instrument must be used in performing retrospective hedge effectiveness testing.

The last paragraph of IAS 39 IG F5.5 explicitly states that this method is not acceptable, as it has the effect of measuring ineffectiveness on only a portion of the derivative. IAS 39 does not permit the bifurcation of a derivative for the purposes of assessing effectiveness.

Sensitivity analysis method

A6.10.172 This method is applied to assess the effectiveness of a hedge prospectively. The method consists of measuring the effect of a hypothetical shift in the underlying hedged risk (for example, a 10 per cent shift in the foreign currency exchange rate being hedged) on both the hedging instrument and the hedged item.

Regression analysis

A6.10.173 Regression analysis is a statistical technique used to analyse the relationship between one variable (the dependent variable) and one or more other variables (known as independent variables). A common application of regression analysis is to build a model using past information that can be used to predict, say, the value of the dependent variable (for example, current year revenue of a particular retail outlet) for a new observation of the independent variable (for example, local employment). However, in the context of hedge effectiveness test, the method investigates the extent to which changes in the hedged item (the independent variable) and the hedging instrument (the dependent variable) are highly and negatively correlated and, thus, supportive of the assertion that there will be a high degree of offset in fair values or cash flows achieved by the hedge.

A6.10.174 For purposes of the hedge accounting effectiveness test, the analysis usually involves a *simple* linear regression that involves determining a 'line of best fit' and then assessing the 'goodness of fit' of this line. *Multiple* linear regression analysis examines the relationship between a dependent variable and two or more independent variables. The linear equation estimated in a simple regression is commonly expressed as:

$$Y = a + bX + e$$

Y: The dependent variable
X: The independent variable
a: The intercept, where the line crosses the Y axis
b: The gradient of the line
e: The random error term

The values of the X and Y variables are plotted and a 'best fit' line is drawn as illustrated below.

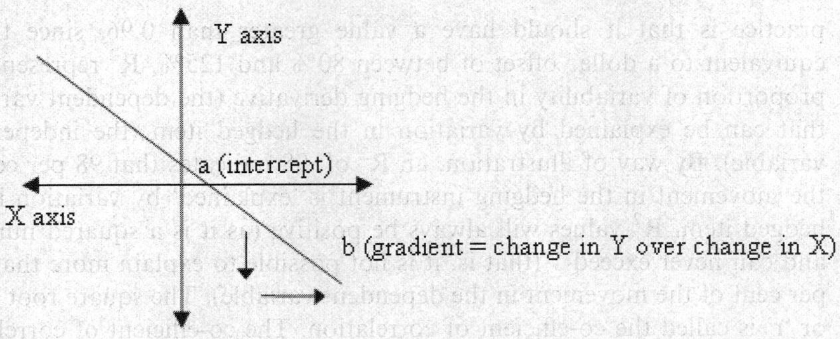

A6.10.175 There are three critical test statistics to determine an effective hedge relationship when using regression analysis. These are as follows:

- Gradient of the line (b) must be negative and in the range -0.8 < b < -1.25.

  The gradient that the regression analysis determines 'best fits' the data, is the ratio of the change in Y value over the change in X value (assuming the model is developed using the hedging derivative as Y or the dependent variable and the hedged item as X or the independent variable). The gradient is a very important component when developing a highly effective hedging relationship and represents the variance-minimising hedge ratio. A gradient of -1 means that for a C1 increase (decrease) in the hedged item, the derivative will generally decrease (increase) by C1, which represents a perfect hedge. The gradient should be negative because the derivative is expected to offset changes in the hedged item. Therefore, if the regression analysis is performed using equal units of the hedging instrument and the hedged item, the gradient b can be used to determine the optimal hedge ratio (that is, the optimal volume of derivative that should be transacted to maximise expected effectiveness). This ratio can then be used by the entity to determine how many units of the hedging instrument it should transact to best mitigate the risk for the particular position being hedged. For example, if the gradient = -0.95, a hedge ratio based on 95 units of the hedging instrument to 100 units of the hedged item will maximise expected effectiveness.

  Once the hedge ratio has been determined and the hedge transacted, the regression analysis is re-performed using the actual quantities of the hedging instrument and the hedged item. The gradient is used when assessing the effectiveness of the actual hedge relationship. The gradient must be negative and fall within the range of -0.8 to -1.25. If the gradient is positive, there is no hedge relationship (that is, the hedging instrument does not mitigate the hedged risk). If the gradient is negative but outside of the range of -0.8 to -1.25, there is some hedge relationship, but it is not strong enough to pass the effectiveness test. Hedge accounting is not permitted in either case.

- The co-efficient of determination (R^2) > 0.96

  The co-efficient of determination (R^2) measures the degree of explanatory power or correlation between the dependent and independent variable. Best practice is that it should have a value greater than 0.96, since this is equivalent to a dollar offset of between 80% and 125%. R^2 represents the proportion of variability in the hedging derivative (the dependent variable) that can be explained by variation in the hedged item (the independent variable). By way of illustration, an R^2 of .98 indicates that 98 per cent of the movement in the hedging instrument is 'explained' by variation in the hedged item. R^2 values will always be positive (as it is a squared number) and can never exceed 1 (that is, it is not possible to explain more than 100 per cent of the movement in the dependent variable). The square root of R^2 or 'r' is called the co-efficient of correlation. The co-efficient of correlation can be either positive or negative depending on the underlying relationship between the dependent and independent variables. Whereas values of R^2 are easily interpreted, 'r' does not have a clear-cut operational interpretation. It should be noted that although it is best practice to have a value of $R^2 > 0.96$, a value of 0.8 (used under US GAAP) maybe acceptable, provided the other regression statistics are also met. In other words, $R^2 > 0.8$ is not, on its own, sufficient.

- The statistical validity of the overall regression model (the F-statistic) must be significant.

  The F-statistic is a standard output from the statistical model. It is a measure of the statistical significance of the relationship between the dependent variable and the independent variable (that is, whether the derivative relationship, relative to the hedged risk, is a statistically valid relationship). A non-significant F-statistic indicates there is no statistically significant relationship between the dependent and independent variables. The F-statistic varies with the number of data points used. It can be obtained from statistical tables. The F-statistic should be significant at a 95 per cent or greater confidence level.

A6.10.176 It is important to note that in order to be deemed highly effective, a regression analysis of a hedging relationship must yield acceptable levels for all three factors as noted above. For example, a regression analysis may produce an $R^2 = 0.96$, but an F-statistic that is not significant at the 95 per cent threshold. In this situation, it is not possible to conclude that there is a statistically significant relationship between the hedged item and the hedging derivative and, therefore, the hedging relationship is not considered effective. Another example is where an entity establishes a 1 for 1 hedge and the regression analysis results in an $R^2 = 0.96$, an F-statistic that is significant at the 95 per cent threshold, but a gradient of only -0.7. In this situation, the hedge relationship would be ineffective, because, on average, it would achieve a dollar offset of only 70 per cent of the hedged item. However, if the entity adjusted its hedge ratio from 1 to 1 to reflect the gradient of -0.7 in order to achieve a higher dollar offset, hedge accounting would be permitted.

A6.10.177 When using regression analysis to test the effectiveness of a hedge, it is important to use a sufficient number of matched paired data points to ensure a statistically valid analysis. Generally speaking, the higher the sample size, the more robust will be the analysis and more reliable the conclusion drawn from the model's output. For statistically reliable results, hedge effectiveness should be based on more than 30 observations. However, as a rule of thumb, no less than 12 observations should be used.

A6.10.178 In using regression or other statistical analysis, it also will be necessary for an entity to determine the interval between data points – for example, whether to use daily, weekly, monthly, or quarterly changes in prices in assessing effectiveness. Generally, the selection frequency would depend on:

- The nature of the hedged item.
- The nature of the hedging derivative.
- Whether certain data points will most appropriately represent the interaction of the hedged item versus the hedging instrument.
- The availability of the data.

Ideally, the entity should try to incorporate as much *relevant* information as possible. Determining what is relevant requires considerable judgment. For instance, it would not be appropriate to use past data that is no longer representative of the current or future market conditions. In those circumstances, it may be appropriate to use a shorter more recent data set consisting of say, daily or weekly frequency period that more faithfully represents the current hedging relationship. On the other hand, too short a period might be equally problematic. If, say, interest rates remained stable over the past few months, a regression analysis based over this short time span would provide a poor indication of how the hedge will perform when interest rates become more volatile.

A6.10.179 When a regression analysis is first performed (at the inception of the hedging relationship), an entity may need to determine that the hedging relationship will be highly effective on a prospective basis. This analysis may use historical data to determine valuations for the proposed derivative and the hedged item. The historical data observation would *typically* (but not necessarily) cover the same period as the length of the hedging relationship. For example, assume an entity issues a three-year fixed rate debt instrument today and enters into an interest rate swap to hedge the fair value exposure to changes in interest rate. The entity should use last three year's data as input for a regression analysis to test whether, at inception, given the terms of the loan and the swap, the hedge is likely to be highly effective on a prospective basis. Conversely, if the last three years' data were not representative of the next three years', use of regression analysis would not be appropriate.

A6.10.180 As the standard requires that effectiveness should be assessed at a minimum at the time an entity prepares its annual or interim financial statements, the entity would carry out both prospective and retrospective hedge effectiveness testing at the subsequent measurement date. If one method is being used for both prospective and retrospective analyses, the same number of data points should be used in the subsequent assessment. Assuming that the entity has chosen monthly data points, the regression analysis at the next annual reporting date would also include 36 data points (12 monthly actual data after inception and the 24 monthly data before inception). As such, 12 months of the oldest data is excluded from the regression analysis. Accordingly, the regression analysis will always contain the same number of data points. It should be noted that the method outlined is not the only acceptable method to determine inputs for regression analysis. Instead of using discrete monthly data, the entity could use a cumulative retrospective evaluation as long as the same number of data points is included in the analysis.

A6.10.181 From an accounting perspective, regression analysis proves whether or not the relationship is sufficiently effective to qualify for hedge accounting. It does not calculate the amount of any ineffectiveness, nor does it provide the numbers necessary for the accounting entries where the analysis demonstrates that the 'highly effective' test has been passed. The accounting entries are based on the dollar-offset method of measuring the changes in the fair values of the derivative and in the hedged risk of the hedged item, both calculated using actual rates at the test date as explained in paragraph A6.10.189 below.

Comparison between regression analysis and dollar offset method

A6.10.182 There may be circumstances where the results from regression analysis support the use of hedge accounting, but the dollar offset measurement indicate that the hedge would not be highly effective if the dollar offset method had been used. Indeed, it would not be unusual for this to happen, as the two methods are very different. Therefore, in a period where the dollar offset accounting measurement indicates that the accounting results are slightly outside of the 80 to 125 per cent range, hedge accounting would still be appropriate assuming that there was a sound statistical regression analysis supporting the use of hedge accounting for that period. However, if the dollar offset accounting measurements indicate that the hedging relationship was significantly outside of the 80 to 125 per cent range, then the validity and soundness of the regression analysis would be called into question. In that situation, the entity should seek to ascertain the causes for such differences. It may be that small changes in the values of either the hedged item or the hedging instrument cause the dollar offset method to be outside the range based on current hedge designation. In that situation, continuation of hedge accounting may be appropriate. However, continual failure to achieve high effectiveness under the dollar offset method for reasons other than small dollar differences may invalidate the use of regression analysis for the hedging relationship. In that situation, hedge accounting should be discontinued prospectively unless the entity is able to correct any known deficiencies in the prior model and demonstrate that the new model produces a sound statistical regression result that is representative of the hedging relationship.

Hedge ineffectiveness

Sources of hedge ineffectiveness

A6.10.183 Hedge relationships are seldom perfect. Therefore, ineffectiveness will almost always arise with the result that changes in the fair value or cash flows of the hedged item that are attributable to a hedged risk and the hedging instrument do not offset within a period. Examples of differences that can produce ineffectiveness include:

- Basis differences – the fair value or cash flows of the hedged item depend on a variable that is different from the variable that causes the fair value or cash flows of the hedging instrument to change. For example, an entity designates the benchmark interest rate as the hedged risk when the hedged item uses a different index, such as the prime base rate. The basis difference between those indices would affect the assessment and measurement of hedge ineffectiveness.

- Location differences – the fair value or cash flows of the hedged item and hedging instrument both depend on the price of the same commodity, but are based on the price at different locations. The price of a commodity will be different in different locations, because of factors such as regional supply and demand and transportation costs.

- Timing differences – the hedged item and hedging instrument occur or are settled at different dates. For example, an entity hedges the forecast purchase of a commodity with a derivative that settles at an earlier or later date than the date of the forecast purchase. Another example is a floating rate debt whose variability is hedged with an interest rate swap where the interest rate reset dates on the two instruments are different.

- Quantity or notional amount differences – the hedged item and hedging instrument are based on a different quantities or notional amounts.

- Changes in the fair value or cash flows of a derivative hedging instrument relating to risks other than the specific risk being hedged. For example, an entity hedges the variability in the price of a forecast purchase of a commodity with a derivative whose cash flows are based on the price of a different commodity and this is the only source of ineffectiveness in the relationship.

- Use of off market derivatives – an off market derivative is an existing derivative that has a non-zero fair value. Hedge ineffectiveness can arise when using an off market derivative in a number of common place scenarios such as: documentation of a hedge not completed at inception, attempting to restart hedge accounting following a documentation deficiency, temporary interruption of a hedging strategy, change of method of assessing hedge effectiveness in the middle of a hedge period, hedges acquired in a business combination and renegotiation of terms of the derivative.

Minimising hedge ineffectiveness

A6.10.184 The key to minimising hedge ineffectiveness is the precision in the hedge designation. In many cases, it will be possible to minimise the ineffectiveness in a hedging relationship by the way an entity designates the risk being hedged. This is because under IAS 39 financial assets or liabilities can be hedged with respect to specific risk only (a component of total risk), provided that the exposure to the specific risk component is identifiable and separately measurable (see para A6.10.24 above). Also, it is possible to designate a hedged financial asset or a financial liability with respect to the risks associated with only a portion of its cash flows or fair value (see para A6.10.23 above). For non-financial items only certain risks can be hedged and this is discussed from paragraph A6.10.31. Therefore, considerable ineffectiveness can be eliminated when the risk designated as being hedged matches the risk of the hedging instrument. Consider the following example.

Example – Exclusion of credit risk from interest rate risk

On 1 October 20X5, entity A issues a fixed-interest note at 8% for C1,000. On the same day, entity A enters into an interest rate swap to pay LIBOR and receive interest at 7% based on the same payment terms and with a notional principal of C1,000. At inception entity A designates the swap as a hedge of the variability in fair value of the issued note.

	Fair values		
	1 October 20X5	30 September 20X6	Change
Fixed interest note	(1,000)	(1,048)	(48)
Interest rate swap	–	102	102
Difference			54
The effectiveness of the hedging relationship =	– 102/48 =		213%

Hedge accounting is not permitted, as the results of the effectiveness test are significantly below the minimum required effectiveness of 125%. The main reason for the difference in fair value movements leading to the ineffectiveness is entity A's deteriorating creditworthiness.

IAS 39 permits an entity to designate any portion of risk in a financial asset or liability as the hedged item. Hedge effectiveness is generally significantly easier to achieve if the designated hedged risk matches the hedging instrument as closely as possible. In this case, entity A should re-designate the risk being hedged in order to improve the hedge effectiveness for future periods. As the entity's deteriorating creditworthiness is the major cause of the hedge ineffectiveness, it should exclude this risk going forward and hedge only the changes in the bond's fair value attributable to changes in the risk-free interest rate. The new designation to exclude the bond's credit risk from the hedge relationship will improve hedge effectiveness, because the bond's credit risk is not reflected in the hedge.

6A.10.185 There is normally a single fair value measure for a hedging derivative in its entirety. Therefore, a derivative cannot be split into components representing different risks and designating such components as the hedging instruments. However, as stated in paragraph A6.10.56 above, the interest element of a forward contract and the time value of an option may be excluded from the fair value measurement of the hedging derivative. These exclusions can often improve the hedge's effectiveness as they allow the hedging derivative's risk to match that of the hedged item. In that case, changes in the excluded component, for example, interest element portion of the fair value of the forward exchange contract are recognised in profit or loss. The interest element of a forward contract is never amortised to profit or loss under IAS 39. [IAS 39 para IG F6.4].

A6.10.186 Similarly, when the hedging instrument is an option rather than a forward contract, the option's time value can be excluded from the option's fair value and hedge effectiveness assessed based on the changes in the option's intrinsic value. However, in such situations, the excluded time value, which is not of the hedge relationship, will be recognised in profit or loss as explained in paragraph A6.10.59 above and illustrated in the example below.

Example – Exclusion of time value of option from hedge effectiveness assessment

Entity A owns 100,000 equity shares in a quoted entity B, which it has classified as available-for-sale. The current price of the security is C25. To give itself partial protection against decreases in the share price of entity B, Entity A acquires an at-the-money put option on 100,000 shares of entity B at a strike price of C25 for C10,000. Entity A designates the change in the intrinsic value of the put as a hedging instrument in a fair value hedge of changes in the fair value of its share in entity B.

In this situation, IAS 39 permits entity A to designate changes in the intrinsic value of the put option as a hedge of its equity investment that is consistent with entity A's hedging strategy. The hedge relationship is designated only for the price range when the put option is in-the-money (current market price = strike price), that is, the option provides protection against the risk of variability in the fair value of entity B's 100,000 shares below or equal to the strike price of the put of C25.

Effectiveness is measured by comparing the change in the investment's fair value below the strike price of C25 with changes in the option's intrinsic value. Therefore, when the option is out-of-the-money, no effectiveness measurement is necessary, but prospective assessment is still required. This means that gains and losses on entity B's 100,000 shares for prices above C25 are not attributable to the hedged risk for the purposes of assessing hedge effectiveness and for recognising gains and losses on the hedged item. Therefore, entity A reports changes in the shares' fair value in equity if it is associated with variation in its price above C25. [IAS 39 paras 55, 90]. Changes in the fair value of the shares associated with price declines below C25 form part of the designated fair value hedge and are recognised in profit or loss. [IAS 39 para 89(b)]. Assuming the hedge is effective, those changes are offset by changes in the intrinsic value of the put, which are also recognised in profit or loss. [IAS 39 para 89(a)].

Since the option is at-the-money at inception, the premium paid of C10,000 is all attributable to the option's time value. Changes in the put option's time value are not included in the assessment of hedge effectiveness and are recognised in profit or loss. [IAS 39 para 55(a)]. The option's fair value may change due to factors such as volatility of the share price, the passage of time and risk free rate. As such factors do not affect the option's intrinsic value (current price – strike price), they form part of the time value component.

6A.10.187 Another issue in connection with ineffectiveness arises when assessing the effectiveness of hedging instruments such as interest rate swaps. In an interest rate swap, the payments are usually set at the beginning of a period and paid at the next interest reset date. Where hedge effectiveness assessments are undertaken between two re-pricing dates, the effect of interest accrual will affect the swap's fair value. Accordingly, the corresponding changes in the swap's fair value will not fully offset changes in the bond's fair value. However, it is possible to improve the hedge's effectiveness by using the swap's 'clean' fair value rather than the 'dirty' fair value that includes the accrued interest. Using the clean fair value in effectiveness testing often decreases the ineffectiveness, as it excludes the accrued interest on the swap's variable leg that will not have any offsetting component in the bond.

Measuring hedge ineffectiveness

A6.10.188 High effectiveness must be achieved initially and on an ongoing basis in order for a hedging relationship to qualify for hedge accounting. High effectiveness does not guarantee, however, that there will be no earnings volatility resulting from hedge ineffectiveness. Where the hedge is highly effective but not perfectly effective (that is, if a dollar-offset test is used the hedge is between 80 and 125 per cent effective, but it is not 100 per cent effective), there will be some volatility in earnings due to the ineffective portion of the hedge. Equally, the designation of the hedge may be very precise and thus achieves hedge accounting but volatility will be caused by that which has been excluded from the hedge relationship, although this is not 'hedge ineffectiveness'.

A6.10.189 Regardless of whether dollar-offset or regression analysis is used to assess prospective and/or retrospective hedge effectiveness, the dollar offset measurements are used to determine the amount of ineffectiveness that has occurred and that must be recognised in profit or loss in each reporting period. Similarly, where hedge effectiveness is assessed using clean prices of an interest rate swap, the spot component of a forward contract, or the intrinsic value of an option to improve hedge effectiveness, the measurement of the hedging instrument for accounting purposes must still be based on the entire fair value of the derivative that will include accrued interest, forward points or intrinsic value.

A6.10.190 The extent to which hedge ineffectiveness is recognised in profit or loss will depend on whether the hedge is a fair value hedge or a cash flow hedge. In a fair value hedge, any hedge ineffectiveness directly affects profit or loss. This is because the entire change in the fair value of the hedged item (attributable to the hedged risk) and the entire change in the fair value of the hedging instrument are both reflected in profit or loss in each reporting period and the two changes may not perfectly offset each other.

A6.10.191 For cash flow hedges, the measurement of hedge effectiveness is different from a fair value hedge. As explained in paragraph A6.10.116 above, the amount recognised in equity for a cash flow hedge is the lower of the cumulative gain or loss on the hedging instrument from inception of the hedge and the cumulative change in fair value (present value) of the expected future cash flows on the hedged item from inception of the hedge. To the extent that the cumulative gain or loss on the hedging instrument exceeds the cumulative change in fair value of the expected cash flows on the hedged item, the excess is recognised in profit or loss. However, if there is a shortfall, there will be no ineffectiveness recognised in profit or loss.

A6.10.192 The implementation guidance to IAS 39 provides a very comprehensive example of the dollar offset method for cash flow hedges. [IAS 39 IGF5.5]. The example sets out two practical methods for assessing effectiveness and measuring ineffectiveness for cash flow hedge of a forecast issuance of fixed rate debt. These two methods are known as 'the hypothetical derivative method' and the 'change in fair value method'. Although the example is not reproduced here, the way in which the hypothetical derivative and the change in fair value methods work in practice is explained in paragraphs 6.10.168 and 6.10.193 respectively. Regardless of which method is used for the measurement of cash flow hedge effectiveness, an entity must meet the requirements of paragraph A6.10.136 above for designation of a cash flow hedging relationship. That is, in designating a cash flow hedging relationship, an entity must have the expectation, both at inception of the hedge and ongoing, that the relationship will be highly effective at achieving offsetting changes in cash flows.

Change in fair value method

A6.10.193 The change in fair value method is referred to as 'method A' in IAS 39 graph IG F5.5. This method is applicable for determining hedge effectiveness for variable rate financial assets and liabilities and forecast issuance of fixed rate debt. Under this method, the measurement of hedge ineffectiveness is based on a calculation that compares the present value of the cumulative change in expected variable future interest cash flows that are designated as the hedged transactions and the cumulative change in the fair value of the swap designated as the hedging instrument. The discount rates applicable to determining the fair value of the swap designated as the hedging instrument should also be applied to the computation of present values of the cumulative changes in the hedged cash flows. This method will result in ineffectiveness.

Change in variable cash flow method

A6.10.194 The 'change in variable cash flow method' is sometimes proposed as a method to test the effectiveness of a cash flow hedge. For example, an entity may under IAS 39 use a receive-variable, pay-fixed interest rate swap as a cash flow hedge of a variable rate bond. Under the method, the entity would test effectiveness by comparing the present value of the cumulative change in expected future cash flows on the floating rate leg of the swap with the present value of the cumulative change in the expected future interest cash flows on the floating rate liability.

A6.10.195 Although this method is not mentioned in IAS 39, it is an acceptable method for performing prospective, but not for retrospective effectiveness testing. The justification for using this method for prospective effectiveness testing is that it is consistent with the cash flow hedge objective of effectively offsetting the changes in cash flows attributable to the hedged risk. It is the floating rate leg of the swap that achieves this offset. However, the method is not permitted under IAS 39 for retrospective testing, because it has the effect of measuring ineffectiveness on only a portion of the derivative (that is, only the floating rate leg). IAS 39 does not permit effectiveness to be assessed retrospectively using only a portion of a derivative as discussed in para A6.10.56 above.

Portfolio (or macro) hedging

A6.10.196 Portfolio or macro hedging is a technique used to reduce or eliminate the risk of a portfolio of assets and liabilities. Banks and similar financial institutions often use this technique to manage the interest rate risk of a portfolio of assets and liabilities. They did this by hedging the net position (for example, net of fixed rate assets and fixed rate liabilities).

A6.10.197 Prior to the issue of the amended version of IAS 39 (see below), the hedging techniques used by banks were not in accordance with the underlying core principles of IAS 39 of not permitting hedges of a net position of assets and liabilities to qualify for hedge accounting. In addition, many of the assets included in a portfolio are typically pre-payable fixed rate assets, that is, the counterparty has the right to pre-pay the item before its contractual maturity. When interest rates change, the resulting change in the fair value of the pre-payable asset differs from the change in fair value of the hedging derivative (which is not pre-payable), with the result that the hedge would often fail the IAS 39 hedge effectiveness test. Furthermore, many of the liabilities included in a portfolio are repayable on demand or after a notice period (often referred to as core deposits). Including them in a portfolio implies that their fair values change with movements in interest rates, which is against the notion in IAS 39 that the fair value of a demand deposit is not less than the amount repayable on demand, because that amount does not change with movements in interest rates.

A6.10.198 Therefore, when the exposure draft of proposed improvements to IAS 39 was published in June 2002, it did not contain any substantial changes to the requirements for hedge accounting as they applied to a portfolio hedge of interest rate risk. Banks were concerned that portfolio hedging strategies that they regarded as effective hedges would not qualify for fair value hedge accounting under IAS 39. They would either:

- not qualify for hedge accounting at all, with the result that profit or loss would be volatile; or

- qualify only for cash flow hedge accounting with the result that equity would be volatile. This is could potentially give rise to genuine problems for some banks because of capital adequacy requirements imposed by prudential regulators.

A6.10.199 The banks' concerns found considerable political sympathy and the IASB was strongly encouraged to come to an agreement with them. As a result, after much deliberation, in March 2004, the IASB published an amendment to IAS 39, 'Fair value hedge accounting for portfolio hedge of interest rate risk'. Unfortunately, not all of the banks' concerns were addressed. In particular, significant restrictions for hedging deposits with a demand feature still remained. As a result, the version of IAS 39 that was endorsed by the EU had a carve-out that primarily allows banks to apply fair value hedge accounting to hedges of the interest rate risk in their portfolio of demand or core deposits for interest rate risk, which is prohibited by the full IAS 39 as noted in paragraph A6.10.197 above. It also removed the need for banks to recognise ineffectiveness in the income statement as a result of under hedging that may arise in certain circumstances in fair value hedge accounting for a portfolio hedge of interest rate risk.

A6.10.200 IAS 39 sets out in paragraphs AG114-AG132 a series of procedures that an entity would need to comply with for achieving hedge accounting for a fair value hedge of interest rate risk associated with a portfolio of financial assets or financial liabilities. It should be noted, however, that in the EU carve-out version some of the above paragraphs were amended and some deleted. The implementation guidance to IAS 39 also sets out a series of issues that an entity should consider when applying cash flow hedge accounting to a portfolio hedge of interest rate risk. [IAS 39 IG F6.2]. A very comprehensive example of applying the approach discussed in IG F6.2 is also included [IAS 39 IG F6.3]. As the topic of macro hedging is of little interest to entities other than banks and other financial institutions, it is not dealt with in this section.

Comprehensive examples

A6.10.201 Three detailed illustrations of how hedge accounting can be applied in practice are given below. The objective is to present the mechanics of applying IAS 39 requirements, starting with the entity's risk management and effectiveness testing policies, working through the necessary designation and effectiveness testing and culminating with the accounting entries.

A6.10.202 The three examples illustrate some of the most common hedging strategies used in practice. They cover the three types of hedges recognised for accounting purposes by IAS 39 (fair value hedges, cash flow hedges and net investment hedges). The issues addressed are summarised in the table below:

	Type of hedge and hedged risk	Hedged item and hedging instrument	Effectiveness testing		Other key points of the illustration
			Prospective	Retrospective	
Illustration 1					
'Conversion' of fixed rate debt into variable rate debt using an interest rate swap	Fair value hedge – Interest rate risk	Fixed rate debt – Interest rate swap	Dollar offset using clean market values, sensitivity analysis approach	Dollar offset on a cumulative basis using clean market values, benchmark approach	Credit risk not hedged
Illustration 2					
Hedge of highly probable foreign currency forecast purchases	Cash flow hedge – Foreign exchange risk	Highly probable forecast transaction – Forward contract	Dollar offset, sensitivity analysis approach	Dollar offset on a cumulative basis, hypothetical derivative approach	Spot/spot rate designation – Change in timing of cash flows – Basis adjustment
Illustration 3					
Foreign currency hedge of a net investment in a foreign operation	Net investment hedge – Foreign exchange risk	Net investment – Borrowing	Dollar offset using dirty market values, sensitivity analysis approach	Dollar offset on a cumulative basis using dirty market values, benchmark approach	Credit risk in borrowing excluded – Effect of losses

A6.10.203 Despite the range of approaches covered, these illustrations do not set out all of the ways of complying with IAS 39's hedging requirements. Other approaches to hedge accounting may meet IAS 39's requirements. One issue not covered in the illustrations is the discontinuance of hedge accounting. This is covered earlier in the section. The underlying calculations in some of the illustrations have been performed using more decimal places for interest rates and discount factors than are presented. If the calculations are reperformed using the data presented, some minor differences in the numbers may arise. Finally, at various points 'helpful hint' boxes have been included. These highlight important issues, give additional guidance and contain tips relating to the illustrations.

Fair value hedge of fixed rate debt

Company A is a UK company with a £ functional currency. Company A's reporting dates are 30 June and 31 December.

On 15 March 20X5, company A issues at par a £10m four-year debt with the following characteristics:

Type	Issued debt
Principal amount	£10m
Start date	15 March 20X5
Maturity date	15 March 20X9
Interest rate	7%
Settlement date	15 March, 15 June, 15 September and 15 December each year

No transaction costs are incurred relating to the debt issuance. On the date on which the debt was issued, consistent with its risk management policies, company A enters into a four-year pay three-month £ LIBOR receive five per cent interest rate swap. The variable leg of the swap is pre-fixed/post-paid on 15 March, 15 June, 15 September and 15 December each year. The fixing of the variable leg for the first three-month period is 4.641 per cent.

> **Helpful hint**
> A pre-fixed/post-paid interest rate swap is an interest rate swap in which the variable coupon is determined based on the market interest rate at the beginning of each period and is paid at the end. The variable coupon on the interest rate swap determined on 15 March is paid on 15 June, and so on.

The cash flows on the debt and the swap can be represented as follows:

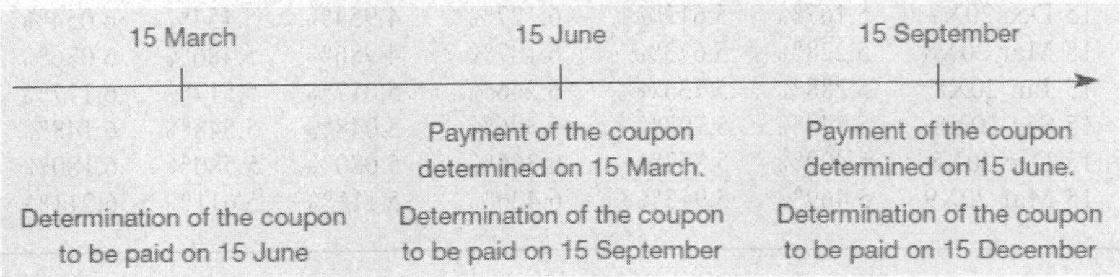

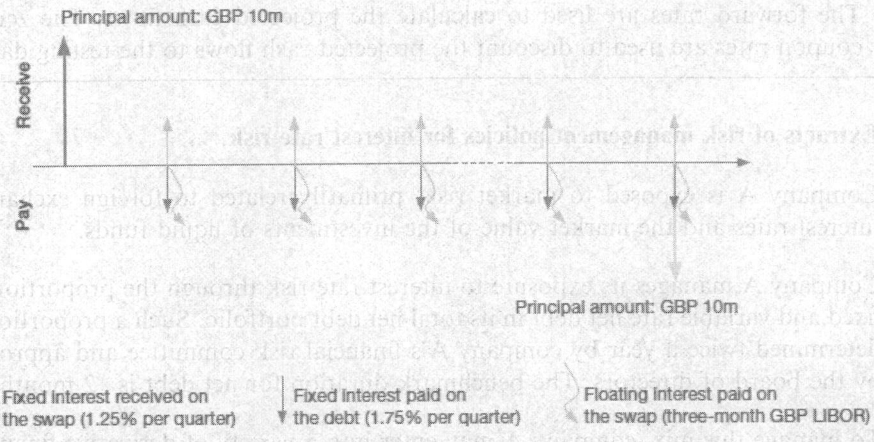

Three-month £ LIBOR rate at various dates when the swap is reset is as follows:

15 Mar 20X5	4.562%
15 Jun 20X5	5.080%
15 Sep 20X5	5.280%
15 Dec 20X5	5.790%

The forward rates derived from the £ LIBOR swap yield curve and the implied zero coupon rates at the dates of testing effectiveness are as follows:

	Forward rates for testing dates			Zero coupon rates for testing dates		
	15 Mar 20X5 (YC1)	30/6/20X5 (YC2)	31/12/20X5 (YC3)	15 Mar 20X5 (ZC1)	30/6/20X5 (ZC2)	31/12/20X5 (ZC3)
15 Jun 20X5	4.562%	–	–	4.641%	–	–
15 Sep 20X5	4.623%	5.069%	–	4.672%	5.172%	–
15 Dec 20X5	4.684%	5.130%	–	4.704%	5.204%	–
15 Mar 20X6	4.744%	5.191%	5.705%	4.735%	5.235%	5.835%
15 Jun 20X6	4.805%	5.251%	5.767%	4.766%	5.266%	5.866%
15 Sep 20X6	4.865%	5.311%	5.827%	4.798%	5.298%	5.898%
15 Dec 20X6	4.926%	5.371%	5.887%	4.829%	5.329%	5.929%
15 Mar 20X7	4.986%	5.432%	5.947%	4.860%	5.360%	5.960%
15 Jun 20X7	5.046%	5.492%	6.007%	4.892%	5.392%	5.992%
15 Sep 20X7	5.107%	5.552%	6.067%	4.923%	5.423%	6.023%
15 Dec 20X7	5.167%	5.612%	6.127%	4.954%	5.454%	6.054%
15 Mar 20X8	5.228%	5.673%	6.187%	4.986%	5.486%	6.086%
15 Jun 20X8	5.288%	5.733%	6.246%	5.017%	5.517%	6.117%
15 Sep 20X8	5.348%	5.793%	6.306%	5.048%	5.548%	6.148%
15 Dec 20X8	5.409%	5.853%	6.366%	5.080%	5.580%	6.180%
15 Mar 20X9	5.469%	5.913%	6.426%	5.111%	5.611%	6.211%

Helpful hint
The forward rates are used to calculate the projected cash flows. The zero-coupon rates are used to discount the projected cash flows to the testing date.

Extracts of risk management policies for interest rate risk

Company A is exposed to market risk, primarily related to foreign exchange, interest rates and the market value of the investments of liquid funds.

Company A manages its exposure to interest rate risk through the proportion of fixed and variable rate net debt in its total net debt portfolio. Such a proportion is determined twice a year by company A's financial risk committee and approved by the board of directors. The benchmark duration for net debt is 12 months.

To manage this mix, company A may enter into a variety of derivative financial instruments, such as interest rate swap contracts.

Extracts of hedge effectiveness testing policies

Strategy 1A Hedges of interest rate risk using interest rate swaps for fair value hedges

Prospective effectiveness testing

Prospective effectiveness testing should be performed at the inception of the hedge and at each reporting date. The hedge relationship is highly effective if the changes in fair value or cash flow of the hedged item that are attributable to the hedged risk are expected to be offset by the changes in fair value or cash flows of the hedging instrument.

Prospective effectiveness testing should be performed by comparing the numerical effects of a shift in the hedged interest rate (£ LIBOR zero coupon curve) on both the fair value of the hedging instrument and the fair value of the hedged item.

This comparison should normally be based on at least three interest rate scenarios. However, for hedges where the critical terms of the hedging instrument perfectly match the critical terms, including reset dates of the hedged item, one scenario is sufficient.

$$\text{Effectiveness} = \frac{\text{Change in clean fair value of hedging instrument when zero coupon curve is shifted}}{\text{Change in clean fair value of hedged item when zero coupon curve is shifted}}$$

Change in the clean fair value of a swap is the difference between the clean fair value of the projected cash flows of the swap discounted using the zero coupon curve derived from the swap yield curve at the date of testing, and the clean fair value of the projected shifted cash flows discounted using the shifted zero-coupon rates.

Change in the clean fair value of a bond is the difference between the clean fair value of the cash flows on the bond excluding the credit spread discounted using the zero coupon curve derived from the swap yield curve at the date of testing, and the clean fair value of the same cash flows discounted using the shifted zero coupon rates.

The scenarios that should be used in the effectiveness test are:

(1) a parallel shift (upwards) of 100 basis points of the zero coupon curve;

(2) a change in the slope of the zero coupon curve of a 5% increase in the rate for one year cash flows, a 10% increase in the rate for two year cash flows, and a 15% increase in the rate for three and more year cash flows; and

(3) a change to a flat zero coupon curve at present three-month LIBOR.

> **Helpful hint**
> The number of scenarios needed to assess prospectively the effectiveness of a hedge when using the dollar offset method will vary depending on the terms of the hedge. When the critical terms of the hedging instrument (start date, end date, currency, fixed payment date, interest rate re-set date, fixed interest rate, principal amount) do not match those of the hedged item, or the hedged item contains a feature – such as optionality – that is likely to cause ineffectiveness, several scenarios should be used, including scenarios that reflect the mismatch in terms or optionality.
>
> The pre-fixed/post-paid feature of the swap that is not present in the bond prevents the use of the critical terms method, as there will be some ineffectiveness. Three scenarios should be used to test effectiveness prospectively, consistent with the entity's policy. The example below shows only the first of these three scenarios.
>
> The dirty fair value is the fair value including accrued interest. The clean fair value excludes accrued interest. Using the clean fair value in effectiveness testing often decreases the ineffectiveness, as it excludes the accrued interest on the variable leg of the swap that will not have any offsetting component in the bond.

Retrospective effectiveness testing

Retrospective effectiveness testing should be performed at each reporting date using the dollar offset method on a cumulative basis. Hedge effectiveness is demonstrated by comparing the cumulative change in the clean fair value of the hedging instrument with the cumulative change in the clean fair value of the hedged item attributable to the hedged risk and showing that it falls within the required range of 80%-125%.

$$\text{Effectiveness} = \frac{\text{Cumulative change in clean fair value of hedging instrument}}{\text{Cumulative change in clean fair value of hedged item}}$$

Change in the clean fair value of a swap is the difference between:

(a) the clean fair value of the projected cash flows of the swap based on the original yield curve discounted using the zero coupon curve derived from the yield curve at the beginning of the hedge; and

(b) the clean fair value of the projected cash flows of the swap based on the yield curve at the date of testing discounted using the zero coupon curve derived from the yield curve at the date of testing.

Change in the clean fair value of a bond is the difference between:

(a) the clean fair value of the cash flows on the bond, excluding the credit spread discounted using the zero coupon curve derived from the yield curve at the beginning of the hedge; and

(b) the clean fair value of the same cash flows discounted using the zero coupon curve derived from the yield curve at the date of testing.

> **Helpful hint**
> In a fair value hedge, the carrying amount of the hedged item, in this case the debt, is adjusted for changes in value attributable to the hedged risk only. This might not be the same as the total changes in the fair value of the debt. Fair value changes attributable to credit or other risks that are not hedged are not included in the adjustment of the carrying amount of the hedged item.

Hedge designation

Company A's hedge documentation is shown below.

1 Risk management objective and strategy

For the current period, company A's approved strategy in accordance with its risk management policies is to maintain a ratio of fixed:floating rate net debt of between 40:60 and 50:50. In order to achieve this ratio, management has selected this debt to be swapped from fixed to floating.

2 Type of hedging relationship

Fair value hedge: swap of fixed to floating interest rates.

3 Nature of risk being hedged

Interest rate risk: change in the fair value of debt number C426M attributable to movements in the £ LIBOR zero coupon curve. Credit risk on the debt is not designated as being hedged.

4 Identification of hedged item

Transaction number: reference number C426M in the treasury management system.

The hedged item is a four-year, £10m, 7% fixed rate debt, which pays interest quarterly.

5 Identification of hedging instrument

Transaction number: reference number L1815E in the treasury management system.

The hedging instrument is a four-year interest rate swap, notional value £10m, under which fixed interest of 5% is received quarterly and actual three-month LIBOR is paid with a three-month reset.

Hedge designation: the fair value movements on the full notional £10m of the swap L1815E is designated as a hedge of fair value movements in the debt C426M attributable to movements in £ LIBOR zero coupon curve (see point 3 above).

6 Effectiveness testing

Testing shall be performed using hedging effectiveness testing strategy 1A in the effectiveness testing policy.

Description of prospective test

Dollar offset method, being the ratio of the change in the clean fair value of the swap L1815E, divided by the change in clean fair value of the bond C426M attributable to changes in £ LIBOR zero coupon curve.

The critical terms of the swap do not perfectly match the critical terms of the hedged debt. The prospective tests will therefore, as required by the risk management policies, be performed based on three scenarios. (Only scenario 1, the 100 basis point increase, is illustrated below; all three would be performed in practice.)

Frequency of testing: at inception of the hedge and at each reporting date (30 June and 31 December).

Description of retrospective test

Dollar offset method, being the ratio of the change in the clean fair value of swap L1815E, divided by the change in the clean fair value of the bond C426M attributable to changes in the £ LIBOR zero coupon curve on a cumulative basis.

Frequency of testing: at every reporting date (30 June and 31 December) after inception of the hedge.

Effectiveness tests and accounting entries

1 Prospective effectiveness test on 15 March 20X5

Company A's management should assess prospectively the effectiveness of the hedge, as required by IAS 39.

Based on the hedge documentation, the prospective effectiveness test consists of comparing the effects of a 100 basis points shift upwards of the zero coupon curve on the clean fair value of the swap and the clean fair value of the hedged item.

A coupon of 7% per annum is paid on the debt (that is, £175,000 per quarter), which can be split into an AA interest rate of 5% and a credit spread of 2%. For effectiveness testing purposes, only the cash flows relating to the AA interest rate (that is, £125,000 per quarter) are taken into account. The credit risk associated with the debt is not part of the hedge relationship; the credit spread of 2% in the coupon is, therefore, excluded from the tests.

Prospective effectiveness test on 15 March 20X5

	15 Jun 20X5	15 Sep 20X5	15 Dec 20X5 ...	15 Dec 20X8	15 Mar 20X9	Total
Cash flows on the swap						
Fixed leg	125,000	125,000	125,000 ...	125,000	125,000	
Variable leg*	(114,059)	(115,573)	(117,088)...	(135,221)	(136,729)	
Net cash flows	10,941	9,427	7,912 ...	(10,221)	(11,729)	
Discounted CF @ ZC1	10,818	9,214	7,644 ...	(8,488)	(9,609)	**0**
Shifted zero coupon curve						
Fixed leg	125,000	125,000	125,000 ...	125,000	125,000	
Variable leg + 1%	(114,059)	(139,640)	(141,144)...	(159,148)	(160,646)	
Net cash flows	10,941	(14,640)	(16,144)...	(34,148)	(35,646)	
Discounted CF @ ZC1 + 1%	10,792	(14,242)	(15,486)...	(27,368)	(28,117)	**(315,574)**
						(315,574)
Cash flows on the debt						
Cash flows	(125,000)	(125,000)	(125,000)...	(125,000)	(10,125,000)	
Discounted CF at ZC1**	(123,590)	(122,178)	(120,764)...	(103,804)	(8,294,694)	**(10,000,000)**
Discounted CF @ ZC1 + 1%	(123,297)	(121,599)	(119,906)...	(100,182)	(7,986,407)	**(9,660,676)**
						339,324
Effectiveness						**-93.0%**

* The variable leg of the swap is the projected cash flow according to forward rates derived from the swap yield curve. As an example, the 15 Sep 20X5 projected cash flow is calculated as 10 million £* 4.623%/4 = 115,573, as the swap has quarterly reset and settlement.

** The discounted cash flows are calculated using the zero coupon rate for the relevant point on the implied zero coupon curve using the normal discounting formula cf/(1 + r)^(d/360), where cf is the undiscounted cash flow, r is the relevant zero coupon rate and d is the number of days remaining to the cash flow (on 360 day basis). As an example, the discounted cash flow on 15 Sep 20X5 is calculated as 125,000/(1.0467)^(180/360) = 122,178.

Conclusion: The hedge is expected to be highly effective.

Helpful hint

The ineffectiveness in the prospective test comes from the change in the fair value of the variable leg of the swap that occurs when projected cash flows are changed. The change in fair value of the fixed leg of the swap perfectly offsets changes in the fair value of the bond.

2 Accounting entries on 15 March 20X5

The debt is recognised at the proceeds received by company A, which represents its fair value on the issuance date. The debt is classified as other financial liabilities and will subsequently be measured at amortised cost.

	Dr	Cr
Cash	10,000,000	
Other financial liabilities – debt		10,000,000
Issuance at par of a £10m four-year debt with a fixed coupon of 7%		

The swap entered into by company A is recognised at fair value on the balance sheet. The fair value of the swap is nil at inception, as it is issued at market rate. The floating rate for the first period is set to 4.562%, which is the three-month swap rate.

	Dr	Cr
Derivative instruments	nil	
Cash		nil
Recognition of the interest rate swap at fair value (nil)		

3 Accounting entries on 15 June 20X5

On 15 June, the first coupon on the loan is paid and the first period of the swap is settled.

Recognition of interest on the debt

	Dr	Cr
Finance costs – interest expense	175,000	
Cash		175,000
Interest on the debt at 7% for three months		

Cash settlement of the swap

	DR	CR
Finance costs – interest expense	114,059	
Finance costs – interest expense		125,000
Cash		10,941
Settlement of the swap: receive 5% and pay 4.562% for three months		

These two transactions result in a total charge of £164,059 to finance cost, which is equivalent to 6.562% interest for the period (that is, the rate on the variable leg of the swap of 4.562% + 2% credit spread). The variable rate on the swap for the following quarter is set at the three-month swap rate of 5.080%.

> **Helpful hint**
> In order to increase clarity, we have chosen to show the entry gross (that is, with the effects of the pay and receive legs of the swap shown separately). This entry is often made on a net basis.
>
> The charge to interest expense has been made without performing an effectiveness test, as no effectiveness test is required until 30 June. In the event that the next effectiveness test is failed, the entries will have to be reversed out of interest expense, as hedge accounting is not permitted for the period after the last successful test. The entries could be to 'other operating income and expense'.

4 Retrospective effectiveness test on 30 June 20X5

IAS 39 requires the effectiveness of a hedging relationship to be assessed retrospectively as a minimum at each reporting date. Based on company A's risk management policies, the effectiveness of the hedge must be assessed using the dollar offset method.

The dollar offset method consists of comparing the effects of the change in £ LIBOR swap yield curve between 15 March and 30 June (in this case, a parallel shift of 0.5%) on the clean fair values of the hedged item and the hedging instrument.

Retrospective effectiveness test on 30 June 20X5

	15 Sep 20X5	15 Dec 20X5	15 Mar 20X6 ...	15 Dec 20X8	15 Mar 20X9	Total
Cash flows on the swap						
Fixed leg	104,167	125,000	125,000 ...	125,000	125,000	
Variable leg at YC2	(105,833)*	(128,257)	(129,765) ...	(146,327)	(147,830)	
Net cash flows	(1,667)	(3,257)	(4,765) ...	(21,327)	(22,830)	
Discounted CF at ZC2	(1,649)	(3,182)	(4,596) ...	(17,676)	(18,646)	**(161,184)**
Clean fair value at original yield curve						**0**
Change in clean fair value (cumulative)						**(161,184)**
Cash flows on the debt						
Cash flows	(104,167)**	(125,000)	(125,000) ...	(125,000)	(10,125,000)	
Discounted CF at ZC2	(103,078)	(122,127)	(120,563) ...	(103,600)	(8,269,357)	**(9,839,030)**
Clean fair value at original yield curve						**(10,000,000)**
						160,970
Effectiveness						**-100.1%**

* The variable rate for the first period is set to 5.08%. The rest of the variable cash flows are projected according to the forward rates derived from the current swap yield curve (YC2), as they have not yet been set.

** The effect of accruals needs to be removed, as the test is based on the clean fair value. 75 days of the next coupon have not yet been accrued; the amount of the first coupon included in the test is, therefore, the cash flow 125,000*75/90.

Conclusion: The hedge has been highly effective for the period ended 30 June 20X5.

> **Helpful hint**
> Based on company A's risk management policies, the retrospective effectiveness test above uses the clean fair values of the swap and the debt. Accrued interest for the current period as well as the fair value changes due to the passage of time on the original swap yield curve are excluded from the tests.
>
> The relationship is ineffective because the variable leg of the swap is pre-fixed/post-paid. As the interest on the variable leg of the swap is determined at the beginning of the period (15 June) it is fixed until the next re-pricing date and, therefore, has an exposure to changes in its fair value. If the variable leg of the swap had been post-fixed/post-paid, then the ineffectiveness would have been lower.

5 Accounting entries on 30 June 20X5

Recognition of accrued interest on the bond

Accrued interest for 15 days on the loan is recognised.

	Dr	Cr
Finance costs – interest expense	29,167	
Accrued interest		29,167
Interest on the debt at 7% for 15 days		

Recognition of fair value changes of the swap

The recorded change in dirty fair value of the swap can be reconciled to the clean fair value of the swap as follows:

Clean fair value on 30/6/20X5	(161,184)
Accrued interest on receive fixed 5% for 15 days (discounted)	20,617
Accrued interest on pay variable 5.080% for 15 days (discounted)	(20,947)
Dirty fair value	**(161,514)**

The swap is recorded at the dirty fair value (that is, including the accrued interest).

	Dr	Cr
Other operating income and expense – ineffectiveness	161,184	
Finance costs – interest expense	330	
Derivative instruments		161,514
Fair value hedge – change in fair value of the swap including accrued interest		

Fair value adjustment to the hedged item

All the criteria for hedge accounting are met for the period ended 30 June 20X5, and fair value hedge accounting can be applied. The carrying amount of the debt is adjusted for the fair value change of the hedged risk (that is, the changes in the clean fair value of the debt attributable to changes in the zero coupon curve). The entry is as follows:

	Dr	Cr
Other operating income and expense – ineffectiveness		160,970
Other financial liabilities – debt	160,970	
Fair value hedge – change in fair value of the debt attributable to the hedged risk		

As the hedge is not 100% effective, the ineffectiveness of £214 (£161,184 – £160,970) is recognised in profit or loss. Best practice is to present the ineffectiveness in 'other operating income and expense', as illustrated above.

6 Prospective effectiveness test on 30 June 20X5

The same method is used as at the inception of the hedge.

Prospective effectiveness test on 30 June 20X5

	15 Sep 20X5	15 Dec 20X5	15 Mar 20X6 ...	15 Dec 20X8	15 Mar 20X9	Total
Cash flows on the swap						
Fixed leg	104,167	125,000	125,000 ...	125,000	125,000	
Variable leg @ YC2	(105,833)	(128,257)	(129,765)...	(146,327)	(147,830)	
Net cash flows	(1,667)	(3,257)	(4,765)...	(21,327)	(22,830)	
Discounted CF @ ZC2	(1,649)	(3,182)	(4,596)...	(17,676)	(18,646)	**(161,184)**
Shifted zero coupon curve						
Fixed leg	104,167	125,000	125,000 ...	125,000	125,000	
Variable leg @ YC2 + 1%	(105,833)	(152,234)	(153,731)...	(170,177)	(171,669)	
Net cash flows	(1,667)	(27,234)	(28,731)...	(45,177)	(46,669)	
Discounted CF @ ZC2 + 1%	(1,646)	(26,493)	(27,526)...	(36,241)	(36,807)	**(451,850)**
						(290,666)

Cash flows on the debt							
Cash flows	(104,167)	(125,000)	(125,000)	. . .	(125,000)	(10,125,000)	
Discounted CF @ ZC2	(103,078)	(122,127)	(120,563)	. . .	(103,600)	(8,269,357)	**(9,839,030)**
Discounted CF @ ZC2 + 1%	(102,875)	(121,599)	(119,758)	. . .	(100,277)	(7,985,352)	**(9,528,668)**
							310,362
Effectiveness							**-93.7%**

Conclusion: The hedge is expected to be highly effective.

7 Accounting entries on 1 July 20X5

The accrual of the interest on the debt is reversed.

	Dr	Cr
Finance costs – interest expense		29,167
Accrued interest	29,167	
Interest on the debt reversed at 7% for 15 days		

The accrual on the swap is reversed.

	Dr	Cr
Finance costs – interest expense		330
Other operating income and expense – ineffectiveness	330	
Accrued interest on the swap reversed for 15 days		

8 Accounting entries on 15 September 20X5

On 15 September the coupon on the loan is paid and the second period of the swap is settled.

Recognition of interest on the debt

	Dr	Cr
Finance costs – interest expense	175,000	
Cash		175,000
Interest on the debt at 7% for three months		

Cash settlement of the swap

	Dr	Cr
Finance costs – interest expense	127,000	
Finance costs – interest expense		125,000
Cash		2,000
Settlement of the swap: receive 5% and pay 5.080% for three months		

These two transactions result in a total charge of £177,000 to finance cost, which is equivalent to 7.08% interest for the period (that is, the variable rate of 5.08% plus 2% credit spread).

The floating rate on the swap for the following quarter is set at the three-month swap rate of 5.28%.

9 Accounting entries on 15 December 20X5

On 15 December the coupon on the loan is paid and the third period of the swap is settled.

Recognition of interest on the debt

	Dr	Cr
Finance costs – interest expense	175,000	
Cash		175,000
Interest on the debt at 7% for three months		

Cash settlement of the swap

	Dr	Cr
Finance costs – interest expense	132,000	
Finance costs – interest expense		125,000
Cash		7,000
Settlement of the swap: receive 5% and pay 5.28% for three months		

These two transactions result in a total charge of £182,000 to finance cost, which is equivalent to 7.28% interest for the period (that is, the variable rate of 5.28% plus 2% credit spread).

The floating rate on the swap for the following quarter is set at the three-month swap rate of 5.79%.

10 Retrospective effectiveness test on 31 December 20X5

The same method for retrospective testing is used as on 30 June 20X5. As required in company A's risk management policies, the effectiveness test is done using the dollar offset method on a cumulative basis.

Retrospective effectiveness test on 31 December 20X5

	15 Mar 20X6	15 Jun 20X6	15 Sep 20X6	...	15 Dec 20X8	15 Mar 20X9	Total
Cash flows on the swap							
Fixed leg	104,167	125,000	125,000	...	125,000	125,000	
Variable leg at YC3	(120,625)	(144,165)	(145,666)	..	(159,157)	(160,654)	
Net cash flows	(16,458)	(19,165)	(20,666)	..	(34,157)	(35,654)	
Discounted CF at ZC3	(16,265)	(18,671)	(19,844)	..	(28,605)	(29,386)	**(308,922)**
Clean fair value at original yield curve							**0**
Change in clean fair value (cumulative)							**(308,922)**
Cash flows on the debt							
Cash flows	(104,167)	(125,000)	(125,000)	..	(125,000)	(10,125,000)	
Discounted CF at ZC3	(102,943)	(121,776)	(120,028)	..	(104,681)	(8,345,128)	**(9,692,833)**
Clean fair value at original yield curve							**(10,000,000)**
Change in clean fair value (cumulative)							**307,167**
Effectiveness							**-100.6%**

Conclusion: The hedge has been highly effective for the period ended 31 December 20X5.

11 Accounting entries on 31 December 20X5

Recognition of accrued interest on the bond

Accrued interest for 15 days on the loan is recognised.

	Dr	Cr
Finance costs – interest expense	29,167	
Accrued interest		29,167
Interest on the debt at 7% for 15 days		

Recognition of fair value changes of the swap

Clean fair value of the swap	(308,922)
Accrued interest on receive fix 5% for 15 days	20,589
Accrued interest on pay variable 5.79% for 15 days	(23,842)
Dirty fair value of the swap on 31 December 20X5	(312,175)
Dirty fair value of the swap on 30 June 20X5	(161,514)
Change in fair value to be recognised on 31 December 20X5	**(150,661)**

The swap is recorded at the dirty fair value (that is, including the accrued interest).

	Dr	**Cr**
Other operating income and expense – ineffectiveness	147,408	
Finance costs – interest expense	3,253	
Derivative instruments		150,661
Fair value hedge – change in fair value of the swap		

Fair value adjustment to the hedged item

All the criteria for hedge accounting are met for the period ended 31 December 20X5, and fair value hedge accounting can be applied.

Fair value adjustment on debt on 30 June 20X5	160,970
Fair value adjustment on debt on 31 December 20X5	307,167
Change in the clean fair value of the debt	**146,197**

As the hedge is not 100% effective, the ineffectiveness of £1,211 (£147,408 – £146,197) is recognised in profit or loss. Best practice is to present the ineffectiveness in 'other operating income and expense', as illustrated above.

12 Prospective effectiveness test on 31 December 20X5

The same method is used as at the inception of the hedge.

Prospective effectiveness test on 31 December 20X5

	15 Mar 20X6	15 Jun 20X6	15 Sep 20X6 ...	15 Dec 20X8	15 Mar 20X9	Total
Cash flows on the swap						
Fixed leg	104,167	125,000	125,000 ...	125,000	125,000	
Variable leg at YC3	(120,625)	(144,165)	(145,666) ...	(159,157)	(160,654)	
Net cash flows	(16,458)	(19,165)	(20,666) ...	(34,157)	(35,654)	
Discounted CF at ZC3	(16,265)	(18,671)	(19,844) ...	(28,605)	(29,386)	**(308,922)**
Shifted zero coupon curve						
Fixed leg	104,167	125,000	125,000 ...	125,000	125,000	
Variable leg at YC3 + 1%	(120,625)	(168,030)	(169,520) ...	(182,917)	(184,403)	
Net cash flows	(16,458)	(43,030)	(44,520) ...	(57,917)	(59,403)	
Discounted CF at ZC3 + 1%	(16,233)	(41,740)	(42,466) ...	(47,176)	(47,511)	**(556,044)**
						(247,122)
Cash flows on the debt						
Cash flows	(104,167)	(125,000)	(125,000) ...	(125,000)	(10,125,000)	
Discounted CF at ZC3	(102,943)	(121,776)	(120,028) ...	(104,681)	(8,345,128)	**(9,692,833)**
Discounted CF at ZC3 + 1%	(102,742)	(121,253)	(119,231) ...	(101,818)	(8,097,959)	**(9,426,135)**
						266,698
Effectiveness						**-92.7%**

Conclusion: The hedge is expected to be highly effective.

The testing and accounting entries are carried out in the same manner throughout the remaining life of the hedge relationship.

	Balance sheet			Income statement		
	Derivative instruments	**Accrued interest**	**Other financial liabilities – debt**	**Cash**	**Finance cost – interest expense**	**Other operating income and expense – ineffectiveness**
15/3/20X5						
Debt			(10,000,000)	10,000,000		
Swap						
15/6/20X5						
Interest on debt				(175,000)	175,000	
Settlement of swap				10,941	114,059	
					(125,000)	
30/6/20X5						
Accrued interest on debt		(29,167)			29,167	
Fair value change of swap	(161,514)				330	161,184
Hedge adjustment to debt			160,970			(160,970)

1/7/20X5						
Accruals reversed on debt		29,167			(29,167)	
Accruals reversed on swap					(330)	330
15/9/20X5						
Interest				(175,000)	175,000	
Settlement of swap				(2,000)	127,000	
					(125,000)	
15/12/20X5						
Interest				(175,000)	175,000	
Settlement of swap				(7,000)	132,000	
					(125,000)	
31/12/20X5						
Accrued interest on debt		(29,167)			29,167	
Fair value change of swap	(150,661)				3,253	147,408
Hedge adjustment to debt			146,197			(146,197)

Cash flow hedge of a highly probable forecast purchase in foreign currency

Background and assumptions

Company C is a Swedish company with a SEK functional currency. Its reporting dates are 30 June and 31 December.

Company C produces and sells electronic components for the automotive industry and is planning to launch a new electronic component that it expects to be more reliable and cheaper than the existing alternatives.

Production is scheduled to start in June 20X6. Company C's management expects to purchase a significant amount of raw material in May 20X6 for the start of production. An external company based in Spain will supply the raw material. Based on C's production plans and the prices that the supplier is currently charging, Company C's management forecasts that 500,000 units of raw material will be received and invoiced on 1 May 20X6 at a price of EUR 50 per unit. The invoice is expected to be paid on 31 August 20X6.

On 1 January 20X5, Company C's management decides to hedge the foreign currency risk arising from its highly probable forecast purchase. C enters into a forward contract to buy EUR against SEK. On that date, the forecast purchase is considered as highly probable, as the board of directors has approved the purchase, and negotiations with the Spanish supplier are far advanced.

The foreign currency forward contract entered into as a hedge of the highly probable forecast purchase is as follows:

Hedge accounting

Type	European forward contract
Amount purchased	EUR 25,000,000
Amount sold	SEK 192,687,500
Forward rate	EUR 1 = SEK 7.7075
Start date	1 January 20x5
Maturity date	31 August 20x6

Exchange rates on various dates during the hedge are as follows:

	1/1/20X5	30/6/20X5	31/12/20X5	30/6/20X6	31/7/20X6	31/8/20X6	31/10/20X6
SEK/EUR spot rate	7.6900	7.6500	7.7500	7.8100	7.9000	8.1500	8.0500
SEK/EUR forward rate*	7.7075	7.6622	7.7574	7.8118	7.9008	8.1500	
Forward points	**0.0175**	**0.0122**	**0.0074**	**0.0018**	**0.0008**	**0.0000**	

* For a forward maturing on 31 August 20X6.

Annualised interest rates applicable for discounting a cash flow on 31 August 20X6 at various dates during the hedge are as follows:

	1/1/20x5	30/6/20x5	31/12/20x5	30/6/20x6	31/7/20x6	31/8/20x6
SEK interest rate	1.3550%	1.3850%	1.3670%	1.3850%	1.4240%	1.4030%
EUR interest rate	1.4916%	1.5213%	1.5100%	1.5200%	1.5470%	1.5170%

Extracts of risk management policies for foreign currency risk

Foreign currency risk

Company C's functional and presentation currencies are the SEK (Swedish krona). Company C is exposed to foreign exchange risk because some of its purchases and sales are denominated in currencies other than SEK. It is therefore exposed to the risk that movements in exchange rates will affect both its net income and financial position, as expressed in SEK.

Company C's foreign currency exposure arises from:

- highly probable forecast transactions (sales/purchases) denominated in foreign currencies;
- firm commitments denominated in foreign currencies; and
- monetary items (mainly trade receivables, trade payables and borrowings) denominated in foreign currencies.

Company C is mainly exposed to EUR/SEK and GBP/SEK risks. Transactions denominated in foreign currencies other than EUR and GBP are not material.

Company C's policy is to hedge all material foreign exchange risk associated with highly probable forecast transactions, firm commitments and monetary items denominated in foreign currencies.

Company C's policy is to hedge the risk of changes in the relevant spot exchange rate.

Hedging instruments

Company C uses only forward contracts to hedge foreign exchange risk. All derivatives must be entered into with counterparties with a credit rating of AA or higher.

Extracts of effectiveness testing policies for interest rate risk

Strategy 2A: Cash flow hedges of foreign currency exposure in highly probable forecast transactions

Prospective effectiveness testing for cash flow hedges

Prospective effectiveness testing should be performed at the inception of the hedge and at each reporting date. The hedge relationship is highly effective if the changes in fair value or cash flow of the hedged item that are attributable to the hedged risk are expected to be offset by the changes in fair value or cash flows of the hedging instrument.

Prospective effectiveness testing should be performed by comparing the numerical effects of a shift in the exchange rate (for example, EUR/SEK rate) on: the fair value of the hedged cash flows measured using a hypothetical derivative; and the fair value of the hedging instrument. Consistent with Company C's risk management policy, the hedged risk is defined as the risk of changes in the spot exchange rate. Changes in interest rates are excluded from the hedge relationship (for both the hedging instrument and the hedged forecast transaction) and do not affect the calculations of effectiveness. Only the spot component of the forward contract is included in the hedge relationship (that is, the forward points are excluded).

At least three scenarios should be assessed unless the critical terms of the hedging instrument perfectly match the critical terms of the hedged item, in which case one scenario is sufficient.

Retrospective effectiveness testing for cash flow hedges

Retrospective effectiveness testing must be performed at each reporting date using the dollar offset method on a cumulative basis. The hedge is demonstrated to be effective by comparing the cumulative change in the fair value of the hedged cash flows measured using a hypothetical derivative; and the fair value of the hedging instrument. A hedge is considered to be highly effective if the results of the retrospective effectiveness tests are within the range 80%-125%.

$$\text{Effectiveness} = \frac{\textbf{Cumulative change in fair value of hedging instrument}}{\textbf{Cumulative change in fair value of hedged item (hypothetical derivative)}}$$

Change in the fair value of the spot component of the hedging instrument (the forward contract) is the difference between the fair value of the spot component at the inception of the hedge, and the end of the testing period based on translating the foreign exchange leg of the forward contract at the current spot rate and discounting the net cash flows on the derivative using the zero-coupon rates curve derived from the swap yield curve.

Change in fair value of the hedged cash flows of the hedged item (hypothetical derivative) is the difference between the value of the hypothetical derivative at the inception of the hedge, and the end of the testing period based on translating the foreign exchange leg of the hypothetical derivative at the current spot rate and discounting the net cash flows on the hypothetical derivative using the zero-coupon rates curve derived from the swap yield curve.

> **Helpful hint**
> The fair value of a foreign exchange forward contract is affected by changes in the spot rate and by changes in the forward points. The latter derives from the interest rate differential between the currencies specified in the forward contract. Changes in the forward points may give rise to ineffectiveness if the hedged item is not similarly affected by interest rate differentials.

Hedge designation

Company C's hedge documentation is as follows:

1 Risk management objective and strategy

In order to comply with Company C's foreign exchange risk management strategy, the foreign exchange risk arising from the highly probable forecast purchase detailed in 5 below is hedged.

2 Type of hedging relationship

Cash flow hedge: hedge of the foreign currency risk arising from highly probable forecast purchases.

3 Nature of risk being hedged

EUR/SEK spot exchange rate risk arising from a highly probable forecast purchase denominated in EUR that is expected to occur on 1 May 20X6 and to be settled on 31 August 20X6.

4 Identification of hedged item

Purchase of 500,000 units of raw material for EUR 50 per unit.

5 Forecast transactions

Hedged amount: EUR 25,000,000

Nature of forecast transaction: purchase of 500,000 units of raw material

Expected timescale for forecast transaction to take place:

- delivery: 1 May 20X6
- cash payment: 31 August 20X6

Expected price: EUR 50 per unit.

Rationale for forecast transaction being highly probable to occur:

- production of electronic component is scheduled to start in June 20X6;
- purchase has been approved by the board of directors; and
- negotiations with supplier are far advanced.

Method of reclassifying into profit and loss amounts deferred through equity: in accordance with Company C's chosen accounting policy, the gains or losses recognised in equity will be included in the carrying amount of the inventory acquired (that is, basis adjustment).

6 Identification of hedging instrument

Transaction number: reference number K1121W in the treasury management system.

The hedging instrument is a forward contract to buy EUR 25,000,000 with the following characteristics:

Type	European forward contract
Amount purchased	EUR 25,000,000
Amount sold	SEK 192,687,500
Forward rate	EUR 1 = SEK 7.7075
Spot rate at inception	EUR 1 = SEK 7.6900
Spot component of notional amount	SEK 192,250,000
Start date	1 January 20X5
Maturity date	31 August 20X6

Hedge designation: the spot component of forward contract K1121W is designated as a hedge of the change in the present value of the cash flows on the forecast purchase identified in 5 above that is attributable to movements in the EUR/SEK spot rate, measured as a hypothetical derivative.

7 Effectiveness testing

Hedge accounting strategy 2A should be applied (see hedge effectiveness testing policy). The hypothetical derivative that models the hedged cash flows is a forward contract to pay EUR 25,000,000 on 31 August 20X6 in return for SEK. The spot component of this hypothetical derivative is SEK 192,250,000 (that is, EUR 25,000,000 at the spot rate on 1 January 20X5 of 7.6900).

Description of prospective testing

Dollar offset method, being the ratio of the change in the fair value of the spot component of forward contract K1121W, divided by the change in present value of the hedged cash flows (hypothetical derivative) attributable to changes in spot EUR/SEK rate.

Frequency of testing: at inception of the hedge and then at each reporting date (30 June and 31 December).

Description of retrospective testing

Dollar offset method, being the ratio of the change in fair value of the spot component of the forward contract, divided by the change in present value of the hedged cash flows (hypothetical derivative) attributable to changes in spot EUR/SEK rate, on a cumulative basis.

Frequency of testing: at every reporting date (30 June and 31 December) after inception of the hedge.

Effectiveness tests and accounting entries

1 Prospective effectiveness test on 1 January 20X5

On 1 January 20X5, the forward EUR/SEK exchange rate is 7.7075. On that date, the spot EUR/SEK exchange rate is 7.6900. Company C's management should assess prospectively the effectiveness of the hedge, as required in IAS 39.

Based on the hedge documentation, the prospective effectiveness test consists of comparing the effects of a 10% shift of the spot EUR/SEK exchange rate on both the fair value of the spot component of the hedging instrument and on the hedged cash flows (hypothetical derivative).

Hedged item and hedging instrument (spot components)

The EUR leg of both the hypothetical derivative (hedged item) and the forward contract (hedging instrument) are translated into SEK using the shifted spot exchange rate (8.459), then discounted back using the current SEK interest rate (1.3550%) for a cash flow due on 31 August 20X6. The SEK leg is discounted back using the current SEK interest rate. The difference between the present values of each leg represents the fair value of the spot component. As the fair value of this spot component is nil at inception, the change in fair value is equal to its fair value.

Hedged item Hypothetical derivative – spot component			**Hedging instrument** Spot component		
Notional amount	(25,000,000)	EUR	25,000,000	EUR	Notional amount
Spot rate + 10%	8.4590		8.4590		Spot rate + 10%
Notional amount in SEK	(211,475,000)	SEK	211,475,000	SEK	Notional amount in SEK
Discount factor*	0.9776		0.9776		Discount factor
FV of the EUR leg (spot) (A)	(206,729,957)	EUR	206,729,957	SEK	FV of the EUR leg (spot) (A)
Spot component of notional	192,250,000	SEK	(192,250,000)		Spot component of notional
Discount factor	0.9776		0.9776		Discount factor
FV of SEK leg (spot) (B)	187,936,324	SEK	(187,936,324)	SEK	FV of SEK leg (spot) (B)
(A-B) FV of the hypothetical derivative (spot)	**(18,793,632)**	**SEK**	**18,793,632**	**SEK**	**(A-B) FV of the derivative (spot)**
Effectiveness	**-100%**				

* The discount factor has been derived from the annualised SEK interest rate on 1 January for cash flows on 31 August 20x6 and has been calculated as 1/(1.0355)^(607days/360).

Conclusion: the hedge is expected to be highly effective.

Helpful hint

As the critical terms of the forward perfectly match the critical terms of the forecast purchase, a quantitative test is not necessarily required. A qualitative test consisting of a comparison of the critical terms of the hedging instrument and the hedged item may be used as long as it is consistent with Company C's risk management policies.

2 Accounting entries on 1 January 20X5

No entry, as the fair value of the forward contract is nil, as shown below:

Derivative		
Notional amount in EUR	25,000,000	EUR
Forward rate	7.7075	
Notional amount in SEK	192,687,158	SEK
Discount factor	0.9776	
FV of the EUR leg	188,363,673	SEK
Notional amount in SEK	(192,687,158)	SEK
Discount factor	0.9776	
FV of the SEK leg	(188,363,673)	SEK
FV of the derivative	0	SEK

3 Retrospective effectiveness test on 30 June 20X5

IAS 39 requires the effectiveness of a hedging relationship to be assessed retrospectively as a minimum at each reporting date. Based on Company C's risk management policies, the effectiveness of the hedge is assessed using the dollar offset method on a cumulative basis.

The dollar offset method consists of comparing the effects of the change in spot EUR/SEK exchange rate (from 7.69 to 7.65) on the fair value of the spot component of the hedging instrument and the hypothetical derivative (hedged cash flows).

Hedged item Hypothetical derivative – spot component			**Hedging instrument** Spot component		
Notional amount	(25,000,000)	EUR	25,000,000	EUR	Notional amount
Spot rate at test date	7.6500		7.6500		Spot rate at test date
Notional amount in SEK	(191,250,000)	SEK	191,250,000	SEK	Notional amount in SEK
Discount factor	0.9838		0.9838		Discount factor
FV of the EUR leg (spot) (A)	(188,155,087)	EUR	188,155,087	SEK	FV of the EUR leg (spot) (A)
Spot comp of notional at inception	192,250,000	SEK	(192,250,000)		Spot comp of notional at inception
Discount factor	0.9838		0.9838		Discount factor

FV of SEK leg (spot) (B)	189,138,905	SEK	(189,138,905)	SEK	FV of SEK leg (spot) (B)
(A-B) FV of the derivative (spot)	**983,817**	**SEK**	**(983,817)**	**SEK**	**(B-A) FV of the derivative (spot)**
Effectiveness	**-100%**				

Conclusion: the hedge has been highly effective for the period ended 30 June 20X5.

Helpful hint
Ineffectiveness can arise from a number of causes, including changes in the date of the forecast transaction and changes in the credit risk or liquidity of the forward contract.

4 Accounting entries on 30 June 20X5

All the criteria for hedge accounting are met for the period ended 30 June 20X5. Cash flow hedge accounting can therefore be applied. The hedge is 100% effective; the change in the fair value of the spot component of the hedging instrument is therefore recognised in equity. The full fair value of the hedging instrument includes the forward points. The change in the fair value of the forward points component is recognised in the income statement.

Derivative		
Notional amount in EUR	25,000,000	EUR
Forward rate	7.6622	
Notional amount in SEK	191,554,154	SEK
Discount factor	0.9838	
FV of the EUR leg	188,454,319	SEK
Notional amount in SEK	(192,687,158)	SEK
Discount factor	0.9838	
FV of the SEK leg	(189,568,988)	SEK
FV of the derivative	**(1,114,669)**	**SEK**

The entry is as follows:

	Dr	Cr
Derivative (financial liability)		1,114,669
Cash flow hedge reserve (equity)	983,817	
Interest expense (income statement)	130,852	
Cash flow hedge – change in fair value of the forward contract		

Helpful hint
The forward points represent the interest rate differential between the currencies of the forward contract. It is common to recognise fair value movements on the forward points component as interest income or expense, although they could also be recognised as 'operating income and expense'.

5 Prospective effectiveness test on 30 June 20X5

The same method is used as at the inception of the hedge.

Hedged item Hypothetical derivative – spot component			Hedging instrument Spot component		
Notional amount	(25,000,000)	EUR	25,000,000	EUR	Notional amount
Spot rate + 10%	8.4150		8.4150		Spot rate + 10%
Notional amount in SEK	(211,475,000)	SEK	210,375,000	SEK	Notional amount in SEK
Discount factor	0.9838		0.9838		Discount factor
FV of the EUR leg (spot) (A)	(206,970,596)	EUR	206,970,596	SEK	FV of the EUR leg (spot) (A)
Spot component of notional	191,250,000	SEK	(191,250,000)		Spot component of notional
Discount factor	0.9838		0.9838		Discount factor
FV of SEK leg (spot) (B)	188,155,087	SEK	(188,155,087)	SEK	FV of SEK leg (spot) (B)
(A-B) FV of the hypothetical derivative (spot)	**(18,815,509)**	**SEK**	**18,815,509**	**SEK**	**(A-B) FV of the derivative (spot)**
Effectiveness	**-100%**				

Conclusion: the hedge is expected to be highly effective.

6 Retrospective effectiveness test on 31 December 20X5

Change in timing of expected cash flow

In December 20X5, management decides to delay the start of production by two months, due to the late delivery of an essential machine. The production will now start in August 20X6, and the raw materials will be purchased in July. The invoice for the raw materials is expected to be paid on 31 October 20X6.

Annualised interest rates applicable for discounting a cash flow on 31 October 20x6 at various dates during the hedge are as follows:

	31/12/20X5	30/6/20X6	31/7/20X6	31/8/20X6
SEK interest rate	1.3920%	1.4060%	1.4420%	1.4030%

The dollar offset method consists of comparing the effects of the cumulative change in spot EUR/SEK exchange rate (from 7.69 to 7.75) on the fair value of the spot component of the hedging instrument and the hedged cash flow (hypothetical derivative). As the hedged cash flow has been delayed, it is discounted from the revised payment date. The payment date on the hedging instrument and the associated discount factor remain unchanged.

Hedged item Hypothetical derivative – spot component			**Hedging instrument** Spot component		
Notional amount	(25,000,000)	EUR	25,000,000	EUR	Notional amount
Spot rate at test date	7.6500		7.7500		Spot rate at test date
Notional amount in SEK	(193,750,000)	SEK	193,750,000	SEK	Notional amount in SEK
Discount factor*	0.9884		0.9909		Discount factor**
FV of the EUR leg (spot) (A)	(191,501,389)	EUR	191,982,442	SEK	FV of the EUR leg (spot) (A)
Spot comp of notional at inception	192,250,000	SEK	(192,250,000)	SEK	Spot component of notional at inception
Discount factor*	0.9884		0.9909		Discount factor**
FV of SEK leg (spot) (B)	190,018,798	SEK	(190,496,126)	SEK	FV of SEK leg (spot) (B)
(A-B) FV of the derivative (spot)	**(1,482,591)**	**SEK**	**1,486,316**	**SEK**	**(A-B) FV of the derivative (spot)**
Effectiveness	**-100.25%**				

* Discount factor calculated based on changed timing of cash flows.
** Discount factor calculated based on original timing of cash flows.

Conclusion: the hedge has been highly effective for the period ended 31 December 20X5.

7 Accounting entries on 31 December 20X5

The full fair value of the hedging instrument is as follows:

Derivative		
Notional amount in EUR	25,000,000	EUR
Forward rate	7.7574	
Notional amount in SEK	193,934,664	SEK
Discount factor	0.9909	
FV of the EUR leg	192,165,421	SEK
Notional amount in SEK	(192,687,158)	SEK
Discount factor	0.9909	
FV of the SEK leg	(190,929,296)	SEK
FV of the derivative	**1,236,126**	**SEK**

All the criteria for hedge accounting are met for the period ended 31 December 20X5. Cash flow hedge accounting can therefore be applied. The hedge is not, however, 100% effective and therefore the amount recognised in equity is adjusted to the lesser of (a) the cumulative change in the fair value of the spot component of the hedging instrument, and (b) the cumulative change in the fair value of the spot component of the hypothetical derivative.

	Derivative (full fair value)	Hedging instrument (spot component)	Hedged item hypothetical derivative (spot component)	Effective portion	Ineffective portion
30/6/20X5	(1,114,669)	(983,817)	983,817	983,817	–
31/12/20X5	1,236,126	1,486,316	(1,482,591)	1,482,591	3,725
Change	2,350,795	2,470,133	(2,466,409)	2,466,409	3,725

The difference between the full fair value of the forward contract and the amount deferred in equity is charged to the income statement. The portion relating to the forward points is recognised in 'interest expense' and the ineffectiveness (SEK 1,486,316 – SEK 1,482,591 = SEK 3,725) is recognised in 'other operating income and expense'.

Helpful hint

The forward points reflect an interest element and can therefore be included in interest income and expense. Alternatively all fair value movements in excess of the effective portion may be recognised in 'other operating income and expense'.

The entry is as follows:

	Dr	Cr
Derivative (financial asset)	2,350,795	
Cash flow hedge reserve (equity)		2,466,409
Interest expense (income statement)	119,339	
Other operating income and expense		3,725
Cash flow hedge – change in fair value of the forward contract		

8 Prospective effectiveness test on 31 December 20X5

The same method is used as at the inception of the hedge.

Hedged item Hypothetical derivative – spot component			**Hedging instrument** Spot component		
Notional amount	(25,000,000)	EUR	25,000,000	EUR	Notional amount
Spot rate + 10%	8.5250		8.5250		Spot rate + 10%
Notional amount in SEK	(213,125,000)	SEK	213,125,000	SEK	Notional amount in SEK
Discount factor	0.9884		0.9909		Discount factor
FV of the EUR leg (spot) (A)	(191,501,389)	EUR	211,180,686	SEK	FV of the EUR leg (spot) (A)
Spot comp of notional at inception	193,750,000	SEK	(193,750,000)	SEK	Spot component of notional
Discount factor	0.9884		0.9909		Discount factor**
FV of SEK leg (spot) (B)	210,651,528	SEK	(191,982,442)	SEK	FV of SEK leg (spot) (B)
(A-B) FV of the derivative (spot)	**(19,150,139)**	**SEK**	**19,198,244**	**SEK**	**(A-B) FV of the derivative (spot)**
Effectiveness	**-100.25%**				

Conclusion: the hedge is expected to be highly effective.

9 Retrospective effectiveness test on 30 June 20X6

The dollar offset method consists of comparing the effects of the change in spot EUR/SEK exchange rate (from 7.69 to 7.81) on the fair value of the spot component of the hedging instrument, and the hypothetical derivative (hedged cash flows). As the hedged cash flow has been delayed, it is discounted from the revised payment date. The payment date on the hedging instrument and the associated discount factor remain unchanged.

Hedged item Hypothetical derivative – spot component			**Hedging instrument** Spot component		
Notional amount	(25,000,000)	EUR	25,000,000	EUR	Notional amount
Spot rate at test date	7.8100		7.8100		Spot rate at test date
Notional amount in SEK	(195,250,000)	SEK	195,250,000	SEK	Notional amount in SEK
Discount factor	0.9952		0.9976		Discount factor
FV of the EUR leg (spot) (A)	(194,320,802)	EUR	194,775,116	SEK	FV of the EUR leg (spot) (A)
Spot comp of notional at inception	192,250,000	SEK	(192,250,000)	SEK	Spot component of notional at inception
Discount factor	0.9952		0.9976		Discount factor
FV of SEK leg (spot) (B)	191,335,079	SEK	(191,782,413)	SEK	FV of SEK leg (spot) (B)
(A-B) FV of the derivative (spot)	**(2,985,723)**	**SEK**	**2,992,703**	**SEK**	**(A-B) FV of the derivative (spot)**
Effectiveness	**-100.23%**				

Conclusion: the hedge has been highly effective for the period ended 30 June 20X6.

10 Accounting entries on 30 June 20X6

The full fair value of the hedging instrument is as follows:

Derivative		
Notional amount in EUR	25,000,000	EUR
Forward rate	7.8118	
Notional amount in SEK	195,293,907	SEK
Discount factor	0.9976	
FV of the EUR leg	194,820,007	SEK
Notional amount in SEK	192,687,158)	SEK
Discount factor	0.9976	
FV of the SEK leg	(192,218,507)	SEK
FV of the derivative	**2,601,500**	**SEK**

All the criteria for hedge accounting are met for the year ended 30 June 20X6. Cash flow hedge accounting can therefore be applied. The hedge is not however 100% effective; the amount recognised in equity is therefore adjusted to the lesser of (a) the cumulative change in the fair value of the spot component of the hedging instrument, and (b) the cumulative change in the fair value of the spot component of the hypothetical derivative.

	Derivative (full fair value)	**Hedging instrument (spot component)**	**Hedged item hypothetical derivative (spot component)**	**Effective portion**	**Ineffective portion**
31/12/20X5	1,236,126	1,486,316	(1,482,591)	1,482,591	3,725
30/6/20X6	2,601,851	2,992,703	(2,985,723)	2,985,723	6,980
Change	1,365,374	1,506,387	(1,503,132)	1,503,132	3,255

The difference between the full fair value of the forward contract and the amount deferred in equity is charged to the income statement. The portion relating to the forward points is recognised in 'interest income' and the ineffectiveness is recognised in 'other operating income and expense'.

The entry is as follows:

	Dr	**Cr**
Derivative (financial asset)	1,365,374	
Cash flow hedge reserve (equity)		1,503,132
Interest expense (income statement)	141,013	
Other operating income and expense		3,255
Cash flow hedge – change in fair value of the forward contract		

11 Prospective effectiveness test on 30 June 20X6

The same method is used as at the inception of the hedge.

Hedged item Hypothetical derivative – spot component			Hedging instrument Spot component		
Notional amount	(25,000,000)	EUR	25,000,000	EUR	Notional amount
Spot rate + 10%	8.5910		8.5910		Spot rate + 10%
Notional amount in SEK	(214,775,000)	SEK	214,775,000	SEK	Notional amount in SEK
Discount factor	0.9952		0.9976		Discount factor
FV of the EUR leg (spot) (A)	(213,752,882)	EUR	214,252,628	SEK	FV of the EUR leg (spot) (A)
Spot comp of notional at inception	195,250,000	SEK	(195,250,000)	SEK	Spot component of notional
Discount factor	0.9952		0.9976		Discount factor
FV of SEK leg (spot) (B)	194,320,802	SEK	(194,775,116)	SEK	FV of SEK leg (spot) (B)
(A-B) FV of the derivative (spot)	**(19,432,080)**	**SEK**	**19,477,512**	**SEK**	**(A-B) FV of the derivative (spot)**
Effectiveness	**-100.23%**				

Conclusion: the hedge is expected to be highly effective.

12 Retrospective effectiveness test on 31 July 20X6

The dollar offset method consists of comparing the effects of the change in spot EUR/SEK exchange rate (from 7.69 to 7.90) on the fair value of the spot component of the hedging instrument, and the hedged cash flows (hypothetical derivative). As the hedged cash flow has been delayed, it is discounted from the revised payment date. The payment date on the hedging instrument and the associated discount factor remain unchanged.

Hedged item Hypothetical derivative – spot component			Hedging instrument Spot component		
Notional amount	(25,000,000)	EUR	25,000,000	EUR	Notional amount
Spot rate at test date	7.9000		7.9000		Spot rate at test date
Notional amount in SEK	(197,500,000)	SEK	197,500,000	SEK	Notional amount in SEK
Discount factor	0.9963		0.9988		Discount factor
FV of the EUR leg (spot) (A)	(196,778,708)	EUR	197,259,676	SEK	FV of the EUR leg (spot) (A)
Spot comp of notional at inception	192,250,000	SEK	(192,250,000)	SEK	Spot component of notional
Discount factor	0.9963		0.9988		Discount factor
FV of SEK leg (spot) (B)	191,547,882	SEK	(192,016,064)	SEK	FV of SEK leg (spot) (B)
(A-B) FV of the derivative (spot)	**(5,230,826)**	**SEK**	**5,243,612**	**SEK**	**(A-B) FV of the derivative (spot)**
Effectiveness	**-100.24%**				

Conclusion: the hedge has been highly effective for the period ended 31 July 20X6.

Helpful hint
Although IAS 39 does not explicitly require it, an effectiveness test is performed when the hedged highly probable forecast transaction occurs in order to determine the amount to be reclassified into the carrying amount of the hedged item.

13 Accounting entries on 31 July 20X6

Recognition of the purchase

	Dr	Cr
Inventory	197,500,000	
Trade payable		197,500,000
Purchase of EUR 25m at spot rate of 7.90		

As the trade payable is short-term and EUR interest rates are low, Company C has determined that the effect of discounting is not material. The trade payable is therefore recognised at its face value, as permitted in IAS 39.

Recognition of the change in the fair value of the derivative

The full fair value of the hedging instrument is as follows:

Derivative		
Notional amount in EUR	25,000,000	EUR
Forward rate	7.9008	
Notional amount in SEK	197,520,232	SEK
Discount factor	0.99878	
FV of the EUR leg	197,279,883	SEK
Notional amount in SEK	(192,687,158)	SEK
Discount factor	0.99878	
FV of the SEK leg	(192,452,690)	SEK
FV of the derivative	**4,827,194**	**SEK**

All the criteria for hedge accounting are met as at 31 July 20X6. Cash flow hedge accounting can therefore be applied. The hedge is not however 100% effective; the amount recognised in equity is therefore adjusted to the lesser of (a) the cumulative change in the fair value of the spot component of the hedging item, and (b) the cumulative change in the fair value of the spot component of the hypothetical derivative.

	Derivative (full fair value)	Hedging instrument (spot component)	Hedged item hypothetical derivative (spot component)	Effective portion	Ineffective portion
30/6/20X6	2,601,851	2,992,703	(2,985,723)	2,985,723	6,980
31/7/20X6	4,827,194	5,243,612	(5,230,826)	5,230,826	12,786
Change	2,226,343	2,250,909	(2,245,103)	2,245,103	5,806

The difference between the full fair value of the forward contract and the amount deferred in equity is charged to the income statement. The portion relating to the forward points is recognised in 'interest expense' and the ineffectiveness is recognised in 'other operating income and expense'.

The entry is as follows:

	Dr	Cr
Derivative (financial asset)	2,226,343	
Cash flow hedge reserve (equity)		2,245,103
Interest expense (income statement)	24,566	
Other operating income and expense		5,806
Cash flow hedge – change in fair value of the forward contract		

Basis adjustment

Company C's accounting policy is that the gain on the hedging derivative is included in the carrying amount of the inventory acquired. The gain is reclassified to profit or loss when the inventory affects profit or loss (that is, on sale of the goods containing the hedged components or impairment of the inventory).

	DR	CR
Cash flow hedge reserve (equity)	5,230,826	
Inventory		5,230,826
Reclassification of gains recognised in equity into the carrying amount of the inventory acquired by Company C		

Helpful hint

The 'basis adjustment' approach is not required. It can be used only if the hedged item is non-financial (for example, a forecast purchase of inventory) and only if its use is consistent with the Company's chosen accounting policy. If Company C's management had chosen not to adjust the carrying amount of the inventory acquired, the amount accumulated in the cash flow hedge reserve would have remained in equity until the inventory affects the income statement (for example, when it is sold or impaired).

14 Retrospective effectiveness test on 31 August 20X6

The spot EUR/SEK exchange rate is 8.15. Company C's management assesses the effectiveness of the hedge retrospectively. The same method is used as at 30 June 20X6. As required in Company C's risk management policies, the effectiveness test uses the dollar offset method on a cumulative basis.

Hedged item Hypothetical derivative – spot component					Hedging instrument Spot component
Notional amount	(25,000,000)	EUR	25,000,000	EUR	Notional amount
Spot rate at test date	8.1500		8.1500		Spot rate at test date
Notional amount in SEK	(203,750,000)	SEK	203,750,000	SEK	Notional amount in SEK
Discount factor	0.9976		1.0000		Discount factor
FV of the EUR leg (spot) (A)	(203,265,719)	EUR	203,750,000	SEK	FV of the EUR leg (spot) (A)
Spot comp of notional at inception	192,250,000	SEK	(192,250,000)	SEK	Spot component of notional
Discount factor	0.9976		1.0000		Discount factor
FV of SEK leg (spot) (B)	191,793,053	SEK	(192,250,000)	SEK	FV of SEK leg (spot) (B)
(A-B) FV of the derivative (spot)	**(11,472,666)**	**SEK**	**11,500,000**	**SEK**	**(A-B) FV of the derivative (spot)**
Effectiveness	**-100.24%**				

Conclusion: the hedge has been highly effective for the period ended 31 August 20X6.

15 Accounting entries on 31 August 20X6

Translation of the trade payable at the spot rate

The trade payable is a monetary item denominated in a foreign currency that must be retranslated at the spot rate under IAS 21, with the resulting currency gain or loss recognised in profit or loss.

The calculation of the gain or loss is as follows:

Trade payable translated at 31 July at 7.90	197,500,000
Trade payable translated at 31 August at 8.15	203,750,000
Foreign exchange loss to be recognised in profit or loss	**6,250,000**

The accounting entry is as follows:

	Dr	Cr
Other operating income and expenses – foreign exchange loss	6,250,000	
Trade payable		6,250,000
To recognise the foreign exchange loss on retranslating the trade payable		

All the criteria for hedge accounting are met as at 31 August 20X6. Cash flow hedge accounting can therefore be applied. The hedge is not however 100% effective; the amount recognised in equity is therefore adjusted to the lesser of:

(a) the cumulative change in the fair value of the spot component of the hedging instrument less the basis adjustment recognised in the previous period; and

(b) the cumulative change in the fair value of the spot component of the hypothetical derivative (hedged item) less the basis adjustment recognised in the previous period.

	Derivative (full fair value)	**Hedging instrument (spot component)**	**Hedged item hypothetical derivative (spot component)**	**Effective portion (recognised as basis adjustment)**	**Ineffective portion**
31/7/20X6	4,827,194	5,243,612	(5,230,826)	5,230,826	12,786
31/8/20x6	11,062,500	11,500,000	(11,472,666)	11,472,666	27,334
Change	6,235,306	6,256,388	(6,241,840)	6,241,840	14,548

The difference between the full fair value of the forward contract and the amount deferred in equity is charged to the income statement.

The entry is as follows:

	Dr	Cr
Derivative (financial asset)	6,235,306	
Cash flow hedge reserve (equity)		6,241,840
Interest expense (income statement)	21,082	
Other operating income and expense		14,548
Cash flow hedge – change in fair value of the forward contract		

Settlement of derivative

Under the terms of the forward contract, Company C receives EUR 25m at 7.7075 (SEK 203,750,000) and pays SEK 192,687,500. The difference is the fair value of the derivative (SEK 11,062,842).

The accounting entry is as follows:

	DR	CR
Cash in EUR	203,750,000	
Cash in SEK		192,687,500
Derivative (financial asset)		11,062,500
Settlement of the derivative in cash		

Reclassification of gains and losses from equity to profit or loss

The amount deferred in equity is recycled to the income statement

	DR	CR
Other operating income and expenses – foreign exchange gain		6,241,840
Cash flow hedge reserve (equity)	6,241,840	
Reclassification of gains recognised in equity to profit or loss		

Company C decides to keep the euro amount received in a euro account until payment of the invoice.

Helpful hint
Hedge accounting is not always necessary when a company is hedging the foreign currency risk arising from short-term monetary items such as foreign currency payables and receivables.

A similar result to that achieved under hedge accounting would have been achieved had Company C de-designated the hedge relationship when the purchase was recognised, as:

1 the derivative, not being designated as a hedging instrument, would have been measured at fair value through profit or loss; and
2 the receivable, which is a monetary item, would have been revalued using the spot exchange rate at the balance sheet date.

16 Accounting entries on 31 October 20X6

The trade payable and the euro bank account are revalued using the closing rate (8.05).

	Dr	Cr
Trade payable	2,500,000	
Other operating income and expenses – foreign exchange gain		2,500,000
Euro bank account		2,500,000
Other operating income and expenses – foreign exchange gain	2,500,000	
Revaluation of trade payable and bank account (both EUR 25m)		

Finally the trade payable is settled.

	Dr	Cr
Trade payable	201,250,000	
Euro bank account		201,250,000
Reclassification of gains recognised in equity to profit or loss		

Summary of accounting entries

	Balance sheet					Income statement	
	Derivative instrument	Equity	Payable	Inventory	Bank account (SEK and EUR)	Interest expense	Other operating income and expense – foreign exchange gains and losses
1/1/20X5							
No entry							
30/6/20X5							
CFH accounting	(1,114,669)	983,817				130,852	
31/12/20X5							
CFH accounting	2,350,795	(2,466,409)				119,339	(3,725)
30/6/20X6							
CFH accounting	1,364,725	(1,503,132)				141,662	(3,255)
31/7/20X6							
Purchase of inventory			(197,500,000)	197,500,000			
CFH accounting	2,226,343	(2,245,103)				24,566	(5,806)
Basis adjustment		5,230,826		(5,230,826)			
31/8/20X6							
Foreign currency reval. of payable			(6,250,000)				6,250,000
CFH accounting	6,235,649	(6,241,840)				21,082	(14,548)
Reclassification		6,241,840					(6,241,840)
Settlement of derivative	(11,062,842)				11,062,842		
31/10/20X6							
Revaluation			2,500,000		(2,500,000)		
Settlement of payable			201,250,000		(201,250,000)		

Net investment hedge in a foreign operation

Background and assumptions

Company K, a Swiss company with a CHF functional currency, has an Italian subsidiary, Company D, whose functional currency is EUR. Company K's reporting dates for its consolidated financial statements are 30 June and 31 December. The group's presentation currency is CHF.

On 1 January 20x5, Company K issues a two-year floating rate debt with the following characteristics:

Type	Issued debt
Principal amount	EUR 100m
Start date	1 January 20X5
Maturity date	31 December 20X6
Interest rate	Six-month EURIBOR
Settlement dates	30 June 20X5, 31 December 20X5, 30 June 20X6, 31 December 20X6

No transaction costs are incurred relating to the debt issuance. K's management has chosen to issue euro-denominated debt to hedge K's net investment in Company D. It wishes to reduce the consolidated balance sheet volatility arising from EUR/CHF fluctuations by designating the debt as a hedge of the net investment. On 1 January 20X5, the net investment in Company D is EUR 100m. It is not expected to fall below EUR 100m, as Company D has been a profitable company for many years and its forecasts for the next two years, as approved by Company K's board of directors, show it continuing to make material profits.

Exchange rates on various dates during the hedge relationship are as follows:

Helpful hint

A net investment in a foreign operation is the amount of the reporting entity's interest in the net assets of the operation, including goodwill. If the entity is financed through an inter-company loan that will not be repaid in the foreseeable future (quasi-equity), this loan is included in the net investment.

A hedge of a net investment is a hedge of an accounting exposure (that is, the variability in equity arising from translating the net investment at different exchange rates).

Average exchange rates for the six-month periods during the hedge are as follows:

	1/1/20X5	**30/6/20X5**	**31/12/20X5**	**30/6/20X6**	**31/12/20X6**
EUR/CHF spot rate	1.5000	1.5800	1.6000	1.6200	1.6500
EUR/CHF forward rate	1.5667	1.6343	1.6364	1.6383	1.6500
Forward points	**0.0667**	**0.0543**	**0.0364**	**0.0183**	**0.0000**
		30/6/20X5	**31/12/20X5**	**30/6/20X6**	**31/12/20X6**
EUR/CHF average rate		1.5400	1.5900	1.6100	1.6400

Annual interest rates on various dates during the hedge are as follows:

	1/01/20X5	30/6/20X5	31/12/20X5	30/6/20X6	31/12/20X6
CHF interest rate	3.5500%	3.6200%	3.6500%	3.5750%	3.6450%
EUR interest rate	1.3505%	1.3500%	1.3750%	1.3250%	1.3550%

For the purpose of this illustration, the yield curve (that is, interest rate) at each reporting period end is assumed to remain the same through the term of the hedge designation (that is, the yield curve is flat at all times). This simplification does not have any impact on the effectiveness test in this example, as the reset dates of the loan coincide with the effectiveness testing date. With a non-flat yield curve, the calculation of the fair value of the variable rate debt will still give a fair value equal to the face value, as the variable coupons will be at market rate.

Extracts of the risk management policies for foreign currency risk

Background to the group

The group is an international retailer operating around the world, particularly in Western Europe (Switzerland, Italy and the UK) and the US. The biggest subsidiary is based in Italy.

Foreign currency risk

The group's presentation currency is CHF. Foreign currency risk arises from transactions denominated in foreign currencies and net investments in foreign operations.

Investments in foreign operations (translation foreign currency risk)

A foreign currency exposure arises from net investments in group entities whose functional currency differs from the group's presentation currency (CHF). The risk is defined as the risk of fluctuation in spot exchange rates between the functional currency of the net investments and the group's presentation currency. This will cause the amount of the net investment to vary. Such a risk may have a significant impact on the group's financial statements.

This translation risk does not give rise to a cash flow exposure. Its impact arises only from the translation of the net investment into the group's presentation currency. This procedure is required in preparing the group's consolidated financial statements.

Hedging instruments

The group uses derivatives (such as forward contracts and purchased options) and cash instruments (non-derivatives such as foreign currency borrowings) to hedge foreign currency risk. All derivatives must be entered into with counterparties with a credit rating of AA or higher.

Extracts of hedge effectiveness testing policies

Strategy 2C: Hedge of a net investment for foreign currency risk with a debt instrument.

Prospective effectiveness testing for net investment hedges

Prospective effectiveness testing should be performed at the inception of the hedge and at each reporting date. For hedges where the hedging instrument is a cash instrument, the hedge relationship is highly effective if the foreign currency gains and losses on the hedged item (net investment) that are attributable to the hedged risk (changes in spot exchange rates) are expected to be offset by the foreign currency gains and losses on the hedging instrument (cash instrument).

Prospective effectiveness testing must be performed by comparing the numerical effects of an upward shift in the benchmark exchange rate (EUR/CHF spot exchange rate) on both the value of the hedging instrument and the value of the hedged item.

- **The value of the hedging instrument:** when the hedging instrument is a cash instrument (for example, a debt instrument), this value is determined by discounting the future cash flows, including interest payments, on the debt and translating the result at the spot exchange rate. Accrued interest (if any) is excluded from the calculation.
- **The value of the net investment being hedged:** this is determined by translating the amount of the net investment into the group's presentation currency using the spot exchange rate.

This test should normally be performed using at least three currency scenarios. However, for hedges where the critical terms of the hedging instrument perfectly match the critical terms of the hedged item, one scenario is sufficient.

Retrospective effectiveness testing for net investment hedges

Retrospective effectiveness testing should be performed at each reporting date using the dollar offset method on a cumulative basis. The hedge is demonstrated to be effective under this method by comparing the cumulative foreign currency gains and losses on the hedging instrument with the cumulative foreign currency gains and losses on the net investment being hedged, and showing that it falls within the required range of 80%-125%.

- **Foreign currency gains and losses on the hedging instrument:** when the hedging instrument is a cash instrument (for example, a debt instrument), such foreign currency gains and losses are determined by discounting the future cash flows (using the current euro interest rate) on the debt and translating the result at the spot exchange rate. Accrued interest (if any) is excluded from the calculation.

- **Foreign currency gains and losses on the net investment being hedged:** such gains and losses are determined by translating the amount of the net investment into the group's presentation currency using the spot exchange rate.

Hedge designation

Company K's hedge documentation is as follows:

1 Risk management objective and strategy

In order to comply with Company K's foreign currency risk management strategy, the foreign currency translation risk arising on the net investment in Company D is hedged.

2 Type of hedging relationship

Net investment hedge.

3 Nature of risk being hedged

In accordance with the group's risk management policies, the hedged risk is the risk of changes in the EUR/CHF spot exchange rate that will result in changes in the value of the group's net investment in Company D when translated into CHF. The risk is hedged from 1 January 20X5 to 31 December 20X7.

4 Identification of hedged item

The group's net investment in EUR in Company D on 1 January 20X5 is EUR 100m. EUR 100m of the net investment is designated as the hedged item.

5 Identification of hedging instrument

Transaction number: reference number G0901Z in the treasury management system.

The hedging instrument is a two-year floating rate debt with the following characteristics:

Type	Issued debt
Principal amount	EUR 100m
Start date	1 January 20X5
Maturity date	31 December 20X6
Interest rate	Six-month EURIBOR
Settlement dates	30 June 20X5, 31 December 20X5, 30 June 20X6, 31 December 20X6

Hedge designation: the foreign currency exposure of debt G0901Z is designated as a hedge of the change in the value of the net investment identified in 4 above that is attributable to movements in the CHF/EUR spot rate.

6 Effectiveness testing

Effectiveness testing strategy 2C will be applied.

Description of prospective effectiveness testing

Dollar offset method, being the comparison of the numerical effects of a shift in the benchmark exchange rate (EUR/CHF spot exchange rate) on both the value of the hedging instrument and the value of the hedged item.

As permitted in the risk management policies, one scenario is used for assessing prospectively the effectiveness of the hedge relationship (a 10% upward shift of the EUR/CHF spot exchange rate), as the critical terms of the hedging instrument perfectly match the critical terms of the hedged item.

Frequency of testing: at inception of the hedge and then at each reporting date (30 June and 31 December).

Description of retrospective effectiveness testing

Dollar offset method, being the ratio of the cumulative foreign currency gains and losses on the debt (G0901Z), divided by the foreign currency gains and losses on the net investment being hedged.

Foreign currency gains and losses on the debt are the change in the present value of cash flows of the debt (interest and principal repayment) attributable to change in the EUR/CHF spot exchange rate.

Foreign currency gains and losses on the net investment being hedged are the change in the value of the net investment being hedged using the EUR/CHF spot exchange rate.

Frequency of testing: at every reporting date (30 June and 31 December) after inception of the hedge.

Effectiveness tests and accounting entries

1 Prospective effectiveness test on 1 January 20X5

At inception of the hedge, the forward EUR/CHF exchange rate is 1.5667 and the six-month EURIBOR is at 1.3505%. On that date, the spot EUR/CHF exchange rate is 1.5000.

Company K's management assesses the effectiveness of the hedge prospectively, as required by IAS 39. Based on the hedge documentation, the prospective effectiveness test consists of comparing the effects of a 10% shift of the EUR/CHF spot exchange rate on the net investment and the debt instrument.

Prospective effectiveness test on 1 January 20X5

	30/6/20X5	31/12/20X5	30/6/20X6	31/12/20X6	Total
Cash flows on the debt					
Expected cash flows at 1.3505% (EUR)	(675,250)	(675,250)	(675,250)	(100,675,250)	
Discount factor	0.99332	0.98653	0.97990	0.97344	
Discounted cash flows (EUR)	(670,736)	(666,153)	(661,675)	(98,001,436)	
EUR/CHF spot exchange rate	1.5000	1.5000	1.5000	1.5000	
Discounted cash flows (CHF)	**(1,006,104)**	**(999,229)**	**(992,513)**	**(147,002,154)**	**(150,000,000)**
Expected cash flows at 1.3505% (EUR)	(675,250)	(675,250)	(675,250)	(100,675,250)	
Discount factor	0.99332	0.98653	0.97990	0.97344	
Discounted cash flows (EUR)	(670,736)	(666,153)	(661,675)	(98,001,436)	
10% shift in EUR/CHF spot exchange rate	1.6500	1.6500	1.6500	1.6500	
Discounted cash flows (CHF)	**(1,106,714)**	**(1,099,152)**	**(1,091,764)**	**(161,702,370)**	**(165,000,000)**
				Change	**(15,000,000)**
Net investment					
Net investment in EUR				100,000,000	
EUR/CHF spot exchange rate				1.5000	
Net investment in CHF				150,000,000	**150,000,000**
Net investment in EUR				100,000,000	
10% shift in EUR/CHF spot exchange rate				1.6500	
Net investment in CHF				165,000,000	**165,000,000**
				Change	**15,000,000**
				Effectiveness	**100%**

Conclusion: the hedge is expected to be highly effective.

2 Entries on 1 January 20X5

The debt is recognised at the proceeds received by Company K, which represents its fair value on the issuance date. The debt is classified as other financial liabilities and will subsequently be measured at amortised cost.

	Dr	Cr
Cash	100,000,000	
Other financial liabilities – debt		100,000,000
Issuance at par of a EUR 100m two-year debt		

3 Retrospective effectiveness test on 30 June 20X5

IAS 39 requires the effectiveness of a hedging relationship to be assessed retrospectively as a minimum at each reporting date. Based on Company K's risk management policies, the effectiveness of the hedge is assessed using the dollar offset method. The dollar offset method consists of comparing the effects of the change in EUR/CHF spot exchange rate on the hedged item (net investment) and the hedging instrument (cash instrument).

Retrospective effectiveness test on 30 June 20X5

	30/6/20X5	31/12/20X5	30/6/20X6	31/12/20X6	Total
Cash flows on the debt					
Expected cash flows at 1.3505% (EUR)	(675,250)	(675,250)	(675,250)	(100,675,250)	
Discount factor	0.99332	0.98653	0.97990	0.97344	
Discounted cash flows (EUR)	(670,736)	(666,153)	(661,675)	(98,001,436)	
EUR/CHF spot exchange rate at inception	1.5000	1.5000	1.5000	1.5000	
Discounted cash flows (CHF)	(1,006,104)	(999,229)	(992,513)	(147,002,154)	**(150,000,000)**
Expected cash flows at 1.3500% (EUR)		(675,000)	(675,000)	(100,675,000)	
Discount factor		0.99317	0.98650	0.98002	
Discounted cash flows (EUR)		(670,389)	(665,885)	(98,663,726)	
EUR/CHF spot exchange rate at testing date		1.5800	1.5800	1.5800	
Discounted cash flows (CHF)		(1,059,215)	(1,052,098)	(155,888,687)	**(158,000,000)**
				Change	**(8,000,000)**
Net investment					
Net investment in EUR				100,000,000	
EUR/CHF spot exchange rate at inception				1.5000	
Net investment in CHF at inception				150,000,000	**150,000,000**
Net investment in EUR				100,000,000	
EUR/CHF spot exchange rate at testing date				1.5800	
Net investment in CHF at testing date				158,000,000	**158,000,000**
				Change	**8,000,000**
				Effectiveness	**100%**

Conclusion: the hedge has been highly effective for the period ended 30 June 20X5.

Helpful hint

In practice, both the prospective and retrospective effectiveness tests may be performed by:

1 translating the principal amount of the debt into CHF using the relevant EUR/CHF spot exchange rates (for the retrospective test, the rates at the beginning and end of the period); and

2 comparing the difference with the foreign currency gains and losses on the net investment.

This 'short cut' gives the same results, as shown below.

	EUR
Principal amount of the debt (in EUR)	100,000,000
EUR/CHF spot exchange rate at inception	1.5000
	CHF
	150,000,000
	EUR
Principal amount of the debt (in EUR)	100,000,000
EUR/CHF spot exchange rate at testing date	1.5800
	CHF
	158,000,000
	CHF
Difference (+gain/-loss):	**(8,000,000)**
Foreign currency gain on the net investment (see table above)	**CHF 8,000,000**
Effectiveness	**100%**

3 Accounting entries on 30 June 20X5

Recognition of interest on the debt

Interest for the first six months (EUR 675,000) is paid on 30 June. The payment is translated using the spot rate on 30 June. The interest expense is translated at the average rate for the six month period as interest accrues over time. The difference in translation rates gives rise to a loss that is recorded as 'other operating income and expense'.

	Dr	Cr
Finance costs – interest expense	1,039,500	
Other operating income and expense	27,000	
Cash		1,066,500
Payment of interest on the debt at 1.35% for six months		

Net investment hedge accounting

As the hedge has been fully effective for the period, the entire foreign currency loss on the debt is recognised in equity, and there is no ineffectiveness to recognise in profit or loss.

	Dr	Cr
Translation reserve (equity)	8,000,000	
Debt instrument		8,000,000
Net investment hedge		

Helpful hint
A gain of CHF 8 million will also be recognised in the translation reserve from the translation of the hedged net investment in the Italian subsidiary. As a result, the net change in the translation reserve for the six months ended 30 June 20X5 is nil.

4 Prospective effectiveness test on 30 June 20X5

The same method is used as at the inception of the hedge.

Prospective effectiveness test on 30 June 20X5

	30/6/20X5	31/12/20X5	30/6/20X6	31/12/20X6	Total
Cash flows on the debt					
Expected cash flows at 1.3505% (EUR)	(675,250)	(675,250)	(675,250)	(100,675,250)	
Discount factor	0.99332	0.98653	0.97990	0.97344	
Discounted cash flows (EUR)	(670,736)	(666,153)	(661,675)	(98,001,436)	
EUR/CHF spot exchange rate	1.5800	1.5800	1.5800	1.5800	
Discounted cash flows (CHF)	(1,059,763)	(1,052,522)	(1,045,447)	(154,842,269)	**(158,000,000)**
Expected cash flows at 1.3500% (EUR)		(675,000)	(675,000)	(100,675,000)	
Discount factor		0.99317	0.98650	0.98002	
Discounted cash flows (EUR)		(670,389)	(665,885)	(98,663,726)	
10% shift in EUR/CHF spot exchange rate		1.7380	1.7380	1.7380	
Discounted cash flows (CHF)		(1,165,137)	(1,157,308)	(171,477,556)	**(173,800,000)**
				Change	**(15,800,000)**
Net investment					
Net investment in EUR				100,000,000	
EUR/CHF spot exchange rate				1.5800	
Net investment in CHF				158,000,000	**158,000,000**
Net investment in EUR				100,000,000	
10% shift in EUR/CHF spot exchange rate				1.7380	
Net investment in CHF				173,800,000	**173,800,000**
				Change	**15,800,000**
				Effectiveness	**100%**

Conclusion: the hedge is expected to be highly effective.

5 Retrospective effectiveness test on 31 December 20X5

The forward EUR/CHF exchange rate is 1.6364 and the six-month EURIBOR is at 1.3750%. On that date, the spot EUR/CHF exchange rate is 1.6000. The method used is the same as at 1 January 20X5.

Retrospective effectiveness test on 31 December 20X5

	30/6/20X5	31/12/20X5	30/6/20X6	31/12/20X6	Total
Cash flows on the debt					
Expected cash flows at 1.3505% (EUR)	(675,250)	(675,250)	(675,250)	(100,675,250)	
Discount factor	0.99332	0.98653	0.97990	0.97344	
Discounted cash flows (EUR)	(670,736)	(666,153)	(661,675)	(98,001,436)	
EUR/CHF spot exchange rate at inception	1.5000	1.5000	1.5000	1.5000	
Discounted cash flows clean (CHF)	(1,006,104)	(999,229)	(992,513)	(147,002,154)	**(150,000,000)**
Expected cash flows at 1.3750%			(687,500)	(100,687,500)	
Discount factor			0.99316	0.98639	
Discounted cash flows (EUR)			(682,796)	(99,317,205)	
EUR/CHF spot exchange rate at testing date			1.6000	1.6000	
Discounted cash flows clean (CHF)			(1,092,473)	(158,907,527)	**(160,000,000)**
				Change	**(10,000,000)**
Net investment					
Net investment in EUR				100,000,000	
EUR/CHF spot exchange rate at inception				1.5000	
Net investment in CHF at inception				150,000,000	**150,000,000**
Net investment in EUR				100,000,000	
EUR/CHF spot exchange rate at testing date				1.6000	
Net investment in CHF at testing date				160,000,000	**160,000,000**
				Change	**10,000,000**
				Effectiveness	**100%**

Conclusion: the hedge has been highly effective for the period ended 31 December 20X5.

6 Accounting entries on 31 December 20X5

Recognition of interest on the debt

Interest for six months (EUR 687,500) is paid on 31 December. The payment is translated using the spot rate on 31 December. The interest expense is translated at the average rate for the six-month period as interest accrues over time. The difference in translation rates gives rise to a loss that is recorded as 'other operating income and expense'.

	Dr	Cr
Finance costs – interest expense	1,093,125	
Other operating income and expense	6,875	
Cash		1,100,000
Payment of interest on the debt at 1.375% for six months		

Net investment hedge accounting

As the hedge has been fully effective for the period, the entire foreign exchange loss on the debt is recognised in equity and there is no ineffectiveness to recognise in profit or loss.

	Dr	Cr
Translation reserve (equity)	2,000,000	
Debt instrument		2,000,000
Net investment hedge		

Cumulative foreign exchange loss on the debt on 31 December 20X5	(10,000,000)
Cumulative foreign exchange loss on the debt on 30 June 20X5	(8,000,000)
Foreign exchange loss to be recognised in translation reserve	**(2,000,000)**

7 Prospective effectiveness test on 31 December 20X5

The same method is used as at the inception of the hedge.

Prospective effectiveness test on 31 December 20X5

	30/6/20X5	31/12/20X5	30/6/20X6	31/12/20X6	Total
Cash flows on the debt					
Expected cash flows at 1.3505% (EUR)	(675,250)	(675,250)	(675,250)	(100,675,250)	
Discount factor	0.99332	0.98653	0.97990	0.97344	
Discounted cash flows (EUR)	(670,736)	(666,153)	(661,675)	(98,001,436)	
EUR/CHF spot exchange rate	1.6000	1.6000	1.6000	1.6000	
Discounted cash flows (CHF)	(1,073,178)	(1,065,845)	(1,058,680)	(156,802,298)	**(160,000,000)**
Expected cash flows at 1.3750% (EUR)			(687,500)	(100,687,500)	
Discount factor			0.99316	0.98639	
Discounted cash flows (EUR)			(682,796)	(99,317,205)	
10% shift in EUR/CHF spot exchange rate			1.7600	1.7600	
Discounted cash flows (CHF)			(1,201,720)	(174,798,280)	**(176,000,000)**
				Change	**(16,000,000)**
Net investment					
Net investment in EUR				100,000,000	
EUR/CHF spot exchange rate				1.6000	
Net investment in CHF				160,000,000	**160,000,000**
Net investment in EUR				100,000,000	
10% shift in EUR/CHF spot exchange rate				1.7600	
Net investment in CHF				176,000,000	**176,000,000**
				Change	**16,000,000**
				Effectiveness	**100%**

Conclusion: the hedge is expected to be highly effective.

8 Retrospective effectiveness test on 30 June 20X6

On 30 June 20X6, Company K's net investment has decreased to EUR 98.5m because Company D made unexpected losses. The spot EUR/CHF exchange rate on 30 June 20X6 is 1.6200 and the six-month EURIBOR is 1.3250%. Effectiveness is tested using the same method as is described on 31 December 20X5.

Retrospective effectiveness test on 30 June 20X6

	30/6/20X5	31/12/20X5	30/6/20X6	31/12/20X6	Total
Cash flows on the debt					
Expected cash flows at 1.3505% (EUR)	(675,250)	(675,250)	(675,250)	(100,675,250)	
Discount factor	0.99332	0.98653	0.97990	0.97344	
Discounted cash flows (EUR)	(670,736)	(666,153)	(661,675)	(98,001,436)	
EUR/CHF spot exchange rate at inception	1.5000	1.5000	1.5000	1.5000	
Discounted cash flows clean (CHF)	(1,006,104)	(999,229)	(992,513)	(147,002,154)	**(150,000,000)**
Expected cash flows at 1.3250%				(100,662,500)	
Discount factor				0.99342	
Discounted cash flows (EUR)				(100,000,000)	
EUR/CHF spot exchange rate at testing date				1.6200	
Discounted cash flows clean (CHF)				(162,000,000)	**(162,000,000)**
				Change	**(12,000,000)**
Net investment					
Net investment in EUR				98,500,000	
EUR/CHF spot exchange rate at inception				1.5000	
Net investment in CHF at inception				147,750,000	**147,750,000**
Net investment in EUR				98,500,000	
EUR/CHF spot exchange rate at testing date				1.6200	
Net investment in CHF				159,570,000	**159,570,000**
				Change	**11,820,000**
				Effectiveness	**101.5%**

As illustrated above, the hedge is no longer fully effective because the carrying value of the hedged net investment is lower than the principal amount of the hedging debt instrument. However, the hedge remains highly effective.

Conclusion: the hedge has been highly effective for the period ended 30 June 20X6.

9 Accounting entries on 30 June 20X6

Recognition of interest on the debt

Interest for six months (EUR 662,500) is paid on 30 June. The payment is translated using the spot rate on 30 June. The interest expense is translated at the average rate for the six month period as interest accrues over time. The difference in translation rates gives rise to a loss that is recorded as 'other operating income and expense'.

	Dr	Cr
Finance costs – interest expense	1,066,625	
Other operating income and expense	6,625	
Cash		1,073,250
Payment of interest on the debt at 1.325% for six months		

Net investment hedge accounting

As the hedge has not been fully effective for the period, ineffectiveness must be recognised in profit or loss.

Cumulative foreign exchange loss on the debt on 30 June 20X6	(12,000,000)
Cumulative foreign exchange loss on the debt on 31 December 20X5	(10,000,000)
Foreign exchange loss on the debt for the period (A)	**(2,000,000)**
Translation reserve balance on 30 June 20X6	11,820,000
Translation reserve balance on 31 December 20X5	10,000,000
Difference (B)	**1,820,000**

As the change in the hedging instrument (the debt) is greater than the change in the hedged item (the net investment), it is not fully absorbed by the hedged item. The difference must therefore be recognised in the income statement as ineffectiveness.

	Dr	Cr
Other operating income and expense (A + B)	180,000	
Translation reserve (equity)	1,820,000	
Debt instrument		2,000,000
Net investment hedge		

10 Prospective effectiveness test on 30 June 20X6

The same method is used as at the inception of the hedge. In addition, Company K's management does not expect its Italian subsidiary to make further losses for the remaining life of the hedge (until 31 December 20X6).

Prospective effectiveness test on 30 June 20X6

	30/6/20X5	31/12/20X5	30/6/20X6	31/12/20X6	Total
Cash flows on the debt					
Expected cash flows at 1.3505% (EUR)	(675,250)	(675,250)	(675,250)	(100,675,250)	
Discount factor	0.99332	0.98653	0.97990	0.97344	
Discounted cash flows (EUR)	(670,736)	(666,153)	(661,675)	(98,001,436)	
EUR/CHF spot exchange rate	1.6200	1.6200	1.6200	1.6200	
Discounted cash flows (CHF)	(1,086,592)	(1,079,168)	(1,071,914)	(158,762,326)	**(162,000,000)**
Expected cash flows at 1.3250% (EUR)				(100,662,500)	
Discount factor				0.99342	
Discounted cash flows (EUR)				(100,000,000)	
10% shift in EUR/CHF spot exchange rate				1.7820	
Discounted cash flows (CHF)				(178,200,000)	**(178,200,000)**
				Change	**(16,200,000)**
Net investment					
Net investment in EUR				98,500,000	
EUR/CHF spot exchange rate				1.6200	
Net investment in CHF				159,570,000	**159,570,000**
Net investment in EUR				98,500,000	
10% shift in EUR/CHF spot exchange rate				1.7820	
Net investment in CHF				175,527,000	**175,527,000**
				Change	**15,957,000**
				Effectiveness	**101.5%**

Conclusion: the hedge is expected to be highly effective, although some ineffectiveness is expected because the carrying value of the hedged net investment is smaller than the principal amount of the hedging debt instrument.

Helpful hint

This ineffectiveness could be avoided by re-designating the hedge, so that the hedging instrument is designated as 98.5% of the debt instrument (that is, an amount that matches the reduced net investment). In this example, in which the losses are relatively small, such re-designation would make no difference to the accounting entries, as the hedge remains highly effective. However, had the losses been so big as to cause the hedge to fail the effectiveness test, re-designating the hedge in this way may allow the company to apply hedge accounting for future periods.

Helpful hint
What will happen if the hedged net investment is sold? If Company D is sold or otherwise disposed of, the hedging gains or losses on the debt previously accumulated in the translation reserve (equity) will be transferred to profit or loss as part of the gain or loss on disposal.

Summary of accounting entities

	Balance sheet			Income statement	
	Debt instrument	Cash	Translation reserve (equity)	Other operating income & expense	Finance cost
01/01/20X5					
Recognition of the debt	(100,000,000)	100,000,000			
30/6/20X5					
Interest on the debt		(1,066,500)		27,000	1,039,500
Debt re-translation	(8,000,000)		8,000,000		
31/12/20X5					
Interest on the debt		(1,100,000)		6,875	1,093,125
Debt re-translation	(2,000,000)		2,000,000		
30/6/20X6					
Interest on the debt		(1,073,250)		6,625	1,066,625
Debt re-translation	(2,000,000)		1,820,000	180,000	

Section 11

Presentation and disclosure

Presentation of financial instruments

A6.11.1 The principles for presenting financial and other assets and liabilities, and any related income and expense, are set out in IAS 1, 'Presentation of financial statements'. This standard's requirements are considered in detail in chapter 4. The paragraphs that follow consider only the presentation of financial assets and liabilities as current or non-current.

Presentation as current or non-current

A6.11.2 IAS 1 states that an entity should present current and non-current assets, and current and non-current liabilities, as separate classifications on the face of the balance sheet, except when a presentation based on liquidity provides information that is reliable and is more relevant. When that exception applies, all assets and liabilities should be presented broadly in order of liquidity. [IAS 1 para 51].

Current and non-current assets

A6.11.3 Where an entity presents assets and liabilities as either current or non-current, IAS 1 defines a current asset as an asset that satisfies any of the following criteria:

- It is expected to be realised in, or is intended for sale or consumption in, the entity's normal operating cycle.
- It is held primarily for the purpose of being traded.
- It is expected to be realised within 12 months after the balance sheet date.
- It is cash or a cash equivalent (as defined in IAS 7, 'Cash flow statements') unless it is restricted from being exchanged or used to settle a liability at least 12 months after the balance sheet date.

[IAS 1 para 57].

A6.11.4 It follows from the above definition that financial assets classified as held for trading should be presented as current assets. [IAS 1 para 59]. Similarly, trading derivative assets should also be presented as current assets. However, in May 2007, IFRIC was asked to provide guidance on whether derivatives that are classified as held-for-trading in accordance with IAS 39 should be presented as current or non-current in the balance sheet. This was in relation to those derivatives that may be settled more than one year after the balance sheet date. This issue arose because IAS 39 sets out requirements on the recognition and measurement of financial instruments, but it does not address how financial instruments should be presented in the balance sheet. Consequently, some believed that the held-for-trading classification under IAS 39 is solely for measurement purposes.

A6.11.4.1 IAS 1 sets out the requirements for the presentation of an asset or a liability as current or non-current in the balance sheet and paragraph 56 specifically states that the presentation should be in such a format that it provides useful information about the liquidity and solvency of an entity. On the other hand paragraph 62 implies that financial liabilities that are classified as held-for-trading in accordance with IAS 39 are required to be presented as current.

A6.11.4.2 The IFRIC did not take this issue on to its agenda, but recommended the IASB to remove the implication in IAS 39 that such derivatives must be presented as current as part of its annual amendment process.

A6.11.4.3 The treatment of hedging derivatives is less clear. Where a portion of a financial asset is expected to be realised within 12 months of the balance sheet date, that portion should be presented as a current asset; the remainder of the financial asset should be shown as a non-current asset. This suggests that hedging derivatives should be split into current and non-current portions. However, as an alternative, the full fair value of hedging derivatives could be classified as current if the hedge relationships are for less than 12 months and as non-current if those relationships are for more than 12 months.

A6.11.5 Financial assets, other than derivatives and those classified as held for trading, should only be presented as current assets if realisation within 12 months is expected. Other financial assets should be classified as non-current assets, although any portion that is expected to be realised within 12 months of the balance sheet date should be presented as a current asset.

Current and non-current liabilities

A6.11.6 Where an entity presents assets and liabilities as either current or non-current, IAS 1 defines a current liability as a liability that satisfies any of the following criteria:

- It is expected to be settled in the entity's normal operating cycle.
- It is held primarily for the purpose of being traded.
- It is due to be settled within 12 months after the balance sheet date.
- The entity does note have an unconditional right to defer the liability's *settlement* for at least 12 months after the balance sheet date.

[IAS 1 para 60].

A6.11.6.1 Under IAS 32, the equity and liability components of financial instruments must be classified separately as financial liabilities, financial assets or equity instruments. [IAS 32 para 28]. The liability component of financial instruments should be classified as current or non-current, depending on the terms of the contract.

A6.11.6.2 The IFRIC was asked to consider whether the liability component of a convertible financial instrument should be presented as current or non-current, when the instrument is convertible to equity at any time within the next 12 months, but if not converted, is repayable in cash only beyond 12 months. Such instruments would have an equity component, being the holders' right to convert the instrument into a fixed number of equity instruments of the issuer any time before the maturity date; and a liability component, being the entity's obligation to deliver cash to holders at the maturity date, which is more than one year after the balance sheet date.

A6.11.6.3 The IFRIC did not reach a definitive conclusion and stated that the IASB should provide clarification. However until the IASB provides clarification on the classification, we believe that the liability component of the convertible debt should be classified as non-current. When applying IAS 1's requirements, components of an instrument that are classified as equity should be ignored. In the case of a convertible instrument, ignoring the conversion option leaves a debt component that is not re-payable within 12 months. Ignoring any equity components when classifying the liability component reflects that the equity components are not part of the liability for accounting purposes. Any equity components are accounted for in the same way as if they had been issued as separate instruments. It follows that the presentation should be the same as if they had been issued as separate instruments.

A6.11.6.4 In contrast, consider puttable debt that is puttable by the holder within the next 12 months but, if not put, is repayable only beyond 12 months. In this case, the puttable debt should be classified in its entirety as current, irrespective of whether IAS 39 requires the put option to be accounted for as a separated embedded derivative and, if it does, of whether the host debt contract is reported in a separate balance sheet line item from the embedded derivative. This reflects that the put option could cause the entire instrument to be settled in a manner that is regarded as a liability under IAS 32.

A6.11.7 The presentation of financial liabilities as current or non-current would take account of similar considerations to financial assets (see para A6.11.4 above). However, IAS 1 provides additional guidance for financial liabilities that have been renegotiated or refinanced. Specifically, the standard requires that a financial liability should be presented as current when it is due to be settled within 12 months after the balance sheet date, even if:

- the original term was for a period longer than 12 months; and

- an agreement to refinance, or to reschedule payments, on a long-term basis is completed after the balance sheet date and before the financial statements are authorised for issue.

[IAS 1 para 63].

A6.11.8 The current or non-current classification of financial liabilities is governed by the condition of those liabilities at the balance sheet date. Where rescheduling or refinancing is at the lender's discretion, and it occurs after the balance sheet date, it does not alter the liability's condition at that date. Accordingly, it is regarded as a non-adjusting post balance sheet event and it is not taken into account in determining the current/non-current classification of the debt. On the other hand where the refinancing or rescheduling is at the entity's discretion and the entity can elect to roll over an obligation for at least one year after the balance sheet date, the obligation must be classified as non-current, even if it would otherwise be due within a shorter period. However, if the entity expects to settle the obligation within 12 months, despite having the discretion to refinance for a longer period, then the debt should be classified as current. [IAS 1 para 64].

Example – rolling over bank facilities

A company has entered into a facility arrangement with a bank. It has a committed facility that the bank cannot cancel unilaterally and the scheduled maturity of this facility is 3 years from the balance sheet date. The company has drawn down funds on this facility and these funds are due to be repaid 6 months after the balance sheet date. The company intends to roll over this debt through the three year facility arrangement. How should this borrowing be shown in the company's balance sheet?

Would the answer be different if the facility and existing loan were with different banks?

The borrowing should be shown as non-current. Although the loan is due for repayment within six months of the balance sheet date, the company is entitled to 'rollover' this borrowing into a 'new loan'. The substance is, therefore, that the debt is not repayable until 3 years after the balance sheet date when the committed facility expires. In addition, the entity expects to rollover the debt, so does not expect to repay it within 12 months.

The position would be different if the facility was with a different bank or if the loan was in the form of commercial paper. In the first case, the company would have a loan repayable in six months, but would be entitled to take out a new loan to settle its existing debt. These two loans are separate and the new loan is not, either in substance or in fact, an extension of the existing. Similarly if the loan was in the form of commercial paper, which typically has a maturity of 90 to 180 days, it would be classified as a current liability as it is likely that the back up facility would be provided by a different bank.

6A.11.9 It is common practice for financial institutions to include borrowing covenants in the terms of loans. Under these borrowing covenants a loan which would otherwise be long-term in nature becomes immediately repayable if certain items related to the borrower's financial condition are breached. Typically, these items are measures of liquidity or solvency based on ratios derived from the entity's financial statements. Where the borrower has breached the borrowing covenant by the balance sheet date, or ends less than 12 months from the balance sheet date but the lender agrees, after the balance sheet date but before authorisation of the financial statements, not to require immediate repayment of the loan, the agreement of the lender is regarded as a non-adjusting post balance sheet event. Since, at the year end, the agreement of the lender had not been obtained, the condition of the borrowing at the balance sheet date was that it was immediately repayable and should, therefore, be shown as a current liability. [IAS 1 para 65]. An example of disclosure of a breach of covenant disclosed in an interim report and events subsequent to the interim reporting date is given in Table 6.11.1.

Table 6.11.1 – Breach of covenant resulting in loans restated as current at period end, post the balance sheet refinancing

First Technology plc – Interim report – 31 October 2005

14. Bank overdrafts and loans

	Six months ended 31st October 2005	Six months ended 31st October 2004	Year ended 30th April 2005
	£'m	£'m	£'m
Bank overdrafts	0.3	2.8	1.0
Bank loans	112.4	111.4	105.3
	112.7	114.2	106.3
Repayable:			
On demand or within one year			
In the second year	112.7	48.9	47.0
In the third year	–	8.1	7.8
In the forth year	–	8.1	7.8
In the fifth year	–	41.2	37.5
	112.7	114.2	106.3
Less: Amount due for settlement within 12 months (shown under current liabilities)	(112.7)	(7.9)	(6.2)
Amounts due for settlement after more than 12 months		106.3	100.1

The Group's principal source of debt at 31st October 2005 was a multi-currency syndicated bank loan ('the Facilities') entered into with a group of seven banks in May 2004 in connection with the Group's offer for BWT. The Facilities comprised three tranches: a US$75 million revolving credit facility; a term loan of up to US$75 million and a US$100 million revolving credit facility. The Facilities were repayable between May 2006 and May 2009. The Facilities were unsecured and initially carried interest at a margin of 1.5% over LIBOR (or EURIBOR for amounts advanced in Euros), plus mandatory costs. The applicable margin was variable (ranging from a minimum of 0.875% up to a maximum of 1.75%) according to the ratio of consolidated net borrowings to EBITDA.

The Facilities were subject to three financial covenants, which were tested quarterly. On 17th August 2005, First Technology PLC informed its bankers that it had failed to meet one of these covenants with respect to the test for the period ended 26th July 2005. As a result of the covenant breach, the Facilities technically became repayable on demand.

> On 12th December 2005, the Group signed an agreement for a new bank loan ('the new Facility') with its two principal bankers, HSBC Bank plc and The Royal Bank of Scotland plc, the proceeds of which are being used to repay the existing Facilities. The new Facility comprises two tranches: a US$80 million revolving credit facility and a US$140 million term loan, each available until December 2006. Both tranches, under certain circumstances, can be extended at the Company's option for a further twelve months to December 2007. The new Facility carries interest at a margin of 1.5% over LIBOR, plus mandatory costs. The new Facility is unsecured, although certain of First Technology PLC's wholly-owned subsidiaries have given guarantees with respect to First Technology PLC's obligations under the agreement. However, in the event that the offer announced on 19th December, or any other offer, for the entire issued share capital of the Company does not become wholly unconditional or that the Company has not completed an equity issue raising proceeds of at least £40 million and used such amount to repay the new Facility, the Company will be required to give security by 30th September 2006. Any net proceeds of an equity issue must be applied to repay the new Facility. If the amount prepaid is more than £40 million, the Company has the option to extend the new Facility for an additional one year term. Under all circumstances, the Company retains the flexibility to re-finance this new Facility.
>
> In July 2004, First Technology PLC entered into an interest rate swap to fix the rate of interest that it would pay under the US$75 million term loan tranche of the syndicated loan. The interest rate swap fixed for the whole term the rate of interest at 3.605% plus the applicable margin for this element of the Group's debt. This swap is now being used to fix the rate of interest payable under a proportion of the new Facility.

A6.11.10 However, following a breach of a borrowing covenant, lenders often agree to a period of grace during which the borrower agrees to rectify the breach. The lender agrees not to demand repayment during this time but, if the breach is not rectified, the debt would become immediately repayable at the end of the period of grace. If, before the balance sheet date, the lender has agreed to such a period of grace and that period ends at least 12 months after the balance sheet date, then the liability should be shown as non-current. [IAS 1 para 66]. If the breach of the borrowing covenant occurs after the balance date, then the liability would still be shown as non-current, unless the breach was so serious that the financial statements could no longer be prepared on a going concern basis. However, if the breach occurred before the balance sheet date, but the period of grace was not granted until after the balance sheet date, then the liability would be classified as current. The key to this approach is that the loan's presentation is dictated by the loan's condition as at the balance sheet date. Events after the balance sheet date may give evidence of that condition but they do not change it. This is consistent with IAS 10, 'Events after the balance sheet date'.

A6.11.11 The standard's approach to breaches of borrowing covenants focuses on the legal rights of the entity rather than on the intentions of either of the parties to the loan. In dealing with situations where the entity has the discretion to roll over or refinance loans, the entity's expectations on the timing of settlement play a part in deciding the liability's classification. The liability's classification is, however, unaffected by the entity's intentions in the case of a breach of a loan agreement. If the entity breaches the loan agreement before the balance sheet date and the lender grants a period of grace of more than 12 months from the balance sheet date, then the loan is classified as non-current even if it is the entity's intention to repay the loan within 12 months of the balance sheet date. In many cases, however, the period of grace will be a matter of negotiation between the borrower and the lender and will match the borrower's intentions in any event. In addition, breaches of loan agreements occur most often in entities that are experiencing financial difficulties and these entities are unlikely to wish to repay the loan earlier than required by the lender.

A6.11.12 Although post balance sheet events may not alter the liability's classification, they may require disclosure as a non-adjusting event. IAS 1 paragraph 67 states that, in respect of loans classified as current liabilities, the following events must be disclosed as non-adjusting events in accordance with IAS 10, if they occur between the balance sheet date and the date of authorisation of the financial statements:

- Refinancing on a long-term basis.
- Rectification of a breach of a long-term loan agreement.
- The receipt from the lender of a period of grace to rectify a breach of a long-term loan agreement ending at least 12 months after the balance sheet date.

A6.11.13 IAS 1 does not specify any disclosures for non-adjusting post balance sheet events in respect of loans classified as non-current liabilities. However, IAS 10 requires that an entity should disclose the following for each material category of non-adjusting event after the balance sheet date:

- The nature of the event.
- An estimate of its financial effect, or a statement that such an estimate cannot be made.

[IAS 10 para 21].

A6.11.14 Further disclosure of defaults and breaches of loan agreements is required by IFRS 7 (see para A6.11.61 below).

Offsetting a financial asset and a financial liability

General principle

A6.11.15 A financial asset and a financial liability should be offset when, and only when, both of the following conditions are satisfied:

- The entity currently has a legally enforceable right to set off the recognised amounts.
- The entity intends either to settle on a net basis, or to realise the asset and settle the liability simultaneously.

[IAS 32 para 42].

A6.11.16 Where the above offset conditions are satisfied, the entity has the right to receive or pay a single net amount and intends to do so, it has, in effect, only a single financial asset or financial liability. In that situation, the financial asset and the financial liability are presented on the balance sheet on a net basis. Where the offset conditions are not satisfied, the financial asset and the financial liability are presented separately from each other, consistently with their characteristics as the entity's resources or obligations. [IAS 32 para 43].

A6.11.17 However, in accounting for a transfer of a financial asset that does not qualify for derecognition, the entity should not offset the transferred asset and the associated liability (see section 8). This is because offsetting a recognised financial asset and a recognised financial liability and presenting the net amount is different from the derecognition of a financial asset or a financial liability. The derecognition of a financial instrument not only results in the removal of the previously recognised item from the balance sheet, but also may result in recognition of a gain or loss. Offsetting does not give rise to recognising a gain or loss. [IAS 32 paras 42, 44].

Legal right of set-off

A6.11.18 IAS 32 defines a right of offset as *"a debtor's legal right, by contract or otherwise, to settle or otherwise eliminate all or a portion of an amount due to a creditor by applying against that amount an amount due from the creditor"*. Because the right of offset is essentially a legal right, the conditions supporting the right may vary from one legal jurisdiction to another and, therefore, the laws applicable to the relationships between the parties would need to be considered carefully. [IAS 32 para 45]. It follows that instruments such as receivables and payables with the same counterparty would fall to be offset if a legal right of offset is agreed between the parties (and the entity intends to settle net or simultaneously).

A6.11.19 In unusual circumstances, a debtor may have a legal right to apply an amount due from a third party against the amount due to a creditor provided that there is an agreement between the three parties that clearly establishes the debtor's right of set-off. [IAS 32 para 45].

Intention to settle on a net basis

A6.11.20 It is clear from the general principle in paragraph A6.11.15 above that, in order to achieve offset, an entity must have both the right and the intention to do so. It is not sufficient to have one and not the other. Although the existence of an enforceable legal right of offset affects the entity's rights and obligations associated with a financial asset and a financial liability and may affect its exposure to credit and liquidity risk, it is, by itself, not a sufficient basis for offsetting. This is because, in the absence of an intention to exercise the right or to settle simultaneously, the amount and timing of the entity's future cash flows are not affected. However, if, in addition to the legal right, the entity clearly intends to exercise the right or to settle simultaneously, it is, in effect, exposed to a net amount, which reflects the timing of the expected future cash flows and the risks to which those cash flows are exposed. Similarly, an intention by one or both parties to settle on a net basis without the legal right to do so is not sufficient to justify offsetting because the rights and obligations associated with the individual financial asset and financial liability remain unaltered. [IAS 32 para 46].

A6.11.21 An entity's intentions with respect to settlement of particular assets and liabilities may be influenced by its normal business practices, the requirements of the financial markets and other circumstances that may limit the ability to settle net or to settle simultaneously. When an entity has a right of offset, but does not intend to settle net or to realise the asset and settle the liability simultaneously, the effect of the right on the entity's credit risk exposure is disclosed in accordance with paragraph A6.11.83 below.

Simultaneous settlement

A6.11.22 IAS 32 states that realisation of a financial asset and settlement of a financial liability are treated as simultaneous only when the transactions occur at the same moment. For example, the operation of a clearing house in an organised financial market or a face-to-face exchange will facilitate simultaneous settlement of two financial instruments. In these circumstances the cash flows are, in effect, equivalent to a single net amount and there is no exposure to credit or liquidity risk. In other circumstances, an entity may settle two instruments by receiving and paying separate amounts, becoming exposed to credit risk for the full amount of the asset or liquidity risk for the full amount of the liability. Such risk exposures, though brief, may be significant and therefore, net presentation is not appropriate. [IAS 32 para 48].

Situations where offset is usually inappropriate

A6.11.23 IAS 32 sets out the following specific situations where the offset criteria in paragraph A6.11.15 above are not met.

- Several different financial instruments are used to emulate the features of a single financial instrument (a 'synthetic instrument'). For example, a floating rate long-term debt combined with an interest rate swap that involves receiving floating payments and making fixed payments synthesises a fixed rate long-term debt. Each of the individual financial instruments that together constitute a 'synthetic instrument':
  - represents a contractual right or obligation with its own terms and conditions;
  - may be transferred or settled separately;
  - is exposed to risks that may differ from the risks to which other financial instruments are exposed.

  Accordingly, when one financial instrument in a 'synthetic instrument' is an asset and another is a liability, they are not offset and presented on an entity's balance sheet on a net basis unless they meet the criteria for offsetting in paragraph A6.11.15 above.

- Financial assets and financial liabilities arise from financial instruments having the same primary risk exposure (for example, assets and liabilities within a portfolio of forward contracts or other derivative instruments), but involve different counterparties.
- Financial or other assets are pledged as collateral for non-recourse financial liabilities.
- Financial assets are set aside in trust by a debtor for the purpose of discharging an obligation without those assets having been accepted by the creditor in settlement of the obligation (for example, a sinking fund arrangement).
- Obligations incurred as a result of events giving rise to losses are expected to be recovered from a third party by virtue of a claim made under an insurance contract.

[IAS 32 para 49].

Master netting agreements

A6.11.24 An entity that undertakes a number of financial instrument transactions with a single counterparty may enter into a 'master netting arrangement' with that counterparty. Such an arrangement creates a right of set-off that becomes enforceable and affects the realisation or settlement of individual financial assets and financial liabilities only following a specified event of default or in other circumstances not expected to arise in the normal course of business. These arrangements are commonly used by financial institutions to provide protection against loss in the event of bankruptcy or other circumstances that result in a counterparty being unable to meet its obligations. In the event of default on, or termination of, any one contract, the agreement provides for a single net settlement of all financial instruments covered by the agreement. [IAS 32 para 50].

A6.11.25 Where an entity has entered into such an agreement, the agreement does not provide a basis for offsetting unless both of the criteria in paragraph A6.11.15 above are satisfied. This is because the entity's right of set off under such an agreement is conditional and enforeable only on the occurrence of some future event, usually a default of the counterparty. To offset a financial asset and a financial liability, an entity must have a currently enforceable legal right to set off the recognised amounts. Thus, such an arrangement does not meet the conditions for offset. [IAS 32 para 50].

A6.11.26 When financial assets and financial liabilities subject to a master netting arrangement are not offset, the effect of the arrangement on an entity's exposure to credit risk is disclosed in accordance with paragraph A6.11.83 below.

Disclosure of financial instruments

A6.11.27 In recent years, there have been significant developments in risk management concepts and practices. New techniques have evolved for measuring and managing exposures to risks arising from financial instruments. As a result, the need for more relevant information and greater transparency about an entity's exposures arising from financial instruments and how those risks are managed has become greater. Financial statement users and other investors need such information to make more informed judgements about risk that entities run from the use of financial instruments and their associated returns. However, it became clear that the disclosures in IAS 30 (disclosure requirements for banks and similar financial institutions) and IAS 32 were not in keeping with such developments and there was a need to revise and enhance the disclosure framework for risks arising from financial instruments. IFRS 7, issued in August 2005, is the product of that revision.

A6.11.28 IFRS 7 contains all the disclosure requirements related to financial instruments and supersedes IAS 30 and the disclosure requirements in IAS 32. IFRS 7 incorporates many of the requirements previously contained in IAS 30 and IAS 32, but some have been amended, some made less prescriptive and new ones added. IAS 32 now deals only with presentation matters, including classification of financial liabilities and equity, compound financial instruments, offsetting and treasury shares.

A6.11.29 At the same time as the IASB published IFRS 7, it also published an amendment to IAS 1. The amendment to IAS 1 adds requirements for all entities to provide information about level of capital and how the entity manages capital. These are important factors for users to consider in assessing the entity's risk profile and its ability to withstand unexpected adverse events. IAS 1's requirements are considered in chapter 4.

Scope of IFRS 7

A6.11.30 IFRS 7 applies to all types of financial instruments except those that are specifically covered by another standard such as interests in subsidiaries, associates and joint ventures, acquirer's interest in contracts for contingent consideration in a business combination, employers' rights and obligations arising from employee benefit plans, share based payments and insurance contracts. IFRS 7 applies to both recognised and unrecognised financial instruments within its scope, even if the financial instrument may not be recognised under IAS 39 (for example, some loan commitments). It applies to contracts to buy or sell a non-financial item that are within IAS 39's scope. [IFRS 7 paras 3-5]. Although, finance leases are mostly outside the scope of IAS 39, they remain within the scope of IFRS 7. Operating leases are not regarded as financial instruments and, therefore, are not in the scope of IFRS 7, except for those individual payments which are currently due and payable. [IAS 32 para AG 9].

A6.11.31 Consistent with IAS 32 and IAS 39, the standard applies to all entities, not just those in the financial services sector. This means that it applies to a manufacturing entity whose only financial instruments may be cash, bank loans and overdrafts, trade debtors and creditors as well as to a bank with many and complex financial instruments. It also applies to subsidiaries of a consolidated group, even though in most large groups risks are managed at the consolidated level.

A6.11.31.1 There is no scope exemption for the financial statements of subsidiaries or, as yet, for small and medium-sized companies. The application of IFRS 7 to subsidiaries may present a challenge to companies that are members of a consolidated group, as they often manage risk at a consolidated or group level.

Objectives of IFRS 7

A6.11.32 IFRS 7's objective is to provide information to users of financial statements about an entity's exposure to risks and how the entity manages those risks. To this end, the standard requires an entity to provide disclosures in its financial statements that enable users to evaluate:

- the significance of financial instruments for the entity's financial position and performance; and
- the nature and extent of risks arising from financial instruments to which the entity is exposed (quantitative disclosure) and how the entity manages those risks (qualitative disclosures).

[IFRS 7 paras 1, 7, 31].

A6.11.33 The first bullet point above covers disclosures about the figures in the balance sheet and the income statement. These disclosures incorporate many of the requirements previously in IAS 32, but IFRS 7 requires additional disclosures of categories of financial instruments and hedging activities. In addition the standard also requires various disclosures by 'class' of financial instruments (see para A6.11.39).

A6.11.34 The second bullet point covers disclosure of qualitative and quantitative information about an entity's exposure to risks arising from financial instruments and in this regard, IFRS 7 takes a very different approach from the previous standards. IFRS 7 expands the qualitative disclosure to include information on the process that an entity uses to manage and measure risk. IFRS 7 introduces new quantitative risk disclosures that should be given 'through the eyes of management', that is, based on information provided internally to key management personnel. Certain minimum disclosures are also required to the extent they are not already covered by the 'through the eyes of management' information. Entities are required to communicate to the market how they perceive, manage and measure risk.

A6.11.34.1 This change to a 'through the eyes of management' approach and will bring financial reporting more closely into line with the way management run their businesses. Their internal measures have not previously been provided under IFRS or local accounting principles. This could enhance a company's ability to demonstrate the strengths of its control environment, but equally it could also expose any flaws. It will also enable the market to better evaluate the strength (or otherwise) of an entity's risk management activities.

A6.11.35 IFRS 7 includes mandatory application guidance that explains how to apply the standard's requirements. It is also accompanied by non-mandatory implementation guidance that describes how an entity might provide the necessary disclosures.

Effective date and transition to IFRS 7

A6.11.36 IFRS 7 is effective for annual periods beginning on or after 1 January 2007. Earlier application is encouraged but not required. If an entity applies IFRS 7 for a period beginning before 1 January 2007, that fact should be disclosed. The amendment to IAS 1 referred to in paragraph A6.11.29 above is also effective for annual periods beginning on or after 1 January 2007.

A6.11.37 To encourage early adoption, the standard provides certain transitional relief from disclosure. There are different transition rules depending on whether the entity is an existing IFRS user preparing its second or subsequent IFRS financial statements or a first-time adopter. These rules are described in the standard's implementation guidance. [IFRS 7 para IG 41].

A6.11.38 In summary, existing IFRS users must present full comparative information, unless IFRS 7 is adopted for periods beginning before 1 January 2006, in which case, the entity is exempt from presenting comparative qualitative and information about the nature and extent of risks arising from financial instruments (see second bullet point in para A6.11.32 above). [IFRS 7 para 44]. These disclosures are discussed from paragraphs 6.11.77. Such entities must still present comparative information for the requirements dealt with in the first bullet point in paragraph A6.11.32 above, as this is largely based on requirements previously in IAS 32. Similarly, a first-time adopter must present full comparative information, unless IFRS 7 is adopted for periods beginning before 1 January 2006, in which case the entity is exempt from presenting comparative information for any of the disclosures required by IFRS 7.

General matters

Classes of financial instruments

A6.11.39 IFRS 7 requires certain disclosures to be given by class of financial instruments, for example, the reconciliation of an allowance account (see para A6.11.56). The standard itself does not provide a prescriptive list of classes of financial instruments. However, IFRS 7 states that a class shall contain financial instruments of the same nature and characteristics. In addition, an entity should provide sufficient information to permit reconciliation to the line items presented in the balance sheet. [IFRS 7 para 6].

A6.11.40 A 'class' of financial instruments is not the same as a 'category' of financial instruments. Categories are defined in IAS 39 as financial assets at fair value through profit or loss, held-to-maturity investments, loans and receivables, available-for-sale financial assets, financial liabilities at fair value through profit or loss and financial liabilities measured at amortised cost. Classes should be determined at a lower lever than the measurement categories and reconciled back to the balance sheet. [IFRS 7 para 6]. The level of detail for a class should be determined on an entity specific basis. However, in determining classes of financial instrument, an entity should, at a minimum:

- Distinguish instruments measured at amortised cost from those measured at fair value.
- Treat as a separate class or classes those financial instruments outside IFRS 7's scope.

[IFRS 7 App B para 2].

A6.11.41 As classes of financial instruments should be determined by the entity and reconciled back to the balance sheet, the level of detail will vary from entity to entity. For example, in the case of banks, the category 'loans and receivables' would comprise more than one class, unless the loans have similar characteristics. In that situation, it may be appropriate to group financial instruments into the following classes:

- types of customers, for example, commercial loans and loans to individuals; or
- types of loans, for example, mortgages, credit cards, unsecured loans and overdrafts.

However, in some cases, 'loans to clients' can be one class if all the loans have similar characteristics (for example, a saving banks providing only one type of loan to individuals).

A6.11.41.1 Similarly, 'available-for-sale' assets could be split into bond and equity investment classes. The equity investments could be further subdivided into those that are listed and those that are unlisted.

Location, level of disclosure and aggregation

A6.11.42 An entity is permitted to disclose the information required by the standard either in the notes or on the face of the balance sheet or on the income statement. [IFRS 7 paras 8, 20]. Some entities might present some of the information required by IFRS 7, such as the nature and extent of risks arising from financial instruments and the entity's approach to managing those risks, alongside the financial statements in a separate management commentary or business review. This is permissible where the information is incorporated by cross-reference from the financial statements and is made available to users of the financial statements on the same terms as the financial statements and at the same time. [IFRS 7 App B para 6].

A6.11.43 An entity should decide, in the light of its own circumstances, how much detail it should provide, how much emphasis it should place on different aspects of the disclosure requirements and how much aggregation it should undertake to satisfy the standard's requirements. Obviously, a significant amount of judgement is required to display the overall picture without combining information with different characteristics. A balance should be maintained between providing excessive detail that may not assist users of financial statements and obscuring important information as a result of too much aggregation. For example, an entity should not obscure important information by including it amongst a large amount of insignificant detail. Similarly, an entity should not disclose information that is so aggregated that it obscures important differences between individual transactions or associated risks. [IFRS 7 App B para 3].

Risks arising from financial instruments

A6.11.44 IFRS 7 requires a significant amount of qualitative and quantitative disclosure about risks associated with financial instruments. In the context of financial instruments, risk arises from the uncertainty in cash flows, which in turn affects the future cash flows and fair values of financial assets and liabilities. The following are the types of financial risk that are related to financial instruments:

- Market risk – the risk that the fair value or cash flows of a financial instrument will fluctuate, because of changes in market prices. Market risk embodies not only the potential for loss, but also the potential for gain. It comprises three types of risk as follows:
  - Interest rate risk – the risk that the fair value or future cash flows of a financial instrument will fluctuate because of changes in market interest rates.
  - Currency risk – the risk that the fair value or future cash flows of a financial instrument will fluctuate because of changes in foreign exchange rates.
  - Other price risk – the risk that the fair value or future cash flows of a financial instrument will fluctuate because of changes in market prices (other than those arising from interest rate risk or currency risk), whether those changes are caused by factors specific to the individual financial instrument or its issuer, or factors affecting all similar financial instruments traded in the market.

- Credit risk – the risk that one party to a financial instrument will cause a financial loss for the other party by failing to discharge an obligation.
- Liquidity risk – the risk that an entity will encounter difficulty in meeting obligations associated with financial liabilities.

[IFRS 7 App A].

A6.11.44.1 Operational risk disclosures, on the other hand, are not within IFRS 7's scope.

Balance sheet disclosures

A6.11.45 The carrying amounts of each of the following categories, as defined in IAS 39, should be disclosed, either on the face of the balance sheet or in the notes:

- Financial assets at fair value through profit or loss, showing separately:
  - those designated as such upon initial recognition; and
  - those classified as held for trading in accordance with IAS 39.
- Held-to-maturity investments.
- Loans and receivables.
- Available-for-sale financial assets.
- Financial liabilities at fair value through profit or loss, showing separately:
  - those designated as such upon initial recognition; and
  - those classified as held for trading in accordance with IAS 39.
- Financial liabilities measured at amortised cost.

[IFRS 7 para 8].

A6.11.46 Table 6.11.2 shows the analysis of financial assets and financial liabilities by class and by categories as defined in IAS 39. Another example is given in Table A6.11.12 in paragraph A6.11.75 below.

Table 6.11.2 – Analysis of financial assets and financial liabilities by class and by categories

Nordea Bank AB (publ) – Annual Report – 31 December 2006

Note 49:
Classification of financial instruments (extract)

Group EURm, 31 Dec 2006	**Loans and receivables**	**Held to maturity**	**Held for trading**	**Assets at fair value through profit or loss**	**Derivatives used for hedging**	**Available for sale**	**Non-financial assets**	**Total**
Financial assets								
Cash and balances with central banks	2,104							2,104
Treasury bills and other eligible bills	10		6,668					6,678
Loans and receivables to credit institutions	15,718		11,074					26,792
Loans and receivables to the public	176,738		8,345	28,902				213,985
Interest-bearing securities		1,482	8,340	19,199		45		29,066
Financial instruments pledged as collateral			10,496					10,496
Shares			3,701	10,873		11		14,585
Derivatives			23,652		555			24,207
Fair value changes of the hedged items in portfolio hedge of interest rate risk	-37							-37
Investments in associated undertakings							398	398
Intangible assets							2,247	2,247
Property and equipment							307	307
Investment property							3,230	3,230
Deferred tax assets							382	382
Current tax assets							68	68
Retirement benefit assets							84	84
Other assets	10,680						46	10,726
Prepaid expenses and accrued income	1,365						207	1,572
Total	**206,578**	**1,482**	**72,276**	**58,974**	**555**	**56**	**6,969**	**346,890**

Group EURm, 31 Dec 2006	Held for trading	Liabilities at fair value through profit or loss	Derivatives used for hedging	Other financial liabilities	Non-financial liabilities	Total
Liabilities						
Deposts by credit institutions	5,939			26,349		32,288
Deposits and borrowings from the public	2,329			124,123		126,452
Liabilities to policyholders	2,220				28,821	31,041
Debt securities in issue	3,327	23,251		56,839		83,417
Derivatives	24,062		877			24,939
Fair value changes of the hedged items in portfolio hedge of interest rate risk				-401		-401
Current tax liabilities					263	263
Other liabilities	6,325			15,618	234	22,177
Accrued expenses and prepaid income				1,459	549	2,008
Deferred tax liabilities					608	608
Provisions					104	104
Retirement benefit obligations					495	495
Subordinated liabilities				8,177		8,177
Total	**44,202**	**23,251**	**877**	**232,164**	**31,074**	**331,568**

Financial assets or liabilities at fair value through profit or loss

A6.11.47 If the entity has designated a loan or receivable (or group of loans or receivables) as at fair value through profit or loss, it should disclose:

- The maximum exposure to credit risk of the loan or receivable (or group of loans or receivables) at the reporting date (see para A6.11.88 below).
- The amount by which any related credit derivatives or similar instruments mitigate that maximum exposure to credit risk.
- The amount of change, during the period and cumulatively, in the fair value of the loan or receivable (or group of loans or receivables) that is attributable to changes in the financial asset's credit risk, determined either
  - as the amount of change in its fair value that is not attributable to changes in market conditions that give rise to market risk; or
  - using an alternative method the entity believes more faithfully represents the amount of change in its fair value that is attributable to changes in the asset's credit risk.

  Changes in market conditions that give rise to market risk include changes in an observed (benchmark) interest rate, commodity price, foreign exchange rate or index of prices or rates (see para A6.11.49 below).
- The amount of the change in the fair value of any related credit derivatives or similar instruments that has occurred during the period and cumulatively since the loan or receivable was designated as at fair value through profit or loss.

[IFRS 7 para 9].

[The next paragraph is 6.11.49.]

A6.11.49 Where an entity discloses the information required by the third bullet point in the above paragraph, it should also disclose the methods used to comply with the disclosure requirements. However, where the entity believes that the disclosure it has given to comply with the requirements does not faithfully represent the change in the financial asset's fair value attributable to changes in its credit risk, it should disclose the reasons and the factors it believes are relevant in reaching that conclusion. [IFRS 7 para 11].

A6.11.50 If the entity has designated a financial liability as at fair value through profit or loss, it should disclose:

- The amount of change, during the period and cumulatively, in the financial liability's fair value that is attributable to changes in the credit risk of that liability determined either:
  - as the amount of change in its fair value that is not attributable to changes in market conditions that give rise to market risk; or
  - using an alternative method the entity believes more faithfully represents the amount of change in its fair value that is attributable to changes in the asset's credit risk.

  Changes in market conditions that give rise to market risk include changes in an observed (benchmark) interest rate, the price of another entity's financial instrument, a commodity price, a foreign exchange rate or an index of prices or rates. For contracts that include a unit-linking feature, changes in market conditions include changes in the performance of the related internal or external investment fund (see para A6.11.52 below).
- The difference between the financial liability's carrying amount and the amount the entity would be contractually required to pay at maturity to the holder of the obligation.

[IFRS 7 para 10].

A6.11.51 As stated in the first bullet point in paragraph A6.11.50 above, an entity is required to disclose the amount of change in a liability's fair value that is attributable to changes in the liability's credit risk. Although quantifying such changes might be difficult in practice, the IASB concluded that disclosure of such information would be useful to users and would help alleviate concerns that users may misinterpret the profit or loss changes in credit risk, especially in the absence of disclosures. Consequently, the standard provides a relatively easy method of computing the amount to be disclosed, as illustrated in the example below. The method assumes that the only relevant change in market condition for the liability is a change in the observed benchmark interest rate. Changes in fair value arising from factors other than changes in the instrument's credit risk or changes in interest rates are assumed not to be significant.

Example – Fair value change attributable to changes in a liability's credit risk

On 1 January 20X1, an entity issues a 10 year bond with a par value of C150,000 and an annual fixed coupon rate of 8%, which is consistent with market rates for bonds with similar characteristics. The entity uses LIBOR as its observable (benchmark) interest rate.

The entity assumes a flat yield curve, all changes in interest rates result from a parallel shift in the yield curve, and the changes in LIBOR are the only relevant changes in market conditions. It is also assumed that changes in the fair value arising from factors other than changes in the bond's credit risk or changes in interest rate are not significant.

At the date of inception of the bond, LIBOR was 5%. At the end of the first year, LIBOR has decreased to 4.75%. The bond's fair value is C153,811, consistent with a market interest rate of 7.6% for the bond. The market rate reflects the bond's credit rating at the end of the first year (see below).

The entity estimates the amount of change in the bond's fair value that is not attributable to changes in market conditions that give rise to market risk as follows:

- Calculate the instrument-specific component of the bond's internal rate of return:

  At inception, the internal rate of return for the 10 year bond is 8%. Since LIBOR at inception was 5%, the instrument-specific component of the internal rate of return is 3% (8% – 5%).

- Determine the discount rate to be used to calculate the present value of the bond at the end of year 1 using the bond's contractual cash flows:

  Since the only relevant change in the market conditions is that LIBOR has decreased to 4.75% at the end of the year, the discount rate for the present value calculation is 7.75% (4.75% + 3%).

- Calculate the present value at the end of year 1 using the above discount rate and the bond's contractual cash flows as follows:

		C
PV of C12,000 interest payable for 9 years (year 2 – 10) =	$\frac{12{,}000 \times [1 - (1 + 0.0775)^{-9}]}{0.0775}$	75,748
PV of C150,000 payable in year 10 =	$150{,}000 \times (1+0.0775)^{-9}$	76,619
Total PV		152,367

- Calculate the present value at the end of year 1 using the market rate and the bonds contractual cash flows as follows:

		C
PV of C12,000 interest payable for 9 years (year 2 – 10) =	$\frac{12{,}000 \times [1 - (1 + 0.076)^{-9}]}{0.076}$	76,226
PV of C150,000 payable in year 10 =	$150{,}000 \times (1 + 0.076)^{-9}$	77,585
Observed market value of liability		153,811

- Calculate change in fair value that is not attributable to the change in the benchmark interest rate

	C
Observed market value of bond	153,811
PV of bond as calculated above	152,367
Change in fair value not attributable to changes in the observed benchmark rate	1,444

The change in fair value not attributable to changes in the observed benchmark rate is a reasonably proxy for the change in fair value that is attributable to changes in the liability's credit risk, since the difference in present values calculated at 7.75% and 7.6% is assumed to reflect changes in the instrument's credit risk. Thus, the amount to be disclosed is C1,444. [IFRS 7 para IG 11].

6A.11.52 Where an entity discloses the information required by the first bullet point in paragraph A6.11.48 above, it should also disclose the methods used to comply with the disclosure requirements. However, where the entity believes that the disclosure it has given to comply with the requirements does not faithfully represent the change in the fair value of the financial asset attributable to changes in its credit risk, it should disclose the reasons and the factors it believes are relevant are relevant in reaching that conclusion. [IFRS 7 para 11].

A6.11.53 Table 6.11.4 shows an example of financial liabilities designated as at fair value through profit or loss.

Table 6.11.4 – Financial liabilities designated as at fair value through profit or loss
Nordea Bank AB (publ) – Annual Report – 31 December 2006

Note 49 (extract)
Classification of financial instruments (extract)

Financial liabilities designated at fair value through profit or loss
Changes in fair values attributable to changes in credit risk
Issued mortgage bonds in the fully owned Danish subsidiary Nordea Kredit Realkreditaktieselskab are measured at fair value. The amount of change in the fair value that is attributable to changes in credit risk of the liabilities are for 2006 EUR 0.0m (EUR 0.0m). The cumulative change since designation are EUR 0.0m (EUR 0.0m). The method used is to calculate the fair value changes that are attributable to changes in market conditions based on relevant benchmark interest rates.

The amount of change in the fair value of loans in Nordea Kredit Realkreditaktieselskab that is attributable to changes in credit risk is for 2006 EUR 0.7m (EUR 0.3m). The cumulative change since designation are EUR 1.0m (EUR 0.3m).

Comparison of carrying amount and conractual amount to be paid at maturity

	Group		**Parent company**	
2006, EURm	**Book value**	**Amount to be payed at maturity**	**Book value**	**Amount to be payed at maturity**
Financial liabilities at fair value through profit or loss	23,251	24,044	-	-

Other sundry balance sheet disclosure

Re-classification

A6.11.54 If the entity has re-classified a financial asset as one measured:

- at cost or amortised cost, rather than at fair value; or
- at fair value, rather than at cost or amortised cost,

it should disclose the amount re-classified into and out of each category and the reason for that re-classification (see section 6). [IFRS 7 para 12].

Derecognition

A6.11.55 An entity may have transferred financial assets in such a way that part or all of the financial assets do not qualify for derecognition (see section 8). In that situation, the entity should disclose for each class of such financial assets:

- The nature of the assets.
- The nature of the risks and rewards of ownership to which the entity remains exposed.
- When the entity continues to recognise all of the assets, the carrying amounts of the assets and of the associated liabilities.
- When the entity continues to recognise the assets to the extent of its continuing involvement, the total carrying amount of the original assets, the amount of the assets that the entity continues to recognise and the carrying amount of the associated liabilities.

[IFRS 7 para 13].

Collateral

A6.11.56 An entity should disclose:

- The carrying amount of financial assets it has pledged as collateral for liabilities or contingent liabilities, including amounts that have been re-classified in circumstances where the transferee has the right to sell or pledge the transferred asset. [IAS 39 para 37(a)].
- The terms and conditions relating to its pledge.

[IFRS 7 para 14].

A6.11.57 When an entity holds collateral (of financial or non-financial assets) and is permitted to sell or repledge it in the absence of default by the owner of the collateral, it should disclose:

- The fair value of the collateral held.
- The fair value of any such collateral sold or repledged, and whether the entity has an obligation to return it.
- The terms and conditions associated with its use of the collateral.

[IFRS 7 para 15].

A6.11.58 An example of how an entity has disclosed the necessary information about assets pledged and held as collateral is given in Table 6.11.5 below.

Table 6.11.5 – Assets pledged and held as collateral

Deutsche Bank plc – Annual Report – 31 December 2006

18 Trade and other receivables (extract)

Assets charged as security for liabilities

Trade and other receivables amounting to EUR 1,165 million (December 31, 2005: EUR 1,324 million) were pledged in connection with ABS transactions and other sales of receivables, and collateral in the form of cash deposits amounting to EUR 125 million (December 31, 2005: EUR 154 million) was pledged to third parties outside the Group. The latter have been recognized as receivables under other financial assets (see Note 24).

In 2006, Deutsche Telekom accepted cash collateral of EUR 7 million (2005: EUR 6 million) as securities for receivables arising from the marketing of mobile communications services and EUR 25 million as securities for the payment of outstanding other invoices. By the reporting date this cash collateral had neither been sold nor transferred as collateral.

Allowance amount for credit losses

A6.11.59 When financial assets are impaired by credit losses and the entity records the impairment in a separate account (for example, an allowance account used to record individual impairments or a similar account used to record a collective impairment of assets) rather than directly reducing the asset's carrying amount, it should disclose a reconciliation of changes in that account during the period for each class of financial assets. [IFRS 7 para 16]. This requirement, which is imported from IAS 30, now applies to all financial assets and not only for loans, as previously required by IAS 30, and to all entities, not just banks. In addition this is one of the disclosures required to be presented by 'class'.

Compound financial instruments with multiple embedded derivatives

A6.11.60 If an entity has issued an instrument that contains both a liability and an equity component (see section 6) and the instrument has multiple embedded derivatives whose values are interdependent (such as a callable convertible debt instrument), it should disclose the existence of those features. [IFRS 7 para 17].

Defaults and breaches

A6.11.61 An entity is required to disclose information on defaults and breaches of loans payable (that is, financial liabilities other than short-term trade payables on normal credit terms) and other loan agreements. Such disclosures provide relevant information about the entity's creditworthiness and its prospects for obtaining future loans. Any defaults or breaches may affect the liability's classification as current or non-current in accordance with IAS 1 (see para A6.11.9 above).

A6.11.62 For loans payable recognised at the reporting date, an entity should disclose:

- Details of any defaults during the period of principal, interest, sinking fund, or redemption terms of those loans payable.
- The carrying amount of the loans payable in default at the reporting date.
- Whether the default was remedied, or the terms of the loans payable were renegotiated, before the financial statements were authorised for issue.

[IFRS 7 para 18].

A6.11.63 If, during the period, there were breaches of loan agreement terms other than those described in the above paragraph, an entity should disclose the same information as above if those breaches permitted the lender to demand accelerated repayment, unless the breaches were remedied, or the loan's terms were renegotiated, on or before the reporting date. [IFRS 7 para 19].

A6.11.63.1 The above requirements would apply if the terms were renegotiated after the balance sheet date but before the signing of the financial statements. However, the disclosure need not include short-term trade payables on normal credit terms as these do not meet the definition in the standard of loans payable. [IFRS 7 App A].

Income statement and equity disclosures

Items of income, expense, gains or losses

A6.11.64 An entity should disclose the following items of income, expense, gains or losses, either on the face of the financial statements or in the notes:

- Net gains or net losses on:
  - Financial assets or financial liabilities at fair value through profit or loss, showing separately those on financial assets or financial liabilities designated as such upon initial recognition and those on financial assets or financial liabilities that are classified as held-for-trading in accordance with IAS 39. Where these financial instruments accrue interest income or expense, the standard allows an accounting policy

choice on how to disclose these. The interest income, interest expense and dividend income can be reported as part of net gains or net losses on these financial instruments or can be disclosed separately as part of interest income and expenses. [IFRS 7 App B5(e)]. In addition, it is possible to adopt one treatment for interest income and expense and a different treatment for dividend income as no such prohibition exists in IFRS 7. However, different treatments cannot be adopted for interest income and interest expense.

Note that if the dividend income is significant, regardless of how it is disclosed here, it will also need to be disclosed separately in the notes. [IAS 18 para 35(b)(v)].

  - Available-for-sale financial assets, showing separately the amount of gain or loss recognised directly in equity during the period and the amount removed from equity and recognised in profit or loss for the period.
  - Held-to-maturity investments.
  - Loans and receivables.
  - Financial liabilities measured at amortised cost.

- Total interest income and total interest expense (calculated using the effective interest method) for financial assets or financial liabilities that are not at fair value through profit or loss.
- Fee income and expense (other than amounts included in determining the effective interest rate) arising from:
  - Financial assets or financial liabilities that are not at fair value through profit or loss.
  - Trust and other fiduciary activities that result in the holding or investing of assets on behalf of individuals, trusts, retirement benefit plans and other institutions.
- Interest income on impaired financial assets accrued in accordance with paragraph AG93 of IAS 39, which requires an entity to continue to recognise interest income using the rate of interest used to discount the future cash flows for the purposes of measuring the impairment loss (see section 9).
- The amount of any impairment loss for each class of financial asset.

[IFRS 7 para 20].

A6.11.65 The disclosure requirements of the above paragraphs are illustrated in Tables 6.11.6 below.

Table 6.11.6 – Items of income, expense, gains or losses

Deutsche Telekom AG – Annual Report – 31 December 2006

7 Finance costs

millions of €	2006	2005	2004
Interest income	297	398	377
Interest expense	(2,837)	(2,799)	(3,657)
	(2,540)	**(2,401)**	**(3,280)**
Of which: from financial instruments in the measurement categories in accordance with IAS 39:			
Loans and receivables	202	220	178
Held-to-maturity investments	14	3	13
Available-for-sale financial assets	27	36	57
Financial liabilities carried at amortized cost[1]	(2,636)	(2,510)	(3,402)

[1] Interest expense calculated using the effective interest method and adjusted for accrued interest from derivatives that were used as hedging instruments against interest-rate-based changes in the fair values of financial liabilities carried at amortized cost in the reporting period for hedge accounting in accordance with IAS 39 (2006: interest income of EUR 29 million, interest expense of EUR 13 million; 2005: interest income of EUR 120 million, interest expense of EUR 35 million).

The year-on-year increase in finance costs in 2006 was primarily due to a positive one-time effect in the second quarter of 2005 that resulted from an adjustment to the book value of financial liabilities to reflect the changes in the present value of the estimated future payments. The changes in estimated future payments were triggered by a downward adjustment in interest rates relating to these financial liabilities following an upgrade of Deutsche Telekom's credit rating by rating agencies in the second quarter of 2005.

Accrued interest payments from derivatives (interest rate swaps) that were designated as hedging instruments in a fair value hedge in accordance with IAS 39 are netted per swap contract and recognized as interest income or interest expense depending on the net amount. Finance costs are assigned to the categories on the basis of the hedged item; only financial liabilities were hedged in the reporting period.

Other disclosures

Accounting policies

A6.11.66 IAS 1 requires an entity to disclose, in the summary of significant accounting policies, the measurement basis (or bases) used in preparing the financial statements and the other accounting policies used that are relevant to an understanding of the financial statements. [IAS 1 para 108; IFRS 7 para 21]. For financial instruments such disclosure may include:

- For financial assets or financial liabilities designated as at fair value through profit or loss:
  - The nature of the financial assets or financial liabilities the entity has designated as at fair value through profit or loss.

  - The criteria for so designating such financial assets or financial liabilities on initial recognition.
  - How the entity has satisfied the conditions for such designation, including, where appropriate, a narrative description of the circumstances underlying the measurement or recognition inconsistency that would otherwise arise, or how designation at fair value through profit or loss is consistent with the entity's documented risk management or investment strategy.

- The criteria for designating financial assets as available for sale.
- Whether regular way purchases and sales of financial assets are accounted for at trade date or at settlement date (see section 9).
- When an allowance account is used to reduce the carrying amount of financial assets impaired by credit losses:
  - The criteria for determining when the carrying amount of impaired financial assets is reduced directly (or, in the case of a reversal of a write-down, increased directly) and when the allowance account is used.
  - The criteria for writing off amounts charged to the allowance account against the carrying amount of impaired financial assets.
- How net gains or net losses on each category of financial instrument are determined, for example, whether the net gains or net losses on items at fair value through profit or loss include interest or dividend income.
- The criteria the entity uses to determine that there is objective evidence that an impairment loss has occurred.
- When the terms of financial assets that would otherwise be past due or impaired have been renegotiated, the accounting policy for financial assets that are the subject of renegotiated terms.

[IFRS 7 App B para 5].

A6.11.67 IAS 1 also requires entities to disclose, in the summary of significant accounting policies or other notes, the judgements, apart from those involving estimations, that management has made in the process of applying the entity's accounting policies and that have the most significant effect on the amounts recognised in the financial statements. [IAS 1 para 113].

Hedge accounting

A6.11.68 An entity should disclose the following separately for each type of hedge described in IAS 39 (that is, fair value hedges, cash flow hedges and hedges of net investments in foreign operations).

- A description of each type of hedge.
- A description of the financial instruments designated as hedging instruments and their fair values at the reporting date.
- The nature of the risks being hedged.

[IFRS 7 para 22].

A6.11.69 For cash flow hedges, an entity should disclose:

- The periods when the cash flows are expected to occur and when they are expected to affect profit or loss.
- A description of any forecast transaction for which hedge accounting had previously been used, but which is no longer expected to occur.
- The amount that was recognised in equity during the period.
- The amount that was removed from equity and included in profit or loss for the period, showing the amount included in each line item in the income statement.
- The amount that was removed from equity during the period and included in the initial cost or other carrying amount of a non-financial asset or non-financial liability whose acquisition or incurrence was a hedged highly probable forecast transaction.

[IFRS 7 para 23].

A6.11.70 An entity should disclose separately:

- In fair value hedges, gains or losses on:
  - The hedging instrument.
  - The hedged item attributable to the hedged risk.

  The requirement here relates to the current reporting period only and not to a disclosure on a cumulative basis (since the inception of the hedge designation).
- The ineffectiveness recognised in profit or loss that arises from cash flow hedges.
- The ineffectiveness recognised in profit or loss that arises from hedges of net investments in foreign operations.

[IFRS 7 para 24].

A6.11.71 Disclosure of information on fair value hedges, cash flow hedges and hedges of *net investments* is given in Table 6.11.9 below.

Table 6.11.9 – Income statement, hedge ineffectiveness, fair value hedges, amounts recycled from equity, interest

National Grid Plc – Annual Report – 31 March 2007

9. Finance income and costs

	2007	2006*	2005*
	£m	£m	£m
Pensions – expected return on scheme assets	**926**	901	881
Interest income on financial instruments	**218**	135	64
Interest income and similar income	**1,144**	1,036	945
Pensions – interest on scheme liabilities	**(869)**	(889)	(880)
Interest expense on financial liabilities held at amortised cost	**(817)**	(742)	(818)
Exceptional debt redemption and B share issue costs	**(45)**	(49)	–
Interest on derivatives	**(54)**	(49)	–
Unwinding of discounts on provisions	**(21)**	(18)	(14)
Less: interest capitalised	**70**	60	63
Interest expense	**(1,736)**	(1,687)	(1,649)
Net gains/(losses) on derivative financial instruments:			
Ineffectiveness on derivatives designated as fair value hedges	**18**	(10)	–
Ineffectiveness on derivatives designated as cash flow hedges	**–**	17	–
Ineffectiveness on derivatives designated as net investment hedges	**25**	(25)	–
On undesignated forward rate risk relating to derivatives designated asnet investment hedges	**(82)**	36	–
On derivatives not designated as hedges or ineligible for hedge accounting	**(114)**	(12)	–
Financial element of remeasurements on commodity contracts	**(19)**	(14)	–
Net losses on derivative financial instruments and commodity contracts	**(172)**	(8)	–
Interest expense and other finance costs	**(1,908)**	(1,695)	(1,649)
Net finance costs	**(764)**	(659)	(704)
Comprising:			
Interest income and similar income	**1,144**	1,036	945
Interest expense and other finance costs			
Before exceptional items and remeasurements	**(1,691)**	(1,638)	(1,649)
Exceptional items and remeasurements	**(217)**	(57)	–
	(764)	(659)	(704)

*Comparatives have been adjusted to reclassify amounts relating to discontinued operations

Interest income on financial instruments comprises interest income from bank deposits and other financial assets £214m (2006: £130m; 2005: £59m), interest receivable on finance leases £3m (2006: £4m; 2005: £5m) and gains, transferred from equity, on disposal of available-for-sale investments £1m (2006: £1m; 2005: £nil).

Interest expense on financial liabilities held at amortised cost comprises interest on bank loans and overdrafts £48m (2006: £33m; 2005: £45m), interest on other borrowings £768m (2006: £708m; 2005: £770m) and interest on finance leases £1m (2006: £1m; 2005: £3m).

Interest on funding attributable to assets in the course of construction was capitalised during the year at a rate of 5.6% (2006: 5.5%; 2005: 5.6%).

> Interest expense and other finance costs include £45m (2006: £39m; 2005: £12m) relating to losses incurred on the repurchase of debt and £nil (2006: £10m; 2005: £nil) associated with the issue of B shares.
>
> Derivative net gains on fair value hedges comprise a net loss on the hedging instruments of £100m (2006: £11m; 2005: £nil) offset by a net gain of £118m (2006: £1m; 2005: £nil) from the fair value adjustments to the carrying value of debt.
>
> Net losses on derivatives not designated as hedges or ineligible for hedge accounting includes a loss of £126m (2006: £nil) relating to pre-tax losses on investment related derivative financial instruments that offset on a post-tax basis.

Fair value

A6.11.72 Except as set out in paragraph A6.11.77 below, for each class of financial assets and financial liabilities (see para A6.11.39 above), an entity should disclose the fair value of that class of assets and liabilities in a way that permits it to be compared with its carrying amount. [IFRS 7 para 25].

A6.11.72.1 Where an entity has issued a convertible bond and has under IAS 32 accounted for it as a compound instrument, the equity component will not need to be fair valued. This is because the above requirement is only for financial assets and financial liabilities and the equity component does not meet the definition of a financial asset or a financial liability.

A6.11.73 In disclosing fair values, an entity should group financial assets and financial liabilities into classes, but should offset them only to the extent that their carrying amounts are offset in the balance sheet. [IFRS 7 para 26].

A6.11.74 An entity should disclose:

- The methods and when a valuation technique is used, the assumptions applied in determining fair values of each class of financial assets or financial liabilities. For example, if applicable, an entity should disclose information about the assumptions relating to pre-payment rates, rates of estimated credit losses and interest rates or discount rates.
- Whether fair values are determined, in whole or in part, directly by reference to published price quotations in an active market or are estimated using a valuation technique (see section 9).
- Whether the fair values recognised or disclosed in the financial statements are determined in whole or in part using a valuation technique based on assumptions that are not supported by prices from observable current market transactions in the same instrument (that is, without modification or repackaging) and not based on available observable market data. For fair values that are recognised in the financial statements, if changing one or more of those assumptions to reasonably possible alternative assumptions would change fair value significantly, the entity should state this fact and disclose the effect of those changes. For this purpose, significance should be

judged with respect to profit or loss, and total assets or total liabilities, or, when changes in fair value are recognised in equity, total equity.

- Where the previous bullet point applies, the total amount of the change in fair value estimated using such a valuation technique that was recognised in profit or loss during the period.

[IFRS 7 para 27].

A6.11.75 The fair value disclosure of financial assets and financial liabilities for a bank is shown in Table 6.11.12 and that of a non-banking company is shown in Table 6.11.13 below.

Table 6.11.12 – Disclosure of financial assets and liabilities of a bank

Danske Bank A/S – Annual Report – 31 December 2005

39 Fair value of financial instruments

Financial instruments are carried on the balance sheet at their fair value or at amortised cost. The interest rate risk on certain financial instruments measured at amortised cost is hedged by derivatives (see note 16). These hedging derivatives are recognised in accordance with the provisions governing fair value hedge accounting, i.e. at amortised cost less the fair value of the hedged interest rate risk. The table below shows the fair value of all financial instruments and the carrying amount on the balance sheet.

The fair value is the amount for which a financial asset could be exchanged, or a financial liability settled, between knowledgeable, willing parties. If an active market exists, the market price is applied. If an active market does not exist, which is the case for a number of financial assets and liabilities, generally accepted estimation and valuation techniques based on market conditions at the balance sheet date are used instead, including the discounted cash flow method.

Generally, the Group applies valuation techniques to OTC derivatives, unlisted trading portfolio assets and liabilities as well as unlisted financial investment securities. The most frequently used valuation and estimation techniques include the pricing of transactions with future settlement, swap models that apply present value calculations, credit pricing models and options models, such as Black & Scholes formulas.

The fair value approximation of financial instruments with variable interest rates is amortised cost less impairment losses. This means that the fair value does not necessarily reflect changes in credit quality.

Most of the Group's financial assets and liabilities measured at fair value are recognised on the basis of publicly quoted prices or market conditions on the balance sheet date. For a description of the recognition of mortgage loans at fair value please see note 14. Financial investment securities (see note 17) include unlisted shares measured at fair value using the valuation guidelines of EVCA (the European Private Equity & Venture Capital Association). These guidelines are based on the estimated fair value of unlisted shares, which is calculated as the price at which an asset could be exchanged between knowledgeable, willing parties.

	Carrying amount 2005	Fair value 2005	Carrying amount 2004	Fair value 2004
Financial assets				
Cash in hand and demand deposits with central banks	13,881	13,881	7,741	7,741
Due from credit institutions and central banks	274,918	274,918	230,690	230,690
Trading portfolio assets	444,521	444,521	422,547	422,547
Financial investment securities	28,712	28,696	31,505	31,505
Bank loans and advances	829,603	829,603	615,238	615,238
Mortgage loans	569,092	569,092	524,428	524,428
Assets under pooled schemes and unit-linked investment contracts	35,676	35,676	29,207	29,207
Assets under insurance contracts	188,342	188,342	163,205	163,205
Total	2,384,745	2,384,729	2,024,561	2,024,561
Financial liabilities				
Due to credit institutions and central banks	476,363	476,363	353,369	353,369
Deposits	631,184	631,184	487,863	487,863
Trading portfolio liabilities	212,042	212,042	215,807	215,807
Issued mortgage bonds	438,675	438,675	432,399	432,399
Deposits under pooled schemes and unit-linked investment contracts	42,287	42,287	35,944	35,944
Liabilities under insurance contracts	211,834	211,834	191,149	191,149
Other issued bonds	251,099	254,677	190,255	197,470
Subordinated debt	43,837	46,107	33,698	35,461
Total	2,307,321	2,313,169	1,940,484	1,949,462

Table 6.11.13 – Disclosure of financial assets and liabilities of a non-banking company

Telstra Corporation Limited and controlled entities – Annual report for the year ended 30 June 2007

2.23 Fair value estimation

The fair value of our derivatives and some financial assets and financial liabilities must be estimated for recognition and measurement or for disclosure purposes. Valuation techniques include where applicable, reference to prices quoted in active markets, discounted cash flow analysis, fair value of recent arm's length transactions involving the same instruments or other instruments that are substantially the same, and option pricing models.

We calculate the fair value of our forward exchange contracts by reference to forward exchange market rates for contracts with similar maturity profiles at the time of valuation.

The net fair values of our cross currency and interest rate swaps and other financial assets and financial liabilities that are measured at fair value (apart from our listed investments) are determined using valuation techniques which utilise data from observable markets. Assumptions are based on market conditions existing at each balance date. The fair value is calculated as the present value of the estimated future cash flows using an appropriate market based yield curve, which is independently derived and representative of Telstra's cost of borrowing. The net fair values of our listed investments are determined by reference to prices quoted on the relevant stock exchanges where the securities are traded.

Unless there is evidence to suggest otherwise, the nominal value of financial assets and financial liabilities less any adjustments for impairment with a short term to maturity are considered to approximate net fair value.

34. Financial and capital risk management

(a) Financial assets, financial liabilities and gearing

The carrying amounts, fair values and face values of our financial assets and financial liabilities are shown in Table A and Table B below:

	As at 30 June 2007			As at 30 June 2006		
	Carrying amount $m	Fair value $m	Face value $m	Carrying amount $m	Fair value $m	Face value $m
Financial assets – current						
Cash at bank and on hand *	241	241	241	238	238	238
Bills of exchange and commercial paper *	582	582	584	451	451	453
Trade receivables	2,756	2,756	2,917	2,561	2,561	2,714
Accrued revenue	966	966	966	1,027	1,027	1,027
Other receivables	92	92	92	113	113	113
Finance lease receivable *	46	46	46	20	20	20
Bank deposits with maturity greater than 90 days *	31	31	31	-	-	-
Cross currency swap hedge receivable *	38	38	38	20	20	16
Forward contract asset *	3	3	3	1	1	2
	4,755	4,755	4,918	4,431	4,431	4,583
Financial assets – non current						
Trade and other receivables	62	62	62	73	73	78
Amounts owed by jointly controlled and associated entities	38	38	221	14	14	229
Finance lease receivable*	90	90	90	59	59	59
Cross currency swap hedge receivable *	25	25	37	222	222	255
Interest rate swap asset *	224	224	-	169	169	-
	439	439	410	537	537	621
	5,194	5,194	5,328	4,968	4,968	5,204

Financial liabilities – current						
Trade and other creditors	1,145	1,145	1,145	975	975	975
Accrued interest and other accrued expenses	3,052	3,052	3,052	2,472	2,472	2,472
Deferred consideration for capital expenditure	10	10	10	123	123	123
Promissory notes *	1,435	1,442	1,456	1,457	1,481	1,490
Bank loans *	-	-	-	111	111	111
Offshore loans *	1,273	1,275	1,272	394	396	392
Finance leases *	35	35	35	20	20	20
Cross currency swap hedge payable *	165	165	169	6	6	6
Interest rate swap payable *	3	3	-	-	-	-
Forward contract liability *	9	9	10	6	6	7
	7,127	7,136	7,149	5,564	5,590	5,596
Financial liabilities – non current						
Other creditors	61	61	61	70	70	70
Deferred consideration for capital expenditure	134	134	293	127	127	287
Telstra bonds and domestic loans *	2,991	2,968	3,024	2,613	2,658	2,649
Offshore loans *	8,545	8,552	8,699	8,748	8,940	8,730
Finance leases *	83	83	83	81	81	81
Cross currency hedge payable *	1,051	1,051	982	612	612	548
Interest rate swap payable *	277	277	-	156	156	-
	13,142	13,126	13,142	12,407	12,644	12,365
	20,269	20,262	20,291	17,971	18,234	17,961

A6.11.76 If the market for a financial instrument is not active, its fair value is established using a valuation technique. [IAS 39 paras AG 74-79]. The best evidence of fair value at initial recognition is the transaction price (that is, the fair value of the consideration given or received), unless the fair value of that instrument is evidenced by comparison with other observable current market transactions in the same instrument (that is, without modification or repackaging) or based on a valuation technique whose variables include only data from observable markets as described in paragraph AG 76 of IAS 39. There could be a difference between the fair value at initial recognition and the amount that would be determined at that date using the valuation technique. If such a difference exists, an entity should disclose, by class of financial instrument:

- Its accounting policy for recognising that difference in profit or loss to reflect a change in factors (including time) that market participants would consider in setting a price. [IAS 39 para AG 76A].

- The aggregate difference yet to be recognised in profit or loss at the beginning and end of the period and a reconciliation of changes in the balance of this difference.

[IFRS 7 para 28].

A6.11.77 Disclosure of fair values is not required:

- When the carrying amount is a reasonable approximation of fair value, for example, for financial instruments such as short-term trade receivables and payables.
- For an investment in equity instruments that do not have a quoted market price in an active market, or derivatives linked to such equity instruments, that measured at cost in accordance with IAS 39, because their fair value cannot be measured reliably.
- For a contract containing a discretionary participation feature (as described in IFRS 4) if the fair value of that feature cannot be measured reliably.

[IFRS 7 para 29].

A6.11.78 In the cases described in the second and third bullet points above, an entity should disclose information to help users of the financial statements make their own judgements about the extent of possible differences between the carrying amount of those financial assets or financial liabilities and their fair value, including:

- The fact that fair value information has not been disclosed for these instruments because their fair value cannot be measured reliably.
- A description of the financial instruments, their carrying amount, and an explanation of why fair value cannot be measured reliably.
- Information about the market for the instruments.
- Information about whether and how the entity intends to dispose of the financial instruments.
- If financial instruments whose fair value previously could not be reliably measured are derecognised, that fact, their carrying amount at the time of derecognition and the amount of gain or loss recognised.

[IFRS 7 para 30].

Financial instrument risk disclosures

A6.11.79 An entity should disclose information that enables users of its financial statements to evaluate the nature and extent of risks arising from financial instruments to which the entity is exposed at the reporting date. [IFRS 7 para 31].

A6.11.80 The disclosures described from paragraph A6.11.83 onwards focus on the risks that arise from financial instruments and how they have been managed.

These risks typically include, but are not limited to, credit risk, liquidity risk and market risk as discussed in paragraph A6.11.44 above. [IFRS 7 para 32].

A6.11.81 When an entity uses several methods to manage a risk exposure, it should disclose information using the method or methods that provide the most relevant and reliable information. [IFRS 7 App B para 7].

A6.11.82 The disclosures should be given either in the financial statements or incorporated by cross-reference from the financial statements to some other statement, such as a management commentary or risk report, that is available to users of the financial statements on the same terms as the financial statements and at the same time. Without the information incorporated by cross-reference, the financial statements are incomplete. [IFRS 7 App B para 6].

Qualitative disclosures

A6.11.83 For each type of risk arising from financial instruments, an entity should disclose:

- The exposures to risk and how they arise.

  Information about risk exposures might describe exposures both gross and net of risk transfer and other risk-mitigating transactions.

- Its objectives, policies and processes for managing the risk and the methods used to measure the risk. This might include, but is not limited to:

  - The structure and organisation of the entity's risk management functions, including a discussion of independence and accountability.
  - The scope and nature of the entity's risk reporting or measurement systems.
  - The entity's policies for hedging or mitigating risk, including its policies and procedures for taking collateral.
  - The entity's processes for monitoring the continuing effectiveness of such hedges or mitigating devices.
  - The entity's policies and procedures for avoiding excessive concentrations of risk.

- Any changes in the above for the period.

  Entities should disclose the reasons for the change. Such changes may result from changes in exposure to risk or from changes in the way those exposures are managed. An entity may have disclosed a change in its 2006 financial statements if it applied IAS 32. This entity will not need to make any further disclosure regarding that change in 2007. However, if such disclosures were not made in the 2006 financial statements and the change was significant then it should be disclosed in the 2007 financial statements in accordance with IFRS 7.

[IFRS 7 paras 33, IG 15-16].

A6.11.84 An example of a company that has included the above disclosure requirements in its risk management policy is given in Table 6.11.14 below. Another example of risk management policy is given in Table 6.11.15 below.

Table 6.11.14 – Qualitative risk analysis
DnB NOR ASA – Annual Report – 31 December 2006

Notes (extract)

Risk management in DnB NOR

The Board of Directors of DnB NOR ASA has a clearly stated goal to maintain a low risk profile, which is reflected in the DnB NOR Bank Group's aim to maintain at least an Aa level rating for ordinary long-term debt. The profitability of DnB NOR will depend on the Group's ability to identify, manage and accurately price risk arising in connection with financial services.

Organisation and authorisation structure

- *Accountability*. All executives are responsible for risk within their own area of responsibility and must consequently be fully updated on the risk situation at all times.
- *Risk reporting*. Risk reporting in the Group must ensure that all executives have the necessary information about current risk levels and future developments. To ensure high-quality, independent risk reports, responsibility for reporting is assigned to units that are independent of the operative units.
- *Capital assessment*. A summary and analysis of the Group's capital and risk situation is presented in a special risk report to the Board of Directors.
- *Use of risk information*. Risk is an integral part of the management and monitoring of business areas. Return on risk-adjusted capital is reflected in product pricing, profit calculations and in monitoring performance in the business areas.

Monitoring and use

- *Accountability*. All executives are responsible for risk within their own area of responsibility and must consequently be fully updated on the risk situation at all times.
- *Risk reporting*. Risk reporting in the Group ensures that all executives have the necessary information about current risk levels and future developments. To ensure high-quality, independent risk reports, responsibility for reporting is assigned to units that are independent of the operative units.
- *Capital assessment*. A summary and analysis of the Group's capital and risk situation is presented in a special risk report to the Board of Directors.
- *Use of risk information*. Risk is an integral part of the management and monitoring of business areas. Return on risk-adjusted capital requirement is reflected in product pricing, profit calculations and in monitoring performance in the business areas.

Relevant risk measures

- *A common risk measure for the Group*. The Group's risk is measured in the form of risk-adjusted capital requirement, calculated for main risk categories and for all of the Group's business areas.
- *Supplementary risk measure*. In addition, risk is followed up through supplementary risk measures adapted to operations in the various business areas, for example monitoring of positions relative to limits, key figures and portfolio risk targets.

A further description of risk management and internal control in the Group can be found under section "Management in DnB NOR" in the annual report.

More about risk in Vital

Risk within life insurance comprises market risk and insurance risk. Market risk is the risk that the return on financial assets will not be sufficient to meet the guaranteed rate of return specified in insurance policies. Otherwise, inadequate returns will have to be covered by applying the securities adjustment reserve, additional allocations, representing buffer capital built up from profits in previous years, or the shortfall could be charged to equity. The company is subject to government regulations on investment management, including risk diversification requirements and limitations on investment options. In addition, the company has to meet statutory capital adequacy and solvency margin requirements. Insurance risk relates mainly to changes in future insurance obligations due to changes in policyholders' life expectancy and disability rate.

Operations in Vital are different from operations in the rest of the Group, and risk in Vital is therefore managed separately. The purpose of risk management is to achieve the highest possible return for policyholders and the owner in the long term, subject to an acceptable risk level. The Board of Directors of Vital Forsikring has stipulated a risk level that is subject to continual monitoring through management models, operative rules and reporting requirements.

As part of regular reporting, stress tests are implemented based on the following assumptions: a 20 per cent decline in share prices, a 1 percentage point rise in interest rates, a 10 per cent appreciation of the Norwegian krone and a 5 per cent reduction in property values. Results of the stress tests were at a satisfactory risk level in 2006.

Note 43-45 specifies market risk for the DnB NOR Group, including risk linked to financial instruments in Vital. Additional information concerning risk associated with operations in Vital is presented in notes 44, 45 and 48.

Risk categories

For risk management purposes, DnB NOR distinguishes between the following risk categories:

- *Credit risk* is the risk of losses due to failure on the part of the Group's counterparties (customers) to meet their payment obligations towards the DnB NOR Group. Credit risk refers to all claims against customers, mainly loans, but also liabilities in the form of other extended credits, guarantees, leasing, factoring, interest-bearing securities, approved, undrawn credits, as well as counterparty risk arising through derivatives and foreign exchange contracts. Settlement risk, which arises in connection with payment transfers as not all transactions take place in real time, also involves counterparty risk. Note 46 contains an assessment of the Group's credit risk at year-end 2005 and 2006.
- *Market risk* arises as a consequence of the Group's open positions in the foreign exchange, interest rate and capital markets. The risk is linked to variations in financial results due to fluctuations in market prices or exchange rates. Notes 43 to 45 contain an assessment of the Group's market risk at year-end 2005 and 2006.
- *Liquidity risk* is the risk that the Group will be unable to meet its payment obligations. Note 47 contains an assessment of the Group's liquidity risk at yearend 2005 and 2006.
- *Insurance risk* relates to changes in future insurance obligations due to changes in policyholders' life expectancy and disability rate. Note 48 contains an assessment of the Group's insurance risk at year-end 2005 and 2006.
- *Operational risk* is the risk of losses due to deficiencies or errors in processes and systems, errors made by employees or external events.
- *Business risk* is the risk of losses due to external factors such as the market situation or government regulations. This risk category also includes reputational risk.

DnB NOR uses a total risk model to quantify risk and calculates risk-adjusted capital requirements for individual risk categories and for the Group's overall risk. Risk-adjusted capital requirements should cover unexpected losses which may occur in operations in exceptional circumstances. Quantifications are based on statistical probability calculations for the various risk categories, using historical data.

Risk measurement is a field in constant development, and measurement methods and tools are subject to continual improvement. No significant changes were made in routines and procedures for risk monitoring in 2006.

Concentrations of risk

Concentrations of financial risk arise when financial instruments with identical characteristics are influenced in the same way by changes in economic or other factors. The identification of risk concentrations is subject to discretionary assessment. The general purpose of risk management in the Group is to reduce and control risk concentrations. With respect to credit risk, this is reflected in the requirement to maintain a credit portfolio with a sound sectoral and geographical balance and a syndication policy that guides the exposure to individual customers and industries, cf. note 4 and 21. With respect to market risk, concentration risk is restricted by limits ensuring that exposure is divided among a number of instruments, ensuring sound diversification to meet changes in share prices, exchange rates and interest rate levels. The concentration of credit risk as at 31 December 2006 for international bonds in the trading portfolio and commercial paper and bonds held by Vital is shown in note 25 and note 4, respectively. The concentration of credit risk for commercial paper and bonds held to maturity is shown in note 30. Currency risk is specified in notes 4 and 45. Concentrations of interest rate risk are presented in note 44. The Group's investments in shares, mutual funds and PCCs are specified in note 27. The Group has no material risk concentrations apart from those referred to above.

Table 6.11. 15 – Risk management policy

Diageo plc – Annual Report – 30 June 2006

Risk management

The group's funding, liquidity and exposure to interest rate and foreign exchange rate risks are managed by the group's treasury department. The treasury department uses a combination of derivative and conventional financial instruments to manage these underlying risks.

Treasury operations are conducted within a framework of board-approved policies and guidelines,which are recommended and subsequently monitored by the finance committee. This committee is described in the corporate governance report. These include benchmark exposure and/or hedge cover levels for key areas of treasury risk. The benchmarks, hedge cover and overall appropriateness of Diageo's risk management policies are reviewed by the board following, for example, significant business, strategic or accounting changes. The framework provides for limited defined levels of flexibility in execution to allow for the optimal application of the board-approved strategies. Transactions giving rise to exposures away from the defined benchmark levels arising on the application of this flexibility are separately monitored on a daily basis using value at risk analysis. These derivative financial instruments are carried at fair value and gains or losses are taken to the income statement as they arise. At 30 June 2006 gains and losses on these transactions were not material.

The finance committee receives bi-monthly reports on the activities of the treasury department, including any exposures away from the defined benchmarks.

Currency risk The group publishes its consolidated financial statements in sterling and conducts business in many foreign currencies. As a result, it is subject to foreign currency exchange risk due to exchange rate movements which will affect the group's transaction costs and the translation of the results and underlying net assets of its foreign operations.

Hedge of net investment in foreign operations The group hedges a substantial portion of its exposure to fluctuations on the translation into sterling of its foreign operations by holding net borrowings in foreign currencies and by using foreign currency swaps and forwards. The group's policy where a liquid foreign exchange market exists is to seek to hedge currency exposure on its net operations before net borrowings at approximately the following percentages – 90% for US dollars, 90% for euros and 50% for other significant currencies. This policy leaves the remaining part of the group's net operations before net borrowings subject to currency movements. Diageo introduced from 1 July 2005 additional processes to determine,monitor and document the effectiveness of these hedges in the context of the underlying exposure under IAS 39. Exchange differences arising on the retranslation of relevant foreign currency borrowings (including foreign exchange swaps and forwards), to the extent that they are in an effective hedge relationship, are recognised in the statement of recognised income and expense, in accordance with IAS 39.

Transaction exposure hedging For currencies in which there is an active market, the group seeks to hedge between 80% and 100% of forecast transactional foreign exchange rate risk, for up to a maximum of 21 months forward, using forward foreign currency exchange contracts. The effective portion of the gain or loss on the hedge is recognised in the statement of recognised income and expense to the extent it is highly effective, and recycled into the income statement at the same time as the underlying hedged transaction affects the income statement. Under IFRS, the degree of confidence in forecast future cash flows required to achieve hedge accounting has increased. This has led to a reduction in the coverage levels initially placed up to 21 months in advance, but with coverage levels being increased nearer to the forecast transaction date. Under IAS 39 hedges are documented and tested for hedge effectiveness on an ongoing basis. Diageo expects hedges entered into to continue to be highly effective and therefore does not expect the impact of ineffectiveness on the income statement to be material.

Interest rate risk The group has an exposure to interest rate risk, arising principally on changes in US dollar, sterling and euro interest rates. To manage interest rate risk, the group manages its proportion of fixed to variable rate borrowings within limits approved by the board, primarily through issuing long term fixed rate bonds, medium term notes and commercial paper, and by utilising interest rate swaps. The profile of fixed rate to floating rate net borrowings is targeted according to a duration measure that is equivalent to an approximate 50% fixed and 50% floating amortising profile. The number of years within the amortising profile depends on a template approved by the board. These practices serve to reduce the volatility of the group's reported financial performance. Following the implementation of IAS 39 from 1 July 2005 the majority of Diageo's existing interest rate hedges are designated as hedges under IAS 39. Designated hedges are expected to be highly effective, and therefore the impact of ineffectiveness on the income statement is not expected to be material.

Liquidity risk The group's policy with regard to the expected maturity profile of group financing companies' borrowings is to limit the proportion of such borrowings maturing within 12 months to 50% of gross borrowings less money market demand deposits and the level of commercial paper to 30% of gross borrowings less money market demand deposits. In addition, it is group policy to maintain backstop facility terms from relationship banks to support commercial paper obligations.

Credit risk The group monitors its credit exposure to its counterparties via their credit ratings (where applicable) and through its policy, thereby limiting its exposure to any one party to ensure that they are within board approved limits and that there are no significant concentrations of credit risk. The counterparties to the financial instruments transacted by the group are major international financial institutions. Group policy is to enter into such transactions only with counterparties with a long term credit rating of A or better. The notional amounts of financial instruments used in interest rate and foreign exchange management do not represent the credit risk arising through the use of these instruments. The immediate credit risk of these instruments is generally estimated by the fair value of contracts with a positive value. The maximum exposure to credit risk for receivables and other financial assets is represented by their carrying amount.

Commodity price risk The group uses commodity futures and options to hedge against price risk in certain commodities. All commodity futures and options contracts hedge a projected future purchase of raw material. Commodity futures or options are then either closed out at the time the raw material is purchased or they are exchanged with the company manufacturing the raw material to determine the contract price. Commodity contracts are held in the balance sheet at fair value and to the extent that they are considered as an effective hedge under IAS 39, fair value movements are recognised in the statement of recognised income and expense. Gains and losses realised in the year in respect of open contracts at the balance sheet date were not significant.

Insurance The group purchases insurance for commercial or,where required, for legal or contractual reasons. In addition, the group retains insurable risk where external insurance is not considered an economic means of mitigating these risks.

Quantitative disclosures

A6.11.85 For each type of risk arising from financial instruments, an entity should disclose:

- Summary quantitative data about its exposure to that risk at the reporting date. This disclosure should be based on the information provided internally to the entity's key management personnel (as defined in IAS 24, 'Related party disclosures'), for example, the entity's board of directors or chief executive officer. An entity with two distinct operations (for example, a retail division and a manufacturing division) may be monitored by management separately as two divisions. All disclosures should normally be provided on a consolidated basis. However, those disclosures that are based on management reporting could be presented separately for both the divisions as that is the way management monitors the financial risks, unless there were material transactions between the divisions, in which case separate disclosures could be misleading.
- The disclosures described in paragraphs 6.11.86 to 6.11.118, to the extent not provided in the previous bullet point, unless the risk is not material. [IFRS 7 para 34(b)]. These, in other words, are IFRS 7's minimum disclosure requirements, regardless of whether management uses this information to manage the entity's risks. In terms of determining whether a risk is material consider the following example. An entity invests in a foreign currency bond maturing in one year and simultaneously enters into an foreign currency forward contract with a corresponding maturity to offset the foreign currency risk. In this case, the materiality of the foreign currency risk on the bond is assessed without the foreign currency forward contract. The bond and the forward are dissimilar items and, therefore, the materiality assessment of the foreign currency risk is performed without considering the forward contract. If it is established that the foreign currency risk is material, the disclosure required in the sensitivity analysis (see para A6.11.106) is based on the net foreign currency exposure; that after offsetting the foreign currency bond against the forward contract. The same approach would apply for the assessment of credit risk, liquidity risk and other market risk.
- Concentrations of risk if not apparent from the previous two bullet points (see para A6.11.86 below).

[IFRS 7 para 34].

A6.11.86 Concentrations of risk arise from financial instruments that have similar characteristics and are affected similarly by changes in economic or other conditions. The identification of concentrations of risk requires judgement taking into account the entity's circumstances. Disclosure of concentrations of risk should include:

- A description of how management determines concentrations (see para A6.11.87 below).
- A description of the shared characteristic that identifies each concentration (for example, counterparty, geographical area, currency or market).
- The amount of the risk exposure associated with all financial instruments sharing that characteristic.

[IFRS 7 App B para 8].

A6.11.87 Concentrations of credit risk may arise from:

- Industry sectors.

  Thus, if an entity's counterparties are concentrated in one or more industry sectors (such as retail or wholesale), it would disclose separately exposure to risks arising from each concentration of counterparties.

- Credit rating or other measure of credit quality.

  Thus, if an entity's counterparties are concentrated in one or more credit qualities (such as secured loans or unsecured loans) or in one or more credit ratings (such as investment grade or speculative grade), it would disclose separately exposure to risks arising from each concentration of counterparties.

- Geographical distribution.

  Thus, if an entity's counterparties are concentrated in one or more geographical markets (such as Asia or Europe) it would disclose separately exposure to risks arising from each concentration of counterparties.

- A limited number of individual counterparties or groups of closely related counterparties.

[IFRS 7 para IG18].

A6.11.88 Similar principles apply to identifying concentrations of other risks, including liquidity risk and market risk. For example, concentrations of liquidity risk may arise from the repayment terms of financial liabilities, sources of borrowing facilities or reliance on a particular market in which to realise liquid assets. Concentrations of foreign exchange risk may arise if an entity has a significant net open position in a single foreign currency, or aggregate net open positions in several currencies that tend to move together. [IFRS 7 para IG18].

A6.11.89 If the quantitative data disclosed as at the reporting date are unrepresentative of an entity's exposure to risk during the period, an entity should provide further information that is representative. [IFRS 7 para 35]. To meet this requirement, an entity might disclose the highest, lowest and average amount of risk to which it was exposed during the period. For example, if an entity typically has a large exposure to a particular currency, but at year-end unwinds the position, the entity might disclose a graph showing the exposure at various times during the period, or disclose the highest, lowest and average exposures. [IFRS 7 para IG20]. In addition consider the following examples:

Example 1 – Year end credit risk exposure unrepresentative due to seasonal fluctuations

Entity Y is producing seeds for the agricultural industry. The main season for planting is the spring. 75% of entity Y's markets are in the northern hemisphere; 25% are in the southern hemisphere. Entity Y's account receivables are approximately C400 million in June and C100 million in December. Entity Y has a December year end. Does entity Y have to disclose additional information about its exposure to credit risk on the receivables that is representative of its exposure to risk during the year?

In this case, the December year end exposure to credit risk is unrepresentative of the entity's exposure during the period. Entity Y should provide further information that is representative, such as a description (with amounts) of how the exposures vary during the year, or the average (or highest) exposure to credit risk during the year.

Example 2 – Year end credit risk exposure unrepresentative due to a major acquisition

On 30 November 20X6, entity A (€ functional currency) acquires a major competitor. Due to the acquisition, the US$ denominated receivables increased from $100 million to $300 million and variable interest rate debt doubled from €200 million to €400 million compared to the balances as at 30 June 20X6. Entity A has a December year end. The balances as of 31 December 20X6 are considered to be representative of the next year(s). Does entity A have to disclose additional information that is representative of its exposure to risk during the year?

In this scenario, entity A should disclose additional information because the quantitative data as at 31 December 20X6 is not representative of the financial period 20X6. A mere statement that the data is not representative is not sufficient. To meet IFRS 7's requirement the entity might disclose the highest, lowest and average amount of risk to which it was exposed during the period. However, a full high/low/average analysis might not be required if the exposure at the year end is representative for future periods and if sufficient explanations of the facts and circumstances are provided.

Credit risk

A6.11.90 IFRS 7 requires an entity to disclose information about its exposure to credit risk by class of financial instrument. Financial instruments in the same class share economic characteristics with respect to the risk being disclosed (in this case, credit risk). For example, an entity might determine that residential mortgages, unsecured consumer loans, and commercial loans each have different economic characteristics. The information an entity should disclose by class of financial instrument is as follows:

- The amount that best represents its maximum exposure to credit risk at the reporting date without taking account of any collateral held or other credit enhancements (for example, netting agreements that do not qualify for offset in accordance with IAS 32 – see para A6.11.26 above).

- In respect of the amount disclosed above, a description of collateral held as security and other credit enhancements (see para A6.11.93 below).
- Information about the credit quality of financial assets that are neither past due nor impaired (see para A6.11.95 below).
- The carrying amount of financial assets that would otherwise be past due or impaired whose terms have been renegotiated. This disclosure should be given only in the year when the renegotiation took place, that is, in the year in which the asset's contractual terms were changed. In subsequent years the asset is considered based on the new (renegotiated) terms and disclosure would only be required if renegotiated again.

[IFRS 7 para 36].

A6.11.90.1 The above disclosures do not apply to an entity's holdings of equity investments. This is because the definition of equity in IAS 32 requires that the issuer has no obligation to pay cash or transfer other assets. Therefore, such equity investments are subject to price risk, not credit risk. The only exception relates to impaired financial assets as described in paragraph A6.11.95.

A6.11.91 In respect of the first bullet point above, the amount that best represents the entity's maximum exposure to credit risk relating to financial assets is typically the gross carrying amount, net of:

- any amounts offset in accordance with IAS 32 (see para A6.11.15 above); and
- any impairment losses recognised in accordance with IAS 39.

[IFRS 7 App B para 9].

A6.11.92 Activities that give rise to credit risk include, but are not limited to:

- Granting loans and receivables to customers and placing deposits with other entities. In these cases, the maximum exposure to credit risk is the carrying amount of the related financial assets.
- Entering into derivative contracts (for example, foreign exchange contracts, interest rate swaps and credit derivatives). When the resulting asset is measured at fair value, the maximum exposure to credit risk at the reporting date will equal the carrying amount.
- Granting financial guarantees. In this case, the maximum exposure to credit risk is the maximum amount the entity could have to pay if the guarantee is called on, which may be significantly greater than the amount recognised as a liability.
- *Making a loan* commitment that is irrevocable over the life of the facility or is revocable only in response to a material adverse change. If the issuer cannot settle the loan commitment net in cash or another financial instrument, the maximum credit exposure is the commitment's full

amount. This is because it is uncertain whether the amount of any undrawn portion may be drawn upon in the future. This may be significantly greater than the amount recognised as a liability.

[IFRS 7 App B para 10].

Collateral and other credit enhancements

A6.11.93 In respect of the second bullet point in paragraph A6.11.83 above, an entity's description about collateral held as security and other credit enhancements might include:

- The policies and processes for valuing and managing collateral and other credit enhancements obtained.
- A description of the main types of collateral and other credit enhancements (examples of the latter being guarantees, credit derivatives and netting agreements that do not qualify for offset in accordance with IAS 32).
- The main types of counterparties to collateral and other credit enhancements and their creditworthiness.
- Information about risk concentrations within the collateral or other credit enhancements.

[IFRS 7 para IG22].

A6.11.94 When an entity obtains financial or non-financial assets during the period by taking possession of collateral it holds as security or calling on other credit enhancements, and such assets meet the recognition criteria in other IFRSs, an entity should disclose:

- The nature and carrying amount of the assets obtained.
- When the assets are not readily convertible into cash, its policies for disposing of such assets or for using them in its operations.

[IFRS 7 para 38].

Financial assets that are either past due or impaired

A6.11.95 A financial asset is past due when the counterparty has failed to make a payment when contractually due. As an example, an entity enters into a lending agreement that requires interest to be paid every month. On the first day of the next month, if interest has not been paid, the loan is past due. Past due does not mean that a counterparty will never pay, but it can trigger various actions such as renegotiation, enforcement of covenants, or legal proceedings. [IFRS 7 para IG 26]. An entity should disclose by class of financial asset:

- An analysis of the age of financial assets that are past due as at the reporting date but not impaired. The purpose of this disclosure is to provide users of the financial statements with information about those financial assets that are more likely to become impaired and to help users to estimate the level of future impairment losses. Thus, the entire balance which relates to the amount past due should be disclosed, rather than only the amount that is past due, as this is the amount that would be disclosed as the amount of the impaired financial assets if impairment crystallises.

Other associated balances due from the same debtor are not included if the debtor has not yet failed to make a payment on these balances when contractually due.

In preparing such an age analysis of financial assets, an entity uses its judgement to determine an appropriate number of time bands. For example, an entity might determine that the following time bands are appropriate:

  - Not more than three months.
  - More than three months and not more than six months.
  - More than six months and not more than one year.
  - More than one year.

- An analysis of financial assets that are individually determined to be impaired as at the reporting date, including the factors the entity considered in determining that they are impaired. These disclosures are not only given in the year of impairment, but also in each subsequent reporting period during which the fair value of a financial asset is below its historical cost and, therefore, considered 'impaired'. Such an analysis might include:

  - The carrying amount, before deducting any impairment loss.
  - The amount of any related impairment loss.
  - The nature and fair value of collateral available and other credit enhancements obtained. This is the only disclosure relating to credit risk that must be made in respect of an entity's equity investments.

- In respect of each of the amounts disclosed above, a description of collateral held by the entity as security and other credit enhancements and unless impracticable, an estimate of their fair value (see 6.11.93 above).

[IFRS 7 paras 37, IG28-29].

A6.11.96 In respect of the third bullet point in paragraph A6.11.90 above, information about credit quality of financial assets that are neither past due nor impaired might include:

- An analysis of credit exposures using an external or internal credit grading system.

  Where an entity manages its credit exposures using an external credit grading system, an entity might disclose information about:

- The amounts of credit exposures for each external credit grade.
- The rating agencies used.
- The amount of an entity's rated and unrated credit exposures.
- The relationship between internal and external ratings.

Where an entity manages its credit exposures using an internal credit grading system, an entity might disclose information about:

- The internal credit ratings process.
- The amounts of credit exposures for each internal credit grade.
- The relationship between internal and external ratings.

- The nature of the counterparty.
- Historical information about counterparty default rates.
- Any other information used to assess credit quality.

[IFRS 7 paras IG23-25].

An example of a company that has given credit risk disclosures for a class of its financial assets (trade receivables) is given in Table 6.11.16 below.

Table 6.11.16 – Trade and other receivables

Telstra Corporation Limited and controlled entities – Annual report – 30 June 2007

34(a) Trade receivables and allowance for doubtful debts

The ageing of trade receivables at 30 June 2007 is detailed below:

	As at 30 June			
	2007		2006	
	Gross	**Allowance**	Gross	Allowance
	$m	**$m**	$m	$m
Not past due (i)	**1,765**	**-**	1,664	(14)
Past due 0 – 30 days	**677**	**(3)**	678	(2)
Past due 31 – 60 days	**186**	**(11)**	166	(13)
Past due 61 – 90 days	**82**	**(13)**	70	(10)
Past due 91 – 120 days	**72**	**(21)**	63	(16)
Past 120 days	**188**	**(113)**	144	(103)
	2,970	**(161)**	2,785	(158)

The movement in the allowance for doubtful debts in respect of trade receivables is detailed below:

	Year ended 30 June	
	2007	2006
	$m	$m
Opening balance	**(158)**	(159)
– additional provisions	**(27)**	(23)
– addition due to acquisition	**(1)**	(2)
– reduction due to disposal	**1**	-
– amounts used	**16**	7
– amounts reversed	**7**	19
– foreign currency exchange differences	**1**	-
Closing balance	**(161)**	(158)

Our policy requires customers to pay us in accordance with agreed payment terms. Depending on the customer segment, our settlement terms are generally 14 to 30 days from date of invoice. All credit and recovery risk associated with trade receivables has been provided for in the balance sheet.

Our trade receivables include our customer deferred debt and White Pages® directory charges. Our customer deferred debt allows eligible post paid mobile customers the opportunity to repay the cost of their mobile handset and approved accessories monthly over 12, 18 or 24 months. The loan is provided interest free to our mobile postpaid customers. Similarly, the White Pages® directory entries can be repaid over 12 months.

Trade receivables have been aged according to their original due date in the above ageing analysis, including where repayment terms for certain long outstanding trade receivables have been renegotiated.

We hold security for a number of trade receivables in the form of guarantees, deeds of undertaking, letters of credit and deposits. During fiscal 2007 and 2006, the securities we called upon were insignificant.

We have used the following basis to assess the allowance loss for trade receivables:

- a statistical approach to determine the historical allowance rate for each debt tranche, and applying this allowance rate to the debt tranches at the end of the reporting period;
- an individual account by account assessment based on past credit history; and
- any prior knowledge of debtor insolvency or other credit risk.

Liquidity risk

A6.11.97 An entity should disclose:

- A maturity analysis for financial liabilities that shows the remaining contractual maturities (see para A6.11.99 below).
- A description of how it manages the liquidity risk inherent in point one above.

[IFRS 7 para 39].

A6.11.98 *The factors that the entity might consider in providing the above disclosure include, but are not limited to, whether the entity:*

- Expects some of its liabilities to be paid later than the earliest date on which the entity can be required to pay (as may be the case for customer deposits placed with a bank).
- Expects some of its undrawn loan commitments not to be drawn.
- Holds financial assets for which there is a liquid market and that are readily saleable to meet liquidity needs.
- Has committed borrowing facilities (for example, commercial paper facilities) or other lines of credit (for example, stand-by credit facilities) that it can access to meet liquidity needs.
- Holds financial assets for which there is not a liquid market, but which are expected to generate cash inflows (principal or interest) that will be available to meet cash outflows on liabilities.
- Holds deposits at central banks to meet liquidity needs.
- Has very diverse funding sources.
- Has significant concentrations of liquidity risk in either its assets or its funding sources.

[IFRS 7 para IG31].

A6.11.99 In preparing the contractual maturity analysis for financial liabilities, an entity uses its judgement to determine an appropriate number of time bands. For example, an entity might determine that the following time bands are appropriate:

- Not later than one month.
- Later than one month and not later than three months.
- Later than three months and not later than one year.
- Later than one year and not later than five years.

[IFRS 7 App B para 11].

A6.11.100 When a counterparty has a choice of when an amount is paid, the liability is included on the basis of the earliest date on which the entity can be required to pay. For example, financial liabilities that an entity can be required to repay on demand (for example, demand deposits) are included in the earliest time band. [IFRS 7 App B para 12].

A6.11.101 When an entity is committed to make amounts available in instalments, each instalment is allocated to the earliest period in which the entity can be required to pay. For example, an undrawn loan commitment is included in the time band containing the earliest date it can be drawn down. [IFRS 7 App B para 13].

A6.11.102 The amounts disclosed in the maturity analysis are the contractual undiscounted cash flows (including principal and interest payments), which may differ from the amounts included in the balance sheet, for example:

- Gross finance lease obligations (before deducting finance charges).
- Prices specified in forward agreements to purchase financial assets for cash. This means that the pay leg of all gross-settled foreign exchange forward contracts should be included, whether or not the derivative's fair value is negative.
- Net amounts for pay-floating receive-fixed interest rate swaps for which net cash flows are exchanged.
- Contractual amounts to be exchanged in a derivative financial instrument (for example, a currency swap) for which gross cash flows are exchanged.
- Gross loan commitments.

[IFRS 7 App B para 14].

A6.11.102.1 There is no requirement to reconcile the amounts disclosed in the maturity analysis to the amounts included in the balance sheet.

A6.11.103 If appropriate, an entity should disclose the maturity analysis of derivative financial instruments separately from that of non-derivative financial instruments. For example, it would be appropriate to distinguish cash flows from derivative financial instruments and non-derivative financial instruments if the cash flows arising from the derivative financial instruments are settled gross. This is because the gross cash outflows may be accompanied by related inflows. [IFRS 7 App B para 15].

A6.11.104 When the amount payable is not fixed, the amount disclosed is determined by reference to the conditions existing at the reporting date. For example, when the amount payable varies with changes in an index, the amount disclosed may be based on the level of the index at the reporting date. [IFRS 7 App B para 16]. However, for floating rate financial liabilities and foreign currency denominated instruments, the use of a forward interest rates and forward foreign exchange rates may be conceptually preferable. Which ever approach is adopted, current rate or forward rate at the reporting date, it should be applied consistently.

A6.11.104.1 IFRS 7 requires a maturity analysis only for financial liabilities. An entity may choose to disclose also a maturity analysis for financial assets as part of its description of how it manages liquidity risk. However, it is not obligatory. The same principle follows for derivatives with the exception of gross settled derivatives (see para A6.11.104.3 below).

A6.11.104.2 In practice, entities may disclose a maturity analysis of financial assets and financial liabilities showing expected maturity, if this is the information provided to key management personnel to manage the business. [IFRS 7 para 34(a)]. However, a maturity analysis based on the remaining contractual maturity for financial liabilities should always be disclosed.

A6.11.104.3 IFRS 7 requires that prices specified in forward agreements to purchase financial assets for cash are included in the maturity analysis. [IFRS 7 App B para 14]. This means that the pay leg of all gross settled derivatives should be included, whether or not the fair value of the derivative is negative. While the standard only requires the gross cash outflows to be included in the maturity analysis, a separate disclosure of the inflows in conjunction with the outflows may make the information more meaningful (see para A6.11.104.2 above). In addition, this disclosure is required where gross cash flows are exchanged under a derivative contract and where the cash flows are exchanged simultaneously.

A6.11.104.4 The examples that follow illustrate how a maturity analysis may be prepared for some typical financial instruments.

Example 1 – Floating rate notes

On 1 January 20X6 entity A issued two-year, US$30m floating rate notes that pay interest of 6m LIBOR plus 2%. The notes mature on 31 December 20X8.

Principal is redeemable at maturity. The carrying amount at the balance sheet date is US$30m (C21.6m).

The functional currency of the entity is C (currency units).

The spot rate at the balance sheet date is US$ = C0.72

The 6m LIBOR at the balance sheet date is 5% per annum.

Scenario 1 – Contractual cash flows of the notes (using spot rates at the balance sheet date)

	30 Jun 20X7	**31 Dec 20X7**	**30 Jun 20X8**	**31 Dec 20X8**	**Total**
Principal (US$)	-	-	-	30,000	**30,000**
Interest payments (LIBOR + 2%)	1,050	1,050	1,050	1,050	**4,200**
Total (in US$)	**1,050**	**1,050**	**1,050**	**31,050**	**34,200**
US/C spot rate as at 31 Dec 20X6	0.72	0.72	0.72	0.72	0.72
Total cash flows (in C)	**756**	**756**	**756**	**22,356**	**24,624**

Scenario 2 – Contractual cash flows of the notes (using forward rates available at the balance sheet date)

6m LIBOR yield curve	5.25%	5.50%	5.75%	5.40%	
6m LIBOR yield curve + 2% per annum	7.25%	7.50%	7.75%	7.40%	
	30 Jun 20X7	**31 Dec 20X7**	**30 Jun 20X8**	**31 Dec 20X8**	**Total**
Principal (US$)	-	-	-	30,000	**30,000**
Interest payments (LIBOR + 2%)	1,088	1,125	1,163	1,110	**4,486**
Total (in US$)	**1,088**	**1,125**	**1,163**	**31,110**	**34,486**
US/C forward rate as at 31 Dec 20X6	0.75	0.78	0.79	0.76	
Total cash flows (in C)	**816**	**878**	**919**	**23,644**	**26,257**

Liquidity analysis

Solution 1 (based on spot rates)

Financial liabilities as at 31/12/20X6	**Less than 1 month**	**Between 1 and 3M**	**Between 3M and 1Y**	**Between 1 and 5Y**	**Over 5Y**	**Balance sheet amounts**
Floating rate notes	-	-	1.512	23,112	-	21,600

Alternative answer based on forward rates

Financial liabilities as at 31 Dec 20X6	**Less than 1 month**	**Between 1 and 3 months**	**Between 3 months and 1 year**	**Between 1 and 5 years**	**Over 5 years**	**Balance sheet amounts**
Floating rate notes	-	-	1,694	24,563	-	21,600

Either the spot rate or the forward rate could be used for the interest rate cash outflow calculation. The forward rate would be based on a yield curve (which will show by how much the LIBOR is expected to move each quarter/six months).

Both alternatives are acceptable provided they are properly disclosed and applied consistently.

In addition, the sum of all the amounts in the maturity analysis does not reconcile to balance sheet amount. This is because the liquidity analysis is based on the undiscounted cash flows.

Example 2 – Interest rate swap

Entity A entered into a two-year interest rate swap, notional value C10m, under which fixed interest of 5% p.a. is received quarterly and actual three-month LIBOR is paid. The contract is settled on a net basis. The swap has a negative fair value of C0.071m at the balance sheet date.

Estimated cash flows on the swap (C'000)

	31 Mar 20X7	30 Jun 20X7	30 Sept 20X7	31 Dec 20X7	31 Mar 20X8	30 Jun 20X8	30 Sept 20X8	31 Dec 20X8	Total
Fixed leg (receives fixed)	125	125	125	125	125	125	125	125	
Variable leg (pays 3 month LIBOR)	-110	-122	-136	-150	-155	-160	-172	-186	
Undiscounted net cash flows	15	3	-11	-25	-30	-35	-47	-61	-191
Discounted cashflows	13	2	-7	-14	-14	-15	-17	-19	-71

In the case of net settled derivatives, only derivatives with negative fair value (financial liabilities), at the balance sheet date should be included in the liquidity analysis. The cash flows to be included are the undiscounted cash flows at each reporting date, whether they result in net inflow or outflow for the entity.

Liquidity analysis (based on forward rates)

Financial liabilities as of 31/12/20X6	**Less than 1 month**	**Between 1 and 3M**	**Between 3M and 1Y**	**Between 1 and 5Y**	**Over 5Y**	**Balance sheet amounts**
Interest rate swaps		- 15	33	173		71

Example 3: Gross settled derivative

Entity A entered into the following forward contract to buy US$ against C on 31/12/20X6.

Type	European forward contract
Amount purchased	C35 million
Amount sold	US$50 million
Forward rate (US$/C)	0.76
Spot rate at the balance sheet date	0.72
Maturity	31 December 20X8
Settlement	Gross basis
Settlement date	31 December 20X8

Presentation and disclosure

The fair value of is forward contract is zero at the balance sheet date.

US$ amount to be sold at 31 December 20X8:	C'000
Retranslated using spot rate at the balance sheet date	36,000
Retranslated using forward rate at the balance sheet date	38,000

As this derivative settles on a gross basis, entity A is required to disclose the pay leg, irrespective whether the fair value of the derivative is positive or negative at the balance sheet date. This disclosure may be more meaningful if the associated cash inflow is disclosed as well. The cash inflow is C35 million and the cash outflow is C38 million (calculated as US50 million x forward rate at the balance sheet date).

Entity A entered into the derivative at the balance sheet date. Thus, the derivative's fair value is zero at the balance sheet date. However, because the two legs disclosed in the liquidity analysis are undiscounted, there is a difference of C3 million between them.

Liquidity analysis

Financial liabilities as of 31 December 20X6	**Less than 1 month**	**Between 1 and 3M**	**Between 3M and 1Y**	**Between 1 and 5Y**	**Over 5Y**	**Balance sheet amounts**
Outflow	-	-	-	(38,000)	-	
Inflow	-	-	-	35,000	-	0

6A.11.104.5 Another issue in preparing a maturity analysis is the treatment of perpetual bonds where the debtor/issuer has a call option to redeem the bond. In this case, the debtor/issuer has discretion over the repayment of the principal. Until the option is exercised, the bond's contractual terms are that it is non-redeemable perpetual bond. Once the call option is exercised, the bond's contractual terms are changed and the bond has a maturity date. If the call option was not exercised, then the undiscounted cash flows are going to be paid in perpetuity. This raises the question of what amount should be shown in the last time band. The standard does not deal explicitly with such a situation so a number of alternative approaches could be applied. One would be to include the principal amount in the last time band. An other option would be not to include any cash flows in the last time band, but disclose the principal amount in time band entitled 'no maturity'. Whatever form of disclosure is chosen, this is an area where it will important to provide a clear narrative description of the instrument's terms.

A6.11.105 An entity that has provided a comprehensive disclosure of its liquidity risk is shown in Table 6.11.17 below.

Table 6.11.17 – Liquidity risk

Novartis Group – Annual report – 31 December 2006

Note 15 Liquidity risk is defined as the risk that the Group could not be able to settle or meet its obligations on time or at a reasonable price. Group Treasury is responsible for liquidity, funding as well as settlement management. In addition, liquidity and funding risks, related processes and policies are overseen by management. Novartis manages its liquidity risk on a consolidated basis based on business needs, tax, capital or regulatory considerations, if applicable, through numerous sources of finance in order to maintain flexibility.

December 31, 2006	Due or due not later than one month USD millions	Due later than one month but not later than three months USD millions	Due later than three months but not later than one year USD millions	Due later than one year but not later than five years USD millions	Due after 5 years USD millions	Total USD millions
Current assets						
Marketable securities	16	42	929	1 726	1 390	4 103
Derivative financial instruments and accrued interest on derivative financial instruments	12	24	1			37
Cash and cash equivalents	3 014	801				3 815
Total current assets	**3 042**	**867**	**930**	**1 726**	**1 390**	**7 955**
Non-current liabilities						
Financial debts				656		656
Total non-current liabilities				**656**		**656**
Current liabilities						
Financial debts	3 438	1 352	1 770			6 560
Derivative financial instruments	47	5	23	8		83
Total current liabilities	**3 485**	**1 357**	**1 793**	**8**		**6 643**
Net liquidity of continuing operations	-443	-490	-863	1 062	1 390	656

Market risk

Sensitivity analysis

A6.11.106 Unless an entity complies with paragraph A6.11.114 below, it should disclose:

- A sensitivity analysis for each type of market risk to which the entity is exposed at the reporting date, showing how profit or loss and equity would have been affected by changes in the relevant risk variable that were reasonably possible at that date. Note that the standard requires this disclosure based on reasonably possible changes and not on a 'worst case scenario' or 'stress test'. Risk variables that are relevant to disclosing market risk include, but are not limited to:

- The yield curve of market interest rates. It may be necessary to consider both parallel and non-parallel shifts in the yield curve.
- Foreign exchange rates.
- Prices of equity instruments.
- Market prices of commodities.

- The methods and assumptions used in preparing the sensitivity analysis.
- Changes from the previous period in the methods and assumptions used and the reasons for such changes.

[IFRS 7 para 40].

A6.11.107 In providing the sensitivity analysis for each type of market risk, an entity should decide how it aggregates information to display the overall picture without combining information with different characteristics about exposures to risks from significantly different economic environments. Entities are not required to disclose the effect for each change within a range of reasonably possible changes of the relevant risk variable. Disclosure of the effects of the changes at the limits of the reasonably possible range would be sufficient. [IFRS 7 App B paras 18 to 19]. For example, an entity that trades financial instruments might disclose this information separately for financial instruments held for trading and those not held for trading. Similarly, an entity would not aggregate its exposure to market risks from areas of hyperinflation with its exposure to the same market risks from areas of very low inflation. Conversely, if an entity has exposure to only one type of market risk in only one economic environment, it would not show disaggregated information. [IFRS 7 App B para 17].

A6.11.107.1 In addition, where there are changes in volatility, an entity should not restate the prior year disclosures. For example, where the reasonable possible change in an exchange rate changes from 5 per cent in the prior year to 8 per cent in the current year, the prior year disclosures should not be restated. An entity could, however, present additional sensitivity information for the comparative period.

A6.11.108 For the purposes of disclosing the effect on profit or loss and equity of reasonably possible changes in the relevant risk variable, for example interest rate risk, as required by the first bullet point of paragraph A6.11.106 above, an entity might show separately the effect of a change in market rates on:

- Interest income and expense.
- Other line items of profit or loss (such as trading gains and losses).
- When applicable, equity.

[IFRS 7 para IG34].

A6.11.109 An entity might disclose a sensitivity analysis for interest rate risk for each currency in which the entity has material exposures to interest rate risk. Similarly, a sensitivity analysis is disclosed for each currency to which an entity has significant exposure. [IFRS 7 paras IG34, App B para 24].

A6.11.109.1 This disclosure would also be relevant to those instruments where an entity has effectively hedged the interest rate risk, as illustrated in the following example.

Example – A bond hedged for variable interest rate risk

An entity hedges its exposure to variable interest rate risk on an issued bond. The hedge is designated as a cash flow hedge. The bond and the hedging instrument (interest rate swap) have a five-year remaining life. The variable leg of the swap exactly matches the variable interest of the bond (causing no ineffectiveness).

The high effectiveness of the hedge does not necessarily mean that there would be no impact on equity or profit or loss due to changes in interest rate risk. The accounting for a cash flow hedge means that the fair value movement related to the effective part of the hedging instrument is included in equity. Amounts deferred in equity are recycled in profit or loss when the hedged transaction occurs. Hence, reasonably possible movements in the interest rate risk exposure have an impact on both profit or loss and equity.

At the same time, reasonably possible movements in the interest rate risk exposure on the outstanding bond would impact profit or loss, as the bond was a recognised financial liability at the balance sheet date.

If the effects of recycling and ineffectiveness are not material, the entity could consider the following disclosure as an approximation for the sensitivity analysis: *"The movements related to the bond and the swap's variable leg are not reflected as they offset each other. The movements related to the remaining fair value exposure on the swap's fixed leg are shown in the equity part of the analysis"*.

A6.11.110 It should be noted that for the purposes of disclosing a sensitivity analysis for foreign currency risk, translation related risk is not taken into account. This is because foreign currency risk can only arise on financial instruments that are denominated in a currency other than the functional currency in which they are measured. [IFRS 7 App B para 23]. Translation exposures arise from financial and non-financial items held by an entity (for example, a subsidiary) with a functional currency different from the group's presentation currency. Therefore, translation-related risks are not taken into consideration for the purpose of the sensitivity analysis for foreign currency risks. This also includes quasi-equity loans (foreign currency inter-company loans that are part of the net investment in a foreign operation). However, foreign currency denominated inter-company receivables and payables would be included in the sensitivity analysis for foreign currency risks, because even though they cancel in the consolidated balance sheet, the effect on profit or loss of their revaluation under IAS 21 is not fully eliminated.

A6.11.111 Because the factors affecting market risk vary depending on the specific circumstances of each entity, the appropriate range to be considered in providing a sensitivity analysis of market risk varies for each entity and for each type of market risk. [IFRS 7 para IG35].

A6.11.112 However, an entity is not required to determine what the profit or loss for the period would have been if relevant risk variables had been different. Instead, it should disclose the effect on profit or loss and equity at the balance sheet date, assuming that a reasonably possible change in the relevant risk variable had occurred at the balance sheet date and had been applied to the risk exposures in existence at that date. For example, if an entity has a floating rate liability at the end of the year, the entity would disclose the effect on profit or loss (that is, interest expense) for the current year if interest rates had varied by reasonably possible amounts. [IFRS 7 App B para 18(a)].

A6.11.113 Furthermore, an entity is not required to disclose the effect on profit or loss and equity for each change within a range of reasonably possible changes of the relevant risk variable. Disclosure of the effects of the changes at the limits of the reasonably possible range would be sufficient. [IFRS 7 App B para 18(b)].

A6.11.114 If an entity prepares a sensitivity analysis, such as value-at-risk (VaR), that reflects interdependencies between risk variables (for example, interest rates and exchange rates) and uses it to manage financial risks, it may use that sensitivity analysis in place of the analysis described above. However, a precondition for disclosing sensitivity in such a format (VaR) is that the company uses VaR in managing its financial risks. It cannot choose just to apply VaR for disclosures purposes but continue to manage each risk variable separately. In addition, it is likely that outstanding intercompany foreign currency receivables and payables at the year end are not considered in the VaR model. If this is the case, the entity will need to prepare additional sensitivity disclosures for these amounts (see para A6.11.110 above). The entity should also disclose:

- an explanation of the method used in preparing such a sensitivity analysis, and of the main parameters and assumptions underlying the data provided; and
- an explanation of the objective of the method used and of limitations that may result in the information not fully reflecting the fair value of the assets and liabilities involved.

[IFRS 7 para 41].

A6.11.115 An example of a company that has provided an analysis of market risk sensitivity is given in Table 6.11.18 below.

Table 6.11.18 – Analysis of market risk sensitivity
Deutsche Telekom – Annual report – 31 December 2006

Extract from note 43
Currency risks

For the presentation of market risks, IFRS 7 requires sensitivity analyses that show the effects of hypothetical changes of relevant risk variables on profit or loss and shareholders' equity. In addition to currency risks, Deutsche Telekom is exposed to interest rate risks and price risks in its investments. The periodic effects are determined by relating the hypothetical changes in the risk variables to the balance of financial instruments at the reporting date. It is assumed that the balance at the reporting date is representative for the year as a whole.

Currency risks as defined by IFRS 7 arise on account of financial instruments being denominated in a currency that is not the functional currency and being of a monetary nature; differences resulting from the translation of financial statements into the Group's presentation currency are not taken into consideration. Relevant risk variables are generally all non-functional currencies in which Deutsche Telekom has financial instruments.

The currency sensitivity analysis is based on the following assumptions:

Major non-derivative monetary financial instruments (liquid assets, receivables, interest-bearing securities and/or debt instruments held, interestbearing liabilities, finance lease liabilities, liabilities arising from ABS transactions, non-interest-bearing liabilities) are either directly denominated in the functional currency or are transferred to the functional currency through the use of derivatives. Exchange rate fluctuations therefore have no effects on profit or loss, or shareholders' equity.

Non-interest-bearing securities or equity instruments held are of a nonmonetary nature and therefore are not exposed to currency risk as defined by IFRS 7.

Interest income and interest expense from financial instruments are also either recorded directly in the functional currency or transferred to the functional currency by using derivatives. For this reason, there can be no effects on the variables considered in this connection.

In the case of fair value hedges designed for hedging currency risks, the changes in the fair values of the hedged item and the hedging instruments attributable to exchange rate movements balance out almost completely in the income statement in the same period. As a consequence, these financial instruments are not exposed to currency risks with an effect on profit or loss, or shareholders' equity either.

Cross-currency swaps are always assigned to non-derivative hedged items, so these instruments also do not have any currency effects.

Deutsche Telekom is therefore only exposed to currency risks from specific currency derivatives. Some of these are currency derivatives that are part of an effective cash flow hedge for hedging payment fluctuations resulting from exchange rate movements in accordance with IAS 39. Exchange rate fluctuations of the currencies on which these transactions are based affect the hedging reserve in shareholders' equity and the fair value of these hedging transactions. Others are currency derivatives that are neither part of one of the hedges defined in IAS 39 nor part of a natural hedge. These derivatives are used to hedge planned transactions. Exchange rate fluctuations of the currencies, on which such financial instruments are based, affect other financial income or expense (net gain/loss from remeasurement of financial assets to fair value).

If the euro had gained (lost) 10 percent against the U.S. dollar at December 31, 2006, the hedging reserve in shareholders' equity and the fair value of the hedging instruments would have been EUR 125 million lower (higher) (December 31, 2005: EUR 68 million higher (lower)).

If the euro had gained (lost) 10 percent against all currencies at December 31, 2006, other financial income and the fair value of the hedging instruments would have been EUR 29 million higher (lower) (December 31, 2005: EUR 3 million lower (higher)). The hypothetical effect on profit or loss of EUR +29 million results from the currency sensitivities EUR/USD: EUR –14 million; EUR /AED: EUR +1 million; EUR/GBP: EUR +8 million; EUR/HUF: EUR +8 million; EUR/PLN: EUR +22 million; EUR/SKK: EUR +4 million.

Interest rate risks

Deutsche Telekom is exposed to interest rate risks, mainly in the euro zone, in the United Kingdom, and in the United States of America. To minimize the effects of interest rate fluctuations in these regions, Deutsche Telekom manages the interest rate risk for net financial liabilities denominated in euros, sterling, and U.S. dollars separately. Once a year, the Board of Management stipulates the desired mix of fixed- and variable-interest net financial liabilities for a future period of three years. Taking account of the Group's existing and planned debt structure, Treasury uses interest rate derivatives to adjust the interest structure for the net financial liabilities of the composition specified by the Board of Management.

Due to the derivative hedges, an average of 66 percent (2005: 67 percent) of the net financial liabilities in 2006 denominated in euros, 60 percent (2005: 80 percent) of those denominated in sterling, and 61 percent (2005: 85 percent) of those denominated in U.S. dollars had a fixed rate of interest. The average value is representative for the year as a whole.

Interest rate risks are presented by way of sensitivity analyses in accordance with IFRS 7. These show the effects of changes in market interest rates on interest payments, interest income and expense, other income components and, if appropriate, shareholders' equity. The interest rate sensitivity analyses are based on the following assumptions:

Changes in the market interest rates of non-derivative financial instruments with fixed interest rates only affect income if these are measured at their fair value. As such, all financial instruments with fixed interest rates that are carried at amortized cost are not subject to interest rate risk as defined in IFRS 7.

In the case of fair value hedges designed for hedging interest rate risks, the changes in the fair values of the hedged item and the hedging instrument attributable to interest rate movements balance out almost completely in the income statement in the same period. As a consequence, these financial instruments are also not exposed to interest rate risk.

Changes in the market interest rate of financial instruments that were designated as hedging instruments in a cash flow hedge to hedge payment fluctuations resulting from interest rate movements affect the hedging reserve in shareholders' equity and are therefore taken into consideration in the equity-related sensitivity calculations.

Changes in market interest rates affect the interest income or expense of non-derivative variable-interest financial instruments, the interest payments of which are not designated as hedged items of cash flow hedges against interest rate risks. As a consequence, they are included in the calculation of income-related sensitivities.

Changes in the market interest rate of interest rate derivatives (interest rate swaps, cross-currency swaps) that are not part of a hedging relationship as set out in IAS 39 affect other financial income or expense (net gain/loss from remeasurement of the financial assets to fair value) and are therefore taken into consideration in the income-related sensitivity calculations.

Currency derivatives are not exposed to interest rate risks and therefore do not affect the interest rate sensitivities.

If the market interest rates had been 100 basis points higher (lower) at December 31, 2006, profit or loss would have been EUR 254 million (December 31, 2005: EUR 158 million) lower (higher). The hypothetical effect of EUR -254 million on income results from the potential effects of EUR -206 million from interest rate derivatives and EUR -48 million from non-derivative, variable-interest financial liabilities. If the market interest rates had been 100 basis points higher (lower) at December 31, 2006, shareholders' equity would have been EUR 27 million higher (lower).

Other price risks

As part of the presentation of market risks, IFRS 7 also requires disclosures on how hypothetical changes in risk variables affect the price of financial instruments. Important risk variables are stock exchange prices or indexes.

As of December 31, 2006, Deutsche Telekom did not hold any material investments to be classified as "available-for-sale".

Table 6.11.19 – Market risk sensitivity analysis (foreign currency risk)

Telstra Corporation Limited – Annual Report – 30 June 2007
Note 34(b)(ii) Foreign currency risk

Foreign currency risk refers to the risk that the value of a financial commitment, recognised asset or liability will fluctuate due to changes in foreign currency rates. Our foreign currency exchange risk arises primarily from:

- borrowings denominated in foreign currencies;
- firm commitments or highly probable forecast transactions for receipts and payments settled in foreign currencies or with prices dependent on foreign currencies; and
- net investments in foreign operations.

We are exposed to foreign exchange risk from various currency exposures, primarily with respect to:

- United States dollars;
- British pounds sterling;
- New Zealand dollars;
- Euro;
- Swiss francs;
- Hong Kong dollars;
- Chinese renminbi;
- Japanese yen;
- Swedish krona; and
- Singapore dollar.

Our economic foreign currency risk is assessed for each individual currency and for each hedge type, calculated by aggregating the net exposure for that currency for that hedge type.

We minimise our exposure to foreign currency risk by initially seeking contracts effectively denominated in Australian dollars where possible and economically favourable to do so. Where this is not possible we manage our exposure as follows.

Foreign exchange risk that arises from firm commitments or highly probable transactions are managed principally through the use of forward foreign currency derivatives. We hedge a proportion of these transactions (such as international telecommunications traffic transactions and asset purchases settled in foreign currencies) in each currency in accordance with our risk management policy.

Cash flow foreign currency risk arises primarily from foreign currency overseas borrowings. We hedge this risk on the major part of our foreign currency denominated borrowings by effectively converting them to Australian dollar borrowings by entering into cross currency swaps at inception to maturity. A relatively small proportion of our foreign currency borrowings are not swapped into Australian dollars where they are used as hedges for foreign exchange exposure such as translation foreign exchange risk from our offshore business investments.

Foreign currency risk also arises on translation of the net assets of our non Australian controlled entities which have a different functional currency. The foreign currency gains or losses arising from this risk are recorded through the foreign currency translation reserve. We manage this translation foreign exchange risk with forward foreign currency contracts, cross currency swaps and/or borrowings denominated in the currency of the entity concerned.

Where a subsidiary hedges foreign exchange transactions it designates hedging instruments with the Treasury department as fair value hedges or cash flow hedges as appropriate. External foreign exchange contracts are designated at the group level as hedges of foreign exchange risk on specific assets, liabilities or future transactions.

Sensitivity analysis

The following Table K shows the effect on profit and equity after tax as at 30 June from a 10 percent adverse/favourable movement in exchange rates at that date on a total portfolio basis with all other variables held constant, taking into account all underlying exposures and related hedges.

Adverse versus favourable movements are determined relative to the underlying exposure. An adverse movement in exchange rates implies an increase in our foreign currency risk exposure and a worsening of our financial position. A favourable movement in exchange rates implies a reduction in our foreign currency risk exposure and an improvement of our financial position.

A sensitivity of 10 per cent has been selected as this is considered reasonable given the current level of exchange rates and the volatility observed both on an historical basis and market expectations for future movement. Comparing the Australian dollar exchange rate against the United States dollar, the year end rate of 0.84885 would generate a 10 per cent adverse position of 0.93374 and a favourable position of 0.77168. This range is considered reasonable given the historic ranges that have been observed, for example over the last five years, the Australian dollar exchange rate against the US dollar has traded in the range 0.8522 to 0.5263.

Our foreign currency risk exposure from recognised assets and liabilities arises primarily from our long term borrowings denominated in foreign currencies. There is no significant impact on profit from foreign currency movements associated with these borrowings as they are effectively hedged.

The net gain in the cash flow hedge reserve reflects the result of exchange rate movements on the derivatives held in our cash flow hedges which will be released to the income statement in the future as the underlying hedged items affect profit.

For the Telstra Group, our foreign currency translation risk associated with our foreign investments results in some volatility to the foreign currency translation reserve. The impact on the foreign currency translation reserve relates to translation of the net assets of our foreign controlled entities including the impact of hedging. We hedge our net investments in TelstraClear Limited and Hong Kong CSL Limited in New Zealand dollars and Hong Kong dollars respectively, where the amount hedged is in the range of 40% to 50%. The net loss of $235 million (2006: $211 million) in the foreign currency translation reserve takes into account the related hedges and represents the impact of the unhedged portion. For the Telstra Entity there is a gain of $75 million (2006: $78 million) resulting from the hedging instruments used to hedge our net foreign investments. This amount is transferred to the foreign currency translation reserve in the Telstra Group and hence there is no impact on profit for the Telstra Group.

	Equity (foreign currency translation reserve) As at 30 June		Equity (cash flow hedging reserve) As at 30 June	
	2007	2006	**2007**	2006
	$m	$m	**$m**	$m
If there was a 10% adverse movement in exchange rates with all other variables held constant - increase/(decrease)	**(235)**	(211)	**38**	43
If there was a 10% favourable movement in exchange rates with all other variables held constant - increase/(decrease)	**288**	211	**(32)**	(43)

Other market risk disclosures

A6.11.116 When the sensitivity analyses disclosed in accordance with paragraphs 6.11.98 or 6.11.106 above are unrepresentative of a risk inherent in a financial instrument (for example because the year-end exposure does not reflect the exposure during the year), the entity should disclose that fact and the reason it believes the sensitivity analyses are unrepresentative. [IFRS 7 para 42].

A6.11.117 As noted above, the sensitivity analysis might be unrepresentative of a risk inherent in a financial instrument where the year end exposure does not reflect the exposure during the year. Other circumstances include the following:

- A financial instrument contains terms and conditions whose effects are not apparent from the sensitivity analysis, for example options that remain out of (or in) the money for the chosen change in the risk variable. In such a situation, additional disclosure might include:
  - the terms and conditions of the financial instrument (for example, the options);
  - the effect on profit or loss if the term or condition were met (that is, if the options were exercised); and
  - a description of how the risk is hedged.
- Financial assets are illiquid, for example, when there is a low volume of transactions in similar assets and an entity finds it difficult to find a counterparty. In such a situation, additional disclosure might include the reasons for the lack of liquidity and how the entity hedges the risk.
- An entity has a large holding of a financial assets that, if sold in its entirety, would be sold at a discount or premium to the quoted market price for a smaller holding. In such a situation, additional disclosure might include:
  - The nature of the security (for example, entity name).
  - The extent of holding (for example, 15 per cent of the issued shares).
  - The effect on profit or loss.
  - How the entity hedges the risk.

[IFRS 7 para IG37-40].

A6.11.118 An entity should provide sensitivity analyses for the whole of its business, but may provide different types of sensitivity analysis for different classes of financial instruments. [IFRS 7 App B para 21].

A6.11.119 The sensitivity of profit or loss (that arises, for example, from instruments classified as at fair value through profit or loss and impairments of available-for-sale financial assets) is disclosed separately from the sensitivity of equity (that arises, for example, from instruments classified as available for sale). [IFRS 7 App B para 27]. For example, where the fair value of a non-monetary available-for-sale asset is close to the impairment threshold, an entity should distinguish between profit or loss and equity effects, taking into consideration its impairment policy. In cases where the asset is already impaired, the downward shift (due to the impairment) should be shown as affecting the profit or loss while the upward shift should be shown as affecting equity.

A6.11.120 Financial instruments that an entity classifies as equity instruments are not remeasured. Neither profit or loss nor equity will be affected by the equity price risk of those instruments. Accordingly, no sensitivity analysis is required. [IFRS 7 App B para 28].

Section 12

Companies Act 1985 requirements

UK.A6.12.1 The Companies Act 1985 (International Accounting Standards and Other Accounting Amendments) Regulations 2004 (SI 2004/2947), which came into effect for accounting periods commencing on or after 1 January 2005, amended the Act to clarify which parts of the Act do and do not apply to those companies applying EU-adopted IFRS (under the EU's 2005 Regulation or voluntarily). In particular, Schedule 4 (which contains accounting requirements) does not apply to companies preparing their financial statements under EU-adopted IFRS, whereas Schedule 7 (which contains requirements for the directors' report) applies to all companies.

UK.A6.12.2 The Statutory Instrument amended Schedule 4 to introduce new rules for fair value accounting, presentation and disclosure of financial instruments, but these rules do not apply to companies reporting under EU-adopted IFRS. The Statutory Instrument also amended Schedule 7 to require certain disclosures in respect of financial instruments to be given in the directors' report and, as noted above, Schedule 7 applies to all companies, including those preparing their financial statements under EU-adopted IFRS. (This is considered in detail in section 3 of the Manual of Accounting – Management reports and governance.) Accordingly, all companies (except small companies as defined in the Act) must give the following disclosures in the directors' report relating to the use of financial instruments:

- The financial risk management objectives and policies of the company and its consolidated subsidiaries, including the policy for hedging each major type of forecasted transaction for which hedge accounting is used.
- The exposure of the company and its consolidated subsidiaries to price risk, credit risk, liquidity risk and cash flow risk.

[CA85 7 Sch 5A].

UK.A6.12.3 This disclosure is not required where the information is not material for the assessment of the assets, liabilities, financial position and profit or loss of the company and its consolidated subsidiaries. Also, where similar disclosures are made in the financial statements, they can be incorporated by cross-reference into the directors' report.

Companies Act 1985 requirements

UK.A6.12.4 The above requirements will be replaced by the Companies Act 2006 while the new rules for fair value accounting, presentation and disclosure of financial instruments will be effective from 6 April 2008. However, this will lead to minimal change in terms of companies preparing their financial statements under EU-adopted IFRS. They will continue giving the required disclosures as described above in the directors' report.

First-time adoption of IFRS

UK.A6.13.1 Applicability of IFRS in the UK is considered in detail in section 2. First-time adoption of IFRS, including the rules relating to financial instruments, is considered in detail in section 3. A summary of the main points for UK first-time adopters of IFRS is given in the following paragraphs.

UK.A6.13.2 Points to consider in respect of initial recognition and classification of financial instruments for UK first-time adopters of IFRS are as follows:

- On first-time adoption, an entity will classify all its financial assets and financial liabilities in accordance with IAS 39, irrespective of their classification under UK GAAP.
- Many financial assets will be measured at fair value where they were previously carried at cost under UK GAAP.
- On first-time adoption, entities should consider whether or not to designate financial assets or liabilities as 'at fair value through profit or loss' (if permitted) or as 'available-for-sale'.
- All derivatives must be measured at fair value.
- Any embedded derivatives that are not closely related to a host contract, where the contract is not carried 'at fair value through profit or loss', will need to be separated out, fair valued and separately accounted for.
- Entities will have to work out how much to record in the available-for-sale reserve within equity.

UK.A6.13.3 Points to consider in respect of derecognition of financial instruments for UK first-time adopters of IFRS are as follows:

- In whatever financial year IAS 32 and IAS 39 are applied, the derecognition rules apply only to transactions that took place after 1 January 2004. Where non-derivative financial assets or liabilities have been derecognised as a result of a transaction that took place before 1 January 2004, then unless they qualify for recognition as a result of a later event or transaction they should remain derecognised.
- Retrospective application from an earlier chosen date is allowed if the required accounting information is available.

- Linked presentation is not available under IAS 39.

UK.A6.13.4 Points to consider in respect of subsequent measurement, fair values and impairment of financial instruments for UK first-time adopters of IFRS are as follows:

- Impairment methodology is likely to be different from that used under UK GAAP. In particular, general provisions are not permitted and all impairment of debt instruments (including trade debtors) must be measured using a discounted cash flow methodology.

- Many financial instruments will need to be fair valued, with no adjustments for blockage or liquidity provisions if they are quoted in an active market.

- Amortised cost at the date of transition will need to be calculated, using effective interest rates as set out in IAS 39. This will apply to both financial assets and financial liabilities that are subsequently measured at amortised cost.

UK.A6.13.5 Points to consider in respect of hedge accounting for UK first-time adopters of IFRS are as follows:

- An entity must consider what its hedging strategy will be under IAS 39.

- All hedge relationships that existed under UK GAAP are recognised in the opening balance sheet if they qualify as a type of hedge that would be allowed under IAS 39.

- If hedge relationships do not meet the conditions for hedge accounting under IAS 39, the entity will apply the IAS 39 provisions to discontinue hedge accounting prospectively.

- Any hedge relationship that was not designated under UK GAAP cannot be retrospectively designated as a hedge, even if it meets all the IAS 39 criteria.

- To qualify for hedge accounting prospectively under IAS 39, strict hedging criteria must be met, including extensive hedge documentation, designation and effectiveness testing.

UK.A6.13.6 In respect of the disclosure of financial instruments for UK first-time adopters of IFRS, systems and processes need to be put in place to gather the information needed for the additional disclosure requirements in IAS 32 or, from 2007, IFRS 7. For example, the disclosures relating to impairments/bad debt provisions on financial assets, maturity analyses for financial liabilities, basis and assumptions made in calculating fair values (to name a few) will need consideration.

Chapter 7

Foreign currencies

	Page
Introduction	7001
SSAP 20	7003
Scope	7003
Objectives	7003
Procedures	7003
The individual company stage	7004
Reporting in local currency	7004
Change in local currency	7005
General rules for translation	7006
Date of transaction	7006
Determining the average rate	7006
Dual rates or suspension of rates	7007
Treatment of monetary items	7008
Treatment of non-monetary items	7009
Treatment of exchange gains and losses	7010
Settled transactions	7010
Unsettled transactions	7012
Transactions between group companies	7014
The consolidation stage	7014
Introduction	7014
Closing rate/net investment method	7015
Illustration of the closing rate/net investment method	7017
The temporal method	7021
Illustration of the temporal method	7023
Foreign branches	7027
Other matters	7028
Determining the average rate	7028
Dual rates or suspension of rates	7030
Local currency	7030
Change from the temporal method to the closing rate method or vice-versa	7031
Intercompany dividends	7032
Intra-group trading transactions	7034
Unrealised profit on stocks	7035
Intra-group long-term loans and deferred trading balances	7038
Translation of subsidiary's non-coterminous accounts	7042
Goodwill arising on consolidation	7042
Foreign equity investments financed by foreign borrowings	7045
Treatment in individual company	7045
Offset restriction	7046

Borrowing restriction. 7047
Consistent accounting treatment 7049
Hedging by means of upstream loans. 7049
Termination of hedging during the year. 7050
Borrowings taken out before or after the investment 7051
Carrying value of foreign equity investment 7054
Partial hedges. 7054
Intermediate holding companies 7055
Treatment in consolidated financial statements. 7058
Goodwill on consolidation. 7060
UITF Abstract 19 7061
Hedging transactions. 7064
Identification of a hedge. 7064
Forward exchange contracts. 7065
Forward exchange contracts taken out at the transaction date. 7067
Hedging an existing asset or liability with forward exchange contract 7068
Hedging a foreign currency commitment. 7070
Hedging a net investment. 7073
Hedging future results of foreign investments. 7073
Speculative forward contracts 7074
Foreign currency options as a hedge. 7075
Disclosures 7077
Requirements of the Act. 7077
Requirements of the standard 7077
Effect that foreign currency translation has on distributable profits 7080
Hyper-inflation. 7083
Multi-currency share capital. 7086
Financial statements in foreign currencies 7088
Annex 7089

Chapter 7

Foreign currencies

Introduction

7.1 Businesses conducted by UK companies are not simply confined within national boundaries. The globalisation of markets for goods and services as well as capital makes it imperative for companies to engage in international trade, cross-border alliances and joint ventures if they are to survive and grow in today's competitive business environment. The ways in which companies enter the international market place are varied. First, companies directly undertake transactions of buying goods and services from overseas suppliers and selling goods and services to overseas customers. Secondly, they may extend their international business by conducting their affairs through overseas subsidiaries, branches and associates.

7.2 In the first situation, transactions undertaken by the UK company will often be expressed in foreign currencies and the results of these transactions will need to be translated into sterling for financial reporting purposes. In the second situation, it is usual for the foreign enterprise to maintain its accounting records in its local currency. In order to prepare consolidated financial statements, the complete financial statements of the foreign enterprise will need to be translated into sterling.

7.3 Accounting for foreign currencies is primarily concerned with the translation process whereby financial data denominated in one currency is expressed in terms of another currency. It is important to note that the translation process in no way changes the essential characteristics of the assets and liabilities measured. It merely restates assets and liabilities, initially valued in a foreign currency unit, to a common currency unit by applying a rate of exchange factor, a translation rate. It does not restate historical cost.

7.4 There are different translation rates that may be used depending on circumstances. These are:

- The historical rate — the rate of exchange ruling at the date the transaction occurred.
- The closing rate — the rate ruling at the balance sheet date.
- The average rate ruling during the year.

7.5 The average rate is generally confined to income and expenditure items. The rates used for balance sheet items will depend on the types of assets and liabilities being translated in individual company financial statements and upon the method of translation used for branches or consolidation of subsidiaries, namely the closing rate/net investment method or the temporal method. These methods are discussed in detail later in this chapter.

7.6 In addition to the difficulties in choosing an appropriate translation method, the treatment of exchange differences that arise on translation raises a number of questions, such as: the extent to which exchange gains and losses from different sources can be offset; whether some exchange differences should be recognised immediately whilst others should be deferred; and whether the recognition should be through the profit and loss account or through reserves. These and other vexing issues, such as the extent to which inflation in overseas countries should be taken into account in the translation process, are considered in this chapter.

7.7 Since its publication in 1983, SSAP 20, 'Foreign currency translation', has been successful in narrowing the range of permissible alternatives by stipulating that the closing rate/net investment method or, in some situations, the temporal method should be used for translating the financial statements of foreign enterprises. In spite of this, the standard is flexible and offers a range of choices both in the selection of exchange rates and in the treatment of the exchange differences in individual and consolidated financial statements.

7.8 SSAP 20 does not cover all the problem areas in accounting for foreign currencies. For example, it fails to provide adequate guidance on accounting for forward contracts and the treatment of hyper-inflation, both of which are adequately covered in IAS 21 and IAS 29. The latter shortcoming has, to some extent, been rectified by the publication of UITF Abstract 9, 'Accounting for operations in hyper-inflationary economies'.

7.9 The international equivalent to SSAP 20 is IAS 21, 'The effects of changes in foreign exchange rates' and the international equivalent to UITF Abstract 9 is IAS 29, 'Financial reporting in hyperinflationary economies'. As part of its convergence with IFRS, in 2004 the ASB issued FRS 23, 'The effects of changes in foreign exchange rates' and FRS 24, 'Financial reporting in hyperinflationary economies'. FRS 23 and FRS 24 are identical to IAS 21 and IAS 29 respectively. FRS 23 and FRS 24 must be applied by UK companies from the same date that FRS 26, 'Financial instruments: Measurement', is applied. SSAP 20 and UITF 9 are superseded by FRS 23 and FRS 24. For those entities not applying FRS 26, SSAP 20 and UITF 9 remain applicable, un-amended. Guidance on the application date of FRS 26 is given in chapter 6.

7.10 This chapter deals with the provisions of SSAP 20 and UITF Abstract 9. It covers many of the problem areas that are not adequately dealt with in SSAP 20, in particular, accounting for hedged transactions with forward contracts and currency options. This is an important area as many companies now manage their exposure to foreign exchange risks by adopting hedging strategies. However, this chapter does not deal with other currency instruments and derivative products which are discussed in chapter 6.

7.11 Accounting under FRS 23 is considered in the Annex to this chapter and companies that have adopted FRS 26 should refer to this.

SSAP 20

Scope

7.12 SSAP 20 sets out the standard accounting practice for foreign currency translation and applies to any entity that comes within the scope of statements of standard accounting practice and engages in foreign currency operations. The standard does not deal with the method of calculating profits or losses arising from a company's normal currency dealing operations. Consequently, all currency forward contracts, currency buying and selling activities, and cash balances that are associated with those activities are excluded from the standard's scope. However, when accounting for its currency dealing operations, a company should comply with the spirit of SSAP 20. It may be appropriate also to consider the requirements of FRS 26, which will apply in the future although not concurrently with SSAP 20. The standard does not deal with how to determine distributable profits, although applying its provisions could give rise to problems with respect to distributability. This is considered further from paragraph 7.149.

Objectives

7.12.1 The translation objectives of SSAP 20 are as follows:

- To produce results that are generally compatible with the effects of rate changes on a company's cash flows and its equity.
- To reflect in consolidated financial statements the financial results and relationships as measured in the foreign currency financial statements prior to translation.
- To ensure that the financial statements present a true and fair view of the management's actions.

[SSAP 20 para 2].

The above objectives may appear to be relatively simple, but their achievement, in practice, is fraught with difficulties. In some situations, these objectives may well conflict as will be apparent later in this chapter.

[The next paragraph is 7.13.]

Procedures

7.13 SSAP 20 deals with the procedures that should be adopted when accounting for foreign currency operations in two stages, namely:

- The translation of foreign currency transactions by individual companies.
- The translation of foreign currency financial statements for consolidation purposes.

[SSAP 20 para 3].

The individual company stage

Reporting in local currency

7.13.1 SSAP 20 defines 'local currency' as the currency of the primary economic environment in which the entity operates and generates cash flows. [SSAP 20 para 39]. In order to meet this definition, a company that adopts (say) the euro as its local currency will be expected to have the majority of its income, expenses, assets and liabilities denominated in euro. In certain cases, however, it is likely that companies may invoice in euro and be invoiced by suppliers in euro, while most of their other expenses, particularly wages, salaries and rent, remain in sterling.

7.13.2 FRS 23 uses the term 'functional currency' rather than 'local currency', but the definition is very similar. FRS 23 provides guidance in the form of indicators that are required to be considered in determining the functional currency. The primary indicators are given more weight whilst the secondary indicators provide additional supporting evidence of the functional currency. FRS 23 goes on to state that, where the facts in a given situation do not clearly identify the functional currency, the determination rests on the judgement of management. FRS 23 is considered further in the Annex to this chapter. The following lists some of the indicators to consider in deciding whether or not the euro is the functional currency:

- Cash flow indicators – the currency of the company's principal cash flows.
- Sales price indicators – whether sales prices are determined principally by local competition or by exchange rate changes. For instance, if price changes are determined not by exchange differences between sterling and the euro, but by competition between companies pricing in euro, this might indicate that the functional currency is the euro.
- Sales market indicators – the entity may have a significant market in those countries where the euro is the principal currency, rather than having its principal market in a non-euro economy.
- Expense indicators – the denomination of the entity's costs of production (labour and materials etc).
- Financing indicators – whether financing is in euro or in domestic currency.

7.13.3 Application of the above indicators may mean that companies with extensive European operations will determine that the euro is their functional currency. In some cases the decision might depend on the weighting given to one indicator relative to another. For instance, a company that makes most of its sales in euro, but incurs the majority of its costs in sterling, may give more weight to the sales price and sales market indicators in order to determine that the functional/local currency is the euro.

Change in local currency

7.13.4 Once the local currency is determined, it is not changed unless there is a change in the underlying transactions, events and circumstances that are relevant to the entity.

7.13.5 Where a company changes its local currency, the change should be accounted for *prospectively* from the date of change. This means that all items must be translated into the new local currency using the exchange rate at the date of the change. The resulting translated amounts for non-monetary items, even where they were originally purchased in the former local currency, are treated as their historical cost (or valuation for revalued assets).

7.13.6 Where a change occurrs during the year, it may not be practicable to determine the date of change precisely at a point during the year. It is also likely that the change may have occurred gradually during the year. Where this is the case, we consider that it may be appropriate, for pragmatic reasons, to account for the change as of the beginning of the period in which the change takes place (unless a specific event during the year gave rise to the change).

Example – Change in local currency

A UK company previously prepared its financial statements in US$ as the US dollar was its local currency. During the year, there has been a significant change in the nature of the company's operations and its local currency is now sterling. How should the company account for the change in local currency?

The closing balance sheet for the previous period, prepared in US$, should be retranslated into sterling by applying the US$/£ closing rate at the end of the previous year to preserve the relationship of the numbers.

Assume that on 1 January 20X0 the UK subsidiary purchased an asset for £50,000 with a useful life of 10 years when the exchange rate was £1 = US$2.00. Therefore, the US dollar equivalent cost was $100,000. On 31 December 20X4, the equipment has a net book value of US$50,000 and a historical sterling book value of £25,000. As a result of the change in functional currency from US dollars to sterling on 1 January 20X5 (exchange rate at 31 December 20X4 is £1 = US$1.6), the functional currency amount of the asset should be carried at £31,250 (US$50,000 @1.6), which becomes its new historical cost rather than the previous historical value of £25,000. However, in this situation an impairment review should be carried out if the indications are that the recoverable amount is less than £31,250.

In relation to the current year profit and loss account, any US$ transactions will be translated at the US$/£ rate that applies at the date of the transaction. Comparative figures in the profit and loss account will be translated using the US$/£ closing rate at the end of the previous year.

General rules for translation

7.14 The general rules that a company should follow in recording foreign currency transactions undertaken during an accounting period are as follows:

- Each asset, liability, revenue or cost arising from a transaction denominated in a foreign currency should be translated into the company's local currency at the exchange rate in operation on the date on which the transaction occurred.
- If rates do not fluctuate significantly, an average rate for a period *may* be used as an approximation.
- Where the transaction is to be settled at a contracted rate, that rate should be used.
- Where a trading transaction is covered by a related or matching forward contract, the rate of exchange specified in the contract *may* be used.

[SSAP 20 para 46].

The above rules appear to be relatively straightforward, but their application in practice may create a number of problems, for instance: determining the date of transaction may not always be that obvious; determining an average rate as an approximation to the actual rate; and the selection of an appropriate rate for translating foreign currency transactions where there is more than one rate in operation.

Date of transaction

7.15 There is no specific guidance in SSAP 20 as to whether the transaction date should be taken as the date on which the contract for the purchase or sale was signed, or the date of delivery, or the date when the invoice is received, or the date of payment. However, the standard does state that a difference may arise if a transaction is settled at a rate that is different from that used when the transaction was initially recorded. [SSAP 20 para 7]. It seems reasonable to assume, therefore, that the date on which a transaction is recorded under normal accounting rules should be taken as the transaction date. FRS 23 supports this, as it defines the transaction date as *"the date on which the transaction first qualifies for recognition in accordance with Financial Reporting Standards"*.

Determining the average rate

7.16 The standard permits the use of an average rate for a period for recording foreign currency transactions as a proxy to the actual rate prevailing at the date of each transaction, provided that there is no significant change in rates during that period. An average rate is unlikely to be used by companies undertaking few transactions in a foreign currency. It is also unlikely to be used for translating large, one-off transactions which would be recorded at the actual rate as illustrated in Table 7.1 below. The flexibility allowed in the standard is likely to be most beneficial to companies that enter into a large number of transactions in different currencies, or that maintain multi-currency ledgers. However, no guidance is provided in the standard as to how such a rate should be determined.

Table 7.1 — Trafalgar House Public Limited Company — Report and Accounts — 30 September 1994

Principal accounting policies (extract)

c) Foreign currencies

Trading results denominated in foreign currencies are translated into sterling at average rates of exchange during the year except for material exceptional items which are translated at the rate on the date of the transaction.

Assets and liabilities are translated at the rates of exchange ruling at the year end except where rates of exchange are fixed under contractual arrangements.

Differences on exchange arising from the translation of the opening net assets of foreign subsidiaries and branches and ships denominated in foreign currency and of any related loans are taken to reserves together with the differences between profit and loss accounts translated at average rates and rates ruling at the year end. Other exchange differences are taken to the profit and loss account when they arise.

7.17 The determination of an average rate and its use in practice will depend on a number of factors, such as: the nature of the company's accounting systems; the frequency and value of transactions undertaken; the period over which the rate will apply; and the acceptable level of materiality. The choice of the period to be used for calculating the average rate will depend on the extent to which daily exchange rates fluctuate in the period selected. If exchange rates are relatively stable over a period of say, one month, then the average exchange rate for that month can be used as an approximation to the daily rate. If, however, there is volatility of exchange rates, it may be appropriate to calculate an average rate for a shorter period such as a week. Whatever period is chosen, materiality is likely to be an important consideration.

7.18 Depending on the circumstances, a company may use an actual average rate or an estimated average rate. An actual average rate is likely to be used where there is some delay between the date when the transactions occurred and the date when they are recorded. In other situations, it may be necessary for a company to use an estimated average rate for a period rather than wait for the period to end in order to calculate an actual average rate. This estimate may be based on the average of daily exchange rates for the previous period or the closing rate of the previous period. Whichever basis is used, it will be necessary to ensure than the estimated average rate is a close approximation of the actual rates prevailing during the period. If it is not, the rate should be revised accordingly.

Dual rates or suspension of rates

7.19 Some countries may operate more than one exchange rate. In that situation, the question arises as to which rate should be used to translate and record the transaction. SSAP 20 provides no guidance. Obviously, where there is a marginal difference between the two rates, it does not matter which rate is used. But where the difference is considered to be significant, we suggest that companies should consider following the relevant provision in FRS 23. This states that *"when several exchange rates are available, the rate used is that at which the future cash flows represented by the transaction or balance could have been settled if those cash flows had occurred at the measurement date"*. In some situations, it may be prudent to use the less favourable rate.

Example – Use of an autonomous rate

The Nigerian budget in January 1995 made changes to the foreign exchange market. From that date all commercial foreign exchange transactions take place at the autonomous rate of exchange (say Niara 65 to US$1) rather than at the official rate of exchange (say Niara 22 to US$ 1). This means that all imports and exports and remittances of profits, dividends and technical services and other fees will take place at the autonomous rate of exchange.

Therefore, when retranslating foreign exchange transactions and monetary amounts receivable and payable in the financial statements of an individual company, the autonomous rate rather than the official rate of exchange should be used. This would also apply to the translation of the results and net assets of Nigerian subsidiary companies in consolidated financial statements.

7.20 From time to time, countries may experience economic conditions that affect the free-market convertibility of the local currency. As a result, the exchangeability between two currencies may be temporarily lacking at the transaction date or a subsequent balance sheet date. SSAP 20 is silent on this point, but FRS 23 requires companies to use the rate on the first subsequent date at which exchanges could be made.

[The next paragraph is 7.23.]

Treatment of monetary items

7.23 Monetary items, as the name implies, are money held and amounts to be received or paid in money. [SSAP 20 para 44]. Obvious examples include cash and bank balances, loans, debtors and creditors. Monetary items can be categorised as short term or long term. Short-term monetary items are those that fall due within one year of the balance sheet date and long-term monetary items are those that fall due more than one year after the balance sheet date.

7.24 SSAP 20 requires that a company should translate its monetary assets and liabilities denominated in foreign currencies outstanding at the end of the year using the closing rate. [SSAP 20 para 48]. An example is given in Table 7.1. The closing rate is the exchange rate for spot transactions ruling at the balance sheet date and is the mean of the buying rate and the selling rate at the close of business on the day for which the rate is to be ascertained. [SSAP 20 para 41]. Where, however, the rate of exchange is fixed under the terms of the relevant contract, the company should use that rate. Where an outstanding trading transaction is covered by a related or matching forward contract, the rate specified in that contract may be used. [SSAP 20 para 48]. An example of a company that uses forward contracted rates is given in Table 7.2 below.

Table 7.2 — BAE SYSTEMS plc — Annual Report — 31 December 2002

Notes to the accounts

1 Accounting Policies (extract)

Foreign currencies
Transactions in overseas currencies are translated at the exchange rate ruling at the date of the transaction or, where forward cover contracts have been arranged, at the contracted rates. Monetary assets and liabilities denominated in foreign currencies are retranslated at the exchange rates ruling at the balance sheet date or at a contracted rate if applicable and any exchange differences arising are taken to the profit and loss account.

For consolidation purposes the assets and liabilities of overseas subsidiary undertakings and joint ventures are translated at the closing exchange rates. Profit and loss accounts of such undertakings are consolidated at the average rates of exchange during the year. Exchange differences arising on foreign currency net investments are taken to reserves.

Treatment of non-monetary items

7.24.1 Non-monetary items are all items other than monetary items. Non-monetary items are generally physical in nature, such as properties, plant and equipment, stocks and equity investments. In some instances, however, it may not be readily apparent whether an item should be regarded as a monetary item or a non-monetary item. The ambiguity can usually be resolved if it is considered whether the item represents an amount to be received or paid in money, in which case it would fall to be treated as a monetary item. Otherwise, it should be treated as a non-monetary item.

7.24.2 SSAP 20 requires that where a non-monetary item has been translated at the rate ruling when it was originally recorded, no subsequent translation of the asset is normally required [SSAP 20 para 47]. This effectively means that such assets are recorded at historical cost. However, in certain circumstances, this treatment will not apply to foreign equity investments. These special circumstances are considered from paragraph 7.80 below.

Example – Foreign exchange gains and losses on investment in preference shares

A UK company, which prepares its financial statements in sterling, has purchased 6% preference shares in an unrelated company for US$5 million. It has financed the investment from cash, converted to US$ at the spot rate. It intends to hold the investment for the long-term, but is unsure whether it should retranslate the preference shares at each year end.

The accounting treatment would depend on whether the preference share investment should be classified as a monetary or a non-monetary asset. This will depend on the nature and terms of the preference shares. The two scenarios are considered below.

(a) Preference shares treated as a monetary asset

SSAP 20, 'Foreign currency translation', defines monetary items as 'money held and amounts to be received or paid in money'. To determine this, the terms of the preference shares and the individual facts and circumstances should be considered. If the terms indicate that the preferences shares rank for a fixed amount of dividends and are redeemable, then clearly they meet the definition of a monetary asset. Such investments should initially be recorded at the spot rate at the date of purchase and retranslated at each balance sheet date, with the exchange gains and losses recognised in the profit and loss account.

(b) Preference shares treated as a non-monetary asset

However, if the terms indicate that the shares are non-redeemable then clearly they cannot be classed as 'amounts to be received in money' and, therefore, should be treated as non-monetary assets. These should not be retranslated if the company applies the historical cost convention. However, if the company adopts a policy of regular revaluation of its foreign currency non-monetary investments under the alternative accounting rules, then the revaluation movements are recognised in the statement of total recognised gains and losses.

Treatment of exchange gains and losses

7.25 An exchange gain or loss will arise if a currency transaction is settled during an accounting period at an exchange rate which differs from the rate used when the transaction was initially recorded, or, where appropriate, the rate that was used at the last balance sheet date. An exchange gain or loss will also arise on unsettled transactions if the rate of exchange used at the balance sheet date differs from that used previously. All exchange gains and losses, whether arising on settled transactions or on unsettled transactions, should be reported as part of the profit or loss for the year from ordinary activities. There are two exceptions to this rule. An exchange difference on a currency transaction that is itself treated as an extraordinary item should be included as part of that item, but such items will be very rare following the issue of FRS 3, 'Reporting financial performance'. The other exception is that, in the special circumstances considered further from paragraph 7.79, exchange gains and losses arising, where a foreign currency borrowing is used to hedge a foreign equity investment, may be taken to the STRGL. The classification of exchange differences in the profit and loss account formats is dealt with in paragraph 7.147.

Settled transactions

7.26 Where a transaction is *settled* at an exchange rate that differs from the rate used when the transaction was initially recorded, the exchange difference will be recognised in the profit and loss account of the period in which the settlement takes place. The rationale for this treatment is that, as the exchange difference will have been reflected in the cash flow at the time of the settlement, it is appropriate to recognise such exchange differences as part of the profit or loss for that year.

Example 1 – Purchase of plant in a foreign currency with settlement after transaction date

In March 20X4, a UK company purchases plant for use in the UK from a Danish company for DK 425,000. At the date the company purchases the plant, the exchange rate is £1 = DK 8.50. The purchase price is to be settled in three months time, although delivery is made immediately. The UK company should record the plant in its accounting records at £50,000. The company will not need to translate the plant again. At the settlement date, the exchange rate is £1 = DK 8.75 so the actual amount the UK company pays is £48,571. The company should include the gain on exchange of £1,429 (that is, £50,000 — £48,571) in arriving at its profit or loss on ordinary activities.

Example 2 – Purchase of plant at a contracted foreign currency rate

In March 20X4, a UK company purchases plant for use in the UK from a Canadian company for C$ 750,000. The transaction is contracted to be settled at £1 = C$ 2.50. The UK company should record the plant in its accounting records at £300,000. The company will not need to translate the plant again, and no exchange differences will arise.

Example 3 – Sales transaction in foreign currency with a specific related forward cover contract

In January 20X5, a UK company sells goods to an Australian company for A$ 405,000. The Australian company pays for the goods in March 20X5. At the time of the sale, the exchange rate is £1 = A$ 2.7, and at the time of the payment, the exchange rate is £1 = A$ 2.9. The UK company, however, covers the transaction by a matching forward contract to sell Australian Dollars. The exchange rate specified in the forward contract is £1 = A$ 2.75. The relevant translations are as follows:

A$ 405,000 at A$ 2.7 (transaction rate) =	£150,000
A$ 405,000 at A$ 2.9 (settlement rate) =	£139,655
A$ 405,000 at A$ 2.75 (forward contract rate) =	£147,273

The UK company could record the sale in one of the following ways:

- It could record the sale and the debtor at £150,000, that is, at the exchange rate ruling at the date of the sale. Because the company has entered into a matching forward contract, the amount received from the debtor is A$ 405,000 which is sold for £147,273. Consequently, the company would have a loss on exchange on the transaction of £2,727 (that is, £150,000 — £147,273) to include in its profit or loss on ordinary activities.

- It could record the sale and the debtor at £147,273, that is, at the exchange rate specified in the matching forward contract. Because the company has entered into a matching forward contract, the amount receivable and ultimately received from the debtor is £147,273. Consequently, the company would not recognise a loss on exchange on the transaction.

Whichever method the company chooses to record the sale (that has been settled in the same period), its profit or loss on ordinary activities will be the same.

It should be noted that under FRS 23 neither of the above treatments are permitted. Under FRS 23, the sale and receivable would be recorded at the transaction rate. The settlement of the debtor would be accounted for separately from the forward contract. Consequently, the company would have an exchange loss on the transaction of £10,345 (that is £150,000 — £139,655). FRS 26 would govern the accounting for the forward contract. FRS 26 would require that the contract is initially measured at cost (usually zero) and subsequently at its fair value immediately before settlement. Assuming the transaction was entered into and settled in the same period the movement in carrying value of the forward contract would be recorded in the profit and loss account where it would offset the exchange loss on the transaction. The detailed requirements of FRS 23 are considered in the Annex to this chapter while those of FRS 26 are considered in chapter 6.

Forward contracts are dealt with in more detail from paragraph 7.125.

Example 4 – Translation of foreign currency convertible loan stock

A company has a convertible loan stock in issue, which is denominated in dollars. Each year it is retranslated at closing rate and exchange differences are charged to the profit and loss account. On conversion the price of the shares to be issued is fixed and so is the rate of exchange (which is the rate prevailing when the loan stock was originally issued). The rate of exchange for conversion is different from the rate of exchange used for the translation of the loan stock in the balance sheet immediately prior to conversion. The difference is equal to the net exchange gains and losses charged over the period in which the loan stock has been in issue. Should these differences be written back to profit and loss account on conversion?

We consider that the consideration for the issue of the shares is the amount at which the loan stock is stated in the balance sheet immediately prior to conversion. This is despite the fact that there is a fixed rate of exchange stipulated in the conversion terms.

The net exchange gains or losses that have been charged to profit and loss in the past are properly to be regarded as part of the cost of financing the loan stock. Together with the interest paid they constitute the total cost of finance.

Even if legally the exchange gains or losses are not required to be taken to share premium they should be taken to an undistributable reserve as, in economic terms, the current sterling carrying value (that is, dollars at closing rate) is the equity's opportunity cost. The pre-determined rate specified in the contract is not relevant. (We consider that this is also consistent with FRS 4, 'Capital instruments').

Unsettled transactions

7.27 Where the transaction remains *outstanding* at the balance sheet date, an exchange difference arises as a consequence of recording the foreign currency transaction at the rate ruling at the date of the transaction (or when it was translated at a previous balance sheet date) and the subsequent retranslation to the rate ruling at the balance sheet date. Such exchange differences arise on monetary items (for example, foreign currency loans, debtors and creditors). To the extent that exchange differences relate to short-term monetary items, they will soon be reflected in cash flows and, therefore, they should be reported as part of the profit or loss for the year from ordinary activities.

Example –Treatment of an unsettled foreign creditor at balance sheet date

In January 20X4, a UK company purchases equipment from an overseas company for FC 11,250,000 (FC being a fictional currency). At the date the company takes delivery of the equipment, the exchange rate is £1 = FC 225. Therefore, the company initially records both the equipment and the creditor at £50,000 (FC 11,250,000 @ 225). At 31 March 20X4, the balance sheet date, the creditor is still outstanding. No further translation of the equipment is necessary, but the creditor should be retranslated using the rate of exchange at the balance sheet date, which is £1 = FC 240. The company should include the gain on exchange of £3,125 (that is, £50,000 — £46,875) in its profit or loss on ordinary activities.

7.28 Where exchange differences arise on the retranslation of unsettled long-term monetary items, SSAP 20 requires that these exchange differences should be reported as part of the profit or loss for the year on ordinary activities, even though they may not be reflected in cash flows for a considerable time. SSAP 20 argues that the treatment of these long-term items on a simple cash movements basis would be inconsistent with the accruals concept and goes on to state:

> *"Exchange gains on unsettled transactions can be determined at the balance sheet date no less objectively than exchange losses; deferring the gains whilst recognising the losses would not only be illogical by denying in effect that any favourable movement in exchange rates had occurred but would also inhibit fair measurement of the performance of the enterprise in the year. In particular, this symmetry of treatment recognises that there will probably be some interaction between currency movements and interest rates and reflects more accurately in the profit and loss account the true results of currency involvement."* [SSAP 20 para 10].

7.29 Paragraph 12 of Schedule 4 to the Act states that *"only profits realised at the balance sheet date shall be included in the profit and loss account"*. Paragraph 65 of SSAP 20 implies that exchange gains that arise on long-term monetary items are not realised profits, but SSAP 20 still requires them to be recognised in the profit and loss account, which would involve a departure from paragraph 12 of Schedule 4. However, as discussed in paragraph 7.151, in March 2003, ICAEW and ICAS issued guidance in Tech 7/03, 'Guidance on the determination of realised profits and losses in the context of distributions under the Companies Act 1985'. This states that a profit is realised where it arises from the translation of a monetary asset which comprises qualifying consideration, or a liability denominated in a foreign currency. [Tech 7/03 para 16]. Consequently, unless there are doubts as to the convertibility or marketability of the currency in question (see below), foreign exchange profits arising on the retranslation of monetary items are realised, irrespective of the maturity date of the monetary item. [Tech 7/03 para 34]. The impact of foreign currency translation on distributable profits is dealt with from paragraph 7.149.

7.30 In certain exceptional situations, however, a company may have doubts as to either the convertibility or the marketability of the currency of a long-term monetary item outstanding at the end of the year. Where this is so, on the grounds of prudence such a company should restrict the amount of any gain (or the amount by which any gain exceeds past exchange losses on the same item) that it recognises in its profit and loss account. [SSAP 20 para 50].

7.31 Doubts as to convertibility may arise if, for example, a UK company makes a long-term currency loan to, say, an overseas supplier, but restrictions on the remittance of funds are imposed by the overseas country sometime prior to the maturity of the loan. Such restrictions would probably arise if there is political upheaval or severe exchange control regulations in the overseas country. In that situation, the company should consider the loan's realisable value in the light of such restrictions and limit any exchange gains arising on the retranslation that is taken to the profit and loss account. The following example illustrates this type of situation.

Example – Impact of convertibility of foreign currency on recognition of foreign exchange gains or losses

In April 20X4, company A, which is incorporated in the UK, used surplus currency to make a long-term loan of FC 20m to its overseas supplier. The loan was made when the exchange rate was £1 = FC 5.00. Initially, the loan would be translated and recorded in company A's books at £4m. The amount that company A will ultimately receive will depend on the rate of exchange ruling on the date when the loan is repaid.

At 31 March 20X5, company A's year end, the exchange rate is £1 = FC 4.00. If the loan of FC 20m was translated at this rate it would give an asset of £5m and an exchange gain of £1m. There are, however, doubts as to the convertibility of FC. Therefore, company A considers that, on the grounds of prudence, it should limit the gain so that the sterling value of the loan is shown at its present estimated realisable value of £4,500,000. Accordingly, company A restricts the exchange gain that it includes in its profit and loss account for the year ended 31 March 20X5 to £500,000.

Transactions between group companies

7.32 Where transactions take place between companies in a group, exchange differences are likely to arise in one or other company since the transaction is likely to be carried out in the local currency of one of the companies in question. SSAP 20 requires that exchange gains and losses arising on such transactions should normally be reported in the individual company's financial statements as part of the profit or loss for the year in the same way as gains and losses arising from transactions with third parties. [SSAP 20 para 12].

The consolidation stage

Introduction

7.33 Translation of foreign currency financial statements is necessary so that the financial statements of overseas subsidiaries may be consolidated with the holding company's sterling financial statements. The method of translation in consolidated financial statements should be such as to reflect the financial and other operational relationships that exist between the investing company and its foreign enterprises. In this context, a foreign enterprise includes not only a foreign subsidiary, but also an associated company or branch whose operations are based in a currency other than that of the investing company or whose assets and liabilities are denominated mainly in a foreign currency. [SSAP 20 para 36].

7.34 The standard requires that, normally, a company should use the 'closing rate/net investment' method for translating the financial statements of its foreign enterprises. However, where the operations of the foreign enterprises are direct extensions of the investing company's trade, the temporal method should be used. [SSAP 20 para 14].

Closing rate/net investment method

7.35 The closing rate/net investment method is based on the premise that a foreign enterprise generally operates as a separate or quasi-independent entity. Such an entity normally conducts its day to day affairs in its local currency, is likely to be financed wholly or partly by local currency borrowings, and is not normally dependent on the investing company's reporting currency. If a foreign enterprise is relatively independent then what is at risk from the investing company's perspective is the net worth of the investment rather than the individual assets and liabilities of that enterprise. The investing company may or may not receive regular dividend income, but the net investment remains until the business is liquidated or the investment is sold.

7.36 Accordingly, it is important to retain the financial and operational relationships existing in the foreign entity's financial statements prior to translation in order to produce results that are meaningful at the consolidation stage. Use of a constant rate of exchange for all items maintains such a relationship in the retranslated financial statements of the reporting currency as existed in the foreign currency financial statements. Therefore, for example, fixed assets would be the same proportion of long-term liabilities.

7.37 This method is widely supported both in the UK and internationally.

7.38 Proponents of the closing rate/net investment method claim that the method acknowledges the fact that operations which are conducted in currencies and in economic environments other than those of the parent are essentially different from the parent's own operations. Accordingly, it clearly reflects the true economic facts, because stating all items at the closing rate presents the foreign enterprise's true earnings at that time, particularly since from the investor's point of view the only real earnings are those that can actually be distributed. The translation of the historical cost financial statements at closing rates is merely a restatement of assets and liabilities for the purposes of consolidation and does not constitute a revaluation.

7.39 Under the closing rate/net investment method:

- All items in a foreign subsidiary's balance sheet at the year end should be translated at the closing rate of exchange into the parent's reporting currency.
- On consolidation, the exchange differences that arise when the parent retranslates its opening net investments in the foreign subsidiary to the closing rate should be treated as a movement on consolidated reserves. Exchange differences may also arise where the closing rate differs from that ruling on the date of a subsequent capital injection (or reduction). Such

exchange differences should also be dealt with as a movement in reserves. The rationale for taking such exchange differences to reserves is explained in paragraph 19 of SSAP 20, which states:

> *"If exchange differences arising from the retranslation of a company's net investment in its foreign enterprise were introduced into the profit and loss account, the results from trading operations, as shown in the local currency financial statements, would be distorted. Such differences may result from many factors unrelated to the trading performance or financial operations of the foreign enterprise; in particular, they do not represent or measure changes in actual or prospective cash flows. It is therefore inappropriate to regard them as profits or losses and they should be dealt with as adjustments to reserves."*

SSAP 20, unlike FRS 23, does not require companies to maintain a separate reserve for exchange differences, but some companies do so.

- The profit and loss account of a foreign subsidiary may be translated either at the closing rate or at an average rate for the period. Although the use of a closing rate is more likely to achieve the objective of translation, stated in paragraph 7.12.1 above, of reflecting the financial results and relationships as measured in the foreign currency financial statements prior to translation, the use of an average rate reflects more fairly the profits or losses and cash flows as they accrue to the group throughout the period. Therefore, the standard permits the use of either method, provided that the one selected is applied consistently from period to period. [SSAP 20 para 17]. It should be noted that FRS 23 does not permit the use of closing rate. SSAP 20 requires that where the average rate is used, the company should record, as a movement on consolidated reserves, the difference between translating the profit and loss account at the average rate and translating it at the closing rate. [SSAP 20 para 54].

An example of a company that uses the closing rate/net investment method is given in Table 7.4 below.

Table 7.4 — The Peninsular and Oriental Steam Navigation Company — Annual Report and Accounts — 31 December 2000

Accounting Policies (extract)

Foreign currencies
Transactions in foreign currencies are recorded at the rate of exchange ruling at the date of the transaction. Profits and losses of subsidiaries, branches joint ventures and associates which have currencies of operation other than sterling are translated into sterling at average rates of exchange except for material exceptional items which are translated at the rate ruling on the date of transaction. Assets and liabilities denominated in foreign currencies are translated at the year end exchange rates.

> Exchange differences arising from the retranslation of the opening net assets of subsidiaries, branches joint ventures and associates which have currencies of operation other than sterling and any related loans are taken to reserves together with the differences arising when the profit and loss accounts are translated at average rates and compared with rates ruling at the year end. Other exchange differences are taken to the profit and loss account.

7.40 The net investment which a company has in a foreign enterprise is its effective equity stake and comprises its proportion of such foreign enterprise's net assets; in appropriate circumstances, intra-group loans and other deferred trading balances may be regarded as part of the effective equity stake. [SSAP 20 para 43]. It follows from the above definition that the net investment is the amount at which the group states the net assets of the subsidiary in the consolidated balance sheet. It is not (for example) the amount at which the net assets are recorded in the subsidiary's financial statements which may be different if the group has restated the assets at fair value at the time of acquisition. Nor is it the market value of the foreign subsidiary.

Illustration of the closing rate/net investment method

7.41 The closing rate/net investment method is illustrated by the following example.

Example – Use of the closing rate/net investment method

Company A, a UK company, whose accounting period ended on 30 September 20X4, has a wholly-owned US subsidiary, S Corporation, which was acquired for US$ 500,000 on 30 September 20X3. The fair value of the net assets at the date of acquisition was US$ 400,000. The exchange rate at 30 September 20X3 and 20X4 was £1 = US$ 2.0 and £1 = US$ 1.5 respectively. The weighted average rate for the year ended 30 September 20X4 was £1 = US$ 1.65.

The summarised profit and loss account of S Corporation for the year ended 30 September 20X4 and the summarised balance sheets at 30 September 20X3 and 20X4 in dollars and sterling equivalents, are as follows:

S Corporation: Profit and loss account for the year ended 30 September 20X4

		Closing rate	Average rate
	$'000	£'000	£'000
Exchange rate £1 =		$1.50	$1.65
Operating profit	135	90.0	81.8
Interest paid	(15)	(10.0)	(9.0)
Profit before taxation	120	80.0	72.8
Taxation	(30)	(20.0)	(18.2)
Profit after taxation	90	60.0	54.6
Dividends paid in the year	(14)	(9.3)	(8.5)
Retained profit	76	50.7	46.1

Balance sheets of S Corporation

	20X4 $'000	20X3 $'000	20X4 £'000 P&L closing	20X4 £'000 P&L average	20X3 £'000
Closing exchange rate £1 =			$1.50	$1.50	$2.00
Fixed assets:					
Cost (20X4 additions: $30)	255	225	170.0	170.0	112.5
Depreciation (20X4 charge: $53)	98	45	65.3	65.3	22.5
Net book value	157	180	104.7	104.7	90.0
Current assets:					
Stocks	174	126	116.0	116.0	63.0
Debtors	210	145	140.0	140.0	72.5
Cash at bank	240	210	160.0	160.0	105.0
	624	481	416.0	416.0	240.5
Current liabilities:					
Trade creditors	125	113	83.3	83.3	56.5
Taxation	30	18	20.0	20.0	9.0
	155	131	103.3	103.3	65.5
Net current assets	469	350	312.7	312.7	175.0
Loan stock	150	130	100.0	100.0	65.0
Net assets	476	400	317.4	317.4	200.0
Share capital	200	200	100.0	100.0	100.0
Retained profits	276	200	217.4	217.4	100.0
	476	400	317.4	317.4	200.0

The analysis of retained profits under the closing rate and the average rate method is as follows:

	$'000	Closing rate £'000	Average rate £'000
Exchange rate £1 =		$1.50	$1.65
Pre-acquisition profit brought forward	200	100.0	100.0
Profit for the year	76	50.7	46.1
Exchange difference	–	66.7	71.3
Retained profits	276	217.4	217.4
Analysis of exchange difference:			
Arising on retranslation of opening net investments:			
at opening rate — $400,000 @ $2 = £1		200.0	200.0
at closing rate — $400,000 @ $1.5 = £1		266.7	266.7
Exchange gain on net investment		66.7	66.7
Exchange gain arising from translating profit and loss account at average rate (£46.1) rather than closing rate (£50.7)		–	4.6
Total exchange difference		66.7	71.3

Note: On consolidation, the above exchange differences will be included in consolidated reserves and shown in the statement of total recognised gains and losses (STRGL). This requirement is the same as that in FRS 23. However, unlike SSAP 20, FRS 23 requires that on disposal of the foreign entity the cumulative amount of exchange differences, which have been recognised in the STRGL in relation to that entity, should be 'recycled' through the profit and loss account. [FRS 23 para 48].

It is further assumed that parent company A does not trade on its own and its only income is dividends received from S Corporation. The summarised balance sheets of company A at 30 September 20X3 and 20X4 are as follows:

Company A — Balance Sheets	20X4 £'000	20X3 £'000
Investments in subsidiary ($500,000 @ 2.0)	250	250
Cash	208	200
Net assets	458	450
Share capital	450	450
P&L account (dividend received: $14,000 @ 1.75*)	8	–
	458	450

* actual rate on date dividend received

Where company A uses the closing rate/net investment method, it may use either the closing rate or the average rate for translating the results of S Corporation. The summarised consolidated profit and loss account for the year ended 30 September 20X4 drawn up on the two bases and the summarised consolidated balance sheet at that date are as follows:

Consolidated profit and loss account for the year ended 30 September 20X4

	Closing rate	Average rate
	£'000	£'000
Operating profit of S Corporation	90.0	81.8
Operating profit of company A	8.0	8.0
	98.0	89.8
Elimination of inter company dividend*	(9.3)	(8.5)
Net operating profit	88.7	81.3
Interest paid	(10.0)	(9.0)
Profit before taxation	78.7	72.3
Taxation	(20.0)	(18.2)
Retained profit	58.7	54.1

* The exchange difference arising on the inter-company dividend, being the difference between the dividend calculated at the date of receipt and at the closing rate or at the average rate, is included in the profit and loss account.

Consolidated balance sheet at 30 September 20X4

	Closing rate	Average rate
	£'000	£'000
Fixed assets	104.7	104.7
Current assets:		
Stocks	116.0	116.0
Debtors	140.0	140.0
Cash (S Corporation £160; company A £208)	368.0	368.0
	624.0	624.0
Current liabilities:		
Trade creditors	83.3	83.3
Taxation	20.0	20.0
	103.3	103.3
Net current assets	520.7	520.7
Loan stock	100.0	100.0
Net assets	525.4	525.4
Share capital	450.0	450.0
Reserves:		
Retained profit	58.7	54.1
Exchange difference on opening net assets	66.7	66.7
Exchange difference on P&L account	–	4.6
Goodwill written off (pre — FRS 10) ($100,000 @ 2.0)	(50.0)	(50.0)
	525.4	525.4

In the above illustration goodwill has been translated at the rate ruling on the date of acquisition on the grounds that it arises only on consolidation and is not part of the net assets of the foreign enterprise. An alternative treatment is to regard the goodwill as a currency asset which is retranslated at the closing rate. In this situation, an exchange difference would arise on the opening net investment including the goodwill. The alternative treatment, regarding goodwill as a currency asset, is consistent with FRS 10 which no longer permits goodwill to be written off directly to reserves as it has been in the above illustration (see further para 7.78). Furthermore, the alternative treatment is the method required by FRS 23, 'The effects of changes in foreign exchange rates'.

7.41.1 The above illustration included a wholly-owned subsidiary. Where the parent holds less than 100 per cent of the issued share capital, the minority's share of the assets and liabilities should also be included at year end rate. FRS 2, 'Accounting for subsidiary undertakings', states in paragraph 80 that the effect of the existence of minority interests on the returns to investors in the parent undertaking is best reflected by presenting the net identifiable assets attributable to minority interests on the same basis as those attributable to group interests. Accordingly, the minority's share of the exchange difference should be allocated to them in the balance sheet and only the amount of the exchange difference attributable to the group should be shown in the statement of total recognised gains and losses.

7.41.2 If a foreign subsidiary holds monetary assets such as cash in the currency of the parent, for example, sterling, such balances will be translated to the subsidiary's local currency under SSAP 20 at the year end. This will result in an exchange difference in the overseas subsidiary's financial statements, which will be taken to the profit and loss account of the overseas subsidiary. If this subsidiary is consolidated using the closing rate method, the exchange difference reported in the subsidiary's profit and loss account will be translated into sterling and remain in the consolidated profit and loss account. In addition, an equal and opposite exchange difference attributable to the sterling cash balance arising as part of the retranslation of the opening net assets (which includes the sterling cash balance) of the overseas subsidiary will also be included in reserves.

The temporal method

7.42 As stated in paragraph 7.34 above, SSAP 20 acknowledges that the use of the closing rate/net investment method may not be appropriate in certain circumstances. The circumstances relate to situations where the foreign enterprise's operations are so closely interlinked with those of the investing company that it no longer seems appropriate to regard the foreign currency as being that on which the foreign enterprise is dependent. In such a situation, the foreign enterprise's local currency is deemed to be that of the investing company and the temporal method should be used for translating the foreign enterprise's financial statements. Under the temporal method all of the foreign enterprise's transactions are treated as if they had been entered into by the investing company itself and all of the foreign enterprise's assets and liabilities are treated as though they belong directly to the investing company.

7.43 SSAP 20 acknowledges that it is not possible to select one factor which would indicate the temporal method should be used. All available evidence must be considered in determining which currency is the local currency (referred to in FRS 23 as the 'functional currency') of each foreign enterprise respectively.

7.44 The standard specifies a number of factors that need to be taken into consideration in determining the dominant currency. The factors, which are listed below, should be considered both individually and collectively before deciding on the appropriate method of translation. In those situations, where the indicators are mixed and the dominant currency is not obvious, considerable management judgment will be required.

- The extent to which the cash flows of the enterprise have a direct impact upon those of the investing company, for example, whether there is regular and frequent transfer of funds between the two companies or whether there are only occasional remittances of dividends.
- The extent to which the functioning of the enterprise is dependent directly upon the investing company, for example, whether major decisions are taken by the parent company, whether pricing decisions are based on local competition and costs or are part of a worldwide decision process.
- The currency in which the majority of the trading transactions are completed, for example, the sales market is mostly in the parent's country of origin or sales invoices are denominated in the parent's currency.
- The major currency to which the operation is exposed in its financing structure, for example whether the operation is dependent on finance raised locally or from the parent.

[SSAP 20 para 23].

7.45 Examples of situations where the temporal method may be appropriate are where the foreign enterprise:

- Acts as a selling agency receiving stocks of goods from the receiving company and remitting the proceeds back to the company.
- Produces a raw material or manufactures parts or sub-assemblies which are then shipped to the investing company for inclusion in its own products.
- Is located overseas for tax, exchange control or similar reasons to act as a means of raising finance for other companies in the group.

[SSAP 20 para 24].

It should be noted that the above are extreme situations where the use of the temporal method is rather obvious. In practice, this will rarely be so and determining the local currency will need to be made in the light of the above factors and the management's judgement.

Example – Subsidiary used for depositing surplus cash

A group has surplus cash and is investing it by way of subscription for shares denominated in Yen, in a newly formed subsidiary, in say, the Channel Islands. The subsidiary will place the money on deposit (in Yen) and will have no other business, nor does the group have any Yen denominated activities. When preparing consolidated financial statements should the group account for the subsidiary's net assets using the temporal method or the closing rate method under SSAP 20? At first sight it would appear that the subsidiary would qualify under SSAP 20 as a foreign enterprise, as the definition in SSAP 20 implies that a subsidiary whose assets and liabilities are in a foreign currency is a foreign enterprise. However, on closer inspection it appears that the subsidiary's only business is to hold the deposit. Indeed, the parent entity itself could have made the investment directly in Yen. Therefore, the temporal method should be used.

7.46 SSAP 20 states that the mechanics of the temporal method are identical to those used in preparing the financial statements of an individual company. [SSAP 20 para 22]. This is probably true to a degree, but applying this method in practice requires detailed and additional record keeping that is not required under the closing rate method and is far more complicated as illustrated in the example below. The similarity of the temporal method with the method used in individual financial statements implies that under the temporal method:

- All transactions should be translated at the rate ruling at the transaction date or at an average rate for the period if this is not materially different.
- Non-monetary items, such as fixed assets and stocks measured at historical cost or valuation, are translated at the exchange rate in effect at the date to which the historical cost or valuation pertains. They are not retranslated at each balance sheet date.
- Monetary items, whether short-term or long-term, are translated using the closing rate at the balance sheet date.
- All items in the profit and loss account are translated at the historical rate. An average rate may be used where it is not materially different from the rate ruling at the transaction date, except for depreciation and stocks which must be included at historical rate.
- All exchange gains and losses including those arising on the retranslation of opening monetary items should be taken to the profit and loss account for the year as part of the profit or loss from ordinary operations.

[The next paragraph is 7.48.]

Illustration of the temporal method

7.48 The way in which the temporal method is used in practice is illustrated by the following example.

Example – Use of the temporal method

The facts and the data are the same as that used in the closing rate method in paragraph 7.41 above, except that further details on exchange rates at the dates of acquisition of fixed assets and stocks are given, together with an analysis of operating profit.

Company A, a UK company, whose accounting period ended on 30 September 20X4, has a wholly-owned US subsidiary, S corporation, that was acquired for US$ 500,000 on 30 September 20X3. The fair value of the net assets at the date of acquisition was US$ 400,000. The exchange rate at 30 September 20X3 and 20X4 was £1 = US$ 2.0 and £1 = US$ 1.5 respectively. The weighted average rate for the year ended 30 September 20X4 was £1 = US$ 1.65.

S Corporation: Profit and loss account for the year ended 30 September 20X4

	$'000	Exchange rate	£'000
Sales	3,760	Average — $1.65	2,278.8
Opening stock	126	Historical — $2.0	63.0
Purchases	3,620	Average — $1.65	2,193.9
Closing stock	(174)	Historical — $1.6	(108.8)
Cost of sales	3,572		2,148.1
Gross profit	188		130.7
Depreciation	53	Historical — $2.0/1.85*	26.8
Operating profit	135		103.9
Interest paid	(15)	Average — $1.65	(9.1)
Exchange gain	–	Balance	16.8
Profit before taxation	120		111.6
Taxation	(30)	Average — $1.65	(18.2)
Profit after taxation	90		93.4
Dividends paid in the year	(14)	Actual	(8.5)
Retained profit	76		84.9

* The charge for depreciation is translated as follows; on original assets ($45,000 @ 2 = £22,500) and on additions ($8,000 @ 1.85 = £4,300) = £26,800.

Balance sheets of S Corporation

	19X4 $'000	Exchange Rate	19X4 £'000	19X3 $'000	Exchange Rate	19X3 £'000
Fixed assets:						
Cost (i)	255	$2.0/1.85	128.7	225	$2.0	112.5
Depreciation (ii)	98	$2.0/1.85	49.3	45	$2.0	22.5
Net book value	157		79.4	180		90.0
Current assets:						
Stocks	174	$1.6	108.8	126	$2.0	63.0
Debtors	210	$1.5	140.0	145	$2.0	72.5
Cash at bank	240	$1.5	160.0	210	$2.0	105.0
	624		408.8	481		240.5

Current liabilities:						
Trade creditors	125	$1.5	83.3	113	$2.0	56.5
Taxation	30	$1.5	20.0	18	$2.0	9.0
	155		103.3	131		65.5
Net current assets	469		305.5	350		175.0
	626		384.9	530		265.0
Loan stock	150	$1.5	100.0	130	$2.0	65.0
Net assets	476		284.9	400		200.0
Share capital	200	$2.0	100.0	200	$2.0	100.0
Retained profits	276	Balance	184.9	200	Balance	100.0
	476		284.9	400		200.0

(i) Fixed assets are translated at the historical rate which, in this example, will be the exchange rate at the date of acquisition (£1 = $2.0) or, for subsequent additions, the actual rate at the transaction date (say £1 = $1.85). The translated amount at 30 September 20X4 is ($225,000 @ 2.0 = £112,500) + ($30,000 @ 1.85 = £16,200) = £128,700.

(ii) Cumulative depreciation is translated as follows; on original assets ($90,000 @ 2.0 = £45,000) and on additions ($8,000 @ 1.85 = £4,300) = £49,300.

Analysis of exchange difference included in the profit and loss account

	Opening monetary items $'000	Closing monetary items $'000
Debtors	145	210
Cash at bank	210	240
Trade creditors	(113)	(125)
Taxation	(18)	(30)
Loan stock	(130)	(150)
	(94)	(145)
Opening monetary items at opening rate — $94 @ $2	47.0	
Opening monetary item at closing rate — $94 @ $1.5	62.7	15.7
Increase in monetary items at closing rate — $51 @ $1.5	34.0	
Increase in monetary items at average rate — $51 @ $1.65	30.9	3.1
Exchange gain		18.8
Exchange difference arising on acquisition of fixed asset:		
Cash outflow on non-monetary items at actual rate $30 @ 1.85	16.2	
Cash outflow on non-monetary items at average rate $30 @ 1.65	18.2	
Exchange loss		(2.0)
Total exchange difference included in profit and loss account		16.8

It is further assumed that parent company A does not trade on its own and its only income is dividends received from S Corporation. The summarised balance sheets of company A at 30 September 20X3 and 20X4 are as follows:

Company A — Balance Sheets	20X4 £'000	20X3 £'000
Investments in subsidiary ($500,000 @ 2.0)	250	250
Cash	208	200
Net assets	458	450
Share capital	450	450
P&L account (dividend received: $14,000 @ 1.75*)	8	–
	458	450

* actual rate on date dividend received

The summarised consolidated profit and loss account for the year ended 30 September 20X4 drawn up on the temporal method and the summarised consolidated balance sheet at that date are as follows:

Consolidated profit and loss account for the year ended 30 September 20X4	£'000
Profit before taxation of S Corporation	111.6
Profit before taxation of company A	8.0
	119.6
Elimination of inter company dividend	(8.5)
Net operating profit	111.1
Taxation	(18.2)
Retained profit	92.9

Consolidated balance sheet at 30 September 20X4	Average rate £'000
Fixed assets	79.4
Current assets:	
Stocks	108.8
Debtors	140.0
Cash (S Corporation: £160; company A £208)	368.0
	616.8
Current liabilities:	
Trade creditors	83.3
Taxation	20.0
	103.3
Net current assets	513.5

Total assets less current liabilities	592.9
Loan stock	100.0
Net assets	492.9
Share capital	450.0
Reserves:	
Retained profit	92.9
Goodwill written off ($ 100,000 @ 2.0)	(50.0)
	492.9

Calculation of Goodwill	£'000
Consideration £500,000 @ 2.0	250.0
Net assets per balance sheet at date of acquisition	200.0
Goodwill written off (pre-FRS 10)	50.0

Foreign branches

7.49 Where a UK company conducts its foreign operations through a foreign branch, the translation method adopted would depend on the nature of the branch operations. A foreign branch may be a legally constituted enterprise located overseas or a group of assets and liabilities which are accounted for in foreign currencies. [SSAP 20 para 37]. Where the foreign branch operates as an extension of the company's trade and its cash flows have a direct impact upon those of the company, the temporal method described in paragraphs 7.42 to 7.48 above should be used. Where the foreign branch operates as a separate business possibly with local finance it should be accounted for under the closing rate/net investment method. [SSAP 20 para 25]. This applies in the individual entity financial statements in addition to the consolidated financial statements.

7.50 The following are examples of situations given in TR 504, 'Statement by the ASC on the publication of SSAP 20 — Foreign currency translation', where a foreign branch consists of a group of assets and liabilities that should be accounted for under the closing rate/net investment method:

- A hotel in France financed by borrowings in French francs (now euros).
- A ship or aircraft purchased in US dollars — with an associated loan in US dollars — which earns revenue and incurs expenses in US dollars.
- A foreign currency insurance operation where the liabilities are substantially covered by the holding of foreign currency assets.

7.51 In each of the above situations the local operation's currency is not the investing company's currency, since the branch operates as a separate business with local finance. Therefore, it is not appropriate to use the temporal method and the closing rate/net investment method should be used. The net investment is likely to be represented by a Head Office Account with the branch which should be translated using the closing rate. Any exchange differences arising from this retranslation process will be taken to reserves. An example of the accounting treatment followed by British Airways, which treats aircraft financed by foreign currency borrowings as a separate group of assets and liabilities is given in Table 7.5 below.

Table 7.5 — British Airways Plc — Report & Accounts — 31 March 2001

ACCOUNTING POLICIES

Tangible fixed assets (extract)

Aircraft which are financed in US dollars, either by loans, finance leases or hire purchase arrangements, are regarded together with the related assets and liabilities as a separate group of assets and liabilities and accounted for in US dollars. The amounts in US dollars are translated into sterling at rates ruling at the balance sheet date and the net differences arising from the translation of aircraft costs and related US dollar loans are taken to reserves.

7.51.1 This treatment would not be appropriate in cases where the income is earned in sterling. In such cases, the aircraft fails to qualify as a foreign branch and no corresponding gain or loss on the 'value' of the asset will be recognised. Therefore, the exchange movements on the foreign currency borrowings should be taken to the profit and loss account as they arise.

Other matters

7.52 This section deals with a number of important practical matters that arise at the consolidation stage, but which are not adequately dealt with in SSAP 20. Where relevant guidance or treatment in the UK is lacking or non-existent, appropriate references have been made to SFAS 52.

Determining the average rate

7.53 As stated in paragraph 7.39 above, SSAP 20 permits the profit and loss account of a foreign enterprise to be translated at an average rate for the period. SSAP 20 intentionally does not prescribe any definitive method of calculating the average rate on the grounds that the appropriate method may justifiably vary as between individual companies. However, the standard suggests that the determination of an appropriate average rate will include such matters as the company's internal accounting system, the extent of any seasonal trade variation and the desirability of using a weighting procedure. [SSAP 20 para 18].

7.54 There are a large number of methods under which an average rate can be calculated, ranging from simple monthly or quarterly averages to more sophisticated methods using appropriate weighting that reflects changes both in exchange rates and in the volume of business. Where the results of an overseas subsidiary are affected by seasonal factors, it may be necessary to weight the average exchange rate used in the calculation by applying an average rate for a shorter period than the whole year. But whatever method a company uses, it should calculate it by the method it considers is most appropriate to the foreign undertaking's circumstances. [SSAP 20 para 54]. An example of an averaging method employed in practice is given in Table 7.6 below.

Table 7.6 — The Boots Company PLC — Report and Accounts — 31 March 2001
Accounting Policies (extract)

Foreign currencies (extract)
The results and cash flows of overseas subsidiaries and the results of joint ventures are translated into sterling on an average exchange rate basis, weighted by the actual results of each month. Assets and liabilities including currency swaps are translated into sterling at the rates of exchange ruling at the balance sheet date.

7.55 In recent years many companies have moved away from using the closing rate to using an average rate for translating the profit and loss accounts of foreign enterprises. In fact, a large majority of companies now use the average rate method. The fact that the use of an average rate reflects more fairly the results and cash flows as they arise throughout the accounting period and permits aggregation of interim results appears to outweigh the relative simplicity of the closing rate method. Where a company decides to change from the closing rate method to the average rate method, the change in method represents a change of accounting policy and not a refinement of accounting policy in view of the conceptual difference between the two methods. As a consequence, a prior year adjustment is required in accordance with FRS 3 if the amounts involved are material. It may be reasonably easy for a company to justify changing its accounting policy to move to an average rate of exchange on the grounds that it is using a more appropriate method, particularly given that FRS 23 does not permit the use of the closing rate for translating the profit and loss accounts of foreign entities. However, it would generally be much harder for such a company to justify a move back to year end rates, especially where the move to an average rate has only occurred recently. An example of a company that changed from the closing rate method to the average rate method is given in Table 7.7 below.

Table 7.7 — The Peninsular and Oriental Steam Navigation Company — Annual report and accounts — 31 December 1994

Notes to the accounts

2 Change in accounting policy for foreign currencies

Profits and losses of subsidiaries, branches and associates which have currencies of operation other than sterling are translated into sterling at average rates of exchange except for material exceptional items which are translated at rates ruling on the date of transaction. Previously such profits and losses were translated at the exchange rates ruling at the year end. The accounting policy has been changed because the directors consider the new policy gives a fairer presentation of the Group's results and cash flows as they arise during the course of an accounting period. The effect of this change in accounting policy on the results for the year ended 31 December 1994 is to increase operating profit by £2.0m (1993 £1.5m decrease), increase the interest charge by £1.1m (1993 £0.3m decrease) and increase profit before tax by £0.9m (1993 £1.3m decrease).

Dual rates or suspension of rates

7.56 The problems of dealing with dual rates or suspension of rates in the context of individual financial statements have already been discussed in paragraph 7.19 above. The same principles also apply to consolidated financial statements when determining which rate should be used to translate results of foreign enterprises using the closing rate/net investment method. There is no guidance on this subject in SSAP 20. FRS 23, however, states that where several exchange rates are available, the rate used is that at which the future cash flows represented by the transaction or balance could have been settled if those cash flows had occurred at the measurement date. [FRS 23 para 26]. The rate applicable to dividend remittances is considered more meaningful than any other rate, because this is the rate indicative of ultimate cash flows from the entity to the investing company.

Local currency

7.57 The definition of local currency as discussed in paragraph 7.13.1, is also relevant at the consolidation stage. Where the closing rate/net investment method is used, the currency of the country in which the foreign enterprise operates will usually be its local currency. Similarly, where the temporal method is used, the investing company's currency will usually be the local currency. However, this will not always be the case.

7.58 In some circumstances, a foreign entity's local currency might not be the currency of that country. For example, a UK company may have a subsidiary in Amsterdam that deals in oil. Since the international oil market is conducted in US dollars, it is likely that the US dollar is the currency in which the subsidiary operates and generates net cash flows. If the majority of the transactions are recorded locally in US dollars rather than the euro or pound sterling, no particular problem arises as the US dollar financial statements can be translated into sterling using the closing rate/net investment method. However, where the transactions are recorded in euros, it would be necessary to first restate the financial statements in US dollars using the temporal method and then retranslate the US dollar financial statements to pounds sterling using the closing/rate net investment method.

7.58.1 Many entities reporting under SSAP 20 are studying previous decisions regarding local currency and are considering the impact of FRS 23.

Example – Local currency of an integral entity

A UK company has US$ denominated share capital and an inter-company receivable also denominated in US$. It currently has a US$ local currency under SSAP 20. However, as it is an integral part of its parent's sterling operations, it is included in the consolidated financial statements using the temporal method under SSAP 20. If the UK company had been applying the guidance on functional currency in FRS 23, it would have the same functional currency as its parent, that is, sterling. Given that the definitions of local currency in SSAP 20 and functional currency in FRS 23 are so similar, could the UK company change its local currency under SSAP 20 to sterling in its entity financial statements before it was required to adopt FRS 23?

Given that the ASB has expressed its intent to bring IFRS into UK GAAP for most (if not all) UK GAAP companies, then a case may be made for early adopting the guidance on functional currency within FRS 23 to determine local currency under SSAP 20. This reflects the lack of specific guidance in SSAP 20 and such developments in practice.

The FRS 23 approach to determining local currency could be adopted before FRS 23 becomes mandatory. It does not mean adopting the whole of FRS 23 early, or even that the entity has to be in the scope of FRS 26. However, such a change in the way in which SSAP 20 is interpreted would need to result in the most appropriate accounting taking into account an entity's particular circumstances for the purpose of giving a true and fair view (FRS 18 para 17). Further guidance on selecting accounting policies is given in chapter 2. A change of local currency under SSAP 20 in such circumstances would be treated as a change in accounting policy and applied retrospectively. This differs from a change in local currency due to a change in the entity's underlying transactions, events and conditions, which should be applied prospectively as noted in paragraph 7.13.4.

Change from the temporal method to the closing rate method or vice-versa

7.59 A company can change the basis of translating the financial statements of a foreign enterprise from the temporal method to the closing rate method or vice versa if the financial and other operational relationships that exist between the investing company and its foreign enterprises change so as to render the method currently used inappropriate. However, as the change is brought about by changed circumstances, it does not represent a change in accounting policy and, therefore, a prior year adjustment under FRS 3 is not necessary. It follows that the effect of the change should be accounted for prospectively from the date of change. Our view is that if this date is difficult to determine, the change may be accounted for generally as from the beginning of the period as an approximation of the date of change.

7.60 A practical solution would be that where a company changes from the temporal method to the closing rate method, the adjustment attributable to translating non-monetary items, previously included at historical rate, to the closing rate should be dealt with as a reserve movement.

Example – Change from the temporal method to the closing rate method

A foreign subsidiary of a UK parent purchases an equipment having an useful life of 10 years for FC 100,000 in 1 January 20X0 when the rate of exchange was FC 8 = £1. Under the temporal method, the asset would be recorded in the consolidated financial statements at £12,500. At 31 December 20X4, the equipment has a net book value of FC 50,000 in the subsidiary's books and £6,250 in the parent's consolidated financial statements.

On 1 January 20X5 the subsidiary acquires a significant local operation financed by borrowings raised locally. Under these circumstances, the parent considers that the temporal method is no longer appropriate and changes to the closing rate method. The fixed asset remains in the subsidiary's financial statements at FC 50,000, but on consolidation the asset will have to be retranslated at the closing rate of say FC 10 = £1, which is £5,000. The difference in the carrying value using the historical exchange rate and the closing rate, that is an exchange loss of £1,250, should be debited to consolidated reserves.

7.61 Where a company changes from the closing rate method to the temporal method, because the operations of the foreign subsidiary has become significantly dependent on the parent's reporting currency, the translated amounts for non-monetary assets at the end of the prior period become the accounting basis for those assets in the period of the change and in subsequent periods. This means that there is no need to restate non-monetary assets at rates ruling when those assets were originally acquired by the foreign enterprise. Any cumulative exchange adjustments for prior periods that have been taken to reserves remain in reserves and need not be reflected in the profit and loss account of the period of change.

Intercompany dividends

7.62 Where a foreign subsidiary pays a dividend to its parent company, the dividend income should be recorded by the parent company at the rate of exchange ruling at the date when the dividend is payable. An exchange gain or loss will arise if the rate of exchange moves between the date on which the dividend becomes payable and the payment date. This exchange difference will be reported in the parent's profit and loss account as a normal inter-company transaction exchange gain or loss.

7.63 Where the temporal method is used in the group financial statements, the dividend payment should be translated at the same rate, that is, the rate of exchange ruling at the date of declaration (or proposal at the year end). This means that both the dividend payment and receipt and the related exchange differences will be eliminated on consolidation.

7.64 Under the closing rate method, it is likely that the dividend, particularly an interim dividend that is a liability of the subsidiary under its local law and is recorded in the financial statements of the foreign subsidiary will be translated either at the closing rate or at an average rate. On consolidation, the translated amount recorded in the subsidiary's profit and loss account will not cancel with the amount at which the dividend is recorded in the parent's profit and loss account because of the exchange difference. Consider the following example:

Example – Payment of intercompany dividends

A foreign subsidiary declared an interim dividend of FC 100,000 on 30 June 20X4. At that date, under local law, it was a legal liability of the subsidiary. The interim dividend was paid on 15 July 20X4. The parent prepares consolidated financial statements for the year ended 31 December 20X4 and uses the average rate for translating the results of the foreign subsidiary. The relevant exchange rates are as follows:

30 June 20X4	FC 1.50 = £1
15 July 20X4	FC 1.60 = £1
31 December 20X4	FC 1.75 = £1
Average for the year	FC 1.55 = £1

The interim dividend will be recorded in the translated profit and loss account of the foreign subsidiary and in the parent as follows:

Subsidiary's translated financial statements	£
Profit and loss account	
Interim paid FC 100,000 at average rate — FC 1.55	64,516
In parent's profit and loss account	
Initially recorded at rate when dividend is declared — FC 1.5	66,667
Exchange loss in the profit and loss account	(4,167)
Amount recorded at rate when interim dividend paid — FC 1.6	62,500
On consolidation	
Parent's P&L — dividend received	66,667
Subsidiary's P&L — dividend paid	64,516
Exchange gain on consolidation	2,151

The overall exchange difference in the consolidated financial statements is a loss of £2,016 comprising the loss of £4,167 in the parent's financial statements and the gain of £2,151 arising on cancellation of the inter-company dividends.

As can be seen from the above example, the cancellation of the inter-company dividends on consolidation gives rise to a further exchange difference, in this example, a gain of £2,151. Some argue that in order for the consolidated financial statements to retain the same financial relationships shown in the subsidiary's own financial statements, the results of the subsidiary should be translated at an average rate and the exchange gain arising on cancellation of the dividends should be taken to reserves. However, we prefer the argument that the exchange difference should be taken to the consolidated profit and loss account. This means that the consolidated profit and loss account reflects the economic effect, namely:

- Profits distributed by the subsidiary are included at the sterling amount remitted. The net exchange loss of £2,016 in the consolidated profit and loss account reflects the difference between the amount remitted translated at an average rate (£64,516) and the actual rate (£62,500).
- Profits retained by the subsidiary are translated at an average exchange rate.

[The next paragraph is 7.66.]

7.66 Given that exchange differences can arise on any transaction where the settlement date is different from the date when the transaction is recorded, it may be appropriate, particularly where there is a likelihood of an exchange loss arising, to ensure that inter-company dividends are paid on the same date as they become a legal liability. In practice, this may not always be possible, so it is not uncommon for a parent company to mitigate exchange differences arising by taking out appropriate forward contracts.

Example – Treatment of forward cover of intercompany dividends

A company has an overseas subsidiary that declares a dividend that is a legal liability under its local law at the year end. At that date the parent takes out a forward contract to sell foreign currency equal in amount to the dividend that will be remitted, thereby hedging the remittance. The forward sale will be deliverable at the same date as the remittance. Considering the treatment in the parent's financial statements:

- The parent could record the dividend receivable both in the profit and loss account and in the balance sheet at the contracted rate in which case no exchange difference will arise when the cash is received, which is clearly the reason for taking out the forward contract.

- The parent could record the dividend receivable at the year end rate in the profit and loss account, but the debtor at the contracted rate. The exchange difference arising is then taken to profit and loss account.

Although the dividend recorded in the profit and loss account is not the same under the above methods, the overall effect on the profit and loss account is the same. Since the purpose of taking out the forward contract is to eliminate the effect of exchange fluctuations on the overall profit for the year, both methods achieve this objective and are, therefore, acceptable.

In the consolidated financial statements there may still be an exchange difference when the dividends are eliminated on consolidation, depending upon the translation policy. If the parent records the dividend receivable at the contracted rate and translates the results of its subsidiaries at an average rate then there will be a difference on consolidation which, as explained in the example in paragraph 7.64, we believe should be included in the consolidated profit and loss account.

Intra-group trading transactions

7.67 Where normal trading transactions take place between group companies located in different countries, exchange differences will arise which will not be eliminated on consolidation. As the transactions will probably be recorded in the local currency of one of the companies in question, exchange differences will arise, which should be reported in the profit and loss account of the enterprise in the same way as gains or losses on transactions arising with third parties. On consolidation, the net exchange gain or loss will have affected group cash flows and, therefore, it is proper that it should be included in consolidated results for the year. The exchange difference arising simply reflects the risk of doing business with a foreign party, even though that party happens to be a group member.

Example – Elimination of intra-group trading transaction where the inventory is no longer owned by the group

A UK parent company has a wholly-owned subsidiary in the US. During the year ended 31 December 20X4, the US company purchased plant and raw materials to be used in its manufacturing process from the UK parent. Details of the transactions are as follows:

	Exchange rate
Purchased plant costing £500,000 on 30 April 20X4	£1 = US$ 1.48
Paid for plant on 30 September 20X4	£1 = US$ 1.54
Purchased raw materials costing £300,000 on 31 October 20X4	£1 = US$ 1.56
Balance of £300,000 outstanding at 31 December 20X4	£1 = US$ 1.52
Average rate for the year	£1 = US$ 1.55

The following exchange gains/losses will be recorded in the profit and loss account of the US subsidiary for the year ended 31 December 20X4.

	US$	US$
Plant costing £500,000 @1.48	740,000	
Paid £500,000 @ 1.54	770,000	
Exchange loss	(30,000)	(30,000)
Raw materials costing £300,000 @1.56	468,000	
Outstanding £300,000 @1.52	456,000	
Exchange gain	12,000	12,000
Net exchange loss recorded in P&L account		(18,000)

The inter-company creditor of US$ 456,000 in the US subsidiary's balance sheet will be translated into sterling at the closing rate to £300,000 and will be eliminated against the debtor recorded in the UK parent's inter-company account. The net exchange loss of US$ 18,000 will either be translated at the average rate or the closing rate depending on whether the UK parent uses the average rate or the closing rate to translate the profit and loss account of the US subsidiary. The resulting sterling figure for exchange losses will not be eliminated on consolidation and will be reported as part of the consolidated results of the group.

Unrealised profit on stocks

7.68 It is generally accepted that intra-group profit arising from the transfer of assets between companies in the group should be eliminated in full where such assets are still held in the undertakings included in the consolidation at the balance sheet date, because it does not represent profit to the group. No specific guidance is given in SSAP 20 or in FRS 23 as to the exchange rate at which the profit should be eliminated, although SFAS 52 requires elimination at the actual rate ruling at the date of the transaction or at a weighted average rate.

Example – Elimination of intra-group transactions where the inventory is still owned by the group

The facts are the same as in the previous example except that the raw materials purchased for £300,000 by the US subsidiary are still in stock at 31 December 20X4. These goods cost the UK parent £270,000.

Therefore, unrealised profit of £30,000 would need to be eliminated on consolidation. However, elimination of this unrealised profit of £30,000 will not necessarily result in the stocks being included in the consolidated balance sheet at cost to the group where the closing rate method is used as illustrated below.

The amount for raw materials included in stock in the balance sheet of the US company at the transaction date is US$ 468,000. Under the closing rate method, the stock would be retranslated at the year end rate of 1.52 to £307,895. Therefore, the stock will be recorded in the consolidated balance sheet as follows:

	£
Cost of stock US$ 468,000 @ 1.52	307,895
Unrealised profit	(30,000)
Stock carried in consolidated balance sheet	277,895

The difference of £7,895 represents the exchange difference arising on the retranslation of the stock in the subsidiary's financial statements to the year end rate under the closing rate/net investment method, that is, £307,895 less the cost to the subsidiary of £300,000.

If, on the other hand, the parent has purchased the raw materials from the US subsidiary for US$ 468,000 at 31 October 20X4, which cost the US subsidiary US$ 421,200, and these items were still in the parent's stock at the year end, a problem arises as to what rate the unrealised profit of US$ 46,800 should be eliminated.

As stated above, if the guidance in SFAS 52 is followed, the profit will be eliminated at the actual rate and the stock will be recorded in the consolidated balance sheet as follows:

	£
Cost of stock US$ 468,000 @ 1.56	300,000
Unrealised profit US$ 46,800 @1.56	(30,000)
Stock carried in consolidated balance sheet	270,000

The amount of stock recorded in the balance sheet represents the original cost to the group of US$ 421,200 translated at the rate ruling at the date of the intra-group transaction. This is the method required by SFAS 52 that can be applied under FRS 23, but it will only be appropriate for a company applying SSAP 20 if the results of the subsidiary are translated at weighted average rates (that is, approximating to actual rates).

This method will not be appropriate for a company applying SSAP 20 if the results of the subsidiary are translated at closing rate. In this situation the amount of profit to be eliminated is that attributable to the subsidiary in the group profit and loss account, that is, US$ 46,800 @ 1.52 = £30,789.

	£
Cost of stock US$ 468,000 @ 1.56	300,000
Unrealised profit US$ 46,800 @ 1.52	(30,789)
Stock carried in consolidated balance sheet	269,211

In practice, a majority of companies use an average rate for translating the results of foreign operations under the closing rate/net investment method. In this situation, the amount of profit to be eliminated should be calculated using that average rate.

	£
Cost of stock US$ 468,000 @ 1.56	300,000
Unrealised profit US$ 46,800 @ 1.55	(30,194)
Stock carried in consolidated balance sheet	269,806

In any event, the amount of stock recorded in the consolidated balance sheet under the closing rate/net investment method will not be the same as the actual cost to the group.

Under the temporal method, the transaction would be recorded at actual rates and, therefore, any intra-group profit eliminated will automatically bring the amount of the stock back to its cost to the group.

7.69 Even if intra-group transactions do not give rise to intra-group profit, there could still be an effect on asset values as the following example illustrates.

Example – Intra-group trading transaction at cost

A UK parent has a wholly-owned subsidiary in Pololand where the currency is Pols. The net assets of the group at 31 March 20X4 are £54,000; consisting of cash £24,000, held in the UK parent and stock held in the Pololand subsidiary costing Pols 3m, which was included in the consolidated balance sheet at the closing rate of £1 = Pols 100. On 30 September 20X4, the subsidiary transfers the goods to its UK parent at cost price when the rate of exchange is £1 = Pols 125. The transaction is settled in cash and the goods are included in parent's stock at £24,000. At 31 March 20X5, the goods are still in stock. The Polos has weakened further against sterling and the exchange rate at the balance sheet date is £1 = Pols 150.

No gain or loss is recorded by either company on the transfer, hence, there are no inter-company profits to be eliminated.

		31 March 20X4 £
Net assets:		
Stock 3m @ 100 (held by sub)		30,000
Cash (held by parent)		24,000
		54,000

		31 March 20X5 £
Net assets:		
Stock (held by parent)		24,000
Cash 3m @ 150 (held by sub)		20,000
		44,000
Exchange difference on retranslation of opening net assets of foreign subsidiary:		
3m @ 100 =	30,000	
3m @ 150 =	20,000	10,000
		54,000

In this example, no exchange difference falls to be included in the consolidated profit and loss account as there is no trading gain or loss, but the effect of switching stock round the group affects the carrying value of the assets. If the stock had not been transferred the net assets would still have to be decreased by £10,000 but the reduction would have been entirely in the stock value with the cash balance unchanged. However, the result of moving the stock around the group is that there is a decrease of £6,000 in the stock value and a decrease of £4,000 in the group's cash position. This reflects the fact that the group's foreign currency exposure is centred on different assets.

Intra-group long-term loans and deferred trading balances

7.70 The recording of intra-group loans made by one group member to another in a currency which is different from the local currency of the borrower is no different from the recording of any other foreign currency monetary items. The borrower will initially record the foreign currency loan at the rate of exchange ruling at the date the loan is made. At each balance sheet date thereafter, until it is repaid, the loan will be translated at the closing rate and any exchange difference will be reported in the profit and loss account. On consolidation, the intra-group loan account will cancel out, but the exchange difference reported in the borrower's profit and loss account will flow through in the consolidated profit and loss account. The same principles apply to an unsettled inter-company account that arises from trading transactions, for example, where a parent finances the acquisition of a fixed asset by the foreign subsidiary through the inter-company account.

7.71 In certain circumstances, however, the parent may decide, because of tax or other benefits, to finance a foreign subsidiary with long-term loans and deferred trading balances rather than wholly with equity. In those situations, it may not be appropriate to treat such financing as an ordinary monetary item and to include the resulting exchange differences in the consolidated profit and loss account when exchange difference arising on equivalent financing with equity capital would be taken to consolidated reserves. SSAP 20 recognises this situation and states:

> *"Although equity investments in foreign enterprises will normally be made by the purchase of shares, investments may also be made by means of long-term loans and inter-company deferred trading balances. Where financing by such means is intended to be, for all practical purposes, as permanent as equity, such loans and inter-company balances should be treated as part of the investing company's net investment in the foreign enterprise; hence exchange differences arising on such loans and inter-company balances should be dealt with as adjustments to reserves."* [SSAP 20 para 20].

The definition of net investment is stated in paragraph 7.40 and includes long-term loans and deferred trading balances.

7.72 The inclusion of long-term loans and deferred trading balances as part of net investment is only permitted where the parent regards them as being as permanent as equity. The parent will effectively regard them as permanent if there is no intention that such balances will be repayable in the foreseeable future. In practice it is likely that a long-term loan of say, 15 to 20 years, would be designated by the parent as being part of the effective equity stake in the foreign enterprise. It is also likely that a short-term loan that is allowed to be continuously rolled over and not intended to be repaid, whether or not the subsidiary is able to repay it, would be regarded for all practical purposes as permanent as equity. The same principle applies to inter-company balances arising from normal trading transactions. Where it is not intended that such balances will be settled in cash for the foreseeable future, they could be regarded as part of the effective equity stake.

7.73 Where exchange differences on long-term loans and deferred trading balances which are regarded as permanent are taken to reserves on consolidation, the question arises as to whether a similar treatment can be adopted in the financial statement of the individual company. Consider the following example:

Example — Currency loan made by parent to overseas subsidiary

A UK parent is preparing its financial statements to 30 June 20X5. It has a loan receivable from its overseas subsidiary of FC 1m which has been outstanding for some time. The parent notified the overseas subsidiary at the previous year end that no repayment of the amount will be requested for the foreseeable future.

The relevant exchange rates are as follows:

		30 June 20X4	30 June 20X5
£1	=	FC 2.45	FC 2.20

In the financial statements of the parent company, the following exchange difference will arise if the loan is retranslated at the closing rate:

UK parent:	£
Exchange difference on long-term loan	
FC 1m @ 2.45	408,163
FC 1m @ 2.20	454,545
Exchange gain	46,382

On consolidation, the retranslated long-term loan will be regarded as part of the net investment in the foreign subsidiary and, therefore, the related exchange gains will be taken to reserves under the closing rate/net investment method. It should be noted that there will also be a corresponding exchange loss included in reserves, arising as part of the retranslation of the net assets (which include the FC loan creditor) of the overseas subsidiary.

The question arises as to how the long-term loan should be treated in the financial statements of the parent company. Some take the view that the loan should be regarded as a monetary item and any exchange difference taken to the profit and loss account. This is because the definition of net investment in SSAP 20 applies to consolidated and not entity accounts. However, we consider that this is a restrictive interpretation.

The parent is exposed to foreign currency risk on the FC loan but, as it does not expect any repayment for the foreseeable future or until the investment is sold, the exchange risk is potentially eliminated. If the long-term loan can be regarded as a permanent investment on consolidation then it is reasonable to treat it in a similar manner in the parent's financial statements. This means that the long-term loan will not be retranslated in the books of the parent, but will be carried at the historical rate of exchange such that no exchange difference arises in the parent's financial statements. This reflects the substance of the loan. Note that this approach of retaining the long-term loan at historical rates is not permitted by FRS 23.

The situation is more complicated if the long-term loan is financed by foreign borrowings in the parent company in which case the long-term loan would be retranslated to offset currency differences on the borrowings. This is dealt with in detail from paragraph 7.79.

Another problem that might arise is the appropriate treatment that should be adopted in the year in which the parent decides to designate any long-term loans or deferred trading balances as effective equity stakes. In the above example, the long-term FC loan was designated as being part of the parent's net investment in the overseas subsidiary from the beginning of the accounting period. If the parent did this part way during the year, say, at 31 December 20X4, it would be appropriate for the parent to treat the long-term loan as a monetary item up to that date and take any exchange difference arising to its profit and loss account. The exchange rate at the date that the loan is designated as permanent equity will be regarded as the historical rate for the purpose of translating the non-monetary asset and so no further exchange differences on the long-term loan will arise in the parent's financial statements.

7.74 In the above example, where the foreign currency loan is regarded as being as permanent as equity, there is no exchange difference in the profit and loss account of the parent company or in the group profit and loss account. However, the situation will differ where the loan is denominated in sterling such that it is the subsidiary that is exposed to the currency risk as there will be an exchange difference in the subsidiary's profit and loss account. Consider the following example:

Example — Sterling loan made by parent to overseas subsidiary

A UK parent is preparing its financial statements to 30 June 20X5. It has a deferred trading balance of £200,000 owed by its overseas subsidiary.

The relevant exchange rates are as follows:

		30 June 20X4	30 June 20X5
£1	=	FC 8.14	FC 7.71

In the financial statements of the individual companies, the following exchange differences will arise if the deferred trading balance is retranslated at the closing rate.

UK parent

There is no exchange difference in the parent's financial statements in respect of the deferred trading balance as this is denominated in sterling.

Overseas subsidiary		
Exchange difference on deferred trading balance		
£200,000 @ 8.14	FC	1,628,000
£200,000 @ 7.71	FC	1,542,000
Exchange gain	FC	86,000
Exchange gain translated at closing rate (@ 7.71)		£11,154

The exchange gain of FC 86,000 on the deferred trading account should be taken to the profit and loss account of the overseas subsidiary. This is because the trading transactions were originally carried out in the parent's currency and the subsidiary was exposed to the foreign currency risk. Therefore, it is appropriate to take the exchange difference to the subsidiary's profit and loss account.

On consolidation, the exchange gain in the subsidiary's profit and loss account will be translated into sterling (£11,154 assuming that the group uses the closing rate to translate its subsidiaries' results). The normal treatment would be to include this exchange gain in the consolidated profit and loss account. However, as the long-term loan is regarded as part of the net investment in the subsidiary, the exchange gain of £11,154 should be taken to reserves in the consolidated financial statements. There will be a corresponding exchange loss included in reserves arising as part of the retranslation of the net assets of the overseas subsidiary. The effect is that the consolidated profit and loss account will not reflect any exchange difference on the deferred trading balance, which is consistent with the fact that the deferred trading balance has no impact on group cash flows.

7.75 The two examples above consider the accounting implications when a loan is made by the parent company to an overseas subsidiary. In the case of a foreign currency upstream loan, that is, a borrowing by a UK parent company from the subsidiary in the subsidiary's local currency, the treatment of exchange differences in the consolidated financial statements will depend on the treatment in the parent company's own financial statements. Such loans are often regarded as hedging transactions because they reduce the net foreign currency investment in the subsidiary (see further para 7.90). If the borrowing is accounted for in the parent's financial statements as a hedge under the SSAP 20 offset procedure (see para 7.81 for details of the SSAP 20 offset procedure) then exchange differences on the borrowing are taken to reserves (insofar as they offset exchange differences on the investment being hedged) and do not appear in the parent company's profit and loss account. A similar treatment will apply in the consolidated financial statements.

Translation of subsidiary's non-coterminous accounts

7.75.1 The question may arise as to what exchange rate should be used when a foreign subsidiary's results are prepared up to a different date than that of the parent. FRS 2, 'Accounting for subsidiary undertakings', permits the use of financial statements for a period ending not more than three months before the parent's year end, where it is impracticable to prepare interim financial statements to the parent's year end. Therefore, the rate should be the year end date at which the subsidiary's financial statements are prepared. However, FRS 2 also requires that any changes that have taken place in the intervening period that materially affect the view given by the group's financial statements should be taken into account by adjustments in the preparation of the consolidated financial statements. In such cases, if the foreign exchange movements in the intervening period materially affect the consolidated financial statements, the rate as at the group's year-end should be used as a consolidation adjustment.

Goodwill arising on consolidation

7.76 Goodwill may arise on consolidation where a company acquires the equity share capital of a foreign subsidiary. Under SSAP 22, this goodwill may have been either written off to reserves or capitalised as an intangible asset and amortised through the profit and loss account over its useful economic life. Where the foreign investment is accounted for under the closing rate/net investment method, the question arises as to whether or not the goodwill, once calculated at acquisition, should be retranslated each year at closing rate.

7.77 In the example illustrating the application of the closing rate method in paragraph 7.41 above, goodwill is translated at the rate ruling on the date of acquisition and written off to reserves. It is not included in the retranslation of the opening net assets on the grounds that it arises only on consolidation and is not part of the net assets of the foreign enterprise. This view would appear to be supported by the ASC when it issued TR 504 on the publication of SSAP 20. Paragraph 21 of TR 504 indicates that the goodwill element of an investment would not be treated as a foreign currency asset for the purpose of the offset procedure in consolidated financial statements. Under this view the goodwill is regarded as a sterling asset whose carrying amount does not fluctuate when the rate of exchange changes.

7.78 However, following the publication of FRS 10, which requires goodwill to be capitalised as an intangible asset and amortised through the profit and loss account over its useful economic life, most companies would regard goodwill as a foreign currency asset and include it in the retranslation of the opening net investment. Furthermore, the view that goodwill is a sterling asset that is not part of the net assets of the foreign enterprise was probably justified when goodwill was allowed to be written off to reserves, but does not appear to be credible any longer because FRS 11 requires capitalised goodwill to be attributed or apportioned to income generating units for the purposes of carrying out impairment reviews. The combination of FRS 10 and FRS 11 provides strong support for regarding goodwill as a currency asset that is very much a part of the net assets of the foreign investment. Accordingly, the exchange difference arising on foreign currency borrowings used to finance or provide a hedge against the foreign investment, that otherwise would have been taken to the profit and loss account had goodwill not been retranslated, will be available for offset against the exchange difference arising on the retranslated goodwill.

7.78.1 Furthermore, treating goodwill as a currency asset and retranslating it at the closing rate is the method required by FRS 23, 'The effects of changes in foreign exchange rates'.

7.78.2 An example of a company that has treated goodwill as a currency asset for hedging purposes is given in the Table 7.8 below.

Table 7.8 — Automated Security (Holdings) PLC — Report and Financial Statements — 30 November 1994

Accounting Policies (extract)

10. FOREIGN EXCHANGE

Foreign currency assets and liabilities of Group companies are translated into sterling at the rates of exchange ruling at the balance sheet date. The trading results of overseas subsidiaries and associated undertakings are translated at the average exchange rate ruling during the year, with the adjustment between average rates and the rates ruling at the balance sheet date being taken to reserves. The difference arising on the restatement of the opening net investment, including goodwill, to overseas subsidiary and associated undertakings, and of matching foreign currency loans and foreign currency swap facilities, are dealt with as adjustments to other reserves. All other exchange differences are dealt with in the profit and loss account.

NOTES TO THE FINANCIAL STATEMENTS

21. RESERVES (extract)	Group £'000	Company £'000
(d) OTHER RESERVES		
At 1st December 1993	(87,560)	80
Goodwill in the year written off (note 24)	(20,193)	–
Goodwill of associated undertakings transferred to profit and loss account	17,365	–
Exchange adjustments on:		
Net investments including goodwill	(6,945)	–
Hedging arrangements	2,136	–
Goodwill	4,516	–
At 30th November 1994	(90,681)	80

24 GOODWILL	Cost of goodwill eliminated £'000	Exchange adjustments £'000	Total £'000
Eliminated to 30th November 1993	196,496	7,482	203,978
Acquisitions in the year			
- Associated undertakings	17,466	–	17,466
- Other businesses acquired	1,769	–	1,769
Adjustments to previous year's acquisitions	535	–	535
Share of goodwill movements of associated undertakings	423	–	423
	20,193	–	20,193
Transferred to profit and loss account	(17,365)	–	(17,365)
Exchange adjustments (note 21 (d))	–	(4,516)	(4,516)
Eliminated to 30th November 1994	199,324	2,966	202,290

7.78.3 Further complexities arise where goodwill was written off to reserves (pre FRS 10).

Example – Treatment of retranslated goodwill on disposal of foreign subsidiary

A company treats goodwill written off to reserves as a currency item and re-translates it each year at the closing rate. (The goodwill all related to overseas acquisitions). As a result the disclosed figure for goodwill written off changes each year. The company has disposed of a subsidiary. Should it take the previously written off goodwill through the profit and loss account at the historical amount or at the most recently retranslated amount?

If the company has consistently retranslated goodwill, and the annual disclosure of cumulative goodwill is on the retranslated basis, then goodwill passed through profit and loss account on disposal should also be on this retranslated basis.

[The next paragraph is 7.79.]

Foreign equity investments financed by foreign borrowings

Treatment in individual company

7.79 As stated in paragraph 7.24.2, in certain circumstances the normal rule that non-monetary items should be carried in the balance sheet at their historical cost at the exchange rate ruling when they were originally acquired without further retranslation, does not apply to foreign equity investments. The exception arises in circumstances where a company or a group has used foreign currency borrowings to finance foreign equity investments, or to provide a hedge against the exchange risk associated with existing foreign equity investments.

7.80 If the normal rules of translation of monetary and non-monetary items are applied to the circumstances mentioned above, any exchange gain or loss on the borrowings would be taken to the profit and loss account, while no exchange gain or loss would arise on the equity investments. SSAP 20 recognises that in such circumstances, as no economic gain or loss would in fact arise where there is a movement in exchange rates, it would be inappropriate to recognise any accounting profit or loss. [SSAP 20 para 28].

7.81 Therefore, provided the conditions set out in paragraph 7.82 below apply, the company *may* denominate its equity investments in the appropriate foreign currency. This means that the investment will be regarded as a currency investment and the company will need to translate the carrying amount at the closing rate each year for inclusion in its financial statements. Where a company treats investments in this way, it should take direct to reserves any exchange differences that arise when the investments are retranslated. It should also take the exchange differences on the related foreign currency borrowings to reserves and not to the profit and loss account to be offset against those exchange differences. [SSAP 20 para 51]. This is known as the 'cover' method or 'offset' procedure.

7.82 The conditions for offset under SSAP 20, all of which must apply, are as follows:

- In any accounting period, exchange gains or losses arising on the borrowings may be offset only to the extent of exchange differences arising on the equity investments.

- The foreign currency borrowings, whose exchange gains or losses are used in the offset process, should not exceed, in the aggregate, the total amount of cash that the investments are expected to be able to generate, whether from profits or otherwise.

- The accounting treatment adopted should be applied consistently from period to period.

[SSAP 20 para 51].

Offset restriction

7.83 The first condition deals with situations where there is not an exact match between the borrowings and the investments (either in amount or currency or both) and greater exchange gains or losses arise on the loans than are available for offset against the investments. Since the excess gains or losses are deemed to be speculative in nature they are not allowed to be used for offset in reserves and must be taken to the profit and loss account. Therefore, only that portion of the total gains or losses on the loans which is matched by an opposite exchange movement on the investments falls to be taken to reserves for offset purposes.

7.84 Whilst it is to be expected that for the cover to operate, exchange gains or losses on the borrowings would be matched by opposite exchange losses or gains arising on the investments, it is possible, particularly where investments are managed on a pool basis and financed by a basket of loans in different currencies, for both the borrowings and the investments to show either exchange gains or losses. In this context, it should be noted that the cover method need not be restricted to individual investments and borrowings. It can also be applied to a group of investments financed by a variety of different currencies. However, where an investment or a number of investments has been financed by a specific borrowing the offset should be applied on an individual matched basis, rather than putting them in a general pool.

Example – Illustration of the offset restriction when foreign equity investments are denominated in the relevant foreign currency

A UK company is preparing its financial statements for the year ended 30 June 20X5. On 31 December 20X4 it raised a loan of US$ 2m in order to finance two equity investments, one in Denmark costing DK 1,500,000 and the other in Canada costing C$ 2,500,000. The relevant exchange rates are:

31 December 20X4	£1 = US$ 1.48 = DK 8.89 = C$ 2.45
30 June 20X5	£1 = US$ 1.55 = DK 8.39 = C$ 2.54

	Exchange difference	P&L account	Reserves
	£	£	£
Exchange difference on investment in Danish company			
31/12/X4 — DK 1,500,000 @ 8.89	168,729		
30/06/X5 — DK 1,500,000 @ 8.39	178,784		
Exchange gain	10,055		
Exchange difference on investment in Canadian company			
31/12/X4 — C$ 2,500,000 @ 2.45	1,020,408		
30/06/X5 — C$ 2,500,000 @ 2.54	984,252		
Exchange loss	(36,156)		

Net exchange loss on equity investments	(26,101)		(26,101)
Exchange difference on US$ loan			
31/12/X4 — US$ 2m @ $1.48	1,351,351		
30/06/X5 — US$ 2m @ $1.55	1,290,323		
Exchange gain	61,028	34,927	26,101

In this example, the amount of the exchange gain on the loan that the company can offset as a reserve movement against the exchange loss on the investments is limited to £26,101. The excess gain of £34,927 is deemed to be speculative and, therefore, is taken to the profit and loss account.

7.85 If, in the example, there had been a loss on exchange on the loan for the year ended 30 June 20X5 of, say, £65,000 and a net gain on exchange on the investments of, say, £35,000, the amount of the exchange loss on the loan that the company could have offset as a reserve movement against the exchange gain on the investment would have been limited to £35,000. The company would have had to include the balance of the exchange loss on the loan (that is, £30,000) in its profit or loss on ordinary activities for the year.

7.86 On the other hand, if in the example there had been either a net gain on exchange on the retranslation of the equity investments as well as an exchange gain on the loan (or a net loss on exchange on the retranslation of the equity investments as well as an exchange loss on the loan) the company would have had to take the whole of the gain or loss on exchange on the equity investments to reserves and the whole of the gain or loss on the loan to its profit or loss on ordinary activities for the year. This is because the offset conditions place no limit on the amount of gain or loss on investments that may be taken to reserves, but limit the amount of the gain or loss on borrowings that may be taken to reserves to the amount of the loss or gain on the investments.

Borrowing restriction

7.87 The second condition is designed to ensure that the hedge is genuine by requiring that the borrowing is not greater than the total amount of cash generated from the investment. However, no guidance is given as to how the cash generation is to be measured or how long the foreign undertaking is given to generate profits. The condition should not cause any undue problem where a borrowing that is invested in a profitable company is sufficiently long-term to enable that company to generate sufficient profits to cover the borrowing. However, where the foreign enterprise is unprofitable or earns negligible profits not sufficient to cover the cash outflows on the borrowings, the expected cash generated will be represented by the net realisable value of the investment at the balance sheet date. To the extent that the net realisable value is less than the book value of the investment, the borrowing used for offset should be restricted accordingly. Restriction might also apply where the foreign enterprise is subject to severe exchange control restrictions such that the expected cash generated from the investment is considered to be insufficient to cover the borrowing. The next example illustrates this provision.

Example – Illustration of the borrowing restriction when foreign equity investments are denominated in the relevant foreign currency

Some years ago, a UK company raised a foreign currency loan in Argentina to finance the acquisition of a company in that country. Both at 31 March 20X4 and at 31 March 20X5, the loan amounted to Peso 5m, and the equity investment amounted to Peso 7m. The company is preparing its financial statements to 31 March 20X5 and considers that the total amount of cash that the investment is able to generate will be 4m Argentinean Pesos. The exchange rates are as follows:

31 March 20X4 £1	= Peso 1.6
31 March 20X5 £1	= Peso 1.4

In this example, the maximum amount of borrowings that can be used for offset purposes is limited to the net realisable value of the investment.

	Exchange difference	P&L account	Reserves
	£	£	£
Exchange difference on loan			
31/03/X4 — Peso 5m @ 1.6	3,125,000		
31/03/X5 — Peso 5m @ 1.4	3,571,429		
Exchange loss	(446,429)	(89,286)	(357,143)
But restricted to net realisable value of investment			
31/03/X4 — Peso 4m @ 1.6	2,500,000		
31/03/X5 — Peso 4m @ 1.4	2,857,143		
Exchange gain			357,143

In this example, the amount of the exchange loss arising on the loan that can be offset in reserves against the exchange gain arising on the investment is £357,143. The remaining exchange loss on the loan of £89,286 must be taken to the profit and loss account.

In addition, the company will also have to write down the investment for permanent diminution in value of Peso 3m as illustrated below.

		P&L account
	£	£
Equity investment		
Opening carrying value Peso 7m @ 1.6	4,375,000	
Permanent diminution Peso 3m @ 1.6	(1,875,000)	1,875,000
	2,500,000	
Retranslation gain (taken to reserves)	357,143	
Realisable value Peso 4m @ 1.4	2,857,143	

Therefore, the total charge in the profit and loss account for the year is £1,964,286 comprising permanent diminution of £1,875,000 and excess exchange loss on retranslation of the loan of £89,286.

7.88 Although, in the above example, it has been assumed that the company is able to determine the amount of the cash which the investment is expected to generate, in practice, it may be difficult or impractical to forecast the total cash to be generated from the investment, both from profits and from its ultimate realisation because of the speculative nature of long-term cash flow projections. It may also be that the investment cash flows are never converted into the currency of the borrowing because they are expected to be reinvested. In that situation, as a practical expediency the alternative would be to consider the amount that would be raised if the investment were sold immediately. If this amount is equal to the book value of the investment, then the whole of the book value is available for use in the offset calculation.

Consistent accounting treatment

7.89 Given that the application of the cover method is fairly flexible the third condition outlined in paragraph 7.82 above is simply designed to ensure that a company does not change its accounting treatment depending on the way in which exchange rates move, but adopts a consistency policy as laid down in FRS 18. For example, where exchange rate movements give rise to exchange losses on borrowings, and the first two conditions apply, it is obviously advantageous for a company to be able to use the offset procedure. If, however, in a subsequent year, exchange rate movements give rise to exchange gains on those borrowings, and the first two conditions still apply, the company must still use the offset procedure. It cannot include the exchange gains in its profit on ordinary activities.

Hedging by means of upstream loans

7.90 It is sometimes appropriate for a UK direct or indirect parent company to borrow from its overseas subsidiary. If the borrowing is in the subsidiary's local currency and the borrowed funds are converted into sterling or invested elsewhere in the business, this reduces the group's net assets in the foreign currency and, therefore, has the same effect that an external borrowing in the currency, used in the same way, would have had. This means that in the parent's individual accounts, the intra-group borrowing can be treated as a hedge against the equity investment under the provisions of paragraph 51 of SSAP 20, that is, exchange differences on the loan can be offset (subject to the criteria in the standard) against exchange differences on the investment which is treated as a currency asset and retranslated. Companies entering into such transactions with their overseas subsidiaries should seek specialist taxation advice as the rules in this area are complex.

Termination of hedging during the year

7.91 The application of the consistency principle becomes particularly relevant where hedging is terminated during the year following either the repayment of the foreign currency borrowing or the sale of the foreign equity investment. In those situations, the offset procedure should be applied up to the date of repayment of the loan or the date of sale of the investment and not stopped at the previous year end. Termination of a hedge is considered in the example below.

Example – Termination of hedging during the year and the impact of the consistency principle

A UK company, which prepares its financial statements to 30 June each year, borrowed US$ 2m to finance the acquisition of a company in Hong Kong costing HK$ 12m (£1,049,869) some years ago. The company's accounting policy is to take unrealised exchange differences on long-term borrowings that are matched with currency equity investments, direct to reserves. On 31 December 20X4, the company repaid the borrowing which resulted in an exchange gain. How should the gain arising on the repayment be treated in its financial statements for the year ended 30 June 20X5 and at what value should the equity investment be recorded in the balance sheet at 30 June 20X5?

The relevant exchange rates are as follows:

30 June 20X4	£1 = US$ 1.54	£1 = HK$ 11.93
31 December 20X4	£1 = US$ 1.56	£1 = HK$ 12.10
30 June 20X5	£1 = US$ 1.59	£1 = HK$ 12.31

	Exchange difference £	P&L account £	Reserves £
Equity investments			
30/06/X4 — HK$ 12m @ 11.93	1,005,868		
31/12/X4 — HK$ 12m @ 12.10	991,736		
Exchange loss	(14,132)		(14,132)
Loan			
30/06/X4 — US$ 2m @ 1.54	1,298,701		
31/12/X4 — US$ 2m @ 1.56	1,282,051		
Exchange gain	16,650	2,518	14,132

Given that the hedging continues up to the date of repayment of the borrowing and ceases thereafter, the company should continue with its consistent policy of taking the exchange gain on the loan to reserves to be matched with the exchange loss on the equity investment until 31 December 20X4. Since the amount of the exchange gain to be offset in reserves is limited to £14,132, the balance of £2,518 should be included in the profit and loss account for the year.

As far as the carrying value of the investment at 30 June 20X5 is concerned, the investment should be recorded at £991,736, its carrying value at the date when cover ceased (that is, 31 December 20X4). The rationale is that after the cover has been removed the investment ceases to be a currency asset and should thereafter be treated as a non-monetary asset without any further retranslation until such time as another loan is taken out to provide a hedge.

Some would argue that the investment should be recorded at the carrying value at the previous balance sheet date, that is, £1,005,868 on the grounds that, as there are no borrowings at the year end, the cover is deemed to have ceased at the beginning of the period. But this treatment fails to recognise the fact that the hedging continued until the date of repayment of the loan. Others might opt to record the investment at its historical cost of £1,049,869. The effect of this would be to reverse cumulative exchange differences of £58,133 (£1,049,869 — £991,736) on the investment that had been taken to reserves. This treatment ignores the fact that hedging on the investment ever took place.

7.92 If the foreign currency investment is sold, but the borrowing is retained, no particular problem arises. The company should apply the offset procedure up to the date of sale of the investment and not stop at the previous year end. At the date of sale, the borrowing changes its nature and becomes a borrowing that is not a hedge. Therefore, any movement from that date to the balance sheet date should be taken to the profit and loss account. Even if that were to show a loss while a hedge, and a profit while not a hedge, that would still be the proper treatment.

Borrowings taken out before or after the investment

7.93 The standard permits the cover method to apply to borrowings that have been taken out before or after the investment is made, because they can be designated as hedges against a new investment or an existing equity investment. In these situations, the period during which the borrowings are in place is different from the period during which the investments are held. Although no guidance is provided in the standard as to how the cover method should operate in these circumstances, it would appear that for the cover method to operate sensibly, the exchange differences on the borrowings that may be offset against the investments should be those that arise during the period when the hedge is effective.

Example – Borrowings taken out after the foreign equity investment in a subsidiary

Some years ago, a UK company acquired all the share capital of an overseas company for FC 10m when the rate of exchange was £1 = FC 10. The investment was carried at historical cost of £1m. On 30 June 20X4, the directors considered the investment to be worth FC 12m and took out a long-term loan of FC 12m to provide a hedge against the investment. The proceeds of the loan were used to reduce an existing sterling borrowing. The relevant exchange rates at 30 June 20X4 and 31 December 20X4 are £1 = FC 8.4 and £1 = FC 8.00 respectively. How should the company apply the cover method for the year ended 31 December 20X4?

The company can apply the cover method in the following ways:

The most straightforward method and the one which recognises the economic rationale of taking out the hedge is to record the investment at directors' valuation of FC 12m (£1,428,571) at 30 June 20X4. The difference between this value and the historical cost, that is, £428,571 is taken to the revaluation reserve. Since the investment and the borrowing are now perfectly matched after 30 June 20X4, the exchange differences arising on the retranslation of both the investment and the loan will cancel out in reserves and no exchange difference on the loan will fall to be taken to the profit and loss account. Note that in order to record the investment at the directors' valuation, the alternative accounting rules in Schedule 4 to the Companies Act must be applied. The implications of this are considered in chapter 6.

Alternatively, if the company does not wish to record the investment at the directors' valuation of FC 12m then, under the approach set out in paragraph 7.93 above, the exchange difference on the investment that arises during the period in which it is hedged is regarded as being available for offset against the exchange differences arising on the loan during the same period. To achieve this, the investment is first treated as a currency asset at 30 June 20X4, the date the loan was taken out, and recorded at £1,190,476 (FC 10m @ 8.4), the exchange gain of £190,476 being taken directly to reserves as it represents a revaluation surplus. Once the investment has been established as a currency asset and its value determined for offset purposes, no further problem arises and the normal rules apply as indicated below.

	Exchange difference	P&L account	Reserves
Equity investment	£	£	£
30/06/X4 — FC 10m @ 8.4	1,190,476		
31/12/X4 — FC 10m @ 8.0	1,250,000		
Exchange gain	59,524		59,524
Loan			
30/06/X4 — FC 12m @ 8.4	1,428,571		
31/12/X4 — FC 12m @ 8.0	1,500,000		
Exchange loss	(71,429)	(11,905)	(59,524)

It can be seen that a proportion of the exchange loss on the loan remains unutilised and is taken to the profit and loss account. If the directors had revalued the investment to FC 12m and followed the first approach outlined above, all of the exchange difference would have been taken to reserves. The first approach is considered to be superior as it better reflects the transaction's underlying purpose.

7.94 The situation where a borrowing is taken out before the investment is made is relatively straightforward. The cover should only apply for the period when the hedge is effective. This means that any exchange difference arising on the borrowing prior to the date that the investment is made should be taken to the profit and loss account. Thereafter, the normal rules of offset apply.

Carrying value of foreign equity investment

7.95 Paragraph 51(a) of SSAP 20 allows exchange gains and losses on foreign currency borrowings to be offset in reserves only to the extent of exchange differences arising on the foreign equity investments. Therefore, where companies use foreign currency borrowings to finance or provide a hedge against foreign equity investments, it may be necessary to consider the accounting policy for the carrying value of those investments. Furthermore, as this is likely to have taxation implications and the rules are complex in this area, specialist tax advice may be necessary.

7.96 The appropriate accounting policy is likely to be influenced by the treasury policy, for instance whether the company chooses to hedge against the investment's cost, the subsidiary's underlying net assets or the underlying fair value. A company applying SSAP 20 as opposed to FRS 26 has a number of choices of policy for the carrying value include the following:

- Cost (reduced to recoverable amount in the event of impairment).
- Net asset value (annual revaluation). It should be noted that if this policy is adopted, the carrying amount of the investment immediately after an acquisition will be reduced by any amount relating to goodwill. It may, however, be an appropriate policy if the subsidiaries were acquired a number of years ago or were set up by the parent, such that the net asset values being hedged are significantly in excess of original cost.
- Directors' valuation (periodic as required). This could be based on cost plus retained post-acquisition profits, or an estimate of the realisable value in the market place.

7.97 Whichever policy is adopted, it must be applied consistently from year to year. Any change in policy would have to be justified on the grounds that the new policy is preferable to the one it replaces, because it will give a fairer presentation of the reporting entity's results and financial position. [FRS 3 para 62; FRS 18 paras 30 to 49].

7.98 Where an investment is designated as a foreign currency asset and is carried at a valuation, it will be necessary to analyse separately the effect of exchange rate movements on the opening value of the investment and the effect of a revaluation of the foreign currency carrying value.

Example – Analysis of the impact in changes in foreign exchange rates on the opening value and the impact of revaluation of the investment

A UK company has an investment in a US subsidiary which is financed by US$ borrowings. It continues to apply SSAP 20 as opposed to FRS 26 and adopts a policy of net asset value for the carrying value of the investment.

	31 December 20X0	31 December 20X1
Net asset value of subsidiary	$100m	$110m
Exchange rate	2.0	1.67
Net asset value in sterling	£50m	£66m

The increase in value of £16m is analysed as follows:

	£m
Exchange gain on retranslation of opening net assets ($100m @ 1.67 — $100m @ 2.0) — taken to reserves for offset with exchange loss on borrowings	10
Gain on revaluation at the year end ($110m — $100m = $10m @ 1.67) — taken to revaluation reserves	6
	16

In the above example, it has been assumed that the whole of the increase in net assets of $10m arising from the increase in profits arose at the end of the year. In practice, however the profits will arise throughout the year. Therefore, it may be possible to split the $10m increase between a real revaluation gain that is taken to the revaluation reserve and a further exchange difference that recognises the fact that the increase in net assets occurs not on the last day of the year, but over the course of the year. For example, if the average exchange rate is £1 = $1.85, the increase in the value of £16m could be analysed as follows:

	£m
Exchange gain on retranslation of opening net assets ($100m @ 1.67 — $100m @ 2.0) — taken to profit and loss reserves for offset with exchange loss on borrowings	10.0
Exchange gain arising on the increase in net assets from use of average rate ($10m @ 1.67 — $10m @ 1.85) — taken to profit and loss reserves for offset with exchange loss on borrowings	0.6
Gain on revaluation = increase in net assets at average rate ($10m @ 1.85) — taken to revaluation reserves	5.4
	16.0

Although the effect of the above calculation is to squeeze out a further amount of exchange difference from the overall revaluation increase that may properly be taken to profit and loss account reserve for offset against the exchange loss on the borrowings, there is nothing in the standard to suggest that this treatment is inappropriate. Indeed, it makes good sense and is consistent with what actually happens in practice, that is, the company is hedging its net investments at the end of each year, provided of course the offset and the borrowing restrictions discussed above are not breached.

Partial hedges

7.99 Paragraph 51 of SSAP 20 refers to a company using foreign currency borrowings to finance its foreign equity investments, but it is not specific as to the extent to which an asset has to be financed in this way. We consider that the general interpretation should be that the investment is entirely or mostly financed by foreign currency borrowings as it would be contrary to the spirit of the standard if a low level of borrowings, say five per cent of the asset amount, could result in the asset being regarded as a foreign currency asset and, consequently, the exchange differences on the borrowings being taken to reserves rather than to the profit and loss account.

7.100 However, there may be circumstances where a less restrictive interpretation is appropriate. For instance, if a group has an overall balance sheet gearing of say 30 per cent and as a matter of policy wants to borrow, for all major subsidiaries, 30 per cent of the asset's carrying value in the relevant currency, then it would seem reasonable to regard the investment as a foreign currency asset. The question then arises as to the appropriate treatment for translation of the partially hedged investment.

7.101 One view is that the whole amount of the partially hedged investment is regarded as a foreign currency asset even though the borrowing in the relevant currency is only, say, 30 per cent of the carrying value of the investment. The effect of regarding such investments as foreign currency assets is that differences on the retranslation of the whole investment go to reserves, but they are only partially matched by differences on a smaller amount of borrowings. Some take the view that this is preferable to the alternative of regarding 30 per cent of the investment as a foreign currency asset and 70 per cent as a sterling asset.

7.102 However, there is also an argument in favour of this alternative treatment which is that the purpose under the offset procedures of retranslating the investment is solely to allow the exchange difference on the borrowings to be relieved, to reflect the fact that there is no economic risk. Taking this view, it would, therefore, make sense to limit the exchange difference recognised on the investment to that on the borrowing. We believe that either method is acceptable provided that it is consistently applied to all investments that are partially hedged.

Intermediate holding companies

7.103 A UK parent company may hold shares in an overseas intermediate holding company that holds investments in further overseas subsidiaries in various countries. A common example is for an intermediate holding company to be based in the Netherlands. If the UK parent company has taken out foreign currency borrowings to finance or hedge its investment then the SSAP 20 offset procedures will apply. At first sight, the UK parent would have a euro investment. However, economically, the investment is a multi-currency asset, that is, its value depends on fluctuations of the currencies in which the underlying subsidiaries operate. In this situation, the investment in the overseas intermediate holding company can be accounted for as a multi-currency asset such that exchange differences on foreign currency borrowings used as hedges can be offset against the exchange differences on each component of the multi-currency asset.

Example – Hedging of intermediate holding companies

A UK company holds subsidiaries in Canada, Hong Kong and Australia through an intermediate Dutch Holding company. The original cost of the investment in the Dutch company was €135m (equivalent to £90m). The Dutch company has no assets other than shares in the three subsidiaries. The UK company borrows C$ 150m to hedge the Canadian subsidiary and HK$ 360m to hedge the Hong Kong subsidiary, but does not hedge the investment in the Australian subsidiary. The relevant figures are as follows:

	Canadian Co C$ m	Australian Co A$ m	Hong Kong Co HK$ m
Cost	100	80	400
Net asset value			
- on acquisition	70	40	350
- post acquisition retained profits	100	10	(30)
- total	170	50	320
Financed by borrowings	150	–	360

All the assets of the Dutch company are shares in the overseas subsidiaries and, therefore, the investment in the Dutch company can be regarded as a multi-currency asset. In order to offset the exchange differences on the borrowings, it will be necessary for the UK company to establish a multi-currency carrying value in the relevant currencies by looking through the Dutch company and building up the carrying value by reference to the appropriate carrying value of the subsidiaries. Possible choices include the following:

- Cost — this would be C$ 100m + A$ 80m + HK$ 400m (reduced to a lower value if the reduction in reserves is regarded as representing a permanent diminution in value). However, a carrying value of cost is insufficient to allow the exchange differences on the whole of the C$150m borrowing to be taken to reserves.

- Net asset value — this would be C$ 170m + A$ 50m + HK$ 320m. However, this policy does not allow exchange differences on the whole of the HK$ 360m borrowing to be taken to reserves.

- Directors' valuation — a number of different bases could be adopted as a policy, for example, a valuation based on net asset value, cost plus retained post-acquisition reserves or a valuation based on the earnings stream.

In this example, the Australian investment is not hedged, and the implications of this need to be considered. If the UK company directly held the three subsidiaries then the C$ and HK$ investments that are hedged could be regarded as foreign currency assets whereas the A$ investment would remain a sterling investment. Where there is a Dutch intermediate holding company that has no other assets then it is possible to look through this company and split the investment into its component parts so that the same result is obtained as if the subsidiaries were directly held.

If the UK company's policy is to record investments at cost, the C$ and HK$ investments would retain a fixed cost in C$ and HK$ but this would be retranslated each year into varying sterling amounts and exchange differences would be taken to reserves (offset against exchange differences on the related borrowings). The A$ investment would retain a fixed sterling cost.

If the UK company's policy is to record investments at a valuation, say, net asset value, the above distinction between currency and sterling investments does not seem to apply. For the C$ *and HK$* investments, the net assets figure would be a C$ or HK figure and this would be retranslated into sterling for the purpose of the UK company's entity financial statements. For the (unhedged) A$ investment, the objective would be to establish an up to date sterling figure for net asset value. But this could only sensibly be done by considering the net assets in A$ and translating them into sterling at the closing rate. The process seems to be the same. This is odd given that two are regarded as foreign currency investments and one regarded as a sterling investment, but appears not to matter.

If we assume that the UK company adopts a policy of cost plus retained post-acquisition profits for the carrying value of its investments and that during the year the retained profits are C$ 20m, A$ 10m and HK$ 15m, the opening and closing positions will be as follows:

	C$	A$	HK$	Total £m
Opening exchange rate	2.2	2.4	11.0	
Closing exchange rate	2.4	2.0	12.0	
Opening carrying value in currency	200	90	370	
Closing carrying value in currency	220	100	385	
Opening carrying value in £	90.9	37.5	33.6	162.0
Closing carrying value in £	91.7	50.0	32.1	173.8
Increase/(decrease) in carrying value	0.8	12.5	(1.5)	11.8

As the A$ investment is a sterling asset, the whole increase in value is regarded as a revaluation gain and taken to revaluation reserve. However, it will be necessary to split the changes in value of the currency assets between revaluation gains and exchange differences in order to offset the exchange differences on the borrowings.

		C$ £m	HK$ £m
Revaluation gains (increase in currency value @ closing rate)		8.3	1.3
Exchange losses on investments (opening net assets retranslated at closing rates)	[A]	(7.5)	(2.8)
		0.8	(1.5)
Currency borrowing		C$ 150.0	HK$ 360.0
Opening value in £		68.2	32.7
Closing value in £		62.5	30.0
Exchange gains on borrowings	[B]	5.7	2.7
Net exchange loss taken to reserves [A — B]		1.8	0.1

7.104 The above example uses the illustration of an overseas intermediate holding company. This is a foreign equity investment that is regarded as being denominated in different currencies than the actual currency of the shares in which the investment is made. However, where the intermediate holding company is a UK company, it is not itself a foreign equity investment. The question then arises as to whether the SSAP 20 offset procedures can be applied where the ultimate parent has currency borrowings taken out to finance the overseas subsidiaries held by the UK intermediate holding company. Our view is that where the UK intermediate holding company has no other assets and liabilities other than the investments in the overseas subsidiaries, it can be regarded as a foreign equity investment and valued by reference to its multi-currency component parts.

Treatment in consolidated financial statements

7.105 The offset procedure described above is available also in consolidated financial statements. Within a group, foreign currency borrowings are often used either to finance, or to provide a hedge against, equity investments in foreign undertakings. Where this is so and also the conditions set out below have been complied with exchange differences on the borrowings *may* be offset, as a movement on consolidated reserves, against exchange differences that arise when the opening net investment in the foreign subsidiary is retranslated for consolidation purposes. But the offset procedure is optional and, if it is not used, the effect is that exchange differences on the net investment are taken to reserves, whilst those arising on the borrowings used to finance the investment are taken to the profit and loss account. Our view is that where a group is covered in economic terms and not exposed to any exchange risk, it is preferable to adopt the offset procedure and, indeed, arguably inappropriate to record an accounting profit or loss when exchange rates change.

7.106 The conditions for offset under SSAP 20, all of which must apply, are as follows:

- The relationships between the investing company and the foreign undertakings concerned should justify the use of the closing rate/net investment method of translation for consolidation purposes.
- In any accounting period, exchange differences on the borrowings may be offset only to the extent of the exchange differences arising on the net investments in foreign enterprises.
- The foreign currency borrowings, whose exchange gains or losses are used in the offset process, should not exceed, in aggregate, the total amount of cash that the net investments are expected to be able to generate from profits or otherwise.
- The accounting treatment adopted should be applied consistently from period to period.

[SSAP 20 para 57].

7.107 The last three conditions stated above are similar to those relating to the offset conditions for individual companies as set out in paragraph 7.82 above. These conditions are explained above and the explanations apply equally to consolidated financial statements. The first condition is necessary because the offset applies to any foreign equity investments at the entity level, but applies only to those foreign enterprises that fall to be accounted for under the closing rate/net investment method at the consolidation level. It is for this reason that where a foreign investment is accounted for under the temporal method, the offset rules cannot be applied to that investment on consolidation and all exchange gains and losses on the foreign borrowings must be taken to the profit and loss account.

7.108 Despite the similarities between the offset conditions that apply in the individual company's financial statements and that apply on consolidation, it will usually be necessary to reverse the entries made at an entity level and recompute the adjustments on a consolidated level for the following reasons:

- At the entity level, the offset applies to *all* foreign equity investments, whereas on consolidation foreign enterprises accounted for under the temporal method are excluded. For these investments, exchange differences on foreign borrowings that have been taken to reserves in the individual company's financial statements must be reversed and reflected in the consolidated results for the year.
- At the entity level, only borrowings of the investing company may be used for offset purposes, whereas on consolidation borrowings of any group company may be included.
- At the entity level, the exchange difference arising each year on the carrying value of the investment translated at the closing rate is used for offset, whereas on consolidation the exchange difference used is that arising through retranslation of the opening net investment.

7.109 There is one situation in which there is no need to reverse the entry. The standard states that in the case of a foreign enterprise that is neither a subsidiary nor an associated company the same offset procedure that has been applied in the individual company's financial statements may be applied in the consolidated financial statements. [SSAP 20 para 58]. This is logical, as it merely acknowledges that where there is a genuine hedge of a simple equity investment at the entity level the hedge does not cease to exist at the consolidation level. Despite this, there may nonetheless be occasions where there is a different treatment on consolidation. An example would be where there was a relevant borrowing in the group, but not one in the investing entity.

7.110 As the next example shows, even where offset procedures are used, it does not always follow that the whole of the exchange difference on the borrowing can be offset in reserves against an exchange difference on the net investment.

Example – Recognition of some exchange differences in profit or loss when applying the offset procedures

A UK company is preparing its consolidated financial statements for the year ended 30 June 20X5. On 31 December 20X4 it raised a loan of US$ 2m in order to finance two wholly-owned subsidiaries, one in Denmark costing DK 1,500,000 and the other in Canada costing C$ 2,500,000. The net assets of the two subsidiaries at the date of acquisition are DK 2m and C$ 2,750,000. The relevant exchange rates are:

31 December 20X4	£1	=	US$ 1.48	=	DK 8.89	=	C$ 2.45
30 June 20X5	£1	=	US$ 1.55	=	DK 8.39	=	C$ 2.54

	Exchange difference £	P&L account £	Reserves £
Exchange difference on net assets in Danish company at acquisition			
31/12/X4 — DK 2m @ 8.89	224,972		
30/06/X5 — DK 2m @ 8.39	238,379		
Exchange gain	13,407		
Exchange difference on net assets in Canadian company at acquisition			
31/12/X4 — C$ 2,750,000 @ 2.45	1,122,449		
30/06/X5 — C$ 2,750,000 @ 2.54	1,082,677		
Exchange loss	(39,772)		
Net exchange loss on net investments	(26,365)		(26,365)
Exchange difference on US$ loan			
31/12/X4 — US$ 2m @ 1.48	1,351,351		
30/06/X5 — US$ 2m @ 1.55	1,290,323		
Exchange gain	61,028	34,663	26,365

In this example, the amount of the exchange gain on the loan that the company can offset as a reserve movement against the exchange loss on the net investments is limited to £26,365. The excess gain of £34,663 is deemed to be speculative and, therefore, is taken to the consolidated profit and loss on ordinary activities for the year.

Goodwill on consolidation

7.111 As stated in paragraph 7.78 above, there is some support among UK companies for regarding goodwill arising on consolidation as a currency asset residing in the foreign enterprise, so that any exchange difference arising on its retranslation is included with those arising on the retranslation of the opening net investment and taken to consolidated reserves. In the context of the cover method, the question arises as to whether the exchange difference arising on the goodwill is available for offset against exchange differences on group borrowings. The question is relevant because the availability of any exchange gain arising on the goodwill element may reduce or even eliminate exchange losses on borrowings not fully covered by exchange gains on the opening net investment, which would otherwise have been taken to the profit and loss account.

7.112 If goodwill is regarded as a currency asset, there is no reason why the exchange difference arising on the goodwill cannot be used in applying the cover method. This is consistent with economic reality that the group is covered in economic terms against any movements in exchange rates. The cover method can be applied even if goodwill on acquisition has been written off to reserves (pre-FRS 10), insofar as it would not have been amortised had a policy of capitalisation and amortisation been adopted, as the write off is a consequence of following an accounting policy not because of the fact that the goodwill has lost its value.

UITF Abstract 19

7.113 Under current tax legislation, exchange gains and losses on foreign currency borrowings and derivatives that are used by a company to finance or hedge its investment in a foreign enterprise are generally not taxable. This is based on the requirements of SI 2004/3256, 'The Loan Relationships and Derivative Contracts (Disregard and bringing into account of profits and losses) Regulations 2004', (as amended by SI 2005/2012), which are intended to preserve the tax treatment, and restore mandatory matching, as it exists under current UK GAAP even where a company accounts under modified UK GAAP (for example, FRSs 23, 25 and 26) or IFRS. Broadly, the conditions are that the instrument is designated as a hedge of exchange rate risk or is intended to reduce or eliminate the economic risk attributable to fluctuations in exchange rates. Therefore, even if the strict requirements for hedge accounting under FRS 26 or IFRS are not met, providing the borrowing or derivative is intended to reduce the foreign exchange risk, the tax will be deferred or 'matched'.

7.113.1 However, some examples of circumstances where tax may be payable are as follows:

- The hedging is structured such that foreign exchange gains and losses are *not* 'matched' with shares and are therefore *not* disregarded. For example, the foreign investment and the borrowings may be located in different companies in a group and, although an economic hedge may exist for consolidated financial statements, the Disregard Regulations conditions are not met. Similarly, if the investment is financed using debt and not shares, the disregard conditions may not be met.
- The liability exceeds the carrying value of the foreign investment. Under the current tax regulations, a liability or derivative hedging shares is matched by the shares at any time only to the extent that the carrying value of the liability or the value of the currency obligation under the derivative does not exceed the carrying value of the asset at the time the liability is entered into or, if later, the asset is acquired.

7.114 The question then arises as to how the tax effects of any such exchange gains and losses on the borrowings should be recognised. The borrowings may have been offset in reserves (to an extent) under the SSAP 20 offset procedure and reported in the statement of total recognised gains and losses. Alternatively, if the company or group is using modified UK GAAP or IFRS then any exchange gains or losses will only be offset in reserves in the consolidated financial statements not in the entity's financial statements, but any amounts taxable in the entity accounts will still need to be reflected in the consolidated financial statements.

7.115 It was already current practice to account for the tax effects of transactions recognised directly in reserves also in reserves when the UITF adopted this principle in Abstract 19, 'Tax on gains and losses on foreign currency borrowings that hedge an investment in a foreign enterprise', which was issued on 20 February 1998. The Abstract states that where exchange differences on foreign currency borrowings that have been used to finance, or provide a hedge against, equity investments in foreign enterprises are taken to reserves and reported in the STRGL, in accordance with paragraphs 51, 57 and 58 of SSAP 20 and paragraph 27 of FRS 3, tax charges and credits that are directly and solely attributable to such exchange differences should also be taken to reserves and reported in that statement. This treatment was incorporated into FRS 16, 'Current tax'. (FRS 16 para 6) and is also in line with the treatment in IAS 12, 'Income taxes'. [IAS 12 para 61].

7.116 The UITF also considered how such tax effects reported in the statement of total recognised gains and losses and in reserves would impact on the restriction on the amount of exchange differences on foreign currency borrowings that can be offset in reserves in accordance with paragraphs 51(a) and 57(b) of SSAP 20. The Abstract concludes that the restriction should be applied after taking account of any tax attributable to those exchange differences — that is, the net-of-tax exchange difference on borrowings should be offset only to the extent of exchange difference arising on the equity investment. The offset restriction is considered in detail from paragraph 7.83. Similarly, the comparison with the total amount of cash that the investments are expected to be able to generate and the exposure created by the borrowings (paragraphs 51(b) and 57(c) of SSAP 20) should be considered in after-tax terms.

7.117 Consistent with SSAP 20's requirement to disclose the amount of exchange gains or losses on borrowings that are taken to the statement of total recognised gains and losses, the abstract requires disclosure of any related tax charges and credits accounted for as described above, in addition to the gross amount of the exchange differences.

7.118 The way in which UITF Abstract 19 is likely to apply in practice is illustrated in the following example.

Example – Tax on foreign exchange differences of borrowings hedging an investment in a foreign enterprise

A UK company's financial year ends on 31 March.

Option A) On 31 March 20X5 it raised a loan of C$ 840,000 to finance an equity investment in Canada costing C$ 840,000.

Option B) The loan of C$ 840,000 was taken out by a Treasury company elsewhere in the group but is still intended to be a hedge at a consolidated level.

Option C) Instead of raising a loan of C$ 840,000 the company raised a loan of C$ 1,000,000 to finance the equity investment and to ensure that it had sufficient C$ liquidity for other Canadian trading activities. The additional loan funding is not used for any other hedging purposes.

Assume UK tax rate is 30%. The relevant exchange rates are as follows:

31 March 20X5 £1 = C$ 2.80

31 March 20X6 £1 = C$ 2.90

The company is still on old UK GAAP and adopts the offset procedure in SSAP 20 in its financial statements for the year ended 31 March 20X6. Therefore the exchange difference on the C$ borrowing that is offset in reserves before considering any tax consequences is as follows:

31 March 20X5 — C$ 840,000 @ 2.80	= £300,000
31 March 20X6 — C$ 840,000 @ 2.90	= £289,655
Gain on borrowing	£10,345

Under option A, there will be no further exchange difference on the loan to be accounted for.

The Disregard regulations apply as the company has used the borrowing to hedge its investment in the Canadian subsidiary. Therefore, under option A, there are no tax consequences. This is because the sterling carrying value of the liability is fully matched by the sterling carrying value of the asset and the exchange gain on the loan is fully matched with the exchange loss in reserves.

Under option B, the Treasury company will record the exchange movement on the borrowing in its profit and loss account and the equity investment will be held at historic cost in the investing company. On consolidation the group will use the offset procedure in SSAP 20 and therefore the exchange movements on the borrowing can be transferred to reserves.

The Disregard regulations do not apply even though hedging is available in the consolidated accounts as the borrowing is not intended to be a hedge in the Treasury or Investing company. Therefore the company would have to pay tax of £3,104 at 30% on the exchange gain of £10,345. Applying UITF Abstract 19, the group would offset £10,345 — £3,104 = £7,241 of net exchange gain on the borrowing against the exchange loss of £10,345 in reserves in the consolidated accounts. Both the exchange difference of £10,345 and the attributable tax of £3,104 would be disclosed.

Under option C, the exchange gain on the excess borrowing of £1,970 (C$160,000 × 2.8 — C$160,000 × 2.9) will be reported in the profit and loss account at an entity and consolidated level. The Disregard regulations will not apply to this excess borrowing and therefore the exchange gain will be taxed. The tax of £591 will be recorded in the profit and loss account.

7.119 The above example is fairly simple and does not demonstrate the complications that can arise in the tax treatment of exchange gains and losses. The tax rules on financial instruments and matching are complex and specialist taxation advice should be sought.

Hedging transactions

Identification of a hedge

7.120 Companies enter into hedging transactions primarily to reduce risks, including those associated with exchange rate movements that can have an adverse effect on their financial position and results. A diverse range of financial instruments, such as forward exchange contracts, futures contracts, currency swaps and currency options, are available for reducing foreign exchange risk. These instruments are often referred to as 'derivative products' because their values are derived from an underlying security, an index, an interest rate, or another financial instrument.

7.121 The word *hedge* is used in a variety of ways by derivatives traders, accountants and regulators and there appears to be no single accepted definition. However, most definitions are based on the notion of reducing exposure to price risk, interest rate risk or currency risk.

7.122 Hedging in an economic sense concerns the reduction or elimination of the effects of market risk, interest rate risk or currency risk, each of which may be present to some extent in a financial instrument. It involves entering into a transaction in the expectation that it will reduce an enterprise's exposure to loss from price risk, often with the additional consequence of reducing the potential for profit. A financial instrument is generally viewed as a hedge when an enterprise has a specifically identified position that is exposed to the risk of loss as a result of adverse price changes in financial markets and the effect of holding the instrument is to mitigate that risk of loss. A hedge is achieved by taking a position exposed to effects of price changes that move inversely and with a high degree of correlation with the effects of price changes on an existing or expected position.

7.123 A position to be hedged can be interpreted fairly broadly. A financial instrument may be accounted for as a hedge when it has an exposure to price risk that is equal but opposite to that of a group of financial instruments or a portion of one instrument. Furthermore, it is not necessary for hedges to be specifically matched with individual items being hedged. However, because different types of assets and liabilities have substantially different exposures to potential gain or loss, the items constituting a group of financial instruments must be similar at least to the extent of the common price risk being hedged.

7.124 Until recently, there was no measurement standard in the UK that dealt with the recognition and measurement of derivatives, nor was there a UK standard that dealt specifically with hedge accounting. In December 2004, the ASB issued FRS 25 and FRS 26, which deal with the accounting for financial instruments and hedge accounting. The requirements are almost identical to IAS 32 and IAS 39. The effective dates of these standards are complex and are covered in detail in chapter 6. For a company that is not applying those standards (and hence, is applying SSAP 20) there is no mandatory UK guidance in this area. In the context of foreign exchange transactions, the paragraphs that follow consider the appropriate accounting treatment, under the current UK historical cost accounting framework, for two hedging tools that are commonly in use that are not dealt with in SSAP 20. These are forward exchange contracts and currency options.

Forward exchange contracts

7.125 A forward exchange contract is a legal agreement under which a company contracts to buy or sell a specified amount of foreign currency at a specified exchange rate (which is the forward rate), but with delivery and settlement at a specified future date. One of the parties to a forward contract assumes a long position and agrees to buy the underlying currency on a specified future date at the forward rate. The other party assumes a short position and agrees to sell the currency on the same date for the same forward rate.

7.126 The duration of the contract is usually fixed, for example, one month, three months or six months. The forward rate specified in the contract is stated at a premium or discount to the spot rate based upon current market conditions and expectations, but it is not an estimate of what the spot rate will be at the end of the contract. Since the alternative to a forward contract is to buy (or sell) the required currency now, the amount of the premium or discount to the spot rate is principally based on:

- The interest rate differentials between the relevant currencies.
- The duration of the contract.

The following example (simplified) illustrates how forward exchange rates are calculated:

Assumptions	
UK interest rate	9%
US interest rate	6%
Spot rate at beginning of year	£1 = US$1.55
One year forward rate	To determine
Company borrows £1m for one year	£
Amount payable	
Principal	1,000,000
Interest @ 9% for one year	90,000
Total payable	1,090,000

Company converts £1m to US dollars at the spot rate, invests the dollars for one year and takes out a one year forward contract to sell the original dollars and interest for sterling.	
Amount payable	US$
Principal £1m @1.55	1,550,000
Interest @ 6%	93,000
Total payable	1,643,000

Ignoring any transaction costs, the one year forward rate at inception of the contract would be calculated on the basis that the company is indifferent between choosing the above two strategies. For this to occur, the one year forward rate must be US$ 1,643,000/£1,090,000 = 1.50734. In fact, the forward rate can be determined arithmetically by applying the interest rate differential ruling between the two currencies in question to the spot rate.

$$\text{Forward rate} = 1.55 \times \frac{1.06}{1.09} = 1.50734$$

A further factor would need to be built into the calculation if the period was other than one year.

Forward rates are usually quoted as being either at a discount or premium to the spot rate. To arrive at the forward rate for US dollars the discount is added to the spot rate and a premium is deducted from the spot rate.

7.127 Forward exchange contracts are frequently used by companies to protect them from experiencing exchange gains or losses from existing positions and on anticipated transactions. They offer the advantage that they can be specifically tailored in terms of amount, currency and maturity date to any hedging situation. There is no initial deposit or margin to pay and settlement is made at maturity. The disadvantage is that there is no benefit from favourable exchange rate movements.

7.128 Accounting for forward contracts is dealt with only briefly in SSAP 20. Two viewpoints have been advanced to account for foreign exchange contracts under the current UK historical cost framework:

- All aspects are viewed as part of a single transaction (the 'one transaction' view). That is, the commitment to buy or sell currency necessary to settle a foreign currency payable or receivable is viewed as part of the purchase or sale transaction and the forward contract rate is used to record that transaction. This is the approach specifically adopted in SSAP 20.
- The transaction to settle a foreign currency payable or receivable is treated separately from the forward contract (the 'two transaction' view). In addition, the premium or discount on the forward contract is accounted for

separately and spread over the life of the contract. The forward contract *is* marked to market as the contract progresses (for example, at the balance sheet date it is marked to the rate effective on that day).

The above viewpoints are illustrated below in some of the typical situations where a company enters into a forward contract for hedging purposes.

Forward exchange contracts taken out at the transaction date

7.129 This is the only situation that is dealt with in SSAP 20. The standard states that the rate specified in the forward contract *may* be the appropriate rate to use for the translation of trading transactions denominated in a foreign currency (or the monetary assets or liabilities arising from such transactions) where these are covered by a related or matching forward contract. This treatment recognises that the purpose of such a transaction is to hedge any exchange risk involved in foreign currency operations and that no economic gain or loss will therefore arise. Therefore, under this approach, the premium or discount on a forward contract is immediately recognised in the profit and loss account.

Example – Accounting for forward cover entered into at transaction date

A company is preparing its financial statements to 31 December 20X5. In October 20X5, the company sells goods to an overseas company for FC 405,000. The overseas company pays for the goods in March 20X6. At the time of the sale, the exchange rate is £1 = FC 2.7, and at the balance sheet date the exchange rate is £1 = FC 2.9. The UK company, however, covers the transaction by a matching forward contract to sell FC. The exchange rate specified in the six month forward contract is £1 = FC 2.6. The relevant translations are as follows:

10/X5 — FC 405,000 @ 2.7 (transaction rate) =	£150,000
12/X5 — FC 405,000 @ 2.9 (balance sheet rate) =	£139,655
03/X6 — FC 405,000 @ 2.6 (forward contract rate) =	£155,769

The UK company could record the sale in one of the following ways:

- It could record the sale and the debtor at £155,769, that is, at the exchange rate specified in the matching forward contract. Because the company has entered into a matching forward contract, the amount receivable and ultimately received from the debtor is FC 405,000 which is sold for £155,769. Consequently, the company would not recognise a loss on exchange on the transaction and no further accounting entries are required. This approach is permitted by SSAP 20.

- A second method is to view the sale and the debtor separately from the commitment to sell foreign currency under the six month forward contract. Therefore, the sale and the debtor would be initially recorded at £150,000. At 31 December 20X5, the debtor would be translated at the exchange rate ruling at that date, that is £139,655. The loss on exchange of £10,345 would be taken to the profit and loss account. This would be matched by an equivalent gain on the forward contract, which is computed by taking the difference between the foreign currency amount of the forward contract translated at the spot rate at the date of inception of the forward contract (FC

405,000 @ 2.7 = £150,000) and the amount translated at the balance sheet date (FC 405,000 @ 2.9 = £139,655).

In addition, the premium or discount on the contract should be accounted for separately. This will give rise to a profit or loss on the forward contract, calculated by taking the difference between the foreign currency amount of the forward contract translated at the spot rate at the date of inception of the forward contract (FC 405,000 @ 2.7 — £150,000) and the contracted forward rate (FC 405,000 @ 2.6 = £155,769). In this situation, there is a profit of £5,769 which should be amortised over that period. Accordingly, £2,885 should be taken to the profit and loss account for the year ended 31 December 20X5 and the balance should be recognised in the following year.

The effect of the two methods can be summarised as follows:

	Method 1 £	Method 2 £
Balance sheet at 31 December 20X5		
Debtor	155,769	139,655
Forward contract	–	13,230
Profit and loss account for year ended 31 December 20X5		
Included in profit on sale of goods	5,769	–
Exchange loss on retranslation of debtor	–	(10,345)
Exchange gain on forward contract	–	10,345
Amortisation of profit on forward contract	–	2,885
	5,769	2,885
Profit and loss account for year ended 31 December 20X6		
Amortisation of profit on forward contract	–	2,884

7.130 Although SSAP 20 allows the first method, it does not rule out the use of the alternative method discussed above. The advantage of the first method is its simplicity, whilst the second method takes a completely different approach and is perhaps theoretically correct. It treats the forward contract as a separate instrument and attributes a value to it. The rationale for this treatment is that the revenue is determined by the original sale transaction and not by any subsequent agreement to exchange currencies.

Hedging an existing asset or liability with forward exchange contract

7.131 Companies may sometimes enter into a forward exchange contract to hedge an existing monetary asset or a liability.

Example – *Forward cover* of an existing loan and interest *payments*

A company is preparing its financial statements to 31 December 20X4. It took out a foreign currency loan of FC 1m at fixed interest rate of 10% on 1 July 20X4 with a maturity date of one year. Interest is payable on 31 December and 30 June. The company immediately enters into two forward contracts as follows

Contract No 1, to purchase FC 50,000 (half-yearly interest on FC 1m) for payment on 31 December 20X4 at a fixed contract price of £1 = FC 1.50.

Contract No 2, to purchase FC 1,050,000 (principal of FC 1m + half-yearly interest of FC 50,000) for payment on 30 June 20X5 at a fixed contract price of £1 = FC 1.46.

The relevant spot rates are as follows:

1 July 20X4 £1 = FC 1.54

31 December 20X4 £1 = FC 1.47

The illustration that follows views the loan and the commitment to purchase foreign currency under the forward contracts separately.

		P&L account	Balance sheet
Loan	£	£	£
Exchange difference on loan			
1/7/X4 — FC 1m @ 1.54 (transaction rate)	649,351		
31/12/X4 — FC 1m @ 1.47 (balance sheet rate)	680,272		(680,272)
Exchange loss	(30,921)	(30,921)	
Forward contracts			
Exchange gain on forward contract No 1			
31/12/X4 — Value at settlement FC 50K @ 1.47	34,014		
1/7/X4 — Value at inception date FC 50K @1.54	32,467		
Exchange gain on settled contract*	1,547	1,547	
Premium payable on contract No 1			
1/7/X4 — FC 50,000 @ 1.54 (spot rate)	32,467		
1/7/X4 — FC 50,000 @ 1.50 (forward rate)	33,333		
Premium payable*	(866)	(866)	
Interest FC 50,000 @ 1.47 paid on 31/12/X4		(34,014)	
		(33,333)	
Forward contract No 2			
Exchange gain on forward contract (principal amount only)			
31/12/X4 — Value at year end FC 1m @ 1.47	680,272		
1/7/X4 — Value at inception date FC 1m @ 1.54	649,351		
Exchange gain on outstanding contract	30,921	30,921	30,921
Premium payable on contract No 2			
1/7/X4 — FC 1.05m at @ 1.54 (spot)	681,818		
1/7/X4 — FC 1.05m at @ 1.46 (forward)	719,178		
Premium payable (half deferred)	(37,360)	(18,680)	(18,680)

Cash			
Loan proceeds	649,351		
Interest paid	(34,014)		
Net settlement on contract No 1 (gain — premium)*	681		
Cash balance	616,018		616,018
Net charge to P&L account		(52,013)	52,013
			–

* The net settlement on contract No 1 amounting to £681 can also be calculated as the difference between the forward contract amount at the spot rate at the date of settlement, being £34,014 (FC 50,000 @ 1.47) and the contracted rate, being £33,333 (FC 50,000 @ 1.50).

As can be seen from the above table, the exchange loss on the loan is matched by an equivalent gain on the outstanding forward contract No 2. This gain is calculated on the principal amount of FC 1m. The balance of the forward contract (FC 50,000) is not included because it is hedging a future commitment. This is dealt with in detail from paragraph 7.132.

As contract No 1 matured during the year, the premium payable is taken to the profit and loss account. The premium payable on contract No 2 is amortised over its life, half the amount being charged during the year ended 31 December 20X4. As stated earlier, the above approach is theoretically correct as it attributes a value to the contract.

If the treatment permitted by SSAP 20 is followed, the half-yearly interest charged to the profit and loss account is translated at the forward rate being £33,333 (FC 50,000 @ 1.5). The loan is translated at the forward rate at the balance sheet date, being £684,932 (FC 1m @ 1.46) and the difference between this amount and the amount at which it was initially recorded (£649,351), being an exchange loss of £35,581 is taken to the profit and loss account. This exchange loss represents the total premium on the portion of the forward contract relating to the loan principal, that is FC 1m @ 1.46 (contract rate) less FC 1m @ 1.54 (inception). Under this method no part of this premium is deferred.

Hedging a foreign currency commitment

7.132 Companies may also use forward exchange contracts to hedge anticipated future transactions, such as a foreign currency payable or receivable, or to a hedge a foreign currency commitment, such as an agreement to buy goods from or sell goods to a foreign entity at some time in the future. In these situations, the gain or loss arising on the forward contract is deferred until the actual date the commitment is fulfilled. This is an example of the 'one transaction' approach (see para 7.128) because both the transaction and the forward contract taken out to hedge it are future commitments. The example illustrated below deals with a future commitment. An anticipated future foreign currency payable or receivable would be treated in a similar manner.

Example – Forward cover of a financial commitment

A company's financial year ends on 31 December 20X1. It intends to renovate part of its plant and enters into an agreement with a foreign supplier on 30 September 20X1 to purchase an improved version of the equipment for FC 1m. The equipment is to be delivered on 31 March 20X2 and the price is payable on 30 June 20X2. In order to hedge the commitment to pay FC 1m, the company enters into a forward contract on 30 September 20X1 to purchase FC 1m on 30 June 20X2 at a fixed exchange rate of £1 = FC 1.51.

The relevant spot rates are as follows:

Inception date	30 September 20X1	£1 = FC 1.54
Year end date	31 December 20X1	£1 = FC 1.47
Transaction date	31 March 20X2	£1 = FC 1.45
Settlement date	30 June 20X2	£1 = FC 1.43

As before, there are two possible treatments:

Method 1

If the treatment permitted by SSAP 20 is followed, then no accounting entries are required at the year end and the company will simply disclose the financial commitment in its balance sheet. On 31 March 20X2, both the equipment and the liability to pay the supplier will be recorded at the forward contract rate, being £662,252 (FC 1m @ 1.51).

Method 2

Method 2 is based on the two transaction approach. No entries are made in respect of the equipment at 31 December 20X1. At 31 March 20X2, the equipment and the liability to the supplier would be initially recorded at £689,655 (FC 1m @ 1.45 — transaction rate). The amount payable to the supplier at 30 June 20X2 is £699,301 (FC 1m @ 1.43 — spot rate at settlement). The exchange loss of £9,646 arising on the settlement will be charged in the profit and loss account for the year ended 31 December 20X2, but will be offset by a corresponding gain on the forward contract (see below).

The forward contract would be accounted for as a separate transaction as follows:

Exchange gain on forward contract	£
Gain up to balance sheet date	
30/09/X1 — FC 1m @ 1.54 (spot — inception date)	649,351
31/12/X1 — FC 1m @ 1.47 (spot — balance sheet date)	680,272
Gain on forward contract	30,921
Gain from balance sheet date to transaction date	
31/12/X1 — FC 1m @ 1.47 (spot — balance sheet date)	680,272
31/03/X2 — FC 1m @ 1.45 (spot — transaction date)	689,655
Gain on forward contract	9,383
Total gain to transaction date (deferred)	40,304

Gain from transaction date to settlement date	
31/03/X2 — FC 1m @ 1.45 (spot — transaction date)	689,655
30/06/X2 — FC 1m @ 1.43 (spot — settlement date)	699,301
Gain on forward contract	9,646
Total exchange gain on forward contract	49,950
Premium payable on forward contract	
30/09/X1 — FC 1m @ 1.54 (spot rate at inception)	649,351
30/09/X1 — FC 1m @ 1.51 (forward rate)	662,252
Premium payable	12,901

The gain or loss arising on the forward contract from the date of inception up to the transaction date is not recognised in the profit and loss account, but is deferred. The amount deferred at 31 December 20X1 is £30,921. The total amount deferred at the transaction date as indicated above is £40,304 and this amount will subsequently be reflected in the asset value.

During the hedging period, between the transaction date and the settlement date, the exchange gain arising on the contract matches the exchange loss arising on the liability to the supplier, reflecting that the position is hedged. These exchange differences are offset in the profit and loss account.

As far as the premium on the contract is concerned, there are two possible treatments that will have an effect on asset values. The first treatment is to amortise the premium payable over the life of the contract. Therefore, half the premium, that is £6,451, would be charged to the profit and loss account for the year ended 31 December 20X1, the balance will be deferred and charged in the following year. If this treatment is followed, only the gain on the forward contract will have an effect on the asset value. The effect is that the asset will be recorded in 20X2 at the spot rate ruling at the date the forward contract was taken out as indicated below.

Asset	£
Initially recorded at transaction date — FC 1m @1.45	689,655
Less deferred gain on forward contract	(40,304)
Value — FC 1m @ 1.54 (spot rate at inception of contract)	649,351

Alternatively, the premium that relates to the commitment period may be deferred and included in the related foreign currency transaction. The effect is that the asset will be recorded at the forward rate as indicated below.

Asset	£
Initially recorded at transaction date — FC 1m @1.45	689,655
Less deferred gain on forward contract	(40,304)
Plus deferred premium	12,901
Value — FC 1m @ 1.51 (forward rate)	662,252

Although both treatments are acceptable, it is preferable to use the second alternative as the company 'locked in' the cost of the equipment at £662,552 by entering into the forward contract.

Hedging a net investment

7.133 A company may decide to hedge against the effects of changes in exchange rates in the company's net investment in a subsidiary. This may be done by taking out a foreign currency borrowing to hedge a foreign equity investment, which is recognised by SSAP 20 and discussed from paragraph 7.105. However, SSAP 20 does not deal with the situation of using forward exchange contracts to hedge foreign equity investments. The question then arises as to how the forward contract should be dealt with in the consolidated financial statements.

7.134 To be consistent with the treatment of the exchange differences on borrowings that are taken out as a hedge, we consider that any gain or loss arising on a forward contract may be taken to reserves to match the movement in the net investment being hedged. This treatment is sensible as it recognises the economic rationale of taking out the forward contract. The premium on the contract should be taken to the profit and loss account, because it represents the interest rate differential between the currencies being exchanged.

Hedging future results of foreign investments

7.135 A company can also take out a forward contract as a hedge against the future results of a foreign subsidiary. Where this is done, the gain or loss on the contract should be included in the profit and loss account for the period being hedged. If the results are translated at the closing rate and the contract is for the whole year, the inclusion of the gain or loss on the contract will ensure that the results are stated at the contracted rate. Where the contract is not for a full year, the results up to the date of contract will effectively be hedged and reflected at the contracted rate. If the contract remains outstanding at the end of the year, the gain or loss on the contract from the date of inception up to the balance sheet date should be recognised in the profit and loss account and the related value of the contract included in the balance sheet. If the results are translated at an average rate and the contract is for less than a year, it may be appropriate to translate the results of that part of the year covered by the contract at the contracted rate and the balance at the average rate.

7.136 Where a company takes out a forward contract to hedge the future results of a foreign subsidiary (for example, the results of the following year) or where there is a rolling hedge so that at the year end there are contracts outstanding to hedge future results, a considerable degree of prudence should be observed in assessing whether or not the future results will be sufficient to ensure that the contract is not an excessive hedge. If projections of the results of the foreign subsidiary are too optimistic or the subsidiary suffers deterioration in its performance, some of the contract could become speculative with the result that any potential loss should be provided for immediately. Consider the following example:

Example – Forward cover of future trading results

A company has forward contracts outstanding at the year end for the sale of FC 20m at a contract rate of FC 1.60. The future trading results of the subsidiary for next year were originally estimated at FC 21m but at the year end have been revised to FC 15m. The relevant spot rate at the year end is FC 1.40.

The revised forecasts indicate that the company will have to purchase FC 5m in order to meet its commitment under the sales contract. At the exchange rates current at the year end, this will result in a loss of £446,429 (FC 5m @ 1.40 less FC 5m @ 1.60) which should be provided for in accordance with FRS 12.

7.137 Some take the view that hedge accounting may not be appropriate for forward contracts that are taken out to hedge future results and that such contracts are in fact speculative. In fact FRS 26 does not permit hedge accounting for this type of hedging relationship.

Speculative forward contracts

7.138 A speculative forward contract is a contract that does not hedge an exposure. Because of the risks involved, companies do not normally enter into such speculative contracts and it is inadvisable for them to do so. However, where a company does enter into a forward contract as a speculative transaction, a gain or loss will arise during the period from inception to maturity. If this period straddles the company's year end it is necessary to deal with the gain or loss that arises for the year. Again SSAP 20 does not deal with this situation. For trading companies, such gains or losses can be regarded as contingent and, consequently, provision should be made for losses, whereas gains would normally be deferred until they crystallise. Other companies (for example, banks) that have a policy of marking to market would recognise both gains and losses. Two possible methods of accounting for the contract are illustrated in the example below.

Example – Speculative foreign exchange contract

A company is preparing its financial statements to 31 December 20X1. It enters into a forward contract on 1 October 20X1 to purchase FC 1m 180 days forward on 31 March 20X2 at a contracted rate of £1 = FC 1.52. At the year end, the 90 day forward is £1 = FC 1.46. The relevant spot rates are as follows:

1 October 20X1	£1 = FC 1.54
31 December 20X1	£1 = FC 1.47

Method 1

Exchange gain on speculative forward contract	£
Gain up to balance sheet date	
01/10/X1 — FC 1m @ 1.54 (spot — inception date)	649,351
31/12/X1 — FC 1m @ 1.47 (spot — balance sheet date)	680,272
Gain on forward contract	30,921
Premium payable on forward contract	
01/10/X1 — FC 1m @ 1.54 (spot rate at inception)	649,351
01/10/X1 — FC 1m @ 1.52 (forward rate)	657,895
Premium payable	(8,544)
Proportion recognised (half)	(4,272)
Net amount taken to P&L account	26,649

This method is the same as that used for a forward contract that is taken out as a hedge. It has the effect of recognising the exchange gain to 31 December 20X1, but deferring part of the premium.

Method 2

No separate recognition is given to the premium on the speculative contract and instead the gain or loss is calculated by taking the difference between the foreign currency amount of the forward contract at the forward rate at the balance sheet date for the remaining maturity of the contract and the contracted forward rate (or the forward rate last used to measure an earlier gain or loss on the contract).

Gain on speculative forward contract	£
Gain up to balance sheet date	
FC 1m @ 1.52 (forward rate — contracted)	657,895
FC 1m @ 1.46 (forward rate — remaining maturity)	684,932
Gain on forward contract	27,037

The second method has the effect of anticipating all the gain on the contract in the year to 31 December 20X1. The first method has the effect of only recognising the gain to 31 December 20X1 but carrying forward part of the premium. Either approach appears acceptable as presumably if the contract was closed out at 31 December 20X1 a gain would arise. As stated above, trading companies would normally defer any gain until it crystallised on maturity of the contract.

Foreign currency options as a hedge

7.139 An option is a contract conveying the right, but not the obligation, to buy (call) or the right to sell (put) a specified item at a fixed price (known as the strike or exercise price). A foreign currency option, therefore, is a right to buy or sell a foreign currency. A company acquiring an option will have to a pay a non-refundable premium to the option seller in exchange for the right to buy or sell a fixed amount of currency. The option premium represents the market's perception of the value of the option, which essentially consists of two parts:

- Intrinsic value — which for a call option is the excess of the market price of the underlying item over the option's strike price.
- Time value — which is the difference between the price paid for the option (the premium) and the intrinsic value.

The intrinsic value represents the benefit to the holder if the option was exercised immediately. The time value is associated with the remaining term to maturity of the option and reflects the income foregone from not holding the underlying item, the cost avoided by not having to finance the underlying item and the value placed on the possibility that the option's intrinsic value will increase prior to its maturity due to future volatility in the fair value of the underlying item.

7.140 If the spot exchange rate is lower than the strike rate, a foreign exchange call will not be exercised and the option is said to be 'out-of-the-money'. If it is advantageous to exercise the option, it is said to be 'in-the-money'. Where the strike rate is equal to the spot rate, the option is said to be 'at-the-money'. Therefore, unlike a forward foreign exchange contract, an option buyer will be able to gain from favourable exchange rate movements.

7.141 Accounting for currency options is not dealt with in SSAP 20. The general principle is that losses in the underlying item being hedged are offset by gains in the option position. It should be noted, however, that the maximum loss that the company can incur on an option is the premium as it will not exercise the option if the exchange rate movements are unfavourable. Due to the nature of a currency option, it would not be appropriate to record the item being hedged at the rate in the related currency option as it may never be exercised. Therefore, the asset or liability being hedged should be treated separately from the premium. The premium should initially be recorded as an asset. At the balance sheet date, the underlying currency amount under the option should be translated at the current rate and compared with the amount translated at the option rate. The resulting gain or loss should be treated as follows:

- If there is a gain, the gain less the cost of the option may be recognised provided that the loss on the item being hedged is also recognised. If a corresponding loss is not recognised, for instance, because the option is hedging a future transaction, then the gain should be carried forward to be matched with the loss when this is recognised.

  If the option is speculative, that is, it is not taken out as a hedge, the gain would normally be deferred unless the company adopts a policy of marking to market. However, it is generally accepted that entering into speculative option contracts is inadvisable as companies have suffered losses in the past where they have taken out such contracts.

- If there is a net loss, the whole of the premium should be written off. If the loss is less than the premium paid then the premium should be written off to the extent of the loss.

7.142 Alternatively, the premium on the hedging option could be 'marked to market' to the current premium at the balance sheet date. If the premium has increased in value there is a gain on the contract indicating that the option is in the money. On the other hand if the premium has fallen in value such that the option is unlikely to be exercised, there will be a loss on the contract.

Disclosures

Requirements of the Act

7.143 The Act does not include any provisions that deal with either the translation of foreign currency transactions or the translation of foreign currency financial statements, other than to require the basis on which sums are translated into sterling to be stated. [4 Sch 58(1)]. The Act does require disclosure of financial commitments to the extent that they are relevant to a proper understanding of the company's state of affairs. [4 Sch 50(5)]. Therefore, where a company has outstanding forward contracts the amounts outstanding under the forward contracts should be disclosed. Note that for accounting periods beginning on or after 1 January 2005, SI 2004/2947, 'The Companies Act 1985 (International Accounting Standards and Other Accounting Amendments) Regulations 2004', has brought in additional disclosure requirements applicable for companies applying the fair value accounting rules to financial instruments, for example, under FRS 26. These disclosure requirements are considered further in chapter 6.

Requirements of the standard

7.144 In addition to the above disclosure, SSAP 20 requires a number of other disclosures which are considered below. Furthermore, following the guidance on publication of the 'Operating and financial review', the disclosure requirements of FRS 13, 'Derivatives and other financial instruments; disclosures' and the requirement to comment in the Directors' report on the principal risks and uncertainties facing the company, companies now tend to give much more information on their foreign currency operations. Guidance on the preparation of an OFR and a directors' report is contained in chapters 2 and 3 of the Manual of Accounting – Management reports and governance respectively. The following paragraphs deal with the disclosures required by SSAP 20 and FRS 13 to be made both in individual financial statements and in consolidated financial statements.

7.145 The methods used in translation of the financial statements of foreign enterprises and the treatment accorded to exchange differences should be disclosed in the financial statements. [SSAP 20 para 59]. These disclosure requirements are illustrated in Table 7.10 below.

Table 7.10 — Reuters Group plc — Annual Report and Accounts — 31 December 2001
Accounting Policies (extract)

Foreign currency translation

Where it is considered that the functional currency of an operation is sterling the financial statements are expressed in sterling on the following basis:

a. Fixed assets are translated into sterling at the rates ruling on the date of acquisition as adjusted for any profits or losses from related financial instruments.

b. Monetary assets and liabilities denominated in a foreign currency are translated into sterling at the foreign exchange rates ruling at the balance sheet date.

c. Revenue and expenses in foreign currencies are recorded in sterling at the rates ruling for the month of the transactions.

d. Any gains or losses arising on translation are reported as part of profit.

For other operations, associated undertakings and joint ventures, assets and liabilities are translated into sterling at the rates ruling at the balance sheet date. Revenue and expenses in foreign currencies are recorded in sterling at the rates ruling for the month of the transactions and gains or losses arising on translation are dealt with through reserves.

Treasury

Reuters receives revenue and incurs expenses in more than 60 currencies and uses financial instruments to hedge a portion of its net cash flow and operating profit. Profits and losses from hedging activities are matched with the underlying cash flows and profits being hedged. Those relating to trading cash flows are reported as part of profit and those relating to capital expenditure programmes are adjusted against the cost of the assets to which they relate.

Reuters uses financial instruments to hedge a portion of its interest exposure. Profits and losses on financial instruments are reported as part of profit for the period to which they relate.

Financial instruments hedging the risk on foreign currency assets are revalued at the balance sheet date and the resulting gain or loss offset against that arising from the translation of the underlying asset into sterling.

7.146 The standard requires disclosure of the net amount of exchange gains and losses on foreign currency borrowings less deposits, identifying separately:

- The amount offset in reserves under the provisions of paragraphs 51, 57 and 58 of SSAP 20. This applies to exchange differences included in the offset process. Examples of this disclosure are included in Table 7.11 and Table 7.12 below.

- The net amount charged/credited to the profit and loss account.

In addition, disclosure is required of the net movement on reserves arising from exchange differences. [SSAP 20 para 60].

Table 7.11 — Reckitt & Colman plc — Report & Accounts — 31 December 1994

Notes to the accounts

32 OTHER RESERVES

	Group £m	**Subsidiary undertakings £m**	**Parent £m**
At beginning of year as previously reported	**542.32**	**395.74**	**146.58**
Prior year adjustment for post-retirement benefits other than pensions	(35.38)	(35.38)	–
At beginning of year restated	**506.94**	**360.36**	**146.58**
Movements during the year:			
Profit for the financial year	81.89	27.54	54.35
Ordinary dividends	(75.99)	–	(75.99)
Net exchange loss on foreign currency loans	(0.35)	–	(0.35)
Exchange differences arising on translation of net investments in overseas subsidiary undertakings	(22.58)	(13.83)	(8.75)
Dividend adjustment (Note 8)	3.09	–	3.09
Goodwill and acquisition costs written off	(206.41)	(206.41)	–
Goodwill reinstated	6.54	6.54	–
	293.13	**174.20**	***118.93**

As permitted by s.230 of the Companies Act 1985, no profit and loss account is presented for Reckitt & Colman plc.

The cumulative amount of goodwill written off to reserves since 1984 in respect of the acquisition of continuing businesses is £536m (1993, £336m).

* The reserves of subsidiary undertakings have generally been retained to finance their businesses. There were statutory or other restrictions on the distribution of £109m (1993, £81m) of the reserves of subsidiary undertakings at 31 December 1994.

Table 7.12 — Imperial Chemical Industries PLC — Annual report and accounts — 31 December 1994

notes relating to the accounts

23 Reserves (extract)

	Share premium account £m	Revaluation £m	Associated undertakings £m	Profit and loss account £m	**1994 Total £m**	1993 Total £m
GROUP						
Reserves attributable to parent company						
At beginning of year as previously stated						3,572
Prior year adjustment (note 2)						(89)
At beginning of year as restated	561	46	66	2,493	**3,166**	3,483
Profit/(loss) retained for year			(63)	52	**(11)**	(433)

Amounts taken direct to reserves						
Share premiums	8				**8**	59
Goodwill				(48)	**(48)**	80
Exchange adjustments		(6)	(11)	(79)	**(96)**	(23)
Share of other reserve movements of associated undertakings and other items			(9)	2	**(7)**	–
	8	(6)	(20)	(125)	**(143)**	116
Other movements between reserves		(3)	77	(74)		
At end of year	569	37	60	2,346	**3,012**	3,166

In the Group accounts, £33m of net exchange gains (1993 losses £26m) on foreign currency loans have been offset in reserves against exchange losses (1993 gains) on the net investment in overseas subsidiaries and associated undertakings.

7.147 Apart from the item mentioned in paragraph 7.146, there is no requirement to disclose the amount of exchange gains and losses taken to the profit and loss account. Nonetheless, the profit and loss account formats in Schedule 4 to the Act distinguish between operating income and expenses and other income and expenses. Therefore, a company will need to consider the nature of each exchange difference. A company should normally show gains and losses that arise from trading transactions as 'other operating income/charges'. Where arrangements that can be considered as financing give rise to exchange gains and losses, a company should disclose these separately as part of 'other interest receivable and similar income' or as part of 'interest payable and similar charges'. Exchange gains and losses that arise from events that are disclosed as exceptional items should be included as part of such items. Similarly, exchange gains and losses that arise from events that fall to be treated as extraordinary items should be included as part of such items (though, in practice these will be rare following the introduction of FRS 3).

7.148 FRS 13 introduced narrative disclosure requirements relating to identification of the financial risks arising in the entity and discussion relating to how these risks have been managed. For companies reporting under FRS 25's disclosure requirements, FRS 13 is superseded by FRS 25. Financial risk includes currency risk. [FRS 13 para 11; FRS 25 para 52]. A number of the numerical disclosure requirements in each standard relate to currency exposure. Further consideration of the narrative and numerical disclosure requirements contained in FRS 13 and in FRS 25 are given in chapter 6.

Effect that foreign currency translation has on distributable profits

7.149 Companies can only make a distribution to their shareholders out of profits that are available for that purpose. The amount of distributable profits is calculated by reference to the financial statements of an individual company and the rules differ for private and public companies. The rules relating to calculating distributable profits are considered in detail in chapter 23. In order to determine distributable profits, it is necessary to distinguish between realised and unrealised profits and losses.

7.150 In an individual company, the exchange gains and losses that arise both on the currency transactions that the company completes during the year and on its outstanding short-term monetary items (as defined in para 7.23), are taken to the profit and loss account. Paragraph 12 of Schedule 4 to the Act states that *"…only profits realised at the balance sheet date shall be included in the profit and loss account"*. Where exchange gains and losses arise on short-term monetary items, their ultimate cash realisation can normally be assessed with reasonable certainty. For companies that prepare financial statements in accordance with Schedule 4, monetary items should be categorised as either short-term or long-term items. Short-term monetary items are those that fall due within one year of the balance sheet date. Therefore, gains and losses on such items are considered to be realised gains and losses in accordance with FRS 18 paragraph 28. Accordingly, the inclusion of these gains in the profit and loss account does not conflict with paragraph 12 of Schedule 4 to the Act.

7.151 Paragraph 65 of SSAP 20 implies that exchange gains that arise on outstanding long-term monetary items are not realised profits, but as discussed in paragraph 7.28, SSAP 20 requires these gains to be included in the profit and loss account. If the gains were unrealised, this would involve a departure from paragraph 12 of Schedule 4. However, since SSAP 20 was issued in 1983, the currency markets have become more sophisticated and companies have a greater ability to crystallise exchange profits on long-term monetary items. In March 2003, ICAEW and ICAS issued guidance in Tech 7/03, 'Guidance on the determination of realised profits and losses in the context of distributions under the Companies Act 1985'. This states that a profit is realised where it arises from the translation of a monetary asset which comprises qualifying consideration, or a liability denominated in a foreign currency. [Tech 7/03 para 16]. Qualifying consideration includes cash, or an asset that is readily convertible to cash and an amount receivable in cash where the debtor is capable of settling the receivable within a reasonable period of time, there is a reasonable certainty that the debtor will be capable of settling when called upon to do so and there is an expectation that the receivable will be settled. [Tech 7/03 para 18 as amended by Tech 2/07]. Consequently, unless there are doubts as to the convertibility or marketability of the currency in question (see para 7.30), foreign exchange profits arising on the retranslation of monetary items are realised, irrespective of the maturity date of the monetary item. [Tech 7/03 para 34]. This has been confirmed by the issue by the ICAEW and ICAS in August 2007 of Tech 2/07, 'Distributable profits — implications of recent accounting changes'. The new guidance does not impact on any of the discussion in this section.

[The next paragraph is 7.154.]

7.154 Where the exchange difference on a long-term monetary item such as a borrowing is a loss, SSAP 20 requires this to be included in the profit and loss account, unless the foreign currency borrowing is being used to finance or provide a hedge against a foreign equity investment (and the conditions in paragraph 51 of SSAP 20 are met). This means that a loss charged to the profit and loss account should be treated as a realised loss. This is because it is the current best estimate of the probable loss that will be incurred when the borrowing is repaid.

7.155 Where an individual company has a foreign currency borrowing that is being used to finance or provide a hedge against a foreign equity investment held by that same company then SSAP 20 permits the exchange gain/loss on the borrowing to be offset in reserves against the exchange loss/gain on the investment (subject to the conditions in paragraph 51 of SSAP 20 being met). Tech 7/03 includes guidance in respect of hedging. It states:

> *"Where a hedged asset or liability and a hedging instrument are accounted for as a hedge, the treatment as realised of any profit or loss is determined in accordance with the criteria in this guidance solely by reference to the net exposure on the hedged asset or liability."*
> [Tech 7/03 para 33].

7.156 The guidance in Tech 7/03 takes the line that where a hedged asset or liability and a hedging instrument are accounted for as a hedge, it is the net exposure on the hedged asset or liability that determines whether any profit or loss arising is realised or unrealised. Therefore, it is not necessary to consider whether the gain/loss on the borrowing and the loss/gain on the investment are themselves realised or unrealised. Instead, the net position is considered as illustrated in the example below.

Example – Impact of hedged investment in foreign subsidiary on distributable profits

If Company A has an investment in a US subsidiary of $100 million and the investment is partially hedged by a US dollar borrowing of $80 million, the relevant amount for the purpose of determining the impact on realised profits is the foreign currency gain or loss on the $20 million net exposure on the investment in the US subsidiary.

If there is a foreign currency gain on the $20 million net exposure on the investment in the US subsidiary, this will be an unrealised profit. Paragraph 16(d) of Tech 7/03 states that a profit is realised where it arises from the translation of a monetary asset that comprises qualifying consideration. As the investment is a non-monetary item, the profit is regarded as unrealised.

If there is a foreign currency loss on the $20 million net exposure on the investment in the US subsidiary, this will generally be regarded as an unrealised loss. Paragraph B28 of Tech 7/03 states that if an asset is revalued downwards below its recoverable amount, as defined in FRS 11, then the difference between that revalued amount and recoverable amount is treated as an unrealised loss as it reflects a revaluation adjustment rather than a provision under paragraphs 88 or 89 of Schedule 4. A similar principle applies to the retranslation of a non-monetary item. If the investment is not impaired and if the foreign currency loss is only recognised as a result of the accounting policy for the SSAP 20 offset (SSAP 20 para 51), then the foreign currency loss would be regarded as unrealised. This is consistent with paragraph 66 of SSAP 20.

[The next paragraph is 7.160.]

7.160 In practice, the financing and hedging of foreign equity investments can be complicated and may involve a number of group companies. For instance, the external borrowing may be held by the ultimate parent company, which then makes loans to an intermediate parent company that holds the foreign investments. It is necessary to consider the impact of the treasury arrangements on the distributable profits of each entity.

Hyper-inflation

7.161 Where a foreign subsidiary or an associate operates in a country in which a very high rate of inflation exists, the closing rate/net investment method is not considered to be suitable for translating the financial statements of the foreign enterprise for inclusion in the consolidated financial statements. This is because an asset acquired in foreign currency is worth very little in sterling terms at a time of high inflation when the foreign currency has weakened considerably against sterling, leading to a large debit to group reserves. At the same time, the results of the foreign enterprise are included at an inflated amount in the group's profit and loss account (whether from high interest income on deposits in a rapidly depreciating foreign currency or from trading operations which could be considered to reflect unrealistically high profitability).

7.162 The above problems were recognised by SSAP 20 which states:

> *"Where a foreign enterprise operates in a country in which a very high rate of inflation exists it may not be possible to present fairly in historical cost accounts the financial position of a foreign enterprise simply by a translation process. In such circumstances the local currency financial statements should be adjusted where possible to reflect current price levels before the translation process is undertaken."* [SSAP 20 para 26].

7.163 SSAP 20 does not provide guidance on what is meant by a high rate of inflation and when or how this guidance should be applied in practice. As a result, the UITF considered this matter and issued Abstract 9, 'Accounting for operations in hyper-inflationary economies', in June 1993. The question of what constitutes hyper-inflation is judgemental. There is some guidance in FRS 24 which describes a number of characteristics of the economic environment of a country that indicate hyper-inflation. These are as follows:

- The general population prefers to keep its wealth in non-monetary assets or in a relatively stable foreign currency. Amounts of local currency held are immediately invested to maintain purchasing power.
- The general population regards monetary amounts not in terms of the local currency but in terms of a relatively stable foreign currency. Prices may be quoted in that currency.

- Sales and purchases on credit take place at prices that compensate for the expected loss of purchasing power during the credit period, even if the period is short.
- Interest rates, wages and prices are linked to a price index.
- The cumulative inflation rate over three years is approaching, or exceeds, 100 per cent.

7.164 The UITF reached a consensus that adjustments are required where the distortions caused by hyper-inflation are such as to affect the true and fair view given by the group financial statements. In any event adjustments must be made where the cumulative inflation rate over three years is approaching, or exceeds, 100 per cent and the operations in the hyper-inflationary economies are material. [UITF 9 para 5].

7.165 The Abstract is not clear whether the word 'cumulative' is intended to mean that the three-year inflation rate should be calculated by simply adding up the inflation rates for each of the three years or by computing the compound inflation rate over the three years. Consider the following example:

Example – Assessment of an economy as hyper-inflationary or not

The following data are relevant to a country operating in a hyper-inflationary economy:

	20X1	20X2	20X3	20X4
Inflation rate		30%	28%	34%
General price level	120	156	200	268

Based on simple addition the cumulative inflation rate for the years 20X2 to 20X4 is 92% (30 + 28 + 34).

Compounded annually (using the index at the end of 20X1 as the base), the cumulative inflation for 20X2 to 20X4 is (268 — 120) ÷ 120 = 123%.

In our view, the cumulative three-year inflation rate should be compounded, because it provides a measure of inflation for the three years taken as a whole.

7.166 The determination of whether a country has experienced cumulative three-year inflation of approximately 100 per cent or more should be based on an internationally or locally recognised general price-level index for that country. At the time of writing, countries that had recently experienced cumulative three-year inflation of 100 per cent or more, included amongst others, Angola, Dominican Republic, Turkey, Uzbekistan and Zimbabwe. Information on inflation rates in various countries is available in International Financial Statistics, issued monthly by the Bureau of Statistics of the International Monetary Fund.

7.167 Although SSAP 20 suggested the use of a local price-level index for adjusting the financial statements of a local enterprise before translation, it may not always be possible to obtain a reliable local index. UITF Abstract 9, therefore, allows an alternative method, of using a relatively stable currency as the functional currency of the relevant hyperinflationary economy, which is similar to the method required by SFAS 52 although not permitted by FRS 24. The two methods specified in UITF 9, that are now considered to be acceptable and, therefore, consistent with SSAP 20 are as follows:

- Adjust the local currency financial statements to reflect current price levels before the translation process is undertaken as suggested in paragraph 26 of SSAP 20. This includes taking any gain or loss on the net monetary position through the profit and loss account.

- Using a relatively stable currency (which would not necessarily be sterling) as the functional currency (that is, the currency of measurement) for the relevant foreign operations. For example, in certain businesses operating in Eastern Europe the US dollar or the euro acts effectively as the functional currency for business operations. The functional currency would in effect be the 'local currency' as defined in paragraph 39 of SSAP 20. In such circumstances, if the translations are not recorded initially in that stable currency, they must first be remeasured into that currency by applying the temporal method described in SSAP 20 (but based on the dollar or other stable currency rather than sterling). The effect is that the movement between the original currency of record and the stable currency is used as a proxy for an inflation index.

[UITF 9 para 6].

7.168 If neither of the above methods is considered appropriate for material operations, then the reasons should be stated and alternative methods to eliminate the distortions should be adopted. [UITF 9 para 7]. In practice, companies tend to follow one or the other method described above as illustrated in the examples below.

7.169 Where group operations in areas of hyper-inflation are material in the context of group results or net assets, the accounting policy adopted to eliminate the distortions of such inflation should be disclosed. [UITF 9 para 8].

Table 7.14 — Courtaulds plc — Report and Accounts — 31 March 1995

Statement of accounting policies (extract)

Foreign currencies

The accounts of overseas subsidiaries are translated into sterling at the rates at which the currencies could have been sold at the date of the Group balance sheet. Gains or losses arising on these transactions are dealt with in reserves. Other assets and liabilities denominated in foreign currencies are translated into sterling at year end rates and differences arising are dealt with in the profit and loss account. The results of subsidiaries in hyper-inflationary economies are dealt with in accordance with UITF 9 using the US$ as the functional currency.

Table 7.15 — Reckitt Benckiser plc — Annual Report & Accounts — 31 January 2001
Accounting policies (extract)

Foreign currency translation
Transactions denominated in foreign currencies are translated at the rate of exchange on the day the transaction occurs or at the contracted rate if the transaction is covered by a forward exchange contract.

Assets and liabilities denominated in a foreign currency are translated at the exchange rate ruling on the balance sheet date or, if appropriate, at a forward contract rate. Exchange differences arising in the accounts of individual undertakings are included in the profit and loss account except that, where foreign currency borrowing has been used to finance equity investments in foreign currencies. Exchange differences arising on the borrowing are dealt with through reserves to the extent that they are covered by exchange differences arising on the net assets represented by the equity investments.

The accounts of overseas subsidiary undertakings are translated into Sterling on the following basis:

Assets and liabilities at the rate of exchange ruling at the year end date.

Profit and loss account items at the average rate of exchange for the year.

Exchange differences arising on the translation of accounts into Sterling are recorded as movements on reserves.

The accounts of subsidiaries operating in hyper-inflationary environments are adjusted where possible to reflect current price levels before being translated into Sterling.

The currencies that most influence these translations and the relevant exchange rates are:

	2001	2000
Average rates:		
£/Euro	**1.6074**	1.6417
£/US Dollar	**1.4404**	1.5260
Closing rates.		
£/Euro	**1.6353**	1.5843
£/US Dollar	**1.4546**	1.4935

7.169.1 Determining whether a subsidiary operates in a hyperinflationary economy per UITF 9 is not a policy choice but rather a change in circumstances (inflation rising or falling). Therefore, the revised accounting method should be applied prospectively and comparatives should not be adjusted. However, the accounting policy note should indicate whether UITF 9 has been applied or no longer applies to the relevant subsidiaries.

Multi-currency share capital

7.170 It is not uncommon for a UK company to issue shares in a currency other than sterling. The legal aspects are dealt with in chapter 23. The question arises as to how such foreign currency share capital should be translated for reporting purposes at the company's year end. This is not dealt with either in SSAP 20 or in FRS 25, 'Financial instruments: Disclosure and presentation'. There are two possible treatments:

- The shares could be maintained at the historical rate at the date the shares were issued.
- The shares could be retranslated at each year end at the closing rate of exchange.

In the latter case, exchange differences would normally be taken directly to reserves (but see example below). Overall, both methods have the same effect on shareholders' funds.

7.171 For equity shares either method is acceptable. For non-equity shares the substance of the instrument should be considered. For accounting periods beginning on or after 1 January 2005, the amendments to the Companies Act effected by SI 2004/2947 require the substance of these instruments to be considered. This is also required by FRS 25. Non-equity shares such as redeemable preference shares are in substance long-term debt and are accounted for as such. Long-term debt is retranslated at the closing rate at each year end under SSAP 20. This is considered further in the following example:

Example — US Dollar preference shares issued by a UK company

A company has issued preference shares denominated in dollars. These are redeemable at par in 20X9. How should the shares be recorded in the company's sterling financial statements and how should the exchange differences, if any, be dealt with under the Companies Act 1985 and also FRS 25?

The redeemable preference shares are economically similar to debt. Long-term debt is normally retranslated by using the closing rate of exchange at each year end, with exchange gains and losses taken into the profit and loss account. The most appropriate treatment, therefore, is to retranslate the preference shares at each year end at the closing rate.

FRS 4 requires the finance costs for non-equity shares to be calculated on the same basis as the finance costs for debt. Exchange gains or losses on debt or non-equity shares would fall within the definition of finance costs in FRS 4. In addition, paragraph 68 of SSAP 20 indicates that exchange differences on debt should be disclosed separately as part of interest payable and similar charges.

Since these shares are accounted for as debt under the Companies Act amendments and under FRS 25, the exchange gains or losses are taken to the profit and loss account and are charged or credited in arriving at the profit for the year.

An exception to the treatment described above is where the preference shares were issued to finance or provide a hedge against, for example, an equity investment in the US. In those circumstances it would be acceptable to use the offset method in SSAP 20. Under this method the investment would be designated as a dollar asset. Both the investment and the preference shares would then be retranslated at each year end at the closing rate. The exchange differences on the preference shares would then be offset, as a reserve movement, against the exchange differences on the investment. Application of the conditions for offset in paragraphs 51 and 57 of SSAP 20 would result in exchange gains or losses on the preference shares being offset only to the extent of exchange differences arising on the foreign equity investments. Any surplus exchange differences on the preference shares would then be shown as a charge or credit in the profit and loss account as described above.

Financial statements in foreign currencies

7.172 Financial statements may be prepared in a foreign currency if that currency is the 'local currency' of that company. SSAP 20 implicitly requires a company to prepare its financial statements in its local currency. Therefore, if the local currency is the dollar, the financial statements should be prepared in dollars. It is generally not appropriate for a company to publish its annual financial statements in a currency different to its local currency

[The next paragraph is 7.176.]

7.176 Although not specifically dealt with in the Companies Act, the Registrar of Companies accepts annual financial statements prepared in a foreign currency, provided that the currency exists legally and the exchange rate to sterling at the balance sheet date is disclosed in the notes to the financial statements.

[The next paragraph is 7.188.]

Annex

7.188 The annex to this chapter reproduces the chapter from the Manual of Accounting – IFRS for the UK that deals with accounting for foreign currencies under IAS 21. As the requirements of FRS 23 and FRS 24 are almost identical to the requirements of IAS 21 and IAS 29, respectively, the accounting for foreign currencies will be the same under UK GAAP as under IFRS.

7.189 The text in the annex contains references to IFRSs. For these to be applied in the UK context, the following should be noted:

- The references to paragraphs in IAS 21 and IAS 29 are identical to the paragraph numbers in FRS 23 and FRS 24, respectively.
- References to other international standards should be read as referring to the equivalent UK standards, as issued by the ASB.
- The transitional provisions for first time adopters of IFRS insofar as they relate to the first time adoption of IAS 21 have been incorporated by the ASB into FRS 23.

Annex — Foreign currencies

Contents

	Page
Introduction	7093
Objectives	7094
Scope	7095
The functional currency approach	7095
Introduction	7095
Determining the functional currency	7096
Illustrative examples	7101
Entity with multiple operations	7101
Different functional currencies for entities in the same country	7101
Accounting records not maintained in functional currency	7102
Change in functional currency	7102
Foreign currency transactions	7103
Introduction	7103
Initial recognition	7103
Determining the average rate	7104
Multiple exchange rates	7114
Suspension of rates	7114
Subsequent measurement	7115
Translation of monetary items	7115
Translation of non-monetary items	7116
Recognition of exchange differences	7117
Monetary items	7119
Non-monetary items	7119
Foreign currency translation of financial statements	7120
Introduction	7120
Translation to the presentation currency	7121
Determining the average rate for translating the income statement	7123
Consolidated financial statements	7123
Translation of a foreign operation	7123
Different reporting dates	7127
Minority interest	7128
Goodwill and fair value adjustments arising on an acquisition	7128
Intra-group trading transactions	7130
Unrealised profit on inventories	7131
Monetary items forming part of net investment in a foreign operation	7134
Inter-company dividends	7140
Disposal or partial disposal of a foreign operation	7142
Hedging a net investment	7146
Foreign operations in hyperinflationary economies	7147
Presentation and disclosure	7149
General	7149
Accounting policies	7149

Disclosure 7151
Convenience translation 7154
Other disclosures 7155
Other matters 7156
Tax effects of all exchange differences 7156
Cash flow statements 7156
First-time adoption of IFRS 7156

Introduction

A7.1 Companies conduct businesses that are not simply confined within national boundaries. The globalisation of markets for goods and services as well as capital makes it imperative for companies to engage in international trade, cross-border alliances and joint ventures if they are to survive and grow in today's competitive business environment. The ways in which companies enter the international market place are varied. First, companies directly undertake transactions of buying goods and services from overseas suppliers and selling goods and services to overseas customers. Secondly, they may extend their international business by conducting their affairs through overseas subsidiaries, branches and associates.

A7.2 In the first situation, transactions undertaken by a company will often be expressed in foreign currencies and the results of these transactions will need to be translated into the company's functional currency for financial reporting purposes. In the second situation, it is usual for the foreign operation to maintain its accounting records in the currency of the primary economic environment in which it operates. Because it is not possible to combine, add or subtract measurements expressed in different currencies, it is necessary to translate the foreign operation's results and financial position into the currency in which the reporting entity presents its consolidated financial statements.

A7.3 Accounting for foreign currencies is, therefore, primarily concerned with the translation process whereby financial data denominated in one currency is expressed in terms of another currency. It is important to note that the translation process in no way changes the essential characteristics of the assets and liabilities measured. It merely restates assets and liabilities, initially valued in a foreign currency unit, to a common currency unit by applying a rate of exchange factor, a translation rate. It does not restate historical cost.

A7.4 There are different translation rates that may be used depending on the circumstances. These are:

- The historical rate — the rate of exchange ruling at the date the transaction occurred.
- The closing rate — the rate ruling at the balance sheet date.
- The average rate ruling during the year.

The average rate is generally confined to income and expenditure items. The rates used for balance sheet items (historical or closing) will depend on the types of assets and liabilities – monetary or non-monetary. These methods are discussed in detail later in this chapter.

A7.5 The treatment of exchange differences that arise on foreign currency transactions is different from those that arise on foreign currency translation. Furthermore, foreign currency translation also raises a number of questions, such as: the extent to which exchange gains and losses from different sources can be offset; whether some exchange differences should be recognised immediately whilst others should be deferred; and whether the recognition should be through the income statement or through reserves. These and other vexing issues, such as the extent to which inflation in overseas countries should be taken into account in the translation process, are considered in this chapter.

A7.6 The current (2003) standard IAS 21, 'The effects of changes in foreign exchange rates', replaces the previous version of IAS 21 (revised in 1993). This version was developed by the IASB as part of its project on improvements to international accounting standards. The standard provides additional guidance on the translation method and on determining the functional and presentation currencies but excludes from its scope foreign currency derivatives and hedge accounting that are now within the scope of IAS 39, 'Financial instruments: Recognition and measurement'.

A7.7 In 2005, the IASB issued a limited amendment to IAS 21 to include guidance explaining that an entity's net investment in a foreign operation includes loans between fellow subsidiaries ('sister company loans'). The amended IAS 21 also permits intercompany items denominated in any currency to be part of a net investment in a foreign operation. The 2003 version of IAS 21 required such items to be denominated in the currency of one of the parties to the transaction. The amendment is effective for accounting periods beginning on or after 1 January 2006.

[The next paragraph is A7.23.]

Objectives

A7.23 IAS 21's objectives are to prescribe how to:

- Include foreign currency transactions and foreign operations in an entity's financial statements.
- Specify which exchange rates to use and how to report the effects of changes in exchange rates in the financial statements.
- Translate the financial statements into a presentation currency.

[IAS 21 paras 1, 2].

The above objectives may appear to be relatively simple, but their achievement, in practice, is fraught with difficulties, as will be apparent later in this chapter.

Scope

A7.24 IAS 21 sets out the standard accounting practice for foreign currency translation and applies to any entity that comes within its scope and engages in foreign currency operations. The standard should be applied in:

- Accounting for transactions and balances in foreign currencies, except for those derivative transactions and balances that are within the scope of IAS 39, 'Financial instruments: Recognition and measurement'.
- Translating the results and financial position of foreign operations that are included in the entity's financial statements by consolidation, proportionate consolidation or by equity accounting.
- Translating an entity's results and financial position into a presentation currency.

[IAS 21 para 3].

A7.25 Accounting for foreign currency derivatives is included in IAS 39 and, therefore, is scoped out of this standard. Foreign currency derivatives that may be embedded in various contracts and that require separate accounting under IAS 39 are scoped out of IAS 21, but embedded foreign currency derivatives that do not require separate accounting under IAS 39 are included in IAS 21. However, IAS 21 applies to translation of foreign currency derivatives from a functional currency to a presentation currency. [IAS 21 para 4].

A7.26 The standard does not apply to hedge accounting for foreign currency items, including the hedging of a net investment in a foreign operation. These issues are dealt with in IAS 39. [IAS 21 para 5]. See further chapter 6.

The functional currency approach

Introduction

A7.27 IAS 21 requires each individual entity to determine its functional currency and measure its results and financial position in that currency.

A7.28 The requirement to identify each entity's functional currency is the initial and key feature of IAS 21, as the functional currency serves as the basis for determining whether the entity is engaging in foreign currency transactions. This is because IAS 21 defines foreign currency as a currency other than the functional currency. [IAS 21 para 8]. Additionally, the selection of the functional currency has a direct impact on the treatment of exchange gains and losses arising from the translation process and, thereby, the reported results as will be evident later. IAS 21 provides guidance on determining the functional currency, which is considered from paragraph A7.31 below.

Example – identification of foreign currency transactions

An entity trades in crude oil and has a US dollar functional currency, because substantially all of its sales and purchases are in US dollars. The entity is located in London and, therefore, has significant transactions in sterling. It has issued euro-denominated share capital to its Dutch parent. Transactions with the parent are denominated in euros.

The sterling transactions and euro transactions are foreign currency transactions. The entity's physical location and the denomination of its share capital do not change the treatment of sterling and euro denominated transactions. This is because the entity has a US dollar functional currency and, therefore, all transactions in other currencies are foreign currency transactions.

[The next paragraph is A7.31.]

Determining the functional currency

A7.31 An entity's functional currency is, in principle, a matter of fact. In some cases, the facts will clearly identify the functional currency, in other cases they will not. IAS 21, therefore, provides guidance on how to determine an entity's functional currency.

A7.31.1 An entity's functional currency is the currency of the primary economic environment in which it operates. [IAS 21 para 8]. It should, therefore, be determined at the entity level. An entity includes a foreign operation, that is, a subsidiary, associate, branch or joint venture whose activities are based or conducted in a country or currency other than that of the reporting entity.

A7.31.2 An individual entity (including a foreign operation) for these purposes may not correspond to a legal entity (for example, a company). For example, a branch that is part of a single legal entity may be a foreign operation. Judgment is required in determining an entity's functional currency based on individual facts and circumstances.

A7.31.3 For a group comprised of multiple entities, the functional currency of each entity is identified for the purpose of defining that entity's foreign currency exposure. Different entities within a multinational group, therefore, often have different functional currencies. The group as a whole does not have a functional currency.

A7.32 The primary economic environment in which an entity operates is normally the economic environment in which an entity primarily generates and expends cash. [IAS 21 para 9]. Ordinarily, the functional currency is the currency of the country in which the entity is located. It may, however, be a different currency. In addition, circumstances might indicate that the foreign operation's functional currency is the same as the reporting entity's functional currency. For this purpose, a foreign operation is defined as an entity that is a subsidiary, associate, joint venture or a branch of the reporting entity, the activities of which are based or conducted in a country or currency other than that of the reporting entity. [IAS 21 para 8]. Hence, there is no longer a need to distinguish between foreign operations that are integral to the reporting entity's operations and foreign entities, which was the requirement under the previous version of IAS 21. The features now are some of the indicators of an entity's functional currency.

A7.33 IAS 21 provides guidance that takes the form of primary and secondary indicators of salient economic factors and circumstances that should be considered in determining the functional currency. Primary indicators are closely linked to the primary economic environment in which the entity operates and are given more weight. Secondary indicators provide additional supporting evidence to determine an entity's functional currency. Both of these indicators and the factors needing consideration are shown in the table below.

Primary indicators of functional currency (IAS 21 para 9)

Indicators	**Factors to be considered by the entity in determining the functional currency**
Sales and cash inflows	(a) The currency that *mainly influences* sales prices for its goods and services. This will often be the currency in which sales prices for goods and services are denominated and settled. [IAS 21 para 9(a)(i)]. In other words, where an active local sales market exists for the entity's products that are also priced in the local currency and revenues are collected primarily in that local currency, then this indicates that the local currency is the functional currency. However, the standard gives greater emphasis than SIC 19 gave to the currency of the economy that determines the pricing of transactions, as opposed to the currency in which transactions are denominated.
	(b) The currency of the country whose competitive forces and regulations *mainly determine* the sales prices of its goods and services. [IAS 21 para 9(a)(ii)]. Therefore, where sales prices of the entity's products are determined by local competition and local government regulations rather than worldwide competition or by international prices, then this indicates that the local currency is the functional currency. For example, aircraft manufacturers often price aircraft in US dollars or in euros, but the legal and regulatory environment of the country in which the manufacturer is located may inhibit the entity's ability to pass hard currency costs to its customers. Thus, while the business is influenced by the hard currency, its ability to generate revenue is determined by the local environment, which may indicate that the local currency is the functional currency.
Expenses and cash outflows	The currency that *mainly influences* labour, material and other costs of providing goods and services. This will often be the currency in which such costs are denominated and settled. [IAS 21 para 9(b)]. For example, where labour, material and other operating costs are primarily sourced and incurred locally, then this points to the local currency being the functional currency, even though there also might be imports from other countries.

Secondary indicators of functional currency (IAS 21 para 10)	
Indicators	**Factors to be considered by the entity in determining the functional currency**
Financing activities	The currency in which funds from financing activities (for example, issuing debt and equity instruments) are generated. [IAS 21 para 10(a)]. For example, where financing is raised in and serviced by funds primarily generated by the entity's local operation, in the absence of other indicators to the contrary this may indicate that the local currency is the functional currency.
Retention of operating income	The currency in which receipts from operating activities are usually retained. [IAS 21 para 10(b)]. This is the currency in which the entity maintains its excess working capital balance, which would generally be the local currency.

A7.34 Note that the above primary and secondary indicators for determining of the functional currency must be considered by all entities. If the entity is a foreign operation, the standard specifies four additional factors that should be considered in determining the functional currency and whether it is the same as that of the reporting entity. These additional factors are shown in the table below and set out the conditions that point to whether the foreign operation's functional currency is the same as, or different from, the reporting entity (the reporting entity, in this context, being the entity that has the foreign operation as its subsidiary, branch, associate or joint venture). Where indicators are mixed, judgement should be exercised to determine the functional currency. However, in the determination of functional currency management should give priority to the primary indicators. [IAS 21 para 12].

Additional indicators for foreign operations (IAS 21 para 11)

Indicators	**Conditions pointing to functional currency being *different from* that of the reporting entity**	**Conditions pointing to functional currency being the *same as* that of the reporting entity**
Degree of autonomy	Activities are carried out with a significant degree of autonomy. An example is when the operation accumulates cash and other monetary items, incurs expenses, generates income and arranges borrowings, all substantially in its local currency.	No significant degree of autonomy – activities are carried out as an extension of the reporting entity. An example is when the foreign operation only sells goods imported from the reporting entity and remits the proceeds to it. It follows that such an entity (which would be regarded an integral foreign operation in the previous version of IAS 21) must have the same currency as the reporting entity. This is because it would be contradictory for an integral foreign operation that *"carries on business as if it were an extension of the reporting entity's operations"* to operate in a primary economic environment different from its parent. [IAS 21 para BC6].
Frequency of transactions with reporting entity	Few inter-company transactions with the reporting entity.	Frequent and extensive inter-company transactions with the reporting entity.
Cash flow impact on reporting entity	Mainly in local currency and do not affect reporting entity's cash flows	Directly impact the reporting entity's cash flows and are readily available for remittance to the reporting entity.
Financing	Primarily in the local currency and serviced by funds generated by the entity's operation.	Significant financing from or reliance on the reporting entity to service existing and normally expected debt obligations.

A7.35 In practice, the relative importance of the various indicators will vary from entity to entity. For example, the primary and secondary indicators apply to the generality of entities that provide goods and services and, therefore, they may not be directly relevant in certain situations. In those situations, management may need to consider the additional indicators stated in paragraph A7.34 above when determining the functional currency.

A7.36 In assessing the indicators' relative importance, management may find it useful to consider the following aspects of each indicator:

- The significance of that indicator to the entity's operation. For example, the existence of sterling denominated debt in a foreign entity of a UK parent may not be significant if the foreign entity is primarily self-financing through retained earnings.
- How clearly the indicator identifies a particular currency as the functional currency. For example, if the same entity purchases raw materials both from the UK and locally, the 'expenses' indicator may be rather inconclusive.

In contrast, if, for the same entity, the majority of sales occur in the host country at prices determined by local conditions, the 'sales' indicator might then be regarded as the key determinant in concluding that the local currency is the functional currency.

A7.37 It may be that after considering all the factors, the functional currency is still not obvious. The operation may be diverse, with cash flows, financing and transactions occurring in more than a single currency. In those situations where the indicators are mixed and the functional currency is not obvious, considerable management judgement is required in determining the functional currency that most faithfully represents the economic effects of the underlying transactions, events and conditions. In exercising that judgement, the standard states that management must give priority to the primary indicators before considering the secondary indicators and the additional factors set out above. [IAS 21 para 12].

A7.38 The reason why the standard gives greater emphasis to the primary indicators is that, as stated above, these indicators are closely linked to the primary economic environment in which the entity operates. The currency of the economy in which the entity operates generally determines the pricing of transactions and this is considered to be more important and influential than the currency in which the transactions are denominated and settled. This is because transactions can be denominated and settled in any currency management chooses, but since the pricing of the transaction is normally done by reference to the economy of the country whose competitive forces and regulations affect the transaction, then the currency of that economy, by definition, becomes the functional currency. In other words, the currency of the country whose economy drives the business and which determines the gains and losses that fall to be recognised in the financial statements most faithfully reflects the economic effects of the underlying transactions, events and conditions.

A7.39 The standard's intention that the primary and secondary indicators should be looked at as a hierarchy is intended to avoid practical difficulties in determining an entity's functional currency. For example, if after careful consideration, all the primary indicators, which should be considered together, clearly identify a particular currency as the functional currency, there is no need to consider the secondary indicators. Secondary indicators mainly serve to provide additional supporting evidence in determining an entity's functional currency. [IAS 21 para BC9].

Illustrative examples

A7.40 The determination of the functional currency depends on the specific facts and circumstances. The following examples are for illustrative purposes only and should not be used as solutions for specific situations.

Example 1 – functional currency of a real estate entity operating in Russia with leases denominated in US dollars

A real estate entity operates in Russia. It owns several office buildings in Moscow and St Petersburg that are rented to Russian and foreign companies. All lease contracts are denominated in US dollars, but payments can be made in either US dollars or in Russian roubles. However, almost all of the lease payments are settled in roubles. This has also been the historical pattern of payment.

On first analysis, the 'sales and cash inflows' indicators appear to produce a mixed response, because the currency that mainly influences the pricing of the lease contracts is the US dollar, whereas the cash inflows are in roubles. Also, cash outflows such as the principal operating costs, management of properties, insurance, taxes and staff costs are likely to be incurred and settled in roubles, which would indicate that the functional currency is the Russian rouble.

Although the lease payments are denominated in US dollars, the US dollar is not considered to be significant to the entity's operation because (a) most of the collection is in roubles, which is subject to short-term changes in US dollar/rouble exchange rate (b) it is the local conditions and circumstances in Russia, not the US, that determine the rental yields of properties in Moscow and St Petersburg that mainly influence the pricing of the lease contracts, which are merely denominated in US dollar.

It follows from the above that it is the currency of the Russian economy, rather than the currency in which the lease contracts are denominated, that most faithfully represents the economic effects of the real estate activity in Russia.

Example 2 – functional currency of an oil refinery in Saudi Arabia

Entity A operates an oil refinery in Saudi Arabia. All of the entity's income is denominated and settled in US dollars. The oil price is subject to the worldwide supply and demand and crude oil is routinely traded in US dollars around the world. Around 45% of entity A's cash costs are imports or expatriate salaries denominated in US dollars. The remaining 55% of cash expenses are incurred in Saudi Arabia and denominated and settled in riyal. The non-cash costs (depreciation) are US dollar denominated since the initial investment was in US dollars.

In this case, the functional currency of entity A is the US dollar. The crude oil sales prices are influenced by global demand and supply. Crude oil is globally traded in US dollars around the world. The revenue analysis clearly points to the US dollar. The cost analysis is mixed. Depreciation (or any other non-cash expenses) is not considered, because the primary economic environment is where the entity generates and expends cash. Operating cash expenses are influenced by the riyal (55%) and the US dollar (45%). Management is able to determine the functional currency as the US dollar, because the revenue is clearly influenced by the US dollar and expenses are mixed.

Example 3 – functional currency of an intermediate parent with some operating activities

Parent (P) is a manufacturing business located in the UK with sterling as the functional currency. P invests US dollars in an intermediate parent (IP) which then invests in three separate US dollar operating subsidiaries (S1, S2 and S3). IP undertakes no 'operating' activities of its own, however, it acts as the holding company of the US subsidiaries – heading up the US group. It has a dedicated management team and staff that carry out the head office functions, including the US group's payroll, cash management and preparation of a sub-consolidation package. Its management team report monthly to P's board on the results of the US group. Its key cash inflows are the dividends from its subsidiaries (which it remits up directly to P), and inter-company balances from its subsidiaries (that are used to settle both IP's own administration costs and those costs incurred directly by IP on behalf of its subsidiaries, that is payroll costs, computer services, maintenance etc). All of its cash inflows and outflows are denominated in US dollar. IP is a US registered company.

In this situation, IP does have operating activities in that it provides local management services to its subsidiaries. It incurs local costs and then will either recharge these to its subsidiaries or it will retain dividend income from its subsidiaries to pay for these costs. All the costs incurred are incurred in US dollar and will be reimbursed in US dollar.

IP does not raise finance so consideration of the currency in which funds from financing activities are generated is not directly applicable. However, the funding of its costs through dividends and inter-company balances is in US dollar. Consideration of the currency in which receipts from operating activities are usually retained would indicate a US dollar functional currency.

Looking to the additional factors in paragraph 11 of IAS 21 revised:

- The IP does have a significant degree of autonomy here – it has its own management team and staff. It has a budget for which it is responsible and has discretion over its head office functions.
- It has a number of transactions with parties outside the group.
- The cash flows of the IP do not directly affect the parent, that is, IP is not merely acting as a conduit here.

Consideration of 11(d), *"whether cash flows from activities of the foreign operation are sufficient to service existing and normally expected debt obligations without funds being made available by the reporting entity"* is not applicable.

Unlike example 4, IP is carrying out operating activities of its own, albeit not in the traditional trading sense. Applying paragraphs 9 and 10 of IAS 21 revised, it is clear that the costs IP incurs and any receipts retained from operating activities are in US dollar. IP in this example is not merely acting as a conduit/cash box for P. It is carrying out management activities and does have a significant degree of autonomy. It has an active management team and exercises discretion over the US group's operations. The US group has been structured in this way for operational, as well as for tax reasons. This suggests that the functional currency of IP should not necessarily be that of P. In these circumstances the functional currency of IP would be US dollar.

Example 4 – functional currency of an intermediate parent with no operating or financing activities of its own

Parent (P) is a manufacturing business located in the UK with sterling as the functional currency. P invests US dollar in an intermediate parent (IP), which then invests in a US dollar operating subsidiary (S) on behalf of P. IP undertakes no operating or financing activities. Its key cash inflows are dividends from S, which it remits up directly to parent P. IP is a US registered company.

In this example, IP undertakes no operating or financing activities. Any investing activity that is undertaken by IP is not carried out as a separate stand-alone activity, but at the behest of its parent. Consequently, considering the 'sales and cash inflow' indicator is not relevant. The 'expenses and cash outflow' indicator may be relevant as it is more likely than not that IP will incur some local costs, but that indicator, by itself, is not considered significant to IP's operations, nor does it clearly identify the US dollar as the functional currency.

It is also clear that the secondary indicators do not clearly identify the US dollar as the functional currency as IP does not raise any finance from external local sources – any finance raised is primarily from its parent or otherwise from sterling sources. Nor does IP retain any funds for own use, which are all remitted to the parent. Consideration of all the additional factors also points to the fact that the US dollar is not the currency that most faithfully represents IP's activities of receiving dividend income from S in US dollars and remitting the same to its parent.

It follows that IP is simply a device or a shell corporation for holding investments that could readily have been done by P itself. Hence, the functional currency of IP is the same as its parent, that is, sterling.

Some argue that an alternative analysis can be advanced in this example as follows. IP does not undertake any operating activities in the sense of conducting businesses with third parties. Therefore, although the primary indicator, 'sales and cash inflows', is not directly relevant, nevertheless IP invests in US dollar in its operating subsidiary and receives cash inflows in the form of dividends from its subsidiary, also in US dollar. In other words, the results of IP are dependent on the economic activities of its subsidiary whose functional currency is the US dollar. Therefore, the cash inflow indicator would appear to suggest that the US dollar is significant to its investing activity.

Since IP is located in the US, it is likely that any local expenses, although not stated in the question, are also incurred and settled in US dollar. Therefore the 'expenses and cash outflow' indicators appear to point to US dollar as the functional currency.

It appears from analysis of the primary indicators that the economic environment in which the IP primarily generates and expends cash is the US. Hence its functional currency would be the US dollar.

However, consideration of the secondary indicators does not seem to provide supporting evidence that the US dollar is the functional currency. This is because IP does not raise any finance from external local sources – any finance raised is primarily from its parent or otherwise from sterling sources. Nor does IP retain any funds for its own use, which are all remitted to the parent.

On the other hand, consideration of the additional factors would appear to support the US dollar as the functional currency. For instance, the investing activity of IP is unlikely to be regarded as an extension of the manufacturing activities of P; other than the remittance of dividends once or twice a year there are few, if any, transactions between IP and P and, furthermore, the occasional remittance of dividends in US dollar is unlikely to have any significant impact on P's cash flows.

Where the indicators are mixed, the standard suggests that management should exercise judgement in determining the currency that most faithfully represents IP's activities. In exercising this judgment, greater weight should be given to the primary indicators. In our view, the primary indicators, whilst they indicate the US dollar, are not strong. In this example, IP is a shell intermediate holding company that merely holds the investment and receives occasional dividends, passing them on to the parent, so it is appropriate to regard it as carrying out a function that the parent could equally carry out. Our view is that in such circumstances, sterling is the functional currency of the IP.

Example 5 – functional currency of a company raising finance for the group in a foreign currency compared to the other entities in the group

A French listed parent has significant French, UK and US operating subsidiaries, but no Japanese operations. The French parent creates a new subsidiary incorporated and resident in France, Newco SA. Newco issues in yen, 1bn of equity capital to French parent, receiving yen 1bn of cash. Newco also raises yen100m of external financing and places the yen1.1bn total cash on deposit with a bank in Japan, earning 0.1% interest per annum. The cash will be reinvested in yen denominated financial instruments such as bonds and commercial paper. Newco has few staff that manage the entity's investing activities and incurs sterling operational costs that are insignificant compared to the interest paid on its yen borrowing. Like any wholly-owned subsidiary, the retained profits are under the parent's control.

In this example, Newco does not undertake any key operating activities on its own. Therefore, consideration of the currency that mainly influences sales and costs is not directly relevant. Newco does incur expenses in euro, but these are not significant by themselves to suggest that euro is the functional currency. There, it is necessary to look at the secondary indicators.

Newco does raise finance by issuing its own equity instruments to the parent in a currency that is different from the parent, but the proceeds are invested in yen-denominated assets at the behest of the parent. The external funds raised through the issue of debt instruments are insignificant compared to the issue of equity shares to the parent. The question is silent as to whether the income generated from the investments is reinvested in other yen denominated assets or whether it is wholly passed on to the parent. Whatever that may be, the decision to reinvest or distribute is under the parent's control.

Consideration of the other additional factors appears to suggest that Newco is merely a 'cash box' type company with no independent management/activity. Newco is simply a conduit for the parent entity that could readily invest the yen directly. It may be that the only reason the parent entity has invested the yen through Newco is in the hope that its exposure to changes in the euro/yen exchange rate is reported in equity through the translation of its net investment in Newco, rather than in the income statement that would be the case if the yen deposits were treated as directly belonging to the parent. The 'autonomy factor' points to euro as the functional currency in that Newco is merely an extension of the activities of the parent. This would point to the functional currency being the same as that of its parent, that is, euro in this example. This would be the answer if Newco carried out only the activities described.

Some argue that an alternative analysis can be advanced in this situation. That is, Newco's only source of revenue is from interest received on its yen deposit. Although the primary indicator 'sales and cash inflows' is directed towards entities that are engaged in the provision of goods and services, nevertheless it is clear that the currency of the country whose competitive forces and regulations mainly determine that revenue is the yen. This is because if the Japanese economy picked up and the market interest rate in Japan rose, Newco's income would increase from the initial 0.1%. Improvement or deterioration of the French economy is unlikely to have any effect on yen cash flows.

Similarly, the 'expenses and cash outflow' indicator points to the yen as the functional currency as Newco's interest payments in yen on its yen borrowing are significant compared to the other costs incurred in sterling.

Hence, both the primary indicators clearly identify the yen as the functional currency that most faithfully represents the economic activities undertaken by Newco. Consideration of the two secondary indicators – 'financing' (raising some funds locally) and 'retention of income' (reinvestment of investment income – not strictly necessary) provides additional evidence that yen is the functional currency.

However, we do not believe that this alternative analysis is valid based on the facts given in this example. The investing activity could easily have been done by the parent rather than the subsidiary and, therefore, the functional currency of the parent should determine the functional currency of the foreign entity.

Example 6 – functional currency of an offshore holding company

A group of companies is organised as follows:

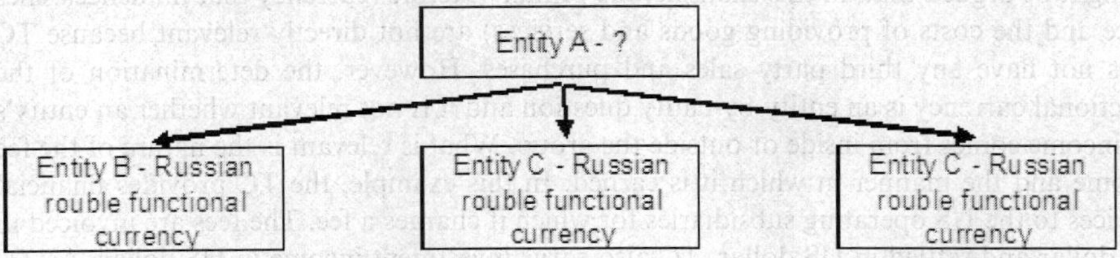

Entity A is a reporting entity and management has concluded on the functional currency of each operating subsidiary (entities B, C and D). All three subsidiaries are incorporated in Russia and management has reached the conclusion that the functional currency of each subsidiary should be the local currency. It is assumed that management's conclusion is appropriate.

Entity A is the holding company and has been set up by institutional investors in Cyprus. Entity A has obtained equity and loan financing and has invested in Russia. It pools cash from all group entities, invests excess cash and obtains external financing, according to the Group's needs. The majority of its financing is drawn in US dollars and all of its assets are denominated in US dollars.

Entity A's functional currency is the Russian rouble. The currency that reflects the economic substance of the underlying economic events is the Russian rouble, because all of the subsidiaries of the holding entity are operating in Russia and the primary source of income of entity A will be Russia. The ability of entity A to service debts and pay dividends to shareholders is dependant on the Russian economy.

Example 7 – functional currency of separate treasury centres in different geographical areas

A Swiss multi-national company with swiss franc as its functional currency has operating subsidiaries in the US and Europe whose functional currencies are the US dollar and the euro respectively. It has established a treasury centre (TC) in each of the above geographical regions. The activities of the two TCs are identical in that each provides financial and risk management services to its relevant operating subsidiaries. All transactions (for example, management of liquid funds, borrowings and hedging activities) between a TC and its respective operating subsidiaries are carried out either in US dollar or euros.

Each TC earns dividends and income from cash management activities in US dollar and euros respectively. Each TC charges a monthly fee for providing such financial services to its operating subsidiaries that is denominated either in US dollar or euros, depending on its area of operation. Similarly all operating costs, such as staff costs payable to treasury and financial management specialists and other administrative and running costs, are incurred and settled by each TC in US dollar or euros. Both TC's short and long-term financing are provided by the Swiss parent in the form of swiss franc loans. The TCs do not retain any US dollar or euros generated from their operation for their own use. After meeting local expenses, the US dollar or euros are either used to settle the inter-company payables to the operating subsidiaries or any surplus is distributed to the parent as dividends.

This response deals only with the US dollar TC; the considerations for the euro TC are the same.

It might be argued that, in this example, the primary factors (currency that influences sales price and the costs of providing goods and services) are not directly relevant because TC does not have any third party sales and purchases. However, the determination of the functional currency is an entity-by-entity question and it is not relevant whether an entity's fee income comes from inside or outside the group. What is relevant is the nature of the fee income and the manner in which it is earned. In this example, the TC provides financial services to the US operating subsidiaries for which it charges a fee. The fees are invoiced in US dollar and settled in US dollar. TC also earns investment income in US dollar. As TC earns its revenue and income in US dollar and the underlying US economy determines the pricing of TC's fee income to the US operating subsidiaries, the 'sales and cash inflow' indicator clearly identifies that the US dollar as the functional currency of TC. Also, as all administrative and local expenses are incurred and settled in US dollar, the 'expenses and cash outflow' indicator also provides strong evidence that the US dollar is the functional currency of the TC. It follows that the primary economic environment in which the TC generates and expends cash is the US, and, hence, its functional currency is the US dollar.

Given that the primary indicators are clear, there is no need to consider the secondary indicators even if these seem to provide evidence that Swiss franc is the functional currency (for example, TC's short and long-term financing is primarily in the form of Swiss franc loans from the parent).

Example 8 – functional currency of a treasury centre that pools resources in the group

A UK multi-national company with sterling as its functional currency has set up a treasury centre (TC) in Switzerland. TC borrows US dollars, euros and sterling in the euro-market and lends the proceeds to its parent and other operating subsidiaries with the loans denominated in the borrowing entity's functional currency. As part of its cash management operations, it pools the liquid resources of the parent and the operational units and invests them temporarily in the euro-market. It also manages foreign exchange and interest rate risks of operating units by executing derivative contracts with third parties and/or with operating units.

TC earns dividends and income from cash management activities in US dollar, euros and sterling. It charges a monthly fee for providing such financial services to its parent and operating subsidiaries that is denominated in the relevant entity's functional currencies. All operating costs, such as staff costs payable to treasury and financial management specialists and other administrative and running costs are incurred and settled in Swiss francs. However, TC's short and long-term financing needs are provided by its parent in the form of sterling loans.

In this example, TC provides financial services to group companies for which it charges a fee. However, the fees are invoiced in the functional currencies of the group companies and settled in those currencies. This is done to ensure that the risk of non-functional currency transaction gains and losses on all inter-company transactions with the TC are effectively passed on from the operating units to the TC for centralised management and control. TC also earns investment income in US dollar, euros and sterling. As TC earns its revenue and income in different currencies, the 'sales and cash inflow' indicator fails to identify a particular currency that is significant in its own right as the functional currency of TC. Furthermore, there is no explicit or implicit evidence to suggest that the underlying Swiss economy determines the pricing of TC's fee income to the group companies.

On the other hand, as all administrative and local expenses are incurred and settled in Swiss francs, the 'expenses and cash outflow' indicator provides strong evidence that Swiss franc is the functional currency.

Therefore, as the primary indicators are not sufficiently conclusive in identifying the functional currency, it is necessary to consider the secondary indicators.

Consideration of the secondary indicators seems to provide evidence that sterling is the functional currency. This is because TC does not raise any finance from external local sources for meeting the cost of its operations in excess of its operating income, but relies on short and long-term financing needs on its parent. Furthermore, since cash inflows from operations occur in various currencies that are used to meet local expenses, retention of cash indicator is not significant in determining TC's functional currency.

Consideration of the additional factors would also appear to support sterling as the functional currency. For instance, the 'autonomy indicator' appears to suggest that the UK parent has set up the TC to achieve overall financial efficiency of its international operations through centralised control and effective management of cash and financial risk. The volume of inter-company transactions is large due to the regular transfer of foreign currency cash balances from and to the parent. Consequently, the cash flows of the TC directly impact the parent's cash flows on a regular basis. The financing indicator also identifies sterling as the functional currency.

The above analysis suggests that the primary indicators do not by themselves provide any conclusive evidence that the local currency of the country in which TC operates is its functional currency. However, the secondary indicators appear to support sterling as the functional currency. Overall, the evidence is mixed and in these circumstances management should exercise judgement in determining the currency that most faithfully represents the economic effects of TC's activities. There are a number of possible solutions, depending on the judgement about the overall balance of evidence. One indicator may be that TC has been set up primarily as a conduit to undertake the treasury operations of the entire multinational group headed by the UK parent and, hence, the currency of the country that most faithfully represents TC's operations is the functional currency of the UK parent, that is, sterling. Another factor to consider is whether any of the three major currencies (dollars, euros, sterling) is dominant. A further factor, especially if no clear currency is suggested by the previous factors, and especially if the TC's operating expenses are significant, is that the Swiss franc may be the TC's functional currency.

Example 9 – functional currency of a foreign subsidiary importing products from parent for local distribution

A foreign subsidiary located in Spain imports a product manufactured by its US parent at a price denominated in US dollars. The product is sold throughout Spain at selling prices denominated in euros that are determined primarily by competition with similar locally produced products. All selling and operating expenses are incurred locally and paid in euros. The operation's long-term financing is primarily in the form of US dollar loans from the parent. Like any subsidiary, the distribution of profits is under the parent's control.

In this example, the 'sales and cash inflows' indicators suggest that the foreign subsidiary's functional currency is the euro, because that is the currency in which the sales prices are denominated and settled. Furthermore, the sales prices for the foreign entity's products are not primarily responsive on a short-term basis to changes in exchange rates, but are determined by local competition and the local government regulation. Hence, this indicator provides strong evidence that the functional currency is that the euro.

The 'expenses and cash outflows' indicators appear to provide a mixed response. This is because cost of sales is primarily denominated and settled in US dollar, whereas local expenses, including selling expenses, are denominated and settled in euros. Given that a significant part of the expenses are settled in US dollars, this indicator does not provide conclusive evidence that the euro is the functional currency.

Therefore, it would appear that the primary indicators produce a mixed response, although overall more in favour of the euro. Hence, it is necessary to look at the secondary indicators.

Consideration of the secondary indicators seems to provide supporting evidence that US dollar is the functional currency. This is because the foreign subsidiary's long-term financing is primarily in the form of US dollar loans from the parent and the subsidiary does not raise any finance from external local sources. Furthermore, it appears that the foreign subsidiary does not retain any euros generated from its operations for its own use.

After meeting local expenses, the euros are either used to settle the inter-company payables to the parent or any surplus is probably distributed to the parent as dividends.

If the 'autonomy' indicator suggests that the foreign subsidiary is simply acting as an agent for its US parent by selling parent produced goods to customers in Spain, collecting the proceeds and remitting the same to the US parent, the functional currency would be US dollar. The volume of inter-company transactions is large as the foreign subsidiary imports goods from its US parent and settles the proceeds on a regular basis. Consequently, the subsidiary's cash flows directly impact the parent's cash flows on a regular basis.

However, if the foreign subsidiary's operations were carried out with a significant degree of autonomy (that is, local management has a significant degree of authority and responsibility, such as to borrow loans, invest excess cash, modify prices or grant discounts, hire and fire staff), the functional currency would need to be determined independently from the parent. In that case, management would conclude that the functional currency is the euro, as the primary indicators of paragraph 9 are, although mixed, overall in favour of the euro.

Example 10 – functional currency of a special purpose entity ('SPE')

Entity A is a US bank with a US dollar functional currency. Entity A establishes an SPE in a European country in order to invest in a European bond portfolio. Entity A has funded the SPE with equity and inter-company debt denominated in euros. The SPE uses the financing to purchase a portfolio of euro government bonds. There is no intention that the SPE should perform any activities other than holding the bond portfolio. The directors are all employees of the US parent and the SPE has no active management of its own.

The functional currency of the SPE is US dollar as the entity has no operations and does not provide any services. Therefore, the primary indicators are not applicable. The 'financing' indicator appears to support the euro, as all financing is in euro. However, the financing is all inter-company and entity A could denominate the financing in any currency it wanted. Considering the 'autonomy' indicator, it is clear the SPE is not autonomous. It is a shell company, has no independent activities and no active management of its own.

Example 11 – different functional currencies for stand-alone accounts and for group reporting purposes?

Entity A is an autonomous foreign operation of reporting entity Z. Entity A operates in a country where the US dollar is frequently used because the local currency has been inflationary in the past.

Entity A primarily operates in the local market and is requested to prepare statutory stand-alone financial statements in accordance with IFRS. Local regulations require entity A to use the local currency as presentation currency for the statutory accounts. Management has determined that the local currency should be the functional currency for the stand-alone financial statements. Entity A is also required to prepare an IFRS reporting package for entity Z. Management believes that entity A should use the US dollar as the functional currency for group reporting purposes, because the US dollar is frequently used in the local economy and because the group presentation currency is US dollar.

An entity can have only one functional currency. The functional currency is the currency of the primary economic environment and this is the same for stand-alone financial statements and for group reporting purposes. Entity A should use the local currency as its functional currency for both statutory and group reporting purposes.

Example 12 – functional currency after a group restructuring

A group has been restructured inserting a new parent at the top of the group structure. Should the functional currency of the new parent be reassessed after the group restructuring?

Yes. The functional currency of the new parent company should be reassessed to determine whether the previous IAS 21 functional currency determination is impacted by the group restructuring. For example, when the ownership of an operating company is transferred to a holding company with limited or no other activities, IAS 21 will likely require the holding company to have the same functional currency as that of the newly acquired operating company.

Entity with multiple operations

A7.41 An entity might have more than one distinct and separable operation, such as a division or a branch, in which case each operation may be considered a separate entity for the purposes of this standard. For example, a foreign entity might have one operation that acts as a selling agent receiving inventories of goods from the parent entity and remitting the proceeds back to the company and another operation that manufactures and sells products locally. If those two operations are conducted in different economic environments, they may well have different functional currencies.

A7.42 However, the foreign entity must determine its functional currency and measure its results and financial position in that currency before it can be included in the reporting entity when it prepares its financial statements. In situations such as above, it may be appropriate to designate the predominant currency of the foreign entity as its functional currency. Once the foreign entity's functional currency is determined, the results and financial position of its branches having different functional currencies will be included in the foreign entity using the translation method set out in paragraph A7.76 below.

Different functional currencies for entities in the same country

A7.43 It is also possible for an entity to have two or more foreign operations in a given country and determine different functional currency for those entities. For example, a UK entity could have a sales branch and an operating subsidiary in the same country, thus justifying different functional currencies. Another example that may occur in practice is where the UK entity has a subsidiary in a foreign country that manufactures and sells goods locally and another subsidiary in that same country whose operations are fundamentally different. For each of these entities, it would be necessary to determine the appropriate functional currency using the guidance discussed from paragraph A7.31 above.

Accounting records not maintained in functional currency

A7.44 If a foreign operation's books or records are not maintained in its functional currency, remeasurement into its functional currency is required. That remeasurement is required at the time the foreign operation prepares its financial statements before they are translated into the presentation currency of the reporting entity. The remeasurement into the functional currency, that should be carried out using the translation method set out in paragraph A7.76 below, would produce the same amounts in the functional currency as would have occurred had all the items been recorded in the functional currency in the first place. For example, monetary items are translated into the functional currency using the closing rate, and non-monetary items that are measured on a historical cost basis are translated using the exchange rate at the date of the transaction that resulted in their recognition. [IAS 21 para 34].

Change in functional currency

A7.45 Once the functional currency of a foreign operation is determined, it should be used consistently, unless significant changes in economic facts, events and conditions clearly indicate that the functional currency has changed. For example, a foreign operation that was carried out as an extension of the reporting entity's business may, as a result of changed circumstances, become primarily regional in nature.

A7.46 It follows from the above that a change in functional currency should be accounted for *prospectively* from the date of change. In other words, an entity should translate all items into the new functional currency using the exchange rate at the date of change. [IAS 21 para 37]. The reason for this is that as the change was brought about by changed circumstances, it does not represent a change in accounting policy and, therefore, a retrospective adjustment under IAS 8, 'Accounting policies, changes in accounting estimates and correction of errors', is not relevant. As all items are translated using the exchange rate at the date of change, the resulting translated amounts for non-monetary items are treated as their historical cost. Exchange differences that arose from the translation of the foreign operation and that were recognised in equity remain in equity and are only recognised in profit or loss on the foreign operation's disposal. [IAS 21 para 37].

A7.47 It may not be practicable to determine the date of change precisely at a point during the year. It is also likely that the change may have occurred gradually during the year. Where this is the case, we consider that it may be appropriate, for pragmatic reasons, to account for the change as of the beginning or end of the accounting period in which the change occurs, whichever more closely approximates the date of change.

Example 1 – change in functional currency

A UK entity operates a foreign branch in France with sterling as its functional currency. A significant change in trading operations and circumstances occurred during the first quarter of the financial year ended 30 June 20X6, which indicated that, going forward, sterling could no longer faithfully represent the underlying transactions, events and conditions of the foreign branch. The UK management decided that the euro should be the functional currency of its foreign operation and that all transactions undertaken from the beginning of the financial year 30 June 20X6 should be recorded in euros.

As stated in paragraph A7.46 above, the foreign branch's financial statements at 30 June 20X5, which were previously prepared in sterling, should be translated to euros at the rate of exchange ruling at the date of change, which in this situation is first day of the current financial year, that is, 1 July 20X5. This means all items in the balance sheet should be translated at the rate of exchange ruling at 30 June 20X5, which approximates to the date of change. Since the change in functional currency should be accounted for prospectively, retrospective application is not permitted. If the foreign branch also chooses to change its presentation currency to the euro, the income statement for the year ended 30 June 20X5 should be translated at the actual rates or at rates that approximate the average rate for the year ended 30 June 20X5.

Example 2 – change in functional currency: impact on a depreciated asset

The facts are the same as in the previous example, except that the foreign branch purchased on I January 20X0 an asset for €164,000 having a useful life of 10 years when the rate of exchange was £1 = €1.64. Since the foreign branch's functional currency was sterling, the asset would be recorded at the sterling equivalent cost of £100,000. At 31 December 20X5, the equipment has a net book value of £50,000 and a historical euro book value of €82,000.

As a result of the change in functional currency from sterling to euros on 1 January 20X6 (exchange rate at 31 December 20X5 is £1 = €1.45), the functional currency amount of the asset should be carried at €72,500 (£50,000 @ 1.45), which becomes its new historical cost rather than the previous historical value of €82,000. However, if as a result of exchange movements, the new historical cost exceeded the previous historical value at the date of change, an impairment review may be necessary if the indications are that the recoverable amount is less than €82,000. [IAS 21 para 25].

Foreign currency transactions

Introduction

A7.48 Foreign currency transactions are transactions denominated in a currency other than the entity's functional currency. Foreign currency transactions may produce receivables or payables that are fixed in terms of the amount of foreign currency that will be received or paid. For example, an entity may buy or sell goods or services in a foreign currency; borrow or lend money in a foreign currency; acquire or dispose of assets; or incur and settle liabilities in a foreign currency.

Initial recognition

A7.49 A foreign currency transaction should initially be recorded, on initial recognition in the functional currency, by applying to the foreign currency amount the spot exchange rate between the functional currency and the foreign currency at the date of the transaction. [IAS 21 para 21]. This process is known as translation whereby financial data denominated in one currency is expressed in terms of another currency. Translation includes not only the expression of individual transactions in terms of another currency, but also the expression of a complete set of financial statements prepared in one currency in terms of another currency (see further para A7.76).

A7.50 The date of transaction is the date on which the transaction first qualifies for recognition in accordance with IFRS. [IAS 21 para 22]. The spot exchange rate is the exchange rate for immediate delivery. [IAS 21 para 8]. For revenues, expenses, gains and losses, the spot exchange rate at the dates on which those elements are recognised should be used. Because translation at the actual exchange rate at the dates the numerous revenues, expenses, gains and losses are recognised is generally impractical, a rate that approximates to the actual rate, for example an average rate, may be used.

A7.51 The above rules appear to be relatively straightforward, but their application in practice may create a number of problems. They include amongst others: determining the date of transaction, which may not always be that obvious; determining an average rate as an approximation to the actual rate; and the selection of an appropriate rate for translating foreign currency transactions where there is more than one rate in operation.

Determining the average rate

A7.52 The standard permits the use of an average rate for a period for recording foreign currency transactions as a proxy to the actual rate prevailing at the date of each transaction, provided that there is no significant change in rates during that period. An average rate is unlikely to be used by companies undertaking few transactions in a foreign currency. It is also unlikely to be used for translating large, one-off transactions that would be recorded at the actual rate. The flexibility allowed in IAS 21 is likely to be most beneficial to companies that enter into a large number of transactions in different currencies, or that maintain multi-currency ledgers. However, no guidance is provided in the standard as to how such a rate should be determined.

A7.53 Determining an average rate and its use in practice will depend on a number of factors, such as: the nature of the company's accounting systems; the frequency and value of transactions undertaken; the period over which the rate will apply; and the acceptable level of materiality. The choice of the period to be used for calculating the average rate will depend on the extent to which daily exchange rates fluctuate in the period selected. If exchange rates are relatively stable over a period of say, one month, then the average exchange rate for that month can be used as an approximation to the daily rate. If, however, there is volatility of exchange rates, it may be appropriate to calculate an average rate for a shorter period such as a week. Whatever period is chosen, materiality is likely to be an important consideration.

A7.54 Depending on the circumstances, a company may use an actual average rate or an estimated average rate. An actual average rate is likely to be used where there is some delay between the date when the transactions occurred and the date when they are recorded. In other situations, it may be necessary for a company to use an estimated average rate for a period rather than wait for the period to end in order to calculate an actual average rate. This estimate may be based on the average of daily exchange rates for the previous period or the closing rate of the previous period. Whichever basis is used, it will be necessary to ensure than the estimated average rate is a close approximation of the actual rates prevailing during the period. If it is not, the rate should be revised accordingly.

Multiple exchange rates

A7.55 Some countries may operate more than one exchange rate. In that situation, the question arises as to which rate should be used to translate and record the foreign currency transactions and balances. IAS 21 states that when several exchange rates are available, the rate used is that at which the future cash flows represented by the transaction or balance could have been settled if those cash flows had occurred at the measurement date. [IAS 21 para 26].

Example – use of an autonomous rate

On 1 January 20X4, the government of country A announced that with effect from that date all commercial exchange transactions would take place at the autonomous rate of exchange (say £1 = FC 65 where FC is the foreign currency of country A) rather than at the official rate of exchange (say £1 = FC 50). This means that all imports and exports and remittances of profits, dividends and technical services and other fees will take place at the autonomous rate of exchange.

Therefore, when retranslating foreign exchange transactions and monetary amounts receivable and payable in the financial statements of an individual company, the autonomous rate rather than the official rate of exchange should be used. This would also apply to the translation of the results and net assets of subsidiary companies operating in country A for inclusion in the UK parent's consolidated financial statements.

Suspension of rates

A7.56 From time to time, countries may experience economic conditions that affect the free-market convertibility of the local currency. As a result, the exchangeability between two currencies may be temporarily lacking at the transaction date or a subsequent balance sheet date. In this situation, IAS 21 requires companies to use the rate on the first subsequent date at which exchanges could be made. [IAS 21 para 26].

A7.57 Doubts as to convertibility may arise if, for example, a UK company makes a long-term currency loan to, say, an overseas supplier, but restrictions on the remittance of funds are imposed by the overseas country sometime prior to the maturity of the loan. Such restrictions may arise as a result of political upheaval or severe exchange control regulations in the overseas country or currency devaluation. In that situation, the company should use the rate on the first subsequent date at which exchanges could be made following restoration of normal conditions. The following example illustrates this type of situation.

Example – suspension of foreign exchange rates

In October 20X3, company A, which is incorporated in the UK, used surplus currency to make a long-term loan of FC 15m to its overseas supplier. The loan was made when the exchange rate was £1 = FC 5.00 and is repayable on 30 September 20X5, company A's year-end. Initially, the loan would be translated and recorded in company A's books at £3m. The amount that company A will ultimately receive will depend on the rate of exchange ruling on the date when the loan is repaid.

On 28 September 20X5, a few days before the due date of the loan's repayment, the exchange rate was £1= FC 6. However, on the same date the local government announced that a devaluation was to occur on 2 October 20X5 and all foreign exchange transactions were to be suspended until 3 October 20X5. On 2 October 20X5, foreign exchange transactions were executed, but left unsettled until the following day when a new rate was to be established. On 3 October 20X5 a new rate of £1 = FC 7.5 was established and was effective for transactions left unsettled the previous day.

In the above example, an official exchange rate at 30 September 20X5 is temporarily lacking and not available. In this situation, the exchange rate was temporarily lacking and the rate established on 3 October 20X5, the first subsequent date, is the appropriate rate to use for translating the monetary asset at the balance sheet date of 30 September 20X5. Therefore, company A would record the loan receivable at £2m and recognise an impairment loss of £1m in the income statement.

Subsequent measurement

A7.58 A foreign currency transaction may give rise to assets and liabilities that are denominated in a foreign currency. The procedure for translating such assets and liabilities into the entity's functional currency at each balance sheet date will depend on whether the assets and liabilities are monetary or non-monetary in nature.

Translation of monetary items

A7.59 Monetary items, as the name implies, are units of currency held and assets and liabilities to be received or paid in fixed or determinable number of units of currency. [IAS 21 para 8]. Therefore, the essential feature of a monetary item is a right to receive (or an obligation to deliver) a fixed or determinable number of units of currency. Obvious examples are financial assets such as cash, bank balances and receivables and financial liabilities such as debt, provisions that are settled in cash, pensions and other employee benefits to be paid in cash, deferred taxes and cash dividends that are recognised as a liability. Derivative financial instruments, such as forward exchange contracts, foreign currency swaps and options, are also monetary items as they are settled at a future date. Short-term monetary items are those that fall due within one year of the balance sheet date and long-term monetary items are those that fall due more than one year after the balance sheet date.

A7.60 In some instances, however, it may not be readily apparent whether an item should be regarded as a monetary item or a non-monetary item. The ambiguity can usually be resolved if it is considered whether the item represents an amount to be received or paid in money, in which case it would fall to be treated as a monetary item. For example, where an entity is required to make progress payments under a long-term contract to purchase a specialised piece of machinery from a foreign supplier, the contract's terms may stipulate whether the payments made on specified dates are refundable (monetary) or non-refundable (non-monetary).

A7.61 It is also not necessary, for an item to qualify as a monetary item, for it to be recovered or settled in cash. A contract to receive (or deliver) a variable number of an entity's own equity instruments or a variable amount of asset in which the fair value to be received (or delivered) equals a fixed or determinable number of units of currency is also a monetary item. [IAS 21 para 16]. In other words, an entity's own equity instruments can be used 'as currency' in a contract that can be settled at a value equal to a fixed or a determinable amount. Such a contract is not an equity instrument, but a monetary financial asset or a liability. It should be noted that not all financial assets would fall to be treated as monetary items. For example, an equity instrument that is classified as an available for sale financial asset is not a monetary item. [IAS 39 para AG83].

A7.62 IAS 21 requires that an entity should translate its foreign currency monetary items outstanding at the end of balance sheet date using the closing rate. [IAS 21 para 23(a)]. The closing rate is the spot exchange rate at the balance sheet date. [IAS 21 para 8]. A rate of exchange that is fixed under the terms of the relevant contract cannot be used to translate monetary assets and liabilities. Translating a monetary item at the contracted rate under the terms of a relevant contract is a form of hedge accounting that is not permitted under IAS 39. IAS 39 details strict criteria that must be fulfilled before hedge accounting can be applied and specifies the appropriate accounting treatment for foreign currency hedged items and hedging instruments where hedge accounting is permitted. The treatment of the resultant exchange difference that arise on translating a monetary item at the balance sheet date is considered from paragraphs A7.67 below.

Translation of non-monetary items

A7.63 Non-monetary items are all items other than monetary items. In other words, the right to receive (or an obligation to deliver) a fixed or determinable number of units of currency is absent in a non-monetary item. Typical examples are intangible assets, goodwill, property, plant and equipment, inventories, amounts pre-paid for goods and services (pre-paid rent), equity investments and provisions that are to be settled by the delivery of a non-monetary asset. [IAS 21 para 16].

A7.64 Translation of non-monetary items depends on whether they are recognised at historical cost or at fair value. For example, property, plant and equipment may be measured in terms of historical cost or fair value in accordance with IAS 16, 'Property, plant and equipment'.

A7.65 Non-monetary items that are measured in terms of historical cost in a foreign currency should be translated using the exchange rate at the date of the transaction. [IAS 21 para 23(b)]. This effectively means that such assets are recorded at historical cost and no retranslation of the asset is required at subsequent balance sheet dates. However, if the asset is impaired the recoverable amount is translated at the exchange rate ruling at the date when that value was determined (for example the closing rate at the balance sheet date). Comparing the previously recorded historical cost with the recoverable amount may result in recognising an impairment loss in the functional currency. For example, suppose an entity's functional currency is the pound sterling and a foreign currency asset costing FC 925,000 is recorded at the date of purchase at £500,000 when £1 = FC 1.85. At a subsequent balance sheet date, the asset's recoverable amount in foreign currency is FC 787,500 when £1 = FC 1.5. In this situation, although there is impairment loss in foreign currency, no impairment loss is recognised, because the recoverable amount at the balance sheet date of £525,000 is higher than the carrying value.

A7.66 Non-monetary asset that are measured at fair value in a foreign currency should be translated using the exchange rates at the date when the fair value was determined. [IAS 21 para 23(c)]. For example, a UK entity has a euro denominated investment property located in France that is carried at fair value with gains and losses from changes in fair value recognised in profit or loss for the period in which they arise, in accordance with IAS 40. In this situation, the fair values measured initially in euros due to the property's appreciation in value would be translated to sterling at the exchange rate ruling at the relevant measurement dates. The resulting change in fair value in sterling would include foreign exchange differences arising on the retranslation of the opening euro carrying value. This exchange difference is recognised as part of the change in fair value in profit or loss for the period.

Recognition of exchange differences

Monetary items

A7.67 Exchange differences arising on the settlement of monetary items or on translating monetary items at rates different from those at which they were translated on initial recognition during the period or in previous financial statements, should be recognised in profit or loss in the period in which they arise, except as described in paragraph A7.70 below. [IAS 21 para 28].

A7.68 When monetary items arise from a foreign currency transaction and there is a change in exchange rate between the transaction date and the date of settlement, an exchange difference results. Where a transaction is *settled* within the same accounting period at an exchange rate that differs from the rate used when the transaction was initially recorded, the exchange difference will be recognised in the income statement of the period in which the settlement takes place. [IAS 21 para 29]. The rationale for this treatment is that, as the exchange difference will have been reflected in the cash flow at the time of the settlement, it is appropriate to recognise such exchange differences as part of the profit or loss for that year.

Example – treatment of a foreign currency denominated purchase of plant

In March 20X5, a UK company purchases plant for use in the UK from an overseas company for FC 1,980,000 (FC being a fictional currency). At the date the company purchases the plant, the exchange rate is £1 = FC 1.65. The purchase price is to be settled in three months time, although delivery is made immediately. The UK company should record both the plant and the monetary liability at £1,200,000 (FC 1,980,000/£1.65). The company will not need to translate the plant again. At the settlement date, the exchange rate is £1 = FC 1.75 so the actual amount the UK company will pay to settle the liability is £1,131,429. The company should include the gain on exchange of £68,751 (that is, £1,200,000 — £1,131,429) in arriving at its profit or loss.

A7.69 Where, however, a monetary item arising from a foreign currency transaction remains *outstanding* at the balance sheet date, an exchange difference arises as a consequence of recording the foreign currency transaction at the rate ruling at the date of the transaction (or when it was translated at a previous balance sheet date) and the subsequent retranslation of the monetary item to the rate ruling at the balance sheet date. Such exchange differences should be reported as part of the profit or loss for the year.

A7.69.1 Foreign exchange gains or losses on monetary assets classified as available-for-sale in accordance with IAS 39 are recognised in the income statement. [IAS 21 paras 11(a), 15]. However, other fair value gains and losses on available-for-sale monetary financial assets are required to be recognised in equity. [IAS 39 para 55(b)]. A detailed example of the treatment of foreign exchange gains and losses on monetary available-for-sale assets is included in chapter 6.

A7.70 Not all exchange differences on monetary items are reported in the income statement. There are number of exceptions. These are:

- A monetary item that is designated as a hedging instrument in a cash flow hedge. In this situation, any exchange difference that forms part of the gain or loss on the hedging instrument is recognised directly in equity through the statement of changes in equity. [IAS 39 para 95].
- A monetary item that is designated as a hedge of a net investment *in consolidated financial statements*. In this situation, any exchange difference that forms part of the gain or loss on the hedging instrument is recognised directly in equity through the statement of changes in equity. [IAS 39 para 102]. See further from paragraph A7.108 onwards below.

- A monetary item that forms part of the net investment in a foreign operation in the consolidated financial statement. See further from paragraph A7.93 onwards below.

Non-monetary items

A7.71 When a gain or loss on a non-monetary item is recognised directly in equity, any exchange component of that gain or loss should be recognised directly in equity. [IAS 39 para 30]. For example, an entity may purchase equity securities denominated in a foreign currency that are classified as available for sale. Under IAS 39, the equity securities are carried at fair value. Any changes in fair value that are recognised directly in equity through the statement of changes in equity will also include any related foreign exchange element. [IAS 39 paras 55(b), AG83]. Another example is where a property denominated in a foreign currency is revalued. Any exchange difference arising when the property is translated at the rate of exchange ruling at the valuation date is reported directly in equity along with other changes in value. Consider the following example.

Example – translation of a revalued foreign asset

A UK entity, with a sterling functional currency, has a property located in the US, which was acquired at a cost of US dollar 1.8m when the exchange rate was £1= US$1.6. At the balance sheet date the property was revalued to US dollar 2.16m. The exchange rate at the balance sheet date was £1= US$1.8.

Ignoring depreciation, the amount that would be reported directly to equity is:

	£
Value at balance sheet date = US$2,160,000m @ 1.8 =	1,200,000
Value at acquisition date = US$1,800,000 @1.6 =	1,125,000
Revaluation surplus recognised in equity	75,000
The revaluation surplus may be analysed as follows:	
Change in fair value = US$360,000 @ 1.8 =	200,000
Exchange component of change = US$1,800,000 @ 1.8 — US$1,800,000 @ 1.6	(125,000)
Revaluation surplus recognised in equity	75,000

A7.72 On the other hand, when a gain or loss on a non-monetary item is recognised in profit or loss, any exchange component of that gain or loss is also recognised in profit or loss. [IAS 21 para 38]. Consider the following example:

Example – translation of an impaired foreign asset

A UK entity with a sterling functional currency has a property located in the US which was acquired at a cost of US$1.8m when the exchange rate was £1=

US$1.6. The property is carried at cost. At the balance sheet date the recoverable amount of the property as a result of an impairment review amounted to US$1.62m. The exchange rate at the balance sheet date was £1 = US$1.8.

Ignoring depreciation, the impairment loss that would be reported in the income statement as a result of the impairment is:

	£
Carrying value at balance sheet date – US$1,620,000m @ 1.8 =	900,000
Historical cost – US$1,800,000 @ 1.6 =	1,125,000
Impairment loss recognised in profit or loss	(225,000)
The impairment loss may be analysed as follows:	
Change in value due to impairment = US$180,000 @ 1.8 =	(100,000)
Exchange component of change = US$1,800,000 @ 1.8 — US$1,800,000 @ 1.6	(125,000)
Impairment loss recognised in profit or loss	(225,000)

Foreign currency translation of financial statements

Introduction

A7.73 Accounting for transactions in foreign currencies that are directly undertaken by an entity and which must be measured and expressed in the entity's functional currency has already been discussed earlier in this chapter. However where foreign activities are undertaken through foreign operations, the financial statements of those foreign operations must be translated so that they can be included in the reporting entity's financial statements by consolidation, proportional consolidation or the equity method. The process of translation addresses the appropriate exchange rates to use for translating the income statement and the balance sheet of the foreign operation and how the financial effects of changes in exchange rates are recognised in the reporting entity's financial statements.

A7.74 The standard permits an entity to present its financial statements in a currency other than its functional currency. The currency in which the financial statements are presented is referred to as the 'presentation currency'. [IAS 21 para 8]. It is rather strange that there is no compulsion in the standard for an entity to present its financial statements in its functional currency that most faithfully portrays the economic effect of transactions and events on the entity. The IASB's reasons for permitting an entity to present its financial statements in any currency are adequately explained in paragraphs BC10 to BC14 of the Basis for Conclusions of IAS 21 and are not repeated here.

A7.75 Although an entity has a free choice in the selection of the presentation currency, in general, it is likely to use its functional currency, the currency used for measurement, as the presentation currency. If an alternative currency is used, disclosure is required of the reasons for selecting a different currency. Therefore, by implication, there must be substantive and valid reasons for choosing an alternative presentation currency. For example, in some countries, an entity may be required by local and legal regulations to present its financial statements in the local currency even if this is not its functional currency.

Translation to the presentation currency

A7.76 Selecting a presentation currency that is different from the functional currency will require a translation from the functional currency into the presentation currency. For example, when a group contains individual entities with different functional currencies, the results and financial position of each entity must be expressed in a common currency so that consolidated financial statements may be presented. IAS 21 has prescribed a translation methodology for translating from the functional currency to a different presentation currency. This translation methodology seeks to ensure that the financial and operational relationships between underlying amounts established in the entity's primary economic environment and measured in its functional currency are preserved when translated into a different measurement currency. The translation method is described in the next paragraph. A different translation methodology applies to an entity whose functional currency is the currency of a hyperinflationary economy and this method is described from paragraph A7.109 below.

A7.77 The translation methodology referred to above prescribes that an entity's results and financial position whose functional currency is not the currency of a hyperinflationary economy should be translated into a different presentation currency using the following procedures:

- Assets and liabilities for each balance sheet presented (including comparatives) should be translated at the closing rate at the date of that balance sheet.

  Use of a constant rate of exchange for all items on the balance sheet maintains the relationship in the retranslated financial statements as existed in the foreign operation's financial statements. Therefore, for example, fixed assets would be the same proportion of long-term liabilities.

- Income and expenses for each income statement (including comparatives) should be translated at exchange rates at the dates of the transactions. For practical reasons, a rate that approximates the exchange rates at the dates of the transactions, for example an average rate for the period, is often used to translate income and expense items. However, if exchange rates fluctuate significantly, the use of the average rate for a period is inappropriate (see further para A7.81 below).

It should be noted that although the use of a closing rate is more likely to preserve the financial results and relationships that existed prior to translation, the use of an actual or average rate reflects more fairly the profits or losses and cash flows as they accrue to the group throughout the period.

- All resulting exchange differences should be recognised as a separate component of equity.

[IAS 21 paras 39, 40].

A7.77.1 The standard is silent on how to translate equity items. Management, therefore, has a policy choice of using either the historic rate or the closing rate. The chosen policy should be applied consistently. If the closing rate is used, the resulting exchange differences are recognised in equity and thus the policy choice has no impact on the amount of total equity. In some jurisdictions, the regulatory framework may mandate one treatment in which case the policy choice does not apply.

A7.78 The exchange differences referred to in the last bullet point above comprises:

- Differences arising from translating the income statement at exchange rates at the dates of the transactions or at average rates and assets and liabilities at the closing rate. Such exchange differences arise on items recognised in the income statement as well as in equity.

- Differences arising on the opening net assets' retranslation at a closing rate that differs from the previous closing rate.

[IAS 21 para 41].

A7.79 The above exchange differences are not recognised in the income statement, because to do so would distort the results from trading operations as shown in the functional currency financial statements. Such differences, which primarily result from a translation process, are unrelated to the foreign operation's trading performance or financial operations; in particular, they do not represent or measure changes in actual or prospective cash flows. They do have an impact on the net investment that may be realised upon sale or liquidation, but that effect is related to the net investment and not to the investee's operations. It is, therefore, inappropriate to regard them as profits or losses and, hence, they are properly recognised in a separate component of equity.

UK.A7.79.1 It should be noted that under SSAP 20, UK entities are not required to recognise these exchange differences in a separate component in equity, although some entities do.

A7.80 The IASB chose the translation method described in paragraph A7.77 because, for a multinational group comprising operations with a number of functional currencies, it means that the operations can be translated into the presentation currency directly without having to determine a 'functional currency' for the group first. The method also results in the same amounts in the presentation currency regardless of whether the financial statements of a foreign operation are first translated into the functional currency of the parent and then into the presentation currency or translated directly into the presentation currency. [IAS 21 para BC18].

UK.A7.80.1 It should be noted that the translation method described above is identical to the 'closing rate/net investment method' that is used in the UK standard SSAP 20 for translating the result of a foreign operation, although the term is not mentioned in IAS 21.

Determining the average rate for translating the income statement

A7.81 As stated in paragraph A7.77 above, the standard permits a foreign operation's income statement to be translated at an average rate for the period. IAS 21 intentionally does not prescribe any definitive method of calculating the average rate, probably because the appropriate method may justifiably vary between individual companies. Determining an appropriate average rate will include such matters as the company's internal accounting system, the extent of any seasonal trade variation and the desirability of using a weighting procedure.

A7.82 There are a large number of methods under which an average rate can be calculated, ranging from simple monthly or quarterly averages to more sophisticated methods using appropriate weighting that reflects changes both in exchange rates and in the volume of business. Where an overseas subsidiary's results are affected by seasonal factors, it may be necessary to weight the average exchange rate used in the calculation by applying an average rate for a shorter period than the whole year. But whatever method a company uses, it should result in a rate that approximates the exchange rates at the dates of the transaction and that is most appropriate to the foreign operation's circumstances.

Consolidated financial statements

Translation of a foreign operation

A7.83 Translating foreign currency financial statements into the presentation currency is necessary so that the foreign operation's financial statements may be included in the reporting entity's financial statements by consolidation, proportional consolidation or the equity method. The method of translation in consolidated financial statements should be such as to reflect the financial and other operational relationships that exist between the reporting entity and its foreign enterprises. As stated in paragraph A7.76, this objective is achieved by following the closing rate/net investment method described in paragraph A7.77. This translation method is illustrated by the following example. Once the foreign operation's financial statements have been translated into the reporting entity's presentation currency, its incorporation into the reporting entity's consolidated financial statement follows normal consolidation procedures.

Example – translation of a foreign subsidiary

Company A, a UK company, whose accounting period ended on 30 September 20X5, has a wholly-owned US subsidiary, S Corporation, which was acquired for US$500,000 on 30 September 20X4. The fair value of the net assets at the date of acquisition was US$400,000 giving rise to goodwill of US$100,000. The exchange rate at 30 September 20X4 and 20X5 was £1 = US$2.0 and £1 = US$1.5 respectively. The weighted average rate for the year ended 30 September 20X5 was £1 = US$1.65. During the year, S corporation paid a dividend of US$14,000 when the rate of exchange was £1 = US$1.75.

Note that the foreign currency movements in this example have been exaggerated. In reality, if exchange rates were this volatile an entity would not be permitted to use average rates for translating the income statement. [IAS 21 para 40].

The summarised income statement of S Corporation for the year ended 30 September 20X4 and the summarised balance sheets at 30 September 20X3 and 20X4 in dollars and sterling equivalents, are as follows:

S Corporation: Income statement for the year ended 30 September 20X5

	$'000	Exchange rate	£'000
Operating profit	135	1.65	81.8
Interest paid	(15)	1.65	(9.0)
Profit before taxation	120		72.8
Taxation	(30)	1.65	(18.2)
Profit after taxation	90		54.6

Balance sheets of S Corporation

	20X5 $'000	20X4 $'000	20X5 £'000	20X4 £'000
Closing exchange rate £1 =			$1.50	$2.00
Property, plant and equipment				
Cost (20X5 additions: $30)	255	225	170.0	112.5
Depreciation (20X5 charge: $53)	98	45	65.3	22.5
Net book value	157	180	104.7	90.0
Current assets:				
Inventories	174	126	116.0	63.0
Debtors	210	145	140.0	72.5
Cash at bank	240	210	160.0	105.0
	624	481	416.0	240.5
Current liabilities:				
Trade creditors	125	113	83.3	57.5
Taxation	30	18	20.0	9.0
	155	131	103.3	65.5

Net current assets	469	350	312.7	175.0
Loan stock	150	130	100.0	65.0
Net assets	476	400	317.4	200.0
Share capital	200	200	100.0	100.0
Retained profits	276	200	217.4	100.0
	476	400	317.4	200.0

Analysis of retained profits

	$'000	£'000
Pre-acquisition profit brought forward	200	100.0
Profit for the year	90	54.6
Dividends paid in the year *	(14)	(8.0)
Exchange difference	–	70.8
Retained profits	276	217.4

* Dividend paid during the year is translated at the actual rate $1 = $1.75

Analysis of exchange difference:

Arising on retranslation of opening net assets (excluding goodwill – see below)	
at opening rate — $400,000 @ $2 = £1	200.0
at closing rate — $400,000 @ $1.5 = £1	266.7
Exchange gain on net assets	66.7
Exchange gain arising from translating retained profits from average to closing rate — $90,000 @1.5 — £54.6	5.4
Exchange loss arising from translating dividend from actual to closing rate — $14,000 @1.5 — £8.0	(1.3)
Total exchange difference arising on translation of S corporation	70.8
Exchange difference on goodwill of US$100,000 treated as a currency asset (see para A7.86 below)	
at opening rate — US$100,000 @ $2 = £1	50.0
at closing rate — US$100,000 @ $1.5 = £1	66.7
Exchange gain on goodwill included in consolidation	16.7
Total exchange difference included in consolidated balance sheet as a separate component of equity (see below)	87.5

It is further assumed that parent company A's functional currency is the pound sterling. It has received a dividend from S Corporation during the year. The summarised balance sheets of company A at 30 September 20X4 and 20X5 are as follows:

Company A — Balance sheets	**20X5**	**20X4**
	£'000	**£'000**
Investments in subsidiary S ($500,000 @ 2.0)	250	250
Cash	208	200
Net assets	458	450
Share capital	450	450
Retained profits (dividend received: $14,000 @ 1.75*)	8	–
	458	450

*actual rate on date dividend received

The summarised consolidated income statement for the year ended 30 September 20X5 and the consolidated balance sheet as at date prepared under the closing rate/net investment method are as follows:

Consolidated income statement for the year ended 30 September 20X5	
	£'000
Operating profit of S Corporation	81.8
Operating profit of company A	8.0
	89.8
Elimination of inter-company dividend*	(8.0)
Net operating profit	81.8
Interest paid	(9.0)
Profit before taxation	72.8
Taxation	(18.2)
Retained profit	54.6

Consolidated balance sheet as at 30 September 20X5	
	£'000
Goodwill	66.7
Property, plant and equipment	104.7
	171.4
Current assets:	
Inventories	116.0
Debtors	140.0
Cash (S Corporation: £160; company A £208)	368.0
	624.0
Current liabilities:	
Trade creditors	83.3
Taxation	20.0
	103.3
Net current assets	520.7
Loan stock	100.0
Net assets	592.1

Capital and reserves	
Share capital	450.0
Retained profit	54.6
Cumulative translation adjustment	87.5
	592.1

Different reporting dates

A7.84 Where a foreign subsidiary's financial statements are drawn up to a date that is different from that of the parent, the foreign subsidiary often prepares additional financial statements as of the same date as the parent for inclusion in the parent's financial statements. Therefore, in this situation, the foreign subsidiary's financial statements should be translated at the exchange rate at the parent's balance sheet date. Where additional financial statements are not prepared, IAS 27 allows the use of a different reporting date that is not more than three months before or three months after the reporting entity's balance sheet date. In that situation, the foreign subsidiary's financial statements should be translated at the exchange rate ruling at the foreign operation's balance sheet date. However, if significant transactions or events occur between the date of the subsidiary's financial statements and the date of the parent's financial statements, adjustments must be made. [IAS 27 para 27]. This may include changes to the exchange rate, as shown in the next example.

Example – translation of a foreign subsidiary with a different reporting date to that of the parent

Entity A prepares its annual financial statements at 31 January. However, local regulations require one of its subsidiaries, entity B, to prepare its financial statements at 31 December. Entity A uses entity B's results for the 12 months to 31 December for consolidation purposes, rather than have a second set of results audited to 31 January.

The exchange rate between the US dollar (used for group reporting) and entity B's local currency was US$1: LC15,000 at 31 December 20X2 and US$1: LC18,000 at 31 January 20X3. There were no significant transactions or other events at entity B during January 20X3. Entity B's net assets at 31 December 20X2 were LC234 million.

The net assets of entity B at 31 December 20X2 using the exchange rate of 31 December 20X2 are US$15,600.

The change in exchange rates between 31 December 20X2 and 31 January 20X3 is significant. Therefore, entity A should use the exchange rate of 31 January 20X3 for consolidation purposes.

Accordingly, management should translate entity B's balance sheet as at 31 December 20X2 using the 31 January 20X3 exchange rate. This results in the consolidation of a balance sheet with net assets of US$13,000.

The same approach is used for foreign associates and joint ventures. [IAS 21 para 46].

Minority interest

A7.85 As explained in paragraph A7.77 above, exchange differences arise on the retranslation of the foreign subsidiary's financial statements that are accumulated in equity. Where the foreign subsidiary is not wholly-owned, the exchange differences that are attributable to minority interest should be allocated to and reported as part of the minority interest in the consolidated balance sheet. [IAS 21 para 41].

Goodwill and fair value adjustments arising on an acquisition

A7.86 Goodwill arising in a business combination is measured as the excess of the cost of combination over the acquirer's interest in the net fair value of the acquiree's identifiable assets, liabilities and contingent liabilities. On the acquisition of a foreign operation, the question arises as to whether goodwill and fair value adjustments, once calculated at the rate of exchange ruling at the date of acquisition, should be subject to retranslation at each balance sheet date. The previous version of IAS 21 allowed a choice. Goodwill and fair value adjustments could be recorded at the historical rate without retranslation on the grounds that they are effectively part of the acquisition price paid and, hence, are part of the acquirer's assets and liabilities. Alternatively, they could be regarded as part of the acquired entity's assets and liabilities and subject to annual retranslation on the grounds that goodwill has no existence apart from the foreign operation and that fair value adjustments clearly relate to the acquired entity's identifiable assets and liabilities.

A7.87 As part of its project on improvements to international accounting standards, the IASB reconsidered the choice and decided to eliminate the first option. The IASB's reasons for treating goodwill as a currency asset that should be subject to retranslation at each balance sheet date are adequately explained in paragraphs BC26 to BC32 of IAS 21 and are not reproduced here. Accordingly:

- Any goodwill arising on the acquisition of a foreign operation and any fair value adjustments to the carrying amounts of assets and liabilities arising on a foreign operation's acquisition should be treated as the foreign operation's assets and liabilities.

- They should be expressed in the foreign operation's functional currency and should be translated at the closing rate in accordance with paragraphs A7.77 above where the functional currency is not the currency of a hyperinflationary economy and in accordance with paragraph A7.109 below where the functional currency is the currency of a hyperinflationary economy.

[IAS 21 para 47].

A7.88 Therefore, where a parent entity acquires a multinational operation comprising businesses with many different functional currencies, the goodwill arising on acquisition should be allocated to the level of each functional currency of the acquired foreign operation. This means that the level at which goodwill is allocated for foreign currency translation purposes may be different to the level at which goodwill is tested for impairment in accordance with IAS 36, 'Impairment of assets'. [IAS 36 para 83].

Example – translation of goodwill and fair value adjustments

On 30 June 20X5, a UK parent company with sterling as the functional currency acquired a multi-national group with operations in Canada, US and Europe. All foreign operations are highly profitable. The functional currencies of the foreign operations are their respective local currencies. The total purchase consideration amounted to £3,000m. The UK parent financial year ends on 31 December 20X5.

The fair values of the net assets of the acquired businesses including fair value adjustments and the relevant exchange rates at the date of acquisition and at the balance sheet date are given below. The UK parent has decided to allocate the purchased goodwill to the acquired businesses on the basis of their relative adjusted fair values of the net assets acquired.

Business acquired	**Canada**	**US**	**Europe**	**Total**
Exchange rate at acquisition £1 =	2.19	1.66	1.42	
Exchange rate at balance sheet date £1 =	2.29	1.80	1.45	
	C$000	**$'000**	**€'000**	**£'000**
Net assets – book value	1,200	1,500	2,000	
Fair value adjustments	150	50	(100)	
Adjusted fair values	1,350	1,550	1,900	
Allocation of goodwill				
Translated at exchange rate at date of acquisition	£616	£934	£1,338	2,888
Purchase consideration				3,000
Goodwill allocated on the basis of adjusted fair values	£24	£36	£52	112
	C$'000	**$'000**	**€'000**	
Adjusted net assets as above	1,350	1,550	1,900	
Goodwill treated as currency asset	53	60	74	
Adjusted fair value + goodwill	1,403	1,610	1,974	
Translation adjustment on opening net assets	**£'000**	**£'000**	**£'000**	**£'000**
Adjusted net assets + goodwill @ closing rate	613	894	1,361	2,868
Adjusted net assets + goodwill @ opening rate	640	970	1,390	3,000
Exchange loss taken to equity on consolidation	(27)	(76)	(29)	(132)

Consolidated balance sheet at 31 December 20X5				
Goodwill at closing rate	23	33	51	107
Net assets at closing rate	590	861	1,310	2,761
Cash outlay				(3,000)
Consolidated net assets				(132)
Translation adjustments in equity	(27)	(76)	(29)	(132)

Intra-group trading transactions

A7.89 Where normal trading transactions take place between group companies located in different countries, the transactions give rise to monetary assets (liabilities) that may either have been settled during the year or remain unsettled at the balance sheet date. As the transactions will probably be recorded in the functional currency of one of the companies in question, exchange differences will arise, which should be reported in the entity's income statement in the same way as gains or losses on transactions arising with third parties as explained from paragraph A7.67 above. Where the monetary asset or liability is settled during the year, the exchange gain or loss will have affected group cash flows and, therefore, it is proper that it should be included in consolidated results for the year. The exchange difference arising simply reflects the risk of doing business with a foreign party, even though that party happens to be a group member. Even where the transaction remains unsettled at the balance sheet date and the monetary asset (liability) in one group company is eliminated against the corresponding liability (asset) in another group company, the exchange difference reported in the group company's own income statement continues to be recognised in consolidated profit or loss. This is because the monetary item represents a commitment to convert one currency into another and exposes the reporting entity to gain or loss through currency fluctuations. [IAS 21 para 45].

Example – elimination of intra-group trading transactions where the inventory is still owned by the group

A UK parent company has a wholly-owned subsidiary in the US. During the year ended 31 December 20X5, the US company purchased plant and raw materials to be used in its manufacturing process from the UK parent. Details of the transactions are as follows:

	Exchange rate
Purchased plant costing £500,000 on 30 April 20X5	£1 = US$1.48
Paid for plant on 30 September 20X5	£1 = US$1.54
Purchased raw materials costing £300,000 on 31 October 20X5	£1 = US$1.56
Balance of £300,000 outstanding at 31 December 20X5	£1 = US$1.52
Average rate for the year	£1 = US$1.55

The following exchange gains/losses will be recorded in the US subsidiary's income statement for the year ended 31 December 20X5.

	US$	US$
Plant costing £500,000 @ 1.48	740,000	
Paid £500,000 @ 1.54	770,000	
Exchange loss – settled transaction		(30,000)
Raw materials costing £300,000 @ 1.56	468,000	
Outstanding £300,000 @ 1.52	456,000	
Exchange gain – unsettled transaction		12,000
Net exchange loss recorded in income statement		(18,000)

The exchange loss of US$30,000 that arises as the inter-company creditor for plant purchase is settled during the year will flow through on consolidation when the US subsidiary's results are incorporated in the consolidated accounts. The inter-company creditor of US$456,000 in the US subsidiary's balance sheet that remains outstanding will be translated into sterling at the closing rate to £300,000 and will be eliminated against the debtor recorded in the UK parent's inter-company account. However, the exchange gain of US$12,000 will not be eliminated on consolidation and will be reported as part of the consolidated results of the group. The rationale of keeping this gain in the group's result is that to repay the creditor balance, the US subsidiary will some day have to expend the amount of its local currency necessary to acquire the required amount of the reporting currency. This exposes the group to a gain or loss on reconversion.

A7.90 The same treatment that applies to an unsettled inter-company monetary item arising from trading transactions also applies to intra-group loans made by one group member to another in a currency that is different from the borrower's functional currency. That is, the borrower will initially record the foreign currency loan at the rate of exchange ruling at the date the loan is made. At each balance sheet date thereafter, until it is repaid, the loan will be translated at the closing rate and any exchange difference will be reported in the borrower's income statement. On consolidation, the intra-group loan account will cancel out, but the exchange difference reported in the borrower's income statement continues to be recognised in profit or loss.

Unrealised profit on inventories

A7.91 IAS 27, 'Consolidated and separate financial statements', requires that intra-group profit arising from the transfer of assets between entities in the group should be eliminated in full where such assets are still held in the undertakings included in the consolidation at the balance sheet date, because it does not represent profit to the group (see further chapter 24). No specific guidance is given in IAS 21 as to the exchange rate at which the profit should be eliminated, although SFAS 52 requires elimination at the actual rate ruling at the transaction date or at a weighted average rate.

Example – elimination of intra-group trading transactions where the inventory had been sold outside the group

The facts are the same as in the example in paragraph A7.89 except that the raw materials purchased for £300,000 by the US subsidiary are still in inventory at 31 December 20X5. These goods cost the UK parent £270,000.

Therefore, unrealised profit of £30,000 (£300,000 — £270,000) that the parent entity made on the inter-company sale would need to be eliminated on consolidation. However, elimination of this unrealised profit of £30,000 will not necessarily result in the inventories being included in the consolidated balance sheet at cost to the group where the closing rate method is used as illustrated below.

The amount for raw materials included in inventory in the US company's balance sheet at the transaction date is US$468,000. Under the closing rate method, the inventory would be retranslated at the year end rate of 1.52 to £307,895. Therefore, the inventory will be recorded in the consolidated balance sheet as follows:

	£
Cost of inventory US$468,000 @ 1.52	307,895
Unrealised profit	(30,000)
Inventory carried in consolidated balance sheet	277,895

The difference of £7,895 represents the exchange difference arising on the retranslation of the inventory in the subsidiary's financial statements to the year end rate under the closing rate/net investment method, that is, £307,895 less the cost to the subsidiary of £300,000.

If, on the other hand, the parent has purchased the raw materials from the US subsidiary for US 468,000 at 31 October 20X5, which cost the US subsidiary US$421,200, and these items were still in the parent's inventory at the year end, a problem arises as to what rate the unrealised profit of US$46,800 should be eliminated.

As stated above, if the guidance in SFAS 52 is followed, the profit will be eliminated at the actual rate ruling at the transaction date and the inventory will be recorded in the consolidated balance sheet as follows:

	£
Cost of inventory US$468,000 @ 1.56	300,000
Unrealised profit US$46,800 @ 1.56	(30,000)
Inventory carried in consolidated balance sheet	270,000

The amount of inventory recorded in the balance sheet represents the original cost to the group of US$421,200 translated at the rate ruling at the date of the intra-group transaction, that is, US$421,200 @ 1.56 = £270,000. This is the method required by SFAS 52, which can be applied under IAS 21.

In practice, it is likely that the UK parent will use an average rate for translating the results of foreign operations. In this situation, the amount of profit to be eliminated should be calculated using that average rate. Use of an average rate is permissible where it approximates the exchange rate at the date of the transaction.

	£
Cost of inventory US$468,000 @ 1.56	300,000
Unrealised profit US$46,800 @ 1.55	(30,194)
	269,806

In any event, the amount of inventory recorded in the consolidated balance sheet under the closing rate/net investment method will not be the same as the actual cost to the group.

A7.92 Even if intra-group transactions do not give rise to intra-group profit, there could still be an effect on asset values as the following example illustrates.

Example – intra-group trading transaction at cost

A UK parent has a wholly-owned subsidiary in Pololand where the currency is Pol. The net assets of the group at 31 March 20X5 are £54,000; consisting of cash £24,000, held in the UK parent and inventory held in the Pololand subsidiary costing Pol 3m, which was included in the consolidated balance sheet at the closing rate of £1 = Pol 100. On 30 September 20X5, the subsidiary transfers the goods to its UK parent at cost price when the rate of exchange is £1 = Pol 125. The transaction is settled in cash and the goods are included in the parent's inventory at £24,000. At 31 March 20X6, the goods are still in inventory. The Pol has weakened further against sterling and the exchange rate at the balance sheet date is £1 = Pol 150.

No gain or loss is recorded by either company on the transfer, hence there are no inter-company profits to be eliminated.

		31 March 20X5
		£
Net assets:		
Inventory 3m @ 100 (held by subsidiary)		30,000
Cash (held by parent)		24,000
		54,000
		31 March 20X6
		£
Net assets:		
Inventory (held by parent)		24,000
Cash 3m @ 150 (held by subsidiary)		20,000
		44,000
Exchange difference on retranslation of opening net assets of foreign subsidiary:		
3m @ 100 =	30,000	
3m @ 150 =	20,000	10,000
		54,000

In this example, no exchange difference is included in the consolidated income statement as there is no trading gain or loss, but the effect of switching inventory around the group affects the asset's carrying value. If the inventory had not been transferred, the net assets would still have decreased by £10,000, but the reduction would have been entirely in the inventory value with the cash balance unchanged. However, the result of moving the inventory and cash around the group is that there is a decrease of £6,000 in the inventory value and a decrease of £4,000 in the group's cash position. This reflects the fact that the group's foreign currency exposure is centred on different assets.

Monetary items forming part of net investment in a foreign operation

A7.93 The net investment that a reporting entity has in a foreign operation is its interest in the net assets of that operation. [IAS 21 para 8]. In appropriate circumstances discussed in paragraph A7.95 below, a monetary item that is receivable from or payable to a foreign operation such as long-term loans and receivables and long-term payables may be regarded as an extension of, or reduction, in the reporting entity's net investment in that foreign operation. In those situations, it may not be appropriate to include the resulting exchange differences arising on the retranslation of such monetary items in consolidated profit or loss when exchange difference arising on equivalent financing with equity capital would be taken to equity on consolidation.

A7.94 IAS 21 recognises the above situation and requires exchange differences arising on a monetary item that forms part of a reporting entity's net investment in a foreign operation that is a subsidiary, associate or joint venture to be treated as follows:

- In the separate financial statements of the reporting entity or the individual financial statements of the foreign operation as appropriate, such exchange differences should be recognised in the income statement.
- In the financial statements that include the foreign operation and the reporting entity (for example, consolidated financial statements when the foreign operation is a subsidiary), such exchange differences should be recognised initially in a separate component of equity and recognised in the profit or loss on disposal of the net investment (see further para A7.106).

[IAS 21 para 32].

A7.95 The inclusion of long-term loans and receivables as part of the net investment in the foreign operation is only permitted where settlement is neither planned nor likely to occur in the foreseeable future. [IAS 21 para 15]. In other words, the parent must regard them as permanent as equity. For example, a loan to a foreign entity that is repayable on demand may seem to be a short-term item, rather than part of capital. However, if there is demonstrably no intent or expectation to demand repayment (for example, the short-term loan is allowed to be continuously rolled over and not intended to be repaid, whether or not the subsidiary is able to repay it), the loan has the same economic effect as a capital contribution. On the other hand, a long-term loan with a specified maturity (say 10 to 15 years) would not automatically qualify to be treated as being part of the net investment simply because it is of a long duration, unless management has expressed its intention to renew the note at maturity. The burden is on management to document its intention to renew by auditable evidence, such as board minutes. Otherwise, absent management's intention to renew, the note's maturity date implies that its settlement is planned in the foreseeable future.

A7.96 Some may argue that inter-company accounts of a trading nature should qualify for the same treatment as above because, although individual transactions are settled, the account's aggregate balance never drops below a specified minimum. In other words, as a minimum amount is permanently deferred, an appropriate amount of the resulting exchange difference should also be deferred in equity. This treatment is not permitted as the standard prohibits its application to trade receivables and payables. [IAS 21 para 15]. The rationale is that as each individual transaction included in the overall inter-company balance is actually settled and replaced by a new transaction, settlement is always contemplated and, therefore, exchange gains and losses arising on such active accounts as described above would not qualify for deferral treatment.

A7.97 The example below illustrates a number of scenarios setting out the treatment that should be followed on consolidation when inter-company loans are made between various members of a group.

Group structure

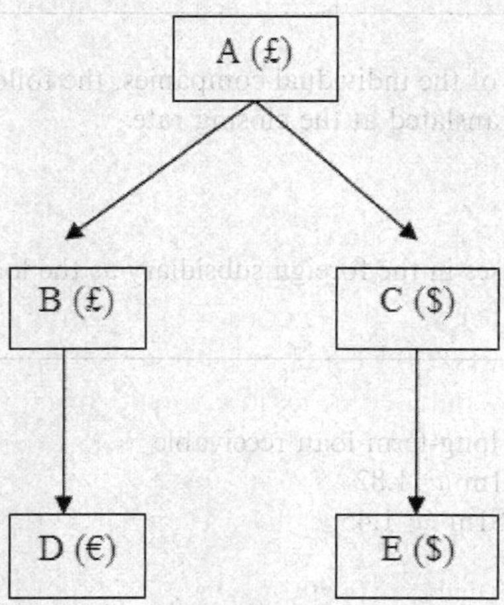

Parent A is the reporting entity that has two subsidiaries B and C, which themselves have subsidiaries D and E. The functional currencies of each of the entities are as noted next to the letters designating the entities.

In all the scenarios that follow, loans made between group companies are effectively permanent in nature (that is, settlement is neither planned nor likely to occur).

Scenario 1

Parent A has a loan receivable from or payable to its foreign subsidiary C that is denominated in either sterling or the dollar.

The loan would be regarded as an extension to or a reduction of entity A's net investment in entity C as appropriate. An exchange difference will be recognised in entity A's income statement if the loan receivable or payable is denominated in dollars. Similarly, an exchange difference will be recognised in entity C's income statement if the loan receivable or payable is denominated in sterling. In all situations, any exchange difference recognised in either entity's profit or loss would be reclassified to a separate component in equity on consolidation. The above situation is dealt with in the numerical examples below.

Example — currency loan made by parent A to foreign subsidiary C

Parent A with sterling as its functional currency is preparing its financial statements to 30 September 20X5. It has a loan receivable of US$1m from its foreign subsidiary C that has been outstanding for some time. The parent notified the overseas subsidiary at the beginning of the financial year that no repayment of the amount will be requested for the foreseeable future.

The relevant exchange rates are as follows:

	30 September 20X5	30 September 20X4
£1 =	US$1.82	US $ 1.45

In the financial statements of the individual companies, the following exchange differences will arise if the loan is retranslated at the closing rate:

Foreign subsidiary C

No exchange difference arises in the foreign subsidiary as the loan payable is denominated in its functional currency.

UK parent A	
Exchange difference on long-term loan receivable	£
On closing rate — US$1m @ 1.82	549,450
On opening rate — US$1m @ 1.45	689,655
Exchange loss	140,205

In the parent entity's separate financial statement, the loan is regarded as a monetary item and any exchange difference is taken to the profit or loss in accordance with paragraph A7.94 above. [IAS 21 para 32].

On consolidation, the retranslated long-term loan would be regarded as part of the net investment in the foreign subsidiary and, therefore, the related exchange loss would be transferred to a separate component in equity in accordance with paragraph A7.94 above. [IAS 21 para 32]. It should be noted that there would also be a corresponding exchange gain included in equity, arising as part of the retranslation of the net assets (which include the US dollar loan creditor) of the overseas subsidiary under the closing rate/net investment method.

Example — sterling loan made by parent A to overseas subsidiary C

The facts are the same as the above example, except that parent A has a loan receivable from its overseas subsidiary of £200,000 that has been outstanding for some time. The loan is treated by the parent entity as forming part of its net investment in the overseas subsidiary.

In the financial statements of the individual companies, the following exchange differences will arise if the loan is retranslated at the closing rate.

UK parent A

There is no exchange difference in the parent's financial statements in respect of the loan as it is denominated in sterling.

Subsidiary C	
Exchange difference on long-term loan payable	US$
On closing rate — £200,000 @ 1.82	364,000
On opening rate — £200,000 @ 1.45	290,000
Exchange loss	74,000
Exchange loss translated at the closing rate @ 1.82	£40,659

As stated above the exchange loss of US$74,000 on the sterling loan should be recognised in the foreign subsidiary C's income statement, because the subsidiary is exposed to the foreign currency risk.

On consolidation, the inter-company loan will cancel out. However, as the long-term loan is regarded as part of the net investment in the subsidiary, the exchange loss of £40,659 should be taken to a separate component in equity in the consolidated financial statements. There would be a corresponding exchange gain included in equity arising as part of the retranslation of the net assets of the overseas subsidiary. The effect is that the consolidated income statement will not reflect any exchange difference on the loan, which is consistent with the fact that the loan has no impact on group cash flows, unless the investment is sold.

The two examples above consider the accounting implications when a loan is made by the parent company to an overseas subsidiary. In the case of a foreign currency upstream loan, that is, a borrowing by a parent company from its subsidiary in the subsidiary's local currency, the treatment of exchange differences in the consolidated financial statements will depend on whether the loan is regarded as part of the net investment in the subsidiary. If that is the case, the treatment will be the same as identified above. That is, the exchange difference arising on the currency loan's retranslation in the parent's income statement would be classified to a separate component of equity in the consolidated financial statements. On the other hand, if the loan is not regarded as part of the net investment, the exchange difference will continue to be recognised in consolidated profit or loss.

Scenario 2

Subsidiary B makes a loan denominated in sterling to subsidiary C ('sister-company loans')

In this situation, subsidiary C will recognise an exchange difference in its own income statement. The question is whether the exchange difference can be reclassified to equity on consolidation.

Some would argue that since subsidiary B is under the control of parent A, it makes no difference whether A or B makes the loan as long as B has the same functional currency as A, the loan is made either in sterling or dollars and it is of a permanent nature.

However, under the 2003 version of IAS 21, there was a view that loans between two fellow (sister) subsidiaries (B and C) could not be treated as part of A's net investment in C. This was because the wording in paragraph 15 of IAS 21 implied that the entity that is the lender or the borrower must have the net investment in a foreign operation. In this case, B, the lender, does not have a net investment in C.

The IASB considered this issue in 2005 and concluded that the treatment of a monetary item that meets the criteria to be part of an entity's net investment in a foreign operation should not depend on which entity within the group conducts the transaction with the foreign operation.

IAS 21 was amended to include clarification in paragraph 15A that it is not necessary for the lender or the borrower to have the net investment in the foreign operation for the exchange differences on translation of the monetary item to be classified within entity. The entity that has the monetary item receivable from or payable to a foreign operation may be any member of group

A7.98 The above examples deal with situations where a monetary item forming part of the net investment was denominated in the functional currency of either the reporting entity or the foreign operation. The question then arises as to whether a similar treatment is permissible in circumstances where a monetary item forming part of the net investment in a foreign operation is denominated in a currency that is different from the functional currency of either the reporting entity or the foreign operation.

A7.99 The 2003 version of IAS 21 required the monetary item to be denominated in the functional currency of either the reporting entity or the foreign operation. In 2005, the IASB considered this issue and noted that a monetary item that meets the criteria to be part of an entity's net investment in a foreign operation is similar to an equity investment in a foreign operation. Hence, the accounting treatment in the consolidated financial statements should not be dependent on the currency in which the monetary item is denominated. Accordingly, it decided to amend paragraph 33 of IAS 21 to require that exchange differences on translation of such a monetary item should be reclassified within equity in the consolidated financial statements, irrespective of the currency of the monetary item.

A7.99.1 Consider the situation in the group structure set out in paragraph A7.97 above where parent A, whose functional currency is the pound sterling, makes a loan denominated in euros to subsidiary C, whose functional currency is the US dollar. In this situation, if the euro loan meets the criteria to be regarded by A as part of its net investment in C, the exchange differences that arise from retranslating the loan receivable in sterling in A's income statement or the loan payable in dollars in C's income statement are reclassified as a separate component of equity in the financial statements that include the foreign operation and the reporting entity (that is, A's consolidated financial statements). [IAS 21 (2005) para 33].

A7.100 Another issue that might arise is the appropriate treatment that should be adopted in the year in which the parent decides to designate any long-term loans and receivables as part of its net investment in the foreign operation. Consider the first example in scenario 1 above where the long-term US dollar loan made by parent A was designated as being part of its net investment in the foreign subsidiary C from the beginning of the accounting period. If the parent did this part way during the financial year ended 30 September 20X5, say, at 31 March 20X5, the parent should recognise any exchange difference arising in profit or loss up to that date and reclassify any exchange difference that arises subsequently following the designation to the separate component in equity in the consolidated financial statements.

A7.101 Although not dealt with in the standard, the designation of an inter-company loan as part of the net investment in a foreign operation should be periodically reassessed. This is because management's expectations and intent may change due to a change in circumstances. Such changes in circumstances should be carefully evaluated to determine that management's previous assertions for not requiring repayment remain valid. For example, the change in circumstances may be such that it could not have been anticipated at the time of initial designation or the change in circumstances could be outside management's control.

A7.102 Where, as a result of a change in circumstance, a previously designated 'net investment' loan is intended to be settled, the loan should be de-designated. As the loan is no longer regarded as part of the net investment, a partial disposal of the net investment is deemed to have taken place in the same way that would have occurred had there been a partial repayment of share capital (see further para A7.106). In that situation, the amount of any exchange gains or losses included in equity and attributable to the part disposed of should be recognised in profit or loss. Exchange gains and losses that arise on the retranslation of the inter-company loan subsequently until eventual repayment should be recorded in the income statement.

A7.102.1 There is no explicit guidance in IAS 21 about the timing of recycling in the circumstances described in the previous paragraph. Should it occur when the loan is no longer considered to form part of the net investment in the foreign operation, or when the loan is actually repaid? Either approach may be adopted as an accounting policy choice. The selected policy should be applied consistently to all of the entity's 'net investment' loans, and all of its investments in foreign operations.

Inter-company dividends

A7.103 Where a foreign subsidiary pays a dividend to its parent company, the dividend is charged directly to equity in its financial statements. Since the dividend is paid in the functional currency of the foreign subsidiary no exchange difference arises. However, if the dividends are payable in a currency that is different from the entity's functional currency, exchange rate fluctuations prior to remittance will produce foreign exchange gains or losses impacting profit or loss.

A7.104 In the parent entity's financial statements, the dividend is translated at the rate in effect upon declaration (that is, the transaction date). An exchange gain or loss will arise if the rate of exchange moves between the date of declaration and the payment date. This exchange difference will be reported in the parent's income statement as a normal inter-company transaction exchange gain or loss that will also be reported in the consolidated financial statements. Consider the following example:

Example – treatment of foreign exchange gains or losses on inter-company dividends

A foreign subsidiary declared a dividend of FC 100,000 on 31 August 20X5 for the year ended 31 December 20X5. The dividend was appropriately authorised and, accordingly, was recognised by the subsidiary as a liability at 31 August 20X5. The parent prepares consolidated financial statements for the year ended 31 December 20X5. The following exchange rates are relevant:

31 August 20X4	FC 1.50 = £1
15 September 20X4	FC 1.60 = £1
31 December 20X4	FC 1.75 = £1
15 January 20X5	FC 1.80 = £1

Scenario 1 – Dividend paid on 15 September 20X5

The dividend will be recorded as follows:

	£
In subsidiary's retained earnings	
The dividend paid of FC 100,000 will be charged directly to equity. However, on consolidation, the dividend paid will be translated at the year end rate as part of the translation process, that is, FC 100,000 @ 1.75	57,142
In parent's income statement	
Amount recorded at rate when dividend paid — FC 1.6	62,500

In theory, the dividend should actually be recorded at the transaction date, which is the date when it was declared, that is, at £66,667 (FC 100,000 @ 1.5). However, since the dividend was declared and paid in the same year, any exchange difference arising between declaration date and settlement date would also be recorded in parent's income statement. The effect is that the income is recorded in the parent's income statement at the exchange rate at which it is received.

In parent's consolidated income statement

In the parent's consolidated financial statement the dividend received of £62,500 would be reclassified to consolidated reserves and will offset the dividend paid in the subsidiary's retained earnings that is translated at the year end rate @ 1.75 = £57,142. The difference of £5,358 (£62,500 — £57,142) comprises the exchange loss that arises as a result of the reduction in the net assets of the subsidiary due to the dividend payment from settlement date to the balance sheet date, that is, (FC 100,000 @ 1.6 – FC 100,000 @ 1.75).

Scenario 2 – Dividend paid on 15 January 20X6

In this situation, the dividend remains outstanding at the balance sheet date. The dividend will be recorded in the subsidiary's and parent's separate and consolidated financial statements as follows:

In subsidiary's balance sheet	
	£
Dividend payable – FC 100,000 @ 1.75	57,142
In parent's income statement	
Initially recorded at rate when dividend is declared — FC 1.5 (transaction date)	66,667
Exchange loss on receivable recognised in the income statement	(9,525)
In parent's balance sheet – Dividend receivable at year end rate — FC 1.75	57,142

In parent's consolidated income statement

In the parent's consolidated financial statements the dividend receivable of £66,667 would be reclassified to consolidated retained earnings and will offset the dividend payable in the subsidiary's retained earnings that is translated at the year end rate @ 1.75 = £57,142. The difference of £9,525 (£66,667 — £57,142) comprises a loss recorded in the parent's income statement and no further exchange difference arises. The inter-company receivable and payable cancel out.

Some may argue that the exchange difference of £9,525 included in the parent's income statement should be removed from consolidated income and reclassified to equity as it relates to dividends that are initially charged to equity. We believe that this treatment is not appropriate since the exchange difference arises on a monetary asset and would affect group cash flows when it is settled. Therefore, it is proper that such an exchange difference should remain in consolidated income.

A7.105 Given that exchange differences can arise on any transaction where the settlement date is different from the date when the transaction is recorded, it may be appropriate, particularly where there is a likelihood of an exchange loss arising, to ensure that inter-company dividends are paid on the same date as they are declared as liabilities. In practice, this may not always be possible, so it is not uncommon for a parent company to mitigate exchange differences arising by taking out appropriate forward contracts so as to hedge the future remittance. However, as stated in paragraph A7.26 above, IAS 21 does not apply to hedge accounting for foreign currency items as this is dealt with in IAS 39, 'Financial instruments: Recognition and measurement'. Hedge accounting is considered in detail in chapter 6.

Disposal or partial disposal of a foreign operation

A7.106 As discussed in paragraph A7.77, the cumulative amount of exchange differences deferred in a separate component of equity is carried forward in equity, until there is a disposal of the foreign operation. On the foreign operation's disposal, such exchange differences are recognised in profit or loss (that is, recycled) when the gain or loss on disposal is recognised. [IAS 21 para 48]. Disposal may occur either through sale, liquidation, repayment of share capital or abandonment of all, or part of, the entity.

A7.107 In the case of partial disposals, only the proportionate share of the related accumulated exchange difference is included in the gain or loss. [IAS 21 para 49]. Events that may lead to a reduction in the foreign investment's carrying value are many and varied, but not all of them would qualify as a partial disposal.

A7.107.1 The payment of a dividend is considered a partial disposal if it constitutes *a return of the investment,* for example when the dividend is paid out of pre-acquisition profits. [IAS 21 para 49]. The situation is complicated when a payment is legally deemed to be a return of capital, but where the operation has sufficient post-acquisition reserves to cover the payment. Here the substance of the transaction should be assessed and if the payment is a return of the investment, recycling occurs even if there are sufficient reserves available to cover that payment. In some jurisdictions where dividends and returns of capital are subject to regulatory processes designed to protect the interests of shareholders and creditors, it is likely that the substance and the form of a payment will be the same.

A7.107.2 In group situations, determining whether a dividend received from an intermediate holding company is paid out of pre- or post-acquisition reserves can be complex. Therefore, the group's parent has an accounting policy choice for determining pre- and post-acquisition reserves for the purpose of recycling the cumulative amount of exchange difference deferred in equity. The entity can choose either:

- the 'narrow entity' approach – determination is based solely on the pre- and post- acquisition reserves of the separate foreign entity that pays the dividend; or
- the 'wider entity' approach – determination is based on the pre- and post-acquisition reserves of the foreign entity that pays the dividend *and* that entity's sub-holdings.

A7.107.3 The transition to IFRS can create problems as illustrated in the following example.

Example – impact of the transition to IFRS on recycling of exchange differences recognised in equity

Entity A is a Swiss company with a Swiss franc functional currency and presentation currency. Entity B is a foreign subsidiary of entity A with the local currency (LC) as functional currency.

Entity A acquired entity B before 1995 and goodwill was written off directly against equity in accordance with the international accounting standards existing at that time. Entity B has negative equity under IFRS for this reason. Such transactions are 'grand-fathered' under IFRS. Entity B has capitalised goodwill in its statutory financial statements prepared under local GAAP and has positive equity. Entity B has been profitable ever since it was acquired by entity A and has paid dividends every year. Management of entity A has decided to repatriate funds in the form of a partial repayment of entity B's share capital rather than as a dividend for the current year.

Management should recycle a proportionate share of the cumulative exchange differences recognised in equity. The repayment of share capital constitutes a partial disposal of entity B and a proportionate share of cumulative translation adjustments deferred in equity should be transferred to profit or loss. The balance of the separate component in equity will decrease and management should define an appropriate method to calculate the proportion of related cumulative exchange differences to be recycled.

A7.107.4 A write-down of the carrying amount of a foreign operation does not constitute a partial disposal. Accordingly, no part of the deferred foreign exchange gain or loss is recognised in profit or loss at the time of a write-down. [IAS 21 para 49]. Where the write-down arises from an impairment assessment as a result of a planned sale or liquidation (for example, where the foreign subsidiary is treated as a disposal group in accordance with IFRS 5, 'Non-current assets held for sale and discontinued operations'), the write-down should also not be treated as a partial disposal. [IFRS 5 BC 37, 38]. Therefore, any exchange difference attributable to that write-down should not be recognised in the income statement. Recycling will occur when the foreign operation is sold.

A7.107.5 A group restructuring can often raise questions as to whether exchange differences recognised in equity should be recycled to profit or loss, as illustrated in the following example.

Example – recycling of cumulative exchange differences due to a group restructuring

In a group restructuring, a foreign operation is transferred from one intermediate holding company to another. The group continues to hold a 100% interest in that foreign operation. No third parties are involved with the group restructuring. Should the cumulative exchange differences be recycled in the group's consolidated financial statements?

The key question is whether the restructuring results in an economic change from the group's perspective that constitutes a partial or full disposal. In this case, the foreign operation continues to be part of the consolidated group and the restructuring is not a disposal event from the group's perspective.

However, if the intermediate holding company that disposes of the foreign operation prepares consolidated financial statements under IFRS, the cumulative translation adjustments deferred in equity (if any) that arise at that intermediate reporting level would be recycled to profit or loss.

A7.107.6 A foreign operation may issue additional shares in the form of scrip dividends or rights issue that are not fully taken up by the parent. As a result the parent's ownership interest in the foreign operation may be reduced giving rise to a deemed disposal. Although deemed disposals are not specifically dealt with in IFRS, we believe that a profit or loss should be recognised on a deemed disposal. In that situation, we believe that the cumulative exchange difference attributable to the reduction in the parent's interest should be included as part of the gain or loss arising on the deemed disposal. Deemed disposals are dealt with in chapter 26.

A7.107.7 Simultaneous transactions can confuse the issues relating to recycling. However, the substance of the transactions should always be considered.

Example – simultaneous transactions triggering a recycling of cumulative differences

A parent company increases its equity investment in a foreign operation and the foreign operation simultaneously repays a 'net investment' loan. The two transactions result in a net increase in the investment in the foreign operation. Should cumulative translation adjustments deferred in equity be recycled on the repayment of the 'net investment' loan?

The answer is that it depends. Separate transactions are aggregated and treated as a single transaction when the transactions result, in substance, in a single arrangement. Indicators of a single arrangement include:

- The transactions are entered into at the same time and in contemplation of one another.
- The transactions are with the same counterparty.
- The transactions relate to the same risk.
- There is no apparent economic need or substantive business purpose for structuring the transactions separately that could not also have been accomplished in a single transaction.

Judgment is applied when determining whether two or more transactions are linked.

In the case of a repayment of a 'net investment' loan and an increase in equity investment, if the two transactions occur simultaneously, this is a strong indication that the transactions are, in substance, one arrangement. The substance of the arrangement appears to be the swapping of the legal form of an investment from a debt instrument to an equity instrument. This is not a disposal event under IAS 21 and no recycling occurs for the exchange differences recognised in equity.

When there is a delay between the two transactions, the facts and circumstances surrounding the delay should be reviewed when considering whether the transactions should be linked. A significant delay between the increase in the investment and the repayment of the 'net investment' loan is an indication that the two contracts are not linked and should be accounted for as separate transactions. If the transactions are accounted for separately, the repayment of the 'net investment' loan is a partial disposal that triggers recycling of the proportionate share of the exchange differences recognised in equity.

A7.107.8 The cessation of hedge accounting of a net investment as the hedge no longer meets the criteria for the hedge accounting in IAS 39 is not a disposal. Therefore, the effective portion of the hedge previously recognised in equity remains in equity until the disposal, or partial disposal, of the foreign operation.

A7.107.9 The conversion of a 'net investment' loan to an equity instrument as defined in IAS 32 would also not result in recycling. The reason for this is that the conversion of the loan is the swapping of the legal form of an investment from a debt instrument to an equity instrument so no disposal has occurred. No further exchange differences will arise on the equity investment, as it is now a non-monetary item. (However, exchange differences would continue to arise on the net assets of the foreign operation.) The exchange differences from the 'net investment' loan recognised in equity are recycled to profit or loss on the disposal, or partial disposal, of the net investment in the foreign operation. The re-denomination of a 'net investment' loan also does not constitute a disposal or partial disposal of the foreign operation. It does not change the parent's net investment in the foreign operation, there is no cash movement and the loan is essentially still the same. Therefore, no gains or losses are recycled from equity to the income statement.

A7.107.10 As highlighted above, the tracking of cumulative exchange differences can be onerous. For a parent with more than one foreign operation, it could be tempting to aggregate these exchange differences related to all the net investments in one currency together, with the recycling of these exchange differences on the disposal (or partial disposal) of some of those foreign operations being calculated proportionately based on the whole investments portfolio. However, since IAS 21 requires recycling whenever there is a disposal, or partial disposal, of a foreign operation, the cumulative translation adjustments are required to be tracked on an individual net investment basis.

Hedging a net investment

A7.108 A net investment in a foreign operation is defined as *"the amount of the reporting entity's interest in the net assets of that operation"*. [IAS 21 para 8]. A company may decide to hedge against the effects of changes in exchange rates in the company's net investment in a foreign operation. This may be done by taking out a foreign currency borrowing or a forward contract to hedge the net investment. Because the net assets of the foreign operation are reported in the reporting entity's consolidated financial statements, hedging a net investment in a foreign operation can only be carried out at the consolidation level. However, as stated in paragraph A7.26 above, this standard does not apply to hedge accounting for foreign currency items including the hedging of a net investment in a foreign operation. IAS 39 applies to hedge accounting. Under IAS 39, the hedging documentation and criteria set out in paragraph 88 of IAS 39 must be met, and any exchange differences recognised in equity relating to the foreign operation and the related borrowing must be recognised in profit or loss on disposal of the foreign operation. This issue is further dealt with in greater detail in chapter 6.

A7.108.1 Therefore, where a reporting entity has a foreign currency borrowing that is designated as a hedge of its net investment in a foreign operation and all the conditions in paragraph 88 of IAS 39 are met, the exchange gain or loss on the foreign currency borrowing would be reported in the reporting entity's separate income statement, but would be reclassified to equity in the reporting entity's consolidated financial statements as stated above.

A7.108.2 IAS 27, 'Consolidated and separate financial statements', states that in a parent's separate financial statements, investments in subsidiaries, jointly controlled entities and associates that are included in the consolidated financial statements should be carried at cost or accounted for in accordance with IAS 39. This means that the equity investment can be designated as 'available for sale' or 'at fair value through profit or loss' (if permitted by IAS 39). IAS 27 requires that the same accounting be applied for each category of investment. However, in some countries parent companies normally record their investments in subsidiaries, associates and joint ventures at cost in their separate financial statements. A question, therefore, arises as to whether a foreign currency borrowing can be designated as a hedge of the entity's foreign equity investment in its separate financial statements where the foreign equity investment is recorded at cost. Although this issue is not specifically dealt with in IAS 39, we believe that the reporting entity can designate the foreign currency borrowing as a fair value hedge of foreign currency risk attributable to its foreign equity investment. In those circumstances, the foreign equity investment would be retranslated at each balance sheet date and exchange difference arising on the retranslation will be recognised in the income statement to offset the exchange difference arising on the retranslation of the foreign currency borrowings. It should be noted, however, that the hedging criteria set out in paragraph 88 of IAS 39 must still be met in order to achieve fair value hedge accounting in the reporting entity's separate financial statements. Whether, in practice, such a parent entity would apply hedge accounting in its separate financial statements is a moot point that may well depend on the tax treatment of undertaking such hedging activities.

[The next paragraph is A7.109.]

Foreign operations in hyperinflationary economies

A7.109 Where a foreign entity operates in a country in which a very high rate of inflation exists and its functional currency is the local currency, the closing rate/net investment method is not considered to be suitable for translating the foreign entity's financial statements for inclusion in the consolidated financial statements. This is because an asset acquired in a currency that is the currency of a hyperinflationary economy may be worth very little at a time of high inflation, when the foreign currency has weakened considerably against the reporting entity's functional currency, leading to a large debit to consolidated reserves. At the same time, the results of the foreign entity are included at an inflated amount in the consolidated income statement (whether from high interest income on deposits in a rapidly depreciating foreign currency or from trading operations which could be considered to reflect unrealistically high profitability). Therefore, as money loses purchasing power in a hyperinflationary economy, the reporting of operating results and financial position in the local currency without adjustment to reflect current price levels is misleading.

A7.110 Accordingly, when an entity's functional currency is the currency of the hyperinflationary economy, the entity should restate its financial statements in accordance with IAS 29, 'Financial reporting in hyperinflationary economies' before applying the closing rate/net investment method referred to in paragraph A7.77 above, except where the comparative amounts are translated into a currency of a non-hyperinflationary economy.

A7.111 IAS 29 describes a number of characteristics of a country's economic environment that indicate hyperinflation. These are as follows:

- The general population prefers to keep its wealth in non-monetary assets or in a relatively stable foreign currency. Amounts of local currency held are immediately invested to maintain purchasing power.
- The general population regards monetary amounts not in terms of the local currency, but in terms of a relatively stable foreign currency. Prices may be quoted in that currency.
- Sales and purchases on credit take place at prices that compensate for the expected loss of purchasing power during the credit period, even if the period is short.
- Interest rates, wages and prices are linked to a price index.

- The cumulative inflation rate over three years is approaching, or exceeds, 100 per cent.

[IAS 29 para 3].

A7.112 IAS 29 is, however, not clear whether the word 'cumulative' in the last point above is intended to mean that the three-year inflation rate should be calculated by simply adding up the inflation rates for each of the three years or by computing the compound inflation rate over the three years. Consider the following example:

Example – assessment of an economy as hyperinflationary or not

The following data are relevant to a country operating in a hyperinflationary economy:

	20X2	20X3	20X4	20X5
Inflation rate		30%	28%	34%
General price level	120	156	200	268

Based on simple addition the cumulative inflation rate for the years 20X3 to 20X5 is 92% (30 + 28 + 34).

Compounded annually (using the index at the end of 20X2 as the base), the cumulative inflation for 20X3 to 20X5 is (268 — 120) ÷ 120 = 123%.

In our view, the cumulative three-year inflation rate should be compounded, because it provides a measure of inflation for the three years taken as a whole.

A7.113 The translation procedure that should be followed in translating the foreign entity's restated financial statements into a different presentation currency is as follows:

- all amounts (that is, income and expenses, assets and liabilities, and equity items including comparatives) should be translated at the date of the most recent balance sheet; except that
- when amounts are translated into the currency of a non-hyperinflationary economy, comparative amounts should be presented as current year amounts in the relevant prior year financial statements (that is, not adjusted for subsequent changes in the price level or subsequent changes in exchange rates).

[IAS 21 para 43].

A7.113.1 The IFRIC issued IFRIC 7, 'Applying the restatement approach under IAS 29, Financial reporting in hyperinflationary economies' in November 2005. IFRIC 7 clarifies IAS 29's requirements relating to two issues:

- How comparative amounts in financial statements should be restated when an entity identifies the existence of hyperinflation in the economy of its functional currency.
- How deferred tax items in the opening balance sheet should be restated.

A7.113.2 On the first issue, the IFRIC clarified that in these cases the comparative amounts in financial statements should be restated as if the economy has always been hyperinflationary. Therefore, non-monetary items in the opening balance sheet are restated to reflect the effect of inflation from the date the assets were acquired and any resulting liabilities were incurred or assumed, or any revalued amounts determined, until the closing balance sheet date of the reporting period.

A7.113.3 The restatement of the opening balance of deferred tax is determined by remeasuring the deferred tax items based on the restatements of the non-monetary items as described above, adjusted for the change in the measuring unit from the date of the opening balance sheet of the reporting period to the closing balance sheet date of that period.

A7.113.4 After the restatement of the previous financial statements, all corresponding figures for a subsequent reporting period, including deferred tax items, are restated by applying the change in the measuring unit for that subsequent reporting period only to the restated financial statements for the previous reporting period.

A7.114 In recent years, inflation rates in countries that used to be considered highly inflationary countries have significantly decreased compared to those of the mid 1980s and early 1990s. When the economy ceases to be hyperinflationary and the entity no longer restates its financial statements in accordance with IAS 29, it should use as the historical costs for translation into the presentation currency the amounts restated to the price level at the date the entity ceased restating its financial statements. [IAS 21 para 43].

Presentation and disclosure

General

A7.115 The paragraphs that follow deal with IAS 21's disclosure requirements that apply to both individual financial statements and consolidated financial statements. IAS 32, 'Financial instruments: Disclosure and presentation' and IFRS 7, 'Financial instruments: Disclosures', require significant additional disclosures about foreign currency transactions and activities. The requirements of IAS 32 and IFRS 7 are dealt with in chapter 6.

Accounting policies

A7.116 There is no specific requirement in IAS 21 to disclose accounting policies in respect of foreign currency transactions. This is because IAS 1, 'Presentation of financial statements', requires disclosure of significant policies that are relevant to an entity's financial statements. [IAS 1 para 108]. In respect of foreign currency transactions, the accounting policy note should state, as a minimum, the methods used in translating foreign currency transactions and the financial statements of foreign operations including those operating in hyperinflationary economies, and the treatment accorded to exchange differences. The following is an example of a foreign currency accounting policy.

Table A7.1 – Accounting policy for foreign currency

Svenska Cellulosa Aktiebolaget SCA – Report and accounts – 31 December 2006

Translation of foreign currency

Functional currency and presentation currency

The companies in the Group prepare their financial reports in the currency used in the primary economic environment in which they operate. This is known as the functional currency. These reports provide the basis for the consolidated accounts. The consolidated accounts are prepared in Swedish kronor (SEK) which is the Parent Company's functional currency and therefore the presentation currency of both the Parent Company and the Group.

Translation of foreign group companies

Balance sheets and income statements for all group companies whose functional currency is not the presentation currency are translated into the Group's presentation currency using the following procedures:

- assets and liabilities for each balance sheet presented are translated at the closing rate at the date of the balance sheet;
- income and expenses for each income statement presented are translated at the average exchange rate for the respective year;
- all exchange differences that arise are reported as a separate component directly in consolidated equity.

Exchange differences arising on the financial instruments held to hedge these net assets are also taken directly to consolidated equity. When a foreign operation is disposed of, both of these exchange differences are reported in the income statement as part of the gain or loss on disposal. SCA has chosen to apply the exemption in IFRS 1, First-time Adoption of IFRS, which allows these translation differences to be disclosed in equity from the date of transition to IFRS, i.e. from 1 January 2004. Goodwill and fair value adjustments that arise on acquisition of a foreign operation are treated as assets and liabilities of the operation and translated according to the same principles as the foreign operation. The financial reports of a subsidiary in a hyperinflationary country are adjusted for inflation using the price index for the country in question before these reports are included in the consolidated accounts.

Transactions and balance sheet items in foreign currency

Transactions in a foreign currency are translated to a functional currency using the exchange rate at the date of the transactions. Monetary receivables and liabilities in foreign currency are remeasured at closing day rates at each balance sheet date. Exchange gains or losses that arise from such remeasurement and on payment of the transaction are recognized in the income statement, except for, in accordance with IAS 39, approved hedging transactions relating to cash flows or net investment where the gain or loss is recognized in equity. Gains and losses on operating receivables and liabilities are reported net and reported within operating profit. Gains and losses on borrowing and financial investments are reported as other financial items. Change in fair value of monetary securities issued in foreign currency and classified as financial assets available for sale is analyzed and the change attributable to changed exchange rates is reported in the income statement, while other unrealized change is reported in equity.

Translation differences for non-monetary financial assets and liabilities valued at fair value through profit or loss are reported as part of the fair value gain or loss. Translation differences for non-monetary financial assets, classified as assets available for sale are taken directly to equity. Non-monetary assets and liabilities recognized at historical cost are translated at the exchange rate prevailing on the transaction date.

Disclosure

A7.117 In respect of exchange differences, IAS 21 requires disclosure of:

- The amount of exchange differences recognised in profit or loss except for those arising on financial instruments measured at 'fair value through profit or loss' in accordance with IAS 39.
- Net exchange differences classified in a separate component of equity, and a reconciliation of the amount of such exchange differences at the beginning and end of the period.

[IAS 21 para 52].

A7.118 The disclosure required above is on an aggregate net basis. The total amount of exchange differences recognised in the income statement would include exchange differences recognised on subsequent settlement and restatement to closing rate on balances arising on foreign currency transactions. However, the standard is silent as to where in the income statement they should be included. A cue can be taken from IAS 12, 'Income taxes', which states that exchange differences arising on foreign deferred tax assets and liabilities may be included as part of the deferred tax expense (income) if that presentation is considered to be the most useful to financial statement users. Therefore:

- Foreign exchange differences arising from trading transactions may be included in the results of operating activities.
- Foreign exchange differences arising from financing may be included as a component of finance cost/income.

A7.118.1 The following examples illustrate the disclosure of the recognition of exchange differences in profit or loss and as a separate component in equity.

Table A7.2 – Disclosure of exchange differences recognised in profit or loss

Associated British Foods plc – Report and accounts – 16 September 2006

2. Operating costs and gross profit (extract)

		Total	
		2006	**2005**
	Note	**£m**	**£m**
Operating costs are stated after charging/(crediting):			
Employee benefits expense	3	848	779
Amortisation of intangibles		41	25
Depreciation of owned property, plant & equipment		177	161
Operating lease payments under property leases		57	31
Operating lease payments for hire of plant & equipment		6	6
Other operating income		(33)	(20)
Research and development expenditure		12	11
Impairment of trade receivables		(1)	3
Foreign exchange gains on operating activities		(3)	(15)
Foreign exchange losses on operating activities		5	15

4. Financial income

	Note	2006 £m	2005 £m
Interest income on bank deposits and investments		31	44
Gain on remeasurement of other current investments at fair value through profit and loss		1	5
Foreign exchange gains on financing activities		1	–
Expected return on pension scheme assets	13	116	113
		149	162

5. Financial expenses

	Note	2006 £m	2005 £m
Interest expense on bank loans		29	18
Interest expense on other loans		16	16
Foreign exchange losses on financing activities		2	–
Interest expense on finance leases		1	–
Interest charge on pension scheme liabilities	13	103	103
		151	137

Table A7.3 – Disclosure of exchange differences recognised in a separate component of equity Xstrata plc – Report and accounts – 31 December 2005

Other reserves

US$m	Other reserves	Net unrealised gains	Foreign currency translation	Total
At 1 January 2004	1,240.7		1,739.6	2,980.3
Hedge on net investment			40.9	40.9
Foreign currency translation of subsidiaries			537.5	537.5
Recycled foreign currency translation net gains			(68.6)	(68.6)
At 31 December 2004	1,240.7		2,249.4	3,490.1
First time adoption of IAS 32 and IAS 39:				
Available-for-sale financial assets		1.3		1.3
Cash flow hedges		12.2		12.2
Deferred tax		(11.0)		(11.0)
At 1 January 2005	1,240.7	2.5	2,249.4	3,492.6
Available-for-sale financial assets		397.5		397.5
Cash flow hedges		(185.4)		(185.4)
Recycled foreign currency translation net gains			(67.2)	(67.2)
Deferred tax		(24.2)	18.2	(6.0)
Foreign currency translation of subsidiaries		4.0	(582.0)	(578.0)
At 31 December 2005	1,240.7	194.4	1,618.4	3,053.5

Other reserves

This reserve principally originated during 2002 from the merger of Xstrata AG into Xstrata plc (US$279.4 million) and the issue of shares from the acquisition of the Duiker and Enex Group's of US$934.8 million.

Net unrealised gains/(losses) reserve
This reserve records the re-measurement of available-for-sale financial assets to fair value (refer to note 5, 6 and 23) and the effective portion of the gain or loss on cash flow hedging contracts (refer to note 5, 6, 24, 32 and 39). Deferred tax is provided on the re-measurement at tax rates enacted or substantively enacted.

Foreign currency translation reserve
This is used to record exchange differences arising from the translation of the financial statements of foreign subsidiaries. It is also used to record the exchange differences from the translation of quasi equity inter-company loans used to acquire investments in foreign operations.

A7.119 As stated in paragraph A7.74 above, the standard permits a reporting entity to present its financial statements in a currency that is different from its functional currency. In this situation, the following should be disclosed:

- The fact that the presentation currency is different from the functional currency.
- The disclosure of the functional currency.
- The reasons for using a different presentation currency.

[IAS 21 para 53].

In these cases the entity should provide the foreign currency risk disclosures required by IAS 32/IFRS 7 in reference to its functional currency rather than its presentation currency. The entity's exposure to currencies other than the functional currency will affect its future performance, and it is details of these exposures that should be provided in the financial statements.

Table A7.4 – Presentation currency differs from functional currency

OAO Baltika Brewery – Report and accounts – 31 December 2006

2. Basis of preparation (extract)

(c) Functional and presentation currency
The national currency of the Russian Federation is the Russian Rouble ("RUR"), which is the Company's functional currency and the functional currency of the majority of the Company's subsidiaries, because it reflects the economic substance of the underling events and circumstances of the Group.

These consolidated financial statements are presented in euro ("EURO") since management believes that this currency is more useful for the users of the consolidated financial statements. All financial information presented in EURO has been rounded to the nearest thousand.

The RUR is not a readily convertible currency outside the Russian Federation and, accordingly, any conversion of RUR to EURO should not be construed as a representation that the RUR amounts have been, could be, or will be in the future, convertible into EURO at the exchange rate disclosed, or at any other exchange rate.

A7.120 When there is a change in the functional currency of either the reporting entity or a significant foreign operation, that fact and the reason for the change in functional currency should be disclosed. [IAS 21 para 54]. As changes in functional currency may be due to a number of reasons, it is not possible to say what disclosure might be required in a particular case. However, it will certainly require a more substantial disclosure than, for example, 'this currency was chosen because it gives the most appropriate presentation'.

Table A7.5 – Change of functional currency

Royal Dutch Shell plc – Report and accounts – 31 December 2005

3 Accounting policies (extract)
Change in functional currency
Following Royal Dutch Shell becoming the parent company of Royal Dutch and Shell Transport on July 20, 2005 and through Royal Dutch and Shell Transport, of the rest of the Shell Group, the Directors have concluded that the most appropriate functional currency of the Company is dollars. This reflects the fact that the majority of the Shell Group's business is influenced by pricing in international commodity markets, with a dollar economic environment. The previous functional currency of the Company was the euro.

On the date of the change of functional currency all assets, liabilities, issued capital and other components of equity and income statement items were translated into dollars at the exchange rate on that date. As a result the cumulative currency translation differences which had arisen up to the date of the change of functional currency were reallocated to other components within equity (refer to Note 13).

As a result of the change in functional currency the Company's functional and presentation currency are now the same.

13 Other reserves (extract)
Cumulative currency translation differences
Cumulative currency translation differences represents the currency differences which arose as a result of translating the financial statements from the Company's previous functional currency of euro to the reporting currency of dollars.

The impact of the change in functional currency was the reallocation at that date of the cumulative currency translation differences of $15 million to issued capital.

A7.121 When an entity presents its financial statements in a currency that is different from its functional currency, it should describe the financial statements as complying with International Financial Reporting Standards only if they comply with all the requirements of each applicable standard and each applicable Interpretation of those standards including the translation method set out in paragraphs A7.77 and A7.109 above.

Convenience translation

A7.122 IAS 21 does not prohibit an entity from providing, as supplementary information, a 'convenience translation'. Such a convenience translation may display financial statements or other financial information (such as five year summaries) in a currency that is not its functional currency or its presentation currency, as convenience to some users. Convenience translations are normally prepared by applying a single exchange rate to all amounts appearing in financial statements presented in the entity's functional or presentation currency. In doing so, the relationships among amounts in the financial statements do not change. Thus, convenience translation fails to account for the effects of changes in foreign exchange rates and, therefore, does not comply with the translation procedures set out in paragraphs A7.77 above. Therefore, where an entity displays its financial statements or other financial information in a currency that is different from either its functional currency or its presentation currency and the requirements of paragraph A7.121 above are not met, it should:

- Clearly identify the information as supplementary information to distinguish it from the information that complies with International Financial Reporting Standards.
- Disclose the currency in which the supplementary information is displayed.
- Disclose the entity's functional currency and the method of translation used to determine the supplementary information.

[IAS 21 para 57].

Table A7.6 – Disclosure for convenience translation

OJSC RBC Information Systems – Report and accounts – 31 December 2005

2 Basis of preparation (extract)

(c) Functional and presentation currency

The national currency of the Russian Federation is the Russian Rouble ("RUR") which is the Company's functional currency and the currency in which these consolidated financial statements are presented. All financial information presented in RUR has been rounded to the nearest thousand.

(d) Convenience translation

The Company's functional currency is RUR because it reflects the economic substance of the underlying events and circumstances of the Company. In addition to presenting the consolidated financial statements in RUR, supplementary information in USD has been presented for the convenience of users of the consolidated financial statements.

All amounts in the consolidated financial statements, including comparatives, are translated from RUR to USD at the closing exchange rate at 31 December 2005 of RUR 28.7825 to USD 1. All financial information presented in USD has been rounded to the nearest thousand.

Other disclosures

UK.A7.122.1 The Companies Act 1985 (Operating and Financial Review and Directors' Report etc.) Regulations 2005 (SI 2005/1011) introduced a statutory requirement for quoted companies to prepare an operating and financial review (OFR) as part of their annual report and accounts for financial years beginning on or after 1 April 2005. In January 2006, the legislation for a mandatory OFR was repealed, although the requirement to prepare a business review still apply to all except small companies for periods beginning on or after 1 April 2005. The ASB's Reporting Statement Operating and Financial Review recommends that the directors of quoted companies give a balanced and comprehensive analysis of their business, including a number of disclosures that may be relevant to foreign currency operations. In particular, the Reporting Statement recommends that the reporting company should give a description of the principal risks and uncertainties facing the company and its subsidiary undertakings as well as a description of the capital structure, treasury policies and objectives and liquidity of the company and its subsidiary undertakings. Such descriptions are likely to include foreign currency risks (including the effect of changes in exchange rates), factors that may have a major effect on future results (possibly including exchange rate fluctuations), management of currency risk and the extent to which foreign currency net investments are hedged by currency borrowings and other hedging instruments.

UK.A7.122.2 A recommendation to provide the above information is unlikely to cause any problems to listed companies as they already disclose the ways in which they manage their foreign currency exposures and treasury activities in accordance with the ASB's previous statement 'Operating and financial review', issued in January 2003 and the previous UK standard, FRS 13, 'Derivatives and other financial instruments – disclosures', which included many of these disclosure requirements. The OFR is covered in detail in the Manual of Accounting – Management reports and governance.

[The next paragraph is A7.126.]

Other matters

Tax effects of all exchange differences

A7.126 Gains and losses on foreign currency transactions and exchange differences arising on the translating the results and financial position of an entity (including a foreign operation) into a different currency may have tax effects. IAS 12, 'Income taxes', applies to these tax effects, and the issues are considered in chapter 13.

Cash flow statements

A7.127 Cash flows arising from transactions in foreign currency and cash flows of a foreign subsidiary should be translated at the exchange rates between the functional currency and the foreign currency at the dates of the cash flows. IAS 7, 'Cash flow statements', applies to foreign currency cash flows, which is considered in chapter 30.

[The next paragraph is A7.130.]

First-time adoption of IFRS

A7.130 There are specific rules in respect of first-time adoption of IFRS, set out in IFRS 1, 'First-time adoption of International Financial Reporting Standards'. In particular, IFRS 1 includes an exemption allowing the cumulative translation difference on retranslation of subsidiaries' net assets to be set to zero (for all subsidiaries) at the date of transition to IFRS. This means it does not have to be separately disclosed and recycled to the income statement on the subsidiaries' disposal. However, translation differences arising from the date of transition would be included in equity and recycled to the income statement on the investment's disposal.

A7.131 Furthermore, the requirement to retranslate goodwill and fair value adjustments as if they are assets and liabilities of the acquired entity, considered in paragraph A7.86 onwards, does not have to be applied retrospectively to business combinations that occurred before the date of transition to IFRS. Therefore, these goodwill and fair value adjustments are already expressed in the acquiring entity's functional currency or they are non-monetary foreign currency items from the acquiring entity's point of view, reported using the exchange rate applied under the entity's previous GAAP.

A7.132 These exemptions and other implications of IAS 21 for first-time adopters of IFRS are considered in detail in chapter 3.

subsidiaries) at the date of transition to IFRS. This means it does not have to be separately disclosed and recycled to the income statement on the subsidiaries' disposal. However, translation differences arising from the date of transition would be included in equity and recycled to the income statement on the investment's disposal.

A7.131 Furthermore, the requirement to retranslate goodwill and fair value adjustments as if they are assets and liabilities of the acquired entity, considered in paragraph A7.86 onwards, does not have to be applied retrospectively to business combinations that occurred before the date of transition to IFRS. Therefore, these goodwill and fair value adjustments are already expressed in the acquiring entity's functional currency or they are non-monetary foreign currency items from the acquiring entity's point of view, reported using the exchange rate applied under the entity's previous GAAP.

A7.132 These exemptions and other implications of IAS 21 for first-time adopters of IFRS are considered in detail in chapter 3.

Chapter 8

Reporting financial performance

Page

Introduction 8001
Profit and loss account formats — an overview 8003
  Layered format 8003
  Operating profit 8004
  Allocation of interest and taxation 8007
  Exceptional items 8008
Discontinued operations 8008
  Definition 8008
  Discontinued compared to discontinuing 8009
  Meaning of 'ceased permanently' 8010
  Materiality and separability of activities 8011
  Disposal of subsidiary with retained interest 8013
  Operations discontinued by sale 8015
  Profits and losses on sale 8016
    Provisions for losses on sale of operations 8016
  Treatment of goodwill on disposals 8020
  Operations discontinued by closure 8022
    Provisions for losses on termination 8023
Acquisitions 8026
  Mergers 8029
Exceptional items 8029
  Definition 8029
  Non-operating exceptional items 8030
  Profits or losses on the sale or termination of an operation 8031
  Fundamental reorganisation or restructuring 8033
  Profits or losses on disposals of fixed assets 8036
    Impairments 8039
  Other exceptional items 8040
  Tax attributable to exceptional items 8049
Extraordinary items 8050
Statement of total recognised gains and losses 8050
  Purchased goodwill 8053
  Movements in reserves 8054
Note of historical cost profits and losses 8054
Reconciliation of movements in shareholders' funds 8056
Prior period adjustments 8058
  Introduction 8058
  Changes in accounting policies 8060
    Disclosures 8061

Fundamental errors 8064
Changes to estimation techniques 8065

Chapter 8

Reporting financial performance

Introduction

8.1 FRS 3, 'Reporting financial performance', was published in October 1992. It superseded SSAP 6, 'Extraordinary items and prior year adjustments', which was first published in 1974 and revised in 1986. The establishment of the ASB in August 1990 coincided with a general feeling of dissatisfaction with several of the accounting standards that were in force at the time, including SSAP 6. In particular, there was evidence that SSAP 6 was not effective, either because of non-compliance or because of a lack of clarity in its provisions, or both.

8.2 An objective of SSAP 6 had been to ensure that, with certain exceptions, all profits and losses were included in the profit and loss account. It divided such profits and losses between ordinary activities and extraordinary activities. The distinction between ordinary and extraordinary was critical, because one of the more widely used measures of performance, earnings per share, *included* profits on ordinary activities, but *excluded* extraordinary items.

8.3 Despite the standard setters' attempts to define 'ordinary activities' and 'extraordinary items' in such a way as to give clear guidance to preparers and users, the distinction between ordinary and extraordinary was frequently blurred. A particular example of this was reorganisation and restructuring costs. SSAP 6 had made it quite clear that the costs of reorganising a continuing business segment were part of ordinary activities. However, some companies, who had carried out what they termed a 'fundamental restructuring' took the view that such a restructuring was extraordinary in nature. In some instances this was because the restructuring involved closures of certain business segments as well as reorganisation of continuing segments and it was considered that it was not possible or meaningful to isolate the costs of the closures (extraordinary) from the other reorganisation (exceptional). As a result of the distinction between ordinary and extraordinary becoming blurred, inconsistencies developed between companies. Because earnings per share excluded extraordinary items, its value as a measure of performance also suffered.

8.4 Furthermore, the frequency with which extraordinary items appeared in companies' profit and loss accounts meant that in practice there was nothing rare or extraordinary about their occurrence. Disillusionment with SSAP 6 gradually increased and pressure grew for eliminating extraordinary items completely. The UITF made a limited attempt to patch up SSAP 6 by issuing UITF Abstract 2, 'Restructuring costs', in October 1991. The UITF's statement referred to preventing *"a perceived drift towards the inclusion of more and more items as extraordinary"*. However, this interim measure was short-lived since the ASB's project on reporting financial performance was already well underway.

8.5 A second important problem with SSAP 6 was that it dealt principally with the profit and loss account and required only that the note disclosing movements on reserves should either follow the profit and loss account or that a cross-reference should be made to where in the notes the reserves summary could be found. It became apparent as a result of several specific cases that items taken directly to reserves, for example, exchange losses on re-translation of opening net assets of overseas subsidiaries, were not always given the importance they merited by shareholders and analysts. This was possibly because the reserves note was often 'hidden' in the body of the financial statements.

8.6 FRS 3's principal purpose was to produce a more effective set of rules for presenting statements of financial performance. To do this the ASB adopted a twofold approach. First, it broadened the range of information that needs to be given both in terms of the amount of detail required and in terms of prominence given to the information. Secondly, it removed the emphasis placed on individual measures of performance by preparers and users by, in particular, reducing the importance of earnings per share. The main reforming measures in FRS 3 were as follows:

- Two primary statements of financial performance are required. These are the profit and loss account and the statement of total recognised gains and losses. These formats are intended to provide an 'information set' that captures all recognised changes in shareholders' funds arising from a company's activities, except for capital contributed by shareholders, distributions and capital repaid to shareholders and (prior to FRS 10 coming into force) purchased goodwill eliminated on consolidation.
- The profit and loss account should disclose separately the results of a company's operations attributable to continuing operations, acquisitions as a component of continuing operations and discontinued operations.
- The definition of ordinary activities was drawn so widely that extraordinary items have all but disappeared from UK companies' profit and loss accounts.
- A framework for disclosing exceptional items was introduced, with rules to control their positioning in the profit and loss account formats.
- The emphasis on earnings per share as a single measure of performance was diminished. Since it is based on a company's profit or loss for the year after all exceptional charges and credits, including those that would previously have been treated as extraordinary, it is a more volatile measure and does not attempt to capture any underlying trends in a company's operating performance. However, alternative earnings per share figures may be disclosed in the notes to the financial statements provided that a reconciliation between the two figures is given (chapter 14 contains a guide to earnings per share.)
- The statement of total recognised gains and losses includes in one place all the gains and losses of the year, whether recognised in the profit and loss

account or taken directly to reserves. Its purpose is to show the year's total financial performance. In addition to the profit for the financial year, the statement includes unrealised revaluation surpluses, exchange gains and losses on translation of net assets of overseas subsidiaries and other gains and losses recognised in the year.

8.7 Thus, FRS 3 requires statements of performance that, taken together, give an information set that depicts the major elements of a company's performance, including all gains and losses of the period whether accounted for in the profit and loss account or in reserves. The aim of this approach is to give analysts and other users sufficient information to enable them to make judgements about a company's past performance and to assist them in forming a basis for predicting future trends in performance.

[The next paragraph is 8.9.]

Profit and loss account formats — an overview

8.9 FRS 3 requires that the profit and loss account should include all gains and losses recognised in the financial statements for the period, except those that are specifically permitted or required by the FRS or by other accounting standards to be taken directly to reserves, or (in the absence of a relevant accounting standard) specifically permitted or required by law to be taken directly to reserves. [FRS 3 para 13]. Gains and losses that go directly to reserves must be included in the statement of total recognised gains and losses, together with the profit or loss for the year.

Layered format

8.10 FRS 3 sets out a layered format for the profit and loss account that is designed to highlight a number of important components of financial performance. These are:

- Results of continuing operations, including separate disclosure of the results of acquisitions, where material.
- Results of discontinued operations.
- Certain types of income or expense that are required to be shown on the face of the profit and loss account after operating profit, but before interest. These include:
  - Profits or losses on the sale or termination of an operation.
  - Costs of a fundamental reorganisation or restructuring having a material effect on the nature and focus of the reporting entity's operations.
  - Profits or losses on the disposal of fixed assets.

  Provisions made in respect of these items should also be included.

8.11 Exceptional items, other than those that fall into the category of post-operating profit items listed above, should be shown under the statutory format headings to which they relate, either in the notes or on the face of the profit and loss account if this is necessary in order to give a true and fair view. [FRS 3 para 19].

8.12 FRS 3 supplements the requirements of the Companies Act 1985 as to the form and content of the profit and loss account. The Act provides a choice of four formats — of the two formats most commonly used by UK companies, Format 1 analyses operating expenses by function, Format 2 by type. These formats are fully described in chapter 4. The Companies Act 2006 ('the 2006 Act') received Royal Assent in November 2006 and is being implemented in stages. Parts 15 and 16 of the 2006 Act, 'Accounts and Reports' and 'Audit' respectively, will replace Part VII of the 1985 Act, 'Accounts and Audit', with effect from financial years beginning on or after 6 April 2008. The 2006 Act, including Part 15, gives the Secretary of State the power to make regulations in specified areas. At the time of writing, these regulations have not been finalised. In particular, the schedules that will replace Schedules 4, 4A, 9 and 9A have yet to be finalised but will be provided through secondary legislation in time for the commencement of Part 15 of the 2006 Act.

Operating profit

8.13 The standard requires that turnover and operating profit should be shown separately on the face of the profit and loss account split between: continuing operations; acquisitions as a component of continuing operations; and discontinued operations. [FRS 3 para 14]. As standards deal only with material items, the requirement to disclose results of acquisitions applies if those results are material in aggregate and the requirement to disclose results of discontinued operations similarly depends on those results being material in aggregate. FRS 6 added the requirement that the results of each material acquisition should be shown separately. [FRS 6 paras 23, 28].

8.14 Where operations that have been sold or terminated are classified as discontinued in the profit and loss account, the comparative profit and loss account figures are restated in order to show the previous year's results attributable to those operations as discontinued. Consequently, the results shown under the heading of continuing operations for both the current year and the previous year are attributable to the operations that are continuing at the end of the current year. This presents something of a track record of the operations that are continuing.

8.15 Analysis of other format headings between turnover and operating profit (under Format 1 these are: cost of sales; gross profit or loss; distribution costs; administrative expenses; and other operating income) should also be given, but this analysis may be by way of note, rather than on the face of the profit and loss account. [FRS 3 para 14].

8.16 The standard uses the term 'operating profit' as an important element of performance although there is no such heading in the statutory profit and loss account formats of Schedule 4 to the Companies Act 1985. The term is described, however, in the standard as being normally the profit before income from shares in group undertakings. In consolidated financial statements, this would mean profit before income from interests in associated undertakings, although the standard acknowledges that, in certain situations, income from associated undertakings or from other participating interests may be considered to be part of the operating profit. In fact, FRS 9, 'Associates and joint ventures', introduced a new requirement that the group's share of operating results of associates and joint ventures should be included immediately after the group's operating result (see further chapter 27). [FRS 9 paras 21, 27].

8.17 A comparison of the two formats is given below, down to the operating profit line.

	Format 1		**Format 2**
1	Turnover	1	Turnover
2	Cost of sales	2	Change in stocks of finished goods and in work in progress
3	Gross profit or loss	3	Own work capitalised
4	Distribution costs	4	Other operating income
5	Administrative expenses	5a	Raw materials and consumables
6	Other operating income	5b	Other external charges
7	Operating profit or loss	6	Staff costs
			(a) wages and salaries
			(b) social security costs
			(c) other pension costs
		7a	Depreciation and other amounts written off tangible and intangible fixed assets
		7b	Exceptional amounts written off current assets
		8	Other operating charges
		9	Operating profit or loss

As explained above 'Operating profit or loss' is not an item in either of the formats, but has been included to show where the requirement for analysis ends.

8.18 The illustrative examples in the FRS are prepared using Format 1, but the examples section explains that *equivalent information* should be shown if any of the other statutory formats are used. Turnover and operating profit or loss would, as for Format 1 companies, be analysed on the face of the profit and loss account, with the remainder of the analysis being permitted to be given in the notes.

8.19 Two basic styles of profit and loss account analysis are envisaged in the illustrative examples in FRS 3. A multi-column approach isolates figures relating to continuing operations, acquisitions and discontinued operations into separate columns. A single-column approach lists such figures in a vertical analysis, with sub-totals providing further analysis. Table 8.1 shows an example of a multi-column analysis; Table 8.2 shows a single-column analysis. The multi-column approach has also been used increasingly to isolate exceptional items included in operating results (see para 8.128 below).

8.19.1 The examples below do not give a sub-total of acquisitions and other continuing operations, which arguably FRS 3 would require, but this point is unclear as the multi-column example given at the end of FRS 3 itself does not include such a sub-total. We would recommend that such a sub-total be given.

Table 8.1 — Coats Viyella Plc — Annual report and accounts — 31 December 1994

CONSOLIDATED PROFIT AND LOSS ACCOUNT (extract)

	Notes	Continuing operations		Discontinued operations	Total	Total
			Acquisitions			
		1994	1994	1994	1994	1993
		£m	£m	£m	£m	£m
For the year ended 31 December 1994						
Turnover	1&2	**2,154.2**	**29.7**	**404.6**	**2,588.5**	2,443.8
Cost of sales	1	**(1,464.0)**	**(22.2)**	**(323.3)**	**(1,809.5)**	(1,702.6)
Gross profit		**690.2**	**7.5**	**81.3**	**779.0**	741.2
Distribution costs	1	**(362.2)**	**(3.9)**	**(50.8)**	**(416.9)**	(398.0)
Administrative expenses	1	**(168.7)**	**(1.8)**	**(19.9)**	**(190.4)**	(179.8)
Other operating income	1&3	**8.2**	–	**0.2**	**8.4**	8.3
Operating profit	1,2&3	**167.5**	**1.8**	**10.8**	**180.1**	171.7
Profit on sale of fixed assets	1	**1.3**	–	–	**1.3**	14.8
Provision for loss on sale or termination of operations	1	–	–	**(51.0)**	**(51.0)**	–
Gains/(losses) on sale or termination of operations	1	**2.3**	–	**0.1**	**2.4**	6.4
Profit/(loss) on ordinary activities before interest	2	**171.1**	**1.8**	**(40.1)**	**132.8**	192.9
Share of profits of associated companies					**0.8**	1.3
Interest receivable and similar income	6				**15.6**	21.5
Interest payable and similar charges	7				**(44.1)**	(65.4)
Profit on ordinary activities before taxation					**105.1**	150.3

Table 8.2 — Pearson plc — Directors' Report and Accounts — 31 December 1994

Consolidated Profit and Loss Account (extract)
for the year ended 31 December 1994

	Notes	1994 £m	1993 £m
Sales turnover			
Continuing operations		**1,469.9**	1,319.6
Acquisitions		**80.2**	
Discontinued operations		–	550.5
	2	**1,550.1**	1,870.1
Cost of sales	3	**(775.8)**	(1,005.6)
Gross profit		**774.3**	864.5
Net operating expenses			
– normal	3	**(533.2)**	(628.4)
– exceptional	3	**31.3**	(20.0)
Operating profit			
Continuing operations		**265.1**	190.3
Acquisitions		**7.3**	
Discontinued operations		–	25.8
	2	**272.4**	216.1
Continuing operations			
Profit on sale of fixed assets	3	**26.4**	4.4
Discontinued operations			
Profit/(loss) on sale of businesses	3	**15.2**	(68.4)
Write back of provision on investment in BSkyB		–	71.4
Profit before interest		**314.0**	223.5
Net interest payable	4	**(16.2)**	(14.9)
Profit before taxation	7	**297.8**	208.6

Allocation of interest and taxation

8.20 The standard explains that the analysis of results is only required down to the operating profit line, because an analysis of the interest cost and taxation charge between continuing, discontinued and acquired operations would normally be too subjective to be reliable. However, analysis of interest and taxation may also be given provided that the method and assumptions used in making the analysis are disclosed. In practice, such further analysis is rarely given. One example is shown in Table 8.3.

Table 8.3 – Glynwed International plc – Report & Accounts – 31 December 1994

notes to the accounts (extract)

1. Accounting Policies (extract)

Discontinued activities

The principle used in allocating interest is that the interest cost or credit on discontinued activities is the additional interest cost or credit arising during the period as a result of retaining the discontinued activity up to the date of discontinuance. The taxation charge or credit on discontinued activities is that which directly arises as a result of their trading operations and discontinuance.

8.21 Some of the issues that arise in respect of the allocation of interest to discontinued operations and acquisitions are:

- Allocating group interest costs where operations acquired or discontinued are funded by intra-group borrowings rather than external borrowings. One method has been to allocate interest to intra-group funding at a rate of interest that represents an average cost of group borrowings.

- Allocating interest costs in respect of new borrowings raised to finance acquisitions. The issue is whether the incremental borrowing costs should be allocated to the group's continuing operations (excluding acquisitions) or to the results of acquisitions. Either method would probably be acceptable. Allocating to the group's continuing operations excluding acquisitions emphasises the *actual results* of the acquired operations, whilst allocating to the acquisitions column emphasises the *effect* of the acquisition.

Exceptional items

8.22 Exceptional items charged or credited in arriving at operating profit should be analysed between continuing or discontinued operations as appropriate. [FRS 3 para 19]. Furthermore, the three categories of exceptional items that are required to be presented after operating profit (disposals of operations, fundamental reorganisations and disposals of fixed assets) should also be attributed to continuing and discontinued operations. [FRS 3 para 20]. The latter analysis is illustrated in Tables 8.1 and 8.2 above.

8.23 The treatment of exceptional items is considered from para 8.79 below.

Discontinued operations

Definition

8.24 Discontinued operations are defined as those operations that satisfy all of the following conditions:

- The sale or termination is completed either in the period or before the earlier of three months after the commencement of the subsequent period and the date on which the financial statements are approved.

- If a termination, the former activities have ceased permanently.

- The sale or termination has a material effect on the nature and focus of the reporting entity's operations and represents a material reduction in its operating facilities resulting either from its withdrawal from a particular market (whether class of business or geographical) or from a material reduction in turnover in the reporting entity's continuing markets.

- The assets, liabilities, results of operations and activities are clearly distinguishable, physically, operationally and for financial reporting purposes.

[FRS 3 para 4].

Discontinued compared to discontinuing

8.25 The ASB deliberately chose the term 'discontinued' rather than 'discontinuing' because it considered that there must be a cut off point to avoid manipulation. If it had chosen 'discontinuing' it would have left the way open for a company to declare that it intended to discontinue a loss making activity in the future and thus to separate out the results of that activity. The company would thereby be able to focus attention on the remaining profitable activities.

8.26 The explanatory note to the standard emphasises that any income and costs relating to a sale or termination that has not been completed within the prescribed period after the financial year end should be included in the continuing category. However, it then states that it may be appropriate in some cases to disclose separately in a note to the profit and loss account the results of operations which, although not 'discontinued', are in the process of discontinuing. They should not be classed as discontinued, but might be a subdivision of continuing operations. Such analysis would enable a company to enhance the predictive value of its financial statements by giving additional disclosure of its results exclusive of those activities that are not expected to be there at the next year end. An example of such a note is given in Table 8.4.

Table 8.4 – BM Group PLC – Annual Report – 30 June 1993

Notes to the financial statements (extract)

2 Continuing operations

As detailed in the Financial Review and Note 28, the Group has disposed of various subsidiary undertakings after the year end. The requirements of Financial Reporting Standard No. 3 (FRS 3) only permit those companies disposed of prior to 30th September 1993 to be classified for the purposes of these financial statements as a discontinued operation. The analysis below provides additional information regarding those companies which have been sold prior to the approval of these financial statements but after 30th September 1993 or are proposed to be disposed of as part of the Group's reorganisation plan. Continuing operations can be further analysed as follows:

	Turnover		Trading profit	
	1993	1992	**1993**	1992
	£000	£000	**£000**	£000
Businesses to be retained	**153,959**	111,812	**11,703**	16,593
Businesses to be sold	**301,831**	293,246	**6,088**	23,134
	455,790	405,058	**17,791**	39,727

Businesses to be retained for the year to 30th June 1992 include four months turnover and trading profit in respect of Thomas Robinson Group companies.

Meaning of 'ceased permanently'

8.27 For an operation that is closed down to qualify as discontinued, its former activities must have 'ceased permanently' within the prescribed time limit. In many situations this is clear-cut because all sources of revenues and costs have been terminated and all assets disposed of. In other situations, it is less clear-cut whether activities have ceased permanently. For example, whilst all revenue earning activities may have ceased, there may be run-off costs still to be incurred and assets still to be sold or scrapped. In those situations it is necessary to consider the nature of the costs still to be incurred (and, if applicable, the credits still to be received) and to form a judgement as to whether they comprise an activity.

Example 1

A company carried out a pharmaceutical wholesaling business which it operated from several leasehold premises throughout the country. The business has been closed, all stocks have been disposed of and employees made redundant before the end of three months into the next financial year. At that time some debtors remain to be collected and costs will continue to be incurred in respect of the vacated premises until the leases are disposed of.

In this example the former activity of pharmaceutical wholesaling has ceased permanently. The outstanding future transactions do not constitute the continuation of the activity and, consequently, the operation has been discontinued.

Example 2

A group is closing its household insurance underwriting business. No new policies are being written. A few staff have been retained to handle claims made on the existing policies. Has the activity ceased permanently when the revenue earning activity ceased or will it be when the last claim is paid?

In our view the complete cessation of carrying on the revenue earning activity is the most meaningful criterion. This is notwithstanding the possibility that the financial effect of settling as yet unknown liabilities may be significant to the results of future periods.

Example 3

A group has announced it is closing an engineering contracting segment. Although no new contracts are being undertaken, all existing contracts will be completed and the business will be run down accordingly.

In our view the operation will have ceased permanently when the contracting activity has been completed, that is, at the end of the last contract. In the period during which existing contracts are completed, the group is continuing to carry out a revenue earning activity, albeit that the activity is being wound down.

Materiality and separability of activities

8.28 The standard's definition of discontinued operations (see para 8.24) requires business disposals and closures to satisfy a high threshold of materiality if they are to be classified as discontinued in the profit and loss account. In addition, the operations discontinued must be clearly separable from the rest of the reporting entity's operations.

8.29 However, this does not mean that the discontinued activity has to constitute a complete business segment for the purposes of SSAP 25, 'Segmental reporting'. This is because the definition of discontinued operations also includes a material reduction in operating facilities resulting from a material reduction in turnover in the entity's *continuing* markets. This means that, although the activity should be *separate* from the rest of the entity's operations, it does not necessarily have to be *different*.

Example

A group had two subsidiaries of equal size, each operating in the field of car leasing. The sale of one of the subsidiaries would not be the disposal of the whole car leasing segment as defined for the purposes of SSAP 25. However, if it materially affected the nature and focus of the entity's operations (for example, if the disposal were made to release funds for investing in a different business such as a road haulage business, that materially changed the nature and focus of the group's operations) it would constitute a discontinued operation for the purposes of FRS 3, because it is a material reduction in operating facilities and causes a material reduction in turnover in the group's continuing markets. In addition, the assets, liabilities, results and activities can be distinguished physically, operationally and for financial reporting purposes. The nature of the operations disposed of is *not* different from that of the rest of the group, but that is not a test that has to be satisfied under the standard in order for the disposal of the subsidiary to qualify as a discontinued operation.

8.30 The nature and focus of a reporting entity's operations refers to the positioning of its products or services in their markets including the aspects of both quality and location. The example of a material change in the nature and focus of operations given in the standard is a hotel group which disposes of all its hotels in the US and buys instead hotels in Europe. Another example relating to products rather than geographical markets might be a property company, involved in development and investment properties, that decided to withdraw from the development activity and to hold only investment properties.

8.31 The standard makes it clear that unless there is a material effect on the nature and focus of operations any disposals should be treated as continuing operations. For example, a sale or termination that is undertaken primarily to achieve productivity improvements or other cost savings is part of an entity's continuing operations. In the example in paragraph 8.29 of a company with two car leasing subsidiaries, the disposal of one subsidiary might be regarded as part of continuing operations if it were not sold, but instead was closed primarily to achieve cost savings to the group, with its business and markets being transferred to the other subsidiary.

8.32 The following example combines several elements of the treatment of discontinued operations.

Example

The facts in this example are:

(a) The company's year end is 31 December 20X1.

(b) The directors approve the financial statements for the year to 31 December 20X1 in May 20X2.

(c) In the year to 31 December 20X1 the company sold subsidiary A and closed a surplus warehouse.

(d) The company achieved a reduction in its workforce of 5% through voluntary and compulsory redundancies.

(e) Before the year end the company decided to close subsidiary B and this was completed on 31 March 20X2. It also announced the decision to close subsidiary C, but this was not completed until April 20X2. It also announced, before the year end, a strategic withdrawal from one of its business segments that was to take place over the next two years.

(f) After the year end it decided to sell subsidiary D and found a buyer for a quick sale that was completed by February 20X2.

The various items would be treated under FRS 3 as follows:

- Sale of subsidiary A — assuming the disposal materially affected the nature and focus of the group's operations and represented a material reduction in its operating facilities, it should be shown as discontinued operations, because the sale was completed in the year.

- Closure of warehouse — if the assets, liabilities, results of operations and activities cannot be clearly distinguished, physically, operationally and for financial reporting purposes, then this would be classed as continuing operations. If they could be clearly distinguished, but the closure has neither a material effect on the nature and focus of the company's operations nor represents a material reduction in its operating facilities resulting from a withdrawal from a particular market or from a material reduction in turnover of continuing markets, then again it would be disclosed as continuing operations. It is most probable that as the warehouse was surplus it would not satisfy the latter condition and the costs would be shown as continuing operations.

- Reduction in workforce of 5% — assuming that no sale or closure was involved this would be shown as continuing, but exceptional if material.

- Closure of subsidiary B — assuming that this could be clearly distinguished and materially affected the nature and focus of operations and represented a material reduction in operating facilities, it should be classed as discontinued. This is because it also satisfies the condition of having been completed by the earlier of three months after the year end or the date of approval of the financial statements.

- Closure of subsidiary C — whether or not this satisfies all the other conditions it does not satisfy the condition of being completed by the earlier of three months after the year end or the date of approval of the financial statements. Therefore, it should be classed as continuing. As the announcement of the closure was made before the year end a provision for loss on closure of C should be made. The provision would be disclosed as a non-operating exceptional item, under continuing operations.
- Strategic withdrawal — this must be classed as continuing, but FRS 3's requirements for disclosing any provisions should be followed, and the company could analyse continuing operations between continuing and discontinuing in a note.
- Sale of subsidiary D — this would be treated as discontinued (assuming the materiality conditions are satisfied), irrespective of the decision date, because the sale has been completed by the earlier of three months after the year end or the date of approval of the financial statements.

8.33 FRS 3 only requires the analysis of results down to the 'operating profit' level. One of the criteria for qualifying as a discontinued operation is that the operating results of the operation that has been sold or terminated must be clearly distinguishable for financial reporting purposes from the rest of the group's activities. This implies that its turnover and operating costs must be readily identifiable from the accounting records. Nevertheless, there are still allocation issues to be dealt with in practice, in particular, in respect of central overheads. For example, the parent company of a group may allocate its head office overheads to all its subsidiaries on some *pro rata* basis. If an operation is disposed of, the relevant central overheads may not decrease, at least in the short term. In these circumstances, it seems logical to attribute the whole of the central overheads to continuing operations in the group's profit and loss account, because the costs are not being taken out of the group by the disposal.

Disposal of subsidiary with retained interest

8.34 A company may dispose of a controlling interest in a subsidiary and retain an interest that is treated either as a trade investment or as an associate. The question arises as to whether the turnover and operating profit of the subsidiary up to the date of disposal should be included as continuing operations or discontinued operations in the consolidated profit and loss account (assuming the subsidiary is material to the group). Where the retained interest is accounted for as an associate the group's share of associate's results will in future be brought into the consolidated profit and loss account on an equity accounting basis, but the full amount of turnover and operating profit of the associate will not be shown in the group profit and loss account because it is no longer a subsidiary.

8.35 We consider that the results of the subsidiary should be classified as discontinued if the retained interest is not regarded as being subject to significant influence by the group. This would be if the retained interest is accounted for as a trade investment rather than as an associate.

8.36 If, however, the remaining interest qualifies as an associate then we consider that it would be appropriate to show the subsidiary's results as continuing operations up to the date of disposal. The group's share of the associate's operating results would then be included on the equity basis in the group's profit and loss account from the date it ceases to be a subsidiary. A note giving details of the subsidiary's results that are included in the profit and loss account in these circumstances would be appropriate. An example of such disclosure is given in Table 8.5. (As mentioned in paragraph 8.19.1 above it is arguable that a total column for continuing operations should also be given.)

Table 8.5 — Dobson Park Industries plc — Annual Report — 2 October 1993

Consolidated Profit and Loss Account (extract)

		Continuing operations	Acquisitions	Discontinued operations	Total
For the 52 weeks ended 2 October 1993	*Note*	1993 £000	1993 £000	1993 £000	1993 £000
Turnover	*2*	98,628	9,359	15,451	123,438
Cost of sales		(62,265)	(4,765)	(10,790)	(77,820)
Gross profit		36,363	4,594	4,661	45,618
Distribution costs		(15,797)	(1,429)	(1,217)	(18,443)
Administration expenses		(14,664)	(2,410)	(3,526)	(20,600)
Operating profit		5,902	755	(82)	6,575
Share of profits of associated companies		2,945	–	–	2,945
Net operating income	*2*	8,847	755	(82)	9,520

Notes on the Accounts (extract)

1 Mining Equipment (extract)

With effect from 18 January 1993, Dobson Park's Mining Equipment Division was merged with Meco International Limited to form Longwall International Limited (LIL).

As a result of this transaction, the Company acquired a 50% interest in the ordinary share capital of LIL together with certain preference shares having a redemption value of £2m.

Prior to the formation of LIL, the turnover and trading results of the Mining Equipment Division have been included in the consolidated profit and loss account within continuing operations. After that date, Dobson Park's interest in LIL's trading results has also been included within continuing operations although LIL's turnover has been excluded from the consolidated profit and loss account thus adopting the accounting convention for associated companies.

In the 9 month period to 2 October 1993, LIL's turnover and pre-tax profits were £169.3m and £4.4m respectively. LIL's net assets at 2 October 1993 were £31.6m comprising fixed assets £28.3m, other net assets £35.1m and borrowings £31.8m.

The profit before tax of the Mining Equipment Division for the 52 weeks ended 2 October 1993 comprises:

	£000
Trading profits for the period to 18 January 1993	1,153
Share of profits of LIL for the period from 19 January to 2 October 1993	2,723
Other fees and rents, after depreciation, received from LIL	606
	4,482

Operations discontinued by sale

8.37 Where an operation that qualifies as discontinued is sold, its results up to the date of sale should be disclosed as part of the normal profit and loss account captions under the heading 'discontinued operations'. The profit or loss on sale should be shown as an exceptional item after operating profit and before interest and should also be disclosed as 'discontinued operations'. Any reorganisation or restructuring of continuing operations resulting from the sale should be treated as part of continuing operations.

8.38 Where the operation is sold after the financial year end, that is, by the earlier of three months after the year end and the date of approval of the financial statements, only the operating results up to the year end should be included in the profit and loss account for that year as discontinued operations. In the subsequent year when the operation is actually sold, the operating results up to the date of sale will be shown as discontinued operations in that year.

Example

A group sells a subsidiary which had turnover and operating profits in 20X1 of £30,000 and £6,000 respectively in the previous year. Up to the date of sale in 20X2 it had turnover and operating profit of £8,000 and £2,000 respectively. It is sold for £15,000. Goodwill previously written off directly to reserves on acquisition (prior to FRS 10) was £4,000. Net assets at the date of sale were £5,000. The borrowings of the subsidiary were £7,000 on which it paid interest of £700 in the previous year and £200 in the current year up to the date of sale. The tax rate is 30%.

The sale would be accounted for as follows:

Profit and loss account (extract)		**20X2**	**20X1**
	£	**£**	**£**
Turnover			
Discontinued operations		8,000	30,000
Cost of sales (say)		(5,000)	(20,000)
Gross profit		3,000	10,000
Net operating expenses		(1,000)	(4,000)
Operating profit — discontinued operations		2,000	6,000
Profit on disposal of discontinued operations –			
surplus over net assets	10,000		
less: goodwill previously written off directly to reserves	(4,000)	6,000	–
Interest payable		(200)	(700)
Profit on ordinary activities before tax		7,800	5,300
Tax on profit on ordinary activities		(2,340)	(1,590)
Profit on ordinary activities after taxation		5,460	3,710

Note: the further analysis of net operating expenses and tax required by the standard would be given in a note.

Profits and losses on sale

8.39 In the above example, the re-classification of operating results as discontinued and the profit on disposal of the operation are recognised in the same period. Under FRS 2, 'Accounting for subsidiary undertakings', the date on which an undertaking ceases to be another undertaking's subsidiary is the date on which control passes (see further chapter 24). Where control is transferred by public offer, the relevant date is usually when an offer becomes unconditional. Where it is transferred by private treaty, the date is usually when an unconditional offer is accepted. Therefore, if the date on which the company ceases to be a subsidiary is after the year end, the operating results up to the disposal date and the profit on disposal would be recognised in the profit and loss account in the following year, classified as discontinued.

8.40 Where an operation in the process of being sold is trading profitably and is expected to be sold at a profit, those profits will be recognised as they arise. Where the operation is loss-making or a loss on sale is expected, the rules are somewhat different. Provision for such expected losses may sometimes be recognised earlier than they arise. FRS 3 introduced rules aimed at controlling the recognition of provisions for future losses.

Provisions for losses on sale of operations

8.41 Where a decision has been taken to dispose of an operation, whether by sale or closure, the standard requires provision to be made for expected future losses if, but not before, the company is *"demonstrably committed to the sale or termination"*. In the case of a sale, the standard requires evidence of the commitment by the existence of a *"binding sale agreement"* that obliges the company to complete the sale. [FRS 3 para 18]. This requirement conflicts with the requirement in FRS 12 that provision should not be made for future losses unless they result from an onerous contract. Although FRS 12 is the later standard, we consider that the FRS 3 requirement was intended to be retained because the amendments to paragraph 18 of FRS 3 were made consequential upon the introduction of FRS 12 but this requirement was retained.

8.42 For most practical purposes, the date of a binding agreement as envisaged in FRS 3 would be the same as the date on which control passes, as defined in FRS 2 (see para 8.39 above), when a subsidiary ceases to be consolidated.

8.43 FRS 3 states that any provision should cover the following:

- The direct costs of the sale.
- Any operating losses of the operation up to the date of the sale.

In both cases, the provision should take account of the aggregate profit, if any, to be recognised in the profit and loss account from the future profits of the operation. [FRS 3 para 18]. It should be noted that FRS 3 was amended by FRS 12, 'Provisions, contingent liabilities and contingent assets', to preclude profits on disposals of assets from being taken into account in measuring such provisions.

8.44 The explanatory section of the standard deals with the situation where a decision to sell an operation has been made, but no legally binding sale agreement exists. In such circumstances, the standard says that no obligation has been entered into by the reporting entity and so provision for the direct costs of the decision to sell and for future operating losses should not be made.

8.45 Although it may not be appropriate to provide for a loss on sale, any impairments in asset values, including any capitalised goodwill, should be recognised regardless of whether a binding sale agreement has been entered into for the sale of the operation. Such impairments should be calculated in accordance with FRS 11, 'Impairment of fixed assets and goodwill'. If the carrying values of the net assets and capitalised goodwill of a business for sale exceed in aggregate their recoverable amount (which would usually be based on the expected sale proceeds), the assets are impaired. FRS 11 requires that, unless specific assets can be identified as having been impaired, the impairment loss should be allocated first to any capitalised goodwill, thereafter to any capitalised intangible assets and finally to tangible assets on a *pro rata* or more appropriate basis. [FRS 11 para 48].

8.46 If, say, a subsidiary was acquired several years ago and goodwill was written off to reserves, it would also be appropriate, if the goodwill is now worth little or nothing, to make a provision in the profit and loss account in respect of that goodwill in advance of any binding agreement, as the goodwill would in any event have to be included in the loss on sale when the disposal is accounted for (see para 8.54 below).

Example

A parent company carries its investments in subsidiaries at net asset value in its individual financial statements. It has decided to sell a subsidiary, but has no legally binding agreement for sale. The price it expects is below the net asset value of the subsidiary.

The parent company should provide for the impairment of the investment in the subsidiary. In the consolidated profit and loss account, no provision for loss on sale is made per se. However, the subsidiary's assets are impaired, because the carrying value of its net assets exceeds their recoverable amount (which would be based on the subsidiary's expected selling price). The impairment loss should, in accordance with FRS 11, be allocated to write down the consolidated carrying values of the subsidiary's assets in the following order: first, any attributable goodwill; secondly, any capitalised intangible assets; and finally, other assets on a *pro rata* or more appropriate basis.

[The next paragraph is 8.48.]

8.48 FRS 3 also allows some degree of hindsight because it states that a binding contract entered into after the balance sheet date may provide additional evidence of asset values and commitments at the balance sheet date. [FRS 3 para 45].

8.49 The following example illustrates the accounting for the sale of an operation that takes place after the year end.

Example

A group decides before the year end to sell a subsidiary. The sale will take place after the year end and after the financial statements of the group are signed. The subsidiary's net assets at the year end are £300,000 and the book value of the attributable purchased goodwill is £100,000. The subsidiary makes a loss of £110,000 from the year end to the date the financial statements are signed. The group expects the company to make further losses up to the possible date of sale estimated to be £20,000. The group is negotiating the sale at the time of signing the financial statements and expects the proceeds on sale will be £150,000.

As mentioned above, where there is no binding sale agreement, no provision for loss on sale should be made, but the value of the subsidiary's net assets consolidated will still have to be considered to determine whether an impairment loss needs to be recognised. If no impairment losses were recognised in respect of the net assets and goodwill amounting to £400,000, the group would expect to incur losses of £250,000 in the subsequent year, comprising the subsidiary's expected future losses of £130,000 and an estimated loss on sale of £120,000, as illustrated below:

	£'000	£'000
Net assets		300
Goodwill		100
Assets to be reviewed for impairment		400
Loss up to date of sale	(110)	
	(20)	(130)
Estimated net assets at date of sale		270
Expected proceeds on sale		150
Estimated loss on sale		(120)

It is clear in this example that the subsidiary's net assets plus attributable goodwill are impaired, because their carrying value is not recoverable. The recoverable amount (being the higher of net realisable value and value in use) at the balance sheet date should be determined for the subsidiary in accordance with the methods specified in FRS 11. The calculation would be based on the present value of the estimated future cash flows of the subsidiary, including the net proceeds expected from its ultimate disposal. These cash flows would include the net cash outflows in respect of the expected future losses. The impairment loss would be calculated as the amount of the shortfall between the estimated recoverable amount and the carrying value of the subsidiary's net assets, and would be allocated first to write off the goodwill of £100,000 and secondly among the subsidiary's assets.

The impairment loss would be included in the results of the group's continuing operations; the loss would not be categorised as a discontinued operation because in the example the sale is not completed before the earlier of three months after the year end and the date on which the financial statements are approved.

8.50 The above example demonstrates that, whereas FRS 3 restricts the circumstances where provisions for losses on sale can be recognised, FRS 11 has increased the emphasis on recognising impairments of assets at an earlier point in time.

8.51 Paragraph 18 of FRS 3 specifies, and illustrates, how any future loss provisions set up in one year in advance of a sale of an operation should be disclosed in the next year when they are utilised, that is, when the sale is completed (but note that this does not apply to any impairment losses recognised before a disposal). The results of the operation in the subsequent period should be presented under the normal profit and loss account headings and should be described as 'discontinued operations' if they qualify as such. Any part of the preceding year's provision that related to trading losses should be credited and separately disclosed under the actual operating loss incurred. Although the standard actually states that the provision should be separately highlighted under the operating loss, the examples in the appendices show it as being deducted from the heading 'net operating expenses'. Therefore, it seems reasonable to interpret the requirement as being to match the provision with the costs with which it is associated under the appropriate format heading, although either presentation is acceptable. The actual loss on sale should be disclosed after operating profit and before interest, again under the 'discontinued' heading if applicable. The balance of the provision relating to the loss on sale should be credited and separately disclosed under the actual loss on sale.

8.52 The standard could be interpreted as implying that the accounting described above is only required for operations that qualify as 'discontinued'. That is because paragraph 18 uses the words *"...when the operation does qualify as discontinued, the provisions should be used to offset the results of the operation in the discontinued category"*. However, we consider that it was not intended to restrict the treatment only to discontinued operations and that such treatment should also be used where the results of operations sold in the subsequent year are shown as part of the group's continuing operations, because they do not meet all the conditions described in paragraph 8.24 above.

8.53 An example showing loss provisions created in one year and utilised the next is given in Table 8.6.

Table 8.6 – The Davis Service Group Plc – Annual Report and Accounts – 31 December 1993
Consolidated profit and loss account (extract)

	Note	*1993* *£000*	*1992* *£000*
Turnover			
Continuing operations		**225,325**	213,291
Acquisition		**46,681**	
		272,006	
Discontinued operations		**7,987**	34,155
	2	**279,993**	247,446
Cost of sales	3	**177,597**	172,627
Gross profit		**102,396**	74,819
Other operating expenses		**(82,089)**	(55,404)
Other operating income		**2,483**	2,359
Operating profit			
Continuing operations		**19,050**	19,221
Acquisition		**3,740**	
		22,790	
Discontinued operations		**(611)**	2,553
Less utilisation of 1992 provision	2	**611**	
		22,790	21,774
(Loss)/profit on disposal of discontinued operations	4	**(889)**	72
Less utilisation of 1992 provision	4	**889**	
Provision for loss on operations to be discontinued	4	**–**	(1,500)
Profit on sale of properties in continuing operations	4	**50**	73
Profit on sale of properties in discontinued operations	4	**291**	–
Profit on ordinary activities before interest		**23,131**	20,419

Treatment of goodwill on disposals

8.54 The previous section referred to provisions for losses on operations being sold and to impairments in asset values. Where goodwill relating to a previously acquired operation has been capitalised (shown separately among intangible fixed assets) on the balance sheet, the goodwill is subject to the same impairment rules as apply to other fixed assets. When the operation is disposed of, the unamortised carrying value of attributable goodwill is eliminated from the balance sheet and forms part of the calculation of the profit or loss on disposal.

8.54.1 Where goodwill relating to a previously acquired operation remains eliminated against reserves, special rules apply to disposals. FRS 10, 'Goodwill and intangible assets', requires any acquisition goodwill that has previously been eliminated against reserves and has not been charged in the profit and loss account to be credited in reserves and debited in the profit and loss account as part of the profit and loss on disposal. This requirement has the effect of treating purchased goodwill as an asset with continuing value, even though it is debited to reserves during the period of ownership of the acquired operation.

8.55 Where provision is made in accordance with paragraph 18 of FRS 3 for a loss on disposal that occurs after the year end, the question arises whether a provision should be made for impairment of the attributable goodwill that has been eliminated against reserves. This question can be extended further to the situation where the write-off of such goodwill turns an expected profit on disposal into a loss — should provision be made for part of the goodwill that has been lost? FRS 10, 'Goodwill and intangible assets', does not deal with the issue of whether provisions should be made in respect of purchased goodwill eliminated against reserves that has lost its value, that is, before the actual disposal occurs. In addition, FRS 11's rules for recognising and measuring impairments of fixed assets and goodwill do not apply to pre-FRS 10 goodwill that remains eliminated against reserves. [FRS 11 para 7]. We believe that, in both situations, the attributable goodwill should be written off. This also has the desirable effect that the whole of the write-down relating to the impending disposal is recognised in the same period.

8.56 The same principle could be applied where a decision has been made to dispose of a business, but there is no binding contract at the date the financial statements are approved. If the directors consider that the value of attributable goodwill that remains eliminated against reserves has been lost, It is common practice for the write-off to be recognised in such circumstances as an impairment loss before the disposal occurs. Table 8.7 shows an example where a company has written off goodwill in anticipation of a loss on disposal. The write-off of attributable goodwill would be shown under the relevant FRS 3 paragraph 20 heading (after operating profit) if there was evidence of a commitment to sell. For example, the business would probably be being actively marketed and it would be reasonable to expect that the disposal would be completed before the next interim accounts and in any event before the end of the next financial year (see para 8.115). If a company has a policy of recognising a loss in the value of goodwill in the profit and loss account in other circumstances (that is, where a disposal is not involved), the loss would be charged in arriving at operating profit.

Table 8.7 – Cable and Wireless plc – Report and accounts – 31 March 1995

Consolidated profit and loss account (extract)

for the year ended 31 March	Note	1995 £m	1994 £m
Operating profit	4	1,133.7	1,091.2
Other exceptional items			
Profits less losses on sale and termination of operations	9	(17.7)	–
Losses on disposal of fixed assets	9	(43.7)	–
Provision for goodwill charge on impending sale of a business	9	(178.0)	–
Profit on ordinary activities before associated undertakings and minorities		894.3	1,091.2

Note 9 Exceptional items (extract)

The exceptional charge of £178m relates to goodwill associated with the acquisition of Telephone Rentals plc (TR) in 1988. This acquisition was made in order to achieve rapid growth in Mercury's business customer base which continues to be reflected in the overall business. The Group has now decided to focus Mercury's activities on service provision and is seeking purchasers for the non-strategic elements of the former TR activities in the UK. The provision reflects the expected outcome of the disposal at the current time and is in accordance with accepted accounting practice.

8.57 Where goodwill that has been eliminated against reserves is written off in the profit and loss account in the period before the disposal occurs, a further question is whether the profit and loss account of the next period in which the disposal occurs should show the actual loss on sale including the goodwill, with the utilisation of the provision set against it, or whether, once written off in the profit and loss account, the goodwill does not re-enter the calculation of the loss on sale (or the provision set against it). The net effect on profit is the same in both cases. We believe that either treatment is acceptable. The latter treatment would be automatic where the goodwill had been capitalised.

Operations discontinued by closure

8.58 Where an operation that qualifies as discontinued is closed, its results up to the date of closure should be shown as part of the normal profit and loss account captions, under the 'discontinued operations' heading. The profit or loss on closure should be shown as an exceptional item after operating profit and before interest and should also be described as 'discontinued operations'. Any reorganisation or restructuring of continuing operations resulting from the closure should be treated as part of continuing operations.

8.59 FRS 3 states that the profit or loss on termination should only include revenue and costs that are directly related to the termination. [FRS 3 para 20]. Whilst this is not explained in more detail in the standard, the exposure draft (FRED 1) stated that such items should be limited to redundancy costs and profits or losses arising from the disposal of fixed assets. Certainly these items may be included, but it may also be appropriate to include other items (see para 8.65

for examples). Trading losses and profits from the date of the decision should, however, not be included in the loss on closure. They should be included as stated above under the appropriate format headings under the discontinued heading.

Provisions for losses on termination

8.60 Where a closure of an operation is completed within an accounting period there will be no need to consider the question of provisioning for losses on closure at the year end. However, where a decision has been made by the year end to close, but the closure is not made until the following period, a provision will be necessary for future losses to be incurred if the company is committed to the closure at the balance sheet date.

[The next paragraph is 8.62.]

8.62 FRS 3 requires a provision to be made if, but only if, a decision to close has been made *and* the decision is evidenced by a detailed formal plan for termination from which the reporting entity cannot realistically withdraw. [FRS 3 para 18]. Where a business termination is contemplated but no demonstrable commitment has been made by the company, no obligation has been incurred and, therefore, there is no liability to be provided for. This is echoed by FRS 21, 'Events after the balance sheet date'. [FRS 21 para 22(b)]. This rule applies in respect of all terminations and not just those that are so significant to the reporting entity that they will qualify as discontinued operations.

8.63 FRS 3 gives two examples of what might be regarded as sufficient evidence of a demonstrable commitment, that is, they would effectively oblige the company to complete the termination. These are:

- Public announcement of specific plans.
- Commencement of implementation.

[FRS 3 para 45].

In practice, the point at which a management decision to close an operation becomes a demonstrable commitment is less objectively determinable than where a sale is involved.

8.64 The provision required by the standard should include:

- Direct costs of the termination.
- Operating losses to be incurred by the operation between the year end and the date of termination.

In both cases, the provision should take into account the aggregate profit, if any, to be recognised in the profit and loss account from the future profits of the operation. [FRS 3 para 18]. FRS 3 was amended by FRS 12 to preclude profits on disposals of assets from being taken into account in measuring such provisions.

Any such profits from disposal of assets should be accounted for separately when they arise. This may, in some cases, mean that a provision is made in one period (say for redundancies), but profits from the disposal of assets are not recognised until future periods when a binding contract for their sale is entered into. Where there are assets that will be sold at a large profit in future periods the effect may be that a provision that would have been relatively small before the amendment introduced by FRS 12 (because the potential gain on the assets was taken into account) is now much larger in the earlier period (because the potential sale is not taken into account) with the gain of the sale of the assets falling into a future period.

8.65 The standard does not give details of the costs that are intended to be included as direct costs of the termination. It would appear reasonable for the following items to be included:

- Redundancy costs (net of government contributions).
- Costs of retaining key personnel during the run-down period.
- Losses arising from the disposal of fixed assets and stocks.
- Ongoing costs relating to facilities being closed, such as rent, rates and security.
- Pension costs attributable to the termination.
- Bad and doubtful debts arising from the decision to close.
- Any losses due to penalty clauses in contracts relating to early termination.

8.66 The provision for loss on closure should be included as an exceptional item in the profit and loss account after operating profit. This applies whether the operation to be closed falls to be treated as discontinued in the current period, in the following period when it is closed (although it could be described in the notes to the financial statements as 'discontinuing' within the category of continuing operations), or whether it remains within continuing operations because it does not satisfy the threshold to be categorised as a discontinued operation.

8.67 It should be noted that where the closure commitment is made in one financial year, but the closure is completed in the following year, the items that may be included in the provision for loss on closure are different from those that may be included in the actual loss on closure where the whole closure process is completed within one financial year. Where a closure is completed within a period the trading results *up to the date of closure* should be shown under each of the profit and loss account headings used in arriving at operating profit. This means that trading losses between the commitment date and the date of closure would *not* be included in the profit or loss on sale, nor would on-going normal costs, such as rent and rates. They would form part of the operating profits or losses included as discontinued, but under the normal format headings up to the date of closure. In contrast, trading losses included in a provision for a closure that spans the year end do not reduce operating profits, because the element of the provision for such losses charged in one period (a non-operating charge) is credited back in the next period as an operating item to offset the operating loss in that period.

8.68 The disclosure requirements relating to the utilisation in a subsequent year of provisions for operations to be terminated are the same as for provisions for losses on sales (see para 8.51 above). The treatment described applies irrespective of whether the operation being terminated qualifies as a 'discontinued operation' or whether its results are included under continuing operations (see para 8.52 above which applies to terminated operations as well as sales).

8.69 The following example illustrates the accounting for provisions for losses on termination.

Example

In 20X1 a company announced a decision to close a subsidiary. The announcement was made three months before the year end, but the closure is not expected to take place until six months into the following year. The subsidiary had turnover and operating losses of £15,000 and £4,000 respectively up to the date of the announcement and had turnover of £3,000 and operating losses of £2,000 between the date of the announcement and the year end. It is expected to have turnover of £6,000 and operating losses of £3,000 in the first six months of next year up to the date of disposal. In addition, there will be stock write downs of £2,000 and fixed asset write downs of £4,000 resulting from the decision to close.

Strictly speaking, under the standard a provision should be established at the date of the announcement. However, if the operating losses were provided from the date of the announcement to the year end, the financial statements to the year end would still have to show the subsidiary's turnover and operating profit up to the year end under the appropriate headings and the reversal of the provision alongside them, which would be pointless. It is, therefore, more appropriate to make the provision as at the year end. The provision will contain the expected operating loss from the year end to the subsidiary's date of closure together with the write downs of stocks and fixed assets amounting in total to £9,000. In this example it is assumed that there was no goodwill written off to reserves on the subsidiary's acquisition. If there had been, it would be included in the provision.

The relevant extract from the profit and loss account will be as follows:

Profit and loss account – year 1

	20X1
	£
Turnover	
Continuing operations	18,000
Cost of sales (say)	(22,000)
Gross loss	(4,000)
Net operating expenses	(2,000)
Operating loss – continuing operations	(6,000)
Provision for loss on operations to be discontinued	(9,000)
Loss on ordinary activities before taxation	(15,000)

In the notes the analysis may be given of continuing operations between 'continuing' and 'discontinuing' as the standard permits this where an operation, although not qualifying as 'discontinued' is, nevertheless, 'discontinuing'.

In the following year the losses prove to have been underestimated and turnover and operating losses from the balance sheet date to the date of closure are £12,000 and £7,000 respectively. However, stock and plant write downs only amount to £5,000 in total. The figures in the profit and loss account in year two are:

Profit and loss account – year 2		20X2	20X1
	£	£	£
Turnover			
Discontinued operations		12,000	18,000
Cost of sales (say)		(15,000)	(22,000)
Gross loss		(3,000)	(4,000)
Net operating expenses		(4,000)	(2,000)
Less: release of provision made in 20X1		3,000	–
Operating loss			
Discontinued operations		(4,000)	(6,000)
Provision for loss on operations to be discontinued		–	(9,000)
Loss on disposal of discontinued operations	(5,000)		
Less: release of provision made in 20X1	6,000	1,000	–
Loss on ordinary activities before taxation		(3,000)	(15,000)

Although the provision is wholly included after operating profit in 20X1 it has to be allocated in 20X2 between operating profit and loss on disposal in 20X2. The total loss provided for in 20X1 was £9,000, but the actual loss incurred was £7,000 operating loss plus £5,000 loss on closure, which gives rise to the additional overall loss of £3,000 before taxation in 20X2. Note that 20X1 turnover and operating profit, which in the 20X1 financial statements were classified as continuing, are classified as discontinued in 20X2. Details of taxation on the loss on disposal would be given in the notes. In 20X2 the provision made for losses up to the date of termination of £3,000 has been released against net operating expenses as it is considered that this is the appropriate statutory format heading. Had the provision been in respect of increased cost of sales it would have been released against that heading. Alternatively, the provision could have been released against the total operating loss which would then be shown as an operating loss of £7,000 less provision released of £3,000.

Acquisitions

8.70 Acquisitions are defined in FRS 3 as those operations of the reporting entity that are acquired in the period. [FRS 3 para 3]. The results of acquisitions, excluding those that are also discontinued in the period, should, if material, be disclosed separately in aggregate as a component of continuing operations. As with the other continuing operations the minimum analysis given on the face of the profit and loss account should be turnover and operating profit. The analysis of each of the other profit and loss account headings between turnover and operating profit may be given in a note, instead of on the face of the profit and loss account. [FRS 3 para 14].

8.71 The standard recognises that sometimes it may not be possible to determine an operation's post-acquisition results to the end of the period. This might occur, for instance, where the business of an acquired subsidiary is transferred to another group company and merged with the existing business of that company shortly after the acquisition. If the results of the acquisition cannot be obtained, the standard requires an indication to be given of the acquisition's contribution to turnover and operating profit of the continuing operations in addition to the information required by the Companies Act 1985. [FRS 3 para 16]. The indication might take the form of a general statement, such as that shown below:

Example

The effect of the acquisition is that the plastics division, into which it has been integrated, has been able to reduce costs relative to turnover. In addition, the acquisition has enabled the group to lift turnover in the division by 25% and the division's operating profit has increased by 15%.

8.72 Where an indication of the contribution of an acquisition cannot be given, that fact and the reason should be explained as illustrated below. [FRS 3 para 16].

Example

No indication can be given of the contribution to turnover and operating profit of XYZ Limited, which was acquired in the year. This is because the business and assets of XYZ Limited were divided up between and integrated into the group's existing subsidiaries immediately after acquisition and it is not now possible to identify the separate results or turnover of each of the separate parts of the business.

8.73 The requirements of FRS 3 concerning the reporting of the results of acquisitions are repeated in FRS 6, 'Acquisitions and mergers'. However, FRS 6 has added an important new interpretation of the requirements as summarised above. It requires the post-acquisition results of businesses acquired in the financial year to be disclosed separately for each material acquisition and for other acquisitions in aggregate. [FRS 6 para 23]. FRS 3 only requires such disclosures in aggregate. An example of the enhanced disclosure required by FRS 6 is given in Table 8.8.

Table 8.8 — Allied Domecq PLC — Report & Accounts — 31 August 1995

	Note	18 months to 31 August 1995 £m	Year to 5 March 1994* £m
Turnover	2		
Continuing operations		**6,954**	4,627
Acquired operations			
— Domecq		**998**	–
— Other		**40**	–
		7,992	4,627
Discontinued operations		**933**	899
		8,925	5,526
Operating costs	4	**(7,878)**	(4,796)
Operating profit	2		
Continuing operations		**950**	682
Restructuring and other costs in continuing operations	7	**(90)**	–
Acquired operations			
— Domecq		**146**	–
— Other		**1**	–
		1,007	682
Discontinued operations		**40**	48
		1,047	730

[The next paragraph is 8.75.]

8.75 FRS 6 incorporates and extends the disclosures required by the Companies Act 1985 in respect of companies acquired. (It is expected that these legal disclosure requirements will be re-enacted in the secondary legislation that will support the 2006 Act.) It also requires disclosures about post-acquisition performance that are intended to make the post-acquisition profit and loss account of a group that has made a substantial acquisition more transparent. These disclosures cover exceptional profits and losses that arise from acquisition accounting and, in particular, post-acquisition reorganisation and integration costs. Disclosures for acquisition accounting are considered fully in chapter 25.

8.76 The information required by FRS 3 and FRS 6 in respect of the post-acquisition operating results of acquisitions may be of limited practical use where the acquisition has taken place late in the financial year. That is, because the standards only require the results to be shown separately in the financial year in which the acquisition occurs. FRS 3 suggests that, in some circumstances, it would be useful for the company to disclose voluntarily in the notes the operating results for the first full financial year for which the acquisition is included. [FRS 3 para 38]. Such disclosure would provide a more useful track record of recent acquisitions and would complement the disclosure of pre-acquisition results required by FRS 6. Table 8.9 provides an example of such additional disclosure;

in fact, the company has shown the results of acquisitions made in both the current year and the previous year on the face of the profit and loss account.

Table 8.9 — Arjo Wiggins Appleton p.l.c. — Directors' Report and Financial Statements — 31 December 1992

Consolidated profit and loss account (extract)

Note			1992		1991
		£m	£m	£m	£m
	Turnover				
	Continuing operations (excluding acquisitions in 1991 and 1992)	**2,476.4**		2,456.8	
	Acquisition in 1991	**79.1**		29.9	
	Acquisitions in 1992	**67.1**		–	
2			**2,622.6**		2,486.7
3	Operating expenses		**(2,429.6)**		(2,239.9)
	Operating profit				
	Continuing operations (excluding acquisitions in 1991 and 1992)	**196.8**		245.9	
	Acquisition in 1991	**(4.8)**		0.9	
	Acquisitions in 1992	**1.0**		–	
			193.0		246.8

Mergers

8.77 Where a business combination is accounted for as a merger in the consolidated financial statements of the parent company that heads the new group, those financial statements are prepared as if the acquiring group and the new subsidiary had been combined throughout the current period, the previous period and at the previous balance sheet date. The reporting entity is, therefore, restated as an enlarged group that includes the new subsidiary throughout. FRS 3 defines acquisitions as operations of the reporting entity that are acquired in the period. Under merger accounting principles there is deemed for reporting purposes to be no acquisition in the period. Consequently, the results of the combined operations of the enlarged group would be shown as continuing without any separate analysis of acquisitions relating to the results of the new subsidiary.

8.78 FRS 6 requires extensive analysis of the results of the enlarged group that is formed by a merger. These disclosures are considered in chapter 28.

Exceptional items

Definition

8.79 Exceptional items are defined in FRS 3 as:

> *"Material items which derive from events or transactions that fall within the ordinary activities of the reporting entity and which individually or, if of a similar type, in aggregate, need to be disclosed by virtue of their size or incidence if the financial statements are to give a true and fair view."* [FRS 3 para 5].

8.80 The definition is very similar to that previously given in SSAP 6, but it is FRS 3's definition of 'ordinary activities' that brings within the scope of exceptional items all those items that under SSAP 6 would have been extraordinary. This is because the definition of ordinary activities includes almost every conceivable activity or event that occurs in a company's life.

8.81 The definition of ordinary activities is:

> *"Any activities which are undertaken by a reporting entity as part of its business and such related activities in which the reporting entity engages in furtherance of, incidental to, or arising from, these activities. Ordinary activities include the effects on the reporting entity of any event in the various environments in which it operates, including the political, regulatory, economic and geographical environments, irrespective of the frequency or unusual nature of the events."* [FRS 3 para 2].

8.82 The last sentence of the definition appears to be all embracing and, therefore, even the effects of events such as a war (political environment), a natural disaster (geographical environment), a devaluation (economic environment) or a fundamental change in the basis of taxation (regulatory environment) would be exceptional items.

8.83 In relation to the last of these examples, a fundamental change in the basis of taxation, the standard specifically covers this situation and states that such a change should be included in the tax charge or credit for the period and separately disclosed on the face of the profit and loss account. [FRS 3 para 23].

Non-operating exceptional items

8.84 The standard sets down rules for presenting exceptional items. Three types of profit or loss must, where material, be shown on the face of the profit and loss account after operating profit and before interest and described as continuing or discontinued, as appropriate. These profits and losses will normally be exceptional items, but need not always be so, as they may not always meet the definition of exceptional items given in the standard. However, for convenience they are referred to as non-operating exceptional items in this text (they are sometimes also referred to as 'super-exceptional'). The three are:

- Profits or losses on the sale or termination of an operation.
- Costs of a fundamental reorganisation or restructuring having a material effect on the nature and focus of the reporting entity's operations.

- Profits or losses on the disposal of fixed assets.

Only revenues and costs directly related to the items in question should be included in calculating the profit or loss in respect of these items. The recognition of provisions in respect of these items are considered to be direct costs and should be included. When the net amount of the first or third bullet points above is not material, but the gross profits or losses are material, the relevant heading should still appear on the face of the profit and loss account with a reference to a related note analysing the profits and losses. [FRS 3 para 20].

8.85 The reason for requiring these items to be disclosed *after* operating profit is probably because they would distort the operating profit line if included above it. Disposals of operations and certain fixed assets are in a sense capital transactions that involve either dealing in the operations themselves or in the assets that support them. Often the figures involved are very material — all the more so as profits or losses on the disposal of operations have to take account of goodwill previously written off direct to reserves. Furthermore, the operations or assets may have been held for a long time. Consequently, such transactions can be distinguished from profits and losses generated by the underlying operating activities and so it is reasonable to exclude them from operating profit.

8.86 The rationale for including costs of a fundamental reorganisation or restructuring in the non-operating exceptional item category is less obvious. The treatment of fundamental restructurings, that is, where the line was to be drawn between exceptional and extraordinary, was a contentious issue under SSAP 6 and was also dealt with by the UITF in UITF Abstract 2 (since withdrawn). It is probable that they are given such prominence in FRS 3 because a fundamental restructuring should occur only very infrequently and the costs are so material that a separate classification is necessary to give a true and fair view.

8.87 Table 8.1 and Table 8.2 above show extracts from published profit and loss accounts containing non-operating exceptional items.

[The next paragraph is 8.90.]

Profits or losses on the sale or termination of an operation

8.90 The accounting and presentation issues relating to the sale of an operation are considered from paragraph 8.39 above; those relating to terminated operations are considered from paragraph 8.58. The standard requires profits or losses on the sale or termination of an operation to be included under the appropriate heading of continuing or discontinued operations.

8.91 FRS 10 requires disclosure of the profit or loss on each material disposal of a previously acquired business or business segment. [FRS 10 para 54]. In respect of goodwill on past acquisitions that remains eliminated against reserves under FRS 10's transitional arrangements, FRS 10 requires the amount of such goodwill attributable to an operation sold or terminated and included in the calculation of the profit or loss on disposal to be separately identified as a component of the profit or loss on disposal, either on the face of the profit and loss account or in the notes. [FRS 10 para 71(c)]. Where goodwill attributable to the disposed operation has been capitalised, there is no requirement in FRS 10 to disclose the amount separately as part of the profit or loss on disposal (although the figures can be worked out in aggregate from the note reconciling the balance sheet movements, including disposals, of goodwill).

8.92 In December 1992, the ASB took the unusual step of issuing a statement emphasising that companies should be guided by the spirit and reasoning of UITF Abstracts. This statement was prompted by what the UITF considered *"the unsatisfactory application"* of UITF 3 (now superseded by FRS 10) by a small minority of companies. The statement cited two approaches regarding goodwill on disposals that the UITF had found unacceptable. These approaches, which had attempted to mitigate the presentational impact of charging goodwill in the profit and loss account, were as follows:

- Goodwill should not be debited in the profit and loss account separately from, rather than as part of, the profit or loss on disposal. For example, the goodwill should not be distanced from the profit or loss on disposal as a separate item. A caption such as 'loss on sale of subsidiary' should not be used to describe an item that does not take account of related goodwill.
- The corresponding release of goodwill from reserves should not be credited in arriving at the profit or loss for the year or in the statement of total recognised gains and losses. It should be shown as a credit adjustment in the reconciliation of movements in shareholders' funds.

[ASB Statement 'The Application of UITF Abstracts' Dec 1992].

8.93 Table 8.10 illustrates one method of disclosing a loss on disposal, including the goodwill write-off.

Table 8.10 — Dixons Group plc — Annual Report — 30 April 1994

Consolidated Profit and Loss Account (extract)
for the 52 weeks ended 30 April 1994

		1993/94			1992/93
	Note	**Before exceptional charges £million**	**Exceptional charges £million**	**Total £million**	Total £million
Discontinued operations — exceptional charges (extract)					
(Loss)/surplus on disposal of operations		–	**(19.4)**	**(19.4)**	1.9
Goodwill previously written off to reserves		–	**(191.1)**	**(191.1)**	(2.9)
Net loss on disposal	6	–	**(210.5)**	**(210.5)**	(1.0)

Notes to the Financial Statements (extract)

	1993/4 £million	1992/93 £million
6 Disposal of operations		
Loss on disposal of Dixons US Holdings, Inc.	**(19.4)**	–
Surplus on disposal of Supasnaps Limited	–	1.9
Goodwill previously written off to reserves	**(191.1)**	(2.9)
	(210.5)	(1.0)

The sale of Dixons US Holdings, Inc., the parent company of Silo Holdings, Inc., to Fretter, Inc. in exchange for common and preferred stock in the enlarged Fretter group was completed on 3 December 1993. The loss on disposal represents the difference between the book value of assets disposed of and the directors' valuation of the investment in Fretter, Inc. at that date.

Fundamental reorganisation or restructuring

8.94 Apart from indicating that it should have *"a material effect on the nature and focus of the reporting entity's operations"*, FRS 3 does not give any further guidance on how to identify a fundamental reorganisation. Some companies may feel under pressure to describe costs as part of a fundamental reorganisation in order to exclude them from operating profit.

8.95 From the dictionary definition of 'fundamental' it could be assumed that the ASB intends that to qualify as fundamental, a reorganisation must go to the root of the company's or group's operations and must involve a change in the basic operations. The 'nature and focus' test is discussed in FRS 3 in the context of discontinued operations. The standard states: *"the nature and focus of a reporting entity's operations refers to the positioning of its products or services in their markets including the aspects of both quality and location"*. [FRS 3 para 42]. An example is given of a hotel company which traditionally served the lower end of the hotel market selling its existing chain and buying luxury hotels. While remaining in the business of managing hotels the group would be changing the nature and focus of its operations.

8.96 We consider that a fundamental reorganisation is likely to be restricted to one that satisfies the following conditions:

- The reorganisation costs must be material.
- The reorganisation should go to the root of and should encompass the whole or a substantial part of the company's or group's total operations (and not be a reorganisation of only one among many different operations).
- The reorganisation, to affect materially the nature and focus of operations, must achieve more than cost savings which leave the existing operations intact.

- The reorganisation must involve a material change in the nature and focus of the group's operations, resulting in the repositioning of its products or services.

[The next paragraph is 8.98.]

8.98 Tables 8.11 and 8.12 give two examples of disclosures relating to group reorganisations that have been treated as fundamental.

Table 8.11 – TSB Group plc – Report to Shareholders and Accounts – 31 October 1993

CONSOLIDATED PROFIT AND LOSS ACCOUNT (extract)

Note		**1993** **£m**	1992 restated (note 1) £m
	Operating profit	**366**	40
7	Reorganisation costs	**(70)**	2
	Profit before sale or termination of activities	**296**	42
8	Profit/(loss) on sale or termination of activities, including goodwill written off	**5**	(37)
4	Profit before taxation	**301**	5

Notes to the Accounts (extract)

Note 7 Reorganisation costs

Reorganisation costs of £70m (the major part being redundancy costs) relate to the implementation of the Group's announced policy of fundamentally reorganising TSB Retail Banking and Insurance and Hill Samuel Bank. In TSB the management, sales force and administration of TSB Retail Banking and TSB Insurance are being integrated to create a "bancassurance" business. Hill Samuel Bank has withdrawn from a number of areas of business, including branch banking, in order to focus on its merchant banking activities. This involves a reduction in its balance sheet and capital employed together with the consequent reduction in support operations.

In the year ended 31 October 1992, as a result of the decision to integrate the TSB Retail Banking and Insurance businesses, the value of long-term life assurance and pension businesses no longer required a provision for commission payable to TSB Retail Banking. As a result £30m (before taxation) was released to the profit and loss account and included as an offset against reorganisation costs (£28m).

Table 8.12 – Unigate PLC – Report and Accounts — 31 March 1995

Group Profit and Loss Account
for the year ended 31 March (extract)

	1995		
	Before exceptional items £m	**Exceptional items (note 7) £m**	**Total £m**
Total operating profit	**108.2**	–	**108.2**
Income from associated undertakings	**20.9**	**(2.5)**	**18.4**
Continuing operations			
– Fundamental restructuring of dairy businesses	–	**(55.1)**	**(55.1)**
– Profit on sale of fixed assets	–	–	–
Discontinued operations			
– Loss on disposal of businesses	–	**(0.7)**	**(0.7)**
– Release of 1991 provision	–	–	–
Profit on ordinary activities before interest	**129.1**	**(58 3)**	**70.8**

Notes to the Financial Statements (extract)

7 Exceptional items (extract)

a The costs of the fundamental restructuring of the dairy-related businesses comprise

	Cash spend **£m**	Asset write-off **£m**	Total **£m**
Dairies	**15.4**	**16.6**	**32.0**
Fresh Foods	**9.6**	**10.6**	**20.2**
Wincanton	**2.8**	**0.1**	**2.9**
	27.8	**27.3**	**55.1**

The background to, and basis of, the fundamental restructuring costs are set out in the Financial Review on page 19.

Financial Review (extract)

Exceptional Items Exceptional items principally comprise a charge for the fundamental restructuring of the Group's dairy-related activities in response to the upheaval in milk procurement in the UK, and our share of the extraordinary items reflected in the accounts of our associate, Nutricia.

As discussed in the Chief Executive's Review on page 7, the change in milk procurement arrangements and resultant milk cost increases, together with the changing pattern of milk sales away from doorstep to supermarket customers, which has been exacerbated by the milk cost increases, has necessitated a radical review and restructuring of the Group's dairy-related activities. The cost of this restructuring is £55.1 million before tax (£40.1 million after tax), and is separately identified as an exceptional cost as required by FRS 3. The provision comprises £27.8 million of cash costs and £27.3 million of asset write-off allocated across the Group's businesses as shown in Note 7 to the financial statements.

The restructuring plans envisage a 40 per cent reduction in liquid milk bottling capacity over the next three years, as well as rationalisation of our dairy products' activities. Also included are the costs of restructuring Wincanton's milk haulage operations. The cash costs analysed by year of expected implementation and the planned benefits are as follows:

Year ended 31 March	Cash spend	Planned cost reductions (cumulative)
	£m	**£m**
1995	**3.1**	–
1996	**14.5**	**7.9**
1997	**7.3**	**16.6**
1998	**2.9**	**24.7**
	27.8	

£18.6 million of the £24.7 million total planned cost reductions arise in the Group's liquid milk operations and will mitigate the impact on profitability of the switch from doorstep to wholesale and supermarket customers.

8.99 When a reorganisation is related to an acquisition, FRS 6 makes it clear that the reorganisation is not fundamental unless it is fundamental to the enlarged group. This issue is considered in chapter 25.

[The next paragraph is 8.103.]

Profits or losses on disposals of fixed assets

8.103 The third type of item that must be disclosed after operating profit is profits or losses on the disposal of fixed assets. This is intended to include profits or losses on sales of major assets, such as properties. It is not intended to include profits or losses on disposal that are in effect no more than normal adjustments to depreciation previously charged. Those adjustments would be included in operating profit as part of the normal depreciation charge.

8.104 The standard requires that the profit or loss on disposal of an asset should be accounted for in the profit and loss account for the period in which the disposal occurs as the difference between the net sale proceeds and the net carrying amount, whether carried at historical cost or at a valuation. [FRS 3 para 21].

8.105 This requirement was new in UK accounting because before FRS 3 it had been quite acceptable to calculate the profit or loss on a previously revalued asset *either* on the above basis *or* by reference to the asset's depreciated historical cost. The difference between the two bases is that under the latter basis the previous revaluation surplus is transferred to the profit and loss account on disposal whereas under the former basis it is not.

8.106 It should be noted that the requirement introduced by FRS 3 applies to all assets and not just to fixed assets.

8.107 The reasoning behind the change stems from the ASB's approach to the presentation of statements of financial performance. As described earlier, the ASB considers that performance should be viewed by reference to the profit and loss account *taken together with* the statement of total recognised gains and losses. A valuation surplus in one year is a recognised gain of that year and is part of the performance of that year. It is shown as an unrealised gain in the statement of total recognised gains and losses. When that gain is realised in a future year it makes no sense, under the ASB view of performance, to recognise it again in the profit and loss account, because it is not part of the performance of that year. It was part of the performance of earlier years.

8.107.1 However, the prohibition on 'recycling' gains and losses from the statement of total recognised gains and losses (STRGL) to the profit and loss account is relaxed by a limited amendment to FRS 3 for accounting periods beginning on or after 1 January 2007, with early adoption permitted. This amendment permits gains and losses originally recognised through the STRGL in accordance with FRS 26, 'Financial instruments: Recognition and measurement', and FRS 23, 'The effects of changes in foreign exchange rates', to be recycled to the profit and loss account on disposal of the related financial asset or foreign operation. Such recycling is a requirement of those standards and the rule in paragraph 21 of FRS 3 requiring the profit or loss on disposal to be calculated on the carrying amount of the asset created a contradiction between the standards. The ASB remains against recycling as a principle for the reasons stated above and does not wish to promote the concept. The amendment applies only to entities within FRS 26's scope, and for those entities, only to the limited cases of disposals of financial instruments and to disposals of foreign operations under FRS 23. Entities that are outside FRS 26's scope are not affected by the amendment; neither are FRS 26-compliant entities that have disposals of non-financial assets or disposals of domestic operations. When an item is recycled to the profit and loss account from the STRGL, a corresponding adjustment is made in the STRGL for the period (see para 8.148).

8.108 When first introduced, the FRS 3 prohibition on recycling was controversial because many people did not accept the ASB concept of 'performance' as measured by both principal statements referred to above. They considered that the profit and loss account was *the* primary statement which should include all gains *realised* in the year, whether or not they have previously been recognised as unrealised. To some extent this view stemmed from a more prudent view of performance, because it took no account of unrealised profits, but on the other hand it still allowed for the recognition of revaluation gains in the balance sheet before they were realised.

8.109 The ASB acknowledged the difference of view and, therefore, also required a note of historical cost profits or losses for the period to be presented immediately following the profit or loss account or the statement of total recognised gains and losses, where there is a material difference between the result as disclosed in the profit and loss account and the result on an unmodified historical cost basis (see para 8.169).

8.110 The following example illustrates the treatment of revaluation surpluses on the sale of an asset.

Example

A company has a property which cost £100,000. In year one it revalued it to £150,000. In year three it sells the property for £170,000. Taxation and depreciation are ignored.

In year one the asset is written up to £150,000 and the surplus of £50,000 is credited to revaluation reserve and appears in the statement of total recognised gains and losses. In year three the profit is calculated by reference to the carrying amount of £150,000 and is recorded as £20,000 in the profit and loss account (as an exceptional item after operating profit and before interest). Before FRS 3 the company could have calculated the profit by reference to historical cost of £100,000 and recorded a profit of £70,000 in the profit and loss account by transferring the revaluation reserve to profit and loss account. Under FRS 3, the previous revaluation surplus of £50,000 is taken to profit and loss account *reserve* and only the £20,000 is shown in the profit and loss account for the year.

In this example, if the taxation is calculated on the full surplus of £70,000 then the taxation attributable to the previous revaluation surplus of £50,000 would be charged in the statement of total recognised gains and losses.

8.111 The standard states that profits *and* losses are to be calculated by reference to carrying amount. Where fixed assets have been revalued downwards below cost, and the diminution in value is not considered to be an impairment (because, say, their value in use at the date of the revaluation is considered to be greater than their current market value), this could have the following effect:

Example

A company revalues all its fixed assets and there is a net surplus of £100,000 which is transferred to the revaluation reserve and shown in the statement of total recognised gains and losses. However, the net surplus is made up of a surplus of £150,000 above cost on one property and a diminution in value below cost on another property of £50,000. (If the diminution was an impairment it would have to be charged to profit and loss account.) There is no intention to sell the property with the diminution at the year end.

Three years later the company receives an offer for the second property and sells it for the revalued amount, that is, cost less the diminution of £50,000. As the profit or loss is calculated on the carrying value there is no profit or loss on sale. Thus, the loss calculated by reference to historical cost never passes through the profit and loss account. Instead there is a transfer from the revaluation reserve to the profit and loss account *reserve* in the reserves note. This is consistent with the ASB's view of performance, as the loss was recognised in the year of revaluation in the statement of total recognised gains and losses. It emphasises the need, however, to make a clear distinction between diminutions that are impairments and diminutions that are downward revaluations.

A similar result would be obtained if, instead of the asset being sold in year three, the board decided that the asset was now impaired (that is, its recoverable amount had fallen to its carrying value). Under the law the impairment (as a permanent diminution in value) should be charged to the profit and loss account. However, as it has already been recognised (albeit as a downward revaluation) in one of the primary statements of performance (the STRGL), it is not shown in the profit and loss account for that year. Instead, under FRS 3 it would be charged to profit and loss account reserve by means of a reserve transfer in the reserves note.

8.112 A loss that arises on sale of a previously revalued asset must be recorded in the profit and loss account even if the loss arises wholly from the reversal of a previous revaluation surplus.

Example

A company revalues an asset costing £100,000 in year one to £150,000. The surplus of £50,000 is shown in the statement of total recognised gains and losses. The revaluation reserve is credited with £50,000 and the asset written up by that amount. In year five the asset is sold for £130,000. The loss on sale should be accounted for in the profit and loss account for the period as the difference between the net sale proceeds and the net carrying amount. This means that there will be a loss on sale of £20,000 recorded in the profit and loss account. The fact that the profit and loss account never recorded a *surplus* of £50,000 in the past is not relevant under the ASB approach, which looks at the profit and loss account and the statement of total recognised gains and losses *together* in assessing performance.

There will, of course, be a transfer from the revaluation reserve to profit and loss account reserve of £50,000 as the previous revaluation surplus is now realised. In the profit and loss account *reserve* the result will be a net gain of £30,000, but the profit and loss account will, in the year of disposal, record only the loss of £20,000, because the unrealised gain of £50,000 was recognised in the statement of total recognised gains and losses in year one.

[The next paragraph is 8.114.]

Impairments

8.114 FRS 3 requires losses on disposals of fixed assets or operations (including provisions in respect of them) to be charged after operating profit and before interest. [FRS 3 para 20]. FRS 11 requires impairment losses recognised in the profit and loss account to be charged in operating profit under the appropriate statutory heading. [FRS 11 para 67]. For example, Format 2 has a heading 'Depreciation and other amounts written off tangible and intangible fixed assets'. Impairment losses would be separately disclosed as exceptional items, if material. If FRS 11 was interpreted in isolation, most losses recognised in connection with asset disposals would be impairments (charged against operating profit) rather than losses on disposals (non-operating exceptional items). That is because in most cases any previously unidentified shortfall between an asset's carrying value and its recoverable amount that is identified as a result of a decision to sell or terminate would be an impairment, not a loss on disposal.

8.115 We consider that the requirements of FRS 3 and FRS 11 taken together should be interpreted as follows. Impairment losses in respect of fixed assets and businesses that are to be retained must be charged in arriving at operating profit. Impairment losses that, in FRS 3 terms, are provisions for losses on disposals (that is, they are recognised as a result of a decision to dispose of the assets or business concerned) should be shown under the relevant one of the three headings in paragraph 20 of FRS 3. In the latter case, if the disposal has not occurred before the balance sheet date, the company would be expected to be able to provide evidence that the asset or operation would not be retained. For example, the asset or business would probably be being actively marketed and it would be reasonable to expect that the disposal would be completed before the next interim accounts and in any event before the end of the next financial year.

8.116 This apparent inconsistency between FRS 3 and FRS 11 gives rise to some anomalies. If an asset is put up for sale and has not previously been reviewed for impairment, the loss on sale is presented in accordance with paragraph 20 of FRS 3. If, however, an impairment loss is identified earlier as a result of carrying out an impairment review in circumstances required by FRS 11, the loss would be presented as part of operating profit in accordance with FRS 11. An exception is for investment properties (which are outside the scope of FRS 11), where impairment losses recognised in the profit and loss account would usually be charged after operating profit under a caption that corresponds to 'amounts written off investments' in the Formats (that is, after operating profit and before interest payable).

[The next paragraph is 8.121.]

Other exceptional items

8.121 All exceptional items, other than the three described above, should be shown within the statutory format headings to which they relate. In practice, this means that almost all other exceptional items (except any exceptional item relating to finance costs, investment income, amounts written off investments or the tax charge) would be shown in arriving at operating profit. The amount of each exceptional item, either individually or in aggregate (if they are of a similar type), should be disclosed separately by way of a note or on the face of the profit and loss account if that is necessary in order to give a true and fair view. [FRS 3 para 19].

8.122 The format 1 headings used in arriving at operating profit are:

- Turnover.
- Cost of sales.
- Gross profit.
- Distribution costs.
- Administrative expenses.
- Other operating income.

8.123 This is a relatively small number of headings to absorb every single type and description of exceptional item that may occur. Some types of exceptional items are relatively straightforward, for instance, a provision for loss on a contract in a construction company might well be exceptional and would be shown under the 'cost of sales' heading. The proceeds of an insurance claim for loss of profits could be accommodated under the 'other operating income' heading. Provisions for redundancy and reorganisation costs might have to be allocated among several headings however. If, for instance, the reorganisation involved a relocation, the costs of that might be put under administrative costs, but any redundancy costs might have to be allocated to several headings (according to where the salary costs of those made redundant were charged). Costs of disposing of delivery vans and sub-contracting the distribution of goods to outside hauliers would be an exceptional distribution cost.

8.124 Some items may, at first, not appear to have an appropriate statutory format heading. One example would be the expropriation of assets by a foreign government. If this is the case, then it may well fit within one of the three categories of exceptional item that must be shown after operating profit. If the expropriation results in a loss on disposal of assets, or of a business, it should be shown separately after operating profit.

8.125 Costs incurred in connection with acquisition activities, such as abortive bid costs incurred by a company that launched a failed takeover bid would be shown as exceptional administrative costs, that is, charged in arriving at operating profit, because they relate to the company's attempt to expand its operations by acquisition (see, for example, Table 8.14). Listing costs or abortive listing costs are also shown as operating exceptionals under the appropriate format heading.

8.126 The following example illustrates the treatment of exceptional items.

Example

A group disposed of a subsidiary during the year making a profit on disposal (after goodwill) of £500,000. A leakage of toxic chemicals from one of its factories caused damage to nearby farmland which cost £1m to clean up. The group was fined £300,000. As part of a reorganisation programme 5% of the employees in the administrative function were made redundant at a cost of £250,000 and plant and machinery with a carrying value of £200,000 was scrapped. The group sold certain patents which were not reflected in its financial statements at a profit of £100,000 in order to raise working capital. The group also obtained a listing for its shares in Luxembourg and the costs of the listing were £150,000. The operating profit of the group prior to these items was £1m as follows:

	£'000
Turnover	8,000
Cost of sales	(5,000)
Gross profit	3,000
Net operating expenses	(2,000)
Operating profit	1,000

After accounting for the exceptional items the figures would be as follows:

	£'000	£'000
Turnover		8,000
Cost of sales	5,000	
Exceptional items:		
Plant write down	200	
Cost of environmental damage	1,300	(6,500)
Gross profit		1,500
Net operating expenses	2,000	
Exceptional operating expenses	400	2,400
Operating loss		(900)
Profit on sale of discontinued operations		500
Profit on sale of patents		100
Interest		–
Loss on ordinary activities before taxation		(300)

Clearly each company will have to decide which heading is appropriate for each exceptional item and the above is only a guide to illustrate how the disclosure might appear.

In the notes the net operating expenses and exceptional net operating expenses would be analysed to show the split between distribution costs and administrative expenses and other operating income.

The costs of listing would be administrative expenses and the costs of redundancy of the employees in the administrative function would also be under the administrative expenses heading.

The profit on sale of patents would be a post operating profit exceptional item on the basis that whilst the patents were not reflected in the balance sheet, they are in the nature of fixed assets and would have been shown as such, had they been recognised.

All of the above exceptional items would be shown under the heading of continuing activities except for the profit on disposal of the subsidiary.

The exceptional item in respect of the costs of environmental damage would need to be shown on the face of the profit and loss account in order to give a true and fair view. Because the balance of the exceptional cost of sales has to be shown separately, it has also been described on the face of the profit and loss account, but it could be relegated to a note.

In practice, the total of exceptional items in respect of net operating expenses might not be shown on the face of the profit and loss account. Instead net operating expenses might be shown as £2,400,000 and the exceptional element would be analysed only in the notes. This is because it may not be considered necessary to the true and fair view to show the amount separately on the face of the profit and loss account.

The tax effect of the profit on disposal of the subsidiary and the profit on disposal of patents would be shown in a note as required by the standard.

[The next paragraph is 8.128.]

8.128 Since FRS 3 was introduced, considerable experimentation has taken place with the presentation of operating exceptional items on the face of the profit and loss account. Various approaches have been adopted as some companies have sought to highlight operating profit before exceptional items as a key performance indicator and a measure of underlying operating performance excluding the distortive and volatile effect of significant one-off charges or credits. The approaches include:

- Multi-column analysis to segregate operating exceptionals as well as discontinued operations (see example in Table 8.13).
- Single-column analysis with imaginative use of boxes or sub-totals to highlight operating profit before and after operating exceptionals (see example in Table 8.14).
- Separate column to segregate operating exceptionals, whilst all other continuing operations, acquisitions and discontinued operations are analysed under a single column (see example in Table 8.15).
- Straightforward disclosure of operating exceptionals under the statutory caption on the face of the profit and loss account, perhaps with additional commentary or analysis in the operating and financial review (see example in Table 8.16).

Table 8.13 — Manweb plc — Annual Report & Accounts — 31 March 1995

Consolidated Profit and Loss Account (extract)

FOR THE YEAR ENDED 31 MARCH 1995

		Continuing Businesses				
	Note	Before Exceptional Items 1995 £ million	Exceptional Items 1995 £ million	Total 1995 £ million	Discontinued Businesses 1995 £ million	1995 £ million
Turnover	1	**850.1**	–	**850.1**	**28.5**	**878.6**
Operating costs		**(719.9)**	–	**(719.9)**	**(30.8)**	**(750.7)**
Reorganisation and restructuring costs		–	**(26.9)**	**(26.9)**	–	**(26.9)**
Total operating costs		**(719.9)**	**(26.9)**	**(746.8)**	**(30.8)**	**(777.6)**
Operating profit	2	**130.2**	**(26.9)**	**103.3**	**(2.3)**	**101.0**

Table 8.14 — Anglo United plc — Annual Report — 31 March 1993

Consolidated Profit and Loss Account (extract)

For the year ended 31 March 1993

Notes		1993 £000	(Restated) 1992 £000
1	Turnover from continuing operations	544,742	555,959
	Cost of sales (including exceptional items) from continuing operations	(463,224)	(458,291)
	Gross profit	81,518	97,668
2	Net operating expenses (including exceptional items)	(80,009)	(63,943)
	Operating profit before exceptional items	20,313	34,345
3	Exceptional items	(18,804)	(620)
	Operating profit from continuing operations	1,509	33,725

Notes to the Accounts (extract)

3 Exceptional items

	Cost of Sales £000	**Distribution Costs £000**	**Administrative Expenses £000**	**1993 Total £000**	1992 Total £000
Legal, professional and banking fees in respect of debt restructuring	–	–	**8,894**	**8,894**	–
Costs in connection with aborted disposals and acquisitions	–	–	**2,360**	**2,360**	–
Future discounted rents receivable	–	–	**(1,370)**	**(1,370)**	–
Reorganisation and restructuring costs of ongoing businesses	**1,450**	**720**	**4,853**	**7,023**	–
Write-off of loan to Employees' Share Ownership Plan Trust*	–	–	**1,367**	**1,367**	–
Professional costs in respect of environmental matters	–	–	**530**	**530**	620
	1,450	**720**	**16,634**	**18,804**	620

The comparative cost for 1992 relates wholly to administrative expenses.

In order to assist in understanding the Group's results for the year, and in view of the unusual materiality of exceptional items to the current year's results, the directors believe that it is appropriate to show separately the operating profit of the Group before exceptional items on the face of the profit and loss account as additional information.

* Note: For periods ended on or after 22 June 1995, the assets and liabilities of the Employee Share Ownership Plan are required to have been reflected in the financial statements as assets and liabilities of the sponsoring company, hence a write-off of a loan to an Employee Share Ownership Plan would not occur. This example does, however, demonstrate the disclosures of exceptional items.

Table 8.15 — Booker plc — Annual Report and Financial Statements — 31 December 1994

Consolidated Profit and Loss Account (extract)

for the fifty-two weeks ended 31 December 1994

	note	Before exceptional items £m	Exceptional items (Note 3) £m	1994 £m
Turnover:				
Continuing operations		3,688.7		3,688.7
Acquisitions		10.5		10.5
		3,699.2		3,699.2
Discontinued operations		23.1		23.1
Total turnover		3,722.3	–	3,722.3
Operating costs	2	(3,620.1)	(20.8)	(3,640.9)
Operating profit				
Continuing operations		98.1	(18.3)	79.8
Acquisitions		1.6	(2.5)	(0.9)
		99.7	(20.8)	78.9
Discontinued operations		2.5	–	2.5
Total operating profit		102.2	(20.8)	81.4

Notes to the Financial Statements (extract)
2. OPERATING COSTS (extract)

	Continuing operations £m	Acquisitions £m	Discontinued operations £m	Pre-exceptional items £m	Exceptional items £m	Total 1994 £m
Cost of sales	3,459.0	7.4	18.9	3,485.3	14.8	3,500.1
Distribution costs	63.3	0.8	1.9	66.0	0.5	66.5
Administrative expenses	66.4	0.7	1.7	68.8	5.5	74.3
Total operating costs	3,588.7	8.9	22.5	3,620.1	20.8	3,640.9
Income from investments	–	–	–	–	–	
Total operating costs *less* other income	3,588.7	8.9	22.5	3,620.1	20.8	3,640.9
Gross profit as defined by the Companies Act 1985	229.7	3.1	4.2	237.0	(14.8)	222.2

Table 8.16 — Cable and Wireless plc — Report and accounts — 31 March 1995

Consolidated profit and loss account (extract)

for the year ended 31 March	Note	1995 £m	1994 £m
Turnover	3,4	**5,132.8**	4,699.2
Operating costs before exceptional items	5	**(3,938.6)**	(3,608.0)
Exceptional items: charged against operating costs	5,9	**(60.5)**	–
Total operating costs		**(3,999.1)**	(3.608.0)
Operating profit	4	**1,133.7**	1,091.2

Note 5. Operating costs (extract)

	1995 After Exceptional items £m	1995 Exceptional items therein £m	1994 £m
Outpayments to other telecommunications administrations and carriers	**1,564.6**	–	1,459.9
Employee costs	**799.2**	**30.3**	686.6
Pension costs* (Note 8) — principal schemes	**51.1**	–	48.6
– other schemes	**8.9**	–	11.2
Rental of transmission facilities	**71.5**	–	58.9
Hire of plant and machinery	**19.9**	–	20.7
Other operating lease rentals	**23.0**		21.3
Other operating costs	**942.1**	**30.2**	833.6
Depreciation of owned tangible fixed assets	**510.9**	–	461.1
Depreciation of tangible fixed assets held under finance leases	**6.3**	–	4.5
Auditors' remuneration — for audit services	**1.6**	–	1.6
	3,999.1	**60.5**	3,608.0

Having regard to the special nature of the Group's business an analysis of operating costs in the manner prescribed by the Companies Act 1985 is not meaningful. In the circumstances therefore the Directors have, as required by paragraph 3(3) of schedule 4 to the Companies Act 1985, adapted the prescribed format to the requirements of the Group's business.

Note 9. Exceptional items (extract)

Exceptional items are as follows:	1995 £m	1994 £m
Mercury reorganisation costs		
Shown as:		
Charge to operating profit	**60.5**	–
Profit less losses on sale and termination of operations	**17.7**	–
Losses on disposal of fixed assets	**43.7**	–
	121.9	–

The exceptional pre-tax charge of £121.9m relates to the Mercury reorganisation announced in December 1994 to streamline its operations and strengthen its competitive position in the UK telecommunications market. Applicable to this exceptional charge is a tax credit of £13.2m relating to the operating cost element of the charge, and a minority interest share of £21.7m.

* Note: Cable and Wireless plc, in its 1995 financial statements applied SSAP 24, 'Pension costs', which has been superseded by FRS 17, 'Retirement benefits'.

[The next paragraph is 8.130.]

8.130 There are different schools of thought on segregation of exceptional items in the profit and loss account.

8.131 One view is that such treatment is consistent with the 'information set' approach that FRS 3 promulgates, because each component of performance is presented fully in the way management believes is most useful for and understandable to shareholders. Investors are particularly interested in analysing the quality of maintainable underlying profits and, hence, growth and dividend prospects. Prominent disclosure of exceptional items is sometimes argued to be an essential part of the overall picture.

8.132 A different view is that excessive emphasis on underlying or maintainable earnings after stripping out unusual items is a flawed concept that reintroduces the problems caused by extraordinary items in the pre-FRS 3 regime. Focus on operating profit before exceptionals can encourage the over-use of the exceptional items category, presenting them in a way that leads them to be discounted by the market.

8.133 We believe that such treatment remains within the spirit of the standard if the exceptionals warrant that degree of prominence and provided that the overall position, including relevant commentary, is presented in an unbiased way and is not misleading.

8.134 Although the above examples illustrate that there is considerable room for experimentation with formats, companies should take great care that they comply with the letter of the standard that requires exceptional items to be shown on the profit and loss account under the statutory format headings to which they relate. The FRRP published a statement on this issue in May 1994. Following an investigation by the FRRP of the financial statements of BET plc for the year ended 27 March 1993, in which FRS 3 was adopted early, the company restated within its 1994 financial statements the presentation of the 1993 comparative exceptional items. The FRRP had concluded that the 1993 presentation *"did not fulfil the requirement of the standard that these items should be shown on the profit and loss account under the statutory format headings to which they relate"*.

8.135 Relevant extracts from the 1993 financial statements are shown in Table 8.17. The problem was that, although the operating exceptional items totalling £76 million were analysed between cost of sales, distribution costs and administrative expenses in the notes, they were not included in the totals shown under the format headings. The FRRP's quibble on this point seemed to many commentators to be rather pedantic, but showed that it was determined to enforce the new standards rigorously.

Table 8.17 — BET Public Limited Company — Annual Report — 27 March 1993

Consolidated profit and loss account (extract)

for the year ended 27th March 1993	Notes	Continuing Operations £m	Discontinued operations £m	1993 Total £m
TURNOVER	1	2,003.2	173.0	2,176.2
Cost of sales		(1,533.2)	(125.8)	(1,659.0)
Gross profit		470.0	47.2	517.2
Distribution costs		(187.5)	(32.2)	(219.7)
Administrative expenses		(231.0)	(20.9)	(251.9)
Other operating income		19.3	1.2	20.5
Income from interests in associated undertakings	4	8.1	–	8.1
OPERATING PROFIT/(LOSS) BEFORE EXCEPTIONAL ITEMS	1&2	78.9	(4.7)	74.2
Permanent diminution in asset values		(42.0)	–	(42.0)
Reorganisation costs		(34.0)	–	(34.0)
Deferred costs		–	–	–
OPERATING EXCEPTIONAL ITEMS	3	(76.0)	–	(76.0)
OPERATING PROFIT/(LOSS)		2.9	(4.7)	(1.8)

Note 3 Exceptional items (extract)

The operating exceptional items referred to above can be categorised as follows:

1993	Cost of sales £m	Distribution costs £m	Administrative expenses £m	Total £m
Permanent diminution in asset values	35.7	–	6.3	42.0
Reorganisation costs	24.5	–	9.5	34.0
	60.2	–	15.8	76.0

8.136 Extracts from the restated comparatives in the 1994 financial statements are shown in Table 8.18.

Table 8.18 — BET Public Limited Company — Annual Report — 2 April 1994

Consolidated profit and loss account (extract)

For the year ended 2nd April 1994	Notes	**Continuing operations £m**	**Discontinued operations £m**	**1994 Total £m**	1993 Restated (see page 36) £m
TURNOVER	1	**1,785.1**	**188.9**	**1,974.0**	2,176.2
Cost of sales		**(1,318.7)**	**(154.7)**	**(1,473.4)**	(1,719.2)
Gross profit		**466.4**	**34.2**	**500.6**	457.0
Distribution costs		**(170.1)**	**(14.5)**	**(184.6)**	(219.7)
Administrative expenses		**(202.6)**	**(23.2)**	**(225.8)**	(267.7)
Other operating income / (expense)		**(0.5)**	**1.1**	**0.6**	20.5
Income from interests in associated undertakings	4	**5.6**	**0.2**	**5.8**	8.1
OPERATING PROFIT/(LOSS)	1	**98.8**	**(2.2)**	**96.6**	(1.8)

Note 3 Exceptional items (extract)

The following operating exceptional items are included within the statutory format headings on the face of the profit and loss account. In 1993 they were disclosed as separate line items on the face of the profit and loss account.

	1994 £m	1993 £m
OPERATING EXCEPTIONAL ITEMS		
Permanent diminution in asset values	–	(42.0)
Reorganisation costs	–	(34.0)
	–	(76.0)

In the previous year a provision was made for reorganisation costs of £34.0 million. This has been fully utilised in the current year (see note 19). The £42.0 million operating exceptional item in 1993 provided for a permanent diminution in the value of land and buildings of £10.5 million, other fixed assets of £21.2 million and current assets of £10.3 million.

The operating exceptional items referred to above are categorised as follows:

	1994			1993		
	Cost of sales £m	**Administrative expenses £m**	**Total £m**	Cost of sales £m	Administrative expenses £m	Total £m
Permanent diminution in asset values	–	–	–	35.7	6.3	42.0
Reorganisation costs	–	–	–	24.5	9.5	34.0
	–	–	–	60.2	15.8	76.0

Tax attributable to exceptional items

8.137 The taxation relating to the three types of exceptional item that are required to be disclosed after operating profit must be shown in a note to the profit and loss account. [FRS 3 para 23]. The three items again are:

- Profits or losses on sale or termination of an operation.
- Costs of a fundamental reorganisation or restructuring having a material effect on the nature and focus of the reporting entity's operations.
- Profits or losses on the disposal of fixed assets.

Provisions in respect of such items should also be included.

8.138 The related tax is required to be shown only in aggregate and not for each individual item, unless the effect of the tax on each of the items differs, when further information should be given, where practicable.

8.139 There is no requirement to disclose taxation relating to other exceptional items.

8.140 The amount of tax attributable to exceptional items falling within any of the three categories set out above should be calculated by computing the tax on the profit or loss on ordinary activities as if the items did not exist and comparing this notional tax charge with the tax charge on the profit or loss for the period. Any additional tax charge or credit (including deferred tax) should be attributed to the items. [FRS 3 para 24].

8.141 If there were both exceptional items and extraordinary items in the same period, the tax on the items combined should be calculated and then apportioned between them in relation to their respective amounts, unless a more precise basis is available. If the latter basis is adopted the method of apportionment should be disclosed. [FRS 3 para 24]. In practice, this requirement is largely academic because extraordinary items have been virtually eliminated by FRS 3.

8.142 Although the FRS states that the tax attributable to the above types of exceptional item should be disclosed in a note, there could be no objection to disclosing the tax separately within the tax charge on the face of the profit and loss account, as the items are themselves disclosed there.

8.143 Further commentary is included in chapter 13.

Extraordinary items

8.144 As mentioned earlier, extraordinary items have all but disappeared from UK financial reporting. In our view there should be no extraordinary items under FRS 3, however unusual the transaction or event may be.

Statement of total recognised gains and losses

8.145 The statement of total recognised gains and losses (STRGL) was a major innovation in UK accounting and is fundamental to the concept of 'performance' embraced by the ASB in FRS 3.

8.146 As explained earlier in this chapter, the ASB's aim was to turn attention away from particular numbers and to encourage users to make their own judgements about a company's performance, based on an 'information set'. Part of that information set is the statement of total recognised gains and losses.

8.147 Several accounting standards permit amounts to be taken direct to reserves and the law requires certain amounts to be so treated. In particular, the law does not permit a company to recognise an unrealised profit in the profit and loss account, except where the company adopts the fair value accounting provisions in Section D of Schedule 4. [CA85 4 Sch 12(a), 34E(2)]. In the past a casual reader of financial statements could be forgiven for not being aware of such amounts, as they were often only disclosed in a reserves note that was not prominently displayed, but instead appeared only a long way into the financial statements. SSAP 6 required the reserves note either to be immediately following the profit and loss account or a cross-reference to be made to it on the face of the profit and loss account. In practice, the cross-reference often consisted only of a note number.

8.148 Because amounts taken directly to reserves are often important in assessing a company's performance, in FRS 3 the ASB required such amounts to be shown in a new primary statement 'The statement of total recognised gains and losses'. This statement, which should have equal prominence to the other primary statements includes the profit for the year (from the profit and loss account) and other amounts taken directly to reserves, including the following principal items:

- Exchange gains and losses on retranslation of opening net assets of overseas subsidiaries. (These would be offset by any exchange gains or losses on foreign currency borrowings that hedge those investments.)
- Revaluation surpluses and certain unrealised revaluation deficits. (Examples of how revaluation surpluses and deficits are to be treated in the statement are given from para 8.110 above.)
- Actuarial gains and losses on defined benefit pension arrangements.
- Unrealised gains resulting from sales of assets to associated companies or joint ventures.
- Tax attributable to gains or losses recognised in the statement.

8.149 Where a company 'recycles' a gain or loss previously recognised in the STRGL to the profit and loss account, in the limited circumstances permitted by the ASB's amendment of FRS 3 (see para 8.107.1), it will be necessary for the STRGL to include a separate line item to reverse the amount previously recognised in the STRGL so that the total recognised gains and losses are not mis-stated.

8.150 The 'total recognised gains and losses' are the gains and losses arising from a company's activities as distinct from capital introduced or withdrawn by shareholders. Consequently, they do not include payments to shareholders in respect of capital redeemed or inflows of new capital from shareholders, nor do they include dividends to shareholders. These items are not elements of a company's performance, and so instead are recorded in the reconciliation of movements in shareholders' funds.

8.151 One of the compelling reasons for bringing the effects of reserve accounting into greater prominence through this new statement was the case of Polly Peck. After the collapse of that company, considerable attention was focused on the very large exchange movements that had been shown in its reserves. Although these movements had been disclosed in the notes, their size and the circumstances at the time emphasised the importance of bringing such movements prominently to the attention of users of financial statements. This idea was, however, by no means a radical one, as it had long been argued by users and preparers of financial statements that the statement of reserves should be prominently displayed. Indeed, until SSAP 6 was revised in 1986, it had been a requirement of that standard that a statement of reserves should immediately follow the profit and loss account.

8.152 What *was* new in FRS 3 was the introduction of the figure of total gains and losses for the year, which was intended in due course to have as much importance to readers and analysts as the figure of profit for the financial year.

8.153 An example of a statement of total recognised gains and losses is given in Table 8.19.

Table 8.19 — Grand Metropolitan Public Limited Company — Annual Report — 30 September 1994

Statement of Total Recognised Gains and Losses

For the year ended 30th September 1994	1994	*1993*
	£m	*£m*
Profit for the financial year	450	*410*
Deficit on revaluation of properties in associate	(10)	*(80)*
Exchange adjustments	(47)	*(39)*
Total recognised gains and losses for the financial year	393	*291*
Prior year adjustment (note 1)	(21)	
Total gains and losses recognised since last annual report	372	

8.154 Where a reporting entity has no recognised gains and losses in a period, other than the profit or loss for the period, it should state this fact immediately below the profit and loss account. [FRS 3 para 57].

8.154.1 FRS 9 requires that the investor's share of total recognised gains and losses of its associates and (separately) joint ventures should be shown separately under each heading, if material, either in the statement or in a note that is referred to in the statement. The above example highlights a share of a deficit on revaluation in an associate that is material (this assumes that all other amounts attributable to associates are not material for the purpose of this example).

Purchased goodwill

8.155 Goodwill that was written off directly to reserves on acquisition before the adoption of FRS 10 was not permitted to be included in the STRGL in the year when it was written off. There is a footnote in FRS 3 to this effect. [FRS 3 para 27].

[The next paragraph is 8.157.]

8.157 When a business is disposed of or closed and there has been goodwill written off directly to reserves on acquisition of the business in the past, FRS 10 requires that the profit or loss on disposal should take account of that goodwill. Thus the goodwill will, on disposal, be part of the profit or loss for the financial year and in this way will be a recognised loss, but only when the business is disposed of or the goodwill is otherwise written off in the profit and loss account. The credit to reserves that results from reinstating the goodwill on disposal will *not* be a recognised gain, in the same way that the original write off was not a recognised loss (see also para 8.92 above).

8.158 The following example illustrates the treatment of goodwill on the disposal of a subsidiary where the goodwill remained eliminated against reserves.

Example

A company bought a subsidiary before the application of FRS 10 and goodwill of £200m arose, which was written off directly to reserves. The goodwill was not shown as a recognised loss in the statement of total recognised gains and losses. In the current year the subsidiary is sold. The profit or loss on sale is calculated as the difference between the proceeds of sale and the net assets at the date of sale plus goodwill previously written off. The subsidiary is sold for net asset value and, therefore, a loss on sale of £200m is incurred. This loss on sale forms part of the profit or loss for the current financial year, which is also reported in the statement of total recognised gains and losses. In order to reinstate the goodwill there was a credit to reserves and a debit to profit and loss account. Whilst the debit forms part of the profit or loss on sale and is a recognised loss, the credit is not a recognised gain and does not appear in the statement of total recognised gains and losses.

8.159 A second example showing the treatment when goodwill was capitalised and amortised is as follows:

Example

A company buys a subsidiary and goodwill arises of £200m which is capitalised and amortised over ten years. In years one to six a charge for amortisation of £20m per year is made in the profit and loss account and is thus a recognised loss in the statement of total recognised gains and losses (because it is included in the profit or loss for the financial year). In year six the subsidiary is sold. Only the *unamortised* goodwill of £80m is included in the calculation of the profit or loss on sale and this £80m is also recognised in the statement of total recognised gains and losses, as it forms part of the profit or loss for the financial year.

Movements in reserves

8.160 The statement of total recognised gains and losses does not include movements between reserves. These are shown in a reserves note which is required by Schedule 4 to the Companies Act 1985.

8.161 The Act's requirements in relation to reserves are that where any amounts are transferred to or from reserves that are required to be shown separately in the balance sheet the following information has to be given:

- The amount of the reserves at the beginning and end of the year.
- The amounts transferred to or from the reserves during the year.
- The source and application of any amounts so transferred.

[CA85 4 Sch 46].

8.162 This means, for example, that the reserves note is required to show movements between the revaluation reserve and the profit and loss account reserve in respect of previous revaluation surpluses realised in the year. Although the standard does not require the note to be given the same prominence as, for instance, the statement of total recognised gains and losses, it remains an important note to the financial statements.

8.163 Because the reserves note is required by law to show movements in each reserve and movements between reserves, it is not possible to substitute for such movements in the reserves note a figure, such as, the total recognised gains and losses figure for the year from the statement of total recognised gains and losses. That figure, which summarises several different types of reserve movements must be broken down into its component parts in the reserves note and transfers between reserves must also be shown in the note.

8.164 Many of the respondents to the exposure draft, FRED 1, considered that the statement of total recognised gains and losses should be extended to include other reserve movements and to provide a reconciliation between opening and closing shareholders' equity. The ASB did not amend its proposals, but instead introduced in FRS 3 the requirement for an additional statement or note reconciling movements in shareholders' funds (see para 8.183).

[The next paragraph is 8.169.]

Note of historical cost profits and losses

8.169 FRS 3 requires that a note of historical cost profits and losses for the period should be presented immediately following the profit and loss account or the statement of total recognised gains and losses, in those instances where there is a material difference between the result as disclosed in the profit and loss account and the result on an unmodified historical cost basis.

8.170 The standard gives the reasons for requiring this note. First, it is argued that for so long as discretion exists on the scale and timing of revaluations included in financial statements, the unmodified historical cost basis will give the reported profits or losses of different enterprises on a more comparable basis. Secondly, certain users wish to assess the profit or loss on sale of fixed assets based on their historical cost rather than, as the standard requires, on their revalued carrying amount.

8.171 The lack of comparability referred to occurs, for instance, where two companies have similar assets costing £100,000 each. The second company revalues the asset to £150,000 and the gain is shown in the statement of total recognised gains and losses in year one. In year two the companies sell the assets for £150,000. The first company will record a profit of £50,000 in the profit and loss account whilst the second will record neither gain nor loss.

8.172 Under the ASB's view of performance, the second company's gain occurs in year one and is recognised in the picture of performance given by the profit and loss account taken together with the statement of total recognised gains and losses. Nonetheless, the two companies' results in year one are not comparable because the first company has not revalued and, therefore, shows no gain. The same lack of comparability occurs in the second year, because the first company reports a profit and the second does not.

8.173 The note of historical cost profits remedies this. In the second company in year two adjustments are made in the note to show the profit on an unmodified historical cost basis and these results can then be fairly compared with those of the first company.

[The next paragraph is 8.178.]

8.178 The note also includes adjustments to the reported profit to remove depreciation charged on the revalued element of fixed assets and to restate profits and losses on sale of assets onto the historical cost basis.

8.179 Investment and dealing companies that apply FRS 26, 'Financial instruments: Recognition and measurement', and carry certain financial assets at fair value, taking the movements to the profit and loss account are not required by the standard to make adjustments in the note of historical cost profits and losses to eliminate gains taken to profit and loss account as a result. This is because the standard's explanation section states that where marking to market is an established industry practice it is not considered to be a departure from the historical cost convention for the purposes of the note of historical cost profits and losses. FRS 3 has now been amended, to extend this principle to the effects of fair value accounting under FRS 26, 'Financial instruments: Recognition and measurement', to hyperinflation adjustments under FRS 24, 'Financial reporting in hyperinflationary economies', and to UITF 9, 'Accounting for operations in hyper-inflationary economies', so that the effects of these items on historical cost profit or loss are not required to be included in the reconciliation. But this omission should be noted. This amendment is effective for accounting periods beginning on or after 1 January 2007 with early adoption permitted.

8.180 Companies holding investment properties, which are required by SSAP 19 to be revalued annually in the financial statements, generally do not include a depreciation adjustment in the note of historical profits and losses. That is because it is probable that either no depreciation would have been charged on a revalued or historical cost basis, so there is no difference to record or it is not possible to quantify depreciation on a revalued or historical cost basis.

8.181 Other companies that do not maintain records of historical costs may instead use the earliest available values. The standard specifically states that where full historical cost information cannot be obtained without unreasonable expense or delay, the earliest available values should be used.

8.182 An example of a note of historical cost profits and losses is given in Table 8.20.

Table 8.20 – Grand Metropolitan Public Limited Company – Annual Report –30 September 1994

NOTE OF HISTORICAL COST PROFITS AND LOSSES

for the year ended 30th September 1994

	1994 £m	*1993 £m*
Profit on ordinary activities before taxation	654	*625*
Realisation of property revaluation gains of prior years	429	*6*
Difference between the historical cost depreciation charge and the actual depreciation charge for the year calculated on the revalued amount	1	*2*
Asset provisions created/(utilised) not required on an historical cost basis	26	*(7)*
Historical cost profit on ordinary activities before taxation	1,110	*626*
Historical cost profit for the year retained after taxation, minority interests and dividends	614	*142*

Reconciliation of movements in shareholders' funds

8.183 There was concern among commentators on FRED 1 that the statement of total recognised gains and losses did not completely achieve the desired effect of bringing into a primary statement all the important movements in shareholders' funds that have hitherto been included only in the notes to the financial statements.

8.184 The ASB's reaction to this concern was to keep the statement of total recognised gains and losses as a primary statement containing only gains and losses — that is, as a statement of performance — but to introduce a new note or primary statement that reconciles the opening and closing totals of shareholders' funds. The reconciliation is not a statement of performance, but just brings together all items that affect shareholders' funds as reported in the financial statements, that is:

- Profit for the year.
- Other recognised gains and losses relating to the year (included in the statement of total recognised gains and losses).
- Other items that are not part of performance such as: dividends; the net proceeds of new share issues; payments for the redemption or repurchase of shares; and reversal on disposal of purchased goodwill previously eliminated against reserves.

8.185 As the reconciliation may be either in the form of a note or in the form of a primary statement, considerable flexibility is given as to where the reconciliation appears in financial statements and thus to the prominence or lack of prominence given to it. If included as a primary statement, however, it must be shown separately from the statement of total recognised gains and losses.

8.186 The reconciliation should include the components of the total recognised gains and losses of the year. The example in the standard shows dividends deducted from profit for the financial year rather than from total recognised gains and losses. This must be correct as dividends cannot be paid out of unrealised profits. The reconciliation should also include share capital subscribed or repaid. Other items could include amounts written off against the share premium account where permitted by law.

8.187 An example is shown in Table 8.21.

Table 8.21 — Marks and Spencer Group p.l.c. — Annual Report and Financial Statements — 30 March 2002

26. Reconciliation of movements in Group shareholders' funds

	Group	
	2002 £m	2001 As restated £m
Profit/(loss) attributable to shareholders	153.0	(5.5)
Dividends	(238.9)	(258.3)
	(85.9)	(263.8)
Other recognised gains and losses relating to the year	0.6	11.6
New share capital subscribed	8.9	7.1
Issue/redemption expenses	(9.3)	–
Amounts added to profit and loss account reserve in respect of shares issued to the QUEST	2.5	–
Redemption of B shares	(1,717.9)	–
Purchase of own shares	(52.0)	(20.3)
Goodwill transferred to profit and loss account on sale/closure of businesses	368.2	(1.3)
Net reduction in shareholders' funds	(1,484.9)	(266.7)
Opening shareholders' funds as previously stated	4,645.4	4,905.3
Prior year adjustment (see note 7)	(79.6)	(72.8)
Opening shareholders' funds as restated	4,565.8	4,832.5
Closing shareholders' funds	3,080.9	4,565.8

Prior period adjustments

Introduction

8.188 FRS 3 requires that prior period adjustments should be accounted for by restating the corresponding primary statements and notes for the preceding period and adjusting the opening balance of reserves accordingly. In the statement of total recognised gains and losses the cumulative effect of the adjustments should also be noted at the foot of the current year column, as shown in Tables 8.19 above and Table 8.22 below. [FRS 3 para 29].

Table 8.22 — Trafalgar House Public Limited Company — Report and Accounts — 30 September 1994

Statement of total recognised gains and losses

for the year ended 30 September 1994

	1994 £m	1993 £m *(restated)*
Profit for the year	30.0	(366.6)
Surplus on revaluation	6.3	(38.9)
Exchange translation differences	(3.3)	(5.2)
Total recognised gains and losses relating to the year	33.0	(410.7)
Prior year adjustment (as explained in note 1)	(2.7)	
Total gains and losses recognised since last annual report	30.3	

1 Changes in accounting policy and in presentation (extract)

(a) Changes in accounting policy

Comparative figures have been restated to reflect two changes of accounting policy:

(i) Trading results denominated in foreign currencies are translated into sterling at average rates of exchange. Previously trading results were translated at the rates of exchange ruling at the year end. The accounting policy has been changed because the directors consider the new policy gives a fairer presentation of group's results and cash flows as they arise during course of accounting period.

(ii) Sales of UK residential property are recognised on legal completion. Previously, sales were recognised when contracts were exchanged. The accounting policy has been changed because the new policy is adopted by most other UK housebuilders.

As a result, comparative figures for the year ended 30 September 1993 have been adjusted as follows:

	Loss for the year after dividends £m	Net assets £m
As previously reported	(402.1)	290.2
Effect of the change from year end average rates	1.5	–
Effect of the change in the timing of recognition of UK residential property sales	(1.3)	(2.7)
As restated	(401.9)	(287.5)

Current year profit before is reduced by £0.9 million following the changes in the foreign exchange policy and reduced by £0.6 million following the change in policy for the recognition of UK residential property sales.

8.189 Normally, items relating to prior periods arise from the corrections and adjustments that are the natural result of estimates inherent in accounting and in the periodic preparation of financial statements. Therefore, they should be dealt with in the profit and loss account of the period in which they are identified. The only types of prior period items that should be adjusted against opening reserves are those that arise from a change of accounting policy or from the correction of fundamental error. The tax effect of a prior year adjustment, whether it arises from a change in accounting policy or from a fundamental error, should be dealt with as part of the prior year adjustment against opening reserves, rather than as part of the current year tax charge.

Changes in accounting policies

8.190 FRS 18, 'Accounting policies', defines accounting policies as the principles, bases, conventions, rules and practices for recognising, selecting measurement bases for, and presenting assets, liabilities, gains, losses and changes to shareholders' funds. [FRS 18 para 4]. FRS 18 distinguishes accounting policies from estimation techniques, which are methods used to estimate monetary amounts corresponding to selected measurement bases. A change of accounting policy requires a prior year adjustment. A change to an estimation technique should not give rise to a prior year adjustment, unless it reflects the correction of a fundamental error. Accounting policies and estimation techniques are discussed in chapter 2.

8.191 FRS 18 gives several examples of items that should be treated as changes of accounting policies or changes of estimation techniques. They are analysed according to the components of the definition of accounting policies, namely recognition, measurement bases and presentation.

8.192 The following would be changes to accounting policies as a result of different recognition policies:

- Changing from writing-off to capitalising interest relating to the construction of fixed assets.
- Changing from writing-off to capitalising development expenditure.
- Changing revenue recognition practices regarding the sale of goods and services.

8.192.1 The following would be changes to accounting policies as a result of different measurement bases:

- Changing from measuring a class of fixed assets at depreciated historical cost to a policy of regular revaluation.
- Changing from measuring deferred tax liabilities on an undiscounted basis to measuring them on a discounted basis.
- Changing from translating the results of foreign subsidiaries at closing rates to translating them at average rates for the year.

8.192.2 FRS 18 also regards as a change of accounting policy a change in the way an item is presented in the balance sheet or profit and loss account, such as classifying depreciation charges within cost of sales instead of administrative expenses. However, the only effect is to restate comparative amounts on a comparable basis.

8.192.3 A change in the basis of absorbing overheads into a stock or work-in-progress valuation is not a change of accounting policy. SSAP 9 requires overheads that are attributable to bringing a product to its present location and condition to be included in cost. In a historical cost setting, SSAP 9 does not allow a choice of accounting policies relating to the recognition and measurement of attributable overheads. Consequently, the change must be a change of estimation technique (the method of estimating the cost of stocks). Similarly, a change of depreciation methods for a class of fixed assets is not a change of accounting policy. The change of depreciation methods is regarded as a change of estimation technique used to measure the unexpired portion of the assets' economic benefits – there is no change to the historical cost or current value measurement basis being used.

8.193 A significant proportion of accounting policy changes are brought about by the introduction of new accounting standards. Others are changes voluntarily adopted by the directors. FRS 18 requires accounting policies to be reviewed regularly to ensure that they remain the most appropriate. [FRS 18 para 45]. It follows from the general requirement to adopt the most appropriate policies that a change in accounting policy can only be justified if the new policy is judged more appropriate than the one it replaces. [FRS 3 para 62].

8.194 FRS 3 notes that, where an accounting policy is introduced to account for transactions or events that are clearly different in substance from those previously occurring (that is, where no policy previously existed), that is not a change of accounting policy. For example, a subsidiary might operate in an economy that becomes hyper-inflationary as defined in FRS 24, 'Financial reporting in hyper-inflationary economies'. The subsidiary's financial statements would then have to be adjusted for hyper-inflation before the closing rate/net investment method of translation in SSAP 20, 'Foreign currency translation', (or FRS 23, 'The effects of changes in foreign exchange rates') is applied. Similarly, inflation adjustments will no longer be required when the economy ceases to be hyper-inflationary. No change of accounting policy is involved in either situation.

Disclosures

8.195 A change of policy must be adequately explained and justified in the financial statements. The Act requires that where there is a change of accounting policy (that is, a departure from the consistency principle) the financial statements must disclose *"particulars of the departure, the reasons for it and its effect"*. [CA85 4 Sch 15].

8.196 Changes in accounting policies have interested the Financial Reporting Review Panel. Three of its published findings have referred to policy changes. In the first of these, Associated Nursing Services PLC, the Panel examined the adequacy of the explanation provided in respect of a change of policy. Although the Panel concluded that it was satisfied with the explanations provided, it stated that it *"welcomes the intention of the directors to ensure that future notes of changes in accounting policy will include reiteration of the former policy as well as a description of the new policy"*.

8.197 In the second case, Ptarmigan Holdings PLC, the Panel investigated a change of policy in respect of purchased goodwill from immediate write-off to reserves to capitalisation and amortisation. The Panel concluded that, although it was satisfied that the company had special reasons for making the change, it considered the reasons for the change had not been adequately disclosed in the financial statements.

8.197.1 More recently, in 2006 the FRRP investigated a change of policy made by Sanctuary plc in their financial statements for the year ended 30 September 2005. The Panel concluded that policies applied previously had been inappropriate and that the revisions made had been to correct fundamental errors (see para 8.203) and not changes in accounting policy.

8.197.2 Where accounting policy changes are brought about by new accounting standards, the reason is self-evident if the old policy is no longer permitted. Consequently, only a simple statement to this effect should normally be necessary. However, where a company voluntarily changes an accounting policy, the reasons for the change need to be clearly and fully disclosed.

8.198 The Companies Act 1985 requires disclosure of the *effect* of a change of policy (see para 8.195 above). FRS 3 requires the effect of the change on the results for the preceding period to be disclosed where practicable. [FRS 3 para 29]. The FRS 3 requirement is satisfied by quantifying the adjustment to the comparative figures as a result of changing from the old policy to the new policy.

[The next paragraph is 8.200.]

8.200 The disclosure requirements of FRS 18 go further than either FRS 3 or the Companies Act 1985. It requires details of any changes to accounting policies including:

- A brief explanation of why each new accounting policy is thought more appropriate.
- Where practicable, the effect of a prior period adjustment on the results of the preceding period (as in FRS 3).
- Where practicable, an indication of the effect of a change in accounting policy on the results for the current period (formerly in UITF 14, see para 8.199).

[FRS 18 para 55(c)].

The last bullet point is particularly relevant because users may be interested to know how much more or less profit the company has made this year as a result of changing its accounting policies.

8.200.1 Where it is not practicable to disclose the effect on the previous year's or the current year's results, FRS 18 requires that fact, together with the reasons, to be disclosed. Non-disclosure of the effect on the previous year's results is rare, since the comparatives have to be restated as part of the prior period adjustment. Sometimes when new accounting standards are adopted it is impracticable to give the effect of changes on the current period's results, especially where the policies use different measurement bases.

8.201 Table 8.22 above shows the financial statement disclosures in respect of two voluntary changes of accounting policy: a change from the closing rate method to the average rate method for translating the results of foreign subsidiaries; and a change relating to revenue recognition on property sales. This example discloses the effect of the change on both the current and previous year.

8.202 Table 8.23 shows the disclosures relating to a change in accounting policy stemming from a new accounting pronouncement, in this case a change from a cash basis to an accruals basis of accounting for post-retirement medical benefits. This example also shows the effect of adopting the new policy on the results of both years.

Table 8.23 — Imperial Chemical Industries PLC — Annual Report and Accounts — 31 December 1994

statement of group total recognised gains and losses
for the year ended 31 December 1994

	Notes	**1994 £m**	1993† £m
Net profit for the financial year		**188**	129
Currency translation differences on foreign currency net investments and related loans		**(96)**	(23)
Share of other reserve movements of associated undertakings and other items		**(7)**	–
Total recognised gains and losses relating to the year		**85**	106
Prior year adjustment	2	**(95)**	
Total gains and losses recognised since last annual report		**10**	

†restated (note 2)

notes relating to the accounts (extract)

2 Basis of presentation of financial information (extract)

The results reflect the initial adoption of the accounting requirements of pronouncement UITF 6 "Accounting for Post-retirement Benefits other than Pensions". The cumulative cost of the benefits relating to previous years has been recognised in the accounts as a prior year adjustment and comparative figures for 1993 have been restated. The effect on continuing operations of implementing this new accounting policy was to reduce trading profit for the year by £12m (1993 £10m), to reduce the tax charge by £4m (1993 £4m) and to reduce the value of Group reserves at 1 January 1994 by £95m (1993 £89m) (Company £3m, 1993 £3m).

23 Reserves (extract)

	Share premium account £m	Revaluation £m	Associated undertakings £m	Profit and loss account £m	**1994 Total £m**	1993 Total £m
GROUP						
Reserves attributable to parent company						
At beginning of year as previously stated						3,572
Prior year adjustment (note 2)						(89)
At beginning of year as restated	561	46	66	2,493	**3,166**	3,483

Fundamental errors

8.203 Fundamental errors are those that are of such significance as to destroy the true and fair view and hence the validity of financial statements. [FRS 3 para 63]. The correction of such errors should not be included in the current year's profit and loss account. Instead, they should be adjusted by restating previous years' results and adjusting the opening balance of retained profits.

8.204 In practice, this means that if the error had been known about at the time the previous year's financial statements were about to be approved, it would have been corrected prior to approval. Equally, if the error came to light between the approval of the prior year's financial statements and the date of preparation of the current year's financial statements, the directors could have withdrawn the previous financial statements and revised them voluntarily under the Act (but this does not mean that every such revision is necessarily a fundamental error).

Changes to estimation techniques

8.205 Where the effect is material, FRS 18 requires a change to an estimation technique to be described and its effect on the current period's results to be disclosed. [FRS 18 para 55(d)]. Disclosure of the effect on the current period's results is important because changes are recognised entirely in the current period. This does not necessarily mean that the effect of changes in assumptions underlying the estimation techniques need to be disclosed if there is no change in the estimation technique. Yet other standards may require it. For example, FRS 15 requires disclosure of the effect of changing from one depreciation method to another (change to estimation technique) and of the effect of revising assets' useful economic lives or residual values (change to the underlying assumptions). Estimation techniques are discussed in chapter 2.

Chapter 9

Revenue recognition

	Page
Introduction	9001
Basic principles	9003
Definition of revenue	9003
Identifying the transaction	9005
Timing of recognition	9006
What activities constitute performance?	9007
Measurement of revenue	9009
Variable consideration	9013
Within customer's control	9013
Within seller's control	9013
Within control of neither seller nor customer	9014
Sale of goods	9014
Transfer of significant risks and rewards of ownership	9015
Bill and hold sales	9015
Payments in advance	9018
Goods despatched subject to conditions (sale or return; consignment)	9019
Continuing managerial involvement	9023
Warranties	9024
Initial warranty	9024
Extended warranty	9025
Installation fees	9026
Shipping and handling charges	9027
Sale of property	9028
Sale of software	9030
Sale of services	9035
Performance over time	9035
Accounting for incomplete contractual performance	9035
Determining the stage of completion of performance	9038
Contracts containing significant acts	9040
Contracts with milestone payments	9041
Inception fees	9043
Subscriptions	9043
Admission fees	9044
Tuition fees	9044
Multiple element transactions	9045
Separation of components	9045
Allocation of consideration	9045
Linked transactions	9049
Measurement of revenue — specific issues	9050

Agency arrangements 9050
Advertising agency commissions 9054
Two-way trading arrangements 9055
Volume or settlement discounting 9058
Barter transactions 9060
Capacity transactions 9062
Sale of an asset or a service? 9063
Presentation in the performance statements 9064
Exchange and reciprocal transactions 9065
Vouchers and coupons 9067
Vouchers or coupons granted for consideration 9067
Vouchers granted as part of sales transaction (vouchers) 9068
Vouchers granted without consideration 9071
Free products 9071
Loyalty programmes (point schemes) 9072
Other benefit schemes similar to point schemes 9074
Dividends, royalties and other practical applications 9075
Dividends 9075
Shares for services 9076
Licensing and royalties 9078
Royalties 9078
Licence income 9079
Franchise fees 9081
Grants 9082
Distinction between capital and revenue 9086
Financial services fees 9087
Fees that are an integral part of the effective interest rate 9087
Fees earned as a result of providing services 9088
Fees earned upon the execution of a significant act 9088
Presentation and disclosure 9089
Accounting policies 9089
Turnover 9090
Trading activities 9090
Commissions and agency fees 9090
Other operating income 9091
Government grants 9092

Chapter 9

Revenue recognition

Introduction

9.1 The issue of revenue recognition is fundamental to the reporting of performance. Evidence of this was dramatically shown a few years ago by a series of high profile accounting restatements in the US and, to a lesser extent, in the UK, which severely damaged investor confidence at the time. Key areas of change included barter sales (for example, in advertising), 'round trip' trades, transactions with off balance sheet partnerships and other special purpose entities, network capacity swaps, recognition of sales to distributors before on-sale by the distributors and recording sales in advance of signing customer contracts.

9.2 As can be seen from the above list (which is by no means comprehensive), the area of revenue recognition is one where the capacity and temptation for manipulation is considerable. It is, therefore, one of the most important areas on which accounting standard setters are focussing.

9.3 In November 2003 the ASB issued 'Amendment to FRS 5, 'Reporting the substance of transactions': Revenue recognition' (Application note G). The ASB noted that there was no UK standard on revenue recognition and that in practice UK preparers had looked for guidance to the international standard IAS 18, 'Revenue', and to US requirements, including SAB 101 (now SAB 104). Despite this, there was evidence that in the UK different entities and industries were following inconsistent policies and practices.

9.4 The ASB's Application note G to FRS 5 sets out basic principles of revenue recognition relating to the supply of goods or services. It sets out basic principles for revenue recognition that should be applied in all cases and gives specific guidance on five types of transactions that give rise to turnover and that have been subject to different interpretations in practice. The five types of transactions are dealt with in the application note under the following headings:

- Long-term contractual performance.
- Separation and linking of contractual arrangements.
- Bill and hold arrangements.
- Sales with rights of return.
- Presentation of turnover as principal or as agent.

[FRS 5 App G para G1].

9.5 The application note does not apply to arrangements:

- Resulting from transactions in financial instruments.
- Arising from insurance contracts.
- Dealt with more specifically elsewhere in FRS 5 or in other accounting standards.

[FRS 5 App G para G2].

9.6 The application note is not a full accounting standard and focuses principally on turnover as a subset of revenue. Nonetheless, it sets out important principles and guidance that now provide the primary authority in UK GAAP for revenue recognition. These principles and guidance are discussed and explained in this chapter together with guidance from IAS 18, which remains useful supplementary guidance for UK preparers and users, where it covers areas not dealt with by the application note.

9.7 Even after Application note G was issued, there remained controversy surrounding its practical application to service contracts, particularly contracts for professional services. To clarify the situation, the UITF issued Abstract 40, 'Revenue recognition and service contracts', in March 2005.

9.7.1 The scope of revenue recognition and its relationship to other areas is illustrated by the following example.

Company D is a diverse business and has four projects at various stages of progress at the year end. How should these projects be accounted for?

The projects are:

(a) A contract for the construction of a hospital for £10m (expected costs are £8m).

(b) The development of a bespoke computer system, in accordance with contractual specifications for a hospital for £200,000 (expected costs are £180,000 and it is expected to take two years to develop).

(c) The manufacture of a new type of hand disinfectant that has been developed and received all necessary regulatory approval.

(d) Monthly servicing of the hospital's X-ray machines for five years.

(a) Under UK GAAP, this falls within the scope of SSAP 9, 'Stocks and long-term contracts'. The accounting for the contract will require both contract revenue and expenses to be recognised by reference to the stage of completion of the contract at the balance sheet date. This results in the profit being recognised as the contract progresses. To the extent that costs incurred on the contract are not recognised in profit or loss, they should be recognised on the balance sheet as contract work-in-progress. See chapter 20.

(b) The accounting for the development of bespoke IT software, which will fall into two or more accounting periods, falls within the scope of SSAP 9 and the accounting uses the same principles as in (a).

(c) Company D is manufacturing the disinfecting handwash for general stock. The stock falls within the scope of SSAP 9 and is recognised on the balance sheet, measured at the lower of cost and net realisable value and sales revenue is recognised when the handwash has been delivered to customers in return for valuable consideration, in accordance with FRS 5 Application note G, 'Revenue recognition'.

(d) UITF Abstract 40, 'Revenue recognition and service contracts', clarifies that a contract for the monthly servicing of a hospital's X-ray machines does not meet the definition of a long-term contract in SSAP 9; instead it should be accounted for using the principles of FRS 5 Application note G. In substance, the contract is for the performance of a separate service each month and not for one long-term service. Because the contract is for 60 separate services, 1/60th of the contractual revenue should be recognised each month once the X-ray machines have been serviced. FRS 5 does not deal with the recognition of the costs associated with the contract. So entity D will recognise expenses as they are incurred.

9.8 This chapter deals mainly with the issues relating to the recognition of revenue. It considers:

- The basic principles of revenue recognition.
- The recognition of revenue from sales of goods.
- The recognition of revenue from sales of services.
- Multiple element transactions.
- Specific measurement issues.
- Vouchers and coupons.
- Dividends, royalties and other practical applications.
- Financial services fees.
- Presentation and disclosure issues.
- Companies Act requirements and the realisation of profits.
- Differences between IFRS and UK GAAP.

Basic principles

Definition of revenue

9.9 Neither company law nor Application note G to FRS 5 define revenue. The application note does, however, set out principles for its recognition.

9.10 The ASB's Statement of principles defines gains and losses in broad terms as all increases or decreases in ownership interests not resulting from contributions from or distributions to owners. It states that the term 'gains' includes items that are commonly referred to as 'revenue'. The definitions of gains and losses rest on those for assets and liabilities.

9.11 IAS 18, 'Revenue recognition', paragraph 7 defines revenue as "*...the gross inflow of economic benefits during the period arising in the course of the ordinary activities of an entity when those inflows result in increases in equity, other than increases relating to contributions from equity participants*". The IASB and the FASB in the US currently have a joint project on revenue recognition as a result of which the definition in IAS 18 may be amended.

9.12 The IAS 18 definition enables a distinction to be made between 'gains', which are all increases in equity not resulting from contributions from owners, and 'revenue', which includes only gains that arise in the course of an entity's ordinary activities.

9.13 In Application note G, revenue from ordinary activities is broken down between revenue that results from the supply of goods and services that is part of an entity's normal business (turnover) and other gains. The definition of turnover (which may also be called 'sales' in the financial statements of the seller) is *"the revenue resulting from exchange transactions under which a seller supplies to customers the goods or services that it is in business to provide"*. [FRS 5 App G para G11]. The application note describes these transactions as being part of the seller's operating activities and distinguishes them from other transactions by stating: *"A seller may enter into other exchange transactions such as the sale of fixed assets. Such transactions do not normally give rise to turnover, as they do not normally fall within the class of transactions set out in paragraph G11"*. [FRS 5 App G para G12]. It notes that, for example, gains or losses on sale of fixed assets are required by FRS 3 to be shown after operating profit.

9.14 The distinction between turnover and other gains is not always clear. Determining whether a transaction should result in recording turnover will depend on the facts surrounding the business and the transaction itself. Consider the following examples:

Example 1

A car dealership has demonstration cars available that can be used by potential customers for test drives. The cars are used for more than one year and then sold as used. The dealership sells both new and used cars. Does the sale represent the sale of a fixed asset, as the car was used by the dealership for the purpose of securing sales, or is the sale of the car the sale of an item of inventory, as the dealership is in the business of selling new and used cars, which would result in the recording of turnover?

The car dealership is in the business of selling new and used cars. As selling used cars is part of the dealership's normal business, the sale of the cars would represent turnover.

Example 2

A company has received a £1 million payment from a developer for an 18 month option to purchase its premises at a price of £40 million. The option payment has been received by the company at the year-end and is non-refundable. Can it be taken to income in the year?

Application Note G to FRS 5, paragraphs G11 and G12 (see para 9.13) make it clear that the sale of the company's premises would not give rise to revenue to be included in turnover. Instead, under paragraph 20 of FRS 3, 'Reporting financial performance', the gain or loss on sale of fixed assets is shown after operating profit.

The option payment is similar to a non-refundable deposit and should not be recognised in the profit and loss account until performance has occurred, that is, until either the option is exercised or lapses. It is not considered appropriate to recognise this amount rateably over the year since the right to consideration is not earned until the option period lapses. Furthermore, in circumstances where a breach of contract occurred, a full refund could be pursued through the courts. If the developer purchases the property the £1m will form part of the proceeds on disposal. If the developer does not purchase the property the option fee would be recorded as other operating income when the option period ends.

9.15 Similarly, interest receivable may constitute turnover for some entities, but not for others. The interest charged by banks on loans made to customers is turnover. The interest represents a gross inflow of economic benefits arising from the bank's ordinary course of business. Conversely, interest charged by a manufacturing company on delinquent customer receivables is not turnover. Deriving interest income is not part of a manufacturing company's ordinary activities.

Identifying the transaction

9.16 Revenue has a variety of names: sales, turnover, fees, interest, dividends, royalties and rents. Many transactions are straightforward, but some can be highly complex. Outsourcing contracts, barter transactions, service contracts, contracts with multiple elements and contracts with milestone payments often provide challenges in understanding what the transaction entails, how much revenue should be recognised and when it should be recorded.

9.17 Revenue should be recognised in accordance with the substance, not the form, of a transaction. Application note G to FRS 5 sets out factors to consider in assessing a transaction's substance, for example in accounting for bill and hold arrangements or in presenting turnover as a principal or as an agent.

9.18 The substance will be determined based on the contractual terms, or the combination of the contractual terms of linked transactions, not only on the transaction's immediately visible effects. Contracts, while inherently form-driven, often provide strong evidence of the intent of the parties involved, as the contract is generally how the parties to the transaction protect their interests. Other factors, such as local legal frameworks and business practices, will also need to be taken into consideration, as well as any side agreements to the contract or other agreements between the parties.

9.19 Understanding a transaction's substance requires more than a high-level knowledge of the business deal. It is often a lack of understanding of the details of contracts or the existence of items such as side letters or verbal agreements that leads to difficulties in properly understanding the transaction. Only once the transaction has been properly understood, can the questions of when and how much revenue to recognise be addressed.

Timing of recognition

9.20 FRS 5 Application note G states that a seller should recognise revenue under an exchange transaction with a customer, when, and to the extent that, it obtains the right to consideration in exchange for its performance. At the same time, it normally recognises a new asset, usually a debtor. [FRS 5 App G para G4].

9.21 This principle incorporates the basic elements of performance and rights to consideration, which are both necessary for revenue recognition. Performance on its own is insufficient for revenue recognition, because no asset is created by performance alone. A right to consideration is not sufficient on its own because, although the right creates an asset, there is a corresponding liability for future performance and no revenue is recognised until such performance takes place.

9.22 Performance is defined in the application note as *"the fulfilment of the seller's contractual obligations to a customer through the supply of goods and services"*. The right to consideration is defined as *"a seller's right to the amount received or receivable in exchange for its performance"*. [FRS 5 App G para G3]. The application note continues *"This right does not necessarily correspond to amounts falling due in accordance with a schedule of stage payments which may be specified in a contractual arrangement. Whilst stage payments will often be timed to coincide with performance, they may not correspond exactly. Stage payments reflect only the agreed timing of payment, whereas a right to consideration arises through the seller's performance"*. [FRS 5 App G para G3].

9.23 When a seller receives payment from a customer in advance of performance, it recognises a liability equal to the amount received (often referred to as deferred revenue), representing its obligations under the contract. When the seller performs its obligations and, thereby obtains the right to consideration, it reduces the liability and recognises that reduction as revenue. [FRS 5 App G para G5].

9.24 This principle again demonstrates the link between performance and right to consideration. Both are essential before revenue can be recognised. It also establishes the principles for measuring the obligation for future performance. Revenue is not recognised in advance of performance, but rather the consideration received is deferred as a liability and the amount of the deferral is the full amount received in respect of future performance, not the cost of providing the goods or services.

9.25 A seller may obtain the right to consideration when it has fulfilled some, but not all, of its contractual obligations. Where the seller has only partly fulfilled its contractual obligations, it recognises revenue to the extent that it has obtained the right to consideration through its performance. [FRS 5 App G para G6].

9.26 This principle again links the elements of performance and rights to consideration. However, it establishes a hierarchy that places rights to consideration above performance. This is because in a situation where a seller may have performed ninety per cent of its obligations, but has obtained rights to only fifty per cent of the total consideration, revenue recognition would be limited to that fifty per cent. It is the right to consideration that determines the amount of revenue that can be recognised not the degree of performance. In practice, partial performance of contractual obligations will normally earn the same proportion of the total right to consideration in a contract. However, there may, for instance, be contracts with trigger clauses where no rights to consideration are obtained until performance is substantially complete (see further para 9.133).

What activities constitute performance?

9.27 Given that revenue may be recognised as performance takes place under a contract (provided there are no trigger events) the question arises as to what constitutes performance.

9.28 Consider two contrasting scenarios. A manufacturer may make standard items of stock that are not specific to any customer or items that are customer-specific. For example, contrast a stationery supplier who contracts with a stationery manufacturer for a lorry load of plain white photocopier paper (which is one of the manufacturer's main lines) with a customer who contracts with a stationery supplier for delivery of 50 reams of paper headed with its address and logo (the stationery supplier does the printing in house).

9.29 In the first of these two cases, it is likely that if the stationery supplier cancelled its order for white paper the manufacturer could claim only nominal damages, because it can easily sell the paper elsewhere. However, in the second case, if the customer cancels the order for printed stationery, the stationery supplier will be unable to sell the paper elsewhere and will seek damages from the customer for the full value of the order.

9.30 The difference between the two examples is that the stationery manufacturer would have manufactured the photocopier paper irrespective of the order from the paper supplier. The stationery supplier, however, would not have printed the 50 reams of paper for its customer without the customer's specific order.

9.31 The general principle drawn from this example is that an activity will constitute part of a contract's performance only if it is a necessary part of the contract, in that it is specific to the customer and would not have taken place had the contract not existed. This means that manufacturing a generic product for general sale is not 'performance' in respect of a contract, but manufacturing is part of the performance of a contract where, and to the extent that, it is a necessary part of the contract, because it is specific to the customer.

9.32 Thus, a manufacturing activity that is specific to a customer should be distinguished from one that is merely specified by a customer from a range of alternatives that are standard. For example, when purchasing a new car a customer may specify certain choices, for example, colour, optional extras and accessories. Because these are not specific to the customer, but are merely selections from a standard range, they are not treated as part of performance of the contract. However, if a customer were to order a house built to the customer's own specification, that activity would be specific to a customer.

9.33 Administrative, indirect and pre-contract activities and expenditure do not form part of the contract's performance. They are not, therefore, taken into account in determining the extent to which revenue should be recognised. This is not to imply, however, that associated costs must be written off as expenses as they are incurred. They may be recognised as assets if they satisfy the necessary recognition criteria. The most obvious example is the manufacture of generic stocks. That manufacture is not part of a specific contracted performance, but the assets are recognised until such time as they are sold or otherwise appropriated to a contract. See further chapter 20.

9.34 Just as revenue should not be recognised where performance has not occurred, revenue should only be deferred where there remains an obligation to perform in respect of the deferred element. Consider two examples:

- Sale of right to use software for £10,000. There is no time limit on the use of software and no obligation on the part of the vendor to upgrade the software or to provide any further services or support whatsoever.
- Sale of the right to use the same software for £9,900 but only for five years. Again, there is no obligation on the vendor to upgrade the software or provide further services or support whatsoever.

9.35 The reason for the difference in price being very small is that the value of the software is expected to be very low after five years. Looked at another way the customer who pays £10,000 is only paying £100 for the right to use the software from year five onwards.

9.36 In neither case does the vendor have any obligation to the customer for any performance after the software is delivered. Application note G requires revenue to be recognised when the seller performs. In the second of the above examples, a time period is stipulated over which the customer can use the software, but the income should not be spread over that five year period because, after delivery, there is no requirement for the seller to perform.

9.37 This illustrates the fact that the presence in a contract of a time element does not necessarily change the contract's substance.

9.38 It is possible to use variants of the examples above to illustrate that two questions need to be asked when evaluating when a supplier's performance occurs and when consideration should be recognised.

9.39 The first of these is *"what is the subject of the contract, that is, what is the customer obliged to pay for?"* In the second example above the contract was for the customer to use the software for five years and the customer was obliged to pay for this, whether it used the software or not. If instead the contract had been that the customer had to pay £6,000 for two years but could cancel after two years or renew for a further three years for £3,900, then the revenue to be recognised initially would have been £6,000 only and the £3,900 could not be recognised until the end of the second year and then only if the customer renewed.

9.40 Having identified the economic benefits that are the subject of the contract the second question is *"to what extent have they been transferred to the customer"*, and conversely, *"to what extent does the customer's access to them depend on the supplier's future performance?"* In both of the original examples above control has passed to the customer and performance has occurred. This is contrasted, however, with the situation where a customer pays for one year's hire of a bank safety deposit box, but where the customer remains dependent on the bank for access. Control, therefore, remains with the bank and full performance has not occurred at the outset. Performance occurs over the 12 month period and revenue is, therefore, recognised over that period. Another way of looking at this is that the bank still has unfulfilled promises under the agreement that it will breach if it fails to give the customer access at the times and for the period specified in the contract.

9.41 Another example would be the lease of a car for a year. Although the customer has control of the car for that year, the lessor can repossess if the rentals are not made and the lessee can claim a refund if the car is not roadworthy at any time in the year. As a result, control remains with the lessor over the period and revenue is recognised over that period.

Measurement of revenue

9.42 Revenue should be measured at the fair value of the right to consideration. Normally this will be the price specified in the contract, net of discounts, value added tax and similar sales taxes. [FRS 5 App G para G7].

9.43 Fair value is defined as the amount at which goods or services could be exchanged in an arm's length transaction between informed and willing parties, other than in a forced or liquidation sale. [FRS 5 App G para G3]. As noted above, the fair value of consideration is normally the price specified in the contract. However, there are situations where the amount of the contract price will need to be adjusted to arrive at the fair value and thus the amount to be recognised as revenue. These situations are described below.

9.44 Where the effect of the time value of money is material to reported revenue, the amount of revenue recognised should be the present value of the cash inflows expected to be received from the customer in settlement. The unwinding of the discount should be included in finance income, because it represents a gain from a financing transaction. [FRS 5 App G para G8].

9.45 Discounting may be necessary if goods are sold on extended credit. Normal terms of settlement (say, 30 days) are unlikely to give rise to a material difference if the consideration is discounted over that normal credit period. However, if the period of credit is unusually long, the effect of discounting may be material and this principle then requires the consideration to be split between the fair value of the consideration for the goods sold (recognised as revenue) and the consideration for the grant of extended credit (recognised as finance income).

Example

A company sells goods on extended credit. The goods are sold for £1,200 on 1 January 20X1, receivable on 1 January 20X3. The customer can borrow at 4.5 % a year.

Management should determine the fair value of the revenue by calculating the present value of the cash flows receivable. On the transaction date, revenue of £1,099 is recorded, being £1,200 discounted for two years. The discounted receivable should be updated at each balance sheet date to reflect the passage of time. The resulting increase in the receivable represents finance income and should be recognised as such over the period from the date of sale to the expected date of receipt of cash.

9.46 If, when entering into a transaction, there is significant risk that there will be default on the amount of consideration due and the effect is material to reported revenue, an adjustment to the price specified in the contract is necessary to arrive at the amount to be recognised as revenue. [FRS 5 App G para G9].

9.47 In practice, we consider that the application note should be interpreted in the same way as IAS 18. That is, revenue should be recognised to the extent that it is probable that the transaction's economic benefits will flow to the entity. This treatment rests on the fact that the approach in the application note is based on the 'assets and liabilities' concept. This concept would not permit revenue to be recognised, unless at the same time an asset was created or a liability reduced. Under FRS 5, assets are defined as *"rights or other access to future economic benefits controlled by an entity as a result of past transactions or events"*. [FRS 5 para 2]. Control is *"the ability to obtain the future economic benefits relating to an asset and to restrict the access of others to those benefits"*. [FRS 5 para 3]. Assets should be recognised if there is sufficient evidence of the existence of the item (including, where appropriate, evidence that a future inflow of benefit will occur) and the item can be measured at a monetary amount with sufficient reliability. [FRS 5 para 20]. Where there is significant risk of default the adjustment required by the application note could often be such as to reduce the revenue recognised to nil.

9.48 In practice we expect adjustments of this nature to be extremely rare. It is hard to envisage circumstances where an entity would enter into a transaction with another party and at the time of the transaction be aware of a significant risk of default. However, the following two examples illustrate the point.

Example 1

A water company supplies water to domestic customers. A number of customers are unable to pay their bills and have not paid them for some time. However, the water company is barred by statute from cutting off their supply. As the water company continues to supply these known customers, it is aware at the time of entering into the transaction that there is a significant risk of default. Therefore, paragraph G9 of Application note G requires that the revenue should be adjusted to reflect the risk of default. In this circumstance, the adjustment is likely to bring the revenue to nil or, where a specially discounted rate has been negotiated, that rate should be used.

Example 2

An Eastern European state has a telecom company with a monopoly on the supply of the state's telephone services. Certain members of the government are provided with the service free of charge. A decision is taken to privatise the company and move to commercial billing arrangements for all customers. Post privatisation the government members are billed for the services they use on normal commercial terms. A number of the government members have ignored the post privatisation billing arrangements and have never paid their bills. Their names are recorded on a special list and they are known as VIP customers. Whilst the company continues to bill these VIP customers, management have taken the decision that they do not wish to pursue them for payment.

Again in this example the company knows at the time it enters into the transaction that there is a significant risk of default. Therefore, revenue should be adjusted to reflect the amount of consideration the company expects to receive.

9.49 A feature of both the above examples is that the supplier can identify the individual customers that carry a significant risk of default in advance of entering into the transaction. This is distinct from the situation where a company knowingly transacts with a portfolio of customers with a relatively high credit risk and expects to suffer bad debts of approximately ten per cent of revenue but does not know which customers will default. In this circumstance, no adjustment would be made to revenue, instead the bad debt expense would be recorded as an operating expense. Paragraph G9 of Application note G deals only with the rare circumstances when a company knows at the time of entering into a particular transaction with a known customer that there is a significant risk of default.

9.50 There may also be circumstances where the risk of default is less clear-cut. The transaction may involve future cash flows that are uncertain because of the time period over which they are expected to be received and the customer's credit profile. In these circumstances, the risk of default may be accounted for by adjusting the likely cash flows or by adjusting the discount rate applied to the deferred consideration for risk. IAS 18 envisages situations where there is doubt about the customer's credit standing. It requires that the discount rate used to arrive at the present value of deferred consideration should be the more clearly determinable of:

- the prevailing rate for a similar instrument of an issuer *with a similar credit rating*; or
- a rate of interest that discounts the instrument's nominal amount to the current cash sales price of the goods or services.

[IAS 18 para 11].

9.51 The principles of the application note could be applied using the same approach as in the first bullet point above, that is, the discount rate could be adjusted for credit risk applicable to the customer. Alternatively, the cash flows could be adjusted to reflect the risk and discounted using the risk free rate. This is the most common approach in practice.

9.52 Subsequent adjustments to a debtor as a result of changes in the time value of money and credit risk should not be included within revenue. [FRS 5 App G para G10].

9.53 This principle is consistent with the reversal of the discount being presented in finance income. Whilst the application note does not specifically say so, we consider that changes in the adjustment for credit risk that have been built into the discount rate should be reflected in finance income in the same way as the unwinding of the discount related to the time value of money. In substance, this reflects a gain or loss from providing extended credit, rather than from the sale of goods or services.

9.54 In summary, we consider that the principles of the application note as regards discounting above should be interpreted in the same way as the corresponding provisions of IAS 18. IAS I8 summarises succinctly the treatment of uncertainties about collection of consideration as follows:

> *"Revenue is recognised only when it is probable that the economic benefits associated with the transaction will flow to the entity. In some cases, this may not be probable until the consideration is received or until an uncertainty is removed. For example, it may be uncertain that a foreign governmental authority will grant permission to remit the consideration from a sale in a foreign country. When the permission is granted, the uncertainty is removed and revenue is recognised. However, when an uncertainty arises about the collectability of an amount already included in revenue, the uncollectable amount or the amount in respect of which recovery has ceased to be probable is recognised as an expense, rather than as an adjustment of the amount of revenue originally recognised."*

[IAS 18 para 18].

9.55 Note that removal of an uncertainty in respect of revenue that has not previously been recognised because of that uncertainty, results in revenue recognition. This contrasts with the situation where revenue has been recognised, but an adjustment has been made for credit risk. As explained above changes in the adjustment for credit risk are not treated as revenue.

Variable consideration

9.56 Where there is uncertainty about the total amount of revenue receivable under a contract, at least the minimum amount receivable under the contract should be recognised when performance has taken place and the right to consideration has been obtained, with a higher amount being used only if that is a better estimate and its receipt is within the seller's control.

Within customer's control

9.57 An example of the situation where variable amounts are within the customer's control is where a customer of an estate agent agrees to pay a fixed amount for the agent to advertise the property for a fixed period. Additionally, there may be a contingent variable fee, dependent on the property being sold and on the price at which it will be sold. Once the estate agent has performed the service of advertising the property for the fixed period it should record the fixed fee receivable. The variable contingent fee would normally be recognised only when the property has been sold. The principle here is that once the seller has performed the contractual services, it should recognise the minimum that the customer is obliged to pay. The estate agent has no right to the variable element of the consideration until the property has been sold. The variable amount should not be recognised until the sale has occurred and the estate agent has a right to it.

Within seller's control

9.58 Generally the only situations where consideration is within the seller's control is where the seller is paid according to its performance or an aspect of performance.

9.59 An example might be a construction contract where completion of the contract by a certain date may give rise to a bonus payment, or where non-completion by a certain date gives rise to a penalty or deduction from an agreed consideration.

9.60 Where performance is incomplete, such that it is not known whether bonuses or penalties (or neither) will arise, a fair estimate of the outcome should be made. This method involves predicting the actual outcome and adjusting it for risk.

Within control of neither seller nor customer

9.61 Consider the sale of a piece of land, where the seller will receive additional consideration if planning permission is subsequently granted on the land. The seller has fully performed at the time of sale, however, some of the consideration will only be paid upon the granting of planning permission. This is an event that neither party can control.

9.62 Application note G of FRS 5 is clear that revenue should be recognised when the seller has obtained the right to consideration as a result of its performance. In this example performance is complete at the time of sale, however the seller does not have the right to all the future consideration as it only obtains this right after the occurrence of a contingent future event.

9.63 The additional consideration should, therefore, only be recognised as the right to consideration arises, that is, upon the granting of planning permission. Revenue should only be recognised when the contingent event is no longer contingent, that is, it has occurred or become virtually certain. However, the seller would need to consider whether it has a contingent asset, which should be disclosed under FRS 12, 'Provisions, contingent liabilities and contingent assets'.

Sale of goods

9.64 The principles set out above are sufficient for the most straightforward of transactions. For example, a contract for the sale of goods will normally give rise to revenue recognition when all the criteria for revenue recognition have been satisfied. That is, usually when delivery of the goods to the customer takes place. The example below illustrates the application of the revenue recognition principles and also illustrates how the application of the assets and liabilities approach and the matching concept can give the same result.

Example

In this example various scenarios are set out and the application of the basic principles examined.

Scenario 1
Goods costing £5,000 are purchased in year 1 and are sold (and delivered) for £8,000, also in year 1.

Scenario 2
Goods costing £5,000 are purchased in year 1 and are sold (and *Scenario 3*
Goods costing £5,000 are purchased in year 1, a customer orders the goods in year 2 and pays £2,000 in advance. Delivery takes place in year 3 with the balance of £6,000 paid by the customer in that year.

Revenue recognition would be as follows:

Scenario 1
There is a contract for sale in year 1 and the conditions for recognition of revenue are fulfilled in year 1 on delivery of the goods. Therefore, revenue of £8,000 is recognised. At the end of the year, the £5,000 spent on purchasing the goods does not qualify as an asset as it does not give rights to future economic benefits (as those benefits have already been received in the form of the sale consideration). Therefore, the £5,000 is written off to profit and loss as a cost of sale.

Scenario 2
At the end of year 1, there is no contract for sale (or sale transaction) so there is no revenue recognised. The cost of the goods (£5,000) qualifies as an asset, because it provides a right or other access to future economic benefit controlled by the entity as a result of a past transaction. Therefore, £5,000 is recorded as an asset – stock.

In year 2, revenue of £8,000 is recognised as there is a contract for sale and the conditions for recognising revenue are fulfilled on delivery. At the same time the stock is de-recognised, because there are no longer any future economic benefits to be derived from it and the £5,000 is charged as a cost of sale.

Scenario 3
At the end of year 1, there is no contract for sale (or sale transaction) so no revenue is recognised. The cost of the goods (£5,000) qualifies as an asset, because it provides a right or other access to future economic benefits controlled by the entity as a result of a past transaction. Therefore, £5,000 is recorded as an asset – stock.

In year 2, an order for the stock is received, so there is a contract. However, because the conditions for recognising revenue (the example assumes they are only met on delivery) have not been met by the end of year 2 no revenue can be recognised. The customer has, however, paid £2,000 in advance. This amount should be recorded as a liability until such time as it is discharged (by delivery of the goods) and this applies whether or not the amount is refundable.

In year 3, delivery has occurred and revenue of £8,000 is recognised (£2,000 is released from liabilities and £6,000 is received in the year). The asset of £5,000 is derecognised, because there are no longer any future economic benefits to be derived from it and the £5,000 is charged as a cost of sale.

Transfer of significant risks and rewards of ownership

Bill and hold sales

9.65 Bill and hold sales are those where a customer obtains title to goods, but physical delivery is deferred until the customer requests delivery or collects the goods. [FRS 5 App G para G43].

9.66 Normally, revenue on sale of goods is only recognised when the performance conditions have been satisfied and the right to consideration has been obtained. One such performance condition is usually delivery of the goods to the buyer.

9.67 The issue, therefore, arises as to whether in the absence of delivery, the seller should recognise revenue and a right to consideration or whether it should continue to recognise the stock. [FRS 5 App G para G44].

9.68 The response would appear to depend on whether or not there has been substantive performance of the contractual obligations and whether the seller has obtained the right to consideration. Normally, for example, a customer might place an order for goods and then take delivery. Revenue would be recognised at the point of delivery. However, if the supplier agreed to offer a discount to the customer to accept title to the goods before delivery and to request a delay in delivery, the substance of the arrangement has not changed, but it could be argued that the arrangement is now a 'bill and hold' sale.

9.69 Clearly it would be wrong to advance income recognition as the result of an artificial arrangement such as that described above. Therefore, some specific conditions are needed to distinguish bill and hold sales from mere executory contracts. Goods cease to be assets of a seller and become assets of a customer when the seller transfers to the customer access to the significant risks and benefits of the asset and in exchange receives the rights to consideration. The principal benefits and risks for the customer are:

Benefits

- The right to take possession of the goods as and when required.
- The sole right to the goods for their sale to a third party and the right to the future cash flows from such a sale.
- No exposure to changes in prices made by the seller subsequent to the date of the bill and hold arrangement. (For example, changes to the seller's standard price list.)

Risks

- Slow movement, resulting in increased costs of financing and holding the stock and obsolescence risk.
- Risk of being obliged to take delivery of the goods even if they have become obsolete or not readily saleable, with the consequence that there may be no onward sale or that such onward sale can only be made at a reduced price.

[FRS 5 App G para G45].

9.70 The application note states that, in order for the seller to have the right to recognise changes in its assets or liabilities and turnover, arising from its right to consideration in respect of a bill and hold arrangement, the contract should have all of the following elements:

- The goods should be complete and ready for delivery.

- The seller should not have retained any significant performance obligations other than storing the goods safely and arranging for their despatch when the customer requests it.

- Subject to any rights of return, the seller should have the right to consideration whether or not the goods are delivered in due course to the customer. Where there are rights of return, the arrangement's commercial substance, particularly in respect of transfer of risk, must be carefully considered to determine whether revenue may be recognised. Rights of return are considered from paragraph 9.75 below.

- The goods must be separately identified from the seller's other stock and should not be capable of being used to fill other orders that are received between the date of the bill and hold sale and delivery of the goods to the customer.

- The terms of the bill and hold sale should be in accordance with the customer's commercial objectives and not those of the seller (although, in many cases, the commercial objectives of the seller and customer will be mutually compatible). An example where the arrangement will be in line with the customer's commercial objectives is where the delay in delivery is to meet the customer's need for flexibility in the timing and location of delivery.

[FRS 5 App G para G46].

9.71 In relation to the fourth bullet point above, the reason for the requirement for the goods to be separately identified from the seller's other stocks is as follows. In a normal sales contract the passing of economic benefits and risks occurs on delivery, when specific goods are appropriated to the contract and passed to the customer. Until then, if the goods are of a general sort manufactured by the seller, the goods are not specific. The seller can still sell stocks that are earmarked for the customer and substitute similar stocks when it comes to delivery. Only if the goods are separately identified and unable to be used to fill other orders should the customer be deemed to have secured the stock's economic benefits on passing of title. 'Separately identified' would include (but would not be confined to) stocks that are so specific to the customer that they are unable to be replaced from the other general stocks of the seller. Examples of such stock might be stationery that is printed with the customer's name or goods manufactured to a customer's specification and not otherwise made by the seller or obtainable by the seller from other sources.

9.72 Where the conditions listed above are satisfied and the stock is considered to be the customer's asset, the seller should recognise the changes in its assets and liabilities and revenue. Where any of the conditions are not satisfied, the stock will continue to be the seller's asset and retained on its balance sheet. Any amounts received from the customer should be included in creditors as they represent the seller's liability to fulfil its contractual obligations. [FRS 5 App G paras G47, G48].

Payments in advance

9.73 Payments received in advance of performance do not represent revenue, because they have not been earned. Until the seller performs, the increase in cash is matched by an increase in liabilities, representing an obligation to supply goods or services or to make a refund.

Example 1

A company manufactures and supplies reproduction furniture. Since the choice of the final colouring and polishing of the furniture is left to the customer, the company takes a large non-refundable deposit from the customer at the time of the initial order. In some situations, the piece ordered is in stock and only needs finishing before it can be despatched to the customer, in other cases the item needs to be completely manufactured.

At first sight,it might appear as though there are many points along the production process at which revenue could be recognised: when the deposit is received provided the item only needs finishing; or when the goods have been despatched to the customer and the invoice has been raised.

However, revenue must not be recognised when there is simply an intention to acquire or manufacture the goods in time for delivery regardless of whether payment has been received. Revenue cannot be considered to be earned until the manufacturing process is complete, including the finishing, and the goods have been delivered and all risks and rewards have been transferred, since this is a significant part of the process. Indeed, recognition may need to be delayed until the customer has accepted the goods if the conditions of sale allow the customer to return furniture if the final colour and polish are unsatisfactory and the incidence of such returns cannot be assessed and provided for. If acceptance is unlikely to cause difficulty, then revenue can be recognised on despatch of the completed items.

Example 2

A distiller has obtained a contract to supply whisky at a later date for which the purchaser has made part payment at the time the contract was signed. The contract is for the sale of 600,000 gallons, but the distiller only has a stock of 200,000 gallons. The contract contains specific instructions with regard to the timing and location of the delivery.

For the 400,000 gallons that are not in stock, there can be no recognition of a sale; revenue cannot be recognised when there is merely an intention to acquire goods in time for delivery. The 200,000 gallons that are in stock may fall under the provisions outlined in paragraphs 9.65 to 9.72 above with regard to 'bill and hold' sales, in which delivery is delayed at the buyer's request, but the buyer takes title and accepts billing.

Example 3

A company supplies furniture to customers. In the past it has recognised income when goods are delivered. It now wants to change the policy to recognise income when deposits (35 per cent of sales price) are received and before goods are delivered, on the grounds that the deposits are non-refundable.

Application Note G to FRS 5 on revenue recognition states in paragraph G4 that *"a seller recognises revenue under an exchange transaction with a customer, when, and to the extent that, it obtains the right to consideration in exchange for its performance. . . .".* In relation to amounts received in advance, paragraph G5 states *"When a seller receives payment from a customer in advance of performance, it recognises a liability equal to the amount received, representing the obligation under the contract. When the seller obtains the right to consideration through its performance, that liability is reduced and the amount of the reduction in the liability is simultaneously reported as revenue".* In this situation, it is not enough that revenue has been received, it should also be earned through performance before recognition takes place. Income in this case is not earned, we consider, until the goods are delivered. This is so, even though the deposit is non-refundable. Application Note G states in the 'Development of the application note' section (para 39): *". . .the principle as to when the seller should recognise turnover in respect of a fee does not necessarily depend on whether or not a fee is refundable. Whilst the fact that a fee is stated to be non-refundable may suggest that the seller has no further performance obligations in respect of that fee, in some cases an obligation to provide goods or services may remain".* In this case, the whole obligation to provide goods remains until the goods are delivered and so no revenue should be recognised until that point.

9.74 When an event is held at a particular time, income and costs may be received and incurred in advance. For example, exhibitions and conferences or courses may involve delegates paying in advance of attending and certain of the costs, such as advertising, may also be incurred in advance. Since performance does not occur and revenue is thus not earned until the exhibition is held or the course is given, the payments in advance represent a liability, which can be released to the profit and loss account when the event takes place. A stringent review of the costs incurred before the event is necessary because such costs should only be carried forward if they are directly related costs and they qualify for recognition as an asset under FRS 5. Table 9.1 gives an example of such an accounting policy for exhibition income and expenditure.

Table 9.1 – Emap plc – Annual Report and Accounts – 31 March 2007

Accounting Policies (extract)

Exhibition income

Exhibition income is recognised when the event has taken place.

Goods despatched subject to conditions (sale or return; consignment)

9.75 Some contracts may give the customer the right to return goods that they have purchased and obtain a refund or release from the obligation to pay. [FRS 5 App G para G49]. This occurs more often than in the obvious example where goods are held by a customer on a sale or return basis. For example, retailers often have a policy of giving refunds on returned goods, whether or not the goods are defective, provided only that the goods (for example, clothes) have not been used. Rights of return can be explicit or implicit in contractual arrangements and can also arise through statutory requirements. [FRS 5 App G para G50].

9.76 Application note G provides an analysis to determine the effect of rights of return on the recognition by a seller of changes in its assets and liabilities and turnover. It notes that rights of return in a contractual arrangement may affect the quantification of the seller's right to consideration compared to an arrangement that does not include any rights of return, but which is otherwise identical. The existence of rights of return may also affect the timing of revenue recognition. The reason for this is that the right of return imposes an obligation on the seller to transfer economic benefits to the customer should the customer return the item. Such a transfer of economic resources would normally be in the form of a refund or credit note. In some cases, the existence of the right of return would oblige the seller to defer recognition of the sales transaction for as long as the seller retains substantially all the risks associated with the goods. [FRS 5 App G paras G51, G52].

9.77 The sales transaction and the right of return that creates an obligation to transfer economic benefits to the customer in the event that the goods are returned are linked transactions. The seller should, therefore, account for changes in its assets and liabilities and turnover so as to reflect both the sale and any loss expected to arise from the rights of return. Thus, turnover should exclude the sales value of expected returns. [FRS 5 App G para G53].

9.78 A seller will normally be able to estimate reliably the sales value of returns. In doing so, it should consider the risk that returns will be made, which will in normal situations be less, and probably considerably less, than the seller's maximum potential obligation. The estimates of the risk of returns may be derived from the seller's historical experience of the amount of similar goods that have been returned in the past as a proportion of total sales of the product that have been made on a sale or return basis. [FRS 5 App G para G54].

9.79 Where the seller is unable to estimate reliably the sales value of future returns, it should calculate the maximum possible amount that it could be required to repay to the customer, in accordance with its contractual arrangement. This amount should then be excluded from turnover. [FRS 5 App G para G55]. To the extent that cash or other consideration has been received from the customer, a liability would be recorded up to the maximum amount that could be refundable. Conceivably, the maximum possible amount could be the whole, or substantially all, of the consideration for the original sale and, hence, the seller would have retained substantially all the risks associated with the goods.

9.80 Where the risk of return is so significant that the seller retains substantially all of the risks associated with the goods, the seller would not be able to recognise changes in its assets and liabilities or turnover, because it would not have earned the right to consideration. Hence, the seller should retain the goods on its balance sheet and recognise any amounts received from the customer as payments in advance (that is, as a liability). [FRS 5 App G para G56].

9.81 The application note sets out the appropriate accounting treatment. It states that:

- A seller should record changes in its assets and liabilities and turnover to the extent that its performance has earned it the right to consideration, taking account of the expected loss from returns. The amount of turnover recognised should exclude the sales value of expected returns.
- At each reporting date, the seller should re-estimate the amount of expected returns, taking account of changes in expectations and the expiry of rights of return. Adjustments to the estimate of returns should be recorded as revenue.
- Where a seller has been unable to recognise changes in its assets and liabilities and turnover, because substantially all the risks associated with the goods have not been transferred to the customer, the seller should recognise such changes and turnover on the earlier of:
- The date when it is able to estimate reliably the level of returns.
- The date when the right of return expires or is given up.

[FRS 5 App G paras G57 to G59].

9.82 In relation to rights of return, a contrast may be drawn between the example of a clothing retailer, which would expect customers to exercise the option to return clothing only in a minority of cases, and a wine merchant, which might supply glasses for functions, but expect the majority of the glasses to be returned with only those that are broken or lost resulting in actual sales.

9.83 In the former case, based on the analysis above, the most appropriate treatment would be to recognise revenue less an appropriate allowance for returns, whereas in the second case it would be more appropriate not to recognise revenue until the right of return expires (by which time most of the glasses would be returned with the result that little revenue is recognised).

Example

A clothing retailer sells T-shirts at a price of £10. The T-shirts cost the retailer £5 to purchase. Customers have the right to return T-shirts within 28 days of purchase, provided that the T-shirts are unworn and undamaged. Based on past experience, the retailer expects that 10% of T-shirts will be returned, of which half will be subsequently resold by the retailer.

Because the retailer expects only a minority of T-shirts to be returned and it can reliably measure the level of returns, revenue can be recognised when the sale is made, adjusted for the expected level of returns. Thus for each T-shirt sold, £9 will be recognised as revenue, with the remaining £1 of consideration recognised as a provision. Cost of sales recognised on each sale will be £4.75, with the remaining £0.25 (5/10 × 50%) of the reduction in stock partially offsetting the provision for returns. This adjustment reflects the impact of the returned goods in measuring the provision in accordance with FRS 12, 'Provisions, contingent liabilities and assets'.

9.84 Table 9.2 illustrates a policy for returns in respect of book sales.

Table 9.2 – Pearson plc – Annual Report– 31 December 2004
Accounting policies (extract)
d. Sales (extract)
Sales represent the amount of goods and services, net of value added tax and other sales taxes, and excluding trade discounts and anticipated returns, provided to external customers and associates.
Revenue from the sale of books is recognised when title passes. Anticipated returns are based primarily on historical return rates.

9.85 Consignment sales or items despatched on a sale or return basis are also covered by the principle of ensuring that performance must have taken place and the right to consideration obtained, before recognising revenue. If the purchaser of goods on consignment has undertaken to sell the items on the seller's behalf, then revenue should not be recognised until the purchaser has sold the goods to a third party. This recognition point is the same for goods sold on a sale or return basis or sales to distributors or dealers where the purchaser is merely acting as an agent for the seller.

Example 1

A company imports sports clothing and has a number of distributors. It gives its distributors an extended credit deal whereby it supplies new fashion items worth £10,000 to each distributor for sale to third parties in order to encourage a market in these new items. The distributor does not have to pay for the goods until payment from the third party to which they are sold has been received. If they are not sold within six months of receipt, the distributor can either return them to the company or pay for them and keep them.

Revenue should not be recognised by the company until the earlier of the distributor receiving payment for the sale of the goods to a third party or six months after the distributor receives them, provided that they are not returned. It is only at this point that the company can determine whether performance under the sales contract has occurred and the risks and rewards of ownership have passed to the distributor, because until then the goods may be returned to the company. Until it is known whether the goods have been sold, the goods should continue to be treated as the company's stock.

Example 2

A furniture company offers goods for sale on deferred payment terms (over three years). The company does not charge interest on these deferred payment sales. It has been agreed that the company should account for the notional interest element on the sale of the goods.

The notional interest should be accounted for as an increase in cost of sales by debiting cost of sales and crediting deferred income initially and then debiting deferred income and crediting interest receivable over the three year period.

Which is the most appropriate treatment?

It would appear that where sales are made on extended credit there should be an amount attributed to notional interest. This is certainly true where the credit period is two to three years as in this case, although where the period is less than a year the issue is more problematical and will depend on the materiality of the effect of the discount given. Paragraph G8 of Application Note G to FRS 5, states:

> *"Where the effect of the time value of money is material to reported revenue, the amount of revenue recognised should be the present value of the cash inflows expected to be received from the customer in settlement. The unwinding of the discount should be credited to finance income as this represents a gain from a financing transaction."*

Thus, reducing turnover by the amount of the notional interest and then accounting for it by debiting debtors and crediting interest over the three year period is the correct treatment in this case.

A possible alternative of treating the notional interest as an increase in cost of sales by debiting cost of sales and crediting deferred income initially and then debiting deferred income and crediting interest receivable over the three year period is not in accordance with Application Note G and would leave turnover overstated by the amount of the notional interest.

Continuing managerial involvement

9.86 Application note G does not specifically consider the concept of continuing management involvement, however, the definition of an asset in the ASB's Statement of principles is *"rights or other access to future economic benefits controlled by an entity as a result of past transactions or events"*. [Statement of principles para 4.6]. It, therefore, follows that if an entity retains significant control over the asset, the transaction is not a sale and revenue is not recognised. This is similar to the guidance in IAS 18, which lists continuing managerial involvement to the degree usually associated with ownership or retention of control as one of the criteria to be considered in determining whether revenue should be recognised. [IAS 18 para 14].

9.87 Continued managerial involvement to the degree usually associated with ownership is less straightforward than control, but it is highly unlikely that an entity would retain such involvement without retaining also the asset's economic benefits. Nor is it likely that a buyer would allow such involvement if it had given fair consideration for the asset. Therefore, commercially, continuing involvement to the degree envisaged should not normally occur if a genuine sale has taken place. If it does, it is likely that there are other features of the arrangement that would need to be considered.

9.88 Examples in which a seller has retained continuing managerial involvement or effective control include:

- The seller can control the future price of the item.

- The seller is responsible for the management of the goods subsequent to the sale.
- The terms of the transaction allow the buyer to compel the seller, or give an option to the seller, to repurchase the item.
- The seller guarantees the return of the buyer's investment or a return on that investment for a limited or extended period.
- The transaction's substance is merely an option to purchase the item.

Example

Entity A sold a racehorse to entity B, but continued to house and train the horse, determine which races to enter and set stud fees for the horse. Should entity A recognise revenue on the sale of the horse to entity B?

If a proper training agreement was in place that provided a commercial fee for the services entity A provides and any winnings or fees achieved by the horse going to the buyer, it may be appropriate to recognise revenue on the sale. However, it would also be necessary to consider whether entity A had given any guarantees or incurred other obligations that would indicate it had not disposed of the significant risks and rewards of ownership of the horse.

[The next paragraph is 9.90.]

Warranties

Initial warranty

9.90 A warranty is often provided in conjunction with the sale of goods. Warranties represent guarantees made by the seller that a product will perform as specified for a period of time. Warranties should not be confused with general rights of return. A warranty only permits a customer to return or exchange a product if the product does not meet the specified performance criteria. Warranty costs represent additional costs that the seller may have to incur in relation to the product it has sold.

9.91 When a company sells a product subject to warranty, it must first determine whether the warranty represents a separable component of the transaction. (Multiple element arrangements are considered further from para 9.145). When a warranty is not a separate element and represents an insignificant part of the transaction, the seller has completed substantially all the required performance and can recognise the full consideration received as revenue, on the sale of the product. The expected future costs to be incurred related to the warranty should not be recorded as a reduction of revenue but rather should be recorded as a cost of sale, as the warranty does not represent a return of a portion of the sales price. The costs of warranties should be determined at the time of the sale, and a corresponding provision for warranty costs recognised. Warranties and similar costs can normally be measured reliably because entities have historical evidence of the costs associated with various products. However, if such costs cannot be measured reliably, revenue should not be recognised until the warranty period has expired and the related warranty costs are identified.

Example

A manufacturer of televisions sells them to retailers for £300 with a one year manufacturer's warranty. The manufacturer does not sell the televisions without this warranty, nor does any manufacturer of a similar product. The manufacturer expects claims to be made on one in every 100 televisions sold, with repairs costing an average of £100.

The warranty is not separable from the sale of the television. As a result, the revenue recognition criteria must be applied to the transaction as a whole. On making the sale to the retailer, the manufacturer has completed substantially all of its required performance, retaining only an insignificant interest in the risks of holding the stock. Thus, on the sale of the television the manufacturer should recognise revenue of £300 and make a provision of £1 against cost of sales for the expected cost of repair.

Extended warranty

9.92 An extended warranty is an agreement to provide warranty protection in addition to the scope of coverage of a manufacturer's original warranty, or to extend the period of coverage provided by the manufacturer's warranty. They are often sold separately from the original product but, where warranties included in the price of a product provide protection in excess of that provided by the normal terms and conditions of sale for the relevant product, the transaction's substance is that the entity has sold two products. This might be the case if similar warranties are sold separately by the entity or by competitors of the entity, or if the customer is able to purchase the same product with no equivalent warranty.

9.93 If a company sells an extended warranty, the revenue from the sale of the extended warranty should be deferred and recognised over the period covered by the warranty, as an extended warranty is similar in nature to a short-duration insurance contract. No costs should be accrued at the inception of the extended warranty agreement.

Example 1

Company A sells electrical goods. The goods come with a manufacturer's 1 year warranty. Company A also offers customers the option of purchasing an extended warranty to cover years 2 to 5.

The sales price of the extended warranty is £100 and company A typically receives valid warranty claims from 4% of customers during the extended warranty period. The average cost of repairing or replacing the goods under the warranty is £600 per valid claim.

As this is an extended warranty, management should defer the revenue and recognise it on a straight-line basis over years 2 to 5, which is the period over which the extended warranty is provided.

The costs incurred under the warranty should be charged to cost of sales as incurred and management should not recognise a provision for the expected costs of the warranty, but should monitor the arrangements to ensure that the expected future cost of the warranty does not exceed the amount of unamortised deferred revenue. The warranty contract will be onerous if, at any time, the expected future costs of meeting the warranty obligations exceed the unamortised warranty revenue. Management should recognise a provision to the extent that the future warranty costs are estimated to exceed the unamortised warranty revenue (see chapter 21).

Example 2

X plc is a retailer of domestic appliances and sells washing machines. Each of a particular model of washing machine is sold with a three-year extended warranty at no extra cost to the customer. X plc sells this washing machine for £399 in its stores, while its competitor, Y plc, sells an identical washing machine without an extended warranty for £379 and an unrelated insurer offers an equivalent warranty for £60.

How should X plc account for its income from the sale of the washing machine and the warranty?

Paragraph 13 of IAS 18, 'Revenue', requires for companies accounting under IFRS that, where a single transaction is made up of two or more separately identifiable components, it may be appropriate to recognise the revenue earned in respect of each component of the transaction separately (Refer to 9.145).

The substance of this transaction is that X plc has sold two products: the washing machine and the extended warranty. Where two or more components of a contractual arrangement operate independently from each other, they should be 'unbundled' and the revenue earned on the sale of each product recognised separately in accordance with the principles of Application note G.

X plc will need to attribute a fair value to each component of the bundle. Where the bundle of goods is sold at less than the aggregate of the fair values of each component, the discount should be allocated to the components on a reasonable basis.

For X plc, one calculated fair value of the washing machine is £344 (being £399 x £379/(£379 + £60)). It will be appropriate to recognise this revenue because X plc has fulfilled its contractual performance obligation relating to the supply of the washing machine in full.

The calculated fair value of the extended warranty is £55. This should be recognised over the three years over which it is earned by X plc.

Installation fees

9.94 Application note G requires that *"A seller recognises revenue under an arrangement with a customer, when and to the extent that, it obtains the right to consideration in exchange for its performance"*. [FRS 5 App G para G4]. Consideration received for the sale of a product may include amounts attributable to the product's installation. Where installation is incidental to the product's sale, installation fees are recognised when the goods are sold as the entity's remaining performance obligations are negligible. If installation is not incidental to the product's sale, and represents a separate component of the transaction (see further from para 9.145), the installation fees should be recognised as performance occurs. This applies the same principles as are applied to accounting for warranties.

9.95 Determining whether installation is incidental to the sale of a product or not is often difficult. In the case of a telephone line, for example, it can be argued that the installation is usually straightforward.

9.96 Where installation is more complicated, for example, in a contract to supply a computer system, the contract may be broken down into separate components one of which would be the installation. However, this approach would only be possible where a reliable fair value could be ascertained for the installation component (see para 9.145 onwards for further consideration of multiple element transactions). Alternatively, if a fair value could not be obtained, revenue would be recognised according to the stage of completion of the whole contract.

Shipping and handling charges

9.97 Where a company sells items either FOB (free on board) or CIF (cost, insurance, freight), this may affect the timing of revenue recognition. If the company is responsible for carriage, insurance and freight, these form part of the company's performance and result in retention of the risks and rewards of the item sold until delivery to the client site has occurred. The timing of revenue recognition will usually be different where an item has been sold on an FOB basis, in which case recognition on despatch of the item is likely to be acceptable. In addition, if the seller is acting only as an agent in respect of the carriage and insurance, then revenue may be recognised upon despatch provided no other risks and rewards are retained by the seller.

9.98 Shipping and handling charges are common in many industries. Charges may be levied to customers based on:

- Specific amounts dependent upon general geographic region.
- A single specified amount irrespective of the geographic location of the customer.
- The actual amount incurred to ship the item to the specific customer.

9.99 There is no specific guidance within UK GAAP that addresses accounting for shipping and handling charges. However, the application note is clear that amounts collected on behalf of third parties are not revenue. [FRS 5 App G para G68]. As such, shipping and handling charges should not be included as part of revenue if the seller is acting as an agent on behalf of the shipper. Where the entity is able to determine the additional margin it will receive from the shipment (or the additional cost it is willing to bear), this indicates that the entity is not acting as an agent. This will normally be the case in the first two situations highlighted above. Where the seller is acting as an agent, as might be the case in the third bullet point above, revenue should be recognised net of any shipping or handling charge (see para 9.161 onwards for further consideration of agency transactions).

Sale of property

9.100 Transactions involving the sale of property often straddle a financial year end. For example, a contract may be exchanged before the year end and completed after the year end. The legal documentation surrounding the sale should clarify when rights to the property are transferred and legal advice may be necessary in specific cases. In general, however, where an unconditional and irrevocable contract has been entered into for the sale of a property, the profit arising on the sale can be recognised at the time when the contract is exchanged (see Table 9.3).

Table 9.3 – Kingfisher plc – Annual report and financial statements – 29 January 2005

Accounting policies (extract)

Disposal of land and buildings

Profits and losses on disposal of land and buildings represent the difference between the net proceeds and the net carrying value at the date of sale. Sales are accounted for when there is an exchange of unconditional contracts.

9.101 It is appropriate to recognise the income when an unconditional and irrevocable contract has been entered into, because the equitable and the beneficial interests already vest in the purchaser, who has a legal commitment for the outstanding purchase consideration. The situation is, therefore, no different from goods sold on credit. If, however, the contract is conditional, recognition should be delayed until the last material condition is satisfied. It is only when all the material conditions have been satisfied that the gain can be considered to be earned.

Example

A company sold land to a developer. At the company's year-end contracts had been exchanged, but completion was set for two years hence. The developer negotiated the delay in completion to allow time for its plans to be approved. The price of the land is fixed in the contract and is in no way contingent on planning being approved.

The company's accounting policy in respect of land sales is to recognise revenue on exchange, provided that the contract is unconditional and irrevocable. In this situation whilst the completion is delayed, the contract is not conditional on planning approval being obtained or on any other factor and in all respects meets the criteria of being unconditional and irrevocable.

Application note G of FRS 5 requires that revenue should be recognised when performance has occurred and a right to consideration is obtained. It further requires that revenue is recognised at fair value and that where at the time revenue is recognised there is a significant risk of default, on the amount of consideration due, an adjustment is made to the reported revenue.

The fact that there is a delay in completion may mean that there is an increased risk of default. In determining the amount of revenue that should be reported, regard should be had to risk factors such as the financial standing of the developer, the likelihood that it will still be in existence in two years time and whether there are any financial guarantees in place. If the company believes it is probable that economic benefit will flow to the entity as a result of this transaction, it is appropriate to recognise the revenue, discounted for the time value of money if this is considered material. Alternatively, the decision may be reached that the risk factors are of such significance that it is not probable, at the reporting date, that the economic benefits associated with the transaction will flow to the entity. In which case, revenue recognition should be deferred until such time as it becomes probable that economic benefit will flow to the entity.

9.102 Property is often sold subject to planning consent being obtained. In these situations, the vendor may be involved in obtaining the required planning consent and may incur costs in submitting planning applications and attending planning hearings. Obtaining the required planning permission is a material contract condition. Therefore, even if the vendor has performed all the tasks necessary to obtain consent before the year end, the sale cannot be recognised until the condition is satisfied and the consent has been granted. If such consent is received after the year end, then the sale should be recognised the following year when the material condition is fulfilled.

9.103 Therefore, revenue should only be recognised on sales of property in a year if a binding and unconditional contract has been entered into before the year end or if the last material condition on a conditional contract has been satisfied before the year end. If the contract is entered into after the year end or if a condition is only fulfilled after the year end, then that sale represents the next year's revenue since it is only in the following year that it has been earned.

9.104 Many companies do not take credit for sales, commonly of private houses, until legal completion has taken place, as is illustrated in Table 9.4. This policy is, therefore, more conservative than recognising revenue on the exchange of unconditional contracts. The property industry has historically taken a more prudent approach to the sale of homes to individual buyers. However, the choice of either of these methods will usually depend on the circumstances of the sale.

Table 9.4 – Tarmac PLC – Annual Report – 31 December 2000
Principal Accounting Policies (extract)

Turnover

Turnover represents the net amount receivable, excluding value added tax, for goods and services supplied to external customers and, in respect of long term contracting activities, the value of work executed during the year. Sales of newly constructed private houses are included in turnover on legal completion.

9.105 Some property companies enter into transactions in which they build properties for particular customers (following the customer's detailed plans) rather than building speculative developments. The properties built may be effectively pre-sold so that the contract has been entered into before construction begins and all the terms and conditions of the sale are known. In such situations, the transaction may be a long-term contract which should be accounted for in accordance with SSAP 9, with profit being recognised according to the percentage of completion of the development, provided that the outcome can be assessed with reasonable certainty. However, selling 'off plan' does not mean it needs to be accounted for under SSAP 9.

Sale of software

9.106 In the software industry, revenue recognition poses a number of problems which combine elements of sale of goods and sale of services. Software houses normally earn their revenue from three principal sources:

- Sale of off-the-shelf or ready made software where the licensing arrangement gives the customer the right to use the software for a specified period.
- Sale of customised software developed for specific application by the customer.
- Sale of software support services related to either own software or customised software.

9.107 Selling software is different from selling a tangible product, since what is being sold is the right to use a piece of intellectual property, rather than the actual computer disk or other media on which the programme is held. The physical delivery of the product in the form of the computer disk may, therefore, appear to be less important than it is where other types of goods are sold. If there is any risk that the customer may reject the software and the product is sold subject to customer satisfaction, then revenue recognition may need to be delayed until after delivery and acceptance by the customer. For example, an off-the-shelf package may require tailoring to meet the customer's specifications. In this situation, if the supply does not qualify as a long-term contract, revenue may not be earned until after delivery, set up and the subsequent testing of the software by the customer.

9.108 The sale of a completely standard package such as a word processor or spreadsheet package may, therefore, need to be treated differently from software that needs to be individually tailored for each customer. Companies that sell standard off-the-shelf packages generally treat their sales no differently than the sale of a physical product and recognise revenue on delivery. For example, Merant's accounting policy adopts this approach (see Table 9.6).

Table 9.6 – Merant plc – Annual Report – 30 April 2002

NOTES TO THE FINANCIAL STATEMENTS (extract)

Licence fees: the Company's standard end user licence agreement for the Company's products provides for an initial fee to use the product in perpetuity up to a maximum number of users. The Company also enters into other types of licence agreement, typically with major end user customers, which allow for the use of the Company's products, usually restricted by the number of employees, the number of users, or the licence term. Licence fees are recognised as revenue upon product shipment, provided a signed agreement is in place, fees are fixed or determinable, no significant vendor obligations remain and collection of the resulting debt is deemed probable. Fees from licences sold together with consulting services are generally recognised upon shipment provided that the above criteria have been met and payment of the licence fees is not dependent upon the performance of the consulting services. Where these criteria have not been met, both the licence and consulting fees are recognised under the percentage of completion method of contract accounting.

Maintenance subscriptions: maintenance agreements generally call for the Company to provide technical support and software updates to customers. Revenue on technical support and software update rights is recognised over the term of the support agreement on a pro-rata basis. Payments for maintenance fees are generally made in advance and are non refundable

Training and consulting: the Company recognises revenues from consulting and education as the services are performed.

9.109 Where a product is sold subject to continuing obligations under the agreement or the provision of updates free of charge, it will be necessary to determine whether the contract can be broken down into separable components. If it can, revenue will be recognised as the separable components are performed – see discussion on multiple element transactions from paragraph 9.145. Where the product's acceptance is in doubt, revenue should be delayed until acceptance.

Example

A company sells software packages that may be modified to meet the customer's exact requirements. The sequence of the transaction is: order; invoice and delivery; and acceptance by the customer. The order, invoice and delivery may be before the year end, but the acceptance may be after the year end.

Where acceptance is subject to installation and inspection the following principles may be relevant. If the installation process is simple in nature – for example, requiring unpacking and connecting only – then it is acceptable to recognise revenue immediately upon delivery. In general, however, where the installation process is more substantial, recognition should be delayed until the installation and inspection processes are complete and customer acceptance has occurred. For many types of software packages, it is acceptable to recognise revenue when delivery has taken place by the year end. However, when there is a risk that the customer may not accept the package, sufficient evidence must be obtained of the acceptance before revenue can be recognised. Unlike most goods sold, software bears more risk of customer rejection and, therefore, acceptance is often required to give reliable evidence of a completed sale.

9.110 The creation of software specifically developed for use by a customer usually meets the definition of a long-term contract in SSAP 9 and revenue should normally be recognised in accordance with the principles outlined in that standard. Consequently, the software house should recognise revenue in a manner appropriate to the contract's stage of completion, provided that the outcome can be assessed with reasonable certainty. The requirements of SSAP 9 are discussed in detail in chapter 20.

9.111 The procedure to recognise profit is to include an appropriate proportion of total contract value as turnover in the profit and loss account as the contract activity progresses. The costs incurred in reaching that stage of completion should be matched with this turnover, resulting in the reporting of results that can be attributed to the proportion of work completed. Where, however, the outcome cannot be assessed with reasonable certainty before the contract's conclusion, or where the contract is of a relatively short duration, the completed contracts method should be applied and, accordingly, revenue should be recognised when final completion takes place. Tables 9.7 and 9.8 give examples of accounting policies in this area.

Table 9.7 – MISYS plc – Annual Report – 31 May 2005

Accounting Policies (extract)

REVENUE RECOGNITION

Turnover represents amounts invoiced to customers for goods and services, net of sales taxes.

Revenue on certain larger composite contracts is recognised on a percentage of completion basis over the period from delivery of the product to customer acceptance. The degree of completion of a contract is measured using the costs incurred to date or milestones reached, depending upon the nature of the individual contract and the most appropriate measure of the percentage of completion. Losses on contracts are recognised as soon as a loss is foreseen by reference to the estimated costs of completion.

For all other contracts, revenue from system sales is recognised when a signed contract exists, delivery to a customer has occurred with no significant vendor obligations remaining and where the collection of the resulting receivable is considered probable. In instances where a significant vendor obligation exists, revenue recognition is delayed until the obligation has been satisfied. No revenue is recognised for multiple deliveries or multiple element products if an element of the contract remains undelivered and is essential to the functionality of the elements already delivered.

Maintenance fees are recognised rateably over the period of the contract. EDI and remote processing services (transaction processing) are recognised as the services are performed.

Revenue from professional services, such as implementation, training and consultancy, is recognised as the services are performed.

Within Sesame, commission revenue received from insurers based on gross premiums written is presented gross of commission payable to Independent Financial Advisers (IFAs) and is recognised when earned. Annual fees received from certain IFAs for industry training, compliance support and access to the Misys network's listing of insurance providers and products are recognised over the relevant subscription period.

Table 9.8 – LogicaCMG plc – Annual Report and Accounts – 31 December 2004

Report of the directors (extract)

Principal activities

Throughout the year group companies, including branches, were in the business of providing information technology services, concentrating on:

- the marketing, design, production, integration and maintenance of custom-built software and associated hardware systems
- consultancy, applications management and project management in the field of information technology
- the design, development, implementation and marketing of software products and the reusable elements of applications software, called systems kernels
- the outsourcing of information technology services.

Accounting policies (extract)

Recognition of profits

Profit on contracts for the supply of professional services at pre-determined rates is recognised as and when the work is performed, irrespective of the duration of the contract.

Profit is taken on fixed price contracts while the contract is in progress, having regard to the proportion of the total contract which has been completed at the balance sheet date and estimated costs by reference to the costs incurred to date versus total estimated costs to completion. Provision is made for all foreseeable future losses.

9.112 When the project involves the provision of hardware as well as software, the contract will need to be carefully reviewed to ensure that income is not recognised before it is earned, that is, before performance has occurred and a right to consideration obtained.

Example

A company is developing a computer system for a customer. It has sold the hardware to the customer for a profit and this has been installed on the site where it will be eventually used, but the company is still working on developing the necessary software. The customer has the right to return the hardware if the software does not work. The company does not anticipate any problems with the software development which should take 12 months.

It seems that there is one contract for the supply of both hardware and software. If this is the case then the treatment in SSAP 9 should be followed. The contract is a long-term contract, revenue and profit would be recognised as the contract progresses, provided that the outcome can be assessed with reasonable certainty. The extent of profit recognition will depend on the degree of certainty over the contract's outcome rather than the margin on the hardware in isolation. If the outcome of the project or the costs of creating software of the required standard cannot be assessed with reasonable certainty, then no profit should be reflected in the profit and loss account.

Even if the contract for the supply of the hardware could be separated from the supply of the software there would still be an argument for delaying recognition of the sale of the hardware. If there is uncertainty about the possibility of return, revenue should only be recognised when the goods have been formally accepted by the customer or the goods have been delivered and the time allowed for their possible rejection has passed. Therefore, until the software has been installed and tested to the customer's satisfaction, revenue should not be recognised and any payments received for the hardware should be included in the financial statements as a liability.

9.113 Where a software house provides maintenance services or other after sales support it is necessary to determine if this can be regarded as a separable component. If it can, (see from para 9.145) then revenue under the separable component method is recognised as performance occurs. For example, maintenance revenue will be recognised as the service is provided. See Table 9.9.

Table 9.9 – Total Systems plc – Annual Report & Accounts – 31 March 2005

Accounting Policies (extract)

Software maintenance (extract)

For own software covered by maintenance contracts, income is credited to the profit and loss account over the period to which the contract relates. Costs associated with these contracts are expensed as incurred.

9.114 FRS 5 Application note G includes guidance on separation and linking of contractual arrangements (see from para 9.145) and illustrates the guidance with two examples relating to sales of software and related maintenance services. In the first example a customer purchases 'off the shelf' software from a seller who also offers a support service comprising helpline assistance and advice about the operation of the software package. Analysis of the arrangement shows that the customer has no obligation to purchase the support service and that the support service is not needed to enable the software to operate satisfactorily. In this case, there are two components of the contract and the seller should recognise turnover separately for each. [FRS 5 App G para G33]. The example is simplistic and should also consider two important criteria: (i) the seller must be able to determine fair values for each component; and (ii) the two components should operate independently of each other. For the meaning of 'operate independently', see paragraph 9.147.

9.115 The second example in the application note concerns the sale and maintenance of bespoke software and the customer's right to future upgrades for a period of three years. Analysis of the arrangement shows that the maintenance and upgrades are required to ensure that the software continues to operate satisfactorily throughout the three year period. These upgrade and maintenance services are offered only by the seller of the (bespoke) software. The application note concludes that the commercial substance is that the customer is paying for a three year service agreement and that the seller should treat all three components of the transaction (software, upgrades and maintenance) as linked and recognise turnover on a long-term contract basis. [FRS 5 App G para 34]. This conclusion was reached because the components do not operate independently of one another (that is, they cannot be sold separately and none of the components is available from another supplier) and fair values are not available for the individual components. It is key that this transaction involved the sale of 'bespoke' software. In other situations, the sale of ancillary services (and particularly maintenance) would normally be available for sale separately and/or as optional extras from the same or other suppliers.

Sale of services

Performance over time

Accounting for incomplete contractual performance

9.116 Full performance, that is fulfilment of contractual obligations, may not always occur immediately. Two examples where performance is not immediate are where performance of a single contract with only one component occurs over a period of time, and where performance of separate components of a contract are completed at different times (see further guidance on multiple element transactions from para 9.145 onwards).

9.117 Where performance of a single contractual obligation takes place over time and the right to consideration is obtained over that period, then revenue should be recognised as performance takes place. For example, under a maintenance contract for 12 months, revenue should be recognised over the 12 months as the service is provided over that period. It is not acceptable to record all the revenue upfront and provide for the costs expected to be incurred in providing the services, this is because to do so would be to recognise revenue before the seller had performed any part of the contract and before the seller has obtained the right to consideration.

9.118 Application note G of FRS 5 deals specifically with revenue recognition in relation to long-term contractual performance. It notes particularly that the seller should recognise changes in its assets and liabilities, and turnover, in accordance with the stage of completion of its contractual obligations, which reflects the extent to which it has obtained the rights to consideration. [FRS 5 App G para G6].

9.119 Following controversy surrounding the interpretation of Application note G to professional services firms, the UITF issued Abstract 40, 'Revenue recognition and service contracts'. Although the main controversy surrounded the revenue recognition of professional services firms, UITF Abstract 40 applies to all contracts for services.

9.120 The Abstract concludes that:

- Where a contract is for the provision of a single service or a number of services that constitute one project and the performance of that service or those services falls into more than one accounting period, the contract should be accounted for as a long-term contract in accordance with SSAP 9. [UITF 40 paras 24, 25].
- Where a contract is not a long-term contract, but the seller's contractual obligations are performed over time, revenue should be recognised as the contract progresses to reflect the seller's partial performance. The amount of revenue recognised should reflect the seller's right to consideration by reference to the value of the work performed. [UITF 40 para 26].
- Where the right to consideration does not arise until the occurrence of a critical event (a trigger event), the revenue should be recognised when that trigger event occurs. [UITF 40 para 27].

9.120.1 The principles of UITF 40 are illustrated in the following example.

Example

A celebrity, Miss C, has agreed with a TV company to make a guest appearance in an episode of a programme to be broadcast on the TV company's network. Miss C is entitled to a fee of £10,000 when her appearance is filmed and a further £2,000 each time the programme is repeated on the TV company's channels.

When considering how Miss C should record her earnings, reference needs to be made to UITF 40, which requires that when a contract is for the performance of a single service, the revenue earned under that contract should be recognised in the period in which the service is performed. Only where the contract is for a single service and the contract activity falls into two or more accounting periods should the revenue be recognised as the contract progresses.

However, where the substance of the arrangement is that the seller does not have a right to revenue until the occurrence of a 'trigger event' outside the seller's control, then revenue should not be recognised until the trigger event has occurred.

Therefore, when Miss C makes her appearance and is filmed (fulfilling her contractual performance and thereby giving her the right to consideration), £10,000 of revenue should be recognised. The airing of a repeat by the TV company is outside Miss C's control and is an event that triggers the payment of additional revenue of £2,000. This additional revenue should be recognised as and when the show is repeated.

9.121 Although Application note G considers accounting for long-term contracts, it does not change SSAP 9, but does suggest an important and overriding principle in how that standard is applied. Prior to the issue of Application note G the 'costs incurred as a proportion of total costs' method of determining the stage of completion was probably the most common method in use. The application note does not prevent use of this method, but it points out that this method will not always be appropriate. The application note states that the amount of turnover should be derived from the proportion of costs incurred only where these provide evidence of the seller's performance and hence of the extent to which it has obtained the right to consideration. [FRS 5 App G para G21]. To use the proportion of costs incurred as a basis for recognising turnover requires the seller to be able to demonstrate that costs incurred provide reliable evidence of performance of the contract terms and the right to consideration.

9.122 SSAP 9, 'Stocks and long-term contracts', contains principles for the recognition of revenues and costs on long-term contracts. These principles and the guidance in the application note that relates to long-term contracts are more fully described and discussed in chapter 20.

9.123 Where revenue from a contract is spread evenly over the period of a contract, because the service is provided evenly over that period, there is sometimes a problem if the up-front costs of securing the contract are written off as they are incurred. This is because the recognition of such costs may mean that the contract is loss making in the early stages and profitable later.

9.124 Because the approach in the Statement of principles, FRS 18 and Application note G to FRS 5 on revenue recognition is to apply the 'assets and liabilities' approach, it is not acceptable either to advance revenue recognition or to defer expense recognition (unless they meet the definition of an asset). The requirement in the application note that the right to consideration must be obtained before revenue may be recognised clarifies this, because such rights would not normally be obtained from incurring such up-front costs. Revenue should, therefore, not be advanced, but should be spread evenly if the service is performed and rights to consideration are obtained on that basis. Instead of advancing revenue it is necessary to look at whether any of the up-front costs would qualify for recognition as an asset, so that they could be carried forward and expensed as the future economic benefits that relate to that asset are recognised (as revenue).

9.125 The most common assets recognised as a result of expenditure in the early stages of a contract are stocks and tangible fixed assets. The criteria for recognition of such assets are considered in chapters 20 and 16 respectively.

9.126 In addition, Private Finance Initiative (PFI) contracts may raise specific issues and problems relating to asset recognition and, to some extent, revenue recognition. Accounting for PFI contracts is dealt with in chapter 3.

Determining the stage of completion of performance

9.127 SSAP 9 requires that turnover should be ascertained in a manner appropriate to the contract's stage of completion, the business and the industry in which it operates. [SSAP 9 para 28]. With regard to recognising revenue based on the stage of completion of performance IAS 18 is not dissimilar from SSAP 9 and contains additional guidance that can assist with SSAP 9's application.

9.128 According to IAS 18, the stage of completion of performance may be determined by a variety of ways depending on the nature of the service being provided. If the service consists of an indeterminate number of acts over a specified period of time, for example, the provision of a maintenance contract, then the revenue should be recognised on a straight line basis over the contract's duration, unless there is evidence that another basis more accurately reflects the stage of completion. If one particular act in the contract's performance has a much greater significance than any of the other acts, then the revenue recognition should be postponed until the significant act is completed.

9.129 In general, the methods that might be used to determine the stage of completion would include those recommended by IAS 18:

- Surveys of work performed.
- Services performed to date as a percentage of total services to be performed.
- The proportion that costs incurred to date bear to the estimated total costs of the transaction. Only costs that reflect services performed to date are included in costs incurred to date. Only costs that reflect services performed or to be performed are included in the estimated total costs of the transaction.

[IAS 18 para 24].

9.129.1 Application of these methods is considered in the the following example:

Example

A company provides consultation services, for example maintenance, IT support, marketing and general advice to a number of service providers. The service providers bring together buyers and sellers of agricultural produce and earn revenue from this. The company earns a non-refundable flat fee of £8,000 annually, receivable in advance, from each service provider, plus an additional 50 per cent of the revenue that each service provider earns from its transactions above a cumulative £10,000.

As the £8,000 fee is for a service during a year, it should be recognised evenly over the year. The remaining incremental fees should only be recognised as they are earned. This is because until they are earned, there is no guarantee that a further amount will be receivable. That is, the incremental revenue is only recognised when the service provider has earned revenue in excess of £10,000 and then only to the extent of 50 per cent of the excess over £10,000.

9.130 The application of the 'percentage of completion' basis where the provision of services straddles a year end is considered in the following examples.

Example 1

A company has entered into fixed rate contracts with local authorities to inspect and report on local property values. Valuation reports were completed and sent out before the year end, but due to administrative problems, invoicing was delayed until after the year end.

Since the work has been completed as evidenced by the submission of the valuation reports and since the contracts are fixed rate, it is acceptable to recognise the revenue and profits on the work performed before the year end.

Example 2

The facts are the same as in example 1 except that the valuation reports were not completed until after the year end.

UITF Abstract 40 clarifies that this is a long-term contract that falls to be accounted for in accordance with SSAP 9. UITF Abstract 40 states that a contract for services should be accounted for as a long term contract where contract activity falls into different periods and it is concluded that the aggregate effect is material for all such contracts. [UITF Abstract 40 para 25]. It will, therefore, be appropriate to recognise revenue to the extent to which the contract is completed, provided the outcome can be assessed with reasonable certainty.

On the other hand, if writing and submitting the reports formed the majority of the work required to complete the contracts, then it would be appropriate to delay recognition until the reports were completed.

9.131 Until the outcome of a transaction can be estimated reliably, revenue should only be recognised to the extent of the costs incurred that are expected to be recoverable. If it is not probable that the costs can be recovered, then they should be written off immediately.

9.132 In other situations, determining the stage of completion may be more a matter of determining the degree of performance completed and whether a contract may be broken down into separate components. For example, in the shipping industry, ships may be engaged in journeys to more than one port, which are not completed at the year end. In these circumstances, revenue is often recognised by reference to the last leg of the journey completed before the year end, as long as there is no doubt that payment will be received. This would be on the basis that the contract is capable of being broken into separable components. Similarly, a tour operator may have a package tour that departs before the year end, but which does not return until after the year end. It could be argued that revenue should not be recognised until the package tour has been completed, since it is only then that the service has been provided. However, in practice, many tour operators recognise revenue on departure provided that all the costs of the package are known and have been accrued. The basis for this would be that by departure performance is substantially complete. Table 9.10 provides an example of recognition of revenue upon completion of holidays, rather then on departure.

Table 9.10 – Carnival plc – Annual Report and Accounts – 30 November 2005

Revenue and expense recognition (extract)

Turnover comprises sales to third parties (excluding VAT and similar sales and port taxes). Guest cruise deposits represent unearned revenues and are initially recorded as customer deposit liabilities when received. Customer deposits are subsequently recognised as cruise revenues, together with revenues from onboard and other activities and all associated direct costs of a voyage, upon completion of voyages with durations of ten nights or less and on a pro rata basis for voyages in excess of ten nights.

Contracts containing significant acts

9.133 In some situations, a contract or a component of a contract may contain a 'trigger event' clause. This may provide that, before the occurrence of the trigger event, the customer has no obligation to pay anything, even if the seller has fulfilled some of its contractual obligations under the contract, until the trigger event occurs. Where this is so, the seller should not recognise revenue until it has fulfilled its contractual obligations *and* the trigger event has occurred. This is because the seller does not obtain the right to consideration until the event has happened. Although performance may have occurred to some extent, Application note G requires (and UITF Abstract 40 clarifies) that, before revenue is recognised, the seller should have obtained the rights to consideration.

Example 1

A professional services company provides advice to a bidder in a takeover situation. Fees are charged on a time basis, but will not be payable unless the bid is declared unconditional. The company normally bills its fees monthly. When should revenue be recognised?

The trigger event is the bid being declared unconditional. Until that point, no revenue should be recognised by the professional services company, even though it may have provided services. This is because, until that point, the company has no rights to consideration (revenue is not receivable) and if that trigger point is not achieved, no revenue will be received.

Example 2

A football club had a coach under contract that gave the club the option to renew the contract for a further year. Another club has paid £100,000 to secure the coach's release from the contract. Should this be recognised immediately or deferred over the next year?

Application Note G to FRS 5, states in paragraph G4: *"A seller recognises revenue under an exchange transaction with a customer, when, and to the extent that, it obtains the right to consideration in exchange for its performance. ..."*. Therefore, the income should be recognised immediately, as, having released the coach from the contract, there are no further performance conditions to be met in earning the income.

Contracts with milestone payments

9.134 Contracts in certain industries, particularly pharmaceutical and biotechnology, are often structured to provide for the payment of cash upon the achievement of certain 'milestones' identified in the contract. Such contracts often relate to research and development of new product offerings and contract terms often include significant up-front payments or payments early on in the contract that in substance represent a form of financing, as opposed to compensation for services provided. Accounting for such contracts can be complex and the appropriate revenue recognition will vary depending on the substance of the arrangements.

9.135 Consideration should be given to a number of factors when determining the appropriate accounting for revenue in a milestone arrangement, including:

- The reasonableness of the payments compared to the effort, time and cost to achieve the milestones. If payments bear no relation to performance under the contracts, then revenue recognition in accordance with the payment profile would not be appropriate.
- The nature of royalty or licence agreements relating to the product being developed. Where a contract includes within it royalty or licence agreements, some of the payments under the contract will often relate to the royalty or licence element in the contract and not to the provision of services and should be accounted for accordingly (see further para 9.255 onwards).
- The existence of any cancellation clauses. Contracts may include cancellation clauses requiring the repayment of amounts received under the contract to date upon cancellation by either party, such cancellation clauses may indicate that recognition of amounts received as revenue is not appropriate.

- The risks associated with achievement of milestones. If payments are dependent upon the achievement of certain milestones, and there is doubt as regards the achievement of the milestones, then revenue should not be recognised until the relevant milestone has been achieved (see further para 9.133 which deals with accounting for contracts containing significant acts).

- Any obligations that must be completed to receive payment or the existence of penalties for failure to deliver. Again, all obligations under a contract must be considered in assessing the extent to which an entity has performed under a contract. The existence of penalty clauses for failure to deliver may reduce the revenue that can be recognised as performance occurs if delivery is not probable or in the control of the entity.

Example

Company A, a small pharmaceutical company, contracts with the much larger company B to develop a new medical treatment for cancer, which is expected to take five years. Company A will periodically have to update company B with the results of its work. Company B has exclusive rights over any development results. Company B will make an up-front payment of £1m on contract signature and five equal annual payments of £500,000 provided company A demonstrates compliance with the development programme. In addition, upon the successful testing of the treatment in clinical trials, company B will pay a further £1.5m. Company A's management estimates the total cost of the contract will be £3m.

Company A incurs costs of £600,000 in year one, in line with its original estimate. Company A is in compliance with the research agreement, including the provision of updates from the results of its work.

How should company A recognise the payments it receives from company B to conduct development?

The contract involves the rendering of pharmaceutical development services. As such, the principles in UITF Abstract 40 should be applied. Company A should recognise the revenue for the payments in accordance with the percentage of completion model, based on an estimate of total costs or on a straight-line basis, whichever provides the most appropriate recognition of revenue. A percentage of completion model based on the estimate of total costs appears to be the most appropriate in the circumstances.

In applying the percentage of completion model, the £1.5m payment upon the successful testing of the treatment in clinical trials will be excluded from any calculation. This is because the payment depends upon a significant act which is not in the control of company A, as successful testing cannot be assured.

In year one, company A has met its obligations, the project is developing in line with the estimates and is forecast to be profitable, so company A should recognise revenue of £700,000 ((1m + 2.5m) ÷ 5), costs of £600,000 (3m ÷ 5) and profit of £100,000. The consideration received in excess of the revenue recognised of £800,000 (1.5m — 700,000) will be recognised as a liability on company A's balance sheet, representing a liability for future performance.

Inception fees

9.136 Application note G describes inception fees as arising from contractual arrangements that require the payment of a fee at inception that permits the customer to purchase goods or services over a period of time. [FRS 5 App G para G35]. The application note's development section notes that such fees may or may not be refundable. However, the principle concerning when the seller should recognise the inception fee as revenue does not necessarily depend on whether or not it is refundable. Although the fact that a fee is non-refundable may suggest that the seller has no further performance obligations in respect of the fee, in some cases an obligation to provide goods or services may remain. [FRS 5 App G Dev para 39].

9.137 In determining whether or not the fee should be recognised as revenue at inception, it is necessary to determine whether or not the fee and the charges for subsequent goods or services operate independently of each other. [FRS 5 App G para G35]. This involves determining whether the components of the contractual arrangement (that is, the inception fee and the subsequent supply of goods or services) should to be treated as linked or as separable components for the purpose of revenue recognition (see further from para 9.145).

9.138 The application note states that often the inception fee together with the charges for subsequent goods or services will provide the seller's return on the contract as a whole. This may be so where the inception fee's payment entitles the customer to purchase subsequent goods or services at a discount to the prices that would otherwise be payable. Where this is the case, the inception fee is not separable from the subsequent supply of goods and services and should be recognised over the period during which the discounted goods or services are expected to be provided to the customer. The inception fee should be recorded as a liability to the extent that it has not been included in revenue. The liability would then be released to revenue on a systematic basis over the period during which the discounted goods or services are provided. [FRS 5 App G para G36].

9.139 Where, however, it can be demonstrated that the seller has no further obligations in respect of the fee once it has been received, the seller should recognise the fee on the date that it becomes entitled to receive it. The seller may have no further obligations in respect of the fee if the customer has to pay the full commercial price for all future goods or services. [FRS 5 App G para G37].

Subscriptions

9.140 The concept that performance must have occurred and the right to consideration obtained before revenue can be recognised in the profit and loss account is also relevant to other types of sales, where payment is received in advance of supply, such as subscriptions. If the subscription consists of the provision of items of a similar value over its duration, such as a typical magazine subscription, then the income should be recognised over the life of the subscription on a straight line basis. If the items provided vary in value, such as a wine of the month club, then the income should be recognised on the basis of the sales value despatched in relation to the total estimated sales value of all the items covered by the subscription. Table 9.11 illustrates an accounting policy where subscription income is recognised on a straight line basis.

Table 9.11 – Pearson plc – Annual Report – 31 December 2004

Accounting policies (extract)

d. Sales (extract)

Subscription revenue is recognised on a straight-line basis over the life of the subscription.

Admission fees

9.141 Admission fees from, for example, artistic performances, banquets and other special events are recognised when the event takes place. IAS 18 contains specific guidance in relation to such fees and states that when a subscription to a number of events is sold, the fee is allocated to each event on a basis that reflects the extent to which services are performed at each event. [IAS 18 App para 15]. The treatment would be the same applying the principles of Application note G, recognising revenue as performance occurs.

9.142 When an event is held at a particular time, income and costs may be received and incurred in advance. For example, exhibitions, conferences and courses may involve delegates paying in advance of attending and certain costs, such as advertising, may also be incurred in advance. Since performance does not occur and revenue is not earned until the exhibition is held or the course is given, the payments received in advance represent a liability, which can be released to the profit and loss account when the event takes place. A stringent review of the costs incurred before the event is necessary, since such costs should only be carried forward if they directly relate to the event being held and qualify for recognition as an asset.

Tuition fees

9.143 Tuition fees should usually be recognised as revenue over the period of instruction, that is, as performance occurs.

9.144 Whilst this deals with the straightforward situation where a single session of tuition is given over a fixed time period, some instruction courses are structured differently. For example, a course may be structured as a number of modules, each of which having repeated tuition sessions staged at regular intervals, with the student able to choose to attend and complete a module at any time within, say, a two-year period. In such a situation it would be more appropriate to recognise revenue as the modules are attended and completed by the student, that is, as the service is provided to the student.

Multiple element transactions

Separation of components

9.145 In some cases a single contractual arrangement may require a seller to provide a number of different goods or services ('components'). These components may be unrelated and capable of being sold individually. [FRS 5 App G para G22].

9.146 Application note G analyses the circumstances where a seller should (or should not) recognise changes in its assets and liabilities and turnover for each component separately. [FRS 5 App G para G24].

9.147 The application note states that a contractual arrangement with two or more components should be accounted for as two or more separate transactions only where the commercial substance is that the individual components operate independently of one another. In this context, components operate independently where each component represents a separable good or service that the seller also provides to customers on a standalone basis or as an optional extra. Alternatively, components operate independently where one or more component can be provided by another supplier. This separation of components of a contract is known as 'unbundling'. [FRS 5 App G para G25].

Allocation of consideration

9.148 For unbundling to be possible the seller should normally be able to attribute a fair value to each component by reference to individual transactions, that is, transactions in which the components are sold separately. [FRS 5 App G para G27]. However, in some situations fair value will only be available for some of the components. Where that happens unbundling of the components is still possible and is discussed further below.

9.149 The application note considers this situation in the context of a contract where there are completed and uncompleted components. As explained in paragraph 9.147 above, it must be demonstrated that these components are capable of operating independently if they are to be unbundled. In determining whether or not the contract can be successfully unbundled, the application note states that where a seller cannot attribute fair values to all components it may be possible to unbundle the arrangement where a fair value can be attributed to either the completed or to the uncompleted components. Where a fair value can be obtained only for the uncompleted components, the seller may be able to calculate a fair value for the completed components by deducting from the total consideration the fair value of the uncompleted components. The same applies in reverse where a fair value can only be obtained for the completed components. However, in that case the application note warns that care should be taken to ensure that turnover is not overstated for the completed components. [FRS 5 App G paras G28, G30]. This is because the total contract price may be at a discount to the sum of the individual fair values of the completed and uncompleted components when sold separately (see para 9.155 below).

9.150 If a contract comprises more than two components and fair values can be attributed only to groups of completed or uncompleted components, those groups should be accounted for as separate components. For example, if a contract consists of three components A, B and C and a fair value can be attributed only to components B and C combined, those components should be treated as a single composite component. Component A may be treated as a separate component because a fair value can be attributed to it by deducting the combined fair value of B and C from the total contract consideration. [FRS 5 App G para G31].

9.151 The application note also deals with contracts that have multiple components, where the components do not operate independently of one another. In such a situation, the seller should account for them as a single contract. Where the contract meets the definition of a long-term contract under SSAP 9 it should be accounted for in accordance with that standard and the guidance in the application note relating to long-term contractual performance. [FRS 5 App G para G32]. Whilst the application note does not say so specifically, components should also be accounted for as one contract where fair values cannot be attributed to any one component or group of components.

9.152 A simple example of a contract with two components might be where a mobile phone company packages within a single sales contract a handset and pre-paid calls. If these two elements are also available for sale separately, their standalone prices may be a good guide as to how the contract price could be allocated between the two components. At the start of the contract, the handset will have been delivered, but provision of the calls will be outstanding. Thus, the revenue from the calls will be deferred and recognised on a usage basis.

9.153 Sometimes, when a contract has been broken down into separate components, some of those components are immaterial. In such a case it may be reasonable to recognise all the revenue when the contract has been substantially performed, that is, ignoring whether the immaterial element has been completed or not.

9.154 In some cases a measurement issue may arise. If the contract value exceeds the sum of the fair value of the separable components it may be that the additional contract value is attributable to some other factor, such as the activity of managing the two contract components. In that case, the management activity will only be performed when the separable components, and thus the full contract, are substantially complete. Therefore, it is at this point that the additional revenue attributable to the management element is recognised.

9.155 The contract value, on the other hand, may be less than the fair value of the separable components. This may indicate some double-counting of components, for example there may be set up time that would be incurred were the components to be performed separately, but which is only needed once when the components are part of the same contract. Another example might be where the seller gives a discount because the customer buys several goods or services (components) together rather than individually. Such double-counting or discounting should be eliminated by apportioning it between the separable components pro rata to their fair values. [FRS 5 App G paras G23, G27]. (Any loss on the overall contract should be recognised at the outset).

Example 1

A company supplies equipment and in addition provides a maintenance service for a year. The price of the equipment and the maintenance package is £100,000. The company also provides maintenance services and equipment sales separately. The price of maintenance contracts is £10,000 per annum, and the cost of the equipment when sold separately is £95,000. Therefore, the equipment and maintenance, if purchased separately, would cost £105,000. How should the sale of the equipment and maintenance package be accounted for?

It is possible to purchase the equipment and the maintenance separately, therefore, the contract has two separable components, the equipment sale and the maintenance contract. The 'discount' of £5,000 should be applied rateably to the fair values of the components so that the equipment should be attributed a value of £100,000 × £95,000 ÷ £105,000 or £90,476 and the maintenance contract would be attributed a value of £100,000 × £10,000 ÷ £105,000 or £9,524 totalling £100,000. The £90,476 of revenue for the sale of equipment would be taken to the profit and loss account on delivery, whilst the £9,524 would be taken to the profit and loss account over the 12 month period of the maintenance contract.

Note: In this example the 'discount' has been allocated between the elements in proportion to the fair value of the revenue estimated for each component. Other methods may be appropriate given different facts and circumstances.

Example 2

A company normally carries out site clearance activities as its sole activity. However, it agrees to clear a site and then order and install two prefabricated buildings for use as temporary offices.

It charges £50,000 for the whole contract. This can be broken down into £10,000, which is the charge it would normally make for the site clearance, and £38,000 for the two prefabricated buildings (cost of £30,000 to the company plus a normal mark-up on such buildings based on its normal profit margins). The balance of £2,000 is attributable to the management of the contract and is a fair price for such services.

The revenue recognition pattern will allow the revenue from the site clearance to be recognised when the work has been performed and right to consideration for that component has been earned. The revenue for the installation of buildings and for management of the contract would then be recognised when the buildings are delivered and installed and the contract is, therefore, complete.

Example 3

A company sells boats for £30,000 each. The company also provides mooring facilities for £2,000 per annum. If a purchaser of a boat also contracts to purchase mooring facilities for a year, there is a five per cent discount on the whole package. Thus the 'package' costs £32,000 less five per cent or £30,400. How should revenue be recognised?

The discount in this case is £1,600. The normal sales price (fair value) of the boat is £30,000 and the normal sales price of the mooring is £2,000.Therefore, the element of the discount attributable to the boat is £1,500 (£1,600 × £30,000 /£32,000) and the element of the discount attributable to the mooring is £100 (£1,600 × £2,000/£32,000). The revenue recognised on the sale of the boat should, therefore, be £30,000 — £1,500 or £28,500 which would be recognised on delivery. The revenue recognised on the moorings would be £2,000 — £100 or £1,900 which would be recognised evenly over the year for which the mooring facility is provided.

Example 4

Company A sells a copy machine in December 20X7 and will provide maintenance services for one year; the total consideration received for both the sale and the maintenance activity is £1,200. Costs expected to be incurred in order to meet the requirements of the sale contract are £700 for the machine and £200 for the maintenance activity; the relative fair values are £1,050 and £150, respectively.

If the entity were to apply a relative fair value approach, this would result in a loss on the maintenance component of the contract. However this would not be appropriate since the contract as a whole is profitable. An alternative policy would be to apply a 'cost plus a reasonable margin' approach.

Having agreed on the overall profit of £300 (for example, for £250 on the machine and for £50 on the maintenance service), this amount is allocated between the two elements of the agreement:

December 20X7	Dr	Cr
Cash	£1,200	
Deferred revenue		£250
Revenue		£950
Cost of sales	£700	
Inventory		£700

9.156 Table 9.12 illustrates an accounting policy for transactions where there are separable components.

Table 9.12 – ARM Holdings PLC – Annual Report – 31 December 2001

1/Principal accounting policies (extract)

Turnover. Turnover (excluding VAT) comprises the value of sales of licences, royalties arising from the resulting sale of licensed products, revenues from support, maintenance and training, and consulting contracts and the sale of boards and software tool kits.

Each licence is designed to meet the specific requirements of each customer. Delivery generally occurs within a short time period after signing. Licence fees are invoiced according to an agreed set of milestone payments. Typically the first milestone is on signing of the contract, the second is on delivery of the customised technology and the third is related to acceptance of the technology by the licensee. Where agreements involve multiple elements, the entire fee from such arrangements has been allocated to each of the individual elements based on each element's fair value. Vendor specific objective evidence of fair value is determined by reference to licence agreements with other customers where elements are sold separately. Revenue from the sale of licences is recognised on a percentage to completion basis over the period from signing of the licence to customer acceptance. Under the percentage to completion method, provisions for estimated losses on uncompleted contracts are recognised in the period in which the likelihood of such losses is determined. The percentage to completion is measured by monitoring progress using records of actual time incurred to date in the project compared with the total estimated project requirement, which corresponds to the costs of earned revenues.

Agreements including rights to unspecified products are accounted for using subscription accounting, revenue from the arrangement being recognised over either the term of the arrangement or an estimate of the economic life of the products offered, beginning with the delivery of the first product.

In addition to the licence fees, contracts generally contain an agreement to provide post contract support. Fees for post contract support, which take place after customer acceptance, are specified in the contract. The fees are determined based on the group's price list as if sold separately. The price list is established and regularly reviewed by management. Revenue for post contract support is recognised on a straight-line basis over the period for which support and maintenance is contractually agreed by the group with the licensee.

The excess of licence fees invoiced over revenue recognised in respect of such fees is recorded as deferred income.

Revenue from consultancy is recognised when obligations are fulfilled; revenue from the sale of development systems is recognised when goods are delivered; and royalty revenue is recognised when notification is received from the customer of product sales, normally quarterly in arrears. Where necessary, the costs associated with providing post contract support on development system sales have been accrued.

[The next paragraph is 9.158.]

Linked transactions

9.158 Application note G also deals with the situation where the commercial substance of two or more separate contracts may require them to be accounted for as a single transaction. This is referred to as the 'bundling' of a contractual arrangement. [FRS 5 App G para G26].

9.159 The application note does not elaborate further on this. However, the issue is dealt with in the main body of FRS 5, paragraph 14 of which states:

> *"A reporting entity's financial statements should report the substance of the transactions into which it has entered. In determining the substance of a transaction, all its aspects and implications should be identified and greater weight given to those more likely to have a commercial effect in practice. A group or series of transactions that achieves or is designed to achieve an overall commercial effect should be viewed as a whole."*

9.160 The main principles of FRS 5, including the above principle from paragraph 14 of the standard, are dealt with in chapter 3. Two examples of where separate contracts may need to be combined are given below. Combination of contracts is also discussed in chapter 20. Combination of contracts that involve sales and purchases from a single third party are discussed in the section 'Two way trading arrangements' below.

Example

A retailer has signed a contract lasting 12 months to purchase certain stocks from a supplier on an exclusive basis (that is, it will not purchase from any other supplier). On signing the contract the company has received from the supplier a 'marketing support' payment. The contract is not entirely specific as to what the payment is for, but it does require that the retailer does not purchase from other suppliers of the same product, does not sell products that are produced by the supplier's competitors, must display the products prominently in the stores and must make purchases at the same level as in the previous year. Can the payment be taken to income immediately or should it be spread over the contract term?

In this case there are two elements to the contract, first an agreement to purchase stocks and secondly an 'exclusivity' agreement. These two elements should be accounted for as part of one overall arrangement. The income in respect of the exclusivity agreement is earned over the period and is subject to significant performance conditions being satisfied, for example, the company must display the supplier's products, not sell competitors' products and so on. It could be argued that until all of these conditions have been satisfied none of the payment has been earned and that it ought, therefore, to be deferred in total until the conditions have been satisfied. However, the satisfaction of the conditions is within the company's control and so it is reasonable that it should spread the income over the period so long as it intends to abide by the conditions for the full period. It would not be acceptable, however, to accrue all the income on day one as the transaction extends over the period of one year and on day one no part of it has been completed.

A second question is where should the revenue be shown in the profit and loss account? The income should not be shown in the turnover line, but should be shown as a reduction in cost of sales, or as a reduction in marketing costs or apportioned between those two categories if such apportionment is practicable. This is because the two elements of the contract need to be considered together (see para 9.159). The substance of the two elements is that the company obtains supplies at a reduced price in return for agreeing to buy exclusively from the supplier, displaying the suppliers' products and so on. Therefore, in substance, the income is in part a discount on purchases (cost of sales) and in part a subsidy of the company's marketing costs (reduction in marketing costs).

Measurement of revenue — specific issues

Agency arrangements

9.161 This issue concerns whether the company is functioning as:

- An agent acting as an intermediary, earning a fee or commission in return for arranging the provision of goods or services on behalf of a principal.

- A principal acting on its own account when contracting with customers for the supply of goods or services in return for consideration.

[FRS 5 App G paras G60, G61].

9.162 Application note G analyses the factors that determine whether a seller is acting as a principal in an exchange transaction or as an agent in relation to a transaction between its principal and the principal's customer. [FRS 5 App G para G62]. In order for a seller to account for a transaction as a principal it should normally have exposure to all the significant benefits and risks associated with at least one of the following:

- The selling price – that is, the ability, within economic constraints, to set the selling price with the customer. The price may be established directly or, where the selling price is fixed, indirectly by providing additional goods or services or adjusting the terms of a linked transaction.
- Stock – that is, exposure to the risks of damage, slow movement and obsolescence, and changes in suppliers' prices.

[FRS 5 App G para G63].

9.163 Other factors that indicate that a seller may be acting as a principal would include:

- Where the seller performs part of the services provided or modifies the goods supplied.
- Where the seller has or assumes the credit risk.
- Where the seller has discretion in selecting suppliers.

[FRS 5 App G para G65].

9.163.1 The following example illustrates some of these principles.

Example

A retailer sells a number of products whose prices are determined by the supplier. The products can be split into two broad categories: electronic (including mobile phone e-top up) and tangible (including mobile phone top up cards, stamps and newspapers). As the retailer has no influence over the price, should the retailer account for sales of these products as principal or agent?

In the transactions being considered, the retailer has no influence over the price, does not modify the goods, bears minimal credit risk (because transactions are routinely for cash, credit card or guaranteed cheque) and has no discretion over supplier selection (as each product is sold by only one supplier, the mobile phone top ups being specific to a mobile phone network). The only exposure that the retailer may have relates to the stock. Where the product sold is electronic and there is no stock of any worth, the retailer is acting as an agent and will recognise its sales commission as turnover.

Where the product sold is tangible and the retailer bears the significant stock risks of obsolescence, damage or theft, then it will be acting as principal and should recognise the sale price as turnover and the associated costs as a cost of sale. However, where the retailer does not bear the significant stock risks, then it will be acting as an agent and will recognise its sales commission as turnover.

9.164 Where a seller acts as an agent it will usually not be exposed to the significant risks and benefits associated with the exchange transaction. Normally, where the seller acts as an agent the agency arrangements will include the following features:

- The seller discloses the fact that it is acting as an agent.
- When the seller has confirmed the customer's order with a third party (usually the supplier who may be the principal), the seller will have no further involvement in the performance of the supplier's contractual obligations.
- The amount that the seller earns is fixed in advance and is either a fixed fee per transaction or a stated percentage of the amount invoiced to the customer.
- The seller bears no stock or credit risk, except where it receives additional consideration from the ultimate supplier (who may be the principal) in return for assuming the risk.

[FRS 5 App G para G66].

9.165 The application note states that where the seller has not disclosed that it is acting as agent there is a rebuttable presumption that it is acting as a principal. [FRS 5 App G para G64].

9.166 When the substance of a transaction is that a seller is acting as a principal it should recognise revenue based on the gross amount received or receivable in respect of its performance under the sales contract with the customer. [FRS 5 App G para G67].

9.167 When the substance is that the seller is acting as agent it should recognise as revenue only the commission or other amounts received or receivable in return for its performance under the contract. In this case the contract in question is usually the agency agreement with its principal rather than the sales contract with the customer. Any amounts received from the customer that have to be paid to the principal should not be included in the agent's turnover. [FRS 5 App G para G68].

9.168 The application note encourages disclosure by agents, where practicable, of the gross value of sales throughput as additional, non-statutory information. Where an agent gives such disclosure it should give a brief explanation of the relationship between recognised turnover and the gross value of sales throughput. [FRS 5 App G para G72].

9.169 The application note includes three examples illustrating how these principles should be applied in particular situations. In the first example, a building contractor has a contract with a customer. Analysis of the contract shows that the contractor negotiates the price, bears any credit risk of customer default and has primary responsibility for the work carried out, including work done by subcontractors. The contractor is, therefore, acting as principal in this transaction. The second example is of a travel agent that acts as an intermediary between holiday companies and customers. The travel agent does not set the price of the holidays and its terms of business exclude any liability to customers after it has put them in touch with a holiday company. The agent receives a fee for each customer that it puts in touch with a holiday company, but has no further involvement after that point. In this situation the travel agent is acting as an agent and should only record the fees as turnover. [FRS 5 App G paras G69, G70].

9.170 In the third example the application note deals with trading concessions operated in department stores. The application note's development section explains that there is a wide variety of potential arrangements between department stores and concessionaires, but that where the department store is not acting as principal in an exchange transaction with the concessionaire's customers it should not include the value of the concessionaire's sales in its own revenues. In the example in the application note, the department store provides space for concessionaires and receives a fixed rental income in return. Analysis of the arrangement shows that the concessionaires are acting as principals in their dealings with customers. In these circumstances, the concessionaires should include as revenue the amounts receivable from sales to customers. The department store should not include in its revenue the value of sales made by the concessionaire. [FRS 5 App G paras G71, Development para 51].

9.171 Another, more complicated example relating to concessions is as follows.

Example

A department store contains concession outlets. Under the terms of a concession agreement, the department store provides the concessionaire with serviced space in the store, sales staff, point of sale equipment and stock-room space. The concessionaire pays the department store a fixed contractual amount of £100,000 each month plus five per cent of the outlet's revenue. The concessionaire determines the stock lines sold and the prices charged to customers and has the right to move stock between its concessions in different stores. At the end of a season, the concessionaire must take back any unsold stock. The agreement between the concessionaire and the department store is not for a fixed term, but is cancellable by the concessionaire at three months' notice and by the department store at six months' notice. How should the department store account for this arrangement?

SSAP 21, 'Leases and hire purchase contracts', defines a lease as *"a contract between a lessor and a lessee for the hire of a specific asset. The lessor retains ownership of the asset but conveys the right to the use of the asset to the lessee for an agreed period of time in return for the payment of specified rentals. The term "lease" as used in this statement also applies to other arrangements in which one party retains ownership of an asset but conveys the right to the use of the asset to another party for an agreed period of time in return for specified payments"*. [SSAP 21 para 14].

The arrangement between the department store and the concessionaire has the substance of a lease. The store retains ownership, but conveys the right to use a specified area of serviced, staffed and networked space to the concessionaire.

The lease is likely to be classified as an operating lease: it is unlikely that substantially all the risks and rewards of ownership of that area of the department store have been transferred to the concessionaire. Furthermore, the minimum contractual lease payments to which the department store is entitled are only for three months' rent, which is unlikely to amount to substantially all of the fair value of the leased space.

SSAP 21 requires that operating lease income is recognised on a straight-line basis over the period of the lease, unless another basis is more appropriate. We consider it most appropriate for the flat monthly rent of £100,000 to be recognised on a straight-line basis.

The revenue-based rent is contingent rent. SSAP 21 contains no guidance on the recognition of contingent rent in operating leases. However, the G4+1 Position Paper, 'Leases: implementation of a new approach', states that contingent rentals should be recognised only when the contingency criteria are met. [G4+1 PP para 11.11(c)]. Thus, the revenue-based rent should be recognised by the department store when the store is unconditionally entitled to it.

The guidance contained in Application note G to FRS 5 requires that the seller recognises the gross revenue. The seller is the entity that is the principal in the sales transaction, having exposure to all significant benefits and risks associated with the selling price and/or the stock. In this example, the concessionaire is able to determine the selling price of each item and bears the significant stock risks of damage and obsolescence. Consequently, the concessionaire will recognise the gross revenue and recognise the rent paid to the department store as a cost.

The department store is, in substance, acting as agent in selling to the customer and is receiving 'commission' (the substance of which is rent) in consideration for the service that it is performing for the concessionaire (making available space in the department store). It should not recognise the gross revenue of the concession. Instead it should report the 'commission' receivable as revenue.

As noted in paragraph 9.168 above, the application note does, however, encourage disclosure in the agent's financial statements of the gross value of sales throughput where the seller is acting as agent. Where such non-statutory information is given a brief explanation of the relationship of recognised turnover to the gross value of sales throughput should be given.

Advertising agency commissions

9.172 Revenue should only be recognised on transactions, including advertising commissions, when the service is completed. The income of advertising agencies may consist of media commissions, which relate to the advertisement appearing before the public and production commissions, which relate to production of the advertisement. Recognition should occur for media commissions when the advertisement appears before the public and for production commissions when the project is completed, for example, as in Table 9.13.

Table 9.13 – WPP Group plc – Annual Report – 31 December 2004
Accounting policies (extract)

Turnover, cost of sales and revenue recognition (extract)

Advertising and Media investment management
Revenue is typically derived from commissions on media placements and fees for advertising services. Traditionally, the Group's advertising clients were charged a standard commission on their total media and production expenditure. In recent years, however, this has tended to become a matter of individual negotiation. Revenue may therefore consist of various arrangements involving commissions, fees, incentive-based revenue or a combination of the three, as agreed upon with each client.

Revenue is recognised when the service is performed, in accordance with the terms of the contractual arrangement. Incentive-based revenue typically comprises both quantitative and qualitative elements; on the element related to quantitative targets, revenue is recognised when the quantitative targets have been achieved; on the element related to qualitative targets, revenue is recognised when the incentive is received/receivable.

[The next paragraph is 9.176.]

Two-way trading arrangements

9.176 Sometimes an issue can arise where one company sells one product to another company and that other company sells a different product to the first company. The Application note G guidance on separation and linking of contractual arrangements (see para 9.145 above), whilst principally concerned with segregation of components of sales contracts or linking of two or more sales contracts, is relevant to this situation and is taken into account in the following paragraphs. Provided the two transactions are not connected and operate independently of each other no problem arises. However, if the commercial substance is that the two contracts do not operate independently of each other, they should be considered together. 'Operate independently' is defined in paragraph 9.147 above.

9.177 Examples where problems may arise are:

- Company A may sell a product to company B which company B uses in the manufacture of a product that is then purchased by company A.
- A retailer may buy goods from a manufacturer and the manufacturer may pay the retailer to promote those products, for example by displaying advertising material round its stores.

9.178 In the first of these examples the issue to decide is whether or not the two transactions should be regarded as two separate contracts or together as one larger contract. The latter will be the case if the contracts are legally or economically conditional or dependent on each other, for example if company A is obliged to purchase the finished product from company B. However, if the contracts are genuinely independent of each other they will be treated as two contracts and company A will recognise profit on the first sale to company B and record the price paid for the product purchased from company B as the cost of that purchase. Generally, the arrangement's individual circumstances will need to be analysed but signs that the contracts are independent would include:

- Company B selling the product manufactured from products supplied by company A to other third parties.
- Company A having no obligation to purchase the product from company B.
- Arm's length market prices for each transaction with price risk resting with company B between the first transaction and the second.

9.179 In relation to the second example above, where a supplier pays a retailer to advertise its products and the retailer purchases goods from the supplier, the same principle applies if the transactions are to be accounted for as separate transactions. That is, the transactions must not be legally or commercially conditional or dependent on each other. This may be so if the prices are arm's length and if the retailer is not obliged to make a certain level of purchases from the supplier in order to obtain the advertising revenue.

9.180 In this second example, if the two transactions are treated as one (possibly because the two conditions detailed above are not met) then it may be necessary to determine whether there is an element of barter, that is goods being exchanged for advertising. In that case it will be necessary to determine the fair value (market price) to the advertiser of the promotional activity in order to determine:

- the extent, if any, to which promotional activity should be seen as giving rise to service revenue for the retailer; and
- the extent to which the promotional payment should be treated as a reduction in the price of the products bought by the retailer.

9.181 Application note G requires that: *"Where a contractual arrangement consists of various components that do not operate independently of each other, the seller should account for them together to reflect the seller's performance of its obligations as a whole in obtaining the right to consideration. ..."*. [FRS 5 App G para G32].

Example 1

A retailer enters into an arrangement with a supplier to purchase goods. The supplier proposes that if the retailer purchases a minimum of £100,000 of goods and undertakes to display advertising for the goods on advertising boards in the retailer's stores for a period of one month the supplier will pay the retailer £10,000. The fair value of this advertising is estimated to be £5,000 based on what the retailer charges other suppliers for equivalent advertising in its stores. How should these transactions be accounted for?

The two transactions are clearly linked in this case. The purchases should be recorded in the normal way, but no revenue from the sale of advertising to the supplier should be recognised. When the trigger event (purchases of £100,000) has been reached and if the performance condition has been satisfied (display of advertising for one month) the retailer should recognise £5,000 as a rebate on the goods purchased from the supplier (that is, a reduction in cost of sales) and £5,000 as revenue for advertising.

Where the £100,000 purchases have been made before the month's advertising has been provided, no revenue should be recognised (until one month has lapsed). However, if the contract was different and specified that the £10,000 would be paid when the £100,000 purchases had been made and would be reduced by up to 50 per cent to the extent that the advertising is not provided, the answer would be different. If that were the case and the £100,000 purchases had been made and half a month's advertising given, £5,000 would be recognised in the income statement, being £2,500 as a rebate for cost/purchases and £2,500 in respect of 50 per cent of the income relating to the provision of advertising.

Example 2

Company A sells materials for making door frames to a manufacturer who assembles the frames and puts glass in the door. Company A then repurchases the doors and sells them to a house builder for installation in homes. It is argued that the sale of the frames and the purchase of the doors are not linked because:

- The manufacturer buys material for the frames regardless of whether the doors can be sold to company A, as the manufacturer has other markets to which it can and does sell assembled doors.
- Company A is not committed to buy doors from this manufacturer as it could and does use other suppliers.
- The price of the door is not fixed at the time the frame is sold and so the manufacturer takes risk on whether or not and at what price it can sell.

Should the sale of the materials for the door frames to the manufacturer be accounted for separately from the purchase of doors from the same manufacturer, or should the transactions be regarded as linked and conditional on each other for accounting purposes?

In any transaction involving a sale to and purchase from a single third party the detailed conditions need to be examined to determine whether or not the sale and purchase should be accounted for separately or as a linked transaction.

In this case, the details indicate that the transactions are not conditional on each other, because the manufacturer takes the risk on the manufactured doors, both in terms of price and because company A does not have to buy any doors from that manufacturer. Therefore, the sales and purchases should be accounted for as separate, distinct transactions.

However, if the facts had been different then the accounting might have been different too. For example, if company A sold the materials (which cost it £5) for £10 per frame and at that time agreed to buy back the materials made up into a finished door with glass fitted for £100, then the two transactions would be linked. This is because the sale carries a corresponding commitment to repurchase the materials in the future at a fixed price. For that reason, company A should not record a sale of the £10 materials (or a profit on that sale). Instead the cost of the materials should be retained in stock and the £10 received from the manufacturer should be recorded as a liability. When the door is repurchased the additional net £90 paid by company A will be recorded as stock, giving a stock value for the completed door of £95.

9.182 Transactions whereby cash is paid by party A to party B are sometimes related to transactions that require party B to pay cash to party A. These transactions have to be carefully analysed to determine if they should be viewed as separate transactions or a single transaction accounted for on a net basis. Factors to consider (in addition to those outlined above) that might lead to a net presentation include:

- The arrangements are entered into in close time proximity to each other and/or their mutual existence is acknowledged in the separate agreements.
- Sufficient verifiable objective evidence does not exist to support the assertion that the amount being charged for the product or service in each transaction is its fair value.
- The party to the transactions that receives the greater amount of cash inflows does not have a clear immediate business need for the product or service it is purchasing.

9.183 The latter point is even more problematic if the party had received cash before it had to pay cash. These types of transactions can be particularly troublesome if they involve what is, in reality, a barter transaction, such as advertising for advertising which is discussed under 'Barter transactions' below (see from para 9.187).

9.184 The UITF considered this subject further when it issued Abstract 36, 'Contracts for sales of capacity', in March 2003. Although aimed principally at transactions involving capacity in the telecommunications and electricity industries, the effect is to allow a gross presentation of two-way trading arrangements only where the assets or services in question have a readily ascertainable market value as defined in FRS 10, 'Goodwill and intangible assets'. The requirements of Abstract 36 are discussed further under 'Capacity transactions' below (see from para 9.201).

Volume or settlement discounting

9.185 Suppliers may offer customers discounts for either achieving a minimum threshold of purchases (volume discounts) or for prompt settlement of outstanding receivables (settlement discounts). In either case, Application note G requires that the amount of revenue recognised under the transaction is reduced by the amount of the discount at the time of sale.

9.186 In order to calculate the appropriate revenue to be recognised, it may be necessary for an entity to estimate the volume of sales or the expected settlement discounts to be taken. The revenue recognised would then be reduced by this estimate, such that the revenue recognised represents the fair value of the right to consideration. The need to estimate the amounts of discounts expected to be taken does not preclude the reduction of revenue for these discounts. However, if no reliable estimate can be made then the revenue recognised on the transaction should not exceed the amount of consideration that would be received if the maximum discounts were taken.

Example 1

A paint manufacturer with a 31 December year end offers several large customers stepped rebates on sales based on the following volumes:

Up to 100,000 litres – no discount
Between 100,000 litres and 250,000 litres – 5% discount on all sales
Over 250,000 litres – 10% discount on all sales

Rebates are paid to customers after the end of their contract year.

At 31 December 20X3, a particular customer has purchased 140,000 litres of paint. That customer has a past history of purchasing over 250,000 litres of paint each contract year (which runs from 1 July to 30 June), spread evenly during the year.

At 31 December 20X3, the manufacturer has a contractual liability to pay the customer a rebate of 5% on all sales to date, because the volume threshold of 100,000 litres has been exceeded. However, based on all the available evidence, it is probable that the customer will also exceed the 250,000 litre threshold and that the manufacturer will pay a rebate of 10% on all sales. Consequently, the adjustment to revenue (and the resultant provision made) would be based on 10% of the sales to date.

Example 2

A food manufacturer sells canned food and has 100 customers. The delivery of the goods is made on the last day of each month. Standard payment terms require settlement within 45 days of delivery. The entity's policy is to grant a settlement discount of 2% to customers who pay within 15 days of delivery. Experience shows that 45% of customers normally pay within 15 days. How much should the food manufacturer recognise as revenue upon a month end delivery with an invoice value of £1,000?

The food manufacturer should recognise revenue of £991. This amount is calculated by deducting from the total invoiced value the expected amount of discounts to be taken of £9 (£1,000 × 45% × 2%).

Example 3

A manufacturer of cars pays various discounts, rebates and incentives to dealers and customers. There is a 2% trade discount on initial sale to the dealer, a further rebate of 5% if the dealer meets certain targets and other bonuses to fleet customers of 3% if certain targets are met. How should these be accounted for if it is considered likely that the dealers and customers will meet the targets?

These are all payments that are related to turnover (that is, to the number of vehicles sold) and should, therefore, be treated as a reduction of turnover. The company (manufacturer) would credit turnover with 90% of the sales value (total value less initial discount and best estimate of rebates/incentives), credit liabilities with the best estimate of the rebates (8%), and debit cash with 98% received initially. If the rebates and other bonuses are paid they will be charged to the liabilities. To the extent that they are not paid the liability is released (to turnover).

Barter transactions

9.187 Companies usually trade for cash or the right to receive cash. Sometimes, however, transactions are undertaken that involve the swapping of goods or services. These are known as barter transactions.

9.188 In terms of determining the point at which a sale should be recognised the accounting for barter transactions is no different from accounting for transactions that are settled in cash.

9.189 Measurement of the value of or consideration for barter transactions is, however, much more difficult than measurement of the consideration for transactions undertaken for cash or the right to receive cash.

9.190 In order to address these, the UITF issued Abstract 26, 'Barter transactions for advertising'. This concluded that, where advertising services are provided in exchange for advertising received, the arrangement provided little or no evidence of the value of the services provided. As the ASB Statement of Principles for financial reporting requires (a) sufficient evidence and (b) measurement at a monetary amount with sufficient reliability for recognition, the UITF concluded that turnover and costs in respect of advertising barter transactions should only be recognised if there was persuasive evidence of the value at which, if the advertising had not been exchanged, it would have been sold in a similar transaction. The Abstract lays down stringent conditions that need to be satisfied in order to conclude that there is evidence of the cash value of the advertising exchanged. In practice, in most cases the evidence will not be sufficient and the Abstract then requires that turnover and costs are not recognised in respect of the barter transaction.

9.191 When UITF Abstract 26 was issued, there was significant practice in barter advertising in one internet company's space for advertising in the counterparty internet company's space, that is, advertising for advertising barter. The Abstract provides guidance on the application of the Statement of Principles to one specific type of transaction, but its principles may be applied to other barter transactions.

9.192 The Abstract states that it is appropriate to recognise revenue and costs in respect of barter transactions for advertising only if there is persuasive evidence of the value at which, if the advertising had not been exchanged, it would have been sold for cash in a similar transaction. The UITF believed that such circumstances would be rare.

9.193 The Abstract applies specifically to barter transactions for advertising, whether on the internet, on television, in magazines, on poster sites or by another medium.

9.194 The Abstract states that persuasive evidence of the value of advertising exchanged will exist only where it can be demonstrated that similar advertising has been sold for cash. This will be the case only where the entity has a history of selling similar advertising for cash and where substantially all of the revenue from advertising within the accounting period is represented by cash sales.

9.195 To provide evidence of the value of advertising exchanged, cash sales of advertising must be similar in all significant respects. This requires that the cash sales are of advertising space in the same vehicle (for example, the same web site or magazine) as that exchanged, and must have taken place within a reasonably short period of the exchange transaction (in no case more than six months before or after it). [UITF 26 paragraph 12]. There must also be no other factors that would be expected to make the value of the advertising sold for cash significantly different from that exchanged. Specific factors set out in the Abstract that should be considered include:

- Circulation, exposure, or saturation within an intended market.
- Timing (time of day, day of week, daily, weekly, 24 hours a day/seven days a week and season of the year).
- Prominence (page on web site, section of periodical, location on page and size of advertisement).
- Demographics of readers, viewers, or customers.
- Duration (length of time advertising will be displayed).

[UITF 26 para 12].

The above list is not meant to be exhaustive.

9.196 Even where similar advertising has been sold for cash, the Abstract states that it is necessary to consider whether, in the light of all available information, there is persuasive evidence of the value at which the advertising exchanged would have been sold if not exchanged. Specific factors that may be relevant include:

- The entity's practice in setting prices for the advertising it provides and the circumstances in which discounts are offered.
- The probability that, if the advertising were not exchanged, a cash sale would have taken place.
- The value to the entity of the advertising received in exchange, and the evidence that the entity would have been willing to buy that advertising for cash if it had not been able to obtain it through an exchange transaction.

[UITF 26 para 13].

9.197 Entities should disclose in the notes to the financial statements the total amount of barter transactions for advertising that is included in turnover. Entities are encouraged to disclose information on the volume and type of such transactions and other kinds of barter transaction (whether or not included in turnover).

9.198 The difficulty of ascertaining a reliable value for the consideration in advertising barter transactions is typical of most barter transactions.

9.199 Table 9.14 is an example of a company which states its policy on advertising barter transactions.

Table 9.14 – Freeserve plc – Report and accounts – 29 April 2002

1.2 Turnover (extract)

Advertising revenues are recognised rateably over the period in which the advertisement is displayed provided that no significant obligations remain at the end of the period and collection of the resulting debt is probable. Freeserve occasionally takes part in barter advertising deals whereby partners' banner advertisements are shown in unsold space on Freeserve sites, in exchange for Freeserve banners appearing in unsold space on their sites. Both the revenue and cost elements of these transactions are deemed to be nil.

[The next paragraph is 9.201.]

Capacity transactions

9.201 In some network-based industries, such as telecommunications and electricity, entities enter into transactions for the sale or purchase of network capacity. For example, a telecommunications company may sell excess capacity on its trans-Atlantic cables. The company would probably retain ownership of the network assets, but would convey an indefeasible right of use (usually referred to as an IRU) to the buyer for an agreed period of time.

9.202 Occasionally, an entity may sell capacity to another party in exchange for receiving capacity on that other party's network. Arrangements such as these have received significant media attention, it being argued that there is not always a valid commercial reason for the transaction. Where there is no valid commercial purpose, exchange transactions have come to be known as 'hollow swaps'. An example could be where the telecommunications company described above had exchanged its excess capacity for another company's excess capacity on the same route.

9.203 Transactions involving the sale of capacity bear some similarity to lease transactions accounted for under SSAP 21. However, varying interpretations of SSAP 21 and FRS 5, as well as adverse media comment concerning 'hollow swaps', led the UITF to issue Abstract 36, 'Contracts for sales of capacity'.

9.204 UITF Abstract 36 addresses three issues:

- Should a transaction be reported as an immediate sale of an asset or as the delivery of a service over time? (See para 9.206 onwards.)

- How should gains and losses be presented in the performance statements? (See para 9.208 onwards.)
- How should exchange or reciprocal transactions be accounted for? (See para 9.214 onwards.)

[UITF 36 para 3].

9.205 With regard to 'hollow swaps', the UITF stated that *"no accounting recognition should be given to transactions that are artificial or lacking in substance"*. [UITF 36 para 23].

Sale of an asset or a service?

9.206 Contracts that convey rights of use are, in many respects, akin to leases. The definition of a lease in SSAP 21 explains that the term *"also applies to other arrangements in which one party retains ownership of an asset but conveys the right to the use of the asset to another party for an agreed period of time in return for specified payments"*. [SSAP 21 para 14]. Hence, the principles of SSAP 21 are relevant when determining whether a transaction should be reported as a sale of an asset or as the delivery of a service over time. Further guidance on categorising leases is given in chapter 19.

9.207 UITF Abstract 36 concludes that contracts for rights of use cannot be treated as a sale, unless a specific asset component can be identified as having been 'sold' and substantially all the risks and rewards of ownership of that asset have been transferred from the seller to the buyer. In other words, the contract has the substance of a finance lease. In determining whether there has been a transfer of risks and rewards, the Abstract requires that the following criteria are satisfied:

- The purchaser's right of use is exclusive and irrevocable such that no other party, including the seller, would have the right to use the capacity that is the subject of the contract, even if the buyer is not using it.
- The asset component is specific and separable (such that the buyer's exclusivity is guaranteed and the seller has no right to substitute other assets). Where the capacity 'sold' is part of a larger infrastructure, it may be difficult to measure its cost or carrying value reliably, with the result that any gain or loss that would be recognised would be uncertain. Where the cost or carrying value cannot be measured reliably, the Abstract concludes that a specific asset component cannot be identified. [UITF 36 para 8].
- The contract's term is for a major part of the asset's useful economic life.
- The attributable cost or carrying value can be measured reliably.
- No significant risks are retained by the seller. Such risks include:
    - Risk of changes in asset value.
    - Risk of obsolescence or changes in technology.

- Risk of damage.
- Risk of unsatisfactory performance (arising, for example, from performance guarantees).
- Risks relating to the seller's obligations to provide continuing access by operating and maintaining the assets. For example, if the company described in paragraph 9.201 was contractually obliged to operate and maintain the cable, the transaction could not be treated as a sale.

[UITF 36 para 20].

Presentation in the performance statements

9.208 Where it has been determined that the transaction's substance is the delivery of a service, income is recognised over the life of the contract. If, on the other hand, the substance is the sale of an asset, the presentation in the profit and loss account will depend on whether the asset sold was a fixed asset or a current asset (that is, stock). Some entities acquire or build capacity both for use within their business and for resale. Accordingly, an entity may present its investment in capacity as both fixed assets and current assets.

9.209 Paragraph 20 of FRS 3 requires that profits or losses on the disposal of fixed assets are shown separately on the face of the profit and loss account after operating profit and before interest. Income and expenses arising on the sale of current assets are included within operating result, generally as turnover and cost of sales. However, UITF Abstract 36 contains a restriction regarding the latter treatment.

9.210 Where an entity intends to dispose of a fixed asset, that asset is no longer intended for use on a continuing basis in the entity's activities. Consequently, it may be inferred that the asset no longer satisfies the criteria for classification as a fixed asset. Accordingly, in such circumstances, it may at first appear appropriate to reclassify some fixed assets as current assets. However, this is not permitted by the Abstract, which provides that the proceeds of sale may be included within turnover only where *"the assets were designated as held for resale (and classified as stock) when they were acquired or on completion of construction"*. Furthermore, capacity may not be transferred from fixed assets to stock, even if it becomes surplus to requirements and is being actively marketed for sale. [UITF 36 paras 12, 21].

9.211 An example of an accounting policy that distinguishes sales of fixed assets from sales of current assets is shown in Table 9.15 below.

Table 9.15 – COLT Telecom Group plc – Annual Report – 31 December 2004

Accounting policies (extract)

Turnover (extract)
Turnover attributable to infrastructure sales in the form of indefeasible rights-of-use ("IRUs") with characteristics which qualify the transaction as an outright sale, or transfer of title agreements, are recognised at the time of delivery and acceptance by the customer. Proceeds from the sale of infrastructure qualify as turnover where the infrastructure was designated as built for resale at the outset and the associated costs of construction have been classified as inventory for future sale. Where the infrastructure was not designated for resale and was classified as tangible fixed assets, the proceeds from these infrastructure sales are recorded net of costs as a gain or loss on the disposals of a fixed asset.

9.212 Where transactions are reported as asset sales within operating results, the Abstract requires that there is separate disclosure of the amounts included in revenue and operating profit. [UITF 36 para 21].

9.213 The guidance in UITF Abstract 36 presumes that any profit arising on the sale of capacity will be realised. However, this may not be the case, for example in most exchange transactions (see from para 9.214). Where a profit is not realised, it should not be recognised in the profit and loss account. Instead it should be recorded in the STRGL. UITF Abstract 31, 'Exchanges of businesses or other non-monetary assets for an interest in a subsidiary, joint venture or associate', deals with this issue in the context of exchanges of business and other non-monetary assets. It requires that any unrealised profit arising on an exchange should be reported in the STRGL (see chapter 26). Although UITF Abstract 36 is silent on the subject, a similar treatment of unrealised profits on the sale of capacity is appropriate.

Exchange and reciprocal transactions

9.214 An entity may sell capacity on a network in exchange for receiving capacity on another entity's network. In some cases the two capacities are of a similar value and little or no cash is exchanged. In other cases, capacity is sold wholly or in part for cash (or the right to receive cash) and a separate agreement is entered into with the buyer at approximately the same time to purchase capacity of a similar value. Such cases are referred to in UITF Abstract 36 as 'reciprocal transactions' where this reflects the transaction's substance, even though the agreements may contain no reference to reciprocity.

9.215 The recognition criteria in the ASB's 'Statement of principles for financial reporting' require:

- sufficient evidence; and
- measurement at a monetary amount with sufficient reliability.

[SoP chapter 5].

9.216 In the case of reciprocal transactions, reliable measurement of the fair value of the asset or services exchanged may not be possible, even where there has been an exchange of cash between the transacting parties.

9.217 UITF Abstract 36 provides that revenue or gains in respect of reciprocal capacity transactions should be recognised only if the assets or services provided or received have a readily ascertainable market value as defined in FRS 10. This means that the value is established by reference to a market where:

- the asset belongs to a homogeneous population of assets that are equivalent in all material respects; and
- an active market, evidenced by frequent transactions, exists for that population of assets.

[FRS 10 para 2].

9.218 In practical terms, this means that revenue and gains in respect of reciprocal transactions will rarely, if ever, be recognised. In the case of a simple exchange of capacity, there will be no accounting entries in respect of the exchange itself. Revenues from the ongoing use of the capacity acquired will be recognised as earned. Where a reciprocal transaction involves an exchange of cash, the accounting will be similar if those cash amounts are equal. In substance, the movement of cash is ignored. However, the accounting is less straightforward where the cash amounts are not equal, as shown in the example below.

Example

Company A and company B have entered into a reciprocal transaction, the terms of which are as follows:

- Company A provides capacity for five years (with a book value of £300) and £1,000 cash.
- Company B provides capacity for the same period (with a book value of £400) and £800 cash.

There is no readily ascertainable market value for the capacity so, in accordance with UITF Abstract 36, revenue and gains are not recognised. However, company A has made a net payment of £200 while company B is a net recipient of the same amount. These net cash flows need to be accounted for. The accounting treatment will depend on the nature of the individual sale and purchase transactions.

If, for the reasons specified from paragraph 9.207 above, the transactions represent immediate sales and purchases of network assets, the net payment made by company A should be treated as an addition to the cost of its assets. The amount of the net payment should, therefore, be capitalised and, if the asset in question is a fixed asset, amortised over its useful life. As regards the net receipt by company B, this represents a part disposal of its network asset, which should be presumed to be at neither a gain (as this is not permitted by UITF Abstract 36) nor a loss (unless there are indicators that the network asset itself may be impaired).

If the transactions represent the delivery of a service over time, the net cash flows should be treated as payments and receipts in advance, which should be deferred and released to the profit and loss account over the periods of the contracts.

Vouchers and coupons

Vouchers or coupons granted for consideration

9.219 Vouchers or coupons for which separate consideration is received give a customer the right to enter into a future transaction on particular terms. One such example would be the purchase by a customer of a store voucher: the customer is paying to have the option of presenting the voucher to the store in order to receive goods at a later date.

9.220 FRS 5 Application note G does not deal specifically with vouchers for which consideration is received separately from the sale of goods or services. However, it does state that *"when a seller receives payment from a customer in advance of performance, it recognises a liability equal to the amount received, representing its obligation under the contract. When the seller obtains the right to consideration through its performance, that liability is reduced and the amount of the reduction is simultaneously reported as revenue"*. [FRS 5 App G para G5]. The application note does deal with other types of voucher and states in the context of recording the liability: *"Regard should also be paid to the proportion of vouchers that are expected to be redeemed"*. It also states: *"At each reporting date the seller should review its estimated liability for outstanding vouchers having regard to the experience of the proportion that are redeemed and expire. Adjustments to the estimate should be included within revenue"*. [FRS 5 App G paras G39, G41]. Thus, the revenue received on the sale of the voucher should be deferred and recognised when the seller performs.

9.221 Although the sale of a voucher or coupon is a contract with the customer, it needs to be considered together with the further contract that arises if and when the rights under that contract are exercised, because the two are inter-dependent. Application note G states that *"...the commercial substance of two or more separate contracts may require them to be accounted for as a single transaction. ..."*. [FRS 5 App G para G26]. The revenue from the sale of the voucher or coupon will generally be accounted for when the seller performs under the further contract – that is when the seller supplies the goods or services on exercise of the voucher or coupon.

9.222 Revenue from the sale of vouchers that were sold for cash should be recognised on the earlier of:

- The date of exercise (that is, the date on which the customer uses the voucher and the supplier completes its performance).

- The expiry of the voucher or coupon (that is, the date from which it is no longer legally valid and the supplier no longer has an obligation to supply 'contractual performance').

Where vouchers have no expiry date, the revenue should not be recognised if the supplier has not completed its contractual performance. Instead, the consideration received for the voucher should be deferred and recognised as a liability until it can be reliably demonstrated that it is unlikely the voucher will ever be presented. This determination must be made for each individual voucher (or group of vouchers in an ageing profile) and not to the whole portfolio of vouchers.

Vouchers granted as part of sales transaction (vouchers)

9.223 Application note G provides specific guidance on vouchers, under the heading 'Separation and linking of contractual arrangements' (see also from para 9.145 above). In the application note the term 'vouchers' is intended to cover all types of arrangement where the seller is committed to perform in the future at a reduced price. [FRS 5 App G Dev para 37]. The term, therefore, includes a wide range of arrangements, including air miles and points schemes. The reason why vouchers are considered as part of the guidance relating to linking and separation of contractual arrangements is that often vouchers are issued as part of a single transaction that includes the sale of goods or services and the issue of the vouchers.

9.224 The application note deals only with situations where vouchers are redeemable against future purchases from the seller. The application note does not specifically mention situations where vouchers may be redeemable against purchases from other sellers, which is a feature of many points schemes, but this is also considered below from paragraph 9.240 in the light of the principles in the application note for vouchers.

9.225 The application note states that where vouchers are issued as part of a sales transaction and are redeemable against future purchases from the seller, the substance is that this is a 'bundled' transaction and the customer is buying both goods or services and a voucher at the same time. Thus, the principles of 'unbundling' which are discussed from paragraph 9.145 should be applied.

9.226 Using the principles of 'unbundling', it is necessary to allocate the consideration received from the customer across the transaction's components. Therefore, revenue should be reported at the amount of the consideration received or receivable less the voucher's fair value. The voucher's fair value represents a liability for future performance that is extinguished and recognised as revenue when the voucher is redeemed as part of the consideration for the future purchase by the customer. [FRS 5 App G para G38].

9.227 Where a voucher is accounted for separately, its fair value will often be less than its face value. Application note G sets out some of the factors that should be taken into consideration in determining the voucher's fair value including:

- The range of goods or services that the customer can obtain on the voucher's redemption.
- The discount the customer obtains when redeeming the voucher compared to the discount that could be obtained by customers who do not redeem vouchers.
- The length of time before the right to use the voucher expires.
- The extent to which the voucher is similar to other vouchers that are distributed to customers free of charge.
- Regard should also be paid to the proportion of vouchers that are expected to be redeemed.

[FRS 5 App G para G39].

Example

An item is sold for £10, together with a voucher entitling the bearer to a £3 discount on a subsequent purchase of the same item. The retailer has historical experience that for every two vouchers issued, one is redeemed.

Hence, for every voucher that is redeemed, three sales have occurred: two in which vouchers were sold and one in which a voucher is redeemed. For each of the two initial sales, the seller received £10 cash and sold one item and one voucher. Although each voucher has a face value of £3, only half are used. This, combined with the other factors listed in paragraph 9.227 may give a fair value of each voucher of £1.

Therefore, when each of the two initial sales of goods and vouchers are made, the accounting for each would be as follows:

Dr Cash	£10 (£20 in total)	
Cr Revenue		£9 (£18 in total)
Cr Deferred revenue		£1 (£2 in total)

Upon redemption, the accounting would reflect the fact that only half of all vouchers are redeemed. Therefore, when the third sale is made and a voucher is redeemed the following entries would be made:

Dr Deferred revenue	£2	
Dr Cash	£7	
Cr Revenue		£9

[The next paragraph is 9.232.]

9.232 Another possible outcome is that after considering the factors set out in paragraph 9.227 above, it may be determined that the fair value of a voucher is not significant, therefore no adjustment to revenue is required at the time the voucher is issued. In such circumstances the voucher may be an inducement to enter into a future transaction, rather than representing a separable component of the original transaction. [FRS 5 App G para G40].

9.233 Examples of how some of the factors in paragraph 9.227 above might be considered are as follows (in the same order as the bullet points):

- A seller includes with a popular line of goods a voucher giving money off a subsequent purchase of a line of goods that are not popular with customers or that are close to their sell-by date. The fair value of the vouchers will be relatively lower if the seller is likely to have to offer other similar discounts to all customers in order to dispose of the goods.

- A tour operator sells a holiday and offers £50 off the list price of a subsequent holiday taken with the tour operator between certain dates. If the operator has in the past offered or is likely to offer similar discounts on holidays between those dates to all customers, new or returning, the fair value of the £50 offer is most likely an amount below £50.

- A voucher for money off the next purchase of a certain item expires before it is likely that the first item will have been used by the customer. (For example, 50 per cent off the next purchase of anti-freeze included in sales made in August and expiring in December). In such cases the likelihood of exercise of the voucher is reduced and thus the value of the voucher may be insignificant.

- A supermarket sells a product with a voucher for money off the next purchase of that item, but at the same time regularly sends customers sheets of free coupons that they can use to purchase those and other goods at the same discounted price. In such a situation, the value of the voucher could again be lower than its face value.

9.234 The seller should review the estimated liability for outstanding vouchers, taking account of the proportion of vouchers that have been redeemed or have expired. The seller should make any adjustments necessary and include them in revenue. [FRS 5 App G para G41].

9.235 For companies applying FRS 26, 'Financial instruments: Recognition and measurement', vouchers that may be redeemed for cash meet the definition of a financial liability under that standard. As a result, any liability may not be derecognised until the derecognition criteria of FRS 26 are met. Furthermore, the liability may not be measured at an amount less than the cash redemption value. [FRS 26 para 49]. See further chapter 6 for recognition and measurement of financial liabilities.

9.236 Sometimes the provision of money-off coupons might result in a future sale appearing to be made at a loss. In such a case it is often unnecessary to provide for any future loss if, when the total consideration is apportioned between the linked transactions there is no loss. This is illustrated in the following example.

Example

A company buys a particular product at £5 and normally sells it for £8. It gives an offer of 50% off a second item if a customer buys one at a later date. How should this be accounted for?

If, in the first sale, the voucher is not recognised, there is a gain on the first item of £3 (£8 — £5) and a loss on the second item of £1 (£4 — £5). However, if the fair value of the voucher is considered significant to the transaction, part of the consideration from the first sale, representing the fair value of the voucher, should be recorded as a liability. If this were to be done the fair value of the voucher may be £2. The proceeds of the first sale would be recorded as revenue of £6 and the revenue for the second sale plus the sale of the voucher would also be £6 (£4 + £2).

Vouchers granted without consideration

9.237 Some vouchers may be granted for no consideration separately from a sales transaction. An example of where a voucher is granted without consideration is where a supermarket, service provider or manufacturer issues money-off coupons or vouchers that can be redeemed in the future for goods or services. These are often included as part of marketing circulars or newspaper advertisements.

9.238 Application note G prescribes the treatment for this situation, where vouchers are distributed free of charge and independently of another transaction. It states that such vouchers do not give rise to a liability, except where redemption of the vouchers will result in products (or services) being sold at a loss. Where this is the case the seller has entered into an onerous contract and provision will need to be made in accordance with FRS 12, 'Provisions, contingent liabilities and contingent assets'. When the vouchers are redeemed, the seller should recognise revenue at the amount received for the product, after deducting the discount granted on exercise of the vouchers from the normal selling price. [FRS 5 App G para G42]. In essence, this type of voucher is no different from sales reductions in price made during an annual or seasonal sale.

Free products

9.239 Some sales promotions are described as 'buy one, get one free' or 'two for the price of one', or a vendor may price products below cost to attract volume. In the past, some have argued that the cost of the free product or the negative margin on a 'loss leader' is a marketing expense or that revenues, cost of sales and marketing expense should be grossed-up to reflect the normal selling price of the 'free' product. We do not consider that this argument is appropriate. The revenue is the actual sales proceeds and the purchase or production cost of the 'free' product and 'loss leader' is always a cost of sale. On the other hand, the cost of relatively insignificant promotional give-aways that are not part of the vendor's normal product offerings (for example, a 'free' bookmark with the purchase of a book, or a 'free' T-shirt bearing the logo of the vendor if you purchase £50 of merchandise) might be appropriately classified as a marketing expense. These principles are illustrated in the following examples.

Example 1

A retailer is offering a special 'buy one get one half price' deal whereby customers who purchase one box of chocolates are then entitled to purchase another box at the same time and obtain the second box for half the price. How should the retailer record the transaction?

The revenue recognised is the cash consideration received for the two boxes of chocolates. The additional cost from offering the second box at a discount to the normal price is recorded as a cost of sales, not as a marketing expense.

Example 2

A company is a start-up, selling an electronic product. It is attracting a customer base by allowing the customer to have the first product free. The customer is under no obligation to take further products. The company has recorded the normal selling price for the free product as turnover and an equivalent amount together with the actual cost of the product to the company as a marketing expense. Is this acceptable?

No, this is not acceptable. No sale has been made and, therefore, no turnover should be recorded. The only amount to be charged is the cost of the product to the supplier, which may be charged as a marketing cost in this case, not cost of sales, as no sale has been made.

Loyalty programmes (point schemes)

9.240 Some companies offer point schemes. Examples are airlines that offer 'free' air miles and supermarkets that offer loyalty cards that amass points that can then be used to reduce the cost of future purchases either from the same or a different supplier or may sometimes be redeemable for cash.

9.241 The rules in the application note described in the previous section apply equally to points schemes. Where points are awarded on sale of goods or services, revenue should be recorded at the amount of the consideration received or receivable less the fair value of the points awarded. Hence, the full fair value of the points awarded is deducted from the consideration received on the initial purchase and carried forward as a liability.

9.242 With points schemes it is also less likely that many of the factors listed in the application note for consideration when determining fair value (see para 9.227) will significantly reduce the fair value, with the exception of the proportion of points expected to be redeemed. This is because the range of goods or services that can be purchased with points is usually either very broad or not restricted. In addition, the discounts that points give rise to are usually over and above any discounts that are generally available to customers who do not have points, that is, the points are like cash. Nor is the length of time in which points may be redeemed usually restricted in such a way that their fair value is affected. Points are sometimes awarded as a 'bonus', but normally only to existing or new cardholders. They are not similar to other vouchers that are distributed to customers free of charge, but are incremental awards to cardholders or members.

Example

A company gives away 80 points with each purchase of goods valued at £100. These points can be exchanged for goods supplied either by the company or by a third party. For every 1,000 points, goods with an average fair value of £5 can be obtained. If the company provides these goods itself its cost is 80p. What is the 'exchange rate' of 100 points?

The exchange rate is 50p being the fair value of goods obtainable for 100 points. It is not 8p as that is the cost to the company of providing the goods. The total consideration received for the original purchase of goods should, therefore, be allocated as to £100 less eight-tenths of £5 (£4) making £96 for the goods and £4 for the points. The £4 should then be treated as a liability until the points are redeemed.

9.243 In some cases the points scheme may be run by a third party on behalf of the selling company, who makes a payment to the third party in respect of points granted by the third party. In principle this should not alter the way in which the company accounts for the points scheme, but in practice the payments to the third party may be close to the fair value of the points to the customer and it may be more practicable to use the payments to the third party (the operator) as a substitute for the fair value of the points.

9.244 If the agency relationship between the selling company and the operator is disclosed, the operator will normally be acting as principal and the customer will not have recourse to the selling company for unredeemed points. The selling company's only liability will be to make the necessary payment to the operator and the liability for this will be recorded when the goods that give rise to the points are sold. The selling company's income in respect of the points will not be the consideration received (which it has to pay over to the operator), but instead will be any commission it receives from the principal (the operator).

9.245 If the agency is undisclosed, the selling company will usually be acting as principal and the revenue from the sale of points will belong to the selling company. However, as noted above in that case the proceeds will be treated as a liability of the selling company until the points are redeemed. The selling company will also usually have to pay a fee to the operator for providing the service of operating the scheme.

Example

Company A runs a loyalty card scheme independently from any retailers. Company A has contracts with each retailer and the retailer can take any one of the following different roles:

- Be an issuer of points.

- Be a redeemer of points.
- Both issue and redeem points.

The customer holds a loyalty point card that is issued by company A and allows the customer to earn points at a given list of retailers and use points at other retailers. The face value of the point issued is £1 and for each point issued, the issuing retailers will pay £0.98 to company A and in doing so earn £0.02 of commission income. Once the issuing retailer has paid company A, it has no further obligation to the customer. When a retailer redeems points with a face value of £1, it will receive compensating cash from company A of £0.91. Company A's margin is the difference between the redemption price and the issue price. Where a retailer both issues and redeems points, there is no netting of cash flows: cash is paid to company A for points issued and cash is received from company A for points redeemed. The benefits for the participating retailers being:

- There is no need to administer the scheme.
- There is no obligation in respect of outstanding points and the retailer can exit the scheme.
- The fair value for the customer will be higher if the points are redeemable at a variety of stores.

The accounting for such as scheme is as follows. When the retailer makes a sale of £10, it issues points with face value of £1:

Dr	Cash	£10	
Cr	Revenue		£9
Cr	Commission income		£0.02
Cr	Liability to A		£0.98

When the risks and rewards associated with the points are immediately passed to company A, the liability is offset:

Dr	Liability	£0.98	
Cr	Cash		£0.98

When the points are redeemed, the redeeming retailers will recognise the revenue made by the points with a face value of £1 at £0.91:

Dr	Receivable from company A	£0.91	
Cr	Revenue		£0.91

Other benefit schemes similar to point schemes

9.246 Other schemes that are similar to points schemes are where customers become entitled to benefits (such as free products) when they have satisfied certain criteria. Such criteria might be achieving a certain level of purchases or they might be time based, for example continuing to be a member of a scheme for a specified period.

9.247 Where benefits are based on achieving a level of purchases, the fair value of the benefit should be recognised by the supplier as the purchases occur. That is, part of the revenue equal to the fair value of the benefit to the customer should be deferred. This should be deferred until the free products are given (and matched against any costs thereof which are then charged).

Example

A DVD rental outlet stamps a card each time a customer hires a DVD. If the customer collects ten stamps and presents the completed card, this entitles the customer to one free DVD rental. In these circumstances, part of the consideration for each of the first ten rentals should be deferred and recognised as revenue when the customer presents the completed card and receives the free DVD rental.

9.248 Where a benefit is given in the form of a cash rebate the payment should be charged against the revenue that has been deferred, so that only the net revenue is recorded. This makes sense because reported revenue should not exceed amounts paid by the customer.

9.249 For those who receive rebates or free products on the attainment of certain targets the benefit should not be recognised until the targets are reached and receipt of the benefit is virtually certain.

9.250 Where criteria are based on a time factor, for instance on remaining a member for a specified period, consideration needs to be given as to whether the customer needs to complete any act of performance or whether the criteria are genuinely time based. Criteria that are time based with no act of performance are likely to be extremely rare. Generally, there will be some act of performance such as payment of a membership fee or subscription. In such cases, part of the fee or subscription should be treated as deferred revenue and recognised when the free products or other benefits are claimed (and any other associated costs are recognised). Where the benefits are genuinely time based only with no act of performance required, the obligation arises immediately and provision would need to be made (as there is no associated revenue there is no revenue to defer) and discounted if necessary to reflect the fact that the benefit may not be claimable until some later time.

Dividends, royalties and other practical applications

Dividends

9.251 Treatment of dividends in a recipient's financial statements will follow that in the paying company, that is, dividends receivable will be recognised when the shareholder's right to receive payment is established. The right to receive payment is established, for interim dividends, when they are paid and, for final dividends, when they are approved by shareholders at an Annual General Meeting. See further chapter 23.

9.252 A related issue concerning some dividends is whether the credit should be regarded as a revenue or capital item. One example of this is the treatment of dividends paid by a subsidiary to its parent. Before the Companies Act 1948 was amended by the Companies Act 1981, when a subsidiary paid a dividend out of pre-acquisition profits to its parent, the parent was required to reduce the carrying value of its investment in the subsidiary by this amount. The parent could not treat this amount as realised and could not distribute it; the dividend received was, therefore, a capital item rather than revenue. Following the 1981 Act, when a dividend is paid out of pre-acquisition profits by a subsidiary it need not be applied in reducing the value of the investment in the subsidiary in the parent's books. It can be taken to the profit and loss account. Only if the underlying value of the subsidiary is impaired following the payment of the dividend, does the parent have to make a provision against its investment.

9.253 Bonus issues of shares by a subsidiary to its parent do not transfer any value from the subsidiary to the parent. There are more shares in issue, but there is no economic significance to the transaction. Therefore, a bonus issue does not give the parent a reason to recognise a gain, realised or unrealised, by increasing the carrying value of its investment in the subsidiary.

Shares for services

9.254 Other revenue recognition issues that create particular difficulties have arisen in respect of start-up companies where the practice of issuing shares for services or accepting equity stakes in exchange for services is particularly common. The following questions and suggested responses illustrate some of these difficulties.

Example

A company provides corporate finance services (for example, assistance in preparing for eventual flotation) to start-up companies and proposes to take equity stakes in the start-up companies instead of fees. In relation to revenue recognition, consider the outcome based on the following facts:

- In some cases securities received will be listed and in other cases they will be unlisted.
- Some securities will be marketable, whereas others may not be marketable.
- The company intends to hold the securities for the medium to long-term.
- There may be restrictions placed on the company's ability to dispose of the securities for a period.

The reason for the proposed arrangements is for the company to share in the success of the start-up companies it advises and to assist them by enabling them to obtain advice without having to pay substantial fees.

Application note G, states that revenue should be measured at the fair value of the right to consideration. However, compliance with company law is also necessary.

Company law (currently CA85 4 Sch 12) permits only realised profits to be included in the profit and loss account.

Listed or marketable shares

If the shares received are listed or marketable, there is a liquid market and the company was capable of readily disposing of the shares and it could do so without curtailing or disrupting its business, then the value of the shares can be regarded as revenue and, hence, as a realised profit and taken to the profit and loss account.

If, however, there are restrictions over the disposal of the shares, then this does not give rise to a realised profit (and no profit could be included in the profit and loss account) until the restrictions are lifted. This is because until the restrictions are removed the company could not have disposed of the shares. However, if the value of the shares can be reliably measured they should be recognised in the balance sheet and any gain taken to the STRGL.

Non-marketable shares

If the shares are not marketable, their receipt does not give rise to a realised profit and so no revenue is included in the profit and loss account. However, an unrealised gain could be recognised.

Whether the shares should be recorded at a value and an unrealised gain recognised will depend on whether the value (and the gain) can be measured reliably. If the investee company had a track record, then recognition at a value might be possible. The unrealised gain would be treated as a revaluation gain and shown in the STRGL. However, given that the company is a start-up, there is likely to be uncertainty as to the investment's value and it should not be included at a value (that is it should be treated as having nil cost, with disclosure of the facts). This is because in the absence of reliable measurement neither the value of the investment nor the gain can be recognised.

If subsequently a basis for reliable measurement of the value of the equity stake is established (such as where the investee company is floated or where other investors subscribe for shares) the company could revalue its investment and show the gain in the STRGL.

Cost of providing the services

The company will have incurred costs in providing the services in return for an equity stake. Where no value is able to be placed on the equity stake received for work done, any costs incurred to the date of billing the client should be written off to the profit and loss account.

Where the value of equity stake can be reliably measured and the stake is readily marketable the value can be recognised in the profit and loss account. The costs incurred should also be charged to the profit and loss account as soon as the work is billed.

Where the value of the equity stake can be reliably measured, but the value is recognised in the STRGL to the extent that the costs are 'covered' by the value of the equity that is recognised, the costs should be included in the carrying value of the investment. This is because the costs qualify for recognition as an asset from which future economic benefits are expected and which can be measured reliably. Here, only the net gain (value of equity stake less cost) is taken to the STRGL. To the extent that costs exceed the value attributable to the equity stake they should be written off to the profit and loss account. Comparison of costs to value of equity stakes for this purpose should be made on a case-by-case basis. Applying a portfolio of costs and matching it to a portfolio of investments is not appropriate.

It would also not be appropriate to capitalise the whole of the cash equivalent fee since it is includes an element of profit. Instead, only such costs as would be included in work in progress should be capitalised. By deciding to accept equity instead of fees, the company has effectively converted a revenue transaction into a capital transaction.

Licensing and royalties

Royalties

9.255 Royalties include other fees for the use of assets such as trademarks, patents, software, copyright, record masters, films and TV programmes. The terms of an agreement will normally indicate when the revenue has been earned. In general, revenue may be recognised on a straight line basis over the life of the agreement or another systematic basis such as in relation to sales to which the royalty relates (see Table 9.16).

Table 9.16 – Chrysalis Group PLC – Annual Report and Accounts – 31 August 2002

Notes to the Accounts (extract)

1 Accounting policies (extracts)

Record royalties (excluding music publishing royalties and record producer services)

Royalty income is included on a receivable basis calculated on sales of records arising during each accounting period as reported by licensees. Royalties payable are expensed on an accruals basis. Royalty advances payable are expensed on a paid basis except that they are carried forward and recognised as an asset where such advances relate to current unreleased products and where it is estimated that sufficient future royalties will be earned for recoupment from those products.

Advances received in respect of individual albums are carried forward and recognised as income over the expected life of each individual licence.

Music publishing royalties and record producer services

Music publishing royalties are accounted for on a notified earnings basis, with any unrecouped royalty advances carried forward until the end of the relevant contract period. This accounting policy was changed with effect from the year ended 31st August 2001, full details of which are set out in the Annual Report and Accounts for 2001. Royalties received for record producer services are accounted for on a cash basis. Royalties payable are expensed on an accruals basis except that music publishing royalty advances are carried forward and recognised as an asset where such advances relate to proven artists or songwriters and where it is estimated that sufficient future royalties will be earned for recoupment of these advances.

Film and broadcasting licensing and distribution income

Revenue from the licensing or distribution of film, broadcast or exhibition rights is recognised from the date of release for distribution or broadcast.

Television productions

Turnover and attributable profits on television programmes produced for commissioning broadcasters are recognised on television production contracts which are incomplete at the end of the year in the proportion that costs incurred to date bear to estimated ultimate costs after making provision for anticipated losses.

Investment in television rights

Investment in television rights is stated at cost and included in intangible assets in the Group balance sheet. They are amortised in the profit and loss account in the proportion that revenue bears to the estimated ultimate revenue after making provision for any anticipated shortfall.

Deferred television programme development expenditure

Pre-contract development expenditure is written off in the period in which it is incurred except where it relates to a clearly defined project, the outcome of which has been assessed with reasonable certainty as to its success and commercial viability. In such cases the expenditure is deferred to the extent that its recovery can be reasonably regarded as assured and the cost is written off against revenue over the period of the contract.

Licence income

9.256 In general, revenue should not be recognised under licensing agreements until performance under the contract has occurred and the seller has a right to consideration.

Example 1

Company A grants a licence to a customer to use its website, which contains proprietary databases. The licence allows the customer to use the website for a two year period (1 January 20X1 to 31 December 20X2). The licence fee of £60,000 is payable on 1 January 20X1.

The agreement's substance is that the customer is paying for a service that is delivered over time. Although company A will not incur incremental costs in serving the customer, it will incur costs to maintain the website.

Hence, the revenue from the licence fees should be accrued over the period of the agreement that reflects the provision of the service. The entity has an obligation to provide services for the next two years, therefore, the fee of £60,000 received on 1 January 20X1 should be recognised as a liability. Each month for the period January 20X1 to December 20X2, an amount of £2,500 should be released from the liability and recognised as income to reflect the service that is delivered.

Example 2

A film distributor grants a licence to a cinema operator. The licence entitles the operator to show the film once for consideration of the higher of a non-refundable guarantee or a percentage of the box office receipts.

The film distributor should recognise the revenue on the date the film is shown. It is only when the film is shown that the revenue has been earned.

Example 3

A computer games software house grants two different licences to arcade games machine manufacturers to use the software for a certain game. The annual licence, which has a fee of £100,000, allows the software to be used for one year and can be renewed annually. The perpetual licence, which has a fee of £400,000, allows the software to be used indefinitely with the licensee entitled to upgrades free of charge, although the software house is under no obligation to upgrade the software and does not expect to incur significant costs in performing any upgrades.

Under the perpetual licence there may be a commercial or at least a constructive obligation to upgrade the software and there is some cost in doing so. This is also supported by the fact that the perpetual licence costs more than the annual licence. In this situation, there is a strong argument for spreading the licence fee over the expected life of the game in order to match it with the costs of providing the upgrades. The annual licence fee, on the other hand, does not carry any further obligations on the part of the software house and may, therefore, be recognised immediately.

9.257 In some situations, a licensing agreement may be recognised as an outright sale. For example, if a non-refundable one-off fee has been received for the foreign exhibition rights to a film that allows the licensee to use the rights at any time in certain countries without restriction, then it may be appropriate to recognise the income when the fee is received. Since the licensor has no control over any further use or distribution of the product and has no further action to perform under the contract he has effectively sold the rights detailed in the licensing agreement.

9.258 An example of a company that has adopted 'best in class' policies for revenue recognition on sale and distribution of programmes is given in Table 9.17.

Table 9.17 – HIT Entertainment plc – Annual Report – 31 July 2004

Turnover

- Consumer products

The Group policy is to recognise licensing revenue by spreading the total guaranteed minimum value of a contract over the term, only recognising actual licensing income receivable once it exceeds the apportionment of the total guaranteed minimum contract value. In addition recognition of revenue and associated royalty expenses will only begin once the following criteria are met:

(a) a licence agreement has been executed by all parties; and

(b) the licence term has commenced.

Any licence fees received in advance which do not meet all of the above criteria, are included in deferred income until the above criteria are met.

Associated royalties on consumer products sales are recognised when the related turnover is recorded.

- **Home entertainment**

Revenues and associated costs of goods sold and royalty expenses from home entertainment revenues are recognised on the date that the products are made widely available for sale by the Group's retailer customers.

- **Television**

Income recognised on HIT-owned television programme series and from the distribution of other television programmes represents the invoiced value of licence fees including withholding tax but excluding value added tax. The Group's policy is to recognise the income and associated royalty payable when all of the following criteria are met:

(a) a licence agreement has been executed by both parties;

(b) the programme has substantially met all necessary technical quality requirements;

(c) delivery to the broadcaster has occurred;

(d) the licence term has commenced;

(e) the arrangement is fixed or determinable; and

(f) collection of the arrangement fee is reasonably assured.

Any licence fees received in advance, which do not meet all of the above criteria, are included in deferred income until the above criteria are met.

- **Stage show**

Turnover from stage shows is based on the invoiced value of the goods and services provided in the year excluding sales tax. Any licensing revenue related to stage show activity is accounted for in accordance with the consumer product policies above.

Franchise fees

9.259 Franchise agreements may provide for the supply of initial services such as training and assistance to help the franchisee set up and operate the franchise operation, subsequent services and the supply of equipment, stocks and other tangible assets and know-how. Therefore, these agreements may generate different types of revenue such as initial franchise fees, profits and losses from the sale of fixed assets and royalties as illustrated in Table 9.18.

Table 9.18 – Diageo plc – Annual Report and Accounts – 30 June 2001
Accounting policies (extract)

Franchising
Franchising generates initial franchise fees, as well as profits or losses arising from the franchising of developed or purchased outlets previously operated by the group, and ongoing royalty revenues based on sales made by franchisees. Income from franchising is included in operating profit, apart from any property element which is treated as a disposal of fixed assets.

9.260 In general, franchise fees should be recognised on a basis that reflects the purpose for which they were charged. For example, revenue from the supplies of assets should be recognised when the items are delivered or title passes, whereas fees charged for the use of continuing rights granted by a franchise agreement or for other continuing services provided during the period of the agreement should be recognised as the service is provided or the rights are used.

9.260.1 Where the agreement provides for the supply of more than one type of good or service, this will be a multiple element arrangement (see para 9.145). This means that the total consideration received under the agreement must be allocated to the components and recognised when goods or services are delivered.

9.261 Sometimes, franchise agreements require an upfront payment by the franchisee. Where the franchise agreement also provides for the franchiser to supply equipment, stocks or other assets at a price lower than that charged to others, or at a price that does not allow the franchiser to make a reasonable profit on the supplies, that part of the initial fee should be deferred. The amount of the initial fee deferred should be sufficient to cover the estimated costs in excess of the price charged to the franchisee for any assets and to allow the franchiser to make a reasonable profit on these sales. This deferred income can then be recognised over the period the goods are likely to be provided. The balance of the initial fee should be recognised when the initial services have been substantially accomplished. This approach is consistent with the accounting for inception fees (see from para 9.136) and based on the fact that the initial fee, in these circumstances, is unlikely to be capable of being treated as a separable component.

9.262 Similarly, if there is no separate fee for the supply of continuing services after the initial fee, then part of the initial fee should also be deferred and recognised as the subsequent services are provided.

Grants

9.263 Gifts in the form of grants may be given to a company to help finance a particular asset or specific profit and loss account expenditure. When these grants are given by government, including inter-governmental agencies and EU bodies, guidance on the accounting treatment is contained in SSAP 4, 'Accounting for government grants', which differentiates between the treatment for revenue and capital based grants. The treatment of revenue grants is discussed below. The treatment of capital grants is discussed in chapter 16. Payments given to companies from sources other than government should be subject to similar analysis since SSAP 4 is indicative of best practice for accounting for grants and assistance from other sources. Thus, for example, a non-refundable payment by a third party franchiser to assist the franchisee with the purchase of specific assets would be more in the nature of a grant than a capital contribution.

9.264 The 'accruals' concept, which is the key principle underlying SSAP 4, implies that government grants should be recognised in the profit and loss account to match them with the expenditure towards which they are intended to contribute. The relationship between the grant and the related expenditure is, therefore, of paramount importance in establishing the accounting treatment to be adopted. Grants made as contributions to revenue expenditure should be credited to the profit and loss account of the period in which the related expenditure is incurred. For example, see Westland Group plc's accounting policy in Table 9.19.

Table 9.19 – Westland Group plc – Annual Report – 1 October 1993

Accounting policies (extract)

8 Research, development, launching costs and launch aid
To the extent that design, development and learning costs are not recoverable under specific contracts, including risk sharing contracts, they are written off as incurred, net of any launch aid recovered under the Civil Aviation Act 1982. Learning costs are the estimated excess cost of manufacturing initial production batches.

Launch aid from H.M. Government is credited in full against the initial research, development and learning costs in the year in which it is receivable. Additional research, development and learning costs required under launch aid agreements in excess of launch aid receivable are charged against revenue as incurred.

9.265 Government grants should not be recognised until the conditions for their receipt have been complied with and there is reasonable assurance that the grant will be received. In the event that a grant appears likely to have to be repaid, provision should be made for the estimated liability.

9.266 Difficulties of matching may arise where the terms of the grant do not specify precisely the expenditure towards which it is intended to contribute. For example, grants may be awarded to defray project costs comprising both revenue and capital expenditure. Project grants are normally awarded on this basis and may be related to the project's capital expenditure costs and the number of jobs created or safeguarded. In such circumstances, the expenditure eligible for grant aid may be all the costs incurred that are directly attributable to the project. The terms of the grant itself often need to be carefully examined to establish whether the intent is to defray costs or to establish a condition relating to the entire amount of the grant.

Example

A company obtains a grant from an Industrial Development agency for an investment project in Scotland. The project is a building to house a manufacturing plant. The principal terms are that the grant payments relate to the level of capital expenditure and the intention of the grant is to help ensure that imports of the product can be replaced with products from sources in the UK to safeguard 500 jobs. The grant will have to be repaid if there is an underspend on capital or if the jobs are not safeguarded until 18 months after the date of the last fixed asset purchase.

This grant is related to capital expenditure. The employment condition should be seen as an additional condition to prevent replacement of labour by capital, rather than as the reason for the grant. If the grant was revenue it would be related to revenue expenditure such as a percentage of the payroll cost or a fixed amount per job safeguarded.

9.267 SSAP 4 states that where the terms of the grant do not specify precisely the expenditure it is intended to meet, the most appropriate accounting may be achieved by assuming that the grant is contributing towards the expenditure that forms the basis for its payment, that is, the expenditure included on the claim form. It will then be possible to account for the grant according to the different types of expenditure towards which it is intended to contribute. If the grant is paid when evidence is produced that certain expenditure has been incurred, then the grant should be recognised simultaneously with that expenditure.

Example

Company A is awarded a government grant of £100,000 on 1 January 20X1 towards the construction of a manufacturing plant. The plant's useful life is estimated at 10 years. The entity took two years to construct the plant. At 1 January 20X3 the entity started to use the plant for manufacturing products. The entity has a December year end.

The £100,000 grant relates to the construction of an asset and should be initially recognised as a liability in the balance sheet. The liability should be recognised as income in line with the asset's depreciation.

The entity should recognise a liability on the balance sheet for the years ending 31 December 20X1 and 31 December 20X2. Once the plant starts being used in the manufacturing process, other operating income of £10,000 should be recognised in each year of the asset's 10 year useful life to match depreciation.

9.268 In certain circumstances, however, the actual expenditure the grant is intended to contribute towards may differ from the expenditure that forms the basis of its payment. For example, the grant may relate to a total project expenditure that may include, in addition to capital expenditure, working capital costs, training costs and removal costs. However, the grant may become payable in instalments on incurring specific amounts of capital expenditure as the project progresses. In this situation, it would be wrong to treat the whole grant as a capital expenditure grant. The most appropriate treatment, therefore, would be to match the grant received rateably with the expenditure towards which the grant is assisting, that is, the grant would have to be spread rateably over the constituent parts of the project expenditure. This treatment is in accordance with SSAP 4 which provides that where such evidence exists and is sufficiently persuasive, then it is appropriate to match grants received with identified expenditure and this approach should always be preferred.

9.269 Sometimes grants may be payable on a different basis, for example on the achievement of a non-financial objective. In such situations, the grant should be recognised simultaneously with the identifiable costs of achieving that objective. Such costs must be identified or estimated on a reasonable basis. For example, if a grant is given on condition that jobs are created and maintained for a minimum period, the grant should be recognised in the same period as the cost of providing the jobs for that period. As a result, a greater proportion of the grant may fall to be recognised in the early stages of the project because of higher non-productive and set-up costs.

Example

Company A is awarded a government grant of £60,000 receivable over three years (£40,000 in year 1 and £10,000 in each of years 2 and 3), contingent on creating 10 new jobs and maintaining them for three years. The employees are recruited at a cost of £30,000, and the wage bill for the first year is £100,000, rising by £10,000 in each of the subsequent years.

The income of £60,000 should be recognised over the three-year period to match the related costs.

In year 1, £21,667 of the £40,000 received from government will match the related costs of £130,000 incurred during the year, and should therefore be recognised as income. The amount of the grant that has not yet been credited to income (that is, £18,333, being £40,000 of cash received less £21,667 credited to income) should be reflected in the balance sheet as such.

Year	Labour cost	CreditGrant	Grant calculations	Credit balance sheet Deferred income	Calculations
1	130 000	21 667	(130/360) x 60 000	18 333	(40 000 – 21 667)
2	110 000	18 333	(110/360) x 60 000	10 000	(50 000 – 40 000)
3	120 000	20 000	(120/360) x 60 000	—	
	360 000	60 000			

9.270 In certain circumstances, government grants may be awarded unconditionally without regard to the entity's future actions, or requirement to incur further costs. Such grants may be given for the immediate financial support, or assistance of an entity, or for the reimbursement of costs previously incurred. They may also be given to finance the general activities of an entity over a specified period, or to compensate for a loss of income. In some instances, the extent of these grants may constitute a major source of revenue for the entity. Where grants are awarded on such a basis, they should be recognised in the profit and loss account of the period in respect of which they are paid, or, if they are not stated to be paid in respect of a particular period, in the profit and loss account of the period in which they are receivable. The presentation and disclosure requirements of SSAP 4 are detailed from paragraph 9.293.

Example

Company A incurred expenses of £5,000 that related to training employees during the period May 20X1 to September 20X1. The employee training was required by government. Company A entered into negotiations with the government for compensation for the training expenses incurred in December 20X1. In February 20X2 the government agreed that it would compensate the entity for the expenses incurred for the year ended 31December 20X1.

Although company A incurred the expenses for the year ended 31 December 20X1, it should recognise the income received from the government for the year ended 31 December 20X2. The grant of £5,000 will only become receivable for the year ended 31 December 20X2, that is the year in which the government agreed to compensate A for the training expenses.

[The next paragraph is 9.275.]

Distinction between capital and revenue

9.275 The Statement of principles excludes from its definition of gains (and, hence, revenue) changes in shareholders' funds, which relate to contributions from or distributions to owners.

9.276 Contributions from owners are defined in the statement of principles as *"...increases in ownership interest resulting from transfers from owners in their capacity as owners"*. [SoP chapter 4]. Such contributions are usually in the form of cash, but may also occur when other assets are transferred into the business or when equity is accepted in satisfaction of a liability. Such gifts of a capital amount are often made by parent companies to their subsidiaries. What constitutes a capital contribution might be difficult to determine in practice. A genuine gift without condition from a third party unconnected with the receiving company and, therefore, not in the capacity of an owner, should generally be treated as a gift and reported as a profit in the year of receipt. In addition, a receipt by a company might not be a capital contribution where it is repaid shortly thereafter other than by way of distribution and this was envisaged at the time the contribution was made. (But it should be remembered that contributions in kind, rather than in cash, do not give rise to a distributable profit.) Such a payment would be a loan, if, in effect, there is an obligation to transfer economic benefits as the contribution is made on the basis that it will be repaid. On the other hand, a contribution that is made without conditions, but is subsequently repaid by a distribution at the discretion of the receiving company, would be a capital contribution rather than a loan.

9.277 In the year in which it is received, the capital contribution should be credited to reserves by the receiving company and reported in its reconciliation of movements in shareholders' funds because it is not a gain, but the receipt from a transaction with shareholders. Nevertheless, it appears that where the amount is received in cash, it is legally a realised profit and as such can be taken into account in determining whether a company has sufficient distributable reserves to pay a dividend. Where, however, a contribution is in the form of an asset (for example, shares in a subsidiary) that is not cash or readily convertible into cash the contribution is not a realised profit and may not, therefore, be taken into account in determining distributable profits. It is best recorded in a separate reserve to distinguish it from other reserves, because of its different nature.

9.278 It seems logical that in the paying company (in a group of companies) the opposite accounting treatment should be adopted. Therefore, the contribution should not be recorded as an expense in the profit and loss account, but should be added to the cost of the investment in the subsidiary. Only if there is an impairment in the underlying value of the investment in the subsidiary would the investing company need to make a provision against its carrying value.

Financial services fees

Fees that are an integral part of the effective interest rate

9.279 In many situations, the actual rate of interest charged by a lender will be the same as the effective rate (that is, the rate required to discount the expected future income streams over the life of the loan to its initial carrying amount). Other transactions may include elements both of interest and of other financial service fees. For these transactions it is necessary to differentiate between fees that are part of the transaction's effective yield and fees that are earned for performing a certain act.

Example

Company A grants a loan to entity B for £100,000 on 1 January 20X1. The loan is repayable at 31 December 20X5. Interest of 8% that is equal to the market rate is payable annually. The loan origination fees amount to £2,000 and are paid by entity B to company A on 1 January 20X1.

Loan origination fees charged by company A are an integral part of establishing a loan. These fees are deferred and recognised as an adjustment to the effective yield. The effective yield is the interest needed to discount all the cash flows (£8,000 for 5 years and the principle amount of £100,000) to the present value of £98,000. In this case, the effective yield obtained by a discounted cash flow calculation is approximately 8.51% and, therefore, the entity recognises a finance cost at 8.51% on the carrying amount in each period.

Table 9.20 gives The Royal Bank of Scotland's accounting policy for loan origination fees.

Table 9.20 – The Royal Bank of Scotland Group Plc – Annual Report and Accounts – 31 December 2004

Accounting policies (extract)

2 Revenue recognition (extract)

Loan origination fees: up-front lending fees are recognised as income when receivable except where they are charged in lieu of interest or charged to cover the cost of a continuing service to the borrower, in which case they are credited to income over the life of the advance.

9.280 The appendix to IAS 18 gives guidance on accounting for different types of financial service fees that can be applied in the UK. Reviewing the borrower's credit rating or registering charges, for example, are necessary and integral parts of the lending process. Fees for performing such services should be deferred and recognised as an adjustment to the effective interest rate. Commitment fees that are charged by the lender when it is probable that a specific transaction will take place should similarly be included in the effective interest rate (where the loan commitment is outside IAS 39's scope, which is the same as FRS 26), but if the commitment expires without the transaction taking place, then the fee may be recognised as revenue on expiration. For companies applying FRS 26 (see chapter 6), loan commitments that are within FRS 26's scope are accounted for as derivatives and measured at fair value.

Fees earned as a result of providing services

9.281 Other types of financial service fees are earned as the service is provided. For example, commitment fees that are charged by a lender when it is unlikely that a lending arrangement will be entered into should be recognised on a time apportioned basis over the commitment period (where the loan commitment is outside the scope of FRS 26). Fees for servicing a loan should also be recognised as the service is provided.

Fees earned upon the execution of a significant act

9.282 A third type of financial service fee relates to performing a particular significant act. Commissions received on the allotment of shares or placement fees for arranging a loan between a borrower and an investor are examples of such significant acts. Revenue should be recognised when the act has been performed, for example when the shares have been allotted or the loan arranged. However, fees earned for the completion of a significant act must be distinguished from fees that relate to future performance or to any risk retained. A loan syndication fee, for example, may be earned when the transaction takes place, if the entity that arranges the loan either has no further involvement or retains part of the loan package at the same effective interest rate for comparable risk as the other participants. Such a fee is recognised as revenue when the syndication has been completed.

9.282.1 It is common within the investment management industry that a financial broker will receive an upfront payment from a fund manager for signing up a new customer. When the financial broker is also the fund manager, the question arises as to whether a non-refundable upfront fee can be recognised as revenue. The outcome has been debated at length under IFRS by IFRIC and in January 2007, it conceded that the accounting for many of these arrangements would depend on the facts and circumstances of the particular case. In the absence of any other guidance in the UK, the limited guidance from IFRIC (in the form of a rejection) is the best that is available in helping to determine whether an upfront fee could be recognised as revenue:

- Fees may be recognised as revenue only to the extent that services have been provided.

- Whilst the proportion of costs incurred in delivering services may be used to estimate the transaction's stage of completion, incurring costs does not by itself imply that a service has been provided.

- The receipt of a non-refundable initial fee does not, in itself, give evidence that an upfront service has been provided or that the fair value of the consideration paid in respect of any upfront services is equal to the initial fee received.

- To the extent that:

  - an initial service can be shown to have been provided to a customer;

  - the fair value of the consideration received in respect of that service can be measured reliably; and

  - the conditions for the recognition of revenue in Application note G have been met,

  upfront and ongoing fees may be recognised as revenue in line with the provision of services to the customer.

Presentation and disclosure

9.283 Company law requires the profit and loss account of a company or a group to comply with one of four formats. FRS 3 also affects the disclosure requirements of the profit and loss account. These requirements and the format requirements are set out in detail in chapter 4. The remainder of this chapter will deal with the different types of income that may be included in the turnover and other operating income lines of the profit and loss account and the disclosure requirements relating to grants.

Accounting policies

9.283.1 FRS 18 requires disclosure in the notes to the financial statements of "*a description of each of the accounting policies that is material in the context of the entity's financial statements*". [FRS 18 para 55(a)].

9.283.2 The purpose of the disclosure of accounting policies is to enable users to understand the financial statements. This is discussed further in chapter 2.

9.283.3 Application note G does not prescribe any specific accounting policies that must be followed, so a detailed description of those policies will be required. It is expected that an entity's revenue recognition accounting policy will address as a minimum, for each principal source of revenue:

- The timing of the recognition of revenue.
- The measurement of revenue.
- The treatment of discounts offered to customers.

- The method of allocation of revenue between different components of the same transaction (where different recognition policies are applied to the components).

9.283.4 In October 2007, the FRRP noted in its activity report for the period from 1 April 2006 to 31 March 2007 that several companies' revenue accounting policies were lacking. This was also a theme in the equivalent 2006 report and is, therefore, still a matter that needs to be improved. It noted that this was a particular issue for companies with a range of revenue streams. The FRRP stated that specific questions were raised in connection with the accounting treatment of advanced royalties, installation costs, research and development and licence fees.

Turnover

9.284 Company law specifies the amount a company must include in its profit and loss account under the heading of 'Turnover.' This comprises the amounts a company derives from providing goods and services that fall within its ordinary activities, after deducting trade discounts, VAT and any other taxes based on the amounts it so derives. [CA85 Sec 262(1); CA06 Sec 474(1)]. The definition accords with the requirement in SSAP 5 that turnover should exclude VAT on taxable outputs.

Trading activities

9.285 Since the income created by the ordinary trading activities of a company is by definition its turnover, the nature of the company's business will dictate what is included in turnover rather than the nature of the income. For most companies, other types of income or gains such as the profit on disposal of a subsidiary or interest receivable which is ancillary to the company's main business activities would be reported in the profit and loss account, but not in the turnover line. Other recognised gains, such as those relating to holding non-trading assets such as buildings which have increased in value may be reported as revaluation movements in the statement of total recognised gains and losses. Groups with diverse activities have turnover from different sources that may be subject to different recognition criteria.

Commissions and agency fees

9.286 Where a company acts as an agent or broker, such as a travel agent, insurance broker or stock broker, it should not include the gross value of the contracts in its turnover, but only the commission or margin that it charges on each deal. The exclusion of such amounts in turnover is consistent with Application note G, which excludes amounts collected on behalf of third parties from its definition of revenue. An estate agent, for example, should only recognise the commission that is earned on each property sold. This is illustrated in Table 9.21.

Table 9.21 – Debenham Tewson & Chinnocks Holdings plc – Report & Accounts – 30 April 1994

Notes to the accounts (extract)

1. Accounting policies (extract)

Turnover
Turnover comprises commissions and fees receivable exclusive of sales related taxes. Agency commissions are recognised on completion of the transaction.

9.287 Further discussion regarding criteria that may be relevant to determining whether companies are acting as agents or principals and accordingly whether they should report turnover gross or net are contained considered from paragraph 9.161.

9.288 As noted in paragraph 9.168 above, FRS 5 Application note G encourages disclosure by agents, where practicable, of the gross value of sales throughput as additional, non-statutory information. Where an agent gives such disclosure it should give a brief explanation of the relationship between recognised turnover and the gross value of sales throughput. [FRS 5 App G para G72].

Other operating income

9.289 'Other operating income' will include income that is associated with a company's normal activities, but that falls outside the definition of revenue. An item is not included in 'other operating income' just because it is small. For example, the revenue of the company's smallest division would nevertheless be included in turnover. Amounts shown in 'other operating income' are typically both incidental to the main activities of the company and are different in nature from amounts included in turnover.

9.290 For example, a manufacturing company that receives a small amount of royalty income may wish to include it in 'other operating income' rather than in turnover since to add it to turnover may overstate the company's margin if the royalty has no associated cost of sales.

9.291 In certain circumstances, commissions may also fall to be treated as 'other operating income'. This analysis is illustrated in the following example.

Example

A retail business sells National Lottery tickets in addition to confectionery, tobacco and newspapers. Customers say which numbers they want and the retailer obtains them via the computer provided by the National Lottery. Then the customers pay for their tickets and the retailer pays this amount less a commission to the National Lottery.

Since turnover, as defined in company law, is amounts derived from the provision of goods and services falling within the company's ordinary activities (see para 9.284), this commission could be seen as more of an incidental activity. If this is the case it may be more appropriate to include the commission under 'other operating income' rather than as turnover. This would prevent the fact that there is no cost of sales attributable to the income from distorting the gross margins, especially if these commissions are not disclosed as a separate segment in the segmental analysis of turnover and profit. On the other hand, the distribution of lottery tickets could be seen as a service to customers in which case it may be appropriate to include the commission in turnover. The category into which the commission falls should be determined based on how significant the provision of lottery tickets is to the activities of the business.

9.292 In addition, 'other operating income' could include rents from land, unless the company involved were a property company that derived income from the renting of property.

Government grants

9.293 Company law specifically does not allow income to be set off against expenditure [currently CA85 4 Sch 5]. In general, therefore, income that is received in compensation for expenditure incurred should not be netted off against the related expenditure. For example, a government grant that is received for employing a certain number of people for a certain length of time should be recognised on a basis that matches the costs of employing the people, but should not be used to reduce those employment costs. Such a grant is not revenue so, therefore, should be included in other operating income.

9.294 Where an enterprise receives government grants, the disclosures required by SSAP 4, 'Accounting for government grants', are as follows:

- The accounting policy adopted for government grants.
- The effects of government grants on the results and/or the financial position of the entity.
- Where an entity is in receipt of government assistance other than grants that have a material effect on its results, the nature of the assistance and, where possible, an estimate of the financial effects.
- Where applicable, the potential liabilities to repay grants.

[SSAP 4 para 28].

9.295 The accounting policy note should include the period or periods over which grants are credited to the profit and loss account. Where an entity is in receipt of various types of grants, it will normally be sufficient to give a broad indication of the period or periods over which they will be credited to the profit and loss account.

9.296 Where an entity is in receipt of a government grant that has a material effect on its results for the period and any future periods, the most practical way of identifying the effect of the grant on reported earnings may be to disclose the total amount credited in the profit and loss as an exceptional item.

9.297 Any unamortised deferred income relating to the grant will be included under the heading 'Accruals and deferred income'. Where the amount of unamortised deferred income is material, it may also be appropriate to identify this amount separately in a note to the balance sheet. It will provide readers of the financial statements with an indication of the extent to which future results may be expected to benefit from grants already received. Another way of showing the effect could be to include a statement of the changes during the period in the amount of the deferred income carried forward, showing: grants received; grants credited to the profit and loss account; and grants repaid, if any. For example, see Table 9.22.

Table 9.22 – Pilkington plc – Directors' Report and Accounts – 31 March 2002

Notes on the financial statements (extract)

	2002		**2001**	
30 Deferred Income	**Group £m**	**Company £m**	Group £m	Company £m
At beginning of year	19	6	**19**	**9**
Exchange rate adjustments	4	—	**3**	—
Investment grants receivable				
	23	6	**22**	**9**
Released to profit and loss account in the year:	(3)	(3)	**(3)**	**(3)**
At end of the year	20	3	**19**	**6**

9.298 Where government assistance is given in a form other than grants, SSAP 4 requires that the nature and, where measurable, the effects of the assistance should be disclosed. Similar disclosures should be given for significant assistance received from a source other than the government as discussed in paragraph 9.270.

9.299 Once a grant is recognised, any related contingency, such as the requirement to repay the grant in certain circumstances, should be treated in accordance with FRS 12, 'Provisions, contingent liabilities and contingent assets'. These requirements are detailed in chapter 21.

Chapter 10

Segmental reporting

Page

Introduction 10001

The regulatory framework 10001

Statutory requirements and exemptions 10001

SSAP 25 10003

Scope and exemptions 10003

Truth and fairness implications 10006

Other accounting standards 10007

General guidance 10007

Determining segments 10007

Classes of business 10008

Geographical segments 10010

Significant business segments 10018

Allocation of costs 10019

Disclosure requirements 10021

Legislative requirements 10021

Additional disclosures required by the standard 10022

Turnover and inter-segment sales 10024

Segment result 10026

Segment net assets 10032

Associates and joint ventures 10035

Joint arrangements 10038

Reconciliation of figures 10038

Comparative figures 10039

Other disclosure requirements 10039

Cash flow statements 10039

Subsidiary undertakings 10042

Acquisitions and discontinued operations 10043

Exceptional items 10046

Voluntary segmental disclosures 10049

Introduction 10049

Employees 10049

Fixed assets and capital expenditure 10051

Depreciation 10053

Research and development 10053

Annex — Comparison of segmental reporting requirements 10055

Chapter 10

Segmental reporting

Introduction

10.1 For companies that operate in a variety of classes of business or in a number of different geographical locations, the availability of segmental information, (also called 'disaggregated information'), setting out meaningful analyses of turnover and profits, is essential for good management. Such information is essential if management is to be able to detect trends in performance and sales within its specific business and geographical regions. Armed with such information, management is better placed to devise strategies and focus actions towards countering adverse trends or exploiting opportunities in specific business lines or market places.

10.2 The form of segmental information that is of use in a business depends to a great extent on how the management of the business is organised. A business may be managed on a product basis, a geographical basis, or on a mixture of both. Where a business is managed on a geographical basis, the information that may be most useful is a geographical analysis of turnover and profits. An analysis by class of business may be difficult to obtain because, for instance, different classes of business within a geographical segment may be financed as one operation and may share resources. Where a business is managed on a product basis, an analysis of turnover and profits by product will be more important. The management structure of the majority of international companies, however, includes both geographical and product structures. Therefore, segmental information by product and by geographical region is relevant to most companies.

10.3 The value of segmental information is not limited to its application as an internal management tool. It also has an important role in external reporting, since by providing segmental information in financial statements, the management of a company can explain to readers many of the factors which have contributed to the result for the year. These factors might be developments instigated by management, such as the expansion of products or markets, or events outside management's control, such as political disturbances abroad.

[The next paragraph is 10.6.]

The regulatory framework

Statutory requirements and exemptions

10.6 The Companies Act 1985 requires all companies to include certain information analysed by both class of business and geographical market in the notes to the profit and loss account. The specific disclosures are considered in detail in paragraphs 10.68 to 10.73. However, disaggregated information need not be disclosed where the directors have determined that such disclosure would be seriously prejudicial to the company's interests. Where this exemption is utilised, however, the financial statements must state that disaggregated information has not been disclosed.

10.7 An example of the circumstances that might result in the directors deciding to utilise the exemption is where a company or a group supplies customers in two countries only. If these companies are politically opposed to each other, to publish a geographical split of turnover could be considered to be prejudicial to the interests of the company or the group. Provided that the notes to the profit and loss account disclose the fact that this analysis has not been given, no further information is required to be published. In practice, the prejudicial exemption is applied by surprisingly few reporting entities. Further, where prejudice is claimed, it is frequently limited to specific segmental disclosures rather than the whole range.

10.8 The fact that the Act gives the directors the responsibility for determining whether segmental information should be reported is a matter of note. This is because they alone determine:

- Whether two or more classes of substantially different business have been carried out by the company.
- Whether turnover has been generated in two or more substantially different geographical markets.
- Whether non-disclosure on the grounds of seriously prejudicing the company's interests is appropriate.

However, it is implicit that, in making their decisions on reportable segments, the directors should act in good faith.

10.9 Small companies (and groups headed by a small company) have been granted a specific exemption from the disclosure requirements of the Act. They need not give details of segmental information by market, as required by paragraph 55 of Schedule 4 to the Act, if they have taken advantage of the exemptions contained in Schedule 8 to the Act in drawing up their financial statements. However, if the company or group has supplied geographical markets outside the UK (turnover by destination), the notes must state the percentage of turnover (but not profit or loss) attributable to those markets. The analysis made for these purposes must still have regard to the manner in which the company's activities are organised. [CA 85 8 Sch 49]. The disclosure requirements applicable to small companies are considered in detail in chapter 32.

[The next paragraph is 10.13.]

SSAP 25

10.13 SSAP 25, 'Segment reporting', was issued in July 1990, since then the ASB has issued a number of subsequent standards that also have implications for segmental-type reporting. IAS 14 and its replacement IFRS 8, 'Operating segments', (which at the time of going to print had not been approved by the EU) are very different from SSAP 25.

Scope and exemptions

10.14 Insofar as they repeat the requirements of paragraph 55 of Schedule 4 to the Companies Act 1985, the segmental disclosure requirements of SSAP 25 apply to all entities preparing Companies Act financial statements as defined by the Act.

10.15 SSAP 25, however, sets out additional requirements that apply to certain entities only. In effect, smaller companies are excluded from the standard's disclosure requirements, other than where those requirements are also prescribed by the Act. However, exempt entities can, and are encouraged to, adopt these additional disclosures on a voluntary basis.

10.16 The entities to which the additional disclosures apply on a mandatory basis are:

- All public companies or parent companies that have a public company as a subsidiary.
- Banking and insurance companies and groups.
- All other entities that exceed two of the three criteria for defining a medium-sized company under section 247 of the Companies Act 1985 multiplied in each case by ten.

10.17 The three criteria referred to in the paragraph above and as multiplied by ten result in the following cut-off points:

- Turnover in excess of £228 million.
- Balance sheet total in excess of £114 million.
- Number of employees in excess of 2,500.

10.18 The three criteria for turnover, balance sheet total and number of employees are amended from time to time by statutory instrument. However, their impact is intended to ensure that larger companies present the full segmental disclosures required by the standard. Conversely, all companies below that size are left with the freedom to choose what, if any, additional segmental disclosures they might make beyond those required by the Act.

10.19 In addition to the exemption available to smaller companies, there is a further exemption from complying with the non-statutory aspects of the standard.

This exemption is intended to be a practical one, in that it seeks to avoid the need for voluminous disclosures by subsidiaries, where the group financial statements provide full segmental disclosures in accordance with the standard. Accordingly, where a subsidiary undertaking is neither a public company, nor a banking or insurance company, it need not comply with the provisions of the standard provided that its parent provides segmental information in compliance with the standard.

10.19.1 Where a subsidiary's parent prepares its financial statements in accordance with IFRS and reports segmental information as required by IAS 14, 'Segment reporting', that subsidiary can only take advantage of the subsidiaries' exemption where the parent's IAS 14 disclosure is compliant with the requirements of SSAP 25. In November 2006, the IASB issued IFRS 8, 'Operating segments', which will be applicable for periods beginning on or after 1 January 2009. At the time of this chapter going to print, this standard had not been endorsed by the EU and, therefore, may not be applied by those entities in the EU that report under IFRS.

10.19.2 Where the reportable segments in the parent's (consolidated) IFRS financial statements are compliant with the requirements of SSAP 25, then the IAS 14 (or IFRS 8) information reported may be adequate to ensure compliance with SSAP 25, or additional disclosure may be included in the parent's IFRS financial statements to achieve compliance with SSAP 25, thus enabling its subsidiaries to take advantage of the exemption.

10.19.3 If, however, the segment's reported under IAS 14 are not compliant with the requirements of SSAP 25, this will be more difficult to achieve.

10.19.4 Within a group it is unlikely that every company will be required to disclose segmental information. Consider the following example.

Example

The group headed by T plc has the following structure:

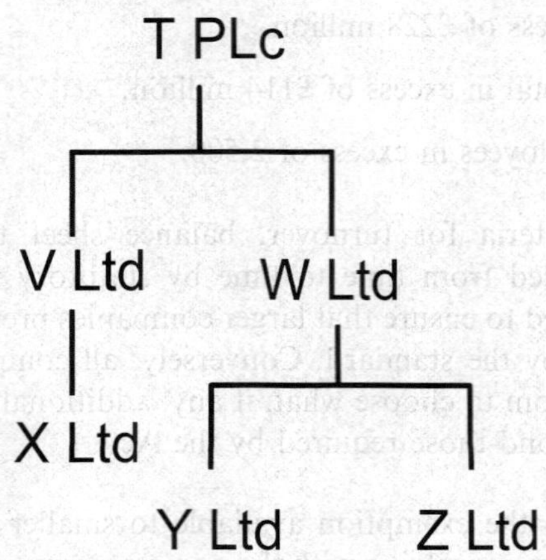

All companies except T plc and W Limited are trading companies engaged in retail operations and are more than ten times the size criteria for a medium-sized company. T plc prepares its consolidated financial statements in accordance with IFRS. All other companies in the group prepare Companies Act financial statements.

T plc prepares segmental information for the group in accordance with IAS 14. This information is not compliant with the requirements of SSAP 25.

V Limited is unable to take advantage of any exemptions contained in SSAP 25 and reports segmental information.

X Limited is able to take advantage of the subsidiary exemption outlined in paragraph 10.19 because its parent (V Limited) has presented segmental information in compliance with SSAP 25. However, unless V Limited has prepared consolidated financial statements, we consider that it is best practice for X Limited to disclose segmental information.

W Limited is non-trading and falls outside the scope of SSAP 25.

Y Limited and Z Limited are unable to take advantage of any exemption in SSAP 25 and are required to report segmental information.

10.20 It should be emphasised that, whether or not companies are exempt from the requirements of the standard, as a minimum, all companies still have to comply with the legal requirements contained in the Act. Thus, a subsidiary undertaking that takes advantage of the exemptions described in paragraph 10.19 will still be required to disclose the segmental information required by the Act, unless it can also take advantage of the Act's exemptions not to disclose segmental information.

10.21 It is not totally clear why subsidiary undertakings engaged in banking and insurance activities have been selected for special treatment, particulary now that FRS 2, 'Accounting for subsidiary undertakings', prohibits the exclusion of a subsidiary from the consolidation on the basis of dissimilar activities. Thus, in most circumstances, segmental information will have been provided at a group level, presumably with financial service operations disclosed as a separate segment or segments. Consequently, there seems little benefit in requiring fuller segmental information in the subsidiaries' financial statements unless it is undertaking a wide spread of financial activities. For insurance groups this situation is compounded by UK insurers being required to submit annual returns to the DTI. The returns set out detailed revenue account analyses by insurance class in a prescribed format. The information contained therein seems likely to be of far greater benefit to analysts, than the more limited segmental information disclosed within statutory financial statements.

10.22 There is a further limitation on the scope and application of the standard in that the standard repeats the exemption contained in paragraph 55(5) of Schedule 4 to the Act in the wider context of the standard. Thus where, in the opinion of the directors, the disclosure of any information required by the standard would be seriously prejudicial to the interests of the company, that information need not be disclosed. However, like the Act, the standard requires the fact that any such information has not been disclosed to be stated. [SSAP 25 para 6]. Few companies now take advantage of this exemption in respect of all the segmental disclosures required by the Act and the standard. Several, however, provide some segmental information, but apply the prejudicial override clause to limit certain types of segmental disclosures. For example, Inspec Group plc, a chemicals manufacturer, provides segmental analysis of turnover by origin and destination, but does not provide a segmental analysis of net assets by class of business or geographical area of origin or an analysis of results by geographical origin, on the grounds that to disclose such information would be seriously prejudicial to the group's interests.

Table 10.1 — Inspec Group plc — Annual Report — 31 December 1997

Notes to the Accounts (extract)

2 SEGMENTAL INFORMATION (extract)
In the opinion of the directors the disclosure of segmental information relating to the business categories of net assets and the geographical origin of results and net assets would be seriously prejudicial to the interests of the Group and has not therefore been provided.

[The next paragraph is 10.24.]

Truth and fairness implications

10.24 Where an entity takes advantage of the exemption referred to in paragraph 10.22 above not to make segmental disclosures on the grounds that they would be seriously prejudicial, the question arises as to the impact of such non-disclosure on the truth and fairness of the financial statements as a whole.

10.25 The standard allows non-disclosure where the information, if disclosed, would be seriously prejudicial to the company. As noted above, this is based on an equivalent provision in the Act. The standard implies that, in such a situation, segmental information is not essential to the true and fair view.

10.26 The Foreword to Accounting Standards is helpful in this regard. It indicates that the prescription of information to be contained with financial statements does *"...not override exemptions from disclosure given by law to, and utilised, by certain kinds of entity"*. [Foreword to Accounting Standards para 15].

10.27 Auditors have to decide whether failure to provide segmental information should result in qualifying their opinion on financial statements on the grounds that the truth and fairness of those financial statements is affected. Clearly, if such information is not disclosed, but there are no grounds on which disclosure could be considered to be seriously prejudicial, then the auditor should state that the financial statements have not been properly prepared in accordance with the Act. If the auditor considers that the non-disclosure is so material as to affect the truth and fairness of the financial statements, it will be necessary to qualify the opinion given on their truth and fairness.

10.28 However, if disclosure is not made and there is reason to believe that disclosure would be seriously prejudicial, then clearly the auditor could state that the financial statements had been properly prepared in accordance with the Act. The omission of the information would also be in accordance with the standard and, therefore, qualification of the audit opinion on the truth and fairness of the financial statements would not be appropriate.

10.29 A similar issue potentially arises in the situation where small companies take advantage of exemptions not to provide the same level of segmental information disclosures as are prescribed for large and public companies. In essence, if detailed segmental information is considered necessary for a true and fair view to be given by those types of entity, how can smaller entities be said to give a true and fair view, unless they mirror that level of segmental disclosure?

10.30 The matter of limited disclosure exemptions permitted to certain types of entity has been addressed in Counsel's opinion, reproduced in the Appendix to the Foreword to Accounting Standards. This indicates that, while it is a question of law as to whether financial statements give a true and fair view, the courts will look to the requirements of accounting standards in reaching their decision. It can be inferred from this that, if accounting standards permit exemptions to certain categories or sizes of company, the courts would not interpret these exemptions as detracting from the true and fair view.

Other accounting standards

10.31 Subsequent to the publication of SSAP 25 in 1990, the ASB has published a number of financial reporting standards that have an impact on segmental disclosures. The disclosure implications of these standards, in terms of segmental reporting, are considered in paragraphs 10.116 to 10.142 below.

General guidance

Determining segments

10.32 For financial statements that disclose segmental information to readers to have real value, a high level of consistency of approach across reporting entities is required. This is particularly important in terms of how directors determine what constitutes a reportable segment, so that different companies apply similar principles in determining what should be reported. This should enable readers of financial statements to make better comparisons of performance and prospects across reporting entities.

10.33 Both the Act and the standard clearly view reportable segments in terms of either class of business segments or geographical segments and both conclude that the determination of a company's classes of business and geographical segments must depend on the judgement of the directors. Thus, it is the directors — and they alone — who decide whether the company operates in more than one class of business or geographical segment. However, as this could lead to inevitable inconsistencies across boards of companies, the standard sets out additional guidance on the matter.

10.34 The advice given by the standard emphasises how the directors should have regard to the overall purpose of presenting segmental information, in making their judgements about reportable segments. Of primary concern to the directors in their deliberations should be the question of whether the provision of segmental information is likely to be helpful and informative to users of financial statements.

10.35 The emphasis of the standard is that, for segmental reporting to be of real value to users of financial statements, the segmental information reported needs both to reflect the company's risk and reward profile and to inform users of the nature of that profile. This sentiment is reiterated in the explanatory note to the standard, which discusses the circumstances where the provision of segmental information may enhance a reader's understanding of the financial statements. Where an entity operates in more than one class of business or more than one geographical market, the circumstances described above arise where businesses:

- Earn a return on the investment that is out of line with the return earned by the remainder of the business.
- Are subject to different degrees of risk.
- Have experienced different degrees of growth.
- Have different potentials for future development.

[SSAP 25 para 8].

10.36 It follows from the above that in determining business or geographical segments, products or services (or a related group of products or services), with significantly differing risks, rewards and future prospects should not be combined together to create a reportable segment. Instead, they should be treated as separate segments and reported as such, provided that they are of sufficient materiality to justify separate disclosure.

10.37 The standard also emphasises the need for the directors to reconsider segment definitions periodically and re-define them where appropriate. [SSAP 25 para 10]. This means that the directors should reconsider the position on each occasion that financial statements are produced.

[The next paragraph is 10.42.]

Classes of business

10.42 When the directors of a reporting entity consider the provision of segmental analysis in that entity's financial statements, they are inevitably faced with the question of whether the entity has distinct business segments and, if so, how these are to be identified.

10.43 In the past, a number of different approaches to defining business segments have been proposed. For instance, a number of approaches were considered by an IASC steering group in developing the revised international accounting standard, IAS 14 'Segment reporting'. The approaches include:

- Defining business segments by products or services grouped together on an industry basis according to a national or international industry or product classification system. Although this could enhance consistency across reporting entities in terms of segment identification, it is not generally considered an appropriate approach. This is because it could result in very broad segments and may not adequately consider differences in risks and rewards within an entity.
- Defining business segments as distinct components of an enterprise that are capable of sale or separation from the rest of the entity without affecting other business segments. A problem with this approach is that it does not necessarily reflect the risk and reward profile of the reporting entity.
- Defining business segments by way of a management approach, whereby financial reporting is based on the major operating units of the reporting entity. In effect, reportable segments constitute organisational units for which financial results are maintained and analysed by management as an integral part of their management and control procedures. This approach has been adopted by the national standard setting body in the US. However, it is arguable that where organisational groupings combine products and services with significantly different risk and reward profiles, this method of reporting fails to achieve the objective of segmental reporting, because the user of the financial statements is not provided with information on a risk and reward basis.
- Defining a business segment as a distinguishable component that provides a product or service, or a group of related products or services; where that distinguishable component is subject to different risks and rewards from other business segments of the entity. This risk and reward approach is the one underlying SSAP 25.

10.44 The UK accounting standard appears to acknowledge the last two approaches. Having defined 'class of business' in paragraph 30 of the standard, as *"...a distinguishable component of an entity that provides a separate product or service or a separate group of related products or services"*, it moves on to provide guidance on identification. In assessing whether the reporting entity has different classes of products or services, the standard suggests that directors should consider the following factors:

- The nature of the products or services.
- The nature of the production processes.
- The markets in which the products or services are sold.
- The distribution channels for the products.

- The manner in which the entity's activities are organised.
- Any separate legislative framework relating to part of the business, for example, a bank or an insurance company.

[SSAP 25 para 12].

10.45 Most of the criteria above are consistent with the risks and reward approach in that they look to the separability of products and services. However, the reference to the way in which activities are organised is more indicative of the management approach. In fact, for operating and management reporting purposes, directors often use the above criteria for organising corporate entities into divisions, branches or subsidiaries. In such situations, the management approach referred to in paragraph 10.43 also acknowledges risk and reward considerations. Consequently, in these instances class of business analysis based on risk and reward considerations will also reflect the organisation structure of the reporting entity.

10.46 Although the standard explains the criteria for identifying whether separate business segments exist, this explanation is merely guidance. The directors have to exercise their own judgement in this area based on the particular circumstances of their reporting entity. In effect, the standard recognises that no one set of characteristics can claim universal application, nor can any individual characteristic claim to be determinative in every situation. Consequently, although different boards might reach different decisions on identifiable and reportable segments, by providing guidance on types of segment and their characteristics, the standard should reduce the degree of difference, so long as boards act in good faith.

Geographical segments

10.47 When directors consider the reporting of segmental information, both the Act and the standard require them to give such information by geographical segments. As for business segments, judgement is required by the directors, who have responsibility for determining whether distinct geographical segments exist and for identifying them.

10.48 The standard's definition of geographical segment indicates that it is "*. . .a geographical area comprising an individual country or group of countries in which an entity operates, or to which it supplies products or services*". [SSAP 25 para 31]. This is helpful insofar as it clearly envisages aggregations of groups of countries to form one geographical segment for reporting purposes. In addition, it emphasises that geographical analysis needs to consider two distinct aspects:

- Analysis by operating location (origin basis).
- Analysis by destination of sale or service (destination basis).

[SSAP 25 para 14].

10.49 The standard defines both origin of turnover and destination of turnover. The former term comprises *"…the geographical segment from which products or services are supplied to a third party or to another segment"*. [SSAP 25 para 32]. The latter term is identified as *"…the geographical segment to which products or services are supplied"*. [SSAP 25 para 33].

10.50 Beyond the above, the guidance given by the standard is very limited, insofar as criteria for determining the choice of geographical segments is concerned. In emphasising that the groupings selected should reflect the overriding purpose of presenting segmental information, the standard suggests that they should indicate to the reader the extent to which a company's operations are subject to factors such as:

- Expansionist or restrictive economic climates.
- Stable or unstable political regimes.
- Exchange control regulations.
- Exchange rate fluctuations.

[SSAP 25 para 15].

10.51 These suggestions indicate that the different risk environments in which a reporting entity operates are an important factor in determining segments. A multi-national operation might take account of its geographical risk profiles, for example, by treating Western Europe as a single geographical market, Eastern Europe as a second and the Far East as a third. On the other hand, an operation which trades out of, or sells into, four overseas countries only, may well treat each of those as a distinct geographical segments. This might be irrespective of whether all or the majority of them are, say, Western European, provided that each of them is significant to the results and future prospects of the reporting entity as a whole.

10.52 A number of examples of segmental disclosures are set out below. The General Electric Company p.l.c provides a wealth of geographical segmental analysis as Table 10.2 illustrates. Not only are turnover, profit and net assets analysed by territory of origin, but turnover is also analysed by territory of destination. The analysis provided enables the reader to understand that:

- The UK is the major originator of sales, but exports a significant proportion of its production. The company's UK-based operations are also responsible for approximately half of the group's worldwide profit.
- France is the other major European originator of sales and also exports a large proportion of its production. It appears to achieve this from a negative local asset base.
- While the rest of Europe represents a material element of The General Electric Company p.l.c's business, no individual European country, other than the UK and France, is considered to constitute a segment in its own

right. However, this geographical segment purchases more The General Electric Company p.l.c products than it produces.

- The Americas constitutes another major originator of sales. However, in 1994, the segment was a net importer of The General Electric Company p.l.c products and services, since total sales within the segment slightly exceeded the value of sales originated therein. This is a reversal of the position that was reported for 1993.
- Although three other segments are identified, namely Australasia, Asia and Africa, they are relative immaterial in terms of their local production, asset levels and impact on profit. However, when considered from a destination perspective, they are clearly important to The General Electric Company p.l.c as notable importers of its products and services originating out of other geographical segments.

Table 10.2 — The General Electric Company p.l.c. — Annual Report and Accounts — 31 March 1994

Notes to the Accounts (Extract)

1 PRINCIPAL ACTIVITIES, PROFIT CONTRIBUTIONS, MARKETS AND NET ASSETS EMPLOYED (extract)

Analysis of turnover by classes of business

	To customers in the United Kingdom		To customers overseas	
	1994	1993	**1994**	1993
	£ million	£ million	**£ million**	£ million
Electronic Systems	**930**	943	**1,819**	1,774
Power Systems	**535**	596	**2,568**	2,539
Telecommunications	**715**	759	**335**	253
Consumer Goods	**236**	233	**23**	20
Electronic Metrology	**139**	132	**350**	281
Office Equipment & Printing	**17**	16	**306**	287
Medical Equipment	**3**	–	**671**	568
Electronic Components	**94**	107	**197**	195
Industrial Apparatus	**207**	236	**126**	106
Distribution & Trading			**351**	290
Other	**59**	77	**13**	20
Intra-Activity sales	**(83)**	(93)	**(68)**	(41)
	2,852	3,006	**6,691**	6,292

Analysis of turnover by territory of destination

	1994	1993
	£ million	£ million
United Kingdom	**2,852**	3,006
France	**1,122**	1,068
Rest of Europe	**1,618**	1,793
The Americas	**2,044**	1,886
Australasia	**341**	310
Asia	**1,353**	1,038
Africa	**213**	197
	9,543	9,298

Analysis of profit, turnover and net assets by territory of origin

			Turnover		Net assets	
	1994	1993	**1994**	1993	**1994**	1993
	£ million	£ million	**£ million**	£ million	**£ million**	£ million
United Kingdom	**344**	367	**4,425**	4,364	**650**	983
France	**93**	85	**1,846**	1,914	**(180)**	(104)
Rest of Europe	**82**	108	**976**	1,032	**143**	231
The Americas	**142**	116	**1,884**	1,620	**506**	473
Australasia	**12**	9	**273**	246	**65**	69
Asia	**6**	5	**115**	100	**7**	6
Africa	**5**	5	**24**	22	**20**	21
	684	695	**9,543**	9,298	**1,211**	1,679

10.53 The General Electric Company p.l.c extract is also notable for the analysis it provides of turnover by class of business. Where many companies provide such analysis on a total basis, The General Electric Company p.l.c sub-analyses such turnover between:

- Sales to UK customers.
- Sales to overseas customers.

10.54 In Table 10.3, Coats Viyella Plc also provides geographical analysis on both location and destination bases. In so doing, it treats *"Rest of Europe"* as a distinct geographical segment, but, identifies *"North America"* and *"South America"* as two separate segments. It also has a further segment described as *"Africa, Asia, Australasia"*, rather than employing the term, *"Rest of World"* adopted by many companies. Whether these three continents can be said to have similar risk and reward characteristics is open to question. The merging together of miscellaneous, individually non-material, geographical territories into a 'catch all' segment is practical. However, drawing conclusions about such segments needs to be undertaken with care.

Table 10.3— Coats Viyella Plc — Annual report and accounts — 31 December 1993

NOTES TO THE ACCOUNTS (extract)

	Turnover		Operating profit		Net assets	
2 Analysis of turnover, operating profit and net assets continued,	**1993**	1992	**1993**	1992	**1993**	1992 Restated
	£m	£m	**£m**	£m	**£m**	£m
Geographical analysis by location:						
United Kingdom	**1,049.2**	1,008.5	**55.7**	60.0	**369.5**	334.9
Rest of Europe	**516.2**	462.3	**24.0**	31.7	**189.2**	202.3
North America	**440.2**	369.7	**51.1**	41.3	**248.1**	222.9
South America	**116.2**	106.9	**3.7**	(3.9)	**97.6**	96.9
Africa, Asia, Australasia	**322.0**	162.4	**37.2**	17.1	**193.7**	131.6
	2,443.8	2,109.8	**171.7**	146.2	**1,098.1**	988.6
Other items			**21.2**	9.7		
Profit before interest			**192.9**	155.9		
Associated companies					**3.9**	17.9
					1,102.0	1,006.5
Net borrowings					**(266.3)**	(404.8)
Other fixed and current asset investments					**24.6**	24.6
Net assets per consolidated balance sheet					**860.3**	626.3
Acquisitions in the year have been included in the following segments:						
United Kingdom	**0.7**		–		**(0.6)**	
Rest of Europe	**51.4**		**7.6**		**15.0**	
North America	**15.0**		**1.5**		**14.2**	
Africa, Asia, Australasia	**132.9**		**19.3**		**61.0**	
	200.0		**28.4**		**89.6**	
Geographical analysis of sales by destination:						
United Kingdom	**968.2**	913.5				
Rest of Europe	**551.4**	506.9				
North America	**459.7**	378.3				
South America	**118.2**	109.4				
Africa, Asia, Australasia	**346.3**	201.7				
	2,443.8	2,109.8				

Notes
Associated companies are principally Thread and Fabrics businesses based in Asia.

10.55 Although identifying geographical segments by risk and reward profile may be the preferred approach, multi-nationals that operate in a very large number of countries appear to find it either impractical to adopt or not their primary consideration. In practice, decisions may be influenced by the volume of disclosure that the basis chosen leads to. For example, consider a global entity that operates out of the majority of African countries. The directors will need to consider whether they should analyse these individually or in small risk groupings to reflect the different circumstances of each. Alternatively, they may decide that an aggregation as 'Africa' is the most sensible presentation. In any event, in making their judgements, the directors will need to take account of the significance of individual countries, aggregations of countries and the continent as a whole to the results and financial status of the reporting entity.

10.56 A further point of interest in this area is the way in which some companies redefine their chosen geographical segments for disclosing segmental information by origin, when they disclose turnover information on a destination basis. This is understandable where a reporting entity sells significant volumes of business into a geographical location where it has no production capacity or minimal physical representation, but this does not appear to be the only determining factor. Examples of this approach include Pilkington plc, which treats *"Europe (excluding United Kingdom)"*, as one segment in disclosing information by origin, but splits it into two segments, *"EEP"* and *"Non EEP"* for disclosure of turnover on a destination basis. Similarly, the *"Rest of the World"* segment on an origin basis becomes three segments for the destination basis: *"Australasia"*, *"South America"* and *"Rest of the World"* (see Table 10.4).

Table 10.4 — Pilkington plc — Directors' Report and Accounts — 31 March 1994

Notes on the Financial Statements (extract)

	1994			1993		
1 Segmental analysis of Continuing Operations	**Turnover £m**	**Operating profit/ (loss) £m**	**Net operating assets £m**	Turnover £m	Operating profit/ (loss) £m	Net operating assets £m
Flat and safety glass–						
Europe	**1,321.7**	**33.2**	**948.3**	1,196.7	42.8	975.6
North America	**691.6**	**26.8**	**372.1**	626.7	5.0	393.6
Rest of the World	**337.0**	**49.7**	**235.3**	304.6	39.0	227.2
Total	**2,350.3**	**109.7**	**1,555.7**	2,128.0	86.8	1,596.4
Other trading companies	**164.5**	**(0.5)**	**158.3**	171.4	(1.0)	153.4
Group technology management	**0.3**	**4.8**	**(16.3)**	1.1	7.0	9.0
Group operations	**–**	**(22.8)**	**(4.6)**	–	(16.3)	18.4
	2,515.1	**91.2**	**1,693.1**	2,300.5	76.5	1,777.2
United Kingdom	**453.8**	**17.4**	**293.3**	331.3	(1.7)	277.3
Europe (excluding United Kingdom)	**925.5**	**14.2**	**754.7**	936.1	37.8	791.2
North America	**780.3**	**25.1**	**427.7**	712.9	5.1	450.9
Rest of the World	**355.2**	**52.5**	**238.3**	319.1	44.6	230.4
Group operations/technology management	**0.3**	**(18.0)**	**(20.9)**	1.1	(9.3)	27.4
	2,515.1	**91.2**	**1,693.1**	2,300.5	76.5	1,777.2

Comparative figures have been restated in accordance with FRS 3 and to take account of the repositioning of Pilkington Aerospace from other trading companies to flat and safety glass, and float process/product development costs from flat and safety glass to Group technology management.

The Companies Act 1985 requires the analysis of profit before tax but the analysis of operating profit is considered by the directors to be more meaningful.

Turnover derived from intra-segmental transactions is not material

Net operating assets are analysed in note 4.

2 Segmental Analysis of Discontinued Operations	**1994 Turnover £m**	**Operating profit/ (loss) £m**	**Net operating assets £m**	1993 Turnover £m	Operating profit/ (loss) £m	Net operating assets £m
Flat and safety glass						
Europe	–	–	–	4.0	(3.6)	–
North America	–	–	–	–	–	–
Rest of the World	–	–	–	–	–	–
Total	–	–	–	4.0	(3.6)	–
Other trading companies	**222.3**	**13.0**	**56.1**	268.0	15.1	191.4
	222.3	**13.0**	**56.1**	272.0	11.5	191.4
United Kingdom	**95.1**	**0.5**	**57.0**	92.2	2.3	76.1
Europe (excluding United Kingdom)	**29.8**	**2.4**	–	47.7	0.3	27.2
North America	**67.8**	**5.3**	**(0.9)**	93.4	3.1	52.1
Rest of the World	**29.6**	**4.8**	–	38.7	5.8	36.0
	222.3	**13.0**	**56.1**	272.0	11.5	191.4

Net operating assets are analysed in note 4.

3 Geographical Analysis of Turnover by Markets	**1994 Group £m**	**%**	1993 Group £m	%

This analysis of turnover shows the markets in which the Group's products are sold, whereas the regional analysis in notes 1 and 2 relate to the domicile of the Group undertakings making the sales.

Continuing Operations				
United Kingdom	**376.6**	**15**	268.0	12
Europe (excluding United Kingdom)				
– EEC	**768.9**	**31**	792.3	34
– Non EEC	**179.6**	**7**	165.0	7
North America	**770.2**	**31**	702.4	30
Australasia	**197.8**	**8**	180.4	8
South America	**156.7**	**6**	130.9	6
Rest of the World	**65.3**	**2**	61.5	3
	2,515.1	**100**	2300.5	100

Discontinued Operations				
United Kingdom	**92.9**	**42**	87.9	32
Europe (excluding United Kingdom)				
– EEC	**27.5**	**12**	44.1	16
– Non EEC	**3.2**	**1**	6.5	2
North America	**67.9**	**31**	93.5	34
Australasia	**8.6**	**4**	11.1	4
South America	**6.1**	**3**	9.7	4
Rest of the World	**16.1**	**7**	19.2	8
	222.3	**100**	272.0	100

	Continuing Operations		Discontinued Operations	
	1994	1993	**1994**	1993
4 Net Operating Assets	**£m**	£m	**£m**	£m
The net operating assets referred to in notes 1 and 2 comprise the following:				
Tangible assets	**1,618.4**	1,634.0	**44.8**	97.9
Stocks	**382.5**	391.3	**13.2**	86.9
Debtors	**435.7**	424.9	**16.8**	61.8
Creditors — falling due within one year	**(430.1)**	(370.4)	**(13.7)**	(52.3)
— falling due after more than one year	**(16.8)**	(11.7)	**(0.7)**	(2.9)
Provisions	**(296.6)**	(290.9)	**(4.3)**	–
	1,693.1	1,777.2	**56.1**	191.4

Creditors exclude loans and overdrafts, taxation on profits, finance leases and dividends. Debtors exclude taxation recoverable. Provisions exclude deferred taxation.

10.57 Enterprise Oil plc's 1994 Report and Accounts provides a further illustration of this point, as Table 10.5 demonstrates. In terms of turnover, the analysis by production location reveals two significant geographical segments, the UK and Norway. A 'catch all' category, described as *"Rest of World"*, is introduced to produce an analysis of total entity turnover. However, this segment is responsible for generating less than two per cent of total turnover in the current or prior year. When the company analyses its turnover by geographical area of destination, it identifies its markets as *"UK"*, *"Europe, excluding UK"*, *"North America"* and *"Asia — Pacific"*. Unusually, the geographical destination disclosures are made on a percentage basis, rather than on a monetary value basis.

Table 10.5 — Enterprise Oil plc — Annual Report and Accounts — 31 December 1994

Notes to the financial statements (extract)
for the year ended 31 December 1994

1. TURNOVER AND GEOGRAPHICAL ANALYSIS

The group's activities predominantly comprise oil and gas exploration and production. The geographical analysis of the group's turnover (by location of production) and profit before tax and net assets is as follows:

	Turnover		Profit before tax		Net assets	
	1994 £m	1993 £m	**1994 £m**	1993 £m	**1994 £m**	1993 £m
UK	**528.0**	391.5	**180.4**	91.2	**1,058.0**	1,123.2
Norway	**118.5**	144.0	**32.8**	42.1	**121.6**	69.2
Rest of World	**4.8**	10.6	**(32.2)**	(43.5)	**93.1**	77.4
	651.3	546.1	**181.0**	89.8	**1,272.7**	1,269.8
Costs and expenses of the offer for LASMO plc			**(5.7)**	–	–	
Equity in associated undertaking			**(19.6)**	2.1	**59.8**	74.3
Investment in LASMO plc			**(18.1)**	–	**141.9**	–
Net interest/net debt and loan to associate			**(43.7)**	7.9	**(538.1)**	(392.8)
			93.9	99.8	**936.3**	951.3

	1994	1993
Analysis of turnover by geographical area of destination:	%	%
UK	36.1	62.8
Europe, excluding UK	46.0	28.4
North America	17.7	7.6
Asia-Pacific	0.2	1.2
	100.0	100.0

Significant business segments

10.58 The problems that can arise when a reporting entity operates out of, or sells into, a large number of different countries have been referred to above. Similarly, when an entity is organised into a large number of relatively small business units or produces an extensive product range, the identification of reportable segments requires careful consideration and judgement. It is, in effect, a balancing act, between providing too little analysis and supplying so much that it obscures the reader's understanding.

10.59 The explanatory notes to the standard are of some assistance in this respect, in that they attempt to set out size criteria for determining whether a segment should be considered significant enough to justify separate identification and reporting. The standard suggests that a segment would normally be regarded as significant if:

- its third party turnover is ten per cent or more of the entity's total third party turnover; or

- its segment result, whether profit or loss, is ten per cent or more of the combined result of all segments in profit or of all segments in loss, whichever combined result is the greater; or
- its net assets are ten per cent or more of the entity's total net assets.

[SSAP 25 para 9].

10.60 The term 'net assets' is discussed later in this chapter in paragraphs 10.91 to 10.99. Although the second of the criteria set out above is tortuously worded, it means that, if a group makes an overall loss of £100, with some segments making losses amounting to £600 and others making profits amounting to £500, an individual segment that makes a profit or loss of £50 is not significant, whereas a segment that makes a profit or loss of £60 is significant.

[The next paragraph is 10.62.]

Allocation of costs

10.62 Reporting entities that provide detailed segmental information face further practical difficulties in dealing with cost allocation and attribution. These difficulties include dealing with costs that have been incurred on behalf of a number of reportable segments or that have been incurred on a segment's behalf by another party.

10.63 In principle, segment costs should be determined by their nature rather than by the location where they are incurred. For example, where costs are incurred at head office level solely on behalf of one specific business segment, it seems equitable in such circumstances to include them within that segment's results for segmental reporting purposes. This treatment will present a true picture of that segment's performance to the reader.

10.64 A similar situation arises where a head office or one segment incurs costs that relate to a number of segments. Such costs are normally referred to as common costs. The guidance given in the standard is that common costs should be treated in the way that the directors consider most appropriate. For example, where these costs are apportioned across different segments for the purposes of internal reporting, it may be appropriate to apportion them in a like manner for external segmental reporting purposes. However, the guidance acknowledges that some companies may not wish to apportion common costs, because any such apportionment might be done on an arbitrary basis and, therefore, could be misleading. Consequently in such circumstances, the common costs should be deducted from the total of the segment results.

10.65 In practical terms, the allocation of common costs is a particular area of difficulty, because the basis of allocation may significantly affect the reported segmental results. This is demonstrated by the following example:

Example

A company has three distinct business segments, A, B and C. Prior to the allocation of any common costs to these segments, the financial position of these segments is as follows:

	A	B	C
	£m	£m	£m
Net assets	2,000	300	800
Turnover	5,000	2,000	3,000
Profit before common costs	200	40	100

On the assumption that the common costs total £100m, the allocation of such costs on the basis of the turnover of each segment as a percentage of total turnover would lead to the following depiction of segment results:

	A	B	C
	£m	£m	£m
Profit before common costs	200	40	100
Allocation of common costs	50	20	30
Profit after common costs	150	20	70

This contrasts with the situation where common costs are allocated on the basis of the individual segment's proportion of total net assets. In this instance, the results would be as follows:

	A	B	C
	£m	£m	£m
Profit before common costs	200	40	100
Allocation of common costs	64	10	26
Profit after common costs	136	30	74

Thus, the basis of allocation chosen may have a material effect on the segment result that is reported. Despite this, the standard does not require disclosure of the basis of allocation, although voluntary disclosure is permissible.

10.66 If it is not possible to determine a reasonable basis for allocation, the standard allows common costs to be shown separately as a deduction from the total of segment results. [SSAP 25 para 23]. In practice it may be possible to allocate some of the common costs, but not others. For instance, if a group bears the costs of managing group properties centrally, it should be possible to allocate such costs reasonably fairly to each segment, on a basis that takes account of the type, age and value of properties used by each segment. Similarly, central administrative overheads in respect of personnel might be allocated on the basis of the number of employees in each segment. If more than one basis is appropriate for different types of common cost, it would be reasonable to apply each of these bases in allocating the respective costs. However, costs which cannot be allocated (except on an arbitrary basis), should be shown as a separate, unallocated, figure deducted from the total of segment results.

Disclosure requirements

10.67 The specific disclosure requirements of the Act, SSAP 25 and other financial reporting standards are considered in detail below. In addition, a summary of the requirements of the Act and SSAP 25 is set out in the annex to this chapter.

Legislative requirements

10.68 Although the disclosure requirements of the Companies Act 1985 in respect of segmental information are few in number, they apply to all reporting entities. Indeed, except for the very limited exemptions granted to small companies by Schedule 8, all companies must comply with the Act's disclosure requirements, subject only to the specific exemptions allowed by it. Thus, unless they adopt the prejudicial override clause, as referred to in paragraph 10.6, or take advantage of the exemptions available to small companies, the notes to the profit and loss account must include certain specified information, analysed by both class of business and geographical market.

10.69 Specifically, the Act requires that, where a company has carried on two or more classes of business during the financial year in question, and these, in the directors' opinion, differ substantially from each other, the notes to the financial statements must give:

- A description of each class of business.
- The amount of turnover that is attributable to each class of business.

[CA85 4 Sch 55(1)].

10.70 'Turnover' comprises the amounts a company derives from providing goods and services that fall within its ordinary activities, after deducting trade discounts, VAT and any other taxes based on the amounts it so derives. In this context, turnover will include that of both continuing and discontinued operations, as defined by FRS 3, 'Reporting financial performance'.

10.71 Under the Act, where a company has supplied goods or services to two or more markets during the financial year in question, the turnover must also be disaggregated between markets. This is necessary, however, only if the directors believe that the markets differ substantially. For this purpose, 'market' means a market delimited by geographical bounds. [CA85 4 Sch 55(2)].

10.72 The Act states that, in determining the turnover attributable to each class, the directors must have regard to the way in which the company's activities are organised. [CA85 4 Sch 55(3)]. Where classes of business do not, in the directors' opinion, differ substantially, they are to be treated as one class. Similarly, where the directors believe that markets do not differ substantially, those markets are to be treated as one market. [CA85 4 Sch 55(4)]. In interpreting these matters the directors should have regard to the practical issues discussed in paragraphs 10.32

to 10.66. They should also re-evaluate the position on each occasion that segmental information is published, to ensure that previous decisions on segmental determination remain valid.

10.73 Details of the limited exemptions available to small companies, in respect of the Act's disclosure requirements, are set out in paragraph 10.9 above. In addition, details of exemptions available because segmental analysis would be prejudicial to the reporting entity, irrespective of its size, are set out in paragraph 10.6 above.

Additional disclosures required by the standard

10.74 SSAP 25 does not limit itself to a repetition of the requirements of the Act. Instead it imposes additional, mandatory, segmental disclosure requirements on public and large companies and all banking and insurance companies, unless they avoid disclosure by taking advantage of the prejudicial override exemption. Thus, while smaller companies are never required to make disclosures beyond those specified in the Act, public and large companies and all banking and insurance companies are required to provide the additional, wider disclosures specified by the standard.

10.75 Under the standard, where such companies have two or more classes of business, or operate in two or more geographical segments which differ substantially from each other, the following information should be disclosed in the financial statements in respect of each class of business or geographical segment:

- Turnover.
- Result, before accounting for taxation, minority interests and extraordinary items.
- Net assets.

[SSAP 25 para 34].

10.76 The directors of the entity are responsible for defining:

- Their identified classes of business.
- Their identified geographical segments.

[SSAP 25 para 34].

10.77 Furthermore, as indicated earlier, the standard requires the directors to *"...re-define the segments when appropriate"*. [SSAP 25 para 39]. Thus, as the classes of business or geographical segments of a reporting entity change over time, the financial statements are required to reflect those changes. In this event, the nature of and reason for the change(s) must be explained, as well as the effect of the change(s) being disclosed. Where this occurs, the standard states that the previous year's figures should be re-stated to reflect the change.

10.78 As an illustration of this in practice, in its 1994 financial statements, Lonrho Plc re-defined certain of its classes of business, to reflect the changing circumstances of the group. The segmental analysis, as set out in Table 10.6, highlights this.

Table 10.6 — Lonrho Plc — Annual Report and Accounts — 30 September 1994

Notes to the accounts (extract)

2 Turnover

Turnover represents sales of goods and services outside the Group net of discounts, and allowances and value added taxation and includes commission earned.

Due to the reduction in significance of the contribution from financial services this activity is now included in general trade whereas it was previously separately disclosed.

Turnover by origin is analysed by activity below:—

	1994			1993		
	Group	**Associates**	**Total**	Group	Associates	Total
				Restated	*Restated*	*Restated*
	£m	**£m**	**£m**	£m	£m	£m
Motor and equipment distribution	**578**	**8**	**586**	526	7	533
Mining and refining	**281**	**92**	**373**	249	95	344
Manufacturing	**346**	**6**	**352**	410	5	415
Hotels	**237**	**16**	**253**	227	15	242
General trade	**240**	**9**	**249**	224	14	238
Agriculture	**142**	**9**	**151**	112	8	120
Discontinued operations				258	572	830
	1,824	**140**	**1,964**	2,006	716	2,722

Turnover by origin is analysed by geographical area below:—

	1994			1993		
	Group	**Associates**	**Total**	Group	Associates	Total
				Restated	*Restated*	*Restated*
	£m	**£m**	**£m**	£m	£m	£m
United Kingdom	**781**	**2**	**783**	728	4	732
East, Central and West Africa	**346**	**112**	**458**	368	106	474
Southern Africa	**424**	**5**	**429**	406	15	421
The Americas	**160**	**16**	**176**	163	16	179
Europe and Other	**113**	**5**	**118**	83	3	86
Discontinued operations				258	572	830
	1,824	**140**	**1,964**	2,006	716	2,722

Turnover by destination is analysed below:—

United Kingdom	**679**	**1**	**680**	626		626
East, Central and West Africa	**333**	**23**	**356**	361	26	387
Southern Africa	**320**	**3**	**323**	293	15	308
The Americas	**220**	**16**	**236**	210	16	226
Europe and Other	**272**	**97**	**369**	258	87	345
Discontinued operations				258	572	830
	1,824	**140**	**1,964**	2,006	716	2,722

10.79 Similarly, Pilkington plc, which provided segmental analysis under continuing and discontinued operation categorisations in its 1994 financial statements, indicated that it had undertaken restatements not merely to meet FRS 3 requirements, but also to take account of the segmental *"repositioning"* of certain of its activities (see Table 10.4).

[The next paragraph is 10.81.]

Turnover and inter-segment sales

10.81 The financial statements must distinguish between:

- Turnover derived from external customers.
- Turnover derived from other segments.

[SSAP 25 para 34.]

10.82 In providing this analysis, geographical turnover should be disclosed on both an origin and a destination basis, unless there is no material difference between the two bases. In effect, therefore, where no material difference between the two bases exists, disclosure by origin will be sufficient. In making this distinction the standard recognises that the origin basis is generally considered to be more important than the destination basis of disclosure. This is logical, since disclosure of other segment information about results and net assets can often be provided only on the origin basis. As Table 10.4 indicates, Pilkington plc's 1994 financial statements provided geographical analyses on an origin basis for both continuing and discontinued businesses at turnover, operating profit and net operating assets levels. However, information on the geographical destination basis is given only for turnover.

10.83 By disclosing turnover on the origin basis, it is possible to assess turnover, results and net assets on a consistent basis and relate all three to the perceived risks and opportunities of the segments. Where turnover on the destination basis is not disclosed, because the amount is not materially different from turnover on an origin basis, the fact that there is no material difference must be stated. [SSAP 25 para 34]. In this context, the probability of origin and destination bases not being materially different is likely to be substantially influenced by the nature of the entity's operating activities. As an example, Johnson Group Cleaners PLC (see Table 10.7) is principally engaged in dry cleaning services and workwear and towel rental, operating nationwide in the UK and US. Identified business segments are dry cleaning and rental; while geographical markets are the UK and the US. The services the members of the group offer are not by nature exportable, so geographical markets are serviced by local operating units. In effect, therefore, the UK business segment sells into the UK and the US segment services the US. Accordingly, the financial statements note that *"...there is no material difference between turnover by origin and destination"*. On the other hand, where a company is structured with operations in a limited number of different countries, but these are export bases for servicing a large number of other locations, the origin and destination basis will be materially different and disclosure under both bases will be required.

Table 10.7 — Johnson Group Cleaners PLC — Annual Report — 31 December 1993

SEGMENTAL INFORMATION RESULTS (EXTRACT)

	1993		1992	
	TURNOVER £000	PROFIT £000	TURNOVER £000	PROFIT £000
GEOGRAPHICAL REGION				
United Kingdom	99,542	16,076	96,457	14,971
United States	65,623	2,871	54,376	2,572
Group	165,165	18,947	150,833	17,543
CLASS OF BUSINESS				
Drycleaning	120,036	8,873	109,839	8,818
Rental	45,129	10,074	40,994	8,725
Group	165,165	18,947	150,833	17,543
Profit on sales of property		77		(76)
Deficit on a property valuation		–		(689)
Profit before interest		19,024		16,778
Net interest payable		814		1,663
PROFIT ON ORDINARY ACTIVITIES BEFORE TAXATION		18,210		15,115

There is no material difference between turnover by origin and by destination.

	1993 £000	1992 £000
NET ASSETS		
GEOGRAPHICAL REGION		
United Kingdom	69,199	66,561
United States	22,064	21,521
Group	91,263	88,082
CLASS OF BUSINESS		
Drycleaning	61,481	60,576
Rental	29,782	27,506
Group	91,263	88,082
Unallocated net liabilities	(23,315)	(25,170)
Group share of net assets of associated undertakings	482	438
Net assets	68,430	63,350

10.84 Inter-segmental turnover is only required to be shown in the segmental disclosure of turnover by origin. It is not required to be disclosed by destination. [SSAP 25 para 34]. In practice, where inter-segmental sales are not material in the context of the reporting entity as a whole, companies state that fact and avoid the need to provide further analysis. Pilkington plc adopt this approach in their 1994 financial statements (see Table 10.4).

10.85 Disclosure of segmental analysis of turnover need not be given where it is not required by law. An example of this is the turnover of a banking company attributable to banking. The fact that such turnover has not been disclosed should be stated. [SSAP 25 para 44].

Segment result

10.86 The standard requires the financial statements to analyse the result by class of business and geographical segment. In this context, the result is defined as being before taxation, minority interests and extraordinary items. Normally, it will also be before accounting for interest. However, this will depend on the nature of the business. In effect, where the nature of the business is such that interest income and expense are central to the business, the segment result should be shown after interest. In the majority of companies, however, segments will be financed by a mixture of debt and equity. In such situations, interest earned or incurred will be the result of the company's overall financial policy rather than reflecting the result of individual segments. For this reason, segment result should normally be disclosed before interest, with interest shown separately. [SSAP 25 para 34].

10.87 Pilkington plc, as noted above, discloses operating profit or loss before investment income and interest. (See Table 10.4.) Similarly, in Table 10.3, Coats Viyella Plc analyses operating profit before *"other items"* and interest.

10.88 As Table 10.8 demonstrates, British Aerospace Public Limited Company provides an interesting set of segmental disclosures in that it provides segmental analysis by class of business on the two following bases:

- Profit/(loss) before interest and exceptional items.
- Profit/(loss) before tax on ordinary activities.

Table 10.8 — British Aerospace Public Limited Company — Annual Report — 31 December 1993

2 Segmental Analysis (extract)

Following the implementation of FRS3, the comparative figures for 1992 have been restated to include exceptional items (note 7).

	Sales		Profit/(loss) before interest	
	1993	1992	1993	1992
Continuing operations	**£m**	£m	**£m**	£m
Defence	**3,963**	4,003	**345**	352
Commercial aircraft	**1,580**	1,485	**(162)**	(337)
Motor vehicles	**4,301**	3,684	**56**	(49)
Property development	**166**	88	**(17)**	(2)
Other businesses and headquarters	**347**	332	**(13)**	(38)
	10,357	9,592	**209**	(74)

Discontinued operations				
Construction	**947**	792	**28**	14
	11,304	10,384	**237**	(60)
Less: intra-group				
Continuing operations	**(211)**	(181)	**–**	–
Discontinued operations	**(333)**	(226)	**–**	–
Exceptional items	**–**	–	**(288)**	(1,015)
	10,760	9,977	**(51)**	(1,075)

Sales include rental income from operating leases of £46 million (1992 £93 million).

Included within loss before interest of Other businesses and headquarters in 1992 is a charge of £36 million in respect of full provision against the carrying value of the Group's investment in DAF NV. The Group disposed of all its investment in DAF NV during 1993.

	Profit and loss before tax on ordinary activities		Assets employed	
	1993 £m	1992 £m	1993 £m	1992 £m
Continuing operations				
Defence	**513**	533	**1,731**	1,416
Commercial aircraft	**(224)**	(410)	**(248)**	(133)
Motor vehicles	**(9)**	(115)	**1,389**	1,444
Property development	**(31)**	(26)	**152**	130
Other businesses and headquarters	**(12)**	(40)	**282**	428
	237	(58)	**3,306**	3,285
Discontinued operations				
Construction	**31**	23	**–**	181
Exceptional items	**(308)**	(1,015)	**–**	–
Unallocated Interest and borrowings	**(197)**	(151)	**(1,575)**	(1,448)
	(237)	(1,201)	**1,731**	2,018

7 Exceptional Items

The **exceptional recourse provision** of £250 million represents an additional provision at net present value for the expected level of financial exposure arising over the lifetime of aircraft finance arranged by the Group or by third parties in respect of turboprop aircraft. A deferred tax asset of £30 million has been established in respect of this provision.

The **exceptional loss on sale or termination of operations** of £38 million arises in respect of the disposal of the Group's interest in Ballast Nedam.

The Ballast Nedam group of construction companies was disposed of on 30th December, 1993 for a cash consideration equivalent to £175 million. The proceeds net of disposal costs approximated to the net assets of the Ballast Nedam construction companies at the date of disposal. The disposal therefore had no impact upon shareholders' funds, however inclusion of £38 million of goodwill previously written off against capital reserves on acquisition has resulted in an accounting loss of £38 million being disclosed in the profit and loss account. There was no tax charge or credit arising in respect of this disposal.

Corporate Jets was disposed of with effect from 6th August, 1993. Completion accounts remain under discussion; no profit or loss has been recognised in these accounts in respect of this disposal.

The disposal of the Group's communications business in 1992 gave rise to a loss of £15 million. There was no tax charge or credit arising in respect of this disposal.

The **exceptional reorganisation provision** of £1,000 million in 1992 was in respect of the Group's Regional Aircraft activities. The provision was dealt with in the 1992 accounts as £830 million within provisions for liabilities and charges* and £170 million within stocks. A deferred tax asset of £250 million was established in respect of these costs. In view of the long term nature of these liabilities, the provision was calculated on a net present value basis, and accordingly, an **interest charge** of £20 million has been included in 1993.

* Note that for years beginning on or after 1 January 2005, the Companies Act 1985 (as amended by Companies Act (International Accounting Standards and Other Accounting Amendments) Regulations 2004) line item is 'provisions for liabilities' and not 'provisions for liabilities and charges'.

10.89 Amortisation of goodwill is included in operating profit and accordingly the segmental analysis of results should be given after taking account of goodwill amortisation. However, several companies have given additional disclosure of results before goodwill amortisation. An example is Table 10.9, United News & Media plc. A more simplified example is Pearson, which shows as additional information the result before exceptional items and goodwill amortisation, see Table 10.10.

Table 10.9 — United News & Media plc — Report & Accounts — 31 December 1998

Notes to the financial statements (extract)

	Group 1998 £m	Group share of joint ventures 1998 £m	Group share of associates 1998 £m	Subtotal 1998 £m	Exceptional items 1998 £m	Total 1998 £m
1. BUSINESS ANALYSIS (continued)						
*** Operating profit before amortisation of goodwill by division**						
Continuing operations						
Business services	**157.3**	**11.1**	**1.9**	**170.3**	**(12.2)**	**158.1**
Consumer publishing	**65.0**	**4.6**	**1.1**	**70.7**	**(4.2)**	**66.5**
Broadcasting and entertainment (excluding new ventures)	**67.4**	**1.0**	**12.2**	**80.6**	**(3.5)**	**77.1**
	289.7	**16.7**	**15.2**	**321.6**	**(19.9)**	**301.7**
Broadcasting and entertainment — new ventures	–	**(4.6)**	**(12.3)**	**(16.9)**	–	**(16.9)**
Continuing operations	**289.7**	**12.1**	**2.9**	**304.7**	**(19.9)**	**284.8**
Discontinued operations						
Consumer publishing	**5.6**	–	–	**5.6**	–	**5.6**
Garban business	**40.1**	**0.1**	**0.7**	**40.9**	**(0.8)**	**40.1**
Discontinued operations	**45.7**	**0.1**	**0.7**	**46.5**	**(0.8)**	**45.7**
Operating profit before amortisation of goodwill	**335.4**	**12.2**	**3.6**	**351.2**	**(20.7)**	**330.5**
Amortisation of goodwill	**(153.3)**	**(7.3)**	**(6.4)**	**(167.0)**	–	**(167.0)**

Operating profit						
Continuing operations						
Business services	**86.2**	**10.9**	**1.9**	**99.0**	**(12.2)**	**86.8**
Consumer publishing	**52.1**	**4.6**	**1.3**	**58.0**	**(4.2)**	**53.8**
Broadcasting and entertainment (excluding new ventures)	**(1.9)**	**1.0**	**5.6**	**4.7**	**(3.5)**	**1.2**
	136.4	**16.5**	**8.8**	**161.7**	**(19.9)**	**141.8**
Broadcasting and entertainment — new ventures	–	**(11.7)**	**(12.3)**	**(24.0)**	–	**(24.0)**
Continuing operations	**136.4**	**4.8**	**(3.5)**	**137.7**	**(19.9)**	**117.8**
Discontinued operations						
Consumer publishing	**5.6**	–	–	**5.6**	–	**5.6**
Garban businesses	**40.1**	**0.1**	**0.7**	**40.9**	**(0.8)**	**40.1**
Discontinued operations	**45.7**	**0.1**	**0.7**	**46.5**	**(0.8)**	**45.7**
Operating profit	**182.1**	**4.9**	**(2.8)**	**184.2**	**(20.7)**	**163.5**
Non-operating exceptional items						**277.9**
Net interest expense						**(40.6)**
Profit on ordinary activities before tax						**400.8**
by geographic market						
United Kingdom	**48.3**	**(5.9)**	**(9.6)**	**32.8**	**(12.8)**	**20.0**
North America	**105.3**	**1.8**	–	**107.1**	**(7.3)**	**99.8**
Europe and Middle East	**19.3**	**8.2**	**3.6**	**31.1**	**(0.5)**	**30.6**
Pacific	**9.2**	**0.8**	**3.2**	**13.2**	**(0.1)**	**13.1**
Operating profit	**182.1**	**4.9**	**(2.8)**	**184.2**	**(20.7)**	**163.5**
Non-operating exceptional items						**277.9**
Net interest expense						**(40.6)**
Profit on ordinary activities before tax						**400.8**

* Includes income from other participating interests.

Discontinued operations comprise United Provincial Newspapers, UPN España and United Southern Publications (all part of consumer publishing) and the demerged Garban businesses. Non-operating exceptional items of £277.9 million in 1998 comprise a profit of £298.1 million relating to consumer publishing and a loss of £20.2 million relating to the Garban businesses. Non-operating exceptional items of £50.6 million in 1997 comprise a profit of £57.3 million relating to broadcasting and entertainment and a loss of £6.7 million relating to business services. Operating exceptional items are described in note 5.

Segmental reporting

	As restated Group 1997 £m	As restated Group share of joint ventures 1997 £m	As restated Group share of associates 1997 £m	As restated subtotal 1997 £m	As restated Exceptional items 1997 £m	As restated Total 1997 £m
*** Operating profit before amortisation of goodwill by division**						
Continuing operations						
Business services	155.1	6.7	1.1	162.9	–	162.9
Consumer publishing	66.0	4.3	0.5	70.8	–	70.8
Broadcasting and entertainment (excluding new ventures)	58.8	0.3	15.4	74.5	7.5	82.0
	279.9	11.3	17.0	308.2	7.5	315.7
Broadcasting and entertainment — new ventures	–	–	(21.3)	(21.3)	–	(21.3)
Continuing operations	279.9	11.3	(4.3)	286.9	7.5	294.4
Discontinued operations						
Consumer publishing	36.3	–	–	36.3	–	36.3
Garban businesses	45.8	0.1	2.3	48.2	–	48.2
Discontinued operations	82.1	0.1	2.3	84.5	–	84.5
Discontinued profit before amortisation of goodwill	362.0	11.4	(2.0)	371.4	7.5	378.9
Amortisation of goodwill	(157.1)	(0.1)	(6.7)	(163.9)	–	(163.9)
Operating profit						
Continuing operations						
Business services	81.0	6.6	1.1	88.7	–	88.7
Consumer publishing	54.8	4.3	0.5	59.6	–	59.6
Broadcasting and entertainment (excluding new ventures)	(9.9)	0.3	8.7	(0.9)	7.5	6.6
	125.9	11.2	10.3	147.4	7.5	154.9
Broadcasting and entertainment new ventures	–	–	(21.3)	(21.3)	–	(21.3)
Continuing operations	125.9	11.2	(11.0)	126.1	7.5	133.6
Discontinued operations						
Consumer publishing	33.3	–	–	33.3	–	33.3
Garban businesses	45.7	0.1	2.3	48.1	–	48.1
Discontinued operations	79.0	0.1	2.3	81.4	–	81.4
Operating profit	204.9	11.3	(8.7)	207.5	7.5	215.0
Non-operating exceptional items						50.6
Net interest expense						(56.5)
Profit on ordinary activities before tax						209.1
By geographic market						
United Kingdom	53.2	4.0	(15.5)	41.7	7.5	49.2
North America	109.2	1.5	–	110.7	–	110.7
Europe and Middle East	28.8	4.9	3.2	36.9	–	36.9
Pacific	13.7	0.9	3.6	18.2	–	18.2
Operating profit	204.9	11.3	(8.7)	207.5	7.5	215.0
Non-operating exceptional items						50.6
Net interest expense						(56.5)
Profit on ordinary activities before tax						209.1

* Includes income from other participating interests

Table 10.10 — Pearson plc — Annual Report — 31 December 1998

Notes to the financial statements (extract)

2a) Analysis of sales and operating profit

	1998			1997	
ALL FIGURES IN £ MILLIONS	SALES	OPERATING PROFIT BEFORE GOODWILL & OTHER ITEMS	OPERATING PROFIT AFTER GOODWILL & OTHER ITEMS	SALES	RESTATED OPERATING PROFIT
Business sectors					
FT Group	683	118	114	676	108
Pearson Education	702	99	(34)	563	60
The Penguin Group	523	48	46	525	58
Pearson Television	343	61	61	247	26
Lazard	–	42	42	–	43
Continuing operations	2,251	368	229	2,011	295
Discontinued operations	144	21	21	282	33
	2,395	389	250	2,293	328
Geographical markets supplied					
United Kingdom	497	51	48	487	54
Continental Europe	461	114	111	382	77
North America	1,078	181	54	916	134
Asia Pacific	161	16	11	179	23
Rest of World	54	6	5	47	7
Continuing operations	2,251	368	229	2,011	295
Discontinued operations	144	21	21	282	33
	2,395	389	250	2,293	328

NOTE: *In 1998 'other items' comprises exceptional items of £120m and Year 2000 costs of £7m.*

- *Exceptional items of £120m comprise integration costs following the acquisition of Simon & Schuster. These all relate to the Pearson Education business sector.*
- *1997 Operating profit is stated after restructuring costs of £34m which were classified as exceptional within operating activities. These related to FT Group, £14m, Pearson Education, £12m, Pearson Television, £4m, and discontinued businesses, £4m, and are shown mainly within United Kingdom, £16m, and North America, £17m. In 1998 operating restructuring costs of £11m were incurred of which £6m were in the FT Group and £5m in the Penguin Group.*
- *1997 has been re-analysed to reflect expanded business groups.*
- *Discontinued operations relate to the withdrawal of the Group from the consumer software business following its disposal of Mindscape Inc. in March 1998, the withdrawal of the Group from the consumer magazine business following its disposal of Pearson New Entertainment in April 1998 and the withdrawal of the Group from the visitor attractions business following its disposal of The Tussauds Group in October 1998.*
- *1997 has been restated to reflect the adoption of FRS 9 'Associates and Joint Ventures' (see note 1).*
- *Analyses of the profits of associates are shown in note 13.*

10.90 The standard suggests that in most cases the disclosure of results by segment should be based on the areas from which products or services are supplied (that is, the origin basis). [SSAP 25 para 21].

Segment net assets

10.91 Companies that have to comply with the segmental reporting disclosure requirements of the standard must disclose the net assets of each business segment and geographical segment. In this context, the standard explains that in most cases net assets will be the non-interest bearing operating assets less the non-interest bearing operating liabilities. This is consistent with the standard's general emphasis on looking at operational performance. However, where segment result has been disclosed after accounting for interest, because investment policy is a principal business activity of the segment and, therefore, a fair measure of the segment's performance, the corresponding interest bearing operating assets and liabilities should be included in net assets. [SSAP 25 para 34].

10.92 The standard provides further guidance on the allocation of assets and liabilities to segments. It indicates that a segment's assets and liabilities may include not only assets and liabilities relating exclusively to that segment, but also an allocated portion of assets and liabilities that are shared by it with other segments. The standard also states that assets and liabilities that are shared by segments should be allocated to those segments on a reasonable basis. [SSAP 25 para 25].

10.93 The words *"reasonable basis"* are not further explained in the standard. However, the guidance on the allocation of common costs, which is discussed from paragraphs 10.62 above, would seem equally relevant to the allocation of shared assets and liabilities. Accordingly, if the entity apportions such assets and liabilities for the purpose of internal reporting, it may be reasonable for such assets and liabilities to be similarly apportioned for external reporting purposes. If apportionment of such assets and liabilities would be misleading, however, it would seem sensible not to apportion them, but, instead, to show them separately. It would, however, be rare for an entity to be unable to find some reasonable basis for allocating shared assets and liabilities, and a preferable method of avoiding any possibility of the allocation being misleading would be to quantify the amount of such assets and liabilities and disclose the basis of allocation.

10.94 The standard also indicates that assets and liabilities that are not used in the operations of any segment should not be allocated to any segment. [SSAP 25 para 25]. These would be shown as a separate figure in reconciling the total of net assets to the balance sheet. Furthermore, operating assets of a segment should not normally include loans or advances to, or investments in, another segment, unless interest on them has been included in arriving at the results of the first segment. Operating assets should include capitalised goodwill, which should not be shown as a reconciling item, but should be allocated to the segments to which it relates. Table 10.11 includes £826.3 million of goodwill in the total of £1,563.3 million of net operating assets, which is analysed by segment.

Table 10.11 — United News & Media plc — Report & Accounts — 31 December 1998

Notes to the financial statements (extract)

	1998	As restated 1997
	£m	£m
Net operating assets by division		
Business services	**781.5**	850.7
Consumer publishing	**289.1**	411.4
Broadcasting and entertainment	**492.7**	558.5
Garban businesses	–	(3.6)
	1,563.3	1,817.0
by geographic market		
United Kingdom	**998.1**	1,131.6
North America	**382.2**	423.4
Europe and Middle East	**153.8**	224.2
Pacific	**29.2**	37.8
	1,563.3	1,817.0
Reconciliation of net operating assets to net assets		
Net operating assets	**1,563.3**	1,817.0
Investments	**147.9**	215.4
Corporation tax	**(72.1)**	(49.6)
Deferred tax	–	(0.4)
Net borrowings	**(703.2)**	(1,155.0)
Proposed dividend*	**(61.1)**	(66.2)
Net assets	**874.8**	761.2

The Garban businesses were previously reported as part of the financial services division, but have been shown separately and comparative amounts restated in order to be consistent with the demerger of those businesses. The financial services division also previously included certain properties, and the financial information business previously included within business services, has been demerged within the Garban businesses. The impact of redefining the segment on the group turnover, operating profit and net assets of the Garban businesses compared to financial services previously reported at 31 December 1997 is an increase of £6.3 million, an increase of £1.0 million and a reduction of £19.0 million respectively.

* Note that for years beginning on or after 1 January 2005, FRS 21 prohibts the recognition of proposed dividends as a liability.

10.95 Pilkington plc's 1994 financial statements include segmental information structured on an operating basis. For consistency, the segmental disclosures of net assets are given on an equivalent operating basis to that used in disclosing operating result. This means that not all of the assets employed by the group are included therein, so a helpful summary of net operating assets is provided in a separate note (see Table 10.4).

10.96 The Mersey Docks And Harbour Company's approach in its 1993 financial statements, as set out in Table 10.12, was to provide business segment information both gross and net of intra-segment sales. It also provided segmental analysis of profit on ordinary activities before interest and taxation, indicating by this treatment that interest could not be attributed on a fair basis to individual business segments. In disclosing segmental information on net assets, it excluded interest bearing assets and liabilities, which were then shown separately in the note, effectively reconciling the segmental net assets to the balance sheet.

Table 10.12 — The Mersey Docks and Harbour Company — Annual Report & Accounts — 31 December 1993

Notes to the Accounts
for the year ended 31 December 1993

2. SEGMENTAL ANALYSIS BY CLASS OF BUSINESS
The analysis by class of business of the Group's turnover, profit before taxation and net assets is set out below.

TURNOVER

		1993			1992	
	Total sales	**Inter-segment sales**	**External sales**	Total sales	Inter-segment sales	External sales
	£000	**£000**	**£000**	£000	£000	£000
Port operations	**71,716**	**(3,685)**	**68,067**	64,867	(2,574)	62,293
Irish Sea subsidiaries	**35,113**	**(1,630)**	**23,482**	18,378	(1,621)	16,757
Property and property development	**2,674**	**(460)**	**2,314**	2,605	(500)	2,105
Non-port activities	**5,673**	**(980)**	**4,693**	6,189	(982)	5,207
	105,175	**(6,755)**	**98,430**	92,039	(5,677)	86,362

PROFIT ON ORDINARY ACTIVITIES BEFORE TAXATION

	1993	1992 as restated
	£000	£000
Port operations	**18,054**	12,496
Irish Sea subsidiaries	**1,321**	1,243
Property and property development	**1,698**	1,583
Non-port activities	**590**	287
	21,663	15,609
Net interest	**(798)**	(449)
	28,865	15,160
NET ASSETS(LIABILITIES)		
Port operations	**124,739**	102,690
Irish Sea subsidiaries	**1,372**	597
Property and property development	**20,005**	20,316
Non-port activities	**(693)**	(344)
	145,323	123,259
Interest bearing assets	**14,938**	9,478
Interest bearing liabilities	**(10,093)**	(8,656)
	150,161	124,081

Turnover and profit are predominantly derived from U.K. operations.

Turnover and profit before taxation for Liverpool Conservancy were £2,922,000 (1992: £2,837,000) and £8,000 (1992: loss £188,000) respectively.

Turnover for Liverpool Pllotage services was £3,859,000 (1992: £4,173,000). **The aggregate expenditure incurred in providing Liverpool Pllotage services was £3,827,000** (1992: £3,753,000).

10.97 In both of the above examples, the amount of net assets attributed to the identified segments is less than the sum of the total net assets in the balance sheet.

However, the items excluded can be separately identified to facilitate a full reconciliation to the financial statements. This contrasts with the disclosure approach adopted by British Aerospace Public Limited Company (see Table 10.8) and Johnson Group Cleaners PLC (see Table 10.7) in their 1993 financial statements. These companies analyse total net assets between segments and then deduct unallocated net liabilities in total to reconcile back to the net assets stated in the balance sheet. This is less helpful to the reader in understanding the real level of net assets used in individual segments, but probably cannot be avoided.

10.98 In disclosing the net assets employed by individual segments, most reporting entities base the disclosures on the balance sheet at the accounting reference date. The standard is silent on this matter and it is possible to base disclosure on the average position for the year. This may be particularly appropriate in the context of evaluating the return on capital employed, in instances where the year end position is materially different from the average position. This may occur in an industry of a seasonal nature, where the balance sheet date may coincide with either a trading peak or trough and where stock, debtor and creditor levels are reflective of that situation. BTR plc is one company that has made disclosure on the basis of average net assets (see Table 10.13).

Table 10.13 – BTR plc – Annual Report and Accounts – 31 December 1997

Notes (extract)

1 Analysis of sales, profit before tax and average operating net assets (extract)

Average operating net assets represent, in the opinion of the Directors, the best estimate of net asset utilisation by the Business Groups, and exclude taxation, dividends*, net debt and provisions for liabilities and charges.†

* Note that for years beginning on or after 1 January 2005, recognition of dividends receivable as payable will be rare because FRS 21 prohibits the recognition of interim dividends until they are paid and final dividends until they are approved by shareholders. See further chapter 22.

† Note that for years beginning on or after 1 January 2005, the Companies Act 1985 (as amended by SI 04/2947, 'The Companies Act 1985 (International Accounting Standards and Other Accounting Amendments) Regulations 2004) line item is 'provisions for liabilites' and not 'provisions for liabilities and charges'.

10.99 The segmental analysis of net assets will usually be based on the areas from which goods are supplied. This is a practical application, for in many instances the provision of such information on a destination basis would be difficult to obtain and its value dubious.

Associates and joint ventures

10.100 SSAP 25 and FRS 9 set out the segmental information to be disclosed in respect of associates and joint ventures. These requirements apply unless publication of such information would be prejudicial to the business of the associate or joint venture. Where disclosure is not made for this reason, the reason for non-disclosure should be stated in the notes, together with a brief description of the omitted business or businesses. [SSAP 25 para 36]. SSAP 25 also allows segmental information concerning associates or joint ventures not to be given if it is unobtainable. [SSAP 25 para 36]. But following the publication of FRS 9 and the increased emphasis on the investors in associates and joint ventures being able to exercise in practice significant influence or joint control (respectively), it seems unlikely that such information would be unobtainable, except in very unusual circumstances. In such circumstances the reason for non-disclosure and a brief description of the omitted business or businesses should also be given.

10.101 FRS 9 required that joint ventures are accounted for using the 'gross equity' method of accounting, which entails investors disclosing additionally their share of joint ventures' turnover and gross assets and liabilities. In addition, the standard requires that the share of the joint ventures' turnover should be included in the segmental analysis and should be clearly distinguished from the turnover of the group itself. [FRS 9 para 21]. Furthermore, an investor can, if it so wishes, disclose its share of its associates' turnover as a memorandum item in the profit and loss account where it considers that this is helpful in giving an indication of the group's size. But where this voluntary disclosure is made, the segmental analysis of turnover should, in addition, clearly distinguish between that of the group and that of associates. [FRS 9 para 27].

10.102 SSAP 25 also requires additional segmental information of results and net assets for associates and joint ventures but only where they form a significant part of a reporting entity's results or assets. In this regard, it notes that associate (including joint venture) undertakings are considered significant if, in total, they account for at least 20 per cent of the total result or 20 per cent of the total net assets of the reporting entity. There is nothing in SSAP 25 or FRS 9 which suggests this threshold should be applied separately for associates and joint ventures (although the additional disclosures in FRS 9 apply on this basis) and so it appears that it can be applied in aggregate. But it appears that the required disclosures should separate joint ventures from associates, following the general requirement to do so in FRS 9, which is also implied in paragraphs 21 and 27 of FRS 9.

10.103 The information required in respect of associates and joint ventures is a segmental analysis of both of the following:

- The reporting entity's share of profits or losses of associates and joint ventures before accounting for taxation, minority interests and extraordinary items (although the latter have been all but eliminated by FRS 3 – see further chapter 24).

- The reporting entity's share of the net assets of associates and joint ventures (including goodwill to the extent that it has not been written off) stated, where possible, after attributing fair values to the net assets at the date of acquisition of the interest in each associate or joint venture.

[SSAP 25 para 36].

10.104 FRS 9 requires that, the share of associates' and joint ventures' operating results, interest, non-operating exceptional items and taxation is required to be disclosed for each of those line items. Consequently, if the reporting group analyses its segment result before charging interest, for the reasons discussed in paragraph 10.86, it will be able to disclose segment information for its associates and joint ventures on an equivalent basis.

10.105 The General Electric Company p.l.c, who adopted FRS 9 early, also provides segmental analysis of its interests in joint ventures as Table 10.15 indicates. Again the analysis is provided on both a business and geographical segment basis.

Table 10.15 — The General Electric Company, p.l.c. — Annual Report and Accounts — 31 March 1998

Notes to the Accounts (extract)

11 Fixed asset investments — joint ventures, associates and other (extract)

	Profit		Turnover		Net assets at 31st March	
	1998	1997	**1998**	1997	**1998**	1997
	£ million	£ million	**£ million**	£ million	**£ million**	£ million
By classes of business						
Marconi Electronic Systems	**36**	38	**568**	646	**(16)**	(62)
Marconi Communications	**8**	8	**30**	22	**18**	13
Industrial Group — Rest of World	**25**	19	**298**	265	**44**	48
Alstom	**180**	169	**3,618**	3,505	**125**	(145)
Other	**–**	11	**–**	–	**–**	–
	249	245	**4,514**	4,438	**171**	(146)
Exceptional items in respect of continuing operations	**(21)**	(80)				
Non-operating exceptional items	**28**	–				
Interest bearing assets and liabilities	**36**	72			**572**	955
Unallocated net liabilities					**(4)**	(55)
	292	237	**4,514**	4,438	**739**	754
By territory of origin						
United Kingdom	**86**	58	**1,439**	1,202	**258**	126
France	**93**	126	**1,841**	2,111	**536**	294
Rest of Europe	**43**	52	**730**	772	**(572)**	(564)
The Americas	**14**	4	**275**	166	**(47)**	–
Africa, Asia and Australasia	**13**	5	**229**	187	**(4)**	(2)
	249	245	**4,514**	4,438	**171**	(146)

10.106 A further example of disclosure in respect of associates and joint ventures is Table 10.9 (United News & Media plc) above.

Joint arrangements

10.107 Joint arrangements are contractual arrangements under which the participants engage in joint activities that do not create an entity, because it would not be carrying on a trade or business of its own. [FRS 9 para 4]. FRS 9 requires that such arrangements should not be accounted for following the equity method of accounting, but participants should account for their own assets, liabilities and cash flows, measured according to the terms of the agreement governing the arrangement. Although SSAP 25 does not cover this type of entity, it seems appropriate that the amounts of the arrangement accounted for under FRS 9 should also be included within the segmental analysis. Joint arrangements are considered in more detail in chapter 27.

Reconciliation of figures

10.108 The standard requires the reporting entity to provide a reconciliation where the total of the amounts disclosed by segment does not agree with the related total in the financial statements. In this situation, the difference between the two figures should be identified and explained. [SSAP 25 para 37]. The issue of reconciling segmental net assets to total reported net assets has been discussed in paragraphs 10.91 to 10.99. Table 10.16 shows a helpful example of a company, The Rank Organisation Plc, reconciling the major areas of segmental disclosures to the figures reported in its primary statements.

Table 10.16 — The Rank Organisation Plc — Directors' Report and Accounts — 31 October 1994

Notes to the Accounts (extract)

1 SEGMENTAL INFORMATION

Analysis by division

	Turnover		Profit before tax		Year end net assets		Net cash flow	
	1994	1993	**1994**	1993	**1994**	1993	**1994**	1993
	£m	£m	**£m**	£m	**£m**	£m	**£m**	£m
Film and Television	**680.1**	571.7	**66.9**	49.4	**335.1**	357.1	**78.1**	29.2
Holidays	**459.9**	424.5	**57.0**	52.0	**485.6**	462.1	**39.5**	47.3
Recreation	**729.5**	692.1	**69.0**	64.0	**511.4**	493.5	**51.4**	54.7
Leisure	**281.7**	269.4	**47.7**	49.1	**334.7**	313.8	**3.5**	13.0
Other	**17.9**	17.1	**(10.8)**	(6.8)	**9.6**	8.6	**(13.2)**	(6.3)
Continuing operations	**2,169.1**	1,974.8	**229.8**	207.7	**1,676.4**	1,635.1	**159.3**	137.9
Discontinued operations	**30.3**	132.0	**(2.8)**	(7.3)	**31.7**	122.1	**58.8**	101.9
	2,199.4	2,106.8	**227.0**	200.4	**1,708.1**	1,757.2	**218.1**	239.8

Share of associated undertakings:						
Rank Xerox	**151.5**	151.2	**606.9**	586.5	**61.5**	72.1
Universal Studios Florida	**11.4**	13.0	**171.1**	199.9	**22.7**	24.4
Other	**(0.3)**	(1.5)	**31.8**	26.4	**(6.7)**	(19.7)
	162.6	162.7	**809.8**	812.8	**77.5**	76.8
	389.6	363.1	**2,517.9**	2,570.0	**295.6**	316.6
Non-operating items	**(30.6)**	2.0				
Interest	**(75.0)**	(88.5)			**(85.1)**	(57.3)
Profit before tax	**284.0**	276.6				
Tax and dividends*			**(102.3)**	(17.0)	**(83.0)**	(135.1)
Other non-operating liabilities (net)			**(50.0)**	(64.9)		
Net borrowings			**(759.0)**	(955.3)		
			1,606.6	1,532.8	**127.5**	124.2

* Note that for years beginning on or after 1 January 2005, FRS 21 prohibits the recognition of proposed final dividends until they have received shareholder approval (see further chapter 22).

[The next paragraph is 10.110.]

Comparative figures

10.110 The standard requires the provision of comparatives figures unless it is the first occasion on which an entity produces a segmental report. In that situation, if the necessary information to produce comparative figures is not readily available, then they need not be provided. [SSAP 25 para 38].

[The next paragraph is 10.116.]

Other disclosure requirements

10.116 Since SSAP 25's publication in 1990, the ASB has published many new standards. Although none of these standards and pronouncements relate specifically to segmental reporting, some of them have an impact upon the nature of segmental disclosures in financial statements. A number of these instances are considered below.

Cash flow statements

10.117 FRS 1, 'Cash flow statements', encourages, but does not require, entities to provide segmental breakdown of cash flows. [FRS 1 para 8]. While segmental cash flow information might be useful to readers of financial statements, by helping them to understand the relationship between the cash flows of the reporting entity as a whole and those of its constituent segments, the FRS is silent on how segmental cash flow information might be given. This contrasts with the position in the earlier exposure draft, ED 54, 'Cash flow statements', which proposed that, as a minimum, an enterprise should give an analysis of the most important elements of operating cash flows between the major reportable segments. An example of a company giving a segmental breakdown of its operating cash flows is shown in chapter 30.

10.118 There are some examples of reporting entities providing segmental analysis of cash flows. While Pearson plc discloses operating cash flows for each of its main business lines (newspapers, books, television and visitor attractions) in its OFR, it does not provide segmental cash flow analysis in the main body of the audited financial statements. The Rank Organisation plc, which provides a segmental analysis of cash flow, appears to be the exception rather than the rule (see Table 10.16).

10.119 One situation where segmental reporting of cash flows has been disclosed is where consolidated financial statements include subsidiary undertakings with a wide variety of activities. The extracts from B.A.T. Industries plc financial statements, set out in Table 10.17, provide an illustration of this.

Table 10.17 — B.A.T Industries p.l.c. — Directors' Report and Accounts — 31 December 1993

Accounting Policies

1 The Group accounts have been prepared in accordance with applicable accounting standards and combine the accounts of Group undertakings at 31 December. As permitted by the Companies Act 1985 the accounts formats have been adapted, as necessary, to give a true and fair view of the state of affairs and profit of the commercial activities of the Group and to present the insurance activities in accordance with the provisions of that Act applicable to insurance companies. The accounts are on an historical cost basis as modified to include certain insurance assets at market value.

The accounts formats have been developed to reflect more appropriately the operations of the Group. All the assets and liabilities of the Group's businesses are included in the consolidated balance sheet. To equity account for either tobacco or financial services would not give a true and fair view of the total Group. However, given the differences between the two main businesses of the Group and the constraints of the regulatory environment within which insurance companies operate, the assets and liabilities are shown separately under headings covering commercial and corporate activities, financial services general business and financial service life business. This approach has been reflected in preparing separate cash flow statements for the three businesses as the regulatory environment in insurance limits the availability of cash flows between businesses. The Directors are of the opinion that this approach, where it differs from the Companies Act 1985 and applicable accounting standards as described further in the Directors' Report on page 1, is necessary to present a true and fair view of the Group.

Group Cash Flow Statements
for the year ended 31 December

COMMERCIAL AND CORPORATE ACTIVITIES	NOTES	**1993 £m**	1992 £m
Net cash inflows from commercial operating activities	13	**977**	1,165
Dividends from—financial services subsidiary undertakings			
–general		**114**	137
–life		**119**	114
–associates		**59**	44
Net cash inflows from operating activities	13	**1,269**	1,460
Investment income		**113**	129
Interest paid		**(226)**	(239)
Dividends to B.A.T. Industries' shareholders		**(276)**	(528)
Dividends to minorities		**(46)**	(30)
Net cash outflows from returns on investments and servicing of finance		**(435)**	(668)
Taxation paid		**(288)**	(396)
Capital expenditure		**(338)**	(278)
Sale of fixed assets		**16**	26
Purchase of other investments	14	**(21)**	(8)
Sale of other investments	14	**42**	59
Subsidiary and associated undertakings			
–purchases	14	**(8)**	(42)
–sales	14		26
Investment in Farmers' insurance exchanges			(128)
Net cash outflows from Investing activities		**(309)**	(345)
Other cash outflows with financial services activities	15	**(15)**	(342)
Net cash inflow/(outflow) before external financing (from above items)		**222**	(291)
Proceeds from issue of shares		**5**	5
Commercial paper		**(1,296)**	76
Bank and other loans		**(38)**	58
Medium term debt issues		**727**	286
Eurobond issues		**595**	
Net cash (outflows)/inflows financing activities	16	**(7)**	425
Increase in cash and cash equivalents	16	**215**	134

Certain comparative figures have been restated as explained in accounting policy 1 on page 8 and details of these changes are given in the individual notes to which they relate.

FINANCIAL SERVICES	Notes	GENERAL 1933 £m	GENERAL 1992 £m	LIFE 1993 £m	LIFE 1992 £m
Net cash inflows from operating activities excluding investment gains	17	**558**	330	**495**	337
Dividend to — Group companies		**(114)**	(137)	**(119)**	(114)
— minority shareholders		**(2)**	(2)		
Interest paid		**(49)**	(28)		
Net cash outflows from servicing of Finance		**(165)**	(167)	**(119)**	(114)
Taxation paid		**(193)**	(56)		
Sale of investments		**2,886**	1,494	**667**	362
Less: purchase of investments		**(3,090)**	(1,884)	**(1,088)**	(567)
Sale proceeds less reinvestments	19	**(204)**	(390)	**(421)**	(205)
Capital expenditure		**(51)**	(42)	**(21)**	(21)
Sale of fixed assets		**7**	2	**9**	7
Proceeds on sale at subsidiary undertakings	18		119	**17**	
Investment in life fund					(102)
Investment in Farmers' insurance exchanges					100
Net cash outflows from investing activities		**(248)**	(311)	**(416)**	(421)
Other cash flows with the life funds			18		
Other cash flows between Group businesses	15	**(24)**	176	**39**	166
Other cash flows with commercial activities and financial services businesses		**(24)**	194	**39**	166
Net cash outflows before external financing (from above items)		**(72)**	(10)	**(1)**	(32)
Borrowings		**3**	59		
Issue of shares				**1**	4
Net cash Inflows from financing activities	19	**3**	59	**1**	4
(Decrease)/increase in cash and cash equivalents		**(69)**	49		(28)

The life business cash flows above exclude flows of the Allied Dunbar and Eagle Star life funds.

10.120 Cash flow statements are considered in more detail in chapter 30.

[The next paragraph is 10.122.]

Subsidiary undertakings

10.122 FRS 2, 'Accounting for subsidiary undertakings', indicates that parent undertakings should consider how best to provide segmental information for their group. It suggests that the ensuing disclosures should indicate the different risks and rewards, growth and prospects of the different parts of the group. In this regard, the requirements of SSAP 25 should be seen as the minimum disclosure level, rather than as the maximum. [FRS 2 para 94].

10.123 Although FRS 2 recognises the importance of segmental reporting in consolidated financial statements, it does not introduce any specific new requirements. However, it does suggest two situations where segmental information could supplement consolidated financial statements, namely:

- In respect of subsidiary undertakings whose activities differ from those of the rest of the group.
- In respect of disclosures relating to minority interests.

[FRS 2 para 94].

[The next paragraph is 10.126.]

10.126 It is likely that a subsidiary whose activities are dissimilar from those of the rest of the group will meet the definition of a reportable segment in its own right if it is material in the context of the group. Nonetheless, the suggestion that groups explain the impact of subsidiaries with dissimilar activities by way of segmental reporting remains.

Acquisitions and discontinued operations

10.127 FRS 3, 'Reporting financial performance', comments that an appreciation of the impact of changes on material components of the business is essential, if a reader is to obtain a thorough understanding of the results and financial position of a reporting entity. In this regard, the standard states that *"...if an acquisition, a sale or a termination has a material impact on a major business segment ... this impact should be disclosed and explained"*. [FRS 3 para 53]. To promote this understanding, FRS 3 requires reporting entities to analyse and disclose turnover, operating profit and exceptional items, as set out in the profit and loss account, between continuing and discontinued operations.

10.128 In making this distinction between continuing and discontinued operations, the standard requires that, for a component of a reporting entity's operations to be reported as discontinued, its *"...assets, liabilities, results of operations and activities of an operation must be clearly distinguishable, physically, operationally and for financial reporting purposes"*. In addition, *"...a sale or termination should have resulted from a strategic decision by the reporting entity either to withdraw from a particular market (whether class of business or geographical) or to curtail materially its presence in a continuing market (i.e. 'downsizing')"*. [FRS 3 paras 43, 44].

10.129 Since FRS 3 requires a detailed analysis of aggregate financial information, it is important to understand its relationship with SSAP 25. In this regard, for a business to be analysed and disclosed as discontinued in accordance with FRS 3, it does not necessarily have to constitute a complete business segment for the purposes of SSAP 25. This is because the definition of discontinued operations also includes a sale or termination that has a material effect on the nature and focus of a reporting entity's operations and represents a material reduction in operating facilities resulting either from its withdrawal from a particular market (whether class of business or geographical) or from a material reduction in turnover in the entity's continuing markets. In effect, therefore, what constitutes a discontinued operation for FRS 3 purposes may only be part of a segment for SSAP 25 reporting purposes.

10.130 An example of the above distinction between FRS 3 and SSAP 25 could be in the case of a group with two equally-sized subsidiaries, each operating in the field of car leasing.The sale of one of the subsidiaries would not be the disposal of the whole car leasing segment as defined for the purposes of SSAP 25. However, if it materially affected the nature and focus of the entity's operations (for example, if the disposal were made to release funds for investing in a different business, such as a road haulage business, that materially changed the nature and focus of the group's operations) it would constitute a discontinued operation for the purposes of FRS 3, because it is a material reduction in operating facilities and results from a material reduction in turnover in the group's continuing markets. In addition, the assets, liabilities, results and activities can be distinguished physically, operationally and for financial reporting purposes. The nature of the operations disposed of is not different from that of the rest of the group, but that is not a test that has to be satisfied under FRS 3 in order for the disposal of the subsidiary to qualify as a discontinued operation.

10.131 In practice, some entities, that have had material sales or terminations, have disclosed the impact of these in their financial statements by analysing continuing and discontinued operations by segment. Pilkington plc adopts this approach, providing detailed business segment and geographical segment analysis for both categories. Even its additional note analysing net operating assets by balance sheet category is disclosed on a continuing and discontinued basis (see Table 10.4).

10.132 In Table 10.18 Grand Metropolitan Public Limited Company also provides segmental information on this basis.

Table 10.16 — Grand Metropolitan Public Limited Company — Annual Report — 30 September 1994

Notes (extract)

2 SEGMENT ANALYSIS

	1994			1993		
	Turnover	Profit	Net assets	Turnover	Profit	Net assets
Class of business:	£m	£m	£m	£m	£m	£m
Continuing operations						
Food — branded	3,267	267	2,007	3,066	227	2,226
— retailing	1,104	230	1,353	1,153	175	1,378
Drinks	3,371	520	1,657	3,418	563	1,856
	7,742	1,017	5,017	7,637	965	5,460
Discontinued operations	38	6	–	483	77	658
	7,780		5,017	8,120		6,118

Operating profit before exceptional items		1,023			1.042	
Associates before exceptional items		45	729		24	620
Exceptional items		(291)			(286)	
Interest		(123)			(155)	
Profit before taxation		654			*625*	
Capital employed			5,746			*6,738*
Net borrowings			(2,159)			(3,025)
Net assets			3,587			3,713
Geographical area by country of operation						
United Kingdom	815	101	339	1,245	173	975
Rest of Europe	1,613	180	627	1,648	210	685
United States of America	4,644	677	3,714	4,499	582	4,140
Rest of North America	173	26	116	214	26	151
Africa and Middle East	183	315	32	182	15	31
Rest of World	352	24	189	332	36	136
	7,780		5,017	8,120		6,118
Operating profit before exceptional items		1,023			1,042	
Associates before exceptional items		45		729	24	620
Exceptional items		(291)			(286)	
Interest		(123)			(155)	
Profit before taxation		654			625	
Capital employed			5,746			6,738
Net borrowings			(2,159)			(3,025)
Net assets			3,587			3,713

Profit before interest relates to the following activities and geographical areas: Food — branded £214m, Food — retailing £183m, Drinks £351m, and discounted businesses £29m (1993 — £184m, £85m, £560m, and £23m respectively, and a £50m charge in respect of a write down of the group's UK properties); United Kingdom £71m, Rest of Europe £81m, United States of America £556m, Rest of World £69m (1993 — £117m, £136m, £458m and £91m respectively).

The group interest expense is arranged centrally and is not attributable to individual activities or geographical areas. The analysis of capital employed by activity and geographical area is calculated on net assets excluding associates, cash and borrowings.

Turnover between the above classes of business is not material.

Following the disposal of The Chef & Brewer Group, Burger King and Pearle are now disclosed as a separate segment of the Food sector and the loans to IEL are included in associates. Discontinued operations comprise The Chef & Brewer Group and, in the prior period, Express Foods; both businesses operated almost exclusively in the United Kingdom. On 19th September 1994, the group announced the sale, subject to regulatory approval, of ALPO Petfoods; the sale was not completed by 1st December 1994 and ALPO Petfoods has been classified as a continuing operation in these accounts.

The weighted average exchange rate used in translation of US dollar profit and loss accounts was £1 = $1.51 (1993 — £1 = $1.52). The exchange rate used to translate US dollar assets and liabilities at the balance sheet date was £1 = $1.58 (1993 — £1 = $1.50).

3 TURNOVER			**1994**			1993
	Continuing	**Discontinued**	**Total**	*Continuing*	*Discontinued*	*Total*
	£m	**£m**	**£m**	*£m*	*£m*	*£m*
Geographical area by destination:						
United Kingdom	**741**	**38**	**779**	*724*	*483*	*1,207*
Rest of Europe	**1,610**	–	**1,610**	*1,641*	–	*1,641*
United States of America	**4,546**	–	**4,546**	*4,389*	–	*4,389*
Rest of North America	**219**	–	**219**	*239*	–	*239*
Africa and Middle East	**210**	–	**210**	*221*	–	*221*
Rest of World	**416**	–	**416**	*423*	–	*423*
	7,742	**38**	**7,780**	*7,637*	*483*	*8,120*

Exports from the United Kingdom were £297m (1993 — £298m).

10.133 Although FRS 3 does not define a business segment, best practice would seem to be to disclose the effect of acquisitions and discontinued activities on both a business class and geographical location basis by segment. In the case of the geographical disclosures, these would be made on both a source and a destination basis. Comparative information would also be provided.

10.134 FRS 3 also requires that the results of acquisitions, excluding those that are also discontinued in the period, should be disclosed separately in aggregate as a component of continuing operations. As with the other continuing operations the minimum analysis given on the face of the profit and loss account should be turnover and operating profit. The analysis of each of the other profit and loss account headings between turnover and operating profit may be given in a note, instead of on the face of the profit and loss account.

10.135 In practice, some companies have disclosed separate, detailed segmental information in respect of acquisitions. For example, Coats Viyella's 1993 financial statements provide analyses of the turnover, operating profit and net assets of its acquisitions, by both product category and geographical location (see Table 10.3).

Exceptional items

10.136 FRS 3 identifies exceptional items as "*. . .material items which derive from events or transactions that fall within the ordinary activities of the reporting entity and which individually or, if of a similar type, in aggregate, need to be disclosed by virtue of their size or incidence if the financial statements are to give a true and fair view*".

[The next paragraph is 10.138.]

10.138 FRS 3 does not give specific guidance on the effect of the 'exceptional' items on segmental reporting, other than by stating that the effect of such items on segment results should be disclosed where material. We consider that the effect can be shown in one of several ways:

- Analyse 'profits after exceptional items but before interest', and then disclose the effect of the exceptionals in narrative form.
- Analyse operating profit (that is before super-exceptionals) and then show these exceptionals as one figure in the reconciliation to profit before tax, again with narrative explanation of their effect on individual segments.
- Analyse operating profit by segment and then give a separate column analysing the non-operating exceptionals by segment.

10.139 The important point is that the segmental analyses published must provide sufficient disclosure to enable the reader to understand the impact of exceptional items on business and geographical segments, and to be able to distinguish operating profit before exceptional items from operating profit after exceptional items.

10.140 Practical examples of companies providing segmental information in respect of exceptional items include Trafalgar House Public Limited Company, which, in addition to a detailed analysis of exceptional items in the notes to the financial statements, sets out a business segment analysis of their effect on operating (loss)/profit (see Table 10.19).

Table 10.19 — Trafalgar House Public Limited Company — Report and Accounts — 30 September 1994

Notes to the Accounts

3 Analysis by geographical area and class of business

Exceptional items charged to operating (loss)/profit analysed by class of business:

	Rationalisation costs 1994 £m	Rationalisation costs* 1993 £m (restated)	**Asset write downs and other items 1994 £m**	Asset write downs 1993 £m (restated)	**Total 1994 £m**	Total restated 1993 £m (restated)
Engineering	**(21.8)**	(45.8)	**(15.2)**	(21.1)	**(37.0)**	(66.9)
Construction	**(1.5)**	(10.1)	–	(6.2)	**(1.5)**	(16.3)
Residential Property	**(0.4)**	(6.3)	**5.7**	(17.4)	**5.3**	(23.7)
Commercial Property	**(0.7)**	(2.9)	**(6.6)**	(129.2)	**(7.3)**	(132.1)
Hotels	–	–	**1.9**	(12.5)	**1.9**	(12.5)
Shipping	–	(1.5)	–	(15.5)	–	(17.0)
Other activities	–	–	–	(57.2)	–	(57.2)
	(24.4)	(66.6)	**(14.2)**	(259.1)	**(38.6)**	(325.7)

*1993 rationalisation costs include directors' compensation of £1.3 million.

10.141 AMEC p.l.c. analyses profit or loss by business and geographical segment gross of exceptional items, showing the gross amount of exceptional items as an aggregate one-line deduction. However, in a note analysing exceptional items, it provides various analyses including by class of business and by geographical area (see Table 10.20).

Table 10.20 — AMEC p.l.c. — Annual Report and Accounts — 31 December 1993

Notes to the accounts (extract)

2 Analysis by class of business and geographical origin

	Turnover 1993 £million	Turnover 1992 £million	Profit (loss) 1993 £million	Profit (loss) 1992 £million	Assets employed 1993 £million	Assets employed 1992 £million.
By class of business						
Building and civil engineering	704.8	674.7	9.6	22.7	30.4	11.0
Mechanical and electrical engineering	1,361.1	1,361.9	22.8	18.0	62.7	83.9
Housing and development	138.1	109.1	(7.6)	(17.1)	150.0	176.2
	2,204.0	2,145.7	24.8	23.6	243.1	271.1
Internal trading	(19.8)	(24.0)	—	—	—	—
Exceptional items (note 7)	—	—	—	(114.6)	—	—
Loss on disposals of operations	—	—	(2.2)	—	—	—
Net interest	—	—	(1.6)	2.8	—	—
Unallocated net liabilities	—	—	—	—	(2.7)	(28.9)
	2,184.2	2,121.7	21.0	(88.2)	240.4	242.2
By geographical origin						
United Kingdom	1,751.4	1,838.4	28.0	37.3	196.0	220.8
Europe	201.4	106.0	3.7	3.2	24.2	17.8
Americas	132.0	117.6	(6.1)	(2.6)	21.6	31.3
Middle East Asia and Australasia	119.2	83.7	(0.8)	(14.3)	1.3	1.2
	2,204.0	2,145.7	24.8	23.6	243.1	271.1
Internal trading	(19.8)	(24.0)	—	—	—	—
Exceptional items (note 7)	—	—	—	(114.6)	—	—
Loss on disposal of operations	—	—	(2.2)	—	—	—
Net interest	—	—	(1.6)	2.8	—	—
Unallocated net liabilities	—	—	—	—	(2.7)	(28.9)
	2,184.2	2,121.7	21.0	(88.2)	240.4	242.2

FRS 3 has been adopted in preparing the consolidated profit and loss account.

Certain businesses have been disposed of or terminated during the year none of which falls within the materiality definition of discontinued operations.

The results of businesses acquired during the year have not had a significant impact on the profit for the year.

Accordingly information disclosed in the consolidated profit and loss account includes the results of business disposals and acquisitions during the year.

The analysis of turnover by geographical market is not materially different from that by geographical origin.

7 Exceptional items

There were no exceptional items in 1993

	1992
Exceptional items in 1992 are made up as follows	£million
Housing and development — write down of value of land and work in progress	63.0
Construction — Trafalgar Place Brighton — contract loss	15.9
Losses relating to investment in Power Corporation Plc	18.0
Closure and reorganisation costs	17.7
	114.6
Analysis by statutory profit and loss account format heading	
Cost of sales	85.1
Administrative expenses	11.5
Share of results of associated undertakings	18.0
	114.6
Analysis by class of business	
Building and civil engineering	20.7
Mechanical and electrical engineering	12.7
Housing and development	81.2
	114.6
Analysis by geographical area	
United Kingdom	88.3
Rest of Europe	20.0
Americas	0.8
Middle East, Asia and Australasia	5.5
	114.6

10.142 Table 10.9 above shows columnar analysis of operating exceptionals by segment and narrative explanation of non-operating exceptional items.

[The next paragraph is 10.144.]

Voluntary segmental disclosures

Introduction

10.144 There are many other types of segmental disclosure given by companies in practice. A number of examples are given below. While none of them are required by the standard, all are potentially useful and informative for the reader and analyst.

Employees

10.145 The Companies Act 1985 requires the average number of employees to be disclosed. This disclosure should be both in total and by category of employee, with the categories being determined by the directors, having regard to the manner in which the company's activities are organised. [CA85 sec 231A]. Various types of disclosure have been adopted by companies, including by geographical region and by business segment. Lonrho Plc, for example, adopts the geographical basis approach, with further analysis between employees of the group and employees of associates (see Table 10.21).

Table 10.21 — Lonrho Plc — Annual Report and Accounts — 30 September 1994

Notes to the Accounts (extract)

5 Staff Numbers

The average number of persons employed during the year was as follows:—

	1994			1993		
	Group	**Associates**	**Total**	Group	Associates	Total
United Kingdom	**7,815**		**7,815**	8,246		8,246
East, Central and West Africa	**59,203**	**25,283**	**84,486**	56,710	26,708	83,418
Southern Africa	**22,637**	**35**	**22,672**	23,160	14	23,174
The Americas	**4,796**	**969**	**5,765**	4,881	949	5,830
Europe and Other	**5,662**	**1,050**	**6,712**	5,822	979	6,801
Discontinued operations				490	2,085	2,575
	100,113	**27,337**	**127,450**	99,309	30,735	130,044

10.146 Grand Metropolitan Public Limited Company, on the other hand, provides analysis by business segment. This analysis separates out full-time and part-time employees, distinguished between continuing and discontinued businesses (see Table 10.22).

Table 10.22 — Grand Metropolitan Public Limited Company — Annual Report — 30 September 1994

Notes (extract)

11 Employees

The average number of employees during the year was

	1994			1993		
	Full time	**Part time**	**Total**	*Full time*	*Part time*	*Total*
Continuing operations						
Food — branded	**19,074**	**1,950**	**21,024**	20,293	2,047	22,340
— retailing	**11,554**	**18,498**	**30,052**	13,422	22,083	35,505
Drinks	**11,464**	**335**	**11,799**	11,612	342	11,954
	42,092	**20,783**	**62,875**	45,327	24,472	69,799
Discontinued operations	**595**	**830**	**1,425**	7,391	9,973	17,364
	42,687	**21,613**	**64,300**	52,718	34,445	87,163

10.147 In contrast to the two above examples, The BOC Group plc provides segmental analysis on both a business and a territorial basis (see Table 10.23).

Table 10.23 — The BOC Group plc — Report and Accounts — 30 September 1994

Notes on Financial Statements (extract)

6 Employees **a) Number of employees by business**	1994 Year end	 Average	1993 Year end	 Average
Gases & related products	**26,551**	**26,686**	27,615	26,037
Health Care	**5,754**	**6,002**	6,228	6,459
Vacuum Technology & Distribution Services	**6,880**	**6,470**	6,193	5,723
Corporate	**236**	**232**	230	215
	39,421	**39,390**	40,266	38,434

b) Number of employees by region	1994 Year end	 Average	1993 Year end	 Average
Europe	**13,849**	**13,601**	13,506	12,746
Africa	**8,427**	**7,944**	7,602	7,493
Americas	**8,858**	**9,201**	9,691	9,760
Asia/Pacific	**8,287**	**8,644**	9,467	8,435
	39,421	**39,390**	40,266	38,434

Fixed assets and capital expenditure

10.148 There is a view that segmental disclosure of expenditure on tangible fixed assets assists readers in assessing the growth potential and possible on-going capital needs of individual segments. While a number of reporting entities, including The BOC Group plc, as Table 10.24 shows, provide analyses of capital expenditure by either or both of business segment and/or geographical segment, few companies have extended this analysis so as to provide detailed segmental analyses of their tangible fixed assets. The British Petroleum Company p.l.c. is one of the exceptions, as it provides such an analysis by business segment (see Table 10.25).

Table 10.24 — The BOC Group plc — Report and Accounts — 30 September 1994

Notes on Financial Statements (extract)

b) Business analysis	Gases and Related Products £million	Health Care £million	Vacuum Technology and Distribution Services £million	Corporate £million	Total £million
1994					
Operating profit before exceptional items	**331.9**	**54.6**	**51.0**	**(2.1)**	**435.4**
Exceptional restructuring costs	**(25.0)**	**(60.0)**	**–**	**–**	**(85.0)**
Capital employed	**2,404.8**	**338.9**	**233.9**	**(12.1)**	**2,965.5**
Capital expenditure[4]	**341.6**	**22.3**	**49.9**	**1.8**	**415.6**
1993					
Operating profit	304.6	**86.2**	33.0	(3.0)	420.8
Capital employed	2,325.5	**381.0**	200.2	(0.5)	2,906.2
Capital expenditure[4]	331.0	**48.9**	28.8	2.2	410.9

c) Regional analysis	Europe £million	Africa £million	Americas £million	Asia/Pacific £million	Total £million
1994					
Operating profit before exceptional items	**151.9**	**56.0**	**95.2**	**132.3**	**435.4**
Exceptional restructuring costs	**(48.4)**	**–**	**(26.7)**	**(9.9)**	**(85.0)**
Capital employed	**1,035.3**	**191.4**	**823.9**	**914.9**	**2,965.5**
Capital expenditure[4]	**135.6**	**27.7**	**105.8**	**146.5**	**415.6**
1993					
Operating profit	130.6	52.3	128.0	109.9	420.8
Capital employed	980.3	158.9	901.7	865.3	2,906.2
Capital expenditure[4]	149.8	30.0	94.1	137.0	410.9

[4] includes capital expenditure of related undertakings of £59.3 million (1993: £51.1 million) mainly in Gases and Related Products and Asia/Pacific region.

Table 10.25 — The British Petroleum Company p.l.c. — Annual Report and Accounts — 31 December 1994

15 Tangible assets — property, plant and equipment [extract]

	Exploration and Production	Refining and Marketing	Chemicals	Other business and corporate	Total	£million of which: Assets under Construction
Cost						
At 1 January 1994	25,986	9,329	3,159	1,030	39,504	1,791
Exchange adjustments	(730)	124	–	6	(600)	(27)
Additions	1,157	655	110	32	1,954	1,409
Transfers	121	31	8	(38)	122	(801)
Deletions	(400)	(426)	(78)	(527)	(1,431)	(399)
At 31 December 1994	**26,134**	**9,713**	**3,199**	**503**	**39,549**	**1,973**

Depreciation						
At 1 January 1994	12,907	4,343	1,735	565	19,550	
Exchange adjustments	(421)	92	(4)	6	(327)	
Charge for the year	1,248	489	205	48	1,990	
Transfers	2	8	7	(15)	2	
Deletions	(341)	(262)	(61)	(395)	(1,059)	
At 31 December 1994	**13,395**	**4,670**	**1,882**	**209**	**20,156**	
Net book amount						
At 31 December 1994	**12,739**	**5,043**	**1,317**	**294**	**19,393**	**1,973**
At 31 December 1993	13,079	4,986	1,424	465	19,954	1,791
Principal rates of depreciation	*	2-25%	5-12%	3-25%		
* Mainly unit-of-production						
Assets held under finance leases, capitalised interest and land at net book amount included above:			Leased assets			Capitalised interest
	Cost	Depreciation	Net	Cost	Depreciation	Net
At 31 December 1994	**1,420**	**506**	**914**	**1,518**	**814**	**704**
At 31 December 1993	1,442	448	994	1,519	746	773
			Freehold land			Leasehold land
					Over 50 years unexpired	
						Other
At 31 December 1994			**677**		**20**	**44**
At 31 December 1993			704		10	57

[The next paragraph is 10.150.]

Depreciation

10.150 In addition to the segmental disclosure of capital expenditure referred to above, a number of companies also give segmental disclosures for depreciation. This enables readers to assess the impact of the employment of fixed assets during the period on the segment result and asset base. The British Petroleum Company p.l.c.'s full analysis of fixed assets by business segment *per se* means that it gives this segmental depreciation information.

[The next paragraph is 10.152.]

Research and development

10.152 This is another category of expenditure where companies can provide useful segmental information to readers of financial statements. Readers could, thereby, better understand the levels of investment in research and development made by different business and geographical segments. Indeed, in industries such as the pharmaceutical industry, many fledgling companies are likely to have a substantial proportion of their total assets invested in research and development activities, generating from this relatively little turnover and, in many instances, operating losses. In such circumstances, the directors may form the view that research and development is actually a separate business segment.

Annex — Comparison of segmental reporting requirements

	Companies Act 1985	SSAP 25	
Description of segments	✓	✓	
Turnover			
Origin basis		✓	
Destination basis	✓	✓	
Class of business	✓	✓	
Inter-segment turnover		✓	
Profit before tax			
Class of business		✓	(1)
Geographical segment		✓	(1)
Net assets/capital employed			
Class of business		✓	(2)
Geographical segment		✓	(2)
Associated company profit before tax			
Class of business			✓
Geographical segment			✓
Associated company net assets			
Class of business			✓
Geographical segment			✓

Notes:

(1) Before or after interest.

(2) Including or excluding interest bearing assets and liabilities dependent or whether or not profit before tax is analysed before or after interest.

Chapter 11

Retirement benefits

	Page
Introduction	11001
Types of pension scheme	11001
Defined contribution schemes	11002
Defined benefit schemes	11003
Funded schemes	11003
Unfunded schemes	11003
Scope of FRS 17	11004
Accounting objective of FRS 17	11004
Defined contribution schemes	11005
Definition	11005
Accounting	11005
Disclosure	11006
Multi-employer and group schemes	11006
Disclosure of multi-employer and group schemes	11011
Defined benefit schemes	11012
Scheme assets and scheme liabilities	11012
Scheme assets	11012
Scheme liabilities	11013
Reflecting defined benefit schemes in the balance sheet	11015
Measurement of scheme assets	11016
Measurement of scheme liabilities	11018
Frequency of valuations	11020
Reporting performance	11021
Current service cost	11022
Interest cost and expected return on assets	11024
Past service costs	11026
Settlements and curtailments	11028
Actuarial gains and losses	11032
Limit on pension asset	11033
Benefit improvements	11034
Required accounting	11035
Taxation	11038
Acquisitions	11039
Disclosures	11040
Disclosures — before December 2006 amendment	11040
Comparatives	11043
Aggregation of schemes	11044
Disclosures — December 2006 amendment	11045
Aggregation of schemes	11049
Best practice disclosures	11050

Relationship between the reporting entity and the trustees of defined benefit schemes 11051
Information about the principal assumptions 11051
Sensitivity analysis for principal assumptions 11051
How defined benefit liabilities are measured
Future funding obligations in relation to defined benefit schemes 11052
Nature and extent of the risks and rewards arising from financial instruments held by defined benefit schemes 11052
Reserves relating to defined benefit schemes 11053
Distributable reserves 11053
Composition of reserves 11055
Pensions Act 2004 implications 11058
The Pension Protection Fund ('PPF') 11058
The Pensions Regulator 11059
The 'moral hazard' provisions 11059
The 'statutory funding objective' 11059
Employers ceasing to participate in a pension scheme 11061
Accounting treatment 11065

Chapter 11

Retirement benefits

Introduction

11.1 Pensions and other retirement benefits is one of the most difficult topics in accounting. For many years accountants across the world have struggled to reach a consensus on how defined benefit pension schemes should be reflected in the employers' financial statements.

[The next paragraph is 11.5.]

11.5 FRS 17, 'Retirement benefits', was published on 30 November 2000. The accounting model for defined benefit schemes in FRS 17 approaches pension cost accounting from a balance sheet perspective. It works from the premise that a surplus or deficit in a pension scheme (measured by reference to the fair values of the scheme assets and liabilities) should be shown on the employer's balance sheet. The overall figures in the performance statements reflect the changes in those fair values year on year.

11.6 As part of the ASB's aim of moving UK GAAP closer to IFRS, an amendment to FRS 17 was issued in December 2006, which is effective for accounting periods beginning on or after 6 April 2007. This amendment changed the disclosure requirements of FRS 17 to those of IAS 19, subject only to ensuring internal consistency in terminology within FRS 17. See paragraph 11.148.1 onwards. The only measurement change made was in paragraph 16 to the basis of calculating the fair value of scheme assets. The original version requires that for quoted securities, mid-market value be taken as fair value for scheme assets. The amendment changes this 'mid-market value' to 'current bid value'. References to FRS 17 paragraphs revised by the December 2006 amendment are shown in this chapter as 'FRS 17R'.

11.7 The ASB was concerned that by making this change some valuable disclosures might be lost. As a result, a reporting statement 'Retirement benefits – disclosures' was published in January 2007. The statement is not mandatory and aims to create best practice for retirement benefit disclosures in the UK. It has no commencement date and is equally applicable to entities reporting under IFRS as well as under UK GAAP. The statement is discussed in more detail from paragraph 11.148.13 onwards.

[The next paragraph is 11.12.]

Types of pension scheme

11.12 There are three basic types of pension arrangement in the UK:

- The state scheme.
- Occupational pension schemes.
- Personal pension and stakeholder schemes.

11.13 The state scheme consists of two elements, the basic pension and the earnings related pension. All employers and employees make contributions towards the state scheme through their national insurance payments. The earnings related scheme is the State Second Pension (S2P), to which all employees pay, unless they choose to 'contract out'. Contracting out is possible if the employee is a member of an occupational pension scheme or contributes to a stakeholder or personal pension.

11.14 In a contracted out occupational scheme, both employer and employee pay a lower rate of national insurance contributions. The occupational scheme is then used to provide employees with benefits which replace part of their state earnings related benefits. The broad intention is that the pension provided by a contracted out scheme is at least as good as the pension that would have been available from S2P. On retirement, the employee receives a state basic pension and a pension from the occupational scheme.

11.15 Occupational pension schemes are not required to contract out of S2P and many do not. Where a scheme is 'contracted in' to S2P, employer and employee pay the full rate of national insurance contributions. The responsibility for payment of S2P remains with the state. On retirement, the employee receives a state basic and earnings related pension, together with a pension from the occupational scheme.

11.16 Personal pension and stakeholder schemes are pension arrangements available to the self-employed, employees with no company scheme, employees with non-pensionable earnings and those who wish to contract out of S2P or opt out of an occupational pension scheme. These are defined contribution schemes.

11.17 Accounting for the cost of providing pension benefits is particularly affected by the type of benefits that are promised by a scheme and by the way in which the employer's obligations in respect of such benefits are funded. The broad classifications used in pensions terminology are summarised in the following paragraphs. Each involves a cost to the employer insofar as it is obligated to contribute towards the cost of the benefits receivable by its employees or their dependants.

Defined contribution schemes

11.18 Defined contribution schemes (often referred to as money purchase schemes) are pension schemes where the benefits are determined directly by the value of contributions paid in respect of each member and the investment performance achieved on those contributions. Normally, the rate of contribution to be paid by the employer company will be specified in the scheme's rules. If the investments have performed well the individual will obtain a higher pension than if the investments have performed badly. In such schemes the risk of poor investment performance lies with the individual.

Defined benefit schemes

11.19 Defined benefit schemes are pension schemes where the rules specify the benefits to be paid, typically by reference to final salary levels, and such schemes are financed accordingly. The majority of these schemes define benefits in relation to an employee's final salary (typically the pension will be based on 1/60th of final salary for each year of pensionable service, up to a maximum of 40 years). In the UK, they are often referred to as final salary schemes. Another form of defined benefit scheme that is becoming increasingly common is the average salary scheme where the pension is calculated by reference to average pay over an extended period. In defined benefit schemes the risk of poor investment performance lies with the sponsoring company.

Funded schemes

11.20 Funded pension schemes are schemes where the future liabilities for pension benefits are provided for in advance by the accumulation of assets held externally to the employing company's business. The assets are usually placed under the control of trustees, who administer the scheme in accordance with the provisions of trust law and the terms of the trust deed governing the particular scheme. Employer and employee contributions paid to the trust are invested by the trustees; pensions are paid out of the accumulated funds of the trust.

11.21 Most funded schemes in the UK that are established under trusts enjoy considerable tax benefits through Inland Revenue recognition as exempt approved schemes.

11.22 Effective from 1 April 2005, the Finance Act 2004 introduced a limit on the transfer value of an employee's accrued benefit, limiting the total accrued benefit that employees may be entitled to, rather than the increase in accrued benefit that they may become entitled to in each year.

Unfunded schemes

11.23 Unfunded pension schemes are schemes where pension benefits are paid directly by the employer. No assets are set aside in advance to provide for future liabilities; instead pension liabilities are met out of the employer's own resources. Such schemes are not common in the private sector in the UK but are found in the public sector. However, the incidence of unfunded arrangements in the UK has increased.

Scope of FRS 17

11.24 FRS 17 applies to all types of benefits that an employer is committed to providing after employees have completed their service, including pensions and post-retirement healthcare benefits. The standard covers statutory and contractual commitments to provide retirement benefits in exchange for services rendered, together with commitments that are implicit in an employer's actions. The same accounting principles apply whether retirement benefits are funded or unfunded.

11.25 The standard does not apply to termination benefits that become payable because an employer decides to terminate an employee's employment before the normal retirement date or because an employee decides to accept voluntary redundancy. These are excluded from the definition of retirement benefits. [FRS 17 para 2].

11.26 There is no concession to multinational groups in respect of overseas schemes that have been accounted for under a different accounting standard. All schemes should be accounted for consistently in compliance with FRS 17 and so adjustments are required, where necessary, to convert retirement benefits accounting from local GAAP to a measurement and recognition basis that complies with the FRS.

11.27 FRS 17 includes within its scope other post-retirement benefits, including post-retirement private medical insurance benefits, which are commonly provided in the US by UK groups with US subsidiaries.

Accounting objective of FRS 17

11.28 FRS 17 approaches pensions accounting from a balance sheet perspective. The approach reflects the trend in accounting standards to base the accounting on the definitions of assets and liabilities and to make more use of fair value measurements for financial assets and liabilities. So the first stated objective of FRS 17 is to ensure that an employer's financial statements reflect at fair value the assets and liabilities arising from its retirement benefit obligations and any related funding. [FRS 17 para 1].

11.29 The next objective deals with recognising the cost of retirement benefits in the performance statements. It is to ensure:

- Operating costs are recognised in the accounting periods in which they are earned by the employees (not when they are due to be paid).
- Finance costs and any other changes in the value of the assets and liabilities are recognised in the accounting periods in which they arise.

[FRS 17 para 1].

This implies there is no scope for smoothing costs by spreading forward gains and losses into future accounting periods.

11.30 The third objective relates to disclosures, to ensure that adequate disclosure is provided about the cost of providing retirement benefits and the related gains, losses, assets and liabilities. [FRS 17 para 1]. FRS 17 has been revised to incorporate the disclosures required by IAS 19 and is applicable for accounting periods beginning on or after 6 April 2007. See paragraphs 11.148.1 onwards. Additionally, a reporting statement 'Retirement benefits – disclosures' was issued in January 2007 aiming to improve disclosure of retirement benefit schemes in UK financial statements, whether prepared under UK GAAP or IFRS (see paragraphs 11.148.13 onwards).

Defined contribution schemes

Definition

11.31 FRS 17 defines a defined contribution scheme as *"A pension or other retirement benefit scheme into which an employer pays regular contributions fixed as an amount or as a percentage of pay and will have no legal or constructive obligation to pay further contributions if the scheme does not have sufficient assets to pay all employee benefits relating to employee service in the current and prior periods"*. [FRS 17 para 2]. In a defined contribution scheme, the employer's liability is limited to the contributions it has agreed to pay. The employee takes the investment risk because the value of the employee's retirement benefits is determined by the value of contributions paid into the scheme during the employee's service life and the investment return achieved on those contributions.

11.32 The definition notes that a defined contribution scheme may also provide death-in-service benefits. It explains that death-in-service benefits are not deemed to relate to employee service in the current and prior periods. Therefore, the provision of death-in-service benefits does not change a defined contribution scheme into a defined benefit scheme.

11.33 With the exception of some multi-employer schemes, all other schemes are deemed to be defined benefit schemes and the defined benefit scheme accounting and disclosure rules apply.

11.34 Some schemes contain features of both defined contribution and defined benefit schemes. For example, there are schemes that provide money purchase benefits, but with an underlying final salary guarantee. The FRS requires such schemes to be accounted for as defined benefit schemes if the employer has a potential liability to pay further contributions.

Accounting

11.35 Except for contributions outstanding or prepaid, an employer has no assets or liabilities in respect of a defined contribution scheme. FRS 17's accounting objective is met by charging to operating profit the contributions payable to the scheme for the accounting period. [FRS 17 para 7].

Disclosure

11.36 The following disclosures are required:

- The nature of the scheme (that is, defined contribution).
- The cost for the period.
- Any outstanding or prepaid contributions at the balance sheet date.

[FRS 17 para 75].

Multi-employer and group schemes

11.37 FRS 17 addresses the accounting by individual entities that participate in multi-employer pension schemes, including group schemes. FRS 17 requires, *"Where more than one employer participates in a defined benefit scheme the employer should account for the scheme as a defined benefit scheme..."*. [FRS 17 para 9]. Therefore, an entity that participates in a defined benefit scheme should account for the scheme in the first instance as a defined benefit scheme in accordance with paragraphs 11.43 onwards. For defined benefit schemes, two situations are envisaged where individual participating employers would account as though the scheme was a defined contribution scheme rather than a defined benefit scheme.

11.38 The first situation is where the employer's contributions are set to cover the cost of the benefits earned in the current period only and are not affected by any surplus or deficit in the scheme relating to past service. So if a deficit arises, the employer has no obligation to increase its contributions to fund it. Similarly, if a surplus arises, the employer has no right to reduce its contributions. In this situation, the scheme is a defined contribution scheme from the individual employer's perspective. To qualify for defined contribution accounting, there must be clear evidence that a third party rather than the employer has an obligation to fund any deficit. [FRS 17 para 10]. Such schemes are likely to be rare – possibly non-existent – in the private sector.

11.39 The second situation is where an employer's contributions are affected by any surplus or deficit in the scheme, but *"the employer is unable to identify its share of the underlying assets and liabilities in the scheme on a consistent and reasonable basis"*. [FRS 17 para 9]. The standard gives as an example the situation where contributions are set at a common level for the scheme as a whole, rather than reflecting the characteristics of the workforces of individual employers. Each employer is, therefore, exposed to actuarial risks associated with other entities. In this situation, the employer should treat the scheme as a defined contribution scheme and recognise only the contributions payable each year. [FRS 17 para 11]. Additional disclosures are, however, necessary as set out in paragraph 11.42.

11.40 Some employers participate in industry-wide pension schemes, which provide centralised pension arrangements for identifiable groups of unrelated employers. Examples in the UK include the merchant navy pension funds for seafaring employees, the Electricity Supply Pension Scheme and schemes in the coal industry. Sometimes each employer has its own separate fund within the industry scheme. Where the arrangements are of the defined benefit type, each employer should follow the defined benefit accounting rules of FRS 17 if the assets and accrued pension liabilities in the scheme can be allocated to individual participating employers. Each employer would recognise an asset or liability relating to its share of the scheme assets less liabilities, and measure components of pension cost in the same manner as an entity that operates its own scheme. In other cases, each employer should treat the scheme as a defined contribution scheme, where the accounting is determined by the contributions payable for each period – no surplus or deficit, or actuarial gain or loss is recognised.

11.41 This part of the FRS is particularly relevant to group pension schemes. Group schemes often apply common contribution rates across the group as a whole. There are several scenarios where it may be difficult for a group company to determine its share of the pension scheme's underlying assets and liabilities on a reasonable basis. For example:

- The allocation of assets and liabilities relating to non-active members may be impossible, in particular for mature schemes where historical information is not readily available.
- Even if it were possible to allocate non-active members across subsidiaries based on last day of employment, members may have worked for more than one subsidiary. Therefore, it may not be possible to identify to whom the liability (and corresponding asset) for successive periods of employment belongs.
- Groups may have changed over the years, with various restructuring exercises, disposals and acquisitions to consider. This can make any allocation exercise extremely complex and perhaps meaningless. For example, a group scheme may have past service liabilities for pensioners and deferred pensioners of former subsidiaries that are no longer part of the group.

11.41.1 Where the structure of the scheme does not enable any of the individual group companies (that is, the parent or subsidiaries) to identify their share of the scheme's underlying assets and liabilities, the parent company as well as the participating subsidiaries should adopt the defined contribution treatment in their individual financial statements. [FRS 17 para 12]. The defined benefit accounting rules would be used only at the consolidation level. A consolidation adjustment will be required to replace the total of the pension costs in the companies' financial statements (based on contributions payable) with the specified components of pension cost for a defined benefit scheme. In addition, any surplus or deficit in the group scheme will be recognised as an asset or liability in the consolidated balance sheet only. In those circumstances the figures in the consolidated financial statements will not be the same as the total of the figures shown in the individual group companies' financial statements.

11.41.2 However, the requirements of the Pensions Act 2004 mean that, where a defined benefit scheme has insufficient assets to cover its liabilities, the trustees must establish a recovery plan setting out how the statutory funding objective (SFO) is to be met and over what period (see para 11.179). In detailing the steps to be taken in order to meet the SFO, the recovery plan will specify the contributions sought from each participating company. Although this deals with cash payments rather than each company's share of assets and liabilities, it is through adjustments to normal levels of contribution that the surplus or deficit (being determined as the net sum of the scheme's assets and liabilities) is often recovered or settled. So it is arguable that a contribution schedule as set out in the scheme's recovery plan provides evidence, on a reasonable and consistent basis, as to how the scheme surplus or deficit (and, hence, the relevant share of scheme assets and liabilities) should be allocated. It, therefore, follows that application of defined benefit accounting in each participating company is appropriate.

11.41.3 Further to this, for accounting periods ended on or after 6 April 2006 the rules for employers deducting pension contributions for tax purposes changed. The more general tax 'wholly and exclusively' test applies, so that deductions are allowed only for contributions made wholly and exclusively for the purposes of the employer's trade or profession. In the context of group schemes, where contributions to a group pension scheme are made by the holding company in the group with each employing subsidiary company in the group being recharged an appropriate amount relating to its employees, the intra-group recharge may be accepted as being a contribution paid by the employer to the registered scheme. More importantly, the contribution paid by the holding company on behalf of each subsidiary company must be recharged to each subsidiary company on a reasonable basis (so as to meet the 'wholly and exclusively' test) in order for a tax deduction to be available. This further increases the likelihood that group plans in the UK will have in place an agreement that allows participating companies to identify their share of assets and liabilities on a reasonable and consistent basis, such that defined benefit accounting is appropriate for each participating company.

11.41.4 A further consideration is where the ultimate parent of a group prepares its individual entity financial statements under IFRS. Whilst some differences do exist between the wording of IAS 19 and FRS 17 and differing treatments may be appropriate under the two standards, FRS 17 only requires an entity to be able to identify its share of the underlying assets and liabilities of the scheme on a consistent and reasonable basis. Therefore, if an entity can identify its share of assets and liabilities under IAS 19, it would seem likely that this allocation would form a consistent and reasonable basis for the purposes of FRS 17. We would, therefore, expect to see full defined benefit accounting in all participating companies in a group scheme under both FRS 17 and IAS 19 in these circumstances. Adoption of IFRS by individual companies within a group such as a parent company may result in a change in the treatment of a defined benefit scheme in the subsidiary companies still reporting under UK GAAP, as demonstrated in the following example.

Example

A listed group has a number of subsidiaries and one defined benefit scheme, to which employees of all subsidiaries belong. The scheme is currently in deficit under both FRS 17 and IAS 19. In the past, under FRS 17, it has been determined that the scheme assets and liabilities cannot be identified on a 'consistent and reasonable basis'. [FRS 17 para 9(b)]. The group prepares its consolidated financial statements and the parent entity financial statements in accordance with IFRS (applying IAS 19).

If there is a contractual agreement or stated policy for charging the net defined benefit cost for the plan as a whole to participating entities, the entity should, in its separate or individual financial statements, recognise the net defined benefit cost so charged (this would equate to the application of defined benefit accounting in each participating entity). Where a group has no contractual agreement or stated policy for charging the net defined benefit cost for the plan as a whole to individual group entities, IAS 19 requires that the entire scheme is recognised in the financial statements of the 'sponsoring employer'. [IAS 19 para 34A].

The group has considered IAS 19 and concluded that, in the absence of such a contractual agreement or policy, the parent entity would be the sponsoring employer. Given the resulting impact on distributable profits of the parent arising from recognising of the whole deficit in this company, the group forms a policy for charging the net defined benefit pension cost to the individual entities.

The formulation of this 'stated policy' means that, when considering the equivalent guidance under FRS 17 (see para 11.37), there is now a 'consistent and reasonable basis' for allocating the scheme assets and liabilities between the participating entities under FRS 17 and that the subsidiaries cease to qualify for the multi-employer exemption.

11.41.5 The application of defined benefit accounting in the individual financial statements of subsidiary companies participating in a group defined benefit scheme may be appropriate where different contribution rates are applied to different members of the group.

11.41.6 If a high percentage of contributions to the scheme come from one company, then it may be that that company is most likely to benefit or suffer from any surplus or deficit in the scheme as a whole, including those generated by non-active members. This could be sufficient evidence to support a reasonable allocation, although this conclusion may not be reached if surpluses are applied to award benefit improvements to non-active members who are not attributable to that company.

11.41.7 Determining what constitutes a 'high percentage' is a matter of judgement. We consider that it should be presumed for anything above 90 per cent while there should be careful inspection of the directors' justification for non-allocation where one company contributes over 75 per cent.

11.41.8 Set out below are other examples of situations where it is considered more likely that a group's scheme assets and liabilities could be allocated on a consistent and reasonable basis.

- Where most of the scheme liabilities relate to active members, who can be identified with individual group entities, it is reasonable to allocate on the basis of this active membership.
- It is generally, although not always, easier to allocate unfunded schemes as there are no assets to be dealt with.
- Where the scheme's trust deed and rules specify what would happen on sale of a participating employer (for example, share of fund), these principles may be applied. The documentation might set out a rational manner in which to allocate the assets and liabilities.

11.41.9 Taking into account all the above factors, we believe it is becoming more difficult to defend the use of defined contribution accounting for group schemes. Defined benefit accounting should become increasingly common, and should be the expected default position. The following table summarises some common situations.

Over 90 per cent of the deficit relates to subsidiary A.	A reasonable allocation under FRS 17 might be to allocate the entire deficit to Company A.
There is an agreed allocation of contributions split between group companies for tax purposes.	Where tax deductions are allowed only for contributions made wholly and exclusively for the purposes of the employer's trade or profession, this increases the likelihood that group plans in the UK will have in place an agreement on how contributions are allocated. This agreement might present a reasonable basis for participating companies to allocate the assets and liabilities, such that defined benefit accounting would be applied. Therefore, arguments that the split for tax purposes does not provide a reasonable basis for accounting purposes would have to be justified.
The scheme's trust deed and rules specify what would happen on sale	The documentation might set out a rational manner in which to

of a participating employer (for example, share of fund).	allocate the assets and liabilities under FRS 17.
Acquisitive company, with large proportion of orphan members and it is difficult to trace to which company these orphan members relate.	DC accounting will be acceptable if reasonable arguments are provided.

In a few years time, we envisage that all groups always have to apply defined benefit accounting. Under UK GAAP, unless arising from a specific event such as a group reconstruction, the change from defined contribution to defined benefit accounting for group schemes will be a change in accounting policy and, therefore, result in an adjustment to opening reserves.

Disclosure of multi-employer and group schemes

11.42 In the situation covered by paragraph 11.39, the individual company financial statements should disclose that the scheme is a defined benefit scheme, state that defined benefit accounting is not used (that is, because the employer is unable to identify its share of the underlying assets and liabilities) and disclose *"any available information about the existence of the surplus or deficit in the scheme and the implications"* for that company – for example, the effect on future contribution rates or a provision for the funding by the company of a deficit within the multi-employer scheme if a 'financial support direction' is imposed by the regulator under the Pensions Act 2004 (see further para 11.177). [FRS 17 para 9(b)]. The December 2006 amendment to FRS 17 extends the disclosures above to also include an explanation of why sufficient information is not available, and details of the basis used to determine the surplus or deficit.

11.42.1 The disclosure of information about the existence and implications of the surplus or deficit in the scheme has to be given in the subsidiary's financial statements. It cannot be dealt with by means of a cross-reference to the consolidated financial statements, as the subsidiary's financial statements have to comply with FRS 17 on a stand-alone basis.

11.42.2 Furthermore, in situations where the group is reporting under IFRS and the IAS 19 surplus or deficit is the only information available to a subsidiary company, then disclosure of the IAS 19 information would meet the requirements of paragraph 9(b) in respect of any available information about the existence of the surplus or deficit in the scheme. In these circumstances, the wording of the disclosure should explain that a valuation of surplus or deficit at a group level on an FRS 17 basis is not performed and, therefore, the surplus or deficit calculated in accordance with IAS 19 has been disclosed.

Defined benefit schemes

Scheme assets and scheme liabilities

Scheme assets

11.43 FRS 17 does not provide a definition of 'scheme assets'. Identifying scheme assets is important because the accounting for them is quite different from the accounting for other investments that are not scheme assets. This applies to both the balance sheet and the performance statements. In the balance sheet, scheme assets less scheme liabilities are shown as a net item. In the performance statements, the profit and loss account is credited each period with the expected long-term rate of return (income plus capital growth) on the scheme assets; differences between the expected and actual return are recognised as actuarial gains or losses in the statement of total recognised gains and losses (STRGL).

11.44 There are several references in the FRS to scheme assets being assets held by the scheme. Furthermore, the ASB's rationale for the 'net' treatment of scheme assets and liabilities is that such assets are held in trust and are controlled by the scheme trustees rather than the employer. [FRS 17 App IV para 25]. In the UK, scheme assets should usually be apparent from the way funded pension schemes are constituted. The assets are usually placed under the control of trustees, who administer the scheme in accordance with the provisions of trust law and the terms of the trust deed governing the particular scheme. The FRS notes that for its purposes notional funding of a pension scheme does not give rise to assets in a scheme. [FRS 17 para 19].

11.45 In some other countries, the identification of scheme assets may not be so clear cut. IAS 19 provides the following definition, which is useful guidance for UK groups with overseas schemes:

> *"Assets held by a long-term employee benefit fund are assets (other than non-transferable financial instruments issued by the reporting entity) that:*
>
> *(a) are held by an entity (a fund) that is legally separate from the reporting entity and exists solely to pay or fund employee benefits; and*
>
> *(b) are available to be used only to pay or fund employee benefits, are not available to the reporting entity's own creditors (even in bankruptcy), and cannot be returned to the reporting entity, unless either:*
>
> *(i) the remaining assets of the fund are sufficient to meet all the related employee benefit obligations of the plan or the reporting entity; or*
>
> *(ii) the assets are returned to the reporting entity to reimburse it for employee benefits already paid."*

[IAS 19 para 7].

Scheme liabilities

11.46 Scheme liabilities are defined as *"the liabilities of a defined benefit scheme for outgoings due after the valuation date"*. They reflect the benefits that the employer is committed to provide for employees' service up to the valuation date and comprise:

- Benefits promised under the formal terms of the scheme.
- Further benefits (if any) that the employer has a constructive obligation to provide as a result of a public statement or past practice that has created a valid expectation in the employees that such benefits will be granted.

[FRS 17 paras 2, 20].

11.47 The components of scheme liabilities specified above reflect the characteristics of a 'present obligation' in FRS 12. The recognition of a provision stems from the existence of a present obligation. A present obligation may be legal or constructive. A constructive obligation may be more difficult to discern in practice than a legal obligation as it derives from the employer's actions. FRS 12 defines a constructive obligation as:

"An obligation that derives from an entity's actions where:

(a) by an established pattern of past practice, published policies or a sufficiently specific current statement, the entity has indicated to other parties that it will accept certain responsibilities; and

(b) as a result, the entity has created a valid expectation on the part of those other parties that it will discharge those responsibilities."

[FRS 12 para 2].

11.48 An example of a constructive obligation is a practice of granting annual increases to pensions in payment and deferred pensions (over and above any increases that may be required by law) that are on paper discretionary, but are in practice customarily granted as a measure of protection against inflation. The cost of such increases should be factored into both the annual current service cost (so that the operating cost is charged as it is earned through employees' service) and the measurement of the scheme liability at each year-end.

11.49 An employer may in the past have granted occasional discretionary increases to pensions without creating an expectation of similar increases in the future. The cost of such increases would have resulted in additional past service liabilities when they were granted (see para 11.93). If the employer's practice changes such that a valid expectation of future increases is created, the cost of future increases should also be provided for at the valuation date.

11.50 Scheme liabilities may also include obligations to pay death-in-service and incapacity benefits. Such benefits are often calculated by reference to salary at the date of death or incapacity rather than the period of an employee's service. FRS 17 requires that:

> *"A charge should be made to operating profit to reflect the expected cost of providing any death-in-service or incapacity benefits for the period. Any difference between that expected cost and amounts actually incurred should be treated as an actuarial gain or loss.*
>
> *Where a scheme insures the death-in-service costs, the expected cost for the accounting period is simply the premium payable for the period. Where the costs are not insured, the expected cost reflects the probability of any employees dying in the period and the benefit that would then be paid out."*

[FRS 17 paras 73, 74].

11.51 Hence, by applying these paragraphs, the liability for death-in-service and incapacity benefits would include the estimated cost of paying benefits only in respect of employees that have died or become incapacitated by the reporting date.

11.52 However, the general principle of FRS 17 views the obligation to pay retirement benefits as arising over the entire period of employees' service. The scheme liability at the balance sheet date represents an accrual of a portion of those total benefits. If this principle was applied to accounting for death-in-service and incapacity benefits that are provided through a defined benefit pension scheme, the scheme liability would need to include a portion of the estimated cost of paying benefits in respect of employees who are expected to die or become incapacitated between the reporting date and the date of leaving service. This is inconsistent with paragraphs 73 and 74 of the Standard.

11.53 The UITF considered this issue and in May 2002 issued UITF 35, 'Death-in-service and incapacity benefits'. The UITF took the view that, unless there is insurance, death-in-service and incapacity benefits form part of the total pension promise, so where those benefits are provided through a defined benefit pension scheme and are uninsured they should be included in the calculation of scheme liabilities. In performing valuations, actuaries will make assumptions regarding mortality and will allow for a resultant reduction in future pension payments. The UITF concluded that it would be inconsistent for the benefits that would then become payable to be excluded from the valuation.

11.54 Hence, the provisions of paragraphs 73 and 74 will only apply where death-in-service and incapacity benefits are provided through a defined contribution scheme or through a defined benefit scheme but are wholly insured. Where benefits are provided through a defined benefit pension scheme and are not wholly insured, the uninsured scheme liability and the cost for the accounting period should be measured in the same way as other pension obligations, that is by the projected unit method. Measurement of pension liabilities is considered further from paragraph 11.68.

Reflecting defined benefit schemes in the balance sheet

11.55 As noted earlier, FRS 17's first objective is to ensure that an employer's financial statements reflect at fair value the assets and liabilities arising from its retirement benefit obligations and any related funding. To achieve this, the scheme liabilities and (in the case of a funded scheme) the scheme assets are measured at each balance sheet date. The scheme assets are measured at fair value. The scheme liabilities are measured on an actuarial basis. The difference between the fair value of the scheme assets and the actuarial value of the scheme liabilities is a surplus or deficit that, subject to certain conditions, should be recognised as an asset or liability on the employer's balance sheet.

11.56 A surplus is regarded as an asset to the extent that the employer can benefit from it. A deficit is regarded as a liability to the extent that the employer has a legal or constructive obligation to make it good – this will nearly always be the case. In an unfunded scheme, the employer has a direct obligation to pay the retirement benefits and so the employer recognises as a liability the gross amount of the scheme liabilities. In a funded scheme, the employer does not have access to or control of the scheme assets, nor does it have a direct obligation to pay the retirement benefits, and so the employer recognises as an asset or liability the net surplus or deficit.

11.57 The FRS avoids implying that a surplus in a defined benefit pension scheme is 'owned' by the employer. But conceptually an employer does not have to own a surplus in order to recognise an asset. It is sufficient that the employer has access to future economic benefits that it controls via, for example, the ability to reduce future employer contributions. Consequently, a surplus should be recognised as an asset to the extent that the employer is able to recover it through reduced future contributions or refunds. Recoverability of a surplus is considered from paragraph 11.115.

11.58 With the exception of any outstanding contributions payable, assets and liabilities in respect of defined benefit schemes should be shown separately on the balance sheet after all other assets and liabilities. They should also be shown net of attributable deferred tax. The standard does not suggest that this adaptation of the Act's formats involves a true and fair override of those formats. The FRS's note on legal requirements states that the ASB has received legal advice that the requirement does not contravene the Act. [FRS 17 App II para 6]. Defined benefit assets and liabilities are sometimes significant in relation to other net assets and the method of calculating them will often lead to large variations in the balances year on year – but the figures are transparent and clearly visible as a separate category on the face of the balance sheet.

11.59 Where an entity operates more than one scheme, some schemes may be in surplus and some may be in deficit. Where this is the case, aggregate amounts of assets and aggregate amounts of liabilities (less attributable amounts of deferred tax in each case) should be shown separately on the face of the balance sheet. [FRS 17 paras 47, 49].

11.60 To illustrate the presentation, the consolidated balance sheet in Format 1 of Schedule 4 and 4A of the Companies Act 1985 would be adapted as follows. At the time of printing, the new Schedules to the Companies Act 2006 had not yet been released, although it is not anticipated that they will change significantly.

Consolidated balance sheet – Format 1

A	Called up share capital not paid
B	Fixed assets
C	Current assets
D	Prepayments and accrued income
E	Creditors: amounts falling due within one year
F	Net current assets (liabilities)
G	Total assets less current liabilities
H	Creditors: amounts falling due after more than one year
I	Provisions for liabilities
J	Accruals and deferred income
	Minority interests (alternative position after K)
	Defined benefit assets
	Defined benefit liabilities
K	Capital and reserves
	Minority interests (alternative position after J)

11.61 Any contributions owing to the scheme as at the employer's balance sheet date are reflected in the scheme assets (as a current asset receivable) and shown as a normal creditor in the employer's balance sheet.

11.61.1 Where a company has a pension asset, it will not be able to present its balance sheet by equating total assets less current liabilities, on the one hand, with the aggregate of creditors falling due after more than one year, provisions for liabilities, and capital and reserves, on the other, as this would include the pension asset within liabilities. Further guidance on sub-totalling in the balance sheet is included in chapter 4.

Measurement of scheme assets

11.62 Scheme assets should be measured at their fair value at the balance sheet date. Fair value is defined in other accounting standards as the amount at which an asset could be exchanged in an arm's length transaction between informed and willing parties, other than in a forced or liquidation sale. The FRS gives the following guidance for determining fair values of scheme assets:

- Quoted securities – use mid-market value prior to the December 2006 amendment to FRS 17, which is effective for accounting periods beginning on or after 6 April 2007, and current bid price once this amendment has been adopted. The transitional accounting for this amendment is discussed in para 11.148.7.
- Unquoted securities – make an estimate of fair value.
- Unitised securities – use the average of the bid and offer prices.

- Property – use open market value or another appropriate basis of valuation sanctioned by the Royal Institution of Chartered Surveyors' Appraisal and Valuation Manual.
- Insurance policies that exactly match benefits payable – use the same value as the related obligations.
- Other insurance policies – use a valuation method that gives the best approximation to fair value.

[FRS 17 paras 14–18].

11.63 Current assets of the scheme (such as contributions receivable at the valuation date) should be included in the valuation of the scheme assets. Creditors and accruals of the scheme should be deducted from the valuation of the scheme assets. [FRS 17 para 15]. That is because the valuation of the scheme liabilities includes only liabilities to pay pensions and other retirement benefits in the future. Other liabilities of the scheme will include current liabilities such as amounts owing to professional advisers and investment managers, and any borrowings of the scheme, and should be offset against scheme assets.

11.64 In the UK and the Republic of Ireland, the SORP, 'The financial reports of pension schemes', sets out recommended accounting practice for funded defined benefit pension schemes, including the form and content of their financial statements. The financial statements include a net assets statement that discloses the size and disposition of the scheme's net assets at the end of the scheme's financial year. The net assets statement comprises all the assets and liabilities of the scheme (other than liabilities to pay pensions and other retirement benefits in the future). As a general principle, the SORP requires a scheme's investments to be included in the net assets statement at their market value. It gives more detailed guidance on valuing various types of investments. The composition and valuation of a scheme's net assets for the purpose of the SORP is, therefore, broadly comparable to that required by FRS 17.

11.65 The SORP gives some guidance on property valuation from the perspective of pension fund trustees. It notes the following circumstances in which open market value may not be the appropriate basis of valuation (the same guidance was included in FRED 20, but has not been retained in the FRS):

- Properties in the occupation of the pension scheme, which should be valued on the basis of the existing use value.
- Properties held fully equipped as operational entities, which should be valued having regard to trading potential.
- Properties under construction or in the course of development or redevelopment, reconstruction or refurbishment which, depending upon the circumstances, including the stage of construction reached, should be valued either on the basis of open market value of the land and buildings in

their existing state or on the basis of open market value of the land plus the cost of development incurred.

11.66 SSAP 19, FRS 15 and the pension scheme SORP all have requirements for properties to be measured at their open market value. None of those statements requires all properties to be fully revalued each year by external valuers, but each sets out guidelines for ensuring valuations are kept up to date in the financial statements. That guidance is useful for establishing reliable valuation policies for the purpose of FRS 17. For example, the SORP recommends that where property comprises a significant proportion of total investments, valuations should be carried out by independent valuers at least at the same frequency as actuarial valuations of the fund (normally every three years). It recommends that in other cases, properties may be included on the basis either of an annual valuation by an internal or external valuer or, where the proportion of property assets within total investments justifies a less frequent valuation, on a rolling basis over three or five years by an internal or external valuer, with an independent valuation of the entire property portfolio at least every five years. The SORP notes that more frequent valuations may be necessary in the case of properties in the course of development, redevelopment or refurbishment where there is a risk of cost overrun.

11.67 FRS 17 differs from the SORP in the treatment of insurance policies that are purchased to match specifically the benefits of particular members – for example, pensions in payment. FRS 17 indicates that such polices should be included in the valuation of the scheme assets at the same value as the related liabilities, that is, the gross value of the related liabilities are included in both the scheme liabilities and scheme assets. [FRS 17 para 18]. For the pension scheme financial statements, the relevant legislation in the UK does not require insurance policies to be included at their market value (or an estimate) where the policies are specifically allocated to provide benefits for particular members and they provide all the benefits payable under the scheme to those members. The SORP recommends that in such cases, where the trustees have in effect discharged their full liability to the particular members or beneficiaries by purchasing matching policies, the policies should be included at nil value in the net assets statement (in the Republic of Ireland, regulations permit them to be excluded altogether).

Measurement of scheme liabilities

11.68 FRS 17 requires scheme liabilities to be measured on an actuarial basis using the projected unit method. [FRS 17 para 20]. The projected unit method considers promised benefits for pensioners and deferred pensioners and accrued benefits for members in service taking into account projected earnings.

11.69 The objective of the valuation is to make the best estimate of the future cash outflows that will arise in respect of the benefits earned by employees at the valuation date. This normally requires the expertise of an actuary. The ground rules regarding the assumptions underlying the valuation of accrued liabilities are:

- The assumptions should be mutually compatible and provide the 'best estimate' of the future cash outflows.
- The directors, who are responsible for the assumptions used in preparing the financial statements, should take advice from an actuary.
- The financial assumptions that are affected by economic conditions should reflect market expectations at the balance sheet date.
- The assumptions should reflect expected future events that will affect the cost of the benefits to which the employer is committed at the balance sheet date.

[FRS 17 paras 23–27].

11.70 Demographic and financial assumptions underlying an actuarial valuation of pension scheme liabilities should take account of all existing legal and constructive obligations. Demographic assumptions include statistical matters such as:

- Mortality rates (before and after retirement).
- Age, sex and marital status of membership.
- Rates of leaving employment before retirement (employee turnover).
- Early retirements.
- Members' surviving spouses and dependants covered by the scheme.

11.71 The main financial assumptions relate to inflation, that is, general price inflation, salary inflation, inflation in pensions in payment and deferred pensions. The valuation of scheme assets and scheme liabilities needs to be internally consistent. Therefore, each of the inflation assumptions should reflect the same level of general price inflation that is reflected in the discount rate at the balance sheet date.

11.71.1 The choice of assumptions is a difficult area of judgement, because relatively small changes in certain key assumptions, such as mortality rates and the rate of growth in pensionable earnings, can have a material impact on the amount of the defined benefit obligation. It is not unusual for the assumptions that are made for a funding strategy to differ from an actuary's 'best estimates' that are applied for the purposes of FRS 17. For example, there may be a deliberate policy of funding very conservatively, so that the members' benefits are given a high degree of security.

11.72 Similar actuarial methodologies are followed to value the accrued liabilities of other types of retirement benefits, such as post-retirement medical plans. They consider claims experience for the population concerned and factor in assumptions about inflation in medical costs and future changes in medical practices.

11.73 To take account of the time value of money, the estimated accrued liabilities should be discounted to their present value at the current rate of return on a high quality corporate bond of a currency and term that matches the scheme liabilities. This should be taken to be an AA-rated bond.

Frequency of valuations

11.74 Full actuarial valuations are not required as at the employer's balance sheet date. The FRS stipulates that full actuarial valuations should be obtained at intervals of no more than three years. If the latest full valuation predates the employer's balance sheet date, that valuation should be updated to reflect current conditions. [FRS 17 para 35].

11.75 The employer's and the pension scheme's financial statements often have different accounting periods. In practice, it is likely that two full three-yearly actuarial valuations will be required for funded pension schemes: one for FRS 17 accounting and one (on a funding basis) for the pension scheme trustees. That is because the funding valuation may use different, possibly more conservative, assumptions in relation to the liabilities. The FRS 17 valuation need not necessarily be done as at the employer's balance sheet date. It could be done at an earlier date, or the same date as the valuation required by the trustees, as suits the employer's reporting timetable. In fact, the guidance for actuaries published by the Institute and Faculty of Actuaries concerning FRS 17 (GN 36, 'Accounting for retirement benefits under Financial Reporting Standard 17') indicates that a triennial valuation as at an employer company's year end would not normally be available when the FRS 17 figures are required for the company's financial statements. For example, a company with a December year-end may have a pension scheme with a March year-end and obtain actuarial valuations as at 31 March. The full valuation would then have to be updated to each company year-end, including the one immediately following the date of the full valuation.

11.76 An update is in effect an estimate of a full valuation. The FRS indicates that some aspects of the valuation should be updated at each balance sheet date of the reporting employer. The scheme assets should in any case be revalued at market values at the balance sheet date. The financial assumptions underpinning the valuation of the scheme liabilities should also be updated to reflect changes in market conditions. Thus the discount rate should always be the current rate of return on the appropriate bond at the employer's balance sheet date. A change in the discount rate may also require other financial assumptions, such as the inflation assumption, to be updated. Other aspects of the valuation of the liabilities can be estimated from the previous full valuation by rolling the valuation forward and updating it for changes to the scheme, such as benefit improvements. Assumptions that are not directly affected by changes in market conditions (for example, mortality rates) need not be updated annually. The guidance for actuaries concerning liability updates under FRS 17 notes that reflecting changes in asset values and discount rates may dominate the calculation, but the actuary should also normally consider, as a minimum, the actual pension and salary increases awarded.

11.77 Individual circumstances will dictate whether a full valuation is required in between the normal triennial valuations or whether an update is sufficient. If the latest full valuation was a long time ago and many changes have occurred since, the actuary may not be confident that an update will produce a reliable current estimate of the scheme liabilities. The guidance for actuaries indicates that the actuary should advise the company how confident he or she is that the approximate figures fall within the materiality limits for the company's financial statements.

Reporting performance

11.78 Since the scheme assets and liabilities are re-measured at each year end, the performance statements reflect the changes in the surplus or deficit except, that is, for contributions paid into the scheme. The FRS analyses the changes in the scheme assets and scheme liabilities into various components and specifies where they should be reported in the profit and loss account or STRGL, as follows:

Profit and loss account		**STRGL**
Operating	**Financing**	
Current service cost (capital cost of benefits earned in current period).	Interest cost (interest on the accrued pension liabilities).	Differences between the actual and expected return on scheme assets.
Past service costs (capital cost of benefit improvements).	Less: expected return on the assets held by the pension scheme.	Experience changes affecting scheme liabilities.
Gains and losses on curtailments and settlements (for example, early retirements, bulk transfers from scheme) – except for FRS 3 para 20 items.		Effect of changes in actuarial assumptions.

11.79 Under FRS 17, with very limited exceptions, no credit (debit) is reflected in the operating costs for any surplus (deficit) in the scheme and so the operating cost is unrelated to whether, or how, the scheme is funded. The exceptions arise in situations where part of a surplus has not previously been recognised, because it was not considered to be recoverable (see para 11.115).

11.80 The following example illustrates the double-entry for reporting the changes in a surplus or deficit in the performance statements.

Example

The actuarial valuation of a company's pension scheme at 31.12.20X1 showed a surplus of £39m. The profit and loss charge for 20X2 is £66m (that is, the aggregate of current service cost, interest cost and expected return on assets, which is not analysed here into different components). After consulting with its actuaries, the company decided to reduce its employer contributions for 20X2 to £50m. At 31.12.20X2 the surplus in the scheme was measured at £15m.

The double-entry for the year 20X2 would be as follows:

Dr Profit and loss account (net pension cost)	66	
Cr Defined benefit asset		66
Dr Defined benefit asset	50	
Cr Cash (contributions paid)		50
Dr Pension reserve – STRGL (actuarial loss)	8	
Cr Defined benefit asset		8

The movements in the pension asset are as follows:

Asset b/f	39
Pension cost (profit and loss account)	(66)
Contributions paid	50
Actuarial loss (STRGL)	(8)
Asset c/f	15

The asset of £39m at 31.12.20X1 is increased by contributions of £50m during 20X2 and reduced by the pension cost of £66m. At 31.12.X2 an asset of £15m is recognised reflecting the current surplus of £15m. This means there has been an actuarial loss of £8m. The surplus was expected to be reduced to £23m, not to £15m, but £15m is the right figure. This loss of £8m should be reported in the STRGL. It is important to note that the actuarial loss of £8m is not a balancing figure – it needs to be analysed into various components, as explained later (see para 11.110).

Current service cost

11.81 Current service cost is defined as *"the increase in the present value of the scheme liabilities expected to arise from employee service in the current period"*. [FRS 17 para 2]. It represents the actuarially calculated present value of the pension benefits earned by the active employees in each period and is supposed to reflect the true economic cost relating to each year based on current market conditions. This cost is determined independently of the funding of the scheme. In principle, therefore, for a given set of employees and benefit formula, the current service cost (shown as an operating cost) should be the same irrespective of whether the scheme is in surplus, in deficit or unfunded. The current service cost is not necessarily a stable percentage of pensionable pay year-on-year. For example, current service cost will vary if the discount rate changes. It will increase year-on-year as a proportion of pay if the average age of the workforce is increasing, as is likely where the scheme is closed to new entrants.

11.82 The valuation of the scheme liabilities and, hence, the calculation of current service cost for each year should be based on the scheme's benefit formula.

An exception is where a disproportionate amount of total benefits relates to later years of service, in which case the benefit should be allocated on a straight-line basis over the period in which it is earned. [FRS 17 para 22]. Current service cost is reduced by employee contributions.

11.83 The following example illustrates the mechanics of the calculations. It should be noted that, for illustrative purposes, the example is extremely simplified to reflect the liability in respect of a single employee with a short service period.

Example

An employee will receive a retirement benefit of 5% of final salary for each year of service, payable as a lump sum on retirement. The scheme is non-contributory. Starting salary is £60,000 and is estimated to increase by 6% per year. The employee is expected to retire after 4 years service. The discount rate is 7%. Based on assumptions at the beginning of year 1, it is expected that a benefit of £14,292 will become payable at the end of year 4 (20% of expected final salary £71,461). That benefit is allocated on a straight-line basis to each year's service and discounted to its present value. Using a simple discounting model, the following table shows the estimated current service cost, scheme liability and interest cost attributable to each year.

Year	Estimated salary (6% growth)	Current service cost (not discounted)	Current service cost (discounted at 7%)	Liability B/f	Interest cost (7%)	Liability C/f
	£	£	£	£	£	£
1	60,000	3,573	2,917	0	0	2,917
2	63,600	3,573	3,121	2,917	204	6,242
3	67,416	3,573	3,339	6,242	437	10,018
4	71,461	3,573	3,573	10,018	701	14,292
		14,292	12,950		1,342	

11.84 The current service cost should be based on the most recent actuarial valuation at the beginning of the year. The financial assumptions underlying the calculation of the present value of the benefits earned (that is, the rate used to discount liabilities, rate of inflation, rate of salary increase, and rates of pension and deferred pension increases) should be current as at the beginning of the year. [FRS 17 para 51]. Although the current service cost for the year is based on the financial assumptions set at the beginning of the year, the financial assumptions should be updated at the end of the year for the purpose of re-measuring the scheme liabilities. The adoption of new assumptions at the end of the year does not affect the current service cost for the past year, but it sets the assumptions underlying the current service cost for the next year. Therefore, the financial assumptions on which the current service cost for 20X2 is based (that is, those at the beginning of 20X2) should already have been updated in the valuation of the scheme liabilities at the end of financial year 20X1 and will also have been disclosed in the financial statements for 20X1.

Interest cost and expected return on assets

Interest cost

11.85 Interest cost is defined as *"the expected increase during the period in the present value of the scheme liabilities because the benefits are one period closer to settlement"*. [FRS 17 para 2]. The interest cost represents the unwinding of the discount on the scheme liabilities. As for the current service cost, the interest cost is determined independently of the funding of the scheme. The discount rate applicable to any financial year, being the appropriate high quality corporate bond rate at the beginning of the year, is the same as the rate at which the scheme liabilities are measured at the end of the previous year.

11.86 The interest cost needs to reflect the liability at the beginning of the year and movements during the year. For example, the current service cost, past service costs relating to benefit improvements and transfers into the scheme will increase the liability during the year; benefits paid to pensioners and transfers out of the scheme will reduce the liability during the year. [FRS 17 para 53].

Expected return on assets

11.87 The expected return on assets component of the pension cost reflects the funding of a scheme. It is the actuarial forecast of total return (that is, income and gains) on the actual assets in the scheme. The profit and loss account is credited each period with the expected long-term rate of return on the scheme assets, based on their market values at the beginning of the year. Where applicable – for example, equities and properties – the rate of return will include expected capital growth as well as income from dividends and rents. The treatment in the employer company's profit and loss account is, therefore, unrelated to the realisation of income and capital gains in the pension scheme itself. The scheme assets are revalued to fair value at each balance sheet date. The difference between the fair value and the 'expected' value of the assets – that is, the value that has accrued by crediting the expected rate of return – is recognised as an actuarial gain or loss in the STRGL. Thus the amount credited each year in the profit and loss account should be a relatively stable long-term return, whereas short-term volatility in equity and other asset values is shown in the STRGL.

11.88 Users can be expected to pay considerable attention to the assumed rates of return; FRS 17 before the December 2006 amendment requires financial statements to disclose the rates set for the following year as well as the rates set at the beginning of the current year and the beginning of the comparative year. The amended FRS 17 does not require the disclosure of expected rates of return at all, although such disclosure would be considered best practice.

11.89 For each class of asset, the calculation needs to reflect the market value at the beginning of the year and movements during the year – for example, contributions received, pensions paid and transfers of assets in and out. Assumptions need to be made about where contributions are invested and from where benefit payments are sourced. The FRS does not require changes during the year in the portfolio mix or risk profile to be taken into account in the calculations, so the effect of such changes would in general be reflected as actuarial gains or losses reported in the STRGL rather than as adjustments to the expected long-term rate of return reported in the profit and loss account. However, if the pension scheme trustees significantly changed the risk profile of the portfolio mid-year (for example, making a significant switch from equities to bonds), it might be appropriate for the calculations to reflect this.

11.89.1 The definition of expected rate of return on assets in paragraph 2 of FRS 17 states that the rate of return is net of scheme expenses. Nevertheless, FRS 17 does not provide further guidance in this area. In our view, expenses will be included in the measurement of the defined benefit obligation where they reflect a present obligation (for example, to administer and pay pension benefits that have already been earned) and not where they reflect future obligations (for example, the production of annual financial statements). This raises the question as to which expenses should be included in the measurement of the obligation and which should be deducted from the return on scheme assets. In our view, expenses should be accounted for in accordance with their substance. Hence, investment management and similar expenses should be deducted from the return on scheme assets, while expenses in respect of commitments to administer the plan should be included in the measurement of the defined benefit obligation.

11.89.2 Sometimes administration expenses may be incurred by the sponsoring employer on behalf of a pension scheme, with or without a recharge to the scheme. The principles described in the previous paragraph will continue to apply, so:

- If the employer recharges pension administration costs, the scheme will be in the same position as where it makes payments to third parties. Hence, the measurement of the defined benefit obligation would take account of administration costs as described above.
- If the employer does not make a recharge, it should make a provision for future administration expenses and add this to the defined benefit obligation. In substance, the fact that the expenses are incurred by the employer rather than the scheme makes no difference to the accounting.

Profit and loss presentation

11.90 The net of the interest cost and the expected return on assets is shown as other finance costs (or income) adjacent to interest. [FRS 17 para 56]. The net figure in the profit and loss account is affected by how the scheme is funded. It will be a net credit if the expected return on the scheme assets exceeds the interest cost on the scheme liabilities. This is likely to occur if a scheme is in surplus on the accounting measurement basis and/or if a higher rate of return is applied to the scheme assets than the discount rate applied to the scheme liabilities. A higher rate of return on assets is inherent in the basis on which the respective rates are calculated – for example, any expected equity risk premium relating to an equity portfolio is reflected in the investment return, but is precluded from being recognised in the interest cost. As UK schemes hold a majority of scheme assets in equities, the profit and loss account will benefit from equities' expected long-term out-performance of bonds.

11.91 The note on legal requirements (paragraph 6 of Appendix II) makes it clear that FRS 17 has introduced a new format heading 'other finance costs (or income)' into the profit and loss account. The ASB received legal advice that this new heading was necessary and that it should be shown adjacent to, but separate from, the heading 'interest payable and similar charges'. FRS 17 before the December 2006 amendment requires that the two components of the item 'other finance costs (or income)', which are the 'interest cost' and the 'expected return on assets' should be disclosed separately in the notes. [FRS 17 para 84]. The amended FRS 17 requires that the total P&L expense recognised in respect of both interest cost and the expected return on scheme assets (among other P&L items) is disclosed, along with the line items on the face of the P&L account in which they are included. [FRS 17 para 77 (f)].

[The next paragraph is 11.93.]

Past service costs

11.93 Past service costs are defined as *"the increase in the present value of the scheme liabilities related to employee service in prior periods arising in the current period as a result of the introduction of, or improvement to, retirement benefits"*. [FRS 17 para 2].

11.94 Benefit improvements may produce both an increase in the cost of future service relating to active members (reflected in a higher annual current service cost) and an increased liability for past service relating to current and ex-employees. The cost (that is, the capitalised present value) of the element of all benefit improvements that relates to past service and that have not previously been allowed for in the valuation of the scheme liabilities should be charged to the profit and loss account on a straight-line basis over the vesting period. [FRS 17 para 60]. Often the improvements will vest immediately they are granted and so the whole cost is charged immediately to operating profits. This treatment applies irrespective of whether the additional past service liability relates to pensioners, deferred pensioners or current employees, or whether the benefit improvements are funded by a surplus or give rise to a deficiency.

11.95 Where benefit improvements have been awarded but some have not yet vested, the FRS requires only the vested portion to be recognised in the reporting employer's financial statements. The unrecognised past service cost (that is, the cost that will be recognised in future periods when the benefits vest) should be deducted from the scheme liabilities in arriving at the asset or liability to be recognised in the balance sheet. [FRS 17 para 60]. The FRS implies, therefore, that the full past service cost (vested and unvested) will be included in the actuarial valuation of the scheme liabilities and that the existence of unrecognised past service costs will give rise to a difference between the surplus or deficit in the scheme and the asset or liability that is recognised in the reporting employer's balance sheet. The FRS also requires such a difference to be explained in the notes (see para 11.143). [FRS 17 para 88 pre December 2006 amendment, FRS 17R para 77(e)(i) after December 2006 amendment]. The difference will gradually be eliminated as the benefit improvements vest and the cost and liability are recognised in the financial statements.

11.96 It is important to distinguish between past service costs and experience losses. Past service costs are charged to operating profit; experience losses are charged in the STRGL. A larger than expected increase in pensionable salaries, for example, will increase the scheme liabilities relating to past service. The FRS indicates that this is an actuarial loss rather than a past service cost, since it is a re-measurement of the existing commitment to pay retirement benefits based on final salary. Similarly, the cost of a higher than anticipated increase to pensions in payment will generally be regarded as an experience loss, being a re-measurement of the employer's existing commitment to provide cost of living increases. On the other hand, the introduction of a new or additional commitment to protect pensions from inflation, where none previously existed, would give rise to a past service cost, because such pension increases would not previously have been allowed for in the valuation of the scheme liabilities.

11.97 Conceptually, the distinction between operating losses and STRGL losses is quite blurred in this area. Changes in estimates of other types of provisions generally are reflected in the profit and loss account rather than the STRGL. The rationale for the treatment of actuarial losses as explained in the development section of the FRS is that STRGL items reflect gains and losses that are caused by general changes in economic conditions. [FRS 17 App IV para 38]. Normal variations in assumed rates of salary inflation would fall into this category. On the other hand, if an employer gave large salary increases to certain employees shortly before retirement, this might well be regarded as a benefit improvement in substance. If so, the pension cost would be regarded as a past service cost rather than an actuarial loss.

11.98 Where the scheme rules or an established pattern of past practice requires the employer to share a surplus with the members, the amount that will be passed to members (probably as a benefit improvement) should be treated as increasing the scheme liabilities. [FRS 17 para 21]. In these circumstances, any past service cost to which the employer is committed by virtue of a surplus would already have been anticipated in the recognition of a smaller surplus and a smaller actuarial gain – and no past service cost would arise.

11.98.1 On the other hand, where benefit improvements are awarded on an ad hoc basis as a result of a surplus arising in the scheme, the fact that they are funded out of a surplus does not result in there being no cost to the employer if the surplus was potentially recoverable by the employer – the use of the surplus for benefit improvements means that the employer cannot then benefit from it in other ways. [FRS 17 para 63].

11.99 FRS 17's definition of 'retirement benefits' specifically excludes benefits that become payable as a result of the early termination of an employee's employment. Therefore, where employees made redundant are granted enhanced pension benefits (say, for early retirement) in lieu of, or in addition to, redundancy payments, the cost of the enhanced pension benefits are in effect treated as redundancy payments rather than past service costs. Some such benefits might relate to the termination of an operation or fundamental reorganisation and be shown as FRS 3 paragraph 20 items outside operating profit.

Settlements and curtailments

11.100 Settlements and curtailments are events that materially change the liabilities relating to a scheme and that are not covered by the normal actuarial assumptions.

11.101 A settlement is defined as *"an irrevocable action that relieves the employer (or the defined benefit scheme) of the primary responsibility for a pension obligation and eliminates significant risks relating to the obligation and the assets used to effect the settlement"*. [FRS 17 para 2]. Settlements have the effect of extinguishing a portion of the scheme liabilities, usually by transferring scheme assets to or on behalf of scheme members – for example, when a subsidiary is sold or when assets and liabilities are transferred into a defined contribution scheme.

11.102 A curtailment is defined as *"an event that reduces the expected years of future service of present employees or reduces for a number of employees the accrual of defined benefits for some or all of their future service"*. [FRS 17 para 2]. Curtailments have the effect of reducing the obligations relating to future service, usually as a result of a significant reduction in the number of employees – for example, on the termination of an operation – or as a result of a reduction in future benefits – for example, following an amendment to the scheme rules such that employees only qualify for reduced benefits in future.

11.103 Calculating the gain or loss arising from a settlement or curtailment event requires a 'before' and 'after' measurement. The gain or loss is in principle the resulting change in the surplus or deficit (that is, the scheme assets less the scheme liabilities) attributable to the reporting employer.

11.104 The FRS specifies the date when the employer should measure and recognise the gain or loss arising:

- Losses – when the employer becomes demonstrably committed to the transaction.

- Gains – when all parties whose consent is required are irrevocably committed to the transaction.

[FRS 17 para 64].

11.104.1 Whether the entity is demonstrably committed is a matter of judgment but it should be noted that this is not as high a hurdle as being irrevocably committed. A management or Board decision alone is not sufficient to meet the definition of demonstrably committed. Communication or action outside of the entity is required. By analogy with FRS 12 paragraphs 80-81, which consider when a constructive obligation for restructuring exists, it is our view that to meet the demonstrably committed criterion, the entity would also have to:

(a) have communicated the decision to the employees affected by it (such that they would expect the settlement or curtailment transaction to go ahead);

(b) have commenced negotiations with any other third party involved, for example, with an insurer buying out a scheme liability as to the specific amounts to be settled bought out, or with an acquirer as to the terms of any transfer of benefits from the entity's scheme to the acquirer's scheme.

11.104.2 It is our view that an entity is only irrevocably committed to a transaction when the amended scheme terms become contractually binding. This is illustrated in the example below:

Example – Timing of curtailment

Company A announced its intention to curtail a pension scheme. Future employee service will give rise only to a pension of 0.8% for each year worked compared to the current plan under which employees earn a pension of 1% for each year worked.

Company A published amended terms of the pension scheme on its web site on 20 December 20X3. The entity's human resource department prepared amended employment contracts in early January 20X4 and sent them to employees for signature. All amended employment contracts were signed by the end of January 20X4. The amendment is not contractually binding under local legislation until signed by the employee.

The curtailment should not be recognised before the amended terms become contractually binding. The terms of a defined benefit scheme were amended in January 20X4 when the new terms became contractually binding through signature of the employees. Company A should account for the effects of the curtailment in January 20X4. The date from which arrangements are contractually binding will vary depending on local legislation.

11.104.3 It is possible that an entity might be demonstrably but not irrevocably committed to a course of action at a year-end. In this case, the settlement loss should be measured and recognised in the profit and loss at the date the entity becomes demonstrably committed. The settlement itself, that is, the derecognition of the pension liability, should not be accounted for in the Balance Sheet as the entity still has the obligation to settle.

Example – Demonstrably but not irrevocably committed at the year-end

Company B announced its intention to settle a pension scheme in deficit to the tune of 330 by giving a lump sum cash payment to scheme participants in exchange for their rights to receive benefits. In order to encourage the employees to take the cash payment, the lump sum represents an enhancement of 90 to the value of their accrued benefits. Any employee not accepting the offer remains as a deferred member in the scheme.

Company B published the terms of the proposed settlement on its web site on 20 November 20X4. The entity's human resource department prepared amended employment contracts and sent them to employees for signature in late December 20X4. All amended employment contracts were signed by the end of March 20X4. The amendment is not contractually binding under local legislation until signed by the employee.

At company B's December 20X4 year-end, the company is demonstrably committed to the settlement because it has communicated its terms to the employees affected and announced the decision publicly. It is not, however, irrevocably committed as the employees affected had not yet agreed the revised terms. Company B should record a settlement loss at the year-end as follows:

Dr	Profit and loss account — settlement loss	90	
	Cr Balance sheet – pension deficit		90

The pension deficit has, therefore, increased because company B is demonstrably committed to the settlement, but the deficit is not removed from the balance sheet until the cash is paid.

Once the employee contracts have been signed, and assuming that all employees accept the offer, the settlement is recognised and the pension deficit is eliminated as follows:

Dr	Balance sheet – pension deficit	330	
Dr	Balance sheet – provision for scheme settlement	90	
	Cr Cash		410

11.105 The measurement of any settlement or curtailment gain or loss may not be straightforward. It is unfortunate, from a practical viewpoint, that the measurement dates are potentially different for gains and losses since, until the scheme is valued, it may not be certain whether a gain or a loss has arisen. Furthermore, the FRS does not specify whether the surplus or deficit at the measurement date should be measured using the actuarial assumptions at the beginning of the year (for example, the discount rate for liabilities) or at the later measurement date. Nor does not it indicate whether the value of the scheme assets should be updated to their fair values at the measurement date or based on their fair values at the beginning of the year. This issue is relevant because for both assets and liabilities, unrecorded actuarial gains or losses may have occurred between the beginning of the year and the measurement date. How the calculation is performed will affect the allocation of total gains and losses during the year between those relating to the settlement or curtailment event (reported in the profit and loss account) and other actuarial gains and losses (reported in the STRGL).

11.106 IAS 19 is more specific and requires the employer to re-measure the scheme liability and scheme assets using current actuarial assumptions. This means that a new discount rate should be used to measure the change in liabilities if the discount rate has changed since the beginning of the year and current market prices should be used to measure the change in assets. This approach makes sense, because the gain or loss attributed to the settlement or curtailment event is then based on fair values at the date of such event.

11.107 Where a subsidiary or other operation is sold, it should be remembered that any pre-existing surplus or deficit relating to that subsidiary will already have been recognised in the consolidated financial statements of the parent (although not in the subsidiary if it is using defined contribution accounting in respect of a group scheme). If the surplus or deficit is transferred to the purchaser, a corresponding settlement loss or gain will be reflected in the calculation of the profit or loss on disposal of the subsidiary, since it forms part of the attributable net assets disposed of.

Example

A wholly-owned subsidiary is sold for £100m. The book value of the subsidiary's net assets on the date of the sale was £70m. The subsidiary participated in the group defined benefit pension scheme, but adopted defined contribution accounting in its own financial statements in accordance with FRS 17 paragraph 9. At the date of the sale, the scheme was in surplus by £35m. The surplus was recognised as an asset in the consolidated financial statements. As part of the sale agreement, a bulk transfer of scheme assets was made to the purchaser's pension scheme. The 'before' and 'after' measurements in the group scheme are as follows:

	Before disposal £m	After disposal £m	Settlement loss £m
Scheme assets	175	145	(30)
Scheme liabilities	(140)	(115)	25
Scheme surplus	35	30	(5)

The profit on sale is as follows:

	£m	£m
Sale proceeds		100
Less:		
– subsidiary's net assets at date of sale	(70)	
– settlement loss	(5)	(75)
Profit on sale		25

11.108 Gains and losses on settlements and curtailments should be included in operating results, unless they attach to an FRS 3 paragraph 20 exceptional item shown after operating results, that is, the sale or termination of an operation or a fundamental reorganisation or restructuring. If the settlement or curtailment is attributable to one of those items, the gain or loss is reported as part of the profit or loss relating to that item, as in the previous example. Under FRS 17 before the December 2006 amendment, gains and losses on settlements and curtailments that are included in FRS 3 paragraph 20 items should be disclosed separately in the notes. [FRS 17 para 83]. There is no such requirement in the amended FRS 17.

Actuarial gains and losses

11.109 FRS 17 defines actuarial gains and losses as:

"Changes in actuarial deficits or surpluses that arise because:

(a) events have not coincided with the actuarial assumptions made for the last valuation (experience gains and losses) or

(b) the actuarial assumptions have changed."

[FRS 17 para 2].

11.110 Actuarial gains and losses arise when the values of scheme assets and scheme liabilities are re-measured at the balance sheet date. They result from unexpected increases or decreases in the fair value of the scheme assets or the present value of the scheme liabilities, including the effects of changes in actuarial assumptions. Actuarial gains and losses are recognised immediately in the STRGL, and are not recognised again in the profit and loss in subsequent periods. [FRS 17 paras 57 and 59]. The STRGL, therefore, picks up most of the short-term volatility in asset and liability values. Under FRS 17 before the December 2006 amendment, the following components of actuarial gains and losses have to be disclosed separately in the notes:

- The difference between the expected and actual return on scheme assets.
- Experience gains and losses on the scheme liabilities.
- The effect of changes in demographic and financial assumptions underlying the valuation of the scheme liabilities.

[FRS 17 para 85].

11.110.1 The above specific requirements no longer exist under the amended FRS 17, although the following do need to be disclosed:

- The expected rates of return on scheme assets. [FRS 17R para 77 (m) (ii)].
- The actual return on scheme assets. [FRS 17R para 77 (l)].
- Actuarial gains and losses affecting the movement in scheme liabilities and scheme assets. [FRS 17R para 77 (b) (iv) and (d) (ii)].

- The total and cumulative amounts of actuarial gains and losses recognised in the STRGL. [FRS 17R para 77 (g) (i) and (h)].

11.111 The expected return on scheme assets is credited in the profit and loss account, based on the yield expected at the beginning of the year (see para 11.87). The difference between the expected and actual return, which is worked out when the assets are re-measured at market values at the end of the year, is treated as an actuarial gain or loss and is recognised in the STRGL.

11.112 Experience gains and losses relating to the scheme liabilities arise where actual events during the year differ from the actuarial assumptions in the previous valuation. They result from factors such as unexpectedly high or low rates of employee turnover, early retirements or mortality during the year and increases in pensionable salaries, pensions or medical costs that differ from previous assumptions. As described earlier, a full actuarial valuation is required at least every three years and the valuation should be updated at balance sheet dates between the full valuations (see para 11.74). Owing to the limitations of the interim updates, it is likely that experience gains and losses will be identified more fully in the years in which full actuarial valuations are performed.

11.113 The effects of changes in actuarial assumptions underlying the annual valuations of the scheme liabilities are also recognised in the STRGL. As noted earlier, the actuary's update at balance sheet dates between full valuations focuses mainly on financial assumptions reflecting current market conditions (see para 11.76). Thus the discount rate should always be updated to the current rate of return on the appropriate bond. Last year's discount rate will have been used to measure the scheme liabilities last year and the interest cost this year. Therefore, the effect of changes in the discount rate will feed into the STRGL each year. Demographic assumptions (such as leaving and mortality rates) are not necessarily updated between full valuations and so changes in those assumptions will tend to be identified only in the years in which full actuarial valuations are performed.

11.114 In addition to the items described above, the required accounting where the recoverability restriction on the recognition of defined benefit assets comes into effect will sometimes result in gains and losses that should be treated as actuarial gains and losses (see para 11.122). [FRS 17 paras 58(c), 67(d), 70].

Limit on pension asset

11.115 In some situations, a surplus in a scheme may be so large that the scheme is in effect 'self-financing', because the return on assets exceeds the total of the current service cost and the interest cost on the scheme liabilities. If the surplus was recognised in an unrestricted way, a potentially ever-increasing asset could result (and corresponding credits in the profit and loss account), some of which could never be realised. The FRS therefore caps the recognisable asset to the amount of the surplus that is recoverable. [FRS 17 para 37].

11.115.1 The amount of surplus recognised as an asset is limited to the amount that the employer can use to generate future economic benefits. The asset should not exceed the present value of the amounts that the employer can recover through reduced contributions, together with refunds that have been agreed by the trustees at the balance sheet date. [FRS 17 paras 38, 42].

11.115.2 The ASB believe that it is likely that an employer will be able to control the use of a surplus, as it is unlikely that the employer can be forced to make contributions when a surplus exists, and also because the employer is usually free to use the surplus to award benefit improvements to scheme members. [FRS 17 para 38].

11.115.3 FRS 17 has a harsher test for recognising surpluses compared to IAS 19. Under IAS 19 paragraph 58, and IFRIC 14 paragraph 11, a surplus may be recognised if economic benefits areavailable in the form of future contribution reductions or refunds to which the entity has an unconditional right. Under FRS 17, as well as being recoverable, refunds also have to have been *agreed* by the pension scheme trustees by the balance sheet date.

11.116 The calculation at each year end of the surplus that is recoverable through reduced contributions should assume a static (or, if applicable, declining) number of active scheme members. No increase in the number of active scheme members may be anticipated. [FRS 17 para 41]. It will be necessary to assume a declining active membership and, hence, a lower recoverable surplus, where a scheme is closed to new entrants. If the number of active members subsequently increases above what was assumed in the previous calculations, the value of the potential future contribution holiday and, hence, the recoverable surplus may increase. The FRS requires the increase to be credited to operating profit when it occurs (see para 11.124). [FRS 17 para 68].

11.117 The FRS makes it clear that the calculations of the recoverable accounting surplus should be based on the accounting assumptions rather than the funding assumptions, which may be more conservative. Even though reductions in contributions are typically agreed with trustees based on funding assumptions, over the life of any scheme, the accounting and funding contributions come together. [FRS 17 App IV para 27]. In addition, the same discount rate should be used to measure the present value of the reduction in future contributions as is used to measure the defined benefit liability. [FRS 17 para 41].

Benefit improvements

11.118 The required accounting for a surplus has an important effect on the treatment of the cost of benefit improvements in the profit and loss and STRGL. Where a surplus arises that is wholly recoverable, the cost of benefit improvements relating to past service (that is, past service cost) is charged as an operating cost over the period in which the increases in benefits vest. [FRS 17 para 60]. An actuarial gain that gives rise to the surplus is credited in the STRGL when it arises. The past service cost cannot be offset against the actuarial gain where the surplus is recoverable by the employer. Where a surplus arises, it may be used partly to fund the cost of benefit improvements, thereby reducing the amount that the employer can recover through reduced contributions. Such a use of a surplus should be treated as a past service cost when it occurs and not anticipated by reducing the amount recognised as an asset. This ensures that the employer recognises a cost to reflect the fact that it can no longer benefit from the surplus in other ways such as through reduced contributions. [FRS 17 paras 45 and 63].

11.119 An exception is where the scheme rules or an established pattern of past practice requires the employer to share a surplus with the members. In that situation, the amount that will be passed to members should be treated as increasing the scheme liabilities. [FRS 17 para 21]. When that occurs, any past service cost to which the employer is committed by virtue of a surplus to be shared with employees would be anticipated in the recognition of a smaller surplus and smaller actuarial gain – and no past service cost would arise.

11.120 A different treatment arises where the amount of surplus that is recognised as an asset has been restricted; the amounts recognised in the performance statements are adjusted. The operating cost of benefit improvements should be offset by the surplus to the extent that the cost is covered by an *unrecognised* surplus, as illustrated in the second example in para 11.123 below.

Required accounting

11.121 Where the recoverability restriction comes into effect, the opening and closing balance sheet figures are determined by calculating the maximum recoverable amount of surplus, using assumptions as described above. The rules for measuring the impact of restricting the asset on the components in the performance statements are complex. The existence of an unrecognised surplus may result in there being no net cost to the employer during the year, but the separate debit and credit components in the profit and loss account have to be measured and disclosed on a systematic basis.

11.122 The FRS specifies the following sequence for recognising amounts in the performance statements:

- Any refund from a previously unrecognised surplus should be credited to the profit and loss account under the heading 'other finance income' when the refund is agreed with the trustees. (Conversely, refunds from schemes where the whole surplus is regarded as recoverable do not give rise to gains. The cash received simply reduces the balance sheet asset.)

- Any past service costs or losses on settlements or curtailments arising during the year should be offset by recognition of any previously unrecognised surplus.

- The expected return on assets is restricted so that the recognised surplus does not exceed the amount that is deemed to be recoverable. Therefore, it is limited to the total of:
  - Current service cost.
  - Interest cost.
  - Any past service cost and losses on settlements and curtailments that have not been covered by the unrecognised surplus.
  - Any increase in the recoverable surplus.
- Any further adjustment necessary should be treated as an actuarial gain or loss.

[FRS 17 paras 58(c), 67].

11.123 Many different scenarios are possible, as illustrated in the following examples.

Example 1

The following table illustrates the simple case where a recognised surplus is the same at the beginning and end of the year, no past service benefits are awarded, no curtailments or settlements occur, no actuarial gains or losses arise in the scheme and no employer contributions are paid during the year.

	Surplus in scheme	**Recoverable surplus and P&L account**
Surplus at beginning of year	350	180
Current service cost	(20)	(20)
Interest cost	(25)	(25)
Expected return on assets	60	45
Net finance income	35	20
Net pension credit	15	Nil
Surplus at end of year	365	180

The 'surplus in scheme' column shows the actual surplus in the scheme and the components of performance before any restriction on the asset. The surplus in the scheme has increased by 15 from 350 to 365, but the recognised surplus is restricted to 180 at the beginning and end of the year.

This example illustrates that the system set out in paragraph 11.122 works as follows.

- Current service cost (operating charge) is unaffected by the existence of the surplus. It cannot be offset under any circumstances.
- Interest cost is calculated as normal on the gross amount of the scheme liability.

- Expected return on scheme assets absorbs the effect of the irrecoverable surplus. In the example, the expected return on the gross assets in the scheme is 60. The credit recognised in the profit and loss account is restricted so that it does not exceed the current service cost and interest cost in aggregate, that is 45.
- The overall profit and loss charge is nil. No further adjustment is necessary in the STRGL. The actual surplus in the scheme has increased by 15, but that increases the irrecoverable (unrecognised) surplus.

Example 2

The following table adds some more features and becomes more complex. At the beginning of the year benefit improvements were granted out of the surplus, which vested immediately, giving a past service cost of 200. At the end of the year the recoverable surplus was estimated to have increased to 190 as a result of a reduced discount rate; the actual surplus in the scheme was valued at 210. The amounts recognised in the performance statements are shown below. The first column shows the amounts as if the surplus in the scheme was recognised in full. The second column shows the restricted amounts recognised in the employer's financial statements.

	Surplus in scheme	Recoverable surplus and components of performance
Surplus at beginning of year	350	180
Current service cost	(20)	(20)
Past service cost (gross)	(200)	(200)
Less: unrecognised surplus	–	170
Past service cost (net)	(200)	(30)
Operating cost	(220)	(50)
Interest cost	(25)	(25)
Expected return on assets	60	60
Net finance income	35	35
Net pension cost (P&L)	(185)	(15)
Actuarial gain (STRGL)	45	25
Surplus at end of year	210	190

First, in calculating the past service cost to the employer, credit is taken for the previously unrecognised surplus in the scheme. Therefore, the gross past service cost of 200 is reduced by 170 (that is, total scheme surplus 350 less surplus already recognised on the balance sheet 180). The separate components of the net past service cost of 30 do not have to be shown on the face of the profit and loss account. Paragraph 82 (c) of FRS 17 before the December 2006 amendment requires any previously unrecognised surplus deduced from the past service costs to be disclosed in the notes. Paragraph 77 (e) (i) of the amended FRS 17 requires disclosure of any past service cost not recognised in the balance sheet. As noted earlier, the current service cost cannot be reduced in this way.

Secondly, the expected return on the scheme assets is 60. The amount credited in the profit and loss account cannot exceed the total of the current service cost (20), interest cost (25) and the net past service cost (30). As the total of these amounts exceeds the expected return on the actual scheme assets, no restriction is required.

Thirdly, any further adjustment necessary to increase the recoverable surplus should be credited in the STRGL as an actuarial gain. In this example, there is an actuarial gain of 45 in the valuation of the surplus in the scheme. In the company's financial statements an actuarial gain of 25 is recognised in the STRGL, bringing the recognised asset to 190.

11.124 As noted earlier, no increase in the number of active scheme members can be anticipated in the calculation of the recoverable surplus at each year end. Therefore, where a scheme has a surplus that is partly unrecognised by the employer, the recoverable amount of the surplus is likely to increase year on year if there is an increase in the number of active members. The FRS requires the portion of any increase in recoverable surplus that is attributable to an increase in the number of active members to be shown as an operating gain. [FRS 17 para 68].

11.125 An acquisition could give rise to an increase in the active membership of the acquirer's scheme. This might occur where employees of the acquired business are transferred to the acquirer's scheme and assets are transferred reflecting transfer values of their accrued pension benefits. In these circumstances, whilst there may be no increase in the surplus in the acquirer's scheme resulting from the transfer, the portion that is deemed to be recoverable may increase. A similar effect may occur where a scheme in an acquired group is merged with the acquirer's scheme. Consistent with FRS 7, the effect of such changes should be reflected in the acquirer's post-acquisition operating results rather than as adjustments in the fair value exercise. [FRS 17 para 69].

11.126 The amount of surplus previously regarded as recoverable may decrease year on year if there is a decrease in the number of active members compared with the number assumed in the previous calculation of recoverable surplus. If the decrease is related to a settlement or curtailment event (such as a disposal or closure of an operation), the loss should be reported in the profit and loss account as a loss arising on settlement or curtailment (as operating or post-operating, as applicable). In most other cases the decrease should be treated as an actuarial loss (reported in the STRGL), because it would be regarded as the effect of a change in the actuarial assumptions underlying the valuation of the surplus regarded as recoverable. [FRS 17 para 70].

Taxation

11.127 In the UK, tax relief on employers' pension contributions is usually given in the period in which they are paid rather than when the costs are recognised in the financial statements. In an unfunded scheme, and in the case of provisions for unfunded benefits such as post-retirement healthcare, the tax relief is given when the pensions or other benefits are paid. Where the total of the pension costs recognised under FRS 17 differs from the actual contributions (or unfunded benefits) paid, the resulting asset or liability recognised in the balance sheet is a timing difference for deferred tax purposes.

11.128 With some exceptions (none of which are applicable to pensions), FRS 19 requires deferred tax to be provided in full on all timing differences that have originated but not reversed by the balance sheet date. Deferred tax assets (which relate to defined benefit liabilities recognised under FRS 17) should be recognised to the extent that they are regarded as recoverable (see further chapter 13).

11.129 Under FRS 17, various components of pension cost are reported in the profit and loss account; actuarial gains and losses are reported in the STRGL. So in any period, pension cost accounting may give rise to current tax (tax relief on contributions) and deferred tax (on the timing differences between contributions and costs). FRS 16 requires current tax to be recognised in the profit and loss account, except where it is attributable to a gain or loss that has been recognised directly in the STRGL, in which case the attributable tax should also be recognised directly in the STRGL. Similarly, FRS 19 requires deferred tax to be recognised in the profit and loss account, except where it is attributable to a gain or loss that has been recognised directly in the STRGL. Normally, there is no direct relationship between the components of pension cost reported in the performance statements and the contributions and benefits paid in a period and so FRS 17 specifies a hierarchy for allocating current tax between the profit and loss account and the STRGL. This is dealt with in detail in chapter 13.

[The next paragraph is 11.135.]

Acquisitions

11.135 Arrangements for transferring defined benefit pensions obligations when an acquisition takes place are many, varied and often complex. They may include the acquisition of all schemes in an acquired group or, in the case of a business acquisition, the transfer of assets from the vendor's scheme to the purchaser's scheme reflecting transfer values of the accumulated pension rights of individual employees transferred. The value of the assets of an acquired scheme may differ from the value of the scheme's liabilities at the date of acquisition. In acquisition accounting, the surplus or deficit should generally be recognised as an asset or liability in the fair value exercise.

11.136 FRS 7 requires that a surplus or deficit as at the date of acquisition is measured consistently with how the acquirer would measure it under FRS 17. [FRS 7 para 71]. The accounting where an acquisition takes place is consistent with the normal (pre-acquisition) accounting for such pension schemes under FRS 17, as surpluses and deficits will be recognised on the balance sheet.

11.137 FRS 7 does not permit the valuation of a surplus or deficit at the date of acquisition to take into account the cost of any retrospective changes in benefits and membership that are decided on by the acquirer. Such costs should be reflected in the acquiring group's post-acquisition performance statements. [FRS 7 para 73]. Examples are:

- Costs of benefit improvements following the acquisition (treated as past service costs – charged in the profit and loss account over the period in which the benefits vest, which may be immediately).
- Pension effect of a significant reduction in the number of employees following a post-acquisition reorganisation (treated as a gain or loss on curtailment – recognised immediately in the profit and loss account).
- Cost of enhanced pensions initiated by the acquirer to induce early retirement (charged immediately in the profit and loss account).

Disclosures

11.138 In December 2006, the ASB published an amendment to FRS 17 that aligns the disclosure requirements of FRS 17 with those contained in IAS 19, 'Employee benefits', its international equivalent. The amendment is effective for periods beginning on or after 6 April 2007, and early adoption is encouraged.

Disclosures — before December 2006 amendment

11.139 The disclosures that apply *before* the amendment is adopted (for example for December 2007 year-end companies that choose *not* to early-adopt the amendment) are set out below:

- Background data relating to the scheme:
  - Nature of the scheme (that is, defined benefit).
  - Date of the most recent full actuarial valuation on which the amounts recognised in the financial statements are based. If the actuary is an employee or officer of the reporting employer, or of the group of which it is a member, this fact should be disclosed.
  - Contributions paid and any agreed contribution rates for future years.
  - Note of the fact that under the projected unit method, where schemes are closed to new entrants or have a significantly ageing active membership, the current service cost will increase as members approach retirement.

  [FRS 17 para 76].
- Main financial assumptions (individually) used at the beginning of the period and at the balance sheet date including inflation, rate of increase in salaries, increase for pensions in payment and deferred pensions and liability discount rate. [FRS 17 para 78].
- Fair value of assets at the beginning and end of the period analysed between equities, bonds and other; expected rate of return for each class for the period and the subsequent period. [FRS 17 para 80].
- Components of the profit and loss charge:

  - Operating profit (including separate disclosure of current service cost, past service costs, gains and losses on settlements and curtailments). Any previously unrecognised surplus deducted from past service costs and (separately) from settlement and curtailment losses should also be disclosed. [FRS 17 para 82].
  - Gains and losses on settlements and curtailments that are post-operating exceptional items under FRS 3 para 20. [FRS 17 para 83].
  - Other finance costs or income (interest cost and expected return on scheme assets). [FRS 17 para 84].

- Components of actuarial gains and losses recognised in STRGL:
  - Difference between expected and actual return on scheme assets.
  - Experience gains and losses on scheme liabilities.
  - Effect of changes in actuarial assumptions (demographic and financial) on scheme liabilities.

  [FRS 17 para 85].

- Five-year history of amounts recognised in the STRGL, showing:
  - The difference between the expected and actual return on assets (amount and percentage of scheme assets at balance sheet date).
  - Experience gains/losses on the scheme liabilities (amount and percentage of present value of scheme liabilities at balance sheet date).
  - Total actuarial gain or loss (amount and percentage of present value of scheme liabilities at balance sheet date).

  [FRS 17 para 86].

- The fair value of the scheme assets, the present value of the scheme liabilities and the resulting surplus or deficit in the scheme. [FRS 17 para 88].
- Analysis of the movements during the year in the surplus or deficit and, if applicable, a reconciliation of the surplus or deficit in the scheme to the asset or liability in the balance sheet (see para 11.143). [FRS 17 para 88].
- Analysis of reserves to distinguish the amount relating to the defined benefit asset or liability (net of deferred tax) (see para 11.149). [FRS 17 para 90].

11.140 Users can be expected to pay considerable attention to assumed rates of return on scheme assets, since they determine the amount of investment income that is credited in the profit and loss account. The differences between actual and assumed expected rates of return pass through the STRGL. Users will be able to spot if one company appears to be out of line with others as regards the expected rates of return that have been assumed. The expected rates of return assumed for the subsequent period do not affect any of the figures in the current period's financial statements (as these figures are based on last year's closing expected rates of return), but they are important assumptions relating to next year's profit and loss account. The requirement to disclose them up front prevents those important assumptions from being manipulated with hindsight in the following year.

11.141 The purpose of the five-year record of amounts recognised in the STRGL is to monitor and expose the reasonableness of the annual assumptions underlying the pension cost figures that pass through the profit and loss account. Differences between the expected costs that pass through the profit and loss account and actual history pass through the STRGL as actuarial gains and losses. A continuing trend of debits or credits in the STRGL could open the actuarial assumptions to challenge. [FRS 17 para 87].

11.142 For amounts recognised in the STRGL in respect of the scheme liabilities, experience gains and losses and the effect of changes in actuarial assumptions should be disclosed separately in the notes. However, the disclosure requirement relating to the five-year record refers only to experience gains and losses and does not include gains and losses relating to changes in assumptions.

11.143 There should be few sources of differences between the asset or liability recognised in the employer's balance sheet and the surplus or deficit in the scheme as measured under the FRS, because in most respects the surplus or deficit in the scheme should be recognised in full. Differences will occur as a result of:

- Attributable deferred tax balance netted off surplus or deficit in the balance sheet.
- Past service costs not yet recognised in the financial statements, because they have not yet vested.
- Part of a surplus is not recognised in the balance sheet, because it is not recoverable.
- Members being required to share the funding of a deficit, in which case the liability recognised by the employer is reduced by the present value of the additional contributions payable by the members.

Example

Fair value of scheme assets	350
Present value of scheme liabilities	(150)
Surplus in the scheme	200
Past service costs not yet vested	20
Irrecoverable surplus	(40)
Recognised pension asset	180
Related deferred tax liability	(54)
Net pension asset	126

11.143.1 The FRRP carried out a review of defined benefit pension disclosures made in the financial statements of a sample of 10 large private companies to evaluate the completeness and clarity of disclosures about pension obligations under FRS 17.The financial statements reviewed were mostly 31 December 2004 year ends and all of the companies had taken advantage of the transitional provisions of FRS 17 to continue to account under SSAP 24, supplemented by the transitional disclosures required by FRS 17. The most common omission under FRS 17 was a failure to provide prior years' information where required. The transitional provisions allowed companies to build up comparative numbers over several years and by 2004 companies should have been reporting three years' data for some items. All companies should be reporting a full 5 year history as required by the standard by their June 2006 or later year-ends. The [illegible] also noted a number of other minor omissions, which are described below:

- The omission of any information on future contribution rates, even where there was a statement that future rates had been agreed between the company and pension fund trustees (see para 11.139).

- No statement in respect of closed schemes and those in which the age profile of the active membership is rising significantly where the scheme is stated to be closed. In these circumstances, the company should disclose that the current service cost will increase as the members of the scheme approach retirement (see para 11.139).

- No sub-analysis of the 'other' category of plan assets where the amount was material (see para 11.139). In other cases, however, supplementary analysis was provided, usually of property or cash held.

- No analysis of reserves to distinguish the amount relating to the defined benefit asset or liability net of related deferred tax. In another case, an analysis of shareholders' funds was given, rather than reserves (see para 11.139).

- Where a company has more than one defined benefit scheme, disclosures may be made in total, separately, or in such groupings as are considered to be most useful. Whilst the standard does allow disclosures to be made in total, the grouping of assumptions into ranges to cover different geographic areas as found in one case (for example, discount rate 2.8% — 6.3%) would not appear to be particularly useful (see para 11.146).

Comparatives

11.144 The FRS has specific requirements relating to comparatives that result in the following disclosures being required for the position at three year-ends, that is the current year-end, the previous year-end and the beginning of the comparative period:

- The main financial assumptions used by the actuary (inflation, rate of increase in salaries, increase for pensions in payment and deferred pensions, liability discount rate).

- The expected rate of return on each class of scheme assets.

- The fair value of each class of scheme assets.

[FRS 17 para 91].

11.145 For the above ms, the information relating to the position at the beginning of the com rative period is relevant to understanding the pension costs for that peri since they were based on the assumptions set at the beginning of the od.

Aggregation hemes

11.146 re an employer operates more than one scheme, the FRS permits the disclo to be made in total for all schemes, separately for each scheme, or sch may be grouped in the way that provides the most useful information. para 92]. For multi-national groups that operate many pension schemes her types of retirement benefit schemes in various parts of the world, some ee of aggregation is necessary to avoid disclosures of excessive length and tail. Where schemes are grouped, the groupings might be based on geographical operations (for example, distinguishing UK schemes from overseas schemes), types of benefits with different risk profiles (for example, pension schemes and retirement medical healthcare schemes), or a combination of features as is considered to be most useful.

11.147 As noted earlier, the main financial assumptions underlying the valuation of schemes' liabilities and the expected rate of return on each class of scheme assets have to be disclosed. Where schemes are aggregated, the FRS requires the assumptions to be stated as weighted averages for the schemes concerned or as relatively narrow ranges – any assumptions outside those narrow ranges should be disclosed separately.

11.148 The FRS does not permit surpluses and deficits to be netted off in arriving at the assets and liabilities that are disclosed on the face of the balance sheet. Where an entity operates more than one scheme, some schemes may be in surplus and some may be in deficit. Where this is the case, aggregate amounts of assets and aggregate amounts of liabilities (which include any unfunded benefits), less attributable amounts of deferred tax in each case, should be shown separately on the face of the balance sheet. [FRS 17 para 47]. A consequence of this requirement is that at least some of the footnote disclosures have to be disaggregated into schemes that have given rise to assets in the balance sheet and schemes that have given rise to liabilities. This is necessary, for example, in order to comply with the requirement to reconcile scheme surpluses or deficits to balance sheet assets and liabilities (see para 11.143). [FRS 17 para 88]. To comply with that reconciliation requirement, say where deferred tax and irrecoverable surpluses arise, the following would have to be disclosed as a very minimum, but a further breakdown of the total assets and liabilities may also be necessary for a proper understanding of the net position.

Total schemes' assets	400			
Total schemes' liabilities	380			
Net surpluses	20			
Comprising:		**Surplus not recoverable**	**Related deferred tax**	**Net pension asset (liability)**
Surpluses	50	(10)	(12)	28
Deficits	(30)		9	(21)
	20	(10)	(3)	7

Disclosures — December 2006 amendment

11.148.1 The amendment to FRS 17 that aligns the disclosure requirements of FRS 17 with those contained in IAS 19, 'Employee benefits' is effective for periods beginning on or after 6 April 2007, and early adoption is encouraged. The first wave of companies to apply the new disclosure requirements are those with June 2008 year-ends, and the last wave those with March 2009 year-ends.

11.148.2 The significant additional disclosures required by the amendment to FRS 17 include:

- Information that enables users of the financial statements to evaluate the nature of the entity's participation in defined benefit schemes and the financial effects of changes in those schemes. FRS 17 previously required the nature of schemes to be disclosed.
- The principal actuarial assumptions used as at the balance sheet date. FRS 17 previously only required information regarding the main financial assumptions. The most significant change this is likely to result in is the requirement to disclose mortality rates where these are considered to be a material assumption.
- An analysis of the opening and closing scheme liabilities and scheme assets showing separately, if applicable, the movements in scheme assets and scheme liabilities.
- An analysis of scheme liabilities into amounts arising from schemes that are wholly unfunded and amounts arising from schemes that are wholly or partly funded.

11.148.3 The following disclosures are no longer required once the amendment has been adopted:

- The date of the most recent full actuarial valuation and if the actuary is an employee or officer of the company.
- The effects of changes in the demographic and financial assumptions underlying the present value of the scheme liabilities.
- The financial assumptions at the beginning of the period.

- An analysis of reserves in the notes to the financial statements distinguishing the amount relating to the defined benefit asset or liability net of the related deferred tax.

- For closed schemes and those in which the age profile of the active membership is rising significantly, the fact that under the projected unit method the current service cost will increase as the members of the scheme approach retirement.

- The fair value of the assets held by the pension scheme at the beginning and end of the period analysed into classes of assets and disclosed together with the expected rate of return assumed for each class.

11.148.4 FRS 17 previously required an entity to disclose the main financial assumptions used at the beginning of the period and at the balance sheet date. In contrast the amended FRS 17 requires assumptions used at the balance sheet date. As a consequence, an entity will no longer be required to disclose assumptions for a three year period. This change includes the expected rate of return which will no longer be required as at the balance sheet date.

11.148.5 An entity will no longer be required to disclose, for the accounting period and previous four periods, the difference between the expected and actual return on assets. In contrast, the amended FRS 17 requires for the current annual period and previous four annual periods the present value of the defined benefit obligation, the fair value of the scheme assets and surplus or deficit arising in the scheme; and experience adjustments arising on the assets and liabilities of the scheme expressed either as: (1) an amount; or (2) a percentage of the scheme assets at the balance sheet date.

11.148.6 The disclosures that apply *after* the amendment is adopted are set out in full below:

- Background information on the nature of the company's defined benefit schemes, including a general description of the type of schemes, as well as the financial effects of changes in those schemes during the period. [FRS 17R para 76-77(a)]. The description should distinguish, for example, flat salary pension schemes from final salary pension schemes and from retirement healthcare schemes, and should include informal practices that give rise to constructive obligations. [FRS 17R para 78].

- A reconciliation of opening and closing balances of the present value of scheme liabilities showing separately, if applicable, the effects during the period attributable to each of the following:

  - current service cost;
  - interest cost;
  - contributions by scheme participants;
  - actuarial gains and losses;

- foreign currency exchange rate changes on schemes measured in a currency different from the entity's presentation currency;
- benefits paid;
- past service cost;
- business combinations;
- curtailments; and
- settlements.

[FRS 17R para 77(b)].

- An analysis of scheme liabilities into amounts arising from schemes that are wholly unfunded and amounts arising from schemes that are wholly or partly funded. [FRS 17R para 77(c)].

- A reconciliation of the opening and closing balances of the fair value of scheme assets showing separately, if applicable, the effects during the period attributable to each of the following:
  - expected rate of return on scheme assets;
  - actuarial gains and losses;
  - foreign currency exchange rate changes on schemes measured in a currency different from the entity's presentation currency;
  - contributions by the employer;
  - contributions by scheme participants;
  - benefits paid;
  - business combinations; and
  - settlements.

[FRS 17R para 77(d)].

- A reconciliation of the present value of scheme liabilities and the fair value of the scheme assets in to the assets and liabilities recognised in the balance sheet, showing at least:
  - any past service cost not recognised in the balance sheet;
  - any amount not recognised as an asset, because of a limit to the recoverability of that asset through refunds or reductions in future contributions; and
  - any other amounts recognised in the balance sheet.

[FRS 17R para 77(e)].

- The total expense recognised in profit or loss for each of the following, and the line item(s) in which they are included: current service cost, interest cost, expected return on scheme assets, past service cost, the effect of any curtailment or settlement and the effect of the limit to the extent to which an asset can be recognised. [FRS 17R para 77 (f)].

- The total amounts recognised in the statement of total recognised gains and losses for actuarial gains and losses and the effect of the limit to the extent to which an asset can be recognised. [FRS 17R para 77 (g)].

- The cumulative amount of actuarial gains and losses recognised in the statement of total recognised gains and losses. [FRS 17R para 77(h)].

- For each major category of scheme assets, which shall include, but is not limited to, equity instruments, debt instruments, property, and all other assets, the percentage or amount that each major category constitutes of the fair value of the total scheme assets. [FRS 17R para 77(i)].

- The amounts included in the fair value of scheme assets for each category of the entity's own financial instruments and any property occupied by, or other assets used by, the entity. [FRS 17R para 77(j)].

- A narrative description of the basis used to determine the overall expected rate of return on assets, including the effect of the major categories of scheme assets. [FRS 17R para 77(k)].

- The actual return on scheme assets. [FRS 17R para 77(l)].

- The principal actuarial assumptions used as at the balance sheet date, including, when applicable:

  - the discount rates;

  - the expected rates of return on any assets of the scheme for the periods presented in the financial statements;

  - the expected rates of salary increases;

  - retirement healthcare cost trend rates; and

  - any other material actuarial assumptions used.

[FRS 17R para 77(m)].

- The effect of an increase of one percentage point and the effect of a decrease of one percentage point in the assumed retirement healthcare cost trend rates on the aggregate of the current service cost and interest cost components of net periodic retirement healthcare costs and the accumulated retirement healthcare obligation for healthcare costs. For the purposes of this disclosure, all other assumptions shall be held constant. [FRS 17R para 77(n)].

- The amounts for the current accounting period and previous four accounting periods of:

- the present value of the scheme liabilities, the fair value of the scheme assets and the surplus or deficit in the scheme; and

- the experience adjustments arising on the scheme liabilities and assets expressed either as (1) an amount or (2) a percentage of the scheme liabilities or assets respectively at the balance sheet date.

[FRS 17R para 77(o)].

- The employer's best estimate, as soon as it can reasonably be determined, of contributions expected to be paid to the scheme during the accounting period beginning after the balance sheet date. [FRS 17R para 77(p)].

11.148.7 Paragraph 77 (o) of the amended FRS 17 requires a 5 year history of the fair value of scheme assets. Paragraph 95C of the amended standard clarifies that it is not necessary to restate corresponding amounts for the first two of those periods to take account of the new requirement to value quoted securities at current bid price as opposed to mid market value.

Aggregation of schemes

11.148.8 Where an employer operates more than one scheme, the FRS permits the disclosures to be made in total for all schemes, separately for each scheme, or schemes may be grouped in the way that provides the most useful information. [FRS 17 para 79]. For multi-national groups that operate many pension schemes and other types of retirement benefit schemes in various parts of the world, some degree of aggregation is necessary to avoid disclosures of excessive length and detail. Where schemes are grouped, the groupings might be based on geographical operations (for example, distinguishing domestic schemes from overseas schemes), types of benefits with different risk profiles (for example, distinguishing flat salary pension schemes from final salary pension schemes and retirement medical healthcare schemes), or a combination of features as is considered to be most useful.

11.148.9 As noted earlier, the main assumptions underlying the valuation of schemes' liabilities and the expected rate of return on each class of scheme assets have to be disclosed. Where schemes are aggregated, the FRS requires the assumptions to be stated as weighted averages for the schemes concerned or as relatively narrow ranges – any assumptions outside those narrow ranges should be disclosed separately.

11.148.10 Paragraph 82 of the amended FRS 17 requires an entity to disclose information about contingent liabilities arising from retirement benefit obligations in accordance with FRS 12, 'Provisions, contingent liabilities and contingent assets'. Similarly, paragraph 94 of FRS 12 requires the nature of contingent assets, where an inflow of the economic benefits is probable, to be disclosed. In accordance with the provisions of FRS 12 an entity should therefore disclose contingent assets and contingent liabilities, including guarantees, arising from retirement benefit obligations.

11.148.11 Where required by FRS 8, 'Related party disclosures' information about related party transactions with retirement benefit schemes should be disclosed.

11.148.12 The FRS does not permit surpluses and deficits to be netted off in arriving at the assets and liabilities that are disclosed on the face of the balance sheet. Where an entity operates more than one scheme, some schemes may be in surplus and some may be in deficit. Where this is the case, aggregate amounts of assets and aggregate amounts of liabilities (which include any unfunded benefits), less attributable amounts of deferred tax in each case, should be shown separately on the face of the balance sheet. [FRS 17 para 47]. A consequence of this requirement is that at least some of the footnote disclosures have to be disaggregated into schemes that have given rise to assets in the balance sheet and schemes that have given rise to liabilities. This is necessary, for example, in order to comply with the requirement to reconcile scheme surpluses or deficits to balance sheet assets and liabilities (see para 11.143). [FRS 17 para 88]. To comply with that reconciliation requirement, say where deferred tax and irrecoverable surpluses arise, the following would have to be disclosed as a very minimum, but a further breakdown of the total assets and liabilities may also be necessary for a proper understanding of the net position.

Total schemes' assets	400			
Total schemes' liabilities	380			
Net surpluses	20			
Comprising:		**Surplus not recoverable**	**Related deferred tax**	**Net pension asset (liability)**
Surpluses	50	(10)	(12)	28
Deficits	(30)		9	(21)
	20	(10)	(3)	7

Best practice disclosures

11.148.13 The ASB considered that IAS 19 and the amended FRS 17 address many, but not all, concerns about the adequacy of defined benefit pension scheme disclosures. Specifically, financial statements should contain sufficient information to allow users to obtain a clear view of the cost of providing retirement benefits, the related gains, losses, assets and liabilities, the risks and rewards arising from defined benefit schemes, and the entity's future funding obligations. The ASB therefore issued a new best practice reporting statement, 'Retirement benefits – disclosures', which is intended to have persuasive rather than mandatory force. The reporting statement applies to both UK GAAP and IFRS reporters, and complements the disclosures required by FRS 17 and IAS 19.

11.148.14 The reporting statement sets out six principles (rather than requirements) to be considered when providing disclosures for defined benefit schemes, and these are considered below.

Relationship between the reporting entity and the trustees of defined benefit schemes

11.148.15 The relationship between the reporting entity and the trustees (managers) will determine how an entity manages and arranges its affairs with regard to the defined benefit scheme. This includes the investment strategy for the assets held by the scheme and the principles for funding the scheme, including how contribution levels to the scheme are agreed. The management and arrangement of affairs may be affected by the powers vested in the trustees.

11.148.16 In recognition of this, the reporting statement recommends that financial statements disclose the arrangements between the trustees of the scheme and the reporting entity, setting out any powers of the trustees that have a material financial effect on the reporting entity and that are both significant and unusual in relation to the legal and regulatory framework in which the entity operates.

Information about the principal assumptions

11.148.17 The reporting statement recommends that financial statements should include sufficient information about the principal assumptions used to measure scheme liabilities to allow users to understand the inherent uncertainties affecting the measurement of scheme liabilities. These assumptions should include mortality rates, even if not explicitly required by FRS 17. Disclosure should be given of the number of years post retirement it is anticipated pensions will be paid to members of the scheme, as this is often more useful than details of a mortality standard table or cohort factor. Where the number of years assumed alters depending on geographical, demographical or other significant reasons, the different mortality rates should be separately disclosed.

Sensitivity analysis for principal assumptions

11.148.18 Financial statements should disclose a sensitivity analysis for the principal assumptions used to measure the scheme liabilities, showing how the measurement of scheme liabilities would have been affected by changes in the relevant assumption that were reasonably possible at the balance sheet date. For the purposes of this disclosure, all other assumptions would be held constant. No further guidance is provided on how the sensitivity analysis would be undertaken other than an illustrative disclosure example in the appendix to the reporting statement.

How defined benefit liabilities are measured

11.148.19 There are alternative approaches to the projected unit credit method for measuring defined benefit scheme liabilities, as required by FRS 17. One such approach is measuring scheme liabilities on a buy-out basis, that is, the cost of buying out benefits at the balance sheet date with a suitable insurer. Where the cost of buying out benefits is made available to trustees and or members of a scheme, then the reporting statement recommends that it is disclosed.

Future funding obligations in relation to defined benefit schemes

11.148.20 FRS 17 requires the employer's best estimate, as soon as it can reasonably be determined, of contributions expected to be paid to the scheme during the annual period beginning after the balance sheet date. Scheme liabilities are, however, often of a long term nature and contributions expected to be paid in the next annual period may not provide sufficient information to allow the users of the financial statements to understand how the scheme liabilities affect the economic resources available to the entity, including its cash-flow.

11.148.21 Given this, the reporting statement recommends that the financial statements should disclose the following:

- The rates or amounts of contributions which have been agreed with the trustees (managers) of the scheme and are payable to the scheme by or on behalf of the reporting entity.
- The funding principles the entity has agreed or operates with regard to defined benefit schemes.
- Where a defined benefit scheme is in deficit and the entity has entered into an agreement with the trustees (managers) of the scheme to make additional contributions to reduce or recover the deficit, separate disclosure of such additional contributions, and the number of years over which it is anticipated the additional contributions will be paid.
- The duration of scheme liabilities allowing users to see the period of time over which the liabilities of the defined benefit scheme mature.
- Information that allows users to understand the projected cash flows of defined benefit schemes.

Nature and extent of the risks and rewards arising from financial instruments held by defined benefit schemes

11.148.22 Disclosures should be made to enable users to evaluate the nature and extent of the risks and rewards arising from the financial instruments held by defined benefit schemes. For each type of risk arising from financial instruments held by retirement benefits schemes, the reporting statement recommends the following disclosure:

(a) the exposures to risk and how they arise;

(b) the objectives, policies and processes undertaken by the defined benefits scheme or the entity for managing the risk and the methods used to measure the risk; and

(c) any changes in (a) or (b) from the previous period.

11.148.23 An entity may disclose a sensitivity analysis, such as value-at-risk, for types of risks to which the assets of the defined benefit scheme are exposed. Where an entity discloses such a sensitivity analysis it should also disclose the method and assumptions used in preparing this analysis and any changes from the previous period in the methods and assumptions used.

11.148.24 As well as disclosing the percentage or amount of the fair value of total scheme assets that each major category of assets constitutes, in accordance with FRS 17, the entity should also disclose the expected rate of return assumed for each category for the period presented.

Reserves relating to defined benefit schemes

11.149 Retirement benefits costs find their way into reserves via the profit and loss account and STRGL (actuarial gains and losses). The FRS does not specify to which reserves amounts passed through the STRGL should be debited or credited. The disclosure example in Appendix 1 to the FRS indicates a pension asset that is reflected in its entirety in the profit and loss reserve (net of attributable deferred tax). Some may prefer to take the cumulative actuarial gains to a separate pension or retirement benefits reserve.

Distributable reserves

11.150 FRS 17 is silent on the question of whether pension assets and liabilities give rise to realised or unrealised gains and losses. The issue only arises in respect of assets and liabilities recognised in the financial statements of individual companies, not groups. Under sections 264 and 270 of the Companies Act 1985 (sections 831 and 836 of the Companies Act 2006), the recognition of a deficit as a liability might affect the ability of a public company to make a distribution (because public companies must take into account unrealised losses).

11.151 Appendix IV to FRS 17 indicates that a distribution problem will arise only where individual company financial statements show a deficit so large that it reduces distributable reserves to below that needed to cover any intended distribution. [FRS 17 App IV para 58]. The possibilities of an unexpected decline in distributable profits are mitigated, however, by FRS 17's rules relating to group defined benefit schemes. Where a scheme that covers more than one company does not enable the individual companies to identify their share of the scheme's assets and liabilities, the FRS requires each company (including the parent) to treat the scheme as a defined contribution scheme. [FRS 17 paras 9, 12]. Each individual company should, therefore, recognise only the employer contributions payable to the scheme for each accounting period. The defined benefit accounting would be used only at the consolidation level (see further para 11.37 onwards). In these circumstances, distributable profits of the individual companies are not hit unless and until additional contributions become payable to fund the deficit. Nevertheless, note that the implications of the Pensions Act 2004, changes in tax rules and the use of IFRS at a group level may all impact the applicability of this exemption (see paras 11.41.2 to 11.41.4).

11.152 In November 2004, the ICAEW and ICAS published guidance in the form of Tech 50/04, 'Guidance on the effect of FRS 17 'Retirement benefits' and IAS 19 'Employee benefits' on realised profits and losses'. This guidance concludes that the existence of a pension surplus or deficit is not the sole factor relevant to determining distributable profits. This is because a pension asset or liability recognised in an entity's balance sheet will also be affected by net contributions paid to the scheme and any balances introduced as a result of a business combination. The Companies Act defines a company's distributable profits not in terms of its assets and liabilities, but as its accumulated, realised profits less its accumulated, realised losses. [CA85 Sec 263(3), CA06 Sec 830(2)]. Accordingly, it is the cumulative profit or loss credited or debited to reserves in respect of a pension surplus or deficit that is important. This is illustrated in the following example.

Example

Company A established a new defined benefit pension scheme at the beginning of 20X5. During 20X5 there is a net pension expense of £4m (encompassing items reflected in both the profit and loss account and the statement of total recognised gains and losses), but contributions to the scheme amount to £5m. Hence, at the end of 20X5 there is a surplus in the scheme, and an asset on the balance sheet of £1m (both taxation and questions over recoverability of the asset are ignored for the purpose of this example). However, the impact on distributable profits is not a credit of £1m, as represented by the surplus in the scheme, but a debit of £4m in respect of the net pension expense. Considered another way, the impact on reserves is derived by deducting the contributions to the scheme from the surplus.

11.153 As regards the question of whether cumulative profits or losses in reserves in respect of a pension surplus or deficit are realised (regardless of whether they were first recognised in the profit and loss account or the statement of total recognised gains and losses), the guidance concludes as follows:

- A cumulative net debit in reserves is a realised loss. Tech 7/03, 'Guidance on the determination of realised profits and losses in the context of distributions under the Companies Act 1985', provides that all losses are realised losses except to the extent that the law, accounting standards or Tech 7/03 provide otherwise. Specifically, it goes on to say that provisions are treated as realised losses. Hence, the conclusion was reached in Tech 50/04 that a cumulative net debit in reserves in respect of a pension scheme is a realised loss.
- A cumulative net credit in reserves is a realised profit only to the extent that it is represented by an asset to be recovered by agreed refunds in the form of qualifying consideration (as defined in Tech 7/03 – see chapter 23). Any further cumulative net credit (in excess of agreed funds) is not covered by qualifying consideration so is treated as unrealised, although it will become realised in subsequent periods to the extent that it offsets subsequent net debits to reserves that are treated as realised losses.

The ICAEW, in Tech 02/07, 'Distributable profits – implications of recent accounting changes', have confirmed that, despite the release of Tech 02/07, the Companies Act 2006 and the increased use of IFRS, the basic principles set out in Tech 7/03, for the determination of realised profits and losses, have not changed since that guidance was issued in 2003. Tech 50/04 is expected to be consolidated with Tech 02/07 in due course.

11.154 Where an entity operates more than one defined benefit scheme, it should assess the impact of a surplus or deficit on its distributable profits separately for each scheme. In other words, schemes should not be aggregated or offset to reach a single net realised profit or loss.

11.155 As regards defined contribution schemes, the expense recognised in profit or loss is equal to the contributions payable to the scheme for the accounting period and is a realised loss. Some entities, however, account for their participation in a multi-employer defined benefit scheme as if it was a defined contribution scheme (see para 11.37). Where a scheme meets the criteria for this treatment in FRS 17, the position as regards realised profits and losses will be the same as for any other defined contribution scheme.

11.156 The guidance also considers the impact of deferred tax. It clarifies that the deferred tax impact of pension accounting generally relates to the pension asset or liability and not the cumulative net debit or credit in reserves. However, it also clarifies that the debit for deferred tax liability may be offset against an unrealised net credit in reserves in respect of the pension asset.

[The next paragraph is 11.162.]

Composition of reserves

11.162 In practice, a pension asset or liability will often arise from better or worse than expected investment performance or other actuarial gains and losses. But this will not be the only reason. An asset will arise in acquisition accounting where the acquired entity has a pension scheme in surplus. Similarly, a deficit (or unfunded liability) may have arisen as part of accounting for an acquisition. More generally, in a funded scheme, the amount of contribution payments will affect the composition of any asset or liability. A recognised asset or liability is normally attributable to shareholders – and, hence, in a broad sense, reflected in capital and reserves. An exception is where, in consolidated financial statements, part of the asset or liability relates to minority interests in a subsidiary. Where a defined benefit scheme is operated by a less than wholly-owned subsidiary, the whole of the surplus or deficit is recognised as an asset or liability in the consolidated balance sheet, but only the group's share is reflected in shareholders' funds (the minority's share being reflected in minority interests). Consequently, properly speaking only the group's share of the defined benefit asset or liability would be disclosed under paragraph 90 of the FRS before the December 2006 amendment.

11.163 The following example illustrates the double entry and the effect on reserves where a defined benefit asset arises from actuarial gains and from overfunding (tax is ignored).

Example

At the beginning of the year, a scheme has no surplus or deficit, the assets and liabilities each being measured at 400.

The pension cost for the year is as follows:

Current service cost	(70)
Interest cost (7%)	(28)
Expected return on assets (8%)	32
Net finance income	4
Total profit and loss charge	(66)
Contributions paid during the year were 80.	

At the end of the year, a scheme surplus of 39 is measured. Actuarial gains (net) of 25 arise and are recognised in the STRGL. The double-entry would be as follows.

Dr Profit and loss account (net pension cost)	66	
Cr Defined benefit asset/liability		66
Dr Defined benefit asset/liability	80	
Cr Cash (contributions paid)		80
Dr Defined benefit asset/liability	25	
Cr Pension reserve – STRGL (actuarial gain)		25

The pension asset arises as follows:

Asset b/f	nil
Pension cost (profit and loss account)	(66)
Contributions paid	80
Actuarial gain (STRGL)	25
Asset c/f	39

The composition of the pension asset could be analysed as follows:

Amount	**Nature of asset**	**Component of reserves**
14	Prepaid contributions	P&L reserve
25	Actuarial gain	Pension reserve

In this analysis, the pension asset of 39 is regarded as comprising two components:

- A 'prepayment' of 14, being the difference between the profit and loss charge (66) and the contributions paid (80). This might be regarded as an investment of profits already made.
- An actuarial gain of 25, which has been credited to reserves (either profit and loss reserve or, as in this example, a separate pension reserve). Since this is in the nature of a revaluation gain, it would be regarded as unrealised.

11.164 The next example extends the previous one into the following year.

Example

The profit and loss charge is again 66. Contributions are, however, reduced to 50 as a result of the surplus. At the end of the year, a scheme surplus of 15 is measured. The double-entry would be as follows.

Dr Profit and loss account (net pension cost)	66	
Cr Defined benefit asset		66
Dr Defined benefit asset	50	
Cr Cash (contributions paid)		50
Dr Pension reserve – STRGL (actuarial loss)	8	
Cr Defined benefit asset		8

The movements in the pension asset are as follows:

Asset b/f	39
Pension cost (profit and loss account)	(66)
Contributions paid	50
Actuarial loss (STRGL)	(8)
Asset c/f	15

The movements in the components of the reserves relating to the asset could be analysed thus:

	Pension reserve (cumulative actuarial gains)	Profit and loss reserve (prepayment)
B/f	25	14
Reduction in contributions	(2)	(14)
Actuarial loss	(8)	–
C/f	15	–

In this analysis, the pension asset of 15 is now equal to the cumulative actuarial gains (less losses):

- The difference of 16 between the profit and loss charge (66) and the contributions paid (50) results in a 'claw-back' of the 'prepayment' (14) and the realisation of part of the cumulative actuarial gain (2).

- The actuarial loss of 8 is debited to the pension reserve and reported in the STRGL. Net cumulative actuarial gains carried forward of 15 would be regarded as unrealised.

[The next paragraph is 11.170.]

Pensions Act 2004 implications

11.170 The Pensions Act 2004 became law in November 2004. It was followed by a web of supporting regulations, codes of practice and other guidance, much of which came into force from April 2005.

11.171 From an accounting perspective, the most significant provisions of the Pensions Act are in the following areas:

- The launch of the Pension Protection Fund (see para 11.173 onwards).
- Increased powers to the new Pension Regulator (see para 11.176 onwards).
- Revised rules for employers ceasing to participate in a pension scheme (see para 11.184 onwards).

11.172 The following paragraphs summarise only the main accounting implications of the new legislation and do not attempt to explore the rules in detail.

The Pension Protection Fund ('PPF')

11.173 The Pension Protection Fund (PPF), which came into force from April 2005, is designed to protect pension scheme members in the event that the sponsoring employer becomes insolvent. Broadly, the PPF will fund current pensions in payment as well as up to 90 per cent of the benefits of active and deferred scheme members when an 'insolvency event' occurs. The term 'insolvency event' encompasses the administration, administrative receivership or liquidation of the sponsoring employer.

11.174 The PPF is funded in part by the assets of the schemes it takes over and in part by a levy on all schemes covered by the PPF. Initially, the levy was based on factors related to scheme size (number of members, value of liabilities, etc) but in subsequent years it will include a risk-based element that will take account of funding levels and the likelihood of the employer's insolvency. Thus, for the 2006/7 year, 80 per cent of the levy is risk-based with the amount reflecting the level of scheme underfunding (the worst funded schemes pay a higher levy) and the viability of the sponsoring employer (the lower a company's Dun & Bradstreet rating, the higher the levy).

11.175 The introduction of the levy represents another cost of maintaining a defined benefit pension scheme. Although not literally an administration cost, the levy's accounting treatment should mirror that of other costs incurred by the scheme.

The Pensions Regulator

11.176 A new regulator (the Pensions Regulator) replaced the previous regulator (OPRA), inheriting all of its powers and functions along with several new powers. In our view, there are two areas in which the new regulatory regime may influence the financial statements:

- The 'moral hazard' provisions (see para 11.177 onwards).
- The 'statutory funding objective' (see para 11.179 onwards).

The 'moral hazard' provisions

11.177 The 'moral hazard' provisions in the Pensions Act are designed to prevent employers from rearranging their affairs so as to avoid their pension obligations. The provisions permit the regulator to impose:

- Contribution notices on people that have been party to an act, or a deliberate failure to act, aimed at avoiding pension obligations.
- Financial support directions on associated or connected parties where the employer is either 'insufficiently resourced' or a service company (that is, a company the turnover of which is solely or principally derived from amounts charged for the provision of employee services to other group members). A financial support direction is a requirement to put financial support in place within a specified time period and to ensure that that support remains in place while the scheme is in existence.
- Restoration orders where the regulator is of the opinion that a transaction has been made at undervalue. Such orders require that a pension scheme's financial position is restored to its pre-transaction position.

11.178 The existence of these powers could influence the judgement of whether a scheme should be treated as defined contribution or defined benefit as they may indicate that an entity could have an obligation to provide funding where one was not thought to exist previously. It will also be necessary to determine whether the risk that the regulator may impose a notice represents a contingent liability (see further chapter 21).

The 'statutory funding objective'

11.179 With effect from September 2005, the previous minimum funding requirement ('MFR') was replaced by a statutory funding objective ('SFO'). This means that all defined benefit schemes have to have 'sufficient and appropriate assets' to cover their liabilities. Where a scheme has insufficient assets to cover its liabilities, the trustees must establish a recovery plan setting out how the SFO is to be met and over what period. Any failure to do this, or to reach agreement with the employer on a funding strategy for the scheme, must be reported to the regulator, who may take any of the following courses of action:

- Modify the scheme in relation to future accrual of benefits.
- Fix the period over which a shortfall is to be made up.
- Impose a schedule of contributions.

11.180 The impact of the above is that levels of contribution to defined benefit pension schemes seem likely to increase. However, of greater significance to the financial statements may be the valuation of a scheme in wind-up, which will be based on the buyout of all accrued benefits. This makes it more expensive to wind up a pension scheme and, taken with the moral hazard provisions described above, almost impossible for a solvent company to walk away from its pension obligations. Employers can become liable to the trustees of a defined benefit scheme for a debt if there is a deficit in a defined benefit scheme. This can apply on:

- the winding-up of a scheme;
- the insolvency of an employer; or
- an employer ceasing participation in a multi-employer scheme (see para 11.184 onwards).

11.181 In situations where a buy-out valuation exceeds the defined benefit liability recognised under FRS 17, there should be consideration as to whether there ought to be disclosure in the financial statements. The ASB's best practice reporting statement on pension disclosures recommends that where the cost of buying out benefits is made available to trustees (managers) and/or members of defined benefit schemes, then the financial statements should also disclose the cost of buying out benefits. [ASB RS para 17].

11.182 Where there is a funding plan in place, FRS 17 requires disclosure of the contribution rate agreed for future years. [FRS 17 para 76(c) (original version); FRS 17R para 77(p) (amended version, applicable to accounting periods beginning on or after 6 April 2007)]. However, in the absence of an agreed funding plan, we consider that there should be disclosure of the potential implications of any action by the regulator. Furthermore, where a scheme is in wind-up, we consider that there should be disclosure of the fact that the buy-out obligation exceeds amounts recognised under FRS 17. In some circumstances, it may be appropriate to recognise these additional obligations.

11.183 Although not arising for the reasons described in paragraph 11.181 above, MFI Furniture Group plc made disclosure in its 2004 interim statement of a potential requirement to make additional contributions to its pension scheme following a failure to equalise properly the retirement ages of men and women. This extract from the company's interim statement shows the type of disclosure that may be appropriate in the context of obligations arising out of the Pensions Act.

Table 11.18 – Obligation to make further contributions

MFI Furniture Group plc – interim report – 12 June 2004

Notes to the financial statements (extract)

12 Pensions (extract)

On 6 May 2004 the Group announced that it had received actuarial and legal advice following a thorough review of an issue arising within its UK pension plans. This issue is liable to result in the Group recognising higher pension obligations than previously identified. The issue has its origins in a failure, back in 1994, effectively to properly equalise the pension age for men and women at age 65 for an employee's service from 17 November 1994. Although announcements to this effect were made at the time to plan members, the relevant trust documentation was not properly amended. This is liable to result in the part of the benefits earned by employee members over a period from 1994 to 2004 having to be calculated using a normal retirement date of age 60 rather than at age 65. Plan rules have now been amended to cap liability in relation to future service.

The Board has sought legal advice on the scope for correction and an independent actuarial assessment of the additional liabilities, which might arise, and of the contributions required to fund them. It appears far from certain that the situation can be corrected, in which case some £40 million of additional liabilities (before tax) will arise. This figure is assessed on the same actuarial assumptions as currently used for funding the UK pension plans and accounting for them under SSAP24 (see note 23 to the Group's 2003 financial statements). Under FRS 17, which the Group has not yet adopted, this figure would be approximately £50 million (before tax).

Under the pensions accounting standard SSAP24, the impact on future profits of the Group will depend on the period over which additional liabilities are recognised. At this stage the funding position has not yet been resolved and is uncertain. Given the current degree of uncertainty in the outcome of the discussions with the Trustees there is no recognition of any additional charge in these interim financial statements.

The Board and the Trustees will be reviewing the funding position in the light of further advice to be received and will then discuss how best to proceed. The Trustees will need to be satisfied both as to the period over which contributions are paid and the date from which contributions commence. The Board expects that the funding position will become clearer in the second half of the financial year and that this would be reflected in the year end accounts.

The Board continues to take advice from leading counsel as to the actions required to obtain recovery from the third parties on whose advice the Group and the Trustees of the plan relied in relation to this issue.

Employers ceasing to participate in a pension scheme

11.184 For a single-employer pension scheme, section 75 of the Pensions Act 1995 (as amended by the Pensions Act 2004) ensures that a debt can be placed on the pension scheme's sponsoring employer if the value of the scheme's assets is less than its liabilities. The debt is triggered if:

- the scheme winds-up; or
- on a relevant event (for example, the employer becomes insolvent).

11.185 Section 75A was inserted into the Pensions Act 1995 by the Pensions Act 2004 to modify the existing section 75 as it applies to multi-employer schemes. For these schemes, the debt is triggered if:

- the scheme winds-up;
- on a relevant event (for example, insolvency) for any one or more companies; or
- on a withdrawal of an individual employer from a multi-employer scheme (referred to as an 'employment-cessation event').

11.186 When an employer ceases to participate in an under-funded defined benefit multi-employer scheme from 2 September 2005, but other employers continue to participate, its exit debt will be calculated on a 'buy-out basis' (that is, the full cost of securing its liabilities with annuities, including an estimate of expenses) – see further paragraph 11.189 below. (Prior to this the debt was calculated on the MFR basis.) However, if the trustees agree and the Pensions Regulator approves, a withdrawal arrangement may be entered into that allows for a lower amount than the buy-out debt to be paid, with further payments contingent on specified future events (see para 11.193 below).

11.187 A multi-employer scheme is a scheme in relation to which more than one employer is exposed to the scheme. 'Employer' in relation to an occupational pension scheme, means the employer of persons in the description or category of employment to which the scheme in question relates. Multi-employer schemes do not include, for the purposes of the section 75 rules, sectionalised schemes where:

- contributions payable by an employer are allocated to that employer's section;
- a specified part of the scheme's assets is attributable to each section and cannot be used for any other section; and
- there is only one employer in each section.

In such cases, section 75 will apply as if each section of the scheme were a separate scheme.

11.188 A liability is triggered when an 'employment-cessation event' occurs. In general, this event takes place when a participating employer ceases to have any employees who are members of the scheme and at least one participating employer remains. This could occur if:

- A company leaves the corporate group and, therefore, ceases to be a participating employer in the pension scheme.

- A company's business is sold, leaving it with no remaining employees.
- A company ceases to be employer of any individuals who are active members of the scheme (for example, a group restructuring).
- A company's employees cease employment through redundancy or resignation.
- Future accruals cease for that company.

This is a complex area and professional advice is likely to be needed.

11.189 When an 'employment-cessation event' occurs, part of the total deficit in a multi-employer scheme has to be apportioned to the withdrawing employer. The apportionment is by reference to the position at the date that the employer ceases to participate in the scheme. The total deficit is calculated on a buy-out basis (that is, based on the full cost of securing the scheme's liabilities with annuities, including an estimate of expenses). The total deficit is apportioned according to the scheme's trust deed and rules, but if the rules are silent then the legislation specifies the calculation.

11.190 Under the legislation, the amount of the employer's debt is:

- the proportion of the buy-out deficit that is attributable to employment with that employer; and
- the expenses attributable to the employer ceasing to participate.

11.191 Depending on what is set out in the scheme's own trust deed and rules, the withdrawing employer has to pay not only the buy-out deficit attributable to its own employees, but also a share of the orphan liabilities. 'Orphan liabilities' are material liabilities that are attributable to companies that have already left the scheme, including any liabilities that cannot be attributed specifically to any of the remaining employers. Unless the scheme rules state otherwise, the other employers share any exposure relating to these liabilities.

11.192 In simplified terms, the liability of the withdrawing employer is calculated as follows:

$$\frac{\text{buy-out liabilities for withdrawing employer}}{\text{buy-out liabilities for withdrawing employer + remaining employers}} \times \text{buy-out deficit for the scheme}$$

11.193 As noted in paragraph 11.186 above, the legislation for multi-employer schemes includes provision for 'withdrawal arrangements', under which the immediate liability of a withdrawing employer can be reduced (or at least deferred) if all the following conditions are met:

- A guarantee is provided – this can be by another entity, such as a parent company.
- The trustees agree to the arrangement.
- The arrangement is approved by the Pensions Regulator.

11.194 Where a withdrawal arrangement applies, the withdrawing employer must initially pay a partial debt to the scheme, with the balance of the full buy-out debt left to the guarantor(s). Further payments from the guarantors are then contingent on specified future events and can be either a fixed amount or a floating liability, depending on the terms of the withdrawal agreement.

11.195 Where the guarantors' payments comprise a fixed amount, this will be the withdrawing employer's share of the buy-out debt at the date of the employer cessation event, less the initial amount paid by the employer and any liabilities transferred to another scheme. Where the guarantors' payments comprise a floating liability, this will be the withdrawing employer's share of the buy-out debt calculated as at the time the guarantor(s) are asked to make payment (see para 11.197).

11.196 The guarantor(s) can be any party, but will generally be one or some of the following:

- One of the remaining employers in the scheme.
- A party connected with the withdrawing employer or remaining employers.
- The withdrawing employer.
- The purchaser in a sale situation.

11.197 Payment by the guarantor(s) is triggered by the earliest of:

- The scheme beginning to wind-up.
- An event occurring as a result of which there is no solvent employer.
- The Pensions Regulator issuing a notice that the guarantor(s) must pay their debt. In reaching this decision, the Pensions Regulator will take into account:
  - whether the guarantor(s) have taken reasonable steps to comply with the agreement;
  - whether the guarantor(s) have complied with their obligations to notify the Pensions Regulator of any notifiable events; and
  - the financial circumstances of the guarantor(s).

11.198 The Pensions Regulator may also bring a withdrawal arrangement to an end without demanding payment if it feels that the arrangement is no longer required (for instance, if the further payments are a floating amount and the scheme moves into surplus) or if it is replaced by another approved withdrawal arrangement.

Accounting treatment

11.199 As noted in paragraph 11.185, a situation that will trigger measurement of the defined benefit obligation on a buy-out basis is where a participating employer ceases to participate in a multi-employer scheme. This may typically arise within group schemes where, for example, a subsidiary within a group is sold. Such an event will trigger a debt on the participating employer, being the amount of the employer's defined benefit pension obligation measured on a buy-out basis, under section 75 of the Pensions Act 1995. In the case where the employer ceases participation in the scheme, payment of the section 75 debt equates to a settlement event having the effect of extinguishing the participating employer's share of the scheme liabilities (see para 11.101). The examples below illustrate this further. For the purpose of these examples it is assumed that no withdrawal arrangements deferring payment of part of the debt (see para 11.193) are entered into.

Example 1 – section 75 payment made by withdrawing employer

Company B is wholly owned by company A. The employees of company B participate in the group A defined benefit pension scheme (other companies owned by company A, as well as company A itself also participate in this scheme). All companies that participate in the group A pension scheme are able to identify their share of the scheme's assets and liabilities on a consistent and reasonable basis such that defined benefit accounting is applied in each company's financial statements (see para 11.37). Company A subsequently sells company B to a third party purchaser.

Following the disposal of company B, the employees of company B remain in the group A pension scheme as deferred members. Company A now assumes responsibility for any liabilities arising in respect of these deferred members. Nevertheless, as company B itself is ceasing to participate in the group A pension scheme, this is determined to trigger a section 75 payment.

The group A pension scheme is in deficit at the time of the disposal and the share of the deficit relating to company B's employees (measured on an FRS 17 basis) amounts to £5m. On a buy-out basis, the share of the deficit relating to company B's employees is £9m (being the value of the section 75 payment). Following the section 75 payment, a surplus of £4m under FRS 17 arises on company B's share of the scheme. All companies in group A have a year end date of 31 December 20X6 and by this date, the disposal and section 75 payment have occurred.

In company B's individual financial statements, a settlement loss of £4m is recognised (see para 11.101) as company B has ceased to participate in the group A pension scheme and company B's liability in respect of the pension scheme has been extinguished (through the transfer of the obligation to company A). The settlement loss of £4m reflects the fact that company B had to make a payment of £9m (being the section 75 payment) in order to exit the group A pension scheme where the deficit attributable to company B's employees, previously recognised and measured on an FRS 17 basis, was £5m.

In company A's consolidated financial statements, no settlement loss is recognised as, whilst company B has ceased to participate in the scheme, company B's employees still remain in the scheme, albeit as deferred members. Hence, from the perspective of the group, the liabilities associated with company B's employees (£5m) have not been extinguished and the section 75 payment (£9m) will increase scheme assets, resulting in a surplus for this part of the scheme of £4m. In addition, a curtailment gain may arise as company B's employees are now deferred members resulting in a reduction in their future benefit entitlement (see para 11.102).

Furthermore, as defined benefit accounting is applied at an entity level, the surplus of £4m in respect of company B's employees needs to be allocated to the participating employers. As company A has assumed responsibility for any liabilities relating to the deferred members, it would appear reasonable for the £4m surplus to be allocated to company A. It will be recognised in company A's individual financial statements if it meets the criteria in paragraphs 37 to 42 of FRS 17 (see para 11.115 onwards). The basic rule is that the amount of surplus recognised as an asset should not exceed the present value of the amounts that the employer can recover through reduced contributions, together with refunds that have been agreed by the trustees at the balance sheet date. Recognition of the surplus in respect of company B's deferred members may depend on whether company A has active employees in the scheme for which it recognises a deficit and for which it can benefit from reduced contributions in the future. If the surplus is recognised in company A's individual financial statements, it will be included as part of the calculation of profit or loss on disposal of company B.

The table below summarises the position in respect of company B's employees (ignoring any curtailment gains):

	Company B (subsidiary) £'m	Company A (parent) £'m	Group £'m
Company B's deficit as at date of disposal	(5)	-	(5)
Section 75 payment *	9	-	9
Group transfer:			
Settlement loss in company B	(4)	-	-
Credit (included in profit or loss on disposal of company B) in company A	-	4	-
Surplus arising after section 75 payment to group A scheme **	-	4	4

* The section 75 payment forms part of the settlement loss calculation in company B's profit and loss account, but increases scheme assets in the group's consolidated financial statements.

** As company A now assumes responsibility for any liabilities arising in respect of the deferred members, it would recognise the surplus of £4m in its individual financial statements if it meets the recognition criteria in FRS 17 (see comments above).

11.200 The above example is based on the situation where the companies that participate in the group pension scheme have been able to identify their share of the scheme's assets and liabilities on a consistent and reasonable basis, such that defined benefit accounting is applied in each company's financial statements. In some cases, section 75 payments will become payable by companies that have not previously been able to identify their share of the scheme's assets and liabilities and which have, therefore, used defined contribution accounting in their individual financial statements as permitted by paragraph 9 of FRS 17 (see para 11.37 onwards). In such cases, the settlement loss in the withdrawing employer's individual financial statements will be the amount of the section 75 payment (that is, £9m in the example above). Under defined contribution accounting, there is no deficit previously recognised in the balance sheet and so the loss is recognised on the basis of contributions payable (in this case, the section 75 payment) in the period. Note that the consolidated financial statements of company A will always apply defined benefit accounting.

11.201 In the situation where the individual companies in the group have used defined contribution accounting on the grounds that it has not been possible to allocate the scheme's assets and liabilities, it will be necessary to consider if this is still applicable for the remaining companies where an allocation is made for the purposes of section 75 when one of the companies leaves the group. Depending on the specific circumstances, it may be that the remaining companies are now able to allocate the scheme's assets and liabilities on a consistent and reasonable basis, such that the exemption for group schemes is no longer applicable. See further paragraph 11.37 onwards.

11.202 The above example in paragraph 11.199 illustrates a relatively straightforward scenario. However, calculation of the section 75 payment often takes time and it may be the case that calculation of the payment is not completed until after the year end date. The following example illustrates this scenario.

Example 2 – section 75 payment made by withdrawing employer after the year end

The facts are as for example 1 in paragraph 11.199 and company A has taken over responsibility for the deferred members at the balance sheet date, but for administrative reasons company B has not made the payment at the balance sheet date, as the amount to be paid is only finalised after the balance sheet date (being £9m as in the previous example).

Similar to example 1, in company B's individual financial statements, a settlement loss of £4m is recognised as company B has ceased to participate in the group A pension scheme (through the transfer of the obligation to company A). This settlement loss of £4m represents the difference between the section 75 liability of £9m and the deficit, previously recognised and measured on an FRS 17 basis, of £5m. The unpaid section 75 settlement payment is included in creditors in company B's balance sheet replacing the previously recognised FRS 17 liability).

Again, similar to example 1, in company A's consolidated financial statements, no settlement loss is recognised as, whilst company B has ceased to participate in the scheme, company B's employees still remain in the scheme, albeit as deferred members. Hence, from the perspective of the group, the liabilities associated with company B's employees (£5m) have not been extinguished. At the balance sheet date, company B is no longer part of the group and so the creditor for the unpaid section 75 debt (£9m) will not be included in the group's consolidated balance sheet. However, it is taken into account in determining company B's net assets (which will be net assets excluding pensions less the section 75 creditor) in the calculation of the profit or loss on disposal of company B and so it has been recognised by the group. The unpaid section 75 contribution would be shown as part of scheme assets (as it is a current asset receivable by the scheme – FRS 17 para 15), resulting in a surplus of £4m. In addition, a curtailment gain may arise as company B's employees are now deferred members resulting in a reduction in their future benefit entitlement (see para 11.102).

Furthermore, as defined benefit accounting is applied at an entity level, the surplus of £4m in respect of company B's employees needs to be allocated to the participating employers. As company A has assumed responsibility for any liabilities relating to the deferred members, it would appear reasonable for the £4m surplus to be allocated to company A. It will be recognised in company A's individual financial statements if it meets the criteria in paragraphs 37 to 42 of FRS 17 (see further example 1). If the surplus is recognised, it will be included as part of the calculation of profit or loss on disposal of company B.

The table below summarises the position in respect of company B's employees (ignoring any curtailment gains):

	Company B (subsidiary) £'m	**Company A (parent) £'m**	**Group £'m**
Company B's deficit as at date of disposal	(5)	-	(5)
Unpaid section 75 payment *	9	-	9
Group transfer:			
Settlement loss in company B	(4)	-	-
Credit (included in profit or loss on disposal of company B) in company A	-	4	-
Surplus arising after section 75 amount payable to group A scheme **	-	4	4

* Note that the unpaid section 75 payment is recognised as a creditor and forms part of the settlement loss calculation in company B's individual financial statements. In the consolidated financial statements, the section 75 creditor is taken into account in determining company B's net assets in the calculation of the profit or loss on disposal of company B and the debit increases scheme assets in the group's consolidated financial statements as explained above.

** As company A now assumes responsibility for any liabilities arising in respect of the deferred members, it would recognise the surplus of £4m in its individual financial statements if it meets the recognition criteria in FRS 17 (see comments in example 1 above).

11.203 In the above example, the parent company has taken over responsibility for the deferred members at the balance sheet date, but the subsidiary has not made the section 75 payment at the balance sheet date for administrative reasons. The situation could be more complicated where the settlement itself has not been finalised at the year end, such that the subsidiary is still responsible for the employees. Losses arising on a settlement should be measured at the date on which the employer becomes demonstrably committed to the transaction and recognised in the profit and loss account covering that date. Gains arising on a settlement should be measured at the date on which all parties whose consent is required are irrevocably committed to the transaction and recognised in the profit and loss account covering that date. [FRS 17 para 64]. Therefore, the accounting treatment for settlements that straddle the balance sheet date will depend on the specific circumstances and whether there is a gain or a loss on settlement. See further paragraph 11.100 onwards.

11.204 The above two examples illustrate the appropriate accounting where the departing employer makes the section 75 payment. Nevertheless, it may be the case that the parent company agrees to pay the section 75 payment. The accounting impact is considered further in the following example.

Example 3 – section 75 payment made by the withdrawing employer's parent

The facts are as for example 1 in paragraph 11.199, but company A agrees to make the £9m section 75 payment. This amount is not repayable by company B.

In company B's individual financial statements, a settlement gain of £5m is recognised. As company B did not make payments in respect of the section 75 debt, but has ceased participation in the scheme, the settlement gain of £5m reflects the release of company B's share of the deficit (previously recognised and measured on an FRS 17 basis).

Similar to example 1, in company A's consolidated financial statements, no settlement loss is recognised (although a curtailment gain or loss may arise) as, whilst company B has ceased to participate in the scheme, company B's employees still remain in the scheme, albeit as deferred members. Hence, from the perspective of the group, the liabilities associated with company B's employees (£5m) have not been extinguished and the section 75 payment (£9m) will increase scheme assets, resulting in a surplus for this part of the scheme of £4m.

In company A's individual financial statements, the £5m deficit (measured on an FRS 17 basis) in respect of the liabilities that company A has taken over should be recognised, with a corresponding loss in respect of the transfer in the profit and loss account (as part of the calculation of profit or loss on disposal of company B). The payment of £9m into the scheme would be treated as a contribution to the pension scheme given that company A participates in the group A pension scheme and has taken over the responsibility for funding the obligation for these deferred members. As such, company A would increase the value of the scheme assets it recognises by £9m, resulting in a surplus of £4m (if the recognition criteria in paragraphs 37 to 42 of FRS 17 are met (see further example 1).

The table below summarises the position in respect of company B's employees (ignoring any curtailment gains):

	Company B (subsidiary) £'m	Company A (parent) £'m	Group £'m
Company B's deficit as at date of disposal	(5)	-	(5)
Section 75 payment *	-	9	9
Group transfer:			
Settlement gain in company B	5	-	-
Loss (included in profit or loss on disposal of company B) in respect of liabilities taken over	-	(5)	-
Surplus arising after section 75 payment to group A scheme **	-	4	4

* The section 75 payment increases scheme assets recognised in both company A and in the group's consolidated financial statements.

** As company A now assumes responsibility for any liabilities arising in respect of the deferred members, it would recognise the surplus of £4m in its individual financial statements if it meets the recognition criteria in FRS 17 (see comments in example 1 above).

11.205 A further situation that may arise is where there is also a bulk transfer of a subsidiary's share of the scheme into a new scheme. The accounting impact of this situation is considered further in the following examples.

Example 4 – section 75 payment made by withdrawing employer (+ bulk transfer out)

The facts are as for example 1 in paragraph 11.199 (that is, company B makes the section 75 payment), but in addition a bulk transfer is made of the assets and liabilities relating to company B's employees to the pension scheme of company B's new parent. Following the section 75 payment, a surplus of £4m arises on company B's share of the scheme. For the purposes of the bulk transfer of company B's share of the scheme, it is agreed that the value of the surplus to be transferred into the new parent's pension scheme will be £3m. It is decided that any surplus remaining after the bulk transfer will be allocated to company A.

In company B's individual financial statements, the section 75 payment of £9m (in respect of a recognised deficit of £5m measured on an FRS 17 basis) initially results in a surplus of £4m. Of this, £3m is transferred to a new pension scheme and remains on company B's balance sheet as an asset. The remaining £1m represents a settlement loss as company B has ceased to participate in the group A pension scheme and company B's liability in respect of that pension scheme has been extinguished.

In company A's consolidated financial statements, a settlement loss of £3m is recognised in respect of the bulk transfer to the new pension scheme (as part of the calculation of profit or loss on disposal of company B), leaving a surplus of £1m in the group A pension scheme.

Furthermore, as defined benefit accounting is applied at an entity level, the remaining surplus of £1m is recognised in company A's individual financial statements if it meets the criteria in paragraphs 37 to 42 of FRS 17 (see example 1). If the surplus is recognised, it will be included as part of the calculation of profit or loss on disposal of company B.

The table below summarises the position in respect of company B's employees:

	Company B (subsidiary) £'m	Company A (parent) £'m	Group £'m
Company B's deficit as at date of disposal	(5)	-	(5)
Section 75 payment *	9	-	9
	4	-	4
Bulk transfer to new scheme (settlement loss)	-	-	(3)
Group transfer:			
Settlement loss in company B	(1)	-	-
Credit (included in profit or loss on disposal of company B) in company A	-	1	-
Surplus arising after section 75 payment to group A scheme **	-	1	1
Surplus in new scheme	3	-	-

* The section 75 payment initially increases scheme assets recognised in both company B and in the group's consolidated financial statements (prior to the bulk transfer).

** In this example, any surplus remaining after the bulk transfer has been allocated to company A.

Example 5 – section 75 payment made by withdrawing employer's parent (+ bulk transfer out)

The facts are as for example 1 in paragraph 11.199, but company A agrees to make the £9m section 75 payment (and it is not repayable by company B). In addition, a bulk transfer is made of the assets and liabilities relating to company B's employees to the pension scheme of company B's new parent. Following the section 75 payment, a surplus of £4m arises on company B's share of the scheme. For the purposes of the bulk transfer of company B's share of the scheme, it is agreed that the value of the surplus to be transferred into the new parent's pension scheme will be £3m. It is decided that any surplus remaining after the bulk transfer will be allocated to company A.

In company B's individual financial statements, a total settlement gain of £8m arises. Company B did not make payments in respect of the section 75 debt, but has ceased to participate in the group A pension scheme and company B's liability in respect of that pension scheme has been extinguished. The gain of £8m comprises £5m in respect of the release of company B's share of the deficit (measured on an FRS 17 basis) and £3m in respect of the surplus (funded by company A) transferred to a new pension scheme (assuming that this is recognised on company B's balance sheet as an asset).

In company A's consolidated financial statements, a settlement loss of £3m is recognised in respect of the bulk transfer to the new pension scheme (as part of the calculation of profit or loss on disposal of company B), leaving a surplus of £1m in the group A pension scheme.

Similar to example 3 in paragraph 11.204, in company A's individual financial statements, the payment of £9m into the scheme is treated as a contribution to the pension scheme. However, as £8m of this contribution has been transferred out of the scheme as a result of the bulk transfer, it represents a loss in company A's books and it will be included in the profit or loss on disposal of company B reported in company A's profit and loss account. The remaining surplus of £1m is recognised in company A's balance sheet if it meets the criteria in paragraphs 37 to 42 of FRS 17 (see example 1).

The table below summarises the position in respect of company B's employees:

	Company B £'m	Company A £'m	Group £'m
Company B's deficit as at date of disposal	(5)	-	(5)
Section 75 payment *	-	9	9
			4
Bulk transfer to new scheme:			
Settlement gain/(loss)	8	-	(3)
Loss (included in profit or loss on disposal of company B) in company A	-	(8)	-
Surplus arising after section 75 payment to group A scheme **	-	1	1
Surplus in new scheme	3	-	-

* The section 75 payment initially increases scheme assets recognised in both company A and in the group's consolidated financial statements (prior to the bulk transfer).

** The surplus remaining after the bulk transfer is recognised in company A (if it meets the criteria in FRS 17) as this company made the section 75 payment.

11.206 As discussed in paragraph 11.203, the situation will be more complicated where the settlement and/or the bulk transfer straddle the balance sheet date.

Chapter 12

Share-based payment

	Page
National insurance contributions on share options gains	12001
Background	12001
Reimbursement or transfer of the liability	12002
Disclosure	12004
Employee share ownership plans (ESOPs)	12004
Background	12004
Accounting for ESOP trusts	12006
Legal considerations	12009
Impact on distributable profits	12009
Additional considerations for public companies	12011
Illustrative examples	12013
Gains made by ESOPs	12014
Trustee company	12014
Disclosures in respect of ESOP trusts	12015
QUESTs and share symmetry arrangements	12015
Simultaneous funding by the parent company	12017
Simultaneous funding by a subsidiary company	12018
Pre-funding by the parent company	12019
Pre-funding by a subsidiary company	12020
Cash payments to employee trusts	12020
Illustrative examples	12023
Transitional provisions	12024
Grants to which FRS 20 does not apply	12028
Annex	12030

Chapter 12

Share-based payment

National insurance contributions on share options gains

Background

12.1 UK employers are required to pay National Insurance Contributions (NIC) on the exercise of certain share options granted after 5 April 1999. The NIC charge applies to share options issued under unapproved share schemes (that is, those not approved by the Inland Revenue) where the shares are 'readily convertible assets', that is, they can be sold on a stock exchange or there are arrangements in place that allow the employees to obtain cash for the shares acquired under the option scheme.

12.2 The charge is based on the intrinsic value of the options at the date of exercise (intrinsic value is the excess of the market price of the shares over the exercise price). Previously, NIC was payable on the grant of an option not its exercise. The change in basis raised the question as to how to account for the NIC obligation between the date of grant and the date of exercise. This matter was addressed by the UITF in 2000 when it issued UITF Abstract 25. In this abstract, the UITF considered whether NIC on share option gains meet the recognition criteria under FRS 12 and also the basis for calculating the estimated liability in advance of the exercise date. FRS 12 requires a provision to be recognised when:

- An entity has a present obligation (legal or constructive) as a result of a past event.
- It is probable that a transfer of economic benefits will be required to settle the obligation.
- A reliable estimate can be made of the amount of the obligation.

[FRS 12 para 14].

12.3 The UITF regards the granting of the option as the past event that gives rise to a present obligation to pay NIC at some point in the future (that is, when the option is exercised). [UITF 25 para 4]. The amount of the obligation is uncertain as it depends on future share prices, but FRS 12 requires that the amount recognised as a provision should be the best estimate of the present obligation at the balance sheet date. [FRS 12 para 36]. The market price of the shares at the balance sheet date provides a reliable basis for estimating the provision. [UITF 25 para 4].

12.4 The UITF concluded that provision should be made for NIC on outstanding share options that are expected to be exercised. [UITF 25 para 10].

Therefore, in assessing the potential charge, it is necessary in the case of performance related options to estimate the degree to which the performance conditions are likely to be met in the future.

12.5 The provision should be calculated by applying the latest enacted national insurance rate to the difference between the market value of the underlying shares at the balance sheet date and the option exercise price. The provision should be allocated over the period from the date of grant to the end of the performance period. This is illustrated in the example in paragraph 12.59 below. Where there is no performance period full provision should be made immediately. [UITF 25 para 10].

12.6 The performance period is the period during which the employee performs the services necessary to become unconditionally entitled to the options. [UITF 25 para 6]. This might involve satisfying performance criteria or service conditions and so in this respect, the term 'performance period' in UITF Abstract 25 is consistent with the term 'vesting period' in FRS 20.

12.7 From the end of the performance period to the date of actual exercise the provision should be adjusted by reference to the current market value of the shares. [UITF 25 para 10].

12.8 As noted in paragraph 12.3, the abstract requires the NIC provision to be determined on the basis of the period end share price. However, it is first necessary to determine the number of options expected to be exercised and, in order to do this, it might be necessary to take account of post balance sheet events. This is because FRS 12 requires that where the amount of a liability will be affected by future events, those events should be taken into account in estimating a provision if there is sufficient objective evidence that they will occur. In some cases the estimation necessarily involves a degree of hindsight.

12.9 For example, if a fall in share prices meant that it was clear that options would not be exercised and no NIC would be payable, a provision would not be made. This would be the case if the fall was so large that the options were 'out of the money' (that is, the exercise price is higher than market price) and the exercise period had expired prior to approval of the financial statements.

[The next paragraph is 12.36.]

Reimbursement or transfer of the liability

12.36 Since 2000, it has been permissible for employers and employees to agree that the employee can pay the employer's NIC on share options. The employee can bear the employer's NIC charge arising on share option gains in one of two ways:

- First, the employer and the employee can make an agreement that some or all of the employer's NIC liability can be recovered from the employee.

- Secondly, the employer and the employee may make a joint election to legally transfer the liability for the secondary NIC to the employee.

The agreements are only valid if made on or after 19 May 2000, but are not valid for gains made prior to 28 July 2000.

12.37 Where there is an agreement between the employer and employee under which the employee agrees to reimburse all or part of the employer's NIC, FRS 12 requires a provision for the full amount to be made and the expected reimbursement to be treated as a separate asset if receipt is virtually certain, with a net presentation permitted in the profit and loss account. [FRS 12 para 56-61].

12.38 Where there is a joint election by employer and employee under which the liability is formally transferred to the employee no liability appears in the employer's financial statements.

12.39 The following example illustrates the application of the requirements of UITF Abstract 25.

Example

The company's year end is 31 December. 20,000 share options are granted at 1 July 20X0, when the market value is £1, at an exercise price of £1, dependent upon performance from 1 July 20X0 to 30 June 20X2. The options are exercisable from 1 July 20X2 to 1 July 20X3.

Employer's national insurance contributions, currently at 12.8%, are payable on exercise of the options.

31 December 20X0
The market value of a share is £2.10. It is estimated that the maximum entitlement of options will be exercised.

National Insurance charge for the year: One-quarter of 12.8% of 20,000 × (£2.10 – £1) = £704.

31 December 20X1
The market value of a share is £2.75. It is expected that 18,000 share options will be exercised.

National Insurance cumulative charge: Three-quarters of 12.8% of 18,000 × (£2.75 – £1) = £3,024.
Charge for the year: £3,024 – £704 = £2,320.

31 December 20X2
The market value of a share is £2.50. Only 15,000 share options vested; none of these have been exercised.

National Insurance cumulative charge: 12.8% × 15,000 × (£2.50 – £1) = £2,880.
Credit for the year: £3,024 – £2,880 = £144.

31 December 20X3
The 15,000 share options were exercised in May 20X3 when the market value of a share was £2.60.

The National Insurance liability was, therefore: 12.8% × 15,000 × (£2.60 – £1) = £3,072.
Charge for the year: £3,072 – £2,880 = £192.

Disclosure

12.40 FRS 12 requires, for each class of provision, disclosure of an indication of the uncertainties about the amount or timing of the eventual transfer of economic benefits and, where necessary to provide adequate information, the major assumptions made concerning future events. [FRS 12 para 90]. In the case of a provision for national insurance on share options, disclosure of the share price and of the effect of a significant movement in that price may be necessary to provide a full understanding of these factors. [UITF 25 para 7].

12.41 An example of a company that has provided for NIC on share options and disclosed the unprovided amount based on year end share prices is Baltimore Technologies plc, in Table 12.1 below.

Table 12.1 — Provision for NIC on share options
Baltimore Technologies plc — Annual Report — 31 December 1999

Notes to the consolidated financial statements (extract)

23 CONTINGENT LIABILITIES (extract)

Share options granted subsequent to 5 April 1999 under unapproved schemes are subject to employers' and employees' national insurance on the gain made on exercise of such options by UK employees.

An accrual of £426,000 has been made at 31 December 1999 based on the year end share price of £51.25 and the elapsed portion of the relevant vesting periods.

Based on the year-end share price there is a further contingent liability of approximately £4.4 million arising by the end of the vesting period that has not been provided for in these Financial Statements.

Employee share ownership plans (ESOPs)

Background

12.42 Employee share ownership plans (ESOPs) are usually designed to enable employees to purchase shares in their employing company. The structures of ESOPs vary, but typically they are arrangements whereby a trust is set up by a sponsoring company to acquire shares in that company for the benefit of its employees, who generally acquire them at a later stage through share option schemes, profit sharing arrangements or other share incentive schemes. The commercial reasons for establishing an ESOP include the following:

- It allows a share scheme to be extended to new participants without diluting existing shareholders' interests, because it can operate by acquiring and distributing shares that are already in issue rather than by requiring new shares to be issued.
- It can provide a private company with a market in its shares in order to operate an employee share scheme, by buying shares from departing employees and other shareholders, warehousing them and then distributing them to new and continuing employees.
- It can facilitate employee participation in connection with a management buyout, privatisation or flotation of a private company.
- In cash flow terms, a company can hedge its obligations in respect of options issued under share option schemes by avoiding exposure to increases in the market value of shares between the dates of granting the options and the dates of exercising those options.

ESOPs have to comply with a number of regulations including those of the Companies Act, the Financial Services and Markets Act and, where the company is listed, the Listing Rules.

12.43 The vehicle used to hold the shares in an ESOP is a discretionary employee benefit trust set up by the sponsoring company for the benefit of all, or most, of its employees. For capital gains tax purposes, the trustee will normally be resident outside the UK and a subsidiary of the sponsoring company will often act as a corporate trustee. The trust buys shares with funds provided by way of cash or loans from the sponsoring company or by a loan from a third party (which will be guaranteed by the company). The shares held by the trust are typically distributed to employees through an employee share scheme. The trust's beneficiaries can only include the company's or group's employees or former employees and certain of their close relations. Generally the sponsoring company will have no beneficial interest in the trust's residual assets.

12.44 The detailed structures of individual ESOP trusts are many and varied. However, the main features are often as follows:

- The trust provides a warehouse for the sponsoring company's shares, for example, by acquiring and holding shares that are to be sold or transferred to employees in the future. The trust will normally purchase the shares with finance provided by the sponsoring company (by way of cash contributions or loans), or by a third party bank loan, or by a combination of the two. Loans from the company are usually interest free.
- Where the trust borrows from a third party, the sponsoring company will often guarantee the loan, that is, it will be responsible for any shortfall if the trust's assets are insufficient to meet its debt repayment obligations. The

company will also generally make regular contributions to the trust to enable the trust to meet its interest payments (to make good the shortfall between the dividend income of the trust and the interest payable). As part of this arrangement, the trustees sometimes waive their right to dividends on the shares the trust holds.

- Shares held by the trust are distributed to employees through an employee share scheme. There are many different arrangements, which include: the purchase of shares by employees when exercising their share options under an executive share option scheme; the purchase of shares by the trustees of an approved profit sharing scheme for allocation to employees under the scheme's rules; or the transfer of shares to employees under an incentive scheme.

12.45 An example of the structure of an ESOP trust is given in Table 12.2.

Table 12.2 – SmithKline Beecham plc – Annual Report – 31 December 1994

NOTES TO THE FINANCIAL STATEMENTS (extract)

33 SHARE OPTION PLANS (extract)

Employee Share Ownership Trust. An Employee Share Ownership Trust (ESOT) was established on 9 March 1992. The ESOT has purchased the Company's A Shares in the open market, which are held on trust for employees participating in the 1991 share option plan. The ESOT has purchased 15.7 million A Shares at a cost of £86 million. The ESOT has borrowed £83 million from third party banks which is guaranteed by the Company and the Company has also lent £3 million to the ESOT. The Company gifts payments to the ESOT to pay the interest on the loans. These payments to third parties amounted to £4.7 million (1993 £1.5 million) and the Company also incurred further interest charges of £3.4 million in 1993. The ESOT has waived its rights to dividends. The external borrowings of the ESOT are now included on the balance sheet (see accounting policies page 48).

Accounting for ESOP trusts

12.46 FRS 20 does not deal with the accounting where an entity's shares are held by an ESOP trust. However, the UITF has considered ESOPs and related matters on a number of occasions. The current guidance is contained in UITF Abstract 38, 'Accounting for ESOP trusts'. This abstract draws on the principles of FRS 5, 'Reporting the substance of transactions', when it concludes that an entity should account for an ESOP trust that it sponsors in accordance with its substance and not merely its legal form. Vehicles other than an ESOP trust established to hold shares for employee remuneration purposes acting in a similar way to an ESOP may also be caught by UITF Abstract 38.

12.47 Although the trustees of an ESOP trust must act under the trust deed at all times in accordance with the beneficiaries' interests, most ESOP trusts (particularly those set up to remunerate employees) are specifically designed to serve the sponsoring entity's purposes and to ensure that there will be minimal risk of any conflict arising between the trustees' duties and the entity's interest. In substance, the sponsoring entity has *de facto* control of the ESOP trust and reaps the benefits or bears the risks associated with its assets and liabilities. For example:

- Where the ESOP trust has unallocated shares, the benefit of increases in value will accrue to the sponsoring entity because, for example, it can pass increased benefits to its employees without using its other resources. Conversely, if the shares fall in value, the sponsoring entity may have to use its other resources to make good the benefits promised to its employees.
- If the shares are under option, the employees' asset is the options rather than the shares themselves and the risks associated with any fall in value below the option price remains with the sponsoring entity.
- When shares are conditionally gifted to the employees, the sponsoring entity retains an interest in the shares, because the benefits and risks associated with them remain with the sponsoring entity until the conditions are fulfilled.
- In many ESOP trusts, dividends on the shares held by the trust are waived until they vest with employees. In other trusts dividends continue to be paid and these will accrue to the trust thereby benefiting the sponsoring entity by either defraying the trust's costs or by reducing the cost of future employee incentive arrangements, which are ultimately borne by the sponsoring entity.

12.48 Where this type of arrangement exists, the UITF considers that the sponsoring company has *de facto* control of the ESOP and, as a consequence, certain of the ESOP's assets and liabilities should be brought back onto the sponsoring company's balance sheet to accord with the transaction's substance. This is on the basis that, for all practical purposes, the sponsoring company is in the same position as if it had purchased the shares directly and, therefore, should account for them in a similar way.

12.49 The consensus reached in UITF Abstract 38 is that FRS 5's principles require an ESOP trust's sponsoring company to recognise the trust's assets and liabilities as its own where the sponsoring company has *de facto* control of the assets and liabilities of the ESOP trust and reaps their benefits or bears their risks. This will generally be the case where the trust is established to hold shares for an employee remuneration scheme. Where this type of trust exists, the shares held by the ESOP trust should be treated in a similar way to that if the sponsoring company had acquired the shares itself. FRS 25 (IAS 32), 'Financial instruments: disclosure and presentation' requires an entity to deduct the consideration paid in acquiring its own shares in arriving at shareholders' funds. [FRS 25 para 33]. Consistent with this, UITF Abstract 38 requires that, until such time as the share held by an ESOP trust vest unconditionally in employees, the consideration paid for those shares should be deducted in arriving at the sponsoring company's shareholders' funds. Other assets and liabilities of the ESOP trust should be recognised as assets and liabilities of the sponsoring company. [UITF 38 paras 10(a),(b)].

12.50 The treatment of own shares described in the previous paragraph appears to contradict the requirements of the balance sheet formats set out in Schedule 4 to the Companies Act 1985. These formats include sub-headings for 'own shares' in both fixed and current assets, which suggests that investments in own shares are to be presented as assets. This is unfortunate, as there are other requirements in both UK and international standards for own shares to be deducted in arriving at shareholders' funds. For example, paragraph 33 of FRS 25 requires that where shares are repurchased or redeemed, equity should be reduced by the value of the consideration given. The approach in UITF Abstract 38 is consistent with this other guidance, but it is hard to ignore the requirements of the formats. Any amount described on the face of the balance sheet as investment in own shares would need to be presented in accordance with those requirements. Accordingly, in our view, the amount deducted in arriving at shareholders' funds should not be presented separately on the face of the balance sheet, but should be deducted from reserves, usually the profit and loss reserve.

12.51 Consistent with the principle that an entity's purchase of its own shares is a transaction with owners in their capacity as such, no gain or loss should arise. Accordingly, UITF Abstract 38 requires that no gain or loss should be recognised in either the profit and loss account or statement of total recognised gains and losses on the purchase, sale, issue or cancellation of a company's own shares. Instead, consideration paid or received should be presented as separate amounts in the reconciliation of movements in shareholders' funds. [UITF 38 paras 10(c),(d)]. This means that the following items will not be recognised in either of the performance statements:

- Charges or credits reflecting the difference between the cost of the shares acquired by the ESOP trust and the amounts to be received from employees on the exercise of options.
- Provisions for permanent or temporary diminution in the value of the shares.

12.52 Finance costs and administrative expenses should be charged as they become due and not as funding payments are made to the ESOP trust. [UITF 38 para 10(e)]. Interest costs incurred on external funding should be shown as interest paid in the company's financial statements and not as staff costs.

12.53 Any dividend income arising on own shares held by the ESOP trust should be excluded in arriving at profit before tax and deducted from the aggregate of dividends paid and proposed. The deduction should be disclosed if material. Under FRS 22, 'Earnings per share', the shares are treated as if they were cancelled when calculating earnings per share. [UITF 38 para 10(f)]. (The calculation of earnings per share is considered in detail in chapter 14.)

12.54 It must be remembered that the above principles relate to the accounting for shares (and other assets and liabilities) held by an ESOP trust. They have no impact on the recognition or measurement of the expense in respect of a share-based payment arrangement, which is dealt with in accordance with FRS 20.

Legal considerations

12.55 UITF Abstract 38 is based on the principles in FRS 5 and makes it clear that this is not intended to affect the legal characterisation of a transaction, or to change the situation at law achieved by the parties to it. Thus, shares acquired by an ESOP trust and deducted in arriving at shareholders' funds are not treasury shares as defined by section 162A(3) of the Companies Act 1985 (as amended by The Companies (Acquisition of Own Shares) (Treasury Shares) Regulations 2003) (section 724(5) of the Companies Act 2006). Neither does the accounting treatment imply that the shares have been purchased by the company as a matter of law nor that they are required to be cancelled, which would be the consequence of such a purchase except for treasury shares (under sections 162(2) and 160(4) of the Companies Act 1985 (sections 706 and 688 of the Companies Act 2006)).

Impact on distributable profits

12.56 The issue of the impact of the accounting required by UITF 38 on a company's profits available for distribution is addressed in Tech 64/04, 'Guidance on the effect on realised and distributable profits of accounting for employee share schemes in accordance with UITF Abstract 38 and revised UITF Abstract 17', issued by the ICAEW in December 2004. The guidance confirmed, for public companies (where the top plc company is the sponsoring company), deduction of the shares held in an ESOP trust in arriving at shareholders' funds will restrict profits available for distribution by the amount of consideration paid for those shares. Therefore, we consider that own shares held through an ESOP trust should be deducted from the profit and loss reserve, thereby reflecting the reduced profits available for distribution.

12.57 Section 270 of the Companies Act 1985 (section 836 of the Companies Act 2006) requires that a company's 'relevant accounts' for the purposes of determining profits available for distribution are properly prepared under the Act. This means, for a company applying UK GAAP, that they comply with UK accounting standards and UITF Abstracts, so it follows that the financial statements of the combined sponsoring entity and ESOP trust are the relevant accounts for the purposes of determining profits available for distribution. Therefore, transactions entered into by an ESOP trust should be considered in the same way as if they had actually been entered into by the sponsoring entity itself.

12.58 UITF Abstract 38, states that, *"the acquisition of shares by an ESOP does not, of itself, affect the company's realised profits or realised losses. The accounting treatment required by this Abstract, which requires a deduction in arriving at shareholders' funds and that no gain or loss should be recognised in the profit and loss account, is consistent with this analysis"*. [UITF 38 Legal considerations]. This means that the acquisition of shares by an ESOP trust does not give rise to an immediate realised loss. However, if the shares are subsequently to be transferred to employees for less than their purchase price, the difference between the purchase price and the consideration to be received from the employees, if any, will be treated as a realised loss, recognised over the vesting period.

12.59 Similar principles were applied to goodwill written off against reserves prior to the introduction of FRS 10, 'Goodwill and intangible assets'. Appendix V to FRS 10 states that where goodwill is written off on acquisition as a matter of accounting policy, rather than because of an actual diminution in value, this does not represent a realised loss. However, goodwill should be treated as reducing distributable profits over its useful economic life so as to achieve the same result as if the goodwill had been amortised through the profit and loss account.

12.60 Sometimes an ESOP trust may hold shares that are not allocated to a specific share scheme. Although under UITF 38 own shares held by an ESOP trust are not treated as assets, it will be necessary to apply the same principles to determine whether any notional diminution should be taken into account in determining distributable profits.

12.61 FRS 11, 'Impairment of fixed assets and goodwill', applies to investments in subsidiaries, associates and joint ventures, but investments in own shares are outside the scope of that standard. Nevertheless, the principles of FRS 11 (including the impairment indicators) and its methodology for determining impairment may be useful and relevant in measuring any diminution in value of shares held by an ESOP trust. Impairment of assets is considered further in chapter 18.

12.62 Where an ESOP trust has disposed of surplus shares, this may give rise to a profit to be recognised in the trust's own accounts. This profit will not be recognised in the profit and loss account of the sponsoring entity. Instead, the proceeds from sale will be credited directly to equity. Nevertheless, in the accounts of both the trust and the sponsoring entity there will be a net credit in equity, so it must be determined whether this credit is distributable by the sponsoring entity. Tech 64/04 concludes that, where the consideration received by an ESOP trust for the sale of shares is in the form of cash or other qualifying consideration, as defined in Tech 7/03 (see chapter 23), the resultant profit will be a realised profit from the perspective of the sponsoring entity. However, before making a distribution of such profits, the directors should have regard to their fiduciary duties, for example to ensure that the company is in a position to settle its debts as and when they fall due. Accordingly, Tech 64/04 suggests that it may not be prudent to distribute an amount represented by assets retained by an ESOP trust that are not available for the general purposes of the sponsoring entity. This reflects the fact the ESOP trusts are generally established to be for the benefit of the sponsoring entity's employees. However, if, in the future, the cash representing the gain is used to defray an expense of the sponsoring entity for which the trust is permitted to use its assets, an equivalent amount of the gain should at that time be treated as distributable.

12.63 Tech 64/04 also deals with the impact on distributable profits of any expenses recognised in accordance with FRS 20. All expenses and losses should be regarded as realised losses, except to the extent that the law or accounting standards provide otherwise. However, it is arguable that an expense recognised in respect of an equity-settled share-based payment transaction is not a loss at all because it does not result in a reduction in recorded net assets. Nevertheless, even if the expense is regarded as a realised loss, Tech 7/03 makes it clear in other contexts (such as revaluation reserves) that an unrealised reserve will be treated as having become realised by the amortisation or writing down of the related asset. Therefore, assuming that the expense has been included in the profit and loss account rather than capitalised as part of the cost of an asset, the credit entry to equity will be treated as a realised profit so there will be no impact on distributable reserves.

Additional considerations for public companies

12.64 Public companies face additional restrictions on their ability to make distributions. Section 264 of the Companies Act 1985 (section 831 of the Companies Act 2006) requires that a public company may only make a distribution if:

- at that time, the amount of its net assets is not less than the aggregate of its called-up share capital and undistributable reserves; and
- the distribution does not reduce the amount of those assets to less than that aggregate.

[CA85 Sec 264; CA06 Sec 831].

12.65 When a public company acquires its own shares through an ESOP trust, this will have the effect of reducing net assets. However, there will be no corresponding impact on undistributable reserves. This is because the deduction from equity in respect of an acquisition of shares by an ESOP trust is not, as a matter of law, a loss (see from para 12.58). Since the deduction is not a loss at all, it follows that it is neither a realised nor an unrealised loss. Accordingly, the deduction from equity for ESOP shares has no immediate effect on the balance of undistributable reserves. Hence, with net assets reduced, but share capital and undistributable reserves unaffected, the purchase of ESOP shares immediately restricts distributable profits under section 264 of the Companies Act 1985 (CA06 Sec 831).

12.66 When the employees finally acquire their shares, the receipt of proceeds will increase net assets without a corresponding increase in share capital and undistributable reserves. Hence, distributable profits will be restored to the extent of those proceeds.

12.67 Where there is a new issue of shares to an ESOP trust, there will be no change in net assets, but there will be an increase in called-up share capital (and an increase in undistributable reserves if the shares are issued at a premium). Hence, the amount of a listed company's distributable profits will be restricted by the proceeds of the share issue. This means that, regardless of whether an ESOP trust acquires its shares in the market or through a new issue, the amount paid for the shares will immediately restrict distributable profits.

12.68 The financial assistance rules may also cause problems for public companies. Section 154(1) of the Companies Act 1985 (section 682 of the Companies Act 2006) provides that a public company may only give financial assistance for the acquisition of its own shares if the net assets of the company are not thereby reduced or, to the extent that net assets are reduced, the company has sufficient distributable profits to cover the full amount of the assistance. For this purpose, net assets are defined as: the amount by which the aggregate of the company's assets exceeds the aggregate of its liabilities (taking the amount of both assets and liabilities *"to be as stated in the company's accounting records immediately before the financial assistance is given)"*. [CA85 Sec 154(2)(a); CA06 Sec 682(4)(a)]. This is in contrast to section 264 of the Companies Act 1985 (CA06 Sec 831) where, by reason of section 270 of the Companies Act 1985 (CA06 Sec 836), net assets are determined by reference to the company's relevant accounts. Although subtle, this is an important distinction. As noted in paragraph 12.57 above, relevant accounts are the financial statements of the combined sponsoring company and ESOP trust. However, there is no requirement for the company's accounting records to reflect the adjustments that would be necessary for these financial statements to be prepared in accordance with the requirements of UITF Abstract 38. Thus, in the absence of any such requirement, the company's assets and liabilities should be given their natural meaning, namely the assets and liabilities of the company as a separate legal entity, excluding the ESOP trust. Accordingly, for the purposes of section 154 of the Companies Act 1985 (CA06 Sec 682), it is necessary to determine whether the manner in which a public company has funded an ESOP trust will reduce net assets. The assets of the trust itself and their treatment in the sponsoring company's financial statements have no relevance for a consideration of section 154 of the Companies Act 1985 (CA06 Sec 682). The following example illustrates this point.

Example

A public company sponsors an ESOP trust. The trust does not currently hold any shares in the sponsoring company, but needs to acquire 100,000 shares in order to satisfy the requirements of an employee share plan. In order to enable the trust to make the purchase, the sponsoring company could provide funding by way of a gift, a loan or a combination of both.

As explained above, for the purposes of section 154 of the Companies Act 1985 (CA06 Sec 682), the sponsoring company is considered in isolation (sometimes referred to as the 'narrow entity') and not in combination with the ESOP trust (the 'extended entity'). Hence, transactions between the company and the trust are considered in the same way as any other transactions involving the company and a third party. A gift to the trust is clearly an immediate realised loss (as it reduces the net assets of the narrow entity) and hence reduces the distributable profits of the sponsoring company. On the other hand a loan, provided it is considered recoverable (that is, sufficient cash is expected when employees exercise their rights to the shares), would not be a realised loss. However, any write down in the value of the loan (caused by a question over its recoverability) would be a realised loss.

12.69 Tech 64/04 makes it clear that where a company has reduced its distributable profits on the provision of financial assistance and shares have been acquired by an ESOP trust, section 264 of the Companies Act 1985 (CA06 Sec 831) does not require a further reduction in distributable profits equal to the amount of the reduction in net assets calculated under section 154 of the Companies Act 1985 (CA06 Sec 682). This is because section 154 and section 264 are directed to different objectives. Section 154 determines the legality of the provision of financial assistance from the perspective of the company in isolation, whereas section 264 considers the combined company and ESOP trust as presented in the relevant accounts. On the latter basis, the assistance provided to the ESOP trust will be ignored as the assets and liabilities of the company and the trust are aggregated. Distributable profits for the purposes of section 264 are not diminished until the shares are purchased, at which point the net assets are restricted by the consideration paid. (Throughout this paragraph, references to sections 264 and 154 of the Companies Act 1985 should be read also to refer to sections 831 and 682 of the Companies Act 2006 respectively.

Illustrative examples

12.70 The examples that follow illustrate UITF Abstract 38's principles and include the examples in appendix II to the abstract.

Example 1

The ESOP trust holds unallocated shares costing £100,000, funded by a bank loan. The sponsoring company undertakes to make contributions to the trust whenever the loan-to-value ratio falls below a set figure. At the reporting date the market value is at least £100,000.

The company deducts the consideration paid for the shares of £100,000 in arriving at shareholders' funds. The company also recognises a liability of £100,000 in respect of the bank loan. Interest expense is accrued in the usual way. The amount of the reduction in shareholders' funds (£100,000) and the market value of the shares held should be disclosed.

Example 2

The facts are the same as in example 1, except that the market value of the shares falls to £80,000 by the company's year end.

The fall in the market value of the shares does not give rise to a recognised loss. As in example 1, the amount of the reduction in shareholders' funds (£100,000) and the market value of the shares held should be disclosed.

Example 3

The facts are the same as in example 1, but options are granted over the shares at £80,000 when the market value is £100,000.

The company recognises an expense over the option vesting period in accordance with FRS 20. The reduction to shareholders' funds of £100,000 in respect of the consideration paid for the shares, and the market value of the shares, are disclosed until the shares vest unconditionally in employees. When the options are exercised, the receipt of £80,000 is credited to shareholders' funds.

Example 4

A company is a co-operative, owned by its employees. All of its shares are held in a trust for the employees' benefit collectively and the trust receives dividends from the company which are distributed to employees in accordance with the trust deed's provisions. The shares never vest in individual employees. The company does not have de facto control of the trust's shares.

The shares held by the trust are not in substance the company's own shares and are not accounted for as such.

Gains made by ESOPs

12.71 There are situations where ESOP trusts make gains, for instance on the sale of surplus shares (where previous awards have lapsed) or where the exercise price exceeds the cost of the shares. UITF Abstract 38 requires that no gain or loss should be recognised in the profit and loss account or statement of total recognised gains and losses on the purchase, sale, issue or cancellation of a company's own shares. [UITF 38 para 10(d)]. This means that the consideration received for the sale of own shares by an ESOP trust should be credited to shareholders' funds, but this raises the question as to whether a gain made by an ESOP trust is distributable by the sponsoring company. This is considered further in paragraph 12.62 above.

Trustee company

12.72 The above sections deal with the financial statements of the sponsoring company. In groups of companies, it is common for a non-trading subsidiary company to act as trustee to the ESOP. The accounting implications for the trustee company are considered in the example below.

Example

A group operates an employee share scheme. A subsidiary of the group has been set up to act as a corporate trustee. What should the subsidiary include in its own entity financial statements?

The corporate trustee for an ESOP trust normally holds legal title to the trust's assets, but if these are held on trust such that the trustee has no beneficial interest (that is, the trustee's interest is limited to its fiduciary or custodial interest) then under FRS 5 they are not its assets. Therefore, the trustee company itself does not account for the assets (and likewise, the liabilities and transactions) of the ESOP. These would be reported in the financial statements of the ESOP trust (and under UITF Abstract 38 in the financial statements of the sponsoring company and group).

The trustee company may well be a dormant company with a nominal share capital. Even if the trustee company is not dormant (for instance, if it charges the trust a fee for its services), this does not change the fact that its financial statements do not normally include the transactions and balances of the trust.

Disclosures in respect of ESOP trusts

12.73 UITF Abstract 38 requires the following information to be disclosed concerning the ESOP trust:

- A description of the ESOP trust's main features, including the arrangements for distributing shares to employees.
- The amounts of reductions to shareholders' funds and the number and (for companies that have shares listed or publicly traded on a stock exchange or market) market value of shares held by the ESOP trust that have not yet vested unconditionally in employees.
- The extent to which the shares are under option to employees or have been conditionally gifted to them.

[UITF 38 para 11].

12.74 The object of these disclosures is to enable the readers of the financial statements to understand the significance of the ESOP trust in the context of the sponsoring company. Where this is not achieved by disclosing the above information, the sponsoring company should give additional information to achieve this objective.

QUESTs and share symmetry arrangements

12.75 A QUEST (qualifying employee share ownership trust) is a trust that is often used to assume a company's obligation to deliver shares under an approved sharesave plan. Similar arrangements, often known as 'share symmetry arrangements' exist for other types of share schemes (such as unapproved or discretionary schemes).

12.76 Until 2003, the cost of shares issued cheaply to employees via a sharesave scheme did not normally attract tax relief for a company. However, under the Finance Act 1989, a company that used a QUEST could obtain a statutory tax deduction for the difference between the market value of shares issued by the company and the option price paid by the employees of the company (or another company that it controls). Alternative structures, such as share symmetry arrangements, generally relied on case law to obtain the company's tax deduction.

12.77 The Finance Act 2003 introduced a statutory tax deduction for most employee share schemes, thus reducing the attractiveness of QUESTs. Nevertheless, many companies do have such structures in place.

12.78 A QUEST may be either simultaneous or pre-funded. A simultaneous QUEST is one in which the company issues shares to the QUEST at the same time as the employees exercise their options. The QUEST immediately transfers the shares to employees to satisfy the exercised options. The company receives a tax deduction on the amount of the gift which tops up the option proceeds to the market value of the shares. The steps involved in a simultaneous quest are as follows:

- UK company establishes the QUEST in accordance with the requirements of Finance Act 1989.
- The trustees of the QUEST agree to take over UK company's liability to deliver shares under its existing sharesave options.
- UK company grants a back-to-back option to the trustees of the QUEST to subscribe for the same number of shares, but with the exercise price being the market value at the date of exercise of the sharesave options.

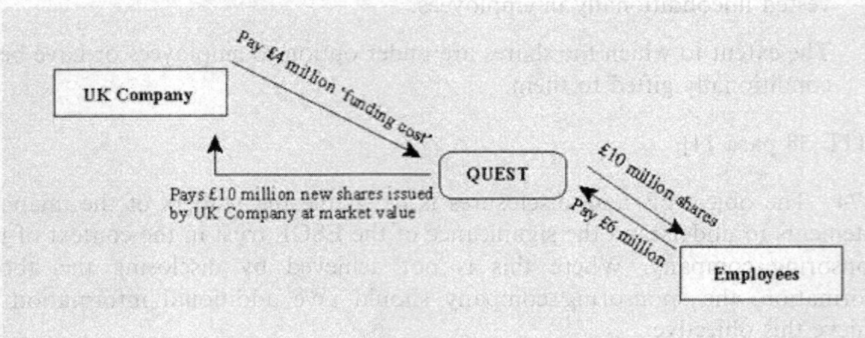

- When the employees exercise their options, they pay the exercise price to the QUEST rather than to UK company.
- UK company contributes the balance required to enable the QUEST to subscribe for newly issued shares at market value (the 'funding cost').
- The QUEST uses the aggregate sums to subscribe for shares at market value (that is, by exercising the back-to-back option) and immediately transfers those shares to employees.
- UK company claims a statutory tax deduction for the funding cost.

12.79 The company should obtain a legal opinion as to whether the scheme constitutes financial assistance as this can be an issue for some arrangements. This legal opinion should include advice as to whether the scheme does not entail giving financial assistance, for instance, because it qualifies for exemption under section 153(4)(b) or (bb) of the Companies Act 1985 (section 682(2)(b) or (c) of the Companies Act 2006), as an 'employee share scheme' (as defined in section 743 of the Companies Act 1985 (section 1166 of the Companies Act 2006)).

12.80 In a pre-funded QUEST, the company provides finance to the QUEST by means of a loan to the value of the subscription monies receivable from employees when they exercise their options together with a contribution to the QUEST equal to the difference between the market price at the time of the funding and the exercise price of all outstanding sharesave options.

12.81 The QUEST would then subscribe for the shares within nine months subsequent to the year end (being the maximum period in which the QUEST must acquire the shares to allow the company to claim the tax deduction for that year).

12.82 Although this structure would result in an earlier tax cash flow advantage for the company, it may result in earlier and potentially greater share capital dilution than would have occurred in the absence of the QUEST.

12.83 Some companies use an alternative to the full pre-funding described above, where the amount of pre-funding is restricted to the difference between the market price at date of issue and the option exercise price. The QUEST then uses this funding to subscribe for shares at market price. The remaining shares are subscribed for at a later date using the proceeds from employees when the options are exercised.

12.84 The paragraphs that follow describe the accounting for the various types of QUEST. It must be remembered that these principles have no impact on the recognition or measurement of the expense in respect of a share-based payment arrangement, which is dealt with in accordance with FRS 20.

Simultaneous funding by the parent company

12.85 When employees exercise their share options, the company makes a gift to the QUEST of an amount equal to the difference between the market value of the shares at the date of exercise and the amount receivable from the employees. The company then issues shares to the QUEST at market value at date of issue. Under UITF Abstract 38 principles, the company is regarded as the sponsoring company of the QUEST, that is, the QUEST is regarded as part of the company.

12.86 At the date the options are exercised, the company will account for the issue of shares at the amount subscribed by the QUEST, which will be their market price at that date. The company will credit share capital with the nominal value of the shares issued and credit share premium with the difference between the market value and the nominal value of the shares.

12.87 Although the transactions are initially recorded in the individual legal entity (that is, company and QUEST) books they are combined for the purpose of statutory reporting. As the QUEST is regarded as part of the company, there is no profit and loss account charge as a cost has not been incurred (that is, the gift made by the company and the gift received by the QUEST are eliminated). In accordance with the principles of UITF Abstract 38, the consideration paid for the issue of the shares is deducted in arriving at shareholders' funds, namely the profit and loss reserve, while the consideration received on the exercise of the options should be credited to shareholders' funds. The net impact of these entries is that the part of the subscription price funded by the company is charged to profit and loss account reserve in the company's statutory accounts – in substance a capitalisation issue by the company reducing its distributable profits.

12.88 Consider the following example.

Example – simultaneous QUEST funded by the company that issues shares

Number of shares under option	1,000,000
Nominal value of shares	10p
Market price of shares at date of grant	£6
Option exercise price	£6
Market price of shares at date of exercise	£10

Taxation is ignored for the purpose of this illustration.

- Employees exercise options and pay £6m to QUEST (£6 × 1m shares).
- The company pays £4m to the QUEST ((£10 – £6) × 1m shares).
- The QUEST subscribes for 1,000,000 newly issued shares in the company at the market price of £10.

The company will record share capital of £100,000 (1m shares × 10p) and share premium of £9.9m (1,000,000 shares × proceeds of £10 = £10m less nominal value of £0.1m).

The £10m consideration paid by the QUEST is deducted from equity and the £6m received from employees is credited to equity.

The overall effect is that the company's net assets are increased by the £6m cash received from employees. The effect on the company's balance sheet can be summarised as:

	£m
Net assets	
Cash	**6.0**
Capital and reserves	
Share capital	0.1
Share premium	9.9
Profit and loss account reserve	(4.0)
	6.0

If the company is the parent of a group then the treatment in the consolidated financial statements is the same as the treatment in the parent company's own financial statements.

Simultaneous funding by a subsidiary company

12.89 The above analysis deals with the situation where an individual company (or parent of a group) operates a QUEST. There are further complications in a group situation, for instance, if the payments are made by a subsidiary company.

If a subsidiary company makes a payment to the QUEST for the difference between the issue price and the option price, it will be recognised as a deduction from the subsidiary's equity.

Pre-funding by the parent company

12.90 The accounting for a pre-funded QUEST follows the same principles as a simultaneous QUEST. That is, the amount paid by the QUEST on the issue of shares is deducted in arriving at the sponsoring company's shareholders' funds, while the amount received from employees on the exercise of options is credited to shareholders' funds.

12.91 An example where a QUEST is pre-funded by the company that issues the shares is considered below.

Example – QUEST fully pre-funded by company that issues the shares

Number of shares under option	1,000,000
Nominal value of shares	10p
Market price of shares at date of grant	£6
Option exercise price	£6
Market price of shares at date of issue	£10

Taxation is ignored for the purpose of this illustration.

- The company pays £10m to the QUEST comprising a loan of £6m and a gift of £4m ((£10 – £6) × 1m shares).
- The QUEST subscribes for 1,000,000 newly issued shares in the company at the market price of £10 (1m shares).
- The company will record share capital of £100,000 (1m shares × 10p) and share premium of £9.9m (1m shares × proceeds of £10 = £10m less nominal value of £0.1m).

As in the previous example, the QUEST is included in the company's financial statements and the loan from the company to the QUEST eliminates as it is intra-entity. The amount paid by the QUEST for the purchase of the shares is deducted from the sponsoring company's equity.

	Company (incorporating the QUEST)
	£m
Net assets	
Loan	–
	–
Capital and reserves	
Share capital	0.1
Share premium	9.9
Profit and loss account reserve	(10.0)
	–

When the options are exercised, the employees will pay £6m to the QUEST and the shares will be transferred in consideration. The £6m cash will be used by the QUEST to repay the loan to the company. In the sponsoring company's financial statements, £6m will be credited to equity. The overall effect is that the company's net assets are increased by the £6m cash received from employees.

If the company is the parent of a group then the treatment in the consolidated financial statements is the same as the treatment in the parent company's own financial statements.

Pre-funding by a subsidiary company

12.92 The above sections deal with the situation where an individual company (or parent of a group) operates a QUEST. There are further complications in a group situation, for instance, if the payments are made by subsidiary companies. It will be necessary to determine which company is the sponsoring company of the QUEST. Normally, where the parent company sets up the QUEST and determines the arrangements then it will be regarded as the sponsoring company even if it requires its subsidiary companies to contribute funding in respect of their employees. However, there might be situations where it is considered appropriate for a subsidiary company to be regarded as the sponsoring company for the purpose of applying UITF Abstract 38 and determining which company should include the QUEST in its financial statements. This might be a situation where the QUEST is funded by a large trading subsidiary.

12.93 The treatment of payments by a subsidiary to a QUEST will depend on which company is the sponsoring company.

- Parent is the sponsoring company — where the parent is the sponsoring company, the treatment is similar to a simultaneous QUEST as described in paragraph 12.90.
- Subsidiary is the sponsoring company — the QUEST is included in the subsidiary's own financial statements. As the shares held by the QUEST are not the subsidiary's own shares (they are its parent's shares), they should be treated as investments. This will have no impact on the recognition or measurement of the expense in respect of the share-based payment transaction, which will be accounted for in accordance with FRS 20.

Cash payments to employee trusts

12.94 Difficulties arise in regard to intermediate payment arrangements where an entity makes a payment to a trust for the benefit of the entity's employees. The trust then uses the assets accumulated from those payments to pay the entity's employees for some or all of the services rendered by the employee.

12.95 The main issue concerns where cash is paid into an employee benefit trust prior to the year end and the question arises as to whether the payment should be treated as an expense. Similar problems arise where an employee benefit trust is formed around the end of a company's accounting year. An amount is transferred into that trust after the year end and the question arises as to whether it should be accrued as a liability and an expense in the financial statements of the previous year. These types of arrangements did not fall precisely within FRS 17, 'Retirement benefits', so to clarify the UITF issued Abstract 32, 'Employee benefit trusts and other intermediate payment arrangement', in December 2001. This abstract applies to all intermediate payment arrangements other than those dealt with in UITF Abstract 38 or FRS 17. The abstract considers the issue of payments not only to trusts, but to other intermediaries with similar features, for example:

- Although such arrangements are most commonly used to pay employees, they are sometimes used to compensate suppliers of goods and services other than employees. Sometimes the sponsoring entity's employees and other suppliers are not the only beneficiaries of the arrangement. Other beneficiaries may include past employees and their dependants and the intermediary may be entitled to make charitable donations.

- Usually, the precise identity of the persons or entities that will receive payments from the intermediary, and the amounts that they will receive, are not agreed at the outset.

- The relationship between the sponsoring entity and the intermediary may take different forms. For example, when the intermediary is constituted as a trust, the sponsoring entity will not have a right to direct the intermediary's activities. However, in these and other cases the sponsoring entity may give advice to the intermediary or may be relied on by the intermediary to provide the information it needs to carry out its activities. Sometimes, the way the intermediary has been set up gives it little discretion in the broad nature of its activities.

- Often, the sponsoring entity has the right to appoint or veto the appointment of the intermediary's trustees (or its directors or the equivalent).

- The payments made to the intermediary and the payments made by the intermediary are often cash payments, but may involve other transfers of value.

[UITF 32 para 3].

12.96 The abstract focuses on two issues:

- Whether the sponsoring entity's payments to the trust represent an immediate expense.

- If the payments do not represent an immediate expense, what the nature and extent of the sponsoring entity's assets and liabilities are after making the payments to the trust.

[UITF 32 para 4].

12.97 An immediate expense to the sponsoring entity will occur only if the payment neither results in the acquisition of another asset nor the settlement of a liability. As the settlement of a liability is a matter of fact, the abstract focuses on whether there is an acquisition of an asset. When determining whether an entity has an asset, FRS 5 requires that you should look beyond the transaction's structure and look at its substance. Based on this, the UITF has taken the view that when an entity transfers funds to a trust, there should be a rebuttable presumption that the sponsoring entity will obtain future economic benefit from the amounts transferred. The entity has control of the rights or other access to the future economic benefits of those amounts and hence has an asset. Consequently, the exchange of one asset for another does not lead to an immediate expense. [UITF 32 para 18].

12.98 In order to rebut the presumption, the abstract requires the sponsoring entity to demonstrate that either:

- the sponsoring entity will not obtain future economic benefit from the amounts transferred. For example, it may be that the only beneficiaries of the intermediary are registered charities or a benevolent fund that is in no way linked to amounts otherwise due from the entity; or

- the sponsoring entity does not have control of the rights or other access to the future economic benefits it is expected to receive. This will involve evidence that the payments made by the intermediary are not habitually made in a way that is in accordance with the sponsoring entity's wishes.

[UITF 32 para 10].

12.99 The abstract makes it clear that the presumption of future economic benefit would not be rebutted where payments are made by the intermediary that relieve the sponsoring entity from paying for items such as retirement benefits or benefits in kind. However, the presumption would be rebutted at the time the payment is made to the intermediary if at that time the assets transferred vest unconditionally in identified beneficiaries. [UITF 32 paras 11, 12].

12.100 In determining the nature and extent of the assets and liabilities, the UITF came to the same conclusion as it has under UITF Abstract 38, that the assets and liabilities of the trust are under *de facto* control of the sponsoring entity and hence the assets and liabilities should be accounted for as an extension of the sponsoring entity's business. When an entity recognises the assets and liabilities held by a trust on its balance sheet, it should disclose sufficient information in the notes to its financial statements to enable readers to understand any restrictions relating to those assets and liabilities. [UITF 32 para 19, 20].

12.101 Where a trust is included in the sponsoring company's financial statements, the issues as regards accruing a liability and expense are the same as if no transfer into the trust had been made.

- If, by the end of the year, the company or the trust has paid money to employees as, for example, bonuses, then those amounts would be properly charged as expenses.
- If at the end of the year, no cash has been paid (or cash has simply been transferred from the company to the trust) then in general, no liability or expense would be recorded. That is, the resources held in the company or transferred to the trust would be carried forward as an asset. This is so even though there may be restrictions as to the uses to which any assets transferred into a trust may be put. An exception arises and an expense should be recognised if:
  - an amount has been promised to employees in respect of the year in question, that is, the board has approved the amount and employees have been notified;
  - the obligation to pay employees in respect of the year in question can be inferred from an established pattern of paying bonuses (even if each one is *ex-gratia*); or
  - even if there is no established pattern, there is clear documentation that an amount is transferred after the year end, but relates to a bonus scheme for the previous year (evidence for this would be that the amounts would be paid, either directly from the company or *via* the trust, to employees, expressly as bonuses for the previous year, and paid during the first few months of the subsequent year).

12.102 The above rules are to some extent a reflection of long-standing practice, but were tightened following the introduction of FRS 12 on accounting for provisions. Some of the consequences are:

- If an amount is paid into a trust that is in practice much larger than could reasonably relate to bonuses for the first year and is likely to be used as a source for paying bonuses over a number of years or may be used in place of salary increases for the following year, then it should be treated as an expense over the years to which the expenditure relates; not charged entirely in the first year.
- If an amount is paid into a trust and is not paid out to employees in the form of bonuses etc, but rather is loaned back to certain employees, then, subject to normal recoverability tests, the asset would remain an asset of the trust and, by virtue of UITF Abstract 38 an asset of the company/group. (If the amounts are loaned back to directors, then questions of legality under the Companies Act need to be considered).

Illustrative examples

12.103 The examples that follow illustrate UITF Abstract 32's principles in relation to payments to a trust for the benefit of the company's employees.

Example 1

The sponsoring company pays £60,000 into the trust, but no bonus is awarded at that stage to employees.

The sponsoring company has exchanged one type of asset (cash) for another asset (cash held in trust). As the trust has been set up for the benefit of the company's employees, the company has *de facto* control of the trust. Consequently, the trust's assets are included on the sponsoring company's balance sheet and there would be no charge at that stage to the profit and loss account. Disclosure of the fact that the cash is restricted would need to be given. Any subsequent bonus awarded will not be a share-based payment.

Example 2

The facts are the same as example 1, except that a bonus is awarded to the employees. This bonus vests unconditionally after three years provided that certain performance conditions have been met.

As for example 1, the sponsoring company will record the asset of cash paid to the trust on its balance sheet. A liability, however, will also be recorded as the sponsoring company has an obligation to transfer economic benefit in the future. The value of the liability should follow the normal FRS 12 rules and be based on the likely outcome of the performance conditions being met.

Example 3

The facts are the same as example 1, except that one third of the balance is awarded as a bonus to employees and vests immediately.

In this case, one third of the cash would be an immediate expense to the company as it relates to an award to the employees and has vested unconditionally with them. The remaining two thirds of the bonus would be treated as in example 1, that is no charge in the profit and loss account as the company has *de facto* control of the trust. Consequently, the assets of the trust are included in the sponsoring company's balance sheet.

Transitional provisions

12.104 The requirements of FRS 20 should be applied by listed entities for accounting periods beginning on or after 1 January 2005 and by unlisted entities for accounting periods beginning on or after 1 January 2006. Of course, all listed companies were required to apply EU-adopted international financial reporting standards in their consolidated financial statements for accounting periods beginning on or after 1 January 2005 so, in effect, FRS 20 only applied to listed entities that do not prepare consolidated financial statements or that prepare their own financial statements under UK GAAP alongside consolidated financial statements prepared under IFRS.

12.105 For the purpose of determining when FRS 20 applies, FRS 20 defines a listed entity as *"an entity that has in issue one or more securities that are admitted to trading on a regulated market of any Member State within the meaning of Article*

1(13) of Council Directive 93/22/EEC of 10 May 1993 on investment services in the securities field". [FRS 20 App A]. This definition encompasses entities with either listed shares or listed debt but, importantly, excludes companies listed on the Alternative Investment Market (AIM), which is not a regulated market as defined above. (It should be noted that, for years beginning on or after 1 January 2007, AIM listed companies will be required to prepare their financial statements in accordance with IFRS – see further chapter 2.) It also excludes companies listed outside the EU.

12.106 When FRS 20 is applied for the first time, it should be treated as a change in accounting policy requiring a prior year adjustment. However, the standard contains transitional provisions that provide some relief from the need to apply its requirements to awards granted many years ago. Broadly, the requirements of FRS 20 are to be applied to grants of equity instruments made since ED 2 was issued (that is, 7 November 2002) that have not vested by the standard's effective date and to liabilities in respect of cash-settled share-based payment transactions outstanding at the standard's effective date. Entities are encouraged, however, to apply the requirements of FRS 20 to other transactions, although this option is somewhat restricted. The transitional provisions are illustrated in the table below.

Application of FRS 20	**Equity-settled transactions [FRS 20 paras 53-57]**	**Cash-settled transactions [FRS 20 paras 58-59]**
Required	The requirements of FRS 20 apply to all grants of shares, share options or other equity instruments made after 7 November 2002, that have not yet vested by the effective date of the standard (that is, accounting periods beginning on or after 1 January 2005 for listed entities and accounting periods beginning on or after 1 January 2006 for unlisted entities). Modifications to the terms and conditions of a grant of equity instruments to which FRS 20 has not been applied fall within the scope of FRS 20 if that modification occurs after the standard's effective date. This is the case even if the equity instrument in question was originally granted before 7 November 2002. For all grants of equity instruments to which FRS 20 has not been applied, the information required by paragraphs 44 and 45 of FRS 20 must still be disclosed. These disclosures are described from paragraph A12.211.	The requirements of FRS 20 apply to all liabilities arising from share-based payment transactions that exist at the effective date of the standard.

Encouraged	Apply the requirements of FRS 20 to other grants of equity instruments only if the fair value of those instruments, determined at the measurement date as defined by FRS 20 has previously been disclosed publicly.	Apply the requirements of FRS 20 to other liabilities arising from share-based payment transactions, for example those that were settled during the comparative period.

12.106.1 The requirements of UITF Abstract 41 (IFRIC interpretation 8), 'Scope of FRS 20 (IFRS 2)', should be applied by entities for accounting periods beginning on or after 1 May 2006, but early adoption is encouraged. An entity should apply the abstract retrospectively in accordance with the requirements of FRS 3, 'Reporting financial performance', subject to the transitional provisions of FRS 20 detailed in table above. Application of the abstract is considered from paragraph A12.49.1.

12.106.2 UITF Abstract 44 (IFRIC interpretation 11), 'FRS 20 (IFRS 2) – Group and treasury share transactions', is effective for accounting periods beginning on or after 1 March 2007, with early adoption encouraged. The abstract should be applied retrospectively.

12.107 The application of the above requirements is illustrated in the following examples.

Example 1 – listed company with a December year end

Company A has a December year end and prepares its own financial statements under UK GAAP. Its first financial statements prepared in accordance with the requirements of FRS 20 are for the year ending 31 December 2005.

The requirements of FRS 20 will apply to all grants of shares, share options or other equity instruments made after 7 November 2002 that have not yet vested by 1 January 2005. Similarly, liabilities in respect of cash-settled transactions should be measured in accordance with the requirements of FRS 20 if they have not been settled by 1 January 2005.

Example 2 – listed company with a September year end

Company B has a September year end and prepares its own financial statements under UK GAAP. Its first financial statements prepared in accordance with FRS 20 are for the year ending 30 September 2006.

FRS 20's requirements will apply to all grants of shares, share options or other equity instruments made after 7 November 2002 that have not vested by 1 October 2005. Similarly, liabilities in respect of cash-settled transactions should be measured in accordance with the requirements of FRS 20 if they have not been settled by 1 October 2005.

Example 3 – unlisted company with a June year end

Company C has a June year end and prepares its own financial statements under UK GAAP. Its first financial statements prepared in accordance with the requirements of FRS 20 are for the year ending 30 June 2007. The requirements of FRS 20 will apply to all grants of shares, share options or other equity instruments made after 7 November 2002 that have not vested by 1 July 2006. Similarly, liabilities in respect of cash-settled transactions should be measured in accordance with the requirements of FRS 20 if they have not been settled by 1 July 2006.

Example 4 – modification of terms and conditions

Company A (as described in example 1) made an award of share options to certain of its key management on 1 April 2002. Information in respect of the award is shown below:

- Number of awards – 100 (all of which are expected to vest).
- Number of options per award – 1,000.
- Exercise price – £1.20.
- Market price of shares at date of grant – £1.20.
- Fair value of option at date of grant – 60p.
- Vesting period – 5 years.

Following a period of declining share prices, the exercise price of the options was reduced to 80p on 1 April 2005. The fair value of the original award on that date was 20p and the fair value of the re-priced option was 50p.

As the original grant of options was made before 7 November 2002, company A does not need to apply FRS 20 to that grant. It must, however, account for the re-pricing in accordance with FRS 20. The incremental fair value of each re-priced option is 30p (that is, 50p – 20p) so this amount is recognised over the remaining two years of the award. On the assumption that all of the awards do vest, the amount recognised in each accounting period will be as follows:

Year ending 31 December 2005 – £11,250 (100 × 1,000 × 0.30 × 9/12)

Year ending 31 December 2006 – £15,000 (100 × 1,000 × 0.30 × 12/24)

Year ending 31 December 2007 – £3,750 (100 × 1,000 × 0.30 × 3/24)

12.108 The requirement in paragraph 54 of FRS 20 for previous public disclosure of the fair value of equity instruments granted means that few UK companies will be permitted to apply FRS 20 to awards granted before 7 November 2002 or awards that have vested before the standard's effective date. One example of a company that has disclosed the fair value of its employee options is BP Plc as shown in the example below.

Table 12.3 – Disclosure of fair value

BP Plc – Annual Report – 31 December 2003

34 Employee share plans (extract)

BP does not recognize an expense in respect of share options granted to employees. If the fair value of options granted in any particular year is estimated and this value amortized over the vesting period of the options, an indication of the cost of granting options to employees can be made. The fair value of each share option granted has been estimated using a Black Scholes option pricing model with the following assumptions:

	2003	2002
Risk-free interest rate	**3.5%**	4.0%
Expected volatility	**30%**	26%
Expected life in years	**1 to 5**	1 to 5
Expected dividend yield	**4.00%**	3.75%
Weighted average fair value of options granted ($)	**1.44**	1.64

The additional expense that would have been recognized in 2003 on this basis would be $79 million ($90 million) and the impact on earnings per share would be 1 cent (1 cent).

12.109 Other companies with shares listed in the US may have disclosed the fair value of equity instruments granted in accordance with FAS 123(R), 'Share-based payment', for the purposes of US reporting.

Grants to which FRS 20 does not apply

12.110 For all grants of equity instruments to which the recognition and measurement requirements of FRS 20 have not been applied, the information required by paragraphs 44 and 45 of FRS 20 must still be disclosed. [FRS 20 para 56]. These disclosures come under the heading of information that enables the users of the financial statements to understand the nature and extent of share-based payment arrangements that existed during the period.

12.111 This leaves the question as to how awards to which FRS 20 has not been applied should be accounted for. FRS 20 gives no guidance in this regard. However, the ASB's notes on the standard's application in the UK and the Republic of Ireland states that *"the normal approach to changes of accounting policy should apply"*. [FRS 20 para N26]. This suggests that there should be a prior year adjustment to restate comparatives except to the extent that FRS 20 provides relief from the requirement to restate certain transactions. Hence, grants of equity instruments to which FRS 20 does not apply should continue to be accounted for in accordance with UITF Abstract 17.

12.112 As regards cash-settled transactions, the requirements of FRS 20 apply to all liabilities arising from share-based payment transactions that exist at the effective date of the standard. In example 1 in paragraph 12.107, company A is required to measure cash-settled transactions in accordance with the requirements of FRS 20 if they have not been settled by 1 January 2005. FRS 20 gives no guidance as to what company A should do with transactions settled during the comparative period (although it is encouraged to apply FRS 20). In ED 2, the IASB proposed that vested liabilities should be measured at their settlement amount (that is, the amount that would have been paid on settlement of the liability had the counterparty demanded settlement at the measurement date), but this proposal has not been included in FRS 20. In our view, where FRS 20 is not applied to a cash-settled share-based payment transaction, the principles of FRS 12 will apply, so the liability should be measured at the best estimate of the expenditure required to settle the obligation at the balance sheet date. [FRS 12 para 36]. As fair value measurement is not required, we consider that this best estimate will be represented by the intrinsic value of the award. Hence, company A will measure transactions settled during 2004 on the basis of the intrinsic value as at 1 January 2004, with subsequent re-measurement to the amount actually paid when settlement occurs. Changes in the amount of the liability between 1 January 2004 and settlement date will be included in profit or loss for the year ended 31 December 2004.

Annex

12.113 Attached is the chapter from the Manual of Accounting – IFRS for the UK that deals with accounting for share-based payment under IFRS 2. As the requirements of FRS 20 are almost identical to the requirements of IFRS 2, the accounting for share-based payment and related issues will be the same under UK GAAP as under IFRS. However, there are exceptions to this principle, particularly where the UITF has issued a consensus dealing with particular issues in a UK context. Hence, the following sections of the IFRS 2 chapter are not relevant to a consideration of UK GAAP.

- National insurance contributions on share option gains. [Para 12.69].
- Employee share ownership plans. [Para 12.172].
- First-time adoption of IFRS. [Para 12.226].

Annex – Share-based payment

Contents

	Page
Introduction	12035
Objective and scope	12035
Business combinations, private equity deals and sweet equity	12043
Leaver provisions	12046
Drag along and tag along clauses	12047
Recognition of share-based payment transactions	12048
Timing of recognition	12049
Group situations – location of share-based payment charge	12050
The credit entry	12051
Equity-settled share-based payment transactions	12051
Measurement of equity-settled share-based payment transactions	12052
Grant date	12055
Awards conditional on IPO	12059
Vesting conditions	12062
Illustrative examples	12066
Social security contributions on share options gains	12073
Background	12073
Treatment of social security contributions under IFRS	12073
Reimbursement or transfer of the liability	12076
Modifications, cancellations and settlements	12077
Modifications and re-pricing	12077
Transitional provisions	12084
Cancellations and settlements	12084
Measuring the fair value of equity instruments	12086
Valuation techniques	12087
Inputs to an option pricing model	12089
Life of the option	12089
Expected volatility	12090
Expected dividends	12094
Risk-free rate	12094
Selection of an option pricing model	12095
The Black-Scholes formula	12095
The binomial model	12096
Monte-Carlo simulation	12098
Cash-settled share-based payment transactions	12098
Measurement of cash-settled share-based payment transactions	12099
Transactions with settlement alternatives	12101
The counterparty may choose the settlement method	12101
Discounting	12104
The entity may choose the settlement method	12104
Practical implications	12106
Group situations and IFRIC 11	12106

Share-based payment arrangements involving an entity's own equity instruments 12107
Share-based payment arrangements involving equity instruments of the parent 12107
Parent grants rights over its equity instruments to the employees of its subsidiary 12108
Subsidiary grants rights over equity instruments of its parent to its employees 12108
Funding arrangements between parent and its subsidiary 12109
Timing of the recharge 12110
Cash-settled awards in group situations 12117
Effective date 12119
Equity incentive plans 12119
Free shares 12119
Matching shares 12120
Dividend shares 12120
Share incentive plans (SIPs) — UK 12121
Free shares 12122
Partnership shares — with accumulation period 12122
Matching shares 12123
Dividend shares 12123
Deferred bonus plans 12123
Employee share purchase plans 12124
Vesting conditions 12125
Cancellations 12125
Additional guidance and implementation 12126
Employee share ownership plans (ESOPs) 12126
Background 12126
Accounting for ESOP trusts 12127
Gains made by ESOPs 12131
Trustee company 12132
Disclosure 12132
Nature and extent of share-based payments 12133
Disclosures for grants made before 7 November 2002 12134
Determination of fair values 12135
Impact on profit or loss 12136
Example 12137
Directors' emoluments disclosure 12141
Related party disclosures 12141
Cash flow statements 12141
Materiality 12141
First-time adoption of IFRS 12142
Effective date of recent interpretations (IFRIC 8 and IFRIC 11) 12144
Companies Act requirements 12144
Impact on distributable profits 12145
Expenses in respect of equity-settled share-based payment transactions 12146
ESOP trusts 12146

Introduction

A12.1 For some years, many companies have used share option schemes for the purpose of employee remuneration, either as a management incentive or through employee share purchase plans that are available to all employees. A more recent development is the increasing use of share awards, either through annual bonuses or long-term incentive plans (LTIPs) as an alternative, or in addition to share option plans. In such schemes the amount of the award is normally based on performance criteria; if these criteria are partially achieved, but not met in full, participants may be entitled to a proportion of the full award. Often, the shares are awarded to employees at nominal value or at nil cost (for instance, where an employee share ownership plan (ESOP) subscribes for shares at nominal value).

A12.2 In addition to the employee context, share-based payments are also used as a method by which entities procure other goods or services.

A12.3 IFRS 2 applies to accounting periods beginning on or after 1 January 2005. The requirements for first-time adoption are considered in detail in chapter 3 (see also para A12.226).

[The next paragraph is A12.26.]

Objective and scope

A12.26 The stated objective of IFRS 2 is *"to specify the financial reporting by an entity when it undertakes a share-based payment transaction. In particular, it requires an entity to reflect in its profit or loss and financial position the effects of share-based payment transactions, including expenses associated with transactions in which share options are granted to employees"*. [IFRS 2 para 1]. Behind this objective is the IASB's strongly held view that an entity should recognise all goods or services it obtains, regardless of the form of consideration. Where goods or services are obtained for cash or other financial assets, the accounting is generally straightforward. IFRS 2 starts from the premise that goods or services obtained in a share-based payment transaction should be recognised and measured in a similar way.

A12.27 The standard applies to all share-based payment transactions, not just employee share schemes. Share-based payment transactions are considered to fall into one of three categories:

- *Equity-settled share-based payment transactions* – Transactions in which an entity receives goods or services, including employee services, as consideration for its own equity instruments. Such transactions include employee share option and share incentive plans.
- *Cash-settled share-based payment transactions* – Transactions in which an entity acquires goods or services by incurring liabilities (typically to be settled in cash), but where the amount paid is based on the value of the

entity's shares or other equity instruments. Typical examples include 'phantom' options schemes, share appreciation rights and certain long-term incentive schemes.

- Transactions in which an entity acquires goods or services and either the entity or the counter-party may *choose* settlement in the form of cash (or other assets) or equity instruments of the entity.

[IFRS 2 para 2].

A12.28 Consistent with the objectives discussed in paragraph A12.26 above, the requirements of IFRS 2 apply to any transactions in which an entity receives goods or services in exchange for a transfer of its own equity instruments, even if that transfer is made by an existing shareholder rather than by the entity itself. Only when a transfer is clearly for a purpose other than payment for goods or services would it be outside IFRS 2's scope. Furthermore, IFRS 2 will apply where goods or services are obtained by an entity in exchange for equity instruments of its parent or another member of the group. [IFRS 2 para 3]. Group situations are considered further in paragraph A12.152 onwards.

A12.28.1 The scope of an equity-settled share-based payment transaction has been extended with the publication of IFRIC 8, 'Scope of IFRS 2', published by the IFRIC in January 2006. The interpretation requires that an entity should recognise any unidentified goods or services within its financial statements. This situation arises where the fair value of equity instruments granted is greater than the fair value of the goods or services received or where the goods or services received cannot be identified. The interpretation is considered further from paragraph A12.49.1. The interpretation is effective for accounting periods beginning on or after 1 May 2006, however, early adoption is encouraged.

A12.28.2 Associates and joint ventures are more complicated. For example, in situations where employees of a joint venture are granted the right to equity instruments over one or both joint venturer's equity instruments, such a transaction in the joint venture would be outside IFRS 2's scope. This is because the joint venture is not part of a group as defined by IAS 27, 'Consolidated and separate financial statements'. Although the shareholders of the joint venture are transferring equity instruments in exchange for employee services to the joint venture, the fact that the equity instruments are not the joint venture's means the awards are not in the scope of IFRS 2. [IFRS 2 para 3]. The position for associates is the same. Note that investors would be within IFRS 2's scope for their own financial statements as they are indeed issuing their own equity in return for services (possibly unidentified services addressed by IFRIC 8).

A12.28.3 In the situation described in the previous paragraph, the associate or joint venture entity would need to apply the hierarchy within IAS 8, 'Accounting policies, changes in accounting estimates and errors', to determine the appropriate accounting treatment, and apply the principles of IAS 8 paragraph 11. In such a situation, the entity is likely to determine that either IFRS 2 or IAS 19, 'Employee benefits', (refer to chapter 11) is the most appropriate standard. This would be a policy choice that the entity would make under IAS 8, and would have to be applied consistently (see further example 8 in para A12.29 below). See from paragraph A12.152 for details of how to apply IFRS 2 in this situation.

A12.29 There are few exclusions from IFRS 2's scope. These relate to transactions dealt with in more detail by other International Financial Reporting Standards, namely:

- Business combinations to which IFRS 3, 'Business combinations', applies, notwithstanding the fact that such a transaction may be equity-settled (see further para A12.31.1 below). However, equity instruments granted to employees of the acquiree in their capacity as employees (for example, to encourage them to remain in the employ of the acquiree after the acquisition) do fall within the scope of IFRS 2. [IFRS 2 para 5]. Similarly, the cancellation, replacement or modification of existing share-based payment arrangements as result of a business combination should be accounted for in accordance with IFRS 2.
- Contracts for the purchase of goods, such as commodities, other than to satisfy the reporting entity's expected purchase or usage requirements and to which IAS 32, 'Financial instruments: Disclosure and presentation', and IAS 39, 'Financial instruments: Recognition and measurement', apply. [IFRS 2 para 6]. This is illustrated in the following examples.

Transaction within the scope of IFRS 2

Example 1 – Purchase of non-financial item expected to be used by the entity

Entity A enters into a contract to purchase silver for use in its jewellery manufacturing business, whereby it is required to pay cash to the supplier in an amount equal to the value of C1,000 of entity A's shares at the date the silver is delivered. This meets the definition of a cash-settled share-based payment transaction (entity A has acquired goods in exchange for a payment the amount of which will be based on the value of its shares).

IAS 32, 'Financial instruments: Presentation', and IAS 39, 'Financial instruments: recognition and measurement', apply to those contracts to buy or sell a non-financial item that can be settled net in cash or another financial instrument, or by exchanging financial instruments, as if the contracts were financial instruments, with the exception of contracts that were entered into and continue to be held for the purpose of the receipt or delivery of the non-financial item in accordance with the entity's expected purchase, sale or usage requirements. [IAS 32 para 8; IAS 39 para 5]. Regardless of whether this contract may be settled net, as it was entered into for the purpose of taking delivery of the silver for use in entity A's business and entity A has a history of doing this, it does not fall within the scope of IASs 32 and 39. Hence, it does fall within the scope of IFRS 2 as a cash-settled share-based payment transaction.

Example 2 – Definition of goods or services

Entity B is developing a new product and purchased a patent from entity C. The parties agreed a purchase price of 1,000 of entity B's shares. These will be issued to entity C within

60 days of finalising the legal documentation that transfers the patent from entity C to entity B.

This is an equity-settled share-based payment. IFRS 2 is applicable to a share-based payment for a patent. The goods to which IFRS 2 applies include inventories, consumables, property, plant and equipment, intangible assets and other non-financial assets.

Example 3 – Business combination and continued employee service

Entity D acquires 90% of the share capital of entity E. As part of the acquisition, entity D grants entity E's employees share options that vest after 2 years.

In this transaction, equity instruments are granted to employees of the acquiree in their capacity as employees and so fall within IFRS 2's scope. [IFRS 2 para 5].

Example 4 – Award of parent entity shares by a shareholder

An individual with a 40% shareholding in entity F awards 2% of his shareholding in entity F to a director of entity F's subsidiary, entity G.

The award is within IFRS 2's scope. A shareholder of entity G has transferred equity instruments of entity G's parent to a party that has supplied services to the entity. [IFRS 2 para 3]. The award will be reflected in both entity F's financial statements and entity G's consolidated financial statements.

Transactions outside the scope of IFRS 2

Example 5 – Commodity contracts

Entity H enters into a contract to purchase 100 tonnes of cocoa beans. The purchase price will be settled in cash at an amount equal to the value of 1,000 of entity H's shares. However, the entity may settle the contract at any time by paying an amount equal to the current market value of 1,000 of its shares less the market value of 100 tonnes of cocoa beans. The entity has entered into the contract as part of its hedging strategy and has no intention of taking physical delivery of the cocoa beans.

As in example 1, the transaction meets the definition of a cash-settled share-based payment transaction (entity H has acquired goods in exchange for a payment the amount of which will be based on the value of its shares). However, unlike example 1, the contract may be settled net and has not been entered into in order to satisfy entity H's expected purchase, sale or usage requirements. Accordingly, the transaction is outside IFRS 2's scope and is instead dealt with in accordance with the requirements of IASs 32 and 39.

Example 6 – Cash payments dependent on earnings multiple

A non-quoted entity issued share appreciation rights (SARs) to its employees. The SARs entitle the employees to a payment equal to any increase in the entity's share price between the grant date and the vesting date. The arrangement's terms and conditions define the share price used to calculate payments to employees as five times EBITDA divided by the number of shares in issue.

IFRS 2 is unlikely to be applicable to this transaction because a multiple of EBITDA is not likely to reflect the fair value of the entity's share price. If it does not, management should apply IAS 19 to this deferred compensation arrangement.

Example 7 – Scheme investing in other entity shares

Entity I is implementing an unusual share option incentive scheme. Entity I will lend C1m to an employee share trust, which will purchase shares in a number of publicly listed companies (but not in entity I). These companies may be suppliers, customers or competitors. Entity I's employees are granted options over 'units' held by the employee share trust. The units are an amalgam of the shares held by the trust. The options are granted at market value at the date of the grant and held over a three year period. When employees exercise their option over the units, they are paid the difference in cash between the market price of the units at the date of the grant (the exercise price) and the market value at the date of exercise. To fund the cash payment the trust sells the shares relating to the exercised units. It then repays the relevant portion of the loan from entity I and also pays the gain to employees.

This transaction is outside IFRS 2's scope as the rights are over shares of companies other than the reporting entity, or companies within the entity's group.

Under SIC 12, 'Consolidation – special purpose entities', equity compensation plans should be consolidated when the entity controls the trust (see further from para A12.183). In this situation, the shares are held for the benefit of the employees, and entity I takes the risks and rewards of the movement in the price of the shares. Consequently, the trust should be consolidated.

Accounting for the changes in value of the assets in the trust will depend on how the assets are classified. If they fall into the definition of a plan asset under paragraph 7 of IAS 19 then they should be accounted for in line with IAS 19. Otherwise, the assets should be treated as available-for-sale financial assets in line with IAS 39. The related liability will be within IAS 19's scope.

UK implications

Under UK GAAP, consistent with IFRS 2, the transaction is outside the scope of FRS 20 (IFRS 2), 'Share-based payment', as the rights are over shares of companies other than the reporting entity, or companies within entity I's group.

Under UITF 38, 'Accounting for ESOP trusts', the trust would be considered part of entity I, because there will be an obligation on the trust (and, therefore, entity I) to pay the increase in the value of the units over the market price on the date of grant to the employees in cash. However, the trust will not be holding 'own shares' of the sponsoring entity, and so the shares will be presented as an asset of the entity, rather than as a deduction in arriving at shareholders' funds. [UITF 38 para 10(b)].

Therefore, entity I will be required to provide for the cost (the increase in value of the units) in line with FRS 12, 'Provisions, contingent liabilities and contingent assets'. The charge should be based on the difference between the market price of the units at the end of the year and the exercise price of the options.

> However, when employees exercise their options and the trust sells the shares a corresponding gain will be recognised in the entity's profit and loss account. The charge under FRS 12 is made each year, but the shares may not be sold until later when the employee exercises the option. Therefore, the charge and the gain may not match in any one year. The only way to achieve such a matching would be for the trust to sell the shares each year to realise a gain that matches the charge (taking market risk so that the gain can be regarded as realised) and then for the trust to repurchase the shares (the period before buyback must be at least two days). This could achieve a matching each year in the profit and loss account, but the entity takes market risk.

Example 8 – Share options in a joint venture

Entity J is a joint venture between entities K and L. Entity K grants senior employees of entity J options over its own shares without making any charge to entity J.

Entity J's financial statements

IFRS 2 includes within its scope transfers of equity instruments of an entity's parent or of an entity in the same group in return for goods or services. [IFRS 2 para 3]. However, entity K is a joint venture investor and is not entity J's parent, nor is it in the same group (defined in IAS 27 as being 'a parent and all its subsidiaries') as entity J. Therefore, on initial consideration, from entity J's perspective, the award in entity J of share options in entity K is not within IFRS 2's scope.

The arrangement also falls outside IAS 19's scope. IAS 19 applies to all employee benefits, but defines those as *"all forms of consideration given by an entity in exchange for service rendered by employees"*. Because no consideration is given by entity J, this does not meet the definition of an employee benefit.

However, IAS 8 requires entities to apply a hierarchy when determining their accounting polices. Where there is no IFRS governing a transaction, IAS 8 requires management to look first to any IFRS standard or interpretation dealing with similar or related issues. Paragraph 10 of IAS 8 states that in the absence of a standard or interpretation that specifically applies to a transaction, "*management shall use its judgment in developing and applying an accounting policy*". Furthermore, paragraph 11 of the standard clarifies that in making such a judgement, management should consider "*the requirements and guidance in standards and interpretations dealing with similar and related issues*". While it is not a formal requirement, it is our view that the most appropriate treatment will be for entity J to apply the principles of IFRS 2 to this equity-settled share-based payment. This is further supported by IFRIC 11, 'IFRS 2 — Group and treasury share transactions', which clarifies the treatment where a parent entity grants options over its own shares to those of its subsidiary. In this case, while entity K does not meet the definition of a parent company, in the absence of any other guidance, it would be appropriate to apply IFRIC 11.

UK implications

The equivalent guidance to IAS 8 under UK GAAP is FRS 18, 'Accounting policies'. Paragraph 14 of FRS 18 states that "*an entity should adopt accounting policies that enable its financial statements to give a true and fair view. Those accounting policies should be consistent with the requirements of accounting standards, Urgent Issues Task Force (UITF) Abstracts and companies legislation*". In this case, while it is not a formal requirement, it is our view that, consistent with IFRS, the most appropriate approach would be to apply the principles of FRS 20 and recognise an expense for what is in nature a share-based payment. This is further supported by UITF 44 (IFRIC 11), 'FRS 20 (IFRS 2) – Group and treasury share transactions', the identical UK interpretation to IFRIC 11.

Entity J should apply the approach that is considered to be most appropriate in accordance with IAS 8. Where the principles of IFRS 2 are not applied, consideration should still be given as to whether disclosure is necessary under IAS 24, 'Related party disclosures'. Whichever approach is adopted, the accounting policy should be clearly disclosed and consistently applied.

Entity K's financial statements
Under IFRIC 8, 'Scope of IFRS 2', entity K has an equity-settled share-based payment arrangement and should measure the services received in accordance with IFRS 2 as appropriate. Thus, in its separate financial statements, entity K should consider whether any unidentifiable services have been or will be received and measure these at fair value at the date of grant.

Entity K's consolidated financial statements should also recognise the share-based payment expense. However, if entity J applies the principles of IFRS 2, entity K's consolidated financial statements would recognise its share via the joint venture accounting entries and so entity K would restrict any additional share-based payment charge so that the total charge recognised equals 100% of entity K's share.

Entity L's financial statements
Other than the fact that entity L will need to account for its joint venture in entity J, there will be no impact on entity L's separate and consolidated financial statements.

[The next paragraph is A12.31.]

A12.31 In some cases, the number of equity instruments to which a counterparty is entitled varies. For example, share appreciation rights may be settled in shares such that the number of shares issued to employees varies according to the appreciation of the employer's share price over a period of time. If the requirements of IAS 32 were applied to transactions such as these, an obligation to issue equity instruments would be classified as a liability (a variable number of shares issued for a fixed amount – see further chapter 6). This would have implications for the basis of measurement of the transaction as discussed later in this chapter. For example, equity-settled transactions involving employees are measured at the date on which awards are granted and are not re-measured, whereas liabilities in respect of cash-settled transactions are re-measured at each balance sheet date. The IASB concluded that different considerations applied in developing IFRS 2 and the standard inserts an amendment to IAS 32 that exempts from its scope any transactions to which IFRS 2 applies (except as discussed in paragraph A12.29 above). [IAS 32 para 4(f)].

A12.31.1 The following examples consider some practical issues when determining whether a transaction is within the scope of IFRS 2.

Example 1 – Bonus with past history of cash settlement

An entity agrees to pay its employees a bonus. The entity has a choice of settlement, either cash or shares with a value equivalent to the value of cash payment. The entity has a past practice of settling in cash and is considering whether the transaction should be accounted for under IFRS 2.

It could be argued that by applying the principles of IAS 32, shares issued for a fixed amount would be accounted for as a liability and, hence, this type of award should be in the scope of IAS 19 and not IFRS 2. However, in March 2006, the IFRIC concluded that IFRS 2 defines a share-based payment transaction as a transaction in which the entity receives goods or services as consideration for equity instruments of the entity or amounts that are based on the price of an equity instrument of the entity. [IFRS 2 para 2]. This definition does not require the amounts to be linked to the share price of the entity. The IFRIC confirmed that IFRS 2 was clear that such a transaction should be accounted for as a share-based payment transaction. Furthermore, as the entity has a choice that allows it to settle the award using equity instruments or cash, the transaction is a share-based payment with a settlement choice (refer to paras A12.148 to A12.151).

Example 2 – Variable number of shares for goods

Entity A signed a contract with a construction entity to acquire a new building for C1m with ownership transferring to entity A when the construction work is complete. The purchase price will be settled by entity A issuing a variable number of its own shares with a total market value of C1m.

As the purchase price is being settled in shares, the transaction is within IFRS 2's scope and is excluded from the scope of IAS 32.

Example 3 – Loan enabling counterparty to purchase shares

An entity lends C100 to an employee to purchase the entity's shares. The loan is interest free and only has recourse to the shares. Dividends paid on the shares must be used to reduce the loan. The employee must pay back the balance of the loan, or return the shares at the earlier of three years or resignation.

In November 2005, the IFRIC confirmed that this transaction would fall within the scope of IFRS 2. The IFRIC stated that the loan is considered to be part of a share-based payment transaction, which in substance is an option with a three year exercise window where the exercise price is reduced by any dividends. The employee is not exposed to any downside risk in the movement of the share price over the three year period as he/she can repay the loan or surrender the shares. Hence, the option would be exercised on the date the loan is repaid. In this example the option would vest immediately as the employee could leave on day one, repay the loan and be fully entitled to the shares. Vesting conditions are considered in detail from paragraph A12.59.

Business combinations, private equity deals and sweet equity

A12.31.2 The scope exclusion in respect of business combinations concerns those combinations to which IFRS 3 applies. However, some business combinations are excluded from IFRS 3's scope, so the wording of paragraph 5 of IFRS 2 might give the impression that those combinations are within IFRS 2's scope. This issue was discussed by the IASB at its September 2004 meeting, where it was confirmed that IFRS 2 was not intended to apply to business combinations that are outside the scope of IFRS 3. Instead, the intention was to exclude from the scope of IFRS 2 business combinations as *defined* in IFRS 3. Furthermore, the IASB noted that some of the IFRS 3 scope exclusions represent an interim measure pending completion of phase II of the business combinations project. Accordingly, where a transaction meets the definition of a business combination in IFRS 3 (that is, the bringing together of separate entities or businesses into one reporting entity) it should be considered to be outside IFRS 2's scope, regardless of whether it is also outside IFRS 3's scope. This principle is illustrated in the examples below. Business combinations are considered further in chapter 25.

Example 1 – Formation of a joint venture

Entity A and entity B are brought together to form a joint venture.

While joint ventures are outside IFRS 3's scope, this transaction meets the definition of a business combination.

The combination of separate entities or businesses to form a joint venture involves the issue of shares for the purpose of forming a joint venture, not the acquisition of goods or services. As such, the transaction is outside IFRS 2's scope.

Example 2 – Common control transactions

A business combination occurs between two entities that are under common control. The transaction is outside IFRS 3's scope. [IFRS 3 para 3(b)].

The primary purpose of the issue of shares in a common control transaction is likely to be to reorganise the legal or managerial structure of a business or to transfer a business, rather than to acquire goods or services. The shares are issued in exchange for a business that is an integrated set of activities and assets conducted and managed for the purpose of providing a return to investors, or lower costs or other economic benefits directly and proportionately to policyholders or participants. [IFRS 3 App A]. As such, the transaction is outside IFRS 2's scope.

A12.32 Transactions with employees in their capacity as holders of equity instruments are also outside IFRS 2's scope. [IFRS 2 para 4]. For example, if a entity makes a bonus issue of shares to all of its shareholders, and these include certain of the entity's employees, this will not represent a share-based payment transaction to be dealt with in accordance with IFRS 2. However, there could be a situation where an employee invests in an entity which is working towards a stock market listing or a trade sale. In these cases there could be a venture capital entity or similar investor involved in the transaction and the employee will subscribe for the shares at the same amount as the other investors. The issue is whether the employee is acting as a shareholder or an employee. Often the interested parties (including directors, management and other shareholders) have acquired shares for a 'fair' value, which may not equate to fair value for the purposes of IFRS 2 and would typically be tax driven. It is important to note that a fair value determined for tax purposes is generally discounted and, therefore, lower than the IFRS 2 fair value.

A12.32.1 It could be that there are no conditions or incentives attached to the acquired shares and, therefore, the employee is purely acting as a shareholder. However, in the majority of situations there are likely to be service conditions or leaver provisions such that the arrangement would be accounted for as a share-based payment transaction under IFRS 2. The shares in question are often referred to as 'sweet' or 'sweat' equity depending on whether they are offered at an advantageous price or in return for services rather than cash.

Example 1 – Employees acting in capacity as shareholders

Entity A made a rights issue to all of its shareholders, entitling them to purchase one new share for each five shares owned at a price of C10. The shareholders include 20 people who are also employees. No other conditions are attached to the rights issue.

In this example, shares are being issued to employees in their capacity as shareholders, and not in exchange for their services. Furthermore, the employees are not required to complete a period of service in exchange for the new shares. As such the transaction is outside IFRS 2's scope.

Example 2 – Capital contribution of a building in settlement of a rights issue

Entity B made a rights issue to all shareholders. Shareholders are entitled to acquire one new share for each share owned at a fixed price of C4 at the date of the rights issue. Entity C owns 1 million of entity B's shares, that is, 10% of the share capital. Entity C subscribed to 1 million of entity B's new shares. Following the subscription, entity C proposed to entity B to settle the purchase price of the new shares by transferring an office building it owns to entity B. Entity B agreed to accept the building as settlement for the new shares.

IFRS 2 is not applicable to this transaction because it is a rights issue to all shareholders. The method of payment is a transaction with shareholders in their capacity as shareholders; the transfer of the building is, therefore, outside IFRS 2's scope. The subscription established a right to receive a fixed payment of C4m from entity C. The transfer of the building was agreed after the receivable was established and is in settlement of the C4m receivable.

Example 3 – In-kind capital contribution by existing shareholder

Entity D needs a new office building and has arranged to acquire it from an existing shareholder. The purchase price will be settled by the entity issuing 1,000 new shares. For legal purposes, the transaction is considered an in-kind capital contribution of a building.

The counterparty did not act in its capacity as shareholder, but as a supplier of the office building. As such, the in-kind capital contribution is within IFRS 2's scope. This would mean that the office building is recognised at its fair value with equity being credited by the same amount for the share issue.

A12.32.2 There are a number of issues that need to be considered before reaching a conclusion that such transactions are not within the scope of IFRS 2 including:

- Whether the instrument that the employees are entitled to is an equity instrument or linked to an equity instrument, as defined by the standard. [IFRS 2 App A]. If the instrument is an equity instrument or linked to an equity instrument and the value varies depending on the extent to which the employee provides services the transaction would be within IFRS 2's scope as a share-based payment.

- Whether the rights/interests of employee shareholders differ from those of other investor shareholders (for example, venture capitalists). Employees may have the right to additional shares with other investor shareholders giving up their rights – a ratchet mechanism. This ratchet usually depends on the business' performance and hence employees get more shares if the business does well. This would qualify as a performance condition, as services from employees contribute towards the company meeting the performance targets and, hence, the transaction is within IFRS 2's scope.
- Whether holders have different rights following an exit event. Through the articles, employees may be given different rights (cash or shares) if an investor exits through a flotation rather than trade sale. This provides evidence of a performance condition (achieving different rights to cash or shares depending on the exit event that occurs) which would scope the arrangement into IFRS 2.

- Leaver conditions (the articles or terms and conditions may define good leavers and bad leavers). In this situation the employees may lose their right to shares by leaving the entity, either by the shares being repurchased or cancelled. Hence, employees may only earn their right to the shares if they stay with the company or, for example, in the event of an IPO. This would also be considered a service condition and, hence, the arrangement is in IFRS 2's scope.

- Whether additional services are being provided. As noted above, employees will often lose their rights to shares if they leave the company. There is often a service requirement, for example, to stay in employment for a number of years or until a change in control. However, this may not always be the case and some employees may have the right to shares whether they stay or leave. This does not automatically scope the arrangement out of IFRS 2, because IFRIC 8 would still require determination of whether additional services are being provided by the shareholders in their capacity as employees, by reference to the fair value of the shares at the date of grant (refer to para A12.49.1 onwards).

- Whether a trust is involved in the arrangement. The existence of an employee benefit trust to buy back and warehouse shares for the benefit of other employees could well imply that shares are being issued as an incentive and, hence, the arrangement is in IFRS 2's scope.

The above list is not exhaustive. However, it highlights some of the areas that should be considered in order to determine if the transaction is within IFRS 2's scope.

Example – Purchase of shares at fair value, with service condition

A CEO is offered the opportunity to buy 100,000 shares in entity A at C1 each, the same price paid by the venture capital investor that holds 40% of entity A's shares. If the CEO resigns within two years he must give the shares back to the entity in return for a payment of the lower of his subscription price and the fair value of the shares.

This transaction is in IFRS 2's scope as in purchasing the shares the CEO accepts a service condition that must be satisfied before he is fully entitled to the risks and rewards of the shares (that is, there is a vesting period of two years).

Leaver provisions

A12.32.3 Some share-based payment arrangements include good and bad leaver provisions. A good leaver is often defined as an individual who leaves the entity due to injury, disability, death, redundancy or on reaching normal retirement age. A bad leaver is usually defined as any other leaver. The following example considers the scope implications in relation to typical leaver provisions.

Example – Exit event with good and bad leavers

Entity A's directors have been given an incentive in the form of share options that will vest when an exit event occurs (the entity is unlisted). Each director has paid an up front exercise price of C10 per share and will become unconditionally entitled to shares in the entity if he or she is still in service when an exit event occurs.

'Exit event' is defined in the scheme's terms and conditions as a trade sale, a listing or other change in control. An exit event is expected to occur in the form of a trade sale in three years' time.

The terms and conditions also set out provisions for good and bad leavers. For every share option held, a 'bad leaver' will receive cash equal to the lower of the amount paid (C10) and the market value of the share (market value will be determined by independent valuation consultants). A 'good leaver' will receive cash equal to the higher of the amount paid and the market value in respect of each share option held.

As any director can choose to leave the entity at any time triggering a contractual 'bad leaver' cash payment that the entity cannot avoid, entity A has a liability under IAS 32 in respect of all directors, that is, for the total number of share options granted. The liability will be measured at the lower of C10 per share and the market value of the share. The payments by the directors are in effect an advance payment of an exercise price due when the awards vest.

In addition to the bad leaver liability, the arrangement in respect of good leavers and directors who are still in service at the time of the trade sale falls within the scope of IFRS 2.

The fair value of share options (which will be incremental to the amount that has already been provided in case each individual becomes a bad leaver) awarded to any director expected to be a good leaver before the exit event occurs will be treated as a cash-settled share-based payment (see from para A12.62.2 in relation to non-market vesting conditions).

The fair value of share options that are expected to vest as a result of the trade sale will be treated as an equity-settled share-based payment (this will be incremental to the amount that has already been provided in case each individual becomes a bad leaver and will not include amounts in repect of any individual who is expected to become a good leaver). Note that if the share options do vest as a result of the trade sale, the bad leaver liability in respect of each individual for whom the award vests will be transferred into equity.

Drag along and tag along clauses

A12.32.4 Some arrangements include 'drag along' and 'tag along' clauses. For example, if an existing majority shareholder chooses to sell his investment in an entity, a drag along clause in an arrangement's terms and conditions may state that the shareholder can force employee shareholders or share option holders to sell their holdings at the same price/date. Alternatively, in the event of a sale of an entity, a tag along clause may allow employees to force an acquirer to purchase their holdings at the same price/date.

Example – Settlement by an acquirer in cash

Entity A grants its employees restricted shares. The articles state that the shares will remain restricted until entity A is acquired. At the date that the entity is acquired, a drag along clause will be invoked such that the employees will be required to sell their shares to the acquirer.

In entity A's financial statements, the award of restricted shares is an equity-settled share-based payment under IFRS 2 because the entity will settle the award in shares. Although the employees can only receive cash for their shares, the cash will be paid by the acquirer to the employees as shareholders. Under no circumstances will entity A be required to settle in cash.

A12.33 There is no exemption from the scope of IFRS 2 for employee share purchase plans or similar broad-based employee share schemes. In drafting IFRS 2, the IASB did consider including an exemption for plans similar to employee share purchase plans (like save as you earn ('SAYE') plans in the UK and employee share option plans ('ESOPs') in the US) and other broad-based employee share schemes, but, they concluded that the accounting for such plans should be no different from other employee share schemes. The IASB also rejected the suggestion that schemes should be exempted if the discount available to employees is small so that its impact is likely to be immaterial.

Recognition of share-based payment transactions

A12.34 The goods or services acquired in a share-based payment transaction should be recognised, either as an expense or as an increase in assets, when they are received. [IFRS 2 paras 7, 8].

A12.35 This is the aspect of IFRS 2 that has caused most controversy, primarily in respect of employee share and share option schemes. Many respondents to ED 2, and the discussion paper before IFRS 2, argued that it was wrong to recognise an expense in respect of such schemes, raising a number of conceptual and practical concerns. For example:

- The effect of an employee share transaction is that existing shareholders transfer some of their ownership interests to employees. Hence, the reporting entity is not involved in the transaction.

- Employees do not provide services in consideration for an award of shares or options. They are instead rewarded in cash.

- There is no cost to the entity in an equity-settled transaction as there is no transfer of cash or other assets. Furthermore, an expense recognised in respect of an equity-settled transaction would not be consistent with the IASB's 'Framework for the preparation and presentation of financial statements', which states in paragraph 70 that *"expenses are decreases in economic benefits during the accounting period in the form of outflows or depletions of assets or incurrences of liabilities that result in decreases in equity, other than those relating to distributions to equity participants"*. It is argued that as there is no outflow or depletion of assets, there can be no expense.

- By reducing earnings and increasing the number of shares (or potential shares) in issue, the impact of an equity settled transaction is to 'hit' earnings per share twice.

- The expense in respect of an employee share or share option scheme cannot be measured reliably.

- To require recognition (or greater recognition) of expenses in respect of employee share and share option schemes could have adverse economic consequences as it might discourage entities from introducing or continuing with such schemes.

A12.36 The basis for conclusions section of IFRS 2 discusses these concerns in detail. The rationale for recognising all types of equity-settled share-based payment transactions, irrespective of whether the equity instrument is a share or a share option, and irrespective of whether the equity instrument is granted to an employee or to some other party, is that the entity has engaged in a transaction that is in essence the same as any other issue of equity instruments. In other words, the entity has received resources (goods or services) as consideration for equity instruments. It should, therefore, account for the inflow of resources (goods or services) and the increase in equity. Subsequently, either at the time of receipt of the goods or services or at some later date, the entity should also account for the expense arising from the consumption of those resources. Hence, the issue of equity instruments and the consumption of resources are to be considered separately. The former results in an increase in equity while the latter is reflected as an expense.

Timing of recognition

A12.37 As noted above, the goods or services acquired in a share-based payment transaction should be recognised when they are received. Typically it will be a question of fact as to when this occurs. However, sometimes, as in the case of employee services, this will be less obvious. For example, a company may grant share options to its employees. Certain performance conditions need to be satisfied over, say, the next three years for the options to be exercisable and even then they may only be exercised after a further year has elapsed. Should an expense be recognised when the award is granted, over the three-year performance period or over the longer period until the options vest (that is, the employees become unconditionally entitled to exercise the options)?

A12.38 IFRS 2 concludes that where equity instruments, such as options awarded to employees, vest immediately, in the absence of evidence to the contrary, an entity should presume that they represent consideration for services already rendered. Accordingly, the entity should recognise the employee services received in full on the date on which the options are granted. [IFRS 2 para 14].

A12.39 On the other hand, if the options do not vest until the employees have completed a specified period of service, the entity should presume that services are to be rendered over that period. [IFRS 2 para 15]. This is referred to as the vesting period. No distinction is drawn in IFRS 2 between vesting periods during which employees have to satisfy specific performance conditions and vesting periods during which there are no particular requirements other than to remain in the entity's employ. Hence, in the example in paragraph A12.37 above, the period over which employee services should be recognised is the four-year period until the options vest and employees become unconditionally entitled to them and not the shorter period during which the employees must satisfy specific performance conditions.

A12.40 The treatment of vesting conditions is considered in greater detail from paragraph A12.59.

Group situations – location of share-based payment charge

A12.40.1 In certain circumstances it may not be immediately clear which entity or entities within a group should bear the IFRS 2 charge. This may be, for example, where an award has been granted to employees who provide services to a number of entities within a group. It may be that employees are remunerated by a service company for services to a number of operating entities. Alternatively, individuals may be directors of both the parent company and an operating subsidiary. The charge should be borne by the entity that is in substance the employer.

A12.40.2 It will be necessary to assess the facts and circumstances surrounding each situation by considering a range of factors, including the following:

- Which entity obtains the benefits associated with the employee. For example, where an individual is a director of both the parent company and an operating subsidiary, consider whether the director is being rewarded for services to the group as a whole (contributing to strategic decisions for the group, or perhaps implementing a restructuring programme) or whether the director is being rewarded for services to the operating subsidiary's business.
- Whether there is a service company arrangement in place. For example, where an individual performs services for a large number of group operating entities and the time spent at each entity varies (or may change) from time to time, this may indicate that a service company is the employer.
- Which entity ultimately bears the employment cost. While one entity may physically pay the employee, the cost may be recharged to another group entity that receives services from the employee. The IFRS 2 charge would generally be expected to follow other employee costs.
- The nature of any management recharges. For example:
  - Whether management costs (such as wages and salaries, overheads and other administrative expenses) are charged back individually (such that the entity's income statement includes each cost as a separate line item) or as part of a larger 'block' management recharge.
  - Whether the employee's costs are recharged to another entity at a margin.
- Which entity sets the employee's salary, appraises the employee and determines any bonus.
- Which entity has issued the employee's contract and which entity the employee considers to be their employer.
- The nature of the employee's contract. For example, whether the employee's contract states that he/she may be required to work for a number of group entities or whether an employee is temporarily seconded to a specific operating entity.

[The next paragraph is A12.41.]

The credit entry

A12.41 The treatment of the credit entry in respect of a share-based payment transaction will depend on whether it is accounted for as an equity-settled or as a cash-settled transaction. In the case of an equity-settled transaction, there is no obligation to transfer economic benefits so the credit entry should be recognised as an increase in equity. A cash-settled transaction, on the other hand, does give rise to an obligation so a liability should be recognised. [IFRS 2 para 7].

A12.42 As regards equity-settled transactions, IFRS 2 does not stipulate where in equity the credit entry should be recognised. In our view, subject to any statutory constraints, it would be permissible for the credit to be to the profit and loss reserve. This is a complicated area and companies may need to take legal advice to comply with local legislation.

UK.A12.42.1 In the UK it is acceptable to present the credit in the profit and loss reserve. Indeed, this is where it is commonly seen. The credit could be taken to a separate share-based payment reserve, but not the share premium account, which is determined by the amount of cash subscribed for the shares by the employees (or the ESOP trust as the case may be).

A12.42.1 The credit to equity will be presented in the statement of changes in equity. It will not be presented in a statement of recognised income and expense, as it reflects the issue of an equity instrument and does not represent a gain.

Equity-settled share-based payment transactions

A12.43 Equity-settled share-based payment transactions are transactions in which an entity receives goods or services as consideration for its own equity instruments. Examples include the following:

- Employee share option schemes.
- Employee share schemes, including employee share purchase plans and share incentive plans.
- Transactions in which an entity obtains goods or services in exchange for its own equity instruments. For example, start-up companies may obtain consultancy and similar services in exchange for shares, thus preserving scarce cash resources and giving the supplier an opportunity to share in the company's success.

A12.44 In each case, IFRS 2 requires an entity to measure the goods or services received and the corresponding increase in equity at fair value. Fair value is defined as *"the amount for which an asset could be exchanged, a liability settled, or an equity instrument granted could be exchanged, between knowledgeable, willing parties in an arm's length transaction"*. [IFRS 2 App A].

Measurement of equity-settled share-based payment transactions

A12.45 Ideally, the fair value of the goods or services obtained by an entity will be measurable directly. However, if the fair value of the goods or services cannot be measured reliably, the standard requires that it should be measured by reference to the fair value of the equity instruments granted as consideration. [IFRS 2 para 10]. This is sometimes referred to as the 'indirect method'. In these circumstances, the fair value of the equity instruments represents the best surrogate for the price of the goods or services.

A12.46 The principle described in the previous paragraph is best illustrated in the context of employee services. Shares and share options are often granted to employees as part of their remuneration package, in addition to a cash salary and other employment benefits. Usually, it is not possible to measure directly the services received for particular components of an employee's remuneration package. Furthermore, options or shares are sometimes granted as part of a bonus arrangement, rather than as an element of basic remuneration. By granting options, in addition to other remuneration, the entity is paying additional remuneration to obtain additional benefits. Estimating the fair value of those additional benefits is likely to be difficult. Therefore, IFRS 2 requires an entity to measure the fair value of the employee services received by reference to the fair value of the equity instruments granted. [IFRS 2 para 11].

A12.46.1 Employees are individuals who:

- Render personal services to the entity and are regarded as employees for legal or tax purposes.
- Work for the entity under its direction in the same way as individuals considered employees for legal or tax purposes.
- Render services that are similar to those rendered by employees.

[IFRS 2 App A].

Example – Who are employees?

An oil company hired an external consultant to assess its oil reserves. The service was provided over a five month period and will be settled by the entity issuing 100 shares to the consultant, valued at C40,000 when the contract was awarded. The entity estimated the cash fair value of the service to be C38,000, based on bids from other consultants. The consultant was considered an employee for tax purposes.

The consultant is considered an employee for the purpose of IFRS 2. Management should, therefore, recognise the service at the fair value of the granted equity instruments, that is, C40,000.

IFRIC 8 may also be relevant, for example if another bid for the contract had been C42,000, there could be an IFRIC 8 charge of C2,000 (see para A12.491).

A12.47 In the case of transactions with parties other than employees, it is presumed that it will be possible to measure the fair value of goods or services reliably. [IFRS 2 para 13]. However, this may sometimes not be possible, in which case the presumption should be rebutted and the fair value should be measured indirectly by reference to the fair value of the equity instrument granted as consideration.

A12.48 Where the fair value of goods or services (other than those received from employees) is capable of direct measurement, it should be measured at the date on which the goods are received or the services are rendered. [IFRS 2 para 13]. With the publication of IFRIC 8 (see para A12.49.1) an entity will be required to consider if there are any unidentifiable goods or services received or to be received by the entity. This should be calculated as the fair value of the equity instruments granted, less the fair value of goods or services received. When the fair value of goods or services is measured by reference to the fair value of equity instruments granted, measurement should be at either:

- The date on which the equity instruments are granted, in the case of employee services or where the goods or services are unidentifiable.
- The date on which the goods are received or the services are rendered, in all other cases.

[IFRS 2 paras 11, 13; IFRIC 8 para 12].

A12.49 The measurement of fair value at grant date is considered further from paragraph A12.95. Measurement of fair value when the goods or services are received is illustrated in the following examples:

Example 1 – Measurement of fair value by the direct method

Entity A is a small start-up entity. To assist it in developing its business, it receives consultancy services from entity B. The entities have agreed that, as entity A has scarce cash resources, the consideration for the consultancy services will be in the form of entity A's ordinary shares. The agreed rate is one share for each hour of consultancy services. Entity B has a publicised schedule of scale rates and the amount charged for a project of this nature is normally C100 per hour. Therefore, subject to the guidance noted in paragraphs A12.49.1 to A12.49.3 below, an expense and an increase in equity of C100 should be recognised by entity A for each hour of consultancy services received.

Example 2 – Measurement of fair value by the indirect method

The facts are similar to example 1, except that further shares are issued to entity B as it assists entity A in respect of a particular project, with 100 shares being awarded if the project is successful.

In this case, it may not be possible to measure reliably the fair value of the consultancy services themselves. The value of the transaction and shares received may have little to do with the value derived from the time spent by the consultants. Instead, the fair value should be measured as the services are rendered by reference to the fair value of the shares offered as consideration.

A12.49.1 As noted in paragraph A12.28.3, the measurement of an equity-settled share-based payment transaction has been extended with the publication IFRIC 8, 'Scope of IFRS 2', published by the IFRIC in January 2006. It is applicable for accounting periods beginning on or after 1 May 2006 with earlier adoption encouraged. The interpretation addressed accounting for share-based payment transactions where it is difficult to demonstrate that goods or services have been (or will be) received. For example, an entity may grant shares to a charitable organisation for nil consideration. It is usually not possible to identify the specific goods or services received in return for such a transaction. A similar situation might arise in transactions with other parties. [IFRIC 8 para 2]. In such a situation, the interpretation would require the entity to measure the unidentifiable goods or services that have been (or will be) received in accordance with IFRS 2 by using the fair value of the equity instruments granted.

A12.49.2 The interpretation also addresses the situation where the consideration for goods or services received (if any) appears to be less than the fair value of the equity instruments granted or liability incurred. The interpretation states that, in these cases, other consideration (being unidentifiable goods or services) has been (or will be) received. [IFRIC 8 para 9]. If this is the case then the unidentified goods or services should be recognised.

A12.49.3 The interpretation seems to be an almost generic rebuttal of the presumption for non-employee goods or services that the fair value of the goods or services can be more reliably measured than the fair value of the equity instrument. The argument is that if the goods or services cannot be identified then clearly they cannot be reliably measured. As a result of IFRIC 8, far more exercises will be required to determine the fair value of awards made. The following examples illustrate the application of IFRIC 8.

Example – Measurement of fair value where services are unidentifiable

An entity granted shares with a total fair value of C100,000 to parties other than employees who are from a particular section of the community (historically disadvantaged individuals), as a means of enhancing its image as a good corporate citizen. The economic benefits derived from enhancing its corporate image could take a variety of forms, such as increasing its customer base, attracting or retaining employees (who may prefer to work for an entity that supports such 'good causes'), or improving or maintaining its ability to tender successfully for business contracts.

The entity cannot identify the specific consideration received. For example, no cash was received and no service conditions were imposed. Therefore, the identifiable consideration (nil) is less than the fair value of the equity instruments granted (C100,000). The circumstances indicate that unidentifiable goods or services have been (or will be) received and, therefore, IFRS 2 applies.

The rebuttable presumption in IFRS 2, that the fair value of the goods or services received can be estimated reliably, does not apply here. The entity should instead measure the goods or services received by reference to the fair value of the equity instruments granted. [IFRS 2 para 13].

Example 2 – Measurement of fair value where fair value of license cannot be reliably estimated

An entity grants 10% of its shares to the local government for nil consideration in exchange for an indefinite-lived license to operate in that country. The fair value of the license is not determinable.

The entity is expected to receive a benefit from the license and, thus, the transaction would fall within the scope of IFRS 2. As the license is an identifiable good, the share-based payment should be recognised at the date when the license is received. As the fair value of the license received cannot be estimated reliably, the entity should instead measure the license received by reference to the fair value of the equity instruments granted.

Note that if the fair value of the license is determinable and less than the fair value of the shares, there may be unidentifiable goods or services to be accounted for, as IFRIC 8 would still apply.

A12.50 IFRS 2 envisages that it will normally be possible to estimate the fair value of equity instruments granted. However, it is acknowledged that there may be situations (for example, where equity instruments are granted by some unlisted companies) in which it is not possible to estimate fair value reliably. In these circumstances, IFRS 2 requires the following approach.

- The equity instruments granted should be measured at their intrinsic value, both initially and subsequently at each reporting date and at the date on which the award is finally settled. For a grant of share options, the award is finally settled when the options are exercised, forfeited or lapse. Any change in intrinsic value is recognised in profit or loss.

- The amount recognised as an expense should be based on the number of equity instruments that ultimately vest or, in the case of options, are ultimately exercised.

[IFRS 2 para 24].

A12.51 We believe that it will rarely be the case that the fair value of equity instruments granted cannot be estimated reliably. If in this rare situation it is the case that the fair value cannot be measured, the entity would measure the transaction using an intrinsic value measurement method. However, specialist advice should be sought if this measurement method is to be followed.

Grant date

A12.52 Grant date is defined in IFRS 2 as *"the date at which the entity and another party (including an employee) agree to a share-based payment* *arrangement, being when the entity and the counterparty have a shared understanding of the terms and conditions of the arrangement. At grant date the entity confers on the counterparty the right to cash, other assets, or equity instruments of the entity, provided the specified vesting conditions, if any, are met. If that agreement is subject to an approval process (for example, by shareholders), grant date is the date when that approval is obtained".* [IFRS 2 App A].

A12.53 Often it will be clear as to when the parties involved in a share-based payment arrangement have a shared understanding of the arrangement's terms and conditions. Sometimes, however, certain of the terms may need to be confirmed at a later date. For example, if a entity's board of directors agrees to issue share options to senior management, but the exercise price of those options will be set by the remuneration committee that meets in three months' time, grant date is when the exercise price is set by the remuneration committe even though the service period starts when the awards are offered to senior management.

A12.54 Similar questions are raised when equity instruments are granted subject to an approval process. This is considered in the following example.

Example – Grant subject to approval process

Directors of an entity customarily include in letters to new employees the offer of options to subscribe for shares in the entity. In February 20X5 the entity offered new employees options over 10,000 shares at the then market price of C10 per share. The letters stated that the board of directors supported the offer. The awards were approved by the shareholders in June 20X5, by which time the market price of the entity's shares had risen to C15 and the fair value of the options had also increased. What is the grant date for the purposes of IFRS 2? The possibilities are:

- The date on which the original offers were made – February 20X5.
- The date on which the awards were approved by shareholders – June 20X5

The allotment of shares or rights to shares in general has to be authorised by shareholders in general meeting or by the entity's articles. In this case, the award of options was subject to shareholder approval so the grant date is the date on which that approval was obtained (that is, June 20X5). However, in practice many companies have in place a pre-existing authorisation from shareholders to cover potential awards of equity instruments to employees before the next AGM. If such pre-authorisation were to exist, in this case, the grant date would generally be considered to have been February 20X5. The situation might differ where the board of directors, as majority shareholders, controls the entity. Where the directors' shareholding gives them the necessary power to authorise the award, for example if there is no shareholders' agreement or similar that requires the consent of the minority, the directors might be able to regard their meeting as being a properly constituted shareholders' meeting for this purpose and should, as a matter of good practice, record themselves as meeting in that form.

A12.55 In the previous example, if grant date is considered to be June 20X5, employees may have already begun to provide services to the entity before that date. As IFRS 2 requires the entity to recognise an expense as employee services are received, an expense will sometimes be recognised in respect of a share-based payment arrangement in advance of the grant date. In this situation, the grant date fair value of the equity instruments should be estimated, for example, by reference to the fair value of the equity instruments at the balance sheet date. An expense will then be based on an estimated amount until the date of grant has been established. At that point, the entity should revise the earlier estimates so that the amounts recognised for services received in respect of the grant are ultimately based on the grant date fair value of the equity instruments.

A12.55.1 The following examples provide further illustrations in determining the grant date when applying IFRS 2. It is vital that the grant date is correctly established as this is the point at which the fair value of the equity-settled share-based payment is measured.

Example 1 – Award subject to shareholder approval

An award is communicated to individual employees on 1 December 20X5, subject to shareholder approval. The award is then approved by shareholders on 1 February 20X6, with the same terms as had initially been communicated to employees. A letter to formalise the award is sent to individual employees on 1 March 20X6.

As the award is subject to an approval process (in this example, by shareholders), the grant date is the date when that approval is obtained. The letter to formalise the award is mainly administrative, both the employees and the employer have a shared understanding on 1 February 20X6 and, therefore, this is the grant date.

Example 2 – Individual notification of award

An award is approved by the board/shareholders on 1 December 20X5. The general terms and conditions of the award (but with insufficient information to determine each employee's share) are posted to the website on 31 December 20X5. The employees are individually informed of their shares on 1 February 20X6.

The grant date is when both parties agree to a share-based payment arrangement. The word 'agree' is used in its usual sense, which means that there must be both an offer and acceptance of that offer. Hence, the date at which one party makes an offer to another party is not always the grant date. In some instances, the counterparty explicitly agrees to the arrangement, for example, by signing a contract. In other instances, agreement might be implicit for example, for many share-based payment arrangements with employees, the employees' agreement is evidenced by their commencing to render services'. Therefore, in this example the grant date is 1 February 20X6.

Example 3 – Services received before grant date

A new compensation package for key employees is announced on 1 January 20X5. The plan covers the calendar year 20X5, incorporates the results of the previous year's annual appraisal process and includes a new share option scheme. The option scheme is subject to approval by shareholders. The shareholders approved the scheme on 28 February 20X5.

The fair value of the share options is measured at the grant date, 28 February 20X5. If the agreement between the entity and its employees is subject to an approval process (for example, by shareholders), the grant date is the date on which that approval is obtained. However, IFRS 2 requires the entity to recognise employee services as they are received and in this case the expense will be recognised in advance of the grant date from 1 January 20X5 when the employees begin rendering services. [IFRS 2 paras 7, IG 4]. The entity should estimate the grant date fair value for the purpose of recognising the expense during the period between the service commencement date and the grant date. Management should revise the earlier estimate once the grant date has been established. The recognised expense is based on the actual grant date fair value of the equity instruments.

Where, at the date the financial statements are signed, the grant date has not occurred and, therefore, the actual fair value of a share award at the grant date is not known, it should be estimated (for example, by reference to the equity instrument's fair value at the date when the original offers were made or at the balance sheet date) and an expense based on that estimate recognised. When the fair value of the awards at grant date is known, the entity should revise the earlier estimate of fair value and recognise the impact of that change in estimate prospectively.

Example 4 – Bonus scheme with services received before grant date and settlement in both cash and shares

Note that this example also illustrates the impact of vesting conditions (see further from para A12.59).

On 1 January 20X5 an entity announced a bonus subject to exceeding the revenue target for 20X5.

C500 of the bonus will be paid in cash on 31 March 20X6 whether or not the employee remains in service at that date. The other part of the bonus will be settled in share options provided that the employee is still in service on 31 March 20X6. The exercise price and number of options will be approved by management on 31 March 20X6. Management expect that the revenue target will be met and that no employees will leave between 31 December 20X5 and 31 March 20X6. At 31 December 20X5 the estimated grant date fair value is C500.

The entity should accrue a liability of C500 for the cash part of the bonus at 31 December 20X5, because the revenue target was met and employees are entitled to the payment even if they leave by 31 March 20X6.

The entity should also recognise an estimated expense of C400 (12/15ths of C500) and a corresponding increase in equity for the part of the bonus that is to be settled in share options subject to the service vesting condition.

As for example 3 above, the share options did not have a grant date on 31 December 20X5, because the parties did not have a shared understanding of the arrangement's terms and conditions. However, IFRS 2 requires the entity to recognise the services when received and, therefore, the fair value at the grant date, 31 March 20X6, must be estimated.

Once the terms of the options are fixed on the grant date, 31 March 20X6, the actual fair value can be calculated and, if necessary, the cumulative charge should be revised.

Example 5 – Award at the discretion of remuneration committee

Employees have been awarded share options that will vest subject to achieving a total shareholder return (TSR) performance target over a three year period. However, at the end of the three year period, where the remuneration committee is not satisfied that the TSR position achieved is supported by the underlying performance of the business the committee has discretion to refuse the award.

Where the remuneration committee has discretion to override an award, despite a performance condition being achieved, there is no shared understanding at the date the award is made. The grant date does not occur until the remuneration committee operates its overriding discretion at the end of the vesting period. The fair value of the award would, therefore, be estimated at each reporting date from the date that services are provided and final measurement would occur at the end of the vesting period. As a result, this may give rise to significantly greater charges in the income statement than where the grant date occurs when the award is made.

In certain circumstances it may be possible to conclude that grant date has been achieved when the award is made. For example, where a remuneration committee has discretion to alter the award but only where the value of each individual's award is not adversely affected, grant date may have been achieved for the guaranteed element of the award. Alternatively, where, in practice, the remuneration committee has never exercised its discretion to override and the entity can prove that it will not do so in the future (and employees share this understanding), it may be possible to conclude that grant date has occurred. It should be noted, however, that this is likely to be difficult to achieve where a discretion clause is set out in the articles.

The circumstances surrounding the award should be carefully assessed and the situation explained in the financial statements where it is concluded that the grant date has occurred when the award is made. Where material, it should be disclosed as a significant accounting policy judgement under IAS 1, 'Presentation of financial statements'. [IAS 1, para 113].

Awards conditional on IPO

A12.56 IFRS 2 does not deal explicitly with awards that are conditional on an initial public offering (IPO). As noted above, an expense in respect of an award of, say, options is recognised immediately if the award vests immediately, or over the vesting period if one exists. [IFRS 2 paras 14,15]. In the case of an IPO (or similar exit event), the award will generally not vest until the IPO occurs so it is reasonable to conclude that the vesting period will be the period from the grant date until the date of the IPO. However, this raises two questions:

- What will the grant date be?
- How can the date of a future IPO be estimated reliably?

A12.57 As regards grant date, the facts of individual awards will vary. Sometimes, an award will be subject to approval at the time of the IPO, in which case grant date would correspond with the date of the IPO. On other occasions, shareholder approval will have been obtained when the award is made or at some other time in advance of the IPO. Nevertheless, IFRS 2 requires that an expense is recognised as employee services are received, regardless of when grant date is determined to occur. Accordingly, as described in paragraph A12.55, where the grant date falls after the employees have begun to provide services, the fair value of the award should be estimated and then revised at the grant date.

A12.58 The more difficult question concerns how the date of a future flotation can be estimated reliably. Paragraph 15(b) of IFRS 2 requires that where the length of the vesting period varies, depending on when a performance condition is satisfied, an estimate must be made on the basis of the most likely outcome. Practically, some companies may find it extremely difficult to estimate the date of a flotation. Nevertheless, a reasonable estimate must be made, although this may then be revised if necessary. This is illustrated in the following example.

Example

The directors of an entity with a June year end are contemplating a listing of the entity's shares. On 31 March 20X5 an award of options is made to employees, but these are exercisable only in the event of a flotation. Furthermore, employees leaving the entity before this occurs will lose their entitlement to the options.

When the award is made, the directors estimate that a stock market listing will be achieved in three years' time. However, during the remainder of 20X5 and the first half of 20X6 the entity performs well and, following discussions with the entity's bankers, the directors decide to seek a listing by the end of 20X6. Due to unforeseen circumstances this target is not achieved, but the shares are finally listed on 31 August 20X7.

Assuming that the directors have the authority to make the award of options to the employees, grant date in this example will be 31 March 20X5 and the fair value of the award will be measured on that date. If the award is subject to shareholder approval at the date of the flotation, fair value will be estimated (for example, by reference to the fair value of the options at each balance sheet date) and revised at grant date when the shareholder approval is obtained.

When the award is made the directors estimate that the listing may be achieved in three years time so an expense in respect of employee services will initially be recognised over this period. By 30 June 20X6, the directors have revised their estimate of the date of listing to the end of 20X6, so the recognition of the expense would be accelerated. By 30 June 20X7, the listing has not yet occurred, but the process has commenced and the directors are able to estimate that it will be achieved within two months. Hence, the expense for the year ending 30 June 20X7 will be based on this estimate. So for the three financial years ending 30 June 20X7, the estimated vesting period for the award of options for the purposes of recognising an expense in accordance with IFRS 2 will be as follows:

Year	**Vesting period**
30 June 20X5	Three years ending 31 March 20X8
30 June 20X6	One year and nine months ending 31 December 20X6
30 June 20X7	Two years and five months ending 31 August 20X7

The accounting for changes in estimates such as these under IFRS 2 is illustrated in example 3 in paragraph A12.68.

A12.58.1 Where awards vest only on an exit event such as flotation, and an exit event is not deemed to be probable, no expense would be recognised. Alternatively it may be determined that some of the awards will vest in another way. These points are illustrated in the following example.

Example – Interaction with other vesting conditions

As in the example in paragraph A12.58, the directors of an entity are contemplating a listing of the entity's shares. On 31 March 20X5 the entity made an award of options to ten employees. The grant date was achieved on this date.

The award is exercisable in full on flotation. Alternatively, where, on leaving the entity, an employee is determined to be a good leaver before flotation has occurred, he/she may exercise options on a *pro rata* basis (based on the length of time the employee has served since the award was granted as a proportion of the maximum 5 year period that the award may be in existence). The arrangement's terms and conditions define a good leaver as someone who is made redundant, dies, or retires on reaching normal retirement age.

There is a cut-off date such that unvested awards will lapse after 5 years, on 31 March 20Y0.

On 30 June 20X5, the directors estimate that a listing will be achieved on 31 March 20X8. One employee is expected to be a good leaver before 31 March 20X8, reaching normal retirement age on 31 December 20X6. All other employees are expected to remain with the entity beyond 31 March 20X8.

On 30 June 20X6, following a change in the entity's fortunes, the directors are of the view that the entity is unlikely to float before 31 March 20Y0. A restructuring programme is underway and it is anticipated that three employees will be made redundant on 31 December 20X6.

For the entity's 30 June 20X5 year end, the award will be treated in two tranches. Awards are expected to vest on 31 March 20X8 for nine employees. The fair value of their awards will be spread over the 3 year vesting period, that is 3 out of 36 months of the charge will be taken in the period to 30 June 20X5. The fair value of the award for the good leaver will be spread over the 21 month vesting period to 31 December 20X6, that is, 3 out of 21 months' charge will be taken in the period to 30 June 20X5. The calculation for the good leaver will also take into account the fact that vesting will be on a *pro rata* basis, that is, based on 21 out of 60 months' service.

At 30 June 20X6, a reversal of the charge in respect of the nine awards no longer expected to vest on flotation will be necessary, however, this will only be a partial reversal in respect of the three employees who will be made redundant. The charge in respect of these good leavers will now be spread over the shorter 21 month period from the grant date to 31 December 20X6 and will be adjusted for the fact that it will vest on a *pro rata* basis. A charge will continue to be made for the employee expected to retire on 31 December 20X6.

[The next paragraph is A12.59.]

Vesting conditions

A12.59 As explained in paragraph A12.39, where a counterparty to a share-based payment arrangement is required to complete a specified period of service before its equity instruments vest, the goods or services obtained by the reporting entity are recognised over that period. [IFRS 2 para 15]. For example, an entity grants options to its employees with a fair value of C300,000. These options vest in three years' time with the only condition being that the employees remain in the entity's service for that period. Assuming that all of the options do vest (that is, none of the employees leave the entity), the amount charged as an expense each year will be C100,000. This will be the case regardless of any movements in the price of the entity's shares. So, even if the options have an intrinsic value of, say, C500,000 when they are exercised, the amount charged as an expense will be unchanged. Having determined the 'price' of employee services when the options were granted, this remains fixed.

A12.60 In reality, employee share option plans, indeed equity-settled share-based payment transactions generally, are seldom that simple. Typically, there will be performance conditions that must be satisfied before employees are absolutely entitled to the equity instruments. For example, the number of options to which employees are entitled under a bonus plan may depend on a certain increase in profit or growth in the entity's share price. Even in the simple example described in the previous paragraph, the amount charged as an expense in each period will vary depending on the latest estimate of the likely number of employees who will remain for three years and, hence, the number of options that will vest. Although the fair value of equity instruments granted is not re-measured, the estimate of the number of equity instruments that is likely to vest is revised, if necessary, until the instruments actually do vest.

A12.61 Conditions that must be satisfied before a counterparty becomes unconditionally entitled to the equity instruments it has been granted are referred to as vesting conditions. IFRS 2 defines vesting conditions as: *"the conditions that must be satisfied for the counterparty to become entitled to receive cash, other assets or equity instruments of the entity, under a share-based payment arrangement. Vesting conditions include service conditions, which require the other party to complete a specified period of service, and performance conditions, which require specified performance targets to be met (such as a specified increase in the entity's profit over a specified period of time)"*. [IFRS 2 App A]. It follows that the vesting period is the period during which all the specified vesting conditions are to be satisfied. The following example illustrates the period over which all specified vesting conditions are to be satisfied, which could be different for different employees in the same share award scheme.

Example 1 – Award exercisable on chosen retirement date

An employee is currently 58 years old and is granted some options that vest over 5 years if he continues in employment. This employee, however, has the option to retire anytime between 60 and 65 (inclusive) without requiring the employer's consent. If the employee chooses to retire at the age of 60, the employee is able to keep the options, which become exercisable at that date. In this example the vesting period for this individual is two years as he becomes entitled to and can walk away with the options at the age of 60, whether he chooses to continue working beyond that date or not.

Example 2 – Options awarded instead of annual bonus

An entity normally awards options annually instead of an annual bonus. The entity grants options representing an annual bonus in 20X4, in respect of the year to December 20X3. The award is not exercisable for three years and the employee must remain with the entity throughout this period.

In this situation, there is an expectation on the part of the employees that they will receive a bonus each year. Consequently, employees are providing services in 20X3 to earn the right to equity instruments. However, there is an additional period of service that the employee is required to complete until the equity instrument vests unconditionally with them. Therefore, the expense should be over the performance period (20X3) and the service period (20X4 to 20X6). The vesting period is a total of four years.

It should be noted that if the employee was not required to remain with the entity for the three year period, the vesting period would be one year (20X3) and the three year delay until the award is exercisable would simply be a post-vesting restriction.

A12.61.1 The IASB is considering a proposal to amend IFRS 2 such that vesting conditions will be restricted to service conditions and performance conditions (see further from para A12.171). A near-final draft of the amendment was published in May 2007. However, at the time of writing this manual the proposals have not been finalised.

A12.61.2 Share awards may have more than one vesting period, which an employee is required to perform to be entitled to the share award, as illustrated in the example below.

Example – Employee choice of settlement

An entity agreed the details of an award with its employees on 1 January 20X6. Under the terms, employees can choose on 31 March 20X6 either:

- cash payment of 25%–50% of salary, depending on specified performance measures, at 31 March 20X7; or
- shares with value equivalent to 150% of the cash payment, but the employee must remain in service for a further 3 years.

The grant date would be 1 January 20X6, as this is the date both parties involved have a shared understanding of the terms and conditions including the formula that would be used to determine the amount of cash to be paid (or the number of shares to be delivered).

The entity has granted the employee the right to choose whether a share-based payment transaction is settled in cash or by the entity issuing equity instruments. The entity has granted a compound financial instrument, which includes a debt component (that is, the counterparty's right to demand cash payment) and an equity component (that is, the counterparty's right to demand settlement in equity instruments). (See paras A12.142 to A12.147.)

The entity should account separately for the goods or services received or acquired in respect of each of the compound instrument's components. [IFRS 2 para 38]. The vesting period of the equity component and that of the debt component should be determined separately and the vesting period of each component may be different. In the above example, the vesting period for the debt component is 1.25 years (1 January 20X6 – 31 March 20X7) and the vesting period for the equity component is 4.25 years (1 January 20X6 – 31 March 20Y0), because employees are entitled to shares only if they complete a 4.25-year service period.

A12.62 The treatment of vesting conditions will vary depending on whether or not any of those conditions relate to the market price of the entity's equity instruments. Such conditions, which IFRS 2 defines as 'market conditions', are taken into account when determining the fair value of the equity instruments granted, so they are ignored for the purposes of estimating the number of equity instruments that will vest. [IFRS 2 para 21]. Market conditions are considered further from paragraph A12.104.

A12.62.1 The following table illustrates some of the more common market and non-market conditions associated with share-based payment arrangements.

Market conditions (Affecting the fair value of the award)	**Non-market conditions** (Affecting the number of awards that vest)
Achieve a minimum share price by a specified date.	Remain in employment for a specified period of time.
Achieve a total shareholder return target.	Achieve earnings per share or profit targets.
Out perform a share price index.	Complete a particular project.
	Successful flotation (see para A12.56).

A12.62.2 For conditions other than market conditions, an entity should recognise the goods or services it has acquired during the vesting period based on the best available estimate of the number of equity instruments expected to vest. It should revise that estimate, if necessary, when subsequent information indicates that the number of equity instruments expected to vest differs from previous estimates. Finally, on vesting date, the entity should revise the estimate to equal the number of equity instruments that ultimately vested. [IFRS 2 paras 19-20].

A12.63 Some share options contain a reload feature. This provides for an automatic grant of additional options ('reload options') whenever the option holder exercises previously granted options using the entity's shares, rather than cash, to satisfy the exercise price. This is illustrated in the following simple example. An entity has issued 100 options to one of its directors. The total

The amount recognised as an expense in each year will be as follows:

Year	Expense for the year	Cumulative expense	Calculation of cumulative expense
31 December 20X5	C90,000	C90,000	54 (that is, 60 × 90%) × 1,000 × 5 × $\frac{1}{3}$
31 December 20X6	C100,000	C190,000	57 (that is, 60 × 95%) × 1,000 × 5 × $\frac{2}{3}$
31 December 20X7	C85,000	C275,000	55 × 1,000 × 5

Example 2 – Grant of equity instruments with a specific performance condition (growth in earnings per share)

On 1 January 20X5, entity B made an award of shares to each of its 50 employees. The number of shares to which each employee will become entitled depends on growth in earnings per share (EPS). If EPS increases by an average of 10% over the next three years, each employee will receive 100 shares. If EPS increases by an average of 15%, each employee will receive 200 shares. If EPS increases by an average of 20%, each employee will receive 300 shares. No shares will be awarded if EPS increases by less than 10%. The recipients of the award must also remain in the employ of entity B for three years. The fair value of each share at 1 January 20X5 is C12.

EPS is a non-market condition as it is not dependent upon share price. The condition is, therefore, relevant in determining the number of awards that will vest.

In the year ended 31 December 20X5, entity B's EPS increased by 16% and management forecast similar growth for the next two years. Hence, management predicted that each employee would receive 200 shares. However, 20X6 was a comparatively poor year and EPS increased by just 12% resulting in an average for the two-year period of 14%. Management cut back its forecast as a result, predicting growth of 14% for 20X7. On this basis, each employee would receive 100 shares. 20X7 was actually a much better year and EPS increased by 17% resulting in an average for the three-year period of 15% so each employee did, in fact, receive 200 shares.

During 20X5, five employees left the entity and management predicted a similar level of departures for the next two years, so 35 awards would vest. Six employees departed during 20X6, but management maintained its forecast of five departures in 20X7, so 34 awards would vest. However, only three employees left during 20X7, so 36 awards actually vested.

The amount recognised as an expense in each year will be as follows:

Year	Expense for the year	Cumulative expense	Calculation of cumulative expense
31 December 20X5	C28,000	C28,000	35 × 200 × 12 × $\frac{1}{3}$
31 December 20X6	(C800)	C27,200	34 × 100 × 12 × $\frac{2}{3}$
31 December 20X7	C59,200	C86,400	36 × 200 × 12

This example illustrates how the impact of 'truing up' the cumulative expense in each period may result in the reversal of amounts previously changed.

Example 3 – Grant of equity instruments in which the length of the vesting period varies

On 1 January 20X5, entity C granted 1,000 shares to each of its 500 employees, conditional upon the employees remaining in the employ of entity C throughout the vesting period. The shares will vest at the end of 20X5 if the entity's earnings increase by more than 20%; at the end of 20X6 if the entity's earnings increase by more than an average of 15% over the two-year period; and at the end of 20X7 if the entity's earnings increase by more than an average of 10% over the three-year period. The fair value of each share at 1 January 20X5 is C6.

During 20X5, earnings increased by 16% and 25 employees left the entity. Management forecast that earnings would grow at a similar rate in 20X6 so the share awards would vest at the end of 20X6. Management also estimated that a further 25 employees would leave the entity, so 450 awards would vest.

During 20X6, earnings increased by only 10% resulting in an average for the two-year period of 13% so the awards did not vest. However, management forecast that earnings growth for 20X7 would be at least 4%, thereby achieving the average of 10% per year. 30 employees left the entity during 20X6 and management estimated a similar level of departures for 20X7, so 415 awards would vest.

During 20X7, earnings increased by 10% (resulting in an average over the three-year period of 12%) and 27 employees left the entity.

The amount recognised as an expense in each year will be as follows:

Year	Expense for the year	Cumulative expense	Calculation of cumulative expense
31 December 20X5	C1,350,000	C1,350,000	450 × 1,000 × 6 × ½*
31 December 20X6	C310,000	C1,660,000	415 × 1,000 × 6 × $\frac{2}{3}$
31 December 20X7	C848,000	C2,508,000	418 × 1,000 × 6

* ½ not $\frac{1}{3}$ as at the end of 20X5 management expected the award to vest at the end of 20X6

Example 4 – Grant of equity instruments in which the exercise price varies

On 1 January 20X5, entity D made an award of 1,000 share options to each of its 50 senior employees. The recipients of the award must remain in entity D's employ for three years. The exercise price of each option is C10, but this will drop to C8 if EPS increases by an average of 10% over the next three years. If EPS increases by an average of 15% or more, the exercise price will drop to C6. The fair value of each option 1 January 20X5 is C6 if the exercise price is C10; C9 if the exercise price is C8 and C12 if the exercise price is C6.

In the year ended 31 December 20X5, entity D's EPS increased by 16% and management forecast similar growth for the next two years. However, 20X6 was a comparatively poor year and EPS increased by just 12% resulting in an average for the two-year period of 14%. Management cut back its forecast as a result, predicting growth of 14% for 20X7. 20X7 was actually a much better year and EPS increased by 17% resulting in an average for the three-year period of 15%, so the options were exercisable at C6.

During 20X5, five employees left the entity and management predicted a similar level of departures for the next two years, so 35 awards would vest. Six employees departed during 20X6, but management maintained its forecast of five departures in 20X7, so 34 awards would vest. However, only three employees left during 20X7, so 36 awards actually vested.

Because the exercise price varies depending on the outcome of a performance condition that is not a market condition, the effect of that performance condition (that is, the possibility that the exercise price might be C10, C8 or C6) is not taken into account when estimating the fair value of the share options at grant date. Instead, the fair value of the options is estimated under each scenario and the accounting in each period reflects the most likely outcome. Hence, the amount recognised as an expense in the first year is based on the assumption that the exercise price will be C6 so the fair value of each option is C12. For 20X6, it is forecast that the exercise price will be C8, so the fair value of each option is C9. In both cases, the fair value is as measured at grant date.

The amount recognised as an expense in each year will be as follows:

Year	Expense for the year	Cumulative expense	Calculation of cumulative expense
31 December 20X5	C140,000	C140,000	$35 \times 1{,}000 \times 12 \times \frac{1}{3}$
31 December 20X6	C64,000	C204,000	$34 \times 1{,}000 \times 9 \times \frac{2}{3}$
31 December 20X7	C228,000	C432,000	$36 \times 1{,}000 \times 12$

Example 5 – Expected life of option depends on non-market vesting condition

On 1 January 20X5, entity E granted 1,000 share options to employees. Each option entitles the employee to purchase one share at a fixed price. The options are exercisable between 1 January 20X7 and 31 December 20X7 if the entity meets its EPS target for 20X5 and 20X6, or on 1 January 20X7 if any of the 20X5 and 20X6 EPS targets are not met. The options' grant date fair values are C1.20 if the options are exercisable on 1 January 20X7, and C2 if the options are exercisable between 1 January 20X7 and 31 December 20X7.

Management determined at 31 December 20X5 that the 20X5 EPS target was met and management expected to meet the 20X6 EPS target. However, the 20X6 EPS target was not met. No employees left the entity, and all 1,000 options ultimately vested.

Entity E should recognise an expense of C1,000 for 20X5 (1,000 options × C2 × 50% of the vesting period), because it met its 20X5 EPS target and at the balance sheet date expected to meet the 20X6 target. At 31 December 20X6, management should convert from the grant date fair value of C2 to C1.20 because the non-market EPS condition was not met. It should recognise an expense of C200 for 20X6 (1,000 options × C1.2 × 100% of the vesting period, less C1,000 expensed in 20X5), thus bringing the total expense recognised over the two years to C1.20.

Example 6 – Grant of equity instruments with a market condition

On 1 January 20X5, entity F made an award of 10,000 options to each of its 50 senior management employees, conditional upon the employees remaining in the entity's employ until the end of 20X7. However, the share options cannot be exercised unless the share price has increased from C10 at the beginning of 20X5 to at least C17.50 at the vesting date.

If the share price is at least C17.50 at 31 December 20X7, the share options can be exercised at any time during the next two years.

At grant date, the fair value of each option (which takes into account the possibility that the share price will be at least C17.50 at 31 December 20X7) is C4.

At the date of the award, management estimated that 10% of employees would leave the entity before the end of three years. Hence, 45 awards would vest. During 20X6 it became apparent that more employees than expected were leaving so management revised its estimate of the number of awards that would vest to 42. At the end of 20X7, awards to 40 employees actually vested.

Where awards are granted with market conditions, paragraph 21 of IFRS 2 requires an entity to recognise the services received from a counterparty who satisfies all other vesting conditions, irrespective of whether the market conditions are satisfied. In other words, it makes no difference whether share price targets are achieved – the possibility that a share price target might not be achieved has already been taken into account when estimating the fair value of the options at grant date. Therefore, the amounts recognised as an expense in each year will be the same regardless of whether the share price has reached C17.50 by the end of 20X7.

The amount recognised as an expense in each year will be as follows:

Year	Expense for the year	Cumulative expense	Calculation of cumulative expense
31 December 20X5	C600,000	C600,000	$45 \times 10{,}000 \times 4 \times \frac{1}{3}$
31 December 20X6	C520,000	C1,120,000	$42 \times 10{,}000 \times 4 \times \frac{2}{3}$
31 December 20X7	C480,000	C1,600,000	$40 \times 10{,}000 \times 4$

In the previous example, the amount recognised as an expense was the same regardless of whether the market condition is satisfied. The impact of market conditions is considered further in the following example.

Example 7 – Vesting conditions relate to share price growth

The facts are the same as in example 3, except that the vesting condition concerns the growth in entity C's share price rather than its earnings. Hence, the shares will vest at the end of 20X5 if the share price increases by more than 20%; at the end of 20X6 if the share price increases by more than an average of 15% over the two-year period; and at the end of 20X7 if the share price increases by more than an average of 10% over the three-year period.

As in example 3 the fair value of each share is C6, but this takes into account the possibility that the share price target will be achieved during the next three years as well as the possibility that it will not be achieved. At grant date, management estimated that the most likely outcome of the market condition was that the share price target would be reached by the end of 20X6. Management also estimated that 450 awards would vest. However, the target was actually reached in 20X7 and 418 awards vested at 31 December 20X7.

Paragraph 15(b) of IFRS 2 provides that where the length of the vesting period may vary, depending on when a performance condition is satisfied, an entity should base its accounting on an estimate of the expected length of the vesting period, based on the most likely outcome of the performance condition. This is illustrated in example 3. However, if the performance condition is a market condition, the estimate of the length of the expected vesting period should be consistent with the assumptions used in estimating the fair value of the options granted and should not be subsequently revised. Accordingly, in this example entity C should treat the award as if it did vest at the end of 20X6 (when 445 employees remained in employment). The fact that the award actually vested at the end of 20X7, after a further 27 employees had left the entity, is ignored.

The amount recognised as an expense in each year will be as follows:

Year	**Expense for the year**	**Cumulative expense**	**Calculation of cumulative expense**
31 December 20X5	C1,350,000	C1,350,000	450 × 1,000 × 6 × ½
31 December 20X6	C1,320,000	C2,670,000	445 × 1,000 × 6

Example 8 – Earnings per share hurdle

Entity G granted share options to employees in exchange for services on 1 January 20X5. The options become exercisable if entity G achieves its earnings per share (EPS) target of C0.23 per share for 20X5 and 20X6. The options' fair value on grant date, ignoring this condition, was C100,000.

Management assessed the probability of meeting the EPS targets as 60%, and fair value of the options, including the EPS conditions as C65,000. The EPS target was met for 20X5 and management also expects to meet the 20X6 target.

The EPS targets are a non-market vesting condition. Management should recognise an expense of C50,000 in 20X5 based on an expectation that 100% of the options will vest at the end of 20X6.

The outcome of the EPS condition can only be that either all options vest or that no options vest. The 60% probability of meeting the EPS condition means that management expect 100% of the options to vest.

Example 9 – Vesting subject to exit event

On 1 January 20X7, entity H granted share option awards to senior management. The awards vest when an exit event (defined in the articles as a listing or change in control) occurs. The number of option awards that vest depends upon the date that the exit event occurs, as follows:

Date of exit event	**Number of awards that vest**
1 January 20X7 – 31 December 20X7	25%
1 January 20X8 – 31 December 20X8	50%
1 January 20X9 – 31 December 20X9	75%
1 January 20Y0 – 31 December 20Y0	100%

At the 31 December 20X7 reporting date, management concluded that a listing was probable and expected to occur on 30 June 20X9.

The IFRS 2 charge should, therefore, be taken over the period from 1 January 20X7 to 30 June 20X9 based upon the expectation that 75% of the awards will vest. The IFRS 2 charge should not be front loaded (see example 10 below).

Example 10 – Staged vesting

Entity I grants 1,000 share options to employees on 1 January 20X7. If an exit event (defined in the articles as a listing or change in control) occurs at any time during the period from 1 January 20X7 to 31 December 20Y0, and employees are still in service at the date of exit, the employees will be entitled to exercise all of their outstanding options. Additionally, until the date of exit, 25% of the options vest each year (provided that the employee is in service at that particular year end) as follows:

Tranche	Date	Number of awards that vest	Cumulative number of vested awards
a	31 December 20X7	250	250
b	31 December 20X8	250	500
c	31 December 20X9	250	750
d	31 December 20Y0	250	1,000

At the 31 December 20X7 reporting date, management concluded that a listing was probable and expected to occur after three and a half years, on 30 June 20Y0.

The expense will be calculated in award tranches, resulting in a front loaded IFRS 2 charge. Assuming that no employees are expected to leave the entity and that the anticipated date of exit does not change, the charge for the first two years of the arrangement will be determined as follows:

Year end	Calculation of expense for year	Cumulative expense to date
31 December 20X7	FV tranche a option × 250 × 1	FV tranche a option × 250 × 1
	FV tranche b option × 250 × 1/2	FV tranche b option × 250 × 1/2
	FV tranche c option × 250 × 1/3	FV tranche c option × 250 × 1/3
	FV tranche d option × 250 × 1/3.5	FV tranche d option × 250 × 1/3.5
31 December 20X8	n/a	FV tranche a option × 250 × 1
	FV tranche b option × 250 × 1/2	FV tranche b option × 250 × 2/2
	FV tranche c option × 250 × 1/3	FV tranche c option × 250 × 2/3
	FV tranche d option × 250 × 1/3.5	FV tranche d option × 250 × 2/3.5

Social security contributions on share options gains

Background

UK.A12.69 UK employers are required to pay National Insurance Contributions (NIC) (social security contributions) on the exercise of certain share options granted after 5 April 1999. The NIC charge applies to share options issued under unapproved share schemes (that is, those not approved by the Inland Revenue) where the shares are 'readily convertible assets', that is, they can be sold on a stock exchange or there are arrangements in place that allow the employees to obtain cash for the shares acquired under the option scheme.

UK.A12.70 The charge is based on the intrinsic value of the options at the date of exercise (that is, the excess of the market price of the shares over the exercise price).

[The next paragraph is A12.75.]

Treatment of social security contributions under IFRS

A12.75 There is no specific standard within IFRS that governs the accounting for social security contributions, as there is for income taxes. When considering under which standard social security costs should be accounted for, IAS 19 concludes that in the context of short-term employee benefits, social security contributions (such as NIC in the UK or FICA in the US) are employee benefits and should be considered in the same way as wages, salaries and so on. [IAS 19 para 8(a)]. This suggests that the social security contributions payable in connection with a grant of share options should be considered as an integral part of the grant itself. Hence, the accounting for the social security contributions will be dictated by IFRS 2 and the charge will be treated as a cash-settled transaction. Cash-settled share-based payment transactions are discussed in detail from paragraph A12.134.

A12.76 The accounting for social security contributions as a cash-settled share-based payment transaction means:

- A liability should be recognised in respect of social security contributions payable in the future when options are exercised.
- The amount of the liability will depend on the number of options that are expected to be exercised (that is, vesting conditions are taken into account).
- The expense should be allocated over the period from the date of grant to the end of the vesting period. From the end of the vesting period to the date of actual exercise the liability should be adjusted by reference to the current market value of the shares.

A12.77 The important difference is that the liability will be based on an estimate of fair value, as if it represented an element of a cash-settled share-based payment transaction, rather than the market price of the shares at the balance sheet date. This is illustrated in the following example.

Example – Treatment of social security contributions

The facts are the same as example 1 in paragraph A12.68. On 1 January 20X5, entity A made an award of 1,000 options to each of its 60 employees. The only condition associated with the award was that recipients must remain in the employ of entity A for three years. At the date of the award, management estimated that 10% of employees (that is, 6 employees) would leave the entity before the end of three years. On 31 December 20X6, management revised their estimate of leavers to 5% (that is, 3 employees). However, awards to 55 employees actually vested on 31 December 20X7. All options must be exercised by the end of 20X9. On 31 December 20X8, when the intrinsic value of each option was C10, ten employees exercised their options. The remaining 45 employees exercised their options on 31 December 20X9 when the intrinsic value of each option was C14. The fair value of an option at each year end is shown below:

Year	Fair value at year end
31 December 20X5	6
31 December 20X6	8
31 December 20X7	9
31 December 20X8	12
31 December 20X9	14

Assuming the rate for employers' social security contributions throughout this period is 12.8%, the amount to be paid by entity A will be 12.8% of the intrinsic value of options exercised. For example, the amount payable at 31 December 20X8 is C12,800 (being 12.8% × 10 × 1,000 × 10). However, the amount recognised as a liability at each period end should be based on an estimate of the fair value of an option at that date. Hence, the amount recognised as an expense in each year and as a liability at each year end will be as follows:

Year	Expense	Liability	Calculation of liability
31 December 20X5	C13,824	C13,824	54 × 1,000 × 6 × 12.8% × $\frac{1}{3}$
31 December 20X6	C25,088	C38,912	57 × 1,000 × 8 × 12.8% × $\frac{2}{3}$
31 December 20X7	C24,448	C63,360	55 × 1,000 × 9 × 12.8%
31 December 20X8	C18,560	C69,120	45 × 1,000 × 12 × 12.8% Expense reflects extent to which social security contributions paid (C12,800) exceeds the liability at the previous year end in respect of the ten employees who exercised their options (C11,520) plus an adjustment to the liability of C17,280 (that is, 45 × 1,000 × (12−9) × 12.8%).
31 December 20X9	C11,520	C0	Liability extinguished. Expense reflects extent to which social security contributions paid exceeds the liability at the previous year end (45 × 1,000 × 14 × 12.8% = C80,640).

A12.78 The accounting treatment described above differs from that applied when accounting for the corporation tax effects of equity-settled share-based payments. IFRS 2 includes a consequential amendment to IAS 12, 'Income taxes', that specifies that if the amount allowed as a tax deduction in future periods is dependent upon an entity's share price at a future date, the measurement of the deductible temporary difference should be based on the entity's share price at the end of the period. [IAS 12 para 68B]. Hence, the accounting for deferred tax is based on the year end intrinsic value rather than an estimate of the fair value of the equity instrument. It is unclear from the basis of conclusions why the IASB concluded that an intrinsic value basis is appropriate for deferred tax accounting, although it is emphasised that an estimate of the fair value of an equity instrument is not intended to represent an estimate or forecast of a future share price. Nevertheless, in view of IAS 19's inclusion of social security contributions within the definition of employee benefits, in our opinion they should be considered an element of the share-based payment transaction and accounted for accordingly.

A12.78.1 A question arises as to how events after the balance sheet date affect the measurement of the liability in respect of social security contributions. This is illustrated in the following example.

Example – Social security contributions on share options — post year end fall in share price

An entity has outstanding employee share options that will attract a social security liability when exercised. The option exercise price is C10 and the market price of the entity's shares at the year end was C50. Since the year end there has been a large fall in share prices in the sector and the entity's share price has dropped to C15. In addition, 30 per cent of the employees to whom options were granted have left and forfeited their options.

Can the entity take those subsequent events into account when calculating the liability at the balance sheet date?

As described from paragraph A12.75 above, a liability is required for the social security contribution on outstanding option grants expected to vest. The liability is derived from the *fair value* of the equity instrument granted, re-measured at each reporting date and spread over the period from the date the options were granted to the end of the vesting period. It is clear, therefore, that where options are expected to be exercised, the provision recognised at the balance sheet date should not be adjusted for subsequent changes in the market price of the entity's shares. The liability should be calculated at each balance sheet date to reflect the *fair value* of the liability at that date. Although market prices may fluctuate widely after the year-end, such fluctuations are disregarded, as with movements in foreign exchange rates that occur after the balance sheet date.

At each balance sheet date the entity needs to estimate the number of options that will ultimately be exercised. Where future events will affect the liability that will ultimately be payable, IAS 37, 'Provisions, contingent liabilities and contingent assets', requires those events to be taken into account in estimating the provision where there is sufficient objective evidence that they will occur. In some cases the estimation necessarily involves a degree of hindsight. We believe the subsequent forfeiture of a substantial number of options should be taken into account when estimating the number of options expected to be exercised.

Reimbursement or transfer of the liability

A12.79 In some countries, such as the UK, it is permissible for employers and employees to agree that the employee can pay the employer's social security contributions on share options. The employee can bear the employer's social security charge arising on share option gains in one of two ways:

- First, the employer and the employee can make an agreement that some or all of the employer's social security liability can be recovered from the employee.
- Secondly, the employer and the employee may make a joint election to legally transfer the liability for the secondary social security contribution to the employee.

A12.80 Where there is an agreement between the employer and employee under which the employee agrees to reimburse all or part of the employer's social security contributions, a liability will be recognised by the employer as set out in paragraph A12.76. When considering the presentation of the reimbursement from the employee, IAS 19 would only permit recognition of the right to reimbursement as a separate asset if the receipt was virtually certain, with a net presentation permitted in the income statement. [IAS 19 para 104A].

A12.81 Where there is a joint election by employer and employee under which the liability is formally transferred to the employee, no liability appears in the employer's financial statements.

Modifications, cancellations and settlements

Modifications and re-pricing

A12.82 An entity might modify the terms and conditions on which equity instruments were granted. For example, in recent years, during which equity markets have been somewhat volatile, many companies have reduced the exercise price of options to restore some of the perceived value of share option plans to their employees.

A12.83 The approach taken in IFRS 2 to the accounting for such modifications is to view them as instruments in their own right. Where a modification increases the fair value of the equity instruments granted (for example, by reducing the exercise price of share options), an entity should include the incremental fair value granted in the measurement of the amount recognised for the services received over the remainder of the vesting period. The incremental fair value is the difference between the fair value of the modified equity instrument and that of the original equity instrument, both estimated as at the date of the modification. An expense based on the incremental fair value is recognised in addition to any amount in respect of the original instrument, which should continue to be recognised over the remainder of the original vesting period (unless there is a failure to satisfy vesting conditions – see from para A12.59). [IFRS 2 para 27].

A12.84 Guidance on how to apply the above requirements is given in Appendix B to the standard. In addition to modifications that increase the fair value of equity instruments granted (such as reductions in the exercise price of options), the principles of paragraph 27 of IFRS 2 also apply to other modifications that are otherwise beneficial to the employees. Examples include:

- An increase in the number of instruments granted.
- A reduction in the vesting period.
- The modification or elimination of a performance condition.

A12.85 If a modification increases the number of equity instruments granted, the entity should include the fair value of the additional equity instruments, measured at the date of the modification, in the measurement of the amount recognised for services received in a similar way to that described in paragraph A12.83. [IFRS 2 para B43(b)].

A12.86 If an entity modifies the vesting conditions associated with an award (for example, by reducing the vesting period or eliminating a performance condition, other than a market condition), this should be taken into account when considering the estimate of the number of equity instruments expected to vest. [IFRS 2 para B43(c)].

A12.87 The period over which the impact of a modification is recognised will depend on when it occurs and any vesting conditions it imposes. For example, if the modification described in paragraph A12.83 (reduction in option exercise price) occurs during the vesting period, the incremental fair value granted is included in the measurement of the amount recognised for services received over the period from the modification date until the date when the modified equity instruments vest. IFRS 2 does not, however, specify whether, in the case of a modification that reduces the vesting period, the change in vesting period should be accounted for prospectively or retrospectively. We believe that either approach is acceptable, for the reasons set out in example 3 of paragraph A12.89. If the modification occurs after the vesting date, the incremental fair value granted is recognised immediately, or over the revised vesting period if the employee is required to complete an additional period of service. [IFRS 2 para B43(a)].

A12.88 Sometimes an entity may modify the terms and conditions of a grant of equity instruments in a manner that reduces the arrangement's total fair value or is not otherwise beneficial to the employee. The accounting treatment of such modifications is similar to that described above insofar as the entity should continue to account for the original grant as if the modification had not occurred. However:

- If the modification reduces the fair value of the equity instruments granted, this should be ignored. The entity should not recognise reduced expense as a consequence of the modification.
- If the modification reduces the number of equity instruments granted, this should be accounted for as a cancellation of that portion of the grant (see para A12.91).
- If an entity modifies the vesting conditions associated with an award (for example, by increasing the vesting period or adding a performance condition), this should *not* be taken into account when considering the estimate of the number of equity instruments expected to vest.

[IFRS 2 para B44].

A12.89 The accounting treatment of modifications to terms and conditions is considered further in the following examples.

Example 1 – Reduction in option exercise price

On 1 January 20X5, entity A made an award of 1,000 options to each of its 60 employees. The only condition associated with the award is that recipients must remain in the employ of entity A for three years. The fair value of each option is C5.

Towards the end of 20X5, entity A's share price dropped so, on 1 January 20X6, management chose to reduce the exercise price of the options. At the date of the re-pricing, the fair value of each of the original share options granted was C1 and the fair value of each re-priced option was C3. Hence, the incremental fair value of each modified option was C2.

At the date of the award, management estimated that 10% of employees would leave the entity before the end of three years (that is, 54 awards would vest). During 20X6 it became apparent that fewer employees than expected were leaving so management revised its estimate of the number of leavers to only 5% (that is, 57 awards would vest). At the end of 20X7, awards to 55 employees actually vested.

The amount recognised as an expense in each year will be as follows:

Year	Expense for the year	Cumulative expense	Calculation of cumulative expense
31 December 20X5	C90,000	C90,000	$54 \times 1{,}000 \times 5 \times \frac{1}{3}$
31 December 20X6	C157,000	C247,000	$57 \times 1{,}000 \times ((5 \times \frac{2}{3}) + (2 \times ½))$
31 December 20X7	C138,000	C385,000	$55 \times 1{,}000 \times (5 + 2)$

Example 2 – Increase in the number of options granted

The facts are similar to example 1, except that instead of reducing the option exercise price on 1 January 20X6, the number of options to which each employee was entitled was increased to 1,500. The fair value of each of these additional options was C1.

The amount recognised as an expense in each year will be as follows:

Year	Expense for the year	Cumulative expense	Calculation of cumulative expense
31 December 20X5	C90,000	C90,000	$54 \times 1{,}000 \times 5 \times \frac{1}{3}$
31 December 20X6	C114,250	C204,250	$57 \times ((1{,}000 \times \frac{2}{3} \times 5) + (500 \times ½ \times 1))$
31 December 20X7	C98,250	C302,500	$55 \times ((1{,}000 \times 5) + (500 \times 1))$

Example 3 – Reduction in the vesting period – prospective versus retrospective adjustment

On 1 January 20X6, entity B awarded an employee 100 share options subject only to the employee remaining in service for three years. At 1 January 20X6, the fair value of each option was C6.

On 1 December 20X6, entity B decides to reduce the service requirement from three years to two years, thereby reducing the vesting period to two years.

It is assumed that the employee remains in service beyond 31 December 20X6.

We believe that entity A has a policy choice for accounting for modifications of equity-settled awards occurring part way through a reporting period that reduce the vesting period by either using a retrospective or a prospective treatment.

Retrospective treatment
The modification may be accounted for retrospectively to reflect the best estimate available as at that date of awards that are expected to vest. This is supported by paragraph 19 of IFRS 2 which states that "*...the amount recognised for goods or services received as consideration for the equity instruments granted shall be based on the number of equity instruments that eventually vest*". Where there is a change in estimate of the period over which the awards are expected to vest and that change occurs during the year, the cumulative expense may be 'trued up' at the balance sheet date to reflect the best estimate of awards expected to vest as of that date. On this basis, the expense each year as a result of the modification would be as follows:

Year	Expense for the year	Cumulative expense	Calculation of cumulative expense
31 December 20X6	C300	C300	100 × C6 × ½
31 December 20X7	C300	C600	100 × C6

Prospective treatment
Alternatively, the modification may be accounted for prospectively from the date of modification (1 December 20X6). While paragraph 19 of IFRS 2 states that the expense should be recognised based on the best estimate available, it does not specify the point at which changes in those estimates should be accounted for.

An analogy may be made to IAS 8 and the treatment of changes in estimates where a change in estimate is accounted for prospectively from the date of change. [IAS 8 para 36].

Furthermore, accounting for the change in vesting period prospectively would be consistent with the principle set out in paragraph B43 of IFRS 2, where other types of modifications are accounted for prospectively. In addition, paragraph 15 of IFRS 2 requires that where equity instruments do not vest until the counterparty completes a specified service period, the entity should account for those services as they are rendered by the counterparty over the specified vesting period. Prior to modification, employee services received as consideration were presumed to be received over a 3 year period and as such, the expense would be recognised on this basis. The presumption changes from 3 years to 2 years when the vesting period is modified hence it would be appropriate to account for the modification prospectively and amend the recognition of expense from the modification date as follows:

Year	Expense for the year	Cumulative expense	Calculation of cumulative expense
31 December 20X6	C215	C215	Original charge, 11 months to 1 December 20X6: 100 × C6 × 1/3 × 11/12 = 183 Modification occurs 1 December 20X6. Expense over remaining 13 months to 31 December 20X7: 600 – 183 = 417 Expense for December 20X6: 417/13 = 32 Therefore, total expense for year to 31 December 20X6: 183 + 32 = 215
31 December 20X7	C385	C600	100 × C6

Whichever approach is followed, the policy should be clearly explained and consistently applied.

It should be noted that where vesting is conditional upon an exit event of some kind such as IPO, the estimated time until the exit event should be reassessed at each reporting date with adjustments made retrospectively. Prospective treatment would not be appropriate, because any adjustment would be a change in estimate, not a modification.

Example 4 – Reduction in the vesting period during final year of award with true up for actual vested awards

The facts are similar to example 1, except that instead of reducing the option exercise price on 1 January 20X6, the vesting period was shortened to two years during what will become the final year of the award (see further example 3 above in relation to situations where the vesting period is shortened at any other time during an award). At the end of 20X6, awards to 58 employees actually vested.

The amount recognised as an expense in each year will be as follows:

Year	Expense for the year	Cumulative expense	Calculation of cumulative expense
31 December 20X5	C90,000	C90,000	54 × 1,000 × 5 × $\frac{1}{3}$
31 December 20X6	C200,000	C290,000	58 × 1,000 × 5

Example 5 – Modification that is not beneficial to employees

An entity granted 100 share options to employees at an exercise price of C10 per share. The grant date is 1 January 20X4 and the options are subject to a two-year vesting period. The grant date fair value of each option was C50. The entity modified the options at

31 December 20X4 by extending the vesting period to 30 June 20X6. At 31 December 20X4 management expected that the number of options outstanding at 31 December 20X5, the original vesting date, would be 90. The actual number of options outstanding at 31 December 20X5 was 85, of which only 80 vested on 30 June 20X6. The modification did not increase the options' fair value.

The extension of the vesting period should be ignored. Modification of vesting conditions in a manner that is not beneficial to employees should not be taken into account when determining amounts to be recognised.

The expense and corresponding increase in equity recognised for 20X4 is C2,250; C50 × 90 options × 50% of the original two-year vesting period. The expense for 20X5 is C2,000; C50 × 85 options × 100% of the original two-year vesting period less C2,250, the amount expensed in 20X4. No expense is recognised in 20X6.

Example 6 – Re-priced options and extension of vesting period

Management granted 100 share options at an exercise price of C10 per share to employees in exchange for services. The grant date is 1 January 20X4 and the options are subject to a two-year vesting period. The grant date fair value of the options was C5,000 and all options are expected to vest.

The options were modified on 1 January 20X5 by reducing the exercise price to C5 per share and extending the vesting period by six months to 30 June 20X6. The fair value of the options at 1 January 20X5 was C8,000 prior to the modification and C9,500 after the modification. All options were expected to vest at the date of the modification.

The original grant date fair value is recognised over the original vesting period. The expense for 20X4 is C2,500; C5,000 × 50%. The expense for 20X5 is C3,700; C5,000 × 50% plus the incremental fair value of the modification of C1,500 × 80%. The incremental fair value is recognised over the vesting period from 1 January 20X4 to 30 June 20X6; 80% of this period passed by the balance sheet date. The incremental fair value is the difference between the fair value of the re-priced options immediately before and after the modification, that is, C9,500 less C8,000. The expense for 20X6 is C300; C1,500 × 20%.

Example 7 – Existing options rolled into new scheme

An entity has previously operated a share option scheme with the option exercise price equal to the market price of the shares at the date of grant. Management decide to roll the options into a new scheme. The entity, therefore, cancels the original option scheme and issues share options under the new scheme. The new options are granted at the same exercise price and on the same terms as the original options (that is, they have the same exercise date). However, the market price of the shares has risen since the date of grant of the initial scheme so that the exercise price is now below the market price of the shares at the date of grant of the new options.

This would not be treated as a cancellation and a new award, but instead as a modification. This is because the entity has indicated that the new award replaces a cancelled award and, therefore, under paragraph 28(c) of IFRS 2 it is treated as if the original award had been modified. Consequently, the entity would be required to account for the incremental fair value of the new award (compared with the existing award) at the date of modification and spread this over the vesting period of the new award. This would be in addition to the entity continuing to charge for the original award over the original vesting period. Note that replacement awards are sometimes structured with similar terms to those of the original award and it may, therefore, be possible that there is no incremental fair value.

It is also worth noting that if the entity had not identified the new award as a replacement award at the date the new options were granted, the cancellation and new award would be unrelated and there would be a requirement to accelerate the vesting of the original award and recognise immediately the amount that otherwise would have been recognised for services received over the remainder of the vesting period. Additionally, there would be a fair value charge for the new award over the new vesting period.

Example 8 – Modification as a result of acquisition

Entity C granted share options to its employees on 1 May 20X5. The options were exercisable subject to the completion of three years' service from that date. The terms of the scheme stated that if entity C was acquired during the three year period, the awards would vest on a *pro rata* basis (for example, if an acquisition occurs on 30 April 20X7, two thirds of the share options will vest).

On 30 April 20X7, entity D acquired entity C. The award did not vest on a *pro rata* basis on this date because the terms of the scheme were modified. The modified terms state that employees will be entitled to shares in entity D at the end of the original three year period as opposed to shares in entity C. The modified terms make clear that entity D, the acquirer, has granted, and has the obligation for, the replacement award. The terms of the scheme are otherwise unchanged.

Entity C's financial statements

Entity C originally granted an equity-settled share-based payment award to its employees. At the date of acquisition, the scheme's terms were modified and the new parent entity, D, has the obligation to settle the award. In accordance with IFRIC 11, the award will continue to be treated as equity-settled in subsidiary entity C's financial statements (see further from para A12.152).

The remainder of the original IFRS 2 charge (measured on 1 May 20X5) will continue to be spread over the vesting period to 30 April 20X8. In addition, if the modification has increased the award's fair value (measured as the difference between the award's fair value immediately before and after the modification), the incremental fair value will be spread over the remaining period to 30 April 20X8. [IFRS 2 para B43].

Entity D's separate and consolidated financial statements

From 30 April 20X7, entity D, as the acquirer, has granted an equity-settled award in its own shares to the employees of its subsidiary, entity C. This will be accounted for as a new award in both entity D's separate and consolidated financial statements. The award's fair value will be measured at the grant date, 30 April 20X7, and spread over the period to 30 April 20X8.

At the 30 April 20X8 year end, the entries in the consolidated financial statements will be:

Dr Income statement (fair value of award measured at 30 April 20X7)

Cr Equity

Further guidance on the treatment in entity D's separate financial statements is provided from paragraph A12.152.6. Based on this guidance, the entries in entity D's separate financial statements on 30 April 20X8 will be:

Dr Investment in subsidiary (fair value of award measured at 30 April 20X7)
Cr Equity

Transitional provisions

A12.90 IFRS 2's transitional provisions require additional consideration when an award granted before 7 November 2002 is modified. As discussed in paragraph A12.226, entities are encouraged, but not required, to apply IFRS 2 to equity instruments granted before 7 November 2002, if they have disclosed publicly the fair value of those equity instruments, determined at the measurement date. [IFRS 2 para 54]. Where a modification occurs after IFRS 2's effective date to equity instruments to which the IFRS was not originally applied, modification accounting in accordance with IFRS 2 is required. [IFRS 2 para 57].

Example 1 – Modification before IFRS 2's effective date

An entity granted share options to employees for services on 1 January 2003. Each option entitles an employee to purchase one of the entity's shares at a fixed price. The options have vesting conditions.

Management decided on 5 November 2004 to modify the terms and conditions and to accelerate vesting. The options vest on 31 December 2004. The entity, an existing IFRS preparer, adopted IFRS 2 on 1 January 2005.

IFRS 2 is not applicable to this grant of share options. The options vested before IFRS 2's effective date (1 January 2005). The entity should disclose information about the nature and extent of share-based payment arrangements that existed during the comparative period in its 2005 financial statements. [IFRS 2 paras 44, 45].

Example 2 – Modification after IFRS 2's effective date

An entity granted share options to employees on 1 January 2002 subject to a five year service condition. Management modified the terms and conditions on 31 December 2005, increasing the number of options awarded to each employee. The entity, an existing IFRS preparer, adopted IFRS 2 on 1 January 2005.

Where an award granted before 7 November 2002 is modified after IFRS 2's effective date, the modification should be accounted for in accordance with paragraphs 26 to 29 of the standard. This means that any incremental fair value (measured as the difference in the fair value of the award calculated immediately before and immediately after modification) should be expensed. In this case, the expense will be spread over the remainder of the vesting period, to 31 December 2006.

Cancellations and settlements

A12.91 If an entity cancels or settles a grant of equity instruments during the vesting period, it should treat this as an acceleration of vesting and recognise immediately the amount that otherwise would have been recognised for services received over the remainder of the vesting period. [IFRS 2 para 28(a)].

A12.92 Any payment made to a counterparty on the cancellation or settlement of a grant of equity instruments, even if this occurs after the vesting date, should be accounted for as a repurchase of an equity interest (that is, as a deduction from equity), except to the extent that the payment exceeds the fair value of the equity instruments repurchased, measured at the repurchase date. Any such excess should be recognised as an expense. [IFRS 2 paras 28(b), 29].

Example – Cancellation during vesting period

The facts are similar to example 1 in paragraph A12.88, except that the grant of options was cancelled on 31 December 20X5 and the 60 employees received a payment of C1.20 per option as consideration. The fair value of each option on that date was C1. No employees left the entity during 20X5, but at the end of the year management continued to estimate that 10 per cent (6 employees) would leave by the end of 20X7.

The amount recognised as an expense during 20X5 before taking account of the cancellation was C90,000. Paragraph 28(a) requires that a cancellation is treated as an acceleration of vesting. This might suggest that an expense should be measured on the basis of the number of awards outstanding at the cancellation date, that is, 60. On the other hand, paragraph 28(a) goes on to require that the amount recognised as an expense should be the amount that otherwise would have been recognised for services received over the remainder of the vesting period. This suggests that the expense should be measured on the basis of the number of awards that management expected to vest immediately before the cancellation, that is, 54. We believe that paragraph 28(a) is clear and awards that actually vest should be expensed. At this stage, when the award is cancelled, any adjustment for future expectations is no longer relevant. Accordingly, on the basis of the number of awards outstanding at the cancellation date, the amount to be recognised immediately as an expense is C210,000 (that is, (60 × 1,000 × 5) – 90,000). Hence, this amount should be recognised immediately as an expense on the date of cancellation.

The payment made to the employees of C1.20 per option exceeds the fair value of the options on the date of repurchase. Hence, only an amount equal to the fair value (C1 per option) is treated as the repurchase of an equity instrument. The excess of C0.20 is recognised as an expense. This means that C60,000 (that is, 60 × 1,000 × 1) is deducted from equity while C12,000 (that is, 60 × 1,000 × 0.20) is recognised as an expense.

[The next paragraph is A12.94.]

A12.94 Sometimes an entity may grant new equity instruments as consideration for the cancellation or settlement of an old grant. When this occurs and, on the date when those new equity instruments are granted, the entity identifies the new equity instruments as replacements for the cancelled equity instruments, the entity should treat this as a modification, as described from paragraph A12.82 above. Hence, the incremental fair value granted is the difference between the fair value of the replacement equity instruments and the net fair value of the cancelled equity instruments, at the date the replacement equity instruments are granted. For this purpose, the net fair value of the cancelled equity instruments is their fair value, immediately before the cancellation, less the amount of any payment made to the counterparty that is accounted for as a deduction from equity as described in paragraph A12.92 above. If the entity does not identify the new equity instruments as a replacement for the cancelled instruments, it should account for those new equity instruments as a new grant. [IFRS 2 para 28(c)].

Measuring the fair value of equity instruments

A12.95 Under IFRS 2, where the fair value of goods or services is measured by the indirect method (see para A12.45), the fair value of the equity instruments granted should be estimated at the relevant measurement date (see para A12.48). However, IFRIC 8 requires entities to measure the fair value of the equity instruments granted for goods or services received. If the fair value of the equity instruments granted is greater than the fair value of the goods or services received or to be received (measured using the direct method as at the grant date), the difference, being the unidentifiable goods or services received, must be recognised by the entity. As with the indirect method, the fair value of the equity instrument granted should be estimated at the relevant measurement date (see para A12.48).

A12.96 Fair value should be based on market prices, if available, taking into account any terms and conditions associated with the grant of the equity instruments. [IFRS 2 para 16]. For example, where employees have been granted an award of shares, but they are not entitled to receive dividends during the vesting period, this factor should be taken into account when estimating fair value. Similarly, if the shares are subject to restrictions on transfer after the vesting date, that factor shall be taken into account, but only to the extent that the post-vesting restrictions affect the price that a knowledgeable, willing market participant would pay for that share. If the shares are actively traded in a deep and liquid market, post-vesting transfer restrictions may have little, if any, effect on the price. [IFRS 2 para B3].

Example – Fair value implications for options that vest only on IPO

An entity grants share options to employees that will vest only if the entity achieves a stock exchange listing within two years.

Management are aware that one of the inputs into the option pricing model to determine the award's fair value is the current price of an entity's shares (see further para A12.101). When determining the current share price for an unlisted entity, a discount to the share price would normally be made to reflect the fact that there is not a market for the shares in the same way that there would be for a comparable entity with listed shares. Should the current share price of the entity's shares be discounted for illiquidity?

The standard requires that the estimated market price of an entity's shares is adjusted to take into account the terms and conditions upon which an award is granted. [IFRS 2 paras B2, B3]. In this case, the award vests only on listing and, therefore, employees will only ever be able to receive a listed share. Therefore, the input to the option pricing model would be the entity's current share price without a marketability discount, that is the entity's current share price as if for a listed share.

Note that this logic would apply similarly if vesting occurred as a result of a trade sale or takeover, as the acquiror would be paying a control premium for the shares.

A12.97 Some shares and most share options are not traded on an active market so alternative valuation techniques must be considered. The objective is to derive an estimate of what the price of those equity instruments would have been at the relevant measurement date in an arm's length transaction between knowledgeable, willing parties. [IFRS 2 para 17]. Sometimes, it may be possible to make an estimate of market price based on prices of traded shares or options with similar terms and conditions, although this is unlikely in the case of executive options with specific performance criteria. It is more likely that an alternative valuation technique will need to be applied. Many pricing models are available and IFRS 2 does not specify which should be used. It does, however, describe the factors that should be taken into account when estimating fair value. It also requires the model used to be consistent with generally accepted valuation methodologies for pricing financial instruments.

A12.98 It should be remembered that the purpose of deriving a fair value for the equity instruments granted is to measure, indirectly, the fair value of the goods or services acquired by the entity. Accordingly, once the fair value of the equity instruments has been estimated at the relevant measurement date, so the 'price' of the goods or services has been determined, it is not re-measured.

Valuation techniques

A12.99 Option pricing models are based on the premise that it is possible to hedge an option exactly by buying (and continually adjusting) a portfolio of the shares over which the option has been granted. Setting up and adjusting the 'hedge portfolio' has a cost. In theory, this hedging cost will be the same, whatever happens to the share price. Given that the option can be hedged precisely at a fixed cost, it follows that this cost will be the market value of the option.

A12.100 In practice, real markets do not always follow the idealised behaviour of financial models and there are limits to how frequently a portfolio can be rebalanced. However, investment banks do, as a matter of fact, hedge option contracts using dynamically traded hedge portfolios. These portfolios are constructed in line with the theoretical models, which have proven robust in practice, despite their imperfections.

A12.101 All option pricing models take into account, as a minimum, the following factors:

- Exercise price of the option.
- Current price of the underlying share.
- Life of the option.
- Expected volatility of the share price.

- Dividends expected on the underlying shares.
- Risk-free interest rate over the life of the option.

A12.102 The first two items define the 'intrinsic value' of the option. The remaining four are relevant to its 'time value'. The time value of an option reflects the right of the holder to participate in future gains, if any. The valuation does not attempt to predict what the future gain will be, only the amount that a buyer would pay at the valuation date to obtain the right to participate in any future gains. In other words, option pricing models estimate the value of the share option at the measurement date, not the value of the underlying share at some future date.

A12.102.1 All other things being equal, a change in the expected volatility of the share price will have the greatest impact of the input assumptions listed in paragraph A12.101 on the option's fair value (an increase in volatility increases the fair value). A change to either the option's exercise price or its life has the next greatest impact on the option's fair value (an increase in the option's exercise price decreases the option's fair value and an increase in the option's expected life increases the option fair value). This will be the case irrespective of the option pricing model used.

A12.103 Other factors that knowledgeable, willing market participants would consider in setting the price should also be taken into account. Some of these are described in paragraph A12.96. In addition, many employee options have long lives, are exercisable during specified periods (usually between vesting date and the end of the life) and are often exercised early. Furthermore, the act of exercising the options at a price below the market price at that date might itself reduce the share price. However, vesting conditions (other than market conditions) and reload features are not taken into account in the valuation. Instead, these are dealt with as described from paragraph A12.59.

A12.104 Paragraph 21 of IFRS 2 requires that market conditions are taken into account when estimating fair value. Arguably, all conditions associated with a grant of equity instruments will influence the fair value of those instruments. This was the view taken by the IASB in developing ED 2. The exposure draft proposed that all conditions (market related or otherwise) should be taken into account when determining fair value. However, respondents to ED 2 raised a variety of concerns about the practicality and subjectivity of including non-market conditions in a valuation. In response, IFRS 2 draws a distinction between market and non-market conditions, with only the former being taken into account when estimating fair value. Broadly speaking a market condition is one that is dependent on share price.

A12.105 Market conditions include target share prices and requirements to achieve a certain level of total shareholder return (that is, the sum of dividends and increases in share price). There are various means by which they may be taken into account when estimating fair value, and some valuation models are better suited to dealing with their effects than others. This is a complex area and specialist advice may need to be obtained.

Inputs to an option pricing model

A12.106 The exercise price of the option and the current market price of the underlying share will usually be readily available. However, estimating the other inputs to an option pricing model can be a complex and time consuming exercise.

Life of the option

A12.107 Holders of traded options generally have a choice between exercising, keeping or selling their options at any point in time during the option's contractual life. As the sale of options realises both their intrinsic and time value, this will usually be a more attractive proposition than exercising, so the real choice becomes between keeping or selling. A traded option would only be exercised (or lapse) at the end of its contractual term. The vast majority of employee options, on the other hand, cannot be traded, so employees only have the choice of either keeping or exercising their options. However, exercising is the only way in which an employee can realise value. In addition, it is common for the contractual life of the option to be cut short if the employee leaves the entity. This means that most employee share options are exercised much earlier than their contractual term. Accordingly, when estimating the fair value of an employee option, it is the expected life rather than the contractual life of the option that is considered.

A12.108 Appendix B to IFRS 2 describes a number of factors that should be taken into account when estimating the expected life of an option. These are:

- The length of the vesting period, because the share option typically cannot be exercised until the end of the vesting period. Hence, determining the valuation implications of expected early exercise is based on the assumption that the options will vest.
- The average length of time for which similar options have remained outstanding in the past.
- The price of the underlying shares. Experience may indicate that the employees tend to exercise options when the share price reaches a specified level above the exercise price.
- The employee's level within the organisation. For example, experience might indicate that higher-level employees tend to exercise options later than lower-level employees.
- Expected volatility of the underlying shares. On average, employees might tend to exercise options on highly volatile shares earlier than on shares with low volatility.

[IFRS 2 para B18].

A12.109 Other factors that could be considered include the following:

- The general state of the equity market, or the economy. Employees might be more inclined to hold on to their options where markets are climbing, or they might exercise their options once they see a gain if markets are performing poorly.
- The dividend yield on the underlying share. Where no dividend is paid, the option holder does not lose by not exercising. Where the dividend yield is high, the dividends lost by not exercising could outweigh the risk-free return available on the cash thus encouraging early exercise.
- The tax treatment of the benefits. In some jurisdictions, a tax charge may crystalise on vesting so employees may have to exercise their options to meet their tax liability.

A12.110 When estimating the expected life of share options granted to a group of employees, the entity could base that estimate on an appropriately weighted average expected life for the entire employee group, or on appropriately weighted average lives for subgroups of employees, based on more detailed data about employees' exercise behaviour. The distinction is likely to be important. Option value is not a linear function of option term – value increases at a decreasing rate as the term lengthens. For example, although a two-year option is worth more than a one-year option, it is not worth twice as much. That means that calculating estimated option value on the basis of a single weighted average life that includes widely differing individual lives would overstate the total fair value of the share options granted. Separating options granted into several groups, each of which has a relatively narrow range of lives included in its weighted average life, reduces that overstatement.

Expected volatility

A12.111 Expected volatility is a measure of the amount by which the price of the underlying share is expected to fluctuate during the option's life. The measure of volatility used in option pricing models is the annualised standard deviation of the continuously compounded rates of return on the share. Volatility is typically expressed in annualised terms, regardless of the time period used in the calculation, for example, daily, weekly or monthly price observations.

A12.112 Standard deviation is a statistical measure of how tightly data are clustered around a mean – the more tightly clustered the data, the smaller the standard deviation. Standard deviation is measured as the square root of the variance, which in turn is measured as the average squared difference between each observation and the mean. This is shown in the following example.

Example – Calculation of standard deviation

Data	Difference between data and mean	Difference^2
53	(2.2)	4.84
58	2.8	7.84
52	(3.2)	10.24
56	0.8	0.64
57	1.8	3.24
Mean = 55.2		Mean = 5.36

The variance (that is, the average squared difference between each number and the mean) is 5.36 so the standard deviation is 2.32, being the square root of the variance.

A12.113 In the previous example, the data represents the entire population. However, the calculation of standard deviation will normally involve a sample of data from a population, in which case the calculation is amended slightly. The formula used in these situations is expressed in one of the ways shown below.

$$\sigma = \sqrt{\frac{\Sigma(x - \bar{x})^2}{n - 1}} \quad \text{or} \quad \sigma = \sqrt{\frac{n\Sigma x^2 - (\Sigma x)^2}{n(n - 1)}}$$

Where: σ = standard deviation
x = an observation
$\bar{x}$ = the mean observation
n = the number of observations

Many spreadsheet packages and scientific calculators are able to calculate the standard deviation for a given series of data.

A12.114 An added complication when considering the volatility of rates of return is that the probability distribution of returns is considered to be lognormal rather than normal. This means that it is the logarithm of the returns that is normally distributed, rather than the returns themselves. This implies a smaller probability of significant deviations from the mean than is usually the case in practice. Consider now a more realistic example.

The market price of an entity's shares over a six week period fluctuated as follows:

Date	Share price
Week 1	C5.00
Week 2	C5.20
Week 3	C5.30
Week 4	C5.10
Week 5	C5.35
Week 6	C5.30

Hence, the return on the entity's shares each week, and the logarithm of those returns, is as shown below:

Date	Weekly return	Relative price change	Logarithm of relative price change
Week 1	–	–	–
Week 2	4.0%	1.040	0.03922
Week 3	1.9%	1.019	0.01882
Week 4	(3.8%)	0.962	(0.03874)
Week 5	4.9%	1.049	0.04784
Week 6	(0.9%)	0.991	(0.00904)

The standard deviation of the logarithm of the weekly return, and hence the weekly volatility, calculated using the formulae above, is 0.036. However, as noted above, the measure of volatility used in option pricing models is the annualised volatility. To derive this figure, it is necessary to multiply the weekly volatility by the square root of 52. This gives an annualised volatility of 0.258, normally expressed as 25.8%.

A12.115 So, what does this mean? Statistically, when data are distributed normally, one standard deviation lies within 68 per cent of the mean. Hence, the expected annualised volatility of a share is the range within which the continuously compounded annual rate of return is expected to fall 68 per cent (or approximately two-thirds) of the time. For example, if a share has an expected rate of return of 12 per cent and a volatility of 30 per cent, this means that the probability that the actual rate of return on the share will be between minus 18 per cent (12 per cent − 30 per cent) and 42 per cent (12 per cent + 30 per cent) is approximately two-thirds. This is illustrated in the diagram below.

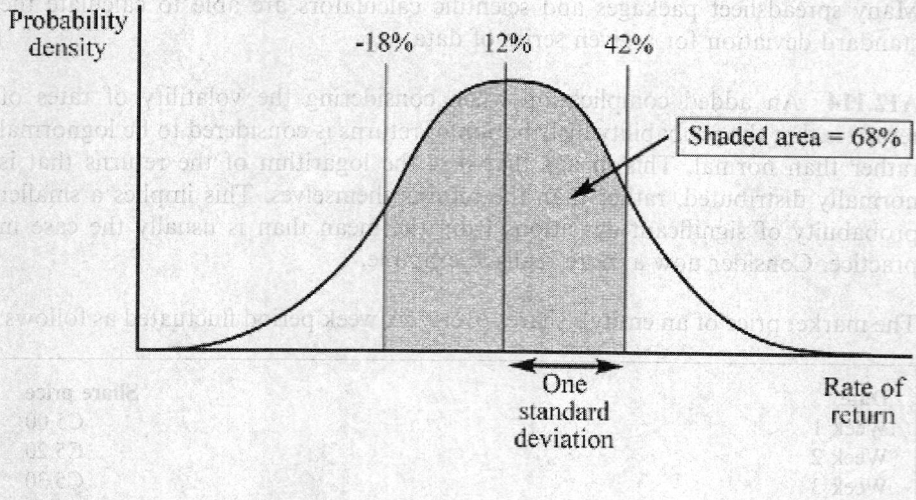

A12.116 Appendix B to IFRS 2 describes a number of factors that should be taken into account when estimating expected volatility. These are:

- The implied volatility from traded share options on the company's shares, or other traded instruments that include option features (such as convertible debt).
- The historical volatility of the share price over the most recent period that is generally commensurate with the expected term of the option.
- The length of time a company's shares have been publicly traded. Unlisted and recently listed companies are considered further below.
- The tendency of volatility to revert to its long-term average and other factors indicating that historical volatility may be an unreliable indicator of expected future volatility. For example, if a company's share price was extraordinarily volatile for a short period because of a failed takeover bid or a major restructuring, that period could be disregarded in computing historical average annual volatility.
- Appropriate and regular intervals for price observations. The price observations should be consistent from period to period. For example, a company might use the closing price for each week or the highest price for the week, but it should not use the closing price for some weeks and the highest price for other weeks.

[IFRS 2 para B25].

A12.117 An unlisted entity will not have historical data on which to base an estimate of expected future volatility. IFRS 2 suggests alternative methods by which an estimate may be made:

- If the entity regularly issues options or shares to employees (or other parties), it might have set up an internal market for its shares. The volatility of those share prices could be considered.
- The historical or implied volatility of similar listed entities, for which share price or option price information is available, could be used. This would be appropriate if the entity has also based the value of its shares on the share prices of similar listed entities.
- If the entity has not based its estimate of the value of its shares on the share prices of similar listed entities, but has instead used another valuation methodology, it could derive an estimate of expected volatility consistent with that valuation methodology. For example, the entity might value its shares on an earnings basis so it could consider the expected volatility of those earnings.

[IFRS 2 paras B28-B30].

A12.118 A newly listed entity may also not have sufficient information on historical volatility on which to base an estimate of expected future volatility. Nevertheless, it should compute historical volatility for the longest period for which trading activity is available. It could also consider the historical volatility of similar entities following a comparable period in their lives. For example, an entity that has been listed for only one year and grants options with an average expected life of five years might consider the pattern and level of historical volatility of entities in the same industry for the first six years in which the shares of those entities were publicly traded.

Expected dividends

A12.119 Whether expected dividends should be taken into account when measuring the fair value of an option depends on whether the counterparty is entitled to dividends on the underlying shares. For example, if employees were granted options, but are not entitled to dividends on the underlying shares between grant date and exercise date, they will have effectively 'lost' those dividends. Hence, the grant date valuation of the options should take expected dividends into account. That is to say, the fair value of the option will be reduced.

A12.120 The concept is easier to understand in the case of grants of shares. When estimating the fair value of the shares, the fair value should be reduced by the present value of dividends expected to be paid, and hence 'lost' by the employees, during the vesting period. Conversely, no adjustment is required for expected dividends if the counterparty is entitled to receive dividends during the vesting period.

A12.121 Option pricing models generally call for expected dividend yield, although they may be modified to use instead an expected dividend amount. If the latter is used, the historical pattern of increases in dividends must be taken into account. For example, if an entity's policy has generally been to increase dividends by around three per cent per year, its estimated option value should not assume a fixed dividend amount throughout the option's life, unless there is evidence to support that assumption.

A12.122 Generally, expected dividends should be based on publicly available information. An entity that does not pay dividends and has no plans to do so should assume an expected dividend yield of zero. However, an emerging entity with no history of paying dividends might expect to begin paying dividends in the near future. Such an entity could use an average of its past dividend yield (that is, zero) and the dividend yield of an appropriately comparable peer group.

Risk-free rate

A12.123 Typically, the risk-free interest rate is the yield currently available on zero-coupon government bonds of the country in whose currency the exercise price is expressed, with a remaining term equal to the expected term of the option being valued. It may be necessary to use an appropriate substitute, if no such bonds exist or circumstances indicate that the yield on zero-coupon government bonds is not representative of the risk-free rate (for example, in high inflation economies). Also, an appropriate substitute should be used if market participants would typically determine the risk-free rate by using that substitute.

A12.123.1 All other things being equal, an increase in the risk-free rate would result in an increase in the option's fair value.

Selection of an option pricing model

A12.124 As noted above, IFRS 2 does not specify which model should be used to estimate the fair value of an equity instrument. Frequent reference is made to the Black-Scholes-Merton formula (more commonly known as the Black-Scholes formula) but other models such as the binomial model or Monte-Carlo simulation may sometimes be more suitable. Each of these models is described and considered in the following paragraphs.

The Black-Scholes formula

A12.125 The most widely used model for valuing straightforward options was published by Fischer Black and Myron Scholes in 1973 and is commonly known as the Black-Scholes formula. This model depends on several assumptions:

- Future returns are independent both of past returns and the current share price.
- Volatility and interest rates both remain constant throughout the option's life.
- The probability distribution of returns is lognormal.
- No transaction costs.

A12.126 Based on these assumptions, the price of a European call option (that is, an option that may only be exercised at the end of its life regardless of the country in which it is issued) is estimated by the following formula:

$$C = SN(d_1) - Xe^{(-rt)}N(d_2)$$

Where:

C = Price of an option (£)
S = Current share price (£)
X = Option exercise price (£)
D = Dividend yield on underlying share (%)
t = Time to expiry
s = Expected volatility (%)
r = Risk-free rate over the life of the option
$N(d_n)$ = Value of d found from standard normal distribution curve

And

$$d^1 = \frac{Ln(Se^{rt}/X) + \sigma^2 t/2}{\sigma\sqrt{t}}$$

$$d_2 = \frac{Ln(Se^{rt}/X) - \sigma^2 t/2}{\sigma\sqrt{t}}$$

A12.127 Although the Black-Scholes formula is widely used, it has several limitations in the context of employee options. For example:

- It does not allow for market conditions or other terms and conditions that are relevant for determining fair value.
- The option is assumed to be exercised at the end of its life. Early exercise can only be taken into account by use of an expected life rather than a contractual life.
- Inputs (such as expected volatility) cannot be varied over the option's life.

A12.128 Nevertheless, for many of the simpler employee options, the Black-Scholes formula can give a reasonably reliable estimate of fair value.

The binomial model

A12.129 The binomial model applies the same principles as decision tree analysis to the pricing of an option. At each point, the possible outcomes are simplified to the possibility that prices may increase by a certain percentage or decrease by a certain percentage. On this basis, a 'tree' or 'lattice' is created. Depending on the relative probabilities of each path, an expected outcome may be estimated. This is illustrated in the following simple example.

Example — The binomial model

A entity has granted options that may be exercised in three year's time. The exercise price of the options is C5, which equates to the current market price of the entity's shares.

Management has estimated that there is a probability of p that the market price of the entity's shares will increase by 10% per year and a probability of (1 – p) that it will reduce by 10%. In order to estimate the value of p, management can equate the expected outcome of owning a share to the known outcome of earning a risk-free rate of interest on a cash deposit. If the risk free rate is assumed to be 6%, the value of a C5 investment after one year will be C5.30. Hence, as regards the share, the value of p may be calculated from the following:

$p \times 5.50 + (1 - p) \times 4.50 = 5.30$

Hence, p is 0.8, or 80%.

On this basis, the possible outcomes and their relative probabilities for each of the next three years may be estimated as shown below:

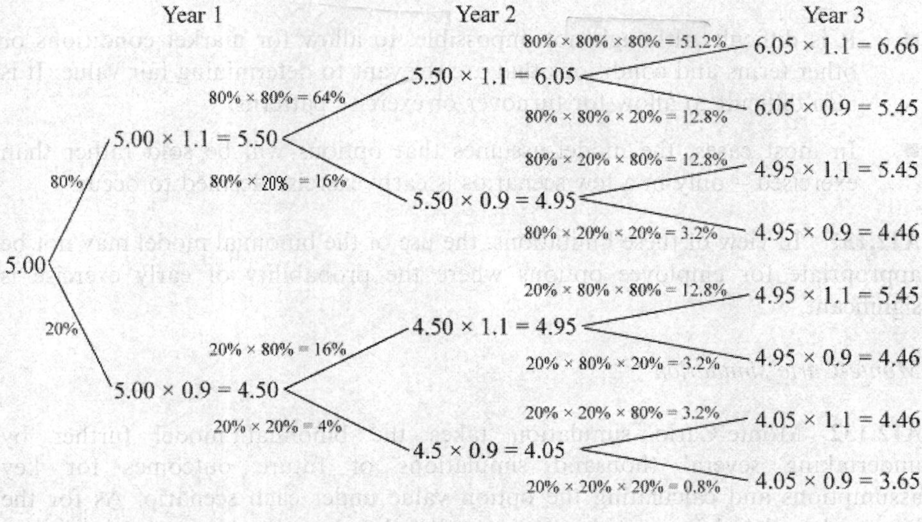

This means, for example, that there is a probability of 51.2% (that is, 80% × 80% × 80%) that the value of a share will be C6.66 in three year's time.

As the exercise price of an option is C5, it will only have value if the market price of the share exceeds C5 at the end of three years. Considering the top path of the tree, if a share is worth C6.66 then the option would be worth C1.66. This represents the intrinsic value of the option. However, considering the bottom path, if the share is worth C3.65 then an option with an exercise price of C5 will be worthless. On this basis, the expected value of the option in three years time may be derived.

Outcome	**Option value (A)**	**Probability (B)**	**A × B**
6.66	1.66 (6.66 – 5)	51.2% (80% × 80% × 80%)	0.85
5.45	0.45 (5.45 – 5)	12.8% (80% × 80% × 20%)	0.06
5.45	0.45 (5.45 – 5)	12.8% (80% × 20% × 80%)	0.06
4.46	0	3.2% (80% × 20% × 20%)	0
5.45	0.45 (5.45 – 5)	12.8% (20% × 80% × 80%)	0.06
4.46	0	3.2% (20% × 80% × 20%)	0
4.46	0	3.2% (20% × 20% × 80%)	0
3.65	0	0.8% (20% × 20% × 20%)	0
Expected value			1.03

If the expected value of an option in three year's time is C1.03, the current price will be the present value of this expected outcome. Hence, the estimated fair value at grant date is C0.865 (that is, $1.03/(1.06)^3$).

A12.130 The model sounds simple, but its application can prove complex. For example, the calculation of the probabilities of particular price movements is highly subjective. Nevertheless, the model is widely used and it can often be a more flexible solution than the Black-Scholes formula. However, like the Black-Scholes formula, the binomial model suffers from limitations, including:

- It is difficult, although not impossible, to allow for market conditions or other terms and conditions that are relevant to determining fair value. It is also difficult to allow for turnover or exercise patterns.
- In most cases, the model assumes that options will be sold rather than exercised – only in a few scenarios is early exercise deemed to occur.

A12.131 In view of these limitations, the use of the binomial model may not be appropriate for employee options where the probability of early exercise is significant.

Monte-Carlo simulation

A12.132 Monte-Carlo simulation takes the binomial model further by undertaking several thousand simulations of future outcomes for key assumptions and calculating the option value under each scenario. As for the binomial model, the expected outcome is then discounted to give an option value.

A12.133 Monte-Carlo models can incorporate even the most complex performance conditions, turnover and exercise patterns, such as those that are a function of gain or time since grant date. Consequently, they are generally the most reliable models for valuing employee options. The only drawback is their complexity, although this is rarely a problem with modern computing technology.

Cash-settled share-based payment transactions

A12.134 Some transactions are 'share-based', even though they do not involve the issue of shares, share options or any other form of equity instrument. Cash-settled share-based payment transactions are defined in IFRS 2 as transactions *"in which the entity acquires goods or services by incurring a liability to transfer cash or other assets to the supplier of those goods or services for amounts that are based on the price (or value) of the entity's shares or other equity instruments of the entity"*. [IFRS 2 App A].

A12.135 The most common examples of cash-settled share-based payment transactions are employee incentive plans, such as share appreciation rights and 'phantom' share schemes. These plans involve the payment of an amount based on the price of the employing entity's shares after a period of time.

A12.136 Sometimes, transactions that are actually settled in shares may be treated as cash-settled if this is more reflective of their substance. For example, an entity might grant to its employees a right to shares that are redeemable, either mandatorily (such as upon cessation of employment) or at the employee's option. As the entity has an obligation to make a cash payment, the transaction would be treated as cash-settled.

Example 1 – Repurchase of shares on termination of employment

Entity A is the sponsoring entity of a trust that administers an employee share-based compensation scheme. Entity A issues new shares to the trust. The trust issues these shares to employees who satisfy the scheme's vesting conditions. The shares are non-transferable while employees remain in entity A's employ and each employee has an obligation to sell the shares acquired through the scheme back to the trust on termination of employment. The trust buys the shares back at market price when returned.

Entity A prepares consolidated financial statements and, therefore, under SIC 12, 'Consolidation – special purpose entities', the trust should be consolidated. When employment is terminated, the award is settled in cash based on entity A's share price and, therefore, the transaction should be accounted for as a cash-settled award under IFRS 2.

Example 2 – Funding of award – shares purchased by trust

Entity B awarded its employees rights to obtain its shares subject to a three year vesting period. Local legislation does not allow the entity either to issue new shares to employees or to buy its own shares. The entity will establish a trust that will purchase the entity's shares from third parties and transfer those shares to entitled employees. The entity will pay the trust the cash required to purchase those shares.

Entity B prepares consolidated financial statement and, therefore, as in example 1, the trust will be consolidated under SIC 12. The fact that the group, *via* the trust, must buy shares from third parties in order to satisfy the obligation to deliver shares does not change the nature of the award. Employee services will ultimately be settled in shares. As such, the transaction should be treated as an equity-settled transaction under IFRS 2 (and any share purchase would be treated as a treasury share transaction in the consolidation).

Measurement of cash-settled share-based payment transactions

A12.137 Like share options and other equity instruments, the fair value of share appreciation rights and other cash-settled share-based payment transactions includes both their intrinsic value (the increase in the share price to date) and their time value (the value of the right to participate in future increases in the share price, if any, that may occur between the valuation date and the settlement date). Accordingly, many of the principles described previously for the measurement of equity-settled transactions apply equally to cash-settled transaction. So:

- The objective is to measure the goods or services acquired and the liability incurred at fair value.
- Fair value is determined using an option pricing model, taking into account the terms and conditions of the award.
- The goods or services are recognised as they are received by the entity.
- Vesting conditions should be taken into account when determining the number of rights to payment that will vest.

[IFRS 2 paras 30, 32, 33].

A12.138 There is, however, an important difference. For cash-settled transactions, the fair value of the liability is re-measured at each reporting date and at the date of settlement. Any changes in fair value are recognised in profit or loss for the period. [IFRS 2 para 30]. This is illustrated in the following example.

Example – Cash-settled award

On 1 January 20X5, an entity granted 1,000 share appreciation rights (SARs) to each of its 40 management employees. The SARs provide the employees with the right to receive, at the date the rights are exercised, cash equal to the appreciation in the entity's share price since the grant date. All of the rights vest on 31 December 20X6. They can be exercised during 20X7 and 20X8. Management estimates that, at grant date, the fair value of each SAR is C11, and that 10% of the employees will leave evenly during the two-year period. The fair values of the SARs at each year end are shown below.

Year	**Fair value at year end**
31 December 20X5	12
31 December 20X6	8
31 December 20X7	13
31 December 20X8	12

10% of employees did leave before the end of 20X6. On 31 December 20X7, when the intrinsic value of each SAR was C10, six employees exercise their options, while the remaining 30 employees exercise their options at the end of 20X8 (when the intrinsic value of each SAR was equal to the fair value of C12). The amount recognised as an expense in each year and as a liability at each year end will be as follows:

Year	**Expense**	**Liability**	**Calculation of liability**
31 December 20X5	C216,000	C216,000	36 × 1,000 × 12 × ½
31 December 20X6	C72,000	C288,000	36 × 1,000 × 8
31 December 20X7	C162,000	C390,000	30 × 1,000 × 13. Expense comprises an increase in the liability of C102,000 and cash paid to those exercising their SARs of C60,000 (6 × 1,000 × 10).
31 December 20X8	(C30,000)	C0	Liability extinguished. Previous cost reversed as cash paid to those exercising their SARs of C360,000 (30 × 1,000 × 12) was less than the opening liability of C390,000.

A12.139 For cash-settled transactions, it is perhaps more difficult to comprehend the difference between the fair value of a right and its intrinsic value. In the previous example, the fair value of each right at 31 December 20X7 was C13. However, the amount paid to each employee who exercised rights on that day was only C10 (that is, the intrinsic value). The reason for the higher fair value is the same for cash-settled transactions as for equity-settled transactions. The fair value of each SAR at 31 December 20X7 is made up of its intrinsic value (reflected by the current market price of the entity's shares) and its time value. The time value reflects the fact that the holders of the SARs have the right to participate in future gains. At 31 December 20X8, all of the outstanding SARs must be exercised so holders have no right to participate in future gains. Hence, the fair value (C12) at that date is made up entirely of the intrinsic value.

A12.140 Prior to applying IFRS 2, some territories may have measured the cash-settled share-based payment using the intrinsic value. Applying IFRS 2 requires measurement at fair value, so for some territories a change to IFRS will necessitate re-measurement of liabilities. Although the IASB did consider the use of intrinsic values to measure cash-settled share-based payment transactions, it concluded that such a method was not consistent with the overall fair value objective of its share-based payment standard.

Transactions with settlement alternatives

A12.141 Some share-based payment transactions give either the entity or the counterparty the choice as to whether to settle in cash or equity instruments. IFRS 2 establishes a principle that an entity should account for such a transaction as cash-settled if, and to the extent that, it has incurred a liability to settle in cash or other assets, or otherwise as equity settled. [IFRS 2 para 34]. In practice, the accounting is driven by determining which party appears to have the choice of settlement method.

The counterparty may choose the settlement method

A12.142 If the counterparty may choose the method of settlement, the entity is considered to have issued a compound financial instrument. This means that it has issued an instrument with a debt component (to the extent that the counterparty has a right to demand cash) and an equity component (to the extent that the counterparty has a right to demand settlement in equity instruments by giving up their right to cash). [IFRS 2 para 35].

A12.143 IAS 32, 'Financial instruments: Disclosure and presentation', requires that when valuing a compound financial instrument, an entity first establishes the value of the debt component. The equity component is then measured at the difference between that amount and the value of instrument as a whole. [IAS 32 para 31]. IFRS 2 applies similar measurement principles.

A12.144 For transactions in which the fair value of goods or services is measured directly, the fair value of the equity component is measured as the difference between the fair value of the goods or services received and the fair value of the debt component. [IFRS 2 para 35].

A12.145 For other transactions in which the fair value of goods or services is measured indirectly by reference to the fair value of the instruments granted, it is necessary to estimate the fair value of the compound instrument as a whole. [IFRS 2 para 36]. To do this, it will be necessary to value the debt and equity components separately, taking into account the fact that the counterparty must forfeit its right to receive cash in order to receive the equity instrument. Transactions are often structured such that the fair value of each settlement alternative is the same. For example, the counterparty might have the choice of receiving either share options or cash-settled share appreciation rights. In order to receive the options, the counterparty would have to 'give up' a cash award of equivalent fair value so, by deduction, the fair value of the equity component will be zero. However, where the fair value of the equity component is greater than zero, it will be necessary to account for each component separately. The debt component will be accounted for as a cash-settled share-based payment transaction as described from paragraph A12.134, while the equity component will be accounted for as an equity-settled share-based payment transaction as described from paragraph A12.43. [IFRS 2 para 38].

A12.146 At the date of settlement, the liability in respect of the debt component should be re-measured at fair value. The method of settlement actually chosen by the counterparty will then determine the accounting, as shown in the table below.

Method of settlement	Accounting implications
Cash	The payment is applied to settle the liability in full. Any equity component previously recognised in equity will remain there, although there may be a transfer from one component of equity to another. [IFRS 2 para 40].
Equity	The balance on the liability is transferred to equity as consideration for the equity instrument. [IFRS 2 para 39].

A12.147 The above requirements are illustrated in the following example.

Example 1 – Compound instrument – mutually exclusive alternatives

An entity established a bonus scheme on 1 January 20X5. The employees have a right to choose between a cash payment equal to the market value of 100 shares at 31 December 20X5 or to receive 100 shares on the same date. At the grant date, the fair value of the right to cash is C5,000 and the fair value of the right to shares is C5,000. The value of the two alternatives is the same at any point in time.

The equity component is determined as the difference between the fair value of the compound instrument as a whole and the fair value of the liability.

The fair value of the compound instrument as a whole is C5,000, as the cash and share alternatives are mutually exclusive. The equity component is, therefore, zero, being the difference between the C5,000 fair value of the compound instrument and the C5,000 fair value of the debt component. This reflects the arrangement's economic substance where there is no benefit to the employee from choosing shares or cash.

See further paragraph A12.147.1 below regarding discounting.

Example 2 – Compound instrument – determining the equity component

On 1 January 20X5, an entity granted to its chief executive the right to choose either 10,000 phantom shares (that is, the right to receive a cash payment equal to the value of 10,000 shares) or 15,000 shares. The grant is conditional upon the completion of two years of service. If the chief executive chooses the share alternative, he must keep the shares for a period of five years. The entity's share price at grant date and at subsequent year end is as follows:

Year	**Share price**
1 January 20X5	7
31 December 20X5	9
31 December 20X6	15

After taking into account the effects of the post-vesting transfer restrictions, management estimates that the grant date fair value of the share alternative is C6.50 per share. Hence, the fair value of the share alternative at grant date is C97,500 (that is, 15,000 × C6.50). The fair value of the cash alternative at grant date is C70,000 (that is, 10,000 × C7) so, by deduction, the fair value of the equity component of the compound financial instrument awarded to the chief executive is C27,500. (See further para 147.1 below regarding the impact of discounting, which has not been considered in this example.) In simple terms, in order to obtain an equity instrument worth C97,500, the chief executive must surrender a right to C70,000 of cash. Thus, the fair value of the equity component is the difference between these amounts. The amount recognised as an expense in each year and as either an increase in equity or a liability at each year end will be as follows:

Year	**Expense**	**Equity**	**Liability**	**Explanation**
31 December 20X5	C13,750	C13,750		C27,500 × ½
31 December 20X5	C45,000		C45,000	10,000 × 9 × ½
31 December 20X6	C13,750	C27,500		C27,500 × ½
31 December 20X6	C105,000		C150,000	10,000 × 15

The chief executive exercises his rights on 1 January 20X7 (on which date the share price is the same as on 31 December 20X6).

If he chooses to receive cash, he will receive a payment of C150,000. This will settle the outstanding liability in full. The amount recognised within equity (C27,500) will remain there, although there may be a transfer from one component of equity to another.

If he chooses the share alternative, the balance on the liability of C150,000 is transferred to equity as consideration for the shares. Once again, the amount already recognised within equity (C27,500) will remain there, although there may be a transfer from one component of equity to another.

Example 3 – Compound instrument – determining the equity component

An entity granted a bonus to its employees on 1 January 20X5. The bonus is due in five years, when each employee will have a right to choose between a cash payment of C1,000 or obtaining 100 shares of the entity. The share price on 1 January 20X5 is C5 per share. There are no vesting conditions. The appropriate discount rate is 5% per year.

The entity should recognise the debt component on 1 January 20X5 at its fair value of C784. Fair value is determined as the present value of the future cash outflow, C1,000/1.05^5 (see further para 147.1 below). The entity should then measure the equity alternative, taking into consideration that the employee has to forfeit the right to C1,000 in cash to obtain the shares. The equity alternative is, in substance, a share option with an exercise price of C10 per share and a term of five years. The fair value of the share options was determined as C25 at 1 January 20X5. A corresponding increase in equity should be recognised on 1 January 20X5.

The entity should re-measure the liability component to its fair value at each subsequent balance sheet date and recognise the changes in the fair value in the income statement. The amounts recognised for the equity component are not subject to subsequent re-measurement.

Example 4 – Compound instrument – settlement in shares

Consider the award granted in example 3 if the share price turned out to be C17 on 31 December 20X9.

A rational employee would select settlement in shares because this alternative has a higher fair value (1,700; 17 × 100 shares). The entity should accrete the liability to its fair value of C1,000 on the exercise date through the income statement. Total interest expense of C216 (1,000 – 784) on a cumulative basis is recognised between 1 January 20X5 and 31 December 20X9. The liability of C1,000 is transferred to equity as the shares are issued.

An employee may choose the cash alternative, despite the higher fair value of the settlement in shares. The entity first accretes the liability to its fair value of C1,000 on the exercise date through the income statement. Total interest expense of C216 on a cumulative basis is recognised between 1 January 20X5 and 31 December 20X9. It subsequently records the payment of C1,000 cash against the liability. The cumulative charge of C25 recognised in respect of the equity component is not adjusted.

Discounting

A12.147.1 As mentioned in example 3 above, the fair value of a liability component is determined as the present value of the future cash outflow. In practice, however, the impact of discounting may not be material.

The entity may choose the settlement method

A12.148 If the entity may choose the method of settlement, it should determine whether, in substance, it has created an obligation to settle in cash. This may be, for example, if:

- The choice of settlement in equity instruments has no commercial substance (for example, because the entity is legally prohibited from issuing shares).
- The entity has a past practice or stated policy of settling in cash.

- The entity generally settles in cash whenever the counterparty requests it. [IFRS 2 para 41].

A12.149 If an obligation to settle in cash does exist, the entity should account for the transaction as a cash-settled share-based payment transaction as described from paragraph A12.134. Otherwise, the transaction should be treated as an equity-settled share-based payment transaction as described from paragraph A12.43. [IFRS 2 paras 42, 43].

A12.150 If the transaction is accounted for as equity-settled, the accounting on settlement depends on which alternative has the greater fair value as at the settlement date, as shown in the table below. [IFRS 2 para 43].

Settlement method	**Settlement method with the higher fair value**	
	Cash	**Equity**
Cash	The amount of payment equal to the fair value of the equity instruments that would otherwise have been issued is accounted for as the repurchase of an equity interest and is deducted from equity. The excess over this amount is recognised as an expense.	The payment is accounted for as the repurchase of an equity interest and is deducted from equity.
Equity	No further accounting is required.	The excess of the fair value of the equity instruments issued over the amount of cash that would otherwise have been paid is recognised as an expense.

A12.151 The above requirements are illustrated in the following example, although in practice it is rare for the alternatives to have different values when the entity has the choice of settlement method.

Example – Entity choice of settlement

An entity has granted to its chief executive the right to either 10,000 phantom shares (that is, the right to receive a cash payment equal to the value of 10,000 shares) or 15,000 shares. The entity may choose the settlement method. It has never made an award of this nature and it is free to select either settlement method (that is, there is no restriction over its ability to issue shares). Accordingly, management does not consider that the entity has established an obligation and the transaction is accounted for as equity-settled. An expense is measured on the basis of the fair value of the 15,000 shares at grant date. The opposing credit is recognised in equity.

On the settlement date, the entity's share price is C10. Hence, the fair value of the phantom shares is C100,000 while the fair value of the shares themselves is C150,000. If the entity chooses to settle the transaction in cash, being the settlement method with the lower fair value, the payment of C100,000 is deducted from equity. In substance it represents the re-purchase by the entity of its own shares so no further expense is recognised. However, if the entity chooses to settle the transaction by issuing shares, the excess of the fair value of the shares over the amount of cash that would otherwise have been paid (that is, C50,000) is recognised as an expense.

If the facts were different, such that at settlement date the fair value of the phantom shares was C150,000 while the fair value of the shares was C100,000, the accounting would be as follows. If the entity chose to settle the transaction by issuing shares, being the settlement method with the lower fair value, no further accounting would be required. If the entity chose to settle the transaction in cash, C100,000 (being the fair value of the equity instruments that would otherwise have been issued) would be deducted from equity. The excess of the amount actually paid over the amount deducted from equity (that is, C50,000) is recognised as an expense.

In summary, if the award is treated as equity-settled it should be accounted for in the same way as any other equity-settled transaction until the point of settlement. On settlement, the accounting is straight forward provided the entity chooses the method of settlement with the lower fair value at that date. If, however, it chooses the settlement method with the higher fair value at that date, the excess is treated as an additional expense. In the first scenario described above (settlement in shares when cash settlement has a lower fair value) the double entry on settlement would be as follows:

		C	C
Dr	Equity	100,000	
Dr	Income statement	50,000	
	Cr Share capital/Equity		150,000

In the second scenario (settlement in cash when equity settlement has a lower fair value) the double entry on settlement would be as follows:

		C	C
Dr	Equity	100,000	
Dr	Income statement	50,000	
	Cr Cash		150,000

Practical implications

Group situations and IFRIC 11

A12.152 As described in paragraph A12.27, the scope of IFRS 2 is broad. Share-based payment transactions include not only transactions settled in an entity's own shares, but also transactions settled in equity instruments of the entity's parent or any other entity in the same group. [IFRS 2 para 3]. This means that if the employees of a subsidiary are awarded options over the shares of the parent, the subsidiary will recognise an expense in respect of the employee services received. However, IFRS 2 does not give any explicit guidance regarding how the expense should be measured in the individual financial statements of the subsidiary (as equity-settled or cash-settled) nor how any recharges should be treated.

A12.152.1 The above questions, and some related topics, were considered by the IFRIC, which issued an interpretation, IFRIC 11, 'IFRS 2 – Group and treasury share transactions', on 2 November 2006. Although the interpretation focuses on transactions with employees, it also applies to similar transactions with suppliers of goods or services other than employees. The interpretation addresses the following issues:

- Clarification on how to account for share-based payment arrangements where an entity receives goods or services as consideration for its own equity instruments (see further para A12.152.2).
- Guidance on how to account in a subsidiary for share-based payment arrangements involving equity instruments of the parent. This includes the situation where a subsidiary has an obligation to provide its employees with parent equity instruments for the services it receives from its employees (see from para A12.152.3 below).

Share-based payment arrangements involving an entity's own equity instruments

A12.152.2 IFRIC 11 clarifies that where an entity receives goods or services as consideration for its own equity instruments, this should be accounted for as an equity-settled arrangement. This would apply regardless of whether the entity chooses or is required to buy those equity instruments from another party to satisfy its obligation to its employees. Whether the employee's rights to the entity's equity instruments were granted or settled by the entity or by the entity's shareholders, the arrangement would be accounted for as an equity-settled share-based payment.

Share-based payment arrangements involving equity instruments of the parent

A12.152.3 The accounting for arrangements involving equity instruments of the parent is dependent upon which entity grants the award.

A12.152.4 Many of the responses to the draft interpretation, D17, were critical of the proposals because the distinction drawn between awards granted by a parent and awards granted by a subsidiary is one that cannot clearly be drawn in practice. In a change from D17, the final interpretation considers not only who granted the award, but also which entity has an obligation to provide the employees with equity instruments. The example in paragraph A12.152.6 considers only the simple situation in which a parent makes a grant of shares directly to a subsidiary's employees.

A12.152.5 This requirement applies irrespective of how the subsidiary funds the arrangement and, therefore, it is necessary to identify which entity grants the awards to determine the accounting in the subsidiary. IFRIC 11 provides clarity that it is now necessary to consider which entity has the obligation to settle.

Parent grants rights over its equity instruments to the employees of its subsidiary

A12.152.6 IFRIC 11 clarifies that when a parent entity grants rights over its equity instruments to the employees of its subsidiary, as long as the share-based payment arrangement is accounted for as equity-settled in the consolidated financial statements, the subsidiary should treat the arrangement as an equity-settled arrangement. The following example considers only the simple situation in which a parent makes a grant of shares direct to a subsidiary's employees.

Example – Options over parent's shares granted to employees of subsidiary

An entity is a subsidiary of a listed parent. The parent has granted options over its shares with a fair value of C100,000 to the subsidiary's employees. There are no vesting conditions associated with the award.

In the subsidiary's financial statements, an expense of C100,000 will be recognised immediately. As for any equity-settled share-based payment transaction, the credit entry will be recognised in equity. In substance this represents a capital contribution by the parent to fund the subsidiary's employee costs.

The parent has issued equity instruments (the options) so, in its separate financial statements, it will also increase its equity by C100,000. The debit will represent an increase in the investment in the subsidiary (see further para from A12.153.1 below).

The consolidated financial statements will include both the expense in respect of employee services and the increase in equity.

A12.152.7 IFRIC 11 states that where an employee transfers employment from one subsidiary to another during the vesting period (the vesting period could be, for example, a service period), each subsidiary should measure the services received from the employee by reference to the fair value of the equity instrument at grant date, and not re-measure at the date of transfer. If, after transferring between group entities, the employee fails to meet a non-market vesting condition (for example, a service condition) each subsidiary should adjust the amount previously recognised in respect of the services received from the employee.

Subsidiary grants rights over equity instruments of its parent to its employees

A12.152.8 Where a subsidiary grants rights over the parent's equity instruments to the subsidiary's employees, the subsidiary is required to account for the transaction as cash-settled. That is, the subsidiary should recognise a liability (re-measured at each balance sheet date) for the other side of the IFRS 2 charge.

Funding arrangements between parent and its subsidiary

A12.153 The illustrative example attached to IFRIC 11 clarifies that where the parent grants rights over its equity instruments to the employees of its subsidiary (accounted for as an equity-settled share-based payment), the debit would be recognised in the subsidiary's income statement and a credit to equity (as a capital contribution) recognised over the vesting period of the share-based payment arrangement.

A12.153.1 The accounting within the parent entity for the capital contribution is not addressed by IFRIC 11. D17 indicated that the parent entity would debit its investment in subsidiary and credit equity for the equity instruments it has granted (if it is satisfying the obligation). The final interpretation does not address this issue as the basis for conclusions notes that the IFRIC *"did not wish to widen the scope of the Interpretation to an issue that relates to the accounting for intra-group payment arrangements"* generally. [IFRIC 11 BC12]. We believe that it was this wider issue that resulted in the deletion of the D17 text, as opposed to a flaw in the thinking. The only alternatives to the parent debiting its investment in subsidiary would seem to be recognising nothing or recognising an expense, neither of which are attractive. There is no indication in IFRIC 11 that the accounting treatment set out in the draft interpretation would be inappropriate and, therefore, we believe it should continue to be applied. The accounting implications are considered in the examples in paragraph A12.153.5 below.

A12.153.2 Sometimes, a parent company makes a recharge to the subsidiary in respect of share options granted to the subsidiary's employees. IFRIC 11 does not address how to account for such intra-group payment arrangements for share-based payment transactions. However, the illustrative example in the draft interpretation D17 did consider the issue. It concluded that an inter-company charge payable by a subsidiary entity should be offset against the capital contribution in the individual or separate financial statements of the subsidiary entity and the parent entity. We believe that this is particularly appropriate where there is a clear link between the recharge and the share-based payment, for example where the recharge is based on the intrinsic value or market value of the shares when they vest. Consistent with the principle of shareholder distributions, if the amount of the inter-company charge exceeded the capital contribution, that excess should be treated as a distribution from the subsidiary to its parent. We consider this to be an appropriate treatment for such a recharge.

A12.153.3 We believe that it is important that management are able to justify a clear link between the recharge and the share-based payment charge in order to apply the principle of shareholder distributions described in paragraph A12.153.2. If there is no clear link between the recharge and the share-based payment we believe that the payment between the subsidiary and its parent should be treated in a manner consistent with management recharges. This would result in an expense recognised in the income statement for the amount recharged. Note that this would result in a 'double debit' to the income statement since the subsidiary would have already recorded the services received under IFRS 2.

Timing of the recharge

A12.153.4 When a subsidiary is recharged by its parent for a share-based payment, the question arises as to when (if at all) a liability should be recorded for the amount that is expected to be recharged in the future, for example, when the award vests in employees or the employees exercise their options. Our view is that recharges should not be accrued, but should be recognised when paid (or when they are virtually certain to be paid), for the following reasons:

- IASs 32 and 39 scope out financial instruments, contracts and obligations under share-based payment transactions to which IFRS 2 applies, except for contracts that can be net settled and in relation to the disclosure of treasury shares. [IAS 32 para 4(f); IAS 39 para 2(i)]. Our view is that these scope exclusions should be read broadly and that recharges clearly related to a share-based payment can be considered outside of the scope of IASs 32 and 39.
- While there is no scope exclusion for share-based payment arrangements under IAS 37, under IAS 37, such recharge payments would not generally meet the recognition criteria to be recorded as liabilities until paid because:
  - The subsidiary does not have a present obligation as a result of a past event. In order for there to be a clear link between a share-based payment and a recharge, in most cases the recharge will generally be linked to employees exercising their options. Options cannot be exercised until they have vested and employees are likely to exercise their options once they are in the money. Therefore, there is unlikely to be a present obligation on the entity until all vesting conditions have been satisfied and until it is probable that employees will exercise their options (for example, where the options are in the money). This is further supported by the fact that distributions (such as dividends) are only provided for when an entity has a present obligation and, as discussed above, an analogy may be drawn between such recharges and distributions to shareholders. There is no present obligation since the distribution is conditional upon an uncertain future event (such as employees providing services or choosing to exercise their options) that is not wholly within the control of the entity.
  - It is not probable that an outflow of economic resources will be required. We consider that the point in time at which it becomes probable that there will be an outflow of economic resources would only be reliably known when the options are close to being exercised.

In most cases, therefore, we believe that a subsidiary entity would account for a recharge when the payment is made to the parent. The recharge would be disclosed as a contingent liability during the time that the recharge payment is not recognised as a liability. It may be appropriate to recognise a liability for a recharge before the payment is made, for example once an award has vested and the options to be exercised are deeply in the money.

A12.153.5 Where there is no link between the share-based payment and the future payment by the subsidiary (that is, the double debit treatment discussed in para A12.153.3), it would be necessary to consider whether the entity has a present obligation in a manner similar to that of a management recharge.

Example 1 – Recharge from parent company in respect of share options

The facts are the same as in the example under paragraph A12.152.6 above, except that the parent makes a recharge to the subsidiary on exercise of the options. The recharge is clearly linked to the share-based payment, being the difference between the option price and the market price of the shares at the date of exercise of the options.

From the subsidiary's perspective, this will still be an equity-settled share-based payment transaction. The requirement for the subsidiary to make a cash payment to the parent does not make this a cash-settled share-based-payment transaction. This is because the subsidiary's obligation is to its parent while the providers of goods or services (that is, the employees) receive equity instruments. Accordingly, the accounting for the share-based payment transaction will be the same as in the previous example. (The subsidiary will recognise an expense and an increase in equity of C100,000.)

Although a recharge such as in this example may be made for a number of reasons, it is often made to enable the parent to acquire shares in the market so as to satisfy the award. In substance, therefore, the payment by the subsidiary to the parent could represent the repurchase of an equity instrument, which would be recorded directly in equity. This would certainly be true for a payment of up to Dr C100,000. However, D17 proposed that any payment in excess of the amount of capital contribution initially recognised should be treated as a distribution from the subsidiary to its parent. The rationale for this proposal was not explained in D17's basis for conclusions, but in view of IFRS 2's basic premise that the recognised expense reflects the fair value of goods or services received, any cash recharge in excess of this fair value could be viewed as a payment for employee services at above fair value. Normally, such a payment would be treated in substance as a distribution. Hence, if the amount of the recharge in this example is Dr C150,000, the double entry in the individual financial statements of the subsidiary would be as follows:

		C	C
Dr	Equity — repurchase of equity instrument	100,000	
Dr	Equity — distribution	50,000	
	Cr Cash		150,000

The subsidiary will not make a provision for the recharge during the vesting period, because it does not have a present obligation and it is not probable that there will be an outflow of economic resources until the options vest. The subsidiary will, however, disclose a contingent liability.

It should be noted that certain entities may wish to show the recharge debit entry within the income statement as opposed to equity and we believe that this approach would also be acceptable, provided that it is applied consistently (this does lead to a 'double debit' in the income statement given that the IFRS 2 charge will also be recognised). In addition, where there is no clear link between the share-based payment and the recharge from the parent, we believe that it would be most appropriate to record a second debit through the income statement.

As regards the parent's separate financial statements, the double entry would be as follows:

		C	C
Dr	Cash	150,000	
	Cr Investment in subsidiary		100,000
	Cr Other income		50,000

Some entities may wish to take the full credit entry as other income rather than reducing the parent's investment in subsidiary and we believe that this approach would also be acceptable, provided that the payment is made from the subsidiary's post-acquisition reserves and the policy is applied consistently. In addition, where there is no clear link between the share-based payment and the recharge from the parent, and the payment is made from the subsidiary's post-acquisition reserves, it would be acceptable to record the credit through the income statement. Where a credit is taken to other income, the parent entity should ensure that it has considered whether its investment in subsidiary is impaired.

Note that, in certain jurisdictions, the impact of accounting for group share-based payment transactions could impact the ability for an entity to pay dividends. Therefore, legal advice may need to be sought.

Example 2 – Settlement in parent's shares with an advance recharge

Employees of a subsidiary are granted options to acquire 100 shares in the parent entity at a fixed price of C10 per share in exchange for services. The grant date is 1 January 20X6. The award is subject to a two year vesting period and performance conditions. The options will vest if the total shareholder return exceeds 5% per annum during 20X6 and 20X7.

The parent entity agreed to issue new shares to entitled employees when the options are exercised. At the grant date the subsidiary paid the parent an option premium in exchange for the parent agreeing to satisfy the obligation to employees. The amount paid to the parent is the fair value of the options granted to employees as determined on 1 January 20X6, C100.

As discussed in paragraph A12.152.6, the subsidiary should treat the transaction as an equity-settled share-based payment. A liability must be incurred to the supplier of the goods or services in order for the transaction to be classified as cash-settled. [IFRIC 11 para 8]. The subsidiary should record the following:

Year ended 31 December 20X6

		C	C
Dr	Employee benefits expense	50	
	Cr Equity		50
Dr	Equity	100	
	Cr Cash		100

Year ended 31 December 20X7

		C	C
Dr	Employee benefits expense	50	
	Cr Equity		50

In its separate financial statements, the parent entity will treat the transaction as an equity-settled share-based payment and record the following:

Year ended 31 December 20X6

		C	C
Dr	Investment in subsidiary	50	
	Cr Equity		50
Dr	Cash	100	
	Cr Equity		100

In its separate financial statements, the parent entity records the exercise price received from employees when the options are exercised on 31 December 20X7 as follows:

Year ended 31 December 20X7

		C	C
Dr	Investment in subsidiary	50	
	Cr Equity		50
Dr	Cash (100 shares at C10 each)	1,000	
	Cr Equity		1,000

The payment by the subsidiary is in substance an advance payment on the capital contribution the parent intends to make in the future. Whether the subsidiary makes a payment to its parent in advance or at a later date (such as when employees exercise their awards) does not affect the classification in the subsidiary or the parent accounts.

A subsidiary entity may wish to show the debit side of the cash payment as an additional expense, for example for tax purposes (again, this leads to a double debit). Similarly, a parent entity may wish to show the cash payment as income. We believe that these approaches would also be acceptable, provided that they are applied consistently. In addition, where there is no clear link between the share-based payment and the recharge from the parent, we believe that it would be most appropriate to record a second debit through the income statement in the subsidiary (provided that there are sufficient post-acquisition reserves) and as a credit through the income statement in the parent.

Example 3 – Options over subsidiary's shares that are convertible into parent's shares

A group has a fast growing subsidiary and intends to incentivise the employees of that subsidiary by granting them options over shares in the subsidiary. The options will be granted at the market price of the subsidiary's shares, say C1. The holding company is listed and its own share price at present is C4.50 per share.

Additionally, in order to provide the employees with an 'exit route' the parent has agreed to issue one share in the parent for every two shares of the subsidiary into which the employees' options are converted. Based on market prices at the date of grant this would give the employees C4.50 worth of shares in the parent for every C2 they invested at that date, an immediate gain of C2.50.

This is an equity-settled share-based payment arrangement, granted to the subsidiary's employees. Therefore, the equity instrument should be fair valued at the date of grant and charged to the subsidiary's profit and loss account over the vesting period.

In this case, the equity instruments to be fair valued would include the right to the parent's shares in compensation for the subsidiary's shares. However, the charge would only be included in the profit and loss account of the subsidiary, as it is the subsidiary that is receiving the services from the employees. This follows the key principle of IFRS 2, which requires a company to recognise a charge for the goods and services received for a share-based payment transaction.

The accounting in the parent's separate financial statements would follow that described in paragraph A12.153.1

Example 4 – Implications for intermediate holding companies

Parent entity P, owns 100% of an intermediate holding company (entity H1). Entity H1 in turn owns 100% of another intermediate holding company (entity H2), entity H2 owns 100% of trading subsidiary entity S.

Entity P grants, and has the obligation to settle, equity-settled options over its shares to employees of entity S. The fair value of the award, which has a two year vesting period, is C200,000. Should the accounting entries described in paragraph A12.153.1 be passed down through each intermediate holding company or can entity P recognise an investment in its indirectly held subsidiary, entity S?

The transaction is between entity P and the employees of entity S. Our view is that it is appropriate for entity P to recognise an investment in entity S. There will be no impact on the separate financial statements of entity H1 and entity H2. This is acceptable on the basis that it is possible for an indirectly-held subsidiary and its ultimate parent to transact directly without involving intermediate parent companies. The double entry in parent entity P's separate financial statements at the end of each year would be to recognise a capital contribution to entity S as follows:

		C	C
Dr	Investment in subsidiary entity S	100,000	
	Cr Equity		100,000

Trading subsidiary entity S's will recognise the IFRS 2 charge in its separate financial statements:

		C	C
Dr	Income statement	100,000	
	Cr Equity		100,000

A12.153.6 Prior to IFRIC 11's publication, our view was that there were at least two alternative approaches for entities reporting under IFRS to account for share-based payment arrangements involving the equity instruments of the parent. One view was that the accounting treatment should be the same regardless of whether the parent or the subsidiary grants shares to the subsidiary's employees, as there is no difference between the substance of either transaction. The alternatives suggested were as follows:

- To look at the transaction from the subsidiary's point of view, regardless of who grants the equity instrument. If it is the subsidiary's equity instrument then the share-based payment is accounted for as an equity-settled share-based payment and if it is another entity's, such as the parent, it is treated as a cash-settled share-based payment in the subsidiary's financial statements; or
- To push down to the subsidiary the accounting used by the group. Where the parent entity grants the award, this results in the same treatment as that specified by IFRIC 11.

Whichever of the accounting treatments is used by the group, the group should choose an appropriate accounting policy and apply this consistently.

A12.153.7 While the alternatives continue to be available until IFRIC 11's effective date (see para A12.229 below), it is important to bear in mind that early adoption of the interpretation is permitted and when adopted, IFRIC 11 is applied retrospectively.

UK.A12.153.7.1 The UITF issued UITF Abstract 44, 'FRS 20 (IFRS 2) – Group and treasury share transactions', in February 2007. UITF 44 has the effect of implementing IFRIC 11 for UK GAAP reporters. It is important to bear in mind not only that early adoption of the abstract is encouraged (and when adopted, UITF 44 is applied retrospectively), but also that an entity is encouraged under FRS 18, 'Accounting policies', to take account of recently issued standards in judging whether its present accounting policies are still the most appropriate to its particular circumstances. In addition, an entity should ensure wherever possible that where it is necessary to implement a new accounting policy, the new accounting policy is in accordance with recently issued standards. [FRS 18 para 46]. The group should choose an appropriate accounting policy and apply this consistently.

A12.153.8 The accounting treatment for the two alternative approaches is considered in the following examples.

Example 1 – Issue of subsidiary's own shares

A group consists of a parent and two subsidiaries. Subsidiary A is 60% owned by the parent and listed. Subsidiary B is wholly owned by the parent and not listed.

Listed subsidiary A grants shares to employees. The shares vest over 2 years. Subsidiary A is unable to issue new shares and has a policy and practice to buy its shares from the market (on the date when the shares vest) for transfer to its employees.

In the subsidiary's financial statements the award is treated as an equity-settled share-based payment, as the subsidiary receives services as consideration for equity instruments of the subsidiary. An expense for the fair value of the option is recognised over the vesting period with a credit recognised in equity.

The parent is not involved in the transaction and there is no impact on the minority interest as the subsidiary buys the shares back from the market, therefore, there is no accounting impact in the parent.

Within the consolidated financial statements the transaction is treated as an equity-settled share-based payment as the group has received services in consideration for equity instruments.

Example 2 – Issue of parent's shares from the subsidiary's point of view

Instead of granting rights over its own equity instruments, subsidiary A grants rights over the parent's shares to subsidiary A's employees. The shares vest over 2 years. When the shares vest, the parent issues its shares direct to subsidiary A's employees. The parent levies a charge equal to the fair value of its shares at the issue date.

In subsidiary A's financial statements the award is treated as a cash-settled share-based payment based on the subsidiary's policy of accounting. An expense would be recognised in the income statement over the vesting period, with a liability being recorded as the other side of the entry. This liability is re-measured at each reporting date until settlement, in accordance with the accounting for cash-settled awards.

The above transaction has no impact on the parent's financial statements until the date of settlement of the award when the parent will record the issue of the shares and cash receipt from the subsidiary. Up until that date, the contract has no value (and, therefore, would not be recognised) as the parent has agreed to issue shares to the subsidiary at fair value.

In the consolidated financial statements the transaction is treated as an equity-settled share-based payment as the group has received services in consideration for the group's equity instruments. An expense is recognised in the income statement for the fair value of the share-based payment over the vesting period, with a credit recognised in equity.

Example 3 – Push down accounting, resulting in IFRIC 11 treatment

The parent grants its shares directly to subsidiary A and subsidiary B employees. The shares vest immediately at grant date. The parent will not charge subsidiaries A and B for the transaction. The subsidiaries have adopted IFRIC 11, which, in this case, results in the subsidiary adopting the same accounting approach that is used in the group consolidated financial statements for the share-based payment, that is an equity-settled share-based payment transaction.

An expense for the grant date fair value of the option is recognised over the vesting period with a credit recognised in equity. The credit to equity is treated as a capital contribution as the parent is compensating the subsidiaries employees with no expense to the subsidiaries. In this example the shares vest immediately, therefore, an expense is recognised in the income statement in full based on the grant date fair value and a credit to equity.

In the parent's financial statements the award is accounted for as an equity-settled share-based payment as the shares vest immediately. The debit is recognised as an increase in the investment in the subsidiaries as a capital contribution from the parent and a credit to equity.

In the consolidated financial statements the transaction is treated as an equity-settled share-based payment as the group has received services in consideration for the group's equity instruments. An expense is recognised in the income statement for the fair value of the share-based payment over the vesting period, with a credit recognised in equity.

Cash-settled awards in group situations

A12.153.9 While IFRIC 11 provides guidance for equity-settled awards on consolidation there is no guidance for cash-settled awards that will be paid by an entity that does not employ the employees who receive the awards. In addition, IFRS 2 itself does not address cash-settled awards granted by one entity to another entity's employees. The standard's scope paragraphs refer only to amounts based on the price (or value) of the *entity's* equity instruments and while there is reference to transfers of equity instruments of another entity in the same group as the entity, there is no reference to transfers of cash or other assets in this context. [IFRS 2 paras 2(b), 3].

A12.153.10 Consider a situation where a parent entity grants a cash-settled share-based payment award to the employees of its subsidiary. This will be treated as a cash-settled award in both the parent entity and consolidated financial statements (the parent entity would take the debit to its investment in subsidiary as discussed in para A12.152.6). From the subsidiary's perspective it has not granted an award, has no obligation to make payments to its employees and the payments are not based on the price of the subsidiary's equity, hence, the definition of a cash-settled award is not met and IFRS 2 does not apply.

A12.153.11 Our view is that in such circumstances the subsidiary has an accounting policy choice. IAS 8 requires the subsidiary to determine an appropriate accounting policy taking into account current IFRS. As this award is an employee benefit (employees receive cash benefits as a direct result of their employment) the relevant standards are IAS 19 or IFRS 2. It would not be appropriate to apply a policy that conflicts with either of these standards. IAS 19 follows a 'cost to the entity' approach, therefore, if the subsidiary is not bearing a cost, no entries would be required (although related party disclosures would be necessary). In contrast, IFRS 2 uses a 'services incurred' model and, therefore, an expense would be recognised.

> **UK.A12.153.11.1** Under UK GAAP the subsidiary faces a similar accounting policy choice, however, in this case there is no equivalent to IAS 19 and, therefore, while the equivalent standard to IFRS 2, FRS 20, 'Share-based payment', does not apply, it is more difficult to argue against applying the principles of FRS 20. The entity will need to demonstrate that the accounting policy chosen gives a true and fair view of the circumstances.

A12.153.12 The IFRIC discussed the issue in July 2007, considering the following situations:

- Employees of a subsidiary entity will receive cash based on the price of the subsidiary entity's equity instruments. The parent entity is obliged to settle the award.
- Employees of a subsidiary entity will receive cash based on the price of the parent entity's equity instruments. The parent entity is obliged to settle the award.

The IFRIC agreed that in both situations, the award should be within IFRS 2's scope. In the case of the second bullet point where there will be no recharge from the parent entity, the proposal is for the subsidiary entity to follow the principles of cash-settled measurement, that is, measuring the fair value of the award at each reporting date, but with the credit entry being taken to equity.

A12.153.13 In September 2007 the IFRIC concluded that IFRIC 11 should be amended to explain the accounting in the subsidiary entity in the above arrangements. In addition, the IFRIC recommended that the IASB clarify IFRS 2's scope (and in particular paragraph 3).

A12.153.14 Until further guidance is issued, our view is that there is an accounting policy choice for the subsidiary, with four possible ways of accounting for such an award:

- Apply the principles of IFRS 2 and treat the award as equity-settled. The subsidiary has no obligation to settle the award and, therefore, by analogy to IFRIC 11, the award would be treated as equity-settled with the fair value measured at grant date. This would reflect the capital contribution that the subsidiary is, in effect, receiving from the parent.
- Apply the principles of IFRS 2 and treat the award as equity-settled, but with a fair value 'true-up' at each reporting date. Similar to the approach described in the first bullet point above, the subsidiary has no obligation to settle the award, and, therefore, by analogy to IFRIC 11, the award would be treated as equity-settled, reflecting the capital contribution that the subsidiary is, in effect, receiving from the parent. However, unlike the approach described above, the approach would use fair values consistent with those used in the consolidated financial statements where cash-settled accounting would be applied.

- Apply the principles of IFRS 2 and treat the award as cash-settled. By applying a 'push-down' approach to mirror the accounting treatment that would be followed in the consolidated financial statements, the subsidiary would recognise a liability over the vesting period. When the award is settled by the parent, the subsidiary would transfer the liability to equity, recognising the capital contribution provided by the parent to settle the obligation.

- Apply the principles of IAS 19. As IAS 19 is a 'cost to the entity' based standard, no accounting entries would be made in the subsidiary's financial statements. However, related party disclosures under IAS 24 would be necessary

A12.153.15 The subsidiary entity should apply the approach that is considered to be most appropriate in accordance with IAS 8. Given the IFRIC's recent discussions on the matter, described in paragraph A12.153.12, it would appear most appropriate to follow the second approach in paragraph A12.153.14 above (particularly where an entity has not previously had such an arrangement), that is, the award should be treated as equity-settled in the subsidiary entity's financial statements, with a fair value 'true-up' at each reporting date. Until further guidance is issued, however, it may be possible to identify one of the other approaches as the most appropriate in accordance with IAS 8. Whichever approach is adopted, the accounting policy should be clearly disclosed and consistently applied.

Effective date

A12.153.16 Details of the effective date of IFRIC 11 are provided from paragraph A12.229 below.

Equity incentive plans

A12.154 Certain equity incentive plans offer organisations an opportunity to widen share ownership as part of their overall reward strategy. These incentive plans may include one or all of the following awards:

- *Free shares* – employers gift shares to employees.

- *Matching shares* – employers match shares which have already been purchased by employees provided the employee continues to provide services for a specified period of time.

- *Dividend shares* – employers offer dividend reinvestment in additional shares with shares held by employees in another plan.

Free shares

A12.154.1 When the award of free shares is not subject to a performance condition and the shares are not forfeitable, an expense will be recognised immediately. This expense will be based on the fair value of the shares at the date that the award is granted. Where the award is subject to vesting conditions, the expense will be recognised over the vesting period.

A12.154.2 In the situation where recipients of an award may retain their entitlements, even if they leave employment, the award would have vested at the point they retain entitlement. At this point, any remaining charge would be accelerated. This is considered in the example following paragraph A12.154.3.

Matching shares

A12.154.3 The accounting for matching shares should be similar to that of a free share award (see para A12.154.1 above), that is, the expense would be recognised over the vesting period. Where awards are part of an ongoing arrangement under which the employee can purchase shares and, consequently, receive matching shares, the charge should be made over the relevant vesting period. This is considered in the following example.

Example – Matching shares with a service condition

An entity operates an equity incentive plan for all of its employees. As part of the arrangement, employees have a right to matching shares when they apply for shares, although they must hold their purchased shares and remain with the entity for three years before the matching shares vest unconditionally. However, 'good' leavers (for example, death, injury, disability, transfer and retirement) would not forfeit their rights to the matching shares.

In the case of good leavers, it is assumed that the matching shares must have vested at the point they become a good leaver (as there are no service conditions to be satisfied for them to receive the shares). Hence, any remaining charge should be accelerated when a good leaver leaves. For bad leavers, on the other hand, due to the fact they have forfeited their rights to the shares by failing to meet the service condition, there should be a reversal of the related charge to the extent they were not anticipated.

Therefore, at the date of grant the matching shares are granted, it is necessary not only to assess the likely number of leavers and when they are going to leave, but also to split these into good and bad leavers. For those expected to be good leavers the estimated vesting period will be reduced to the likely date of their departure, for example, on retirement. However, it would be difficult to estimate vesting for death and/or disability events and these amounts may not be material. Where such events are unlikely to be material vesting for these conditions might not be adjusted until the event takes place.

Dividend shares

A12.154.4 Dividends paid on shares that have vested with employees (perhaps through another plan) accrue to the benefit of the employee. Clearly, these dividends will be included within dividends paid by the company.

A12.154.5 In some situations the shares have not vested (for example, where shares are subject to forfeiture) but dividends on those shares do vest (either by being paid to the employee or by reinvestment in dividend shares that are not forfeitable). This is a complex area and specialist advice may need to be obtained.

Share incentive plans (SIPs) — UK

UK.A12.154.6 UK-specific equity incentive plans are called 'share incentive plans' (SIPs). Participation in such a plan must be offered to all employees, although employers can set a minimum service requirement of up to 18 months.

UK.A12.155 Employees can obtain shares in four ways under a SIP. All shares that are obtained under a SIP must, initially, be held in a UK resident employee benefit trust. Concerns raised by many employers have been addressed by including innovative features such as tax advantages for dividends reinvested in SIP shares and a forfeiture mechanism to deal with shares held by employees who cease employment. Examples of the four ways employees can obtain shares in the employing company under a SIP are:

- *Free shares* – employers can gift up to £3,000 of free shares to each employee each year. Employers can award all or some of the free shares on different bases to different employees. The performance targets used for each different group must be broadly comparable and be set in such a way that each employee in the group has a similar chance of meeting them. Employers can award shares to recognise, for example, individual, team or divisional performance.
- *Partnership shares* – subject to certain limits employees can purchase up to £1,500 of partnership shares each year out of their pre-tax income. Employers may allow for either the purchase of shares using deductions from employees' pay within 30 days of the deduction, or an accumulation period of up to 12 months, where the salary deductions are rolled up and the shares allocated to employees within 30 days of the end of that period. Since April 2003, employees have also been permitted to invest in partnership shares on a 'one-off' basis rather than through monthly savings. The method chosen by the employer will have an effect on whether or not there is an IFRS 2 charge. This will depend on the grant date fair value compared with the amount paid by the employee. There would be no IFRS 2 charge where the employee paid an amount equal to the grant date fair value.
- *Matching shares* – employers can match partnership shares purchased by employees at a ratio of up to 2:1, that is, the employer can gift matching shares with a value of up to £3,000. These shares may be subject to forfeiture provisions linked to the withdrawal of the associated partnership shares or to the cessation of employment within a given period from the date of award.
- *Tax-free reinvestment of dividends* – the SIP allows employers to offer tax-free dividend reinvestment in further shares for employees with shares in

the plan. Up to £1,500 of dividends may be reinvested in shares tax-free each year. The reinvestment must be within 30 days of the date the dividends become payable. Dividend shares are not forfeitable, that is, they must be given to the employee even if he leaves. However, this will not have an IFRS 2 impact.

UK.A12.156 The employer will be entitled to a statutory deduction in computing profits for income tax purposes for the cost of setting up and administering the SIP, for the market value of any free or matching shares allocated to employees and for the amount of the employee's gross salary used to buy shares. Depending on the circumstances, further income tax deductions may also be available to the company.

UK.A12.157 The following accounting analysis is intended to show how the various components of a SIP may be treated under IFRS 2. It is, however, only intended to be indicative and companies will need to consider the appropriate accounting treatment in the light of the specific plan rules.

Free shares

UK.A12.158 The accounting for an award of free shares is consistent with that covered in paragraphs A12.154.1 and A12.154.2 above.

UK.A12.159 The accounting is more complicated where recipients of an award may retain their entitlements even if they leave employment. This is considered in the example following paragraph A12.154.3.

Partnership shares — with accumulation period

UK.A12.160 The purchase price of the shares (used to determine the number of partnership shares that the employee can purchase) is the lower of:

- the market price at the beginning of the accumulation period; and
- the market price at the end of the accumulation period.

UK.A12.161 The accounting for partnership shares is a complex area given the fact that the employee can save different amounts during the accumulation period and given the variability of the exercise price. Each arrangement needs to be looked at on a case by case basis to determine the most appropriate accounting treatment.

[The next paragraph is UK.A12.165.]

Matching shares

UK.A12.165 The accounting for matching shares is covered in paragraph A12.154.3 above.

Dividend shares

UK.A12.166 The accounting for dividend shares is covered in paragraph A12.154.4 and A12.154.5 above.

[The next paragraph is A12.167.]

Deferred bonus plans

A12.167 A deferred bonus plan is a type of share incentive plan that is common in some territories. Terms are varied and often complex, but the following are typical features:

- A bonus is awarded to employees based on individual and company performance over one year.
- At the end of the year, employees may elect to receive a portion of their bonus in the form of shares rather than cash.
- If an employee elects to receive shares:
  - the shares are restricted insofar as they cannot be sold for three years; and
  - if the individual is still an employee at the end of the three year period, they receive an allocation of matching shares (see paras A12.154 and A12.154.3).

A12.167.1 However, the entitlement to matching shares introduces a degree of complexity as there are, in substance, two awards. The first, which may be settled in cash or shares, vests at the end of the first year. The second (the entitlement to matching shares) does not vest until the end of the fourth year and only then if the employee has chosen shares rather than cash at the end of the first year. This means that an expense should be recognised over one year for the first award and over four years for the second.

A12.167.2 As regards measurement, the grant date value of the cash alternative is clearly the agreed amount of the bonus. The value of the equity alternative is made up of two components, namely the restricted shares (the value of which may be slightly less than the cash alternative if it is appropriate to reduce the value as a result of the sale restriction – see para A12.96) plus the matching shares.

A12.167.3 If at the end of the first year an employee chooses the cash alternative they will not receive the equity alternative or the matching shares. One acceptable method of accounting for this could be as the employee selecting the cash option of an award with employee choice. No further expense would be recognised, but at the same time any expense recognised in respect of the equity alternative remains in equity (see further from para A12.142). [IFRS 2 para 40]. An alternative method (which will become the only method if the current draft amendment to IFRS 2 is approved) is for the above employee election to be treated as a cancellation of the matching share award with an acceleration of any unregonised grant date fair value (see further from para A12.91 on cancellations and from para A12.171 on the draft amendment). [IFRS 2 para 28(a)].

A12.167.4 On the other hand, if the employee chooses the equity alternative, the balance on the liability is transferred to equity and the company will continue to recognise the balance of the expense in respect of the matching shares over the remaining three years. If, having taken the equity alternative, an employee leaves after, say, two years, this will represent failure to satisfy a vesting condition, so the cumulative expense recognised in respect of the matching shares will be reversed. The expense recognised in the first year in respect of the restricted shares will not be reversed, as the former employee will normally be entitled to retain the shares.

Employee share purchase plans

A12.168 In some territories, sharesave plans are plans through which employees are given the opportunity to subscribe for shares often at a discount to the market price. This may be paid for from a reduction of payroll over a period rather than a lump sum payment.

UK.A12.168.1 In the UK, save as you earn (SAYE) plans are Inland Revenue approved plans through which employees are given the opportunity to subscribe for shares at a discount of up to 20 per cent of the market price. Typically the plans have a term of three, five or seven years. In the case of three or five year arrangements, employees must make regular savings throughout the term. In the case of a seven-year term, savings made under a five year agreement are left to increase in value for a further two years. The amount that can be invested is up to £250 per month across all plans to which an employee belongs. If an employee ceases saving, they receive a reimbursement of all amounts saved to date, plus interest, but they must withdraw from the plan.

[The next paragraph is A12.170.]

A12.170 As described in paragraph A12.33, employee share purchase plans (for instance SAYE plans in the UK) do fall within the scope of IFRS 2. Hence, they should be treated like any other equity-settled share-based payment arrangement. However, unlike many other arrangements, some employee share purchase plans, such as those in the UK, impose a condition on their members that requires regular saving. If an employee ceases saving, they forfeit their right to subscribe for shares. Hence, it would appear that the requirement to save could be considered a vesting condition (see para A12.61).

A12.171 In December 2004, the IFRIC published a draft interpretation (D11, 'Changes in contributions to employee share purchase plans') containing guidance on accounting for employee share purchase plans. The IFRIC's proposals were controversial and many respondents disagreed with the draft interpretation. In April 2005, after the IFRIC failed to conclude on the D11 proposals, the issue was passed to the IASB to consider whether there should be an amendment to IFRS 2.

A12.171.1 The IASB issued an exposure draft for consultation in February 2006. Over a year later, in May 2007, a near final draft of proposed amendments to IFRS 2 was published consistent with the IFRIC's original proposals, the near final draft sets out the following changes to IFRS 2:

- Vesting conditions should be restricted to service conditions (requirements to complete a specified period of service) and performance conditions (requirements to meet specified performance targets).
- All cancellations, whether by the entity or by other parties, should receive the same accounting treatment.

Vesting conditions

A12.171.2 IFRS 2 currently states that vesting conditions include service conditions and performance conditions, but the standard is silent on whether other features of a share-based payment arrangement (such as a requirement to hold shares as part of a matching share award or a requirement to make regular payment into a plan as a part of a SAYE scheme) are vesting conditions. The near-final draft amendments clarify that only service conditions and performance conditions are vesting conditions.

A12.171.3 The proposals make clear that where vesting conditions are restricted to service and performance conditions, it will not be possible to treat requirements to make regular plan contributions over a specified period and to hold shares for a specified period as vesting conditions. Instead, non-vesting conditions for equity-settled awards should be included in the calculation of fair value at grant date.

Cancellations

A12.171.4 Under IFRS 2, a failure to meet a condition, other than a vesting condition, is a cancellation. Currently, IFRS 2 only specifies the accounting treatment of cancellations by the entity and does not give guidance on the treatment of cancellations by parties other than the entity (for example, the counterparty or the shareholders). Cancellation by an entity is accounted for as an acceleration of vesting, such that the entity should recognise immediately the amount that otherwise would have been recognised for services over the remainder of the vesting period (see from para A12.91 for further details). The amendment proposed that cancellations by parties other than the entity should be accounted for in the same way as cancellations by the entity.

Additional guidance and implementation

A12.171.5 The near-final draft of proposed amendments includes a worked example illustrating the accounting where an employee stops paying contributions to a plan. There is also a table categorising various vesting and non-vesting conditions. The table explains the implications of each condition on the fair value calculation and sets out the accounting treatment in the event that the condition is not met.

A12.171.6 The near-final draft states that entities should apply the amendments retrospectively in financial statements for periods beginning on or after 1 January 2008, with earlier application permitted. However, at the time of writing this manual the IASB had not concluded on the proposed amendments. Until such time as the amendments to IFRS 2 are finalised (and within Europe endorsed by the EU), accounting practice in respect of employee share purchase plans is likely to be mixed. Consequently, an entity should describe its accounting policy clearly.

Employee share ownership plans (ESOPs)

Background

A12.172 Employee share ownership plans (ESOPs) are usually designed to enable employees to purchase shares in their employing company. The structures of ESOPs vary, but typically they are arrangements whereby a trust is set up by a sponsoring company to acquire shares in that company for the benefit of its employees, who generally acquire them at a later stage through share option schemes, profit sharing arrangements or other share incentive schemes. The commercial reasons for establishing an ESOP include the following:

- It allows a share scheme to be extended to new participants without diluting existing shareholders' interests, because it can operate by acquiring and distributing shares that are already in issue rather than by requiring new shares to be issued.
- It can provide a private company with a market in its shares in order to operate an employee share scheme, by buying shares from departing employees and other shareholders, warehousing them and then distributing them to new and continuing employees.
- It can facilitate employee participation in connection with a management buyout, privatisation or flotation of a private company.
- In cash flow terms, a company can hedge its obligations in respect of options issued under share option schemes by avoiding exposure to increases in the market value of shares between the dates of granting the options and the dates of exercising those options.

A12.173 The vehicle used to hold the shares in an ESOP is a discretionary employee benefit trust set up by the sponsoring company for the benefit of all, or most, of its employees. For tax purposes, the trustee may be resident in a different country and a subsidiary of the company will often act as a corporate trustee. The trust buys shares with funds provided by way of cash or loans from the company or by a loan from a third party (which will be guaranteed by the company). The shares held by the trust are typically distributed to employees through an employee share scheme. The trust's beneficiaries usually only include the company's or group's employees or former employees and certain of their close relations.

A12.174 The detailed structures of individual ESOP trusts are many and varied. However, the main features are often as follows:

- The trust provides a warehouse for the sponsoring company's shares, for example, by acquiring and holding shares that are to be sold or transferred to employees in the future. The trust will normally purchase the shares with finance provided by the sponsoring company (by way of cash contributions or loans), or by a third party bank loan, or by a combination of the two. Loans from the company are usually interest free.

- Where the trust borrows from a third party, the sponsoring company will often guarantee the loan, that is, it will be responsible for any shortfall if the trust's assets are insufficient to meet its debt repayment obligations. The company will also generally make regular contributions to the trust to enable the trust to meet its interest payments (that is, to make good the shortfall between the dividend income of the trust and the interest payable). As part of this arrangement, the trustees sometimes waive their right to dividends on the shares the trust holds.

- Shares held by the trust are distributed to employees through an employee share scheme. There are many different arrangements, which include: the purchase of shares by employees when exercising their share options under an executive share option scheme; the purchase of shares by the trustees of schemes approved by taxation authorities for allocation to employees under the scheme's rules; or the transfer of shares to employees under an incentive scheme.

A share nominee company could be used by an entity as opposed to an ESOP trust. A share nominee company is used by entities to hold shares and other securities on the entity's behalf to satisfy their obligation for employee share awards.

[The next paragraph is A12.176.]

Accounting for ESOP trusts

A12.176 IFRS 2 does not deal with the accounting for an entity's shares held by an ESOP trust.

> **UK.A12.176.1** This is similar to the position in the UK, where there has never been an accounting standard on the subject of ESOP trusts. However, the UITF did issue UITF Abstract 13, 'Employee share ownership plans', which was superseded in 2003 by UITF Abstract 38, 'Accounting for ESOP trusts'. For further details, see the Manual of Accounting – UK GAAP.

[The next paragraph is A12.183.]

A12.183 SIC 12, 'Consolidation – special purpose entities', concludes that an entity should consolidate a special purpose entity ('SPE') where the substance of the relationship between the parties indicates that the SPE is controlled by the entity. [SIC 12 para 8]. SIC 12 was amended in November 2004 to remove the exclusion from its scope of an equity compensation plan, such as an ESOP trust and consequentially ESOPs are now caught by this interpretation. (The amendment does not change the scope exclusion for employee benefit trusts, which continue to be accounted for under IAS 19.) The interpretation goes on to give examples of circumstances in which an SPE may be consolidated. These include the following:

- The activities of the SPE are being conducted on behalf of the entity according to its specific business needs so that the entity obtains benefits from the SPE's operation.
- The entity has rights to obtain the majority of the benefits of the SPE and, therefore, may be exposed to risks incident to the activities of the SPE.

[SIC 12 paras 10(a), 10(c)].

A12.183.1 Although the trustees of an ESOP trust must act under the trust deed at all times in accordance with the beneficiaries' interests, most ESOP trusts (particularly those set up to remunerate employees) are specifically designed to serve an entity's purposes, (otherwise known as the sponsoring entity), and to ensure that there will be minimal risk of any conflict arising between the trustees' duties and the entity's interest. In substance, the sponsoring entity has control of the ESOP trust and reaps the benefits or bears the risks associated with its assets and liabilities. In order to determine whether a sponsoring company does control the ESOP here follows a number of examples where control may occur:

- Where the ESOP trust has unallocated shares, the benefit of increases in value of those shares will accrue to the sponsoring entity because, for example, it can pass increased benefits to its employees without using its other resources. Conversely, if the shares fall in value, the sponsoring entity may have to use its other resources to make good the benefits promised to its employees. Therefore, the sponsoring entity benefits from the activities of the trust and will need to make decisions about how many shares, at any point in time, the ESOP should hold. It is also worth noting that shares in an ESOP that have been allocated to employees but have not vested unconditionally (for example, where the employee is still required to pay an exercise price), would result in the sponsoring entity retaining the benefits and risks associated with holding the shares. Therefore, the ESOP would still be controlled by the sponsoring entity and hence consolidated.

- At the point when shares are conditionally gifted to the employees, the sponsoring entity retains an interest in the shares, because the benefits and risks associated with them remain with the sponsoring entity until the conditions are fulfilled and the shares have been exercised by the employees. Therefore, again by taking the risks with respect to the number of shares the sponsoring company continues to control the ESOP. The benefits and risks associated with shares that have been allocated to employees that have conditionally vested with the employee could still remain with the sponsoring entity if the ESOP has ownership of the shares as it could have a liability to the employee to repurchase the shares.

- In many ESOP trusts, dividends on the shares held by the trust are waived until they vest with employees. In other trusts dividends continue to be paid and these will accrue to the trust thereby benefiting the sponsoring entity by either defraying the trust's costs or by reducing the cost of future employee incentive arrangements, which are ultimately borne by the sponsoring entity. Hence, the sponsoring entity has power to govern the financial and operating decisions of the ESOP by determining how the additional dividend income should be allocated.

- In many ESOP trusts, the sponsoring entity will fund the ESOP to purchase shares in the market place. These loans are effectively a gift to the trust, which will then be used to satisfy the sponsoring company's employee share remuneration schemes. Hence, financing decisions as well as how funds are used are controlled by the sponsoring company.

A12.184 Thus, an ESOP trust that is controlled by its sponsoring entity should be consolidated into the financial statements with the sponsoring company. If the shares held by the ESOP are those of the group's parent, then the requirements of IAS 32 to treasury shares should be used. [SIC 12 para BC15C].

Example 1 – Treatment of ESOP trust

Parent entity P has a subsidiary entity S, which is the sponsoring company of an ESOP trust. Entity S does not prepare consolidated financial statements, but prepares separate financial statements.

The ESOP trust is required by SIC 12 to be included in the consolidated financial statements of entity P, but not in the separate financial statements of entity S.

A12.185 The impact on the consolidated financial statements, in which an ESOP trust should be accounted, is as follows:

- Until such time as shares in the sponsoring entity held by an ESOP trust vest unconditionally in employees, the consideration paid for those shares should be deducted from consolidated equity. This would be the case even if the shares vest unconditionally with the employee, but the shares are yet to transfer to the employee.

- No gain or loss is recognised in the income statement on the purchase, sale, issue or cancellation of those equity instruments. Instead, any consideration paid or received by the ESOP trust is recognised directly in equity.
- Other assets and liabilities, including borrowings, of the ESOP trust should be recognised as assets and liabilities of the group.
- External finance costs and administrative expenses should be charged as they become due and not as funding payments are made to the ESOP trust.
- Any dividend income arising on own shares held by the ESOP trust should be excluded from profit or loss and should not be reported as dividends paid or payable by the sponsoring entity.
- Shares held by the ESOP trust should be excluded from the calculation of earnings per share. The calculation of earnings per share is considered in detail in chapter 14.

UK.A12.185.1 Consolidation of an ESOP trust represents a difference to UK GAAP. Under UITF 38, individual assets and liabilities of such a trust are treated as if they were assets and liabilities of the sponsoring entity itself (that is, they are aggregated with the sponsoring company's own assets and liabilities in its separate financial statements). However, there is no GAAP divergence at a consolidated level: aggregation of a trust's assets and liabilities in consolidated financial statements under UK GAAP gives a similar effect to the consolidation of a trust under SIC 12 under IFRS.

[The next paragraph is A12.187.]

A12.187 The examples that follow illustrate the above principles.

Example 1 – Unallocated shares funded by a bank loan

An ESOP trust holds unallocated shares costing C100,000, funded by a bank loan. The trust's sponsoring entity undertakes to make contributions to the trust whenever the loan-to-value ratio falls below a set figure. At the reporting date the market value is at least C100,000. The entity deducts the consideration paid for the shares of C100,000 from equity in its consolidated financial statements. A liability of C100,000 in respect of the bank loan is also recognised. Interest expense is accrued in the usual way.

Example 2 – Reduction in the market value of shares

The facts are the same as in example 1, except that the market value of the shares falls to C80,000 by the entity's year end.

As in example 1, consideration paid for the shares of C100,000 is deducted from equity. The fall in the market value of the shares does not give rise to a recognised loss. Hence, there are no accounting entries to reflect the fall in the market value of the shares.

Example 3 – Market value of shares is in excess of exercise price

The facts are the same as in example 1, but options are granted over the shares at C80,000 when the market value is C100,000.

The entity recognises an expense over the option vesting period in accordance with IFRS 2. As in example 1, consideration paid for the shares of C100,000 is deducted from equity. When the options are exercised, the receipt of C80,000 is credited to equity.

Example 4 – Use of surplus shares for new award

An entity's ESOP trust purchased a number of its shares in the market some years ago when the share price was £1. The original share option awards have lapsed and the shares are to be used to satisfy new awards. The shares have been carried at cost. The share price has since risen to £4 and the entity proposes to grant options over those shares to employees at an exercise price of £1.

Under IFRS 2, the share-based payment charge is based on the fair value of the award at the date of grant and, therefore, awarding the options gives rise to an income statement charge. The award's fair value would be charged over the vesting period of the award. In the consolidated financial statements, the own shares held through the trust would be deducted from equity at cost, in line with SIC 12 and, therefore, would not change with the new award.

A12.187.1 An entity could use a share nominee company as opposed to an ESOP trust. A share nominee company is used by entities to hold shares and other securities on the entities' behalf to satisfy their obligation for employee share awards. An ESOP would be acting on behalf of one entity, whereas a share nominee company would be providing a service to a number of entities. In such a situation, the shares are in the possession of the nominee company, but not under its control. Consideration would need to be given as to whether the entity consolidates part of the nominee company applying the principles of SIC 12, or accounts for the holding of shares that the entity has beneficial holding of and not the investment in the nominee company. This is a complex area that requires consideration on a case by case basis.

A12.188 It must be remembered that the above principles relate to the accounting for shares (and other assets and liabilities) held by an ESOP trust. They have no impact on the recognition or measurement of the expense in respect of a share-based payment arrangement, which is dealt with in accordance with IFRS 2.

Gains made by ESOPs

A12.189 There are situations where ESOP trusts make gains, for instance on the sale of surplus shares (where previous awards have lapsed) or where the exercise price exceeds the cost of the shares. As noted above, no gain or loss should be recognised on the purchase, sale, issue or cancellation of an entity's own equity instruments. However, to the extent that the consideration received on the sale of surplus shares exceeds their cost, there will be a net credit in consolidated equity.

UK.A12.189.1 Under UK GAAP, this credit arises in the sponsoring company's own equity so there is a question as to whether this is distributable. Under IFRS, however, the credit arises only at group level so it has no impact on the sponsoring company's ability to make distributions.

Trustee company

A12.190 The above sections deal with the financial statements of the sponsoring company. In groups of companies, it is common for a non-trading subsidiary company to act as trustee to the ESOP. The accounting implications for the trustee company are considered in the example below.

Example – Treatment of ESOP by corporate trustee

A group operates an employee share scheme. A subsidiary of the group has been set up to act as a corporate trustee. What should the subsidiary include in its own entity financial statements?

The corporate trustee for an ESOP trust normally holds legal title to the trust's assets, but if these are held on trust such that the trustee has no beneficial interest (that is, the trustee's interest is limited to its fiduciary or custodial interest) then they are not, in substance, its assets. Therefore, the trustee company itself does not account for the assets (and likewise, the liabilities and transactions) of the ESOP. These would be reported in the financial statements of the ESOP trust and, as described from paragraph A12.176 above, in the financial statements of the group.

The trustee company may well be a dormant company with a nominal share capital. Even if the trustee company is not dormant (for instance, if it charges the trust a fee for its services), this does not change the fact that its financial statements should not normally include the transactions and balances of the trust.

[The next paragraph is A12.210.]

Disclosure

A12.210 IFRS 2 requires extensive disclosure under three broad headings:

- The nature and extent of share-based payment arrangements that existed during the period.
- How the fair value of the goods or services received or the fair value of the equity instruments granted during the period was determined.

- The effect of expenses arising from share-based payment transactions on the entity's profit or loss for the period.

[IFRS 2 paras 44, 46, 50].

A12.211 Furthermore, if the information that IFRS 2 requires to be disclosed is insufficient to enable users of the financial statements to understand each of these matters, further information should be provided. [IFRS 2 para 52].

Nature and extent of share-based payments

A12.212 Paragraph 44 of IFRS 2 requires disclosure of information that enables users of the financial statements to understand the nature and extent of share-based payment arrangements that existed during the period.

A12.213 To satisfy this objective, IFRS 2 requires disclosure of the following:

- A description of each type of share-based payment arrangement that existed at any time during the period, including the general terms and conditions of each arrangement, such as:
  - Vesting requirements.
  - The maximum term of options granted.
  - The method of settlement (for example, whether in cash or equity).

  An entity with substantially similar types of share-based payment arrangements may aggregate this information, unless separate disclosure of each arrangement is necessary for users to understand properly the nature and extent of share-based payment arrangements.

- The number and weighted average exercise prices of share options for each of the following groupings of options:
  - Outstanding at the beginning of the period.
  - Granted during the period.
  - Forfeited during the period.
  - Exercised during the period.
  - Expired during the period.
  - Outstanding at the end of the period.
  - Exercisable at the end of the period.
  - IFRS 2 only requires the above disclosure for share options. However, as share awards are equivalent to share options with a zero exercise price it would be appropriate to give disclosure consistent with the above requirements for share awards.

- For share options exercised during the period, the weighted average share price at the date of exercise. If options were exercised on a regular basis throughout the period, the entity may instead disclose the weighted average share price during the period.
- For share options outstanding at the end of the period, the range of exercise prices and weighted average remaining contractual life. If the range of exercise prices is wide, the outstanding options should be divided into ranges that are meaningful for assessing the number and timing of additional shares that may be issued and the cash that may be received upon exercising those options.

[IFRS 2 para 45].

A12.213.1 IFRS 2 requires the above disclosure to be given for share options. However, as share awards are equivalent to share options with a zero exercise price, it would be appropriate to give disclosure consistent with the above requirements for share awards as well as share options.

Disclosures for grants made before 7 November 2002

A12.213.2 As explained in paragraph A12.226, IFRS 2 does not require a charge in respect of equity instruments granted before 7 November 2002. However, certain disclosures are required for such awards as set out in the following example.

Example – Disclosures for option award granted before 7 November 2002

An entity granted 100 share options at an exercise price of C10 per share to employees for services. The grant date was 1 January 2002 and the options were subject to a five year vesting period.

An IFRS 2 charge in respect of the share options is not required because they were granted before 7 November 2002. [IFRS 2 para 53]. However, the entity must disclose information that enables the reader to understand the nature and extent of the share-based payment arrangement. This includes disclosure of:

- A description of the share-based payment arrangement:
- The general terms and conditions.
- Vesting requirements.
- The maximum term of options granted.
- The number and weighted average exercise prices of share options:
- Outstanding at the beginning of the period.
- Granted during the period.
- Forfeited during the period.
- Exercised during the period.

- Expired during the period.
- Outstanding at the end of the period.
- Exercisable at the end of the period.
- The weighted average share price at the date of exercise.
- The range of exercise prices and weighted average remaining contractual life for share options outstanding at the end of the period.

[IFRS 2 para 56, 44, 45].

[The next paragraph is A12.214.]

Determination of fair values

A12.214 Paragraph 46 of IFRS 2 requires disclosure of information that enables users of the financial statements to understand how the fair value of the goods or services received, or the fair value of the equity instruments granted, during the period was determined. The level of disclosure will vary depending on whether the fair value of the goods or services was determined directly or indirectly (see from para A12.45).

A12.215 In the case of transactions with parties other than employees, there is a rebuttable presumption that the fair value of goods or services will be measured directly. [IFRS 2 para 13]. Where the presumption is rebutted, for example where IFRIC 8 leads to a conclusion that unidentifiable goods or services have been provided and the fair value of the goods or services is measured indirectly by reference to the fair value of the equity instruments granted as consideration, the entity should disclose that fact and explain why the presumption has been rebutted. [IFRS 2 para 49].

A12.216 Where the fair value of goods or services has been measured directly, the entity should disclose how this fair value was determined. [IFRS 2 para 48]. For example, the fair value may have been determined by reference to a published list of prices or scale rates.

A12.217 Where the fair value of goods or services has been measured indirectly by reference to the fair value of the equity instruments granted as consideration, the entity should disclose the number and weighted average fair value of those equity instruments at the relevant measurement date together with information on how the fair value was measured. [IFRS 2 para 45(b)(ii), 47(a), 47(b)].

A12.218 Information on how the fair value was measured will vary depending on the type of equity instruments granted. For share options granted during the period, the information will include the following:

- The option pricing model used and the inputs to that model. These will include, at least on a weighted average basis:
  - Price of the underlying share.

  - Price of the option.
  - Expected volatility of the share price.
  - Life of the option.
  - Dividends expected on the underlying shares.
  - Risk-free interest rate over the life of the option.
  - The method used and the assumptions made to incorporate the effects of early exercise.
- How expected volatility was determined, including an explanation of the extent to which expected volatility was based on historical volatility.
- Whether and how any other features of the option grant were incorporated into the measurement of fair value (for example, market based vesting conditions).

[IFRS 2 para 47(a)].

A12.219 For other equity instruments granted during the period, information on how fair value was measured will include the following:

- If fair value was not measured on the basis of an observable market price, how it was determined.
- Whether and how expected dividends were incorporated into the measurement of fair value.
- Whether and how any other features of the equity instruments granted were incorporated into the measurement of fair value.

[IFRS 2 para 47(b)].

A12.220 Where there has been a modification to a share-based payment arrangement during the period, the following should be disclosed:

- An explanation of the modification.
- The incremental fair value granted.
- Information on how the incremental fair value was measured, consistent with the requirements set out in paragraphs A12.218 or A12.219 as appropriate.

[IFRS 2 para 47(c)].

Impact on profit or loss

A12.221 Paragraph 50 of IFRS 2 requires disclosure of information that enables users of the financial statements to understand the effect of share-based payment transactions on the entity's profit or loss for the period and on its financial position.

A12.222 To satisfy this objective, IFRS 2 requires disclosure of the following:

- The total expense recognised in the period in respect of share-based payment transactions, with separate disclosure of the portion of the expense that relates to transactions accounted for as equity-settled. In satisfying this requirement, only expenses in respect of goods or services that did not qualify for recognition as an asset are considered. Therefore, depreciation of an asset acquired in a prior-year share-based payment transaction does not need to be disclosed.
- For liabilities arising from share-based payment transactions:
  - the total carrying amount at the end of the period; and
  - the total intrinsic value at the end of the period of liabilities for which the counterparty's right to cash or other assets has vested.

[IFRS 2 para 51].

Example

A12.223 Table A12.3 is an example of IFRS 2 disclosures in respect of equity-settled share-based payments.

Table A12.3 – IFRS 2 share-based payment disclosures

British Sky Broadcasting Group plc – Annual Report – 30 June 2007
7. Employee benefits and key management compensation (extract)

(a) Group employee benefits

	2007	2006	2005
	£m	£m	£m
Wages and salaries	**451**	362	327
Social security costs	**48**	38	32
Costs of employee share option schemes (i)	**35**	23	25
Contributions to the Group's pension schemes (ii)	**20**	16	14
	554	439	398

(i) £33 million relates to equity-settled share-based payments (2006: £23 million; 2005: £25 million) and £2 million relates to cash-settled share-based payments (2006: nil; 2005: nil). At 30 June 2007, the total expense relating to non-vested awards not yet recognised was £39 million which is expected to be recognised over a weighted average period of 1.1 years. At 30 June 2007, £2 million was recognised as liabilities arising from share-based payment transactions (2006: nil), none of which related to awards for which the counterparty's right to cash had vested by the end of the year.

(ii) The Group operates defined contribution pension schemes. The pension charge for the year represents the cost of contributions payable by the Group to the schemes during the year. The Group's amount payable to the schemes at 30 June 2007 was £2 million (2006: £2 million).

23. Share capital (extract)
Share option and contingent share award schemes

The Company operates various equity-settled share option schemes (the "Schemes") for certain employees.

The number of newly issued shares which may be allocated under the Schemes on any day shall not, when aggregated with the number of newly issued shares which have been allocated in the previous ten years under the Schemes and any other employee share scheme adopted by the Company, exceed such number as represents five percent of the ordinary share capital of the Company in issue immediately prior to that day. In determining this limit no account shall be taken of any newly issued shares where the right to acquire the newly issued shares was released, lapsed, cancelled or otherwise became incapable of exercise. Options and awards which will be satisfied by ESOP shares do not fall within these headroom limits.

The share awards outstanding can be summarised as follows:

	2007 Number of ordinary shares	2006 Number of ordinary shares
Executive Share Option Scheme options (i)	**24,909,710**	36,289,000
Sharesave Scheme options (ii)	**5,795,544**	5,149,576
Management LTIP awards (iii)	**11,306,811**	4,103,306
LTIP awards (iv)	**7,965,417**	6,073,333
Key Contributors Plan ("KCP") awards (v)	**14,237**	917,518
Equity Bonus Plan ("EBP") awards (vi)	**–**	235,000
	49,991,719	52,767,733

(i) Executive Share Option Scheme options
Included within the total Executive Share Option Scheme options outstanding at 30 June 2007 are 22,955,210 options (2006: 34,094,411) which may be exercised in the final year before their lapsing date, regardless of meeting performance criteria, provided that the employee remains in employment with the Group. Where performance criteria are achieved, the options may be exercised immediately following the end of the vesting period (being the term over which the performance criteria are required to be met). The remaining 1,954,500 options (2006: 2,194,589) have no performance criteria attached, other than the requirement that the employee remains in employment with the Group. The contractual life of all Executive Share Option Scheme options is ten years.

Grants under the Executive Share Option Scheme were made on an annual basis to selected employees, with the exercise price of options being equal to the Company's share price on the date of grant. For those options with performance conditions, growth in EPS has to exceed growth in the Retail Prices Index plus 3% per annum in order for awards to vest. Options vest on an accelerated basis over a period of up to four years from the date of grant.

(ii) Sharesave Scheme options
All Sharesave Scheme options outstanding at 30 June 2007 and 30 June 2006 have no performance criteria attached, other than the requirement that the employee remains in employment with the Group. Options granted under the Sharesave scheme must be exercised within six months of the relevant award vesting date.

The Sharesave Scheme is open to all employees. Options are normally exercisable after either three, five or seven years from the date of grant. The price at which options are offered is not less than 80% of the middle-market price on the dealing day immediately preceding the date of invitation. It is the policy of the Group to make an invitation to employees to participate in the scheme following the announcement of the end of year results.

(iii) Management LTIP awards

All Management LTIP awards outstanding at 30 June 2007 and 30 June 2006 vest only if performance conditions are met. Awards granted under the Management LTIP must be exercised within one year of the relevant award vesting date.

The Company grants awards to selected employees under the Management LTIP. Awards under this scheme mirror the LTIP, with the same performance conditions. Awards exercised under the Management LTIP can only be satisfied by the issue of market-purchased shares.

(iv) LTIP awards

All LTIP awards outstanding at 30 June 2007 and 30 June 2006 vest only if performance conditions are met. Awards granted under the LTIP must be exercised within one year of the relevant award vesting date.

The Company operates the LTIP for Executive Directors and Senior Executives. Awards under the scheme are granted in the form of a nil-priced option, and are satisfied using market-purchased shares. The awards vest in full or in part dependent on the satisfaction of specified performance targets. 30% of the award vests dependent on TSR performance over a three year performance period, relative to the constituents of the FTSE 100 at the time of grant, and the remaining 70% vests dependent on performance against operational targets.

(v) KCP awards

All KCP awards outstanding at 30 June 2007 and 30 June 2006 vest only if performance conditions are met. The contractual life of all KCP awards is ten years.

Designated managers participated in the KCP, which was a replica scheme of the LTIP, with the same performance conditions. Awards exercised under the KCP can only be satisfied by the issue of shares purchased in the market.

(vi) EBP awards

All EBP awards outstanding at 30 June 2006 vested only if performance conditions were met. The contractual life of these awards was ten years.

The EBP operated for Executive Directors and Senior Executives. Awards under the plan were made in the form of a contingent right to acquire the Company's shares, for nil consideration, which are acquired in the market, and were subject to performance achieved in the financial year of award.

The movement in share awards outstanding is summarised in the following table:

	2007 Number of shares under option	**2007** Weighted average exercise price	2006 Number of shares under option	2006 Weighted average exercise price
Outstanding at 1 July	52,767,733	£4.96	58,446,794	£5.64
Granted during the year	13,478,079	£0.62	8,390,285	£0.80
Exercised during the year	(8,343,434)	£4.47	(4,160,336)	£3.85
Forfeited during the year	(7,768,714)	£4.63	(9,906,234)	£5.90
Expired during the year	(141,945)	£4.93	(2,776)	£4.85
Outstanding at 30 June	49,991,719	£3.93	52,767,733	£4.96

The weighted average market price of the Group's shares at the date of exercise for share options exercised during the year was £5.94 (2006: £5.48). The middle-market closing price of the Company's shares at 30 June 2007 was £6.40 (2006: £5.735). The following table summarises information about share awards outstanding at 30 June 2007:

Range of exercise prices	**2007 Number**	**2007 Weighted average remaining contractual life**	2006 Number	2006 Weighted average remaining contractual life
£0.00-£1.00	**19,286,465**	**2.2 years**	11,329,157	4.5 years
£2.00-£3.00	**277,874**	**1.2 years**	295,355	2.2 years
£3.00-£4.00	**2,305,099**	**1.7 years**	2,630,543	2.7 years
£4.00-£5.00	**2,888,496**	**3.2 years**	1,722,925	3.2 years
£5.00-£6.00	**8,976,001**	**6.2 years**	16,744,201	6.8 years
£6.00-£7.00	**6,789,744**	**5.0 years**	8,547,034	6.0 years
£7.00-£8.00	**5,154,316**	**4.4 years**	6,285,648	5.4 years
£8.00-£9.00	–	–	26,668	5.4 years
£9.00-£10.00	**4,176,903**	**3.4 years**	4,964,142	4.4 years
£10.00-£11.00	–	–	21,842	3.9 years
£11.00-£12.00	**12,247**	**3.0 years**	57,860	4.1 years
£12.00-£13.00	**124,574**	**3.0 years**	142,358	4.0 years
	49,991,719	**3.7 years**	52,767,733	5.4 years

The exercise prices of options outstanding at 30 June 2007 ranged from nil to £12.98 (2006: nil to £12.98). The weighted average remaining contractual life of the 19,501,864 options which were exercisable at 30 June 2007 (2006: 21,519,271) was 4.5 years (2006: 5.0 years), and their weighted average exercise price was £7.28 (2006: £7.40).

Information for awards granted during the year

The weighted average fair value of equity-settled share options granted during the year, as estimated at the date of grant, was £4.02 (2006: £3.27; 2005: £2.37). This was calculated using the Black-Scholes share option pricing model, except for awards which have market-based performance conditions, where a Monte-Carlo simulation model was used, and for grants of nil-priced options, which were treated as the award of a free share.

The Monte-Carlo simulation model reflected the historical volatilities of the Company's share price and those of all other companies to which the Company's performance would be compared, over a period equal to the vesting period of the options. The fair value of nil-priced options granted during the year was measured on the basis of the market-price of the Company's shares on the date of grant, discounted for expected dividends which would not be received over the vesting period of the options.

Weighted average fair value assumptions

The following weighted average assumptions were used in these option pricing models:

	2007	2006	2005
Share price	**£5.51**	£5.13	£4.93
Exercise price	**£0.62**	£0.80	£3.57
Expected volatility	**23.8%**	25.9%	41.5%
Expected life	**3.0 years**	2.0 years	3.5 years
Expected dividends	**2.2%**	1.8%	1.0%
Risk-free interest rate	**4.8%**	4.3%	4.8%

Expected volatility was determined by calculating the historical volatility of the Company's share price, over a period equal to the expected life of the options. Expected life was based on the contractual life of the options and adjusted, based on management's best estimate, for the effects of exercise restrictions and behavioural considerations.

1. Accounting policies (extract)

The Group issues equity-settled and cash-settled share-based payments to certain employees which must be measured at fair value and recognised as an expense in the income statement, with a corresponding increase in equity in the case of equity-settled payments, and liabilities in the case of cash-settled awards. The fair values of equity-settled payments are measured at the dates of grant using option-pricing models, taking into account the terms and conditions upon which the awards are granted. Cash-settled share-based payments are measured at their fair value as at the balance sheet date. The fair value is recognised over the period during which employees become unconditionally entitled to the awards, subject to the Group's estimate of the number of awards which will lapse, either due to employees leaving the Group prior to vesting or due to non-market based performance conditions not being met. Where an award has market-based performance conditions, the fair value of the award is adjusted for the probability of achieving these via the option pricing model. The total amount recognised in the income statement as an expense is adjusted to reflect the actual number of awards that vest, except where forfeiture is due to the failure to meet market-based performance measures.

In accordance with the transitional provisions in IFRS 1, and IFRS 2, the recognition and measurement principles in IFRS 2 have only been applied to options and awards granted after 7 November 2002 that had not vested by 1 January 2005.

Directors' emoluments disclosure

UK.A12.224 IFRS 2 does not deal with the disclosure of directors' emoluments. Disclosure requirements for long-term incentive schemes and other share-based payment transactions involving directors are contained in Schedule 6 of the Companies Act 1985 (section 412 of the Companies Act 2006), Schedule 7A of the Companies Act 1985 (section 420 of the Companies Act 2006) and in the Listing Rules. Details of these requirements are covered in chapter 5 of the Manual of Accounting – Management Reports and Governance.

Related party disclosures

A12.225 IAS 24, 'Related party disclosures', contains a requirement to disclose compensation payable to key management personnel, which includes share-based payment. [IAS 24 para 16]. This requirement is discussed further in chapter 29.

Cash flow statements

A12.225.1 IAS 7, 'Cash flow statements', requires an entity to report cash flows from operating activities. Employee share-based payment transactions that are equity-settled should be adjusted for in reporting the cash flows from operating activities as this represents a non-cash item that is operating in nature. [IAS 7 paras 19, 20].

Materiality

A12.225.2 IAS 8 confirms that accounting policies set out in IFRSs do not need to be applied where the effect of applying them is immaterial. [IAS 8 para 8]. Both the quantitative and qualitative impact of an entity's share-based payment transactions should be assessed in order to determine the impact of applying IFRS 2. It will also be necessary to consider whether the impact of share-based payment transactions is likely to become material in the future. If the impact of applying IFRS 2 is determined to be either quantitatively or qualitatively material, the standard should be applied in full.

A12.225.3 Where IFRS 2 is not applied, certain disclosures in relation to share-based payment transactions may be required under local legislation or listings rules (such as gains on directors' share options or shares receivable under long-term incentive schemes). It would be appropriate to explain, particularly in these circumstances, that the standard has not been applied in the financial statements, particularly where disclosures provided under local legislation indicate that the entity has share-based payment transactions in place.

First-time adoption of IFRS

A12.226 There are specific rules in respect of first-time adoption of IFRS, set out in IFRS 1, 'First-time adoption of International Financial Reporting Standards'. When IFRS 2 was published in February 2004, IFRS 1 was amended to introduce a further exemption from full retrospective application for share-based payment transactions. Broadly, the requirements of IFRS 2 are to be applied to grants of equity instruments made since ED 2 was issued (that is, 7 November 2002) and to liabilities in respect of cash-settled share-based payment transactions outstanding at the date of transition to IFRS. First-time adopters are encouraged, however, to apply IFRS 2's requirements to other transactions, although this option is somewhat restricted. The requirements for first-time adoption are considered in detail in chapter 3.

Example 1 – Previous fair value presentation of share-based payment awards

Entity A, a quoted company, has operated an employee share scheme for a number of years. The scheme has been granting options with a three year performance period to employees on an annual basis. The directors are aware that on transition to IFRS the requirements of IFRS 2 may be applied only to equity-settled share-based payments that are granted after 7 November 2002, that have not vested at the later of 1 January 2005 and the date of transition.

The directors are concerned that as IFRS 2 will not be applied to all outstanding awards, there will be a step up of the IFRS 2 charge over the next two years. They have asked whether they can apply the IFRS 2 principles to all outstanding awards.

The amendment to IFRS 1 (made when IFRS 2 was published) states that if an entity has previously publicly disclosed the fair value of equity instruments that were granted on or before 7 November 2002, it may apply IFRS 2 to such equity instruments.

Therefore, if the entity publicly discloses the fair value of all outstanding equity-settled share-based payment arrangements, before it adopts IFRS, and those fair values are determined at the date of grant, then it is able to apply the standard's requirements retrospectively. Note, however, that the fair value needs to be at the measurement date and, therefore, the inputs used for calculating fair value at the measurement date must not include the benefit of hindsight.

Example 2 – Restatement of comparatives for cash-settled schemes prior to 7 November 2002

An entity granted share appreciation rights (SARs) to a director on 1 January 2000. The SARs entitle the director to a cash payment equal to the appreciation in the entity's share price between 1 January 2000 and 31 December 2005. The entity adopted IFRS 2 in its financial statements for the year ended 31 December 2004 and is presenting two years of comparatives: 2003 and 2002. The entity wishes to comply with IFRS 2's minimum requirements and does not wish to restate information prior to 7 November 2002.

IFRS 2 is applied retrospectively to liabilities existing at the standard's effective date of 1 January 2005 (or an earlier date if IFRS 2 is adopted early). The entity should restate comparatives for these liabilities, including adjusting the opening balance of retained earnings in the earliest period presented for which comparative information has been restated. The entity is not required to restate comparative information to the extent that it relates to a period or date before 7 November 2002. [IFRS 2 para 58]. Management should determine the fair value of the SAR liability as of 7 November 2002 and adjust liabilities and retained earnings as of that date. The expense reported in the 2002 comparatives should represent the change in the SARs liability from 7 November 2002 to 31 December 2002.

Example 3 – Effective date of early adopter

An entity granted 100 share options at an exercise price of C10 per share to employees for services. The grant date was 1 December 2002 and the options vest on 31 December 2004 if the entity meets its three year revenue growth target.

The entity early adopted IFRS 2 in its financial statements for the year ended 31 December 2004.

The effective date is the beginning of the period in which the entity first applies IFRS 2. The entity should, therefore, apply IFRS 2 to the grant of the 100 share options that are not yet vested at 1 January 2004 and restate comparatives for 2003.

UK.A12.226.1 In the UK, all listed companies (that is, those whose securities are admitted to trading on a regulated market) are required by an EU Regulation (EC No.1606/2002) to prepare their consolidated financial statements in accordance with EU-adopted International Financial Reporting Standards for accounting periods beginning on or after 1 January 2005. In addition, the Companies Act 1985 has been amended to extend the EU Regulation on a voluntary basis to all companies (except charitable companies) in their individual and/or consolidated financial statements for accounting periods beginning on or after 1 January 2005 (this is also included in the Companies Act 2006) (see further chapter 2).

[The next paragraph is A12.228.]

Effective date of recent interpretations (IFRIC 8 and IFRIC 11)

A12.228 The requirements of IFRIC 8 should be applied by entities for accounting periods beginning on or after 1 May 2006, but early adoption is encouraged. If an entity applies IFRIC 8 to a period beginning before 1 May 2006, it should disclose that fact. An entity should apply the interpretation retrospectively in accordance with the requirements of IAS 8, subject to the transitional provisions of IFRS 2 detailed in chapter 3. [IFRIC 8 paras 13, 14].

UK.A12.228.1 UITF 41, the equivalent interpretation for companies reporting under UK GAAP has the same effective date.

A12.229 IFRIC 11, which should be applied retrospectively subject to the transitional provisions of IFRS 2, is effective for annual periods beginning on or after 1 March 2007. Earlier application of the interpretation is permitted provided that the fact that it is being adopted early is stated. Where an entity has not previously applied the guidance in the draft interpretation D17, a change in accounting policy will be required.

A12.230 If an entity chooses not to apply the interpretation early, IAS 8, 'Accounting policies, changes in accounting estimates and errors' would require the entity to disclose the fact that the interpretation has not yet been adopted in its financial statements. Additionally, disclosure of the impact the interpretation will have on the entity's financial statements in the period of initial application is required.

UK.A12.231 Consistent with IFRIC 11, the equivalent interpretation for UK GAAP reporters, UITF Abstract 44 is effective for accounting periods beginning on or after 1 March 2007. Earlier adoption is encouraged.

UK.A12.232 Entities are required to apply UITF 44 retrospectively in accordance with FRS 3 and subject to the transitional provisions of FRS 20 (as set out in paragraphs 53 to 59 of the standard).

[The next paragraph is UK.A12.237.]

Companies Act requirements

UK.A12.237 The Companies Act 1985 and the Companies Act 2006 contain no accounting requirements regarding share-based payment transactions. There are, however, extensive disclosure requirements for options and share awards made to directors. Details of these requirements are covered in chapter 5 of the Manual of Accounting – Management Reports and Governance.

UK.A12.238 As regards shares acquired and held by an ESOP trust, the note of legal considerations attached to UITF Abstract 38 makes it clear that the accounting treatment described in paragraph A12.185 (that is, deduction of the cost of the shares from equity) does not affect the legal characterisation of the transaction, or change the situation at law achieved by the parties to it. Thus, shares acquired by an ESOP trust and deducted from equity are not treasury shares as defined by the Companies Act 1985 (as amended by The Companies (Acquisition of Own Shares) (Treasury Shares) Regulations 2003) (or the Companies Act 2006). Neither does the accounting treatment imply that the shares have been purchased by the company as a matter of law nor that they are required to be cancelled, which would be the consequence of such a purchase except for treasury shares (under sections 162(2) and 160(4) of the Companies Act 1985 (sections 688 and 724 of the Companies Act 2006)). [UITF 38 Legal considerations].

[The next paragraph is A12.239.]

Impact on distributable profits

A12.239 International Financial Reporting Standards do not concern themselves with how to determine distributable profits. Such matters are dealt with in national law (and are considered in greater detail in chapter 24). In the case of share based-payment (and the related topic of ESOP trusts), several questions are raised:

- Does the expense in respect of an equity-settled share-based payment transaction represent a realised loss?
- Does the opposing credit entry to equity represent a realised profit?
- What is the impact on distributable profits of deducting the cost of acquiring shares through an ESOP trust from equity?
- If an ESOP trust makes a profit on the sale of surplus shares, is this distributable by the sponsoring entity?

A12.240 The answers to the above questions should be dealt with in accordance with national law.

UK.A12.240.1 In the UK these questions are considered in Tech 64/04, 'Guidance on the effect on realised and distributable profits of accounting for employee share schemes in accordance with UITF Abstract 38 and revised UITF Abstract 17', issued by the ICAEW in December 2004. Although, as the title suggests, this guidance focuses on UK GAAP, paragraph I-5 states that the implications for distributable profits are likely to be similar for entities reporting under FRS 20 and, therefore, its conclusions are also relevant to determining distributable profits under IFRS.

Expenses in respect of equity-settled share-based payment transactions

UK.A12.241 All expenses and losses should be regarded as realised losses, except to the extent that the law or accounting standards provide otherwise. It is arguable that the expense in respect of an equity-settled share-based payment transaction is not a loss at all because it does not result in a reduction in recorded net assets. However, even if the expense is regarded as a realised loss, Tech 7/03, 'Guidance on the determination of realised profits and losses in the context of distributions under the Companies Act 1985', makes it clear in other contexts (such as revaluation reserves) that an unrealised reserve will be treated as having become realised by the amortisation or writing down of the related asset. Therefore, assuming that the expense has been included in the profit and loss account rather than capitalised as part of the cost of an asset, the credit entry will be treated as a realised profit so there will be no impact on distributable reserves.

ESOP trusts

UK.A12.242 Under UK GAAP, the accounting treatment of ESOP trusts results in a sponsoring entity including the assets, liabilities and transactions of an ESOP trust in its own financial statements as if the trust were an extension of the entity. These financial statements (that is, the combined entity and trust) are the relevant accounts for the purposes of determining profits available for distribution in accordance with section 270 of the Act. It follows, therefore, that transactions entered into by an ESOP trust will have an impact on the sponsoring entity's distributable profits in the same way as if they had actually been entered into by the sponsoring entity itself.

UK.A12.243 Under IFRS, as described from paragraph A12.176, an ESOP trust would be consolidated rather than aggregated with the sponsoring entity's individual assets and liabilities. Accordingly, as the ESOP trust's individual transactions, assets and liabilities are not reflected in the sponsoring entity's relevant accounts, they do not affect the sponsoring entity's distributable profits, for an entity that has adopted IFRS within its individual financial statements.

UK.A12.244 In determining the impact of an ESOP trust on a sponsoring entity's distributable profits it will be necessary to consider the nature of transactions and balances between the two parties. An entity may fund an ESOP trust by making a gift, a loan or a combination of both. A gift to the trust is clearly an immediate realised loss (as it reduces the net assets of the sponsoring entity). On the other hand a loan, provided it is considered recoverable (that is, sufficient cash is expected when employees exercise their rights to the shares), would not be a realised loss. However, any impairment in the value of the loan (caused by a question over its recoverability) *would* be an immediate realised loss and, hence, would reduce the sponsoring entity's distributable profits.

UK.A12.245 Public companies may face additional problems in respect of the financial assistance rules. Section 154(1) of the Companies Act 1985 (section 682 of the Companies Act 2006) provides that a public company may only give financial assistance for the acquisition of its own shares if the company's net assets are not thereby reduced or, to the extent that net assets are reduced, the company has sufficient distributable profits to cover the full amount of the assistance.

Chapter 13

Taxation

	Page
Introduction	13001
Corporation tax	13002
General principles	13002
The imputation tax system	13003
FRS 16 — Current tax	13004
Recognition of current tax charge	13005
Tax credits, withholding and underlying taxes	13006
Outgoing dividends and other interest payable	13007
Incoming dividends and other interest receivable	13008
Underlying tax	13008
Income and expenses subject to non-standard rates of tax	13010
Measurement of the current tax charge	13012
Recoverability of ACT	13013
Uncertain tax positions	13014
Expenses associated with taxation	13017
Interest and penalties on uncertain tax positions	13017
Professional fees linked to tax expense	13017
Deferred tax	13018
Introduction	13018
Method of computation	13018
Income statement liability method	13019
FRS 19 — Deferred tax	13022
Objectives	13022
General principles	13023
Timing differences	13024
Accounting for some specific timing differences	13026
Accelerated capital allowances	13026
Industrial building allowances	13028
Infrastructure assets	13029
Provisions	13030
Deferred revenue expenditure	13030
Government grants	13031
Leases	13033
Post-retirement benefits	13035
Share-based payment transactions	13042
Equity-settled transactions	13042
Cash-settled transactions	13044
Revaluation of non-monetary assets	13045
General rule	13045
Subsequent depreciation	13046

Subsequent devaluation and impairment 13046
Marked to market assets 13047
Rollover and holdover reliefs 13048
Deferred tax assets 13050
General rule 13050
Suitable taxable profits 13051
Tax planning opportunities 13051
Recovery of deferred tax assets against deferred tax liabilities 13055
Recovery of deferred tax assets against future taxable profits 13056
Trading losses 13057
Capital losses 13058
Effect of a going concern uncertainty 13059
Reassessment of recoverability 13059
Measurement issues 13060
Introduction 13060
Average rates 13060
Change in tax rates 13061
Discounting 13062
Introduction 13062
Mechanics of the discounting calculation 13064
Scheduling the cash flows to be discounted 13065
Scheduling timing differences in respect of marked to market assets 13067
Discount rates 13067
Worked examples 13068
Treatment of tax in consolidated financial statements 13074
General principles 13074
Tax effects of consolidation adjustment 13075
Fair value adjustments 13076
Goodwill 13079
Unremitted earnings of subsidiaries, associates and joint ventures . . 13080
Foreign exchange differences 13080
Deemed disposals 13081
Presentation and disclosures 13082
General 13082
Accounting policies 13082
Profit and loss account 13083
Presentation and disclosures required by the Act 13083
Presentation required by the accounting standards 13084
Disclosures in the notes 13084
Analysis of current tax 13084
Analysis of deferred tax 13085
Tax on non-operating exceptional items 13087
Statement of total recognised gains and losses 13088
Disclosure in the notes 13089
Changes in the carrying amounts of deferred tax assets and liabilities 13089

Balance sheet 13090
Presentation and disclosures required by the Act 13090
Presentation required by the accounting standards. 13091
Offset of deferred tax assets and liabilities. 13092
Presentation of material balances 13093
Disclosure required by accounting standards. 13094
Analysis of deferred tax balance 13094
Disclosure of deferred tax asset. 13096
Circumstances affecting current and future tax charges. 13096
Circumstances affecting current tax charge 13097
Circumstances affecting future tax charge 13100
Groups of companies 13102
Group relief 13102
No payments made for group relief 13103
Payments made for group relief. 13104
Payment represents the amount of tax saving 13105
Payment is less than the amount of tax savings 13106
Payment is less than the gross amount of the loss surrendered. 13106
Payment represents the gross amount of the loss surrendered 13108

Chapter 13

Taxation

Introduction

13.1 Accounting for tax is based on the premise that tax is an expense incurred as a result of doing business. As tax is levied by national government, it is an expense that is quite different from all other expenses appearing in the financial statements. In the UK, companies pay corporation tax at a single rate on taxable profits, regardless of whether those profits are distributed to the shareholders or retained in the business. However, the amount of tax payable on the taxable profits of a particular period often bears little relationship to the amount of income and expenditure appearing in the financial statements. This is because the computation of accounting profit is governed by the application of generally accepted accounting principles and company law, whereas the computation of taxable profit is governed by the application of tax law. For example, certain items of income appearing in the financial statements may be tax free, whilst others may be taxable in a different period. Similarly, certain items of expenditure may be disallowable for tax, whilst others may fall to be tax deductible in a period different from that in which they were recognised in the financial statements.

13.2 If the profit and loss account tax charge were based simply on the amount of tax payable on taxable profits, it would be inconsistent with the accruals concept, the basis on which all other expenses are stated in the financial statements. Therefore, it is generally accepted that the tax charge in the profit and loss account should include not only the current tax charge based on taxable profit that takes into account the effects of tax-free income and disallowable expenses, but also an amount that recognises the tax effects of transactions appearing in the financial statements in one period, but which fall to be taxed or tax deductible in a different period. This additional amount, comprising the tax effects of what are generally referred to as 'timing differences' resulting from the difference between fiscal and accounting rules, ensures that the correct tax expense is recognised in the financial statements in the same periods as the income and expenditure to which it relates. The recognition of this additional amount gives rise to deferred taxation either payable or recoverable in a subsequent accounting period. Therefore, the tax charge in the profit and the loss account comprises deferred tax as well as current tax. Deferred tax was conceived and developed as a means of recognising the tax effects of the difference between accounting and taxable profit.

13.3 Although the concept of deferred taxation can be explained in the context of matching income and expenditure with their tax effects, it can also be viewed from the perspective of accounting for a liability and indeed, as the debate on deferred tax has progressed, this has become a preferable way of understanding deferred tax. Given that a future liability would arise through the tax effects of timing differences, the principles of accounting require that provision should be made in full for this known liability. On the other hand, taxation deferred as a result of timing differences could be permanently deferred under a tax system that gives initially high tax reliefs, for example, where capital allowances claimed in a period always exceed the depreciation charged in that period. In that situation, the accepted principle of not accounting for remote contingencies becomes relevant.

13.4 This chapter deals with accounting for current and deferred taxation in the light of the provisions contained in the Companies Act, FRS 16, 'Current tax', and FRS 19, 'Deferred tax'. There is also a further accounting standard SSAP 5, 'Accounting for value added tax', but as accounting for value added tax, although extremely complicated to administer in practice, poses few technical accounting problems, it is not dealt with in this chapter.

[The next paragraph is 13.8.]

Corporation tax

General principles

13.8 A UK resident company is, in general, chargeable to corporation tax on its profits wherever they arise, other than dividends received from other UK companies. Corporation tax is assessed on a company's profits, whether distributed or retained, at the end of each accounting period. The tax charge is calculated by applying the current basic rate of corporation tax to the taxable profit for the period. The general rate of corporation tax for the fiscal year 2007 (year commencing on 1 April 2007) is 30 per cent. This has been reduced to 28 per cent from the 2008 financial year onwards (commencing on 1 April 2008). This basic rate is reduced for smaller companies to a small company rate, which is 19 per cent for the 2007 fiscal year. The small company rate is being increased to 22 per cent on a phased basis and will reach 22 per cent by the 2009 financial year. The taxable profit is arrived at by applying relevant tax laws and rules and is rarely the same as the accounting profit disclosed in the financial statements. Differences between taxable and accounting profit form the basis of accounting for deferred taxation, which is considered later in this chapter.

13.9 Although the rate of corporation tax is set for a fiscal year, it should be noted that the assessments are made on the basis of the company's actual accounting period. If a company prepares financial statements for a year which straddles 31 March, and the rate of corporation tax is different for different fiscal years, an average rate will have to be computed and applied in the tax computation as illustrated in paragraph 13.50 below.

The imputation tax system

13.10 In many countries around the world, it is usual for a company's profits to be taxed and any dividends paid out of them treated as taxable income in the hands of shareholders. This means that, in effect, the same profits are taxed twice – once in the hands of the company and again in the hands of the shareholder. In contrast, the UK operates a system under which a company's profits and any corporation tax paid on them are 'imputed' to the shareholder. In other words, the shareholder is liable to pay income tax on any distributed profits at the applicable personal tax rate, but such income tax is reduced by deemed corporation tax already paid on those profits. The economic effect of such a system is that profits are taxed only once in the hands of a shareholder. This is known as the 'imputation system'.

13.11 The corporation tax 'imputed' to the shareholder is given as a tax credit to the shareholder. Shareholders could then set off this tax credit against their liability to tax on those dividends. Taxpayers chargeable at the basic rate on other income are chargeable only at the lower rate that is 10 per cent on gross dividend income inclusive of the tax credit (equivalent to one-ninth of the net dividends). These taxpayers, therefore, do not have to pay any further tax in respect of UK dividend income after taking account of the tax credit given in respect of the dividends they receive. If the shareholder is chargeable to tax at a higher rate, then he/she will still have a tax liability at the higher rate and will be assessed on the amounts of dividend income declared in his/her tax return and the tax credit attributed to the dividend will be set against that liability. The tax credits are not repayable to shareholders with no tax liability.

13.12 Until April 1999, a company paid Advance Corporation Tax (ACT) when it paid a dividend. This tax could be set off, within a limit, against the corporation tax liability of the accounting period. The remaining tax liability was called 'mainstream' corporation tax. One purpose of ACT was to finance the tax credit that the exchequer made available to the shareholder receiving the dividend. As stated above the tax credit could be set against the shareholder's income tax liability on the dividend or, until the payment of tax credit was abolished for non-taxpayers and exempt institutions (pension schemes, unit trusts etc), the credit would be paid to the shareholder.

13.13 However, ACT was abolished as from 6 April 1999. This means companies paying a dividend (or other distribution of profits) after that date no longer have to pay any ACT.

13.14 With the abolition of ACT, a system of quarterly instalment payments for corporation tax was introduced for large companies starting with accounting periods ending on or after 1 July 1999, the same period for which self-assessment for companies was introduced. The first instalment became due in month seven of the accounting period with further instalments due in months 10, 13, and 16 with any balance to be paid nine months after the end of the period. In fact, the due dates are day 14 of the month. Since companies do not have to pay their quarterly instalments until they are at least six months into their accounting periods, this gives them sufficient time to estimate reasonably accurately their corporation tax liability for the period under the system of self-assessment for companies.

13.15 Medium-sized companies (currently those with profits between £300,000 and £1,500,000) and small companies (currently those with profits up to £300,000) are not affected and they will continue to pay all of their corporation tax nine months after the end of their accounting period.

13.16 Although ACT is abolished, UK dividends still carry tax credits, at the rate of one-ninth of the net dividends from 6 April 1999, which shareholders will continue to be able to set off against their liability to tax on dividends as stated in paragraph 13.11 above. UK companies (other than financial traders who pay tax on the net dividends on shares treated as trading assets) continue to be treated as before and generally have no obligation to pay corporation tax themselves on dividends they receive from other UK companies.

[The next paragraph is 13.18.]

FRS 16 — Current tax

13.18 FRS 16, 'Current tax', deals with the recognition and disclosure of current tax.

13.19 The objective of FRS 16 is *"to ensure that reporting entities recognise current taxes in a consistent and transparent manner"*. [FRS 16 para 1]. The standard is very wide in scope, covering all financial statements giving a true and fair view, except those prepared by smaller entities applying the FRSSE.

13.20 As stated above, FRS 16 specifies how current tax, in particular withholding tax and tax credits, should be reflected in financial statements. The standard defines current tax as *"the amount of tax estimated to be payable or recoverable in respect of the taxable profit or loss for a period, along with adjustments to estimates in respect of previous periods"*. [FRS 16 para 2]. The standard deals with the following matters:

- Recognition of current tax charge in the profit and loss account and the STRGL.
- The treatment of tax credits, withholding and underlying taxes in the context of dividends and other income payable and receivable.
- Income and expenses subject to non-standard rates of tax.
- Measurement of current tax charge.
- Recoverable ACT.
- Disclosure of current tax.

Apart from the last item which is considered from paragraph 13.236 below, the above matters are discussed in the paragraphs that follow. In addition, uncertain tax positions are dealt with from paragraph 13.50.10 onwards.

Recognition of current tax charge

13.21 FRS 16 requires that current tax should be recognised in the profit and loss account for the period, except to the extent that it is attributable to a gain or loss that is or has been recognised directly in the STRGL. [FRS 16 para 5]. Where a gain or loss is or has been recognised in the STRGL, the tax relating to that gain or loss should also be recognised in that statement. [FRS 16 para 6].

13.22 Because a UK company pays corporation tax on all its profits including those that may be reported in the STRGL, it may sometimes be difficult to determine the amount of current tax that is attributable to the amount of gain reported in the STRGL. In those circumstances, the standard permits the attributable tax to be calculated on a reasonable *pro rata* basis, or another basis that is more appropriate in the circumstances. [FRS 16 para 7]. Consider the following examples:

Example 1

A parent company made a trading profit of £1,500,000 during the year. The parent has a foreign currency loan on which an exchange loss of £500,000 arose and on which tax relief is given in this instance. The corporation tax rate for the year is 30%. Therefore, the parent's tax liability for the year is £300,000 (profit before tax of £1,000,000 @ 30%). On consolidation, the loan held by the parent is treated as hedging the net assets of its foreign subsidiary so that the exchange loss of £500,000 is reported in the STRGL. The total tax charge of £300,000 that should be allocated between the profit and loss account and the STRGL is as follows:

	£'000
Tax on trading profit (£1.5m @ 30%)	450
Tax relief on exchange loss (£500,000 @ 30%)	(150)
Total tax charge	300

The profit and loss account would bear a tax charge of £450,000, with £150,000 of tax relief being credited to the STRGL.

Example 2

A company sold a plot of land during the year for £10m. The land was acquired ten years ago for £4m and the carrying value prior to sale was £6m (following a revaluation three years ago). The tax value of the land after allowing for indexation relief is £5m. No deferred tax was provided on the earlier revaluation on the grounds that there was no commitment to sell the land at that time. Assuming that the corporation tax rate is 30% and rollover relief is not available, the tax payable on the gain of £5m is £1.5m (sale proceeds £10m less tax indexed cost of £5m @ 30%).

As the standard is not very specific as to how the tax of £1.5m on the total accounting gain of £6m (sale proceeds of £10m less cost of £4m) should be allocated between the gain of £4m (£10m – £6m) reported in the profit and loss account and the revaluation gain of £2m reported previously in the STRGL, one method would be to allocate the tax in proportion to the gain reported in the respective performance statement, that is, in the ratio 2:1. On this basis, the allocation would be as follows:

	Profit and loss account	STRGL	Total
	£'000	£'000	£'000
Total accounting gain	4,000	2,000	6,000
Total tax	1,000	500	1,500

An alternative method would be to reflect the fact that the purpose of indexation relief is to exclude from taxation purely inflationary gains. In principle, such gains form part of the holding gain dealt with in the STRGL. On this basis, the allocation would be as follows:

	Profit and loss account	STRGL	Total
	£'000	£'000	£'000
Total accounting gain	4,000	2,000	6,000
Indexation allowance	–	(1,000)	(1,000)
Taxable gain	4,000	1,000	5,000
	1,200	300	1,500

If the indexation allowance were sufficient to cover all the gain dealt with in the STRGL, any balance would be attributed to the profit and loss account. Furthermore, if the gain dealt with in the profit and loss account contained a significant holding gain, it may be appropriate to allocate part of the effect of the indexation allowance on an appropriate basis. For instance, in this example, it would be possible to attribute £300,000 (3/10 × £1m) of the indexation allowance of £1m to the profit and loss account on the grounds that this proportion of the inflationary gain arose subsequent to the revaluation that took place three years prior to sale. Although this method is arguably the most accurate method, it is also unnecessarily complex and in practice, companies are likely to choose between the first two approaches outlined above.

[The next paragraph is 13.24.]

Tax credits, withholding and underlying taxes

13.24 Dividends paid by UK companies carry tax credits, currently at the rate of one-ninth of the net dividends (see para 13.11). The credit is given to acknowledge that the income out of which the dividend has been paid has already been charged to tax, *rather than* as a tax that has been deducted at source. UK dividends received with a tax credit fall outside the corporation tax computation altogether for companies and there is no basic rate liability on them for individuals (and partnerships). Tax credits are not repayable. FRS 16 defines tax credit as *"the tax* *credit given under UK tax legislation to the recipient of a dividend from a UK company".*

13.25 Withholding tax does not arise on UK dividends, but it is relevant in the context of dividends received by a UK company from its investments located overseas. FRS 16 defines withholding tax as *"tax on dividends or other income that is deducted by the payer of the income and paid to the tax authorities wholly on behalf of the recipient".* [FRS 16 para 2].

13.26 Apart from the fact that withholding tax is tax that is actually paid by (or at least on behalf) of the recipient of the dividends, there is a fundamental difference in the way dividend and other income subject to withholding tax is treated for tax purposes from dividends and other income received with an imputed tax credit. Income subject to tax credit is essentially tax free in the hands of the recipient and no further tax is payable. In contrast, dividends or other income received after deduction of withholding tax are not tax free receipts, but are charged to corporation tax based on the gross amount inclusive of the withholding tax. So further tax is usually payable in addition to the withholding tax, unless (unusually) the amount of withholding tax is sufficient to discharge the full tax liability.

13.27 The above differences are considered to be sufficiently significant for FRS 16 to require different accounting treatments for dividends and other income subject to tax credit (notional and should not be taken into account) from those that are subject to withholding tax (real and should be taken into account). In doing so, the standard harmonises the tax treatment of incoming and outgoing dividends and other income payable and receivable.

Outgoing dividends and other interest payable

13.28 Accordingly, FRS 16 requires that outgoing dividends, interest and other amounts payable should be recognised at an amount that:

- Includes any withholding taxes
- Excludes any other taxes, such as attributable tax credits, not payable wholly on behalf of the recipient.

[FRS 16 para 8].

13.29 This is logical as the imputed tax credit is not part of the cost of the dividend. It is more concerned with the taxes paid by the payer of the dividend, rather than those paid by (or on behalf of) the recipient.

13.30 The requirement to include withholding tax in interest and other amounts payable by an UK company is not specifically relevant to the UK. However, under current tax rules UK companies are sometimes required to deduct UK income tax on interest payable to third parties. As UK income tax deducted at source is very similar in substance to withholding tax, we believe that interest payable should be shown gross in the profit and loss account, that is, inclusive of the income tax deducted.

Incoming dividends and other interest receivable

13.31 Similarly, FRS 16 requires that incoming dividends, interest and other income receivable should be recognised at an amount that:

- Includes any withholding taxes.
- Excludes any other taxes, such as attributable tax credits, not payable wholly on behalf of the recipient.

[FRS 16 para 9].

13.32 The standard's requirement to show income at an amount inclusive of the withholding tax is consistent with its nature, which is tax actually suffered by the company as explained in paragraph 13.25 above. Withholding taxes normally arise on dividends received from investments located overseas. Such dividends are also subject to UK corporation tax on the gross amount of the foreign dividend received. However, a UK company is often able to obtain relief to mitigate the double tax charge. Where in accordance with paragraph 13.31 above, the income is reported gross of the foreign withholding tax, the standard requires the withholding tax suffered to be shown as part of the tax charge. [FRS 16 para 9].

13.33 Similarly, where tax has been deducted at source on interest income and paid by the payer of the interest to the tax authorities on behalf of the recipient, the interest income should be recorded gross of the tax deducted at source. The tax should be shown as part of the tax charge.

[The next paragraph is 13.35.]

Underlying tax

13.35 In some situations, relief is also available for foreign 'underlying tax' (that is, tax on the company's profits out of which the dividends are paid). Often double tax agreements between the UK government and the overseas government provide that a UK resident company in receipt of foreign dividends is entitled to a tax credit for underlying tax if a specified percentage (usually ten per cent) of the voting control of the overseas company is held by the UK company. However, many treaties are silent on this point, in which case unilateral relief for underlying overseas tax is provided for in section 790 of the Taxes Act 1988. This is subject also to a requirement of ten per cent voting control of the paying company. The double taxation relief is normally obtained by setting the overseas tax first against the gross corporation tax liability calculated on the gross dividend (grossed up for the withholding and underlying tax).

13.36 Notwithstanding the fact that a company can claim double tax relief for both withholding and underlying tax, the standard makes it clear that dividends or other income received should not be grossed up for the underlying rate of tax. [FRS 16 para 10]. This is because the underlying tax is the liability of another entity (the payer of the dividend) and is not tax that has been suffered by the recipient. The underlying tax rate is simply used by the UK tax authority to calculate the UK corporation tax due on the dividend income and to work out the total relief that should be given for the double tax suffered as explained above. The only tax that the recipient suffers is the withholding tax, which is a 'real tax', as opposed to the underlying tax which, from the perspective of the recipient, is a 'notional tax'.

13.37 A UK company is normally able to obtain double tax relief against UK corporation tax but this depends on whether the overseas tax rate (withholding and underlying) is less than the UK corporation tax rate. Where, however, the rate of overseas tax exceeds the rate of UK corporation tax, a proportion of the overseas tax can remained unrelieved. The amount of overseas tax unrelieved cannot be carried forward and falls to be written off in the profit and loss account. This write off need not be disclosed separately as it is included within overseas taxation in the profit and loss account taxation charge. Consider the following example:

Example

A UK company has a US subsidiary. The US subsidiary generated taxable profits of £100,000 on which it paid US income tax @ 35% amounting to £35,000. It distributed the remaining after tax profit of £65,000 to the UK parent after deducting 5% withholding tax amounting to £3,250. The UK parent received a cash dividend of £61,750. The rate of UK corporation tax is 30%.

UK corporation tax computation	£	£
Cash dividend of £61,750 grossed up for overseas taxes		100,000
Corporation tax @ 30%		30,000
Less double tax relief:		
Total overseas tax paid	38,250	
Relief restricted to UK tax payable	(30,000)	(30,000)
Unrelieved overseas tax	8,250	
UK corporation tax liability		Nil

Parent company's individual profit and loss account

	£	£
Gross dividend received (grossed up for withholding tax)		65,000
Tax charge:		
UK corporation tax	–	
Overseas tax paid (withholding tax)	3,250	
Total tax charge		3,250
Profit after tax		61,750

Parent company's consolidated profit and loss account

	£	£
Profit before tax		100,000
Tax charge:		
UK corporation tax	30,000	
Less: double tax relief	30,000	
	–	
Overseas tax paid*	38,250	
Total tax charge		38,250
Profit after tax		61,750

* Total tax charge is effectively UK tax of £30,000 and unrelieved overseas tax of £8,250 = £38,250

Income and expenses subject to non-standard rates of tax

13.38 It is necessary to distinguish income that is received after deduction of tax as discussed in paragraph 13.31 from income that is taxable at non-standard rates. It is not uncommon for companies to enter into transactions that give rise to income or expense that is not subject to the standard rate of corporation tax. Examples include some leasing transactions and advances and investments made by financial institutions. In some situations, the transaction may, after taking account of the financing cost, result in a pre-tax loss and a post-tax profit. Consider the following example:

Example

A financial institution borrows £10m which bears interest at 9% per annum. The proceeds are immediately invested in an instrument that yields 8% per annum, but the income is taxable at 20%. The standard rate of corporation tax is 33%. The company makes a pre-tax loss of £100,000, but the transaction is profitable after tax effects are taken into account as shown below:

Profit and loss account	£'000	£'000
Investment income @ 8%		800
Less: interest expense		(900)
Pre-tax loss		(100)
Taxation:		
On income @ 20%	(160)	
Tax relief on interest @ 33%	297	
Tax credit		137
Post-tax profit		37

13.39 Banks and other institutions enter into such transactions precisely because it is profitable on an after tax basis. However, they may contend that the presentation shown above is misleading, because it makes it difficult to interpret the profit and loss account and inhibits comparison between different companies, especially as pre-tax profits are seen as an important measure of performance. They may advocate that income subject to the non-standard rate of tax should be presented on a grossed-up basis as shown below to eliminate the distortion between pre and post-tax profits by reporting tax at the standard rate.

Profit and loss account (grossed-up)	£'000
Investment income (grossed up): 640/(100%–33%)*	955
Less: interest expense	(900)
Pre-tax profit *	55
Tax charge @ 33% †	(18)
Post-tax profit	37

*Includes notional income of £155
†Includes notional tax charge of £155

13.40 However, grossing up, because it is notional, fails to report the true nature of the transaction. If a transaction results in a pre-tax loss and a tax benefit it is necessary that it is reported as such in order to achieve a faithful representation. Grossing up reports a false amount both as pre-tax profits and as the tax charge for the year. The tax treatment of the transaction should have no bearing on the way in which the transaction is reported for financial reporting purposes.

13.41 On this basis, income and expenses should be reported in the pre-tax results on the basis of the income or expenses actually receivable or payable. No adjustment should be made to reflect a notional amount of tax that would have been paid or relieved in respect of the transaction if it had been taxable, or allowable for tax purposes, on a different basis. [FRS 16 para 11].

13.42 Companies whose results are significantly affected by transactions that are subject to tax other than at a standard rate should disclose the full effects of such transactions in their financial statements. Indeed, both the Act and FRS 3 require disclosure of any special circumstances that affect the tax charge or credit during the period. These disclosure requirements are considered from paragraph 13.236.

13.43 FRS 16 makes it clear that the requirement applies only to notional tax. It is not intended to reverse the normal accounting treatment followed in some specialised industries, such as leasing and life insurance, of allocating profits to accounting periods on a post-tax basis and then grossing up those post-tax profits by the actual effective tax rate to arrive at the pre-tax profit and the tax charge. [FRS 16 para 13].

Measurement of the current tax charge

13.44 FRS 16 requires current tax to be measured at the amounts expected to be paid (or recovered) using the tax rates and laws that have been enacted or substantially enacted by the balance sheet date. [FRS 16 para 14].

13.45 A UK tax rate is taken as 'substantially enacted' if it is included in either:

- a Bill that has been passed by the House of Commons and is awaiting only passage through the House of Lords and Royal Assent; or
- a resolution having statutory effect that has been passed under the Provisional Collection of Taxes Act 1968 (PCTA 1968).

[FRS 16 para 15].

13.46 The parliamentary resolution under the PCTA 1968 is, in effect, a temporary enactment of tax changes relating to certain taxes that persists and has full statutory force for a limited period. During that period a permanent statutory provision is made with full parliamentary procedures and in the normal course of events the temporary statute falls away when the permanent one is enacted.

13.47 In the UK, changes in tax laws and rates are normally announced in a Finance Bill on Budget day. Therefore, where a company's accounting reference period ends on a date that straddles the Budget date and the date on which the process of enactment is regarded as substantively complete (for instance, when the Bill has been passed by the House of Commons), the substantively enacted rate would be the rate that is currently in force at the balance sheet date and current and deferred tax should be measured using that rate.

13.48 In practice, however, the above guidance is unlikely to make any difference since UK corporation tax rates are set by reference to a financial year and a year in advance. For instance, the main rate of corporation tax for the financial year 2008 (the year beginning 1 April 2008) was set at 28 per cent at the 2007 Budget on 21 March 2007. The Finance Bill 2007 received Royal Assent on 26 June 2007 and became the Finance Act 2007. Therefore, this is the substantively enacted rate for the financial year 2008 and later years to be reflected in the financial statements for accounting periods ending on or after 26 June 2007. In periods ending prior to this date, taxes will be measured with reference to the previous tax rate of 30 per cent.

13.49 The standard's requirement to use a tax rate that has been substantially enacted by the balance sheet date rather than the date of approval of the financial statements means that the subsequent receipt of information about rates of taxation is not an adjusting post balance sheet event (see further chapter 22).

13.50 Of more significance is the situation where a company prepares its financial statements for a period that straddles 31 March and the enacted tax rates or substantially enacted rates are different for different financial years. In that situation, the company may need to compute an effective tax rate. An example is given below:

Example

A company has an accounting period ending on 30 October 20X8 and the rates of corporation tax for the financial years 20X7 and 20X8 are 30% and 28% respectively. The effective rate of tax that should be disclosed for the current tax in the financial statements is calculated as follows:

Period 1 November 20X7 to 31 March 20X8 (FY 20X7)	5/12 @ 30%	12.50%
Period 1 April 20X8 to 30 October 20X8 (FY 20X8)	7/12 @ 28%	16.33%
Effective rate of corporation tax		28.83%

Furthermore, the accounting period for corporation tax purposes can never exceed 12 months. If the financial statements cover a period longer than 12 months, the first 12 months constitute one accounting period and the remainder of the period constitutes the second accounting period for tax purposes.

Recoverability of ACT

13.50.1 Following the abolition of Advance Corporation Tax (ACT) from April 1999 (see para 13.13), there has been no further build-up of unrelieved or surplus ACT. However, companies are able to recover past surplus ACT built up in the periods prior to the abolition of ACT. This is achieved through a system of 'shadow ACT'.

13.50.2 Although ACT can be carried forward indefinitely, if necessary, in each year there is an overriding restriction on the use of ACT for set-off imposed by the shadow ACT system. The shadow ACT system is designed to be no more generous than the old ACT system. Its effect is to ensure that ACT that was previously irrecoverable becomes recoverable only to the extent that it would have become recoverable under the old ACT system. [FRS 16 App II para 2].

13.50.3 The way in which shadow ACT works is illustrated by the following simple example.

Example

A company has surplus ACT of £100,000 as at 31 March 1999. During its accounting period to 31 March 2000, it expects to have taxable profits of £200,000 and pay a dividend of £60,000. In this situation:

- The limit on ACT set off is 20% of £200,000 = £40,000.
- If ACT was not abolished, the company would have to pay ACT on the dividend = 25% of £60,000 = £15,000. This ACT of £15,000 is referred to as shadow ACT.

- The effect of the shadow ACT is to restrict the set off of past surplus ACT to £25,000 (£40,000 – £15,000).
- As a result, the company's corporation tax liability will be reduced by £25,000, as is the figure for past surplus ACT carried forward to the next accounting period, which is £75,000.

The above is a simple example and ignores the effect of any carry back of shadow ACT of future periods. The actual rules on shadow ACT are extremely complex and tax advice should be sought in calculating the amount by which the corporation tax liability can be reduced.

13.50.4 The detailed accounting rules for ACT are contained in Appendix II to FRS 16, rather than in the main body of the standard.

13.50.5 Under FRS 16, ACT is regarded as recoverable where the amount of the ACT previously paid on outgoing dividends could either be:

- Set off against a corporation tax liability on the profits of the period under review or of previous periods.
- Properly set off against a credit balance on the deferred tax account.
- Expected to be recoverable taking into account expected profits and dividends – normally those of the next accounting period only.

13.50.6 ACT should be offset against a credit balance on the deferred tax account only if, in the period in which the underlying timing differences are expected to reverse, the reversal will create sufficient taxable profits to enable ACT to be recovered under the shadow ACT system. [FRS 16 App II para 4].

13.50.7 In the absence of a deferred tax liability against which it can be offset, ACT recoverable should be shown as a deferred tax asset. [FRS 16 App II para 5].

13.50.8 If ACT that was previously regarded as recoverable becomes irrecoverable, it should be charged in the profit and loss account as a separately disclosed component of the tax charge. [FRS 16 App II para 6].

13.50.9 Where ACT written off as irrecoverable in the past becomes recoverable under the shadow ACT system, the write back should be made in the year in which the ACT is actually recovered. Such ACT is required to be credited in the profit and loss account as a separately disclosed component of the tax charge. [FRS 16 App II para 8].

Uncertain tax positions

13.50.10 There may be situations when an entity's tax position is uncertain. Examples are where the tax treatment of an item of expense, or a structured transaction, may be challenged by the tax authorities. Uncertainties in current taxes are not addressed specifically in FRS 16. FRS 12, 'Provisions, contingent liabilities and assets', excludes taxes from its scope (as these are covered by another standard) and is not used to measure uncertain tax positions. The general measurement principles in paragraph 14 of FRS 16 should, therefore, be applied: *"Current tax should be measured at the amounts expected to be paid (or recovered) using tax rates and laws that have been enacted or substantively enacted by the balance sheet date"*. The unit of account and measurement method are not specified in FRS 16, so there is diversity in practice.

13.50.11 We believe the unit of account is an accounting policy. An entity may choose to consider uncertain tax positions at the level of the individual uncertainty or group of related uncertainties. Alternatively, it may choose to consider tax uncertainties at the level of its total tax liability to each relevant taxing authority.

13.50.12 When an entity elects to consider uncertain tax positions at the level of each uncertainty, it should first consider whether each position taken in the tax return is probable of being sustained on examination by the taxing authority. A liability should be recognised in connection with each item that is not probable of being sustained. The liability is measured using either an expected value (weighted average probability) approach or a single best estimate of the most likely outcome. The current tax liability would be the aggregate liability in connection with uncertain tax positions.

13.50.13 When an entity elects to consider uncertain tax positions at the level of its relationship with the taxing authority, the key issue is the measurement of the tax liability. It is usually probable that an entity will pay tax, so the recognition threshold has been met. The entity should determine the total amount of current tax it expects to pay, taking into account all the tax uncertainties, using either an expected value (weighted average probability) approach or a single best estimate of the most likely outcome.

13.50.14 The examples below are prepared on the assumption that the entity has elected to consider tax uncertainties at the level of each uncertainty. The examples illustrate that the liability determined using the two acceptable measurement methodologies referred to in paragraph 13.50.11 above may be materially different. In all cases, it is assumed that it is probable (more likely than not) that tax will be payable.

Example 1

Entity K has included deductions in a tax return that may be subject to challenge by the tax authorities resulting in an uncertain tax position. Entity K and its tax consultants estimate the probability of the potential outcomes for additional tax payable as follows:

Potential tax payable £	Individual probability	Cumulative probability	Probability-weighted calculation £
800	15%	15%	120
600	30%	45%	180
400	20%	65%	80
200	20%	85%	40
0	15%	100%	0
			420

- Most likely outcome £600.
- Probability weighted outcome £420.

Example 2

Entity K takes a deduction in a tax return that may be subject to challenge by the tax authorities. It is estimated that there is a 40% probability that additional tax of £120 will be payable and a 60% probability that additional tax of £80 will be payable.

- Most likely outcome £80.
- Probability weighted outcome £96 (£120 × 40% + £80 × 60%).

Example 3

A deduction of £100 may be subject to challenge. Entity K and its tax consultants estimate the probability of the potential outcomes for additional tax payable as follows:

Potential tax payable £	Individual probability	Cumulative probability	Probability-weighted calculation £
100	45%	45%	45.00
80	10%	55%	8.00
50	25%	80%	12.50
0	20%	100%	-
			65.50

- Probability weighted outcome £65.5.
- It would not be logical to use £100 as the most likely outcome in this case, as it is more likely than not that some of the deductions will be accepted by the tax authorities. Whilst there is a 45% chance that the full amount of £100 will be payable, there is a 55% change of reduced tax being payable on the basis of the information given above. In this scenario, measurement using the probability weighted average method would be appropriate.

Expenses associated with taxation

Interest and penalties on uncertain tax positions

13.50.15 An entity may incur interest or penalties in relation to taxation, for example as a result of uncertain tax positions that have been successfully challenged by the tax authorities. FRS 16 does not specifically address the treatment of uncertain tax positions or associated interest and penalties. The liability for the uncertain tax position is for a tax based on taxable profits and is, therefore, a current tax liability. This liability is recognised and measured in accordance with FRS 16 (see further para 13.50.10 onwards above).

13.50.16 There is a strong argument that interest and penalties are different from tax liabilities. This is because these items are not measured and settled by the tax authorities on the basis of taxable profits. This suggests that interest and penalties should be presented as provisions under FRS 12, 'Provisions, contingent liabilities and assets', and as finance or other operating expense, respectively, in the profit and loss account. This is because:

- such obligations are not based on taxable profit or loss and fall outside FRS 16's scope; and
- the economic substance of reducing or delaying a tax payment is not different from any other financing arrangement. Interest that increases with time and is in substance a financing cost of the liability is interest expense; other penalties represent operating costs.

13.50.17 There is, however, diversity in practice with regard to these items. In some cases, interest and penalties may be rolled up into a lump sum settlement and it may not be possible to separate them from the taxes. To the extent that such amounts are not identified separately from tax payable on taxable profits, it may be acceptable to conclude that they are within FRS 16's scope. In that case, any associated charge would be shown within the tax line in the profit and loss account and the liability would be included within the tax liability on the balance sheet.

Professional fees linked to tax expense

13.50.18 A company may incur expenses that are indirectly linked to the current tax expense, for example fees payable to tax consultants that are based upon a percentage of savings made under a specific tax scheme. The fees paid to tax consultants are not 'tax on profit on ordinary activities', the format line in the profit and loss account formats in Schedule 4 of the Companies Act 1985. They should be charged in arriving at operating profit, probably under the administrative expenses heading.

Deferred tax

Introduction

13.51 Most transactions and events recorded in the financial statements have a tax consequence. A classic example is an acquisition of an asset that is deductible for tax purposes in the current and future periods.

13.52 The future tax consequences of transactions and events that have occurred by the balance sheet date cannot be avoided; whatever happens in the future, the entity will have to pay less or more tax than it would have done if those transactions and events did not happen. Therefore, it is necessary to recognise the tax effects of all income and expenditure, gains and losses, assets and liabilities in the same period in which they are recognised themselves and not in the period in which they form part of taxable profit. This matching of transactions and events with their tax effects gives rise, not only to current tax, but also to deferred tax balances that meet the definitions of, and recognition criteria for, assets and liabilities.

Method of computation

13.53 Notwithstanding its origin as a means of matching income and expenditure with their tax effects, deferred tax balances represent assets or liabilities. A deferred tax liability relating to an asset represents an obligation to refund a temporary cash flow advantage obtained by claiming capital allowances on that asset. Therefore, the tax effects of accelerated capital allowances should be reported as liabilities for taxes. Similarly, a deferred tax asset relating to a liability, for example pension costs, represents tax relief that is expected to be received when the pension liability is settled. Therefore, the tax effects of timing differences relating to pension costs should be reported as assets representing future tax recoverable.

13.54 The objective of the liability method is to recognise the expected tax effects of timing differences either as liabilities for taxes payable in the future or as assets recoverable in the future. Under this method, deferred tax on the timing differences originating in the period is provided using the rate of tax expected to apply when the asset is recovered or the liability is settled. Since the rate at which the timing difference will reverse is not normally known, the current rate of tax is taken as the best approximation to the rate that will apply in the future. This means that the deferred taxation account is always maintained at the current rate of tax and the movement in the balance sheet amounts is reflected as a deferred tax charge or credit, usually in the profit and loss account or STRGL. It follows that whenever there is a change in the rate of tax, the balance on the deferred taxation account is adjusted to that current rate with the result that the charge for deferred tax in the profit and loss account and STRGL (where applicable) will include the effects of any such change in rate, which is applied to the opening balance of cumulative timing differences. FRS 19 requires that deferred tax is determined using a method based on the 'income statement liability method' (see para 13.63).

Income statement liability method

13.55 In most countries, including the UK, profits disclosed in the company's financial statements form the basis for the computation of taxable profits on which the company's liability to tax is calculated. In practice, however, many governments introduce various incentives and disincentives in their fiscal policy for economic and social reasons. As a consequence, the taxable profits of a particular period often bear little relationship to the accounting profits disclosed in the financial statements.

13.56 The differences between accounting and taxable profits can be analysed into two categories: permanent differences and timing differences. Permanent differences arise because certain types of income appearing in the financial statements are not taxable, whilst certain types of expenditure are not tax deductible. Timing differences, on the other hand, arise from items that are either taxable or tax deductible, but in periods different from those in which they are dealt with in the financial statements. Therefore, such items are included in the measurement of both accounting and taxable profits, but in different periods. These differences are said to 'originate' in one period and are capable of 'reversal' in one or more subsequent periods.

13.57 It follows from the nature of permanent and timing differences that, over time, cumulative taxable and accounting profits are the same, except for permanent differences. Because permanent differences are the inevitable result of the differences between accounting and tax rules and do not give rise to any accounting entries, they do not represent an accounting problem. They merely give rise to effective tax charges that differ from the statutory rate. However, the question arises as to whether and to what extent the tax effects of timing differences between accounting and taxable profits should be recognised in the financial statements.

13.58 Since timing differences originating in one period reverse in a later period, the tax charged in the later periods is affected by transactions or events that have taken place in a previous period. As a result, future tax assessments (whatever their amount in absolute terms) will be lower or higher than they would have been if those timing differences had not arisen. These known increases or decreases in future tax liabilities, that is, the company's obligation to pay less or more tax in the future are recognised in the balance sheet as deferred tax assets and liabilities.

13.59 Therefore, the objective of the income statement liability method is to recognise the expected tax effects of timing differences either as liabilities for taxes payable in the future or as assets recoverable in the future. Under this method, deferred tax on the timing differences originating in the period is provided using the rate of tax expected to apply when the asset is recovered or the liability is settled. No deferred tax is provided on permanent differences.

13.60 The way in which deferred taxation is calculated under the income statement liability method is illustrated below.

Example

A company prepares its financial statements to 31 December each year. The company makes an annual profit of £100,000 and incurs the following capital expenditure.

Machine purchased on 1 January 20X1: Cost £100,000, residual value £nil, life 5 years.

Machine purchased on 1 January 20X3: Cost £230,000, residual value £20,000, life 7 years.

Depreciation is charged on a straight line basis and amounts to £20,000 per annum for the first machine and £30,000 per annum for the second machine. The rate of capital allowances is 25% per annum on a reducing balance basis. The rate of corporation tax for 20X1 and 20X2 is 50% and falls to 30% in 20X3 and remains at that level.

The calculation of the deferred tax charge and the balance arising are shown in the table below.

	20X1	20X2	20X3	20X4	20X5
Per financial statements	£	£	£	£	£
Carrying value b/f	–	80,000	60,000	240,000	190,000
Addition	100,000	–	230,000	–	–
Depreciation	(20,000)	(20,000)	(50,000)	(50,000)	(50,000)
Carrying value c/f	80,000	60,000	240,000	190,000	140,000
Per tax computation					
Pool b/f	–	75,000	56,250	214,687	161,015
Addition	100,000	–	230,000	–	–
Capital allowances	(25,000)	(18,750)	(71,563)	(53,672)	(40,254)
Pool c/f	75,000	56,250	214,687	161,015	120,761
Timing differences					
Capital allowances allowed	25,000	18,750	71,563	53,672	40,254
Depreciation charged	(20,000)	(20,000)	(50,000)	(50,000)	(50,000)
Originating (reversing)	5,000	(1,250)	21,563	3,672	(9,746)
Cumulative timing differences	5,000	3,750	25,313	28,985	19,239
Deferred tax balances					
Tax on opening cumulative difference	–	2,500	1,875	7,594	8,696
Tax on closing cumulative difference	2,500	1,875	7,594	8,696	5,772
Tax provided (released)	2,500	(625)	5,719*	1,102	(2,924)

* Includes impact of change in tax rate during year (see below)

In 20X3, when the tax rate changes from 50% to 30%, the deferred tax liability includes an adjustment of £750 under the liability method. The adjustment is simply due to the effect of the change in rate on the opening balance of cumulative timing difference of £3,750 × (50% – 30%) = £750, which is reflected in the tax charge under the liability method (but would be ignored under the deferral method referred to in para 13.55). The effect of this adjustment is to ensure that deferred tax liability or asset in the balance sheet is always maintained at the current rate as indicated in the table above.

13.61 It is also evident from the above table that the deferred tax liability at the end of 20X5 amounting to £5,772 comprises tax on the whole of the cumulative timing difference of £19,239 at 30 per cent that would crystallise when the timing difference reverses. This basis of providing in full for deferred tax on all timing differences is referred to as 'full provision' or 'comprehensive allocation'.

13.62 The profile of timing differences in the above example also indicates that in years 20X1, 20X3 and 20X4 originating timing differences exceed reversing timing differences, thus leading to an increase in the deferred tax liability for that year. It follows that whenever new timing differences originating in later periods more than offset the effect of timing differences reversing in those periods, the balance on the deferred tax account will keep on increasing. This may lead to the accumulation of large liabilities since their settlement is indefinitely postponed. This is particularly true in times of high inflation or under a tax system offering tax reliefs in the form of high capital investment allowances.

13.63 FRS 19 is based on the income statement liability method. However, it takes a different view on how an approach based on timing differences should be implemented. FRS 19 takes the view that deferred tax should be recognised only if it meets the strict criteria for recognition of a liability in its own right – 'obligations to transfer economic benefits as a result of past transactions or events'. Under this approach, the entity will provide deferred tax where the transaction and events giving rise to an obligation to pay tax in the future (the obligating events) are past events, that is, have occurred at the balance sheet date. Therefore, deferred tax would be provided for most types of timing differences where the obligating events have happened by the balance sheet date and the entity has no discretion to avoid the future reversal of a timing difference.

13.64 On the other hand, no deferred tax would be provided where the obligating events have not occurred by the balance sheet date or any of the events that have still to take place are under the entity's control and the entity retains discretion to avoid them. For example, an entity may revalue a property at the balance sheet date that has no tax consequence in the UK until the property is sold. Because the event that gives rise to the future tax payable – the sale of the asset – is under the entity's control and the entity retains a discretion to avoid the sale in order not to crystallise the liability, no deferred tax would be provided at the balance sheet date, unless an obligating event such as a binding agreement to sell the property exists at the balance sheet date. The ASB labelled this approach the 'incremental liability' approach and believes that it gives rise to deferred tax balances that are more meaningful and economically realistic. This method is conceptually different from the balance sheet liability approach that forms the basis of both IAS 12, 'Income taxes', and SFAS 109, 'Accounting for income taxes', and significant GAAP differences can arise.

[The next paragraph is 13.90.]

FRS 19 — Deferred tax

Objectives

13.90 The objectives of FRS 19 are to ensure that:

- Future tax consequences of past transactions and events are recognised as liabilities or assets in the financial statements.
- The financial statements disclose any other special circumstances that may have an effect on future tax charges.

[FRS 19 para 1].

13.91 The first objective is based on the definition of liabilities as 'obligations of an entity to transfer economic benefits as a result of past transactions or events' in the Statement of Principles. A liability for deferred tax should be recognised only for past transactions or events that give rise to an obligation to pay more tax in the future.

13.92 Past transactions and events will have future tax consequences only if they fall to be recognised as timing differences that have originated but not reversed at the balance sheet date. Since timing differences originating in one period reverse in a later period, the tax charged in the later period is affected by transactions or events that have taken place in a previous period. As a result, future tax assessments (whatever their amount in absolute terms) will be lower or higher than they would have been if those timing differences had not arisen. These known increases or decreases in future tax liabilities, that is, the company's obligation to pay more tax or the right to pay less in the future are recognised in the balance sheet as deferred tax assets and liabilities. This is the case whether or not future transactions occur that would reduce or increase the tax assessments in those periods.

13.93 In other words, an entity will have an obligation to pay more tax or a right to pay less tax where it has no discretion to avoid the future reversal of a timing difference, notwithstanding that it may have discretion to originate a new timing difference at the same time, which may have the effect of postponing the tax payable or recoverable. The reversal of an existing timing difference and the origination of a new timing difference at the same time are seen as two separate events. Only the first one is a consequence of a past event. The second originating timing difference does not prevent the first one from reversing.

13.94 Thus, a deferred tax asset or liability is recognised for the future tax consequences of past events. If the transactions or events have not occurred by the balance sheet date or any of the events that have still to take place are under the entity's control and the entity retains a discretion to avoid them, then no deferred tax asset or liability will fall to be recognised. For example, an entity may carry a property at the balance sheet date at a revalued amount in excess of cost. Because the event that gives rise to the future tax payable – the sale of the asset – is under the entity's control and the entity retains a discretion to avoid the sale in order not to crystallise the liability, no deferred tax would be provided at the balance sheet date.

13.95 The ASB labelled this approach the 'incremental liability' approach to deferred tax and believes that it is consistent with the Statement of principles. Although FRS 19 is based on full provision for deferred tax, it is significantly different (including conceptual differences) from both the International and US models.

General principles

13.96 FRS 19 states that deferred tax:

- Should be recognised in respect of all timing differences that have originated but not reversed by the balance sheet date.
- Should not be recognised on permanent differences.

[FRS 19 para 7].

13.97 The general rule is that deferred tax should be provided on timing differences that have originated but have not reversed by the balance sheet date where transactions or events that result in an obligation to pay more tax in the future or a right to pay less tax in the future have occurred at the balance sheet date. This is because, as stated above, the entity will not have the discretion to avoid the future reversal of a timing difference that has occurred by the balance sheet date. Permanent differences, on the other hand, are the opposite of timing differences. They simply affect current tax and not future taxes. So no deferred tax is recognised on permanent differences. The general rule is subject to certain exceptions that are considered in the paragraphs that follow.

13.98 Under FRS 19, there is no need to prepare budgets and projections or consider future events to determine the extent to which timing differences originating by the balance sheet date will reverse in future in order to estimate the amount of tax liability or asset that will crystallise and should be provided for. It is also not necessary to determine the specific period or periods in which an originating timing difference would reverse, unless the entity has chosen to adopt a policy of discounting deferred tax. It is sufficient to identify timing differences that have originated and not reversed by the balance sheet date by reference to the nature and the tax treatment of items of income or expenditure to which they relate and provide deferred tax accordingly. Each individual timing difference should initially be considered in isolation to determine whether it gives rise to a deferred tax asset or a liability. The individual assets and liabilities can be offset in accordance with the rules considered from paragraph 13.258 below. This is consistent with the FRS 19's incremental liability approach that relies fundamentally on an item by item view of deferred tax. In other words, the reversal of a timing difference leads to a settlement or extinguishment of a liability even though it may be offset before it crystallises by a new originating timing difference.

13.98.1 Deferred tax should be measured at the average tax rates that are expected to apply in the period in which the timing differences are expected to reverse, based on the tax rates and laws that have been enacted or substantively enacted by the balance sheet date. [FRS 19 para 37]. See further paragraph 13.171 onwards.

Timing differences

13.99 Timing differences are defined in FRS 19 as differences between an entity's taxable profits and its results as stated in the financial statements that arise from the inclusion of gains and losses in tax assessments in periods different from those in which they are recognised in the financial statements. Timing differences originate in one period and are capable of reversal in one or more subsequent periods. [FRS 19 para 2].

13.100 It follows from the above definition that there are only two situations under which timing differences can arise, as illustrated below:

- An item of income or expenditure is included in accounting profit of the period, but recognised in taxable profit in later periods. For example, income receivable might be accrued in the financial statements in one year, but fall to be taxed in the subsequent year when received. Similarly, provisions might be made for restructuring costs in the financial statements in one period, but would qualify for tax deduction at some later period when the expenditure is incurred.
- An item of income or expenditure is included in taxable profit of the period, but recognised in accounting profit in later years. For example, development expenditure might be tax deductible in the year in which it is incurred, but capitalised and amortised over a period for financial reporting purposes. Similarly, income received in advance might be taxed in the period of receipt, but treated as earned in the financial statements in a later period.

13.101 A timing difference is said to 'originate' when a transaction is first reflected in the financial statements, but not yet in the tax computation (or vice versa). It is said to 'reverse' when in due course the transaction is reflected in the tax computation or the financial statements either wholly or partly as the case may be. It is not necessary for a timing difference to originate in the financial statements and reverse in the tax computation (or vice versa). A timing difference can also originate in the financial statements of one period and reverse in the financial statements of a subsequent period without ever having been reflected in the tax computations. An example is a general provision for bad debts made in one year, but written back as not required in the following year. Similarly, a transaction might be reflected in the tax computation of one period and reverse in the tax computation of a later period, without ever having been reflected in the financial statements, although such situations are rare.

13.102 FRS 19 provides the following list of timing differences:

- Tax deductions for the cost of a fixed asset (including deductions for expenditure on infrastructure assets capitalised and depreciated using renewals accounting) are accelerated or decelerated, that is, received before or after the cost of the fixed asset is recognised in the profit and loss account.
- Pension liabilities are accrued in the financial statements but are allowed for tax purposes only when paid or contributed at a later date.
- Interest charges or development costs are capitalised on the balance sheet but are treated as revenue expenditure and allowed as incurred for tax purposes.
- Intragroup profits in stock, unrealised at group level, are reversed on consolidation.
- An asset is revalued in the financial statements, but the revaluation gain becomes taxable only if and when the asset is sold.
- A tax loss is not relieved against past or present taxable profits, but can be carried forward to reduce future taxable profits.
- The unremitted earnings of subsidiary and associated undertakings and joint ventures are recognised in the group results but will be subject to further taxation only if and when remitted to the parent undertaking.

[FRS 19 para 2].

13.103 A number of the timing differences in the above list would be short-term timing differences, that is, those that usually reverse in the accounting period following the one in which they originate (hence the name). There are other timing differences that do not reverse within a year of their origination. A classic example is 'accelerated capital allowances'. Accounting for some specific timing differences are considered in the following paragraphs.

13.103.1 In some situations, it may not be clear whether a timing difference exists. This may occur if there is uncertainty with regards to the tax position. For example, the entity may have incurred certain costs that have been capitalised and will be recognised in the profit and loss account over time for accounting purposes. Management may have claimed these costs as tax deductions in a tax return and these claims could be subject to challenge by the tax authorities. In this case, it is not clear whether a timing difference exists. In such a scenario, we consider that management should judge what they expect the outcome of any uncertainty to be and determine the deferred tax on that basis. If it is more likely than not that the uncertain item will be accepted by the tax authorities, it is management's expectation that a timing difference exists and deferred tax should be recognised. If it is more likely than not that the tax authorities will disallow the deduction, the expectation is that the amounts recognised in the profit and loss account over time will be permanent differences and no deferred tax should be recognised.

Accounting for some specific timing differences

Accelerated capital allowances

13.104 In the UK, tax relief in respect of capital expenditure on plant and machinery is given by means of capital allowances that are a form of standardised tax depreciation. Since capital allowances are deducted from accounting profit to arrive at taxable profit, the amount of depreciation charged in the financial statements is always disallowed in the tax computation. Although depreciation for taxation and accounting purposes will be the same over the life of the asset, they will differ from year to year, thus giving rise to timing differences. In many cases, the capital allowances depreciate the asset at a faster rate for tax purposes than the rate of depreciation charged in the financial statements. For this reason, the timing differences created are often referred to as 'accelerated capital allowances'. The following example illustrates the creation of the timing differences:

Example

A company purchases a machine in 20X1 for £100,000. The asset is expected to be sold at the end of its useful life of five years for £10,000. Depreciation is charged on a straight line basis for accounting purposes and amounts to £18,000 ((£100,000 – £10,000)/5) per annum. The rate of capital allowances is 25% per annum on a reducing balance basis.

The timing difference will arise as follows:

Per financial statements	20X1 £'000	20X2 £'000	20X3 £'000	20X4 £'000	20X5 £'000
Carrying value of asset	100	82	64	46	28
Depreciation charge	18	18	18	18	18
Book written down value	82	64	46	28	10
Per tax computation					
Carrying value of asset	100	75	56	42	32
Capital allowance	25	19	14	10	8
Tax written down value	75	56	42	32	24
Timing difference					
Capital allowance allowed	25	19	14	10	8
Depreciation charged	18	18	18	18	18
Originating (reversing)	7	1	(4)	(8)	(10)
Cumulative	7	8	4	(4)	(14)

The table shows that a timing difference of £7,000 originates in the first year, but this gradually reverses from year three onwards. Over the useful life of the asset depreciation charged exceeds capital allowances by £14,000. For the first two years, capital allowances exceed depreciation and, hence, the tax assessed and provided in the profit and loss account as current tax payable is less than the tax that would eventually become payable on the profit reported in the financial statements. This early benefit of lower taxation gradually reverses from year three onwards when capital allowances have fallen below depreciation. In those years, the tax assessed and, hence, provided in the profit and loss account as current tax is higher than the amount due on the profit reported in the financial statements. The cumulative timing difference at the end of 20X5 of £14,000 will either gradually reverse from 20X6 onwards if the asset is included in the pool for capital allowance purposes, or it will give rise to a balancing allowance if the asset is sold in 20X6 for £10,000.

13.105 The description of accelerated tax deductions for the cost of fixed assets set out in the first bullet point in paragraph 13.102 above has been made more general by FRS 19 to clarify that it applies to tax deductions received before or after the *cost* of the fixed asset is recognised in the profit and loss account. The definition reflects the fact that the cost of a fixed asset is recognised in the profit and loss account either through depreciation or, if not depreciated, on sale of the asset. This means that the reversal of accelerated capital allowances occurs as the asset is consumed through use or on disposal.

13.106 The definition of accelerated capital allowances has wide implications in practice. For instance, many items of plant and machinery such as, standby electrical generators, air-conditioning plant and passenger and goods lifts that form part of investment properties are normally included in the overall valuation of the investment property and are not depreciated. Under FRS 19, if an asset is not depreciated (and has not otherwise been written down to a carrying value less than cost), a timing difference equal to the amount of the capital allowances claimed arises. [FRS 19 para 10]. This means that deferred tax should be provided on the timing difference. Therefore, in general, deferred tax should be provided on all tax deductible assets irrespective of whether or not they are depreciated. In the absence of depreciation or a write down for impairment, the timing difference will reverse on the asset's disposal, by way of a balancing charge.

13.106.1 In the 2007 budget, the Chancellor of the Exchequer announced major changes to the capital allowances regime in the UK. This will reduce the number of different types of allowance, based on the economic life of the asset. The main changes announced were as follows:

- The rate of writing down allowances (tax depreciation) on plant and machinery in the general pool is to be reduced from 25 per cent per annum to 20 per cent per annum from 1 April 2008.
- The rate of writing down allowances are further reduced for certain fixtures integral to buildings to 10 per cent per annum from 1 April 2008.
- The rate of writing down allowances on long-life assets is to be increased from 6 per cent per annum to 10 per cent per annum from 1 April 2008.
- There are also changes to the capital allowances rules for small enterprises.

13.106.2 It is currently expected that the changes in timing of capital allowances will be introduced in the Finance Bill 2008. The impact of the changes should be accounted for once the changes have been substantively enacted and so will remain a potential disclosure item until that Bill is approved by the House of Commons (see para 13.98.1 above).

Industrial building allowances

13.107 As a general rule, capital allowances on fixed assets become repayable through a balancing charge if the asset is not consumed, but is instead sold for more than its tax written-down value at the time of sale. However, allowances on certain buildings are currently subject to a different regime of Industrial Building Allowances (IBAs). As part of the 2007 budget statement, various amendments were proposed to the regime, the impact of which is discussed in paragraph 13.109 onwards.

13.108 Under the original rules, IBAs on factories, warehouses, hotels and commercial buildings in enterprise zones did not need to be repaid if they were retained in the business for a qualifying holding period of 25 years following purchase. After 25 years, no balancing charge arose even if an industrial building was sold for more than its tax written-down value, which could be the entire sales proceeds if the industrial building was located in an enterprise zone and qualified for 100 per cent initial allowance.

13.109 Deferred tax attributable to capital allowances of all types should be recognised until all the conditions for retaining those allowances have been met. Under the original IBA regime this meant that, in many cases, a deferred tax liability was held on balance sheet in relation to IBAs as accounting depreciation was booked at a slower rate than the IBAs (tax depreciation) were received. Once the conditions for retaining the allowances were met, that is, there was no longer any possibility that the allowances could be clawed back as a balancing charge on sale, the timing difference relating to the accelerated capital allowances became permanent and any deferred tax liability previously recognised was reversed. [FRS 19 para 9]. In practice, this meant that the deferred tax liabilities were released at the end of year 25.

13.109.1 In the 2007 budget, two key changes were announced to the IBA regime as follows:

- Balancing adjustment provisions and those that recalculate writing-down allowances for buyers are withdrawn for balancing events (such as disposals) occurring on or after 21 March 2007
- IBAs are to be phased-out gradually from 2008/2009 onwards. The rate will drop in successive years from 4 per cent to 3 per cent to 2 per cent to 1 per cent with the allowances being eliminated thereafter.

13.110 Deferred tax is measured using the tax rates and laws that are enacted or substantively enacted at the balance sheet date. [FRS 19 para 37]. The removal of the IBAs balancing adjustment was included in the Finance Act 2007, which was substantively enacted on 26 June 2007. Therefore, this change should be accounted for in periods ending on or after that date (including interims). The phased withdrawal of IBAs is not expected to be substantively enacted until the Finance Bill 2008 is approved by the House of Commons (and will remain a potential disclosure item until that Bill is approved). Therefore, the impact of the accounting for the changes to IBAs may impact on more than one accounting period.

13.110.1 The fact that balancing adjustments will no longer arise means that any deferred tax liability will never be 'clawed back' by the tax authorities even if a balancing event occurs before the end of the 25 year time period. Under paragraph 9 of FRS 19, if and when all conditions for retaining IBAs have been met, any deferred tax liability previously recognised should be reversed. Therefore, the removal of the balancing adjustment (and with it, the removal of the qualifying period for retaining allowances) means that allowances received prior to the removal will become a permanent difference. This will result in the release of any existing deferred tax liabilities. In the remaining years when reduced IBAs are available, the allowance will be treated as a permanent difference as it arises.

13.110.2 The situation may differ if a company has a deferred tax asset with respect to industrial buildings. This will occur if the accumulated accounting depreciation at the balance sheet date is greater than the IBAs received. The general principle is to consider whether the deferred tax asset is recoverable under the applicable tax rules. If the expectation is that the building will continue to be used, it will be necessary to determine if sufficient IBAs will be received to cover the timing difference. In this situation, the elimination of the balancing adjustment by the Finance Act 2007 has no effect. The recoverability of the deferred tax asset could be impacted by the phasing out of IBAs, which is expected to be introduced by the 2008 Finance Bill. It could be the case that there will be insufficient IBAs in the future for the full timing difference to reverse. In this situation, all or part of the deferred tax asset should be written off, as appropriate. The write off should be made in the first accounting period ending on or after the date of substantive enactment of the rules phasing out the IBAs (and will remain a potential disclosure item until that period).

13.110.3 When recognising adjustments to deferred tax balances as a result of a change in tax laws, consideration must be given as to whether the adjustment should be recognised in the profit and loss account or in the STRGL (or a combination of the two). This is considered in more detail in paragraph 13.249 below.

Infrastructure assets

13.111 Infrastructure assets can be defined as groups of assets which together form an integrated system. Such a system could not be effectively operated if individual components were removed. Systems typically falling within this category include gas, water, railways, roads as well as electricity distribution systems.

13.112 Traditionally, depreciation accounting has been the method under which the consumption of service potential of fixed assets is recognised in financial statements. Renewals accounting emerged as an alternative method of recognising consumption of service potential of long-lived assets such as infrastructure assets. The renewals accounting approach is most applicable to that part of the networks or systems where the system as a whole is be maintained indefinitely at a particular level of service potential by the continuous replacement and refurbishment of its components. When renewals accounting is adopted, the level of annual expenditure required to maintain the operating capacity of the infrastructure asset is treated as the depreciation charged in the period. The actual expenditure incurred each year to maintain the asset is capitalised.

13.113 Under FRS 19, tax deductions for expenditure on infrastructure assets capitalised and depreciated using renewals accounting are included within the definition of accelerated capital allowances noted in paragraph 13.102 above. Therefore, deferred tax should be provided on the timing difference between the actual expenditure qualifying for tax relief and the assessed level of planned expenditure treated as depreciation. [FRS 19 App V para 62].

Provisions

13.114 Provisions, such as those made for refurbishment, or for plant closures following a reorganisation, or those arising on pensions and unfunded retirement benefits usually give rise to timing differences in that tax relief is obtained when the expenditure is actually incurred and not when it is recognised in the financial statements. It follows that such provisions will always give rise to a deferred tax asset, because taxable profits are higher than accounting profits in the year in which the provisions are made. The tax asset will be recovered in the year in which the actual expenditure is incurred, but for some provisions, like pensions and other post-retirement benefits, recoverability of the tax benefit may take many years (see further para 13.126 onwards).

[The next paragraph is 13.116.]

Deferred revenue expenditure

13.116 Deferred revenue expenditure, on the other hand, gives rise to deferred tax liabilities. In this situation, tax relief is typically obtained on the full amount of the expenditure in the year in which it is incurred, but only a proportion is recognised in the financial statements, the balance being carried forward as an asset to be charged to income over a period of time. The difference between book and tax treatment gives rise to a deferred tax liability to reflect the fact that the company has obtained full tax benefit on expenditure of which only a proportion has passed through the profit and loss account in the year.

13.117 Capitalisation of interest gives rise to similar tax considerations and is one of the examples of timing differences noted in FRS 19 (see para 13.102 above). The full interest incurred in the year is allowed for tax, but for accounting purposes the tax benefit is effectively recognised over the years in which the interest capitalised in the financial statements is charged through depreciation of the asset in the profit and account. Even where the asset is not depreciated, such as in the case of investment properties, deferred tax should be provided because the reversal of the timing difference (the interest charge in the performance statement) will arise when the asset is sold or the property is impaired. The deferred tax liabilities will be reversed when the costs are taken to the profit and loss account.

Government grants

13.118 The accounting treatment of government grants and their treatment for tax purposes may give rise to timing differences. SSAP 4, 'Accounting for government grants', requires grants to be treated as deferred income and amortised either over the periods in which the related revenue expenditure is recognised or, if the grant is made as a contribution towards capital expenditure, over the expected useful life of the related asset. In the latter situation, an alternative treatment of deducting the grant from the capital cost of the asset is permitted for entities not preparing their financial statements in accordance with Schedule 4 to the Act (see further chapter 16). Grants given as a contribution towards the cost of acquisition of an asset may be non-taxable, although some are in effect taxed by reducing the cost of fixed assets for capital allowances purposes. Other grants, such as revenue-based grants, are usually taxable on a cash received basis.

13.119 If the grant is not taxable, it gives rise to a permanent difference between accounting and taxable profits. Non-taxable revenue-based grants do not have any deferred tax consequences, because the amortised credit to the profit and loss account is simply a permanent difference in arriving at taxable profits of each year. Similarly, receipts of non-taxable capital-based grants do not give rise to deferred tax adjustments, except that accelerated capital allowances will need to be calculated as the difference between the net book value of the asset (gross cost less accumulated depreciation calculated on the gross cost) and the tax written down value (gross cost less tax allowances claimed). This applies even if the asset is stated in the financial statements net of the grant since the balance sheet presentation permitted by SSAP 4 for entities that do not report under Schedule 4 to the Companies Act 1985 does not affect the deferred tax calculation.

13.120 If the grant is taxable, a timing difference will arise between the taxable profits and the accounting profits. Revenue-based grants that are taxed on receipt, but amortised over a period for financial reporting purposes, give rise to a timing difference on which a deferred tax asset may need to be set up on the unamortised balance carried forward in the financial statements. The deferred tax asset will fall to be recoverable in subsequent accounting periods as the deferred credit unwinds through amortisation. Where a grant that has been taxed on receipt becomes repayable, the repayment will qualify for tax relief in the year in which the repayment is made. In that situation, any deferred tax asset previously carried forward should be immediately written off as part of the tax charge.

13.121 Where a taxable grant is received as a contribution towards expenditure on a fixed asset, the nature of the deferred tax adjustment will depend on how the grant is treated for tax and accounting purposes. If the grant is deducted from the cost of fixed assets both for financial reporting and tax purposes, the deferred tax calculation is relatively straightforward as accelerated capital allowances are calculated on a reduced cost. On the other hand, if the grant is treated as a deferred credit for financial reporting purposes, but deducted against the cost of the asset for capital allowances purposes, the deferred tax calculation will consist of two components. A deferred tax debit balance will arise on the unamortised grant, which will be netted off against the deferred tax credit balance arising on the accelerated capital allowances. In practice, the balance on the deferred income account is netted off against the book value of the asset for the purposes of calculating the timing difference. Consider the following example:

Example

A company purchases a fixed asset for £120,000. The asset qualifies for a grant of £20,000 which is treated in the financial statements as a deferred credit. The asset has a useful economic life of five years. The company claims capital allowances, but these are restricted by the amount of the grant. The timing differences for deferred tax purposes are calculated as follows:

Per financial statements	20X1	20X2	20X3	20X4	20X5
	£	£	£	£	£
Cost of asset	120,000	96,000	72,000	48,000	24,000
Depreciation	(24,000)	(24,000)	(24,000)	(24,000)	(24,000)
Net book value	96,000	72,000	48,000	24,000	–
Unamortised deferred income	16,000	12,000	8,000	4,000	–

Per tax computation	20X1 £	20X2 £	20X3 £	20X4 £	20X5 £
Cost of asset	120,000				
Less grant	(20,000)				
Cost net of grant/pool	100,000	75,000	56,250	42,187	31,640
Capital allowances @ 25%	(25,000)	(18,750)	(14,063)	(10,547)	(7,910)
Tax written down value	75,000	56,250	42,187	31,640	23,730
Timing difference					
Capital allowances	25,000	18,750	14,063	10,547	7,910
Depreciation	(24,000)	(24,000)	(24,000)	(24,000)	(24,000)
Accelerated capital allowances	1,000	(5,250)	(9,937)	(13,453)	(16,090)
Amortisation of grant	4,000	4,000	4,000	4,000	4,000
Net timing difference	5,000	(1,250)	(5,937)	(9,453)	(12,090)
Net book value of fixed asset	96,000	72,000	48,000	24,000	–
Unamortised grant	(16,000)	(12,000)	(8,000)	(4,000)	–
	80,000	60,000	40,000	20,000	–
Tax written down value	(75,000)	(56,250)	(42,187)	(31,640)	(23,730)
Cumulative timing difference	5,000	3,750	(2,187)	(11,640)	(23,730).

The timing difference profile will be the same if the grant is deducted directly from the cost of the asset and the net amount written off over the five year period.

Leases

13.122 Many companies enter into lease and hire purchase contracts under which they obtain the right to use or purchase assets. In the UK there is normally no provision in a lease contract for legal title to the leased asset to pass to the lessee. A hire purchase contract has similar features to a lease, except that the hirer may acquire legal title by exercising an option to purchase the asset upon fulfilment of certain conditions (normally the payment of a specified number of instalments). Current tax legislation provides that capital allowances may be claimed by a lessor under a lease contract in most circumstances, but by a hirer under a hire purchase contract. Since 1 April 2006, capital allowances are claimed by the lessee on longer leases of plant and machinery (whether they are accounted for as finance leases or operating leases) if they meet certain conditions and are essentially financing transactions. Such leases are known as 'long funded leases' for tax purposes.

13.123 Assets acquired under leases and hire purchase contracts give rise to timing differences between the amounts recorded in the profit and loss account and the amounts recorded in the tax computations. Where the asset is purchased under a hire purchase agreement or a 'long funded lease', the hirer will normally account for the acquisition of the fixed asset in question and will be able to claim the capital allowances. Therefore, no particular deferred tax problems arise. Similarly, no deferred tax problems normally arise in accounting for an operating lease. This is because the amount that is charged to rentals in the profit and loss account for financial reporting purposes is likely to be the same as the amount charged in arriving at the taxable profit. The only exception to this will arise where there are accrued rentals that may give rise to a potential short-term timing difference.

13.124 A timing difference will arise in circumstances where the lessee enters into a finance lease that is accounted for under the provisions of SSAP 21 and that is not a 'long funded lease'. In that situation, the asset acquired under a finance lease will be recorded as a fixed asset with a corresponding liability for the obligation to pay future rentals. The asset is then depreciated over the lease term or the useful life of the asset, whichever is shorter. Rents payable are apportioned between the finance charge and a reduction of the outstanding obligation for future amounts payable. The total finance charge is allocated to accounting periods during the lease term so as to produce a constant periodic rate of charge on the remaining balance of the obligation for each accounting period. A reasonable approximation is permitted (see further chapter 19).

13.125 If the finance lessee does not qualify for capital allowances, but is able to obtain a tax deduction for the whole of each rental payment, a timing difference arises if tax relief is given on the rentals paid, as a result of the differing treatment for accounting and tax purposes. In some situations, the Inland Revenue may accept the SSAP 21 treatment for tax purposes, in which case there are no deferred tax consequences. However, in principle, a timing difference arises and this is illustrated in the following example:

Example

A company leases a fixed asset under a finance lease over a five year period. The annual lease payments amount to £12,000 per annum. The asset is recorded at the present value of the minimum lease payments of £48,000 and is depreciated at £9,600 per annum.

The timing difference arising is calculated as follows:

	Year 1	Year 2	Year 3	Year 4	Year 5
	£	£	£	£	£
Rentals	12,000	12,000	12,000	12,000	12,000
Finance cost @ 7.93%	(3,806)	(3,158)	(2,455)	(1,699)	(882)
Capital repayment	8,194	8,842	9,545	10,301	11,118
Timing difference					
Tax computations: rentals	12,000	12,000	12,000	12,000	12,000
Profit and loss account:					
Finance cost	3,806	3,158	2,455	1,699	882
Depreciation	9,600	9,600	9,600	9,600	9,600
	13,406	12,758	12,055	11,299	10,482
Timing difference	(1,406)	(758)	(55)	701	1,518
Net book value of fixed asset	38,400	28,800	19,200	9,600	–
Outstanding obligation (capital)	39,806	30,964	21,419	11,118	–
Cumulative timing difference	(1,406)	(2,164)	(2,219)	(1,518)	–

Finance leases capitalised under SSAP 21, therefore, tend to produce an originating negative timing difference (deferred tax asset) as greater finance charges are allocated to earlier years to reflect the reducing capital amount owed under the lease.

13.125.1 In the UK, the tax treatment of leases usually follows their legal form rather than the economic reality adopted for accounting purposes. Thus in most cases, it is the lessor not the lessee who is generally entitled to capital allowances on the leased asset that is set off against the gross rental earnings (except for 'long funded leases' – see para 13.122 above). The lessee as the user rather than the owner of the leased asset is granted relief for the rentals payable under the lease agreement. Given that the lease payments specified under the lease contracts are generally deductible for tax purposes, lessees, depending on their particular circumstances, began to structure their leases for tax purposes so that they were able to accelerate the tax relief through large initial rentals or defer it through final balloon rentals, even though for accounting purposes each period's rentals were apportioned effectively between the finance charge (calculated at a constant periodic rate on the remaining balance of the carrying amount of the liability) and depreciation representing the consumption of the leased asset.

13.125.2 In order to prevent the above practice of timing the tax relief in a manner that suited the lessees, the Inland Revenue issued a Statement of Practice (SP 3/91) in 1991, which deals with how a lessee should obtain tax relief for his rental obligations. In general terms, SP 3/91 sets out to ensure that, irrespective of when they are due to be paid, rental payments are spread so that a finance lessee secures relief for them over the estimated useful economic life of the leased asset. To achieve this, the Statement suggests that tax deductions will be allowed for the amount of the accounting depreciation plus the finance charge as booked in the profit and loss account in each accounting period. If this is the case, there will be no timing difference.

13.125.3 As noted in paragraph 13.106.1 above, changes to the capital allowance regime in the UK were announced in the 2007 budget statement. These changes (in addition to the changes in tax rates discussed in para 13.48 above) will have implications for lessees and lessors where leases have a 'change of tax law' clause, as the capital allowances available to lessors under affected leases will be different to that assumed at the time the lease was entered into and could trigger changes to lease rentals.

Post-retirement benefits

13.126 In the UK, tax relief on employers' pension contributions is often given in the period in which they are paid, rather than when the costs are recognised in the financial statements (with the exception of some large contributions, where tax relief is spread over a period). In an unfunded scheme, and in the case of provisions for unfunded benefits such as post-retirement healthcare, the tax relief is often given when the pensions or other benefits are paid. In the financial statements, on the other hand, pension costs and other post-retirement benefits are recognised as service is provided by the employee, in accordance with the principles set out in FRS 17, 'Retirement benefits'. Where the total of the pension costs recognised under FRS 17 differs from the actual contributions (or unfunded benefits) paid, the resulting asset or liability recognised in the balance sheet is a timing difference for deferred tax purposes. This is the case whether the defined benefit scheme is in a net deficit or a net surplus position.

13.126.1 In the UK, the corporate tax rules for deductions and spreading of tax relief on employer pension contributions changed with effect from the first corporation tax period ending on or after 6 April 2006. Employer pension contributions will now only be deducted as an expense provided they are incurred *"wholly and exclusively for the purposes of the employer's trade or profession"*. Tax relief is, therefore, no longer automatic and entities should consider this when accounting for tax in respect of pension schemes. In addition, where tax relief is obtained, tax deductions on any significant contributions may be subject to spreading rules. This will occur when 'relevant excess contributions' (RECs) are made. The implications of spreading of tax deductions on RECs are discussed in paragraph 13.126.12 below. This is a complex area and consultation with a tax specialist is advised.

13.126.2 FRS 19 defines timing differences as differences between an entity's taxable profits and its results as stated in the financial statements that arise from the inclusion of gains and losses in tax assessments in periods different from those in which they are recognised in financial statements. Timing differences originate in one period and are capable of reversal in one or more subsequent periods. Consider an actuarial gain. The actuarial gain is reflected in the entity's financial statements in the year it arises. If contributions are reduced in future years as a result of the surplus, the pension asset will be recovered because the pension cost accrued each year will exceed the contributions payable.

13.126.3 An actuarial gain does give rise to a timing difference. The gain is not taxed in the year it arises (when the timing difference originates), but in a sense it is taxed in future years as the surplus is recovered (when the timing difference reverses). In those future years, the accounting profits are adjusted to taxable profits by replacing the pension costs with the reduced contributions payable, the difference being the amount of surplus that is recovered in the year.

Example

A company's defined benefit pension scheme is in surplus as a result of an actuarial gain and because contributions paid were greater than pension costs. In accordance with FRS 17, 'Retirement benefits', the surplus is recognised as an asset on the company's balance sheet. Management has queried whether it is appropriate to recognise a deferred tax liability as the pension surplus is not taxable. Should a deferred tax liability be recognised?

The key here is to determine whether the pension asset represents a timing difference.

Paragraph 37 of FRS 17 specifies that a pension asset should be recognised only to the extent that it is recoverable through reduced contributions in the future or through refunds from the scheme. This means that, for the pension asset to be recognised, there must be an expectation that it will be recovered.

Normally, contributions will be reduced in future years as a result of the surplus and the pension asset will thus be recovered.

The entity's taxable profits are arrived at after deducting the employer's pension contributions payable each period, rather than reflecting the pension gains and losses that are recognised in the financial statements.

In future years, the current tax deductions received will be lower as a result of the reduced contributions payable. Pension costs will be greater than the contributions and the surplus will be recovered. That difference in effect reflects the inclusion in the later period's tax assessment of a gain that has been recognised in an earlier period's financial statements. Hence it is necessary to build up a deferred tax liability as the surplus arises and to reverse that liability as the surplus is recovered.

13.126.4 With some exceptions (none of which are applicable to pensions), FRS 19 requires deferred tax to be provided in full on all timing differences that have originated but not reversed by the balance sheet date. In most cases, these timing differences will reverse, albeit over a long time scale. Deferred tax assets (which relate to defined benefit liabilities recognised under FRS 17) should be recognised to the extent that they are regarded as recoverable.

13.126.5 A deferred tax asset should be recognised to the extent that it can be regarded as more likely than not that there will be suitable taxable profits from which the future reversal of the underlying timing differences can be deducted. [FRS 19 para 23]. The question arises as to whether deferred tax liabilities resulting from taxable timing differences can be taken into account in determining the recoverability of the deferred tax asset relating to pensions. Recovery of deferred tax assets against existing deferred tax liabilities is dealt with in paragraph 13.156 onwards. A deferred tax asset in respect of a pension obligation cannot be recognised simply because there are sufficient taxable timing differences at the balance sheet date. The timing of reversal of the timing differences giving rise to liabilities also needs to be taken into account.

13.126.6 Therefore, some scheduling of the reversal of timing differences may be required to ensure that the reversal of the deductible timing differences would allow the company to carry the deferred tax asset against the profits arising on reversal of the taxable timing differences. The company must have plans in place to eliminate the pension deficit – simply paying the normal regular cost will not eliminate the deficit. Therefore, the recognition of a tax asset in respect of the pension obligations should take into account the expected timing of contributions necessary to eliminate the deficit.

13.126.7 Also, if the company has incurred losses in the past and has incurred losses in the current period as well, this will impact on the extent to which tax assets can be recognised. For example, if say the company continues to make losses in the next few years before a turnaround is anticipated, but the amount of the reversal of the existing taxable timing differences in those years is not enough to create taxable profits such that any pension contributions made in those years simply add to the tax loss, then the deferred tax asset may not be recoverable. The assessment of the likelihood that taxable profits will arise when there has been a history of trading losses is discussed in paragraph 13.158 onwards.

13.126.8 Under FRS 17, various components of pension cost are reported in the profit and loss account; actuarial gains and losses are reported in the STRGL. So in any period, pension cost accounting may give rise to current tax (tax relief on contributions) and deferred tax (on the timing differences between contributions and costs). FRS 16 requires current tax to be recognised in the profit and loss account, except where it is attributable to a gain or loss that has been recognised directly in the STRGL, in which case the attributable tax should also be recognised directly in the STRGL (see para 13.21). Similarly, FRS 19 requires deferred tax to be recognised in the profit and loss account, except where it is attributable to a gain or loss that has been recognised directly in the STRGL (see para 13.237). Normally, there is no direct relationship between the components of pension cost reported in the performance statements and the contributions and benefits paid in a period and so FRS 17 specifies a hierarchy for allocating current tax between the profit and loss account and the STRGL. Deferred tax will normally arise on the balance of costs and credits in each statement.

13.126.9 Tax relief on contributions should be allocated on the basis that the contributions cover profit and loss items first and actuarial losses (STRGL items) second, unless it is clear that some other allocation is more appropriate. If contributions exceed those items, tax relief relating to the excess should be credited in the profit and loss account, again unless it is clearly more appropriate to allocate it to the STRGL. The standard gives an example where an alternative method of allocation may be appropriate – when a special contribution is made to fund a deficit arising from an identifiable cause, say an actuarial loss, in which case the tax relief should be allocated to the STRGL. However, in the absence of a clear link between the contribution and the items recognised in the performance statements, the allocation above should be followed. [FRS 17 para 71].

13.126.10 The allocation of current and deferred tax is illustrated in the following table, which shows the movements in a surplus during the year. A tax rate of 30 per cent is assumed.

Example 1 – Defined benefit asset

	Change in defined benefit asset	Current tax relief (30%)	Deferred tax liability (30%)
	£	£	£
B/f	120		(36)
Contributions	70	(21)	
P&L – net pension cost	(60)	18	–
STRGL – actuarial loss	(20)	3	3
	(80)	21	3
C/f	110	–	(33)

Current tax relief arises on contributions paid of £70. This is allocated first to cover the pension cost of £60 reported in the profit and loss account (resulting in a credit of £18 in the tax charge in the profit and loss account). The balance of the contributions paid, £10, is allocated to the actuarial loss and hence current tax of £3 is credited in the STRGL. Deferred tax of £3 is attributable to the balance of the actuarial loss, £10 and is credited in the STRGL.

It should be noted that FRS 17 requires the deferred tax to be offset against the defined benefit asset in the balance sheet (see para 13.257).

Example 2 – Defined benefit liability

	Change in defined benefit liability	Current tax relief (30%)	Deferred tax asset (30%)
	£	£	£
B/f	(200)		60
Contributions paid	80	(24)	
P&L – net pension cost	(70)	21	–
STRGL – actuarial loss	(20)	3	3
	(90)	24	3
C/f	(210)	–	63

Current tax relief of £24 arises on contributions paid of £80. This is allocated first to cover the pension cost of £70 reported in the profit and loss account (resulting in a credit of £21 in the tax charge in the profit and loss account). The balance of the contributions paid of £10 is allocated to the actuarial loss and hence current tax of £3 is credited in the STRGL. Deferred tax of £3 is attributable to the balance of the actuarial loss of £10 and is credited in the STRGL.

Example 3 – Defined benefit liability

If, in the above example, there was an actuarial gain rather than an actuarial loss, the whole of the current tax relief of £24 would be credited in the profit and loss account. None of the current tax credit can be allocated to the STRGL as there is no debit to the STRGL. Thus the initial £21 (30% of £70) is allocated to the profit and loss account, nil is allocated to the STRGL and the excess of £3 is allocated to the profit and loss account. Deferred tax attributable to the actuarial gain would be charged in the STRGL. This is illustrated below.

	Change in defined benefit liability	**Current tax relief (30%)**	**Deferred tax asset (30%)**
	£	£	£
B/f	(200)		(60)
Contributions	80	(24)	
P&L – net pension cost	(70)	24	(3)
STRGL – actuarial gain	20	–	(6)
	(50)	24	(9)
C/f	(170)	–	51

13.126.11 The allocation is more complicated if a large contribution is made in the period, say to reduce an existing pension deficit. Assume that, in example 2 above, an additional contribution of £100 was paid and that tax deductions were received in the period.

Example

	Change in defined benefit liability	**Current tax relief (30%)**	**Deferred tax asset (30%)**
	£	**£**	**£**
B/f	(200)		60
'Normal' contributions paid	80	(24)	
Additional contribution paid	100	(30)	
P&L account – net pension cost	(70)	21	
STRGL:			
Current year actuarial loss	(20)	3	3
Relating to previous actuarial losses	–	30	(30)
	(90)	54	(27)
C/f	(110)	–	33

Therefore, if tax deductions on the normal contribution of £80 and the additional contribution of £100 are all received in the period (that is, no spreading of deductions), then the current tax relief of £24 on the 'normal' contributions is allocated first against the pension cost in the profit and loss account and then the balance is allocated against the actuarial loss.

Further, current tax deductions of £30 are received on the additional contribution. There is, therefore, an excess deduction to be considered. Under the allocation hierarchy in paragraph 13.126.9, this excess would go to the profit and loss account, unless another method of allocation is more appropriate. The treatment of the deferred tax in relation to the additional contribution will depend on why that contribution was made. In this case, it is likely that the additional contribution is funding past actuarial losses, in which case it is necessary to backwards-trace the items in the performance statement to determine where the underlying items giving rise to the deficit that is being funded were originally recognised.

It will be necessary to backwards-trace further if the deductions received in the year exceed the current and prior year actuarial losses that had not been allocated current tax deductions. Assuming that it is possible to establish, using backwards-tracing, that the tax deductions relate to prior year actuarial losses, the excess tax deductions will be recognised in the STRGL, with a corresponding reversal of deferred tax, as shown above.

Alternatively, if the additional contribution was made to fund current year actuarial losses as well as previous actuarial losses, £3 would be allocated to the STRGL (to cover the £10 of actuarial loss made in the current year not yet tax effected). There is then an excess deduction of £27 after allocating to the net pension cost in the profit and loss account and any actuarial losses in the STRGL. Again, in this case, it would be appropriate to allocate this to the STRGL if the contribution was made to fund the accumulated actuarial losses. Notably, this has the same outcome as the allocation method illustrated in the table above. An element of judgement will be necessary when considering why the additional contribution was made.

Note that the fact that a pension liability recognised on transition to FRS 17 was charged to reserves does not necessarily mean that any current tax deductions or subsequent changes in any related deferred tax asset will also be recognised in reserves (see further para 13.249 below).

13.126.12 If tax deductions are spread across more than one accounting period then this will impact on the deferred tax calculation, as the deduction received in the current year will be lower. Assume that in the example in paragraph 13.126.11 above the additional contribution of £100 meets the definition of a REC (see para 13.126.2 above) and is thus spread over, say, three periods (that is only one-third of the relief on the additional contribution is received in the current period).

Example

	Change in defined benefit liability	**Current tax relief (30%)**	**Deferred tax asset (30%)**
	£	£	£
B/f	(200)		60
'Normal' contributions paid	80	(24)	
Additional contribution paid	100	(10)	
P&L account – net pension cost	(70)	21	–
STRGL:			
Current year actuarial loss	(20)	3	3
Relating to previous actuarial losses	–	10	(10)
	(90)	34	(7)
C/f	(110)	–	53

Note that in this example, the deferred tax balance at the period end is not 30% of the pension balance.

Assuming that a deferred tax asset has been recognised in relation to the pension liability at the beginning of the period, part of this deferred tax asset reverses as a result of the tax deductions received in the period. However, if the contributions paid do not receive tax relief in the period, then a corresponding portion of the deferred tax asset on the opening pension liability will continue to be carried forward (assuming the recognition criteria are met) and will reverse in the future when the tax deductions are received.

The deferred tax asset can be summarised as:

	£
On pension liability at year end (£110 × 30%)	33
Outstanding deductions on contributions made (£100 × 30% × 2/3)	20
Total deferred tax asset	53

A deferred tax asset should be recognised to the extent that it is regarded as more likely than not that the deferred tax asset will be recovered. Under FRS 17, it is presented as a deduction from the net pension deficit recorded in the balance sheet (see para 13.257). This applies even if part of the deferred tax asset relates to deductions to be received through spreading. In some cases, this may give an odd result, for example, where the deferred tax asset exceeds the pension deficit. Our view is that the deferred tax asset should still be shown with the related pension deficit. In this situation, it would be appropriate to make clear that there is not a pension asset, which may be achieved by expanding the disclosure to show both the pension deficit and the related deferred tax asset on the face of the balance sheet, with a sub-total.

13.126.13 FRS 16 requires the current tax charged or credited in the profit and loss account and the STRGL to be disclosed separately. In addition, FRS 19 requires the deferred tax charged or credited in the profit and loss account and the STRGL to be disclosed separately.

Share-based payment transactions

Equity-settled transactions

13.127 FRS 20, 'Share-based payment', requires companies to recognise the cost of equity-settled share-based awards (for example, share options) on the basis of the fair value of the award at the date of grant, spread over the vesting period (see further chapter 12). However, the amount of the deduction available for tax purposes in the case of equity-settled transactions does not often correspond to the amount charged to the profit and loss account in accordance with FRS 20.

13.127.1 Under current UK tax law, which came into effect on 1 January 2003, a tax deduction in connection with an employee share option scheme is available at the date of exercise, measured on the basis of the share option's intrinsic value at that date (being the difference between the share's market price at the date of exercise and the option's exercise price).

13.127.2 When the FRS 20 charge (based on the share option's fair value at the date of grant) is recognised in the profit and loss account, there is a timing difference between the recognition of this cumulative charge and the related deduction for tax purposes that will be received in the future. This timing difference results in a deferred tax asset, which will be recognised if it meets FRS 19's criteria for recognition. On the basis of all available evidence it must be regarded as more likely than not that there will be suitable taxable profits against which the deferred tax asset can be utilised (see para 13.142 onwards), in order to meet these criteria.

13.127.3 It will also be necessary to consider whether the share options will be exercised and the implications of any changes in the market price. If the FRS 20 charge is revised as a result of a change in the number of options expected to vest, there will be a corresponding adjustment to the deferred tax asset. If it appears that the share options will not be exercised because they are out of the money, then it is likely that any deferred tax asset recognised should be written off. In addition, assuming the share options are likely to be exercised, if the option's intrinsic value falls below the option's fair value at the date of grant, then the carrying value of the deferred tax asset may not be recoverable and should be reviewed.

13.127.4 If the deduction for tax purposes that will be obtained (based on the share option's intrinsic value at the date of exercise) exceeds, or is expected to exceed, the total expected accounting charge based on the option's fair value at date of grant, the excess is regarded as a permanent difference under FRS 19 and is accounted for when it crystallises, that is, when the share options are exercised.

13.127.5 Both current and deferred tax should be recognised in the profit and loss account for the period, except to the extent that the tax is attributable to a gain or loss that is or has been recognised directly in the STRGL (in which case, the related tax is also recognised in the STRGL). [FRS 16 para 5; FRS 19 para 34]. If the tax deduction exceeds the cumulative amount of the FRS 20 charge, this indicates that the tax deduction relates not only to the FRS 20 charge recognised in the profit and loss account, but also to an equity item. However, as this excess amount is not recognised in the STRGL, the related tax is required to be included in the profit and loss account and so, under UK GAAP, the full amount of tax relating to the deduction is recognised in the profit and loss account.

13.127.6 The accounting for deferred tax on an equity-settled share-based award is illustrated in the following example.

Example

On 1 January 20X3, 100,000 options are issued with a fair value of £360,000. The vesting period is 3 years and all the share options are expected to be exercised. All of the share options are exercised in year 4. The tax rate is 30%. The intrinsic value of the share options (being market value of the underlying shares less exercise price) at the date of exercise in year 4 is £400,000.

The total staff cost recognised in each year of the three year period is £120,000 (£360,000/3), resulting in a deferred tax charge each year of £36,000 (£120,000 x 30%).

The actual current tax benefit obtained on exercise of the options in year 4 is £120,000 (30% of £400,000 intrinsic value at the date of exercise).

	Profit and loss account Dr (Cr)			Balance sheet Dr (Cr)	
Year	**Expense**	**Current tax**	**Deferred tax**	**Current tax**	**Deferred tax**
	£	**£**	**£**	**£**	**£**
1	120,000		(36,000)		36,000
2	120,000		(36,000)		72,000
3	120,000		(36,000)		108,000
	360,000		(108,000)		108,000
4	–	(120,000)	108,000	120,000	(108,000)
Total	360,000	(120,000)	–	120,000	–

The deferred tax asset of £108,000 (£36,000 x 3) at the end of year 3 is reversed through the profit and loss account in year 4, giving a net tax credit of £12,000 (120,000 – 108,000).

In years 1 to 3, since there is no current tax deduction in relation to the profit and loss account expense, this should be noted in the reconciliation of the current tax charge required by FRS 19.

In year 4, since there is no profit and loss account expense in relation to the current tax deduction of £120,000, the credit should be explained in the reconciliation of the current tax charge.

13.127.7 It should be noted that the accounting for deferred tax on equity-settled share-based payments under UK GAAP differs from the accounting under IFRS. Under IAS 12, a deductible temporary difference arises on the difference between the tax base of the employee services received to date (being the amount the tax authorities will permit as a deduction in future periods) and the carrying amount of nil in the balance sheet. As the future tax deduction depends on the share price at the date of exercise, the tax base of the employee services received is remeasured at the end of each period, with a resulting adjustment to the deferred tax asset. Therefore, the tax on the deduction relating to the excess over the IFRS 2 charge is recognised over the period to exercise under IFRS. In addition, a further difference is that the tax relating to this excess amount is recognised in equity, rather than the profit and loss account.

Cash-settled transactions

13.127.8 Cash-settled share based payment transactions, such as share appreciation rights issued to employees, give rise to a liability and not a credit to equity. The fair value of the liability is remeasured at each reporting date until the liability is settled. A timing difference arises on the cumulative difference between the share-based payment charge (remeasured to fair value) in the profit and loss account and the related deduction for tax purposes where that will be received in the future, resulting in a deferred tax asset (subject to FRS 19's recognition criteria). The tax effects of such transactions are recognised through the profit and loss account.

[The next paragraph is 13.128.]

Revaluation of non-monetary assets

General rule

13.128 Many companies revalue their non-monetary assets such as land and buildings. In the UK, revaluation of assets *per se* does not give rise to a timing difference, because taxable profits are not affected and no future tax liability arises as a result of the revaluation. However, to the extent that the valuation exceeds net book value, a potential timing difference arises, in that a balancing charge or tax on a chargeable gain may be payable if the asset is sold at its revalued amount.

13.128.1 Under FRS 19's incremental liability approach, an obligation for the deferred tax arises when the reporting entity enters into a binding sale agreement and not when the reporting entity decides, in principle, to sell the asset. An intention to sell, however compelling, is not sufficient for recognising deferred tax on a revaluation (under FRS 19). There must be a binding agreement that leaves the entity with no realistic chance of withdrawing from the sale and avoid paying tax. An asset that has been purchased with a view to resale such as stock does not create a binding sale agreement, even though the company in effect is committed to sell the stock. In other words, there must be an unconditional and irrevocable sales contract. Accordingly, FRS 19 requires that deferred tax should not be recognised on timing differences arising when non-monetary assets (other than those that are marked to market – see para 13.132 below) are revalued, unless, by the balance sheet date, the reporting entity has:

- entered into a binding agreement to sell the revalued assets; and
- recognised the gains and losses expected to arise on sale.

[FRS 19 para 14].

13.129 Where an unconditional and irrevocable contract has been entered into for the sale of a property before the year end, revenue and hence any profit arising on sale would also have been recognised at the time of exchange of contracts. It follows that any tax payable on the gain should similarly be recognised if the entity does not expect to claim rollover relief (see further para 13.137). Indeed, in practice, where an unconditional contract for the sale of a property has been exchanged before the year end but legal completion takes place after the year end, any tax payable on the gain would be provided as part of current tax, because under the tax rules a disposal for capital gains tax arises on the date when the contract is made. To the extent that the tax payable on the gain is not recognised as part of current tax, it should be recognised as part of deferred tax. On the other hand, if the contract is conditional, no profit on the sale and hence no tax payable would be recognised until all conditions have been satisfied.

13.130 It should be noted that to the extent that a revaluation gain that was previously recognised in the STRGL becomes realised as a result of the sale, any tax attributable to the gain should be charged to the STRGL as stated in paragraph 13.249 below.

Subsequent depreciation

13.130.1 When an asset has been revalued upwards, subsequent depreciation charges are based upon the revalued amount as opposed to original historical cost. Where there is no binding agreement to sell these revalued buildings no deferred tax is provided on the revaluation gains. However, a further question arises as to whether the deferred tax on the timing difference between capital allowances and accounting depreciation should be measured with reference to the historical cost depreciation or revalued depreciation.

13.130.2 Deferred tax should normally be provided on the difference between the capital allowances and the accounting depreciation charged to the profit and loss account. This is because a timing difference arises when tax deductions for the cost of a fixed asset are received before or after the cost of the fixed asset is recognised in the profit and loss account. In this case, however, the depreciation of the revaluation gain does not enter into the calculation of a timing difference, because there will never be a tax deduction for the revalued element of the building. The excess depreciation is an additional accounting cost and represents a permanent difference between the company's taxable and accounting profits. Consequently, deferred tax should be calculated using the 'historical' accounting depreciation, that is, in this case, the depreciation based on the building's original cost.

Subsequent devaluation and impairment

13.130.3 When a policy of revaluation is adopted, assets that have previously been subject to upward revaluation may subsequently be revalued downwards. If this devaluation takes the building below its original historical cost, management will need to judge whether this represents a clear consumption of economic benefit (an impairment) or whether the devaluation is temporary in nature. If there is a clear consumption of economic benefit an impairment loss will be recognised. FRS 19 does not appear to distinguish between revaluation gains and losses so it is not immediately clear how this impairment should be tax effected.

13.130.4 Paragraph 14 of FRS 19 applies equally to revaluation gains and losses. However, the standard does not define or clarify what it means by a 'revaluation'. We believe that the term revaluation should be interpreted in the normal way, that is, change in the carrying value of an asset as a result of value changes. Following the principles in FRS 11, 'Impairment of fixed assets and goodwill', and FRS 15, 'Tangible fixed assets', the tax effects of upward and downward changes in value that are reflected through the STRGL should not be tax effected, unless there is a binding agreement to sell the property and the gain or loss expected to arise on sale is recognised. All other changes in value (for example, impairments in the carrying value of assets that are dealt with through the profit and loss account) should be tax effected if the impairment represents a timing difference.

13.130.5 Where the revaluation loss is a clear consumption of economic benefits, it will be taken in full to the profit and loss account. The impairment will be treated as additional depreciation for accounting purposes, but the tax deductions will continue to be received on the cost of the building on a straight-line basis. Again it is necessary to go back to the principles set out above and to compare the extent to which the tax deductions on the cost of the building are received before or after the cost of the building is recognised in the profit and loss account. The amount of the impairment below depreciated historical cost will be treated as if it were depreciation on the historical cost; that is, it will reduce the difference between the tax written down value and the historical cost written down value and this will result in a partial reversal of deferred tax. To the extent that the reduction in value reverses a previous revaluation gain, this is a permanent difference, which is not tax effected.

Marked to market assets

13.131 In the past, companies sometimes adopted a policy of 'marking to market' current asset investments under which changes in fair values were reported in the profit and loss account, rather than in the revaluation reserve. Marking to market was adopted as a matter of course by certain financial institutions and companies in the securities industry even though there was no binding agreement to sell the investments. This accounting policy ('fair valuing through profit or loss') is now included in FRS 26, 'Financial instruments: Recognition and measurement', and is required for certain types of financial assets and permitted for others if specified conditions are met. In many circumstances, the gains and losses would be subject to current tax when they are recognised and no timing difference (and hence no deferred tax) would arise. The question arises as to what would be the appropriate accounting treatment in circumstances where the gains and losses are not taxed until realised at a later date.

13.132 FRS 19 states that deferred tax *should* be recognised on timing differences arising when an asset is continuously revalued to fair value with changes in fair value being recognised in the profit and loss account. [FRS 19 para 12].

13.133 The above requirement is an exception to the general rule discussed in paragraph 13.128 above that deferred tax should be provided only when there is a binding agreement to sell the asset. The exception was introduced to address the concerns that it was wrong not to provide deferred tax on assets that are marked to market. There is an implicit assumption in the accounting treatment that trading assets and investments that are marked to market with gains and losses recognised in the profit and loss account will be sold in the future. In other words, the commitment to dispose of the asset is implied. This made these assets different from assets that are used in the business. Consequently, it is inappropriate to fail to recognise any deferred tax on the contingent capital gains simply because no binding agreement has been made to sell the revalued assets. The alternative treatment, to provide no deferred tax, would produce an incorrect answer in practice with the gain reported in the profit and loss account in one period and the tax on the gain reported in a subsequent period.

13.134 The limited exception ensures sensible results in the present tax and financial reporting regimes for those companies that adopt a policy of fair valuing through profit or loss account, without significantly altering the basic approach of the standard. As a corollary, the above requirement does not apply to other current asset investments that are revalued under the alternative accounting rules with gains and losses arising from the valuation reported in the revaluation reserve. No deferred tax should be provided on them, unless they meet the criteria set out in paragraph 13.128 above.

13.135 The above requirement only applies when non-monetary assets are continuously fair valued with fluctuations being recognised in the profit and loss account. It would not apply, for instance, to situations where a one off downward revaluation of an asset, which is above historical cost but which is caused by a clear consumption of economic benefit, is recognised in the profit and loss account.

13.135.1 FRS 26 has also introduced the concept of available-for-sale (AFS) financial assets. The accounting for these assets is dealt with in chapter 6. It results in fluctuations in the fair value of such assets being recognised in reserves, through the STRGL (although interest, foreign exchange and impairment losses are still taken directly to the profit and loss account). Similarly to those assets where the accounting policy is 'fair value through profit or loss', in many circumstances the fair value movements on AFS assets will be taxed immediately, so no deferred tax will arise. Where the fair value movements are not taxed as they arise (for example, certain overseas financial instruments), FRS 19's rules for revaluations apply and no deferred tax should be provided, unless the conditions in FRS 19 are met (see para 13.128 onwards).

13.135.2 In the UK, the tax rules with regards to gains and losses on financial instruments are complex. Depending on the elections made under the 'Disregard regulations', fair value gains and losses may either be taxable as they accrue for accounting purposes or may be taxable when realisation occurs at a later date. Consultation with a tax specialist is recommended in this area.

Rollover and holdover reliefs

13.136 On the disposal of certain assets used for trading purposes, such as properties, it may be possible to defer immediate payment of the tax arising on the chargeable gain provided the proceeds of the sale are reinvested within certain time limits (at present, within three years on the sale of the original asset) in other qualifying assets. This relief, known as 'rollover relief', reduces the 'base cost' of the replacement asset by the chargeable gain 'rolled over' so that (subject to intervening period indexation) correspondingly higher tax may become payable when the replacement asset is sold. It is also possible to claim rollover relief on the gain arising on the sale of the replacement asset such that payment of the tax is further postponed. This situation can continue indefinitely.

13.137 FRS 19, therefore, states that deferred tax should not be recognised on timing differences arising when non-monetary assets (other than those referred to in para 13.132 above) are revalued or sold if, on the basis of all available evidence, it is more likely than not that the taxable gain will be rolled over, being charged to tax only if and when the assets into which the gain has been rolled over are sold. [FRS 19 para 15].

13.138 It is, therefore, important to take account of the possibility of obtaining rollover relief when assessing whether a tax liability will arise on the sale of an asset. This is because the relief has the effect of deferring the reversal of any timing differences arising on the revaluation of an asset beyond the sale date, or of creating a timing difference on the sale of an asset that has not been revalued, or a combination of the two. Consequently, where it is more likely than not that rollover relief will be claimed, then no deferred tax should be provided on the gain arising on disposal. However, there is a requirement in paragraph 13.286 to disclose the potential liability as rollover relief merely postpones, but does not extinguish the liability altogether. Even where an asset that has not been revalued is sold at a profit, there is no need to provide for the tax if the tax payable has been deferred by the operation of rollover relief, although again there is a need to disclose the potential liability.

13.139 Capital gains may also be 'held over' for a maximum of ten years with the result that tax payable on the gain is postponed for up to ten years. In that situation, as the tax is merely postponed and not permanently deferred, a timing difference arises and deferred tax on the gain should be provided in the normal way. Problems may arise, even in the tenth year, where under the tax rules the held-over gains are converted into rollover relief provided that qualifying assets are acquired in the 10-year hold over period. To the extent that the deferred tax liability remains unsettled, the company may need to review the position at each year end to determine whether any qualifying assets have been purchased against which the held-over gains can be rolled over. Where this is the case, any deferred tax previously recognised should be reversed by a credit to the profit and loss account.

13.140 Judgement is required to determine whether it is more likely than not that rollover relief would be available. However, no judgement is required and, therefore, no deferred tax would be provided if, in accordance with the tax rules, the company intends to roll the gain over onto a replacement asset that has been acquired or has entered into an unconditional contract to acquire the replacement asset within 12 months prior to the disposal of the existing asset. But judgement is required where the entity intends to invest the proceeds of sale in qualifying replacement assets within the period allowed under the tax rules, which is currently three years following sale. All available evidence, including the existence of approved budgets for capital expenditure, past pattern of claiming rollover relief, tax planning strategies and subsequent events should be considered to determine whether it is more likely than not that rollover relief would be claimed. If necessary, specialist tax advice should be sought to determine eligibility. If no deferred tax had been provided on sale and it subsequently transpires that no rollover relief would be claimed or that the terms of claiming the relief are unlikely to be met, any unprovided deferred tax should be provided immediately in the year as a change in estimate.

[The next paragraph is 13.142.]

Deferred tax assets

General rule

13.142 Timing differences may give rise to deferred tax assets. Common examples are tax losses carried forward and timing differences arising on provisions such as those made for refurbishment or those arising on pensions and retirement benefits where tax deductions are obtained only when the expenditure is actually incurred and not when the expense is recognised in the financial statements.

13.143 FRS 19 states that deferred tax assets should be recognised to the extent that they are regarded as recoverable. They should be regarded as recoverable to the extent that, on the basis of all available evidence, it can be regarded as more likely than not that there will be suitable taxable profits from which the future reversal of the underlying timing differences can be deducted. [FRS 19 para 23].

13.144 In order to recover a deferred tax asset, an entity would have to do more than simply *not make losses* in future: it would have to *make sufficient taxable profits*. Further, the need for prudence would suggest that more evidence of the likelihood of future profits was needed for recognition of a deferred tax asset than for recognition of a deferred tax liability. For these reasons, the FRS permits deferred tax assets to be recognised only when, on the basis of available evidence, it is more likely than not that there will be taxable profits in future against which the deferred tax asset can be offset. In other words, if it is more likely than not that either all or only a portion of the deferred tax asset will be recovered, a deferred tax asset should be recognised for the whole or the part that will be recovered.

13.145 The term 'more likely than not' is not defined in FRS 19, but paragraph 23 of FRS 12 suggests that it should be taken to mean that *"the probability that the event will occur is greater than the probability that it will not"*. In the US standard FAS 109, 'Income taxes', more likely than not is taken to mean a likelihood of more than 50 per cent. In IAS 12, a deferred tax asset is recognised if it is *probable* that the asset will be recovered. In IAS terminology, an event is regarded as probable if it is more likely than not to occur. Therefore, the more likely than not interpretation makes it clear that anything above 50 per cent qualifies for recognition.

13.146 However, paragraph 13.143 above also mentions that all available evidence has to be considered to justify recognition of deferred tax assets. This means both favourable and unfavourable evidence. If there is no unfavourable evidence, and the entity has historically been profitable and paid taxes, we believe FRS 19 permits an assumption that the situation will continue *in the absence of knowledge of facts to the contrary*. Reliance could be placed on expected future taxable profit in concluding that recording a deferred tax asset is appropriate. However, any unfavourable evidence must be considered carefully. Unfavourable evidence can usually be objectively verified, because it is a past event. However, estimates of future taxable profits can rarely be objectively verified; therefore, future taxable profits would be assigned lesser weight in assessing the appropriateness of recording a deferred tax asset when there is other unfavourable evidence.

Suitable taxable profits

13.147 As noted above, the future realisation of deferred tax assets ultimately depends on the expectation of sufficient taxable profit of the appropriate type (trading profit or capital gain). Sources of suitable taxable profit from which the future reversal of timing differences could be deducted are those that are:

- Generated in the same taxable entity (or in an entity whose taxable profits would be available for offset, for example under group relief rules) and assessed by the same taxation authority as the income or expenditure giving rise to the deferred tax asset.
- Generated in the same period as that in which the deferred tax asset is expected to reverse, or in a period to which a tax loss arising from the reversal of the deferred tax asset may be carried back or forward.
- Of a type (such as capital or trading) from which the taxation authority allows the reversal of the timing difference to be deducted.

[FRS 19 para 24].

13.148 In essence, the suitable taxable profits referred to above will be those against which the tax authority would permit the underlying timing difference in respect of the deferred tax asset to be offset.

Tax planning opportunities

13.149 The ASB acknowledges that entities sometimes take advantage of tax planning opportunities to reduce their future tax liabilities. FRS 19, therefore, permits an entity to create suitable taxable profits by undertaking tax planning opportunities. [FRS 19 para 25]. At first sight this may seem at odds with the general thrust of the standard that no account should be taken of future events. However, putting in place a tax scheme that may reduce future expenses or create additional income is, in substance, no different from procuring orders that will result in future sales. Both actions will create future taxable profits necessary for the recovery of the deferred tax asset.

13.150 A tax planning opportunity is an action that the entity would not normally take, but would do so to prevent, say, an unused tax loss from expiring. Such actions could include:

- Accelerating taxable amounts or deferring claims for writing down allowances to recover losses being carried forward (perhaps before they expire).
- Changing the character of taxable or deductible amounts from trading gains or losses to capital gains or losses or *vice versa*.
- Switching from tax-free to taxable investments.

[FRS 19 para 25].

13.151 Tax planning strategies should only be considered in determining the extent to which a deferred tax asset will be realised. They cannot be used to avoid recognition of, or reduce, a deferred tax liability (see para 13.154). The prudence and feasibility of the strategy would have to be assessed based on the individual facts and circumstances of each case. Whatever tax planning opportunities are considered, management must be capable of undertaking them and must have the ability to implement them.

13.152 A company may incur various expenses as a result of implementing a tax planning opportunity. A question arises as to whether the tax benefit of the expenses could be included in the carrying amount of any deferred tax asset recognised as a result of the plan's implementation, or included in current tax expense. We believe that any deferred tax asset recognised as a result of implementing a tax planning opportunity should be recorded net of the tax effects of any expenses or losses expected to be incurred as a result of the strategy, because that is the net amount by which future tax payments will be reduced as a result of implementing it. Consider the following example.

Example

A company has gross timing differences of £1,000 in respect of a deferred tax asset which is not recognised in the balance sheet. The tax rate is 30% and the unrecognised deferred tax asset is, therefore, £300. As a result of implementing a tax planning strategy, the company expects to generate taxable profits of at least £1,000. However, the cost of implementing the strategy is expected to be £200. Therefore, only £800 of future taxable profits would be available against which the deferred tax asset can be offset. A maximum deferred tax asset of £240 (£800 @ 30%) would qualify for recognition. The remaining £60 will remain unrecognised. In other words, the deferred tax asset of £300 is reduced by £60, being the tax benefit of the expenses expected to be incurred as a result of implementing the tax planning strategy.

13.153 Similarly, where a tax planning opportunity is being used to support realisation of unused tax losses in a business combination that is an acquisition, the same principles apply, that is the benefit of any deferred tax asset recognised should also be reduced by the tax effects of any expenses or losses incurred to implement a tax planning opportunity.

13.154 Tax planning strategies should never be used to reduce a deferred tax liability. For instance, a company cannot avoid recognising an existing deferred tax liability on the grounds that future tax losses will prevent the transfer of economic benefits.

13.155 Two examples of possible tax planning opportunities are considered below:

Example 1 – Sale of appreciated assets when operating losses are projected

A company has experienced a history of operating losses over the last five years with accumulated tax losses of £20m giving rise to a potential unrecognised deferred tax asset of £6m. Based on the introduction of a new product line, the company is currently projecting that for the next three years it will experience losses of approximately £5m in aggregate before it 'turns the corner' and becomes profitable. Due to appreciation in the real estate market, the company's investment in a shopping mall property is now valued at approximately £500,000 more than the carrying amount in the balance sheet. The company proposes to recognise a deferred tax asset of £150,000 (£500,000 × 30%) based on a tax planning opportunity to sell the investment. The shopping mall is not a 'core' asset of the entity, and management asserts that it would sell the shopping mall property, if necessary, before it would permit the unused tax losses to expire.

We believe that there is no case for recognising a deferred tax asset because of the above tax planning opportunity. A tax planning opportunity to sell appreciated assets constitutes a subset of the broader source of future taxable profit from operations. Thus, it would not be appropriate to recognise a deferred tax asset when it appears that the tax planning opportunity will merely reduce an expected future loss. In the above case, based on (1) the entity's history of losses, (2) an unproved new product line, and (3) the fact that the entity does not anticipate being profitable for at least three years, little weight can be assigned to the projection of profitability. Accordingly, there is no *incremental* tax benefit (at least for the foreseeable future), as the potential gain on the sale of the shopping mall property would only reduce what would otherwise be a larger operating loss.

Example 2 – Acquisition of a profitable company

A company that has incurred losses for many years proposes a tax planning opportunity to support its deferred tax asset related to unused tax losses. The company will use a portion of the cash balances it received from a recent public share offering to acquire a company that generates significant taxable profits. Could such a tax planning opportunity be considered for the recognition of the deferred tax asset?

No. We believe that a proposed business combination and, hence the availability of sufficient taxable profits, should not be anticipated for purposes of supporting a deferred tax asset. Until the acquisition of the company is irrevocable and there are no further statutory or regulatory impediments, the acquirer requires the co-operation of others to make the tax planning opportunity effective. That is, the acquirer does not control an essential part of the tax planning opportunity (the target company). Consequently, the tax effects of such an event (for example, the acquisition of a company) should not be recognised before the event has occurred. However, once the acquisition has taken place, the acquirer can recognise a deferred tax asset as a credit to the tax charge in the post-acquisition period in accordance with paragraph 22 of FRS 7 (as amended by paragraph 71 of FRS 19).

Example 3 – Unused tax losses in an acquiree

Company B has unrecognised deferred tax assets related to unused tax losses. Company C bought company B in December 20X3.

Company C's management intends to integrate company B's operations into company C in the first quarter of 20X4 in order to take advantage of the tax losses. Company C has a track record of generating taxable profits and management expects this to continue for the foreseeable future.

In this situation, management should recognise a deferred tax asset in the consolidated financial statements in respect of the unused tax losses, provided that it is probable that management will carry out the integration and it is probable that company C will generate enough taxable profit to absorb company B's unused tax losses. This will impact the goodwill calculation in the consolidated financial statements.

This contrasts with the situation in example 2 above as both the newly-acquired entity holding the losses (company B) and the profitable entity (company C) are part of the same group at the balance sheet date.

Example 4 – Strategy to implement an exit plan

A company has a history of recent losses. Management has developed an exit plan in which a loss-making activity will be discontinued. Management intends to implement the measures from March 20X4. The current date is January 20X4 and the plan has not yet been made public.

Management expects to reverse the losses over the two years following the implementation of the exit plan and proposes that a deferred tax asset in respect of the losses is recognised in the 31 December 20X3 financial statements, using the exit plan to justify the recognition of the deferred tax asset.

A deferred tax asset should be recognised in respect of the losses to the extent that it is probable that future taxable profit will be available against which the unused tax losses can be utilised.

The assessment of whether future taxable profits are probable should be undertaken based on circumstances as at the balance sheet date.

Consideration should be given to the following factors as at the balance sheet date:

- the probability that management will implement the plan;
- management's ability to implement the plan (for example, obtaining concessions from labour unions or regulatory approval); and
- the level of detailed analysis and sensitivity analysis that management has prepared.

Judgment will be required to establish whether it is probable that the exit plan will go ahead and that taxable profits will be earned. If, at the balance sheet date, management has not yet finalised its decision to sell, it may be difficult to argue that it is more likely than not that the exit plan will be implemented.

In contrast to example 2, in this case, the subsidiary that management plan to dispose of is part of the group that holds the losses at the balance sheet date. As such, we consider that tax planning opportunities in relation to that subsidiary may be taken in account when assessing the recoverability of deferred tax assets.

Recovery of deferred tax assets against deferred tax liabilities

13.156 It can be assumed that the future reversal of any timing differences relating to deferred tax liabilities recognised at the balance sheet date will give rise to taxable profits. To the extent that those profits will be suitable for the deduction of the reversing deferred tax asset, the asset can always be regarded as recoverable. [FRS 19 para 26]. Therefore, where deferred tax liabilities exceed deferred tax assets and the reversal periods are consistent, recognition of the entire deferred tax asset is justified. The recoverability assessment becomes problematic, however, where there are insufficient deferred tax liabilities against which the deferred tax asset can be offset. In that situation, it is necessary to consider the likelihood of there being other suitable taxable profits as indicated in the following example.

Example

A company has timing differences of £80,000 in respect of deferred tax liabilities that are expected to be included in taxable income at a rate of £20,000 a year in years one through four. The company also has a warranty provision of £40,000 that is expected to be deductible for tax purposes as follows: £30,000 and £10,000 in years two and three respectively. In addition to warranty provisions, the company has unused tax losses of £60,000. A schedule of the reversal of timing differences and the utilisation of tax losses carried forward is shown below:

	Year 1	Year 2	Year 3	Year 4
	£	£	£	£
Timing differences — deferred tax liabilities				
Opening balance	80,000	60,000	40,000	20,000
Recognised in taxable income	(20,000)	(20,000)	(20,000)	(20,000)
Closing balance	60,000	40,000	20,000	–
Timing differences — deferred tax assets				
Warranty provisions				
Opening balance	40,000	40,000	10,000	–
Deducted for tax purposes	–	(30,000)	(10,000)	–
Closing balance	40,000	10,000	-	-
Tax losses				
Opening balance	60,000	40,000	50,000	40,000
Increase (utilisation) in year	(20,000)	10,000	(10,000)	(20,000)
Closing balance	40,000	50,000	40,000	20,000
Total timing differences — deferred tax assets	80,000	60,000	40,000	20,000

At the end of year 1, the company would recognise a deferred tax asset in respect of at least £60,000 of timing differences at the appropriate tax rate. This is because there are timing differences in respect of deferred tax liabilities of the same amount that are expected to be included in taxable income and against which the expected reversal of the timing differences in respect of deferred tax assets can be utilised.

For similar reasons, a deferred tax asset in respect of at least £40,000 and £20,000 of timing differences would be recognised at the end of years 2 and 3 respectively, if circumstances remained the same at those dates.

However, in order to recognise a deferred tax asset in any of the years 1 to 4 with respect to the £20,000 of tax losses that remain unutilised, the company may have to look for other sources of taxable profit, other than reversals of timing differences, as indicated below.

Recovery of deferred tax assets against future taxable profits

13.157 As illustrated in the example in paragraph 13.156, to the extent that the deferred tax asset cannot be recovered against the reversal of deferred tax liabilities, it is necessary to consider other persuasive and reliable evidence suggesting that suitable taxable profits will be generated in future. This consideration becomes difficult where the deferred tax asset arises from unrelieved trading losses, because the very existence of such losses may indicate significant uncertainty about the availability of future taxable profit. It is because of this uncertainty that the standard calls for the disclosure of the amount of deferred tax asset and the nature of the evidence supporting its recognition in the absence of profits arising from the reversals of existing timing differences (see para 13.272 below).

13.157.1 When projecting future taxable profits, the question is raised as to whether such profits should be calculated after adjusting for depreciation and the deduction of capital allowances arising on new acquisitions of fixed assets in the future periods. The accounting profits of future periods should not take into account any timing differences originating on new fixed assets. Therefore, taxable profits in future periods that will be available for absorbing deferred tax assets would include reversing/originating capital allowances on assets existing at the current balance sheet date, accounting profits adjusted for permanent differences and any expected tax planning opportunities that have been formulated at the current balance sheet date and which will generate taxable profits in the following period.

Trading losses

13.158 Where a company incurs a trading loss for tax purposes, that loss, which is determined after the deduction of any capital allowances given in that trade, may be set off against other profits (including chargeable gains) made in the same accounting period. To the extent that it cannot be used against the current period's profits, it can be carried back against profits of the preceding year. Any trading losses of a company that are not relieved by offset against current profits or profits of the previous period can be carried forward to be set off against the first available profits of the same trade for subsequent accounting periods.

13.159 Therefore, where a company has tax losses that can be relieved against a tax liability for a previous year, it is appropriate to recognise those losses as an asset, because the tax relief is recoverable by refund of tax previously paid. This asset can be shown either separately in the financial statements as a debtor, or offset against an existing deferred tax balance.

13.160 Where tax losses can be relieved only by carry-forward against taxable profits of future periods, a timing difference arises. [FRS 19 para 2]. If the company is maintaining a deferred tax account that will result in future tax payable, then the tax losses will be recoverable by offset against taxable income that arises when those timing differences will reverse. Accordingly, losses carried forward can be set off against deferred tax liabilities carried in the balance sheet.

13.161 To the extent that the deferred tax liabilities are not sufficient to absorb all the tax losses, it is necessary to consider other 'persuasive and reliable evidence' suggesting that suitable taxable profits will be generated in future. [FRS 19 para 29]. In the case of unrelieved trading losses, such evidence may exist if both of the following conditions are satisfied:

- The loss resulted from an identifiable and non-recurring cause.
- The reporting entity has been consistently profitable over a long period, with any past losses being more than offset by income in later periods.

[FRS 19 para 30].

13.162 A strong earnings history will provide the most objective evidence in assuming future profitability when assessing the extent to which a deferred tax asset can be recognised. This justification becomes stronger if the tax loss arises from identifiable causes that are unlikely to recur as stated above. Hence, there would be less need for profitable companies to consider the pattern and timing of the reversals of existing timing differences.

13.163 The very existence of losses will often provide strong evidence that they may not be recovered. The ASB's reasons for setting a 'more likely than not' threshold for the recognition of all deferred tax assets are set out in Appendix V, paragraphs 78 and 79 of FRS 19.

13.164 For companies with no record of profit in recent years a more rigorous assessment is required of the probability that taxable profit will be available against which unrelieved tax losses can be utilised. If it is expected that it will take some time for tax losses to be relieved, the recoverability of the resulting deferred tax asset is likely to be relatively uncertain. In such circumstances, it may not be appropriate to recognise the deferred tax asset at all. [FRS 19 para 32].

Capital losses

13.165 Whereas trading losses can be offset against chargeable gains, capital losses cannot be offset against trading profits. Where a company makes capital losses in an accounting period, those losses can generally be set off only against chargeable gains which it makes in the same period. If those capital losses are greater than the chargeable gains, they may be set off against gains of a later accounting period.

13.166 A capital loss that is available to relieve against chargeable gains creates a timing difference. However, as a deferred tax asset in respect of a capital loss cannot be offset against deferred tax liabilities arising from trading items, because of the offset rules in tax legislation, a deferred tax asset in respect of a capital loss will be recognised only if there is strong evidence that it will be recoverable against any available chargeable gains. Such evidence will exist only if:

- A potential chargeable gain not expected to be covered by rollover relief is present in assets, but has not been recognised as a deferred tax liability.
- Plans are in place for the sale of these assets.
- The carried-forward loss will be offset against the resulting chargeable gain for tax purposes.

[FRS 19 para 31].

In the context of the second point above, it is not necessary to have a binding sale agreement, only adequate evidence that it is more likely than not that a sale will take place.

Effect of a going concern uncertainty

13.167 FRS 18, 'Accounting policies', paragraph 61, requires disclosure when management concludes that uncertainty exists regarding an entity's ability to continue as a going concern for a reasonable period of time (usually understood to be at least one year from the date of approval of the financial statements). The inclusion of such disclosure would, in almost all situations, constitute significant unfavourable evidence under FRS 19 and recognition of all or a portion of a deferred tax asset would not be justified, unless realisation is assured by either (a) carry-back to prior tax years or (b) reversals of existing timing differences. However, the absence of such disclosure does not, by itself, constitute favourable evidence about the realisation of deferred tax assets.

13.168 In addition to going-concern considerations, there are certain entities that, by their nature, would not ordinarily recognise deferred tax assets not supported through either carry-back or reversals of existing timing differences. Examples of such entities include development stage enterprises, start-up businesses and entities emerging from a financial reorganisation or bankruptcy.

Reassessment of recoverability

13.169 The carrying amount of a deferred tax asset should be reviewed at each balance sheet date. This means that an entity would need to assess whether a net deferred tax asset recognised in the balance sheet is still recoverable and has not been impaired. For example, an entity may have recognised a deferred tax asset in respect of tax losses in a previous period based on information then available. A year later circumstances may have changed such that it is no longer probable that the entity would earn sufficient future taxable profits to absorb all the tax benefit. In that situation, the asset has suffered an impairment and should be written down. If circumstances giving rise to the previous write down no longer apply or it is probable that sufficient future taxable profit will be available, the reduction should be reversed.

13.170 Similarly, where an entity has been unable to recognise a deferred tax asset because of the unavailability of sufficient taxable profit, it should review the situation at each subsequent balance sheet date to ascertain whether some or all of the unrecognised balance should now be recognised. For example, an improvement in trading conditions or the acquisition of a new subsidiary might make it more likely that a previously unrecognised tax loss in the acquiring entity will be recovered. The recognition of a previously unrecognised deferred tax asset is a change in estimate that should be reflected in the results for the year as required by FRS 3, 'Reporting financial performance'. [FRS 19 para 33]. See further paragraph 13.252.1 onwards below.

Measurement issues

Introduction

13.171 FRS 19 requires deferred tax to be measured at the average tax rates that are expected to apply in the periods in which the timing differences are expected to reverse, based on tax rates and laws that have been enacted or substantively enacted by the balance sheet date. [FRS 19 para 37].

13.172 Timing differences may reverse over many years and, since the rate of tax will not normally be known in advance of those years, FRS 19 requires the use of a rate that has been enacted or substantively enacted by the balance sheet date. Enacted means that the rate is part of tax law. The meaning of substantively enacted is considered in paragraph 13.45 above.

Average rates

13.173 It will normally be necessary to calculate an average tax rate only if the enacted or substantively enacted tax rates are graduated, that is, if different rates apply to different levels of taxable income. [FRS 19 para 38]. For instance, if the first five million of profit is taxed at the rate of 20 per cent and profit thereafter at 30 per cent, an average tax rate is used for measuring deferred tax liabilities and assets. This average rate is the rate that is expected to apply to taxable profit (or loss) in the years in which the liability or the asset is expected to be settled or recovered. To calculate the average tax rate it is necessary to estimate the levels of profits expected in the periods in which the timing differences reverse. [FRS 19 para 38]. In the above example, the estimated average rate will need to be calculated where the entity expects to earn annual taxable profit in excess of five million in the future. In order to determine a single average rate, which would be greater than 20 per cent but less than 30 per cent, it would be necessary to estimate future annual taxable profits, including reversing timing differences. Although a detailed analysis to determine the net reversals of timing differences in respect of deferred tax assets and liabilities is usually not warranted, consideration should be given to the effect of an abnormal level of taxable profit or any abnormally large timing difference that may reverse in a single future year and cause the average rate to be distorted.

13.174 The above situation may well arise in the UK for companies whose profits fall within the 'marginal bands' above the small companies rate. For periods ending prior to 1 April 2008, profits up to £300,000 are taxed at the small companies rate of 19 per cent. Profits in excess of £1,500,000 are taxed at the normal corporation tax rate of 30 per cent. As a result of marginal relief, profits falling between £300,000 and £1,500,000 are taxed at an effective rate of 32.75 per cent (to claw back the benefit of the small companies' rate by the time the upper profits limit is reached). Therefore, these companies should generally provide deferred tax at the rate used in the past on the assumption that profits would continue at a comparable level. Where future profits are expected to be higher and there is reliable evidence to support this level of profit, it may be appropriate to use the rate applicable to that rate of profit. Where it is impossible to determine whether marginal relief will apply, it would be prudent to measure deferred tax at the standard corporation tax rate. For periods ending after 1 April 2008, the changes to the UK tax rates as introduced by the Finance Act 2007 will apply (see further detail in para 13.48 above).

13.175 The requirement to calculate an average tax rate is not intended to lead to averaging of different rates expected to apply to different types of taxable profit or in different tax jurisdictions. If different rates of tax apply to different types of taxable profits (for example, trading profits and capital gains), the rate used will reflect the nature of the timing difference. The rates used for measuring deferred tax arising in a specific tax jurisdiction will be the rates expected to apply in that jurisdiction. [FRS 19 para 39].

Change in tax rates

13.175.1 The tax rate applicable to an entity may change as a result of changes in relevant legislation. The impact of such changes in tax rate will vary depending on the nature and timing of the legislative changes made. Any impact of the changes will be recognised in accounting periods ending on or after the date of substantive enactment (and may be disclosable prior to that date). In many cases, changes in tax rates will be prospective and thus there will be no impact on current tax assets and liabilities that have arisen prior to the effective date of the change. However, deferred tax balances are likely to be affected. Professional advice from tax advisors on how the changes impact on the company's tax position is likely to be necessary.

Example

As noted in paragraph 13.48 above, the Chancellor of the Exchequer announced various changes to UK tax legislation in the 2007 budget. Included in this budget were provisions to reduce the standard rate of UK corporation tax from 30 per cent to 28 per cent with effect from 1 April 2008. This change became substantively enacted upon the third reading and approval of the Finance Bill 2007, which took place in the House of Commons on 26 June 2007.

The change of tax rates will have no impact on current tax assets or liabilities arising prior to the effective date of the change. However, the measurement of deferred tax assets and liabilities will be impacted for accounting periods (including interim periods) ending on or after 26 June 2007.

Deferred tax balances will need to be analysed to determine when they are expected to reverse and the tax rate that will be applicable in the period of reversal. The reduction in tax rate will not impact on deferred tax that is expected to reverse prior to 1 April 2008. However, it will impact on subsequent reversals and will be further complicated for companies with a financial year that straddles 1 April 2008 as, in that situation, the company will need to compute an effective tax rate for reversals in the financial year in which the change takes effect.

In accounting for the impact of this reduction in tax rate, it will be necessary to consider whether the impact will be reflected through the profit and loss account or the STRGL (see further para 13.249 below).

For accounting periods ending prior to 26 June 2007, the change in tax rate would be disclosable as a non-adjusting post-balance sheet event in accordance with paragraph 22(h) of FRS 21, 'Events after the balance sheet date', to the extent that the impact is material.

Discounting

Introduction

13.176 Perhaps the most significant aspect of FRS 19 is the option for entities to adopt a policy of discounting deferred tax balances. FRS 19 states that reporting entities are permitted but not required to discount deferred tax assets and liabilities to reflect the time value of money. [FRS 19 para 42].

13.177 Discounting is also not permitted by any other major standard setters and specifically prohibited in IAS 12.

13.178 The arguments for and against discounting and the reasons why discounting has been made optional are set out in great detail from paragraph 85 in Appendix V of FRS 19. However, on closer inspection, the discounting methodology set out in the standard may not be so simple in its effect. It could give rise to practical difficulties that make the discounted liability a more subjective figure.

13.179 Where it is necessary to choose between accounting policies, an entity should select whichever of those accounting policies is judged by the entity to be most appropriate to its particular circumstances for the purposes of giving a true and fair view. [FRS 18 para 17]. The FRS, therefore, provides the following list of factors that are likely to be especially relevant to the selection process:

- How material the impact of discounting would tend to be to the overall results and position reported in the entity's financial statements.
- Whether the benefits of discounting to users would outweigh the costs of collating the necessary information and performing discounting calculations.
- Whether there is an established industry practice, adherence to which would enhance comparability.

[FRS 19 para 43].

13.180 In practice, however, the effect of discounting accelerated capital allowances (arguably the most complex discounting calculation) is most likely to be material where:

- The reporting entity invests heavily in long-life fixed assets that are eligible for capital allowances early in their lives (for example, assets located in certain enterprise zones that qualify for 100 per cent first year allowances).
- The prevailing interest rate is high.
- The effect of discounting has been material to the financial statements as a whole in previous periods.

An example of a company that has considered the likely impact of discounting deferred tax liabilities in respect of accelerated capital allowances is given in the Table 13.2 below.

Table 13.2 – Severn Trent plc – Annual Report & Accounts – 31 March 2001

Notes to the financial statements (extract)

17 Provisions for liabilities and charges (extract)

The accounting standard FRS 19, requiring full provision for deferred tax, will be adopted by the group in the year ended 31 March 2002. It is intended that, where material, the group will adopt a policy of discounting. If FRS 19 had been adopted for the year ended 31 March 2001, the tax charge would have been increased by £52.6 million, and a deferred tax liability of £324.1 million would have been reflected in the balance sheet as follows:

	2001
	£m
Origination and reversal of timing differences	65.1
Increase in discount	(12.5)
Total deferred tax charge	52.6

The provision for deferred tax would be disclosed as follows:

	2001	2000
	£m	£m
Accelerated capital allowances	750.0	685.3
Tax losses/other reliefs carried forward	(50.5)	(56.2)
Undiscounted provision for deferred tax	699.5	629.1
Discount	(375.4)	(362.9)
Discounted provision for deferred tax	324.1	266.2
Provision at start of period	266.2	
Deferred tax charge for period (above)	52.6	
Movements arising on acquisition of businesses	5.3	
Provision at end of period	324.1	

* *Note that, for years beginning on or after 1 January 2005, SI 2004/2947, 'The Companies Act 1985 (International Accounting Standards and Other Amendments) Regulations 2004', renamed the statutory line item, 'provisions for liabilities'.*

13.181 All the above factors mentioned in paragraph 13.179 above and the way they interact with each other would need to be considered. It is impossible to single out one variable that would be significant enough to merit performing discounting calculations. Therefore, notwithstanding this guidance, the choice of whether to discount or not is unlikely to be an easy one. In practice, companies may well need to perform the calculations and consider the results before deciding whether to adopt a policy of discounting.

13.182 It should be noted that discounting would have the effect of making the effective tax rate (total tax charge as a percentage of profit before tax) volatile. This is because, as explained in paragraph 90 of Appendix V of FRS 19, under discounting, the benefit of receiving capital allowances on the acquisition of an asset will give rise to an instant credit in the profit and loss account. Undiscounted full provision, on the other hand, would produce a constant effective tax rate if permanent differences were ignored. Therefore, it would be necessary to carry out the trial calculation over a period and not just at a point in time to consider the implications that discounting would have on the stability of the effective tax rates. It may well be that most companies conclude that the complexity of the calculation, the cost involved and the volatile result outweigh the benefit of recording a lower liability.

13.183 Where a reporting entity adopts a policy of discounting, FRS 19 requires that all deferred tax (and recoverable advance corporation tax) balances that have been measured by reference to undiscounted cash flows and for which the impact of discounting is material should be discounted. [FRS 19 para 44].

13.184 Discounting deferred tax assets and liabilities is only valid if the timing differences underlying those assets and liabilities give rise to future cash flows that are not already measured at their present value. This would apply, for example, to deferred tax arising on assets that are continuously marked to market and accelerated capital allowances. For some items, it would not be appropriate to discount the tax effects of the underlying timing differences that are already stated at their present values. Typical examples are long-term provisions measured on a discounted basis under FRS 12 and pension accruals.

Mechanics of the discounting calculation

13.185 In order to perform the discounting calculation, it is first necessary to schedule out or forecast the timing of the future tax cash flows that the deferred tax represents. For some items in the financial statements (for example, finance lease obligations) the dates and amounts of cash flows are known in advance. Where deferred tax is concerned, however, there is no equivalent pre-determined payment schedule and, therefore, it is necessary to determine what in principle are the future cash flows to which discounting should be applied.

13.186 Two approaches were considered by the ASB as noted in paragraph 106 of Appendix V of FRS 19. These are:

- *The full reversal method* under which the future cash flows are treated as occurring when the timing differences constituting the deferred tax balance at the year end are expected to reverse. In other words, as every individual reversing timing difference has the effect of increasing or decreasing the amount of tax cash flow in the year of reversal, the reversals of all timing differences at the balance sheet date are scheduled on a year-by-year basis. The tax effects on those reversals are calculated and discounted.

- *The net reversal method* under which the future cash flows are treated as occurring when the timing differences as a whole (that is, after taking account of new timing differences to replace those that reverse) are expected to reduce. In other words, the estimated payments of deferred tax (after taking account of the tax effects of likely future transactions) are discounted based on their expected year of payment.

13.187 The full reversal approach is appropriate to deferred tax calculated on a full provision basis as it does not take into account the tax effects of future transactions. It is, therefore, the approach adopted under the standard. The net reversal approach is rejected on the grounds that it can only be justified within a partial provision framework (see paras 107 and 108 in App V of FRS 19 for a fuller explanation).

Example

The company has estimated the following tax losses and profits:

Year 0	Year 1	Year 2	Year 3
(100)	(100)	100	100

The company is satisfied that it is 'more likely than not' that there will be suitable taxable profits. The losses are due to an identifiable and non-recurring cause and the reporting entity has otherwise been consistently profitable over a long period, with any past losses being more than offset by income in later periods. A deferred tax asset is, therefore, being recognised in year 0. Is the discount period for the asset to year 2 or to year 3?

Paragraph 47 of FRS 19 says that in scheduling the reversal of the timing differences no account should be taken of future tax losses, that is a full reversal rather than a net reversal basis should be used. Therefore, the tax losses in year 1 should be ignored and the reversal of the losses in year 0 should be taken to occur in year 2 from which date the asset should be discounted. This is also true of the asset to be recognised at the end of year 1, being discounted to year 3.

13.188 Once the cash flows have been scheduled out, the discounted amount is then calculated by applying an appropriate discount rate to the undiscounted cash flows. FRS 19 provides detailed guidance as to how the discounting calculations should be performed.

Scheduling the cash flows to be discounted

13.189 In scheduling the cash flows to be discounted, the following factors should be considered:

- The discount period(s) should be the number of years between the balance sheet date and the date(s) on which it is estimated that the underlying timing differences will reverse. [FRS 19 para 47].

  In practice, a round number of years should be used rather than the date on which the implicit tax cash flows occur, which under the quarterly payments system will be in months 7,10,13 and 16 following the start of the accounting periods. The assumption that timing differences would reverse at the end of each period is generally consistent with normal discounting calculation and is unlikely to introduce any material difference in the calculation.

- Assumptions made when estimating the date(s) of reversal should be consistent with those made elsewhere in the financial statements. [FRS 19 para 47].

  Certain assumptions would have to be made when scheduling the reversals of the timing differences. For instance, the assumptions about future depreciation charges and residual values should be consistent with those used to account for the related fixed asset. Again, this is a simplification because in practice, residual values used in estimating depreciation rates are based on prices prevailing at the date of purchase (or revaluation) and these are unlikely to be the same as sales proceeds that may crystallise a balancing charge/allowance or reduce the capital allowance pool on which future capital allowances are received.

- The scheduling of the reversal(s) should take into account the remaining tax effects of transactions that have already been reflected in the financial statements. However, no account should be taken either of other timing differences expected to arise on future transactions or of future tax losses. [FRS 19 para 47].

  The requirement to schedule the reversals by taking account of the 'remaining tax effects' of transactions is crucial to the discounting calculation. The implication is that both reversing timing differences that have arisen at the balance sheet date and further originating timing differences that will arise in the future in respect of past transactions would have to be included in the scheduling. In the context of accelerated capital allowances, this means taking account of the remaining capital allowances to be received on assets 'held at the balance sheet date' on which timing differences have arisen, but without taking into consideration timing differences that might arise from future capital expenditure that is only appropriate under a partial provision model.

  It was suggested that the remaining capital allowances should be ignored on the grounds that they were future events that created further timing differences (rather than delaying the reversal of the existing timing differences). The existing timing differences would be viewed as reversing as soon as further depreciation occurred. However, the Board did not view the remaining capital allowances as arising from future events. Rather it regarded the allowances, like depreciation, as one of the expected consequences of a past event (the purchase of an asset) that had to be taken into account in measuring the tax liability arising from that event [FRS 19 App V para 109].

> The reversal of timing differences may occur in periods in which it is also expected that the entity will make tax losses. Any tax payments arising on the reversal of timing differences will, therefore, be postponed until the tax losses themselves are relieved. Since it would be difficult to forecast patterns of future losses reliably, especially those expected to arise in later years, (that is, those for which discounting would be most relevant), the scheduling of reversals should be carried out without taking account of the incidence of future tax losses. [FRS 19 para 49].

13.190 FRS 19 indicates that if a policy of discounting is chosen, all deferred tax balances that have been measured by reference to undiscounted cash flows and for which the impact of discounting is material, should be discounted. If a company has a very large fixed assets base, the question arises as to whether it is acceptable to group like assets together, and discount the deferred tax relating to the groups rather than to individual assets. Paragraph 48 of FRS 19 states (in relation to future depreciation charges and residual values of fixed assets) that *"it may be possible to use approximations or averages to simplify the calculations without introducing material errors"*. In addition, the example in Appendix 1 of FRS 19, which deals with discounting, uses an example that relates to a pool of plant and machinery. This implies that the FRS permits grouping of assets and use of approximations and averages where this does not produce material error. Clearly the selection of groups needs to avoid introducing material error into the calculations, but it would appear to be permitted by the standard.

Scheduling timing differences in respect of marked to market assets

13.191 The present value of any additional tax payable on the sale of an asset that is continuously revalued to fair values (through the profit and loss account) would depend on the timing of the tax cash flow. Since it would not be possible for an entity to identify when that tax would be payable, estimates would have to be made. It would be necessary for the company to examine the past pattern of sales, average portfolio churn etc to determine a reasonable estimate. [FRS 19 para 51]. It may be that in practice the portfolio is churned over a fairly short period, in which case the impact of discounting may not be material.

Discount rates

13.192 In determining a suitable discount rate, FRS 19 states that the discount rates should be the post-tax yields to maturity that could be obtained at the balance sheet date on government bonds with maturity dates and in currencies similar to those of the deferred tax assets or liabilities. [FRS 19 para 52]. (See further FRS 19 App V paras 113–119.)

13.193 Yields to maturity (redemption yields) of UK gilts are published daily. They are categorised under shorts (lives up to five years), five to ten years, ten to fifteen years and over fifteen years. The redemption yields quoted are gross redemption yields and, therefore, it would necessary to obtain the post-tax yield (quoted yield less tax at the enacted or substantially enacted rate) for discounting purposes. [FRS 19 para 53].

13.194 It should be possible to obtain a gilt yield with the same maturity as the period over which the underlying timing differences reverse. For instance, if the timing differences reverse before the earliest period for which a quote is available, it would be acceptable to use the earliest quoted rate. Where quoted yields are not available for particular maturity periods, it should be possible to derive an estimated rate by simple linear interpolation without introducing any significant error in the calculation. Where the rest of the discounting period is large, it would be acceptable to group the periods into short-term, medium-term and long-term and use a single discount rate for each period without introducing material differences in the discounting calculation. In the case of very long-lived assets (for example, infrastructure assets with lives of over 30 years), there may not be any UK gilt with maturity dates that correspond with the period over which the timing differences reverse. In that situation, the redemption yield for gilts with the longest maturity date available (likely to be 30 years) should be used. In other words, all timing differences reversing in years 30 onwards are treated as reversing in year 30. This is because the effect of estimating a rate for reversals beyond 30 years is unlikely to be material to the overall calculation.

13.195 For multinational groups adopting a policy of discounting, it would be necessary to match the discount rate with the maturity date and currency of the deferred tax asset or liability arising in each different tax jurisdiction. Therefore, the government bond rates should be those of the countries in which the timing difference arises. Bond yields of varying maturities for major economies are also found in the World bond prices section of the FT. In practice, for consolidation purposes, the group reporting packs would probably require foreign subsidiaries to provide data on their local government bond yield rates for various maturity dates for the discounting calculation to be performed at the group level.

Worked examples

13.196 The following examples illustrate the principles of the discounting methodology discussed above.

Example 1

A company has timing differences of £100,000 in respect of deferred tax liabilities at 31 December 20X0. These timing differences are expected to be included in taxable income at £40,000 in 20X3 and at £60,000 in 20X5. The tax rate is 30%. The three year and five year redemption yield on UK Treasury gilts are as follows:

Description of gilt	Years to maturity	Redemption yield %	Post-tax (yield less tax at 30%)
Tr 6½pc 'X3	3	5.21	3.65
Tr 8½pc 'X5	5	5.15	3.61

Without discounting

In the absence of discounting, the company would provide deferred tax of £30,000 (£100,000 @ 30%). This amount would reduce to £18,000 (£60,000 @ 30%) at 31 December 20X3 following reversal of £40,000 of timing differences. The liability would reduce to nil by 31 December 20X5 when the remaining timing difference of £60,000 reverses.

With discounting

The following table shows the discounted liability on the assumption that all future reversals occur at the end of the year:

Table 1 — Computation of discounted deferred tax liability as at 31 December 20X0

	31 December 20X3	31 December 20X5	Total
Reversing timing differences	£40,000	£60,000	£100,000
Undiscounted tax @ 30%	£12,000	£18,000	£30,000
Post-tax yield	3.65%	3.61%	
Discount factor	$1/(1+0.0365)^3$ = 0.8981	$1/(1+0.0361)^5$ = 0.8377	
Discounted deferred tax	£12,000 × 0.8981 = £10,777	£18,000 × 0.8377 = £15,078	= £25,855

As can be seen from the above table, the total discounted deferred tax liability is £25,855 which amounts to 86% of the total undiscounted liability. If a reduction of 14% is considered to be material to the financial statements as a whole, discounting would be necessary if the entity has adopted a policy of discounting deferred tax assets and liabilities. It should be noted that each reversing timing difference would need to be discounted separately by reference to the period in which it reverses. So the company would need to keep track of each reversal. This tracking becomes important since the unwinding effect of the discounting would need to be calculated for each reversal by reference to the same Treasury gilt yield for one year less as shown in the table below:

Table 2 — Computation of the unwinding of the discount for the year ended 31 December 20X1	31 December 20X3	31 December 20X5	Total
Reversing timing differences	£40,000	£60,000	£100,000
Undiscounted tax @ 30%	£12,000	£18,000	£30,000
Post-tax yield	3.65%	3.61%	
Discount factor — one year less than maturity period	$1/(1+0.0365)^2$ = 0.9308	$1/(1+0.0361)^4$ = 0.8679	
Discounted deferred tax	£12,000 × 0.9308 = £11,170	£18,000 × 0.8679 = £15,622	= £26,792
Discounted deferred tax as previously calculated in Table 1	= £10,777	= £15,078	= £25,855
Unwinding of the discount	£393	£544	£937

The unwinding of the discount of £937 would be reported as part of the tax charge and not as part of the interest cost (see para 13.198 below). In practice, however, the unwinding effect could be calculated simply by applying the previous post-tax discount rate to the opening discounted deferred tax liability in respect of each reversal as shown below:

Opening discounted deferred tax for 20X3 reversal	£10,777 × 3.65% = £393
Opening discounted deferred tax for 20X5 reversal	£15,078 × 3.61% = £544
Total effect of unwinding of the discount for 20X1	£937

Obviously, the treasury gilt yield rates are unlikely to remain constant over the terms of the reversals. Therefore, the discounted deferred tax liability would change as the discount rate changes. In addition, for the year ended 31 December 20X1, the maturity periods of the reversals would reduce by one year. As a result, the appropriate discount rates would be the 2 year and 4 year post-tax Treasury gilt redemption yields as at 31 December 20X1.

Suppose the 2 year and the 4 year redemption yield on UK Treasury gilts are as follows:

Description of gilt	Years to maturity	Redemption yield %	Post-tax (yield less tax at 30%)
Tr 6½pc 'X3	2	5.24	3.67
Tr 8½pc 'X5	4	5.18	3.63

Table 3 shows the discounted liability at 31 December 20X1 calculated by reference to above gilt yields. It would be acceptable in practice to use a single discount rate where the rates applicable to each reversing period are close to each other (see also para 13.194).

Table 3 — Computation of discounted deferred tax liability as at 31 December 20X1	31 December 20X3	31 December 20X5	Total
Reversing timing differences	£40,000	£60,000	£100,000
Undiscounted tax @ 30%	£12,000	£18,000	£30,000
Post-tax yield	3.67%	3.63%	
Discount factor — one year less than maturity period	$1/(1+0.0367)^2$ = 0.9305	$1/(1+0.0361)^4$ = 0.8677	
Discounted deferred tax	£12,000 × 0.9305 = £11,166	£18,000 × 0.8677 = £15,619	= £26,785

The movement of £26,785 – £25,855 (from Table 1) = £930 for the year ended 31 December 20X1 comprises:

Unwinding of the discount on opening timing differences (as these are now one year closer to reversal)	£937
Change in discount rate at which opening deferred tax is discounted	£ (7)
Total change in discounted liability reflected in the tax charge for 20X1	£930

The reduction in the opening discounted liability is due to the effect of an increase in the discount rates. In this example, the amount representing the change in the discount rate is small because only a small increase in the discount rate was assumed. The effect would be more pronounced had the discount rate changed by a bigger amount and a longer time period was involved.

13.197 It may so happen that, in addition to the change in discount rates, the company finds at 31 December 20X1 that the reversal of £100,000 is now likely to take place over 3 years — £25,000 in 20X3, £25,000 in 20X4 and the remaining £50,000 in 20X5. As the amount and timing of the reversals have changed, the company would need to discount the reversals of three separate timing differences by reference to three Treasury gilts redemption yields with maturity dates corresponding to the periods of reversals. A similar calculation as above would need to be performed and, in this case, the total movement would comprise three elements — (a) unwinding of the discount; (b) change in discount rate; and (c) change in timing and amount of reversing timing differences, not including the change that would arise if the tax rate itself changes.

13.198 Fortunately, it is not necessary to calculate the separate components. This is because the standard simply requires disclosure of the changes in the amounts of discounts deducted in arriving at the deferred tax balance (see further para 13.240 below). Therefore, only the net movement needs to be disclosed as part of the tax charge. This amount would be obtained simply by calculating the discounted deferred tax liability at the balance sheet date by reference to prevailing discount rates and future reversal of timing differences, which may have changed as to amount and timing compared with the previous estimate, and deducting the opening discounted deferred tax liability.

13.199 The discounting calculation becomes complicated for deferred tax arising from accelerated capital allowances and could, in certain circumstances, produce an odd result. As stated in paragraph 13.189 above, the discounting calculation is performed by scheduling out, by year, the future movements in accelerated capital allowances on assets — without regard to the effect of future asset purchases. It is important to appreciate that the scheduling of the future movements in accelerated capital allowances should include not only reversing timing differences, but also any further originating timing differences that would arise as a result of claiming the remaining capital allowances on the existing asset. In other words, the accelerated capital allowances build up to a maximum amount before starting to reverse. The way in which the scheduling and the discounting calculation should be performed is set out in great detail in the discounting example in Appendix 1 to FRS 19.

13.200 In certain circumstances, especially in the early years, an undiscounted deferred tax liability could, with discounting, turn into a deferred tax asset. The reason for this is relatively straightforward to understand. When an asset is purchased on which capital allowances are claimed, there are future originating and future reversing timing differences, which, over the life of the asset, will sum to zero or add up to a small net ouflow on an undiscounted basis. In the early years, however, the originating differences (proxies for cash inflows) dominate the reversing timing differences (proxies for cash outflows). As these early inflows are less affected by discounting than later outflows, it is possible that the net effect of discounting results in a net inflow, giving rise to a deferred tax asset. Consider the following example:

Example 2

On 1 January 20X0, a company acquires an asset costing £10,000, which has a life of 20 years. Depreciation is provided on a straight line basis and the asset qualifies for capital allowances of 25% on a reducing balance. The discount rate, for simplicity is assumed to be 6%, which remains constant over the life of the asset. At the end of the asset's life, the asset is scrapped and any capital allowances outstanding are claimed as a balancing allowance. The tax rate is 30%.

At 31 December 20X0:

Net book value of the asset	= £9,500
Tax written-down value	= £7,500
Timing difference at that date	= £2,000

The timing difference of £2,000 is expected to reverse over the remaining 19 years as follows:

Year	Depreciation	Capital allowances	Reversal of timing difference/ (further originating timing difference)	Undiscounted deferred tax liability/ (asset) (being column 4 × 30%)	Discounted deferred tax liability/ (asset)
1	500	1,875	(1,375)	(413)	(389)
2	500	1,406	(906)	(272)	(242)
3	500	1,055	(555)	(166)	(140)
4	500	791	(291)	(87)	(69)
5	500	593	(93)	(28)	(21)
6	500	445	55	17	12
7	500	334	166	50	33
8	500	250	250	75	47
9	500	188	312	94	55
10	500	141	359	108	60
11	500	106	394	118	62
12	500	79	421	126	63
13	500	59	441	132	62
14	500	45	455	137	60
15	500	33	467	140	58
16	500	25	475	142	56
17	500	19	481	144	54
18	500	14	486	146	51
19	500	11	489	147	49
20	-	31	(31)	(10)	(3)
Total	9,500	7,500	2,000	600	(142)

13.201 As can be seen from the above table, an undiscounted deferred tax liability of £600 at the end of 31 December 20X0 becomes, on discounting, a deferred tax asset of £142. This is because the early years' amounts are less affected by discounting than the later years' amounts and so they predominate giving rise to a deferred asset. In accounting terms, this means that the discounted deferred tax asset of £142 is not simply the discounted equivalent of the undiscounted liability of £600 that represents the liability to pay back the upfront tax relief received to date. Rather, it also includes the right to receive further upfront tax relief before both the upfront tax relief received to date plus any upfront tax relief still to be received are paid back, again all discounted. In other words, if we view the accelerated capital allowances as an interest-free loan from the government, then the effect of discounting may be to value not just the interest free loan received upfront, but also the right to receive any further interest-free loans in the future. The profile for undiscounted and discounted liability over the life of the asset is shown below.

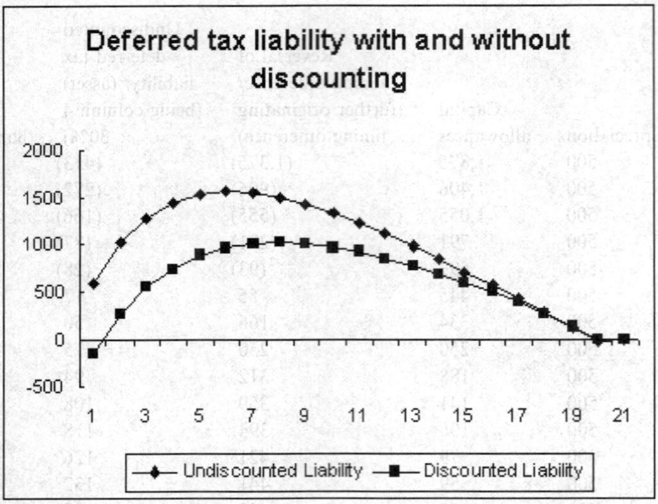

13.202 In practice, however, the above results are unlikely to show up in the generality of situations since most companies would have a portfolio of assets with different ages and the cumulative effect of the individual timing differences may prevent the liability/asset switch from occurring. It could, however, occur in start-up situations. If this were to happen in practice, a deferred tax asset should be recognised in the early years subject to meeting the recognition criteria. The apparent ambiguity would need to be explained in the financial statements.

Treatment of tax in consolidated financial statements

General principles

13.203 The treatment of taxation in the consolidated financial statements involves considerations that are different from those that apply to individual financial statements. In a group, the tax positions of the individual group members are unlikely to be similar. Some group members may be profitable, whilst others may be loss making, leading to different tax considerations. Some may operate in the same tax jurisdiction, whilst others may operate in different tax jurisdictions. Given that consolidated financial statements are prepared as if the parent company and its subsidiary undertakings were a single entity, it follows that the group's tax position has to be viewed as a whole.

13.204 It is a requirement of the Act and FRS 2 that a group should follow uniform accounting policies in preparing consolidated financial statements. This may result in appropriate adjustments being made at the consolidation level where a subsidiary has not followed uniform group policies in preparing its own financial statements, because of local requirements. Adjustments are also required to eliminate various intra-group transactions for the group to be treated as a single entity.

13.205 The total tax liability of a group is determined by aggregating the actual tax liability assessed under local tax laws and borne by individual group members. Consolidation adjustments may have tax consequences. In order to avoid distorting the group's tax charge, the tax effect of consolidation adjustments should be reflected therein without affecting the group's total tax liability. This can only be achieved if those tax effects are recognised as part of the deferred tax account of the group. The effect is that consolidation adjustments are treated as giving rise to timing differences, even though they do not appear in the tax computations of any group members. Nevertheless, they do have the effect of deferring or accelerating tax when viewed from the perspective of treating the group as a single entity. Therefore, the provisions of FRS 19 apply equally to consolidated financial statements.

Tax effects of consolidation adjustment

13.206 FRS 19 regards the reversal of intragroup profits in stock, unrealised at the group level, as a timing difference that should be tax effected. Assuming that a subsidiary sells goods costing £50,000 to its parent company for £60,000 and these goods are still held in stock at the balance sheet date, a consolidation adjustment is required to eliminate the profit of £10,000 from the consolidated profit and loss account. The subsidiary would have provided tax of £3,000 (£10,000 @ 30 per cent) as part of its current tax liability.

13.207 The tax provided by the subsidiary is eliminated on consolidation through recognition of a deferred tax asset at the group level. Under FRS 19, a deferred tax asset is recognised following elimination of any intragroup profits in stock held at the group level at the supplying company's tax rate. (This differs to IAS 12, which requires recognition of a deferred tax asset at the receiving company's tax rate.) The deferred tax asset would be recovered when the goods are sold to third parties.

13.208 Therefore, consolidation adjustments that have the effect of deferring or accelerating tax when viewed from the perspective of the group as a whole give rise to timing differences and should be accounted for as part of the deferred tax position of the group.

Example

A company is preparing consolidated financial statements. In one of its overseas sub-groups there was a transfer of assets from one subsidiary to another giving rise to a large profit in the transferor (which is taxable in the overseas country). The transferor company has paid the tax in the year. On consolidation the intra-group profit is eliminated but the tax charge remains. Can the group reverse this charge and set up a deferred tax asset on consolidation?

This is clearly a timing difference under FRS 19 so far as the consolidated financial statements are concerned. If the assets were sold outside the group there would be a different tax base for the value of assets sold compared to the value of the assets in the consolidated financial statements. Therefore, under FRS 19, provided the conditions in paragraph 23 of the standard are satisfied (that is, provided that the deferred tax asset is regarded as recoverable) the tax charge should be treated as a deferred tax asset on consolidation.

13.208.1 Another example is where borrowing costs incurred to finance the creation of a fixed asset for use by the group are expensed by a subsidiary, but capitalised on consolidation. As the subsidiary has already benefited from the tax deduction on the interest expense in the current period, but the group would recognise the interest expense as part of the subsequent depreciation or sale of the asset, a timing difference is created from the perspective of treating the group as a single entity. Consequently, a deferred tax liability should be set up to eliminate the benefit from the tax deduction arising as there is no associated interest charge in the consolidated financial statements.

Fair value adjustments

13.209 FRS 19 treats fair value adjustments as if they were timing differences in the acquired entity's own financial statements. For example, a non-monetary asset, such as a building of the acquired entity would be valued on acquisition at its market value. Any tax that would be payable if the asset were sold at that value would be provided for only if, before the acquisition, the acquired entity had itself entered into a binding agreement to sell the asset and rollover relief was not available. [FRS 7 para 74, as amended by FRS 19 para 71]. In general, if the acquired company's assets are fair valued upwards on acquisition, it is treated as being the same as revaluations and no deferred tax should be provided, unless the conditions in FRS 19 are met (see para 13.128).

13.210 Another way of looking at fair value adjustments on consolidation is to treat them as if they had been policy adjustments in the acquired entity. For instance, assume that the acquired entity has a number of outstanding forward currency contracts taken out to hedge committed transactions, which, at the date of acquisition, are sitting at a considerable loss. In accordance with FRS 7, the forward contracts would be fair valued on acquisition with a consequent adjustment to goodwill. However, if both the acquirer and the acquired entity apply SSAP 20 rather than FRS 23 and neither has a policy of fair valuing derivatives, any gains or losses arising are deferred until the contracts mature. The question arises as to whether it is appropriate to provide deferred tax on the fair value adjustments on consolidation under these circumstances. The answer will be impacted by the tax position of the entity. This will vary depending on the entity's elections under the 'Disregard regulations' (see further paras 13.135.2 and 13.217). If the entity had a policy to fair value derivatives and fair value gains and losses are not taxable until their subsequent realisation, this would give rise to a timing difference on which deferred tax would have been provided in the entity's own financial statements. Consequently, as fair values are used in the consolidated financial statements, it is appropriate to recognise the tax effects of the adjustment on consolidation also.

13.210.1 If the acquirer is applying FRS 23 and FRS 26 (see further chapters 7 and 6 respectively), then its accounting policy must be that derivatives are marked to market with fair value movements being recognised in the profit and loss account. To the extent that the fair value movements are not taxed until their subsequent realisation, it is appropriate to recognise deferred tax on those fair value movements on consolidation.

13.211 A similar situation arises where the acquired entity has current asset investments and the group has an accounting policy of carrying these at cost, but which are fair valued at the date of acquisition. As stated above, we would treat the fair value adjustment as if it was a policy adjustment in the acquired entity. Unless the group applies FRS 26 (see below) a policy of revaluation for current asset investments would be effected through the STRGL and no deferred tax would be provided on the fair value adjustments, unless there was a binding commitment, see paragraph 13.209.

13.211.1 If the acquirer applies FRS 26 in its consolidated financial statements, it may account for equity investments (other than investments in subsidiaries, associates and joint ventures) either at cost or at fair value. The accounting treatment depends on the designation of the investment (see further chapter 6). The following table outlines for each category of investment held by the acquired entity, whether deferred tax should be recognised on acquisition or not.

Category of investment	Accounting for investment	Recognise deferred tax?
Held to maturity	Cost	No – the reasons given in paragraph 13.211 apply
Available for sale	Fair value, with movements recognised in STRGL	No – see paragraph 13.209
At fair value through profit or loss	Fair value with movements recognised in profit or loss	Yes – see paragraph 13.132

13.211.2 The examples below consider the deferred tax implications when assets are written down in a fair value exercise.

Example 1

A group made an acquisition during the year. The acquired company had stock stated in its books at cost (£l0 million). As part of the fair value exercise, the stock has been written down to its net realisable value of £8 million. This adjustment does not reflect the acquiring company's intentions, but rather reflects conditions at the date of acquisition. Should deferred tax be provided on the fair value adjustment?

Paragraph 18 of FRS 19 states that *"stock may be adjusted to its fair value on the acquisition of a business. However, even where such stock has been manufactured under the terms of a binding contract, that contract will generally be treated as an executory contract. The rights and obligations under that contract (and hence the gain on sale) will not have been recognised. In adjusting the value of the stock, the entity is merely recognising a movement in the replacement cost of the stock. In such circumstances the FRS does not allow a provision to be made for deferred tax on the adjustment"*. This would suggest that no adjustment should be made for deferred tax when a fair value adjustment is made to stock.

This part of the FRS deals with upward revaluations of stock for the purpose of fair valuing and is consistent with the principle that adjustments to record the acquired entity's assets and liabilities are treated in the same way as they would be if they were timing differences arising in the entity's own financial statements. [FRS 19, para 71]. Upward revaluations on the cost of stock would not be permitted in the acquired entity's own historical cost financial statements under SSAP 9, 'Stocks and long-term contracts', and even if they were allowed, deferred tax would not be provided under FRS 19. Paragraph 14 states that deferred tax should not be provided on timing differences arising when non-monetary assets are revalued, unless there is a binding commitment to sell and the entity has recognised the gains and losses expected on sale.

However, we consider that the provisions of paragraph 18 of FRS 19 do not apply in circumstances where a fair value adjustment is made to write an asset down to its net realisable value (where this write down has not been made in the acquired entity's own financial statements) and that in this case deferred tax should be provided on the difference between cost of £10m and fair value of £8m, as part of the fair value exercise. This is consistent with the principle described above: the acquired entity would have recognised a deferred tax asset in respect of the write-down if it had been made in the entity's own financial statements. It follows that FRS 7, 'Fair values in acquisition accounting', as amended by FRS 19, requires deferred tax to be recorded on acquisition in this situation.

Example 2

Should deferred tax be recognised on fair value adjustments to write down plant and machinery to its fair values?

Yes, FRS 19 amended FRS 7 and states that deferred tax on adjustments to fair values should be recognised in accordance with FRS 19. Where assets are revalued upwards to fair value in a fair value exercise there would normally be no deferred tax to provide, unless the company was committed to dispose of the assets. However, in this case the assets are being written down and this is like additional depreciation. As a result depreciation going forward will be reduced and this will affect the calculation of deferred tax relating to capital allowances resulting in a reduction of the deferred tax liability going forward.

13.212 One fair value adjustment often made before FRS 19 amended FRS 7 was to recognise a deferred tax asset in respect of unrelieved tax losses of the acquired subsidiary that were not regarded as recoverable, but, as a result of the acquisition, became recoverable within the enlarged group. Given that FRS 7's previous treatment of recognising deferred tax from the enlarged group's perspective is no longer appropriate, the question arises as to whether companies can recognise a deferred tax asset in respect of an acquisition of a loss-making company, especially where a large proportion of the purchase price related to the losses. The ASB took the view that, notwithstanding the amendment to FRS 7, the recognition of a deferred tax asset for the unrelieved tax losses was consistent with the recognition criteria for contingent assets under paragraph 37 of FRS 7. That paragraph states that certain contingent assets and liabilities that crystallise as a result of the acquisition would be recognised, provided that the underlying contingency was in existence before the acquisition. Consequently, where a loss-making company is acquired, that company has a contingent asset in the form of future tax benefit attributable to the unrelieved tax losses. Such future tax benefits should be recognised as a fair value adjustment provided the group has sufficient taxable profits. Therefore, as a general rule, deferred tax assets of the acquired entity should be included in the fair value exercise, even if they had not been recognised before the acquisition, provided they meet the recognition criteria for deferred tax assets as set out in paragraph 13.143 above.

13.213 On the other hand, if the losses had arisen in the acquiring group and had remained unrelieved at the date of acquisition, FRS 19 would not permit recognition of a deferred tax asset in the fair value exercise even though the group is able to utilise the benefit of its unused tax losses against the future taxable profit of the acquired entity. This is because those losses are not the losses of the acquired entity and hence would not be recognised in the fair value exercise. [FRS 19 para 71; FRS 7 para 75]. Rather, as a result of the acquisition, the acquiring group is expected to be more profitable in future. FRS 19, therefore, requires unrecognised deferred tax assets of the acquirer or other entities existing at the date of acquisition that fall to be recoverable against the future taxable profits of the acquired entity to be recognised as a credit to the tax charge in the post acquisition period. [FRS 19 para 71; FRS 7 para 22].

Goodwill

13.213.1 In some jurisdictions outside the UK (and where goodwill arises in the UK on the acquisition of trade and assets), tax relief is available on goodwill (the goodwill being amortised for tax purposes over a pre-determined life or in accordance with any amortisation for accounting purposes). Where the goodwill is amortised over the same period for accounting purposes, then there is no timing difference. However, where a different period is used for tax purposes then deferred tax will arise. For example, it is common in the UK for companies to make an election to claim annual deductions at four per cent, thus deductions are received over a 25 year period whilst, for accounting purposes, the period over which amortisation is recognised is unlikely to be greater than 20 years (see further chapter 25). Additionally, a particular issue arises where goodwill that relates to acquisitions made before 1998 remains eliminated against reserves under the transitional arrangements in FRS 10, 'Goodwill and intangible assets'. Under FRS 19, the tax deductions for the goodwill's cost create timing differences in the consolidated financial statements as the tax relief is received before the cost is recognised in the profit and loss account. Whereas the tax deduction is obtained systematically over a pre-determined life, the goodwill is not charged in the profit and loss account until the business to which it relates is sold or closed (or earlier if the group's policy is to reinstate the goodwill when it is impaired and write it off through the profit and loss account). Under FRS 19, deferred tax should be provided on this timing difference.

13.213.2 For example, if goodwill costing £100 is being amortised for tax purposes over 20 years (that is, amortisation of £5 per annum), the tax written-down value at the end of, say, year eight would be £60 (£100 – £5 × 8). The goodwill was eliminated against reserves prior to 1998, but this was a matter of accounting policy rather than an accounting loss. A deferred tax liability should be provided on the timing difference of £40. The liability is increased each year up to 20 years as further timing differences of £5 originate, unless the goodwill is charged in the profit and loss account (for instance, on disposal of the business), when the timing difference would reverse and the provision would be released.

13.213.3 In the consolidated profit and loss account, the current tax charge reflects the benefit of the annual tax deductions. The tax-deductible goodwill is a reconciling item in FRS 19's reconciliation of the current tax charge to the charge that would result from applying the standard rate of tax to the profit on ordinary activities before tax (see further para 13.276 below).

Unremitted earnings of subsidiaries, associates and joint ventures

13.214 Earnings of subsidiaries, associates and joint ventures that are not remitted to the parent/investor do not normally suffer UK corporation tax. However, if such profits are remitted by way of dividends, they may suffer tax. Therefore, unremitted earnings of such entities that have been recognised in the consolidated financial statements are potentially timing differences which reverse when they are distributed or a commitment to distribute them exists. Accordingly, FRS 19 states that tax that could be payable (taking account of any double taxation relief) on any future remittance of the past earnings of a subsidiary, associate or joint venture should be provided for only to the extent that, at the balance sheet date:

- Dividends have been accrued as receivable; or
- A binding agreement to distribute the past earnings in future has been entered into by the subsidiary, associate or joint venture.

[FRS 19 para 21].

13.215 Therefore, there must be a binding agreement in place rather than simply an intention to remit profits, thus eliminating any degree of subjectivity. The standard acknowledges that, in practice, a binding agreement to remit profits is unlikely to arise. [FRS 19 para 22].

Foreign exchange differences

13.216 Gains or losses arising on the translation of the financial statements of overseas subsidiaries and associated companies are not regarded as creating a timing difference. However, gains or losses arising on the translation of an enterprise's own overseas assets (including investments in subsidiaries and associated companies) and liabilities may give rise to timing differences depending on whether or not the gains or losses have a tax effect. In addition, where gains and losses on foreign currency borrowings that have been used to finance or hedge foreign equity investments are offset and reported in the STRGL, then, in accordance with UITF Abstract 19, any tax effects that may arise on the exchange gains or losses on the borrowings because they are not deferred or matched for tax purposes, should also be reported in the STRGL (see also paragraph 13.239 below). See further chapter 7.

13.217 In the UK, the tax rules with regards to foreign exchange gains and losses are complex. Depending on the elections made under the 'Disregard regulations', exchange gains and losses may either be taxable as they accrue for accounting purposes or may be taxable when realisation occurs at a later date. Consultation with a tax specialist is recommended in this area.

Deemed disposals

13.218 When a profit or loss is made on a deemed disposal, the question arises as to whether deferred tax should be recognised.

Example

A company has a subsidiary that has issued shares for cash in a flotation. The shares were issued for a value that exceeds the share of net assets per share. Therefore, whilst the company's percentage holding has reduced, its attributable share of net assets has increased giving rise to a profit on the deemed disposal under FRS 2, 'Accounting for subsidiary undertakings'. Because this profit is represented by increased cash it is reflected in the group's profit and loss account. Should the company provide for deferred tax on this profit given that no actual tax arises at this stage, because the company has not actually sold any shares in the subsidiary?

If the parent were to sell the subsidiary at a later date there would be a gain based on the difference between the original cost to the parent and the proceeds. In the consolidated financial statements (ignoring goodwill) this gain would be represented by (a) retained profits since acquisition, (b) gain on deemed disposal and (c) actual gain between the proceeds and the carrying value of net assets at the date of sale. In the group only (c) would be recognised on disposal as (a) and (b) would already have been recognised. There is clearly a timing difference between the recognition in the consolidated financial statements of the retained profits and the gain on deemed disposal and their taxation on disposal of the shares in the subsidiary. However, FRS 19 does not permit deferred tax to be recognised on the sale of the subsidiary until there is a commitment to sell. This is implied because the recognition of retained profits and gain on deemed disposal of the subsidiary is like a revaluation and paragraph 14 of FRS 19 does not allow deferred tax on a revaluation to be provided, unless the entity has a binding agreement to sell and has recognised the gains expected to arise on sale. The conclusion, therefore, is that the gain on deemed disposal should be treated as a revaluation for FRS 19 purposes and no provision for tax made until there is a commitment to sell.

[The next paragraph is 13.234.]

Presentation and disclosures

General

13.234 It is generally accepted that, however they have been calculated, tax effects should be shown in the financial statements separately from the items or transactions to which they relate. It is not surprising, therefore, that a considerable number of disclosure requirements in respect of taxation are contained both in the Act and the relevant accounting standards, although there is significant overlap between the two. Most of the disclosure requirements apply to the financial statements of individual companies as well as to consolidated financial statements. However, small companies preparing annual financial statements under the modified formats are permitted to omit many of the statutory disclosure requirements relating to taxation (see further chapter 32). The paragraphs that follow deal with the disclosure requirements of corporation tax as well as deferred tax.

Accounting policies

13.235 There is no specific requirement in FRS 16 and FRS 19 to disclose accounting policies in respect of current and deferred tax. This is because a description of each of the accounting policies that is material in the context of the entity's financial statements is now required by FRS 18 and by the Act. [CA85 4 Sch 36, FRS 18 para 55(a)]. In respect of deferred tax the policy note should state the basis on which deferred tax has been recognised. It should also state whether deferred tax is measured on a discounted or undiscounted basis. Examples of accounting policy on deferred tax are given in Table 13.4 and 13.5 below.

Table 13.4 – British Vita PLC – Annual Report & Accounts – 31 December 2000

NOTES ON THE ACCOUNTS
1 Accounting policies (extract)

Deferred taxation
Deferred tax is recognised in respect of all timing differences that have originated but not reversed at the balance sheet date where transactions or events that result in an obligation to pay more tax in the future or a right to pay less tax in the future have occurred at the balance sheet date. Timing differences are differences between the Group's taxable profits and its results as stated in the financial statements.

Deferred tax is recognised in respect of the retained earnings of overseas subsidiaries and associates only to the extent that, at the balance sheet date, dividends have been accrued as receivable or a binding agreement to distribute past earnings in future has been entered into by the subsidiary or associate.

Deferred tax is measured at the average tax rates that are expected to apply in the periods in which the timing differences are expected to reverse, based on tax rates and laws that have been enacted or substantially enacted by the balance sheet date. Deferred tax is measured on a non-discounted basis.

Table 13.5 – Costain Group plc – Annual Report and Accounts – 31 December 2000

1 Accounting Policies (extract)
Taxation
Deferred taxation has been recognised as a liability or asset if transaction have occurred at the balance sheet date that give rise to an obligation to pay more taxation in future, or a right to pay less taxation in future. An asset is not recognised to the extent that the transfer of economic benefits in future is uncertain. Deferred tax assets and liabilities recognised have not been discounted.

No provision is made to cover any further liability to taxation that would arise in respect of the distribution of profits retained by overseas subsidiary undertakings and joint ventures.

Profit and loss account

Presentation and disclosures required by the Act

13.236 The requirements in the Companies Act 1985 in relation to the presentation of taxation in the profit and loss account are as follows:

- There must be disclosed separately 'tax on profit or loss on ordinary activities' and 'tax on extraordinary profit or loss'. The latter is unlikely to arise following publication of FRS 3. These are separate headings included in each of the four profit and loss account formats. In addition, all the profit and loss account formats include a further heading 'other taxes not shown under the above items'. As the Act does not indicate the type of information that must be included under this heading and as no such 'other taxes' are presently collected in the UK, this heading in the format appears to be superfluous for the time being.
- The taxation charge in the profit and loss account should be analysed, distinguishing between:
  - UK corporation tax, both before and after double tax relief.
  - UK income tax.
  - Overseas tax.

  [CA85 4 Sch 54(3)].
- Particulars are required of any special circumstances that affect the overall tax charge or credit for the period or that may affect those of future periods, whether in respect of profits, income or capital gains. [CA85 4 Sch 54(2)]. This requirement is also contained in FRS 3 which is discussed in paragraph 13.274.

References throughout this chapter are to schedules to the Companies Act 1985. At the time of writing, the schedules to the Companies Act 2006 have still to be published.

Presentation required by the accounting standards

13.237 Both current and deferred tax should be recognised in the profit and loss account for the period, except to the extent that it is attributable to a gain or loss that is or has been recognised directly in the STRGL. [FRS 16 para 5, FRS 19 para 34]. All such amounts should be recognised as part of 'tax on profit and loss on ordinary activities'. This requirement is implicit within FRS 16, but explicitly stated in paragraph 59 of FRS 19 in respect of deferred tax.

Disclosures in the notes

13.238 A considerable amount of information relating to both current tax and deferred tax falls to be disclosed in the profit and loss account under the provisions contained in FRS 3, FRS 16 and FRS 19. These disclosure requirements have been grouped under appropriate headings for ease of reference and examples from published financial statements to illustrate the disclosure requirements of the Act and accounting standards are included where relevant.

Analysis of current tax

13.239 FRS 16 requires that the current tax charge or (credit) reported in the profit and loss account should be analysed between UK tax and foreign tax. Each of these components should be further analysed to distinguish tax for the current period and adjustments recognised in respect of prior periods. The total UK tax should also be shown before and after double taxation relief. [FRS 16 para 17]. An example of a non-mandatory format, capturing all the disclosure requirements of paragraph 17 relating to the profit and loss account, is given in Appendix I to the standard and is reproduced below:

	£'000	£'000
UK corporation tax		
Current tax on income for the period	a	
Adjustments in respect of prior periods	b	
	c	
Double taxation relief	d	
		e
Foreign tax		
Current tax on income for the period	f	
Adjustments in respect of prior periods	g	
		h
Tax on profit on ordinary activities		i

Analysis of deferred tax

13.240 In addition to the disclosure of the major components of current tax considered above, the notes to the financial statements should disclose the amount of deferred tax charged or credited within tax on ordinary activities in the profit and loss account, separately disclosing material components, including those attributable to:

- Changes in deferred tax balances (before discounting, where applicable) arising from:
  - The origination and reversal of timing differences.
  - Changes in tax rates and laws.
  - Adjustments to the estimated recoverable amount of deferred tax assets arising in previous periods.
- Where applicable, changes in the amounts of discount deducted in arriving at the deferred tax balance.

[FRS 19 para 60(a)].

13.241 The above disclosure requirements are illustrated in the example in FRS 19 Appendix II. The single figure of the originating and reversing timing differences disclosed within the deferred tax charge in the profit and loss account is likely to include the tax effects of accelerated capital allowances, material provisions, utilisation of unrelieved tax losses, capitalised interest and other timing differences. It would appear from the requirement of the above paragraph that further analysis of the single figure for the originating and reversing timing is not required, although such an analysis could be computed from the available information in the tax note. Indeed, the example in Appendix II simply discloses a single figure for the original and reversal of timing differences without providing further analysis. An example of a company that has followed the above disclosure requirements is given in Table 13.6 below.

Table 13.6 – Scottish Power plc – Annual Report & Accounts – 31 March 2001

Notes to the Group Profit and Loss Account (extract)

6 Tax on profit on ordinary activities (extract)

	Before exceptional item 2001 £m	Exceptional items 2001 £m	2001 £m	Before exceptional items 2000 £m	Exceptional items 2000 £m	2000 £m	1999 £m
Current tax:							
UK corporation tax at 30% (2000 30% and 1999 31%)	145.6	–	145.6	135.6	56.0	191.6	141.6
Double taxation relief	(61.2)	–	(61.2)	–	–	–	–
UK Corporation tax liability	84.4	–	84.4	135.6	56.0	191.6	141.6
Foreign taxation	5.7	(8.7)	(3.0)	26.1	–	26.1	–
Total current tax	90.1	(8.7)	81.4	161.7	56.0	217.7	141.6
Deferred tax:							
Origination and reversal of timing differences	51.0	(37.2)	13.8	45.2	–	45.2	33.5
Total deferred tax	51.0	(37.2)	13.8	45.2	–	45.2	33.5
Total tax on profit on ordinary activities	141.1	(45.9)	95.2	206.9	56.0	262.9	175.1

13.242 In addition to the disclosure of adjustments to deferred tax balances arising from changes in the tax rates and laws as stated above, the effect of a fundamental change in the basis of taxation, if applicable, should be included in the tax charge for the period and separately disclosed on the face of the profit and loss account. [FRS 3 para 23].

13.243 The standard simply calls for the disclosure of the total amount of discount that has been deducted in arriving at the deferred tax balance. As stated in paragraph 13.198 above, the total amount of discount charged in the profit and loss account would consist of the unwinding of discount, the effect of changes in discount rates and the effect of changes in timing and amount of reversing timing differences. It would have been consistent with FRS 12 if the unwinding of the discount was included as other finance costs adjacent to interest with the other components shown as part of the tax charge. The ASB believes this to be the correct approach in principle, but nevertheless requires the unwinding of the discount to be presented as part of the tax charge. The reason is that profit and loss account formats require all of the tax consequences of pre-tax profits to be shown separately, below the sub-total 'profits on ordinary activities before taxation'. The unwinding of a discount on a deferred tax balance, whether viewed conceptually as part of the tax expense or as a finance item, is not part of profits before tax. Hence, it is shown after the subtotal of profits before tax. [FRS 19 App V para 122]. Therefore, all the effects of discounting deferred taxes are recorded within the same tax line. On the other hand, interest charged on overdue tax or received in respect of overpayments are considered to be proper finance costs and should be included within interest in the profit and loss account.

13.244 There is no requirement to disclose the discount rate. This is sensible since there is little subjectivity involved in determining gilt redemption rates as they are all obtained from published information and objectively verifiable. Furthermore, users are more interested in determining the impact that discounting has on the undiscounted deferred tax balance and such information is readily obtained from other disclosures.

Tax on non-operating exceptional items

13.245 The amount of tax attributable to the three non-operating exceptional items described in paragraph 20 of FRS 3 (sometimes referred to as 'super-exceptionals') should be disclosed in a note. The three items are: profits or losses on sale or termination of an operation; costs of a fundamental reorganisation or restructuring having a material effect on the nature and focus of the reporting entity's operations; and profits or losses on the disposal of fixed assets (and provisions in respect of each of these). The related tax is required to be shown only in aggregate and not for each individual item, unless the effect of the tax on each of the items differs, when further information should be given, where practicable. An example of the relevant disclosure required under FRS 3 is shown in Table 13.8 above. Although the FRS states that the tax attributable to the above types of exceptional item should be disclosed in a note, there could be no objection to disclosing the tax separately within the tax charge on the face of the profit and loss account, as the items are themselves disclosed there.

13.246 FRS 3 recognises that the above disclosure can be useful in understanding the period's charge or credit in respect of taxation. In support of this disclosure requirement, paragraph 50 of FRS 3 states:

> *"It is recognised that analysing an entity's total taxation charge between component parts of its result for a period can involve arbitrary allocations that tend to become less meaningful the more components there are. However, in respect of items such as disposal profits or losses the tax can often be identified with the exceptional item concerned and the relationship between the profit or loss and the attributable tax may be significantly different from that in respect of operating profits or losses. In such circumstances it is relevant to identify the tax charge or credit more specifically."*

13.247 FRS 3 then goes on to stipulate the way in which tax attributable to exceptional items falling within any of the three categories set out above should be calculated for accounting disclosure purposes. The amount of tax attributable to the exceptional items should be calculated by computing the tax on the profit or loss on ordinary activities as if the items did not exist and comparing this notional tax charge with the tax charge on the profit or loss for the year (after extraordinary items if any). Any additional tax charge or credit (including deferred tax) that arises should be attributable to the items. If there are both non-operating exceptional items and extraordinary items in the same period, the tax attributable to the items combined should be calculated and then apportioned between the two groups in relation to their respective amounts. If a more appropriate basis is adopted the method of apportionment must be disclosed. [FRS 3 para 24]. In practice, it is unlikely that under FRS 3 there will be extraordinary items and so the apportionment of tax between the two categories should not arise.

13.248 The following examples illustrate some of the difficulties that may arise in calculating the taxation that relates to the non-operating exceptional items described above:

Example 1

Apportionment of tax where losses brought forward absorb a profit on ordinary activities

A group makes a profit on ordinary activities (excluding non-operating exceptionals) and there is an exceptional loss of the same amount. The group has sufficient tax losses brought forward which can be surrendered to relieve the tax charge on the profit on ordinary activities, or it can use the taxable loss arising from the exceptional item. It uses the former. The question arises as to whether or not the notes to the financial statements should assume a taxation charge on the profit on ordinary activities and show a taxation credit attributable to the exceptional item? The overall tax charge is nil.

In this situation, if the exceptional item were ignored, the tax charge on the profit on ordinary activities would still be nil, as the group would have used taxable losses to eliminate the tax charge. Therefore, the notes should not assume a tax charge on ordinary activities and should not show a tax credit on exceptional items. However, there will still be tax losses carried forward and the notes could disclose that part of the losses brought forward have been utilised to relieve the taxable profit of the group leaving other taxable losses attributable to the exceptional item to be carried forward.

Example 2

Apportionment of tax where goodwill previously written off is treated as non-operating exceptional item

A company makes a profit before non-operating exceptional items and then has an exceptional loss on disposal of a subsidiary. The exceptional loss arises wholly because of the inclusion, in the calculation of the loss, of goodwill previously written off to reserves on the acquisition of the subsidiary. After taking account of the exceptional loss the result before tax is neither a profit nor loss, but there is a substantial tax charge. This is wholly attributable to the profit excluding exceptional items and accordingly there is no taxation attributable to the exceptional item. In this case, however, there would need to be an explanation in the notes of the reasons for an apparently high tax charge relative to the profit on ordinary activities before tax.

Statement of total recognised gains and losses

13.249 Where a gain or loss is or has been recognised directly in the STRGL, both current and deferred tax attributable to that gain or loss should also be recognised directly in that statement [FRS 16 para 17, FRS 19 para 35].

13.250 Because a UK company pays corporation tax on all its profits including any that are reported in the STRGL, it may sometimes be difficult to determine the amount of deferred tax attributable to the amount of gain or loss reported in the STRGL. In those circumstances, both standards permits the attributable current and deferred tax to be calculated on a reasonable pro-rata basis, or another basis that is more appropriate in the circumstances. [FRS 16 para 7, FRS 19 para 36]. The practical implications of this are considered in paragraph 13.23.

Disclosure in the notes

13.251 Both FRS 16 and FRS 19 contain requirements for additional disclosures of the single line item disclosed in the STRGL.

13.252 FRS 16 requires that the current tax charge or (credit) reported in the STRGL should be analysed between UK tax and foreign tax. Each of these components should be further analysed to distinguish tax for the current period and adjustments recognised in respect of prior periods. The total UK tax should also be shown before and after double taxation relief. [FRS 16 para 17]. Similarly, FRS 19 requires separate disclosure of the material components of the tax charge or credit reported directly in the STRGL, including those listed in paragraph 13.240 above. [FRS 19 para 60].

Changes in the carrying amounts of deferred tax assets and liabilities

13.252.1 The carrying value of deferred tax assets and liabilities can change even though there is no change in the timing difference. Such changes may arise as a result of:

- a change in tax rates or laws; or

- a re-assessment of the recoverability of deferred tax assets (see para 13.169).

In such situations, the resulting change in deferred tax should be recognised in the profit and loss account, except to the extent that it relates to items that were previously recognised in the STRGL (see further para 13.249). [FRS 19 para 35].

Example

An entity has a defined benefit pension scheme that is in deficit at the period end. A deferred tax asset has been recognised in relation to the timing difference that exists in relation to the pension deficit.

The rate of corporation tax has been changed from 30% to 28% with an effective date of 1 April 20X8. This change has been substantively enacted at the balance sheet date and will impact the reversal of the temporary difference from 1 April 20X8 onwards, reducing the deferred tax asset.

Management will need to consider what transactions gave rise to the timing difference and trace the impact of the change in tax rate to the same place. In this case, the pension deficit may have arisen as a result of service costs or other profit and loss account charges, actuarial losses recognised directly in the STRGL or, potentially, a combination of the two.

Depending on how the pension deficit arose, and thus how the deferred tax asset was originally booked, the reduction in the deferred tax asset will be recognised either solely in the profit and loss account, solely in STRGL or split between the two performance statements.

The backwards tracing for the change in tax rates should be consistent with the approach used for allocating tax deductions (see para 13.126.7). The deferred tax asset, which is impacted by the tax rate change, represents the amounts against which tax deductions have not yet been allocated. To the extent that amounts in the performance statements are covered by deductions received on contributions, no deferred tax arises. The deferred tax arises on any excess amounts in the performance statements and the backwards tracing should be carried out on that basis.

The fact that a pension liability recognised on transition to FRS 17, 'Retirement benefits', was charged to reserves does not necessarily mean that subsequent changes in the related deferred tax asset will also be recognised in reserves. Instead, it is necessary to determine where the items on which the original deferred tax arose would have been recognised if FRS 17 had been applied in the prior periods.

Where it is not possible to assess where the items on which the original deferred tax arose would have been recognised, the changes in the deferred tax should be taken, by default, to the profit and loss account.

Balance sheet

Presentation and disclosures required by the Act

13.253 The requirements of the Act which relate specifically to the presentation of taxation in the balance sheet are as follows:

- Liabilities, as opposed to provisions, for taxation must be included in the balance sheet heading 'other creditors including taxation and social security', with the liability for taxation and social security being shown separately from 'other creditors'. [Note 9 to the balance sheet formats]. 'Other creditors including taxation and social security', like other categories of creditors, has to be split between amounts that will fall due within one year and amounts that will fall due after more than one year. [Note 13 to the balance sheet formats]. However, as all companies are due to pay corporation tax within nine months of the financial year end no corporation tax balances payable in over one year should arise.

- The provision for deferred taxation should be included under the balance sheet heading 'Provisions for liabilities' as part of the provision for 'Taxation, including deferred taxation', and stated separately from any other provision for other taxation. [Balance sheet formats 1 and 2, 4 Sch 47].

- Where there has been a transfer to or from any provision in respect of tax other than a transfer from that provision for the purpose for which it was set up, the following information should be disclosed:
  - The aggregate amount of the provision at both the beginning and end of the financial year.
  - Any amounts transferred either to or from the provision during the financial year.
  - The source and the application of any amounts so transferred.

  [4 Sch 46(1)(2)].
- The tax treatment of amounts credited or debited to the revaluation reserve should be disclosed. [4 Sch 34(4)].

Presentation required by the accounting standards

13.254 FRS 16 does not contain any specific requirements for the presentation of current tax in the balance sheet, presumably because it is adequately covered by the Act as stated above. The paragraphs that follow deal with the presentation of deferred tax in the balance sheet in accordance with FRS 19.

13.255 With the exception of deferred tax relating to a defined benefit asset or liability recognised in accordance with FRS 17, 'Retirement benefits', which is considered in paragraph 13.257 below:

- Net deferred tax liabilities should be classified as provisions for liabilities.
- Net deferred tax assets should be classified as debtors, as a separate sub-heading of debtors where material.

[FRS 19 para 55].

13.256 The above requirement is consistent with the Act's requirement for including net deferred tax provisions under the balance sheet heading 'Provisions for liabilities' as stated in paragraph 13.253 above. However, there is no heading in the balance sheet formats for taxation recoverable, but the second point in paragraph 13.255 above clarifies that net deferred tax assets should be classified as debtors and shown as a separate sub-heading of debtors, where material. The Act permits an item of asset or liability that is not covered by any of the prescribed formats to be shown separately. [4 Sch 3(2)]. See further paragraph 13.263 below.

13.257 FRS 19 specifically excludes deferred tax assets and liabilities in respect of defined benefit schemes from being included with other deferred tax assets or liabilities. Instead, deferred tax relating to a defined benefit asset or liability is offset against the related asset or liability in accordance with FRS 17. The resulting defined benefit asset or liability, net of the related deferred tax is then presented separately on the face of the balance sheet (see further chapter 11).

Offset of deferred tax assets and liabilities

13.258 An entity may have a large number of different timing differences, giving rise to deferred tax assets and liabilities, arising during a period. Although these deferred tax assets and liabilities are measured separately, the ability to offset assets against liabilities depends on the nature of the balances (for example, deferred tax relating to capital losses cannot be offset against deferred tax liabilities in respect of accelerated capital allowances) and whom they are due to or due from.

13.259 The ASB's Statement of principles states that:

> *"If a right to receive future economic benefits and an obligation to transfer future economic benefits exist and the reporting entity has the ability – which is assured – to insist on net settlement of the balances, the right and obligation together form a single net asset or liability regardless of how the parties intend to settle the balances."*

13.260 The ASB acknowledges that if the above principle is applied, offset of deferred tax balances could take place only if the timing differences giving rise to a deferred tax asset reverse before or at the same time as those giving rise to a deferred tax liability. (If those giving rise to the liability reverse first, there will be a requirement to pay tax before any entitlement to recover tax.) The ASB felt that the need to schedule the timings of the reversals to measure the extent to which the balances should be offset would be impractical and unnecessarily costly. [FRS 19 App V para 124 to 127].

13.261 As a result the standard takes a pragmatic approach and requires offset of deferred tax debit and credit balances within the above headings set out in paragraph 13.255 to the extent, and only to the extent, that they:

- Relate to taxes levied by the same tax authority.
- Arise in the same taxable entity or in a group of taxable entities where the tax losses of one entity can reduce the taxable profits of another.

[FRS 19 para 56].

13.262 The above requirement effectively precludes offset of deferred tax assets and liabilities relating to different tax jurisdictions in consolidated financial statements. It also means that presenting a net group tax liability by offsetting group tax assets on the grounds of a group tax planning opportunity is not possible, unless the opportunity relates to taxes levied by the same tax authority on different group members and the entities are treated as a group for tax purposes.

13.262.1 The application of the rules of offset can be more complicated in consolidated financial statements when deferred tax arises as a result of a consolidation adjustment (see further para 13.208 above).

Example

Within a group, a UK subsidiary sells stock to a French fellow subsidiary. On consolidation, the elimination of unrealised profit in stock gives rise to a deferred tax asset, which meets the criteria for recognition. Should it be offset against other deferred tax liabilities in the balance sheet?

Paragraph 56 of FRS 19 states that deferred tax debit and credit balances should be offset to the extent that they relate to taxes levied by the same tax authority and arise in the same taxable entity, or in a group of them, where one entity's tax losses can reduce another's taxable profits.

In other words, provided that a group tax-pooling regime is in operation under each tax authority, deferred tax assets and liabilities should be offset if they arise within the same tax authority. However, deferred tax assets and liabilities arising in different tax jurisdictions cannot be offset.

It is, therefore, possible to have both deferred tax liabilities and deferred tax assets in the same group balance sheet. Deferred tax liabilities are included in provisions for liabilities, whereas deferred tax assets are recognised within debtors.

Here, the deferred tax asset arises on consolidation only. The UK subsidiary has a current tax charge in respect of the profit it made on the stock sold to the French subsidiary. However, the French subsidiary still holds the stock at the balance sheet date. Therefore, from a group perspective, the UK profit has not yet been recognised. This leads to the recognition of a deferred tax asset at the UK subsidiary's tax rate on consolidation, to eliminate the tax charge on the unrealised profit.

Although the deferred tax asset will reverse when the French subsidiary has sold the stock to a third party, it should not be offset against any of that company's deferred tax liabilities. This is because the deferred tax asset relates to tax already paid (or payable) to the UK tax authorities by the UK subsidiary. Hence it should properly be offset against any deferred tax liabilities that arise within the UK companies in the group that are part of the same tax group as the UK subsidiary.

Presentation of material balances

13.263 FRS 19 does not require separate presentation of all material deferred tax balances on the face of the balance sheet. In the ASB's view such a requirement would simply add clutter. Instead, the ASB has followed the consensus reached in UITF Abstract 4 in respect of any long-term debtor included within current assets. Accordingly, deferred tax liabilities and assets should be disclosed separately on the face of the balance sheet if the amounts are so material in the context of the total net current assets or net assets that, in the absence of such disclosure, readers may misinterpret the financial statements. [FRS 19 para 58].

13.264 It is not clear, however, whether the above requirement applies to the net deferred tax balance or to its gross components. We believe that the requirement applies to the net balance. For instance, a net deferred tax asset would normally fall to be disclosed within debtors with separate disclosure within that sub-heading in the notes as required by paragraph 13.255 above. However, where it is considered to be material in the context of total net assets or net assets it should, in accordance with the above requirement, be shown on the face of the balance sheet to avoid possible misinterpretation.

13.265 As a corollary, it is difficult to see how deferred tax liabilities could be material in the context of total net current assets or for that matter net current liabilities since they would normally be shown as a provision under long-term liabilities. A sensible interpretation would be to show deferred tax liabilities on the face of the balance sheet where they are material in the context of net assets and deferred tax assets on the face of the balance sheet under current assets where they are material in the context of total net current assets or net assets.

Disclosure required by accounting standards

13.266 FRS 16 contains no additional disclosure requirements in respect of current tax shown as a liability on the balance sheet. A significant amount of additional disclosures is required by FRS 19 in support of the deferred tax balances reported either net or as separate assets or liabilities in the balance sheet. As with disclosures in the profit and loss account, examples from published financial statements are given to illustrate the disclosure requirements of the Act and the accounting standards.

Analysis of deferred tax balance

13.267 FRS 19 requires the following disclosures to be given in the notes to the financial statements in respect of deferred tax included in the balance sheet:

- The total deferred tax balance (before discounting, where applicable), showing the amount recognised for each significant type of timing difference separately.

- The impact of discounting on, and the discounted amount of, the deferred tax balance.

- The movement between the opening and closing net deferred tax balance, analysing separately:

  - The amount charged or credited in the profit and loss account for the period.
  - The amount charged or credited directly in the STRGL for the period; and
  - Movements arising from the acquisition or disposal of businesses.

  [FRS 19 para 61].

An example of a company giving the above disclosures is shown in Table 13.7 below:

Table 13.7 – Scottish Power plc – Annual Report & Accounts – 31 March 2001

Notes to the Group Balance sheet (extract)

Deferred tax provided in the Accounts is as follows:	**Provided**	
	2001	2000
	£m	£m
Accelerated capital allowances	**1,963.1**	1,999.7
Other timing differences	**(337.8)**	(387.6)
	1,625.3	1,612.1

	£m
At 1 April 1998 – as previously stated	–
Prior year adjustment for FRS 19	709.6
At 1 April 1998 – as restated	709.6
Charge to profit and loss account	33.5
Deferred tax provided at 1 April 1999	743.1
Charge to profit and loss account	45.2
Movements arising from acquisition	818.1
Exchange	5.7
Deferred tax provided at 1 April 2000	1,612.1
Charge to profit and loss account	13.8
Movements arising from revisions to fair values	(98.5)
Exchange	97.9
Deferred tax provided at 31 March 2001	**1,625.3**

13.268 The significant type of timing difference that will generally fall to be disclosed separately will include, amongst others, accelerated capital allowances, short-term timing differences, tax losses carried forward etc. These items should then be added to show a gross undiscounted amount from which the discount, if any, recognised on this total should be deducted to arrive at the discounted amount. There is no further requirement to analyse the discount or the discounted amount by significant type of timing difference. The standard supports this approach as is evident from the illustrative disclosure given in Appendix II to FRS 19.

13.269 In the case of multinational groups, it is likely that the balance sheet will show a net deferred tax asset of say £4 million (net of short-term liability of £6 million) as well as a net deferred tax liability of £10 million (net of short-term asset of £4 million). The same type of short-term timing difference, but of opposite signs, may be included in both the asset and the liability amounts because they arise in different tax jurisdictions and do not qualify for offset. However, for the purpose of the above analysis they would need to be included in the same category and offset (that is, a short-term liability of £2 million). Similar type of timing differences included in both assets and liabilities may need to be grouped together before they are all added to show a net deferred tax liability of £6 million before discounting.

13.270 The above disclosure may require modification where certain timing differences such as those arising on long-term liabilities or a lessor's investment in finance leases also exist. Since these timing differences are measured by reference to cash flows that have already been discounted, the deferred tax provisions to which they give rise already incorporate discounting. As a result, they should be presented after the discounted figure (if there is one).

[The next paragraph is 13.272.]

Disclosure of deferred tax asset

13.272 The amount of the deferred tax asset and the evidence supporting its recognition should be disclosed where an entity has incurred a tax loss in the current or preceding period and the recovery of the deferred tax asset is dependent on future taxable profits in excess of those arising from the reversals of deferred tax liabilities. [FRS 19 para 62].

13.273 The reasons for the disclosure requirements are noted in paragraph 13.157 above. The evidence supporting the recognition of the deferred tax asset is the specific circumstances that make it reasonable to forecast that there will be future profits against which the deferred tax assets can be recovered. [FRS 19 para 63]. Such circumstances are discussed from paragraph 13.157 above and are also likely to include tax planning strategies as explained from paragraph 13.149 above.

Circumstances affecting current and future tax charges

13.274 As stated in paragraph 13.236 above, the Act requires details of 'any special circumstances' affecting the tax charge or credit for the period or that may affect those of future periods, whether in respect of profits, income or capital gains. [4 Sch 54(2)]. This requirement is also contained in FRS 3, which requires quantification of the individual effects of any special circumstances. Such disclosures should include any special circumstances affecting the tax attributable to the exceptional items. [FRS 3 para 23]. Special circumstances could also include, for example, the effect of tax losses utilised, significant tax-free income and significant disallowables such as goodwill amortisation arising on consolidation.

13.275 The above requirements have been codified in FRS 19, which requires significant disclosures in respect of circumstances that affect the current and total tax charges or credits for the current period or may affect the current and total tax charges or credits in future periods. [FRS 19 para 64]. These requirements are considered in the paragraphs that follow.

Circumstances affecting current tax charge

13.276 A number of matters may have a significant effect on the current tax charge for the period. FRS 19 contains a standard treatment as to how these should be disclosed. The standard's requirements are as follows:

- A reconciliation of the current tax charge or credit on ordinary activities for the period reported in the profit and loss account to the current tax charge that would result from applying a relevant standard rate of tax to the profit on ordinary activities before tax.
- Either the monetary amounts or the rates (as a percentage of profits on ordinary activities before tax) may be reconciled.
- Where material, positive amounts should not be offset against negative amounts or *vice versa*: they should be shown as separate reconciling items.
- The basis on which the standard rate of tax has been determined should be disclosed.

[FRS 19 para 64(a)].

13.277 It should be noted that FRS 19 requires a reconciliation of the *current* tax charge or credit to the current tax charge or credit that would result from applying the standard rate of tax to the profit on ordinary activities before tax. In the past, many companies already provided an explanation of the special circumstances affecting the tax charge as required by the Act and FRS 3 by way of a reconciliation between the expected tax charge (the profit before tax multiplied by the statutory rate) to the *total* tax charge (current and deferred). Both IAS 12 and FAS 109 require a reconciliation of the total tax charge for the period to a standard rate of charge.

13.278 The ASB, however, chose to focus the reconciliation on the *current* tax charge instead, because it believed that that was the element of the total tax charge that was of most importance to users. A reconciliation based on the current tax charge was the clearest and most direct way of providing information on the factors that might affect future current tax charges. [FRS 19 App V para 134].

13.279 Notwithstanding the ASB's reasons, a reconciliation of the current tax charge would obviously be more transparent, because it would provide users with a complete picture of the factors (both permanent and timing differences) that had influenced the current tax charge for the period. However, a lot of tax planning transactions are based upon delaying the payment of tax and so creating timing differences. These would all be highlighted in the reconciliation of the current tax charge required under FRS 19, notwithstanding that deferred tax would have been provided on these timing differences. It seems rather superfluous to provide further disclosure of timing differences that have already been tax effected thereby calling into question the reasons for providing deferred tax in the first place. This situation would not arise in a reconciliation of the total tax charge required by

IAS 12 that would simply highlight permanent differences and other items such as adjustments related to prior year and unrecognised deferred tax. One would have expected that, at least in this disclosure requirement, a divergence from international practice was unnecessary.

13.280 The standard requires that material positive and negative reconciling items should not be offset, but shown separately in the reconciliation. This is rather obvious as aggregating material items into a single figure defeats the object of the reconciliation, which is to provide an explanation of the current tax charge. An analysis of the factors included in the reconciliation will serve as a final check on the tax computations made and will help management explain the effects of the tax provisions to others including the Inland Revenue.

13.281 The standard provides significant guidance as to how the 'standard' rate of tax should be calculated. For a UK group, the relevant rate is the standard rate of corporation tax. This rate should be used even if some of the group's operations are conducted in other countries. In that situation, the impact of different rates of tax applied to profits earned in other countries would appear as a reconciling item. [FRS 19 para 65]. However, where a UK group carries out its operations mainly outside the UK, the standard rate of corporation tax is of limited relevance. For such a group, the standard recommends use of an average tax rate (weighted in proportion to accounting profits) as illustrated below:

Example

Determination of 'standard' rate for a group with significant overseas subsidiaries

Country	Profit	Tax rate		Weighted average
UK	100	30%	100/2030 × 30% =	1.48
US	600	40%	600/2030 × 40% =	11.82
France	500	35%	500/2030 × 35% =	8.62
Germany	450	38%	450/2030 × 38% =	8.42
Australia	380	33%	380/2030 × 33% =	6.18
Total	2,030		Average rate =	36.52

The above average rate of 36.52% should be used in the tax reconciliation. The basis on which the rate has been calculated should also be disclosed as stated in paragraph 13.276.

13.282 Alternatively, multi-nationals may find it more meaningful to aggregate separate reconciliations prepared using the applicable tax rate in each individual jurisdiction, rather than provide a reconciliation to a single applicable tax rate for the whole group. Such information would normally be requested as part of the group reporting packs and would greatly simply the presentation of the tax reconciliation in the consolidated financial statements. Examples of companies that have presented the reconciliation using monetary amounts and tax rates are shown in Tables 13.8 and 13.9 below.

Table 13.8 – Costain Group plc – Annual Report – 31 December 2000

Notes to the Accounts (extract)

8 Taxation (extract)

	2000	1999
		(restated)
	£m	£m
On profit for the year:		
United Kingdom corporation tax at 30% (1999: 30.25%)	–	–
Overseas taxation	**(0.3)**	(0.2)
Adjustments in respect of prior years	**0.3**	–
	–	(0.2)
Deferred taxation	**(1.2)**	(1.3)
Adjustments in respect of prior years	**(0.2)**	–
	(1.4)	(1.5)

	2000	1999
		(restated)
	£m	£m
Tax reconciliation:		
Profit before taxation	**6.5**	6.4
Tax at 30% (1999: 30.25%)	**(2.0)**	(1.9)
Rate adjustments relating to overseas profits	**0.5**	0.3
Profit relieved by capital losses and sundry disallowed expenses	**0.7**	0.3
Unrelieved overseas taxation	**(0.3)**	(0.1)
Timing differences relating to the pension asset	**1.0**	1.3
Other timing differences	**(0.1)**	–
Exchange differences	**(0.1)**	(0.1)
Adjustments in respect of prior years	**0.3**	–
Tax charge for current year	–	(0.2)

Table 13.9 – Scottish Power plc – Annual Report & Accounts – 31 March 2001
Notes to the Group Profit and Loss Account (extract)
6 Tax on profit on ordinary activities (extract)
The rate of current tax charge on profit on ordinary activities before exceptional items and goodwill amortisation varied from the standard rate of corporation tax in the UK due to the following factors:

	Before exceptional items	Before exceptional items	
	2001	2000	1999
	%	%	%
UK corporation tax rate	**30.0**	30.0	31.0
Permanent differences	**(9.8)**	(2.6)	(1.9)
Net effect of different rates of tax in overseas businesses	**2.3**	0.7	–
Advance corporation tax written back	–	–	(2.0)
Effective tax rate on ordinary activities	**22.5**	28.1	27.1
Effect of deferred tax	**(8.1)**	(6.1)	(5.2)
Effective current tax rate on ordinary activities	**14.4**	22.0	21.9

Circumstances affecting future tax charge

13.283 FRS 19 requires a number of disclosures that provide information about the tax charge or credit that may arise in future periods. These requirements are considered below.

13.284 Where assets have been revalued in the financial statements without deferred tax having been recognised on the revaluation gain or loss or where the market values of assets that have not been revalued have been disclosed in a note, the following information should be disclosed:

- An estimate of tax that could be payable or recoverable if the assets were sold at the values shown.
- The circumstances in which the tax would be payable or recoverable.
- An indication of the amount that may become payable or recoverable in the foreseeable future.

[FRS 19 para 64(b)].

13.285 Although the above unprovided deferred tax represents neither a liability nor a contingent liability, users are entitled to know the possible tax effects of a sale at the revalued amounts either recognised or disclosed in the financial statements. The above disclosures would apply to fixed and current asset investments carried in the balance sheet at a valuation under the alternative accounting rules and where the year end market values have been disclosed in a note (or in the directors' report) because they differ materially from their book amounts. It would also apply to fixed assets whose values have been 'frozen' under the transitional provisions of FRS 15 and to investment properties carried in accordance with SSAP 19.

13.286 Where the reporting entity has sold (or entered into a binding agreement to sell) an asset but has not recognised deferred tax on a taxable gain because the gain has been or is expected to be rolled over into replacement assets, the following information should be disclosed:

- The conditions that will have to be met to obtain the rollover relief.
- An estimate of the tax that would become payable if those conditions were not met.

[FRS 19 para 64(c)].

13.287 The above disclosures apply in circumstances where deferred tax is not recognised, because it is regarded as no more than a contingent liability for as long as it appears more likely than not that the entity will be able to roll over the gain. In this respect, the above disclosures are consistent with those required by FRS 12 on contingent liabilities — its nature, an indication of the uncertainty affecting whether it will become payable and an estimate of the financial effect.

13.288 Where there is insufficient evidence that a deferred tax asset will be recoverable, the FRS does not permit that asset to be recognised. In those circumstances the following information should be disclosed:

- The amount that has not been recognised.
- The circumstances in which the asset would be recovered.

[FRS 19 para 64(d)].

13.289 If a deferred tax asset has not been recognised on the grounds of insufficient evidence of recoverability, it indicates that the entity is currently loss making and the recoverability of the asset is contingent on the entity improving its trading performance. In such circumstances, any statements made to explain the circumstances in which the asset would be recovered should be balanced, realistic and consistent with the other disclosures made in the financial statements, particularly in the OFR. References to any profit forecasts etc should be avoided as far as possible.

13.290 The following disclosure should be given in respect of any other deferred tax that has not been recognised in the financial statements:

- The nature of the amounts not recognised.
- The circumstances in which the tax would become payable or recoverable.
- An indication of the amount that may become payable or recoverable in the foreseeable future.

[FRS 19 para 64(e)].

The above disclosure would apply to deferred tax not provided on the unremitted earnings of subsidiaries, associates and joint ventures.

Example

A group made an acquisition and has fair valued fixed assets. The fair values are in excess of original cost to the acquired company. There is no binding agreement to sell these assets so no deferred tax has been provided. Is there a requirement in FRS 19 to disclose the potential tax payable if the asset is sold at the fair value?

Paragraph 64(e) of FRS 19 requires such disclosure as it states that if any other deferred tax has not been recognised, the circumstances and an estimate of the tax payable should be disclosed. It states that disclosure should include "*if any other deferred tax has not been recognised – the nature of the amounts not recognised, the circumstances in which the tax would become payable or recoverable and an indication of the amount that may become payable or recoverable in the foreseeable future*". This means that where properties are stated in the group financial statements at fair value (that is, 'cost to the group') and sold at that value, tax would become payable if that value is above the tax base (that is, 'original cost'). Since the future tax payable is not recognised it falls to be disclosed under paragraph 64(e) of FRS 19.

Groups of companies

Group relief

13.291 Subject to meeting detailed provisions in the tax legislation, trading profits and losses arising in the same accounting period may be offset for tax purposes between companies in the same group by way of group relief. For example, a subsidiary that incurred a loss during an accounting period may surrender that loss to another group member that made a profit during the same accounting period. The tax rules allow the profitable subsidiary (the claimant company) to pay to the loss making subsidiary (the surrendering company) any amount up to the full amount of the loss surrendered by way of group relief, without giving rise to any tax impact in either company.

13.292 Whether payment should or should not be made is a matter for the group to decide and does not affect the granting of the relief. However, non-payment or underpayment for group relief received may be objectionable if there are minority interests in the company. The reason for this is that if a company that has minority shareholders surrenders its losses for group relief purposes without receiving an adequate compensation payment, the minority shareholders' interests will be impaired. Likewise, overpayment for group relief may be objectionable if there are minority interests in the receiving company. Therefore, it is advisable that a fair payment should be made where there are minority interests in either the surrendering company, or the receiving company.

13.293 Where a payment is made to the surrendering company, the payment may take one of the following forms:

- The payment may be of the amount of the corporation tax saving by reason of group relief. In this situation, the claimant company pays as group relief what it would have paid as corporation tax at the applicable rate in force and the surrendering company receives the benefit of losses relieved at the same time.
- The payment may be made of any other amount up to a maximum of the gross amount of the loss surrendered by way of group relief. For example, it could be for an amount that is less than the amount of tax savings, or it could be more than the amount of tax savings, but less than the gross amount of the losses surrendered.
- The payment may be equal to the gross loss, that is the loss that has been incurred and surrendered by way of group relief, but no more than that. Any part of a payment in excess of the tax relief on the loss surrendered by way of group relief (for example, to finance the balance of the underlying loss) is not a payment in respect of group relief and it should not be dealt with as such in the financial statements.

13.294 Different accounting considerations arise in the financial statements of the claimant company and the surrendering company depending on whether payment is made for group relief or not. For the purposes of illustrating the impact of group relief made with or without payment, the tax computations of two wholly-owned fellow subsidiary undertakings, company X and company Y, for the year ended 31 December 20X1 are given in the table below. The rate of corporation tax is 33 per cent and is expected to remain constant for the foreseeable future.

Tax computations	Company X 31 December 20X1	Company Y 31 December 20X1
	£	£
Profit (loss) before tax	(90,000)	180,000
Timing differences	(10,000)	(30,000)
	(100,000)	150,000
Group relief	100,000	(100,000)
Taxable profit (loss) chargeable to tax	–	50,000
UK corporation tax @ 33%	–	16,500

No payments made for group relief

13.295 In the financial statements of company X, the surrendering company, losses surrendered without payment being received are of no value to the company and, therefore, no credit can be taken in the profit and loss account. However, part of the losses surrendered may relate to timing differences, as indicated in the example. In that situation, a deferred tax liability should be set up with a corresponding debit to the profit and loss account tax charge even if there is no current corporation tax charge. This is because the surrendering company has lost the benefit of these losses which could have been utilised by offset against future trading profits created by the reversal of the timing difference. As a result, the losses cannot be taken into account in the deferred tax calculation.

13.296 Where the surrendering company has been advised by its parent to surrender losses without receiving payment, the taxation note to the profit and loss account should disclose the fact and the financial impact. An appropriate note is included in the profit and loss account presentation below.

Company X – The surrendering company		31 December 20X1
		£
Loss on ordinary activities before taxation		(90,000)
Taxation:		
UK corporation tax @ 33%	–	
Deferred tax	3,300	(3,300)
Loss for the financial year		(93,300)

Note on taxation:

The company has surrendered the benefit of tax losses amounting to £100,000 to a fellow subsidiary undertaking without receiving any payment. Accordingly, no tax losses are available for carry-forward and the company has provided deferred tax amounting to £3,300 in respect of timing differences of £10,000 included in the losses surrendered.

13.297 In the financial statements of the claimant company, different considerations apply. Group relief received without payment is effectively a gift as far as the claimant is concerned. As the relief is included in arriving at the taxable profit of the claimant, it will reduce, or sometimes completely eliminate, the claimant's liability to current corporation tax. As a result, there could be a significant difference between the actual effective tax rate (tax charge as a percentage of profit before tax) and the prevailing corporation tax rate. In that situation, the difference will have to be explained and quantified as *"special circumstances affecting the liability to taxation for the current year"* to comply with the requirements of the Act and FRS 3 (see para 13.236 above). The presentation in the profit and loss account of the claimant company will be as follows:

Company Y – The claimant company		31 December 20X1
	£	£
Profit on ordinary activities before taxation		180,000
Taxation:		
UK corporation tax @ 33%	16,500	9,900
Deferred tax		26,400
Profit on ordinary activities after taxation		153,600
Effective current tax rate		9.17%

Note on taxation:
The corporation tax charge for the year has been reduced by £33,000 because of losses surrendered by a fellow subsidiary undertaking. No payment for this surrender is to be made by the company.

The explanation can also be provided by way of a reconciliation between the actual rate of 33% and the effective rate of 9.17% as follows:

Actual UK corporation tax rate	33.00%
Group relief received without payment	(18.33)%
Deferred tax on timing difference	(5.50)%
Effective tax rate	9.17%

Workings:
Group relief received £33,000 ÷ £180,000 = 18.33%.
Deferred tax £9,900 ÷ £180,000 = 5.5%

Payments made for group relief

13.298 Where a payment passes between the companies concerned, the accounting treatment in the financial statements of the claimant and the surrendering company will depend upon the nature of the payment as illustrated in the various situations discussed below.

Payment represents the amount of tax saving

13.299 In the financial statements of the surrendering company, the payment received or receivable will be credited as part of the tax charge with a corresponding debit to cash or amounts receivable from group companies. The treatment is similar to the repayment of tax. In some situations, it may not be prudent to take credit until the group's tax affairs have been finalised and the appropriate group election has been made. An appropriate note should be included in the tax note as illustrated below.

Company X – The surrendering company		31 December 20X1
	£	£
Loss on ordinary activities before taxation		(90,000)
Taxation:		
Amount receivable from a fellow subsidiary in respect of group relief	33,000	
Deferred taxation	(3,300)	29,700
Loss for the financial year		(60,300)

Note on taxation:
The company has surrendered the benefit of tax losses to another group company for a consideration of £33,000 which will be receivable on 30 September 20X2. Accordingly, no tax losses are available for carry-forward and the company has provided deferred tax amounting to £3,300 in respect of timing differences of £10,000 included in the losses surrendered.

13.300 As far as the claimant company is concerned, no particular problem arises because payment of tax is being made to a group member, rather than to the Inland Revenue. Therefore, the payment made should be dealt with as part of the tax charge to bring this into proper relationship with the profits, but suitably described as payment made for group relief. The presentation in the profit and loss account for the claimant company will be as follows:

Company Y – The claimant company		31 December 20X1
	£	£
Profit on ordinary activities before taxation		180,000
Taxation:		
UK corporation tax @ 33%	16,500	
Amount payable to a fellow subsidiary in respect of tax saved by group relief	33,000	
Deferred tax	9,900	59,400
Profit on ordinary activities after taxation		120,600

Note on taxation:
The corporation tax payable for the year has been reduced by £33,000 because of group relief received from a fellow subsidiary for which a payment of £33,000 will be made on 30 September 20X2.

Payment is less than the amount of tax savings

13.301 Where the group relief payment is for an amount that is less than the amount of the tax saving, the payment should be shown as part of the tax charge in the financial statements of the claimant company. Assuming that the claimant makes a payment of £20,000 in consideration for tax savings of £33,000, the disclosure in the financial statements of the claimant company would be as follows.

Company Y – The claimant company		31 December 20X1
	£	£
Profit on ordinary activities before taxation		180,000
Taxation:		
UK corporation tax @ 33%	16,500	
Amount payable to a fellow subsidiary in respect of tax saved by group relief	20,000	
Deferred tax	9,900	46,400
Profit on ordinary activities after taxation		133,600

Note on taxation:
The corporation tax charge for the year has been reduced by £13,000 because of group relief received from a fellow subsidiary for which no payment has been made.

A symmetrical treatment is followed in the financial statements of the surrendering company as indicated below:

Company X – The surrendering company		31 December 20X1
	£	£
Loss on ordinary activities before taxation		(90,000)
Taxation:		
UK corporation tax @ 33%	–	
Amount receivable from a fellow subsidiary in respect of group relief	20,000	
Deferred tax	(3,300)	16,700
Loss on ordinary activities after taxation		(73,300)

Note on taxation:
The company has surrendered the benefit of tax losses of £100,000 to another group company for a consideration of £20,000 which will be receivable on 30 September 20X2. Accordingly, no tax losses are available for carry-forward and the company has provided deferred tax amounting to £3,300 in respect of timing differences of £10,000 included in the losses surrendered.

Payment is less than the gross amount of the loss surrendered

13.302 Where the payment is of any amount greater than the tax saving, but less than the gross amount of the group relief, the consideration in respect of the group relief might be dealt with in arriving at the profit before taxation. Assuming that the claimant makes a contribution of £60,000 in consideration for financing only part of the surrendering company's tax loss of £100,000, the payment should be suitably described and the effect on the tax charge amplified by a note, as shown below. An alternative treatment, that is also acceptable, would be to treat the payment for the amount of tax savings as part of the tax charge and any excess payment as part of operating profit. This treatment results in a higher tax charge (as indicated below) and this will need to be explained.

Company Y – The claimant company

	£	31 December 20X1 £
Operating profit		180,000
Contribution towards loss of a fellow subsidiary payable by way of group relief		(60,000)
Profit on ordinary activities before taxation		120,000
Taxation:		
UK corporation tax @ 33%	16,500	
Deferred tax	9,900	26,400
Profit on ordinary activities after taxation		93,600

Note on taxation:
The charge for taxation has been reduced by £13,200 (being, £40,000 @ 33%) by reason of group relief receivable in addition to that appropriate to the contribution towards the loss of a fellow subsidiary that is charged against operating profit.

Alternative treatment

		£
Operating profit		180,000
Contribution towards loss of a fellow subsidiary in excess of tax saved by way of group relief		(27,000)
Profit on ordinary activities before taxation		153,000
Taxation:		
UK corporation tax @ 33%	16,500	
Amount payable to a fellow subsidiary in respect of tax saved by way of group relief	33,000	
Deferred tax	9,900	59,400
Profit on ordinary activities after taxation		93,600

As can be seen, in this situation, the tax charge is 38.8% of profit before tax, which is not very easy to understand unless the view is taken that the £27,000 is made in respect of financing losses and, therefore, disallowed for tax. This will need to be explained in the tax note.

Company X – The surrendering company

	£	31 December 20X1 £
Operating loss		(90,000)
Contribution receivable from a fellow subsidiary		60,000
Loss on ordinary activities before taxation		(30,000)
Taxation:		
UK corporation tax @ 33%	–	
Deferred tax	3,300	3,300
Loss for the financial year		(33,300)

Note on Taxation:
The company has surrendered the benefit of tax losses of £100,000 to another group company for a consideration of £60,000 which will be receivable on 30 September 20X2. Accordingly, no tax losses are available for carry-forward and the company has provided deferred tax amounting to £3,300 in respect of timing differences of £10,000 included in the losses surrendered.

In the above example, it has been assumed that the claimant has paid £60,000 in consideration for receiving tax losses of a value amounting to £100,000. It is possible for the surrendering company to surrender only part of the loss, leaving the balance to absorb any deferred tax on timing differences that are likely to crystallise in the future.

An alternative treatment similar to the one illustrated above may also be adopted in the financial statements of the surrendering company, but the tax credit for the loss will be out of line with the pre-tax loss and this will need to be explained.

Payment represents the gross amount of the loss surrendered

13.303 Where the claimant company makes a payment equal to the whole of the loss surrendered, the effect would be to take out of charge to corporation tax an equivalent amount of profit for both financial reporting and tax purposes. Consequently, the payment would be dealt with in arriving at profit before taxation, and it should be disclosed as shown below.

Company Y – The claimant company

	£	31 Dec 20X1 £
Operating profit		180,000
Amount payable to a fellow subsidiary in respect of group relief		(100,000)
Profit on ordinary activities before taxation		80,000
Taxation:		
UK corporation tax @ 33%	16,500	
Deferred tax	9,900	26,400
Profit for the financial year		53,600

An alternative treatment would be to split the payment of £100,000 between the actual tax relief of £33,000, which would be included within the tax charge in the profit and loss account and include the excess payment for £67,000 within operating profit as expenses incurred in financing the losses of the surrendering company.

13.304 A symmetrical treatment should also be adopted in the financial statements of the surrendering company. That is, the amount received or receivable should be credited in arriving at profit before taxation. However, in this situation, the surrendering company receives payment for the full amount of the timing differences included in the loss surrendered and this creates a book profit. Although no tax loss is available for carry-forward, a deferred tax charge is required in respect of the timing differences included in the surrendered loss if it is concluded that the timing differences are likely to reverse as illustrated below.

Company X – The surrendering company

	31 Dec 20X1 £		£
Operating loss			(90,000)
Contribution receivable from a fellow subsidiary			100,000
Profit on ordinary activities before taxation			10,000
Taxation:			
UK corporation tax @ 33%		–	
Deferred tax		3,300	3,300
Profit for the financial year			6,700

Note on taxation:
The company has surrendered the benefit of tax losses to another group company for a consideration of £100,000 which will be receivable on 30 September 20X2. Accordingly, no tax losses are available for carry-forward and the company has provided deferred tax amounting to £3,300 in respect of timing differences of £10,000 included in the losses surrendered.

Again the alternative presentation discussed in paragraph 13.302 may be adopted.

13.305 Where a payment for group relief is brought into account in a year subsequent to that to which it relates, because the group relief position and group election for the current year were not finalised by the time the financial statements were approved, it should be appropriately described (depending upon the nature of the payment) as set out in the examples above, with the addition of words indicating that it relates to previous years. If the tax relief relating to the payment is brought to account at the same time, that too should be described appropriately.

Chapter 14

Earnings per share

	Page
Background	14001
Business combination accounted for as a merger	14003
Annex	14005

Chapter 14

Earnings per share

Background

14.1 Earnings per share (EPS) is a ratio that is widely used by financial analysts, investors and others to gauge the profitability of a company and to value its shares. Its purpose is to indicate how effective a company has been in using the resources provided by the equity shareholders. The allocation of earnings accruing to other providers of finance, such as non-equity shareholders (for example, preference shareholders) is a prior charge and is often fixed. Therefore, the income remaining after making allocations to those parties is attributable to equity shareholders. This amount, when presented on the face of the profit and loss account on a pence per share basis, assists the equity shareholders to gauge the company's current net earnings and changes in its net earnings from period to period. It can, therefore, be relevant as a measure of company performance and in evaluating management's effectiveness. Another reason for the popularity of EPS is that it forms the basis for calculating the 'price-earnings ratio', which is a standard stock market indicator. Price-earnings ratios relating to both past and prospective profits are widely used by investors and analysts in valuing shares.

14.2 EPS is simply a ratio of the numerator – *earnings measured in terms of profits available to equity shareholders* – to the denominator – *the number of equity shares*. Therefore, it is very simple in concept, but it is the determination of the numerator and, in particular, the denominator that can make the calculation of this ratio rather complex in practice. Also if the ratio is to be meaningful it must be calculated on a similar basis for every entity so as to facilitate comparisons between different accounting periods for the same entity and between different entities in the same period. It is for this reason that the original standard, SSAP 3, 'Earnings per share', was issued in February 1972 with the objective of providing a minimum standard of measurement and disclosure of EPS in financial statements of listed companies.

14.3 SSAP 3 had been working reasonably well in the UK. On the international front, however, the IASC had been co-operating with the FASB in the US to develop a new international standard on earnings per share. The FASB was already working on a project to improve and simplify its existing guidance on earnings per share that had become unduly complicated. Early in 1996, the two standard setting bodies published exposure drafts on earnings per share which contained proposals that were considerably closer to the current UK requirement than to US GAAP. The ASB's support for international harmonisation of accounting standards and the recognition that EPS is a popular statistic that has international appeal, gave it the opportunity to bring the UK guidance in line with an internationally acceptable method for calculating and presenting earnings per share data.

14.4 The IASC issued IAS 33, 'Earnings per share', in February 1997 at the same time as the FASB issued a substantially similar but more detailed standard (FAS 128) in the US. In June 1997, the ASB issued FRED 16 which adopted, with minimal exceptions, the requirements and to a large extent the text of IAS 33. Comments on the FRED, however, highlighted a need to customise the international requirements to minimise inconsistencies between UK law and other accounting standards. Several commentators also requested guidance on how some of the general principles of IAS 33 would apply, in practice, to a number of areas. As a result of these comments, the ASB issued a final standard FRS 14, 'Earnings per share', which includes specific guidance on some aspects, in particular contingently issuable shares, employee share schemes and special dividends, which were either not adequately dealt with or considered in the 1997 version of IAS 33.

14.5 In December 2003, the IASB issued a revised version of IAS 33. The revised standard includes additional guidance on more complex matters, such as the effects of contingently issuable shares, contracts that may be settled in ordinary shares or cash, written put options and participating securities.

14.6 In December 2004, as part of its strategy of convergence of UK GAAP with IFRS, the ASB issued FRS 22, 'Earnings per share', which is almost identical to the 2003 revised version of IAS 33 and supersedes FRS 14.

14.7 Attached as an annex to this chapter is the chapter from the Manual of Accounting – IFRS in the UK that deals with the measurement and presentation of earnings per share under IAS 33 (2003). As the requirements of FRS 22 are almost identical to those of IAS 33 (2003), the issues will be the same under UK GAAP as under IFRS.

14.8 The text in the annex contains references to IFRS. For these to be applied in the UK context, the following should be noted:

- The references to paragraphs in IAS 33 (2003) are identical to the paragraph numbers in FRS 22.
- References to other international standards should be read as referring to the equivalent UK standards, as issued by the ASB.
- Because it is permitted under UK GAAP for business combinations to be accounted for as mergers, FRS 22 contains guidance surrounding the impact of that on the calculation of earnings per share. Such guidance is not included in IAS 33 (2003) because under International Financial Reporting Standards it is not generally permitted for business combinations to be accounted for using merger accounting.

14.9 The remainder of this chapter considers the calculation of earnings per share when the reporting entity has been a party to a business combination that has been accounted for as a merger during the year.

Business combination accounted for as a merger

14.10 Where a business combination is accounted for as a merger, the financial statements of the combined entity are presented as if the combined entity had always existed. This means that the acquired subsidiary's results for both the current and the previous year are included in full in the current and in the corresponding amounts shown in the consolidated profit and loss account. Therefore, EPS computations should be based on the aggregate of the weighted average number of ordinary shares of the combined entity, adjusted to equivalent shares of the entity whose shares are outstanding after the combination for all periods presented. [FRS 22 App C para C1].

Annex

14.11 The chapter from the Manual of Accounting – IFRS for the UK that deals with IAS 33 is included as an annex to this chapter. Because FRS 22 is identical to IAS 33 (2003), the accounting and practical issues are the same.

14.12 The text in the annex contains references to IFRSs. For these to be applied in the UK context, the following should be noted:

- The references to paragraphs in IAS 33 should be read as references to FRS 22, whose paragraph numbers are identical.
- References to other international standards should be read as references to their UK GAAP equivalents.

Annex — Earnings per share

Contents

	Page
Introduction	14009
Objectives and scope of IAS 33	14010
Objectives	14010
Scope	14010
Basic earnings per share	14011
Measurement	14011
Computation of earnings	14012
Preference dividends	14012
Other appropriations and adjustments in respect of preference shares	14013
Participating securities and two-class ordinary shares	14015
Computation of number of ordinary shares	14120
Purchase and holding of own shares and ESOPs	14122
Contingently issuable shares	14123
Shares issued as consideration in a business combination	14124
Mandatorily convertible instruments	14124
Bonus issue (stock dividends), share split and share consolidation	14124
Issue of shares at full market price	14126
Rights issue	14126
Issue of shares at less than market price	14130
Dividends payable in shares or cash	14130
Special dividend followed by share consolidation	14131
Diluted earnings per share	14137
Measurement	14137
Computation of earnings	14138
Computation of number of ordinary shares	14140
Partly paid shares	14141
Convertible securities	14141
Share warrants, options and other potential ordinary shares	14148
Calculating diluted EPS	14154
EPS for interim periods	14160
Securities of subsidiaries, joint ventures and associates	14161
Employee share and incentive plans	14163
Contingently issuable ordinary shares	14165
Contracts that may be settled in ordinary shares or cash	14171
Purchased options	14174
Written put options	14175
Restatement of EPS data	14175
Post balance sheet changes in capital	14176
Prior period adjustments	14176
Presentation and disclosure	14179
Presentation of basic and diluted EPS	14179
Additional disclosures	14180
Volatility of published EPS	14184

Additional earnings per share 14184
Financial statistics in the historical summary 14189
First time adoption of IFRS 14191

Introduction

A14.1 Earnings per share (EPS) is a ratio that is widely used by financial analysts, investors and others to gauge a company's profitability and to value its shares. Its purpose is to indicate how effective a company has been in using the resources provided by the ordinary shareholders (described as ordinary equity holders in IAS 33). The allocation of earnings accruing to other providers of finance, such as preference shareholders is a prior charge and is often fixed. Therefore, the income remaining after making allocations to those parties is attributable to ordinary shareholders. This amount, when presented on the face of the profit and loss account on a pence per share basis, assists the ordinary shareholders to gauge the company's current net earnings and changes in its net earnings from period to period. It can, therefore, be relevant as a measure of company performance and in evaluating management's effectiveness. Another reason for the popularity of EPS is that it forms the basis for calculating the 'price-earnings ratio', which is a standard stock market indicator. Price-earnings ratios relating to both past and prospective profits are widely used by investors and analysts in valuing shares.

A14.2 EPS is simply a ratio of the numerator – earnings measured in terms of profits available to ordinary shareholders – to the denominator – the number of ordinary shares. Therefore, it is very simple in concept, but it is the determination of the numerator and, in particular, the denominator that can make the calculation of this ratio rather complex in practice. Also if the ratio is to be meaningful it must be calculated on a similar basis for every entity so as to facilitate comparisons between different accounting periods for the same entity and between different entities in the same period.

[The next paragraph is A14.4.]

A14.4 The IASC issued IAS 33, 'Earnings per share', in February 1997. However, in 2003, as part of its improvements project, the IASB revised IAS 33. IAS 33 (revised 2003) includes additional guidance and illustrative examples on a number of matters. Additional matters covered in the revised IAS 33 and reflected in this chapter include specific guidance on:

- Contingently issuable shares.
- Potential ordinary shares of subsidiaries, joint ventures or associates.
- Participating equity instruments.
- Written put options.
- Purchased put and call options.
- Mandatorily convertible instruments.

Additional clarification is also included on employee share options and share consolidations combined with special dividends. The revised IAS 33 is effective for accounting periods beginning on or after 1 January 2005. In this chapter, references to IAS 33 are to the revised standard, unless otherwise stated.

> **UK.A14.4.1** In the past, the equivalent UK standard was FRS 14, 'Earnings per share', which was issued in October 1988. This included guidance on many of the additional matters listed in paragraph A14.4 above and was substantially the same as IAS 33 in the method adopted to calculate earnings per share amounts. In December 2004, the ASB issued a new UK standard, FRS 22 (IAS 33), 'Earnings per share', which is effective for accounting periods beginning on or after 1 January 2005. FRS 22 is based on IAS 33 and is almost identical to that standard. A comparison of the rules in the revised IAS 33 with those in FRS 22 is given at the end of this chapter for information purposes.

[The next paragraph is A14.40.]

Objectives and scope of IAS 33

Objectives

A14.40 IAS 33 specifies the way in which earnings per share data should be calculated, presented and disclosed in the financial statements of entities. In doing so, it focuses primarily on determining the number of shares to be included in the denominator of the earnings per share calculation. [IAS 33 para 1].

A14.41 Although it is accepted that earnings per share data may have limitations because of the different accounting policies used for determining 'earnings', a consistently calculated denominator will improve the comparison of the performance of different entities in the same period and of the same entity in different accounting periods. Furthermore, a denominator calculated in accordance with international consensus will go a long way in enhancing global comparison of earnings per share data in spite of different national methods for determining 'earnings'.

Scope

A14.42 The standard applies to entities whose ordinary shares or potential ordinary shares (for example, convertible debt, warrants etc) are publicly traded. [IAS 33 para 2]. Therefore, entities whose securities are listed on a recognised stock exchange (for example, London Stock Exchange, Luxembourg Stock Exchange, NASDAQ) or are otherwise publicly traded, will have to calculate earnings per share data in accordance with the standard. Furthermore, entities that are in the process of issuing ordinary shares or potential ordinary shares in public markets (that is, not private placings) are also required to comply with the standard. [IAS 33 para 2].

A14.43 When both the parent's separate and consolidated financial statements are presented, the disclosures are required only on the basis of consolidated information. Users of the financial statements of a parent are normally concerned with, and need information on, the results of operations of the group as a whole. Where an entity chooses voluntarily to present earnings per share based on its entity financial statements as well as earnings per share based on the consolidated financial statements, the entity earnings per share figures may be shown only on the face of the entity income statement. They must not be shown in the consolidated financial statements. [IAS 33 para 4].

A14.44 Entities whose securities are not publicly traded are not required to disclose earnings per share data because, generally, they have a smaller number of ordinary shareholders. However, where such entities choose to disclose earnings per share data, to maintain comparability in financial reporting, they should comply with the standard's provisions. [IAS 33 para 3]. Such entities are likely to be those that intend to establish a track record before seeking entry to the public market at a future date.

[The next paragraph is A14.46.]

Basic earnings per share

Measurement

A14.46 Entities that fall within the standard's scope must calculate basic (and diluted) EPS for the profit or loss attributable to the parent entity's ordinary equity holders. Basic (and diluted) EPS should also be calculated for profit or loss from continuing operations if this is presented. [IAS 33 para 9]. Where an entity has no operations that qualify as discontinued under IFRS 5, 'Non-current assets held for sale and discontinued operations', the profit or loss for the year will all be attributable to continuing operations and so calculation of an additional EPS figure for continuing operations will be unnecessary. Where an entity has operations that qualify as discontinued under IFRS 5, however, it has to give separate disclosure of the results of such operations. IAS 33 then requires the basic (and diluted) EPS for profit or loss attributable to continuing operations to be calculated. The standard requires disclosure of these EPS figures for each class of ordinary shares that has a different right to share in profit for the period – see 'Presentation and disclosure' from paragraph A14.173 below. The following paragraphs describe the EPS calculation for profit or loss for the period attributable to ordinary equity holders, but the principles are the same for calculating EPS for profit or loss from continuing and discontinued operations.

A14.47 Basic EPS should be calculated by dividing the profit or loss for the period attributable to the parent entity's ordinary equity holders by the weighted average number of ordinary shares outstanding during the period. [IAS 33 para 10].

A14.48 The term 'ordinary share' is defined as an equity instrument that is subordinate to all other classes of equity instrument. An equity instrument is any contract that evidences a residual interest in the assets of an entity after deducting all of its liabilities. [IAS 33 para 5; IAS 32 para 11].

A14.49 Ordinary shares participate in profit only after other types of shares such as preference shares have participated. [IAS 33 para 6]. Indeed preference shares that provide for mandatory redemption by the issuer for a fixed or determinable amount at a fixed or determinable future date or that give the holder the right to require such redemption are treated as liabilities under IAS 32, 'Financial instruments: Disclosure and presentation'. [IAS 32 para 18(a)]. An entity may have more than one class of ordinary share (see further para A14.59 below). Ordinary shares of the same class will have the same rights to receive dividends. [IAS 33 para 6].

A14.50 The computation of the EPS figure requires a calculation of the earnings as the numerator and the relevant number of ordinary shares as the denominator. If no adjustments are required to the numerator or the denominator, the profit or loss attributable to the ordinary equity holders and the relevant number of ordinary shares can be obtained directly from the financial statements and the figure computed. However, in practice the numerator or to the denominator or both may need to be adjusted. The circumstances in which such adjustments should be made and the reasons are considered in the paragraphs that follow.

Computation of earnings

A14.51 For the purposes of calculating basic EPS, the profit or loss from continuing operations and the profit or loss for the period attributable to the parent entity's ordinary equity holders are the profit or loss after tax and minority interest and after adjusting for the after tax effects of preference dividends, differences arising on settlement of preference shares and other similar effects of preference shares classified as equity under IAS 32. [IAS 33 paras 12, A1]. In the absence of any preference shares, it is relatively simple to calculate the earnings figure for EPS purposes. However, where the entity has preference shares in issue, some further adjustments as stated above may be necessary. The ways in which such adjustments are likely to affect earnings for the purposes of calculating basic EPS are considered below.

Preference dividends

A14.52 Where an entity has preference shares in issue, those shares will be classified as financial liabilities or equity under IAS 32, depending on the terms of the shares. Where preference shares are classified as liabilities in accordance with IAS 32 (see para A14.49 above) any dividends or other appropriations in respect of such preference shares (for example, a premium payable on redemption) will be treated as finance costs in arriving at profit or loss for the period. [IAS 32 paras 35, 36]. However, where preference shares are classified as equity, any dividends and other appropriations would be debited directly to equity and an adjustment is, therefore, needed to deduct it from the profit for the period to arrive at the profit attributable to ordinary equity holders for the purpose of calculating EPS. [IAS 33 para 12].

A14.53 Where preference shares carry the right to a fixed dividend, then those dividends can either be cumulative or non-cumulative. If the preference dividends are cumulative, the dividend for the period should be taken into account, whether or not it has been declared. [IAS 33 para 14(b)]. Thus, in a year in which the company is unable to pay or declare a cumulative preference dividend, because of insufficient distributable profits (for example, the company has accumulated losses), the undeclared amount of the cumulative preference dividend (net of tax, if applicable) should still be deducted in arriving at earnings for the purposes of the EPS calculation. In the year in which these arrears of preference dividends are paid, they should be ignored in the EPS calculation for that year. [IAS 33 para 14(b)]. On the other hand, if the preference dividends are non-cumulative, only the amount of dividends declared in respect of the year should be deducted in arriving at the profit attributable to ordinary shareholders. [IAS 33 para 14(a)].

Other appropriations and adjustments in respect of preference shares

A14.54 Under IAS 32 (see para A14.49 above) and IAS 39, 'Financial instruments: Recognition and measurement', the charges made in the profit and loss account in respect of preference shares that are treated as financial liabilities will include not only the preference and/or participating dividends, but also other elements such as the amortisation of transaction costs and accrual for any premium payable on redemption. [IAS 39 paras 47, IAS 32 paras 35, 36]. It follows that these other elements should continue to be deducted in arriving at profit for the financial year and the earnings available to ordinary equity holders. In the year in which the preference shares are redeemed, any premium payable on redemption should be ignored in calculating EPS for that year to the extent that it has been accrued (and, therefore, already taken into account) in earlier years.

A14.55 In respect of preference shares classified as equity the following adjustments should also be made:

- Any original discount or premium that is amortised to retained earnings using the effective interest method is treated as a preference dividend for the purposes of calculating EPS. [IAS 33 para 15]. An example is non-convertible, non-redeemable preference shares that have been issued at a discount to compensate for non-payment of dividends in earlier years, the discount being amortised to retained earnings. Such shares are often referred to as 'increasing rate preference shares'. (See illustrative example 1 in IAS 33.)
- On the repurchase of preference shares, any excess of the fair value of consideration given over the carrying amount of the shares is a charge to retained earnings and is deducted in determining the profit, or added in

determining the loss, available to ordinary equity holders for the purpose of calculating EPS. [IAS 33 para 16].

- Where preference shares are converted early on favourable terms, the excess of the fair value of ordinary shares or other consideration paid over the fair value of ordinary shares or other consideration payable under the original terms is deducted in determining the profit, or added in determining the loss, available to ordinary equity holders for the purpose of calculating EPS. [IAS 33 para 17].

- Any excess of the carrying amount of preference shares over the fair value of the consideration paid to settle them is added in determining the profit, or deducted in determining the loss, available to ordinary equity holders for the purpose of calculating EPS. [IAS 33 para 18].

A14.56 The treatment of preference shares in the EPS calculation is illustrated in the following example:

Example

An entity has the following preference shares in issue at the end of 20X4:

■ 5% Redeemable, non-cumulative preference shares, these shares are classified as liabilities under IAS 32. During the year a dividend was paid on the 5% preference shares.	C100,000
■ Increasing rate, cumulative, non-redeemable preference shares issued at a discount in 20X0 with a cumulative dividend rate from 20X5 of 10%. The shares were issued at a discount to compensate the holders, as dividend payments will not commence until 20X5. The accrual for the discount in the current year, calculated using the effective interest method amounted to, say, C18,000. These shares are classified as equity under IAS 32.	C200,000
■ 8% Non-redeemable, non-cumulative preference shares. At the beginning of the year the entity had C100,000 8% preference shares outstanding, but at 30 June 20X4, it repurchased C50,000 of these at a discount of C1,000.	C50,000
■ 7% Cumulative, convertible preference shares (converted in the year). These shares were classified as equity, until their conversion into ordinary shares at the beginning of the year. No dividend was accrued in respect of the year, although the previous year's dividend was paid immediately prior to conversion. To induce conversion, the terms of conversion of the 7% convertible preference shares were also amended and the revised terms entitled the preference shareholders to an additional 100 ordinary shares on conversion with a fair value of C300.	CNil

The profit attributable to ordinary equity holders for the year 20X4 is C150,000. Adjustments for the purpose of calculating EPS are made as follows:

	C	C
Profit for the year attributable to the ordinary equity holders		150,000
Amortisation of discount on issue of increasing rate preference shares	(18,000)[1]	
Discount on repurchase of 8% preference shares	1,000[2]	
		(17,000)
Profit attributable to ordinary equity holders for basic EPS		133,000

Notes

1 The original discount on issue of the increasing rate preference shares has been amortised to retained earnings, so must be treated as preference dividends for EPS purposes and adjusted against profit attributable to the ordinary equity holders. [IAS 33 para 15]. There is no adjustment in respect of dividends as these do not commence until 20X5. Instead, the finance cost is represented by the amortisation of the discount in the dividend-free period. In future years, the accrual for the dividend of C20,000 will be deducted from profits. [IAS 33 para 14(b)].

2 The discount on repurchase of the 8% preference shares has been credited to equity so must be added to profit. [IAS 33 para 18].

3 The dividend on the 5% preference shares has been charged to the income statement as the preference shares are treated as liabilities, so no adjustment is necessary to profit.

4 No accrual for the dividend on the 8% preference shares is required as they are non-cumulative. Had a dividend been declared for the year it would have been deducted from profit for the purpose of calculating basic EPS as the shares are treated as equity and the dividend would have been charged to equity in the financial statements. [IAS 33 para 14(a)].

5 As the 7% preference shares were converted at the beginning of the year, there is no adjustment in respect of the 7% preference shares as no dividend accrued in respect of the year. The payment of the previous year's cumulative dividend is ignored for EPS purposes as it will have been adjusted for in the prior year. [IAS 33 para 14(b)]. Similarly, the excess of the fair value of additional ordinary shares issued on conversion of the convertible preference shares over fair value of the ordinary shares to which they would have been entitled under the original conversion terms would already have been deducted from profit attributable to the ordinary shareholders and no further adjustment is required.

Participating securities and two-class ordinary shares

A14.57 Sometimes, preference shares may be given the right to participate in the profit with ordinary shares according to a predetermined formula, but with an upper limit or cap on the extent of participation by the preference shares. Such participation is usually in addition to a fixed dividend. Participating preference shares would be treated as either financial liabilities or equity instruments under IAS 32, dependent on their terms. Where participating preference shares are classified as liabilities, both the fixed and the participating element would have been charged in arriving at profit or loss attributable to the parent entity and no further adjustments are necessary. Where participating preference shares are classified as equity instruments, IAS 33 contains further guidance that is considered below.

A14.58 IAS 33 describes instruments that would include participating preference shares as 'participating equity instruments'. It notes that such instruments include instruments that participate in dividends with ordinary shares according to a predetermined formula (for example, two for one) with, sometimes an upper limit on participation (for example, up to a specified amount per share, but no more). [IAS 33 para A13(a)]. An example might be a participating preference share that receives a fixed dividend of 3 per cent and a variable participation of 20 per cent of the dividend on an ordinary share up to a maximum of 50 pence per participating preference share. Therefore, the total earnings would need to be calculated by reference to the fixed and the participating element in order to calculate the EPS attributable to the participating preference shares.

A14.59 In addition to participating equity instruments, an entity could have a class of ordinary shares with a different dividend rate from that of another class of ordinary shares, but without prior or senior rights. [IAS 33 para A13(b)]. IAS 33 describes such instruments as 'two-class ordinary shares'. Where this is the case, the earnings for the period should be apportioned over the different classes of equity shares in issue in accordance with their dividend rights or other rights to participate in undistributed earnings. [IAS 33 para A14]. This means that a company could disclose a number of EPS figures, each attributable to different classes of equity shares and participating equity instruments.

A14.60 The steps that should be followed in allocating earnings for the purposes of calculating basic EPS where an entity has different classes of ordinary shares and participating equity instruments that are not convertible into ordinary shares are as follows:

- Profit or loss attributable to ordinary equity holders is adjusted by the amount of dividends declared in the period for each class of shares and by the contractual amount of dividends that must be paid for the period (for example, unpaid cumulative dividends).
- The remaining profit or loss is allocated to ordinary shares and participating equity instruments to the extent that each instrument shares in earnings or losses. The allocation is made as if all the profit or loss has been distributed. The total profit or loss allocated to each class of equity instrument is determined by adding together the amount allocated for dividends and the amount allocated for the participation feature.
- The total amount of profit or loss allocated to each class of equity instrument is divided by the number of outstanding instruments to which the profits or losses are allocated (that is, the instruments in that class) to determine the EPS for that class of instrument.

[IAS 33 para A14].

A14.61 Where participating equity instruments (participating preference shares) are convertible into ordinary shares, conversion is assumed if the effect is dilutive. Where this is so, the conversion shares should be included in outstanding ordinary shares for the purposes of calculating diluted EPS (see below under 'Diluted earnings per share'). [IAS 33 para A14].

A14.62 The illustrative examples accompanying IAS 33 include a worked example illustrating how the allocation would be done. The following example is based on that example.

Example

An entity has two classes of shares in issue:

5,000 Non-convertible preference shares

10,000 Ordinary shares

The preference shares are entitled to a fixed dividend of C5 per share before any dividends are paid on the ordinary shares. Ordinary dividends are then paid in which the preference shareholders do not participate. Each preference share then participates in any additional ordinary dividend above C2 at a rate of 50% of any additional dividend payable on an ordinary share.

The entity's profit for the year is C100,000 and dividends of C2 per share are declared on the ordinary shares.

The calculation of basic EPS using the allocation method described in the previous paragraph is as follows:

	C	C
Profit		100,000
Less dividends payable for the period:		
Preference (5,000 × C5)	25,000	
Ordinary (10,000 × C2)	20,000	(45,000)
Undistributed earnings		55,000

Allocation of undistributed earnings:
Allocation per ordinary share = A
Allocation per preference share = B where B = 50% of A

(A × 10,000) + (50% × A × 5,000) = C55,000
A = 55,000 / (10,000 + 2,500) A = C4.4
B = 50% of A
B = C2.2

The basic per share amounts are:	Preference shares C per share	Ordinary shares C per share
Distributed earnings	5.00	2.00
Undistributed earnings	2.20	4.40
Totals	7.20	6.40

Proof: (5,000 × C7.2) + (10,000 × C6.4) = C100,000

A14.63 IAS 33 implies that the EPS attributable to the participating preference shares (participating equity instrument in IAS 33 terminology) should be disclosed even though only one of its two elements (the participating element) is subordinate to all other classes of equity instrument.

A14.64 Table A14.1 illustrates disclosure of EPS for different classes of shares – preferred shares and ordinary shares. The equity note describes the respective dividend rights of the shares.

Table A14.1 — EPS for different classes of shares

Volkswagen AG — Annual Report and Accounts — 31 December 2004

INCOME STATEMENT OF THE VOLKSWAGEN GROUP FOR THE PERIOD JANUARY 1 TO DECEMBER 31 2004 (EXTRACT)

	Note	2004	2003
Earnings per ordinary share (€)	(10)	**+1.75**	**+2.54**
Diluted earnings per ordinary share (€)	(10)	**+1.75**	**+2.54**
Earnings per preferred share (€)	(10)	**+1.81**	**+ 2.60**
Diluted earnings per preferred share (€)	(10)	**+1.81**	**+ 2.60**

(10) EARNINGS PER SHARE

Basic earnings per share are calculated by dividing the portion of earnings attributable to the shareholders of Volkswagen AG by the weighted average number of ordinary and preferred shares outstanding during the fiscal year. Earnings per share are diluted by 'potential shares'. These include stock options, although these are only dilutive if they result in the issuance of shares at a value below the average market price of the shares. There was no dilutive effect because the average price of Volkswagen ordinary shares was below the conversion price for the exercise of conversion rights.

Quantity shares	Ordinary 2004	Ordinary 2003	Preferred 2004	Preferred 2003
Weighted average number of shares outstanding — basic	278,570,587	278,570,587	105,238,280	105,238,280
Dilutive potential ordinary shares stock option plan	–	–	–	–
Bonds with warrants	–	–	–	–
Weighted average number of shares outstanding — diluted	278,570,587	278,570,587	105,238,280	105,238,280

million €	**2004**	**2003**
Profit after tax	716	1003
Minority interests	39	23
Profit attributable to shareholders of Volkswagen AG	677	980
Basic earnings of which relating to:		
— ordinary share	487	707
— preferred share	190	273
Diluted earnings of which relating to:		
— ordinary share	487	707
— preferred share	190	273

€	2004	2003
Earnings per share — basic		
Ordinary share	1.75	2.54
Preferred share	1.81	2.60
Earnings per share — diluted		
Ordinary share	1.75	2.54
Preferred share	1.81	2.60

22 equity (extract)

The subscribed capital of Volkswagen AG is denominated in euros. The shares are no-par value bearer shares. Each share has a notional value of €2.56. As well as ordinary shares, there are preferred shares that entitle the bearer to a €0.06 higher dividend than ordinary shares, but do not carry voting rights. The subscribed capital is composed of 320,289,940 no-par value ordinary shares and 105,238,280 preferred shares, and amounts to €1,089 million (previous year: €1,089 million).

Based on the resolution by the Annual General Meeting on June 7, 2001, authorized capital of up to €130 million, expiring on June 6, 2006, was approved for the issue of new ordinary bearer shares. Based on the resolution by the Annual General Meeting on April 22, 2004, further authorized capital of up to €400 million, expiring on April 21, 2009, was approved.

	shares 2004	shares 2003	€ 2004	€ 2003
Balance at January 1	425,528,220	425,528,220	1,089,352,243	1,089,352,243
Issued shares (bonds with warrents)	–	–	–	–
Balance at December 31	425,528,220	425,528,220	1,089,352,243	1,089,352,243

Of the ordinary shares, 41,719,353 were held by the wholly owned subsidiary Volkswagen Beteiligungs-Gesellschaft mbH at December 31, 2004.

Computation of number of ordinary shares

A14.65 The denominator of the basic EPS is calculated using the weighted average number of those ordinary shares that are outstanding during the period under review. [IAS 33 para 19].

A14.66 Where there have been no changes in capital structure during the year, the relevant denominator is the number of ordinary shares outstanding at the year end. However, if additional ordinary shares have been issued during the year, it would not give a fair presentation to apportion the earnings for the whole of the year over the larger equity base. This is because the capital invested through the issue of the additional shares was available to the entity to increase its earnings only for part of the year. Similar considerations apply where shares have been bought back during the year. In order to take these factors into account, and to permit comparison of EPS with the previous period when there may have been no such change in the issued equity capital, it is necessary to use an average of the number of shares weighted by the number of days outstanding (a 'weighted average ordinary share capital') in the calculation of the denominator. The time-weighting factor should generally be the number of days that the specific shares are outstanding as a proportion of the total number of days, although a reasonable approximation of the weighted average is adequate in most circumstances. [IAS 33 para 20].

A14.67 An example of how the weighted average number of shares should be calculated is given below. The example is derived from the illustrative example in IAS 33.

	Shares issued	Treasury shares	Shares outstanding
1 Jan 20X1 Balance at beginning of year	2,400	–	2,400
31 May 20X1 Issue of new shares for cash	800	–	3,200
1 Dec 20X1 Purchase of shares for cash	–	(200)	3,000
31 Dec 20X1 Balance at end of year	3,200	(200)	3,000

Computation of weighted average:
(2,400 × 5/12) + (3,200 × 6/12) + (3,000 × 1/12) = 2,850 shares
or
(2,400 × 12/12) + (800 × 7/12) — (200 × 1/12) = 2,850 shares

A14.68 The general principle under IAS 33 is that shares should be included in the weighted average calculation from the date the consideration is receivable (which is generally the date of their issue). [IAS 33 para 21]. Therefore, shares issued for cash are brought into the calculation from the date the cash is receivable. Where shares are issued as consideration for the acquisition of an asset or a satisfaction of a liability, the shares are included in the averaging calculation from the date the asset is recognised or the liability is settled. In other situations, the date of inclusion should be determined from the terms and conditions attaching to the issue. The substance of any contract associated with the issue should also be considered. The standard provides a number of examples illustrating the timing of inclusion of ordinary shares in the weighted average calculation. These examples are listed below:

- Ordinary shares issued in exchange for cash are included when cash is receivable.
- Ordinary shares issued on the voluntary reinvestment of dividends on ordinary or preference shares are included when dividends are reinvested.
- Ordinary shares issued as a result of the conversion of a debt instrument to ordinary shares are included as of the date when interest ceases accruing.
- Ordinary shares issued in place of interest or principal on other financial instruments are included as of the date when interest ceases accruing.
- Ordinary shares issued in exchange for the settlement of a liability of the entity are included as of the settlement date.
- Ordinary shares issued as consideration for the acquisition of an asset other than cash are included as of the date on which the acquisition is recognised.
- Ordinary shares issued for the rendering of services to the entity are included as the services are rendered.
- Ordinary shares issued as part of the cost of a business combination are included from the acquisition date (see para A14.76).

[IAS 33 paras 21, 22].

A14.69 The general rule that shares should be included in the basic EPS calculation from the date consideration is receivable does not apply to shares that are issued in partly paid form. Partly paid shares are treated as fractions of shares (payments received to date as a proportion of the total subscription price) and included in the averaging calculation only to the extent that they participate in dividends for the period. [IAS 33 para A15]. Partly paid shares that do not participate in dividends are excluded from the basic EPS calculation, but included in the calculation of diluted EPS (see further para A14.110).

Example

A company issues 100,000 ordinary shares of C1 each for a consideration of C2.50 per share. Calls amounting to C1.75 per share were received by the balance sheet date. The partly paid shares are entitled to participate in dividends for the period in proportion to the amount paid. The number of ordinary share equivalents that would be included in the basic EPS calculation on a weighted basis is as follows:

$$100{,}000 \times \frac{C1.75}{C2.50} = 70{,}000 \text{ shares}$$

A14.70 Whenever changes in ordinary shares occur during the accounting period, an amendment is necessary to the number of shares used in the EPS calculation. In some situations, the EPS in prior periods will also have to be adjusted. Some of the ways in which a company can change its ordinary share capital and the consequential effect on the number of shares used in the EPS calculation are considered below.

Purchase and holding of own shares and ESOPs

A14.71 Where a company has purchased its own ordinary shares during the year, there will be a lesser number outstanding after the repurchase. Such repurchases should be reflected in the weighted average number of shares outstanding during the period from the date shares are repurchases as illustrated in paragraph A14.67. Any premium payable on the purchase of a company's own ordinary shares will be charged against reserves and will not affect earnings for the year. No adjustments should be made to the prior year's EPS.

A14.72 A company may sometimes hold its own shares in treasury. This situation may arise where it has acquired them in the market, or by forfeiture, or by surrender in lieu of forfeiture, or by way of a gift. Shares held uncancelled in treasury are accounted for as a deduction from shareholders' funds. [IAS 32 para 33; IAS 33 para 20]. Another not uncommon group situation is where a subsidiary continues to hold the shares in the parent that were acquired before it became a group member. Since such shares are no longer available in the market, they are excluded from the weighted average number of ordinary shares for the purpose of calculating EPS. [IAS 33 para 20].

[The next paragraph is UK.A14.74.1.]

UK.A14.74.1 In the UK, a company may hold its own shares where the shares are held as treasury shares under 'The Companies (Acquisition of Own Shares) (Treasury Shares) Regulations 2003' (SI 2003/1116). These Regulations came into force on 1 December 2003 and amended the Companies Act 1985 to permit companies with *'qualifying shares'* to purchase such shares out of distributable profits and hold them in treasury for resale, transfer or cancellation at a later date. 'Qualifying shares' are defined as shares that:

- are included in the official list (that is, listed on the London Stock Exchange);
- are traded on AIM;
- are officially listed in another EEA State; or
- are traded on a market established in an EEA State, which is a regulated securities market.

[Sec 162(4) as inserted by SI 2003/1116].

A14.75 Another common situation where a company holds its own shares arises where it operates an Employee Share Ownership Plan (ESOP) for the benefit of its employees. For the purpose of calculating EPS these outstanding shares should also be excluded from the calculation to the extent that they have not vested unconditionally in the employees.

A14.76 An example where a company has excluded treasury shares for the purposes of determining the weighted average number of shares for calculating EPS is given in Table A14.2 below. In this example there were no other issues of shares in the year.

Table A14.2 — Treatment of treasury shares in EPS calculation

Telkom SA Limited — Annual Report and Accounts — 31 March 2005

9. Earnings per share (extract)

	2003 Rm	2004 Rm	2005 Rm
Basic earnings per share (cents)	292.3	812.0	**1,241.8**

The calculation of earnings per share is based on profit attributable to equity holders of Telkom SA Limited for the year of R6,724 million (2004: R4,523 million; 2003: R1,628 million) and 541,498,547 (2004: 556,994,962; 2003: 557,031,819) weighted average number of ordinary shares in issue.

Reconciliation of weighted average number of ordinary shares			
Ordinary shares in issue	557,031,819	557,031,819	**557,031,819**
Weighted average number of treasury shares	–	(36,857)	**(15,533,272)**
Weighted average number of shares outstanding	557,031,819	556,994,962	**541,498,547**
Diluted earnings per share (cents)	292.3	812.0	**1,239.4**

The calculation of diluted earnings per share is based on earnings for the year of R6,724 million (2004: R4,523 million; 2003: R1,628 million) and 542,537,579 (2004: 556,994,962; 2003: 557,031,819)

Contingently issuable shares

A14.77 Contingently issuable shares are ordinary shares that are issuable for little or no cash or other consideration if and when specified conditions in a contingent share agreement have been met. [IAS 33 para 5]. In other words, the consideration for the shares has effectively been received, but the shares remain to be issued – a typical example is contingent consideration on an acquisition payable in shares. Contingently issuable shares are considered to be outstanding and are included in the calculation of basic EPS from the date when all the necessary conditions have been satisfied, that is, the events have occurred. Shares that are issuable solely after the passage of time are not contingently issuable shares, because the passage of time is a certainty and should, therefore, be included in the calculation from inception of the contract. Outstanding ordinary shares that are contingently returnable (that is, subject to recall) are not treated as outstanding, that is they are excluded from the calculation of basic EPS until the date when the shares are no longer subject to recall. [IAS 33 para 24]. Contingently issuable shares are discussed further from paragraph A14.145.

Shares issued as consideration in a business combination

A14.78 Where ordinary shares are issued during the financial year as part of the cost of a business combination (for example, in exchange for a majority interest in the equity of another company) – that is, as non-cash consideration, the results of the new subsidiary are included in the consolidation from the acquisition date. Therefore, the shares issued as consideration to obtain those earnings should be included in the EPS calculation on a weighted average basis from the same date. [IAS 33 para 22].

Mandatorily convertible instruments

A14.79 An entity may issue a loan note or a preference share that is convertible into ordinary shares of the entity. The instrument may either be mandatorily convertible or convertible at the option of the issuer or holder into a fixed number of shares. Where an instrument is mandatorily convertible, the issue of ordinary shares is solely dependent on the passage of time. Consequently, ordinary shares that are issuable on conversion of a mandatorily convertible instrument should be included in basic EPS from the date that the contract is entered into. [IAS 33 para 23]. On the other hand, debt that is convertible at the option of the holder contains an obligation to issue a fixed number of shares *if* the conversion option is exercised. Such shares are treated as potential ordinary shares as they may never be issued if the conversion option is not exercised. Consequently, such potential shares are not considered outstanding for purposes of calculating basic EPC, but are included in the calculation of diluted EPS (see para A14.114 below).

Example

A company has issued debt that is mandatorily convertible into a fixed number of shares in five years time. Neither the issuer nor the holder has any option to require settlement in cash. Interest is payable (in cash) until conversion. How does it affect EPS?

For the purpose of EPS the potential ordinary shares that will be issued on conversion are included in the weighted average number of ordinary shares used in the calculation of basic EPS (and, therefore, also diluted EPS) from the date of issue of the instrument, since their issue is solely dependent on the passage of time. There is no adjustment to the profit or loss attributable to the ordinary equity holders for consequential interest savings, because the shares are treated as if they had already been issued. The interest relates to a separate liability for the interest payments that remain payable.

Bonus issue (stock dividends), share split and share consolidation

A14.80 The weighted average number of ordinary shares outstanding during the period and for all periods presented should be adjusted for events, other than the conversion of potential ordinary shares, that have changed the number of ordinary shares outstanding, without a corresponding change in resources (see further para A14.169). [IAS 33 para 26]. Where a company issues new shares by way a bonus issue or stock dividend during the period, the effect is to increase only the number of shares outstanding after the issue. There is no effect on earnings as there is no flow of funds as a result of the issue. Consequently, the shares should be treated as outstanding as if the issue had occurred at the beginning of the earliest period reported. This means that the earnings for the year should be apportioned over the number of shares after the capitalisation. The EPS figure disclosed for the previous year should be recalculated using the new number of shares in issue. [IAS 33 para 28].

A14.81 Similar considerations apply where ordinary shares are split into shares of smaller nominal value (a share of C1 nominal value is divided into four shares of 25c each C1 = 100c) or consolidated into shares of a higher nominal amount (four shares of 25c each are consolidated into one share of C1). In both these situations, the number of shares outstanding before the event is adjusted for the proportionate change in the number of shares outstanding after the event. [IAS 33 para 27].

A14.82 The impact on the EPS figure of a bonus issue of shares is illustrated in the following example:

Example

On 31 December 20X7, the issued share capital of a company consisted of £1,000,000 in ordinary shares of 25c each and C500,000 in 10% cumulative preference shares of C1 each. On 1 October 20X8, the company issued 1,000,000 ordinary shares fully paid by way of capitalisation of reserves in the proportion of 1:4 for the year ended 31 December 20X8.

	20X8 C'000	20X7 C'000
Calculation of earnings		
Profit for the year	550	450
Less: preference dividend	(50)	(50)
Earnings	500	400
Number of ordinary shares	No	No
Shares in issue for full year	4,000	4,000
Capitalisation issue at 1 October 20X8	1,000	1,000
Number of shares	5,000	5,000
Earnings per ordinary share of 25c	10.0c	8.0c

The comparative earnings per share for 20X7 can also be calculated by adjusting the previously disclosed EPS in 20X7, in this example 10p, by the following factor:

$$\frac{\text{Number of shares before the bonus issue}}{\text{Number of shares after the bonus issue}}$$

$$\text{Adjusted EPS for 20X7: } 10c \times \frac{4{,}000}{5{,}000} = 8.0c$$

The above ratio should also be used to restate previous years' EPS and other financial ratios (for example, dividend per share) disclosed in the historical summary.

Issue of shares at full market price

A14.83 Where new ordinary shares are issued during the year for cash at full market price, the earnings should be apportioned over the average number of shares outstanding during the period weighted on a time basis.

Example

On 31 December 20X7, the issued share capital of a company consisted of C1,000,000 in ordinary shares of 25c each and C500,000 in 10% cumulative preference shares of C1 each. On 1 October 20X8, the company issued 1,000,000 ordinary shares at full market price in cash for the year ended 31 December 20X8.

	20X8 C'000	20X7 C'000
Calculation of earnings		
Profit for the year	550	450
Less: preference dividend	(50)	(50)
Earnings	500	400
Weighted average number of ordinary shares	No	No
Shares in issue for full year	4,000	4,000
Issued on 1 October 20X8 (1,000,000 × 3/12)	250	–
Number of shares	4,250	4,000
Earnings per ordinary share of 25c	11.8c	10.0c

The calculation of earnings per share is based on earnings of C500,000 (20X7: C400,000) and on the weighted average of 4,250,000 ordinary shares in issue during the year (20X7: 4,000,000).

[The next paragraph is A14.85.]

Rights issue

A14.85 Companies sometimes raise additional capital during the year by issuing shares to existing shareholders on a *pro rata* basis to their existing holdings in the form of a rights issue. The rights shares may either be offered at the current market price or at a price that is below the current market price. Where shares are issued at full market price, the weighting is carried out on a time basis as discussed in paragraph A14.83 above. However, where ordinary shares are issued during the year by way of a rights issue at a discount to the market price, the weighting calculation must reflect the fact that the discount is effectively a bonus (stock dividend) given to the shareholders in the form of shares for no consideration and must, therefore, be taken into account in calculating the weighted average number of shares. [IAS 33 para A2]. In fact, it can be demonstrated (see example below) that a rights issue is equivalent to a capitalisation issue of part of the shares for no consideration and an issue of the remainder of the shares at full market price. The notional capitalisation issue reflects the bonus element inherent in the rights issue and is measured by the following fraction:

$$\frac{\text{Fair value per share immediately before the exercise of rights}}{\text{Theoretical ex-rights fair value per share}}$$

A14.86 The fair value per share immediately before the exercise of rights is the *actual* closing price at which the shares are quoted on the last date inclusive of the right to subscribe for the new shares. This is often referred to as the 'cum-rights price', being the price on the last day of quotation cum-rights. The 'ex-rights price', on the other hand, is the *theoretical* price at which, in a perfect market and without any external influences, the shares would trade after the exercise of the rights. Where the rights themselves are publicly traded separately from the shares themselves, as is the case in some countries, the fair value for the purpose of the above calculation is established at the close of the last day on which the shares are traded together with the rights. [IAS 33 para A2].

A14.87 The above factor should be used to adjust the number of shares in issue before the rights issue in order to correct for the bonus (stock dividend) element in the rights issue. This correction should be made both for the current period prior to the rights issue and the previous period. The way in which EPS should be calculated following a rights issue and the adjustment that should be made to the comparative EPS figure are considered in the example below.

Example

At 31 December 20X7, the issued capital of a company consisted of 1.8m ordinary shares of 10c each, fully paid. The profit for the year ended 31 December 20X7 and 20X8 amounted to C630,000 and C875,000 respectively. On 31 March 20X8, the company made a rights issue on a 1 for 4 basis at 30c. The market price of the shares immediately before the rights issue was 60c.

Calculation of theoretical ex rights price

	No		c
Initial holding	4	Market value	240
Rights taken up	1	Cost	30
New holding	5	Theoretical price	270
Theoretical ex rights price	$\frac{270}{5}$ = 54c		

The market price is the fair value of the shares immediately prior to the exercise of rights, that is, the actual cum-rights price of 60c.

Cost is the amount payable for each new share under the rights issue.

Calculation of bonus element

The bonus element of the rights issue is given by the fraction:

$$\frac{\text{Market price before rights issue}}{\text{Theoretical ex-rights price}} \quad \frac{60}{54} = \frac{10}{9}$$

This corresponds to a bonus issue of 1 for 9. The bonus ratio will usually be greater than 1, that is the market price of the shares immediately prior to the exercise of rights is greater than the theoretical ex-rights price. If the ratio is less than 1 it may indicate that the market price has fallen significantly during the rights period, which was not anticipated when the rights issue was announced. In this situation, the rights issue should be treated as an issue of shares for cash at full market price (see para A14.83 above).

As stated in paragraph A14.85 above, it can be demonstrated, using the figures in the example, that a rights issue of 1 for 4 at 30c is equivalent to a bonus issue of 1 for 9 combined with an issue of shares at full market price of 54c per share. Consider an individual shareholder holding 180 shares.

	No	Value	C
Original holding	180	Value at 60c per share	108.00
Rights shares (1:4)	45	Value at 30c per share	13.50
Holding after rights issue	225	Value at 54c per share	121.50

The additional 45 rights shares at 30p can be shown to be equivalent to a bonus issue of 1 for 9 on the original holding followed by an issue of 1:8 at full market price of 54c following the bonus issue as follows:

	No	Value	C
Original holding	180	Value at 60c per share	108.00
Bonus issue of 1 for 9	20	Value nil	nil
	200	Value at 54c per share	108.00
Issue of 1 for 8 at full price	25	Value at 54c per share	13.50
Total holding	225	Value at 54c per share	121.50

The shareholder is, therefore, indifferent as to whether the company makes a rights issue of 1 for 4 at 30c per share or a combination of a bonus issue of 1 for 9 followed by a rights issue of 1 for 8 at full market price of 54c per share.

Having calculated the bonus ratio, the ratio should be applied to adjust the number of shares in issue before the rights issue both for the current year and for the previous year. Therefore, the weighted average number of shares in issue for the current and the previous period, adjusted for the bonus element would be:

Weighted average number of shares		
	20X8	20X7
Number of actual shares in issue before rights	1,800,000	1,800,000
Correction for bonus issue (1:9)	200,000	200,000
Deemed number of shares in issue before rights issue (1.8m × 10/9)	2,000,000	2,000,000
The number of shares after the rights issue would be: 1.8m × 5/4 = 2,250,000		
Therefore, the weighted average number of shares would be:		
2.0m for the whole year		2,000,000
2.0m × 3/12 (before rights issue)	500,000	–
2.25m × 9/12 (after rights issue)	1,687,500	–
Weighted average number	2,187,500	2,000,000
Calculation of EPS following a rights issue		
	20X8	20X7 (as previously stated)
Basic EPS	C875,000	C630,000
	2,187,500	1,800,000
	40.0c	35.0c
Basic EPS for 20X7 (as restated)		C630,000
		2,000,000
		31.5c

The restated EPS for 20X7 can also be calculated by adjusting the earnings per share figure of the previous year by the *reciprocal* of the bonus element factor as shown below.

$$35c \times 9/10 = 31.5c$$

In practice, the EPS for the corresponding period can be adjusted directly using the reciprocal of the bonus element factor above.

A14.88 A question arises as to whether the averaging calculation in a rights issue made during the year should be performed from the announcement date, or from the last date of acceptance of the subscription price, or from the share issue date following despatch of the share certificates. Depending on the circumstances of each case, there is often a delay of between 60 to 80 days between the date of announcement of the rights issue and the share issue date. Following the principle in paragraph 21 of IAS 33 that shares should generally be included from the date consideration is receivable, it follows that the averaging calculation should be performed from the day following the last date of acceptance of the subscription price, which is also the date when the rights are legally exercised. This is because the company begins to generate income from all the proceeds received from that date, which is often midway between the announcement date and the share issue date. Therefore, the new shares should be included in the EPS calculation from the day following the last date on which proceeds are received and not from the announcement date or from the date when the new shares are actually issued.

Issue of shares at less than market price

A14.88.1 Sometimes shares may be issued at a discount to the market price, such as for the acquisition of an asset or the cancellation of a liability. Although the standard does not specifically deal with this situation, it would be appropriate to calculate the inherent bonus element in the issue for the purposes of adjusting the number of shares before the issue. This treatment is implicit in the wording in paragraph 27(b) of IAS 33, which makes reference to a bonus element in *any other issue*.

Dividends payable in shares or cash

A14.89 Where a company pays its dividends in the form of shares or gives the shareholder the option to receive a dividend in either cash or shares (sometimes referred to as scrip dividends or enhanced scrip dividends), the shares issued increase the weighted average number of shares used in the EPS calculation.

A14.90 Under IAS 33, paragraphs 5 and 7 and paragraphs 58 to 61 'Contracts that may be settled in ordinary shares or cash', scrip dividends may be regarded as potential ordinary shares (see para A14.98 below) that entitle the recipient to ordinary shares. These potential ordinary shares are converted into ordinary shares when the scrip shares are issued, which is after the balance sheet date. Since shares are included in the weighted average from the date consideration is receivable, ordinary shares issued on the voluntary reinvestment of dividends on ordinary or preference shares should be included on a weighted average basis at the date when the dividends are reinvested. [IAS 33 para 21(b)]. In practice, for scrip dividends, this is the dividend payment date.

A14.91 Furthermore, the cash dividend foregone by the shareholders electing to take a scrip dividend of shares is taken to be the consideration paid for those shares, which is normally equivalent to the current market value of the shares. The rationale for this is that the cash dividend foregone by the shareholders electing to take shares instead of cash is effectively reinvested in the company as fully paid up shares at market value. As a result, the earnings figure in the numerator already reflects the income generated by the additional cash retained from the dividend payment date. Consequently, for the purposes of the EPS calculation the issue of scrip shares should be treated as an issue at full market price and the relevant number of shares should be included in the denominator on a weighted basis from the dividend reinvestment date.

[The next paragraph is A14.93.]

Special dividend followed by share consolidation

A14.93 Companies sometimes return surplus cash to shareholders. This is normally effected by means of a share repurchase or by a synthetic share repurchase that is achieved by the payment of a special dividend to shareholders followed by a consolidation of share capital, for example, changing five 20c shares into four 25c shares.

A14.94 IAS 33 deals specifically with the effect on EPS of a special dividend accompanied by a share consolidation. Where a share consolidation is combined with a special dividend and the overall effect of the combined transaction is a share repurchase at fair value the reduction in the number of ordinary shares outstanding is the result of a corresponding reduction in resources. The weighted average number of ordinary shares outstanding for the period in which the combined transaction takes place is adjusted for the reduction in the number of ordinary shares from the date the special dividend is recognised. [IAS 33 para 29].

Example

A company has in issue 10,000 shares with a nominal value of 10c each. At the beginning of 20X8, it decides either to launch a share repurchase of 1,000 shares at the current market price of C1 per share or pay a special dividend of 10c per share (net) followed by a share consolidation of 9 new shares for 10 old shares. The profit after tax for 20X7 and 20X8 (before the effect of the share transactions) is C2,000. Interest rates are 8% per annum and the company pays corporation tax at 31%.

	Balance sheet before transactions	Repurchase of 1,000 shares at c1 per share	Special dividend of 10c per share followed by share consolidation of 10:9
	C	C	C
Net assets	5,000	4,000	4,000
Share capital 10,000 shares at 10c each	1,000		
9,000 shares at 10c each		900	
9,000 shares at 11.1c each			1,000
Capital redemption reserve		100	
Profit and loss account	4,000	3,000	3,000
	5,000	4,000	4,000
Net assets per share	C0.50	C0.44	C0.44

Effect on earnings per share — share repurchase

	20X8	20X7
	C	C
Profit for the year	2,000.00	2,000.00
Loss of interest on cash paid out (£1,000 × 0.08 × 0.69)	55.20	–
Earnings	1,944.80	2,000.00
Number of shares in issue	9,000	10,000
EPS	21.61c	20.00c

Effect on earnings per share — special dividend followed by share consolidation

The total nominal value of the shares remain unchanged, but whereas before there were 10,000 shares of 10p each there are now 9,000 shares of 11.1c each.

	20X8	20X7
	C	C
Profit for the year	2,000.00	2,000.00
Loss of interest on cash paid out (C1,000 × 0.08 × 0.69)	55.20	–
Earnings	1,944.48	2,000.00
Number of shares in issue (unadjusted)	9,000	10,000
EPS unadjusted (correct treatment)	21.61c	20.00c
Number of shares in issue (adjusted for consolidation)	9,000	9,000
EPS adjusted (incorrect treatment)	21.61c	22.22c

A14.95 As can be seen from the above example, the economic effect, in terms of net asset per share, of an actual share repurchase is identical to a synthetic share repurchase that is achieved by the combination of a special dividend with a share consolidation. It follows that the earnings per share figures for the two transactions should also be identical. If an adjustment were made to the previous year's EPS for the share consolidation as shown above, there would be an apparent dilution of 2.75 per cent ((22.22 – 21.61)/22.22) that would make the share repurchase look significantly more attractive than the special dividend route. But this would be misleading as the economic effect of the two transactions is identical. Therefore, no adjustment to prior year's EPS should be made for the share consolidation. [IAS 33 para 29].

A14.96 In the above example, it was assumed for simplicity that the combined transaction took place at the beginning of the year and so the new shares were treated as outstanding for a full year. If the combined transaction takes place part way through the year, the weighted average number of ordinary shares outstanding for the period in which the combined transaction takes place should be adjusted for the reduction in the number of shares from the date the special dividend is paid, that is, when resources leave the entity. [IAS 33 para 29]. An example of a company that has treated the payment of an exceptional dividend and a share consolidation carried out at the same time as equivalent to a share buy-back is given in the Table A14.3 below. The company is an investment company and also shows net assets per share (based on shares in issue at the period end).

Table A14.3 — Effect on EPS of special dividend and share consolidation

3i Group plc — Interims — 30 September 2005

Consolidated reconciliation of movement in equity
for the six months to 30 September 2005

	Notes	**6 months to 30 September 2005 (unaudited) £m**	6 months to 30 September 2004 (as restated)* (unaudited) £m	12 months to 31 March 2005 (as restated)* (unaudited) £m
Total equity at start of period		**3,699**	3,294	3,294
Total recognised income and expense for the period		**447**	224	501
Share-based payments		**4**	3	6
Ordinary dividends	6	**(56)**	(53)	(85)
Special dividends	6	**(245)**	–	–
Issues of shares		**5**	2	5
Share buy-backs		**(151)**	–	–
Own shares		**8**	5	(22)
Total equity at end of period		**3,711**	3,475	3,699

* As restated for the adoption of IFRS, as explained within the Basis of preparation.

6 Dividends

	6 months to 30 September 2005 (unaudited) £m p per share	6 months to 30 September 2004 (as restated)* (unaudited) £m p per share	12 months to 31 March 2005 (as restated)* (unaudited) £m p per share
Declared and paid during the period			
Ordinary shares			
Final dividend	**9.3**	8.9	8.9
Special dividend	**40.7**	–	–
Interim dividend	–	–	5.3
	50.0	8.9	14.2
Proposed dividend	**5.5**	5.3	9.3

The Directors have proposed an interim dividend of 5.5c per share.

	6 months to 30 September 2005 (unaudited) £m	6 months to 30 September 2004 (as restated)* (unaudited) £m	12 months to 31 March 2005 (as restated)* (unaudited) £m
Declared and paid during the period			
Ordinary shares			
Final dividend	**56**	53	53
Special dividend	**245**	–	–
Interim dividend	–	–	32
	301	53	85
Proposed dividend	**30**	32	56

5 Per share information

The earnings and net assets per share attributable to the equity shareholders of the Company is based on the following data:

Earnings per share	**6 months to 30 September 2005 (unaudited)**	6 months to 30 September 2004 (as restated)* (unaudited)	12 months to 31 March 2005 (as restated)* (unaudited)
Basic	**79.6p**	36.9p	82.6p
Diluted	**77.0p**	36.3p	81.0p
Earnings (£m)			
Profit for the year attributable to equity holders of the Company	**462**	223	498
Effect of dilutive potential ordinary shares	**5**	5	11
	467	228	509

	6 months to 30 September 2005 (unaudited) Number	6 months to 30 September 2004 (unaudited) Number	12 months to 31 March 2005 (unaudited) Number
Number of shares			
Weighted average number of shares in issue	**580,583,146**	604,250,584	603,240,340
Effect of dilutive potential ordinary shares			
Share options	**1,697,906**	381,696	119,980
Convertible Bonds	**24,750,000**	24,750,000	24,750,000
Diluted shares	**607,031,052**	629,382,280	628,110,320

Net assets per share

	6 months to 30 September 2005 (unaudited)	6 months to 30 September 2004 (as restated)* (unaudited)	12 months to 31 March 2005 (as restated)* (unaudited)
Basic	**679p**	574p	615p
Diluted	**677p**	574p	614p
Net assets (£m)			
Net assets attributable to equity holders of the Company	**3,711**	3,475	3,699

	6 months to 30 September 2005 (unaudited) Number	6 months to 30 September 2004 (unaudited) Number	12 months to 31 March 2005 (unaudited) Number
Number of shares			
Number of shares in issue	**546,363,945**	605,010,144	601,912,869
Effect of dilutive potential ordinary shares			
Share options	**1,952,013**	538,649	1,007,723
	548,315,958	605,548,793	602,920,592

No adjustment has been made to the opening number of shares used in the above calculations for the share consolidation on 8 July 2005.

*As restated for the adoption of IFRS, as explained within the Basis of preparation.

	30 September 2005 (unaudited) Number	**30 September 2005 (unaudited) £m**	30 September 2004 (unaudited) Number	30 September 2004 (unaudited) £m	31 March 2005 (unaudited) Number	31 March 2005 (unaudited) £m
Authorised						
Ordinary shares of 50p	–	–	820,000,000	410	820,000,000	410
Ordinary shares of 531/8p	**771,764,704**	**410**	–	–		
Unclassified shares of 10p	**1,000,000**	–	1,000,000	–	1,000,000	–
Issued and fully paid						
Ordinary shares of 50p						
Balance at the beginning of the period	**614,409,167**	**307**	613,479,159	307	613,479,159	307
Share options	**268,792**	–	358,324	–	930,008	
Share consolidation	**(614,677,959)**	**(307)**	–	–	–	–
Closing balance —	–	–	613,837,483	**307**	614,409,167	307

During the period to 8 July 2005, the Company issued shares for cash on the exercise of share options at various prices from 467p to 664p per share. The Company repurchased 400,452 shares at 683p per share. These shares were cancelled after the Company consolidated its share capital on 8 July 2005. The Company consolidated its share capital by issuing 16 531/8p shares for every 17 50p shares held. This coincided with the payment of a special dividend of 40.7p per share (see note 6).

	30 September 2005 (unaudited) Number	**30 September 2005 (unaudited) £m**	30 September 2004 (unaudited) Number	30 September 2004 (unaudited) £m	31 March 2005 (unaudited) Number	31 March 2005 (unaudited) £m
Ordinary shares of 531/8p						
Balance at the beginning of the period	–	–	–	–	–	–
Share consolidation	**578,520,432**	**307**	–	–	–	–
Share options	**523,503**	–	–	–	–	–
Shares cancelled	**(21,256,896)**	**(11)**	–	–	–	–
Closing balance	**557,787,039**	**296**	–	–	–	–

Since 11 July, the Company issued shares for cash on the exercise of share options at various prices from 467p to 664p per share. The Company repurchased 20,880,000 shares at an average price of 712p per share. These shares, and those purchased before the share consolidation, were cancelled and a transfer made to the capital redemption reserve equal to the nominal value of the shares repurchased.

Diluted earnings per share

Measurement

A14.97 As discussed from paragraph A14.65 above, the basic EPS is calculated on the number of ordinary shares outstanding in respect of the period. Sometimes companies may have 'potential ordinary shares' in issue. The standard defines a 'potential ordinary share' as a financial instrument or other contract that may entitle its holder to ordinary shares. [IAS 33 para 5]. Examples given in the standard are:

- Financial liabilities or equity instruments, including preference shares, that are convertible into ordinary shares.
- Options (including employee share options) and warrants.
- Shares that would be issued on satisfaction of certain conditions that result from contractual arrangements, such as the purchase of a business or other assets.

[IAS 33 para 7].

A14.98 In addition IAS 33, clarifies that contracts that may result in the issue of ordinary shares of the entity to the holder of the contract at the option of the issuer or the holder are potential ordinary shares. [IAS 33 paras 58 to 61]. Such contracts are dealt with from paragraph A14.159 below.

A14.99 In each of these situations, the effect of the conversion into ordinary shares may be to dilute future EPS. It should be noted that not all potential ordinary shares in issue will have a diluting effect (see further para A14.126). Any potential dilution, however, is of considerable interest to existing ordinary shareholders. This is because it indicates the possible reduction in current earnings that may be distributed to them by way of dividends in the future and the possible increase in the number of shares over which the total market value of the company may be divided.

A14.100 The standard, therefore, requires the calculation of diluted EPS, in addition to the basic EPS (see para A14.46), for profit or loss attributable to the parent entity's ordinary equity holders and separately for each of continuing and discontinued operations where these are presented in accordance with IFRS 5, 'Non-current assets held for sale and discontinued operations'. For the purpose of calculating diluted EPS, the profit or loss for the period attributable to ordinary equity holders adjusted for the effects of all dilutive potential ordinary shares should be divided by the sum of the weighted average number of ordinary shares used in the basic EPS calculation and the weighted average number of shares that would be issued on the conversion of all the dilutive potential ordinary shares into ordinary shares. [IAS 33 paras 30 to 32, 36].

A14.101 It should be noted that although existing ordinary shareholders are interested in future dilution, the diluted EPS figure calculated in accordance with the standard is not intended to be a predictor of dilution, or a forward-looking number. It is seen as an additional historical measure. The IASB and the FASB concluded that as the objective of basic EPS is to measure performance over the reporting period, the objective of diluted EPS should be consistent with that objective while giving effect to all dilutive potential ordinary shares that were outstanding during the period. A past performance method of computing diluted EPS will aid comparison between diluted EPS of different periods. In addition, presenting diluted EPS with undiluted EPS that are calculated on a consistent basis will enable users to view the spread between the two figures as representing a reasonable estimate of the potential dilution that exits in the entity's capital structure.

Computation of earnings

A14.102 For the purpose of calculating diluted EPS, the profit or loss attributable to the parent entity's ordinary equity holders should be adjusted for the after-tax effect of:

- Dividends or other items related to dilutive potential ordinary shares that have been deducted in arriving at profit attributable to ordinary equity holders for the purpose of calculating basic EPS, such as dividends on dilutive convertible preference shares.
- Interest recognised in the period on dilutive potential ordinary shares, such as interest on dilutive convertible debt.
- Any other changes in income or expense that would result from the conversion of the dilutive potential ordinary shares.

[IAS 33 paras 32(a), 33].

A14.103 Once potential ordinary shares are converted into ordinary shares during the period, the dividends, interest and other expense associated with those potential ordinary shares will no longer be incurred. The effect of the conversion, therefore, is to increase profit (or reduce losses) attributable to ordinary equity holders as well as the number of shares in issue. This is illustrated in paragraph A14.114 dealing with convertible securities. Adjustments to profit or loss attributable to ordinary equity holders also include any transaction costs, discounts or premiums on potential ordinary shares that are allocated to periods in accordance with the effective interest method in paragraph 9 of IAS 39, that is, the adjustment to earnings should add back the issue costs (or similar) amortised in the period, in addition to the interest/dividend cost.

A14.104 The adjustments to earnings include not only the direct savings in debt servicing cost or dividends and other appropriations and adjustments in respect of convertible preference shares and the related tax effects, but also any other consequential changes in other income or expense arising as a result of the conversion. A situation that often arises in practice is where the equity conversion option in a foreign currency convertible bond, which is treated as a liability, is marked to market through profit or loss. The marked-to-market adjustment needs to be removed from profit or loss for the purposes of calculating diluted EPS. IAS 33 also mentions, as an example, an increase in an employee non-discretionary profit sharing plan as a result of the savings in after-tax interest cost following conversion of convertible debt. [IAS 33 paras 34, 35]. The example given below illustrates such an adjustment. When calculating tax for the purposes of diluted EPS the standard tax rate rather than the entity's effective tax rate should be used. This is because the effective tax rate may be influenced by factors (such as group relief) that affect the entity's results other than the expenses associated with the potential ordinary shares.

Example

Entity A has in issue 25,000 4% debentures with a nominal value of C1. The debentures are convertible to ordinary shares at a rate of 1:1 at any time until 20X9. The entity's management receives a bonus based on 1% of profit before tax.

Entity A's results for 20X2 showed a profit before tax of C80,000 and a profit after tax of C64,000 (for simplicity a tax rate of 20% is assumed in this example).

For the purpose of calculating diluted EPS, the earnings should be adjusted for the reduction in the interest charge that would occur if the debentures were converted and for the increase in the bonus payment that would arise from the increased profit.

This is illustrated below:

	C
Profit after tax	64,000
Add: Reduction in interest cost[1]	
25,000 × 4%	1,000
Less tax expense 1,000 × 20%	(200)
Less: Increase in management bonus	
1,000 × 1%	(10)
Add tax benefit 10 × 20%	2
Earnings for the purposes of diluted EPS	64,792

[1] Note that for simplification, this example does not illustrate the classification of the components of the convertible debenture as liabilities and equity as required by IAS 32.

A14.105 It should be noted that the requirement in paragraph A14.102 above refers to adjusting the profit attributable to ordinary equity holders. This figure is after deducting dividends on convertible preference shares and is the figure used for the purpose of calculating basic EPS. In some cases those dividends will be charged as finance costs in arriving at profit for the year (preference shares treated as a financial liability under IAS 32) and no adjustment will be necessary to arrive at profit attributable to ordinary shareholders. In other cases they will be classified in equity (preference shares treated as equity instruments under IAS 32) and an adjustment will be made to profit for the year to arrive at profit attributable to ordinary equity holders. In either case, however, if the convertible preference shares are dilutive, the profit attributable to ordinary shareholders for the purpose of calculating diluted EPS is before deducting the preference dividend.

Computation of number of ordinary shares

A14.106 As noted in paragraph A14.100, the denominator of diluted EPS should be calculated as the sum of the weighted average number of ordinary shares used in the basic EPS calculation and the weighted average number of ordinary shares that would be issued on the conversion of all the dilutive potential ordinary shares into ordinary shares. [IAS 33 para 36].

A14.107 Entities may have more than one type of potential ordinary share in issue at the reporting date. Whether all these potential ordinary shares actually will be converted into ordinary shares in the future is usually not determinable at the reporting date. The standard requires the assumption that all potential ordinary shares have been converted into ordinary shares at the beginning of the period or, if not in existence at the beginning of the period, the date of the issue of the financial instrument or the granting of the rights by which they are generated. [IAS 33 para 36]. This is sometimes referred to as the 'if converted' method. However, where an instrument has variable conversion terms (that is, it is convertible at different rates over its life – see para A14.115 below), the conversion rate at the end of the period in effect is used to determine the number of shares that would be issued on conversion.

A14.108 The conversion into ordinary shares should be determined from the terms of the financial instrument or the rights granted and this determination should assume the most advantageous conversion rate or exercise price from the standpoint of the holder of the potential ordinary shares. [IAS 33 para 39]. The effect is to ensure that the diluted EPS is based on the maximum number of new shares that would be issuable under the instrument's terms. In practice, it may be that not all conversion rights or warrants are exercised, in which case the dilutive effect in reality would be less than the diluted figure suggests.

A14.109 Potential ordinary shares are included in the diluted EPS calculation on a weighted basis only for the period they were outstanding. Therefore, potential ordinary shares that are issued during the year are included on a weighted basis from the date of issue to the balance sheet date. Where potential ordinary shares that are outstanding at the beginning of the period are converted during the year, they are included on a weighted average basis from the beginning of the year to the date of conversion. This is illustrated in the examples in paragraph A14.115. The new ordinary shares that are issued on conversion are included from the date of conversion in both basic and diluted EPS on a weighted basis. The same principles apply where potential ordinary shares, instead of being converted, are cancelled or allowed to lapse during the reporting period. [IAS 33 para 38].

A14.110 In computing diluted EPS, only potential ordinary shares that are dilutive are considered in the calculation. Potential ordinary shares should be treated as dilutive when, and only when, their conversion to ordinary shares would decrease profit per share or increase loss per share from *continuing operations* attributable to ordinary equity holders. [IAS 33 para 41]. The effects of antidilutive potential ordinary shares are ignored in calculating diluted EPS. [IAS 33 para 43]. Where a company has a number of different types of potential ordinary shares in issue, each one would need to be considered separately rather than in aggregate. The way in which this should be done is considered further from paragraph A14.126 below.

[The next paragraph is A14.112.]

A14.112 As noted in paragraph A14.110, potential ordinary shares are either dilutive or antidilutive based on profit or loss from continuing operations attributable to ordinary equity holders. If the potential ordinary shares are dilutive at this level they must be treated as dilutive for all other EPS calculations (that is, total EPS, discontinued operations EPS and any additional EPS given) whether or not they are actually dilutive at the relevant level of profit (see further para A14.126). [IAS 33 para A3].

Partly paid shares

A14.113 As stated in paragraph A14.69, partly paid shares are included in the computation of basic EPS to the extent that they rank for dividends during the period. Partly paid shares that do not rank for dividends during the period — for example, they do not rank until they are fully paid — are regarded as the equivalent of share options and warrants. That is, the unpaid balance should be assumed to be the proceeds used to purchase shares under the treasury stock method (see further para A14.117). The number of shares included in diluted EPS is the difference between the number of partly paid shares already in issue and the number of shares assumed to be purchased at average market price during the period. [IAS 33 para A16].

Convertible securities

A14.114 Where a company has issued instruments in the form of debentures, loan stocks or preference shares that are convertible into ordinary shares of the entity, the instrument's terms will specify the dates, the number of shares and, in effect, the conversion price or prices at which the new shares will be issued. Convertible preference shares are dilutive when the amount of dividend on such shares declared or accrued in the period per ordinary share obtainable on conversion is below basic EPS for continuing operations (where it exceeds basic EPS, the convertible preference shares are antidilutive). Convertible debt is dilutive when the interest, net of tax and other changes in income or expense, per ordinary share obtainable on conversion is lower than basic EPS for continuing operations (where it exceeds basic EPS, the convertible debt is antidilutive). [IAS 33 para 50]. However, see paragraph A14.130 for situations where there is more than one class of potential ordinary share.

A14.115 A convertible security is a particularly good example to illustrate the application of the principles discussed from paragraphs A14.102 to A14.110 above for calculating diluted EPS.

Example 1

No conversion during the year

At 30 June 20X1, the issued share capital of a company consisted of 1,500,000 ordinary shares of C1 each. On 1 October 20X1 the company issued C1,250,000 of 8% convertible loan stock for cash at par. Each C100 nominal of the loan stock may be converted at any time during the years ended 20X6/X9 into the number of ordinary shares set out below:

30 June 20X6 135 ordinary shares
30 June 20X7 130 ordinary shares
30 June 20X8 125 ordinary shares
30 June 20X9 120 ordinary shares

If the loan stocks are not converted by 20X9, they would be redeemed at par. Because the convertible loan is convertible into a variable number of shares, it would fall to be classified wholly as a liability under IAS 32. In that situation, the written equity conversion option is treated as a derivative and marked to market through profit or loss. The change in the options' fair value reported in 20X2 and 20X3 amounted to a loss of C2,500 and C2,650 respectively. It is assumed that there are no tax consequences arising from these losses.

The profit before interest and taxation for the year ended 30 June 20X2 and 20X3 amounted to C825,000 and C895,000 respectively and relate wholly to continuing operations. The rate of tax for both periods is 33%.

	20X3	20X2
Trading results	C	C
Profit before interest and tax	895,000	825,000
Interest on 8% convertible loan stock		
(20X2: 9/12 × C100,000)	(100,000)	(75,000)
Change in fair value of embedded option	(2,650)	(2,500)
Profit before tax	792,350	747,500
Taxation @ 33%	(262,350)	(247,500)
Profit after tax	530,000	500,000
Calculation of basic EPS		
Number of equity shares outstanding	1,500,000	1,500,000
Basic EPS	C530,000 / 1,500,000	C500,000 / 1,500,000
	35.3c	33.0c
Calculation of diluted EPS		

Test whether convertibles are dilutive:

The saving in after-tax earnings resulting from the conversion of C100 nominal of loan stock amounts to C100 × 8% × 67% + C2,650/12,500 = C5.36 + C0.21 =

C5.57. There will then be 135 extra shares in issue. Therefore, the incremental earnings per share = 4.12c (that is, C5.57/135). As this incremental earnings per share is less than the basic EPS at the continuing level, it this will have the effect of reducing the basic EPS of 35.3c. Hence the convertibles are dilutive (see further para A14.131).

	20X3	20X2
Adjusted earnings	C	C
Profit for basic EPS	530,000	500,000
Add: interest and other charges on earnings saved as a result of the conversion	102,650	77,500
Less: tax relief thereon	(33,000)	(24,750)
Adjusted earnings for equity	599,650	552,750

Adjusted number of shares

From the conversion terms, it is clear that the maximum number of shares issuable on conversion of C1,250,000 loan stock after the end of the financial year would be at the rate of 135 shares per C100 nominal, that is, 1,687,500 shares.

	20X3	20X2
Number of equity shares for basic EPS	1,500,000	1,500,000
Maximum conversion at date of issue 1,687,500 × 9/12	–	1,265,625
Maximum conversion after balance sheet date	1,687,500	–
Adjusted capital	3,187,500	2,765,625
Diluted EPS	C599,650 / 3,187,500	C552,750 / 2,765,625
	18.8c	20.0c

Example 2

Partial conversion during the year

The facts are the same as set out in the previous example, but at 1 January 20X6, the holders of half the loan stock exercised their right of conversion.

	20X6	20X5
Trading results	C	C
Profit before interest and tax	1,220,000	1,000,000
Interest on 8% convertible loan stock *	(75,000)	(100,000)
Change in fair value of embedded option	(2,750)	(5,000)
Profit before tax	1,142,250	895,000
Taxation @ 33%	(377,850)	(297,000)
Profit after tax	764,400	598,000

*Interest = (C1,250,000 × 8% × ½) + (C625,000 × 8% × ½) = C75,000

Calculation of basic EPS		
Adjusted number of shares:		
Number outstanding before conversion	1,500,000	1,500,000
Weighted average shares issued on conversion at 1 January 20X6 = 843,750/2	421,875	–
Adjusted number of shares	1,921,875	1,500,000
Basic EPS	C764,400 / 1,921,875	C598,000 / 1,500,000
	39.8c	39.9c
Calculation of diluted EPS		
Adjusted earnings	C	C
Profit for basic EPS	764,400	598,000
Add: and other charges on earnings saved as a result of conversion	77,500	105,000
Less: tax relief thereon	(24,750)	(33,000)
Adjusted earnings	817,400	670,000
Adjusted number of shares		
Number of equity shares for basic EPS	1,921,875	1,500,000
Assumed conversion of C1,250,000 loan stock outstanding at the beginning of the year at the maximum rate of 135 shares per C100 of stock up to 1 January 20X6 (6 months)	843,750	–
Assumed conversion of C625,000 of remaining stock outstanding at 30 June 20X6 at the maximum rate of 135 shares per C100 of stock (6 months)	421,875	–
Maximum conversion after balance sheet date at the rate of 135 shares per £100 of stock	–	1,687,500
Adjusted number of shares	3,187,500	3,187,500
Diluted EPS	C817,400 / 3,187,500	C670,000 / 3,187,500
	25.6c	21.0c

Example 3

Final conversion during the year

The facts are the same as set out in the previous example, but the holders of half of the loan stock had exercised their right of conversion on 1 January 20X6 at 135 shares per C100 stock and the remaining stock was converted on 30 June 20X7 at 130 shares per C100 stock.

	20X7	20X6
Trading results	C	C
Profit before interest and tax	1,450,000	1,220,000
Interest on 8% convertible loan stock *	(50,000)	(75,000)
Change in fair value of embedded option	(3,500)	(2,750)
Profit before tax	1,396,500	1,142,250
Taxation @ 33%	(462,000)	(377,850)
Profit after tax	934,500	764,450

*Interest = C625,000 × 8% = C50,000

Calculation of basic EPS

Adjusted number of shares:		
Number outstanding before conversion	1,500,000	1,500,000
Weighted average shares issued on conversion at 1 January 20X6	843,750	421,875
Weighted average shares issued on conversion at 30 June 19X7		–
Adjusted number of equity shares	2,343,750	1,921,875
Basic EPS	C934,500 / 2,343,750	C764,400 / 1,921,875
	39.9c	39.8c

Calculation of diluted EPS

Adjusted earnings	C	C
Profit for basic EPS	934,500	764,400
Add: interest and other charges on earnings saved as a result of conversion	53,500	77,750
Less: tax thereon	(16,500)	(24,750)
Adjusted earnings	971,500	817,400
Adjusted number of shares		
Number of equity shares for basic EPS	2,343,750	1,921,875
Assumed conversion of C1,250,000 loan stock outstanding at the beginning of the year at the maximum rate of 135 shares per C100 of stock up to 1 January 20X6 (6 months)	–	843,750
Assumed conversion of £625,000 of remaining stock outstanding at 30 June 20X6 at the maximum rate of 135 shares per C100 of stock (6 months)	–	421,875
Assumed conversion of C625,000 of stock outstanding at the maximum rate of 130 shares per C100 of stock†	812,500	–
Adjusted number of shares	3,156,250	3,187,500

† Deemed to be outstanding for the whole year because the remaining loan stock of C625,000 was redeemed on the last day of the financial year, that is, on 30 June 20X7.

Diluted EPS	C971,500 / 3,156,250	C817,400 / 3,187,500
	30.8c	25.6c

A14.116 Table A14.4 shows the presentation of adjustments made for the purpose of diluted EPS that result from dilutive convertible debt. The extract also illustrates disclosure of continuing, total and discontinued EPS, the treatment of own shares held and the effect on diluted EPS of share options issued by a subsidiary, Genentech (see para A14.134).

Table A14.4 – Effect of potential ordinary shares on diluted EPS

Roche Holding Ltd – Annual Report and Accounts – 31 December 2005

32. Earnings per share and non-voting equity security

Basic earnings per share and non-voting equity security
For the calculation of basic earnings per share and non-voting equity security, the number of shares and non-voting equity securities is reduced by the weighted average number of its own non-voting equity securities held by the Group during the period.

Basic earnings per share and non-voting equity security

	Continuing businesses		Group	
	2005	2004	2005	2004
Net income (millions of CHF)	5,799	4,304	5,787	6,606
Number of shares (millions)[31]	160	160	160	160
Number of non-voting equity securities (millions)[31]	703	703	703	703
Weighted average number of own non-voting equity securities held (millions)	(18)	(22)	(18)	(22)
Weighted average number of shares and non-voting equity securities in issue used to calculate basic earnings per share (millions)	845	841	845	841
Basic earnings per share and non-voting equity security (CHF)	6.86	5.12	4.40	7.86

Diluted earnings per share and non-voting equity security
For the calculation of diluted earnings per share and non-voting equity security, the net income and weighted average number of shares and non-voting equity securities outstanding are adjusted for the effects of all dilutive potential shares and non-voting equity securities.

Potential dilutive effects arise from the convertible debt instruments and the employee stock option plans. If the outstanding convertible debt instruments were to be converted this would lead to a reduction in interest expense and an increase in the number of shares which may have a net dilutive effect on the earnings per share. The exercise of outstanding vested employee stock options would have a dilutive effect. The exercise of the outstanding vested Genentech employee stock options would have a dilutive effect if the net income of Genentech is positive. The diluted earnings per share and non-voting equity security reflects the potential impacts of these dilutive effects on the earnings per share figures.

Diluted earnings per share and non-voting equity security	Continuing businesses		Group	
	2005	2004	2005	2004
Net income (millions of CHF)	5,799	4,304	5,787	6,606
Elimination of interest expense, net of tax, of convertible debt instruments, where dilutive (millions of CHF)	43	15	43	15
Increase in minority share of Group net income, net of tax, assuming all outstanding Genentech stock options exercised (millions of CHF)	(58)	(25)	(58)	(25)
Net income used to calculate diluted earnings per share (millions of CHF)	5,784	4,294	5,772	6,596
Weighted average number of shares and non-voting equity securities in issue (millions)	845	841	845	841
Adjustment for assumed conversion of convertible debt instruments, where dilutive (millions)	13	8	13	8
Adjustment for assumed exercise of equity compensation plans, where dilutive (millions)	2	–	2	–
Weighted average number of shares and non-voting equity securities in issue used to calculate diluted earnings per share (millions)	860	849	860	849
Diluted earnings per share and non-voting equity security (CHF)	6.73	5.06	6.71	7.77

31. Equity attributable to Roche shareholders (extract)

Share capital

As of 31 December 2005, the share capital of Roche Holding Ltd, which is the Group's parent company, consisted of 160,000,000 shares with a nominal value of 1.00 Swiss franc each, as in the preceding year. The shares are bearer shares and the Group does not maintain a register of shareholders. Based on information supplied to the Group, a shareholders' group with pooled voting rights owns 50.0125% (2004: 50.0125%) of the issued shares. This is further described in Note 34. Based on information supplied to the Group, Novartis International Ltd, Basel, and its affiliates own 33.3330% (participation below 331/3%) of the issued shares (2004: 33.3330%).

Non-voting equity securities *(Genussscheine)*

As of 31 December 2005, 702,562,700 non-voting equity securities were in issue as in the preceding year. Under Swiss company law these non-voting equity securities have no nominal value, are not part of the share capital and cannot be issued against a contribution which would be shown as an asset in the balance sheet of Roche Holding Ltd. Each non-voting equity security confers the same rights as any of the shares to participate in the net profit and any remaining proceeds from liquidation following repayment of the nominal value of the shares and, if any, participation certificates. In accordance with the law and the Articles of Incorporation of Roche Holding Ltd, the Company is entitled at all times to exchange all or some of the non-voting equity securities into shares or participation certificates.

Own equity instruments (extract)

Holdings of own equity instruments *in equivalent number of non-voting equity securities*

	31 December 2005	31 December 2004
Non-voting equity securities	–	87,386
Low Exercise Price Options	14,233,945	21,080,081
Derivative instruments	7,233,454	4,723,565
Total own equity instruments	21,467,399	25,891,032

Own equity instruments are recorded within equity at original cost of acquisition.

11. Discontinued businesses (extract)

Earnings per share and non-voting equity security from discontinued businesses for 2005 were – 0.01 CHF (basic and diluted). The equivalent amounts in 2004 were 2.74 CHF and 2.73 CHF, respectively.

Share warrants, options and other potential ordinary shares

A14.117 Where a company has issued warrants to subscribe for shares at fixed prices on specified dates in the future or granted share options to directors and employees, these and other potential ordinary shares should be taken into account in the calculation of diluted EPS if they are dilutive. [IAS 33 para 45]. Warrants or options are defined as financial instruments that give the holder the right to purchase ordinary shares. [IAS 33 para 5]. They are dilutive when they would result in the issue of ordinary shares for less than the average market price of ordinary shares during the period. Under IAS 33, the expected proceeds from the exercise of the dilutive share warrants and options are deemed to be used by the company in purchasing as many of its ordinary shares as possible in the open market, using an average market price for the period. Since these shares are fairly priced and are neither dilutive or antidilutive, they are ignored in the diluted EPS calculation. They are, therefore, deducted from the number of shares to be issued under the options or warrants to give the number of shares deemed to be issued at no consideration. As these shares are dilutive, they are added to the number of ordinary shares outstanding in the computation of diluted EPS. [IAS 33 paras 45 to 47].

A14.118 The method reflects more dilution as the value of options and warrants increases relative to the value of the underlying share. That is, as the average market price for the underlying share increases, the assumed proceeds from exercise will buy fewer shares, thus increasing the number of shares issued for nil consideration and, hence, the denominator. This method of accounting for share warrants and options and other share purchase agreements is often referred to as 'the treasury stock method'. However, although increases in the share price over a number of periods may increase the dilutive effect, the standard makes it clear that previously reported EPS figures are not retrospectively adjusted to reflect changes in share prices. [IAS 33 para 47].

A14.119 It should be noted that the fair value of share options and warrants under the treasury stock method should always be calculated on the basis of the average price of an ordinary share for the period rather than the period end market price. The use of the average stock price is consistent with the objective of diluted EPS to measure earnings per share for the period based on period in formation and that use of end-of-period data or estimates of the future is inconsistent with the objectives as discussed in paragraph A14.101 above. The standard indicates that a pragmatic basis of calculation, such as a simple average of weekly or monthly prices should be adequate for calculating the average price for the period. Also, closing market prices are adequate for calculating the average market price, but where prices fluctuate wildly an average of the high and low prices generally produces a more representative price. The method should be used consistently, unless it becomes unrepresentative due to changed market conditions. For example, an entity that had used closing market prices to calculate the average market price during several years of relatively stable prices might change to using an average of high and low prices, if prices began to fluctuate wildly and closing prices no longer produced a representative average price. [IAS 33 paras A4, A5].

A14.120 Paragraph 41 of IAS 33 says that potential shares are treated as dilutive when they decrease profit or increase loss per share from continuing operations attributable to ordinary equity holders. Where an entity is making profits from continuing operations, share options will always be additionally dilutive if the exercise price is below the average of the share price during the period (that is, the options are 'in the money'). However, where an entity has incurred a loss from continuing operations, options that are in the money would only be dilutive if they increased the loss per share from continuing operations, that is, made the loss per share more negative. But as the effect of bringing in more shares will be to increase the denominator and therefore reduce the loss per share, in the money options will be anti-dilutive and so are not included in the diluted EPS.

A14.121 An example that illustrates the mechanics of calculating diluted EPS where a company has granted options is given below.

Example

At 31 December 20X7 and 20X8, the issued share capital of a company consisted of 4,000,000 ordinary shares of 25c each. The company has granted options that give holders the right to subscribe for ordinary shares between 20Y2 and 20Y3 at 70c per share. Options outstanding at 31 December 20X7 and 20X8 were 630,000. There were no grants, exercises or lapses of options during the year. The profit after tax attributable to ordinary equity holders for the years ended 31 December 20X7 and 20X8 amounted to C500,000 and C600,000 respectively (wholly relating to continuing operations).

Average market price of share:

Year ended 31 December 20X7 = C1.20
Year ended 31 December 20X8 = C1.60

Calculation of basic EPS		
	20X8	20X7
Basic EPS	C600,000	C500,000
	4,000,000	4,000,000
	15.0c	12.5c
Calculation of diluted EPS		
Adjusted number of shares		
Number of shares under option:		
Issued at full market price:		
(630,000 × 0.70) ÷ 1.20		367,500
(630,000 × 0.70) ÷ 1.60	275,625	
Issued at nil consideration — dilutive	354,375	262,500
Total number of shares under option	630,000	630,000
Number of equity shares for basic EPS	4,000,000	4,000,000
Number of dilutive shares under option	354,375	262,500
Adjusted number of shares	4,354,375	4,262,500
Diluted EPS	C600,000	C500,000
	4,354,375	4,262,500
	13.8c	11.7c
Percentage dilution	8.00%	6.40%

Note – If options had been granted or exercised during the period, then the number of 'nil consideration' shares in respect of these options would be included in the diluted EPS calculation on a weighted average basis for the period prior to exercise.

A14.122 Table A14.5 illustrates the disclosure of the effect of options on diluted EPS.

Table A14.5 – Effect of share options on diluted EPS

Syngenta AG – Annual Report and Accounts – 31 December 2004

Consolidated Income Statement (extract)

(for the years ended December 31, 2004, 2003 (adjusted) and 2002 (adjusted))

(US$ million, except per share amounts)	**Notes**	**2004**	**2003 (adjusted)**	**2002 (adjusted)**
Continuing operations				
Basic earnings/(loss) per share				
From continuing operations	9	5.16	2.41	(0.71)
From discontinued operations	9	(0.79)	0.05	0.07
Total	9	4.37	2.46	(0.64)
Diluted earnings/(loss) per share				
From continuing operations	9	5.12	2.40	(0.71)
From discontinued operations	9	(0.78)	0.05	0.07
Total	9	4.34	2.45	(0.64)
Weighted average number of shares				
Basic		105,208,929	101,682,672	101,541,119
Diluted		106,015,369	101,799,899	101,586,435

9. Earnings per share

2003 and 2002 comparatives have been adjusted to apply retroactively the changes in accounting policy described in Note 2.

(US$ million, except per share amounts)	**2004**	**2003 (adjusted)**	**2002 (adjusted)**
Basic and diluted earnings:			
Net income/(loss) from continuing operations	536	248	(68)
of which:			
Attributable to Syngenta AG shareholders	543	245	(72)
Net income/(loss) from discontinued operations	(108)	6	9
of which:			
Attributable to Syngenta AG shareholders	(83)	5	7
Net income/(loss)	428	254	(59)
of which:			
Attributable to Syngenta AG shareholders	460	250	(65)
Weighted average number of shares			
Weighted average number of shares — basic	105,208,929	101,682,672	101,541,119
Adjustments for dilutive potential ordinary shares:			
Grants of options over Syngenta AG shares	672,031	62,069	45,316
Grants of Syngenta AG shares	134,409	55,158	–
Weighted average number of shares — diluted	106,015,369	101,799,899	101,586,435

Treasury shares are deducted from total shares in issue for the purposes of calculating earnings per share.

A14.123 Although the standard does not specifically say so, it should be assumed that the average price for the period means the average price during the period covered by the financial statements. However, where options are issued during the period the average price should be taken to be the average price during the period for which the options were in issue. This may affect whether the options are dilutive or anti-dilutive.

Example

An entity issued share options on 1 January 20X3. The share options are exercisable upon issue. The exercise price of the share options is 20c. The average share price during the year was as follows:

Average share price 1 January 20X3 to 30 June 20X3	8c
Average share price 1 July 20X3 to 31 December 20X3	22c
Average share price for the year to 31 December 20X3	15c

Management is preparing the financial statements for the year ended 31 December 20X3 and is considering the effect on diluted EPS of the following two scenarios for year-end share prices:

(a) the share price is 18c at 31 December 20X3; or

(b) the share price is 23c at 31 December 20X3.

(a) The fact that the year end share price is less than the exercise price is not relevant because the standard requires the comparison to be made between the exercise price and the average market price of the shares for the period, not with the price at the year end. [IAS 33 para 45]. The share options should not be included in the diluted EPS calculation as they are out-of-the money, that is, the exercise price (20c) is higher than the average price of the ordinary shares for the period (15c).

(b) Similarly the fact that the year end share price is more than the exercise price is not relevant. There is no change in the answer from that given in (a) above, because the extent of dilution is calculated by reference to the exercise price and the average share price during the period. The exercise price is 20c and the average fair value of the shares is 15c and, therefore, the options are still out of the money for the purpose of the diluted EPS calculation.

The answer would change, however, if the options had been issued at 1 July 20X3. The average price of the shares during the second half of the year (22c) was above the exercise price of the options (20c), so that the share options would be included in the diluted EPS calculation.

A14.124 The basic method of including options or warrants in the EPS computation is the treasury stock method described in paragraph A14.117 above. However, the treasury stock method may not always be applicable for calculating the dilutive effects of options or warrants. Sometimes options or warrants may require or permit the tendering of debt or other securities of the entity in payment of all or part of the exercise price. In computing diluted EPS:

- Those options or warrants are assumed to be exercised and the debt or other securities are assumed to be tendered.
- Interest (net of tax) on any debt assumed to be tendered is added back as an adjustment to the numerator.
- If tendering cash would be more advantageous to the option holder or warrant holder and the contract permits tendering cash, the tendering of cash should be assumed.

[IAS 33 para A7].

Example

An entity issued 50,000 warrants at the beginning of the year. Each warrant may be exercised to purchase 10 ordinary shares by tendering either C100 cash or C100 nominal of outstanding 6% debentures of the entity. The market value of the debentures at the balance sheet date is C92 and the average market price of the entity's share for the period and at the balance sheet date is C9.50 and C9.60 respectively.

In the calculation of diluted EPS, it is first necessary to consider whether the warrants are dilutive. The warrants would be dilutive if either:

(a) The warrants are exercised for cash and the average market price of the related ordinary shares for the period exceeds the exercise price. This is not the case here as the average share price of C95 (10 shares @ C9.50) is less than the exercise price of C100.

(b) The warrants are exercised by tendering the entity's debentures and the selling price of the debenture to be tendered is below that at which the debenture may be tendered under the warrant agreement and the resulting discount establishes an effective exercise price below the market price of the ordinary shares obtained upon exercise. This is the case here as the market value of the debentures of C92 (nominal value C100) is less than the market price of the shares obtained of C96 at the balance sheet.

Therefore, the warrants are dilutive, and it is assumed that debentures will be tendered because it will be more advantageous to the warrant holder to surrender the entity's debentures that have a market value of C92 rather than pay cash of C100 to obtain 10 ordinary shares with a market value of C96.

For the purposes of calculating diluted EPS, the company will increase the numerator by the after-tax interest saved of C210,000 (C5m @ 6% less tax @ 30%) on effectively repurchasing C5m (C100 nominal for each 50,000 warrants) of the entity's outstanding debentures. In addition, the full amount of 500,000 shares to be issued following the exercise of warrants, (rather than the number computed under the treasury stock method using an effective exercise price equal to the market value of C92 for the debenture and an average share price of C9.50), is included in the denominator. This treatment reflects the fact that a repurchase of debt with the warrant/option proceeds followed by an issue of shares under the warrant/option agreement is in substance equivalent to a traditional or conventional debt instrument that is convertible into a fixed number of shares.

On the other hand, if the tendering of cash is considered to be more advantageous to the warrant holder, for instance, if cash tendered in the above example was C90 for each warrant, tendering of cash would be considered to be dilutive as the exercise price is less than the average share price. In that situation, the number of dilutive shares included in the denominator would be calculated under the treasury stock method in the normal way for options and warrants.

Furthermore, where both cash and debt instruments are tendered, the number of dilutive shares included in the denominator would be the sum of (a) the amount calculated using the treasury stock method to the cash proceeds and (b) the amount calculated by the treating the debt tendered as a conventional convertible debt.

A14.125 In some circumstances, the proceeds from the exercise of options or warrants may be required to be applied to redeem the entity's existing debt instruments. Upon the assumed exercise of such options or warrants, the proceeds are applied to purchase the debt at its market price rather than to purchase ordinary shares under the treasury stock method. The treasury stock method is applied, however, for the excess proceeds received from the assumed exercise of the options or warrants over the amount used for the assumed purchase of debt. Interest, net of income tax, on any debt assumed to be purchased is added back as an adjustment to the numerator. [IAS 33 para A9].

Example

An entity granted 500,000 new options at the beginning of the year to its debenture holders that also own all of the entity's 6% redeemable 20,000 nominal C100 debentures. The exercise price of the option is C6.50. The terms of the options require the company to use the proceeds received from the exercise of options to repurchase the company's outstanding debentures. The average market price of nominal C100 debenture and an ordinary share for the period are C105 and C8 respectively.

For the purposes of calculating diluted EPS, the above options are assumed to be exercised and the proceeds of C3,250,000 (500,000 @ 6.50) are applied to purchase all the outstanding 20,000 nominal debentures at the average price of C105 for C2,100,000. The excess proceeds of C1,150,000 are deemed to be applied to purchase shares in the market at C8 per share, that is, 143,750 shares. Therefore, the number of dilutive shares that are included in the denominator under the treasury stock method is 500,000 – 143,750 = 356,250.

In addition, the entity would increase the numerator by the after-tax interest saved on the assumed repurchase of the debentures, that is, C84,000 (C2m @ 6% less tax @ 30%).

The incremental earnings per share = C84,000 ÷ 356,250 = C0.24.

The options would be included in the diluted EPS calculation if the incremental earnings per share of C0.24 is less than the basic EPS at the continuing operations level.

Calculating diluted EPS

A14.126 As stated in paragraph A14.110 above, only potential ordinary shares that are dilutive are considered in the calculation of diluted EPS. Potential ordinary shares should be treated as dilutive when, and only when, their conversion to ordinary shares would decrease profit or increase loss per share from continuing operations attributable to ordinary equity holders. [IAS 33 paras 41, 43]. The profit from continuing operations is the profit for the period after deducting preference dividends (and other appropriations and adjustments in respect of preference shares) and excluding items relating to discontinued operations. This means that the entity would need to calculate a basic earnings per share from continuing operations. A potential ordinary share would be dilutive if its assumed conversion results in reducing this earnings per share from continuing operations below the basic level. On the other hand, if the effect is to increase this earnings per share above the basic level, the security is not dilutive and should be excluded from the diluted EPS calculation. [IAS 33 para 42].

A14.127 It follows from the above that on no account should the dilution be tested by reference to whether the conversion of a potential ordinary share reduces the standard basic EPS calculated on the total profit or loss for the period. The reason for choosing, as a control number, the 'profit from continuing operations' is because this level of profit, unaffected by discontinued operations, is likely to remain stable over time and reflect the earnings that will exist in the future when the dilution occurs. This is a sensible approach for the following reason. If there is a loss from discontinued operations and this turns the overall earnings per share attributable to ordinary equity holders into a loss per share, the exercise of, say, an option will increase the denominator and result in a lower overall loss per share. This is because the loss is 'shared' among a higher number of shares. In that situation, the option is antidilutive at this level, but may well be dilutive at the continuing operations level.

Example

A company has a profit from continuing activities, but a loss for the year overall because of losses on discontinued operations. Options are dilutive when considered at continuing operations profit level as the diluted EPS at that level decreases profit per share. However, at the overall loss for the year level, applying the dilution caused by the options decreases loss per share. Is it still correct to show the effect of the options in the diluted EPS?

Yes. If the options are dilutive at the profit from continuing operations level then they should be included in the diluted EPS calculation at the loss for the year level. If that reduces loss per share then so be it, but the company should explain the circumstances. A form of explanation might be *"Options are dilutive at the profit from continuing operations level and so, in accordance with IAS 33, have been treated as dilutive for the purpose of diluted earnings per share. The diluted loss per share is lower than basic loss per share because of the effect of losses on discontinued operations"*.

In addition to disclosing basic and diluted EPS for the overall loss for the year, the entity would also be required to disclose basic and diluted EPS at the continuing operations level on the face of the income statement and the basic and diluted EPS for discontinued operations either on the face of the income statement or in the notes (see further para A14.173 onwards). [IAS 33 paras 66, 68].

[The next paragraph is A14.130.]

A14.130 In order to determine whether a particular convertible instrument, option or warrant will have a diluting effect, it is necessary to consider each of them separately rather than in aggregate. This consideration is complicated and involves the following steps:

- The entity first calculates the profit from continuing operations attributable to ordinary equity holders.
- The entity next calculates the earnings per incremental share for each type of potential ordinary share. The earnings per incremental share is the increase in profit (or less commonly the decrease) that would result from the exercise or conversion of the security divided by the weighted average increase in the number of ordinary shares that would result from the conversion.
- The entity next ranks all potential ordinary shares from the most dilutive (lowest earnings per incremental share) to the least dilutive (highest earnings per incremental share). Options and warrants are generally included first because they do not affect the numerator of the calculation and, hence, are most dilutive.
- The entity then calculates a basic EPS using profit from continuing operations attributable to ordinary equity holders as the numerator.
- The most dilutive potential ordinary share with the lowest earnings per incremental share is then included and a new EPS as indicated above is calculated. If this new figure is lower than the previous one, the entity recalculates EPS including the potential shares with the next lowest earnings per incremental share.
- The above process of including increasingly less dilutive shares continues until the resulting EPS figure increases or there are no more potential ordinary shares to consider.
- Any potential ordinary share that has the effect of increasing the cumulative EPS from continuing operations is considered to be antidilutive and is excluded from the diluted per share calculation.
- All other potential ordinary shares with higher rankings are considered to be dilutive potential ordinary shares and are included in the diluted EPS calculation in the normal way.

[IAS 33 para 44].

A14.131 The sequence of including each issue or series of potential ordinary shares from the most dilutive to the least dilutive guarantees that the final diluted EPS figure expresses maximum dilution of the basic EPS. A numerical example depicting the above steps is shown below.

Example

The issued share capital of C plc at 31 December 20X7 and 20X8 comprises 2,000,000 ordinary shares of 10c each. The company granted options over 100,000 ordinary shares in

20X6. The options can be exercised between 20X9 and 20Y1 at 60c per share. The average market price of C plc's shares during 20X8 was 75c.

In addition, C plc has 800,000 8% C1 convertible cumulative preference shares (treated as an equity instrument under IAS 32) and C1,000,000 5% convertible bonds in issue throughout 20X8. Each preference share and bond is convertible into 2 ordinary shares.

The company's results for the year ended 31 December 20X8 comprised operating profit from continuing operations of C300,000 and operating profit from discontinued operations of C100,000. Interest and tax at 30% amounted to C100,000 and C90,000 respectively. The profit for the year was C210,000.

The necessary steps to calculate C plc's diluted earnings per share for 20X8 are set out below. Comparative figures for 20X7 have not been included in this example.

1 Calculation of profit from continuing operations

	Total C	Continuing operations C	Discontinued operations C
Operating profit from continuing operations	300,000	300,000	
Operating profit from discontinued operations *	100,000		100,000
Profit before interest	400,000	300,000	100,000
Interest **	100,000	76,000	24,000
Profit after interest	300,000	224,000	76,000
Tax @ 30% **	90,000	67,200	22,800
Profit	210,000	156,800	53,200
Less: Preference dividend	64,000	64,000	–
Profit attributable to ordinary equity holders	146,000	92,800	53,200

* The above workings are for illustrative purposes and do not show the discontinued operations as they are required to be presented in the income statement by IAS 1, 'Presentation of financial statements' and IFRS 5, ' Non-current assets held for sale and discontinued operations'. The presentation of discontinued operations is dealt with in chapter 8.

** Interest has been allocated to the discontinued operation on the basis of the debt that has been attributed to the discontinued operation. Taxation has been attributed on the basis of the taxation actually payable by the discontinued operation.

2 Determine earnings per incremental share for each class of potential ordinary share and rank them from the most dilutive to least dilutive

	Increase in earnings C	Increase in number of ordinary shares	Earnings per incremental share c	Rank (note)
Options				
Increase in earnings	nil			
Incremental shares issued for nil consideration 100,000 × (75-60)/75		20,000	nil	1
8% Convertible preference shares				
Increase in earnings 8% × C800,000	64,000			
Incremental shares 2 × 800,000		1,600,000	4.00	3
5% Convertible bonds				
Increase in earnings after taxes 1,000,000 × 5% × 70%	35,000			
Incremental shares 1,000,000 × 2		2,000,000	1.75	2

Note: Ranking is in ascending order of earnings per incremental share.

Since the options, convertible preference shares and convertible bonds have been in issue throughout 20X8, the increase in number of ordinary shares is also their weighted average for the year. If options are granted during the year, they are brought into the averaging calculation from the date of grant.

If there were more than one series, say, of options these would have to be ranked by series.

3 Calculate the cumulative dilution effect on profit per share from continuing operations

	Profit from continuing operations C	Weighted average number of shares	Profit from continuing operations per share (c)	
Profit	92,800	2,000,000	4.64	
Options	–	20,000		
	92,800	2,020,000	4.59	Dilutive
5% Convertible bonds	35,000	2,000,000		
	127,800	4,020,000	3.18	Dilutive
8% Convertible preference shares	64,000	1,600,000		
	191,800	5,620,000	3.41	Anti-dilutive

Since diluted earnings per share from continuing operations is increased when taking the convertible preference shares into account (from 3.18 to 3.41), the convertible preference shares are antidilutive and are ignored in the calculation of diluted earnings per share.

4 Calculate diluted earnings per share including only dilutive potential ordinary shares

	Earnings C	Weighted average number of shares	Earnings per share (c)
Profit attributable to ordinary equity holders	146,000	2,000,000	7.30
Options		20,000	–
	146,000	2,020,000	
5% Convertible bonds	35,000	2,000,000	–
Diluted earnings	181,000	4,020,000	4.50

The final diluted EPS is calculated by reference to profit attributable to ordinary equity holders, but the dilution test is carried out by using the profit from continuing operations as the 'control number' (see para A14.132 below) as set out in step three above.

The above example deals only with the calculation of the diluted EPS for the total profit attributable to ordinary equity holders. However, IAS 33 also requires disclosure of the basic and diluted EPS attributable to continuing and to discontinued operations. The figures to be disclosed would be as follows.

	Basic EPS (c)	Diluted EPS (c)
Profit attributable to ordinary equity holders	7.30	4.50
Profit from continuing operations	4.64[1]	3.18[1]
Profit from discontinued operations	2.66[2]	1.32[2]

Notes:

[1] As per step 3 above, Basic = 92,800/2,000,000 = 4.64 ; Diluted = 127,800/4,020,000 = 3.18

[2] Basic = 53,200/2,000,000 = 2.66; Diluted = 53,200/4,020,000 = 1.32

Note that the income statement effect of the convertible bonds is not adjusted against the discontinued operations results, because it relates to continuing operations. The additional shares are taken into account because the discontinued operation EPS is measured as one element of the EPS for the total entity result. Also, the sum of the continuing operations EPS and discontinued operations EPS (for both basic and diluted) equals the EPS calculated on the profit attributable to ordinary equity holders.

A14.132 Paragraph A3 of the standard illustrates the application of the 'control number' with a useful example. The following example is derived from that example.

Example

An entity has a profit from continuing operations of C4m, a loss from discontinued operations of C7m, a loss for the year attributable to equity holders of C3m and C4m ordinary shares and C1m potential ordinary shares outstanding.

The entity's basic EPS for continuing operations is C1 for continuing operations, a (C1.75) loss for discontinued operations and (C0.75) for the loss for the year.

The C1m potential ordinary shares are included in the diluted EPS calculation because (assuming no income statement effect for the potential ordinary shares) their effect on the EPS calculation for continuing operations is dilutive. On that assumption, the resulting diluted EPS for continuing operations is C0.8. Because the profit from continuing operations is the control number, the potential ordinary shares are also included in the calculation of the diluted EPS for loss from discontinued operations and for the total loss for the year attributable to equity holders. The resultant diluted EPS figures are respectively (C1.4) for discontinued operations and (C0.6) for the loss attributable to equity holders. This is despite the fact that these figures are antidilutive to their comparable basic EPS figures of (C1.75) and (C0.75).

EPS for interim periods

A14.133 IAS 33 states that dilutive potential ordinary shares should be determined independently for each period presented. The number of dilutive potential ordinary shares included in the year to date period should not be a weighted average of the dilutive potential ordinary shares included in each interim computation. [IAS 33 para 37]. In other words, the number of dilutive potential ordinary shares should be determined for each interim period based on the year to date position at the end of the interim period.

Example

An example of this principle might be where an entity made an acquisition in the previous year and entered into an agreement to issue 1,000 additional ordinary shares for each C50,000 of consolidated profit in excess of C1,000,000 in the following year, based on the entity's consolidated financial statements. The entity reports quarterly. The results for each quarter are as follows:

		Cumulative
	C	C
First quarter	600,000	600,000
Second quarter	700,000	1,300,000
Third quarter	(200,000)*	1,100,000
Fourth quarter	400,000	1,500,000

*includes a loss from discontinued operations of C300,000.

The company has 100,000 ordinary shares outstanding during the year.

The EPS and diluted EPS for each quarter are as follows:

	Quarter 1	Quarter 2	Quarter 3	Quarter 4	Year
Numerator C	600,000	700,000	(200,000)	400,000	1,500,000
Denominator:					
Ordinary shares	100,000	100,000	100,000	100,000	100,000
Basic EPS*	C6	C7	(C2)	C4	C15
Potential ordinary shares	--	6,000	2,000**	10,000	10,000
Total denominator for diluted EPS	100,000	106,000	102,000	110,000	110,000
Diluted EPS	C6	C6.6	(C1.96)	C3.64	CC13.64

* The potential ordinary shares are not included in the calculation of the basic EPS, because there is no certainty that the condition will be satisfied until the end of the period.

** In quarter 3 there is a profit from continuing operations of C100,000 and a loss from discontinued operations of C300,000 and as the potential ordinary shares are dilutive at the continuing operations level they are taken into account in the diluted EPS, even though they are antidilutive at the total loss level.

The above example demonstrates that the diluted EPS for the year differs from any average or weighted average of the diluted EPS figures reported in the individual quarterly accounts. This is simply because the denominator used in each of the first three quarters differs from the denominator at the year end. Under the rules in the standard the diluted EPS figure for the year should be based on the year to date figures, that is, at the year end the figure should be disclosed as C13.64.

Securities of subsidiaries, joint ventures and associates

A14.134 A subsidiary, joint venture or associate may issue potential ordinary shares to parties other than the parent, venturer or investor. These potential ordinary shares may be convertible into either ordinary shares of the subsidiary, joint venture or associate or they may be convertible into shares of the parent, venturer or investor (the reporting entity). If the potential ordinary shares have a dilutive effect on the reporting entity's basic EPS, they should be included in the calculation of the reporting entity's diluted EPS. [IAS 33 para 40].

A14.135 If the potential ordinary shares issued by a subsidiary enable their holders to obtain ordinary shares in the subsidiary, then those potential ordinary shares should be included in computing the subsidiary's EPS figures (if indeed the subsidiary is calculating an EPS figure). In any event, those earnings per share amounts would be included in the consolidated EPS based on the group's holdings of the subsidiary's securities. On the other hand, if the potential shares issued by the subsidiary enable their holders to obtain ordinary shares in the parent, then these potential ordinary shares should be considered along with the other potential ordinary shares issued by the parent in the computation of consolidated diluted EPS. The same considerations apply where potential ordinary shares issued by an associate or a joint venture are exchangeable into ordinary shares of the associate or joint venture, or into ordinary shares of the reporting entity. They should be included in the EPS computation of the reporting entity if they are considered to be dilutive. [IAS 33 para A11].

Example

A parent entity has profit attributable to ordinary shareholders of C100,000 (excluding any earnings of the subsidiary). There are 10,000 ordinary shares outstanding. The parent owns 800 ordinary shares in the subsidiary representing 80% of the subsidiary's ordinary share capital. It also owns 200 convertible preference shares in the subsidiary representing 50% of the subsidiary's preference share capital (which is treated as an equity instrument under IAS 32). The parent also has 20 warrants exercisable to purchase ordinary shares in the subsidiary.

The subsidiary has profit attributable to ordinary shareholders of C6,000. Its ordinary share capital consists of 1,000 ordinary shares and it has 400 convertible (one for one) preference shares in issue. It has also issued 150 warrants exercisable to subscribe for ordinary shares of the subsidiary, with an exercise price of C5 per warrant. The average market price of one ordinary share of the subsidiary was C10. Dividends on the preference shares are C1 per share. There were no inter-company transactions or eliminations other than dividends. Tax has been ignored for the purposes of this example.

Subsidiary's earnings per share

Basic EPS $\frac{6{,}000 - 400}{1{,}000} = \text{C}5.6$

This is calculated as the subsidiary's profit from which is deducted the preference dividend that had been charged to retained earnings. The result is divided by the number of the subsidiary's ordinary shares.

Diluted EPS $\frac{6{,}000}{1{,}000 + 75 + 400} = \text{C}4.07$

This is the subsidiary's profit (preference dividends are not deducted as they would be saved on conversion of the preference shares) divided by the number of ordinary shares plus the ordinary shares that would be issued on conversion of the preference shares on the basis of one for one and the number of ordinary shares that would be issued for nil consideration on exercise of the warrants calculated as follows:

Proceeds of warrants 150 × C5 = C750.
Number of ordinary shares that could be issued at fair value C750/C10 = 75
Number of ordinary shares that would be issued at nil consideration 150 – 75 = 75

Consolidated earnings per share

Basic EPS $\frac{100{,}000 + 4{,}680}{10{,}000} = \text{C}10.47$

The earnings are calculated as the profit attributable to ordinary shareholders, before taking account of the subsidiary's results that are included in the consolidated financial statements, of C100,000, plus the share of the subsidiary's profits calculated as:

6,000 – 400 = 5,600 × 800/1000 = 4,480 + 200 (share of preference dividend) = 4,680

$$\text{Diluted EPS} \quad \frac{100{,}000 + 3{,}256 + 41 + 814}{10{,}000} = \text{C}10.41$$

The earnings figure comprises:

(a) The profit of parent entity attributable to ordinary shares (excluding dividends from subsidiary) of C100,000.

(b) The share of subsidiary's profit calculated as (800 shares × 4.07) = C3,256. (C4.07 being the diluted EPS of the subsidiary).

(c) The parent's proportionate interest in the subsidiary's earnings attributable to the warrants calculated as (75 shares × 4.07) × 20/150 = C40.7.

(d) The parent's proportionate interest in the subsidiary's earnings attributable to the convertible preference shares calculated as (200 shares × 4.07) = C814.

A14.136 Table A14.4 above discloses the effect on the group diluted EPS of options in a subsidiary that are convertible into shares of the subsidiary.

A14.137 The standard also covers the situation where securities of the reporting entity are issued that are convertible into ordinary shares of a subsidiary, joint venture or associate. In such a situation, the securities are assumed to be converted and the profit or loss attributable to ordinary equity holders of the reporting entity is adjusted, in the normal way, for any changes in dividends, interest or other changes that would result from conversion. The profit or loss is also adjusted for any changes in the reporting entity's share of results of the subsidiary, joint venture or associate that would result from the change in the number of shares in the subsidiary, joint venture or associate held by the reporting entity as a result of conversion. The denominator (number of shares and potential ordinary shares) of the diluted EPS calculation is not adjusted because the number of shares of the reporting entity itself would not change following conversion. [IAS 33 para A12].

Employee share and incentive plans

A14.138 Many companies have in place share options and other share award schemes to remunerate officers and other employees. Under some schemes, share options or share purchase rights are granted solely on the basis that the employees continue to render service for a specified period of time, that is, the award does not specify a performance condition for vesting. In other schemes, vesting of the shares depends on both the employee's rendering service to the employer for a specified period of time and the achievement of a specified performance target, for example, attaining a specified growth rate in return on assets or a specified earnings target.

A14.139 IAS 33 states that employee share options with fixed or determinable terms and non-vested ordinary shares are treated as options in calculating diluted EPS, even though they may be contingent on vesting. They are treated as outstanding on the grant date. Performance-related employee share options are treated as contingently issuable shares (see para A14.145 below) because their issue is contingent on satisfying specified conditions in addition to the passage of time. [IAS 33 para 48].

A14.140 As noted above, performance-related share options are treated as contingently issuable shares and these are dealt with from paragraph A14.145 below. All other awards that do not specify a performance criteria should be regarded as options for the purposes of computing diluted EPS. They should be considered to be outstanding as of the grant date for purposes of computing diluted EPS even though their exercise may be contingent upon vesting. They should be included in the diluted EPS computation even if the employee may not receive (or be able to sell) the stock until some future date. Accordingly, all shares to be issued should be included in computing diluted EPS if the effect is dilutive. The dilutive effect should be computed using the treasury stock method described in paragraph A14.117 above. If the share awards were granted during the period, the shares issuable must be weighted to reflect the portion of the period during which the awards were outstanding. [IAS 33 para 38].

A14.141 For share options and other share-based payment arrangements to which IFRS 2, 'Share-based payment', applies, the assumed exercise price should include the fair value (as calculated on the date the options were granted) of any goods or services to be supplied to the entity in the future under the share option or other share-based payment arrangement. [IAS 33 para 47A]. Therefore, in applying the treasury stock method described in paragraph A14.117 above, the assumed exercise price, for the purpose of determining the incremental number of shares issued for nil consideration, would comprise the amount, if any, the employee must pay upon exercise and the balance of any amounts calculated under IFRS 2 that has not yet been charged to the income statement. The assumed proceeds should not include cost attributable to past service. Neither should any adjustments be made to the numerator in respect of the IFRS 2 charge to the income statement as the charge represents the cost of issuing potential ordinary shares that would not be saved on conversion. The treatment of employee share options that are not related to performance is illustrated in the following example (ignoring tax).

Example

Share option scheme not related to performance

Company A has in place an employee share option scheme that awards share options to employees on the basis of period of service with the company.

The provisions of the scheme are as follows at the 20X0 year end.

Date of grant	1 January 20X0
Market price of option at grant date	C2.10
Exercise price of option	C2.50
Date of vesting	31 December 20X2
Number of shares under option	1 million

Applying IFRS 2, the income statement is charged with 70c per option in each of the three years 20X0-20X2 (that is, C2.10/3).

Profit for year 20X0 (after compensation expense)	C1,200,000
Weighted average number of ordinary shares outstanding	5 million
Average market price of an ordinary share during the year	C5.00
Assumed proceeds per option	C3.90 (being the exercise price of C2.50 and IFRS 2 expense attributable to future service, not yet recognised, of C1.40). Next year C3.20 (being C2.50 + 70c).

Computation of earnings per share	per share	earnings	shares
Profit for year 20X0		C1,200,000	
Weighted average shares outstanding for 20X0			5,000,000
Basic earnings per share	24.0c		
Number of shares under option			1,000,000
Number of shares that would have been issued at fair value: (1 million × C3.90)/C5.00			(780,000)
Diluted earnings per share	23.0c	C1,200,000	5,220,000

[The next paragraph is A14.143.]

A14.143 Sometimes shares to satisfy the company's obligations under share award schemes have already been purchased by an ESOP trust and are held by the trust as pre-funding for options or other performance-related shares. The trust's holding in the company's shares is treated as treasury shares and deducted from equity. [IAS 32 para 33]. Accordingly, the rules relating to treasury shares would apply and those non-vesting shares should be excluded from both basic and diluted EPS as discussed in paragraph A14.75 above. Instead, the calculation of diluted EPS should include non-performance-related shares in the same way as options as set out from paragraph A14.140 above and performance-related shares in the same way as contingently issuable shares as discussed from paragraph A14.145 below.

A14.144 If share based awards are payable in ordinary shares or in cash at the election of either the entity or the employee, the determination of whether such awards are potential ordinary shares should be made in the same way as discussed in paragraph A14.163.

Contingently issuable ordinary shares

A14.145 It is not uncommon for acquisition agreements to include a clause under which the purchaser of an acquired entity is required to make an additional consideration payment in the form of ordinary shares in future. The value of such shares may either be known precisely at the time of the acquisition, or may be contingent upon the future performance or future evaluation of the acquired entity. In the first instance, the acquirer has an obligation to issue ordinary shares in future, but the obligation is simply deferred (deferred consideration). In the second instance an obligation may or may not arise depending on whether or not certain earnings conditions are met (contingent consideration). In any event, the need to issue ordinary shares in future could lead to dilution of EPS. The standard refers to these as 'contingently issuable ordinary shares'. [IAS 33 para 52]. Contingently issuable ordinary shares are defined as *"ordinary shares issuable for little or no cash or other consideration upon the satisfaction of specified conditions in a contingent share agreement"* (see also para A14.77 above). [IAS 33 para 5].

A14.146 The way in which diluted EPS should be calculated to take account of contingently issuable shares is described below:

- Contingently issuable shares are considered outstanding and included in the calculation of diluted EPS as if the conditions of the contingency are deemed to have been met, based on the information available, at the end of reporting period. In effect this means that the diluted EPS computation includes those shares that would be issued under the terms of the contingency, based on the current status of conditions, as if the end of the reporting period was the end of the contingency period. An example would be an estimate of the number of shares that would have been issued under an earn-out if that agreement had terminated at the balance sheet date (see further para A14.148). Ordinary shares issuable under such contingent share agreements are included in the diluted EPS calculation as of the beginning of the period or as of the date of the contingent share agreement, if later. Restatement is not permitted if the conditions are not met when the actual contingency period expires. [IAS 33 para 52].
- Where the conditions relating to the issue have been met (the events occurred) by the end of the period, the relevant shares are included in the computation of both basic and diluted EPS. In effect, this will be when issuing the shares is no longer contingent and when there are no circumstances under which the shares would not be issued. [IAS 33 para 52].

A14.147 The criteria under which additional shares are issuable under contingent consideration agreements are many and varied, although in practice most involve either future levels of earnings or the future share price of the issuing company or a mixture of both. It should be noted, however, that such contingently issuable shares should be included in the diluted EPS calculation only if the effect is dilutive.

A14.148 Where the number of contingently issuable shares depends upon the level of earnings, the diluted EPS computation should include those shares to the extent that that they would be issuable under the agreement based on the current amount of earnings. However, earnings conditions in earn out agreements come in various forms. Sometimes the terms may specify that further shares will be issued if the average profit earned over a period is a specific amount. Sometimes the maintenance of current earnings levels, or the attainment of specified increased level of earnings of the acquired entity for a specified number of years may be the condition. Other earnings conditions may specify the issue of shares when a minimum earnings target is reached, increasing rateably until the maximum earnings target is reached, with a cap on the maximum number of shares that could be issued.

A14.149 IAS 33 deals specifically with one such type of arrangement, where the achievement or maintenance of a specified level of earnings is the condition and that amount has been achieved at the end of the period, but must be maintained for a further period. In such a case the additional ordinary shares are included if dilutive in the *diluted* EPS, because the end of the period is *assumed* to be the end of the contingency period for the purpose of diluted EPS and the level of profit has been achieved at the end of the period. However, the shares are not included in *basic* EPS until the end of the *actual* contingency period, that is, the end of the further period for which the level of earnings must be maintained. This is because there may be losses in that further period that could mean that the contingent condition will not be met at the end of the actual contingency period. [IAS 33 para 53].

A14.150 Whatever the earnings criteria, the guiding principle is that the current level of earnings should be used to determine the number of shares that could be issued under the terms, assuming that the contingency period ended on the balance sheet date. They should be included in the diluted EPS calculation only if dilution results. If in the subsequent period, or until the end of the agreement, there is a decline in earnings such that the contingent shares no longer need to be issued, previous period's diluted EPS should not be restated. Hence, basic EPS should not include any contingently issuable shares, because all the necessary conditions have not been satisfied, but the shares would be included in calculating the diluted figure. The following examples illustrate the application of the above principle.

Example 1

Average earnings condition

On 1 January 20X4, company A acquired the whole of the issued share capital of company B. The total consideration payable in respect of the acquisition comprises initial consideration and deferred contingent consideration. Under the terms of the deferred contingent consideration, company A is required to issue 100,000 shares if company B's profit for the year averages C100,000 over a three year period. Any additional shares will be issued on 1 January 20X7 after the end of the three year contingency period. Company B's profit for the year ended 31 December 20X4 amounted to C120,000.

Given that the terms stipulate the achievement of C100,000 of average profit for the three year period, it would appear at first sight that the contingency condition at the balance sheet date has been met as the profit for the year ended 31 December 20X4 exceeds C100,000. This is not the case as it assumes that the company will earn at least C90,000 for each of the next two years ended 31 December 20X6. Projecting future earnings levels in this way is not permitted under the standard because as stated in paragraph A14.101 above, the standard takes a historical approach and not a predictive or forward-looking approach in measuring dilution. The provisions relating to contingently issuable shares in the standard are quite specific and do not allow an entity to consider the probability of a contingent issue occurring.

The correct analysis is to measure whether performance achieved in the current period is deemed to be that achieved over the whole of the contingency period as if the end of the reporting period was the end of the contingency period. On this basis, an average over a period has the same effect as if it were expressed as a cumulative amount over the period. So in this situation, the contingency condition should be expressed in terms of a cumulative target of C300,000 over the three year period. Since the profit for the year ended 31 December 20X4 is only C120,000, which is less than C300,000, the contingency condition is not met at the balance sheet and no additional shares would be brought into the diluted EPS computation.

Similarly, if the profit for the year ended 31 December 20X5 were to increase to C150,000 again the contingency condition is not met in that year, because the cumulative earnings to date amounts to C270,000. So no additional shares would be included in that year. In the final year ended 31 December 20X6 when the contingency period comes to an end, the company will know for certain whether the contingency conditions have been met or not. If the condition is met in that year, the company will include 100,000 shares in both basic and diluted EPS.

Example 2

Attainment of a specified increased level of earnings

The facts are the same as in the previous example except that the deferred contingent consideration agreement provides for the issue of 1,000 shares for each C1,000 of total profit in excess of C250,000 over the three years ending 20X6.

Using the above principles, the company did not earn C250,000 for the year ended 31 December 20X4. Again projecting future earnings levels (C120,000 for 3 years = C360,000) and including 110,000 ((C360,000 — C250,000)/C1,000 × 1,000) contingent shares in the diluted EPS calculation is not permitted by the standard.

For the year ended 31 December 20X5, the cumulative amount earned to that date is C270,000. As this amount exceeds C250,000, the contingency condition is met in that year and the company will include 20,000 contingently issuable shares in the diluted EPS calculation for that year.

However, no additional shares would be included in basic EPS because there is a possibility that the contingency condition may not be met in 20X6 (for example, there is a loss in 20X6).

A14.151 Similar considerations apply when computing diluted EPS for interim reports. If at 30 June 20X5, the cumulative amount earned to that date was C245,000 (C120,000 to 31 December 20X4 + C125,000 to 30 June 20X5), the contingency provision is not met. Therefore, no contingently issuable shares would be included in calculating the diluted EPS for the half year, even though at the time of preparing the interim report it is apparent that 20,000 shares will be included in the year end diluted EPS calculation.

A14.152 IAS 33 also gives specific guidance for the situation where the number of shares issuable in the future depends on the market price of the shares at the future date. It states that the computation of diluted EPS should reflect the number of shares that would be issued based on the current market price at the end of the reporting period if the effect is dilutive. If the condition is based on an average of market prices over some period of time that extends beyond the end of the reporting period, the average for the period that has elapsed at the period end should be used. Because the market price may change in a future period, basic EPS should not include such contingently issuable shares, because all necessary conditions have not been satisfied. [IAS 33 para 54].

A14.153 Where the number of contingently issuable ordinary shares depends on both future earnings and the future market price of ordinary shares, the number of ordinary shares included in the diluted EPS calculation is based on both conditions. Unless both conditions are deemed to be met (using the guidance in the previous paragraphs) the contingently issuable shares are not included in the diluted EPS. [IAS 33 para 55].

A14.154 In some deferred consideration agreements, the value of the deferred consideration is known, but the number of shares to be issued when the deferred consideration falls due is not known. IAS 33 does not specifically consider this situation. However, we consider that the number of shares to be included in the calculation should be based on the market price at the balance sheet date as if it were the end of the contingency period.

A14.155 IAS 33 also gives guidance for the situation where the contingency is based on a condition other than earnings or market price (for example, opening a certain number of retail stores). It states that the contingent shares should be included in the computation of diluted EPS based on the assumption that the current status (at the period end) of the condition will remain unchanged until the end of the contingency period. So, if during the period only half the required number of new stores that would result in the issue of shares were opened, no contingently issuable shares are included in the diluted EPS computation. [IAS 33 para 56].

A14.156 If the contingency is based on a number of different conditions, we consider that the determination of the number of shares included in diluted EPS should be based on the status of all relevant conditions as they exist at the end of each reporting period. If one of the conditions is not met at the end of the reporting period, no contingently issuable shares should be included in diluted EPS. Though not specifically mentioned in IAS 33 it is implicit in the guidance described in paragraph A14.153 above.

A14.157 Contingently issuable potential ordinary shares that are not covered by a contingent share agreement, such as contingently issuable convertible instruments, should be included in diluted EPS on the following basis:

- It is first necessary to determine whether the potential ordinary shares may be assumed to be issued on the basis of the conditions specified for their issue under the contingently issuable share provisions discussed from paragraph A14.145.
- Depending on the type of those potential ordinary shares, they should be reflected in diluted EPS by following the provisions for convertible securities discussed from paragraph A14.114, the provisions for share options and warrants discussed from paragraph A14.117, and the provisions for contracts that may be settled in ordinary shares or cash discussed from paragraph A14.159.

However, exercise or conversion should not be assumed for purposes of computing diluted EPS, unless exercise or conversion of similar outstanding potential ordinary shares that are not contingently issuable is also assumed. [IAS 33 para 57].

A14.158 An example of contingently issuable potential ordinary shares is given in Table A14.6. This relates to contingent consideration for an acquisition that is subject to a lawsuit.

Table A14.6 – Diluted EPS and contingent consideration payable in shares

Altana AG – Annual Report and Accounts – 31 December 2002

Earnings per share

Basic earnings per share are computed by dividing net income by the weighted average number of shares outstanding for the year. Diluted EPS reflects the potential dilution that could occur if securities or other contracts to issue common stock were exercised or converted into common stock. Diluted earnings per share are calculated by adjusting the weighted average number of shares for the effect of the stock option plans as well as the impact of the DAT lawsuit which is payable in the Company's shares (Note 31). No adjustments to net income were necessary for the computation of diluted earnings per share.

The diluted earnings per share were calculated under the assumption that all potential diluting options are exercised.

	2002	2001
Basic earnings per share:		
Net income	**324,408**	327,937
Weighted average common shares outstanding	**136,622,766**	137,533,720
Basic earnings per share in €	**2.37**	**2.38**
Diluted weighted average shares:		
Net income	**324,408**	327,937
Weighted average shares outstanding	**136,622,766**	137,533,720
Dilution from stock options	**604,546**	607,434
Dilution from DAT lawsuit	**306,391**	306,391
Diluted weighted average shares outstanding	**137,533,703**	138,447,545
Diluted earnings per share in €	**2.36**	**2.37**

31 Litigation
Deutsch-Atlantische Telegraphen AG
In 1988, a group of minority shareholders of DAT brought a legal action against the Company in connection with an exchange offer made to these minority shareholders.

After consideration of the case, both the Landesgericht Köln and the Oberlandesgericht Düsseldorf stated that the 1.3 or 1.4 shares offered to the former shareholders was fair consideration. However, in 1999 the Federal Supreme Court of Germany overturned this ruling stating that the fair value should be determined based on a higher market value for DAT shares.

On March 12, 2001, the German Federal Court of Justice (Bundesgerichtshof, BGH) ruled that the exchange ratio must be based on the average market price of the shares to be exchanged during the three months preceding the approval by majority shareholders of DAT to sell its shares to the Company. The BGH referred the appeal back to a lower court (Landgericht Köln).

The expected settlement is recorded as contingent consideration based on the Company's best estimate of the exchange of 3.45 ALTANA shares for one DAT share. However, since all of the assets of DAT were either sold or written off in connection with the Company's restructuring plan in 1995, the additional consideration was expensed immediately as an impairment expense. As of December 31, 2002, consideration expected to be settled by the Company by issuance of shares has been measured at €13.8 million based on the Company's share price at December 31, 2002. The portion of the settlement expected to be paid in cash is €2.3 million. The estimated total settlement of €16.1 million is recorded as an accrual. The final settlement is subject to change based on the final exchange ratio and the market value of ALTANA's stock on the date of the settlement (Note 32).

In 2001, the addition of the accrual was recorded in other operating expenses. In 2002 the reduction of the accrual (€3.4 million) due to the decrease in the ALTANA's share price at the balance sheet date was recorded in other operating income.

32 Subsequent events (extract)
The management board and the supervisory board of ALTANA AG authorized the issuance of the financial statements as of March 17, 2003.
On January 15, 2003, the federal court decided that the consideration of the former DAT shareholders (Note 31) should be based on a conversion ratio of 3.45 shares of ALTANA for one share of DAT. The Company has appealed against that ruling.

Contracts that may be settled in ordinary shares or cash

A14.159 IAS 33 deals specifically with contracts that may be settled in ordinary shares or cash. The rules differ depending on whether the option is held by the entity (the issuer) or by the holder of the contract, as set out in the following paragraphs.

A14.160 If an entity has issued a contract that may be settled in ordinary shares or in cash at the *entity's option* (but not at the holder's option), IAS 33 lays down the following rules:

- The entity should presume that the contract will be settled in shares, and the resulting potential ordinary shares should be included in diluted EPS if the effect is dilutive.
- When such a contract is presented for accounting purposes as an asset or a liability, or when it has both an equity and a liability component under IAS 32, the entity should adjust the numerator (profit or loss attributable to

ordinary equity holders) for any changes in the profit or loss that would have resulted during the period if the contract had been classified wholly as an equity instrument. This is similar to the adjustments required in paragraph 33 of IAS 33 (see para A14.102 above).

[IAS 33 paras 58, 59].

A14.161 An example of such a contract is a deferred or contingent consideration agreement where the entity has the unrestricted right to settle the consideration in the form of ordinary shares or cash. At the date of acquisition it may not be possible for the entity to determine how the deferred consideration will be settled. It should, therefore, be presumed that the contract will be settled in shares, the more dilutive method, and the resulting potential ordinary shares included in diluted EPS in accordance with the standard's relevant provisions. An example is given in Table A14.7. Another example given in the standard is a debt instrument that, on maturity gives the entity the unrestricted right to settle the liability in cash or in ordinary shares. [IAS 33 para 61].

Table A14.7 – Diluted EPS, contract that can be settled in shares or cash at entity's option

Informa PLC – Interim report – 30 June 2005

9 Earnings per share

Basic
The basic earnings per share calculation is based on a profit on ordinary activities after taxation of £48,769,000 (2004 profit: £15,115,000 six months and £69,836,000 twelve months). This profit (2004: six months profit and twelve months profit) on ordinary activities after taxation is divided by the weighted average number of shares in issue (less those non-vested shares held by employee share ownership trusts) which is 299,335,000 (2004: 193,647,000 six months and 244,928,000 twelve months).

Diluted
The diluted earnings per share calculation is based on the basic earnings per share calculation above except that the weighted average number of shares includes all potentially dilutive options granted by the Balance Sheet date as if those options had been exercised on the first day of the accounting period or the date of the grant, if later, giving a weighted average of 300,900,000 (2004: 195,557,000 six months and 246,713,000. twelve months). In accordance with IAS 33 the weighted average number of shares includes the estimated maximum number of shares payable to the vendors of Routledge Publishing Holdings Limited assuming that there are no claims for compensation by the Group that will reduce this deferred consideration and assuming that the Company does not exercise its option to pay the balance of deferred consideration in cash. The deferred consideration shares are also assumed for the purposes of this calculation to have been issued on 1 January 2005 at the closing mid-market share price on 30 June 2005 of 379p making 335,000 (2004: 314,000 six months and 336,000 twelve months) ordinary shares potentially issued.

The table below sets out the adjustment in respect of diluted potential ordinary shares:

	6 months 2005	6 months 2004	12 months 2004
Weighted average number of shares used in basic earnings per share calculation	299,334,804	193,646,662	244,927,883
Effect of dilutive share options	1,230,032	1,597,198	1,449,594
Shares potentially to be issued or allotted	334,734	313,624	335,629
Weighted average number of shares used in diluted earnings per share calculation	300,899,570	195,557,484	246,713,106

A14.162 For contracts that may be settled in ordinary shares or cash at the *holder's option*, the more dilutive of cash settlement and share settlement should be used in calculating diluted EPS. [IAS 33 para 60]. An example might be an incentive scheme where annual bonuses may be payable in either shares or cash at the election of the employee. In that situation it should be presumed that the contract will be settled by the more dilutive method. Another example given in the standard is a written put option that gives the holder the choice of settling in ordinary shares or cash. [IAS 33 para 61].

A14.163 Whilst the standard does not specifically cover the point if a contract may be settled in cash or shares at either the issuer's or the holder's option, the more restrictive of the above rules, that is those where only the issuer has an option should be applied. In practice the rules in the standard recognise that it is likely that only one party will have the option as otherwise there could be a conflict.

A14.164 The standard includes an example of the calculation of diluted EPS where the entity has in issue a convertible bond that may be settled in ordinary shares or cash at the issuer's option. The example illustrates also the adjustments that may have to be made to the numerator under the second bullet point in paragraph A14.160 above. The example below is based on the example in the standard.

Example

An entity issues 1,000 convertible bonds at the beginning of 20X5. The bonds have a three-year term and are issued at par with a face value of C1,000 per bond, giving total proceeds of C1,000,000. Interest is payable annually in arrears at a nominal annual interest rate of 4%. Each bond is convertible at any time up to maturity into 150 common shares. The entity has an option to settle the principal amount of the convertible bonds in ordinary shares or in cash.

When the bonds are issued, the prevailing market interest rate for similar debt without a conversion option is 9%. At the issue date, the market price of one common share is C3. Income tax is ignored.

Profit 20X5	C1,000,000	
Ordinary shares outstanding	1,200,000	
Convertible bonds outstanding	1,000	
Liability component	C873,434	[see note 1 below]
Equity component	C126,566	
Proceeds of the bond issue	C1,000,000	

Note 1: Present value of the principal and interest discounted at 9% – C1,000,000 payable at the end of three years; C40,000 payable annually in arrears for three years.

The liability and equity components would be determined in accordance with IAS 32, 'Financial instruments: Disclosure and presentation'. These amounts would be recognised as the initial carrying amounts of the liability and equity components presented on the balance sheet. The amount assigned to the issuer conversion option equity element is a permanent addition to equity and is not adjusted.

Basic earnings per share 20X5:

$$\frac{C1{,}000{,}000}{1{,}200{,}000} = C0.83 \text{ per ordinary share}$$

Diluted earnings per share 20X5:

It is presumed that the issuer will settle the contract by the issue of ordinary shares, the dilutive effect is calculated in accordance with paragraph A14.158.

$$\frac{C1{,}000{,}000 + C78{,}609(a)}{1{,}200{,}000 + 150{,}000(b)} = C0.80 \text{ per ordinary share}$$

(a) The initial carrying amount is adjusted for the accretion of the liability using the effective interest rate – that is, C78,609 (C873,434 × 9%).

(b) 150,000 ordinary shares = 150 ordinary shares × 1,000 convertible bonds

[IAS 33 Example 8].

[The next paragraph is A14.166.]

Purchased options

A14.166 The standard notes that contracts such as purchased put options and purchased call options held by an entity over its own ordinary shares are not included in the calculation of diluted EPS. This is because their inclusion would be antidilutive. A put option (defined by IAS 33 as a contract that gives the holder the right to sell ordinary shares at a specified price for a given period) would be exercised only if the option exercise price were higher than the market price and a call option would be exercised only if the option exercise price were lower than the market price. [IAS 33 para 62]. In both instances, the options' effect would be antidilutive under the treasury stock method (see para A14.118 above) and the reverse treasury stock method (see para A14.167 below).

Written put options

A14.167 The standard also deals with written put options. Contracts that require the entity to repurchase its own shares, such as written put options and forward purchase contracts are reflected in diluted EPS if their effect is dilutive. If the contracts are 'in the money' during the period, that is, if the exercise or settlement price is above the average market price for the period, their dilutive effects should be calculated using the 'reverse treasury stock' method. Under that method:

- It should be assumed that at the beginning of the accounting period sufficient ordinary shares will be issued at the average market price for the period to raise the necessary proceeds to satisfy the contracts.
- It should be assumed that the proceeds from this issue are used to satisfy the contract to buy back ordinary shares.
- The incremental ordinary shares, that is, the difference between the number of shares assumed to be issued and the number of shares received (bought back) on satisfying the contract will be included in the calculation of diluted EPS.

[IAS 33 para 63].

Example

Assume an entity has outstanding 160 written put options on 160 of its ordinary shares with an exercise price of C10 per option. The put obligation is, therefore, C1,600. The average market price of the entity's ordinary shares is C8 for the period. In calculating diluted EPS the entity assumes that it issues 200 ordinary shares at C8 per share to raise the proceeds necessary to satisfy the put option. The difference between the 200 ordinary shares assumed to be issued and the 160 ordinary shares that would have been received on exercise of the option, that is 40 shares is added to the denominator (number of shares) in calculating the diluted EPS. No adjustments are made to the numerator (profit attributable to ordinary shareholders) as the shares are deemed issued for nil proceeds. [IAS 33 para A10].

Restatement of EPS data

A14.168 Diluted EPS of any prior period presented should not be restated for changes in the assumptions used (such as for contingently issuable shares) or for the conversion of potential ordinary shares (such as convertible debt) outstanding at the end of the previous period. [IAS 33 para 65]. This is because these factors are already taken into account in calculating the basic and, where applicable, the diluted EPS for the current period. However, in some circumstances, prior period's EPS data should be restated. These circumstances include certain post balance sheet changes in capital (see para A14.169) and prior period adjustments (see para A14.171).

Post balance sheet changes in capital

A14.169 As noted in paragraph A14.80 above, the weighted average number of ordinary shares outstanding for all periods presented (and, therefore, both basic and diluted EPS for all periods presented) should be restated for bonus issues, share splits, share consolidations and other similar events occurring during the period that change the number of shares in issue without a corresponding change in the resources of the entity. [IAS 33 para 26]. In addition, if such events occur after the balance sheet date, but before the financial statements are approved for issue, the basic and diluted EPS figures for the current period and for prior periods should be presented on the basis of the new number of shares. [IAS 33 para 64]. Where the EPS figures reflect such post balance sheet date changes, this fact should be disclosed (see further para A14.181 below).

A14.170 Other post balance sheet changes in capital should not be adjusted for, but disclosure is required of ordinary share transactions or potential ordinary share transactions that would have changed significantly the number of ordinary shares or potential ordinary shares outstanding at the end of the period if they had occurred before the end of the period (see further para A14.182).

Prior period adjustments

A14.171 EPS for all periods presented should be adjusted for the effects of errors and adjustments resulting from changes in accounting policies accounted for retrospectively in accordance with IAS 8, 'Accounting policies, changes in accounting estimates and errors'. [IAS 33 para 64]. That is, the EPS figure for the prior period should be restated as if the restated profit or loss had been reported originally in the prior period or periods.

A14.172 When a change in accounting policy: has an effect on the current period or any prior period; would have such an effect except that it is impracticable to determine the amount of the adjustment; or might have an effect on future periods, an entity should disclose for the current period and each prior period presented, to the extent practicable, the amount of the adjustment for basic and diluted earnings per share. Similarly, for the retrospective correction of material prior period errors, an entity should disclose for each prior period presented, to the extent practicable, the amount of the correction for basic and diluted earnings per share. [IAS 8 paras 28(f)(ii), 29(c)(ii), 49(b)(ii)]. Table A14.8 is an example of disclosure, as noted in the Table the effect on 2005 is not disclosed as it is immaterial.

Table A14.8 – Effect of changes in accounting policy on EPS

Barloworld Limited – Annual Report and Accounts – 30 September 2005

30. CHANGES IN ACCOUNTING POLICY AND DISCLOSURES (extract 1)

30.1 The annual financial statements have been prepared in accordance with International Financial Reporting Standards (IFRS) on a basis consistent with the prior year except for the adoption of the following new or revised Standards and Interpretations:

IAS 8 (Revised) Accounting policies, changes in accounting estimates and errors

The revised IAS 8 is effective for the group from the year ending 30 September 2006. Revised requirements relate to selection of accounting policies, changing of accounting policies and correction of prior period errors as well as disclosures relating to these items. The changes were made in order to reduce or eliminate alternatives, redundancies and conflict with other Standards, to deal with some convergence issues and make other improvements. The group early adopted this Standard in the current year.

IAS 16 (Revised) Property, plant and equipment

The revised IAS 16 is effective for the group from the year ended 30 September 2006. Amendments that impact on the group relate to the components approach to depreciation and the requirement for an annual review of the residual value and useful lives of assets. These changes affect the annual depreciation charge to the income statement. The group early adopted this Standard in the current year.

IAS 36 (Revised) Impairment of assets; IAS 38 (Revised) Intangible Assets; IFRS 3 Business Combinations

The revised IAS 38 and IAS 36 were issued simultaneously with IFRS 3 as part of the first phase of the International Accounting Standards Board's project on business combinations. The changes to IAS 38 mainly relate to clarifying the identifiability of intangible assets, the useful life and amortisation of intangible assets and the accounting for in-process research and development projects acquired in business combinations. None of these issues impact significantly on the accounting for intangible assets in the group.

With the adoption of IFRS 3, amortisation of goodwill has ceased with effect from the beginning of the current financial year. All goodwill is tested for impairment as required by IAS 36 on at least an annual basis and for this purpose is allocated to the appropriate cash generating units. The group adopted these Standards in the current year.

IFRS 4 Insurance contracts

This Standard is effective for the group from the year ending 30 September 2006 and requires certain changes in accounting for contracts that continue to meet the definition of insurance as well as additional disclosures. The requirements do not have a significant impact on the group and the Standard was early adopted in the current year.

IAS 39 (Revised) Financial instruments: recognition and measurement

IAS 39 was originally adopted by the group in the year ended 30 September 2002, followed by subsequent amendments which were adopted when issued. In the current financial year, further amendments to the Standard were issued in April, June and August 2005. These amendments relate to the treatment of cash flow hedges of forecast intragroup transactions, restricting the ability to designate any financial asset or liability to be measured at fair value through profit and loss, and broadening the scope to include financial guarantee contracts issued. These amendments do not have a significant impact on the group and were early adopted in the current year.

IFRIC Interpretation 1: Changes in existing decommissioning, restoration and similar liabilities (IFRIC 1)

IFRIC 1 contains guidance on accounting for changes in decommissioning, restoration and similar liabilities that have previously been recognised both as part of the cost of an item of property, plant and equipment under IAS 16 and as a provision (liability) under IAS 37. The Interpretation addresses subsequent changes to the amount of the liability that may arise from (a) a revision in the timing or amount of the estimated decommissioning or restoration costs or from (b) a change in the current market-based discount rate. It is group policy to account for assets using the cost model. As a result of this, IFRIC 1 requires changes in the initial estimates of rehabilitation and decommissioning costs to be capitalised as part of the cost of the item and depreciated prospectively over the remaining life of the item to which it relates. This is consistent with the treatment under IAS 16 of other changes in estimates relating to property, plant and equipment. This Interpretation is effective from the current year.

IFRIC Interpretation 2: Members' shares in co-operative entities and similar instruments

This Interpretation is effective for the group from the year ending 30 September 2006 and deals with the treatment of members' shares in co-operative entities and similar instruments in terms of its classification as either a financial liability or equity. The requirements of the Interpretation do not have a significant impact on the group and it was early adopted in the current year.

In addition to the accounting policy changes as set out above, the group also changed the treatment of operating leases with fixed escalations, which were previously expensed on a cash basis, to a straight-line basis in terms of circular 7/2005 issued by the South African Institute of Chartered Accountants and in accordance with IAS 17 Leases.

Comparative information has been restated for the effects of adopting IAS 16 and IFRIC 1 as well as for the effect of accounting for operating leases with fixed escalations on a straight-line basis.

30. CHANGES IN ACCOUNTING POLICY AND DISCLOSURES (extract 2)

	Previously stated	Adjustments IAS 16	IFRIC1	IAS 17	Restated
Earnings per share 2003					
Net profit per share (cents)					
– basic	576.4	(1.5)	(0.5)	(2.0)	572.4
– fully diluted	565.0	(1.5)	(0.5)	(2.0)	561.1
2004 Net profit per share (cents)					
– basic	760.9	(1.0)	(0.5)	(2.5)	756.9
– fully diluted	742.9	(1.0)	(0.5)	(2.5)	738.9

Cash flow statement

The restatements have not impacted on cash flows.

With the adoption of IFRS3 Business Combinations, the amortisation of goodwill has ceased with effect from the beginning of the current financial year. As required by the standard no restatement of comparatives has been made. The adoption of the rest of the abovementioned standards has not had a material impact on the group's results for the current year.

Presentation and disclosure

Presentation of basic and diluted EPS

A14.173 An entity should present both basic and diluted EPS on the face of the income statement. The basic and diluted EPS should be presented for profit or loss from continuing operations attributable to the entity's ordinary equity holders and for profit or loss for the period (that is, including both continuing and discontinued operations) attributable to the entity's ordinary equity holders. The basic and diluted EPS should be presented with equal prominence for all periods presented. [IAS 33 para 66]. This applies even if the basic and diluted EPS are the same. If they are the same the entity can disclose just one line described as 'Basic and diluted EPS'. [IAS 33 para 67].

A14.174 In practice, unless an entity has discontinued operations that it must disclose in accordance with IFRS 5, 'Non-current assets held for sale and discontinued operations', the EPS from continuing operations is likely to be identical to total EPS. Accordingly, if the basic EPS for continuing and total EPS is the same and the diluted EPS is the same, the entity could disclose the figures as follows:

Basic EPS for profit from continuing operations and for profit for the year	x
Diluted EPS for profit from continuing operations and for profit for the year	y
If the basic and diluted figures are the same the disclosure could be:	
Basic and diluted EPS for profit from continuing operations and for profit for the year	x

A14.175 The standard also requires disclosure either on the face of the income statement or in the notes of basic and diluted EPS for discontinued operations, where an entity has such operations and is required to disclose them in accordance with IFRS 5. [IAS 33 para 68]. Where an entity has such operations, its EPS from continuing operations will not be the same as its total EPS and so disclosure of three basic and three diluted EPS figures will be required. Assuming that the EPS figures for profit or loss on discontinued operations are disclosed on the face of the income statement the disclosure might be as follows:

	20X5	20X4
Earnings per ordinary share:		
Profit from continuing operations	x	x
Profit from discontinued operations	x	x
Profit for the period	x	x
Diluted earnings per share:		
Profit from continuing operations	x	x
Profit from discontinued operations	x	x
Profit for the period	x	x

An example is also given in Table A14.5 above.

A14.176 Where there is more than one class of ordinary shares in issue with different rights to share in the profit for the period, basic and diluted EPS figures must be calculated and disclosed for each such class of ordinary shares. [IAS 33 para 66]. The way in which such calculations should be performed is considered from paragraph A14.57 above.

A14.177 If a company incurs a loss or the amount it earns for the ordinary equity holders is a negative figure, basic and diluted EPS should be determined in accordance with the rules set out in the standard and shown as a loss per share. [IAS 33 para 69]. Where the diluted loss per share is the same as the basic loss per share, because the company has incurred a loss from continuing operations and all the company's existing potential ordinary shares are not dilutive as they decrease the loss from continuing operations, the entity can disclose these in one line. An example is given in Table A14.9 below. The example illustrates the basic and diluted EPS figures for the loss attributable to ordinary equity holders only and does not illustrate the disclosure for continuing or discontinued operations.

Table A14.9 – Basic and diluted loss per share

Ascom Holding Ltd – Annual Report and Accounts – 31 December 2002

Consolidated Income Statement (extract)

	2002	2001
Loss or diluted loss per share nom. CHF 10	(12.55)	(17.65)
Weighted average number of shares for loss per share	22 398 971	22 411 674
Annual loss attributable to shareholders in CHF million	(281.2)	(395.5)

Additional disclosures

A14.178 The following additional information should be given for both basic and diluted EPS:

- The amounts used as the numerators in calculating the basic and diluted EPS figures. These amounts should also be reconciled with the profit or loss for the period. The reconciliation should include the individual effect of each class of instrument that affects EPS, that is, it should describe and list the adjustments arising from each of the types of potential ordinary share that has affected the basic earnings figure.
- The weighted average number of ordinary shares used as the denominator in calculating the basic and diluted EPS figures. The denominators used in the basic and diluted EPS should also be reconciled to each other. This reconciliation should include the individual effect of each class of instrument that affects EPS, that is, it should list and describe the effects of each of the types of dilutive potential ordinary shares that has affected the basic weighted average number.

[IAS 33 para 70(a)(b)].

A14.179 An example of how a company can give the above information in a concise manner is shown in the table below. The example illustrates the basic and diluted EPS figures for the profit attributable to ordinary equity holders only and does not illustrate the disclosure for continuing or discontinued operations.

Example

	Year ended 31 December 20X5		
	Earnings	Number of shares	Per-share amount
Profit for the year	6,525,000		
Less: preference dividends	75,000		
Basic EPS:			
Earnings available to ordinary shareholders	6,450,000	2,500,000	C2.58
Effect of dilutive securities:			
Options		45,000	
Convertible preferred stock	35,000	255,000	
6% convertible debentures	60,000	60,000	
Diluted EPS:			
Adjusted earnings	6,545,000	2,860,000	C2.29

A14.180 The standard also requires disclosure of instruments, including contingently issuable shares, that could dilute EPS in the future, but that were not included in the computation of diluted EPS in the period (or periods) presented, because they were antidilutive in that period (or those periods). [IAS 33 para 70(c)].

A14.181 As stated in paragraph A14.80, basic and diluted EPS for all periods presented should be restated for bonus issues, share splits, share consolidations and similar events occurring during the period that change the number of shares in issue without a corresponding change in the resources of the entity. If these events occur after the balance sheet date, but before the financial statements are approved for issue, the EPS figures for the current period, and those of any prior periods, should be based on the new number of shares issued (see para A14.169). As a result, the number of shares used in the EPS calculation will not be consistent with that shown in the balance sheet. Therefore, disclosure should be made to that effect. [IAS 33 para 64]. An example of a share split that occurred in the year is Table A14.10 (only the figures for basic EPS are reproduced in the table).

Table A14.10 – EPS adjusted for share split in the year

STADA Arzneimittel AG – Report and Accounts – 31 December 2004

2.18. Earnings per share (extract)

Earnings per share	2004	Previous year
Net income distributable to shareholders of STADA Arzneimittel AG in € 000s	48,484	43,869
Average number of shares	53,348,910[1,2]	43,327,286[1,2]
Earnings per share in €	0.91[2]	1.01[2]

Basic earnings per share are calculated according to IAS 33.10 by dividing net income distributable to the shareholders of STADA Arzneimittel AG by the average number of shares outstanding, less treasury stock.

[1] Please refer to the notes on shareholders' equity (see note 3.12) regarding the change in the number of shares.

[2] Pursuant to IAS 33.20 in conjunction with IAS 33.22, a capital increase from existing funds changes the average number of shares without any concomitant change in the level of resources. The number of common shares in issue prior to the capital increase is adjusted in accordance with the proportional change in the number of outstanding common shares after the share issue as if the event (the de facto 1:1 stock split) had occurred at the beginning of the period under review. For the purposes of historical comparison, the historical figure for the average number of shares in each fiscal year ending prior to the conversion date will be doubled to adjust for the stock split when calculating the earnings per share.

3.12. Share capital (extract)

As of the balance sheet date, share capital consisted of 53,390,820 common shares, each with an arithmetical par value of € 2.60 (prior year: 26,695,290).

The increase in the number of shares in 2004 is almost entirely due to the de facto 1:1 stock split that took place in the year under review and only to a very small extent due to the increase in shares resulting from the initial exercise of options from STADA warrants 2000/2015. STADA executed the de facto 1:1 stock split resolved by the Annual Shareholders' Meeting on June 15, 2004 after close of trading on Friday, July 30, 2004, once the capital measure had been entered into the commercial register.

STADA shareholders received one bonus share for every registered bearer share of restricted transferability they already held (ISIN DE0007251803, WKN 725180). The Company's share capital thereby increased to €138,816,132.00. As a total of 26,695,410 bonus shares were issued, the number of STADA shares also doubled, arithmetically reducing its share price by half. This capital measure therefore constitutes a de facto 1:1 stock split. The bonus shares created by this capital increase from the Company's own funds were automatically credited to STADA shareholders' custody accounts with a value date of August 2, 2004. Shareholders holding their own shares were requested to effect the credit of the bonus shares to which they were entitled via a bank by submitting profit participation certificate no. 11 as proof of entitlement. The text of the official notification to shareholders was also published on STADA's website, www.stada.de.

A14.182 Entities are required to disclose details of all material ordinary share transactions or potential ordinary share transactions entered into after the balance sheet date, other than those described in the preceding paragraph. Such transactions should be disclosed where they would have significantly changed the number of ordinary or potential ordinary shares outstanding at the balance sheet date if the transactions had occurred before the end of the reporting period. [IAS 33 para 70(d)]. EPS for the period is not adjusted for such post balance sheet transactions, because they do not affect the amount of capital used to produce the profit or loss for the period. Such transactions include:

- Issue of shares for cash.
- Issue of shares where the proceeds are used to repay debt or preference shares outstanding at the balance sheet date.
- Redemption of ordinary shares.
- Conversion of potential ordinary shares outstanding at the balance sheet date into ordinary shares.
- Issue of warrants, options or convertible securities.
- Achievement of conditions that would result in the issue of contingently issuable shares.

[IAS 33 para 71].

A14.183 Most of these transactions would fall to be disclosed anyway as material non-adjusting post balance sheet events under IAS 10, 'Events after the balance sheet date'. An example of disclosure is Table A14.11.

Table A14.11 – Disclosure of post balance sheet changes in capital

Swisscom AG – Annual Report and Accounts – 31 December 2004

41 Post balance sheet events (extract)
Approval by the Board of Directors

Swisscom Board of Directors approved these consolidated financial statements on March 7, 2005.

Dividend
At the General Meeting of Shareholders on April 26, 2005, a dividend of CHF 14 per share, amounting to a total income distribution of CHF 861 million, is to be proposed for 2004. In these financial this dividend payable is not disclosed as a liability. It is accounted for as a dividend contribution against shareholders' equity in 2005. The dividends declared at the 2004 General Meeting of Shareholders in respect of 2003 was CHF 861 million (previous year: CHF 794 million).

Share buy-back
In 2005 the Board of Directors decided to launch a share buy-back scheme in the amount of around CHF 2 billion in order to distribute the entire equity free cash flow.

Convertible bond of the Swiss Confederation on Swisscom shares
About one third of the convertible bonds of the Swiss Confederation related to Swisscom shares, which mature at the end of February 2005, were exercised by the maturity date. According to the Swiss Confederation authorities, of the 2.67 million shares included in the convertible bond, around 915,000 shares were converted. As a result of the conversion the share of the Confederation in Swisscom fell from 62.7% to 61.4%. On April 26, 2005 the Board of Directors applied to the Shareholders' Meeting for a capital reduction. Taking this into account the share of Confederation in Swisscom is now 66.1%.

A14.184 The standard also encourages companies to disclose the terms and conditions of financial instruments and other contracts generating potential ordinary shares if disclosure is not already required by IAS 32 or IFRS 7. Such disclosure may help users to understand the extent to which these instruments are dilutive and, if so, the effect they have on the disclosed diluted EPS data. Disclosure of the terms and conditions are particularly relevant for those antidilutive securities that are not included in the computation of diluted EPS. [IAS 33 para 72].

Volatility of published EPS

A14.185 The EPS figure, which is based on the profits available to ordinary equity holders, is an 'all inclusive' figure and may be volatile. This is because profits or losses of a period may be affected by certain unusual (exceptional) items, such as: profits or losses on the sale or termination of an operation; reorganisation costs; and profits and losses on the disposal of fixed assets. As a result, the presence or absence of such items will affect the EPS figure from one period to another. The requirement to disclose EPS figures for continuing and discontinued operations goes some way to explaining the volatility caused by disposing of operations. However, many companies prefer also to report an adjusted EPS that removes profits and losses of an unusual nature that do not relate to the entity's trading activities. An adjusted EPS is also popular with analysts.

[The next paragraph is A14.187.]

Additional earnings per share

A14.187 IAS 33 recognises that there may be instances where a company would wish to disclose additional EPS figures calculated on a level of earnings other than one required by the standard. It, therefore, permits companies to disclose an additional EPS using a reported component of the income statement other than profit or loss for the period, profit or loss for continuing operations and profit or loss for discontinued operations attributable to ordinary equity holders. Such EPS data should, however, be calculated using the weighted average number of ordinary shares determined in accordance with the standard. This means that the weighted average number of ordinary shares used in the calculation of this additional EPS should be the same as the number used in the basic and diluted EPS figures required by the standard. Entities should indicate the basis on which the numerator, that is, the income statement figure, is determined, including whether amounts per share are before or after tax. In addition, if a component of the income statement is used that is not reported as a line item in the income statement, a reconciliation should be provided between the component used and a line item that is reported in the income statement. Additional basic and diluted per share amounts should be disclosed with equal prominence and should be presented in the notes to the financial statements. The requirement that such figures should be presented in the notes means that they should not be shown on the face of the income statement as has often been the practice in the past, before the 2003 revision to IAS 33. [IAS 33 para 73].

A14.188 In November 2005 the Committee of European Securities Regulators (CESR) issued a recommendation on disclosure of alternative performance measures (APMs), which were defined as including 'operating earnings', 'cash earnings', 'earnings before one-time charges', 'EBITDA – earnings before interest, taxes, depreciation, and amortisation' and similar terms denoting adjustments to line items of income statement, balance sheet or cash flow statement. Thus, for example, they would include additional EPS figures. The recommendation included the following points:

- Under the IAS Framework, there are four qualitative characteristics that make the information provided in financial statements useful to users: understandability, relevance, reliability and comparability. CESR believes that issuers should always follow these principles for preparation and presentation of financial information including the preparation of alternative performance measures.

- Issuers should define the terminology used and the basis of calculation adopted (that is, defining the components included in an alternative performance measure). Clear disclosure is key to the understandability of any alternative performance measure and its relevance. Where relevant, investors should be made aware of the fact that alternative performance measures are not prepared in accordance with the accounting standards applied to audited financial statements. Alternative performance measures should be given meaningful names reflecting their basis of preparation in order to avoid misleading messages.

- Where possible, issuers should present alternative performance measures only in combination with defined measures (for example GAAP measures). Furthermore, issuers should explain the differences between both measures. This might be through a reconciliation of figures to provide investors with enough information to fully understand the company's results and financial position.

- Comparatives should be provided for any alternative performance measure presented.

- Alternative performance measures should be presented consistently over time.

- To ensure that investors are not misled, alternative performance measures should not be presented with greater prominence than defined GAAP measures. Where alternative performance measures are derived from audited financial statements and resemble defined performance measures, but do not actually have the characteristics of the defined measures (such characteristics include being audited, based on an identified reporting framework, consistent and comparable with performance measures of other enterprises), CESR recommends that defined measures should be given greater prominence than the alternative performance measures.

- Issuers may internally use alternative performance measures for measuring and controlling the company's profitability and financial position.

Generally, issuers explain this as the reason for presenting alternative performance measures to investors. CESR expects issuers to give an explanation of the internal use of alternative performance measures in order to make investors understand the relevance of this information. This explanation is useful only when presented in direct relation to the alternative performance measures.

[CESR Recommendation on Alternative Performance Measures].

A14.189 In practice, most of these recommendations would normally be observed under IFRS in any case. For example, a requirement for consistency of presentation is contained in IAS 1 'Presentation of financial statements', and it would normally be logical to explain the reason for presenting additional EPS numbers. The recommendation for a reconciliation is to a large extent covered by the IAS 33 requirement that if components of profit are used that are not reported in the income statement there should be a reconciliation to a line item in the income statement.

A14.190 Where a company has disclosed an EPS that is additional to the ones required by IAS 33, the requirements stated in paragraph A14.187 above should be followed. An example where a company has followed the standard's requirements where an additional EPS is presented (as explained in para A14.187) is shown in Table A14.12 below. In this example there are no discontinued operations and basic and diluted continuing and total EPS figures are the same.

Table A14.12 – Disclosure of additional EPS figures

Barloworld Limited — Annual Report and Accounts — 30 September 2005

GROUP INCOME STATEMENTS (extract)
for the year ended 30 September 2005

	Notes	**2005** **Rm**	2004* Rm	2003* Rm
Net profit per share (cents)				
– basic	24	**897.4**	756.9	572.4
– fully diluted	24	**877.3**	738.9	561.1

* *Restated – refer note 30*

24. NET PROFIT AND HEADLINE EARNINGS PER SHARE

24.1 Fully converted weighted average number of shares

	2005	2004	2003
Weighted average number of ordinary shares (net of share buy-back)	**207 366 842**	199 374 681	196 027 500
Increase in number of shares as a result of unexercised share options	**4 749 836**	4 837 422	3 410 348
	212 116 678	204 212 103	199 437 848
Increase in number of shares assuming conversion of the convertible bond			3 022 242
Fully converted weighted average number of shares	**212 116 678**	204 212 103	202 460 090

Account is taken of the number of ordinary shares in issue for the period in which they are entitled to participate in the net profit of the group.

	2005 Cents	2004 Cents	2003 Cents	**2005**	2004	2003
24.2 Net profit per share (basic)						
Net profit for the year (R million)				**1 861**	1 509	1 122
The weighted average number of ordinary shares				**207 366 842**	199 374 681	196 027 500
Net profit per share (basic)	**897.4**	756.9	572.4			
Net profit per share (fully diluted)						
Net profit for the year (R million)				**1 861**	1 509	1 122
Adjusted for: After-tax interest saving assuming conversion of convertible bond where effect is dilutive						14
Net profit for the year adjusted for diluted calculation (R million)				**1 861**	1 509	1 136
Fully converted weighted average number of shares (note 24.1)				**212 116 678**	204 212 103	202 460 090
Net profit per share (fully diluted)	**877.3**	738.9	561.1			
Percentage dilution	**2.2**	2.4	2.0			

24.3 Headline earnings per share (basic)						
Net profit for the year (R million)				**1 861**	1 509	1 122
Profit on disposal of properties, investments and subsidiaries				**(25)**	(108)	(123)
Impairment of assets				**21**	108	45
Goodwill amortisation					148	113
Realisation of translation reserves on liquidation of offshore subsidiary					57	
Interest in associate goodwill amortisation					6	9
Profit on sale of plant and equipment excluding rental assets				**(2)**	(15)	(6)
Other exceptional items						4
Taxation on exceptional items				**(6)**	(7)	(11)
Attributable exceptional items of associates (impairment losses)					3	
Interest of outside shareholders in exceptional items				**4**		1
Headline earnings (R million)				**1 853**	1 701	1 154
The weighted average number of ordinary shares				**207 366 842**	199 374 681	196 027 500
Headline earnings per share (basic)	**893.6**	853.2	588.7			
Headline earnings per share (fully diluted)						
Headline earnings (R million)				**1 853**	1 701	1 154
After-tax interest saving assuming conversion of convertible bond where effect is dilutive						14
Headline earnings adjusted for diluted calculation (R million)				**1 853**	1 701	1 168
Fully converted weighted average number of shares (note 24.1)				**212 116 678**	204 212 103	202 460 090
Headline earnings per share (fully diluted)	**873.6**	833.0	576.9			
Percentage dilution	**2.2**	2.4	2.0			

A14.191 Directors should carefully consider what profit measure to choose when calculating additional EPS figures and what information they would wish those figures to convey. This is because whatever profit measure is chosen it must be used consistently (see para A14.189 above). It is not possible to choose a profit measure to present a particular aspect of a company's performance in one year, because performance at that level is good, and then to ignore that measure in the following year when performance at that level is not so good.

[The next paragraph is A14.200.]

Financial statistics in the historical summary

A14.200 Entities often publish a historical summary, usually covering at least five years. IAS 33 does not deal specifically with adjustments to historical summaries, but the following guidance is relevant in such situations. In order to present a fair comparison of EPS figures published in such a summary, the basic EPS figure will need to be adjusted for subsequent changes in capital as set out below:

- Where a capitalisation issue or share split has taken place during a financial year, all previously published EPS figures should be adjusted by the bonus factor as explained in paragraph A14.80 above.
- Where a rights issue at less than full market has taken place during a financial year, all previously published EPS figures should be adjusted by the reciprocal of the bonus element inherent in the rights issue as explained from paragraph A14.85 above.

Where there is more than one capitalisation or rights issue during the year, both these factors will operate cumulatively. The cumulative effect of all the above events should be taken into account. The resultant figures should be described as restated EPS and should be set out separately from the other financial data that is not so adjusted.

A14.201 Where there has been a bonus or rights issue in the period covered by the summary, the ordinary dividend actually paid in those periods should be set out in the form of pence per share and similarly adjusted by the same factors used in restating EPS. This adjustment is necessary to ensure that the ordinary dividends and EPS data are comparable. The adjusted dividend per share should be described as restated. In practice, the adjusted EPS and the adjusted dividend per share are normally presented next to each other.

A14.202 Sometimes companies also disclose a dividend cover, which is the number of times a dividend is covered by current earnings. Some companies even disclose price/earnings ratios, high and low share prices or market capitalisation.

A14.203 An example of disclosure in a historical summary is Table A14.13. This example includes adjustment of earlier years for a bonus issue (see para A14.200 above).

A14.204 IFRS 1 requires at least one year of comparative information prepared under IFRS in an entity's first IFRS financial statements. [IFRS 1 para 36]. The IFRS does not require earlier years in a historical summary (that is, the years before the current and previous year) to comply with IFRS. However, those earlier years, if not presented in compliance with IFRS, must be clearly labelled as not being prepared under IFRS. In addition the nature of the main adjustments that would make those earlier years comply with IFRS should be disclosed. An entity need not quantify those adjustments. [IFRS 1 para 37]. IFRS 1's requirements are considered in detail in chapter 3.

A14.205 In Table A14.13, Huhtamaki Oyj, presents the latest two years of the historical summary in accordance with IFRS and earlier years in accordance with Finnish GAAP, but gives the 2002 figures for the year of transition to IFRS under both Finnish GAAP and IFRS. Elsewhere in the financial statements it includes a detailed description of the differences between accounting policies applied under Finnish GAAP and IFRS (not reproduced in Table A14.13).

Table A14.13 – EPS in historical summaries

Huhtamaki Oyj – Annual Report and Accounts – 31 December 2003

Per share data
Comparison figures (1999-2001) adjusted for the 3:1 bonus issue in August 2002

			FAS			IFRS	
		1999	**2000**	**2001**	**2002**	**2002**	**2003**
Earnings per share	EUR	0.60	0.65	0.74	0.88	0.86	0.38
Earnings per share (diluted)						0.86	0.38
Dividend, nominal	EUR	0.26	0.28	0.31	0.38	0.38	0.38[1]
Dividend/ earnings per share	%	43.3	43.1	41.9	43.2	44.2	100.0[1]
Dividend yield	%	3.1	3.9	3.5	4.0	4.0	4.1[1]
Shareholders' equity per share	EUR	7.61	8.20	8.64	8.79	8.26	7.85
Share price at December 31	EUR	8.40	7.10	8.88	9.55	9.55	9.35
Average number of shares adjusted for share issue		111,856,128	125,903,852	117,117,696	100,769,970	100,769,970	96,292,220
Number of shares adjusted for share issue at year end		125,903,852	125,903,852	101,215,792	97,547,792	97,547,792	96,161,703
P/E ratio		14.0	10.9	12.0	10.9	11.1	24.6
Market capitalization at December 31 EUR million		1,057.6	893.9	898.3	931.6	931.6	899.1

[1] 2003: Board's proposal.

First time adoption of IFRS

A14.206 There are specific rules in respect of first-time adoption of IFRS, set out in IFRS 1, 'First-time adoption of International Financial Reporting Standards', and these are considered in detail in chapter 3. See also paragraph A14.204.

UK.A14.206.1 In the UK, all listed companies (that is, those whose securities are admitted to trading on a regulated market) are required by an EU Regulation (EC No.1606/2002) to prepare their consolidated financial statements in accordance with EU-adopted International Financial Reporting Standards for accounting periods beginning on or after 1 January 2005. In addition, the Companies Act 1985 has been amended to extend the EU Regulation on a voluntary basis to all companies (except charitable companies) in their individual and/or consolidated financial statements for accounting periods beginning on or after 1 January 2005 (see further chapter 2).

Chapter 15

Intangible fixed assets

	Page
Intangible fixed assets	15001
Introduction	15001
The Act's requirements	15001
Scope of FRS 10	15002
Definition of intangible assets	15003
Separability from goodwill	15004
Control	15006
Readily ascertainable market value	15006
Internally developed intangible assets	15007
Purchased intangible assets	15008
Acquisition accounting	15008
Valuation methods	15009
Relief from royalties	15010
Premium profits	15010
Capitalisation of earnings	15011
Comparison with market transactions	15012
Revaluation of intangible assets	15012
Amortisation and impairment	15012
Useful economic life	15013
Residual values	15015
Methods of amortising intangible assets	15016
Impairment reviews	15016
Useful life 20 years or less — first year review	15017
Useful life 20 years or less — reviews in other years	15017
Detailed impairment review	15017
Disclosures	15018
Intangible assets — other information	15019
Copyrights	15019
Know-how	15020
Licences	15021
Patents and trademarks	15021
Research and development	15021
SSAP 13	15022
Development costs	15024
Capitalisation of development costs	15024
Amortisation	15025
Disclosure	15025
Exemptions from disclosure	15027
Provisions for diminution in value	15027
Effect on realised reserves	15028

Computer software 15029

Chapter 15

Intangible fixed assets

Intangible fixed assets

Introduction

15.1 Accounting for intangible fixed assets, and in particular brands, has been one of the major issues facing the accounting profession for many years. The issue is closely related to the problems of accounting for goodwill. This is because, for many people, brands and certain other intangibles, irrespective of whether purchased or generated internally, are merely a part of goodwill. For others, however, brands are distinct from goodwill and their value can be independently measured.

15.2 The problem of accounting for intangibles was settled with the publication of FRS 10, 'Goodwill and intangible assets'. The ASB found it convenient to deal with both goodwill and intangibles in a single standard, because they are so closely related. The ASB also decided the same accounting rules should apply to both in order to avoid the sort of accounting arbitrage that would otherwise arise from labelling similar items differently on the balance sheet.

The Act's requirements

15.3 Recognition of intangible assets in company balance sheets is specifically permitted by Schedule 4 to the Act. The model formats for the balance sheet include a heading for 'Intangible assets'. Under that heading there are separate sub-headings for:

- Concessions, patents, licences, trademarks, and similar rights and assets.
- Development costs.
- Goodwill.
- Payments on account.

15.4 The balance sheet may include amounts for concessions, patents, licences, trademarks and other similar rights and assets only where either of the following conditions is satisfied:

- They were acquired for valuable consideration in circumstances that do not qualify them to be shown as goodwill.
- They were created by the company itself. (FRS 10, however, restricts the circumstances where costs of self-developed intangibles may be capitalised.)

[Note 2 to the balance sheet formats].

15.5 The Act also permits intangible assets, other than goodwill, to be included in financial statements at their current cost (but FRS 10 is much more restrictive). Goodwill on the other hand may not be revalued. [CA85 4 Sch 31(1)].

15.6 Where capitalised intangible assets (including brands) are acquired or internally generated, they must be amortised over their estimated useful economic lives. [CA85 4 Sch 18]. If the lives are finite, the assets should be depreciated to their residual values. There is, however, an important distinction between the rule that applies to the depreciation of assets generally, and as a consequence to intangible assets, and the specific rule that applies to the amortisation of goodwill. For assets generally, it is acceptable to estimate the asset's residual value and to amortise the asset's cost or valuation down to its residual value over its useful life. However, the equivalent rule for goodwill requires that it is reduced by provisions for depreciation calculated to write it off completely on a systematic basis over a period chosen by the company's directors, which cannot exceed its useful economic life. [CA85 4 Sch 21]. This legal distinction has had important consequences for the development of the amortisation and impairment rules in FRS 10. In effect it is easier to justify carrying certain intangible assets permanently on the balance sheet without amortisation than it is for goodwill.

15.7 The disclosure requirements for intangible fixed assets are governed by paragraph 42 of Schedule 4 to the Act. These requirements are identical to those for tangible fixed assets. The Act requires the information to be given in respect of each of the sub-headings that are preceded in the formats by Arabic numerals. FRS 10 requires detail of the movements to be disclosed for each class of intangible assets.

15.8 Where a company has applied one of the alternative accounting rules (see further chapter 16) to any intangible fixed asset, the notes must disclose the years in which the assets were separately valued (so far as the directors know these) and also the separate values. If any assets are valued during the financial year in question, the notes must also disclose the valuers' names or particulars of their qualifications and the basis of valuation used by them. [CA85 4 Sch 43]. (FRS 10, however, limits the circumstances where intangible assets may be revalued.)

Scope of FRS 10

15.9 In addition to goodwill, FRS 10 applies to all intangible assets except for oil and gas exploration and development costs, research and development costs (covered by SSAP 13) and any other intangible assets that are specifically addressed by another accounting standard.

15.10 The definition of intangible assets (see below) also scopes out items that are financial assets and items included as current assets (including prepaid expenditure).

15.11 FRS 10 deals with the following issues in respect of intangible assets:

- Recognition rules.
  - Intangible assets developed internally.
  - Intangible assets purchased separately.
  - Intangible assets acquired as part of the acquisition of a business.
- Valuation rules.
- Amortisation and impairment rules.
- Financial statement disclosures.

Definition of intangible assets

15.12 FRS 10 defines intangible assets as: *"non-financial fixed assets that do not have physical substance but are identifiable and are controlled by the entity through custody or legal rights"*. [FRS 10 para 2].

15.13 Application of the definition is important, first, to distinguish intangible from tangible assets and, secondly, to distinguish intangible assets from goodwill. These distinctions are important, because different accounting rules apply to each category. In particular, the rules for capitalising and revaluing intangible assets are much more conservative than those for tangible assets.

15.14 In some respects, it is arguable that the distinction between tangible and intangible assets, based on physical or non-physical substance, no longer has much relevance in the modern business world. For example, assets associated with electronic systems do not fit neatly into either category. FRS 10 recognises that software development costs present a problem within this framework and provides a convenient response. It explains that such costs should be treated as part of the cost of the related hardware (and, hence, as a tangible, rather than intangible, asset) where they are "*directly attributable to bringing a computer system or other computer-operated machinery into working condition for its intended use within the business*". [FRS 10 para 2]. Costs that might fall to be treated as tangible assets in this way include the costs of developing electronic dealing systems and web sites.

15.15 There are other examples in practice where the benefit of intangible rights, such as the right to operate a licensed trading activity from specific premises (such as casinos), is treated as an integral part of the physical property rather than as a separate intangible asset (see, for example, Stakis plc in Table 15.1).

Table 15.1 — Stakis plc — Annual Report and Accounts — 28 September 1997

Accounting policies (extract)

Fixed Assets and Valuations
A professional valuation of approximately one-third of the Group's freehold and leasehold properties, excluding health clubs, is carried out annually on a rolling basis and the valuations incorporated in the accounts. In the year of acquisition, properties acquired are included at cost or fair value. Valuation or cost includes the benefit of licences where applicable. All other fixed assets are stated at cost.

Depreciation (extract)
(iii) The element of the carrying value of casino properties attributable to the casino licence is written down only if the trend in maintainable casino profits indicates that such value has reduced.

Separability from goodwill

15.16 Separability is a key component of the definition of an identifiable asset. The Act includes the requirement for separability in the definition of identifiable assets and liabilities that relates to acquisition accounting. [CA85 4A Sch 9(2)]. FRS 10 basically repeats the legal position without adding much to clarify the longstanding issue of whether certain intangibles that have characteristics that make them similar to goodwill are separable or not. FRS 10 states:

> *"An identifiable asset is defined by companies legislation as one that can be disposed of separately without disposing of a business of the entity. If an asset can be disposed of only as part of the revenue-earning activity to which it contributes, it is regarded as indistinguishable from the goodwill relating to that activity and is accounted for as such."* [FRS 10 para 2].

15.17 Some intangibles are more clearly separable than others, but defining the cut remains subjective. The ASB considered that, because intangibles, such as brand names, are in any case very similar to goodwill whether they are separable or not, the most important consideration was that the accounting treatment should be the same. Separability is less of an issue under FRS 10 than it was before, because in general neither intangible assets nor goodwill may be capitalised if they have been developed internally, whereas both purchased intangible assets and purchased goodwill must be capitalised. But there are still differences between the rules for purchased intangible assets and purchased goodwill — for example, non-amortisation of goodwill requires a 'true and fair override' of the Act's specific requirement that goodwill should be amortised to zero over a period that does not exceed its useful economic life, whereas non-amortisation of separable intangible assets does not require a true and fair override.

15.18 Some would consider that many brands and publishing titles do not meet the separability criteria, because they cannot be disposed of without at least reducing the revenue-earning activity that they are part of. However, FRS 10 refers to brands and publishing titles as examples of intangible assets that are unique, and so there is an expectation that they are regarded as identifiable assets at least in some circumstances.

15.19 Many brand names are identified with single products that form only part of a company's business. For example, a particular detergent may have a well known brand name, but the name could be sold and the company would still carry on making the product, even though that product might generate lower profits, because it was no longer 'branded'. Diageo plc provides an example where brands have been recognised separately from goodwill in acquisition accounting. It refers to the fact that the recognised brands could be sold separately from the rest of the business acquired (see Table 15.2).

Table 15.2 — Diageo plc — Annual Report and Accounts — 30 June 2001
Accounting policies (extract)

Brands, goodwill and other intangible assets
When the cost of an acquisition exceeds the fair values attributable to the group's share of the net assets acquired, the difference is treated as purchased goodwill. Goodwill arising from 1 July 1998 is capitalised; prior to that date it was eliminated against reserves, and this goodwill has not been restated.

Acquired brands and other intangible assets which are controlled through custody or legal rights and could be sold separately from the rest of the business are capitalised, where fair value can be reliably measured.

Where capitalised goodwill and intangible assets are regarded as having limited useful economic lives, their cost is amortised on a straight-line basis over those lives – up to 20 years. Where goodwill and intangible assets are regarded as having indefinite useful economic lives, they are not amortised*. Impairment reviews are carried out to ensure that goodwill and intangible assets are not carried at above their recoverable amounts. Any amortisation or impairment write downs are charged to the profit and loss account.

* Note – non-amortisation of goodwill requires a 'true and fair override' of the Companies Act 1985 and disclosure should be made of the override.

15.20 Other brand names cover a range of products or services. Where a product brand name is the same as that of the company itself, it is much less likely that the name could be sold without disposing of a business. It is sometimes argued that names can be exploited by granting licences or franchises to third parties and, hence, that they are identifiable assets not goodwill. For example, a name associated with a particular type of footwear may be exploited by granting a licence for a third party manufacturer of sports clothes to use the name. Another example is where a fast food chain grants franchises to third parties to use the name for their restaurants. In these situations, however, it is difficult to see how the separability criteria are met, because licensing the use of the name does not necessarily imply that it can be disposed of separately from the business; indeed, licensing and franchising may not involve disposals at all.

15.21 The separability test is relevant in the context of distinguishing intangible assets from goodwill when accounting for a business combination. An issue considered by the UITF was whether the definition precluded recognition of certain intangible assets that had been purchased separately from a business (such as mobile telephone licences) but could not be disposed of separately because, for example, they are non-transferable. The UITF clarified in Information Sheet 34 that licences and similar assets that are purchased separately meet FRS 10's definition of intangible assets – it is presumed that if an intangible asset is purchased separately, then in theory it can also be disposed of separately. The implication is that any intangible asset that is purchased separately from a business (that is, without goodwill) is to be regarded as identifiable for the purpose of the definition.

15.22 Interestingly, separability is not a necessary condition for identifying an intangible asset under the equivalent international standard, IAS 38, 'Intangible assets' (revised 2004), if the intangible asset arises from contractual or other legal rights. Under the international standard, an intangible asset is identifiable when it is separable *or* when it arises from contractual of other legal rights, regardless of whether those rights are transferable or separable from the entity or from other rights and obligations. [IAS 38 para 12].

Control

15.23 Another key component of the definition of intangible assets is control. More generally, FRS 5 defines control in the context of an asset as: *"the ability to obtain the future economic benefits relating to an asset and to restrict the access of others to those benefits"*. [FRS 5 para 3]. In the context of intangible assets, FRS 10 says control must be exercised through custody or legal rights.

15.24 In respect of items such as trademarks, patents, copyrights, licences and franchises, control is secured by legal rights that restrict the access of others. The standard also recognises that control could be evidenced without legal rights, but this would be more difficult — for example, the benefits of know-how could be controlled by secrecy.

15.25 According to FRS 10, a company's workforce and clients cannot be recognised as intangible assets. Although they may be extremely valuable to a business, the business does not control them and, hence, their value is part of its goodwill.

[The next paragraph is 15.27.]

Readily ascertainable market value

15.27 FRS 10 identifies a special type of intangible assets — ones that have a readily ascertainable market value — where the accounting rules differ from the rules that apply to all other intangible assets.

15.28 FRS 10 defines readily ascertainable market value as a value that derives from:

- an asset belonging to a homogeneous population of assets that are equivalent in all material respects; and
- an active market in those assets, evidenced by frequent transactions.

[FRS 10 para 2].

15.29 Most intangible assets are unique to the business that controls them. In practice, hardly any intangible assets have a readily ascertainable market value. Possible examples given in the standard are certain operating licences, franchises and quotas. Many of these assets are in practice also unique. Intangible assets that may have a readily ascertainable market include milk quotas, taxi licences and airport landing rights.

15.30 The differences between the accounting rules are summarised in the table below. In effect, intangible assets with readily ascertainable market values are accounted for in the same way as tangible fixed assets, whereas more restrictions are placed on the recognition and valuation of unique intangible assets. The ASB's rationale for the distinction is twofold: first, it considers that many unique intangible assets are similar to goodwill and should be treated similarly; secondly, it considers that the valuation of unique intangible assets is too subjective to allow them to be recognised (other than where they have actually been purchased) or revalued.

	Intangibles with readily ascertainable market value	**Unique intangibles**
Initial recognition (cost or fair value)		
Internally generated	Yes	No
Purchased separately	Yes	Yes
Business acquisition	Yes	Yes; but only if it can be measured reliably and does not create or increase negative goodwill
Subsequent revaluation	Yes, to market value	No
Impairment loss allocation	Not written down below net realisable value	Written down fully before any tangible assets
Impairment loss reversal	Yes, if net realisable value increases above impaired carrying value	Yes, but only if an external event is reversed in a way that was not originally foreseen

Internally developed intangible assets

15.31 An internally developed intangible asset may be capitalised only if it has a readily ascertainable market value. [FRS 10 para 14]. In all other cases, the costs of developing intangible assets must (as for internally developed goodwill) be written off as incurred.

15.32 As noted above, in practice hardly any intangible assets have a readily ascertainable market value. Those that do are in any case unlikely to have been developed internally.

15.33 Capitalisation of internal costs of obtaining copyrights, patents, licences and similar rights is not, therefore, permitted even though they may satisfy the conditions of identifiability embodied in the definition of intangible assets. Here the ASB has taken a very restrictive approach and thus avoided addressing issues that would be associated with a more permissive approach, such as defining which costs should and should not be capitalised.

[The next paragraph is 15.37.]

Purchased intangible assets

15.37 An intangible asset purchased separately from a business should be capitalised at its cost. [FRS 10 para 9].

15.38 One issue that is not altogether clear in the standard is whether external costs of patent applications and external costs of securing other legal rights in respect of products that a company has developed itself should be capitalised or expensed as incurred.

15.39 One view is that these are internally developed, not purchased, intangibles. The costs are incurred to secure legal protection for and, hence, control of intangible assets that the company has developed itself. Under this view, neither internal costs (for example, the salaries of in-house legal people involved in registering legal rights), nor external costs attributable to generating the intangible asset, would be capitalised.

15.40 However, FRS 10 can be interpreted as making a different cut, that is, between internal and external costs. The emphasis is on preventing internally created value from being recognised. Thus internally generated value and internal costs cannot be capitalised. But external costs of securing legal rights may be objectively determined and fall within the category of purchased intangible assets.

Acquisition accounting

15.41 An intangible asset acquired as part of the acquisition of a business should be capitalised separately from goodwill if its value can be measured reliably on initial recognition. [FRS 10 para 10].

15.42 The normal principles for fair valuing the identifiable assets in acquisition accounting (in FRS 7) apply to intangible as well as tangible assets. FRS 7 merely states that where an intangible asset is recognised, its fair value should be based on its replacement cost, which is normally its estimated market value. [FRS 7 para 10]. FRS 10 introduces a third criterion — reliable measurement — over and above the separability and control issues considered earlier.

15.43 The standard makes another accounting distinction between those rare types of intangible assets that have a readily ascertainable market value and those that are unique. Whereas the former should be included at their market value at the date of acquisition, the fair value of the latter should be limited to an amount that does not create or increase any negative goodwill arising on the acquisition (see chapter 25 for further discussion of the interaction between fair valued assets and negative goodwill).

15.44 During the development of FRS 10, the ASB was sceptical about the reliability of valuations of unique intangible assets, such as brands and publishing titles, where there is no market value as such. FRS 10, however, accepts that certain entities that regularly buy and sell them have developed reliable valuation techniques that would allow them to be capitalised separately from purchased goodwill as a result of an acquisition. The price paid for the acquisition of a business as a whole in effect forms a ceiling on the value that may be ascribed to such intangible assets and goodwill in aggregate.

15.45 The wording in FRS 10 on the reliability of measurement issue implies a degree of flexibility as regards the separate recognition of intangibles in acquisition accounting. Those entities that are not in a position that they have developed valuation techniques from their regular involvement in the purchase and sale of unique intangibles may legitimately subsume the value of intangibles within goodwill. [FRS 10 para 13]. The onus is on those entities that wish to capitalise intangibles separately from goodwill to demonstrate that they can measure them reliably.

[The next paragraph is 15.48.]

Valuation methods

15.48 FRS 10 refers briefly to valuation techniques that may be used to estimate fair values of intangible assets at the date of acquisition. It mentions techniques based on 'indicators of value', such as multiples of turnover or present value of royalties that would be payable to license the asset from a third party. [FRS 10 para 12].

15.49 There are a number of methods commonly used by specialist valuers to value intangibles. These are not mutually exclusive — more than one method would normally be used in a valuation exercise and each would be used to cross-check the reasonableness of the valuation. Methods include:

- Relief from royalties.
- Premium profits.
- Capitalisation of earnings.

- Comparison with market transactions.

15.50 FRS 10 requires the method used to value intangible assets to be disclosed in the financial statements. [FRS 10 para 52]. The methods noted above are described briefly below.

Relief from royalties

15.51 Under the royalty method, an attempt is made to determine the value that could be obtained by licensing out the right to exploit the intangible asset to a third party or, alternatively, to determine the royalties that the owner of the intangible asset is relieved from paying by virtue of being the owner rather than the licensee.

15.52 A notional royalty rate is estimated as a percentage of revenue. This is applied to an estimate of the revenue to be generated by the intangible asset. This estimated royalty stream is capitalised, for example, by discounting at a risk-adjusted market rate, to arrive at an estimated market value.

15.53 The methodology is relatively simple, especially if the intangible asset is already subject to licensing agreements. Where this is not the case, the valuer may research licensing arrangements for comparable intangible assets or, where such information is not available, estimate a theoretical royalty rate that would give an acceptable return both to the owner and the licensee.

Premium profits

15.54 The premium profits approach attempts to determine a value that is based on capitalising the additional profits generated by the intangible asset (for example, a brand) over and above the profits achieved by similar businesses that do not benefit from the intangible asset (for example, similar unbranded products).

15.55 This approach is often used for brands. There are various methods of estimating the premium profits contributed by brands. These include calculating a margin differential, identifying the premium price compared with the price of generic equivalents and comparing the rate of return on capital employed of the business that owns the intangible asset with the normal rate of return of a comparable business that does not benefit from the asset.

15.56 The estimated premium profits attributable to the intangible asset are capitalised, for example, by discounting at a risk-adjusted market rate, to arrive at an estimated market value.

15.57 It is important that the premium profits identified are specifically attributable to the brand or other intangible asset and not some other factor, such as an efficient production facility or distribution network, that relates to the business as a whole.

15.58 In determining the value of a brand under this or similar methods, various specific factors may need to be taken into account, which include the following:

- The market sector.

  Brands that are established in a business sector that generates high sales, margins, or both, will clearly have a higher value than those in markets that are restricted in terms of total sales volume or profit margins. Expanding markets for a product will enhance the prospects for exploiting the brand name and will, therefore, increase its value.

- Durability.

  If a brand name has lasted for many years, it is likely to have considerable customer loyalty and will, therefore, support a higher valuation than a name that may be fashionable, but that is in a business sector where fashions change rapidly and brand names are less durable.

- Overseas markets.

  A brand name that is also known in overseas markets and which, therefore, has a larger potential customer base will usually be worth more than a brand that can be sold only in the domestic market.

- Market position.

  A brand that is a market leader will be worth more than one that is not recognised as a leader.

- Advertising support.

  This could be either a negative or a positive factor in valuing a brand. If a brand requires substantial advertising to maintain its place in the market, this could be a sign that the value of the brand is declining. If, however, advertising spend increases sales and/or margins significantly, so that the brand is better known, the value of the brand itself could be enhanced.

- Changes or prospective changes in legislation, or technological advances.

  Many brands are vulnerable to changes in legislation or environmental factors. However, if a brand name has survived such changes, the fact that it is able to adapt to new conditions may enhance its value.

- Competition.

  The introduction of alternatives to the branded product or indications that competitors are likely to increase spending on rival products could also affect the value of brands.

Capitalisation of earnings

15.59 The capitalised earnings method involves estimating the maintainable earnings that accrue to the intangible asset. A capitalisation factor, or earnings multiple, is then applied to the earnings. The multiple should take account of the expected risks and rewards, which include the prospects for future earnings growth and the risks involved.

15.60 This method is often used to value publishing titles and mastheads.

Comparison with market transactions

15.61 This approach considers actual market transactions in similar intangible assets. A multiple of turnover or earnings associated with an intangible asset would be derived from a market transaction and be applied to the asset being valued.

15.62 However, many intangible assets are unique and comparable market transactions may be infrequent. As a result, the scope for making direct comparisons with values actually achieved in the marketplace is limited. Nevertheless, acquisitions and disposals of businesses that include similar intangible assets can sometimes provide useful indicators of value that complement the other valuation methods.

Revaluation of intangible assets

15.63 With the following exception, no intangible assets may be revalued after their initial recognition at cost or fair value on acquisition. The exceptions are those rare intangible assets that have a readily ascertainable market value (see para 15.29 above). Such assets may be revalued to their market value, provided that all such intangible assets of the same class are revalued and that further revaluations are performed on a regular basis to ensure that the carrying value does not differ from the market value at the balance sheet date. [FRS 10 para 43].

15.64 It follows that for most recognised intangible assets, no value created after their acquisition may be recognised on the balance sheet. For example, if an ailing brand is purchased cheaply and relaunched by the new management, the carrying value must continue to be based on the historical cost or fair value. Furthermore, the brand development costs must be written off as incurred. This is consistent with the treatment of purchased goodwill.

[The next paragraph is 15.66.]

Amortisation and impairment

15.66 FRS 10's objective, in relation to capitalised intangible assets, is to ensure that they are charged in the profit and loss account in the periods in which they are depleted. [FRS 10 para 1]. The same amortisation and impairment rules apply whether intangible assets have been purchased separately or have been recognised as a result of fair valuing an acquisition.

15.67 Intangible assets should be amortised quickly, slowly or not at all according to the circumstances:

- Where an intangible asset has a limited useful economic life, it should be amortised systematically over that life.
- There is a rebuttable presumption that the useful economic life does not exceed 20 years.
- A longer life than 20 years, or an indefinite life, may be chosen where the asset can be demonstrated to be more durable.

15.68 Amortisation over more than 20 years or non-amortisation must be supported by annual impairment reviews to ensure that the carrying value of the intangible asset does not exceed its recoverable amount. If the review identifies an impairment, the asset should be written down to its recoverable amount.

15.69 Intangible assets that are amortised over 20 years or less should be reviewed for impairment at the end of the first full financial year following their acquisition. In other years an impairment review is required only if adverse events indicate the amortised carrying value of the asset may not be recoverable and an impairment write-down should be made if the review confirms this.

[The next paragraph is 15.71.]

Useful economic life

15.71 The useful economic life of an intangible asset is defined in FRS 10 as: *"the period over which the entity expects to derive economic benefits from that asset"*. [FRS 10 para 2].

15.72 A useful economic life of more than 20 years, or an indefinite life, may be chosen only if:

- the durability of the intangible asset for the longer (or indefinite) period can be demonstrated; and
- the intangible asset is capable of continued measurement (so that annual impairment reviews will be feasible).

[FRS 10 para 19].

15.73 FRS 10 requires that the useful economic lives should be reviewed at the end of each reporting period and revised if necessary. Where it is considered that previous estimates of useful economic lives need to be revised, the net book values at the date of revision should be amortised prospectively over the revised remaining useful economic lives. [FRS 10 para 33]. UITF Abstract 27, 'Revision to estimates of the useful economic life of goodwill and intangible assets', a change in an asset's useful economic life should be dealt with prospectively by amortising the carrying value over the revised remaining economic life (that is, it should not be dealt with as a prior year adjustment). This applies even if the change results from a decision to no longer rebut the 20 year life presumption.

15.74 One reason for having a presumed arbitrary upper limit on the useful economic life is that it would otherwise frequently be difficult to estimate it. A period of 20 years is a benchmark that has some significance internationally. However, the uncertainty involved in estimating useful economic life does not allow 20 years to be automatically used by default, nor does it allow intangibles to be written off over an unrealistically short period. [FRS 10 paras 21, 22].

15.75 FRS 10 states that the 20 year upper limit *may* be rebutted if the conditions (that is, evidence of durability and continued measurability) are met. The assumptions used in forecasting become more vulnerable the longer the estimated life is. For example, in many industries the pace of developments means that consumer patterns cannot be predicted with much certainty over very long periods. The emphasis in the FRS is, therefore, on being prudent when choosing asset lives, without being unrealistically prudent.

15.76 The second condition for rebutting the 20 year upper limit, that the intangible asset must be capable of continued measurement, is also important. The annual impairment reviews, which must be carried out in accordance with FRS 11, 'Impairment of fixed assets and goodwill', have to be feasible. FRS 10 states that intangible assets will not be capable of continued measurement if the cost of such measurement is viewed as being unjustifiably high. This clearly invites directors to opt not to rebut the presumption of a 20 year life if they judge that the cost of carrying out annual impairment reviews outweighs the benefits. This may be so where, for example, an acquisition comprises a large number of publishing titles that individually are not material. [FRS 10 para 23].

15.77 FRS 10 gives examples of factors that contribute to the durability of intangible assets and goodwill. These factors refer to the nature of the business, the stability of the industry, the effects of future competition, the typical lifespan of the products involved and (in respect of business acquisitions) the extent to which the acquisition overcomes market entry barriers that will continue to exist.

15.78 These factors often combine to present an overall picture of durability. A long life (20 years plus) will generally require a business, industry and products with a long track record of stability and achievement and having high barriers to market entry. Added to this, of course, is the commitment of the new management to continue to invest for the long term to extend the period over which the intangible asset is expected to continue to provide economic benefits. Long or indefinite lives may be justified for certain long established brands and publishing titles that have demonstrated their ability to survive changes in the economic environment. Lives much shorter than 20 years may be appropriate for other brands and publishing titles that are relatively new and operate in more volatile sectors, where they are more likely to be affected by changes in fashions or technology.

15.79 In addition to the economic factors outlined above, for certain intangible assets useful economic lives are also restricted by the period for which legal rights are held. For some intangible assets, the legal rights either remain in force indefinitely or can be continually renewed (for example, trademarks that secure brand names). For others, the legal rights that protect a product's position in the market expire after a fixed period (that is, they are non-renewable), when competitors can introduce similar products (for example, drug patents). In other situations, a licence may give an entity the right to carry out a business activity for a fixed period and, although the entity can apply for renewal, there is no guarantee that it will be renewed (for example, broadcasting licences).

15.80 FRS 10 states that where legal rights are granted for a finite period, the useful economic life of the related intangible asset cannot extend beyond that period unless *"the legal rights are renewable and renewal is assured"*. [FRS 10 para 24]. In other cases, the useful economic life is restricted by the expiry date of the existing legal right. The FRS also limits the circumstances in which the renewal of a legal right may be regarded as assured to those where:

- The value of the intangible asset does not reduce as the expiry date approaches (or reduces only by the cost of renewal).
- There is evidence that the legal rights will be renewed.
- There is no evidence that any conditions that have to be complied with in respect of renewal have been or will be breached.

[FRS 10 para 26].

15.81 If the capitalised cost of an intangible asset includes costs that will recur each time the legal right is renewed, the amortisation period for that element of the cost should not extend past the renewal date. [FRS 10 para 24].

Residual values

15.82 Before FRS 10, two arguments were sometimes advanced to demonstrate that, in certain circumstances, no amortisation was required. Some companies stated that the lives of brands and publishing titles were indefinite and, therefore, no amortisation charge was necessary. Others considered that expenditure on advertising and other brand support costs meant that the brand's or publishing title's residual value was always equal to or greater than its cost and this was put forward as an alternative reason for not amortising.

15.83 Under FRS 10, a residual value at the end of the asset's useful economic life may be assumed only if it can be measured reliably. [FRS 10 para 28]. In practice, an intangible asset is only likely to have a significant residual value that can be measured reliably where a company has a legal or contractual right to receive an amount of cash when its right to use the asset expires, or in those rare cases where there is a readily ascertainable market value for the residual asset. [FRS 10 para 29]. This was confirmed by the FRRP Ruling in respect of Equator Group Plc for the year ended 31 December 1999, which held that the group's firm libraries should be amortised without regard to any estimate of residual value. This means that in practice a low or nil amortisation charge must generally be justified in terms of a long or indefinite useful economic life rather than the maintenance of a high residual value, although in many respects they amount to the same thing.

Methods of amortising intangible assets

15.84 FRS 10 states that the method of amortising an intangible asset should reflect the expected pattern of its depletion. However, a straight-line method should be chosen, unless another method can be demonstrated to be more appropriate. [FRS 10 para 30]. An example of an alternative amortisation method is a unit of production method in respect of a licence to produce a fixed quantity of output. [FRS 10 para 31]. The FRS also requires disclosure of the methods used. [FRS 10 para 55]. Although arbitrary, specifying straight-line as a benchmark method is a practical means of dealing with the difficulty of measuring depletion and it does promote comparability. The FRS also explains that it is unlikely that methods that are less conservative than the straight-line method could be justified with sufficient evidence. Furthermore, FRS 10 specifically prohibits amortisation methods that aim to produce a constant rate of return on the carrying value on an intangible asset, such as the 'reverse sum of digits' method and the annuity method. [FRS 10 para 32].

15.85 A company may conceivably wish to change its method of amortising intangible assets, say, to revert to the straight-line method from some other method. Where this occurs, FRS 10 requires the reason and the effect, if material, to be disclosed in the year of change. [FRS 10 para 57]. The effect of a change is the difference between the amortisation charge that results from applying the previous and the revised amortisation methods (that is, how much more or less profit a company records as a result of changing amortisation methods).

Impairment reviews

15.86 The requirements for impairment reviews on intangible assets are integrated with those for capitalised goodwill, which are explained in more detail in chapter 18. The details of impairment reviews for tangible and intangible fixed assets and goodwill are contained in a separate standard FRS 11, 'Impairment of fixed assets and goodwill'. The requirements for impairment reviews differ according to whether an intangible asset is attributed a useful live of more or less than 20 years, as illustrated below.

Useful life 20 years or less	**Useful life more than 20 years**
End of first full year (simplified review)	Every year (detailed review)
Other years — high level check for impairment indicators detailed review only if impairment indicators are present	

15.87 Where intangible assets or goodwill are carried permanently as assets or amortised over very long periods, there is a greater risk of impairment in the future. Where they are written off over shorter periods, there is less risk of impairment, because their net book value in any case diminishes more quickly. A threshold of 20 years has been chosen, below which the impairment reviews are less onerous than for longer periods.

Useful life 20 years or less — first year review

15.88 Intangible assets should be reviewed for impairment at the end of the first full year after their acquisition. Most recognised intangible assets are acquired through business acquisitions and the timing of this review corresponds with the end of the investigation period in FRS 7, when the fair value exercise on the assets and liabilities of the acquired business should be completed.

15.89 The first year review has two stages. The first stage in effect requires management formally to consider whether the acquisition has lived up to expectations. This is done by comparing post-acquisition performance with the forecasts used in the acquisition appraisal and by considering whether there have been any other unexpected adverse events or changes in circumstances that throw doubt on the recoverability of the intangible asset or capitalised goodwill. If the acquisition passes this test, there is no need to go on to the second stage.

15.90 The second stage, which is a full impairment review, is only necessary if the first stage indicates that there may be an impairment problem. [FRS 10 para 40].

Useful life 20 years or less — reviews in other years

15.91 After the first full year, management has to consider whether events or changes in circumstances indicate that the amortised carrying value of intangible assets or goodwill may not be recoverable. If there are no such indicators, no further work is required. FRS 11 and the impairment indicators are discussed in chapter 18.

[The next paragraph is 15.94].

Detailed impairment review

15.94 A detailed impairment review is required in the following situations:

- Where intangible assets or goodwill are amortised over more than 20 years or carried permanently without amortisation: at each year end automatically (including the end of the year in which the acquisition took place).
- Where intangible assets or goodwill are amortised over 20 years or less:
  - At the end of the first full year following the acquisition, *only* if there is an indicator of impairment or if the first year review indicates that the

post-acquisition performance has failed to meet pre-acquisition expectations.

- In other years, *only* if there is an indicator of impairment.

15.95 The details of the impairment review are contained in FRS 11. An impairment review is a recoverable amount check on individual assets or groups of assets that may comprise tangible and intangible assets and capitalised goodwill. It follows the long-established principle that an asset's balance sheet carrying value should not exceed its recoverable amount, which is measured by reference to the future cash flows that can be generated from its continued use (value in use) or disposal (net realisable value), whichever is higher. To the extent that an asset's carrying value exceeds its recoverable amount, it is impaired and should be written down to the higher of its net realisable value or value in use. The requirements of FRS 11 are considered in chapter 18.

Disclosures

15.96 FRS 10 requires the following disclosures in respect of intangible assets:

- The method of valuation. [FRS 10 para 52].
- For each class of intangible asset:
  - The cost or revalued amount at the beginning and end of the period.
  - The cumulative provisions for amortisation or impairment at the beginning and end of the period.
  - A reconciliation of the movements, showing additions, disposals, revaluations, transfers, amortisation, impairment losses and reversals of past impairment losses.
  - The net carrying amount at the balance sheet date. [FRS 10 para 53].
- The methods and periods of amortisation and the reasons for choosing those periods. [FRS 10 para 55].
- The reason for, and effect of, changing useful economic lives. [FRS 10 para 56].
- The reason for, and the effect of, changing amortisation methods. [FRS 10 para 57].
- Where an intangible asset is amortised over more than 20 years or is not amortised, the reasons for rebutting the 20 year presumption. (This should be a reasoned explanation based on the specific factors contributing to its durability). [FRS 10 para 58].
- The following details where a class of assets has been revalued:
  - The year in which the assets were valued, the values and the bases of valuation.

- The original cost or fair value of the assets and the amount of any provision for amortisation that would have been recognised if the assets had been valued at their original cost or fair value. [FRS 10 para 61].

- The name and qualifications of the person who valued any intangible asset that has been revalued during the year. [FRS 10 para 62].

15.97 In respect of the last two bullet points above concerning revaluations, it should be noted that FRS 10 only permits revaluation (to their market value) of those intangible assets that have a readily ascertainable market value.

15.98 Two of the above disclosure points refer to a 'class of intangible assets'. The most commonly encountered will be the second bullet point, which requires the analysis and movements on intangible assets to be shown separately for each class. A class of intangible assets is defined in FRS 10 as: *"a category of intangible assets having a similar nature, function or use in the business of the entity"*. The explanatory paragraph to the definition indicates that items such as licences, quotas, patents, copyrights, franchises and trademarks may be treated as separate classes, as may intangible assets that are used within different business segments. Further sub-division may be appropriate where there are different types of licences, etc, which have different functions within the business. [FRS 10 para 2]. For entities that recognise several types of intangible assets, the analysis has, therefore, to be given under several headings.

[The next paragraph is 15.100.]

Intangible assets — other information

15.100 In practice, given the lack of authoritative guidance on intangibles before FRS 10, the range of intangibles in addition to brands and publishing titles capitalised in financial statements has been relatively extensive and includes:

- Copyrights.
- Know-how.
- Licences.
- Patents and trademarks.

Copyrights

15.101 Copyrights are designed to provide the holder with the exclusive right to produce copies of, and control over, an original musical, artistic or literary work. They are granted by law for a specified number of years, which in the UK was, until 1 January 1996, 50 years from the date of the author's or composer's death. A statutory instrument, the Duration of Copyright and Rights in Performances Regulations 1995 (SI 1995/3297), enacting an EC Directive to harmonise the term of protection of copyright and related rights, has altered the period of copyright.

For literary (including compilations and computer programs), dramatic, musical and artistic works, copyright expires 70 years from the end of the calendar year in which the author died. Where such a work is computer generated, the period of copyright is 50 years from the end of the calendar year in which the work was made. Copyright in films will generally expire 70 years from the last to die of the director, authors of the screenplay and dialogue and composer of any specially created music. Copyright in sound recordings expires 50 years from the end of the calendar year in which it is made or is released.

15.102 There are complex transitional provisions of which the following is a very brief summary. The new provisions apply to new works and existing copyright works. However, the period of copyright existing before 1 January 1996 will continue to apply to an existing work if this period would expire later than the new period. The provisions may also apply to existing works in which copyright expired before 31 December 1995 where the authors died between 1925 and 1945. Consequently, some copyright which had expired may be revived under these provisions. As such, where companies acquire a copyright for exclusive rights to publish an author's or composer's work, it is done in the expectation of receiving future income streams. The copyright is an intangible asset which will result in potential financial benefits to a company over a considerable number of years.

15.103 In practice, a number of different accounting policies have been adopted, varying from those companies that amortise the asset over a few years, to those that do not amortise unless a permanent fall in value occurs.

Know-how

15.104 Know-how is, in effect, a technical aptitude or skill. As such, it may be people-reliant or process-reliant; it may be purchased by acquisition of, say, a specialist service unit; or it may be internally generated. Its nature and characteristics suggest that it is more nebulous than say a copyright and, therefore, more difficult to measure or prone to greater subjectivity in terms of both identification and valuation.

15.105 As an example, a company that acquires a specialist testing unit is likely to acquire few tangible assets and, therefore, the difference between the price it pays and the fair value of the tangible assets acquired could be significant. Many commentators would argue that what the company is buying is: the tangible assets; the know-how in terms of methodologies and personnel; and future trading opportunities. While the third of these equates to goodwill, the second does not. In effect, a prime element of the difference between the purchase price and the fair value of tangible fixed assets would be the bespoke testing procedures acquired and the specialist personnel taken on, or, put another way, know-how.

15.106 Under FRS 10, any value attributed to purchased know-how could not be recognised separately as an intangible asset, unless it is controlled through custody or legal rights. This is unlikely to be the case where, for example, the know-how is essentially related to specific people who have freedom of movement in the labour market, but it could be the case if the know-how relates to a secret process.

Licences

15.107 Licences are agreements that a reporting company enters into with a third party which enable it to carry out certain trading functions. Examples may be brewing concerns, which operate out of licensed premises, or bookmakers, who are required to obtain a gaming licence. Similarly, companies may purchase licences allowing them to use software and technology developed by third parties.

15.108 As with copyrights, licences are generally acquired to obtain access to benefits that may continue for many years. Under FRS 10, the cost of licences should be capitalised if they have been purchased separately from a business. If they have been acquired through the acquisition of a business, they should be capitalised separately from goodwill if their fair value can be measured reliably. They should generally be amortised over the life of the licences.

15.109 Some companies have included the benefit of licences within tangible fixed assets where they operate from licensed premises, that is, as part of the valuation of the properties that carry on the licensed activity.

Patents and trademarks

15.110 A patent is in effect a document granted by the government assuring an inventor of the sole right to make, use and sell his invention for a determined period. Registering a trademark provides legal protection to the name or symbol used to differentiate the products supplied by a manufacturer or authorised distributor from those of competing manufacturers and dealers. Brands are likely to be secured by trademarks. Such protection is clearly of vital importance to entities that invest in product development (such as pharmaceutical companies), to ensure that their competitors do not merely copy their commercially successful inventions. The legal rights may be granted for long periods (17 or 18 years for drug patents) or may be renewable indefinitely (some trademarks).

15.111 Under FRS 10, the cost of patents and trademarks should be capitalised if they have been purchased separately from a business. If they have been acquired through the acquisition of a business, they should be capitalised separately from goodwill if their fair value can be measured reliably. They should generally be amortised over the period covered by the legal rights or the period for which the owner expects to derive economic benefits, if shorter.

Research and development

15.112 The Act permits development costs to be capitalised in certain circumstances. [CA85 4 Sch 20(1)]. In contrast, however, research costs, whether pure or applied, must be written off to the profit and loss account as they are incurred. [CA85 4 Sch 3(2)(c)].

SSAP 13

15.113 The Act does not define development. However, SSAP 13, 'Accounting for research and development', defines development as *"use of scientific or technical knowledge in order to produce new or substantially improved materials, devices, products or services, to install new processes or systems prior to the commencement of commercial production or commercial applications, or to improving substantially those already produced or installed"*. [SSAP 13 para 21]. Therefore, development is the work a company performs after it has planned or designed a new or substantially improved product or service until the time that this is ready either to be manufactured or to be put into operation commercially.

15.114 In making this definition of development, the standard distinguishes it from pure and applied research, which are defined as follows:

- Pure or basic research is *"experimental or theoretical work undertaken primarily to acquire new scientific or technical knowledge for its own sake rather than directed towards any specific aim or application"*.
- Applied research is *"original or critical investigation undertaken in order to gain new scientific or technical knowledge and directed towards a specific practical aim or objective"*.

[SSAP 13 para 21(a),(b)].

15.115 The standard also specifically indicates that where companies enter into firm contracts to carry out development work on behalf of third parties, on terms such that the related expenditure will be fully reimbursed, then expenditure that has not been reimbursed at any period end is contract work-in-progress and not development expenditure. A similar situation occurs where companies contract to develop and manufacture at an agreed price calculated to reimburse expenditure on development as well as on manufacture. [SSAP 13 para 17].

15.116 Racal Electronics Plc and Oxford Instruments plc disclose accounting policies that show examples of this, as Tables 15.3 and 15.4 indicate.

Table 15.3 — Racal Electronics Plc — Annual Report and Accounts — 31 March 1995
Statement of Accounting Policies (extract)

7 RESEARCH AND DEVELOPMENT

Private venture research and development expenditure is written off in the year in which it is incurred. Uninvoiced research and development fully funded by customers is carried forward as work in progress.

Table 15.4 — Oxford Instruments plc — Report and Accounts — 31 March 2004

Notes on the Financial Statements (extract)

1 Accounting policies (extract)

Research and development

Research and development expenditure, net of the relevant proportion of grants receivable, is charged to the profit and loss account in the year in which it is incurred, unless it is recoverable under a customer contract when it is carried forward as work in progress at the lower of cost and net realisable value.

15.117 SSAP 13 also provides examples of activities that would normally be *included* in research and development. The examples are:

- Experimental, theoretical or other work aimed at the discovery of new knowledge, or the advancement of existing knowledge.
- Searching for applications of that knowledge.
- Formulation and design of possible applications for such work.
- Testing in search for, or evaluation of, product, service or process alternatives.
- Design, construction and testing of pre-production prototypes and models and development batches.
- Design of products, services, processes or systems involving new technology or substantially improving those already produced or installed.
- Construction and operation of pilot plants.

[SSAP 13 para 6].

15.118 The standard also gives examples of activities typically *excluded* from research and development activities:

- Testing and analysis either of equipment or product for purposes of quality or quantity control.
- Periodic alterations to existing products, services or processes even though these may represent some improvement.
- Operational research not tied to a specific research and development activity.
- Cost of corrective action in connection with breakdowns during commercial production.
- Legal and administrative work in connection with patent applications, records and litigation and the sale or licensing of patents.

- Activity, including design and construction engineering, relating to the construction, relocation, rearrangement or start-up of facilities or equipment other than facilities or equipment whose sole use is for a particular research and development project.
- Market research.

[SSAP 13 para 7].

15.119 The original standard, prior to revision in 1989, specifically permitted market research to be capitalised, if it was incurred in order to determine whether a product under development was commercially viable in terms of market conditions, public opinion and consumer and environmental legislation. Its exclusion from expenditure that can be carried forward under the revised version, represents a tightening of the rules.

Development costs

15.120 The types of development costs that may be capitalised are not defined either in the Act or in the revised standard. However, IAS 38 does give some guidance on the type of costs that may be capitalised. It indicates that development costs may include:

- The costs of materials and services used or consumed in generating the intangible asset.
- The cost of employee benefits (as defined in IAS 19, 'Employee benefits') arising from the generation of the intangible asset.
- Fees to register a legal right.
- The amortisation of patents and licences.
- Interest, in accordance with the criteria of IAS 23, 'Borrowing costs'.

[IAS 38 para 66].

Capitalisation of development costs

15.121 The Act permits development costs to be capitalised, but only in 'special circumstances'. However, as it does not define the term 'special circumstances', it is necessary to look to SSAP 13 for guidance. We interpret this to imply that, if all the conditions set out in paragraph 25 of SSAP 13 are met, special circumstances exist and so development costs may be capitalised. However, if any one of the conditions is not met, then development costs must be written off as they are incurred.

15.122 Paragraph 25 of SSAP 13 lays down the following conditions, all of which must all be satisfied if development expenditure is to be capitalised:

- There is a clearly defined project.

- The related expenditure is separately identifiable.
- The outcome of the project has been assessed with reasonable certainty as to both its technical feasibility and its ultimate commercial viability, considered in the light of factors such as likely market conditions (including competing products), public opinion, and consumer and environmental legislation.
- The aggregate of the deferred development costs, any further development costs, and related production, selling and administration costs, is reasonably expected to be exceeded by related future sales or other revenues.
- Adequate resources exist, or are reasonably expected to be available, to enable the project to be completed, and to provide any consequential increases in working capital.

15.123 Where these conditions are satisfied, a company can defer development expenditure, but only until commercial production begins. SSAP 13 requires a company to amortise the expenditure it has capitalised from the time that commercial production of the product or service begins. Where a company is developing a product, commercial production begins when the company is manufacturing the product with a view to selling it commercially. [SSAP 13 para 28].

[The next paragraph is 15.125.]

Amortisation

15.125 Amortisation of development expenditure must be allocated to each accounting period on a systematic basis. This can be done by reference to the sales or the use of the product or the service, or by reference to the period over which the product or service is expected to be sold or used. However, the period of amortisation may be difficult to determine. In determining this period, the directors must establish a realistic and prudent number of years over which they expect the development expenditure to produce a benefit. They must decide also whether they expect the benefit to occur evenly over these years.

Disclosure

15.126 SSAP 13 requires the following disclosures to be made in the financial statements where development costs are deferred and are shown as an asset in the balance sheet:

- The accounting policy should be stated, as required by FRS 18, and explained.
- The total amount of research and development expenditure written off to the profit and loss account in the period should be disclosed, analysed between the current year's expenditure and amounts amortised from deferred expenditure.

- Movements on deferred development expenditure and the amount carried forward at the beginning and the end of the period should be disclosed. Deferred development expenditure should be disclosed under the heading of 'intangible assets' in the balance sheet. [SSAP 13 paras 30-32].

15.127 In addition, the Act requires that further disclosure should also be made of the period over which the amount of those costs that were originally capitalised is being, or is to be, written off, together with the reasons for capitalising the development costs in question. [CA85 4 Sch 20(2)].

15.128 Capitalising development cost is an option and, in practice, many companies write off all research and development expenditure as it is incurred, rather than attempt to justify capitalising development expenditure under the SSAP 13 rules. However, in Table 15.5, the 1994 financial statements of Dobson Park Industries plc provide an example of a company that does capitalise development expenditure. The charge to the profit and loss account is analysed between amortisation of the capitalised development costs and the immediate write-off of other non-capitalised research and development expenditure.

Table 15.5 — Dobson Park Industries plc — Annual Report & Accounts — 1 October 1994

Accounting Policies (extract)

Research and Development Expenditure
Expenditure on research and development is charged to the profit and loss account in the year in which it is incurred with the exception of expenditure on the development of certain major new product projects where the outcome of those projects is assessed as being reasonably certain as regards viability and technical feasibility. Such expenditure is capitalised and amortised over a period not longer than five years commencing in the year sales of the product are first made.

Notes on the accounts (extract)	**1994**	1993
	£000	£000
5. Profit on Ordinary Activities Before Taxation		
Stated after Charging:		
Depreciation of tangible fixed assets	**3,385**	4,431
Amortisation of intangible fixed assets	**370**	–
Research and development expenditure	**5,172**	5,594
Auditors' remuneration (including expenses)	**205**	252
Other fees paid to the auditors in the UK	**243**	295
Operating lease rentals — plant and machinery	**479**	630
Operating lease rentals — other assets	**1,857**	1,792

11. Intangible Fixed Assets	The Group
	£000
Development Expenditure:	
Cost	
At 2 October 1993	1,488
Incurred during the year	363
At 1 October 1994	1851
Amortised in year	370
Net Book Value	
At 1 October 1994	1481
At 2 October 1993	1488

Development expenditure is the amount incurred by IRD Mechanalysis in respect of "IQ 2000", a major new product launched in the latter part of 1993. These costs are being amortised over a period of five years from 3 October 1993.

Exemptions from disclosure

15.129 SSAP 13 has exempted some smaller companies from certain of its disclosure requirements. Thus, a company that satisfies two of the three criteria for defining a medium-sized company under section 247 of the Act, *multiplied by ten* need not disclose the total amounts of research and development charged in the profit and loss account, unless it is:

- A public limited company.
- A banking company or an insurance company.
- A parent company that has either a public limited company or a banking or an insurance company as a subsidiary.

Guidance on determining small and medium-sized companies and groups is given in chapter 32.

15.130 As a result, most private companies will not have to disclose the research and development expenditure charged in the profit and loss account. However, they will still have to disclose their accounting policy for research and development and any amounts of deferred development expenditure carried forward in intangible assets.

Provisions for diminution in value

15.131 A company should review at the end of each accounting period the development expenditure it has capitalised. Where the circumstances that justified the original deferral of the expenditure no longer apply, or are considered doubtful, the company should write off immediately the expenditure to the extent that the company considers it to be irrecoverable. [SSAP 13 para 29]. Consequently, a company will have to consider the conditions outlined in paragraph 25 of the standard at each year end in order to establish whether it should write off all or some of the previously capitalised development expenditure.

15.132 Where the directors expect the diminution in value of the development expenditure to be permanent, the Act, SSAP 13 and FRS 11 require that provision should be made for the asset's diminution in value or impairment. However, the directors may consider that a diminution in value of development expenditure is only temporary. For example, when the financial statements are prepared, the directors may no longer be able to show that the development project is technically feasible, but they may believe that the company will find a solution to the feasibility problem in the future. However, they would need to provide for the diminution in value of the development expenditure in accordance with SSAP 13 and FRS 11, even though such a provision may not generally be required to be made under the Act.

15.133 Once development costs have been written off, the question arises whether they can be reinstated if the uncertainties which led to their write off no longer apply. SSAP 13 does not deal with this issue. However, development costs that are capitalised as intangible fixed assets are within the scope of FRS 11's rules regarding the recognition and reversal of impairment losses. FRS 11 does not permit impairment losses to be reversed unless (a) an external event caused the original impairment loss; and (b) subsequent external events clearly and demonstrably reverse the effects of that event in a way that was not foreseen in the original impairment calculations. [FRS 11 para 60]. Situations where development costs could be reinstated within those criteria are likely to be rare. In the situation described above, for example, the problem that led to the write-off is an internal one. If the company subsequently finds a solution to the technical problem, the expenditure written off cannot be reinstated even though it may once more be considered to be recoverable.

Effect on realised reserves

15.134 Where development expenditure is deferred by capitalising it, and the unamortised development expenditure is not treated as a realised loss, the notes to the financial statements must also state:

- The fact that the amount of unamortised development expenditure is not to be treated as a realised loss for the purposes of calculating distributable profits.

- The circumstances that the directors relied upon to justify their decision not to treat the unamortised development expenditure as a realised loss.

[CA85 Sec 269(2); CA06 Sec 844 (2) and (3)].

Computer software

15.135 There is considerable diversity in practice in respect of accounting for the costs of computer software, both as regards software for internal use and software that is incorporated into products under development. In the past, many companies wrote off the cost of their computer software immediately to the profit and loss account. However, an increasing number of companies have capitalised their computer software costs as either tangible fixed assets or intangible fixed assets.

15.136 FRS 10 has an important bearing on the treatment of the costs of internal-use software. The FRS does not permit internally developed intangible assets to be capitalised (except for those that have a readily ascertainable market value, which in practice is few, if any). Therefore, the FRS would not permit any internal costs of developing computer software for internal use to be capitalised as an intangible fixed asset. FRS 10 recognises that the rules restricting the recognition of internally developed intangible assets potentially create a problem for computer software costs. It explains that such costs should be treated as part of the cost of the related hardware (and, hence, as a tangible, rather than intangible, asset (see chapter 16) where they are *"directly attributable to bringing a computer system or other computer-operated machinery into working condition for its intended use within the business"*. [FRS 10 para 2].

15.137 Computer software development costs may arise in several ways. Consider the following four situations:

- A company purchases computer software externally (including, for example, packages for applications such as payroll, or general ledger or other similar packages to be used on the company's own computer). The company should capitalise the cost of such software as a tangible fixed asset. This is because the software complies with the Act's definition of a fixed asset, as the company will generally purchase it to use on a continuing basis in the company's activities.

  The company should depreciate this software, in common with its other fixed assets, over its estimated useful life. Where a company purchases a software package specifically to run on a particular computer, the software's estimated useful life should generally not exceed the computer's remaining useful life.

  Where a company incurs subsequent expenditure to upgrade or enhance the software (so that its service potential is increased), it must decide if this additional expenditure gives rise to an asset. If so, then the costs should be capitalised, otherwise they should be expensed as incurred. If this expenditure is capitalised it should be written off over the remaining useful life of the software package. However, where the improvement costs lead to an extension of the software's useful life, the company will need to revise the depreciation charge, because the asset's life has been extended.

- A company employs programmers to develop software for the company's own use. In this situation, two problems exist, namely that:

  - The company will need to analyse the programmers' time and other expenses in order to identify the costs of developing the software.
  - If the software is not operational at the time the financial statements are prepared, the company will have to provide evidence to demonstrate that the software will be completed successfully and have a value to the business.

  Provided that it can overcome both of these problems, a company should capitalise this type of computer software cost as a tangible fixed asset if it meets the criteria in FRS 15 (see chapter 16). If the software is to be capitalised, but is not fully developed, it may be included under the balance sheet heading of 'Payments on account and assets in the course of construction'.

  SSAP 13 criteria are not relevant in assessing whether this expenditure should be capitalised, because the expenditure is not part of a commercial project. The company is merely producing its own fixed assets. However, it will be necessary to ensure that the definition of an asset is met, namely that the expenditure provides access to future economic benefits — which means that the development must be capable of being assessed as viable. Costs that might fall to be treated as tangible assets in this way include the costs of developing electronic dealing systems and web sites, where ongoing activities are associated with those assets. Web site costs are dealt with in UITF Abstract 29, 'Website development costs', (see chapter 16).

- A company buys computer software to incorporate into a product that it is developing. This could include software that an external software house writes and that the company will include in computer-controlled equipment it will produce and sell.

  This expenditure is a form of development expenditure and so the question of whether this can be capitalised is covered by the criteria included in SSAP 13. Provided that these criteria are satisfied, the company may capitalise the expenditure and amortise it over the product's estimated useful life.

- A company's own programmers write software that the company will include in its products. The question of capitalisation will again depend on whether the criteria set out in SSAP 13 are satisfied.

15.138 An example of a company that capitalises major software purchases is The Automobile Association (Table 15.6).

Table 15.6 — The Automobile Association — Annual Report and Accounts — 31 December 1996

Accounting policies (extract)

Software

Software costs are written off as incurred, except for purchases from third parties in respect of major systems. In such cases, the costs are written off over a maximum of five years from the date of implementation.

Chapter 16

Tangible fixed assets

	Page
Introduction	16001
Background — fixed assets generally	16001
Defining fixed assets	16002
Categories of fixed asset under the Act	16002
Specifically excluded items	16003
Tangible fixed assets	16004
Introduction	16004
Pre-FRS 15	16004
'Cherry-picking' revaluations	16004
Start-up costs	16005
Capitalisation of interest	16006
FRS 15 and FRS 12 — component depreciation	16006
Non-depreciation	16006
Objective of FRS 15	16007
Scope of FRS 15	16007
Initial recognition	16008
Definition of tangible fixed assets	16008
Classification of tangible fixed assets	16008
Payments on account and assets under construction	16009
Transfers to fixed assets	16011
Initial measurement	16012
Introduction	16012
Cost	16012
Directly attributable costs	16013
Labour costs	16015
Incremental costs	16016
Software development costs	16017
Decommissioning costs	16021
Decommissioning costs arising later in the asset's life	16022
Changes in estimate	16022
Period of capitalisation of directly attributable costs	16023
Start-up costs	16023
Donated assets	16025
Unknown purchase price or production cost	16026
Recoverable amount and impairments	16026
Capitalisation of finance costs	16027
Introduction	16027
Definition of finance costs	16027
Accounting treatment	16028
Period of capitalisation of finance costs	16029

Specific borrowings 16031
General borrowings 16032
Group situations 16033
Tax on capitalised finance costs 16034
Disclosures 16034
Subsequent expenditure 16036
Introduction 16036
Accounting treatment 16036
Previously assessed standard of performance 16037
Replacing components 16038
Major inspections and overhauls 16042
Revaluing tangible fixed assets 16044
Introduction 16044
Class of assets 16045
Frequency of revaluations 16046
Qualified valuers 16047
Properties 16047
Other tangible fixed assets 16048
Material changes in value 16049
Bases of valuation 16049
Tangible fixed assets used in the business 16051
Tangible fixed assets surplus to requirements 16051
Open market value 16053
Existing use value 16053
Depreciated replacement cost 16054
Value of plant and machinery to the business 16055
Disclosures 16057
Frozen valuations 16061
Revaluation gains and losses 16062
Introduction 16062
Gains on revaluation 16062
Revaluation losses 16063
Treatment of accumulated depreciation when assets are revalued . . 16066
Revaluation reserve 16067
Taxation consequences 16069
Depreciation 16070
Introduction 16070
Definition of depreciation 16070
Determination of useful economic life and residual value 16071
Methods of depreciation 16073
Straight line method 16073
Reducing balance method 16074
Sum of the digits (or 'rule of 78') 16074
Unit-of-production method 16074
Annuity method 16075
Depreciation of revalued assets 16076
Component depreciation 16078
Non-depreciation of certain assets 16078

Tangible fixed assets other than non-depreciable land 16079
Non-depreciable land 16081
Renewals accounting 16081
Change in estimate of useful economic life 16083
Change in estimate of residual value 16084
Change in method of providing depreciation 16084
Disclosures 16085
Disposals of tangible fixed assets 16086
Introduction 16086
Reporting gains and losses on disposal 16087
Revalued assets 16087
Intended disposal of fixed assets 16089
Capital grants 16089
SSAP 4 16089
Disclosure requirements 16091
Grants on non-depreciable fixed assets 16092

Chapter 16

Tangible fixed assets

Introduction

16.1 This chapter considers the accounting treatment and disclosure of the standard categories of tangible fixed assets (as governed by FRS 15, 'Tangible fixed assets') and of capital grants. With the exception of impairments, which are dealt with in detail in chapter 18, this chapter covers the following matters:

- Initial measurement, based on historical cost.
- The concept and methods of depreciation.
- The alternative accounting rules, including bases of valuation.

[The next paragraph is 16.3.]

Background — fixed assets generally

16.3 The key accounting issues relating to fixed assets are, first, what assets should be treated as fixed assets and, secondly, how should they be measured. The first question is largely answered by the legal definition, as set out in paragraph 16.9.

16.4 As regards the second issue—measurement—various options are available. Companies can present financial statements which are:

- prepared under the historical cost convention;
- prepared under the historical cost convention as modified by the revaluation of certain assets; or
- prepared under the current cost convention.

16.5 There has long been controversy about the basis on which financial statements are drawn up in the UK and much of this has surrounded the valuation issue. The question of whether a balance sheet should present costs or values is a very fundamental one and the present position is an unhappy compromise between these two approaches. However, the point at issue is not restricted to the balance sheet, but also fundamentally affects the measurement of income.

16.6 Chapter 6 of the ASB's Statement of principles, 'Measurement in financial statements', discusses in detail the 'larger' questions surrounding the basis on which financial statements may be prepared. The Statement discusses the various bases of valuation used and the capital maintenance concepts that may be applied in preparing financial statements. It envisages that the present system based on a mixture of historical costs and current values will continue to be used. The Statement of principles is discussed in chapter 2.

16.7 The UK accounting model is based on historical cost. The Companies Act 1985, based on the EC 4th Directive, sets out the 'historical cost accounting rules' as the principal framework, but also includes the 'alternative accounting rules', which are optional under the directive. The use of the alternative accounting rules has been patchy. Many companies stick to historical cost accounting, but many have also revalued at least some assets. The extent of this is very varied. Despite intense debate in the late 1970s and early 1980s about various forms of accounting for the effects of changing prices, very few companies now use a comprehensive system of inflation accounting. Much more common has been to revalue assets selectively. It has been quite common, for example, for companies to revalue properties held as fixed assets, but fairly uncommon to revalue plant and vehicles.

16.8 This mixture of approaches made the balance sheets of many UK companies hard to interpret and, in particular, hard to compare with each other. The ASB published FRS 15, 'Tangible fixed assets', in February 1999, which addressed some of the concerns relating to previous revaluation practice. One of these concerns was that there had been no requirement for valuations to be kept up to date. Another was that previously an entity could 'cherry-pick' those assets which it revalued, that is, it could have revalued only some out of a class of fixed assets. FRS 15 requires that, where a tangible fixed asset is revalued, the whole of that class of asset should be revalued as well.

Defining fixed assets

16.9 In terms of definition, the Act gives only limited assistance, because its guidance is of a general nature. The Schedule 4 formats indicate that all assets are either fixed or current. The Act says that assets are fixed assets where they "*...are intended for use on a continuing basis in the company's activities*". Consequently, current assets are "*...assets not intended for such use*". [CA85 Sec 262(1); CA06 Sec 835(6)].

Categories of fixed asset under the Act

16.10 Schedule 4 to the Act provides further guidance, in that it sets out standard presentation formats. These formats are to be adopted, in respect of fixed assets, so far as is relevant to their individual circumstances, by reporting entities governed by the Act. The balance sheet formats identify the following sub-classifications of fixed assets and their constituent parts:

- Intangible assets:
  - Development costs.

  - Concessions, patents, licences, trademarks and similar rights and assets.
  - Goodwill.
  - Payments on account.
- Tangible assets:
  - Land and buildings.
  - Plant and machinery.
  - Fixtures, fittings, tools and equipment.
  - Payments on account and assets in course of construction.
- Investments:
  - Shares in group undertakings.
  - Loans to group undertakings.
  - Participating interests.
  - Loans to undertakings in which the company has a participating interest.
  - Other investments other than loans.
  - Other loans.

16.11 The Act requires companies to use the headings and sub-headings prescribed in the formats other than in certain instances where the special nature of the company's business requires their adaptation. Some companies have changed the headings used on the face of the balance sheet. Examples of this are given in Tables 16.1 and 16.2.

Specifically excluded items

16.12 In addition to the guidance on asset recognition referred to in paragraphs 16.9 and 16.10 the Act specifically states that the following three items cannot be treated as assets — either fixed or current — in any company's balance sheet:

- Preliminary expenses.
- Expenses of, and commission on, any issue of shares or debentures.
- Costs of research.

[CA85 4 Sch 3(2)].

16.13 In view of the Act's prohibition, the above items should not be capitalised. Historically, they have been written off to the profit and loss account, except where a company had a share premium account, in which case, the first two items could be written off to that account. [CA85 Sec 130(2); CA06 Sec 610(2)(3)].

However, this treatment has been amended by FRS 4, 'Capital instruments', insofar as issue costs connected with such instruments are concerned. [FRS 4 para 76]. This is considered further in chapter 6.

Tangible fixed assets

Introduction

Pre-FRS 15

16.14 Before the publication of FRS 15, 'Tangible fixed assets', in February 1999, there had never been an accounting standard in the UK that specifically dealt with the measurement and valuation of tangible fixed assets. Depreciation was dealt with in SSAP 12, 'Accounting for depreciation', which was published by the Accounting Standards Committee (ASC), the ASB's predecessor body in December 1977.

16.15 In addition, there were, and still are, rules for accounting for tangible fixed assets and, more generally, fixed assets, within the Act. These rules, however, permit a fair degree of flexibility which has led to inconsistencies on application, as well as opportunities for abuse.

'Cherry-picking' revaluations

16.16 The alternative accounting rules in Schedule 4 to the Act, which stem from the EC's 4th Directive, permit a company to use either a current value or a historical cost accounting system for its statutory financial statements. These rules, however, can be applied selectively and as such the law has been used by some companies in the past to enable particular assets to be revalued and determine when those revaluations are reflected in the financial statements (commonly called 'cherry-picking').

16.17 In particular, in the late 1980s, when the property market was at its peak, many companies chose to revalue some of their properties, so boosting net asset values. However, because there was no requirement for valuations to be updated in subsequent accounting periods, when the property market fell so spectacularly at the beginning of the 1990s, the fall in value was often not reflected in the financial statements on the grounds it was believed to be only temporary.

16.18 The ASB first tackled these issues with a discussion paper, 'The role of valuation in financial reporting', issued in March 1993. This paper considered the wider question of whether the present hybrid modified historical cost system should be developed into one more clearly founded on principles embracing current values or alternatively whether the system should be pruned back to one rigorously based on principles of historical cost. The ASB concluded that although the present modified historical cost system involving both the retention of historical costs and irregular revaluation was clearly unsatisfactory, the approach should be evolutionary rather than revolutionary. Accordingly, it was proposed that the present modified historical cost system should continue, but an attempt should be made to remove some of the existing anomalies by requiring revaluations of certain assets on a more consistent basis.

16.19 The ASB subsequently published another discussion paper, 'Measurement of tangible fixed assets', in October 1996, which covered the initial measurement, valuation and depreciation of tangible fixed assets. Rather than impose mandatory valuation requirements, at least for large or listed companies with significant property portfolios, the discussion paper proposed to continue the present practice of optional revaluations, but with consistent rules that should be applied by those entities that decide to revalue their assets.

16.20 The discussion paper noted that replacing the cost of a tangible fixed asset with a valuation provided more relevant information to the user of the financial statements. However, the relevance of that information diminished over time as it no longer reflected the current value of the asset. Furthermore for current values to be meaningful and comparable from year to year, similar assets should be treated consistently. Therefore, it was proposed that if a policy of revaluation is adopted, it should be applied to all assets of the same class and those valuations should be kept up to date. These proposals were designed to reduce the scope for 'cherry-picking' and to increase the relevancy of valuations. They formed the basis for the eventual valuation requirements in FRS 15.

Start-up costs

16.21 In some industries, for example hotel and retail industries, it had become fairly common practice to capitalise start-up costs associated with new or expanding businesses, as part of the cost of the related tangible fixed asset, such as a new hotel or store.

16.22 The ASB's view was that whilst essential commissioning costs to prepare an asset for use were valid costs of a tangible fixed asset, other start-up costs were not costs of the physical asset, but rather operating costs associated with the setting up of a new business. Such start-up costs include marketing and advertising costs, staff recruitment and training costs and operating costs associated with initial slack periods because demand for the product or service has not yet built up. This issue was, therefore, tackled in FRS 15, which prohibits such costs from being capitalised as part of a tangible fixed asset. This was subsequently followed by UITF Abstract 24 in June 2000, which clarified the treatment of start-up costs that cannot be capitalised under FRS 15.

16.23 As well as addressing start-up costs, FRS 15 also tightened up the regime for the capitalisation of costs generally, providing a definition of directly attributable costs, and the period of production over which costs should be capitalised.

Capitalisation of interest

16.24 The capitalisation of interest has caused some debate in the past. As mentioned in the ASB's discussion paper, 'Measurement of tangible fixed assets', ideally the capitalisation of interest should be either mandatory or prohibited on the grounds of consistency. In the end, it was acknowledged that the arguments for each approach were finely balanced and, therefore, the compromise of allowing the optional adoption of a policy of interest capitalisation prevailed in the FRS. This, at least, is consistent with the current version of IAS 23, 'Borrowing costs', which permits the capitalisation of interest as an alternative to a treatment of non-capitalisation.

16.25 To avoid introducing different terminology, FRS 15 uses the term 'finance costs', as defined in FRS 4, 'Capital instruments' paragraph 8, rather than 'interest' or 'borrowing costs'.

FRS 15 and FRS 12 — component depreciation

16.26 FRS 12, 'Provisions, contingent assets and contingent liabilities', introduced strict rules about the costs it is appropriate to provide for. One of the consequences of FRS 12 is that entities are, in the main, no longer permitted to provide for the cost of major capital maintenance expenditure over the period that the related asset is in use. This is because the entity has no obligation to a third party in relation to the expenditure until it has been carried out. Despite this, the entity clearly benefits from that expenditure over a period of time that the related asset is in use and not just in the period that the maintenance takes place.

16.27 Therefore, in conjunction with the development of FRS 12, proposals were developed for inclusion in FRS 15 introducing the concept of 'component depreciation'. Rather than provide for the cost of major capital maintenance, part of the tangible fixed asset (a component) that will be replaced, restored or overhauled by the major capital maintenance expenditure is depreciated over the period until the expenditure is needed. In this way the depreciation of the asset more accurately reflects the consumption of the economic benefits of the asset as it is being used. When the capital maintenance expenditure takes place, it is capitalised as part of the cost of the asset, since it restores or replaces the previously depreciated component.

Non-depreciation

16.28 Although FRS 15 superseded SSAP 12, the key principles of SSAP 12 remained largely unchanged in the new standard. However, as highlighted by the ICAEW review of SSAP 12 in 1992 (FRAG 2/92, 'Review, for major practical problems, of SSAP 12'), an increasing number of entities were not depreciating their buildings, often for reasons that were inconsistent with SSAP 12. It was noted that this possibly stemmed from a misunderstanding of the nature and purpose of depreciation.

16.29 Consequently, FRED 17 proposed that subsequent expenditure on a tangible fixed asset did not negate the need for depreciation. In addition, it proposed that there should be an assumption that residual values were materially different from the carrying amount of the asset, hence forcing depreciation charges. This proposal was not generally supported by respondents to FRED 17 on the grounds that in certain circumstances it did not reflect the economic reality of the situation.

16.30 In FRS 15, therefore, the ASB acknowledged that there may be exceptional circumstances where depreciation is genuinely immaterial (because of either long useful economic lives or high residual values). However, to prevent the abuse of non-depreciation, FRS 15 contains a requirement for annual impairment reviews whenever depreciation is not charged (with the exception of land), or where the remaining useful economic life of an asset is expected to be greater than 50 years.

Objective of FRS 15

16.31 The objectives of FRS 15 reflect many of the concerns outlined above. They are to ensure that:

- Consistent principles are applied to the initial measurement of tangible fixed assets.
- If an entity adopts a policy of revaluation, the valuation is performed, and revaluation gains and losses are recognised, on a consistent basis, and valuations are kept up-to-date.
- Depreciation is calculated in a consistent manner and recognised as the economic benefits of the assets are consumed over their useful economic lives.
- Adequate disclosures are given concerning the impact of the entity's policies for the treatment of tangible fixed assets on the entity's financial position and performance.

[FRS 15 para 1].

Scope of FRS 15

16.32 FRS 15 applies to all tangible fixed assets, with the notable exception of investment properties, whose accounting treatment continues to be governed by SSAP 19. [FRS 15 paras 3, 4]. However, properties in the course of construction and development, including development properties, are not covered by SSAP 19 and, therefore, fall within the scope of FRS 15.

16.33 Whilst the standard deals with the initial measurement, valuation and depreciation (superseding SSAP 12) of tangible fixed assets, it does not deal with their impairment, because this falls within the scope of FRS 11, 'Impairment of fixed assets and goodwill'.

16.34 Accordingly, this section does not cover the accounting treatment of either investment properties (see further chapter 17), nor the impairment of tangible fixed assets (see further chapter 18).

Initial recognition

Definition of tangible fixed assets

16.35 The Act distinguishes between current and fixed assets, as noted in paragraph 16.9, but does not define tangible fixed assets. FRS 15 defines tangible fixed assets as:

> *"Assets that have physical substance and are held for use in the production or supply of goods or services, for rental to others, or for administrative purposes on a continuing basis in the reporting entity's activities."* [FRS 15 para 2].

16.36 Note that, as well as having physical substance and being used on a continuing basis in the business, a tangible fixed asset must also be an *asset*. This means that it must also satisfy the general definition of an asset, which is given in FRS 5, 'Reporting the substance of transactions', as "*rights or other access to future economic benefits controlled by an entity as a result of past transactions or events*".

16.37 The definition of a tangible fixed asset is important in distinguishing tangible from intangible fixed assets, because the accounting treatments for tangible and intangible fixed assets differ quite significantly. Intangible fixed assets are discussed in chapter 15.

Classification of tangible fixed assets

16.38 The Act sub-analyses tangible fixed assets into the following four categories:

- Land and buildings.
- Plant and machinery.
- Fixtures, fittings, tools and equipment.
- Payments on account and assets in course of construction.

16.39 However, many companies face practical problems when categorising their tangible fixed assets into these four fairly restrictive headings. In particular, some companies find it difficult to decide whether certain assets should be described as 'plant and machinery' or 'fixtures, fittings, tools and equipment'. Some companies also have difficulty in deciding the category in which to include motor vehicles.

16.40 In practice, companies categorise their assets according to the nature of their particular business. As a general rule, companies treat major manufacturing assets (including motor vehicles involved in the manufacturing process — for example, fork-lift trucks and cranes) as plant and machinery. They include other assets not involved in the manufacturing process in 'fixtures, fittings, tools and equipment'.

16.41 Because the Act allows a company to show any item in greater detail than the formats require, a company may, for example, disclose the amount for motor vehicles as a subdivision of either plant and machinery or fixtures, fittings, tools and equipment. [CA85 4 Sch 3(1)]. However, where an asset does not fall under any of the headings given in the formats, paragraph 3(2) of Schedule 4 allows a company to include the amount of it under a separate heading. Consequently, motor vehicles could be included in the balance sheet as a separate item, a presentation format adopted by Caradon plc in Table 16.1.

Table 16.1 — Caradon plc — Annual Report & Accounts — 31 December 1998

Notes to the accounts (extract)
10 Tangible fixed assets (extract)

	Land and buildings						
	Freehold	Long leasehold £m	Short leasehold £m	Motor vehicles £m	Fixtures and fittings £m	Plant machinery and tools £m	Group total £m
Cost or valuation							
At 1 January 1998	179.6	20.3	7.1	46.0	105.9	663.7	1,022.6
Currency translation	2.4	(0.1)	(0.3)	(0.1)	1.1	0.3	3.3
Reclassification	0.8	(0.8)	–	0.1	1.2	(1.3)	–
Additions	5.1	0.2	0.9	4.8	9.6	50.1	70.7
Disposals	(7.0)	–	(0.6)	(7.3)	(6.8)	(38.7)	(60.4)
Divestments	(6.2)	–	–	(0.9)	(2.8)	(34.0)	(43.9)
At 31 December 1998	**174.7**	**19.6**	**7.1**	**42.6**	**108.2**	**640.1**	**992.3**

16.42 Furthermore, FRS 15 requires disclosures to be given for each class of assets, which may be narrower than the Act's categories of assets. As discussed from paragraph 16.158 below, a class of assets is defined as *"a category of tangible fixed assets having a similar nature, function or use in the business of the entity"*. [FRS 15 para 2].

Payments on account and assets under construction

16.43 The category of payments on account and assets in course of construction is in effect a suspense categorisation, pending the transfer of the assets to one of the other categories.

16.44 'Payments on account' represent payments a company has made in respect of tangible assets for which it has not yet taken delivery. As the assets are not yet being employed by the entity, it would seem inappropriate in most circumstances to depreciate them until they are received and utilised. However, in exceptional circumstances where their value is perceived to have been impaired, FRS 11 would require a provision to be made to reduce their carrying amount. This situation could occur, for example, where a company has contracted and paid for specialised machinery with a lead-time for delivery and where adverse changes in the company's circumstances or in technology during the lead-time mean that the intended use either disappears or is seriously reduced.

16.45 'Assets in course of construction' represent the cost of purchasing, constructing and installing tangible fixed assets ahead of their productive use. As a category of asset, it seems more prevalent in published financial reports than 'payments on account'. It is a category of a temporary nature, pending completion of the asset and its transfer to the appropriate and permanent category of tangible fixed assets. The timing of the transfer of an asset from this category to the appropriate heading will vary. Unless the exceptional circumstance described in paragraph 16.44 occurs, a company will not normally charge depreciation on, or impair, an asset that is in the course of construction until it is completed and it is transferred to an asset heading that is appropriate.

16.46 In Table 16.2, the BOC Group plc provides an illustration of a company with assets under construction and clearly sets out the nature of the assets reclassified during the reporting period. In addition, its accounting policies state that *"no depreciation is charged on ... construction in progress"*.

Table 16.2 — The BOC Group plc — Report and Accounts — 30 September 1998

Notes to the financial statements (extract)

7. Fixed assets — tangible assets

a) Group summary	Land and buildings[1] £ million	Plant machinery and vehicles £ million	Cylinders £ million	Construction in progress £ million	Total £ million
Gross book value					
At 1 October 1997	703.0	3,545.0	550.2	406.2	5,204.4
Exchange adjustment	(69.2)	(290.3)	(47.8)	(41.8)	(449.1)
Capital expenditure[2]	32.4	311.2	25.9	226.7	596.2
Revaluations	1.6	–	–	–	1.6
Disposals	(10.2)	(106.4)	(5.9)	–	(122.5)
Transfers	8.2	145.7	7.0	(160.9)	–
Acquisitions and disposals of businesses	(61.4)	(198.0)	5.8	(22.7)	(276.3)
At 30 September 1998	**604.4**	**3,407.2**	**535.2**	**407.5**	**4,954.3**

Depreciation					
At 1 October 1997	191.3	1,860.9	198.5	–	2,250.7
Exchange adjustment	(13.5)	(143.4)	(16.9)	–	(173.8)
Provided during the year	19.3	224.1	24.5	–	267.9
Impairment	5.4	44.7	–	–	50.1
Revaluations	(0.4)	–	–	–	(0.4)
Disposals	(2.4)	(76.2)	(4.1)	–	(82.7)
Transfers	(2.1)	2.1	–	–	–
Acquisitions and disposals of businesses	(21.2)	(138.1)	–	–	(159.3)
At 30 September 1998	**176.4**	**1,774.1**	**202.0**	**–**	**2,152.5**
Net book value at 30 September 1998[3]					
Owned assets	389.3	1628.8	328.8	407.5	2,754.4
Leased assets	38.7	4.3	4.4	–	47.4
	428.0	**1,633.1**	**333.2**	**407.5**	**2,801.8**

1. Net book value of land and buildings at cost was £356.8 million (1997: £242.9 million).
2. Capital expenditure of joint ventures and associates is given in note 1.
3. Net book value includes net interest capitalised of £59.0 million (1997: £52.1 million).

Transfers to fixed assets

16.47 Most of the time, an item initially recognised as a tangible fixed asset will not have been previously recognised elsewhere in the balance sheet. However, occasionally an event may occur such that an item previously recognised as a current asset is transferred to tangible fixed assets. For example, a car dealer may decide to redeploy some of its stock as company cars for its employees. Those cars would then be transferred from current assets (stock) to tangible fixed assets, as they are now being used in the business on a continuing basis.

16.48 This issue is addressed in UITF Abstract 5, 'Transfers from current assets to fixed assets'. The abstract states that the transfer from current to fixed assets should be recognised in the financial statements at the date of management's change of intent. [UITF 5 para 4].

16.49 Furthermore, the UITF took the view that any diminution in value (or impairment) of a current asset that had taken place before the effective date of transfer of that asset to fixed assets should be charged in the profit and loss account, reflecting the loss to the entity while the asset was held as a current asset. In other words the asset should be transferred at the lower of cost and net realisable value. [UITF 5 para 5].

[The next paragraph is 16.51.]

Initial measurement

Introduction

16.51 The basic principle in FRS 15 that tangible fixed assets should be initially measured at cost is consistent with the requirement in the Act that fixed assets should be shown at either purchase price or production cost.

16.52 Experience has shown that, in particular for self-constructed assets, different practices have arisen on application of this principle. For example, one company may only capitalise external costs incurred on the construction of a building, whereas another company may also capitalise the direct and indirect costs of its own employees working on the asset. Both are acceptable under the Act's requirements. FRS 15, however, tightens the general rules in the Act, by requiring that directly attributable costs (but only those costs) be capitalised and defines what is meant by directly attributable costs.

16.53 Furthermore, FRS 15 gives detailed requirements about the period over which costs related to the constructed asset should be capitalised. It aims to prevent the capitalisation of costs relating to periods where no construction activity is taking place, in particular in the period after the asset is physically complete but before it has been put to full use.

16.54 FRS 15, therefore, ensures greater consistency over which costs, should be capitalised on the initial recognition of an asset and for what period capitalisation is allowed.

Cost

16.55 FRS 15, requires that a tangible fixed asset should initially be measured at cost, which should include only those costs directly attributable to bringing the asset into working condition for its intended use. [FRS 15 paras 6, 7]. This is based on the historical accounting rules in the Act, which require fixed assets to be shown at either their purchase price or their production cost, less any provision for depreciation or diminution in value. [CA85 4 Sch 17].

16.56 The FRS states that cost is purchase price (less trade discounts and rebates) plus directly attributable costs. [FRS 15 para 8].

16.57 This is the case even if assets were acquired at a bargain and, therefore, the purchase cost does not reflect the full value of the asset. However, except in exceptional circumstances, donated assets received by charities should be recognised at their current value, see from paragraph 16.90.

16.58 The Act also defines purchase price, in relation to an asset of a company or any raw materials or consumables used in the production of such an asset, as including any consideration (whether in cash or otherwise) given by the company in respect of that asset or those materials or consumables, as the case may be. [CA85 Sec 262(1)]. It is ascertained by adding to the actual price the company paid for the asset any expenses that were incidental to its acquisition. [CA85 4 Sch 26(1)]. These incidental expenses include, for example, the expenses that the company had to incur in order to get the asset to its present location and into its present condition.

16.59 The amount to be shown as the production cost of an asset is ascertained by adding the following amounts:

- The purchase price of the raw materials and consumables the company used in producing the asset.
- The direct costs of production the company incurred (excluding distribution costs in the case of current assets).

[CA85 4 Sch 26(2)].

16.60 The Act also *permits* the following costs to be included, although FRS 15 further stipulates when and in what circumstances these permitted costs should be included in the cost of tangible fixed assets if at all, as discussed in greater detail below.

- A reasonable proportion of indirect overheads, to the extent that they relate to the period of production.
- Interest on any capital the company borrowed in order to finance the production of that asset, to the extent that it relates to the period of production. Where such interest has been included in the production cost, the fact that it has been included and its amount must be stated in the notes to the financial statements.

[CA85 4 Sch 26(3)].

Directly attributable costs

16.61 Directly attributable costs are:

- Labour costs of the entity's own employees (for example, construction workers, architects and surveyors employed by the entity) arising in the construction or acquisition of the tangible fixed asset.
- Incremental costs to the entity that would have been avoided only if the tangible asset had not been constructed or acquired.

[FRS 15 para 9].

16.62 The standard gives some examples of directly attributable costs which include:

- Acquisition costs (such as stamp duty, import duties and non-refundable purchase taxes).
- The cost of site preparation and clearance.

- Initial delivery and handling costs.
- Installation costs.
- Professional fees (such as legal, architects' and engineers' fees).
- The estimated cost of dismantling and removing the asset and restoring the site, to the extent that it is recognised as a provision under FRS 12 (see para 16.75 below).

[FRS 15 para 10].

16.63 The FRS also identifies expenditure that should not be included. For example:

- Administrative and other general overheads.
- Employee costs not related to the specific asset (such as site selection activities).
- Abnormal costs arising from inefficiencies (such as costs relating to design errors, industrial disputes, idle capacity, wasted materials, labour or other resources and production delays).
- Other costs such as operating losses that occur because a revenue activity has been suspended during the construction of a tangible fixed asset.

[FRS 15 paras 9, 11].

16.64 In addition, intra-group profits or losses should be excluded from cost in the consolidated financial statements of a group.

16.65 It is worth mentioning here that the standard does not allow entities to be selective about which directly attributable costs should be capitalised. All those costs (subject to materiality) that meet the FRS 15 definition of a directly attributable cost must be capitalised, whilst those costs that fall outside the definition cannot be capitalised. The capitalisation of all directly attributable costs could result in an initial cost of an asset that is greater than its recoverable amount. In that case the asset should be immediately written down to recoverable amount, in accordance with FRS 11.

Example 1

A company has a number of retail stores. It has been refurbishing two of the stores and they were shut for 3 months whilst the refurbishment took place. However, the company has still incurred staff salaries, paid staff a retention bonus and paid to bus them to other stores to work. Can any of these costs be capitalised as part of the refurbishment?

None of these costs can be capitalised as they relate to retaining staff during the refurbishment and, consequently, must be expensed. FRS 15 specifically states that a tangible fixed asset should be measured at cost, but only those costs that are directly attributable to bringing the asset into working condition for its intended use can be capitalised. Therefore, the standard does not permit such costs to be capitalised. [FRS 15 paras 6-7].

Example 2

A company is introducing a loyalty card scheme in a number of its stores. It has a policy of capitalising software costs of the scheme, but can it also capitalise other costs such as call centre costs, consultants' costs and printing costs?

Software development and fixed asset costs can be capitalised under FRS 15. However, UITF 24 on start-up costs needs to be considered to determine whether these other costs can be capitalised. As they are not costs that the business usually incurs, also FRS 15, FRS 10 or SSAP 13 need to be considered to determine if they can be capitalised. As they do not satisfy the criteria of any of these standards, the company cannot capitalise the other costs referred to above, hence they should be written off.

Labour costs

16.66 The standard clarifies that only those labour costs that relate to the time spent by employees on constructing or acquiring the specific asset should be capitalised. Therefore, time spent on other potential acquisitions or developments cannot be included. For example, an internal surveyor may carry out surveys on five different properties as part of the process to determine which one of those properties the company will buy. However, only the surveyor's time in respect of the survey on the successful property should be capitalised as part of the tangible fixed asset.

16.67 Furthermore, if a site engineer spends 30 per cent of his time on a particular development project, then only 30 per cent of his employee costs should be capitalised as part of the cost of the asset. Other overhead costs should not be capitalised unless they are incremental costs to the company that would have been avoided only if the tangible fixed asset had not been constructed. Therefore, it is not permitted to capitalise in tangible fixed assets 30 per cent of the indirect overheads that could be apportioned to the engineer (for example, an allocation of the office rent or secretarial costs). (This contrasts with the position under SSAP 9 when certain indirect overhead costs may be allocated to stock, as discussed in chapter 20.) However, the costs of a temporary office on the site of the development, that would not have been incurred but for the project, should be capitalised.

Example

A company is capitalising software development costs. The software is for own use and so is classified as a tangible fixed asset to which FRS 15 applies. Directly attributable staff costs will be capitalised in accordance with paragraph 9 of FRS 15. Do such costs include national insurance and pension costs of the staff who are developing the software?

FRS 15 paragraph 7 states that costs that are directly attributable to bringing the asset into working condition for its intended use should be included in its measurement. Paragraph 9 states that directly attributable costs include the labour costs of own employees (for example site workers, in-house architects and surveyors) arising directly from the construction or acquisition of the specific tangible fixed asset. Employers' national insurance and pension costs are both part of staff costs and so fall within the meaning of labour costs in this context. Therefore, they should be included in the amount capitalised under FRS 15.

Pension costs are governed by FRS 17, 'Retirement benefits'. This standard makes specific reference to this situation in paragraph 51 which says that the current service cost should be included within operating profit in the profit and loss account (except insofar as the related remuneration is capitalised in accordance with another standard). The pension costs capitalised will require disclosure under paragraph 82 of FRS 17. On 7 December 2006, the ASB published an amendment to FRS 17, 'Retirement benefits', which removes this disclosure requirement.

Note that only the current service cost which is normally included in operating profit may be considered as a staff cost eligible for capitalisation (as per FRS 17 paragraph 51). Other elements of the pension cost included after operating profit, for example the finance cost, are costs of financing the pension scheme and are not eligible for capitalisation.

Incremental costs

16.68 External professional fees incurred in finding a suitable asset, which is then acquired or constructed, may be capitalised, as they are incremental costs to the entity that would have been avoided only if the tangible fixed asset had not been constructed or acquired. This contrasts with the treatment of labour costs of own employees in searching for suitable sites or assets, which cannot be included within the costs to be capitalised. However, costs such as external professional fees should only be capitalised as part of the cost of an asset when they relate directly to the acquisition or construction of the asset. Therefore, costs on speculative projects and costs of aborted plans should not be capitalised.

16.69 The definition of directly attributable costs in FRS 15 (see para 16.61) should be used in conjunction with the black letter requirement in FRS 15 that only costs directly attributable to bringing the tangible fixed asset into working condition for its intended use should be included in the cost of the asset. [FRS 15 para 7]. Therefore, although constructing or acquiring a new asset may result in other incremental costs that would have been avoided only if the asset had not been constructed or acquired, these should not be included in the cost of the asset if they do not bring the asset into working condition for its intended use.

16.70 For example, a mobile phone operator may be setting up a new network in a new territory, involving the construction of the network system (new transmitter towers etc). There will be incremental costs that would have been avoided only if the physical network system had not been constructed, as without the physical infrastructure in place there can be no business, but not all of these fall to be capitalised, because some are not directly attributable to bringing the physical asset into working condition. Costs that do not relate to the construction of the physical asset, but rather relate to setting up the new business as a whole, even though they are incurred during the construction phase of the new network (for example, market research, accounts staff, advertising, head office costs during the construction phase) do not qualify to be capitalised as part of the cost of the tangible fixed asset.

16.71 Another type of cost not specifically mentioned in the FRS, but sometimes put forward as a candidate for capitalisation, is the cost of training operatives for new machinery or computer equipment. Such costs should not be capitalised as they are operating costs rather than directly attributable to the tangible fixed asset. As operatives may leave at short notice, their training costs would not meet the definition of an asset and, therefore, may not be capitalised, since the access to future economic benefits is not controlled by the entity.

Example

The company has an existing freehold factory property that it intends to knock down and redevelop. During the redevelopment period the company will move its production facilities to another (temporary) site. As a result the following incremental costs will be incurred, set up costs £50,000, rent £150,000 and removal costs £30,000. Can these costs be capitalised into the cost of the new building under FRS 15?

Although constructing or acquiring a new asset may result in incremental costs that would have been avoided only if the asset had not been constructed or acquired, they should not be included in the cost of the asset if they do not bring the asset into working condition for its intended use. This is because the black letter standard in paragraph 7 of FRS 15 specifically says that only costs directly attributable to bringing the asset into such working condition may be capitalised. Although paragraph 9 of FRS 15 then includes incremental costs as 'directly attributable', this is subject to the overriding condition for capitalisation set out in paragraph 7, which states that such costs must be attributable to bringing the asset into working condition. The costs to be incurred by the company do not meet that requirement of FRS 15 and cannot, therefore, be capitalised.

Software development costs

16.72 Computer software development costs may arise in several ways as discussed in more detail in chapter 15. However, only those directly attributable software development costs that are associated with computer hardware for the entity's own use that has been capitalised should be capitalised as a tangible fixed asset.

16.73 This is consistent with FRS 10, 'Goodwill and intangible assets', which does not allow any internal costs of developing computer software for internal use to be capitalised as an intangible fixed asset. Instead, FRS 10 prescribes that such costs should be capitalised as part of the cost of the related hardware (and, hence, as a tangible, rather than intangible, asset), where they are *"directly attributable to bringing a computer system or other computer-operated machinery into working condition for its intended use within the business"*. [FRS 10 para 2]. Table 16.3 gives an example.

Table 16.3— Laura Ashley Holdings plc — Annual Report — 31 January 2004

Accounting policies (extract)

Fixed assets

Depreciation of property, plant and equipment and vehicles is calculated at rates estimated to write off the cost of the relevant assets, less any estimated residual value, by equal amounts over their expected useful lives.

The principle lives used are:

Freehold buildings and long leasehold property:	50 years
Short leasehold property:	Period of lease
Leasehold improvements:	Period of lease
Plant and machinery:	10 years
Vehicles:	5 years
Fixtures, fittings and equipment:	
Computer systems:	5 years
Shop fixtures and fittings:	5 years
Other equipments, fixtures and fittings:	5 to 10 years

Key money on properties which is paid in certain European countries is written down by 25% over 10 years to its estimated recoverable amount. Software development costs are capitalised as computer system expenditure.

16.74 One issue that caused considerable debate in the past was whether costs of developing a web site may be capitalised. In response to this the UITF issued an Abstract, UITF Abstract 29, 'Website development costs', in February 2001, which was effective for accounting periods ended on or after 23 March 2001. The Abstract details the factors that should be taken into account.

16.74.1 The Abstract divides the costs into four types:

(a) *Planning costs* – including, for example, the costs of feasibility studies, determining the objectives and functionalities of the web site, exploring how to achieve the desired functionalities, identifying appropriate hardware and Web applications and selecting suppliers and consultants.

(b) *Application and infrastructure development costs* – including the costs of registering a domain name and of buying or developing hardware and operating software for the site (for example, updateable content management systems and e-commerce systems, including encryption software, and interfaces with other IT systems used by the entity).

(c) *Design costs* – expenditure on the design and appearance of individual web site pages.

(d) *Content costs* – expenditure incurred on preparing, accumulating and posting the web site content, including graphics.

16.74.2 The Abstract states that planning costs do not give rise to future economic benefits that are controlled by the entity. Such costs should not, therefore, be capitalised as an asset, but should be charged to the profit and loss account as incurred. However, the other types of cost referred to above in paragraphs (b), (c) and (d) could give rise to an asset, which should be capitalised if the relationship between the expenditure and the future economic benefits is sufficiently certain.

16.74.3 But, there is often substantial uncertainty regarding the viability, useful economic life and value of a web site. The UITF took the view that amounts spent on the design and content of a web site should be capitalised only to the extent that they created an enduring asset and there were reasonable grounds for supposing that future economic benefits in excess of the amounts capitalised would be generated by the web site. This would be the case only if the web site was capable of generating revenues directly, for example by enabling orders to be placed.

16.74.4 The UITF considered that web site development costs were of the type that FRS 10 envisaged should be treated as tangible fixed assets. The UITF consensus was accordingly that:

- Web site planning costs should be charged to the profit and loss account as incurred.
- Other web site development costs should be capitalised as tangible fixed assets, in accordance with the requirements of FRS 15, 'Tangible fixed assets', subject to the *proviso* on design and content costs set out in the next paragraph below.
- Expenditure to maintain or operate a web site once it has been developed should be charged to the profit and loss account as incurred, in accordance with the requirements of FRS 15.

[UITF 29 para 11].

16.74.5 The *proviso* on design and content development costs is that they should be capitalised only to the extent that they lead to the creation of an enduring asset delivering benefits at least as great as the amount capitalised. This will be the case only to the extent that:

- The expenditure is separately identifiable.
- The technical feasibility and commercial viability of the web site have been assessed with reasonable certainty in the light of factors such as likely market conditions (including competing products), public opinion, and possible legislation.
- The web site will generate sales or other revenues directly* and the expenditure makes an enduring contribution to the development of the revenue-generating capabilities of the web site.
- There is a reasonable expectation that the present value of the future cash flows (that is, future revenues less attributable costs) to be generated by the

web site will be no less than the amounts capitalised in respect of that revenue-generating activity.

- Adequate resources exist, or are reasonably expected to be available, to enable the web site project to be completed and to meet any consequential need for increased working capital.

[UITF 29 para 12].

* For not-for-profit entities, the Abstract should be interpreted as permitting capitalisation only to the extent that the primary purpose of the web site is to provide a means of delivery of the specific services offered by the entity in fulfilment of its principal objectives.

16.74.6 If there is not sufficient evidence on which to base reasonable estimates of the economic benefits that will be generated in the period until the design and content are next updated, the costs of developing the design and content should be charged to the profit and loss account as incurred. [UITF 29 para 13].

16.74.7 Revenues that may be treated as arising directly from the website could include those attributable to orders placed *via* the website, amounts paid by subscribers for access to information contained on the website or advertising revenues obtained by selling advertising space on the web site. If a web site is used only for advertising or promotion of the entity's own products or services, it is unlikely to be possible to provide sufficient evidence to demonstrate that future sales or revenue will be generated directly by the web site. [UITF 29 para 14].

16.74.8 Revenues expected to arise directly from the web site might include some that would have been achieved by other means in the absence of the web site. Where this happens, it will be necessary to consider whether other fixed assets have become impaired as a result of the development of the web site. [UITF 29 para 15].

16.74.9 Capitalised web site development costs should be reviewed for impairment in accordance with FRS 11 if events or changes in circumstances indicate that the carrying amount may not be recoverable. [UITF 29 para 16].

16.74.10 Capitalised web site development costs should be depreciated over their estimated useful economic life, which should be reviewed each period in accordance with the requirements of FRS 15. Because of the rapid rate of technological innovation, the useful economic life of a web site is likely to be short. Also, where the design or content of a web site has to be replaced more frequently than the web site as a whole, it may be appropriate to select a depreciation period for the cost of the design or content that is shorter than the depreciation period selected for the remainder of the asset. [UITF 29 para 17].

[The next paragraph is 16.75.]

Decommissioning costs

16.75 As mentioned in paragraph 16.62 above, an example given in the FRS of a directly attributable cost for capitalisation as part of a tangible fixed asset is the estimated cost of dismantling and removing the asset and restoring the site ('decommissioning costs'), to the extent recognised as a provision under FRS 12, 'Provisions, contingent liabilities and contingent assets'. [FRS 15 para 10]. This is consistent with the requirement in FRS 12 that when a provision or a change in a provision is recognised, an asset should also be recognised when (but only when) the obligation incurred gives access to future economic benefits. [FRS 12 para 66].

16.76 At first glance it seems odd to capitalise decommissioning costs that are not going to emerge until later in the asset's life. However, where a provision is recognised in accordance with FRS 12 as a direct consequence of acquiring or constructing a tangible fixed asset, the entity has an obligation at that point to incur further costs in the future that it cannot avoid in connection with the acquisition or construction of the asset. Therefore, it is argued that the decommissioning costs at the end of the asset's life are just as much a cost of acquiring or constructing the asset as the costs incurred at the start of the asset's life.

16.77 Decommissioning or similar costs such as dilapidation expenditure can often arise in connection with operating leases and leasehold improvements. For example, the terms of an operating lease may allow the tenant to tailor the property to meet their specific needs by building an additional internal wall, say, but on condition that the tenant returns the property at the end of the lease in its original state. This will entail dismantling the internal wall. On building the internal wall, the tenant creates an obligation to remove the wall, which it cannot avoid, and, therefore, must recognise a provision for that obligation in accordance with FRS 12. The cost to the tenant, therefore, of the leasehold improvement is not only the cost of building the wall, but also the cost of restoring the property at the end of the lease. As such, both costs are capitalised when the internal wall is built and will be recognised in the profit and loss account over the useful economic life of the asset (generally the lease term) as part of the depreciation charge.

16.78 Other examples of decommissioning costs that may be capitalised as part of the cost of the asset typically arise in oil and gas and electricity industries where environmental damage is caused by, say the construction and commissioning of the facility (for example, the oil platform or nuclear plant). Similar costs are incurred in other industries such as: abandonment costs in the mining and extractive industries; clean up and restoration costs of landfill sites; and environmental clean up costs in a number of industries. Decommissioning and abandonment are considered in more detail in chapter 21.

Decommissioning costs arising later in the asset's life

16.79 Sometimes the obligation in respect of such decommissioning costs does not arise until, or only becomes apparent, later in the asset's life, due, for example, to a change in legislation in respect of environmental damage. If these costs meet the recognition criteria under FRS 12 for a provision, then FRS 15 says that these costs should still be capitalised as part of the cost of the asset to the extent that they related to the installation, construction or acquisition of the asset. [FRS 15 para 10].

16.80 In contrast, provisions that arise during an asset's life as a result of damage incurred through the use of the asset are production costs and should not be capitalised as part of the cost of the asset. For example, provisions arising in respect of the wear and tear of a leasehold property, which must be rectified at the end of the lease under the lease terms, are costs of using the property and, therefore, the related debit is a revenue, rather than a capital item and accordingly should be recognised in the profit and loss account.

16.81 Where such a provision is a cost related to the construction, acquisition or addition of a tangible fixed asset, there are two ways of determining the amount of the provision to be capitalised as an asset. Suppose an asset has a life of 30 years and, due to a change in legislation, after ten years an obligation arises in respect of decommissioning costs relating to the installation of the asset for which a provision of £900,000 has been recognised. Either:

- the whole £900,000 is capitalised as part of the cost of the asset and depreciated over the remaining useful economic life of 20 years (subject to recoverability); or
- only £600,000 of the provision is capitalised and depreciated over the remaining useful economic life of 20 years. The remainder of the provision of £300,000, which is the amount that would have been recognised as depreciation in the first ten years of the asset's life had the obligation been in existence then, is recognised immediately in the current year's profit and loss account.

16.82 The standard does not tell us which of these two approaches to use. However, the first approach is more appropriate, because the change arises from new information and developments and does not relate to past periods. In addition, it is consistent with the requirements for revisions to useful economic lives and residual values (see from para 16.302).

Changes in estimate

16.83 Inevitably, there are likely to be significant changes in the initial (and subsequent) estimates of decommissioning costs of an asset, particularly where asset lives are long. These changes in estimate may be due to changes in legislation, technology, timing of the decommissioning, management's assumptions etc. The question is how should these changes in estimates be reflected when such obligations had previously been recognised as a provision and the cost capitalised as part of the cost of the asset. These issues together with the problems associated with discounting are considered further in chapter 21.

Period of capitalisation of directly attributable costs

16.84 Consistent with paragraph 26(2) of Schedule 4 to the Act, the FRS allows capitalisation of costs to take place only in respect of the period in which the activities necessary to bring the asset into use are in progress. Thus, capitalisation should cease when substantially all the activities necessary to get the tangible fixed asset ready for use are complete, even if the asset has not yet been brought into use. [FRS 15 para 12]. 'Ready for use' means when *"physical construction is complete"*. [FRS 15 para 13].

Start-up costs

16.85 FRS 15 states that costs associated with a start-up or commissioning period should be included in the cost of a tangible fixed asset only where the asset is available for use, but incapable of operating at normal levels without such a start-up or commissioning period. [FRS 15 para 14].

16.86 A distinction is drawn between a commissioning period for plant, where the plant cannot yet physically operate at normal levels, and a start-up period, where plant can operate at normal levels, but it is not doing so because demand has not yet built up. The costs of an essential commissioning period, as in the former case, are capitalised, whilst the machinery is run in and equipment is tested. In the latter case, where the asset is ready for use, but demand has not yet built up, costs should not be capitalised. [FRS 15 paras 15, 16].

16.87 An example of where costs should not be capitalised is given in the FRS. This is a new hotel or bookshop, which could operate at normal levels almost as soon as it has been constructed or opened, but where demand usually builds up slowly and full use or sales levels will be reached only after several months. In such a case initial operating losses in the start-up period are not costs that may be capitalised.

16.88 Similarly marketing and similar costs associated with generating demand for the services of the tangible fixed asset may not be capitalised as part of the tangible fixed asset.

16.89 FRS 15 does not, however, specify how costs that cannot be included in the cost of a tangible fixed asset should be accounted for. In response to this, the UITF issued Abstract 24 on accounting for start-up costs in June 2000.

16.89.1 Abstract 24 does not attempt to give a precise definition of costs, but instead takes a takes a broad view, indicating that it covers costs (that is, expenses and losses incurred both before and after opening) arising from those one-time activities related to:

- Opening a new facility.
- Introducing a new product or service.
- Conducting business in a new territory.
- Conducting business with a new class of customer.
- Initiating a new process in an existing facility.
- Starting a new operation.
- Relocating or reorganising all or part of an entity.
- Establishing and organising a new entity.

16.89.2 The Abstract concludes that start-up costs should be accounted for on a basis consistent with the accounting treatment of similar costs incurred as part of the entity's on-going activities. However, where there are no such similar costs, start-up costs that do not meet the criteria for recognition as assets under a relevant accounting standard should be recognised as an expense as they are incurred.

16.89.3 Therefore, costs associated with a start-up situation should not be deferred as a current asset, unless they meet the conditions for recognition as an asset and it is the company's policy to defer similar costs that are incurred on an ongoing basis. Further discussion on prepayments and cost deferral is contained in chapter 21.

Example

A new store is being developed on a rented site. Can the rentals incurred before the store is opened be capitalised and then be amortised over the period of the lease?

Under SSAP 21, 'Leases and hire purchase contracts', operating lease rentals payable are normally charged as period expenses over the lease term (that is, from lease inception) rather than over the period the leased asset is actually in use. The rule in UITF Abstract 24 is that costs incurred in a start-up period should be treated consistently with the treatment of similar costs incurred at any other time in the business cycle. UITF Abstract 24 states that start-up costs include expenses incurred both before and after opening a new facility. Therefore, under UITF Abstract 24, there is no basis for capitalising operating lease rentals, despite the fact that the store has not yet been opened.

16.89.4 All other costs associated with an activity should be expensed as incurred, except where they can be capitalised as part of another asset as permitted by FRS 15, 'Tangible fixed assets', FRS 10, 'Goodwill and intangible assets', SSAP 13, 'Accounting for research and development', SSAP 9, 'Stocks and long-term contracts', and SSAP 21, 'Accounting for leases and hire purchase contracts'.

16.89.5 Where such costs have been expensed, they may fall within the definition of an exceptional item under FRS 3, 'Reporting financial performance', by virtue of their size or incidence. If so, the disclosures required by FRS 3 should be given, as set out in chapter 8, including an adequate description in the notes to the accounts to enable the nature of the item to be understood. In addition, the Abstract encourages companies to discuss the impact of activities and costs incurred in the operating and financial review, as recommended in paragraphs 16-18 of the ASB's statement (paragraph 23 of the revised statement – see chapter 2 of the Manual of Accounting – Management Reports and Governance).

[The next paragraph is 16.90.]

Donated assets

16.90 The FRS deals briefly with the receipt of donated assets by charities. Donated assets effectively have a nil cost to the recipient. However, rather than record the asset at nil cost, the FRS states that the initial carrying amount of tangible fixed assets received as gifts and donations by charities should be the current value of the assets at the date on which they are received. [FRS 15 para 17]. Unless the asset is impaired, the current value of the asset is its replacement cost for existing use (see from para 16.177).

16.91 Whilst the FRS lays down this general rule it acknowledges that there may be measurement difficulties and even where the value of a donated asset can be measured the cost of measurement may outweigh the benefits. The standard, therefore, permits alternative approaches to the measurement of assets in such circumstances provided that disclosure of the reason for the different treatment, and of the age, nature and scale of the assets is given in the notes to the financial statements. The FRS notes that this also applies where the FRS is first applied to tangible fixed assets that were not previously capitalised and reliable estimates of cost or value are not available. It refers to the industry specific guidance that is in the Statement of recommended practice (SORP) for charities. [FRS 15 para 18]. A revised SORP, 'Accounting and reporting by charities: Statement of recommended practice', was issued in 2005 and applies for all accounting periods beginning on or after 1 April 2005, with earlier adoption encouraged. The SORP recommends that the amount at which gifts in kind (including donated tangible fixed assets) are included in the Statement of Financial Activities should be either a reasonable estimate of their gross value to the charity or the amount actually realised as in the case of second-hand goods donated for resale. [SORP para 130].

16.92 Although donated assets should be recorded at their current value the FRS makes clear that this does not constitute a 'revaluation' for the purposes of the standard. Therefore, there is no need for further revaluations of the asset, or for other assets of the same class to be revalued as well. The revised SORP also makes this clear. [SORP para 263].

16.93 The standard does not state where the gain on recognition of the donated asset should be recognised in the financial statements. For charities preparing a statement of financial activities, the credit would be recognised in that statement, in the same way that a cash donation would be recognised, that is as incoming resources. Where a charity is an incorporated entity, it may then need to produce a separate income and expenditure account which would exclude the unrealised gain on the donation, as such unrealised gains may not be included in the profit and loss account under the Companies Act 1985. [SORP paras 423-425].

Unknown purchase price or production cost

16.94 The Act deals with circumstances where purchase price and production cost are unknown. In certain circumstances, an asset's purchase price or production cost is to be taken as the value the company ascribed to the asset in the earliest available record of its value that the company made on or after it either acquired or produced the asset. These circumstances are where there is no record of either of the following:

- The actual purchase price or the actual production cost.
- Any price, any expenses or any costs that are relevant for determining the purchase price or the production cost.

16.95 This exemption applies also where the relevant record is available, but it could be obtained only with unreasonable expense or delay. [CA85 4 Sch 28].

16.96 Where a company has determined, for the first time, an asset's purchase price or production cost according to its earliest known value, the company must disclose this fact in the notes to its financial statements. [CA85 4 Sch 51(1)].

Recoverable amount and impairments

16.97 The general rule that an asset should be held at no more than its recoverable amount (see chapter 18) also applies on the initial recognition and measurement of a tangible fixed asset. [FRS 15 para 32].

16.98 In all cases, all directly attributable costs that fall to be capitalised as part of the cost of the asset (including finance costs, where the entity has a policy of capitalising finance costs) should be capitalised before considering whether the asset is impaired. Generally an asset is unlikely to be impaired on initial recognition, as this indicates that, from an economic perspective, the entity should not have acquired or constructed the asset in the first place. It is only necessary, therefore, to consider impairment if there is an indication of impairment, as set out in FRS 11, 'Impairment of fixed assets and goodwill'. [FRS 15 para 33].

16.99 Where an impairment has been identified on initial measurement, the carrying amount of the asset should be immediately written down to recoverable amount (that is, the higher of value in use and net realisable value). The impairment loss should be recognised in the profit and loss account.

Capitalisation of finance costs

Introduction

16.100 Views differ on whether finance costs should be included in the production cost of an asset or whether they should be expensed as incurred. Some regard such costs as forming part of the cost of the particular asset with which they can be either directly or indirectly identified. Others regard them as essentially period costs that should be charged to income regardless of how the borrowing is applied.

16.101 Both FRS 15 and the Act (as mentioned in para 16.60 above) permit either treatment. FRS 15 introduces further new requirements where a policy of capitalisation of finance costs is adopted. A description of the main features of these requirements is given below.

Definition of finance costs

16.102 Finance costs are defined in FRS 15 as:

> *"The difference between the net proceeds of an instrument and the total amount of payments (or other transfers of economic benefits) that the issuer may be required to make in respect of the instrument".* [FRS 15 para 2].

16.103 This definition is the same as that in FRS 4, 'Capital instruments'. As noted in FRS 15, finance costs include:

- Interest on bank overdrafts and short and long-term debt.
- Amortisation of discounts and premiums relating to debt.
- Amortisation of ancillary costs incurred in connection with the arrangement of debt.

[FRS 15 para 2].

16.104 The presentation requirements of FRS 25, which deal predominantly with the classification of financial liabilities and equity instruments, must be applied by all UK GAAP reporting entities (except those applying the current version of the FRSSE) in any accounting period commencing on or after 1 January 2005. Subsequent to the amendment of FRS 4 in January 2005, on the adoption of the presentation requirements of FRS 25, the treatment of interest, dividends, losses and gains in the profit and loss account follows the classification of the related instrument as debt or equity. To comply with paragraph 26 of Schedule 4 to the Act, only items that would otherwise be charged to the profit and loss account (and are not appropriations of profit) are eligible for capitalisation as part of the cost of a tangible fixed asset. Therefore, the actual or implied costs (including issue costs) of equity instruments are not eligible for capitalisation. Dividends on equity instruments are not finance costs since their payment is up to the discretion of the issuer.

16.105 The FRS is silent on whether or not foreign currency exchange differences on funds borrowed to finance construction of a fixed asset are included in finance costs. The international accounting standard IAS 23, 'Borrowing costs', states that such exchange differences are included in borrowing costs to the extent that they are regarded as an adjustment to interest costs. In addition, SSAP 20, 'Foreign currency translation', suggests that, to ensure the format of the profit and loss account complies with Schedule 4 to the Companies Act 1985, exchange gains or losses from financing should be disclosed as part of interest payable and similar charges. Because UK companies applying FRS 23, 'The effects of changes in foreign exchange rates', are also required to comply with Schedule 4, the same principle applies. Exchange differences that are in effect an adjustment to interest costs would, in general, be included in finance costs, as defined by FRS 4.

16.105.1 However, in the preface to FRED 29, 'Property, plant and equipment and borrowing costs', which the ASB issued in May 2002, the ASB stated, *"FRS 15's definition of finance costs does not include exchange differences. The ASB does not believe that capitalisation of exchange differences is appropriate and proposes to omit exchange differences from the UK standard's definition of borrowing costs"*. FRED 29 is an exposure draft that was designed to replace FRS 15 with the international accounting standards IAS 16 and IAS 23 with minor modifications, such as the one referred to above. However, its implementation has been delayed as there is a separate revaluations project that is likely to result in further changes to international standards and the ASB does not intend to replace FRS 15 until the basis of valuation to be used under IFRS is clear. Until then, however, we consider that, in the absence of specific prohibition in FRS 15, exchange differences, to the extent that they are regarded as an adjustment to interest costs, may be regarded as finance costs under FRS 15.

Accounting treatment

16.106 The arguments for and against capitalisation of finance costs are set out in the 'The development of the FRS' section of FRS 15. The conclusion reached is that the arguments for and against are evenly balanced and that entities should be permitted to choose whether or not to capitalise finance costs on fixed assets that take a substantial period of time to bring into service.

16.107 Once a policy has been selected it should be applied consistently to all relevant assets, whether financed by specific or general borrowings. [FRS 15 para 20]. Relevant assets are assets that are constructed by the entity itself, or by third parties for the entity, to whom the entity is paying progress or stage payments. It also includes additions to existing fixed assets (for example, store refurbishment costs incurred by retailers), where material. However, only finance costs relating to the expenditure on the additions should be capitalised. Finance costs should not be capitalised on the carrying amount of the underlying asset, even if it is suspended from use during the period of the addition.

16.108 FRS 15 states that only directly attributable finance costs should be capitalised. 'Directly attributable' means those finance costs that would have been avoided (for example, by avoiding additional borrowings or by using the funds paid out for the asset to repay existing borrowings) if there had been no expenditure on the asset. [FRS 15 paras 19, 21].

16.109 A limit is placed on the amount of finance costs that may be capitalised. The amount should not exceed the total amount of finance costs incurred by the entity in that period. [FRS 15 para 19]. Therefore, 'notional' finance costs (that is, 'lost' interest on cash deposits used to finance the asset) may not be capitalised. This treatment is consistent with FRS 4, which requires all finance costs to be charged in the profit and loss account, but states that where appropriate, such costs may be capitalised as part of the cost of an asset by way of simultaneous transfer from the profit and loss account. [FRS 4 para 76].

16.110 The standard does not state whether this limit is in respect of gross or net finance costs that would otherwise be recognised in the profit and loss account. However, it would be consistent with the treatment of finance costs on borrowings specific to the asset, if the limit was based on gross finance costs payable, without offsetting interest receivable.

Example

A company with a policy of capitalising finance costs, constructs an asset. The actual physical construction takes a month to complete and the weighted average carrying amount of the asset (before finance costs) is £1m. The company has general borrowings during the period of £750,000, on which the company pays an average interest rate of 10% per annum. The notional finance costs incurred on the asset is, therefore, £8,333 (10% on £1m for one month). However, the company has only actually incurred finance costs of £6,250 (10% on £750,000 for one month) during the period of construction and, therefore, the company can only capitalise finance costs of £6,250 as part of the cost of the asset.

Period of capitalisation of finance costs

16.111 FRS 15 gives quite specific rules regarding which period should be used to determine the finance costs to be capitalised. It states:

> *"Where finance costs are capitalised, capitalisation should begin when:*
>
> *(a) finance costs are being incurred; and*
>
> *(b) expenditures for the asset are being incurred; and*
>
> *(c) activities that are necessary to get the asset ready for use are in progress."*

[FRS 15 para 25].

16.112 Therefore, where borrowings have been incurred specifically to fund the construction of an asset, finance costs on those borrowings cannot be capitalised in the period before activities necessary to get the asset ready for use are in progress. These activities would often coincide with the commencement of the physical construction of the asset. However, activities that are necessary to get the asset ready for use also includes other activities before construction starts such as drawing up site plans and obtaining planning permission.

16.113 FRS 15 also states that *"capitalisation of finance costs should be suspended during extended periods in which active development is interrupted"*. [FRS 15 para 27]. This means, for example, that finance costs should not be capitalised while land acquired for building purposes is held without any development activity taking place.

16.114 FRS 15 also determines when capitalisation should stop:

> *"Capitalisation of finance costs should cease when substantially all the activities that are necessary to get the tangible fixed asset ready for use are complete. When construction of a tangible fixed asset is completed in parts and each part is capable of being used while construction continues on other parts, capitalisation of finance costs relating to a part should cease when substantially all the activities that are necessary to get that part ready for use are completed."* [FRS 15 para 29].

16.115 This is consistent with the requirements for the cessation of capitalisation of other directly attributable costs.

16.116 Where assets are capable of being completed in parts, then finance costs associated with each part should cease being capitalised when each part is capable of being used, even if it has not yet been put into use. However, this does not apply to a part of an asset that is not capable of being put into use without the completion of another part. For example, an out of town store may be constructed in three phases: the first phase is the construction of the core building and the main car park closest to the store; the second phase is the construction of the internal fixtures and fittings; and the final phase is the completion of the overflow car park. The first phase, the basic building and initial car park, is not capable of being used as a store until the internal store fixtures and fittings are complete and, therefore, capitalisation of finance costs in respect of phases one and two should cease when both phases are complete, but before phase three is complete. In addition, where the development activities necessary to get an asset ready for its use are interrupted, costs of holding partially completed assets do not qualify for capitalisation during the interruption. [FRS 15 paras 26, 28].

16.117 These requirements in FRS 15 are also consistent with the requirement in the Companies Act 1985 that *"...there may be included in the production cost of an asset ...interest on capital borrowed to finance the production of that asset, to the extent that it accrues in respect of the period of production"*. [4 Sch 26(3)].

Specific borrowings

16.118 FRS 15 gives guidance on how finance costs to be capitalised should be determined. If a particular borrowing can be specifically associated with expenditure on constructing or producing the asset, the amount of finance costs capitalised is limited to the actual finance costs incurred on that borrowing during the period in respect of expenditure to date on the asset. This means, for example, that if the borrowings are temporarily invested before being expended on the fixed asset, neither the finance cost during that investment period nor the investment income are taken into account in determining the amount of finance costs that may be capitalised.

Example

A company has borrowed £1m specifically to finance the cost of constructing a new head office and has a policy of capitalising finance costs. The loan is drawn on 1 February and during the year the company pays interest on that loan at a rate of 12% until 1 November when the interest rate is increased to 13% due to a rise in LIBOR. Construction on the building does not begin until 1 September and continues without interruption until after the year end on 31 December. During the period of construction the company incurs directly attributable costs of £100,000 in September and £250,000 in each month from October to December (for simplicity it is assumed that these costs are incurred on the first of each month). The borrowings that have not been used to pay for the building works are reinvested and earn interest at a rate of 5% per annum.

During the year ended 31 December, the company, therefore, incurs interest on the £1m loan totalling £111,667 and earns interest on the reinvested portion of the loan of £37,917.

However, only the interest paid on the borrowings actually used to finance the expenditures on the construction of the asset can be capitalised as part of the cost of the asset. Therefore, the total amount of finance costs capitalised is calculated as follows:

	£
Interest on expenditures of £100,000 at 12% for September	1,000
Interest on total expenditures of £350,000 (100,000 + 250,000) at 12% for October	3,500
Interest on £600,000 (350,000 + 250,000) at 13% for November	6,500
Interest on £850,000 (600,000 + 250,000) at 13% for December	9,208
Total interest to be capitalised	20,208

Therefore, £91,459 of the total interest payable on the loan of £111,667 is reported in the profit and loss account and £20,208 is capitalised and depreciated in future years as part of the cost of the asset. The total interest receivable of £37,917 on the funds that were temporarily reinvested is recognised in the profit and loss account.

IFRS difference

Under IAS 23, the amount of borrowing costs that may be capitalised on specific borrowings is slightly different. To the extent that borrowings are raised specifically for obtaining a qualifying asset, the amount of borrowing costs that may be capitalised is the actual costs during the period less any investment income on the temporary investment of the borrowings. [IAS 23 para 15]. Under IAS 23, therefore, £32,917 would be capitalised, being interest paid of £41,667 from 1 September to 31 December less interest received of £8,750 from 1 September to 31 December.

16.119 Where construction of the asset spans more than one financial period, in subsequent periods the finance costs capitalised in respect of the construction of the asset in earlier periods should be included in the total expenditure on the asset upon which the current period's finance costs available for capitalisation are to be calculated. (Whilst this principle may be applied on a monthly basis, in practice this is often not done (as in the above example) on grounds of expediency and materiality.) This is the case regardless of whether the related borrowings are specific or general.

16.120 FRS 15 states that finance costs in respect of leased tangible fixed assets should continue to be accounted for in accordance with SSAP 21, 'Accounting for leases and hire purchase contracts'. [FRS 15 para 22]. Finance costs in respect of leased tangible fixed assets under construction should be capitalised in accordance with the above rules, where a policy of capitalisation of finance costs is adopted.

General borrowings

16.121 Where funds are borrowed generally and used for financing the construction or production of the asset, the amount of finance costs eligible for capitalisation should be determined by applying a capitalisation rate to the expenditure on that asset. The capitalisation rate should be the weighted average of the rates applicable to the borrowings of the entity that are outstanding during the period, other than borrowings made specifically for the purpose of constructing or acquiring other tangible fixed assets (such as lease liabilities) or for other specific purposes (such as loans used to hedge foreign investments). The 'expenditure' on the asset is the weighted average carrying amount of the asset during the period including finance costs previously capitalised. [FRS 15 paras 22, 23].

Example

As in the previous example, a company constructs a new head office building commencing on 1 September, which continues without interruption until after the year end on 31 December. Directly attributable expenditure on this asset is £100,000 in September and £250,000 in each of the months of October to December. Therefore, the weighted average carrying amount of the asset during the period is £475,000 ((100,000 + 350,000 + 600,000 + 850,000)/4).

The company has not taken out any specific borrowings to finance the construction of the asset, but has incurred finance costs on its general borrowings during the period of construction. During the year the company had 10% debentures in issue with a face value of £2m and an overdraft of £500,000, which increased to £750,000 in December on which interest was paid at 15% until 1 October, when the rate was increased to 16%. The capitalisation rate of the general borrowings of the company during the period of construction is calculated as follows:

	£
Finance cost on £2m 10% debentures during September — December	66,667
Interest at 15% on overdraft of £500,000 in September	6,250
Interest at 16% on overdraft of £500,000 in October and November	13,333
Interest at 16% on overdraft of £750,000 in December	10,000
Total finance costs in September — December	96,250

Weighted average borrowings during period $= \dfrac{(2\text{ million} \times 4) + (500{,}000 \times 3) + (750{,}000 \times 1)}{4}$

= £2,562,500

Capitalisation rate = total finance costs in period/weighted average borrowings during period

= 96,250/2,562,500

= 3.756%

The capitalisation rate, therefore, reflects the weighted average cost of borrowings for the four month period that the asset was under construction. On an annualised basis 3.756% gives a capitalisation rate of 11.268% per annum, which is what would be expected based on the borrowings profile.

Therefore, the total amount of finance costs to be capitalised

= weighted average carrying amount of asset × capitalisation rate

= £475,000 × 3.756%

= £17,841

Group situations

16.122 In calculating which general borrowings to include in the weighted average, judgement is needed in a group situation. It may be appropriate in some cases to include all borrowings of a parent and its subsidiaries when calculating the weighted average of finance costs, particularly where the treasury function is managed centrally within the group. In other cases, for example where each subsidiary is responsible for managing its own treasury function, it may be appropriate for each subsidiary to calculate the weighted average applicable to its own borrowings. [FRS 15 para 24].

16.123 In consolidated financial statements the limitation applied is the consolidated amount of finance costs, because the Act requires consolidated financial statements to be prepared so far as possible as if they were the financial statements of a single company. The limitation on capitalisation of finance costs, described above, is sometimes objected to by companies that have little borrowing, but which are using cash resources to finance the construction of fixed assets. The argument put forward is that cash being used to finance the construction could otherwise have been used to earn interest and it is, therefore, fair to attribute a notional finance cost representing the deprival cost of the cash employed in financing the construction of the asset. FRS 15 does not accept this argument and acknowledges in the 'Development of the FRS' section that the inability to capitalise notional interest was one of the reasons for not requiring compulsory capitalisation of interest. A further reason for rejecting the argument is that the Act refers to 'interest' and not to 'notional interest' and, therefore, capitalisation of notional interest would be contrary to the law. [CA85 4 Sch 26(3)(b)].

16.124 Some groups of companies with little or no borrowing have subsidiaries that are engaged in constructing assets. In such circumstances, it is possible for the subsidiary to capitalise interest in its own financial statements on finance provided by another group company, even though at the consolidated financial statements level such intra-group interest must be eliminated, because the group as a whole has not incurred interest on those borrowings. But where another group member borrows externally and on lends to the construction subsidiary, any interest capitalised will remain on consolidation.

Tax on capitalised finance costs

16.125 FRS 15 requires that finance costs should be capitalised gross of tax. [FRS 15 para 21]. Whilst the argument for capitalising net of tax relief is based on the matching concept which suggests that the tax relief should be treated in the same way as the interest, the reason for gross capitalisation is that all other costs are capitalised gross, so there is no reason for interest capitalisation to be any different. As the costs are capitalised on a gross basis, a deferred tax liability should be set up where it fulfils the conditions in FRS 19, 'Deferred tax', in the particular circumstances of the entity and is released to the profit and loss account over the life of the asset, (that is, as the capitalised finance costs are recognised in the profit and loss account as part of the depreciation).

Disclosures

16.126 Where a policy of capitalisation of finance costs has been adopted, FRS 15 requires disclosure of the following in financial statements:

- The entity's policy concerning the capitalisation of finance costs on tangible fixed assets.
- The amount of finance costs capitalised during the period.
- The amount of finance costs recognised in the profit and loss account during the period.

- The aggregate amount of finance costs included in the costs of tangible fixed assets.
- The capitalisation rate used to determine the amount of finance costs capitalised in the period.

[FRS 15 para 31].

16.127 The disclosures required by FRS 15 duplicate the requirements in the Act, where finance costs are capitalised, to disclose in the notes the fact that interest is included in determining the production cost of particular assets and the amount of interest so included. [CA85 4 Sch 26(3)]. In addition, the Listing Rules require listed companies to disclose the amount of interest capitalised by the group in the year together with an indication of the amount and treatment of any related tax relief. [LR 9.8.4 R(1)].

16.128 FRS 4 states that where finance costs are capitalised by way of simultaneous transfer from the profit and loss account, this should be separately disclosed. [FRS 4 para 76]. As a result the finance cost shown on the face of the profit and loss account would be the net amount and in the notes this would be expanded to show the gross amount with the amount capitalised deducted.

16.129 An example of disclosures in respect of the capitalisation of finance costs is given in Table 16.4. Comparing with the FRS 15 disclosure requirements listed above, note that disclosure of the capitalisation rate is a new requirement of FRS 15 and is not given in the example.

Table 16.4 — Safeway plc — Annual Report and Accounts — 28 March 1998

5.0 Net interest payable	**1998 £m**	1997 £m
Interest payable:		
Loans repayable by instalments within five years	**(1.7)**	(2.9)
Bank overdrafts and loans repayable other than by instalments within five years	**(48.4)**	(26.8)
Loans not wholly repayable within five years	**(11.5)**	(13.0)
	(61.6)	(42.7)
Interest capitalised on freehold and long leasehold developments	**8.6**	8.1
	(53.0)	(34.6)
Interest receivable on money market investments and deposits	**2.0**	2.9
	(51.0)	(31.7)

The interest element of charges payable under finance leases amounted to £1.1 million (1997 — £2.2 million).

Interest payable includes £17.9 million due to the full year effect of the share capital buy-back in July 1996 (1997 — £10.8 million).

Interest costs relating to the financing of freehold and long leasehold developments are capitalised at the weighted average cost of the related borrowings up to the date of completion of the project.

11.0	**Tangible fixed assets (extract)**
11.1.5	Interest capitalised on freehold and long leasehold developments included in additions during the year amounted to £8.6 million (1997 — £8.1 million). The cumulative amount of interest capitalised in the total cost above amounts to £124.0 million (1997 — £116.9 million).
8.0	**Tax on profit on ordinary activities (extract)***

The principal reasons for the lower than standard tax charge are tax relief for capital allowances on fixed assets exceeding related depreciation by £4.1 million (1997 — £11.6 million) and tax relief for interest capitalised on freehold and long leasehold developments of £2.7 million (1997 — £2.7 million).

* Note that, for years ended on or after 23 December 2002, FRS 19 requires a reconciliation between the expected tax charge (being the group's profit before tax at the relevant standard rate of tax) and the current tax charge for the year.

Subsequent expenditure

Introduction

16.130 Once a tangible fixed asset has been recognised and capitalised in the books, a company may incur further expenditure on that asset at a later date.

16.131 Often it is easy to tell whether expenditure is capital or revenue in nature and, therefore, whether it should be capitalised or expensed. For example, the cost of adding a new wing to a hotel should be capitalised as the additional rooms increase the revenue earning capacity of the hotel. Similarly the cost of cleaning the hotel should be expensed as incurred, since it merely maintains the standard of the hotel.

16.132 However, sometimes it is difficult to distinguish whether expenditure on improvements and repairs should be capitalised or expensed, for example hotel room refurbishment. FRS 15 provides more guidance and rules in this area and introduces the concept of 'component depreciation' as explained below.

Accounting treatment

16.133 FRS 15 requires that, as a general rule, subsequent expenditure on a tangible fixed asset should be written off to the profit and loss account as incurred. Such expenditure is generally of a repairs and maintenance nature and does not improve the asset beyond the standard of performance previously expected of it. [FRS 15 para 34].

16.134 There are three exceptions to this general rule. In each of the following circumstances subsequent expenditure should be capitalised:

- Where the subsequent expenditure provides an enhancement of the economic benefits of the asset in excess of the previously assessed standard of performance.

- Where a component of a tangible asset that has been treated separately for depreciation purposes (see para 16.143 below), and depreciated over its individual useful economic life, is replaced or restored.

- Where the subsequent expenditure relates to a major inspection or overhaul of the tangible fixed asset that restores the economic benefits of the asset that have been used up by the entity and that have already been reflected in the depreciation charge.

[FRS 15 para 36].

Previously assessed standard of performance

16.135 The treatment of subsequent expenditure depends upon the previously assessed standard of performance expected from an asset and how that has been reflected in the depreciation of that asset.

16.136 Consider a new tangible fixed asset. Before the asset is depreciated, an assessment must be made of the standard of performance expected from it, in order to determine the appropriate useful economic life, residual value and depreciation method to use. In doing so, it will be expected that there will be certain costs associated with the asset in order to keep the asset in a good enough condition to achieve that expected level of performance, such as routine maintenance and repairs. Expenditure that merely maintains the expected performance levels expected from the asset is written off to the profit and loss account as it is incurred. For example, a head office may have a useful economic life of 25 years. However, in order to provide the level of performance expected from it, the company must repaint the property every five years. Such expenditure is expensed as incurred, since it maintains the expected condition of the property.

16.137 Other expenditure may enhance the economic benefits of an asset in excess of its expected standard of performance by:

- Increasing the capacity or capability of the asset.
- Extending the useful economic life of the asset.
- Improving the quality of the asset's output.
- Significantly reducing the operating costs of the asset.

16.138 Examples of subsequent expenditure that results in the enhancement of economic benefits given in FRS 15 are:

- Modification of an item of plant to extend its useful economic life or to increase its capacity.

- Upgrading machine parts to achieve a substantial improvement in the quality of output.

[FRS 15 para 37].

16.139 Subsequent expenditure that enhances the economic benefits of an asset beyond that previously expected of it should be capitalised as an addition to the cost of the asset. Sometimes expenditure will both maintain and enhance the asset. Only that element that enhances the asset should be capitalised.

16.140 Subsequent expenditure that enhances the economic benefits of an asset may also result in a revision to the useful economic life, residual value or depreciation method of the asset. For example, increasing the size of the memory of a PC may allow it to be used for a year longer than previously expected, in which case the cost of increasing the memory bank is capitalised and the useful economic life of the whole asset is extended by a year. Another example is the conversion of a store room at the back of a shop into more retail space. This increases the sales capacity of the shop and, therefore, the cost of the conversion is capitalised. It does not increase the useful economic life of the shop, but may increase its residual value. Other expenditure may enhance the economic benefits expected from the asset, but may not result in a revision to its useful economic life, residual value or depreciation method.

16.141 Other developments and new information, as well as subsequent expenditure, may give rise to a revision of the originally assessed standard of performance of an asset. This reassessment may result in a revision to the useful economic life, residual value or depreciation method of the asset, or an impairment of the asset's carrying amount. In such cases, the capitalisation of further expenditure should depend upon the revised assessment of the standard of performance of the asset.

16.142 For example, a company estimated that an automated plant would have a useful economic life of ten years when it was acquired. However, due to falling market demand for the product produced by the plant, its useful economic life and residual value were revised downwards, resulting in increased depreciation charges. A year later, the company paid for the plant to be reconfigured, so that it could be used to produce an alternative product with a longer useful economic life. As this expenditure enhanced the previously assessed useful economic life of the asset, it should be capitalised and the useful economic life of the asset revised. If, however, the plant was modified at the point at which it was realised that the existing product had a shorter life than previously expected and, therefore, the useful economic life and residual value of the plant was not revised, then the costs of modifying the machine would be expensed as incurred as they merely maintained the standard of performance expected from the asset.

Replacing components

16.143 An asset may consist of several different physical components. FRS 15 states that, if a tangible fixed asset comprises two or more major components, with substantially different useful economic lives, then each component should be treated separately for depreciation purposes (that is, as if each component was a separate asset in its own right) and depreciated over its individual useful economic life. [FRS 15 para 83]. It follows, therefore, that when a component is replaced or restored, the old component is written off, to avoid double counting, and the new component capitalised.

16.144 An example of a component of an asset that might have a different life from the rest of the asset, and thus might be depreciated separately, is the lift or escalator within a head office. Another example is given in Table 16.5 below.

Table 16.5 — James Fisher and Sons PUBLIC LIMITED COMPANY — Annual Report and Financial Statements — 31 December 1998

1. Accounting policies (extract)

A summary of the more important accounting policies which have been applied consistently, throughout the year and the preceding year, with the exception explained in note 28, is set out below.

Tangible fixed assets

Tangible fixed assets are stated at cost, net of depreciation and any provision for impairment.

The inherent refit element in cost of ships is shown separately and is amortised over 30 months. Subsequent refit costs are capitalised and amortised over the 30 month period.

Depreciation is provided to write-off the cost of tangible fixed assets in annual instalments over their estimated useful lives. The principal rates used are:

Ships:	
owned	4% to 10%
under period charter	Over life of charter
Freehold property	2.5%
Leasehold property	
long term	2.5%
short term	Over the period of lease
Plant and equipment	5% to 20%

No depreciation is charged on assets under construction.

The calculation of depreciation on owned ships takes into account their estimated residual value.

Refit costs

For vessels held by the group under operating leases, where there is a contractual obligation to maintain the ships, provision is made on a straight line basis as the vessels are used, towards the future cost of refits to the end of the lease. The provision is utilised as expenditure is incurred.

For vessels owned by the group, and for which the group is responsible for maintenance, the accounting policy is detailed within the tangible fixed assets accounting policy earlier.

16. Tangible fixed assets

	Analysis of ships		Total	Assets under	Freehold & leasehold	Plant &	
	ships	Refit	Ships	construction	property	equipment	Total
	£000	£000	£000	£000	£000	£000	£000
GROUP							
Cost:							
At 1 January 1998	79,956	–	79,956	26,991	3,364	4,533	114,844
Prior year adjustment (note 28)	(2,224)	2,911	687	–	–	–	687
At 1 January 1998 as restated	77,732	2,911	80,643	26,991	3,364	4,533	115,531
Additions	6,336	1,947	8,283	5,009	3	290	13,585
Acquisition of subsidiary undertaking	–	–	–	–	336	580	916
Transfer	31,421	460	31,881	(31,881)	–	–	–
Disposals	(27)	–	(27)	–	(1,289)	(1,159)	(2,475)
At 31 December 1998	**115,462**	**5,318**	**120,780**	**119**	**2,414**	**4,244**	**127,557**
Depreciation:							
At 1 January 1998	16,780	–	16,780	–	2,567	2,839	22,186
Prior year adjustment (note 28)	(234)	1,219	985	–	–	–	985
At 1 January 1998 as restated	16,546	1,219	17,765	–	2,567	2,839	23,171
Provided during the year	5,551	1,307	6,858	–	34	475	7,367
Disposals	(27)	–	(27)	–	(745)	(1,011)	(1,783)
At 31 December 1998	**22,070**	**2,526**	**24,596**	–	**1,856**	**2,303**	**28,755**
Net book value:							
At 31 December 1997 as restated	61,186	1,692	62,878	26,991	797	1,694	92,360
At 31 December 1998	**93,392**	**2,792**	**96,184**	**119**	**558**	**1,941**	**98,802**

Included in ships are assets with a cost of £567,000 (1997 £554,000) and accumulated depreciation of £189,000 (1997 £94,000) which are held for use in operating leases. Included in tangible fixed assets is aggregate interest capitalised of £2,612,000 (1997 £1,924,000).

16.145 This approach was primarily adopted in response to FRS 12, 'Provisions, contingent liabilities and contingent assets'. The argument in that FRS revolved around the question of whether future maintenance constitutes a liability of the entity. The FRS concluded that even where there will in due course be a legal or constructive obligation the appropriate accounting treatment is to recognise depreciation to take account of the actual consumption of the asset's economic benefits. Thus, for example, where a separate component of an asset wears out more quickly than the rest, it is depreciated over a shorter period and subsequent expenditure on restoring the component is then capitalised. This replaces the previous general practice of depreciating such components over the same period as the rest of the asset, but providing in advance for the maintenance/replacement of the component.

16.146 Where the depreciation of an asset does not allow for the wearing out of a component of the asset, subsequent expenditure that restores or replaces a component is recognised in the profit and loss account as incurred. This approach, however, results in a lumpy charge to the profit and loss account and does not match the expense of replacing a component with the benefit of the use of that component.

Example

A small manufacturing company has recently acquired a new factory, which cost £1 m for the freehold and has a residual value of £100,000. This factory has a flat roof which needs replacing every ten years at a cost of £100,000. Before FRS 12, the company would have depreciated the whole factory over its estimated useful economic life of 30 years on a straight line basis, charging the profit and loss account £30,000 depreciation per annum. In addition, for the first 20 years it would have provided for £10,000 every year, which would be utilised in years 10 and 20 for the cost of the replacement roof.

However, in accordance with FRS 12, the company may not provide for the cost of replacing the roof. The company, therefore, has two choices:

- To depreciate the whole factory over its useful economic life of 30 years, charging £30,000 per annum and to write off the £100,000 cost of replacing the roof to the profit and loss account as incurred, in years 10 and 20.
- To depreciate the cost of the roof of £100,000 over 10 years, giving a depreciation charge of £10,000 per annum and to depreciate the remainder of the factory of £900,000 down to its residual value of £100,000 over 30 years, giving a depreciation charge of £26,667. In year 10, when the roof is replaced, the original, fully written down roof is written off and the cost of the new roof is capitalised and depreciated over its useful economic life of 10 years.

The second approach more accurately reflects the company's consumption of economic benefits of the factory, resulting in an even charge to the profit and loss account of £36,667 per annum, over the 30 years of the useful economic life of the factory.

16.147 Whether to identify separate components of an asset in this way will be a matter of judgement and will depend on:

- The degree of irregularity in the replacement expenditure required.
- The materiality of the component.
- The materiality of the effect of separately depreciating the component.
- Whether the useful economic life of the component is substantially different from that of the rest of the asset.

16.148 In practice, a commonsense approach should be applied, so that separate components will only be identified where there is a material impact on the profit and loss account. For example, it is unlikely that an entity with a large number of properties would separately depreciate the roofs of each property, since the cost of replacing the roofs results in a similar size charge to the profit and loss account each year. However, an entity with just one major property may depreciate the roof of that property separately, as otherwise the cost of replacing the roof would distort the profit and loss account when it was incurred.

16.149 Where components of an asset have been separately identified, the components need not be disclosed separately in the fixed asset table in the notes to the financial statements as they do not constitute separate classes of assets.

Major inspections and overhauls

16.150 Sometimes a tangible fixed asset may require periodic major inspections or overhauls. The FRS applies a similar 'component' approach to major inspection and overhaul costs, even though the cost of a major inspection or overhaul is not a physical component of an asset.

16.151 An aircraft, for example, may be required by law to be overhauled every three years. In such a case the FRS permits a proportion of the cost of the asset equivalent to the expected overhaul cost to be depreciated over the period to the next overhaul. If this is done the actual cost of the overhaul or inspection is then capitalised (because it restores the economic benefits, usage of which has been reflected in depreciation). This overhaul cost is then depreciated over the period to the next overhaul. The cost and depreciation attributed to the overhaul originally is removed from the balance sheet once the cost of the new overhaul has been capitalised to avoid double counting. [FRS 15 para 39]. The remainder of the asset is depreciated over the full useful economic life of the asset, on the basis that the appropriate overhauls will be carried out as they are due. As shown in Table 16.6 PowerGen plc adopted this approach in their 1998 financial statements.

Table 16.6 — PowerGen plc — Report — Nine months ended 31 December 1998

Principal Accounting Policies (extract)

Overhaul of generation plant
Prior to the adoption of Financial Reporting Standard 12 'Provisions, Contingent Liabilities and Contingent Assets' from 30 March 1998, charges were made annually against profits to provide for the accrued proportion of the estimated costs of the cyclical programme for the major overhaul and maintenance of generation plant. Since that date overhaul costs have been capitalised as part of generating assets and depreciated on a straight-line basis over their estimated useful life, typically the period until the next major overhaul. That period is usually between four and six years. As a result of this change in accounting policy, prior year figures have been restated (see note 4).

Notes to the Accounts (extract)
for the financial period ended 3 January 1999

4 Prior year adjustment

Financial Reporting Standard 12 'Provisions, Contingent Liabilities and Contingent Assets' (FRS 12) was adopted from 30 March 1998. This has necessitated adjustment to provisions made in prior periods, principally relating to major overhaul and decommissioning of generation plant.

Prior to the adoption of FRS 12 charges were made annually against profits to provide for the accrued proportion of the estimated costs of the cyclical programme for the major overhaul and maintenance of generation plant. Since that date overhaul costs have been capitalised as part of generating assets and depreciated on a straight-line basis over the period until the next major overhaul. That period is usually between four and six years. As a result of this change in accounting policy, prior year figures have been restated.

In addition, a fixed asset has been recognised in respect of the estimated total discounted cost of decommissioning which is being depreciated over the remaining useful economic life of the associated power stations. The provision for decommissioning has also been increased to reflect the estimated total discounted cost. Prior year figures have been restated.

16.152 The decision to adopt this approach to overhaul expenditure may depend on:

- Whether the period until the next overhaul is substantially different from the useful economic life of the rest of the asset.
- The degree of irregularity in the level of expenditure on overhauls.
- The materiality of the expenditure in the context of the financial statements.

16.153 Where the 'separate components' method has not been adopted or part of the asset is not depreciated over a shorter timescale to allow for major overhaul expenditure as described above, the cost of replacements or overhauls should be charged to the profit and loss account as incurred. [FRS 15 para 41]. This is the approach adopted by BAA plc, as shown in Table 16.7.

Table 16.7 — BAA plc — Annual report — 31 March 1999

Accounting policies (extract)

3 Depreciation

Depreciation is provided on operational assets, other than land, to write off the cost of the assets by equal instalments over their expected useful lives as set out in the table below.

Fixed asset lives

Terminal building, pier and satellite structures	50 years
Terminal fixtures and fittings	5 — 20 years
Airport plant and equipment:	
Baggage systems	15 years
Screening equipment	7 years
Other plant and equipment including runway lighting and building plant	5 — 20 years
Tunnels, bridges and subways	100 years
Runways, taxiways and aprons	up to 100 years

Airport transit systems:	
Rolling stock	20 years
Track	50 years
Railways:	
Rolling stock	30 years
Tunnels	100 years
Track	10 — 50 years
Signals and electrification work	40 years
Motor vehicles	4 — 8 years
Office equipment	5 — 10 years
Computer equipment	4 — 5 years
Computer software	3 — 7 years
Short leasehold properties	Over period of lease

Major periodic maintenance expenditure on runways, taxiways and aprons is charged to the profit and loss account as incurred except where the expenditure represents an asset improvement when the cost is capitalised and written off over the asset's estimated useful economic life.

Revaluing tangible fixed assets

Introduction

16.154 Having acquired or constructed a tangible fixed asset and recorded it in the books at cost, an entity can choose whether to subsequently revalue that asset.

16.155 The alternative accounting rules in Schedule 4 to the Act permit replacing the historical cost of a tangible fixed asset with a market value (as at the date of its last valuation) or its current cost. [CA85 4 Sch 31(2)]. Legally, companies may adopt all or any or none of the alternative accounting rules. So, for example, a company could include some of its plant and machinery in its balance sheet at current cost and include every other item on an historical cost basis. However, although it might appear reasonable for a company to include certain assets at a valuation, if it mixed the historical cost rules and the alternative accounting rules indiscriminately it might produce meaningless financial statements.

16.156 Whilst FRS 15 continues to permit the optional adoption of a policy of revaluation, it tightens up the application of the alternative accounting rules to tangible fixed assets by setting out the conditions that apply when determining:

- Which tangible fixed assets (if any) should be revalued.
- When those assets should be revalued.
- The valuation basis to be used.

16.157 To prevent 'cherry picking' of which assets are revalued and when, the FRS requires that, if a policy of revaluation is adopted, it must be applied to all assets within an individual class of assets, and the valuations must be kept up-to-date at current values. [FRS 15 paras 42, 43]. These aspects are considered in more detail below.

Class of assets

16.158 When an entity values its assets in accordance with the alternative accounting rules in the Act it must value each asset separately, in order to comply with the separate valuation principle contained in paragraph 14 of Schedule 4. However, FRS 15 requires that if a single tangible fixed asset is revalued, then all the fixed assets of the same class should also be revalued, although the policy need not be applied to all classes of tangible fixed assets. [FRS 15 para 42]. This reduces the scope for picking out individual assets for revaluation, just because they happen to have significantly increased in value. However, this requirement means that adopting a policy of revaluation may be more onerous and involve more complex record keeping than before.

16.159 There is an exception to this general rule, however, which is that where an asset held outside the UK or Republic of Ireland cannot be revalued, it may be excluded from the class of assets to be revalued. This is expected to be rare in practice, although in certain parts of the world, assets (in particular properties) cannot be valued for a variety of reasons. For example, there may not be any suitably qualified valuers in a particular location, or there may be government controls over property ownership so that it is impossible to put a value on an asset. The existence of such a constraint does not prevent all the other assets in its class from being revalued. However, in such cases the carrying amount of the tangible fixed asset that has not been revalued and the fact that it has not been revalued must be disclosed. [FRS 15 para 61].

16.160 The Act already defines quite broad categories or classes of assets, as follows:

- Land and buildings.
- Plant and machinery.
- Fixtures, fittings, tools and equipment.
- Payments on account and assets in the course of construction.

[CA85 4 Sch 7, 8].

16.161 However, for valuation purposes, an entity may adopt other, narrower, classes of assets, provided that they meet the following definition:

> *"A category of tangible fixed assets having a similar nature, function or use in the business of the entity."* [FRS 15 para 2].

16.162 Other than ruling out classes of assets determined on a geographical basis, this definition is reasonably flexible, so that an entity can adopt meaningful classes that are appropriate to the type of business and assets held by an entity. However, when determining which classes of assets to adopt, it is worth bearing in mind that separate disclosures must be made for each class of assets. For example, as noted from paragraph 16.309, each class of assets must be presented as a separate category in the table of movements in tangible fixed assets in the notes to the financial statements. [FRS 15 para 100]. In practice, this effectively prevents the adoption of many narrowly defined classes of assets.

16.163 Although property is often revalued, a class of assets for revaluation need not be confined to property. For example, Associated British Ports Holdings PLC revalues operational land, but holds other operating tangible fixed assets, such as buildings, dock structures and plant and equipment at historical cost, as can be seen in Table 16.8. Other examples of classes of assets include:

- All retail properties.
- Specialised or non-specialised properties.
- Short or long leasehold, or freehold properties.
- Art and antiques.

Table 16.8 — Associated British Ports Holdings PLC — Annual Report & accounts — 31 December 2001

1 Accounting policies (extract)
Basis of preparation (extract)

The financial statements have been prepared on a going concern basis in accordance with applicable accounting standards and under the historical cost convention as modified by the revaluation of operational land, investment properties, land at ports held for development and investments in subsidiary and associated companies.

Frequency of revaluations

16.164 One of the requirements of FRS 15 is that valuations should remain up-to-date, as old valuations that do not reflect current values are meaningless. However, FRS 15 does not require valuations to be performed every year. Indeed to do so would be rather onerous, particularly if values have not materially changed from one year to the next. The specific requirements in respect of properties and other tangible fixed assets are set out from paragraph 16.169 below, although the FRS acknowledges that for cost-benefit reasons, charities and other not-for-profit organisations may adopt alternative approaches. Of course, other entities may undertake more rigorous valuation procedures than recommended in the standard, should they believe it appropriate to do so.

Qualified valuers

16.165 The guidance in FRS 15 is also concerned with the reliability of the valuations and, therefore, specifies the involvement of qualified valuers and whether and when they should be external to the entity.

16.166 A qualified valuer is a person who:

- Holds a recognised and relevant professional qualification.
- Has recent relevant post-qualification experience.
- Has sufficient knowledge of the state of the market in the location and category of the tangible fixed asset being valued.

[FRS 15 para 2].

16.167 In the UK a qualified valuer would usually be a member of the Royal Institution of Chartered Surveyors (RICS). As well as valuing properties, some members specialise in the valuation of plant and machinery and fine art and antiques. However, the above definition of a qualified valuer does not preclude non-RICS members from carrying out valuations where appropriate.

16.168 An internal valuer is defined as being a director, officer or employee of the entity. In contrast, an external valuer cannot be a director, officer or an employee of the entity, nor have a significant financial interest in the entity. [FRS 15 para 2].

Properties

16.169 The guidance in FRS 15 states that for each property subject to a policy of revaluation:

- A full valuation should be performed at least every five years.
- An interim valuation should be carried out in the third year after the full valuation.
- Interim valuations should be carried out in the intervening years only where it is likely that there has been a material change in value.

[FRS 15 para 45].

16.170 However, for portfolios of non-specialised properties, the need for an interim valuation in the third year after the full valuation, regardless of whether it is likely that there has been a material change in value, is dispensed with, provided that:

- A full valuation is performed on a rolling basis designed to cover all the properties over a five-year (or more frequent) cycle.

- An interim valuation is carried out on the remaining four-fifths of the portfolio where it is likely that there is a material change in value.
- The portfolio either consists of a broadly similar range of properties, which are likely to be affected by the same market factors, or can be divided on a continuing basis into five groups of a broadly similar spread.

[FRS 15 para 46].

16.171 FRS 15 summarises the main requirements of the RICS's Appraisal and Valuation Standards regarding the basic procedures to be carried out in respect of full and interim valuations, although ultimately the exact work needed will depend upon the individual circumstances and be down to the professional judgement of the valuer. [FRS 15 paras 47, 49].

16.172 FRS 15 states that for all properties being revalued:

- The five yearly full valuation should be performed by either:
  - a qualified external valuer; or
  - a qualified internal valuer, provided that the valuation performed by the internal valuer has been appropriately reviewed by a qualified external valuer. In the case of properties, such a review should involve the valuation of a sample of the properties, so that the external valuer can give an opinion on the overall accuracy of the valuations performed.
- Interim valuations should be performed by a qualified valuer, who may be either internal or external to the entity.

[FRS 15 paras 48, 49].

Other tangible fixed assets

16.173 For tangible fixed assets other than properties (for example, plant and machinery, vehicles, art and antiques), where a policy of valuation is adopted, a qualified internal or external valuer is required to perform:

- A valuation at least every five years, which should be subject to review by a qualified external valuer if performed by an internal valuer.
- An update of the valuation three years after the original valuation.
- Further updates of the valuation in intervening years if it is likely that there has been a material change in value.

[FRS 15 para 50].

16.174 There is an exception to this general rule, however. In particular circumstances, the FRS acknowledges that the directors may be able to establish an asset's value with reasonable reliability, without going to the length of using a qualified valuer. Therefore, where there is an active market or appropriate indices for the assets concerned (such as in second hand cars), the valuation may instead be performed by the directors. In such cases, the directors should revalue the asset on an annual basis. [FRS 15 para 50]. Where the directors use an index it should be appropriate to the class of asset, to its location and condition and should take account of technological change. The index should have a record of regular publication and be expected to continue to be available in the foreseeable future. [FRS 15 para 51].

Material changes in value

16.175 The need for interim valuations in intervening years often relies upon an assessment of whether it is likely that there has been a material change in value. This is to avoid the need for unnecessary valuations each year when it is obvious that there has been no material change in value, but should ensure that material changes, when they occur, are reflected in the balance sheet.

16.176 FRS 15 states that a material change in value is one that *"would reasonably influence the decisions of a user of the accounts"*. [FRS 15 para 52]. It is a matter of judgement, which is ultimately the responsibility of the directors. However, in making that judgement, the directors would probably consult their valuers and consider, amongst other things, factors such as changes in the general market, the condition of the asset, changes to the asset and its location. In coming to their decision, the directors should consider the combined effect of all the relevant factors, as it is possible that the effect of one factor may be offset by other factors.

Bases of valuation

16.177 The Act specifies that tangible fixed assets may be included in the balance sheet at a market value determined as at the date of their last valuation or at current cost. However, it does not define current cost, nor does it give further details about the bases to be used to determine market value. FRS 15, however, gives more definitive requirements in respect of the valuation bases to be used.

16.178 The general requirement in FRS 15 is that tangible fixed assets subject to a policy of revaluation should be carried at current value. [FRS 15 para 43]. Current value is defined in FRS 15 as the lower of replacement cost and recoverable amount, where, as set out in FRS 11 'Impairment of fixed assets and goodwill', recoverable amount is the higher of net realisable value and value in use. [FRS 15 para 2; FRS 11 para 2]. This is illustrated diagrammatically below.

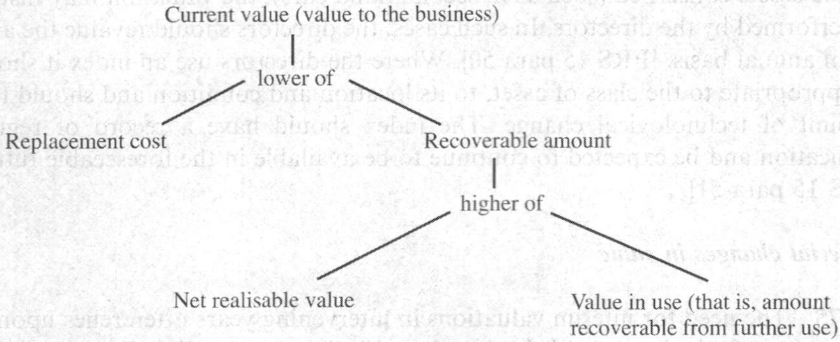

16.179 This definition of current value is based on the value to the business model. Under this model, the value of an asset to a business is the most relevant value when making economic decisions, that is, it is the loss that the entity would suffer if it were deprived of that asset.

16.179.1 The value to the business model is not used under IFRS, which also permits an entity to adopt a policy of revaluation. Under IAS 16, if a policy of revaluation is adopted, the basis of valuation used is 'fair value'. Fair value under IFRS is much the same as 'open market value' and is defined in IAS 16 as *"…the amount for which an asset could be exchanged between knowledgeable, willing parties in an arm's length transaction"*. The effect of this difference in approach is that properties used in the business would be valued under IFRS at fair value (that is, open market value), whereas under FRS 15 existing use value would be used (see para 16.185 below). An important practical effect of the difference is where OMV is higher than EUV because, for example, it reflects the possibility of the property being developed for an alternative use. FRS 15 would not permit the higher value for alternative use to be reflected in an entity's balance sheet if the property were being used in the business, although it would require information about the higher OMV to be disclosed in the notes.

[The next paragraph is 16.180.]

16.180 A profit-making entity would only invest in an asset (or project) if it expected that the asset (or project) would generate profitable returns — in other words, if the asset's recoverable amount exceeded its cost of investment. If deprived of the asset in such circumstances then, from an economic view point, the entity would choose to replace it as this generates the most profitable return. Hence, the current value of the asset is its current replacement cost.

16.181 If, on the other hand, the cost of replacing the asset exceeds its recoverable amount (that is, the value of the asset in its most profitable use), then the entity would not replace that asset if deprived of it. Instead the asset's current value to the entity is its recoverable amount (that is, the greatest value obtainable from either continuing to use the asset or selling it).

16.182 Most of the time tangible fixed assets are used in profitable businesses and, therefore, replacement cost is usually the relevant measure of value to the business. In any event, FRS 11, 'Impairment of fixed assets and goodwill', requires an asset to be written down to its recoverable amount where the asset is impaired and recoverable amount falls below replacement cost. FRS 15, therefore, directs entities to use replacement cost when revaluing a tangible fixed asset, except where the asset is impaired, in which case FRS 11 should be followed.

16.183 As noted in FRS 15, a revalued asset should be recorded at the lower of its revalued amount (determined as set out in paras 16.185 and 16.189 below) and recoverable amount. Because recoverable amount is the higher of net realisable value and value in use, where the revalued amount of the asset is not materially different from its net realisable value, any further consideration of impairment is not generally necessary. [FRS 15 para 54].

16.184 FRS 15 specifies the valuation bases that provide the best approximation to replacement cost in the different circumstances. These valuation bases are defined by the Royal Institution of Chartered Surveyors (RICS) and are described in greater detail below from paragraph 16.190 onwards. The RICS publishes the RICS Appraisal and Valuation Standards, which include Practice Statements (PSs) and Guidance Notes that apply to valuations for incorporation in company financial statements and other financial statements that are subject to audit which should be applied. It should be noted that since the publication of FRS 15, The RICS definition of 'open market value' has been discarded and replaced by 'market value'. Appendix 1 of FRS 15 contains the RICS definition of open market value extant at the date of publication of the standard and we consider this should be applied.

Tangible fixed assets used in the business

16.185 For tangible fixed assets that are not surplus to an entity's requirements, FRS 15 requires that:

- Non-specialised properties are valued on the existing use value basis with the addition of notional directly attributable acquisition costs where material. Where the open market value differs materially from existing use value, the open market value and the reasons for the difference should be disclosed.
- Specialised properties are valued on the depreciated replacement cost basis.
- Tangible fixed assets other than properties are valued using market value, where possible. Material notional directly attributable acquisition costs should be added. If market value is not obtainable, assets should be valued on the basis of depreciated replacement cost, with the assistance of a qualified valuer.

[FRS 15 paras 53, 59, 60].

16.186 Specialised properties are defined in the RICS Appraisal and Valuation Standards as those properties that, because of their specialised nature, are rarely, if ever, sold in the market, except by way of a sale of the business or entity of which it is part, due to uniqueness arising from its specialised nature and design, its configuration, size, location or otherwise. See from paragraph 16.197 for greater detail. All other properties (that is, the majority of properties) are, therefore, non-specialised properties.

16.187 Notionally directly attributable acquisition costs are not included in market value or existing use value as defined by the RICS. However, they are added to the valuation where material, because they form part of the cost to the entity of replacing the asset. Notionally directly attributable acquisition costs include normal dealing costs such as professional fees, non-recoverable taxes and duties. They do not include costs incurred to enhance site value, such as site improvements, costs of obtaining planning permission, site clearance and preparation or other costs already included in the existing use value. [FRS 15 para 55]. In practice, notionally directly attributable acquisition costs are often not material and are, therefore, ignored. However, where they are included in the carrying amount of a revalued asset, their total amount must be separately disclosed. [FRS 15 para 74].

16.188 Some entities make structural changes to their properties or include special fittings within the properties (for example, shop or bank facias). These changes are referred to as adaptation works, which may have a low market value, because they are particular to the present owner. In such cases, the adaptation works and the shell of the building may be treated as separate components with only the shell of the building being revalued on the existing use basis. The adaptation works are then held at depreciated replacement cost (if revalued) or at depreciated historical cost, if not revalued. [FRS 15 para 57].

Tangible fixed assets surplus to requirements

16.189 Tangible fixed assets surplus to requirements would not be replaced by an entity and, therefore, replacement cost is irrelevant in these circumstances. Instead the current value of such assets to the business is their net realisable value. This is determined as follows:

- Properties surplus to an entity's requirements are valued on the open market value basis, with expected directly attributable selling costs deducted where material.
- Tangible fixed assets other than properties that are surplus to requirements are valued using market value, or depreciated replacement cost if market value is not available, with expected selling costs deducted if material.

[FRS 15 paras 53, 60].

Open market value

16.190 Open market value, not qualified by any reference to existing use or alternative use, implies the value for *any* use to the extent to which that value is reflected in the price obtainable in the open market.

16.191 Open market value means the best price at which the sale of an interest in property would have been completed unconditionally for cash at the valuation date assuming:

- A willing seller.
- A reasonable period, prior to the date of valuation, for the proper marketing of the interest, for agreement of price and terms and for the completion of the sale.
- That the state of the market, level of values and other circumstances were, on any earlier assumed date of exchange of contracts, the same as on the date of valuation.
- That no account is taken of any additional bid by a prospective purchaser with a special interest.
- That both parties to the transaction had acted knowledgeably, prudently and without compulsion.

[FRS 15, App I].

16.192 Open market value is the only basis of valuation that is appropriate for investment properties and properties that are surplus to a company's requirements.

Existing use value

16.193 The existing use value has a similar definition to that in paragraph 16.191, but additionally reflects the use of the property for the same or similar purposes as hitherto and assumes vacant possession on completion. It ignores any alternative use for the property, any 'hope value' for an alternative use, any value attributable to goodwill and any other possible increase in value due to special transactions, such as a sale and leaseback. This basis should be used for all non-specialised owner occupied properties (except those that are surplus to requirements), as it reflects the cost that the entity would suffer if it were to replace the tangible fixed asset with another, equivalent asset for the same use. An example of its use is given in Table 16.9.

Tangible fixed assets

Table 16.9 — Kingfisher plc — Annual Report and Accounts — 29 January 2000

Notes to the accounts (extract)

Tangible fixed assets (extract)

During each of the last five years a representative sample of the freehold and long leasehold properties owned by Chartwell Land plc, the Group's property subsidiary, have been valued by external qualified valuers. CB Hillier Parker, has carried out a valuation of a representative sample as at 31 December 1999 and based upon the results of these valuations there have been internal valuations by qualified valuers employed by the Group of the remainder of Chartwell Land's portfolio.
Properties with any element of Group occupancy are valued on an existing use basis which does not take account of formal lease arrangements with Group companies or the Group's occupation of the premises. Properties without Group occupancy are valued on the basis of open market value. These valuation bases comply with the RICS Appraisal and Valuation Manual.

16.194 An example of the distinction between the open market value (unqualified) basis and the existing use value basis is where a company operates a factory on the outskirts of a town. The site on which it operates might have a considerably increased value if it were to be sold for redevelopment. In such a case, the financial statements of the company should reflect any valuation on an existing use value basis, because it is intending to continue to operate the site as a factory and the additional value that could be obtained from closing the factory and selling the site for redevelopment should not be reflected in the valuation. However, as mentioned in paragraph 16.185, the company must disclose the open market value in the notes to the financial statements and explain the reasons for the difference. (See also para 16.179.1 above regarding the difference between FRS 15 and IAS 16 in this situation.)

16.195 Certain types of non-specialised property that are equipped as operational entities in their own right are valued with regard to trading potential. Existing use value that is determined on this basis includes the value of the trading potential that runs with the property, but should not include any goodwill that has been created by the owner, which would not remain with the property should it be sold. This basis applies to land and buildings that invariably change hands in the open market at prices based directly on trading potential for a strictly limited use. [FRS 15 para 56].

16.196 Examples of such properties include hotels, private hospitals and nursing homes, public houses, cinemas, theatres, bingo clubs, gaming clubs, petrol filling stations, licensed betting offices and specialised leisure and sporting facilities.

Depreciated replacement cost

16.197 The depreciated replacement cost (DRC) basis of valuation is used for specialised properties, as there is no means of ascertaining a market value for such properties. As noted in paragraph 16.186, such properties are rarely, if ever sold in the market, except by way of a sale of the business or entity of which it is part.

16.198 Such specialised properties might include:

- Oil refineries and chemical works where, usually, the buildings are no more than housings or claddings for highly specialised plant.
- Power stations and dock installations.
- Properties of such construction, arrangement, size or specification that there would be no market (for sale to a single owner occupier for continuation of existing use) for the properties.
- Standard properties of abnormal size in particular geographic areas that are isolated or remote from main business centres and which are located there for business or operational reasons, such that there is no market there for the properties.
- Schools, colleges and research establishments where there is no market for such properties from other competing organisations in the area.
- Hospitals, health centres and leisure centres where there is no competing market demand in the area.
- Museums, libraries and other similar public sector properties.

16.199 For a property, calculating DRC involves estimating the value of land in its existing use and the gross replacement cost of buildings and other site works. From this appropriate deductions ('depreciation') are made to allow for age, condition and economic or functional obsolescence and other factors which might result in the existing property being worth less than a new replacement. DRC is often calculated by applying relevant indices to both cost and depreciation.

16.200 Because of the nature of DRC valuations a valuer will qualify all valuations on this basis as being subject to the adequate potential profitability of the business compared with the value of the total assets employed. However, for properties in public ownership, or not occupied primarily for profit, where the test of adequate potential profitability is not available, DRC is expressed as subject to the prospect and viability of the continuance of the occupation and use.

Value of plant and machinery to the business

16.201 Where plant and machinery is valued the valuation is the price at which the plant and machinery could have been transferred at the valuation date assuming:

- Continuation of the present uses in the business.
- Adequate potential profitability of the business, or continued viability of the undertaking, having regard to the value of total assets employed and to the nature of the operation.

- Transfer of the plant and machinery is part of an arm's length sale of the business wherein both parties acted knowledgeably, prudently and without compulsion.

[FRS 15, App I].

16.202 Where suitable market evidence is not available, plant and machinery and other non-property tangible fixed assets are normally valued on a DRC basis. Therefore, the cost of replacing an existing asset with an identical or substantially similar new asset having similar production or service capacity is depreciated to reflect the value attributable to the remaining portion of the total useful economic life of the asset. In assessing the DRC of an asset, account should be taken of the age, condition, economic and functional obsolescence and environmental and other factors, including residual value at the end of the asset's useful economic life.

16.203 In practice, the actual determination of value will depend upon the individual circumstances and evidence available. Table 16.10 shows the valuation methods used by BG plc.

Table 16.10— BG plc — Annual Report and Accounts — 31 December 1998

Principal accounting policies (extract)

Accounting principles (extract)
These accounts have been prepared in accordance with applicable accounting standards, under modified historical cost principles. Under these principles the Group values regulatory assets at depreciated replacement cost (see Tangible fixed assets below) or, where lower, the estimated value in use (see Impairment of regulatory fixed assets below). Regulatory assets are those assets which are included in that part of the asset base which is subject to a regulatory regime. Revalued assets include operational land and buildings, mains, services, meters, storage and other plant and machinery in Great Britain.

Tangible fixed assets (extract)
Regulatory tangible fixed assets in Great Britain are included in the balance sheet at depreciated replacement cost or, where lower, the estimated value in use (see Impairment of regulatory fixed assets below). Investment properties are carried at valuation. All other categories of tangible fixed assets are carried at depreciated historical cost.

a) Modified historical cost
i) land and buildings — Great Britain regulatory assets — based upon periodic valuation by chartered surveyors employed by the Group, determined on the basis of open market value for existing use; land and buildings — investment properties — based upon periodic valuation by chartered surveyors employed by the Group, determined on the basis of open market value. Valuations take into account estimated non-statutory decontamination costs;
land and buildings — other — based upon historical cost;
ii) distribution mains, services and meters — Great Britain regulatory assets — based upon application of calculated average unit replacement costs to the physical lengths or quantities in use; distribution mains, services and meters — other — based upon historical cost;
iii) transmission mains, plant and machinery, and gas storage — Great Britain regulatory assets — based upon engineering assessments of the cost of replacing existing assets; transmission mains, plant and machinery and gas storage — other — based on historical cost;
iv) exploration and production tangible fixed assets — based upon historical cost; and

> v) other tangible fixed assets — Great Britain regulatory assets — based upon indexation of historical cost using appropriate indices;
> other tangible fixed assets — other — based upon historical cost.

Disclosures

16.204 The RICS Appraisal and Standards set out in Practise Statement 5 (PS 5) minimum disclosures that should be made in a published document, such as a company's financial statements that make reference to a valuers report. The disclosure requirements of FRS 15 broadly encompass and expand on those laid down by the RICS and those of the Act, but should be given for each class of revalued assets. In addition to the disclosure requirements mentioned in paragraphs 16.159 and 16.185 above, the disclosure requirements in respect of valuations are:

- The name and qualification of the valuer or the valuer's organisation and a description of its nature. [FRS 15 para 74; CA85 4 Sch 43; PS 5.11].
- Whether the valuer is internal or external. [FRS 15 para 74; PS 5.11].
- The date of the valuation. [FRS 15 para 74; CA85 4 Sch 43; PS 5.11].
- The amounts of the valuation. [FRS 15 para 74; CA85 4 Sch 43].
- The basis or bases of valuation (including whether notional acquisition costs have been included or expected selling costs deducted). [FRS 15 para 74; CA85 4 Sch 33(2), 43]. The RICS Appraisal and Valuation Standards require the valuation basis together with any special assumptions made. [PS 5.11].
- For revalued properties, the total amount of notional directly attributable acquisition costs included (or the total amount of expected selling costs deducted), where material. [FRS 15 para 74].
- Where properties have been valued as fully equipped operational entities and having regard to their trading potential, a statement to that effect and the carrying amount of the properties (see para 16.195 above). [FRS 15 para 74].
- Comment on the extent to which the values were determined directly by reference to market evidence or were estimated using other valuation techniques. [PS 5.11].
- Where appropriate, confirmation that the valuation has been made in accordance with the RICS Appraisal and Valuation Standards, or the extent of and reasons for departure from those standards. [PS 5.11].
- Where the directors are not aware of any material change in value and, therefore, the valuation has not been updated by an interim valuation as specified from paragraph 16.164 above, a statement to that effect. [FRS 15 para 74].

- Where the valuation has not been updated, or is not a full valuation, the date of the last full valuation. [FRS 15 para 74].
- Where historical cost records are available, the net carrying amount that would have been shown under the historical cost method less depreciation (see also from para 16.206 below). [FRS 15 para 74; CA85 4 Sch 33(3)].

16.205 The RICS Appraisal and Valuation Standards include useful examples of disclosures in Appendix 5.2 to the Practice Statements. One example is as follows:

"The company's freehold and leasehold properties were valued on 31 December 2004 by an External Valuer, Joe Smith, FRICS of Alpha, Chartered Surveyors. The valuations were in accordance with the requirements of the RICS Appraisal and Valuation Standards and FRS 15. The valuation of each property was on the following bases and assumptions:

i *For owner occupied property: Valued to Existing Use Value (EUV) assuming that the property would be sold as part of the continuing business.*

ii *For investment property: Valued to Market Value assuming that the property would be sold subject to any existing leases.*

iii *For surplus property and property held for development: Valued to Market Value assuming that the property would be sold with vacant possession in its existing condition."*

Actual examples of disclosure are given above in Tables 16.10 and 16.11.

16.206 The Act requires either the balance sheet or the notes to disclose, in respect of every item affected by the alternative accounting rules (except stocks), one or other of the following amounts:

- The comparable amounts determined according to the historical cost convention.
- The differences between those comparable amounts and the actual amounts shown in the balance sheet.

[CA85 4 Sch 33(3)].

16.207 For this purpose, 'comparable amounts' means the aggregate amount the company would have shown if it had applied the historical cost convention and the aggregate amount of the cumulative provisions for depreciation or diminution in value that would have been permitted or required in determining those amounts according to that convention. [CA85 4 Sch 33(4)].

16.208 As noted in paragraph 16.204, FRS 15 requires the net amounts required by the first bullet point in paragraph 16.206 above but in greater detail, because it requires it for each class of revalued assets. [FRS 15 para 74].

16.209 To illustrate the requirement in paragraph 16.206, consider the following example:

Example

Details of a company's fixed assets are as follows:

	Cost	Valuation
	£	£
Fixed assets	10,000	15,000
Accumulated depreciation	6,000	4,000
	4,000	11,000

If the company records the fixed assets in the balance sheet at valuation, the effect of the Act's provisions is to require the balance sheet or the notes to the financial statements to state either the comparable amounts (namely, cost £10,000 and depreciation £6,000) or the difference between the comparable amounts and the amounts at which they are actually stated (namely, £5,000 and £2,000 respectively).

The historical cost net book amount (namely, £4,000) or the difference between the comparable net book amounts (namely, £7,000) is another interpretation of the amounts that are required to be disclosed. This latter disclosure is arguable because the Act refers to the amounts stated in the balance sheet and the amounts so stated will be the net book amounts of the assets.

16.210 As a result of this requirement, a company that has revalued its fixed assets has to maintain records of both the historical cost and the valuation of those fixed assets. In addition, the company has to calculate depreciation on the historical cost as well as on the valuation.

16.211 Table 16.11 shows how a company complied with these disclosure requirements.

Table 16.11 — Lonrho plc — Annual Report and Accounts — 30 September 1998

Notes to the Accounts (extract)

11. Tangible assets (extract)

Assets shown below at valuation were valued by independent professional valuers or by the Directors after advice from independent professional advisers in the year shown, on the basis of open market value for existing use.

	Land and buildings	Leasehold					
	Freehold	Long term	Short term	Mining assets	Plant and machinery	Fixtures fittings and equipment	Total
Group	£m	£m	£m	£m	£m	£m	£m
Up to 1994				67			67
1998				6			6
Valuation				73			73
Cost	19		1	548	8	39	615
	19		1	621	8	39	688
Capital work in progress							5
At 30 September 1998							**693**
Depreciation:							
Valuation				14			14
Cost				68	4	32	104
At 30 September 1998				**82**	**4**	**32**	**118**
Historical cost of revalued assets							
Cost				14			14
Depreciation				5			5
Net historical cost at 30 September 1998				**9**			**9**
Cost	70	12	2	19	2	4	109
Depreciation	1			6	1	1	9
Net historical cost at 30 September 1997	69	12	2	13	1	3	100

The Directors have valued the following asset after taking account of the advice of the independent professional adviser listed below:

Property valued	Independent professional adviser	Qualification
Corsyn Consolidated Mines	Northland Mining services 1991 Ltd	Chartered Engineers

16.212 In addition, the FRS highlights that paragraph 1(2) of Schedule 7 to the Act also requires disclosure in the directors' report of any substantial differences between the market value of properties and their carrying value, if the directors think the difference is of such significance that members should be made aware of it. [FRS 15 para 76]. This difference is likely to be significant where, for example:

- Land and buildings are held at historical cost (or frozen at their pre-FRS 15 valuations, see para 16.212.1) and market values have significantly increased or decreased since the date of acquisition (or last valuation).
- Owner-occupied property is valued at existing use value, but the property has a more valuable alternative use, such that open market value is significantly greater than the carrying value.
- The open market value of a property is significantly less than existing use value, for example, where restrictive alienation clauses in the headlease, planning consents that are personal to the present occupier, or known contamination do not affect the existing use of a property, but would result in a significantly lower market value.

Frozen valuations

16.212.1 Where an entity decided not to adopt a policy of revaluation on the implementation of FRS 15, but had tangible fixed assets that had previously been recorded at valuation, it could either:

- Retain the assets at their book amounts (subject to the requirement to test them for impairment if an indication exists that impairment may have occurred). In such circumstances the entity should disclose that it has taken advantage of the transitional provisions of the FRS and that the valuation has not been updated. It should also disclose the date of the last valuation.
- Restate the assets to historical cost (less depreciation), as a change of accounting policy.

[FRS 15 para 104].

16.212.2 An entity could adopt the transitional arrangement in the first bullet point above only on first application of the FRS and not thereafter. [FRS 15 para 105].

16.212.3 If advantage was taken of this transitional arrangement, for the purposes of FRS 15 the 'frozen' book values are treated as though they were historical cost. However, in terms of the Act, the company still has revalued assets and so the disclosure requirements for the alternative accounting rules under the Act must be complied with on an ongoing basis. The Act's disclosure requirements are:

- The amounts of fixed assets held at valuation, the years of valuation, and the basis adopted.
- The historical cost equivalents for revalued assets.
- The amount of a revaluation reserve and any transfers from that reserve to realised reserves.

[CA85 4 Sch 33, 34, 43].

In addition, a note of historical cost profits and losses should be given as required by FRS 3.

[The next paragraph is 16.213.]

Revaluation gains and losses

Introduction

16.213 A revaluation gain or loss arises on the revaluation of a tangible fixed asset. It is the difference between the revalued amount and the carrying amount of the asset (net of cumulative depreciation) immediately before the revaluation.

16.214 Part or all of a revaluation gain or loss may be an impairment or a reversal of an impairment. Both of these fall to be recognised in the profit and loss account. The remaining gain or loss on revaluation is required by FRS 3 and the Act to be transferred to the revaluation reserve *via* the statement of total recognised gains and losses.

16.215 The tricky part is determining the split between the profit and loss account and the statement of total recognised gains and losses in practice and FRS 15 provides specific rules to ensure consistency of application.

Gains on revaluation

16.216 FRS 15 requires that revaluation gains should be recognised in the statement of total recognised gains and losses (that is, treated as a transfer to revaluation reserve). The only exception is where a gain reverses a revaluation loss (which may have been an impairment) on the same asset that was previously recognised in the profit and loss account. In such a case the gain (to the extent that it reverses the loss after adjusting for subsequent depreciation) is recognised in the profit and loss account. [FRS 15 para 63]. Therefore, the net charge to the profit and loss account over time would be the same as if the downward revaluation had not been recognised in the profit and loss account in the first place. The mechanics of this are best illustrated by means of an example.

Example

A company has a policy of revaluing its tangible fixed assets. An asset cost £1,000 at the start of year one. It has a useful economic life of ten years and is being depreciated on a straight line basis to nil residual value. It was revalued downwards at the end of year one to £850, which was assumed to be the asset's recoverable amount. The loss on revaluation in year one is recognised in the profit and loss account, because it is a fall in value below depreciated historical cost.

At the end of the following year (year two) market values had risen to £1,050. The revaluation gain and loss are recognised as follows:

	Year 1	Year 2
Cost/valuation brought forward	1,000	850
Depreciation charge (opening balance divided by remaining useful economic life)	(100)	(94)
	900	756
(Loss)/gain on revaluation — profit and loss	(50)	44
Gain on revaluation — STRGL	–	250
Carrying amount carried forward	850	1,050

Of the £294 gain on revaluation in year two, £44 is recognised in the profit and loss account. This reverses the £50 loss previously recognised in the profit and loss account, adjusted for depreciation of £6 (that is, £50 divided by 9), which is the additional depreciation charge that would have been recognised in year two had the opening balance been £900, that is, if the £50 loss had not been recognised in year one.

Note that the adjustment to depreciation of £6 is also the difference between depreciation that would have been charged of £100 (that is, 1,000 divided by 10) on the original cost of £1,000, and the depreciation actually charged for the year of £94.

Revaluation losses

16.217 FRS 15 requires revaluation losses caused by a clear consumption of economic benefits to be recognised in the profit and loss account in their entirety. Where there is no clear consumption of economic benefits, revaluation losses should be recognised as follows:

- In the statement of total recognised gains and losses until the carrying amount falls to depreciated historical cost.
- In the profit and loss account for falls in value below depreciated historical cost, except where it can be demonstrated that the recoverable amount is greater than the revalued amount, in which case the fall in value below recoverable amount is recognised in the statement of total recognised gains and losses.

[FRS 15 para 65].

16.218 The above rules seem rather complex. This is because the FRS is trying to differentiate between downward revaluations that are due to a consumption of economic benefits and those that are due to other factors such as a general change in prices. The general principle is that downward revaluations due a consumption of economic benefits are akin to depreciation and should be recognised in the profit and loss account. However, downward revaluations due to general price changes are not losses from operations and so should be recognised in the statement of total recognised gains and losses and ultimately in the revaluation reserve.

16.219 This approach is consistent with that taken in FRS 11 for impaired assets that have been revalued, as set out in chapter 18. Given that an impairment is defined as a reduction in the recoverable amount of a fixed asset below its carrying amount, it is possible that a downward revaluation of a tangible fixed asset may comprise, at least in part, an impairment loss. [FRS 11 para 2; FRS 15 para 2].

16.220 Where there is a clear consumption of economic benefits, for example due to physical damage to, or contamination or obsolescence of, the asset or a deterioration in the quality of service provided by the asset, then both FRS 11 and FRS 15 require the fall in value to be taken to the profit and loss account in its entirety. No part of it should be taken to the statement of total recognised gains and losses. [FRS 11 para 63; FRS 15 para 65]. Whilst FRS 15 uses the term 'revaluation loss' rather than 'impairment', in this case the two terms refer to the same type of loss.

16.221 However, where there is no clear consumption of economic benefits, it may be difficult, in practice, to distinguish between these different types of losses. The approach taken by the standard, however, makes this less of an issue, because in such circumstances the standard requires downward revaluations of an asset to be recognised in the statement of total recognised gains and losses, until the carrying amount reaches depreciated historical cost. Thereafter, the balance of the downward revaluation is recognised in the profit and loss account. [FRS 11 para 63; FRS 15 para 65].

16.222 Note, however, that an asset cannot be impaired where its carrying amount is less than its recoverable amount. Since recoverable amount is the higher of net realisable value and value in use, it is possible that revaluing a tangible fixed asset may result in a revalued amount that is both less than the previous carrying amount and recoverable amount. In such circumstances, where recoverable amount is known, the difference between the recoverable amount and the (lower) revalued amount cannot be an impairment and, therefore, should be recognised in the statement of total recognised gains and losses, as illustrated in the example following paragraph 16.225. [FRS 15 para 65]. This would lead to a negative balance in the revaluation reserve for that asset.

16.223 FRS 15 does not require an impairment test and calculation of recoverable amount to be performed every time an asset is revalued downwards. As noted in paragraph 16.183, a newly revalued asset can only be impaired below its revalued amount if either net realisable value or value in use is materially less than the revalued amount (which would generally be replacement cost). If recoverable amount is not known then the full revaluation loss below depreciated historical cost should be recognised in the profit and loss account (that is, it is assumed that recoverable amount is the same as the revalued amount — see also the chart in para 16.178, which shows that current value is the lower of recoverable amount and replacement cost).

16.224 All impairments of tangible fixed assets that are charged to the profit and loss account under the rules of FRS 11 and FRS 15 represent permanent diminutions in value under the Act and should be charged in arriving at operating profit, generally under the same statutory format headings as depreciation. One exception is where the impairment is effectively a provision for a loss on disposal, as noted from paragraph 16.325.

16.225 For the purpose of determining in which performance statement gains and losses on revaluation should be recognised, material gains and losses on individual assets in a class of asset should not be aggregated. [FRS 15 para 67].

Example

A tangible fixed asset cost £100 and is depreciated over ten years on a straight-line basis, with nil residual value. At the end of year one the asset is revalued to £135. The revaluation gain of £45 (£135 less £90 (that is, £100 less £10 depreciation)) is recognised in the statement of total recognised gains and losses.

At the end of year two, the asset's value has fallen to £50, however an impairment review has revealed that the recoverable amount of the asset is £60. After depreciation for the year of £15 (£135 divided by 9), there is a revaluation loss of £70 (£120 – £50).

(a) If there is a clear consumption of economic benefits (for example, the asset was damaged by fire), then all the fall in value down to recoverable amount, that is, £60 (£120 – £60) in this example, is recognised in the profit and loss account as an impairment. The remaining revaluation loss of £10 being the fall in value from recoverable amount (£60) to the revalued amount (£50) is recognised in the statement of total recognised gains and losses.

(b) If, however, there is no obvious consumption of economic benefits, then only the fall in value below depreciated historical cost (£80) to recoverable amount (£60), that is, £20, is assumed to be an impairment loss to be recognised in the profit and loss account. The remaining revaluation loss of £50 is recognised in the statement of total recognised gains and losses. This revaluation loss comprises the fall in value to depreciated historical cost of £40 (£120 – £80) and the fall in value below recoverable amount of £10 (£60 – £50), as follows:

	£
Carrying amount at beginning of year 2	135
Depreciation for year	(15)
Carrying amount at end of year 2 just before revaluation	120
Fall in value to depreciated historical cost — recognised in STRGL	(40)
Depreciated historical cost at end of year 2	80
Fall in value to recoverable amount — recognised in profit and loss	(20)
Recoverable amount at end of year 2	60
Fall in value to replacement cost (revalued amount) — recognised in STRGL	(10)
Carrying amount (revalued amount) at end of year 2	50

Treatment of accumulated depreciation when assets are revalued

16.226 In the past, before the revision of SSAP 12 in January 1987 and the introduction of FRS 15, companies adopted one or other of two different ways of treating their existing accumulated depreciation when they revalued fixed assets.

16.227 The first method, the only one allowed under SSAP 12 and FRS 15, which replaces SSAP 12, is the simple one of comparing the revalued amount with the net book amount immediately before revaluation and taking the difference to the profit and loss account or statement of total recognised gains and losses as discussed from paragraph 16.216 above. This method is illustrated by the following simple example:

Example

Details of a fixed asset before revaluation are as follows:	£
Fixed asset at cost	1,000
Accumulated depreciation	400
Net book amount	600
The asset is revalued to	1,500
Details of the fixed asset after revaluation are as follows:	£
Fixed asset at cost	1,000
Gain on revaluation	500
Fixed asset at revalued amount	1,500
Accumulated depreciation	400
Gain on revaluation	(400)
Nil depreciation after revaluation	–

The gain on revaluation, which is recognised in the statement of total recognised gains and losses and transferred to the revaluation reserve, is £900 (namely, £1,500 – £600). This includes £400 of accumulated depreciation.

16.228 For assets revalued using depreciated replacement cost, rather than market value, the gain or loss on revaluation is calculated in the same way (that is, as the difference between the net book amount immediately before revaluation and the revalued amount). However, the cost and accumulated depreciation carried forward after the revaluation may, alternatively, reflect the gross cost and accumulated depreciation used to determine depreciated replacement cost. [FRS 15 para 101].

Example

As previously, but the fixed asset is revalued to £1,500 on a depreciated replacement cost (DRC) basis, consisting of £3,000 gross cost and £1,500 depreciation.

Details of the fixed asset after revaluation on a DRC basis are as follows:	£
Fixed asset at cost	1,000
Gain on revaluation	2,000
Fixed asset at revalued gross replacement cost	3,000
Accumulated depreciation	400
Loss (that is, additional depreciation) on revaluation	1,100
Accumulated depreciation after revaluation	1,500

The gain on revaluation, which is recognised in the statement of total recognised gains and losses and transferred to the revaluation reserve, is again £900 (namely, £2,000 – £1,100).

16.229 The second approach, which is prohibited by FRS 15, was to write back the accumulated depreciation of £400 to the profit and loss account and to transfer the difference between the revalued amount of the asset and its historical cost or previous valuation to the revaluation reserve.

16.230 Although the FRS makes clear that the reversal of accumulated depreciation should be credited to the revaluation reserve (and to the statement of total recognised gains and losses), it is unclear as to whether or not the amount thus credited in respect of the depreciation represents a realised profit or not. In our view the amount should not be assumed to be a realised profit and if a company wished to treat it as such it should seek legal advice.

Revaluation reserve

16.231 The Act specifies that any difference between the amount of any item that a company has determined according to one of the alternative accounting rules, and the amount that the company would have disclosed if it had adhered to the historical cost convention, must be credited or debited (as applicable) to a 'revaluation reserve'. [CA85 4 Sch 34(1)].

16.232 In determining the amount of this difference, a company should take account, where appropriate, of any provisions for depreciation or diminution in value that it made otherwise than by reference to the value it determined under the alternative accounting rules. It should also take account of any adjustments of any such provisions that it made in the light of that determination. [CA85 4 Sch 34(1)]. This wording seems simply to mean that the figures on the historical cost basis and the figures on the basis of the alternative accounting rules should be compared net of any depreciation. For example, if an asset shown under the historical cost rules at cost of £100 less depreciation of £40 (net carrying amount £60) were revalued to a gross figure of £150 less cumulative depreciation £60 (net revalued amount under the alternative accounting rules £90), the credit to the revaluation reserve should be £30 (that is, £90 – £60).

16.233 As required by FRS 3, 'Reporting financial performance', this transfer to the revaluation reserve should be recognised in the statement of total recognised gains and losses. Compliance with the requirements of FRS 15, as explained above from paragraph 16.216, will ensure that the Act's requirements are met.

16.234 The Act restricts the circumstances in which a company can transfer an amount from the revaluation reserve. It can do this only where one of the following circumstances exists.

- An amount may be transferred to the profit and loss account if the amount in question was previously charged to that account or represents a realised profit. [CA85 4 Sch 34(3)(a)].
- An amount may be transferred to capital on capitalisation. Capitalisation means applying the amount standing to the credit of the revaluation reserve wholly or partly to paying up unissued shares in the company to be allotted to the company's members as fully or partly paid shares, thereby allowing bonus and scrip issues to be made out of the revaluation reserve. [CA85 4 Sch 34(3)(a)].
- Furthermore, it is possible to transfer from the revaluation reserve an amount in respect of the taxation relating to any profit or loss credited or debited to that reserve. [CA85 4 Sch 34(3)(b)]. This applies for example to the tax relating to a previously recognised revaluation gain.

16.235 The implications of the first bullet point above are that when an entity charges the whole of the depreciation based on the revalued assets to the profit and loss account, it may also transfer an amount equal to the excess depreciation from the revaluation reserve to the profit and loss account reserve. However, such a transfer is not compulsory.

16.236 The transfer should be made between reserves in the notes. Where such an adjustment is made, the revaluation reserve is systematically reduced over the asset's life and, consequently, if the asset is sold any net profit on the sale that is credited to the profit and loss account reserve will ultimately be the same whether the asset has been revalued or not.

16.237 In addition, the revaluation reserve must be reduced to the extent that the amounts transferred to it are no longer necessary for the purpose of the valuation method that the company has adopted. [CA85 4 Sch 34(3)]. An example of this would be where an asset with a previous revaluation surplus, which has not already been transferred to the profit and loss account reserve, has been sold. On realisation, the revaluation gain held in the revaluation reserve should be transferred from the revaluation reserve to the profit and loss account reserve. This gain should not be recognised in the profit and loss account, because it has already been recognised in the statement of total recognised gains and losses on revaluation.

16.238 Schedule 4 paragraph 34(3)), which was introduced by the Companies Act 1989, states that the revaluation reserve shall not be reduced except as mentioned above. This means that it is no longer available, for example, to write off goodwill, which companies had sometimes done prior to the 1989 Act. This prohibition does not, however, affect goodwill write offs made before the introduction of the Companies Act 1989. However, for companies that became subsidiaries because of the changes in the definitions in the Companies Act 1989, the provisions of that Act apply and consolidated goodwill is prohibited from being written off to the revaluation reserve. Following the introduction of FRS 10, which is effective for periods ending on or after 23 December 1998, it is no longer permissible to write goodwill off immediately to reserves.

16.239 The revaluation reserve must be shown on the face of the balance sheet as a separate amount, although it need not be shown under that name. [CA85 4 Sch 34(2)]. This concession is necessary for several reasons. For example, where current cost financial statements are being prepared the revaluation reserve may be described as the unrealised current cost reserve.

16.240 It should also be noted that sometimes a company's articles of association will govern the way in which the company operates its revaluation reserve and these articles may stipulate also the name of the reserve. Consequently, the company should use that name in its financial statements. Articles of this nature are commonly found in investment companies and pension funds.

16.241 The question of whether a revaluation surplus or deficit is realised or unrealised is considered in chapter 23.

Taxation consequences

16.242 The Act requires the taxation implications of a revaluation to be noted in the financial statements. [CA85 4 Sch 34(4)].

16.243 This does not mean that there must be a statement of whether the amount is taxable or allowable under tax legislation. It means that there must be an explanation of the tax effect of the revaluation.

16.244 The tax effect will often be deferred until a later period. FRS 19 says that a timing difference will arise when an asset is revalued in the financial statements, but the revaluation gain becomes taxable only if and when the asset is sold. However, deferred tax should not be recognised unless, by the balance sheet date, the reporting entity has entered into a binding agreement to sell the revalued asset and has recognised the gain or loss expected to arise on sale. Deferred tax should not be recognised when the asset is revalued or sold if, on the basis of all available evidence, it is more likely than not that the taxable gain will be rolled over, being charged to tax only if and when the asset into which the gain has been rolled is sold. [FRS 19 paras 2, 14, 15].

16.245 Where, in accordance with FRS 19, provision has not been made on revalued assets because the conditions for providing, as described above, have not been met, a company should disclose an estimate of the tax that could be payable or recoverable if the assets were sold at the values shown, the circumstances in which the tax would be payable or recoverable and an indication of the amount that might be payable or recoverable in the foreseeable future. Where deferred tax has not been provided, because rollover relief is expected to be available, this disclosure is replaced by disclosure of the conditions that will have to be met to obtain the rollover relief and an estimate of the tax that would become payable if those conditions were not met. [FRS 19 para 64].

16.246 Compliance with the disclosure requirements of FRS 19 will ensure compliance with paragraph 34(4) of Schedule 4.

Depreciation

Introduction

16.247 Both FRS 15 and the Act require the depreciation of tangible fixed assets. The objective is to reflect in operating profit the cost of use of the tangible fixed assets in the period.

16.248 Depreciation applies to all tangible fixed assets, whether held at historical cost or current value, with two exceptions:

- Investment properties, which are not depreciated in accordance with SSAP 19, 'Accounting for investment properties', by invoking the true and fair override of the Act's requirements.
- Tangible fixed assets where it can be demonstrated that depreciation is immaterial.

Definition of depreciation

16.249 Although depreciation is not defined in the Act, it is defined in FRS 15 as:

> *"The measure of the cost or revalued amount of the economic benefits of the tangible fixed asset that have been consumed during the period."*

As explained in FRS 15:

> *"Consumption includes the wearing out, using up or other reduction in the useful economic life of a tangible fixed asset whether arising from use, effluxion of time or obsolescence through either changes in technology or demand for the goods and services produced by the asset."* [FRS 15 para 2].

16.250 Further guidance is given in FRS 15 about the factors to be taken into account when determining the depreciation of a tangible fixed asset, as follows:

- The expected use of the asset by the entity. This is the principal factor and is generally assessed by reference to the asset's expected capacity or physical output.
- The expected physical deterioration of the asset through use or the passing of time (that is, 'wear and tear'), when the asset is both in use and idle. This will depend upon how well the asset is maintained and repaired throughout its life.
- Economic and technological obsolescence. The asset itself or the product or service generated by the asset may become economically or technologically obsolete by being superseded by new or more advanced products. Similarly, changes in market demand may render an asset economically obsolete, for example changes in fads and trends or competitor actions.
- Legal or similar limits on the use of the asset, for example the expiry of a patent, licence or lease.

[FRS 15 para 80].

16.251 Notably, FRS 15 does not mention the financing of an asset as a factor that should be taken into account when determining its depreciation.

Determination of useful economic life and residual value

16.252 Depreciation is calculated by allocating the cost or revalued amount of a tangible fixed asset less its estimated residual value (that is, its 'depreciable amount') on a systematic basis over its useful economic life. [CA85 4 Sch 18; FRS 15 paras 2, 77].

16.253 The allocation of depreciation to a period is recognised in the profit and loss account, as part of operating profit, unless it is permitted to be included in the carrying amount of another asset. This will only occur when depreciation is included in stock or work-in-progress as part of an allocation of overheads, in accordance with SSAP 9, 'Accounting for stock and long-term contracts', or when it forms part of the cost of a tangible fixed asset. For example, a mining company may purchase earth moving equipment for the purpose of excavating a new mine. It is, therefore, a directly attributable cost of the mine and the depreciation charge of the equipment should be capitalised as part of the cost of the mine.

16.254 Useful economic life is defined in FRS 15 as *"...the period over which the entity expects to derive economic benefit from that asset"*. [FRS 15 para 2]. Note that if an entity intends to hold a tangible fixed asset for the asset's whole economic life, then the asset would only be good for scrap, that is, it will have nil or a residual scrap value. However, the useful economic life of a tangible fixed asset to an entity may be less than the asset's total economic life, in which case the value of the asset at the end of that life will reflect the remaining economic life of the asset. This may occur because the asset has an alternative use at the end of the useful economic life to the entity, or because it is the entity's policy to dispose of its assets before they reach the end of their economic lives.

16.254.1 The requirement to allocate depreciation over the useful economic life was underlined by the FRRP in 2001 when it criticised the accounts of Wyevale Garden Centres plc. The FRRP press notice stated: *"The company's stated accounting policy in respect of short leasehold properties was not to provide any depreciation until the last ten years of the lease from which point the depreciable amount was written off over the remainder of the useful life of the lease. In respect of plant and equipment it was the company's policy not to commence depreciation until the accounting year following that in which the assets were acquired. In the Panel's view, neither of these policies complied with the requirements of FRS 15 as they did not result in depreciation charges throughout the economic lives of the assets"*.

Example

A company has a policy of not providing for depreciation on tangible assets capitalised in the year until the following year, but provides for a full year's depreciation in the year of disposal of an asset. Is this acceptable?

This is not acceptable as the requirement of FRS 15 is to allocate the depreciable amount of a tangible fixed asset on a systematic basis over its useful economic life. The depreciation method should reflect as fairly as possible the pattern in which the asset's economic benefits are consumed by the entity. This means that depreciation should commence as soon as the asset is brought into use. The same applies to amortisation of intangible fixed assets and goodwill. FRS 10 states *"Where goodwill and intangible assets are regarded as having limited useful lives, they should be amortised on a systematic basis over those lives"*. It goes on to say that the method of amortisation should be chosen to reflect the expected pattern of depletion of the goodwill or intangible asset.

[The next paragraph is 16.255.]

16.255 Residual value is defined in FRS 15 as *"...the net realisable value of an asset at the end of its useful economic life. Residual values are based on prices prevailing at the date of the acquisition (or revaluation) of the asset and do not take account of expected future price changes"*. [FRS 15 para 2].

16.256 The effect of this definition is that future inflation should not be taken into account when calculating an asset's residual value. Strictly, therefore, the value of the asset in question should be considered at the end of its useful economic life, but expressed in pounds of the date of acquisition or latest revaluation.

Example 1

An asset is bought for £1,000. Its estimated useful economic life is six years and its estimated residual value, based on prices prevailing at the date of acquisition, is £100. However, if future inflation is taken into account, the estimated residual value would be £400. The rule in FRS 15 would lead to a company making annual provisions for depreciation of £150 (assuming the straight-line method is used). At the end of the useful economic life, the asset would be written down to £100 and, if estimates proved correct, it would be sold for £400, resulting in a profit on sale of £300. Under the alternative (but not permissible) method — taking inflation into account — depreciation would have been charged at the rate of £100 a year and there would have been no profit or loss reported on sale.

The effect of the rule in the standard is that, in an inflationary environment, assets should be depreciated at a rate which is higher than the rate necessary to produce no profit or loss in the year of disposal. This effect may seem strange, although in support of the method required by the standard, it must be acknowledged that there is considerable difficulty in estimating future inflation and its effect on residual values, particularly in the present economic environment where some industries are experiencing deflation. It can also be argued that the gain (or loss) on disposal is a holding gain (or loss) on a fixed asset that should not be recognised in historical cost accounts until it is realised.

Example 2

The facts are the same as in the above example, except the company has a policy of revaluing its fixed assets. The asset is bought for £1,000 and its useful economic life is estimated at six years. The residual value is expected to be £100 based on prices prevailing at the date of acquisition, but if future inflation is taken into account the residual value is estimated to be £400. In this example, however, the asset is revalued in year three. The written down value at that point is £700 and the revalued amount is £900. Based on prices prevailing at the time of the revaluation the residual value is expected to be £150. Accordingly, depreciation for year three will be based on the revalued amount of £900 less the revised residual value of £150 divided by the remaining useful life. Depreciation for the year would, therefore, be £187. The increase in the depreciation charge of £37 is equal to the revaluation surplus of £200 less the increase in the residual value of £50 divided by the remaining life of four years, that is, £37.

Methods of depreciation

16.257 FRS 15 notes that there is a range of acceptable depreciation methods. Management should select the method regarded as most appropriate to the type of asset and its use in the business so as to allocate depreciation as fairly as possible over the useful economic life to reflect the pattern in which the economic benefits of the asset are consumed. [FRS 15 para 77]. This section describes some of the most common methods.

16.258 The FRS warns that the method chosen should result in a depreciation charge throughout the asset's useful economic life and not just towards the end of its useful economic life or when the asset is falling in value. [FRS 15 para 81]. Therefore, it is not acceptable (except where depreciation in the earlier years would be immaterial — see from para 16.279) just to depreciate a leasehold property, mine or landfill site in, say, the last 20 years of its useful economic life. This is because the asset is being used throughout the whole useful economic life and the allocation of depreciation should reflect that.

Straight line method

16.259 This is the most common method used in practice and should be used whenever the pattern of consumption of an asset's economic benefits is uncertain. The cost (or revalued amount — see para 16.268 below) less the estimated residual value is allocated over the useful economic life so as to charge each accounting period with the same amount.

Reducing balance method

16.260 This method is designed to charge higher amounts of depreciation in the earlier years of an asset's use, as follows:

Example

	£
Cost	125
Depreciation charge (20%)	25
Carrying amount at end of year 1	100
Depreciation charge (20% of 100)	20
Carrying amount at end of year 2	80
Depreciation charge (20% of 80)	16
Carrying amount at end of year 3	64
and so on	

16.261 This method is appropriate when the economic benefits of an asset decline as they become older, for example because the asset becomes less reliable and more likely to break-down, less capable of producing a high-quality product or less technologically advanced. Furthermore, where charges for repairs and maintenance of assets are higher in later years, the lower depreciation charge in the later years offsets the higher repair and maintenance costs.

Sum of the digits (or 'rule of 78')

16.262 This method is similar in its effect to the reducing balance method although the mechanics are different. If an asset is expected to last, say, 12 periods (years, months, etc), the digits 1 to 12 are added (total 78); the first period is charged with 12/78, the next period with 11/78 and so on — hence, the name 'rule of 78'.

Unit-of-production method

16.263 This method relates depreciation to the estimated production capability of an asset. The rate of depreciation per hour of usage or unit of production is given by dividing the depreciable amount by the estimated total service capability of the asset, measured in terms of hours or units. This method is sometimes employed when the usage of an asset varies considerably from period to period because, in these circumstances, it matches cost against revenue more satisfactorily. Examples of the types of asset that are often depreciated in this way are: for hourly rates — airline engines; and for unit of production — mineral resources.

Example 1

A machine cost £100,000 and its expected residual value is £10,000. The total usage of the machine is expected to be 500,000 hours. The depreciation rate per hour's usage is, therefore, £0.18 (£100,000 – £10,000 divided by 500,000).

Example 2

Exploration costs amounting to £5m are incurred in finding mineral reserves. The reserves are expected to be 5m tonnes. The rate of depreciation to be applied to the exploration costs is worked out as £1 per tonne. In the first year of production 200,000 tonnes are extracted and depreciation charged at £1 per tonne is £200,000.

Annuity method

16.264 The annuity method is not a commonly used method of depreciation and is rarely appropriate. It results in a depreciation charge that increases over time. Whilst paragraph 32 of FRS 10 specifically prohibits such methods for the amortisation of goodwill at present, FRS 15 is silent in respect of the use of the annuity method for the depreciation of tangible fixed assets.

16.265 The annuity method may be appropriate where an entity's rate of consumption of the economic benefits of an asset increases over its life. An example is where production begins at a low level, but builds up over time. However, such cases are rare in practice. In any event, the unit-of-production method of depreciation is probably more appropriate in these circumstances, as it reflects the consumption of an asset's economic benefit, since each homogeneous unit produced by the asset has the same value to the entity.

16.266 In certain circumstances, for example where an asset is leased to a third party under an operating lease, the economic benefits consumed by the lessor are not related to the units of production (or services) obtained from the physical asset. Instead, the profile of economic benefits of such an asset to the lessor is akin to that of a financial asset, in which case the overall performance may be more usefully measured using a method of depreciation that treats the asset as a monetary, as opposed to non-monetary, asset. Using the annuity method of depreciation produces results that, economically, are closer to the net constant rate of return on capital invested. This approach, however, is only permitted under the Finance & Leasing Associations' SORP, 'Accounting issues in the asset finance and leasing industry', provided that:

- The asset is let on a lease that is for a significant portion of the total economic life of the asset.
- The terms of the lease adequately protect the lessor against early cancellation.
- Adequate income is retained in the lease to cover future uncertainties in respect of the realisation of residual values.

[FLA SORP para 5.3.34].

The restrictions placed on the use of this method by the SORP mean that generally the method would not be appropriate for, say, assets held for short-term rentals such as motor vehicles or plant on hire.

16.267 It is sometimes argued, in respect of a wider range of assets, that the depreciation profile of an asset should reflect the cost of capital or, alternatively put, the time value of money, as well as the consumption of economic benefits of the asset. Where the entity consumes the economic benefits of an asset evenly over its useful economic life (for example, produces the same units of production each year), then the annuity method achieves the aim of also reflecting the effect of the cost of capital or time value of money in the depreciation profile of that asset. However, the appropriateness of such an approach has been a matter of hot debate under existing GAAP. As a consequence, the ASB issued an exposure draft of an amendment to FRS 15 and FRS 10 in June 2000, proposing to prohibit the use of interest methods of depreciation, such as the annuity method, for both tangible and intangible fixed assets, except in the limited circumstances described in paragraphs 16.265 and 16.266 above. The responses to this exposure draft are being considered by the ASB as part of its project on lease accounting.

Depreciation of revalued assets

16.268 With the exception of investment properties (see chapter 17), depreciation is required, by both FRS 15 and the Act, to be charged on revalued tangible fixed assets. The rules relating to depreciation of fixed assets that have been valued under the alternative accounting rules are essentially the same as those described above with the revalued amount being substituted for historical cost. The application of the rules for revalued assets is described in the following paragraphs.

16.269 Where an entity has revalued a tangible fixed asset in accordance with the alternative accounting rules in the Act, that value (rather than the historical cost) is to be (or else is to be the starting point for determining) the amount at which it discloses that asset in its financial statements. Accordingly, any references to cost in the Act's depreciation rules must be substituted by a reference to the value determined by the alternative accounting rules the company applied. [4 Sch 32(1)]. This means that, in determining the amount to be written off systematically over a tangible fixed asset's useful economic life, an entity must have regard to the asset's value determined according to the latest application of the alternative accounting rules, rather than to its historical cost.

16.270 FRS 15 states that ideally the average value of the asset for the period should be used as the basis for calculating the year's depreciation charge, but that in practice either the opening or closing balance may be used instead, provided that it is used consistently in each period. [FRS 15 para 79]. It is common to use the opening balance, together with the cost of subsequent additions, for determining the year's depreciation charge, which avoids the need to recalculate depreciation charged in the earlier part of the year, used, for example in interim reports. On this basis some might argue that until the year end valuation *"the* *most recently determined value"* would be the valuation carried out at the last year end and if depreciation is deemed to accrue evenly over the life of an asset, depreciation should be charged on that opening value plus additions throughout the year until the next valuation at the year end.

16.271 But the Act says that where the value of any fixed asset has been determined according to the alternative accounting rules, the amount of any provision for depreciation to be charged in the profit and loss account may be either the amount based on the valuation of the asset, or the amount based on its historical cost. However, where the amount so charged is based on historical cost, the difference between that charge and the charge based on the asset's valuation must be disclosed separately. It must be so disclosed either on the face of the profit and loss account or in the notes. [CA85 4 Sch 32(2),(3)]. This might appear to allow a company to either debit or credit the difference (as appropriate) direct to the revaluation reserve. This is, however, prohibited by FRS 15. [FRS 15 para 77].

16.272 FRS 15 echoes the Act's rules in most respects, but it requires that where an entity revalues assets, and gives effect to the revaluation in its financial statements, it should base the profit and loss charge for depreciation on the revalued amount. [FRS 15 para 79]. No depreciation previously charged should be written back to the profit and loss account on revaluation of an asset. The FRS states also that an increase in the value of an asset does not remove the necessity for a company to charge depreciation even where the market value of an asset is greater than its carrying amount. [FRS 15 para 78].

16.273 Consequently, it is clear that FRS 15 requires an entity to charge depreciation on the carrying amount of the revalued asset in the balance sheet and to charge it in its entirety to the profit and loss account. Thus, it is appropriate where a company revalues its assets at its year end to base the depreciation charge for the period on that revised amount.

16.274 The practice of 'split depreciation' where depreciation on the historical cost is charged to the profit and loss account, and depreciation on the revaluation is charged to the revaluation reserve is prohibited under FRS 15. [FRS 15, 'The development of the FRS, paras 42 to 47].

16.275 Whilst chapter 23 considers realised reserves and distributable profits in detail, it should be noted that section 275(2) of the Act has a bearing on the way in which companies should treat depreciation on revalued assets. This section says that if the revaluation of an asset produces an unrealised profit, then an amount equal to any excess depreciation charged as a result of the revaluation may be treated as a realised profit. This section is concerned only with the determination of distributable profits (and not with the accounting treatment of excess depreciation). Despite this, it means that where a company properly charges the whole of the depreciation based on the revalued assets to the profit and loss account, it may also transfer an amount equal to the excess depreciation from the revaluation reserve to the profit and loss account reserve, as noted in paragraph 16.235 above. Because the amount transferred from the revaluation reserve to the profit and loss account reserve represents a realised profit, this treatment does not contravene paragraph 34(3) of Schedule 4.

Component depreciation

16.276 FRS 15 requires that where a tangible fixed asset comprises two or more major components with substantially different useful economic lives, each component should be accounted for separately for depreciation purposes and depreciated over its useful economic life. The FRS makes it clear that this is a requirement in the case of assets where the components are clearly distinguishable such as land and buildings. In that example it states that land, with certain exceptions, normally has an indefinite useful life and is not depreciated, whereas buildings have a finite life and are depreciated. In other cases, where it is not so clear that an asset has separable components, there appears to be more choice. For example, the FRS states that another example of separable components that may have substantially different lives is the structure of a building and items within the structure such as general fittings. There is, therefore, a need for entities to review whether or not an asset has such separable components. If it decides it has, then separable components should be depreciated individually over their useful lives. [FRS 15 para 84].

16.277 Another example of the separable components approach is described above under 'subsequent expenditure' (see from para 16.130), where an example is of the lining of a blast furnace or major overhaul expenditure. In cases such as these, however, there is discretion given to the entity's management to decide whether or not to adopt the separate components approach, based on an analysis of various factors such as the materiality of the component and the degree of irregularity of replacement or overhaul expenditure.

16.278 The FRS notes, however, that it would not be appropriate to treat the trading potential associated with a property valued as an operational entity, such as a public house or hotel, as a separable component, where the trading potential is inherently inseparable from the asset to which it attaches. [FRS 15 para 85].

Non-depreciation of certain assets

16.279 Investment properties other than short leaseholds (20 years or less) are not depreciated. This is a requirement of SSAP 19, 'Accounting for investment properties', and is discussed in chapter 17.

16.280 However, for other tangible fixed assets, one issue that has caused debate and variations in practice over many years is whether, in some circumstances, it is appropriate to omit annual charges for depreciation in respect of certain assets. The issue is generally discussed in the context of buildings.

16.281 SSAP 12 was silent on the question of non-depreciation. However, in the accompanying Technical Release, the ASC referred to the general principle of SSAP 12 — that where a fixed asset has a finite useful economic life, its cost (or revalued amount) less residual value should be depreciated over that life — and acknowledged that there might be circumstances where following the principle rendered any depreciation charge unnecessary.

Example

A property costing £1m is bought in 19X6. Its estimated total useful economic life is 50 years. However, the company considers it likely that it will sell the property after 20 years. The estimated residual value in 20 years' time, based on 19X6 prices, is (a) £1m, (b) £900,000. A residual value that is the same as or close to original cost is likely to be rare, as it assumes that in 20 years' time potential purchasers would pay, for a 20 year old property, an amount similar to what they would pay for a new property.

In case (a), the company considers that the residual value will equal the cost. There is, therefore, no depreciable amount and depreciation is correctly zero.

In case (b) the company considers that the residual value will be £900,000 and the depreciable amount is, therefore, £100,000. Annual depreciation (on a straight line basis) will be £5,000 (1m — 900,000/20). Depending on the context, the annual depreciation charge of £5,000 may be immaterial and it may, therefore, be acceptable not to provide for depreciation of the property on those grounds. It is, however, necessary to consider the materiality of the cumulative depreciation as well as the depreciation in the year.

16.282 This example demonstrates two points mentioned in paragraphs 16.254 and 16.256 above.

- The useful economic life is defined in terms of the present owner; therefore, 20 years rather than 50 years is the relevant period.
- Residual value is defined as being based on prices prevailing at the date of acquisition (or revaluation), that is, excluding the effects of future inflation.

16.283 In this example, maintaining the asset to a high standard is not assumed. Maintenance is of course one of the factors that determines the estimated residual value and in practice is almost invariably quoted as the reason why the residual value of particular assets is expected to be at least as high, in terms of prices prevailing at the date of acquisition or revaluation, as the present carrying value. As explained in paragraph 16.288 below consideration should now also be given to whether the asset is likely to suffer from technological and economic obsolescence and whether, in practice, such assets have been sold in the past for at least the expected residual value, based on prices prevailing at the date of acquisition or revaluation.

Tangible fixed assets other than non-depreciable land

16.284 In the 'Development of the FRS' section of FRS 15, the ASB stated that it did not accept that the estimate of a tangible fixed asset's useful economic life could be extended without limit by maintenance. This is because the physical life of a tangible fixed asset other than non-depreciable land, cannot be infinite. At some point it will be more economic to scrap the physical asset and replace it with a new one. On the other hand, the standard acknowledges that for some, exceptional, assets the useful economic life may be extended to such a degree that any depreciation charge would be immaterial (for example, heritage properties and fine art). The FRS states that immateriality is the only permissible grounds for not charging depreciation.

16.285 For this reason the FRS contains two provisions. First, it states that subsequent expenditure (for example, maintenance) that maintains or enhances the previously assessed standard of performance does not remove the need to charge depreciation. [FRS 15 para 86]. Where subsequent expenditure extends the useful life or adds to the previously assessed economic benefits, the expenditure may be capitalised, but it is then depreciated over its useful economic life. [FRS 15 para 88]. The circumstances in which subsequent expenditure may be capitalised are described under 'Subsequent expenditure' above (see from para 16.130).

16.286 Secondly, the FRS introduces a requirement for impairment tests to be performed on a tangible fixed asset (other than non-depreciable land) in accordance with FRS 11 at the end of each reporting period where either:

- No depreciation charge is made, because it would be immaterial (either because of the length of the estimated remaining useful economic life or because the estimated residual value (as defined in para 16.255 above) of the tangible fixed asset is not materially different from the carrying amount of the tangible fixed asset).

- The estimated remaining useful economic life of the tangible fixed asset exceeds 50 years.

[FRS 15 para 89].

[The next paragraph is 16.288.]

16.288 In order to justify that depreciation is immaterial, reasonable assumptions and estimates of useful economic lives and residual values need to be made. The FRS states that conditions that might give rise to immaterial depreciation include:

- When the entity has a policy of regular maintenance and repair (charges for which are made to the profit and loss account) such that the tangible fixed asset is retained at its previously assessed standard of performance.

- When the tangible fixed asset is unlikely to suffer from technological or economic obsolescence (due to changes in demand for its products or services).

- Where estimated residual values are material:
  - the entity has a policy and practises the policy of disposing of similar assets well before the end of their useful lives; and

- the disposal proceeds of similar assets (excluding inflationary effects since acquisition or later revaluation) have not historically been materially less than their carrying values.

[FRS 15 para 91].

16.289 Furthermore, the FRS requires that where depreciation is judged to be immaterial the aggregate depreciation should be considered as well as the depreciation on individual assets. This would include considering the effect of cumulative uncharged depreciation on the balance sheet. [FRS 15 para 91]. The FRS states that the depreciation charge and the accumulated depreciation are only immaterial if they would not reasonably influence the decisions of a reader of the financial statements. [FRS 15 para 90].

16.290 The impairment reviews may be performed on groups of assets, forming income generating units, if it is impracticable to perform them on individual assets. After the first review, subsequent reviews need only be updated. [FRS 15 para 92]. It is only necessary to carry out enough work to justify that the assets are not impaired (that is, that recoverable amount is at least as much as the carrying amount). For example, if it is known that the net realisable value of an asset is greater than its carrying amount, then there is no need to perform value in use calculations.

16.290.1 On the introduction of FRS 15 many companies, which previously did not depreciate properties on the grounds of having maintained them to a high standard, began to depreciate their properties. The UITF in Abstract 23 clarified that a prior year adjustment to identify and separately depreciate components of an asset (on implementation of FRS 15) did not extend to the remainder of the asset. In respect of the remainder of the asset a change in useful economic life or residual value should be accounted for prospectively (see further paras 16.340 to 16.346 below).

[The next paragraph is 16.291.]

Non-depreciable land

16.291 Land is normally considered to be a non-depreciable asset, because it does not generally have a limited useful economic life. Therefore, annual impairment reviews are not required. Mineral bearing land, however, comprises two elements: the mineral reserves and the land itself. Mineral reserves are depreciated as they are extracted, whilst the land itself is not depreciated.

[The next paragraph is 16.293.]

Renewals accounting

16.293 A major problem which the ASB faced when developing FRS 12 and FRS 15 concerned the application of the principles in those standards to large infrastructure systems or networks, as typically found in the water industry.

Traditionally such networks had not been depreciated and instead provisions for maintenance had been established, which were designed to ensure that the infrastructure or network's useful economic lives were extended indefinitely. The charge to this renewals provision was based on the planned level of annual expenditure required to maintain the operating capacity or service capability of the infrastructure system. The provision, therefore, indicated the actual under spend, compared to plan. A prepayment indicated an overspend compared with planned expenditure.

16.294 This caused the standard setters problems, because FRS 12 prohibits provisions for future maintenance and FRS 15 requires assets with finite lives to be depreciated. However, if such provisions were not made the results shown for entities with large infrastructure or network assets would reflect a pattern of expenditure that would not match the actual plans and assumptions that underlay their economic performance.

16.295 A pragmatic solution is set out in FRS 15, which lays down detailed rules for accounting for tangible fixed assets within an infrastructure system or network. It is based on the principle that in a steady state system, the average level of expenditure to maintain the system is the best means available for determining the cost of consumption of economic benefits of the system to the entity, that is, depreciation.

16.296 Where major tangible fixed assets or components of fixed assets within such an infrastructure system or network have determinable finite lives the assets should be accounted for separately and depreciated over their useful economic lives. [FRS 15 para 97].

16.297 For the remaining tangible fixed assets within the infrastructure system or network, renewals accounting may be used to estimate the depreciation to be charged. This treatment may, however, only be adopted where:

- The infrastructure system or network as a whole is intended to be maintained at a specified level of service potential by continuing replacement and refurbishment of its components.
- The level of annual expenditure required to maintain the operating capacity or service capability of the infrastructure system is calculated from an asset management plan, which is certified by a person who is appropriately qualified and independent.
- The system or network is in a mature or steady state.

[FRS 15 para 97].

16.298 Where renewals accounting is adopted the level of annual expenditure that is needed to maintain the operating capacity or service capability of the infrastructure system is treated as depreciation for the period and is charged to the profit and loss account. The amount is then deducted from the carrying amount of the system and shown in arriving at accumulated depreciation. Actual expenditure is capitalised as part of the cost of the system. [FRS 15 para 98].

16.299 The treatment described above would risk overstating both cost and accumulated depreciation in the long run, if the carrying amount of that part of the infrastructure that is replaced or restored by subsequent expenditure is not removed. The standard, therefore, requires that this should be done. [FRS 15 para 99]. This will generally be achieved by applying estimates based on the percentage of the system that is replaced each year.

16.300 Where the renewals method is not adopted expenditure on maintaining the system should be charged to profit and loss account or capitalised as appropriate under the other provisions in the FRS. [FRS 15 para 99].

[The next paragraph is 16.302.]

Change in estimate of useful economic life

16.302 FRS 15 requires that the useful economic lives of assets should be reviewed at the end of each reporting period and, when necessary, revised. The net book amount is then written off over the revised remaining useful life. [FRS 15 para 93]. FRS 15, therefore, prohibits the practice of taking an adjustment to accumulated depreciation (commonly called 'backlog' depreciation) to the profit and loss account in the current period, where future results would be materially distorted.

16.303 An example that illustrates this treatment is as follows:

Example

A company purchased an asset on 1 January 19X0 for £100,000, and the asset had an estimated useful life of ten years and a residual value of nil. The company has charged depreciation using the straight-line method at £10,000 per annum. On 1 January 19X4, when the asset's net book value is £60,000, the directors review the estimated life and decide that the asset will probably be useful for a further four years and, therefore, the total life is revised to eight years. The company should amend the annual provision for depreciation to charge the unamortised cost (namely, £60,000) over the revised remaining life of four years. Consequently, it should charge depreciation for the next four years at £15,000 per annum.

16.304 An example of a company that has changed the useful economic lives and is depreciating the balance of the assets over the remaining useful life is given in Table 16.12.

Table 16.12— Cable & Wireless plc — Report and Accounts — 31 March 1993

Financial Overview (extract)

Depreciation

Our depreciation policies are reviewed on a regular basis against the background of rapidly changing technology and competitive developments. In recent years, there have been significant changes in submarine cable technology and markets. This is reflected in significantly lower unit costs and capacity availability. The Group has considerable investments in both analogue and digital cable systems which were being depreciated over a 25 year estimated useful economic life. In the case of analogue cables, revised lives have been established having regard to both known plans to lay digital cables over similar routings and the view that it would be prudent for all existing analogue cables to be fully depreciated by the year 2000. With regard to digital cables, depreciation will be based upon an estimated economic life of 15 years. This takes account of anticipated cost trends and the related cost benefit economics that will influence future cable replacement decisions.

14 Tangible fixed assets (extract)

During the year the Group revised the life of its cables and repeaters to take account of technological changes. The effect of this revision is an increase in the depreciation charge for the year of £11.6m.

16.305 If a tangible fixed asset is carried at valuation the FRS states that, particularly if it is valued at depreciated replacement cost, a reassessment of useful economic life may require that the asset be revalued. The revalued asset should then be depreciated over its revised useful economic life. [FRS 15 para 94].

Change in estimate of residual value

16.306 The FRS also requires that where residual value is material, it should be reviewed at the end of each reporting period to take account of reasonably expected technological changes, based on prices prevailing at the date of acquisition or subsequent revaluation. Any change in the estimate of residual value should be accounted for prospectively over the remaining useful life, unless, and to the extent that, the asset has been impaired at the balance sheet date (when the impairment should be charged to profit and loss account immediately). [FRS 15 para 95].

Change in method of providing depreciation

16.307 If there is a change from one *method* of providing depreciation to another, the remaining undepreciated cost (that is, the net carrying amount) of the asset should be written off over the remaining useful life on the new basis, commencing with the period in which the change is made. A change from one method of providing depreciation to another is permitted only if the new method will give a fairer presentation of the entity's results and financial position. A change of method does not constitute a change of accounting policy and, therefore, a prior period adjustment is not permissible. [FRS 15 para 82].

16.308 Consequently, in the example given above (but assuming that the life remains as ten years) the company may decide that, from 1 January 19X4, the sum-of-the-digits method of calculation would give a fairer presentation than the straight-line method. If so, the depreciation charge for 19X4 would be £17,143 (namely, £60,000 × 6/6+5+4+3+2+1), because the asset still has a remaining useful life of six years.

Disclosures

16.309 The disclosure requirements in FRS 15 incorporate the Act's disclosure requirements to give a table that explains the movements in cost, or revalued amount and depreciation. However, FRS 15 requires disclosures to be given for each class of tangible fixed assets adopted, which may result in a greater volume of disclosures particularly where a revaluation policy has been adopted.

16.310 FRS 15 requires the following disclosures for each class of assets:

- The depreciation methods used (for example, straight-line method or reducing balance method).
- The useful economic lives or the depreciation rates used.
- Total depreciation charged for the period.
- Where material the financial effect of a change during the period of either the estimate of useful economic lives or the estimate of residual values.
- Where there has been a change in the depreciation method used, the effect, if material, and the reason for change should be disclosed in the year of change.
- The cost or revalued amount at both the beginning and end of the financial year.
- The cumulative amount of provisions for depreciation or impairment at the beginning and end of the financial year.
- A reconciliation of the movements, separately disclosing additions, disposals, revaluations, transfers, depreciation, impairment losses, and reversals of past impairment losses written back in the period.
- The carrying amount (that is, net book amount) at the beginning and end of the financial year.

[FRS 15 paras 100, 102].

16.311 The Act also requires that disclosures in respect of land and buildings should include an analysis of freehold, long leasehold and short leasehold. [CA85 4 Sch 44]. For this purpose, a lease includes an agreement for a lease. It will be a long lease if it still has 50 years or more to run at the end of the financial year in question. Otherwise, it will be a short lease. [CA85 4 Sch 83]. Table 16.13 also illustrates these disclosures.

16.312 Although FRS 28, 'Corresponding amounts', requires comparative figures to be provided for every item included in a note to the financial statements, this requirement does not apply in respect of the disclosures discussed in paragraph 16.310. [FRS 28 para 11].

16.313 In addition, disclosures are required in respect of impairment, as set out in chapter 18, finance costs (from para 16.126), valuations (from para 16.204).

16.314 An example of the accounting policy note explaining the depreciation methods, useful economic lives or depreciation rates used is given in Table 16.13.

Table 16.13— Thorn Plc — Annual Report and Accounts — 31 March 1998

ACCOUNTING POLICIES (extract)
Depreciation (extract)

Depreciation of tangible fixed assets (other than rental equipment) is calculated on cost at rates estimated to write off the cost less the estimated residual value of the relevant assets by equal annual amounts over their expected useful lives; effect is given, where necessary, to commercial and technical obsolescence.

The annual rates used are:

Freehold buildings and long-term leasehold property	2%
Short-term leasehold property	Period of lease
Plant, equipment and vehicles	10 — 33 1/3%

Rental equipment (other than that on rent-to-own agreements) is depreciated at rates estimated to write off the cost to nil residual value by equal annual amounts over its estimated useful life, from the month of installation. Once commenced, depreciation is not suspended during off-lease periods. The estimated useful lives of rental equipment (other than that on rent-to-own agreements) are:

Colour television sets	5 — 6 years
Video recorder equipment	5 years
Domestic appliances	5 years
Personal computers	3 years

Rental equipment placed on rent-to-own agreements is fully depreciated over the expected life of those agreements, which range from one to five years.

Disposals of tangible fixed assets

Introduction

16.315 The treatment of the disposal of tangible fixed assets is set out in FRS 3, 'Reporting financial performance', and repeated in FRS 15. As well as dealing with the disposal of tangible fixed assets, this section also considers the treatment of intended disposals of tangible fixed assets.

Reporting gains and losses on disposal

16.316 FRS 15 repeats the requirement in FRS 3 (which is discussed in greater detail in chapter 8) that the profit or loss on disposal of a tangible fixed asset is the difference between the net sale proceeds and the net carrying amount, whether carried at historical cost or at a valuation. The profit or loss on disposal should be recognised in the profit and loss account for the period in which the disposal occurs. [FRS 3 para 21; FRS 15 para 72].

16.317 Profits or losses on disposal should be recognised in the profit and loss account as an exceptional item after operating profit. When the net amount is not material, but the gross profits or losses are material, the relevant heading should still appear on the face of the profit and loss account with a reference to a related note analysing the profits and losses. [FRS 3 para 20]. However, profits or losses on disposal that are in effect no more than normal adjustments to depreciation previously charged should be included in operating profit as part of the normal depreciation charge. [FRS 3 para 46].

16.318 FRS 15 also gives an example that relates to an asset that is destroyed, but for which insurance proceeds are received, which are used to buy a new asset. In such a case the destroyed asset is removed from the balance sheet and the resulting gain or loss (the difference between carrying amount and insurance proceeds) is recognised. The replacement asset is capitalised at cost in the normal way. [FRS 15 para 73]. A further example is given below.

Example

A company had plant and machinery in its books at £200,000. These were destroyed by fire. However, the assets were insured under a 'new for old' policy and were replaced by the insurance company with new machines that cost £2m. The machines were acquired directly by the insurance company and the company did not actually receive the £2m in cash.

This situation is, in substance, the same as if the company had received cash and invested it in new machinery, because the insurance company has merely acted as agent for the company, effectively buying the new assets on behalf of the company, with the company's cash. The company has earned the profit through paying premiums for the 'new for old' insurance policy. Therefore, the profit on disposal of the destroyed assets of £1.8m (that is, the difference between the £2m insurance proceeds and the carrying amount of the destroyed plant and machinery of £200,000) should be recognised in the profit and loss account as an exceptional item separately identified immediately after operating profit. The new machines are capitalised at £2m.

Revalued assets

16.319 As noted above, the treatment for revalued assets is the same as that for assets held at historical cost. Therefore, the profit and loss on disposal of a revalued asset (that is, the difference between sales proceeds and carrying amount) is recognised in the profit and loss account. Whilst being consistent with the treatment of assets held at historical cost, this leads to some peculiarities.

16.320 Consider, for example, an asset that is revalued each year based on current market values. Since acquisition the asset has only increased in value and, therefore, on each revaluation, a revaluation gain is recognised in the statement of total recognised gains and losses (in accordance with the requirements explained in para 16.216). In the year of disposal, the asset has increased in value even further, but rather than recognising this element of the gain in the statement of total recognised gains and losses, as in previous years, it is required to be recognised in the profit and loss account. This seems at odds with the fact that both the revaluation gains and the gain on disposal arose solely as a result of the entity holding onto the asset and price movements.

16.321 The proposals in FRED 17, 'Measurement of tangible fixed assets', that preceded FRS 15, attempted to resolve this peculiarity, by proposing that an asset should be revalued to the anticipated disposal proceeds just prior to its disposal. Accordingly, the resulting gain or loss from this 'deathbed' revaluation would be recognised in the profit and loss account or the statement of total recognised gains and losses as though it were simply a gain or loss on revaluation. However, this proposal did not survive in the final FRS, mainly because it led to further inconsistencies elsewhere.

16.322 Paragraph 34(3) of Schedule 4 allows a company to make a transfer from the revaluation reserve to the profit and loss account where the amount transferred represents a realised profit. Consequently, when a company sells a revalued asset, the Act permits it to credit the profit on the sale (including the amount of the realised revaluation surplus) to the profit and loss account. This would have the effect that the profit or loss on disposal would be the same as that recognised had the asset not been revalued, but held at historical cost. However, this treatment is prohibited by FRS 3. This is because under FRS 3 performance is measured by reference to total recognised gains for the year, which includes the profit or loss for the year and the other gains and losses which have been taken direct to the statement of total recognised gains and losses. Therefore, if a gain has been recognised when an asset was initially revalued, that gain should not be recognised a second time in either the profit and loss account or the statement of total recognised gains and losses, when the asset is sold.

16.323 Any revaluation surplus in the revaluation reserve that is realised on sale should, therefore, be transferred directly to the profit and loss account reserve and not to the profit and loss account for the year. This is in accordance with the requirement to reduce the revaluation reserve where it is no longer necessary for the purpose of the valuation method that the company has adopted, as noted in paragraph 16.237 above. [CA85 4 Sch 34(3)].

16.324 In order to deal with the wishes of some users to see what profits or losses on disposals of revalued assets would be if measured by reference to historical cost, the ASB introduced a requirement in FRS 3 for a note of historical cost profits and losses, where the effect was material. The information provided in such a note enables users to see what profits and losses have been made measured against historical costs rather than revalued amounts.

Intended disposal of fixed assets

16.325 Where a company intends to dispose of a fixed asset, the asset is no longer intended for use on a continuing basis in the company's activities. Consequently, it may be inferred that the asset no longer satisfies the criteria for classification as a fixed asset. Accordingly, in such circumstances, some entities consider that the asset needs to be reclassified as a current asset.

16.326 Where assets are transferred from fixed to current assets, it is not appropriate to include the asset in the balance sheet at an amount that exceeds cost, unless it is disclosed as a current asset investment. This is because the alternative accounting rules can only be adopted for stocks and current asset investments and not other current asset items. [CA85 4 Sch 31(4),(5)]. However, SSAP 9 does not allow stocks to be stated at current cost in either historical cost financial statements or financial statements modified to include the revaluation of only certain assets.

16.327 Not all companies that intend to dispose of fixed assets follow the transfer to current assets approach. As an alternative treatment, some companies consider it more appropriate to retain the asset within fixed assets under a new sub-heading 'assets held for resale'. Moreover, in many situations assets that are disposed of quickly, rather than held for disposal for some time, are simply retired from the sub-heading in which they have been held during their life.

16.328 Deciding to dispose of an asset by itself, or as part of a larger reorganisation or disposal of a business, may trigger an impairment review. If the asset held for disposal is impaired then the question arises as to whether the resultant loss is treated as though it were a loss on disposal or simply as an impairment. As discussed in chapter 18, if an impairment loss is first identified when the asset is put up for sale and is attributable to that decision, then the loss is treated as a loss on disposal and presented as an exceptional item immediately after operating profit. However, if the impairment loss is identified earlier, that is before the asset was intended for disposal, then the loss would be presented as part of operating profit as an impairment loss.

Capital grants

16.329 The accounting options available in respect of grants are dealt with in detail in discussing revenue recognition in chapter 9. This chapter, therefore, considers only grants awarded to companies because of their investment in fixed assets.

SSAP 4

16.330 Grants received against capital investment are dealt with in SSAP 4, 'Accounting for government grants'. The original version of the standard, as published in 1974, was developed following the introduction of Regional Development Grants by the Industry Act 1972. As such, however, its scope was relatively limited, with its main requirement being that companies should credit the grant received to revenue over the useful life of the related asset. In effect, this could be achieved in one of two ways:

- The grant could be deducted from the cost of the asset thereby reducing the depreciation charged to revenue (but see discussion below on legal requirements now prohibiting this treatment for Schedule 4 companies).

- The grant could be treated as a deferred credit of which a proportion would be credited to revenue annually. In this situation, the amount of the deferred credit should be shown separately on the balance sheet if material.

16.331 SSAP 4 was revised in 1990, following the issue of ED 43 in 1988 whose proposals it broadly adopted. One of the main reasons for the revision was the proliferation of types of grant that had occurred since the standard's original publication. In particular, there had been a growth not only in the range of both capital and revenue grants, but also in hybrid varieties whereby a grant might be partly capital and partly revenue in nature. The revised standard, therefore, sought to provide broader guidance on the area of grant recognition and accounting.

16.332 When the ASC first published ED 43, it proposed to remove the option to account for capital grants by deducting them from the cost of the related asset. This was proposed partly to further the ASC's objective of narrowing the differences in accounting treatment and partly on an interpretation of company law.

16.333 Schedule 4 to the Act requires that (subject to any provision for depreciation or diminution in value) fixed assets should be stated, under the historical cost accounting rules, at their purchase price or production cost. The statutory definitions of purchase price or production cost make no provision for any deduction from that amount in respect of a grant or subvention from a third party. The references are to paragraphs 17 and 26 of Schedule 4 respectively. These requirements could be read as prohibiting the deduction of capital-based grants from the cost of fixed assets, a treatment previously permitted by SSAP 4. In addition, the general rule that amounts in respect of items representing assets or income may not be set off against amounts in respect of items representing liabilities or expenditure can be interpreted as specifically forbidding this practice.

16.334 The proposal in ED 43 had the DTI's support, which expressed the view that the deduction from the cost method is contrary to paragraph 17 of Schedule 4. The DTI also indicated that the 'true and fair override' could not be held to apply, since the deferred income method is capable of giving a true and fair view. In effect, the override could only be invoked in specific, exceptional circumstances where the deferred income method failed to give a true and fair view, rather than in a blanket fashion to circumvent a particular legal problem.

16.335 Reactions to ED 43 were generally unfavourable, with many commentators opposing the proposal to remove the option allowed in the original version of SSAP 4. Their rationale was that the deduction from cost method was both expedient and generally acceptable in practice, while the interpretation of company law was also considered to be questionable.

16.336 In the face of this opposition, the ASC decided that the proposal in ED 43 to remove the option in SSAP 4 should be withdrawn. Consequently, the existing provisions, whereby both the deferred income and deduction from cost methods were permitted, were retained. In adopting this stance, the ASC recognised that, from a practical perspective, not all reporting entities are governed by Schedule 4. Thus, there was no legal reason why those other entities should not retain the option. However, the ASC also recognised that most reporting entities are governed by Schedule 4 to the Act, so Counsel's opinion on the legality of the deduction from cost method was sought to clarify the position for such entities.

16.337 Counsel reiterated the DTI's opposition to the deduction from cost method and concluded that this treatment is not justifiable for companies that follow Schedule 4, even as a permitted option. Nor would the Act's requirements be satisfied by the disclosure in the notes to the financial statements of the gross cost of the related asset before deduction of the grant, together with the amount of the grant deducted.

16.338 As a result, the revised standard was issued in a way that continues to allow both treatments as being acceptable in practice and capable of giving a true and fair view. However, the standard also warns that Counsel's opinion is that the deduction from cost method is unlawful and cannot be used by enterprises to which Schedule 4 to the Act applies.

Disclosure requirements

16.339 Where an enterprise receives grants, SSAP 4 (revised) requires the following disclosures:

- The accounting policy adopted for government grants.
- The effect of government grants on the results and/or the enterprise's financial position.
- Where an enterprise is in receipt of government assistance other than grants that have a material effect on its results, the nature of the assistance and, where possible, an estimate of the financial effects.
- Where applicable, the potential liabilities to repay grants.

[SSAP 4 paras 28, 29].

16.340 In this context, 'government' is defined in the broader context to include government and inter-governmental agencies and similar bodies whether local, national or international. [SSAP 4 para 21]. Thus, the basic requirements of the standard are interpreted to encompass grants made by such organisations as the National Lottery, the Foundation for Sport and the Arts and the Football Trust.

Grants on non-depreciable fixed assets

16.341 While the general rule is that tangible fixed assets are depreciated over their estimated useful life to reduce them to their residual value, there are instances where assets are not depreciated on the grounds that they do not have a finite life. The commonest asset to which this applies is freehold land.

16.342 The essential difficulty facing such companies is that, should they receive grants on such assets, it would not make sense to employ the deferred income method of accounting. This is because such assets have an infinite life and, therefore, there is no appropriate method for releasing the grant. In effect, it would never be released. The deferred income figure on the balance sheet would simply get bigger and bigger and would become meaningless. Faced with this situation, recipients of grants appear to have no alternative to employing the deduction from cost method of accounting. In so doing they are, in effect, invoking the true and fair override.

16.343 A similar situation arises with certain large infrastructure assets (for example, utility networks). Where the depreciation charge on these assets is calculated using renewals accounting (see para 16.293 onwards) and the assets do not have determinable finite lives, then no basis exists on which to recognise the grants as deferred income. Consequently, grants relating to these infrastructure assets are deducted from the cost or valuation of those assets, with use of the true and fair override.

Chapter 17

Investment properties

	Page
Introduction	17001
SSAP 19	17001
Accounting requirements	17001
Balance sheet presentation	17005
Interaction with the Companies Act 1985	17006
Measurement at market value	17006
True and fair override	17007
Investment revaluation reserve	17008
Investment properties — diminutions in value	17009
Investment properties — temporary diminutions in value	17009
Investment properties — permanent diminutions in value	17009
Negative revaluation reserves	17011
Owner-occupied properties	17011
Disclosures	17011

Chapter 17

Investment properties

Introduction

17.1 The objective of SSAP 19 is to set out the requirements for the accounting treatment and disclosures for investment property and these are the areas this chapter covers.

[The next paragraph is 17.3.]

SSAP 19

17.3 While the Act does not use the term 'investment property', SSAP 19 defines it as an interest in land and/or buildings, where:

- the construction work and development have been completed; and
- the interest is held for its investment potential, with any rental income being negotiated at arm's length.

[SSAP 19 para 7].

17.4 In addition to this definition, the standard indicates that the following properties should not be treated as investment properties:

- A property that is owned and occupied by a company for its own purposes.
- A property that is let to, and occupied by, another group company.

[SSAP 19 para 8].

17.5 On the other hand, the standard is relatively generous in terms of its scope, since it does not limit its application to companies such as investment trusts and property investment companies, whose main or sole activity is the holding of investments. Rather it also brings into its scope any investment properties held by companies whose main activity is other than investment holding and management.

Accounting requirements

17.6 The key requirements of the standard are that:

- Investment properties should not be depreciated, but should be included in the balance sheet at their open market value. The exception to this occurs when the investment properties are held on leases that have less than twenty years to run. In such instances, they should be depreciated over the remaining term of the lease. [SSAP 19 paras 11, 12]. Note that FRS 15 excludes investment properties from its scope and, therefore, the exemption from depreciation in SSAP 19 is still applies.

- The carrying value of investment properties and the investment valuation reserve should be displayed prominently in the financial statements. [SSAP 19 para 15].

- Changes in the value of investment properties should not be taken to the profit and loss account, but should be taken to the investment revaluation reserve. This is subject to an exception which is discussed from paragraph 17.17. [SSAP 19 para 13].

17.7 SSAP 19's requirement to include investment properties in the balance sheet at their open market value has been modified by the publication of UITF Abstract 28, 'Operating lease incentives'. Operating lease incentives are sometimes given to a lessee by a lessor to encourage the lessee to enter into a rental agreement with the lessor. These incentives take a variety of forms including rent free periods and contributions towards fit-out costs. The abstract, which is discussed more fully in chapter 16, requires lessors to treat the aggregate cost of operating lease incentives as a reduction of rental income. Therefore, the cost of the incentives should be allocated over the lease term or a shorter period ending on a date from which it is expected that the prevailing market rental will be payable. [UITF 28 para 15]. Any accrued rent receivable would be recognised as a separate asset.

17.8 Also the open market valuation of an investment property may also take into account the benefit of any such incentives. To avoid double-counting the same benefit in the balance sheet, the abstract, therefore, requires that the value at which the investment property is stated in the balance sheet should be adjusted so that it excludes any amount that is reported as a separate asset under the abstract. [UITF 28 para 16]. The result of this is that an investment property would be recognised in the balance sheet at an amount equal to open market value less the accrued rent receivable debtor.

Example

An investment property is leased to a tenant for 10 years. A rent free period is granted for the first year of the lease, as an incentive, and the rent is fixed at £1.11m per annum for the remaining nine years of the lease. This is equivalent to a rent receivable of £1m per annum for 10 years. Therefore, at the end of the first year, the lessor would have recognised rental income of £1m and accrued a rent receivable debtor of £1m, in accordance with Abstract 28. The open market value of the property at the end of year one will reflect the income stream under the lease of £1.11m per annum for nine years and the residual value of the property at the end of the lease period. For simplicity ignoring the residual value of the property at the end of the lease and the effects of discounting, the open market value of the property at the end of year one would be £10m to reflect the future cash inflows from the lease. However, in the balance sheet the investment property would be revalued to £9m, to reflect the £1m that has already been recognised as a separate asset. If the open market value of the property at the beginning of the lease was £10m, this would represent a downward revaluation, which, unless it was regarded as a permanent diminution in value, would be recognised in the STRGL.

17.9 In practice arriving at the open market value of a property is a complex and judgmental exercise. It will, therefore, be necessary to understand how the valuation has been derived and how the effect of any incentive has been reflected in the valuation to determine whether, and for how much, the valuation needs adjusting to compensate for the separate accrued rent receivable asset.

17.10 In Table 17.1, Hammerson plc's 1997 financial statements provide an illustration of investment property accounting in practice (before the introduction of UITF Abstract 28).

Table 17.1 — Hammerson plc — Annual Report — 31 December 1997

Notes to the Accounts (extract)

12 LAND AND BUILDINGS (extract)

	Book value		Cost	
	1997	1996	**1997**	1996
	£m	£m	**£m**	£m
Investment properties				
Fully developed properties	**1,840.5**	1,776.9	**1,401.5**	1,518.7
Properties held for or in the course of development	**94.6**	63.3	**94.6**	63.3
	1,935.1	1,840.2	**1,496.1**	1,582.0

Fully developed properties are stated at market value as at 31 December 1997, valued in each region by professionally qualified external valuers, Jones Lang Wootton, Chartered Surveyors. In the United Kingdom the valuation was performed jointly with Donaldsons, Chartered Surveyors, who also acted in the capacity of external valuers. The valuations have been prepared in accordance with the Appraisal and Valuation Manual of The Royal Institution of Chartered Surveyors.

As at 31 December 1997 the market value of properties held for development was £121.3m (1996: £66.6m). The total amount of interest included in development properties at 31 December 1997 was £3.6m (1996: £2.3m). Included within properties held for development is the group's 50% share in The Oracle Limited Partnership, a joint arrangement with Abu Dhabi Investment Authority for the development of The Oracle Shopping Centre, Reading.

Should the group's properties be sold at their market value a tax liability of approximately £83m (1996: £78m) would arise. No provision for this contingent liability has been made as it is not expected that any liability will arise in the foreseeable future.

A geographical analysis of the group's properties is provided on page 59.

	Freeholds £m	Long leaseholds £m	Short leaseholds £m	Total £m
Movements in the year				
Balance 1 January 1997	1,084.4	750.9	4.9	1,840.2
Exchange adjustment	(41.2)	—	(0.2)	(41.4)
Additions at cost	63.7	38.7	—	102.4
Disposals at valuation	(87.6)	(24.8)	—	(112.4)
Development outgoings capitalised	1.9	0.5	—	2.4
Revaluation surplus	41.4	101.3	1.2	143.9
Balance 31 December 1997	**1,062.6**	**866.6**	**5.9**	**1,935.1**

20 RESERVES

	Share premium account £m	Revaluation reserve £m	Other reserves £m	Profit and loss account £m
Balance 1 January 1997	524.2	212.0	1.5	292.3
Exchange adjustment	—	4.8	—	(10.4)
Premium on issue of shares	2.0	—	—	—
Adjustment in respect of scrip dividends	(0.3)	—	—	5.4
Surplus arising on revaluation of properties	—	140.0	—	—
Revaluation of properties in associated undertaking	—	(1.2)	—	—
Transfer to profit and loss account on disposal	—	35.5	—	(35.5)
Retained profit for the year	—	—	—	11.1
Balance 31 December 1997	**525.9**	**391.1**	**1.5**	**262.9**

17.11 SSAP 19 requires the names of the persons making the valuation, or particulars of their qualifications, to be disclosed, accompanied by an explanation of the bases of valuation applied. [SSAP 19 para 12]. Where the impact of UITF Abstract 28 is material this should be reflected in the explanation of the bases of valuation applied. Furthermore, although not a specific requirement, entities may wish to consider disclosing the amount of the rent receivable debtor so that the full open market value of their investment property portfolio can be derived from the information given in the financial statements. [SSAP 19 para 12].

17.12 Moreover, in accordance with SSAP 19, where the valuer is an officer or employee of the company or group which owns the property, that fact should be disclosed. Hence, whilst the standard does not require the valuation to be made by qualified or independent valuers, there is an underlying assumption that the persons responsible for making the valuation are sufficiently knowledgeable about property valuation principles to enable them to undertake the valuation in a competent manner. The explanatory note to the standard indicates that where investment properties represent a substantial proportion of the total assets of a major company (for example, a listed company), the valuation should normally be carried out:

- Annually by persons holding a recognised professional qualification and having recent post-qualification experience in the location and category of properties concerned.
- At least every five years by an external valuer.

[SSAP 19 para 6].

Balance sheet presentation

17.13 A further issue that arises with investment properties is whether they should be treated as tangible fixed assets or as fixed asset investments. While the description of such properties as 'investment' and their non-depreciation for that reason might suggest that they should be included within the 'investments' category, neither the Act nor SSAP 19 gives any clear guidance on this question. Consequently, both practices are adopted in practice. In Table 17.2, Great Universal Stores P.L.C, for example, includes its investment properties with fixed assets as part of its property portfolio, specifying also the valuation of investment properties and the names of the valuers.

Table 17.2— The Great Universal Stores P.L.C. — Annual Report — 31 March 1999

NOTES TO THE FINANCIAL STATEMENTS (extract)

15. TANGIBLE FIXED ASSETS	*Freehold properties*	*Leasehold properties*		*Plant vehicles & equipment*	*Assets in course of construction*	*Total*
		Long leasehold	*Short leasehold*			
The Group	*£m*	*£m*	*£m*	*£m*	*£m*	*£m*
Cost or valuation						
At 31 March 1998	242.7	20.9	24.9	741.8	8.8	1,039.1
Movements in year:						
Difference on exchange	2.7	0.5	0.9	6.8	0.4	11.3
Acquisition of subsidiaries	24.6	53.6	0.9	275.6		354.7
Additions	19.2	5.8	5.0	204.0	23.3	257.3
Transfers	5.1		5.8	(4.2)	(6.7)	–
Sales	(6.6)	(0.3)	(0.9)	(98.0)		(105.8)
Transfer to revaluation reserve	(0.1)	0.3	(5.0)			(4.8)
At 31 March 1999	287.6	80.8	31.6	1,126.0	25.8	1,551.8
Cost	158.2	67.9	30.6	1,126.0	25.8	1,408.5
Valuation — trading properties (1996)	120.5	9.8	1.0			131.3
Valuation — trading properties (1998)	3.4					3.4
Valuation — investment properties (1999)	5.5	3.1				8.6
	287.6	80.8	31.6	1,126.0	25.8	1,551.8

Depreciation						
At 31 March 1998	43.5	2.1	10.3	433.6	–	489.5
Movements in year:						
Difference on exchange	1.2	0.1	0.4	5.1		6.8
Acquisition of subsidiaries	3.7	15.1		158.7		177.5
Transfers	0.2		3.0	(3.2)		–
Provided in year	5.1	2.9	3.0	141.5		152.5
Sales	(21)	(0.1)	(0.7)	(69.9)		(72.8)
Transfer to revaluation reserve			(0.7)			(0.7)
At 31 March 1999	51.6	20.1	15.3	665.8	–	752.8
Net Book Value at 31 March 1999	236.0	60.7	16.3	460.2	25.8	799.0
Net Book Value at 31 March 1998	199.2	18.8	14.6	308.2	8.8	549.6

Assets of £155.8m (1998 £135.9m) are held for hire under operating leases, comprising cost or valuation of £216.2m (1998 £181.6m) and related depreciation of £60.4m (1998 £45.7m).

The net book value of plant, vehicles and equipment at 31 March 1999 includes £40.1m (1998 £65.3m) acquired under finance leases.

Investment properties were revalued as at 31 March 1999, in accordance with the Group's accounting policy, by external valuers, Colliers Erdman Lewis Limited, Chartered Surveyors. This valuation was carried out in accordance with the Royal Institution of Chartered Surveyors Appraisal and Valuation Manual.

On the historical cost basis the net book value of properties carried at valuation is £80.6m (1998 £78.7m), comprising cost of £104.4m (1998 £102.6m) and related depreciation of £23.8m (1998 £23.9m).

17.14 A number of other companies account for such properties within investments. This seems to be the common practice of entities such as general insurers with large investment portfolios and relatively small levels of tangible fixed assets for consumption by the business.

Interaction with the Companies Act 1985

Measurement at market value

17.14.1 The Companies Act 1985 permits tangible fixed assets (which include investment properties) to be measured under the alternative accounting rules at *"a market value determined as at the date of their last valuation or at their current cost*". [CA85 4 Sch 31(2)]. The Act requires that, where the alternative accounting rules are applied, gains and losses resulting from movements in the assets' value are recognised in the revaluation reserve. [CA85 4 Sch 34(1)]. This is consistent with the requirements of SSAP 19.

17.14.2 SI 2004/2947, 'The Companies Act 1985 (International Accounting Standards and Other Amendments) Regulations 2004', introduced provisions into UK GAAP to allow investment properties to be measured at *fair value* with movements in fair value recognised in the profit and loss account. However, this accounting is not consistent with the requirements of SSAP 19 (it was introduced to facilitate the convergence of UK GAAP with IFRS) and so should not be applied.

[The next paragraph is 17.15.]

True and fair override

17.15 Although non-depreciation of investment properties is required by SSAP 19, it may be a departure from the Act in certain circumstances. Such circumstances would include where the amount of depreciation would be material. FRS 18, 'Accounting policies', sets out the disclosure requirements in financial statements where the true and fair override has been applied. These are fully discussed in chapter 2. The key disclosures are:

- A clear statement that there has been a departure from the Act and that the departure is necessary to give a true and fair view.
- A statement of the treatment which the Act would normally require in the circumstances and a description of the treatment actually adopted.
- A statement as to why the treatment prescribed would not give a true and fair view.
- A description of how the position shown in the financial statements is different as a result of the departure, normally with quantification, except:
  - where quantification is already evident in the financial statements themselves (an example of which might be a presentation rather than a measurement matter, such as an adaptation of the headings in the Act's format requirements not covered by para 3(3) of Schedule 4); or
  - whenever the effect cannot reasonably be quantified, in which case the directors should explain the circumstances.

[FRS 18 para 62.]

17.16 In Table 17.3, Trafalgar House Public Limited Company's 1994 financial statements provide a clear example of such a disclosure, including a statement that the effect of non-depreciation cannot be quantified.

Table 17.3 — Trafalgar House Public Limited Company — Report and Accounts — 30 September 1994

Principal accounting policies (extract)

d) Fixed assets (extract)

Investment properties

Investment properties are included in the balance sheet at their open market value at the balance sheet date on the basis of an annual professional valuation.

e) Depreciation (extract)

Depreciation is not provided on investment properties. This treatment, as regards certain of the company's investment properties, may be a departure from the requirements of the Companies Act concerning depreciation of fixed assets. However, these properties are not held for consumption but for investment and the directors consider that systematic annual depreciation would be inappropriate. The accounting policy adopted is therefore necessary for the accounts to give a true and fair view. Depreciation or amortisation is only one of the many factors reflected in the annual valuation and the amount which might otherwise have been shown cannot be separately identified or quantified.

Investment revaluation reserve

17.17 The standard states that:

"Subject to paragraph 14 below, changes in the market value of investment properties should not be taken to the profit and loss account but should be taken to the statement of total recognised gains and losses (being a movement on an investment revaluation reserve), unless a deficit (or its reversal) on an individual investment property is expected to be permanent, in which case it should be charged (or credited) in the profit and loss account of the period. In the special circumstances of investment companies as defined in companies legislation (as mentioned in paragraphs 31 and 66 of FRS 3 'Reporting Financial Performance') and of property unit trusts it may not be appropriate to deal with such deficits in the profit and loss account. In such cases they should be shown only in the statement of total recognised gains and losses." [SSAP 19 para 13].

17.18 Paragraph 14 of the standard confirms that:

"Paragraph 13 does not apply to the financial statements of:

(a) insurance companies and groups (and consolidated financial statements incorporating such entities) where changes in the market value of investment properties (including those comprising assets of the long-term business) are included in the profit and loss account;

(b) pension funds where changes in the market value of investment properties are dealt with in the relevant fund account."

[The next paragraph is 17.20.]

Investment properties — diminutions in value

17.20 The rules in SSAP 19 relating to diminutions in value and described in paragraph 17.18 above differ from the rules relating to impairments in FRS 11 and FRS 15, which apply to other tangible fixed assets. The SSAP 19 rules retain the terminology of temporary and permanent diminutions used in the Act and follow the Act's requirements. The rules are described below.

Investment properties — temporary diminutions in value

17.21 When a company applies the alternative accounting rules of the Act, it *must* debit to the revaluation reserve those deficits that arise from a *temporary diminution* in value of a fixed asset (other than a fixed asset investment, see chapter 6). This is because it would seem that the Act does not permit such revaluation deficits to be charged to the profit and loss account (see chapter 16). The deficit would instead be disclosed in the statement of total recognised gains and losses.

17.22 On a revaluation that gives rise to deficits which are *temporary* (for example, the situation when a diminution arises as part of an annual revaluation exercise and there are no indications that any of the deficit is permanent), it is possible for these deficits to be taken to the revaluation reserve and, in effect, netted off against surpluses on other assets. If the net of surpluses and deficits results in an overall deficit on the revaluation reserve it used to be the case that this overall deficit was charged in the profit and loss account on the grounds of prudence. This is consistent with the treatment prescribed in SSAP 19, 'Accounting for investment properties'.

17.23 As noted above, SSAP 19 requires all changes in the market value of investment properties (including deficits) to be taken to the statement of total recognised gains and losses unless a deficit on an individual investment property was expected to be permanent, in which case it should be charged to the profit and loss account. As a result it is possible to have a negative investment revaluation reserve (see para 17.32).

Investment properties — permanent diminutions in value

17.24 The treatment of permanent diminutions in value of previously revalued assets is governed by paragraph 32 of Schedule 4 which, as described in chapter 16, requires that the rules relating to permanent diminutions should be applied by substituting the revalued amount for the historical cost of the asset.

17.25 The effect of this is that the amount of the permanent diminution includes not only the diminution below cost, but also the diminution in value between cost and revalued amount. Thus, for example, if an asset costing £100 has subsequently been revalued to £150 and then suffers a permanent diminution to £70, the amount of the permanent diminution under paragraph 32 of Schedule 4 is £80 (that is, £150 – £70) and not £30.

17.26 One view which follows from this is that the whole of the permanent diminution in value should be charged to the profit and loss account. Any previous revaluation surplus relating to the asset would then be transferred through reserves from the revaluation reserve to the profit and loss account reserve up to the amount of the permanent diminution. Thus, in the above example, £80 would be charged to the profit and loss account and the previous revaluation surplus of £50 would be transferred from revaluation reserve to profit and loss account reserve.

17.27 There is an alternative treatment of provisions for permanent diminution in value of previously revalued assets. The effect is that only that element of the diminution that represents the loss below cost is charged to the profit and loss account. There are two different technical routes through which this alternative treatment can be rationalised.

17.28 One route is to argue that when a permanent diminution occurs, it can be seen as the result of a valuation process that is governed by the rules in Schedule 4. Under this interpretation, the diminution in value from the previous revalued amount down to cost is seen as the result of a valuation which, in accordance with paragraph 34(1) of Schedule 4, should be taken to the revaluation reserve. Once this is done the asset is stated at cost, but there is still a permanent diminution in value which, under the historical cost accounting rules, must be taken to profit and loss account. [CA85 4 Sch 19(2)].

17.29 The second route is to argue as follows. The full amount of the permanent diminution in value is charged to the profit and loss account (that is, £80 in the example). [CA85 4 Sch 19(2)]. As noted above, paragraph 19(2) applies in the context of the historical cost rules, but it can be argued that it also applies in the context of the alternative accounting rules. However, when the alternative accounting rules are used, Schedule 4 also states that *"an amount may be transferred from the revaluation reserve ... to the profit and loss account if the amount was previously charged to that account or represents realised profits"*. [CA85 4 Sch 34(3)]. In the example, the £50 has been charged to the profit and loss account (as part of the £80) and so paragraph 34(3) allows the relevant amount of the revaluation (that is, £50) to be transferred to the profit and loss account.

17.30 Both of these ways of rationalising the alternative treatment have the same effect, namely that only the diminution below cost of £30 would be charged in the profit and loss account, with the diminution of £50 between original cost and the revalued carrying amount being debited to the revaluation reserve and shown in the statement of total recognised gains and losses.

17.31 We believe that this alternative treatment is acceptable. The first view (see para 17.26) has the disadvantage that the initial uplift in value is credited to reserves and shown in the statement of total recognised gains and losses, whilst the subsequent reversal of the uplift is charged to the profit and loss account. This asymmetrical treatment is avoided in the alternative treatment.

Negative revaluation reserves

17.32 Under SSAP 19, a net deficit on an investment revaluation reserve, provided that it is temporary, is not charged to the profit and loss account, but instead is shown in the STRGL. The standard is silent as to whether a net deficit should remain on the revaluation reserve or whether there should then be a transfer to the profit and loss reserve. The implication appears to be that temporary net deficits can remain on an investment revaluation reserve.

17.33 A further point of note is that, despite the standard referring specifically to the 'investment revaluation reserve', the term is rarely used in practice. In fact, the majority of companies refer simply to the 'revaluation reserve', although other terms are used such as 'property revaluation reserve' and 'unrealised capital account'. Furthermore, as the standard requires the investment revaluation reserve to be displayed prominently in the financial statements, this can be interpreted to mean that where companies with investment properties also revalue other properties, the standard requires the revaluation reserve to provide an analysis of the reserve between investment properties and other revalued assets. However, this is not done very often in practice.

Owner-occupied properties

17.34 Although the standard indicates that a property that is used and occupied by a company for its own purposes is not an investment property, there may be instances where a property is only partially owner occupied. [SSAP 19 para 8]. In such circumstances, where a property is held for its investment potential, but is either partly occupied by the company or partly let to and occupied by another group company, it would normally be appropriate to apportion the property between an 'investment' element and a 'non-investment' element. This apportionment could, for example, be done on the basis of arm's length rentals. However, before a company apportions properties in this way, it should consider materiality. For example, if a company has a number of investment properties and one small 'split' property, all the properties could reasonably be treated as investment properties.

Disclosures

17.35 SSAP 19 requires the carrying value of investment properties and the investment revaluation reserve to be displayed prominently in the financial statements. [SSAP 19 para 15]. In addition, SSAP 19 and the Act both require disclosures about the valuation of investment properties as follows:

- The names of the persons carrying out the valuation, or particulars of their qualifications. [SSAP 19 para 12; CA85 4 Sch 43].
- The bases of valuation used. [SSAP 19 para 12; CA85 4 Sch 33(2), 43].
- Whether the valuer is an employee or officer of the group. [SSAP 19 para 12].
- Comparable amounts determined under the historical cost accounting rules. [CA85 4 Sch 33(2)].
- The year in which the assets were valued. [CA85 4 Sch 43].

17.36 In addition, if a valuation has been performed in accordance with the RICS Appraisal and Valuation Manual and reference is made to that valuation in the financial statements, then various disclosures must be made under Practice Statement 7 (see chapter 16).

17.37 Furthermore, as a fixed asset, the Act's disclosure requirements must also be met:

- The aggregate amount of that item at both the beginning and the end of the financial year in question.
- The effect of any application of the alternative accounting rules during that financial year.
- The amount of any acquisitions and the amount of any disposals, during that financial year.
- The amount of any transfers of assets to, or from, that item during that financial year.
- The cumulative amounts of provisions for depreciation or diminution in value of assets at both the beginning and the end of the financial year in question.
- The amount of any such provisions that have been made during the financial year.
- The amount of any such provisions that have been eliminated during that financial year on the disposal of the fixed asset to which they related.
- The amount of any other adjustments made in respect of any such provisions during that financial year.

[CA85 4 Sch 42(1)(2)(3)].

17.38 The Act also requires that disclosures in respect of land and buildings should include an analysis of freehold, long leasehold and short leasehold. [CA85 4 Sch 44]. For this purpose, a lease includes an agreement for a lease. It will be a long lease if it still has 50 years or more to run at the end of the financial year in question. Otherwise, it will be a short lease. [CA85 4 Sch 83].

17.39 Although FRS 28, 'Corresponding amounts', requires comparative figures to be provided for every item included in a note to the financial statements, this requirement does not apply in respect of the disclosures discussed in para 17.37. [FRS 28 para 11].

Chapter 18

Impairment of fixed assets and goodwill

	Page
Introduction	18001
Scope and objective of FRS 11	18002
Scope of FRS 11	18002
Objective	18002
Identifying assets that may be impaired	18003
Definition of impairment	18003
Deferred tax taken into account	18004
When impairment reviews are required	18005
Impairment indicators	18005
Special rules for goodwill and intangible assets	18007
First year review	18008
Companies Act's requirements	18009
Measuring recoverable amount	18010
General matters	18010
Income-generating units	18011
Identifying income-generating units	18011
Retail establishments	18013
Banks and building society branches	18014
Public houses	18014
Hotels	18014
Petrol stations	18015
Vertically integrated operations	18015
Indefinite-lived intangible assets, for example, brands	18016
Net realisable value	18016
Value in use	18019
Calculating value in use	18020
Composition of cash flow forecasts	18020
Transfer pricing between IGUs	18022
Central overheads	18022
Inflation	18023
Constraints on forecasts	18023
Growth rates	18023
'Look-back' tests	18024
Reorganisation and capital expenditure	18026
Future reorganisation	18027
Future capital expenditure	18030
Newly acquired IGUs	18033
Discount rate	18034
Pre-tax rate	18036
Allocating assets and liabilities to IGUs	18040

Central assets 18041
Purchased goodwill 18042
Guidelines on allocating goodwill 18043
Recognition of impairment losses 18046
Allocation of impairment losses to assets of income-generating units . 18046
Different methods of treating goodwill 18047
Central assets 18050
Integration of acquired businesses with existing operations 18053
Goodwill previously written off to reserves 18057
Impairment and depreciation 18057
Assets held for disposal 18058
Corporate structures — issues for parent companies and subsidiaries. 18060
Parent's investment in subsidiaries 18060
Subsidiaries that are part of larger IGUs 18061
Reversals of impairment losses 18062
General rules 18062
Special rules for goodwill and intangible assets 18067
Presentation and disclosures 18069
Presentation of impairment losses in performance statements 18069
Assets carried at historical cost 18069
Revalued assets 18069
Assets held for disposal 18072
Loss on disposal or impairment loss? 18072
Disposal of previously impaired asset 18073
Other financial statement disclosures 18073
Fixed asset movements 18073
Revalued assets held at market value 18074
Revalued assets held at depreciated replacement cost 18076
Value in use calculations 18077
Reversals 18078
Companies Act disclosures 18078

Chapter 18

Impairment of fixed assets and goodwill

Introduction

18.1 FRS 11, 'Impairment of fixed assets and goodwill', was published by the ASB in July 1998 and applies to accounting periods ending on or after 23 December 1998.

18.2 The principles underlying the standard are not new. Long-established rules in the Companies Act and previous accounting standards (SSAP 12, 'Accounting for depreciation') had the effect that the balance sheet carrying values of fixed assets should not exceed their recoverable amounts, that is, the net cash inflows they are expected to generate for the business. There was, however, little detailed guidance on how to apply those rules — for example, how cash flows could be related to individual assets, whether the cash flows should be measured on a discounted or undiscounted basis or, more generally, when a diminution in value should be regarded as permanent.

18.3 FRS 11 was issued at the same time as the International Accounting Standards Committee published an accounting standard on the same subject, IAS 36, 'Impairment of assets'. A revised version of IAS 36 was published in March 2004.

18.4 FRS 11 evolved in conjunction with the development of the new methods of accounting for goodwill and intangible assets that are found in FRS 10, 'Goodwill and intangible assets', published by the ASB at the end of 1997 and which became effective at the same time as FRS 11. FRS 10 requires purchased goodwill to be treated as an asset and that both purchased goodwill and intangible assets should generally be amortised over a useful economic life not exceeding 20 years. However, FRS 10 also allows for the possibility that purchased goodwill and intangible assets can, in appropriate circumstances, be amortised over longer periods or be carried permanently on the balance sheet without amortisation (where the useful economic life is considered to be indefinite).

18.5 A key feature of FRS 10 is that impairment reviews must be performed in certain circumstances to check whether the carrying values of goodwill and intangibles are recoverable. If a company amortises goodwill or intangibles over more than 20 years or does not amortise them at all, it has to carry out an impairment review annually. An impairment review for long-life goodwill or intangible assets should be a rigorous exercise that would require an entity to demonstrate that, in respect of acquisitions, the present value of the incremental future cash flows was enough to justify the carrying value of the goodwill or intangible assets. Thus the detailed methodology relating to impairment reviews that is contained in FRS 11 evolved from the development of the goodwill standard.

18.6 FRS 11 requires entities to focus more attention on the carrying values of fixed assets than previously. Greater use is made of cash flow projections to support asset values. Less emphasis is placed on the distinction between permanent and temporary diminutions in value because, essentially, the standard is concerned with identifying diminutions in value that should be recognised immediately. The impairment tests are complex and assumptions about future cash flows are inherently subjective.

[The next paragraph is 18.9.]

Scope and objective of FRS 11

Scope of FRS 11

18.9 FRS 11 applies to purchased goodwill that is treated as an asset on the balance sheet and, with the following specific exceptions, to all tangible and intangible fixed assets. The exceptions, which are assets covered by other accounting pronouncements, are:

- Fixed assets within the scope of FRS 13, 'Derivatives and other financial instruments: Disclosures', or FRS 25, 'Financial instruments: Disclosure and presentation', – these include investments that are financial assets, such as investments in equity and non-equity shares and debt instruments. Investments in subsidiaries, quasi-subsidiaries, associates and joint ventures are, however, excluded from the scope of FRS 13 and FRS 25 and thus in effect included in the scope of FRS 11.
- Investment properties within the scope of SSAP 19.
- Costs relating to oil and gas exploration that have been capitalised pending the determination of whether or not economically developable reserves exist, which continue to be accounted for under the Oil Industry Accounting Committee's SORP 2, 'Accounting for oil and gas exploration and development activities'.

[FRS 11 para 5].

18.10 FRS 11 does not apply to current assets; neither does it apply to purchased goodwill that was previously written off to reserves and that remains so under the transitional arrangements of FRS 10. [FRS 11 para 7].

Objective

18.11 FRS 11's objectives are to ensure that:

- The carrying values of fixed assets and goodwill do not exceed their recoverable amount.
- Impairment losses are recognised and measured on a consistent basis.
- Adequate disclosures are given concerning the impact of impairment on an entity's financial position and performance.

[FRS 11 para 1].

18.12 FRS 11 puts in place a detailed methodology for identifying impairments and measuring recoverable amount.

18.13 Although the methodology is complex and recoverable amount calculations may appear to be precise and detailed, it needs to be borne in mind when applying the standard that the calculations are based on best estimates of unknown future events. The forecasts that may be required are inherently judgemental and subjective.

Identifying assets that may be impaired

Definition of impairment

18.14 The basic principle is that a fixed asset may not be carried in the balance sheet at more than its recoverable amount. An impairment is defined in FRS 11 as *"a reduction in the recoverable amount of a fixed asset or goodwill below its carrying amount"*. [FRS 11 para 2].

18.15 An asset's recoverable amount represents its greatest value to the business in terms of the cash flows that it can generate. That is the higher of net realisable value (what the asset could be sold for, net of direct selling expenses) and value in use (the cash flows that are expected to be generated from its continued use in the business, including those from its ultimate disposal). Value in use is explicitly based on present value calculations.

18.16 The theory is that this measurement basis reflects the economic decisions that management makes when assets become impaired — is the business better off disposing of the asset or keeping it in use? An asset is impaired only if both net realisable value and value in use are lower than its carrying value.

18.17 An impairment review involves estimating an asset's recoverable amount and comparing it with its carrying value, as illustrated in the panel below. If net realisable value cannot be estimated reliably, recoverable amount is determined by estimating value in use alone. If the recoverable amount is lower than the carrying value, the asset is impaired and must be written down to the recoverable amount. A write-off cannot be avoided by arguing that the diminution in value is not permanent.

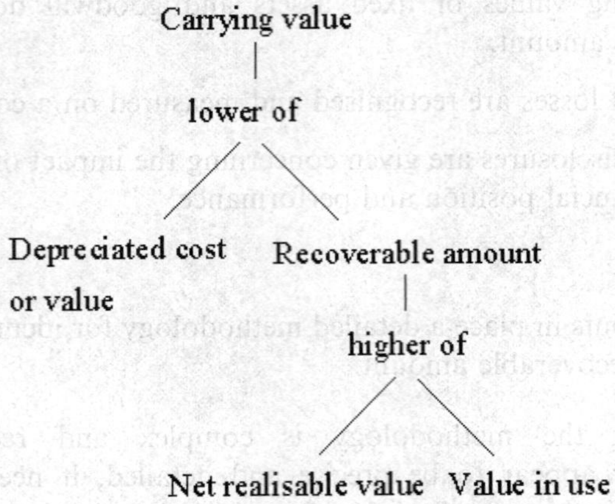

18.18 The standard is written from the perspective of commercial enterprises where fixed assets are employed to generate cash flows for the business. Where fixed assets are not held for the purpose of generating cash flows (such as certain assets held by non-profit making organisations), the value to such organisations of fixed assets acquired for the purpose of carrying out their activities cannot meaningfully be measured in terms of cash flow, because the benefits that derive from their use are not financial. Furthermore, such assets typically do not generate cash flows to cover financing costs or replacement. The normal accounting treatment for such assets is that they are depreciated systematically over their estimated useful lives, that is, as they wear out or as the benefits are otherwise consumed. The standard refers briefly to this issue and explains that it may not be appropriate to write down such assets to their recoverable amount and that *"an alternative measure of its service potential may be more relevant"*. [FRS 11 para 20]. In practice, an impairment of an asset employed in a non-cash generating activity is likely to arise only where the asset suffers impairment in a physical sense, for example, where the asset is physically damaged or where the quality of service that it provides has deteriorated. As long as such assets continue to provide the anticipated benefits to the organisation, the consumption of such benefits will be reflected in regular depreciation charges.

Deferred tax taken into account

18.19 FRS 11 explains that in determining whether recoverable amount (and, hence, the measurement of any impairment losses) should be based on net realisable value or value in use, any deferred tax balances that would arise in each case should be taken into account. [FRS 11 para 19].

18.20 The value of an asset to the business is affected by tax considerations, such as future tax reliefs or capital gains tax liabilities, which would typically be taken into account when deciding whether the business is better off disposing of the asset or keeping it in use. Thus, if a disposal at market value would give rise to a capital gains tax liability, this should be 'netted off' the calculation of net realisable value when comparing it with value in use. However, although the comparison should be made on a 'net of tax' basis, the impaired carrying value of the asset (that is, the estimated recoverable amount), whether it is based on net realisable value or value in use, should be recognised in the financial statements on a 'before tax' basis and any related deferred tax balances should be recognised separately as is normal practice. Similarly, any impairment losses should be recognised on a 'before tax' basis in the profit and loss account and the deferred tax effects are picked up in the tax line.

[The next paragraph is 18.22.]

When impairment reviews are required

18.22 FRS 11 does not require formal impairment reviews to be carried out annually. In general, the full rigours of the standard apply only when there is an indication that assets might be impaired.

18.23 However, there are special rules in FRS 10 and in FRS 15, 'Tangible fixed assets'. FRS 10 requires purchased goodwill and intangible assets to be reviewed for impairment at the end of each reporting period where the amortisation period is more than 20 years; it also requires a special first year impairment review of goodwill and intangible assets relating to new acquisitions (at the end of the first full year following the acquisition). FRS 15 requires tangible fixed assets (other than non-depreciable land) to be reviewed for impairment at the end of each reporting period when either no depreciation is charged on the grounds that it would be immaterial or when the asset's estimated remaining useful economic life is greater than 50 years. Where annual impairment reviews are required, they should be carried out in accordance with FRS 11.

18.24 Where fixed assets or goodwill are being depreciated over relatively short periods, depreciation reduces the risk of impairment, but where assets or goodwill have very long economic lives, the greater is the risk that they may become impaired in the future. FRS 11 states that for tangible fixed assets impairments will be an infrequent addition to depreciation, which is likely to be the case provided that depreciation rates and useful economic lives of assets are determined realistically and reviewed frequently.

Impairment indicators

18.25 FRS 11 requires an impairment review of a fixed asset or goodwill if events or changes in circumstances indicate that the carrying amount of the fixed asset or goodwill may not be recoverable. [FRS 11 para 8].

18.26 FRS 11 includes a list of circumstances which may indicate that there has been an impairment. These are:

- A current period operating loss in the business in which the fixed asset or goodwill is involved or net cash outflow from the operating activities of that business, combined with either past operating losses or net cash outflows from such operating activities or an expectation of continuing operating losses or net cash outflows from such operating activities.

- A significant decline in a fixed asset's market value during the period.
- Evidence of obsolescence or physical damage to the fixed asset.
- A significant adverse change in:
  - Either the business or the market in which the fixed asset or goodwill is involved, such as the entrance of a major competitor.
  - The statutory or other regulatory environment in which the business operates.
  - Any 'indicator of value' (for example, turnover) used to measure the fair value of a fixed asset on acquisition.
- A commitment by management to undertake a significant reorganisation.
- A major loss of key employees.
- A significant increase in market interest rates or other market rates of return that are likely to affect materially the fixed asset's recoverable amount.

[FRS 11 para 10].

18.27 The above list is not exhaustive. Other indicators may be apparent that are relevant to the particular circumstances of a business. If there are any, an impairment review should be carried out. For example, changes in tax regulations or a significant devaluation of the currency in which the business derives its cash flows may require the recoverable amount of its assets to be investigated. Or management's own forecasts may show a significant decline from previous budgets and forecasts. A decision to sell an under-performing business would also give rise to a review of its asset values if impairment losses had not been identified and recognised earlier.

18.28 Most of the examples of impairment indicators are self-explanatory. They reflect adverse events or conditions that affect either the assets directly or the business in which they are employed. They should normally trigger a review for impairment where they are relevant to the measurement of the fixed assets or goodwill. An impairment test should still be performed if there are any impairment indicators. This will be the case even where there are conflicting indicators of impairment.

18.29 Interest rates are identified as an indicator for entities to consider. The effect of calculating an asset's recoverable amount on the present value basis required by FRS 11 is that an asset will be deemed to be impaired unless it can earn sufficient to recover not only its carrying value but also its cost of capital. Therefore, if interest rates rise, the asset may need to earn more to recover a higher cost of capital. However, only significant movements in long-term rates would normally be relevant. FRS 11 emphasises that increases in short-term interest rates would not necessarily trigger an impairment review, because they may not affect the rate of return the market would require on long-term assets. [FRS 11 para 11].

[The next paragraph is 18.33.]

Special rules for goodwill and intangible assets

18.33 For goodwill and intangible fixed assets, the requirements for impairment reviews differ according to whether goodwill is amortised over more or less than 20 years, as illustrated below.

Impairment reviews	
Useful life 20 years or less	**Useful life more than 20 years**
End of first full year (simplified review)	Every year (detailed review)
Other years – high level check for impairment indicators – detailed review only if impairment indicators are present	

18.34 The requirements for impairment reviews are set out in FRS 10. Apart from the first year review (see below), the methodology for performing the reviews set out in FRS 11 should be followed.

18.35 A threshold of 20 years is specified in FRS 10, below which the impairment reviews are less onerous than for longer periods. Where goodwill or an intangible asset is written off over a shorter period, there is less risk of impairment, because its net book value diminishes more quickly.

18.36 A detailed impairment review of goodwill and intangible assets is required in the following situations:

- Where they are treated as having a useful life of more than 20 years, at the end of each reporting period (including the one in which the acquisition took place).
- Where their useful life is 20 years or less:
  - At the end of the first full year following their acquisition, *only* if there is an indicator of impairment or if the first year review (see below) indicates that the post-acquisition performance has failed to meet pre-acquisition expectations.
  - In other years, *only* if there is an indicator of impairment (that is, following the normal procedures for identifying fixed assets that may be impaired).

[FRS 10 paras 34-37].

18.37 Where goodwill has to be reviewed annually for impairment, but is not actually expected to be impaired, the reviews in subsequent years after the first annual review can often be performed by updating the calculations performed for the first review. FRS 10 notes that if there have been no adverse changes since the first review, it may be possible to ascertain immediately that there has been no impairment. [FRS 10 para 38].

First year review

18.38 Where newly acquired goodwill or intangible assets are being amortised over 20 years or less, a first year impairment review is required. Purchased goodwill and most recognised intangible assets are acquired through business acquisitions. No equivalent review is required for newly acquired tangible fixed assets. This review should be carried out at the end of the first full financial year following their acquisition. It is intended to identify factors such as:

- Overpayment.
- Under-performance compared with expectations.
- Material adverse changes to the acquired business in the immediate post-acquisition period.

18.39 The first year review has two stages. The first stage in effect requires management formally to consider whether the acquisition has lived up to expectations. This is done by comparing post-acquisition performance with the forecasts used in the acquisition appraisal and by considering whether there have been any other unexpected adverse events or changes in circumstances that throw doubt on the recoverability of the capitalised goodwill or intangible assets. For all acquisitions that give rise to significant amounts of purchased goodwill or intangible assets, the requirement for the first year review means that management needs to document formally the projections used at the time of the acquisition.

18.40 If the acquisition passes the first stage, there is no need to go on to the second stage. The second stage is a full impairment review, which is only required if the first test is failed or if there is any other indicator of impairment. [FRS 10 para 40]. An example of the disclosures is shown in Table 18.1 below.

Table 18.1—Pearson plc—Annual Report & Accounts—31 December 2001

Financial Review (extract)

Goodwill Impairment

This £61m charge resulted from a review of the carrying value of goodwill on our balance sheet, required under FRS 10 (Goodwill and Intangible Assets) and FRS 11 (Impairment of Fixed Assets and Goodwill), which led to a decision to impair the value of Dorling Kindersley by £50m.

Dorling Kindersley was purchased in May 2000 for a price of £318m plus embedded debt of £49m. Although Dorling Kindersley adds value both to Penguin and our education businesses, and is expected to return to profit in 2002, the integration has taken longer to achieve than we initially envisaged and we have also reduced the revenue base in order to eliminate unprofitable publishing. Taken together with a difficult economic environment,which has affected Dorling

> Kindersley 's travel guides in particular, we thought it prudent to write down the value of goodwill by just under 15%.
>
> We also took a total of £11m in write-downs on various other businesses, the largest of these relating to a Latin American subsidiary. We undertook a detailed review of our 2000 acquisition of NCS but found no reason to reduce the goodwill we carry on our balance sheet as a result

Companies Act's requirements

18.41 The Companies Act's rules on impairments are framed in terms of 'permanent diminutions in value' and 'temporary diminutions in value'. There has often been difficulty in determining what is permanent and what is temporary. The Companies Act requires that a company must make provision if *any* fixed asset (including a fixed asset investment) has diminished in value, and this reduction is expected to be *permanent*. In such a situation, the company must reduce the amount at which it recognises the asset in its financial statements by the amount of this diminution in value. This requirement applies whether or not the asset has a limited useful economic life. [CA85 4 Sch 19(2)].

18.42 FRS 11 does not specifically use the term 'permanent diminution' or contrast this with a temporary diminution. Where an impairment is identified in accordance with the methodology of the standard, the asset should be written down. In the case of fixed assets carried on the historical cost basis, the tests in the standard are designed to identify impairments that should be regarded as permanent. Where assets are carried at revaluation, any impairment identified using the tests in the standard will still be regarded as a loss that must be recognised, but FRS 11 specifies that the presentation of the loss will vary according to whether the impairment arises from:

- a clear consumption of economic benefits; or
- other impairments, for example impairments arising from general changes in prices.

These presentation issues are considered from paragraph 18.252.

18.43 FRS 11 also introduces the concept of the income-generating unit (IGU), which contrasts with the Act's requirements that *"...in determining the aggregate of any item the amount of each individual asset or liability that falls to be taken into account shall be determined separately"*. Whilst the Act, therefore, appears to require each asset or liability to be looked at separately, the standard requires assets and liabilities to be grouped together in some circumstances for the purpose of testing assets for impairment.

18.44 The standard, however, makes it clear that IGUs should be identified by dividing the total income of an entity into as many largely independent income steams as is reasonably practicable. Thus, it aims to ensure that the smallest possible grouping of income-earning assets and liabilities that is independent of the rest of the entity's income is chosen. This aims to come as close to the Act's requirements as is, in practice, possible, whilst at the same time being practical by recognising that assets that are inter-dependent can only be tested as one unit. Nonetheless, the standard emphasises that the value in use of a fixed asset should be estimated individually where reasonably practicable.

Measuring recoverable amount

General matters

18.45 FRS 11 defines recoverable amount as the higher of net realisable value and value in use. This reflects the greatest value of an asset in terms of the cash flows that can be derived from it, either by selling it or by continuing to use it in the business.

18.46 Both net realisable value and value in use can be difficult to determine in practice. It may be possible to determine net realisable value even if an asset is not traded in an active market. Sometimes it will not be possible to make an estimate of net realisable value as there is no basis for making a reliable estimate. In these circumstances, recoverable amount should be determined by estimating the asset's value in use. As explained later in this chapter, estimating value in use is a matter of judgement, requiring estimates of cash flows many years into the future and determining appropriate discount rates to bring them back to their present values. The objective is to make estimates as realistic as possible.

18.47 It is not always necessary to calculate both measures when performing an impairment review. If an asset's net realisable value or its value in use exceeds its carrying amount, there is no need to estimate the other amount. Similarly, if it is clear that net realisable value is lower than value in use, there is no need to estimate the other amount.

18.48 In some circumstances it may be apparent from a quick review of financial data that the value in use of an asset will either exceed its carrying value or be exceeded by its net realisable value, in which case a detailed calculation of value in use is not required. [FRS 11 para 18]. For example, where goodwill has to be reviewed for impairment each year (because its useful life is greater than 20 years) and there was previously substantial leeway between the value in use and the carrying value, a simple check on actual performance against previous estimates may be sufficient to demonstrate that value in use continues to exceed carrying value.

18.49 Where an asset is to be disposed of, its net realisable value and value in use will generally be approximately the same, because value in use then reflects mainly the net cash proceeds expected from the asset's disposal.

Income-generating units

Identifying income-generating units

18.50 In most practical situations, dividing the activities of an enterprise into IGUs is the first key step in carrying out impairment reviews. This establishes the level of aggregation at which impairment reviews should be carried out.

18.51 In general, the higher the level of aggregation the greater is the risk that impairment losses on unprofitable assets might be masked by unrecognised increases in value of profitable ones. Hence, impairment reviews should as a matter of principle be carried out at the lowest level that is practicable.

18.52 FRS 11 indicates that IGUs can be aggregated (that is, groups of similar IGUs can be considered as one IGU) for the purpose of determining value in use, provided that the level of aggregation is reasonable in the circumstances of the impairment review and that material impairments would not escape recognition by such aggregation. The rationale is that the standard is only concerned with identifying material impairments. [FRS 11 para 26]. Aggregation has important practical implications for businesses (such as retailers) that trade through a large number of separate outlets, since it may be impracticable, or at least costly, for businesses to prepare separate cash flow forecasts for large numbers of individual outlets.

18.53 An income-generating unit is defined as:

> *"A group of assets, liabilities and associated goodwill that generates income that is largely independent of the reporting entity's other income streams. The assets and liabilities include those directly involved in generating the income and an appropriate portion of those used to generate more than one income stream".* [FRS 11 para 2].

18.54 IGUs should be identified *"by dividing the total income of the business into as many largely independent income streams as is reasonably practicable in the light of the information available to management".* [FRS 11 para 28].

18.55 An asset or business that is to be disposed of forms an IGU of its own and does not belong to any other IGU. [FRS 11 para 31]. Its recoverable amount consists mainly of the expected net proceeds from disposal and these are independent of the income streams of other assets or businesses.

18.56 For continuing operations, management has discretion to identify IGUs to fit their information systems within the following parameters set out in FRS 11:

- The groups of assets and liabilities should be as small as is reasonably practicable (consistent with the principle that assets should be valued separately).

- The income streams of each IGU should be largely independent of each other and should be capable of being monitored separately.
- IGUs are likely to be identified in a way that is consistent with the way in which management makes decisions about continuing or closing different lines of business.
- IGUs may be identified by reference to major products or services.
- Unique intangible assets (such as brands and mastheads) can often be used to identify IGUs, because they may generate income independently of each other and are usually monitored separately.

[FRS 11 paras 27 to 29].

18.56.1 Care is needed in respect of intangible assets as many do not generate independent cash flows and, hence, despite bing 'unique intangible assets', they do not form an IGU. For example, a manufacturer that has previously acquired a branded competitor will use the brand to support the IGU that is the maintaining facility for the branded product.

18.57 Several commentators on FRED 15 (the exposure draft that preceded FRS 11) referred to the subjectivity involved in identifying IGUs and raised issues as to when income streams are really independent. For example, in businesses that operate large numbers of retail outlets, such as stores, restaurants and financial services, different companies may take different views as to whether an IGU is an individual retail outlet or a group of outlets in a smaller or larger geographical region. Activities can also be cut in different ways — by geographical areas, product lines or in some other way. Much depends on how the operations are managed and how independent or interdependent they are.

18.58 In response to respondents' concerns about this issue, additional guidance was introduced into the FRS in the form of four mini-case studies. Although these are helpful, selection of IGUs remains a very judgmental area, particularly for vertically integrated operations and for businesses with multi-locations in retailing or manufacturing.

18.59 The first example in the FRS is a transport company operating a trunk route fed by supporting routes, which should be combined for the purposes of determining an IGU. The reasons given are that the cash flows of each route are not independent and that economic decisions about continuing or closing the supporting routes are not based on their returns in isolation.

18.60 An analogous situation is where a public transport operator runs a number of unprofitable routes in order to have access to profitable ones — it could not obtain the benefits of the latter without incurring the cost of the former where it may be under contract to provide a specified minimum level of service. Each route may or may not have its own dedicated assets and identifiable revenues and operating costs, but the income of each route is not independent in an economic sense, because management could not decide to discontinue any one route. The IGU for the assets of each route may be the whole franchise.

18.61 The second example in the FRS is a manufacturer that can allocate production across a number of facilities. One facility may be operating with surplus capacity and, hence, might be considered to be impaired if it were reviewed in isolation. However, there is not enough surplus capacity overall to enable any one manufacturing site to be closed. The FRS explains that, in this situation, the IGU should comprise all the sites at which the product can be made, because the cash inflows generated by any one site depend on the allocation of production across all sites. Therefore, the facilities are not reviewed separately, because impairment indicators affect them all together — at the larger IGU level, there may be no impairment.

Retail establishments

18.62 The third example in the FRS is a restaurant chain. The example concludes that each restaurant is a separate IGU, because its income is independent of the income of other restaurants — the cash inflows of each restaurant can be individually monitored and sensible allocations of costs to each restaurant can be made. However, since any impairment of individual restaurants is unlikely to be material, groups of restaurants that are affected by the same economic factors may be reviewed for impairment together for the purpose of identifying material impairments.

18.63 This example is relevant to a large spectrum of retail establishments but, in general, is of limited use in helping to reach a clear-cut view on whether an IGU is an individual site, a group of sites in a region, a country or the whole business. For the majority of modern multi-site retailers some level of aggregation of sites is normally appropriate, whether a larger grouping is treated as an IGU or whether each site is taken to be an IGU, but a pragmatic view of aggregation is taken on grounds of materiality, as in the restaurant example referred to above. Apart from other considerations, in some circumstances it may be impractical (or at least costly) to prepare detailed cash flow forecasts for each individual site — in any case, forecasts may to some extent be based on macro-assumptions about factors that affect larger groupings in a similar way. Some further examples are discussed below.

18.64 Judging which grouping of outlets produces largely independent income streams requires the characteristics of the way the business is managed to be assessed, for example, by considering whether:

- Performance is monitored at individual, regional or other levels — for example, considering the lowest level at which meaningful profitability statements are produced.
- Product offering and investment decisions are made at individual, regional or other grouping levels.

- Individual outlets generate custom for other parts of the network.
- Units are managed on a combined basis sharing systems, centralised purchasing and distribution functions.
- Product pricing is determined locally or on an area or national basis.

18.65 Where regional or other groupings of establishments are taken as the normal basis for carrying out impairment reviews, any specific indicators of impairment affecting a smaller grouping would also need to be taken into account to ensure that material impairments are properly identified. Examples might include the entry of a major competitor into a local area, or the closure of a town's principal employer, both of which could have a long-term effect on the income of establishments in that area. A specific review of the smaller grouping or individual establishment affected by a local impairment indicator would then be necessary.

Banks and building society branches

18.66 Banking and building society branches generally sell a variety of products that are supported by central operations. In many ways the outlets represent a conduit for the central organisation which determines product pricing on a national basis. Whilst it may be possible to look at the income of each branch as being separate from the others, it is likely that very broad assumptions would need to be made to arrive at a measure of profitability, particularly in respect of recurring products such as life policies and savings schemes. In these circumstances it is unlikely that a branch is an IGU, unless for some reason management addresses profitability or contribution at a branch level. It is also unlikely that an individual branch would be material to the organisation.

Public houses

18.67 The income of individual public houses would usually be largely independent of others, and their performance would be capable of being monitored separately. Thus, in the main they would be individual IGUs. However, as with the restaurants example in the FRS, where large numbers are operated it is unlikely that any one public house would be material and so it may be acceptable to consider them in groupings affected by the same economic factors.

Hotels

18.68 Individual hotels would usually generate income that is largely independent of others and their performance would be monitored closely by management on an individual basis. It is, therefore, probable that they form individual IGUs, even if there are central sales and marketing and finance functions. It is conceivable that a hotel chain that markets itself centrally to perhaps mainly commercial customers, might, as part of its business strategy, operate a loss making hotel in a particularly popular higher cost location in order, for example, to secure group wide contracts or a nationally advertised price pledge. On the other hand, a hotel may operate as part of a small cluster of similar quality hotels that are managed as a single operation and frequently refer guests to each other when one is full. In such circumstances, it might be argued that the hotel's income is not independent and, hence, an IGU is a larger grouping.

Petrol stations

18.69 The income of individual petrol stations is likely to be closely monitored by management, for example to determine the relative impact of local pricing differentials, and costs are likely to be able to be determined to arrive at a measure of profitability. If management would consider closing one station depending upon its individual performance, each petrol station may be an IGU — similar to the restaurant example in the FRS. However, it is unlikely that any one station owned by a major operator would be material. Therefore, where a large number of outlets is involved, impairment reviews would normally be carried out on the basis of groupings affected by the same economic conditions. Where establishments combine retail, catering, hotel and petrol outlets the interdependency of these income streams would also need to be taken into account.

Vertically integrated operations

18.70 The fourth example in the FRS illustrates vertical integration. When determining whether a group of assets involved in an intermediate stage in the production process should be treated as an IGU, the most important factor is to consider the extent to which there is an external market and source of supply for its products. This will help to determine whether the income of one facility is dependent on the income of another.

18.71 If there is a deep and liquid external market and source of supply for each stage of production, the income of each process is likely to be independent in the sense that management will monitor and make decisions about retaining or discontinuing it based on its own performance — for example, a line of production might be closed if its output could be sourced more cheaply externally. Similarly, the income generated at the retail end of the business may not be dependent on the fact that its input is supplied internally, if there are alternative sources. In such circumstances, there could be several IGU's within the vertically integrated operation.

18.72 On the other hand, if there is no external market for the output of a facility in the production chain, or the external market is not of sufficient depth to influence management decisions about the production facility itself, its income cannot be independent because the demand for its products depends entirely or substantially on the demand for the products of the facilities further up the line. In extreme cases, the whole enterprise could be a single IGU, because the income generated by each of its activities is entirely dependent on the demand for the end product.

Indefinite-lived intangible assets, for example, brands

18.72.1 Under US GAAP, indefinite-lived intangible assets are required to be tested for impairment separately by re-performing the fair value exercise on acquisition. Typically, the asset category that is most often impacted by this requirement is acquired brands. As noted in paragraph 18.53, an income generating unit is defined as a group of asset, liabilities and goodwill that generate income that is largely independent of other income streams. In many businesses, the brand is used to support production of a branded asset and the revenues from sales of the branded asset are not capable of being split between revenue for the brand and revenue for the costs of production. Hence, under FRS 11, brands are typically not an IGU and should not be tested alone, rather the brand should be tested with the associated manufacturing IGU.

18.72.2 It is, therefore, the case that it is possible for internally generated goodwill to shelter an impairment of a brand which would occur should it be considered in isolation. The principle in question is illustrated in the following example:

Example

Entity A is a manufacturer of consumer electronics. It has several identifiable divisions, including hi-fi, television and games consoles. In 20X1 it purchased the rights to a competitor's hi-fi brand for £300m. Production, development and marketing for the products sold under the new brand are undertaken in the same factories as the existing hi-fi operations. For the 20X2 year end, valuation specialists have been employed and have determined that the recoverable amount of the brand, in isolation, is £250m. This would, at first sight, suggest that an impairment of the brand is required of £50m. However, the recoverable amount of the overall hi-fi division at the end of 20X2 is £1,500m compared to carrying value of its assets (including the purchased brand) of £1,300m. As such, no impairment is required. The internally generated goodwill within the existing hi-fi business has sheltered any impairment on the brand, on the basis that it has been determined that the purchased brand does not generate cash inflows from continuing use that are largely independent to those from other assets.

Net realisable value

18.73 The definition of net realisable value is "*...the amount at which an asset could be disposed of, less any direct selling costs*". [FRS 11 para 2].

18.74 In calculating net realisable value, direct selling costs are deducted. Such costs include, for instance, legal costs and stamp duty or perhaps costs of removing a sitting tenant before selling a building.

18.75 However, costs associated with reducing or reorganising the business, such as costs of making staff redundant, that may be incurred before a factory building could be sold should not be deducted in arriving at net realisable value (nor should any incremental income from changes in capacity be assumed). Those costs are not regarded as part of the costs of selling the asset itself. [FRS 11 para 23]. Provisions for certain reorganisation costs are recognised (as liabilities) when the criteria of FRS 12, 'Provisions, contingent liabilities and contingent assets', are met, that is, when the company has a constructive obligation to carry out the reorganisation. If there is no such obligation at the time the asset is being reviewed for impairment, no provision is made. Either way, the question of whether provisions for reorganisation costs should be made does not affect the calculation of the asset's net realisable value.

18.76 Net realisable value is based on market value where there is an active market. Whilst active markets may exist, for example, in second-hand cars, commercial vehicles, computer equipment, certain plant and machinery and many types of property, they may not exist for specialised plant or buildings. For those assets it may also be difficult to find recent transactions for similar assets to provide reliable evidence of potential sales proceeds.

18.76.1 Where a business or an asset is being sold, the expected sale proceeds may provide reliable evidence of the net realisable value of its recognised net assets and goodwill. For example, a binding sale contract entered into after the balance sheet date would provide the best evidence, but an intended sale where negotiations are in progress may in some cases also provide reliable evidence of net realisable value.

18.77 Where there is an asset for which there is no active market, such as goodwill attaching to a business, then net realisable amount may still be derived using estimation techniques such as a discounted cash flow analysis. Discounted cash flow techniques may be used incorporating assumptions that market participants would use in estimating the asset's fair value. Any estimated net realisable value needs to be reliable in order for the net realisable value to be used. FRS 11 requires that a value in use basis should be used where no realisable estimate of net realisable value can be made. [FRS 11 para 16].

18.77.1 Some of the restrictions imposed by FRS 11 on assumptions inherent in the value in use calculations do not apply to a net realisable value and, hence, a valuation on a net realisable value basis might be higher.

18.77.2 In respect of assessing net realisable value, there are a number of valuation methodologies that are used to assess a businesses' value. More than one methodology is normally used to ensure that the valuations are cross-checked and considered in light of all appropriate market evidence.

18.77.3 In practice, a first assessment of the valuation is performed using cash flows from management. There must be, where appropriate, market evidence to support the key assumptions underpinning the cash flow analysis; for example, growth rates may be considered by benchmarking to industry/analyst reports. If certain of the assumptions used are not those that a market participant would use, those cash flows must be adjusted to take into account the assumptions that are supported by market evidence.

18.77.4 The cashflows to be used in a discounted cashflow prepared to determine net realisable value will also be different to those in a value in use calculation. Any differences in the assumptions in the cash flows used for the net realisable value compared to the cash flow forecasts used in the value in use analysis will also need to be considered for reasonableness. For example, in a net realisable value cashflow working capital and tax cashflows would be included. The assumptions could also include restructurings, reorganisations or future investments. This is because all rational market participants would be expected to undertake these expenditures and reorganisations in order to extract the best value from the purchase and, hence, they would have been factored into the acquisition price.

18.77.5 If comparable transactions in similar assets or businesses are available, they should be used as market evidence. Consideration should be given to the comparability of the acquired asset/business to the asset/IGU being tested. For example, adjustments for factors such as size, growth expectations, profitability, risk will need to be considered. This evidence might arise in the implied multiple of earnings before interest, taxes, depreciation and amortisation ('EBITDA') or revenue that was paid in a comparable transaction which when applied to the current model (and adjusted for points of difference) provides support for the valuation. For example, if there are a number of recent transactions in comparable entities where the price paid is six times EBITDA and management has produced a valuation that is ten times EBITDA, then the external data would appear not to support the assumptions made in the valuation. Care is needed in selecting comparable entities; risk profile and size may well be more important than geography. Care is also needed to avoid selection bias, if one transaction in ten provides some support for the EBITDA multiple, but the same transaction is regarded in the financial press as an over-payment and an isolated example, then it should not be used.

18.77.6 As a cross-check, it will be necessary to benchmark the net realisable value of an IGU to multiples implied by quoted comparable companies, although consideration will need to be given to comparability in terms of size, growth expectations, profitability, risk etc. In the unlikely event that a benchmark or comparable transactions do not exist, any possible external evidence (growth rates, discount rates, etc) will be used to support the cash flow projections prepared by management.

18.77.7 Based upon the above, it is almost always possible to determine net realisable value. If net realisable value is used then the carrying value of the asset or IGU being tested for impairment must be determined on a consistent basis.

18.78 If net realisable value is found to be lower than the carrying amount of the asset, it should not automatically be written down to that value. For example, some assets could be sold only for their scrap value, because no market exists for the particular second-hand asset, and value in use may well be much higher. Before a write-down is booked, the asset's value in use also needs to be estimated in order to determine whether it is higher than its net realisable value. If it is, the impairment write-down, if any, is calculated by reference to value in use.

Value in use

18.79 The definition of value in use is *"the present value of the future cash flows obtainable as a result of an asset's continued use, including those resulting from its ultimate disposal"*. [FRS 11 para 2].

18.80 Where reasonably practicable, the value in use of a fixed asset should be estimated individually.

18.81 Investments that are within the scope of FRS 11 — subsidiaries, associates and joint ventures — generate cash flows as discrete assets and should normally be considered individually. To be consistent with the way such entities are accounted for, their value in use should normally be based on the future net cash flows of the underlying entities that are attributable to the group's interest, rather than on the basis of dividend flows. For associates and joint ventures, the carrying value of the group's interest reflects two elements — the group's share of net assets and any purchased goodwill. Any impairments in the underlying fixed assets should already be picked up in the financial statements of the associate or joint venture.

18.82 Measuring the value in use of most fixed assets (tangible and intangible) is not straightforward, because they do not generate cash flows by themselves. Cash flows are normally generated by groups of assets working together, usually by the whole range of assets used in a business. Goodwill by definition is not a separable asset and always has to be considered as part of a group of assets in a business unit. Therefore, in practice, a degree of aggregation is necessary in order to estimate value in use for complete groups of assets and associated goodwill.

18.83 If value in use cannot be estimated for individual assets, it should be estimated for groups of assets that generate income streams that are largely independent of each other. These are referred to as income-generating units (IGUs). Where an impairment review of an IGU is required, it is intended to cover all its tangible assets, intangible assets and attributable goodwill. The carrying value of each IGU containing the fixed asset or goodwill being reviewed should be compared with the higher of its value in use or net realisable value (if net realisable value can be measured reliably). If net realisable value cannot be measured reliably — which is frequently the case for IGUs — the recoverable amount of an IGU is determined by estimating its value in use alone.

18.84 In summary, the key steps in calculating value in use for groups of assets are:

- Identifying separate IGUs.
- Establishing carrying values for the net assets of each IGU, comprising the assets and liabilities attributable to the IGU, plus allocated goodwill.
- Forecasting the future cash flows of the income-generating unit and discounting them to their present value.

- Comparing the present value of the cash flows with the carrying amounts of the net assets attributable to the income-generating unit and recognising any shortfall as an impairment loss.

The details of the methodology and calculations are considered in the paragraphs below.

18.85 When considering impairment issues, the separate valuation principles and the objective of FRS 11 (that fixed assets should be recorded in the financial statements at no more than their recoverable amount) should always be borne in mind. For example, if an individual asset is clearly no longer providing service potential (say, as a result of physical damage) it obviously has a recoverable amount of zero (or scrap value) and should be written off immediately, irrespective of whether the cash flows of the income-generating unit are sufficient to recover the carrying value of all its assets, including the one that has become redundant.

Calculating value in use

Composition of cash flow forecasts

18.86 Estimating value in use involves identifying the future cash flows that are expected to arise from the fixed asset or IGU (or group of IGUs) being tested for impairment. The cash flows consist of those expected to arise from the continued use of the asset or IGU and those, if any, expected to result from its ultimate disposal.

18.87 Relevant cash flow forecasts should be made on the basis of reasonable and supportable assumptions and should be consistent with the most up-to-date budgets and plans that have been formally approved by management. [FRS 11 para 36]. However, the detailed requirements include a number of exceptions to that principle, which have the effect of constraining the rate of growth and anticipated improvements that may be built into the assumptions. These are considered from paragraph 18.99 below.

18.88 The period covered by cash flow forecasts must obviously relate to the useful lives of the fixed assets or goodwill being reviewed for impairment. However, periods covered by detailed formal budgets and plans will vary in different companies and industries. In some, cash flows cannot be predicted with much certainty beyond short periods. The useful lives of the assets concerned may extend far beyond the period covered by formal budgets and plans. It is then necessary to extrapolate the formal cash flow projections into the future using reasonable and prudent broad assumptions about growth and future prospects. The standard places constraints on those assumptions that should be complied with in most circumstances and controls those assumptions by requirements for disclosure where higher growth rates are assumed.

18.89 Where the carrying value of an IGU includes goodwill or other fixed assets with an indefinite useful economic life, the calculation of value in use will include an estimated value of the IGU's cash flows relating to the indefinite period beyond that covered by detailed cash flow projections. This may be calculated by applying a terminal value multiple to, say, the cash flows expected in the last year ('CF') covered by the company's explicit forecasts, by using the formula $CF \times (1+g)/(r-g)$, where r is the discount rate and g is the estimated longer term annual rate of growth in the cash flows (constraints on long-term growth rates are considered from para 18.130). The terminal value calculated as at the end of the period covered by formal budgets and plans will, of course, have to be discounted to its present value.

18.90 The composition of the cash flows that are used to estimate value in use needs to be considered carefully. It is important, for example, to ensure that they are comparable with the basis on which the carrying amounts of the IGUs have been established, so that omissions or double-countings that would lead to errors in the calculations are avoided.

18.91 The cash flows will include:

- Cash inflows from the use of the asset or the activities of the IGU.
- Cash outflows directly attributable to the asset or IGU.
- Any allocation of cash flows attributable to central overheads.
- Net cash inflows expected from the disposal of assets or IGUs at the end of their useful lives.
- Cash outflows to maintain the operating capacity of existing fixed assets.

18.92 The cash flows should exclude cash flows relating to financing (which include interest payments), since financing items are also excluded from the liabilities attributed to IGUs and because the cost of capital is taken into account by discounting the cash flows. Tax cash flows should also be excluded, because the FRS requires value in use to be calculated on the basis of discounting pre-tax cash flows at a pre-tax discount rate (in practice, however, value in use if often likely to be derived from post-tax cash flows discounted at a post-tax discount rate, as discussed from para 18.131).

18.93 Cash inflows and outflows relating to working capital (that is, items such as trade debtors and creditors that are expected to generate cash flows equal to their carrying amounts) in the balance sheet at the time of the impairment review can be excluded from the calculations if that is easier than allocating the working capital components to individual IGUs. The assets and liabilities are then excluded from the carrying value of the IGU and the respective receipts and payments are also excluded from the value in use calculation. [FRS 11 para 33]. This exclusion of balances purely aids the preparation of the working capital forecasts, and should not make any difference to the impairment calculation. In practice, companies may find it easier to prepare an operating profit forecast for the IGU being tested for impairment and then to convert the operating profit forecast into a cash flow forecast by carrying out the same sort of reconciliation of operating profit to operating cash flow as specified in FRS 1, 'Cash flow statements'.

Transfer pricing between IGUs

18.94 Internal transfer pricing directly affects the cash inflows and operating cash outflows relating to separate IGUs in, say, vertically integrated groups. For example, consider a situation where one IGU transfers part of its output to another IGU in the same group at a price that is lower than the market price for its output. This issue is not addressed directly in FRS 11, however, the fourth mini-case study in the standard that discusses how IGUs are determined in vertically integrated groups (see para 18.70) indicates that the cash inflows of the transferor IGU and the cash outflows of the transferee IGU that are used in the value in use calculations should be adjusted to reflect market prices rather than internal transfer prices.

18.95 This principle of adjusting cash flows to reflect market prices, which is stated more explicitly in IAS 36, is logical if the cash inflows of both business units are properly to be regarded as independent. Otherwise, either the wrong assets (in terms of their true economic value to the business) could be identified as being impaired, or impairments might be avoided altogether purely by making adjustments to internal transfer prices. This is likely to be a subjective area in practice.

Central overheads

18.96 The inclusion in the cash flow forecasts of central overheads is mentioned only briefly in FRS 11, which notes that the cash flows include *"any allocation of central overheads"*. [FRS 11 para 36]. It is reasonable to assume that the cash outflows attributable to an IGU should include sensible allocations of central overheads, in the same way that the carrying values of IGUs should, where practicable, include apportionments of central assets. The assets of an IGU could be considered to be impaired if, for example, its own cash flows did not make a contribution to central overheads that are incurred to support its activities.

18.97 It is important to ensure that central overheads are not omitted altogether in the value in use calculations. It is also important to ensure that central assets and overheads are not double-counted in the impairment review. For example, if part of the carrying value of head office property is allocated to IGUs for the purpose of impairment reviews, any internal management charges that are rendered to IGUs relating to the use of that property should be excluded from their cash outflows — otherwise, the carrying value of the IGU would be increased and its value in use decreased by elements relating to the same item.

Inflation

18.98 Assumptions about inflation can be dealt with in one of two ways. One method is to forecast cash flows in current prices — that is, not to forecast future inflation. The cash flows are then discounted at a real discount rate (that is, a rate of return that excludes inflation). The second method is to forecast cash flows to include estimates of inflation in revenues and costs. The cash flows are then discounted at a nominal discount rate (that is, a rate of return that includes inflation). It is important that inflation is treated consistently in the cash flow projections and the choice of discount rate. [FRS 11 para 46]. It is arguable that the preferred method is to use nominal cash flows and a nominal discount rate. This is because the components of the discount rate are obtained from market data that reflect expectations of future inflation rates. It is difficult to remove the impact of inflation other than in a crude and thus unreliable fashion.

Constraints on forecasts

18.99 FRS 11 imposes several important limitations on the cash flows that may be recognised in the calculation of value in use, including restrictions on the growth assumptions that can be built into long-term cash flow forecasts.

Growth rates

18.100 In the period that is covered by formal budgets and plans, there are no restrictions as long as the period does not exceed five years. Therefore, in that initial period the cash flows will reflect the variability in growth rates that is included in the explicit forecasts.

18.101 However, the cash flows for periods beyond those covered by formal budgets and plans (whether they cover the full five years or a shorter period) should assume a steady or declining growth rate that does not exceed the long-term average growth rate for the country or countries in which the business operates. The UK's post-war average growth in gross domestic product, expressed in real terms (that is, assuming no inflation), is stated in the standard to be 2.25 per cent. Furthermore, the period before the steady or declining growth rate is assumed should not normally exceed five years. Only in exceptional circumstances may this growth constraint be overridden, with appropriate disclosure. [FRS 11 para 36].

18.102 Whilst this restriction is clearly aimed at preventing short-term difficulties from being overridden by over-optimistic long-term forecasts, the theory is that in the long run a business has no right to assume it can out-perform the economy as a whole. It is also prudent in the light of an uncertain future.

18.103 The FRS gives an example of a situation where a higher long-term growth rate may be justified. This is where the specific industry is expected to grow faster than the country's economy in the long-term and the business under review is expected to grow as rapidly as the industry as a whole, taking into account the prospects of increased competition. [FRS 11 para 37]. However, the ASB issues a caution in the development section of the FRS that, in its view, individual businesses in higher growth industries do not necessarily grow as quickly as the industry, because such industries may attract new businesses, reducing the opportunities for high growth rates in existing businesses.

18.104 Where the long-term growth rate assumed in the calculation of value in use for the period beyond that covered by explicit forecasts exceeds the long-term average for the country in which the business operates, the assumed growth rate and the circumstances justifying it must be disclosed. [FRS 11 para 73].

18.105 There may be situations where it would be unrealistic to cap the growth assumptions (that is, defaulting to a restricted steady or declining growth rate) after five years. This might be the case where hi-tech businesses are purchased at high multiples of current earnings, reflecting longer term growth prospects. For example, a recently acquired IGU with products under development may be expected to incur losses for two or three years and be followed by several years of significant growth as the new products reach the market — thus cash flow forecasts with explicit growth assumptions may exceed five years. But the circumstances for overriding the presumed five year cut-off must be clearly exceptional and must be disclosed.

18.106 Where, in the calculation of value in use, the period covered by explicit forecasts and before a steady or declining growth rate is assumed exceeds five years, FRS 11 requires the length of the longer period and the circumstances justifying it to be disclosed. [FRS 11 para 72].

'Look-back' tests

18.107 FRS 11 contains a safety net to safeguard against entities continually using over-optimistic forecasts to defer impairment losses. Where an impairment review has been carried out and recoverable amount has been based on value in use, the standard requires the results of the review to be monitored for the next five years, irrespective of whether or not an impairment loss was booked when the review was carried out. [FRS 11 para 54].

18.108 The actual cash flows should be compared with those forecast in the impairment review. If actual cash flows are significantly less than those previously forecast, the calculations should be re-performed by substituting the actual cash flows for those previously forecast. In this exercise, forecasts of future cash flows should remain as previously forecast in the original impairment review, except for where actual cash flows are lower than previously forecast, because certain cash inflows or outflows have occurred, or will occur, in an earlier or later period than was budgeted. If the reworked calculation identifies a previously unrecognised impairment (or increases a previously recognised impairment), an immediate impairment write-down should be made in the current period.

18.109 The under-performance in the years following the original impairment review might be an indicator of further impairment losses and, hence, a new impairment review will also be required, reflecting *current* budgets and plans. Any further impairment losses identified should be recognised immediately.

18.110 There is, however, an exception to the requirement for an immediate write-down when the exercise described above identifies an impairment. A new impairment review, reflecting *current* budgets and plans, might indicate that the impairment loss identified when the original impairment calculations were re-performed no longer exists. In this situation, an impairment loss is deemed to have arisen (based on the original calculations as reworked) and reversed (based on the new forecasts of value in use). If the reasons for the turnaround meet FRS 11's criteria for reversing previously recognised impairment losses, a write-down is not required. However, the impairment that would have been recognised and its subsequent reversal should be disclosed. [FRS 11 para 71].

18.111 The following example illustrates the calculations.

Example

At 31 December 20X1, an asset with a carrying value of £500,000 and a remaining useful economic life of 5 years was reviewed for impairment. Its recoverable amount was based on value in use of £506,000 and so no impairment loss was recognised.

In years 20X2 and 20X3 the actual net cash flows were significantly lower than forecast. In accordance with FRS 11 (para 54), the original value in use calculations are reworked using the actual net cash flows, as illustrated in the table below. The original value in use is recalculated as £450,000.

The future cash flows have been discounted at a rate of 5%. For simplicity, it has been assumed that the cash flows arise at the end of each year.

		Review at 20X1	**Review re-performed at 20X3**	
	Future net cash flows	Present value	Future net cash flows	Present value
Year	£000	£000	£000	£000
20X2	100	95	90*	85
20X3	110	100	60*	54
20X4	120	103	120	103
20X5	130	106	130	106
20X6	130	102	130	102
Value in use		506		450

*Actual cash flows

The revised calculation of value in use (£450,000) as at 31 December 20X1 indicates an impairment loss of £50,000 compared to the carrying value of £500,000. The impairment loss should be recognised in the year ended 31 December 20X3.

Part of the impairment loss of £50,000 would have been charged as depreciation in years 20X2 and 20X3. FRS 11 does not specify how such depreciation should be taken into account. A suggested method is shown in the table below, which indicates that an impairment loss of £30,000 is required at 31 December 20X3 after adjusting for depreciation, in order to write the asset down from its carrying value of £300,000 to the carrying value that would have been recognised if the impairment loss of £50,000 had been booked at 31 December 20X1.

	Carrying value before impairment £000	Carrying value after impairment £000
31 December X1	500	500
Impairment loss	–	(50)
Depreciation 20X2 and 20X3	(200)	(180)
31 December X3	300	270

It should be noted that a further impairment review may be necessary at 31 December 20X3. Value in use would be calculated using management's latest forecasts of future cash flows. Any further impairment loss thus identified should be recognised immediately.

If the current estimate of value in use exceeds the impaired carrying value of £270,000, the impairment loss should not be reversed, unless the increase in value in use results from a forecast change in economic conditions or in the expected use of the asset. [FRS 11 para 56]. Thus in this example, if management's latest cash flow forecasts for the 3 years to 31 December 20X6 were in line with the previous estimates (£120,000, £130,000 and £130,000 respectively), their present value (that is, value in use) at 31 December 20X3 would be £345,000. Although value in use of £345,000 exceeds the impaired carrying value of £270,000, no reversal of the impairment loss is permitted, because the increase in value in use arises solely from the reduced net cash flows in years 20X2 and 20X3 now having past and from the discounted value of the future cash flows having increased (see further para 18.235).

Reorganisation and capital expenditure

18.112 A key — and controversial — constraint concerning the assumptions in the cash flow forecasts relates to future reorganisation and capital investment. Value in use is supposed to reflect the value of assets or goodwill in their current condition. Hence, the future costs and benefits of future reorganisations should not be recognised in the cash flow forecasts, unless related provisions have been made. Furthermore, the costs and benefits of future capital investment that is intended to improve or enhance the performance of the assets or business should not be taken into account in the cash flow forecasts. [FRS 11 para 38].

18.113 These are severe constraints on the calculations. Impairment reviews should be based on the most recent budgets and plans that have been formally approved by management. Where management has approved reorganisation and capital investment plans, however, the most recent formally approved budgets and plans would typically include both the costs and benefits (such as lower production costs or extra revenues from higher quality output) of the planned reorganisation and capital expenditure. Provisions for reorganisation costs might, however, be recognised in financial statements later than their inclusion in formal budgets and plans — say, after the balance sheet date at which assets are being reviewed for impairment.

18.114 FRS 12, 'Provisions, contingent liabilities and contingent assets', sets out in some detail the conditions that must be complied with before provisions for reorganisations may be recognised in financial statements. In particular, FRS 12 states that a management or board decision to restructure that is taken before the balance sheet date does not give rise to a constructive obligation (the trigger for recognising a provision) unless the entity has, before the balance sheet date (a) started to implement the restructuring, or (b) announced its main features to those affected by it in a sufficiently specific manner to raise a valid expectation in them that the entity will carry out the restructuring.

18.115 If those criteria are met by the balance sheet date and the costs have been provided for in the financial statements, the expenditure and the related benefits (such as savings from lower staff costs) of the reorganisation should also be included in the cash flow forecasts in the appropriate period for determining value in use.

18.116 If, however, those criteria are not met by the balance sheet date and, therefore, no provisions for reorganisation costs have been booked, the costs and benefits of the reorganisation should not be taken into account in the calculation of value in use either. To comply with FRS 11, it is necessary to strip out of the formally approved budgets and plans the planned expenditure on restructuring and the related benefits.

18.117 Stripping out the cash inflows and outflows relating to a planned reorganisation or improvement-type capital expenditure may not be straightforward. For example, it is hypothetical to forecast what future revenues would be if the business remained static rather than being developed in the way that is envisaged and so it may be difficult to adjust a budget to show what the cash flows would be estimated to be if a planned reorganisation or capital expenditure did not take place.

Future reorganisation

18.118 The following example illustrates the treatment of a future reorganisation and the interaction of the impairment calculations with the recognition of reorganisation provisions. The example contrasts the timing of impairment losses and reorganisation costs, which differ according to whether or not the reorganisation is sufficiently advanced in its execution for provisions to be recognised in the financial statements. It also shows how the rules may give rise to the recognition of impairment losses in earlier periods, even though management may expect to avoid impairment by reorganisation, and the reversal of such impairment losses in later periods when the reorganisation is implemented.

Example — future reorganisation planned

At 31 December 20X1, the assets and goodwill of an income-generating unit are being reviewed for impairment. The carrying value of the IGU's net assets is £6,500,000 (excluding any reorganisation provision) and the remaining useful economic life of the recognised assets is 8 years.

Management's approved budgets at 31 December 20X1 include reorganisation costs of £350,000 to be incurred in 20X2; the reorganisation is expected to generate cost savings of £100,000 per annum from 20X3 onwards. Formal budgets have been prepared for the three years to 31 December 20X4; thereafter, for the purpose of the impairment review, a zero growth rate is assumed, because market conditions are extremely competitive and this is expected to continue for the foreseeable future. The future cash flow estimates are set out below, along with figures that exclude from those estimates the cost and benefits of the planned reorganisation. Thus in 20X2 the net cash flows without reorganisation (£870,000) exceed the net cash flows with reorganisation (£520,000) by the amount of the reorganisation costs (£350,000).

The future cash flows (which exclude inflation) have been discounted at a rate of 4%. For simplicity, it has been assumed that the cash flows arise at the end of each year; therefore, the figures in the 'present value' columns for the cash flows (CF) in 'n' years time from 31 December 20X1 are derived from the formula $CF^n/(1+i)^n$, where i (the discount rate) is 0.04.

	With reorganisation		**Without reorganisation**	
	Future net cash flows	Present value	Future net cash flows	Present value
Year	£000	£000	£000	£000
20X2	520	500	870	836
20X3	1,000	925	900	832
20X4	1,050	933	950	845
20X5	1,050	898	950	812
20X6	1,050	863	950	781
20X7	1,050	830	950	751
20X8	1,050	798	950	722
20X9	1,050	767	950	694
Value in use		6,514		6,273

The impairment calculations at 31 December 20X1 differ according to whether or not provision for the reorganisation costs is recognised in the financial statements.

A — Provision for reorganisation costs recognised at 31 December 20X1

If provision has been made for reorganisation costs, the costs and benefits of the reorganisation are taken into account in determining the IGU's value in use. In this example, the post-reorganisation value in use (£6,514,000) exceeds the IGU's carrying value (£6,500,000 less reorganisation provision £350,000). Hence, there is no impairment of the IGU's assets.

In the year to 31 December 20X1, the financial statements reflect the following charges:

Reorganisation provision	£350,000
Impairment loss	Nil

B — No provision for reorganisation costs recognised at 31 December 20X1

If no provision for reorganisation costs is permitted by FRS 12, the costs and benefits of the reorganisation have to be stripped out of the projections in determining the IGU's value in use. In this example, the IGU's carrying value (£6,500,000) exceeds its pre-reorganisation value in use (£6,273,000). Therefore, there is an impairment loss of £227,000.

In the year to 31 December 20X1, the financial statements reflect the following charges:

Impairment loss	£227,000
Reorganisation provision	Nil

In the year to 31 December 20X2, the reorganisation is carried out. Assuming that the cash flow projections at 31 December 20X2 are the same as those previously estimated at 31 December 20X1 (including the benefits of the reorganisation), the calculation of the IGU's value in use at 31 December 20X2 is as follows. Note that the present values of each year's cash flows have increased from the previous table because they are one year closer.

Year	Future net cash flows £000	Present value £000
20X3	1,000	961
20X4	1,050	971
20X5	1,050	933
20X6	1,050	898
20X7	1,050	863
20X8	1,050	830
20X9	1,050	798
Value in use		6,254

As a result of the reorganisation, the IGU's value in use at 31 December 20X2 (£6,254,000) will exceed its impaired carrying value (£6,273,000 less depreciation charged in the year). For example, assume the carrying value of the IGU comprises fixed assets as follows, which are depreciated uniformly over their remaining useful life of eight years.

	Depreciated historical cost before impairment £000	Carrying value after impairment £000
31 December X1	6,500	6,273
Depreciation	812	784
31 December X2	5,688	5,489
Value in use		6,254

The IGU's value in use at 31 December 20X2 exceeds the impaired carrying value by £765,000, therefore the impairment loss of £227,000 should be reversed insofar as permitted by FRS 11. Impairment losses should be reversed in situations where the recoverable amount increases as a result of a reorganisation, the benefits of which had been excluded from the original measurement of value in use. [FRS 11 paras 56, 57]. In this case, the impairment loss should be reversed by increasing the carrying value of the fixed assets to what it would have been had no impairment loss been recognised in the previous year, that is, from £5,489,000 to £5,688,000 — a reversal of £199,000.

In the year to 31 December 20X2, the financial statements reflect the following charges and credits:

Reorganisation costs	£350,000
Reversal of impairment loss	£199,000 Cr

Future capital expenditure

18.119 Future capital expenditure and the related benefits should also be excluded from the calculation of value in use to the extent that the expenditure *"will improve or enhance the income-generating units or assets in excess of their originally assessed standard of performance"*. [FRS 11 para 38]. It should be noted that only improvement-type capital expenditure should be excluded; that which is necessary to maintain an asset or IGU at its originally assessed standard of performance should be included.

18.120 This treatment of capital expenditure needs to be considered carefully. For an individual fixed asset that is being reviewed for impairment, the treatment is relatively straightforward. The value in use takes into account the expenditure that is necessary to maintain the asset for its estimated useful economic life, but it does not anticipate the asset's enhancement or replacement. When those events occur, they result in new capital expenditure being recognised — until then, only the old asset exists.

18.121 FRS 15 codifies the accounting treatment of subsequent expenditure on fixed assets. FRS 15 sets out the circumstances where such expenditure should be capitalised or expensed in the profit and loss account. Repairs and maintenance-type expenditure (that is, expenditure necessary to ensure that an asset maintains its previously assessed standard of performance during its estimated useful life) should be recognised in the profit and loss account as incurred. Such expenditure should be included in the value in use calculations.

18.122 Capitalisation is required in three specific situations. The first is expenditure that enhances the fixed asset in excess of the previously assessed standard of performance. Under FRS 11, the costs and benefits of enhancing assets in excess of the previously assessed standard of performance should be excluded from the impairment calculations.

18.123 The second situation is expenditure that replaces or restores a separate component of the fixed asset (that is, depreciated separately from the rest of the asset). It is highly unlikely that the component would be tested individually for impairment, since it forms part of a larger asset or IGU.

Example

The carrying value of a furnace is being reviewed for impairment. The furnace has a useful life of 20 years and requires relining every 5 years. The lining is treated as a separate asset component under FRS 15. Thus the cost of the lining is depreciated over 5 years; the remainder of the furnace is depreciated over 20 years.

For calculating the furnace's value in use, the net cash flows forecast for the remainder of the furnace's 20 year useful life would include the costs relating to relining the furnace every 5 years, because that expenditure is necessary to maintain the originally assessed standard of performance of the furnace.

18.124 The third situation is expenditure that relates to a major inspection or overhaul of a fixed asset that restores the economic benefits of the asset that have consumed and already reflected in depreciation charges.

Example

An aircraft with a useful life of 20 years requires a major overhaul every 3 years. The value in use of the aircraft would include the costs of each major overhaul (and revenues that assume that the overhauls are carried out and that the aircraft can continue to carry passengers for the whole of its useful economic life).

18.125 The following example illustrates the value in use calculations for an asset where future improvement-type capital expenditure is planned.

Example — improvement-type capital expenditure

A cruise ship is being reviewed for impairment at 31 December 20X1. The ship forms an IGU of its own. Its carrying value is £72,000,000 and its estimated remaining useful life is 10 years, with a residual value estimated at £6,000,000.

Management has approved a major investment plan to increase the ship's passenger capacity and to replace its engines. The work will be carried out in 20X4 and is expected to result in a significant increase in passenger revenues and a decrease in running costs. The remaining useful life is expected to be extended by two years. The estimated cost of the new investment is £8,000,000.

It is assumed that recoverable amount is to be determined by reference to value in use alone. The future cash flow estimates are set out below, along with figures that exclude from those estimates the cost and benefits of the planned capital expenditure. The future cash flows (which exclude inflation) have been discounted at a rate of 6%. For simplicity, it has been assumed that the cash flows arise at the end of each year; therefore, the figures in the 'present value' columns for the cash flows (CF) in 'n' years time from 31 December 20X1 are derived from the formula $CF^n/(1+i)^n$, where i (the discount rate) is 0.06.

	Including new capex		Excluding new capex	
Year	Future net cash flows	Present value	Future net cash flows	Present value
	£000	£000	£000	£000
20X2	8,300	7,830	8,300	7,830
20X3	8,500	7,565	8,500	7,565
20X4	(4,000)	(3,358)	8,500	7,137
20X5	10,500	8,317	8,500	6,732
20X6	10,800	8,070	8,285	6,191
20X7	11,050	7,790	8,078	5,695
20X8	11,250	7,482	7,876	5,238
20X9	11,450	7,184	7,679	4,818
20Y0	10,990	6,505	7,487	4,431
20Y1	10,550	5,891	13,300	7,427
20Y2	10,130	5,336		
20Y3	15,725	7,815		
Value in use		76,427		63,064

For the purpose of the impairment review at 31 December 20X1, the future capital expenditure and the related benefits should be excluded from the calculation of value in use. On this basis, the estimated value in use of the ship in its existing state (£63,064,000) is lower than its carrying value (£72,000,000) and so an impairment loss of £8,936,000 should be recognised.

In the year to 31 December 20X4, the improvement work is carried out. Assuming that the cash flow projections at 31 December 20X4 are the same as those previously estimated at 31 December 20X1, the calculation of the ship's value in use at 31 December 20X4 is as follows.

Year	Future net cash flows	Present value
	£000	£000
20X5	10,500	9,906
20X6	10,800	9,612
20X7	11,050	9,278
20X8	11,250	8,911
20X9	11,450	8,556
20Y0	10,990	7,748
20Y1	10,550	7,016
20Y2	10,130	6,356
20Y3	15,725	9,307
Value in use		76,690

The ship's carrying value at 31 December 20X4 is as follows (straight-line depreciation at 10% per annum to the estimated residual value of £6,000,000 has been assumed).

	Carrying value
	£000
31 December 20X1	63,064
Depreciation 20X2 to 20X4	(17,119)
Capital expenditure	8,000
31 December 20X4	53,945

The ship's value in use following the improvement exceeds its impaired carrying value. In accordance with paragraph 57 of FRS 11, an increase in the recoverable amount as a result of further capital investment (the benefits of which had been excluded from the original measurement of value in use) should result in a reversal of the original impairment loss at 31 December 20X4. The amount of the reversal is restricted to the extent that the carrying value of the ship is increased to what it would have been had the original impairment not occurred, which is calculated as follows, resulting in a reversal of £6,255,000 (£60,200,000 — £53,945,000).

	Carrying value without impairment £000
31 December X1	72,000
Depreciation 20X2 to 20X4	(19,800)
Capital expenditure	8,000
31 December X4	60,200

18.126 Where all the fixed assets and goodwill of an IGU are being reviewed for impairment, the calculation of the IGU's value in use may need to include a level of fixed asset replacement expenditure in the period that is covered by the impairment review. For example, where the assets of an IGU include purchased goodwill with a long estimated useful economic life (in excess of the lives of many of the IGU's fixed assets), the cash flows of the IGU should include a normal level of fixed asset replacement expenditure that is necessary to maintain the operations of the IGU (and, hence, to support its originally assessed revenue-generating capability). However, the value in use of an IGU's existing assets and goodwill does not anticipate the costs of future improvement-type capital expenditure and the related benefits (such as additional revenues or cost savings from the use of more efficient technology). Those items would be factored into an impairment review when the capital expenditure has been incurred and new assets have been recognised, which need to be reviewed for impairment. In practice, the dividing line between maintenance-type and improvement-type capital expenditure is rarely clear-cut, since businesses are not static; the former often includes an element of the latter, especially as regards overhauls and regular refurbishments.

Newly acquired IGUs

18.127 The above rules relating to future reorganisation and capital expenditure are modified for newly acquired IGUs. FRS 11 allows the costs and benefits of planned reorganisation and capital investment relating to a newly acquired IGU to be taken into account for the purpose of impairment reviews in the initial years after the acquisition. In the case of a planned reorganisation, this is irrespective of whether provisions have yet been made in the post-acquisition financial statements (provision for such costs in determining the fair value of the net assets acquired is not permitted by FRS 7). However, the reorganisation or investment that is taken into account in those impairment reviews should be consistent with the budgets and plans that had been formulated by the end of the first full year after the acquisition. [FRS 11 para 39].

18.128 This is a somewhat pragmatic approach for the purpose of reviewing the value of goodwill on a recent acquisition. FRS 10 requires goodwill with a long (more than 20 years) or indefinite life to be reviewed for impairment at the end of each financial year, including the year immediately following the acquisition. Goodwill with a shorter life (20 years or less) should be reviewed for impairment at the end of the first full year following the acquisition. FRS 11's pragmatic approach recognises that purchasers generally share something of the perceived benefits from an acquisition with the vendors. It avoids the situation where goodwill on a new acquisition might be deemed to be impaired (and, hence, written down immediately) solely because the benefits of future reorganisation and investment, which were taken into account by the acquirer in framing its offer, could not be reflected in the impairment reviews over the initial years.

18.129 The FRS goes on to explain that the validity of this treatment would be called into question if the reorganisation or investment does not, in fact, proceed according to the acquisition plan. That situation would itself be an indicator that the assets and goodwill of the acquired business may be impaired and subsequent impairment reviews should then be carried out by excluding the costs and benefits of the originally planned reorganisation or capital investment from the value in use calculations. [FRS 11 para 40].

18.130 The formation of new IGUs in business start-up situations is not addressed in the FRS, but the principles described above from the perspective of acquisitions seem appropriate where, in order to obtain the benefits from initial investment, it is necessary to undertake further capital expenditure. For example, in the early stages of the development of a new project, an impairment loss might be identified if no account were taken of future capital expenditure required to complete the development plan, as it might be loss-making on a 'current condition' basis (that is, until successful completion). Applying the principles of paragraph 39 of FRS 11, if the projections in the development plan (taking account of future capital expenditure required to enable the IGU to reach its originally assessed standard of performance) showed an adequate expected rate of return on the new investment, there would be no impairment. However, if the business subsequently abandoned the development plan, it could no longer be used to support the avoidance of an impairment loss.

Discount rate

18.131 Investment decisions take account of the time value of money and the risks associated with expected future cash flows. These are also reflected in the measurement of an asset's value in use.

18.132 Expected future cash flows are discounted at a rate described as *"an estimate of the rate that the market would expect on an equally risky investment."* [FRS 11 para 41]. This rate reflects both current assessments of the time value of money and the risks specific to the asset concerned. This means that (unless net realisable value is higher) an asset is regarded as impaired if it is not expected to earn a current market-related rate of return on its carrying value.

18.133 The rate of return expected by the market is independent of the way the asset is financed, although the entity's overall cost of capital will sometimes provide a good starting point for estimating a rate.

18.134 The choice of a discount rate is a subjective area. Furthermore, the value in use calculations are sensitive to variations in discount rates. Often there is no directly observable market rate. The FRS suggests the market rate can be estimated by a number of means:

- The rate implicit in market transactions of similar assets.
- The weighted average cost of capital (WACC) for a listed company with a similar risk profile.
- The WACC for the entity, adjusted up or down for the particular risks of the IGU being reviewed for impairment.

[FRS 11 para 42].

18.135 Rates applicable to different business units within a group may vary to reflect any risk factors that are specific to those units. Trading activities and investments in different countries are likely to have different risks, for example, currency and political risks. The rate should be appropriate to the country in which the IGU operates (or in whose currency it derives its major cash flows) rather than the country in which the finance is sourced. Different business sectors also attract different risks — for example, a biotechnology company will carry a greater market risk than a regulated utility. In general, the more uncertain the cash flows are, the more risky the investment is, and the greater the risk adjustment is to increase the discount rate.

18.136 For some companies, the WACC will be an observable rate that they are familiar with. IAS 36 refers to using techniques such as the Capital Asset Pricing Model, which is commonly used in assessing the cost of equity. The FRS notes, however, that if the discount rates are derived from the entity's WACC, the weighted average of the rates applied to each IGU should equal the WACC of the entity as a whole. [FRS 11 para 43]. The FRS does not, however, indicate how this calculation might be performed; proving that the sum of the IGUs' WACCs equals the entity's WACC may be difficult and may not really be relevant if only one IGU is being reviewed for impairment.

18.137 If an impairment loss is recognised and is measured by reference to value in use of a fixed asset or IGU, the FRS also requires the discount rate to be disclosed in the financial statements. As an alternative to using a risk-adjusted discount rate, it may sometimes be more practicable to adjust the expected cash flows (downwards) for risk and to discount those risk-adjusted cash flows at a risk-free discount rate, such as a government bond rate. [FRS 11 para 45]. Where this is done, the FRS requires some indication of the risk-adjustments made to the cash flows to be disclosed. [FRS 11 para 69]. It is important that risk is not double-counted in the calculations; that is, the discount rate should not include a risk weighting if the underlying cash flows have already been adjusted for risk.

18.138 Inflation should also be treated consistently in the present value calculations. If the future cash flows are estimated at current values, the discount rate is a real rate, that is, inflation should be excluded. If the estimated future cash flows include inflation, the discount rate is a nominal rate, that is including inflation.

Pre-tax rate

18.139 FRS 11 requires the discount rate for value in use to be calculated on a pre-tax basis. [FRS 11 para 41]. Thus, an IGU's pre-tax cash flows should be discounted at the determined pre-tax discount rate.

18.140 Where a pre-tax discount rate is available this presents no issues. FRS 11 recognises that in many cases the only observable market rate of return is a *post-tax* rate. This is the case, for example, where the discount rate is derived from an entity's WACC, which many companies would look to when estimating the appropriate discount rate. The FRS requires the post-tax rate to be adjusted to a pre-tax basis.

18.141 The use of pre-tax cash flows and a pre-tax discount rate means that the result is a pre-tax value in use, which will normally differ from the post-tax value in use. If an impairment loss arising from a pre-tax value in use, this creates a taxable temporary difference on which deferred tax should be recognised if required by FRS 19.

18.142 How to calculate the appropriate pre-tax rate from a post-tax starting point is a key practical issue. Unfortunately, it is not simply a matter of grossing up the required post-tax rate of return at the standard or effective rate of tax and discounting the pre-tax cash flows at that grossed up rate. This would only give the correct result if there is no growth in cash flows and no deferred tax. It is necessary to adjust the post-tax rate much more carefully, to reflect the specific amount and timing of the future cash flows.

18.143 Appendix 1 to the standard gives some guidance on how the adjustment to a pre-tax rate might be calculated. It states that the required pre-tax rate is *"the rate of return that will, after tax has been deducted, give the required post-tax rate of return"*. The example given in the standard is over-simplified, but some useful observations can be drawn from it.

18.143.1 The following example illustrates how the pre-tax rate could correctly be derived from the post-tax rate.

Example

An IGU is being tested for impairment at the end of 20X0. The IGU comprises a specific asset, which was purchased two years ago for £2,400. The asset has a ten year useful life for accounting purposes. Tax relief on the asset is available on a straight line basis over the first three years of the asset's life, hence there is a timing difference giving rise to a deferred tax liability. The tax rate is 35%.

Pre-tax profits from the asset are expected to be £125 at the end of 20X1, increasing by 5 for each of the following seven years. The appropriateness of such an increasing rate has been considered and determined reasonable. The results for the seven years in question are, therefore, as follows:

£	**20X1**	**20X2**	**20X3**	**20X4**	**20X5**	**20X6**	**20X7**	**20X8**
Pre-tax profit	125	130	135	140	145	150	155	160
Add back depreciation	240	240	240	240	240	240	240	240
Pre-tax cash flow	**365**	**370**	**375**	**380**	**385**	**390**	**395**	**400**
Tax on profit	(44)	(46)	(47)	(49)	(51)	(53)	(54)	(56)
Post-tax cash flow	**321**	**325**	**328**	**331**	**334**	**338**	**341**	**344**

The post-tax discount rate, determined from the WACC of the company, is 8%.

There are two potential misapplications of the requirements of FRS 11 that are commonly seen. Neither of these give the correct value in use per the requirements of FRS 11.

Misapplication 1: Discount post-tax cash flow at post-tax discount rate of 8%. This gives a value in use of £1,904.

Misapplication 2: Discount pre-tax cash flow at post-tax discount rate grossed up for the tax rate. This rate would be 8%/(1-0.35) = 12.3%. This gives a value in use of £1,866.

These misapplications fail to achieve the correct result, either by not accounting for varying period-on-period cash flows or by ignoring deferred tax. The correct value in use can be achieved by taking the value in use from Misapplication 1 and adjusting for the discounted cash outflows related to deferred tax. This is a complex iterative calculation as the discounted cash outflows in question relate to the pre-tax value in use – hence the result of the calculation feeds back into the calculation itself. The calculation is best solved with the aid of a computer, but the following summarises the final calculation for the above example once the iteration has been completed.

£	**20X0**	**20X1**	**20X2**	**20X3**	**20X4**	**20X5**	**20X6**	**20X7**	**20X8**
Pre-tax VIU (*a*)	1,729	1,513	1,296	1,080	864	648	432	216	0
Tax base (*ß*)	800								
a – ß	*929*	*1,513*	*1,296*	*1,080*	*864*	*648*	*432*	*216*	*0*
Change in *a – ß*		*584*	*(216)*	*(216)*	*(216)*	*(216)*	*(216)*	*(216)*	*(216)*
@ 35% (tax)		204	(76)	(76)	(76)	(76)	(76)	(76)	(76)
Discounted (8%)	(175)								
Post-tax VIU	1,904								
Pre-tax VIU	**1,729**								

The 'pre-tax VIU' number is as calculated in 'Misapplication 1' above. The iterative process will complete when a set of figures for the first line have been derived which, when discounted at 8%, produce the same number as in the bottom 'pre-tax VIU' line.

Having derived the correct pre-tax VIU, and having the correct pre-tax cash flows, it is possible to 'back-solve' to obtain pre-tax discount rate that discounts the latter to the former. In this case this figure is 14.5%.

18.143.2 Deriving a true pre-tax discount rate is a complex exercise. There are some practical methods to use to identify potential impairment losses and estimate the pre-tax impact.

18.143.3 One method is to calculate the post-tax cash flow discounted at the post-tax discount rate, as per Misapplication 1. This calculation should give a reasonable indication of whether there has been an impairment using readily available data. If no impairment is identified, a judgement can then be made with regard to the headroom above carrying value – if the headroom is considered sufficiently high, then it will be possible to infer that the likelihood of an impairment arising on a pre-tax calculation is remote. The pre-tax rate can be estimated for disclosure purposes.

18.143.4 If there is not significant headroom in the post-tax calculation then a pre-tax analysis will be required to identify the correct pre-tax value in use from which the pre-tax impairment loss and the related deferred tax effects can be derived (as can the pre-tax discount rate for disclosure purposes).

18.143.5 An alternative method would be to estimate the correct value in use of Misapplication 2 – estimating the pre-tax discount rate by grossing up the post-tax discount rate by an appropriate tax rate (for example, the estimated future cash tax rate). Care should be taken in this exercise. For instance the estimate made should be adjusted to reflect the effect of special factors that might materially distort the relationship between the post-tax rate and the pre-tax rate — for example, where the timing of the tax cash flows is very favourable to the entity because of accelerated capital allowances. Applying this estimated rate to the the pre-tax cash flows would result in an estimated value in use (and an estimated impairment loss) of the asset or CGU. As above, judgement will be needed to assess the reasonableness of the estimate.

18.143.6 If neither of these approximations is deemed acceptable then a pre-tax analysis will be required. The required pre-tax rate is the rate of return that will, after tax has been deducted, give the required post-tax rate of return. The following example illustrates how the pre-tax rate may be derived from the post-tax rate.

Example

The post-tax market rate of return required from an asset is 14%. Profits are taxed at 30%; there is a capital allowance of 100% of the cost of the asset. All cash flows arise at the end of year 1.

For an asset costing £100, the required post-tax cash flows during year 1 are £114. Pre-tax cash flows of £120 must be earned in order to give the required post-tax return of £114. Pre-tax cash flows of £120 result in a tax charge of £6 — comprising tax on profit before depreciation of £36 (30% of £120) less tax relief on the cost of the asset of £30 (30% of £100). Thus the required pre-tax rate is 20%.

The value in use of £100 of an asset with the above cash flows can be derived either by discounting the post-tax cash flows of £114 at the post-tax rate of 14% or by discounting the pre-tax cash flows of £120 at the derived pre-tax rate of 20%. The same answer is obtained from both methods, because the cost of the asset is fully deductible for tax purposes as a result of the 100% capital allowances and, therefore, does not give rise to any timing differences.

18.144 The above examples demonstrate that the pre-tax rate has to be derived from the post-tax rate and the post-tax cash flows. Therefore, the starting point is a *post-tax* analysis, despite the value in use calculation being labelled as a pre-tax exercise.

18.145 Grossing up from a post-tax rate of 14 per cent to a pre-tax rate of 20 per cent reflects the assumed rate of corporation tax only because of its unrealistic simplicity. The relationship between the post-tax rate and the derived pre-tax rate will deviate from the standard rate as soon as real factors are introduced such as uneven multi-period cash flows, timing differences between pre-tax cash flows and the related tax cash flows and so on.

18.146 The pre-tax discount rate can be derived using the post-tax discount rates directly observable from capital markets by using a two-step iterative calculation process to convert the post-tax discount rate into an implicit pre-tax rate. This is based on: first, discounting the post-tax cash flows using a post-tax discount rate, then determining the implicit pre-tax rate that needs to be applied to pre-tax cash flows to arrive at the same result. Post-tax cash flows should reflect the specific amount and timing of the future tax cash flows.

18.146.1 In theory, discounting post-tax cash flows at a post-tax discount rate should lead to the same result as discounting pre-tax cash flows with a pre-tax discount rate, as long as the pre-tax discount rate is the post-tax discount rate adjusted to reflect the specific amount and timing of the future tax cash flows.

18.146.2 In practice, the following two-step approach can be applied to derive iteratively the implicit pre-tax discount rate from post-tax data. In Step 1, the expected actual tax cash payments are calculated to arrive at post-tax cash flows (after-tax cash flows) from pre-tax cash flow projections. These after-tax cash flows are discounted at an appropriate post-tax discount rate derived using information observable on the capital markets.

18.146.3 As a starting point for the derivation of the post-tax discount rate, the entity's weighted average cost of capital (WACC) could be taken into account (as opposed to entity's incremental borrowing rate or other market borrowing rates), as the WACC is usually a good reflection of the risk specific to the asset/IGU provided that it is similar to the rate a market participant would use. This WACC should be adjusted for specific risks associated with the asset/IGU's estimated cash flows (for example, country/currency/price risk). If such WACC for the entity is not available, it may be necessary to estimate a WACC using peer group data.

18.146.4 In Step 2, the pre-tax discount rate is derived by determining the rate required to be applied to the pre-tax cash flows to arrive at the result obtained in step 1. In practice, the rate is calculated using the same methodology as for the calculation of an internal rate of return.

Allocating assets and liabilities to IGUs

18.147 The carrying amount of each IGU being reviewed for impairment needs to be established. This is done by allocating assets and liabilities to individual IGUs. The carrying amount of an IGU consists of:

- Assets and liabilities that are directly and exclusively attributable to the IGU.
- An allocation of assets and liabilities that are indirectly attributable to more than one IGU (that is, central assets).
- Capitalised goodwill (or negative goodwill).

18.148 The assets and liabilities attributed to IGUs should be consistent with the cash flows that are identified for calculating value in use. Assets in the first category above will include all directly attributable tangible and intangible fixed assets and current assets such as stocks, trade debtors and prepayments. Liabilities will include trade creditors and directly attributable accruals and provisions. However, if it is easier in practice to exclude items of working capital in the IGU's balance sheet at the date of the impairment review (that is, items such as trade debtors and creditors that will generate cash flows equal to their carrying amounts), this is permitted provided, of course, that the receipts and payments are also excluded from the value in use calculation.

18.149 Liabilities that relate to financing the operations of IGUs (including interest-bearing debt, dividends and interest payable) are not allocated, because the related cash outflows are also excluded from the impairment calculations and such items are taken into account in the rate used to discount the future operating cash flows when calculating an IGU's value in use. Similarly, tax balances are not allocated for a value in use calculation, because the discounted cash flow forecasts are prepared on a pre-tax basis. In contrast in a net realisable value calculation current and deferred tax balances and their associated cash flows are taken into account.

18.150 The standard does not specify how leased assets should be treated. Under the standard's impairment review methodology, the approach would be as follows. For finance leases, the carrying value of the leased asset would be included in the carrying value of the IGU; the lease liability and the lease payments would be excluded from the impairment calculations because they relate to financing. For operating leases, no assets would be recognised in the carrying value of the IGU; the lease payments would be treated as operating cash outflows in the calculation of value in use.

Central assets

18.151 Where practicable, FRS 11 requires that assets that contribute indirectly to IGUs (such as corporate head offices, computer centres or research facilities) should be allocated to individual IGUs on a logical and systematic basis that reflects the extent to which those resources are applied to support each IGU. An example is given of pro-rating according to the carrying values of the net assets directly attributable to IGUs. The idea is that the carrying values of all IGUs in a group should add up to the carrying value of the group's net assets in aggregate (excluding tax and financing items) — thus, no assets should escape attention in an impairment review.

18.152 The reason for including central assets (which may not generate any income) is that unless the operating assets or IGUs are expected to generate sufficient cash flows to recover the carrying amounts of all the entity's assets (that is, including the central assets which generate no external income themselves), there is an impairment.

18.153 This treatment of central assets may be problematical if companies' information systems do not readily provide such allocations. In addition, the basis for allocating central costs to operating units will need to be reviewed to ensure that the cash flows used for the impairment reviews are on a basis that is consistent with the basis on which the central assets have been allocated.

18.154 By including allocations of central assets within the IGU's carrying value, the impairment review checks whether or not the IGU's net cash flows (exclusive of any cash outflows relating to the IGU's use of those central assets) are expected to recover the carrying values of the IGU's own assets and the allocated portion of central assets. For example, if an IGU is allocated a portion of the book value of the group's head office, the impairment review compares the IGU's value in use with the carrying value as increased. Any internal charges that are payable relating to the use of the head office would need to be excluded from the IGU's cash flows; otherwise the consumption of head office resources would be double-counted, because the carrying value would be increased and the value in use decreased by the same item.

18.155 FRS 11 permits a simpler alternative approach to be used where central assets cannot readily be allocated on a meaningful basis. The alternative approach permits central assets to be reviewed for impairment on an aggregate basis where there is no reasonable basis for allocating them to individual IGUs. This would require a two-tier impairment review:

- A review at the individual IGU level, where only the assets and liabilities directly involved are reviewed for impairment.

- A review at a higher level, where any central assets that contribute to the relevant IGU are reviewed for impairment in aggregate with all other IGUs to which they contribute. This review compares the aggregate of the net assets of those IGUs and the central assets with their combined value in use.

18.156 A consequence of this approach is that impairment tests encompass certain IGUs irrespective of whether they are displaying characteristics which would trigger an impairment review.

18.157 The two methods described above of dealing with central assets are likely to result in different impairment calculations. The second method of not allocating central assets to IGUs reduces the prospect of impairment losses being identified. The reason is that impairment losses that may otherwise be attributed to individual IGUs (because their carrying values would reflect allocations of central assets) may to some extent be avoided if the carrying amounts of central assets can be recovered from other more profitable IGUs. At the IGU level, there is no impairment of the operating assets as long as they are earning a market-related return on their carrying values. At the combined level, there is no impairment of the central assets as long as the combined operations are in aggregate earning a market-related return on all the assets, including the central assets. An example in paragraph 18.199 illustrates the different calculations.

Purchased goodwill

18.158 For goodwill, the details of the impairment review differ according to whether:

- Goodwill *only* is being reviewed for impairment (for example, the mandatory annual review for goodwill with a useful life of more than 20 years, where there are no indicators of impairment).

- Goodwill *and* other fixed assets are being reviewed for impairment (for example, because there are indicators that an impairment may have occurred).

18.159 The differences relate to the level of aggregation at which groups of assets or businesses are reviewed for impairment. Although impairment reviews for fixed assets, including recognised intangibles, should be carried out at the level of each IGU that is being tested for impairment (subject to possible groupings on materiality grounds), FRS 11 allows a higher level of aggregation for impairment reviews on goodwill.

18.160 IGUs may be combined for testing the recoverability of the related goodwill if:

- they were acquired as part of the same investment; and

- they are involved in similar parts of the business.

[FRS 11 para 34].

18.161 This means that if goodwill relating to the acquisition of a group of companies has to be reviewed annually for impairment only because it is being carried permanently as an asset or is being amortised over more than 20 years, and there are no reasons to suggest that either the goodwill or other assets have actually been impaired, the whole acquisition could be treated as one IGU for the purpose of testing goodwill for impairment if the acquisition comprises similar activities. Thus, the overall goodwill on the acquisition would not have to be sub-divided for the purpose of this impairment review.

18.162 If, however, there are indicators that the carrying values of goodwill or fixed assets may not be recoverable, the normal rules of FRS 11 apply. Individual reviews of each relevant IGU must then be carried out to consider whether fixed assets (other than goodwill) have been impaired.

18.163 If IGUs are combined for testing goodwill, a two-tier impairment review is required, similar to the combined approach for dealing with central assets:

- A review at the individual IGU level, where the assets and liabilities (excluding any allocation of goodwill) are reviewed for impairment. Any impairment loss is attributed to the IGU's assets.

- A review at a higher level to test the recoverability of the goodwill, where all the IGUs to which the goodwill relates are reviewed in aggregate. This review compares the carrying amount of the net assets of those IGUs and the purchased goodwill in aggregate with their combined value in use. Any further impairment loss identified at this level relates to the goodwill.

An example illustrating the two different approaches to treating goodwill is given in paragraph 18.193.

Guidelines on allocating goodwill

18.164 The carrying amount of capitalised goodwill should be allocated either to individual IGUs or, if the alternative approach is taken, to groups of similar IGUs that formed part of the same acquisition. An impairment of goodwill in one business could not be offset against an increase in value of another dissimilar business or one that was acquired at a different time.

18.165 Groups need to keep detailed records of the composition of the aggregate amount of purchased goodwill, that is, to which parts of the group it relates. Apart from the possibility of impairment reviews in the future, allocation of goodwill to business units is necessary to account for subsequent disposals (to determine how much goodwill should be written off when a business is sold) and to keep track of elements of goodwill with different useful economic lives.

18.166 It has always been recognised that there are practical difficulties with attributing goodwill to businesses closed or sold. Tracing purchased goodwill is an issue in complex group structures, particularly where an acquired business quickly loses its separate identity or when businesses undergo change and restructuring. Nevertheless, groups have generally managed to make reasonable allocations of goodwill to disposals.

18.167 As far as is practical and consistent with the requirements of the impairment review, the objective should be to allocate goodwill balances to business units on a basis consistent with the group's management reporting structure.

18.168 There is no real guidance in the accounting standards dealing with goodwill and impairment on how to allocate purchased goodwill to different business units. In principle, goodwill should be allocated based on information and factors existing at the date of acquisition.

18.169 If the acquirer, when framing its offer, had assessed individually the values of different businesses in an acquired group, such valuations should be a good starting point for the allocation of goodwill. Thereafter, various methods could be adopted to apportion goodwill to different IGUs or groups of similar IGUs. The choice should best reflect the basis on which the business would be valued by the market at the time of the acquisition. It should be noted, however, that FRS 10 does not permit purchased goodwill arising on a single acquisition transaction to be divided into components of positive and negative goodwill, because goodwill (positive or negative) is treated as a residual difference that arises from fair valuing the acquisition as a whole. Examples of possible allocation methods are:

- Using discounted cash flow forecasts where these are available at the time of the acquisition.
- Pro-rata on the basis of a price-earnings formula, using cash flows or income streams projected at the acquisition date.
- Pro-rata on net asset value at the acquisition date (probably excluding interest-bearing debt and other financing liabilities).
- Pro-rata using the fair values of the fixed assets at the acquisition date.

18.170 Earnings-based methods may give a very different goodwill allocation from asset-based methods. The choice would be determined by ascertaining how the market rates businesses similar to those acquired — on an earnings or net assets basis. Earnings-based methods are, in general, likely to be appropriate for most acquisitions, because asset-based methods do not generally reflect the relative profitability of different businesses. A cash flow/price-earnings (PE) approach is also consistent with the principles for calculating value in use and is therefore likely to be the most appropriate method to use. An asset value basis would be appropriate for some asset-based acquisitions, such as property companies.

18.171 The choice of a PE ratio could be influenced by considering PE ratios of similar businesses that are listed, although it would not be appropriate to look to PE ratios of those preparing their financial statements on a different basis, such as IFRS. For example, if an acquisition comprised a construction and a transport operation, the allocation would take account of the differing PE ratios relating to those sectors at the acquisition date.

18.172 Where an acquisition gives rise to positive goodwill overall, no goodwill (positive or negative) would be attributed to an IGU where management believe none existed when the group was acquired. For example, where a business is loss-making or operating at a low level of profitability that does not cover the cost of capital, no negative goodwill should be allocated; instead, the overall goodwill on the acquisition would be allocated to those IGUs where it is believed goodwill does exist.

18.173 An example of different allocation methods is illustrated below.

Example — allocation of purchased goodwill

An acquisition of a group comprises three business segments A, B and C. Total purchase consideration was £450m. The fair value of the net assets in aggregate was £350m (as allocated in the table below), leaving goodwill of £100m. Different allocation methods are illustrated in the table below.

Business acquired	**A**	**B**	**C**	**D**
-	-	-	-	-
Profit estimate	20	30	(5)	45
Net assets – fair value	200	100	50	350
Sector PE ratio	12	8		
Goodwill – earnings basis	22	78	Nil	100
Goodwill – net assets basis	67	33	Nil	100

Segment C (which is loss-making) receives a zero allocation of goodwill under both methods. Therefore, all of the goodwill has been allocated to segment A and segment B.

On an earnings basis, segment A and segment B are each valued at £240m (that is, 12 × £20m and 8 × £30m respectively), compared with fair valued net assets of £200m and £100m respectively. The purchased goodwill of £100m is allocated *pro rata* to the amount by which the values of segment A and segment B exceed the fair values of their net assets (£40m and £140m respectively) which results in £22m being allocated to segment A and £78m being allocated to segment B.

On a net assets basis, the purchased goodwill of £100m is allocated *pro rata* to the fair valued net assets of £200m in segment A and £100m in segment B, which results in £67m being allocated to segment A and £33m to segment B.

18.174 In the above example, no goodwill (positive or negative) has been allocated to segment C, which is loss-making. FRS 10 does not allow both positive and negative goodwill to be recognised in respect of a single acquisition.

If the assets of that business are already impaired at the date of acquisition, FRS 7 requires the impairment to be reflected by reducing the fair values on acquisition. [FRS 7 paras 47].

[The next paragraph is 18.184.]

Recognition of impairment losses

Allocation of impairment losses to assets of income-generating units

18.184 Where the recoverable amounts of fixed assets can be estimated individually, the recognition of impairment losses is straightforward. The assets are written down to their individual recoverable amounts (that is, the higher of net realisable value and value in use).

18.185 Where the recoverable amounts of fixed assets or goodwill cannot be estimated individually and, hence, they need to be estimated in aggregate for the IGUs to which they belong, the question arises as to which assets in the IGU should be written down where the carrying value of an IGU's net assets in aggregate exceeds its recoverable amount.

18.186 FRS 11 requires that, unless an impairment is obviously attributable to a specific asset in an IGU, an impairment loss attributable to an IGU should be allocated to write down the assets in the following order:

- Purchased goodwill.
- Capitalised intangibles.
- Tangible assets, on a *pro rata* or more appropriate basis.

[FRS 11 para 48].

The reason for this hierarchy is to ensure that the assets with the most subjective valuations are written off first.

Example

An IGU has attributed net assets of £500m, as set out in the table below. An impairment review estimates the present value of its future cash flows to be £300m. There is an impairment loss of £200m which is written off as shown.

		Write-off
	£m	£m
Purchased goodwill	150	(150)
Intangible assets	30	(30)
Net tangible assets	320	(20)
Net assets	500	(200)
Value in use	300	

18.187 However, within this allocation framework no intangible asset with a readily ascertainable market value or tangible asset with a net realisable value that can be measured reliably should be written down below those values. [FRS 11 para 49]. It should be noted that very few intangible assets have a readily ascertainable market value as defined in the FRS.

18.188 This rule accords with the general principle in the FRS that an asset should not be written down below the higher of its net realisable value or value in use. Whilst the value in use of individual assets in an IGU may not be determinable, their net realisable values may be. For example, individual properties occupied by branches of an integrated financial services operation that is treated as a single IGU for calculating value in use may have determinable market values. Any impairment losses that cannot be allocated on a *pro rata* basis to specific assets because they have higher net realisable values are allocated to other assets in the IGU.

18.189 The allocation process is important because it establishes new carrying values for individual assets that form the basis for subsequent depreciation charges and for accounting for subsequent disposals. However, it is necessarily arbitrary. The allocation between tangible fixed assets in an IGU would normally be made *pro rata* to their individual carrying values. However, management has discretion to adopt a different basis if that is considered to be more appropriate.

Example

The carrying value of an IGU's assets is £130 in aggregate, comprising tangible assets as analysed in the table below. The IGU's property has a market value of £70; the other assets do not have determinable net realisable values. The IGU's value in use is estimated to be £100, resulting in an impairment loss of £30 to be allocated.

The impairment loss is allocated to the assets of the IGU based on their relative carrying values, except that the property is not written down below its net realisable value of £70. Part of the loss that would otherwise be allocated to the property is reallocated to the other fixed assets, as illustrated below.

	Carrying value before impairment review	Impairment loss allocation		Impaired carrying value
		Pro-rata	Reallocated	
Property	80	18	10	70
Plant & equipment	30	7	12	18
Fixtures & fittings	20	5	8	12
	130	30	30	100

Different methods of treating goodwill

18.190 Paragraph 18.64 onwards explains the principles for allocating purchased goodwill to IGUs. Two methods are permitted and these are to some extent optional.

18.191 The first method is to fully allocate purchased goodwill to individual IGUs. Where relevant, the carrying values of IGUs reviewed for impairment then include a share of purchased goodwill.

18.192 The second method allows the purchased goodwill component to be reviewed for impairment at a higher level of aggregation than other assets. IGUs may be combined for testing the recoverability of the related goodwill if:

- they were acquired as part of the same investment; and
- they are involved in similar parts of the business.

[FRS 11 para 34].

18.193 If the second method is adopted, a two-tier impairment review is required, comprising:

- A review at the individual IGU level, where the assets and liabilities (excluding any allocation of goodwill) are reviewed for impairment. Any impairment loss is attributed to the IGU's assets.
- A review at a higher level to test the recoverability of the goodwill, where all the IGUs to which the goodwill relates are reviewed in aggregate. This review compares the carrying amount of the net assets of those IGUs and the purchased goodwill in aggregate with their combined value in use. Any further impairment loss identified at this level relates to the goodwill.

Example

An acquisition made some years ago comprised two IGUs, A and B. There has been an indicator that the carrying value of A may be impaired.

A — Recognition of impairment where goodwill is allocated

The carrying values of the net assets and goodwill of IGUs A and B, and their value in use, are determined as follows:

Income-generating unit	**A**	**B**	**Total**
	£m	**£m**	**£m**
Net assets	220	110	330
Goodwill	40	40	80
Total net assets	260	150	410
Value in use	200	180	380
Impairment	60		

In this example, where purchased goodwill is allocated to the separate IGUs there is an impairment loss of £60m in A, reducing the carrying value of its net assets and goodwill to £200m. The impairment loss is attributed £40m to goodwill and £20m to other fixed assets.

The carrying values after recognising the impairment loss are as follows.

Carrying values after impairment	A	B	Total
	£m	£m	£m
Net assets	200	110	310
Goodwill	–	40	40
Total net assets	200	150	350

B — Recognition of impairment where goodwill is aggregated

If A and B, which were acquired together in one investment, were involved in similar parts of the business, the calculations could be done as follows:

Income-generating unit	A	B	Goodwill	Total
	£m	£m	£m	£m
Net assets	220	110	80	410
Value in use	200	180		380
Impairment	20		10	30

First, IGU A is reviewed for impairment without any allocation of goodwill. The value in use of £200m is compared with the carrying value of its net assets (excluding goodwill) of £220m. There is an impairment loss of £20m, reducing the carrying value of its net assets to £200m.

Secondly, A and B may be combined to assess the recoverability of the goodwill. The value in use of the combined units is now £380m, which is compared with the aggregate carrying value of the net assets and goodwill, which is £390m (that is, £410m less the £20m written off the net assets of unit A). Therefore, a further impairment loss of £10m is recognised to write down the goodwill to £70m.

The carrying values after recognising the impairment loss are as follows.

Carrying values after impairment	A	B	Goodwill	Total
	£m	£m	£m	£m
Net assets	200	110	70	380

18.194 The above example illustrates that significantly different accounting results can be achieved by adopting different approaches to aggregation and also serves to place impairment testing in its context — showing that impairment tests are not exact mathematical exercises. Under the first method, where no aggregation assumed, there is an impairment loss of £60 million. Under the second method, where goodwill is reviewed on an aggregate basis, there is an impairment loss of only £30 million. The second method in effect allows the impairment in the value of the goodwill of the impaired IGU to be partly offset against an increase in the value of the goodwill of the unimpaired IGU since its acquisition. It should be noted that this offset would not be allowed if A and B were involved in dissimilar activities or were acquired in different acquisitions.

18.195 It should also be noted that if A or B were subsequently sold separately, an allocation of the carrying value of goodwill would be necessary to eliminate it from the balance sheet (that is, to write it off as part of the profit or loss on disposal). Where the first method (allocating goodwill to separate IGUs) has been used to account for impairment, this is straightforward. Where the second method has been used, the allocation of goodwill between A and B that previously was not made would have to be made if there is a sale. In the above example, if A were sold, a loss of £30 million would have to be recognised on disposal in respect of purchased goodwill attributable to A that has not previously been written off. The figure of £30 million reflects the purchased goodwill of £40 million that would have originally been allocated to A less the previous impairment of £10 million that would have been attributable to A.

Central assets

18.196 Central assets that provide benefits to two or more IGUs in an enterprise (such as corporate head offices, computer centres or research facilities) should be dealt with in one of two ways.

- First, if possible, their carrying values should be apportioned across the IGUs that they support on a logical and systematic basis. The resulting carrying values of each IGU are then compared with their recoverable amounts.
- Secondly, if it is not possible to apportion central assets meaningfully, they are covered in a two-tier impairment review. The methodology for the two-tier review is similar to that relating to goodwill and permits the central assets to be reviewed in aggregate with all the IGUs that they support.

18.197 However, the two methods are not strictly optional as they may be in some circumstances for goodwill — if central assets can be allocated meaningfully across IGUs, they should be (see para 18.151 for further discussion of allocation methodology).

18.198 As with goodwill, the two methods of dealing with central assets may give different overall impairment results. The 'two-tier' approach could avoid some impairment losses that would be identified in the full allocation approach. The recoverable amount of one IGU might only just exceed the carrying value of its operating assets (without any allocation of central assets), whereas the recoverable amounts of the other IGUs might exceed the carrying values of both their operating assets and the central assets. In such circumstances, the 'two tier' review would not reveal any impairment, whereas the full allocation approach would reveal an impairment in the marginally profitable IGU. The 'two-tier' approach has the effect of allowing central assets to be allocated first to the more profitable IGUs, thus protecting less profitable IGUs from impairment losses. The view would presumably be that the central assets are not impaired as long as the more profitable parts of the business can support their carrying values.

18.199 The following examples illustrate the full allocation and two-tier approaches to dealing with central assets, coupled with the different approaches to the allocation of goodwill.

Example 1 — full allocation of central assets and goodwill to individual IGUs

An entity comprises two IGUs, A and B. The entity has a head office with a book value of £30m.

The following table illustrates the impairment review based on the calculation of value in use assuming that both the head office and purchased goodwill are allocated fully to the two IGUs. The head office is allocated *pro rata* to the other net assets; thus, £20m is allocated to A and £10m is allocated to B. (Note that any intra-group cash flows relating to the use of the head office should be excluded from the IGUs' value in use calculations in order to avoid double-counting).

Income-generating unit	**A**	**B**	**Total**
	£m	**£m**	**£m**
Directly attributable net assets	220	110	330
Head office	20	10	30
Goodwill	40	40	80
Total net assets	280	160	440
Value in use	200	180	380
Impairment	80		80
Net assets as written down	200	160	360

There is an impairment loss of £80m in A. This needs to be allocated between the assets of A — first to the allocated goodwill and thereafter to the tangible fixed assets. Possible methods are illustrated in the following table.

The first method allocates the balance of the impairment loss after goodwill write-off (£40m) *pro-rata* between all the tangible fixed assets attributable to the IGU, including the head office allocation. (The impairment attributable to the head office and the IGU's tangible fixed assets is calculated as 40 × 20/240 and 40 × 220/240 respectively.) The rationale would be that the part of the head office that is dedicated to the unprofitable IGU is impaired.

Some may find it curious to write down a proportion of the head office in this way and may prefer to charge the whole impairment loss against the IGU's operating assets, as in the second method. But it is still necessary (if possible) to allocate the head office asset for the purpose of the impairment calculations, even if impairment losses arising are allocated only to the IGU's assets.

Allocation of impairment loss	**1**	**2**
	£m	**£m**
Goodwill	40.0	40.0
Head office	3.3	–
Directly attributable tangible fixed assets of A	36.7	40.0
	80.0	80.0

A further complication that could arise is where the head office had a market value in excess of its impaired value as calculated on a value in use basis — say, its net realisable value were in excess of £30m. In that situation, because no asset can be written down below its net realisable value, the whole of the impairment loss would have to be allocated to the IGU's tangible fixed assets.

Example 2 — full allocation of central assets; goodwill reviewed in aggregate

The facts are as in example 1. The following table illustrates the impairment review assuming that the head office is allocated to the two IGUs, but goodwill is reviewed in aggregate, because it relates to a single acquisition and the two IGUs are involved in similar parts of the business.

The allocated net assets of A are impaired by £40m and the capitalised goodwill in aggregate is impaired by £20m, giving a total impairment loss of only £60m.

Income-generating unit	**A**	**B**	**Goodwill**	**Total**
	£m	**£m**	**£m**	**£m**
Directly attributable net assets	220	110	80	410
Head office	20	10	–	30
Total net assets	240	120	80	440
Value in use	200	180		380
Impairment	40		20	60
Net assets as written down	200	120	60	380

This method in effect allows the impairment of goodwill that was recognised in example 1 (£40m) to be offset by unrecognised internally generated goodwill of £20m in unit B. This offset would not be allowed if A and B were involved in dissimilar activities.

The impairment loss of £40m attributable to IGU A would be allocated on one of the bases described in example 1. Method 1 is a *pro rata* allocation between the IGU's tangible fixed assets and the allocated portion of the head office; method 2 allocates the whole of the impairment loss after goodwill write-off to the IGU's directly attributable fixed assets.

Allocation of impairment loss	**1**	**2**
	£m	£m
Goodwill	20.0	20.0
Head office	3.3	–
Directly attributable tangible fixed assets of A	36.7	40.0
	60.0	60.0

Example 3 — two-tier review of central assets and goodwill

The facts are the same as in examples 1 and 2. The following table illustrates the impairment review if neither the head office nor purchased goodwill is allocated to the individual IGUs. Instead, two impairment reviews are carried out. The first review is at the individual IGU level, comparing value in use with the carrying value of the net assets directly involved in the businesses (that is, excluding central assets and goodwill). The second review brings in the head office and goodwill at an aggregate level.

The first review shows an impairment loss of £20m in IGU A.

The second review compares the aggregate value in use (£380m) with the aggregate net asset value recognised after the first impairment review (£420m), comprising the impaired net assets of unit A (£200m), the net assets of unit B (£110m), the head office (£30m) and the capitalised goodwill (£80m). This results in a further impairment loss of £40m, which is allocated to the goodwill.

Income-generating unit	**A £m**	**B £m**	**Head office £m**	**Goodwill £m**	**Total £m**
Directly attributable net assets	220	110	30	80	440
Value in use	200	180			380
Impairment	20			40	60
Net assets as written down	200	110	30	40	380

The impairment loss of £20m attributable to IGU A would be allocated *pro rata* to its tangible fixed assets. The overall impairment loss would be allocated as follows.

Allocation of impairment loss	**1 £m**	**2 £m**
Goodwill	40.0	40.0
Head office	1.7	–
Directly attributable tangible fixed assets of A	18.3	20.0
	60.0	60.0

18.200 The three examples above illustrate how different approaches to allocating central assets and goodwill can result in either different impairment losses or different allocations of impairment losses as between operating assets, central assets and goodwill. A further issue is to ensure that cash flows relating to central overheads are treated consistently in the calculation of value in use, that is, that they are neither omitted from nor double-counted in the impairment review. For example, in example 3 above, where no allocation of the head office carrying value was made to the IGUs, the inclusion of any compensating cash outflows relating to the head office property in the calculation of the IGUs' value in use would also affect the impairment calculations. Thus any rent payable to the parent company in relation to the head office would reduce the IGUs' value in use and, as a result, any impairment losses attributable to the IGUs would be correspondingly increased. The message is that the calculations can be significantly affected by subjective allocations of central assets or central costs.

Integration of acquired businesses with existing operations

18.201 FRS 11 addresses a specific issue relating to purchased goodwill. The situation is where an acquired business that resulted in the recognition of purchased goodwill is integrated with other operations of the acquiring group and, as a result, loses its separate identity. As the benefits from many acquisitions lie in the cost savings and other synergies that can be gained from merging the acquired operations with an existing unit, this is a common practice.

18.202 Where operations are merged in this way, the assets and purchased goodwill of the acquired business may then form part of the carrying value of a larger IGU that includes assets of pre-existing operations. If an impairment review of the larger IGU is required, its value in use would be compared with its carrying value. The IGU's carrying value comprises the carrying values of the recognised net assets of the acquired and pre-existing operations, together with the carrying value of the purchased goodwill relating to the acquired business. The IGU's value in use will reflect the value of any internally generated goodwill in the existing business, this internally generated goodwill is not permitted to be recognised as an asset. If impairment reviews were carried out on this basis, an impairment relating to the acquired business could be avoided to the extent that it was offset by unrecognised internally generated goodwill in the existing business with which the acquired business was merged.

18.203 FRS 11 sets out a method that should be applied to a combined IGU that contains both (capitalised) purchased goodwill relating to the acquired business and (unrecognised) internally generated goodwill that relates to the existing business. This method notionally preserves a distinction between the two types of goodwill in the IGU, and requires impairment losses to be allocated between them in order to prevent a potential impairment of the purchased goodwill from being avoided.

18.204 FRS 11 requires the internally generated goodwill of the existing business to be estimated at the date of merging the businesses. This exercise requires the existing business to be valued separately before the integration (that is, its value in use should be estimated). The internally generated goodwill should be calculated by deducting the fair value of the net assets (and any purchased goodwill) of the existing business from its estimated value in use before combining the businesses. [FRS 11 paras 50 to 52].

18.205 The internally generated goodwill as calculated should be added to the carrying value of the net assets of the combined IGU for the purpose of the impairment review as illustrated below (note that the internally generated goodwill is not actually recognised in the financial statements). The internally generated goodwill is assumed to be amortised on the same basis as the purchased goodwill.

Notional carrying value of integrated income-generating unit		
	Net assets	**Goodwill**
New acquisition	Fair value	Purchased
Existing business	Carrying value*	Internally generated
		Purchased (re previous acquisitions by the existing business, if any)

* that is, existing book value, but note that fair values are used to calculate the internally generated goodwill when the businesses are integrated

18.206 FRS 11 states that this exercise should be carried out whenever an acquisition that gives rise to goodwill is merged with an existing business. [FRS 11 para 52]. Even if a full-scale impairment review is not required (say, because there is no indicator that the carrying amounts of fixed assets or goodwill may not be recoverable), the calculations are still necessary to create the records that would be required to carry out a full impairment review later if, say, an indicator of impairment arose some years after the integration of businesses. This is a requirement of FRS 11 that is easy to forget as it is not directly related to a current impairment. It is, however, very important to avoid significant difficulties in any impairment calculations required in the future.

18.207 At the time when the businesses are integrated, if the aggregate carrying value of the net assets and goodwill, including the notional internally generated goodwill as illustrated above, exceeds the recoverable amount of the combined IGU, the impairment should be allocated wholly to the capitalised purchased goodwill relating to the acquired business and, hence, recognised in full in the consolidated profit and loss account. This is because any impairment of the existing business will have been identified and recognised when the exercise to calculate the internally generated goodwill of the existing business (that is, when calculating fair values of the net assets) was carried out. By definition, therefore, if a further impairment arises when the review of the combined business is carried out, it must relate to the purchased goodwill of the acquired business. This should ensure that any overpayment for the acquisition is identified and written off and is not offset against the unrecognised goodwill of the existing business.

18.208 Any goodwill impairments identified in subsequent years should be apportioned on a *pro rata* basis between the carrying value of the purchased goodwill and the notional carrying value of the internally generated goodwill. Only the impairment allocated to the capitalised purchased goodwill would be charged in the profit and loss account.

Example

The combined balance sheet of an IGU formed by integrating an acquired business with an existing business is set out in the following table. The figures in italics are those that include the notional value of (unrecognised) internally generated goodwill in the existing business. The actual recognised net assets and purchased goodwill of the combined IGU amounts to £400m. Added to this is unrecognised internally generated goodwill in the existing business of £500m (which derives from the value that was estimated when the businesses were merged, after deducting notional amortisation since that date), making a notional total of £900m.

Impairment review of combined IGU	**Acquisition**	**Existing business**	**Combined**
Net assets	80	100	180
Goodwill	220	*500*	*720*
Total	300	*600*	*900*
Value in use			750
Impairment	46	*104*	*150*

An impairment review of the combined IGU compares its value in use of £750m with its aggregate (notional) net assets of £900m.

Assuming that this impairment review takes place some years after the integration of the acquired business, the impairment loss of £150m is allocated *pro rata* between the purchased goodwill (acquisition) and the internally generated goodwill (existing business). This allocates £46m to the former and £104m to the latter.

Only the impairment loss of £46m allocated to the capitalised purchased goodwill is written off in the consolidated profit and loss account.

If, however, the impairment was identified when the businesses were integrated, the whole loss of £150m would be allocated to the capitalised purchased goodwill relating to the acquisition and, hence, written off in the consolidated profit and loss account (see para 18.207).

It should be noted that if this *pro rata* exercise were not required, in the above example no impairment loss would be recognised in the profit and loss account. That is because there would be no impairment of the combined IGU's recognised net assets and purchased goodwill, which amount only to £400m. The impairment of the goodwill in the acquired business would in effect be offset against the unrecognised internally generated goodwill (£500m) in the existing business. Hence, the recoverable amount of the combined IGU would have to fall below £400m before any impairment loss were recognised in the consolidated profit and loss account.

18.209 This is a complicated approach and somewhat artificial. It was developed alongside the rules for capitalising and amortising purchased goodwill in FRS 10 and appears to be a consequence of the possibility of carrying goodwill permanently as an asset or amortising it over very long periods (more than 20 years). FRS 10 requires such long-life purchased goodwill balances to be reviewed annually for impairment in order to demonstrate formally that they are recoverable. The ability to perform annual impairment reviews on purchased goodwill balances is a pre-condition for rebutting FRS 10's presumption that goodwill should be amortised against profits over a period of no more than 20 years. Unless there was some standardised basis for measuring the recoverable amount of purchased goodwill in situations where the acquired business had lost its separate identity through the merging of operations, it might appear that it would not be possible to carry out an impairment review on the capitalised goodwill relating to the original acquisition. Groups that subsumed their acquisitions would then be less likely to be in a position to rebut FRS 10's presumption that the useful economic life does not exceed 20 years than those groups that ran their acquisitions as stand-alone businesses.

Goodwill previously written off to reserves

18.210 A further complication arises where the balance sheet of the existing business includes some purchased goodwill that was previously written off to reserves before capitalisation of purchased goodwill became mandatory and remains written off as permitted by the transitional provisions of FRS 10. Such goodwill is not internally generated goodwill of the existing business and so it should be treated in the impairment calculations as purchased goodwill within the existing business. This would mean that the notional balance sheet created for the purpose of allocating impairment losses would include three elements in respect of goodwill: purchased goodwill that has been capitalised; purchased goodwill that has been written off to reserves; and notional internally generated goodwill.

18.211 When it comes to allocating impairment losses to goodwill, it would seem logical to allocate the impairment *pro rata* to these three elements. The impairment relating to the element of goodwill remaining in reserves may or may not be recognised in the profit and loss account at that time (in addition to the impairment attributed to the capitalised purchased goodwill), depending on the group's policy for recognising such impairments. If the group's policy is not to account for goodwill written off to reserves until the business is disposed of, then no impairment relating to that goodwill would be recognised until disposal, when all the attributable goodwill that has not previously been written off in the profit and loss account would be written off as part of the profit or loss on disposal.

Impairment and depreciation

18.212 When a fixed asset or purchased goodwill has been impaired, the remaining carrying value (if any) should be amortised over the remaining useful economic life. The remaining useful economic life and, where applicable, estimated residual value, should also be reviewed and, if necessary, revised. [FRS 11 para 21]. (Note that FRS 10 does not permit any residual value to be assigned to goodwill.)

18.213 This requirement reiterates the normal principle in accounting for fixed assets that asset lives and residual values should be regularly reviewed to ensure they are realistic and be revised if this is not the case in the light of experience or changed circumstances. An impairment warrants particular attention, because it may indicate that previously estimated asset lives are unrealistically long and may need to be shortened.

Assets held for disposal

18.214 If a decision is made to sell an asset, a practical issue is when should the expected sale proceeds be factored into the value in use calculation in place of the cash flows from continued use. This may affect the timing and measurement of any impairment losses.

18.215 FRS 11 para 31 states: *"The income stream of a fixed asset to be disposed of will be largely independent of the income stream of other assets. Such an asset therefore forms an income-generating unit of its own and does not belong to any other income-generating unit."* This suggests that the measurement of recoverable amount would normally anticipate the disposal when it is formally factored into management's cash flow projections. Value in use (which includes the estimated cash flows from the asset's ultimate disposal) would then be similar to net realisable value; hence, the future cash flows of the IGU to which the asset may have formerly belonged are no longer taken into account.

18.216 Similarly, where a decision is made to sell or terminate a business, the amounts expected to be recoverable from the sale or closure of the business would then provide the basis for measuring the recoverable amount of its fixed assets and goodwill. In the case of a business for sale, if the carrying values of the net assets and capitalised goodwill exceeded in aggregate their recoverable amount (which would be based on the expected sale proceeds), the assets are impaired.

18.217 It is also useful to consider how the requirements of FRS 11 interact with FRS 3 and FRS 12 where losses are expected to be incurred in respect of disposals of fixed assets or businesses. FRS 3 and FRS 12 prohibit recognition of provisions for liabilities in respect of sales or terminations of businesses until (a) in the case of a sale, there is a binding sale agreement; or (b) in the case of a termination, a constructive obligation has been incurred (requiring a detailed formal plan and evidence that implementation has started or that the plan has been communicated to those affected).

18.218 Provisions do not include amounts written off assets. The expression that is sometimes used 'provision for loss on disposal of fixed assets' is not a provision in the sense of FRS 12 and any such loss should not be shown as a provision or liability. Both FRS 3 (para 45) and FRS 12 (para 84) refer to the need for asset values to be reviewed for impairment before any provisions are recognised. For example, FRS 3 states that where a decision has been made to sell an operation, but there is no binding contract or other demonstrable commitment to the sale at the reporting date, no provisions for future costs or losses should be made but any impairments (formerly permanent diminutions) in asset values should be recorded.

18.219 Thus impairment losses should be recognised as soon as a disposal is envisaged, if they have not been identified and recognised earlier. The following example illustrates the accounting for the sale of an operation that takes place after the year end.

Example

A group decides before the year end to sell a subsidiary. The sale will take place after the year end and after the financial statements of the group are signed. The carrying values of the subsidiary's fixed assets and purchased goodwill at the year end are £300,000 and £100,000 respectively. Working capital is assumed to be zero.

The subsidiary makes a loss of £110,000 before depreciation from the year end to the date the financial statements are signed. Further losses up to the date of sale are estimated to be £20,000. The group is negotiating the sale at the time of signing the financial statements and expects the proceeds on sale will be £150,000. It is assumed that the group does not fund the subsidiary's losses after the balance sheet date.

As mentioned above, where there is no binding sale agreement, no provision for loss on sale should be made, but the value of the subsidiary's net assets consolidated will still have to be considered to determine whether an impairment loss needs to be recognised. If no impairment losses were recognised in respect of the fixed assets and goodwill amounting to £400,000, the group would expect to incur losses of £250,000 in the subsequent year, comprising the subsidiary's expected future losses of £130,000 and an estimated loss on sale of £120,000, as illustrated below:

	£'000	£'000
Fixed assets		300
Goodwill		100
Assets to be reviewed for impairment		400
Loss up to date of sale	(110)	
	(20)	(130)
Estimated net assets at date of sale		270
Expected proceeds on sale		150
Estimated loss on sale		(120)

It is clear in this example that the subsidiary's assets are impaired, because their carrying values are not recoverable. The subsidiary's net assets and goodwill would form a separate IGU, because the subsidiary is to be disposed of. The recoverable amount is £150,000, which is the cash inflow expected from ultimate disposal and represents the subsidiary's value in use to the group (discounting has been ignored for simplicity). It is assumed that net realisable value at the balance sheet date would be similar.

The impairment loss is, therefore, £250,000, which would be allocated first to write-off the goodwill of £100,000 and secondly to write down the subsidiary's fixed assets by the balance of £150,000. The impairment loss of £250,000 is the same amount that might have been provided for as a provision for loss on disposal had there been a binding sale agreement at the balance sheet date.

After the impairment loss of £250,000 has been recognised, the amounts to be included in the group's profit and loss account in the subsequent year in respect of the subsidiary would be:

	£'000
Operating losses	(130)
Profit on disposal	130
Net profit or loss	nil

The profit on disposal is calculated as follows:

	£'000
Fixed assets (as impaired)	150
Goodwill	nil
	150
Operating losses	(130)
Net assets at date of sale	20
Proceeds on sale	150
Profit on sale	130

18.220 The above example demonstrates that, whereas FRS 3 and FRS 12 restrict the circumstances where provisions for losses on sale can be recognised, FRS 11 has increased the emphasis on recognising impairments of assets at an earlier point in time. Issues concerning the presentation of such losses in the profit and loss account — whether the loss should be treated as an impairment (charged against operating profit) or as a loss on sale (charged as a non-operating exceptional item) are considered in paragraph 18.263.

Corporate structures — issues for parent companies and subsidiaries

Parent's investment in subsidiaries

18.221 Where capitalised goodwill on consolidation is written down as a result of impairment, the carrying value of the parent company's investment in the relevant subsidiary should also be reviewed for impairment. [FRS 10 para 42].

18.222 The recoverable amount (if determined by value in use) of an investment in a subsidiary would normally be based on the present value of the subsidiary's estimated cash flows.

18.223 The goodwill and other net assets in the consolidated financial statements that are attributable to an impaired subsidiary will usually differ from the subsidiary's carrying value in the parent's balance sheet as time goes by after the acquisition. The likelihood that the parent's investment has also been impaired will depend partly on its accounting policy, which may be:

- Cost less provision for impairment.
- Cost (excluding share premium qualifying for merger relief or group reconstruction relief) less provision for impairment.

- Net asset value (including unamortised goodwill).

Subsidiaries that are part of larger IGUs

18.224 For groups, FRS 11 is principally targeted at identifying and recognising impairment losses from a group perspective. Thus, the whole group as a reporting entity is divided into separate IGUs for the purpose of impairment reviews, such that the IGUs in aggregate cover the whole group and are non-overlapping.

18.225 Individual subsidiaries may also be separate reporting entities, but the allocation of a group's activities between separate companies within a group does not necessarily coincide with the way the group's IGUs are defined.

18.226 Issues arise where a subsidiary's activities form part of a larger IGU in the group. In particular, the cash flows of an individual subsidiary may appear not to support the carrying values of its fixed assets, yet from a group perspective there is no impairment, because the subsidiary is part of a profitable IGU.

18.227 Such situations may be numerous where wholly-owned subsidiaries are concerned and can be illustrated by reference to the examples in the standard that discuss how IGUs are identified. For example, a low-return supporting route operated by a transport group may reside in a separate subsidiary company, yet be part of an IGU that includes a profitable trunk route that is fed by the supporting route. Another example is where a factory owned by a subsidiary company is operating with surplus capacity, but the IGU comprises this and a number of other sites (owned by other subsidiary companies) at which the product can be made — overall there is no impairment, because demand is such that there is not enough surplus capacity to close any one site.

18.228 Transfer pricing also creates difficulties. A subsidiary may be only breaking even because it sells its output to a fellow subsidiary at cost, yet they are part of the same IGU from a group perspective. Where subsidiaries are separate IGUs, one subsidiary may be unprofitable, because it sells output to a fellow subsidiary at below-market prices. Conversely, the transferee subsidiary might be profitable, because it buys goods and services from its fellow subsidiary at below-market prices. The standard indicates (from a group's perspective) that the cash inflows of the transferor IGU and the cash outflows of the transferee IGU that are used in the value in use calculations should be adjusted to reflect market prices rather than internal transfer prices. Consequently, where there is an impairment in the consolidated financial statements the situation could arise where the assets of the 'profitable' subsidiary, rather than those of the 'unprofitable' subsidiary, might be impaired after such adjustments have been made to their respective cash flow forecasts.

18.229 In situations such as those outlined above, it cannot automatically be assumed that the allocation of impairment losses in subsidiaries' own financial statements would follow the way they are allocated in the consolidated financial statements. This is because FRS 11 has to be applied individually to all financial statements that are intended to give a true and fair view of a reporting entity's financial position and profit or loss. Therefore, in general, if the recoverable amount of an asset to a subsidiary (that is, the present value of the future cash flows obtainable by the subsidiary) does not support its carrying value, it should be treated as impaired in the subsidiary's financial statements. However, where wholly-owned subsidiaries enter into transactions at transfer prices that differ significantly from market prices (and such market prices are freely available), it does not make much sense to treat an asset as being impaired in a subsidiary if the carrying value in the subsidiary is supported when its cash flows are re-based to external market prices. In cases where a subsidiary is not earning an economic return on its assets in terms of its separate cash flows, the absence of any impairment loss should require explanation in the subsidiary's financial statements in order to give a true and fair view.

Reversals of impairment losses

General rules

18.230 FRS 11 requires impairment losses recognised in previous periods to be reversed in certain circumstances where the recoverable amount of the assets concerned subsequently increases. This corresponds to the requirement in the Companies Act that where a company has made provision for a diminution in value, but the factors that gave rise to it no longer apply to any extent, then the company must write back the provision to that extent. [CA85 4 Sch 19(3)].

18.231 For tangible fixed assets and investments in subsidiaries, associates and joint ventures, the reversal of an impairment loss should be recognised where the recoverable amount increases *"because of a change in economic conditions or in the expected use of the asset"*. [FRS 11 para 56]. This rule is based on the premise that the original impairment is caused by the inability of the asset to generate sufficient returns to recover its carrying amount. Once there is a change in economic conditions or in the expected use of the asset that enables the asset to recover its former carrying amount, the reason for the impairment ceases to apply. For intangible assets and goodwill the criteria for reversing impairment losses are stricter than for other assets (see para 18.242 below).

18.232 The amount of any reversal that can be recognised is restricted to increasing the carrying value of the relevant assets to the carrying value that would have been recognised had the original impairment not occurred (that is, after taking account of normal depreciation that would have been charged had no impairment occurred). [FRS 11 para 56]. In respect of depreciable assets, therefore, any reversals of impairment losses will tend not to be as large as the original impairment loss.

18.233 Indicators that impairment losses may have reversed are the reverse of those that indicated the impairment loss in the first place. Companies should consider whether there have been favourable events or changes in circumstances since the impairment loss was recognised that would indicate that the impairment loss no longer exists or may have decreased. If there are indicators, the recoverable amount of the relevant assets or IGUs should be estimated again. Such changes include situations where the recoverable amount increases as a result of further capital investment or a reorganisation, the benefits of which had been excluded from the original measurement of value in use (see paras 18.118 and 18.125 for examples showing how the recognition and reversal rules operate in respect of future reorganisation and capital investment).

18.234 It should be borne in mind that this exercise would only be undertaken if there is evidence of a significant improvement in actual performance or future prospects that would give rise to a material reversal of an impairment loss. As with the original impairment calculations, amounts recognised in respect of reversals are likely to be broad estimates; in fact, it could be positively misleading in terms of reporting performance to have regular impairment losses and reversals resulting from imputing spurious accuracy into the calculations.

18.235 The standard explains that increases in value in use should not be recognised as reversals of impairment losses if they arise simply from:

- The passage of time, resulting from the unwinding of the discount rate that was applied to arrive at the present value of expected future cash flows.
- The occurrence of forecast cash outflows — once the forecast cash outflows have happened they are no longer part of the value in use calculation and the value in use, therefore, increases.

[FRS 11 para 58].

18.236 The reason why the two events described in the previous paragraph do not give rise to the reversal of an impairment loss is because, whilst the value in use admittedly increases, the underlying reasons for the original impairment have not been removed. All that has happened is that time has passed and the expected cash flows have occurred — the service potential of the asset has not increased. The effect is illustrated in the following example:

Example

An asset cost £100 on 1 January 20X0. Its expected useful life is 5 years; depreciation is on a straight-line basis. An impairment review is carried out as at 31 December 20X0 when the carrying value is £80. The projected cash flows are as follows:

	20X1	20X2	20X3	20X4
Cash flows (nominal total 82; present value 64)	13	22	23	24

Using a discount rate of 10%, the present value of the cash flows (value in use) at 31 December 20X0 is £64. Thus an impairment loss of £16 is recognised.

The impaired carrying value of £64 is then depreciated on a straight-line basis over the remaining 4 years of its expected useful life. Assuming the cash flows materialise as projected in the impairment calculation, the carrying value and value in use (present value of remaining cash flows discounted at 10%) at each year end are as follows:

	20X0	20X1	20X2	20X3	20X4
Carrying value	64	48	32	16	–
Value in use	64	57	41	22	–

It can be seen that the value in use at 31 December 20X1, 20X2 and 20X3 exceeds the carrying amount. The reason is a combination of the unwinding of the discount (as the future cash flows get nearer, their present value increases) and the fact that the cash flows themselves increase during the life of the asset. But there is no reversal of the original impairment loss.

The profit and loss accounts for the remaining life of the asset are as follows (ignoring any timing differences between cash flows and profit):

	20X1	20X2	20X3	20X4
Profit before depreciation	13	22	23	24
Depreciation	(16)	(16)	(16)	(16)
Profit (loss) before interest	(3)	6	7	8

The effect of discounting is that a profit before interest of £18 emerges over the remaining 4 years' life of the asset. Discounting the cash flows in the first place reduced the value in use from the nominal amount of £82 to a present value of £64. The corollary of this is that the discount of £18 unwinds over those 4 years, in effect leaving an operating profit to cover the cost of capital. Of course, this profit does not accrue in any even pattern, because (a) the cash flows themselves are uneven; and (b) depreciation is on an arbitrary straight-line basis.

18.237 It should be noted, however, that where a reversal of an impairment loss is recognised because economic conditions have changed, the FRS does not suggest that any increase in value in use that is due to 'the passage of time' should be estimated as a separate component and excluded from the reversal. In most practical situations this would be quite unrealistic.

18.238 To illustrate accounting for reversals, consider the following example:

Example

The history of a company's fixed assets is as follows:

	Investment in subsidiary £'000	Tangible fixed assets £'000
Cost at 1 January 20X1	10	6
Value at 31 December 20X1	8	5
Value at 31 December 20X2	*5	*3
Value at 31 December 20X3	9	4

* only these decreases in value are impairments. All other diminutions in value have arisen from a general fall in prices.

Ignoring the normal depreciation rules for the purposes of this example (and assuming historical cost rules apply), FRS 11 and the Companies Act apply as follows:

- At 31 December 20X1 both the investment and the fixed asset have fallen in value, but this is due solely to a general fall in prices. It is determined, following an impairment review that the recoverable amount of the investment and the fixed asset remain at £10,000 and £6,000 respectively. In these circumstances, the directors *could* (if they wish) write down the amount of the investment in subsidiary to £8,000. (This is because the Act permits, but does not require, provision to be made for the diminution in value of a fixed asset *investment* that the directors consider to be only temporary). However, the directors could not write down the value of the tangible fixed asset to £5,000 under the historical cost rules. (This is because the Act allows tangible fixed assets to be written down in value only in circumstances where the diminution in value is expected to be *permanent*. Also, in FRS 11 terms, there has been no impairment of the fixed asset.)

- At 31 December 20X2 a change in economic circumstances has occurred which leads the directors to believe that the recoverable amounts of the investment and the fixed asset have fallen to £5,000 and £3,000 respectively. Accordingly, the directors must write down the amount of the investment in subsidiary to £5,000 (whether or not they wrote it down to £8,000 at 31 December 20X1). In addition, they *must* write down the value of the tangible fixed asset to £3,000. This is because the fall in value of each of them is expected to be *permanent* and because in FRS 11 terms there has been an impairment loss.

- At 31 December 20X3, due to a further change in economic circumstances the recoverable amounts have been restored to £9,000 and £4,000 respectively and the reasons for the original impairment have disappeared. Therefore, the directors must write back £4,000 in respect of the investment in subsidiary and £1,000 in respect of the tangible fixed asset. This is because the reasons that gave rise to the provision for diminution in value/impairment loss on each of them have ceased to apply to that extent. Had the increase in the recoverable amount occurred only because of the passage of time (unwinding of discount) or because forecast cash outflows had occurred, the impairment losses could not be written back, because the reasons for the original impairment would not have ceased to apply.

18.239 Accounting for the reversal of an impairment loss should be consistent with the treatment adopted when the impairment was recognised. Where the asset is held at historical cost, the reversal should be recognised in the current year's profit and loss account, since the original loss would have been charged in the profit and loss account.

18.240 For a revalued asset, the reversal of an impairment loss should be recognised in the profit and loss account to the extent that the original impairment loss (adjusted for subsequent depreciation) was recognised in the profit and loss account. Any remaining balance of the reversal of an impairment loss should be recognised in the statement of total recognised gains and losses, since part of the original impairment loss would have been charged there. [FRS 11 para 66].

18.241 The reversal calculations for revalued assets can be rather complex, as illustrated in the following example.

Example — recognition and reversal of impairment loss on revalued asset

At 31 December X1 an asset was purchased for 100. Its expected useful economic life is 20 years. Three years later it was revalued to 136.

At 31 December X6 the asset was reviewed for impairment and written down to its recoverable amount of 50.

The following table shows the movements in the asset's book value on a depreciated historical cost basis and as actually recognised in the financial statements.

	Depreciated historical cost	**Revalued carrying value**
31 December X1 – cost	100	100
Depreciation (3 years)	(15)	(15)
Revaluation	–	51
31 December X4	85	136
Depreciation (2 years)	(10)	(16)
31 December X6	75	120
Impairment loss	(25)	(70)
31 December X6 after impairment loss	50	50

The impairment loss of 70 at 31 December X6 is not caused by a clear consumption of economic benefits, and so the loss is charged in the statement of total recognised gains and losses until the carrying amount reaches depreciated historical cost and thereafter in the profit and loss account, as follows:

Statement of total recognised gains and losses	45
Profit and loss account	25
Impairment loss	70

At 31 December X8 economic conditions have improved and the asset's recoverable amount is estimated to be 90.

If no impairment loss had been recognised, the carrying value at 31 December 1998 would have been 104 (120 at 31 December X6 less 2 years of further depreciation of 16), which is greater than the recoverable amount of 90. Therefore, the whole of the increase in the carrying value can be treated as a reversal of the previous impairment loss. It should be noted that if the carrying value had been increased to more than 104, the excess would be treated as a revaluation, not a reversal of the impairment. [FRS 11 para 59].

The impairment loss should be reversed, as indicated in the following table.

	Depreciated historical cost Before impairment	After impairment	Carrying value
31 December X6	75	50	50
Depreciation (2 years)	(10)	(7)	(7)
31 December X8	65	43	43
Reversal of impairment loss	–	22	47
31 December 98 after reversal	65	65	90

The reversal of the impairment loss of 47 is recognised as follows:

Profit and loss account	22
Statement of total recognised gains and losses	25

The profit and loss account figure of 22 represents the amount of the original impairment loss that was charged in the profit and loss account of 25 less an adjustment for the additional depreciation that would have been charged had the asset been carried at depreciated historical cost of 3. The balance of the reversal of 25 is credited in the statement of total recognised gains and losses.

Special rules for goodwill and intangible assets

18.242 Impairment losses relating to capitalised goodwill and intangible assets may be reversed only in limited circumstances. These are where (a) an external event caused the original impairment loss; and (b) subsequent external events clearly and demonstrably reverse the effects of that event in a way that was not foreseen in the original impairment calculations. [FRS 11 para 60]. FRS 11 makes an exception to this rule for intangible assets with a readily ascertainable market value, where impairment losses may be reversed to the extent that the net realisable value (based on market value) subsequently increases to above the impaired carrying value. [FRS 11 para 60]. However, there are very few intangible assets in that category.

18.243 For goodwill, the objective of restricting reversals of impairment losses is to prevent a goodwill write-off from being credited back to the profit and loss account if the credit is in effect attributable to the generation of new non-purchased goodwill. The accounting rules generally for goodwill and intangible assets are similar. Consequently, situations that justify reversals are likely to be rare and in most cases amounts written off goodwill or intangible assets will stay written off. The reason given for the different approaches to tangible and intangible assets is that tangible fixed assets can in any case be revalued, whereas goodwill and most intangible assets cannot.

18.244 An example of a situation that would meet the reversal criteria for an intangible asset is as follows.

Example

A brand name had previously been written off because a product had been withdrawn from the market as a result of a health scare that raised concerns about its safety. The safety concerns subsequently prove to be unfounded and the health authorities approved the product's reintroduction. The company's management had assumed that the product's withdrawal would be permanent when they recognised the impairment loss.

In this example, the impairment loss was caused by an external event (the health scare). An external event (the removal of the safety concerns and the permission to reintroduce the product to the market) clearly and demonstrably has reversed the effects of the external event that caused the impairment loss in a way that was not foreseen in the original impairment calculations. Consequently, the impairment loss should be reversed to the extent that the brand's recoverable amount has increased above its current written down value (assuming that the brand regains some value after the health scare).

18.245 An example of originating and reversing external events that would meet the reversal criteria for goodwill is the introduction of a new law that damages profitability (resulting in a goodwill write-off) and that is subsequently repealed by a new government. Another example is the confiscation of assets in an overseas territory (resulting in a goodwill write-off) that are subsequently released to allow the business to continue its operations. In both of these examples the original goodwill has been reclaimed.

18.246 The recoverable amount of an acquired business may increase in subsequent years after an impairment loss has been recognised, but the improvement will often be unrelated to the circumstances that gave rise to the original impairment. One example is where goodwill has been written off because a competitor has introduced a better product to the market; some years later, the company launches a new product of its own and develops a different market. Another example is where a business has been reorganised to curtail underperforming operations, resulting in a write-off of goodwill; in later years, the business may expand again as new market opportunities arise. In neither of these examples would the turnaround justify reversing the impairment loss relating to the goodwill even though the recoverable amount of the business has increased above the balance sheet value of its net assets and goodwill. This is because the higher value of goodwill that now exists includes goodwill that has been generated internally since the original impairment.

18.247 If, however, the reason for an impairment write-down was a competitor coming into the market and a reversal of the impairment was attributable to the competitor subsequently withdrawing from the market (or modifying its pricing policy in a way that was not foreseen), the criteria for recognising the reversal of the impairment loss in respect of goodwill would be met.

18.248 It should be noted that if the net assets of a business included impaired carrying values for both purchased goodwill and tangible fixed assets, the situation may occur where some impairment loss reversals are permitted (for tangible fixed assets) and others are not (for goodwill and most intangible fixed assets). This situation may occur with business restructurings. Goodwill and tangible fixed assets of businesses in need of reorganisation may have to be written down (there is a concession, though, for recent acquisitions — see para 18.127); if their values are restored as a result of reorganisation, only the impairment losses relating to the tangible fixed assets may be written back.

18.249 The amount that can be written back to reverse an impairment loss is restricted to an amount that increases the carrying value of the goodwill or intangible asset to the carrying value that would have been recognised had the original impairment not occurred (that is, after taking account of normal depreciation that would have been charged had the impairment not occurred). [FRS 11 para 61].

Presentation and disclosures

Presentation of impairment losses in performance statements

Assets carried at historical cost

18.250 FRS 11 requires impairment losses recognised in the profit and loss account to be included within operating profit under the appropriate statutory heading, and disclosed as an exceptional item if appropriate. [FRS 11 para 67]. This applies to goodwill as well as fixed assets.

18.251 The formats in Schedule 4 to the Act prescribe the headings under which depreciation and other amounts written off tangible and intangible fixed assets are to be included in the profit and loss account. Under Format 1, where expenses are classified by function, an impairment loss would generally be charged under the same format heading as depreciation of (or other amounts written off) the relevant assets. Under Format 2, where expenses are classified by type, there is a separate heading 'depreciation and amounts written off tangible and intangible fixed assets'.

Revalued assets

18.252 For revalued assets, FRS 11 introduces rules for recognition of impairment that are more conservative than the Act's requirements in respect of temporary diminutions in value.

18.253 Although FRS 11 does not use the term 'temporary diminutions in value' it distinguishes two types of impairments. These are impairments arising from:

- A clear consumption of economic benefits.
- Other impairments of revalued fixed assets.

18.254 The FRS requires that the former of these two types of impairment should be recognised in the profit and loss account in its entirety, because it is similar to depreciation. No part of it should be taken to the statement of total recognised gains and losses. [FRS 11 para 63]. Examples of clear consumption of economic benefits are physical damage, contamination, obsolescence, deterioration in quality of service — often something wrong with the asset itself.

18.255 Other impairments are accounted for by recognising them in the statement of total recognised gains and losses, until the carrying amount reaches depreciated historical cost. Thereafter, the balance of the impairment is recognised in the profit and loss account. [FRS 11 para 63].

18.256 This category is intended to cover impairments caused by a general fall in prices, for example a general slump in the property market. However, the FRS recognises that in many cases it will be unclear whether an impairment loss is the result of a consumption of economic benefits or some other cause — for example, when there is a fall in demand for an asset's output or services. The development appendix explains that where there is doubt whether the impairment is caused by a reduction in the quantum of an asset's service potential, it should be treated as falling into the other category, that is, the loss is recognised in the statement of total recognised gains and losses, until the carrying amount reaches depreciated historical cost. [FRS 11 App IV para 20].

18.257 An asset's recoverable amount may be reduced by specific factors that do not necessarily affect the general market, say, the establishment of a local competitor to a retail store. Whereas, there may be no physical impairment of the asset, there may be evidence that the impairment has not been caused by a general fall in prices and thus it could be argued that the impairment has been caused by a reduction in its service potential. But rarely will such situations be clear cut.

18.258 The FRS appears to acknowledge that a downward revaluation of a previously revalued asset may constitute partly an impairment due to consumption of economic benefits and partly an impairment due to general price changes. It may be difficult, in practice, to determine whether or not this is the case. The prudent approach taken by the standard, however, makes this less of an issue, because the standard requires all impairments of an asset below depreciated historical cost to be taken to the profit and loss account. (Note, however, that the standard does not apply to investment properties).

18.259 Impairment losses recognised in the profit and loss account should be included in operating profit under the appropriate statutory heading and disclosed as exceptional if appropriate. Impairment losses recognised in the statement of total recognised gains and losses should be disclosed separately on the face of that statement. [FRS 11 para 67].

18.260 It should be noted that if a company's policy is to carry assets at market value and market value is below recoverable amount, the shortfall is not an *impairment under* FRS 11. The additional write-down would be recognised in the statement of total recognised gains and losses as a revaluation deficit.

18.261 Where, therefore, the revaluation of a fixed asset results in a revalued amount that is below the previous carrying value and is below the value in use of that asset, FRS 11 only requires the asset to be written down, if necessary, to the value in use figure. The difference between the value in use figure and the (lower) revalued amount is simply a valuation adjustment which is then shown in the statement of total recognised gains and losses.

Example

A tangible fixed asset cost £100 and is subject to a revaluation policy to reflect its current market value. Its previous revalued carrying amount was £150, with the surplus of £50 taken to the statement of total recognised gains and losses and the revaluation reserve.

In the current year the fixed asset is revalued and the revalued amount is £80 (in this example, for simplicity, depreciation has been ignored).

An impairment review is done on the asset and the recoverable amount (higher of net realisable value and value in use) is determined to be £90.

The following describes how the revaluation deficit of £70 (£150 — £80) should be accounted for:

(a) If the impairment of £60, that is, the difference between carrying value of £150 and recoverable amount of £90, is considered to have arisen due to a clear consumption of economic benefits, it should be charged in its entirety to the profit and loss account and shown under the appropriate statutory heading in arriving at operating profit.

The previous revaluation surplus of £50 in the revaluation reserve may then be transferred through reserves (but not through the statement of total recognised gains and losses) to profit and loss reserves.

(b) If the impairment of £60 is considered not to have arisen from a clear consumption of economic benefits, it should be charged as to £50 to the statement of total recognised gains and losses and £10 to the profit and loss account, again under the appropriate heading in arriving at operating profit. The charge of £50 to the statement of total recognised gains and losses should be shown on the face of that statement.

(c) In both cases, that is whether the impairment loss is due to a clear consumption of economic benefits or not, the remaining revaluation adjustment of £10 to reduce the asset from its recoverable amount of £90 to its revalued amount of £80 is shown in the statement of total recognised gains and losses. This is because it corresponds to a temporary diminution under the Companies Act rules and such diminutions should be taken, via the statement of total recognised gains and losses, to the revaluation reserve.

18.262 In the above example, a diminution in value of £10 below cost was charged in the statement of total recognised gains and losses rather than the profit and loss account, because that amount was purely a market value adjustment and not an impairment. Consider the presentation in the following year if a further impairment is identified.

Example

The facts are as in the previous example. In the following year the fixed asset's market value has fallen from £80 to £50. A further impairment review is carried out and the recoverable amount is estimated also to be £50 (that is, it has fallen from £90 to £50).

The impairment loss in the following year is £40 (£90 less £50). However, the loss to be recognised in the year (in the profit and loss account) is only £30, because a loss of £10 was charged in the previous year (in the statement of total recognised gains and losses) as a revaluation deficit. In effect that revaluation deficit of £10 has become an impairment loss. But, in accordance with FRS 3, as the loss of £10 has already been recognised in the statement of total recognised gains and losses (albeit not as an impairment loss), it is not shown again in the profit and loss account. Instead, that part of the impairment loss would be charged to profit and loss account reserve by means of a reserve transfer in the reserves note (that is, crediting revaluation reserve and debiting profit and loss account reserve by £10).

Assets held for disposal

Loss on disposal or impairment loss?

18.263 FRS 3 requires losses on disposals of fixed assets or operations (including provisions in respect of them) to be charged after operating profit and before interest. [FRS 3 para 20]. FRS 11 requires impairment losses recognised in the profit and loss account to be charged in operating profit under the appropriate statutory heading. [FRS 11 para 67]. If FRS 11 was interpreted in isolation, most losses recognised in connection with asset disposals would be impairments (charged against operating profit) rather than losses on disposals (non-operating exceptional items). That is because in most cases any previously unidentified shortfall between an asset's carrying value and its recoverable amount that is identified as a result of a decision to sell or terminate would be an impairment, not a loss on disposal.

18.264 The apparent conflict may be interpreted as follows when the requirements of FRS 3 and FRS 11 are considered together. Impairment losses in respect of fixed assets and businesses that are to be retained must be charged in arriving at operating profit. Impairment losses that, in FRS 3 terms, are provisions for losses on disposals (that is, they are recognised as a result of a decision to dispose of the assets or business concerned) should be shown under the relevant one of the three headings in paragraph 20 of FRS 3. In the latter case, if the disposal has not occurred before the balance sheet date, the company would be expected to provide evidence that the asset or operation would not be retained. For example, the asset or business would probably be being actively marketed and it would be reasonable to expect that the disposal would be completed before the next interim accounts and in any event before the end of the next financial year.

18.265 This apparent inconsistency between FRS 3 and FRS 11 gives rise to some anomalies. If an asset is put up for sale and has not previously been reviewed for impairment, the loss on sale is presented in accordance with paragraph 20 of

FRS 3. If, however, an impairment loss is identified earlier as a result of carrying out an impairment review in circumstances required by FRS 11, the loss would be presented as part of operating profit in accordance with FRS 11.

18.266 A similar issue arises where a company undertakes a fundamental reorganisation having a material effect on the nature and focus of its operations. FRS 3 requires the costs incurred to be shown after operating profit under a separate caption. Costs incurred often involve write-offs of assets and goodwill, which are regarded as impairments under FRS 11, as well as other reorganisation costs. In such circumstances, it is logical to present all the costs of the fundamental reorganisation, including the impairments, under the relevant FRS 3 caption.

Disposal of previously impaired asset

18.267 Where a previously impaired fixed asset is sold and the proceeds exceed the impaired carrying value, the gain should be recognised in the profit and loss account. A question arises whether the whole of the gain should be shown under the heading 'profits or losses on the disposal of fixed assets' (after operating profit) or whether at least part of the gain should be recognised as a reversal of the past impairment and be included in operating profit.

18.268 Paragraph 21 of FRS 3 requires the profit on disposal to be accounted for in the profit and loss account of the period in which the disposal occurs as the difference between the net sale proceeds and the net carrying amount, whether carried at historical cost (less any provisions made) or at a valuation. Therefore, the whole of the gain should be shown after operating profit (except where the gain is in effect no more than a marginal adjustment to depreciation previously charged).

18.269 However, where a previously impaired fixed asset has increased in value and has not been disposed of by the year end, paragraph 56 of FRS 11 requires the asset's carrying value to be increased if its recoverable amount has increased because of a change in economic conditions or in the expected use of the asset. The reversal of an impairment loss should be recognised in the profit and loss account to the extent that (a) the original impairment loss was charged in the profit and loss account; and (b) the reversal increases the carrying amount up to the amount that it would have been had the original impairment not occurred. It is logical that the reversal of the impairment loss should be credited under the same statutory heading that the original impairment loss was charged, that is, included within operating profit.

Other financial statement disclosures

Fixed asset movements

18.270 In the notes showing fixed asset movements, impairment losses should be disclosed as follows:

- For assets held at historical cost, the impairment loss should be included within the cumulative depreciation. The cost of the asset should not be reduced.
- For revalued assets held at market value (that is, existing use value or open-market value) the impairment loss should be included within the revalued carrying amount and not shown within any cumulative depreciation.
- For revalued assets held at depreciated replacement cost, an impairment loss charged to the profit and loss account should be included within cumulative depreciation. The revalued carrying amount of the asset should not be reduced. An impairment loss charged to the statement of total recognised gains and losses should be deducted from the revalued carrying amount of the asset.

[FRS 11 para 68].

18.271 FRS 10, which applies to goodwill and intangible assets and FRS 15, which applies to tangible fixed assets, are rather more specific on detailing the movements. They require impairment losses, and reversals of past impairment losses, to be disclosed separately in the note that reconciles the movements between the opening and closing balances for goodwill and each class of intangible and tangible asset. [FRS 10 para 53; FRS 15 para 100].

Revalued assets held at market value

18.272 For revalued assets held at market value, revaluations are usually reflected in the reconciliation of fixed asset movements by adjusting the gross revalued carrying amount (that is, before depreciation) to the new market value. Accumulated depreciation charged up to the date of the new valuation is eliminated from the reconciliation. The disclosure of impairment losses in the reconciliation does not distinguish between impairments that are caused by a consumption of economic benefits (charged to the profit and loss account) and other impairments that are deemed to result from general changes in prices (charged to the statement of total recognised gains and losses). All impairments are deducted from the gross revalued carrying amount before depreciation and, hence, none are shown within accumulated depreciation.

18.273 The treatment of revalued assets held at market value is illustrated in the following example. It shows that all impairment losses are in effect treated as downward valuations in the reconciliation of fixed asset movements.

Example

An asset cost £200 and has a useful life of 20 years; it is depreciated on a straight-line basis. At the end of year 3 it was revalued to £220 (compared with depreciated historical cost of £170).

At the end of year 5, the asset had a carrying value of £194 (comprising the revalued amount of £220 less accumulated depreciation of £26 relating to years 4 and 5). On a depreciated historical cost basis, the carrying value would have been £150 (comprising cost of £200 less accumulated depreciation of £50 relating to years 1 to 5).

At the end of year 5, as a result of an impairment review of the IGU to which the asset contributes, the recoverable amount of the IGU is found to be lower than its carrying value. The allocation of the impairment loss in accordance with paragraphs 48 and 49 of FRS 11 results in the asset being written down to its net realisable value (which is based on its current market value). The disclosure of the impairment loss in the reconciliation of fixed asset movements is illustrated in three different scenarios:

A Recoverable amount is £150. The impairment loss of £44 (which is equal to the surplus of the revalued carrying value of £194 over the depreciated historical cost of £150) is charged in the statement of total recognised gains and losses (that is, treated as a downward revaluation) because the loss is not considered to have been caused by a consumption of economic benefits.

B Recoverable amount is £150. The impairment loss of £44 is considered to have been caused by a consumption of economic benefits and is charged in the profit and loss account.

C Recoverable amount is £100. The impairment loss of £94 is charged £44 as in A above in the statement of total recognised gains and losses (that is, the surplus of the revalued carrying value of £194 over the depreciated historical cost of £150) and £50 (the balance) in the profit and loss account.

Impairment loss

	A	B	C
Carrying value	194	194	194
Recoverable amount	150	150	100
Impairment loss	44	44	94
Charged:			
STRGL	44	–	44
Profit and loss account	–	44	50
Total	44	44	94

The impairment losses would be disclosed in the reconciliation of fixed asset movements as follows:

Note of fixed asset movements

	A	B	C
Valuation			
At 1 January 05	220	220	220
Impairment	(44)	(44)	(94)
Valuation adjustment	(26)	(26)	(26)
At 31 December 05	150	150	100
Accumulated depreciation			
At 1 January 05	13	13	13
Charge for the year	13	13	13
Valuation adjustment	(26)	(26)	(26)
At 31 December 05	–	–	–
Net book value			
At 31 December 04	207	207	207
At 31 December 05	150	150	100

It should be noted that the valuation adjustment of £26 shown as movements under the 'valuation' and 'accumulated depreciation' headings is necessary to eliminate accumulated depreciation from the reconciliation; thus the recoverable amount at 31 December 05 is treated as a new valuation.

Revalued assets held at depreciated replacement cost

18.274 The treatment of revalued fixed assets carried at market value may be contrasted with the treatment of revalued fixed assets carried at depreciated replacement cost, where impairment losses charged in the profit and loss account should be included within accumulated depreciation. If the revalued asset in the previous example had been valued at depreciated replacement cost, the treatment in the reconciliation of fixed movements would be different, as illustrated in the following example.

Example

The facts are the same as in the previous example, except that the asset was revalued at depreciated replacement cost at the end of year 3. FRS 15 states that both the cost or revalued amount and the accumulated depreciation at the date of revaluation may be restated, so that the carrying amount of the asset after revaluation equals its revalued amount. [FRS 15 para 101]. If this approach was adopted, the valuation of £220 (net replacement cost) would be 'grossed up' to disclose a gross replacement cost and, separately, accumulated depreciation to reflect the portion of the asset's useful life already consumed, as follows:

Cost or valuation	£
Cost b/f	200
Revaluation	59
Gross replacement cost	259
Accumulated depreciation	
B/f	30
Revaluation	9
	39
Net replacement cost	220

The impairment at the end of year 5 would be shown as follows, under each of the three scenarios set out in the previous example.

Note of fixed asset movements			
	A	**B**	**C**
Gross replacement cost			
At 1 January 05	259	259	259
Impairment loss	(44)	–	(44)
At 31 December 05	215	259	215
Accumulated depreciation			
At 1 January 05	52	52	52
Charge for the year	13	13	13
Impairment loss	–	44	50
At 31 December 05	65	109	115
Net book value			
At 31 December 04	207	207	207
At 31 December 05	150	150	100

The impairment losses shown in the above reconciliation can be identified directly with the amounts charged in the profit and loss account (shown under accumulated depreciation) and in the statement of total recognised gains and losses (shown under gross replacement cost).

Value in use calculations

18.275 Where an impairment loss is recognised and has been measured by reference to value in use, the discount rate applied to the cash flows should be disclosed. If a risk-free discount rate is used, some indication of the risk adjustments made to the cash flows should be given. [FRS 11 para 69].

18.276 Where, in measuring value in use, the period before a steady or declining growth rate is assumed extends to more than five years, the financial statements should disclose the length of the longer period and the circumstances justifying it. [FRS 11 para 72].

18.277 Where, in measuring value in use, the long-term growth rate used has exceeded the long-term average growth rate for the country or countries in which the business operates, the financial statements should disclose the growth rate assumed and the circumstances justifying it. [FRS 11 para 73].

18.278 It should be noted that the disclosures referred to in the previous two paragraphs are not limited to circumstances where an impairment loss has actually been recognised. Thus, if a formal impairment review has been carried out and no impairment loss has been recognised, some disclosure of the facts appears to be necessary if the normal constraints on the growth assumptions relating to long-term cash flow forecasts have been exceeded when measuring value in use.

18.279 For the five years following each impairment review, where recoverable amount has been based on value in use, the cash flows achieved should be compared with those forecast. If the cash flows achieved show that an impairment loss should have been recognised in previous periods, that loss should be recognised in the current period, unless it has already reversed. Where an impairment loss would have been recognised in a previous period had forecasts of future cash flows been more accurate, but the impairment has since reversed and the reversal is permitted to be recognised by FRS 11, the impairment now identified and its subsequent reversal should be disclosed. [FRS 11 para 71].

Reversals

18.280 Where a previously recognised impairment loss has been reversed, the reasons for the reversal should be disclosed, including any changes in the assumptions upon which calculation of recoverable amount is based. [FRS 11 para 70].

Companies Act disclosures

18.281 The Companies Act requires that where a company has made any provision for diminution in value, or has written back any provision for diminution in value, it must disclose the amounts involved (either in the profit and loss account or in the notes to the financial statements). [CA85 4 Sch 19]. The amounts to be disclosed are:

- Provisions made in respect of the permanent diminution in value of fixed assets (impairment losses recognised under FRS 11 would normally be regarded as permanent). [CA85 4 Sch 19(2)].
- Provisions made in respect of the temporary diminution in value of fixed asset investments. [CA85 4 Sch 19(1)].
- Amounts written back to the extent that the circumstances that gave rise to the provisions no longer apply. [CA85 4 Sch 19(3)].

18.282 The amounts disclosed must be split between the three headings, but amounts that fall within the same heading may be aggregated. [CA85 4 Sch 19].

Chapter 19

Leases and HP contracts

	Page
Introduction	19001
Classification of leases	19002
Lease term	19003
Minimum lease payments	19005
The interest rate implicit in the lease	19007
The present value calculation	19008
Property leases	19008
Accounting by lessees	19009
Accounting for finance leases	19009
Accounting for operating leases	19012
Lease incentives	19012
Lessee disclosure requirements	19014
Sale and leaseback transactions	19020
Finance leasebacks	19020
Operating leasebacks	19021
Sale and leasebacks with repurchase options	19022
Accounting by lessors	19023
Finance & Leasing Association SORP	19023
Accounting for finance leases	19023
The actuarial after-tax method	19025
Accounting for operating leases	19028
Operating lease incentives	19031
Lessor disclosure requirements	19032
Implications of the Act on the disclosure lessors make	19034
Direct costs	19035
Rental variation	19037
Tax variation clauses	19037
Variations in interest rates	19037
Construction periods	19038
Manufacturer/dealer lessors	19038
Back-to-back and sub-leases	19039
The head lessor	19040
The intermediate party	19040
Residuals	19041
Residuals under operating leases	19042
Residuals under finance leases	19042
Fluctuations in anticipated residual values	19042
Tax-free grants	19043

Chapter 19

Leases and HP contracts

Introduction

19.1 This chapter considers the accounting treatment and disclosure of leased assets in a company's financial statements and discusses some of the practical issues concerning lease accounting. The UK accounting requirements for lease transactions for both lessees and lessors are set out in SSAP 21, 'Accounting for leases and hire purchase contracts'. Additionally, those lease transactions which form part of a complex arrangement or which contains options, conditional provisions and guarantees also fall under the scope of FRS 5. As explained in FRS 5, where a transaction falls under the scope of both FRS 5 and SSAP 21 the standard containing the more specific provision will apply. In general, SSAP 21 contains the more specific provisions, relating to stand-alone leases. The exception to this is in Application Note B of FRS 5, which deals specifically with sale and repurchase transactions including the treatment of options.

19.2 Under SSAP 21, a 'lease' is defined as a contract between the lessor and the lessee for the hire of a specific asset. The lessor retains ownership of the asset, but conveys to the lessee the right to use the asset in return for paying specific rentals. In addition, the definition of a lease in the standard includes other arrangements not described as leases, in which one party retains ownership but conveys to another the right to use the asset for an agreed period of time in return for specific rentals.

19.3 In broad terms, SSAP 21 requires that, where a company finances a significant amount of its capital investment through leasing, its financial statements should properly reflect the commercial effect of those transactions. Thus, where the substance of those transactions is akin to the lessee purchasing the asset, financed by borrowings drawn from the lessor (a 'finance lease'), the standard requires the lessee's balance sheet to show both an asset, reflecting the lessee's rights in the leased asset, and a liability, reflecting the future financial obligations under the lease. However, where the lease does not have the commercial effect of a financing arrangement for the acquisition of an asset (an 'operating lease') the lessee need only account for the rental expense through its profit and loss account.

19.4 Similarly, from the lessor's perspective, leases that have similar characteristics to other forms of lending ('finance leases') are classified in the balance sheet as receivables; whereas assets held for use in operating leases are treated in a similar way to other tangible fixed assets.

19.5 Thus, the accounting treatment of a lease depends on the commercial substance of the lease. The accounting distinction between a finance lease and an operating lease is, therefore, a crucial one.

19.6 The paragraphs below consider the factors to be taken into account when classifying leases. The following two sections consider the appropriate treatment from the perspective of the lessee and lessor, respectively, once the lease has been classified.

Classification of leases

19.7 Under SSAP 21, a finance lease is defined as *"…a lease that transfers substantially all the risks and rewards of ownership of an asset to the lessee"*. [SSAP 21 para 15]. Thus, a finance lease is an arrangement that has the substance of a financing transaction for the lessee to acquire effective economic ownership of an asset.

19.8 An operating lease, under SSAP 21, is simply *"…a lease other than a finance lease"*. [SSAP 21 para 17]. In practice, this means that an operating lease does not pass substantially all the risk and rewards of ownership to the lessee: a significant element of risk must, therefore, remain with the lessor or some party other than the lessee. Consequently, an operating lease is usually for a period substantially shorter than the asset's useful economic life and the lessor will be relying on recovering a significant proportion of his investment from either the proceeds from the asset's sale or the asset's further hire after the end of the lease term.

19.9 Whether or not a lease passes substantially all the risks and rewards of ownership to the lessee will normally be self-evident from the terms of the lease contract and an understanding of the commercial risks taken by each party. Where the lessor takes little or no asset-related risk, other than a credit risk on the lessee, the agreement will obviously be a finance lease. Similarly, where the lessor is exposed to significant levels of risks relating to movements in the asset's market value, utilisation, or performance, such as on a short-term hire agreement, the agreement will be easily classified as an operating lease. The difficulty, therefore, tends to emerge on classifying leases where the lessor recovers most of his investment through the terms of the lease, but retains some element of risk relating to the asset's residual value at the end of the lease term.

19.10 In order to provide guidance on when such risks and rewards could be reasonable presumed to have passed, SSAP 21 sets a simple test:

> *"It should be presumed that such a transfer of risks and rewards occurs if at the inception of a lease the present value of the minimum lease payments, including any initial payment, amounts to substantially all (normally 90 per cent or more) of the fair value of the leased asset"*. [SSAP 21 para 15].

19.11 In essence, the present value test is a measure of the risk that the lessor (or other third party) is taking in relation to the asset's residual value at the end of the lease term. Where the lessor (or other third party) is assuming a significant level of residual value risk (ten per cent or more in present value terms) then it is presumed that substantially all the risks of ownership could not have passed to the lessee. As a yardstick for measuring risk the present value test is somewhat crude, but it was seen as a reasonable test of risk at the time SSAP 21 was introduced. It was, however, never intended to provide a strict mathematical definition of a finance lease. Thus, SSAP 21 provides that the presumption can be overridden where there is demonstrable evidence to support doing so.

19.12 One of the principal criticisms of SSAP 21 is that it led to practices under which lessors would structure leases in a way that apparently gives a present value result below the 90 per cent threshold, often marginally so, in order to provide lessees with a source of off-balance sheet finance. In July 1987, the ICAEW took the unusual step of issuing a Technical Release, TR 664, to clarify the rules in SSAP 21. TR 664 seeks to dissuade preparers of financial statements from standing behind the present value test in determining whether a leased asset should be on- or off-balance sheet by emphasising that the leases should be classified according to an informed judgement as to what is the true substance of the leasing transaction. Thus, while the present value test sets a presumption, it should be overridden where the circumstances justify it.

19.13 The publication of FRS 5, 'Reporting the substance of transactions', in 1994 further reinforces the message of TR 664, because it requires emphasis to be placed on those aspects and implications of a transaction that are likely to have a commercial effect in practice. Moreover, FRS 5 is particularly relevant in interpreting leases containing options, guarantees and conditional provisions where it provides more specific guidance than SSAP 21.

19.14 Consequently, although the present value test may be a useful yardstick for measuring the lessor's risk in a lease, it is by no means conclusive of where the risks and rewards lie. A proper interpretation of the classification of a lease, therefore, requires the exercise of judgement to determine the agreement's true nature. In this matter, the terms dealing with: the contractual lease period, the cancellation provisions, the renewal options and the rights and obligations of each party in relation to the asset at the end of the lease term are particularly important.

Lease term

19.14.1 Under SSAP 21, the lease term includes both of the following:

- The period for which the lessee has a contractual obligation to lease the asset.
- Further periods for which the lessee has the option to continue to lease the asset, with or without further payments, and it is reasonably certain at the inception of the lease that the lessee will exercise that option.

[SSAP 21 para 19].

Those parts of the lease that deal with: the lease's minimum contractual period (sometimes referred to as the 'primary period'); cancellation (or 'break') clauses; exchange and upgrade conditions; and options to extend the lease must, therefore, be considered carefully.

[The next paragraph is 19.15.]

19.15 If a lease contains a clean break clause, that is, where the lessee is free to walk away from the lease agreement after a certain time without penalty, then the lease term for accounting purposes will normally be the period between the inception of the lease and the earliest point at which the break option is exercisable by the lessee. Thus, the inclusion of a break clause can significantly reduce the minimum lease payments for the purpose of the present value test with the effect that the present value of the minimum lease payments falls below the 90 per cent threshold and the lease is classified as an operating lease. This, however, is not an unreasonable result if there is a genuine commercial possibility that the lessee might exercise the option resulting in the realisation of the lessor's unrecovered investment in the leased asset being subject to market risk.

19.16 If a lease contains an early termination clause that requires the lessee to make a termination payment to compensate the lessor (sometimes referred to as the 'stipulated loss value') such that the recovery of the lessor's remaining investment in the lease was assured, then the termination clause would normally be disregarded in determining the lease term.

19.17 Where, however, there are break clauses that transfer some economic risk to the lessor, but at the same time give the lessor some protection from financial loss, the interpretation becomes more difficult. For example, certain computer lessors include right to exchange clauses in leases that would otherwise be classified as finance leases. These give lessees the right to return equipment, or a proportion of the equipment, at certain times during the primary lease term, but normally on condition that a replacement lease is entered into on the new and remaining equipment. These right to exchange clauses need to be considered very carefully.

19.18 On the one hand, the effect may be the replacement of one finance lease by another, analogous to an outright purchase of equipment with a right to trade in for new equipment at a future date. This will be particularly so where the commercial loss on early termination (the difference between market value and the lessor's book value) is effectively rolled into the new lease agreement either through higher rentals or through an extension of the term on the remaining pool of assets not subject to the exchange. On the other hand, if the lessor takes a genuine residual value risk under the exchange conditions and such losses are not passed on to the lessee in the way described, this may justify classification as an operating lease.

19.19 Renewal clauses can cause similar problems of interpretation as break clauses. Where the terms of renewal are set at what is anticipated to be significantly below a fair market rental then it is reasonable to assume that the lessee will act in his own commercial interests and extend the lease. In these situations, the lease term would include both the minimum period and the renewal period. Where, however, the rentals in the secondary period are based on a fair market basis, such that there is no compelling commercial reason why the lessee must extend the lease, then the lease term will normally exclude the secondary period.

19.20 Other factors that may need to be considered in determining whether secondary periods should be included in the lease term are other forms of commercial compulsion such as penalties. For example, if the lessee is subject to a penalty for failing to renew a lease or exercise a purchase option, or if the return conditions stipulated in the lease are unduly penal, it may be to the lessee's advantage to continue to lease the asset. Similarly, if the lessee's business is dependent on the asset such that the cost of its removal and disruption of business are disproportional to the costs of continuing the lease, the secondary period should be included in the lease term.

Minimum lease payments

19.21 Once the lease term is determined, the lessee's minimum lease payments can be calculated. These are the payments that the lessee is committed to make during the lease term, and include:

- Any initial payment the lessee makes.
- The minimum rentals over the lease term (excluding charges in respect of services, such as maintenance, and VAT).
- Any amounts guaranteed by the lessee, or by a party related to him, to the lessor in respect of the realisation of the asset at the end of the lease term.

[SSAP 21 para 20].

19.22 From the lessor's perspective, the minimum lease payments may be different from that defined above since the lessor's minimum lease payments includes all the above and further amounts that are guaranteed by third parties in relation to the asset's future realisation. Thus, if the manufacturer originally supplying the asset agreed to repurchase the asset from the lessor, or guaranteed the sales proceeds, at the end of the lease term, then this amount would be included in the lessor's minimum lease payments. Consequently, in these circumstances, the lessee and lessor may well classify the lease quite differently.

19.23 The inclusion of 'residual guarantees' in lease agreements and related documentation will have an important impact on the way leases are classified by both lessors and lessees.

19.24 Obviously, if the lessee guarantees the whole of the asset's expected residual value at the end of the lease term the lessor would not be taking any of the risks relating to the performance or market value of the asset and the transaction would be clearly a finance lease. It would also mean that, by definition, the present value of the minimum lease payments would be equal to 100 per cent of the asset's fair value.

19.25 However, it is not uncommon in certain leases for the lessee and lessor to share both the downside risks and potential upside benefits associated with the asset's market value at the end of the lease term such that the lessee is taking some, but not all, the residual risk. For example, in certain leases the terms of the agreement provide for the asset to be sold at the end of the lease term and any profit and loss arising against anticipated values is shared between the lessor and lessee. However, the profit and loss sharing arrangements are usually unevenly balanced between the parties, with the lessee often taking the first tranche of loss up to a stipulated amount, with the lessor (or other third parties) only taking losses beyond that sum. In these circumstances, the amount of losses the lessee guarantees is normally set at such an amount that the inclusion of the guaranteed amount in the minimum lease payments does not cause the 90 per cent test to be breached.

19.26 Interpreting these types of agreement can be particularly difficult. The lessor may have a residual risk of ten per cent in present value terms, but if this implies that residual values have to fall to a level substantially below that anticipated to occur in practice, even under the most pessimistic circumstances, then the lessor's risk is remote and all the real commercial risks must rest with the lessee. In these circumstances, there is a strong argument for overriding the results of the present value test and classifying the lease as a finance lease.

Example

A lease of a car for two years has built into it an assumed residual value for the car of 45% of original cost. The market's perception is that the likely range of the residual value is 40-50% of cost. The terms of the lease provide that the lessee takes the risks and rewards regarding the residual down to a residual of 20% of cost. Below 20%, the lessor bears the loss.

It is clear under the combination of SSAP 21 and FRS 5 that the lessor's taking of risk below 20% of cost should not be taken into account in classifying the lease. The lessee takes the residual risk in all likely outcomes of residual value. Therefore, subject to any other terms in the lease, a finance lease is indicated.

19.27 However, in practice, the facts as illustrated above are rarely so simple. For example, under certain aircraft leases the lessee is offered a range of options under which it can terminate, or not renew, the leasing agreement. If it terminates the lease the residual sharing arrangements can be complex with the residual risk being shared by a number of parties including the lessor, lessee, supplier and residual insurer in a complex series of tranches. Interpreting these types of complex lease arrangements can be particularly difficult and the general principles and specific provisions of FRS 5 will need to be applied to determine the nature of transactions. For example, implementing FRS 5 had a dramatic impact on British Airways' Plc accounting for certain aircraft leases (see Table 19.1).

Table 19.1 – British Airways Plc – Report & Accounts – 31 March 1995

Notes to the accounts

1 CHANGES IN ACCOUNTING POLICIES (extract)

Adoption of new accounting standard (extract)

The Group has adopted the provisions of Financial Reporting Standard 5 'Reporting the Substance of Transactions' with effect from 1 April 1994 and corresponding amounts have been adjusted accordingly. As a consequence, the leases on twenty-four aircraft previously accounted for as operating leases are now accounted for as if they were finance leases and are aggregated with finance leases in the various disclosures in theses accounts. The effect of this change on the balance sheet at 31 March 1995 has been to increase tangible fixed assets by £870 million (1994: £1,006 million) and borrowings by £905 million (1994: £1,041 million) and to reduce opening reserves by £52 million (1994: £45 million). The effect on the results for the year ended 31 March 1995 has been to increase operating profit by £53 million (1994: £43 million) and to increase interest payable by £54 million (1994: £52 million), thereby reducing profit before taxation for the year by £1 million (1994: £9 million).

19.28 In some agreements relating to car fleets, the assessment of the commercial effects of these residual sharing arrangements can be further complicated by terms that mitigate a lessor's risk by providing for any residual losses on individual assets to be pooled against profits on others in the same portfolio. Again, these types of arrangement will need to be considered carefully to determine the nature of the risks borne by the lessor (and other third parties) and those transferred to the lessee. As a general rule, for instance, losses on some assets should not be set against profits on others.

The interest rate implicit in the lease

19.29 The rate of interest used for the present value test should be the interest rate implicit in the lease. This is the discount rate that, when applied at the inception of the lease to the amounts that the lessor expects to receive and retain from his investment in the lease, produces a present value equal to the leased asset's fair value. The amounts that the lessor expects to receive and retain comprise:

- The lessee's minimum lease payments.
- Any further amounts guaranteed by third parties in respect of the asset's residual value.
- The asset's expected residual value at the end of the lease, which is not guaranteed by the lessee or any other party.

- Less any amounts for which the lessor will be accountable to the lessee (for example, a rental rebate at the end of the lease based on the proceeds from the assets' sale).

[SSAP 21 para 24].

19.30 In more simple terms, the interest rate implicit in the lease is the lessor's internal rate of return from the lease taking into account the normal cash price of the leased asset, rentals and the amount he expects to recover from the residual value. In practice, the interest rate implicit in the lease is unlikely to be stipulated in the agreement and, unless the lessor volunteers the information to the lessee, the lessee will need either to derive an estimate of the rate from the information available to him or to use an approximation based on a similar lease.

19.31 A lessee can normally derive a reasonable estimate of the interest rate implicit in a lease where he either knows, or can make a reasonable estimate of, the cost of the asset and the anticipated residual value of the asset at the end of the lease term.

The present value calculation

19.32 The present value calculation is performed by discounting the minimum lease payments and comparing the resulting present value to the fair value of the leased asset. In most circumstances, the fair value will be the normal cash price at which the lessee could otherwise purchase the asset. A potentially misleading result can arise if the comparison is made against an amount that is not representative of the fair value, for example, a list price where substantial discounts are normally given to customers purchasing assets.

19.33 As indicated above, the present value test can also be misleading where the results of the present value test are engineered to provide a result marginally below the 90 per cent threshold. Such engineering can arise through the uses of break clauses, renewal clauses, and residual guarantees. Where there is evidence that the amount of residual risk taken by the lessor (or other unrelated parties) is insignificant or remote then there will be reasons to believe that substantially all the risks and rewards of ownership have passed to the lessee. In these circumstances, the results of the present value test should be overridden and the lease classified as a finance lease.

Property leases

19.34 Under the standard, leases of land and buildings are subject to the same accounting requirements as other leased assets. This means that they should either be classified as finance leases or as operating leases and should be accounted for accordingly. However, the present value test is difficult to apply to property leases and can sometimes be misleading. This is partly because of the practical difficulties of ascertaining the true interest rate implicit in the lease and partly because of the commercial nature of most UK institutional property leases.

19.35 Most UK institutional 'short' leases are for periods up to 25-30 years, and contain clauses that adjust lease payments to market rates at a regular interval (for example, five-yearly or three-yearly rent reviews). The lessor is often an institution that is seeking long-term rental and capital growth and is, therefore, taking most of the risks and rewards associated with changes in the property market. Although part of the investor's return may be protected by 'upward only' rental review clauses the overall return is dependent on market conditions, which may be substantially less or greater than originally anticipated. In this sense, the nature of the lessor's return is very different from a 'lender's return', which is based on the lender's cost of money plus margin.

19.36 However, it does not necessarily follow that all leases that look like institutional 'short' leases are operating leases. There are a number of hybrid leasing structures which, though in the legal form of a short lease, have many of the characteristics of financing arrangements.

19.37 Again the principles of FRS 5 and, in particular, whether the lender achieves a lenders' return, will help determine the true nature of the lease. An example could be a building with a relatively short life, perhaps built to a customer's specification or for a specific use, or certain types of sale and leaseback arrangements where the commercial objective is for the lessee to repurchase the property at an early option date.

19.38 Long leases (usually 99-999 years) are more likely to be finance leases. Such leases often involve the payment of a large lease premium with only a small annual ground rent. In these situations, the lease premium is normally capitalised and depreciated over the lease term. While, strictly, the present value of the ground rent should also be capitalised and an obligation set up, these amounts are often ignored as being immaterial.

Accounting by lessees

Accounting for finance leases

19.39 A finance lease should be recorded in a lessee's balance sheet both as an asset and as an obligation to pay future rentals. At the inception of the lease, the sum to be recorded both as an asset and as a liability should be the present value of the minimum lease payments, derived by discounting them at the interest rate implicit in the lease. [SSAP 21 para 32].

19.40 An asset leased under a finance lease should be depreciated over the shorter of the lease term and its useful life. [SSAP 21 para 36]. The lease term is the period for which the lessee has contracted to lease the asset plus any further optional periods, which are at the lessee's option and which are reasonably certain to be exercised. [SSAP 21 para 19]. With a hire purchase contract that has the characteristics of a finance lease, the asset should be depreciated over its useful life. [SSAP 21 para 36].

19.41 The lease is deemed to commence on the earlier of the date on which the asset is brought into use by the lessee and the date from which rentals first accrue. Therefore, if a lease provides for a rent-free period at the start of the lease, the lessee should treat the inception date as the date on which he started to use the asset.

19.42 Rentals payable should be apportioned between the finance charge and a reduction of the outstanding obligation for future amounts payable. The total finance charge under a finance lease should be allocated to accounting periods during the lease term, so as to produce either a constant periodic rate of charge on the remaining balance of the obligation for each accounting period or a reasonable approximation to it. [SSAP 21 para 35].

Example

Cost of leased asset	£100,000
Lease term	5 years
Rental six-monthly in advance	£12,000
Expected residual on disposal at the end of the lease term	£10,000
Lessee's interest in residual proceeds	97%
Economic life	8 years
Inception date	1 January 20X4
Lessee's financial year end	31 December

In this example, the lease must obviously be a finance lease because the lessor has only a 3% interest in the residual value. There is, therefore, little point in performing the 90% test. The amounts the lessor expects to receive and retain comprise the rentals, plus 3% of the residual at the end of the lease term. These amounts can be used to determine the interest rate implicit in the lease and the present value of the lessee's minimum lease payments as follows:

	Present value factor	Present value at 4.3535%
		£
Lessee's minimum lease payments (10 × £12,000)	8.3170	99,804
Lessor's residual (£10,000 – £9,700)	0.6533	196
Fair value		100,000

The interest rate that amortises these amounts is 4.3535%, compounded on a six-monthly basis.

The amount that is capitalised as both an asset and an obligation at the inception of the lease is, therefore, £99,804. Alternatively, it could be simply assumed that, because the lessor's residual was so immaterial, the fair value was a reasonable approximation of the present value of the lease payments and this would generally be allowed in such a case. If this approach was adopted, the amount that would be capitalised at the inception of the lease as an asset and an obligation would be £100,000.

The finance charge can now be allocated to each accounting period. In this example the actuarial method has been used:

Period commencing	Obligation at start of period	Rental paid	Obligation during period	Finance charge at 4.3535%	Obligation at end of period
	£	£	£	£	£
January 20X4	99,804	(12,000)	87,804	3,823	91,627
June 20X4	91,627	(12,000)	79,627	3,467	83,094
January 20X5	83,094	(12,000)	71,094	3,095	74,189
June 20X5	74,189	(12,000)	62,189	2,707	64,896
January 20X6	64,896	(12,000)	52,896	2,303	55,199
June 20X6	55,199	(12,000)	43,199	1,881	45,080
January 20X7	45,080	(12,000)	33,080	1,440	34,520
June 20X7	34,520	(12,000)	22,520	980	23,500
January 20X8	23,500	(12,000)	11,500	500	12,000
June 20X8	12,000	(12,000)	–	–	–
		(120,000)		20,196	

The finance charges for each year and, by deduction, the capital repayment element of the rental can now be summarised as follows:

	Rental	Finance charges	Capital repayment
	£	£	£
20X4	24,000	7,290	16,710
20X5	24,000	5,802	18,198
20X6	24,000	4,184	19,816
20X7	24,000	2,420	21,580
20X8	24,000	500	23,500
	120,000	20,196	99,804

In this example, the lessee's financial year end coincides with the end of a rental period and so no interest accrual is necessary.

Depreciation can now be calculated as follows:

Lease term = 5 years

Economic life = 8 years

Lessee's interest in the proceeds of the residual = £9,700

Therefore, the depreciation charge on a straight line basis is:

$$\frac{£99{,}804 - £9{,}700}{5 \text{ years}} = £18{,}021 \text{ per annum}$$

Where the lessee's interest in the anticipated proceeds of the residual is immaterial, the residual can be ignored for the purposes of calculating depreciation.

The effects on the lessee's balance sheet and profit and loss account for each year can now be summarised as follows:

	Obligations under finance leases	Net book value of leased assets	Depreciation	Finance charges	Total charges
	£	£	£	£	£
Start	99,804	99,804			
20X4	83,094	81,783	18,021	7,290	25,311
20X5	64,896	63,762	18,021	5,802	23,823
20X6	45,080	45,741	18,021	4,184	22,205
20X7	23,500	27,720	18,021	2,420	20,441
20X8	–	9,700	18,020	500	18,520
			90,104	20,196	110,300

The above example illustrates that, in addition to its impact on the lessee's balance sheet, lease capitalisation may also have a significant impact on the lessee's profit and loss account. For example, the lease rentals are £24,000 per annum, but the combined charge for depreciation and interest varies from £25,311 to £18,520 per annum. These differences between rental payments and profit and loss charges will be more pronounced on assets subject to long economic lives and leases with short primary lease periods, but which may have secondary periods at peppercorn rents.

Accounting for operating leases

19.43 Operating leases should not be capitalised and the lease rental should be charged on a straight-line basis over the lease term, unless another systematic and rational basis is more appropriate. This applies even if the payments are not made on such a basis. [SSAP 21 para 37].

Lease incentives

19.44 Prospective lessees are sometimes given incentives to sign operating leases for office or retail property. These incentives may include either rent-free or reduced-rent periods at the start of the lease or even contributions toward fitting out costs.

19.45 The UITF issued Abstract 28, 'Operating lease incentives', in February 2001. UITF Abstract 28 expands and clarifies the requirements of paragraph 37 of SSAP 21 with regard to incentives for lessees to sign leases from both the lessee's and the lessor's perspective.

19.46 Operating lease incentives may take many different forms. Examples of such incentives include: contributions to relocation or start-up costs; the assumption of liabilities, such as the rentals under the an old lease which would otherwise fall to be a vacant property; or the gift of an asset such as the lessor bearing directly all the costs of fitting out the property to the lessee's specifications or giving rent free or reduced rental periods for an initial period of the lease. However, both abstracts detail the same treatment for all incentives for the agreement of a new or renewed operating lease regardless of their form or cash flow effect. UITF Abstract 28 clarifies that a payment or other transfer of value from a lessor to a lessee (or for its benefit) should be regarded as a lease incentive when that fairly reflects the transaction's substance. Where it does not reflect the transaction's substance then it should not be regarded as an incentive. For example, a lessor may reimburse a lessee for expenditure that enhances the property generally (rather than for fixtures and fittings that are specific to the lessee) such that the lessor, rather than the lessee, will primarily benefit from that expenditure. The benefit to the lessor may be achieved through increases in the market rent of the property at the next rent review or on the termination of the existing lease. Such expenditure should be treated as a reimbursement of expenditure on the property, so that the lessee would simply record the amount owed by, and subsequently received from, the lessor in the balance sheet. [UITF 28 para 3]. An alternative scenario might be where the lessor pays the lessee compensation in respect of a delay in delivery of the leased asset, again provided that the compensation is genuine, it would not be treated as a lease incentive.

19.47 Benefits received and receivable by a lessee as an incentive to sign a lease in whatever form should be spread by the lessee on a straight-line basis over the lease term, or, if shorter than the full lease term, over the period to the review date on which the rent is first expected to be adjusted to the prevailing market rent. [UITF 12 para 8]. This requirement seeks to ensure that the profit and loss account reflects the true effective rental charge for the property irrespective of the particular cash flow arrangements agreed between the two parties. The lessor will seek to recover a market rental over the lease term. Therefore, the existence of an up-front incentive creates the presumption that the subsequent rental levels will be set at higher than the prevailing market level until either the end of the lease or until the review date when the rent is adjusted to the market level. In requiring that the incentive should be spread over the lease term or to the first rent review to market value if earlier, the abstract amended paragraph 16 of the guidance notes to SSAP 21, which had stated merely that incentives should be spread over the period in which the asset is in use.

19.48 UITF Abstract 28 similarly requires that a lessee should recognise the aggregate benefit of incentives as a reduction of rental expense. The benefit should be allocated on a straight-line basis over the shorter of the lease term and the period ending on the date from which it is expected that prevailing market rental will be payable. [UITF 28 para 14].

19.49 UITF Abstract 28 permits systematic bases other than a straight-line basis to be used to allocate the aggregate benefit of incentives, provided that they are more representative of the time pattern of the lessee's benefit from the use of the leased asset. [UITF 28 para 14]. No disclosure of this is required under UITF

Abstract 28, although if material it would require disclosure under the general requirements of FRS 18, as an estimation technique. In practice the use of bases other than straight-line is rare. In particular this is not a permission to recognise all the benefit of the incentive in a start up period with none recognised over the remaining lease period or until the next rent review to market rates, as this is not consistent with the requirement for a 'systematic' basis. For example, a retailer may lease a new store for a five year period, with no rent reviews. Although the retailer may not open the store for the first six months due to a fit-out period, the retailer still has the benefit of the use and enjoyment of the leased property during that initial period, as well as for the rest of the lease, and hence the incentive should be spread over the five years of the lease period from the start of the lease on a straight-line basis. There is no justification for not recognising lease costs for the initial period, as the lessee still has the benefit of use for this period.

19.49.1 The arguments in UITF Abstract 28 for deferring and spreading the recognition of lease incentives received also provide a good starting point for accounting for lease premiums paid. Therefore, where a substantial premium is paid with only nominal rents paid during the lease, the lease payments would never be adjusted to market rates and so the premium would be charged on a straight-line basis over the full lease term. Where there is a provision in the lease for the rents to be adjusted to market rates, it would be consistent with the reasoning in UITF Abstract 28 for the premium to be charged over the shorter period to the rent review date rather than the full lease term.

Lessee disclosure requirements

19.50 In respect of finance leases, SSAP 21 requires the following information to be disclosed in the lessee's financial statements:

- The gross amount, the related accumulated depreciation and the total depreciation allocated for the period, analysed by each major class of asset capitalised under finance leases. [SSAP 21 para 49].
- Alternatively, this information may be included within the totals disclosed by each major class of asset for owned assets. However, where this alternative is adopted, the total of the net amount of assets held under finance leases and the total amount of depreciation allocated for the period in respect of finance leases, need to be disclosed separately. [SSAP 21 para 50]. An example of this disclosure is in Table 19.2.
- The liability for net obligations under finance leases (net of finance charges allocated to future periods), shown separately from other liabilities. This liability should be disclosed either on the face of the balance sheet or in the notes to the financial statements (see Table 19.3). [SSAP 21 para 51].
- The liability for net obligations under finance leases, analysed between amounts payable in the next year, amounts payable in the second to fifth years inclusive from the balance sheet date and the aggregate amounts payable after the fifth year. [SSAP 21 para 52]. For example, Table 19.3

illustrates this disclosure. The detailed disclosure requirements for such creditors are also contained in chapter 6.

- Where the lessee discloses the analysis of obligations under finance leases separately, he may, as an alternative to analysing the net obligations, analyse the gross obligations and show future finance charges as a separate deduction from the total (see Table 19.5). [SSAP 21 para 52].

- The aggregate finance charge allocated to the period. [SSAP 21 para 53]. This disclosure is often made as part of the interest charge for the year as illustrated in Table 19.4.

- The commitments under finance leases existing at the year end that have been entered into, but whose inception occurs after the year end. [SSAP 21 para 54]. This requirement is analogous to the legal requirements in respect of commitments for capital expenditure (see chapter 21). Zeneca Group PLC, for example, includes such disclosure in the leases note (see Table 19.5).

Table 19.2 – British Airways Plc – Report & Accounts – 31 March 1995

Notes to the accounts (extract)

	Group	
£million	**1995**	1994
5 OPERATING PROFIT (extract)		
a Operating Profit is arrived at after charging:		
Depreciation of Group tangible fixed assets		
Owned assets	**263**	258
Finance leased aircraft	**109**	117
Hire purchased aircraft	**63**	48
Other leasehold interests	**23**	24
	458	447

15 TANGIBLE ASSETS (extract)

				Group total	
	Property	Equipment	**1995**	£million 1994	Fleet
Net Book Amounts					
31 March 1995	5,155	801	207	**6,163**	
31 March 1994	5,127	484	200		5,811
Utilisation at 31 March					
Assets in current use					
Owned	1,883	734	165	**2,782**	2,631
Finance leased	1,436			**1,436**	1,623
Hire purchased arrangements	1,445			**1,445**	1,274
Progress payments	377	65	42	**484**	257
Assets held for resale	14	2		**16**	26
	5,155	801	207	**6,163**	5,811

Table 19.3 – Cable and Wireless plc – Report and Accounts – 31 March 1995

Balance sheets (extract)

		Group	
		1995	1994 Restated
at 31 March	Note	**£m**	£m
Creditors: amounts falling due within one year	21		
Loans and obligations under finance leases		**321.4**	359.5
Other creditors		**1,423.8**	1,318.8
		1,745.2	1,678.3
Creditors: amounts falling due after more than one year	22		
Convertible bonds		**149.5**	154.5
Other loans and obligations under finance leases		**1,190.2**	1,022.4
Other creditors		**33.4**	34.2
Provisions for liabilities and charges*			
Deferred taxation	23	**130.0**	126.8
Other provisions	24	**89.5**	28.8
		1,592.6	1,366.7

21. Creditors: amounts falling due within one year (extract)

	Group	
		Restated
	1995	1994
	£m	£m
Loans and obligations under finance leases		
Banks loans and overdrafts	**39.2**	32.6
Bills payable	**15.2**	31.1
Current instalments due on loans	**253.8**	287.4
Obligations under finance leases	**13.2**	8.4
	321.4	359.5

22. Creditors: amounts falling due after more than one year (extract)

		Group
		Restated
	1995	1994
	£m	£m
Loans and obligations under finance leases		
Sterling repayable at various dates up to 2019	**353.2**	161.1
Hong Kong dollars repayable at various dates up to 1995	**200.9**	220.9
US dollars repayable at various dates up to 2041	**775.1**	838.8
Other currencies repayable at various dates up to 1997	**56.7**	63.6
	1,385.9	1,284.4
Less: Current instalments due	**253.8**	287.4
	1,132.1	997.0
Net obligations under finance leases	**71.3**	33.8
Less: Current instalments due	**13.2**	8.4
	58.1	25.4
Total loans and net obligations under finance leases	**1,190.2**	1,022.4
Total loans and net obligations under finance leases are payable as follows:		
Between one and two years	**130.7**	56.7
Between two and five years	**259.6**	289.3
In five or more years	**799.9**	676.4
	1,190.2	1,022.4

* Note that for years beginning on or after 1 January 2005, SI 2004/2947, 'The Companies Act 1985 (International Accounting Standards and Other Amendments) Regulations 2004', replaces the statutory line item 'provisions for liabilities and charges' with 'provisions for liabilities'.

Table 19.4 – Racal Electronics Plc – Annual Report & Accounts – 31 March 1994

Notes on the financial statements (extract)

5 NET INTEREST RECEIVABLE (extract)	**1994**	
	£000	**£000**
Interest receivable:		
Interest receivable on loans and deposits		**12,283**
Interest receivable on finance leases		**3,499**
		15,782
Less interest payable:		
Bank overdrafts, loans and other borrowings repayable within five years	**(13,034)**	
Loans and other borrowings repayable wholly or in part after five years	**(405)**	
Finance charges on hire purchase contracts and finance leases	**(710)**	
		(14,149)
		1,633

Table 19.5 – Zeneca Group PLC – Annual Report and Accounts – 31 December 1994

Notes relating to the accounts (extract)

6 LEASES

The total rentals under operating leases, charged as an expense in the profit and loss account, are disclosed below.

	1994 £m	1993 £m
Hire of plant and machinery	8	6
Other	28	29
	36	35

Commitments under leases to pay rentals during the year following the year of these accounts are given in the table below, analysed to the period in which each lease expires.

	1994 £m	1993 £m
Obligations under operating leases comprise		
Land and buildings		
Expiring within 1 year	3	1
Expiring during years 2 to 5	3	3
Expiring thereafter	4	4
	10	8
Other assets		
Expiring within 1 year	7	4
Expiring during years 2 to 5	6	12
Expiring thereafter	–	–
	13	16
Obligations under finance leases comprise		
Rentals due within 1 year	2	4
Rentals due during years 2 to 5	6	5
Rentals due thereafter	2	2
Less interest element	(2)	(2)
	8	9

Obligations under finance leases are included in other creditors (Note 18).

The Group had commitments totalling £6m (1993 £nil) under finance leases at the balance sheet date which were due to commence thereafter.

19.51 In respect of operating leases, SSAP 21 requires the following information to be disclosed:

- The total of operating lease rentals charged as an expense in the profit and loss account, and analysed between amounts payable both in respect of hire of plant and machinery and in respect of other operating leases. [SSAP 21 para 55]. An example of this disclosure is included in Table 19.5 above.
- The payments that the lessee is committed to make during the next year, analysed between: those in which the commitment expires within that year; those in which the commitment expires within the second to fifth years inclusive; and those in which the commitment expires more than five years after the balance sheet date. This analysis should show the

commitments in respect of land and buildings separately from those of other operating leases. [SSAP 21 para 56]. This requirement is sometimes misunderstood; the intention is to show only the annual commitment not the total amount that will be payable until the end of the lease as illustrated in Table 19.5 above. If the amount to be paid in the next year is significantly different from the amount that will be charged to profit and loss, then details of the difference and the reasons should be given.

19.52 In respect of both finance leases and operating leases, the accounting policies that the lessee has adopted must be disclosed in the financial statements. [SSAP 21 para 57]. For example, Table 19.6 contains such an accounting policy.

Table 19.6 – Cable and Wireless plc – Annual report and Accounts – 31 March 2003

Statement of Accounting Policies (extract)

Leased assets

Where assets are financed by leasing agreements that give rights approximating to ownership, the assets are treated as if they had been purchased outright. The amount capitalised is the present value of the minimum lease payments payable during the lease term. The corresponding lease commitments are shown as obligations to the lessor. Lease payments are split between capital and interest elements using the annuity method. Depreciation on the relevant assets and interest are charged to the profit and loss account. All other leases are operating leases and the annual rentals are charged to operating profit on a straight line basis over the lease term.

19.53 In addition to the standard's disclosure requirements, the Guidance Notes to the standard indicate that other details about a company's leases may need to be disclosed in order to give a true and fair view of the company's state of affairs. These include for example: contingent rentals; profit participation arrangements; significant restrictions on future borrowing or leasing; and contingent liabilities. The information will depend on whether the user's appreciation of the company's state of affairs would be affected if he was aware of that information. The criteria to be applied to that information are no different from those to be applied to any other information about the company's financial affairs.

19.53.1 An up-front payment made under an operating lease would usually be regarded as prepaid rental (that is, presented as a prepayment, which is a current asset) rather than the acquisition of a fixed asset. Leases of property sometimes involve different considerations. Paragraph 144 of the guidance notes to the standard state that "*nothing in the standard precludes the recognition as a fixed asset of an amount paid in the form of a premium as consideration for a leasehold interest*". The payment of a premium to purchase a leasehold interest in a property is traditionally reported as a fixed asset under UK GAAP rather than as prepaid rental, regardless of whether the lease would be classified as a finance lease or an operating lease. To be treated as a fixed asset, the lease term would normally be substantial, the premium paid would be material and would provide the lessee with continuing benefits during the lease term. For example, it is clear that a premium paid on a long lease that gives the lessee the benefit of a peppercorn rental for the lease term is appropriately shown as a fixed asset. On the other hand, if a lease provides for regular rent reviews, and the rent payable is brought up to fair market rates, any premium paid at inception has the characteristics of a prepayment. In such circumstances, the premium would normally be written off over the period until the rent is first expected to be adjusted to market levels.

Sale and leaseback transactions

19.54 A sale and leaseback transaction arises when a vendor sells an asset and immediately re-acquires the use of the asset by entering into a lease with the buyer. Such transactions are a popular method of releasing cash funds for new investment as an alternative to borrowing. Under SSAP 21, the accounting treatment depends on the type of lease entered into. It also depends on whether the sale and the subsequent leaseback are on a strictly arm's length basis.

Finance leasebacks

19.55 Where the seller enters into a finance leaseback, the transaction is essentially a financing operation. In essence, the seller/lessee never disposes of the risks and rewards of ownership of the asset and so he should not recognise a profit or loss on the sale. There are two ways of looking at this situation in accounting terms. SSAP 21's approach was that any apparent profit or loss on the transaction (that is, the difference between the sale price and the previous carrying value) should be deferred and amortised over the shorter of the lease term and the asset's useful life. [SSAP 21 para 46]. This treatment will have the effect of adjusting the overall charge to the profit and loss account for the depreciation of the asset to an amount consistent with the asset's carrying value before the leaseback.

19.56 Normally, a fixed asset's carrying value before a sale and finance leaseback will not be more than the leased asset's fair value. Indeed, if it were, it would need to be tested for impairment under FRS 11. Any such adjustments to the asset's carrying value should be made before determining the apparent profit or loss on the sale and leaseback transaction. The apparent profit or loss that is deferred and amortised over the lease term will then represent the difference between the sale price and the revised carrying value (the fair value). In these circumstances, such a difference would arise only if the sale proceeds and the subsequent rentals were determined other than on an arm's length basis.

[The next paragraph is 19.58.]

19.58 There is, however, a second, and now preferable, way of accounting for a sale and finance leaseback. This method views the transaction as being simply the raising of finance. Hence there is no change to the carrying value of the asset: it is regarded as being retained rather than disposed of and re-acquired. Hence, a sale and finance leaseback is treated not as a sale and repurchase, but simply as a source of finance, like raising a secured loan on an existing asset. Proceeds are then simply credited to a liability account (representing the present value of the obligation under the finance lease), and there is no need to show a disposal and a re-acquisition of an asset. It can be argued that this treatment better reflects the commercial substance of this transaction because it is only the legal form of the transaction that represents a disposal and re-acquisition of the underlying asset. This treatment is, therefore, consistent with the principles underlying FRS 5 (which are considered further in chapter 3).

19.59 A question arises as to whether the revaluation surplus on the asset becomes realised or not on a sale and finance leaseback. The accounting principles upon which SSAP 21 and FRS 5 are based argue that the seller/lessee does not dispose of the risks and rewards of ownership under a sale and finance leaseback arrangement. Section 262(3) of the Companies Act 1985 (CA06 Sec 853) states that whether profits are realised or not depends on"*…principles generally accepted, at the time when the accounts are prepared, with respect to the determination for accounting purposes of realised profits or losses"*. Because in accounting terms there is no genuine disposal of the asset by the seller/lessee, it is considered that the revaluation surplus does not become realised immediately.

Operating leasebacks

19.60 Where the seller enters into a sale and operating leaseback, he effectively disposes of substantially all the risks and rewards of owning the asset in the sale transaction; and may re-acquire some of the risks and rewards of ownership in the leaseback, but does not re-acquire substantially all of them. Accordingly, the transaction should be treated as a disposal and any profit or loss on the transaction should be recognised. It is interesting to note that in this respect the specific requirements of SSAP 21 are different to the general principles of FRS 5. This is because SSAP 21 recognises assets and liabilities on an all or nothing basis. FRS 5, however, will only recognise a disposal of an asset in its entirety when all significant rights or other access to benefits and all exposures to risks have been transferred. However, in a sale and leaseback transaction rights and obligations are retained by the seller-lessee. In this case, however, as SSAP 21 contains the more specific requirements the SSAP 21 treatment would prevail. Under SSAP 21, the calculation of the profit or loss will depend on whether the sale proceeds and the rentals under the subsequent lease were determined on an arm's length basis.

19.61 Where the sale transaction is established at the fair value, any profit or loss on the sale should be recognised immediately. Consequently, no further adjustment is necessary. [SSAP 21 para 47].

19.62 Where the sale price is above the fair value, the excess of the sale price over the fair value does not represent a genuine profit. This is because the rentals payable in future years will almost certainly be inflated above the market value. Accordingly, the excess of the sale proceeds over the fair value should be deferred and amortised over the shorter of the remainder of the lease term and the period to the next rent review. [SSAP 21 para 47]. This treatment will have the effect of reducing the annual expense for rentals to a basis consistent with the fair value of the asset.

19.63 Where the sale price is below the fair value, the standard requires that any profit or loss should be recognised immediately. This requirement recognises the fact that the company, perhaps motivated by the need to raise cash quickly, may simply have negotiated a poor bargain. An exception is made, however, where a loss is compensated by future rentals that are below market levels. In such a circumstance, the standard requires the loss (to the extent that it is compensated by future rentals below market levels) be deferred and amortised over the remainder of the lease term (or, if it is shorter, the period during which the reduced rentals are chargeable). [SSAP 21 para 47]. This practice may seem to go against the prudence principle. In effect, however, it merely reverses the effect of an artificial loss created by establishing, in an artificial way, the sale price and the subsequent rental. Rather strangely perhaps, the standard does not require a similar adjustment where the profit that is made is lower than would be expected if the sale proceeds and the subsequent rentals were established on an arm's length basis.

Sale and leasebacks with repurchase options

19.64 The use of put and call options in sale and leaseback transactions involving properties is a popular method to enable a company to raise medium-term finance to the value of the property that it owns. Under such arrangements, the seller/lessee may have an option to repurchase the property (call option), or the buyer/lessor may have an option to require the seller/lessee to repurchase the property (put option), or there may be a combination of options.

19.65 The substance of the transaction needs to be considered very closely in order to classify the lease correctly as a finance or operating lease. In essence, the objective is to determine whether the commercial effect of the transaction is that of a genuine sale or that of a secured loan.

19.66 If the repurchase price contained in an option to repurchase is the market value of the asset at the date of exercise, it is probable that the buyer/lessor acquires both have the opportunity to benefit from any increase in the value of the asset and the risk of loss if there is a fall in its value. In this situation the option is a 'genuine' option and will not influence the way the lease is classified.

19.67 If, however, the repurchase price is predetermined so that, when exercised it assures the buyer/lessor of a return of his original purchase price together with his required rate of return, this may well be indicative of a finance lease. A key issue will be whether there is a genuine commercial possibility that the option will fail to be exercised and, in that event, what further conditions protect the buyer/lessor's return. For example, if the conditions of the leaseback were such that the rental rate increased to a rate substantially in excess of a commercial rate should the lessee fail to exercise his repurchase option, this could well have the effect of a penalty which would force the exercise of the option. Consequently, it is important to understand properly the commercial objectives for the inclusion of a repurchase option in the leaseback and the commercial effect it will have in practice.

Accounting by lessors

Finance & Leasing Association SORP

19.67.1 The guidance in SSAP 21 on matters such as income recognition and accounting for residual values is limited and does not relate specifically to the types of complex arrangements that may be entered into by, for example, specialist computer lessors.

19.67.2 In April 1994 the ASB approved the Finance & Leasing Association (FLA) for the development of a SORP on lessor accounting. The SORP, 'Accounting issues in the asset finance and leasing industry', was published in April 2000. The SORP supplements, but does not override, the basic accounting requirements of SSAP 21 and FRS 5 as they apply to lessors. It has been developed in order to improve comparability in the accounting practices of lessors and to provide more specific guidance on how SSAP 21 should be interpreted in certain problem areas.

19.67.3 The SORP endorses the requirements of SSAP 21 and FRS 5 that lease transactions should be accounted for and presented in accordance with their substance and not merely their legal form. In determining this substance, the SORP sets out a number of questions which, whilst not intended to be a comprehensive list, the lessor should consider. The SORP also emphasises prudent income recognition practices for lessors and recommends certain additional disclosures that are not required by SSAP 21 in order to make residual value risks more transparent.

19.67.4 The SORP applies to the financial statements of lessors that are members of the FLA and also encourages lessors that are not members of the FLA to follow its recommendations.

[The next paragraph is 19.68.]

Accounting for finance leases

19.68 The amount due from the lessee under a finance lease should be recorded in the lessor's balance sheet as a debtor at the amount of the net investment in the lease, after making provisions for items such as bad and doubtful rentals receivable. [SSAP 21 para 38].

19.69 At the inception of a finance lease, the lessor's net investment in the lease is the cost of the asset to the lessor. Over the lease term, rentals will be apportioned between a reduction in the net investment in the lease and gross earnings.

19.70 At any point in time during the lease term, the net investment in the lease will be represented by the remaining minimum lease payments (the amounts the lessor is guaranteed to receive under the lease from either the lessee or third parties), less that part of the minimum lease payments that is attributable to future gross earnings (namely, interest and the lessor's profit). The lessor's net investment in the lease may also include an unguaranteed residual value. The unguaranteed residual value, which will be small in a finance lease, represents the amount the lessor expects to recover from the value of the leased asset at the end of the lease term that is not guaranteed in any way by either the lessee or third parties.

19.71 SSAP 21 requires that the total gross earnings under a finance lease be allocated to each accounting period during the lease term in such a manner as to produce a constant rate of return (or a reasonable approximation to it) on each period's net *cash* investment. [SSAP 21 para 39]. The net cash investment in a lease represents the total cash invested after taking into account all of the cash flows associated with the lease. It differs, therefore, from the amount of the net investment in the lease that is shown in the balance sheet. This is because it takes account of other cash flows. The most important of these other cash flows relates to the tax effects of the lease.

19.72 One of the reasons why SSAP 21 requires that gross earnings should be allocated to accounting periods on the basis of the net cash investment is that the gross earnings will then be properly matched with the interest costs of funding the net cash investment in the lease. Consequently, SSAP 21 permits alternative methods of allocating gross earnings which allocate gross earnings so that net earnings (gross earnings less estimated interest costs) are recognised on a systematic basis. This means that an allocation of gross earnings is first made to each accounting period to cover the estimated costs of finance. The remaining balance of gross earnings is then allocated to accounting periods on a systematic basis. The FLA SORP, however, seeks to prohibit the general use of methods that allocate gross earnings after interest costs except where the normal treatment of allocating gross earnings before interest is imprudent given the risk profile of the lease. [FLA SORP para 5.3.4].

19.73 The SORP refers to SSAP 21's method of accounting as 'lease accounting incorporating tax cash flows'. It should be used where the tax consequences of the lease form a material and integral part of the overall return from the lease. This is the case where the lessor has the benefit of accelerated capital allowances that result in significant deferrals of tax payments. Where the tax consequences are not material, the SORP notes that a method that ignores the effect of tax may be used, because it will give a reasonable approximation to a constant return on the lessor's net cash investment in the lease. [FLA SORP 5.3.18]. Thus a finance company will normally allocate gross earnings from a hire purchase contract to give a constant periodic rate of return on its net investment (ignoring any tax effects). This is because the tax effects of a hire purchase contract are rarely significant as the lessee takes all of the benefit and so the company's net investment in a hire purchase contract will approximate to its net cash investment in that contract.

19.74 The most popular methods for allocating gross earnings to accounting periods that are used in practice in the leasing industry are the 'actuarial after-tax method' and the 'investment period method'. Below, we briefly describe the actuarial after-tax method and illustrate its application. The FLA SORP prefers this method, but allows the 'investment period method' or the 'sum of digits method' provided that the chosen method gives a reasonable approximation to the 'actuarial after-tax method' and does not result in gross earnings being recognised significantly earlier.

The actuarial after-tax method

19.75 The basis of the actuarial after-tax method is that rentals are allocated between interest (gross earnings) and capital (amortisation) in each accounting period in such a way that the anticipated after-tax profit (gross earnings less interest expense and tax) will emerge as a constant periodic rate of return on the lessor's average net cash investment in the lease. The accounting entries for 'amortisation' and 'gross earnings' for each period during the lease is, therefore, based on the forecast cash flows made at the start of the lease.

Example

Lease term	Seven years from 31 March 20X4
Rental payments	£1,787.00 payable annually in advance
Asset cost	£10,000.00
Lessor's year end date	31 March
Lessor's tax payment date	Nine months after the year end (1 January)
Cost of money	8.5% per annum
Reinvestment rate	3.0% per annum
Interest assumptions	calculated daily in arrear (annual compounding)
Tax rate	33%
Capital allowances	25% writing down allowance
Balancing allowance (assumed)	31 March 20Y1

The first step, is to calculate the after-tax profit-take-out rate using the forecast lease cash flows. This is the rate at which the lessor could theoretically withdraw profit from the lease measured as a constant rate on the average daily net cash investment balance for each period. It is calculated by a computer program using an iterative process that involves a succession of trial-and-error estimates of the rate until the net cash investment balance becomes zero at the end of the cash flows. In this example the profit-take-out rate is calculated at 0.8458% per annum.

Date	Net cash investment start of period £	Rental £	Tax £	Interest paid/ (received) £	Profit taken out £	Net cash investment end of period £
31 March 20X4	10,000.00	(1,787.00)	–	–	–	8,213.00
1 January 20X5	8,213.00	–	(823.38)	–	–	7,389.62
31 March 20X5	7,389.62	(1,787.00)	–	681.04	67.76	6,351.42
1 January 20X6	6,351.42	–	(253.79)	–	–	6,097.63
31 March 20X6	6,097.63	(1,787.00)	–	536.03	53.34	4,900.00
1 January 20X7	4,900.00	–	(51.24)	–	–	4,848.76
31 March 20X7	4,848.76	(1,787.00)	–	415.44	41.34	3,518.54
1 January 20X8	3,518.54	–	104.57	–	–	3,623.10
31 March 20X8	3,623.11	(1,787.00)	–	301.24	29.97	2,167.32
1 January 20X9	2,167.32	–	229.26	–	–	2,396.58
31 March 20X9	2,396.58	(1,787.00)	–	188.97	18.80	817.35
1 January 20Y0	817.35	–	331.57	–	–	1,148.92
31 March 20Y0	1,148.92	(1,787.00)	–	76.62	7.62	(553.84)
1 January 20Y1	(553.84)	–	417.60	–	–	(136.24)
31 March 20Y1	(136.24)	–	–	(13.56)	–	(149.80)
1 January 20Y2	(149.80)	–	152.07	–	–	2.27
1 January 20Y2	2.27	–	1.12	(3.39)	–	–
		(12,509.00)	107.78	2,182.39	218.83	

The lessor's initial net cash investment in the lease is the cost of the leased asset (£10,000).

Interest paid is calculated at 8.5% per annum on the daily net cash investment balances. Similarly profit-taken-out is calculated at the profit-take-out rate of 0.8458% on the daily net cash investment balances. Thus interest of £681.04 and profit-take-out of £67.76 for the period to 31 March 20X5 is based on net cash investment balances of £8,213.00 for 276 days and £7,389.62 for 89 days.

Interest received is calculated at a conservative rate of 3.0% per annum on the daily cash surplus balances. No profit-take-out arises when the net cash investment is in surplus (after 31 March 20Y0).

Tax is payable/receivable on 1 January each year, based on rentals, interest paid, interest received, and capital allowances in the previous accounting year, as follows:

Year to 31 March	Accrued rental £	Capital allowances £	Interest £	Total £	Tax payable (receivable) £
20X4	4.90	(2,500.00)	–	(2,495.10)	(823.38)
20X5	1,786.99	(1,875.00)	(681.04)	(769.05)	(253.79)
20X6	1,787.01	(1,406.25)	(536.03)	(155.27)	(51.24)
20X7	1,787.00	(1,054.69)	(415.44)	316.87	104.57
20X8	1,787.00	(791.02)	(301.24)	694.74	229.26
20X9	1,786.99	(593.26)	(188.97)	1,004.76	331.57
20Y0	1,787.01	(444.95)	(76.62)	1,265.44	417.60
20Y1	1,782.10	(1,334.83)	13.56	460.83	152.07
20Y2	–	–	3.39	3.39	1.12
	12,509.00	(10,000.00)	(2,182.39)	326.61	107.78

In order to simplify the calculations of the tax cash flows, it has been assumed that the amount of expenditure unrelieved after five years' writing-down allowances is relieved in the computation for the year ending 31 March 20Y1. Where the lessor does not anticipate recovering the remaining unrelieved expenditure by the end of the lease term it may be appropriate for him to delay recognising some of his gross earnings.

A further simplification is that the cash flows are deemed to terminate at the last tax payment date relating to the above. Thus interest for the period 1 April 20Y1 to 1 January 20Y2 and tax thereon is deemed to be paid on 1 January 20Y2.

The apportionment of gross earnings to each period for accounting purposes is derived from the cash flows by working backwards from the anticipated after-tax profit as follows:

Year to 31 March	Anticipated after-tax profit	Derived pre-tax profit	Anticipated interest	Derived apportionment of gross earnings
	£	£	£	£
20X4	–	–	–	–
20X5	67.76	101.14	681.04	782.18
20X6	53.34	79.60	536.03	615.63
20X7	41.34	61.70	415.44	477.14
20X8	29.97	44.73	301.24	345.97
20X9	18.80	28.06	188.97	217.03
20Y0	7.62	11.38	76.62	88.00
20Y1	–	–	(16.95)	(16.95)
	218.83	326.61	2,182.39	2,509.00

The anticipated after-tax profit is derived from the cash flows by time apportioning the profit-take-out. In this example, because the lease was written on 31 March and because it has been assumed interest is to be taken daily in arrear, the profit-take out on the cash flow matches the figures accrued for accounting purposes. An alternative basis would be to accrue one day's income and interest expense for the year to 31 March 20X4 and to adjust each year's figures by one day.

The pre-tax profit is derived by grossing-up the anticipated after-tax profit for each period by the appropriate tax rate. The tax rate is 33% and so the factor by which the after-tax profit is grossed up to arrive at the pre-tax profits is 1/(1 – 0.33).

The anticipated interest is derived from the cash flow summary in a similar way. In this example no interest accrual is necessary.

The derived apportionment of gross earnings is simply the sum of the derived pre-tax profit and anticipated interest.

For the purpose of calculating gross earnings for accounting purposes the small amount of interest receivable of £3.39 in the cash flows for the period to 31 March 20Y2 and tax thereon has been treated as arising in the year to 31 March 20Y1. This is a simplification for illustration purposes in order to limit the period over which gross earnings are spread. More sophisticated systems may well spread the gross earnings over a period extending beyond the lease term to take full account of the interest effects associated with tax cash flows arising beyond the end of the lease term.

The effect of allocating gross earnings in this way can be summarised as follows:

Profit & Loss Account

	20X4	20X5	20X6	20X7	20X8	20X9	20Y0	20Y1
	£	£	£	£	£	£	£	£
Rent receivable	4.90	1,786.98	1,787.02	1,787,00	1,787.00	1,786.98	1,787.02	1,782.10
Amortisation	4.90	1,004.80	1,171.39	1,309.86	1,441.03	1,569.95	1,699.02	1,799.05
Gross earnings	–	782.18	615.63	477.14	345.97	217.03	88.00	(16.95)
Interest costs	–	681.04	536.03	415.44	301.24	188.97	76.62	(16.95)
Pre-tax profit	–	101.14	79.60	61.70	44.73	28.06	11.38	–
Tax:								
Current	(823.38)	(253.79)	(51.24)	104.57	229.26	331.57	417.60	153.19
Deferred	823.38	287.17	77.50	(84.21)	(214.50)	(322.31)	(413.84)	(153.19)
Post-tax profit	–	67.76	53.34	41.34	29.97	18.80	7.62	–

Balance sheet

	20X4	20X5	20X6	20X7	20X8	20X9	20Y0	20Y1
	£	£	£	£	£	£	£	£
Assets								
Lease receivables	8,213.00	7,208.18	6,036.81	4,726.95	3,285.92	1,715.95	16.95	–
Group relief	823.38	253.79	51.24	–	–	–	–	–
Cash	–	–	–	–	–	–	553.84	153.19
	9,036.38	7,461.97	6,088.05	4,726.95	3,285.92	1,715.95	570.79	153.19
Liabilities								
Borrowings	8,213.00	6,351.42	4,900.00	3,518.54	2,167.32	817.35		
Deferred tax	823.38	1,110.55	1,188.05	1,103.84	889.34	567.03	153.19	0.00
Current tax	–	–	–	104.57	229.26	331.57	417.60	153.19
	9,036.38	7,461.97	6,088.05	4,726.95	3,285.92	1,715.95	570.79	153.19

For the purpose of illustrating the profit and loss and balance sheet the actual interest charges have been assumed to match precisely those anticipated in the cash flows and the post-tax profit is assumed to be fully distributed. Consequently, in this example the net cash investment balances per the anticipated cash flows will match the borrowing/cash position in the balance sheet. In practice, actual cash flows will almost certainly vary from those forecast, but this will not be sufficient reason by itself, to reassess the allocation of gross earnings.

Lease receivables at 31 March 20X5 of £7,208.18 represents future rentals of £8,935 less future gross earnings of £1,782.12. Alternatively, it can be proven as the cost of the leased asset of £10,000 less accumulated amortisation of £1,009.70 less prepaid rent of £1,782.12.

Accounting for operating leases

19.76 SSAP 21 requires that a lessor should record as fixed assets the assets held for leasing under operating leases. It also requires that the lessor should depreciate those assets over their useful economic lives. [SSAP 21 para 42]. This requirement was not followed by Brammer Plc in its financial statements for the year ended 31 December 1994. In these financial statements, the directors included rental assets, consisting of electronic instruments, in stock at the lower of amortised cost and net realisable value on the grounds that these assets were circulating capital. The FRRP rejected the directors' views and argued that SSAP 21 required such assets to be classified as fixed assets as they were held for use in operating leases. Accordingly, in the company's 1995 Annual Report the rental inventory was reclassified as fixed assets and the 1994 comparative figures were adjusted as indicated in Table 19.7 below.

19.77 Where assets held for use in operating leases are recorded as fixed assets, the lessor should recognise his rental income from operating leases (excluding charges for services such as insurance and maintenance) on a straight-line basis over the period of the lease, irrespective of when the payments are due. This requirement does not apply, however, if another systematic and rational basis is more representative of the time pattern in which the lessor receives the benefit from the leased asset (for example, the time pattern of the related depreciation charge). [SSAP 21 para 43]. UITF Abstract 28 requires a similar treatment for incentives, see paragraph 19.77.7 below.

Table 19.7 – Brammer plc – Annual Report – 31 December 1995

Accounting policies (extract)

Change of accounting policy – rental inventory

As explained in the financial review on page 14, the company has agreed with the Financial Reporting Review Panel that rental inventory, previously classified as current assets, should be reclassified as fixed assets. As a result of effecting this change:

- proceeds from the disposal of previously rented instruments are excluded from turnover and included in the profit on sale of fixed assets in the profit and loss account.

- rental inventory is classified as fixed assets and is valued at cost less depreciation on a straight line basis over the expected economic lives of the assets (generally 2 to 6 years) taking account of estimated residual values, less any necessary provision for permanent diminution in value.

- the depreciation charge for the year on rental inventory is added back to operating profit in arriving at net cash inflow from operating activities in the cash flow statement.

The accounts carrying value of rental inventory is unchanged and, accordingly, the change of classification does not affect the profit for the year in any year or the shareholders' equity at the end of the year. The figures in the 1994 consolidated profit and loss account, balance sheet and cash flow statement have been reclassified as a result of this change.

19.77.1 The FLA SORP gives additional guidance on the choice of depreciation methods. The principle is that the chosen method should best reflect the consumption of the benefits of the leased asset. The principal methods are:

- Straight-line method.
- After-tax methods.
- Annuity method.

19.77.2 The straight-line method is the benchmark method that is appropriate for all operating lease assets, particularly where the pattern of economic benefits is uncertain. This applies where assets are leased for periods that are considerably shorter than their useful economic lives, including all short-term hire agreements. This is consistent with the requirements of FRS 15 relating to depreciation of tangible fixed assets generally. [FLA SORP paras 5.3.27 to 5.3.30].

19.77.3 The SORP recognises, however, that lessors' interests in some operating lease assets have characteristics of financial assets rather than physical fixed assets and so it allows other depreciation methods that do not reflect the consumption of the physical asset but instead reflect the time value of money. These methods have the effect of 'back-loading' depreciation charges such that charges are lower in accounting periods near the beginning of the lease and increase in later accounting periods covered by the lease. These methods are in general only appropriate where the lease is similar to a finance lease.

19.77.4 After-tax methods are generally only suitable for finance leases. The SORP makes an exception, however, where a lessor has a portfolio of leases that comprise finance leases and similar leases that are classified as operating leases. An after-tax method, such as the actuarial after-tax method described earlier, may be used to determine the pattern of profit that is recognised over the term of the relevant operating leases if that reflects more faithfully the substance of the lessor's investments and the similarity between the finance and operating leases in the lessor's portfolio. The annual depreciation charge is calculated so that the profit from the lease produces a constant periodic rate of return on the lessor's net cash investment.

19.77.5 The annuity method calculates the annual depreciation charge by taking into account the cost of financing the asset, such that the aggregate amount of depreciation and interest in each period is constant. Since rental income from operating leases is normally credited on a straight-line basis over the lease term, the effect of using annuity depreciation is that the amount of profit after interest recognised in each period is constant.

19.77.6 The SORP restricts the use of after-tax methods and the annuity method to the following circumstances where the lessor's asset is in substance a quasi-financial asset:

- the asset is let on a lease that is for a significant portion of the total economic life of the asset;
- the terms of the lease adequately protect the lessor against early cancellation; and

- adequate income is retained in the lease to cover future uncertainties in respect of the realisation of residual values.

[FLA SORP para 5.3.34].

Operating lease incentives

19.77.7 When negotiating a new or renewed operating lease, a lessor may provide incentives for the lessee to enter into the agreement. Such incentives may take various forms as discussed in paragraph 19.46. UITF Abstract 28 provides guidance for the treatment of such incentives.

19.77.8 The treatment of operating lease incentives by lessors in UITF Abstract 28 mirrors the accounting treatment by lessees. All incentives, regardless of their nature, form or timing, be it a payment, assumption of liabilities or a rent-free or reduced rent period, given by lessors for the benefit of lessees to sign a new or renewed operating lease should be recognised as an integral part of the net payment agreed for the use of the leased asset. [UITF 28 para 13]. Therefore, the aggregate cost of incentives should be treated as a reduction of rental income and allocated to the profit and loss account over the lease term or a shorter period ending on a date from which it is expected the prevailing market rental will be payable. The allocation should be on a straight-line basis, unless another more systematic basis is more representative of the time pattern in which the benefit from the leased asset is receivable. [UITF 28 para 15]. In practice the use of an allocation basis other than straight-line should be rare.

Example 1

Under a ten year lease agreement, the lessor may give a one year rent free period followed by a fixed rent of £1.11m per annum for nine years. This is equivalent to ten years rent of £1m per annum. The benefit of the incentive should be spread over the period of the lease as there are no rent reviews. Therefore, each year £1m of rental income will be recognised in the profit and loss account. At the end of the first year, the lessor will recognise accrued rent receivable of £1m, which will be reduced by £0.11m each year for the next nine years.

Example 2

Alternatively, the lessor may have agreed with the lessee to make an up front cash payment of £1m to contribute towards the lessee's own fit out costs, with a fixed annual rental of £1.1m per annum for the ten year lease. This is also equivalent to an annual rent of £1m per annum without the incentive. Therefore, £1m will be recognised as net rental income each year of the lease. The £1m incentive will initially be recognised as a debtor (accrued rent receivable), which will be amortised by £0.1m each year to the profit and loss account.

19.77.9 As with any asset, the amount recognised as a debtor in respect of an operating lease incentive should be written down to the extent that it is not recoverable. [UITF 28 para 17]. Furthermore, the debtor is likely to be long-term in nature, in which case UITF Abstract 4, 'Presentation of long-term debtors in current assets', may be relevant.

19.77.10 Investment properties are often leased to tenants under operating leases and incentives are common practice. The abstract states that to avoid double-counting on the revaluation of investment properties, the value recognised in the lessor's balance sheet should not include any amount that is reported as a separate asset, such as accrued rent receivable. [UITF 28 para 16]. This is discussed further in chapter 17.

[The next paragraph is 19.78]

Lessor disclosure requirements

19.78 In respect of finance leases (including hire purchase contracts that have similar characteristics) the following needs to be disclosed:

- The net investment in finance leases and hire purchase contracts at the balance sheet date. [SSAP 21 para 58].
- The costs of assets acquired in the period (whether by purchase, finance lease or hire purchase) for the purpose of letting under finance leases or hire purchase contracts. [SSAP 21 para 60(c)].

Table 19.7A contains an example of these disclosure requirements.

Table 19.7A — Inchcape plc — Annual report & accounts — 31 December 2000

notes to the accounts (extract)

9b Debtors (extract)		**Group**
	2000	**1999**
	£m	**£m**
Net investment in finance leases and hire purchase contracts comprises:		
Total amounts receivable	**90.6**	100.9
Less: Interest allocated to future periods	**(19.8)**	(23.0)
	70.8	77.9

Rentals receivable during the year under finance leases and hire purchase contracts amounted to £33.4m (1999 — £32.6m)

The cost of assets acquired during the year for onwards finance leasing was £18.1m (1999 — £22.1m).

[The next paragraph is 19.80.]

19.80 In respect of both finance leases and operating leases (including hire purchase contracts that have similar characteristics), the following need to be disclosed also:

- The policy adopted for accounting for operating leases and finance leases and, in detail, the accounting policy adopted for recognising finance lease income. [SSAP 21 para 60(a)]. Table 19.9 contains an example of such a policy.

- The aggregate rentals receivable in the accounting period, analysed between amounts receivable under finance leases and amounts receivable under operating leases. [SSAP 21 para 60(b)]. For example, Gestetner Holdings PLC includes this information in the analyses of trading profit (see Table 19.10).

Table 19.9 – Automated Security (Holdings) PLC – Report and Financial Statements – 30 November 1994

ACCOUNTING POLICIES (extract)

2. FIXED ASSETS

The cost of equipment on contract hire installed by Group companies is capitalised. Costs comprise materials, labour and attributable overheads relating to identifiable and recoverable equipment. All other costs are written off as they are incurred.

On the acquisition of installed systems from third parties, a fair value is placed on installed equipment acquired.

6. EQUIPMENT LEASED TO CUSTOMERS

Equipment leased to customers under finance leases is deemed to be sold at normal selling value which is taken to turnover at the inception of the lease. Debtors under finance leases represent outstanding amounts due under these agreements less finance charges allocated to future periods. Finance lease interest is recognised over the primary period of the lease so as to produce a constant rate of return on the net cash investments. Equipment leased to customers under operating leases is capitalised in accordance with 2 above. Operating lease income is accounted for on a straight line basis with any rental increases recognised during the period to which they relate.

Table 19.10 – Gestetner Holdings PLC – Report and Accounts – 31 December 1994

Notes to the accounts (extract)

Note 2 Trading profit (extract)	**1994 £m**	1993 £m
Rental receivable under		
operating leases	**(21.7)**	(24.9)
finance leases	**(10.2)**	(12.3)
Equipment acquired for sale under finance leases	**73.4**	70.0

[The next paragraph is 19.83.]

19.83 The Guidance Notes to SSAP 21 indicate that the lessor may also need to disclose further information about leases and hire purchase contracts that is of particular significance to the users of the financial statements. This includes, for example, details of arrangements that could affect future profitability, such as contingent rentals or new-for-old guarantees.

19.83.1 The FLA SORP includes a number of disclosure recommendations that add to the limited disclosures required by SSAP 21. They are intended to improve users' understanding of the lessor's business and associated risks.

- General description of the lessor's leasing activities and related risks.
- Income recognition policies should be specified in detail.
- Maturity analysis of residual value exposures – for each type of leased asset, a table should be given setting out the carrying value of the lessor's unguaranteed residual interests and the years in which the residual value will be recovered.
- Details of contingent liabilities arising from lease transactions.
- Uncertainties relating to profits or losses arising from transactions that result in partial derecognition of leasing balances (for example, from the sale of a rental stream).
- Initial selling profits recognised by manufacturer or dealer lessors and the basis for determining them.
- State whether the SORP has been complied with and state the reasons for any non-compliance.

[FLA SORP para 5.9.1].

[The next paragraph is 19.84.]

Implications of the Act on the disclosure lessors make

19.84 Although some banks carry out leasing activities themselves, many banks prefer, for tax reasons, to carry out their leasing through separate subsidiaries. Consequently, many lessors, whether they are related to a bank or not, will not be a banking company within the meaning of the Banking Act 1987 and so they will have to comply with the requirements of Schedule 4 to the Companies Act 1985 for the purpose of their own statutory financial statements. However, at the same time those leasing companies with banking parents will need to provide information to their parent companies for consolidation purposes to comply with Schedule 9.

19.85 The balance sheet formats set out in Schedule 4 do not show any specific category for leased assets. Paragraph 3(2) of Schedule 4, however, permits (with certain exceptions) a company's balance sheet or profit and loss account to include an item that is not otherwise covered in the formats. SSAP 21, however, requires that amounts due from lessees under finance leases be recorded as a debtor and assets held for use in operating leases as a fixed asset.

19.86 As a category of debtors, amounts due under finance leases will need to be analysed in the notes to the financial statements between amounts receivable within one year and those receivable after more than one year. However, where the amounts due over one year are particularly material in the context of net current assets such that a reader might misinterpret the financial statements, UITF abstract 4 requires the amounts over one year to be disclosed on the face of the balance sheet (see further chapter 4).

19.87 The turnover of a leasing company will consist of its 'gross earnings' from finance leases and rentals from operating leases.

19.88 Those leasing companies, or parents of leasing companies, that are banks will need to comply with the requirements relating to the form and content of financial statements of banking companies as set out in Parts I to III of Schedule 9 to the Companies Act 1985. Under these formats, finance leases would be shown either under 'Loans and advances to customers' or 'Loans and advances to banks' as appropriate and gross earnings from finance leases would be included under interest receivable. The treatment of operating leases and related income under the formats is less clear. A strict interpretation would be to classify: operating leases under 'Tangible fixed assets'; operating rentals under 'operating income'; and depreciation of operating leased assets under 'Depreciation and amortisation'.

19.89 However, where a bank has significant amounts of operating leases and a significant amount of the bank's interest costs relate to the financing of such activities it could be argued that this treatment gives a misleading picture of the true net interest income from banking activities. Some banks have, therefore, taken the view that operating lease rentals less related depreciation is in effect a form of 'interest receivable' and have treated it in this way. Thus, net interest income will reflect both net income from operating leasing and the related interest expense, while the bank's depreciation expense will reflect only those tangible fixed assets other than operating leases. While this form of presentation has considerable merit there is an element of doubt as to whether it strictly accords with the Act's requirements. The FLA SORP states that Schedule 9 to the Companies Act 1985 requires depreciation to be shown under 'Depreciation and amortisation' and rental income under 'Other operating income' and that a different presentation may be used only where transactions relating to operating leases are immaterial. [FLA SORP para 5.10.2].

Direct costs

19.90 SSAP 21 states that initial direct costs may be apportioned over the period of the lease on a systematic and rational basis (or may alternatively be written off immediately). In allowing either of these treatments SSAP 21 draws no distinction between those initial direct costs from finance leases and those from operating leases.

19.91 SSAP 21 defines initial direct costs as:

> *"...those costs incurred by the lessor that are directly associated with negotiating and consummating leasing transactions, such as commissions,*

legal fees, costs of credit investigations and costs of preparing and processing documents for new leases acquired." [SSAP 21 para 30].

19.92 SSAP 21 gives no further guidance on the interpretation of the words 'directly associated' with these activities, although the Guidance Notes indicate that it is not intended to exclude salespersons' costs. The FLA SORP, however, takes a more restrictive view of the costs that may be deferred. The SORP defines initial direct costs as:

"...costs incurred by the lessor that are:

- *directly associated with negotiating and consummating a lease transaction;*
- *incremental to the lessor and would have been avoided had the transaction not taken place."* [FLA SORP para 4.1].

19.93 Under the SORP's definition, only incremental costs may be deferred whereas internal costs that are not incremental (such as administration and selling expenses) should be written off as incurred. The SORP identifies the following types of initial direct costs:

- External costs such as commission, legal, arrangement and brokers' fees.
- Other commissions and bonuses paid to procure business that are based upon reaching sales volumes (such as dealer volume bonuses, salesman's incentive schemes).

[FLA SORP para 5.4.14]

19.94 The SORP recommends that initial direct costs should be deferred over the lease term (using the same pattern as used for income recognition) provided that the costs are recoverable (that is, the lease is expected to generate a normal commercial return commensurate with the risks involved after taking account of such costs). Otherwise the costs should be written off immediately. [FLA SORP paras 3.27, 5.4.15-16].

19.95 Generally, the most appropriate, systematic and rational basis for deferring initial direct costs will be the same pattern used for recognising income. For finance leases this can be achieved by either deducting initial direct costs from total gross earnings before the net amount is allocated to accounting periods, or recognising sufficient gross earnings in the first year to absorb the costs and allocating the balance of gross earnings over the lease term. For operating leases, a straight-line basis of deferral over the lease term will usually be the most appropriate method.

Rental variation

Tax variation clauses

19.96 Major changes in tax rates can create significant accounting issues for lessors. This is because many finance leases contain tax variation clauses that vary the rental the lessee pays in the event of a tax rate change in order to preserve the lessor's post-tax rate of return.

19.97 In simple terms, if tax rates are reduced lessors pay less future tax, but will instead receive reduced rentals under their existing leases. Under FRS 19, deferred tax is provided on timing differences that have originated, but not reversed by the balance sheet date. Thus, deferred tax is provided at the corporation tax rate at which it is expected to be paid based on tax rates and laws that have been enacted or substantively enacted at the balance sheet date. Consequently, the 'windfall' gain from a reduction in corporation tax rates will be reflected in the tax charge or credit in the profit and loss account in the year in which the tax changes are enacted. However, the related reductions in rentals will generally occur over the remaining periods of the leases and, therefore, reduce future pre-tax income. The reduction in future rental income means that the carrying value of the lease receivable has been impaired. This impairment should be recognised immediately as a charge to pre-tax income. Although the impairment loss may not be exactly offset by the tax credit arising from the reduction in corporation tax rate, the difference may not be significant in terms of preserving the lessor's post-tax rate of return. This treatment will ensure that the lessors do not report material future losses on their leases. The previous practice, widely used in the leasing industry, of 'grossing up' tax savings would not comply with the principles of FRS 16.

[The next paragraph is 19.101.]

Variations in interest rates

19.101 Normally, when a finance lessor apportions his gross earnings, he does this on the basis of the forecast he prepares, at the start of the lease, of his future cash flows under the lease. The amount of gross earnings he releases to the profit and loss account in subsequent periods will then follow the forecast, even though his actual cash flows may vary from those he initially anticipated.

19.102 Minor variations in interest costs from those expected in the original cash flows evaluation will almost certainly occur. The interest charged to the lessor's profit and loss account in the period will be the actual interest cost for the period, thus, any differences from that originally anticipated will be reflected in the profit and loss account in the period in which they occur.

19.103 To mitigate interest rate risk, the lease facility may provide for a specifically calculated periodic adjustment for the difference between the actual rate of interest incurred on the borrowings and the rate of interest initially used in the cash flow to determine the level of lease rentals. Such adjustments are made periodically in arrears by applying, for example, the difference in interest rates on the first day of each quarterly period to the amount of the lessor's cash investment in the lease.

Construction periods

19.104 Often, where a leased asset is constructed over a period of time, the terms of the lease provide for rentals to commence only when the lessee brings the asset into use. In effect, the lessor finances the asset during the period of construction and recovers his costs out of his rentals over the remaining lease term. In order to match his gross earnings from the lease with his interest costs, the lessor will need to spread his gross earnings over the whole lease term (including the construction period). Where he adopts this treatment, however, the lessor will need to consider carefully his potential risks of loss from cancellation or default.

Manufacturer/dealer lessors

19.105 SSAP 21 distinguishes manufacturer/dealer lessors from other lessors. Although the term is not defined in the standard, it is defined in the FLA SORP as:

"......a lessor which either:

(a) manufactures particular equipment which it leases; or

(b) acquires the leased asset as part of its dealing activities where its leasing activities are ancillary to those of distribution and servicing."

[FLA SORP para 4.1].

What makes the manufacturer/dealer lessor different from a normal lessor is the cost at which he acquires an asset for lease. Because he obtains the asset at his cost of manufacture or at a wholesale price his cost will be below a normal arm's length selling price. The accounting issue is whether he should recognise a normal sale profit and this will depend on the accounting classification of the lease.

19.106 Where the manufacturer/dealer enters into an operating lease, he should not recognise a selling profit when he leases the asset. [SSAP 21 para 45]. This is because the risks and rewards associated with the asset's ownership have not passed to the customer. Consequently, the manufacturer/dealer will account for the lease in the same way as any other operating lessor does. He will capitalise the asset at its cost and depreciate it over its remaining economic life. In addition, he will recognise rentals on a straight-line basis over the period of the lease.

19.107 Where a manufacturer/dealer enters into a finance lease with a customer, the manufacturer/dealer may be able to recognise a normal selling profit. This is because the risks and rewards associated with the ownership of the asset have passed to the customer. The gross earnings under the lease (namely, the difference between what the manufacturer/dealer expects to receive and retain and the normal selling price) would be allocated over the lease term in the normal way. For example, the accounting policy of Automated Security (Holdings) indicates that the company takes what it deems the 'normal selling value' to turnover at the inception of the lease (see Table 19.9).

19.108 In most circumstances, where the sales price is known, determining the split between selling profit (recognised immediately) and gross earnings from finance leasing (spread over the lease term) is relatively easy. The FLA SORP specifies that the selling profit should be quantified with reference to the fair market value of the asset, that is the normal sales price at which identical goods are sold for cash. The normal selling price of broadly similar products sold by competitors may be used if the lessor does not normally sell such goods for cash. [FLA SORP para 5.6.3]. Where, however, a manufacturer/dealer does not sell the asset separately he may have difficulty in determining a true arm's length sales price. In these circumstances, some lessors have sought to determine the sales profit by assuming a deemed selling price (of fair value) being the present value of the minimum lease rentals discounted at a commercial rate.

19.109 The practice of calculating the sales profit in this way does not contradict the spirit of the SSAP 21, but can be lead to abuse and excessive front-end profits unless the present values are calculated prudently. For example, understating the true commercial lease rate or including overly optimistic residual values in the present value calculation will overstate sales profit. For this reason, this method needs to be applied with care. The FLA SORP provides some additional guidance. It states that a fair value should be determined by discounting the minimum lease payments and any unguaranteed residual value "*at a rate sufficient to take account of the lessor's borrowing rate, overhead rate and commercial profit return requirements, provided that the payments/residual value are reasonably predictable and certain in amount*". [FLA SORP para 5.6.5]. Unguaranteed residual values should be excluded if they are uncertain.

19.110 Even when the normal sales price is known, it does not necessarily follow that the full normal sales profit should be recognised at the lease's inception. In order to promote sales, a manufacturer/dealer lessor may offer finance leasing arrangements at concessionary rates. When it does this it should restrict its initial selling profit to an amount that will allow it to recognise its gross earnings at the normal commercial rate over the lease term.

Back-to-back and sub-leases

19.111 The term 'back-to-back' can be used to describe a variety of different agreements, each of which has different legal and tax implications. It is, therefore, difficult to prescribe specific accounting treatments for each variation. The Guidance Notes to SSAP 21, however, set out the broad principles that a lessor should follow when accounting for back-to-back leases and sub-leases. In addition, FRS 5 provides the more detailed rules on the treatment of non-recourse finance that can be applied to these types of arrangement (see further chapter 3).

19.112 For convenience, the Guidance Notes terms are used below. These refer to the three parties to a lease agreement as: the head lessor; the intermediate party (who may be either a lessor under a sub-lease to the lessee or merely an agent for the head lessor); and the lessee.

The head lessor

19.113 The head lessor's accounting is straightforward. Unless the original lease agreement between the head lessor and the intermediate party is replaced by a new agreement, the head lessor's accounting should not be affected if the intermediate party enters into a sub-lease.

The intermediate party

19.114 The intermediate party's accounting, however, is more complex. The form it takes will depend on the nature of the intermediate party's contract with the head lessor and the substance of the transaction.

19.115 If the intermediate party's role is genuinely in substance that of a broker or agent for the head lessor, such that the intermediate party has no significant commercial benefits or risks associated with the sub-leases, it should not include either the asset or the obligation on its balance sheet. Such a view would be consistent with the principles for recognising and ceasing to recognise assets set out in FRS 5 and the guidance given in the Guidance Notes to SSAP 21. [FRS 5 paras 20, 22; SSAP 21 para 165].

19.116 Where, however, the intermediate party enters into a lease with the head lessor, and that lease requires him to make payments to the head lessor regardless of whether he receives payments from the lessee under a sub-lease (a full 'recourse' arrangement) or he bears other significant risks such as 'slow payment' risk, he should account for the arrangement as two separate transactions. Such a view is supported by paragraph 21 of FRS 5 and paragraph 166 of the Guidance Notes to SSAP 21. This is because the intermediate party's liability under the head lease remains in effect and needs to be reflected in his accounting treatment. Where the intermediate party's lease with the head lessor is a finance lease, the intermediate party will need to record the obligation as a liability on his balance sheet. He will also need to record an asset on his balance sheet for the sub-lease to the ultimate lessee. Where the sub-lease is a finance lease the intermediate party should record the asset as a receivable. Where the sub-lease is an operating lease he should record the asset as a fixed asset.

19.117 The above explains the accounting treatment where the intermediate party acts purely as an agent or where the head lessor has full recourse to the intermediate party. Between these extremes, there are arrangements that might qualify under paragraphs 23 to 25 of FRS 5 as 'special cases' for partial derecognition or which might qualify under paragraphs 26 and 27 of FRS 5 for 'linked presentation'. These are particularly difficult to interpret. The guidance in FRS 5 is discussed in detail in chapter 3.

19.118 Where the effect of the arrangement is to transfer all the risks and benefits relating to a separately identifiable benefit stream (for example, the rentals) to the head lessor, but retain others (for example, marketing rights); or to transfer a proportion of the benefit stream (for example, the sub-lease rentals less a margin, but no more) to the head lessor, it may be appropriate for the intermediate party to simply recognise a new asset, which reflects his remaining and distinctly separate parcel of rights in the arrangement. Such an approach would only be appropriate where the transaction met the 'special case' conditions of paragraphs 23 to 25 of FRS 5 concerning 'partial de-recognition'.

19.119 The way in which the intermediate party recognises his income will also depend on the nature of the agreement. Where the intermediate party accounts for a separate liability and asset, the treatment he applies both to his gross earnings from his sub-lease and to the finance charges that are due on the head lease, will follow the normal requirements of SSAP 21. Where the intermediate party uses the linked presentation, the 'net' earnings will be included in the profit and loss account with separate disclosures of the gross earnings and finance charges in the notes to the financial statements. Where the intermediate party acts an 'agent', the Guidance Notes state that he should recognise his income on a systematic and rational basis. For example, he could recognise a pure commission immediately, but he should spread a guarantee fee over the period at risk.

Residuals

19.120 Residual values will need to be recognised by lessors when they are a fundamental component to the profitability of the lease transaction. However, it is important that they are recognised prudently. This need for prudence is reflected in the FLA SORP, which states: *"the estimates of residual values should be the amounts that can be safely expected to be realised under anticipated business conditions, net of disposal costs and should reflect any uncertainty."* [FLA SORP para 5.4.2].

19.121 The amount that the lessor 'can safely expect' is difficult to assess. If the lessor is too optimistic in his residual estimates he carries a risk of incurring a loss. If he is excessively conservative in his estimates his rental rates may prove uncompetitive. How he estimates residuals will depend on specific factors:

- The nature of the asset under consideration.
- The known volatility of second-hand values.
- The rate of technological change.
- Competitive conditions.
- The asset's economic life relative to the lease's primary period.
- The degree to which the lessor can spread his risks.

19.122 The accounting treatment of a residual will largely depend on the nature of the lease. This is because SSAP 21 recognises two different types of leases, finance and operating leases, and prescribes a very different accounting treatment for each.

Residuals under operating leases

19.123 Under an operating lease, the lessor's revenue (rental income) is normally allocated over the lease term on a straight-line basis to reflect the time pattern of the performance of the service he is providing. In the lessor's balance sheet, assets leased to customers are shown as fixed assets, which are depreciated over the assets' economic life to their expected residual values. Different estimates of residual value obviously give rise to different levels of depreciation and, therefore, different levels of profit being recognised over the lease term.

19.124 Where the lessor values his future residuals conservatively, an eventual profit is likely to emerge at the end of the lease term on the sale of the asset, which would be represented by the sales proceeds less residual value and related selling costs.

19.125 While depreciation methods can vary, the method most widely used by operating lessors is the straight-line method. Thus, under operating leases, gross profit (rentals less depreciation) is normally recognised on a straight-line basis.

Residuals under finance leases

19.126 While finance leases are treated for accounting purposes by the lessor as though they are financial products akin to lending, there can, of course, still be a small element of residual risk. This risk is often disregarded as it will represent, at most, less than ten per cent of the lessor's investment at the inception of the lease. However, even variations in a component as small as ten per cent of the original investment can have a significant effect on a lessor's profitability because, although the residual is a small part of the total investment, it may amount to a substantial proportion of the expected gross earnings from the lease.

Fluctuations in anticipated residual values

19.127 Where the amount of residual values is significant the lessor will need to monitor the second-hand market closely and continuously. He will need to do this both to ensure that he has based his current rental pricing structure on up-to-date estimates and to ensure that he is accounting for the residual values correctly. Where the lessor identifies market conditions that indicate that there has been a permanent fall in residual values, he will need to account for the deterioration.

19.128 If the lease is an operating lease the lessor should calculate new depreciation rates for his leased assets in order to ensure the remaining book value of the leased asset is amortised to its anticipated residual value over its remaining useful life. In some circumstances, however, the book value of the leased asset may not be recoverable (that is, the present value of the future cash flows expected from the leased asset, including the revised estimate of residual value, may be lower than the book value) Where such a situation arises, the lessor should write down his leased assets to their recoverable amounts immediately, by charging an additional impairment loss in the current period's profit and loss account in accordance with the principles of FRS 11.

19.129 Similarly, if the lease is a finance lease, the lessor may need to write down the future residual value and recalculate the remaining future earnings to be recognised over the lease term. Where the carrying value of the finance lease receivable asset becomes impaired, the loss should be recognised immediately in the profit and loss account.

19.130 Many lessors also adhere to the principle that residual values should not be revised upwards. While this is not a strict requirement of SSAP 21 or FRS 15, it is good practice. The FLA SORP in effect codifies this principle, because it requires that any profit arising through selling the asset, in excess of the residual value that was set at the inception of the lease, should not be recognised until the asset has been sold.

19.131 There are no specific disclosure requirements in SSAP 21 for lessors to provide additional information concerning the quantification of residual value exposures within the financial statements of leasing companies. However, the FLA SORP seeks to make residual value risks more transparent by requiring leasing companies to give additional information in their financial statements so that the users of such financial statements can properly assess the impact of residual exposures on the lessor's financial position. For each type of asset, lessors should provide a maturity analysis of unguaranteed residual values included in the carrying values of finance leases and operating leases. This analysis should indicate the years in which the residual value will be recovered (analysed as between amounts to be recovered within 1 year, between 1-2 years, between 2-5 years, and more than 5 years). The SORP also requires lessors to disclose their policy for monitoring residual value exposure and recognising related impairments. [FLA SORP para 5.9].

Tax-free grants

19.132 Grants are normally paid to the owner of the asset upon which the grant is claimed. When a lessor receives such a grant on an asset that is subject to a finance lease, it is usual for the lessor to pass the benefit of the grant to the lessee either in the form of a lump sum payment (a negative rental) or in lower rentals over the lease term. The benefit of the grant comprises not just the cash amount of the grant, but also the fact that it is non-taxable. The tax benefit arises because, although the grant reduces the net cost of the asset to the lessor, he can still claim capital allowances on the full gross cost of the asset. If the lessor passes the tax benefit of the grant back to the lessee in one of the two ways mentioned above, it could have the effect of reducing the total rentals payable by the lessee below the net cost of the leased asset. Thus the lessor shows an accounting loss in pre-tax terms, but a profit after tax.

19.133 Paragraph 41 of SSAP 21 requires that tax-free grants that are available to the lessor against the purchase-price of assets acquired for leasing should be spread over the period of the lease and dealt with by treating the grant as non-taxable income. [SSAP 21 para 14]. The practice of avoiding showing a pre-tax loss and an after-tax profit by recording the grant as a grossed-up amount as if the grant was a larger taxable amount that suffered a tax charge, and increasing the tax charge accordingly, is not permitted.

Chapter 20

Stocks and long-term contracts

	Page
Introduction	20001
Stocks	20001
Definition of cost of stocks	20001
Determination of cost	20005
Net realisable value of stocks.	20008
Disclosure	20009
Replacement value of stocks	20010
Sale and repurchase of stocks	20012
Consignment stock	20014
Objective of consigning stocks	20015
Principal sources of benefits and risks	20015
Accounting treatment	20017
Example of required analysis	20018
Manufacturer's position	20020
Conclusion	20021
Goods with reservation of title	20021
Long-term contracts	20022
Definition of long-term contracts	20022
Accounting treatment of long-term contracts	20023
Turnover	20023
Recognition of profit	20027
Determination of future costs	20033
Variations and claims	20034
Losses on contracts	20035
Cost of sales	20035
Amounts recoverable on contracts	20036
Disclosure	20037
Turnover exceeds payments on account	20038
Payments on account exceed turnover	20038
Payments on account exceed turnover and balance of costs on contracts	20039
Provision for foreseeable losses	20041

Chapter 20

Stocks and long-term contracts

Introduction

20.1 This chapter deals with the accounting treatment and disclosure of stocks and long-term contracts. In particular, it deals with the carrying value of stocks and complex transactions involving stock, such as consignment stock and sale and repurchase of stocks. It also deals with the treatment of long-term contracts, including the carrying value of the contract and profit recognition and incorporates FRS 5, Application note G, 'Revenue recognition', but only insofar as the application note deals with revenue relating to long-term contracts. Other aspects of the application note are dealt with in chapter 9.

[The next paragraph is 20.3.]

Stocks

20.3 Stocks include goods or other assets purchased for resale, consumable stores, raw materials and components purchased for incorporation into products for sale, products and services in intermediate stages of completion, long-term contract balances and finished goods. [SSAP 9 para 16].

20.4 The amount at which stocks are stated in the financial statements should be the total of the lower of cost and net realisable value of the separate items of stock or of groups of similar items. [SSAP 9 para 26]. These items should be considered individually, as to compare the total realisable value of stocks with the total cost would result in an unacceptable setting off of foreseeable losses against unrealised profits. [CA85 4 Sch 14].

[The next paragraph is 20.8.]

Definition of cost of stocks

20.8 Cost is defined as being that expenditure that has been incurred in the normal course of business in bringing the product or service to its present location and condition. This expenditure should include, in addition to cost of purchase, such costs of conversion as are appropriate to that location and condition. [SSAP 9 para 17]. Cost of purchase comprises purchase price including import duties, transport and handling costs and any other directly attributable costs, less trade discounts, rebates and subsidies. [SSAP 9 para 18].

Example 1

A car distributor values its items of inventory at the year end. Rebates are only received from the car manufacturers once a year and are only known after the year end, but relate to purchases in the current period.

Should the rebates be taken through the income statement as a deduction in the cost of sales without allocation to the items in inventory at the balance sheet date, or, should a proportion of the rebates be allocated to the inventory items at the year end?

A proportion of the rebates should be allocated to the inventory items at the year end. Paragraph 18 of SSAP 9, 'Stocks and long-term contracts', states that the cost of purchase of stock comprises purchase price including import duties, transport and handling costs and any other directly attributable costs, less trade discounts, rebates and subsidies. A proportion of the rebates should be allocated to inventory items at the year end. For example, if purchases during the year are 100 and there is inventory with a cost of 10 at the year end, 10% of the rebate should be applied to the inventory items at the year end and 90% should be taken through the income statement as a deduction in the cost of sales. The reasoning is that the rebates cannot be allocated to particular items in the year, therefore, they should be spread over all the items purchased during the year, sold or unsold.

Example 2

A company is a motor dealer. It receives vehicle-related bonuses from manufacturers when it reaches certain sales targets. It credits the bonuses to income, but is concerned about whether this is still allowed following the FRRP ruling on Northgate plc. In this case, the cars are initially held in inventory, rather than in fixed assets and the sales-related bonuses are received only after the cars have been sold (that is, when they are no longer in inventory).

The bonus from the manufacturers is a contingent asset and should be recognised only when it becomes virtually certain. As it is a sales-related bonus in respect of inventory that has been sold and is not a rebate on the cost of a fixed asset it is appropriate to take the credit to profit and loss account. It should be shown as a reduction in cost of sales as it would not qualify as turnover.

Example 3

A company has development land on which it intends to build houses for sale. It is to pay the local authority to build an access road from A to B, where A is on local authority land and B is on the edge of the land owned by the company. The company will not own the access road or have exclusive rights to use it. However, the company considers that there is an economic benefit from the cost of building the access road, because the homes that it builds on the development site will be more attractive to customers if there is a good road access. Can the cost of building the access road be capitalised? If so is it an intangible asset, a separate asset, or is it added to the cost of the development?

Under SSAP 9, cost should include expenditure that has been incurred in the normal course of business in bringing the product or service to its present location and condition. [SSAP 9 para 17]. The cost of paying the local council to build an access road should be capitalised as part of the development (not as a separate asset), provided that it is clear that the company will gain economic benefits from the access road. This would be so, for example, if the company needs the access road built to obtain planning permission for the development, or if the company can sell the houses more easily or for a higher value.

If, however, the money paid to the local authority resulted in no future economic benefits to the company (for example, if the access road did not lead to the development site) and was more in the nature of a gift or goodwill gesture, then it should be written off to profit or loss.

20.9 Costs of conversion comprise:

- Costs that are specifically attributable to units of production, for example, direct labour, direct expenses and sub-contracted work.
- Production overheads, that is, those incurred in respect of materials, labour or services for production, based on the normal level of activity, taking one year with another.
- Other overheads, if any, attributable in the particular circumstances of the business to bringing the product or service to its present location and condition.

[SSAP 9 para 19].

20.10 The Companies Act 1985 also allows interest to be included in cost if it relates to capital borrowed to finance the production of the asset insofar as it arises in the period of production. [CA85 4 Sch 26(3)(b)]. This is discussed in more detail in chapter 16.

20.11 Paragraph 8 of Appendix 1 to SSAP 9 contains some guidance on the inclusion of overheads in cost of conversion noting that the allocation of overheads included in the valuation of stocks and long-term contracts needs to be based on the company's normal level of activity, taking one year with another. The governing factor is that the cost of unused capacity should be written off in the current year. In determining what constitutes 'normal' the following factors need to be considered:

- The volume of production that the production facilities are intended by their designers and by management to produce under the working conditions (for example, single or double shift) prevailing during the year.
- The budgeted level of activity for the year under review and for the ensuing year.
- The level of activity achieved both in the year under review and in previous years.

Although temporary changes in the load of activity may be ignored, persistent variation should lead to revision of the previous norm. The adoption of a prudent approach to the valuation of stocks has sometimes been used to argue against the inclusion of overheads. SSAP 9 states that prudence will be taken into account in determining net realisable value and is not a reason for excluding overheads from the cost of stock. Having said that, the overheads that should be included are those arising from normal activity. All abnormal conversion costs (such as exceptional spoilage, idle capacity and other losses), which are avoidable under normal operating conditions, should be excluded.

Example

For entity A normal production is 10 and normal overhead (fixed) is £10 so that £1 is allocated to each item. If there are three items in inventory, then £3 of overhead is carried forward. If, however, 15 are actually produced, to include a 'normal' level of overhead in such a case would over value inventory.

The principle in SSAP 9 is that stock is carried at the lower of cost and net realisable value. We consider that allocating £1 to each stock item in the case above, where 15 are produced would mean stock is recorded above cost and so would be against SSAP 9. On the basis that 15 were actually produced only £0.667 (that is £10/15) should be allocated to each item, so if there are 3 items in inventory at end of the year 2 of overheads are carried forward.

20.12 The classification of overheads for the purpose of the allocation takes the function of the overhead as its distinguishing characteristic (for example, whether it is a function of production, marketing, selling or administration), rather than whether the overhead varies with time or with volume. The costs of general management, as distinct from functional management, are not directly related to current production and are, therefore, excluded from cost of conversion.

20.13 The Companies Act 1985 states that distribution costs may not be included in production cost. [CA85 4 Sch 26(4)]. This means that a company should not include external distribution costs such as those relating to the transfer of goods from a sales depot to an external customer. It may, however, include a proportion of the costs that a company incurs in distributing goods from its factory to its sales depot as these are costs incurred in bringing the product to its present location.

20.14 An example of a retail company disclosing its methods of determining cost of sales and distribution costs is illustrated in Table 20.1. Cost of sales includes costs of transfer to the point of sale. For retailers, costs of transfer to the point of sale will often include a proportion of normal warehouse costs. Distribution costs include holding costs at the point of sale and costs of transfer to the customer.

Table 20.1 — Safeway plc — Annual Report and Accounts — 30 March 2002

Statement of Accounting Policies (extract)

Sales and profit

Cost of sales represents the purchase cost of goods for resale and includes the cost of transfer to the point of sale.

Net operating expenses

Distribution costs represent the cost of holding goods at the point of sale, selling costs and the costs of transferring goods to the customer and include store operating expenses.

Determination of cost

20.15 It is often not possible to relate expenditure to specific units of stock and so a near approximation has to be ascertained. This gives rise to two problems:

- The selection of an appropriate method for relating costs to stocks, for example:
  - Job costing.
  - Batch costing.
  - Process costing.
  - Standard costing.

The selection of an appropriate method for calculating the related costs where a number of identical items have been purchased or made at different times.

20.16 The Companies Act 1985 allows companies to use certain methods for arriving at the purchase price or the production cost of stocks and other 'fungible items'. For this purpose, 'fungible items' are those items that are indistinguishable one from another (for example, identical nuts and bolts). [CA85 4 Sch 27(6)].

20.17 Under the Act a company may adopt any of the following methods (but, in order to comply with the requirements of FRS 18, the method chosen must be the one which appears to the directors to be the most appropriate in the circumstances of the company) [FRS 18 para 50]:

- First-in, first-out (FIFO).
- Last-in, first-out (LIFO) (but see para 20.21).
- Weighted average price.
- Any other similar method.

[CA85 4 Sch 27(1)(2)].

20.18 An example of a company using an average cost method is Cadbury Schweppes plc (see Table 20.2).

Table 20.2 – Cadbury Schweppes plc – Annual Report – 30 December 2001

Accounting Policies (extract)

(k) Stocks	**Stocks are valued at the lower of average cost and estimated net realisable value. Cost comprises direct material and labour costs together with the relevant factory overheads (including depreciation) on the basis of normal activity levels.**

20.19 Under the FIFO method, the cost of stock is calculated on the basis that the quantities in hand represent the latest purchases or production. An example of a company using the FIFO method is Bass PLC (see Table 20.3).

Table 20.3 – Bass PLC – Annual Report – 30 September 1994

Accounting Policies (extract)

Stocks

The basis of valuation is as follows:

i) Raw materials, bought-in-goods and consumable stores at the lower of cost and net realisable value on a first in, first out basis.

ii) Work in progress and finished stocks at the lower of cost, which includes an appropriate element of production overhead costs, and net realisable value.

Cost includes all expenditure incurred in bringing each product to its present condition and location. Net realisable value is based on estimated selling prices less further costs expected to be incurred in bringing the stocks to completion and disposal.

20.20 The example below illustrates the calculation of the value of stocks on both a FIFO basis and a weighted average price basis.

Example

Assume that opening stock on 1 March 20X8 is nil. All stock is finished goods, and is of the same type. Details of the stock received and sent out are as shown below.

	Quantity unit	**Unit cost**
		£
Batch 1 received on 1 March 20X8	2	3.00
Batch 2 received on 15 March 20X8	4	4.50
On 25 March 20X8 the entity sold 5 units.		
Closing stock value on 31 March 20X8		

	Quantity unit(1)	Unit cost	Value
		£	£
(a) FIFO	1	4.50 (a)	4.50
(b) Weighted average	1	4.00 (b)	4.00

The quantity of goods remaining is one (2 + 4 — 5) for both of the measurement methods.

(a) FIFO: all units of batch 1 have been sent out first, then three units from batch 2 were sent out. One unit from batch 2 is remaining at £4.50.

(b) Weighted average: the average unit cost of all units received is £4.00 (2 × £3 + 4 × £4.50)/(2 + 4).

20.21 When choosing a method, the directors must ensure that the method they choose provides the fairest practicable approximation to 'actual cost'. SSAP 9 considers that the LIFO method (where the quantities in hand represent the earliest purchases or production) does not usually bear a reasonable relationship to actual cost and so LIFO is not an acceptable method of valuation in the UK.

20.22 Similarly, a base stock method is also not normally an acceptable method of stock valuation as it often results in stocks being stated in the balance sheet at amounts that bear little relationship to recent cost levels. Under this method, the cost of stocks is calculated on the basis that a fixed unit value is ascribed to a predetermined number of units of stock, any excess over this number being valued on the basis of some other method.

[The next paragraph is 22.24.]

20.24 Costs are often allocated to stocks by the use of a standard costing method. The cost of stocks is calculated on the basis of periodically predetermined costs derived from management's estimates of expected levels of costs and operational efficiency. The standard costs should be based on normal levels of operations and any abnormal costs or costs arising from inefficiencies should be written off in the period. Where standard costs are used, they need to be reviewed frequently to ensure that they bear a reasonable relationship to actual costs arising during the period.

20.25 The method of arriving at cost by applying the latest purchase price to the total number of units in stock is unacceptable in principle because it is not necessarily the same as actual cost and, in times of rising prices, will result in the taking of profit that has not been realised.

20.26 One method of arriving at cost is the use of selling price less an estimated profit margin. This is acceptable only if it can be demonstrated that it gives a reasonable approximation of the actual cost. This method is often used by retailers with a large number of rapidly changing individual items in stores, for example, Tesco PLC (see Table 20.5).

Table 20.5 — Tesco PLC — Annual report and financial statements — 22 February 2003

Accounting policies (extract)

Stocks

Stocks comprise goods held for resale and properties held for, or in the course of, development and are valued at the lower of cost and net realisable value. Stocks in stores are calculated at retail prices and reduced by appropriate margins to the lower of cost and net realisable value.

20.27 In industries where the production process results in minor by-products, the costs of the main products are calculated after deducting the net revenue from sales of the by-products. An example of this treatment is found in the accounts of Lonmin Plc (see Table 20.6).

Table 20.6 — Lonmin Plc — Annual Report — 30 September 2001

Statement on accounting policies (extract)

Stocks (extract)

Platinum metal stock is valued by allocating costs to platinum, palladium and rhodium stock based on the annual cost of production, less revenue from by-products, apportioned according to the quantities of each of the three main metals produced.

Net realisable value of stocks

20.28 SSAP 9 requires that the figure of stocks disclosed in the financial statements should be the total of the lower of cost and net realisable value of the separate items of stock or of groups of similar items. [SSAP 9 para 26].

20.29 If there is no reasonable expectation of sufficient future revenue to cover cost incurred, the irrecoverable cost should be charged to revenue in the year under review. Net realisable value is the actual or estimated proceeds from the sale of items of stock (net of trade discounts, but before settlement discounts) less all further costs to completion and less all costs to be incurred in marketing, selling and distributing directly related to the items in question. [SSAP 9 para 5].

20.30 The principal situations in which net realisable value is likely to be less than cost are where there has been:

- An increase in costs or a fall in selling price.
- Physical deterioration of stocks.
- Obsolescence of products.
- A decision as part of a company's marketing strategy to manufacture and sell products at a loss.
- Errors in production or purchasing.

20.31 The initial calculation of write downs to reduce stocks from cost to net realisable value may often be made by the use of formulae based on predetermined criteria. The formulae normally take account of the age, movements in the past, expected future movements and estimated scrap values of the stock, as appropriate. Whilst the use of such formulae establishes a basis for making a write down that can be consistently applied, it is still necessary for the results to be reviewed in the light of any special circumstances that cannot be anticipated in the formulae, such as changes in external market information or in the state of the order book.

20.32 Where a write down is required to reduce the value of finished goods below cost, the stocks of the parts and sub-assemblies held for the purpose of the manufacture of such products, together with stocks on order, need to be reviewed to determine if a write down is also required against such items.

20.33 Events occurring between the balance sheet date and the date of completion of the financial statements need to be considered in arriving at the net realisable value at the balance sheet date (for example, a subsequent reduction in selling prices).

Example

A company supplies car parts to a major manufacturer. At the year end it had a inventory of parts and the carrying value was £1 million. However, after the year end the manufacturer changed the models of the cars and as a result the inventory became obsolete (the part is not interchangeable between models). Should the company provide against the inventory at the year end? It does not wish to provide on the grounds that the manufacturer did not make its decision to switch models until after the company's year end.

The company should write down the inventory (to realisable value). SSAP 9, states in an appendix that events between the balance sheet date and the date of completion of the financial statements should be considered in determining net realisable value. In addition, FRS 21, 'Events after the balance sheet date', refers to the sale of inventories after the balance sheet date as giving evidence of the net realisable value at the balance sheet date.

20.33.1 However, a reduction is not necessary when the realisable value of material stocks is less than the purchase price, provided that the goods into which the materials are to be incorporated can still be sold at a profit after incorporating the materials at cost price.

Disclosure

20.34 The Companies Act 1985 requires that stocks should be analysed between the following four categories:

- Raw materials and consumables.
- Work in progress.
- Finished goods and goods for resale.

- Payments on account — this represents the payments a company makes on account of stocks and not the payments it receives from customers.

[CA85 4 Sch formats].

20.35 A company should follow this categorisation so long as it produces true and fair financial statements. However, in certain circumstances, the special nature of a company's business may mean that the company needs to adapt the formats. Table 20.7 shows a company that has included additional categories for showhomes and part exchange properties within stocks.

Table 20.7 — Bellway p.l.c. — Annual Report — 31 July 2001

Notes to the Accounts

9 Stocks (extract)	**2001**	2000
	£000	£000
Group		
Work in progress and stocks	**639,572**	506,437
Grants	**(8,483)**	(7,383)
Payments on account	**(9,387)**	(16,164)
	621,702	482,890
Showhomes	**14,483**	16,799
Part exchange properties	**8,236**	8,825
	644,421	508,514

20.36 The accounting policy that has been applied to stocks should be stated and applied consistently within the business and from year to year. [SSAP 9 para 32]. Although there is no requirement in SSAP 9 to state the methods used in calculating cost and net realisable value, these are estimation techniques and, if significant, should be disclosed as required by FRS 18, 'Accounting policies'. Examples of disclosure of these estimation techniques are illustrated above in Table 20.2 and Table 20.3.

Replacement value of stocks

20.37 Paragraph 27 of Schedule 4 says that, where the historical cost of stocks or fungible assets is calculated using a method permitted by the Act (for example, FIFO, weighted average or any similar method), and that valuation differs materially from the 'relevant alternative amount' of those items, then the difference should be disclosed in a note to the financial statements.

20.38 The 'relevant alternative amount' will normally be the amount at which the assets would have been disclosed if their value had been determined according to their replacement cost as at the balance sheet date. [CA85 4 Sch 27(4)]. The replacement cost of these types of assets will normally be their current cost. However, a company may instead determine the relevant alternative amount according to the most recent actual purchase price or the most recent actual production cost of assets of that class before that date. But it can do this only where this method gives a more appropriate standard of comparison for assets of the class in question. [4 Sch 27(5)]. The Act leaves it to the company's directors to form an opinion as to whether the method does this. An example of the disclosure of replacement cost is found in the accounts of BP p.l.c. (see Table 20.8).

Table 20.8 — BP p.l.c. Annual Accounts — 31 December 2001
Notes on accounts
22 Stocks

	$ million 2001	**2000**
Petroleum	5,176	**6,933**
Chemicals	953	**1,046**
Other	568	**504**
	6,697	**8,483**
Stores	934	**751**
	7,631	**9,234**
Replacement cost	7,686	**9,392**

20.39 The example below considers the disclosure of the replacement cost of stocks. It uses the details from the previous example:

Example

Two companies, A and B, have identical opening and closing stocks and purchases in a particular year, but company A chooses to determine the value of its closing stocks by the FIFO method, and company B does so by the 'weighted average price' method. In these circumstances, the amount to be included in the balance sheets would be calculated as follows:

Company A:	£3,175
Company B:	£2,825

The value of the stocks at replacement cost is, say, £3,300.

If the difference between the balance sheet value of stocks and their replacement cost is material in the context of their balance sheet value, it must be disclosed under the requirement outlined in paragraph 20.37. The difference for company A is £125 (£3,300 — £3,175), which is unlikely to be considered material. The difference for company B is £475 (£3,300 — £2,825), which is likely to be considered material. If it is, it must be disclosed.

20.40 Counsel has advised that a 'method' is not used when stocks are valued at either their actual purchase price or their production cost. It would appear, therefore, that where companies value their stocks at actual purchase price or production cost, they do not need to disclose, in their financial statements, the difference between this value and the replacement value of those stocks.

20.41 In many situations, it is likely that some items of stocks will be valued by one of the methods mentioned above and that other items will be valued at actual purchase price or production cost. Where a company does this, the company will need to disclose not only the difference between the figure of stocks valued by a method and their replacement cost, but also the actual purchase price or production cost of the stocks it has valued by that method. Otherwise, it could be misleading for the company to disclose the figure that represents the difference, without also giving an indication of the proportion of the total stock value to which this difference relates.

Sale and repurchase of stocks

20.42 Sometimes stock is sold with an option (or obligation) to buy it back. The detailed terms of such options vary and, indeed, the options may sometimes be expressed at market value such that it is by no means certain that the options will be exercised. Perhaps more commonly, however, the option is constructed so that it is reasonably certain that it will be exercised. The arrangement may run for months, or even years, during which time the company that sold the stock will use the sale proceeds as a form of finance. The stock and the related purchase obligation (that is, the liability to repay the finance provided by the temporary holder of the stock) were often excluded from the balance sheet in the past.

20.43 Such arrangements are covered by FRS 5 and are considered in detail in chapter 3. In summary, the true commercial effect of a transaction is a sale if the seller genuinely relinquishes control of significant benefits and transfers the exposure to significant risks associated with the asset to the buyer (for example, if the repurchase price is market value at the date of repurchase). However, a transaction structured so that, in practice, the purchaser secures a lender's return on the purchase price without genuine exposure to, or benefit from, changes in value of the underlying assets (for example, if the repurchase price is pre-determined as original sale price plus an increment based on interest rates applied to the finance provided) should be treated as a financing arrangement.

Example

A company sells stock in year one for £100,000 and at the same time enters into an agreement to repurchase it a year later for £110,000. The £10,000 should not be treated as part of the cost of the stock, but represents interest, and should be charged to the profit and loss account.

If the company's year end fell halfway through the transaction, the company should initially show in its balance sheet stock of £100,000 and a financing liability of £100,000. Interest should be calculated at a constant rate on the carrying value of the liability although, if there was no significant difference, it could be assumed to accrue evenly throughout the period. In this case, interest of £5,000 should be accrued and charged to the profit and loss account.

Consideration would also need to be given as to whether the stock requires a write down to reduce it to net realisable value.

20.44 FRS 5 recognises that, in more complex situations, it may be determined that a sale and repurchase agreement is not, in substance, a financing transaction and that the seller only retains access to some of the benefits of the original asset. In this circumstance, the partial derecognition rules in paragraph 23 of the standard might apply. If, for example, the buyer receives more than merely a lender's return, as other benefits and risks associated with the asset have been transferred to the buyer, the seller will not have retained the original asset. In this situation, the original asset should be derecognised and the analysis should determine whether another asset should be recognised in its place. For example, the seller might have an interest in the asset's residual value at the end of its life, in which case the residual interest should be recognised as an asset and the repurchase obligation as a liability in the seller's balance sheet. An example of this can be found in the accounts of Inchcape plc, where equipment sold with repurchase obligations is included in stocks. (see Table 20.9).

Table 20.9 — Inchcape plc — Annual Report — 31 December 2001

Stocks	**2001**	2000
	£m	£m
Raw materials and work in progress	**2.3**	1.4
Finished goods and merchandise	**517.4**	528.7
	519.7	530.1

Certain subsidiaries have an obligation to repurchase, at a guaranteed residual value, certain vehicles which have been legally sold for leasing contracts. Although the credit risk is passed to the finance house, in substance these vehicles remain as assets of the Group. They have been included in stock at the guaranteed repurchase price less appropriate provisions where the anticipated realisable value is lower. The corresponding cross guaranteed repurchase price liability is included within trade creditors. Stock includes £93.8m (2000 – £110.1m) of such vehicles.

Vehicles held on consignment which are in substance assets of the Group amount to £37.0m (2000 – £29.0m). These have been included in finished goods stock with the corresponding liability included within trade creditors. Payment becomes due when title passes to the Group, which is generally the earlier of six months from delivery or date of sale.

20.45 The notes to the financial statements should include the following information concerning all sale and repurchase transactions:

- The transaction's principal features. [FRS 5 App B paras B19 and B21].
- The asset's status. [FRS 5 App B paras B19 and B21].

  For example, disclosure that an asset has been legally sold to another party, but has been retained on balance sheet.

- The relationship between the asset and the liability. [FRS 5 App B paras B19 and B21].

  Again, where an asset has been legally sold, but has been retained on balance sheet because the transaction is considered to be a financing arrangement, the notes should explain how the finance is connected with the asset (for example, whether it is non-recourse).

20.46 An example of stock retained on balance sheet where it has been legally sold is seen in Table 20.10.

Table 20.10 — Persimmon plc — Report & Accounts — 31 December 1997

NOTES TO THE FINANCIAL STATEMENTS
for the year ended 31 December 1997 (extract)

26 Contingent liabilities (extract)
The company has guaranteed the return to investors in the companies formed under the Business Expansion Scheme and has indemnified the company's bankers who have provided guarantees of up to £40,500,000 in support of these obligations.

27 Properties in Business Expansion Scheme (BES) companies
The group sold properties into BES companies set up under BES assured tenancy schemes from 1989 to 1993.

Persimmon plc has guaranteed the return to investors in the companies formed under the BES (see note 26). Because the company has guaranteed that the BES companies will have sufficient cash resources at scheme maturity to pay the guaranteed return to investors, the proceeds received for the properties are treated as loans under BES advances on the balance sheet. The finance cost implicit in the BES arrangements, calculated by reference to the difference between the sales proceeds received and the guaranteed distribution to investors, is being charged in the profit and loss account over the appropriate term. In addition, the net rental income arising in the BES companies is recognised in the profit and loss account in the appropriate period.

Turnover does not include properties sold to BES companies until the schemes mature, the properties being held at cost on the balance sheet as BES assets until the sale is recognised.

At 31 December 1997 only two schemes now remain, all obligations under the previous schemes having been fulfilled. The maturity dates of the two remaining schemes are 5 March 1998 and 24 January 1999. The company acts on behalf of the BES companies in the sale of the properties prior to the scheme maturity date in accordance with the original scheme rules. The company has the right to exercise its option to repurchase any properties that remain unsold at maturity date in fulfilling its obligations under the guarantees.

20.47 Where the substance of the transaction is that the seller has a different asset, then, in addition to the disclosure set out in paragraph 20.45, the terms of any provision for repurchase (including any options) and of any guarantees should be disclosed. [FRS 5 App B para B21]. Disclosure of repurchase obligations in respect of residual interests in equipment is shown in Table 20.9.

Consignment stock

20.48 Arrangements where goods are supplied from a manufacturer to a dealer on a consignment basis are common in certain industries, particularly in the motor vehicle trade. Application note A to FRS 5 shows how the principles of recognising assets and liabilities should be applied to these arrangements.

Objective of consigning stocks

20.49 The objective of both parties to a consignment stock arrangement is to enable the dealer to sell as many units of the product as possible. The dealer is often given some incentive by the manufacturer through various bonus schemes to ensure that the volume of items sold is as high as possible. The consignment arrangement serves to achieve this objective and benefit both parties.

20.50 However, under such arrangements the manufacturer (or a financier) generally retains title to the goods supplied to the dealer until some predetermined event occurs. This may be when the dealer sells the goods or has held them for a set period, or some other event triggers the dealer's adoption of the goods (that is, when he pays for them and acquires title). But the date that title transfers tends to be some time after the date that the stock item is physically transferred to the dealer. Title will generally pass on receipt of cleared funds (but not to the dealer if he has already sold the vehicle on).

20.51 The standard's application note seeks to determine the point at which the dealer has in substance acquired an asset that should be recognised on its balance sheet (that is, whether it is when legal title passes or at some other time).

Principal sources of benefits and risks

20.52 In practice, the terms of consignment agreements vary considerably in important respects, for example: the right of return by the dealer; the determination of the sale price, known as the transfer price; and the terms under which deposits are required to be made by the dealer to the manufacturer or a requirement for the dealer to pay interest (which is in substance indicative of an advance of finance). These are normally the most important factors to be considered in the analysis. Other aspects of consignment transactions such as rights of inspection, responsibility for damage and loss or theft and related insurance are of less importance.

20.53 The standard analyses the principal benefits and risks associated with consignment stock arrangements from the point of view of the dealer to determine whether the stock should appear on the dealer's balance sheet. The application note identifies four principal sources of benefits and risks, which need to be considered in the analysis:

- Manufacturer's right of return.
- Dealer's right of return.
- Stock transfer price and deposits.
- Dealer's right to use stock.

20.54 These principal sources of benefits and risks are then considered in detail in the application note and the principles stemming from that discussion are summarised in a table. The summary table is reproduced below, but with the principal sources of benefits and risks added as headings; also included are references to the paragraphs of the application note that give the narrative explanation:

Indicates stock is not an asset of the dealer at delivery	Indicates stock is an asset of the dealer at delivery
Manufacturer's right of return [App A para A5].	
Manufacturer can require the dealer to return stock (or transfer stock to another dealer) without compensation, or Penalty paid by the dealer to prevent returns/ transfers of stock at the manufacturer's request.	Manufacturer cannot require dealer to return or transfer stock, or Financial incentives given to persuade dealer to transfer stock at manufacturer's manufacturer's request.
Dealer's right of return [App A para A6].	
Dealer has unfettered right to return stock to the manufacturer without penalty and actually exercises the right in practice. Manufacturer bears obsolescence risk, for example: — obsolete stock is returned to the manufacturer without penalty; or — financial incentives given by manufacturer to prevent stock being returned to it (for example, on a model change or if it becomes obsolete).	Dealer has no right to return stock or is commercially compelled not to exercise its right of return. Dealer bears obsolescence risk, for example: — penalty charged if dealer returns stock to manufacturer; or — obsolete stock cannot be returned to the manufacturer and no compensation is paid by manufacturer for losses due to obsolescence.
Stock transfer price and deposits	
Stock transfer price charged by manufacturer is based on manufacturer's list price at date of transfer of legal title. [App A para A7]. Manufacturer bears slow movement risk; for example: — transfer price set independently of time for which dealer holds stock, and there is no deposit. [App A para A8].	Stock transfer price charged by manufacturer is based on manufacturer's list price at date of delivery. [App A para A7]. Dealer bears slow movement risk, for example: — dealer is effectively charged interest as transfer price or other payments to manufacturer vary with time for which dealer holds stock. [App A para A8]; or — dealer makes a substantial interest-free deposit that varies with the levels of stock held. [App A para A9].

20.55 One of the principal sources of benefits and risks is not dealt with in the table above and that concerns the dealer's right to use the stock. The existence of a right by the dealer to use consignment stock will not normally of itself require the stock to be recorded on the dealer's balance sheet. However, once that right is exercised and the dealer uses the stock (for example, as a demonstration model) and once he has paid for it this generally causes the legal title to be transferred to the dealer and thus the stock to be recognised on its balance sheet.

20.56 The analysis of a consignment stock agreement will often give conflicting indications, as some aspects of the transaction might indicate that the stock should be put on the dealer's balance sheet while other aspects might indicate that it should remain off. In such a circumstance, one of the important factors will be to determine who pays the finance/interest cost of holding the stock. If the dealer pays an interest cost or another charge that varies with the time the stock is held (sometimes referred to by some other name, for example, display charge) then this strongly indicates that the dealer has an obligation and hence a liability that should be recognised in the dealer's financial statements. The related asset may only be an 'interest in consignment stock', but should be recorded as such until the dealer adopts the stock when that interest will convert to recognising the actual consignment stock on balance sheet. These principles are explained more fully in the example in paragraph 20.61.

Accounting treatment

20.57 The accounting treatment in the dealer's books specified in the standard is as follows. If the analysis shows that the asset should be recorded on the dealer's balance sheet then the double entry is:

Dr Stock or interest in stock	£10,000	
Cr Liabilities – trade creditors		£10,000
To record the consignment stock brought onto the dealer's balance sheet.		

20.58 Where the dealer has paid a deposit to the manufacturer for the consignment then this amount should be deducted from the liability to the manufacturer and the balance shown within trade creditors (assuming the asset and liability comply with the offset rules in FRS 5.

20.59 The notes to the financial statements should give the following information:

- An explanation of the nature of the arrangement.
- The amount of the consignment stock.
- The main terms under which the consignment is held.
- The terms of any related deposit.

[FRS 5 App A para A12].

20.60 Where the analysis of the transaction indicates that the stock should remain off the dealer's balance sheet, then the dealer should still give in the notes to the financial statements the information set out in paragraph 20.59. If the dealer has paid a deposit to the manufacturer, then this should be included within 'other debtors' on the balance sheet.

Example of required analysis

20.61 Application Note A does not give any examples of how to apply the analysis, but the example that follows illustrates the types of feature that might underlie a typical consignment arrangement and how the analysis under FRS 5 would determine how to account for the arrangement.

Example

A motor manufacturer enters into an arrangement with its dealers to consign stock to them. The agreement is the same for each dealer in the network. The basic principles of the consignment are as follows:

- The dealer orders and is allocated stock by the manufacturer under a consignment agreement and, in most cases, the stock is physically located at the dealer's premises. The manufacturer can reward or penalise dealers through the allocation of consignment stock.
- Title to the stock does not pass until the dealer has paid for the stock. The obligation to pay will arise on the earlier of:
  - The date of sale of the vehicle to the customer.
  - The date of adoption of stock (for example, as a demonstration model).
  - 180 days.
- A third party finance house has a separate agreement with the manufacturer and dealer, whereby the manufacturer receives a payment from the finance house, by way of a deposit, for all vehicles consigned to the dealer. The dealer has to pay a funding cost to the finance house based on the value of the vehicles consigned to it, which is set at 3% above LIBOR. There is a free stocking period of two months, where there is no finance charge to the dealer for the consignment stock (the finance cost being paid by the manufacturer).
- At any point, until the dealer adopts the stock or sells it or the 180 days has passed, the stock may be returned to the manufacturer, exchanged or transferred to another dealer in the manufacturer's network. This ensures that the dealer has access to the complete range of manufacturer's stock. In practice, stock is rarely returned to the manufacturer (only about 1% of vehicles consigned). In rare circumstances the manufacturer will request the return of a vehicle to fulfil a particular order elsewhere. In this situation no benefit accrues to the dealer. However, as much as 30% of stock is transferred between dealers generally by receiving a similar model in exchange.
- If a model is not selling well, then approaching its adoption date, the dealer can take one of the following actions:
  - Exchange it or transfer it to another dealer who may have a demand for that particular vehicle.
  - Negotiate an extension of the adoption date with the manufacturer.
  - Give an incentive to sell the stock, which might be supported by the manufacturer where the model is performing badly (for example, giving one year's free insurance).

- The transfer price is set at the adoption date by reference to the manufacturer's list price. However, prices on older models may be held to enable the dealer to discount his selling price.

It can be seen that such agreements can be very complex and very difficult to analyse in practice. Considering the principal benefits and risks the transaction can be analysed as follows:

	Off B/sheet	On B/sheet
Manufacturer's right to return Manufacturer can require dealer to return stock or transfer stock without compensation.	✓	
Dealer's right to return Dealer does have a right to return stock to the manufacturer without penalty, but because of the incidence of transfers between dealers, does not need to effect this right often.	✓	
Financial incentives are given by the manufacturer to prevent stock being returned in the event that a model becomes obsolete.	✓	
Regular exchanges or transfers between dealers.	✓	
Consignment period extended with agreement of the manufacturer.	✓	
Stock transfer price and deposits Stock transfer price is based on the manufacturer's list price at the date of adoption of the vehicle.	✓	
After the initial stocking period, which is interest free, the dealer pays the finance house a finance cost which varies with the level of stock held and as a consequence bears slow movement risk.		✓

It is necessary to consider the results of the analysis very carefully. It is not merely a matter of counting the ticks in the left hand column and those in the right hand column to determine which presentation wins. It is a matter of determining which of the parties bears the benefits and risks of ownership. It would appear that the manufacturer has retained the risk of obsolescence in this example, but the risk of slow movement falls to the dealer. This is a real risk as interest is paid following the period of free stocking. Therefore, after the free stocking period is complete (that is, after two months), the dealer has a risk which gives rise to an obligation that needs to be recognised by the dealer. Analysing this risk using the standard's definition of a liability, it is clear that the obligation should be recorded in the dealer's balance sheet as such at the end of the free stocking period and at an amount that equates to the deposit on which the interest is being paid. The corresponding asset could be disclosed as an 'interest in consignment stock' and would be recorded at the same amount. When the consignment stock is adopted it should then be recorded as stock of the dealer. Adoption will either take place for demonstration purposes or for onward sale.

20.62 As illustrated in the example, the interest payments in this particular transaction represent an obligation to transfer economic benefits and, as a consequence, a liability for them arises, which is in substance a loan. Under the standard, the loan should be recognised in the financial statements if it can be measured with sufficient reliability. The 'loan' would, therefore, be recorded in the dealer's balance sheet and an asset recognised which represents the dealer's interest in the consignment stock. In a study carried out for the motor industry on the impact of FRED 4, the exposure draft that preceded FRS 5, this test was seen as the primary test and has been termed the 'liability test'.

20.63 Alternatively, the analysis might have indicated that the dealer bore the risks and rewards of ownership of the stock and, as a consequence, the consignment stock itself (rather than just an interest in it) should be recorded on the dealer's balance sheet and the related finance recorded as a liability (known as the 'asset test'). Consequently, an asset (either the vehicle or an interest in it) and the corresponding liability should be accounted for on balance sheet at the earlier of: (a) the date the asset test is passed; and (b) the date the liability test is passed. However, the figure for the interest in stock recorded following the liability test will not necessarily be the same amount as the consignment stock recognised following the asset test.

Manufacturer's position

20.64 There is no discussion in the standard of the accounting treatment in the manufacturer's financial statements and its treatment cannot be assumed to be the reverse of that adopted in the dealer's books. For example, the manufacturer might recognise the physical stock in its financial statements while the dealer recognises an interest in that stock. Furthermore, there are no specific disclosures required to be given by the manufacturer in its financial statements other than the general requirement of paragraph 30 of FRS 5, which requires that the disclosure should be sufficient to enable the user of the financial statements to understand the transaction's commercial effect.

20.65 Revenue recognition by the manufacturer has to be decided on its own merits. The date that the dealer records the interest in the stock in its financial statements is not necessarily the date from which the manufacturer would recognise its revenue on sale of the stock. In the example in paragraph 20.61, the effect is that:

- In the period prior to the end of the free stocking period the manufacturer holds 'stock' whilst the dealer has no asset. The manufacturer will benefit from the deposit advanced by the finance company and pay interest to the finance company.
- In the period between the end of the free stocking period and the adoption date the manufacturer holds 'stock' whilst the dealer also holds an 'interest in consignment stock'. In this period the manufacturer will benefit from the deposit advanced by the finance company and will not pay interest to the finance company as this is paid by the dealer.
- In the above example, the manufacturer recognises revenue at the date the consignment stock is adopted (which is when all the risks and rewards of

ownership are transferred and the manufacturer has earned the right to the consideration).

Conclusion

20.66 Obviously, as mentioned above, the terms of consignment stock agreements differ significantly. It must be stressed, therefore, that the analysis of these transactions needs to be undertaken very carefully in conjunction with the detailed application note in FRS 5.

Goods with reservation of title

20.67 It is quite common for companies that sell goods to other companies to have reservation of title clauses included in their contracts. This enables the selling company to retain ownership of those goods until the purchaser has paid for them. Such clauses are often known as 'Romalpa clauses' following the Romalpa case (*Aluminium Industrie Vaassen B.V. v Romalpa Aluminium Limited* [1976] 1 WLR 676) in 1976, which was concerned with contractual relationships. The main effect of trading with reservation of title is that the position of the unpaid seller may be improved if the purchaser becomes insolvent. However, whether an effective reservation of title exists depends upon the construction of the particular contract.

20.68 Even if there is an effective reservation of title clause, on a going concern basis it is common practice for the purchaser to recognise such stocks in its balance sheet, although the supplier retains legal title to the goods. The liability to the supplier is also recognised. This was first recommended in guidance issued by ICAEW in 1976, 'Accounting for goods subject to reservation of title'. It is consistent with FRS 5 as it is the purchaser who bears the risks and benefits from the rewards of the asset.

20.69 The ICAEW guidance recommended that where the financial statements are materially affected by the accounting treatment adopted in relation to sales or purchases subject to reservation of title, the treatment should be disclosed and a note indicating the amount of liabilities that are subject to reservation of title clauses be given, where quantifiable. An example of such disclosure is given in Table 20.11.

Table 20.11 – CHARNOS plc – Annual Report and Accounts – 31 December 1988

Notes on the accounts

16 Creditors – amounts falling due within one year (extract)

Part of the amount owing to trade creditors is or may be secured by the reservation by the supplier of legal title to the goods supplied and to the proceeds of their sale. The amount secured in this way depends on the legal interpretation of individual contracts and cannot readily be determined. In the opinion of the directors, the maximum amount likely to be involved is £1,150,000 (group) and £400,000 (company).

20.70 However, in practice, this note is often not given where the purchasing company is a going concern such that the likelihood of the reservation of title clause crystallising is remote. Whether or not disclosure is necessary in order to give a true and fair view will be a matter for judgement. FRS 5 requires sufficient details of a transaction to be given to enable the user to understand its commercial effect. [FRS 5, para 30]. It also requires an explanation where the nature of assets and liabilities differs from those items normally included under the relevant balance sheet headings. An example would be where the company did not have legal title to assets and disclosure of this fact was necessary for a true and fair view to be given.

Long-term contracts

20.71 Long-term contracts need to be considered separately, because of the length of time taken to complete such contracts. The main accounting issue is the allocation of turnover and costs to the accounting periods in which work is carried out. To defer recording turnover and not to take account of profit until completion of the contract may result in the profit and loss account reflecting not so much a fair view of the results of the activity of the company during the year, but rather a view of the results relating to contracts that have been completed in the year. It is, therefore, appropriate to take credit for ascertainable turnover and profit while contracts are in progress.

Definition of long-term contracts

20.72 A 'long-term contract' is defined in SSAP 9 as follows:

> *"A contract entered into for the design, manufacture or construction of a single substantial asset or the provision of a service (or of a combination of assets or services which together constitute a single project) where the time taken substantially to complete the contract is such that the contract activity falls into different accounting periods. A contract that is required to be accounted for as long-term by this accounting standard will usually extend for a period exceeding one year. However, a duration exceeding one year is not an essential feature of a long-term contract. Some contracts with a shorter duration than one year should be accounted for as long-term contracts if they are sufficiently material to the activity of the period that not to record turnover and attributable profit would lead to a distortion of the period's turnover and results such that the financial statements would not give a true and fair view, provided that the policy is applied consistently within the reporting entity and from year to year."* [SSAP 9 para 22].

20.73 A situation where a contract of duration of less than one year might be treated as long-term is, for example, when a company completes a material short-term contract just after the year end, but a substantial amount of work on the contract had been completed before the year end. If an element of turnover and profit is not attributed to the current period, this might distort that period's turnover and results to such an extent that they do not give a true and fair view.

20.73.1 In March 2005 the UITF issued Abstract 40, (see further chapter 9) which noted that contracts for the provision of a professional service, the performance of which falls into two or more accounting periods, should be accounted for as a long-term contract in accordance with SSAP 9.

[The next paragraph is 20.74.]

Accounting treatment of long-term contracts

20.74 Long-term contracts should be assessed on a contract by contract basis and reflected in the profit and loss account by recording turnover and related costs as contract activity progresses. Turnover is ascertained in a manner appropriate to the stage of completion of the contract, the business and the industry in which it operates. [SSAP 9 para 28]. Further guidance on the measurement of revenue (turnover) on long-term contracts is given in FRS 5 Application note G, 'Revenue recognition'.

20.75 Where it is considered that the outcome of a long-term contract can be assessed with reasonable certainty before its conclusion, the prudently calculated attributable profit should be recognised in the profit and loss account as the difference between the reported turnover and related costs for that contract. [SSAP 9 para 29]. This is illustrated in the following example.

Example

A construction company has pre-sold a development to an institution. No work has yet been done on the construction. Profit will arise on proceeds less the cost of the land and the cost of the development, which it will sub-contract.

The contract should be accounted for, in accordance with SSAP 9, as a long-term contract, which means not taking profit until a stage of construction has been reached that enables the eventual outcome to be foreseen and then only taking profit attributable to the work performed at the balance sheet date.

Turnover

20.76 No definition of turnover is provided in SSAP 9; it merely states that turnover is ascertained in a manner appropriate to the stage of completion of the contract, the business and the industry in which it operates. However, amounts taken through the profit and loss account in an accounting period would normally relate to separate or measurable parts of the contract completed within that period. Appendix 1 to the standard states that turnover may sometimes be ascertained by reference to the valuation of work carried out to date. In other situations, there may be specific points during a contract where individual elements of work done will have separately ascertainable sales values, where costs can be identified and, therefore, turnover can be recorded as appropriate. This could be, for example, when delivery or when customer acceptance takes place.

20.76.1 FRS 5 Application note G, 'Revenue recognition', sets out basic principles for revenue recognition that should be applied to all transactions and deals with a number of specific areas. These are dealt with in chapter 9. It also includes guidance on long-term contractual performance and, specifically, on the recognition of turnover derived from such contracts. However, it does not amend the existing requirements of SSAP 9. [FRS 5 App G para G14].

20.76.2 The application note states in relation to long-term contracts that, in accordance with SSAP 9, the seller should recognise changes in its assets and liabilities, and related turnover, that represent the accrual over the course of the contract of its right to consideration. This 'assets and liabilities' approach represented a shift in emphasis away from the 'matching concept' approach, which did, in the past, concentrate on matching revenue and expenses rather than measuring revenue by reference to changes in assets and liabilities. The difference in the approach can result in lower revenue being recognised at interim stages with correspondingly higher costs being carried forward. This does not necessarily give any different result from that which applying SSAP 9 would give, as SSAP 9 does not prescribe any particular method of determining revenue and merely requires that revenue is ascertained in a manner appropriate to the contract's stage of completion and to the business and industry in which the entity operates.

20.76.3 A seller should recognise turnover in respect of performance under a long-term contract when, and to the extent that, it obtains the right to consideration. [FRS 5 App G para G18]. The right to consideration is the right to receive amounts in exchange for its performance. The right does not necessarily correspond to amounts that fall due under a schedule of stage payments, as stage payments may not correspond to performance. Stage payments reflect only an agreed timing of payments whereas a right to consideration arises from a seller's performance. [FRS 5 App G para G3].

20.76.4 The right to consideration and, therefore, turnover under a long-term contract should be ascertained from assessing the fair value of the goods or services provided to the balance sheet date (that is, the stage of completion) as a proportion of the total fair value of the contract. [FRS 5 App G para G18]. Fair value means the amount at which goods or services could be exchanged in an arm's length transaction between informed and willing parties, other than in a forced or liquidation sale. [FRS 5 App G para G3].

20.76.5 In some contracts, the proportion of the total fair value will correspond to the costs to date compared to the total costs incurred and to be incurred on the contract. This is a commonly used basis, if only because it is the most straightforward method of arriving at a reasonable allocation of revenue. However, this method will not always be appropriate and the overriding principle is to consider the stage of completion of the contractual obligations, which reflects the extent to which the seller has obtained the right to consideration. To use the proportion of costs incurred as a basis for recognising turnover requires the seller to be able to demonstrate that costs incurred provide evidence of performance of the contract terms and the right to consideration. The emphasis on rights to consideration as the principal determining factor in revenue recognition means that as a result different stages of a contract may vary in their relative profitability. [FRS 5 App G para G18].

20.76.6 For example, a long-term contract might have a technical development stage and a construction stage. The technical development stage might have relatively low costs compared to the construction stage (because, for example, the seller has already developed the necessary technical expertise on other contracts). However, such development might represent a high proportion of the fair value of the contract and entitle the seller to a higher proportion of the total consideration under the contract than the construction stage. In such a case, as well as giving rise to higher turnover relative to the construction stage, the development phase may also give higher relative profits (subject of course to the overall contract remaining profitable).

20.76.7 The fair values used in determining the right to consideration should be based on the values applicable at the start of the contract. This applies unless the contract specifies that changes in prices will be passed on to the customer, in which case such amendments to the price are taken into account. The application note also contains guidance on separation and linking of contractual arrangements (see chapter 9 and below) and notes that that guidance may also be relevant in attributing fair values to the goods or services that have been provided up to the balance sheet date. [FRS 5 App G para G19, paras G22-G42].

20.76.8 An example of a situation where the application note provisions relating to separation and linking of contractual arrangements might affect attribution of fair values would be where two separate contracts need to be considered together under the provisions of the application note. If the two contracts had been priced artificially, with one contract having a much higher stated value than the other, adjustments would have to be made so that fair values were attributed to the rights to consideration earned under the respective contracts when they are accounted for as components of a single transaction.

[The next paragraph is 20.76.10.]

20.76.10 As noted in paragraph 20.76.2 above, the assets and liabilities approach, whilst consistent with the general principle in SSAP 9 for recognising turnover, basing revenue recognition on costs to date as a proportion of total costs will be valid where, and only where, if it gives an accurate measure of the amounts of consideration to which the seller is entitled as a result of its performance. The key point is that the overriding criterion for determining turnover is not costs incurred, but rather rights to consideration. The application note emphasises these points when it states;

> *"The seller should recognise changes in its assets and liabilities, and turnover, in accordance with the stage of completion of its contractual obligations, which reflects the extent to which it has obtained the right to consideration. The amount of turnover recognised should be derived from the proportion of costs incurred only where these provide evidence of the seller's performance and hence the extent to which it has obtained the right to consideration."*
>
> [FRS 5 App G para G21].

20.76.11 Where payment is received in arrears then it may be necessary to discount the turnover. The application note states that *"where the effect of the time value of money is material to reported revenue, the amount of revenue recognised should be the present value of the cash inflows expected to be received from the customer in settlement. The unwinding of the discount should be credited to finance income as this represents a gain from a financing transaction"*. [FRS 5 App G para G8].

[The next paragraph is 20.77.]

20.77 SSAP 9 requires that the means of ascertaining turnover should be disclosed as an accounting policy. [SSAP 9 para 32]. An example of such disclosure is found in the accounts of George Wimpey PLC (see Table 20.12).

Table 20.12 – George Wimpey PLC – Annual Report – 31 December 1994

ACCOUNTING POLICIES (extract)

Turnover

Contracting turnover comprises the value of work executed during the year including the settlement of claims arising from previous years, amounts received on management fee contracts funded by the client and the Group's share of unincorporated joint venture turnover. Other turnover is based on the invoiced value of goods and services supplied during the year and includes house and land sales completed, trading and investment property sales completed and rental income. Turnover excludes value added tax and intra-group turnover.

Profit

Operating profit comprises the results of contracting, the provision of goods and services, private housing development, land sales, property development and investment. It includes the results attributable to contracts completed and long-term contracts in progress where a profitable outcome can prudently be foreseen, after deducting amounts recognised in previous years and after making provision for foreseeable losses. Claims receivable are recognised as income when received or if certified for payment. Estate development profit is taken on the number of houses of an estate in respect of which legal completions have taken place.

Long-term contracts

The amount of long-term contracts, at costs incurred, net of amounts transferred to cost of sales, after deducting foreseeable losses and payments on account not matched with turnover, is included in work in progress and stock as long-term contract balances. The amount by which recorded turnover is in excess of payments on account is included in debtors as amounts recoverable on long-term contracts. Payments in excess of recorded turnover and long-term contract balances are included in creditors as payments received on account on long-term contracts. The amount by which provisions or accruals for foreseeable losses exceed costs incurred, after transfers to cost of sales, is included within either provisions for liabilities and charges or creditors, as appropriate.

Recognition of profit

20.78 The profit and loss account should only include profit when the outcome of a particular contract can be ascertained with reasonable certainty (that is, where it is reasonable to foresee profits in advance of the completion of a contract). This is often a difficult exercise to undertake in practice. In addition, the standard comments that this judgement of future profitability should be exercised with prudence. [SSAP 9 para 29]. Such prudent judgements are not inconsistent with FRS 18, which requires the directors to achieve the balance between prudence and neutrality by making prudent judgements without systematic overstatements of liabilities and losses and understatement of assets and gains. [FRS 18 para 43].

20.79 In some businesses, long-term contracts for the supply of services or goods exist where the prices are determined and invoiced according to separate parts of the contract. FRS 5 Application note G, 'Revenue recognition', contains guidance on the separation and linking of contractual arrangements and states that a contractual arrangement should be accounted for as two or more separate transactions where the commercial substance is that the individual components operate independently of each other. Operating independently means that each component represents a good or service that the entity can supply separately to a customer either on a standalone basis or as an optional extra. Alternatively, one or more components may be capable of being provided by another supplier. [FRS 5 App G para G25]. This is discussed further in chapter 9.

20.80 Where a contract's individual components operate independently of each other, the most appropriate method of reflecting profits on each component is usually to record revenue and related costs as the right to consideration is earned by performance of the contract's separable parts, treating each such separable part as a separate contract. In such instances, however, future revenues from the total contract need to be compared with future estimated costs and provision made for any foreseeable loss. [SSAP 9 App 1 para 22]. More commonly, the separate stages of a long-term contract will fall to be treated as a single contract, as the separate stages are not independent of each other.

20.81 FRS 5 Application note G does not permit contracts to be 'unbundled' where the component parts do not operate independently of each other. Neither can this be done if reliable fair values cannot be attributed to any of the components individually. In addition, where there is more than one contract, the application note requires them to be treated as one contract where this best reflects the commercial substance. Typically, this would be where there was only one contract when the contracts do not operate independently of each other and reliable fair values cannot be attributed to each contract. [FRS 5 App G paras G26, G32]. This is discussed further in chapter 9. The following example considers how certain contracts should be valued.

Example

A company has a long-term contract for land reclamation. This involves clearing old collieries. As a by-product the company is entitled to sell off any coal that it recovers. On this site there are coal deposits that the company has sold to a third party for £500,000, although it has not yet recovered the coal.

The question is whether the company can take the £500,000 to the profit and loss account as it considers that there will be only minimal costs in recovering the coal. Our view is that the coal sale proceeds should be only one part of the assessment of profitability of the whole contract. It should not be accounted for separately. Therefore, the long-term contract should be accounted for including the coal sale recoveries in accordance with SSAP 9 and profit should only be taken on the contract when it has reached a stage of completion when the outcome can be foreseen and then only in proportion to the work done.

20.82 The procedure to recognise profit is to include an appropriate proportion of total contract value as turnover in the profit and loss account as the contract activity progresses and entitlement to consideration is earned. The costs incurred in reaching that stage of completion are charged to cost of sales, resulting in the reporting of results that can be attributed to the proportion of work completed.

20.83 The turnover recognised on a particular contract will depend on the stage of completion of that contract and the entity's rights to consideration. When, in the contract's early stages, it is not possible to foresee its outcome with reasonable certainty, the related costs incurred that are charged to cost of sales will not be less than the recognised turnover (although they may be more if losses are expected on the contract as a whole or if there has been abortive or wasted expenditure). Therefore, no profit will be recognised in the profit and loss account. However, when in the later stages of a contract, the outcome can be assessed with reasonable certainty, turnover recognised in respect of the rights to consideration that have been earned may exceed the related costs charged giving rise to profit.

[The next paragraph is 20.86.]

20.86 The figures to be included in the year's profit and loss account will be both the appropriate amount of turnover and the associated costs of achieving that turnover, to the extent that these exceed amounts recognised in previous years. The estimated outcome of a contract that extends over several accounting years will nearly always vary in the light of changes in circumstances and for this reason the result of the year will not necessarily represent the profit on the contract which is appropriate to the amount of work carried out in the period. It may also reflect the effect of changes in circumstances during the year that affect the total profit estimated to accrue on completion. This is illustrated in the following example.

Example

A construction contractor has a fixed price contract for £11,500. The initial estimate of costs is £7,500 and the contract is expected to take four years. In year two the contractor's estimate of total costs increases to £8,000. Of the £500 increase, £300 is to be incurred in year three and the remainder in year four.

The contractor determines the stage of completion of the contract by comparing the costs of work to date with the estimated total costs as this is a reliable method of determining the right to consideration earned through performance in the case of this particular contract.

	Year 1 £	Year 2 £	Year 3 £	Year 4 £
Turnover agreed in contract	11,500	11,500	11,500	11,500
Contract costs incurred to date	3,000	4,500	6,675	8,000
Contract costs to complete	4,500	3,500	1,325	–
Total estimated costs	7,500	8,000	8,000	8,000
Estimated profit	4,000	3,500	3,500	3,500
Stage of completion	40%	56.3%	83.4%	100%
	(3,000 ÷ 7,500)	(4,500 ÷ 8,000)	(6,675 ÷ 8,000)	

The amount of turnover, costs and profit recognised in the profit and loss account in the four years is as follows:

	To date	Prior years	Current year	Margin
Year 1				
Turnover (11,500 × 40%)	4,600		4,600	
Costs (7,500 × 40%)	3,000		3,000	
Profit	1,600		1,600	(35%)
Year 2				
Turnover (11,500 × 56.3%)	6,475	4,600	1,875	
Costs (8,000 × 56.3%)	4,504	3,000	1,504	
Profit	1,971	1,600	371	(20%)
Year 3				
Turnover (11,500 × 83.4%)	9,591	6,475	3,116	
Costs (8,000 × 83.4%)	6,672	4,504	2,168	
Profit	2,919	1,971	948	(30%)
Year 4				
Turnover	11,500	9,591	1,909	
Costs	8,000	6,672	1,328	
Profit	3,500	2,919	581	(30%)

The profit margin in year two (that is, 20%) is lower than in the subsequent years (that is, 30%) because it takes account of the fact that in the light of the revised estimates, too much profit has been taken in year one when the total estimated costs (and total expected performance) were lower.

If the initial cost estimates had been £8,000, then the percentage completion at the end of year one would have been 37.5% (that is, 3,000 divided by 8,000). This means that turnover of £4,313 (£11,500 × 37.5%) would have been attributed to the costs incurred to date of £3,000 giving a profit of £1,313 compared with the reported profit of £1,600. The turnover recognised in year two is that attributed to the total costs incurred to date, calculated on the basis of the revised estimates, less the turnover of £4,600 reported in year one. Therefore, the results in year two reflect the fact that an adjustment is necessary in respect of year one.

20.87 Contract costs are usually recognised as an expense in the period in which the work to which they relate is performed. Only if the costs relate to future activity should they be carried forward as work in progress. Equally, if costs incurred to date are used to determine the percentage completion, then turnover attributed to work carried out should not be increased to offset additional costs incurred where these represent inefficiencies. SSAP 9 states that the profit accounted for needs to reflect the proportion of the work carried out at the accounting date and to take into account any known inequalities of profitability in the various stages of a contract. [SSAP 9 para 9]. This is illustrated by the following example.

Example

A construction contractor has a fixed price contract for £11,500. The initial estimate of costs is £7,500. The contract is expected to take four years. In year two the contractor's estimate of total costs increases to £8,000 as a result of inefficiencies in year two.

The contractor determines the stage of completion of the contract by comparing the costs of work to date with the estimated total costs.

Method one

	Year 1	Year 2	Year 3	Year 4
	£	£	£	£
Turnover agreed in contract	11,500	11,500	11,500	11,500
Contract costs incurred to date	3,000	5,000	6,875	8,000
Contract costs to complete	4,500	3,000	1,125	
Total estimated costs	7,500	8,000	8,000	8,000
Estimated profit	4,000	3,500	3,500	3,500
Stage of completion	40%	62.5%	85.9%	100%
	(3,000 ÷ 7,500)	(5,000 ÷ 8,000)	(6,875 ÷ 8,000)	

The amount of turnover, costs and profit recognised in the profit and loss account in the four years under this method would be as follows:

	To date	Prior years	Current year	Margin
Year 1				
Turnover (11,500 × 40%)	4,600		4,600	
Costs (7,500 × 40%)	3,000		3,000	
Profit	1,600		1,600	(35%)
Year 2				
Turnover (11,500 × 62.5%)	7,188	4,600	2,588	
Costs (8,000 × 62.5%)	5,000	3,000	2,000	
Profit	2,188	1,600	588	(23%)
Year 3				
Turnover (11,500 × 85.9%)	9,879	7,190	2,689	
Costs (8,000 × 85.9%)	6,872	5,000	1,872	
Profit	3,007	2,190	817	(30%)
Year 4				
Turnover	11,500	9,879	1,621	
Costs	8,000	6,872	1,128	
Profit	3,500	3,007	493	(30%)

Under this method the profit in year two is reduced as a result of the inefficiencies. However, part of this inefficiency is being spread forward into years three and four as is evident from the reduced profit margins of 30% compared with 35% in the initial estimates.

In view of the fact that the increased costs result from inefficiencies in year two, there is an argument that it is not prudent to spread the effect of this.

Method two

	Year 1 £	Year 2 £	Year 3 £	Year 4 £
Contract costs incurred to date	3,000	5,000	6,875	8,000
Total estimated costs	7,500	8,000	8,000	8,000
Stage of completion (Ignoring inefficiencies of £500)	40%	60%	85%	100%
		(3,000 ÷ 7,500)	(4,500 ÷ 7,500)	(6,375 ÷ 7,500)

The amount of turnover, costs and profit recognised in the profit and loss account in the four years under this method would be as follows:

	To date	Prior years	Current year	Margin
Year 1				
Turnover (11,500 × 40%)	4,600		4,600	
Costs (7,500 × 40%)	3,000		3,000	
Profit	1,600		1,600	(35%)
Year 2				
Turnover (11,500 × 60%)	6,900	4,600	2,300	
Costs: normal (7,500 × 60%)	4,500	3,000	1,500	
inefficiencies	500	–	500	
	5,000	3,000	2,000	
Profit	1,900	1,600	300	(13%)
Year 3				
Turnover (11,500 × 85%)	9,775	6,900	2,875	
Costs: normal (7,500 × 85%)	6,375	4,500	1,875	
inefficiencies	500	500	–	
	6,875	5,000	1,875	
Profit	2,900	1,900	1,000	(35%)
Year 4				
Turnover	11,500	9,775	1,725	
Costs	8,000	6,875	1,125	
Profit	3,500	2,900	600	(35%)

This method is preferred because the inefficiencies are charged to the period in which they are incurred leaving a 'normal' contract profit margin in the subsequent periods.

20.88 No matter what method of determining attributable profit is adopted, it should be applied consistently and from year to year. Paragraph 32 of SSAP 9 requires that the method of ascertaining attributable profits should be stated in the accounting policies. This means that the basis of calculation should be disclosed. An example of a company with an accounting policy note giving details of the method of ascertaining attributable profit is Verson International Group plc which uses the percentage of completion method (see Table 20.13).

Table 20.13 – Verson International Group plc – Annual Report – 31 January 1994

Accounting Policies (extract)

f) *Stocks and long-term contracts*

In the case of long-term contracts where the group's involvement is principally as a manufacturer, rather than contract manager, turnover represents the estimated contract revenues on work during the year. Contract revenues and profits are computed on the percentage of completion method, primarily by reference to labour hours, profits being determined after making reserves against all anticipated costs including possible warranty claims.

Where the group's involvement in a long-term contract is principally as a contract manager, turnover reflects costs incurred to date in establishing and managing the contract plus the directors' best estimate of profits attributable to the work performed to date. For this purpose the directors' estimate of attributable profits will include a proportion of the total profits anticipated to be made on the contract, to the extent that their realisation is reasonably foreseeable, and after making provision for all future costs including all possible warranty claims.

Long-term contract balances included in stocks comprise costs incurred on long-term contracts, net of amounts transferred to cost of sales, after deducting foreseeable losses and related payments on account. Costs include all direct material and labour costs incurred in bringing a contract to its state of completion at the year end, including an appropriate proportion of indirect expenses. Provisions for estimated losses on contracts are made in the period in which such losses are foreseen. Long-term contract balances do not include attributable profit.

The excess of payments received over amounts recorded as turnover is classified under creditors due within one year. Amounts recoverable on contracts, being the amount by which recorded turnover is in excess of payments on account, is classified under debtors.

Other stocks are stated at the lower of cost and net realisable value.

Provision is made for obsolete, slow-moving or defective items where appropriate.

Determination of future costs

20.89 When a company determines the amount of attributable profit to be included in turnover, it should take account of the company's type of business, the nature of the contract and the contractual relationship with its customer. Appendix 1 to SSAP 9 states that when estimating profit:

> *"It is necessary to take into account not only the total costs to date and the total estimated further costs to completion . . . but also the estimated future costs of rectification and guarantee work, and any other future work to be undertaken under the contract. These are then compared with the total sales value of the contract."* [SSAP 9 App 1 para 25].

20.90 The definition of attributable profit requires that it should be calculated, specifically, after estimating 'remedial and maintenance costs'. [SSAP 9 para 23]. In practice, for example, these costs will include the usual snagging clause of a building contract (that is, the clauses covering completion of the finishing touches to a building). They would also include provision for costs incurred under a 'guarantee' period for maintenance that is part of the original contract.

20.91 In considering future costs, it is necessary to have regard to likely increases in wages and salaries, to likely increases in the price of raw materials and to rises in general overheads, so far as these items are not recoverable from the customer under the terms of the contracts. Also, if interest on borrowings financing specific long-term contracts is capitalised (see chapter 16), then the calculation of total cost should include future interest costs.

Variations and claims

20.92 A variation is an instruction by the customer for a change in the scope of the work to be performed under the contract. Examples are changes in the specifications or designs of an asset and changes in the contract's duration.

20.93 Where approved variations have been made to a contract during its course and the amount to be received in respect of these variations has not yet been settled and is likely to be a material factor in the outcome, it is necessary to make a conservative estimate of the amount likely to be received and this is then treated as part of the total sales value. On the other hand, allowance needs to be made for foreseeable claims or penalties payable arising out of delays in completion or from other causes.

20.94 A claim is an amount that the contractor seeks to collect from the customer or another party as reimbursement for costs not included in the contract price. A claim may arise from, for example, errors in the initial specifications and delays caused by the customer.

20.95 The settlement of claims arising from circumstances not envisaged in the contract or arising as an indirect consequence of approved variations is subject to a high level of uncertainty relating to the outcome of future negotiations. In view of this, it is generally prudent to recognise receipts in respect of such claims only when negotiations have reached an advanced stage and there is sufficient evidence of the acceptability of the claim by the customer, with an indication of the amount involved also being available. Trafalgar House Public Limited Company provides an example of an accounting policy for claims on contracts (see Table 20.14). Another example is shown in Table 20.12.

Table 20.14 – Trafalgar House Public Limited Company – Report and Accounts – 30 September 1994

Principal accounting policies (extract)

g) Long-term contracts (extract)

Amounts recoverable on contracts (other than small works) are valued at anticipated net sales value of work done after provision for contingencies and anticipated future losses on contracts. Claims are included in the valuation of contracts and credited to the profit and loss account when entitlement has been established.

Losses on contracts

20.96 If it is expected that there will be a loss on a contract as a whole, all of the loss should be recognised as soon as it is foreseen. [SSAP 9 para 11].

20.97 Foreseeable losses are defined as losses which are currently estimated to arise over the duration of the contract (after allowing for estimated remedial and maintenance costs and increases in costs so far as not recoverable under the terms of the contract). This estimate is required irrespective of:

- Whether or not work has yet commenced on such contracts.
- The proportion of work carried out at the accounting date.
- The amount of profits expected to arise on other contracts.

[SSAP 9 para 24].

20.98 Where unprofitable contracts are of such magnitude that they can be expected to utilise a considerable part of the company's capacity for a substantial period, related administration overheads to be incurred during the period to the completion of those contracts should also be included in calculating the provision for losses. [SSAP 9 para 11].

Cost of sales

20.99 The associated costs of achieving the turnover that is recorded in the profit and loss account on a contract by contract basis is deducted from the total costs incurred to date and charged in the profit and loss account as 'cost of sales'. Consequently, the reported result is attributed to the proportion of work completed.

20.100 Cost of sales will include costs that relate directly to the specific contract and also other costs that can be allocated to the contract. Costs that relate directly to the contract may include:

- Site labour costs.
- Costs of materials used in construction.
- Transport costs of plant and equipment to and from the site.
- Depreciation of plant and equipment used on the site.
- Design and technical costs related to the contract.
- The estimated costs of rectification and guarantee work.

20.101 Other costs that may be allocated to the contract include insurance, construction overheads and supervision costs.

20.102 Cost of sales will also normally include provisions made in respect of a loss making contract. An example of provisions for losses on contracts shown within cost of sales is shown in Table 20.15.

Table 20.15 – Trafalgar House Public Limited Company – Report and Accounts – 30 September 1993

Notes to the Accounts

2 Exceptional items (extract)

Total exceptional items included in continuing operations have been allocated to the following statutory headings:

	Note	1993 £m	1992 £m
Cost of sales			
Current asset write downs			
Commercial developments	*(f)*	**(87.2)**	(0.9)
Residential developments	*(g)*	**(16.7)**	(38.9)

(f) Commercial development properties have been valued by the directors at the lower of cost and net realisable value. The write downs of commercial developments relate principally to the following items:

- US business parks where, during the year, the directors have decided to accelerate the group's withdrawal from this activity and have therefore written down the developments to estimated disposal values expected to be achieved.
- The Paddington Basin developments where the directors believe there is now insufficient certainty that the development can be completed within the timescale previously envisaged and have therefore written down the development to the current value of the group's interests in the site, having regard to the group's obligations under the terms of its developments agreement with British Waterways Board.

(g) The write downs of residential developments reflect the effect of the decision, taken by the directors during the year, to withdraw from the group's activities in Portugal and a provision in respect of UK residential development.

20.102.1 Another issue that arises is in connection with costs incurred before a contract starts. The UITF addressed this matter in Abstract 34, 'Pre-contract costs'. This is discussed further in chapter 3.

Amounts recoverable on contracts

20.103 Amounts recorded as turnover in respect of a contract are treated as debtors to the extent that they are unpaid and amounts recorded as costs of sales are deducted from the balance sheet work in progress figure. This is based on the theory that once a transaction has been recorded as turnover, it cannot then also be carried as stocks and must, consequently, be a receivable.

[The next paragraph is 20.105.]

20.105 A long-term contract bears the characteristics of any legally binding contract so that the contractor may sue for any monies rightfully owed by the customer. This implies that amounts receivable for work completed under a long-term contract can, correctly, be regarded as debtors. In addition, there is no necessity to disclose any further details, such as the profit element included in the debtor, in the notes to the financial statements.

Disclosure

20.106 Long-term contracts should be disclosed in the balance sheet as follows:

- The amount by which recorded turnover is in excess of payments on account should be classified as 'amounts recoverable on contracts' and separately disclosed within debtors.
- The balance of payments on account (in excess of amounts matched with turnover, and offset against long-term contract balances) should be classified as 'payments on account' and separately disclosed within creditors.
- The amount of long-term contracts, at costs incurred (net of amounts transferred to cost of sales) after deducting foreseeable losses and payments on account not matched with turnover, should be classified as 'long-term contract balances' and separately disclosed within the balance sheet heading 'stocks'. The balance sheet note should disclose separately the balances of:
    - Net cost less foreseeable losses.
    - Applicable payments on account.
- The amount by which the provision or accrual for foreseeable losses exceeds the costs incurred (after transfers to cost of sales) should be included within either 'provisions for liabilities and charges' or 'creditors' as appropriate.

[SSAP 9 para 30].

20.107 'Payments on account' are defined as all amounts received and receivable at the accounting date in respect of contracts in progress. [SSAP 9 para 25].

20.108 The accounting policies that have been applied to long-term contracts, in particular the method of ascertaining turnover and attributable profit, should be stated and applied consistently within the business and from year to year. [SSAP 9 para 32]. An example of typical disclosure for long-term contracts is George Wimpey PLC (see Table 20.12).

20.109 Each of the above balance sheet disclosure requirements is illustrated in the examples that follow:

Turnover exceeds payments on account

Example

	£'000
Turnover (value of work done and rights to consideration earned)	52
Cumulative payments on account	45
Excess – *included in debtors*	7
Balance of costs on this contract not transferred to cost of sales – *included in stocks*	10
Balance sheet (extract)	
Stocks	
Work in progress	
Net cost less foreseeable losses	10
Debtors	
Amounts recoverable on contracts	7

20.110 In the above example, the value of work included in turnover for the particular contract exceeds the progress payments received and receivable to date on that same contract. In accordance with SSAP 9, the excess amount is classified as 'amounts recoverable on contracts' and is shown separately under the heading 'debtors' in the balance sheet formats. The balance of costs not transferred to cost of sales is shown as work in progress.

Payments on account exceed turnover

Example

	£'000
Turnover (value of work done and rights to consideration earned)	52
Cumulative payments on account	60
Excess – *reduces stocks*	8
Balance of costs on this contract not transferred to cost of sales – *included in stocks*	10
Balance sheet (extract)	
Stocks	
Work in progress	
Net cost less foreseeable losses	10
Applicable payments on account	(8)
	2

20.111 In this example, there is nothing to be included as 'amounts recoverable on contracts', because all turnover has been invoiced as payments on account and so will either be included in trade debtors or will have been received.

20.112 The amount included in work in progress comprises the total costs incurred to date less:

- Amounts transferred to cost of sales in the profit and loss account in respect of work carried out to date.
- Any foreseeable losses.
- Any applicable payments on account, that is, those in excess of turnover.

The balance sheet note should disclose separately both the net cost less foreseeable losses and the applicable payments on account.

Payments on account exceed turnover and balance of costs on contracts

Example

	£'000
Turnover (value of work done and rights to consideration earned)	52
Cumulative payments on account	60
Excess – *part reduces stocks/and part included in creditors*	8
Balance of costs on this contract not transferred to cost of sales – *included in stocks*	5
Balance sheet (extract)	
Stocks	
Work in progress	
Net cost less foreseeable losses	5
Applicable payments on account	(5)
	–
Creditors	
Payments on account (£8,000 – £5,000)	3

20.113 In the this example, payments on account exceed both the amount of recorded turnover and the balance of costs incurred to date included in stocks. The excess amount is classified as 'payments on account' and separately disclosed in 'creditors'.

20.114 An example of balance sheet disclosure for long-term contracts is provided by George Wimpey PLC (see Table 20.16). The accounting policy note is shown in Table 20.12.

Table 20.16— George Wimpey PLC — Annual Report — 31 December 1994

NOTES ON THE ACCOUNTS

15 Work in Progress and Stock

	Group	
	1994 **£m**	1993 £m
Long-term contract balances		
– net cost less foreseeable losses	**11.8**	11.6
– less applicable payments on account	**(11.2)**	(11.4)
Net valuation	**0.6**	0.2
Land development and construction	**504.8**	473.3
Other stock	**20.6**	20.0
	526.0	493.5

17 Debtors (extract)

	Group		Parent	
	1994 **£m**	1993 £m	**1994** **£m**	1993 £m
Receivable within one year:				
– trade debtors	**80.1**	78.7	–	–
– amounts recoverable on long-term contracts	**62.1**	56.0	–	–
– amounts owed by subsidiary undertakings	–	–	**140.4**	186.6
– amounts owed by associated undertakings	**2.1**	1.7	–	–
– prepayments and accrued income	**8.2**	5.9	**0.2**	–
– corporate taxation	**9.2**	12.2	**2.1**	–
– other	**15.7**	13.1	–	–
	177.4	167.6	**142.7**	186.6

18 Creditors Falling Due Within One Year

	Group		Parent	
	1994 **£m**	1993 £m	**1994** **£m**	1993 £m
Finance debt (Note 20)	**17.3**	14.2	**3.5**	0.3
Trade creditors	**313.5**	309.1	–	–
Payments received on account on long-term contracts	**53.2**	53.7	–	–
Amounts owed to subsidiary undertakings	–	–	**86.7**	173.0
Amounts owed to associated undertakings	**0.4**	0.1	–	–
National insurance, VAT and other taxes	**9.9**	0.1	–	–
Accruals and deferred income	**12.8**	10.6	–	–
Corporate taxation	**36.2**	30.3	**3.4**	5.0
Proposed dividend* (Note 6)	**12.6**	11.7	**12.6**	11.7
Other	**13.4**	11.1	**1.9**	1.6
	469.3	449.9	**108.1**	191.6

* Note that for years beginning on or after 1 January 2005, the recognition of proposed dividends as liabilities is prohibited by FRS 21.

Provision for foreseeable losses

20.115 The amount transferred to the profit and loss account for a particular contract is the costs incurred to date in reaching that contract's stage of completion recognised in turnover. In most circumstances, this amount represents the cost of sales figure for a contract. However, where a provision is made for foreseeable losses, this charge also becomes part of cost of sales.

Example

	£'000
Turnover (value of work done and rights to consideration earned)	52
Cumulative payments on account	45
Excess – *included in debtors*	7
Total costs on this contract	50
Transferred to cost of sales	40
Balance – *included in stocks*	10
Provision/accrual for foreseeable losses – *included in cost of sales in the profit and loss account. In the balance sheet part reduces stocks and part is included in liabilities*	30
Profit and loss account (extract)	
Turnover	52
Cost of sales (£40,000 + £30,000)	(70)
Loss	(18)
Balance sheet (extract)	
Stocks	
Work in progress	
Net cost less foreseeable losses (£10,000 – £10,000)	–
Debtors	
Amounts recoverable on contracts	7
Liabilities	
Provision/accrual (£30,000 – £10,000 deducted from stocks)	20

20.116 In this example, foreseeable losses exceed the total costs incurred after transfers to cost of sales by £20,000 and the excess should be included in either accruals or provisions, as appropriate.

20.117 SSAP 9 provides no guidance on when these losses should be shown as an accrual and when they should be shown as a provision. The treatment used would appear to depend on the contract's state of completion at the time the financial statements are finalised. A provision is defined in the Act as:

> "*...any amount retained as reasonably necessary for the purpose of providing for any liability the nature of which is clearly defined which is either likely to be incurred, or certain to be incurred but uncertain as to the amount or as to the date on which it will arise.*" [CA85 4 Sch 89].

20.118 The definition of a provision given in the Act implies that there is some argument for disclosing a loss as an accrual if a loss can be quantified with certainty. Losses that cannot be calculated with accuracy at the time of signing the financial statements should be disclosed as a provision, with disclosures made in accordance with company law.

Chapter 21

Provisions, contingencies and commitments

	Page
Introduction	21001
Objective and scope of FRS 12	21001
Provisions against assets	21004
Recognition	21004
Provisions v other liabilities	21006
Provisions v contingent liabilities	21008
Definition of provision	21009
Provision recognition rules	21010
Present obligation	21010
Legal obligations	21010
Constructive obligations	21011
Past event	21011
Legal enforcement	21012
Third party expectation	21013
Future operating costs	21014
Two stage test	21014
Probability of a present obligation	21015
Probable transfer of economic benefits	21017
Groups of similar obligations	21017
No reliable estimate	21017
Future events	21018
Provision becomes a creditor	21018
Changes in provisions	21018
Where does the debit go?	21019
Contingent liabilities and contingent assets	21020
Contingent liabilities	21020
Contingent assets	21021
Reimbursements	21023
Measurement	21024
Best estimate	21025
Estimation techniques	21026
Large population of similar claims	21027
Discounting	21027
Adjusting for inflation	21028
Adjusting for risk	21030
Effects of taxation	21033
Selecting an appropriate discount rate	21033
Unwinding the discount	21034
Measurement of related asset	21034
Changes in estimates	21036

Changes in discount rates . . . 21039
Changes in estimate of provisions . . . 21041
Future events . . . 21042
Future operating losses . . . 21043
Restructuring . . . 21044
Restructuring rules in FRS 12 . . . 21044
Definition . . . 21044
Applying the recognition criteria . . . 21045
Board decision . . . 21046
Third party expectation . . . 21046
Restructuring time-frame . . . 21048
Binding sale agreement . . . 21049
Termination of operations . . . 21050
Post balance sheet events . . . 21051
Costs of restructuring . . . 21051
Redundancy provisions . . . 21054
Compulsory redundancies . . . 21055
Situation 1 — redundancy payments made . . . 21055
Situation 2 — employees informed . . . 21055
Situation 3 — employees identified but not informed . . . 21056
Situation 4 — numbers determined but not specific employees . . . 21056
Voluntary redundancies . . . 21056
Onerous contracts . . . 21057
General rules . . . 21058
Interpretation . . . 21059
Expected economic benefits . . . 21059
Assets dedicated to the contract . . . 21059
Illustrative examples . . . 21060
Long-term purchase contracts . . . 21060
Operating leases on property . . . 21062
Measurement of an onerous contract . . . 21064
Other practical applications . . . 21065
Warranties . . . 21066
Refunds . . . 21068
Major repairs and maintenance . . . 21069
Operating leases . . . 21071
Finance leases . . . 21072
Infrastructure renewals . . . 21072
Lease dilapidations . . . 21073
Operating leasehold improvements . . . 21073
Self-insurance . . . 21074
Environmental liabilities . . . 21076
Waste electrical and electronic equipment . . . 21079
The WEEE Regulations in the UK . . . 21081
Scope . . . 21081
Producer obligations . . . 21083
Distributor obligations . . . 21087
End-user obligations . . . 21087

Summary . . . 21088
Emission obligations . . . 21088
Abandonment and decommissioning costs . . . 21097
Litigation . . . 21099
Regulatory fines, compensation and systems rectification . . . 21101
Financial guarantee contracts . . . 21102
Tariff over-recoveries . . . 21104
Disclosure requirements . . . 21105
Provisions for liabilities . . . 21105
Categorising by class . . . 21105
Tabular information . . . 21106
Narrative information . . . 21107
Unwinding of discount . . . 21107
Further rules included in other regulations . . . 21108
Pensions and similar obligations . . . 21108
Taxation provisions . . . 21108
Acquisition provisions . . . 21109
Contingent liabilities . . . 21109
Contingent assets . . . 21110
Guarantees . . . 21110
Exemptions from disclosure . . . 21111
Commitments . . . 21112
General . . . 21112
Capital commitments . . . 21112
Pension commitments . . . 21113
Other financial commitments . . . 21113

Chapter 21

Provisions, contingencies and commitments

Introduction

21.1 Liabilities are defined in FRS 12, 'Provisions, contingent liabilities and contingent assets', as "*obligations of an entity to transfer economic benefits as a result of past transactions or events*". A provision falls within the category of liabilities and is defined as *"a liability of uncertain timing or amount"*. [FRS 12 para 2]. FRS 12 sets out rules on the recognition, measurement and disclosure of provisions. The standard requires that provisions should be recognised only when an entity has an obligation (legal or constructive) to transfer economic benefits as a result of a past event. It is not possible to provide for future expected losses (unless there is an onerous contract). The standard also sets out rules for contingent liabilities and contingent assets.

21.2 Provisions for liabilities are also encompassed within the law. Schedule 4 to the Companies Act 1985, which stems from the EU's 4th Directive, requires that *"all liabilities which have arisen in respect of the financial year to which the accounts relate or a previous financial year shall be taken into account, including those which only become apparent between the balance sheet date and the date on which it is signed on behalf of the board of directors..."*. [CA85 4 Sch 12(b)]. Provisions for liabilities fall within this requirement and are defined in the Act as: *"...any amount retained as reasonably necessary for the purposes of providing for any liability the nature of which is clearly defined and which is either likely to be incurred, or certain to be incurred but uncertain as to amount or as to the date on which it will arise."* [CA85 4 Sch 89].

Furthermore, the Act requires the movements on provisions to be disclosed and details to be given of each provision included in the balance sheet format item 'other provisions'.

21.3 References throughout this chapter are to the Schedules to the Companies Act 1985. At the time of writing the equivalent Schedules to the Companies Act 2006 have still to be published.

[The next paragraph is 21.20.]

Objective and scope of FRS 12

21.20 FRS 12's objective is to ensure that appropriate recognition criteria and measurement bases are applied to provisions, contingent liabilities and contingent assets and to ensure that sufficient information is disclosed in the notes to the financial statements to enable users to understand their nature, timing and amount. [FRS 12 para 1].

21.21 The standard applies to all financial statements that are intended to give a true and fair view (other than those adopting the FRSSE – see para 21.24), in accounting for provisions, contingent liabilities and contingent assets, except:

- Those arising from executory contracts, except where the contract is onerous. [FRS 12 para 3].
- Those arising in insurance entities from contracts with policy holders. The FRS does, however, apply to other provisions, contingent liabilities and contingent assets of insurance companies. [FRS 12 paras 3, 7].
- Those covered by another FRS or SSAP dealing with more specific provisions, contingent liabilities or contingent assets, such as: long-term contracts (SSAP 9); deferred tax (FRS 19); leases (SSAP 21), with the exception of onerous operating leases; and pension costs (FRS 17). [FRS 12 paras 3, 8].
- Those resulting from financial instruments that are carried at fair value (for entities that are not applying FRS 26, 'Financial instruments: Recognition and measurement'). But the standard does apply to those instruments that are not carried at fair value, that is, that are carried at cost, the most obvious example of which is guarantees given by a company not applying FRS 26 (see further chapter 6). [FRS 12 para 3].

21.21.1 For entities that are applying FRS 26 on financial instruments, FRS 12 does not apply to financial instruments (including guarantees) that are within FRS 26's scope. However, for financial guarantees excluded from FRS 26's scope, FRS 12 applies. [FRS 12 para 5 as amended by FRS 26].

21.21.2 Some amounts treated as provisions may relate to the recognition of revenue. FRS 12 does not address the recognition of revenue and does not, therefore, impact on the requirements of Appendix G to FRS 5. Similarly, FRS 12 does not specify whether expenditures are treated as expenses or assets when a provision is made.

21.22 The list in paragraph 21.21 above of exclusions from FRS 12's scope refers to executory contracts, which are contracts under which neither party has performed any of its obligations or both parties have partially performed their obligations to an equal extent. [FRS 12 paras 6]. Executory contracts encompass commitments to purchase goods or to deliver services where performance has not yet happened. Take-or-pay contracts and throughput contracts are examples of executory contracts. In some situations these types of contracts might be onerous and where they are, the rules in FRS 12 concerning onerous contracts should be applied (see further para 21.195).

21.23 The example below considers whether management should recognise a liability following the placement of an order for goods.

Example

Entity P's management has placed two separate orders for 100 units each of components A and B. Both types of component are specific to entity P's production processes and are not widely used by other entities. The contract's terms are such that once the goods are manufactured, the manufacturer will notify entity P, which must arrange for the goods to be collected from the supplier's premises. Entity P is obliged to accept the goods once it has been notified that the goods have been manufactured, or pay a substantial penalty if entity P's management decide to cancel the contract. A penalty is also payable if the contract is cancelled by entity P if it cancels the contract before the components are manufactured.

At the balance sheet date, the supplier has manufactured all 100 of the units of A. The supplier has notified entity P that the components are ready for collection, but entity P has not yet arranged for collection. None of the units of B have been manufactured.

Entity P's management expects to take delivery of all components of A and B that have been ordered. Should management recognise a liability at the balance sheet date?

A liability for the purchase of component A should be recognised. No liability should be recognised in respect of the purchase of component B.

The parties to an executory contract do not have a present obligation in respect of that contract, unless it is onerous. Consequently, the parties to an executory contract should not recognise a liability in respect of the contract. [FRS 12 para 3].

The supplier has performed all of its obligations under the contract to manufacture 100 units of component A. The contract has, therefore, become non-executory and entity P has a present obligation to arrange for collection and pay for the components or to pay the penalty fee.

The supplier has not yet performed its responsibilities under the contract to manufacture 100 units of component B. Despite entity P's intention to take delivery of the goods, the contract remains an executory contract and entity P is not required to recognise a liability. Entity P's intention to take delivery of the goods does not create a present obligation.

If, however, entity P decided (before completion of the manufacture of component B) not to take delivery of that component, because it was no longer needed and entity P judged it to be more rational economically to pay the penalty fee, entity P's contract to purchase component B would then become onerous and a provision for the penalty fee would be required.

(Note: this example does not consider any implications under FRS 26, 'Financial instruments: Recognition and measurement', of any embedded derivatives. This is dealt with in the section on embedded derivatives in executory contracts in chapter 6.)

21.24 In addition to the above exemptions, small companies need only comply with the requirements of the Financial Reporting Standard for Smaller Entities (FRSSE). The FRSSE deals specifically with provisions, contingent liabilities and contingent assets. This guidance is based on the principles set out in FRS 12. For further discussion in this area, see chapter 32.

Provisions against assets

21.25 The word 'provision' is often used to describe amounts that are deducted from assets to arrive at their balance sheet carrying amount. For example, provisions are made for depreciation or amortisation or impairment of assets and provisions are made for bad and doubtful debts. These types of provisions do not fall within FRS 12's scope, because they relate to the measurement of assets and are merely adjustments made to arrive at the asset's appropriate carrying value.

Example

Entity A has some long outstanding receivables and management has determined that some of them are impaired.

In addition, the fall in demand for entity A's products has caused a decline in the utilisation of one of its factories. Management has estimated that the recoverable amount of the factory is below the carrying amount.

Are provisions for impairment of financial and non-financial assets within FRS 12's scope?

The impairment loss on the receivables is not a provision in accordance with FRS 12; it should be presented as a reduction of the financial asset either directly or through the use of an allowance account. [FRS 26 para 63].

Property, plant and equipment should be presented net of the impairment charge, in accordance with FRS 11. An impairment charge is not a probable outflow of economic resources, but a reduction in the cash flows expected from the asset. An impairment charge is not within FRS 12's scope. [FRS 12 para 9].

Recognition

21.26 FRS 12 prohibits provisions from being made in respect of expenses and losses that are likely to arise in the future, but in respect of which no obligation exists at the balance sheet date. Consequently, the rules in FRS 12 have a significant impact on companies:

- Undertaking major restructuring programmes (see para 21.148 onwards).
- In the extractive and nuclear industries, with regard to how they account for decommissioning (see para 21.250 onwards).
- In the water industry, concerning how they account for infrastructure asset maintenance programmes (see para 21.240 onwards).
- In regulated industries with pricing controls (see para 21.275 onwards).
- That have captive insurance subsidiary companies (see para 21.238 onwards).
- That have environmental obligations (see para 21.245 onwards).

- That have outstanding litigation (see para 21.258 onwards), particularly where off-setting insurance cover exists (see para 21.104 onwards).
- That have onerous contracts (see para 21.193 onwards).

21.27 The definition of a liability was first established in FRS 5 and is reiterated in FRS 12. The definition refers to *"obligations of an entity to transfer economic benefits as a result of past transactions or events"*. [FRS 12 para 2]. The rules in FRS 12 concerning provisions hinge on this definition. Basically, there is only one rule that determines when it is necessary to make a provision for an obligation. In other circumstances, generally a contingent liability has to be disclosed unless it is remote. The rules are summarised below.

Provision necessary

- There is a *present obligation* as a result of a past event that *probably* requires a transfer of economic benefits.

Contingent liability should be disclosed

- There is a *present obligation* as a result of a past event:
  - That *probably* requires a transfer of economic benefits, but the obligation *cannot be measured* reliably.
  - That *may, but will probably not*, require a transfer of economic benefits.
- There is a *possible obligation* that will *probably not* require a transfer of economic benefits.

Contingent liability exists but no disclosure required

- There is either a *possible obligation* or a *present obligation, but* the *likelihood* of a transfer of economic benefits is *remote*.

21.28 These possibilities are illustrated in the standard by the use of a flow chart, which is reproduced below.

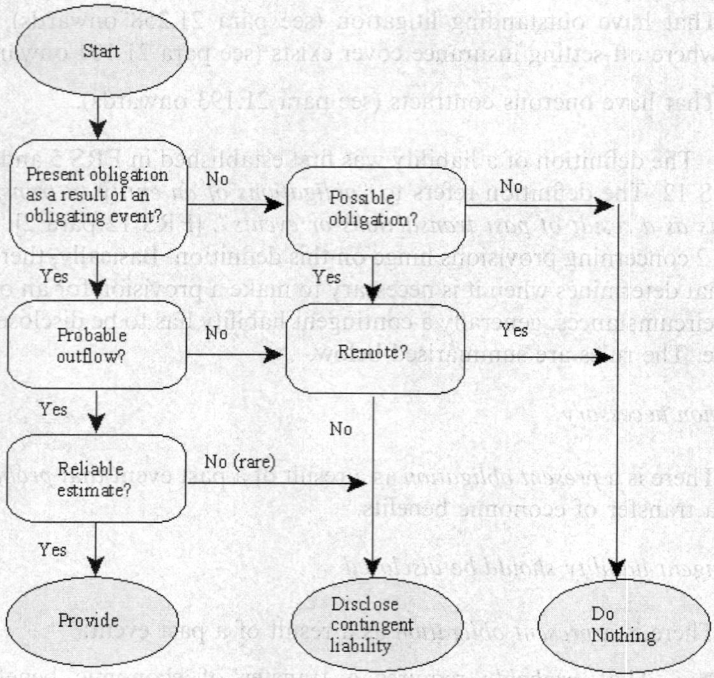

21.29 Creditors, provisions, disclosed contingencies and remote contingencies lie on a spectrum and an obligation might move between all four categories during its existence. At one extreme where an obligation arising is *remote*, no disclosure is required in the financial statements. When the obligation becomes less remote, it might require disclosure as a contingent liability, until it becomes *probable* when it would be required to be recognised and provided for in the financial statements. When the liability becomes *certain* it would move away from being treated as a provision and become a creditor (see further para 21.80).

21.30 The standard makes it clear that a provision may only be used for the purpose for which the original provision was intended. [FRS 12 para 64]. It is not acceptable to set up a provision for, say, committed restructuring costs and then to set other expenses not related to the restructuring (for example, the costs of resurfacing the company's car park) against the provision. The correct treatment where part of the provision is surplus is to release the provision as unused with appropriate disclosure (see para 21.293). Then costs incurred that have nothing to do with the reason for which the provision was made would be taken to the profit and loss account in the normal way.

Provisions v other liabilities

21.31 A provision is simply defined as *"a liability of uncertain timing or amount"*. [FRS 12 para 2]. Consequently, like other liabilities, for a provision to be necessary a company must have an obligation to transfer economic benefits that results from a past transaction or event.

21.32 The standard clearly makes a distinction between provisions and other categories of liabilities and sets detailed measurement and recognition rules that apply to particular types of provisions only, although the basic definition of a liability applies to other categories of creditors as well as to provisions. The only difference between other liabilities and provisions is the degree of uncertainty about the amount of the payment or the timing of the payment. Hence, there is a clear distinction between provisions and other liabilities such as trade creditors and accruals.

21.33 Trade creditors form a separate item in the balance sheet formats in Schedule 4 to the Act and this item should only include liabilities to pay for goods or services that have been received or supplied and that have been invoiced or formally agreed with the supplier. [FRS 12 para 11(a)]. Amounts arising from a contract are formally agreed. So, for example, an operating lease obligation would be a trade creditor. Similarly, a contract to purchase a certain amount of a commodity per month would constitute a creditor at the month end even though an invoice might not have been raised.

21.34 Also, a distinction has to be made between accruals and provisions. There are two format positions for accruals (coupled together with deferred income) in the balance sheet formats specified in the Companies Act. 'Accruals and deferred income' may either be shown as a separate item within 'creditors', split between amounts falling due within one year and amounts falling due after more than one year, or as a separate line item after 'provisions for liabilities'.

21.35 Whereas there is little if any uncertainty relating to the amount of a creditor or the timing of when it becomes due, there is some uncertainty with an accrual, which primarily arises because an invoice has not yet been received at the balance sheet date. But typically, a very good estimate can be made of the amount due at the period end and the timing of the payment is often certain (to within a short period of time). So accruals are a category of liability to pay for goods or services that have been received or supplied where they have yet to be paid for and no invoice has been received or formally agreed with the supplier. [FRS 12 para 11(b)].

21.35.1 A familiar example is the supply of electricity. At the period end the entity can make a very good estimate, or can measure the quantity, of electricity consumed within the business that has not been paid for and either by using current rates or previous bills can calculate the amount that is likely to be due. The amount of the liability is almost certain if the estimate is reliable and the timing of the payment is known to within a few days. Although an accrual is estimated and the timing of the payment is not known exactly, the degree of uncertainty is much less than that associated with a provision.

21.36 Common examples of accruals include goods and services supplied by utility companies such as electricity, water and gas. Rates also fall into this category, but rent should be classified as a creditor, because the obligation arises under a contract and is formally agreed. Amounts due to employees relating to holiday pay should be accounted for as an accrual. For example, a company with a factory that closes for three weeks in the summer would accrue three weeks pay per worker over the year until the summer holiday.

21.37 The following table further identifies the types of liabilities that are usually presented as provisions and those that are presented as other liabilities.

Nature of the obligation	Provision	Other liabilities	Comments
Warranties given for goods or services sold (see para 21.225)	✓		
Refunds given for goods sold (see para 21.228)	✓		
Payments for damages connected with legal cases that are probable (see para 21.258 onwards)	✓		
Dilapidations payable at the end of an operating lease (see para 21.234)	✓		
Interest payments		✓	Accrual – the service has been received and the timing and amount of payment is known.
Holiday pay earned by employees		✓	Accrual – see para 21.36.
Property rentals		✓	Accrual – the service has been received and the timing and amount of payment is known.
Ordinary dividend declared and appropriately authorised before the period end		✓	Recognise as a current financial liability.

Provisions v contingent liabilities

21.38 FRS 12 makes the point that in a general sense, all provisions are contingent because they are uncertain in timing or amount. However, the standard uses the term 'contingent' for liabilities and assets that are not recognised because their existence will be confirmed only by the occurrence or non-occurrence of one or more uncertain future events not wholly within the entity's control (see para 21.92). In addition, the term 'contingent liability' is used for liabilities that do not meet the recognition criteria in the standard. [FRS 12 para 12].

21.39 Contingent liabilities, as defined in FRS 12, are not provided for, but must be disclosed in the notes to the financial statements unless they are remote, in which case, they are not disclosed at all. Contingent liabilities and contingent assets are considered further from paragraph 21.91.

Definition of provision

21.40 A provision is very simply defined in FRS 12 as *"a liability of uncertain timing or amount"*. [FRS 12 para 2]. Provisions for liabilities are also defined in Schedule 4 to the Companies Act 1985 as: *"Any amount retained as reasonably necessary for the purposes of providing for any liability the nature of which is clearly defined and which is either likely to be incurred, or certain to be incurred but uncertain as to amount or as to the date on which it will arise."* [CA85 4 Sch 89].

21.41 The ASB makes the comment in appendix V of the standard that although the Act and FRS 12 define provisions in different terms, it believes that, when taken in their respective contexts, the standard is consistent with the requirements of Schedule 4. It goes on to say that the reference to *"...any amount retained as reasonable necessary for the purposes..."* recognises that the appropriate amount for which provision should be made is often a matter of judgement.

21.42 Paragraph 12(b) of Schedule 4 also states the general requirement that: *"all liabilities which have arisen or are likely to arise in respect of the financial year to which the accounts relate or a previous financial year shall be taken into account, including those which only become apparent between the balance sheet date and the date on which it is signed on behalf of the board of directors in pursuance of section 233 of this Act."*

It is curious that the quotation of this requirement of Schedule 4 included within appendix V of FRS 12 stops after the words *"shall be taken into account"*. But the ASB does recognise in paragraph 16 of FRS 12 that in establishing whether or not a past event has occurred (see para 21.54) the evidence considered should include any additional evidence provided by events occurring after the balance sheet date. [FRS 12 para 16]. In addition, the standard includes specific rules regarding how events occurring after the balance sheet date should affect restructuring provisions (see further from para 21.148).

21.43 As explained in the introduction (see para 21.1), a provision falls within the definition of a liability with the added feature that there is uncertainty over the amount to be paid or the timing of the payment. Liabilities are *"obligations of an entity to transfer economic benefits as a result of past transactions or events"*. [FRS 12 para 2].

21.44 It is clear from the definition of a liability given above, that it does not generally include expected future operating losses. Obviously, the reason future operating losses do not meet the definition of a liability is that they do not stem from a past event (see further para 21.54).

21.45 Where a company is expected to incur future operating losses, rather than indicating that a provision should be made, this might suggest that an impairment review should be carried out on the appropriate income generating unit (IGU) in accordance with the rules in FRS 11, 'Impairment of fixed assets and goodwill', or, where applicable, with the rules in other standards, for example, FRS 26, 'Financial instruments: Recognition and measurement'. Such a review could then expose whether those assets have suffered an impairment and need to be written down.

21.46 Alternatively, expected future trading losses might indicate that a company has an onerous contract. In certain circumstances it is necessary to provide for the onerous element of a contract and the standard's rules in this area are considered from paragraph 21.193. Furthermore, FRS 3, 'Reporting financial performance', requires provision for future operating losses on termination of operations and this is considered from paragraph 21.171.

Provision recognition rules

21.47 Following from these definitions, the standard requires that a provision should only be recognised where the following conditions are met:

- An entity has a present obligation (legal or constructive) as a result of a past event.
- It is probable that a transfer of economic benefits will be required to settle the obligation.
- A reliable estimate can be made of the amount of the obligation.

[FRS 12 para 14].

21.48 In order to comprehend the recognition criteria outlined above, it is first necessary to understand the meaning of the terms 'present obligation' and 'past event'.

Present obligation

21.49 A present obligation can stem from a legal agreement (a 'legal obligation') or may be constructive in nature (a 'constructive obligation').

Legal obligations

21.50 Whether or not a legal obligation exists will usually be relatively easy to establish in practice as it derives either from a contract (through its explicit or implicit terms), or from legislation, or from the operation of the law. [FRS 12 para 2].

21.50.1 A legal obligation can arise, for example, where an entity operates an oilfield in the north sea and its licensing agreement requires that the oil rig it constructs is removed and the seabed is restored at the end of the licence period. The licence forms the contract under which the obligation arises. An obligation can also arise where the Government passes a new Act of Parliament which requires, for example, certain environmental damage which has already been caused to be rectified. But it is important to realise that in such a circumstance the obligation will only arise once the law becomes operative or is virtually certain that it will become law (see further from para 21.57 below).

21.51 Manufacturers' standard warranties given at the time a sale is made are also examples of legal obligations even where the defect arises a number of years later (if the warranty is still effective), as they arise from the contract entered into with the customer at the time the original sale was made. The accounting for warranties is dealt with in more detail in paragraph 21.225 onwards. Obligations arising from onerous contracts (see from para 21.193) are also examples of legal obligations, because they arise from a contractual burden.

Constructive obligations

21.52 A constructive obligation will often be more difficult to discern in practice than a legal obligation as it derives from an entity's actions:

"(a) by an established pattern of past practice, published policies or a sufficiently specific current statement, the entity has indicated to other parties that it will accept certain responsibilities; and

(b) as a result, the entity has created a valid expectation on the part of those other parties that it will discharge those responsibilities."

[FRS 12 para 2].

21.53 Some constructive obligations will be obvious, for example, many retailers have policies of giving cash refunds to dissatisfied customers whether or not the goods they bought are faulty. Such a policy is clearly over and above any legal obligation, but a constructive obligation arises from the retailer's established or published practice. Ad hoc refunds would not be covered. In some circumstances, for example where a company has published its environmental policies, this might also give rise to a constructive obligation, where no legal obligation exists, as there is no law compelling the company to carry out the environmental rectification. Clearly, the essence of a constructive obligation is the entity's commitment to a third party. That commitment arises through the entity's actions, that is, by establishing a pattern of practice or by publishing its policies or by making a statement setting out in detail its intended future actions.

Past event

21.54 In order for there to be a liability and a need to make a provision, it is necessary for something to have happened in the past (a 'past event') to trigger a present obligation. The past event is known in FRS 12 as the 'obligation event'. An 'obligating event' is *"an event that creates a legal or constructive obligation that results in an entity having no realistic alternative to settling that obligation"*. [FRS 12 para 2]. Many obligating events are obvious, for example, the obligating event giving rise to the need to make a warranty provision is the original sale of the warrantied goods. Similarly, with the contamination of land, the obligating event is the original contamination. Some obligating events can occur over a period of time. For example, where an oil rig is built in the north sea to extract oil and gas, an obligating event might arise when the oil rig is first built, which relates to its eventual removal. But other obligating events might arise over time as the oil and gas are extracted if there is a need subsequently to make good any damage caused by that extraction.

21.55 Another example where past events giving rise to obligating events might arise over a period of time is open cast mining. Here, the environmental damage is done as the top soil is removed and coal is dug out. Hence, the obligating event occurs as the damage is caused and provision should be made as the damage is caused for the necessary rectification work that will need to be undertaken in the future to restore the site to its pre-agreed condition.

21.56 The notion of 'no realistic alternative' is at the heart of the definition of an obligating event. It means that if there is a realistic possibility that the entity can avoid settlement, no obligation arises. An entity has no realistic alternative to settling an obligation only where:

- The settlement of the obligation can be enforced by law.
- The event, in the case of a constructive obligation, creates a valid expectation in others that the entity will discharge the obligation.

[FRS 12 para 17].

Legal enforcement

21.57 The first of the bullet points above should be relatively straightforward to put into practice. However, even with legal enforcement problems can arise where, for example, legislation is in the pipeline, but not yet on the statute book or where the law has been passed, but the enforcement date has not yet been reached. For example, with an environmental issue, if there is no current law to require clean-up, but it is virtually certain that one will be passed shortly after the year end, there will be a present obligation which results from a past event (because the law enforcement is virtually certain and the contamination has already taken place). Such an obligation is treated as a legal obligation, because the legislation is virtually certain to be enacted as drafted. [FRS 12 para 22]. On the other hand, where the environmental legislation is still in its infancy (for example, where only a preliminary paper has been issued) no obligation exists, because although the potentially obligating event has taken place (that is the contamination of the land) there is as yet no obligation that can be enforced by law.

21.58 In contrast, an entity might need to operate in a particular way in the future, because of commercial pressure or legal requirements. [FRS 12 para 19]. For example, legislation might exist which requires an entity to fit smoke filters to its chimneys. This requirement, although legal in nature, relates to the entity's future operations. For instance, if legislation exists but the enforcement date has not yet been reached, no obligation arises to fit the smoke filters. Once the enforcement date has been reached, still no obligation arises to fit the filters, but an obligation might arise for any fines for non-compliance with the legislation.

21.59 It is clear from the examples above, that although initially there might be a potentially obligating event a provision is not made, because there is no legal or constructive obligation. But over time the legal position could change and what was originally a potential obligation (see further para 21.91) might become an actual obligation for which provision is required.

21.60 Because of the different legal jurisdictions in which a company might trade, it is very difficult to set specific rules to identify when enactment of a law might be virtually certain. This will be a matter of judgement after considering the legal due process in each particular country. The standard comments that in many cases it will be impossible to be virtually certain of the enactment of a law until it is actually enacted. [FRS 12 para 22].

Third party expectation

21.61 In practice, companies may have more difficulty in determining exactly when a constructive obligation arises from which they cannot realistically withdraw. Here the expectation of other parties is the key. For example, a company's board might have taken a decision to undertake a major restructuring programme, but until its plans are actually being carried out or they have been communicated to others to the extent that the company cannot realistically withdraw from its course of action (that is, when it has no realistic alternative but to carry it through) no obligation exists and no provision for restructuring can be made.

21.62 Although the expectation of other parties is critical, the standard comments that it is not necessary to know the other party's identity for an obligation to arise. [FRS 12 para 20]. This is clearly the case with warranted goods, as a company cannot possibly know which of its customers will claim under a standard warranty, but an obligation still arises from a general commitment to those who buy the product. Similarly, with a restructuring programme, there needs to be a valid expectation created in those affected by it in a *"sufficiently specific manner"* that the company has no alternative but to discharge its responsibilities. [FRS 12 para 20]. Consequently, it is no longer acceptable under FRS 12 to make a provision for restructuring where the company's board has merely decided on such a course of action before its year end, but its plan is not actioned until the new year. Restructuring programmes are specifically dealt with in FRS 12 and are considered in more detail from paragraph 21.148.

21.63 Where a potentially obligating event has taken place (such as environmental damage), but where no legal obligation exists, a constructive obligation could subsequently arise, for example, where the company changes its policy and makes a public statement that in future it will rectify such damage. Again it is necessary that the public announcement carries such weight that it leaves the company no alternative but to carry out the rectification work.

21.64 In practice there will often be situations where it appears that a constructive obligation exists, but because it can be avoided, no obligating event has occurred. For example in the airline industry, the licensing authorities require aircraft to undergo major engine overhauls at regular intervals (say every five years). Without the overhaul, the aircraft cannot renew its licence and continue to fly. Following the rules outlined above, it is not possible to provide for these costs, because no obligating event arises prior to the overhaul taking place. This is because the airline operator can avoid the costs by, for example, selling the aircraft. The proper accounting treatment is either to charge the maintenance as incurred or to identify the cost of the element of the aircraft which will wear out over the five-year period and depreciate this to the profit and loss account. Then when the overhaul takes place, the relevant replacement costs can be capitalised to replace the fully-depreciated original cost, the new cost again being depreciated over the period to the next overhaul (see further para 21.230). Accounting for overhaul costs is dealt with in chapter 16.

Future operating costs

21.65 Because of the fundamental requirement that there must be a past event that gives rise to an obligation before a provision can be made for that liability, it is clear that it is not acceptable under FRS 12 to make provision for costs that will be incurred in order to operate in the future, if those costs could be avoided by the entity's future actions. [FRS 12 para 18].

21.66 This rule would, in principle, seem also to preclude companies from making provisions for restructuring, but the standard has special rules that allow provision to made in specific circumstances as explained from paragraph 21.148.

[The next paragraph is 21.69.]

Two stage test

21.69 As explained in paragraph 21.47 above, before a provision can be recognised, an entity must have a present obligation that arises from a past event and it must be probable that a transfer of economic benefits will take place. Therefore, not only must it be probable that there is a present obligation, but it must also be probable that it will result in the transfer of economic benefits. These two issues are considered in the paragraphs that follow.

Probability of a present obligation

21.70 The standard points out that in rare circumstances where there has been a past event it may not be clear whether there is a *present obligation*. In these situations, a past event is deemed by FRS 12 to give rise to a present obligation if, after taking account of all the available evidence, it is more likely than not that a present obligation exists at the balance sheet date. [FRS 12 para 15].

21.71 The issue here is not to determine whether the *transfer of economic benefits* is probable (which is considered in para 21.74 below), but whether the *past event* gives rise to a *present obligation*. The principal difficulty in this area concerns litigation. Often in a legal case the events might be disputed by the parties. Because of the uncertainty concerning the past event it will be unclear whether or not a present obligation exists. In this type of situation it may be necessary for a company to obtain an expert's opinion in order to determine, after taking into account all the available evidence, whether or not a present obligation arises for which provision is required. The standard requires that on the basis of such information:

- Where it is more likely than not that a present obligation exists at that balance sheet date, the entity should recognise a provision (if the recognition criteria are met).
- Where it is more likely that no present obligation exists at the balance sheet date, the entity should disclose a contingent liability, unless the possibility of a transfer of economic resources is remote, in which case no disclosure is required (see further para 21.91).

[FRS 12 para 16].

21.71.1 An example where there is uncertainty over whether a past event gives rise to a present obligation, is illustrated in the following example.

Example

Entity A has received notice from the governmental environment agency that official investigations will be made into claims of pollution caused by the entity. Neighbours living near entity A's factory claim that its operations have caused ground water contamination. The investigation will only consider whether entity A has caused contamination and, if so, what penalties and fines should be levied on it.

Manufacturing operations have been conducted at the site for 150 years; however, entity A acquired the factory only 50 years ago. Entity A has used toxins at the plant, but only to an extent that is unlikely to cause pollution, according to available records.

However, management is not sure whether it has all the information about the entire 50 years. Therefore, neither management nor external experts are able to assess entity A's responsibility until the investigation is completed.

How should management account for a liability where it is not possible to reliably assess whether a present obligation exists?

FRS 12, paragraph 15, recognises that, in rare cases, it is not clear whether there is a present obligation. In these cases, a past event is deemed to give rise to a present obligation if, taking account of all available evidence, it is more likely than not that a present obligation exists at the balance sheet date. In this case, there is a limitation on the available evidence and management considers all the available evidence in assessing whether or not a present obligation exists. The available evidence does not support a conclusion that a present obligation exists. Therefore, management should disclose the contingent liability for potential penalties and fines that may be imposed if past contamination is proved, but should not recognise a liability for this at the balance sheet date.

The obligating event would be the contamination in the past by entity A, not the future investigation. However, management cannot determine whether the obligating event has occurred until the investigation is complete. In accordance with FRS 21, any new evidence as to the existence of the obligating event, that becomes available after the balance sheet date up to the date of approval of the financial statements, is an adjusting event in assessing whether a present obligation existed at the balance sheet date.

If and to the extent that the entity is obligated at the balance sheet date to meet any costs of the investigation, irrespective of the outcome of the investigation, the entity recognises a liability for such costs at the balance sheet date.

21.72 This requirement introduces probability into assessing whether or not a liability exists. Although not used extensively in UK GAAP, the term 'probable' is used extensively in IFRS. There, probable is often taken to mean that the chance of occurrence is 'likely'. In some countries this has been taken to mean anything more than 50 per cent and in other countries a considerably higher level, in say the 70-80 per cent range. 'More likely than not' would seem to suggest more than 50 per cent. In fact paragraph 23 of FRS 12 confirms this as it says (in considering the term 'probable' as it applies to a transfer of economic benefits) that 'more likely than not' means that the "*...probability that the event will occur is greater than the probability that it will not*".

21.73 Further information might become available between the balance sheet date and the date on which a company's financial statements are finalised. Where this is so, that information should be taken into account in determining whether or not a present obligation exists at the balance sheet date. [FRS 12 para 16]. This also accords with the Companies Act 1985, which requires *"all liabilities which have arisen in respect of the financial year... shall be taken into account, including those which only become apparent between the balance sheet date and the date on which it is signed on behalf of the board..."*. [CA85 4 Sch 12(b)]. For example, in a legal case evidence might come to light after the balance sheet date, which clearly indicates that a past event giving rise to an obligation arose before the balance sheet date. This does not mean to say, however, that a provision can be made at the year end where the obligating event occurs after the balance sheet date (see further para 21.112).

21.73.1 Another instance where post balance sheet evidence is taken into account in determining whether a provision should be recognised is where a company self insures some of its risks. At the balance sheet date provision will be made for claims that have been incurred but are not yet reported (that is, IBNR claims – see further para 21.238). During the period between the company's balance sheet date and the date on which its financial statements are finalised, a number of IBNRs might have surfaced, in which case a firmer estimate for these claims can be made. Of course it will still be necessary to estimate those that have not yet been reported but that are likely to be, where these arise from events that occurred before the balance sheet date and, hence, qualify for provision.

Probable transfer of economic benefits

21.74 Once it has been established that a present obligation exists (that is, it is at least more likely than not to exist) it is then necessary to determine whether this will result in the transfer of economic benefits to settle the obligation. This judgement is similarly determined on the probability of the outcome. The standard says that also in this case *"a transfer of economic benefits or other event is regarded as probable if the event is more likely than not to occur..."* [FRS 12 para 23]. The same thresholds as discussed in paragraph 21.72 apply in this analysis, that is 'more likely than not' means a probability of more than 50 per cent that the transfer will occur. Where the probability of the transfer of economic benefits is below 50 per cent, no provision is necessary, but a contingent liability will exist, which will require to be noted in the financial statements unless the contingency is remote.

21.75 With litigation, not only will there be a need to assess whether or not the evidence supports the fact that a past event has occurred (that is, that there is a case to answer), but there will also be a need to consider whether or not it is probable that a transfer of economic benefits will result from the obligation. Again, it might be necessary to seek the advice of an expert in determining the monetary amount that might have to be settled and for which provision should be made.

Groups of similar obligations

21.76 In applying these rules in practice, it will be necessary to consider obligations arising from a group of similar transactions together. For example, with a warranted product, the chances of a particular customer making a claim resulting in a transfer of economic benefits might be very small (that is, not probable). Here, FRS 12 says that the probability that a transfer of economic benefits will be required in settlement should be determined by considering the class of obligations as a whole. [FRS 12 para 24]. A provision would hence be made for the best estimate (see further para 21.110) of the costs of rectifying the goods sold under warranty.

No reliable estimate

21.77 In extremely rare cases, there will be situations where it will not be possible for even an expert to make a reliable estimate of the obligation such that a provision can be made. In this type of circumstance, because of the uncertainty in the measurement of the obligation, only a contingent liability should be disclosed. [FRS 12 para 26]. (See further the disclosure requirements concerning contingent liabilities from para 21.306.)

21.78 The standard emphasises that, in nearly all cases, an entity will be able to determine a range of possible outcomes and will generally be competent to make an estimate of an obligation that will be sufficiently reliable to use in recognising a provision. [FRS 12 para 25]. The standard does not, however, elaborate further the type of situation where a provision would not be made. Clearly, for those provisions where the amount is uncertain (as opposed to the timing being uncertain) it will always be necessary to make a judgement on the amount that needs to be provided. In many situations this judgement should be relatively easy to reach by using a variety of estimation techniques (see further para 21.117).

Future events

21.79 As explained above, it is not acceptable to provide for obligations that arise after the balance sheet date. It is, therefore, only possible to use hindsight to provide additional evidence that a liability existed at the balance sheet date or to establish the amount for which provision should be made. The use of hindsight in measuring a provision is considered from paragraph 21.112 below.

Provision becomes a creditor

21.80 It is clear from the definition of a provision that it differs from other liabilities, because of the degree of uncertainty surrounding the amount of the settlement or the uncertainty of the timing of that settlement. Once the outcome becomes certain, then the provision will become a normal creditor. For example, with litigation, the uncertainty remains until a judgement is made and accepted (that is, it is not subject to appeal). Once the uncertainty is removed, the provision should be reclassified as a creditor and disclosed as payable under one year or over one year as appropriate until it is paid. A transfer would have to be made out of the specific provision in order to reclassify the item as a creditor (see further FRS 12's disclosure requirements as discussed from para 21.288).

Changes in provisions

21.81 Once a provision has been established, it should be reviewed at each subsequent year end and adjusted if necessary to reflect the current best estimate. [FRS 12 para 62]. Changes in the estimate will result from changes to the discount rate used and different assumptions made concerning the outcome of the obligation which result in a new estimate of the outcome. The measurement implications of changes in estimates are considered from paragraph 21.135 and those relating to changes in discount rates are dealt with from paragraph 21.139.

21.82 Where a provision has been set up in the past, the circumstances of the obligation might change from one year to the next. Where, for example, in a subsequent year it becomes no longer probable that a transfer of economic benefits will arise, the provision should be reversed. [FRS 12 para 62].

21.82.1 A provision should only be used for the expenditures for which it was originally set up and should be reversed when it is no longer required (see also para 21.30). [FRS 12 para 64]. Where the original provision was charged as an expense, any subsequent reversal should be credited to the same line in the profit and loss account in accordance with the principle of consistency. [FRS 18 para 39]. Changes in provisions that were originally recognised as part of the cost of an asset are dealt with in paragraph 21.135. The reversal of a provision is illustrated in the example below.

Example

During 20X1, 15 customers of a food manufacturer suffered from severe food poisoning, allegedly from products the entity sold. Management withdrew the product from supermarket shelves as a precaution. During the year a legal action was brought against the entity. At 31 December 20X1, the entity's lawyers advised management that it was more likely than not to lose the court case. Management recognised a provision for damages in the 31 December 20X1 balance sheet.

At 31 December 20X2, the entity's lawyers advised management that the chances of losing the court case were now negligible as a result of a decision made in a similar case. Lawyers now believe that it is no longer probable that the entity will be found liable. Management has questioned how this change in the assessment of the legal action should be reflected in the financial statements.

Management should reverse the provision and recognise the reversal in the profit and loss account within the same line item in which the original expenditure was charged.

Management should disclose the litigation as a contingent liability, unless the possibility of an outflow of economic benefits is regarded as remote. Management should explain the reasons for the change in the assessment of the legal action and disclose the amount of the reversal.

Where does the debit go?

21.83 The recognition rules considered so far in this chapter all relate to determining whether or not an entity can recognise a provision. What has not been considered in any great detail is what happens to the other side of the double entry. It cannot be assumed that the debit should be charged to the profit and loss account, although this may often be the case. Recognition of a provision could equally be related to an inflow of future economic benefits, which might justify recording an asset as part of the double entry.

21.84 The standard requires that when a provision or a change in a provision is recognised, an asset should also be recognised when (but only when) the obligation incurred gives access to future economic benefits. [FRS 12 para 66]. Where this is not so, the provision should be charged immediately to the profit and loss account.

21.85 For example, if a company builds a nuclear reactor, turning it on gives rise to a decommissioning obligation. The best estimate of the present value of the decommissioning cost should be provided for when the reactor is turned on and a matching asset should be capitalised. The company would recover the cost of the facility and the decommissioning cost over the life of the facility, both aspects of the asset being depreciated over that life.

21.86 The standard gives as an example an obligation for decommissioning costs incurred by commissioning an oil rig. Here, the commissioning of the rig gives access to oil reserves over the years of the oil rig's operation. Therefore, a further element of the cost of the asset — representing the decommissioning cost, which is supported by future access to oil reserves, is recognised at the same time as the provision for decommissioning. [FRS 12 para 67]. The issues stemming from this requirement are considered further from paragraph 21.250.

[The next paragraph is 21.91.]

Contingent liabilities and contingent assets

21.91 Under FRS 12, contingent liabilities are never provided for, but are disclosed, unless they are remote. Contingent assets are only disclosed in the notes to the financial statements where an inflow of economic benefits is probable and are similarly never recognised in the financial statements.

Contingent liabilities

21.92 A contingent liability should not be recognised, but should be disclosed, unless the possibility of a transfer of economic benefits is remote. [FRS 12 paras 27, 28]. Contingent liabilities are not specifically defined in the Companies Act 1985, although the Act does require certain disclosures to be made where a contingent liability exists at the balance sheet date for which provision has not been made in the financial statements. But there is a definition in FRS 12, which states that a contingent liability is:

"(a) *A possible obligation that arises from past events and whose existence will be confirmed only by the occurrence of one or more uncertain future events not wholly within the entity's control; or*

(b) *a present obligation that arises from past events but is not recognised because:*

(i) *it is not probable that a transfer of economic benefits will be required to settle the obligation; or*

(ii) *the amount of the obligation cannot be measured with sufficient reliability."*

[FRS 12 para 2].

21.93 As explained in paragraph 21.27 above and following directly from the definition, contingent liabilities can arise in the following three situations where there is a:

- *Present obligation* as a result of a past event:
  - That *probably* requires a transfer of economic benefits, but where the obligation *cannot be measured* reliably.
  - That *may, but will probably not*, require a transfer of economic benefits.
- *Possible obligation* that will *probably not* require a transfer of economic benefits.

21.94 This contrasts with the need to make a provision, which is only required where a *present obligation* exists that will *probably* require a transfer of economic benefits. On the other hand where the likelihood of a transfer of economic benefits is remote, it is not necessary to refer to the contingency in the financial statements, even where there is no uncertainty over whether or not it exists.

21.95 In certain situations, an entity is jointly and severally liable for an obligation. Joint and several obligations often arise in joint venture arrangements where two or more parties cooperate to build, develop or exploit a particular product. They may also arise in groups of companies where, for example, the group's parent guarantees bank overdrafts or other loans of its subsidiaries. Where joint and several obligations arise, the part of the obligation that is expected to be met by other parties is required by FRS 12 to be treated as a contingent liability. [FRS 12 para 29]. How to account for the part of the obligation that the entity is obligated to in its own right will depend on the normal rules as outlined above. The entity would recognise a provision for any part of the obligation for which a transfer of economic benefits is probable. If a transfer of economic benefits is not probable, a contingent liability is disclosed, unless the likelihood of this arising is remote.

21.96 It is not acceptable to net related contingent assets against contingent liabilities when they are disclosed; they should be shown gross and also before taking into account the effects of taxation.

Contingent assets

21.97 Under FRS 12, contingent assets are not recognised – just as contingent liabilities are not recognised. Contingent assets are required to be disclosed by FRS 12, but only where an inflow of economic benefits is probable. [FRS 12 para 34]. This can be contrasted with the standard's requirement for contingent liabilities as set out above, under which disclosure is given, unless an outflow of economic benefits is remote.

21.98 Contingent assets generally only arise from unplanned or other unexpected events that give rise to the possibility of an inflow of economic benefits to the entity. Contingent assets are, consequently, defined in the standard in the following terms: *"A possible asset that arises from past events and whose existence will be confirmed only by the occurrence of one or more uncertain future events not wholly within the entity's control."* [FRS 12 para 2].

21.98.1 If the existence of a possible asset is not (or is no longer) subject to confirmation by an uncertain future event not wholly within the entity's control, the related asset is not (or is no longer) a contingent asset. It is recognised if there is sufficient evidence of the item's existence (including, where appropriate, evidence that a future inflow of benefit will occur) and the item can be measured with sufficient reliability. [FRS 5 para 20]. If it is not probable that there will be an inflow of economic benefit or it cannot be reliably measured, it is an unrecognised asset, but does not fall within the definition of a contingent asset. This can be contrasted with the definition of a contingent liability, as set out in paragraph 21.92 above, under which, even if there is a present obligation whose existence does not depend on an uncertain future event, the item falls within the definition of a contingent liability if it is not probable that there will be an outflow or if the item cannot be reliably measured.

21.99 The reason for not recognising a contingent asset is that only profits that are realised can be recognised in the profit and loss account. And so it would be wrong to recognise a contingent asset where it is only probable that it exists dependent on the occurrence of an uncertain future event. However, the standard notes that when it becomes virtually certain that an inflow of economic benefits will arise, the asset and the related profit should be recognised in the financial statements in the period in which the change occurs (that is, when the future event occurs and confirms the existence of the asset or, if earlier, when it becomes virtually certain that the future event will confirm the existence of the asset and it is virtually certain the asset will be realised). [FRS 12 para 35].

21.100 Therefore, the spectrum that exists for contingent assets is as follows:

- An inflow of economic benefits is not probable — do not mention in the financial statements.
- An inflow of economic benefits is probable — disclose as a contingent asset (see further para 21.308).
- An inflow of economic benefits is virtually certain — recognise an asset and the related profit in the financial statements.

21.101 Like contingent liabilities, contingent assets may move through this spectrum during their existence. For example, where an entity is pursuing a legal claim against another party through the courts, at the outset of the legal process the probability of winning the case or the other side settling out of court might be slim. In this circumstance, an inflow of economic benefits is not probable so a contingent asset cannot even be noted in the entity's financial statements. Where the entity has been successful and has received a favourable judgment, but the case has been taken to appeal, it will still only be appropriate to note a contingent asset where success by the entity in the court of appeal is probable. Until the final judgment is made, it would be rare for the outcome of the case to be virtually certain. Hence, only when the final judgment is received should the asset be recognised and the related profit be recorded in the financial statements of the period in which the change occurs. [FRS 12 para 35]. In effect, a judgement received after the balance sheet date up to the date of approval of the financial statements is normally a non-adjusting event. The debtor when recognised then becomes subject to normal credit risk evaluation.

21.102 It is not acceptable to net contingent assets against contingent liabilities. Each category of contingencies must be treated separately.

[The next paragraph is 21.104.]

Reimbursements

21.104 FRS 12 includes specific guidance on accounting for reimbursements. Under FRS 12, where some or all of the expenditure required to settle a provision is expected to be reimbursed by another party, the reimbursement should be recognised only when it is virtually certain that reimbursement will be received if the entity settles the obligation. [FRS 12 para 56]. Reimbursements of this nature are required to be treated as separate assets and the standard also comments that the amount recognised for reimbursement should not exceed the amount of the related provision. [FRS 12 para 56].

21.105 In some situations, it may not be clear at the balance sheet date as to whether there is an obligation (and a related reimbursement asset). However, where evidence arises after the balance sheet date that relates to conditions that existed at the balance sheet date, this is an adjusting event under FRS 21, 'Events after the balance sheet date', and would result in recognising of a liability for the obligation. Provided that it is virtually certain at the year end that the reimbursement will be received if the entity settles the obligation – that is, any post year end negotiation in respect of the asset relates to agreement of the final amount to be paid and not to whether the reimbursement will be paid if there is a related liability, then a reimbursement asset would be recognised at the balance sheet date.

Example

An entity had a provision for a legal case that was in progress at the year end. Also at the year end it was negotiating with its insurance company for reimbursement of the amount to be paid out in the legal case, although there was agreement, in principle, with the insurance company that reimbursement would be made if the company lost the legal case. Although the final amount of the reimbursement from the insurer is not agreed at the year end, it is very likely that the amount to be paid in the legal case will be incurred after the year end and that the reimbursement will be agreed with the insurer before the financial statements are approved. If this happens should the asset for the reimbursement be included in the financial statements for the year?

Yes, the asset should be recognised in the financial statements if it is virtually certain at the balance sheet date that reimbursement will be received if the entity settles the obligation. [FRS 12 para 56]. The post year end settlement of the court case confirms the amount of the liability that should be recognised at the balance sheet date. FRS 21 gives as an example of an adjusting event the settlement after the balance sheet date of a court case that confirms that the entity had a present obligation at the balance sheet date. [FRS 21 para 9(a)]. In the same way as a liability would be recognised at the balance sheet date on the basis of post year end evidence that confirms its existence, the related reimbursement asset should be recognised if it is virtually certain to be received.

21.106 Although there is a general prohibition on netting recoveries against related obligations and contingent assets against contingent liabilities, this does not extend to their recognition in the profit and loss account. Here, expenses relating to a provision may be presented net of the amount recognised for a reimbursement. [FRS 12 para 57]. For example, a company might have identified during the year a *present obligation* that *probably* requires a transfer of economic benefits and makes a provision for that obligation. In addition, it might have an insurance contract under which it can claim when the obligation arises. The insurance company has accepted that it will pay-out under the policy. The company can recognise an asset representing the recovery as it is virtually certain that it will receive the amount due from the insurance company. Although the company has to recognise the provision for the obligation and the debtor for the recovery gross, it may net these in the profit and loss account. In practice, this concession has little impact as both the provision and the recovery will often form part of operating profit and, therefore, may only affect the allocation between say administrative expenses and other income.

21.107 In most cases, an entity will remain liable for the whole of an obligation even where it can recover some or all of the loss from another party. But the general prohibition on netting, in effect, does not extend to situations where, for example, the obligation has been extinguished because another party has agreed to assume the obligation or will settle it directly. The key here is that the entity that has transferred the obligation cannot be left with any significant risks and rewards associated with it. (This judgement is based on the rules set out in FRS 5.) In this case, the entity no longer bears, for example, the credit risk associated with the recovery and this risk is passed to the party to whom the obligation is owed. In such cases the entity has no liability for those costs arising under the obligation and they should not be included in the provision. [FRS 12 para 60].

21.108 The practical implications of this is that a company may recognise an obligation (and an expense) before recognising a related insurance recovery. This is because companies must provide for insured risks if these become probable. As explained above, the insurance recovery must be separately assessed.

Measurement

21.109 Provisions, by definition, are uncertain as to either their amount or their timing. Hence, a number of tricky problems can arise with their measurement, which is primarily caused by this uncertainty. Even for those provisions where only the timing is uncertain, problems with measurement can arise due to the passage of time before the obligation is settled. The problems surround how to estimate a provision, whether it will be settled in the near future and whether and, if so, how it should be discounted. These matters are considered in the paragraphs that follow.

Best estimate

21.110 The standard takes a helpful practical stance in determining the amount that should be recognised as a provision. It says that the amount should be the best estimate of the expenditure required to settle the present obligation at the balance sheet date. [FRS 12 para 36]. Clearly, the best estimate of a provision represents the amount that an entity would rationally pay to settle the obligation at the balance sheet date or to transfer it to a third party. In practice, it will seldom be possible to settle the obligation or transfer it in this way, but nevertheless this still remains the best way in which to estimate an obligation.

21.111 Any estimation will be a matter of judgement. Primarily this judgement is the responsibility of management and their best estimate will generally be based on their experience in similar situations. For example, with a warranty obligation, management will often have a track record of the type and number of claims that have been made in the past. From this past experience it will be able to estimate to a reasonable degree of certainty the number and magnitude of claims for which provision is necessary. But in other situations, management might need to seek the advice of an expert. For example, in a litigation case, it might be necessary to seek expert legal advice not only on the likelihood of a liability arising (see para 21.69 onwards), but also on the quantum of any claim.

21.112 Although in order to recognise a provision an obligating event must have taken place before a company's year end, in deciding the amount to be provided the company can take into account any additional evidence provided by events that take place after the balance sheet date. [FRS 12 para 38].

21.113 Although the most likely amount of the liability will generally give the soundest indication of the best estimate of a provision, this might not always be the case. For example, if a company has an environmental obligation to decontaminate some of its land, there might be a number of different ways in which this work can be carried out. Each of these techniques might have different probabilities of success and will cost different amounts. The company might choose the method with the most likely possibility of success, but a provision for a larger amount may be necessary if there is a significant chance that further work will be necessary before success is achieved. [FRS 12 para 40].

21.114 Inevitably, in establishing the amount of any provision judgements have to be made concerning the risks and uncertainties that surround the particular events which give rise to the obligation. These all have an impact on the amount that is recognised. If the estimate is particularly vulnerable to risk, any risk adjustment is likely to increase the amount of the provision. Similarly, where the facts are uncertain caution needs to be taken to ensure that profits or assets are not overstated and equally expenses and liabilities are not understated. But the standard stresses that uncertainty does not justify creating excessive provisions or deliberately overstating liabilities. [FRS 12 para 43]. Management needs, therefore, to make a balanced assessment of amount of a provision and to bear in mind the ASB's assertion that being overly prudent does not result in the financial statements being neutral and having the quality of reliability.

21.115 In addition, it is necessary to make sure that adjustments for risks and uncertainties are not duplicated during the estimation process. This is particularly relevant when estimating a provision by discounting future cash flows, where risk can be taken into account in either the cash flows themselves or the discount rate that is used (see further para 21.124). The disclosures that have to be made concerning uncertainties are considered from paragraph 21.297.

21.116 Provisions are required to be measured before tax with the tax consequences being dealt with in accordance with FRS 19, 'Deferred tax'. Accounting for deferred tax is considered in detail in chapter 13.

21.116.1 The measurement of a provision should not take account of any gains from the expected disposal of assets, even if the expected disposal is closely linked to the event giving rise to the provision. [FRS 12 para 54]. For example, a restructuring provision cannot be reduced by an expected gain on disposal of a factory that is being sold as part of the restructuring. Instead, the gain will be recognised when the factory is sold.

Estimation techniques

21.117 There are a number of different techniques that can be used to arrive at the best estimate of the amount of a provision, where the creditor does not wish to settle and where there is no market in obligations of the kind for which provision is being made. Assuming that it is possible to specify all the possible outcomes and their associated probabilities, the amount to be provided for an obligation could be estimated as:

- The most likely outcome (that is, the outcome with the highest probability). This method, however, ignores other possible outcomes and where it is nil can lead to the wrong conclusion that the entity has no obligation.
- The maximum amount (that is, the highest possible outcome). This can lead to excessive provisions where the possibility of that outcome is remote.
- At least the minimum amount in the range (that is, any amount from the lowest possible outcome to the highest possible outcome). This might result in a wide range of possible estimates and could impair comparability between financial statements.
- The expected value (that is, the amount that takes account of all possible outcomes using probabilities to weight the outcomes). This method provides an estimate that reflects the entire probability distribution, that is, all the possible outcomes weighted by their probabilities. It is particularly suited to situations where there is a large population of similar claims.

The method an entity should use will depend on the particular circumstances. For a provision relating to a large population of items the expected value method may well be the most appropriate. But for provisions for individual obligations or provisions on a small number of items, one of the other methods may be more appropriate.

Large population of similar claims

21.118 Where an entity is trying to establish the amount of a provision for a large population of similar claims the 'expected value' method usually gives the best result and should be used. The example below is based on the example in paragraph 39 of FRS 12, which uses a warranty claim to illustrate how to apply the 'expected value' method.

Example

An entity sells goods with a standard warranty under which customers are covered for the cost of repairs of any manufacturing defects that become apparent within the first six months after purchase. If minor defects were detected in all products sold, repair costs of £1 million would result. If major defects were detected in all products sold, repair costs of £4 million would result. The entity's past experience and future expectations indicate that, for the coming year, 75% of the goods sold will have no defects, 20% of the goods sold will have minor defects and 5% of the goods sold will have major defects.

The expected value of the cost of repairs under the standard warranty is calculated as follows:

	Expected value £
75% × nil	nil
20% × £1,000,000	200,000
5% × £4,000,000	200,000
Total	400,000

Note that in this example, the warranty is a standard manufacturing warranty and it is presumed that it is not a separate element and that it represents an insignificant part of the sales transaction. The accounting for warranties is dealt with in more detail in paragraph 21.225 onwards.

Discounting

21.119 Once the cash flows associated with an obligation have been estimated, it is then necessary to consider whether or not the time value of money has a material effect on the sums to be paid. The standard requires that where the effect of the time value of money is material the amount of a provision should be the present value of the expenditures expected to be required to settle the obligation. [FRS 12 para 45]. Clearly, provisions for cash outflows that arise soon after the balance sheet date are more onerous than those where cash outflows of the same amount arise some time later. But, in practice the standard makes it clear that it only requires cash flows to be discounted, where this is has a material effect. Therefore, for the majority of provisions that will reverse in the short-term, for example, within the next and perhaps in the following financial year, the effects of discounting may be immaterial and are not then required to be made.

21.120 The present value of a provision should be determined based on a pre-tax discount rate that reflects current market assessments of the time value of money and the risks specific to the liability. The discount rate should not reflect risks for which future cash flow estimates have been adjusted. [FRS 12 para 47]. Estimates of cash flows to be paid in the future will be subject to the following factors, which may all have an impact on the discount rate to be used in establishing an obligation's present value:

- Inflation.
- Other risks and uncertainties concerning the amount to be settled.
- The effects of taxation.

Each of these issues is considered below.

Adjusting for inflation

21.121 For the purposes of measuring provisions, cash flows are usually expressed in expected future prices (that is, including inflation) and should, therefore, be discounted using a 'nominal' rate (that is, a rate that includes inflation). Alternatively, where cash flows are expressed in current prices they should be discounted using a 'real' rate (that is, a rate that excludes the effects of inflation). [FRS 12 para 50]. Nominal discount rates are higher than real discount rates (unless there is deflation). Theoretically, discounting cash flows adjusted for price changes using a nominal rate should arrive at the same net present value as using a real rate to discount cash flows that have been adjusted for inflation, as illustrated in the example that follows.

Example

A company has estimated that it needs to pay £1,000 (in current prices) at the end of each of the next three years to settle an obligation. If it takes into account inflation these cash flows will increase to the amounts shown in the table below. The company has established that the nominal discount rate (that is, including inflation) is 4.5%. By discounting the cash flows the net present value works out to be £2,887. By using an estimation process called iteration, it is possible to calculate the discount rate (that is, the real rate) that would have to be applied to the cash flows excluding inflation to arrive at the same present value.

	Net present value	Cash flows Year 1	Year 2	Year 3
	£	£	£	£
Cash flows include inflation of 2.5% per annum				
Nominal discount rate of 4.5%	2,887	1,025	1,051	1,077
Cash flows excluding inflation				
Real discount rate of 1.95%	2,887	1,000	1,000	1,000

The example shows the equivalent real rate is 1.95%. Clearly it would be wrong to discount the cash flows excluding inflation (that is, £1,000 per annum) using the nominal discount rate of 4.5% as this would give an understated net present value of £2,749.

21.122 It can be seen from this example that it is possible to estimate the real rate by deducting the inflation rate from the nominal rate. However, this would only be appropriate where the cash flows arise over a relatively short period of time, for instance, up to five years. Mathematically, the relationship between the nominal rate and the real rate is expressed by the following formula:

$$(1 + \text{real rate}) = \frac{(1 + \text{nominal rate})}{(1 + \text{inflation rate})}$$

Which in the case of the example above gives the following:

$$\text{Real rate} = \frac{(1 + 4.5\%)}{(1 + 2.5\%)} - 1$$
$$= \frac{(1.045)}{(1.025)} - 1$$
$$= 1.0195 - 1$$
$$= 1.95\%$$

21.123 Once a company has established the amount for which provision is to be made (in the example above £2,887) it is necessary to consider how this provision should be adjusted each year. The objective should be to end up in the financial statements with a provision that equals the amount to be settled. In the example, the amounts settled are estimated to be £1,025 at the end of year one, £1,051 at the end of year two and £1,077 at the end of year three. Therefore, it would not be appropriate to inflate the provision each year by the real discount rate (to arrive at the £1,000 amounts in the example); the nominal discount rate is the appropriate rate to use. As explained above, the nominal rate is the real rate adjusted to include an inflation factor. The increase in the provision from one year to the next is recognised as an interest cost. [FRS 12 para 62]. This interest cost is made up of a discount factor (in the example the real interest rate of 1.95 per cent) and an inflation factor (in the example 2.50 per cent). It does not follow that the discount charged each year in the profit and loss account should be split with the inflation adjustment being taken to operating profit and the real interest being included in finance costs. Rather, the full nominal amount of the discount is included as the finance cost consistent with other external borrowing costs.

Adjusting for risk

21.124 The risks and uncertainties about the amounts and timing of cash flows required to meet a provision must be taken into account in reaching the best estimate of the expenditure required to settle the present obligation at the balance sheet date. [FRS 12 para 42]. Although theoretically, this best estimate could be based on a market (fair value) or counterparty-specific (negotiated) estimate of a current settlement amount, usually the best estimate is based on the estimate of outflows of resources required to meet the obligation. To estimate a current settlement amount, the cash outflows are estimated under different possible outcomes, taking account of the various risks and uncertainties. As described in paragraph 21.118, the 'expected value' technique is one means of arriving at a single point estimate of the cash outflows that is particularly relevant when there is a portfolio of similar items. This deals with one aspect of uncertainty, but does not deal fully with the value impact of the variability in the expected outcome. To illustrate this, consider the following example.

Example

Should the following obligations have the same estimated settlement values (ignoring the time value of money and third party handling costs)?

(a) There are three possible outcomes for a particular obligation, which are estimated as follows:

Cash outflow	Probability	Expected value
£1,000	25%	250
£1,500	50%	750
£2,000	25%	500
		£1,500

(b) There is a fixed obligation of £1,500.

It is not likely that the settlement values would be the same. It is easy to see that a third party might accept a payment of £1,500 in exchange for the fixed obligation, but their attitude to the value of the variable obligation would depend on their perspective of the risk of paying out more that they receive. In general, there is a reluctance to take on variable payment obligations in exchange for a fixed payment and a third party might, therefore, generally require an additional payment in excess of the amount that would be accepted for the fixed obligation, even though the expected values are the same – requiring a total payment of, say, £1,600.

However, it does depend on how the other party might be able to use the proceeds of the fixed payment prior to meeting the obligation. If they could match the variability of the outcome by investing in an asset that had counter-variability, they might require little or no risk premium and indeed could even be willing to accept a risk discount if they were willing to share the benefit of the risk premium on the corresponding assets. Usually, however, a risk premium would be required.

21.125 In line with the above example, a risk adjustment is made to the single point best estimate of the liability (arrived at by means of an expected value or other appropriate technique) to reflect variability of outcome. This would usually increase the amount at which a liability is measured. [FRS 12 para 43]. Another way of adjusting for risk is to adjust the discount rate. If this approach is taken, the discount rate should reflect the current market assessment of the risks specific to the liability. [FRS 12 para 47]. However, risk adjustments should not be made to the discount rate if risk adjustments for the same risks have been made to the estimated cash flows, as this would lead to double-counting. [FRS 12 para 49]. Where all risk adjustments are reflected in the cash flows, then the cash flows are discounted at a risk-free rate. The following example illustrates the impact of risk on the risk-adjusted discount rate.

Example

A company's best estimate of its liability in two years time is £1,000. The actual liability could be anything between £950 and £1,050. But at the balance sheet date it knows that it can pass the obligation onto another party for a certain payment in two years time of £1,020. So the company's best estimate is £1,000 (that is, excluding any risk adjustment) and the equivalent certain amount payable in two years time is £1,020 (that is, including an adjustment for risk of £20). Clearly, the obligation that arises at the balance sheet date for which provision is required should be the same net present value amount whether the unadjusted best estimate or the risk-adjusted best estimate equivalent is used as the basis for the measurement. The risk-free rate for 2 year money is 4.5%.

	Net present value £	Cash flows Year 1 £	Year 2 £
Certain cash flow (adjusted for risk)			
Risk-free rate 4.5%	934[1]	0	1,020
Expected cash flow (unadjusted for risk)			
Risk-adjusted rate 3.5%[2]	934	0	1,000

1 Using a risk-free rate of 4.5% on the certain cash flow of £1,020 gives a discounted net present value of £934. This equates to a risk-adjusted rate of 3.5% used to discount the expected cash flow of £1,000.

2 To arrive at the same net present value of £934, this equates to a risk-adjusted rate of 3.5% used to discount the expected cash flow of £1,000.

21.126 As in the example above, risk-adjusted discount rates generally will be lower than risk-free rates when discounting is used to value liabilities. The risk-adjusted rate is very susceptible to changes in the risks associated with the cash flows.

21.127 The standard comments that using a discount rate that reflects the current market assessments of the time value of money and the risks specific to the liability (that is, a risk-adjusted rate) will be the easiest method of reflecting risk. [FRS 12 para 49]. But as can be seen from the above example, a market-based risk-adjusted discount rate might be difficult to obtain and, accordingly, in most situations it is appropriate in practice to reflect risk in determining the cash flows that will arise, rather than adjusting the discount rate used. We do not believe that companies would necessarily find it useful to use the approach of adjusting the discount rate for risk in order to value liabilities, as this may be very difficult to achieve in practice. Indeed, adjusting the discount rate for risk to value liabilities is counter-intuitive as the discount rate usually needs to be reduced (as noted in para 21.126 above), not increased, to allow for the risk.

21.128 The example in paragraph 21.125 also illustrates another anomaly. This concerns how the discount should unwind and to what figure. A discount of £42 (that is, £934 × 4.5%) would be charged in year 1 and a further discount of £44 charged in year 2 to arrive at a provision of £1,020 (the certain cash flow adjusted for risk). If at the end of year 2 the provision is settled for £1,000, then the correct treatment would be to release £20 of the provision at that time as being surplus to requirements.

21.129 As noted in paragraph 21.125 above, where a risk-adjusted discount rate is used (as opposed to adjusting cash flows for risk), the discount rate should reflect the risks specific to the liability. This is illustrated in the following example.

Example

An entity sells a vacuum cleaner, Model A, on which it provides a standard warranty of a three year guarantee for parts and labour. Based on current market assessments, the pre-tax discount rate of the provision of warranty is expected to be 13%.

At the beginning of the year, the entity manufactures a new range of vacuum cleaner, Model B. Model B is a high-end vacuum cleaner and uses the latest technology. The entity also provides a standard warranty of a three year guarantee for parts and labour.

For the purpose of this example, it is presumed that the standard warranty represents an insignificant part of the sales transaction and is not a separate element.

How should the discount rate be determined for warranty provisions?

Management should not use the same discount rate in discounting the warranty provision for Model A to discount the warranty provision for Model B. The provisions are for different products that display different kinds of risk and, therefore, different discount rates should be used, although the nature of both provisions is for warranty repairs. As a starting point, the entity may take into account the discount rate of Model A and adjust it to reflect specific risks of Model B and to exclude specific risks of Model A.

Effects of taxation

21.130 The standard requires that the discount rate applied to future cash flows associated with an obligation should be a pre-tax rate. [FRS 12 para 47]. If, for example, a company has elected to adjust the cash flows themselves for risk and has decided, therefore, to use a risk-free rate, then it should not have to make any further adjustments to that rate for tax. Helpfully, government bond rates, which are risk-free, are also pre-tax (that is, the income received is taxed in the hands of the recipient and is paid gross).

Example

A company has a known cash flow of £1,200 which is payable in two years time. As the cash flow is an allowable expense, tax relief at 30% will be given when it arises. The pre-tax risk-free rate is 4.5%.

			Cash flows	
	Discount	Net present	Year 1	Year 2
	rate	value £	£	£
Pre-tax risk-free rate	4.5%	1,099	–	1,200
Tax relief			–	(360)
			–	840

Initially a provision will be recognised for £1,099. At the end of year one the provision will grow by £49 and this will be charged as a finance cost in the profit and loss account. It will grow by a further £52 in year two to arrive at the final amount to be settled of £1,200. The tax consequences of these changes in provision should also be considered to determine whether a deferred tax asset should be provided in accordance with FRS 19.

Selecting an appropriate discount rate

21.131 Following from the explanation above, the appropriate discount rate to be used when estimating the amount to be provided should be the nominal, risk-free pre-tax rate. Typically, a UK Gilt 'yield' rate (not the coupon rate) disclosed in the Financial Times should be used, as this is a nominal, risk-free pre-tax rate. The yield to redemption rates vary within a small range that depends upon the period of time to redemption. The Financial Times quotes Gilt yield to redemption rates in bands of: up to five years; five to fifteen years; and over fifteen years. Within these bands the rates remain fairly constant. Consequently, in practice it is logical to select a rate that matches the maturity of the liability being discounted. This is relatively straightforward where the amount being discounted is a single payment to be settled in the future, as a Gilt will have a single capital repayment at the end of its term. But where the provision is made up of a string of cash flows arising in different periods, it might be necessary to adjust the discount rate to reflect the different timing of the cash flows.

Unwinding the discount

21.132 As explained in the example in paragraph 21.123 above, the unwinding of the discount should be included as an element of finance costs in the profit and loss account. This amount should be included in a separate profit and loss account line item called 'other finance costs' adjacent to interest (see further para 21.299). [FRS 12 para 48]. The unwinding of the discount is illustrated in the simplified example below.

Example

Entity A has litigation pending. Legal advice is that entity A will lose the case, and costs of £1,200 in two years' time are estimated. The liability is recognised on a discounted basis. The appropriate discount rate is 4.5% and, for the purposes of this example, it is assumed that the discount rate does not change.

How should management calculate the amount of borrowing costs recognised on the unwinding of a discount?

Management should initially recognise a provision for £1,099, being the present value of £1,200 discounted at 4.5% for two years.

	Discount factor at 4.5%	**NPV**	**Cash flows**	**Borrowing cost**
	0.9157	1,099		
Year 1	0.9569	1,148		49
Year 2	1.0000	1,200	1,200	52

At the end of year 1, the provision will increase to £1,148 as management discounts the cash outflow of £1,200 for one year instead of two. The increment of £49 should be recognised as a borrowing cost in the profit and loss account. Similarly in year 2, the provision will increase by £52 to equal the amount due.

The situation is more complicated if the discount rate changes over the period – this is dealt with in paragraph 21.139 onwards.

Measurement of related asset

21.133 In certain circumstances, where recognition of the obligation gives access to future economic benefits, it might be appropriate to recognise an asset rather than charging the costs to be provided to the profit and loss account. This typically arises in oil and gas and generating industries where environmental damage is caused by, say, the construction and commissioning of the facility (for example, the oil platform or nuclear plant). In the circumstances explained from paragraph 21.83 there is often a need to recognise an asset at the outset for an amount equivalent to the decommissioning obligation, which will be recovered from the benefits derived from the facility (for example, the future sale of oil or electricity).

21.134 Obviously, discounting has an important part to play in establishing both the obligation and the equivalent asset to be recognised where decommissioning is unlikely to take place for a number of years. In the case of decommissioning a nuclear facility, the work might not be expected to start for (say) 100 years. With an oil rig the time-frame is likely to be shorter, but could be anywhere between 25 and 50 years. Consequently, the impact of discounting can be significant as illustrated in the next example.

Example

A company has constructed a nuclear facility for £100m. It anticipates that the plant will run for the next 30 years. It has estimated, using existing technology and some expected efficiencies in using that technology, that the cost of decommissioning the plant in 100 years time will be £1 billion in today's pounds. It has been assumed that the obligation arises at the end of year 100.

Present value of obligation	**Discount rate**	**Net present value £'m**	**Cash flows Year 100 £m**
	4.5%	12.26	1,000.00
Unwinding of discount			**Total discount in**
		Discount	**first 10 years £'m**
Year 1		0.55}	
Year 2		0.58}	
Year 3		0.60}	
Year 4		0.63}	
Year 5		0.66}	
Year 6		0.69} =	6.78
Year 7		0.72}	
Year 8		0.75}	
Year 9		0.78}	
Year 10		0.82}	
...		...	
Year 25		1.59	
...		...	
Year 50		4.76	
...		...	
Year 75		14.32	
...		...	
Year 100		43.06	
Total discount		987.74	

It can be seen that the net present value of the decommissioning obligation is only £12.26m using a discount rate of 4.5%. Hence, the facility should be recorded at its original cost of £100m together with the initial cost of the obligation of £12.26m — giving a total cost of £112.26m. This amount should then be amortised over the 30 year operating life of the facility giving an annual amortisation charge using the straight line method of £3.74m (of which £0.41m per annum relates to the capitalised obligation).

The example also illustrates that the increase in the obligation arises solely from the addition of the discount. Although in the opening years the effect is relatively small (for example, at the end of year 1 £0.55m is added to the obligation to bring it to a figure of £12.81m), the discount effect is back-end loaded. In the final year the obligation increases by £43.06m. The oddity is, however, that the reversal of the discount appears as a finance cost whilst the benefits of the asset appear in operating profit.

Although there is a mismatch between the useful life of the facility and the length of time before the decommissioning will take place, in theory this should pose no problem, as long as the entity has retained sufficient funds (that is, it has not over-distributed) to honour the obligation at the end of year 30. In the example, the obligation will be £45.91m at the end of year 30. These funds can then be invested in risk free investments to generate the required risk-free rate (in this case 4.5%) to build up the provision until the obligation crystallises at the end of year 100.

Changes in estimates

21.135 All would be wonderful if life were as simple as outlined in the previous example. However, with such long-tail commitments, there are significant problems with trying to estimate the costs that will arise that far ahead and very significant assumptions have to be made in practice to arrive at an initial estimation of such a decommissioning obligation. It would be naive to think that once that obligation had been assessed that no further amendments would be made to it. Inevitably, because the standard prohibits management from postulating anything other than existing technology (unless the development of new technology is supported by sufficient objective evidence – see para 21.143), changes to the estimate of the obligation and possibly its timing and changes in management's assumptions will be inevitable.

21.136 There is no guidance in the standard concerning how to treat these types of adjustments. The discussion paper on provisions that preceded FRED 14 proposed a simple method whereby, after the initial recognition of a decommissioning provision, if the estimate of its amount changed, the entire change of estimate should be capitalised and charged to the profit and loss account prospectively over the remaining life of the facility and indeed, it is a variation of this method that has become the generally accepted practice and that has been adopted for IFRS in IFRIC 1, 'Changes in existing decommissioning, restoration and similar liabilities' (see further para 21.138.1). However, after the proposal in the discussion paper was made, the ASB carried out some field testing which indicated that changes in the expected life of an oilfield and changes in the expected decommissioning cost could result in a reduction in the necessary provision, which could be significantly greater than the net book value of the decommissioning asset originally capitalised. Therefore, the ASB revised its proposal in FRED 14 and suggested that where subsequent changes are made to the provision, the carrying amount (net of accumulated depreciation) should be recalculated based on current knowledge; and the balance of the change in the provision should be recognised in the profit and loss account. Although this proposal was not included in FRS 12, it might still be appropriate in certain situations as illustrated below.

Example

The facts are the same as in the previous example. At the end of year 10 the obligation stands in the books at £19.04m. The value of the asset is £74.84 (amortisation of £37.42m having been charged — £4.08m relating to the decommissioning element of the asset). Researchers have found a new way of decommissioning which has been tested satisfactorily in the laboratory. It is believed that this new method, which is far safer and less labour intensive, will cost £400m and can be undertaken in a further 75 years time.

Present value of obligation	**Discount rate**	**Net present value £'m**	**Cash flows Year 100 £m**
	4.5%	14.73	400.00
Unwinding of discount		**Discount**	**Total discount in first 10 years £'m**
Year 11		0.66}	
Year 12		0.69}	
Year 13		0.72}	
Year 14		0.76}	
Year 15		0.79}	
Year 16		0.83} =	8.14
Year 17		0.86}	
Year 18		0.90}	
Year 19		0.94}	
Year 20		0.99}	
...		...	
Year 35		1.91	
...		...	
Year 60		5.73	
...		...	
Year 85		17.22	
Total discount		385.27	

The net present value of the obligation needs to be decreased from £19.04m to £14.73m as illustrated in the table below. This is easily done, but a problem then arises as to what to credit. Should the amount of £4.31m be deducted from the depreciated cost of the asset? If the new technology had been in existence when the original provision was made, the provision needed then would have been £9.49m compared to the actual provision made of £12.26m, a reduced amount of £2.77m. The asset capitalised would have been less by this amount and ten years amortisation would have been less by £0.92m.

	Original assessment £'m	Revised assessment £'m	Difference £'m
Provision year 1	12.26	9.49	2.77
Charged to P&L over 10 years	6.78	5.24	1.54
Provision year 10	19.04	14.73	4.31
Asset capitalised year 1	12.26	9.49	2.77
10 years depreciation	4.08	3.16	0.92
Net book value year 10	8.18	6.33	1.85

Therefore, it would be necessary to make the following adjustments in order to restate the provision and asset:

Dr balance sheet provision	£4.31m	
Cr fixed asset		£1.85m
Cr P&L depreciation		£0.92m
Cr P&L discount		£1.54m

As these adjustments are a revision of an estimate rather than a fundamental error, their effect would be recorded in the current year's profit and loss account rather than as a prior year adjustment.

21.136.1 Another way of calculating the adjustment is to consider the proportion of the adjustment that relates to past depreciation. Suppose that when an asset was built a provision for decommissioning costs was estimated to be £100. The £100 was capitalised as part of the cost of the asset and depreciated over the useful economic life of the asset of 20 years. After ten years the estimate of the decommissioning costs was revised and the provision reduced to £40. Ignoring the effects of discounting, the release of the provision of £60 should be recognised in the same place as the original debit associated with the initial provision. £100 was initially capitalised as a tangible fixed asset, but ten years later on, only half of this remains in the carrying amount of the asset in the balance sheet. Therefore, only half of the £60 now being reversed remains in the balance sheet, so £30 should be credited to tangible fixed assets. The remaining £30 was previously recognised in the profit and loss account (*via* depreciation) and, therefore, its reversal should also be reflected in the profit and loss account.

21.136.2 We consider that it is also acceptable when the adjustment decreases the provision to reduce the corresponding asset by the same amount, until the asset's carrying value reaches nil, in which case any remaining credit would be taken to the profit an loss account.

21.137 The example in paragraph 21.136 considers the situation where the revision of the estimate leads to a reduced provision, but the need to increase the original provision will also arise in practice. Where this is the case, similar calculations can be performed to work out what effect the revised assessments would have had on the originally recognised provision and asset. The resulting adjustment would be to increase the provision and asset and charge the adjustment as additional depreciation and discount in the profit and loss account. But it could be argued following the introduction of FRS 15, that a backlog depreciation adjustment of this nature is no longer appropriate.

21.138 The better way of dealing with such adjustments to the provision is merely to add any increase in provision to the carrying value of the asset and depreciate the balance prospectively over its life. Any possible over-valuation caused by adding such adjustments to the carrying value of the asset would be taken care of by carrying out impairment tests to ensure that the asset's carrying value does not exceed its recoverable amount.

21.138.1 Our view is that, although any of the methods outlined above could be argued to be acceptable, we would normally expect companies to adopt the prospective method. This is the method specified in the SORP, 'Accounting for oil and gas exploration, development, production and decommissioning activities', issued by the UK Oil Industry Accounting Committee (OIAC). Furthermore, use of the prospective method is now required under IFRS. In May 2004, the IFRIC issued an interpretation, IFRIC 1, 'Changes in existing decommissioning, restoration and similar liabilities'. This requires that, where the related asset is accounted for under the cost method, changes in the liability that result from changes in the estimated timing or amount of economic benefits required to settle the obligation, or a change in the discount rate, should be accounted for as follows:

- Changes in the liability should be added to, or deducted from, the related asset's cost in the current period. However, the amount deducted from the asset's cost should not exceed its carrying amount. If a decrease in the liability exceeds the asset's carrying amount, the excess should be recognised immediately in profit or loss.

- If the adjustment results in an addition to the asset's cost, the entity should consider whether this is an indication that the new carrying amount of the asset may not be fully recoverable and, if so, should test the asset for impairment.

IFRIC 1 also sets out requirements for where a policy of revaluation is used for the related asset. [IFRIC 1 paras 5, 6].

Changes in discount rates

21.139 The discount rate might change over time, particularly where the rate being used is a nominal rate, which includes the effects of inflation. The rate to be applied in assessing the amount of the provision should be the rate which is current at the year end date. This will mean that different rates might apply at different year ends.

Example

A company has a number of leasehold properties that are empty and not used in the business, but which are sublet for their full term (20 years) at a rental below that which the company is paying. It is providing for these as onerous leases (see further para 21.193), and is doing so by discounting the difference between the rentals payable and the rentals receivable. What discount rate should it use?

The amount of the lease rentals payable and receivable are known in money terms and, therefore, a nominal risk-free rate should be used to discount them (see para 21.131 above). The discount rate should be pre-tax. An appropriate rate would be a government bond rate. In theory, different rates should be applied to the cash flows arising in each year. However, in practice, it is likely that a single rate based on a 20 year bond will give a result that is not materially different.

Each year the company will need to reassess the provision and, if there has been a significant move in interest rates, it will be necessary to recalculate the present value. Note that paragraph 89(e) of FRS 12 requires that the company should disclose separately the increase during the period in the discounted amount arising from the passage of time and the effect of any change in the discount rate.

21.140 The standard includes no guidance on how to deal with changes in the discount rates used to measure the provision. However, whether the discount rate increases or decreases, the resulting adjustment represents a reassessment of the provision. As a consequence the movement should be charged or credited as an operating item rather than as a finance cost.

21.141 If the discount rate goes down in a period, then the liability would increase as illustrated in the following example.

Example

A company has a £1,000 obligation which is due at the end of year 5. It provides now for the net present value of the obligation of £802, which has been arrived at by using a nominal risk-free pre-tax rate of 4.5%. At the end of year three the discount rate has changed to 4%. The obligation at the beginning of the year 3 (measured at a discount rate of 4.5%) is £876. At the end of year 3 it would be stated at £916 if the rate were still 4.5%; but based on a current rate of 4% it needs to be £925. The difference is made up of a finance cost and a change in estimate of the provision. If in the example the rate changed at the beginning of the year, it would be appropriate to charge £35 (that is, £876 × 4%) as discount for the year. This would increase the provision to £911 and the additional amount of £14 to bring the provision to £925 should be charged as an operating item.

			Provision at end of				
		Net present value	**Year 1**	**Year 2**	**Year 3**	**Year 4**	**Year 5**
		£	**£**	**£**	**£**	**£**	**£**
Original discount rate	4.50%	802	839	876	916	957	1,000
Revised discount rate	4.00%				925	962	1,000

21.142 The effect of a change in rates can be much more significant if the remaining period is very long, as in the above decommissioning example.

21.142.1 If the provision relates to a decommissioning obligation, in practice the effect of any changes in rates could be added to (or deducted from) the related asset and the resulting carrying value depreciated prospectively over its remaining life. The carrying value of the asset would be subjected to impairment testing to ensure that it is not overstated, but this would be unlikely as a decrease in a discount rate, which would increase an obligation and cause an addition to the related asset, could also increase the related asset's value in use.

Changes in estimate of provisions

21.142.2 In practice, companies may well re-estimate their provisions at each year end. For example, the graph below shows that a company has estimated a provision at the beginning of the year as 800 and at the end of the year its estimate has increased to 850. It can either make these estimates by discounting risk-adjusted cash flows using a risk-free discount rate or by discounting cash flows, which exclude the effects of risk, by a risk-adjusted discount rate.

21.142.3 In this example, no cash flows have arisen during the period, so all the company has to determine is how to split the increase in the provision of 50 between changes in measurement and the effects of discounting. As explained in paragraph 21.123 above, it is appropriate to inflate the provision each year by the nominal discount rate and this is the amount that should be charged in the profit and loss account as a finance cost. If the opening provision of 800 is inflated by a risk-free pre-tax rate of 4.5 per cent, the provision would have increased by 36 in the year to 836. Therefore, it would be appropriate to charge 36 as a finance cost in the profit and loss account. The difference between the uplifted provision of 836 and the re-estimated amount of 850 (that is, 14) should be charged to the profit and loss account as an operating expense.

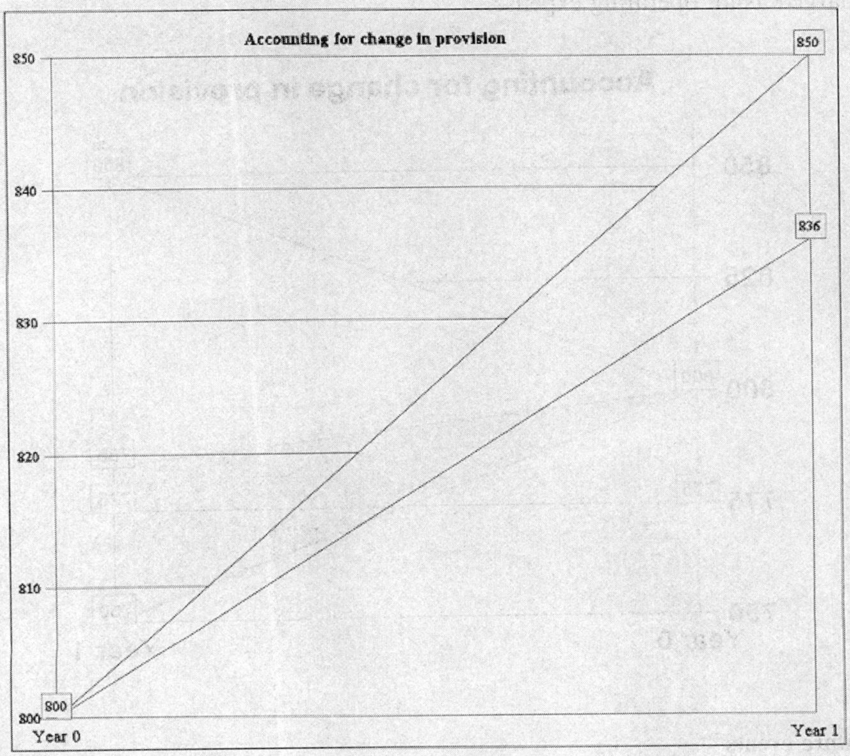

21.142.4 Similarly, if the re-estimate of the provision at the end of year 1 was 820, it would be reasonable to charge 36 as a finance cost in the profit and loss account and credit operating costs with a release of the re-estimated provision of 16.

21.142.5 If this provision related to a decommissioning obligation, then as mentioned in paragraph 21.138.1 above, in practice, it would be acceptable to add, or deduct, the amount related to the re-estimate to, or from, the carrying value of the related decommissioning fixed asset and to amortise the revised balance prospectively over the asset's remaining life.

21.142.6 The same basis can be used where cash flows arise in the period. For example if 50 has been paid in relation to the provision during the year, the provision would have decreased from 800 to 750, without taking into account the effects of discounting. If the repayment had arisen evenly throughout the period, the average provision outstanding during the year would have been 775. The effect of the discount rate of 4.5 per cent on this amount would have been 35 and this amount could be charged as a finance cost in the profit and loss account. Taking into account the repayment of 50 and the increase due to the discount rate of 35, the adjusted provision at the beginning of year 1 is 785. In this case the difference of 65 between this amount and the re-estimated provision of 850 should be charged as an operating expense.

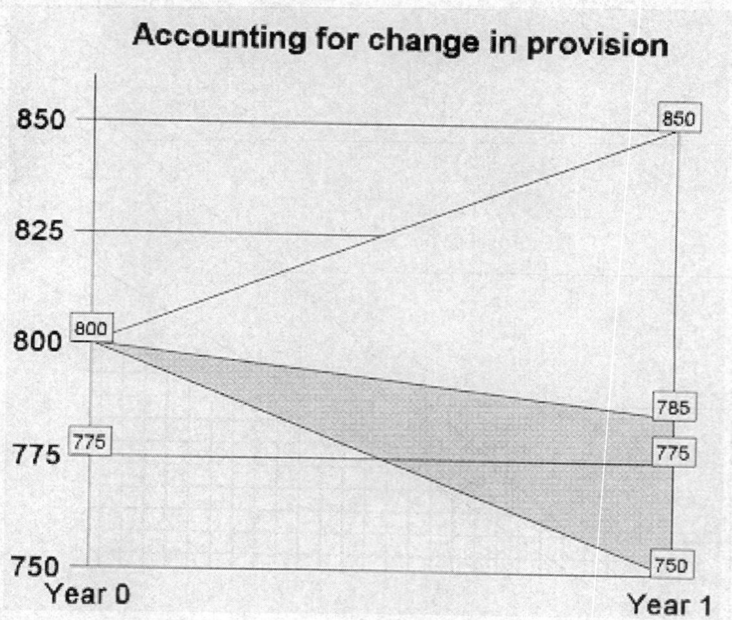

Future events

21.143 Although an obligating event that occurs after the balance sheet date cannot be provided for at the year end, events that occur after the year end can be taken into account and provide evidence to establish the amount for which provision should be made. The standard says that such future events, if they are likely to affect the amount required to settle an obligation, should be reflected in the amount of the provision where there is sufficient objective evidence that they will occur. [FRS 12 para 51].

21.144 An example is given in paragraph 21.73 concerning litigation, where the amount to be settled under a claim might crystallise or be more certain because further evidence comes to light after the entity's period end.

21.145 Sometimes it may be difficult to predict how future developments in (say) technology should impact the amount to be provided. This will typically be so in situations where provision is being made for rectification work that will be incurred a significant number of years into the future. Clearly it would be wrong to assume, for example, in the case of contaminated land, that in 50 years time a clean-up solution will be found that will have minimal cost and, as a consequence, little if any provision is required now. The standard says in these situations that the amount recognised (for both the provision and the asset if one is recognised) should reflect *"a reasonable expectation of technically qualified, objective observers, taking account of all available evidence as to the technology that will be available at the time of the clean-up"*. [FRS 12 para 52]. The standard goes on to explain that it is appropriate to include, for example, *"expected cost reductions associated with increased experience in applying existing technology or the expected cost of applying existing technology to a larger or more complex clean-up operation than has previously been carried out"*. But the standard is also quite clear that it does not mean that the entity can anticipate the development of a completely new technology, unless this is supported by sufficient objective evidence.

21.146 So undoubtedly great care needs to be taken in ascertaining that the changes in technology that are taken into account are appropriate. It is fine to anticipate the use of existing methods with some refinement, adaptation and cost reduction, if there is sufficient evidence that such factors are likely to arise in practice. But it is not acceptable to assume there will be a bright new idea, which will cost significantly less.

Future operating losses

21.147 There is a general rule in FRS 12 that provisions should not be recognised for future operating losses. FRS 12 specifically states that future operating losses do not meet the definition of a liability and the general recognition criteria set out for provisions in the standard (see para 21.47). [FRS 12 paras 68, 69]. The reason that future operating losses do not meet the definition of a liability is that they do not result from a past event (see para 21.54). This is similar to the prohibition on provisions for future operating costs where it is not acceptable under FRS 12 to make provision for costs that will be incurred in order to operate in the future, if those costs could be avoided by the entity's future actions (see para 21.65).

21.147.1 Where a company is expected to incur future operating losses, this is an indication that an impairment review should be carried out on the appropriate income generating unit (IGU) in accordance with the rules in FRS 11, 'Impairment of fixed assets and goodwill'. Such a review would determine whether those assets have suffered an impairment and need to be written down. [FRS 12 para 70]. Alternatively, anticipated future operating losses might indicate that a company has an onerous contract. In certain circumstances it is necessary to provide for the onerous element of a contract and the standard's rules in this area are considered from paragraph 21.193. Furthermore, FRS 3, 'Reporting financial performance', requires provision for future operating losses on termination of operations and this is considered from paragraph 21.171.

Restructuring

21.148 Provisions under FRS 12 are obligations to transfer economic benefits as a result of past transactions or events (that is, liabilities) that are uncertain as to their timing or amount. With a restructuring it is possible to construct an argument which says that although there will be a transfer of economic benefits that is uncertain as to its timing or amount, the restructuring is fundamentally about reshaping the entity's future business and has little if anything to do with the past. Therefore, it is not easy to identify a past event that gives rise to an obligation for which provision is necessary.

21.149 The key elements of the definition of a liability are considered in detail from paragraph 21.40. One of those relates to the need to have an obligating event, which evidences that a past event has taken place. For restructurings, FRS 12 sets down detailed rules that indicate when an obligating event has occurred and when an obligation to restructure arises. The impact of these rules means that it is possible in certain defined circumstances to make restructuring provisions under FRS 12.

21.150 The paragraphs that follow explore the rules that apply when a company proposes to carry out a restructuring programme.

[The next paragraph is 21.152.]

Restructuring rules in FRS 12

21.152 FRS 12 deals with restructuring operations generally and harmonised with and where necessary amended the rules in FRS 3, 'Reporting financial performance', to ensure similar rules apply to provisions made for the termination and discontinuance of operations and for continuing operations.

Definition

21.153 FRS 12 introduces the following definition of a 'restructuring':

"A programme that is planned and controlled by management, and materially changes either:

(a) the scope of a business undertaken by an entity; or

(b) the manner in which that business is conducted."

[FRS 12 para 2].

21.154 The standard gives some helpful examples of situations that fall within the restructuring definition:

- The sale or termination of a line of business.
- The closure of business locations in a country or region or the relocation of business activities from one country or region to another.
- Changes in management structure, for example, eliminating a layer of management.
- Fundamental reorganisations that have a material effect on the nature and focus of the entity's operations.

[FRS 12 para 75].

Applying the recognition criteria

21.155 It is only acceptable to make a provision for restructuring when an obligating event has arisen. Without the existence of an obligating event no obligation can exist. For a restructuring programme, it is unlikely that a liability will arise from a legal obligation as the obligation is more likely to be constructive in nature. As explained in paragraph 21.52 it is often more difficult to discern when a constructive obligation originates, so the standard introduces specific conditions that have to exist before a constructive restructuring obligation can exist. The evidence needed is:

- A detailed formal plan for the restructuring, which identifies at least:
  - The business or part of a business concerned.
  - The principal locations affected.
  - The location, function, and approximate number of employees who will be compensated for terminating their services.
  - The expenditures that will be undertaken.
  - When the plan will be implemented.
- A valid expectation in those affected that it will carry out the restructuring by starting to implement that plan or announcing its main features to those affected by it.

[FRS 12 para 77].

21.156 The standard indicates examples of the type of evidence needed to demonstrate that the entity has started to implement a restructuring plan. This includes:

- Dismantling plant.
- Selling assets.
- Public announcement of the plan's main features.

[FRS 12 para 78].

Board decision

21.157 It is not possible to make a provision where only a management or board decision to restructure has been taken before the balance sheet date, as this does not in itself give rise to a constructive obligation. [FRS 12 para 80]. Furthermore, even if the management or board complete the detailed plan and announce the restructuring after the entity's year end, but before its financial statements are approved by the board, provision for the restructuring should not be made. This is because it does not represent an adjusting post balance sheet event as there is no commitment to restructure at the year end from which the entity cannot withdraw. The entity could, for instance, change its plans completely in the new year. Consequently, the 'obligating event' does not take place until after the year end and should be reported as a non-adjusting post balance sheet event if the restructuring is of such importance that its non-disclosure would affect the ability of the users of the financial statements to make proper evaluations and decisions. [FRS 12 para 80].

21.158 FRS 12 specifies precisely the requirement for a commitment at the year end and makes it clear that even for a sale or termination, the binding sale agreement or the formal plan (the 'obligating event') must exist at the balance sheet date for an obligation to arise. [FRS 12 paras 83, 77]. Examples of disclosure of post balance sheet events involving restructurings are given in chapter 22 'Post balance sheet events and financial commitments'.

Third party expectation

21.159 To be a constructive obligation, a public announcement has to be made in such a way and in sufficient detail (that is, setting out the main features of the plan) that it raises valid expectations in customers, suppliers, employees (or their representatives) and others that the entity will carry out the restructuring. [FRS 12 para 78]. Practically, this means that in order to provide for a restructuring at the balance sheet date the entity must have started to implement its restructuring plan or announced the main features of the restructuring plan to those affected by it in a sufficiently specific manner to raise a valid expectation in them that the entity will carry out the restructuring. [FRS 12 para 80]. This is illustrated in the following example.

Example

Entity A's management has prepared a plan for a reorganisation of its operations. The board has approved the plan, which involves the closure of ten of entity A's fifty retail outlets. Management will conduct further analysis before deciding which outlets to close.

Management has announced its intentions publicly and believes that this has given rise to an obligation that should be recognised as a liability. Should a provision for restructuring costs be recognised?

No, a provision for restructuring should not be recognised. A constructive obligation arises only when an entity has both a detailed formal plan for restructuring and makes an announcement of the plan to those affected by it. The plan to date does not provide sufficient detail that would permit recognition of a constructive obligation.

21.160 Starting to implement the plan means that something must have happened that makes those affected expect that the plan will be carried out. Examples include dismantling plant, selling assets or making a detailed public announcement. Where only an announcement has been made, it must be to a level of detail that raises a valid expectation in customers, suppliers, employees or trade unions, that the entity will actually carry out the restructuring and will not be able to change its mind.

Example

An entity is planning a head office restructuring. The year end is 31 March 20X1. The entity will have made announcements before the year end (say in January 20X1). However, there is a 90 day consultation period and so individual employees will not have been notified by the year end. Can the entity provide for the restructuring costs at 31 March 20X1?

At the balance sheet date there has to be a detailed plan and the entity has to have raised a valid expectation in those affected that it will carry out the restructuring by starting to implement that plan or announcing its main features to those affected by it. Paragraph 78 of FRS 12 states that a public announcement of a detailed plan to restructure constitutes a constructive obligation to restructure only if it is made in such a way and in sufficient detail (that is, setting out the main features of the plan) that it gives rise to valid expectations in other parties such as customers, suppliers and employees (or their representatives) that the entity will carry out the restructuring.

Our view is that it is not necessary for individual employees to have been notified at the year end. If employee representatives have been notified then this would be sufficient. It will be necessary to consider what is involved in the specific consultation, but if it is negotiation of terms rather than something that could change the company's plans (which have already been announced in detail), then provision would be made.

21.161 In some situations, however, a board decision might confirm that an obligation exists. For example, in the situation where employees have been consulted about the restructuring and the restructuring plan has been developed with their participation, board approval will crystallise an obligation when the decision has been made and it has been communicated to the entity's employees. Similarly, where negotiations for the sale of part of the business have been agreed with a purchaser, but the terms of the sale are subject to board approval, once that approval has been gained and this has been communicated to the buyer (see further para 21.168) an obligation will arise, because the agreement will then be unconditional. [FRS 12 para 81].

21.162 Also in certain countries a board decision and a formal plan might be all that is necessary to give rise to an obligation. This might occur, for example, where the board includes worker representatives and management representatives. Or formal communication to management and worker representatives might be required by the local laws of the country concerned. [FRS 12 para 82]. In both these cases, a valid expectation that the entity will carry out the restructuring will be instilled in the entity's employees as soon as the board decision is taken.

Example

A company has prepared a formal plan for a reorganisation involving site closures and redundancies. The plan has been approved by the board at the year end. However, the company does not wish to provide for the reorganisation this year as it is planning a rights issue and does not want to depress the results. Accordingly, it will not implement or announce the reorganisation until after the year end and until after the financial statements are approved and the rights issue document is published.

If the company has not committed itself to the reorganisation or begun to implement it, the company's proposed treatment is acceptable. However, disclosure should be made of the board's plans in the financial statements and the rights issue document in order to give a true and fair view. On the other hand if the board has actually begun to implement the reorganisation by the end of the year, for example, by scrapping plant or informing employees and suppliers of the reorganisation, then there is an obligating event and provision should be made, despite the fact that no formal announcement has been made.

Restructuring time-frame

21.163 Many company reorganisations can take a number of years to complete. Typically a programme can run for two or three years and some might take up to five years. Where a restructuring will take a long time, then it is unlikely that all of the reorganisation will represent an obligation at the first year end following the decision, as the entity will inevitably be able to change its plans. [FRS 12 para 79]

21.164 If it is expected that there will be a long delay before the restructuring begins or that the restructuring will take an unreasonable length of time, it is unlikely that the plan will raise a valid expectation on the part of others that the entity is committed to restructuring.

21.165 For example, a company involved in a retailing business has a significant number of small retail outlets and it has decided to restructure to consolidate its retailing activities into a smaller number of larger outlets. This sort of decision could take a long time to implement in practice and so the company might decide to phase the work. The time-frame will depend on a number of factors some of which will be outside the company's control (for example, the availability of suitable retail outlets of the appropriate size and location). If the time-frame for the plan's implementation is over a number of years, it will be unlikely that the plan can be specific enough initially to make a provision for all of the costs associated with the proposed restructuring. Again the issue here comes back to whether there is a valid obligation from which the company cannot realistically withdraw. Certainly, the early part (say phase one) of a restructuring plan might create a valid expectation such that a provision can be made, but subsequent phases might not do so. In future years as the restructuring progresses it might become appropriate to make a provision for the next phase when there is a valid expectation that this will be carried through.

21.166 Clearly this is an area where there will be considerable debate concerning whether or not a plan is detailed enough and firm enough to create a valid expectation in others that it will be carried through. Any plan that is over one year in length will inevitably be subject to higher scrutiny. For major restructuring programmes this will lead to costs being charged to the profit and loss account over a number of accounting periods during the course of the restructuring programme.

21.167 One of the consequences of the standard is that the costs of a single reorganisation could be charged in different accounting periods and, in the case of reorganisations that are not fundamental, under different profit and loss account headings. Consequently, where this happens it might be useful for the totality of such costs and any related capital expenditure to be disclosed, but it may not be possible to provide for these costs all at once. [FRS 12 para 85].

Binding sale agreement

21.168 Both FRS 12 and FRS 3 require that a binding sale agreement evidencing a commitment to sell part of the business must exist before an obligation to sell can arise. [FRS 12 para 83; FRS 3 para 18]. An entity needs to have found a purchaser and signed unconditional contracts before a legal obligation can arise under which a provision might become necessary. This means that an unconditional sale agreement must be signed before the year end for an obligation to arise at the year end. During the period between the board decision to sell and the date on which the sale becomes unconditional, there might be a need to consider the carrying value of the income generating unit to which the operations relate. For example, if it is envisaged that a loss will arise on the sale of the operations or the operations are loss making, it would generally be necessary to carry out an impairment review in accordance with FRS 11 and this might necessitate a provision for impairment against the assets being sold. Impairment reviews are considered in more detail in chapter 18.

21.169 If a company has announced at its year end that it has put a subsidiary up for sale and if it cannot find a buyer it will close down the entity, the question arises whether or not an obligation exists. In this type of situation it is hard to say that the company is committed to a course of action if it still has options open to it. Therefore, it is unlikely that the company can make provision for the reorganisation costs in this type of circumstance, although it may still have to carry out an impairment review.

21.170 In some situations, the sale of an operation might be a small part of a larger restructuring. Where this is the case, an obligation might arise for other aspects of the restructuring plan for which provision should be made before a formal sale agreement has been reached for the operation being sold. [FRS 12 para 84].

Termination of operations

21.171 Restructurings that involve the termination of an operation are dealt with in FRS 3. In a similar way to FRS 12, that standard requires provision for any losses to be made if a decision to close has been made and the decision is evidenced by a detailed formal plan for termination from which the reporting entity cannot realistically withdraw. [FRS 3 para 18]. Evidence of the commitment might be the public announcement of specific plans, the commencement of implementation or other circumstances effectively obliging the reporting entity to complete the termination.

21.172 The provision required by the standard should include direct costs of the termination and any operating losses of the operation up to the date of termination, after taking account of any future profits of the operation, but not from the disposal of its assets. [FRS 3 para 18 as amended by FRS 12 para 100]. FRS 3 was amended by FRS 12 to preclude profits on disposals of assets from being taken into account in measuring such provisions. [FRS 12 para 100]. Although generally it is not possible under FRS 12's rules to provide for future operating losses, this is not the case for a provision made in accordance with FRS 3 on the termination of an operation. Future operating losses up to the date of termination of an operation may be included in a provision made under FRS 3's rules. Whereas for a sale of an operation, profits arising on its eventual sale cannot be taken into account, if the sale gives rise to a loss this may be provided for. There is no justification given in the standard for allowing provision to be made for future operation losses where an operation is being terminated, but it is possible to surmise that this situation is akin to an onerous contract where provision is required (see further para 21.193). However, often before there is a need to make provision for future losses in this way, assets should be written down for impairment as a result of FRS 11. Provisions for losses on termination of operations are discussed in detail in chapter 8.

Example

A company is closing an operation and by the year end a formal plan has been approved by the board and an announcement has been made. The closure will involve redundancies, but there will be a corresponding gain when the factory is sold. The factory has been valued professionally at above its carrying value and is expected to be sold after the year end, but before the financial statements are approved. Can the provision for redundancies be reduced by the profit on sale of the factory assuming it is sold before the financial statements are approved?

The company has a constructive obligation in respect of the redundancies and should provide for them. The gain on disposal is, however, a contingent gain whose receipt is not virtually certain at the year end. Thus, the gain should not be recognised at the year end, although disclosure may be required.

[The next paragraph is 21.174.]

Post balance sheet events

21.174 Post balance sheet events are dealt with in detail in chapter 22. However, in summary, FRS 21, 'Events after the balance sheet date', requires that an adjusting post balance sheet event should be reflected in the prior year's financial statements. An adjusting event is a post balance sheet event that provides evidence of conditions that existed at the balance sheet date. [FRS 21 para 3(a)].

21.175 Provision should not be made in the current year for non-adjusting post-balance sheet events. FRS 21 lists examples of the types of events that are adjusting events and those that are non-adjusting events. The non-adjusting list includes:

- Reconstructions and proposed reconstructions.
- Announcing a plan to discontinue an operation.

21.176 FRS 21 also deals with going concern. Where management determine after the balance sheet date either that it intends to liquidate the entity or to cease trading, or that it has no realistic alternative but to do so, the financial statements should not be prepared on a going concern basis. [FRS 21 para 14]. Therefore, where a decision to close down an entity's operation is made after the balance sheet date, this may indicate that applying the going concern concept to the entity is not appropriate. As the going concern basis is not appropriate, the financial statements should be prepared on a fundamentally different basis. This is dealt with in chapter 2.

Costs of restructuring

21.177 FRS 12 specifies that a restructuring provision should include only the direct expenditures arising from the restructuring, which are those that are both:

- necessarily entailed by the restructuring; and
- not associated with the ongoing activities of the entity.

[FRS 12 para 85].

21.178 Expenditure allowed in a restructuring provision includes the following:

- Expenditure to be made in the course of the re-organisation, such as the remuneration of employees engaged in dismantling plant and disposing of surplus stocks.
- Costs of making employees redundant (see para 21.182 onwards).
- Costs of terminating leases and other contracts, the termination of which results directly from the reorganisation.
- Costs representing contractual obligations that would either continue after the restructuring with no economic benefit to the entity, for example, where the company is not permitted to cancel the lease and is unable to use the property in its continuing operations. Onerous contracts are discussed in more detail from paragraph 21.193.

The following table distinguishes between costs that should be included in, and those that should be excluded from, a restructuring provision.

Description of costs	**Included**	**Excluded**	**Reason for exclusion**
Voluntary redundancies (see para 21.190 onwards).	✓		
Compulsory redundancies, if the target for voluntary redundancies are not met (see para 21.183 onwards).	✓		
Lease cancellation fees for a factory that will no longer be used.	✓		
Relocation of employees and related equipment from a factory (to be closed) to a factory that will continue to be used.		✓	Costs associated with ongoing activities.
Retraining of remaining employees.		✓	Costs associated with ongoing activities.
Recruitment costs for a new manager.		✓	Costs associated with ongoing activities.
Marketing costs to develop new corporate image.		✓	Costs associated with ongoing activities.
Investments in a new distribution network.		✓	Costs associated with ongoing activities.
Future identifiable operating losses up to the date of a restructuring.		✓	Costs associated with ongoing activities.

Impairment write-down of certain property, plant and equipment.		✓	The impairment provision should be assessed in accordance with FRS 11 and offset against the asset.
Costs of the remaining non-cancellable term of an operating lease after operations cease.	✓		
Consulting fees to identify future corporate strategies and organisational structures.		✓	Costs associated with ongoing activities.
Costs of relocating inventory and equipment that will be used at another location.		✓	Costs associated with ongoing activities.
Acquisition integration costs, for example, integrating the combining companies' computer systems.		✓	Costs associated with ongoing activities.

21.179 FRS 12 states that retraining or relocating continuing staff, marketing, or investment in new systems and distribution networks should not be included in the restructuring provision. [FRS 12 para 86]. This is because these costs relate to the future conduct of the business and, as a consequence, do not represent an obligation arising from a past event. Also, the restructuring provision does not include future operating losses (unless these relate to an onerous contract) as the losses do not result from a past event (see para 21.147). [FRS 12 para 87].

21.180 Therefore, in order to recognise a provision, it is not sufficient to demonstrate that a commitment for future expenditure exists at the balance date, it is also necessary for that expenditure commitment to relate to past operations, not future operations (except in the case of onerous contracts). If expenditure commitments relating to future operations were provided for, then it is likely that an associated asset would also exist, representing the future economic benefits to be derived from the expenditure. Hence, the expenditure commitment would be treated as an asset and a liability, instead of as an expense and a liability. Rather than go down the route of recognising all expenditure commitments (which would entail dealing with the complexities relating to recognising the associated assets), FRS 12 has confined itself to recognising expenditure commitments that relate to past operations — where future economic benefits are unlikely to exist — and onerous contracts — where the expected future benefits to be derived from the contract are less than the expenditure commitment.

Example 1

A company has drawn up a plan to restructure its management and has decided to make a number of its managers redundant. It is also going to bring in a new senior manager to take over responsibility for running the business as part of the overall plan. The new manager is to be recruited from outside the company and the company will pay for the relocation costs for its new employee. There will also be some retraining of the remaining employees in new systems to be introduced.

In this case, redundancy costs and other closure costs associated with terminating any of the company's operations will not yield any future economic benefits. These costs, therefore, should be included in the company's restructuring provision. Staff retraining costs, on the other hand, are likely to generate future economic benefits to the entity's future operations, so are excluded from the restructuring provision. Doubtless, the company would be unlikely to have committed to the appointment of the new manager unless it considered that the future economic benefits to be derived from that appointment exceeded the costs. Hence, no provision should be made to cover these costs as part of the restructuring provision.

Example 2

A company has announced before its year end that it will be closing its offices in London and will be relocating staff to Birmingham after its year end. The company recognises that, normally under FRS 12, a relocation provision would be prohibited. However, in this case, all employees affected have been advised in writing before its year end that if they relocate they will be paid a one off incentive to do so. There is, therefore, either a legal or at least a constructive obligation at the balance sheet date, in that those asked to relocate now have a valid expectation that such payments will be made and that the company is not in a position to withdraw from this.

The company's question is whether it can make a provision for the relocation incentive under FRS 12 based on the current best estimate of the number of employees expected to accept the incentive offer to relocate.

Whilst it appears that the company is far enough down the track to enable provision to be made in principle, it could only make a provision for allowable costs under FRS 12. An incentive to relocate is the same as a relocation cost and, therefore, cannot be provided.

21.181 Gains on the expected disposal of assets are not taken into account in measuring a restructuring provision, even if the sale of assets is envisaged as part of the restructuring. [FRS 12 para 88]. See the example in paragraph 21.172.

Redundancy provisions

21.182 An area that often results in significant provisions and is often associated with reorganisations concerns redundancies. The timing of such provisions is considered below by looking at the various stages involved in the redundancy process.

Compulsory redundancies

21.183 The process of making compulsory redundancies usually involves several stages:

- Initial board decision.
- Identifying the business or part of the business concerned and the principal locations affected.
- Identifying the location, function and approximate number of employees to be made redundant.
- Approval of the detailed formal plan by the board, which includes details of the expenditures to be incurred and the timing of implementation.
- Identifying employees to be made redundant in terms of individuals.
- Informing employees.
- Making the redundancy payments.

Situation 1 — redundancy payments made

21.184 Where all the above steps have been taken by the balance sheet date, the cost of the redundancy programme will be reflected in the financial statements of the year. This is because the liability has been incurred and settled.

Situation 2 — employees informed

21.185 Where the employees have been informed of their redundancies by the balance sheet date, provision should be made in the financial statements for the year, because the company's detailed formal plan is being actioned. A clear obligation has been incurred to specific employees. It is probable that there will be an outflow of resources and the cost can be measured with reliability.

[The next paragraph is 21.187.]

21.187 It is sometimes argued that the liability represents only the amount that is legally payable to employees and that *ex-gratia* amounts, paid over and above the legal minimum, need not be provided. This may be an argument in some cases where it has not been the company's practice in the past to make such *ex-gratia* payments. However, if it is established practice in the company to make *ex-gratia* payments and the decision has been made as part of the detailed formal plan to pay such extra amounts in the particular case, then the additional payment forms part of the constructive obligation. Clearly this would also be the case if the employees had terms in their contracts that provided for the payment of extra amounts, or if the employees included directors who are entitled to such amounts under their service contracts. Generally, the full amount of redundancy payments should be provided and not just the legal minimum.

Situation 3 — employees identified but not informed

21.188 Where the employees have been identified both in terms of numbers and individuals no provision should be made, unless an obligating event has taken place. At this stage in the process, the board has formally approved the detailed formal plan, but it is also necessary for the company to have raised a valid expectation in those affected that it will carry out its proposals. Even where the company has identified the specific employees that it wishes to make redundant, no expectation will have been raised on the part of others that the company will carry out its plans, unless the company has made a formal announcement or has started to implement its plans. Only when such a commitment has been made does an obligating event arise and provision can be made. If, for example, the company has started to implement its plan and has announced its intention to 100 of 300 employees affected, provision will be allowed where this announcement makes it clear that more employees are to be made redundant as part of the plan. Where, however, the announcement only specifies that the 100 told will be made redundant, this does not raise a valid expectation that other redundancies will occur and, consequently, provision cannot be made for the further 200 redundancies still to be announced.

Situation 4 — numbers determined but not specific employees

21.189 In this situation the detailed formal plan has been approved by the board, the numbers to be made redundant have been identified, but not the specific employees. It is likely that no provision can be made for the redundancies at this stage, because it is possible that the board can still change its plans thereby avoiding the potential obligation. However, as the board has approved a detailed formal plan, if it raises a valid expectation in its staff that it will carry out the redundancy programme, by either starting to implement the plan or by announcing its main feature to those affected, it should make provision for the redundancies.

Voluntary redundancies

21.190 The same principles apply to voluntary redundancies. In general, provision should be made for the expected amount of the redundancy payment, but only where the conditions in FRS 12 have been complied with. That is, the company has a detailed formal plan and its main features have been announced to those affected or the plan has started to be implemented. Where a detailed formal plan has been approved, but it has not been communicated to employees, there is no obligating event and no provision can be made. What could happen in practice is that a detailed formal plan might be approved by the balance sheet date to reduce the workforce and this might have been announced, but the board does not know how much of the reduction will come from voluntary redundancies (giving rise to a higher payment), how much from natural wastage (no payment arising) and how much from compulsory redundancies (a lower amount being payable). Hence, it is possible that any liability that arises as a result of the detailed plan decision etc will not be capable of being reliably measured.

21.191 Although this uncertainty might suggest that no provision should be made for the full liability, there may be minimum amounts that can be estimated reliably. For instance, it may be possible to estimate the maximum number of people that could be lost through natural wastage and, therefore, to estimate the numbers who would be made redundant, whether voluntarily or compulsorily. If the latter numbers could be determined it might be possible to quantify the legal minimum that would have to be paid in redundancy pay and provide for that. If on the other hand it is not possible to determine the split between those taking voluntary or compulsory redundancy, then the company should probably, depending on the circumstances, make provision for the maximum amount that will become due under the terms of the voluntary scheme. It should be remembered that the standard says that it will only be in extremely rare circumstances that an entity will not be able to make as estimate of the obligation. [FRS 12 para 25].

21.192 A further factor that may make it impossible to quantify a liability reliably is if the reduction in employees is to take place over an extended period. This could, for instance, affect the numbers of employees who would be lost through natural wastage and thus make more difficult the estimates of how many would be made redundant. In such a case, where the amounts cannot be reliably measured, no provision should be made and the obligation should be disclosed as a contingent liability (see further para 21.92). It may be necessary to make a provision in a subsequent period when the obligation becomes more certain and can be reliably estimated.

Onerous contracts

21.193 FRS 12 contains a specific requirement to make provision for onerous contracts, but only in certain circumstances. The standard requires that where an entity has a contract that is onerous, provision should be made for the present obligation that arises under the contract. [FRS 12 para 71]. Many contracts can be cancelled without any compensation being paid to the other contracting party and clearly as no obligation can arise in this type of situation, such contracts (for example, routine purchase orders) cannot be onerous. But other contracts establish both rights and obligations on each of the contracting parties. It is these types of contract that potentially fall within FRS 12's scope. Where such contracts become onerous, provision should be made for the onerous obligations that arise. It is worth remembering also that the standard excludes from its scope, and hence its rules concerning onerous contracts, contracts that are covered by more specific standards (for example, long-term contracts that fall within SSAP 9).

21.194 Contracts that typically fall into this area are leases of property particularly where the property is being sublet. For example, a sub-lease rental received by an entity for a property might be less than that being paid by it under a head lease for the same property. Clearly, in this circumstance the contract is onerous and it is necessary to make a provision for the onerous element. Where a company has a head lease on a property it has a continuing obligation to pay the landlord for the rents due under the lease. However, if the property is vacant, the company may not be able to recover any of that cost in the future, unless it can find a sub-lessee for the unoccupied premises. Examples of onerous operating leases are covered in paragraph 21.212 below.

21.195 Executory contracts are generally excluded from FRS 12's scope. However, where these types of contracts are onerous the rules in FRS 12 should be applied as outlined below from paragraph 21.199. Executory contracts are defined in the standard as contracts under which neither party has performed any of its obligations or under which both parties have partially performed their obligations to an equal extent. [FRS 12 para 6]. Executory contracts encompass commitments. Also, take-or-pay contracts are examples of executory contracts. In a take-or-pay contract, an entity enters into a long-term contract with a supplier at a predetermined price for the supply of either goods or services and undertakes to pay for a minimum quantity whether or not the quantity is actually required. The advantage for the purchaser is guaranteed delivery of a certain quantity of goods and an ability to negotiate a competitive price, but will lose out if prices subsequently fall. Throughput contracts are also executory contracts and are very similar in nature to take-or-pay contracts. They are common in the oil industry, where more than one company might share, for example, an oil pipe line. The parties to the contract enter into an agreement to share the use of the facility and each party will pay a certain amount which will not necessarily depend on the quantity of oil that they transport through the pipe line.

21.196 Financial instruments that are carried in the financial statements at market value are excluded from the standard's scope. Thus, for an entity applying FRS 26 (see further chapter 6), many financial instruments will fall outside FRS 12's scope. For entities that are not applying FRS 26, certain financial instruments, for example, derivative contracts used for hedging purposes are included within FRS 12's scope. However, it is unlikely that such derivative contracts of that nature would fall to be treated as onerous simply if they are adverse, because the underlying position would also be taken into account (see further from para 21.202 below).

[The next paragraph is 21.199.]

General rules

21.199 The standard requires that where an entity has an onerous contract, the present obligation under that contract should be recognised and measured as a provision. [FRS 12 para 71]. For this purpose FRS 12 defines an onerous contract as *"a contract in which the unavoidable costs of meeting the obligations under it exceed the economic benefits expected to be received under it"*. [FRS 12 para 2]. The question then arises as to what are the 'unavoidable costs' under a contract. The standard comments that these costs represent the least net cost of exiting from the contract, that is the lower of the cost of fulfilling it and any compensation or penalties arising from failure to fulfil it. [FRS 12 para 73].

21.200 FRS 12 has a general prohibition on providing for future operating losses, but this does not contradict the requirement to provide for onerous contracts, which appears directly after the prohibition. This view is based on our interpretation of FRS 12 and on FRED 14, which preceded it. FRED 14 was clearer in this respect than FRS 12, and said *"...provision for future operating losses should not be made. However where an entity has entered into an onerous contract a provision will be required"*.

21.201 Specific assets might be dedicated to a particular contract, in which case before a separate provision for an onerous contract can be made, it is necessary to recognise any impairment loss for those assets in accordance with the rules set out in FRS 11. [FRS 12 para 74].

Interpretation

Expected economic benefits

21.202 It is important in applying the standard's requirements to understand what the words *"...economic benefits expected to be received under [the contract]"* mean in the definition of an onerous contract. The point is important because if this means only the benefits expected from the contract itself, in a narrow sense, then this would be likely to give rise to much larger provisions than if the benefits include the economic benefits to be derived from the use of the goods or services received under the contract in the business of the entity.

21.203 One interpretation of the standard could be that the quantification of the economic benefits of the contract should be limited to the direct benefits measured by reference to market prices for a similar contract. In such a case if the prices under the purchase contract exceeded market prices, the contract could be deemed onerous.

21.204 Another interpretation could be that the quantification of the benefits should include those indirect benefits that are derived by the business (or by the income generating unit (IGU)) that has the contract. Such benefits include using the product or services received under the contract (possibly in conjunction with other 'favourable' contracts) to produce other goods or services. Under this interpretation if the overall benefits from using the contract are more than the overall cost, the contract would not be onerous.

21.205 We consider that the second interpretation is the appropriate one to use. If the former interpretation were accepted, it would mean marking to market and providing for all contracts that showed any level of unfavourable movement when compared with market price.

Assets dedicated to the contract

21.206 The standard requires that before a separate provision for an onerous contract can be made, an entity should recognise any impairment that has occurred on assets *"dedicated to that contract"*. [FRS 12 para 74]. It is then necessary to consider what the words 'dedicated to that contract' mean. For instance, do they mean only assets used for the purpose of fulfilling the contract, or can they, or should they, include the assets of the IGU that has the onerous contract?

21.207 One interpretation is that only assets that are used in fulfilling the contract should be reviewed for impairment. For example, if the contract is for the purchase of oil and the purchaser builds a pipeline that carries only the oil to be supplied under the contract, then the pipeline would be a dedicated asset. Other assets of the business, such as a refinery that uses both the oil received under the contract and oil bought under other contracts would not fall within the term 'dedicated assets'. This view is based on the fact that assets not dedicated to a contract could be used in conjunction with favourable contracts and are, therefore, not intrinsically impaired.

21.208 Another interpretation is that, despite the word 'dedicated', the ASB's intention was not to introduce a rule whereby onerous contracts and their associated assets were provided against by reference only to market values of similar contracts, whilst no account was taken of other 'favourable' contracts and their associated assets. Instead it is more appropriate, and a reasonable interpretation of the words in the standard, to consider impairment in relation to the IGU (as defined in FRS 11) that has the contract. Only if the IGU is impaired, taking account of the benefits, direct and indirect, of all contracts should provision for impairment be made. If the impairment is so great that there remains a loss after all the assets of the IGU have been provided against, provision should then be made for the remaining onerous element of the contract.

21.209 We consider that the latter interpretation is the more appropriate because:

- It reflects the practice that existed prior to the introduction of FRS 12, which we do not believe the ASB intended to change.
- It does not result in unfavourable contracts being provided for whilst no account is taken of favourable contracts.

Illustrative examples

21.210 The principles outlined above are examined further using examples of two types of contracts (long-term purchase contracts and property operating leases) to illustrate different situations that might arise in practice.

Long-term purchase contracts

21.211 The examples that follow illustrate when a contract is onerous, whether or not dedicated assets need to be impaired and how payments to vary contract terms should be dealt with in the financial statements.

Example 1 — contract not onerous

A company has a contract to purchase one million units of gas at 23p per unit giving a contract price of £230,000 and the current market price for a similar contract is 16p per unit giving a price of £160,000. The gas will be used in generating electricity and the electricity will be sold at a profit.

In this case the economic benefits from the contract include the benefits to the entity of using the gas in its business and because the electricity that is produced can be sold at a profit, the contract is not onerous.

Example 2 — impairment of assets

The contract's terms are the same as in example 1, as is the market price. However, when the gas is used to generate electricity, the high cost of the gas means that the electricity is sold at a loss and the entity makes an overall operating loss. (It is assumed that all the gas used by the entity to generate electricity is purchased under the contract.)

In this case, as the entity is making losses, it will be necessary to comply with paragraph 74 of the standard to carry out an impairment test (in accordance with FRS 11) on the IGU that generates the electricity and write down any assets that are impaired. To the extent that there is still an impairment after the assets have been fully written down, the balance should be provided for as a provision for an onerous contract. The impairment test on the IGU should be carried out by reference to the normal time span for impairment testing of IGU's set out in FRS 11 and not by reference to the contract's duration.

Example 3 — sale to third party at below purchase price

The facts are the same as in example 1 with regard to the price of the gas subject to the contract and the market price. However, in this example there is a sales contract to sell the gas on to a third party as it is in excess of the entity's requirements. The sales contract is priced at 18p per unit. The entity would have to pay C55,000 to exit the purchase contract.

In this example the only economic benefits to be derived from the purchase contract costing £230,000 are the proceeds from the sales contract, which are £180,000. Therefore, a provision should be made for the onerous element of £50,000, being the lower of the cost of fulfilling the contract and the penalty cost of cancellation (£55,000).

21.211.1 In practice, a company may decide to terminate an existing contract and incur a penalty, in order to enter into a more beneficial contract. The example below considers the accounting for the termination cost in this situation.

Example

In the year ended 31 December 20X1, an entity has an existing contract with a third party supplier. The entity wishes to terminate this contract in 20X2 even though it will still have two years to run, because they can enter into a cheaper contract with a new supplier. They will incur a charge for terminating the contract.

(a) Do they have to provide in 20X1 for the contract that they will be exiting in 20X2?

If the contract with the existing supplier is an onerous contract (that is, one in which the unavoidable costs of meeting the obligations under it exceed the economic benefits expected to be received under it) then provision should be made under FRS 12 for the least net cost of exiting from it. However, if the business in which the products supplied under the contract are used is profitable, then the contract is not onerous and provision should not be made in 20X1 in advance of termination. Instead, the termination cost should be charged as incurred in 20X2.

(b) The entity argues that as the old contract is being terminated in order to enter the new one (at a lower cost) then they should be permitted to spread the termination payment over the period of the new contract. Can they defer the termination charge to match this against the benefits of the new contract?

Although the decision to terminate the old contract is commercially linked to the decision to enter into the new contract, the cost does not form part of the cost of the new contract. The fact that there will be future benefits from entering the new contract does not mean that they should not show the termination cost of the old contract when it is incurred (comparable with treatment of redundancy costs). The cost of terminating the contract would not qualify for recognition as an asset as there are no future economic benefits specifically attributable to the cost.

Operating leases on property

21.212 The examples that follow illustrate for property leases where a contract becomes onerous, when assets need to be impaired, the treatment of sub-leases and the issues concerning groups of similar properties.

Example 1 — contract not onerous

A company has a 10 year lease on a property at a rental of £50,000 per annum. The market rent is £30,000 per annum. The property is used in the business and the business is profitable.

In this situation the lease is not onerous, because the economic benefits are assumed to include those that derive from the asset's use in the company's continuing business.

Example 2 — impairment of assets

The company has the same lease as in example 1 and the property is used in the business, but the business is loss making.

In this example under FRS 11 there is an indication of impairment in the IGU and the IGU's assets should be reviewed for impairment and written down. If the impairment loss exceeds the assets' value, the company needs to assess the least net cost of exiting from the lease and make provision for the onerous lease. (Clearly in this situation management will need to look at whether or not to close the business.)

Example 3 — temporary closure of retail store

A company has an operating lease on a retail store. The air-conditioning system is unreliable and the company proposes to replace it. The store will be closed while the works are carried out. Can the company provide in advance for the rent that is payable during the closure period?

FRS 12 does not permit provisions to be made for future operating losses. A provision for future operating lease payments cannot be made unless the lease is an onerous contract. An onerous contract is defined as *"a contract in which the unavoidable costs of meeting the obligations under it exceed the economic benefits expected to be received under it"*. In the context of the store's lease, the economic benefits from it include the future cash flows that are expected to be earned from operating the store. The lease would be onerous only if the rentals for its full term could not be recovered (in present value terms) from the future cash flows.

A lease is not onerous merely because an operating loss is expected for a short period during the lease. If, as is probable, the rentals payable over the full lease term (including those relating to the closure period) were expected to be recovered, the lease as a whole is not an onerous contract and so no provision should be made. The company's reported earnings for each period would then show operating losses and profits for the store as they arise.

Example 4 — sub-lease to third party at below head lease cost

The company has an operating lease as in example 1. It no longer occupies the property and it is not used in the business. A sub-lease on the property has been arranged at a rent of £30,000 a year for 10 years. The company has established that the present value of the net cost of continuing with the lease is less than the penalty for exiting the lease.

In this example the maximum benefits to be derived from the contract are £30,000 for 10 years. The cash inflow of £30,000 should be deducted from the cash outflows of £50,000 and the balance of £20,000 each year should be discounted using a risk-free rate (see para 21.217 below) to give the amount that should be provided on the onerous element of the lease.

Example 5 — property is one of many similar properties

The facts are the same as in example 1 with regard to the lease. In addition, the property is empty and is not sublet. However, the company is a bank (or a retailer) and also has lots of other properties where the leases are above market rates. The company does not consider it is fair to provide for this lease, in isolation. It may or may not reopen the property and use it again in its business.

In this example, if it is only a possibility that the property will be used again in the business, the prudent approach would be to provide. However, where the entity plans to use the property again in its business, it is necessary to look at the IGU of which the property forms part. This IGU will not necessarily include all of the company's properties, but only those that form part of the IGU. The IGU is then assessed for impairment taking account of the net cash outflows from the empty property. If the IGU has suffered an impairment then the assets should be written down, if the amount of the impairment is material.

Example 6 — property to be sold or never used

The facts are as in example 5 except that the company intends either never to use the property again and/or to dispose of the lease.

In this instance the property lease cannot be viewed in conjunction with the IGU of which it forms part, because FRS 11 paragraph 31 says that an asset held for sale does not belong to any other IGU, but is an IGU of its own. Provision should, therefore, be made for the onerous element of the lease.

21.213 A question arises in practice as to whether the words *"expected benefits to be received under the contract"* mean only those benefits that are contractually committed or whether they mean those benefits that are expected, although no contract has been entered into that assures their receipt. We consider that the latter approach is acceptable and the example that follows illustrates this for a property lease.

Example — sub-lease negotiation not complete

The lease is the same as in example 1 in paragraph 21.212, that is, the company has a 10 year lease on a property at a rental of £50,000 per annum and the market rent is £30,000 per annum. However, in this example the company no longer uses the property and never will do so again. It is, therefore, going to make a provision for an onerous contract. It has not yet found a sub-lessee, but expects to do so soon. The question is then whether or not it is acceptable for the company to anticipate the future sub-lease in determining the provision to be made.

FRS 12 clearly says in the definition of an onerous contract that the expected benefits to be received under the lease should be taken into account. [FRS 12 para 2]. Consequently, it is reasonable to take account of the expected rent to be received under a sub-lease in determining the provision, provided that the company is actively seeking to sublet the property, there is evidence (from estate agents or similar) that the property can be let, and there is reasonable evidence as to the rent that may be obtained in an open market rental. Alternatively, the least cost could be determined as the cost of negotiating out of the lease with the landlord.

Measurement of an onerous contract

21.214 There are a number of ways of setting up a provision for an onerous contract. For example, a provision could be made for the discounted gross costs under a contract; or the discounted gross costs less the discounted expected benefits provided as a net liability; or the gross costs as a liability and, separately, a discounted asset for the expected benefits. The following paragraphs explore these issues.

21.215 Clearly, setting up a provision for the discounted gross costs without taking account of the expected benefits would overstate the provision and would be overly prudent. On the other hand, grossing up for an asset and liability would be premature when no services or goods had been received under the contract.

21.216 FRS 12 states that the unavoidable costs under a contract reflect the least net cost of exiting from the contract. The explanation of this is "*the lower of the cost of fulfilling it and any compensation or penalties arising from failure to fulfil it*". We interpret this to mean the net cost after taking account of the benefits that can be obtained from resale of the product, or the net cost of negotiating out of the contract with the supplier. In reality the entity will be able to negotiate cancellation of the contract for the net amount, unless the asset is incapable of being sold on (or relet) to a third party. Therefore, we consider that the discounted gross costs less the discounted expected benefits should be provided as a net liability.

21.217 As noted in paragraph 21.119, FRS 12 requires that where the effect of the time value of money is material the amount of a provision should be the present value of the expenditures expected to be required to settle the obligation. [FRS 12 para 45]. This is considered in paragraph 21.139 for leases. Where the amount of the lease rentals payable and receivable are known in money terms, a nominal risk-free rate should be used to discount them (see para 21.131 above). The discount rate should be pre-tax. An appropriate rate would be a government bond rate. In theory, different rates should be applied to the cash flows arising in each year. However, in practice, it is likely that a single rate based on a bond with a term similar to that of the lease term will give a result that is not materially different.

21.218 For companies applying FRS 26, a further consideration with contracts of the type discussed in this section is whether or not they conceal one or more embedded derivatives. See chapter 6 for further detail on embedded derivatives, their identification, recognition and measurement.

[The next paragraph is 21.222.]

Other practical applications

21.222 A number of examples have been used throughout the text to illustrate how each of the specific aspects of FRS 12 is likely to apply in practice. The paragraphs that follow consider how these affect different types of transactions in their entirety. Some of these transactions are also considered in appendix III to FRS 12.

21.223 The rules in FRS 12 that specify when a provision can be made are summarised in the five bullet points below. The paragraphs that follow makes reference to these points. In order for an entity to make provision:

- It must have a present obligation (which can be legal or constructive in nature) that is more likely than not to arise.
- The obligation must arise from an obligating event (that is, a past event) that either can be legally enforced or is an undertaking given to third parties from which the entity cannot realistically withdraw.
- The obligation must not relate to costs that will be incurred in the future as part of the entity's future operations.
- It must be more likely than not that the obligation will result in a transfer of economic benefits.

- It must be possible to make a reliable estimate of the obligation.

21.224 When considering the examples below, it is also helpful to consider what would happen if the entity were to stop trading as of its balance sheet date. Would it have an obligation to incur further expenditure? This simple test often gives a very good indication of whether or not an obligation exists that arises from a past event. This is referred to in the paragraphs below as the 'year end test'.

Warranties

21.225 A warranty is often provided in conjunction with the sale of goods. Warranty costs represent additional costs that the seller may have to incur to rectify defects in, or to replace, the product it has sold. The warranty obligation can arise either through the operation of the law (contract or statute) or through a company's stated policies as explained from paragraph 21.51 onwards.

21.225.1 When an entity sells a product subject to warranty, it must first determine whether the warranty represents a separable component of the transaction. If an item sold proves to have been defective at the time of sale (usually based on evidence coming to light within a standard period), the purchaser may have the right to require the seller to rectify the defect or replace the faulty item. Such a warranty is considered to be a 'standard warranty' that relates to the condition of the item sold at the date of sale. It is not usually considered separable from the sale of goods.

21.226 When the warranty is not a separate element and represents an insignificant part of the sale transaction, generally the full consideration received is recognised as revenue on the sale and a provision is recognised for the expected future cost to be incurred relating to the warranty. An example of such an arrangement is a standard manufacturing warranty given under the normal terms and conditions of sale. Warranties that are not separate elements are dealt with in FRS 12. The principles included in the example given in appendix III to FRS 12 are explained below.

Example 1

A company sells gardening merchandise. On some of its products it warrants at the time the sale is made that it will make good by repair or replacement manufacturing defects that become apparent within one year from the date of sale. Its past experience shows that it does receive warranty claims on these products.

A provision should be made for the best estimate of the obligation for the following reasons:

- A legal obligation exists which is more likely than not to arise.
- The obligating event is the sale of the product and the normal one-year warranty can be legally enforced.
- The related costs of repair do not relate to the company's future operations.

- From past experience, it is more likely than not that the obligation will result in a transfer of economic benefits.

- A reliable estimate of the obligation can be made from the company's previous claims experience.

Using the simple year end test, if the company stopped trading at its year end, it would still be liable for the obligations arising from warranties it has already given. Hence, provision is required. The company should use past experience to estimate reliably the amount of potential claims.

Example 2

The facts are the same as those outlined in example 1, except that the company makes a payment to a third party insurer, which underwrites the risk. In the event of a claim by a customer, the company would claim a corresponding amount from the insurer.

Provision would be made for the warranty for the reasons given in example 1 above. The mere existence of the underwriting agreement does not mean that the company can ignore the warranty obligation. The customer has recourse directly to the company for the warranty. The company in turn has a claim on the insurance company, but this does not offset the company's obligation to its customer.

Hence, the company will have to provide for its best estimate of its warranty obligation. It will have to consider whether or not it can recognise its counter-claim on its insurer. It cannot recognise a separate debtor for such claims, unless it is virtually certain that it will recover the funds from the insurer. If it cannot be this certain, then it should disclose the existence of the contingent asset in the notes to its financial statements.

21.226.1 An example of how to measure a provision for warranty claims is given from paragraph 21.118.

21.227 Where the warranty goes further than a standard warranty, it may well be separable from the sale of goods. An extended warranty is an agreement to provide warranty protection in addition to the scope of coverage of a manufacturer's standard warranty, or to extend the period of coverage provided by the manufacturer's warranty. They are often sold separately from the original product but, where warranties included in the price of a product provide protection in excess of that provided by the normal terms and conditions of sale for the relevant product, the transaction's substance is that the entity has sold two products. If an entity sells a product with an extended warranty, it is treated as a multiple element arrangement and the revenue from the sale of the extended warranty should be deferred and recognised over the period covered by the warranty. No costs should be provided for at the inception of the extended warranty agreement, because the warranty is deemed to relate principally to rectification of defects, the risks relating to which were transferred to the buyer in the sales transaction. Therefore, the obligation to repair or replace only arises for the seller if and when a defect arises, rather than at the time of selling the goods. Provision is recognised for rectification and/or replacement only as defects arise through the warranty period, which differs from the situation with a standard warranty where provision is made at the time of selling the goods (see para 21.226). The entity recognises provisions both for claims received and for IBNR claims.

21.227.1 Accounting for warranties (both standard and extended) is dealt with further in chapter 9.

Refunds

21.228 Many entities have refund policies which are over and above the customers' rights under the Sale of Goods Act. A number of retailers, for example, give cash refunds for products returned whether or not they are defective, whereas others make cash refunds even where the customer does not have the receipt showing when the goods were purchased. Yet these policies have been operated in such a way, and for so long, that the customer has come to accept that they will be honoured.

21.229 FRS 12 includes an example in appendix III which considers how such refund policies should be dealt with under its rules:

Example

A retail company has a policy of refunding purchases by dissatisfied customers, even where it is under no legal obligation to do so. It has adopted this policy for a number of years and it is well known to its customers.

The company should make a provision for the best estimate of its refund obligation for the following reasons:

- It has a present obligation that is constructive in nature, which is more likely than not to arise.
- The obligating event is the sale of the goods, which has raised a valid expectation on the part of its customers from which the entity cannot realistically withdraw.
- The obligation does not relate to costs of future operations.
- Past experience shows that it is more likely than not that the obligation will result in a transfer of economic benefits.
- A reliable estimate of the obligation can be made from past refunds.

Using the simple year end test would arrive at the same conclusion, because if the company did not continue to trade, it would still have an obligation in relation to the sales it had made to date.

21.229.1 A situation where a refund may have to be made is where faulty goods have to be recalled. The example below considers the implication where goods sold prior to the period end are recalled after the period end.

Example

A retailer has to make a product recall on goods sold before its year end, as it has subsequently been found that the goods are faulty. The recall notice was issued after the year end. Costs of the recall can be recovered from the supplier under the retailer's supply contract.

(a) Does the retailer need to make a provision at the year end for the recall costs?

Under FRS 12, provision for the costs of the recall should be made at the year end. The obligating event was the sale of the faulty goods, not the recall notice. At the balance sheet date the company has an obligation to recall the faulty goods.

(b) How should it account for the recovery from the supplier?

Recovery of the costs from the supplier can only be recorded if it is deemed to be virtually certain they will be recovered if the recall expenditure is incurred. If it is not virtually certain, but is probable, it is disclosed as a contingent asset under FRS 12.

Major repairs and maintenance

21.230 Accounting for major repair and maintenance programmes and major inspections and overhauls is dealt with in FRS 15, 'Tangible fixed assets'. See further chapter 16. Under FRS 15 repair and maintenance costs should generally be charged to the profit and loss account when they are incurred. In calculating the useful life of an asset it is assumed that subsequent expenditure (such as the cost of servicing or routine overhaul of plant and equipment) will be incurred to maintain as asset's previously assessed standard of performance. Without such expenditure the depreciation expense would be increased, because the useful economic life or residual value of the asset would be reduced.

21.230.1 However, FRS 15 notes that parts of some items of tangible fixed assets may require replacement at regular intervals. It states that such expenditure should be capitalised where it restores the economic benefits of the asset that have been consumed by the entity and that have already been reflected in depreciation. In these circumstances, the capitalised element of the asset to be replaced/ enhanced by the maintenance should be identified and depreciated typically over the period until the maintenance is carried out. The costs of the major inspection or overhaul are then capitalised when those costs are incurred and depreciated over the period to the next major inspection or overhaul. [FRS 15 para 38]. This method of accounting is required because under FRS 12 no provision can be made for the expected expenditure over the period to the next major overhaul. This treatment matches the consumption of the asset to the revenue being earned from its use.

21.230.2 As general maintenance expenditure is required to be charged to the profit and loss account as incurred, except where it is allowed to be capitalised, it is no longer appropriate in most circumstances to provide for maintenance programmes even where it is known that the related expenditure has to be incurred. FRS 12 includes an example concerning provision for expenditure on a major refit or refurbishment, which is explained below.

Example

A company has a blast furnace which requires its lining to be replaced every five years.

Prior to the company incurring the expenditure, no provision can be made for replacement of the furnace lining, because the company has no present obligation as it does not have to replace the lining. For example, it could avoid the obligation by shutting the blast furnace. This conclusion is confirmed by using the simple year end test, because if the company did not continue to trade beyond the end of (say) year three, there would be no need to incur the future expenditure. But although no provision can be built up over the five years before the expenditure is due to be incurred, the blast furnace lining should be separately identified and depreciated over that period. When the expenditure is incurred to replace the lining, this will be capitalised as part of the cost of the furnace and depreciated over the period until it is next replaced, thus, avoiding any double counting in the profit and loss account.

The cost and depreciation attributed to the blast furnace lining originally should be removed from the balance sheet once the cost of the new blast furnace lining has been capitalised to avoid double-counting in the balance sheet.

21.230.3 Maintenance expenditure in respect of owned assets cannot be provided for in advance of being incurred even if there is an external requirement for maintenance of those assets. This is illustrated in the following example:

Example

An entity has purchased some assets outright and borrowed from a bank to do so. The bank covenants include conditions that the entity should maintain the assets in good condition. Should the entity provide for maintenance on the owned assets that are financed by borrowings that contain the maintenance covenant?

Where an owned fixed asset is used as a security for a loan, and the covenants require that the asset is maintained, there is no penalty as such in respect of non-maintenance. Of course, should the covenant be broken in any way, the bank could call in its loan. If the entity is unable to pay back the loan in cash the bank may repossess the asset and consider this as settlement of the outstanding balance. It may even, in extreme cases, sue the entity for returning the asset in a state of disrepair. However, we do not consider that this would justify providing for maintenance on an ongoing basis. A failure to maintain an asset used for secured lending does no more than trigger a repayment of the lending, which, in any case, has already been recognised as a liability. It does not trigger a claim for compensation for the maintenance work the owner has to carry out.

This is in accordance with FRS 12, which requires that a provision should be made only when there is a present obligation arising from a past event and it is probable that a transfer of economic benefits will be required to settle the obligation. FRS 12 also confirms that maintenance of an owned tangible fixed asset is not a liability. Accordingly, we do not believe that a provision for maintenance on owned assets should be made, even where they have been mortgaged and covenants that require their regular maintenance have been given.

The response would differ for leased assets, where the lease agreement can impose penalties for non-maintenance on the lessee. This is considered further in the following paragraphs.

Operating leases

21.231 Although the owner of a fixed asset cannot provide for major inspection or overhaul costs (because it has discretion over whether to incur the expenditure and could avoid the expenditure, for example, by selling the asset), obligations that arise under an operating lease may give rise to the need for a provision. FRS 12 comments in the development section that in some operating leases the lessee is required to incur periodic charges for maintenance of the leased asset or to make good dilapidations or other damage occurring during the rental period. It goes on to explain that the general principle for fixed assets does not preclude the recognition of such liabilities arising under operating leases once the event giving rise to the obligation under the lease has occurred. [FRS 12, App VII para 39]. The example that follows illustrates the type of situation that can arise in practice.

Example

A company leases an aircraft on an operating lease which includes options to cancel the lease at year four, eight and twelve. Every four years the aircraft has to undergo a major refit and maintenance programme in order to be able to continue to fly. The operating lease specifies that this work must be undertaken every four years and before the aircraft is returned to the operator. In addition, the aircraft has to have its engines serviced about once a year after a certain number of flying hours have been reached, but there is no mention in the operating lease of this obligation.

As the lease is an operating lease, the aircraft does not appear on the lessee's balance sheet. The lessee charges its lease rentals to its profit and loss account as they arise. Furthermore, because it has no asset on its balance sheet, it cannot recognise the wearing out of the asset to be replaced in the major refit over the period before the refit takes place. The operating lease creates an obligation on the company to carry out the major refit. Therefore, it would be appropriate to provide for the major refit and maintenance costs over the four years to the refit for the following reasons:

- The lessee has a legal obligation arising under the lease, which will arise. If the company decided to mothball the aircraft and not to use it or to terminate the lease, the company's action would result in the operating lease becoming onerous and provision for future rental payments would need to be made instead or termination penalties would need to be provided for. (Onerous contracts are considered further from para 21.193.)

- The past event is the action of using and flying the aircraft.

- The costs to be incurred do not relate to the entity's future operations, because it is clear from considering the final period (between years nine and twelve) that the aircraft has to be returned in a maintained state. Therefore, the obligation in the last period clearly arises over the four-year term. Some might argue that the costs incurred at the end of year four and year eight relate to the following four-year terms, but this ignores the underlying obligation created by the lease, which is in effect to put right the damage that is caused through the asset's usage.

- An obligation will result under the lease that will result in a transfer of economic benefits.

- It will be possible to make a reliable estimate of the obligation to be provided each year based on the extent of wear and tear over the period.

The engine service each year is not covered by the lease, although it is an integral part of operating the aircraft. But because the obligation does not arise from the lease agreement, the normal rules in FRS 12 apply and provision cannot be made. These costs will be charged to the company's profit and loss account as they are incurred.

Finance leases

21.232 Major maintenance programmes can also arise under a finance lease and may or may not be specified as part of the lease terms. Because the asset under a finance lease is accounted for as if it is owned by the lessee, it would generally account for major renewal and maintenance programmes in the same was as if it owned the asset outright. See paragraph 21.230.

Example

A company leases a ship under a finance lease for 25 years. In order to be seaworthy it has to obtain a certificate of seaworthiness, which entails the entity carrying out significant maintenance and overhaul work in a dry dock every five years. Without such a certificate the ship cannot operate. This matter is referred to in the finance lease agreement, which requires the ship to be maintained in a seaworthy condition.

Although the ship cannot continue to operate without a certificate of seaworthiness, this in itself does not obligate the company to carry out the required maintenance work. It could, instead decide to lay-up the ship and not continue its operation. The terms of the lease would have to be carefully scrutinised to ensure there were no clauses that could change this conclusion, for example termination clauses might create an obligation. Where no obligation is created by the lease, no provision can be made for these costs. However, if the element of the asset that wears out can be identified at the outset, this cost should be amortised over the five-year term in the same way as if the asset were an 'owned asset'. When the maintenance work is carried out, this may be capitalised if it restores the ship's economic benefits.

If the ship has to be returned fully reinstated and the company is obliged to do the reinstatement, then the finance leased asset is different from an owned equivalent asset. The entity should make provision as the damage is done. This is in effect decommissioning expenditure (see para 21.250).

Infrastructure renewals

21.233 Accounting for infrastructure renewal programmes (such as those in the water and railway industries) is dealt with specifically in FRS 15. Under FRS 15's rules, infrastructure renewals expenditure is capitalised and classified in the fixed asset movement note as an addition with the renewals charged to the profit and loss account being treated as depreciation. As a result the present method of determining the profit and loss charge is unaffected, but there is a change in the balance sheet presentation. The rules are considered further in chapter 16.

Lease dilapidations

21.234 Major repair and maintenance costs in respect of leases in general have been dealt with in paragraphs 21.231 and 21.232 above. Many property leases include tenant repairing clauses. They typically require the tenant to return the property to the landlord at the end of the tenancy in a specified condition. The question then arises as to whether or not it is acceptable to make a provision for the costs relating to dilapidations during the tenancy period or whether these costs have to be borne in the period the work is undertaken. The following example illustrates the type of issues that arise in practice.

Example

The company is currently a tenant of a property and is due to vacate it in five years time. There is a clause in the tenancy relating to dilapidation work which must be undertaken before the property is vacated. In addition, there is also a clause that enables the landlord to recharge the tenant for costs related to repairing the fabric of the building. In this regard, the landlord is intending to replace the cladding on the building and is obtaining quotes for this work.

Provision should be made for the estimated costs of the dilapidation repairs spread over the period of the tenancy for the following reasons:

- The tenant has a present legal obligation, arising from the lease agreement.
- The obligating event is the wear and tear to the property, which arises over the period of the tenancy and its repair can be legally enforced.
- Because the obligation arises from the wear and tear to the property, it is not related to future operating costs.
- It is almost certain that the obligation will result in a transfer of economic benefits.
- It is possible to make a reliable estimate of the yearly obligation arising from the extent of the wear and tear taking place each year. This will not necessarily equate to one fifth of the estimated total.

With regard to repairing the fabric of the building, it should be clear from the lease whether or not an obligation arises. If the damage has already been done to the property, then a provision should be made for the whole of the rectification work when the damage is identified.

Operating leasehold improvements

21.235 Some operating leases allow the tenant to improve the property by adding, for example, additional partitioning, but include obligations on the lessee to return the property at the end of the lease in its original state. Often this will entail dismantling certain aspects of the asset. For example, consider the situation described below.

Example

A company has entered into an operating lease for a warehouse. The company wishes to use the warehouse for office accommodation. It has planning permission to spend £1.5m on building a mezzanine floor and building partitioning for offices. The operating lease is for a period of 15 years and the property must be returned to the lessor in its original condition as this is clearly specified in the lease. The company estimates that it will cost £500,000 in today's pounds to remove the improvements.

The company should capitalise leasehold improvements of £1.5m and depreciate those over the term of the lease in accordance with FRS 15. The company has an obligation under the lease to remove the improvements at the end of the lease term. The obligation arises as the company completes the improvements and this represents a past event. Therefore, if the improvements have been made by the company's year end a provision of the present value of £500,000 in 15 years time should be made for their eventual removal. In addition, an asset of the same amount should be recognised for what is, in effect, decommissioning, which will be recovered from the benefits generated by the business over the term of the lease. The asset should then be depreciated over the remaining lease term.

21.236 The rules applied to the example above are the same as apply to decommissioning an oilwell or a nuclear facility and are considered further from paragraph 21.250 below.

[The next paragraph is 21.238.]

Self-insurance

21.238 If a company takes out insurance to cover potential future losses, the cost is accounted for annually on the basis of the premium paid. However, if a company does not take out insurance cover, but instead decides to self-insure, often by means of a separate captive insurance subsidiary, the question arises as to how this should be accounted for.

21.239 Prior to the introduction of FRS 12, there were different views on accounting for self-insurance. The general view was that if the self-insured losses were likely to occur, then these should be provided for on an on-going basis on the grounds of prudence. The provision made would be an actuarial best estimate, based on previous claims experience. An alternative view was that a group, taken as a whole, did not incur a loss until an incident occurred. In this case provision would only be made for any known or likely claims when an obligation arose. This reflected the fact that the group did not have external insurance cover and, therefore, incurred losses when the event giving rise to the claim occurred. Both of these treatments were found in practice.

21.240 But FRS 12 now only allows a provision to be recognised if there is an obligation at the balance sheet date. The standard gives the example in appendix III of an entity that operates a chain of retail outlets and decides not to insure itself for minor accidents to customers, instead opting to self-insure. Its past experience suggests it will pay £100,000 in respect of such accidents. The standard concludes that in this case, unless an accident has happened, there is no present obligation, because there is no other party involved in insuring the risks. Hence, no provision should be made.

21.241 Rather unhelpfully, the standard makes no mention of incurred but not reported (IBNR) claims. FRED 14 was more helpful in this respect as it explained in the same circumstance that an obligation to another party does not arise until such time as an accident occurs. Clearly, where an accident has happened the retailer might not know of its occurrence, but this in itself does not preclude it from making a provision (see the example below). FRED 14 was clear on this point and commented that because an obligation arose on the occurrence of an accident, it was necessary to provide for the expected cost of all such accidents that occurred before the balance sheet date, including those for which the customer has yet to make a claim. The same conclusion can be reached under FRS 12.

Example

An entity that operates a chain of retail outlets decides not to insure itself for the risk of minor accidents to customers. Instead it opts to self-insure. Its past experience suggests it will pay £200,000 in respect of such accidents.

An obligation to another party does not arise until such time as an accident occurs. This means that under FRS 12's rules a provision of a larger amount than the cost of the actual accidents is not permitted. Therefore, if no accidents have occurred as at the year end, there is no present obligation to another party and hence no provision should be made.

Where an accident has happened the retailer might not know of its occurrence, but this in itself does not preclude it from making a provision. As long as the entity has a track record of claims experience from which it can estimate (probably actuarially) the level of accidents that have occurred but which have not yet been reported (that is, IBNR claims) it may make a provision for its estimate of the obligation.

Therefore, the company should make provision for the expected cost of all accidents that have occurred before the balance sheet date, including those for which the customer has yet to make a claim. During the period between the company's year end and the date on which its financial statements are finalised, a number of IBNRs might have surfaced which means that a firmer estimate for these claims can be made. However, it will still be necessary to estimate those that have not yet been reported but that are likely to be, where these arise from events that occurred before the year end date and hence qualify for provision.

21.242 In summary:

- The entity has an obligation which is legal in nature and its past experience shows it is likely to have arisen by the balance sheet date.
- The obligating event is the occurrence of the accident and the obligation cannot be avoided (unless the risk is passed to a third party for a payment).
- The costs do not relate to future operations.

- From past experience it is probable that an outflow of economic benefits will arise (that is, the settlement of the future claim).
- A reliable estimate can be made by (say) an actuary from the past claims experience.

21.243 The year end test arrives at the same conclusion, because if the company stopped trading, it would still be liable for claims that had been incurred by the balance sheet date but that had not been reported.

21.244 This basis is clearly not the same as building up (say) a reserve for insurance claims and in practice will mean that the expenses of different periods will vary, depending upon the number of accidents that occur. This might contrast with the more constant expense that would arise if the entity's policy had been to insure for these risks with the risks passed onto an insurance company. FRED 14 commented that this variability in expense was a consequence of the company's exposure to risk. Furthermore, even where a company is insured, it might be necessary to recognise the gross amount of an obligation and a recovery where the claim is on the company.

Environmental liabilities

21.245 Environmental damage covers a whole spectrum of problems, including: contamination of land; pollution of rivers and waterways; emission of harmful gases into the atmosphere (see para 21.249 onwards); excavating holes and drilling mines in the ground; and felling trees for logging. Some sensitive areas of the environment are controlled by legislation whereas others are not. Often companies have a moral obligation to rectify environmental damage, but this alone is no longer enough to justify making a provision for the necessary work to be undertaken.

21.246 FRS 12's requirements mean that provisions for environmental liabilities should be recognised when and only when the entity becomes obliged, legally or constructively, to rectify the environmental damage or to perform restorative work on the environment. These rules have a significant impact on the timing of recognising of all environmental liabilities.

21.247 Environmental costs can typically be split into the following four categories:

- Costs incurred at the company's option.
- Costs required to be incurred because of existing or new legislation.
- Costs that have to be incurred because of environmental damage caused by the company.
- Fines relating to environmental damage.

21.247.1 Appendix III to the standard covers these issues in a number of examples which are explored below:

Example 1 – environmental legislation due to be enacted

An oil company causes contamination which it will only clean-up when a law exists in the particular country in which it operates. No laws currently exist in a particular country where it has contaminated some land, but at its year end, it is virtually certain that a draft law requiring clean-up will be enacted shortly.

The company should provide for its best estimate of the clean-up costs because:

- It has a legal obligation that is virtually certain to arise, as it is virtually certain that the legislation will be enacted. [FRS 12 para 22].
- The obligating event is the contamination of the land. Once the law has been passed, clean-up can be legally enforced.
- The related costs do not form part of the entity's future operations.
- It is more likely than not that the obligation will result in a transfer of economic benefits.
- It will be possible to make a reliable estimate of the obligation.

Example 2 – published environmental policy

The facts are the same as in example 1 with the exception that there is no planned environmental legislation. However, in this case the entity has a widely published environmental policy under which it undertakes to clean up all contamination which it causes. The company can demonstrate that it honours its published statement.

In this circumstance, the company should also provide for its best estimate of the clean-up costs as:

- It has a present constructive obligation that arises from its commitment to the public at large by the publication of its environmental policies. It has raised a valid expectation that it will carry them through from which it cannot realistically withdraw.
- The obligation arises from the contamination of the land, which is the obligating event. But the key here is that it must not be able to realistically withdraw from carrying out its stated policy (that is, it cannot be able to change its mind).
- The related costs do not form part of the entity's future operations.
- It is more likely than not that the obligation will result in a transfer of economic benefits.
- It will be possible to make a reliable estimate of the obligation.

Example 3 – legislation in respect of future activity

A new law has been passed which requires smoke filters to be fitted to factories by the middle of the company's next year. The company has not yet fitted the smoke filters.

As the legislation has still to come into operation, there is no present obligation of a legal nature for the company to fit the filters. Furthermore, the company's management have done nothing to suggest that a constructive obligation arises either. Consequently, no provision should be made. Using the year end test arrives at the same conclusion, because if the company stopped trading there would be no obligation to fit the filters, as their fitting relates to reducing future pollution.

Example 4 – legislation in force

The facts are the same as in the previous example, except that the company has now reached its subsequent year end and the law is now operational, but it still has not fitted the filters.

The company should not make a provision for the cost of fitting the filters. Even though at first sight it might appear that there is a present obligation, as the law compelling the filters to be fitted is now operational, no obligation arises for the cost of fitting the filters because no obligating event has taken place (that is, the filters have not yet been fitted). Again using the simple year end test, if the company stopped trading there would be no requirement to fit the filters. Nevertheless, a provision may still be necessary for the cost of paying fines in the following situation:

- An obligation might arise for any penalties that the company might incur for not complying with the legislation to the year end.
- The obligating event giving rise to the liability to pay fines is the fact that the factory does not comply with the law.
- The fines do not relate to costs of future operations, if they have to be paid whether or not the company continues to trade.
- Whether it is more likely than not that the obligation will result in a transfer of economic benefits will depend on an assessment of the probability of incurring the fines. This might depend, for example, on the stringency of the enforcement regime.
- Whether it is possible to make a reliable estimate of the fines, will depend on factors such as whether or not the rates have been published.

Example 5 – legislation in force in respect of past contamination

Health and safety legislation has been introduced that requires asbestos to be removed from all buildings. Asbestos removal is required whether or not the property is in use. The legislation is effective from 31 December 20X2. Entity A owns a 20 year old factory that includes asbestos. The estimated cost of removing the asbestos is £70,000, plus a further £30,000 in lost profits because the factory will not be able to operate at full capacity while the asbestos is being removed. At 31 December 20X2, the work has not commenced in respect of the asbestos removal; however, contracts have been signed with contractors for the work to be performed in the first few months of 20X3.

The Health and Safety legislation has been enacted and there is, therefore, a requirement for the asbestos to be removed. The obligating (past) event is the contamination caused by the presence of the asbestos and the existence of a legal requirement to remove it creates an obligation that should be provided for. Therefore, entity A should recognise a provision for £70,000, being the direct cost of removing the asbestos.

No provision should be made for the operating losses that will be incurred during the period of asbestos removal, because there is no obligation to incur these losses. Management could attempt to reschedule or relocate operations to avoid or minimise the losses. The operating losses are an indirect result of the requirement to remove the asbestos.

The existence of signed contracts does not affect the conclusion of whether to provide for the costs. The contracts are executory contracts, so no liability to the contractor arises until the contractor performs work under the contract.

The introduction of the new law does not create the obligating event on its own. It is the combination of the past contamination and the new law that creates the obligation to remove the asbestos. This can be contrasted with the smoke filters in example 4 above where there is no past contamination and so the obligation created when the legislation comes into force is only for penalties and fines.

Waste electrical and electronic equipment

21.248 The European Union's Directive on Waste Electrical and Electronic Equipment (2002/96/EC) (the 'WEEE Directive'), which regulates the collection, treatment, recovery and environmentally sound disposal of electronic and electrical equipment waste, gave rise to questions about when a liability for the decommissioning of WEEE should be recognised. As a result, in September 2005, the IFRIC issued an interpretation, IFRIC 6, 'Liabilities arising from participating in a specific market – Waste electrical and electronic equipment', to provide guidance regarding what constitutes an obligating event in certain circumstances created by the WEEE Directive.

21.248.1 The WEEE Directive was brought into force in the UK in January 2007 – see further paragraph 21.248.11. As a result, the UITF issued UITF 45, 'Liabilities arising from participating in a specific market – Waste electrical and electronic equipment', which is based on IFRIC 6.

21.248.2 The WEEE Directive distinguishes between 'new' and 'historical' waste and between waste from private households and waste from sources other than private households. New waste relates to products sold on or after 13 August 2005. All equipment sold before that date is deemed to give rise to historical waste for the purposes of the Directive.

21.248.3 The WEEE Directive states that the cost of waste management for historical household equipment should be borne by producers of that type of equipment that are in the market during a specified period (the 'measurement period'). The WEEE Directive states that each Member State should establish a mechanism for producers to contribute to costs proportionately, for example, in proportion to their respective market share by type of equipment.

21.248.4 Member States within the EU will have their own interpretation of the WEEE Directive enacted into their law. The detailed requirements associated with the Directive will, therefore, vary from State to State.

21.248.5 UITF 45 provides guidance on the recognition, in the financial statements of producers, of liabilities for waste management of WEEE in respect of sales of historical household equipment.

21.248.6 The abstract only addresses sales of historical household equipment; it does not address new waste or historical waste from sources other than private households. The UITF considers that the liability for such waste management is covered by FRS 12's general requirements. It notes, however, that if, in national legislation, new waste from private households is treated in a similar manner to historical waste from private households, UITF 45's principles apply. [UITF 45 para 7].

21.248.7 UITF 45 addresses what constitutes an obligating event in accordance with paragraph 14(a) of FRS 12 for the recognition of a provision for waste management costs.

21.248.8 The UITF consensus is that participation in the market during the measurement period is the obligating event. For this reason, a liability for waste management costs for historical household equipment does not arise when the products are manufactured or sold. As the obligation for historical household equipment is linked to participation in the market during the measurement period, rather than to production or sale of the items to be disposed of, there is no obligation unless and until a market share exists during the measurement period. [UITF 45 para 9].

21.248.9 Paragraph BC5 of UITF 45 illustrates the interpretation's requirements with the following example.

Example

An entity selling electrical equipment in 20X4 has a market share of 4% for that calendar year. It subsequently discontinues operations and is thus no longer in the market when the waste management costs for its products are allocated to those entities with market share in 20X7. With a market share of 0% in 20X7, the entity's obligation is nil. However, if another entity enters the market for electronic products in 20X7 and achieves a market share of 3% in that period, then that entity's obligation for the costs of waste management from earlier periods will be 3% of the total costs of waste management allocated to 20X7, even though the entity was not in the market in those earlier periods and has not produced any of the products for which waste management costs are allocated to 20X7.

21.248.10 The timing of the obligating event may also be independent of the particular period in which the activities to perform the waste management are undertaken and the related costs incurred. Incurring costs in the performance of the waste management activities is a separate matter from incurring the obligation to share in the ultimate cost of those activities. [UITF 45 paras 9, BC6].

The WEEE Regulations in the UK

21.248.11 The WEEE Directive aims to minimise the impact of electrical and electronic goods on the environment. It seeks to achieve this by making producers responsible for financing the collection, treatment and recovery of WEEE; and by requiring distributors to allow consumers to return their waste equipment free of charge. The majority of the WEEE Directive's provisions were implemented in the UK by Statutory Instrument, 'The Waste Electrical and Electronic Equipment Regulations 2006' (SI 2006/3290) (the 'WEEE Regulations'), which was laid before Parliament on 12 December 2006 and entered into force on 2 January 2007. Guidance on interpreting the WEEE Directive is available in a Frequently Asked Questions ('FAQ') document on the WEEE Directive published by the EC. Guidance on interpreting the WEEE Regulations is available in Government Guidance Notes ('WEEE Guidance Notes') published by the DTI (now the DBERR) in February 2007.

21.248.12 The legislation creates obligations for producers (see para 21.248.18), distributors (see para 21.248.31) and, in certain circumstances, end-users (see para 21.248.35) of electrical and electronic equipment ('EEE') with respect to the collection, treatment, recovery and environmentally sound disposal ('processing') of waste arising from such equipment in any compliance period from 1 July 2007. This includes the obligation to pay for the processing of such waste. The WEEE Regulations place obligations in relation to WEEE on the producers of EEE from 1 July 2007 (although for certain types of WEEE, provisions for obligations were required to be recognised before that date). Distributor obligations commenced from 1 July 2007. The first WEEE compliance period runs from 1 July 2007 to 31 December 2007. Each subsequent compliance period will run for 12 months from 1 January to 31 December each year.

Scope

21.248.13 The WEEE Regulations relate to electrical and electronic equipment (EEE – see para 21.248.14 below) and apply to the following groups:

- Producers (that is, any business that manufactures, imports or rebrands EEE – see para 21.248.18 below).
- Retailers and distributors (that is, any business that sells EEE to end-users – see para 21.248.31 below).
- Local authorities.
- Waste management industry.
- Exporters and reprocessors.
- Businesses and other non-household users of EEE.

21.248.14 The WEEE Regulations apply to EEE that falls within the ten product categories listed in the WEEE Directive:

- Large household appliances.
- Small household appliances.
- IT and telecommunications equipment.
- Consumer equipment.
- Lighting equipment.
- Electrical and electronic tools.
- Toys, leisure and sports equipment.
- Medical devices.
- Monitoring and control instruments.
- Automatic dispensers.

Annex A to the WEEE Guidance Notes includes examples of products under each of the categories listed above.

21.248.15 For many products, the decision on whether they are included within the WEEE Regulations' scope should be straightforward. However, there are a number of 'grey area' products (particularly in specialised or industrial sectors), where there may be areas of doubt and uncertainty. Annex B to the WEEE Guidance Notes includes a decision tree to assist in determining whether products might come within the WEEE Regulations' scope. However, entities may wish to obtain legal advice supporting their decisions on scope if this is not clear.

21.248.16 The WEEE Regulations recognise two categories of waste, being waste from:

- Private households (that is, consumer use by members of the public – 'household waste').
- Users other than private households (that is, professional, business or official use – 'non-household waste').

Household waste includes waste from other users if it is similar to that from private households by nature or quantity. Annex C to the WEEE Guidance Notes presents the suggested criteria for EEE to be considered as non-household. Entities may wish to seek legal advice in interpreting this in some cases.

21.248.17 As noted in paragraph 21.248.2, the WEEE Directive also distinguishes between 'new' and 'historical' waste. New waste relates to products sold on or after 13 August 2005 and historical waste relates to products sold before that date. Under the WEEE Regulations, the same model of attributing waste management costs is applicable to all WEEE from private households (that is, the Regulations do not distinguish historical waste and new waste for household EEE). However, a distinction is made for non-household WEEE (see para 21.248.25 onwards).

Producer obligations

21.248.18 Under the WEEE Regulations, a 'producer' means:

- a manufacturer of EEE, selling under their own brand in the UK;
- a business based in the UK selling under their own brand EEE manufactured by another person (that is, rebranding);
- a professional importer introducing EEE to the UK market; or
- a business based in the UK that places EEE in other EU Members States by means of distance selling.

21.248.19 The WEEE Guidance Notes explain that 'selling' takes the meaning of 'putting on the market' according to the EC's 'Guide to the implementation of Directives based on the New Approach and the Global Approach'. This is applied to the UK market and relates to making a product available for first use. While this definition is used to determine who would be producers, obligations are based on sales onto the UK market (see para 21.248.23 onwards).

21.248.20 The definition of 'producer' (of equipment) is a wide one and includes many non-manufacturing entities, such as importers and exporters of equipment. Furthermore, the WEEE Guidance notes clarify that a producer that leases EEE, rather than selling it, would be within the WEEE Regulations' scope as they would still be regarded as putting EEE on the market. However, organisations that exclusively provide financing arrangements for EEE are not producers under the WEEE Regulations. Entities may wish to seek legal advice if the definition is unclear in relation to any of their activities.

21.248.21 A producer's obligations under the WEEE Regulations include the following:

- Joining an approved Producer Compliance Scheme (PCS). An entity's obligations in respect of WEEE will be discharged through the PCS for as long as it remains a member of that scheme and the scheme remains approved (see further para 21.248.29).
- Paying the PCS according to its published fee structure and membership rules.
- Providing information to the PCS, including the amounts of EEE that the entity places on the UK market on a quarterly basis, broken down by compliance category and its household or non-household nature.

21.248.22 For an entity that is a producer, membership of a PCS covers obligations to finance the collection, treatment, recycling and environmentally sound disposal for:

- household WEEE arising in each compliance period, as the proportion given by the entity's share of the UK market for EEE in each category (see para 21.248.24 below); and
- non-household WEEE arising in each compliance period, from:
  - EEE the entity placed on the market on or after 13 August 2005 (see para 21.248.27 below); and in addition
  - EEE that was placed on the market before 13 August 2005, regardless of the producer, which the user is replacing with the equivalent new EEE provided by the entity (see para 21.248.28 below).

21.248.23 In some circumstances, the obligation to pay for processing of waste arises for producers from participating in the market during the compliance period ('pay as you go') and, in others, arises for producers, from supply of equipment or, for users (see para 21.248.35), from use of equipment ('specific attribution'). The pay as you go obligations do not arise until the first compliance period (1 July 2007), but there are some specific attribution obligations for which companies will need to assess the costs earlier from 12 December 2006 and at later period ends. The following flowchart summarises when a producer should recognise a provision for the cost of processing waste under the Regulations.

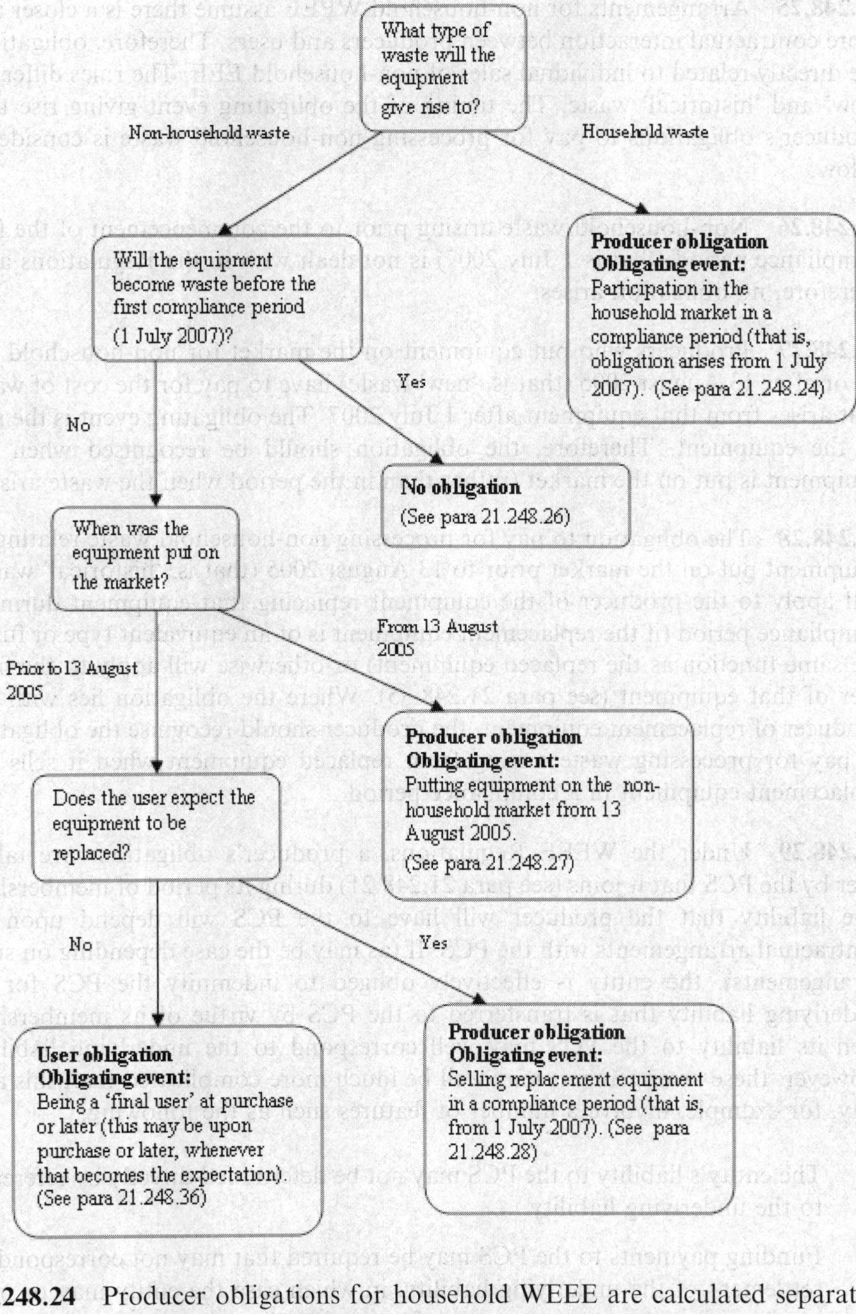

21.248.24 Producer obligations for household WEEE are calculated separately for each compliance category. Each producer will be responsible for a proportion of the cost of processing household WEEE arising in each compliance category in which they place EEE on the UK market during any compliance period (that is, after 1 July 2007), given by the producer's market share of this EEE. In line with the accounting treatment in UITF 45 (see para 21.248.8 above), the obligation should be recognised as equipment is put on the market during the compliance period. No obligation, therefore, arose prior to 1 July 2007.

21.248.25 Arrangements for non-household WEEE assume there is a closer and more contractual interaction between producers and users. Therefore, obligations are directly related to individual sales of non-household EEE. The rules differ for 'new' and 'historical' waste. The timing of the obligating event giving rise to a producer's obligations to pay for processing non-household waste is considered below.

21.248.26 Non-household waste arising prior to the commencement of the first compliance period (that is 1 July 2007) is not dealt with in the Regulations and, therefore, no obligation arises.

21.248.27 Producers who put equipment on the market for non-household use on or after 13 August 2005 (that is, 'new' waste) have to pay for the cost of waste that arises from that equipment after 1 July 2007. The obligating event is the sale of the equipment. Therefore, the obligation should be recognised when the equipment is put on the market (rather than in the period when the waste arises).

21.248.28 The obligation to pay for processing non-household waste relating to equipment put on the market prior to 13 August 2005 (that is, 'historical' waste) will apply to the producer of the equipment replacing that equipment during a compliance period (if the replacement equipment is of an equivalent type or fulfils the same function as the replaced equipment) or otherwise will apply to the final user of that equipment (see para 21.248.35). Where the obligation lies with the producer of replacement equipment, the producer should recognise the obligation to pay for processing waste arising from replaced equipment when it sells the replacement equipment in a compliance period.

21.248.29 Under the WEEE Regulations, a producer's obligations are taken over by the PCS that it joins (see para 21.248.21) during its period of membership. The liability that the producer will have to the PCS will depend upon its contractual arrangements with the PCS. If (as may be the case depending on such arrangements), the entity is effectively obliged to indemnify the PCS for its underlying liability that is transferred to the PCS by virtue of its membership, then its liability to the PCS may well correspond to the underlying liability. However, these arrangements may well be much more complicated than this and may, for example, involve a number of features such as the following:

- The entity's liability to the PCS may not be determined directly by reference to the underlying liability.
- Funding payments to the PCS may be required that may not correspond to settlement of the underlying liability, in which case the entity may or may not have a right to repayments of excess funding payments and/or may obtain an interest in the excess assets of the PCS.
- The entity may be required to provide funding guarantees that may go beyond guaranteeing funding for its own underlying liability.
- Payment of service fees to the PCS.

21.248.30 All such arrangements with a PCS will need to be considered carefully to determine whether and to what extent any assets, liabilities, contingent assets or contingent liabilities arise from such arrangements and when and how such items should be recognised and measured, including under which standards' scope they fall.

Distributor obligations

21.248.31 A 'distributor' means any person (or entity) who provides EEE on a commercial basis to the party who is going to use it ('end-users'). This applies irrespective of the method of sale. Distributor includes wholesalers, retailers, and distance sellers (for example, internet retailers, mail order retailers, and tele-sales businesses) and producers who sell products direct to consumers of EEE.

21.248.32 Distributors are required to provide a free of charge in-store take-back service for household waste customers, unless they are a member of a distributor take-back scheme. Distributors also have various administrative obligations, such as record-keeping and providing returns of certain information. These obligations relate to any sales of new EEE and do not apply to sales of second-hand or reconditioned EEE that has been previously placed on the UK market. As noted in paragraph 21.248.12, distributor obligations arise from 1 July 2007.

21.248.33 The WEEE Regulations entitle distributors to dispose of household WEEE collected through take-back by passing it on to a Producer Compliance Scheme, who cannot charge for accepting it (although a transport fee may be charged).

21.248.34 There are no obligations for distributors in relation to sales of non-household EEE or for the take-back of non-household WEEE.

End-user obligations

21.248.35 Although 'end-user' is not defined by the WEEE Regulations, under a commonsense reading it would mean the person or entity owning it/using it at the time it becomes waste.

21.248.36 If waste from products placed on the market before 13 August 2005 ('historical' waste) is not being replaced by new EEE serving an equivalent function, the end-user is responsible for arranging and financing its collection and treatment themselves in accordance with the WEEE Regulations. The obligation should be recognised at the later of the date when the equipment is purchased, when the entity expects to be the end-user or when the Regulations were enacted (12 December 2006) and should continue to be recognised throughout the remaining life of the equipment, unless the expectations regarding replacement or being the end-user change.

Summary

21.248.37 As noted in paragraph 21.248.6, UITF 45 deals only with sales of historical household equipment under the WEEE Directive. Entities will need to determine appropriate accounting policies for other types of waste in accordance with FRS 18, 'Accounting policies' (see chapter 2) The detailed rules for attributing cost in respect of other types of WEEE may vary between Member States (see para 21.248.4) and where a group operates in more than one location, it will need to consider the legal requirements in different jurisdictions.

Emission obligations

21.249 Many jurisdictions have introduced cap and trade schemes as a way to encourage a reduction in greenhouse gas emissions. The schemes generally involve the allocation of a limited number of allowances at the start of a compliance period and require entities to have sufficient allowances at the end of the compliance period to cover the volume of emissions made. Some schemes permit entities to purchase additional allowances (on top of their free allocation) or to sell any surplus allowances generated from reducing their emissions.

21.249.1 The UK's first emissions trading scheme was launched in March 2002 and ran until December 2006, with final reconciliation in March 2007. This was a voluntary scheme and enabled UK business and other organisations to obtain early experience of emissions trading prior to the introduction of an EU-wide scheme. The EU Emissions Trading Scheme (EU ETS) has been introduced across Europe to reduce emissions of greenhouse gases. Phase I of the Scheme (covering carbon dioxide emissions) began on 1 January 2005 and runs until 31 December 2007. Phase II (which may cover other greenhouse gases) will run from 2008-2012 to coincide with the first Kyoto Protocol commitment period. Further five-year periods are expected subsequently. The EU scheme is different from the voluntary UK scheme, but participants of the UK scheme, as well as those with climate change agreements, were given the opportunity to be excluded from the EU ETS until the end of 2006, or Phase I, respectively.

21.249.2 The EU ETS was introduced into the UK in 'The Greenhouse Gas Emissions Trading Scheme Regulations 2005' (SI 2005/925), which came into force on 21 April 2005. The EU ETS works on a 'cap and trade' basis. EU Member State governments are required to set an emission cap for all installations covered by the scheme. These installations include those carrying out activities in the following areas:

- Energy activities (for example, electricity generation).
- Production and processing of ferrous metals.
- Mineral industries.
- Pulp and paper industries.

21.249.3 The significant elements of Phase I of the EU ETS can be summarised as follows:

- Each installation covered by the scheme is allocated allowances for a particular compliance period (calendar year). The number of allowances allocated to each installation for any given period, (that is, the number of free tradable allowances each installation receives), is set down in a document called the National Allocation Plan (which is approved by the EC).
- Entities have the flexibility to sell any surplus allowances expected to be generated from reducing their emissions below their allocation. This enables other entities to buy additional allowances (on top of their free allocation) to cover any expected shortfalls. The buying and selling of allowances takes place on an EU-wide market.
- After the end of each compliance period (calendar year), entities are required to ensure they have sufficient allowances to cover the actual emissions of their installations for that period. By a specified deadline, the operator of each installation has to surrender a number of allowances equal to the total emissions from that installation during the compliance period.
- If the entity fails to deliver the requisite number of allowances at the end of the compliance period, it may be fined and may face other sanctions, but also remains liable to deliver the requisite number of allowances from later years' allowances supply.

21.249.4 Under cap and trade schemes (such as the EU ETS), the emission of greenhouse gases creates an obligation to deliver allowances. Entities must recognise a liability (and related expense) in respect of this obligation to the extent of emissions made as at the balance sheet date. There are a number of accounting models that can be used for accounting for participation in schemes aimed at reducing greenhouse gas emissions. The liability's measurement will depend on the accounting model used. These are discussed further below.

21.249.5 There is no specific accounting guidance in UK GAAP dealing with accounting for emissions. In December 2004, the IASB's interpretations committee, the IFRIC, published an Interpretation, IFRIC 3, 'Emission rights'. which dealt with the accounting for a 'cap and trade' emission rights scheme. It required that companies should account for the emission allowances they receive from governments as intangible assets, recorded initially at fair value. Where allowances are issued for less than fair value, the difference between the amount paid and the fair value is treated as a government grant. The grant is initially recognised as deferred income in the balance sheet and subsequently taken to income on a systematic basis over the compliance period for which the allowances were issued, regardless of whether the allowances are held or sold. A liability is recognised for the obligation to deliver allowances equal to emissions that have been made. The liability is measured at the best estimate of the expenditure required to settle the present obligation at the balance sheet date (usually, the market price of the number of allowances required to cover emissions made up to the balance sheet date).

21.249.6 IFRIC 3 proved to be a controversial interpretation, as it resulted in a mismatch in performance reporting, due to the different rules on accounting for changes in value of the intangible asset and the related emissions obligation. The UITF issued proposals for emissions accounting similar to those in IFRIC 3, but decided not to proceed with an Abstract as it was considered likely that there would be further changes to accounting in this area. IFRIC 3 was withdrawn by the IASB in June 2005, but despite its withdrawal, it remains a valid accounting model for emissions accounting under UK GAAP. However, its withdrawal indicates that other accounting models are acceptable. Two acceptable accounting models for emission schemes are summarised in the table below (note: this summary does not deal with the accounting for emission allowances by broker/traders).

Acceptable accounting models for emissions accounting		
	'Full market value approach' (similar to IFRIC 3)	**'Cost of settlement approach' ('Initial market value')**
Allowances (asset)		
When to recognise	Recognise when able to exercise control.	Recognise when able to exercise control.
How much to recognise	Measure initially based on the market value at the date of initial recognition.	Measure initially based on the market value at the date of initial recognition.
	Measure subsequently based on either: (i) the amount initially recognised (cost model); or (ii) the revalued amount (revaluation model).	Measure subsequently based on either: (i) the amount initially recognised (cost model); or (ii) the revalued amount (revaluation model).
Government grant		
When to recognise	Recognise at the same time as allowances.	Recognise at the same time as allowances.
How to recognise	Measure initially based on the market value of the allowances at the date of initial recognition.	Measure initially based on the market value of the allowances at the date of initial recognition.
	Amortise over the compliance period on a systematic and rational basis.	Amortise over the compliance period on a systematic and rational basis.

Emissions obligations (liability)		
When to recognise	Recognise when the liability is incurred.	Recognise when the liability is incurred.
How to recognise	Re-measure the liability based on the market value of allowances at each period end, whether they are to be settled using the allowances on hand or to be purchased from the market.	Re-measure the liability at each period end. The liability to be settled using allowances on hand is measured at the carrying amount of those allowances; any excess emission is measured at the market value of allowances at the period end.

21.249.7 The first accounting model in the above table (the 'full market value' approach) is similar to the model set out in IFRIC 3, as summarised in paragraph 21.249.5 above. There are two variants under UK GAAP – the cost model and the revaluation model, depending on whether the intangible asset is revalued on an ongoing basis under FRS 10. The other accounting model is based on a 'cost of settlement approach', under which the liability is measured at the amounts expected to be incurred in settling it, but is otherwise similar to the IFRIC 3 approach. Under the cost of settlement approach, the liability is measured, to the extent allowances are held at the period end, at the carrying amount of those allowances and any excess obligation is measured at the market value of allowances at the period end.

21.249.8 Under both the accounting models in the above table, the emissions allowances held are intangible assets, accounted for in accordance with FRS 10, 'Goodwill and intangible assets', and should be recognised at cost if separately acquired. Allowances that are received free of charge from the government are accounted for in accordance with SSAP 4, 'Accounting for government grants'. Paragraph 16 of SSAP 4 states that where a government grant takes the form of a transfer of non-monetary assets, the amount of the grant is the fair value of the assets transferred. Therefore, allowances received free of charge are recognised at fair value with a corresponding deferred income.

21.249.9 It should be noted that, under UK GAAP, an accounting model that recognises allowances received free of charge at a nominal amount (for example, nil) cannot be used, as this is not consistent with paragraph 16 of SSAP 4, which requires the use of fair value. This differs from IFRS, where IAS 10, 'Accounting for government grants and disclosure of government assistance', permits a government grant received in the form of a non-monetary asset to be recorded at a nominal amount (as an alternative to fair value).

21.249.10 The intangible assets recognised should not be amortised if they have indefinite useful economic lives, but should be reviewed for impairment at the end of each reporting period. [FRS 10 paras 17, 37]. If the intangible assets have limited useful economic lives, they should be amortised on a systematic basis over those lives. In amortising an intangible asset, a residual value may be assigned to that asset if the residual value can be measured reliably. [FRS 10 paras 15, 28]. If residual values can be measured reliably, it is likely that these will be equal to the asset's carrying amount at initial recognition or subsequent revaluation and so there will be no amortisation. Emission allowances recognised as an asset should be tested for impairment, in accordance with the requirements of FRS 11, 'Impairment of fixed assets and goodwill', which is dealt with in chapter 18.

21.249.11 Under the above two models in the table in paragraph 21.249.6, the entity may choose to apply the revaluation model in FRS 10 for the subsequent measurement of the emissions allowances. [FRS 10 para 43]. The revaluation model requires that the carrying amount of the allowances is restated to market value at each balance sheet date with changes to market value recognised directly in equity, except for impairments which are recognised in the profit and loss account. Accounting for intangible assets is considered further in chapter 15.

21.249.12 The balance recognised as deferred income for the government grant is amortised to the income statement on a straight line basis over the compliance period. An alternative to the straight line bases should be used if this can be determined to provide a better reflection of the consumption of the economic benefits of the government grant; this could, for example, be based on the volume of emissions generated.

21.249.13 The accounting policy chosen for emission obligations (which should be consistently applied) will depend on the overall accounting model that is being used for emissions (including allowances) and will impact on the liability's measurement as follows:

- The obligation may be measured at market price at the balance sheet date of the allowances required to cover the emissions made to date (the 'full market value' approach in the table above) – see further paragraph 21.249.14 below.
- The obligation may be measured at the amounts expected to be incurred in settling the liability (the 'cost of settlement' approach in the table above), as follows:

- To the extent that the obligation can be met from allowances already held by the entity – this is measured at the carrying amount of the allowances held (see para 21.249.8 above).

- To the extent that the obligation cannot be met from allowances held, it must be met from allowances purchased in the market – this is measured at the market price of allowances at the balance sheet date.

Entities should make clear in their accounting policy note which approach they are following.

21.249.14 The 'full market value' approach (that is, similar to the method set out in IFRIC 3) is illustrated in the following example.

Example

An entity participates in a 'cap and trade' scheme for emission rights and is allocated on 1 January 20X6, free of charge, allowances to emit 10,000 tonnes of carbon dioxide during the calendar year 20X6, which is also its financial accounting period. The market price of an allowance (equivalent to one tonne of carbon dioxide) at 1 January 20X6 is £10, giving a fair value of £100,000.

At the half year, 30 June 20X6, the entity has emitted 6,000 tonnes of carbon dioxide and expects its emissions for the full year to be 12,500 tonnes. The market price for allowances has risen to £11 (per tonne).

At the year end the entity has emitted the expected 12,500 tonnes and the market price of allowances is £12 (per tonne). How should the entity account for the scheme under the method similar to that set out in IFRIC 3 (the 'full market value' approach), assuming that the entity uses the revaluation model in FRS 10 to measure the intangible asset at fair value after its initial recognition?

The entity would record the initial receipt of allowances at fair value of £100,000, setting up an intangible asset for this amount and recording a government grant as deferred income for the same amount. There would be no depreciable amount as the residual value (as defined in FRS 10) equals the carrying value (fair value) at acquisition.

At the half year stage the entity would record a liability for the emissions to date of £66,000 (6000 tonnes at £11 per tonne). The asset of £100,000 is revalued to £110,000 (10,000 tonnes at £11 per tonne). The deferred income is released in the proportion that emissions to date bear to total emissions expected for the year, that is £100,000 x 6,000/12,500 = £48,000.

At the half year the profit and loss account, therefore, reflects deferred income released of £48,000 less the accrued emission liability expense of £66,000, giving a net charge to the profit and loss account for the period of £18,000. The revaluation surplus of £10,000 on the intangible asset is taken to the revaluation reserve *via* the STRGL.

At the full year (and ignoring the half year entries) the entity records a liability for emissions of £150,000 (12,500 tonnes at £12 per tonne). The asset is revalued to £120,000 (10,000 tonnes at £12 per tonne). All of the deferred income of £100,000 is released.

The effect on the profit and loss account for the full year is to record a liability of £150,000 (based on the market price of allowances at the balance sheet date) in respect of the emission obligation and to release deferred income of £100,000. The revaluation surplus of £20,000 is taken to the revaluation reserve *via* the STRGL. There is a net charge to the profit and loss account of £50,000. Taken together with the revaluation surplus in the STRGL of £20,000 the net total recognised gains and losses of £30,000 (loss) represents the cost to the entity of excess emissions of 2,500 tonnes (over the free allowances granted) multiplied by the market price at the year end of £12 per tonne.

If the cost model in FRS 10 had been used for the intangible asset and, accordingly, it had been measured after its initial recognition at cost less amortisation and/or impairment (cost being fair value on initial recognition for this purpose) there would be no revaluation surplus of £20,000 at the year end and the intangible asset would be stated at £100,000. Because part of the liability of £150,000 would be settled by using allowances stated at £100,000 (but worth £120,000), the entity would need to pay only £30,000. There would remain a balance of the liability of £20,000 that would be released to the profit and loss account when settlement occurs. Thus the net charge in the profit and loss account would be £30,000. Again this represents the cost of the excess emissions of 2,500 tonnes multiplied by £12 per tonne. Therefore, the overall net effect on the performance statements would be the same (£30,000 loss) whether the cost model or the revaluation model in FRS 10 is adopted. However, there will be a timing difference, because, under the cost model, the gain (£20,000) on release of the liability will only be recognised when the liability is settled, which will be after the year end.

21.249.15 In contrast to the above example, entities using the 'cost of settlement' approach will only measure the obligation at the current (that is, balance sheet date) market price of allowances to the extent that emissions made to date exceed the volume of allowances held. If emissions do not exceed allowances held, there is no obligation to purchase additional allowances and, so, no basis to use the current market price under this approach. Therefore, in the example above, under the 'cost of settlement' approach, at the year end the liability would be measured at 10,000 x £10 (for allowances held by the entity) + 2,500 x £12 (for allowances to be purchased on the market), that is, a total liability at the year end of £130,000 (rather than £150,000 under the 'full market value' approach).

21.249.16 There is an additional consideration for entities using the 'cost of settlement' approach, as the measurement of the obligation for which allowances are held will depend on whether the carrying amount of allowances is allocated to the obligation on a FIFO or on a weighted average basis. This is a particular issue, where a balance sheet date is not the end of a compliance period, for example, at an interim balance sheet date (where the financial year is the same as the compliance period), or at a financial year end (where the financial year is not the same as the compliance period).

21.249.17 Entities using the FIFO method should measure the obligation at the carrying amount per unit of emissions, up to the number of allowances (if any) held at the balance sheet date and at the expected cost (the market price at the balance sheet date) per unit for the shortfall (if any) at the balance sheet date (see further para 21.249.20).

21.249.18 Entities using the weighted average method should measure the obligation using the weighted average cost per unit of emission expected to be incurred for the compliance period as a whole. To do this, the entity determines the expected total emissions for the compliance period and compares this with the number of allowance units granted by the government (and/or purchased) and still held by the entity for that compliance period, to determine the expected shortfall (if any) in allowances held for the compliance period. The weighted average cost per unit of emission for the compliance period is the carrying amount of the allowances held plus the cost of meeting the expected shortfall (using the market price at the balance sheet date), divided by the expected total number of units of emission for the compliance period. In other words:

$$\frac{\text{Carrying amount of allowances held + Cost of meeting expected shortfall}}{\text{Expected total units of emission for the compliance period}} = \text{Weighted average cost per unit of emission for the compliance period}$$

21.249.19 The weighted average method is consistent with the approach to measuring items at an interim date, such as tax, bonuses and volume rebates. The general principle under this approach is that where an entity has an obligation, the effective rateable measurement of which is determined by reference to a full period's activities, then measurement is made on the basis of the volume of activity giving rise to the obligation up to the interim date at the expected effective rate for the period (determined on the basis of expected activity for the full year). This principle can be rationalised on the basis that there is a presumption that the entity will continue operating and that the best estimate of the amount the entity expects to pay should recognise this as well as the fact that settlement can in fact only be for a specified period which straddles the interim period.

21.249.20 The following example (using the facts in the example in paragraph 21.249.14) illustrates the difference under the FIFO and weighted average methods of applying the 'cost of settlement' approach to the measurement of an obligation for emissions.

Example – FIFO method

An entity participates in a 'cap and trade' scheme for emission rights and is allocated on 1 January 20X6, free of charge, 10,000 allowances (to cover emissions of 10,000 tonnes of carbon dioxide) during the calendar year 20X6, which is also its financial accounting period. It has recognised these allowances in its balance sheet at fair value (being £100,000 at a fair value of £10 per allowance).

The entity is preparing its interim financial report for the 6 months to 30 June 20X6. At the interim balance sheet date, the entity has generated emissions equivalent to 6,000 allowances. For the full year, the entity expects to require 12,500 emission allowances and, hence, expects to purchase an additional 2,500 allowances from the market. The entity allocates allowances to cover the obligation on a FIFO basis. How should the entity's liability be measured in the interim financial report?

At the interim balance sheet date, the entity has generated an obligation equal to 6,000 allowances. As the entity allocates its allowances on a FIFO basis and has not yet allocated all the emission allowances it holds (10,000 allowances held at £100,000), there is no shortfall of allowances at the interim date. Therefore, the liability will be recognised at the interim date at the carrying amount per unit held at the balance sheet date (£10), that is, 6,000 x £10 = £60,000.

If in the second half of the year, the entity generates the further expected emissions of 6,500 (giving a total of 12,500 for the year) and if the market price of allowances is £12 at the year end balance sheet date, the liability at the end of the year will be measured at 10,000 x £10 = £100,000 (for allowances held by the entity) + 2,500 x 12 = 30,000 (for allowances to be purchased on the market), that is, a total liability at the year end of £130,000, recognising a further cost of £70,000 in the results for the second half of the financial year.

Example – weighted average method

The facts are the same as above, except that the entity allocates allowances on a weighted average basis. The market price of an allowance at the interim balance sheet date is £11 and at the year end is £12.

Again, at the interim balance sheet date, the entity has generated an obligation equal to 6,000 allowances and expects to require 12,500 emission allowances for the full year. It is probable that a portion of the settlement of the obligation for the compliance year as a whole will involve the outflow of economic benefit. This outflow can be estimated by allocating the total expected cost of the additional 2,500 allowances that the entity expects to purchase in the market (using the market price at the interim balance sheet date for estimation purposes) across all emissions expected to be generated during the year.

$$\frac{\text{Carrying amount of allowances held + Cost of meeting expected shortfall}}{\text{Expected total units of emission for the compliance period}} = \text{Weighted average cost per unit of emission for the compliance period}$$

$$\frac{£100,000 + £27,500\ (2,500 \times £11)}{12,500} = £10.2$$

Therefore, at the interim balance sheet date, the liability will be measured at 6,000 x £10.2 = £61,200.

If in the second half of the year, the entity generates the further expected emissions of 6,500 (giving a total of 12,500 for the year), the liability at the end of the year will be measured at 10,000 x £10 = £100,000 (for allowances held by the entity) + 2,500 x £12 = £30,000 (for allowances to be purchased on the market), that is, a total liability at the year end of £130,000 (that is, £10.4 per unit), recognising a further cost of £68,800 in the second half of the financial year.

Comparison of methods

The effect of using the different methods for allocating allowances to the obligation under the 'cost of settlement' approach is that the total expense for the year will be recognised in different periods as shown below. The corresponding figures under the full market value approach are shown below for comparison purposes.

	'Cost of settlement' approach (FIFO)			'Cost of settlement' approach (weighted average)		
	Emissions	Grant1	Net	Emissions	Grant1	Net
	£'000	£'000	£'000	£'000	£'000	£'000
Expense in first half-year	60,000	(48,000)	12,000	61,200	(48,000)	13,200
Expense in second half-year	70,000	(52,000)	18,000	68,800	(52,000)	16,800
Total	130,000	(100,000)	30,000	130,000	(100,000)	30,000

	'Full market value' approach			
			Gain	
	Emissions	Grant	(STRGL)	Net
	£'000	£'000	£'000	£'000
Expense in first half-year	66,000[2]	(48,000)	(10,000)	8,000
Expense in second half-year	84,000	(52,000)	(10,000)	22,000
Total	150,000[3]	(100,000)	(20,000)	30,000

1 The grant has been allocated *pro rata* to expected emissions as for the full market value approach (see para 21.249.14)

2 6,000 x £11 = £66,000

3 12,500 x £12 = £150,000

Under the FIFO method using the 'cost of settlement' approach, if the entity holds sufficient allowances to cover the obligation at the interim period and if those allowances are recognised at a lower cost per unit than the market price prevailing at the period end, there will be a relatively lower expense in the first half year. This contrasts with the weighted average method for the 'cost of settlement' approach, where the cost of meeting the expected shortfall (measured at the market price at the interim balance sheet date) is taken into account in measuring the cost per unit applied to the obligation at the interim balance sheet date.

The emissions charge of £68,800 in the second half of the year under the weighted average approach comprises the cost (of £67,600) in respect of the obligation generated in the second half (6,500 x (£100,000 + (2,500 x £12))/12,500 = £10.4) and the uplift of the obligation for the first half year (cost of £1,200) for the change in market value (= 6,000 x (£10.4 – £10.2)).

The full market value approach is shown above for comparison purposes. Under this approach (with revaluation of the intangible allowances), the net charge in the first half year (including the recognised gain on revaluation) is lower than the cost of settlement (weighted average approach), because the whole of the revaluation gain is recognised in the STRGL (£10,000), rather than just the proportion relating to the allowance units attributable to emissions in the first half year (£10,000 x 6,000/12,500 = £4,800). The net charge in the first half year is, therefore, reduced by the excess interim revaluation of £5,200 (that is, a net charge of £13,200 – £5,200 = £8,000) and the net charge in the second half is correspondingly increased (that is, a net charge of £16,800 + £5,200 = £22,200).

The example above illustrates the accounting where financial statements are drawn up at a date part way through the compliance period (for example, an interim financial report). As noted in paragraph 21.249.16, the above accounting will also be applicable for a financial year end where the financial year is not coterminous with the compliance period.

Abandonment and decommissioning costs

21.250 Abandonment is the term used to describe: the plugging and abandonment of wells; the dismantlement of wellheads; production and transportation facilities; and restoration of producing areas in accordance with the licence requirements and the relevant legislation. It normally commences at the date when the facility ceases to produce, treat, transport or store saleable quantities of oil or gas.

21.251 Similar costs are incurred in other industries such as: decommissioning costs in the electricity and nuclear industries; abandonment costs in the mining and extractive industries; clean up and restoration costs of landfill sites; and environmental clean up costs in a number of industries.

21.252 The underlying issue is whether, on developing a facility (such as drilling an oil well, excavating a mine or commissioning a power station), the liability that will arise in the future to abandon or decommission should be recognised in full as a liability on day one or should be recognised gradually by spreading over a period.

21.253 FRS 12 requires a provision for the liability for abandonment and other similar costs to be made on day one with a corresponding asset set up (see para 21.83).

21.254 Appendix III to FRS 12 includes an example of how the rules apply in practice and this example is explained below.

Example

A company operates an oil field in the North Sea. Its operating licence requires it to remove the oil rig at the end of its production life and to restore the seabed. 90% of the costs of undertaking this work relate to removing the rig and restoring the damage it has caused. A further 10% arise through the extraction of oil. At the balance sheet date the rig has been constructed, but no oil has been extracted.

A provision should be made at the balance sheet date for the discounted cost of removing the rig and restoring the seabed for the following reasons:

- A legal obligation exists which stems from the operating licence and it is more likely than not to arise.
- The obligating event is installing the rig, which has caused the damage.
- The costs to be incurred do not relate to the entity's future operations, as when they are incurred the rig will no longer be operating.
- The obligation will result in a transfer of economic benefits as this is required under the licence.
- The difficult area is whether or not it is possible to make a reasonable estimate of the obligation. This will depend on a number of factors and the standard says that only in exceptional circumstances will it not be possible to make some estimate of the obligation.

The costs provided will be treated as part of the cost of the oil rig to be depreciated over the production life of the rig (see para 21.83).

However, there is no obligation to rectify the damage caused by the extraction of the oil, until that oil is extracted. Hence, the costs of making good this damage (the 10% referred to above) will be accrued as the damage is caused (that is, the oil is extracted).

21.255 The measurement issue of providing for such long-term obligations and how subsequent re-measurement should be accounted for are considered from paragraph 21.133 and from paragraph 21.135 respectively.

[The next paragraph is 21.258.]

Litigation

21.258 Throughout the recognition section of this chapter, litigation has been used to illustrate how certain aspects of FRS 12 apply. These issues are brought together here.

21.259 A company might find that it is taking an action against another party or is defending an action. Whichever side of the fence a company finds itself on, there will be costs associated with the litigation process (that is, primarily lawyers' fees and perhaps fees for expert witnesses) and finally costs (or proceeds) from either settling the action out of court or arising from the court's decision. There may also be, for the party losing the action, an insurance claim and potential insurance recoveries if the action was covered by insurance.

21.260 During the stages of the litigation process, it will be necessary for the company to consider carefully whether or not an obligation arises for which provision is required. Initially, the likelihood of settlement might be remote and, as a consequence, not even a contingent liability requires noting. However, once an action has been started a contingent liability might arise which initially requires disclosures but, as the litigation progresses, becomes firmer and may warrant a provision being made. The outcome will not be assured until the final judgment has been given. Even then, there may still be uncertainties concerning whether claims against insurers will be successful. The example and paragraphs that follow consider a number of these aspects.

Example

A company sells an additive for leaded petrol engines, which allows them to comply with new emission requirements. The company has heard from the representatives of ten customers who claim that the canisters have burst open on use and the additive has burnt their hands. They contend that the canisters were faulty. The company is insured for such liabilities and does not expect to lose any money if the claims succeed.

The first stage in establishing whether a provision should be made is to determine whether there is a present obligation. The past event is the sale to the customer of the potentially faulty goods. A present obligation will arise if the company is found responsible for the canisters bursting. The prosecution will have to prove that a present obligation has arisen from the canisters bursting and that some compensation is then payable. Where it is unclear whether the company is liable, it will be necessary for the company defending the action to determine whether there is a present obligation arising from the past event and this might entail its seeking expert advice. In the example, the company might contend that there is nothing wrong with the canisters and the customers did not follow the company's instruction leaflet, which clearly shows how to avoid the reported problem. If it is more likely than not (that is, greater than a 50% chance) that the company is liable for the canisters bursting, there is a present obligation for which provision should be made.

21.261 Once it has been established whether there is a present obligation, it is then necessary to establish whether a transfer of economic benefits will result from settling the claim. Again, this judgement is based on whether it is more likely than not that a transfer of economic benefits will be made. Often further information might become available between the balance sheet date and the date on which a company's financial statements are finalised. Where this is so, that information should be taken into account in determining whether or not a present obligation arose at the balance sheet date (see para 21.73).

21.262 Where it is established that a transfer of economic benefits is probable, the next step is to decide how much to provide. It is helpful here to consider the simple year end approach. If the company stopped trading at its year end, how much would it have to pay to settle the obligation? This will obviously depend on the outcome of the claim. For example, if the company decided that it was going to settle out of court, it would provide the estimated cost of settlement.

21.263 Where a company does not believe that there is a present obligation (that is, it is more likely than not that the bursting of the canisters does not create a present obligation), it would not recognise a provision, but would disclose a contingent liability (unless the possibility of a transfer of economic benefit is remote).

21.264 If, as in the above example in paragraph 21.260, a present obligation arises, the company would need to make a provision. But in the example, it mentions that the company is insured for such claims. FRS 12 is clear that the obligation and the recovery need to be considered separately. As explained above, a provision for the obligation will be made when it is more likely than not both that an obligation exists and that a transfer of economic benefits will be necessary and if a reliable estimate of the obligation can be established. However, the same rules do not apply to recognition of an insurance recovery. A receivable can only be recognised as an asset where it is virtually certain that it will be received if the entity settles the obligation. If the receipt is not virtually certain, then the notes to the financial statements should merely disclose the amount as a contingent asset. Such a claim would be virtually certain of receipt once it has been accepted by the insurance company or where previous experience indicates that settlement is virtually certain.

21.265 One of the issues which will be important in practice is the sensitivity associated with the disclosures that the standard requires. It might be appropriate for a company to provide for the settlement of a legal claim because it is more likely than not that the obligation will arise, but to give the full disclosures required by the standard could prejudice the case's outcome. In extremely rare cases, the standard allows companies an exemption from disclosure (see from para 21.314) of all the information required as illustrated in Table 21.1.

Table 21.1 — Reflec plc — Annual Report & Accounts — 28 February 1998

Notes forming part of the financial statements (extract)

5 Exceptional items (extract)

The following operating exceptional items are included within the statutory format headings on the face of the profit and loss account and are categorised within administrative expenses other than £200,000 categorised in cost of sales.

	1998 £'000	1997 £'000
Provision for legal fees	750	–
Permanent diminution in value of goodwill	1,875	–
Permanent diminution in asset values	434	–
	3,059	–

Legal fees relate to a provision for the likely cost of defending proceedings taken against a subsidiary undertaking. This litigation relates to a dispute with a competitor in the US which alleges that the subsidiary undertaking has infringed patents in the US. The information required by the recent accounting standard FRS12, "Provisions and Contingent liabilities" is not disclosed on the grounds that it can be expected to prejudice the outcome of the litigation. The directors are of the opinion that the claim can be successfully resisted by the subsidiary undertaking and feel it is commercially desirable to defend the proceedings and therefore provision has been made for the likely legal costs.

Regulatory fines, compensation and systems rectification

21.266 Many regulated industries have their business activities scrutinised and if they do not comply with their regulators' rules may be subject to fines and compensation payments. For example, in the pension industry mis-selling of personal pensions has led to fines on the companies selling inappropriate pensions and to compensation payments to their customers who were affected. Regulators can look at company systems and operations to determine whether an entity is acting in a fit and proper manner to continue its trade. Sometimes, regulators recommend system changes for the future, but can also levy fines for past breaches of their rules. In extreme cases regulators can withdraw licences or close businesses.

21.267 There are different types of costs resulting from these rule breaches. These include: fines paid to the regulators; compensation payments made to customers; and the costs associated with improving systems to ensure compliance in the future. Whether or not a company can provide for these will depend on a number of factors as illustrated in the following example.

Example

A company expects to be fined £250,000 for the time taken in settling its pension mis-selling obligation. At its year end, the company has not paid the fine, but it knows the amount it will have to pay from published rates. It anticipates that it has a pension mis-selling obligation of £5m, but it still needs to calculate how much to repay its customers and who those customers are. In addition, the regulator has requested that it make certain system changes to the way it sells pensions and this is expected to cost the company a further £500,000, £100,000 of which relates to training costs.

The pension mis-selling obligations clearly arise from a past event, which was the original sale of personal pensions to customers. If the simple year end test is applied as if the company discontinued trade at its year end, the company would be responsible for paying the fine of £250,000. In addition, it would have an obligation of £5m to compensate its customers for mis-selling them personal pensions.

Clearly the costs of £400,000 to rectify the company's systems and the £100,000 training costs relate to the company's future operations and are not eligible for provision.

Financial guarantee contracts

21.268 Appendix III to FRS 12 includes an example of a financial guarantee. The accounting treatment for such an item depends on whether the company is applying FRS 26, 'Financial instruments: Recognition and measurement'. If FRS 26 does not apply, then the normal rules in FRS 12 are applied. This is illustrated in the example in paragraph 21.272 below.

21.269 If the entity applies FRS 26, then its scope specifically considers financial guarantee contracts that provide for payment to be made if the debtor fails to make payment when due. FRS 26 defines a financial guarantee contract as:

> *"... a contract that requires the issuer to make specified payments to reimburse the holder for a loss it incurs because a specified debtor fails to make payment when due in accordance with the original or modified terms of a debt instrument"*. [FRS 26 para 9].

21.270 This would, therefore, apply to financial guarantees given by or to financial institutions, but also certain guarantees given by parent companies to their subsidiaries and other intra-group guarantees. Financial guarantee contracts are dealt with in detail in chapter 6, but in summary, such contracts (other than certain specified exemptions – see chapter 6 for details) are required to be accounted for as follows under FRS 26:

- Initially at fair value. If the financial guarantee contract was issued in a stand-alone arm's length transaction to an unrelated party, its fair value at inception is likely to equal the premium received, unless there is evidence to the contrary. [FRS 26 paras 43, AG4(a)].

- Subsequently (unless they are designated as at fair value through profit or loss, if permitted) at the higher of:

- the amount determined in accordance with FRS 12; and
- the amount initially recognised less, when appropriate, cumulative amortisation.

[FRS 26 para 47(c)].

21.271 An exception to the above rules in FRS 26 for financial guarantee contracts is where an issuer has previously asserted explicitly that it regards a financial guarantee contract as an insurance contract and has used accounting applicable to insurance contracts. In that case, the issuer may elect to apply either FRS 26 or continue to use accounting applicable to insurance contracts. The issuer can make that election on a contract by contract basis, but the election for each contract is irrevocable. [FRS 26 para 2(e)].

21.272 As noted above, Appendix III to FRS 12 includes an example dealing with a financial guarantee. The example below, which is based on the example in FRS 12 considers this further, both for entities that are applying FRS 26 and those that are not.

Example

On 31 December 20X2, entity A gives a guarantee of certain borrowings of entity B, whose financial condition at that time is sound. Under the guarantee's terms, entity A will make specified payments to reimburse the holder for any loss it incurs if entity B fails to make payment when due. During 20X3, entity B's financial condition deteriorates and at 30 June 20X3 entity B files for protection from its creditors.

At 31 December 20X2

- The obligating event is the giving of the guarantee, which gives rise to a legal obligation.
- At 31 December 20X2, the financial position of entity B is sound. Therefore, an outflow of economic benefits is not probable at 31 December 20X2.

Entities not applying FRS 26 – No provision is recognised. [FRS 12 paras 14, 23]. The guarantee is disclosed as a contingent liability, unless the probability of any transfer is regarded as remote. [FRS 12 para 91].

Entities applying FRS 26 – The guarantee is initially recognised at fair value. [FRS 26 para 43].

At 31 December 20X3

- The obligating event is the giving of the guarantee, which gives rise to a legal obligation.
- At 31 December 20X3, the financial position of entity B has deteriorated such that it is probable that an outflow of economic benefits will be required to settle the obligation.

Entities not applying FRS 26 – A provision is recognised for the best estimate of the obligation. [FRS 12 paras 14, 23]. Note that this example deals with a single guarantee. If an entity has a portfolio of similar guarantees, it will assess that portfolio as a whole in determining whether a transfer of economic benefit is probable. [FRS 12 para 24].

Entities applying FRS 26 – The guarantee is subsequently measured at the higher of (a) the best estimate of the obligation determined in accordance with FRS 12 and (b) the amount initially recognised less cumulative amortisation. [FRS 26 para 47(c)].

[The next paragraph is 21.275.]

Tariff over-recoveries

21.275 Appendix VII to FRS 12 gives some background on the development of the FRS and paragraph 16 includes some specific guidance on how the standard applies to regulated industries. This paragraph comments that the FRS rules out the recognition of any provision made simply to allocate results over more than one period or otherwise to smooth the reported results. It goes on to say that in a regulated industry the results achieved in the current period may cause the pricing structure in the next period to be adjusted such that the higher the profits in the current year the lower the prices that will be permitted in the next year. FRS 12 does not allow provisions to be made in this situation as there is no past event. The standard says that the purpose of such a provision would be to transfer some of the current year's profit to the following year, which would suffer from lower prices because of the current year's profits. But the standard argues that there is no present obligation that requires the transfer of economic benefits to settle it and nothing to justify recognition of a provision.

21.276 Paragraph 16 of the appendix first appeared when the FRS was issued and was not included in the exposure draft that preceded it. Although not part of the standard itself, the paragraph is indicative of the ASB's thinking and utilities will need to consider how it applies in their particular circumstances.

21.277 Noted below are three instances within the UK regulatory environment for utilities where prior to FRS 12's introduction a utility may have reduced its prices in a future period by reference to its results in an earlier period.

- The utility believed that it may be penalised in a future period by being required to reduce prices and, therefore, prior to FRS 12 deferred an element of income from the current period.
- The utility operated under price cap regulatory control based on predetermined volumes of supply. The predetermined volumes were compared to actual volumes at the end of the tariff year and provision was made for over recoveries of income, which would then be reflected in future tariff periods where volume variances arose.
- The utility operated under price cap control and undershot certain regulatory parameters. The regulator might indicate that the utility should

voluntarily have reduced its tariff in a subsequent year before the next periodic price review.

21.278 In February 2000, the UITF confirmed (in Information Sheet 35) that the principles of FRS 12 should be applied to regulated industries and, consequently, no liability should be recognised for a price reduction or similar regulatory correction factors in subsequent accounting periods required by a regulator. The UITF agreed that liabilities for such items should not be included in financial statements, unless the company had a binding obligation actually to repay amounts to customers at the balance sheet date rather than adjusting prices in the following year.

[The next paragraph is 21.288.]

Disclosure requirements

21.288 FRS 12 contains extensive disclosures that companies have to make when they recognise provisions and have contingent liabilities and assets. Before the publication of FRS 12, the only rules were included in the Companies Act 1985. These rules still apply, but have been supplemented by those in FRS 12. Also, unless specifically exempted, FRS 13 (or FRS 29, for entities applying FRS 26), is applicable to those provisions that meet the definition of financial instruments, but which are accounted for under FRS 12 as they are exempt from FRS 26. The application of FRS 13 and FRS 29 to provisions is discussed in detail in chapter 6.

Provisions for liabilities

Categorising by class

21.289 The Companies Act 1985 requires 'Provisions for liabilities' to be analysed into the following categories:

- Pensions and similar obligations.
- Taxation, including deferred taxation.
- Other provisions.

[CA85 4 Sch formats].

21.290 The Act goes on to say that apart from the categories of provision mentioned above, an item representing a provision that is not covered by the prescribed format may be shown separately. [CA85 4 Sch 3(2)]. FRS 12 ties in with this as it requires each class of provision to be disclosed separately. [FRS 12 para 89].

[The next paragraph is 21.292.]

21.292 In order to determine which provisions can be aggregated together to form a class, it is necessary to consider whether the nature of the items is sufficiently similar for a single statement about them to fulfil FRS 12's disclosure requirements, which are set out below. [FRS 12 para 92]. Examples of different classes of provision include those set up in relation to restructurings, integration of acquisitions, self-insurance, warranties and environmental liabilities. It might, for example, be appropriate to treat warranties for different products as a single class, but the standard comments that it would not be appropriate to treat as a single class amounts relating to normal warranties and amounts that are subject to legal proceedings. Also, the materiality of each class needs to be considered and some aggregation might be necessary where individually provisions are immaterial.

Tabular information

21.293 The Act's requirements concerning how to analyse the movements on provisions are set out in paragraph 46 of Schedule 4 to the Companies Act 1985. But these disclosures are only required where there has been a transfer to or from any provision for liabilities other than a transfer from that provision for the purpose for which that provision was originally established. FRS 12's requirements cover the same types of disclosure as the Act, except that the standard's requirements are more prescriptive and apply whether or not the provision is being used for the purpose it was originally intended. Therefore, putting the two sets of disclosure requirements together, companies now have to give the following information for each class of provision:

- The carrying amount at the beginning and end of the period. [FRS 12 para 89(a); CA85 4 Sch 46(2)(a)].
- Additional provisions made in the period, including increases to existing provisions. [FRS 12 para 89(b); CA85 4 Sch 46(2)(b)].
- Amounts used (that is, incurred and charged against the provision) during the period. [FRS 12 para 89(c); CA85 4 Sch 46(2)(b)].
- Unused amounts reversed during the period. [FRS 12 para 89(d); CA85 4Sch 46(2)(b)(c)].
- The increase during the period in the discounted amount arising from the passage of time and the effect of any change in the discount rate. [FRS 12 para 89(a); CA85 4 Sch 46(2)(a)].

21.294 One of the Act's requirements is not exactly mirrored by the disclosures required by FRS 12. Paragraph 46(2)(c) of Schedule 4 to the Companies Act 1985 requires that disclosure should be made of the source and the application of any amounts transferred to or from provisions. This disclosure, prior to the introduction of FRS 12, was aimed in particular at the situation where a provision was not used for its intended purpose. But following the prohibition in paragraph 64 of FRS 12, provisions can now only be used for their intended purpose. Still the Act requires the source and application of the provision to be disclosed and this can either be mentioned in the description in the table or is probably better dealt with in the narrative disclosures (see para 21.297 below).

21.295 Although comparative information is required for most items included in financial statements, FRS 28, 'Corresponding amounts', contains an exemption from the requirement to disclose an analysis showing the movement between the opening provision and the closing balance in the preceding period. [FRS 28 para 11].

21.296 Where a provision and a contingent liability arises from the same set of circumstances, the entity should make the disclosures required by the standard's paragraphs 89 to 91 in such a way that clearly shows the link between the provision and the contingent liability.

Narrative information

21.297 In addition to the tabular information, the standard requires the following narrative disclosures to be given for each class of provision:

- A brief description of the nature of the obligation and the expected timing of any resulting transfers of economic benefits.
- An indication of the uncertainties about the amount or timing of those transfers of economic benefits. This might necessitate disclosure of the major assumptions made concerning those future events.
- The amount of any expected reimbursement, stating the amount of any asset that has been recognised for that expected reimbursement.

[FRS 12 para 90].

21.298 As mentioned above in paragraph 21.294 the Companies Act 1985 requires that the source and the application should be disclosed of any amounts transferred to or from provisions and this information could be given as part of the narrative disclosure.

Unwinding of discount

21.299 Where the measurement of a provision has been discounted the tabular disclosures described in paragraph 21.293 above require separate disclosure of the increase during the period in the discounted amount arising from the passage of time and the effect of any change in the discount rate. The unwinding of the discount will be charged to the profit and loss account. The standard says that this charge should be included as a financial item. However, in order to ensure that the relationship between an entity's debt and its interest charge is visible, the standard requires that the charge should be shown adjacent to interest. [FRS 12 para 48].

21.299.1 Originally, entities could present the charge for unwinding of a discount either separately on the face of the profit and loss account or in a note to the financial statements. In practice, many companies chose to show one figure for interest payable and similar charges, including the discount, on the face of the profit and loss account whilst showing the split in the notes. However, FRS 17 introduced an amendment to FRS 12 requiring that the unwinding of a discount on provisions is shown as 'other finance costs adjacent to interest'. The legal requirements section of FRS 17 makes it clear that 'other finance costs (or income)' involves a new profit and loss account format heading and that the unwinding of a discount is not now part of the format heading for interest payable and similar charges. [FRS 17 App II para 6]. However, in practice, because all items in the profit and loss account can be aggregated and given in the notes to the financial statements, it is likely that companies will still aggregate 'interest receivable and similar income' and 'interest payable and similar changes' with 'other finance costs (income)' on the face of the profit and loss account, disclosing the three items separately in the notes.

Further rules included in other regulations

21.300 In addition to the requirements in accounting standards, the Companies Act 1985 requires certain additional information to be given with regard to pensions and similar obligations and for taxation including deferred tax, as explained in the paragraphs below.

Pensions and similar obligations

21.301 The Companies Act 1985 requires the following disclosure in respect of pensions provisions:

- Any pension commitments included under any provision shown in the company's balance sheet.
- Any such commitments for which no provision has been made.

[CA85 4 Sch 50(4)].

21.301.1 Such commitments in relation to pensions payable to the company's past directors must be separately disclosed. [CA85 4 Sch 50(4)]. This principally relates to unfunded pension arrangements.

21.302 In addition, FRS 17, contains extensive disclosure requirements in respect of pensions. These are considered in detail in chapter 11.

Taxation provisions

21.303 The Companies Act 1985 also specifies that if a provision for liabilities and charges includes any provision for taxation (excluding deferred taxation) it must be disclosed separately. [CA85 4 Sch 47].

21.304 In addition, deferred taxation should be included under the balance sheet heading 'Taxation, including deferred taxation' within provisions. Both the Act and FRS 19 require any provision for deferred taxation to be shown separately.

The deferred tax balance, its major components, and transfers to and from the deferred tax account are also required by FRS 19, to be disclosed in the notes to the financial statements. [FRS 19 paras 60, 61]. Taxation and deferred tax are considered further in chapter 13.

Acquisition provisions

21.305 FRS 6, 'Acquisitions and mergers', requires movements on provisions or accruals for costs related to an acquisition to be disclosed and analysed between the amounts used for the specific purpose for which they were created and the amounts released unused. [FRS 6 para 32]. Such disclosure should be given separately for each material acquisition and for other acquisitions in aggregate. [FRS 6 para 23]. These rules are consistent with the FRS 12's requirements and indicate that each material acquisition should be treated as a separate class for the purposes of the disclosures required by FRS 12. Acquisition provisions are discussed further in chapter 25.

Contingent liabilities

21.306 As explained in paragraph 21.93, under FRS 12 it is not appropriate to provide for contingent liabilities, but contingencies of this nature are required to be noted, because of the chance that they might turn into an obligation in the future. However, if the likelihood of an obligation arising is remote, no disclosure is required.

21.307 For each class of contingent liability that exists at the balance sheet date an entity should disclose a brief description of the nature of the contingent liability and where practicable:

- An estimate of its financial effect (including the amount or estimated amount of the liabilities, measured under paragraphs 36 to 52 of FRS 12 – see para 21.109 onwards).
- An indication of the uncertainties relating to the amount or timing of any outflow.
- The possibility of any reimbursement.
- Its legal nature.
- Whether any valuable security has been provided by the company in connection with the liability and a description of that security.

[FRS 12 para 91; CA85 4 Sch 50(2)].

21.307.1 In order to meet the requirements in the first two bullet points above, an entity should disclose both:

- an amount for the best estimate measured under paragraphs 36 to 52 of FRS 12, which may, for instance, be:

  - the most likely outcome; or
  - a probability weighted average depending on facts and circumstances; and
- an indication of uncertainties relating to the amount and timing; this may be achieved by disclosing:
  - a range of outcomes, for example, by giving maximum exposure accompanied by a narrative description of the uncertainties; or
  - probabilities used to determine the weighted average amount, which would allow the user to assess the uncertainties of the exposure, accompanied by a narrative description of the uncertainties.

The level of disclosure necessary will depend on the specific facts and circumstances.

Contingent assets

21.308 Contingent assets are required to be disclosed by FRS 12, but only where an inflow of economic benefits is probable. This can be contrasted with the standard's requirement for contingent liabilities, which is to require disclosure of them all, unless they are remote.

21.309 Hence, where an inflow of economic benefits is probable, an entity must disclose a brief description of the nature of the contingent assets at the balance sheet date and, where practicable, an estimate of their financial effect. [FRS 12 para 94]. Because of the higher degree of certainty needed before a contingent asset is even disclosed, it is important that disclosures of contingent assets avoid giving a misleading indication of the likelihood of a profit arising. [FRS 12 para 95].

Guarantees

21.310 FRS 12's scope includes guarantees, other than those falling within the scope of FRS 26 for entities applying that standard – see further chapter 6. These may fall to be disclosed as contingent liabilities and, in certain circumstances, provision might be required where an obligation under the guarantee arises. In addition, the Companies Act 1985 requires the notes to the financial statements to give details of:

- Any charge on the company's assets that has been given in order to secure the liabilities of any other person.
- The amounts so secured (where practicable).

[CA85 4 Sch 50(1)].

21.311 In addition to the requirement to disclose details of any charge on the company's assets, paragraph 50(2) of Schedule 4 to the Companies Act 1985 (other contingent liabilities) requires the notes to disclose whether any valuable security has been provided.

[The next paragraph is 21.314.]

Exemptions from disclosure

21.314 As can be seen from the explanation of the disclosures required to be given under FRS 12 outlined above, significant information is necessary for each class of provision. In certain situations some of this information might not be readily available or might be of a highly sensitive nature. The standard does include some relaxation in these circumstances as explained below.

21.315 Where any of the information required to be disclosed by the standard is not given because it is not practicable to do so, that fact must be stated. [FRS 12 para 96]. The standard does not elaborate on what is meant by 'not practicable' in this context. But it is possible to imagine situations where it might not be possible to ascertain what uncertainties might relate to the timing of a provision or perhaps difficulties with estimating the financial effect. There is no doubt, however, that the ASB's intention is that entities should use their best endeavours to ascertain all of the required information and only whether this is totally impracticable should the facts surrounding the problem be given instead.

21.316 Some information concerning provisions and contingent liabilities and assets, for example, litigation and litigation recoveries (particularly through insurance) might be very sensitive and disclosure could prejudice the outcome of a particular case. The ASB has acknowledged this and concedes in the standard that, in extremely rare cases, disclosure of some or all of the information required by FRS 12 might prejudice seriously the position of the entity in a dispute with other parties on the subject matter of the provision, contingent liability or contingent asset. In such situations the standard accepts that an entity need not comply with the standard's disclosure requirements, unless the particular disclosure is required by law. The disclosures required by law are primarily set out in paragraph 46 of Schedule 4 to the Companies Act 1985.

21.317 Where advantage is taken of this exemption, the standard requires instead disclosure of the general nature of the dispute, together with the fact that, and reason why, the information has not been disclosed. [FRS 12 para 97]. See the example below and Table 21.1 given in paragraph 21.265.

Example

Entity A is in dispute with a competitor, which is alleging that entity A has infringed patents. The competitor is seeking damages of £100 million. Management recognises a provision for its best estimate of the obligation, but does not disclose the information required by paragraphs 89 and 90 of FRS 12 on the grounds that this would be prejudicial to the outcome of the case.

Management should disclose the following in a note to the financial statements:

> Litigation is in process against the entity relating to a dispute with a competitor, which alleges that the entity has infringed patents and is seeking damages of £100 million. The information usually required by FRS 12 is not disclosed, because the directors believe that to do so would seriously prejudice the outcome of the litigation.

21.318 As to what might fall into the category of 'extremely rare' is a matter of judgement. But it is clear that if, for example, disclosure of certain information is likely to change the course of a particular legal action, then this would justify non-disclosure. Whether this would extend to all of the required disclosures would depend on the particular circumstances.

[The next paragraph is 21.336.]

Commitments

General

21.336 The Companies Act 1985 requires the notes to the financial statements to disclose details, where practicable, of:

- Capital commitments.
- Pension commitments.
- Other financial commitments.

[CA85 4 Sch 50(3)-(5)].

Capital commitments

21.337 Where practicable details must be disclosed of the aggregate amount or estimated amount of capital expenditure contracted for, but not provided for, at the balance sheet date. It is no longer necessary to disclose the aggregate amount or estimated amount of capital expenditure authorised by the directors, but not contracted for, at the balance sheet date. [CA85 4 Sch 50(3)].

21.338 In circumstances where a business is highly capital intensive and the capital commitments are of particular significance in the context of the financial statements as a whole, it may be considered appropriate to provide more information as to the extent and nature of the commitments. An example of the more detailed disclosures made by British Airways is illustrated below in Table 21.9.

Table 21.9 — British Airways Plc — Report & Accounts — 31 March 1997

Notes to the accounts (extract)

15 CAPITAL EXPENDITURE COMMITMENTS

Capital expenditure authorised and contracted for but not provided in the accounts amounts to £3,030 million for the Group (1996: £3,788 million) and £2,871 million for the Company (1996: £3,788 million).

The outstanding commitments include £2,539 million which relates to the acquisition of Boeing 747-400 and Boeing 777 aircraft scheduled for delivery during the next four years and £255 million which relates to the acquisition of Boeing 757-200 and Boeing 737-300 aircraft scheduled for delivery during the next year. It is intended that these aircraft will be financed partially by cash holdings and internal cash flow and partially through external financing, including committed facilities arranged prior to delivery.

At March 31, 1997 British Airways had an unused long term secured aircraft financing facility of US$2.31 billion and unused overdraft and revolving credit facilities of £40 million, and undrawn uncommitted money market lines of £229 million and US$45 million with a number of banks. In addition, British Airways had arranged a £150 million bank-guaranteed facility from the European Investment Bank to assist in funding the airline's ongoing longhaul fleet replacement programme.

The Group's holdings of cash and short-term loans and deposits, together with committed funding facilities and net cash flow, are sufficient to cover the full cost of all firm aircraft deliveries due in the next two years.

Pension commitments

21.339 Under the Companies Act 1985, the notes to the financial statements must give details of pension commitments. See further paragraph 21.301.

21.340 The Act does not specify the basis a company should use to measure pension costs or pension commitments that it has not provided for. However, extensive guidance is given by FRS 17 and, except in relation to disclosure of any commitments to pay pensions to past directors, compliance with FRS 17 is considered to be sufficient to meet the Act's requirements. The provisions of FRS 17 are considered in chapter 11.

[The next paragraph is 21.343.]

Other financial commitments

21.343 The Companies Act 1985 requires details to be disclosed of any other financial commitments that:

- Have not been provided for.
- Are relevant to assessing the company's state of affairs.

[CA85 4 Sch 50(5)].

21.344 However, the Act does not define financial commitments nor does it give guidance as to the nature of the commitments that are required to be disclosed.

21.345 Part 4 of SSAP 21, 'Accounting for leases and hire purchase contracts', sets out the Act's requirements that are relevant to that standard's application. The legal requirements referred to include paragraph 50(5) of Schedule 4 to the Act thereby implying that a commitment under a lease is an example of an 'other financial commitment'.

21.346 Commitments that represent an unusual risk to the reporting entity, either because of their nature or their size or duration, are likely to be relevant to an assessment of the reporting entity's state of affairs and, consequently, should be disclosed. Examples of such contracts could include significant long-term purchase contracts and forward exchange or commodity contracts held by an entity that is not applying FRS 26 (see further chapter 6) that do not hedge existing commitments. Examples of companies that disclose details of purchase commitments are shown in Tables 21.10 and 21.11 below.

Table 21.10 — Imperial Chemical Industries PLC — Annual Report and Accounts — 31 December 1997

Notes relating to the accounts (extract)

41 Commitments and contingent liabilities (extract)
Significant take-or-pay contracts entered into by subsidiaries are as follows:

(i) the purchase of electric power, which commended April 1993, for 15 years. The present value of the remaining commitment is estimated at £688m.

(ii) the purchase of electric power, which will commence in the second quarter of 1998, for 15 years. The present value of this commitment is estimated at £141m.

Table 21.11 — PowerGen plc — Report and Accounts — 31 December 2000

Notes to the Accounts (extract)

31 Commitments and contingent liabilities (extract)
c) The Group has in place a portfolio of fuel contracts of varying volume, duration and price, reflecting market conditions at the time of commitment. These contracts are with UK, US and other international suppliers of coal and are backed by transport contracts for rail, road, canal and sea movements. At 31 December 2000 the Group's future commitments for the supply of coal under all its contractual arrangements totalled £798 million.

The Group is also committed to purchase gas under various long-term gas supply contracts including the supply of gas to the Group's UK CCGT power stations. At 31 December 2000 the estimated minimum commitment for the supply of gas under all these contracts totalled £2.660 million.

Chapter 22

Post balance sheet events

	Page
FRS 21	22001
Annex	22003

Chapter 22

Post balance sheet events

FRS 21

22.1 Accounting for post balance sheet events is dealt with in FRS 21, 'Events after the balance sheet date', which is based on the international standard of the same name, IAS 10.

22.2 The chapter from the Manual of Accounting – IFRS for the UK that deals with IAS 10 is included as an annex to this chapter. Because FRS 21 is identical to IAS 10, the accounting and practical issues are the same.

22.3 The text in the annex contains references to IFRSs. For these to be applied in the UK context, the following should be noted:

- The references to paragraphs in IAS 10 should be read as references to FRS 21, whose paragraph numbers are identical.
- References to other international standards should be read as references to their UK GAAP equivalents.

Annex — Post balance sheet events and financial commitments

Contents

	Page
Introduction	22005
Objectives and scope	22005
Adjusting events	22005
Settlement of a court case	22006
Assets sold or purchased before the year end	22007
Information that indicates impairment or provides evidence of net realisable value	22008
Fraud, error and other irregularities	22010
Going concern	22013
Updating disclosures	22016
Non-adjusting events	22017
Acquisitions and disposals	22019
Major restructuring	22021
Changes in foreign exchange rates or asset prices	22023
Changes in tax rates	22024
Breach of debt covenants and subsequent waivers	22025
Dividends payable and receivable	22028
Date of approval of the financial statements for issue	22031
Preliminary announcements	22034
Listing Rules disclosures for post balance sheet events	22036
Financial commitments	22036
First-time adoption of IFRS	22039
Companies Act 1985	22039

Introduction

A22.1 Almost invariably, it will not be practicable for preparers to finalise financial statements without a period of time elapsing between the balance sheet date and the date on which the financial statements are authorised for issue. The question, therefore, arises as to what extent events occurring between the balance sheet date and the date of approval (that is, 'post balance sheet events') should be reflected in the financial statements. Some of these issues are considered in chapter 21 in relation to provisions, whereas this chapter considers the requirements of IAS 10, 'Events after the balance sheet date'.

[The next paragraph is A22.16.]

Objectives and scope

A22.16 IAS 10 applies to the accounting and disclosure of events that happen after the balance sheet date. The standard determines when an event that occurs after the balance sheet date should result in an entity adjusting its financial statements or alternatively, when such events should only be disclosed, but accounted for in the period in which they have occurred. In addition, IAS 10 requires disclosures regarding the date when the financial statements are authorised for issue and who gave that authorisation. The standard also requires that the going concern basis of preparation should not be applied to financial statements if events after the balance sheet indicate that the going concern assumption is no longer appropriate. [IAS 10 paras 1, 2].

A22.17 IAS 10 covers all post balance sheet events up to the date that the financial statements are authorised for issue and distinguishes between events that require changes in the amounts to be included in the financial statements ('adjusting events') and events that only require disclosure ('non-adjusting events'). The classification of an event depends on whether it presents additional information about conditions already existing at the balance sheet date or indicates conditions that arose after the balance sheet date.

Adjusting events

A22.18 A material post-balance-sheet event requires changes in the amounts to be included in financial statements where either of the following applies:

- It is an adjusting event (that is, it is an event that provides additional evidence relating to conditions that existed at the balance sheet date). [IAS 10 paras 3, 8].
- It indicates that it is not appropriate to apply the going concern concept. [IAS 10 para 14].

A22.19 Going concern is dealt with separately below from paragraph A22.31. In certain very limited circumstances, a post balance sheet grant of a 'grace period' to an entity to rectify a breach of debt covenant affects the classification of debt at the balance sheet date. This is primarily dealt with by IAS 1, 'Presentation of financial statements', as explained in paragraph A22.48 below.

A22.20 Examples of adjusting events are given in IAS 10 and include:

- The settlement of a court case after the balance sheet date that confirms that the entity had a present obligation at the balance sheet date. The entity adjusts any existing provision for the obligation or creates a new provision.
- The receipt of information after the balance sheet date indicating that an asset was impaired as at the balance sheet date; for example, the bankruptcy of a customer that occurs after the balance sheet date or the sale of inventories after the year end that gives evidence about their net realisable value at the balance sheet date.
- The determination after the balance sheet date of the consideration for assets sold or purchased before the balance sheet date.
- The determination after the balance sheet date of profit-sharing or bonus arrangements if the entity had an obligation to make such payments as a result of events before the balance sheet date.
- The discovery of fraud or errors that show that the financial statements are incorrect.

[IAS 10 para 9].

Settlement of a court case

A22.21 In relation to the first bullet point in paragraph A22.20 above, IAS 10 requires that an entity should remeasure the amount of a provision for an obligation if the result of a court case after the balance sheet date requires such remeasurement. However, in some cases the result of a court case may also affect the degree of probability of an outflow of economic benefits. For example, an entity may not have recognised a provision at the balance sheet date because it considered that it was not probable that an outflow of future economic benefits would occur. In such situations, the entity should create a new provision as at the balance sheet date if the outcome of the court case clarifies that such an outflow was probable at the balance sheet date. Thus, the standard requires that the result of the court case after the year end is taken into account, not only in determining whether changes in measurements are required, but also in determining, as at the balance sheet date, whether a provision should be recognised. [IAS 10 para 9(a)].

A22.22 This latter requirement is consistent with the requirement of IAS 37 for provisions. Paragraph 16 of IAS 37 notes that in rare cases, for example in a law suit, it may be disputed either whether certain events have occurred or whether those events result in a present obligation. In such a case, an entity determines whether a present obligation exists at the balance sheet date by taking account of all available evidence, including, for example, the opinion of experts. The settlement of a court case after the year end could also provide evidence of conditions existing at the balance sheet date.

A22.23 IAS 10 refers to a present *obligation* at the balance sheet date, but a court case in progress at the balance sheet date might also concern a matter in which the entity was claiming damages. In this situation, under IAS 37, an asset is not recognised unless an inflow of economic benefits is virtually certain at the balance sheet date. Until the final court judgement is made, it would be rare for the outcome of the court case to be virtually certain. Hence, only when the final judgement is received should the asset be recognised and the related profit be recorded in the financial statements of the period in which the change occurs. [IAS 37 para 35]. In effect, a judgement received after the balance sheet date up to the date of approval of the financial statements is normally a non-adjusting event. The debtor when recognised then becomes subject to normal credit risk evaluation.

Assets sold or purchased before the year end

A22.24 Consider the situation where a property is being sold at the balance sheet date and the sale is conditional on planning permission being granted. Planning permission is granted and the sale is completed, with both these events occurring after the balance sheet date, but before the financial statements are approved. In that situation receipt of planning permission does not permit the sale proceeds to be recognised at the year end, because there is no existing condition at the balance sheet date for which the grant of planning permission would provide additional evidence. This is because no sale had taken place at the balance sheet date and the conditional sale would not be recognised at that date. By contrast, in the example in paragraph A22.21, there is an ongoing court case in existence at the balance sheet date that relates to a transaction or event that occurred before the balance sheet date. The outcome of the court case confirms the existence of the liability and resolves the uncertainty about the amount. In the case of the property sale, the planning permission is critical to whether there is a sale – it is a new event that causes the sale.

A22.25 Furthermore, in a different situation the property may have been *sold unconditionally* before the year end and only the amount of the consideration is dependent on whether or not planning permission is obtained. In such a situation, the potential for planning permission would be taken into account in determining the fair value of the receivable at the balance sheet date in accordance with IAS 39, 'Financial instruments: Recognition and measurement'. Any adjustment to the receivable's value resulting from the granting or refusal of planning permission after the balance sheet date would be a non-adjusting event.

Information that indicates impairment or provides evidence of net realisable value

A22.26 Whilst a post balance sheet restructuring and discontinuance of operations by sale or closure are not in themselves adjusting events, as explained in paragraph A22.39 below, they may often provide evidence of impairment at the balance sheet date. Indeed, such impairment may be a cause rather than a consequence of those post balance sheet events. Therefore, it is common for entities to review carrying values of assets in the light of post balance sheet events of this type and make impairment write-downs as appropriate. The example below illustrates the distinction between an impairment indicator regarded as adjusting and an impairment indicator regarded as non-adjusting.

Example

Should management adjust the carrying amount of assets to reflect impairment indicators that arose after the balance sheet date, but before the financial statements were issued?

Management should consider an impairment loss if it becomes aware of conditions after the balance sheet date that must have existed at balance sheet date (adjusting events). The Russian crisis in 1998 is an example of such an event. The poor performance of the Russian economy would have been evident at a balance sheet date before the collapse in the post balance sheet date period. This type of event should be treated as an adjusting post balance sheet date event.

A new impairment indicator arising after the balance sheet date is a non-adjusting event. Destruction of an asset or expropriation of a mine subsequent to the balance sheet date would be an example. The event occurred after the balance sheet date and was not indicative of a condition existing at the balance sheet date. However, management should disclose the nature of such an event and an estimate of its financial effect.

A22.26.1 A post balance sheet restructuring may provide evidence of impairment at the balance sheet date, however, in accordance with IAS 37, provision is not made for future restructuring costs (see further para A22.44 onwards). The example in Table A22.1 below is consistent with IAS 10 and IAS 37. Table A22.9 also illustrates how a post year end restructuring has been taken into account in determining the impairment of assets at the year end.

Table A22.1 – Impairment loss related to post year end restructuring

Carphone Warehouse Group plc – Annual report and accounts – 31 March 2001

Profit and loss on disposal of fixed assets (extract)
In certain non-key markets where the prospects of achieving acceptable financial returns are not evident, the Group has announced its intention to either restructure its operations or to withdraw its involvement.

As such the Group has provided for the loss of £2.9m expected to arise on the disposal of specific fixed assets. The Group anticipates that further restructuring costs of £3.0m will be incurred the period to 30 March 2002.

> **29 Post-balance sheet events**
> As detailed in note 6b, the Group is in the process of restructuring its involvement in certain non-key markets. Whilst provision has been made for the anticipated loss on disposal of certain fixed assets, the Directors expect additional exceptional restructuring costs of £3m to arise in the period ended 30 March 2002.

A22.27 The above example in Table A22.1 illustrates an impairment that applies to fixed assets, but the examples given in the second bullet point of paragraph A22.20 relate to debtors and inventory. Impairments of current assets that become evident as a result of post balance sheet events are usually fairly straightforward to identify and quantify, because they are usually the direct result of an insolvency of a debtor or the sale of inventory. Where either a current or fixed asset is sold at a loss or revalued downwards subsequent to the balance sheet date, this may also provide additional evidence of a diminution in value that existed at the balance sheet date and would indicate that an impairment review should be carried out in accordance with IAS 36, 'Impairment of assets', (see chapter 18).

Example 1

An entity supplies parts to a car manufacturer in respect of a particular model of car. At the balance sheet date the entity has a high level of inventory of parts due to low order levels. After the balance sheet date, the car manufacturer announces that the specific model will no longer be produced. There is no alternative market for the inventory. Does the subsequent event trigger a write-down of inventory to net realisable value?

Estimates of net realisable value are based on the most reliable evidence available at the time the estimates are made. These estimates consider fluctuations of price or cost directly relating to events occurring after the end of the period to the extent that such events confirm conditions existing at the end of the period. [IAS 2 para 30].

The inventory should be written down to net realisable value. The high inventory levels indicated slow demand from the manufacturer. The post balance sheet announcement confirmed the over-supply at year end.

Example 2

Consider the situation where, prior to the approval of the financial statements but subsequent to the balance sheet date, a company in trading difficulties obtained a valuation of its properties for the purpose of providing additional security to its bankers. In view of its trading difficulties, the company is also considering selling certain properties to generate cash. The amount shown by the valuation is materially lower than the amount attributed to the properties at the balance sheet date based on a valuation carried out three years ago. How should this be reflected in the financial statements?

We consider that the valuation provides evidence of an impairment in value that had occurred prior to the balance sheet date. An impairment review should be carried out in accordance with IAS 36 and a provision to write down the properties would be regarded as an 'adjusting event' with the values attributed to the properties in the balance sheet being adjusted accordingly.

A22.28 Where a company terminates a construction contract after the year end due to the customer becoming insolvent, any debtor balance at the year end should normally be adjusted for the impairment, as it is likely that the customer was experiencing problems prior to the year end (unless there is evidence to the contrary). However, an additional issue arises as to whether the company should make provision for costs incurred in relation to the contract subsequent to the year end. Although IAS 10 does not address this issue, IAS 11, 'Construction contracts', states that when it is probable that total contract cost will exceed total contract revenue, the expected loss should be recognised as an expense immediately. This is regardless of the state of completion of the contract. [IAS 11 paras 36, 37]. Therefore, if costs on the contract have been incurred after the balance sheet date and those costs will not be recovered, they should also be provided for at the balance sheet date as an adjusting event, unless they clearly arose from a new event after the balance sheet date.

A22.29 An example of an adjustment required in interim accounts because of the insolvency of a debtor after the end of the interim period is given in Table A22.2 below. There are also instances where losses on current assets are the result of internal control failures prior to the period end, but only discovered after the period end. These types of losses are also adjusting events as the last bullet point in paragraph A22.20 indicates. Some examples are given in the following section.

Table A22.2 – Adjusting event, insolvency of debtor

Carclo plc – Interim report – 30 September 2005
Operating review (extract)

A significant customer in the USA, Delphi Corporation, filed for chapter 11 protection shortly after the period end and a provision of £0.1 million has been reflected in the half year accounts. This provision is lower than previously indicated in the statement made on 10 October due to the recent US court ruling which enabled Delphi to pay up to 75% of outstanding amounts, subject to certain conditions being met.

Fraud, error and other irregularities

A22.30 Fraud, error and other irregularities that occurred prior to the balance sheet date, but only come to light after the balance sheet date are adjusting items. This type of adjusting event sometimes gives rise to uncertainties about the entity's ability to continue its operations (see further para A22.31 on going concern). Often the consequences of failures in internal controls extend back to earlier years, necessitating not only adjustments to the current year figures, but also a prior year adjustment (see further chapter 5). An example which is consistent with IAS 10, is given in Table A22.3. In this example, the irregularities did not extend to earlier years. A further example, which is also consistent with IAS 10, is given in Table A22.4. In this example the entity recognises an asset for the insurance recovery agreed after the year end – see paragraph A22.23 above.

Table A22.3 – Adjustment in respect of internal control failure

Azlan Group plc – Annual report and accounts – 5 April 1997

Chairman and chief executive's statement (extract)

Overview

The financial year to 5 April 1997 has been one of major disappointment.

On 28 April 1997, Azlan announced that the anticipated pre-tax profits for the financial year ended 5 April 1997 would be broadly in line with market expectations at around £14.8 million and that cash flow from operating activities in the second half had improved significantly and was positive for that period. This announcement was based on the unaudited management accounts for that financial year, which showed a pre-tax profit of £15.1 million.

As a result of initial audit work by Azlan's auditors, KPMG Audit Plc, and, inquiries by the new Group Finance Director, Peter Bertram, certain accounting issues were identified which required further investigation and which caused the Board to conclude that the results for the financial year ended 5 April 1997 would be materially lower than previously indicated. Accordingly, the Board requested the suspension of the listing of the Company's Ordinary Shares on 13 June 1997. To assist the audit work, Azlan's Audit Committee appointed a specialist Forensic team from KPMG to investigate certain specific matters. Your Board is now in a position to report on these matters and other issues which came to light during the course of the investigations carried out by the Company and KPMG.

Your Board regrets to inform you that, due principally to a serious failure of management and internal financial controls in the UK operations and at Group level during the financial year ended 5 April 1997, the management accounts which formed the basis of the 28 April 1997 announcement significantly overstated profits. The audited accounts for the financial year ended 5 April 1997, show a loss of £14.1 million before taxation. In addition, the audited accounts show a cash outflow from operating activities of £14.3 million during the financial year and a cash outflow, after financing, of £4.1 million. There has also been a significant cash outflow since 5 April 1997, when the Group had net cash of £7.7 million, the reasons for which are described in more detail below.

In view of the deterioration in your Company's financial position and in order to meet anticipated cash requirements, the Directors have had to seek revised bank facilities. The availability of the new bank facilities is conditional, *inter alia,* upon the receipt by the Company of the net proceeds of the Rights Issue. The Rights Issue has been fully underwritten by SBC Warburg Dillon Read, which is also broker to the Rights Issue.

The adjustments made as a result of the audit and forensic work are summarised below:

Financial year ended 5 April 1997	Turnover £million	Pre-tax profit/ (loss) £million
Per unaudited management accounts	293.4	15.1
Adjustments		
Purchasing and inventory management		(16.6)
UK operations	(0.5)	(4.4)
Central costs		(3.6)
Overseas operations accounting adjustments		(1.7)
Consolidation adjustments		(1.1)
Additional costs and fees		(1.8)
Per audited financial statements	292.9	(14.1)

As the table above shows, the largest category of adjustments, totalling £16.6 million, relates to central purchasing and inventory management in the product business. These adjustments include balances which were incorrectly treated as recoverable from suppliers in respect of: returns of stock (£0.9 million); compensation for adverse product price movements (£2.7 million); and stock rotations, that is "swapping" old stock for new (£3.4 million). Additional provisions of £3.3 million have been made for unreconciled balances on suppliers' statements, including £2.1 million in respect of one supplier alone. Further adjustments of £0.9 million were made to write off other unreconciled balances and £0.6 million to adjust for unrealised stock profits which had been incorrectly recognised in the profit and loss account. Finally, as a result of a thorough post year end review, the stock provision (previously £0.5 million) was increased by £4.8 million to cover slow-moving, excess and obsolete stock.

The table above also shows adverse adjustments of £4.4 million in respect of the management accounts of the UK operations. Of this amount, £2.0 million was to increase provisions in respect of debtors no longer considered to be recoverable, £0.6 million to defer profit from services and training courses which had not been delivered at the year end, and £1.8 million of sundry adjustments.

Central costs were increased by a total of £3.6 million, which includes accruals of £0.9 million for overhead for the extra five days in the financial year, £0.8 million for general under accrual of expenses and the balance of £1.9 million in relation to sundry smaller adjustments, principally in respect of irrecoverable stock and debtor balances. Profits from overseas operations were reduced by £1.1 million reflecting adjustments to inter-company transactions in relation to pace protection and rebates on stock supplied by the Group and a further £0.6 million in respect of other sundry adjustments. Adjustments totalling £1.1 million were necessary principally to remove items which had previously been incorrectly charged against goodwill created on acquisitions. Additional costs and professional fees of £1.6 million have been incurred in respect of the audit and investigations.

Table A22.4 – Asset recognised in respect of post year end insurance recovery

Etam plc – Annual report and accounts – 25 January 1997

Extract from Corporate Governance statement

The Board confirm that they have carried out a review of the effectiveness of the system of internal financial control as it operated through the key procedures, as described above, during the year.

During the course of the year the Board became aware of the existence of serious irregularities within the Group's Property Development Department since 1989 which have resulted in material losses for the Group being recorded. These irregularities arose from the payment of improper invoices to certain third parties and other matters with respect to various property transactions. Following this discovery, the Board has undertaken an extensive investigation into the circumstances which gave rise to these irregularities, and as part of this process, the Board has reviewed the detailed internal controls in place within the Property Department. The Board has subsequently implemented a number of corrective actions and improvements in the system of controls including:

- An entire change of personnel in the property department.
- Outsourcing the property administration function to a specialised firm of property surveyors skilled in the task of managing this function.
- Tightening of controls notably in the area of authorisation levels.

5 Loss on ordinary activities before interest (extract)

	1997
	£000
Net recoveries from property investigation — see note 32	**(1,075)**
Write-down of freehold and long leasehold property — see note 15	**998**

15 Tangible fixed assets (extract)
Although properties are held for the purposes of trade and not for resale, following the discovery in the Group's property department, the Directors considered it appropriate to commission a review and valuation of the Group's property transactions and portfolio. The overall valuation of the Group's freehold and long leasehold stores is slightly in excess of book value.

Despite this overall surplus, the Directors have concluded that certain properties, which are superfluous to the Group's short term requirements, have suffered permanent diminutions in value which may be attributable to the irregularities in the Group's property department. The Directors have therefore made write-downs of £998,000 against the relevant book values as above.

32 Post Balance Sheet Event
On 17th April 1997, the Company obtained a favourable High Court ruling, with regard to the property fraud as referred to in the Chairman's Statement and Report of the Directors. Agreement has also been reached with the Company's insurers and various other defendants. Amounts receivable from the judgement and settlements, net of costs, of £1,075,000 have been recognised in the current period. Whilst further recoveries are being pursued, these are not sufficiently advanced to be quantifiable at this stage.

Going concern

A22.31 Under IAS 1, 'Presentation of financial statements', an entity's management is required to assess, at the time of preparing the financial statements, the entity's ability to continue as a going concern and this assessment must cover the entity's prospects for at least 12 months from the balance sheet date. [IAS 1 paras 23, 24]. This is considered in more detail in chapter 4. IAS 10 makes it clear that an entity should not prepare its financial statements on the going concern basis if management determines *after the balance sheet date* either that it intends to liquidate the entity or to cease trading or that it has no realistic alternative to doing so. [IAS 10 para 14].

A22.32 When the economic condition of an entity deteriorates after the balance sheet date management has to consider whether or not the going concern basis of accounting remains appropriate. [IAS 10 para 15]. If it is not appropriate, then the financial statements should not be prepared on that basis, but instead should be prepared on a fundamentally different basis of accounting. This is dealt with in detail in chapter 4. IAS 1 requires disclosure of certain information where financial statements are not prepared on the going concern basis including:

- The fact that the financial statements are not prepared on a going concern basis.
- Details of the basis used in preparing the financial statements, for example, the realisable value basis.

- The reason why the entity is not regarded as a going concern.

[IAS 1 para 23; IAS 10 para 16(a)].

A22.33 Where a decision to close down an entity's operation is made after the balance sheet date, this may indicate that applying the going concern concept to the entity is not appropriate. Where the going concern basis is not appropriate, the financial statements should be prepared on a fundamentally different basis.

A22.34 Examples of financial statements prepared on a non-going concern basis are fairly rare, but they may occur where an entity's operating licence expires and is not renewed, for example in the television broadcasting or train operating sectors. Or they might arise where an entity's management has decided that shareholder value would be maximised by an orderly realisation of assets as in the example in Table A22.5. In this example, which is consistent with IAS 10, management has put proposals to shareholders after the year end and has included fixed assets in the financial statements at their 'net recoverable amounts' in the extract below.

Table A22.5 – Financial statements prepared on a 'realisable basis'

Property Partnerships plc – Annual report and accounts – 31 March 1998

Report of the Directors (extract)

1 Principal Activities and Future Developments

The company continued to own and develop commercial properties for investment which are mainly situated in East Anglia. Property Partnerships (Hotels) Limited, a wholly owned subsidiary, operated the Hotel Norwich and the Hotel Nelson until 16th January 1998 when the subsidiary's trade and assets were transferred to the company at book value. In February 1998, the Hotel Norwich and an adjoining investment property were sold to Jarvis Hotels plc.

During the year, your Board has developed a policy for enhancing value to shareholders in the manner described in the circular dispatched to shareholders on 28th July 1998. In line with this policy:

(a) The Hotel Norwich was sold to Jarvis Hotels plc in February 1998 for £4,652,000.

(b) Subject to shareholders' approval at the Extraordinary General Meeting to be held on 20th August 1998, the majority of the company's investment property portfolio will be sold to GE Capital Corporation (Wherry GP) Limited and Equity Estates Ventures Limited for cash of £21,500,000, and the Hotel Nelson and two adjoining investment properties will be sold to Swallow Hotels Limited for cash of £11,250,000.

(c) It is the present intention of the directors to effect an orderly disposal of the remaining investment properties as soon as possible, and to return value to the shareholders by means of special dividend and, subject to shareholder approval, a capital distribution through a members' voluntary liquidation. As explained in note 8, on page 20, costs associated with the disposal of the business and returning value to shareholders, which have not been provided for in the financial statements, are estimated to be in the order of £810,000. It is anticipated that these costs will be less than profits and interest income arising in the periods from 1st April 1998 to the dates on which the assets are disposed of and liquidation occurs.

22 Going concern As stated in the note on page 19 describing the basis of preparation of the financial statements, it is the Board's intention to effect an orderly disposal of the group's assets and to return value to shareholders both by means of special dividend and, subject to shareholder approval, a capital distribution through a members' voluntary liquidation. Accordingly, the company's fixed assets have been stated in the financial statements at their estimated net recoverable amounts. Certain estimated costs associated with the decisions to dispose of the business and to liquidate the company have not been provided for in the financial statements as it is anticipated that the costs will be less than operating profits and interest income arising in the periods from 1st April 1998 to the dates on which the assets are disposed of and liquidation occurs. Details of these costs are given in note 8.

Accounting Policies

Basis of Preparation of the Financial Statements (extract)

As explained in paragraph 1 of the Directors' Report on page 7, the Hotel Norwich was sold during the year, and it is intended to dispose of the majority of the group's investment property portfolio and the Hotel Nelson, subject to the approval of shareholders, in August 1998. It is the present intention of the directors to effect an orderly disposal of the remaining investment properties as soon as possible. Following the sale of the investment properties and the Hotel Nelson, the company will have no ongoing trading activities and its assets will consist principally of cash and/or cash equivalents. Assuming the sales of the investment properties and the Hotel Nelson are successfully concluded, the proceeds from the sales will be used, subject to shareholder approval, to increase the company's net funds. The directors intend to return value to shareholders by means of special dividend and, subject to shareholder approval, a capital distribution through a members' voluntary liquidation. In view of this, the costs have not been provided in the financial statements as it is anticipated that the costs will be less than operating profits and interest income arising in the periods from 1st April 1998 to the dates on which the assets are disposed of and liquidation occurs (see note 8).

A22.35 Whilst preparing financial statements on a non-going concern basis is rare, it is more common for there to be uncertainty about whether the going concern basis of accounting is appropriate. This uncertainty may arise because of post balance sheet events. If so, no adjustments are made to the financial statements, that is, they continue to be prepared on the going concern basis, but full disclosure of the uncertainties is required. IAS 1 also requires disclosure of such uncertainties. [IAS 1 para 25; IAS 10 para 16]. An example of disclosure, which is consistent with IAS 10's requirements, is given in Table A22.6. This also includes disclosure of the loss of a major customer.

Table A22.6 – Post year end going concern uncertainties

Cordiant Communications Group plc – Preliminary announcement – 31 December 2002

PRELIMINARY STATEMENT (extract)

INTRODUCTION (extract)

Cordiant was notified on Friday 25 April 2003 by one of its major clients, Allied Domecq plc, of its intention to terminate its contract with Cordiant with effect from October 2003. In the current financial year Cordiant had budgeted for revenue from this global contract of approximately £18.0 million, some 3.4% of the Group's revenue in 2002. The direct impact of this client loss on revenue in 2003 is not expected to be material, although the Group will incur associated restructuring costs in the current year. However, there will be a substantial impact on operating profit from 2004 onwards.

Following Allied Domecq's decision, and particularly with the interests of the Group's clients in mind, the Board of Cordiant is actively investigating alternative strategic options for the Group, in addition to the disposal programme previously announced, which is progressing well.

The financial statements have been presented on a going concern basis. However until the outcome of the Group's evaluation of strategic options, and the implications of this for the Group's future funding structure are known, there is considerable uncertainty about the appropriateness of this basis of presentation. Attention is drawn to Note 1 of this statement which explains the basis of preparation of the financial information and the form of the auditor's report.

NOTES (extract)

1. Accounting policies and presentation (extract)

Basis of preparation (extract)
In February 2003 the Group commenced negotiations with its principal lenders designed to reset the terms of its principal lending facilities consistent with current trading conditions and the planned disposal programme. Prior to the expected agreement of new financing terms on 29 April 2003 with its lenders, one of its major clients, Allied Domecq plc, notified Cordiant of its intention to terminate its contract with the Group with effect from October 2003. Whilst the direct impact of this client loss on revenue in 2003 is not expected to be material, the Group will incur associated restructuring costs in the current year and there will be a substantial impact on operating profit from 2004 onwards.

Following Allied Domecq's decision, Cordiant is now working with its lenders to amend the financing terms and in addition, the Board is also actively investigating its strategic options for the Group which include, amongst other actions, the realisation of value through disposals, and alternative financing arrangements to reflect its revised circumstances.

Discussions with the lenders have progressed well and Cordiant has reached an agreement in principle, subject to contract, for continuing financing arrangements to 15 July 2003 whilst the Board concludes its review of strategic options and agrees new financing terms consistent with the outcome of that process. These financing arrangements incorporate a waiver of existing financial covenants and continued access to existing committed undrawn facilities. Cordiant expects to make a further announcement once documentation has been signed.

The financial information set out in this preliminary announcement has been presented on a going concern basis. However, until the outcome of the Group's evaluation of its strategic options and negotiations with its lenders, and the implications of this for the Group's future funding structure are known, there is considerable uncertainty about the appropriateness of this basis of presentation.

The financial information does not reflect any adjustments which would be required if the going concern assumption was not appropriate. Given the uncertainty described above it is not currently possible to determine the extent and quantification of such adjustments but these might include the reclassification of creditors due in more than one year to less than one year, the write down of the carrying value of goodwill in the balance sheet to the best estimate of its net realisable value on disposal, the write down of certain assets carried on a value in use basis to net realisable value, and the disclosure of or provision for additional liabilities.

Updating disclosures

A22.36 Where information is received after the balance sheet date about conditions that existed at that date, adjustments may be required to the figures at the balance sheet date as described above. However, even where no adjustments are required, disclosures that relate to conditions existing at the balance sheet date may require to be updated to reflect new information received after the balance sheet date. [IAS 10 para 19]. An example given in the standard is where information obtained subsequent to the balance sheet date gives evidence of a contingent liability that existed at the balance sheet date. [IAS 10 para 20]. An example of disclosure, which is consistent with IAS 10, is given in Table A22.7. This includes additional post balance sheet information about a legal action in progress at the balance sheet date. Although no adjustments are required, the information is disclosed to inform shareholders of the progress of the case.

Table A22.7 – Post year end developments relating to legal action

Cable and Wireless plc – Annual report and accounts – 31 March 2003

34 Legal Proceedings (extract)

Class action litigation against Cable and Wireless plc
Between December 2002 and February 2003, ten shareholder class action lawsuits were filed in the United States District Court for the Eastern District of Virginia naming Cable and Wireless plc and several of its officers and directors as defendants.

In March 2003, the court consolidated all of the cases into one action, styled as In re Cable and Wireless plc Securities Litigation, Civil Action No. 02-1860-A. The Court has appointed Ontario Teachers' Pension Plan Board, an institutional investor located in Canada, and Alex Osinski, a U.S. citizen, as co-lead plaintiffs (collectively 'lead plaintiffs') to prosecute on behalf of all plaintiffs.

In May 2003, the lead plaintiffs filed a consolidated complaint that alleges violations of certain sections of the Securities and Exchange Act of 1934 and the rules promulgated thereunder. A central allegation is that the defendants made false and misleading statements about the Company's financial condition by failing to disclose on a timely basis the existence of a tax indemnity and a ratings trigger to place money in escrow until any liability which the Company may have had under the tax indemnity was finally determined. The indemnity and ratings trigger appear in an agreement between the Company and Deutsche Telekom for the sale of the Company's interest in the mobile telephone company that operated under the name One2One.

In addition to the allegations relating to the tax indemnity, the consolidated complaint also alleges that the defendants made false and misleading statements by: (1) failing to disclose certain lease liability commitments and (2) improperly recognising revenue received from sales of capacity to other carriers.

The plaintiffs seek unspecified money damages in their complaints.

Cable & Wireless believes that it has meritorious defences to these claims and intends to vigorously defend itself in this litigation.

Non-adjusting events

A22.37 Adjustments to amounts recognised in the financial statements are not made for material non-adjusting post balance sheet events, but they do require disclosure in the notes to the financial statements. [IAS 10 paras 10, 21]. A non-adjusting event is an event that arises after the balance sheet date concerning conditions that did not exist at that time and is material in that its non-disclosure could influence the users' economic decisions taken on the basis of the financial statements. [IAS 10 para 3].

A22.38 In such circumstances, the information to be disclosed in the financial statements is the nature of the event and an estimate of its financial effect. Where it is not possible to make an estimate of an event's financial effect, that fact must be disclosed. [IAS 10 para 21].

A22.39 Examples of non-adjusting post balance sheet events are given in the standard as follows:

- A major business combination or disposal of a major subsidiary after the balance sheet date.
- The announcement of a plan to discontinue an operation.
- Major purchases of assets, classification of assets as held for sale in accordance with IFRS 5, 'Non-current assets held for sale and discontinued operations', other disposals of assets, or expropriation of major assets by government.
- The destruction of a major production plant by fire after the balance sheet date.
- Announcing or commencing a major restructuring.
- Major ordinary and potential ordinary share transactions after the balance sheet date. IAS 33, 'Earnings per share', requires an entity to give a brief description of such transactions, except when they involve capitalisation or bonus issues, share splits or share consolidations (which are all treated as adjusting events under IAS 33). IAS 33 is dealt with in chapter 14.
- Abnormally large changes after the balance sheet date in asset prices or foreign exchange rates.
- Changes in tax rates or tax laws enacted or announced after the balance sheet date that have a significant effect on current and deferred tax assets and liabilities.
- Entering into significant commitments or contingent liabilities for example by issuing significant guarantees. Commitments are dealt with from paragraph A22.65 below.
- Commencing major litigation arising solely out of events that occurred after the balance sheet date.

[IAS 10 para 22].

A22.40 In addition, IAS 10 notes that IAS 1, 'Presentation of financial statements', requires disclosure of uncertainties about whether the going concern basis of accounting is appropriate. It notes that such uncertainties may emerge after the balance sheet date. Going concern is discussed above from paragraph A22.31. [IAS 10 para 16(b)].

A22.41 In addition, where an entity has breached borrowing covenants at the year end, but the lender subsequently grants a waiver of the breach or a 'grace period' for rectification of the breach, the grace period is in some circumstances treated as an adjusting event and sometimes as non-adjusting. The detailed requirements relating to this situation are set out in IAS 1 and are dealt with in chapter 4. The main principles are also summarised from paragraph A22.48 below to explain how post balance sheet events, such as waivers, should be treated. In addition paragraph A22.50 sets out the disclosures required by IAS 1 where liabilities are classified as current because of breaches and a post balance sheet event such as a refinancing occurs before the financial statements are approved.

A22.42 The appropriate accounting treatment for a post balance sheet event can normally be determined by reference to IAS 10's underlying principle — that is, that events arising after the balance sheet date need to be reflected in financial statements if they provide additional evidence of conditions that existed at the balance sheet date. This principle is illustrated in the following examples.

Acquisitions and disposals

A22.43 Acquisitions and disposals that are made subsequent to the balance sheet date are examples of non-adjusting post balance sheet events that require disclosure in financial statements. In addition, IFRS 3, 'Business combinations', requires specific disclosures in the case of acquisitions after the balance sheet date. [IFRS 3 para 71]. IFRS 5, 'Non-current assets held for sale and discontinued operations', requires specific disclosures in respect of assets classified as held for sale after the balance sheet date. [IFRS 5 para 12]. These requirements are considered below.

A22.43.1 IFRS 3 is dealt with in detail in chapter 25. The standard sets out specific disclosure requirements in respect of business combinations that occur after the balance sheet date. It requires an acquirer to disclose the detailed information required by paragraph 67 of the standard for each business combination effected after the balance sheet date, but before the financial statements are authorised for issue, unless such disclosure would be impracticable (see further chapter 25). If disclosure of any of that information would be impracticable, that fact should be disclosed, together with an explanation of the reason. The information required to be disclosed is similar to that in respect of a business combination that occurs during the reporting period and includes information in respect of:

- General information (the names and descriptions of the combining entities or businesses; the acquisition date; the percentage of voting equity instruments acquired; and details of any operations the entity has decided to dispose of as a result of the combination).

- Cost of the combination.

- Identifiable assets, liabilities and contingent liabilities.
- Goodwill or 'negative goodwill'.
- Post-acquisition activities.

[IFRS 3 para 71].

A22.43.2 An example of disclosure in respect of a post balance sheet acquisition is given in table A22.8 below (although it should be noted that this example pre-dates the publication of IFRS 3 and so does not give all the disclosures referred to above).

Table A22.8 – Post balance sheet acquisition

Coca Cola HBC SA – Annual report and accounts – 31 December 2003

35. Post-balance sheet events

On 28 January 2004, CCHBC completed the acquisition of the Croatian mineral water company Gotalka d.o.o. The acquisition includes a production facility at Budinscina and the mineral water brand Bistra. Total consideration for the acquisition was €7.2m (excluding costs).

Due to the recent closure of the acquisition, the fair values of the significant assets and liabilities assumed are preliminary and pending finalisation of valuations. At this stage the fair values are as follows:

	€ million
Property, plant and equipment	4.1
Cash and cash equivalents	0.2
Other current assets	0.1
Short term borrowings	(0.7)
Other current liabilities	(0.2)
Fair value of net tangible assets acquired	**3.5**
Water rights	0.4
Goodwill arising on acquisition	3.5
Fair value of net assets acquired	**7.4**
Cash paid to former shareholders	7.2
Costs of acquisition	0.2
Total consideration	**7.4**

A22.43.3 IFRS 5 has specific disclosure requirements for non-current assets or disposal groups classified as held for sale and is dealt with in detail in chapter 8. An example of disclosure in respect of a post balance sheet sale of a disposal group that is classified as held for sale (as a discontinued operation) is given in table A22.8.1 below.

Table A22.8.1 – Post balance sheet disposal

Cadbury Schweppes plc – Annual report and accounts – 01 January 2006

39. Events after the Balance Sheet date

On 1 September 2005, the Group announced its intention to sell Europe Beverages. On 21 November 2005, the Group received a binding offer to buy the business from a consortium acting on behalf of the funds managed by Blackstone Group International and Lion Capital LLP. The transaction was conditional upon receiving European Union regulatory approval.

The sale completed on 2 February 2006 for gross proceeds of €1.85 billion (£1.26 billion). Net proceeds after tax and expenses are expected to be £1.15 billion and we anticipate reporting a profit on disposal in 2006 of around £480 million. The proceeds from the disposal will be used to reduce the Group's borrowings and to increase the funding of our defined benefit pension schemes. In accordance with IFRS 5, Europe Beverages has been classified as a discontinued operation in these financial statements. The results of Europe Beverages are included as discontinued operations in the consolidated income statement and the assets and liabilities are classified as held for sale in the consolidated balance sheet as described in Note 32.

On 1 March 2006, the Group announced its intention to repurchase a proportion of the outstanding £400 million 4.875% Sterling Notes due 2010. It is expected that on 14 March 2006 a repurchase of £323 million will take place.

A22.43.4 Entities cannot classify a non-current asset or disposal group as held for sale if it only meets the criteria to be classified as held for sale *after* the balance sheet date. However, if the criteria are met between the balance sheet date and the date that the financial statements are authorised, the entity should give the disclosures described below:

- A description of the asset or disposal group.
- A description of the facts and circumstances of the sale or those leading to an expected disposal and the expected method and timing of the disposal.
- Where applicable, the segment that the non-current asset or disposal group is part of. This applies in all cases where an entity is required to present segmental information.

[IFRS 5 para 12].

Major restructuring

A22.44 As noted in paragraph A22.26, a post balance sheet restructuring may provide evidence of impairment at the balance sheet date, which is an adjusting event. However, in accordance with IAS 37, a provision is not made for future restructuring costs, until a legal or constructive obligation to restructure arises. This is illustrated in the following example.

Example

Should management recognise a provision if it decides subsequent to year-end to restructure its operations?

The facts are that subsequent to the year end and before the financial statements are approved, entity B's management announces that it will restructure entity B's operations. Management plans to make significant redundancies and to close a division of entity B's business; however, there is no formal plan yet.

Management should not recognise a provision in the financial statements, because a constructive obligation did not exist at balance sheet date. The announcement to restructure the operation was made after the year end and no formal restructuring plan existed at the year end.

The announcement is a non-adjusting post balance sheet event that management should disclose in the financial statements. Management's decision to exit the business may be an indicator that the division is not an economically viable one and the assets may have been impaired at balance sheet date. Management should determine the recoverable amount of the division's assets and recognise impairment losses where appropriate.

A22.44.1 A company may commence a restructuring after the balance sheet date, but prior to the approval of the financial statements. In such a situation, the terms of the restructuring are likely to be a post balance sheet event of such significance that non-disclosure could influence the economic decisions of users of the financial statements. Therefore, disclosure of the restructuring is required.

A22.45 Table A22.9 shows an example of disclosure of a restructuring announced after the year end. In this example disclosure is also made of uncertainties that cast doubt on the ability to continue as a going concern as mentioned in paragraph A22.35 above. In addition, the post year end announcement of restructuring has been taken into account in determining impairment, as mentioned in paragraph A22.26.

Table A22.9 – Post balance sheet restructuring and going concern uncertainty

Swiss International Airlines Ltd. – Report and accounts – 31 December 2004

39. Business risks and going concern

The restructuring programme announced in 2003 was implemented in full in 2004. The Group workforce comprised
6 625 full-time equivalents on December 31, 2004 (compared to 8 072 full-time equivalents on December 31, 2003).

In view of the still-difficult market environment, the high cost of aviation fuel and continuing declines in yields, the Board of Directors approved a further package of measures on January 17, 2005 under which the regional aircraft fleet will be reduced by at least 13 aircraft. This action, in association with the corresponding reduction in flying personnel numbers, the renegotiation of all collective labour agreements and supplier contracts and further efficiency enhancements in the administrative field, is intended to reduce net annual costs by a recurring CHF 300 million. These actions will be taken over the next 18 months. The Business Plan envisages a break-even result or better for 2006. Consequently these consolidated financial statements were prepared on a going concern basis.

In the event of unexpected negative developments caused by the impact of unplannable exceptional events which cannot be offset by appropriate corrective action, further restructuring measures may be required. In such an event, the Group's liquidity position and – in a worst case – its going concern ability might be seriously affected within the next 18 to 24 months.

40. Subsequent events

The Group announced restructuring measures on January 18, 2005 which are designed to provide a profitable and competitive basis for its future growth. Under these measures, the fleet will be downsized by at least 13 regional aircraft operating largely from Basel. A large part of the Group's current operations from Basel should be transferred to the operation of partner airlines in the course of 2006, with the Group retaining a presence on these routes as a codeshare partner. The restructuring envisages the elimination of 800 to 1 000 positions over the next 18 months. The Group expects to achieve further cost savings through renegotiations with its unions and suppliers.

These actions are intended to gradually achieve a recurring CHF 300 million improvement in net annual costs, the full effect of which should be effective from 2007 onwards. No restructuring provisions were made for this programme in 2004, but impairment as far as recognisable. The costs of the restructuring will depend on the outcome of the ongoing negotiations with the unions and suppliers, and cannot yet be estimated with any degree of accuracy.

19. Aircraft fleet (extract)

An impairment loss of CHF 154 million had to be recognised in respect of the aircraft fleet. The impairment, which is for part of the fleet, was based on negative results from point-to-point traffic not contributing to the long-haul network. The impairment was made on the estimated net realisable value of the aircraft fleet, based on market studies and comparable transactions. The supplementary depreciation for a further part of the aircraft fleet is based on the values established as a result of the planned use of manufacturers' repurchase guarantees in 2005 and 2006. All aircraft are traded in USD. Part of the impairment loss was based on the weakening of the USD over the past few years.

The results for 2004 include any impairments required in relation to the corporate restructuring communicated in January 2005 as far as they could be estimated. With associated negotiations still under way, the precise extent of such impairments is currently impossible to determine.

Changes in foreign exchange rates or asset prices

A22.46 Changes in currency exchange rates or in asset prices occurring after the balance sheet date do not normally reflect the conditions at the balance sheet date, as the recoverable value at the balance sheet date was defined by the market, that is, by knowledgeable and willing participants. The following two examples illustrate how changes in exchange rates or asset prices after the year end would be treated:

Example 1

Consider the situation where an adverse movement on the foreign exchange rate post year end has had the effect that the exchange differences arising on the retranslation of the bank overdraft that existed at the balance sheet date at the current exchange rate (as compared to the rate at the balance sheet date) exceed the profit for the period under review. How should this be reflected in the financial statements?

Although the bank overdraft existed at the balance sheet date, the conditions that gave rise to the loss did not. The exchange rate fluctuation occurred subsequent to the balance sheet date. Accordingly, we consider that, in normal circumstances, the effect of the exchange rate fluctuations should not be adjusted for in the financial statements. Exchange rate changes are included in the list of non-adjusting post balance sheet events set out in paragraph 22 of IAS 10. The effect of the exchange rate fluctuations should be referred to in the financial statements as a post balance sheet event. If the fluctuations are of such a materiality that non-disclosure could influence the economic decisions of users taken on the basis of the financial statements then they should also be quantified (as at the latest date before the financial statements are authorised for issue by the directors) and disclosed by way of note to the financial statements as a non-adjusting post balance sheet event.

Example 2

A further example that often arises in practice is where the company has a holding of shares in a listed company and these are included in the balance sheet at market value at the balance sheet date. Subsequently, the listed company has disclosed financial problems and the holding is now worth less than at the balance sheet date. Such an event is generally regarded as being non-adjusting, because the loss has arisen subsequently and it would have been possible for the holding to be sold at the balance sheet date for its market value at that date.

A major stock market movement after the balance sheet date would be an example of a decline in value that is considered to have occurred subsequent to the balance sheet date. Such a 'crash' would, therefore, generally be regarded as being a 'non-adjusting' event.

Changes in tax rates

A22.47 Proposed changes in tax rates are not reflected in the financial statements, unless they have been enacted or substantially enacted by the balance sheet date. [IAS 12 para 47]. However, IAS 10 requires disclosure of changes in the tax rates enacted or announced after the balance sheet date that have a significant effect on current or deferred tax. This is illustrated in the following example.

Example

An entity has deferred tax assets recognised in the balance sheet at 31 December 20X1 in respect of unused tax losses that can be used to reduce taxable income in future years. The income tax rate used to calculate the deferred tax asset was 40%, which was the current rate of tax applicable at the balance sheet date. On 1 January 20X2 a new president came to power and on 17 January 20X2 the income tax rate was reduced to 33% with immediate effect. Should management consider this event as a non-adjusting event?

The change in the income tax rate was announced (and enacted) after the balance sheet date, therefore, it is a non-adjusting event. The change in the tax rate is an event that occurred after the year-end. Management should not adjust the amounts recognised in its financial statements because of this event.

If the effect of the new tax rate on the deferred tax asset will be material, management should disclose details of the change in the income tax rate and its related effects on the entity, in the notes to the financial statements. Where applicable, the disclosure should consider the impact on the different performance statements (see para A22.47.1 below).

A22.47.1 It will be necessary to consider whether the accounting impact of a change in tax rates will be reflected through the income statement or in equity (for example, in the current period SORIE for those entities preparing a SORIE).

IAS 12 requires that deferred tax should be recognised in profit or loss for the period, except to the extent that it is attributable to a gain or loss that is or has been recognised directly in equity. This applies to changes in deferred tax resulting from a change in tax rates. [IAS 12 para 60]. Therefore, where the impact is likely to be material for the purpose of the post balance sheet disclosure, companies will need to consider how the transactions that gave rise to deferred tax were accounted for and trace the impact of the change in tax rate to the same place. Backwards tracing of adjustments to deferred tax is considered further in chapter 13.

A22.47.2 Table A22.10 is an example where announced changes in tax rates have been disclosed and the effect has been quantified.

Table A22.10 — Proposed changes in tax rates

Verbund – Annual report and accounts – 31 December 2003

INCOME TAX (9) (extract)

The Austrian federal government has announced that the corporate tax rate will be reduced from 34 % to 25 % with effect from 2005. In accordance with the IFRS provisions, the rate of 34 % is still used as a basis for the calculation of the deferred taxes stated. Under utilization of the new corporate tax rate, deferred tax liabilities as of 31 December 2003 would drop by €18.3 million. The actual relief in fiscal 2004 will depend on the final decision relating to the tax rate, the determination of taxable income and the tax result in 2004.

Breach of debt covenants and subsequent waivers

A22.48 Often, breaches of banking covenants only become evident close to or after the year end when draft financial statements are prepared. Where covenants are breached, usually long-term borrowings will become payable on demand. The question arises as to whether such borrowings should be re-classified and presented as current liabilities where successful re-negotiation of the covenants has taken place after the year end and before the financial statements are authorised for issue. IAS 10 does not address this issue, but it is covered by IAS 1, 'Presentation of financial statements'. It is dealt with in more detail in chapter 4, but in summary, IAS 1 makes clear that a post balance sheet waiver of a covenant breach is a non-adjusting event and the liability that has become payable on demand due to the breach should be presented as a current liability. At the balance sheet date there is no unconditional right for the company to defer payment of the liability for at least 12 months from the balance sheet date and the liability is therefore current. [IAS 1 para 65]. The only exception to this rule is where the lender has agreed *before the balance sheet date*:

- to provide a period of grace ending at least 12 months from the balance sheet date, within which the entity can rectify the breach; and
- that it cannot demand immediate repayment during that 12 months.

[IAS 1 para 60].

A22.49 Post balance sheet waivers do not constitute adjusting events and, even where a period of grace is given in the terms outlined above, it must be given before the balance sheet date if the debt is to be classed as non-current. In effect, this means that the lender must have agreed by the balance sheet date to extend the term of the loan for a further year unconditionally and despite the breach.

A22.50 Where debt is classified as current because of a breach of covenant or other breach of the terms, IAS 1 requires certain post balance sheet events that occur before the financial statements are approved for issue to be disclosed as non-adjusting events in accordance with IAS 10. These events are:

- Refinancing on a long-term basis.
- Rectification of a breach of a long-term loan agreement.
- Receipt from a lender of a period of grace to rectify a breach of a long-term loan agreement ending at least 12 months from the balance sheet date.

[IAS 1 para 67].

A22.51 Table A22.9 is an example of disclosure of a refinancing after the year end whereby debt classed as current has been converted into share capital. In practice, rectification of a breach will not often be possible and usually an entity will instead negotiate amended terms for an existing facility, probably with additional security or undertakings as to future disposals. Such arrangements are also disclosable as refinancings and should be disclosed even if they are on a short-term basis. This is because if they are on a short-term basis there is likely to be uncertainty about the appropriateness of the going concern basis and such uncertainties are also disclosable under IAS 1 – see paragraph A22.35 above. A further, more straightforward, example of a breach of covenant and post balance sheet refinancing is given in Table A22.11.

Table A22.11 – Breach of covenant and post balance sheet refinancing

First technology plc – Interim report – 31 October 2005

14. Bank overdrafts and loans

	Six months ended 31st October 2005 £'m	Six months ended 31st October 2004 £'m	Year ended 30th April 2005 £'m
Bank overdrafts	**0.3**	2.8	1.0
Bank loans	**112.4**	111.4	105.3
	112.7	114.2	106.3
Repayable:			
On demand or within one year	**112.7**	7.9	6.2
In the second year	–	48.9	47.0
In the third year	–	8.1	7.8
In the fourth year	–	8.1	7.8
In the fifth year	–	41.2	37.5
	112.7	114.2	106.3
Less: Amount due for settlement within 12 months (shown under current liabilities)	**(112.7)**	(7.9)	(6.2)
Amounts due for settlement after more than 12 months	–	106.3	100.1

The Group's principal source of debt at 31st October 2005 was a multi-currency syndicated bank loan ("the Facilities") entered into with a group of seven banks in May 2004 in connection with the Group's offer for BWT. The Facilities comprised three tranches: a US$75 million revolving credit facility; a term loan of up to US$75 million and a US$100 million revolving credit facility. The Facilities were repayable between May 2006 and May 2009. The Facilities were unsecured and initially carried interest at a margin of 1.5% over LIBOR (or EURIBOR for amounts advanced in Euros), plus mandatory costs. The applicable margin was variable (ranging from a minimum of 0.875% up to a maximum of 1.75%) according to the ratio of consolidated net borrowings to EBITDA.

The Facilities were subject to three financial covenants, which were tested quarterly. On 17th August 2005, First Technology PLC informed its bankers that it had failed to meet one of these covenants with respect to the test for the period ended 26th July 2005. As a result of the covenant breach, the Facilities technically became repayable on demand.

On 12th December 2005, the Group signed an agreement for a new bank loan ("the new Facility") with its two principal bankers, HSBC Bank plc and The Royal Bank of Scotland plc, the proceeds of which are being used to repay the existing Facilities. The new Facility comprises two tranches: a US$80 million revolving credit facility and a US$140 million term loan, each available until December 2006. Both tranches, under certain circumstances, can be extended at the Company's option for a further twelve months to December 2007. The new Facility carries interest at a margin of 1.5% over LIBOR, plus mandatory costs. The new Facility is unsecured, although certain of First Technology PLC's wholly-owned subsidiaries have given guarantees with respect to First Technology PLC's obligations under the agreement. However, in the event that the offer announced on 19th December, or any other offer, for the entire issued share capital of the Company does not become wholly unconditional or that the Company has not completed an equity issue raising proceeds of at least £40 million and used such amount to repay the new

> Facility, the Company will be required to give security by 30th September 2006. Any net proceeds of an equity issue must be applied to repay the new Facility. If the amount prepaid is more than £40 million, the Company has the option to extend the new Facility for an additional one year term. Under all circumstances, the Company retains the flexibility to re-finance this new Facility.
>
> In July 2004, First Technology PLC entered into an interest rate swap to fix the rate of interest that it would pay under the US$75 million term loan tranche of the syndicated loan. The interest rate swap fixed for the whole term the rate of interest at 3.605% plus the applicable margin for this element of the Group's debt. This swap is now being used to fix the rate of interest payable under a proportion of the new Facility.

Dividends payable and receivable

A22.52 Dividends to holders of equity instruments are recognised when declared (that is, when the dividends are appropriately authorised and no longer at the entity's discretion). Dividends may be payable only with the approval of the entity's directors or may require other levels of approval, for instance by the holders of the equity instruments. Therefore, dividends on equity instruments can be considered under four categories:

- Dividends declared and paid in an accounting period (see para A22.52.2).
- Interim dividends announced by the directors, but unpaid at a balance sheet date (see para A22.52.3).
- Final dividends proposed by the directors, but not declared (see para A22.52.4).
- Final dividends declared (see para A22.53).

[The next paragraph is A22.52.2.]

A22.52.2 Dividends on equity instruments that are declared and paid in an accounting period are recognised in that accounting period and disclosed in accordance with IAS 1, 'Presentation of financial statements', as discussed in chapter 4. Dividends declared after the balance sheet date are not recognised as a liability at the balance sheet date. [IAS 10 para 12].

A22.52.3 Interim dividends announced by the directors but unpaid at a balance sheet date are a liability at that balance sheet date where, and only where, neither the directors nor the shareholders retain an ability to cancel them. This is because the test for recognition in IAS 10 (that is, that they have been declared) means that the dividends are *"appropriately authorised and no longer at the discretion of the entity"*. [IAS 10 para 13]. In many jurisdictions, the directors retain the discretion to cancel interim dividends until such time as they are paid. Hence, they are not 'declared' in the sense attributed to that term in IAS 10 and are, therefore, not recognised until paid.

A22.52.4 In many jurisdictions final dividends for a year are proposed by directors but are then subject to approval by shareholders in general meeting, at which point they become formally declared. In such a situation, final dividends proposed by directors are not a liability of the company until such time as they are declared by the company in general meeting. In practice, final dividends are usually proposed by the directors after the balance sheet date for declaration by the company at the annual general meeting at a date even further removed from the balance sheet date. Were directors to propose the final dividend prior to the balance sheet date, its declaration would not happen until the subsequent general meeting. Lastly, even where there is a past history of paying dividends, this does not give rise to a constructive obligation. Therefore, no liability should ever be recognised at the balance sheet date for proposed final dividends that are subject to shareholders' approval. Disclosure is required in the notes to the financial statements by paragraph 125 of IAS 1. See Table A22.12 for an example.

Table A22.12 – Disclosure of proposed dividends

Coca-Cola HBC SA – Annual report and accounts – 31 December 2006

29. Dividends
The directors propose a dividend of €0.32 per share (totalling €77.5m) for the year ended 31 December 2006. The proposed dividend will be submitted for formal approval at the Annual General Meeting to be held on 20 June 2007. These financial statements do not reflect this dividend payable, which will be accounted for in shareholders' equity as an appropriation of retained earnings in the year ending 31 December 2007.

During 2006, a dividend of €0.30 per share (2005: €0.28 per share) totalling €72.2m (2005: €66.7m) was paid.

[The next paragraph is A22.53.]

A22.53 Final dividends should be recognised as a liability in the period in which they are declared (that is, appropriately authorised and no longer at the discretion of the entity); in many jurisdictions, this binding declaration occurs through the passing of a resolution by the company. They remain as liabilities until such time as they are paid.

A22.54 In the same way that dividends declared after the year end are not recognised by the paying company at the balance sheet date as they do not meet the definition of a liability, the recipient of such dividends cannot recognise them as an asset and, consequently, as income at the balance sheet date. Treatment of dividends in a recipient's financial statements will follow that in the paying company, that is, dividends receivable will be recognised when the shareholder's right to receive payment is established. This may have significant consequences for those companies that depend on dividends from subsidiaries to cover their dividends to shareholders. In jurisdictions where distributable profits are required to cover dividend payments, it will be vital to get the subsidiaries' dividends declared and properly approved prior to the year end so that the parent has the recognised income. Whether or not the recognised income can then be distributed by the parent will depend on the legal rules governing distributions by the parent.

UK.A22.54.1 The law relating to distributions and dividends made by companies governed by the Companies Act 1985 applies to all such companies irrespective of the accounting framework used in preparing their relevant accounts for the purposes of section 270 of the Companies Act 1985. Thus it applies to companies using IFRS in their individual financial statements. The legal position is set out in Appendix B of Tech 7/03, 'Guidance on the determination of realised profits and losses in the context of distributions under the Companies Act 1985', issued in March 2003 by the ICAEW and ICAS and as approved by both English and Scots Counsel. In particular, paragraph B8 states that:

> *"A distribution is made either when a dividend is declared by the company in general meeting and thereby becomes a liability of the company regardless of the date on which it is to be paid; or, in the case of an interim dividend authorised under common form articles of association (for example, Table A), when the dividend is paid."*

UK.A22.54.2 In the UK, the standard articles of association (Table A) stipulate that, subject to the provisions of the Companies Act 1985, directors may declare and pay interim dividends without authorisation from shareholders at a general meeting. As stated in paragraph B8 of Tech 7/03, an interim dividend declared by directors only becomes a liability at the moment it is paid. This is because their resolution is not irrevocable. The directors have discretion over whether the interim dividend is paid; that is, the directors are able to reverse their resolution to pay an interim dividend at any time up to the date of payment. In *Potel v IRC 46 TC 658* it was determined that the directors, by resolution of the board, are authorised to pay 'interim dividends' (Table A, article 103), but that such a resolution of the board can be revoked prior to actual payment, as no debt is created. Under the law, shareholders cannot force the directors to pay a dividend they declare, but subsequently revoke. Hence, an interim dividend declared but unpaid at a balance sheet date should not be recognised as it does not meet the definition of a present obligation under IAS 37, 'Provisions, contingent liabilities and contingent assets'; neither does a past history of paying interim dividends give rise to a constructive obligation. This line of argument is also found in paragraph AG26 of IAS 32, 'Financial instruments: Disclosure and presentation'. Dividends that are declared but unpaid at the balance sheet date should be disclosed in the notes to the financial statements in accordance with paragraph 125(a) of IAS 1.

UK.A22.54.3 Under their common law duties, directors in the UK have to be able to revoke their resolution as they must test for sufficient distributable profits at both the date of declaration and at the date of payment. They may be sufficient at the first date, but if by the latter those profits have been eroded by subsequent losses, the dividend must not be paid. [Tech 7/03 paras B1 to B3]. For example, in the UK, if an interim dividend is declared by the directors on 4 May and is payable on 4 July, but profits available for distribution are insufficient at the date of payment (4 July), the dividend will not be paid and will not be recognised as a liability at either date. Where, however, the dividend is a final dividend, declared by the company in general meeting on 4 May and payable on 4 July, but profits available for distribution are insufficient at the date of payment, the dividend will not be paid, but will remain as a liability of the company until there are sufficient profits available for distribution to allow it to be paid, or until it is waived by the shareholders.

UK.A22.54.4 The guidance in Tech 7/03 is supplemented by guidance on the implications of IAS 10 for dividends in Tech 02/07, 'Distributable profits: Implications of recent accounting changes'. Paragraph 6.58 of Tech 02/07 states:

> *"IAS 10 refers to dividends "declared" after the balance sheet date with the implication that those "declared" before the balance sheet date would be accrued (by both the subsidiary and the parent). However, IAS 10 refers to dividends that are declared as those that are "appropriately authorised and no longer at the discretion of the entity". In the UK, interim dividends do not become a legally binding liability until they are paid and final dividends do not become a legally binding liability until they are approved by a general meeting or, for private companies, by the members passing a written resolution (see TECH 7/03 B8)."*

UK.A22.54.5 It is clear from Tech 02/07, therefore, that interim dividends declared by UK companies are not recognised as liabilities. This is discussed further in chapter 23.

UK.A22.54.6 The position for UK parent companies that rely on dividends from UK subsidiaries to support their own distributions is also considered in chapter 23.

Date of approval of the financial statements for issue

A22.55 IAS 10 requires an entity to disclose the date on which the financial statements are authorised for issue and who gives that authorisation. [IAS 10 para 17]. If, for example, the board approves the financial statements then IAS 10 specifically requires the fact that the board (or similar body for unincorporated entities) gave the approval to be stated. Also, the standard requires that if the entity's owners or other parties have the power to amend the financial statements after issue, that fact should be disclosed. [IAS 10 para 17].

UK.A22.55.1 In practice, in the UK, the financial statements are approved by the board of directors and, therefore, it will normally be the board that is identified as the body that gave approval. In the UK the entity's owners or other parties do not have the power to amend the financial statements so the requirement of paragraph 17 is unlikely to apply.

A22.56 The reason for requiring that the date of authorisation should be disclosed is that the financial statements do not reflect events after this date. [IAS 10 para 18]. Tables A22.12A, A22.12B and A22.12C give examples of disclosure. In the first example the financial statements are subject to approval at the AGM. In the last example the financial statements are submitted to the supervisory board for approval after authorisation by the executive board – see also paragraph A22.61 below.

Table A22.12A – Disclosure of date of authorisation of financial statements

Jelmoli Holding Limited – Report and accounts – 31 December 2005

42 Events after the balance sheet date (extract)
On March 10, 2006 the consolidated financial statements were authorised for issue by the Board of Directors. They are subject to approval by the Annual General Meeting.

Table A22.12B – Disclosure of date of authorisation of financial statements

BP p.l.c. – Report and accounts – 31 December 2005

Accounting policies (extract)
AUTHORIZATION OF FINANCIAL STATEMENTS AND STATEMENT OF COMPLIANCE WITH INTERNATIONAL FINANCIAL REPORTING STANDARDS (extract)
The financial statements of the BP group for the year ended 31 December 2005 were authorized for issue by the results committee on behalf of the board of directors on 6 February 2006 and the balance sheet was signed on the board's behalf by Peter Sutherland and The Lord Browne of Madingley.

Table A22.12C – Disclosure of date of authorisation of financial statements

Deutsche Börse AG – Report and accounts – 31 December 2005

56. Date of approval for publication
Deutsche Börse AG's Executive Board approved the consolidated financial statements for submission to the Supervisory Board on 21 February 2006 . The Supervisory Board is responsible for examining the Consolidated Financial Statements and stating whether it endorses them.

Report of the Supervisory Board (extract – report is dated 30 March 2006)
Adoption of the annual financial statements (extract)
Based on our own examination of the annual financial statements, the management report and the Group management report, we agreed with the results of the audit performed by the auditor. No objections were raised. Today the Supervisory Board approved the annual and consolidated financial statements; the annual financial statements of Deutsche Börse AG are therefore adopted.

A22.57 The standard devotes several paragraphs to situations that may arise in various jurisdictions. It notes that the process of authorisation of financial statements will vary according to the management structure and legal environment in which an entity operates. [IAS 10 para 4]. In some situations an entity has to submit its financial statements to shareholders for approval after they have been authorised for issue by, for example, the board. In such situations the date of authorisation for the issue of the financial statements is the date of the board's authorisation for issue not the date on which the shareholders approve them – see Table A22.12A above. [IAS 10 para 5]. It is the former date that is disclosed under IAS 10.

UK.A22.57.1 In the UK, shareholders do not formally approve the financial statements, but instead the financial statements are 'laid' before the members.

A22.58 The standard notes that sometimes entities have to submit the financial statements to a supervisory board made up of non-executives for approval. In such situations, the financial statements are authorised for issue when management authorises them for issue to the supervisory board – see Table A22.12C above. [IAS 10 para 6]. Table A22.12D below is an unusual situation where notes to the accounts have been changed after they were approved by the Management Board and reviewed by the Supervisory Board. Disclosure is given of the date of approval of the financial statements and of the date of the subsequent changes.

Table A22.12D – Disclosure of date of authorisation of financial statements

Vivendi Universal SA – Report and accounts – 31 December 2005
Notes to the consolidated financial statements (extract)

On February 21, 2006, the Management Board approved the consolidated financial statements for the year ended December 31, 2005. On February 28, 2006, they were reviewed by the Supervisory Board, after their presentation to the Audit Committee on February 22, 2006.

On February 28, 2006 and March 21, 2006, the Management Board met again to modify the notes to the consolidated financial statements relating to the consolidation method used for Elektrim Telekomunikacja (Telco) and PTC (see Note 2.3), the total distribution of dividend for the year 2005 (see Note18.3) and Directors and Officers' compensation (see Note 28.1).

On April 20, 2006, the consolidated financial statements for the year ended December 31, 2005 will be submitted for adoption to Vivendi Universal shareholders at the Annual General Shareholders' meeting.

UK.A22.58.1 In the UK, where there is a unitary board system of executive and non-executive directors, non-executive directors play a major part in reviewing and monitoring financial information, for example, through audit committees. They also have equal responsibility with executive directors for the financial statements. As a result, financial statements are not approved for issue before being seen by non-executive directors. Therefore, the situation envisaged in the standard would not usually arise in the UK.

Preliminary announcements

UK.A22.59 IAS 10 notes that events after the balance sheet date include all events up to the date on which the financial statements are authorised for issue. This applies even if the events occur after the public announcement of profit or other selected financial information. [IAS 10 para 7]. This rather simple fact can sometimes be very significant. Following the implementation by the FSA of the EU Transparency Directive (see chapter 31), the publication of preliminary announcements by UK listed companies is voluntary (for accounting periods beginning on or after 20 January 2007), although any company choosing to publish one, for example, to ensure the timely release of price-sensitive information, must still follow FSA guidance on its preparation and publication. The preliminary announcement may contain figures taken from full financial statements that have been audited and approved for issue or from unaudited full financial statements that have not yet been approved for issue.

UK.A22.60 In the former situation any events that occur after the issue of the preliminary statement based on audited full financial statements are not post balance sheet events in respect of the year, because they occur after the financial statements have been approved for issue. However, if the preliminary statement is based on figures from full financial statements that have not yet been authorised for issue by the board and on which the audit has not yet been completed, any events between the date of the preliminary announcement and the date of authorisation of the full financial statements for issue are post balance sheet events. Such events are accounted for in accordance with the standard, irrespective of the fact that the entity has already announced figures publicly by way of the preliminary statement.

UK.A22.61 Practical difficulties can sometimes arise if significant post balance sheet events occur after the preliminary publication of results for the year before the full financial statements have been authorised for issue. An example might be the announcement of the insolvency of a major debtor, which would require adjustments to the figures previously announced. Other non-adjusting events might only require additional disclosure. In such circumstances, the entity may have to release revised information with the adjusted figures and/or disclosures. An example of restatement of unaudited preliminary figures and reissue of the preliminary statement is given in Table A22.13. The example is from as long ago as 1990, but the incidence of revisions to preliminary announcements for subsequent events is not uncommon even today and the example has been used here because it illustrates the point well, rather than because of a lack of more recent examples. The example is consistent with IAS 10. Table A22.3 above is also an example of revising previously published figures.

Table A22.13 – Revision of previously published figures

Brent Walker Group plc – Preliminary announcement – 31 December 1990

1990 RESULTS AND DIVIDENDS

On 20th May the Group announced its unaudited preliminary results for the year ended 31st December 1990. At that time the Group stated that the net worth of the Group had fallen by £690 million.

In addition, however, the Group indicated the material difference existing in the valuations adopted for the development properties of the Group compared to professional valuations which had been received. Further consideration of the values of these and certain other assets has persuaded the Board that it would be more appropriate to recognise the professional valuations and make other write downs in the accounts for the year ended 31st December 1990.

This has led to a significant restatement of the Group's results for the year, the principal features of which are set out below:

	1990 £million Revised	1990 £million As previously announced	1989 £million Revised
Turnover	1,763.4	1,778.4	572.0
Group Operating Profit	107.2	122.2	112.9
Interest	(116.2)	(116.2)	(44.1)
(Loss)/profit before exceptional items	(5.9)	9.1	72.7
(Loss)/profit for the financial year	(385.5)	(246.8)	119.9
Shareholders' funds	(56.1)	139.0	827.7

A summary of the movements in shareholders' funds is shown in the accounts.

The reduction in Group Operating Profit of £15 million from the figure of £122.2 million reported in the preliminary figures arises because we have not yet concluded the Walker Power transaction announced on 12th April 1991. The current position of this negotiation is referred to below.

In view of the reduction in net worth and the continuing losses, the Board considered it likely that a "serious loss of capital" as defined by S142 of the Companies Act 1985 had occurred. Consequently an extraordinary general meeting was called where the Board stated that the proposed restructuring was the appropriate action to be taken. At that meeting shareholders sanctioned the Group's borrowings exceeding the limit specified in the articles of association.

In the light of these results the Board are unable to recommend the payment of a final dividend on the Ordinary shares or the payment of the dividend on the Preference shares which fell due on 1st July 1991. Interest was due on the 13% Convertible Capital Bond on 23rd May 1991 and, after discussion with the principal holders of the bonds, arrangements were made to defer the payment of their interest subject to the implementation of the financial restructuring. These particular arrangements have since lapsed but are currently the subject of further negotiation.

Listing Rules disclosures for post balance sheet events

UK.A22.61.1 The Listing Rules for UK listed companies require disclosure of any change in directors' interests occurring between the end of the period under review and a date not more than one month prior to the date of the notice of the annual general meeting. Furthermore, if there has been no such change, that fact should be disclosed. [LR 9.8.6 R(1)]. See further chapter 29.

UK.A22.61.2 Similarly, details of certain interests in a company's share capital need to be disclosed as at a date not more than one month prior to the date of the notice of the annual general meeting. If there is no such interest that fact must be stated. [LR 9.8.6 R(2)]. The relevant interests in a company's share capital are those disclosed to the company in accordance with Part 22 of the Companies Act 2006 (information about interests in a company's shares) or DTR 5 (in respect of notifiable shareholdings).

UK.A22.61.3 The Listing Rules also require disclosure of any purchases of own shares (including treasury shares), or options or contracts to make such purchases, entered into since the end of the period covered by the financial statements. The information to be disclosed is equivalent information to that required under Part II of Schedule 7 to the Companies Act 1985 (disclosure required by company acquiring its own shares, etc). [LR 9.8.6 R(4)].

[The next paragraph is A22.65.]

Financial commitments

A22.65 If an entity enters into any significant commitment or contingent liability after the year end, this is a non-adjusting event that requires disclosure. [IAS 10 para 22(i)]. This is the only specific disclosure requirement concerning commitments in IAS 10, however, other international standards require disclosure of commitments that exist at the balance sheet date that will affect future periods.

A22.66 These include:

- Capital commitments (see para A22.67).
- Operating lease commitments (see para A22.68).
- Commitments in respect of investment properties (see para A22.68.1).
- Other commitments (see para A22.69).

A22.67 IAS 16, 'Property, plant and equipment', requires the disclosure of contractual commitments that exist at the balance sheet date to acquire fixed assets. [IAS 16 para 74(c)]. IAS 38, 'Intangible assets', requires disclosure of contractual commitments for the acquisition of intangible assets. [IAS 38 para 122(e)]. In addition, IAS 41, 'Agriculture', requires disclosure of the amount of commitments for the development or acquisition of biological assets. [IAS 41 para 49(b)]. IAS 16, IAS 38 and IAS 41 are dealt with in chapters 16, 15 and 32 respectively, which include examples of disclosure.

A22.68 IAS 17, 'Leases', requires the disclosure of future minimum lease payments for non-cancellable operating leases. These disclosures are required to be split between the periods in which the amounts fall due. [IAS 17 paras 35 and 56]. IAS 17 is dealt with in chapter 19.

A22.68.1 IAS 40, 'Investment property', requires disclosure by an entity that holds investment properties of contractual obligations to purchase, construct or develop investment property or for repairs, maintenance or enhancements. [IAS 40 para 75(h)].

A22.69 IFRS 7, 'Financial instruments: Disclosure', contains extensive disclosure requirements in respect of financial instruments. It applies to both recognised and unrecognised financial instruments within its scope, even if the financial instrument may not be recognised under IAS 39 (for example, some loan commitments). IFRS 7 is dealt with in chapter 6.

A22.70 IAS 31, 'Interests in joint ventures', requires separate disclosure by the venturer of its capital commitments in respect of a joint venture and its share of capital commitments incurred jointly with the other venturers. It is also required to disclose its share of the joint venture's own capital commitments. IAS 31 is dealt with in chapter 28.

A22.71 IAS 34, 'Interim financial reporting', states that interim reports should include any events or transactions that are material to an understanding of the interim period. It gives as one example, commitments for the purchase of property, plant and equipment. [IAS 34 para 17(e)]. Interim reports are dealt with in chapter 31.

A22.72 Commitments that represent an unusual risk to the reporting entity, either because of their nature or their size or duration, are likely to be relevant in assessing the reporting entity's financial position and, consequently, should be disclosed. Examples of such contracts could include significant long-term purchase contracts. An example of disclosure of commitments is given in Table A22.14. This example illustrates disclosure of future capital expenditure and of long-term purchase commitments.

Table A22.14 – Disclosure of financial commitments

National Grid plc – Annual report and accounts – 31 March 2006

35. Commitments and contingencies

a) Future capital expenditure

	2006 £m	2005 £m
Contracted for but not provided	**1,343**	927

b) Lease commitments

Total Group commitments under non-cancellable operating leases were as follows:

	2006 £m	2005 £m
In one year or less	**87**	99
In more than one year, but not more than two years	**80**	91
In more than two years, but not more than three years	**75**	83
In more than three years, but not more than four years	**71**	79
In more than four years, but not more than five years	**67**	77
In more than five years	**451**	501
	831	930

c) Power commitments

At 31 March 2006, the Group had obligations to purchase energy under long-term contracts. The following table analyses these commitments, excluding commodity contracts carried at fair value (notes 28 and 29):

	2006 £m	2005 £m
In one year or less	**1,504**	1,058
In more than one year, but not more than two years	**935**	623
In more than two years, but not more than three years	**753**	583
In more than three years, but not more than four years	**588**	567
In more than four years, but not more than five years	**94**	462
In more than five years	**1,579**	1,622
	5,453	4,915

d) Other commitments, contingencies and guarantees

The value of other Group commitments, contingencies and guarantees at 31 March 2006 amounted to £334m (2005: £349m), including guarantees amounting to £149m (2005: £189m).

Details of the guarantees entered into by the Group at 31 March 2006 are shown below:

(i) performance guarantees of £20m relating to certain property obligations of Group undertakings. The bulk of these expire by December 2025;

(ii) a guarantee of £50m of the obligations of a Group undertaking to make payments in respect of any liabilities under a meter operating contract that runs until May 2008;

(iii) a performance guarantee relating to the construction of the Victoria to Tasmania Interconnector of 48m Australian dollars (A$48m) (£20m). This halved on commissioning in April 2006 and expires in November 2006;

(iv) a guarantee of the payment obligations of a Group undertaking in respect of a Power Connection Agreement amounting to an annual maximum of A$7m, reducing over the term of the contract. This runs until June 2051, but the maximum potential payout is estimated at £5m;

(v) a guarantee of the payment obligations of a Group undertaking in respect of a Nitrogen Supply Agreement amounting to a maximum potential payout of £14m subject to a cap of £1m per annum. This runs until November 2019;
(vi) a guarantee of the payment obligations of a Group undertaking in respect of a Power Connection Agreement amounting to a maximum potential payout of £14m subject to a cap of £7m per annum. This runs until December 2024;
(vii) guarantees in respect of a former associate amounting to £14m, the bulk of which relates to its obligations to supply telecommunications services. This is open-ended; and
(viii) other guarantees amounting to £12m arising in the normal course of business and entered into on normal commercial terms. These guarantees run for varying lengths of time.

e) Amounts receivable under sublease arrangements
The total of future minimum sublease payments expected to be received under non-cancellable subleases is £26m (2005: £23m).

First-time adoption of IFRS

A22.74 There are specific rules in respect of first-time adoption of IFRS, set out in IFRS 1, 'First-time adoption of International Financial Reporting Standards'. In particular, IFRS 1 requires estimates at the date of transition to IFRS to be based on information consistent with that available under previous GAAP, irrespective of recently available evidence. This and other first-time adoption issues (for instance, the treatment of dividends) are considered in detail in chapter 3.

Companies Act 1985

UK.A22.75 The provisions of the Companies Act 1985 relating to post balance sheet events and the disclosure of commitments are mainly contained in Schedule 4 to the Act and these do not apply to companies reporting under EU-adopted IFRS. However, the disclosure requirements in Schedule 7 to the Act, relating to the directors' report, do apply to companies reporting under EU-adopted IFRS. Schedule 7 requires material post balance sheet events to be disclosed in the directors' report, but does not specify to what extent such events should be adjusted for in preparing the financial statements. [CA85 7 Sch 6(a)]. The disclosures required in the directors' report are discussed in chapter 3 of the Manual of Accounting — IFRS and UK supplement.

Chapter 23

Share capital and reserves

Page
Introduction . . . 23001
Share capital . . . 23002
Types of shares . . . 23002
Measuring issued share capital . . . 23005
Called up share capital . . . 23009
Accounting for share capital . . . 23010
Disclosure of share capital . . . 23014
Statutory requirements . . . 23014
Allotment of shares during the financial year . . . 23016
Serious loss of capital . . . 23017
Multi-currency share capital . . . 23018
Treasury shares . . . 23020
General rules . . . 23020
Conditions applying to treasury shares . . . 23021
Sale or cancellation of treasury shares . . . 23022
Delivery of returns to the Registrar of Companies . . . 23023
Accounting treatment for the purchase of own shares (including treasury shares) . . . 23024
Disclosure in respect of treasury shares . . . 23029
Effect on distributable profits . . . 23031
Listing Rule requirements . . . 23032
Buying back shares in prohibited (close) periods . . . 23033
Treasury shares and capitalisation issues . . . 23033
Other Listing Rules requirements on treasury shares . . . 23034
Alteration of share capital . . . 23034
Reduction of share capital . . . 23034
Court confirmation procedure . . . 23035
Redenomination of share capital . . . 23040
Sub-division or consolidation of shares . . . 23042
Reserves . . . 23042
Profit and loss account . . . 23043
Share premium account . . . 23043
Implications of Shearer v Bercain Ltd . . . 23046
Merger relief . . . 23047
Application of merger relief . . . 23049
Relief in respect of group reconstructions . . . 23051
Reduction of share premium account . . . 23054
Capital redemption reserve . . . 23054
Revaluation reserve . . . 23054
Fair value or available-for-sale reserve . . . 23055
Hedging reserve . . . 23056

Companies not using FRS 26 23058
Foreign currency translation reserve 23058
Companies not using FRSs 23 and 26 23059
Capital reserve 23060
Disclosure 23060
Realised and distributable reserves 23060
Statement of movement on reserves 23062
Dividends 23063
Realised profits and losses 23066
General principles 23066
Realised profits 23068
Realised losses 23071
Fair value accounting 23072
Proposed dividends 23073
Intra-group transactions 23074
Other matters 23076
Distributable profits 23077
Definition of distribution 23077
Conditions applying to companies (other than investment companies) 23078
Additional conditions applying to public companies 23079
Provisions relating to investment companies 23082
Effect of revaluations of fixed assets on distributable profits 23084
Depreciation of revalued fixed assets 23085
Subsequent sale of revalued assets 23087
Provision for impairment 23088
Foreign currency translation 23088
Capitalisation of development costs 23090
Goodwill 23091
Transactions within the group 23092
Pre-acquisition profits 23093
Other transactions 23094
Relevant accounts 23094
Treatment of revalued assets in relevant accounts 23098
Interpreting section 275 of the 1985 Act (section 841 of the 2006 Act) 23101
Summary of action relating to section 275 of the 1985 Act (section 841 of the 2006 Act) 23104
Qualified audit reports and distributions 23105
Other matters 23106
Bonus issues 23106
Amounts unpaid on debentures and shares 23107
Profits and losses made before 22 December 1980 23107
Memorandum and articles of association 23107
Accounting for distributions in kind 23108
Liability for an unlawful distribution 23109
The legality of distributions in kind 23110
Aveling Barford 23110
Distributions in kind under the Companies Act 2006 23113
Companies Act 2006 23114

Chapter 23

Share capital and reserves

Introduction

23.1 This chapter deals with the general legal requirements and disclosure requirements for share capital and reserves. It also deals with the rules for treasury shares. It does not deal with shares held by an ESOP trust, which are dealt with in chapter 12. The effect of FRS 25, 'Financial instruments: Presentation', UITF 39, 'Members' shares in co-operative entities and similar instruments', FRS 26, 'Financial instruments: Recognition and measurement') and FRS 4, 'Capital instruments', on the classification and accounting for share capital and shareholders' funds is discussed in detail in chapter 6.

23.1.1 In November 2006, the Companies Act 2006 (the 2006 Act) received Royal Assent. The 2006 Act is being implemented in stages; the provisions affecting share capital and reserves are to be implemented from 1 October 2008. The 2006 Act re-enacts many of the provisions of the Companies Act 1985 (the 1985 Act) but it also introduces a number of new measures designed to simplify and modernise the legislation affecting share capital and reserves. These new measures are described in the relevant sections of this chapter and are summarised from paragraph 23.258. References to 'the Act' encompass both the 1985 and 2006 Acts.

23.2 This chapter also deals with realised and distributable profits. Companies may make a distribution to their shareholders only out of profits that are available for distribution. Part VIII of the 1985 Act, 'Distribution of profits and assets', imposes conditions that companies must satisfy before they can make distributions; these requirements are substantially re-enacted in the 2006 Act under Part 23, 'Distributions'. Some of the conditions in the Act apply only to public companies. Also, special provisions apply to investment companies and insurance companies. In March 2003, the ICAEW and ICAS ('the Institutes') published guidance on realised profits in technical release Tech 07/03, 'Guidance on the determination of realised profits and losses in the context of distributions under the Companies Act 1985'. In August 2007, the Institutes published Tech 02/07, 'Distributable profits: Implications of recent accounting changes', which amends Tech 7/03 and incorporates the draft guidance issued in May 2005 in Tech 21/05, 'Distributable profits: Implications of IFRS' and interim guidance in Tech 57/05, 'Distributable profits: Implications of IAS 10 and FRS 21 for dividends'. Tech 50/04, 'Guidance on the effect of FRS 17 'Retirement benefits' and IAS 19 'Employee benefits' on realised profits and losses', and Tech 64/04, 'Guidance on the effect on realised and distributable profits of accounting for employee share schemes in accordance with UITF abstract 38 and revised UITF abstract 17' complete the current suite of technical releases on the interaction of accounting requirements with the determination of realised and distributable profits. The principles in Tech 64/04 are applicable to FRS 20, 'Share-based payment' and IFRS 2, 'Share-based payment'.

23.2.1 At October 2007, the extant body of guidance on realised and distributable profits comprises: Tech 7/03 (amended), Tech 50/04, Tech 64/04 and Tech 02/07. The Institutes intend to publish a consolidated text of these four technical releases late in 2007 and, subsequently, in 2008 a consolidated text, updated for the 2006 Act references and dealing with the few changes introduced by that Act, such as the new capital reduction by solvency statement procedure for private companies (see para 23.83.21) The regulations dealing with the solvency statement and the nature of any reserve created by the reduction have yet to be enacted and thus the implications for distributable profits have yet to be determined.

23.3 Part VIII of the 1985 Act (Part 23 of the 2006 Act) is concerned with the profits that may legally be distributed by way of dividend or other distribution. The actual payment of dividends or other distributions must be made in accordance with the company's memorandum and articles. The articles may also contain special provisions regarding dividends and other distributions.

23.4 In addition to the statutory rules in Part VIII of the 1985 Act (Part 23 of the 2006 Act), directors may have to consider other restrictions on their ability to make distributions. For example, under the common law, dividends cannot be paid out of capital. The directors must also consider their duty to act in the company's best interests. They must, for example, consider the future cash needs of their company, even if the company has profits that are distributable under Part VIII of the 1985 Act (Part 23 of the 2006 Act). A description of the common law applicable to distributions is set out in appendix B to Tech 07/03 (amended).

Share capital

Types of shares

23.5 Shares can be divided into numerous different types including: ordinary shares, preference shares, non-voting shares, and redeemable shares. Broadly, FRS 25 can result in some shares and their related share premium, in whole or in part, being presented as liabilities. In simple terms, the classification for accounting purposes depends on whether the issuer has discretion over the transfer of economic benefits; where there is no discretion, the instrument will be recorded, wholly or partly, as a liability. Typically, ordinary shares are classified as equity (and referred to as 'equity' shares) because the issuer has discretion over future dividend payments and the shares are non-redeemable. That is, ordinary shares have no contractual obligation to pay cash or other financial assets. The existence of voting rights does not affect the classification of shares. Shares that are redeemable in cash or a variable number of equity shares would be recorded as a liability for accounting purposes. Similarly, shares that allow the holder to put them back to the issuer for cash or another financial instrument ('puttable shares') are generally classified as financial liabilities, unless they meet the conditions in UITF 39 in which case they can be classified as equity. Non-redeemable shares with a mandatory fixed coupon that is at market rate would be classified as liabilities at their net present value. Further details of the effect of FRS 25 and UITF 39 on share capital are dealt with in detail in chapter 6.

23.5.1 The 1985 Act requires all companies to have prior authorisation for the allotment of shares; that is, every company has an authorised share capital [CA85 Sec 2(5)(a)]. This has been changed in the 2006 Act. Companies are no longer required to have an 'authorised share capital' stated in their memoranda, which can be increased by ordinary resolution of members under section 121 of the 1985 Act. For public companies this is subject to the requirement in section 765 of the 2006 Act that requires an 'authorised minimum' amount of share capital (see para 23.43). Section 542 of the 2006 Act makes it clear that a limited company having share capital must have shares that have a fixed nominal value (for example, 1p, £1, $1 or €1) and prevents a company from issuing shares of no par value.

25.5.2 Private companies that only have one class of share capital do not require prior authorisation and are free to allot shares, except to the extent that they are prohibited from doing so by the company's articles. [CA06 Sec 550]. Private companies that have more than one class of share capital and all public companies, irrespective of the number of classes of shares, are required to have prior authorisation to allot shares, either by ordinary resolution of members or in the articles. Prior authorisation is also required for granting rights to subscribe for shares or to convert any security into shares. [CA06 Sec 551].

23.5.3 The Companies Act (and common law) rules apply to all shares, irrespective of their classification for accounting purposes. The interaction of these rules and those in FRS 25 are often complex, particularly when they impact on determining profits available for distribution, as is reflected in Section 5 of Tech 02/07 and its appendix. Failure to comply with the statutory and common law rules relating to shares can involve legal sanctions against companies and their directors. The classification for legal purposes depends on the rights that the shares are given in the company's memorandum and articles of association.

23.6 The Act defines equity share capital as the issued share capital of a company except for any shares that, neither in regard to dividends nor in regard to capital, carry any right to participate beyond a specified amount in a distribution. [CA85 Sec 744, CA06 Sec 548]. In general, ordinary shares meet this legal definition, although it is possible to design preference shares that qualify as equity share capital in terms of the Act. The definition of an equity instrument in FRS 25 is not the same as the definition of equity share capital given in the Act – see chapter 6. Although the legal definition differs from that used for accounting purposes, the *presentation* of shares in financial statements is driven by the accounting definition as in preparing financial statements under UK GAAP 'Companies Act individual accounts' or 'Companies Act group accounts' within the meaning of sections 226 and 227 of the 1985 Act (sections 395 and 403 of the

2006 Act), the law requires compliance with Schedule 4 paragraph 5A; this paragraph requires that the items in the profit and loss account and balance sheet are presented according *"to the substance of the transaction or arrangement, in accordance with generally accepted accounting principles or practice"*.

23.7 For tax purposes, ordinary share capital has a special meaning that differs from the company law definition of 'equity share capital'. Ordinary shares are defined in the Income and Corporation Taxes Act 1988 as *"…in relation to a company, all the issued share capital (by whatever name called) of the company, other than capital the holders of which have a right to a dividend at a fixed rate, but have no other right to share in the profits of the company"*. [ICTA 1988 Sec 832]. Consequently, preference shares cannot be ordinary share capital for tax purposes where they carry the right to a fixed dividend only (that is, a dividend that is set and known in advance).

23.8 FRS 25, which is applicable for years beginning on or after 1 January 2005, has a significant impact both on the classification of shares as equity or liabilities and on their presentation in financial statements. The effect of FRS 25 on share capital is dealt with in detail in chapter 6. Broadly, FRS 25 can result in some shares and their related share premium, in whole or in part, being presented as liabilities.

23.9 There are strict rules in the Act that govern the purchase by a company of its own shares. The rules governing the redemption of redeemable shares are very similar to the rules that apply when a company purchases its own shares. A company may, if authorised to do so by its articles, issue shares that are redeemable at the option of the company or the shareholder. However, a company can only issue such shares where there are also non-redeemable shares in issue. [CA85 Sec 159, CA06 Sec 684]. The classification of redeemable shares under FRS 25 is considered in chapter 6 and the Act's rules concerning the purchase of own shares, including redeemable shares, are detailed in chapter 7 of the Manual of Accounting – Management reports and governance.

23.9.1 In addition to purchasing its own shares, a company may reduce its share capital using the statutory procedure set out in section 135 of the 1985 Act (section 641 of the 2006 Act). This procedure requires a special resolution of the company's members and court confirmation of the reduction (see para 23.83.13). The 2006 Act carries forward the court approval route for all companies but provides an alternative method by permitting a private company to reduce its share capital without court confirmation using a new solvency statement procedure (see para 23.83.21). The solvency statement procedure is not available to public companies; private companies may continue to use the court procedure, instead of the solvency statement procedure, if they wish to do so.

23.10 A situation where certain UK companies may hold their own shares is where the shares are held as treasury shares under sections 162A to 162G of the 1985 Act (sections 724 to 732 of the 2006 Act). These sections of the Act permit companies with 'qualifying shares' (see para 23.47) to purchase such shares out of distributable profits and hold them in treasury for resale, transfer or cancellation at a later date. Treasury shares are dealt with in paragraph 23.46 onwards.

Measuring issued share capital

23.11 Under the 1985 Act, a company's memorandum must state the amount of the nominal share capital and the nominal value of each type of share. Shares can be issued for consideration that is greater than their nominal value. Under the 2006 Act, the memorandum is a simple document evidencing that the subscribers wish to form a company under the 2006 Act, they agree to become members of the company and, in the case of a company that is to have a share capital, to take at least one share each. All other matters relating to the company's constitution are dealt with in the articles which may be drawn up as the company sees fit, but any provision that is contrary to the 2006 Act is void. For companies formed prior to the 2006 Act, the other provisions not designated for the memorandum in the 2006 Act will be deemed transferred to the articles and, if the articles contain a provision for entrenchment, will be regarded as entrenched provisions. (A provision for entrenchment permits companies to provide in their articles that specified provisions may be changed only if conditions are met that are more restrictive than a special resolution, the minimum requirement for a change in the articles.) As indicated in paragraph 23.5.1, the 2006 Act does not require companies to have an 'authorised share capital' but instead requires shares to have a stated nominal value and introduces a requirement for a statement of capital and initial shareholdings to be delivered on registration to the Registrar of Companies (CA06 Sec 542). This provides, *inter alia*, the information that would have been contained in the memorandum for companies formed under previous legislation. The statement of capital and initial shareholdings must state:

- The total number of shares of the company to be taken on formation by the subscribers to the memorandum of association.
- The aggregate nominal value of those shares.
- For each class of shares:
  - Prescribed particulars of the rights attached to the shares.
  - The total number of shares of that class.
  - The aggregate nominal value of shares of that class.
- The amount to be paid up and the amount (if any) to be unpaid on each share (whether on account of the share's nominal value or by way of premium).

[CA06 Sec 10(2)].

23.11.1 With very limited exceptions, whenever a company makes an alteration in its share capital, it will be required under the 2006 Act to file a statement of capital.

23.11.2 Shares can be issued for consideration that is greater than their nominal value. The excess over the nominal amount is the premium that is recognised in the share premium account (unless relief is available, see further from para 23.96). Shares can be traded, either on investment exchanges (for example, the main market on the London Stock Exchange ('LSE')) or on markets such as the LSE's AIM or otherwise, at their market value.

23.11.3 Shares that are classified as equity instruments under FRS 25 are recorded at the net proceeds of issue, irrespective of whether the entity is applying FRS 26. The net proceeds of issue are split between the nominal (par) value of the share and any premium at the date of issue less any directly attributable transaction costs. Net proceeds of issue can be similar to the initial measurement under FRS 26 of financial instruments not carried at fair value, although that standard does not apply to equity instruments. [FRS 26 paras 2(d), 43, AG64]. However, shares can be issued for any amount in excess of their nominal value. Subsequent movements in the fair value (market value) of the equity share do not affect the amount at which it is stated in the financial statements. Where shares and their associated premium (if any) are classified as debt under FRS 25, they are presented as financial liabilities. For those entities applying FRS 26, that standard requires that financial liabilities are initially recognised and measured in accordance with paragraphs 43 and AG64 of FRS 26 and subsequently, they are measured in accordance with paragraph 47, generally at amortised cost. For those entities applying FRS 4, 'Capital instruments', financial liabilities must be stated initially at the net proceeds of issue and, subsequently, their carrying value is increased by the finance cost in respect of the reporting period and reduced by payments made in respect of that period. [FRS 4 para 29]. That is, FRS 4 requires financial liabilities to be measured at amortised cost. In the case of compound financial instruments (that is, instruments that are partly equity and partly debt), the debt component is presented as a financial liability and the equity component is presented as equity. Where the compound financial instrument is a share, for example, a mandatory redeemable, non-cumulative preference share with discretionary dividends, as referred to in paragraph AG37 FRS 25, the debt component will on initial recognition be the net present value of the redemption amount. This comprises the relevant portion of the share's nominal value and associated premium (if any). The debt component is subsequently measured in accordance with FRS 26 (or FRS 4) at amortised cost. The equity component will comprise the balance of the nominal value and associated premium and is not remeasured subsequently. Directly attributable transaction costs are allocated to the debt and equity components in proportion to the allocation of the proceeds. [FRS 25 para 38].

23.11.4 Compound instruments are legally either wholly debt or wholly shares. The law does not contemplate that instruments will be broken into components. Therefore, determining the legal consequences, particularly for distributions and capital maintenance purposes, can be complex. Section 5, and the appendix to, Tech 02/07 provide illustrative examples of the interaction of the accounting and the statutory and common law rules for compound instruments that are either legally debt or legally shares.

23.12 Public or private companies may allot shares, including any premium, for money or for other items which can be valued in money such as fixed assets or know-how. [CA85 Sec 99; CA06 Sec 582]. However, a public company is not permitted to accept as payment an undertaking given by any person that he or another should do work or perform services for the company or any other person. [CA85 Sec 99(2); CA06 Sec 585(1)]. A public company that accepts permitted non-cash consideration is subject to further rules (see para 23.15 below). The Act prevents shares being allotted at a discount to their nominal value. If shares are allotted at a discount by mistake, the allottee must pay the company an amount equal to the discount plus interest. [CA85 Sec 100; CA06 Sec 580].

23.13 Shares do not have to be paid for in full at the time of issue. For a private company there are no rules to determine the minimum amount of consideration that must be paid or how the consideration paid should be divided into the nominal value of share capital and share premium. For example, a private company can issue (say) a 20p nominal value share for £1 and have only 30p paid up. A public company must, however, have paid up at least a quarter of the nominal value plus the whole of any premium. [CA85 Sec 101; CA06 Sec 586]. This amount must be in cash if the shares are taken up as a subscriber to the public company's memorandum in pursuance of an undertaking of his in the memorandum. [CA06 Sec 584]. The meaning of cash is given in section 583 of the 2006 Act (in part previously in section 782 of the 1985 Act). Consequently, in the example, the minimum amount paid up would represent 85p (that is 20p × ¼ + premium of 80p). Shares issued by a public company to the original subscribers to the memorandum, however, must be fully paid in cash including any premium. [CA85 Sec 106; CA06 Sec 584]. The accounting for unpaid amounts on shares and calls for such amounts under FRS 25 and FRS 26 is considered at paragraph 23.26 below.

23.14 As indicated in paragraph 23.12, a public company must not accept an undertaking for work or services to be performed as payment for shares or share premium. If the public company treats the undertaking of services as payment for shares, then the holder of the shares is liable to pay the company an amount equal to the nominal value of the shares and any share premium and also pay interest on this amount. [CA85 Sec 99; CA06 Sec 585(2)].

23.14.1 Under FRS 20, 'Share-based payment', a share-based payment includes transactions in which the entity receives goods or services as consideration for equity instruments of the entity but, in the vast majority of cases, this does not create a difficulty with respect to section 99 of the Act (section 585 of the 2006 Act). FRS 20 includes 'Notes on the standard's application in the UK and in the Republic of Ireland' and these notes deal with legal issues arising on application of the standard. In particular, it is noted that in developing UITF 17, 'Employee share schemes' (which FRS 20 supersedes), the UITF had obtained legal advice on the application of section 99 of the 1985 Act. Although the accounting required by FRS 20 is different from that required by UITF 17, the ASB stated that this legal advice may still have relevance in the context of FRS 20. UITF 17 stated:

"The UITF has received legal advice as to the implications for share premium account when the accounting treatment required by this Abstract is followed. It has been advised that where new shares are issued in connection with an employee share scheme the share premium account will normally have to reflect only the cash subscribed for the shares (e.g. by the employee or by an ESOP). In such cases, any difference between the cash subscribed for the shares (which must be at least as much as the nominal value, as shares cannot be issued at a discount) and the fair value at the date of grant of rights should be credited to reserves other than the share premium account. This is on the basis that the services of the employee do not, as a matter of law, form part of the consideration received for the shares issued, and the Task Force has been advised that this would be the usual legal interpretation of such transactions. Exceptionally, however, the terms of a transaction might be such as to lead to the opposite interpretation, and companies may need to take legal advice on this point. In such a case, the operation of Companies Act 1985 s. 99(2) [prohibition of public company accepting undertaking to perform services in payment up of its shares] and of Companies Act 1985 s. 103 [non-cash consideration to be valued before allotment of shares] would also have to be considered."

[FRS 20 N28].

23.14.2 Further consideration of the law and its implications for the accounting for employee share schemes in the context of the implications for realised profits and profits available for distribution is set out in Tech 64/04 and section 6 (paras 6.124 to 6.131) of Tech 02/07.

23.15 A public company that intends to accept non-cash consideration (other than for work or services) for the allotment of shares must have the consideration independently valued under section 108 of the 1985 Act (sections 593 and 1150 of the 2006 Act). [CA85 Sec 103; CA06 Sec 593]. This valuation report must be made for the company, during the six months before the allotment, by a person qualified to be the company's auditor who may seek assistance from any suitably qualified and independent valuer. [CA85 Sec 108; CA06 Secs 593, 1150]. The valuer's report should contain sufficient information to allow the amount of the paid up share capital and any premium to be readily apparent. The report must state in particular:

- The nominal value of the shares to be wholly or partly paid for by the consideration being valued.
- The amount of any premium payable on the shares.
- The description of the consideration.
- The extent to which the nominal value of the shares and any premium are to be treated as paid up either by the consideration that has been valued or by cash.

[CA85 Sec 108(4); CA06 Sec 596(2)].

The report must also state that, on the basis of the considerations's valuation, together with any cash paid, the amount of the nominal value of the share capital (plus the whole of any premium) that is to be treated as paid is not less than the valued consideration plus any cash paid. [CA85 Sec 108(6)(d); CA06 Secs 596(3), 600(3)]. A copy of the report must be sent to the proposed allottee. [CA85 Sec 103(1)(c); CA06 Sec 593(1)].

23.16 A valuation report is not required where a public company uses the credit balance on a reserve account such as the profit and loss account reserve or a revaluation reserve to allot shares, including any premium on the shares, to any members of the company (known as a bonus issue). [CA85 Sec 103(2); CA06 Sec 593(2)]. Amounts are to be transferred from the reserve to share capital and share premium in accordance with the articles and memorandum and the terms of the issue.

23.17 In addition, a valuation report is not necessary if shares are issued in consideration for the transfer or cancellation of shares in another company (an example being a business combination) provided that the arrangement is open to all the other company's shareholders or all the shareholders of the class of shares in the other company being transferred. [CA85 Sec 103(3)(4); CA06 Sec 594(1) to (5)]. Shares issued in connection with a transaction, where the issuing company will take over all the assets and liabilities of another company in exchange for the issue of shares with or without any cash payment, also do not require a valuation report. [CA85 Sec 103(5); CA06 Sec 595(1) (2)].

Called up share capital

23.18 The amount of issued share capital and the amount of share capital that has been called up may differ. 'Called up share capital' means:

- That proportion of a company's share capital as equals the aggregate amount of the calls made on its shares (whether or not those calls have been paid).
- Any share capital that has been paid up without being called.
- Any share capital that is to be paid on a specified future date under the Articles of Association, or under the terms of allotment, or any other arrangements for paying for those shares.

[CA85 Sec 737(1), CA06 Sec 547].

23.18.1 Hence, share capital is 'called up' or 'paid up', not just when cash is received by the company, but also when there is a schedule of payments due on fixed future dates or there is an undertaking to pay cash to the company at a future date (see para 23.44); that is, 'paid up' share capital may be unpaid. [CA85 Sec 737(1); CA06 Sec 547]. Uncalled share capital is to be construed accordingly. [CA85 Sec 737(2); CA06 Sec 547]. A share in a company is deemed paid up in cash if the consideration received is one of five (previously four) types specified in the legislation, of which the physical receipt of cash is but one. [CA85 Sec 738(2); CA06 Sec 583(2) to (3)(e)].

23.19 Called up share capital is relevant for a number of purposes. These include:

- Accounting for share capital (see para 23.25).
- Serious loss of capital (see para 23.38 onwards).
- The 'net assets' test, restricting distributable profits of a public company (see para 23.165).

Accounting for share capital

23.20 Under FRS 25, 'Financial instruments: Presentation', the classification of a financial instrument between liabilities and equity is based on the substance of the contractual arrangement. [FRS 25 para 15]. FRS 25 is based on IAS 32 and, accordingly, comments made by the IASB or the IFRIC are relevant to the interpretation of the requirements of FRS 25 when no equivalent interpretive comment has been provided by the ASB or the UITF. In the June 2006 edition of IASB Update (as set out under 'IFRIC activities'), the IASB confirmed the 'substance of contractual arrangement approach' (see para 23.20.1). The IASB stressed that IAS 32 does not require or permit factors not within the contractual arrangement to be taken into consideration in classifying a financial instrument (for example, economic obligations). The same approach should, therefore, be taken in respect of FRS 25. As with IAS 32, under FRS 25, the critical test is whether the issuer has discretion over the transfer of benefits (being cash or another financial asset). If the issuer has no discretion over the payment, then the instrument (or a component part) is a liability. As a result there are certain instruments, such as redeemable preference shares, that are shown, in whole or in part, as liabilities. [FRS 25 paras AG25, AG26, AG37].

23.20.1 In its discussions in June 2006, the IASB considered whether economic compulsion should affect the classification of a financial instrument (or a component of a financial instrument) under IAS 32. The IASB noted that for a financial instrument (or a component of a financial instrument) to be classified as a financial liability under IAS 32, the issuer must have a contractual obligation either:

- to deliver cash or another financial asset to the holder of the instrument; or
- to exchange financial assets or financial liabilities with the holder under conditions that are potentially unfavourable to the issuer.

(Different requirements apply to financial instruments that may or will be settled in the issuer's own equity instruments.) The Board confirmed that such a contractual obligation could be established explicitly or indirectly, but it must be established through the terms and conditions of the instrument. Thus, by itself, economic compulsion would not result in a financial instrument being classified as a liability under IAS 32.

23.20.2 This clarification of IAS 32 paragraphs 15 and AG26 is particularly significant as it means that a financial instrument that may appear to be debt, and which an entity may be economically compelled to repay in cash is, nevertheless, classified as an equity instrument. Such a financial instrument might be a perpetual bond that carries a coupon, in respect of which the issuer has the option to defer payment indefinitely. However, if it does defer payment the issuer has to cease payments of dividends on its ordinary shares. The issuer, therefore, has discretion over payment of the coupon; it does not have a contractual obligation. That economically it would be detrimental not to pay the coupon, as it would mean that it is not allowed to pay its ordinary dividends, is economic compulsion not a contractual obligation. Hence, as there is no contractual obligation to repay the principal of the bond (it is perpetual) and no contractual obligation to pay the coupon, the whole financial instrument is classified as equity and the coupons will be dealt with as equity dividends.

23.20.3 Although such financial instruments as illustrated in paragraph 23.20.1 may be treated as equity and the coupons as equity dividends for accounting purposes, they are legally debt. Consequently, they impact distributable profits and capital maintenance as debt and not as shares and dividends. This can be complex. Section 5, and the appendix to, Tech 02/07 provide illustrative examples of the interaction of the accounting and the legal rules (both statutory and common law) for financial instruments that are legally debt.

23.21 A contract that may be settled in an entity's own shares may be a financial liability. For example, a contract is a financial liability if it is to be settled with the entity's own shares and the number of such shares is variable so as to equate in market value to a specified amount (or an amount determined by reference to the value of some other item). This is because the entity uses a variable number of its own shares as 'a currency' to settle the contract and the holder is not exposed to a gain or loss from variation in the equity shares' price. Accordingly, the contract does not evidence a residual interest in the entity's assets after deducting all of its liabilities. [FRS 25 para 21]. Equally, a contract that may be settled in a fixed number of the entity's equity shares for a variable amount in the entity's functional currency is a financial liability. Puttable shares are generally classified as financial liabilities. However, if the holder's right to request redemption for cash or another financial asset is subject to restrictions in local law, regulation or the entity's governing charter (constitution) (articles of association), such shares may be classified as equity. To be classified as equity the redemption must be unconditionally prohibited by local law, regulation or the entity's governing charter (constitution) (articles of association). If the redemption is prohibited only if conditions, such as liquidity constraints, are, or are not, met the shares are not classified as equity. [UITF 39 para 8].

23.22 FRS 25 requires that instruments comprising an equity and a liability component (such as convertible debt) should be split into those respective components and accounted for separately (split accounting). The liability component is measured first and the residual is the equity component. [FRS 25 paras 28 to 32]. If a compound instrument contains an issuer call option that allows the issuer to redeem the compound instrument for cash or another financial asset at its par (nominal) value, the option is considered to attach to the liability component and is included in the measurement of the liability component. The call option is normally considered to be closely related to the debt component and is not bifurcated (that is, split out) and not accounted for as a stand-alone derivative. [FRS 25 para 31]. On the other hand, if the issuer has a call option to redeem the compound instrument at its fair value for cash or another financial asset, this is considered to attach to the equity component, which is likely to mean that the component is not equity but a derivative financial instrument with a settlement option. [FRS 25 para 26]. If this is the case, the whole compound instrument is a financial liability, with an embedded 'equity' derivative.

23.23 Classifying financial instruments between debt and equity is dealt with in detail in chapter 6. That chapter also deals with the initial recognition and subsequent measurement of financial instruments (including shares) that are classified as financial liabilities and those that contain embedded derivatives.

23.23.1 As mentioned in paragraph 23.11.4, compound instruments are legally either wholly debt or wholly shares. The law does not contemplate that instruments will be broken into components. Therefore, determining the legal consequences, particularly for distributions and capital maintenance purposes can be complex. Section 5 of, and the appendix to, Tech 02/07 provide illustrative examples of the interaction of the accounting and the statutory and common law rules for compound instruments that are either legally debt or legally shares.

23.24 FRS 25 includes rules for the repurchase of equity shares (see para 23.64). Although it does not include specific rules on the initial recognition and measurement of shares classified as equity shares. Therefore, generally, the timing of initial recognition of issued shares classified as equity under FRS 25 should follow legal and regulatory requirements. This means that such shares are normally recognised and measured at the net proceeds of issue (see para 23.11.3). This is similar to the initial recognition of a financial liability not at fair value through profit or loss (FVTPL) under FRS 26, albeit financial instruments issued by an entity that meet the definition of an equity instrument in FRS 25 (including options and warrants) are excluded from FRS 26's scope. (They are within the scope of the standard for the holder of the equity instruments.) Certain companies are required to (or elect to) apply FRS 26 to the measurement of financial instruments (see further chapter 6).

23.25 Initial recognition of shares classified as equity occurs when the proceeds of issue are receivable. Paragraph 21 of FRS 22, 'Earnings per share', includes this and other points in providing examples of the timing of inclusion of ordinary shares in the weighted average share calculation for the purposes of calculating basic earnings per share. See chapter 14 for more details. Any tax benefit obtained on the directly attributable transaction costs of an issue of equity shares is also taken to equity. [FRS 25 para 35].

23.26 Shares may be issued fully paid or partly paid. With fully paid equity shares, the cash received by the issuer and recorded as an asset will equate to the amount recognised as an increase in equity, less any directly attributable transaction costs, recorded as share capital and share premium as appropriate. The accounting treatment for partly paid shares is more complex and depends on the terms and conditions of the share issue; in addition, the terms of the company's articles may have a bearing on the accounting treatment. The issuer of an equity share will always record at least the amount received in cash on the partly paid shares as an asset and as a credit to equity (less directly attributable transaction costs). However, the company will also need to consider whether it is appropriate to recognise the balance not yet paid on the shares paid as a receivable.

23.26.1 For example, consider the case where a company issues partly paid shares under a share agreement with a fixed schedule of definite call dates on which the shareholders must pay the outstanding amounts on the shares. The shareholder has rights to full dividends (irrespective of the proportion paid up on the shares) and has no ability to avoid the calls. The company's articles of association will determine whether such a schedule of calls has the effect that the shareholders are legally obliged to make the payments as scheduled. If the shareholder is legally obligated to make the fixed payments as scheduled as a result of the agreement, and they have full rights to dividends, the issuer should recognise, at the date of the share issue, a receivable for the outstanding proceeds of issue. The issuer has a contractual right to receive cash from the shareholder and therefore has a financial asset. For entities applying FRS 26, this receivable is measured at fair value on initial recognition and subsequently at amortised cost (unless designated as at FVTPL). The amortised cost will be calculated using the effective interest rate, such that the receivable will be recorded at the net present value of the future payments. The unwinding of the discount on that receivable will be recognised through the profit and loss account over the expected payment period.

23.26.2 Conversely, it may be that the shareholder has discretion as to whether to make payments on calls, and does not have the right to full dividends on the shares, either because of the terms of the share agreement or because of the company's articles of association. In such cases, the absence of a contractual right to receive cash from the shareholder means that there is no financial asset until such time as the call is made and the shareholder has agreed to meet the call.

23.27 As discussed in paragraph 23.18.1, under the Act, share capital is 'called up' or 'paid up' not just when the cash is received, but when there is a schedule of payments due on fixed future dates or there is an undertaking to pay cash to the company at a future date. Paragraph 12 of Table A provides that calls may be made in respect of moneys unpaid on partly paid shares and that a call may be required to be made in instalments. In addition, paragraph 104 states that *"all* *dividends shall be declared and paid according to the amounts paid up on the shares on which dividend is paid. All dividends shall be apportioned and paid proportionately to the amounts paid up on the shares...".* Where, in respect of the amounts outstanding on the shares, there is a schedule of payments due on fixed future dates or there is an undertaking to pay cash to the company at a future date, those shares will be regarded as fully paid and, accordingly, under Table A, the shareholder will be entitled to full dividends on the shares. In such cases, the accounting treatment will follow that outlined in paragraph 23.26.1 above. On the other hand, where the issuer has discretion over the calls (that is, there is no schedule of payments due on fixed future dates and no undertaking to pay cash to the company at a future date), then the shareholder will not be entitled to full dividends under Table A and the accounting treatment will be as set out in paragraph 23.26.2 above.

23.28 In most circumstances, the aggregate share capital/share premium to be recognised will be the net present value of the future payments (that is, the same value at which the receivable is originally recognised) as this is the fair value of the consideration received. However, depending on the legal terms of allotment of the shares, the discount (credit) recognised from the unwinding of the net present value of the receivable through the profit and loss account may be transferred as a reserves transfer to share premium in order to reflect the legal share premium. On the other hand, if the net present value of the future payments is less than the nominal value of the shares, it will be necessary to debit a reserve (probably profit and loss account reserve) at initial recognition with the amount required to meet the legal requirement not to issue shares at a discount to their nominal value, This debit reserve will gradually be eroded by the unwinding of the discount on the receivable recognised through the profit and loss account over the payment period.

23.29 It should be noted that although the discount unwind will be receivable in cash and is, therefore, in principle, realised, in some instances it may be deemed part of the legal share capital of the company for capital maintenance purposes and, therefore, should not be distributed. The effect on profits available for distribution can be assessed using the principles set out in section 5 of Tech 02/07 and, in particular, whether the initial debit to reserves might cause a restriction (equal to the initial amount of the debit) on profits available for distribution under section 264 of the 1985 Act (section 831 of the 2006 Act).

Disclosure of share capital

Statutory requirements

23.30 The amount of allotted share capital and the amount of called up capital that has actually been paid up must be shown separately in the financial statements. These amounts must be shown either under the heading 'called up share capital' in the balance sheet, or in a note to the financial statements. [Note 12 on the balance sheet formats in Schedule 4 to the 1985 Act].

Example

On 1 January 20X1, a company (with a December year end) issues 500,000 ordinary shares of £1 each fully paid. On 30 November 20X1, the company allots a further 100,000 ordinary shares. By 31 December 20X1, the company has made calls amounting to 75p per share. At 31 December 20X1, the holders of 10,000 shares have not paid the last call of 25p per share, but this is due to be paid shortly after the year end; that is, the shareholder does not have discretion over the payment of the call. Therefore, at the year end, 75p has been paid on 90,000 shares and 50p has been paid on 10,000 shares. The shares are classified as equity shares under FRS 25. In the financial statements at 31 December 20X1, the company would include £575,000 of share capital in equity, calculated as follows:

Allotted share capital	600,000
Called up share capital	575,000
Called up share capital not paid	2,500

23.31 Called up share capital is part of the double entry, and it will appear under capital and reserves (KI in Format 1 or AI in Format 2 of the Schedule 4 to the 1985 Act formats (equivalent formats are expected to be included in The Small Companies and Groups (Accounts and Reports) Regulations 2008 and The Large and Medium-sized Companies and Groups (Accounts and Report) Regulations 2008.) Similarly, called up share capital not paid forms part of the double entry, and it will appear in the balance sheet format either as a separate item (A in Format 1 or 2) or under debtors C II 5 in Format 1 or 2 of the Schedule 4 to the 1985 Act formats (and their expected replacements in the regulations indicated above). Allotted share capital does not form part of the double entry. However, it must still be disclosed either on the face of the balance sheet or in a note to the financial statements.

23.32 The notes to the financial statements must also show the amount of a company's authorised share capital. In addition, where shares of more than one class have been allotted, the notes must show the number and the aggregate nominal value of the shares of each class that have been allotted. [CA85 4 Sch 38(1)]. In practice, companies will generally be able to refer to share capital that is 'allotted, called up and fully paid', because these items will often be the same amount. As the 2006 Act no longer requires a company to have an authorised share capital, it is expected that the disclosure will be amended in the equivalent to Schedule 4 to the 1985 Act that is expected to be included in The Small Companies and Groups (Accounts and Reports) Regulations 2008 and The Large and Medium-sized Companies and Groups (Accounts and Reports) Regulations 2008.

23.33 It is not appropriate to accrue for the issue of shares. The correct time to record the issue is when the shares are allotted. This is because share capital is a residual interest. The normal reasons for making accruals, to allocate a cost or revenue to the correct period or to recognise an asset or a liability at the appropriate time, do not therefore apply.

Example

At its year end, a company had committed itself to issue shares as a result of an underwritten rights issue although it is not known whether the shares will be issued to individuals or the underwriter. How should the 'shares to be issued' be shown in the financial statements?

The financial statements should not show the rights issue in share capital since the shares have not been issued. However, the issue should be disclosed as part of a post balance sheet event note and a proforma balance sheet could be prepared and included in the notes to the financial statements to reflect the issue.

23.34 The Act requires certain information to be disclosed concerning redeemable shares. The notes to the financial statements must show:

- The earliest and the latest dates on which the company may redeem those shares.
- The fact whether or not the company is obliged to redeem those shares, or either it or the holder merely has an option to do so.
- The amount of any premium payable on redemption, or the fact that no such premium is payable.

[CA85 4 Sch 38(2)].

Allotment of shares during the financial year

23.35 The Act requires that where a company has allotted any shares during the financial year, the notes to the financial statements must state:

- The classes of shares allotted.
- The number of shares allotted, their aggregate nominal value, and the consideration received in respect of each class of shares allotted.

[CA85 4 Sch 39].

23.36 Furthermore, information has to be given about any 'contingent rights to the allotment of shares' that may exist. These rights could be options to subscribe for shares, or rights on the conversion of loan stock or any other rights where a person may require the allotment of shares (whether, in the latter case, the rights arise on conversion of any other type of security, or otherwise). The information to be given is:

- The number, the description and the amount of the shares in respect of which the right is exercisable.
- The period during which the right is exercisable.
- The price to be paid for the shares allotted.

[CA85 4 Sch 40].

Hence, the financial statements have to include details of the rights of conversion of convertible loan stock or issues required by share option schemes.

23.37 The disclosure rules referred to in paragraphs 23.30 to 23.36 are expected to be carried forward for the 2006 Act in the equivalent to Schedule 4.

23.37.1 The Listing Rules require disclosure of certain information where a listed company (or its unlisted major subsidiary) has allotted any types of shares for cash and the allotment has neither been made to the company's shareholders in proportion to their shareholdings nor specifically authorised by the company's shareholders. The requirement is for the following information to be disclosed:

- The classes of shares allotted and for each class, the number allotted, their aggregate nominal value and the consideration received.
- The names of the allottees, if less than six in number, and in the case of six or more allottees, a brief generic description of each new class of equity holder (for example, a holder of loan stock).
- The market price of the securities concerned on the date on which the terms of the issue were fixed, together with that date.

[LR 9.8.4 R (7)(8)].

Serious loss of capital

23.38 If the value of a public company's net assets falls to half or less than half of its called up share capital (see para 23.39 below), the directors have a duty to convene a general meeting in order to consider whether any, and if so, what action to take to deal with the situation. Proper notice must be given, and the directors must convene the meeting not later than 28 days from the earliest date the serious loss of capital was known to a director. The meeting itself must be held within 56 days of that earliest date. If the company fails to convene the meeting, each of the directors of the company permitting the failure is liable to a fine.
[CA85 Sec 142; CA06 Sec 656].

23.39 The Act defines a company's called up share capital as including so much of its share capital as equals the aggregate amount of calls made on its shares (whether or not those calls have been paid), any share capital paid up without being called and other paid up share capital to be paid on a specified future date (see further para 23.18). [CA85 Sec 737; CA06 Sec 547]. Depending on the terms on which shares are allotted, the directors may make calls on shares so that shareholders become immediately liable to the nominal value of the shares allotted, together with any premium that the shareholders have agreed to pay. Calls are sometimes paid by instalments. In situations where the dates for payment of calls is specified, the called up share capital would be the same as the nominal value of, and share premium payable on, the shares in question. (See paras 23.36.1 to 23.39).

23.40 However, if shares are issued at a premium, an amount equal to this premium must be transferred to the share premium account. [CA85 Sec 130, CA06 Sec 610]. This implies that the share premium is not part of a company's paid-up share capital. Also, the balance sheet formats in Schedule 4 show separate captions for called up share capital and for the share premium account. Consequently, for the purposes of determining whether a company has suffered a serious loss of capital under section 142 of the 1985 Act (section 656 of the 2006 Act), called up share capital is generally taken in practice to exclude the share premium account.

23.41 Where shares are recognised as liabilities in accordance with FRS 25, this will affect the application of the rule in section 142 of the 1985 Act (section 656 of the 2006 Act). Similarly, the rule in section 264 of the 1985 Act (section 831 of the 2006 Act), applying to public companies, which is also a 'net assets test' is affected by the classification of shares (see further para 23.165). The DTI (now the BERR) has stated in the 'Guidance for British companies on changes to the reporting and accounting provisions of the Companies Act 1985', issued In November 2004 (and revised in 2005) in connection with SI 2004/2947, 'The Companies Act 1985 (International Accounting Standards and Other Amendments) Regulations 2004', that, *"where preference shares are classified as liabilities, they should be treated as such for the purposes of the net asset test, and should not be treated as part of called-up share capital and undistributable reserves for that purpose"*. [DTI Guidance para 6.5]. Although the section 264 (section 831) rules appear in Part VIII of the 1985 Act (Part 23 of the 2006 Act), while section 142 (section 656) appears in Part V of the 1985 Act (Part 15 of the 2006 Act), we believe the same approach should be applied to section 142 of the 1985 Act (section 656 of the 2006 Act). Therefore, where shares are classified as liabilities, they should not, we believe, be included in called up share capital, but should be treated as liabilities, for the purposes of the section 142 (section 656) test. However, as this requires legal interpretation, companies should take legal advice.

Multi-currency share capital

23.42 Companies may issue share capital denominated in a currency that is not their functional currency. When foreign currency share capital is presented as a financial liability in the balance sheet, the liability is initially stated at the spot rate prevailing at the date of issue. Subsequently, the financial liability will be retranslated, as a monetary item, at each balance sheet date in accordance with SSAP 20, 'Foreign currency translation', or, for FRS 26 users, FRS 23, 'The effects of changes in foreign exchange rates'. Equity share capital is initially stated at the spot rate prevailing at the date of issue but is generally not retranslated under SSAP 20 or FRS 23. However, some companies do retranslate their foreign currency share capital and take the translation differences to reserves. This is not specifically precluded by SSAP 20 and while this may seem contrary to FRS 23, the overall effect on equity, taking the retranslated foreign share capital and the cumulative translation differences together, is as if the foreign currency share capital is carried at the original historical spot rate.

23.42.1 In the past, a number of companies have issued share capital denominated in foreign currencies. One of those companies was the Scandinavian Bank Group Plc. In 1986 it petitioned the court for confirmation of a special resolution to cancel part of its existing sterling share capital in order to increase its share capital to £30m, $30m, SFr 30m and DM 30m (see *Re Scandinavian Bank Group plc*, [1987] BCLC 220). The 2006 Act introduces provisions to enable all companies to redenominate shares in a fixed nominal value in one currency to a fixed nominal value in another currency. [CA06 Sec 622].

23.43 The court confirmed that a company can have shares in more than one currency. Any particular share, however, must be denominated in one particular currency, but different shares can be denominated in different currencies. This does not conflict with the requirement in the 1985 Act because section 5(a) states that *"...the memorandum must...state the amount of the share capital...and the division of the share capital into shares of a fixed amount"*. By fixed amount the 1985 Act does not mean a fixed value in sterling terms. The 2006 Act places into statute the common law rule that shares may be denominated in different currencies. [CA06 Sec 542].

23.44 However, sections 117 and 118 of the 1985 Act (sections 761 to 763 of the 2006 Act) require a public company to have an authorised minimum allotted share capital of £50,000. This requirement stems from Article 6 of the EU 2nd Company Law Directive (77/91/EEC). Accordingly, the court held (obiter) that this 'authorised minimum' must be in pounds sterling. Consequently, a private company can have all of its share capital in currencies other than pounds sterling. However, a public limited company must have at least £50,000 of its share capital in pounds sterling. Any share capital above this amount can be in other currencies. The 2006 Act relaxes this rule by permitting public companies to meet the minimum share capital requirements by reference to share capital denominated in sterling or euros, but not a combination of the two. [CA06 Sec 765]. The Secretary of State has the power to create regulations under the 2006 Act to prescribe the euro equivalent of the minimum share capital, which will change from time to time as a result of exchange rate fluctuations.

23.45 A difficulty is encountered where a company that has issued foreign currency share capital comes to redeem or repurchase some or all of those shares. The foreign share capital is generally redeemed or repurchased in the currency in which the shares are denominated. Consequently, the functional currency amount at redemption will only coincidentally be equal to the amount recorded at the issue of the shares. There will be a difference. The question arises as to whether this difference affects distributable profits. It seems logical that it should do so and thus a debit difference will absorb distributable profits. It is equally logical that a credit difference should also be taken to distributable profits, although, in this case it will need to be established that the shares were originally issued for cash or near cash. A second question arises as how much should be transferred out of distributable profits to the capital redemption reserve (assuming that the shares are not redeemed or repurchased out of the proceeds of a fresh issue of shares made for the purpose). There are two legal views on the application of the Companies Act's capital maintenance rules. One is that the transfer to the capital redemption reserve should be the nominal value of the shares concerned translated at the historical exchange rate. The alternative view is that the transfer should be the nominal value translated at the exchange rate ruling on the date of the redemption or repurchase. Consequently, a company that comes to redeem or repurchase its foreign currency share capital should take legal advice.

Treasury shares

23.46 FRS 25 paragraph 33 refers to 'treasury shares' but by this term it means reacquired own *equity instruments* (which is wider than equity shares as it includes other equity instruments, such as share options).

General rules

23.46.1 Under the Act, companies with *'qualifying shares'* are permitted to purchase such shares out of distributable profits and hold them in treasury for resale, transfer or cancellation at a later date.

23.47 'Qualifying shares' are defined as shares that:

- are included in the official list maintained by the FSA (that is, listed on the main market of the LSE or on the Plus-listed market);
- are traded on AIM;
- are officially listed in another EEA State; or
- are traded on a regulated market established in an EEA State.

[CA85 Sec 162(4); CA06 Sec 724(2)].

23.48 In the UK, the regulated securities markets referred to in the last bullet point in paragraph 23.47 above, include:

- LIFFE.
- Regulated Market Segment for SMI securities (operated by Virt-X Exchange).
- Regulated Market Segment for pan-European securities (operated by Virt-X Exchange).
- EDX.

23.49 Companies that acquire shares other than 'qualifying shares' (for example, shares that are not traded, such as unlisted redeemable preference shares) are required to cancel those shares by following the normal legal rules for the acquisition of own shares. These rules are considered in detail in chapter 7 of the Manual of Accounting – Management reports and governance.

23.50 Where qualifying shares are purchased by a company out of distributable profits (see paras 23.163 and 23.165) in accordance with section 162 of the 1985 Act (sections 692(2)(a)(i), 724(1) of the 2006 Act), the company may:

- hold the shares (or any of them) in treasury; or
- deal with any of them, at any time, as follows:
  - sell the shares (or any of them) for cash (see para 23.56);
  - transfer the shares (or any of them) for the purposes of, or pursuant to, an employees' share scheme; or
  - cancel the shares (or any of them) (see para 23.58).

[CA85 Secs 162A(1), 162D(1), CA06 Sec 724(3), 727(1), 729(1)].

Conditions applying to treasury shares

23.51 References to a company holding shares as treasury shares are references to the company holding shares that were (or are treated as having been) purchased by it in circumstances in which section 162A of the 1985 Act (section 724 of the 2006 Act) applies and have been held by the company continuously since they were so purchased. [CA85 Sec 162A(3); CA06 Sec 724(5)].

23.52 Where a company has only one class of shares, the aggregate nominal value of shares held as treasury shares must not at any time exceed 10 per cent of the company's nominal value of the issued share capital at that time. Similarly, where the company has more than one class of shares, the aggregate nominal value of the shares of any class held as treasury shares must not at any time exceed 10 per cent of the nominal value of the issued share capital of the shares in that class at that time. If the limit is exceeded, the excess shares must be disposed of or cancelled within 12 months. [CA85 Sec 162B; CA06 Sec 725].

23.53 The company may not exercise any rights over the treasury shares, including voting rights. Furthermore, no dividend can be paid, and no other distribution of the company's assets (including any distribution of assets to members on a winding up) can be made, to the company in respect of the treasury shares it holds. However, rights over bonus issues or redemption rights (if the shares are redeemable) do still remain. [CA85 Sec 162C; CA06 Sec 726].

23.54 A company may not purchase its shares if as a result of the purchase there would no longer be any member of the company holding shares other than redeemable shares or shares held as treasury shares.
[CA85 Sec 162(3); CA06 Sec 690(2)].

23.55 Where shares are held in treasury, the company must be entered in the register of members as the member holding those shares.
[CA85 Sec 162A(2); CA06 Sec 724(4)].

Sale or cancellation of treasury shares

23.56 As stated in paragraph 23.50 above, one of the ways in which a company can deal with its treasury shares is to sell the shares for cash. In this respect, 'cash' means one of the following:

- Cash (including foreign currency) received by the company.
- A cheque received by the company in good faith that the directors have no reason for suspecting will not be paid.
- A release of a liability of the company for a liquidated sum.
- An undertaking to pay cash to the company within 90 days of the date on which the company agrees to sell the shares.

[CA85 Sec 162D(2), CA06 Sec 727(2)(a)-(d)].

23.57 Under the 2006 Act, the company may sell treasury shares for 'cash consideration' (as opposed to 'cash' under the 1985 Act). The definition of 'cash consideration' includes all of the items listed in paragraph 23.68.2 plus one other item: *"payment by any other means giving rise to a present or future entitlement (of the company or a person acting on the company's behalf) to a payment, or credit equivalent to payment, in cash"*. [CA06 Sec 727(2)(e)]. The Secretary of State has the power to specify by order any particular means of payment as falling within this definition so as to remove uncertainties surrounding other methods of settlement, such as the CREST assured payment system. It will also allow the definition to be updated should other settlement systems be identified or developed in the future. [CA06 Sec 727(3)].

23.57.1 Where treasury shares are sold, if the proceeds are equal to or less than the purchase price paid by the company for the shares, the proceeds are treated as a realised profit. If the proceeds exceed the purchase price, the excess over the purchase price has to be transferred to the share premium account. The purchase price paid by the company for the shares is determined by the use of a weighted average price method. If the shares were allotted to the company as fully paid bonus shares, the purchase price is deemed to be nil.
[CA85 Sec 162F; CA06 Sec 731].

23.58 If the company cancels shares held as treasury shares, the company must reduce the amount of its issued share capital by the nominal value of the cancelled shares. However, the cancellation does not reduce the amount of the company's authorised share capital. [CA85 Sec 162D(4); CA06 Sec 729(4)]. The amount by which the company's issued share capital is diminished on cancellation of shares held as treasury shares is required to be transferred to a capital redemption reserve. [CA85 Sec 170(1); CA06 Sec 733(1), (2) and (4)]. (See further chapter 7 of the Manual of Accounting – Management reports and governance.)

23.59 If shares held as treasury shares cease to be 'qualifying shares', other than when shares are suspended from listing, the company is required to cancel them immediately. [CA85 Sec 162E, CA06 Sec 729].

Delivery of returns to the Registrar of Companies

23.60 Where a company purchases its own shares under the rules for treasury shares set out above, it is required to deliver a return to the Registrar of Companies no later than 28 days after the delivery of shares to it (except where all of the shares have been cancelled immediately), stating with respect to each class of shares purchased (other than any cancelled shares) the number and nominal value of each of those shares that are held as treasury shares and the date on which they were delivered to the company. [CA85 Sec 169(1B); CA06 Sec 707(1) to (3), 708(1)]. The return should also state the aggregate amount paid by the company for the shares and the maximum and minimum prices paid in respect of each class of shares class purchased. [CA85 Sec 169(2), CA06 Sec 707(4)].

23.61 Where a company purchases its own shares under the rules for treasury shares set out above and immediately cancels some or all of these, it is required to deliver a return to the Registrar of Companies with respect to the cancelled shares under the general requirements for a purchase of own shares. [CA85 Sec 169(1A), CA06 Sec 707(1) to (3), 708(1)]. In addition, under the 2006 Act, the company must submit to the Registrar of Companies, a statement of capital stating:

- The total number of shares of the company.
- The aggregate nominal value of those shares.
- For each class of shares:
  - Prescribed particulars of the rights attached to the shares.
  - The total number of shares of that class.
  - The aggregate nominal value of shares of that class.
- The amount to be paid up and the amount (if any) to be unpaid on each share (whether on account of the share's nominal value or its premium).

23.62 Where a company is or was required to make a return as set out in paragraph 23.60 above and the shares have subsequently been cancelled, sold or transferred for the purposes of, or pursuant to, an employees' share scheme, the company is required to deliver another return to the Registrar of Companies no later than 28 days after the date on which the shares are cancelled or disposed of. This return is required to state with respect to each class of shares, the number and nominal value of those shares cancelled or disposed of and the date on which they were cancelled or disposed of. [CA85 Sec 169A, CA06 Sec 728, 730]. Under the 1985 Act, the same returns are made on cancellation of treasury shares but under the 2006 Act, there is an additional requirement to submit a statement of capital stating the items listed above.

Accounting treatment for the purchase of own shares (including treasury shares)

23.63 In 2003, the UITF issued Abstract 37, 'Purchases and sales of own shares', effective for accounting periods ending on or after 23 December 2003. This states that an entity's purchase of its own shares gives rise to a reduction in the entity's ownership interest, not an asset. [UITF 37 para 4].

23.64 In 2004, the ASB issued FRS 25, 'Financial instruments: Disclosure and presentation' (now FRS 25, 'Financial instruments: Presentation'), which contains rules on accounting for 'treasury shares' and supersedes UITF 37 for years beginning on or after 1 January 2005. The rules in FRS 25 include reacquired own equity instruments (which is wider than equity shares as it includes other equity instruments, such as share options) within its scope and states that, if an entity reacquires its own equity instruments, those instruments should be deducted from equity. [FRS 25 para 33].

23.65 The Act's rules in respect of treasury shares apply to all qualifying shares (see para 23.47), irrespective of whether they are classified as liabilities or equity. Where a transaction to reacquire own shares relates to shares classified as a financial liability, the accounting will need to reflect both the removal of the financial liability (see chapter 6) and the legal capital maintenance rules for treasury shares (see para 23.81 onwards). When considering the acquisition of 'treasury shares', it is necessary to understand how the entity has acquired them. It is probable that the entity will have placed a contract with a broker or bank to acquire the shares on its behalf. Such a contract will fall within the rules of paragraph 23 of FRS 25, which states that *"a contract that contains an obligation for an entity to purchase its own equity instruments for cash or another financial asset gives rise to a financial liability for the present value of the redemption amount (for example, for the present value of the forward repurchase price, option exercise price or other redemption amount). This is the case even if the contract itself is an equity instrument"*. The acquisition of the 'treasury shares' is, therefore, accounted for at the inception of the contract rather than when the shares are paid for.

23.66 In accounting for purchases and sales of own equity instruments, FRS 25 generally requires, subject to paragraph 23 of the standard (see para 23.65) the following:

- No gain or loss should be recognised in the profit and loss account or STRGL on the purchase, sale, issue or cancellation of an entity's own equity instruments

- Consideration paid or received for the purchase or sale of an entity's own equity instruments should be recognised directly in equity (that is, shareholders' funds).

[FRS 25 para 33].

23.66.1 However, when paragraph 23 of FRS 25 applies to a contract containing an obligation to reacquire an entity's own shares, such as a forward contract or option to acquire shares for cancellation or to be held in treasury, there may well be gains or losses to be recognised in profit or loss. For those entities applying FRS 26, the financial liability recognised initially under that standard is measured at its fair value (being the present value of the acquisition or repurchase price or redemption amount). The equivalent amount is reclassified from equity (that is, it is a debit to equity). Subsequently, the financial liability is measured in accordance with FRS 26. If the contract only specifies a fixed number of shares without specifying the amount to be spent, the financial liability is initially measured using an estimate of the share price it will have to pay. The best estimate of the share price at inception of the contract is the share price on that day. Subsequently, the financial liability is adjusted applying FRS 26 paragraph AG8 to reflect the movements in the share price. Consequently, there will be gains or losses to be recognised in profit or loss as paragraph AG8 requires any adjustment to be recognised in profit or loss. Paragraph AG8 of FRS 26 applies because the entity has to revise its estimates of the amount it will have to pay as the price and/or the number to be acquired of its shares varies. AG8 requires that the carrying amount of the financial liability is adjusted to reflect actual and revised estimated cash flows.

23.66.2 However, if the contract stipulates the maximum amount that may be spent then the application of FRS 26 to the measurement of the financial liability will be that maximum amount discounted for the time value of money for the period between the inception of the contract and the date of payment. In this case where the amount to be paid is capped, we consider that the effect on profit or loss is limited to the unwinding of the discount.

23.66.3 If the contract expires without delivery or full delivery, the financial liability's carrying amount, or the relevant part thereof, is reclassified to equity. That is, it is credited to equity against the original debit.

23.66.4 Even if the obligation to purchase, reacquire or redeem is conditional on the counterparty exercising a right to redeem (for example, a written put option that gives the counterparty the right to sell an entity's own equity instruments to the entity for a fixed price), the entity still has a contractual obligation to purchase its own equity instruments and this gives rise to a financial liability for the present value of the purchase, reacquisition or redemption amount. [FRS 25 para 23].

23.66.5 The application of paragraph 23 of FRS 25 and the resulting debit to equity on inception of the contract does absorb profits available for distributable. For legal purposes, the purchase, reacquisition or redemption has not yet occurred and thus the accounting is anticipating what will happen when the shares are actually purchased, reacquired or redeemed by the company. Consequently for private limited companies the initial debit to equity does not affect the amount of profits available for distribution until the shares are actually purchased, reacquired or redeemed by the company. However, for public limited companies the initial debit to equity restricts the ability to make distributions by the amount of the debit. This is through the application of section 264 of the 1985 Act (section 831 of the 2006 Act) net assets test. [Tech 02/07 para 5.31].

23.67 FRS 25 notes that own equity instruments may be acquired and held in treasury by the entity or by other members of the consolidated group. [FRS 25 para 33]. Therefore, the deduction of those equity instruments applies to all interests in own equity instruments held by a company itself and, in consolidated financial statements, the parent's equity instruments (for example, shares held by subsidiaries). In the latter case, this applies to all such shareholdings, including those held by subsidiaries that carry on a business of dealing in securities (see further chapter 24). However, in the individual financial statements of a subsidiary that holds shares in its parent, such shares are treated as a financial asset (available-for-sale or financial asset at fair value through profit and loss under FRS 26); that is, 'treasury shares' accounting does not apply as these are not 'own shares' for the subsidiary itself.

23.68 The requirements of paragraph 33 of FRS 25 also apply to 'treasury shares' sold, issued or cancelled in connection with employee share option plans, employee share purchase plans and all other share-based payment arrangements. [FRS 25 para 4]. These are considered in more detail in chapter 12.

23.68.1 Neither a subsidiary (as defined in section 736 of the 1985 Act (section 1159 of the 2006 Act)) nor a subsidiary undertaking (as defined in section 258(2) of the 1985 Act (section 1162(2) of the 2006 Act) (which, therefore, meets the section 736 (section 1159) definition of a subsidiary) is permitted to become a member of its holding company and thus should not acquire its holding company's shares [CA85 Sec 23(1); CA06 Sec 136(1)]. There are exemptions for subsidiaries that carry on a business dealing in securities. [CA85 Sec 23(3); CA06 Sec 141(1) (2)]. An entity that is a subsidiary undertaking by virtue of section 258(4) of the 1985 (section 1162(4) of the 2006 Act) (power to exercise, or actually exercises, dominant influence etc.) is not so prohibited. These will, therefore, fall to be dealt with as 'treasury shares' in their parent undertaking's consolidated financial statements (see para 23.67).

23.69 Under the Act, a company is permitted to hold qualifying shares in treasury (subject to meeting the conditions described in para 23.51 onwards) where these have been purchased out of distributable profits (see para 23.50) Therefore, when the shares are purchased there is a charge to distributable reserves, normally the profit and loss account reserve. As a result, the company will not also show a separate debit reserve on the face of the balance sheet as this would be double-counting. Instead, the amount by which shareholders' funds have been reduced is required to be disclosed (see para 23.75).

23.70 The treatment of treasury shares described in the previous paragraph appears to contradict the requirements of the balance sheet formats set out in Schedule 4 to the 1985 Act (and its equivalent expected to be included in The Small Companies and Groups (Accounts and Reports) Regulations 2008 and The Large and Medium-sized Companies and Groups (Accounts and Reports) Regulations 2008). These formats include sub-headings for 'own shares' in both fixed and current assets, which suggests that investments in own shares are to be presented as assets. This is unfortunate, as FRS 25 requires treasury shares to be deducted in arriving at shareholders' funds. However it is hard to ignore the requirements of the formats. Any amount described on the face of the balance sheet as investment in own shares would need to be presented in accordance with those requirements. Accordingly, in our view, the amount deducted in arriving at shareholders' funds should not be presented separately on the face of the balance sheet, but should be deducted from the profit and loss reserve.

23.71 The accounting for the purchase of equity shares to be held in treasury is illustrated in the following example.

Example

Purchase of treasury shares

Company A (a listed company) has 1,000,000 £1 ordinary shares originally issued at a premium of £9. It buys back 20,000 shares when their market value is £40 per share. The purchase is made out of distributable profits and the company holds the shares in treasury. In this situation, the company does not reduce its issued share capital, but instead will reduce its distributable profits by the consideration paid for the shares (that is, 20,000 × £40 = £800,000), as shown below.

	Before purchase	Purchase of shares	After purchase
	£'000	£'000	£'000
Net assets other than cash	20,000		20,000
Cash	5,000	(800)	4,200
	25,000	(800)	24,200
Share capital	1,000		1,000
Share premium	9,000		9,000
Capital	10,000		10,000
Distributable reserves	15,000	(800)	14,200
	25,000	(800)	24,200

In its notes, Company A should explain that '20,000 £1 ordinary shares with an aggregate nominal value of £20,000 were purchased during the period and are held in treasury. Distributable reserves have been reduced by £800,000, being the consideration paid for these shares'.

The debit to distributable reserves of £800,000 is a realised loss and should be shown in the profit and loss account reserve note. It is not shown in the STRGL, because the charge represents the capital repaid to shareholders and is not, therefore, a recognised loss shown in the performance statements. The reconciliation of movements in shareholders' funds will show the purchase of treasury shares of £800,000.

23.72 Under FRS 25, the directly attributable costs of an equity transaction should be accounted for as a deduction from equity. [FRS 25 para 35]. Therefore, expenses directly relating to the purchase of equity shares to be held in treasury ('treasury shares') should be treated as part of the overall cost of purchase and like the purchase cost itself should be charged to distributable profits and shown in the profit and loss account reserve note (and shown in the reconciliation of movements on shareholders' funds). The treatment of transaction costs of equity instruments is discussed in chapter 6.

23.73 As noted in paragraph 23.50 above, a company can cancel the treasury shares, sell them for cash, or transfer them for the purposes of an employees' share scheme. The accounting treatment for these various scenarios is considered in the examples below (based on the purchase of treasury shares in the example in para 23.71 above).

Example

Scenario A – Cancellation of treasury shares

If the company cancels shares held as treasury shares, it must reduce its issued share capital by the nominal value of the cancelled shares and, in accordance with the Act, transfer this amount to a capital redemption reserve (CRR) (see para 23.58). Therefore, in the above example in paragraph 23.71, if all the treasury shares are subsequently cancelled by the company, the issued share capital would be reduced by the aggregate nominal value of £20,000 and a CRR for this amount would be set up in order to maintain the capital, as shown below.

	After purchase	**Maintain capital**	**After cancellation**
	£'000	£'000	£'000
Net assets other than cash	20,000		20,000
Cash	4,200		4,200
	24,200	–	24,200
Share capital	1,000	(20)	980
Share premium	9,000		9,000
Capital redemption reserve		20	20
Capital	10,000	-	10,000
Distributable reserves	14,200		14,200
	24,200	-	24,200

Scenario B – Sale of treasury shares

Another possibility is that the company subsequently sells the treasury shares for, say, £55 per share (that is, total sales proceeds of £55 × 20,000 = £1,100,000). The sales proceeds are treated as a realised profit up to the amount of the purchase price of the shares of £800,000 (£40 × 20,000). However, as the sales proceeds exceed the purchase price of £40 per share, the excess over the purchase price has to be transferred to the share premium account (see para 23.57). Therefore, an amount of £300,000 ((£55 – £40) × 20,000) is transferred to share premium account, as illustrated below.

	After purchase	Sale of shares	After sale
	£'000	£'000	£'000
Net assets other than cash	20,000		20,000
Cash	4,200	1,100	5,300
	24,200	1,100	25,300
Share capital	1,000		1,000
Share premium	9,000	300	9,300
Capital	10,000	300	10,300
Distributable reserves	14,200	800	15,000
	24,200	1,100	25,300

The realised profit arising on the sale of the shares cannot exceed the amount paid for the purchase of the shares. Therefore, distributable reserves can be restored to their original amount, but cannot be increased overall.

The reconciliation of movements in shareholders' funds will show the sale of treasury shares of £1,100,000.

Scenario C – Transfer for the purposes of an employees' share scheme

A purchase from a company of its treasury shares by its ESOP trust for cash will be a sale of treasury shares for cash (see scenario B above), the accounting for which is governed by UITF Abstract 38, 'Accounting for ESOP trusts'. The accounting for awards of shares to employees, whether those shares have been transferred into an ESOP trust or remain in treasury, is governed by FRS 20, 'Share-based payment' or, (where FRS 20 has not been adopted) UITF Abstract 17, 'Employee share schemes'. The accounting in accordance with FRS 20 is dealt with in chapter 12, while the accounting in accordance with UITF Abstract 17 is dealt with in chapter 12A. The treatment of any consideration received for the shares transferred to an ESOP trust is also dealt with in those chapters.

Disclosure in respect of treasury shares

23.74 The following disclosures are required in the financial statements where shares are held as treasury shares:

- The number and aggregate nominal value of the treasury shares.
- Where more than one class of shares has been allotted, the number and aggregate nominal value of each class of shares held as treasury shares.

[CA85 4 Sch 38(1)(c)].

23.75 FRS 25 requires that the amount of equity treasury shares held by the reporting entity is disclosed separately either on the face of the balance sheet or in the notes. [FRS 25 para 34]. As noted in paragraph 23.69, treasury shares, as defined in the Act, are required to be charged to distributable profits, in which case these shares will not be shown as a separate debit reserve on the face of the balance sheet as this would be double-counting. However, the amount of treasury shares held is still required to be disclosed separately.

23.76 As noted in paragraph 23.75, FRS 25 requires a reporting entity to give disclosure of its shares that are held by the entity or by its subsidiaries or associates. Shares held by the entity, its subsidiaries or associates are the shares of the reporting entity in which those companies have a beneficial interest. Where the shares are held on behalf of others (for example, a financial institution holding its own equity on behalf of a client), there is an agency arrangement and, accordingly, the shares are not included in the companies' balance sheets. [FRS 25 para AG36].

23.77 FRS 25 does not state whether 'the amount held' refers to the number of shares or the financial amount (see para 23.75). However, the FRS 25 disclosure requirement encompasses the entity's shares held by subsidiaries and associates despite the fact that these are not deducted from equity in the parent company's separate balance sheet. (Similarly, in consolidated financial statements, shares held by associates would not be deducted from equity, because associates are not part of the consolidated group.) Therefore, we believe the 'amount held' refers to the number and class of shares held by the entity, its subsidiaries and its associates, rather than the financial amount and is consistent with the Schedule 4 to the 1985 Act (and its expected equivalent under the 2006 Act) disclosure requirement (see para 23.74). Nevertheless, it would be sensible for companies to disclose the financial amount of all treasury shares.

23.78 Where the company has an interest in its own shares, Part II of Schedule 7 to the Act requires the directors' report to include certain information. These disclosures are dealt with in chapter 3 of the Manual of Accounting – Management reports and governance. Furthermore, if the entity reacquires its own equity instruments from related parties then disclosure should be made in accordance with FRS 8, 'Related party disclosures' (see further chapter 29). [FRS 25 para 34].

23.78.1 Chapter 11 of the UKLA's Listing Rules, on related party transactions, requires disclosure in a listed company's annual financial statements of purchases of own equity securities or preference shares from a related party (for example, a director, substantial shareholder or person exercising significant influence or associates of these). (The requirements of chapter 11 of the UKLA's Listing Rules were amended from 6 August 2007 by FSA 2007/40 — Listing, Prospectus and Disclosure Rules (Miscellaneous Amendments) Instrument 2007). This is unless a purchase is made by way of a tender offer to all holders of the class of securities or, in the case of a market purchase pursuant to a general authority granted by shareholders, it is made without prior understanding, arrangement or agreement between the company and any related party. [LR 12.3.1 R]. See chapter 29 and chapter 7 of the Manual of Accounting – Management reports and governance.

23.78.2 The UKLA's Listing Rules also require disclosures in the financial statements of listed companies incorporated in the UK that have a valid authority for the purchase of own shares and have either purchased their own shares or have sold treasury shares for cash in off-market transactions. This disclosure will apply to qualifying shares that are classified as equity or as financial liabilities. The following disclosure is required:

- Details of any shareholders' authority for the purchase by the company of its own shares still valid at the period end.
- For purchases and proposed purchases of own shares made otherwise than through the market or by tender or partial offer to all shareholders during the period under review, the names of the sellers.
- For purchases made otherwise than through the market or by tender or partial offer to all shareholders, or options or contracts to make such purchases, entered into since the end of the period, equivalent information as is required under Part II of Schedule 7 to the Companies Act 1985. (See chapter 3 of the Manual of Accounting – Management reports and governance).
- In the case of sales of treasury shares for cash made otherwise than through the market, or in connection with an employees' share scheme, or otherwise than pursuant to an opportunity that was made available to all holders of a relevant class of the company's securities on the same terms, the names of the purchasers of such shares sold, or proposed to be sold, by the company during the period under review.

[LR 9.8.6 R (4)].

23.79 The AIM Rules require further disclosures in the financial statements of AIM companies that have either purchased or sold treasury shares. Disclosure is required of the following:

- The date of the movement into or out of treasury shares.
- The number of treasury shares of each class transferred into or out of treasury.
- The total number of treasury shares of each class held by the company following such movements.
- The number of shares of each class that the company has in issue less the total number of treasury shares of each class held by the company following such movements.

[AIMR 17].

Effect on distributable profits

23.80 As noted in paragraph 23.69 above, treasury shares are purchased out of distributable profits. Therefore, when a company purchases the shares it will reduce its distributable profits by the amount of consideration paid for the shares (see the example in para 23.71 above).

23.81 As noted in paragraph 23.58 above, if the company cancels treasury shares, it must reduce its issued share capital by the nominal value of the cancelled shares and transfer this amount to a capital redemption reserve. However, this does not impact on distributable profits as the cost of the treasury shares has already been charged to distributable profits (see scenario A in the example in para 23.73 above).

23.82 Where treasury shares are sold for cash (see para 23.56 above), the proceeds are treated as a realised profit up to an amount equal to the purchase price paid by the company for the shares. This reflects the symmetrical treatment when the shares are purchased. If the proceeds exceed the purchase price, the excess over the purchase price has to be transferred to the share premium account (see para 23.57). This is illustrated in the example in paragraph 23.73 above (see scenario B).

23.83 Sometimes an ESOP trust may acquire some or all of a company's holding of treasury shares for cash for the purposes of an employee share scheme. Such a transaction will be considered a sale of treasury shares for cash, so the impact on distributable profits will be the same as described in the previous paragraph. At the same time, the former treasury shares, now held by the ESOP trust, will be accounted for and treated for distributable profit purposes just as if they had been purchased by the ESOP trust from a third party. The impact on distributable profits of shares held within an ESOP trust is considered further in chapter 12 (where the entity has applied FRS 20) or 12A (where it has not).

Listing Rule requirements

23.83.1 The principal UKLA Listing Rules requirements on treasury shares are:

- Sales and transfers of shares out of treasury cannot be made during a prohibited period (see para 23.83.2). This is subject to the exemption in LR 12.2.1: *"The company has in place a buy back programme managed by an independent third party which makes its trading decisions in relation to the company's securities independently of, and uninfluenced by, the company"*.
- A requirement to notify capitalisation issues and sales, transfers and cancellations of treasury shares (see para 23.83.4 and 23.83.5).
- A limit on the discount to market price at which shares can be sold for cash out of treasury in certain situations (see para 23.83.6).

23.83.2 As mentioned in the first bullet point above, sales for cash, or transfers for the purposes of, or pursuant to, an employees' share scheme, of treasury shares cannot be made during a prohibited period; that is, when a company is in a close period or any period when there exists any matter that constitutes inside information. [LR 12.6.1 R]. However, this prohibition does not apply to:

- Transfers of treasury shares arising out of the operation of an employees' share scheme where the transfer facilitates dealings that do not fall within the provisions of the Model Code (section 2(h) to (k)) appended to Listing Rule 9.
- Sales or transfers by the company of treasury shares (other than equity shares) of a class whose price or value would not be likely to be significantly affected by the publication of the information giving rise to the prohibited period. [LR 12.6.2 R – as amended by FSA 2007/40 40 – Listing, Prospectus and Disclosure Rules (Miscellaneous Amendments) Instrument 2007]. (See further chapter 7 of the Manual of Accounting – Management reports and governance).
- A company that has in place a buy back programme managed by an independent third party that makes its trading decisions in relation to the company's securities independently of, and uninfluenced by, the company.

[LR 12.2.1 R].

Buying back shares in prohibited (close) periods

23.83.3 The exemption in Listing Rule 12.2.1 R from the general prohibition on buying back shares in close periods is very useful for those companies that need a full 12 month period in order to complete an announced buy-back programme, although shorter periods are also common, or to gain maximum pricing flexibility while doing so. Listed companies can utilise this permission to buy back shares in their close period by giving the company's broker an authority, prior to the start of a close period, to continue buying shares during the close period. The purchases should be effected pursuant to the annual buy back authority passed at most companies' AGMs in the usual way and, therefore, no new authority should generally be needed. As companies cannot have control over these independent programmes, directors must be satisfied with the authority they invest in their broker before entering into one of these programmes. Further discussion of the legal issues surrounding buying back shares in prohibited (close) periods is given in chapter 7 of the Manual of Accounting – Management reports and corporate governance. The accounting for these type of contracts with banks and brokers is governed by paragraph 23 of IAS 32 and is discussed from paragraph 23.66 above.

Treasury shares and capitalisation issues

23.83.4 If, by virtue of it holding treasury shares, a company is allotted shares as part of a capitalisation issue, the company must notify a Regulatory Information Service as soon as possible (no later than 07.30 am on the following business day). The notification must include:

- The date of the allotment.
- The number of shares allotted.

- A statement as to what number of shares allotted have been cancelled and what number is being held as treasury shares.
- Where shares allotted are being held as treasury shares:
  - The total number of treasury shares of each class held by the company following the allotment.
  - The number of shares of each class that the company has in issue, less the total number of treasury shares of each class held by the company following the allotment.

[LR 12.6.3 R].

23.83.5 Similar notification to a Regulatory Information Service is required where treasury shares are either sold for cash, cancelled or transferred for the purposes of (or pursuant to) an employees' share scheme. The sale or transfer price for each of the highest and lowest prices paid is also required to be notified where relevant. [LR 12.6.4 R].

Other Listing Rules requirements on treasury shares

23.83.6 Where a company makes an issue out of treasury shares any discount on the price of those shares is limited to 10 per cent of the middle market price of those shares. [LR 9.5.10 R].

23.83.7 The prohibition in paragraph UK.23.103 above does not apply if it is under a pre-existing general authority to disapply section 89 of the 1985 Act (section 561 of the 2006 Act) (Offers to shareholders on a pre-emptive basis). [LR 9.5.10 R (3)(b)].

23.83.8 Further information on the requirements in the UKLA's Listing Rules for notifying purchases and sales of treasury shares to a Regulatory Information Service can be found within chapter 7 of the Manual of Accounting – Management reports and governance. The UKLA's Listing Rule disclosure requirements for treasury shares are given in paragraph UK.23.94 below.

Alteration of share capital

Reduction of share capital

23.83.9 A reduction of share capital may be achieved in the following ways, subject to certain conditions:

- Extinguishing or reducing the liability on any of its shares in respect of share capital not paid up.
- Either with or without extinguishing or reducing the liability on any of its shares:

- cancel any paid up share capital that is lost or unrepresented by available assets; or
- repay any paid up share capital in excess of the company's wants.

[CA85 Sec 135(2); CA06 Sec 641(4)].

23.83.10 Companies may reduce their share capital by acquiring their own shares, subject to certain conditions. Acquisition of own shares is discussed in chapter 7 of the Manual of Accounting – Management reports and governance. For the purposes of this chapter, a 'reduction of capital' means a capital reduction achieved by one of the means set out in paragraph 23.83.9.

UK.23.83.11 The paid up share capital of the company for the purposes of a capital reduction is not just the nominal value of the share capital, but also certain of the company's reserves. The share premium account and capital redemption reserve are regarded as part of the company's paid up capital for the purposes of a capital reduction. [CA85 Sec 130(3); 170(4); CA06 Sec 610(4), 733(6)]. Similarly, the redenomination reserve under the 2006 Act (see para 23.83.29) is regarded as part of the company's paid up capital for the purposes of a capital reduction. [CA06 Sec 628(3)].

23.83.12 A limited company, whether public or private, may reduce its share capital by special resolution confirmed by the court. [CA85 Sec 135; CA06 Sec 641(1)(b)]. The 1985 Act requires that the articles contain specific authorisation for such capital reductions; the 2006 Act relaxes this rule by requiring only that the articles do not restrict or prohibit the capital reduction. [CA85 Sec 135(1); CA06 Sec 641(6)]. (In any event, the 1985 Act permits a company to amend its articles by special resolution. [CA85 Sec 9].) For private companies, the 2006 Act introduces a new procedure for capital reductions that requires a special resolution, does not require court confirmation but instead requires the directors to make a 'solvency statement'. [CA06 Sec 641(1)(a)]. Both public and private companies may continue to use the court confirmation procedure.

Court confirmation procedure

23.83.13 Under this procedure, having passed the special resolution, the company must apply to the court for an order confirming the reduction. Every creditor to whom the company owes a debt or claim on a date specified by the court is entitled to object to the reduction of capital. For this purpose, the court must draw up a list of those creditors and may publish notices fixing a day (or days) from which any other creditors will be excluded from the right to object. [CA85 Sec 136(3); CA06 Sec 646]. Any officer of the company who intentionally or recklessly conceals the name of a creditor, or who misrepresents a creditor s debt or claim, commits an offence and is liable to a fine.

23.83.14 The court may then make an order confirming the reduction of capital on such terms and conditions as it thinks fit. In doing so, the court must be satisfied that every creditor who has raised an objection has either consented subsequently or that his debt or claim has been discharged or has determined, or has been secured. [CA05 Sec 137; CA06 Sec 648].

23.83.15 The court order must be delivered to the Registrar of Companies. For capital reductions performed under the 1985 Act, the order must be accompanied by a court approved minute showing in respect of the altered share capital, the amount of the share capital, the number of shares into which it is to be divided (and the amount of each share), and the amount (if any) at the date of registration deemed to be paid up on each share. [CA85 Sec 138(1)]. For those capital reductions performed under the 2006 Act, instead of a court approved minute, a court approved statement of capital must be delivered to the Registrar of Companies. This statement of capital must contain the information set out in paragraph 23.11 in respect of the altered share capital only.

23.83.16 A court approved capital reduction takes effect when the court order and court approved minute (or statement of capital) is registered by the Registrar of Companies, with one exception for capital reductions made under the 2006 Act. A capital reduction that forms part of a compromise or arrangement under Part 26 of the 2006 Act will take effect at the same time as the other aspects of that compromise or arrangement; that is, on delivery of the court order and statement of capital to the Registrar of Companies. [CA06 Sec 649(3)]. Once registered, the Registrar's certificate under section 138 of the 1985 Act (section 649 of the 2006 Act) is conclusive evidence that the company's share capital is as stated in the minute or statement of capital.

23.83.17 One of the grounds mentioned in section 135 of the 1985 Act (section 641 of the 2006 Act) on which a company may reduce its capital is where capital is lost or is unrepresented by available assets. An example would be where the financial statements show a deficit on the profit and loss account. The company must in these circumstances prove to the court that the loss of capital is permanent and not temporary. If the loss is permanent, the court will generally sanction the application without opposition. This is on the basis that the reduction would not affect creditors and no members or class of members would be disadvantaged.

23.83.18 However, to prevent a company reducing its capital more than is necessary the court will generally require it to credit to a special reserve any excess over the amount required to write off the deficit. This reserve will be subject to certain conditions, for instance, that it will be undistributable other than for the specific purposes mentioned.

23.83.19 Where, however, the loss of capital cannot be shown to be permanent, a cancellation of paid-up share capital will prejudice creditors. An example might be where a company writes off an investment in a loss-making subsidiary, but the loss is not proved to be permanent. The court will in these circumstances consider the extent to which the interests of creditors must be fully safeguarded. An undertaking offered by the company may enable the court to dispense with the need to obtain creditors' consent and sanction the reduction.

23.83.20 In addition to the creation of a special reserve as mentioned above, the undertaking may specify that any amounts received in respect of its investment or release of a provision on a subsequent revaluation of assets would need to be credited to the special reserve. This special reserve would generally be made undistributable for so long as there remain outstanding any liabilities of the company that would be admissible in a winding up beginning on the date of the reduction of capital.

Table 23.1.1 – Transfer of special reserve

Trafalgar House Public Limited Company – Report & Accounts – 30 September 1994

26 Reserves Company

	Special Reserve £m	Profit and loss account £m	Total £m
As at 1 October 1993	95.0	102.0	197.0
Special Reserve transfer	(95.0)	95.0	–
Transfer to profit and loss account	–	(20.2)	(20.2)
Arising on scrip dividends		7.3	7.3
As at 30 September 1994	–	184.1	184.1

Following the rights issue and placing on 7 January 1994, the balance of the Special Reserve in the accounts of the company became distributable and has accordingly been transferred to the profit and loss account. This is in accordance with the undertaking given to the Court during the year ended 30 September 1991 whereby the amount standing to the credit of the Special Reserve may be reduced by the amount of any increase in its share capital or share premium as a result of any issue of shares paid up by receipt of new consideration.

Table 23.2 — Cordiant Communications Group plc — Report and Accounts — 31 December 1997

17 Reconciliation of movement in equity shareholders' deficit

Group	Share capital £ m	Share premium £ m	Capital redemption reserve £ m	Special reserve* £ m	Goodwill reserve £ m	Profit and loss account £ m	Total 31 Dec 1997 £ m	Total 31 Dec 1996 £ m
At beginning of year	230.1	137.3	86.5	–	(235.6)	(433.6)	(215.3)	(224.9)
Issues of Ordinary shares net of expenses	0.1	–	–	–	–	–	0.1	0.4
Net goodwill arising in year	–	–	–	–	(1.7)	–	(1.7)	(17.4)
Elimination of goodwill reserves on disposals	–	–	–	–	124.1	(124.1)	–	–
Profit retained for the year	–	–	–	–	–	147.0	147.0	19.8
Translation adjustment	–	–	–	–	–	(15.8)	(15.8)	6.8
Reduction of capital	(119.2)	(137.3)	(86.5)	25.7	–	317.3	–	–
At end of year	**111.0**	–	–	**25.7**	**(113.2)**	**(109.2)**	**(85.7)**	**(215.3)**

Company	Share capital £ m	Share premium £ m	Capital redemption reserve £ m	Special reserve* £ m	Goodwill reserve £ m	Profit and loss account £ m	Total 31 Dec 1997 £ m	Total 31 Dec 1996 £ m
At beginning of year	230.1	137.3	86.5	–	–	34.1	488.0	540.5
Issue of Ordinary shares net of expenses	0.1	–	–	–	–	–	0.1	0.4
Loss for the year	–	–	–	–	–	(202.5)	(202.5)	(48.5)
Demerger dividend	–	–	–	–	–	(128.7)	(128.7)	-
Dividends proposed	–	–	–	–	–	(2.7)	(2.7)	(4.4)
Reduction of capital	(119.2)	(137.3)	(86.5)	25.7	-	317.3	–	–
At end of year	**111.0**	–	–	**25.7**	–	**17.5**	**154.2**	**488.0**

*As part of the demerger the Company applied to the Court to approve a reduction of capital in the form of the deferred shares, the share premium account and capital redemption reserve. Court approval was granted, with effect from 28 November 1997, which permitted the reduction of capital to be applied first to making up the deficit resulting from the pre-demerger reconstruction and then to create distributable reserves in an amount equal to the amount of the demerger dividend. The excess capital was credited to a special reserve which is non-distributable other than for the purpose of paying of shares in a bonus issue of fully paid shares.

18 Reconciliation of operating profit to net cash inflow from operating activities

	1997 £m	1996 £m
Operating profit	55.6	31.5
Depreciation	26.2	25.8
(Gain) loss on sale of tangible fixed assets	(0.8)	0.2
(Increase)/decrease in work in progress	(5.5)	3.5
(Increase)/decrease in debtors	(35.3)	0.2
Increase in creditors	38.5	12.6
Utilisation of property provisions	(19.2)	(16.9)
Exceptional non-cash item – goodwill write off	2.2	–
Net cash inflow from operating activities	61.7	56.9

Solvency statement procedure

23.83.21 The solvency statement procedure is only available to private companies and will only apply to capital reductions occurring on or after 1 October 2008; public companies must continue to use the court confirmation procedure, as must private companies wishing to reduce capital before the implementation date of the solvency statement provisions in the 2006 Act.

23.83.22 Companies electing to use the solvency statement procedure must pass a special resolution supported by a solvency statement made not more than 15 days before the date on which the resolution is passed. A copy of the solvency statement must be made available to all members either at the meeting at which the resolution is to be proposed or, in the case of a written resolution, by being sent to the members at or before the time at which he is sent the proposed resolution. [CA06 Sec 642(2)(3)]. Once the resolution has been passed, the company must deliver a copy of the solvency statement and a statement of capital (as in para 23.83.15) to the Registrar of Companies who must register the documents on receipt at which time the resolution takes effect.

23.83.23 The solvency statement is made by all the company's directors. In the event that a director is unwilling to make the statement, the company will not be able to use the solvency statement procedure unless the dissenting director resigns as a director of the company in which case the remaining directors may make the statement. A solvency statement is a statement that each of the directors:

- Has formed the opinion, as regards the company's situation at the date of the statement, that there is no ground on which the company could then be found to be unable to pay (or otherwise discharge) its debts.
- has also formed the opinion:
    - if it is intended to commence the company's winding up within twelve months of that date, that the company will be able to pay (or otherwise discharge) its debts in full within twelve months of commencing the winding up; or
    - in any other case, that the company will be able to pay (or otherwise discharge) its debts as they fall due during the year immediately following that date.

[CA06 Sec 643(1)].

23.83.24 In forming their opinions, the directors must take into account all the company's liabilities, including contingent and prospective liabilities. A proposed redemption of preference shares treated as liabilities for accounting purposes should be regarded as a contingent or prospective liability. [CA06 Explanatory notes para 961]. A director who makes a solvency statement without having reasonable grounds for the opinions expressed in it commits an offence punishable by imprisonment or a fine, or both.

23.83.25 The Secretary of State has the power to prescribe the form of the solvency statement by regulations or by an order made under the 2006 Act.

Redenomination of share capital

23.83.26 As discussed in paragraph 23.42, it is permissible for companies to issue shares denominated in a foreign currency. However, it has not been possible under the 1985 Act for limited companies to 'convert' easily existing shares from one currency to another; companies would instead have to go through the normal cancellation or buy back or redemption procedures, accompanied by a new issue of shares in the desired currency or convert their paid-up shares into stock and re-convert that stock into paid-up shares of the required denomination (using section 121(2)(c) of the 1985 Act). Unlimited companies having a share capital are able to redenominate their shares if they wish. The 2006 Act simplifies the law to allow limited companies to redenominate their share capital easily. Redenomination is defined in the 2006 Act: *"To redenominate means to convert shares from having a fixed nominal value in one currency to having fixed nominal value in another currency"*. [CA06 Sec 622(1)].

23.83.27 Subject to their being no prohibition or restriction on redenomination contained in the articles, a limited company may by resolution redenominate its share capital or any class of its share capital. The resolution may specify conditions that must be met before the redenomination takes effect.
[CA06 Sec 622(4)].

23.83.28 The conversion must be made at an appropriate exchange rate and the rate must be specified in the resolution. The rate must be either a rate prevailing on the date of the resolution or a rate determined by taking the average of rates prevailing on each consecutive day of a period specified in the resolution. [CA06 Sec 622(3)]. To calculate the new nominal values of the shares, the following procedure must be used:

- Step one – Take the aggregate of the old nominal values of all the shares of that class.
- Step two – Translate that amount into the new currency at the rate of exchange specified in the resolution.
- Step three – Divide that amount by the amount of the number of shares in that class.

[CA06 Sec 623].

23.83.29 Inevitably, this calculation will often result in a new nominal value for shares that is not a round number. The 2006 Act anticipates this situation and makes provision for the reduction of capital and creation of a redenomination reserve to deal with the problem. This is illustrated in the following example:

Example

Company A has 1,000,000 £1 Class A shares in issue and wishes to redenominate these shares as US dollar shares. It passes a resolution to redenominate these shares at an exchange rate of £1 = $2.0132. The company also has 500,000 £1 Class B shares in issue.

Step one: Take the aggregate of the old nominal values of all the shares of that class. This is £1,000,000.

Step two: Translate that amount into the new currency at the rate of exchange specified in the resolution. £1,000,000 at £1 = $2.0132 is $2,013,200.

Step three: Divide that amount by the amount of the number of shares in that class. $2,013,200/1,000,000 gives a new nominal value of $2.0132.

Company A believes that it would be more suitable if the new nominal value were $2 per share; this would mean that the nominal value of the new shares was in aggregate $2,000,000, $13,200 less than the US dollar equivalent of the sterling nominal value. Section 626 of the 2006 Act allows the company to reduce its share capital, provided that it passes a special resolution to that effect within three months of the resolution effecting the redenomination and provided that the amount of the capital reduction is not more than 10% of the company's total allotted share capital immediately after the reduction.

The amount of the reduction in this example is $13,200, equivalent to £6,557 (translated at the rate £1 = $2.0132).

The nominal value of the Class A shares after the reduction expressed in pounds sterling is £993,443. The total allotted share capital in pounds sterling is therefore £1,493,443 (£993,443 + £500,000). £6,557 is less than 10% of £1,493,443 and therefore the capital reduction is permitted.

Section 628 of the 2006 Act requires that the amount of the capital reduction is transferred to a reserve called the redenomination reserve'. Assuming that the company retains a pound sterling functional currency, the following entry will be made:

DR Nominal share capital – $2 Class A shares	£6,557
CR Redenomination reserve	£6,557

The financial statements of Company A will, therefore, show:

Nominal share capital – $2 Class A shares	£993,443
Nominal share capital – £1 Class B shares	£500,000
Redenomination reserve	£6,557

The share capital's nominal value in functional currency terms before the redenomination is, therefore, equal to the sum of the nominal value of the share capital and the redenomination reserve after the redenomination.

23.83.30 The redenomination reserve may be applied by the company in paying up shares to be allotted to members as fully paid bonus shares. [CA06 Sec 628(2)]. The reserve is treated as if it were paid up share capital of the company for the purposes of a reduction in capital. [CA06 Sec 628(3)]. In other words, the redenomination reserve is subject to exactly the same restrictions as the capital redemption reserve.

Sub-division or consolidation of shares

23.83.31 Companies are permitted to sub-divide their shares into shares of a smaller nominal amount or to consolidate their shares into shares of a larger nominal amount. [CA85 Sec 121; CA06 Sec 618]. The 1985 Act requires express permission in the articles for such actions; the 2006 Act requires only a resolution of members (unless the company has prohibitions or restrictions in the articles). The resolution may give the company the power to sub-divide or consolidate the shares at any time in the future, or at certain times by reference to specified dates or circumstances. [CA06 Sec 618(4)]. Under the 2006 Act, companies can no longer consolidate their shares into stock and then split that stock back into shares of a different denomination. [CA06 Sec 540(2)]. However, companies that have stock created before the commencement of Part 17 of the 2006 Act may be reconverted into shares in accordance with section 620 of the 2006 Act. [CA06 Sec 540(3)].

Reserves

23.84 Companies may have any of the following reserves and accounts in the balance sheet. These headings must be shown on the face of the balance sheet:

- Share premium account (see para 23.87).
- Capital redemption reserve (see para 23.119).
- Revaluation reserve (see para 23.120).
- Profit and loss account (see para 23.86).
- Other reserves.

[CA85 4 Sch 8].

23.85 Other reserves include all reserves, both realised and unrealised, that do not fit elsewhere in the formats. If they are material, they should be specifically described. Under the Act, it is permissible to show any format item in more detail. [CA85 4 Sch 3]. Typically, other reserves that are shown separately include:

- Fair value or available-for-sale reserve (see para 23.124.1).
- Hedging reserve (see para 23.124.2).
- Foreign currency translation reserve (see para 23.124.3).

- Capital reserve (see para 23.124.6).

23.85.1 As noted in paragraph 23.83.26, the redenomination of share capital from one currency to another, as permitted under the 2006 Act, may create a 'redenomination reserve'. Companies may also create a 'merger reserve' when it applies the 'fair value' option under section 133 of the 1985 Act (section 615 of the 2006 Act) when it obtains merger relief under section 131 of the 1985 Act (section 612 of the 2006 Act) or group reconstruction relief under section 132 of the 1985 Act (section 611 of the 2006 Act) (see paras 23.96 to 23.112).

Profit and loss account

23.86 Many companies do not use the wording 'profit and loss account'. They use instead terms such as 'revenue reserves', 'profit and loss reserve' or 'retained profits'. The possibility of changing the wording of headings from those prescribed in the formats is discussed in chapter 4.

Share premium account

23.87 The Companies Acts 1985 and 2006 set out rules that relate to the creation of share premium on an issue of shares and also to the way in which that premium may be used. These rules apply to all shares, regardless of how they are classified for accounting purposes. The share premium associated with shares presented as liabilities is presented as part of the liability, but is still subject to the capital maintenance rules. Therefore, for accounting purposes, legal share premium has to be analysed between amounts relating to equity shares and shares that are presented as liabilities (see further para 23.92).

23.88 The basic rule for share premium is detailed in section 130(1) of the 1985 Act (section 610(1) of the 2006 Act), and it says that, where a company issues shares at a premium (whether for cash or otherwise), a sum equal to the aggregate amount or value of the premium must be transferred to a share premium account. Therefore, under the basic rule, where a company issues shares at a value that exceeds their nominal value, a sum equal to the difference between the issue value and the nominal value must be transferred to a share premium account. [CA85 Sec 130(1); CA06 Sec 610(1)]. For example, if a company issues 100,000 £1 shares at £1.50 each, then it must credit £50,000 to a share premium account.

23.89 Once a share premium account has been established, it may only be used for certain purposes specified in the 1985 Act, namely to:

- Pay up fully paid bonus shares.
- Write off a company's preliminary expenses.
- Write off expenses of any issue of shares or debentures.
- Write off commission paid or discount allowed on any issue of shares or debentures.

- Provide for the premium payable on any redemption of debentures.
- Fund the premium on an acquisition of own shares, where those shares were initially issued at a premium and the redemption is made from the proceeds of a new issue of shares.

[CA85 Secs 130(2), 160(2), repealed from 1 October 2008 and replaced by CA06 Sec 610(2)(3), 687(4)(5), 692(3)(4)].

23.90 A company's preliminary expenses that may be written off to share premium under the 1985 Act should be limited to the legal costs and fees relating to a company's incorporation. For example, solicitors' fees, registration fees and the costs of printing the memorandum and articles are expenses that may reasonably be written off to the share premium account. However, other costs, such as pre-incorporation trading losses, should not be written off to the share premium account.

23.90.1 With effect from 1 October 2008, the 1985 Act's rules will be repealed and replaced by those in the 2006 Act. The new Act further restricts the use of the share premium account in that it will no longer be permissible to use the share premium account to write off preliminary expenses. Neither will it be possible to write off expenses or commission paid on the issue of debentures or to provide for the premium payable on redemption of debentures. It will still be permissible to use the share premium account to fund fully paid bonus shares. [CA06 Sec 610(3)]. Although it will still be permissible to use the share premium account to write off share issue expenses and commission paid on the issue of shares, the amount that can be written off will be restricted to the amount of share premium arising on that issue of shares; that is, it will not be permissible to write off the expenses of a share issue against the premium arising on a previous share issue. [CA06 Sec 610(2)]. The 2006 Act continues to permit the use of the share premium account for the purpose of funding the premium on an acquisition of own shares, where those shares were initially issued at a premium and the redemption is made from the proceeds of a new issue of shares. [CA06 Sec 687(4)(5), 692(3)(4)].

23.91 As noted in paragraph 23.89, once a share premium account has been established, it may only be used for certain specified purposes. Apart from these specific uses, the share premium account has to be treated as if it were part of the company's paid-up share capital, other than in the case of a serious loss of capital (see para 23.40). Consequently, the provisions of the Act that apply to the reduction of share capital apply also to the share premium account (see further para 23.113. [CA85 Sec 130(3); CA06 Sec 610(4)].

23.92 As noted in paragraph 23.87 above, the requirements in respect of share premium apply, regardless of how the shares and any related share premium are classified for accounting purposes. This is illustrated in the following example.

Example

A company issues shares for consideration of £1,000. The shares have a nominal value of £100 and so there is a share premium of £900. The shares are non-redeemable and carry a cumulative fixed non-discretionary dividend for the first five years and then dividends are payable at the company's discretion after that period.

The company determines that, under FRS 25, the 5-year coupon on the share is debt and the principal is equity. It determines that the fair values of the two elements at the date the shares were issued are £200 for the debt element and £800 for the equity element. Therefore, at the date of issuing the shares, the company will record the following:

Cr	Cash	£1,000	
	Cr Equity		£800
	Cr Liability		£200

Therefore, in its balance sheet, the company will show a liability of £200 (being £20 nominal value and £180 share premium) and, as components of equity, share capital of £80 and share premium of £720 included in equity (that is, total equity of £800). The share premium of £720 is calculated by taking 9/10ths of the equity element of £800, because the original share premium amount was 9/10ths of the original proceeds.

There will need to be a note to the financial statements stating that (legal) share capital is £100 and share premium £900. The company will have to maintain sufficient records such that in effect it can reconstruct a 'legal' balance sheet, as share capital and share premium are still subject to capital maintenance requirements, irrespective of their classification in the balance sheet, and the £100 share capital and £900 share premium cannot be repaid, unless the requirements of, for example, section 159 of the 1985 Act (section 684 of the 2006 Act) are met.

By way of illustration, if the company repurchases the shares out of distributable profits for £1,000, the following entries are recorded:

Dr Equity – share capital	£80	
Dr Liability	£200	
Dr Equity – Retained earnings	£1,000	
Cr Capital redemption reserve (see para 23.119)		£100
Cr Equity – share premium		£180
Cr Cash		£1,000

The element of the share premium that was previously included in the carrying amount of the debt (that is, £200 × 9/10 = £180) is transferred to the share premium account component of equity once that the debt has been repaid, in order to maintain the company's legal capital.

If, say, the company had retained earnings of £11,000 prior to the repurchase, the company's balance sheets before and after the repurchase of shares would be as follows:

	Actual balance sheet	
	Before repurchase	After repurchase
	£	£
Debt	(200)	–
Cash/assets	12,000	11,000
Net assets	11,800	11,000
Share capital	80	–
Share premium	720	900
Capital redemption reserve	–	100
Retained earnings	11,000	10,000
Total equity	11,800	11,000

A separate memorandum account should also be maintained recording the legal position of the share capital and premium accounts. If, say, the company had retained earnings of £11,000 prior to the repurchase, this would be expected to show the following:

	Memorandum account	
	Before repurchase	After repurchase
	£	£
Share capital	100	–
Share premium	900	900
Capital redemption reserve	–	100
Retained earnings	11,000	10,000
Total equity	12,000	11,000

23.93 Section 130 of the 1985 Act is derived from section 56 of the Companies Act 1948 and, until the Companies Act 1981 came into effect, there was no relief from the provisions of that section. The Companies Act 1981 introduced certain merger and group reconstruction relief provisions that are now set out in sections 131 to 133 of the 1985 Act. These provisions have been carried forward into sections 611 to 615 of the 2006 Act. These reliefs under the 1985 and 2006 Acts are considered in the following sections.

Implications of Shearer v Bercain Ltd

23.94 The tax case of Shearer v Bercain Ltd questioned the construction of section 56 of the Companies Act 1948, which is now section 130 of the Companies Act 1985 (section 610 of the Companies Act 2006). [*Shearer v Bercain Ltd* [1980] 3 AER 295]. The court held that where shares were issued at a premium, whether for cash or otherwise, section 56 of the 1948 Act required the premium to be carried to a share premium account in the issuing company's books, and the premium could be distributed only if the procedure for reducing capital was carried through.

23.95 This judgement gave authority to the interpretation of section 56 of the 1948 Act that required a company to set up a share premium account in any transaction where it acquired another company's shares in return for the allotment of its own shares and the fair value of the shares it acquired exceeded the nominal value of the shares it issued. Following the court's decision, the government introduced legislation that relieved companies, in certain circumstances, from the obligation to carry some, or all, of this share premium to a share premium account. The provisions that give this relief appear in sections 131 to 133 of the 1985 Act (sections 611 to 615 of the 2006 Act).

Merger relief

23.96 The essence of merger relief is that, where appropriate conditions are met, section 130 of the 1985 Act (section 610 of the 2006 Act) does not apply. Merger relief, despite its name, is in effect relief from the need to set up a share premium account. It is a relief that affects the accounting for capital and reserves in the issuing company's own financial statements, but it is not directly concerned with the actual accounting treatment of acquisitions in consolidated financial statements.

23.97 The situations in which companies obtain merger relief are those in which the transaction satisfies the following three conditions (where 'equity share capital' is as defined in para 23.98 below):

- A company (known either as the issuing company or the acquiring company) secures at least 90 per cent of the nominal value of each class of the equity share capital of another company (the acquired company) as a result of an arrangement.
- The arrangement provides for the allotment of equity shares in the issuing company. (Such allotment will normally be made to the acquired company's shareholders.)
- The consideration for the shares so allotted is either: the issue, or the transfer, to the issuing company of equity shares in the acquired company; or the cancellation of those of the equity shares in the acquired company that the issuing company does not already hold.

[CA85 Sec 131(1)(5); CA06 Sec 612(1)].

23.98 In determining whether a particular transaction satisfies the above conditions, the following rules apply:

- 'Equity share capital' is a company's issued share capital, excluding any part that (as regards dividends and capital) does not carry a right to participate beyond a specified amount in a distribution. [CA85 Secs 744, 131(7); CA06

Secs 548, 616(1)]. 'Non-equity shares' are all other shares. In particular, preference shares will generally not form part of a company's 'equity share capital'. (Note that this is the Act's definition. The definition of an equity instrument in FRS 25 is different – see chapter 6.)

- Any shares in the acquired company that are held by other companies in the same group (that is, parent companies, subsidiaries and fellow subsidiaries) as the issuing company, or their nominees, should be treated as being held by the issuing company. [CA85 Sec 131(6); CA06 Sec 613(5)].
- An 'arrangement' means any agreement, scheme or arrangement, including an arrangement that is sanctioned under either section 425 of the Act (company compromise with creditors and members) (Part 26 of the 2006 Act or section 110 of the Insolvency Act 1986 (liquidator accepting shares, etc., as consideration for the sale of the company's property). [CA85 Sec 131(7); CA06 Sec 616(1)].
- A company will be treated as having secured a 90 per cent holding in another company as part of an arrangement, irrespective of whether or not it actually acquired, under that arrangement, all the equity shares that it holds. [CA85 Sec 131(4); CA06 Sec 613(2) and (3)]. This rule means that, in determining whether or not a company has obtained a 90 per cent holding in another company, prior holdings can be taken into account.
- The issuing company is regarded as having secured at least a 90 per cent equity holding in another company if it holds equity shares in that company of an aggregate nominal value equal to 90 per cent or more of the nominal value of that company's equity share capital (excluding any shares in that company held as treasury shares). [CA85 Sec 131(4); CA06 Sec 613(2) and (3)].
- 'Company' includes any body corporate, except where reference is made to the issuing company (the acquiring company). [CA85 Sec 133(4); CA06 Sec 616(1)].
- In any provisions that relate to a company's acquisition of shares in another company, shares that a nominee of a company acquired are to be treated as having been acquired by the company itself. Similarly, the issue, or the allotment or the transfer of any shares to or by a company's nominee is to be regarded as if the shares were issued, or allotted or transferred to or by the company itself. [CA85 Sec 133(2); CA06 Sec 616(2)].
- The transfer of a company's shares includes the transfer of a right to be included in the company's register of members in respect of those shares. [CA85 Sec 133(3); CA06 Sec 616(3)].

23.99 The examples that follow illustrate the application of these provisions:

Example 1

Company A issues equity shares and acquires 90% of company B's equity shares in a share-for-share exchange. This is the most obvious application of the provisions. In these circumstances, company A is entitled to the relief from section 130 of the Act.

Example 2

Company C owns 60% of company D's equity shares. The members of company D agree to a cancellation of the equity shares that company C does not hold, in return for the allotment to them of equity shares in company C. In this situation, also, company C is entitled to the relief from section 130 of the 1985 Act (section 610 of the 2006 Act). There are two reasons for this:

- The effect of cancelling the remaining shares is to increase company C's 60% holding to a 100% holding (and so over the 90% threshold).
- The consideration for the allotment of company C's equity shares is the cancellation of those of company D's shares that it does not already hold.

For this purpose, it is irrelevant that the acquiring company did not acquire the original 60% holding as part of the arrangement. To be entitled to the relief, a company (whether newly formed or otherwise) needs only to acquire shares sufficient either to secure or increase its holding to at least 90%. However, company C is entitled to the relief only on the shares it is now issuing in consideration for the cancellation of the shares in company D that it does not hold. It cannot retrospectively write back any share premium that it set up on any shares it issued when it acquired the 60% holding.

Example 3

Company E acquires all of company F's 'A' equity shares. Company F also has 'B' equity shares in issue, but company E holds none of these. In this situation, company E is not entitled to the relief from section 130 of the 1985 Act, because section 131 (section 613(4) of the 2006 Act) requires the issuer to secure a 90% holding of each class of equity shares in the acquired company. This applies even if the 'B' shares represent in total only 10% or less of the nominal value of company F's equity share capital.

Example 4

Company G acquires 95% of company H's equity shares. The consideration for these shares is, in equal proportions, equity shares in company G and cash. In this situation, company G is entitled to the relief from section 130 (section 610 of the 2006 Act). This is because there is no 'cash limit' criterion in the conditions for relief. The section states only that the consideration received for the shares allotted should be equity shares. It does not stipulate any minimum proportion of the consideration that should consist of shares.

Application of merger relief

23.100 Where an issue of shares satisfies the conditions referred to in paragraph 23.97, the Act provides relief from the application of section 130 of the 1985 Act (section 610 of the 2006 Act). In these circumstances, section 130 (section 610) will not apply to any premium that attaches to the shares that the issuing company allots as part of the arrangement. [CA85 Sec 131(2); CA06 Sec 612(2)].

23.101 In addition, where a transaction satisfies the conditions referred to in paragraph 23.97 the relief will extend to shares issued for either the acquisition, or the cancellation, of non-equity shares. The relief extends to cover an arrangement that provides for the allotment of any shares in the issuing company in return for either of the following:

- The issue or the transfer to the issuing company of non-equity shares in the acquired company.
- The cancellation of any such shares (that is, non-equity shares) in the acquired company that the issuing company does not hold.

In such circumstances, section 130 of the 1985 Act (section 610 of the 2006 Act) will not apply to any premium that attaches to the shares that the issuing company allots for this purpose. [CA85 Sec 131(3); CA06 Sec 612(3)].

23.101.1 Non-equity shares are, for the purposes of relief, defined by the Act not by accounting standards.

23.102 In this connection, it is important to note that where a transaction satisfies those conditions, which as stated in paragraph 23.97 must include the issue of equity shares, the issuing company can also allot any of its shares in return for either the acquisition of non-equity shares or the cancellation of non-equity shares in the acquired company. This means that the issuing company may, itself, also allot non-equity shares for the acquisition of non-equity shares or the cancellation of non-equity shares not held by the issuing company and take merger relief on the non-equity shares that it issues.

23.103 Where it is applicable, the use of section 131 of the 1985 Act (section 612 of the 2006 Act) relief is compulsory. This is based on the wording of section 131(2) of the 1985 Act (section 612(2) of the 2006 Act), which states that *"if the equity shares in the issuing company allotted in pursuance of an arrangement in consideration for the acquisition or cancellation of equity shares in the other company are issued at a premium, section 130 does not apply to the premium on these shares"*. The same wording (other than the use of 2006 Act references) appears in the 2006 Act and the use of merger relief continues to be mandatory.

23.104 Merger relief applies in accounting for capital and reserves in the parent company's separate financial statements. It does not affect the accounting for the acquisition of the subsidiary in the consolidated financial statements, which is dealt with in chapter 25.

Relief in respect of group reconstructions

23.105 Under the basic rule in section 130 of the 1985 Act, the issuing company should transfer any premium on the issue of its shares to a share premium account, not only where a 'third party' acquisition occurs, but also where a group reconstruction occurs. The Act provides some relief from this requirement, but it does not dispense altogether with the requirement to recognise a share premium. The merger relief provisions of section 131 of the 1985 Act (section 612 of the 2006 Act) (which have been discussed in paragraph 23.97 onwards) are not available for group reconstructions. [CA85 Sec 132(8); CA06 Sec 612(4)]. The relief in respect of group reconstructions is contained in section 132 of the 1985 Act. The group reconstructions for which the Act affords relief are different from those as defined in FRS 6, 'Acquisitions and mergers', (see further chapter 25) and are those that satisfy the following conditions:

- A wholly-owned subsidiary (the issuing company) allots some of its shares either to its holding company or to another wholly-owned subsidiary of its holding company. [CA85 Sec 132(1); CA06 Sec 611(1)].
- The allotment is in consideration for the transfer to it of any assets (other than cash) of its holding company or of another wholly-owned subsidiary of its holding company. [CA85 Sec 132(1); CA06 Sec 611(1)].
- 'Company' includes any body corporate except where reference is made to the issuing company (that is, the acquiring company). [CA85 Sec 133(4); CA06 Sec 616(1)].

23.105.1 If the assets being transferred include cash, it must be determined how much of the shares the issuing company has allotted to the cash amount. For those shares section 130 of the 1985 Act (section 610 of the 2006 Act) is not disapplied and the share premium on those shares must be taken to the share premium account. This is because section 132 (section 611) relief only applies to the transfer of 'non-cash' assets. [CA85 Sec 132(1); CA06 Sec 611(1)].

23.106 For example, the allotment may be in consideration for the transfer to the issuing company of shares in another subsidiary (which is not necessarily wholly-owned) that the holding company holds. Diagrammatically, the situation before and after such a reconstruction would be as shown below.

23.107 Where those shares in the issuing company that relate to the transfer are issued at a premium, the issuing company need only transfer to the share premium account an amount equal to the 'minimum premium value'. [CA85 Sec 132(2); CA06 Sec 611(2)]. See further paragraph 23.111.

23.108 For this purpose, the following definitions apply:

- The 'minimum premium value' is the amount, if any, by which the base value of the consideration that the issuing company receives exceeds the aggregate nominal value of the shares that it allots in consideration for the transfer. [CA85 Sec 132(3), CA06 Sec 611(3)].
- The 'base value' of the consideration that the issuing company receives is the amount by which the base value of the assets transferred to it exceeds the base value of any liabilities that the issuing company assumes as part of that consideration. [CA85 Sec 132(4), CA06 Sec 611(4)].
- The 'base value of the assets transferred' is the lower of:
  - The cost to the transferor company of those assets.
  - The amount at which the assets are stated, immediately before the transfer, in the transferor company's accounting records

  [CA85 Sec 132(5)(a), CA06 Sec 611(5)].
- The 'base value of the liabilities' assumed is the amount at which those liabilities are stated, immediately before the transfer, in the transferor company's accounting records. [CA85 Sec 132(5)(b), CA06 Sec 611(5)].

23.109 The following two examples illustrate the method of calculating the relief available under the provisions of the Act:

Example 1

An issuing company (company Y) allots 1,200 £1 ordinary shares (the consideration being valued at the equivalent of £5 per share) to its holding company (company X). In consideration of this allotment, company X agrees to transfer to company Y its 75% holding in a fellow-subsidiary (company Z), which is considered to have a fair value of £6,000. Company X originally paid £3,000 for its 75% holding in company Z. Immediately before the reconstruction, the amount at which that holding was stated in company X's accounting records was £2,000.

In these circumstances, the base value of the shares in company Z is £2,000. This amount is the lower of the cost of the shares to company X (that is, £3,000) and the amount at which the shares are stated in company X's accounting records (that is, £2,000). The nominal value of the shares that company Y allots in respect of the transfer is £1,200. Therefore, the 'minimum premium value' is £800. This amount is calculated as the base value of the shares in company Z (that is, £2,000) less the nominal value of the shares company Y allots (that is, £1,200). Consequently, the amount of £800 (being the 'minimum premium value') must be transferred to company Y's share premium account. (Without the relief given by section 132 of the 1985 Act (section 611 of the 2006 Act), the company would have had to transfer £4,800 to its share premium account. This amount is calculated as the difference between the value of £5 and the nominal value of £1 for each of the 1,200 shares.)

Example 2

A holding company (company H) has a wholly-owned subsidiary (company S). Company H has, as part of its assets, land that originally cost £110,000. This land has subsequently been revalued and it is currently included in the company's accounting records at £175,000.

In addition, the purchase of the land was partly financed by a loan of £40,000 that is secured on the land and is still outstanding. The land is currently valued at £200,000. It is proposed that company S allots to company H 25,000 of its ordinary £1 shares in consideration for the transfer to it of the land that company H currently owns. In addition, company S will assume the liability for the loan of £40,000 that is secured on the land.

If the Act did not provide relief from section 130 of the 1985 Act (section 610 of the 2006 Act) in respect of group reconstructions such as the above, company S would need to transfer £135,000 to a share premium account. This premium is calculated as follows:

	£	£
Nominal value of shares allotted		25,000
Fair value of consideration received:		
Current value of the land	200,000	
less: liability assumed	40,000	160,000
Premium on the shares allotted		135,000

However, because of the relief from section 130 that section 132 of the 1985 Act (sections 610 and 611 of the 2006 Act) gives, the company needs only to transfer £45,000 (which is the 'minimum premium value') to a share premium account. This minimum premium value is calculated as follows:

	£
Base value of the land transferred (being the lower of the original cost of £110,000 and the amount at which it currently stands in company H's books, £175,000).	110,000
Base value of the liability that company S assumes	40,000
Base value of the consideration that company S receives for the shares it allots	70,000
Nominal value of the shares that company S allots	25,000
Minimum premium value	45,000

23.110 The principal difference between the group reconstruction relief and merger relief is that, with group reconstruction relief, the need may arise to recognise a share premium in the share premium account; with merger relief, there is no such requirement.

23.111 In addition, where it is applicable, the use of group reconstruction relief is not regarded as compulsory. This view is based on the wording of section 132(2) of the 1985 Act (section 611(2) of the 2006 Act), which states that "*Where the shares in the issuing company allotted in consideration for the transfer are issued at a premium, the issuing company is not required by section 130 to transfer any amount in excess of the minimum premium value to the share premium account*". The wording in section 132(2) (CA06 Sec 11(2)) does not state that use of section 130 (CA06 Sec 610) is excluded. This is in contrast to the wording in section 131(2) (CA06 Sec 12(2)) (see para 23.103), which requires compulsory use of the merger relief given in section 131 (CA06 Sec 612).

23.112 However, in our view, crediting more to the share premium account than the 'minimum amount' required by section 132 of the 1985 Act (section 611 of the 2006 Act) is unusual and potentially confusing to users of the financial statements. This is because they may infer that the excess amount over the 'minimum amount' is subject to the restrictions of section 130 of the 1985 Act (section 610 of the 2006 Act). We, therefore, recommend that the excess premium over the 'minimum amount' required by section 132 of the 1985 Act (section 611 of the 2006 Act) in group reconstructions is credited to an 'other reserve', often called a 'merger reserve', rather than to the statutory share premium account.

Reduction of share premium account

23.113 Although the share premium account can be used for certain purposes mentioned from paragraph 23.89 above, it is treated as forming part of the company's capital for the purposes of the reduction of share capital. As such it can be reduced under section 135 of the 1985 Act (section 641 of the 2006 Act). This section requires a reduction to be authorised by the company's articles of association and by special resolution of the company. In addition, the company must obtain a court order confirming the reduction. Reductions of share capital are discussed further from paragraph 23.83.9.

[The next paragraph is 23.119.]

Capital redemption reserve

23.119 Unless a private company is making an acquisition of its own shares out of capital, the 1985 and 2006 Acts require companies to maintain their capital after the redemption or purchase of their own shares. This generally means that companies have to make a transfer to a capital redemption reserve of an amount equal to the nominal value of the shares that they acquire, or on cancellation of shares held as treasury shares. [CA85 Sec 170(1); CA06 Sec 733(1), (2) and (4)]. But where the acquisition is funded by an issue of new shares (a 'fresh issue' of shares) made for the purposes of the redemption/repurchase, the amount that is required to be transferred to the capital redemption reserve is the difference between the proceeds of the fresh issue and the nominal value of the shares being purchased if it is greater. [CA85 Sec 170(2); CA06 Sec 733(3)]. In this situation, where the acquisition is funded by a fresh issue, the capital of the company is still maintained, although some of the capital may now be represented by share premium and an amount transferred to the capital redemption reserve. The purchase by a company of its own shares is discussed in detail in chapter 7 of the Manual of Accounting – Management reports and governance.

Revaluation reserve

23.120 Schedule 4 to the 1985 Act includes rules on the transfer of amounts to and from the revaluation reserve. [CA85 4 Sch 3, 3A, 3B].

23.120.1 Where a company has valued an item in accordance with one of the alternative accounting rules, the Act states that the revaluation surplus or deficit must be credited or debited to a revaluation reserve. [CA85 4 Sch 34(1)].

23.121 Furthermore, a company can transfer an amount from the revaluation reserve to the profit and loss account, if the amount was previously charged to that account or represents a realised profit. A company is also permitted to apply the whole or a part of the revaluation reserve in wholly or partly paying up unissued shares in the company to be allotted to the members as fully or partly paid shares. The revaluation reserve will also be reduced by any amounts transferred to it that are no longer necessary for the purpose of the valuation method that the company has adopted. [CA85 4 Sch 34(3)]. Furthermore, it is possible to transfer from the revaluation reserve an amount in respect of the taxation relating to any profit or loss credited or debited to that reserve. [CA85 4 Sch 34(3)(b)]. This applies for example to the tax relating to a previously recognised revaluation gain.

23.122 The revaluation reserve must be disclosed on the face of the balance sheet. It may be described by a different name, although it is generally preferable for companies to keep to the terminology in the Act. [CA85 4 Sch 34(2)].

23.123 Where an amount has been credited or debited to the revaluation reserve, its treatment for taxation purposes must be disclosed in a note to the financial statements (see chapter 13). [CA85 4 Sch 34(4)].

23.124 The revaluation reserve and some of the problems surrounding it are considered in the discussion of the alternative accounting rules in chapter 16.

Fair value or available-for-sale reserve

23.124.1 FRS 26 requires that gains or losses on available for sale financial assets are recognised in equity, through the statement of total recognised gains and losses, except for impairment losses and foreign exchange gains and losses (when they relate to a monetary item), interest and dividends. [FRS 26 paras 55(b) AG83]. These gains and losses must, under the 1985 Act, be included in a separate reserve, (typically known as the fair value or available-for-sale reserve) and are recycled to the income statement on derecognition (for example, when sold) or impairment. [FRS 26 para 55(b)]. FRS 3, 'Reporting financial performance', was amended for accounting periods commencing on or after 1 January 2007, to disapply the prohibition on recycling between the STRGL and profit and loss account for companies using FRSs 23 and 26. [FRS 3 para 12B]. The treatment of available-for-sale financial assets is considered further in chapter 6. Companies not using FRS 26 but that choose to carry investments at market value and take the changes in value to revaluation reserve do so under the 'Alternative accounting rules' of the Act (see para 23.120.1) not the Act's 'Fair value accounting rules'. Companies that take the change in market value of their investments to profit and loss account put themselves within the 'Fair value accounting rules' and, therefore, within FRS 26's scope. [FRS 26 paras 1A and 1B].

23.124.1.1 The profits and losses arising on the remeasurement of available-for-sale (AFS) financial assets are realised or unrealised according to the same principles that apply if the same assets are accounted for at fair value through profit or loss (FVTPL). It would be illogical if the question of whether a profit is realised or unrealised depended on whether the directors designated the particular financial assets as FVTPL on initial recognition. Consequently, profits on remeasurement of AFS financial assets are realised on unrealised irrespective of whether they meet the requirements to be accounted for at FVTPL. [Tech 02/07 para 3.19]. Similarly, losses on remeasurement of AFS financial assets are realised unless they meet both the specific conditions set out in paragraph 30A of Tech 7/03 (as inserted by Tech 02/07 para 3.30). (See para 23.124.1.2 below).

23.124.1.2 In respect of losses, cumulative net losses arising on fair value accounting (both for AFS and FVTPL purposes) are generally realised and can only be unrealised if:

- profits on remeasurement of the same financial asset would be unrealised; and
- the losses would not have been recorded otherwise than pursuant to fair value accounting.

[Tech 7/03 para 30A as inserted by Tech 02/07 para 3.30].

23.124.1.3 With reference to the second condition above, absent fair value accounting, a loss may need to be recorded for a financial asset, for example, on the basis of amortised cost less impairment provisions.

23.124.1.4 If the fair value or AFS reserve is in an overall loss position (that is, it is a net debit), public companies will find that operation of the net assets test in section 264 of the 1985 Act (section 831 of the 2006 Act) will restrict the amount of profits available for distribution by the amount of the net debit balance.

Hedging reserve

23.124.2 FRS 26 requires that the effective portion of gains (profits) and losses (net of tax), arising from the remeasurement of a financial instrument designated as the hedging instrument in a cash flow hedge, be recognised in reserves, through the statement of total recognised gains and losses. [FRS 26 para 95]. The 'Fair value accounting rules' require that these profits and losses are taken to the fair value reserve. [CA06 4 Sch 34E(3)]. However, some companies designate a separate reserve as a hedging reserve. Legally, this is subject to the same rules as the fair value reserve, of which it is, in effect, a sub-set. These gains and losses are subsequently recycled to the profit and loss account in the period (or periods) when the hedged item affects the profit and loss account. [FRS 26 para 100]. FRS 3 was amended for accounting periods commencing on or after 1 January

2007 to allow recycling where the company uses FRSs 23 and 26. [FRS 3 para 12B]. If the hedged cash flows result in the recognition of a non-financial asset or liability on the balance sheet, the entity can choose to adjust the basis (that is, measurement on initial recognition) of the asset or liability by the amount of gains and losses recognised in reserves. [FRS 26 para 98]. However, this 'basis adjustment' is not permitted if the hedged cash flows result in the recognition of a financial asset or liability. In that case, the deferred amount remains in equity and is recycled to profit or loss according to the profile of the effect that the asset or liability has on profit or loss. If the hedging relationship ceases because one of the criteria for hedge accounting is no longer met, the hedge is revoked or the hedging instrument is expired, sold, terminated or exercised, the gains and losses accumulated in equity are either:

- released to the profit and loss account immediately if the hedged item is no longer expected to occur; or
- left in equity until the hedged cash flow occurs at which point they are released to the profit and loss account.

[FRS 26 para 101].

23.124.2.1 Profits and losses deferred in the hedging reserve are unrealised and become realised only when the hedged item affects profit or loss. This is based on the principle set out in paragraph 4.2 of Tech 02/07 that it is necessary to have regard to the combined effect of both sides of the hedging relationship to determine whether there is a realised profit or loss. [Tech 02/07 para 4.9]. To the extent that any ineffective element of the profit or loss on remeasurement of the hedging instrument is recognised in profit or loss, that element should be assessed as to whether it is realised in accordance with the 'readily convertible to cash' test in the amended Tech 7/03. [Tech 02/07 para 4.9].

23.124.2.2 The hedging principle in paragraph 4.2 of Tech 02/07 applies irrespective of whether the profits or losses in question arise from changes in fair value of open contracts or from settled transactions. The amounts taken to the hedging reserve may, for example, include profits or losses on short-term derivative contracts that form part of a rolling-strategy but which have matured. Such profits and losses should be treated as unrealised provided that FRS 26 requires them to remain deferred in equity as part of a cash flow hedging relationship. [Tech 02/07 para 4.10].

23.124.2.3 If the hedging reserve is in an overall loss position (that is, it is a net debit), public companies will find that operation of the net assets test in section 264 of the 1985 Act (section 831 of the 2006 Act) will restrict the amount of profits available for distribution by the amount of the net debit balance. [Tech 02/07 para 4.11].

Companies not using FRS 26

23.124.2.4 Companies that do not use FRS 26 do not use the 'fair value accounting rules' under the Act and thus do not have a fair value or hedging reserve. Such companies account for their hedges on an 'accruals basis', that is, one where the gains and losses on the hedging instruments are generally not recognised until the gains and losses on the hedged items are recognised in the profit and loss account. Where a company carries out net investment hedging under SSAP 20, profits and losses on the hedging instrument (for example, a foreign currency borrowing or a forward foreign exchange contract) are taken to the profit and loss account reserve *via* the STRGL as are the profits and losses on the retranslation of the cost of investment in the subsidiary (in the company's individual financial statements) or the subsidiary's net assets (in the company's consolidated financial statements), where they offset each other.

23.124.2.5 For companies that do not use FRS 26, the effect on the determination of realised and distributable profits of hedge accounting on an 'accruals basis', the principle in paragraph 33 of Tech 7/03 (amended) still applies *"Where hedge accounting is obtained in accordance with the relevant accounting standards, it is necessary to consider the combined effect of both sides of the hedging relationship to determine whether there is a realised profit or loss in accordance with the criteria in this guidance"*. [Tech 7/03 para 33 as amended by Tech 02/07 para 4.2]. Consequently, in a hedging model where profits and losses on the hedging instruments and the hedged items are not recognised until there is a cash realisation, there is normally an automatic set off for the purposes of determining the effect on realised and distributable profits. In circumstances where the strategy is to use a series of 'rolling' instruments the hedging principle above applies irrespective of whether profits or losses have been recognised from settled transactions. Such profits and losses should be treated as unrealised.

Foreign currency translation reserve

23.124.3 Exchange differences that arise on translation of a foreign operation must be recognised through the statement of recognised gains and losses; cumulative net exchange differences so recognised must be separately disclosed, together with a reconciliation of the amount of such differences as at the beginning and end of the period. [FRS 23 para 32, 52]. These differences may arise on the translation of a foreign branch to be included in the entity's separate financial statements or may arise on the translation of a foreign subsidiary to be included in the entity's consolidated accounts. Similarly, gains or losses that arise on hedging instruments that are effective hedges against the effect of exchange rates on the net assets of an operation (a 'net investment hedge') should be included in the consolidated foreign currency translation reserve. Entities need to track separately the translation differences contained within an entity's own equity and its consolidated equity because, on disposal of a foreign branch or operation, the cumulative translation difference relating to that operation must be transferred (recycled) to the profit and loss account and included in the gain or loss on disposal. [FRS 23 para 48]. FRS 3 was amended with effect for accounting periods commencing on or after 1 January 2007 to allow this type of recycling for entities using FRSs 23 and 26. [FRS 3 para 12B]. Such recycling also applies to the required portion of the cumulative translation difference on an actual or deemed partial disposal. [FRS 23 paras 48 and 49]. Accounting for the effects of changes in foreign exchange rates is considered further in chapter 7.

23.124.4 Under FRS 26, net investment hedge accounting of foreign operations arises in consolidated financial statements. These financial statements are not relevant for the purposes of justifying distributions. However, in the case of a foreign branch, net investment hedge accounting can take place in the company's separate financial statements. A net investment hedge is accounted for similarly to a cash flow hedge. The extent to which the profit or loss on remeasurement of the hedging instrument is realised is determined by reference to the loss or profit on the hedged item. In the case of a foreign branch, determining whether the retranslation profits and losses of a branch's assets and liabilities are realised can be complex. Consequently, this has implications for the profits and losses on the hedging instrument. The issues in respect of the hedged item are considered in paragraphs 6.91 to 6.96 of Tech 02/07. [Tech 02/07 para 4.12].

23.124.5 If the foreign currency translation reserve is in an overall loss position (that is, it is a net debit) on retranslation of foreign currency assets and liabilities, public companies will find that operation of the net assets test in section 264 of the 1985 Act (section 831 of the 2006 Act) will restrict the amount of profits available for distribution by the amount of the net debit balance. Where foreign currency denominated shares have been classified as financial liabilities under FRS 25, careful consideration is needed of whether the retranslation gains and losses (whether recognised under FRS 23 (for companies using FRS 26) or SSAP 20 (for companies not using FRS 26)) are gains and losses in law, as it may be that the accounting is made in anticipation of the eventual distribution or capital repayment.

Companies not using FRSs 23 and 26

23.124.5.1 Companies that are not using FRS 26 are not permitted to use FRS 23 and, consequently, continue to use SSAP 20. This standard does not require the maintenance of a cumulative translation reserve nor does FRS 3 (absent the use of FRSs 23 and 26) permit any recycling from reserves through the STRGL to the profit and loss account. Hence translation differences on the cost of investment (individual financial statements) or on net assets (consolidated financial statements) that have previously been taken to reserves are not recycled on disposal or partial disposal of the relevant foreign subsidiaries or other foreign equity investments and thus not included in the gain or loss on disposal reported in the profit and loss account.

23.124.5.2 Net investment hedge accounting for a branch under SSAP 20 is not dissimilar from that under SSAP 20. Accordingly, the issues discussed in paragraph 23.124.4 are equally relevant when considering the impact on determining of realised and distributable profits for a branch.

Capital reserve

23.124.6 Where a company receives consideration from one or more shareholders without a contractual obligation to make any repayment (a gift or a 'capital contribution'), this will represent an increase in equity. Typically, such amounts are recorded in a separate reserve, often known as the 'capital reserve'.

23.124.7 If the gift or 'capital contribution' is received in cash or an asset that is readily convertible to cash, the amount included in the capital reserve will be realised. However, if it is not received in qualifying consideration the amount will be unrealised, although it may become realised if the consideration is converted into qualifying consideration, or the asset is depreciated or sold. [Tech 07/03 para 16(f)].

[The next paragraph is 23.125.]

Disclosure

23.125 Under Schedule 4 of the 1985 Act, certain information must be included in the notes to the financial statements in respect of movements on each reserve that is shown either on the face of the balance sheet or in the notes to the financial statements. This information is as follows:

- The amount of the reserve at the beginning and end of the year.
- The amounts transferred to or from the reserve during the year.
- The source and application of any amounts so transferred.

[CA85 4 Sch 46(1)(2)].

23.126 Companies may either give the information for each reserve in a separate note or prepare a combined note. Combining reserves helps clarify reserves movements when there are transfers between different reserves.

Realised and distributable reserves

23.127 The Companies Act contains no specific requirement for reserves to be disclosed as either realised or unrealised, or as distributable or undistributable. However, there may be differences between the balance on a company's profit and loss account and the amount that is realised (and so is distributable in law). Where there is a material difference between the balance on the profit and loss account and the amount that is legally distributable the financial statements may need to disclose the amounts of distributable and undistributable reserves respectively.

23.127.1 Paragraph 6.133 of Tech 02/07 makes clear that there is no requirement under law or accounting standards for financial statements to distinguish between realised and unrealised profits. Paragraph 6.135 goes on to say that it may be thought helpful to users of financial statements if there is an indication of which reserves are realised in a company's separate financial statements. However, there is generally no need for directors to form a view on whether profits are realised, unless they intend to utilise them to make a distribution.

23.127.2 Paragraph B12 of Tech 07/03 (amended) draws attention to the need for companies to maintain sufficient records to enable them to distinguish between those profits which are available for distribution and those that are not.

23.128 Although distributions are made from the distributable reserves of individual companies, rather than groups, users of financial statements may nonetheless draw inferences from the amount shown on the consolidated profit and loss account reserve. It would be misleading if consolidated financial statements gave the impression that subsidiary companies' distributable profits were readily available for distribution outside the group through payments to the parent when there were significant restrictions on their distribution to the parent. Where there are significant restrictions (for example, resulting from borrowing arrangements or regulatory requirements) on the ability of subsidiaries to transfer funds to the parent in the form of cash dividends or to repay loans or advances, the nature and extent of the restrictions should be disclosed. [FRS 2 para 53]. There is a similar disclosure requirement in respect of associates and joint ventures. [FRS 9 para 54].

23.129 Indeed, users of consolidated financial statements may wish to know how much a parent could distribute if all the subsidiaries in the group were to pay up their realised profits by way of dividends to the parent. In the past, some groups have voluntarily disclosed this amount or state in their reserves note any amounts that are not available for distribution. For example, the financial statements of Coats Viyella include a note that clarifies the reserves that are, or are not, available for distribution by the company. Coats Viyella's note also details the distributable reserves of the group, that is the reserves that would be available if all the subsidiaries paid up their reserves as dividends to the parent company (see Table 23.3).

Table 23.3 — Coats Viyella Plc — Annual Report and Accounts — 31 December 1999

Notes to the accounts (extract)

	Group		Company	
	1999	1998	**1999**	1998
25 Total reserves	**£m**	£m	**£m**	£m
Available for distribution	**223.1**	160.2	**426.0**	331.2
Not available for distribution	**330.5**	324.9	**242.1**	242.1
	553.6	485.1	**668.1**	573.3

23.130 Companies may also consider it necessary to give such disclosure when the size of a dividend paid or proposed is substantial, in the context of the total distributable reserves of the company, and there is the risk that the shareholders may be under the mistaken impression that the same level of dividends can be maintained in the future.

Statement of movement on reserves

23.131 As stated in paragraph 23.125, a reserves note is required by the 1985 Act to show movements in each reserve and movements between reserves. (This requirement is expected to be carried forward into the secondary legislation supporting the 2006 Act). Therefore, it is not possible to substitute for share capital and for the movements in the reserves note a figure such as the total recognised gains and losses for the year. That figure, which summarises several different types of reserve movements, must be broken down into its component parts in the reserves note, and transfers between reserves must also be shown in the note. For example, the reserves note is required to show movements between the revaluation reserve and the profit and loss account reserve in respect of previous revaluation surpluses that have been realised in the year. This movement would not be evident from either the profit and loss account or the statement of total recognised gains and losses.

23.132 FRS 3 requires an additional statement or note reconciling movements in shareholders' funds. This reconciliation between opening and closing shareholders' funds should include the components of the total recognised gains and losses of the year. The reconciliation will also include dividends as a deduction from the profit or loss for the year and other movements in shareholders' funds such as share capital issued or redeemed. Since the reconciliation can be provided in the form of a note or in the form of a primary statement, considerable flexibility is given to where this statement appears and thus to the prominence or lack of prominence given to it.

23.133 It may, however, be appropriate to combine the statement of movements on reserves with the reconciliation of movements in shareholders' funds. This can be done by including a column for the total shareholders' funds brought forward from the previous year and carried forward for the year in the reserves note. Siebe plc provides a reconciliation of movements in shareholders' funds that also serves as the reserves note (see Table 23.4).

Table 23.4 — Siebe plc — Report and Accounts — 1 April 1995

Consolidated Balance Sheet (extract)

		Group		Company	
		1995	1994 Restated Note 1	**1995**	1994
	Notes	**£m**	£m	**£m**	£m
Capital and reserves					
Called up share capital	25	**107.1**	106.9	**107.1**	106.9
Share premium account	26	**393.4**	390.1	**393.4**	390.1
Other reserves	26	**(10.3)**	24.7	**217.3**	222.2
Revenue reserve	26	**476.0**	428.4	**64.1**	59.0
Shareholders' funds — equity		**966.2**	950.1	**781.9**	778.2
Minority interests — equity		**79.0**	63.3	**–**	–
		1,045.2	1,013.4	**781.9**	778.2

26 Reconciliation of movements in shareholders' funds (extract)

	Share capital £m	Share premium account £m	Merger reserve £m	Other reserves: Exchange variation reserve £m	Other reserves: Total other reserve £m	Revenue reserve £m	Total £m	1994 Total £m
Group								
At 3 April 1994	106.9	390.1	–	24.7	24.7	428.4	950.1	742.6
Profit attributes to the members of Siebe plc	–	–	–	(35.0)	(35.0)	160.3	125.3	127.0
Dividends	–	–	–	–	–	(51.9)	(51.9)	(47.1)
Rights issue	–	–	–	–	–	–	–	184.3
New Share capital subscribed	0.2	3.3	–	–	–	–	3.5	3.1
Goodwill written off	–	–	–	–	–	(60.8)	(60.8)	(59.8)
At 1 April 1995	107.1	393.4	–	(10.3)	(10.3)	476.0	966.2	950.1

The cumulative amount of goodwill resulting from acquisition which has been written off between 1 April 1984 and 2 April 1994 is £228.9 million, of which £218.6 million has been charged to Merger Reserve and £10.3 million to Revenue Reserve.

Dividends

23.134 The following items should be disclosed in the notes to the financial statements:

- Any amount set aside or proposed to be set aside to, or withdrawn or proposed to be withdrawn from, reserves.
- The aggregate amount of dividends paid during the year (other than those for which a liability existed at the immediately preceding balance sheet date).
- The aggregate amount of dividends that the company is liable to pay at the balance sheet date.
- The aggregate amount of dividends that are proposed before the date of approval of the accounts, and not otherwise disclosed under the second or third bullet above.

[CA85 4 Sch 35A].

23.135 Where equity dividends are shown on the face of the profit and loss account, they should preferably be shown as a footnote, separate from the profit and loss account itself. Although there is no legal prohibition on presenting equity dividends as a deduction from the profit for the period, such a presentation could be regarded as inconsistent with the accounting for equity dividends. In particular, FRS 25 states:

> *"Interest, dividends, losses and gains relating to a financial instrument or a component that is a financial liability shall be recognised as income or expense in profit or loss. Distributions to holders of an equity instrument*

> *shall be debited by the entity directly to equity, net of any related income tax benefit....*" [FRS 25 para 35].

Coupons on financial instruments that are classified as equity under FRS 25 are taken to reserves, not treated as an expense in the profit and loss account. As equity, dividends are a transaction with equity owners and they are not included within the statement of total recognised gains and losses. Instead, the aggregate amount of equity dividends is dealt with in the reconciliation of movements in shareholders' funds.

23.135.1 Prior to accounting periods beginning on or after 1 January 2005, Schedule 4 of the Companies Act 1985 required dividends to be shown within the profit and loss account as a deduction from profit for the period, but this requirement has been deleted for later accounting periods. Therefore, the legal imperative for adopting such a treatment no longer exists. However, it can be argued that the presentation of equity dividends after profit for the financial year as an appropriation, rather than as an expense, is acceptable under UK GAAP.

23.135.2 The question arises as to when a dividend should be recognised as a liability in a company's statutory accounts, with a consequential reduction of distributable profits. Directors have no discretion to pay final dividends. They can propose a final dividend but it does not become a legally binding liability until it is approved by members of a public company in general meeting (or a when a private company's members' written resolution is passed). Thus a proposed, but not approved, final dividend at the balance sheet date is not a legal obligation to shareholders. Therefore, a proposed final dividend is not booked in the financial statements of the year to which it relates, but is recognised in the following period when it is paid. Where a company's articles provide that interim dividends can be declared by directors, such dividends are never a liability until their actual payment as the directors' resolution to pay a dividend can be revoked by them prior to actual payment; no contractual obligation is created. A past history of paying dividends does not give rise to a contractual obligation nor a constructive obligation. (For further discussion, see chapter 22.) This is consistent with FRS 25 para AG13, which states that *"an issuer of non-puttable ordinary shares assumes a liability when it formally acts to make a distribution and becomes legally obligated to the shareholders to do so"*. Similarly, it is consistent with FRS 12, 'Provisions, contingent liabilities and contingent assets', where there is no obligation at the balance sheet date; a liability is not recorded.

23.136 Dividends on shares treated as liabilities are treated as interest expense and recognised on an accruals basis. Regardless of the accounting treatment, dividends can only be paid if the company has sufficient distributable profits; that is, even where a company has charged the dividend on a preference share as interest expense and therefore reduced its balance sheet profit and loss reserve accordingly, it is still prohibited from paying that dividend if there were insufficient distributable profits for that purpose before the accrual was made. Compound financial instruments are divided into their liability and equity components with a consequential effect on amounts recognised as interest expense and distributions. For example, a non-cumulative preference share that is mandatorily redeemable, but with dividends payable at the discretion of the entity is recognised as a liability in respect of the redemption amount (and the unwinding of the discount is classified as interest expense), whilst the dividends relate to the equity component and are recognised as distributions. [FRS 25 para AG37].

23.136.1 The treatment of shares as financial liabilities or compound instruments for accounting purposes has a complex interaction with the legal rules on distributions and capital repayments. Section 5 of Tech 02/07 and its appendix provide ten key principles, underlying statute and common law in respect of distributions and capital maintenance. These principles should be used for determining distributable profits when dealing with such contracts. They illustrate how the principles are applied in eight scenarios involving shares and compound instruments. The appendix provides the detail of the accounting and capital maintenance book-keeping entries. Principles 1, 2 and 3 are particularly relevant for distributions presented as interest expense. In essence, these principles say that dividends accounted for as interest expense are not losses, as a matter of law; that the accounting is an advanced recognition of a future distribution; and that distributable profits are only consumed by a dividend when it is paid or when it is approved by members and becomes a legal liability. [Tech 02/07 paras 5.7 to 5.15]. Consequently, when directors assess whether their companies have sufficient distributable profits to make a distribution they will have to reverse the accounting for dividends that has been charged as interest expense.

23.137 Dividends per share excludes any attributable tax credit. A distinction is not required to be made between the dividends on different classes of equity share, but it is best practice to do so as it enables dividend per equity share to be compared with the relevant earnings per share. The denominator for the calculation of dividends per share would usually be the number of shares on which the dividends are actually paid. Where a dividend was paid in instalments, and the number of shares varied during the year, a weighted average number of shares should be used. The weighted average number of shares for this purpose should be calculated in the same way as the weighted average number of shares used in earnings per share calculations. The method of calculation is set out in paragraph 20 of FRS 22, 'Earnings per share' (see further chapter 14).

23.138 Many listed companies choose to make arrangements for ordinary shareholders to elect to receive their dividends in the form of additional ordinary shares rather than in cash. The share equivalent is sometimes referred to as a scrip dividend or a stock dividend and consists of shares fully paid up out of the company's profits. An advantage of issuing scrip dividends is that, in the short term, the company's cash position would be improved. Such dividends should be recognised in the financial statements at the amount of the cash alternative and the notes to the financial statements should give a full explanation of the situation.

23.138.1 The Listing Rules for listed companies require particulars to be disclosed of any arrangements under which a shareholder has either waived or agreed to waive any dividends. [LR 9.8.4 R (12)].

Realised profits and losses

General principles

23.139 Although section 263(3) of the 1985 Act (section 831(2) of the 2006 Act) provides that a company's available profits for distribution are *"...its accumulated, realised profits ... less its accumulated, realised losses"*, the exact meaning of the term 'realised' is not defined in the Act (see also section 742(2)). Section 262(3) of the 1985 Act (section 853(4) of the 2006 Act) merely gives an indication of the interpretation of the term. It says that *"...references to realised profits and realised losses, in relation to a company's accounts, are to such profits or losses of the company as fall to be treated as realised in accordance with principles generally accepted, at the time when the accounts are prepared, with respect to the determination for accounting purposes of realised profits or losses"*.

23.140 Not only is the definition somewhat circular, there is also little indication in case law of what is meant by 'realised'. The few cases that there have been mainly relate to tax law, rather than to company law. All that can really be derived from the cases is that the judges have interpreted 'realised' as meaning something wider than 'realised in cash', and also that they, like the legislature, see realisation as an accounting concept rather than a strictly legal concept.

23.141 In March 2003, the Institute of Chartered Accountants in England and Wales (ICAEW) and the Institute of Chartered Accountants of Scotland (ICAS) issued guidance in technical release Tech 7/03, 'Guidance on the determination of realised profits and losses in the context of distributions under the Companies Act 1985', which is now *de facto* GAAP on what constitutes a realised profit. The purpose of Tech 7/03 is to identify, interpret and apply the principles relating to determining realised profits and losses for the purposes of making distributions under the Companies Act 1985. It will have continued application for distributions under the Companies Act 2006 when that comes into force. (see paragraphs 23.143.1). It does not provide guidance on how transactions and arrangements should be accounted for in a company's financial statements.

23.142 Separate supplementary guidance has been issued in respect of employee benefits. In December 2004, Tech 50/04, 'Guidance on the effect of FRS 17, 'Retirement benefits' and IAS 19, 'Employee benefits' on realised profits and losses', was issued to clarify the impact of full adoption of FRS 17 and IAS 19 on profits available for distribution (see further chapter 11). In addition, Tech 64/04, 'Guidance on the effect on realised and distributable profits of accounting for employee share schemes in accordance with UITF Abstract 38 and revised UITF Abstract 17', which was also issued in December 2004, clarifies the impact on distributable profits of presenting own shares held through an ESOP trust as a deduction in arriving at shareholders' funds. The guidance in Tech 64/04 on the effect on realised profits and losses of any expenses recognised in accordance with revised UITF Abstract 17 is, in principle, equally applicable to any expense recognised under FRS 20 'Share-based payment'. [Tech 02/07 para 6.124].

23.143 The ICAEW and ICAS issued further guidance in August 2007, a technical release, Tech 02/07, 'Distributable profits: Implications of recent accounting changes'. This includes the guidance that was published in May 2005 in draft technical release Tech 21/05, 'Distributable profits: Implications of IFRS'. Tech 02/07 provides guidance on the effects of reporting under IFRS (and converged UK GAAP) on realised and distributable profits, including the constraints of the net assets test for public companies (see para 23.165 onwards). It identifies a number of issues that may have an effect on companies' ability to pay dividends. It supplements and, in some cases, amends Tech 7/03, 'Guidance on the determination of realised profits and losses in the context of distributions under the Companies Act 1985'. Pending the finalisation of the guidance in Tech 21/05, in December 2005, the ICAEW and ICAS published interim guidance on proposed dividends and payment of dividends in Tech 57/05, 'Distributable profits: Implications of IAS 10 and FRS 21 for dividends'. This interim guidance has also been incorporated into Tech 02/07 paragraphs 6.55 to 6.67.

23.143.1 Neither Tech 7/03 (amended) nor Tech 02/07 deal with the Companies Act 2006. However, as there are only a few limited changes made by the 2006 Act to the distributions regime, the guidance in the technical releases remains applicable after Part 23 of the 2006 Act comes into force from 6 April 2008. The Institutes plan to issue a consolidated technical release in late 2007 of the four technical releases that currently contain guidance relating to the determination of distributable profits. In 2008, the Institutes expect to re-issue the consolidated technical release updated for references to the 2006 Act and dealing with the few limited changes caused by that Act.

23.144 The guidance in Tech 07/03 (amended) is based on the principle that realised profits are primarily those that are realised in the form of 'cash or of other assets the ultimate cash realisation of which can be assessed with reasonable certainty'. [Tech 07/03 (amended) para 10]. In this context, 'realised' may also encompass profits relating to assets that are readily realisable. This would embrace profits and losses resulting from the recognition of changes in fair values, in accordance with relevant accounting standards, to the extent that they are readily convertible to cash. [Amended by Tech 02/07 para 3.8]. Paragraph 28 of FRS 18 states that it is generally accepted that profits shall be treated as realised for the purpose of applying the definition of realised profits in companies legislation only when realised in this form.

23.145 In assessing whether a company has a realised profit, transactions and arrangements should not be looked at in isolation. A realised profit will arise only where the overall commercial effect on the company satisfies the definition of realised profit set out in the guidance. A group or series of transactions or arrangements should be viewed as a whole, particularly if they are artificial, linked (whether legally or otherwise) or circular. [Tech 07/03 (amended) para 12].

Realised profits

23.146 Tech 7/03 (amended) states that a profit is realised where it arises from:

- A transaction where the consideration received by a company is 'qualifying consideration'. Qualifying consideration is defined as:
  - Cash.
  - An asset that is readily convertible into cash (amended by Tech 02/07 para 3.14) (as defined in para 23.147 below).
  - The release, or the settlement or assumption by another party, of all or part of a liability of the company, unless:
    - the liability arose from the purchase of an asset that does not meet the definition of qualifying consideration and has not been disposed of for qualifying consideration; and
    - the purchase and release are part of a group or series of transactions or arrangements. A realised profit will arise only where the overall commercial effect on the company satisfies the definition of realised profit set out in the guidance.
  - An amount receivable in any of the above forms of consideration where the debtor is capable of settling the receivable within a reasonable period of time, there is a reasonable certainty that the debtor will be capable of settling when called upon to do so and there is an expectation that the receivable will be settled.
- The recognition in the financial statements of a change in fair value, in those cases where fair value has been determined in accordance with the fair value measurement guidance in the relevant accounting standards, and to the extent that the change recognised is readily convertible to cash. [Amended by Tech 02/07 para 3.11].
- An event that results in a company receiving qualifying consideration in circumstances where no consideration is given by the company (for example, a 'capital contribution').
- The recognition in the profit and loss account of the profit arising from the use of the marking to market method of accounting (that is, 'at fair value through profit or loss'), in those cases where the method is properly adopted in accordance with law and generally accepted accounting principles (see para 23.152 onwards).
- The translation of a monetary asset that comprises qualifying consideration or a liability denominated in a foreign currency (see further chapter 7).
- The reversal of a loss previously regarded as realised (for example, writing back a charge for impairment or releasing a provision for a specific loss).

- A profit previously regarded as unrealised that has not been capitalised (for example, a revaluation reserve, merger reserve or other similar reserve) becoming realised as a result of:
  - Consideration previously received by the company becoming qualifying consideration.
  - The related asset being disposed of in a transaction where the company receives qualifying consideration.
  - A realised loss being recognised on the scrapping or disposal of the related asset.
  - A realised loss being recognised on the write-down for depreciation, amortisation, diminution in value or impairment of the related asset.
  - The distribution in *specie* of the asset to which the unrealised profit relates.
  - The receipt of a dividend in the form of qualifying consideration when no profit is recognised because the dividend is deducted from the book value of the related investment (for example as required by IAS 27 in the case of dividends out of pre-acquisition profits of subsidiaries). [Amended by Tech 02/07 para 6.107].

  In such situations, the appropriate proportion of the related unrealised profit becomes a realised profit.

- A reduction or cancellation of capital (for example, share capital, share premium account or capital redemption reserve) that is credited to reserves where the reduction or cancellation is confirmed by the court (except to the extent that, and for as long as, the company has undertaken that it will not treat the reserve arising as a realised profit, or where the court has directed that it shall not be treated as a realised profit).
- A reduction or cancellation of capital (for example, share capital, share premium account or capital redemption reserve) that is undertaken by an unlimited company without confirmation by the court. Any credit to reserves represents a realised profit to the extent that the consideration received for the capital:
  - Was qualifying consideration.
  - Has subsequently become qualifying consideration.
  - Has subsequently been written off (for example, by way of depreciation) and the loss arising has been treated as realised.
  - Was originally paid up either by a capitalisation of realised profits or by a capitalisation of unrealised profits or reserves that, had they not been capitalised, would subsequently have become realised.

[Tech 07/03 (amended) paras 16, 18].

23.146.1 The 2006 Act introduces new legislation in relation to reductions in capital; in particular it creates a new 'solvency statement' procedure (see paragraph 23.83.21) which is available to private companies as an optional alternative to the current court procedure (see para 23.83.13). It is expected that for those companies using the solvency statement procedure, amounts credited to reserves following a reduction in capital will be regarded as a realised profit. It is also expected that a company that has accumulated realised losses prior to the capital reduction by 'solvency statement' procedure will have to use the realised profit created by the capital reduction to offset those realised losses before considering any distribution to members; to the extent that the amount of the capital reduction exceeds the accumulated realised losses, it would be available for distribution. This application of any reserve created by a reduction of capital using the 'solvency statement' procedure is expected to be set out in 'The Companies (Shares, Share Capital and Authorised Minimum) Regulations 2008'.

23.147 As used above, the expression 'asset that is readily convertible into cash' means that:

- A value can be determined at which a transaction in the asset or liability could occur, at the date of determination, in its state at that date, without negotiation and/or marketing, to either convert the asset, liability or change in fair value into cash, or to close out the asset, liability or change in fair value.

- In determining the value, information such as prices, rates or other factors that market participants would consider in setting a price is observable.

- The company's circumstances must not prevent immediate conversion to cash or close out of the asset, liability or change in fair value; for example, the company must be able to dispose of, or close out the asset, liability or the change in fair value, without any intention or need to liquidate, to curtail materially the scale of its operations, or to undertake a transaction on adverse terms.

[Tech 07/03 (amended) para 19].

Further guidance on the application of 'readily convertible to cash' is provided in paragraphs 35 to 40O of Tech 7/03 (amended). The position regarding fair value losses is dealt with at paragraphs 29(f), 30A and 30B of Tech 7/03 (amended). [Amended by Tech 02/07 para 3.16].

23.148 Tech 02/07 amended the previous definition of 'qualifying consideration' to ensure that if an increase in an asset's value would be regarded as a realised profit as a result of fair value accounting (see para 23.152 onwards), any profit represented by the receipt of a similar asset would also be a realised profit (which hitherto may not have been the case). [Tech 02/07 para 3.15].

23.149 In addition to those situations that are readily apparent from the definition of realised profit, the following would constitute a realised profit:

- The receipt or accrual of investment or other income receivable in the form of qualifying consideration.
- A gain arising on a return of capital on an investment where the return is in the form of qualifying consideration.
- A gift (such as a 'capital contribution') received in the form of qualifying consideration.
- The release of a provision for a liability or loss that was treated as a realised loss.
- The reversal of a write-down or provision for diminution in value or impairment of an asset that was treated as a realised loss.

[Tech 07/03 (amended) para 28].

Realised losses

23.150 Losses should be regarded as realised losses except to the extent that the law, accounting standards or the guidance in Tech 07/03 (amended) provide otherwise. [Tech 07/03 (amended) para 17]. Realised losses include:

- A cost or expense (other than one charged to the share premium account) that results in a reduction in recorded net assets.
- A loss arising on the sale or other disposal or scrapping of an asset.
- The writing down, or providing for the depreciation, amortisation, diminution in value or impairment, of an asset (with an exception as detailed in para 23.151 below). Where the asset has been revalued, the appropriate proportion of the related unrealised profit becomes a realised profit, thus mitigating the effect of the realised loss – see paragraph 23.146 above.
- The creation of, or increase in, a provision for a liability or loss that results in an overall reduction in recorded net assets. However, when assets are revalued to their fair value, with any unrealised gain being included in the profit and loss account, the deferred tax on that gain should be treated as a reduction in that unrealised gain rather than as a realised loss.
- A gift made by the company (or the release of all or part of a debt due to the company or the assumption of a liability by the company) to the extent that it results in an overall reduction in recorded net assets.
- A loss arising from the use of the marking to market method of accounting.
- A loss arising from fair value accounting where profits on remeasurement of the same asset or liability would be treated as realised profits. [Amended by Tech 02/07 para 3.25].
- Cumulative net losses arising on fair value accounting, unless both: profits on remeasurement of the same asset or liability would be unrealised; and the

losses would not have been recorded otherwise than pursuant to fair value accounting. [Inserted by Tech 02/07 para 3.30].

[Tech 07/03 para 29, 30A, 30B, 31].

With reference to the last bullet point, absent fair value accounting, a loss may need to be recorded for example, in relation to an asset, on the basis of historical/amortised costs less impairment provisions; and in relation to a liability, under either an amortised cost basis of financial instrument accounting or as an onerous contract liability. [Inserted by Tech 02/07 para 3.30].

23.151 Where a fixed asset is revalued to an amount that is below its 'recoverable amount', paragraph 65(b) of FRS 15 requires the loss below recoverable amount to be reflected in the STRGL (rather than the profit and loss account for the year). Paragraph 70 of FRS 15 states that where the recoverable amount is greater than the revalued amount, the resulting difference is clearly not an impairment; in these circumstances the difference is treated as an unrealised loss. Such a loss would become realised in the event of a subsequent scrapping, disposal or impairment of the asset. [Tech 07/03 (amended) para 30, App B28].

Fair value accounting

23.152 As noted in paragraph 23.146 above, a realised profit includes the profit arising from the use of fair value accounting irrespective of whether the profit is recognised in the profit and loss account (for financial instruments at fair value through profit or loss) or in the fair value or available-for-sale reserve (for available-for-sale financial assets). Similarly, a realised loss includes a loss arising from the use of fair value accounting, unless a cumulative net loss arises where both the profits on remeasurement of the same asset or liability would be unrealised; and the losses would not have been recorded otherwise than pursuant to fair value accounting. [Tech 07/03 (amended) para 30A, as inserted by Tech 02/07 para 3.30]. Special considerations apply to whether the profit or loss on remeasurement of a hedging instrument are realised. [Tech 02/07 Section 4].

23.153 Due to the increased use of fair value accounting under IFRS-based standards (which are being incorporated into UK GAAP), in particular IAS 39, 'Financial instruments: Recognition and measurement', (which has been issued in the UK as FRS 26), Tech 02/07 reconsiders the degree to which profits from fair value accounting are realised or otherwise and has inserted appropriate guidance into Tech 07/03 (amended). [Tech 02/07 Section 3].

23.154 Tech 02/07 has revised the definitions and made other amendments to Tech 07/03, and concludes that fair value accounting profits that are 'readily convertible into cash' will fall to be treated as realised. It is highlighted that the changes in the fair value of many, though not all, financial instruments will fulfil this definition; but some will not, such as unquoted equity investments and investments held for strategic purposes. [Tech 07/03 paras 40C, 40D, inserted by Tech 02/07 para 3.17]. However, changes in the fair value of non-financial assets such as investment property and agricultural and biological assets, will rarely, if ever, fulfil the definition. Questions concerning profits and losses from remeasurement of financial instruments that may be affected by the company's own creditworthiness and block discounts for securities traded in an active market are now addressed in paragraphs 40G to 40H and 40I to 40O of Tech 07/03 (amended) respectively, as inserted by paragraph 3.17 of Tech 02/07.

23.155 Tech 02/07 makes it clear that the performance statement (profit and loss account or STRGL) in which an entity recognises a gain or loss will not, itself, be a driver as to whether that gain or loss is considered to be realised for the purpose of distribution. For example, a company that applies FRS 26 may hold one tranche of listed shares as an available-for-sale (AFS) financial asset and also have a second tranche of those shares designated as 'at fair value through profit or loss' (FVTPL). Fair value gains/losses on the AFS tranche are deferred in equity until sale, but those on the FVTPL tranche are taken directly to the profit and loss account. The fair value of both tranches of shares are determined on the same basis from the quote on the relevant market (for example, the Main Market of the LSE or the Plus-listed market) and meet the 'readily convertible to cash' test. Hence, the movements in fair value are treated as realised. It would be illogical if the treatment of the fair value gains or losses on the two tranches of shares were different merely due to which of the two performance statements they passed through.

23.155.1 The fair value of financial instruments may be volatile even though such fair value is properly determined in accordance with FRS 26. Profits arising from changes in fair values of financial instruments may be realised in accordance with the guidance in Tech 7/03 (as amended by Section 3 of tech 02/07), but are also volatile. Consequently, in the context of fair value accounting, volatility is an aspect where directors will need to consider their fiduciary duties and, thus, whether it is prudent to distribute profits arising from fair value changes of financial instruments. [Tech 02/07 paras 2.13 to 2.15].

23.156 As observed in paragraph 23.154 above, not all fair value adjustments will fall to be treated as realised. The concept of 'readily convertible to cash' embraces an unrestricted ability to convert the asset or the change in the fair value of an asset or liability to cash almost instantaneously at the balance sheet date, that is, without protracted negotiations. This is possible within most financial instruments and commodity markets, but is rarely found in others. For example, fair value gains on investment property will rarely pass the 'readily convertible to cash' test due to the period of marketing/negotiation needed to complete a disposal. Although, agricultural and biological assets (which are also held at fair value) are not specifically addressed in the draft guidance, the treatment of their fair value gains and losses should follow the same principles.

Proposed dividends

23.156.1 Paragraphs 6.55 to 6.67 if Tech 02/07, which incorporate the previous interim guidance in Tech 57/05, 'Distributable profits: Implications of IAS 10 and

FRS 21 for dividends', deal with proposed dividends and intra-group dividends from UK companies. The Institutes have determined that, based on legal advice, companies that rely on dividends from UK subsidiaries to support their own distributions will have to require those subsidiaries to pay or approve those dividends before the year end. Recording a dividend on inter-company account does not necessarily constitute payment. In addition, in determining the amount of the dividend to be proposed in respect of one financial year but to be paid in following financial year, companies must consider the known impact of new accounting standards. Similarly, in paying an interim dividend in the current financial year, companies must consider the known impact of new accounting standards. Proposed dividends are discussed in paragraph 23.156.2 below and intra-group dividends are discussed from paragraph 23.157.1 below.

23.156.2 Tech 02/07 amends previous guidance, in paragraph 22 of the original Tech 07/03, relating to the introduction of a new accounting standard and the application of the common law capital maintenance rule in respect of distributions. Previously, in proposing a dividend, directors did not have to consider the known impact of a new accounting standard being introduced in the subsequent accounting period, provided that the proposed dividend was booked in the period to which it related. For example, a proposed dividend for the year ended 31 December 2004 would have been booked in the 2004 annual financial statements. Tech 02/07 now reflects the position at law where a proposed dividend is booked in the next accounting period, when it is approved by members. For example, a proposed dividend for the year ended 31 December 2007 would be booked in the 2008 annual financial statements. Accordingly, to the extent that proposed dividends are no longer accounted for in the preceding period but in the current period, directors will have to take into account the effect of the accounting standards in force in that current period at the time the dividend is proposed and when it is paid. Where a new accounting standard is implemented in the current year, an interim dividend paid in the current year would have to have regard to the effect of the adoption of that new standard on opening distributable reserves even though the 'relevant accounts' may be those of the prior year prepared prior to the implementation of the new standard or adoption of IFRS.

Intra-group transactions

23.157 The principles set out in Tech 07/03 (amended) apply to profits arising from intra-group transactions. The guidance states that, in particular, the provisions of paragraph 12 relating to artificial, linked or circular transactions or arrangements should be applied. Tech 07/03 (amended) includes an appendix dealing with a number of situations as follows:

- Cash pooling arrangements and group treasury functions.
- Dividend received or receivable on an investment in a subsidiary.
- Dividend by a subsidiary to a parent that provides or reinvests the funds in the subsidiary.

- Dividends received out of pre-acquisition profits.
- Sale of an asset by a parent to its subsidiary.
- Sale of an asset by a subsidiary to a parent, followed by a dividend to the parent of the resulting profit (see also para 23.199 onwards).
- Sale of an asset by a subsidiary to a fellow subsidiary followed by a dividend to the parent of the resulting profit.
- Dividend in *specie*.
- Return of capital contribution.

23.157.1 For accounting periods beginning on or after 1 January 2005, UK companies must comply with FRS 21, 'Events after the balance sheet date', (discussed further in chapter 22). Prior to the implementation of FRS 21, interim dividends were booked, under pre-1 January 2005 UK GAAP, when declared by the directors and final dividends were booked when proposed by the directors. Under FRS 21 and FRS 25, dividends are recognised when a liability to pay the dividend is created. This will mean:

- Interim dividends are booked when paid. As a matter of law, in the UK, interim dividends do not become a legal liability until they are paid. This is because they are at the discretion of directors; it is open to the directors to reverse a decision to pay a dividend at any time up to the date of payment. [Tech 07/03 (amended) para B8].
- Final dividends are booked when they legally become a liability. This is when they are approved, either by the members in general meeting or, for private companies, by the members passing a written resolution. [Tech 07/03 (amended) para B8; Tech 02/07 para 6.58].

23.157.2 Dividends are recognised by a receiving company at the same time as the paying company recognises the liability to pay a dividend. Interim dividends are recognised by the paying company when they are paid. Recording a dividend on inter-company account does not necessarily constitute payment (see below). It is open to companies to 'convert' an interim dividend into a final approved dividend (by approval by members in general meeting or, for private companies, by written resolution); final dividends are recorded when approved.

23.157.3 Under FRS 21, it is not possible to record as income a dividend proposed by a UK subsidiary until that dividend is paid or is approved by members; that is, a proposed but not approved final dividend will not be booked in the financial statements of either the paying or the receiving company until it is approved by members of the paying company. In some jurisdictions, the declaration of a dividend by directors creates a liability for the company, because it would require a members' resolution to cancel the payment of that dividend; that is, the discretion as to whether to pay the dividend is removed from the company and rests with the members and thus the obligation to pay remains. In such cases, the receiving company would recognise the dividend receivable when it is declared by the directors. However, where a parent company relies on dividend income from UK subsidiaries to create distributable reserves from which it will pay its own dividend, it will be necessary to ensure that the dividend is paid or approved by members before the parent company's year end, otherwise it will have to prepare 'interim accounts' (under section 272 of the 1985 Act (section 838 of the 2006 Act)) after the year end to support the distribution. The following items would constitute payment; in scenarios other than those discussed below, the position is more complex and depends on the specific facts and circumstances and companies in doubt as to the position may wish to seek legal advice.

- Payment in cash or other assets. (To support a cash distribution by the parent, the 'other assets' received from the subsidiary would have to be 'qualifying consideration', as defined in Tech 07/03 (amended).)
- Recording the dividend in an inter-company account when the effect of the dividend is to reduce the amount previously owed to the subsidiary by the parent.
- Effecting the dividend via a group treasury function, where the subsidiary company instructs the group treasury function to debit the subsidiary's account and credit the parent's account, would constitute payment.
- If there were no doubt as to the paying subsidiary's ability to pay the dividend, payment in respect of individual dividends could be effected by the execution as a Deed of an acknowledgment of liability to pay the amount entered in the accounting records as a payable by the subsidiary and a receivable by the parent company or the constitution of such liability pursuant to an enforceable contract under Scots law. The effect of this latter arrangement is that the subsidiary has paid the interim dividend and the parent has returned value of the same amount to its subsidiary by way of loan without the need for a cash transaction.

[Tech 02/07 paras 6.61 to 6.66].

Other matters

23.158 Where hedge accounting is obtained in accordance with the relevant accounting standards, it is necessary to consider the combined effect of both sides of the hedging relationship to determine whether there is a realised profit or loss in accordance with the criteria in this guidance. [Tech 7/03 (amended) para 33]. Further guidance is included in Section 4 of Tech 02/07.

23.159 Where an asset is sold partly for qualifying consideration and partly for other consideration (for example, a mixed consideration of cash and a freehold property), any profit arising is a realised profit to the extent that the fair value of the consideration received is in the form of qualifying consideration. This approach is sometimes referred to as 'top-slicing'. For example: if the fair value of consideration received is 10 (4 is cash and 6 is freehold property) and if the depreciated historical cost of the asset sold is 5, the total gain is 5 but the realised profit is limited to 4. [Tech 07/03 (amended) para 32]. Paragraph 40B of Tech 7/03 (amended), as inserted by paragraph 3.17 of Tech 02/07, makes clear that the concept of 'top-slicing' into realised and unrealised elements is not relevant when considering profits and losses on remeasurement of assets and liabilities carried at fair value.

23.160 Tech 07/03 (amended) also provides guidance on a number of other areas including the impact of a change in circumstances on realised profits (Tech 07/03 (amended) para 20); foreign exchange profits and losses (Tech 07/03 (amended) para 34; Tech 02/07 paras 6.89 to 6.96) and goodwill (and negative goodwill) in a company's individual financial statements (Tech 07/03 (amended) paras 41 to 44; Tech 02/07 paras 6.120 to 6.123).

Distributable profits

Definition of distribution

23.161 For the purposes of Part VIII of the 1985 Act (Part 23 of the 2006 Act), 'distribution' is defined as any distribution of a company's assets to its shareholders (whether or not it is made in cash), other than a distribution that is made by way of any one of the following:

- The issue of either fully paid or partly paid bonus shares.
- The redemption or the purchase of any of the company's own shares, either out of capital, or out of the proceeds of a fresh issue of shares, or out of unrealised profits in accordance with Part V, Chapter VII of the Act. (Chapters 3, 4 and 5 of Part 18 of the 2006 Act).
- The reduction of share capital by either of the following means:
    - Extinguishing or reducing the liability in respect of share capital that is not paid up.
    - Repaying paid up share capital.
- The distribution of assets to shareholders on a winding-up.

[CA85 Sec 263(2); CA06 Sec 829(1) and (2)].

23.161.1 Where a company reduces its share capital by means of a court confirmation procedure (23.83.13) there are three possible situations where a payment to shareholders is involved. These are:

- An immediate repayment of capital is made to shareholders. This is not a distribution under section 263 of the 1985 Act (section 829 of the 2006 Act).
- A staged repayment of capital where the staged repayment is effected pursuant to the court order. Here the amount of the capital that is reduced and is to be paid out to shareholders at a later date is converted into debt and not into a reserve under section 263 of the 1985 Act (section 829 of the

2006 Act). Again, the payments to shareholders would not be a distribution. As there is an obligation to repay the shareholders over time this legal debt instrument would be classified as a financial liability under FRS 25.

- The amount of share capital that is reduced is transferred to a reserve. The reserve that is set up is then subject to Part VIII of the 1985 Act (Part 23 of the 2006 Act). Such a reserve qualifies as a realised profit having regard to the decision in *Re Quayle Munro Limited [1994]*, which is reflected in Tech 7/03 (amended), subject to any contrary undertaking given to the court. Absent any undertaking given to the court or when such undertaking is lifted, the company will be able to take this reserve into account in determining the amount of any distribution which may be made in accordance with Part VII of the 1985 Act (Part 23 of the 2006 Act).

23.161.2 An unlimited company is able to repay its share capital by passing a special resolution for that purpose, provided that it has the powers to do so in its articles of association. However, the unlimited company is still subject to the same rules on distribution of profit as a limited company and cannot distribute its profits without reference to Part VIII of the 1985 Act (Part 23 of the 2006 Act) because section 263 of the 1985 Act (section 830 of the 2006 Act) does not distinguish between limited and unlimited companies. Accordingly, if an unlimited company creates a reserve following a reduction of capital, that reserve is subject to the provisions of Part VIII of the 1985 Act (Part 23 of the 2006 Act). However, Tech 7/03 (amended) only allows for this reserve to be a realised profit if the share capital that has been reduced had been paid up in qualifying consideration or the consideration had become so over time (for example, the consideration may have been a property that was subsequently sold for cash). An unlimited company may have unrealised profits that it is not able to distribute. It can, nevertheless, capitalise these profits as share capital, then effect a reduction of capital with immediate or staged repayment to shareholders.

Conditions applying to companies (other than investment companies)

23.162 Any company (whether public or private) may make a distribution only out of *"profits available for the purpose"*. [CA85 Sec 263(1); CA06 Sec 830(1)]. In this sense, the word 'make' means 'pay'. Therefore, a company must have available sufficient profits at the time it pays a dividend not just at the time it declares one.

23.163 For any company other than an investment company or an insurance company, profits available for distribution are the company's accumulated realised profits that have not previously been either distributed or capitalised, less its accumulated realised losses (insofar as they have not been previously written off in either a reduction or a re-organisation of capital). [CA85 Sec 263(3); CA06 Sec 830(2)(3)]. The origin of these profits and losses may be either revenue or capital. [CA85 Sec 280(3); CA06 Sec 853(3)].

23.164 In general, provisions for depreciation or diminution in value of assets and provisions that are necessary to provide for a liability or a loss must be treated as realised losses for the purpose of determining the amount of distributable profits [CA85 Sec 275(1); CA06 Sec 841(1)(2)]. The exception to this rule is where a provision in respect of a diminution in value of a fixed asset is found to be necessary when all the fixed assets of the company (or all the fixed assets other than goodwill) are revalued. This exception is discussed from paragraphs 23.179 and 23.214.

Additional conditions applying to public companies

23.165 In addition to the condition that it can make a distribution only out of profits available for the purpose, a public company can make a distribution only to the extent that the distribution does not reduce the amount of the company's net assets below the aggregate of its called-up share capital (see para 23.18) plus its undistributable reserves (the 'net assets test'). [CA85 Sec 264(1), CA06 Sec 831(1)(6)].

23.166 In this context, 'undistributable reserves' include:

- The share premium account.
- The capital redemption reserve.
- The excess of accumulated unrealised profits that have not previously been capitalised over accumulated unrealised losses that have not previously been written off by a reduction or a reorganisation of capital. For this purpose, capitalisation includes the issuing of bonus shares, but it excludes transfers of profits to the capital redemption reserve that have been made after 22 December 1980.
- Any reserve that the company, for any other reason, is prohibited from distributing. For instance, revaluation reserves in respect of property, plant and equipment are unrealised profits. Also, under the guidance in technical release, Tech 02/07, a cash flow hedge reserve would be an unrealised profit or loss, until the hedged transaction affects profit or loss. A fair value or available-for-sale reserve may, however, be wholly or partly realised, depending on whether the assets fair valued are 'readily convertible into cash'.

[CA85 Sec 264(3); CA06 Sec 831(4)].

23.166.1 Although not specifically mentioned in section 831 of the 2006 Act, the redenomination reserve is also an undistributable reserve. It may be used to pay up fully paid bonus shares, but is otherwise regarded as part of the company's paid up share capital. [CA06 Sec 628].

23.167 The effect of this additional condition for a public company is that whereas a private company can make a distribution provided only that it has realised profits available, a public company can only do so if it has profits available after it has taken into account any net unrealised losses.

23.167.1 Increasingly, the accounting treatment of some classes and portions of share capital as liabilities and some components of compound financial instruments that are legally debt within shareholders' funds is creating debits and credits that are not easy to interpret for determining their effect on the section 264 of the 1985 Act (section 831 of the 2006 Act) net assets test. This makes it difficult to assess whether a public company's profits available for distribution are subject to a restriction. The Institutes, in what is now Section 5 of Tech 02/07 (Issues arising from IAS 32 (and its equivalent, FRS 25)), developed and codified with English and Scottish Counsel some principles for dealing with these items. There are four principles that are set out as Principles 7 to 10 in section 5 of Tech 02/07:

- The treatment of certain shares wholly as liabilities under FRS 25 does not in itself affect the application of the section 264 of the 1985 Act (section 831 of the 2006 Act) net assets test for public companies and thus does not restrict distributable profits. [Tech 02/07 principle 7 para 5.24]. (See para 23.168.)

- A debit to shareholders' funds arising from an advanced recognition of a future distribution or capital repayment does not form part of share capital and undistributable reserves (as defined) for the purposes of section 264 of the 1985 Act (section 831 of the 2006 Act) and thus restricts distributable profits for public companies under that section. [Tech 02/07 principle 8 para 5.31]. This happens, for example, when dividends are treated, and accrued, as interest expense. Legally this is an advanced recognition of the distribution.

- On initial recognition, split accounting for compound financial instruments does not restrict distributable profits for public companies under section 264 of the 1985 Act (section 831 of the 2006 Act). [Principle 9, para 5.35 Tech 02/07]. Split accounting a compound instrument that is legally a share is neutral to the net assets test. However, where the compound instrument is legally a debt, any credit to shareholders' funds reflects an increase in net assets, but not a corresponding increase in "share capital and undistributable reserves". This imbalance has the effect of mathematically reducing any pre-existing restriction on distributable profits. It does not create distributable profits. (See para 5.37 of Tech 02/07).

- The accretion of the liability component of compound financial instruments reduces distributable reserves for public companies under section 264 of the 1985 Act (section 831 of the 2006 Act) unless the instrument is legally a debt. [Tech 02/07 principle 10 para 5.38]. Where a compound financial instrument is legally a share and has been split accounted into its debt and equity components, the 'interest charge' for the accretion of the debt component is not a loss as a matter of law and has no effect on share capital and undistributable reserves. Consequently, the initial credit to shareholders' funds, which is legally share capital (and share premium) cannot absorb the accumulating 'interest charge' debited ultimately to the profit and loss account reserve due to the accretion of the liability. Hence, under the section

264 of the 1985 Act (section 831 of the 2006 Act) net assets test, the amount that a public company can distribute is restricted by the accumulated amount of 'interest charge' debit. This debit over time will cumulatively equal the initial credit to shareholders' funds. (See para 5.39 of Tech 02/07). This problem is not encountered where the compound instrument that has been split accounted is legally debt as the 'interest charge' can be off-set by the initial credit to shareholders' funds and thus does not cause a restriction on a public company's profits available for distribution. (See para 5.40 of Tech 02/07).

23.167.2 Similar issues are confronted with some aspects of share-based payment accounting, Tech 64/04 and paragraphs 6.124 to 131 of Tech 02/07 provide guidance on the impact these have on companies in general and on the section 264 of the 1985 Act (section 831 of the 2006 Act) net assets test for public companies specifically.

23.168 As indicated earlier, under FRS 25, financial instruments are presented according to the substanceof their contractual terms, determined by the principles contained within that standard (see further chapter 6). This will have the effect of increasing or decreasing a company's net assets for the purposes of section 264 of the 1985 Act (section 831 of the 2006 Act). For instance, where preference shares are presented as a liability, net assets will be reduced by that amount. Under section 270 of the 1985 Act (section 836 of the 2006 Act), net assets for the purposes of section 264 of the 1985 Act (section 831 of the 2006 Act) are those shown in the 'relevant accounts' prepared in accordance with applicable accounting standards; that is, the UK GAAP individual financial statements.

23.169 Legally, although some shares and related share premium are shown in two places on the balance sheet, this does not reduce the total share capital and related share premium. However, in accordance with section 270 of the 1985 Act (section 831 of the 2006 Act), the amount of share capital and undistributable reserves for the purpose of applying the 'net asset test' is determined by reference to the amount as stated in the company's relevant accounts. Therefore, the amount of share capital and related share premium that has been presented as a financial liability should be excluded from the amount of share capital and undistributable reserves for the purpose of applying section 264 of the 1985 Act (section 831 of the 2006 Act). This was confirmed in the BERR (formerly the DTI) guidance notes on applying Statutory Instrument 2004/2947, 'The Companies Act 1985 (International Accounting Standards and Other Amendments) Regulations 2004'.

23.170 Consequently, the presentation of preference shares as a liability does not result in an immediate restriction in the amount of profits available for distribution by a public company under section 264 of the 1985 Act (section 831 of the 2006 Act). [Tech 02/07 para 5.24].

23.171 The table below, which sets out extracts from the balance sheets of four companies, gives examples of the method of calculating distributable profits.

Examples of distributable profits in private and public companies

	Company 1		Company 2		Company 3		Company 4	
	£	£	£	£	£	£	£	£
A share capital		1,000		1,000		1,000		1,000
B Unrealised profits	150		150		150		–	
C Unrealised losses	–		(200)		(200)		(200)	
D Net unrealised profits		150		–		–		–
E Net unrealised losses		–		(50)		(50)		(200)
F Realised profits	300		300		300		300	
G Realised losses	–		–		(120)		(120)	
H Net realised profits		300		300		180		180
I Share capital and Reserves		1,450		1,250		1,130		980
Maximum distributable profit:								
Private company (H)		300		300		180		180
Public company (H-E)		300		250		130		Nil

Provisions relating to investment companies

23.172 Investment companies may make a distribution either on the basis of the *capital maintenance* test applicable to all public companies (see para 23.165) or on the basis of an *asset ratio* test (see para 23.175).

23.173 Subject to the conditions listed in paragraph 23.174 below, an investment company may make a distribution at any time out of those of its accumulated realised *revenue* profits that have not previously been either distributed or capitalised, *less* its accumulated *revenue* losses (realised and unrealised, and only insofar as they have not been previously written off in a reduction or re-organisation of capital). The advantage of this is that capital losses may be ignored, although the other side of the coin is that realised capital profits cannot be included and the asset ratio test in paragraph 23.175 below must be satisfied. An investment company is, therefore, able to satisfy the HM Revenue and Customs condition of non-retention of income, because it may make distributions even where the value of its investments has fallen.

23.174 The conditions which must be satisfied before an investment company may make a distribution on this basis are:

- The company's shares must be listed on a recognised investment exchange other than an overseas investment exchange within the meaning of the Financial Services and Markets Act 2000. [CA85 Sec 265(4)(a); CA06 Sec 832(5)].

- During the period beginning with the first day of the accounting reference period immediately preceding that in which the proposed distribution is to be made (or, where the distribution is proposed to be made during the company's first accounting reference period, the first day of that period) and ending with the date of that distribution, the company must not have:

- Distributed any of its capital profits.
- Applied any unrealised profits or capital profits (whether realised or unrealised) in paying up debentures or any amounts unpaid on any of its issued shares. This means that company may not distribute indirectly any amounts that are not available for distribution directly.

[CA85 Sec 265(4)(5); CA06 Sec 832(5)(6)].

- The company must have given the Registrar of Companies notice of its intention to carry on business as an investment company at one of the following times:
  - Before the beginning of the period referred to in the point immediately above.
  - As soon as reasonably practicable after the date on which the company was incorporated.

  [CA85 Sec 265(6); CA06 Sec 832(5)].

  This condition is necessary to prevent companies adopting investment company status merely for a particular distribution and who might then revoke that status only to adopt it again for the purpose of the next distribution.

- The amount of the company's assets must be at least 50 per cent greater than the aggregate of its liabilities. [CA85 Sec 265(1)(a); CA06 Sec 832(1) to (3)]. In this context, 'liabilities' includes any provision other than for depreciation of diminution in the value of assets. [CA85 Sec 265(2), 4 Sch 89; CA06 Sec 832(4)]. However, the company must not include any uncalled share capital as an asset in those financial statements that are used to determine the legality of any distribution. [CA85 Sec 265(3); CA06 Sec 832(7)]. Although 'creditors' is not defined for this purpose in the Act, it is the clear intention of the legislators that this amount should exclude amounts in respect of shares. 'Liabilities to creditors', therefore, excludes amounts in respect of share capital and share premium that have been presented as financial liabilities. It also excludes other amounts due to shareholders in their capacity as such, including accruals for dividends and redemption premiums that have been presented as expenses in the profit and loss account and liabilities in the balance sheet. It does not exclude general accruals, deferred income or deferred tax. [Tech 02/07 para 6.10].

23.175 Where all the above conditions are satisfied, an investment company may make a distribution, but only to the extent that the distribution does not reduce the company's assets below 150 per cent of the aggregate of its liabilities. [CA85 Sec 265(1)(b)], CA06 Sec 832(1) to (3)].

23.176 The following example sets out extracts from the balance sheets of four companies. The example shows how investment companies calculate their distributable profits and contrasts this with how other companies calculate their distributable profits:

Examples of distributable profits in private and public companies

	Company 1		Company 2		Company 3		Company 4	
	£	£	£	£	£	£	£	£
A Share capital		1,000		1,000		1,000		1,000
B Share premium		100		100		100		100
C Unrealised capital profits	600		600		600		600	
D Unrealised revenue profits	–		–		100		100	
E Unrealised Capital losses	–		(700)		(700)		(700)	
F Unrealised revenue losses	–		(250)		(250)		(250)	
G Net unrealised reserves		600		(350)		(250)		(250)
H Realised revenue profits	1,200		1,200		1,200		1,200	
I Realised capital profits	–		–		100		100	
J Realised capital losses	–		–		–		(600)	
K Realised revenue losses	–		–		(150)		(150)	
L Net realised reserves		1,200		1,200		1,150		550

	Company 1	Company 2	Company 3	Company 4
	£	£	£	£
M Share capital and reserves	2,900	1,950	2,000	1,400
N Total liabilities	1,300	1,300	1,300	1,300
O Total assets	4,200	3,250	3,300	2,700
Maximum distributable profits—				
Special rules for an investment company				
(i) per section 265				
The lower of:				
(a) Realised revenue profits (H) less accumulated revenue losses (K + F)	1,200	950	800	800
(b) 150 per cent asset test, O–(1½ × N)	2,250	1,300	1,350	750
Amount distributable	1,200	950	800	750
Normal rules for a public company				
(ii) per section 264 (the lower of L and (L + G))	1,200	850	900	300

Effect of revaluations of fixed assets on distributable profits

23.177 The revaluation of fixed assets can affect the amounts recorded in the profit and loss account and distributable profits in the following ways:

- Depreciation on revalued assets passes through the profit and loss account.
- The profit on revalued assets that are subsequently sold may not pass through the profit and loss account.

- The revaluation itself may involve writing off depreciation that has previously been charged to the profit and loss account.
- Diminutions in value of assets may need to be taken to the profit and loss account.

Depreciation of revalued fixed assets

23.178 When fixed assets are revalued, depreciation charged to the profit and loss account must in accordance with FRS 15 be based on the asset's carrying value of the asset rather than its original cost. Provisions for the depreciation of revalued fixed assets require special treatment to the extent that they *exceed* the amounts that would have been provided if the assets had not been revalued. For the purpose of calculating the amount of profit that is legally available for distribution, a company is required to treat an amount equivalent to the excess depreciation on the revaluation surplus as a realised profit. [CA85 Sec 275(2), CA06 Sec 841(5)]. In this way, the provision for depreciation that is charged in the profit and loss account is reduced to the amount that would have been charged on the asset's original cost.

23.179 As a result, when fixed assets have been revalued, the depreciation of the 'surplus element' will not normally affect the amount of a company's accumulated distributable profits. However, it will affect its annual profits as stated in the published financial statements since the depreciation charge in the profit and loss account will included the 'surplus element'.

Example

Ignoring the effect of taxation, a revaluation would have the following effect on the profit and loss account:

Example of depreciation adjustment for revalued fixed assets

	Cost	Valuation	Difference between cost and valuation
	£	£	£
Fixed assets	1,000	2,500	1,500
Profit before depreciation	5,000	5,000	N/A
Depreciation at 10% a year	100	250	150
Profit after depreciation	4,900	4,750	150

Therefore, without the requirement of section 275(2) of the 1985 Act (section 841(5) of the 2006 Act) to treat an amount equal to the difference between the depreciation of the asset at cost and at a valuation as a realised profit, the distributable profit would be £4,750. This is because the profit in the financial statements is the profit after charging depreciation on the revalued amount. The effect of section 275(2) of the 1985 Act (section 841(5) of the 2006 Act) is to add back the additional depreciation of £150 (that arises because the assets have been revalued) in determining the profits available for distribution.

Without this requirement of the Act, companies might be discouraged from revaluing their fixed assets, because the extra depreciation charged on the revalued amount would have the effect of reducing their profits available for distribution. (Of course, companies might be discouraged from revaluing their assets despite this, because of the effect of the additional depreciation on their reported profits.)

23.180 The difference between the depreciation based on the historical costs and on revalued amounts should also form part of the note of historical cost profits and losses required by FRS 3. This is illustrated in Table 23.5. NFC plc adjusts for the 'surplus depreciation' in both its historical cost profits and losses note and in its reserves note.

Table 23.5 — NFC plc — Annual Report & Accounts — 1 October 1994

Group Historical Cost Profits and Losses

	1994	1993
		As restated
	£m	£m
Profit on ordinary activities before taxation	**105.6**	104.9
Revaluation surpluses realised on sale of properties	**5.1**	3.5
Difference between depreciation based on historical costs and on revalued amounts	**1.2**	1.2
Historical cost profit on ordinary activities before taxation	**111.9**	109.6
Historical cost retained profit for the year	**30.6**	53.7

Notes to the Accounts (extract)

25 Reserves (extract)

	Revaluation reserve £m	Profit and loss account £m
Profit for the financial year	–	73.4
Dividends	–	(49.1)
	–	24.3
Elections for shares under share dividend plans	–	1.4
Unrealised deficit on revaluation of properties	(5.7)	–
Transfer of revaluation surpluses realised on disposals of properties	(5.1)	5.1
Transfer of difference between depreciation based on historical costs and on revalued amounts	(1.2)	1.2
Goodwill written off	–	(13.6)
Translation differences on net investment in non-sterling assets	(0.1)	2.6
Movements in the year	(12.1)	21.0
At 2 October 1993 as previously reported	83.5	144.2
Prior year adjustment (note 9)	–	(1.4)
At 1 October 1994	71.4	163.8

The revaluation reserve arises in respect of the revaluation of certain properties.

Subsequent sale of revalued assets

23.181 Reserve adjustments are also required for items taken to reserves that may properly be included in determining distributable profits. For example, an unrealised profit on a property revaluation will originally be included in the statement of total recognised gains and losses and credited to a revaluation reserve. When the property is subsequently disposed of, the whole profit is clearly realised, notwithstanding the fact that all or part of it may not have been passed through the profit and loss account. However, since the gain was previously recognised in the statement of total recognised gains and losses, it is not recognised again in the profit and loss account when it is realised. The gain or loss on the disposal of the asset must be calculated by reference to its carrying value rather than its original cost in accordance with FRS 3 paragraph 21. (Note that for companies applying FRSs 23 and 26, FRS 3 was amended for accounting periods commencing on or after 1 January 2007 to allow the recycling of gains and losses from reserves through the STRGL to the profit and loss account. [FRS 3 para 12B].)

23.182 The note of historical cost profits and losses provides users of accounts with details of all profits that have been earned in the period based on historical cost figures regardless of whether the profits have previously been recognised as unrealised. Therefore, this note should contain an adjustment to restate profits and losses on the sale of assets onto the historical cost basis. This same adjustment will also need to be made as a transfer between the revaluation reserve and the profit and loss account reserve so that the profit and loss account reserve contains the realised profit. For example, Table 23.5 includes such an adjustment in both its note of historical cost profits and its reserves note. With effect for accounting periods commencing on or after 1 January 2007, paragraph 26 of FRS 3 was amended to read *"The effects of fair value accounting under FRS 26 and hyperinflation adjustments under FRS 24 (IAS 29) Financial Reporting in Hyperinflationary economies and UITF Abstract 9 Accounting for Operations in Hyper-inflationary Economies are not required to be included in this reconciliation, but this omission should be noted"*.

23.183 In addition, where a revalued asset is disposed of, any deficit below cost that has previously been treated as unrealised should be redesignated as a realised loss. For example, if a revaluation of an investment property resulted in a diminution in value below cost that the directors believed was temporary then, in accordance with SSAP 19, the deficit would be taken to the revaluation reserve and reported in the statement of total recognised gains and losses rather than being included in the profit and loss account. When the asset is subsequently sold, the profit or loss on disposal should be calculated based on the carrying value and the deficit on the revaluation reserve relating to the asset should be transferred to the profit and loss account reserve.

Example

An investment property that originally cost £10m was revalued down to £8m in previous years. The directors considered that the decrease in value was temporary and the deficit was included in the revaluation reserve. During the year the property was sold for £9m. The table below shows the profit and loss account and the profit and loss account reserve for the sale of the revalued property and the sale of the property if the revaluation had not taken place.

Loss based on historical cost and revalued amount

	Historical cost	Revalued amount
	£'m	£'m
Proceeds	9	9
Cost/carrying value	10	8
Profit and loss account for the year	(1)	1
Transfer from revaluation reserve	-	(2)
Effect on profit and loss account reserve	(1)	(1)

The realised loss recorded in the profit and loss account reserve of £1m is the same regardless of whether the temporary diminution in value had previously been recorded.

23.184 Where an asset's original cost is not known, or where it is not possible to ascertain it without unreasonable delay or expense, then for the purpose of determining whether the company has made a profit or loss in respect of that asset, its cost is taken to be the value shown in the company's earliest available record of its value. [CA85 Sec 275(3), CA06 Sec 842].

Provision for impairment

23.185 A provision for depreciation or impairment of a fixed asset, to the extent that it does not offset a previous revaluation surplus on that asset, must normally be treated as a realised loss. Such a realised loss cannot be reduced by being offset (either wholly or in part) against revaluation surpluses on other assets (whether or not they are of the same class). There is, however, an exception to this contained in section 275 of the 1985 Act (section 841 of the 2006 Act). The provisions of this section of the Act are complicated and are considered from paragraph 23.214.

Foreign currency translation

23.186 The accounting standard applied by companies preparing their financial statements in accordance with UK GAAP will depend on whether or not they have adopted FRS 26. Those that have adopted FRS 26 are required to apply FRS 23, 'The effects of changes in foreign exchange rate', while those that have not adopted FRS 26 are required to apply SSAP 20, 'Foreign currency translation'. These standards are considered in detail in chapter 7.

23.187 SSAP 20 and FRS 23 both require that a company should translate into its functional currency those of its currency transactions that are outstanding at the end of the year (for example, creditors for fixed assets purchased from overseas and currency loans) using the rate of exchange at the balance sheet date (that is, the closing rate). Where, however, the rate of exchange is fixed under the terms of the relevant transaction, SSAP 20 (but not FRS 23) requires the company to use that rate. [SSAP 20 para 48].

23.188 Exchange gains and losses will arise both on the currency transactions a company completes during the year and on the retranslation to its functional currency of its monetary items in the balance sheet. Tech 07/03 (amended) (see para 23.146) states that a profit is realised where it arises from the translation of a monetary asset which comprises qualifying consideration, or a liability denominated in a foreign currency. [Tech 7/03 (amended) para 16]. This is considered in more detail in chapter 7.

23.189 Under SSAP 20 or FRS 23, where a company has a foreign branch with a functional currency that is different from that of its parent, the exchange differences arising on the translation of the branch's assets and liabilities into the functional currency of the parent are taken directly to reserves via the STRGL. The issue is to what extent are these exchange differences realised or unrealised. Paragraph 6.92 of Tech 02/07 advises that the gross profits and losses should be analysed separately according to the nature of the assets and liabilities on which they arise. A profit that arises on the retranslation of an asset that comprises qualifying consideration, or a liability, is a realised profit in accordance with paragraph 18(d) of Tech 7/03 (amended). However, a profit arising on the retranslation of assets that do not constitute qualifying consideration (for example, property, plant and equipment) is an unrealised profit. A loss arising on retranslation is treated as a realised loss, unless it is the reversal of an unrealised profit. It is, therefore, possible that there is a realised loss to be taken into account when determining profits available for distribution, even though the net amount on the reserve is a profit. [Tech 02/07 para 6.92].

23.189.1 Tech 02/07 warns that the above analysis applies only in straightforward situations where the composition of the foreign branch's assets has not changed significantly during a period. For example, it would not be appropriate to regard the exchange differences related to the amount of the opening cash balance (that is, the beginning to the end of the year exchange difference computed in relation to that part of the opening net assets equal to the opening cash balance) as realised if that cash balance had not existed throughout the period. For example, it might have been invested in a new property, which is not qualifying consideration. Other differences arise when the branch's profit and loss account is translated at the average rate for the year and the profit or loss for the year is translated at closing rate, the profit or loss for the year arises on changes in the amounts and/or composition of the branch's assets and liabilities (for example, on an exchange of inventory for cash). Thus taking together the exchange differences on retranslation of the branch's profit or loss for the year and on its opening net assets, the total amount arises in relation to an asset base that changes throughout the year. To establish whether these exchange differences are realised, partly realised or unrealised takes careful analysis. [Tech 02/07 paras 6.93 to 6.95].

23.189.2 While a company must always measure its foreign currency assets, liabilities and transactions in its functional currency, FRS 23 permits (and SSAP 20 is generally understood not to allow) a company to present its individual financial statements in any currency, referred to as a presentation currency. For example, a company that has pounds sterling as its functional currency may choose to present its financial statements in US dollars or in euros. It is these presentation currency financial statements that are the company's 'relevant accounts' for justifying a distribution and thus it is the presentation currency by which the amount of profits available for distribution is measured. [Tech 02/07 para 6.90]. However, included in the presentation currency financial statement's shareholders' funds are the exchange differences thrown up in the process of translation into the company's presentation currency. These exchange differences are similar to those that arise when dealing with a foreign branch with a different functional currency as described above (see para 23.189.2). Paragraph 6.96 of Tech 02/07 notes that the nature of these exchange differences is complex, but does not address whether they are realised or unrealised. Nevertheless, we believe that directors should be conservative in their consideration of these exchange differences bearing in mind their fiduciary duties.

23.189.3 As noted in paragraph 23.187, where hedge accounting is obtained in accordance with the relevant accounting standards, it is necessary to consider the combined effect of both sides of the hedging relationship to determine whether there is a realised profit or loss in accordance with the criteria in Tech 07/03 (amended). [Tech 07/03 para 33 as amended by Tech 02/07 para 4.2]. Where a company undertakes a fair value hedge of a foreign currency risk, the gross profits and losses on remeasuring the hedging instrument and the hedged item for the hedged risk are both recognised in the profit and loss account. In the case of foreign currencies, these are generally very liquid and active markets, thus both the profit on one side of the hedge relationship and the loss on the other will be realised by reference to the 'readily convertible to cash' criterion and other criteria. In such cases no special consideration of hedging aspects is required (including hedge effectiveness and ineffectiveness). [Tech 02/07 para 4.4]. However, if the currency being hedged is illiquid or inactive, further analysis is required. Paragraphs 4.5 and 4.6 of Tech 02/07 explain how the principle in the amended paragraph 33 of Tech 07/03 is applied when the profit is not realised. Consideration of cash flow and net investment hedges and whether gains and losses in those hedge relationships are realised or unrealised is given in paragraphs 23.124.2 to 23.124.3.

Capitalisation of development costs

23.190 Where development costs are shown as an asset in the financial statements, any amount in respect of those costs should be treated as a realised loss, unless there are special circumstances justifying the directors' decision not to treat the costs as a realised loss and certain statements are made in the notes to the financial statements. [CA85 Sec 269, CA06 Sec 844]. Where development costs are capitalised in accordance with SSAP 13 (see chapter 15), these special circumstances generally exist. The note to the financial statements that states the special circumstances that permit the company to capitalise development costs must state also that the development costs have not been treated as a realised loss and the justification (the special circumstances contained in SSAP 13) the directors used for adopting this treatment. [CA85 Sec 269(2), CA06 Sec 844(2)(3)].

23.191 Tech 07/03 (amended) notes that companies that carry forward costs in accordance with the requirements of accounting standards will normally be able to justify these costs not being treated as a realised loss. [Tech 07/03 (amended) App B29; Tech 02/07 paras 6.116 to 119].

Goodwill

23.192 When goodwill arises on consolidation, there is no effect on the realised and distributable profits because it is individual companies that make distributions not groups. However, where goodwill arises in a company (which would be the case, for example, where the company has purchased an unincorporated business), questions arise as to whether and how any write-off of goodwill would affect distributable profits.

23.193 Where goodwill is capitalised in a company's balance sheet, any amortisation or impairment charges reduce its distributable profits.

23.194 Where goodwill pre-dating FRS 10, 'Goodwill and intangible assets', remains written off to a company's reserves under the standard's transitional arrangements, the goodwill write-off should be transferred from unrealised to realised reserves over its estimated useful economic life. This will reduce realised reserves on a systematic basis in the same way as if the company had capitalised and amortised the goodwill. [FRS 10 App V para 2]. This preserves the treatment that paragraph 42 of Tech 7/03 (amended) advocates when considering the transition from SSAP 22 to FRS 10 under UK GAAP.

23.195 Where negative goodwill pre-dating FRS 10 remains credited to reserves, a company should credit it initially to an unrealised reserve (see further chapter 25). Under the principles in Tech 07/03 (amended), negative goodwill up to the fair values of the non-monetary assets acquired should be treated as being realised in the periods in which the non-monetary assets are recovered, whether through depreciation or sale. Where the negative goodwill exceeds the value of the non-monetary assets, this excess should be treated as being realised in the periods expected to benefit. However, negative goodwill should not be treated as a realised profit in the case of a sale of the non-monetary asset where the consideration received is not qualifying consideration. [Tech 07/03 (amended) para 43, as amended by Tech 02/07 para 6.123].

Transactions within the group

23.196 Where consolidated financial statements are prepared, the relevant distributable profits will be the parent company's realised profits. This is because distributable profits must be established for individual companies and not for groups of companies. Consequently, a situation may arise where the group has sufficient distributable profits in aggregate to make a desired distribution, but the parent company itself has insufficient distributable profits. In this situation, a distribution may not be made to the parent company's shareholders without distributions first being made from the subsidiaries to the parent company to pass the distributable profits to the parent. The parent company must then prepare relevant accounts that account for the receipt of these distributions in order to justify a distribution to its shareholders (see from para 23.203 below). However, these relevant accounts need only include the parent company's financial statements (not the consolidated financial statements), because it is the parent company that will make the distribution.

23.196.1 FRS 21, 'Events after the balance sheet date', impacts on the timing of recognising dividends payable and receivable. This may have significant implications for the distributable profits of some companies. It will not be possible to recognise dividends receivable from subsidiaries and associates that were declared after the balance sheet date. In order to be recognised at the year end, the dividends have to be *"appropriately authorised and no longer at the discretion of the entity"*. Interim dividends do not become a liability of UK companies until they are paid and final dividends do not become a liability until they are approved by a general meeting. [Tech 07/03 para B8] (see further chapter 22). Therefore, companies may need to consider paying up interim dividends before the balance sheet date to ensure that the parent company has adequate distributable reserves to support the expected level of the proposed final dividend. [Tech 02/07 paras 6.55 to 6.67].

23.197 If a parent company or a subsidiary has fixed assets that have been revalued in accordance with the alternative accounting rules, the revaluation surplus taken to revaluation reserve is unrealised. However, if the company sells these revalued assets to another company within the same group for qualifying consideration, essentially cash or cash equivalents, the revaluation surplus attaching to those assets in the company's revaluation reserve is realised. The amount is *prima facie* available for distribution. Similarly, a parent company could sell one of its subsidiaries to another subsidiary at more than its carrying amount for qualifying consideration and thus generate a gain on disposal that would, prima facie, be a realised profit available for distribution. These transactions should be carried out at arm's length and supported by proper legal documentation. (Transactions undertaken at an undervalue are considered from paragraph 23.244.) The fact that a transaction is undertaken between companies in the same group need not prevent the profit on the transaction being realised and therefore distributable. However, a profit arising on an intra-group transaction is unlikely to be a realised profit if, for example, the transaction (and any related arrangements) results in an increase in the inter-company balance between the companies involved. [Tech 7/03 (amended) para 18].

23.197.1 Although a realised profit may be generated in the vendor group company, further consideration is required as to whether any dividend made out of a profit arising on an inter-group transaction is a realised profit for the recipient group company. It may not be a realised profit where the recipient group company has been directly or indirectly involved in funding the inter-group transaction and thus the dividend it receives. This is particularly so when a series of transactions considered in the whole show that there is a circular flow of cash provided by a recipient group company and, as such, there is no incremental cash coming into the recipient group company or its sub-group. Appendix A of Tech 07/03 (amended) considers a number of inter-group transactions and the principles to be applied to determine whether the paying group company has made a realised profit or whether the receiving group company has received an amount that it can treat as a realised profit. In addition, Tech 02/07 gives guidance on what constitutes 'payment' in a group context (see para 23.157.3).

23.198 Furthermore, transactions undertaken at other than fair value and transactions undertaken when one of the parties to the transaction has net liabilities or no distributable reserves may be unlawful. Such transactions are considered from paragraph 23.244.

[The next paragraph is 23.201.]

Pre-acquisition profits

23.201 Pre-acquisition profits are those profits earned by a subsidiary company before it is acquired by a group. Following a change brought about by the Companies Act 1981, in certain circumstances, it is now possible for a parent company to distribute to its shareholders pre-combination profits arising in its subsidiaries (see the example below).

Example

The situation is similar to that described in the example in paragraph 23.200 above, except that the realised profit in the subsidiary represents pre-acquisition reserves. Pre-acquisition reserves are a company's retained earnings at the date on which that company becomes a subsidiary of another company. Before the enactment of the Companies Act 1981, where a subsidiary paid a dividend to its parent company out of its pre-acquisition profits, the parent company would treat the dividend received as a reduction of the cost of its investment in that subsidiary. Consequently, dividends the subsidiary paid to the parent company out of pre-acquisition profits were not available for distribution to the parent company's shareholders.

However, the Companies Act 1981 amended paragraph 15(5) of the then Schedule 8 to the Companies Act 1948. This change had the effect that where a subsidiary now pays a dividend to its parent company out of pre-acquisition profits, that dividend need not necessarily be applied as a reduction in the cost of the investment in the subsidiary.

[FRS 6 App 1 para 16]. Such a dividend should be applied to reduce the carrying value of the investment to the extent that it is necessary to provide for a diminution in value of the investment in the subsidiary as stated in the parent company's financial statements. To the extent that this is not necessary, it appears that the amount received will be a realised profit in the hands of the parent company. However, in this example, on consolidation, any part of the dividend received by the parent company that has not been applied to reduce the cost of the investment, will need to be adjusted on consolidation by taking out of the parent company's realised reserves an amount that will cause the goodwill on consolidation to remain the same as in previous years. If, as in the example in paragraph 23.200, the parent company decides to distribute these funds to its shareholders, the transaction may need to be explained further if the consolidated financial statements are to give a true and fair view.

Other transactions

23.202 A bed and breakfast transaction is one in which a company agrees to sell certain assets (such as securities) to a third party (normally a broker) and arranges to repurchase them, or identical assets, shortly thereafter, usually overnight, for the same price. Such transactions are normally undertaken to crystallise a capital gain or loss for tax purposes. They may also be undertaken in an attempt to turn an unrealised revaluation gain on investments into realised and therefore distributable profits. Bed and breakfast transactions are examples of sale and repurchase transactions to which the provisions of FRS 5 apply. In general, they are unlikely to create realised profits. Chapter 3 considers the implications of such transactions.

Relevant accounts

23.203 The 1985 Act (and the 2006 Act) states that, in order to determine whether a company has profits available, and (if it is a public company) whether the additional condition in paragraph 23.165 above has been satisfied, reference must be made to certain items in the company's 'relevant accounts'. [CA85 Sec 270(2); CA06 Sec 836(1)].

23.204 The items to be referred to in the 'relevant accounts' are:

- Profits, losses, assets and liabilities.
- Provisions of any kind.
- Share capital and reserves (including undistributable reserves).

[CA85 Sec 270(2); CA06 Sec 836(1)].

23.205 The 'relevant accounts' are normally the company's latest audited individual financial statements that have been laid before a public company in general meeting or sent to the members of a private company. [CA85 Sec 270(3); CA06 Sec 836(2), 837(1)]. (See also Tech 02.07 paras 2.9 and 2.10.) However, where a distribution would exceed the amount that is distributable according to the latest audited financial statements, *interim accounts* must be prepared and used in addition to the latest financial statements to justify the payment. These additional financial statements are necessary to enable a proper judgement to be made of the amounts of any of the relevant items referred to in paragraph 23.204. [CA85 Sec 270(4)(a); CA06 Sec CA06 Sec 836(2), 838(1), 839(1)]. These interim accounts are different from the half yearly reports required from listed companies under the UKLA's Disclosure and Transparency Rules.

23.206 Furthermore, *initial accounts* must be prepared and used where a public or private company proposes to make a distribution during its first accounting reference period or before the date on which it lays its first audited financial statements before its shareholders. [CA85 Sec 270(4)(b); CA06 Sec 836(2), 838(1), 839(1)]. These initial accounts must be such as to enable a reasonable judgement to be made of the amounts of the items mentioned in paragraph 23.204.

23.206.1 As mentioned in 23.189.2, the company's directors can choose to present the company's individual financial statements in a currency other than its functional currency, a presentation currency, as permitted by FRS 23. It is those presentation currency financial statements that are sent to members of a private company or laid before members of a public company in general meeting, that are the company's 'relevant accounts'. Hence, any profits available for distribution are measured in that presentation currency. However, the use of a presentation currency creates some complex issues regarding whether the retranslation profits and losses are realised, partly realised or are unrealised.

23.207 The legislation regarding 'relevant accounts', although of importance to all companies, is particularly important for investment trusts because they are required to distribute the majority of their reserves each year. Consequently, an interim dividend is unlikely to be covered by the retained reserves included in their last financial statements. Therefore, generally, such companies will need to prepare interim accounts in order to pay an interim dividend legally.

23.208 The Act lays down strict requirements in respect of the relevant accounts used for the purposes of testing the legality of a distribution. Failure to comply with these requirements will mean that the distribution will be unlawful. [CA85 Sec 270(5); CA06 Sec 836(3) and (4)]. The shareholders cannot agree to waive the requirements. [*Re Precision Dippings Ltd v Precision Dippings Marketing Ltd* [1985] Ch 447]. The requirements set out in paragraph 23.209 do not apply to a private company's interim or initial accounts and, as a consequence, they may use management accounts for this purpose to support a distribution, provided that, as mentioned above, such accounts enable the directors to make a reasonable judgement as to the profits available for distribution. [CA85 Sec 270; CA06 Sec 836]. It may be that the management accounts need to be adjusted for the sort of closing adjustments that are made when preparing the annual financial statements. A private company's interim or initial accounts are not required to be published (that is, filed with the Registrar of Companies).

23.209 The requirements for relevant accounts, that is the published annual financial statements of all companies and the published *interim and initial accounts* of public companies, are as follows:

- They must be 'properly prepared', or they must be so prepared at least to the extent that is necessary in order to decide whether or not a proposed distribution is legal. In particular, the items referred to in paragraph 23.204 above must be determined. [CA85 Secs 271(2), 272(2), 273(2); CA06 Sec 837(2), 838(3), 839(3)].

  For annual financial statements, 'properly prepared' means that they must comply with Part VII of the Act (Part 15 of the 2006 Act). For either *interim or initial accounts,* it means that they must comply with section 226 of the Act (that is, applying that section and sections 226A and 226 B of the 1985 Act (sections 396 and 397 of the 2006 Act) and Schedule 4 to the 1985 Act with such modifications as are necessary, because the accounts are prepared otherwise than in respect of an accounting reference period). These accounts will, therefore, include a balance sheet, income statement and related notes. However, directors' reports (required by Schedule 7 to the 1985 Act) and cash flow statements (which are not required by the Act) need not be included. It also means that the balance sheet comprised in those accounts has to be signed by the directors in accordance with the Act. [CA85 Secs 272(3), 273(3); CA06 Sec 838(4)(5), 839(4)].

- They must give a true and fair view of both the state of the company's affairs (financial position) and its profit or loss. [CA85 Secs 271(2), 272(3), 273(3); CA06 Secs 837(2), 838(4)(5), 839(4)].

- They must not include, for a public company, any uncalled share capital as an asset. [CA85 Sec 264(4); CA06 Sec 831(5)].

- With annual financial statements, the auditors must have given their opinion on them in accordance with section 235 of the 1985 Act (sections 475 and 495 of the 2006 Act). [CA85 Sec 271(3); CA06 Sec 837(3)(4)]. So far as *initial accounts* are concerned, the auditors must have reported whether, in their opinion, those accounts have been properly prepared. [CA85 Sec 273(4); CA06 Sec 839(5)(6)]. *Interim accounts* need not be audited.

- If the auditors have qualified their opinion on annual or initial accounts, they must state, in writing, whether the subject matter of their qualification is material, by reference to the items listed in paragraph 23.204, in determining the legality of the proposed distribution.

  [CA85 Secs 271(3)(4), 273(4)(5); CA06 Secs 837(3)(4), 839(4) — (6)].

- With annual financial statements, this statement will suffice if it relates to distributions of the same description as the distribution proposed (see para 23.223 below). [CA85 Sec 271(5); CA06 Sec 837(5)]. Such statements must have been laid before the shareholders of a public company in general meeting or sent to the members of a private company. [CA85 Sec 271(4); CA06 Sec 837(4)].

- With *initial accounts*, a copy of those accounts, together with a copy of the auditors' report and such statement (where applicable), must have been delivered to the Registrar of Companies before the proposed distribution is made. [CA85 Sec 273(6); CA06 Sec 839(7)].

- With *interim accounts*, a copy of the accounts must be delivered to the Registrar of Companies before the proposed distribution is made. [CA85 Sec 272(4); CA06 Sec 838(6)].

23.210 If any document in a set of accounts that must be delivered to the Registrar of Companies is in a foreign language, a certified translation (see chapter 26 for an explanation) of that document must also be delivered to the Registrar of Companies. [CA85 Secs 242(1), 272(5), 273(7); CA06 Secs 441(1)(2), 445(1)(2), 446(1)(2), 447(1)(2), 838(6), 839(7)].

23.211 A company may find that it does not have sufficient distributable reserves shown in its last relevant accounts to justify paying an interim dividend. Where this is so, the company will have to prepare *interim accounts* and, with a public company, will have to deliver them to the Registrar of Companies (in the way outlined above) to justify the payment of the interim dividend. Also if the company is listed on the Main Market of the LSE or on the Plus-listed market, the company should also release the interim accounts, as soon as they are available, to a Regulatory Information Service as they may contain price-sensitive information. The UKLA's Listing Rules also require that the company notify a Regulatory Information Service of any decision to make a distribution. [LR 9.7.2 R (2)].

23.211.1 It is a relatively common failing for directors of public companies to neglect to send the *interim or initial accounts* to the Registrar of Companies before the proposed distribution is made. If this occurs, it renders the distribution unlawful and remedies have to be put in place to legitimise the dividend. Due to the legal implications for the directors (see section 277 of the 1985 Act (section 847 of the 2006 Act) for the civil penalties), such remedies require legal advice. They may require that the distribution is repaid by the recipients and the whole process started again. Repayment may be an option where the recipient is another group company or only a few individuals. However, for a listed company this is impracticable and other solutions are necessary.

23.212 A particular set of financial statements may have been used to determine whether a distribution can be made. If it is proposed to determine the legality of a subsequent distribution by reference to the same financial statements ('relevant accounts'), the amount of the proposed distribution must be notionally increased by the amount of the earlier distribution. [CA85 Sec 274(1); CA06 Sec 840(1)]. This is to compare the total distributions made by reference to these relevant accounts to the distributable profits contained in them. The object of this requirement is to prevent a company avoiding the restrictions by making several small distributions that are permissible individually, but which, when taken in aggregate, exceed the amount available for distribution.

23.213 Similarly, a set of financial statements used to determine whether a distribution can be made must be adjusted by the amount of financial assistance for the purchase of own shares out of distributable profits or certain payments in respect of, or in connection with, the purchase of own shares if the assistance was provided since the financial statements were prepared. [CA85 Sec 274(2); CA06 Sec 840(1) and (2)].

Treatment of revalued assets in relevant accounts

23.214 Paragraph 23.162 sets out the basic conditions for establishing profits available for distribution, that is, a company's accumulated realised profits less its accumulated realised losses, and that provisions for depreciation of assets must be treated as realised losses. Section 275(1) of the 1985 Act (section 841(1) of the 2006 Act) permits, as an exception, that a provision for depreciation or diminution in value of an asset, to the extent that it does not offset a previous revaluation surplus on that asset, may not need to be treated as a realised loss. However, a company needing to rely on the complicated provisions of section 275 of the 1985 Act (section 841 of the 2006 Act) in order to have sufficient distributable profits to pay a dividend, is likely to have other difficulties and would be well advised to seek legal advice before relying on section 275 of the 1985 Act (section 841 of the 2006 Act). The provisions of these sections of the Acts are complicated and the purpose of the following section is to clarify these requirements.

23.215 Surprisingly, where a company revalues all of its fixed assets (meaning all its assets which are intended for use on a continuing basis in the company's activities)and takes advantage of section 275 of the 1985 Act (section 841 of the 2006 Act), then even where an actual revaluation shows an overall deficit, the diminution in value of the asset that is being accounted for can still be treated as an unrealised loss for distribution purposes, even if it has been accounted for through the profit and loss account for the period. However, the diminution in value of the asset that is being accounted for will reduce a public company's distributable profits if, as a result of the provision, there is a net deficit on the revaluation reserve. This is because a public company's distribution must not reduce its net assets to less than its share capital plus undistributable reserves (see para 23.165 above).

23.216 In determining whether a revaluation of a company's fixed assets has taken place for the purposes of the exception from section 275(1) of the 1985 Act (section 841(1), (2) of the 2006 Act), the directors' *consideration* of the value at any particular time of any fixed asset may be treated as a revaluation. [CA85 Sec 275(4); CA06 Sec 841(4)]. 'Consideration' does not necessarily mean the directors must value each asset as an individual item. It simply means that the directors should have addressed themselves to the question of the asset's value for the purpose of determining the legitimacy of distributions. However, a company may take advantage of the exception from section 275(1) of the 1985 Act (section 841(1), (2) of the 2006 Act) only where the conditions below are satisfied.

23.217 The conditions referred to in paragraph 23.216 above that must be satisfied are as follows:

- All the company's fixed assets (or all those other than goodwill) have been revalued, either by an actual revaluation or by the directors' consideration of their value.
- The directors' consideration of the value of those fixed assets that have not actually been revalued must take place at the same time as, and must consider the value at the same date as, the revaluation that recognised the particular asset's diminution in value.
- Where there has been no actual valuation, the directors are satisfied that the aggregate value of the fixed assets that they have treated as having been revalued by virtue of their considering the assets' value at the time in question, is not less than the aggregate amount at which those assets are, for the time being, stated in the company's financial statements. [CA85 Sec 275(5); CA06 Sec 841(4)]. (See para 23.219 for the statement to be made in the notes to the financial statements.)

23.218 For example, Table 23.6 contains such disclosures made by Berisford International plc as well as a reconciliation of the profit and loss reserve to the distributable reserves.

Table 23.6 — Berisford International plc — Annual Report & Accounts —30 September 1992

Notes to the accounts (extract)

24. Revaluation reserve		**1992**	1991	
	Group £m	**Company £m**	Group £m	Company £m
The movement for the year comprised:				
At 1 October	-	**328.2**	84.2	585.2
Revaluation in year				
investments in subsidiary entities *(Notes 12 & 25)*	-	**(46.7)**	-	(257.0)
tangible fixed assets *(Note 11)*	-	-	(1.0)	-
Transfers to profits and loss account on disposal of subsidiary entities	-	**(4.7)**	(83.2)	-
At 30 September	-	**276.8**	-	328.2

25. Profit and loss account (extract)		**1992**	1991	
	Group £m	**Company £m**	Group £m	Company £m
The movement for the year comprised:				
At 1 October	**81.5**	**(246.7)**	(93.1)	(338.4)
(Loss) profit for the financial year (i)	**(67.1)**	**(20.5)**	62.1	74.8
Currency relignment	**(0.8)**	**(2.3)**	2.9	(10.2)
Transfer from other reserves and revaluation reserve (Notes 23 & 24)	-	**4.7**	114.0	27.1
Share of goodwill written of by associated undertakings	**(1.6)**	-	(4.4)	-
At 30 September	**12.0**	**(264.8)**	81.5	(246.7)

(i) The Directors have revalued the Company's investments in subsidiary entities at 30 September 1992 to their underlying net assets values. The Directors have considered the value of the remaining fixed assets and are satisfied that these are worth, in total, not less than the aggregate amount at which they are stated in the Company's accounts. Accordingly, in accordance with Section 275 of the Companies Act 1985 the aggregate provision does not fall to be classified as a realised loss and therefore distributable reserves of the Company are £12.0m (1991 £81.5m) as analysed below:

	£m	£m
Profit and loss account	(264.8)	(246.7)
Provisions against investment in subsidiary entities	332.4	396.9
Excess of provisions over surpluses on revaluation of investments in subsidiary entities	(55.6)	(68.7)
Distributable reserves	12.0	81.5

23.219 In addition, the directors will not be able to use this consideration to justify treating a provision as unrealised unless the notes to the relevant accounts state that:

- The directors have considered the value of some of the company's fixed assets, without actually revaluing those assets.
- The directors' consideration of the value of those assets that have not been revalued took place at the same time as, and considered the values at the same date as, the revaluation that recognised the particular asset's diminution in value.
- The directors are satisfied that the aggregate value of those assets whose value they have considered was not less than the aggregate amount at which those assets are or were stated in the company's accounts.
- The asset or assets that have diminished in value are recorded in the company's relevant accounts after providing for that diminution in value.

[CA85 Sec 275(6); CA06 Sec 841(4)].

23.220 The examples below serve to illustrate the effect of section 275 of the 1985 Act (section 841 of the 2006 Act) in different situations.

Values of all of a company's fixed assets

	Book value	Market value	Deficit
	£000	£000	£000
Land and buildings	1,000	750	250
	50	40	10
	1,050	790	260

Example 1

The market value of all of the fixed assets has been determined by a professional valuation. The diminutions in value may, therefore, be treated as unrealised losses, even though there is an overall deficit of £260,000. The reason for this is that the deficit results from a revaluation of all the fixed assets. [CA85 See 275(1); CA06 Sec 841(1)(2)].

Example 2

The market value of the land and buildings has been determined by a professional valuation, but the market value of the plant and machinery results from the directors' consideration of its value. Because the aggregate value of the assets that the directors have considered is £40,000, which is less than their book value of £50,000, the directors cannot claim to be satisfied that those assets' aggregate value is not less than their book value. The directors are, therefore, not able to rely on the exception from section 275(1) of the 1985 Act (section 841(1), (2) of the 2006 Act) and so they must treat the deficit on the revaluation of the land and buildings as well as the deficit on the plant and machinery as a realised loss. [CA85 Sec 275(5); CA06 Sec 841(4)]. However, if the directors had *valued* the assets rather than merely considering their value, both deficits would result from a revaluation of all the fixed assets and the diminutions in value would be treated as unrealised losses. [CA85 Sec 275(1); CA06 Sec 841(1)(2)].

Example 3

If the directors considered that the plant and machinery's market value was £60,000 (not £40,000), then they would be able to treat the deficit on the land and buildings of £250,000 as unrealised. This applies even though the fixed assets have an overall deficit of £240,000.

However, in both the first and the third examples, if the company were a public company, it might still be prevented from making a distribution even if it could treat the loss as unrealised. This is because a distribution must not reduce the amount of a public company's net assets below the aggregate of its called-up share capital plus its undistributable reserves. [CA85 Sec 264(1); CA06 Sec 831(1)(6)].

Interpreting section 275 of the 1985 Act (section 841 of the 2006 Act)

23.221 The interpretation of the provisions of section 275 of the 1985 Act (section 841 of the 2006 Act) may cause difficulties in certain circumstances. The responses to the questions discussed below are based on guidance given by Counsel on the application of section 275 of the 1985 Act, which it appears reasonable to read across to section 841 of the 2006 Act. However, the guidance given below should not be relied upon in isolation and directors should take their own legal advice in the light of their company's particular facts and circumstances and on the application of section 841 of the 2006 Act.

Question 1

Where a provision has been charged to realised profits, and it is subsequently released, does this restore the realised profits in question?

Where an asset has been either written down or provided against and it is then written up again, the initial reaction is that the write-up constitutes a profit that *prima facie* appears to be unrealised. However, it seems correct that the write-up should be treated as a realised profit to the extent that the previous reduction was charged to realised profits. (This view is supported by *Bishop v Smyrna and Cassaba Railway Co*. [1895] 2 Ch 596, in particular at 601, and by *Stapley v Read Bros*. [1924] 2 Ch 1.) Furthermore, paragraph 19(3) of Schedule 4 requires a company to write back such a provision no longer required to the profit and loss account. The write-back to the profit and loss account will fall to be treated as realised. It has subsequently been confirmed in paragraph 16(e) of Tech 07/03 (amended) (see para 23.146).

Question 2

In what order should releases of provisions be applied where provisions have been made in previous years, and where some of these have been treated as realised losses and some as unrealised losses?

The principle expressed above is easy enough to apply when all provisions have been charged against the same reserve and where the whole of a particular provision is restored at the same time. It seems that there is no established authority or principle that lays down any rule where the position is less simple. The best solution would seem to be to apply common sense. This approach leads to the conclusion that the more recent parts of the provision should normally be regarded as being released before the earlier parts.

Question 3

What is the meaning of the words 'value' and 'the company's accounts' in sections 275(4) and 275(5) of the 1985 Act respectively?

It seems clear that the word 'value' in section 275(4) of the 1985 Act means market value, and not book value.

The question arises whether the 'company's accounts' that are referred to in section 275(5), are those financial statements (to, say, 30 September 19X5), which are in the course of preparation, and in which the directors have adjusted the assets' book values (by taking into account depreciation, for example), or the previous financial statements (that is, those to 30 September 19X4).

When section 275(4) is relied on, section 275(6) of the 1985 Act deals with the contents of the note to the financial statements where the directors have considered the value of any of the company's fixed assets, without actually revaluing those assets. Section 275(6)(b) requires the notes to state:

> *"That they (the directors) are satisfied that the aggregate value of those assets at the time in question is or was not less than the aggregate amount at which they are or were for the time being stated in the company's accounts."*

This note makes it clear that the company's accounts for the purpose of section 275(5) are those in which the revaluation is incorporated. Thus the directors must compare actual values with the values at which the relevant assets are to be incorporated in the accounts.

This view is supported by the fact that the section 275(4) procedure, including the requirement for a section 275(6) note, applies also to *initial accounts* being prepared.

Question 4

If no dividend is to be paid by reference to the relevant accounts, but the directors have considered the value of the company's fixed assets in accordance with section 275(4) of the 1985 Act, does section 275(6) require that the note that is needed if a distribution is to be made to be included in those relevant accounts?

Relevant accounts are those financial statements that contain the entries that justify a particular distribution, either because they show adequate distributable profits or because they have been specially prepared in order to justify the distribution. (This interpretation seems clear from section 270 generally and, in particular, from subsections (2) and (3) and the introductory words of sections 271(1), 272(1) and 273(1).)

Consequently, it appears to follow that, if a company does not propose to justify a particulars distribution by reference to a particular set of financial statements, section 275(6) does not require those financial statements to contain the special note, because those financial statements are not *relevant accounts*.

Accordingly, it seems that the note that section 275(6) requires need not appear in the financial statements either for the year in which the section 275(4) revaluation took place, or for a subsequent year, unless those financial statements are to be relied upon for the purpose of justifying a distribution.

However, if the note is excluded from the financial statements, the directors cannot use those financial statements to justify a distribution in the future. Although the directors may have no plans at that time to make a distribution, they may wish to do so at some time before the next audited financial statements are prepared. If they have not included the note required by section 275(6) in their last set of financial statements, then they will need to prepare *interim accounts* to justify the proposed distribution. Consequently, it will be sensible to include in the financial statements the note that section 275(6) requires, even where the directors do not intend at that time to make a distribution.

However, for a private company, the note need not appear in the *interim* or the *initial accounts* that the directors rely upon to justify making a distribution. This is because sections 272 and 273 do not apply to private companies.

Question 5

Where the note that section 275(6) of the 1985 Act requires is not included in a company's financial statements, does this omission convert a provision on a revaluation that is made in those financial statements into a realised loss for all future financial statements that are to be used as relevant accounts?

It appears that any financial statements that are used to justify a distribution are *relevant accounts*. And, for the purposes of section 275(6), they are the relevant accounts, even if the directors do not need to rely on the particular section 275(4) revaluation in order to justify a current distribution. Accordingly, if a set of financial statements that does not contain a note relating to a section 275(4) revaluation that took place in either that year or a previous year, become *relevant accounts* (because they are used to justify a distribution), it seems that the provision that is made on that revaluation becomes, and must remain, a realised loss. Where it becomes necessary to rely on section 275(4) to justify a subsequent distribution, it will be too late to include the section 275(6) note in a subsequent set of financial statements.

This last point, however, is a difficult issue and it is still the subject of debate. Consequently, this is another reason why it is advisable to include in any financial statements the note that section 275(6) requires, even where a distribution is not to be made by reference to those financial statements.

Summary of action relating to section 275 of the 1985 Act (section 841 of the 2006 Act)

23.222 To summarise, therefore, when the directors have some of the company's assets valued, and provisions for diminution in value arise that affect the company's ability to pay a dividend, the directors, after taking legal advice, may wish to:

- Consider the value as at the same date of all other assets (excluding goodwill) themselves at the same time that the valuation of the assets that shows the deficit is made.
- Include the note referred to in paragraph 23.219 above in the financial statements for the year in which the valuation took place. The directors should do this even if they do not intend to rely on their consideration of the value to justify a distribution.
- Repeat that note in all subsequent financial statements, because they may become *relevant accounts* for the purpose of making a distribution in the future.

If the directors take these three steps, any provisions that arise from a revaluation of the company's assets may be treated as unrealised for the purpose of ascertaining the profits available for distribution unless the value of the assets considered, but not revalued, by the directors is less than their book value. (see para 23.220 example 2).

Qualified audit reports and distributions

23.223 If the auditors have qualified their opinion and the company is proposing to pay a dividend based on those financial statements as the relevant accounts, the auditors must state in writing whether the subject matter of their qualification is material in determining the legality of the proposed distribution. [CA85 Secs 271(3)(4), 273(4)(5); CA06 Secs 837(3)(4), 838(6)]. This statement must be laid before the company in general meeting. [CA85 Sec 271(4); CA06 Sec 837(4)]. A qualified audit report is a report that is not a report without qualification to the effect that, in the auditors' opinion, the financial statements have been properly prepared in accordance with the Act. [CA85 Secs 271(3), 273(5); CA06 Secs 837(3)(4), 839(6)].

23.224 Therefore, for an audit report that contains an emphasis of matter paragraph, but which is unqualified, there would appear to be no legal requirement for the auditors to make a statement under section 271(4) of the 1985 Act (section 837(4) of the 2006 Act). However, in some instances, if there is an emphasis of matter paragraph about, for example, going concern, it may also be uncertain whether the directors would be acting in the best interests of the company if they pay a dividend and they would be wise to seek legal advice in such circumstances.

23.225 Many companies pay interim dividends and the previous year's annual financial statements that the auditors have reported on will constitute the *relevant accounts* for the purposes of those interim dividends. Accordingly, auditors should, whenever possible, word their statement to cover any future distributions. If the statement is not worded to cover future distributions but only covers the final dividend recommended by the directors in those annual financial statements, the auditors will need to make a further statement in respect of any interim dividends.

23.226 The implication of a qualified audit report may be either *favourable* or *unfavourable*. An audit qualification may be material for distribution purposes, but in a favourable sense. For example, it may be possible to say that if any adjustment was to be made to eliminate the need for the qualification, it could have the effect only of increasing the company's net assets or realised profits. In this situation, the qualification is regarded as *favourable* for distribution purposes. An *unfavourable* qualification means that the profits available for distribution could be less than the amount inferred from the financial statements ('relevant accounts').

23.227 Where the effect of the auditors' qualification is *favourable*, the auditors could include the following additional statement in their report:

"In our opinion, the qualification is not material for the purpose of determining whether any distribution payable by reference to these financial statements is permitted under Sections 263(830) (and 264 (831) for public companies only) of the Companies Act 1985(2006)."

23.228 Where the auditors can quantify the effect of an audit qualification that is *unfavourable* but not material for the purpose of determining a distribution up to a certain amount, they could word the additional statement in their report as follows:

"In our opinion, the qualification is not material for the purpose of determining whether distributions not exceeding £X in total payable by reference to these financial statements are permitted under Sections 263(830) (and 264(831) for public companies only) of the Companies Act 1985 (2006)."

23.229 If the auditors can word their statement on these lines and not restrict it to the legality of the recommended final dividend only, they will not need to make a further statement in respect of the next interim dividend. If, however, the auditors do have to make a further statement, the company will have to hold a general meeting to lay the statement before the shareholders.

Other matters

Bonus issues

23.230 Companies may use the revaluation reserve in order to issue bonus shares. In this situation, the revaluation reserve would be debited with the nominal value of the shares issued and the paid up share capital in equity would be credited with an equivalent amount, if the bonus shares qualify as equity shares under FRS 25. If the bonus shares are not equity shares under FRS 25, they will be recognised as financial liabilities.

23.231 Section 264(3) of the 1985 Act (section 831(4) of the 2006 Act) defines a company's undistributable reserves as including "*the amount by which the company's accumulated unrealised profits, so far as not previously utilised by capitalisation . . . exceed its accumulated, unrealised losses (so far as not previously written off in a reduction or reorganisation of capital duly made)*". Capitalisation is defined as including every description of capitalisation except a transfer of the company's profits to its capital redemption reserve on or after 22 December 1980. (The 2006 Act removes *"on or after 22 December 1980"* from the definition but a saving provision in section 848 retains an equivalent effect.) This definition implies that a company may utilise its undistributable reserves, such as a revaluation reserve, for bonus issues. In addition, there is no specific provision in the Act that requires the revaluation reserve to be reinstated if it has been utilised in a manner the law permits.

23.232 Companies may not make bonus issues unless their articles of association expressly permit them to do so. Therefore, newly-incorporated companies must take express power in their articles to make bonus issues out of unrealised profits (for example, as detailed in article 110 of Table A, as set out in SI 1985/805, for the purposes of the 1985 Act). However, companies that existed before 22 December 1980 need not alter their articles to do this if immediately before that date they had power under their articles to capitalise unrealised profits. With companies that existed at 22 December 1980, this means that a power in the articles to make bonus issues out of profits available for dividend will be deemed to include a power to make bonus issues out of unrealised profits. A saving provision in the 2006 Act retains this position. [CA85 Sec 278; CA06 Sec 848(1)(2)].

Amounts unpaid on debentures and shares

23.233 A company may not apply an unrealised profit to pay up debentures or any amounts that are unpaid on its issued shares. [CA85 Sec 263(4); CA06 Sec 849]. The purpose of this prohibition is to prevent profits that are not available for distribution being made available indirectly for dividend purposes.

Profits and losses made before 22 December 1980

23.234 The commencement date of the 1980 Companies Act was 22 December 1980. This Act introduced statutory distribution rules including concepts of realised and unrealised profits, for the first time. As a result, transitional measures were required.

23.235 Where, after making all reasonable enquiries, the directors are unable to determine whether a profit or a loss that was made before 22 December 1980 is realised or unrealised, they may treat the profit as realised and the loss as unrealised. [CA85 Sec 263(5); CA06 Sec 850(1) to (3)]. This provision prevents problems occurring if no record exists of the original cost of an asset or the amount of a liability.

Memorandum and articles of association

23.236 Distributions are not only influenced by the provisions of the Act: they may also be subject to any enactment, or any rule of law or any provision in the memorandum or articles of association that may restrict either the amounts available for distribution or the circumstances in which a distribution may be made. [CA85 Sec 281; CA06 Sec 852]. For example, investment companies are restricted by their memorandum and articles of association from distributing realised capital profits.

23.237 It is important, therefore, for the directors to have regard to the memorandum and articles, as well as to the statutory rules, before making a distribution. Also, it would probably be unlawful as a matter of common law to pay a dividend if, as a result, the company either became insolvent, or had insufficient working capital to carry on its business in the foreseeable future.

Accounting for distributions in kind

23.238 A company may make a distribution that includes or comprises a non-cash asset. FRS 25 states that distributions to holders of an equity instrument should be debited by the entity directly to equity but the amount to be debited is not specified. [FRS 25 para 35]. The question is whether the paying company should measure the distribution at book value or at fair value of the assets concerned. When the distribution is in the form of cash or a short-term monetary asset the book value and fair value of such assets are likely to be close and, therefore, the distinction between book and fair value treatments does not arise. Where the asset being distributed is carried at fair value, its book and fair value are one and the same. However, the position is less clear when the asset to be distributed is a non-monetary asset, such as an investment in a subsidiary or a property, which is carried at cost. Should the paying company use the historical cost amount or its fair value to measure the amount of the distribution? There are supporting arguments for either a book or a fair value accounting treatment. At the time of writing, both treatments are acceptable.

23.238.1 Where the asset to be distributed has been included in the relevant accounts, and part of the amount at which it is stated represents an unrealised profit (that is, the asset has been revalued and a revaluation surplus has been included in the revaluation reserve), the Act allows that unrealised profit to be treated as realised for the purpose of the distribution. [CA85 Sec 276(a), CA06 Sec 846(1)(2)]. However, the company's articles must contain a power to make distributions in specie (non-cash distributions). Table A, as set out in SI 1985/805, for the purposes of the 1985 Act, contains this power in article 105 and it requires the dividend to be approved at a general meeting. The dividend is declared as a cash amount and it is for the directors to satisfy themselves as to the asset's value.

23.239 The company making the distribution may recognise the dividend at the book value of the asset that is being distributed or at the fair value of the asset being distributed. Where the company's accounting policy is to carry the asset at fair value, the dividend would be shown at fair value. Consequently, a surplus or a deficit (which is the difference between the asset's previous net book value and its fair value) may have to be accounted for in the company's financial statements. Any deficit would be reflected in the company's profit and loss account as an amount written off the assets. A surplus would be recognised in the profit and loss account or STRGL, depending on the asset involved and the company's accounting policy. Similarly, where the company's accounting policy is to carry the asset at cost (less depreciation, if applicable) but the company elects to recognise the dividend at the fair value of the asset distributed, any surplus or deficit (the difference between the asset's net book value and its fair value) will be refected in the profit and loss account or STRGL, in the manner described above.

23.240 Traditionally, book values of the assets being distributed have been used to measure the value of the dividend. For example, in a demerger of a subsidiary, the parent company may record a demerger dividend in *specie* at an amount equal to the book value of the investment and the group may record the same dividend in *specie* at the amount of the net assets of the subsidiary at the date of the demerger. For example, Pearson recorded the demerger of Royal Doulton at different values in the company and in the group. (See Table 23.7). However, there is, particularly under IFRS, a view that the distribution should be measured at the fair value of the assets being distributed. At the time of writing, both treatments are acceptable under both UK GAAP and IFRS.

23.240.1 A dividend or distribution in *specie* from a subsidiary is an unrealised profit in the hands of the parent (even where there is a cash alternative) unless the asset distributed meets the definition of qualifying consideration. However, if the non-cash asset is distributed by the parent then, following section 276 of the 1985 Act (section 846 of the 2006), that unrealised profit would be treated by the parent as a realised profit for the purpose of that onward distribution, provided that the profit was recorded in the relevant accounts. [Tech 07/03 (amended) para A13].

Table 23.7 — Pearson plc — Annual Report & Accounts —31 December 1993

Notes on the accounts (extract)

20 Notes on the company balance sheet (extract)

The company demerger dividend *in specie* of £134.2 million is the historical cost of the investment in Royal Doulton.

The group demerger dividend *in specie* of £111.8 million is the net assets of Royal Doulton at the date of demerger and goodwill written back on disposal.

Liability for an unlawful distribution

23.241 Any shareholder of a company who receives an unlawful distribution is liable to repay it to the company if, at the time he received it, he knew, or had reasonable grounds to believe, that it was made in contravention of the Act. [CA85 Sec 277(1); CA06 Sec 847(1)(2)]. This provision is without prejudice to any other liability of a shareholder to repay distributions that have been unlawfully made to him. [CA85 Sec 277(2); CA06 Sec 847(3)(4)]. In addition, if the directors make an unlawful distribution they may be in breach of their fiduciary duties to the company.

23.242 Even where a distribution has been made that is apparently permitted by the relevant accounts, the directors may be personally liable in respect of payments made out of undistributable reserves. This situation may arise where the company makes a distribution that is covered by the distributable reserves shown in the last relevant accounts, but the company no longer has distributable reserves because they have been consumed by losses the company has made since those accounts were drawn up.

23.243 If the company subsequently goes into liquidation, the liquidator could apply to the court for an order to compel the directors to compensate the company for their having misapplied the company's property by making the unlawful distribution. The directors should not only refer to the relevant accounts when they authorise a dividend: they should also take into account the company's results since the date on which those accounts were drawn up.

The legality of distributions in kind

Aveling Barford

23.244 The judgment given by Hoffmann J in *Aveling Barford v Perion Ltd and others* [1989] BCLC 626 is relevant to transactions not undertaken at market value. In that case, the plaintiff company sold property at considerably less than its fair value to a company controlled by the company's sole shareholder at the time when it had no distributable reserves. In delivering his judgment, the judge stated that:

> *"The sale to Perion was not a genuine exercise of the company's power under its memorandum to sell its assets. It was a sale at a gross undervalue for the purpose of enabling a profit to be realised by an entity controlled and put forward by its sole beneficial shareholder. This was as much a dressed-up distribution as the payment of excessive interest in Ridge Securities or excessive remuneration in Halt Garage. The company had at the time no distributable reserves and the sale was therefore ultra vires and incapable of validation by the approval or ratification by the shareholder."*

23.245 In this case, since the company had large negative reserves, it was not in a position to make a distribution. The sale of property was at a significant undervalue and as the company had no distributable reserves, the sale effectively amounted to an unauthorised return of capital.

23.246 Company distribution rules are dealt with in section 270 of the 1985 Act (section 836 of the 2006 Act). There is an argument that the Act does not permit any transfer of an asset at book value which constitutes a distribution to take place unless the asset is first written up to its full value and section 276 of the 1985 Act (section 846 of the 2006 Act) applies. The contrary view is that a transfer may take place at book value provided care is taken to avoid an unlawful reduction of capital (see para 23.247 below). The position is clarified by the 2006 Act, as discussed in paragraph 23.254. This is still a complex area where legal advice should be sought.

23.247 The Aveling Barford case confirmed that where a company undertakes a transaction at an undervalue at a time when the company has no distributable reserves (or inadequate reserves to cover the shortfall between the fair value and book amount), this amounts to an unlawful reduction in/return of capital. It follows that the transaction is incapable of validation by the approval of, or ratification by, the shareholders. The Aveling Barford case does not discuss the effects on the distribution provisions of the Act.

23.248 A transfer of an asset at a consideration less than its proper value will *prima facie* involve a breach of duty by the directors and the transferor company. But for certain transfers between group companies this might not be so. This may be the case where, for example, the transferor and transferee are UK companies within the same group and wholly owned, the objects of the transferor company allow assets to be disposed of for such a consideration as is thought fit, the transfer is approved by the shareholders of the transferor company and the transaction does not place in any doubt the solvency of any of the parties to it.

23.249 The implications of the Aveling Barford ruling can be summarised as follows:

- Where an asset is transferred at an undervalue for a consideration that is less than its book value when the transferor company does not have sufficient distributable profits to cover the undervalue, then this amounts to an unlawful reduction of capital.
- Where an asset is transferred at an undervalue, but for a consideration at least equal to its book value (such that the transfer does not affect the transferor company's distributable reserves) it is sufficient that the transferor company has some distributable reserves.
- Where an asset is transferred for a consideration less than its market value but equal to or above book value at a time when the transferor company has accumulated losses that exceed the difference between the book value and the transfer value, this amounts to an unlawful reduction of capital because the surplus on realisation of the asset will be insufficient to make good the accumulated losses.
- If a transfer takes place for consideration of more than the market value of the asset, the company receiving the asset must have distributable reserves at least equal to the excess of the consideration over the market value. These distributable reserves would need to be sufficient to allow the asset to be written down to its market value and still leave the company with distributable reserves.

23.250 In addition, depending on the circumstances, the provisions of section 151 of the 1985 Act or section 238 of the Insolvency Act 1986 may apply to transactions not at market value if carried out in connection with the acquisition of its shares. Section 151 of the 1985 Act prohibits a company from giving financial assistance for the acquisition of its own shares. The prohibition does not apply to a lawful dividend. [CA85 Sec 153(3); CA06 Sec 681(1)(2)]. The 2006 Act abolishes the prohibition on private companies giving financial assistance for a purchase of own shares (see chapter 7 of the Manual of Accounting – Management Reports and Governance). Section 238 of the Insolvency Act 1986 applies if an administration order is made in relation to the company or the company goes into liquidation and permits the liquidator or administrator to apply to the court to have a transaction at undervalue (which would include the payment of a dividend) set aside.

23.251 The company law consequences are dependent on the precise circumstances of each situation. In addition to the issues discussed above, a transaction not at market value may also have one or more of the following company law consequences as it may be:

- Ultra vires.
- In breach of the directors' fiduciary duties.
- A fraud on the minority.

23.252 Directors of both the vendor and purchaser companies should, therefore, obtain proper advice as to the value of the assets, as well as appropriate legal advice, before they decide upon implementing a transaction that may not be at market value if the companies involved do not have sufficient distributable reserves. This advice should be obtained even if the vendor and purchaser are wholly-owned members of the same group.

23.253 Examples of typical transactions not undertaken at market value include the following:

- The sale of an asset at an undervalue.
- The purchase of an asset at an overvalue — for example, the transfer of a subsidiary intra-group without warranties and indemnities normally given on third party sales and purchases.
- Book/tax written down value transfers where these do not correspond to market value.
- Sale for debt in certain circumstances, for example, where the debt is not repayable on demand and does not bear interest, or where the purchaser does not have a realistic prospect of settling the debt.
- Capitalising or subordinating debt.
- Waivers of debt.
- Capital contributions — UK company law is silent about such contributions, but essentially these are gifts.
- Interest-free loans or loans with excessive rates of interest.
- Non-payment for the surrender of group relief.
- Assumption of an inherent tax liability under the Taxation of Capital Gains Act 1992, section 171 — when an asset is transferred by one member of a capital gains group to another member, the transferee inherits the transferor's base cost and, therefore, is liable to corporation tax on the increase in value of the asset that accrued during the transferor's period of ownership.

Distributions in kind under the Companies Act 2006

23.254 The 2006 Act seeks to bring clarity to the effect of distributions in kind on distributable profits. Section 845 of that Act inserts a new provision which states:

> *"(1) This section applies for determining the amount of a distribution consisting of or including, or treated as arising in consequence of, the sale, transfer or other disposition by a company of a non-cash asset where —*
>
> *(a) at the time of the distribution the company has profits available for distribution, and*
>
> *(b) if the amount of the distribution were to be determined in accordance with this section, the company could make the distribution without contravening this Part.*
>
> *(2) The amount of the distribution (or the relevant part of it) is taken to be —*
>
> *(a) in a case where the amount or value of the consideration for the disposition is not less than the book value of the asset, zero;*
>
> *(b) in any other case, the amount by which the book value of the asset exceeds the amount or value of any consideration for the disposition.*
>
> *(3) For the purposes of subsection (1)(a) the company's profits available for distribution are treated as increased by the amount (if any) by which the amount or value of any consideration for the disposition exceeds the book value of the asset.*
>
> *(4) In this section "book value", in relation to an asset, means —*
>
> *(a) the amount at which the asset is stated in the relevant accounts, or*
>
> *(b) where the asset is not stated in those accounts at any amount, zero.*
>
> *(5) The provisions of Chapter 2 (justification of distribution by reference to accounts) have effect subject to this section."*

[CA06 Sec 845].

23.255 The Aveling Barford case dealt with a situation where a company making a sale at an undervalue had no distributable profits. It did not deal directly with the effect on distributable profits where a company makes a sale at an undervalue at a time when it has distributable profits. This created uncertainty in that there was a concern that where a company sells an asset at book value and that book value is less that its fair value, the transaction would constitute a distribution requiring the company to have distributable profits sufficient to cover the shortfall. As a consequence of this uncertainty, some companies have resorted to revaluing the assets in question, often at considerable expense and then applying section 276 of the 1985 Act so that the revaluation surplus can be regarded as a realised profit (see para 23.238.1).

23.256 The government's intention is that section 845 of the 2006 Act should not alter the position established in the Aveling Barford case for companies selling assets at an undervalue when they have no distributable profits. Such distributions in kind remain unlawful.

23.257 The position for companies selling assets at an undervalue when it has distributable profits is clarified. Where a company has distributable profits and it wishes to sell an asset at less than book value, this will be legal provided that the company has distributable profits equal to, as a minimum, the shortfall between the book value and the asset's selling price. The asset's fair value is not relevant to the assessment of the legality of a sale at an undervalue as long as the company has distributable profits sufficient to cover this shortfall. This shortfall will be equivalent to a loss that will be recognised in the financial statements on the asset's sale. To the extent that the loss arises as a result of a previous revaluation of the asset (that is, the sale is not made below cost), the revaluation surplus is regarded as realised by virtue of section 846 of the 2006 Act. Consider the following example:

Example

Company A has an investment property that has a book value of £1,000,000, comprising cost of £800,000 and a revaluation surplus of £200,000. Company A decides to sell this property to its parent for £550,000 at a time when company A has distributable profits of £400,000. Is this legal under the 2006 Act?

Yes. The shortfall between the sales price and the book value is £450,000; company A has distributable profits of £400,000. However, £200,000 of the amount at which the asset is stated in the financial statements is an unrealised profit which, by virtue of section 846 of the 2006 Act, is regarded as realised. Total realised profits available for distribution are, therefore, £600,000, sufficient to cover the shortfall of £450,000.

Companies Act 2006

23.258 The changes made by the Companies Act 2006 to the law on share capital and reserves include the following, all of which will apply to transactions occurring on or after 1 October 2008:

- Further restrictions on the use of the share premium account (see para 23.90.1).
- New provisions to enable companies to redenominate their shares in a foreign currency (see para 23.83.26).
- Creation of a 'solvency statement' procedure for reductions in share capital for private companies (see para 23.83.21).

- Requirement to provide a 'statement of capital' to the Registrar (see paras 23.11 and 23.61).
- New provision to permit minimum share capital for public companies to be expressed in sterling or euros. (see para 23.44).
- Relaxation of the rules on sub-division and consolidation of shares (see para 23.83.31).
- New provision to deal with implications related to the Aveling Barford decision (see para 23.254).
- Private companies no longer required to have prior authorisation to allot shares; that is, an 'authorised share capital (see para 23.5.1).

Other changes relating to the acquisition of own shares and secretarial matters are dealt with in the chapter 7 of the Manual of Accounting – Management reports and governance.

23.259 The Companies Act 2006 requires various schedules to support the law contained in the main body of the Act. At the time of writing, many of these schedules have yet to be enacted. The 2006 Act is being implemented in stages and the outstanding supporting schedules relate to parts of the 2006 Act that have yet to be implemented. These schedules include those that will replace Schedules 4, 4A, 5, 6, 8, 8A, 9 and 9A of the 1985 Act, all of which deal with the form and content of accounts and certain disclosures to be made in those accounts as well as schedules 7 and 7A to the 1985 Act that deal with the content of the directors' report and directors' remuneration report. Equivalent schedules to the 2006 Act will be published in due course.

Chapter 24

Consolidated financial statements

	Page
Introduction	24001
Section I — The group and its structure	24001
Concept of the group	24001
Proprietary concept	24002
Parent company concept	24002
Entity concept	24002
Statement of principles	24003
Accounting for investments	24003
Purpose of consolidated financial statements	24004
Scope of the Act's and FRS 2's provisions	24005
Parent and subsidiary undertakings	24005
Requirement to prepare consolidated financial statements	24006
Parent companies	24006
Small and medium-sized groups	24007
Other parent undertakings	24007
Form of consolidated financial statements	24008
Parent's profit and loss account	24009
True and fair view	24010
Exemptions from preparing consolidated financial statements	24011
Intermediate parent exemption	24012
Immediate parent is an EEA company exemption	24013
Parent companies included in non-EEA group accounts exemption	24015
Relevant dates	24019
Certified translations	24020
Application of the exemptions in practice	24020
All subsidiaries excluded from consolidation	24022
Accounting treatment	24023
Disclosure	24023
Suggested wording for exempt parents	24024
Subsidiary undertakings	24025
Introduction	24025
Company Law	24025
Meaning of subsidiary undertaking	24025
Expressions used by unincorporated undertakings	24027
Majority of voting rights	24027
Appointment or removal of majority of board	24029
Dominant influence	24031
Right to exercise a dominant influence	24032
Power to, or actually exercise, dominant influence or control	24033
Definition	24034

Operating and financial policies. 24035
Practical ability and power to control 24035
Power of veto and other reserve powers. 24036
Commercial relationships 24036
Two parents 24036
Ceasing to exercise a dominant influence. 24037
Special purpose entities. 24038
Summary. 24039
Disclosure. 24039
Managed on a unified basis 24039
Control governed by an agreement. 24040
Control contrasted with shared control 24040
Common expressions and interpretations. 24040
Parent and subsidiary undertakings 24041
Provisions concerning rights. 24041
Provisions concerning capital. 24042
Meaning of subsidiary used elsewhere in the legislation. 24043
Examples of practical situations 24043
Subsidiaries excluded from consolidation. 24045
Inclusion not material. 24045
Disproportionate expense or undue delay 24046
Severe long-term restrictions 24046
Basis of exclusion. 24046
Accounting treatment 24049
Interest held exclusively with a view to subsequent resale. 24050
Basis of exclusion. 24050
Accounting treatment 24052
Dissimilar activities 24052
Disclosure for subsidiaries excluded from consolidation 24053
The Act's requirements. 24053
Additional requirements of FRS 2 24054
Aggregation of disclosures 24055
General exemptions from disclosure requirements 24056
Limited partnerships 24056
Consolidation of limited partnerships by general partner — historical approach 24057
Severe long-term restrictions over general partner's control — FRS 9 approach. 24058
Associated undertakings and joint ventures. 24059
Interest more than 50 per cent. 24059
Severe long-term restrictions do not apply. 24059
Accounting for a limited partnership as part of a portfolio 24059
Accounting for a limited partnership's interest in subsidiaries 24060
Implications for the limited partnership's financial statements 24061
Disclosure requirements concerning subsidiaries and investments 24061
Place of origin and reason for consolidation. 24061
Holdings in subsidiary undertakings. 24063
Financial years of subsidiaries. 24063

Company shares held by subsidiaries 24064
Significant investment holdings of the parent or group 24065
Interpretation of 'shares held by the group' 24066
Disclosure 'seriously prejudicial' 24066
Disclosure of excessive information 24067
Disclosure of parent company 24067
Membership of a qualifying undertaking 24071
Other disclosure issues 24073
Realised and distributable reserves 24073
Tax on the accumulated reserves of overseas subsidiaries 24073
Section II — Consolidation rules 24073
Introduction 24073
Generally accepted accounting principles 24074
Procedure for consolidation 24075
Consolidation adjustments 24076
Uniform accounting polices 24076
Other consolidation adjustments 24078
Subsidiary year ends 24078
Interim financial statements 24079
Disclosure where year ends differ 24081
Practical problems 24082
Parent's period differs from group 24084
Elimination of intra-group transactions 24086
Elimination calculations 24087
Profit elimination from fixed assets 24089
Losses 24090
Subsidiaries excluded from consolidation 24090
Section III — Minority interests 24092
Introduction 24092
Definition 24092
Minority or majority interests 24093
Basis of recognising minority interests 24094
Measurement of minority interests 24095
Equity minority interests 24095
Presentation in financial statements of equity minority interests 24095
Balance sheet 24095
Profit and loss account 24097
Stapled shares 24099
Directors' interests 24099
Measurement of minority interests 24100
Profit and loss account calculation 24100
Balance sheet calculation 24101
Indirect holdings 24102
Treatment of minority on acquisition 24104
Acquisition of direct subsidiary 24104
Acquisition of indirect subsidiary 24106
Compulsory acquisition of minority 24107
Acquisition of minority interests 24107

No fair value exercise 24109
Consequences of fair valuing 24111
Loss making subsidiaries 24113
Puts and calls over minority interests 24115

Chapter 24

Consolidated financial statements

Introduction

24.1 Section I of this chapter considers the purpose of consolidated financial statements. It also considers those entities that are required to prepare consolidated financial statements and those entities that are required to be consolidated as subsidiaries. Furthermore, it looks at the reasons parents must exclude certain subsidiary undertakings from their consolidated financial statements and the additional disclosures that then apply. It also sets out the disclosure required in the consolidated financial statements concerning all subsidiary undertakings. Section II deals with the practical aspects of performing a consolidation and section III deals with the measurement and disclosure of minority interests.

24.2 In this chapter the terms 'subsidiary' and 'subsidiary undertaking' are used interchangeably and unless otherwise stated, 'subsidiary' is used to mean 'subsidiary undertaking' as defined in section 258 of the Companies Act 1985 (CA06 Sec 1162) with regard to preparing consolidated financial statements and not as defined in section 736 of the Companies Act 1985 (CA06 Sec 1159). (See further para 24.172.)

[The next paragraph is 24.6.]

Section I — The group and its structure

Concept of the group

24.6 The 'group' is defined in the Act to mean *"a parent undertaking and its subsidiary undertakings"*. [CA85 sec 262(1); CA06 Sec 474(1)]. However, three concepts have evolved since the first consolidations were made that concern how the group is established and how the financial statements of the companies forming the group are consolidated. The three concepts are the:

- Proprietary concept.
- Entity concept.
- Parent company concept.

24.7 Each of these concepts is explained in the paragraphs that follow.

Proprietary concept

24.8 The proprietary concept considers the group as if the parent's members are only concerned with the proportion of the assets and liabilities of the group that they own. Consequently, it takes a very narrow view of the group. The members are, therefore, not concerned with the control they might have over the proportion of assets (and liabilities) that are owned, in effect, by minorities.

24.9 Under this concept the consolidated balance sheet deals only with the proportion of assets and liabilities that the parent owns in a subsidiary. Similarly, the profit and loss account would deal with only an equivalent proportion of revenues and expenses of such a subsidiary. Consequently, no minority interests would be shown in the consolidated financial statements.

24.10 This concept of accounting is not generally used in the UK, although it may be seen as a foundation for the equity method and for proportional consolidation. Equity accounting and proportional consolidation are considered further in chapter 27.

Parent company concept

24.11 The parent company concept requires 100 per cent consolidation of all controlled subsidiaries as its base, even if the parent has less than 100 per cent of the shares in the subsidiary. However, it does recognise that the parent company's members' interest is limited to its shareholding in subsidiaries. Consequently, minority interests are not recognised as shareholders' funds, but are shown separately either before or after shareholders' funds.

24.12 This concept developed in the UK and stems from the early days of consolidation when the consolidated balance sheet was seen as a supplement to the parent company's balance sheet. It is the concept that still underlies UK GAAP. Traditionally, this concept has also been the one embodied within IFRS, but some subtle changes made to the standards in 2003 as part of the improvements project have seen international accounting move towards the entity concept.

Entity concept

24.13 The entity concept considers the group as a single entity. Consequently, any companies that are controlled by the parent would be consolidated. In a similar way to the parent company concept this concept requires 100 per cent consolidation of all subsidiaries.

24.14 Minority interests are sometimes recognised under this concept, but they are treated as part of shareholders' funds, thereby emphasising the control that the parent and its shareholders have over a subsidiary. The entity concept has not traditionally been used in the UK and minority interests have not been traditionally treated as part of shareholders' funds under UK GAAP. However, this concept is now influencing IFRS (see further Manual of Accounting – IFRS for the UK).

[The next paragraph is 24.16.]

Statement of principles

24.16 The Statement of principles (see chapter 2) addresses how a reporting entity is defined and how interests in other entities are reported in consolidated financial statements. It notes that consolidated financial statements present a view of the group, from the perspective of the parent's shareholders, where the gains, losses, assets, liabilities and cash flows of all subsidiaries are reflected in full.

24.17 The boundary of a group (that is, the entities which form the group) which are the subject of a set of consolidated financial statements is set by the extent of control. The statement explains that control is the power to direct and that there are two aspects to control:

- The ability to deploy the economic resources, whether assets or entities.
- The ability to benefit by (or to suffer from) their deployment.

To have control an entity must have both these abilities. An entity has control of another entity where it has the ability to direct the operating and financial policies of that entity with a view to gaining economic benefits from its activities (or the power to do this). This is the essence of control and control of the operating and financial policies forms the basis of the definitions of subsidiaries found in FRS 2, 'Accounting for subsidiary undertakings', as explained below.

Accounting for investments

24.18 At present in the UK there are a number of ways a company may account in its consolidated financial statements for an investment in another undertaking, which depend upon the size of the investment and the control or influence the investing company has over the entity in which it is investing. These different situations are summarised below:

- Where the investing entity does not exercise significant influence over the operating and financial policies of the other undertaking (normally holdings of below 20 per cent), its investment is recorded at:
  - cost unless there is a permanent diminution in its value; or
  - market value.

  (see further chapter 6).
- Where the investing entity does exercise significant influence over the operating and financial policies of the other undertaking (normally holdings of over 20 per cent), its investment is accounted for using equity accounting,

unless the entity is a joint arrangement in which case, another method of accounting should be used (see further chapter 27).

- Where the investing entity controls (or has the power to control) the operating and financial policies of the other undertaking (normally holdings of more than 50 per cent) its investment is consolidated in full and any minority interests are recognised.

24.19 There are, therefore, several ways in which an undertaking can be incorporated into the consolidated financial statements of its investor including:

- Equity accounting — the investing undertaking incorporates its share of the assets and liabilities of the entity in which it has invested on a one line basis in its consolidated balance sheet (netting assets and liabilities). In the consolidated profit and loss account, the investing group's share of operating profit, super-exceptional items, interest and taxation is shown. Only dividends received are recorded in the investing entity's cash flow statement. Where the investing undertaking does not prepare consolidated financial statements the equivalent information has to be given in the notes to the financial statements. Equity accounting is explained in chapter 27.

- Proportional consolidation — in this method, the investing undertaking consolidates into its financial statements its share of assets and liabilities, profits and losses and cash flows of the entity in which it has invested line by line in its consolidated balance sheet, its consolidated profit and loss account and its consolidated cash flow statement, respectively. As only the investing company's share of assets and liabilities are consolidated, this method does not result in recognising any minority interests. Proportional consolidation is mentioned in more detail in chapter 27 in relation to accounting for joint arrangements.

- Full consolidation — the investing undertaking consolidates in full 100 per cent of the assets and liabilities, profits and losses and cash flow of the entity in which it has invested on a line by line basis in its consolidated balance sheet, its consolidated profit and loss account and its consolidated cash flow statement, respectively. Where the investing undertaking's interests is less than 100 per cent, a minority interest is recognised representing the minority's share of assets and liabilities and profits and losses on a net basis. The rules that apply to preparing consolidated financial statements are considered in section II, paragraph 24.303.

Purpose of consolidated financial statements

24.20 The explanatory section of FRS 2 provides the following justification for requiring parents to prepare consolidated financial statements:

"For a variety of legal, tax and other reasons undertakings generally choose to conduct their activities not through a single legal entity but through several undertakings under the ultimate control of the parent undertaking of

that group. For this reason the financial statements of a parent undertaking by itself do not present a full picture of its economic activities or financial position. Consolidated financial statements are required in order to reflect the extended business unit that conducts activities under the control of the parent undertaking." [FRS 2 para 59].

Scope of the Act's and FRS 2's provisions

24.21 The Companies Act 1985 (as amended by the Companies Act 1989) requires *parent companies,* subject to certain exemptions, to prepare consolidated financial statements and it sets out the form that those financial statements should take. [CA85 Sec 227; CA06 Secs 399, 403].

24.22 The provisions of FRS 2 go further and apply to *all parent undertakings*, not just parent companies. Subject to certain exemptions, FRS 2 requires *all parents* preparing financial statements that are intended to give a true and fair view of the financial position and profit or loss of the group to prepare them in the form of consolidated financial statements (see further para 24.37). [FRS 2 para 18].

24.23 FRS 2 also directs a parent that uses one of the exemptions from the requirement to prepare consolidated financial statements, but prepares individual financial statements intended to give a true and fair view, to include certain additional disclosure (see para 24.72). FRS 2 does not otherwise deal with the individual financial statements of a parent.

24.24 FRS 2 was drafted within the framework of the Act and, although it does not conflict with it, there are circumstances where the standard is more restrictive than the Act. Furthermore, the standard states that:

"Parent undertakings that do not report under the Act should comply with the requirements of the FRS, and of the Act where referred to in the FRS, except to the extent that these requirements are not permitted by any statutory framework under which such undertakings report". [FRS 2 para 19].

24.25 By referring to sections of the Act and applying them to parents that are not subject to the Act, the FRS achieves a single set of rules that apply to parents preparing consolidated financial statements, whether or not they are companies.

[The next paragraph is 24.27.]

Parent and subsidiary undertakings

24.27 The Companies Act refers throughout to 'parent undertaking' and 'subsidiary undertaking'. These terms stem directly from the EC 7th Directive. The term 'undertaking' is defined in the Act and FRS 2 as follows:

> *"…a body corporate or partnership, or an unincorporated association carrying on a trade or business, with or without a view to profit."* [CA85 Sec 259(1); CA06 Sec 1161(1); FRS 2 para 16].

24.28 Consequently, a *parent undertaking* could be a partnership or an unincorporated business. However, under the Act consolidated financial statements have only to be prepared where, at the end of a financial year, an undertaking is a parent company. [CA85 Sec 227(1); CA06 Sec 399(2)]. Therefore, parent undertakings that are not companies are not required by the Act to prepare consolidated financial statements, but as explained above they are required to do so in certain circumstances by FRS 2 (see further para 24.37).

24.29 However, *subsidiary undertakings* (including both partnerships and unincorporated associations) are required to be consolidated into the group's consolidated financial statements. Such entities are normally required to be fully consolidated and any minority interests (see section III, paragraph 24.353) are shown separately in the consolidated balance sheet.

24.30 The Act and FRS 2 require as a starting point that all subsidiary undertakings should be included in UK GAAP consolidated financial statements. [CA85 Sec 229(1); CA06 Sec 405(1); FRS 2 para 23]. The FRRP commented in July 1993 that the Report and Accounts of Breverleigh Investments plc for the year ended 30 June 1992 did not include its subsidiary The Banyan Tree of Key West Inc. in its consolidated financial statements. Following discussions with the FRRP this subsidiary was consolidated in accordance with the Act and FRS 2 in the group's consolidated financial statements for the year to 30 June 1993 and comparatives were amended accordingly. There are, however, a number of situations where subsidiary undertakings may, or should, legitimately be excluded from consolidated financial statements and may be accounted for in some other way. These situations are covered in the provisions of both the Act and FRS 2.

24.31 The provisions of both the Act and FRS 2 that relate to the definitions of subsidiary undertakings and the exemptions from the requirement to consolidate certain subsidiary undertakings are considered in detail below (see paras 24.76 and 24.176 respectively).

Requirement to prepare consolidated financial statements

24.32 Whether or not there is a legal or regulatory obligation for a parent to prepare consolidated financial statements will depend on how the parent is constituted.

Parent companies

24.33 As mentioned above, where a *company* is a parent company at the end of a financial year the directors of the company are required by the Act, subject to certain exemptions, to prepare consolidated financial statements as well as individual company to certain financial statements for the financial year.

[CA85 Sec 227(1); CA06 Sec 399(2)]. The consolidated financial statements must comply with the Act's requirements. [CA85 Sec 227(3); CA06 Sec 403(2)].

24.34 Such consolidated financial statements prepared by a parent company are also required by law to give a true and fair view. [CA85 Sec 227A(2); CA06 Sec 404(2)]. In order to comply with the true and fair requirement, the parent should comply with the provisions of FRS 2.

Small and medium-sized groups

24.35 Under the Companies Act 1985 a parent company need not prepare consolidated financial statements if the group headed by it qualifies as a small group or a medium-sized group, provided it is not an ineligible group. [CA85 Sec 248(1)]. The Companies Act 2006 changes this requirement so that a parent company under the small companies regime has the option to prepare consolidated financial statements and any other parent company must prepare consolidated financial statements unless subject to one of the exemptions noted below. [CA06 Secs 398, 399(2)(3)].

24.36 These exemptions available to small and medium-sized groups and the conditions that need to be fulfilled are explained further in chapter 32.

Other parent undertakings

24.37 Whether or not an unincorporated parent undertaking is *required* to prepare consolidated financial statements will depend on the statutory framework under which that undertaking was established. If that framework requires the undertaking to prepare *consolidated* financial statements and to prepare financial statements that give a *true and fair view* (and, as a consequence, require it to comply with FRS 2), then that undertaking will be *required* to prepare consolidated financial statements (providing it is not entitled to an exemption). [FRS 2 para 18].

24.38 For example, a partnership that owns a subsidiary company is not required by the Act to prepare consolidated financial statements as it is not itself a parent *company*. However, if there is a requirement in the partnership deed for the partnership to prepare consolidated financial statements and for it to prepare financial statements that give a true and fair view (and, therefore, comply with FRS 2) the partnership would be required to prepare consolidated financial statements in accordance with FRS 2.

24.39 The basic rule is that any parent preparing consolidated financial statements purporting to give a true and fair view is required to comply with FRS 2, unless it is specifically exempt from preparing such financial statements. [FRS 2 paras 18, 19].

[The next paragraph is 24.41.]

Form of consolidated financial statements

24.41 Both the Act and FRS 2 require the financial statements of a group to be in the form of consolidated financial statements, unless the parent is exempt.

24.42 FRS 2 defines consolidated financial statements as *"the financial statements of a group prepared by consolidation"* and it defines consolidation as *"the process of adjusting and combining financial information from the individual financial statements of a parent undertaking and its subsidiary undertaking to prepare consolidated financial statements that present financial information for the group as a single economic entity"*. [FRS 2 paras 4, 5].

24.43 The Act requires that for parent companies consolidated financial statements should include:

- A consolidated balance sheet dealing with the state of affairs of the parent and its subsidiary undertakings.
- A consolidated profit and loss account dealing with the profit or loss of the parent and its subsidiary undertakings.
- Notes to the consolidated financial statements dealing with additional disclosure requirements.

[CA85 Sec 227A(1)(3); CA06 Sec 404(1)(3)].

These provisions are explained further in chapter 4.

24.44 FRS 3 now also requires the consolidated financial statements to include a consolidated statement of total recognised gains and losses, a consolidated note of historical cost profits and losses and a consolidated reconciliation of movements in shareholders' funds. Entities preparing such consolidated financial statements are not required to publish equivalent statements for the parent entity itself. The provisions of FRS 3 concerning these statements are considered in detail in chapters 4 and 8.

24.45 In addition, subject to certain exemptions, FRS 1 requires all undertakings preparing financial statements that are intended to give a true and fair view to prepare a cash flow statement. Undertakings preparing consolidated financial statements should prepare a consolidated cash flow statement and related notes; they are not then required to prepare an entity cash flow statement. The detailed requirements of FRS 1 are dealt with in chapter 30.

24.46 Both the Act and FRS 2 state that the consolidated financial statements should include the parent and all its subsidiaries, except for those subsidiaries that are required to be excluded. The provisions relating to exclusion of subsidiaries are considered further in paragraph 24.176.

Parent's profit and loss account

24.47 When a parent company prepares consolidated financial statements in accordance with the Act, it is not required to include its own profit and loss account and related notes if the financial statements satisfy the following requirements:

- The notes to the parent company's individual balance sheet show the company's profit or loss for the financial year determined in accordance with the provisions of the Act. [CA85 Sec 230(1)(b); CA06 Sec 408(1)(b)].
- The figure to be given is the profit or loss reported in the parent's profit and loss account format line item 'profit or loss for the financial year', which is before any consolidation adjustments or dividends.
- The parent company's board of directors must approve the company's individual profit and loss account in accordance with the rules concerning approval of the company's financial statements. [CA85 Sec 230(3); CA06 Sec 408(3)].
- The notes to the financial statements disclose the fact that the parent company has taken advantage of this exemption. [CA85 Sec 230(4)]; CA06 Sec 408(4)].

24.48 Where the consolidated financial statements do not include the company's profit and loss account, the consolidated financial statements need not include certain supplementary information when presented to the Board for their approval. [CA85 Sec 230(2)]. The information that can be excluded is specified in paragraphs 52 to 57 of Schedule 4 to the Companies Act 1985, which includes the following:

- Interest and similar charges. [CA85 4 Sch 53].
- Detailed particulars concerning tax. [CA85 4 Sch 54].
- Disaggregated information concerning turnover. [CA85 4 Sch 55].
- Certain miscellaneous matters including:
  - The effect of including any preceding year's items in the current year's profit and loss account.
  - Particulars of extraordinary income or extraordinary charges.
  - The effect of any exceptional items.

  [CA85 4 Sch 57].

The information that can be excluded in financial statements prepared under the Companies Act 2006 is information regarding employee numbers and costs. [CA06 Sec 408(2)].

24.49 Suitable wording for a note to be included in the consolidated financial statements when the parent's profit and loss account is not reproduced would be:

> "*As permitted by section 230 of the Companies Act 1985, the parent company's profit and loss account has not been included in these financial statements and its profit/loss for its financial year amounted to £X.*"

> "*As permitted by section 408 of the Companies Act 2006, the parent company's profit and loss account has not been included in these financial statements and its profit/loss for its financial year amounted to £X.*"

24.50 In certain situations an intermediate parent, for example, might wish voluntarily to prepare consolidated financial statements even though it might comply with the conditions that would allow it not to prepare consolidated financial statements (see para 24.56). In this situation, it might not wish to include its individual company profit and loss account in those consolidated financial statements. However, the wording of section 230 of the Companies Act 1985 (CA06 Sec 408) would only seem to allow the exemption where the company is *required* to prepare consolidated financial statements. The solution to this technical issue is for the intermediate parent deliberately not to comply with one of the conditions outlined in paragraph 24.62. For example, one of those conditions is that the company must disclose that it is exempt from the requirement to prepare consolidated financial statements in its financial statements. If it does not make this disclosure, then it is strictly required by the Act to prepare consolidated financial statements and, therefore, can take the exemption from presenting its own profit and loss account.

True and fair view

24.51 It is an overriding requirement of the Act that a company's consolidated financial statements must give a true and fair view of the state of affairs as at the end of the financial year and of the profit or loss for the financial year, of the undertakings included in the consolidation. [CA85 Sec 227A(2); CA06 Sec 404(2)].

24.52 Where, however, compliance with the disclosure provisions of the Act (including Schedule 4A to the Companies Act 1985) would not be sufficient to give a true and fair view, then additional information should be given in the financial statements or in the notes to the financial statements. [CA85 Sec 227A(4); CA06 Sec 404(4)]. This additional information needs to be of sufficient detail to ensure that its disclosure enables the financial statements to give a true and fair view.

24.53 There is a further provision concerning the true and fair view, which provides that if in 'special circumstances' compliance with the Act's provisions would be inconsistent with the requirement to give a true and fair view, the directors of the company must depart from the Act's provisions. [CA85 Sec 227A(5); CA06 Sec 404(5)]. Where such a departure is necessary, the particulars of the departure, the reasons for it and its effect must be given in a note to the financial statements. [CA85 Sec 227A(6); CA06 Sec 404(5)]. FRS 18 specifically requires the following disclosures, which give a more precise meaning to 'particulars, reasons and effect':

- A statement of the treatment which the Act would normally require in the circumstances and a description of the treatment actually adopted.
- A statement as to why the treatment prescribed would not give a true and fair view.
- 'Its effect' should be interpreted to mean a description of how the position shown in the financial statements is different as a result of the departure, normally with quantification, except where:
  - quantification is already evident in the financial statements themselves; or
  - the effect cannot reasonably be quantified, in which case the directors should explain the circumstances.

[FRS 18 para 62].

These provisions are considered further in chapter 2.

24.54 The true and fair override given by section 227A(5) of the Companies Act 1985 (CA06 Sec 404(5)) cannot be used to justify not consolidating a subsidiary; it merely entitles the directors to depart from the other requirements of the Act with respect to the matters to be included in the consolidated financial statements. In interpreting the Act's provisions the court would be bound to give effect so far as possible to the provisions of the EC 7th Directive. In the EC 7th Directive the true and fair override in article 16(5) (included in section 227A(5) of the Companies Act 1985 (CA06 Sec 404(5))) applies only to specific articles of the directive (that is, articles 17 to 35 and 39). It does not apply to the articles which set out the conditions for consolidation. Therefore, the override cannot be used to override provisions relating to the composition of consolidated financial statements so as to exclude a subsidiary undertaking from consolidation.

24.55 This requirement of the law has been reinforced by the ASB in FRS 2. The ASB consider that for consolidated financial statements to give a true and fair view they must present information about the group that is complete and, for this reason, the conditions set out in the Act for exclusion of subsidiaries from consolidation have been further restricted in the standard. These restrictions are considered from paragraph 24.176 onwards.

Exemptions from preparing consolidated financial statements

24.56 There are three situations where a parent may be exempt from the general requirement to prepare consolidated financial statements. The exemptions are for:

- Parents of small and medium-sized groups (see para 24.35).

- Certain parents that are also subsidiaries (that is, intermediate parents — see para 24.56.1).
- Parents, all of whose subsidiaries are permitted or required to be excluded from consolidation (see para 24.70).

[FRS 2 para 21].

The provisions concerning small and medium-sized groups are explained in chapter 32.

Intermediate parent exemption

24.56.1 Under certain circumstances an intermediate holding company is not required to prepare consolidated financial statements. There are two potential exemptions available. These are found in sections 228 and 228A of the Companies Act 1985 (CA06 Secs 400, 401). The two exemptions differ as their requirements vary depending on the group structure. The exemption under section 228 of the Companies Act 1985 (CA06 Sec 400) is only available if the immediate parent is established under the law of an EEA state. The section 228A of the Companies Act 1985 (CA06 Sec 401) exemption is wider and is available to any company which has a non-EEA parent (not necessarily immediate parent). Section 228A of the Companies Act 1985 (CA06 Sec 401) exemption is, therefore, potentially available to any subsidiary included in the consolidated financial statements of a larger group regardless of political geography.

24.56.2 Depending on the group structure, it may be that a particular intermediate parent company can look to one or both of these sections for its potential exemption. The following flow chart summarises this principle and highlights which exemption might be available in the circumstances in question.

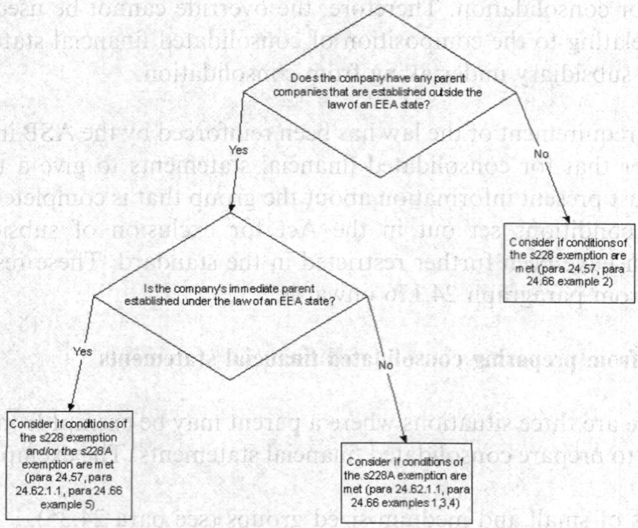

Immediate parent is an EEA company exemption

24.57 An intermediate holding company is not required to prepare consolidated financial statements where it is wholly owned by its immediate parent undertaking, and this immediate parent company is established under the law of an EEA state. [CA85 Sec 228(1)(a); CA06 Sec 400(1)(a)]. However, there are a number of conditions that must apply before the exemption can be taken and these are summarised below in paragraph 24.62.

24.58 In addition to wholly-owned subsidiaries, this exemption extends to the situation where the immediate parent holds more than 50 per cent of the shares by number in the intermediate holding company and no notice has been served on the company to prepare consolidated financial statements. Such notice has to be made by either of the following:

- Shareholders holding in aggregate more than half of the remaining shares in the company.
- Shareholders holding in aggregate five per cent of the total shares in the company.

As with paragraph 24.57, the immediate parent company must be established under the law of an EEA state.

[CA85 Sec 228(1)(b); CA06 Sec 400(1)(b)].

24.58.1 The EEA (European Economic Area) encompasses the member states of the EC and the EFTA countries of Iceland, Liechtenstein and Norway. The member states of the EC are Austria, Belgium, Denmark, Finland, France, Germany, Greece, Republic of Ireland, Italy, Luxemburg, Netherlands, Portugal, Spain, Sweden, United Kingdom, Cyprus, Czech Republic, Estonia, Latvia, Lithuania, Hungary, Malta, Poland, Slovak Republic, Slovenia, Romania and Bulgaria.

24.59 The notice has to be served within six months of the end of the previous financial period (that is, normally within the first six months of the financial year for which the consolidated financial statements are being prepared). [CA85 Sec 228(1); CA06 Sec 400(1)]. Consequently, the onus is clearly on the minority shareholders to serve such notice if they require consolidated financial statements to be prepared for a sub-group.

24.60 FRS 2 extends the scope of the relevant sections of the Act outlined above to apply also to unincorporated parents, hence reference to 'company' should be treated as applying to any undertaking where appropriate. [FRS 2 para 21].

24.61 For the purposes of determining whether the company is wholly owned or whether the parent holds more than 50 per cent of the company's shares, the rules below apply:

- Shares held by directors to comply with their share qualification requirements should be disregarded when determining whether a company is wholly owned in paragraph 24.57. [CA85 Secs 228(4); CA06 Sec 400(5)].

- In determining whether the parent holds more than 50 per cent of the shares of the company in paragraph 24.58, shares held by a parent's wholly owned subsidiary should be attributed to the parent undertaking. Also shares held on behalf of the parent, or by or on behalf of a wholly-owned subsidiary, should be attributed to the parent undertaking. [CA85 Secs 228(5); CA06 Sec 400(3)].

24.62 Both the exemptions outlined above in paragraphs 24.57 and 24.58 only apply, however, where the following conditions have been followed:

- The company is included in the consolidated financial statements of a larger group drawn up to the same date (or an earlier date in the same financial year – see para 24.63) by a parent undertaking established under the law of an EEA state. [CA85 Sec 228(2)(a); CA06 Sec 400(2)(a)]. This parent does not have to be the EEA immediate parent referred to in 24.57, it could be an EEA parent further up the chain. This parent will be referred to henceforth as the 'reporting parent'.

  'Included in' for this purpose means by way of full consolidation. Equity accounting or proportional consolidation is not sufficient.

- The reporting parent's consolidated financial statements and annual report must be drawn up and audited in accordance the law of the EEA state under which it is established, in accordance either:
  - with the provisions of the EC 7th Directive (where applicable as modified by the provisions of the Bank Accounts Directive or the Insurance Accounts Directive); or
  - with IFRS.

- It must be noted in the company's individual financial statements that it is exempt from preparing and delivering to the Registrar of Companies consolidated financial statements. [CA85 Sec 228(2)(c); CA06 Sec 400(2)(c)].

- The reporting parent's name must be noted in the company's individual financial statements stating:
  - The reporting parent's country of incorporation, if it is incorporated outside Great Britain.
  - The address of the reporting parent's principal place of business, where it is unincorporated.

  [CA85 Sec 228(2)(d); CA06 Sec 400(2)(d)].

- The company must deliver to the Registrar of Companies, within the period allowed for delivering its individual financial statements, a copy of the reporting parent's consolidated financial statements and annual report, together with the audit report thereon. [CA85 Sec 228(2)(e); CA06 Sec 400(2)(e)].

- Where any of the documents delivered to the Registrar of Companies in accordance with the previous requirement is not in English (or Welsh for a company registered in Wales), a copy of a translation must be annexed to those documents. The translation has to be certified in the prescribed manner to be a correct translation. [CA85 Sec 228(2)(f); CA06 Sec 400(2)(f)].
- The company cannot have any securities listed on a regulated market in an EEA member state. [CA85 Sec 228(3); CA06 Sec 400(4)]. For this purpose, 'securities' include shares and stocks, debentures (including debenture stock, loan stock, bonds, certificates of deposit and other similar instruments), warrants and similar instruments and certain certificates and other instruments that confer rights in respect of securities. [CA85 Sec 228(6); CA06 Sec 400(6)].

24.62.1 With regard practical application of the requirement in the second bullet point of paragraph 24.62, the national GAAPs of the 27 countries which are members of the EC should have implemented the EC 7th Directive. If the reporting parent is established in another country in the EEA, in order for the exemption to be taken appropriate analysis will be needed to confirm that the GAAP under which the financial statements are prepared is either IFRS or a GAAP that is in accordance with the EC 7th Directive.

Parent companies included in non-EEA group accounts exemption

24.62.1.1 An intermediate holding company is not required to prepare consolidated financial statements where it is wholly owned by a parent undertaking not established under the law of an EEA state. [CA85 Sec 228A(1)(a); CA06 Sec 401(1)(a)]. However, there are a number of conditions that must apply before the exemption can be taken and these are summarised below in paragraph 24.62.6. Note that there is a key difference here to the section 228 of the Companies Act 1985 (CA06 Sec 400) exemption requirement, since the parent undertaking identified need not be the 'immediate parent' of the company, merely a 'parent'.

24.62.2 In addition to wholly-owned subsidiaries, this exemption extends to the situation where the parent holds more than 50 per cent of the shares by number in the company looking to claim the exemption and no notice has been served on the company to prepare consolidated financial statements. Such notice has to be made by either of the following:

- Shareholders holding in aggregate more than half of the remaining shares in the company.
- Shareholders holding in aggregate five per cent of the total shares in the company.

As with paragraph 24.62.1.1, the parent undertaking identified may not be established under the law of an EEA state, but may be any parent of the company, with no restriction to 'immediate parent'.

[CA85 Sec 228A(1)(b); CA06 Sec 401(1)(b)].

24.62.3 The notice has to be served within six months of the end of the previous financial period (that is, normally within the first six months of the financial year for which the consolidated financial statements are being prepared). [CA85 Sec 228A(1); CA06 Sec 401(1)]. Consequently, the onus is clearly on the minority shareholders to serve such notice if they require consolidated financial statements to be prepared for a sub-group.

24.62.4 FRS 2 extends the scope of the relevant sections of the Act outlined above to apply also to unincorporated parents, hence reference to 'company' should be treated as applying to any undertaking where appropriate. [FRS 2 para 21].

24.62.5 For the purposes of determining whether the company is wholly owned or whether the parent holds more than 50 per cent of the company's shares, the rules below apply:

- Shares held by directors to comply with their share qualification requirements should be disregarded when determining whether a company is wholly owned in paragraph 24.62.1. [CA85 Sec 228A(4); CA06 Sec 401(5)].

- In determining whether the parent holds more than 50 per cent of the shares of the company in paragraph 24.62.2, shares held by a parent's wholly-owned subsidiary should be attributed to the parent undertaking. Also shares held on behalf of the parent, or by or on behalf of a wholly-owned subsidiary, should be attributed to the parent undertaking. [CA85 Sec 228A(5); CA06 Sec 401(3)].

24.62.6 Both the exemptions outlined above in paragraphs 24.62.1 and 24.62.2 only apply, however, where the following conditions have been followed:

- The company and all of its subsidiary undertakings are included in the consolidated financial statements of a larger group drawn up to the same date (or an earlier date in the same financial year – see para 24.63) by a parent undertaking. [CA85 Sec 228A(2)(a); CA06 Sec 401(2)(a)]. This group does not have to be the non-EEA parent referred to in paragraph 24.62.1, it could be an alternative parent in the group structure, referred to hence forth as the 'reporting parent'.

  Note that this is a stronger requirement than under section 228 of the *Companies* Act 1985 (CA06 Sec 400), which does not include the requirement *"and all of its subsidiary undertakings"*.

'Included in' for this purpose means by way of full consolidation. Equity accounting or proportional consolidation is not sufficient.

- The reporting parent's consolidated financial statements and annual report must be drawn up in accordance with the provisions of the EC 7th Directive (where applicable as modified by the provisions of the Bank Accounts Directive or the Insurance Accounts Directive) or otherwise in a manner equivalent to consolidated accounts and annual reports so drawn up. [CA85 Sec 228A(2)(b); CA06 Sec 401(2)(b)].

  The financial statements must also be audited by one or more persons authorised to audit accounts under the law under which the parent undertaking which draws them up is established. [CA85 Sec 228A(2)(c); CA06 Sec 401(2)(c)]

- It must be noted in the company's individual financial statements that it is exempt from preparing and delivering to the Registrar of Companies consolidated financial statements. [CA85 Sec 228A(2)(d); CA06 Sec 401(2)(d)].

- The name of the reporting parent must be noted in the company's individual financial statements stating:

  - The reporting parent's country of incorporation, if it is incorporated outside Great Britain.

  - The address of the reporting parent's principal place of business, where it is unincorporated.

  [CA85 Sec 228A(2)(e); CA06 Sec 401(2)(e)].

- The company must deliver to the Registrar of Companies within the period allowed for delivering its individual financial statements a copy of the parent's consolidated financial statements and a copy of the parent's annual report together with the audit report thereon. [CA85 Sec 228A(2)(f); CA06 Sec 401(2)(f)].

- Where any of the documents delivered to the Registrar of Companies in accordance with the previous requirement is not in English (or Welsh for a company registered in Wales), a copy of a translation must be annexed to those documents. The translation has to be certified in the prescribed manner to be a correct translation [CA85 Sec 228A(2)(g); CA06 Sec 401(2)(g)].

- The company cannot have any securities listed on a regulated market in an EEA member state. [CA85 Sec 228A(3); CA06 Sec 401(4)]. For this purpose, 'securities' include shares and stocks, debentures (including debenture stock, loan stock, bonds, certificates of deposit and other similar instruments), warrants and similar instruments and certain certificates and other instruments that confer rights in respect of securities. [CA85 Sec 228A(6); CA06 Sec 401(6)].

24.62.7 A problem that may occur in practice arises from the requirement for the reporting parent's consolidated financial statements and annual report to be drawn up in line with the EC 7th Directive or in a manner equivalent. Paragraph 62.1 above discusses which national GAAPs are 'in accordance with' the Directive. Further to this, the UITF Abstract 42, 'The Interpretation of equivalence for the purposes of section 228A of the Companies Act 1985', gives guidance for determining whether a particular GAAP is 'in a manner equivalent' for the purposes of the section 228A of the Companies Act 1985 exemption. (CA06 Sec 401). It is generally accepted by the UITF that the reference to equivalence in section 228A of the Companies Act 1985 [CA06 Sec 401] does not mean compliance with every detail of the 7th Directive. The UITF believes that a qualitative approach, being one with a focus on compliance with the basic requirements of the Directive and in particular the requirement to give a true and fair view, is more in keeping with the deregulatory nature of the exemption.

24.62.8 With respect IFRS-based financial statements, the UITF notes that there are various varieties of IFRS, each of which has a different treatment with regard equivalence:

- IFRS as adopted by the EU. This will meet the test of equivalence as the procedure for adoption of IFRS by the EU requires a standard to meet the basic requirements of the EU Directives.
- IFRS as issued by the IASB. This will currently meet the test of equivalence as there are currently no standards issued by the IASB which conflict with the basic requirements of the Directives. However if, in future, the European Commission fails to adopt a standard on the grounds that it does not meet the 7th Directive's basic requirements, it will be necessary to consider whether the reasons for the failure to adopt the standard suggest that compliance with that standard will fail to give a true and fair view and will, therefore, fail the test of equivalence.
- IFRS-based GAAPs. These include Australia, South Africa and Hong Kong. It is not practicable to give specific guidance on all of the increasing number of GAAPs that are based on, or are converging with, IFRS. In those cases where they are more restrictive than IFRS by eliminating choices (for example, Australian GAAP) they will currently meet the test of equivalence for the purposes of section 228A. In other cases, it will be necessary to obtain an understanding of how they differ from IFRS and whether those differences might result in a departure from the basic requirements of the 7th Directive.

24.62.9 Furthermore the UITF has considered the specific cases of US, Canadian and Japanese GAAP. It notes that, in most cases, application of these GAAPs will result in financial statements that fulfil the basic principles of the 7th Directive. There are, however, three areas where there is potential for application of these GAAPs to result in financial statements that are not equivalent to the 7th Directive.

- Scope of consolidated accounts. The 7th Directive contains a definition of subsidiary undertakings that is based on a widely defined concept of control and is likely to ensure that many SPEs are included in consolidated financial statements. There may be cases where a country's GAAP does not require the consolidation of an entity in circumstances where the 7th Directive would do so. This could lead to a lack of equivalence where the effect on the consolidated financial statements is material.
- Consistent accounting policies. There are instances where these are not required by the GAAPs in question. To accept the conclusion of equivalence it will be necessary to ensure the consolidated financial statements are drawn up on the basis of consistent accounting policies.
- Any exemptions of modifications to the GAAPs allowed by specialised industry standards that have been applied. The effect of any such modifications would need to be specifically considered with respect to equivalence.

Provided the above points have been addressed, then the three GAAPs in question would be considered equivalent to the 7th Directive

24.62.10 Financial statements prepared using other GAAPs should be assessed for equivalence with the 7th Directive based on the particular facts and circumstances in question. This will include consideration of the similarities to, and differences from, the GAAPs considered specifically above.

Relevant dates

24.63 The relevant dates specified in the exemptions above can cause particular problems in practice as explained in the example that follows:

Example

A parent company acquires the whole of the company S sub-group in June 19X1 during its current financial year and after the acquisition the group has the following structure.

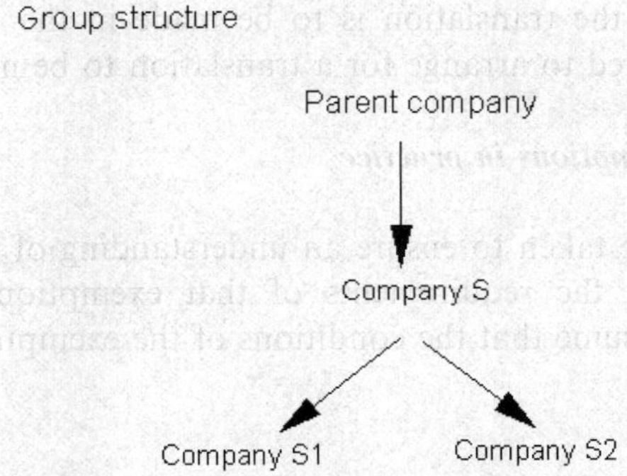

The parent company's year end is 31 December, but the year end of the company S sub-group is 30 September. The question then arises as to whether company S can take

advantage from the exemption to prepare consolidated financial statements for its sub-group (that is including both company S1 and company S2). If it complies with the other conditions of the exemption it will fail on the first condition in the year of acquisition (that is, 19X1). This is because at its year end, 30 September 19X1, it will not have been included in the parent's consolidated financial statements drawn up to the same date (that is, 30 September 19X1) or to an earlier date in company S's financial year. The company S sub-group will only be included in the parent's consolidated financial statement as at 31 December 19X1. In 19X2, company S does comply with this condition, because its results will be consolidated into its parent's financial statements to an earlier date in its financial year to 30 September 19X2 (that is, its parent's consolidated financial statements for the financial year to 31 December 19X1). Therefore, in 19X1 company S will have to prepare consolidated financial statements, but in 19X2 if it complies with the other conditions it will not have to prepare them. The simple way round this problem is for company S to change its year end from 30 September to 31 December.

Certified translations

24.64 The term 'certified translation' used above means a translation made by any of the following:

- A notary public.
- A solicitor if the translation was made in the UK.
- A person authorised in the place where the translation was made to administer an oath or any of the British officials mentioned in section 6 of the Commissioners for Oaths Act 1889 for translations made overseas. This includes British Ambassadors, envoys, ministers, charges d'affaires and secretaries of embassies and every British consul-general, consul, vice-consul, acting consul, pro-consul, consular agent, acting consul-general, acting vice-consul, and acting consular agent exercising his functions in any foreign place, including anyone with the diplomatic rank of counsellor.
- Any person certified by any of the above to be known to him to be competent to translate the document into English.

[SI 1990/572 para 5(1)].

24.65 In practice, if the translation is to be made in the UK, a notary or a solicitor should be asked to arrange for a translation to be made and certified.

Application of the exemptions in practice

24.66 Care should be taken to ensure an understanding of which exemption is being taken and that the requirements of that exemption are fulfilled. The following examples assume that the conditions of the exemptions in question are met.

Example 1

An ultimate parent company is incorporated in Germany and prepares its consolidated financial statements in accordance with EU-adopted IFRS. The German ultimate parent has a wholly-owned subsidiary in the US, which does not prepare consolidated financial statements. The US parent in turn wholly owns a UK company and its subsidiaries.

The section 228 of the Companies Act 1985 (CA06 Sec 400) exemption would not be available to the UK company in this circumstance due to the fact that the immediate parent is not incorporated under the law of an EEA state.

However, since the company has a non-EEA parent (the US company) the section 228A of the Companies Act 1985 (CA06 Sec 401) exemption is available. Since the UK group is included in the consolidated financial statements of its German parent that are prepared in accordance with a variant of IFRS that is consistent with the 7th Directive, it is able to take advantage of the exemption and need not prepare consolidated financial statements.

Example 2

The facts are the same as in example 2, except that there is a Belgian company in the group structure instead of the US company.

In this example the immediate parent company and the reporting parent are both incorporated under the law of an EEA state. Hence the section 228 of the Companies Act 1985 (CA06 Sec 400) exemption is available to the UK company. Since the UK company is included in the consolidated financial statements of its German parent that are prepared in accordance with the 7th Directive, it is able to take advantage of the exemption and need not prepare consolidated financial statements.

The section 228A of the Companies Act 1985 (CA06 Sec 401) exemption would not be available to the UK company in this circumstance due to the fact that all of the UK company's parent undertakings are incorporated under the law of an EEA state.

Example 3

The ultimate parent of a group is incorporated in the US and prepares its consolidated financial statements in accordance with US GAAP. The US ultimate parent has a wholly-owned subsidiary incorporated in Bermuda that prepares and has audited consolidated financial statements in accordance with 'pure' IFRS. The Bermudan subsidiary, in turn, owns a UK company and its subsidiaries.

The section 228 of the Companies Act 1985 (CA06 Sec 400) exemption would not be available to the UK company in this circumstance due to the fact that the immediate parent is not incorporated under the law of an EEA state.

However, since the company has a non-EEA parent the section 228A of the Companies Act 1985 (CA06 Sec 401) exemption is potentially available. As the UK group is included in the consolidated financial statements of its Bermudan parent that are prepared in accordance with IFRS (which per para 24.62.8 is consistent with the 7th Directive), it is able to take advantage of the exemption under section 228A of the Companies Act 1985 (CA06 Sec 401) and need not prepare consolidated financial statements.

Example 4

The facts are the same as in example 2, except that the Bermudan parent does not prepare consolidated financial statements.

The section 228 of the Companies Act 1985 (CA06 Sec 400) exemption would not be available to the UK company in this circumstance due to the fact that the immediate parent is not incorporated under the law of an EEA state.

However, since the company has a non-EEA parent the section 228A of the Companies Act 1985 (CA06 Sec 401) exemption is potentially available. In this case, the UK parent company is included in the consolidated financial statements of its US parent prepared in accordance with US GAAP. It will be necessary to determine whether the US GAAP consolidated financial statements are prepared *"in a manner equivalent to the 7th Directive"*. Such assessment should be made based on the principles in 24.62.9 above. If equivalence is agreed for the circumstances in question, then the UK group may take advantage of the exemption in section 228A of the Companies Act 1985 (CA06 Sec 401) and will not need to prepare consolidated financial statements. If equivalence cannot be agreed then the exemption will not be available.

Example 5

An ultimate parent company is incorporated in the US and prepares its consolidated financial statements in accordance with US GAAP. The US ultimate parent has a wholly-owned subsidiary in France. The French parent in turn wholly owns a UK company and its subsidiaries.

In this example the immediate parent company is incorporated under the law of an EEA state. Hence, the section 228 of the Companies Act 1985 (CA06 Sec 400) exemption is potentially available to the UK company. If the French company prepares consolidated financial statements in accordance with the 7th Directive, it is able to take advantage of the exemption and need not prepare consolidated financial statements.

Since the company has a non-EEA parent the section 228A of the Companies Act 1985 (CA06 Sec 401) exemption is also potentially available. In this case, the UK parent company is included in the consolidated financial statements of its US parent prepared in accordance with US GAAP. It will be necessary to determine whether the US GAAP consolidated financial statements are prepared *"in a manner equivalent to the 7th Directive"*. Such assessment should be made based on the principles in paragraph 24.62.9 above. If equivalence is agreed for the circumstances in question, then the UK group may take advantage of the exemption in section 228A of the Companies Act 1985 (CA06 Sec 401) and will not need to prepare consolidated financial statements. If equivalence cannot be agreed then the 228A of the Companies Act 1985 (CA06 Sec 401) exemption will not be available.

[The next paragraph is 24.70.]

All subsidiaries excluded from consolidation

24.70 Where all of a parent's subsidiaries are permitted or required to be excluded from consolidation by section 229 of the Companies Act 1985 (CA06

Secs 402, 405) (as restricted by FRS 2), that parent is exempt from the requirement to prepare consolidated financial statements. [FRS 2 para 21(f)]. The conditions for exclusion of subsidiaries from consolidation are considered in detail in paragraph 24.176.

Accounting treatment

24.71 Where a parent makes use of any of the above exemptions not to prepare consolidated financial statements, it should treat in its individual financial statements its interests in subsidiaries as fixed asset investments except for those held exclusively with a view to resale. Subsidiaries held exclusively with a view to resale should be recorded as current asset investments at the lower of cost and net realisable value (see further para 24.193).

Disclosure

24.72 Where a parent makes use of any of the exemptions and does not prepare consolidated financial statements, FRS 2 requires that parent to:

- Comply with the disclosure requirements of Part 1 of Schedule 5 to the Companies Act 1985 and also section 231 of the Companies Act 1985 (CA06 Secs 409, 410) in respect of parent companies not required to prepare consolidated financial statements.
- State that its financial statements present information about it as an individual undertaking and not about its group. The statement should include or refer to the note giving the grounds on which the parent undertaking is exempt from preparing consolidated financial statements, as required by Schedule 5 to the Companies Act 1985 paragraph 1(4).

[FRS 2 para 22].

24.73 The disclosure requirements set out in Part 1 of Schedule 5 to the Companies Act 1985 are extensive. They cover the following subjects:

- Reason for not preparing consolidated financial statements.
- Details about subsidiaries including: name; country of incorporation or registration; proportion of shares held; profit/loss for the year; aggregate capital and reserves at the year end; details about non-coterminous year ends; and holdings in shares of the parent.
- Details about significant holdings of greater than 20 per cent in undertakings other than subsidiary undertakings including: name; country of incorporation; proportion of shares held.
- Additional information about significant holdings of greater than 20 per cent in undertakings other than subsidiary undertakings including: aggregate capital and reserves and profit or loss for the year.

- Details about parents including: name of ultimate parent; name of largest group of undertakings for which consolidated financial statements are drawn up of which the undertaking is a member; and the name of the smallest such group.

24.74 The disclosure requirements of Part I of Schedule 5 to the Companies Act 1985 that relate to subsidiaries are explained in detail from paragraph 24.257.

Suggested wording for exempt parents

24.75 In practice, it is likely that many parent undertakings will be exempt from the requirement to prepare consolidated financial statements. Set out below are examples of wording that may be included in the accounting policies of parent undertakings that use one of the exemptions from preparing consolidated financial statements.

Example

Intermediate parent undertaking

Accounting policy extract — company

The financial statements contain information about GAAP UK Limited as an individual company and do not contain consolidated financial information as the parent of a group. The Company is exempt under [section 228 (for EEA immediate parents) (CA06 Sec 400), 228A (for non-EEA parents) (CA06 Sec 401)] of the Companies Act 1985 from the requirement to prepare consolidated financial statements as it and its subsidiary undertakings are included by full consolidation in the consolidated financial statements of its parent, [GAAP (UK) plc/ FRGAAP SA], a company [registered in England and Wales/registered in Scotland/incorporated in (for example) France].

Accounting policy extract — unincorporated undertaking

The financial statements contain information about GAAP & Co as an individual undertaking and do not contain consolidated financial information as the parent of a group. The [Partnership/Trust/ or other undertaking as applicable] is exempt under paragraph 21 [(b), (c), (d) or (e) as applicable] of FRS 2 from the requirement to prepare consolidated financial statements as it is included by full consolidation in the consolidated financial statements of its parent, [GAAP & Co/GAAP (UK) plc, a [partnership whose principal place of business is at [insert address]/company registered in England and Wales].

All subsidiaries excluded from consolidation

Accounting policy extract — company

The financial statements contain information about GAAP UK Limited as an individual company and do not contain consolidated financial information as the parent of a group. The Company is exempt under section 229(5) of the Companies Act 1985 (CA 06 Sec 402) from the requirement to prepare consolidated financial statements as the directors consider that all the company's subsidiaries [may/should] be excluded from consolidation for the reasons set out [below/in note x].

Accounting policy extract — unincorporated undertaking

The financial statements contain information about GAAP & Co as an individual undertaking and do not contain consolidated financial information as the parent of a group. The [Partnership/Trust/ or other undertaking as applicable] is exempt under paragraph 21(f) of FRS 2 from the requirement to prepare consolidated financial statements as the [directors/corresponding officers] consider that all its subsidiaries [may/should] be excluded from consolidation for the reasons set out [below/in note x].

Subsidiary undertakings

Introduction

24.76 Before the parent of a group of companies can start to prepare consolidated financial statements, it is important to decide exactly which undertakings form the group and should, therefore, be included in the consolidation. In addition, it is important to determine whether any subsidiaries should be excluded from the group under the exemptions allowed or required by the legislation and FRS 2.

24.77 Consequently, determining which undertakings are the parent's subsidiaries and should, therefore, be consolidated is fundamental to the preparation of consolidated financial statements and this section considers the rules that govern whether an undertaking is a subsidiary for this purpose.

[The next paragraph is 24.79]

Company Law

24.79 The Companies Act 1985 (International Accounting Standards and Other Amendments) Regulations (SI 2004/2947) introduced an updated EC 7th Directive definition of a subsidiary, removing the requirements for a participating interest to be held and introducing the notion of consolidation due to the 'power' to control. This brings the UK GAAP definition of a subsidiary closer to IAS 27, 'Consolidated and separate financial statements', and may mean that some entities that were previously classified as quasi-subsidiaries and some special purpose entities will become full legal subsidiaries (see further para 24.149.1 onwards).

Meaning of subsidiary undertaking

24.80 As mentioned above, a subsidiary undertaking can mean any of the following undertakings:

- A body corporate.
- A partnership.
- An unincorporated association carrying on a trade or business for profit.

- An unincorporated association not trading for profit.

[CA85 Sec 259(1); CA06 Sec 1161(1); FRS 2 para 16].

24.81 Consequently, any undertakings included in the above list may fall to be consolidated with the parent's financial statements if they are subsidiary undertakings.

24.82 It appears that the definition of 'undertaking' in section 259 of the Companies Act 1985 (CA06 Sec 1161) is wide enough to include trusts. Case law refers to 'association' meaning a combination of persons or of firms carrying on a particular venture, which seems to encompass trusts. The distinction in case law between associations and undertakings is that undertakings carry on business for gain. However, the definition in section 259 of the Companies Act 1985 (CA06 Sec 1161) is not restricted to there being a profit or gain resulting from the association's activities. Therefore, it would seem that generally trusts are associations that fall within the definition of undertaking in section 259 of the Companies Act 1985 (CA06 Sec 1161). These definitions have been amended for years beginning on or after 1 January 2005 for the effect of SI 2004/2947 (see para 24.79 above).

24.83 The Act provides the definitions of parent and subsidiary. FRS 2 uses the same definitions as those given in the Act and builds on them by giving additional guidance on their interpretation. There are six situations where an undertaking may be a subsidiary of a parent undertaking and these are where the parent:

- Holds a majority of the voting rights in the undertaking (see further para 24.89 onwards).
- Is a member of the undertaking and has the right to appoint or remove directors holding a majority of the voting rights at meetings of the board on all, or substantially all, matters (see further para 24.96 onwards).
- Has a right to exercise dominant influence over the undertaking by virtue of provisions either in its memorandum or articles, or in a control contract (see further para 24.125 onwards). (Note that no shareholding is necessary.)
- Is a member of the undertaking and controls alone, pursuant to an agreement with other shareholders or members, a majority of the voting rights in the undertaking (see further para 24.155 onwards).
- Has the power to exercise, or actually exercises, dominant influence or control over the undertaking (see further para 24.130 onwards).
- Is managed on a unified basis with the undertaking (see further para 24.152 onwards).

[CA85 Secs 258(2)(4), 10A Sch 3(1); CA06 Sec 1162(2)(4)].

24.84 The common feature of these definitions is that of control, or power to exercise control, by the parent (or the parent and its subsidiaries) over the subsidiary. The definitions are considered in detail in the paragraphs that follow.

24.85 Where an undertaking is determined not to be a subsidiary undertaking under the Act and FRS 2 it may still be necessary for it to be consolidated if it is a quasi-subsidiary. A quasi-subsidiary is defined in FRS 5 as "*a company, trust, partnership or other vehicle that, though not fulfilling the definition of a subsidiary, is directly or indirectly controlled by the reporting entity and gives rise to benefits for that entity that are in substance no different from those that would arise were the vehicle a subsidiary*". [FRS 5 para 7]. Where a quasi-subsidiary is identified, it is accounted for in the same way as other subsidiaries, that is, by way of full consolidation. Quasi-subsidiaries and how to account for them are considered in chapter 3.

Expressions used by unincorporated undertakings

24.86 Although subsidiaries can include unincorporated undertakings such as partnerships, various parts of the legislation use expressions that are common to companies only. Consequently, the Act provides the following provision:

> "*Other expressions appropriate to companies shall be construed, in relation to an undertaking which is not a company, as references to the corresponding persons, officers, documents or organs, as the case may be, appropriate to undertakings of that description.*" [CA85 Sec 259(3); CA06 Sec 1161(3)].

24.87 This provision will apply in a number of situations, but a good example of its effect concerns the expressions used by limited partnerships. A limited partnership is made up of a 'general partner' and a number of 'limited partners'. The general partner manages the business and the limited partners cannot be involved in the day to day business of the partnership. The partnership itself does not have a board of directors, but the equivalent to the board is the general partner himself. Consequently, if a company is a general partner in a limited partnership, then it will control the board of the limited partnership and the partnership will, therefore, be a subsidiary under section 258(2)(b) of the Companies Act 1985 (CA06 Sec 1162(2)(b)). (See further para 24.212.1 onwards).

24.88 Section 259(3) of the Companies Act 1985 (CA06 Sec 1161(3)) is also important because various disclosure provisions concerning subsidiary undertakings detailed in Schedule 5 to the Companies Act 1985 are expressed using terms that are only relevant to companies. These disclosure requirements are considered further in paragraph 24.213.

Majority of voting rights

24.89 An undertaking is a subsidiary where the parent undertaking holds a majority of its voting rights. [CA85 Sec 258(2); CA06 Sec 1162(2); FRS 2 para 14(a)].

24.90 This is the definition of a subsidiary that is applied most frequently in practice to identify subsidiaries. While ownership (equity) and voting rights are usually held in equal proportions, there are situations where an undertaking may own a majority of the equity in another undertaking and yet not hold a majority of the voting rights in it. In such a situation, the undertaking will not be a subsidiary (unless it is a subsidiary by virtue of one of the other definitions).

24.91 The example that follows illustrates how these provisions work in practice. Company A owns 100 ordinary shares in company B and company C owns 100 five per cent preference shares in company B. Company B has no other share capital.

Example

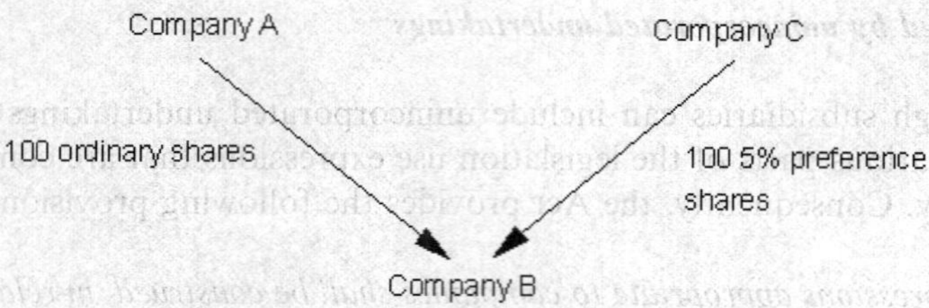

The rights attached to company B's shares are as follows:

- Ordinary shares:
  - 100 £1 ordinary shares.
  - All dividends after payment of preference dividends.
  - Right to all surplus assets on a winding up of the company after repayment of 5% preference shares.
  - Right to vote on all matters at any meetings of the company.
- Preference shares:
  - 100 £1 preference shares.
  - Fixed preference dividend.
  - Right on winding up to the repayment of par value and up to 25% of any sum standing to the credit of the share premium account.
  - No rights to vote at company meetings.

Under the Companies Act 1989 rules the distinction between equity share capital and other share capital is irrelevant in determining whether an undertaking is a subsidiary of another. The definition looks at who controls the 'voting rights' in the undertaking. The preference shares have no voting rights, while the ordinary shares do. Consequently, under the Act's rules, company B is a subsidiary of company A, but is not a subsidiary of company C. This of course ignores the other five tests for potential subsidiaries outlined in paragraph 24.83.

24.92 The Act and FRS 2 provide considerable guidance on the interpretation of the term 'voting rights', both in the context of companies and in the context of unincorporated undertakings.

24.93 'Voting rights' means the rights conferred on shareholders in respect of their shares to vote at the undertaking's general meetings on all, or substantially all, matters. [CA85 10A Sch 2(1); FRS 2 para 17]. Similarly, where an undertaking does not have share capital, voting rights also mean the rights conferred on members to vote at the undertaking's general meetings on all, or substantially all, matters. [CA85 10A Sch 2(1); FRS 2 para 17]. If the undertaking does not have general meetings where matters are decided by exercising voting rights, 'voting rights' will mean having the right under the undertaking's constitution to direct its overall policy, or to alter the terms of its constitution. [CA85 10A Sch 2(2)].

24.94 In determining whether an undertaking holds a majority of the voting rights, certain common rules apply and these are explained further in paragraph 24.165. In particular, options will generally only be taken into consideration, for the purposes of determining whether any party has a majority of voting rights or control of the board, when the option *has been exercised* (see further para 24.167). They may, however, be relevant for consideration of whether the parent has the power to exercise dominant influence over the other party (see further para 24.132).

24.95 In addition, the total voting rights in an undertaking have to be reduced where any rights are exercisable by the undertaking itself. [CA85 10A Sch 10]. This means, for example, that where an undertaking holds any of its own shares they should be excluded from the total voting rights taken into account in deciding whether the undertaking is a subsidiary.

Appointment or removal of majority of board

24.96 An undertaking is a subsidiary where the parent is a member of that undertaking and has the right to appoint or remove a majority of its board of directors. [CA85 Sec 258(2)(b); CA06 Sec 1162(2)(b); FRS 2 para 14(b)]. The meaning of the term 'member' is discussed in paragraph 24.161.

24.97 In this circumstance, *"the right to appoint or remove the majority of the board of directors"* means the right to appoint or remove directors that have a majority of the voting rights at board meetings on all or substantially all matters (without the need for any other person's consent or concurrence, except in the case where no other person has the right to appoint or, as the case may be, remove in relation to that directorship). [CA85 10A Sch 3(1)(3)]. In these circumstances, an undertaking should be treated as having the right to appoint a person to a directorship where:

- The person's appointment follows directly from his appointment as a director of the investing undertaking.
- The directorship is held by the investing undertaking itself.

[CA85 10A Sch 3(2)].

24.98 Certain common rules apply to the expression 'rights' used in paragraph 24.96 above and these are explained further in paragraph 24.165.

24.99 The operation of this definition of subsidiary is illustrated by the example that follows. In this example, the structure is the same as that described in the example in paragraph 24.91 above and illustrated in the diagram. However, in this example the rights attaching to the two different types of share are as follows:

Example

- Ordinary shares:
  - 100 £1 ordinary shares.
  - All dividends after payment of preference dividends.
  - Right to all surplus assets on a winding up of the company after repayment of 5% preference shares.
  - Right to vote on all matters at any meetings of the company.
  - Power to appoint two directors of the company with one vote each.
- Preference shares:
  - 100 £1 preference shares.
  - Fixed preference dividend.
  - Right on winding up to the repayment of par value and up to 25% of any sum standing to the credit of the share premium account.
  - No rights to vote at company meetings.
  - No voting rights, but where the preference dividend payment is passed the shareholders have the power to appoint two directors with two votes each.

Initially, company A holds the majority of the voting rights of company B and by virtue of section 258(2)(a) of the Companies Act 1985 (CA06 Sec 1162(2)(b)) (as explained in para 24.91 above) company B is a subsidiary of company A. However, if the preference dividend is in arrears and, as a consequence, the preference shareholders appoint their two directors, company B becomes a subsidiary of company C by virtue of section 258(2)(b) of the Companies Act 1985 (CA06 Sec 1162(2)(b)), as company C then has the right to appoint or remove directors holding a majority of the voting rights at company B's board meetings.

24.100 The situation described in the example is unusual and it is likely that in this situation as soon as company C is able to control company B's board, company A will lose effective control and will have to exclude company B from its consolidated financial statements. In this regard, FRS 2 states that where more than one undertaking is identified as a parent in such a situation, only one of those parents can have control in practice. [FRS 2 para 62]. In practice, when the arrears of dividend are paid the directors appointed to company B by company C might cease to hold office, in which case control would again reside with company A.

24.101 Where severe long-term restrictions exist on the rights or the ability of one of the parents to exercise control the subsidiary is required under FRS 2 to be excluded from consolidation (see para 24.185). Alternatively, in a situation where there is effectively deadlock in voting rights there might be common control, in which case this might indicate the existence of a joint venture (see chapter 27). [FRS 2 para 63].

24.102 Where an undertaking has the right to appoint a director with a casting vote in the event of a board deadlock and that undertaking controls half of the voting rights on the board, it will effectively control the board as it holds the casting vote and can, therefore, control any board decision.

24.103 In practice a further complication can arise. Many 50/50 joint ventures are set up in the form of companies with each party owning 50 per cent of the equity, holding 50 per cent of the voting rights in general meeting and having the right to appoint directors with 50 per cent of the votes on the board. In order to avoid total deadlock in the event of a disagreement a 'rotating' chairman is appointed with a casting vote. The chairman, who is chosen from the directors, is appointed in alternate years by each party to the joint venture. Therefore, in theory, by virtue of the casting vote, in years one, three and five the undertaking is the subsidiary of one of the venturers while in years two, four and six it is a subsidiary of the other.

24.104 Clearly it does not make sense for each party to consolidate in alternate years. Consequently, using the provision in paragraph 63 of FRS 2 mentioned in paragraph 24.101, such problems can be resolved in practice by considering the substance of the arrangement. It is likely that the arrangement outlined above would be treated as a joint venture with shared control, that is, both parties equity account, their interests.

[The next paragraph is 24.121.]

Dominant influence

24.121 The Act uses the term dominant influence in two of its definitions of subsidiaries. These definitions are as follows; an undertaking is a subsidiary of a parent if the parent:

- Has a *right to exercise a dominant influence* over the undertaking by virtue of provisions either in its memorandum or articles, or in a control contract (see para 24.125).
- Has the *power to exercise, or actually exercises, dominant influence or control* over it (see para 24.130).

24.122 The Act defines the term 'right to exercise a dominant influence', but it does not define 'actually exercises dominant influence' or 'power to exercise dominant influence'. Furthermore, the Act specifically states that its definition of 'right to exercise a dominant influence' should *"not be read as affecting the* *construction of the expression 'actually exercises a dominant influence'* ". [CA85 10A Sch 4(3)]. The right sought in the first bullet point above is a contractual right, whereas with the latter definition, it is the control that the investing entity actually has in practice or the power to exercise dominant influence or control that is important. The contractual right to exercise a dominant influence was introduced into the EC 7th Directive to deal with situations that arose in another EC member state; although it was also included in the UK legislation, it may not be effective in the UK (see further para 24.129).

24.123 FRS 2 first defines 'dominant influence' and then provides definitions for *'right to exercise a dominant influence'*, *'actually exercises dominant influence'* and *'the power to exercise dominant influence'*.

Dominant influence is defined as:

> *"Influence that can be exercised to achieve the operating and financial policies desired by the holder of the influence, notwithstanding the rights or influence of any other party."* [FRS 2 para 7].

24.124 By defining 'dominant influence', as well as the three longer expressions in the Act containing the term, FRS 2 is, in effect, linking the three expressions. The common thread is the implementation by the subsidiary of the operating and financial policies desired by the holder of the influence, that is, the parent.

Right to exercise a dominant influence

24.125 As stated above, an undertaking will be a subsidiary where the parent has the right to exercise a dominant influence in either of the following two ways:

- By provisions contained in the undertaking's memorandum or articles of association.
- By a 'control contract' with the undertaking.

[CA85 Sec 258(2)(c); CA06 Sec 1162(2)(c)].

24.126 A 'control contract' is a contract in writing that confers such a right that is authorised by the memorandum or articles of the undertaking in relation to which the right is exercisable and is permitted by the law under which that undertaking is established. [CA85 10A Sch 4(2)].

24.127 It should be noted that for this definition of a subsidiary the parent need not have an interest in the subsidiary.

24.128 Both the Act and FRS 2 state that the right to exercise dominant influence over another undertaking shall not be regarded as exercisable unless:

"*. . .it has a right to give directions with respect to the operating and financial policies of that other undertaking which its directors are obliged to comply with whether or not they are for the benefit of that other undertaking*." [CA85 10A Sch 4(1); FRS 2 para 7(a)].

24.129 It is thought that 'the right to exercise a dominant influence' is unlikely to apply to UK subsidiary companies as, in the UK, directors have a duty under common law to act in the company's best interests. There is some doubt whether the directors of a UK subsidiary could be obliged to comply with the directions of the holder of the influence if to do so would not be for the benefit of the subsidiary as this might leave them in breach of their duties as directors.

Power to, or actually exercise, dominant influence or control

24.130 An undertaking is a parent in relation to another undertaking, its subsidiary, if it has the *power to exercise, or actually exercises, dominant influence or control* over it. [CA85 Sec 258(4)(a); CA06 Sec 1162(4)(a); FRS 2 para 14(e)].

24.131 This definition of subsidiary, like the others, has been taken from the amended EC 7th Directive. Although implementation of the Directive by Member States into their national laws was optional, it was incorporated initially into the UK legislation by the Companies Act 1989 deliberately to catch a number of off balance sheet schemes that used special purpose entities to avoid consolidation (see further chapter 3). The original definition was *"if it owns a participating interest in the undertaking and actually exercises a dominant influence over it"*. This definition was subsequently amended by the Modernisation Directive (2003/51/EC) to be closer to that used in IFRS. In the UK, SI 2004/2947, 'The Companies Act 1985 (International Accounting Standards and Other Amendments) Regulations 2004' updated the Act for this change and this was also incorporated as an amendment to FRS 2.

24.131.1 As can be seen, a parent is no longer required to have a 'participating interest' in a subsidiary for section 258(4) of the Companies Act 1985 and FRS 2 to apply. [CA06 Sec 1162(4)]. (A participating interest is an interest in the shares of another undertaking held on a long-term basis for the purpose of securing a contribution to its activities by the exercise of control or influence arising from or related to that interest.) The second change is that under the new definition, the *power* to exercise dominant influence *or control* is enough for a company to qualify as a subsidiary. Previously, a company had to actually exercise dominant influence over the undertaking for it to be a subsidiary under this provision of the Act and FRS 2.

[The next paragraph is 24.132.]

Definition

24.132 The 'power to exercise dominant influence' is defined as *"a power that, if exercised, would give rise to the actual exercise of dominant influence"*. [FRS 2 para 7(c)].

24.133 FRS 2 defines 'actual exercise of dominant influence' as follows: *"The actual exercise of dominant influence is the exercise of an influence that achieves the result that the operating and financial policies of the undertaking influenced are set in accordance with the wishes of the holder of the influence and for the holder's benefit whether or not those wishes are explicit. The actual exercise of dominant influence is identified by its effect in practice rather than by the way in which it is exercised."* [FRS 2 para 7(b)].

24.134 The definitions above hinge on the terms 'control' and 'dominant influence'. Control is the ability of an entity to direct the operating and financial properties of another undertaking with a view to gaining economic benefits from its activities. Whereas, dominant influence is defined in FRS 2 in terms of the influence that can be exercised to achieve the operating and financial policies desired by the holder of the influence (see para 24.123). [FRS 2 para 7].

24.135 The term 'power to, or actually exercises, dominant influence or control' can be difficult to interpret in practice, principally because of the degree of judgement involved. However, in many cases it should be relatively obvious where control arises.

Example

Company A owns 5% of company B, but in addition has call options exercisable at any time that would give it all the voting rights in company B. Although company A's management do not intend to exercise the call options, the existence of the options and company A's ability to exercise them at any time to gain control of company B gives company A the power to exercise dominant influence. The presence of the options means that the operating and financial policies are set in accordance with company A's wishes and for its benefit, as the other shareholders of company B are mindful of the options in voting on operating and financial policies, as should company B make a decision not in accordance with company A's wishes, company A has the power to exercise the call options and reverse the decision.

24.136 An illustration of a group that consolidates subsidiaries because of dominant influence is given in Table 24.1.

Table 24.1 — BET Public Limited Company — Annual Report — 2 April 1994

Accounting policies (extract)

(b) Basis of consolidation (extract)

SUBSIDIARY UNDERTAKINGS (extract)
All companies over which the group is able to exercise a dominant influence are consolidated as subsidiary undertakings. Dominant influence is defined as the right to give directions with respect to operating and financial policies.

Operating and financial policies

24.137 The operating and financial policies of an undertaking will normally be set by the board of directors (in the case of a company) or a similar body for unincorporated undertakings. Usually, a parent would have a *right* to control the board by having the power to appoint or remove a majority of the board and would, therefore, be a parent by virtue of section 258(2)(b) of the Companies Act 1985 (CA06 Sec 1162(2)(b)).

24.138 The 'actual exercise of dominant influence' and 'power to exercise dominant influence' definitions of a subsidiary, discussed above, are intended to apply to those undertakings that, although effectively controlled by the parent, are not specifically caught by other definitions of the Act.

24.139 The operating and financial policies over which dominance would be needed in a typical entity would cover (but may not be limited to) the following subjects:

- Overall strategy.
- Financial (including most importantly the dividend policy).
- Marketing.
- Production.
- Personnel.

Practical ability and power to control

24.140 Heavy emphasis is placed on the effect of the influence in practice to ensure that undertakings genuinely controlled by the parent are defined as subsidiaries under this definition. But now powers that are unlikely to be exercised to change the decisions of those in day-to-day control of an entity's and financial policies do come into play. Their mere existence is likely to indicate that an entity has the ability to control (that is, the power to control). It is no longer just what happens in practice that is important, it is now also the ability to do something to gain control that is important as well.

Power of veto and other reserve powers

24.141 A power of veto (or other reserve power) that has the necessary effect in practice may give the holder a basis for actually exercising a dominant influence or the power to exercise dominant influence. However, the nature of the power of veto will be of critical importance.

24.142 For example, if an undertaking has shares carrying less than 50 per cent of the votes, but has over 75 per cent of the equity share capital of a company, it may only be able to block business that requires a special resolution. Such a power of veto is not, alone, sufficient to give the undertaking control, but would clearly have to be taken into account with other factors in determining whether the undertaking has the requisite control over the other party.

Commercial relationships

24.143 Certain undertakings can become very dependent on others by virtue of the commercial relationship between them. Examples include undertakings with:

- Only one customer.
- Only one possible supplier.
- Large borrowings from a bank.

24.144 In each of the above examples there may be situations where the undertaking concerned may be significantly influenced by the desires of the other party. With this in mind FRS 2 states that "*Commercial relationships such as that of supplier, customer or lender do not of themselves constitute dominant influence*". [FRS 2 para 72].

24.145 These relationships will not, generally, give rise to dominant influence unless some other factors are involved. For example, in the situation where undertakings only have one customer or supplier, if the customer or supplier concerned has a substantial participating interest in the undertaking, but it is not quite sufficient to control the undertaking on the grounds of his/her interest alone, the participating interest and the customer/supplier relationship taken together could be sufficient to give the customer/supplier the required control.

Two parents

24.146 The definition of a parent may give rise to an anomaly in that in certain situations it may seem that there are two parents. For example, one company may appear to be exercising dominant influence, yet another may have the power to do so. This situation is likely to arise when the shareholder with the power to exercise dominant influence chooses to be passive and does not prevent the other shareholder from actually exercising dominant influence. Where more than one undertaking appears to be the parent, only one can have control [FRS 2 para 62]. Control is defined as the ability to direct the financial and operating policies of another with a view to gaining economic benefits from its activities. Under the revised definitions in the law and FRS 2 the shareholder with the power to exercise dominant influence has control, despite choosing to be passive.

Example 1

A government has a controlling shareholding in a company, has board representation and is able to cast a majority vote, but in practice permits the other shareholder to govern the operating and financial policies of an entity. The government elects to be passive, voting consistently with the other shareholder appearing only to intervene where necessary to protect the national interest. In this situation, the government's ownership does constitute control as despite being passive and only intervening where necessary to protect the national interest it has the power to intervene. In effect, it has the power to exercise dominant influence as its presence on the board means that the operating and financial policies are set in accordance with the government's wishes and for its benefit.

Example 2

A government does not have a controlling shareholding in a company, but has a golden share that enables it to replace the board of directors with its nominees should the government disagree with the operating and financial policies decisions taken by the other shareholder. Whilst the share exists to enable the government to protect its national interest, the power that this share gives the government extends beyond this as there are no restrictions on the circumstances on which it can intervene. The share gives the government a power to exercise dominant influence as the presence of the share means that the operating and financial policies are set in accordance with the government's wishes and for its benefit. However, if there were restrictions on when the government could intervene, for example only in preventing the issuance of additional shares or the sale of a material ownership interest to foreign shareholders, then this would indicate that the government does not control the company.

Ceasing to exercise a dominant influence

24.147 As interpretation of the terms 'actual exercise of dominant influence' and 'power to exercise dominant influence' is subjective it might be seen as an opportunity, by some, to manipulate profit or gearing. In theory, at least, a parent might consolidate the results of a subsidiary in some years and exclude them in others, on the grounds that the parent either does, or does not, exercise dominant influence in a particular year. FRS 2 recognises that this may cause problems and states that:

> *"Once there has been evidence that one undertaking has exercised a dominant influence over another, then the dominant undertaking should be assumed to continue to exercise its influence until there is evidence to the contrary. However, it is still necessary for the preparation of the consolidated financial statements to examine the relationship between the undertakings each year to assess any evidence of change in status that may have arisen."* [FRS 2 para 73].

24.148 For example, if an undertaking has demonstrated that it actually exercises a dominant influence by vetoing a board decision or removing a chief executive then that undertaking will be presumed to continue to actually exercise dominant influence. This will continue to apply, even if the veto is not exercised again, unless there is some change in status of the relationship between the two undertakings.

24.149 Once an undertaking has been treated as a subsidiary of another, it should continue to be treated as a subsidiary until there is persuasive evidence that the relationship between the two undertakings has changed, such that the parent does not have dominant influence over the subsidiaries.

Special purpose entities

24.149.1 As a result of the introduction of 'power to exercise dominant influence' in 2005, certain entities that were previously considered to be quasi-subsidiaries under FRS 5 could now actually be full legal subsidiaries.

24.149.2 However, this might not always be the case. For example, where a parent gained the majority of the benefits arising from a special purpose entity (SPE) and its operating and financial policies were pre-determined, it would have fallen to be treated as a quasi-subsidiary under FRS 5 and not a full subsidiary under FRS 2. In this case, the changes to the definitions of subsidiaries under the Companies Act and FRS 2 do not impact the classification as a quasi-subsidiary, because the parent's control relationship has not changed. In relation to control FRS 5 says that where arrangements are made for allocating the benefits arising from the activities of an entity such active exercise of control is not necessary. It also says that in these situations no party has direct control and that control is exercised indirectly. Hence it can still be argued that the entity is not a full subsidiary, because the parent does not control or have the power to control (that is, cannot change) the SPE's financial and operating policies as these are predetermined and the SPE is a quasi-subsidiary as it is still caught by the provisions of FRS 5 (see further chapter 3).

24.149.3 Whilst this distinction may seem arbitary, given that the entity in question is consolidated in both circumstances, there were previously potential advantages to designation as a quasi-subsidiary rather than as a full subsidiary. The key advantage was the availability of 'linked presentation' under FRS 5 for the consolidated assets and liabilities. This potential advantage has been removed for those companies applying FRS 26. The amendment to FRS 26 published by the ASB introducing the IAS 39 recognition and derecognition criteria into UK GAAP, removes 'linked presentation' from FRS 5.

[The next paragraph is 24.150.]

Summary

24.150 To decide whether or not, in practice, an undertaking has the power to exercise, or actually exercises, dominant influence or control over another, a number of different factors have to be considered. Therefore, it is important that the full circumstances of each situation are considered, including the effect of any formal or informal agreements between the undertakings. Any decision in this respect is likely to be judgemental and should take into account the following:

- The degree of board representation.
- The degree of day-to-day influence over the undertaking's financial and operating policies.
- The extent of any powers of veto (or other reserve powers) held by the investor.
- Evidence of intervention to ensure that the investor's preferred operational and financial policies are implemented by the undertaking.
- Powers held by other investors or third parties that affect the degree of influence of the investor over the undertaking.
- Evidence of decisions *not* being taken in accordance with the investor's wishes.
- Other contrary evidence that indicates that dominant influence is not held.

Disclosure

24.151 Where an undertaking is a subsidiary only because its parent undertaking has the power to exercise, or actually exercises, a dominant influence or control over it, the consolidated financial statements should disclose the basis of the parent's dominant influence or control. [FRS 2 para 34].

Managed on a unified basis

24.152 An undertaking is a parent in relation to another undertaking, a subsidiary, if it and the undertaking are managed on a unified basis. [CA85 Sec 258(4)(b); CA06 Sec 1162(4)(b); FRS 2 para 14(e)].

24.153 The Act provides no definition of 'managed on a unified basis', however, FRS 2 defines it as follows:

> "*Two or more undertakings are managed on a unified basis if the whole of the operations of the undertakings are integrated and they are managed as a single unit. Unified management does not arise solely because one undertaking manages another.*" [FRS 2 para 12].

24.154 The application of this definition in practice will, as for dominant influence, require considerable judgement. The definition seems to suggest unified management at all levels in the undertakings. Characteristics of unified management could include:

- Adoption of an overall management strategy for the group which includes the undertaking in question.
- The group treating the undertaking as if it were a subsidiary, for example by determining its dividend policy.
- Common management teams, both at board level and operationally.
- Common employees.
- Common administrative functions, for example, accounting, personnel and marketing.
- Common premises.

Control governed by an agreement

24.155 An undertaking will be a subsidiary where the parent is a member of it and controls alone, following an agreement with other shareholders or members of the undertaking, a majority of its voting rights. [CA85 Sec 258(2)(d); CA06 Sec 1162(2)(d); FRS 2 para 14(d)].

24.156 The term 'voting rights' in this context means the same as the term explained in paragraph 24.93 above.

[The next paragraph is 24.159.]

Control contrasted with shared control

24.159 There is an important distinction to be drawn between the control that identifies the parent/subsidiary relationship and shared control. Shared control is the principal feature of a joint venture. A parent that has sole control over its subsidiary's resources can exercise that control to use the subsidiary's resources in a similar way to its own. The ability of an undertaking that shares control of the operating and financial policies of an undertaking is limited by the need to take account of the wishes of the other parties that share control. Shared control may indicate the presence of a joint venture and such ventures are considered further in chapter 27.

Common expressions and interpretations

24.160 In the definitions of subsidiaries explained above there are a number of common expressions and interpretations and these are considered in the paragraphs below.

Parent and subsidiary undertakings

24.161 The subscribers of a company's memorandum are deemed to have agreed to become members of the company and are entered as such in the company's register of members. Every person who agrees to become a member of a company and whose name is entered in its register, is a member of the company. [CA85 Sec 22; CA06 Sec 112]. A person holding preference shares in a company is a member of that company for this reason.

24.162 In the definitions of subsidiaries a parent undertaking is treated as a member of another undertaking if any of the parent's subsidiaries are members of that other undertaking. [CA85 Sec 258(3)(a); CA06 Sec 1162(3)(a); FRS 2 para 14]. Furthermore, this is also so if any shares in the other undertaking are held by a third party on behalf of the parent or its subsidiaries. [CA85 Sec 258(3)(b); CA06 Sec 1162(3)(b); FRS 2 para 14]. These provisions, however, do not extend to the situation where an undertaking is consolidated for the reason that its parent has the power to exercise or actually exercises dominant influence or control over it, or manages it on a unified basis.

Example

A parent's subsidiary company B may be a member of company C. In this circumstance, even where the parent is not a member of company C itself (for the purposes of determining whether company C is a subsidiary of the parent), the parent is treated as a member of company C by virtue of section 258(3) of the Companies Act 1985 (CA06 Sec 1162(3)).

24.163 In addition, where a group has intermediate parent undertakings (which can either be companies or unincorporated undertakings), their subsidiaries will also be regarded as subsidiaries of any parent undertakings further up the group structure. [CA85 Sec 258(5); CA06 Sec 1162(5)]. Consequently, subsidiaries of all parent undertakings within a group are deemed by this provision to be subsidiaries of the ultimate parent company.

24.164 In the situation where an undertaking is not a company, the Act provides no specific guidance on what constitutes membership of that undertaking. The Act does, however, provide general guidance on interpreting expressions used by companies that are not used by unincorporated undertakings. These provisions are discussed in paragraph 24.86.

Provisions concerning rights

24.165 There are a number of common provisions that explain how to treat rights in different situations. These rules apply to voting rights (see para 24.89 and 24.155 above) and rights to appoint or remove the majority of the board of directors (see para 24.96 above).

24.166 In determining whether rights should be attributed to a parent, rights held by a subsidiary undertaking should be treated as if they are held by the parent. [CA85 10A Sch 9(1)].

24.167 Rights exercisable in certain circumstances should only be taken into account when those circumstances have arisen and only for as long as they continue. [CA85 10A Sch 5(1)(a)]. Furthermore, such rights should also be taken into account where the circumstances are in the control of the person having the rights. [CA85 10A Sch 5(1)(b)]. In this respect, it is obvious that where the option *has been exercised* the shares must be taken into account in determining whether any party has a majority of voting rights or control of the board. Where an option to acquire shares has not yet been exercised, but can be freely exercised by its holder (that is, the option is within its exercise period) the rights in the shares under option (such as the voting rights) do not vest with the holder until the option is actually exercised. However, the existence of such an option might indicate that the holder has the power to actually exercise a dominant influence (using FRS 2's definition of that term) and the entity would be a subsidiary under section 258(4) of the Companies Act 1985 (CA06 Sec 1162(4)).

24.168 In addition, rights that the undertaking can normally exercise, but that are temporarily incapable of being exercised, should continue to be taken into account. [CA85 10A Sch 5(2)].

24.169 Rights should not be treated as held by a person (which includes an undertaking) if they are held in a fiduciary capacity. [CA85 10A Sch 6]. Similarly, rights held by a person as nominee should not be treated as held by him. Such rights will be considered held 'as nominee' for another person if they can only be exercised on his instructions or with his consent or concurrence. [CA85 10A Sch 7]. However, this provision cannot be used to require rights held by a parent to be treated as held by any of its subsidiaries. [CA85 10A Sch 9(2)].

24.170 Rights that are attached to shares held as security shall be treated as held by the person providing the security where those rights (excluding any right to exercise them to preserve the value of the security, or to realise it) are only exercisable in accordance with his instructions. This rule applies where the shares are held in connection with granting loans in the normal course of business and, except where they are exercisable to preserve the value of the security or to realise it, the rights are exercised only in the interests of the person providing the security. [CA85 10A Sch 8]. This provision, however, cannot be used to require rights held by a parent to be treated as held by any of its subsidiaries. [CA85 10A Sch 9(2)]. Furthermore, rights should be treated as being exercisable in accordance with the instructions, or the interests of, an undertaking if they are exercisable in accordance with the instructions of, or in the interests of, any group undertaking. [CA85 10A Sch 9(3)].

Provisions concerning capital

24.171 References to shares in an undertaking with a share capital are to allotted shares. [CA85 Sec 259(2)(a); CA06 Sec 1161(2)(a)]. In an undertaking that has capital, but no share capital, shares mean the rights to share in the capital of the undertaking. [CA85 Sec 259(2)(b); CA06 Sec 1161(2)(b)]. For example, in the case of a partnership, this would mean the relevant partners' share in the capital of the partnership. For an undertaking that has no capital, shares mean an interest conferring any right to share in the profits, or to contribute to the losses, of the undertaking. In this situation, it could also mean an interest giving rise to an obligation to contribute to the debts or expenses on winding up the undertaking. [CA85 Sec 259(2)(c); CA06 Sec 1161(2)(c)].

Meaning of subsidiary used elsewhere in the legislation

24.172 Whereas the paragraphs above explain the definitions of subsidiary undertaking used in the Act to determine which undertakings should be included in consolidated financial statements, section 736 of the Companies Act 1985 (CA06 Sec 1159) explains the meaning of 'subsidiary', 'holding company' and 'wholly-owned subsidiary' used elsewhere in the legislation; and the definitions of subsidiary differ. Section 736 of the Companies Act 1985 (CA06 1159) is narrower than section 258 of the Companies Act 1985 (CA06 1162) (which defines the undertakings to be included in the consolidation) in that section 736 of the Companies Act 1985 (CA06 Sec 1159) only includes some of the definitions of subsidiaries discussed above. Section 736 of the Companies Act 1985 (CA06 Sec 1159) does not include the following definitions used for consolidation purposes:

- Rights to direct operating and financial policies (see para 24.125).
- Dominant influence or unified management (see paras 24.130 and 24.152).

24.173 The notion of 'equity share capital' used before the introduction of the Companies Act 1989 as the main criterion in determining whether a company was a subsidiary of another, does not now apply either when determining whether an undertaking is a subsidiary for the purposes of consolidation or as part of the section 736 of the Companies Act 1985 (CA06 Sec 1159) definitions of subsidiary for other purposes within the Act. However, the term remains in the Act as it is used elsewhere in the legislation.

24.174 Loan stock deeds often refer to the parent and its subsidiaries as defined by section 736 of the Companies Act 1985 (CA06 Sec 1159) in determining borrowing restrictions. However, in this particular circumstance, section 144(6) of the Companies Act 1989 will allow the old definition based on equity share capital to remain in operation for trust deeds executed before the Companies Act 1989 came into effect.

Examples of practical situations

24.175 The examples that follow illustrate the type of situations that might arise in practice.

Example 1

A group takes an interest in a company that has £500,000 net liabilities in the hope that it can turn the company around. The group's interest is £100,000 preference shares and the preference shares are convertible at any time at the option of the group into 51% of the company's equity carrying 51% of the company's voting rights. The group also has an option to acquire the other 49% of the company's equity shares.

In this situation it is necessary to establish whether the company has the power to exercise, or actually exercises dominant influence or control over the company, or manages it on a unified basis, before it is deemed to be a subsidiary. The existence of the potential voting rights would *prima facie* give the required control. If it is determined that the undertaking is a subsidiary, the group will consolidate fully the assets and liabilities of the company and will show a significant minority interest. Such a situation could be very confusing for a reader of the financial statements and, as a consequence, some additional disclosure might be necessary.

In contrast, if the preference shares were convertible into the same number of ordinary shares at the option of the issuer, then the group would not have the power to exercise dominant influence or control over the company and, in the absence of any other factors, the company would not be a subsidiary.

Example 2

A UK group has a 50% interest in an overseas joint venture company and the other 50% is held by another overseas company incorporated in the same overseas country. Representation on the board and the share of income is spilt equally. Any disputes are referred to an arbitrator or to the High Court. The joint venture company manufactures goods only for the UK group and sells these goods at a price that is designed to provide a fixed return to the joint venture. The managing director of the joint venture is also an employee of the UK group.

Although the joint venture appears to have been set up as a 'deadlock' company the commercial arrangements suggest that it may be managed on a unified basis with the UK group and that the UK group might have dominant influence over the joint venture. In order to determine the extent of the influence, it would be necessary to establish if the joint venture's board is independent of the UK group. If, for example, the managing director reports to the board of the UK group and that board decides on, for instance, production levels and other management issues, then the joint venture may well be a subsidiary of the UK group.

Example 3

A group decides to dispose of a subsidiary to its management. After the disposal the group retains 49% of ordinary shares, management has 30% and outsiders have 21%. The group, management and outsiders also have convertible shares, which are convertible into the same proportions of ordinary shares. Those of the group are convertible after five years without any conditions, but those of the management are convertible only if certain profit targets are met. If they are not met management's shares will not be converted and the conversion of the group's shares will result in the company becoming a subsidiary again.

It is necessary to decide whether in practice the group has the power to exercise, or actually exercises, dominant influence or manages the subsidiary on a unified basis. If that is so, the company would remain a subsidiary throughout. If the group does not have dominant influence over the company or manage it on a unified basis, a view has to be taken as to whether it is probable and there is reasonable evidence that the profit targets will be met. If it is considered probable that they will be met, the company would not be treated as the group's subsidiary and, consequently, would not be consolidated. However, full details of the conversion rights should be disclosed in the group's consolidated financial statements.

Subsidiaries excluded from consolidation

24.176 As mentioned in paragraph 24.29 above, the general rule under both the Act and FRS 2 requires that all subsidiary undertakings should be included in the consolidated financial statements. [CA85 Sec 229(1); CA06 Sec 405(1); FRS 2 para 23]. The Act *permits* exclusion of a subsidiary from consolidation where:

- Inclusion is not material for the purposes of giving a true and fair view. [CA85 Sec 229(2); CA06 Sec 405(2)].
- The information necessary for the preparation of consolidated financial statements cannot be obtained without disproportionate expense or undue delay. [CA85 Sec 229(3)(b); CA06 Sec 405(3)(b)].
- There are severe long-term restrictions over a parent's rights in respect of a subsidiary. [CA85 Sec 229(3)(a); CA06 Sec 405(3)(a)].
- The parent's interest is held exclusively with a view to resale. [CA85 Sec 229(3)(c); CA06 Sec 405(3)(c)].

24.177 Paragraph 25 of FRS 2 restricts the fourth exemption to allow only when *"the subsidiary has not previously been consolidated in group accounts prepared by the parent undertaking"*.

24.178 The Act formerly required exclusion of a subsidiary from consolidation where its activities were so dissimilar from the rest of the group that inclusion would be incompatible with the obligation to give a true and fair view. This requirement was removed for periods beginning on or after 1 January 2005.

24.179 Within the constraints of the statutory framework set out in the Act, FRS 2 refines the conditions for exclusion so that they identify those undertakings that, though defined by the Act as subsidiaries, are not controlled by the parent in a way that would in principle justify consolidation. Having identified such subsidiaries, FRS 2 *requires* their exclusion from consolidation.

Inclusion not material

24.180 As mentioned above, a subsidiary undertaking need not be consolidated where its inclusion in the consolidation would have an immaterial effect. Two or more undertakings may only be excluded using this provision where taken together they are still not material to the consolidation. [CA85 Sec 229(2); CA06 Sec 405(2)]. As Financial Reporting Standards deal only with material items, this exemption is not found in the main body of FRS 2, but is dealt with and permitted by paragraph 78(a) of the explanatory section of FRS 2. However, materiality needs to be judged carefully, as Alliance Trust was commented on by the Financial Reporting Review Panel (FRRP) in April 1995 for not consolidating its banking subsidiary. In its financial statements for the year to 31 January 1994,

Alliance Trust had excluded its subsidiary on the grounds of immateriality, but has consolidated it in the subsequent year following discussions with the Stock Exchange and the FRRP (see Tables 24.3 and 24.4).

Table 24.3 – The Alliance Trust PLC – Report and Accounts – 31 January 1994

NOTES ON THE ACCOUNTS (extract)

1. ACCOUNTING POLICIES (extract)

f The accounts of Alliance Trust (Finance) Limited have not been consolidated with those of the Company as the directors consider that the amounts involved are not material and that their inclusion would detract from the clarity of the accounts in respect of the principal activity of the Company as an authorised investment trust. A separate statement of the affairs of Alliance Trust (Finance) Limited is on page 23.

Table 24.4 – The Alliance Trust PLC – Report and Accounts – 31 January 1995

REPORT OF THE DIRECTORS (extract)

The consolidated accounts, which are provided for the first time this year, include the results of our banking and savings subsidiary. Alliance Trust (Finance) Limited. These have been produced in the light of developing accounting standards, which will lead shortly to adoption of a Statement of Recommended Practice for investment trusts, and after discussion with the Financial Reporting Review Panel, the Company having raised the issue of consolidation with the Stock Exchange. Full information on the subsidiary has previously been included separately within the accounts. Relevant information continues to be given in note 12.

Disproportionate expense or undue delay

24.181 Although the Act allows a subsidiary that is material in the context of the group to be excluded on the grounds that the information necessary for the preparation of the consolidated financial statements cannot be obtained without disproportionate expense or undue delay, this is not permitted by FRS 2. [CA85 Sec 229(3)(b); CA06 Sec 405(3)(b); FRS 2 para 24]. FRS 2 takes the view that mere expense or undue delay are not sufficient grounds to exclude a material subsidiary and, therefore, in practice this reason for exclusion cannot be used. The ASB's view is that if the subsidiary is material, it must be included and the consolidated financial statements cannot give a true and fair view without its inclusion.

Severe long-term restrictions

Basis of exclusion

24.182 Consolidation of a subsidiary undertaking is *not required* by the Act where severe long-term restrictions substantially hinder the exercise of the parent company's rights over the assets or over the management of the undertaking.

[CA85 Sec 229(3)(a); CA06 Sec 405(3)(a)]. The rights that must be restricted for this exclusion to apply are those that would result in the undertaking being a subsidiary of the parent and without which it would not be a subsidiary (see para 24.165). [CA85 Sec 229(3); CA06 Sec 405(3); FRS 2 para 25(a)]. They include all such rights attributed to the parent undertaking under section 229(3). Table 24.5 illustrates a situation where certain subsidiaries are excluded from consolidation because of severe long-term restrictions.

Table 24.5 – BM Group PLC – Annual Report – 30 June 1993
NOTES TO THE FINANCIAL STATEMENTS (extract)

15. Investments (extract)

The net assets of certain African subsidiaries of the Group have been excluded from consolidation on the basis that severe long term restrictions are in place which hinder the exercise of the Group's rights over the assets employed. The subsidiaries concerned are Blackwood Hodge (Kenya) Ltd, Blackwood Hodge (Cote d'Ivoire) SarL. Blackwood Hodge (Tanzania) Ltd, Blackwood Hodge (Ghana) Ltd (60% owned) and Blackwood Hodge (Sierra Leone) Ltd.

24.183 The ASB considers, however, that where the parent's rights are restricted in this way the subsidiary concerned *should* be excluded from consolidation. The important difference is that the Act *permits* exclusion on these grounds whereas FRS 2 *requires* exclusion. However, FRS 2 states that in order to justify not consolidating a subsidiary the effect of the restrictions must be that the parent does not *control* its subsidiary.

24.184 Furthermore, severe long-term restrictions are identified by their effect in practice rather than by the way in which the restrictions are imposed. For example, a subsidiary should not be excluded because restrictions are threatened or because another party has the power to impose them unless such threats or the existence of such a power has a severe and restricting effect in practice in the long-term on the parent's rights. [FRS 2 para 78(c)].

24.185 There are a number of situations where a parent's control over its subsidiary *may* be subject to severe long-term restrictions. These include situations where the following exist:

- A power of veto is held by a third party.
- Severe restrictions exist over remittances.
- Insolvency or administration procedures are in progress.
- Two parent undertakings are identified under the definitions in the Act, but one does not control the subsidiary undertaking or they exercise joint control.

An example of a situation where a company holds a majority of the subsidiary's voting rights, but its ability to exercise those rights is restricted, is given in Table 24.6.

Table 24.6 – British Steel plc – Report and Accounts – 2 April 1994

ACCOUNTING POLICIES (extract)

1. BASIS OF CONSOLIDATION (extract)

The Company holds a majority of the voting rights in UES Holdings Limited (UES), but is restricted in its ability to exercise those rights under an agreement with the other shareholder. Consequently, the investment has not been consolidated in these accounts but has been included based on the Group's share of its results and net assets.

24.186 In general, restrictions are better dealt with by disclosure rather than by exclusion. However, the overriding principle is that a parent *should not* consolidate a subsidiary that it does not control. Consider the following example, which deals with a power of veto and restrictions over remittances.

Example

A parent has a subsidiary overseas. The subsidiary is owned and managed by the parent, but the host government has the power to:

- Veto the sale of the parent's interest in the subsidiary to an overseas investor.
- Veto any board decisions that are not in the interests of the local community.
- Restrict or prevent the remittance of funds from the subsidiary to the UK.

The parent company does not intend to sell the subsidiary and it has never experienced a veto of a board decision or restrictions of remittances by the host government. In practice, the parent's and the host government's objectives are the same and it is, therefore, extremely unlikely that the veto will be used or the restrictions over remittances imposed.

Although the host government has a power of veto over a sale and certain board decisions and can restrict remittance of funds to the UK, it has never used these powers and it is assumed, from the facts given, that it is unlikely to do so. Furthermore, as the parent's objectives and those of the local government are similar, it is unlikely that the threat of the veto or restrictions have any effect on the manner in which the subsidiary is managed by the parent. This would, therefore, appear to be a situation where the veto and restrictions have little effect in practice and consolidation would be required. The potential restrictions over distributions should then be disclosed in accordance with paragraph 53 of FRS 2.

24.187 FRS 2 specifically considers the situation where a subsidiary undertaking is subject to an insolvency procedure in the UK. Where control over that undertaking has passed to a designated official (for example, an administrator, an administrative receiver or a liquidator), the effect will be that severe long-term restrictions are in force. A company voluntary arrangement does not necessarily lead to loss of control and in some overseas jurisdictions formal insolvency procedures may not amount to loss of control. [FRS 2 para 78(c)].

Example

An intermediate holding company's parent is in administration and is unlikely to produce consolidated financial statements. It therefore appears that the intermediate holding company will have to prepare consolidated financial statements as it will not be able to avail itself of the exemption from preparing consolidated financial statements given in the Companies Act (see para 24.57). Most of the intermediate parent's subsidiaries have been sold since the year end because of the group's need to realise assets. There is also a problem in obtaining information from the purchasers of those companies.

If it can be demonstrated that there are significant restrictions imposed on the intermediate parent by the administrator such that the intermediate parent was unable to exercise its rights over the assets and management of the subsidiaries then that would be a justifiable reason for non-consolidation.

Accounting treatment

24.188 Where a parent's control over a subsidiary is subject to severe long-term restrictions, that subsidiary should be excluded from consolidation and treated as a fixed asset investment. If the subsidiary was acquired with the restrictions, the investment should be carried initially at cost. However, if the restrictions came into force at a later date, the investment should be carried at a fixed amount calculated using the equity method at the date on which the restrictions came into force. While the restrictions are in force the parent should make no further accruals for the profits or losses of the undertaking. But if it continues to exercise significant influence over the undertaking it should account for its investment as an associate using equity accounting (see chapter 27). [FRS 2 para 27].

24.189 A review of the value of subsidiary undertakings subject to severe long-term restrictions should be carried out to assess whether the carrying value of the investment has suffered an impairment. Where any impairment has occurred, this should be reflected by providing against the carrying amount of the relevant subsidiary and charging the provision to the consolidated profit and loss account. It may then be necessary also to make a provision against the carrying value of the investment in the undertaking holding the investment and charge that provision to that undertaking's profit and loss account. In assessing impairment, each subsidiary should be considered individually. The intra-group balances with subsidiary undertakings excluded on the grounds of severe long-term restrictions should also be reviewed and written down, if necessary. [FRS 2 para 27].

24.190 When the severe long-term restrictions cease and the parent undertaking's rights are restored, the amount of the profit or loss for that subsidiary that accrued during the period of restriction should be separately disclosed in the consolidated profit and loss account for the period in which the control is resumed. Any amount previously charged as an impairment that is written back as a result of restrictions ceasing, should be separately disclosed. [FRS 2 para 28]. An example of this situation is given in Table 24.7.

24.191 It should be remembered, however, that where a subsidiary is liquidated during or after the year end, it should still be consolidated up to the point that the restrictions come into force. Such a subsidiary should only be excluded from consolidation after the date on which it has gone into liquidation.

24.192 It is possible that restrictions may lift sufficiently for a subsidiary that has previously been treated as an investment to be equity accounted as an associated undertaking, because the parent now has significant influence over that undertaking, but does not exercise sufficient control to justify full consolidation. In practice this is likely to be rare, but should it occur, the *group's share* of the profit or loss that accrued during the period of the restriction should be dealt with in the consolidated profit and loss account of the period in which significant influence is resumed. The amount should be separately disclosed if it is material.

Interest held exclusively with a view to subsequent resale

Basis of exclusion

24.193 Consolidation of a subsidiary undertaking is *not required* where the interest of the parent company is held exclusively with a view to subsequent resale. [CA85 Sec 229(3)(c); CA06 Sec 405(3)(c)]. In this situation, the 'interests' of the parent company are the interests attributed to it under the definition of 'parent undertaking' (see para 24.161). Again, this exemption is repeated in FRS 2, but with the important difference that the Act *permits* exclusion on these grounds whereas FRS 2 *requires exclusion*. [FRS 2 para 25(b)]. FRS 2 also restricts the circumstances in which a subsidiary held for resale is permitted (and required) to be excluded to those where *"the undertaking has not previously been consolidated in group accounts prepared by the parent undertaking"*. [FRS 2 para 25(b)].

24.194 The standard defines an interest held exclusively with a view to subsequent resale as:

"a An interest for which a purchaser has been identified or is being sought, and which is reasonably expected to be disposed of within approximately one year of its date of acquisition; or

b An interest that was acquired as a result of the enforcement of a security, unless the interest has become part of the continuing activities of the group or the holder acts as if it intends the interest to become so." [FRS 2 para 11].

24.195 FRS 2 gives specific guidance on the interpretation of disposal 'within approximately one year'. An interest for which a sale is not completed within one year of its purchase may still meet the requirement if, at the time the financial statements are signed:

- The terms of sale have been agreed.
- The process of disposing of the subsidiary is substantially complete.

[FRS 2 para 78(d)].

24.196 FRS 2 includes only 'enforcement of a security' and excludes other methods of involuntary acquisition (unless they meet the first definition's requirements). Typically 'enforcement of a security' will apply to banks that have made secured loans to undertakings that have subsequently defaulted on their loans and which are, therefore, controlled by the banks. Provided such an undertaking has not become part of the continuing activities of the bank's group and the bank does not act as if it intends it to become so, the undertaking should not be consolidated.

24.197 FRS 2 draws attention to paragraph 8 of Schedule 10A to the Companies Act 1985 which provides that *rights* that are *"attached to shares held by way of security"* should be treated as held by the 'person providing the security' where those rights are only exercisable in accordance with his instructions. The right of the holder of the security to exercise the rights to preserve the value of the security or to realise it does not affect the above provision. This rule applies where the shares are held in connection with granting loans in the normal course of business and, apart from the purpose of preserving the value of the security or of realising it, the rights are exercisable only in the interests of the provider of the security.

Example

A bank has acquired over 50% of the voting rights of a company as a result of a reconstruction whereby it and other lenders converted debt into equity. The bank intends to dispose of the equity when it gets the opportunity.

The company is technically a subsidiary of the bank, but it would not require to be accounted for on a full consolidation basis in the bank's consolidated financial statements as it is held for resale. It should, therefore, be excluded from consolidation and accounted for in the way described below.

26.197.1 An illustration of a company excluding a subsidiary from consolidation on this ground is given in Table 24.7.

Table 24.7 – Barclays PLC – Report and Accounts – 31 December 1993

Notes to the accounts (extract)

54 Subsidiary and associated undertakings (extract)

Certain subsidiaries not consolidated in previous years are now included in these accounts because, in the opinion of the Directors, the long-term restrictions which hindered the exercise of the rights of the Group over their assets or management have ceased. After allowing for dividends received and foreign exchange adjustments, there were no unrecognised profits or losses accruing during the period of restriction.

During 1992, the Group acquired a 100% interest in Imry Holdings Limited (Imry), a company registered in England, as a result of enforcing security against a loan to Chester Holdings (UK) Limited, the parent company of Imry. The interest is held exclusively with a view to subsequent resale and therefore has not been consolidated. The Group holds all the issued shares of Imry and all of the £100m zero coupon preference shares in its subsidiary, Imry Jersey Limited. The shareholdings were valued at £56m at 31st December 1993 (1992 £56m). At 31st December 1993, the capital and reserves of Imry amounted to £79m (1992 £71m). The profit before taxation of Imry for the year ended 1993 was £8m. There were outstandings of £81m (1992 £85m) due to the Group, secured by a fixed and floating charge on the assets of Imry. During the year, Barclays Mercantile Limited paid £2,147,000 in rentals to Imry under a lease. Imry paid £675,000 to Barclays Bank PLC in exchange for the Bank providing a guarantee for the rental obligations of Barclays Mercantile Limited under its lease, and £385,000 to Barclays Property Holdings on behalf of Barclays Mercantile Limited to cover the cost of repair work required under the terms of the lease. There were no other material transactions between Imry and the Group during the year.

Accounting treatment

24.198 A subsidiary held exclusively with a view to resale and not previously consolidated, although controlled by its parent, does not form part of the group's continuing activities. The parent's control is temporary and is not used to deploy the underlying assets and liabilities of that subsidiary as part of the group's continuing activities and for the parent's benefit. The subsidiary should, therefore, be excluded from consolidation on these grounds and should be treated as a current asset investment, included in the group balance sheet at the lower of cost and net realisable value. [FRS 2 paras 29, 79(b)]. Where the subsidiary has still not been sold within approximately one year of the acquisition, it should be consolidated and fair values attributed to its individual assets and liabilities as at the date of acquisition (see further chapter 25). [FRS 7 para 18]. An example of a subsidiary excluded on these grounds is given in Table 24.8.

Dissimilar activities

24.199 A further exemption from consolidation previously applied where the activities of one or more subsidiaries are so different from those of the other undertakings included in the consolidated financial statements that their inclusion would be *"incompatible with the obligation to give a true and fair view"*. This was repealed under SI 2004/2947, 'The Companies Act 1985 (International Accounting Standards and Other Amendments) Regulations 2004'.

Disclosure for subsidiaries excluded from consolidation

24.200 Schedule 5 to the Companies Act 1985 sets out certain information about subsidiaries that companies that prepare consolidated financial statements have to give; these general requirements are considered in paragraph 24.213 below. Also, companies that do not prepare consolidated financial statements have to give information about their subsidiaries and this information is similarly set out in Schedule 5 to the Companies Act 1985. These provisions are considered in chapter 6.

24.201 The additional disclosure required by Schedule 5 to the Companies Act 1985 and FRS 2 concerning subsidiaries that have been excluded from consolidation where consolidated financial statements are prepared is extensive. Although, in general, the disclosures relate to individual subsidiaries excluded from consolidation, there are circumstances where it may be possible to provide the information on an aggregated basis for some or all of the subsidiaries concerned. FRS 2 extends the Act's disclosure requirements for subsidiaries excluded from consolidation (including those that are unincorporated subsidiaries).

The Act's requirements

24.202 Where a subsidiary is excluded from consolidation, the notes to the consolidated financial statements must disclose:

- The reasons why the subsidiary or the subsidiaries are not dealt with in the consolidated financial statements. [CA85 5 Sch 15(4)]. The reason disclosed would have to be one of those explained above.
- The aggregate amount of the subsidiary's capital and reserves at the end of its relevant financial year and its profit or loss for the period. This information need not be given, however, where either of the following conditions is satisfied:
  - The group's total investment in its subsidiaries' shares is included in the consolidated financial statements by the equity method of valuation (see chapter 27).
  - The undertaking is not required under the Act to file its balance sheet with the Registrar of Companies or publish it in Great Britain or elsewhere. Exemption is only allowed under this provision, however, if the group's holding in the undertaking is less than 50 per cent of the nominal value of that undertaking's shares. [CA85 5 Sch 17(1)(2)].

An example of the type of disclosure required where a subsidiary has been excluded on the grounds of being held exclusively for resale is illustrated in Table 24.8.

Table 24.8 — Airtours plc — Annual report and accounts — 30 September 1993

Notes to the financial statements (extract)

10) Fixed asset investments (extract)

All of the subsidiary undertakings, with the exception of Moon Leasing Limited, have been consolidated in the Group financial statements. The financial statements of Moon Leasing Limited have not been consolidated as it is being held exclusively for resale.

The aggregate amount of the capital and reserves of Moon Leasing Limited was £149,808 at 30th September 1993. The profit for the year was £149,807.

26.202.1 References to 'relevant financial year' above are to the subsidiary's financial year ending with the parent's year end or the last financial year ending before that date. [CA85 5 Sch 17(4)].

26.202.2 The information required by paragraph 17 of Schedule 5 to the Act need not be given if it is not material. [CA85 5 Sch 17(3)].

Additional requirements of FRS 2

24.203 In addition to the disclosures required by Schedule 5 to the Act, the following information should be given in the consolidated financial statements for subsidiaries not included in the consolidation:

- Particulars of the balances between the excluded subsidiaries and the rest of the group.
- The nature and extent of transactions of the excluded subsidiaries with the rest of the group.
- For an excluded subsidiary carried other than by the equity method, any amounts included in the consolidated financial statements in respect of:
  - Dividends received and receivable from that subsidiary (although the adoption of FRS 21 all but prohibits the recognition of dividends receivable at the year end).
  - Any write-down in the period in respect of the investment in that subsidiary or amounts due from that subsidiary.

[FRS 2 para 31].

- Guarantees in respect of subsidiary undertakings excluded from consolidation have to be treated in the same way as guarantees given by members of the group to third parties. [FRS 2 para 79(d)]. The detailed disclosure in respect of commitments and guarantees is set out in paragraph 50 of Schedule 4 to the Act and is discussed in detail in chapter 21.

Aggregation of disclosures

24.204 The general disclosure requirements listed above are required for individual excluded subsidiaries. However, if the information about excluded subsidiaries is more appropriately presented for a sub-unit of the group made up from more than one excluded subsidiary, the disclosures may be made on an aggregate basis. The sub-units for which these disclosures should be given are to be made up from subsidiary undertakings *"excluded under the same sub-section of section 229"*. [FRS 2 para 32]. The three permitted or required exclusions are dealt with in section 229 of the Companies Act 1985 (CA06 Sec 405) as follows:

- Not material (see para 24.180 above).
- Severe long-term restrictions (see para 24.182 above).
- Held for subsequent resale (see para 24.193 above).

24.205 As FRS 2 does not deal with immaterial matters the disclosures are not required for subsidiaries excluded from consolidation on the grounds of immateriality.

24.206 A strict interpretation of paragraph 32 of FRS 2 suggests that aggregation of the information concerning subsidiaries excluded because of severe long-term restrictions and subsequent resale is permitted as they are both dealt with by the Companies Act 1985 in section 229(3) (CA06 Sec 405(3)). However, as the subsidiaries concerned are excluded for different reasons this may lead to some confusion. To avoid such confusion, aggregation might be given under the following headings:

- Severe long-term restrictions.
- Held for subsequent resale.

24.207 However, individual disclosures should be made for any excluded subsidiary, including its sub-group where relevant, that alone accounts for more than 20 per cent of any one or more of the group's:

- Operating profits.
- Turnover.
- Net assets.

[FRS 2 para 32].

24.208 The group amounts in paragraph 24.207 should be measured by including all excluded subsidiaries. [FRS 2 para 32].

General exemptions from disclosure requirements

24.209 The information required to be disclosed under the Act concerning subsidiaries excluded from consolidation outlined above (except for that required by paragraphs 6, 9A, 20 and 28A of Schedule 5 to the Companies Act 1985) need not be disclosed if, in the directors' opinion, its disclosure would be seriously prejudicial to the subsidiary's business or to the business of the parent or any of its subsidiaries. This exemption applies where the particulars relate to a subsidiary that is established under the law of a country outside the UK or where its business is carried on outside the UK. However, the Secretary of State has to agree that the disclosure need not be made and the fact that advantage is taken of this exemption has to be disclosed. [CA85 Sec 231(3)(4); CA06 Sec 409(3)(4)(5)]. It is then questionable whether this exemption extends to disclosures required by FRS 2 and this is considered further in paragraph 24.233.

24.210 An example of an occasion when it would be allowable not to disclose this information would be when a company has trading subsidiaries in two countries and those two countries are either in conflict, or have trade embargoes between them. In these two situations where these subsidiaries are excluded from consolidation on one of the grounds considered above, the disclosure of the UK group's investment in each subsidiary might impair its trading ability in those countries.

24.211 The general exemption from the disclosure requirements of Schedule 5 to the Companies Act 1985 (where certain information is not required if the number of undertakings is such that the resulting disclosure is, in the opinion of the directors, excessively lengthy) does not apply to subsidiaries that are excluded from consolidation. [CA85 Sec 231(5)(b); CA06 Sec 410(2)(b)].

24.212 Note that, where a subsidiary has been excluded from consolidation as outlined from paragraph 24.176 above, the Act requires that the information outlined below from paragraph 24.213 should still be given as there is no exemption in this respect.

Limited partnerships

24.212.1 As mentioned in paragraph 24.87 above a limited partnership is made up of one or more 'general partners' and one or more 'limited partners'. A limited partner that is registered under the Limited Partnership Act 1907 is prevented from taking any active role in the affairs of the entity. If a limited partner does involve itself in the entity's affairs, it will be liable for the debts and obligations of the entity whilst its participation continues. The partnership itself does not have a board of directors, but the nearest equivalent to the board is the general partner. Consequently, if a company is the general partner in a limited partnership, then it will control the equivalent of the board and *prima facie*, under both the Companies Act and FRS 2 the limited partnership should be consolidated in full.

24.212.2 Therefore, the starting point when a group is considering how to account for a limited partnership in which it is the general partner should be to consider whether full consolidation is appropriate. In determining whether full consolidation is necessary, it should be borne in mind that in certain situations the general partner might be liable for all of the debts of the limited partnership in excess of the capital contributed by the limited partners. Consequently, full consolidation might be appropriate, for example where:

- the limited partnership operates a business which could incur losses;
- the limited partnership has external debt additional to partners' capital; or
- the limited partners have only contributed nominal capital.

A similar treatment might be applicable also where there are guarantees given by the limited partnership that might if called fall due to the general partner where the limited partners' capital would not cover the obligation.

Consolidation of limited partnerships by general partner — historical approach

24.212.3 Fully consolidating such limited partnerships can cause particular problems in practice, especially where a company's investment as the general partner in a limited partnership is only nominal in amount and the funding of the limited partnership comes mainly from its limited partners, external funding being minimal. This often arises in the case of venture capital or property asset management companies where the limited partnership route is seen as being the most tax efficient vehicle for some investors. For example, where a company's investment as a general partner is only (say) one per cent of the capital of the limited partnership, full consolidation of the assets and liabilities of the limited partnership would be required and there would be a large minority interest of 99 per cent. Consequently, prior to the publication of FRS 9 (referred to below), many companies in this situation (particularly in the venture capital industry) historically applied a true and fair override to avoid full consolidation. As the 'true and fair override' cannot be used to exclude a subsidiary from consolidation, some companies proportionately consolidated the company's share of the assets and liabilities and profits and losses of the limited partnership (see further chapter 27). This represents an override of the requirement in paragraph 1 of Schedule 4A to the Companies Act 1985, which requires consolidation in full of those results and assets and liabilities. This illustrates the point that a group cannot override those sections of the Act that specify the composition of the group; but it can override the detailed provisions of (in this case) Schedule 4A of the Companies Act 1985 as to how a subsidiary is to be consolidated. Where such an override is used, the particulars, reasons and effect should be given in the notes in accordance with the Act and FRS 18 (see para 24.51 and chapter 2).

24.212.4 Using the true and fair override in this way is no longer considered appropriate in most situations given the guidance available in FRS 9, which is explained in the paragraphs that follow.

Severe long-term restrictions over general partner's control — FRS 9 approach

24.212.5 FRS 9 paragraph 11, recognises that in certain situations an investor may qualify as the parent of an entity under the definition of a subsidiary in the Act and FRS 2, but that contractual arrangements between the parties mean that the other investors in practice control the investee. In such cases, 'severe long-term restrictions' exist over the parent's interests that *"substantially hinder the exercise of the rights of the parent undertaking over the assets or management of the subsidiary undertaking"*.

24.212.6 With a limited partnership, severe long-term restrictions might arise where the general partner's ability to control the partnership is restricted by the rights that the limited partners have. In this type of situation, where the limited partnership is funded mainly by its limited partners, the limited partnership should be excluded from consolidation by the general partner because FRS 2 requires, and the Act permits, exclusion of a subsidiary from consolidation if severe long-term restrictions exist. [CA85 Sec 229; CA06 Secs 405, 402; FRS 2 para 25(a)].

24.212.7 Depending upon the particular circumstances, severe long-term restrictions would probably exist where the limited partners (excluding any related party to the general partner) have the ability to dismiss the general partner within a short notice period. In addition, depending upon the particular circumstances, it might be possible to show that severe long-term restrictions exist over the general partner's ability to exert control where a combination of the following factors arise:

- The involvement of the limited partners in high level strategic decisions (these would have to be prescribed in the partnership deed as limited partners are not permitted to be involved in the day to day running of the partnership).
- Limited partner representation on the board of the general partner.
- Limited partners voting on key decisions (again this would need to be specified in the partnership deed).
- Pre-determined sharing of profits between the partners.
- Active participation by the limited partners in determining the limited partnership agreement.
- Very narrow investment guidelines.

24.212.8 If severe long-term restrictions do apply and the subsidiary is not consolidated, the accounting treatment will then depend on the nature of the investment in the partnership. If the interest is less than 20 per cent, then generally *the investment in the partnership* should be treated as a simple investment and recorded at cost or valuation (unless the investor exercises significant influence).

Associated undertakings and joint ventures

24.212.9 FRS 2 paragraph 79 highlights certain situations where significant influence may be retained even though severe long-term restrictions exist. For example, the general partner may be influential in the decision making process. In such circumstances, the limited partnership should be treated as an associated undertaking in accordance with FRS 9 and accounted for using the equity method of accounting (but see para 24.212.12 below). But this treatment might not be appropriate where the limited partners' have only contributed nominal capital or where there is a substantial amount of debt within the limited partnership. These circumstances indicate that full consolidation would be appropriate.

Interest more than 50 per cent

24.212.10 Where a group holds an interest in a limited partnership that comprises the general partner together with a limited partner interest, such that in aggregate it owns more than 50 per cent of the partnership, there is a presumption that the limited partnership should be consolidated, unless it can be clearly demonstrated that the partnership should be excluded from consolidation on the grounds of severe long-term restrictions. However, the circumstances of each case, including the terms of the partnership agreement or group structure, would need to be considered closely, before the appropriate accounting treatment can be decided.

Severe long-term restrictions do not apply

24.212.11 In cases where severe long-term restrictions do not apply, it will generally be appropriate to fully consolidate the limited partnership, because it will be under the control of the general partner. Where the substance of the arrangement is that there is no significant economic benefit or risk to the general partner group other than a management fee or priority profit share for managing the limited partnership it may, in exceptional circumstances, still be possible to avoid consolidation by using the true and fair override as explained in paragraph 24.212.3 above. However, this option is unlikely to be available if:

- the general partner group has a significant economic interest;
- the interests of the limited partners are nominal in value; or
- there is substantial external debt in the limited partnership; or
- the limited partnership has given significant third party guarantees.

Accounting for a limited partnership as part of a portfolio

24.212.12 A situation that often arises in the asset management industry is where an investor has an interest in a limited partnership (of less than 50 per cent) as part of a portfolio of investments. In this instance, paragraph 49 of FRS 9 requires that the interest is regarded for accounting purposes as being held as part of a basket of investments even when the investor has significant influence or joint control. This would mean accounting for the investment at cost or valuation rather than equity accounting. This conflicts with the Act's provisions which require 'associated undertakings' to be shown by the equity method of accounting when preparing consolidated financial statements. [CA85 4A Sch 22(1)]. The Act defines an 'associated undertaking' as an investment in which the investor has a participating interest and over whose operating and financial policies the investor exercises significant influence, excluding subsidiaries or joint ventures dealt with by proportional consolidation. [CA85 4A Sch 20(1)]. Therefore, where an investor has an investment in a limited partnership as part of a portfolio and accounts for it at cost or valuation in accordance with paragraph 49 of FRS 9 (as opposed to equity accounting), it will need to invoke the true and fair override. This is because compliance with paragraph 49 of FRS 9 requires departure from the accounting rules in the Companies Act. If a true and fair override is used, the particulars, reasons and effect should be given in the notes in accordance with the Act and FRS 18 (see para 24.51 and chapter 2).

Accounting for a limited partnership's interest in subsidiaries

24.212.13 An additional complication arises when the limited partnership itself holds interests in entities that qualify as its subsidiaries. The investor in a limited partnership may have to consolidate not only the partnership, but also that partnership's subsidiaries. For example, where a general partner (the investor) holds a one per cent interest in a limited partnership, which itself has (say) a 51 per cent interest in its subsidiary, then the general partner would have to consolidate 100 per cent of the limited partnership and 100 per cent of its subsidiary, in which it holds (indirectly) an interest of just over half a per cent. This would result in a large minority interest.

24.212.14 It will only be possible to avoid consolidating such a subsidiary where either:

- there are severe long-term restrictions over the ability of the investing company to control the limited partnership (as explained in para 24.212.11 above), in which case it would be appropriate to treat the investment in the limited partnership at cost or valuation if the exemption in paragraph 49 of FRS 9 applies (as explained in para 24.212.12 above); or
- where the limited partnership cannot exercise control over its subsidiary, because there are severe long-term restrictions over its ability to exercise such control.

24.212.15 In the latter situation, if severe long-term restrictions do exist, but the limited partnership still has significant influence, on the face of it equity accounting would be required. However, the exemption from equity accounting in paragraph 49 of FRS 9 would be available to the limited partnership itself if it regards such investments as part of its investment portfolio. These investments would then be recorded at cost or market value as explained in paragraph 24.212.12 above. This would effectively mean that on consolidation the general partner would also record in its investment portfolio its investment in the underlying subsidiary at cost or valuation, rather than by full consolidation.

Implications for the limited partnership's financial statements

24.212.16 The accounting method adopted by the general partner can have implications for the financial statements of the limited partnership itself. As discussed in chapter 8 of the 'Manual of Accounting – Management Reports and Governance', limited companies that are members of a qualifying partnership are required to prepare and append to their own financial statements a copy of the audited financial statements of the partnership. [CA85 5 Sch 28A]. The partners are exempt from this requirement if the limited partnership *"is dealt with on a consolidated basis"* in one of the partners' consolidated financial statements either by consolidation, proportional consolidation or equity accounting. [SI 1993/1820 Reg 7(2)]. For a limited partnership, these provisions apply to the general partner and not to the limited partners. In that case, to avail itself of the exemption from preparing full Companies Act style financial statements for the limited partnership, the general partner has to deal with the partnership on a consolidated basis in its financial statements (or those of its group) by consolidation, proportional consolidation or equity accounting. Clearly, if the partnership is included at cost or valuation, for example, as required by paragraph 49 of FRS 9 where the partnership is part of an investment portfolio, then this exemption is not available, because the partnership is not consolidated or equity accounted in the group's consolidated financial statements. This may cause some difficulty as the partnership's financial statements will then have to comply with all accounting standards and the Companies Act, whereas the accounting requirements (if any) specified in the partnership deed, which would otherwise apply, might be less onerous.

[The next paragraph is 24.213.]

Disclosure requirements concerning subsidiaries and investments

24.213 Certain additional information has to be given for all subsidiaries and this is detailed in Schedule 5 to the Companies Act 1985. Considered below are the disclosure requirements concerning the information required for subsidiaries that are included in consolidation and these requirements are supplemented by FRS 2. The information required about subsidiaries when the parent does not prepare consolidated financial statements is considered in chapter 6.

Place of origin and reason for consolidation

24.214 The Act requires disclosure of the following information concerning subsidiary undertakings:

- Name of each subsidiary undertaking.

- The country of incorporation, if incorporated outside Great Britain.
- The address of the principal place of business if the undertaking is unincorporated.
- Whether the subsidiary is included in the consolidation, and if not, the reasons for excluding it.

[CA85 5 Sch 15(1) to (4)].

These disclosures are illustrated in Tables 24.9 and 24.10.

Table 24.9 – Whitbread PLC – Annual Report and Accounts – 27 February 1999

NOTES TO THE ACCOUNTS (extract)

14 INVESTMENT IN SUBSIDIARY UNDERTAKINGS (extract)

	PRINCIPAL ACTIVITY	COUNTRY OF INCORPORATION OR REGISTRATION	COUNTRY OF PRINCIPAL OPERATIONS	% OF EQUITY AND VOTES HELD
BrightReasons Group Ltd	Restaurants	England	England	100
Churrasco Steak-Restaurant GmbH.*	Restaurants	Germany	Germany	100
Country Club Hotels Ltd.	Hotels	England	England	100
David Lloyd Leisure Ltd	Leisure	England	England	100
The Pelican Group PLC	Restaurants	England	England	100
Whitbread Hotels Ltd	Hotels	England	England	100

Shares in the above are all held directly by Whitbread PLC unless marked with an asterisk. All subsidiary undertakings have the same year end as Whitbread PLC. All the above companies have been included in the group consolidation. The companies listed above include all those which materially affect the amount of profit and the assets of the Group. A full list of subsidiary undertakings, joint ventures and associates will be annexed to the next annual return of Whitbread PLC to be filed with the Registrar of Companies in August 1999.

Table 24.10 – Guinness PLC – Report and accounts – 31 December 1994

Principal subsidiary and associated undertakings and joint ventures (extract)

6. The registered addresses of partnerships in which the group has an interest are:

Schieffelin & Somerset Co	2 Park Avenue, 17th Floor, New York, NY10016, USA.
Asbach GmbH & Co.	AM Rottland 2-10, 65385 Rudesheim am Rhein, Germany.
Bundaberg Rum Company	Whittred Street, Bundaberg, Queensland 4670, Australia.

24.215 Furthermore, it is necessary to disclose the particular definition of 'subsidiary undertaking' that makes an undertaking a subsidiary under the provisions of the Act. [CA85 5 Sch 15(5)]. However, there is an exemption where the undertaking is a subsidiary because the parent holds a majority of its voting rights and it holds the same proportion of shares in the subsidiary as it holds voting rights. This will obviously be the reason for consolidating most subsidiaries and, consequently, disclosure will only be required for other subsidiary undertakings, of which there will be relatively few.

24.216 FRS 2 supplements the above disclosures by requiring the following additional information to be given for subsidiaries:

- The proportion of voting rights held by the parent and its subsidiary undertakings.

- An indication of the nature of the subsidiary's business.

[FRS 2 para 33].

24.217 FRS 2 also requires that where an undertaking is a subsidiary because its parent has the power to exercise or actually exercises dominant influence or control over it (see para 24.130), the financial statements should indicate the basis of the parent's dominant influence or control (for example, see Table 24.1 in para 24.136). [FRS 2 para 34].

Holdings in subsidiary undertakings

24.217.1 The following information has to be given separately (where different) concerning the subsidiary's shares held by the parent and the group:

- The identity of each class of shares held.

- The percentage held of the nominal value of each of those classes of shares.

[CA85 5 Sch 16].

24.218 Shares that are held on the parent's or group's behalf by any other person should be treated for this purpose as if they are held by the parent. [CA85 5 Sch 32(1)(2)(a)(3)]. However, shares held on behalf of a third party other than the parent or the group should be disregarded for this purpose. [CA85 5 Sch 32(3)].

Financial years of subsidiaries

24.219 Where a subsidiary's financial year, for which financial statements are drawn up for consolidation purposes (that is, either statutory financials or management accounts), does not coincide with its parent's financial year, FRS 2 requires that the notes should disclose, for each principal subsidiary that has a different accounting date, its name, its accounting date and the reasons for using a different accounting date. If a principal subsidiary's accounting period is of a different length from that of its parent, this accounting period should also be stated. [FRS 2 para 44].

24.220 The requirements concerning non-coterminous year ends are considered further in paragraph 24.319.

Company shares held by subsidiaries

24.221 A subsidiary company cannot generally own shares in its parent company. [CA85 Sec 23(1); CA06 Sec 136(1)]. This prohibition also applies equally to subsidiaries incorporated overseas. This provision extends to sub-subsidiaries holding shares in their immediate parent companies and also their ultimate parent companies. It also includes any shares held on behalf of the subsidiary by another person as its nominee. [CA85 Sec 23(7); CA06 Sec 144]. However, the prohibition does not apply where the subsidiary is acting as a personal representative for a third party, or as a trustee. This exemption only applies, however, where the subsidiary or a parent company is not beneficially interested under the trust. [CA85 Sec 23(2); CA06 Sec 138(1)(2)]. An exemption is also given to market makers. [CA85 Sec 23(3); CA06 Sec 141(1)(2)].

24.222 For the purposes of section 23 of the Companies Act 1985 (CA06 Sec 136 to 138, 141 to 143), the definitions of holding company and subsidiary given in section 736 of the Companies Act 1985 (CA06 Sec 1159) are relevant and not those given in section 258 (CA06 Sec 1162) (see further para 24.172).

24.223 Where a corporate body became a subsidiary company because of the changes to the definition of subsidiaries included in section 736 of the Companies Act 1985 (CA06 Sec 1159), it may continue to retain any shares that it already held in its parent. However, where shares are held in this way, they will carry no right to vote at company meetings. [CA85 Sec 23(4); CA06 Sec 137(1)].

24.224 In certain situations a subsidiary may find that it does hold shares in its parent. This may arise, for example, where the parent has recently acquired a subsidiary which owned shares in the parent before it became a group member. Before the introduction of the Companies Act 1989, the effect of section 23(1) of the Companies Act 1985 was unclear. Now, section 23 of the Companies Act 1985 (CA06 Secs 136 to 138, 141 to 143) expressly provides that, where a company acquires shares in its parent, but before it becomes a subsidiary of the parent, it may retain those shares. In this circumstance also, those shares will carry no right to vote at company meetings. [CA85 Sec 23(5); CA06 Sec 137(2)].

24.225 The notes to a parent's consolidated financial statements must disclose the number, the description and the amount of any of its shares that subsidiaries or their nominees hold. [CA85 5 Sch 20(1)]. This information is not required, however, where the subsidiary holds the shares as personal representative or as a trustee. [CA85 5 Sch 20(2)]. However, the exemption for a subsidiary acting as a trustee will not be available if the company or any of its subsidiaries is beneficially interested under the trust, unless the beneficial interest is by way of security for the purpose of a transaction entered into by it in the ordinary course of a business which includes the lending of money. [CA85 5 Sch 20(3)]. Additionally, FRS 25 requires separate disclosure, either on the face of the balance sheet or in the notes, of the amount of treasury shares held. [FRS 25 para 34]. See further chapter 6.

24.226 In the past, such shares held by subsidiaries may have been classified as an asset, 'own shares', in the parent's consolidated financial statements. However, UITF Abstract 37, 'Purchases and sales of own shares', effective for accounting periods ending on or after 23 December 2003, required that where shares in a holding company are purchased or held by a subsidiary, the consideration paid should be deducted in arriving at shareholders' funds in the holding company's consolidated financial statements. This was subsequently superceded by FRS 25, which followed the same principle. [FRS 25 para 33].

Significant investment holdings of the parent or group

24.227 Where the parent or any of its subsidiaries has *significant holdings* in undertakings, certain additional information has to be given in the consolidated financial statements. A 'significant holding' means one where the investment in the undertaking concerned amounts to twenty per cent or more of the nominal value of *any class* of shares in the undertaking. [CA5 Sch 23(2)(a), 26(2)(a)]. (Joint ventures and associated undertakings are considered separately in chapter 27.)

24.228 The disclosure is also required where the holding by the parent or its subsidiaries exceeds twenty per cent of the amount of the parent's, or the group's, assets. [CA85 5 Sch 23(2)(b), 26(2)(b)]. The information to be disclosed is as follows:

- The name of the undertaking.
- The country of incorporation of the undertaking, if it is incorporated outside Great Britain.
- The address of its principal place of business, if it is unincorporated.
- The identity of each class of shares held.
- The percentage held of the nominal value of each of those classes of shares.

[CA85 5 Sch 24, 27].

24.229 Furthermore, additional information is required to be disclosed as follows:

- The aggregate amount of the capital and reserves of the undertaking at the end of its 'relevant year'. Relevant year means the year ending with, or last before, that of the company.
- Its profit or loss for the year.

[CA85 5 Sch 25(1)(4), 28(1)(4)].

24.230 This additional information need not be disclosed if the undertaking is not required by the Act to deliver to the Registrar of Companies a copy of its balance sheet and does not otherwise publish it (for example, a partnership). However, this exemption only applies where the company's holding is less than 50 per cent of the nominal value of the undertaking's shares. [CA85 5 Sch 25(2), 28(2)]. Consequently, this exemption is likely to apply to investments in partnerships where the interest in the partnership is less than 50 per cent. The information is also not required if it is immaterial.

24.231 For investments in unincorporated undertakings with capital, 'shares' for the purposes of the paragraphs above means the rights to share in the capital of the undertaking, by virtue of section 259(2)(b) of the Companies Act 1985. [CA06 Sec 1161(2)(b)]. In respect of an undertaking that does not have capital, the term 'shares' refers to any right to share in the profits or liability to contribute to losses of the undertaking, or an obligation to contribute to its debts or expenses on winding up. [CA85 Sec 259(2)(c); CA06 Sec 1161(2)(c)].

Interpretation of 'shares held by the group'

24.232 In the paragraphs above, reference to shares held by the group are to shares held by the parent company or any of its subsidiaries, or to shares held on their behalf. However, such references do not include shares held on behalf of third parties. [CA85 5 Sch 32(3)]. Furthermore, shares held by way of security must be treated as held by the person providing the security where both the following apply:

- The rights attached to the shares are exercisable only in accordance with that person's instructions (apart from the right to exercise them for the purpose of preserving the value of the security or of realising it).
- The shares are held in connection with granting loans as part of normal business activities and the rights attached to the shares are exercisable only in that person's interest (apart from the right to exercise them for the purpose of preserving the value of the security, or of realising it).

[CA85 5 Sch 32(4)].

Disclosure 'seriously prejudicial'

24.233 In certain circumstances, the information required by Schedule 5 of the Companies Act 1985 concerning subsidiaries and other significant holdings in undertakings (summarised above) need not be given where the undertaking is established under the law of a country outside the UK, or carries on business outside the UK. [CA85 Sec 231(3); CA06 Sec 409(3)(4)]. The situations where this exemption will apply are where, in the directors' opinion, disclosing information would be *seriously prejudicial* to the business of that undertaking, or to the business of the parent company, or to any of the parent's subsidiaries. Permission to exclude the information also needs to be obtained from the Secretary of State before advantage can be taken of this exemption. A group that takes advantage of this exemption is required under section 231(4) of the Companies Act 1985 (CA06 Sec 409(5)) to disclose this fact in its financial statements.

24.234 The section 231(4) of the Companies Act 1985 (CA06 Sec 409(5) statement that exemption has been taken is required to be given irrespective of whether the group has taken advantage of section 231(5) of the Companies Act 1985 (CA06 Sec 410(1)(2)) (see para 24.236 below), which only requires information for subsidiaries that principally affect the group's reported figures to be given in its financial statements. Under section 231(5) of the Companies Act 1985 (CA06 Sec 410(1)(2)) the full information for all subsidiaries must be annexed to the company's next annual return, but where the Secretary of State has granted exemption under section 231(3) of the Companies Act 1985 (CA06 Sec 409(3)(4)), this need not include the information regarding the subsidiary excluded on seriously prejudicial grounds.

24.235 The exemption does not apply, however, to the information required by paragraph 20 of Schedule 5 to the Companies Act 1985, which is summarised in paragraph 24.225 above.

Disclosure of excessive information

24.236 There is a further relaxation of the disclosure requirements of Schedule 5 that applies if, in the directors' opinion, the resulting disclosure would be excessively lengthy. This will often be the situation where the group has a significant number of subsidiaries. Where this is so, the directors need only give the required information concerning the undertakings whose results or financial position principally affect the figures shown in the company's annual accounts. [CA85 Sec 231(5); CA06 Sec 410(1)(2)]. However, the directors are required to give the necessary information that relates to undertakings excluded from consolidation, except where they are excluded on the ground of materiality (see para 24.180).

24.237 Where the directors take advantage of this exemption, they have to note in the financial statements that the information given is only in respect of principal subsidiaries and significant investments. [CA85 Sec 231(6)(a); CA06 Sec 410(3)(a)]. In addition, the full information (including that disclosed in the financial statements) has to be annexed to the parent's next annual return. [CA85 Sec 231(6)(b); CA06 Sec 410(3)(b)].

Disclosure of parent company

24.238 The Companies Act 1985 deals with the disclosures concerning a company's parent (or parents) in Schedule 5 to the Companies Act 1985. Part I of Schedule 5 to the Companies Act 1985 sets out the disclosures to be made where a company is not required to prepare consolidated financial statements, whereas Part II deals with the disclosure requirements concerning those companies that are required to prepare consolidated financial statements. These requirements are identical. The paragraphs that follow summarise these disclosures and make reference to the paragraphs of Schedule 5 to the Companies Act 1985 that are duplicated.

24.239 Where, at the end of a financial year, a company is a subsidiary, or where the company is a parent company and is itself a subsidiary, it should disclose concerning its *ultimate parent company* its name and if incorporated outside Great Britain the country of its incorporation (if known). 'Company' includes any corporate body in this context. [CA85 5 Sch 12, 31].

24.240 An example of the disclosures required by the Act is given in Table 24.11.

Table 24.11 – Dunhill Holdings PLC – Report and Accounts – 31 March 1993

NOTES TO THE ACCOUNTS (extract)

28 ULTIMATE HOLDING COMPANY

The Company is a subsidiary of Rothmans International p.l.c., which is incorporated in England and Wales. Copies of the accounts of Rothmans International p.l.c. are available from 15 Hill Street, London, W1X 7FB.

The Directors consider the Company's ultimate holding company to be Compagnie Financière Richemont AG, which is incorporated in Switzerland. Copies of that company's accounts are available from its registered office at Rigistrasse 2, CH-6300 Zug, Switzerland.

24.241 Furthermore, where the parent company is itself a subsidiary, similar information has to be disclosed (whether or not it prepares consolidated financial statements) for the parent undertaking that heads the following:

- The largest group of undertakings that prepares consolidated financial statements and of which the company is a member.
- The smallest group of undertakings that prepares consolidated financial statements and of which the company is a member.

[CA85 5 Sch 11(1), 30(1)].

24.242 The information to be disclosed in respect of both these undertakings is similar to that required by paragraph 24.239 above:

- The name of the parent undertaking.
- The country of incorporation of the undertaking, if it is incorporated outside Great Britain.
- The address of its principal place of business, if it is unincorporated.
- If copies of the undertaking's consolidated financial statements are available for the public, then the address where copies of the financial statements can be obtained.

[CA85 5 Sch 11(2)(3)(4), 30(2)(3)(4)].

24.243 Where the ultimate parent company prepares consolidated financial statements, the information in paragraph 24.242 disclosed in the sub-group parent's financial statements need be given only for the ultimate parent and for the smallest group of undertakings that prepare consolidated financial statements which include the sub-group (if such an undertaking exists) (see for example Table 24.12). [CA85 5 Sch 11(1), 30(1)].

Table 24.12 – The Telegraph plc – Annual Report and Accounts – 31 December 1994

Notes to the accounts (extract)

32. Ultimate parent company

Hollinger Inc., incorporated in Canada and listed on the Toronto, Montreal and Vancouver stock exchanges, is regarded by the directors of the company as the company's ultimate parent company.

The largest group in which the results of the company are consolidated is that of which Hollinger Inc. is the parent company. The consolidated accounts of Hollinger Inc. may be obtained from Montreal Trust Company of Canada, 151 Front Street West, 8th Floor, Toronto, Ontario, Canada M5J 2N1.

The smallest such group is that of which DT Holdings Limited is the parent company, whose consolidated accounts may be obtained from 21 Wilson Street, London EC2M 2TQ. DT Holdings Limited is registered in England and Wales.

24.244 However, where the ultimate parent does not prepare consolidated financial statements, the information in paragraph 24.239 above has to be disclosed in the sub-group parent's financial statements. In addition, the information set out in paragraph 24.242 may also be required to be disclosed concerning the largest and smallest groups that prepare consolidated financial statements which include the sub-group.

24.245 These provisions can be very confusing and are best illustrated by an example. Consider the group structure set out in the diagram below.

Example

Group structure

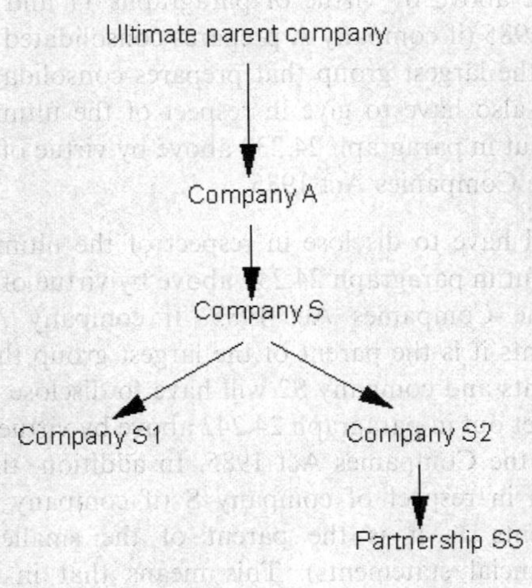

In the situation where the ultimate parent company *does prepare* consolidated financial statements, the following disclosure applies:

- Company A will have to disclose in respect of the ultimate parent company (being the largest group parent) the information set out in paragraphs 24.239 and 24.242 above by virtue of paragraphs 11, 12, 31 and 30 of Schedule 5 to the Companies Act 1985.

- Company S will have to disclose in respect of company A the information set out in paragraph 24.242 above by virtue of paragraphs 11 and 30 of Schedule 5 to the Companies Act 1985 (if company A prepares consolidated financial statements as it is the parent of the smallest group that prepares consolidated financial statements). Company S will also have to give in respect of the ultimate parent company (being also the largest group parent) the information set out in paragraphs 24.239 and 24.242 above by virtue of paragraphs 11, 12, 31 and 30 of Schedule 5 to the Companies Act 1985.

- Company S2 will have to disclose in respect of the ultimate parent company (being also the largest group parent) the information set out in paragraphs 24.239 and 24.242 above by virtue of paragraphs 11, 12, 31 and 30 of Schedule 5 to the Companies Act 1985. If company S prepares consolidated financial statements, then company S2 will also have to disclose in respect of company S (being the parent of the smallest group that prepares consolidated financial statements) the information set out in paragraph 24.242 above by virtue of paragraphs 11 and 30 of Schedule 5 to the Companies Act 1985. Where company S does not prepare consolidated financial statements, then company S2 has to give the same information in respect of company A (if company A prepares consolidated financial statements as it is the parent of the smallest group that prepares consolidated financial statements).

In the situation where the ultimate parent company *does not* prepare consolidated financial statements, the following disclosure applies:

- Company A will have to disclose in respect of the ultimate parent company the information set out in paragraph 24.239 above by virtue of paragraphs 12 and 31 of Schedule 5 to the Companies Act 1985.

- Company S will have to disclose in respect of company A the information set out in paragraph 24.242 above by virtue of paragraphs 11 and 30 of Schedule 5 to the Companies Act 1985 (if company A prepares consolidated financial statements as it is the parent of the largest group that prepares consolidated financial statements). Company S will also have to give in respect of the ultimate parent company the information set out in paragraph 24.239 above by virtue of paragraphs 12 and 31 of Schedule 5 to the Companies Act 1985.

- Company S2 will have to disclose in respect of the ultimate parent company the information set out in paragraph 24.239 above by virtue of paragraphs 12 and 31 of Schedule 5 to the Companies Act 1985. If company A prepares consolidated financial statements it is the parent of the largest group that prepares consolidated financial statements and company S2 will have to disclose in respect of company A the information set out in paragraph 24.242 above by virtue of paragraphs 11 and 30 of Schedule 5 to the Companies Act 1985. In addition, the same information will have to be given in respect of company S (if company S prepares consolidated financial statements as it is the parent of the smallest group that prepares consolidated financial statements). This means that in the situation described, company S2 is required to disclose information concerning three parent companies. Furthermore the situation might arise, for example, where another intermediate parent undertaking exists in the group structure between company S and company A. Even where such an undertaking prepares consolidated financial statements company S2 is still only required to give information concerning company A, company S and its ultimate parent. This is because the legislation only requires the information concerned to be disclosed in respect of the largest and smallest groups preparing consolidated financial statements and is not concerned with other intermediate parents in between that prepare consolidated financial statements.

24.246 In practice in the majority of situations, these provisions will mean that the information required by paragraph 24.242 above will have to be given for the next parent undertaking in the group that prepares consolidated financial statements that included the sub-group, and will also have to be given for the ultimate parent company that prepares consolidated financial statements.

Membership of a qualifying undertaking

24.247 Where at the year end a parent company or group is a member of a qualifying undertaking, it has to give the following information in its financial statements:

- The name and legal form of the undertaking.
- The address of the undertaking's registered office or, if it does not have such an office, its head office.

[CA85 5 Sch 28A(1)(2)].

24.248 In addition, where the qualifying undertaking is a qualifying partnership one of the following must also be stated:

- That a copy of the latest financial statements of the undertaking has been, or is to be, appended to the copy of the company's financial statements sent to the Registrar under section 242 of the Act.
- The name of at least one body corporate (which may be the company) in whose consolidated financial statements the undertaking has been, or is to be, dealt with by the method of full consolidation, proportional consolidation or the equity method of accounting.

[CA85 5 Sch 28A(3)].

24.249 For the purpose of these rules, 'qualifying undertakings' can either be companies or partnerships. A qualifying company (or qualifying partnership) is an unlimited company (or partnership) incorporated in (or governed by the laws of any part of) Great Britain if each of its members is:

- a limited company; or

- another unlimited company, or a Scottish firm, each of whose members is a limited company.

The references to limited company, another unlimited company and Scottish firm also encompass any comparable undertakings incorporated in, or formed under the law of, any country or territory outside Great Britain. [SI 1993/1820 Reg 3, 9].

24.250 The information required to be disclosed in the second bullet point of paragraph 24.248 need not be given if the partnership is dealt with either by consolidation, proportional consolidation or equity accounting in the consolidated financial statements prepared by:

- a member of the partnership that is established under the law of a Member State; or

- a parent undertaking of such a member established in the same way.

[CA85 5 Sch 28A(5); SI 1993/1820 Reg 7(1)].

24.251 The exemption can only be taken, however, where the following two conditions are complied with:

- The consolidated financial statements are prepared and audited under the law of the member State in accordance with the provisions of the 7th Directive.

- The notes to those consolidated financial statements disclose that advantage has been taken of the exemption. An example of the disclosure is given in Table 24.13.

[CA85 5 Sch 28A(5); SI 1993/1820 Reg 7(2)].

Table 24.13 – BP p.l.c. – Annual Report – 31 December 2001

42 Subsidiary and associated undertakings and joint ventures (extract)

The more important subsidiary and associated undertakings and joint ventures of the group at 31 December 2001 and the group percentage of equity capital or joint venture interest (to nearest whole number) are set out below. The principal country of operation is generally indicated by the company's country of incorporation or by its name. Those held directly by the parent company are marked with an asterisk (*), the percentage owned being that of the group unless otherwise indicated. A complete list of investments in subsidiary and associated undertakings and joint ventures will be attached to the parent company's annual return made to the Register of Companies. Advantage has been taken of the exemption conferred by regulation 7 of The Partnerships and Unlimited Companies (Accounts) Regulations 1993 from the requirements to deliver to the Register of Companies and publish the annual accounts of the Ca To Finance V Limited Partnership.

Other disclosure issues

Realised and distributable reserves

24.252 The restrictions on distributions contained in the Act apply to individual companies and not to groups. This is because individual companies make distributions, whereas groups do not. However, users of consolidated financial statements may wish to know the amount the holding company could distribute if all the group's subsidiaries were to pay up their realised profits by way of dividends to the parent company. Some groups specifically disclose the amount of their distributable reserves and this issue is discussed in chapter 23.

24.253 Furthermore, FRS 2 requires that, where significant statutory, contractual or exchange control restrictions exist which materially limit the distributions a subsidiary undertaking can make and, therefore, the parent undertaking's access to distributable profits, the nature and extent of the restrictions should be disclosed. [FRS 2 para 53].

24.254 The parent company's ability to distribute pre-acquisition reserves of its subsidiaries is discussed in chapter 23.

Tax on the accumulated reserves of overseas subsidiaries

24.255 FRS 19, 'Deferred tax', provides some guidance on the treatment of overseas retained earnings. Its provisions require that deferred tax should be computed using the 'incremental liability' approach. The general principle is that deferred tax should be recognised as a liability or asset if the transactions or events that give the entity an obligation to pay more tax in the future or a right to pay less tax in the future have occurred by the balance sheet date. More specifically, FRS 19 paragraph 21 states that tax that could be payable on any future remittance of the past earnings of a subsidiary or joint venture should only be provided in certain situations; and FRS 2 adds to the disclosure requirements. These matters are considered in chapter 13.

[The next paragraph is 24.296.]

Section II — Consolidation rules

Introduction

24.296 Consolidated financial statements must give a true and fair view of the state of affairs and the profit or loss of the company and those of its subsidiaries included in the consolidated financial statements as a whole, so far as concerns the parent company's shareholders. [CA85 Sec 227A(2); CA06 Sec 404(2)]. As with individual financial statements, this is an overriding requirement. This overriding requirement is explained in chapter 2.

24.297 In addition to the overriding requirement to give a true and fair view, the Act and FRS 2 include accounting rules that apply to consolidated financial statements. In general, the Act's provisions correspond to those that apply to an individual company's financial statements. Consequently, consolidated financial statements must comply with the requirements of Schedule 4 to the Companies Act 1985 both as to their form and content and as to the information they must disclose in the notes (to the extent that this Schedule applies to consolidated financial statements).

24.298 Furthermore, the Companies Act 1989 introduced Schedule 4A to the Companies Act 1985. This Schedule details the rules concerning the form and content of consolidated financial statements and introduced into UK company law the majority of the 7th Directive's provisions. One exception to these consolidation rules is that if any member of a group is a banking or an insurance company the Schedule 4 and 4A to the Companies Act 1985 formats are not appropriate. Banks have to comply with Schedule 9 of the Companies Act 1985 which was completely revised by the Companies Act 1985 (Bank Accounts) Regulations 1991 (SI 1991/2705). Insurance companies have to comply with Schedule 9A to the Companies Act 1985 as revised by the Companies Act 1985 (Insurance Companies Accounts) Regulations 1993 (SI 1993/3246). The accounting requirements that apply to banking and insurance companies are not within the scope of this book.

24.299 If, at the end of the financial year, a company has one or more subsidiaries, consolidated financial statements must be prepared in addition to the parent company's individual financial statements. The consolidated financial statements should deal with the state of affairs and the profit or loss of the company and its subsidiaries. [CA85 Sec 227(1); CA06 Sec 399(2)].

24.300 FRS 2 extends the Act's provisions to require that consolidated financial statements should be prepared also where a parent undertaking is an entity other than a company and its financial statements are to give a true and fair view. [FRS 2 para 18].

24.301 The only exceptions to the general rules outlined in paragraph 24.299 above are considered in paragraph 24.176.

24.302 The particular provisions in Schedule 4A to the Companies Act 1985 and the provisions in FRS 2 that form the basic consolidation rules are explained below, together with other rules that have become generally accepted accounting principles through their general use in preparing consolidations.

Generally accepted accounting principles

24.303 Consolidated financial statements have to incorporate all of the information contained in the individual financial statements of the undertakings included in the consolidation. [CA85 4A Sch 2(1)]. However, this provision is subject to adjustments authorised by Schedule 4A to the Companies Act 1985 and to any adjustments that are necessary in order to accord with "*generally accepted accounting principles or practice*". [CA85 4A Sch 2(1)]. Although the term in the Companies Act 1985 incorporates the word 'practice', the term is more often referred to by accountants as 'Generally Accepted Accounting Principles' (GAAP). The term UK GAAP is one that means generally accepted accounting principles that apply to UK companies and groups and that encompass UK law, accounting standards, UITF Abstracts, the FSA's accounting requirements included in the Listing Rules (if appropriate) and other generally accepted accounting practices (see further chapter 2).

24.304 The accounting principles that are used in the consolidation process should be disclosed in the accounting policies note to the consolidated financial statements. This note generally covers the following matters relating to consolidations:

- The methods of accounting used to consolidate new subsidiaries, that is either of the following:
  - Acquisition accounting (see chapter 25).
  - Merger accounting (see chapter 28).
- The treatment of any goodwill arising on consolidation, and the treatment of other differences arising on consolidation (see further chapter 25).
- The translation of overseas subsidiaries' financial statements (see chapter 7).
- How minority interests are dealt with (see para 24.344).
- How associated companies and joint ventures are dealt with (see chapter 27).
- How the trading between non-coterminous year ends of the parent and subsidiary are dealt with (see para 24.322).
- The treatment of intra-group transactions (see para 24.332 below).

Procedure for consolidation

24.305 As mentioned in paragraph 24.303 above, the Companies Act 1985 specifies that the consolidated balance sheet and the consolidated profit and loss account should incorporate in full the information contained in the individual financial statements of the undertakings included in the consolidation, subject to certain consolidation adjustments. [CA85 4A Sch 2(1)]. However, it does not specify how the aggregation of this information should be undertaken.

24.306 FRS 2 makes no comment on the process of consolidation and SSAP 14, its predecessor, only commented that the method for preparing consolidated financial statements on an item basis, eliminating intra-group balances and transactions and unrealised intra-group profit, was well understood and did not deal further with the matter. IAS 27, 'Consolidated and separate financial statements', mentions that, in preparing consolidated financial statements, the financial statements of the parent and its subsidiaries are combined on a line by line basis by adding together like items of assets, liabilities, income and expenses. [IAS 27 para 22]. IAS 27 then goes on to mention some of the steps in the consolidation process. These are very similar in nature to the matters mentioned in paragraph 24.304 above.

24.307 In practice, there are two methods of preparing consolidated financial statements. In the first method the individual financial statements of subsidiaries are aggregated centrally by adding together the profit and loss account and balance sheet figures on a line by line basis. These aggregate figures taken from the subsidiaries' statutory financial statements are then amended to deal with consolidation adjustments. Such adjustments would be necessary in order to:

- Adjust individual figures in the financial statements of subsidiaries to bring them onto common accounting policies (see para 24.310 below).
- Achieve the consolidation by, for example, dealing with goodwill and minority interests (see para 24.317 below).

24.308 A second method, more suitable for large groups, is for each subsidiary to prepare a consolidation return. The consolidation return is made up from the individual subsidiary's financial statements which are:

- Adjusted to common accounting policies.
- Edited into a format and analysis that makes the consolidated process easier.

These returns are then aggregated to form the group's consolidated financial statements. Even using this basis, there may still be a need to make consolidation adjustments. For example, company A would not know how much intra-group profit to eliminate on goods sold to its subsidiary company B, because it would not know how much of that stock company B had sold.

Consolidation adjustments

24.309 There are a number of reasons why a parent may have to make consolidation adjustments to its subsidiaries' financial statements in preparing the group's consolidated financial statements. Some of these reasons and the rules relating to such adjustments are considered in the paragraphs that follow.

Uniform accounting polices

24.310 Except in exceptional situations, which are explained below, uniform group accounting policies should be used to determine the amounts to be included in the consolidated financial statements. This may require adjustment, on consolidation, of the amounts that have been reported by subsidiaries in their individual financial statements. [CA85 4A Sch 3(1); FRS 2 para 40].

24.311 In practice, a group that operates wholly within the UK and prepares UK GAAP financial statements is unlikely to have to make such adjustments, because in situations where UK GAAP permits the use of different accounting policies, the parent is likely to impose the group policy on each of its subsidiaries. See also chapter 2, which deals with consistency of accounting policies in group situations.

24.312 The Companies Act 1985 specifically requires consolidation adjustments to be made where a subsidiary undertaking's assets and liabilities have been valued using accounting rules that differ from those used by the group. [CA85 4A Sch 3(1)]. For example, the need for such an adjustment would arise where a subsidiary values its stocks using a LIFO method of valuation. In the UK LIFO stock valuations are not allowed for UK corporation tax purposes and are considered in SSAP 9 to be likely to be incompatible with the requirement to give a true and fair view. Such valuations are, however, allowed for both tax and accounting purposes in other countries and, consequently, subsidiaries that operate in those countries may value their stocks on that basis. Clearly, when such subsidiaries are consolidated, an adjustment will be required to bring the stock valuations onto a basis acceptable in the UK (for example, FIFO or average cost).

24.313 However, in certain situations, the parent's directors might consider that there are special reasons for retaining the different accounting rules adopted by the subsidiary. Where this is so, the Companies Act 1985's and FRS 2's provisions require that particulars of the departure, the reasons for it and its effect should be disclosed in the notes to the consolidated financial statements. [CA85 4A Sch 3(2); FRS 2 para 41]. FRS 18 sets out the disclosure requirements in such a situation and its implications are considered further in chapter 2.

24.314 It may also be that the accounting policies used by the parent in its individual financial statements differ from those of the group. However, this is less common. While the law does not require the policies of the parent and the group to be the same, it requires disclosure of any differences in the notes to the consolidated financial statements and of the reason for the differences. [CA85 4A Sch 4]. An example of where such a difference could arise is where the parent records its fixed asset land and buildings at historical cost, but the group carries them at revalued amounts, but in practice this is unlikely to happen.

24.315 Where a new subsidiary is acquired by a group and the two have different accounting policies, the new subsidiary has sufficient reason to change its accounting policy and make a prior-year adjustment in accordance with FRS 18. Alternatively, the new subsidiary may continue with its original accounting policy in its entity financial statements, in which case the group would need to make an adjustment on consolidation to reflect the subsidiary's results in accordance with the group's accounting policy.

24.316 Problems can arise with overseas subsidiaries in applying uniform accounting policies. Where the subsidiaries are subject to either company law or tax law that is different from that in the UK, it may not always be practicable for the parent to insist that the subsidiaries change their accounting policies to bring them into line with the group's accounting policies. For example, in many European countries depreciation is calculated in accordance with local tax regulations rather than by reference to the estimated useful life of the asset. However, in order to obtain the tax relief, the tax-based depreciation figure must be shown in the subsidiary's individual financial statements. In order to comply with FRS 2 and the Companies Act 1985 an adjustment must then be made on consolidation to both the depreciation charge for the year and the accumulated depreciation to bring them into line with UK (and the group's) practice. In this situation, an adjustment to deferred taxation may also be required. Table 24.16 illustrates a situation where local legislation prevents the subsidiaries adopting the group's accounting policies.

Table 24.16 — GKN plc — Report & Accounts — 31 December 2000

Notes on the accounts (extract)

1 Basis of Consolidation

Accounting policies

The Group's accounting policies are shown in the notes on pages 47 to 69. Local legislation prevents certain overseas subsidiaries from conforming with the accounting policies adopted by the Group. Adjustments are made on consolidation so that the group accounts are presented on a uniform basis.

Other consolidation adjustments

24.317 Consolidation adjustments are required for a variety of reasons and the group's accounting policies will often describe the areas where adjustments are made as detailed in paragraph 24.304 above. The elimination of pre-acquisition reserves, although it would not generally be dealt with specifically in the accounting policies note, is another adjustment that is fundamental to the consolidation process (see further chapter 25).

24.318 A consolidation adjustment may also be necessary where a material 'subsequent event' occurs in a subsidiary between the date when the subsidiary's directors sign the subsidiary's own financial statements and the date when the holding company's directors sign the consolidated financial statements. If the 'subsequent event' is material to the group and is an 'adjusting event' (which is a post balance sheet event that provides additional evidence of conditions that exist at the balance sheet date), a consolidation adjustment should be made for it in the consolidated financial statements.

Subsidiary year ends

24.319 The financial statements of all subsidiaries to be used in preparing the consolidated financial statements should, wherever practicable, be prepared to the same financial year end and for the same accounting period as those of the parent.

[FRS 2 para 42]. The directors have an obligation under section 223(5) of the Companies Act 1985 (CA06 Sec 390(5)) to secure that the financial year of each of its subsidiary undertakings coincides with the parent company's own financial year, unless in their opinion there are good reasons for this not to be so.

24.320 The Act requires that the financial statements of a subsidiary may not be consolidated if its accounting period ends more than three months before that of its parent. [CA85 4A Sch 2(2)(a)]. If the subsidiary's financial year ends before this period, it has to prepare interim financial statements to coincide with the end of the parent company's financial year. [CA85 4A Sch 2(2)(b)].

Interim financial statements

24.321 However, FRS 2 takes a stricter approach and requires that where the financial year of a subsidiary undertaking differs from that of the parent, interim financial statements should be prepared to the same date as those of the parent for use in preparing consolidated financial statements (see for example Table 24.17). If it is *not practicable* to use such interim financial statements, the subsidiary's financial statements should be used, providing that its year ended not more than three months before the relevant year end of the parent. In this situation, any changes that have taken place in the intervening period that materially affect the view given by the financial statements should be taken into account by adjusting the consolidated financial statements. [FRS 2 para 43]. In certain circumstances, such adjustments might be considered to be immaterial as illustrated in Table 24.18.

Table 24.17 — Abbey National plc — Directors' Report and Accounts — 31 December 2000

Accounting policies (extract)

Basis of consolidation

The Group financial statements comprise the financial statements of the Company and all its subsidiary undertakings. The accounting reference date of the Company and its subsidiary undertakings is 31 December, with the exception of those leasing, investment, insurance and funding companies which, because of commercial considerations, have various accounting reference dates. The financial statements of these subsidiaries have been consolidated on the basis of interim financial statements for the period to 31 December 2000.

Table 24.18 — National Westminster Bank Plc — Annual Report and Accounts — 31 December 1997

Notes to the accounts (extract)

1 PRINCIPAL ACCOUNTING POLICIES (extract)

(ii) **Basis of consolidation (extract)**
To avoid undue delay in the presentation of the Group's accounts, the accounts of certain subsidiary undertaking have been made up to 30 November. There have been no changes in respect of these subsidiary undertakings, in the period from their balance sheet dates to 31 December, that materially affect the view given by the Group's accounts. Details of principal subsidiary undertakings are given in note 25.

24.322 Consolidation adjustments of this nature might be required for settlement of intra-group balances outstanding at the subsidiary's year end, which would obviously have to be dealt with as part of the consolidation process. Other transactions might not be so obvious, such as a post balance sheet event in the subsidiary. For example, an adjustment would have to be made for a substantial loss on a contract undertaken by a subsidiary that has occurred in between the subsidiary's year end and that of its parent. Another example, where the subsidiary is incorporated overseas, is where there has been a devaluation of the currency in which it trades between its year end date and that of its parent.

24.323 FRS 2 is, therefore, restricting the legislation by giving preference to the requirement to prepare interim financial statements and only permitting the use of the subsidiary's own financial statements if the preparation of interim financial statements is *not practicable*. One practical reason sometimes given for having different year ends is to avoid delays in presenting the consolidated financial statements (for example, see Table 24.18 and Table 24.19).

Table 24.19 — Blue Circle Industries PLC — Annual Report & Accounts — 31 December 1999

Accounting Policies (extract)

2 Consolidation

The Group accounts incorporate the results of the Company and its subsidiary and joint venture and associated undertakings. To avoid delay in the presentation of the accounts the accounting period of one overseas subsidiary ends on 30 November. The results of joint ventures and associates are based upon statutory or management accounts for periods ending on either 30 November or 31 December. Where subsidiaries, joint ventures and associates are acquired or disposed of during the year, results are included from the date of acquisition or to the date of sale.

24.324 The example below illustrates the options that are available when consolidating a subsidiary with a non-coterminous year end.

Example

A parent company has a year end of 31 December 20X1. One of its subsidiaries has a year end of 30 June 20X1 and another has a year end of 30 September 20X1. What figures may the parent include in its consolidated financial statements in respect of these subsidiaries?

In the first situation the subsidiary must prepare interim financial statements covering the year ended 31 December 20X1 (that is, coinciding with that of its parent). It may not prepare interim financial statements to, for example 30 November, despite this date being within three months of the parent's year end. Under no circumstances (unless the subsidiary is immaterial) may the parent consolidate the subsidiary's own statutory financial statements as the subsidiary's year end is more than three months before that of the parent.

In the second situation the parent should consolidate interim financial statements prepared by the subsidiary for the year ended 31 December 20X1, but if this is not practicable it may consolidate the financial statements of the subsidiary for the year ended 30 September 20X1 (as it ends no more than three months prior to the parent's year end). If the financial statements for 30 September 20X1 are used, consideration should be given to the requirement to adjust for transactions between the subsidiary's year end and that of the parent.

24.325 The interim financial statements are not required by the Act to be audited. However, they would have to be audited at least to the group materiality to satisfy the requirement that the group's consolidated financial statements have to give a true and fair view.

Disclosure where year ends differ

24.326 The following information should be given for each material subsidiary that is included in the consolidated financial statements on the basis of information prepared to a different date or for a different accounting period from that of the parent:

- Its name.
- Its accounting date or period, including the date on which its last financial year ended.
- The reason for using a different accounting date or period, including why the directors consider that the subsidiary's financial year should not end with that of its parent.

[FRS 2 para 44].

These disclosures are illustrated in Table 24.20.

Table 24.20 — Imperial Chemical Industries PLC — Annual report and accounts —31 December 1994 notes relating to the accounts (extract)

Composition of the Group

The Group accounts consolidate the accounts of Imperial Chemical Industries PLC (the Company) and its subsidiary undertakings, of which there were 363 at 31 December 1994. Owing to local conditions and to avoid undue delay in the presentation of the Group accounts, 62 subsidiaries made up their accounts to dates earlier than 31 December, but not earlier than 30 September; one subsidiary makes up its accounts to 31 March but interim accounts to 31 December are drawn up for consolidation purposes.

principal subsidiary undertakings (extract)

OTHER COUNTRIES (extract)	**Class of capital**	**Held by ICI %**	**Principal activities**
AECI Explosives Ltd Republic of South Africa	Ordinary	51†	Manufacture of industrial explosives and initiating systems
ICI Australia Ltd Australia (Accounting and reporting date 30 September)	Ordinary*	62†	Manufacture and distribution of chemicals and other products including fertilisers and crop care, industrial and specialty chemicals, consumer and effect products, plastics and performance of related services
ICI China Hong Kong and China	Ordinary	100†	Merchanting of ICI and other products
ICI India Ltd India (Accounting date 31 March; reporting date 31 December)	Equity*	51	Manufacture of industrial explosives, paints, agrochemicals, pharmaceutical, polyurethanes, catalysts, rubber chemicals and surfactants

* Listed
† Held by subsidiaries
The country of principal operations and registration or incorporation is stated below each company. The accounting dates of principal subsidiary undertakings are 31 December unless otherwise stated.

Practical problems

24.327 Problems often arise in deciding what accounting periods to include in the consolidation when subsidiaries have different accounting year ends to their parent. The example below illustrates the type of situation that can arise in practice.

Example

A parent whose year end is 31 March has for a number of years consolidated a subsidiary's financial statements drawn up to 31 December. It has now decided to use the subsidiary's management accounts to 31 March 20X2 for consolidation with the group's financial statements to 31 March 20X2. The situation can be illustrated as set out below:

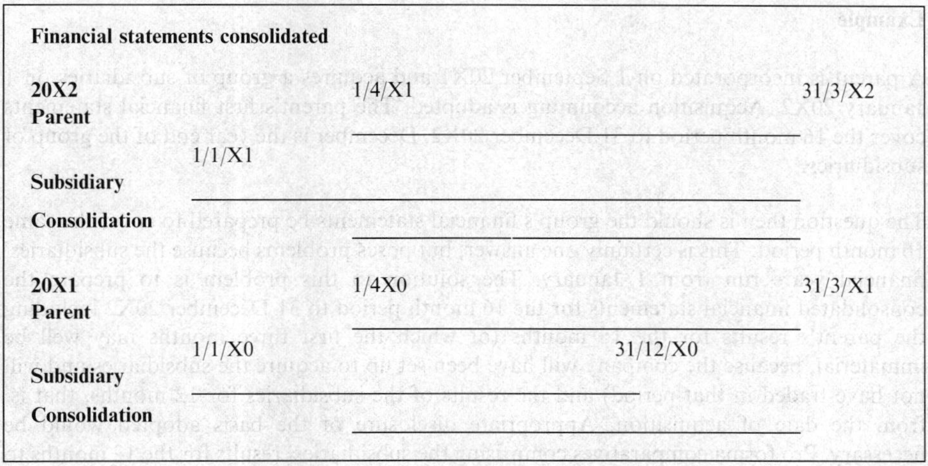

The consolidated financial statements for the year to 31 March 20X2 would include 15 months of the subsidiary's trading. By comparison, the group's published financial statements for the year to 31 March 20X1 include 12 months of the subsidiary's trading ending on 31 December 20X0. Therefore, the consolidated financial statements prepared for the year to 31 March 20X2 include comparatives which are not truly comparable. Also, if the subsidiary was particularly material to the group, it might be misleading to describe the group's consolidated financial statements as representing the group's trading for merely 12 months.

Consequently, if the subsidiary's trading is particularly material to the group, the consolidated financial statements should indicate clearly that they include the financial statements of the parent (and other subsidiaries) for the year to 31 March 20X2, but the result of the material subsidiary for the 15 month period ending on the same date. Then it would be necessary to show the impact that the additional three months has on the reported results. This can be done in a variety of ways, the best approach would be to split the trading into three columns and show the subsidiary's trading for the 3 months to 31 March 20X1 in one column, the trading for the 12 months to March 20X2 (including the subsidiary) in the next column and a total column. The comparatives would remain unchanged. This method gives users clear disclosure of the group's most recent 12 months trading which may assist in their projections of future comparable trading periods. It also satisfies the Act's requirements concerning consolidations. Some would argue that this basis still does not solve the problem as the comparatives are not truly comparable. To resolve this issue it would also be necessary to disclose the subsidiary's trading for the 3 months to 31 March 20X2. The need for this additional disclosure will depend on the individual circumstances.

Parent's period differs from group

24.328 Similar difficulties to those explained above arise where the parent has recently been incorporated and acquires subsidiaries which have different reporting periods to that of the parent.

Example

A parent is incorporated on 1 September 20X1 and acquires a group of subsidiaries on 1 January 20X2. Acquisition accounting is adopted. The parent's first financial statements cover the 16 month period to 31 December 20X2. December is the year end of the group of subsidiaries.

The question then is should the group's financial statements be prepared to cover the same 16 month period. This is certainly one answer, but poses problems because the subsidiaries' financial years run from 1 January. The solution to this problem is to prepare the consolidated financial statements for the 16 month period to 31 December 20X2 including the parent's results for the 16 months (of which the first three months may well be immaterial, because the company will have been set up to acquire the subsidiaries and will not have traded in that period) and the results of the subsidiaries for 12 months, that is, from the date of acquisition. Appropriate disclosure of the basis adopted would be necessary. Pro forma comparatives comprising the subsidiaries' results for the 12 months to 31 December 20X1 may be given for information.

24.329 A similar type of situation arose in Chubb Security Plc, where a new parent was incorporated on 17 August 1992 and acquired Chubb International Holdings Limited (CIHL) on 5 October 1992. The group's financial statements ended 31 March 1993 show pro forma financial statements for 1993 and 1992 as if the group had existed independently for those two years. The statutory financial information is given as a separate column and includes the results of CIHL from the date of its acquisition in October 1992 to 31 March 1993. The balance sheet shows the statutory group balances for the year to 31 March 1993 and pro forma information as comparatives (see Table 24.21).

Table 24.21 — Chubb Security Plc — Annual Report & Accounts — 31 March 1993

Notes to the Accounts

1 **BASIS OF REPORTING**

Chubb Security Plc was incorporated on 17 August 1992. During 1992 all companies within the Security Division of Racal Electronics Plc (Racal) which were not already owned by Chubb International Holdings Limited (CIHL), formerly Racal Security Limited, were transferred into its ownership and companies owned by CIHL which were not part of the Security Division were transferred out of its ownership. CIHL was then transferred into the ownership of Chubb Security Plc which was demerged from Racal on 5 October 1992.

The proforma financial statements include the results for the Group as currently constituted and show the results that would have been presented if Chubb Security Plc had been an independent company throughout the two years ended 31 March 1993. The results for the year ended 31 March 1992 are as previously presented in the Introduction to the Official List (Listing Particulars) circulated to Racal shareholders in September 1992.

The Statutory financial statements for the period ended 31 March include the results for the Group for the 21 weeks from 10 October 1992 (the closest date to the demerger up to which management accounts had been prepared) to 31 March 1993. It was not practical to adjust these management accounts by the results for the period 5 to 9 October 1992.

Consolidated Profit and Loss Account (extract) for the Period and Year Ended 31 March 1993

Note		1993 proforma £000	1992 proforma £000	1993 Statutory £000
2	Turnover	**674,402**	668,943	**330,880**
2 & 3	Operating profit before exceptional items	**75,602**	53,326	**40,078**
4	Exceptional items	**(7,822)**	(5,943)	**(2,248)**
	Trading profit	**67,780**	47,383	**37,830**
5	Group interest payable less investment income	**3,577**	8,311	**1,995**
	Profit on ordinary activities before taxation	**64,203**	39,072	**35,835**

Consolidated Balance Sheet (extract) at 31 March 1993

Note		1993 Statutory £000	1992 proforma £000
	FIXED ASSETS		
13	Tangible assets	**123,671**	121,935
14	Investments	**1,624**	4,154
		125,295	126,089

24.330 In the reorganisation of Rothmans International in 1993, a new parent company was incorporated to acquire the tobacco business of the group, but here the principles of merger accounting were applied (see Table 24.22). In this case, the parent company's accounting period (28 July 1993 to 31 March 1994) was shorter than that of the subsidiaries acquired and group accounts were prepared including the new parent's results for the period 28 July 1993 to 31 March 1994, but incorporating the results of the subsidiaries for their full financial year, that is, for the year to 31 March 1994 in accordance with the principles of merger accounting. Comparatives for the group were the results of the subsidiaries for the year to 31 March 1993.

Table 24.22 — Rothmans International p.l.c. — Annual Report and Accounts — 31 March 1994
DIRECTORS' REPORT (extract)

INCORPORATION AND CHANGE OF NAME The Company was incorporated on 28th July 1993 as New Rothmans plc. On 25th October 1993 the Company changed its name to Rothmans International plc.

STATEMENT OF ACCOUNTING POLICIES (extract)

BASIS OF PREPARATION As part of the amalgamation and reconstruction of the tobacco and luxury goods interests of Rothmans International p.l.c. ('old Rothmans'), Compagnie Financière Richemont AG ('Richemont') and Dunhill Holdings PLC ('Dunhill') in October 1993, the tobacco businesses of old Rothmans and certain tobacco trade marks owned or controlled by Dunhill and by Richemont, were transferred to two new listed companies, Rothmans International plc (formerly New Rothmans plc) and Rothmans International N.V. (together, 'new Rothmans'). Rothmans International plc acquired the UK based tobacco business of old Rothmans and the Dunhill tobacco trade marks. Rothmans International N.V. acquired the non UK based tobacco business of old Rothmans and certain tobacco trade marks owned or controlled by Richemont. The luxury goods interests of old Rothmans, comprising its 58 per cent interest in Dunhill and its 47 per cent indirect interest in Cartier Monde S.A., were transferred to form part of a new separate listed group under the name Vendôme Luxury Group. Shareholders in old Rothmans received units in new Rothmans, each comprising one Rothmans International plc share and one Rothmans International N.V. share, in exchange for their shares in old Rothmans which were transferred to that group, and a payment of cash, representing funds not required by new Rothmans. Units in new Rothmans were also issued to the shareholders in Dunhill and to Richemont representing the tobacco trade marks transferred to new Rothmans. Pursuant to the reconstruction, old Rothmans is in voluntary liquidation.

The consolidated financial statements of the Rothmans International plc group have been prepared using the principles of merger accounting. As a result, although the reconstruction did not take effect until 23rd October 1993, the financial statements are presented as if the reconstruction had taken place on 1st April 1992, except for the exchange of shares, which took place on 23rd October 1993, the return of surplus cash on 1st November 1993 and certain other transactions connected with the reconstruction. The results of the UK based tobacco business of old Rothmans for the year ended 31st March 1993 and for the full year ended 31st March 1994 have been included in these consolidated financial statements except that net dividends received from companies which are now in the Rothmans International N.V. group and dividends received from Dunhill have been excluded from the profit and loss account and are shown as a movement in reserves.

The consolidated accounts include the accounts of Rothmans International plc and its subsidiary undertakings together with the Group's share of the profits and retained post-acquisition reserves of associated undertakings.

24.331 Non-coterminous accounting periods are also considered in chapter 28 which looks at the problems that can arise in merger accounting.

Elimination of intra-group transactions

24.332 *Until* the Companies Act 1989, there were no laid down rules concerning how to eliminate intra-group transactions. Nevertheless, it has been accepted accounting practice to eliminate transactions between group members in the consolidated financial statements. SSAP 14 stated that such eliminations should be made, but did not detail how, apart from stating that the method was well understood. However, the Companies Act 1985 specifically requires "*debts and claims*" (that is, debtors and creditors) between group undertakings to be eliminated on consolidation. Also, income and expenditure relating to transactions between group undertakings should be eliminated on consolidation. [CA85 4A Sch 6(1)].

24.333 Similarly, profits and losses resulting from transactions between group undertakings included in the value of assets retained at the year end should be eliminated. [CA85 4A Sch 6(2)]. The Companies Act 1985, but not FRS 2 (see below), permits the elimination of such profits and losses to be made in proportion to the group's interest in the undertaking's shares. [CA85 4A Sch 6(3)].

24.334 The rules set out in FRS 2 are consistent with the Act except that they are further restricted as follows:

- Profits or losses on any intra-group transactions, to the extent that they are reflected in the book value of assets to be included in the consolidation, should be eliminated in full.
- Intra-group debtors and creditors should be eliminated.
- The elimination of profits or losses relating to intra-group transactions should be set against the interest held by the parent and its other subsidiaries and against the minority interest in proportion to their respective holdings in the undertaking whose individual financial statements recorded the eliminated profits or losses.

[FRS 2 para 39].

24.335 The rationale for full elimination of unrealised profits or losses even where the related transactions are between subsidiary undertakings with minority interests is set out below.

24.336 Transactions between subsidiaries included in the consolidation are wholly within the control of the parent company, whether or not the subsidiaries are wholly-owned. All the assets and liabilities of a subsidiary and transactions between subsidiaries are brought into the consolidation in full, again whether or not they are wholly-owned. Therefore, as the group includes 100 per cent of all the subsidiaries' assets and liabilities, intra-group transactions that give rise to profits or losses that are unrealised at the balance sheet date are wholly unrealised to the group and do not represent any increase or decrease in the group's net assets. They should, therefore, be eliminated in full, even where the transactions involve subsidiaries with minority interests.

Elimination calculations

24.337 The following examples deal with the elimination of intra-group profit on the sale of assets by a subsidiary to its parent and the elimination of intra-group profit on sale of assets by a parent to its subsidiary.

Example 1

A parent owns 60% of a subsidiary. The subsidiary sells some stock to the parent for £70,000 and makes a profit of £30,000 on the sale. The stock is in the parent's balance sheet at the year end.

The parent must eliminate 100% of the unrealised profit on consolidation. The stock will, therefore, be carried in the group's balance sheet at £40,000 (£70,000 – £30,000). The profit and loss account will show a corresponding reduction in profit of £30,000. The minority interest in the profit and loss account for the year will be credited with the minority's share of the unrealised profit, £12,000 (40% × £30,000).

The double entry on consolidation is as follows:

	£'000	£'000
Dr Profit before taxation	30	
Cr Stock		30

Being the elimination of 100% of the unrealised profit from the balance sheet.

Dr Balance sheet minority interest	12	
Cr Profit and loss account minority interest		12

Being the allocation to the minority of its 'share' of the elimination of the unrealised profit.

The effect on the profit and loss account and balance sheet is as follows:

Profit and loss account	Results of sub (say)	Adjustment	Results consolidated
	£'000	£'000	£'000
Profit before taxation	100	(30)	70
Minority interests	(40)	12	(28)
Profit for the financial year	60	(18)	42
Consolidated balance sheet	Before adjustment (say)	Adjustment	After adjustment
Stock	800	(30)	770
Other shareholders' funds	400	—	400
Profit and loss account	275	(18)	257
Minority interests	125	12	113
	800	(30)	770

In other words, from the group's point of view, no profit has been recognised. The stock is retained at cost to the group of £40,000. The profit before tax also does not include any of the profit of £30,000 on the stock in question. This reflects the fact that the group as an entity has not made a profit on selling stock to itself. Since in this method, the objective is to eliminate the entire profit, it is necessary to show the effect of the subsidiary in question earning £30,000 less profit. The effect of this is that the group has earned £18,000 less (60% × £30,000). Hence the adjustment of £12,000 shown above in the minority's line.

Example 2

The situation is as above except that, on this occasion, it is the parent that makes the sale. The parent owns 60% of a subsidiary. The parent sells some stock to the subsidiary for £70,000 and makes a profit of £30,000 on the sale. The stock is in the subsidiary's balance sheet at the year end.

The parent must eliminate 100% of the unrealised profit on consolidation. The stock will, therefore, be carried in the group's balance sheet at £40,000 (£70,000 – £30,000). The profit and loss account will show a corresponding reduction in profit of £30,000. As the minority has no interest in the company that made the profit (the parent) there will be no element of the elimination attributed to the minority.

The double entry on consolidation is as follows:

	£'000	£'000
Dr Profit before taxation	30	
Cr Stock		30

Being the elimination of 100% of the unrealised profit from the balance sheet.

The effect on the profit and loss account and balance sheet is:

Consolidated profit and loss	Before adjustment (say)	Adjustment	After adjustment
	£'000	£'000	£'000
Profit before taxation	100	(30)	70
Minority interests	(40)	—	(40)
Profit for the financial year	60	(30)	30
Consolidated balance sheet	Before adjustment (say)	Adjustment	After adjustment
Stock	800	(30)	770
Other shareholders' funds	400	—	400
Profit and loss account	275	(30)	245
Minority interests	125	—	125
	800	(30)	770

Profit elimination from fixed assets

24.338 The rules explained above apply equally to any profit that might be included in the group's fixed assets (including investments) as a result of one group company selling assets to another group company at a profit. Before the introduction of FRS 2 many companies did not eliminate such profits immediately from their fixed assets, but eliminated them over the life of the asset *via* higher depreciation charges. This method is not acceptable under FRS 2 and such intra-group profits must be eliminated in full.

Losses

24.339 Where a company makes a loss selling assets (at fair value) to another group company, no consolidation adjustment should be necessary at the year end. This is because it would be wrong to reinstate the asset at a value above its recoverable amount.

Subsidiaries excluded from consolidation

24.340 Profits or losses arising on transactions with undertakings excluded from consolidation because they are held exclusively with a view to subsequent resale or because of severe long-term restrictions need not be eliminated, except to the extent appropriate where significant influence is retained and the subsidiary is treated as an associate (that is, equity accounted). However, it is important to consider whether it is prudent to record any profit arising from transactions with subsidiaries excluded on these grounds (see the examples in para 24.342 below). [FRS 2 para 83].

24.341 The adjustments required to eliminate the effects of intra-group trading between a group and an undertaking included in the consolidation by the equity method are straightforward. The elimination of intra-group profits or losses should be in proportion to the group's interest.

24.342 To eliminate the profits or losses of such undertakings in proportion to the group's share is logical as it ensures that only profits that are actually recorded in the profit and loss account are eliminated. It would clearly be wrong to eliminate a greater proportion of profit than was recorded originally. Two examples below deal with whether or not any adjustments are necessary when intra-group profits are made on sales of assets to subsidiaries that have been excluded from consolidation. In the first example, the two subsidiaries have been wholly excluded. In the second example, the subsidiary is equity accounted as significant influence is retained.

Example 1

A group has a subsidiary that manufactures office equipment. It also has two subsidiaries that are not included in the group's consolidated financial statements either by full consolidation or by equity accounting. The first of these subsidiaries is profitable and has not been consolidated as it is being held exclusively with a view to subsequent resale and the second has been excluded due to severe long-term restrictions (remittances to the UK are virtually impossible and are not expected to be in the future, representing a loss of control of financial and operating policy). At the year end the consolidated financial statements show substantial debtor balances due from each of the excluded subsidiaries. Are any consolidation adjustments necessary?

As neither of the debtor balances are with subsidiaries included in the consolidation the balances do not require elimination as intra-group transactions. However, consideration should be given to whether it would be prudent to recognise any element of profit included in those balances.

The first of the subsidiaries is profitable and provided there is no reason to believe that the debt will not be settled there is no reason to make an adjustment to eliminate the profit included in the debtor.

The second subsidiary has been excluded on the grounds that remittances to the UK are virtually impossible. It would clearly be imprudent for the group to recognise a profit on a sale to such a company until the debt was settled. Indeed, in this situation it may be necessary to provide for the whole debt in the group's profit and loss account.

Example 2

Company H prepares its consolidated financial statements to 31 December 20X1. It has a 60% holding in a subsidiary (company S) which has been excluded on the grounds of severe long-term restrictions, but it retains significant influence and accounts for the subsidiary under the equity method of accounting. During the year company H purchased stock amounting to £1 million on which company S made a profit of £500,000. At the year end half of this stock remained unsold to third parties. Company H's consolidated financial statements would initially record its share of this profit under the equity method at £300,000 (60% × £500,000) and the unrealised element of this should be eliminated. The unsold stock amounts to £500,000 on which there is £250,000 unrealised profits. The elimination journal in the consolidation would be to debit share of the subsidiary's profit £150,000 (60% × £250,000), and to credit stock £150,000.

24.343 Where an undertaking that is fully consolidated makes a sale to an undertaking that is included in the consolidation under the equity method, a profit may arise in the group. The undertaking's assets that are equity accounted will be overstated by the profit element if the asset is held at the year end. Consequently, an adjustment is required on consolidation to reduce the group's share of the associate's net assets by the same amount. But in this case, the group's profit will not be eliminated in full as the element of profit which is attributable to the minority's share is not recorded in the balance sheet. This is because under the equity method the group's balance sheet will only include its percentage share of the net assets of the subsidiary. Therefore, for a 60 per cent subsidiary that is equity accounted, 40 per cent of the group's profit on the transaction (that is, the element of the profit that is attributable to the third party shareholders) will be recorded in the consolidated profit and loss account and 60 per cent eliminated.

Example

A parent company sells stock worth £100,000 to a 60% owned subsidiary which has been excluded from consolidation on the grounds of lack of control because of severe long-term restrictions. The profit on the transaction is £20,000 and the subsidiary retains the stock at the year end. The results of the subsidiary are equity accounted with those of the group. The profit to be eliminated is 60% of the £20,000, that is, £12,000. The stock included in the net assets that are equity accounted before the profit elimination would be £60,000 (that is, £100,000 × 60%). The stock would, therefore, be reduced to £48,000. The double entry on consolidation is as follows:

	£'000	£'000
Dr Profit before taxation	12	
Cr Net assets of equity accounted subsidiary		12

Being the elimination of the group's share of 60% of the unrealised profit included in the balance sheet by the equity method of accounting.

Section III — Minority interests

Introduction

24.344 Under the parent company concept of accounting for groups (explained in paragraph 24.6), which is the basis adopted for consolidations in the UK, minority interests are shown separately either before or after shareholders' funds and therefore, unlike under the entity concept, do not form part of shareholders' funds. Minority interests represent the share of net assets of subsidiaries consolidated into the group's consolidated financial statements that are financed by shareholders who are not members of the group and are outside third parties.

24.345 This chapter considers the general accounting and disclosure requirements that apply to minority interests now to be found in the Companies Act 1985 (as amended), FRS 2 and FRS 25. The latter half of this section concentrates on the problems associated with calculating minority interests and considers:

- Measurement of minority interests (see para 24.371).
- Indirect holdings (see para 24.375).
- Treatment of minority interests on acquisition (see para 24.377).
- Acquisition of minority interests (see para 24.380).
- Loss making subsidiaries (see para 24.383).

Definition

24.346 'Minority interests' is defined in the Companies Act 1985 to mean "*the amount of capital and reserves attributable to shares in subsidiary undertakings included in the consolidation held by or on behalf of persons other than the parent company and its subsidiary undertakings*". [CA85 4A Sch 17(2)]. The effect of the legislation is, for example, that where a parent owns 70 per cent of a subsidiary, it has to consolidate 100 per cent of the subsidiary's results and net assets and show minority interests of 30 per cent.

24.347 FRS 2 also defines minority interests based on the Companies Act 1985 definition, but the standard's definition recognises also that a parent need not be a company. It states that the minority interest in a subsidiary is:

> "*The interest in a subsidiary undertaking included in the consolidation that is attributable to the shares held by or on behalf of persons other than the parent undertaking and its subsidiary undertakings.*" [FRS 2 para 13].

24.348 The definition in FRS 2 and the Companies Act 1985 requirements can be seen reflected in companies' accounting policies, for example see Table 24.23 which shows Marconi plc's policy for minority interests.

Table 24.23 — Marconi plc — Annual Report and Accounts — 31 March 2001

Notes to the Accounts (extract)

7 Minority Interests
Equity minority interests represent the share of the profits less losses on ordinary activities attributable to the interests of equity shareholders in subsidiaries which are not wholly owned by the Group.

24.349 The term 'minority interests' was originally introduced into company law at a time when consolidation was based on equity ownership rather than control. Under the current provisions of the Companies Act 1985, where consolidation is based on control, it is possible, although fairly uncommon, for minority interests to be more than 50 per cent. Indeed there are situations where minority interests might be considerably higher than 50 per cent (see further para 24.351).

24.350 With regard to the disclosure of minority interests, Article 21 of the EC 7th Directive on group accounts states that minority interests should be shown as a separate item (with an appropriate heading) in the company's capital, reserves and results brought forward. The Companies Act 1989 brought this requirement into UK law and, therefore, specifies where minority interests should be shown in both the consolidated balance sheet formats and the consolidated profit and loss account formats (see further para 24.357).

Minority or majority interests

24.351 Under the revised definitions of subsidiary brought into company law by SI 2004/2947, 'The Companies Act 1985 (International Accounting Standards and Other Amendments) Regulations 2004', a company has to be treated as a subsidiary where its parent has the power to exercise, or actually exercises, dominant influence or control over it or manages it on a unified basis (see further para 24.130). Consequently, it is quite possible for a parent to own only (say) 20 per cent of the undertaking's equity and exercise dominant influence over it, or manage it on a unified basis, or have the power to control it. Where this is so, it is also quite possible that the minority shareholders will hold (say) 80 per cent of the undertaking's equity. Accordingly, the minority interests shown in the consolidated financial statements will be calculated using this percentage. This could result, for example, in the group consolidating 100 per cent of the assets and liabilities of the subsidiary, but showing also minority interests of 80 per cent of those assets and liabilities. A similar situation could arise where the parent owns a majority of the voting rights, but owns (say) only 20 per cent of the total equity.

24.352 Where these types of situation arise, it is unlikely that this is a good enough reason for the term 'minority interests' to be amended to (say) 'majority interests'. Furthermore, we consider that it is unlikely that circumstances would exist where using the term 'minority interests' would affect the true and fair view and, therefore, justify using another term. In the situation described above, the minority although owning the majority of capital will be in a minority position with regard to controlling the company and, consequently, the term 'minority interests' still describes the outside interest fairly. However, we consider that in this type of situation it is necessary to explain the relationship with the subsidiary fully in the consolidated financial statements in order that they should give a true and fair view. In particular, FRS 2 requires that where the parent has the power to exercise, or actually exercises, a dominant influence or control over it, the consolidated financial statements should disclose this fact and should explain the basis of the parent's dominant influence. [CA85 5 Sch para 15(5); FRS 2 para 34].

Basis of recognising minority interests

24.353 FRS 2 states that the effect of the existence of minority interests on the returns to investors in the parent is best reflected by presenting the net identifiable assets attributable to minority interests on the same basis as those attributable to group interests. The same general approach applies to the balance sheet where the group's assets and liabilities, whether they are attributable to minorities or to the parent, should be presented on a consistent basis. This is logical as the group includes 100 per cent of the assets and liabilities of a subsidiary in its consolidated balance sheet (after consolidation eliminations) whatever the parent's holding in the subsidiary. As explained briefly above, this basis is consistent with the parent company concept.

24.354 Although the basis for recognising minority interests under UK GAAP is consistent with the parent company concept, this consistency of approach does not extend to all of the goodwill of the subsidiary. When a parent purchases a controlling, but not 100 per cent, interest in a subsidiary, goodwill may arise (see chapter 25). The goodwill that arises on consolidation relates only to the parent's share of the subsidiary and not to the minority's share. Although it might be possible to estimate a goodwill figure for minority interests by extrapolation or valuation, it would be inappropriate under existing UK GAAP to include that amount in the balance sheet as the minority is not party to the group's transaction to acquire the subsidiary. To include an amount for goodwill would, from the group's point of view, represent the recognition of inherent goodwill, which is not permitted by the Act or FRS 10. The requirement that goodwill arising on acquisition should only be recognised with respect to the part of the subsidiary undertaking that is attributable to the interest held by the parent and its other subsidiaries is summarised in paragraph 38 of FRS 2. This would be the situation, for example, where company P acquires 70 per cent of sub-group A. The net assets of sub-group A would be fair valued on consolidation (ignoring any goodwill recognised in sub-group A) and the minority would be given their share of those net assets. However, where a subsidiary (company A) of parent (company P) has acquired a sub-subsidiary (company B), any goodwill arising on the acquisition of company B, which in company A's consolidated financial statements is capitalised and amortised, will have an effect on the calculation of any minority interests in company A recognised in the parent's consolidated financial statements (see further para 24.378).

Measurement of minority interests

24.355 As explained above, shares issued by subsidiaries to persons outside the group are normally accounted for as minority interests. But in situations where the minority interest has one or more features that would lead it to fall within the definition of a liability contained in FRS 25, 'Financial instruments: Disclosure and presentation', it should be recognised and measured in accordance with that standard (see further chapter 6). Examples of such features include preference shares with fixed dividends and situations where the group guarantees the payment of the minority's dividends or the repayment of its capital. Prior to FRS 25 classification of a minority interest as a liability was restricted to circumstances where a potential guarantee was in place.

Equity minority interests

24.356 Minority interests that meet the definition of equity under FRS 25, 'Financial instruments: Disclosure and presentation', are no less straightforward than those classified as liablilities. Such minority interests are merely represented by the net proceeds on issue of the shares (that is, net of issue costs) plus the equity minority shareholders' percentage interest in the other reserves of the company. Examples of such calculations follow from paragraph 24.371.

Presentation in financial statements of equity minority interests

Balance sheet

24.357 In the balance sheet Format 1 'minority interests' should be shown either directly above or below 'capital and reserves'. Because it is possible to total the format 1 balance sheet in different positions, it is possible to:

- Draw a total before capital and reserves which includes minority interests.
- Draw a total before capital and reserves and minority interests, showing minority interests either before or after capital and reserves.

Chapter 4 includes a summary of Format 1 which shows the positioning of 'minority interests'.

24.358 In Format 2 the disclosure of 'minority interests' should be made under 'liabilities' between the headings 'capital and reserves' and 'provisions for liabilities'. [CA85 4A Sch 17(1)(2); FRS 2 para 35].

24.359 In determining how the disclosure of minority interests can be changed or adapted in the consolidated balance sheet, the Act states that the item should be treated in the same way as if a letter were assigned to it. [CA85 4A Sch 17(5)(a)]. But in practice even under the Companies Act 1985 strict criteria there are a number of ways of presenting minority interests to emphasise different balance sheet totals as illustrated in the examples that follow. Most commonly the balance sheet shows minority interests after drawing a total for shareholders' interests. By contrast Table 24.24 shows Bass PLC's balance sheet which follows Format 1 of the Act, but it has presented minority interests in the alternative position before capital and reserves and has also totalled net assets to include the deduction for minority interests. This is perfectly acceptable under the Act's rules, because although the order of items in the formats can only be changed within certain defined parameters, there are no rules on where the balance sheet totals can be struck. From Table 24.25 it can be seen that ICI's PLC's balance sheet is also Format 1 and that it has used a similar positioning to Bass PLC, but has totalled in a different place showing 'total assets less current liabilities'.

Table 24.24 – Bass PLC – Annual Report – 30 September 1994

Balance sheets (extract)

		Group		Company	
30 September 1994	Note	**1994 £m**	1993 £m	**1994 £m**	1993 £m
Total assets less current liabilities		**4,942**	4,834	**3,700**	3,685
Creditors: amounts falling due after more than one year	18	**(1,268)**	(1,288)	**(1,286)**	(1,273)
Provisions for liabilities and charges[1]		**(62)**	(85)		
Minority equity interests[2]	19	**(30)**	(48)	**–**	–
Net assets	21	**3,582**	3,413	**2,414**	2,412
Capital and reserves – equity interests					
Called up share capital	22	**218**	217	**218**	217
Share premium account	23	**539**	517	**539**	517
Revaluation reserve	23	**1,007**	1,051	**–**	–
Capital reserve	23	**–**	–	**241**	241
Profit and loss account	23	**1,818**	1,628	**1,416**	1,437
Shareholders' funds		**3,582**	3,413	**2,414**	2,412

1 Note that for years beginning on or after 1 January 2005, SI 2004/2947, 'The Companies Act 1985 (International Accounting Standard and Other Amendments) Regulations 2004', changed the Schedule 4 line item to 'provisions for liabilities'.

2 Note that for years beginning on or after 1 January 2005, the identification of equity and non-equity minority interests is no longer required by FRS 4.

Table 24.25 – Imperial Chemical Industries PLC – Annual Report and Accounts and Form 20-F – 31 December 1999

Balance Sheets (extract) at 31 December 1999

		Group		Company	
		1999	1998	**1999**	1998
	Notes	**£m**	£m	**£m**	£m
Total assets less current liabilities	4	**4,073**	4,647	**5,921**	5,376
Financed by					
Creditors due after more than one year					
Loans	21	**2,252**	2,954	**247**	360
Other creditors	20	**71**	55	**1,256**	2,784
		2,323	3,009	**1,503**	3,144
Provisions for liabilities and charges[1]	22	**1,456**	1,440	**321**	210
Minority interests – equity		**50**	49	–	–
Shareholders' funds – equity					
Called-up share capital	24	**728**	728	**728**	728
Reserves					
Share premium accounts		**588**	587	**588**	587
Associates' reserves		**26**	15	–	–
Profit and loss account		**(1,098)**	(1,181)	**2,781**	707
Total reserves	25	**(484)**	(579)	**3,369**	1,294
Total shareholders' funds (page 51)		**244**	149	**4,097**	2,022
		4,073	4,647	**5,921**	5,376

1 Note that for years beginning on or after 1 January 2005, SI 2004/2947, 'The Companies Act 1985 (International Accounting Standard and Other Amendments) Regulations 2004', change the Schedule 4 line item to 'provisions for liabilities'.

2 Note that for years beginning on or after 1 January 2005, the identification of equity and non-equity minority interests is no longer required by FRS 4.

Profit and loss account

24.360 For the profit and loss account formats the Companies Act 1985 requires two additional lines to be added for minority interests. The first line requires the disclosure of minority interests in the profit or loss excluding extraordinary items, and in Format 1 and Format 2 this item should be included after 'profit or loss on ordinary activities after taxation'. In addition, the Companies Act 1985 specifies that the item should be described 'minority interests'. For Format 3 and Format 4 minority interests should be included under 'charges' or 'income' as appropriate, in the same position after striking the 'profit or loss on ordinary activities after taxation'. [CA85 4A Sch 17(3); FRS 2 para 36]. This presentation can be seen in many of the extracts from the financial statements reproduced in this chapter, for example see Table 24.26.

Table 24.26 – Marks and Spencer p.l.c. – Annual Report and Financial Statements – 31 March 1995

Consolidated profit and loss account (extract)
FOR THE YEAR ENDED 31 MARCH 1995

	Notes	1995 52 weeks £m	1994 53 weeks Restated £m
PROFIT ON ORDINARY ACTIVITIES BEFORE TAXATION	2	**924.3**	851.5
Tax on ordinary activities	6	**(299.5)**	(272.2)
PROFIT ON ORDINARY ACTIVITIES AFTER TAXATION		**624.8**	579.3
Minority interests (all equity)		**(1.0)**	(1.1)
PROFIT FOR THE FINANCIAL YEAR	7	**623.8**	578.2

24.361 The second line required to be disclosed by the legislation is the minority's share of any extraordinary items. [CA85 4A Sch 17(4)]. However, the introduction of FRS 3 (see chapter 8) has, in effect, stopped the use of extraordinary items as a caption for presentation in the profit and loss account. Consequently, the position of the minority's share of extraordinary items is no longer relevant.

24.362 The consolidated profit and loss account disclosure for 'minority interests' under Format 1 is illustrated in chapter 4.

24.363 There is in principle more scope to adapt and combine the minority interests disclosure in the consolidated profit and loss account than there is in the balance sheet. This is because the Act states that minority interests shall be treated as if they have been assigned an Arabic number. [CA85 4A Sch 17(5)(b)]. This means that the minority interests disclosure in the profit and loss account can be adapted where the special nature of the group's business requires such adaptation. [CA85 4 Sch 3(3)]. It is, in practice, difficult to imagine when this particular provision would apply apart from perhaps in the circumstance of stapled stock (see para 24.368).

24.364 FRS 3, 'Reporting financial performance', requires that the notes to the financial statements should include information regarding the effect on any minority interests of the three non-operating exceptional items specified in that standard, which are:

- Profits or losses on the sale of termination of an operation.
- Costs of a fundamental reorganisation or restructuring having a material effect on the nature and focus of the reporting entity's operations.
- Profits or losses on the disposal of fixed assets.

[FRS 3 para 20].

24.365 Table 24.27 shows an extract from Unitech plc's annual report and accounts which has shown the minority's share of a non-operating exceptional.

Table 24.27 — Unitech plc — Annual report and accounts — 31 May 1993
Notes (extract)

2 Segment information (extract)

The gains arising on the sale of buildings include a £1,225,000 gain, less tax of £55,000, on the disposal of buildings owned by Nemic-Lambda in Israel, of which the minority interest share is £578,000.

[The next paragraph is 24.368.]

Stapled shares

24.368 An example of where the minority interests in the balance sheet might need to be shown in another position in order to give a true and fair view is where shareholders in the parent have been issued with shares in a subsidiary that have been 'stapled' with their shares in the parent. This method of share issue is often used where the subsidiary is resident overseas for tax purposes to ensure that distributions from the subsidiary are still treated as distributions of the UK company. Therefore, depending upon the circumstances and the rights attaching to the subsidiary's shares, those shares might, in substance, be more akin to shareholders' funds than to minority interests.

Directors' interests

24.369 It is often a requirement of a company's articles of association for the company's directors to acquire nominee shareholdings in the company's shares. Generally these shareholdings are very small and the directors have no beneficial interest in them. Where such a situation arises in a subsidiary company, clearly the directors' shareholding from the group's perspective does not constitute a minority interest in the company as the shares are normally held on the parent company's behalf.

24.370 Other situations arise in practice where directors have beneficial interests in the company's shares. These situations need to be considered very carefully to determine whether the shareholding constitutes a minority interest or should be recognised for accounting purposes in some other way. For example, if a director is given shares in his/her company and the company's parent arranges to reacquire those shares at a future date, the substance of the transaction might be to remunerate the director. Where this is so, the cost to the company should be charged to the profit and loss account as staff costs over the term of the arrangement in accordance with FRS 20, 'Share-based payments' (see further chapter 12) and disclosed as directors' emoluments. Alternatively, the substance of the transaction could be quite different, for example, it might be a way of acquiring intellectual property rights or expert knowledge that the director has or has some right to. In such a situation it could be argued that the transaction relates to the acquisition of that right or knowledge and as such represents an intangible asset and should be accounted for as such. Clearly, transactions with directors of this nature need to be considered very carefully and inevitably where they are not accounted for as minority interests additional disclosure will be necessary, because the transaction is likely to be material to the director (see further chapter 6 of the Manual of Accounting – IFRS and UK supplement) and it will be a transaction with a related party (see chapter 29).

Measurement of minority interests

24.371 Minority interests included in the consolidated balance sheet should represent the total amount of capital and reserves attributable to shares in the subsidiary held by or on behalf of persons other than the parent and its other subsidiaries. [CA85 4A Sch 17(2)]. Similar wording is also used to indicate how to calculate the minority's interest in the profit and loss for the period. [CA85 4A Sch 17(3)(4)]. In practice, the calculation of minority interests is fraught with complications. These complications can include changes in stake and the treatment of losses. The examples that follow illustrate each of these problems.

Profit and loss account calculation

24.372 The minority interests in a subsidiary's profit for the year is calculated by taking the profit after taxation and calculating the proportion of the profit that is attributable to the minority. Consider the following simple example.

Example

A parent owns 80% of a subsidiary's ordinary share capital (there are no other classes of capital) since the subsidiary's incorporation. The subsidiary's profit and loss account is as follows:

	£'000
Operating profit	1,000
Non-operating exceptional item	1,250
Profit on ordinary activities before taxation	2,250
Tax on profit on ordinary activities	(280)
Retained profit for the financial year	1,970

The figures that would be brought into the consolidated financial statements in respect of the subsidiary (ignoring any intra-group profit elimination) are:

	£'000
Operating profit	1,000
Non-operating exceptional item	1,250
Profit on ordinary activities before taxation	2,250
Tax on profit for the financial year	(280)
Profit on ordinary activities after taxation	1,970
Minority interests (20% × £1,970,000)	(394)
Retained profit for the year	1,576

Balance sheet calculation

24.373 The calculation of the balance sheet minority interests follows directly from the definition. In a simple situation involving only equity shares, the balance of the minority interests at the year end is the minority's interest in the capital and reserves of the subsidiary. An example of the calculation of the balance sheet minority interests is shown below:

Example

Following on from the example above, the subsidiary's balance sheet is as follows:

		£'000
Net assets		3,820
Equity share capital		250
Share premium		500
Revaluation reserve		300
Profit and loss account	800	
Retained profit for the year	1,970	2,770
Equity shareholders' funds		3,820

The minority interests in the capital and reserves of the subsidiary are calculated as follows, assuming that issue costs are immaterial (if they were material the relevant proportion should be deducted from the minorities' equity share capital):

		£'000	£'000
Equity share capital	20% × 250,000		50
Share premium	20% × 500,000		100
Revaluation reserve	20% × 300,000		60
Profit and loss account b/f	20% × 800,000	160	
Minority's interest in the profit after taxation		394	554
Minority interests			764

24.374 This is clearly a very straightforward example and would be made more complicated by, for example, a share structure involving different classes of shares (particularly if one or more of those classes is a share classified as a liability) or where there are intra-group transactions that require elimination.

Indirect holdings

24.375 Where a parent holds an indirect interest in a subsidiary the treatment of minorities becomes more complicated. Before the minority interests can be calculated it is first necessary to establish whether the entity is a subsidiary of the parent and, therefore, should be consolidated.

Example

Consider the following group structure:

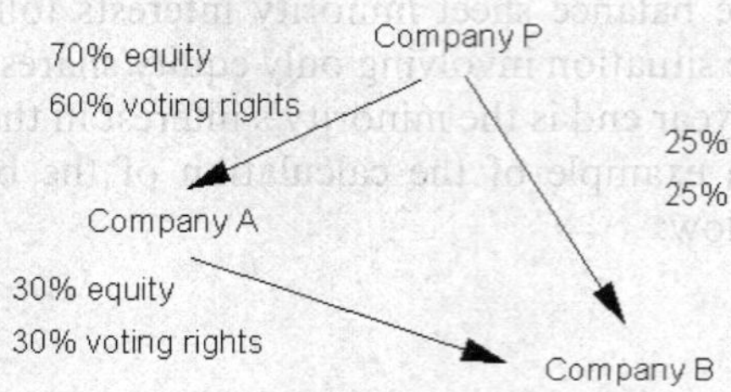

A number of factors have to be considered to determine whether company B is a subsidiary of company P. These matters are fully discussed from paragraph 24.76 onwards. However, in the example company P owns 70% of the equity of company A and 60% of the voting rights of company A. Company A is, therefore, a subsidiary of company P, because company P controls more than 50% of the voting rights of company A.

Company P owns 25% of the equity and voting rights in company B, while company A owns 30% of the equity and voting rights in company B. Company B is not a direct subsidiary of company A as company A only controls 30% of its votes (assuming company B is not a subsidiary of company A for other reasons, for example, dominant influence — see further in para 24.76 onwards). However, company P controls 25% of the votes in company B directly and, by virtue of its control of company A, 30% of the votes in company B indirectly. Company B is, therefore, a subsidiary of company P as company P controls in total 55% of the voting rights in company B. On the other hand, if company A had not been a subsidiary of company P, then company P would not have controlled company B and, as a consequence, company B would not have been a subsidiary of company P either.

The summarised balance sheets of each of the group companies is as follows:

Summarised balance sheets	Company P £'000	Company A £'000	Company B £'000
Investment in subsidiaries	60*	30	-
Net assets	190	120	200
	250	150	200
Equity share capital	100	50	100
Profit and loss account	150	100	100
Equity shareholders' funds	250	150	200

* The investment in subsidiaries represents the investments in company A and company B, which were acquired for their nominal value at incorporation, being 35 for the investment in A (70% × 50) and 25 for the investment in B (25% × 100).

The balance sheet minority interests can be ascertained in two ways: either by considering the minority interest arising when company B is consolidated with company A; or by considering company P's indirect holding in its subsidiaries. Both methods will arrive at the same result unless goodwill has been capitalised (see para 24.378)

Indirect method

The indirect method involves calculating the total minority interests by considering the indirect minority interests from the parent's perspective. In this case there is an indirect minority interest in company B of 54% (100% — (30% x 70% + 25%)) and a direct minority interest of 30% in company A. The minority interests calculated under the indirect method is as follows:

Minority interest in group — indirect method	£'000
Minorities' share of net assets of company A net assets × direct minority interest (£120,000 × 30%)	36
Minorities' share of net assets of company B net assets × indirect minority interest (£200,000 × 54%)	108
	144

Direct method

The direct method of calculating the minority interests involves consolidation of the minority interests of company B with company A and then consolidating company A with company P. The calculation is as follows:

Minority interest in group — direct method	£'000
Company B consolidated into company A	
Equity share capital of company B (£100,000 × 70%)	70
Reserves of company B (£100,000 × 70%)	70
Minority interest in group A	140
Group A consolidated into company P	
Equity share capital of company A (£50,000 × 30%)	15
Reserves of company A (£100,000 × 30%)	30
Reserves of company B ((£100,000 – £70,000) × 30%)*	9
Adjustment to eliminate 25% of company B owned directly by company P†	
Equity share capital of B (£100,000 × 25%)	(25)
Reserves of B (£100,000 × 25%)	(25)
	144

* The minority in group A will take their proportion of the reserves of company B that have been consolidated with company A's reserves.

† The adjustment is necessary because the 70% minority interest in company B consolidated into company A includes the 25% held by company P.

24.376 The two methods arrive at the same result, a minority interest of £144,000. However, the use of the indirect and direct methods would not arrive at the same result when there is goodwill arising on the acquisition of company B by company A and, in such cases, the direct method should be used.

Treatment of minority on acquisition

Acquisition of direct subsidiary

24.377 When a subsidiary is acquired it is necessary to allocate to the minority its share of the net assets of the subsidiary. This is normally done in the consolidation process by allocating to the minority its share of the adjusted capital and reserves of the subsidiary (that is, after fair value adjustments). However, they are not allocated any goodwill (see para 24.354). The example that follows illustrates these principles.

Example

At the end of year 1, company P acquires company S. Immediately before the acquisition the summarised balance sheets of both companies are as follows:

Summarised balance sheets	**Company P £'000**	**Company S £'000**
Net assets	500	100
Equity share capital	200	20
Share premium account	100	–
Profit and loss reserve	200	80
Equity shareholders' funds	500	100

On the acquisition company P issues 10,000 £1 equity shares to the shareholders of company S to acquire 80% of its issued capital. The fair value of the consideration is valued at £150,000 and the fair value of the net assets of company S at the date of acquisition is determined to be £160,000. Consequently, the companies' balance sheets will look as follows after the acquisition:

Summarised balance sheets	**£'000**	**Company P £'000**	**£'000**	**Company S £'000**
Investment in subsidiary		150		–
Other net assets	500		100	
Fair value adjustment	–	500	60	160
		650		160
Equity share capital		210		20
Share premium		240		–
Profit and loss account		200		80
Revaluation reserve		–		60
Equity shareholders' funds		650		160

The goodwill arising on acquisition and the minority interests are calculated as follows:

Cost of control account/goodwill

	£'000		£'000
Investment	150	Equity share capital (£20,000 × 80%)	16
		P&L reserve (£80,000 × 80%)	64
		Revaluation reserve (£60,000 × 80%)	48
			128
		Goodwill	22
	150		150

Minority interests account

	£'000		£'000
Balance	32	Equity share capital (£20,000 × 20%)	4
		P&L reserve (£80,000 × 20%)	16
		Revaluation reserve (£60,000 × 20%)	12
	32		32

The consolidated balance sheet for the group immediately after the acquisition would be as follows:

Summarised consolidated balance sheet	**Group**
	£'000
Goodwill	22
Net assets (£500,000 + £160,000)	660
	682
Equity share capital	210
Share premium account	240
Profit and loss account reserve	200
Equity shareholders' funds	650
Minority interests	32
	682

Acquisition of indirect subsidiary

24.378 When a subsidiary acquires another company and goodwill arises on that acquisition, that goodwill will affect the calculation of the minority interest and goodwill to be shown in the consolidated financial statements of the ultimate parent. Consider the following example:

Example

A parent company (company P) has an 80% owned subsidiary (company S). Company S makes an acquisition for cash of a third company (company A), which it then wholly owns. Goodwill of £100,000 arises on the acquisition of company A. How should that goodwill be reflected in the consolidated financial statements of company P. Should it be reflected as:

(a) 100% of the goodwill with 20% then being allocated to the minority; or

(b) 80% of the goodwill that arises?

Assuming that company S prepared consolidated financial statements, 100% of the goodwill would be recognised on the acquisition of company A in those financial statements.

In company P's consolidated financial statements, the argument for showing £100,000 as goodwill with a minority interest of £20,000 is that the Companies Act defines minority interest as the amount of capital and reserves attributable to shares in the subsidiary undertakings included in the consolidation held by or on behalf of persons other than the parent company and its subsidiary undertaking. [CA85 Sch 4A para 17(2)]. The capital and reserves attributable to the shares in the subsidiaries (or rather the net assets) would include £100,000 of the goodwill on the acquisition of company A by company S, and this would be included in company P's consolidated financial statements if no adjustment were made on consolidation. Therefore, if no adjustment is required, the consolidated financial statements of company P would include goodwill of £100,000 and a related minority interest of £20,000.

However, this raises the question of whether or not any adjustment is required. FRS 2 para 38 states:

> *"However, goodwill arising on acquisition should only be recognised with respect to the part of the subsidiary undertaking that is attributable to the interest held by the parent and its other subsidiary undertakings. No goodwill should be attributed to the minority interest."* [FRS 2 para 38].

This might appear to mean that an adjustment is required to reduce goodwill in company P's consolidated financial statements to £80,000. However, paragraph 82 of FRS 2 explains further:

> *"The FRS requires that the goodwill arising on acquisition of a subsidiary undertaking that is not wholly owned should be recognised only in relation to the group's interest and that none should be attributed to the minority interest. Although it might be possible to estimate by extrapolation or valuation an amount of goodwill attributable to the minority when a subsidiary undertaking is acquired, this would in effect recognise an amount for goodwill that is hypothetical because the minority is not a party to the transaction by which the subsidiary undertaking is acquired."* [FRS 2 para 82].

From this explanation, it is clear that FRS 2 is referring only to direct acquisitions by a parent of a part interest in a subsidiary. This is clear because in such a case the minority is not a party to the transaction. However, in the case of an acquisition of a third company by a partly owned subsidiary, as in the question above, the minority is a party to the transaction. Accordingly, it would appear that the requirement of FRS 2 not to attribute goodwill to the minority applies where the minority is not a party to the transaction, but does not apply where the minority is a party to the transaction. Therefore, company P should reflect 100% of the goodwill and allocate 20% to the minority.

Compulsory acquisition of minority

24.379 In certain situations it might appear that there is a minority to recognise at the year end, where one should not be recognised. Such a situation might arise, for example, where the investing company makes an offer before the year end and receives (say) 90 per cent of acceptances before the year end. If it has given notice to compulsorily acquire the minority and were to acquire the remaining 10 per cent soon after the year end, then it would be acceptable for the group not to record a minority interest in its consolidated financial statements, but explain in the notes the circumstances.

Acquisition of minority interests

24.380 Where a holding company acquires more shares in a subsidiary either by buying them from the minority or by subscribing for a fresh issue of shares in the subsidiary itself, the goodwill arising on the acquisition will need to be recalculated. The identifiable assets and liabilities of the subsidiary should be revalued to fair value and the goodwill arising on the increase in interest should be calculated by reference to those fair values. This revaluation is not required if the difference between net fair values and the carrying amounts is not material.

[FRS 2 para 51]. An example of a group acquiring a minority interest is given in Table 24.28.

Table 24.28 — Tesco PLC — Annual Report and Accounts — 25 February 1995

Notes to the financial statements (extract)

Note 29 Acquisitions

The company acquired a controlling interest in the Hungarian food retailer Global TH ('Global') on 28 June 1994.

On 2 September 1994 the company also acquired the UK food retailer Wm Low & Company PLC ('Wm Low'). Wm Low results from this date until 25 February 1995 have been consolidated within the group profit and loss account. In the year ended 2 September 1994 the Wm Low group made a profit after taxation of £15m (1993 — £17m).

During the year the group also acquired the remaining ordinary share capital of Ets. Catteau S.A. ('Catteau') for a consideration of £9m, increasing its holding from 95% to 100%.

All of the group's acquisitions have been accounted for using acquisition accounting.

The acquisitions of Global, Wm Low and the remaining share capital of Catteau have been consolidated into the Tesco group balance sheet as follows:

	Balance sheet at acquisition			
	Wm Low	**Other**	**Fair value adjustments**	**Fair value balance sheet**
	£m	**£m**	**£m**	**£m**
Fixed assets	240	5	27	272
Working capital	(13)	1	(2)	(14)
Taxation	(2)	–	–	(2)
Net short term borrowings	(51)	19	–	(32)
Minority interests	–	(8)	–	(8)
Shareholders' funds	174	17	25	216
Goodwill				65
Total purchase consideration				281

The purchase consideration for Wm Low includes £181m that was settled by the issue or ordinary shares in Tesco PLC. The remaining consideration for Wm Low and other acquisitions was settled by cash of £100m.

The net outflow of cash and cash equivalents for the purchase of subsidiary undertakings comprises:

	£m
Cash consideration	100
Cash at bank and in hand acquired	(26)
Bank overdrafts of acquired subsidiary undertakings	58
	132

Fair values at acquisition, total purchase consideration and goodwill are analysed as follows:

	Fair value balance sheet £m	Total purchase consideration £m	Goodwill £m
Wm Low	199	257	58
Global	14	15	1
Catteau	3	9	6
	216	281	65

Fair value adjustments

All fair value adjustments relate to the acquisition of Wm Low.

	£m
Revaluation (a)	27
Accounting policy alignment	(1)
Other	(1)
	25

a) The principal adjustment relates to the revaluation of the property portfolio totalling £30m following advice from independent chartered surveyors.

There were no provisions for reorganisation or restructuring made in the accounts of Wm Low in the year ended 2 September 1994.

No fair value exercise

24.381 The example below is a continuation of the example in paragraph 24.377 and considers how to account for a reduction in the minority interests.

Example

On the first day of year 2 company P subscribes for a further 20,000 £1 equity shares in company S for cash amounting to £40,000. The minority interests in the subsidiary are, therefore, reduced from 20% to 10%. During the year company P makes a profit of £200,000. In the same period company S makes a loss of £30,000. Immediately prior to the share issue the fair value of company S's net assets was £180,000 compared with a book value of £170,000. As this difference is not material, company P does not intend to fair value the net assets attributable to company S included in the consolidation.

The balance sheets of company P and company S at the end of year 2 are as follows:

Summarised balance sheets		**Company P**		**Company S**
	£'000	**£'000**	**£'000**	**£'000**
Investment in subsidiary		190		–
Other net assets				
Company P (500 – 40 + 200)		660		–
Company S (160 – 30 + 40)		–		170
		850		170
Equity share capital		210		40
Share premium		240		20
Profit and loss account	200		80	
Profit for the year	200	400	(30)	50
Revaluation reserve		–		60
Equity shareholders' funds		850		170

The goodwill arising on acquisition and the minority interests are calculated below:

Cost of control account/goodwill

	£'000			£'000
Investment		Equity share capital		
(£150,000 + £40,000)	190	(£20,000 × 80%)		16
		Acquired in year		20
		Total capital (£40,000 × 90%)		36
		P&L reserve		
		(£80,000 × 80%)	64	
		(£80,000 × 10%)	*8	72
		Revaluation reserve		
		(£60,000 × 80%)	48	
		(£60,000 × 10%)	*6	54
		Share premium		
		(£20,000 × 90%)		18
				180
Negative goodwill	12	Initial goodwill		22
	202			202

* It is only necessary to bring into the cost of control account pre-acquisition reserves. Consequently, the additional percentage acquired need only be applied to the reserve balances at the date of acquisition, which in the example is the first day of the year. Therefore, the balances at the previous year end date have been used.

Minority interests account

	£'000		£'000
Balance	17	Equity share capital (£40,000 × 10%)	4
		Share premium (£20,000 × 10%)	2
		P&L reserve (£50,000 × 10%)	5
		Revaluation reserve (£60,000 × 10%)	6
	17		17

The consolidated profit and loss account would be arrived at in the following way:

Extract from profit and loss accounts	**Company P**	**Company S**	**Group**
	£'000	**£'000**	**£'000**
Trading profit/(loss)	200	(30)	170
Profit on ordinary activities	200	(30)	170
Minority interest (£30,000 × 10%)	–	–	3
Retained profit	200	(30)	173

The consolidated balance sheet for the group at the end of year 2 would be as follows:

Summarised consolidated balance sheet		**Group**
	£'000	**£'000**
Goodwill	22	
Negative goodwill	(12)	
		10
Net assets (£660,000 + £170,000)		830
		840
Equity share capital		210
Share premium account		240
Profit and loss account reserve	200	
Profit for the year	173	373
Equity shareholders' funds		823
Minority interests		17
		840

Consequences of fair valuing

24.382 The example that follows is exactly the same as the example above in paragraph 24.381, except that immediately prior to the share issue at the beginning of year 2 the fair value of company S's net assets is £330,000 compared with a book value of £170,000. As this difference is material to company P's consolidated financial statements it must fair value the net assets attributable to company S included in the consolidation.

Example

The balance sheets of company P and company S at the end of year 2 are as follows:

Summarised balance sheets	**£'000**	**Company P £'000**	**£'000**	**Company S £'000**
Investment in subsidiary		190		–
Other net assets				
Company P (500 – 40 + 20)		660		–
Company S (160 + 40 – 30 + 160)		–		330
		850		330
Equity share capital		210		40
Share premium		240		20
Profit and loss account	200		80	
Profit for the year	200	400	(30)	50
Revaluation reserve		–		220
Equity shareholders' funds		850		330

The goodwill arising on acquisition and the minority interests are calculated below:

Cost of control account/goodwill

	£'000			£'000
Investment		Equity share capital		
(£150,000 + £40,000)	190	(£20,000 × 80%)		16
		Acquired in year		20
		Total capital (£40,000 × 90%)		36
		P&L reserve		
		(£80,000 × 80%)	64	
		(£80,000 × 10%)	*8	72
		Revaluation reserve		
		(£60,000 × 80%)	48	
		(£220,000 × 10%)	*22	70
		Share premium		
		(£20,000 × 90%)		18
				196
Negative goodwill	28	Initial goodwill		22
	218			218

* See the explanation in the previous example.

Minority interests account

	£'000		£'000
Balance	33	Equity share capital	
		(£40,000 × 10%)	4
		Share premium (20,000 × 10%)	2
		P&L reserve (£50,000 × 10%)	5
		Revaluation reserve	
		(£220,000 × 10%)	22
	33		33

The consolidated profit and loss account is the same as that given in paragraph 24.381. The consolidated balance sheet for the group at the end of year 2 would be as follows:

Summarised consolidated balance sheet

	£'000	£'000
Goodwill	22	
Negative goodwill	(28)	
		(6)
Net assets (£660,000 + £330,000)		990
		984
Equity share capital		210
Share premium account		240
Profit and loss account reserve b/f	200	
Profit for the year	173	373
Revaluation reserve (80% × £160,000)		128
Equity shareholders' funds		951
Minority interests		33
		984

The effect of these entries is that not only is there a fair valuation of the 10% acquired, but also a revaluation of the 80% which represents the share of assets previously owned (credited to the group's revaluation reserve) and a revaluation of the share still attributable to minority interests of 10%.

An alternative approach is that the proportion of assets of the subsidiary held prior to the acquisition of part of the minority (that is, 80%) plus the proportion of assets of the subsidiary attributable to the remaining minority (that is, 10%) need not be revalued when part of the minority is acquired. If this approach is adopted, the result will be that only 10% of the assets will be subject to fair valuing at the date of the acquisition of the 10% minority. 90% of the assets will remain at their cost to the group.

Loss making subsidiaries

24.383 The treatment of minority interests requires special attention for subsidiaries that have made losses in the current year or in previous years. As seen above, minority interests for profitable subsidiaries are shown as a deduction in the profit and loss account and, consequently, reduce the group's profits transferred to shareholders' funds. Conversely, minority interests in a loss making subsidiary are, if recognised, added to the consolidated profit and account, thereby reducing the loss transferred to shareholders' funds.

24.384 The balance sheet minority interests in respect of a loss making subsidiary will be a credit if the subsidiary has net assets and will be a debit if it has net liabilities. Debit minority interests recognised in the balance sheet need careful consideration and FRS 2 requires the group to consider making a provision against such a balance where it arises. A provision should be made to the extent that the group has an obligation (whether formal or implied) to provide finance that may not be recoverable in respect of the accumulated losses attributable to the minority interests. [FRS 2 para 37]. For example, where a parent issues a letter of support to its subsidiary, the existence of the letter would indicate that there is a legal or commercial obligation on the parent to make good the losses of its subsidiary. Consequently, in these circumstances, a provision would need to be made against any debit minority interests arising on consolidation.

24.385 In situations where no provisioning is necessary it is argued that not recognising a debit minority interest balance in the consolidated balance sheet obscures the comparison between the assets and liabilities attributable to the minority interests and those attributable to group interests. This is particularly true where over a period of time accumulated losses accrue and are then made good by subsequent profits. Accumulated losses of this nature do not necessarily require funding by the parent, but, as mentioned above, a provision should be made in the consolidated balance sheet where funding is likely to be required. A debit balance does not represent an amount receivable from a minority, but rather the net liabilities attributable to the shares held by the minorities in that subsidiary.

24.386 FRS 2 makes it clear that the group should provide for any commercial or legal obligation, whether formal or implied, to provide finance that may not be recoverable in respect of the accumulated losses attributable to the minority interests. Any provision made with respect to minority debit balances should be set directly against the minority interests shown in the profit and loss account and in the balance sheet.

24.387 Provisions of this sort would go beyond merely providing against a debit balance and could include the minorities' share of any liability guaranteed by the group, or any liability that the group itself would be likely to settle for commercial or other reasons, if the subsidiary could not do so itself.

24.388 As losses are incurred by a subsidiary the minority's share of these losses will:

- First, be set against the minority's share of the subsidiary's reserves.
- Secondly, be set against the minority's share of the subsidiary's capital.

- Finally, be recognised as a debit balance in the consolidated balance sheet to the extent that the group does not have a commercial or legal obligation in respect of the losses attributable to the minority interests.

The above process should be reversed when profits attributable to the minority start to make good the losses incurred previously.

Puts and calls over minority interests

24.389 A parent may write a put option on shares in an existing subsidiary that are held by minority interests. The put option gives the minority shareholder the right to force the parent entity to purchase the shares subject to the put in accordance with the option's terms and conditions. The put might be created at the time that the parent acquires the controlling interest in the subsidiary or at some later date. The put's exercise price may be a fixed price, fair value or a formula, for example, a multiple of EBITDA. A purchased call option might also accompany the written put. The call option gives the parent entity the right to force the minority shareholder to sell its shares to the parent in accordance with the option's terms and conditions. A common variation on this type of arrangement is a forward purchase contract for the shares in the subsidiary that are held by minority interests.

24.390 The terms of the put and any related call should be analysed in detail to assess whether in substance the minority interest has been acquired. It is necessary to consider whether the minority has retained the risks and rewards associated with the continued ownership of the shares or whether in substance the risks and rewards have been transferred to the parent.

24.391 Typically a put option with an exercise price at the fair value of the shares at the date of exercise will not result in a transfer of the risks and rewards until the put option is exercised. However, a put option with a fixed exercise price, that is accompanied by a similarly priced call option, exercisable at the same future date, will, in substance result in a transfer of risks and rewards of ownership of the shares to the parent from the date the options are written. In this situation, it is virtually certain that either the parent or the minority will exercise the option, as it will be in one of their economic interests to do so. If the share price falls below the fixed strike price the minority will exercise the put option and sell the shares (that is, the parent has retained access to the risks) and if the share price increases above the fixed strike price the parent will exercise the call option and buy the shares (that is, the parent has retained access to the benefits). Even if the minority retains the right to dividends during the put and call exercise period, the risks and rewards of ownership have transferred to the parent as the parent has full control over whether dividends are to be paid to the minority.

24.392 Judgement should be applied in assessing when the risks and rewards of ownership are transferred from the minority interest shareholder to the parent. A fixed price put and a call option with matching exercise prices and dates is economically the same as a forward purchase contract. The accounting for a matching put and call should, therefore, be the same as for a forward purchase contract.

24.393 If the risks and rewards of the shares subject to the put have transferred to the parent, the minority is treated as having been acquired. The minority interest is derecognised and goodwill is calculated on the additional interest acquired (see para 24.380). No amounts are allocated to the minority in respect of the shares subject to the put. A liability is recognised for management's best estimate of the present value of the put option's redemption amount.

24.394 The accretion of the discount on the put liability is recognised as a finance charge in the profit and loss account.

24.395 If the put was written over an existing subsidiary, any adjustments to the expected settlement amount included in the estimated amount of the liability are recognised in the income statement. If the put was written at the time the controlling interest in the subsidiary was acquired (that is, as part of a business combination) the put liability is treated as contingent consideration and, therefore, other than the accretion of discount, any adjustments to the estimated amount of the liability are recognised against goodwill. [FRS 7 para 81].

24.396 If the risks and rewards have not transferred to the parent, then the minority interest is not treated as having been acquired.

24.397 Companies applying FRS 26 are required to account for derivatives on an interest in a subsidiary in accordance with FRS 26, unless the derivative meets the definition of an equity instrument of the entity in FRS 25. [FRS 26 para 2(a)]. FRS 25 applies to all derivatives on interests in subsidiaries, associates and joint ventures and, therefore, this standard determines the debt/equity classification of such derivative interests.

24.398 However, the accounting that results is complex as FRS 2 requires that a minority interest is recognised in respect of the shares subject to the put and FRS 25 additionally requires that a liability is recognised for management's best estimate of present value of the put option's redemption amount. Paragraph 23 of FRS 25 states:

> *"A contract that contains an obligation for an entity to purchase its own equity instruments for cash or another financial asset gives rise to a financial liability for the present value of the redemption amount (for example, for the present value of the forward repurchase price, option exercise price or other redemption amount). This is the case even if the contract itself is an equity instrument."* [FRS 25 para 23].

24.399 Minority interests are presented in the consolidated balance sheet within equity. Therefore, if a parent enters into a contract to purchase the shares of a subsidiary, in the consolidated financial statements, this is a contract to purchase own equity. In addition, when classifying a financial instrument in consolidated financial statements it is necessary to consider whether the group as a whole has an obligation that results in liability classification. [FRS 25 para AG 29]. Shares that are puttable by the minority back to the group are more appropriately classified as a liability rather than equity as the group has no discretion to refuse redemption of the shares should the minority exercise the put option.

24.400 The minority interest continues to be recognised as normal. A liability is recognised in respect of the put, measured at management's best estimate of the redemption amount discounted back from the expected redemption date. [FRS 25 para AG27(b)]. The put liability is recognised by reclassification from parent equity (not minority interest). The accretion of the discount on the put liability is recognised as a finance charge in the income statement. The put liability is re-measured to the final redemption amount and any adjustments to the estimated amount of the liability are recognised in the income statement, also as a finance charge.

24.401 On exercise of the put, the liability is eliminated as paid. The minority interest is derecognised and goodwill is calculated on the additional interest acquired (see further para 24.380). The amounts charged to finance costs (accretion of discount and adjustments in re-measuring the liability) during the exercise period of the put are in effect re-categorised from retained earnings to goodwill (because goodwill is calculated based on the actual cash paid at the date risks and rewards transfer). If the put option lapses unexercised, the liability is derecognised against equity.

Chapter 25

Acquisition accounting

	Page
Introduction	25001
Comparison of acquisition accounting to merger accounting	25001
Section I — Accounting for acquisitions	25003
Merger relief and group reconstruction relief	25003
Summary of accounting rules	25004
Date of changes in group membership	25004
Background	25004
Definition	25004
Effective date post balance sheet	25006
Consolidation of a new subsidiary	25007
Acquisition cost	25007
Fees and expenses of acquisition	25008
Adjusted capital and reserves acquired	25009
Identifiable assets and liabilities	25010
Recording adjustments to fair values	25010
Treatment of goodwill	25011
Date for recognising trading	25011
The parent company's financial statements	25012
Carrying value of investment	25012
Pre-acquisition and post-acquisition reserves	25015
Increases in stake	25016
Introduction	25016
Accounting principles	25016
Practical examples	25019
An investment becomes a subsidiary	25019
An associate becomes a subsidiary	25023
A parent acquires part or all of the minority	25026
Becoming a subsidiary other than by a purchase or an exchange of shares	25029
Disclosure for acquisition accounting	25029
General requirements	25030
Purchase consideration	25031
Fair values of identifiable assets and liabilities	25031
Table of assets and liabilities acquired	25031
Pre-acquisition activities of material acquisitions	25034
Pre-acquisition activities of substantial acquisitions	25034
Post-acquisition activities	25038
FRS 3 layered formats	25038
Exceptional items	25039
Post-acquisition reorganisation and integration	25040

Acquisition provisions 25040
Cash flow statement 25043
Disclosures 25043
Reverse acquisition accounting 25043
Cash alternative 25052
Section II — Fair values 25053
Introduction 25053
Scope and basic principles of FRS 7 25055
Scope 25055
Purchase of business or assets 25055
Objective 25056
Fair value of identifiable assets and liabilities 25056
Overriding principles 25056
Identifying the assets and liabilities acquired 25057
Definitions of assets and liabilities 25057
Inclusion of additional assets and liabilities 25058
Exclusion of certain assets and liabilities 25061
Adjustments for different accounting policies 25061
Examples — identifiable liabilities or post-acquisition costs 25062
Intangible assets 25065
Post-acquisition reorganisation and integration costs 25068
Background 25068
Post-acquisition activities 25069
Anti-avoidance measures 25070
Disclosure of post-acquisition reorganisation costs 25072
Fundamental reorganisation or not 25076
Nature of reorganisation costs 25077
Disclosure of acquisition provisions 25079
Measuring fair values of identifiable assets and liabilities 25080
Meaning of fair value 25080
Period for completing the fair value exercise 25082
Subsequent amendments to fair values 25083
Amendments after investigation period has expired 25083
Amendments within investigation period 25084
Fair valuing fixed assets 25087
Market value 25087
Depreciated replacement cost 25089
Recoverable amount 25090
Fair valuing stocks 25094
Market value 25095
Replacement cost 25096
Net realisable value 25098
Long-term contracts 25099
Disposals of business segments 25100
Fair valuing monetary assets and liabilities 25105
Fair valuing contingencies 25108
Identification of contingencies 25108
Measurement of contingencies 25109

Pensions and other post-retirement benefits . . . 25113
Identification of assets and liabilities . . . 25113
Measurement of assets and liabilities . . . 25114
Deferred taxation . . . 25115
Fair valuing the purchase consideration . . . 25116
Cost of acquisition . . . 25116
Quoted securities . . . 25117
Unquoted securities . . . 25117
Other securities . . . 25118
Non-monetary consideration . . . 25118
Other consideration . . . 25118
Deferred consideration . . . 25121
Deferred cash consideration . . . 25121
Deferred share consideration . . . 25122
Contingent consideration . . . 25123
Discounting contingent cash consideration . . . 25124
Consideration involving settlement options . . . 25126
Disclosure of contingent consideration . . . 25127
Consideration contingent on net assets . . . 25127
Fees and other expenses of acquisition . . . 25129
Section III — Goodwill . . . 25131
Introduction . . . 25131
The move from immediate write-off to capitalisation . . . 25131
Scope of FRS 10 . . . 25133
Definition of purchased goodwill . . . 25133
Accounting for goodwill — summary . . . 25134
Internally generated goodwill . . . 25134
Purchased goodwill . . . 25134
Useful economic life . . . 25135
Definition . . . 25135
Rebuttable presumption of 20 years or less . . . 25136
Factors determining useful economic life . . . 25137
Accounting implications of life above or below 20 years . . . 25139
Indefinite life — true and fair override . . . 25139
Goodwill with more than one useful economic life . . . 25141
Revisions of useful economic lives . . . 25143
Methods of amortising goodwill . . . 25144
Acquisition with contingent consideration . . . 25145
Presentation of amortisation and impairment charges . . . 25147
Reversals of past goodwill write-offs . . . 25148
Allocation of purchased goodwill . . . 25149
Disposals . . . 25150
Impairment reviews . . . 25150
Positive and negative goodwill . . . 25150
Integrated acquisitions . . . 25151
Impairment reviews . . . 25151
Purpose of impairment reviews . . . 25151
When impairment reviews are required . . . 25152

Useful life 20 years or less . . . 25152
First year review . . . 25152
Reviews in other years . . . 25153
Detailed impairment review . . . 25153
Negative goodwill . . . 25153
Pre-FRS 10 goodwill that remains in reserves . . . 25157
Separate goodwill write-off reserve prohibited . . . 25157
Reserves used for write-offs . . . 25158
Profit and loss account . . . 25158
Merger reserve . . . 25158
Other non-distributable reserves . . . 25159
Share premium account . . . 25159
Capital redemption reserve . . . 25160
Revaluation reserve . . . 25160
Effect on distributable profits — groups . . . 25161
Effect on distributable profits — companies . . . 25162
Goodwill on disposals . . . 25163
Impairment of goodwill . . . 25163
Disclosures . . . 25163
Accounting policy . . . 25163
Cumulative amounts written off . . . 25164
Pre-FRS 10 negative goodwill that remains in reserves . . . 25165
Effect on distributable profits — companies . . . 25165
Implementing FRS 10 — transitional arrangements . . . 25166
Options for reinstating goodwill eliminated against reserves . . . 25166
Additions to goodwill in existing subsidiaries . . . 25166
Increases in stake . . . 25166
Earnout consideration . . . 25167

Chapter 25

Acquisition accounting

Introduction

25.1 Under UK GAAP, there are two accounting methods that might be applicable in a business combination. Groups will generally have to use acquisition accounting, but in certain exceptional circumstances merger accounting *must* be used to account for the business combination. There are now strict conditions that must be satisfied before merger accounting may be adopted.

25.2 The Companies Act 1985 contains rules on acquisition accounting and merger accounting, an area which had before the Companies Act 1989 traditionally been left to accounting standards and practices. The 1985 Act states in Schedule 4A that an acquisition should be accounted for by the acquisition method of accounting, unless the conditions for accounting for it as a merger are met and the merger method of accounting is adopted. [CA85 4A Sch 8]. Merger accounting is optional under the Companies Act 1985, but must be used where the merger accounting conditions set out in FRS 6 are met (see further chapter 28).

25.2.1 At the time of writing, Schedule 4A to the Companies Act 1985 still has effect and the equivalent schedule of the Companies Act 2006 has yet to be published. Reference is made throughout this chapter to sections in the Companies Act 2006 that are equivalent to those in the Companies Act 1985.

25.3 Although the criteria for merger accounting in FRS 6 are strict, international standard-setters do not consider that they are sufficient to enable 'true mergers' to be distinguished from business combinations in which one entity obtains control of another entity (or entities). Therefore, in March 2004, the IASB issued IFRS 3, 'Business combinations', which brings IFRS into line with US GAAP by prohibiting merger accounting. It requires the use of acquisition accounting ('the purchase method') for all business combinations within its scope. IFRS 3 represented the completion of the first phase of the IASB's larger project on business combinations. The IASB's second phase, a revised IFRS 3, is due for publication in Autumn 2007.

Comparison of acquisition accounting to merger accounting

25.4 Before considering the detailed accounting requirements that apply to business combinations it is useful to understand the three main differences between acquisition accounting and merger accounting, which are explained in the paragraphs below.

25.5 In acquisition accounting, the consolidated financial statements reflect the acquired company's results from the date of acquisition only. However, in merger accounting, the consolidated financial statements incorporate the combined companies' results as if the companies had always been combined. Consequently, under merger accounting, the consolidated financial statements reflect both companies' full year's results, even though the business combination may have occurred part of the way through the year. Under merger accounting, the corresponding amounts in the consolidated financial statements for the previous year should reflect the results of the combined companies, even though the business combination did not occur until the current year.

25.6 In acquisition accounting, the acquiring group should attribute fair values to the identifiable assets and liabilities of the acquired business at the date of acquisition and these are used as the initial carrying values (or 'cost') in the acquiring group's balance sheet. However, in merger accounting, the group does not restate any assets and liabilities at their fair values. Instead, the group incorporates the assets and liabilities at the amounts recorded in the books of the combined companies, adjusted only to achieve harmonisation of accounting policies.

25.7 Acquisition accounting may give rise to goodwill on consolidation. However, goodwill does not arise in merger accounting. Merger accounting may lead to differences on consolidation. For example, in merger accounting, there may be a difference between the nominal value of the shares issued together with the fair value of any additional consideration given, and the nominal value of the other company's shares that have been acquired. However, such differences are not goodwill as defined in FRS 10, because they are not based on the fair values of both the consideration given and the identifiable assets and liabilities acquired.

25.8 An example that demonstrates the difference between acquisition accounting and merger accounting is given in chapter 28. It is somewhat artificial in that the two methods are not alternatives in accounting for the same transaction and hence it is merely illustrative.

25.9 The rules governing how to account for the acquisition of a subsidiary are now contained in FRS 2, FRS 6, FRS 7, FRS 10 and the Companies Act. This chapter considers the requirements that determine how a company should account for the acquisition of a subsidiary including the disclosure requirements (contained in section I), the fair valuing rules (contained in section II) and accounting for goodwill (contained in section III).

Section I — Accounting for acquisitions

25.10 This section considers primarily the accounting treatment that should be adopted when a subsidiary is acquired and also considers some of the problems that arise with piecemeal acquisitions. Many investments that end up as subsidiaries start out as much smaller interests in the undertakings concerned and may be treated in the group's financial statements in a variety of ways before they actually become subsidiaries. The most common way for an undertaking to become a subsidiary of another is by acquisition. It is also possible for a parent to gain a subsidiary other than by acquisition, for example:

- By gaining the power to control without acquiring a further interest in an undertaking, perhaps by virtue of an agreement with another shareholder.
- By enforcement of a security by a lender where a creditor defaults on a loan.
- By the company purchasing and cancelling its own shares held by third parties.
- By changes to the voting rights attached to shares.

25.11 These issues are fully explained in this section, which also outlines the disclosure that is required in the year that a company acquires a subsidiary. This section also considers the accounting for reverse acquisitions, where it is the acquired company's shareholders and board of directors who effectively control the combined group even though the other party is the legal acquirer.

Merger relief and group reconstruction relief

25.12 It is extremely important in any business combination to understand how merger relief might impact the accounting treatment. Merger relief is a relief given under section 131 of the Companies Act 1985 (CA06 Sec 612) from the need to transfer to a share premium account the difference between the nominal value of any shares issued by the company to acquire shares in another company and the fair value of those issued shares. Merger relief does not only apply to business combinations accounted for as mergers, it also applies to those accounted for using acquisition accounting techniques. By obtaining merger relief a group may be able to distribute pre-acquisition profits which would otherwise be locked in the subsidiary it acquires. The rules as they apply to both acquisitions and mergers are considered in chapter 23.

25.13 Group reconstruction relief is a relief given under section 132 of the Companies Act 1985 (CA06 Sec 611). Group reconstruction relief can be taken in certain situations where assets are transferred around the group and where the subsidiaries concerned are wholly owned. This relief applies to the transfer of both shares in wholly-owned group companies and other assets where the consideration is shares issued by the group company acquiring the assets. Chapter 23 explores this complex area and explains in detail how the minimum premium value is calculated on such transactions, being the amount that it is necessary to credit to the share premium

Summary of accounting rules

25.14 As explained above, there are two methods that a parent company can use to account for a business combination in its consolidated financial statements. The vast majority of business combinations are accounted for using acquisition accounting and only a small minority are required to use merger accounting.

25.15 The rules concerning acquisition accounting are contained in FRS 2, FRS 6, FRS 7 and FRS 10, as well as the Act. These rules, which deal with the determination of the date of acquisition, the method of consolidating a new subsidiary and the accounting treatment for changes in stake, are dealt with in the following section of this chapter.

25.16 Acquisitions of subsidiaries can also arise where a parent sells a subsidiary for shares in another undertaking, which results in that other undertaking becoming a subsidiary of the vendor. Therefore, at the same time as the acquisition there is a disposal. This is addressed by UITF Abstract 31, 'Exchanges of businesses or other non-monetary assets for an interest in a subsidiary, joint venture or associate'. The accounting for these transactions is dealt with in chapter 26.

25.17 Although FRS 6 primarily defines the situations where merger accounting must be used, it does in addition bring together in one standard most of the disclosure requirements that must be followed for all business combinations whether accounted for as acquisitions or mergers (including those required by the Act). However, most of the disclosure requirements concerning goodwill arising on an acquisition are set out in FRS 10.

Date of changes in group membership

Background

25.18 The date on which an undertaking becomes or ceases to be a subsidiary marks the point at which a new accounting treatment for that undertaking in the group's consolidated financial statements applies. The Act does not define the effective date of acquisition or disposal. However, the Act does state that undertakings that the group controls, or has the power to control, should be consolidated and that other undertakings should not be consolidated. FRS 2, therefore, contains a definition which is based entirely on the passing of control (or the power to control).

Definition

25.19 Until recently, both the Act and FRS 2 required consolidation of undertakings over which the company had control. The Act was amended by SI

2004/2947, 'The Companies Act 1985 (International Accounting Standards and other amendments) Regulations 2004', and FRS 2 was amended (in 2005) to change the scope to refer to undertakings that the company has the power to control. These changes were effective for accounting periods beginning on or after 1 January 2005.

25.20 The date of change in group membership is the date on which control of that undertaking passes to its new parent undertaking. Furthermore, this date is said in FRS 2 to be the date of acquisition for the purposes of Schedule 4A paragraph 9 to the Companies Act 1985 (which is the Act's requirement to account for the purchase of a subsidiary using acquisition accounting). [FRS 2 para 45]. The date, therefore, hinges on 'control' (or the power to control) passing and control is defined as:

> *"The ability of an undertaking to direct the financial and operating policies of another undertaking with a view to gaining economic benefits from its activities."* [FRS 2 para 6].

Note that since FRS 2 was amended by SI 2004/2947, gaining the power to control would equally mark a change in group membership. Use of 'control' in the following paragraphs should be taken to mean 'control, or the power to control'.

25.21 The definition of control refers to 'gaining economic benefits'. This is not intended to be interpreted restrictively and covers a wide range of situations in practice, including gaining benefits:

- In the form of current or future profits.
- By preventing another competitor from buying the business.
- By preventing a key supplier or distributor from going out of business.
- By reducing losses of the acquiring group.

For undertakings that are not formed for the purpose of making profits, for example charities, the economic benefits will not necessarily be profit related.

25.22 The date of change in group membership under FRS 2 should also be taken as the date on which an undertaking becomes or ceases to be a subsidiary under section 258 of the Companies Act 1985 (CA06 Sec 1162). In practice, although it may often be difficult to determine, the date on which control passes is a matter of fact and cannot be backdated or artificially altered. [FRS 2 para 84]. Consequently, the definition under FRS 2 applies even if the acquirer has a right to profits from a date earlier than the effective date of acquisition.

25.23 The following factors could, for example, indicate that the acquirer has gained control of an undertaking:

- The acquirer starts to direct the operating and financial policies of the acquired undertaking.
- The acquirer starts to benefit from the economic benefits arising from the undertaking. However, this does not cover the situation where a potential acquirer is given a right to profits from a date which is conditional on the completion of the purchase at some later date. Equally, it does not apply to an agreement giving the acquirer rights to past profits.
- The date the consideration is paid. The payment date for the consideration will often in simple acquisitions be the date on which control passes, but in practice this cannot be assumed, because this date can easily be manipulated. Furthermore, payment of consideration is often made by instalments and, as a consequence, may have little relevance to when control passes.

25.24 In practice, control might pass in a number of ways, which will often depend on whether the offer for the entity is made to the public (a public offer) or is a private sale (a private treaty) or is effected by the issue or cancellation of shares.

25.25 Where control is transferred by a public offer, the date control is transferred is the date the offer becomes unconditional. This will usually be the date on which a sufficient number of acceptances are received to enable the new parent to exercise control over the undertaking. [FRS 2 para 85]. Under a private treaty, the date control is transferred is generally the date an unconditional offer is accepted. [FRS 2 para 85].

25.26 It can be seen that in both a public offer and a private treaty, the key to control passing is dependent on acceptance of *unconditional* terms. The negotiations to purchase or sell a subsidiary may take place over a considerable period and there may be considerable delays between the time when agreement is reached in principle and the time when the legal formalities are completed. Other conditions, such as third party or shareholder approval may also take time to be satisfied. Until such time as agreement is reached and all conditions are satisfied the transaction cannot be regarded as unconditional.

25.27 Where an undertaking becomes a subsidiary through an issue of shares or by a cancellation of shares, the date that control will be transferred is the date on which those shares are issued or cancelled. [FRS 2 para 85].

Effective date post balance sheet

25.28 Where the effective date of acquisition of a subsidiary is after the parent's year end, but before the consolidated financial statements are approved and signed on behalf of the board, the transaction should be treated as a non-adjusting post balance sheet event in accordance with the requirements of paragraph 21 of FRS 21, 'Events after the balance sheet date'. If the group wishes to show the effect that this post balance sheet acquisition will have, it will be necessary for it to prepare proforma accounts in addition to its statutory financial statements.

Consolidation of a new subsidiary

25.29 The Companies Act 1985 sets out the basic requirements for consolidating a subsidiary when it is first acquired. It specifies that:

- The identifiable assets and liabilities of the subsidiary acquired should be included in the consolidated balance sheet at their fair values as at the date of acquisition.
- The income and expenditure of the undertaking acquired should be brought into the consolidated financial statements from the date of the acquisition.
- The interest of the group in the adjusted capital and reserves of the undertaking acquired should be offset against the acquisition cost of the group's interest in the shares of the undertaking. The difference if positive represents goodwill and if negative represents a negative consolidation difference (that is, negative goodwill).

[CA85 4A Sch 9].

25.30 Consequently, on an acquisition it is necessary to ascertain the following elements in respect of the undertaking acquired in order to account for that undertaking as a subsidiary on consolidation:

- Acquisition cost.
- Adjusted capital and reserves.
- Identifiable assets and liabilities.
- Date for recognising profits or losses from operations.

Each of these elements of acquisition accounting is considered in the paragraphs that follow.

Acquisition cost

25.31 Under the Companies Act 1985 the 'acquisition cost' incurred in acquiring a subsidiary includes the amount of any cash consideration paid and the fair value of any other consideration (such as shares and debentures), together with fees and other expenses of the acquisition. [CA85 4A Sch 9(4)]. FRS 7 deals with the fair value issues that arise when determining the cost of acquisition and these issues are considered in detail in section II, paragraph 25.383.

25.32 When a company issues shares as part of the consideration to acquire a subsidiary, the difference between the fair value of the consideration and the nominal value of the shares issued has to be credited to the share premium account, unless the company is eligible for merger relief. Eligibility for merger relief is considered in detail in chapter 23. If the company can obtain merger relief on the issue, then the difference between the fair value of the shares issued and their nominal value is credited to a merger reserve (as opposed to a share premium account) or need not be recorded in the parent company's own financial statements. Where a merger reserve is used, the parent's investment will be recorded in its financial statements at an amount equal to the fair value of the investment.

25.33 Where a merger reserve is not set up on an acquisition, the investment will be recorded in the parent's financial statements at the nominal value of shares issued plus the fair value of any other consideration given in the acquisition. This is discussed further in paragraph 25.49 onwards.

25.34 Where the parent company does not recognise the merger reserve in its own financial statements, the merger reserve will be brought into the consolidated financial statements as part of the consolidation adjustment for goodwill (that is, to include the consideration for the acquisition at fair value).

Fees and expenses of acquisition

25.35 The fees and expenses of an acquisition have to be analysed. Some may relate to the issue of any capital instruments (that is, shares or debt) given as part of the consideration. Issue costs are defined in FRS 4 as:

> *"The costs that are incurred directly in connection with the issue of a capital instrument, that is, those costs that would not have been incurred had the specific instrument in question not been issued."* [FRS 4 para 10].

25.36 However, FRS 4 has been superseded by FRS 26 and, for those companies applying the newer standard (see further chapter 6), the equivalent term is 'transaction costs', which are defined as:

> *"...incremental costs that are directly applicable to the acquisition, issue or disposal of a financial asset or financial liability... An incremental cost is one that would not have been occurred if the entity had not acquired, issued or disposed of the financial instrument."* [FRS 26 para 9].

25.37 The definitions of issue costs are restrictive and their accounting treatment complex: further guidance on issue costs is given in chapter 6.

25.38 Certain fees and expenses of acquisition that do not relate to the issue of capital instruments can be added to the cost of an investment and these are considered further in section II, paragraph 25.426. However, the UITF clarified in Information sheet 35 that costs such as arrangement fees for bridging finance facilities, participation fees and costs of researching alternative financing arrangements for a takeover, that do not qualify as issue costs under FRS 4, are not incremental costs incurred directly in making an acquisition and, therefore, should not be included as part of the cost of the acquisition, but should be written off immediately. Similarly, FRS 26 notes that: *"transaction costs include fees and commissions paid to agents, advisers, brokers and dealers, levies by regulatory agencies and securities exchanges, and transfer taxes and duties. Transaction costs do not include debt premiums or discounts, finance costs or internal administrative or holding costs"*. [FRS 26 para AG13].

Adjusted capital and reserves acquired

25.39 The Companies Act 1985 requires that the adjusted capital and reserves is set off against the acquisition cost of the acquired subsidiary in order to ascertain the figure of goodwill (or negative goodwill) arising on the acquisition. In this context 'adjusted capital and reserves' means the subsidiary's capital and reserves at the date of acquisition after adjusting the undertaking's identifiable assets and liabilities to fair values. [CA85 4A Sch 9(4)]. This is equivalent to 'adjusted net assets'. Consequently, the subsidiary's adjusted capital and reserves will be made up of its capital and reserves disclosed in its books of account adjusted for any changes in the value of net assets determined in fair valuing its assets and liabilities. The following example illustrates this provision of the legislation.

Example

Company A acquires 80% of company B. The acquisition cost is £50m and at the date of acquisition, the reserves of the subsidiary are determined as follows:

Capital and reserves of company B

	£m
Share capital	2
Share premium account	1
Revaluation reserve	10
Profit and loss account	15
Total capital and reserves	28

Company A carries out a fair value exercise on Company B as at the date of acquisition and ascertains that its fixed assets and stocks have values in excess of their book values of £12m and £3.5m respectively.

Adjusted capital and reserves of company B

	£m
Capital and reserves (as above)	28.0
Fair value adjustment	15.5
Total capital and reserves	43.5

Consequently, the difference arising on consolidation (goodwill) would be calculated as follows:

Difference arising on consolidation

	£m
Acquisition cost	50.0
Adjusted capital and reserves (£43.5m × 80%)	(34.8)
Goodwill	15.2

Identifiable assets and liabilities

25.40 The Companies Act 1985 requires that the subsidiary's identifiable assets and liabilities must be included in the consolidated balance sheet at their fair values, as at the date of acquisition. [CA85 4A Sch 9(2)]. For this purpose the Act defines 'identifiable assets and liabilities' to mean the:

> *"...assets or liabilities which are capable of being disposed of or discharged separately, without disposing of a business of the undertaking."* [CA85 4A Sch 9(2)].

FRS 7, which also applies to entities other than companies, contains an equivalent definition.

25.41 The test to establish whether an asset should be included in the category of identifiable assets, is whether the asset can be identified and sold separately without disposing of a business as a whole. In this context, goodwill is clearly not separable from a business as a whole. Such assets, however, may well include other intangible assets (including trade marks and publishing titles) and their valuation is considered in more detail in chapter 15.

25.41.1 There is no guidance in the Act on how to determine the fair values of assets and liabilities, but rules on fair valuing are detailed in FRS 7. Ascertaining the fair values of identifiable assets is very difficult in practice and substantial problems can arise and these issues are considered in detail in section II, paragraph 25.232.

Recording adjustments to fair values

25.42 Although an acquiring company has to carry out a fair value exercise as at the date of acquisition, there is no general requirement to record these values in the books of account of the subsidiary (unless, for example, they relate to impairments of assets). The adjustments would be made in the subsidiary's books of account if they were consistent with the subsidiary's accounting policies. Therefore, a write down of stock to its net realisable value (where this is lower than cost) would be recognised in the subsidiary's books. However, it is not normally possible for UK subsidiaries to record their stocks at a fair value that exceeds cost, because the Act and SSAP 9 require stocks to be valued at the lower of cost and net realisable value. [CA85 4 Sch 23; SSAP 9 para 26].

Treatment of goodwill

25.43 Any difference between the total of the subsidiary's acquisition cost (that is, the fair value of the purchase consideration plus expenses) and the group's share of the subsidiary's adjusted capital and reserves represents purchased goodwill arising on consolidation (or, if negative, negative goodwill, termed a negative consolidation difference in the the Companies Act 1985). [CA85 4A Sch 9(5); FRS 10 para 2; FRS 6 para 20]. The treatment of both goodwill and negative goodwill arising on consolidation is considered in section III, paragraph 25.451.

Date for recognising trading

25.44 The the Companies Act 1985 states that income and expenditure of the subsidiary should only be brought into the consolidated financial statements from the date of acquisition. [CA85 4A Sch 9(3)]. The date of acquisition is discussed under the heading of 'date of changes in group membership' above from paragraph 25.18 onwards. Similarly, FRS 6 requires that the results and cash flows of the acquired company should be brought into the consolidated financial statements only from the date of acquisition. [FRS 6 para 20].

25.45 It is, therefore, necessary on an acquisition to apportion the results between pre-acquisition and post-acquisition on a reasonably accurate basis. In practice, this is often achieved by using the subsidiary's management accounts or completion accounts, if any, prepared as at the date of acquisition. However, there may be rare situations where there is no alternative but to use a time apportionment method. Where such a method is used, however, it will be necessary to identify any profit and loss account items that do not arise evenly over the accounting period. For such items a time apportionment would not be acceptable. For example, this may be the situation with exceptional items. Such items would, therefore, need to be analysed into the period in which they arose and treated accordingly as either being pre-acquisition or post-acquisition.

25.46 Under FRS 3, the operating results of continuing operations have to be shown separately from those of discontinued operations. Furthermore, acquisitions in the period have to be shown separately as a component of continuing operations. As a minimum on the face of the profit and loss account turnover and operating profit have to be analysed between continuing operations, acquisitions as a component of continuing operations and discontinued operations. In addition, this analysis has also to be given in the notes (if not given on the face of the profit and loss account) for each of the profit and loss account format line items between turnover and operating profit. The provisions of FRS 3 are dealt with in detail in chapter 8.

25.47 Although the method of consolidating the results in the profit and loss account outlined above has to be adopted, groups may still wish to give their members an idea of what the results of the new group would have looked like for a whole period's trading. Clearly, the shareholders will not be able to ascertain this picture entirely from the consolidated results as presented, although for 'substantial acquisitions' as defined in FRS 6 a summarised profit and loss account and statement of total recognised gains and losses has to be given for the subsidiary acquired from the beginning of its last accounting reference period to the date of acquisition (see further paragraph 25.109). [FRS 6 para 36]. There is no reason, however, why the group should not also include in its consolidated financial statements a *pro forma* consolidated profit and loss account by way of a note showing the combined results of all subsidiaries for the entire period of trading, regardless of when they were acquired. In addition, the group may wish to disclose a *pro forma* earnings per share by way of note based on the *pro forma* consolidated profit and loss. In this way it is possible for a group to account for its acquisition using acquisition accounting in its statutory financial statements, but retain some of the benefits of the merger accounting principles, namely of reporting the trends of the enlarged group as if the subsidiary has always been combined with the rest of the group.

25.48 Where the group decides to include this type of additional information in its consolidated financial statements, it should not give the *pro forma* accounts more prominence than its statutory accounts.

The parent company's financial statements

Carrying value of investment

25.49 The Companies Act 1985 clarifies the accounting treatment of an investment in an acquired company that should be used in an issuing company's balance sheet where there is:

- Merger relief under section 131 of the Companies Act 1985. [CA06 Sec 612].
- Group reconstruction relief under section 132 of the Companies Act 1985. [CA06 Sec 611].

25.50 In these circumstances, the amount at which the issuing company carries its investment in the acquired company does not need to include an amount corresponding to the premium (or the part of the premium) that the issuing company has not credited to its share premium account. [CA85 Sec 133(1); CA06 Sec 615]. That is, the issuing company has a choice. Disregarding other considerations such as cash, the issuing company can record both the shares it issues and the investment in the new subsidiary at either:

- the nominal value of the shares issued and any minimum premium under section 132 of the Companies Act 1985 (CA06 Sec 611); or
- the fair value of the shares issued, with the premium in excess of any minium premium under section 132 of the Companies Act 1985 (CA06 Sec 611) credited to a merger reserve instead of to a share premium account.

25.51 Although the Act says that the value of the investment shown in the balance sheet need not include the premium, it at first sight appears that for those companies that have not yet adopted FRS 26 the application of FRS 4 would require it to do so, where merger relief or group reconstruction relief is taken, but acquisition accounting is adopted for the business combination. This is because FRS 4 requires that the net proceeds from the issue of equity shares should be credited to shareholders' funds. 'Net proceeds' are defined as *"the fair value of the consideration received on the issue of a capital instrument after deduction of issue costs"*. [FRS 4 para 11].

25.52 This issue does not arise for entities that are applying FRS 26, because FRS 26 (which supersedes FRS 4) excludes from its scope investments in subsidiaries so there is no applicable accounting standard and the permission within the Act is unrestricted.

25.53 Therefore, where acquisition accounting is adopted on consolidation for the business combination, FRS 4 would appear to require the shares issued by the acquiring company to be recorded at fair value. This does not mean that the difference between the nominal value and the fair value would be credited to share premium account. Only the minimum premium value, where group reconstruction relief is taken, would be credited to that account. The balance of the difference (all of it, if merger relief is taken) would be credited to a separate reserve, normally called a merger reserve.

25.54 As the shares issued would then be recorded at fair value it follows that the investment would also have to be recorded at fair value in these circumstances.

25.55 However, where merger accounting is adopted for the business combination, on consolidation the requirements of FRS 4 do not apply to equity shares issued. There is an exception in FRS 4 for equity shares issued as part of a business combination that is accounted for as a merger. At first sight this exception appears only to apply to equity shares that are issued and not to non-equity shares that are issued.

25.56 Despite the apparent requirements of FRS 4 in this regard it has become clear since the issue of FRS 4 that it was not the ASB's intention to restrict the reliefs available under section 133 of the Companies Act 1985 (CA06 Sec 615) where either acquisition or merger accounting is adopted. As evidence of this the Appendix to FRS 6, 'Note on Legal Requirements', states:

> *"The FRS deals only with the method of accounting to be used in group accounts; it does not deal with the form of accounting to be used in the acquiring or issuing company's own accounts and in particular does not restrict the reliefs available under Sections 131-133 of the Companies Act."*

In addition in FRS 7 the ASB has included a paragraph in the legal requirements section stating:

> *"Where (if the merger relief provisions apply) the premiums are disregarded, the cost of investment in the parent company's books will be*

different from the cost of acquisition for the purposes of paragraph 9(4) (of Sch 4A).”

25.57 Therefore, the apparent requirements of FRS 4 may be disregarded both when acquisition accounting and merger accounting is adopted. This does not of course prevent a company recording the shares issued and the investment acquired at fair value where acquisition accounting is adopted, if it wishes, but does leave it a choice.

25.58 Where acquisition (or merger) accounting is adopted on consolidation and the investment shown in the holding company's balance sheet does not include the premium it is debatable whether the investment should be described as being at cost, because the amount shown in the balance sheet may be quite different from the actual cost. It could be argued that the ‘true’ cost of the shares issued is their fair value and not their nominal value. Consequently, the company may need to choose some appropriate wording other than ‘cost’ to describe the investment (for example, ‘at nominal value of shares issued’).

Example

A company owns 40% of another company that it acquired for cash several years ago. It decides to acquire the remaining 60% in an exchange for shares. Merger accounting does not apply, but merger relief is available. The company wonders how it should record its investment in the parent company's financial statements.

Even though merger accounting is not available, the parent can record its investment at the nominal value of the shares it issues in exchange for the 60% interest, plus the existing cost of the investment. Alternatively, the fair value of the shares issued can be added to the previous investment cost. The difference between the fair values of the shares issued and their nominal value would then be shown as a merger reserve (as opposed to share premium).

25.59 Where one company acquires another company, the identifiable assets and liabilities acquired from the point of view of the acquiring company will be the shares in the acquired company, not the individual assets and liabilities of the acquired company. Consequently, when one company acquires another company, purchased goodwill will not arise in the parent's balance sheet.

25.60 However, goodwill will arise on consolidation because the fair value of the consideration given is not in general the same as the aggregate fair value of the acquired company's identifiable assets and liabilities.

25.61 FRS 10 does not require an adjustment to be made in the parent's financial statements to the carrying value of the shares in the subsidiary in respect of any consolidation goodwill written off either in the consolidated financial statements or in the subsidiary's own financial statements. An exception is that, where consolidation goodwill is written off because it is impaired, FRS 10 requires the carrying value of the parent's investment also to be reviewed for impairment.

[FRS 10 para 42]. The parent company will in normal circumstances only write down the investment's carrying value to reflect any impairment.

Pre-acquisition and post-acquisition reserves

25.62 In the past, an important element of consolidations was whether profits of a subsidiary should be treated as pre-acquisition or post-acquisition. In particular, this was important because it had a bearing on how dividends paid by the subsidiary were treated in the parent's financial statements. If, for example, a subsidiary paid a dividend out of pre-acquisition profits to a parent, the parent would reduce its investment in the subsidiary by this amount (assuming that the net worth of the subsidiary had decreased by a similar amount). The parent could not treat this amount as realised and could not distribute it.

25.63 Paragraph 15(5) of the original Schedule 8 to the Companies Act 1948, which was the source of the above treatment, was amended by the Companies Act 1981. As a result of this change, when a cash dividend is paid out of pre-acquisition profits by a subsidiary, it need not be applied in reducing the carrying value of the investment in the subsidiary in the parent's books. It should be taken to the profit and loss account. Only if the underlying value of the subsidiary does not support the amount at which the parent carries its investment in the subsidiary following the dividend does the parent have to make a provision against its investment. This accords with the legal requirements included in paragraph 19(2) of Schedule 4 to the Companies Act 1985 which requires a company to make provision for any permanent diminution in value of any fixed asset. Consider the following example.

Example

Company A has an investment in its subsidiary company B. Company A acquired the subsidiary for £22m. The net assets of the subsidiary at that time were £18m. In the following year, the subsidiary's net assets are £20m and it decides to pay a cash dividend to its parent of £1m. It is unclear whether this dividend is made out of pre-acquisition reserves or post-acquisition reserves. Company A should take the dividend it receives from company B to its profit and loss account. However, company A then has to consider whether it is necessary to make a provision against the carrying value of its investment in company B. This assessment will take into account not only the net asset value of company B (which after the dividend payment has reduced to £19m), but also any additional value that the shares in company B have. When it was acquired, this additional value was £4m, which equates to the goodwill arising on consolidation. If company A considers that the premium on the value of company B's shares has not diminished, then the worth of company B is in excess of £23m. On this basis company A does not need to make a provision against its investment in company B and can treat the dividend received as realised and, consequently, distributable.

This provision as it applies to merger relief is considered in chapter 23.

Increases in stake

Introduction

25.64 Many accounting problems can arise on increasing a stake in an undertaking. Such acquisitions arise where the investing company starts off with a small stake in an undertaking and gradually increases its investment. Initially the interest in the undertaking may be no more than an investment that will be either valued at cost (less any provisions for diminution in value of the investment) or at a valuation (under the alternative accounting rules).

25.65 Once the interest in the undertaking becomes 20 per cent or more of the equity voting rights of a company and the investor actually exercises significant influence, then the investment is likely to have to be treated in the consolidated financial statements as an associate in accordance with the requirements of FRS 9 (see further chapter 27). In certain circumstances an interest in an undertaking can be treated as an associate where the investment is below 20 per cent and equally interests in excess of 20 per cent may, in certain circumstances, be treated as investments.

25.66 If the investor has joint control over an undertaking that has a business of its own, this would be accounted for in the consolidated financial statements as a joint venture in accordance with the requirements of FRS 9 (see further chapter 27).

25.67 Once an interest in the undertaking is over 50 per cent of the voting rights of a company, such that the investor controls the undertaking, then the investment has to be treated in the consolidated financial statements as a subsidiary to accord with the Act and FRS 2. In certain circumstances an interest below 50 per cent might be regarded as a subsidiary, where control over the undertaking is exercised in some other way or the entity has the 'power to control' the undertaking (see chapter 24).

Accounting principles

25.68 The basic principles of accounting for acquisitions set out in the Act apply equally to increases in stake. FRS 2 provides specific guidance on interpreting the Companies Act 1985 in the context of changes in stake. The principles that apply are as follows:

- The identifiable assets and liabilities of the subsidiary acquired should be included in the consolidated balance sheet at their fair values at the acquisition date, that is, the date it becomes a subsidiary. [CA85 4A Sch 9(2); FRS 2 para 50].
- The income and expenditure of the undertaking acquired should be fully consolidated into the consolidated financial statements from the date the undertaking first becomes a subsidiary. [CA85 4A Sch 9(3)].

- The interest of the group in the adjusted capital and reserves of the undertaking acquired should be offset against the acquisition cost of the group's interest in the shares of the undertaking. The difference if positive represents goodwill and if negative represents a negative consolidation difference (that is, negative goodwill). [CA85 4A Sch 9(5)].

25.69 Paragraph 9 of Schedule 4A to the Companies Act 1985 requires goodwill to be calculated as the difference between the following two amounts:

- The fair value, at the date an undertaking becomes a subsidiary, of the group's share of its identifiable assets and liabilities.
- The total acquisition cost of the interests held by the group in that subsidiary.

25.70 This approach, a one-off exercise at the time the undertaking becomes a subsidiary, is required by the Companies Act 1985 even where the interests have been purchased at different dates. FRS 2 points out that that approach will provide a practical means of applying acquisition accounting in most cases, because it does not require retrospective fair value exercises to be performed. [FRS 2 para 89]. However, FRS 2 notes that, in special circumstances, not using fair values at the dates of earlier purchases, while using an acquisition cost part of which relates to earlier purchases, may result in accounting that is inconsistent with the way the investment has previously been treated in the group's consolidated financial statements. It suggests that the inconsistency may lead to the treatment required by the Companies Act 1985 failing to give a true and fair view. [FRS 2 para 89].

25.71 FRS 2 considers two examples of such inconsistency that might lead to failure to give a true and fair view:

- An acquisition of a further interest in an undertaking that has already been treated as an associate by the group is acquired so that the undertaking becomes a subsidiary. Using the method set out above to calculate goodwill will lead to the group's share of post acquisition profits, losses and reserve movements of its associated undertaking being reclassified as goodwill (usually negative goodwill). This situation is considered in detail in paragraph 25.83 below.

- A group has substantially restated an investment that subsequently becomes its subsidiary. For example, where a provision has been made against such an investment for an impairment, the effect of using the Act's method of calculating goodwill would be to increase reserves and create goodwill. This situation is considered in detail in paragraph 25.77 below.

[FRS 2 para 89].

25.72 In such situations, where the calculation of goodwill in accordance with the Act's provisions would be misleading, the FRS states that goodwill should be calculated as the sum of the goodwill arising from each purchase of an interest in the relevant undertaking adjusted as necessary for any subsequent impairment. [FRS 2 para 89]. The goodwill arising on each purchase should be calculated as the difference between the cost of that purchase and the fair value *at the date of that purchase* of the identifiable assets and liabilities attributable to the interest purchased. The difference between the goodwill calculated using the true and fair override and that calculated in accordance with paragraph 9 of Schedule 4A to the Companies Act 1985 is shown in reserves. [FRS 2 para 89].

25.73 Adopting this alternative treatment requires the use of the true and fair override under section 227A(5)(6) of the Companies Act 1985 (CA06 Sec 404(5)) as it does not comply strictly with the requirements of the Act. This section of the Act provides that in this type of situation:

> *"If in special circumstances compliance with any of those provisions is inconsistent with the requirement to give a true and fair view, the directors must depart from that provision to the extent necessary to give a true and fair view. Particulars of any such departure, the reasons for it and its effect must be given in a note to the accounts."*

The disclosures required when the true and fair override is used are set out in FRS 18. Table 25.1 gives an example of such disclosure in respect of accounting for an associated company that has become a subsidiary.

Table 25.1 – THORN EMI plc – Report and accounts – 31 March 1995

Notes to the accounts (extract)
30. Purchase of businesses (extract)

TOEMI — On 3 October 1994, THORN EMI plc increased its shareholding in TOEMI from 50 to 55 per cent. TOEMI became a consolidated subsidiary on this date, having previously been accounted for as an associated company.

The transaction was effected by a redemption of shares owned by the joint venture partner, Toshiba Corporation, and funded by TOEMI's cash reserves in which the Group already had a 50 per cent beneficial interest. The indirect cost to the Group was therefore Yen 3.75 billion (£24.1m).

The Companies Act 1985 normally requires goodwill arising on the acquisition of a subsidiary undertaking to be calculated as the difference between the total acquisition cost of the undertaking and the fair value of the Group's share of the identifiable assets and liabilities at the date it became a subsidiary undertaking.

FRS 2 recognises that, where an investment in an associated undertaking is increased and it becomes a subsidiary undertaking, in order to show a true and fair view goodwill should be calculated on each purchase as the difference between the cost of that purchase and the fair value at the date of that purchase.

If goodwill had been calculated in accordance with the basis set out in the Companies Act 1985, £61.2m of the Group's share of the retained earnings of TOEMI would have been reclassified as goodwill and in total negative goodwill of £63.9m would have been recognised.

Practical examples

25.74 There are three basic situations that might arise with a piecemeal acquisition, as follows:

- An undertaking has an investment in another undertaking and increases its stake in the undertaking so that it becomes a subsidiary.
- An undertaking has an investment in an associate (or a joint venture) and increases its stake in the undertaking so that it becomes a subsidiary.
- A parent has an investment in a subsidiary and acquires part or all of the minority's interest.

Each of these situations is explained in the paragraphs that follow.

An investment becomes a subsidiary

25.75 This is the simplest situation to account for. The rules that apply in determining the date upon which an undertaking becomes a subsidiary are considered from paragraph 25.18.

25.76 The initial investment will be recorded in the parent's accounting records at either its cost (less provisions) or at a valuation (in accordance with the alternative accounting rules). With piecemeal acquisitions, up to the date of acquisition the parent will only have accounted for dividend income received from the undertaking. On acquisition, the goodwill arising on the acquisition has to be ascertained and this will be the difference between the fair value of the consideration given for the subsidiary (including the cost of the investment to date, any revaluation being ignored) and the fair value (at the date the investment becomes a subsidiary) of the parent's share of net assets acquired. Consider the following example:

Example

A group made an investment of 10% in a company in 20X2. The investment cost £2.5m and has subsequently been revalued to £5m. In 20X8 it makes a further investment in the company of 50% to bring its total investment to 60%. The fair value of the consideration given for the 50% is £25m. The net assets of the company acquired stand in its books at the date of acquisition at £20m (including share capital of £5m). The fair value exercise shows that the company's net assets are worth £35m, which is also the adjusted capital and reserves. The goodwill on acquisition and minority interest would be calculated in the following way:

Cost of acquisition	
	£m
Original investment in company (at cost)	2.5
Fair value of consideration given	25.0
Total consideration	27.5
Consolidation goodwill	
Total consideration	27.5
Adjusted capital and reserves (being 60% of £35m)	21.0
Goodwill	6.5
Minority interests	
Share capital (40% of £5m)	2.0
Reserves (40% of £30m)	12.0
Minority interests	14.0

The only additional adjustment that is required in this example, in contrast to a straight acquisition of a subsidiary, is to reduce the value of the original investment from its revalued amount to cost. The entry on consolidation would be to debit the revaluation reserve with £2.5m and credit the investment £2.5m. Whether the parent decides to make this adjustment in its own balance sheet might depend on whether the total cost of the subsidiary including the valuation adjustment exceeds the parent's share of the subsidiary's worth (including goodwill). Consequently, in this example the total consideration paid for the subsidiary together with the book value of the original investments is £30m (that is, £25m + £5m). If 60% of the subsidiary (including goodwill) is worth more than £30m, then no provision will have to be made in the parent's books of account against the carrying value of its investment.

25.77 As already mentioned, a further complication can arise where a provision has been made against an investment for permanent diminution in value. Consider the following example:

Example

A parent acquired a 10% interest in a property company in 20X3 for £11m. At that time the fair value of the net assets of the property company was £100m. The parent has subsequently provided for a permanent diminution in value of its investment and written it down from £11m to £4m. In 20X8 the other shareholder sold its 90% holding to the parent for £40m. At that time the fair value of the net assets of the property company were £50m.

Calculation of goodwill – applying the provisions of paragraph 9 of Schedule 4A of the Companies Act 1985

Cost of acquisition		£m
Original investment 10% in 20X3		11
Final investment 90% in 20X8		40
Total consideration		51
Calculation of goodwill		£m
Total consideration		51
Less: adjusted capital and reserves at date property company became subsidiary		(50)
Goodwill arising on acquisition of subsidiary		1

The double entry on consolidation is as follows:

	£m	£m
Dr Investment	7	
Cr Profit and loss account reserve		7
Being the restatement of the original investment to original cost.		
Dr Capital and reserves of subsidiary	50	
Dr Goodwill	1	
Cr Investment		51
Being the capitalisation of goodwill		

In practice some of the provision for permanent diminution of £7m may be written back through the parent's profit and loss account, as the parent's cost of investment (after provision for permanent diminution in value) is £44m compared to underlying net assets of £50m. Let us suppose, for example, that £6m of the provision is written back through the parent's profit and loss account. The write-back of £6m should then be credited to the consolidated profit and loss account (as it was originally charged to the consolidated profit and loss account) and the remaining £1m credited to the consolidated profit and loss account reserve with the corresponding debit shown as goodwill arising on the acquisition.

25.78 The method just described gives a figure for positive goodwill by, in effect, reinstating the provision for permanent diminution in value and offsetting it against a substantial negative goodwill figure which arose on the second tranche. However, in substance the effects of the transactions are:

- A substantial holding loss on the original investment.
- A purchase at a discount.

25.79 The substance of the transaction is more closely represented by the following approach, which uses the true and fair override in calculating the goodwill arising on consolidation.

Example

Calculation of goodwill – using the true and fair override

Cost of acquisition		£m
Original investment 10% in 20X3		11
Final investment 90% in 20X8		40
Total consideration		51
Consolidation goodwill		
Total consideration		51
Less: adjusted capital and reserves at dates of original investments		
10% × £100m	10	
90% × £50m	45	55
Negative goodwill		(4)

The double entry on consolidation is as follows:

	£m	£m
Dr Investment	7	
Cr Profit and loss account reserve		7

Being the restatement of the original investment to original cost.

Dr Capital and reserves of subsidiary	50	
Cr Cost of investment		51
Cr Negative goodwill		4
Dr Profit and loss account reserve	5	

Being the recognition of negative goodwill arising on consolidation and the reduction in the underlying net assets of £5m attributable to the original 10% investment between its acquisition date in 20X3 and the date the undertaking became a subsidiary (10% × (£100m – £50m)).

As above, in practice, some of the provision for permanent diminution may be written back through the parent's profit and loss account, as the parent's cost of investment (after provision for permanent diminution in value) is £44m compared to underlying net assets of £50m. Again let us suppose that £6m of the provision is written back through the parent's profit and loss account. Only £1m of the £6m provision also reported in the consolidated profit and loss account in previous years could be credited back through the consolidated profit and loss account, because in effect £5m of that provision has already been adjusted to reserves in the calculation to arrive at the goodwill arising on the acquisition of the 10% interest.

25.80 If the true and fair override is adopted, the particulars of the departure from the requirements of paragraph 9 of Schedule 4A to the Companies Act 1985, the reasons for it and its effect should be disclosed in a note to the financial statements. [CA85 Sec 227A(6); CA06 Sec 404(5)]. In addition, the disclosure provisions of FRS 18 must be complied with (see chapter 2).

An associate becomes a subsidiary

25.81 When an associate becomes a subsidiary the accounting treatment is not as straightforward as in the previous example. The main difference lies in the fact that a proportion of the associate's results have already been dealt with in the consolidated profit and loss account and consolidated balance sheet. In addition, goodwill will have been calculated on the acquisition of the interest in the associate and will have been either written off to reserves or amortised over its useful economic life.

25.82 The method set out in the Act still applies and the goodwill arising on the acquisition of the subsidiary should be calculated as the difference between the following two amounts:

- The fair value, at the date an undertaking becomes a subsidiary, of the group's share of its identifiable assets and liabilities.
- The total acquisition cost of the interests held by the group in that subsidiary.

25.83 Using this method to calculate goodwill leads to the group's share of post acquisition profits, losses and reserve movements of its associated undertaking becoming reclassified as goodwill, thus reducing goodwill or creating negative goodwill on the acquisition. FRS 2 recognises that this accounting treatment is inconsistent with the way the investment has previously been treated and that this inconsistency could lead to a failure to give a true and fair view.

Example

A group made an investment of 20% in a company in 20X2. The investment cost £12m and the book value (also fair value) of the associate's net assets at that date was £50m. In 20X8 it makes a further investment in the company of 50% to bring its total investment to 70%. Goodwill on the acquisition of the associate was written off directly against reserves in the year of acquisition which was prior to the implementation of FRS 10. The net assets of the associate stand in its books at £68m on the date it becomes a subsidiary. The associate would be treated as follows up to the date of acquisition:

Acquisition of associate	
	£m
Original investment in company	12.0
Fair value of net assets acquired (20% × £50m)	10.0
Goodwill arising	2.0
Consolidation of associate up to date of increased investment	
Share of net assets	
Date of acquisition	10.0
Post acquisition profits	
(being (£68m – £50m) × 20%)	3.6
	13.6

The fair value of the consideration given for the additional 50% is £42m. The fair value exercise shows that the company's net assets are worth £75m, which is also the adjusted capital and reserves. The group must include the whole amount of the fair value of the subsidiary's net assets in the consolidated balance sheet. The goodwill on acquisition and minority interest would be calculated as follows:

Associate becomes a subsidiary — applying the provisions of the Act

Cost of acquisition as shown in the parent's books

	£m	£m
Original investment in company		12.0
Fair value of consideration given for new investment		42.0
Total investment in subsidiary		54.0
Consolidation goodwill		
Total consideration		54.0
Adjusted capital and reserves		
being 20% of £75m	15	
being 50% of £75m	37.5	52.5
Total goodwill arising on the acquisition		1.5
Goodwill previously written off		2.0
Balance of goodwill (negative)		(0.5)
Minority interests		
Share capital (30% of £5m)		1.5
Reserves (30% of £70m)		21.0
Minority interests		22.5

The problem with this method of calculating the goodwill is that it treats the post acquisition profits and reserve movements of the undertaking while it was an associate of the group as a deduction from goodwill. The amount of the undertaking's profits while it was an associate have to be 'removed' from the profit and loss account reserves as part of the double entry on consolidation, as follows:

	£m	£m
Dr Profit and loss account reserve	3.6	
Cr Investment		3.6

Being the restatement of the original investment to original cost.

This method gives a figure of negative goodwill of £0.5m, which is the difference between the goodwill arising on the acquisition of £1.5m less the goodwill of £2m previously written off on the initial acquisition of the associate interest. However, the goodwill of £1.5m is *understated because the total* interest of 70% has been applied to the fair value of the net assets at the date the undertaking becomes a subsidiary (in compliance with the Act) and does not take into account the fact that when the 20% interest was acquired the fair value of the net assets was less. Therefore, if the difference is material, it is necessary to adopt the

Act's true and fair override in order to arrive at the correct amount of goodwill arising on the acquisition.

Associate becomes a subsidiary — adopting true and fair override

Cost of acquisition as shown in the parent's books	£m	£m
Original investment in company		12.0
Fair value of consideration given for new investment		42.0
Total investment in subsidiary		54.0
Consolidation goodwill		
Total consideration		54.0
Adjusted capital and reserves		
being 20% × £50m	10.0	
being 50% × £75m	37.5	47.5
Goodwill		6.5
Goodwill previously written off		2.0
Balance of goodwill		4.5
Minority interests		
Share capital (30% × £5m)		1.5
Reserves (30% × £70m)		21.0
Minority interests		22.5

In this case, the goodwill figure that emerges is instinctively correct as it reflects the fact that a premium of £4.5m arises on the acquisition of the additional 50% (that is, £42m – (£75m × 50%)). The results since the date of acquisition of the associate are attributable to the group and as such are correctly treated as post-acquisition.

There is one further adjustment that is required to be made on consolidation in this example. There is a difference of £5m between the fair values of the net assets consolidated (that is, £75m) and the adjusted capital and reserves taken into account above (that is, £47.5m + £22.5m = £70m). The amount relates to two items. Part relates to the post acquisition profits of £3.6m taken into account since the acquisition of the associate (that is, 20% × (£68m – £50m)). The other part relates to the increase in net assets of £7m from their book value of £68m to their fair value of £75m. In the above example 30% of that increase is reflected in the minority's interest and 50% is taken into account in calculating goodwill. The other 20% (that is, £1.4m) is the further adjustment that will need to be credited to the consolidated revaluation reserve. This represents a revaluation (not a fair value adjustment) of the assets that were already included in the consolidated balance sheet by virtue of the inclusion of the associate interest.

If the revaluation adjustment is made, the double entry on consolidation is as follows:

	£m	£m
Dr Profit and loss account reserve	3.6	
Cr Investment		3.6
Being the restatement of the original investment to original cost.		
Dr Share capital and reserves	75.0	
Cr Minority interest		22.5
Cr Cost of investment		54.0
Cr Revaluation reserve		1.4
Cr Profit and loss account reserve		3.6
Dr Goodwill written off to reserves *	2.0	
Dr Goodwill capitalised *	4.5	
Being the adjustment necessary to reflect minority interests and goodwill		

*Even though the goodwill arising on the original acquisition of the associate interest was written off to reserves, which was allowed prior to the introduction of FRS 10, the goodwill arising on the further transfer of shares acquired must be capitalised in accordance with FRS 10.

A parent acquires part or all of the minority

25.84 FRS 2 states that when a group increases its interest in an undertaking that is already its subsidiary, the identifiable assets and liabilities of that subsidiary should be revalued to their fair value and goodwill arising on the increase in interest should be calculated by reference to those fair values. This rule is additional to the general rule in FRS 2 that requires a fair value exercise to be carried out when an entity becomes a subsidiary. However, the standard goes on to say that such a revaluation is not required if the difference between net fair values and carrying amounts of the assets and liabilities attributable to the increase in stake is not material. [FRS 2 para 51].

25.85 When a group increases its stake in a subsidiary the consideration it pays may not equal the fair value of the identifiable assets and liabilities acquired from its minority. If the net assets of the subsidiary, which are already included in the consolidation, were not revalued to up to date fair values before calculating the goodwill arising on the change in stake, the difference between the consideration paid and the relevant proportion of the carrying value of the net assets acquired would be made up in part of goodwill and in part of changes in value. For that reason FRS 2 requires that the assets and liabilities of the subsidiary be revalued to their fair value at the date of the increase in stake, unless the difference between the fair values and the carrying amounts of the share of net assets acquired is not material. [FRS 2 para 90].

Example

A parent acquired a 60% interest in an undertaking in 20X2 for £50m. At that time the fair value of the net assets of the subsidiary was £60m. In 20X8 the parent purchased a further 30% interest in the subsidiary for £40m. At that time the fair value of the net assets of the subsidiary was £150m; the increase in fair value of net assets between the original investment date and 20X5 is due to revaluation increases of £70m and profits of £20m.

Assuming that the difference between the fair values and carrying values of the net assets acquired is material the acquisition will be dealt with as follows:

Cost of acquisition	£m	£m
Original investment 60% in 20X2		50
Additional investment 30% in 20X8		40
Total consideration		90
Consolidation goodwill		£m
Total consideration		90
Less: share of adjusted capital and reserves		
60% × £60m	36	
30% × £150m	45	81
Goodwill		9

The profits of the subsidiary company between 20X2 and 20X8 will have already been reflected in the assets and liabilities in the consolidated balance sheet. The treatment of the £70m revaluation element will depend on whether it has already been reflected in the consolidated balance sheet. If the revaluation had been booked prior to the purchase of the second tranche of shares the entries would have been:

	£m	£m
Dr Net assets	70	
Cr Revaluation reserve		42
Cr Minority interests		28

On the acquisition of the additional 30% the minority's share of the revaluation, £21m (30% × £70m) would be transferred from minority interests to the cost of control account together with the other elements of minority interests that relate to the 30% interests (that is, share capital, profit and loss account and other reserves).

If, on the other hand, the revaluation had not been reflected in the consolidated balance sheet the entries to reflect the revaluation would be:

	£m	£m
Dr Net assets	70	
Cr Revaluation reserve		42
Cr Minority interests		7
Cr Cost of control account †		21

† The entries in the cost of control account are shown below:

Cost of control account

Dr		Cr	
Original cost of investment	50	Share of adjusted capital and reserves in 20X2 (£60m × 60%)	36
		Goodwill on original acquisition	14
	50		50
Additional cost of investment	40	Share of adjusted capital and reserves in 20X8 (£60m + £20m × 30%)	24
		Share of revaluation reserve	21
Negative goodwill	5		
	95		95

The effect of these entries is that not only is there a fair valuation of the 30% acquired, but also a revaluation of the 60% which represents the share of assets previously owned (credited to the group's revaluation reserve) and a revaluation of the share still attributable to minority interests of 10%. It can also be seen that the goodwill of £9m is made up of £14m on the original acquisition and negative goodwill of £5m arising on the increase in stake.

An alternative view is that the proportion of assets of the subsidiary held prior to the acquisition of the minority (60% in this case) need not be revalued when the minority interest is acquired. If this approach is adopted the result will be that only the additional 30% of assets acquired will be subject to fair value at the date of acquisition of the 30% minority, the bulk of the assets will be held at their original cost to the group.

Change in stake not material

If the difference between the carrying values of the assets of the subsidiary and their fair values was not deemed to be material and the change in stake was not considered significant there would have been no requirement to revalue the assets of the subsidiary in the consolidation and the calculations would be as follows:

Cost of acquisition		£m
Original investment 60% in 20X2		50
Final investment 30% in 20X8		40
Total consideration		90
Consolidation goodwill		£m
Total consideration		90
Less: share of adjusted capital and reserves		
60% × £60m	36	
30% × (£60m + £20m) net assets in balance sheet prior to revaluation	24	60
Goodwill		30

The goodwill of £30m is made up of £14m on the original acquisition and £16m arising on the increase in stake (cost of £40m less net assets of £24m) attributable to the 30% purchased.

Becoming a subsidiary other than by a purchase or an exchange of shares

25.86 Some investments that end up as subsidiaries start out as much smaller interests in the undertakings concerned and may be treated in the group's financial statements in a variety of ways before they actually become subsidiaries. The most common way for an undertaking to become a subsidiary of another is by acquisition, but it is also possible for a parent to gain a subsidiary other than by acquisition, for example:

- By gaining control or the power to control without acquiring a further interest in an undertaking, perhaps by virtue of an agreement with another shareholder.
- By the default by a creditor on a loan, that gives the lender an option to convert the loan into a holding of shares that is sufficient to make the creditor a subsidiary.
- By the subsidiary company purchasing and cancelling its own shares held by third parties.
- By changes to the voting rights attached to shares.

25.87 Where an undertaking becomes a subsidiary other than as a result of a purchase or exchange of shares, not only should its name be disclosed as required by paragraph 21(a) of FRS 6, but also FRS 2 paragraph 49 requires the circumstances to be explained.

Disclosure for acquisition accounting

25.88 Schedule 4A to the Companies Act 1985 sets out various details that have to be disclosed in the consolidated financial statements in the year that a subsidiary is acquired. These disclosure requirements concern business combinations that are accounted for using either acquisition accounting or merger accounting. In addition, FRS 6 repeats these requirements and includes further disclosure requirements relating both to acquisitions and mergers. Those relating to merger accounting are dealt with in chapter 28. The disclosures related to fair valuing on an acquisition have been consolidated into FRS 6 and include disclosures of post-acquisition reorganisation costs which are discussed in section II, from paragraph 25.208. The disclosures relating to the treatment of goodwill that arises on an acquisition are detailed in section III, from paragraph 25.473. The disclosures required where the group has taken merger relief on the issue of its shares in an acquisition are given in chapter 23. The paragraphs that follow outline the general disclosure requirements that apply to business combinations that are accounted for as acquisitions.

25.89 With the exception of goodwill, the disclosures concerning acquisitions can now be found in one standard, FRS 6. This standard encompasses the disclosure requirements of the Companies Act 1985. FRS 6 also repeats some of the disclosure requirements contained in FRS 1 and FRS 3, and expands the latter in an important respect.

25.90 A group may make several acquisitions in an accounting period. There is no exemption from disclosure on the grounds of excessive information, although information relating to non-material acquisitions can be aggregated. For acquisitive groups the disclosure resulting from FRS 6 and the Companies Act 1985 is extensive.

General requirements

25.91 The acquiring company should disclose certain information in respect of all acquisitions. The parent must disclose in the consolidated financial statements that deal with the period in which the acquisition occurs:

- The names of undertakings acquired during the financial year, or where a group of companies is acquired, the name of the group's parent. [CA85 4A Sch 13(2)(a); FRS 6 para 21(a)].
- That the company has adopted acquisition accounting. [CA85 4A Sch 13(2)(b); FRS 6 para 21(b)].
- The date of the acquisition (that is, the date on which control passes). [FRS 6 para 21(c)].

25.92 As described in the following paragraphs, FRS 6 requires certain additional disclosures to be given in respect of each *material acquisition*, and in aggregate for other acquisitions that are individually not material. Whilst the FRS 6 disclosures encompass those required by the Companies Act 1985, which are required *"in relation to an acquisition which significantly affects the figures shown in the group accounts"*, they go further than the Act. [CA85 4A Sch 13(2)]. FRS 6 indicates that an acquisition should be judged to be material when *"the information relating to the acquisition might reasonably be expected to influence decisions made by the users of general purpose financial statements"*. [FRS 6 para 84]. However, FRS 6 also introduced a new class of *substantial acquisitions*, which are defined by reference to a size test and lead to certain enhanced disclosures.

25.93 If in the directors' opinion the disclosure of any of the information in paragraph 25.91 above and paragraphs 25.94 to 25.102 below that is required by the Companies Act 1985 (relating to an undertaking established under the law of a country, or one that carries on a business, outside the UK) would be seriously prejudicial to the business of the undertaking, its parent or its fellow subsidiaries, it need not be given if the Secretary of State's permission is obtained. [CA85 4A Sch 16].

Purchase consideration

25.94 The following information should be disclosed for each material acquisition and for other non-material acquisitions in aggregate:

- The composition and the fair value of the consideration for the acquisition given by the parent and its subsidiaries. [CA85 4A Sch 13(3); FRS 6 para 24].
- Where applicable, a statement that the attributed fair value of the purchase consideration has been determined on a provisional basis at the end of the accounting period in which the acquisition took place. Any material adjustments in subsequent periods should be disclosed and explained. [FRS 6 para 27].
- The nature of any purchase consideration where settlement is deferred or where the amount is contingent on future events. [FRS 6 para 24].
- The range of possible outcomes and the principal factors that might affect the amount of contingent purchase consideration that may become payable in the future. [FRS 6 para 24].

25.95 Fair valuing the purchase consideration, including deferred and contingent consideration, is considered in section II, paragraph 25.383.

Fair values of identifiable assets and liabilities

25.96 The following information should be disclosed for each material acquisition and for other non-material acquisitions in aggregate:

- A table of assets and liabilities acquired, including a statement of the amount of goodwill or negative goodwill arising on the acquisition (see para 25.97 below). [CA85 4A Sch 13(5); FRS 6 para 25].
- Where applicable, a statement that the attributed fair values at the end of the accounting period in which the acquisition took place are provisional, together with the reasons. Any material adjustments made to those provisional fair values in the next financial statements should also be disclosed and explained. [FRS 6 para 27]. (See section II, from para 25.243.)

Table of assets and liabilities acquired

25.97 The Companies Act 1985 and FRS 6 require the book values and fair values of each class of assets and liabilities of the undertaking or group acquired to be stated in tabular form. The book values to be shown in the table are those recorded in the books of the acquired entity immediately before the acquisition and are before any fair value adjustments. [FRS 6 para 25(a)]. The book values of assets and liabilities of a group acquired must include all the necessary consolidation adjustments within that group. [CA85 4A Sch 13(7)].

25.98 The table should also detail the fair value adjustments of those same categories of assets and liabilities at the date of acquisition. FRS 6 also requires the fair value adjustments to be analysed between the following:

- Revaluations.
- Adjustments to bring accounting polices of the subsidiary onto the same basis as those of the group.
- Any other significant adjustments, including reasons for the adjustments.

[FRS 6 para 25(b); CA85 4A Sch 13(5)].

25.99 The FRRP published a statement in November 1997 in connection with the financial statements of Stratagem Group plc concerning the adequacy of the information and explanations given in respect of fair value adjustments. The Panel was concerned that the company had not analysed such adjustments into the components specified above.

25.100 The table should also include a statement of the amount of goodwill or negative goodwill arising on acquisition. [FRS 6 para 25; CA 85 4A Sch 13(5)]. Table 25.2 gives an example of a fair value table showing a material acquisition separately and other acquisitions in aggregate.

Table 25.2 — Hanson PLC — Annual Report — 30 September 1995

Notes to the accounts (extract)

20 Acquisitions, demerger and disposals (extract)

Acquisitions

Eastern was acquired on September 18, 1995 and included in the consolidated balance sheet at September 30, 1995. For the period since acquisition, sales of £74mn and operating profit of £7mn are included within the consolidated profit and loss account as continuing operations — acquisitions.

On September 18, 1995 the acquisition of Eastern was declared unconditional. The purchase consideration was £2.5bn. The operating assets and liabilities of Eastern, Carter Mining and other acquisitions during the year were as follows:

	Eastern Book value £ million	Others Book value £ million	Total Book value £ million	Total Adjustments £ million	Total Fair value £ million
Fixed assets	1,118	211	1,329	625	1,954
Stock	12	49	61	(1)	60
Debtors	364	16	380	(11)	369
Cash	264	1	265		265
Unlisted investments	251	—	251	295	546
Creditors	(411)	(15)	(426)	—	(426)
Loans and finance leases	(688)	(16)	(704)	—	(704)
Provision for liabilities	(113)	(49)	(162)	(497)	(659)
	797	197	994	411	1,405
Accrued purchase consideration					2,495
Cash consideration					299
Consideration (Eastern £2,496mn and others £298mn)					2,794
Goodwill (Eastern £1,377mn and others £12mn)					(1,389)
					1,405

Of the provisions for liabilities above, £88mn was provided by Eastern for reorganisation costs in the year up to acquisition.

The following fair value adjustments which relate principally to Eastern and Carter Mining were made to the book value of the assets and liabilities of the above acquisitions:

	Eastern £ million	Others £ million	Total £ million
Revaluations			
Tangible fixed assets	242	383	625
Unlisted investments	295	—	295
Alignment of accounting policies			
Liabilities in respect of mining reclamation	—	(94)	(94)
Black lung excise tax liability	—	(183)	(183)
Other			
Liabilities in respect of purchase contracts	(129)	—	(129)
Taxation	(86)	—	(86)
Other liabilities	—	(17)	(17)
	322	89	411

The above figures reflect a preliminary allocation of the purchase consideration to the net assets and liabilities of Eastern and other acquisitions of the year. The preliminary allocation will be reviewed based on additional information up to September 30, 1996. The directors do not believe that any net adjustments resulting from such review would have a material adverse effect on Hanson.

For the year ended March 31, 1995, Eastern reported an audited post-tax profit of £141mn. For the period ended September 18, 1995 the unaudited operating profit before exceptional items was £80mn and the unaudited post-tax loss after exceptional items was £19mn based on its then accounting policies.

25.101 Because of the intention of FRS 7 to curtail provisioning as part of the fair value exercise (as explained in section II, para 25.198), FRS 6 requires that any provisions for reorganisation and restructuring costs which have been included in the liabilities, or related asset write-downs, of the acquired entity to be identified separately in the table. This is, however, only required where the provisions were made in the twelve months up to the date of acquisition. [FRS 6 para 26]. The example in Table 25.2 discloses the existence of such provisions.

25.102 This disclosure is an anti-avoidance measure. To a very limited extent, some reorganisation provisions may be properly regarded as pre-acquisition liabilities of the acquired company where, for example, the acquired company was already committed to the expenditure before the acquisition was in prospect. By requiring separate disclosure of any such provisions in the fair value table, the ASB sought to ensure that the spirit of FRS 7 is observed. The disclosure of such provisions in the fair value table is likely to be a sensitive matter. Accordingly, the directors of the acquiring group may wish to include a statement explaining why the provision is valid.

Pre-acquisition activities of material acquisitions

25.103 For each *material acquisition* (but for *substantial acquisitions*, see para 25.106 below) the notes should disclose the following:

- The profit or loss after tax and minority interests of the undertaking or group acquired for the period from the beginning of its financial year up to the date of acquisition.
- The profit or loss after tax and minority interests of the undertaking or group acquired for its previous financial year.
- The date on which the acquired undertaking's or group's financial year before the acquisition began.

[FRS 6 para 35].

25.104 FRS 6 is silent on the question of whether the disclosed profit or loss of the acquired undertaking should be adjusted to comply with the accounting policies of the acquiring group. It would be consistent with the disclosures for substantial acquisitions (see para 25.111 below) for this information to be reported on the basis of the acquired undertaking's accounting policies prior to the acquisition, although the directors of the acquiring group may wish to disclose additional adjusted figures.

25.105 The above disclosures are not required to be given in aggregate for non-material acquisitions.

Pre-acquisition activities of substantial acquisitions

25.106 The ASB was anxious to meet the concerns of users who were interested in assessing the performance of acquisitions in the acquiring group, by requiring a more detailed analysis of the pre-acquisition results of significant acquisitions than was previously required by the Act. The objective was to enable users to put together something of a track record for the acquisition before and after it enters the group, given that in most acquisitions it is continuing businesses that are acquired. Such information has the effect of complementing the layered format for the profit and loss account required by FRS 3, which provides separate disclosure of the post-acquisition results of acquisitions made during the year.

25.107 FRS 6 requires, for each acquisition that meets the following size tests, disclosure of additional information about the pre-acquisition results of the acquired entity for its financial year in which the acquisition takes place.

25.108 The size tests are:

- 'Class 1' or 'Super Class 1' acquisitions, where the acquirer is listed on the Stock Exchange. It should be noted that the 'Class 1' category was abolished by the Stock Exchange in an amendment to the Listing Rules in August 1995, and the 'Super Class 1' category was redesignated as 'Class 1' with effect from January 1999. UITF Abstract 15, issued in January 1996 and revised in February 1999, confirmed that the size test in FRS 6 should continue to be based on the former 'Class 1' criteria. UITF 15 requires references to Class 1 transactions in FRS 6 to be interpreted as meaning those business combinations in which any of the ratios set out in the Listing Rules for the classification of transactions exceeds 15 per cent (it should be noted that a transaction is a Class 1 transaction under the Listing Rules where any of the ratios is 25 per cent or more). The ratios are specified in Annex 1 to Chapter 10 of the Listing Rules.

- For other acquiring entities, if either of the following conditions are met:
  - The net assets or operating profits of the acquired entity (as shown its last statutory financial statements before the date of acquisition) exceed 15 per cent of those of the acquiring entity. For this purpose, the amount of net assets is determined after adding any purchased goodwill that has been written off to reserves as a matter of accounting policy and not charged in the profit and loss account.
  - The fair value of the consideration given exceeds 15 per cent of the net assets of the acquiring entity.

- Other exceptional cases where an acquisition does not meet the above criteria, but is nevertheless of such significance that the disclosure is necessary in order to give a true and fair view.

[FRS 6 para 37].

25.109 For each substantial acquisition as defined above, the disclosures required in the financial statements of the acquirer for the financial year in which the acquisition took place are:

- For the period from the beginning of the acquired entity's latest financial year to the date of acquisition:
  - A summarised profit and loss account of the acquired entity, disclosing as a minimum the turnover, operating profit, any exceptional items falling within paragraph 20 of FRS 3, profit before taxation, taxation, minority interests, and extraordinary items.
  - A summarised statement of total recognised gains and losses of the acquired entity.
  - The date on which the period began.
- For the acquired entity's previous financial year, the profit or loss after tax and minority interests. This is the same as the disclosure required for each material acquisition (see para 25.103 above).

[FRS 6 para 36].

25.110 The principal components of the statement of total recognised gains and losses would usually be:

- Profit or loss for the period.
- Exchange gains or losses taken direct to reserves.
- Revaluation surpluses or deficits booked in respect of asset revaluations in the period.
- Total recognised gains or losses.

25.111 The information described above may in some situations be of limited practical use to analysts. Firstly, the period for which the more detailed summary of the results of the acquired entity is included will vary according to the timing of the acquisition in relation to the financial year end of the target and may be very short. Secondly, FRS 6 requires the results of the acquired entity to be shown on the basis of its own accounting policies prior to the acquisition. [FRS 6 para 36].

25.112 Where harmonisation of accounting policies on to the acquiring group's own policies gives rise to a material restatement of the results of the acquired company, their disclosure on the old basis may be misleading when compared to the disclosure of post-acquisition performance on the basis of the new policies. However, the standard explains that management may in those circumstances wish voluntarily to disclose, as additional notes, the same information restated on to the basis of the accounting policies of the acquiring group. [FRS 6 para 89]. Although this is sensible, it could give rise to excessive disclosure in the acquirer's consolidated financial statements.

25.113 There may be practical difficulties in complying with the disclosure requirements where a business (for example, the trade and assets of a division) rather than a subsidiary is acquired. Information about pre-acquisition results may not be readily available to the acquirer. Furthermore, profitability may have been distorted by intra-group charges under previous ownership, or matters such as taxation may not have been dealt with at a divisional level. In such circumstances, the acquirer should comply as far as is practically possible. The disclosure note may need to explain how the figures have been derived. Tables 25.3, 25.4 and 25.5 illustrate different solutions to the disclosure problem in practice. In Table 25.5, the acquirer disclosed that the information could not be given.

Table 25.3 — Reckitt & Colman plc — Report and Accounts — 31 December 1994
Notes to the accounts (extract)

27 ACQUISITION OF BUSINESSES

The 1994 full year trading result and statement of recognised gains and losses of L&F Household, as reported on the US accounting basis used by the business as part of Kodak, were as follows:

	1994 US$m
Net sales	**809.13**
Operating profit	**105.87**
object >	
Profit before tax	**101.62**
Taxation	**(40.65)**
Profit after tax	**60.97**
Foreign currency translation adjustments	**3.36**
Other	**4.88**
Total recognised gains and losses relating to the financial year	**69.21**

In 1993 profit after tax was $53.49m. The taxation affairs of L&F Household were treated integrally with those of Kodak, and the above figures include a charge of 40% of profit before taxation. There were no minority interests.

There is no material difference in the result when calculated using Reckitt & Colman's accounting policies.

Table 25.4 — SmithKline Beecham plc — Annual Report & Accounts — 31 December 1994
NOTES TO THE FINANCIAL STATEMENTS (extract)

Acquisitions (extract)
Acquisitions consist of Diversified Pharmaceutical Services, Inc., which was acquired from United HealthCare on 27 May 1994 and the worldwide consumer healthcare business of Sterling Winthrop Inc., which was acquired from Eastman Kodak on 31 October 1994.

From 1 January 1994 to 27 May 1994 Diversified had sales of £74 million and a trading profit of £31 million; profit before taxation was £16 million and taxation £6 million. The profit after tax for Diversified for the year to 31 December 1993 was £17 million. There is no difference between profit after tax and the recognised gains and losses for the period.

From 1 January 1994 to 31 October 1994 Sterling had sales of £379 million and a trading profit of £66 million. The trading profit for Sterling for the year to 31 December 1993 was £80 million. The trading profit is presented before corporate and other charges, interest and taxation, as all financing items and US taxation matters were dealt with on a group basis by Eastman Kodak, and no meaningful allocation of such items can be made.

Table 25.5 — Scottish & Newcastle plc — Annual Report & Accounts — 28 April 1996
NOTES TO THE ACCOUNTS (extract)

25 ACQUISITION OF THE COURAGE BUSINESS (extract)
The Courage business was acquired from the Foster's Brewing Group on 16 August 1995.

Prior to acquisition the Courage business was part of Courage Limited. However, only certain of the assets and liabilities of Courage Limited were acquired. In these circumstances, it is not practical to provide details of profits or recognised gains and losses for the Courage business for financial periods before acquisition. Since acquisition the operations of the Courage business have been integrated into the existing Beer Division. As a result it is impractical to isolate the cashflows of the Courage business.

Post-acquisition activities

FRS 3 layered formats

25.114 FRS 6 repeats the requirements of FRS 3 concerning the reporting of the results of acquisitions made during the financial year of the acquiring group. The results of acquisitions, excluding those that are also discontinued in the period, should be disclosed separately in aggregate as a component of the group's continuing operations. As with the other continuing operations, the minimum analysis given on the face of the profit and loss account should be turnover and operating profit. The analysis of each of the other profit and loss account headings between turnover and operating profit may be given in a note, instead of on the face of the profit and loss account. In addition, where an acquisition has a material impact on a major business segment this should be disclosed and explained.

25.115 FRS 3 recognises that sometimes it may not be possible to determine post-acquisition results of an acquired operation to the end of the period. This might occur, for instance, where the business of an acquired subsidiary is transferred to another group company and merged with the existing business of that company shortly after the acquisition. If the results of the acquisition cannot be obtained the standard requires an indication to be given of the contribution of the acquisition to turnover and operating profit of the continuing operations. If that is also not possible, this fact and the reason should be explained. An illustration of this latter situation is given in Table 25.6, where the operations of the continuing and acquired businesses were merged for the latter part of the reporting period.

25.116 FRS 6 has added an important new interpretation of the requirements of FRS 3 as summarised above. It requires the post-acquisition results of businesses acquired in the financial year to be disclosed separately for each material acquisition and for other acquisitions in aggregate. [FRS 6 para 23]. This new interpretation – FRS 3 only refers specifically to separate disclosure of the aggregate results of acquisitions – is explained, in the appendix to the standard that deals with its development, as a clarification of FRS 3.

25.117 The FRS 3 presentation is considered in more detail in chapter 8, together with examples from published financial statements.

Exceptional items

25.118 The results of acquired companies disclosed for the first period after acquisition may not be entirely indicative of the ongoing performance of such companies. This is because, for example, they may be distorted significantly by fair value adjustments made on acquisition. Alternatively, they may be affected by changes introduced by the acquirer soon after the acquisition. FRS 6 indicates that exceptional profits or losses that arise as a result of fair valuing the assets and liabilities of acquired companies should be disclosed in accordance with FRS 3 and should be identified as relating to the acquisition. Once again, such disclosure should be given separately for each material acquisition and for other acquisitions in aggregate. [FRS 6 para 30].

25.119 The standard gives examples of circumstances where such disclosures may be necessary:

- Abnormal trading margins resulting from the revaluation of stocks to fair values on acquisition.
- Material profits resulting from the acquirer turning a loss-making long-term contract into a profitable contract.
- Material profits or losses resulting from contingent assets or liabilities crystallising at amounts different from their attributed fair values.

[FRS 6 para 85].

25.120 The above examples are considered in the subsections in section II that deal with fair valuing stocks (para 25.295) and contingencies (para 25.350).

Post-acquisition reorganisation and integration

25.121 FRS 6 requires the profit and loss account or notes to the financial statements of periods following an acquisition to disclose the costs incurred in those periods in reorganising, restructuring and integrating the acquisition. [FRS 6 para 31]. Such disclosure should be given separately for each material acquisition, and for other acquisitions in aggregate. [FRS 6 para 23].

25.122 Such costs are restrictively defined in the standard. The practical implications of this requirement are considered in section II, paragraph 25.189.

Acquisition provisions

25.123 FRS 6 requires movements on provisions or accruals for costs related to an acquisition to be disclosed and analysed between the amounts used for the specific purpose for which they were created and the amounts released unused. [FRS 6 para 32]. Such disclosure should be given separately for each material acquisition and for other acquisitions in aggregate. [FRS 6 para 23]. This disclosure is considered in section II, paragraph 25.230.

25.124 Table 25.6 provides extracts from the accounts of Glaxo Wellcome plc and illustrates the extensive profit and loss account disclosure required where a group makes a material acquisition and other acquisitions during the financial year. In addition, the group changed its year end from 30 June to 31 December, thus presenting its results for an 18 month period.

Table 25.6 — Glaxo Wellcome plc — Annual Report and Accounts — 31 December 1995

Consolidated Profit and Loss Account

	Notes	12 months to 30.6.95		6 months to 31.12.95	18 months to 31.12.95			12 months to 30.6.94 (restated)
		Glaxo continuing business	Acquisitions	Merged business	Combined business	Integration	Total	
		£m	£m	£m	£m	£m	£m	£m
Turnover	26	5,834	638	4,018	10,490	–	10,490	5,656
Operating costs	5	3,863	438	2,592	6,893	1,215	8,108	3,839
Trading profit	26	1,971	200	1,426	3,597	(1,215)	2,382	1,817
Profit on disposal of business	7	35	–	–	35	–	35	–
Share of profits/(losses) of associated undertakings	8	(8)	26	39	57	–	57	(3)

Profit before interest		1,998	226	1,465	3,689	(1,215)	2,474	1,814
Net (interest payable)/ investment income	9	130	(96)	(121)	(87)	–	(87)	21
Profit on ordinary activities before taxation	26	2,128	130	1,344	3,602	(1,215)	2,387	1,835
Taxation	10	627	53	417	1,097	(230)	867	524
Profit on ordinary activities after taxation		1,501	77	927	2,505	(985)	1,520	1,311
Minority interests		39	5	18	62	–	62	12
Profit attributable to shareholders		1,462	72	909	2,443	(985)	1,458	1,299
Dividends	12	1,004	–	526	1,530	–	1,530	823
Retained(loss)/ profit	23	458	72	383	913	(985)	(72)	476
Earnings per Ordinary Share	11	47.8p			74.6p		44.5p	42.7p
Weighted average number of shares in issue (millions)		3,056			3,274		3,274	3,040
Dividends per Ordinary Share	12				45.0p		45.0p	27.0p

The basis of analysis between Glaxo continuing business, Acquisitions, Merged business and Integration is set out in Note 1 on the Accounts.

Notes to the Accounts (extract)

1 Presentation of Accounts (extract)

Presentation of Profit and Loss Account

The Company has presented the profit and loss account in columnar form to illustrate the respective effect on the results for the period of the acquisitions during the period and their subsequent integration. This analysis is consistent with the way the business was managed and reported during the period. The analysis by column is defined as follows:

Glaxo continuing business reflects the results of the Glaxo business for the 12 months to 30th June 1995. Net investment income is stated as if Glaxo's investment funds had been available for investment throughout the period.

Acquisitions reflects the trading results of the acquisitions from their respective dates of acquisition to 30th June 1995. Interest payable on acquisitions represents the interest costs on borrowings taken out to finance the acquisitions, as if none of the combined Group's investment funds had been utilised to reduce borrowings. Taxation is stated at the rates applicable to the acquired businesses and to the interest costs.

Merged business reflects the results for the six months from 1st July 1995, from which date the continuing and acquired businesses were effectively merged and managed on a unified basis. It is therefore not feasible to identify and report separately the acquired businesses from 1st July 1995.

Integration reflects the costs charged relating to the integration of the continuing and acquired businesses. Taxation is stated at the rates applicable to integration costs and internal restructuring.

5 Operating costs (extract)

	12 months to 30.6.95		6 months to 31.12.95			18 months to 31.12.95	12 months to 30.6.94 (restated)
	Glaxo continuing business	Acquisitions	Merged business	Combined business	Integration	Total	
	£m	£m	£m	£m	£m	£m	£m
Cost of sales	1,037	115	654	1,806	558	2,364	1,004
Selling, general and administrative expenditure	1,986	227	1,368	3,581	400	3,981	1,988
Research and development expenditure	852	103	585	1,540	257	1,797	858
Other operating income	(12)	(7)	(15)	(34)	–	(34)	(11)
	3,863	438	2,592	6,893	1,215	8,108	3,839

Costs expected to be incurred in integrating the businesses of Glaxo and Wellcome are estimated at £1,215 million, comprising severances and other cash costs of £763 million and losses on disposal of fixed assets of £452 million. Costs of £384 million had been incurred by 31st December 1995 and provision for further costs of £831 million has been made at that date.

Operating and Financial Review (extract)
Acquisitions

The results of Wellcome have been consolidated into the Group results from 16th March 1995. In the period to 30th June 1995 Wellcome sales added £628 million to Group turnover and £204 million to trading profit; this represents a trading margin of 32 per cent.

The consolidation of Glaxo Korea Limited added £10 million to sales in this period but made no contribution to trading profit. The consolidation of Affymax N.V. added £4 million to operating costs.

Integration

Plans and financial targets for integration, as developed by the integration task forces in the period to 30th June 1995, were referred to in the Second Interim Report sent to shareholders in September 1995. The plans and targets were updated in November and December 1995 and form the basis of the figures reflected in this Annual Report and Accounts. Compared with the separate forward plans of Glaxo and Wellcome prior to Glaxo's bid for Wellcome, the new plan for the combined Group envisaged the achievement of cost savings year by year amounting to £700 million per year by the end of 1998, and progress is being made towards this objective.

The costs expected to be incurred in achieving these savings are forecast at £1,215 million. Some £452 million of the costs relate to potential losses on asset disposals resulting from site closures.

Cumulative savings are expected to achieve payback of total costs by around the end of 1997. In terms of the cash costs of £763 million, payback will be achieved earlier. The proceeds of asset disposals will reduce the net cash costs of integration.

> To recognise the impact of integration activities, the anticipated costs of £1,215 million have been charged in the Accounts at 31st December 1995. The charge comprises costs incurred by 31st December 1995 of £384 million, and a provision for a further £831 million of costs. Taxation relief on integration amounts to £230 million. In calculating the attributable taxation, no taxation relief has been assumed on asset write downs.

Cash flow statement

25.125 Where a group acquires a subsidiary, FRS 1 requires the cash flows relating to the purchase consideration to be reported under 'acquisitions and disposals' in the consolidated cash flow statement. The amounts of cash and overdraft acquired should be shown separately along with the gross consideration paid for the acquisition.

25.126 A group's consolidated cash flow statement should be consistent with the rest of its consolidated financial statements, that is, cash flows should be included from the date of acquisition. Recording the gross consideration separately along with the cash and overdraft balances acquired means that the assets and liabilities of the acquired subsidiary at the date of acquisition, excluding cash and overdraft, would need to be eliminated so as to avoid double counting. For example, stock, debtors and creditors acquired would need to be eliminated from the total balance sheet changes in stock, debtors and creditors in the reconciliation of operating profit to operating cash flows.

Disclosures

25.127 FRS 1 requires a significant amount of disclosure to be made in respect of the cash flow effects of subsidiaries acquired during the financial year. These disclosure requirements are also referred to in FRS 6. The information should be disclosed for each material acquisition and for other non-material acquisitions in aggregate. These disclosure requirements are considered in chapter 30.

Reverse acquisition accounting

25.128 Reverse acquisition accounting is a method of acquisition accounting that may, in certain circumstances, be required to give a true and fair view of a business combination. Normally, where one company acquires another, the shareholders of the acquiring company retain the majority holding in the combined group. However, in certain circumstances the positions may be reversed and it is the acquired company's shareholders who effectively control the combined group even though the other party is the legal acquirer. In such circumstances, the acquired company's board will normally dominate the combined group's board, but there could be exceptions to this, for instance if as part of the reverse acquisition there is a change in the acquired company's management.

25.129 An example is where a listed company with little or no business (sometimes called a cash shell) acquires a well-established unlisted trading company, which is much larger in size. The motive for such acquisitions is often that by combining with the cash shell the unlisted trading company obtains a listing for itself. In such circumstances it may not give a true and fair view to account for the combination as the acquisition of the trading company by the cash shell. A true and fair view may require the combination to be accounted for as the acquisition of the cash shell by the trading company, in other words reverse acquisition accounting.

25.130 UK company law and accounting standards do not envisage reverse acquisition accounting and to adopt that approach is a departure from the law and accounting standards. However, such a departure is required by both the Companies Act and accounting standards where it is necessary to give a true and fair view. In such cases the particulars, reasons and effect of the departure have to be given.

25.131 The UITF considered reverse acquisition accounting in an information sheet that it issued in 1996. In this it stated:

> *"Reverse takeovers*
>
> *A reverse takeover occurs when a company that is being acquired issues sufficient voting shares, as consideration for a business combination, for control of it (and hence of the combined enterprise) to pass to the owners of the company whose shares it acquires. In these circumstances IAS 22 'Business Combinations' requires that the enterprise issuing the shares is deemed to be acquired by the other. FRS 6 'Acquisitions and Mergers' notes (in Appendix II) that this accounting, which is sometimes described as 'reverse acquisition accounting', is incompatible with companies legislation in the UK and the Republic of Ireland. It has been suggested that, in the light of the reference in FRS 6, it is not possible to invoke the true and fair override in such cases.*
>
> *The UITF discussed this point and concluded that, whilst each case should be considered on its merits, there are some instances where it would be right and proper to invoke the true and fair override and apply reverse acquisition accounting. It also agreed that, as this is simply an application of the general requirement that the true and fair override may be invoked in the circumstances prescribed by companies legislation, and the point could be clarified by this announcement, no useful purpose would be served by issuing an Abstract on this issue."*

25.132 The UITF referred to IAS 22. This has now been superseded by IFRS 3, 'Business combinations', which states the following concerning reverse acquisitions:

> *"In a business combination effected through an exchange of equity interests, the entity that issues the equity interests is normally the acquirer. However, all pertinent facts and circumstances shall be considered to determine which*

of the combining entities has the power to govern the financial and operating policies of the other entity (or entities) so as to obtain benefits from its (or their) activities. In some business combinations, commonly referred to as reverse acquisitions, the acquirer is the entity whose equity interests have been acquired and the issuing entity is the acquiree. This might be the case when, for example, a private entity arranges to have itself 'acquired' by a smaller public entity as a means of obtaining a stock exchange listing. Although legally the issuing public entity is regarded as the parent and the private entity is regarded as the subsidiary, the legal subsidiary is the acquirer if it has the power to govern the financial and operating policies of the legal parent so as to obtain benefits from its activities. Commonly the acquirer is the larger entity; however, the facts and circumstances surrounding a combination sometimes indicate that a smaller entity acquires a larger entity. Guidance on the accounting for reverse acquisitions is provided in paragraphs B1-B15 of Appendix B."

[IFRS 3 para 21].

25.133 Whilst the UITF therefore, acknowledges that reverse acquisition accounting may be required in certain circumstances, it does not set out in detail how the accounting should work in practice. IAS 22 also did not contain detailed accounting guidance, but some guidance has now been included in an appendix to IFRS 3.

25.134 In practice, under UK GAAP, the accounting on consolidation for reverse acquisitions will normally follow the principles outlined below (the company issuing the shares – the legal acquirer – is referred to as the 'issuer' and the other party – the in substance acquirer – is referred to as the 'acquirer'):

- The assets and liabilities of the legal subsidiary (that is, the 'acquirer' for accounting purposes) will be recognised and measured in the consolidated financial statements at their pre-combination carrying amounts.
- The assets and liabilities of the legal parent (that is, the 'issuer' – the acquiree for accounting purpose) will be fair valued.
- The consideration for the reverse acquisition of the issuer will be taken to be the number of shares of the issuer in issue immediately prior to the reverse acquisition times the market price of those shares at the point in time when the offer goes unconditional. The premium on these shares which is thus derived will be taken to a reverse acquisition reserve.
- Where merger relief is available under section 131 of the Companies Act 2005. [CA06 Sec 612]. No share premium or merger reserve will be recorded on the shares issued by the issuer for the combination with the acquirer.
- The profit and loss reserve, revaluation reserve and 'other' reserves of the acquirer will be shown in place of those of the issuer.

- The share capital, share premium and capital redemption reserves of the issuer (being of a capital nature) will be shown, as these are legal capital reserves and may not be altered.

How this works in practice is illustrated in the following example.

Example 1

Issuer with share capital of 1m 10p shares and net assets of £200,000 (fair value £250,000) combines with acquirer, which has share capital of 20,000 £1 shares and net assets of £5m (fair value £7m). The balance sheets before the reverse acquisition are:

	Issuer £'000	**Acquirer £'000**
Net assets	200	5,000
Share capital	100	20
Share premium	50	580
Capital redemption reserve	20	300
Revaluation reserve	20	600
Profit and loss	10	3,500
Shareholders' funds	200	5,000

The share price of the issuer at the date of acquisition is 30p per share and it issues 30m shares giving a consideration of £9m. However, a true and fair override is adopted and reverse acquisition accounting is used to account for the combination.

The £9m represents the value of acquirer (which legally has been acquired by issuer). However, if acquirer was buying issuer it would pay market value which at the date of acquisition is 1m x 30p per shares and equals £300,000. Therefore, the consideration is determined, not as £9m for the acquisition of acquirer by issuer, but rather as £300,000 being the share capital in issue immediately prior to the combination times the share price of issuer's shares at the date when the offer went unconditional. The £300,000 represents 1m shares at a price of 30p per share.

Immediately after the combination the share capital of the combined group is shown as £3,100,000 being 31m shares at their nominal value of 10p. The share premium is shown at £50,000 because merger relief under section 131 is available for the 30m shares that have been issued and no premium need, therefore, be recognised for those shares. The capital redemption reserve (CRR) is £20,000 as this, like the share premium account, is a statutory capital reserve of the legal parent, the issuer.

The reverse acquisition reserve is credited with the difference between the nominal value of the issuer's share capital immediately prior to the combination and the fair value of those shares based on the market price at the date the offer went unconditional – that is as if the shares had been issued as consideration for the acquisition of the issuer itself. This amount is £300,000 less nominal value of £100,000, that is £200,000.

Goodwill is calculated as the difference between the fair value of the consideration notionally given for the issuer (£300,000) and the fair value of the issuer's assets and liabilities, which is £250,000, giving goodwill of £50,000.

The consolidation, therefore, appears as follows:

	Issuer	Acquirer	Fair value adjustment	Consolidated
	£'000	£'000	£'000	£'000
Net assets (excluding goodwill)	200	5,000	50	5,250
Goodwill				50
Investment	3,000			
Net assets	3,200	5,000		5,300
Share capital	3,100	20		3,100
Share premium	50	580		50
Capital redemption reserve	20	300		20
Revaluation reserve	20	600		600
Profit and loss	10	3,500		3,500
	3,200	5,000		7,270
Difference – reverse acquisition reserve				(1,970)
Shareholders' funds				5,300

As explained above one element of the reverse acquisition reserve is a credit of £200,000. The full amount of the difference can be explained as follows:

	£'000
Premium on issue of shares for issuer (1m shares @ 30p = £300,000 less nominal value £100,000)	200
Difference between reserves of acquirer and issuer included in consolidation (£600,000 + £3.5m – £20,000 – £10,000)	(4,070)
Excess of net assets of acquirer over nominal value of shares issued (£5m – £3m)	2,000
Less excess of net assets of issuer over share capital of issuer at date of acquisition (£200,000 – £100,000)	(100)
Reverse acquisition reserve	(1,970)

The figure of £1.97m is the extent to which the reserves of the acquirer have been capitalised as a result of the combination. Another method of reconciling the reverse acquisition reserve is given in paragraph 25.136 below.

25.135 In the above example if the nominal value of the issuer's 1 million shares was 1p instead of 10p there would have been a different result as follows:

Example 2

	Issuer £'000	Acquirer £'000
Net assets	200	5,000
Share capital	10	20
Share premium	140	580
Capital redemption reserve	20	300
Revaluation reserve	20	600
Profit and loss	10	3,500
Shareholders' funds	200	5,000

The only changes to the figures in the previous example are reducing the share capital of the issuer to £10,000 from £100,000 and increasing the share premium account by £90,000 (that is, assuming the shares were originally issued at a premium of £90,000).

The reverse acquisition is still made for a consideration of £9m, and 30m shares are issued at 30p per share. This gives a nominal value of £300,000 rather than £3,000,000 as in the previous example.

The consolidation is:

	Issuer £'000	Acquirer £'000	Fair value adjustment £'000	Consolidated £'000
Net assets (excluding goodwill)	200	5,000	50	5,250
Goodwill				50
Investment	300			
Net assets	500	5,000		5,300
Share capital	310	20		310
Share premium	140	580		140
Capital redemption reserve	20	300		20
Revaluation reserve	20	600		600
Profit and loss	10	3,500		3,500
	500	5,000		4,570
Difference – reverse acquisition reserve				730
Shareholders' funds				5,300

The reverse acquisition reserve is made up of:

	£'000
Premium on issue of shares for issuer (1m shares @ 30p = £300,000 less nominal value £10,000)	290
Difference between reserves of acquirer and issuer included in consolidation (£600,000 + £3.5m – £20,000 – £10,000)	(4,070)
Excess of net assets of acquirer over nominal value of shares issued (£5m – £300,000)	4,700
Less excess of net assets of issuer over share capital of issuer at date of acquisition (£200,000 – £10,000)	(190)
Reverse acquisition reserve	730

25.136 Another method of reconciling the reverse acquisition reserve in the two examples above is as follows:

		Example 1		Example 2
	£'000	£'000	£'000	£'000
Additional 'premium' recognised re issuer				
Premium on issue of shares for issuer		200		290
Statutory reserves of issuer		(70)		(160)
		130		130
Reverse acquisition difference re acquirer				
Shares issued (nominal value)		(3,000)		(300)
Share capital and statutory reserves:				
Share capital	20		20	
Share premium	580		580	
Capital redemption reserve	300		300	
		900		900
		(2,100)		600
Reverse acquisition reserve		(1,970)		730

25.137 Where reverse acquisition accounting is adopted, a true and fair override of the Companies Act and FRS 6 and FRS 7 is required. The particulars, reasons and effect must be disclosed in accordance with companies legislation and FRS 18.

25.138 The reasons given will normally be that the acquisition results in control passing from the issuer to the acquirer and thus the substance is an acquisition by the acquirer. Particulars will include the fact that the Act and accounting standards would normally require that an acquisition is accounted for as an acquisition by the issuer of the acquirer, but that to reflect the transaction's substance it has been accounted for as the acquisition of the issuer by the acquirer and reverse acquisition accounting has been adopted.

25.139 The effect will include disclosure of the fair value of assets and liabilities and of the goodwill that would have arisen had normal acquisition accounting in accordance with the Act and accounting standards been adopted, together with the effect on reserves of adopting reverse acquisition accounting.

25.140 In the former of the two examples above the goodwill that would have arisen had normal acquisition accounting been adopted would be calculated as follows:

Example 1

	£'000
Consideration at fair value (30m shares @ 30p)	9,000
Fair value of acquirer's net assets	(7,000)
Goodwill	2,000

Reserves under normal acquisition accounting would be:

	£'000
Share capital	3,100
Share premium	50
Merger reserve (30m shares @ 30p – 10p)	6,000
Capital redemption reserve	20
Revaluation reserve	20
Profit and loss	10
Shareholders' funds	9,200
Net assets on consolidation (£7m + £200,000) (excluding goodwill)	7,200
Goodwill	2,000
Net assets	9,200

The reconciliation of reserves between normal acquisition accounting and reverse acquisition accounting would be:

	Note	Normal acquisition accounting £'000	Adjustment £'000	Reverse acquisition accounting £'000
Share capital		3,100		3,100
Share premium		50		50
Merger reserve	1	6,000	(6,000)	–
Capital redemption reserve		20		20
Revaluation reserve	2	20	580	600
Profit and loss	3	10	3,490	3,500
Reverse acquisition reserve	4		(1,970)	(1,970)
Shareholders' funds		9,200		5,300

Notes:

1 Removes merger reserve arising on fair value of consideration for acquirer as acquirer is not treated as being acquired under reverse acquisition accounting.

2 Replaces revaluation reserve of issuer with that of acquirer.

3 Replaces profit and loss reserve of issuer with that of acquirer.

4 Includes notional merger reserve on fair valuing notional consideration for acquisition of issuer (credit of £130,000 – see para 25.136 above) and reflects the difference between the share capital issued as a result of the combination and the share capital and statutory reserves of the acquirer (debit of £2.1m – see para 25.136 above).

25.141 The reverse acquisition reserve, where it is negative, should be applied against the profit and loss reserve. Where it is positive it should be carried as a separate reserve.

25.142 The reconciliation of reserves for the second example above is as follows:

Example 2

	£'000
Goodwill is calculated as above	2,000
Reserves under normal acquisition accounting would be:	
Share capital	310
Share premium	140
Merger reserve (30m shares @30p – 1p)	8,700
Capital redemption reserve	20
Revaluation reserve	20
Profit and loss account	10
Shareholders' funds	9,200
Net assets (excluding goodwill)	7,200
Goodwill	2,000
Net assets	9,200

The reconciliation of reserves would be:

	Normal acquisition accounting £'000	Adjustment £'000	Reverse acquisition accounting £'000
Share capital	310		310
Share premium	140		140
Merger reserve	8,700	(8,700)	–
Capital redemption reserve	20		20
Revaluation reserve	20	580	600
Profit and loss	10	3,490	3,500
Reverse acquisition reserve		730	730
Shareholders' funds	9,200		5,300

Cash alternative

25.143 In some cases a partial cash alternative might be offered by the issuer when making the bid for the acquirer. Such a cash alternative would not form part of the consideration for accounting purposes when adopting reverse acquisition accounting, because it would be paid to the acquirer's shareholders. Instead it would be treated as if it were the repurchase of shares. This can be illustrated as follows.

Example

In the second example above (in para 25.135) 30m shares were issued at 30p per share giving a value of £9m. Suppose there had been a cash alternative of 30p instead of one share and this was taken up such that only 29m shares were issued (value £8.7m) and £300,000 was paid in cash.

In such a case, the share capital in the consolidated financial statements would be £300,000 (that is, 29m shares × 1p = £290,000 + £10,000 of shares already in issue) rather than £310,000. Net assets would be £4.95m (that is, £5.25m less cash paid out of £300,000) and the reverse acquisition reserve would be £440,000 rather than £730,000 as follows:

	Issuer £'000	**Acquirer £'000**	**Fair value adjustment £'000**	**Consolidated £'000**
Net assets (excluding goodwill)	(100)	5,000	50	4,950
Goodwill				50
Investment	590			
Net assets	490	5,000		5,000
Share capital	300	20		300
Share premium	140	580		140
Capital redemption reserve	20	300		20
Revaluation reserve	20	600		600
Profit and loss	10	3,500		3,500
	490	5,000		4,560
Difference – reverse acquisition reserve				440
Shareholders' funds				5,000

Using the two reconciliation methods used in the previous examples, the reverse acquisition reserve can be reconciled as follows:

Method 1

	£'000
Premium on issue of shares for issuer (1m shares @ 30p = £300,000 less nominal value £10,000)	290
Difference between reserves of acquirer and issuer included in consolidation (£600,000 + £3.5m – £20,000 – £10,000)	(4,070)
Excess of net assets of acquirer over nominal value of shares issued and cash paid (£5m – £590,000)	4,410
Less excess of net assets of issuer over share capital of issuer at date of acquisition (£200,000 – £10,000)	(190)
Reverse acquisition reserve	440

Method 2

		£'000
Additional 'premium' recognised re issuer		
Premium on issue of shares for issuer		290
Statutory reserves of issuer		(160)
		130
Reverse acquisition difference re acquirer		
Shares issued (nominal value)		(290)
Share capital and statutory reserves:		
Share capital	20	
Share premium	580	
Capital redemption reserve	300	
		900
Cash paid out for 'repurchase of shares'		(300)
		310
Reverse acquisition reserve		440

Section II — Fair values

Introduction

25.144 Consolidated financial statements are prepared on the principle that the reporting entity and its subsidiary undertakings are a single economic entity. Thus, the activities, assets and liabilities of all the undertakings in a group are included within the consolidation.

25.145 When a group extends its activities through the purchase of a new business entity, the purchase price is seldom negotiated on the basis of the values of the individual assets and liabilities of the entity being acquired. Instead, it is more likely to be determined by reference to the purchase of a stream of future profits or cash flows, so that a value is arrived at for the entity as a whole.

Nevertheless, for the purposes of the consolidated financial statements the transaction has to be 'looked through' in order to determine initial carrying values for the underlying assets and liabilities of the acquired entity. This is sometimes described as a process of allocating the purchase price to the underlying net tangible and intangible assets to arrive at a 'cost' to the group. Establishing initial carrying values for those assets and liabilities, as a proxy for their cost, also provides a basis for reporting the performance of the enlarged group from the date the new entity is acquired.

25.146 The elements of accounting for a typical business acquisition can be demonstrated as follows:

Purchase consideration

Add: Expenses of acquisition

=

Cost of acquisition

Less: Fair valued assets and liabilities

=

Goodwill on acquisition

25.146.1 Fair values are a key part of acquisition accounting because:

- The fair value of the purchase consideration determines the cost of acquisition of the investment to the acquiring company.
- The fair value of the identifiable net assets acquired will be used as the carrying amounts for the newly acquired assets and liabilities in consolidated financial statements.
- The difference between the cost of acquisition and the sum of the fair values of the identifiable assets less liabilities is goodwill.

25.147 The principle of fair valuing assets and liabilities in acquisition accounting has been recognised for many years, both in the UK and internationally. The principle is also recognised in the Companies Act 1985, which requires that a newly acquired subsidiary's identifiable assets and liabilities must be included in the consolidated balance sheet at their fair values, as at the date of acquisition. [CA85 4A Sch 9(2)].

25.148 While the principle is relatively simple, applying it in practice has proved a difficult matter. FRS 7, 'Fair values in acquisition accounting', was issued in 1994 and has brought rigour to the principles to be applied when acquisition accounting.

Scope and basic principles of FRS 7

Scope

25.149 FRS 7 deals with fair value in the context of the acquisition of subsidiary undertakings by a parent company that prepares consolidated financial statements. Acquired subsidiary undertakings can include unincorporated entities, such as partnerships. The principles of the FRS also apply where a group or an individual company acquires the trade and assets of an unincorporated business (including a division of a company). [FRS 7 para 4]. Whether the acquisition is of a subsidiary or a business, it is necessary for the acquirer to account for the cost of acquisition by recognising the underlying assets, liabilities and goodwill of the acquired subsidiary or business. A subsidiary's assets, liabilities and goodwill will be recognised at fair value in the acquiring company's consolidated financial statements. Where a business is acquired the fair values will be reflected in the acquiring company's own financial statements.

25.150 Other transactions that require fair value accounting, and the calculation of goodwill, include:

- The purchase of an additional interest in an existing subsidiary from a minority shareholder. FRS 2 states that when a group increases its interest in an undertaking that is already its subsidiary, the identifiable assets and liabilities of that subsidiary should be revalued to their fair values and goodwill arising on the increase in interest should be calculated by reference to those fair values (except where the effect of changes in value is not material). [FRS 2 para 51]. (See section I, para 25.84.)
- The purchase of interests in associated undertakings and joint ventures which are accounted for under the equity method or gross equity method in accordance with FRS 9. [FRS 9 para 31].

The principles of FRS 7 are relevant to accounting for the above transactions in the acquirer's consolidated financial statements.

Purchase of business or assets

25.151 The definition of an 'acquisition' in FRS 7 derives from the definition of a 'business combination', which is framed as *"the bringing together of separate entities into one economic entity as a result of one entity uniting with, or obtaining control over the net assets and operations of, another"*. [FRS 7 para 2].

25.152 In some purchase transactions, it is necessary to determine whether the substance of the transaction is really the acquisition of a business or simply the purchase of assets or other payment. In the latter case, the transaction does not give rise to goodwill in the acquirer's financial statements, but results in the recording of any identified assets at their cost, as evidenced by the purchase price.

25.153 The above definitions imply that, for acquisition accounting to be applicable, the acquired entity must be more than a collection of assets and liabilities. It would normally be carrying out a continuing trade with an identifiable turnover, which means that the assets and liabilities of the acquired entity interact with each other and, importantly, with the people who operate the assets as a business.

Objective

25.154 The standard's overriding objective is twofold:

- All the assets and liabilities that existed in the acquired entity at the date of acquisition should be brought into the acquirer's financial statements at fair values reflecting their condition at that date.
- All changes to the acquired assets and liabilities, and the resulting gains or losses, that arise after control has passed to the acquirer are reported as part of the post-acquisition financial performance of the acquiring group.

[FRS 7 para 1].

25.155 By restricting the assets and liabilities recognised in the fair value exercise to those that already existed in the acquired entity, and by limiting the extent to which future events may be anticipated in arriving at fair values, the ASB has established a strict framework for determining whether revenues and costs should be treated as pre-acquisition (that is, reported within the pre-acquisition assets and liabilities of the target) or post-acquisition (that is, reported as profits or losses) in the acquirer's consolidated financial statements.

25.156 Consistent with its stated objective, the FRS precludes an acquirer from recognising any costs of planned post-acquisition reorganisation in the fair value exercise and, as a result, in the calculation of purchased goodwill, because they were not liabilities of the acquired entity at the date of acquisition. This framework has introduced a significant change from previous acquisition accounting practices, where it had been accepted that initial fair values could be adjusted to take account of changes anticipated by the acquirer when bidding for control.

Fair value of identifiable assets and liabilities

Overriding principles

25.157 The objective of FRS 7 is reflected in the two stated principles that underpin the standard for determining initial fair values for the assets and liabilities of an acquired entity, which are:

- The identifiable assets and liabilities to be recognised should be those of the acquired entity that existed at the date of the acquisition. [FRS 7 para 5].

- The recognised assets and liabilities should be measured at fair values that reflect the conditions at the date of the acquisition. [FRS 7 para 6].

Identifying the assets and liabilities acquired

Definitions of assets and liabilities

25.158 Identifiable assets and liabilities are defined as:

> *"The assets and liabilities of the acquired entity that are capable of being disposed of or settled separately, without disposing of a business of the entity"*. [FRS 7 para 2].

This definition is for all intents and purposes the same as the definition in the Act. [CA85 4A Sch 9(2)].

25.159 An acquiring company should review its acquisition and determine all the identifiable assets and liabilities as soon as possible after making the purchase. Goodwill is not an identifiable asset, because it cannot be sold separately from a business.

25.160 Definitions of assets and liabilities have been developed by the ASB in its Statement of Principles, and have been incorporated into FRS 5, 'Reporting the substance of transactions'. These definitions are implicitly embodied in the principles of FRS 7. Assets are defined as:

> *"Rights or other access to future economic benefits controlled by an entity as a result of past transactions or events."* [FRS 5 para 2].

Liabilities are defined as:

> *"An entity's obligations to transfer economic benefits as a result of past transactions or events."* [FRS 5 para 4].

25.161 When applied to acquisition accounting the 'entity' is the acquired entity. The past transactions or events giving rise to the rights or obligations (including those that are contingent) of the acquired entity must have occurred before the date of acquisition if they are properly to be regarded as pre-acquisition.

25.162 Therefore, to qualify for recognition in the fair value exercise, FRS 7 requires that, in the case of assets, the rights to future benefits must have been obtained by the acquired entity before the date of acquisition. In the case of liabilities, there must have been a commitment by the acquired entity before the date of acquisition to transfer economic benefits.

25.163 The definitions of assets and liabilities quoted above are wide ranging and encompass most items that would usually be recognised in the balance sheet of an acquired entity under conventional accounting principles. For example, the definition of assets would generally include prepayments, where payments have been made which give the acquired entity rights to obtain future services or access to future benefits. Similarly, the definition of liabilities would generally include, in addition to creditors and accruals, items of deferred income, where the entity has still to incur costs in respect of future obligations relating to payments that have been received. These items, which would normally be recognised in the financial statements of the acquired entity, should also be taken into account in the fair value exercise.

Inclusion of additional assets and liabilities

25.164 Not all items that meet the above definitions of assets and liabilities are necessarily recorded in the financial statements as soon as they are identified. Consequently, some identifiable assets and liabilities may need to be recognised by the acquirer although they have not been recognised in the financial statements of the acquired entity.

25.165 An acquisition requires a fair value allocation to be made, so far as is practically possible, over all the existing assets and liabilities of the acquired entity. Ensuring that all pre-acquisition assets and liabilities are recognised at the acquisition date ensures that the post-acquisition profit and loss account will not include any items relating to the pre-acquisition period, giving more useful post-acquisition performance information.

25.166 Examples of liabilities that may not previously have been booked in the acquired company's financial statements, but would be included as fair value adjustments, include provisions for the following:

- Onerous financial contracts entered into by the acquired company, such as forward, futures and options contracts, where the provision is calculated by reference to current market values of the relevant financial instruments.
- Contingent losses, provided that the contingency was in existence before the acquisition (see para 25.350 for further discussion of contingencies).
- Losses arising from pre-existing contractual arrangements, such as 'poison pill' clauses in shareholder agreements or compensation clauses in directors' service contracts, that are triggered in the event of a change of ownership, that is, where the crystallisation of the liability is independent of any decision or action of the acquirer. This type of identifiable liability is referred to in the explanation section of the standard. [FRS 7 para 37].

25.167 Following the issue of FRS 12, UK entities should have recognised provisions for items such as environmental clean up obligations related to their past activities, or provisions for onerous contracts. However, the principle in FRS 7 requiring recognition of liabilities of the entity at the date of acquisition means that even if such items have not been recognised by the acquired entity (for example, an overseas company), they will be identifiable liabilities for the fair value exercise.

25.168 In each of the above examples, the item meets the criteria for recognition in the fair value exercise because either the obligation had been incurred before the acquisition or the underlying contingency giving rise to the provision was in existence before the acquisition and, in the last case, the outcome was not dependent on the acquirer's intentions. Various practical examples are considered in paragraph 25.177 below.

25.169 FRS 7 makes specific reference to onerous contracts and commitments:

> *"Identifiable liabilities include items such as onerous contracts and commitments that existed at the time of acquisition, whether or not the corresponding obligations were recognised as liabilities in the financial statements of the acquired entity".* [FRS 7 para 38].

Whilst the standard does not define what 'onerous' means, this should generally be interpreted with reference to its basic principles. Firstly, a contract must have been onerous to the acquired entity at the date of acquisition and not have become onerous as a result of the acquirer's actions. Secondly, whether or not a contract is onerous can often reasonably be interpreted as meaning whether or not the obligation exceeds the current (that is, at date of acquisition) market value.

25.170 Examples of potentially onerous contracts include long-term supply contracts for commodities such as oil, gas and electricity, where the price to which the acquired company is committed exceeds the current market price for such contracts. They should usually be capable of being bought and sold in an arm's length transaction. They would not be recognised on the acquired entity's balance sheet unless, unusually, it had a policy of marking such contracts to market or they qualified as onerous contracts under FRS 12. The 'losses' derived from fair valuing such commitments – the value at which a contract for a similar product, a similar amount and for a similar future delivery date could be entered into at the date of acquisition – would be recognised as identifiable liabilities in the fair value exercise.

25.171 Long-term purchase commitments that are onerous contracts under FRS 12 (that is, those that result in loss-making business – see chapter 21), clearly have to be recognised as liabilities in the fair value exercise. However, an important consideration in fair valuing other long-term purchase commitments is that there should be consistency of treatment. This means that where other long-term purchase commitments (that is, those that are unfavourable, but which are used in profitable business) are recognised as identifiable liabilities, all such commitments, whether unfavourable or favourable, should be recognised. Thus where commitments have been entered into at prices lower than current market prices for equivalent commitments, the 'gains' derived from valuing them at fair value should be recognised as assets in the fair value exercise.

25.172 Table 25.7 gives an example of onerous purchase contracts recognised as fair value adjustments.

Table 25.7 — United Utilities PLC — Annual Report & Accounts — 31 March 1996

Notes to the accounts (extract)

12 Purchase of subsidiary (extract)

The Group acquired NORWEB plc on 8 November 1995 and the acquisition method of accounting has been adopted. The analysis of net assets acquired and the fair value to the Group is as follows:

	Book value £m	Revaluation £m	Accounting policy alignment £m	Other £m	Fair value to Group £m
Tangible fixed assets	779.3	234.9	–	–	1,014.2
Investments	147.4	247.6	–	–	395.0
Stocks	68.4	–	(3.7)	–	64.7
Debtors	248.2	–	(14.7)	(21.1)	212.4
Cash and cash equivalents	254.9	–	–	–	254.9
Creditors falling due within one year	(281.0)	(48.0)	–	4.0	(325.0)
Creditors falling due after more than one year	(517,7)	(32.5)	–	–	(550.2)
Provisions for liabilities and charges*	(44.2)	(1.0)	(1.3)	(217.9)	(264.4)
Net assets before special dividend	655.3	401.0	(19.7)	(235.0)	801.6
Special dividend, including advance corporation tax	(195.6)	–	–	–	(195.6
Net assets	459.7	401.0	(19.7)	(235.0)	606.0
Consideration:					
Cash					1,463.2
Shares allotted					197.0
Share option obligations					22.7
Total consideration					1,682.9
Goodwill arising					1,076.9

Explanations of the major fair value adjustments in the above table are given in the financial review on pages 12 and 13.

The fair value adjustment of £217.9 million relating to provisions for liabilities and charges includes £173.2 million in respect of onerous gas and electricity contracts.

The fair value adjustments are provisional and may be subject to revision in the 1996/97 accounts. Any adjustments made will be reflected in the goodwill calculation.

Financial review (extract)

Acquisition of Norweb (extract)

Norweb's net assets acquired, excluding the special dividend and associated advance corporation tax, amounted to £801.6 million. This was after a net increase of £146.3 million for provisional fair value adjustments.

The **distribution network** was revalued upward on the basis of the return being earned on those assets increasing the net book value by £248 million.

The **investments** in the National Grid and Pumped Storage Business were revalued upward by £199.6 million, net of £48.0 million tax provisions, reflecting the net proceeds received on disposal.

Provision was made for **gas and electricity contracts** of £173.2 million mainly in relation to long term power purchase agreements, where the recent collapse in gas prices and reduced capacity costs resulted in onerous conditions compared to prices available in November 1995, the date the fair valuation was made. The provisions are of a long term nature and, in any event, will not be utilised prior to 1998. Also included is a small element relating to short term take or pay gas purchase contracts.

Other adjustments are given in note 12 to the accounts.

The fair value adjustments will be reviewed again during the course of 1996/97 and amended as necessary in the light of subsequent knowledge or events.

* Note that, for years beginning on or after 1 January 2005, SI 2004/2947, 'The Companies Act 1985 (International Accounting Standards and Other Amendments) Regulations 2004', changes this schedule 4 line item to 'provisions for liabilities'.

Exclusion of certain assets and liabilities

25.173 Conversely, certain items recognised by the acquired entity may not be recognised by the acquirer. An obvious example is where purchased goodwill is recognised as an asset in the acquired entity's balance sheet in respect of its previous acquisitions. That purchased goodwill is by definition not an identifiable asset and would be subsumed within the calculation of goodwill arising on the acquisition in the acquirer's consolidated financial statements. Another example is development expenditure capitalised in the accounts of the acquired entity. In the fair value exercise it may, for example, be impossible to arrive at a reliable fair value relating to the balance of unamortised deferred development expenditure; alternatively, deferral of development costs may be inconsistent with the accounting policies of the acquiring group (see 25.175 below). In those circumstances, it would be necessary to reflect the value of all past research and development expenditure in goodwill.

25.174 Where the acquired entity has booked provisions for expenditure not yet incurred, the standard requires the circumstances to be considered very carefully in order to determine whether the provisions are proper pre-acquisition liabilities. It states that "*only if the acquired entity was demonstrably committed to the expenditure whether or not the acquisition was completed would it have a liability at the date of acquisition*". [FRS 7 para 40]. Any provisions that fail this test do not meet the definition of identifiable liabilities and should be added back to the net assets of the acquired entity in the fair value exercise. This issue is considered further in paragraph 25.200.

Adjustments for different accounting policies

25.175 FRS 7 requires that, subject to the detailed rules that apply its principles to specific types of assets and liabilities of an acquired business, recognition and measurement should be determined in accordance with the acquirer's accounting policies for similar assets and liabilities. [FRS 7 para 8].

25.176 Examples where fair value adjustments may be necessary to achieve consistency with the acquirer's accounting policies include: current assets affected by different revenue recognition policies; and deferred tax liabilities where the acquirer has adopted a policy of discounting but the acquiree had not. The purpose of the requirement to base fair values on the acquirer's accounting policies is so that post-acquisition performance is not distorted purely by accounting policy differences.

Examples — identifiable liabilities or post-acquisition costs

25.177 Some examples of items that would be included in pre-acquisition liabilities and items that would be treated as post-acquisition costs are considered below:

Example 1 — Vacant leasehold property

An acquired company has a lease on a property that it no longer occupies. The acquirer decides to move out of one of its existing properties, which it also leases, and occupy the surplus property leased by the acquired company. The acquirer decides to incur the costs of early termination of its existing lease.

FRS 12 considers the general question of whether the rent payable and other expenses of vacant leasehold property should be provided for when such property ceases to be used. FRS 12 requires provision to be made where there is an onerous contract. An example of an onerous lease contract is one where the property is vacant and the company is unable to find a sub-lessee or can only sub-let at a rental less than it is paying under the head lease.

Following the principles of FRS 7 and FRS 12, the acquired company's obligations in respect of the lease on the vacant property is likely to be an identifiable liability that existed at the date of acquisition. If provision is appropriate in the circumstances of the acquired company at the date of acquisition, it should be recognised in the fair value exercise as a liability of the acquired company.

The reoccupation of the property leased by the acquired company and the abandonment of the property leased by the acquirer are part of the post-acquisition reorganisation of the combined group and, therefore, the financial effects of the relocation would be included in the consolidated profit and loss account. Thus any provision recognised as an identifiable liability at the date of acquisition would be written back and the cost of terminating the acquirer's lease would be written off, with both items being treated as post-acquisition.

Example 2 — Property vacated in rationalisation

An acquired company had occupied a rented warehouse. After the acquisition the acquiring group rationalised its distribution facilities and the warehouse occupied by the acquired company was vacated. The group is making provision for the rentals payable under the unexpired lease.

Under FRS 7 the abandonment of the property should be accounted for as a post-acquisition event. The provision for rent payable on the property being vacated should be charged in the profit and loss account as part of the cost of post-acquisition reorganisation.

Example 3 — Property lease at above market rent

An acquired company leases its head office on an operating lease. The rent for the next 15 years is fixed at a level that is in excess of the rents payable on leases of comparable buildings that are on the market at the time of the acquisition. This is not an onerous lease under FRS 12 as the company continues to occupy the property and the business of the acquired company makes adequate profits to absorb the lease costs. Can provision be made in the fair value exercise for the lease, that is, the difference between the committed lease payments over the term of the lease and those that would reflect current market rents?

There are alternative approaches to this question. One view is that operating leases are not recognised as liabilities under standard accounting practice, and FRS 7 does not specifically indicate that they should be recognised in acquisition accounting. SSAP 21 requires rents payable under operating leases to be expensed on a straight-line basis over the term of the lease; the method of expensing is not accelerated (or decelerated) as market rentals fluctuate. Only timing differences between the amount of rentals expensed and rentals paid are normally recognised as accruals or prepayments. Under this view, the 'above-market' element of the lease is not regarded as an identifiable liability, and no provision is recognised in the fair value exercise. The actual lease payments would continue to be expensed in the acquirer's consolidated profit and loss account unless, and until, the acquirer managed to renegotiate the lease.

A different view is that recognising a provision for the 'above-market' element of the lease when accounting for the acquisition is entirely consistent with FRS 7's principles as regards identifying, and measuring at fair value, the acquired company's existing obligations. A leasehold interest will have a negative value where the rent reserved under the lease exceeds the open market rental. By recognising a provision for this commitment's estimated market value, the acquiring group would be reflecting the fact that in effect it would have received an incentive to take on such a lease, in the form of a reduction in the purchase consideration. Under the principles of UITF Abstract 28, 'Operating lease incentives', a cash incentive given to a lessee to take on a lease is recognised as a liability initially and is allocated to reduce the future rental expense over the shorter of the lease term and a period ending on a date from which it is expected the prevailing market rental will become payable.

In our view, it is acceptable for an acquirer to have an accounting policy of fair valuing an acquired company's leases. Of course, if this treatment is adopted, it should be applied consistently by valuing all leasehold interests acquired. Where applicable, any favourable operating leases (that is, where the rent under the lease is below the current open market rentals) should be included as assets in the fair value exercise. Whether or not the acquirer has a policy of fair valuing operating leases, the policy should also be applied consistently to all acquisitions.

An identifiable liability that is recognised in the fair value exercise in respect of the 'above-market' rentals is not a type of provision that is normally recognised under FRS 12 where no acquisition is involved. Instead, the liability established at the acquisition date would in effect be treated as a premium received for taking on the lease. The balance would not be re-measured in subsequent years if market rentals change, but would be amortised to reduce the future rental expense during the lease.

Example 4 — Relocation costs

Company A acquired a subsidiary of company B. The subsidiary occupied premises that it shared with other operations in B's group. As part of the purchase agreement the new subsidiary was required to vacate those premises. Company A is making a provision in the accounts of the subsidiary for the estimated costs of relocation.

Under FRS 7 the relocation costs were not an identifiable liability of the acquired subsidiary at the date of acquisition. The relocation is a post-acquisition event and is not, for example, an action that the subsidiary was committed to whether or not the acquisition was completed, nor the crystallisation of a pre-existing contingent liability. In addition, FRS 12 does not permit costs of relocation to be provided in advance. [FRS 12 paras 85, 86]. The costs of relocation should, therefore, be charged as incurred as a post-acquisition revenue cost in company A's consolidated financial statements.

Example 5 — Golden parachute

The directors of the target company have clauses in their contracts that entitle them to receive twice their basic salary, together with an amount in respect of loss of pension benefits, if they decide to terminate their contracts within 28 days of an offer for more than 50% of the company's share capital being declared unconditional. The company has been taken over and the directors have exercised their rights to terminate their contracts and claim compensation.

In this example, a so-called golden parachute, the acquirer has no control over the decision to terminate the service contracts of the acquired company's directors and incur the consequential costs. As the change of ownership clauses were already in existence before the acquisition took place, those directors had the right to claim compensation regardless of the acquirer's intentions towards the acquired company. It is, therefore, appropriate to treat the compensation costs as identifiable liabilities resulting from the crystallisation of a pre-acquisition contingency, that is, to include them as fair value adjustments under the principle in paragraph 37 of FRS 7.

In contrast, if the acquirer decided to fire the directors of an acquired company where those directors had no such rights to terminate their contracts as a result of an acquisition, it would not be appropriate to accrue for the ensuing compensation costs in the fair value exercise. That is because paragraph 7 of FRS 7 requires changes resulting from the acquirer's intentions or actions after the acquisition to be treated as post-acquisition costs. Similarly, the costs would be post-acquisition if artificial arrangements were made between acquirer and target to put in place such clauses during the negotiations for the acquisition.

Example 6 — Redundancy costs

Company A has acquired company B. Company A has the management capacity to integrate the operations of company B into its own operations without taking on the majority of B's employees. The purchase price for B of £20m has been negotiated in contemplation of redundancy costs of £2m being incurred after the acquisition. The employees to be made redundant, and their costs, had been identified during the course of negotiations and a formal plan had been drawn up and agreed between the acquirer and vendor. The balance sheet in the completion accounts of B included a provision of £2m in respect of the anticipated redundancy costs.

In accordance with paragraph 40 of FRS 7, the redundancy costs of £2m should be treated as post-acquisition costs in company A's consolidated financial statements. Despite the fact that provision was included in the completion accounts of company B, the provision was clearly made for the purposes of reaching an agreed purchase price with company A, and did not reflect expenditure that company B was committed to whether or not the acquisition was completed.

Example 7 — Redundancy costs and vendor refunds

Facts as in the previous example except that, instead of a provision being included in the completion accounts, the purchase price payable on completion is £22m and the vendor has undertaken to refund up to £2m as and when the employees of company B are made redundant after the acquisition. In addition, company B is currently making losses and the agreement says that up to £1m should be refunded in respect of future operating losses of company B.

In accordance with paragraph 7 of FRS 7, both the future redundancy costs and the future operating losses should be treated as post-acquisition in the consolidated profit and loss account of company A because they are not identifiable liabilities of company B at the date of acquisition. Amounts up to £3m refunded by the vendor of company B would be applied by company A to reduce the purchase consideration, that is, the cost of investment in company B and goodwill.

Some accountants would argue that the amounts refunded should be matched with the costs and losses to which they relate, that is, that they should be credited in the profit and loss account. However, the net purchase price of £19m payable to the vendor reflects the fact that the acquired business is loss-making and requires management action to turn it around. Such action involves incurring revenue costs. Following the principles in FRS 7, the short-term operating losses and the costs of reorganisation should all be shown as part of post-acquisition performance.

Intangible assets

25.178 FRS 7 makes only the briefest of references to identifiable intangibles. It merely states that "*where an intangible asset is recognised, its fair value should be based on its replacement cost, which is normally its estimated market value*". [FRS 7 para 10].

25.179 A number of companies have included a variety of intangibles in their fair value exercises in recent years. Such intangibles have included brand names, publishing titles, the embedded value of life insurance, milk quotas and even company names. Intangibles can constitute very significant proportions of a company's consolidated balance sheet. For example, a substantial portion of the capital employed of Reed Elsevier comprises intangibles identified on past acquisitions, see Table 25.8.

Table 25.8 — Reed Elsevier plc — Annual Review — 31 December 1996

Accounting policies (extract)

Intangible fixed assets

Publishing rights and titles, databases, exhibition rights and other intangible assets are stated at fair value on acquisition and are not subsequently revalued. Having no finite economic life, no systematic amortisation is applied, but provision is made for any permanent impairment in value. Internally developed intangibles are not carried on the balance sheet. Intangible assets are only recognised on more significant acquisitions.

Combined Balance Sheet (extract)

£ million	1996
Fixed assets	
Intangible assets *note 13*	2,550
Tangible assets note 13	323
Investments note 14	180
	3,053
Current assets	
Stocks	139
Debtors: amounts falling due within 1 year *note 15*	667
Debtors: amounts falling due after more than 1 year *note 16*	147
Cash and short term investments *note 17*	1,141
	2,094
Creditors: amounts falling due within 1 year *note 18*	(2,146)
Net current (liabilities)/assets	(52)
Total assets less current liabilities	3,001

25.180 This treatment has reflected the increased commercial importance of brands and similar assets in the context of many acquisitions. This is because the most significant value is often in intangible benefits rather than in the tangible assets of the acquired entity. The practice has attracted much attention among preparers and users of financial statements, with the debate centred around two problem areas: first the problem of establishing which intangibles are truly identifiable assets; and secondly the problem of how to value them.

25.181 The problem of accounting for intangibles was eventually settled with the publication of FRS 10. The ASB considered that, because some intangibles, such as brand names, are very similar to goodwill, the most important principle was that the accounting treatment should be the same irrespective of whether intangibles are labelled separately on the balance sheet or subsumed within goodwill.

25.182 Since FRS 10 requires purchased goodwill to be capitalised and accounted for alongside intangible assets, the separate recognition of intangibles has become less of an issue. Nevertheless, the standard sets three thresholds that must be passed before an intangible asset of an acquired business can be capitalised separately from goodwill:

- Separability.
- Control.
- Reliable measurement.

25.183 First, FRS 10's definition of an intangible asset requires it to be identifiable. Identifiability is a basic concept in both FRS 7 and the Act for recognising any asset and liability in an acquisition (see para 25.158). Separability is a key component of the definition of an identifiable asset. FRS 10 explains that an asset is not identifiable if it *"can be disposed of only as part of the revenue-earning activity to which it contributes"*. [FRS 10 para 2].

25.184 These words do little to clarify the issue – some intangibles are more clearly separable than others, but defining the cut remains subjective. In practice, the standard admits a wide range of intangibles such as those specifically mentioned in the balance sheet formats in the Act (concessions, patents, licences, trademarks and similar rights) as well as quotas, publishing titles, franchise rights and brands. But not all such items would necessarily be identifiable in all circumstances; to some extent this depends on how fundamental the intangible item is to the continuation of the acquired business. A business name is much less likely to qualify as identifiable.

25.185 Secondly, an identifiable intangible must be controlled through custody or legal rights that secure an entity's access (and restrict the access of others) to the benefits that are expected to derive from it. In practice, this rules out recognition of items such as a skilled workforce or a customer list because, whilst they may be extremely valuable to a business, the business does not control them and, hence, their value is part of its goodwill.

25.186 Thirdly, an intangible should be recognised if (and only if) its initial fair value can be measured reliably. [FRS 10 para 10]. The FRS refers to two categories of intangibles:

- Intangibles with a readily ascertainable market value.
- Intangibles that are unique to the business.

25.187 In practice, hardly any intangibles fall into the first category. The FRS defines them as belonging to a homogeneous population of assets that are equivalent in all material respects and where there are frequent transactions in an active market. These are very strict conditions, because the FRS also allows intangibles of this type only to be revalued and to be recognised where they have been self-developed. The FRS suggests that some operating licences, franchises and quotas might meet these conditions (although many of these will in fact be unique).

25.188 The ASB has been sceptical about the reliability of valuations of unique intangibles such as brands and publishing titles where there is no market value as such. This is evident in FRS 10, because the standard specifically precludes intangibles (other than those with a readily ascertainable market value) from being recognised to the extent that their valuation would increase the net assets of the acquired business above the purchase price to give rise to negative goodwill. The standard accepts, however, that certain entities that regularly buy and sell them have developed reliable valuation techniques that would allow them to be capitalised separately from purchased goodwill as a result of an acquisition. This implies that those entities that are not in that position may legitimately choose not to attempt to value such intangibles and may subsume them within goodwill. The accounting treatment and valuation of intangibles is discussed in chapter 15.

Post-acquisition reorganisation and integration costs

25.189 FRS 7 specifically requires the following items to be *excluded* from the fair value exercise and treated as post-acquisition items in the acquirer's consolidated financial statements:

- The accounting effects of changes to the acquired entity resulting from the acquirer's intentions or future actions.
- Impairments in asset values, or other changes, resulting from events subsequent to the acquisition.
- Provisions for future operating losses.
- Provisions or accruals for reorganisation and integration costs expected to be incurred as a result of the acquisition, whether they relate to the acquired entity or to the acquirer.

[FRS 7 para 7].

Background

25.190 Prior to FRS 7 there had been much criticism of the use of provisions and the making of excessive asset write-downs in fair valuing acquisitions. By setting up provisions in the fair value exercise, in the post-acquisition period companies could offset subsequent costs that would otherwise have to be charged in the profit and loss account against those provisions. On the other hand, if provisions are not set up as fair value adjustments, these costs of reorganisation will flow through to the profit and loss account in the subsequent periods and will, therefore, adversely affect the earnings per share of the combined group.

25.191 The principal objection that was raised by many companies to the treatment of reorganisation costs in the manner prescribed by FRS 7 was that, in their view, it does not reflect commercial reality. In their view, where an acquiring company has taken account of the costs of future reorganisation in arriving at a price it is prepared to pay, those costs should be reflected as capital costs. They argue that such costs should be included in the fair value exercise and should not be charged as revenue costs in the profit and loss account in subsequent periods. This view was supported by one ASB member in a 'dissenting view' published with the standard. However, the majority view in FRS 7 prevailed.

25.192 One of the ASB's main arguments for the approach taken in FRS 7 has been that financial statements should treat the costs and benefits of reorganisations related to acquisitions in the same manner as reorganisations of continuing operations. The benefits derived from realising synergy, and from implementing other post-acquisition restructuring and investment programmes, add post-acquisition value to the acquiring group by improving its profitability. Consequently, the costs of achieving such improvements should also be treated as post-acquisition. Those costs should be treated as revenue or capital according to normal accounting principles. The ASB has also stated that the approach adopted in FRS 7 is consistent with its Statement of Principles and with the profit and loss account formats introduced by FRS 3.

Post-acquisition activities

25.193 There are many reasons why companies seek to expand by acquisition. These might include:

- Gaining access to new markets.
- Diversification into a new business or a different product line.
- Expanding market share or protecting an existing market position.
- Acquiring production or distribution facilities, market skills or other expertise.
- Achieving economies of scale by rationalising facilities.
- Securing the supply of a key component or service.
- Financial reasons such as securing the utilisation of unrelieved tax losses and allowances.

25.194 A successful acquisition will normally involve:

- A thorough investigation of the target before the acquisition is completed.
- A detailed post-acquisition integration plan for maximising the value of the acquisition to the acquiring group.

25.195 In other words, few companies buy blind. They have commercial and strategic plans underlying their acquisitions, conduct a detailed evaluation and due diligence exercise and develop a strategy for getting the required or best return out of the enlarged operation. Frequently this means that the integration plans are already at an advanced stage of development, even before the acquisition contract is signed.

25.196 The post-acquisition plan would examine how the combining organisations are to be fitted together. It would identify opportunities to:

- Integrate activities, for example by harmonising systems and strategies. This would include activities such as consolidating marketing and advertising functions, financial control systems, data processing and other administrative systems.
- Achieve cost savings by reducing management and other overheads.
- Rationalise activities through closure of facilities that are surplus to the combined group.
- Invest in the development of the target company's business.

25.197 FRS 7 does not permit provisions to be made in the fair value exercise to cover the costs of such post-acquisition activities, even where these costs were taken into account by the acquirer when negotiating the acquisition price, because they were not liabilities of the acquired entity at the date of acquisition. The following are examples of items, as disclosed in companies' financial statements, that have been included as acquisition provisions in arriving at the fair value of net assets acquired, under pre-FRS 7 practices. Under FRS 7 these items should be treated as post-acquisition costs:

- Redundancy costs.
- Closure of head office and certain branches of acquired company.
- Costs of restructuring and strategically realigning operations to acceptable levels of efficiency.
- Cost of implementing strategic changes subsequent to acquisition.
- Costs of implementing the acquirer's quality standards, including training.
- Costs of converting and integrating acquired retail outlets into the acquirer's chain.
- Plant and other fixed assets written off as part of post-acquisition reorganisation.
- Rationalisation and reorganisation of existing business as a consequence of the acquisition.

Anti-avoidance measures

25.198 FRS 7 contains measures specifically addressed at a potential loophole concerning the timing of provisions for future reorganisation. Provisions for the type of expenditure to be incurred in reorganisation plans are generally booked before the relevant expenditure is incurred. Most acquisitions do not involve hostile bids, but are agreed between willing buyers and willing sellers. The ASB has been concerned that, particularly in the case of 'friendly' takeovers, there could be scope for provisions for reorganisation planned by the acquirer to be booked by the acquired company during the course of negotiations with the acquirer, and before the date of acquisition. Those provisions would then be entered as pre-acquisition liabilities when the newly acquired company is consolidated. An example is where reductions in excessive manpower in the acquired company are 'negotiated' during the course of the acquisition. Potentially a significant principle of the standard could relatively easily be circumvented.

25.199 The FRS (together with FRS 6, which contains the relevant disclosure provisions) deals in three ways with the problem of provisions made by the acquired company shortly before the acquisition. The explanation states that:

- Only if the acquired entity was demonstrably committed to the expenditure whether or not the acquisition was completed would it have a liability at the date of acquisition. [FRS 7 para 40].
- If obligations were incurred by the acquired entity as a result of the influence of the acquirer, it would be necessary to consider whether control (or the power to control) had been transferred at an earlier date and, consequently, whether the date of acquisition under FRS 2 should also be taken to be an earlier date. [FRS 7 para 40].
- *Disclosure* is required in the fair value table of any provisions for reorganisation and restructuring costs made within the 12 months preceding the date of acquisition that are included in the identifiable liabilities acquired, together with related asset write-downs. [FRS 7 para 40; FRS 6 para 26].

25.200 As mentioned in paragraph 25.174 above, a pre-condition for inclusion in the identifiable liabilities at the date of acquisition is that the acquired entity must have been *committed* to a particular course of action by the date of acquisition.

25.201 This approach to the recognition of certain liabilities is already embodied in FRS 3, where principles are set out in respect of setting up provisions for losses on businesses to be sold or terminated. That standard requires a provision to be made if, but not before, a decision has been made to close an operation *and* the commitment is evidenced by a detailed formal plan from which the reporting entity cannot realistically withdraw.

25.202 It follows from the above that, if a reorganisation provision set up by the acquired entity before the date of acquisition relates to a reorganisation that is only implemented because of the acquisition, the provision should not be treated as an identifiable liability of the acquired entity in the fair value exercise. This is because the acquired entity is not committed to the expenditure before the acquisition, as it is conditional on the acquisition taking place.

25.203 Similarly, if a reorganisation provision set up by the acquired entity before the date of acquisition relates to its plans as a stand-alone operation, but those plans are subsequently cancelled by the acquirer before they have been implemented, the provision should not be treated as an identifiable liability of the acquired entity. That is because the acquired entity could not have been demonstrably committed to the expenditure regardless of whether or not the acquisition was completed.

25.204 In practice, it may be unlikely that management of a company being acquired could commit the company irrevocably to a particular course of action at the request of an acquiring company unless the completion of the acquisition was a foregone conclusion. If they did bind the acquired company, this might suggest that the acquirer had *de facto* already obtained control.

25.205 If the acquirer has gained control, or has the power to control, the date of acquisition should be brought forward and the new subsidiary should be consolidated from the earlier date. Hence, the profits and losses (including the reorganisation provisions) would be brought into the acquirer's consolidated profit and loss account from that earlier date. Identifying the date of acquisition for the consolidated financial statements is dealt with in FRS 2 and is considered in section I, from paragraph 25.18. It should be stressed that all aspects of the relationship between the acquirer and the target would need to be considered before the date of acquisition is brought forward. Where, for example, completion of the acquisition is conditional on the approval of the shareholders of the acquirer, it is unlikely that, in practice, control could have passed at an earlier date. It is equally unlikely in such a case that the acquired company could, in fact, commit itself irrevocably to the reorganisation.

25.206 The effect of the above anti-avoidance measures is that any commitments entered into by the acquired company at the request of the acquirer may well be deemed to be post-acquisition in substance. However, it is not unusual for a vendor to reorganise a business that is to be put up for sale in order to make the business more attractive to a potential purchaser. The purchase price would then reflect the business in its reorganised or semi-reorganised state. Thus reorganisation costs may be incurred by a company shortly before it is sold and there may be some provisions related to the reorganisation that are properly regarded as pre-acquisition liabilities.

25.207 The ASB also seeks to ensure that the spirit of FRS 7 is observed, in respect of reorganisation provisions, by requiring disclosure, in the fair value table, of any reorganisation provisions that were made by the acquired company in the 12 months immediately preceding the date of acquisition and which are included in its pre-acquisition liabilities.

Disclosure of post-acquisition reorganisation costs

25.208 FRS 7 requires that all post-acquisition reorganisation costs should be charged in the profit and loss account of the acquiring group. The ASB believes that, where they are material, separate disclosure of such costs is important for a proper assessment of post-acquisition performance to be made, particularly in the context of the 'information set' style of the profit and loss account under FRS 3. To some extent these disclosures may mitigate the adverse effect of the accounting requirements in the eyes of preparers.

25.209 All the disclosure requirements relating to acquisitions, including those stemming from FRS 7, are consolidated in FRS 6. FRS 6 *requires* the following disclosure regarding reorganisation costs to be made in the financial statements of an acquiring group for each material acquisition, and for other acquisitions in aggregate:

- The profit and loss account or notes to the financial statements of periods following the acquisition should show the costs incurred in those periods in reorganising, restructuring and integrating the acquisition. [FRS 6 para 31].

- If material, these costs should be shown as exceptional items, and disclosed separately from other exceptional items, whether they relate to a fundamental restructuring or not. [FRS 6 para 86].

25.210 FRS 6 explains that post-acquisition integration, reorganisation and restructuring costs, including provisions in respect of them, would, if material, be reported as exceptional items under FRS 3. If, and only if, a reorganisation or restructuring is fundamental, having a material effect on the nature and focus of the *enlarged* group's operations, would the costs be included as one of the items required by paragraph 20 of FRS 3 to be shown separately on the face of the profit and loss account after operating profit and before interest. [FRS 6 para 86].

25.211 Tables 25.9, 25.10, and 25.11 show examples of different methods that have been used to present acquisition reorganisation costs in the profit and loss account.

Table 25.9 — SmithKline Beecham plc — Annual Report and Accounts — 31 December 1994

CONSOLIDATED PROFIT AND LOSS ACCOUNT (extract)

	Notes	Comparable business £m	Acquisitions (note 1) £m	Business performance £m	One-off items (note 1) £m	**1994 £m**
Sales						
Continuing operations		5,877	194	6,071	–	**6,071**
Discontinued operations		421	–	421	–	**421**
	1	6,298	194	6,492	–	**6,492**
Cost of goods sold		(2,109)	(95)	(2,204)	(243)	**(2,447)**
Gross profit		4,189	99	4,288	(243)	**4,045**
Selling, general and administrative expenses	2	(2,261)	(85)	(2,346)	(320)	**(2,666)**
Research and development expenditure	2	(620)	(1)	(621)	(17)	**(638)**
Trading profit						
Continuing operations	1&2	1,224	13	1,237	(580)	**657**
Discontinued operations	1&2	84	–	84	–	**84**

NOTES TO THE FINANCIAL STATEMENTS (extract)

One-off items

A restructuring provision, to be utilised over three years, of £580 million has been established and is included under a separate column headed 'one-off items' on the profit and loss account. This provision is to cover the cost of closing Sterling's New York headquarters; the integration of the Sterling and existing Consumer Healthcare operations; the establishment of an integrated Pharmaceutical and Consumer Healthcare International business; the creation of shared services across all of the business operations and the reorganisation of the Group's supply chain.

The 'one-off items' column also includes the tax charge arising on the reorganisation of Sterling in connection with the sale by SB of Sterling's North American business and a credit associated with the deferred tax asset arising on the creation of the restructuring provision. (see note 5).

Table 25.10 — Reckitt and Colman plc — Report & Accounts — 31 December 1994

Group profit and loss account (extract)

Notes		1994 £m	1993 £m
3	**Sales to customers:**		
	Continuing operations	**2,070.78**	2,068.09
	Discontinued operations	**8.17**	27.56
	Total sales to customers	**2,078.95**	2,095.65
3	Cost of sales	**(1,073.22)**	(1,048.26)
	Gross profit	**1,005.73**	1,047.39
	Net operating expenses	**(834.67)**	(735.94
3	**Operating profit:**		
	Continuing operations [1]	**169.35**	305.22
	Discontinued operations	**1.71**	6.23
4	**Total operating profit**	**171.06**	311.45

[1]In 1994 operating profit from continuing operations is stated after charging exceptional reorganisation costs of £56.00m in Europe and £83.10m in connection with the L&F Household integration in the USA.

Table 25.11 — Scottish Power plc — Annual Report & Accounts — 31 March 1996

Group Profit and Loss Account (extract)

	Before acquisitions 1996 £m	**Acquisitions 1996 £m**	**Total before reorganisation costs 1996 £m**	**Reorganisation costs 1996 £m**	**Total 1996 £m**	Total 1995 £m
Turnover from continuing operations	**1,832.1**	**439.4**	**2,271.5**	–	**2,271.5**	1,715.8
Cost of sales	**(1,091.3)**	**(283.7)**	**(1,375.0)**	–	**(1,375.0)**	(1,011.8)
Gross profit from continuing operations	**740.8**	**155.7**	**896.5**	–	**896.5**	704.0
Transmission and distribution costs	**(152.4)**	**(49.8)**	**(202.2)**	**(1.0)**	**(203.2)**	(141.9)
Administrative expenses	**(199.6)**	**(28.6)**	**(228.2)**	**(41.7)**	**(269.9)**	(188.0)
Other operating income	**7.8**	**3.1**	**10.9**	–	**10.9**	6.0
Operating profit from continuing operations	**396.6**	**80.4**	**477.0**	**(42.7)**	**434.3**	380.1

The group profit and loss account includes under Acquisitions the results of Manweb for the period 6 October 1995 to 31 March 1996.

25.213 Where a post-acquisition reorganisation does not qualify as fundamental in the context of the operations of the enlarged group, the costs should be charged in arriving at the profit or loss on ordinary activities before tax and shown under the statutory format headings to which they relate. In practice, this means that reorganisation costs that qualify as exceptional items (but are not fundamental) would be shown in arriving at operating profit or loss. In accordance with FRS 3 the amount should be disclosed separately by way of note, or on the face of the profit and loss account if that is necessary to give a true and fair view.

25.214 FRS 6 *suggests* that, for major acquisitions where post-acquisition reorganisation is expected to extend over more than one period, management may wish to disclose in the notes the total expenditure expected to be incurred and the nature of the expenditure. This suggested disclosure analyses the total: between amounts charged in the profit and loss account and further amounts expected to be incurred; and between cash expenditure and asset write-offs. [FRS 6 para 87].

25.215 The above-mentioned suggested disclosures were in response to users who believed that it is important to be able to ascertain the total expected costs relating to an acquisition. They also enable management to present what they believe to be the true total acquisition cost, that is, the consideration given for the acquisition plus, for example, the planned costs of turning the acquisition around and integrating it into the acquiring group. Appendix IV to FRS 6 gives an example of the type of disclosure that the ASB had in mind.

25.216 Many companies already give significant disclosures about the progress of recent acquisitions, details of post-acquisition integration plans and their associated costs in the part of the annual report in which the Board reviews the group's activities for the year. Discussion of post-acquisition reorganisation plans and their likely future benefits, together with the subsequent monitoring of those costs and benefits, often forms an integral part of this disclosure. See further chapter 2 of the Manual of Accounting – Management reports and governance.

[The next paragraph is 25.218.]

25.218 There are two practical issues regarding the disclosure of exceptional post-acquisition reorganisation costs required by FRS 6:

- What is *fundamental* in the context of the enlarged group?
- Which costs should be included in the captions that are required to be separately disclosed as costs of *reorganising, restructuring and integrating the acquisition*?

Fundamental reorganisation or not

25.219 Identifying a fundamental reorganisation under FRS 3 is considered in chapter 8. FRS 6 makes it clear that whether a post-acquisition reorganisation is fundamental must be judged in relation to the enlarged group. It is not automatic that such costs would be shown as a non-operating exceptional item. Clearly, the use of judgement is required to determine whether a particular reorganisation is fundamental or not. However, by requiring the reorganisation to have a material effect on both the nature and focus of the enlarged group's operations, it is implicit that the reorganisation should encompass the whole or a substantial part of the enlarged group's total operations and should not be a reorganisation of only one among many different operations of the enlarged group.

25.220 At one end of the spectrum, a group may acquire a new subsidiary and run it as a stand alone operation. The acquired subsidiary may be reorganised to achieve cost savings, but the existing operations of the subsidiary and the group are essentially left intact. The reorganisation would not be fundamental to the enlarged group, nor even probably to the acquired subsidiary. In this situation, the reorganisation costs should be charged in arriving at operating profit and, if material, separately identified. FRS 3 already requires the profit and loss account of an acquiring group to disclose separately (in aggregate) the operating results attributable to acquisitions made in the year, as a component of the group's continuing operations.

25.221 At the other end of the spectrum, a group may make a substantial acquisition in its core business. Soon after the acquisition the business of the new subsidiary is subsumed into the existing operations of the acquiring group. The post-acquisition plan for the enlarged group involves material expenditure in respect of both integrating the combining operations and repositioning their market focus. This results in the enlarged group withdrawing from certain market sectors and investing in those that are core to the group's future strategy. The restructuring goes to the root of the enlarged group's operations and the repositioning process includes significant asset disposals from both the pre-existing and acquired operations. In these circumstances, the post-acquisition reorganisation is likely to be fundamental and the costs would be shown separately after operating profit.

25.222 However, in the majority of cases it is likely that post acquisition reorganisation costs will be included as part of the acquiring group's operating results and not as fundamental reorganisation or restructuring. Although the integration of combining operations may require significant reorganisation across the enlarged group, this fact alone does not make the reorganisation fundamental. A fundamental reorganisation must involve a material change in the nature and focus of the enlarged group's operations — that is, the combined operations of the acquirer and acquired business after the acquisition — and this would need to result in the repositioning of its products or services in their markets.

Nature of reorganisation costs

25.223 The nature of reorganisation costs is important because requiring post-acquisition reorganisation costs to be shown in the profit and loss account would not, of itself, remove the often publicised possibilities under previous practices for flattering the operating results following an acquisition. In practice, the headline reporting of performance tends to focus on a company's operating results. If the amount shown under exceptional reorganisation costs (in particular, fundamental costs) were inflated by items that should properly be shown as normal operating costs, the operating result would also be inflated.

25.224 FRS 6 gives a strict definition of which costs are permitted, as a matter of principle, to be included in the captions of costs relating to reorganising, restructuring and integrating an acquisition. It states that such costs are those that:

- Would not have been incurred had the acquisition not taken place.
- Relate to a project identified and controlled by management as part of a reorganisation or integration programme set up at the time of acquisition or as a direct consequence of an immediate post-acquisition review.

[FRS 6 para 31].

25.225 Subject to meeting the criteria in the above paragraph, examples of costs that might be included under this definition are:

- Employee redundancy and early retirement costs.
- Costs of relocating facilities as part of an integration plan.
- Contract cancellation costs.
- Plant closure costs, including costs of eliminating duplicate facilities.

- Write-off of fixed assets and stocks relating to the reorganisation.

  (The write-down of assets is mentioned in paragraph 87 of FRS 6 as a potential component of reorganisation costs, which suggests that the profit and loss charge is properly shown under reorganisation costs rather than as, for example, losses on the disposal of fixed assets.)

- Incremental costs incurred in converting branches of the acquired company into the format of the acquiring group.

- Incremental costs incurred in implementing the administrative and management information systems of the acquiring group into the acquired company.

- Costs of retraining the workforce of the acquired company.

25.226 FRS 6 refers to costs of integrating as well as reorganising and restructuring the acquisition. Consequently, it appears that some integration costs admitted under this caption could relate to the acquirer's own business, provided that the costs are incurred as a direct consequence of the acquisition and relate directly to the activities being integrated. Such costs might include the following:

- Costs of closing facilities in the acquiring group that are duplicated in the enlarged group in preference to closing those of the acquired company.

- Costs of redundancies in the acquiring group resulting from the merging of head office functions.

25.227 Where other activities of the acquiring group are reorganised following an acquisition, the costs would not be admitted into the FRS 6 definition.

25.228 The following items would not appear to qualify as costs of reorganising, restructuring and integrating the acquisition. They should be included in the relevant headings in normal operating costs:

- Ongoing salaries of staff to be made redundant, unless they have effectively been made redundant, that is they have ceased to provide services to the group.

- Operating costs of running facilities to be merged or closed pending the implementation of the reorganisation plan.

- Internal management costs relating to time spent on developing and implementing the reorganisation plan.

25.229 It might be argued that some of the above items, for example the 'additional' costs of running two departments rather than one, should be included as reorganisation costs because they are additional costs incurred from the time of the acquisition to the date of the implementation of the reorganisation. Arguments against this are: first, it does not reflect what happened after the acquisition, because the fact is that two departments did exist and their operating costs were incurred; secondly, it is probable that each of the departments in fact carried out a necessary task up to the date that the reorganisation was implemented and, therefore, until that time the costs incurred were not, in fact, 'additional' costs.

Disclosure of acquisition provisions

25.230 FRS 6 *requires* movements on provisions or accruals for costs related to an acquisition to be disclosed and analysed between the amounts used for the specific purpose for which they were created and the amounts released unused. [FRS 6 para 32]. The information should be disclosed separately for each material acquisition and for other non-material acquisitions in aggregate. Inclusion of the word 'accruals' is interpreted to mean that the information should be given in respect of all material costs accrued and shown in the profit and loss account as costs of reorganising, restructuring and integrating an acquisition and not just those that are shown in the balance sheet under the caption of provisions. An example of the disclosure is given in Table 25.12.

Table 25.12 — Glaxo Wellcome plc — Annual Report and Accounts — 31 December 1995

Notes on the Accounts (extract)

19 Provisions for liabilities and charges* (extract)	Integration costs £m	Pensions and other post-retirement benefits £m	Deferred taxation £m	Other provisions £m	Total £m
At 1st July 1994 as previously stated	–	90	139	64	293
Prior period adjustment	–	26	(9)	–	17
At 1st July 1994 restated	–	116	130	64	310
Exchange adjustments	–	3	(3)	2	2
Acquisition of subsidiary undertakings	–	92	187	75	354
Charge/(credit) for the period	1,215	138	(251)	67	1,169
Applied	(384)	(34)	(33)	(67)	(518)
At 31st December 1995	831	315	30	141	1,317

The provision for integration costs at 31st December 1995 represents the costs expected to be incurred in integrating the business of Glaxo and Wellcome.

* Note that, for years beginning on or after 1 January 2005, SI 2004/2947, 'The Companies Act 1985 (International Accounting Standards and other Amendments) Regulations 2004', changed the Companies Act line item to 'provisions for liabilities'.

25.231 FRS 6 and FRS 7 set out requirements for identifying and disclosing post-acquisition reorganisation costs. They do not provide any guidance on the principles for setting up provisions for such costs where they are expected to be incurred over more than one period. Recognition and measurement rules that apply to provisions for restructuring costs generally are contained in FRS 12. These rules affect the amount of 'one-off' acquisition reorganisation provisions that can be charged in the immediate post-acquisition period. Where costs relating to a post-acquisition reorganisation and integration programme are charged over more than one period, FRS 6 suggests that management may wish to disclose the total expected costs, indicating the extent to which they have been charged in the profit and loss account, in order to give a fuller picture of the progress of the post-acquisition plan. [FRS 6 para 87]. Appendix IV to the standard provides an illustration, in tabular form, of how this information might be presented by analysing details of amounts charged and amounts still to be charged.

Measuring fair values of identifiable assets and liabilities

Meaning of fair value

25.232 FRS 7 defines fair value as:

> *"The amount at which an asset or liability could be exchanged in an arm's length transaction between informed and willing parties, other than in a forced or liquidation sale".* [FRS 7 para 2].

25.233 This basic definition of fair value, or similar versions of it, is well recognised in accounting literature. The problem in accounting for business combinations is that many of the assets and liabilities to be recognised in an acquisition are not regularly exchanged in arm's length transactions. Consequently, the definition is of limited practical use in measuring fair values for this purpose.

25.234 Before FRS 7, it had been accepted practice for acquisitions to be fair valued from the perspective of the acquiring company. The perspective of the acquirer was favoured because it took into account the acquirer's plans for the future and its style of operation. It was also consistent with the concept of the acquirer's perspective that provisions for reorganisation costs included in those plans should be taken into account in the fair value exercise.

25.235 The ASB considered that the notion of a 'fair value to the acquiring company' seemed to contradict the basic definition of fair value, which is a market value concept reflecting both buyers and sellers. The ASB also argued that, as a general principle, management intent is not a sufficient basis for recognising changes to an entity's assets and liabilities; and in the context of acquisition accounting, the acquirer's intentions regarding the future use of acquired assets are not necessarily relevant to determining their cost.

25.236 Consequently, FRS 7 rejected the acquirer's perspective as a principle for determining fair values. Instead, the standard attempts to adhere to the definition of fair value by requiring that:

- Fair values should reflect the conditions at the date of acquisition.
- Fair values should *not* reflect:
  - Changes resulting from the acquirer's intentions or future actions.

- Impairments, or other changes, resulting from events subsequent to the acquisition.

[FRS 7 paras 6, 7].

25.237 The basic concept of fair value in FRS 7 is, therefore, free from any particular 'perspective'. It attempts to establish what the price paid for a whole business represented, taking into account the conditions of the acquired business, including its existing cost structures, that existed at the time of acquisition.

25.238 The last part of the definition of fair value in paragraph 25.232 indicates that fair values of individual assets and liabilities should generally be valued on a going concern basis, even if the business was acquired cheaply in a fire sale from, for example, a vendor who was in financial difficulty. In circumstances where the acquirer has obtained a bargain purchase as a result of a forced or liquidation sale, the fair values of the identifiable net assets may well exceed the cost of acquisition, with negative goodwill arising on consolidation.

25.239 The standard provides a detailed framework for establishing fair values for individual categories of assets and liabilities. Although the concept of fair value as described above is intended to prevail, there are several exceptions or modifications to the concept when applied in practice to certain assets and liabilities where market values do not exist. This framework draws heavily on the chapter of the ASB's Statement of Principles, 'Measurement in Financial Statements', that deals with valuations in financial statements generally. This describes the concept of deprival value or 'value to the business' that in many cases corresponds to fair value under FRS 7.

25.240 The overall framework can be summarised as follows:

- Fair values are indicated by market values where similar assets are bought and sold on a readily accessible market.
- Where market values are not available, or are inappropriate to the circumstances of the acquired company, fair values should be based on replacement cost, reflecting the acquired company's normal buying process and the sources of supply and prices available to it (but see below).
- The fair value of an asset should not exceed its recoverable amount. Therefore, where the fair value of an asset is based on its depreciated replacement cost, the recoverable amount will also need to be considered.

  The recoverable amount of an asset is in effect the maximum discounted cash flows that can be obtained from the asset, either by selling it or by continuing to use it (see para 25.280 below).
- A valuation of an asset at recoverable amount should reflect its condition on acquisition, but not any impairments or enhancements resulting from subsequent events or actions of the acquirer.

- The accounting policies of the acquiring group should be adopted where they affect fair values attributed to assets and liabilities.

25.241 The attribution of fair values is not determined from the 'acquirer's perspective', in the sense that the acquirer's intentions for the future use of assets do not affect the valuation of the business as it stood when it was acquired. However, fair values can only be arrived at under the system described in paragraph 25.240 after a detailed investigation of the acquisition by the acquirer. Therefore, in several cases fair values would represent the acquirer's judgement of the worth of the underlying assets in their existing state.

25.242 Examples of situations where considerable judgement needs to be exercised by the acquirer include:

- Review of useful lives of fixed assets, for determining depreciated replacement cost.
- Compilation of cash flow projections for the business being acquired, for determining the recoverable amount of assets where the business is unable to recover the depreciated replacement cost.
- Review of provisions against the value of slow-moving stock, for determining net realisable value.
- Review of the recoverability of debtors.

25.242.1 In carrying out the fair value exercise, it would be appropriate to work at a fairly detailed level and, therefore, to assign fair values to individual assets or small groups of assets. For example, if a property portfolio is being fair valued, it would usually be necessary to carry out the exercise on individual assets. Clearly, this may not be possible where stocks are concerned. Also, where a business of the acquired company is to be resold soon after acquisition, the standard requires the whole business unit to be valued as a single item (see further para 25.322).

Period for completing the fair value exercise

25.243 The standard requires that fair values of assets and liabilities should be based on conditions at the date of acquisition. They should not generally be affected by matters arising after this date. In practice, sufficient time is required to enable an acquirer to examine the acquisition in order to identify all the assets and liabilities existing at the date of acquisition and to perform a full and reliable fair value exercise.

25.244 As far as the assets and liabilities of the acquired company are concerned, the fair value exercise should, if possible, be completed by the date on which the board of the acquirer approves for publication the acquiring group's first annual financial statements following the acquisition. [FRS 7 para 23].

25.245 However, the standard recognises that some acquisitions need more time to be properly investigated. Situations where this is likely to arise include the following:

- The acquisition is complex and is completed late in the financial year of the acquirer.
- The acquired company has assets and liabilities where more evidence is required before they can be valued reliably — examples include evaluating environmental liabilities and contingent liabilities involving legal claims.

25.246 In circumstances where the fair value exercise cannot be completed in time for publication of the acquirer's first post-acquisition financial statements, FRS 7 requires *provisional* fair values to be included. These provisional fair values should be amended, if necessary, in the next financial statements with a corresponding adjustment to goodwill. [FRS 7 para 24].

25.247 The cut-off point for making fair value adjustments is, therefore, the date of approval of the acquirer's second annual financial statements after the acquisition. By basing the investigation period on the financial year of the acquirer rather than on an absolute time limit, there could in practice be significant differences in the time available for completing the fair value exercise in respect of different acquisitions. The time available depends on the timing of an acquisition in relation to the financial year end of the acquirer and could, in theory, extend for over two years.

Subsequent amendments to fair values

Amendments after investigation period has expired

25.248 Amendments may still be necessary to fair values after the investigation period, as described above, has expired. Because the standard does not allow any further goodwill adjustments to be made, the effect of such amendments should, where applicable, be dealt with in the profit and loss account for the year. If material, they may require separate disclosure as exceptional items.

25.249 The only exception to the above treatment is where amendments discovered outside the permitted investigation period result from fundamental errors in the fair value exercise rather than from the normal process of revising estimates that is inherent in financial reporting. An example is where hidden problems relating to past activities of the acquired company are only discovered later by the acquirer. In these circumstances, the fundamental errors would, in accordance with FRS 3, be treated as prior period adjustments, that is, by adjusting the goodwill arising on the acquisition.

25.250 An example of adjustments that have been treated as fundamental errors was contained in the accounts of Ferranti International Signal plc (see Table 25.13).

Table 25.13 — Ferranti International Signal plc — Annual report & accounts (revised) — 31 March 1989

Notes to the accounts (extracts)

1 Basis of accounting

For the reasons given in paragraphs 2 to 4 of the Report of the Directors the accounts of the group and the parent company for the year ended 31 March 1989, despatched to shareholders on 11 August 1989, have been withdrawn and revised to write off assets in respect of certain suspect contracts (as defined in the Report of the Directors) and incorporate a consequential adjustment to the fair value of the net tangible assets of International Signal & Control Group PLC ("ISC") at the date of acquisition by the company, 16 November 1987, and a restatement of the comparative amounts shown for the year ended 31 March 1988. No credit has been taken for any amounts which may be recoverable from third parties in respect of the suspect contracts. The Revised Accounts also reflect other adjustments for post balance sheet events occasioned by the extension of the date of approval of the Accounts from 13 July 1989 to 16 November 1989 and reflecting additional evidence relating to conditions in the group existing at 31 March 1989.

Note 20 Reserves (extract)

	Share premium £M	Merger £M	Revaluation £M	Profit & loss £M	Total £M
Group					
As previously reported at 31 March 1988	3.8	73.5	38.9	152.4	268.6
Adjustment in respect of acquisitions other than ISC		17.0		(17.0)	
Adjustment to the fair value of the net tangible assets of ISC as at the date of acquisition		(90.5)		(50.9)	(141.4)
Adjustment to retained profit:					
Operating profit previously taken on suspect contracts				(13.5)	(13.5)
Consequential tax effects				4.7	4.7
Currency translation effects				12.1	12.1
As restated at 31 March 1988	3.8	–	38.9	87.8	130.5
Deficit for the year				(6.6)	(6.6)
Premium on allotments	1.0				1.0
Goodwill arising on acquisitions (note 21)				(4.0)	(4.0)
Currency translation				(5.0)	(5.0)
At 31 March 1989	4.8	–	38.5	72.2	115.5

Amendments within investigation period

25.251 Where fair values attributed to the assets and liabilities of an acquired company are considered provisional in the acquirer's first post-acquisition financial statements, FRS 6 requires this fact to be stated and the reasons to be given. It also requires any material adjustments made to those fair values in the next financial statements, with corresponding adjustments to goodwill, to be disclosed and explained. [FRS 6 para 27].

25.252 The FRRP published a statement in April 1997 in connection with the financial statements of Reckitt & Colman plc concerning the adequacy of the disclosure of final adjustments to provisional fair values. The Panel noted that in its view this second stage requires a similar level of disclosure and explanation so as to comply with the requirements of paragraph 25 of FRS 6 and paragraph 13(5) of Schedule 4A to the Companies Act 1985 and should include an analysis of the adjustments and an explanation of the reasons for them.

25.253 An example of a provisional fair value allocation and subsequent goodwill adjustment is taken from the accounts of RJB Mining PLC (see Table 25.14).

Table 25.14 — RJB Mining PLC — Annual Report and Accounts — 31 December 1995

NOTES TO THE FINANCIAL STATEMENTS (extract)

23 Goodwill on acquisition of English Coal	Provisional fair value to the Group	Completion and hindsight period adjustments	Final fair value to the Group
	1994	1995	1995
	£'000	£'000	£'000
Fixed assets	643,818	(84,258)	559,560
Stock & WIP			
Coal stock	189,407	6,121	195,528
Stores	54,927	(8.278)	46,649
Work in progress	95,271	(11,781)	83,490
Debtors	2,395	(1,604)	791
Creditors	(28,264)	(1,568)	(29,832)
Provisions for liabilities and charges*			
Concessionary coal	(29,041)	–	(29,041)
Claims	(43,500)	1,673	(41,827)
Surface damage	(28,439)	–	(28,439)
Restoration and closure costs (opencast)	(41,580)	–	(41,580)
Restoration and closure costs (deep mines)	(8,832)	(1,380)	(10,212)
Draglines maintenance	(3,597)	2,508	(1,089)
Deferred taxation	(17,000)	38,441	21,441
	785,565	(60,126)	725,439
Purchase consideration	844,289	(1,074)	843,215
Goodwill written off	58,724	59,052	117,776

The principal adjustments to fair value to the group are in respect of the Asfordby colliery which has been written down to a nominal carrying value following a reassessment due to the difficult geological conditions and consequent operational problems associated with safe and economic extraction of coal from these reserves. The other adjustments to fair value in the hindsight period relate to agreement of the final acquisition cost and to asset and liability valuation and existence assessments in the period.

1. Asfordby	£77.8m
2. Revaluation of deferred opencast assets	£11.5m
3. Other	£8.2m
4. Deferred tax on adjustments	(£38.4m

* Note that, for years beginning on or after 1 January 2005, SI 2004/2947, 'The Companies Act 1985 (International Accounting Standards and other Amendments) Regulations 2004', changed the Companies Act line item to 'provisions for liabilities'.

25.254 FRS 7 indicates that fair values should not be considered provisional in the first post-acquisition financial statements unless it has not been possible to complete the investigation of fair values by then and the fact is disclosed in those financial statements. This would suggest that, where an acquirer has completed its investigation of the acquisition by the date of approval of the financial statements for the year in which the acquisition took place, and obtained all the evidence considered necessary at that time to arrive at reliable estimates of fair values based on information then available, no further adjustments should be made to those fair values (and goodwill) in the subsequent financial year.

25.255 Even if additional information is obtained in the next financial year which causes previous estimates to be changed, those changes would usually be dealt with in the profit and loss account of the period in which they are identified. This principle is consistent with normal practice in financial statements, where items relating to prior periods, which arise from corrections and adjustments that are the natural result of estimates inherent in accounting and in the periodic preparation of financial statements, are dealt with as they arise and are not adjusted retrospectively.

25.256 However, there may be exceptional situations where fair values and goodwill would need to be adjusted retrospectively in the acquirer's second post-acquisition financial statements, even where the fair values attributed to the acquired company at the previous balance sheet date had not been declared provisional in the previous financial statements.

25.257 For example, paragraph 57 of FRS 7 discusses the treatment of exceptional stock profits arising after the date of acquisition. It states that, if exceptional profits appear to have been earned on the realisation of stocks after the date of acquisition, it will be necessary to re-examine the fair values determined on acquisition and, if necessary, to make an adjustment to these values and a corresponding adjustment to goodwill. It goes on to state that if, alternatively, the profit is attributable to post-acquisition events, it should be disclosed as an exceptional item in the post-acquisition profit and loss account.

25.258 Paragraph 57 is clearly addressing a potential source of abuse, because errors made in calculating the fair value of stocks quickly feed through into the profit and loss account. If the fair value attributed to stocks is understated, post-acquisition profits are inflated by their realisation in the post-acquisition period.

Fair valuing fixed assets

25.259 If there are separately identifiable asset transactions in an acquisition, the bargained price would normally provide the initial fair value (that is, actual cost), assuming the price is a proper arm's length value. In other cases, fair values should be estimated using conventional measurement principles (that is, market value, replacement cost or recoverable amount). FRS 7 requires the choice of valuation basis to be determined by a structured analysis of the circumstances, as summarised in paragraph 25.240 above.

Market value

25.260 Where there is a ready market in the types of fixed assets held by the acquired company, market values should generally be used. Such assets would include properties in which an active market exists. Properties that are sometimes referred to as *non-specialised* properties may be included in this category — examples include shops, offices, and general purpose warehouses that could be occupied by a number of different users. Professional valuers would normally be required to value such assets.

25.261 Where assets are sold shortly after the acquisition, the price obtained will often provide the most reliable evidence of fair value at the date of acquisition.

25.262 There may be some confusion as to what market value means, because variants are used in practice when properties are included in accounts at valuations. The most commonly used bases are market value and existing use value. Until a consistent framework or guidelines are established for revaluing properties generally, it is not possible to be dogmatic about the question of market value in the fair value exercise.

25.263 Guidelines for the valuation of property assets for the purposes of financial statements are presently contained in the RICS Appraisal and Valuation Manual, published by the Royal Institution of Chartered Surveyors (RICS).

25.264 Market value, as defined in those statements, reflects the value for any use to the extent to which that value is reflected in the price obtainable in the open market between a willing buyer and a willing seller, assuming that a reasonable period of time is allowed for marketing and selling the asset. This definition corresponds closely to the definition of fair value in FRS 7, and is the basis generally used for valuing investment properties, properties held for future development and surplus properties.

25.265 Existing use value is the basis normally used for valuing properties that are occupied in the company's business and that have not been declared surplus. It is based on market value, but the valuation reflects an important assumption that the property can be used for the foreseeable future only for the existing use. It is intended to represent the cost of replacing the remaining service potential of a property.

25.266 Neither market value nor existing use value include any value attributable to the goodwill generated by the business that occupies the property with the following exception. A variation of existing use value is 'existing use as a fully operational business unit'. This basis applies to properties that invariably change hands in the open market at prices based directly on trading potential for a strictly limited use. Examples of such properties include hotels, private hospitals and nursing homes, public houses, cinemas, theatres, bingo clubs, gaming clubs, petrol filling stations, licensed betting offices and specialised leisure and sporting facilities. The valuation includes the value of the trading potential which runs with the property, but should not include any goodwill which has been created by the owner and which would not remain with the property should it be sold.

25.267 In acquisition accounting, properties that would normally be valued, under the alternative accounting rules, on an existing use value basis in the acquired company's financial statements (that is, those occupied for the purpose of its business) would also usually be valued on this basis in the fair value exercise. That is because FRS 7 requires fair values to reflect the conditions of the acquired company at the date of acquisition. If an acquirer determines to change the use of an acquired property, subsequently carrying out the necessary planning and redevelopment procedures, any resulting change in value is attributable to the acquirer's actions and, consequently, treated as post-acquisition as required by paragraph 7 of FRS 7.

25.268 FRS 7 discusses the use of market values in secondhand assets. It states that where a fair value is based on a market price, it is important to ensure that such price is appropriate to the circumstances of the acquired business. [FRS 7 para 44].

25.269 Fixed assets that can be traded in secondhand markets include cars, commercial vehicles, computer equipment and certain plant and machinery. Where, for example, a company operates a fleet of vehicles, the market price of a used vehicle that is not due for replacement may be irrelevant to the business if, as is usually the case, it would never consider replacing vehicles in the secondhand market. In this situation the standard indicates that the fair value of a vehicle should be taken to be the current purchase price of a new vehicle, depreciated to reflect its age and condition. For certain used assets the depreciated replacement cost could be significantly different from the value in the secondhand market owing to a different pattern of depreciation in value.

25.270 As a general rule, depreciated replacement cost should be used for such assets unless the acquired business is genuinely able to consider the purchase of secondhand equipment as a viable alternative to purchasing new replacement assets.

Depreciated replacement cost

25.271 Where market values are not applicable, FRS 7 explains that depreciated replacement cost should be used as a proxy for fair value, provided it does not exceed the recoverable amount.

25.272 Depreciated replacement cost should reflect the acquired business's normal buying process and the sources of supply and prices available to it. [FRS 7 para 9].

25.273 Depreciated replacement cost is normally used by professional valuers for valuing *specialised* properties. These are defined in the RICS valuation manual as those properties that, because of their specialised nature, are rarely, if ever, sold in the market, except by way of a sale of the business or entity of which it is part, due to uniqueness arising from its specialised nature and design, its configuration, size, location or otherwise. Depreciated replacement cost would also generally be the appropriate basis of valuation of such properties in a fair value exercise. Examples of properties that might be valued on this basis include chemical installations, power stations, docks, breweries and other special purpose factories.

25.274 Depreciated replacement cost is the proper basis for fair valuing most items of plant and machinery. This may be viewed as the cost of replacing an asset with one having a similar service potential.

25.275 In principle, all fixed assets should be fair valued. The carrying value in the financial statements of an acquired company should not be used in the fair value exercise unless there is a reasonable basis for concluding that the current depreciated replacement cost is not materially different.

25.276 The gross replacement cost of an asset may be determined by reference to sources of information such as:

- Suppliers' quotations and current price lists.
- Recent purchases of the same or similar assets.
- Expert knowledge of the industry, which might include expert opinion.
- Relevant specific price indices for indexing historical cost.
- Cost of modern equivalent assets.

25.277 To arrive at the depreciated replacement cost, an appropriate amount of depreciation should be deducted to reflect the age and condition of the asset. FRS 7 explains that when the acquirer is assessing the remaining useful lives and, where applicable, residual values of fixed assets for the purposes of arriving at an estimate of their depreciated replacement cost, the *acquirer's* own policies for determining depreciation rates for similar assets should be used where these differ from the acquired company's. This is consistent with the general principle in FRS 7 that accounting policies should be harmonised by way of fair value adjustments, so that post-acquisition profit and loss accounts are not distorted by this type of non-performance adjustment.

25.278 Where government grants would be available to the acquired company for the replacement of fixed assets, it would be consistent with the principles of FRS 7 for allowance to be made for such grants in the calculation of a depreciated replacement cost to the acquired company. The fair value would be reduced by the notional grant; the amount of grant deducted would normally be calculated as an amortised amount that matches the amount of depreciation deducted from the gross replacement cost in order to reflect the acquired asset's age and condition. (Any deferred income in the books of the acquired company relating to grants previously received for the purchase of fixed assets would be eliminated on consolidation.)

25.279 Fair valuing by one of the techniques referred to above is inherently a process of estimation and as a practical measure it seems acceptable to use an appropriate level of aggregation for valuing groups of similar assets rather than valuing each asset separately.

Recoverable amount

25.280 Although depreciated replacement cost places a cap on the fair values that a purchaser can ascribe, fair value should also not exceed the asset's recoverable amount.

25.281 'Recoverable amount' is defined in FRS 7 as *"the greater of the net realisable value of an asset and, where appropriate, the value in use"*. 'Value in use' is defined as *"the present value of the future cash flows obtainable as a result of an asset's continued use, including those resulting from the ultimate disposal of the asset"*. [FRS 7 para 2]. In other words the fair value attributed to a fixed asset should not exceed the net cash flows the business can recover from the asset, either by disposing of it or by continuing to use it. This is one of the most difficult and subjective areas of valuation in practice.

25.283 FRS 7 explains that an asset is impaired when its replacement cost is not recoverable in full. The recoverable amount should be assessed to reflect the condition of the asset on acquisition, but not any impairments resulting from subsequent events or actions of the acquirer. [FRS 7 para 47]. Thus, for example, if an acquirer decides to close a profitable factory occupied by the acquired company in order to rationalise the enlarged group's manufacturing facilities, any asset write-downs related to the closure (to reduce the assets' carrying values to net realisable value) should be charged in the post-acquisition profit and loss account and should not be included in the attributed fair values.

25.284 Recoverable amount needs to be considered in situations where it is unlikely that a fixed asset would be worth replacing at its current replacement cost because, even with the most efficient and profitable use of the asset, the business could not generate sufficient cash flows to earn an adequate return on the investment. Examples might include businesses owning major infrastructure assets whose replacement cost could not be recovered in full from the cash flows of the acquired business. In such situations, fair values reflecting lower recoverable amounts would need to be estimated.

25.285 The recoverable amount of fixed assets also needs to be reviewed in circumstances where the fair value exercise gives rise to negative goodwill, that is, where the fair values assigned to the identifiable assets and liabilities exceed, in aggregate, the cost of acquisition. FRS 10 requires the fair values of the acquired assets to be tested for impairment and the fair values of the acquired liabilities checked carefully to ensure that none has been omitted or understated. [FRS 10 para 48].

25.286 Where negative goodwill arising on an acquisition is material, after reviewing the assets' recoverable amounts, this may indicate that the acquirer has made a genuine bargain purchase, for example as a result of a distress sale. However, under FRS 7, negative goodwill may arise in other circumstances. For example, the purchase consideration for an acquisition may be lower than the fair value of the net assets acquired, because the acquired business is in need of reorganisation. The purchase price may reflect the fact that the acquirer has to incur reorganisation costs after the acquisition. FRS 7 does not allow the anticipated reorganisation costs to be recognised as an identifiable liability in the fair value exercise; it requires the reorganisation costs to be expensed in the profit and loss account of the acquiring group. The requirement to reassess the fair values of assets and check liabilities implies, however, that negative goodwill may be due to an error in the fair value exercise rather than being the result of a real bargain purchase.

25.287 Where the recoverable amount of an asset is estimated by reference to the 'value in use', that is *via* projected future cash flows, those cash flows should be discounted to their present value. Any valuation based on future cash flows is inherently very subjective.

25.288 One problem is that it is often very difficult to attribute cash flows to individual fixed assets. In estimating future cash flows for determining recoverable amount, FRS 7 allows assets to be considered as a group where they are used jointly. [FRS 7 para 49]. The grouping of assets by reference to cash flows is also inevitably subjective. One approach would be for such grouping to be taken as the smallest group of assets for which cash flows can be identified that are broadly independent of the cash flows of other assets or groups of assets. This approach has been adopted in FRS 11, 'Impairment of fixed assets and goodwill', which specifies methods for measuring value in use when fixed assets are reviewed for impairment. Such impairment reviews are usually carried out at the level of 'income-generating units' which comprise groups of assets, liabilities and associated goodwill that generate cash flows that are largely independent of an entity's other income streams.

25.289 FRS 7 gives no guidance on the choice of discount rate to be applied to the future cash flows in arriving at a value in use. The following two documents contain guidance on discounting and illustrate the emerging methodologies that may be useful for the purposes of estimating fair values of fixed assets by reference to recoverable amounts:

- A working paper entitled 'Discounting in financial reporting' issued by the ASB in April 1997.
- FRS 11 'Impairment of fixed assets and goodwill' published in July 1998.

25.290 The working paper explains the concepts involved in discounting where long-term assets and liabilities are measured by reference to future cash flows. The value of future cash flows is affected not only by the time value of money, but also by the variability (risk) associated with the cash flows. The paper specifically considers the value in use calculations that are required to estimate an asset's recoverable amount. The principle is that value in use represents the cash flows expected by the entity discounted at a market rate that takes account of the riskiness of the cash flows. The risk adjustment should be based on the market's price for risk. In effect, value in use is intended to simulate the market value of the cash flows expected by the entity.

25.291 Although it does not specifically deal with acquisition accounting, FRS 11 sets out in considerable detail the methodology for estimating cash flows and choosing a risk-adjusted discount rate for the purpose of calculating value in use when reviewing fixed assets for impairment. Some relevant points are summarised below.

- All relevant cash flows attributable to the group of assets or operation being valued should be taken into account, including an allocation of central overheads. Interest payments and other costs of capital are not included since these are taken into account in the discount rate.
- Cash flow forecasts should be based on reasonable and supportable assumptions and be consistent with budgets and plans that have been formally approved by management. Beyond the period covered by formal budgets and plans, the projections should generally assume a steady or declining growth rate.
- The cash flows used for estimating the value in use of income-generating units or individual fixed assets in their current condition should not include:
  - the costs or benefits that are expected to arise from a future reorganisation for which provision has not yet been made; or
  - the effects of future capital expenditure that is expected to enhance the assets from their current condition.

- The discount rate should be an estimate of the rate of return that the market would expect on an equally risky investment. Therefore, the riskiness of the cash flows, taking into account any significant uncertainties about their amount or timing, will affect the risk factor built into the discount rate. There may be a variety of means of estimating this rate including reference to:
  - The rate implicit in market transactions of similar assets.
  - The weighted average cost of capital of a listed company whose cash flows have a similar risk profile to those of the asset.
  - The weighted average cost of capital for the entity, but only if adjusted for the particular risks associated with the asset or the operation in which the asset is employed.
- FRS 11 requires that value is use is measured, for the purpose of impairment reviews, using cash flow forecasts that do not include tax cash flows. The pre-tax cash flows are discounted using a pre-tax discount rate.

25.292 The net present value that emerges from the discounted cash flow exercise will represent, in aggregate, the recoverable amount of all the identifiable assets less liabilities of the group of assets that generates the cash flows on which the calculation is based. If the recoverable amount is lower than their aggregate book value immediately before the acquisition, a fair value adjustment is required.

25.293 Any fair value adjustment to reduce aggregate book values to a lower recoverable amount will need to be allocated on a rational basis to the identifiable assets of the acquired business. FRS 11 could be used for guidance in the context of a fair value exercise. It proposes that, unless a specific asset is obviously impaired, assets with the most subjective valuations should be written down first. Any capitalised intangibles would thus be written down first; thereafter, tangible assets would be written down on a pro rata or more appropriate basis. However, no intangible asset that has a reliably ascertainable market value should be written down below its net realisable value; and no tangible asset with a net realisable value that can be measured reliably should be written down below its net realisable value.

25.294 Table 25.15 gives an example where assets acquired (on the acquisition by RJB Mining PLC of the principal coal mining activities of British Coal Corporation in England) have been fair valued at recoverable amounts.

Table 25.15 — RJB Mining PLC — Annual Report and Accounts — 31 December 1994

Notes to the Financial statements (extract)

13 Tangible fixed assets (extract)

	Land and buildings £'000	Mineral rights £'000	Mines and surface works £'000	Assets in course of construction £'000	Plant and machinery £'000	Total £'000
Group						
Cost or valuation						
At 1 January 1994	3,511	4,150	–	420	63,556	71,637
Additions	1,125	–	12,560	11,773	9,759	35,217
Acquired with Monckton	723	–	–	–	6,607	7,330
Acquired with English Coal	52,795	–	412,846	151,774	26,403	643,818
Disposals	(220)	(65)	–	(699)	(6,121)	(7,105)
Reclassification	–	(988)	485	988	(485)	
At 31 December 1994	**57,934**	**3,097**	**425,891**	**164,256**	**99,719**	**750,897**

On acquisition, book values of collieries assets have been adjusted to net recoverable amounts. These amounts have been arrived at, following existing mining plans, by estimating future cash flows, net of all costs of running collieries, including capital expenditure, an allocation of central overheads and closure restoration costs and discounting these to their present values. The discount rate used has been based on the weighted cost of capital and taking into account appropriate risk. The methodology used to value fixed assets on acquisition is in accordance with Financial Reporting Standard 7 and Technical Release 773 issued by the Institute of Chartered Accountants in England and Wales.

Fair valuing stocks

25.295 Fair values of stocks and work-in-progress are determined using the same measurement principles as for fixed assets, that is by reference to market value, replacement cost or net realisable value, according to the circumstances. 'Value in use' is not an issue in the valuation of stocks, because stocks are held for resale and not for their continued use in the business.

25.296 The application of 'value to the business', or deprival value, principles to stocks mean that, in general, the valuation relates to the acquired company as a buyer rather than a seller. Consequently, FRS 7 does not require a profit element to be included in the fair value of finished and partly finished stocks. This means that, where stocks are revalued to market value or replacement cost, the consequent reduction in post-acquisition profits (assuming stock values move up rather than down) when the revalued amounts feed through into cost of sales is limited to the effect of market price or input price changes during the period the stocks were held by the acquired company. Often, where the turnover period is short, the effect of price changes will be immaterial and no revaluation will be necessary. Consequently, the post-acquisition operating profit of the acquired company will not be reduced in the acquirer's consolidated financial statements by the application of replacement cost principles.

25.297 If fair values are attributed to stocks, and these values are in excess of historical cost to the acquired company, it would seem that the provisions of SSAP 9 would not allow the fair values to be incorporated in the financial statements of the acquired company. This is because the standard requires that stocks, other than long-term contracts, should be recorded at the lower of cost and net realisable value. [SSAP 9 para 26]. Fair values should be incorporated in the consolidated financial statements because they represent cost to the group, but not in the acquired company's financial statements if they are in excess of cost to that company.

25.298 It will again be necessary for the group to keep separate records of any stocks that are recorded at fair values in excess of cost to the acquired company. A consolidation adjustment will be necessary to adjust the profits and stocks of the acquired company for the effect of the fair value exercise, for so long as the stocks remain unsold.

25.299 Whether market value, replacement cost or net realisable value is used, FRS 7 stresses that the basis of valuation must be consistent with the circumstances pertaining to the acquired company at the date of acquisition. Thus, for example:

- Market values are relevant where stocks are replaced by purchasing in a ready market to which the acquired entity has access. [FRS 7 para 52].
- Replacement cost should reflect the acquired company's normal buying process, the sources of supply available to it and its current cost of manufacture. [FRS 7 paras 12, 53].
- Estimates of net realisable value should be justified by the circumstances of the acquired entity before acquisition. [FRS 7 para 57]. However, the standard's definition of fair value does not permit stocks to be written down to values that would reflect a forced or liquidation sale.

Market value

25.300 Fair values would normally be based on market values in the following cases:

- Commodity and dealing stocks.
- Land and buildings held as trading stock.
- Land and buildings held for development.

Replacement cost

25.301 FRS 7 explains that for most manufactured stocks, fair value is represented by the current cost to the acquired company of reproducing the stocks. Account should be taken of the way the acquired company purchased or manufactured the stocks. [FRS 7 paras 52, 53].

25.302 The implications for the valuation of raw materials, work in progress and finished goods are as follows:

- Raw materials should be valued at replacement cost, reflecting the acquired company's normal sources of supply and current prices available to it.
- Manufactured work in progress and finished goods should be valued at the current cost of bringing the stocks to their present location and condition, reflecting the acquired company's own cost structures at the date of acquisition. Current standard costs would be used where these are available and reliable.
- Properties in the course of development would usually be valued at the replacement cost to the acquired company of the land and the development at its current stage of completion.
- Bought-in finished goods should be valued at replacement cost, reflecting the acquired company's normal sources of supply and current prices available to it.

25.303 In times of low inflation in manufacturing input prices, it is likely that the difference between historical cost and current replacement cost of most short-term manufactured stocks would not be material. In such circumstances no fair value adjustments would be necessary. There is an existing Companies Act requirement to disclose any material difference between the historical cost of stocks and their current replacement cost. [CA85 4 Sch 27(3)].

25.304 FRS 7 explains how these principles should be applied to determine the replacement cost of certain long-term maturing stocks, such as distillery products and growing timber. As an example, a whisky distiller holds stocks of whisky at different stages of maturity; there is also a market in semi-matured whisky. In a fair value exercise the question is whether such stocks should be valued at a market price or at the acquired company's own replacement cost.

25.305 FRS 7 indicates that market prices should be used if the acquired company normally purchases stocks in the market. If it does not replace stocks by purchasing in the market, then market prices would not be used. Where, as is likely to be the case, there is market trading at the margin, but the market is very thin compared to the volumes of stocks held, the standard indicates that market prices would not be appropriate. Where replacement by manufacture would not be possible in the short term, the standard suggests that a surrogate for replacement cost may be found in the historical cost of the stocks, together with an interest cost in respect of holding the stock. [FRS 7 para 55].

25.306 An example of fair valuing long-term maturing stocks is taken from the financial statements of Guinness PLC when it accounted for the acquisition of Distillers. (Table 25.16.) The policy described appears to correspond to the method suggested by FRS 7.

Table 25.16 — Guinness PLC — Annual Report — 31 December 1986

Notes to the consolidated accounts (extracts)
15 Effect of the acquisition of Distillers on the Consolidated Balance Sheet (extract)

(ii) Stocks

Stocks have been included at fair value which has been determined by taking account of costs of production, including financing costs, and after writing off surplus stocks and providing for costs of realisation.

18 Stocks

	1986 £m	1985 £m
Raw materials and consumables	127	52
Work in progress	11	8
Stocks of maturing whisky	788	82
Finished goods	118	55
Goods purchased for resale	77	55
	1,121	**252**

The estimated replacement cost of all stocks is not materially different from the above figures.

In accordance with the Group's accounting policy, stocks of maturing whisky include an appropriate proportion of financing costs in determining production costs. At 31 December 1986 the total cost of £788m included £360m as a result of the application of this policy, of which £62m arose during the period. The balance of £298m represents the amount remaining of the accumulated financing costs taken into account in the Group's assessment of fair value at date of acquisition and is stated after a reduction of £46m in respect of sales during the period.

The net adjustment to stocks of £16m during the period, resulting from the increase of £62m and the reduction of £46m as set out above, has been credited to the profit and loss account as described in Note 7.

25.307 The emphasis on valuing stocks according to the existing cost structures of the acquired company means that one potential source of fair value adjustment is avoided. An acquiring company might consider that it could reduce the cost base of the acquired company and, accordingly, lower its cost of sales, by reorganising its manufacturing operations and negotiating discounts with its suppliers. Under FRS 7 the acquirer is not allowed to reduce the fair value of the acquired company's stocks if it believes it could have produced those stocks more cheaply. Thus, the benefit of lower cost of sales would not feed into the acquirer's post-acquisition operating results until stocks produced after the post-acquisition reorganisation (that is, at a lower cost) are sold.

Net realisable value

25.308 The principles for determining net realisable value of stocks are set out in SSAP 9. The calculation of provisions to reduce stocks from cost to net realisable value is often subjective and involves the use of different criteria by different companies. Where an acquisition is involved, the acquirer should review the book values of slow-moving, excess or obsolescent stocks and, if necessary, make adjustments to those values to reflect the application of its own criteria as represented by its own accounting policies.

25.309 FRS 7 explains that any material write-down in the fair value exercise should be justified by the circumstances of the acquired company before acquisition. [FRS 7 para 57]. As with any other impaired assets, the fair value attributed to stocks should not reflect any impairments resulting from post-acquisition events, such as stock written off in a post-acquisition reorganisation.

Example 1

The management of a company that is acquired may have certain stocks that are slow moving, but which they hope to sell after conducting an advertising campaign. They may, therefore, value these stocks at cost. The management of the acquirer may decide, on investigating the company, that an advertising campaign would not work and that, consequently, the stocks are unsaleable. The management of the acquirer would, therefore, attribute a lower fair value to the stocks, as the impairment in value existed at the date of acquisition.

Example 2

An acquired company has stock relating to a continuing product range, that has been turning over within a reasonable period. The management of the acquired company considered that the net realisable value exceeded cost. The management of the acquirer decides to discontinue that product range and reduces the selling price of the product in order to achieve a quick clearance of the remaining stocks. A provision is then necessary to reduce the cost of the stocks to their new net realisable value. Under FRS 7 the fall in net realisable value is attributable to the post-acquisition actions of the acquirer and, accordingly, the provision should be charged against post-acquisition profits and not as a fair value adjustment.

25.310 Although the above examples show a clear distinction between a stock provision that is allowed as a fair value adjustment and a stock provision that should be charged against post-acquisition profits, some situations will be less clear cut.

25.311 Paragraph 57 of the explanatory section of FRS 7 indicates that some hindsight should be applied in situations where exceptional margins appear to have been earned in the post-acquisition period, that is, within the period allowed for making fair value and goodwill adjustments. First, the attributed fair values would need to be re-examined in the light of actual experience and adjusted if they are found to have been materially understated. Secondly, if the profits are attributable to post-acquisition events, they may need to be disclosed as an exceptional item as required by paragraph 30 of FRS 6.

25.312 Although the standard discusses the implications of exceptional post-acquisition profits, there is no reason why the same logic should not be used where stocks are realised at a loss in the post-acquisition period, that is, fair values should be re-examined within the permitted hindsight period and adjusted if they are found to have been overstated.

Long-term contracts

25.313 The presentation of long-term contracts under SSAP 9 is convenient for FRS 7, because amounts recorded as turnover in respect of a contract are treated as debtors and not as work-in-progress. Amounts included as work-in-progress are generally very small. Consequently, the application of replacement cost principles is unlikely to be an important issue for long-term contracts in a fair value exercise.

25.314 A 'long-term contract' is defined in SSAP 9 as *"a contract entered into for the design, manufacture or construction of a single substantial asset or the provision of a service... where the time taken substantially to complete the contract is such that the contract activity falls into different accounting periods"*. [SSAP 9 para 22].

25.315 Although such contracts usually extend for more than one year, some contracts with a shorter duration than one year should be accounted for as long-term contracts if they are sufficiently material to the activity of the period that not to record turnover and attributable profit would lead to distortion of the period's turnover and results such that the financial statements would not give a true and fair view, provided that the policy is applied consistently within the reporting entity and from year to year.

25.316 In acquisition accounting, the acquirer first needs to identify those contracts that fulfil the criteria in the definition described above. By applying the principles of accounting for long-term contracts in SSAP 9, the turnover and profit attributable to such contracts are allocated to the pre-acquisition and post-acquisition periods, as well as to discrete financial years, on a basis that matches the progress of the contracts.

25.317 As the guidance in SSAP 9 is very general, methods of calculating turnover and recognising attributable profit (or foreseeable losses) on long-term contracts vary between different companies and different industries and, of course, between different countries. Some companies in the UK take a more prudent approach to profit recognition than others.

25.318 The main source of fair value adjustments under FRS 7 is likely to be in the area of harmonising the methods of accounting in the acquired company with those of the acquirer. If, for example, both the acquiring and acquired companies took a similar approach to identifying long-term contracts, calculating turnover and determining attributable profit, no fair value adjustments would be necessary to the balances shown as amounts recoverable on contracts.

25.319 Additionally, an acquirer would wish to make a critical review of the estimated outcome of each long-term contract, in order to ensure that adequate provisions have been made by the acquired company's management for any foreseeable losses as required by SSAP 9. Fair value adjustments would be made, as necessary, where the acquirer considered existing provisions to be inadequate or excessive, taking into account the circumstances of the acquired company before the acquisition.

25.320 Where exceptional margins or deficits appear to have been earned on acquired long-term contracts post acquisition, the principles described in paragraph 25.311 above should be applied. First, previously attributed fair values should be re-examined and, if necessary, adjusted. Secondly, if the profit or loss is attributed to post-acquisition activities, the acquirer should consider whether the profit or loss should be disclosed as an exceptional item in the profit and loss account. An example of a potential exceptional item given in paragraph 85 of FRS 6 is the release of a provision in respect of an acquired loss-making long-term contract that the acquirer makes profitable.

25.321 The following question sometimes arises in connection with fair valuing long-term contracts, where contracts are acquired that are similar in nature to contracts already being carried out by the acquirer. If the contracts undertaken by the acquired company are less profitable than those of the acquirer, the acquirer may consider that provisions should be made in the fair value exercise so that the contracts acquired will then give similar margins to those of the acquirer. Clearly such a practice would be contrary to the principles of FRS 7 because, even though the contracts may not be as valuable as the acquirer would like, they are not loss-making contracts. Whereas SSAP 9 requires provision to be made for contracts that are expected to result in a loss as soon as the loss is foreseen, it does not permit provision to be made for sub-normal future profits. Consequently, such contracts cannot be identifiable liabilities of the acquired company.

Disposals of business segments

25.322 There have been many examples of acquisitions where the acquirer has subsequently disposed of unwanted portions of the acquired business, sometimes recouping the major part of his initial outlay in the process.

25.323 FRS 2 had already dealt in a limited way with the treatment of interests in subsidiaries held exclusively with a view to subsequent resale. Such an interest is defined as *"an interest for which a purchaser has been identified or is being sought, and which is reasonably expected to be disposed of within approximately one year of its date of acquisition"*. [FRS 2 para 11]. FRS 2 requires such a subsidiary to be excluded from consolidation (provided it has not previously been consolidated) and to be shown in the acquirer's consolidated financial statements as a current asset at the lower of cost and net realisable value. [FRS 2 para 29].

25.324 FRS 7 has extended this treatment to any business operation acquired and held exclusively with a view to subsequent resale, whether a separate subsidiary or not, provided that its assets, liabilities, operating results and activities are clearly distinguishable, physically, operationally and for financial reporting purposes, from the other assets, liabilities, results of operations and activities of the acquired entity. [FRS 7 para 16]. In other words, the treatment only applies to a discrete business unit, including a business that operates as a division of an acquired company, which should be accounted for in the fair value exercise as a single identifiable asset instead of a collection of underlying assets, liabilities and goodwill. Additionally, the operation must be sold as a single unit.

25.325 The accounting treatment described in this section only applies to business operations sold. If an acquirer decides to *close* an operation of the acquired business, the assets, liabilities and results of that operation should be fully consolidated from the date of acquisition. Fair values should be attributed individually to identifiable assets and liabilities according to the normal rules of FRS 7. Closure costs and asset write-downs would have to be charged in the profit and loss account to the extent that they do not relate to identifiable liabilities that already existed or to assets that were already impaired at the date of acquisition. The treatment of disposals by means of sale is, therefore, inconsistent with the treatment of disposals by closure and with the general principles of FRS 7, which do not allow the acquirer's intentions regarding the acquired business to affect the fair valuing process.

25.326 FRS 7 requires the fair value of businesses sold or held exclusively with a view to subsequent resale to be determined as follows:

- Where the business has been sold by the time the first post-acquisition accounts are approved, fair value is based on the net proceeds of the sale, adjusted for the fair value of any assets or liabilities transferred into or out of the business. [FRS 7 para 16].

  Such transfers would include items such as dividends from and capital contributions to the business between the date of acquisition and the date of disposal.

- Where the business has not been sold by the time the first post-acquisition financial statements are approved, fair value is based on the estimated net proceeds of sale. [FRS 7 para 17].

25.327 Where the business has not been sold by the time the first post-acquisition financial statements are approved, for it to be excluded from consolidation the acquirer must be able to demonstrate that:

- A purchaser has been identified or is being sought.

- Disposal is reasonably expected to occur within approximately one year of the date of acquisition.

Otherwise, normal consolidation of the assets, liabilities and results of the business according to the general requirements of FRS 2 and FRS 7 is required.

25.328 The effect of the prescribed period for disposing of the business is that the disposal must have occurred within the period allowed in FRS 7 for completing the fair value exercise, because that period extends for more than one financial year. Any provisional fair value in the first post-acquisition financial statements (based on estimated net proceeds) should be adjusted in the subsequent period, with a corresponding adjustment to goodwill.

25.329 The FRS requires that if the business is not, in fact, sold within approximately one year of the acquisition, it should be fully consolidated, with fair values attributed to the individual assets and liabilities as at the date of acquisition. [FRS 7 para 18]. This means that a prior period adjustment would be necessary, as a change of accounting policy, in order to 'backdate' the consolidation to the date of acquisition, and to re-work the fair value exercise. The prior period adjustment would involve replacing the previously identified single asset. That is, the current asset investment in the subsidiary or business would be replaced by fair values of individual assets and liabilities (and goodwill). The profit and loss account of the previous period would be adjusted to include the results of that operation from the date of acquisition. These accounting adjustments would need to be accompanied by adequate management explanation.

25.330 It is interesting to consider what would happen in the opposite scenario — where an acquired business that was consolidated in the immediate post-acquisition period (because it was not then up for sale) is actually sold in the next financial year and within a year of its acquisition. In that situation, once consolidated, a business would continue to be consolidated right up to the date of disposal, as required by FRS 2, because the exclusion from consolidation of subsidiaries held exclusively for resale does not apply where the subsidiary has previously been consolidated. There is no question of altering the previous treatment and restating comparative figures.

25.331 The choice of net realisable value as fair value at the date of acquisition is justified by the ASB on the grounds that the resale value of a business in an arm's length transaction shortly after the valuation date would normally provide the most reliable evidence of its fair value at the date of acquisition. Otherwise, if a low fair value were placed on a business segment and it were subsequently sold at a profit it would be tempting to try to present the profit as entirely due to the expertise of the new management.

25.332 FRS 7 states that fair value should not be based on net realisable value in the following cases:

- Where the adjusted net proceeds are *demonstrably* different from the fair value at the date of acquisition *as a result of a post-acquisition event*.

- Where the acquirer has made a material change to the acquired business before disposal.
- The disposal is completed at a reduced price for a quick sale.

[FRS 7 paras 16, 69].

25.333 In each of the above circumstances the proceeds from disposal may be materially different from fair value at the date of acquisition as defined in the standard. It would then be necessary to estimate separately fair values at the date of acquisition and record a profit or loss on disposal in the post-acquisition profit and loss account. An example is where there is a collapse in the market for one of the subsidiary's products, which is attributable to an identifiable post-acquisition event.

Example 1

An acquisition of a group of companies included a coffee trading subsidiary that the acquirer intends to sell. Since the acquisition date, but before the first consolidated accounts following the acquisition were completed, the price of coffee has risen by 100%, thus increasing the value of the subsidiary's stocks and the market value of the company.

If there is evidence of a post-acquisition increase in value which is reflected in the price obtained for the subsidiary, the increase should not be included in the fair value attributed to the subsidiary; it should be accounted for as a profit on the sale of an operation in the post-acquisition profit and loss account of the acquiring group.

Example 2

An acquirer has carried out a reorganisation of an acquired subsidiary prior to its resale. In such a case the net realised value would in all likelihood be above the fair value of the subsidiary at the date of acquisition. The costs of reorganisation borne by the subsidiary, and the increase in value that could reasonably be attributed to the reorganisation would (because the subsidiary is excluded from consolidation) in effect be combined and shown as a post-acquisition profit on sale, which would be disclosed as a post-operating exceptional item.

25.334 An explanatory paragraph to FRS 7 also states that where the effect is material, the net proceeds from disposal would be discounted to obtain their present value at the date of acquisition. [FRS 7 para 65]. The effect of discounting is to shelter the post-acquisition profit and loss account from any notional or actual interest cost in respect of financing the purchase of the subsidiary or business operation during the period it is held by the group. It may, therefore, be appropriate to discount the net proceeds at a debt rate of interest.

25.335 An example of an acquisition including businesses held for resale is shown in Table 25.17.

Table 25.17 — De La Rue plc — Annual Report — 31 March 1995

Notes to the Accounts (extract)

23 **Acquisitions (extract)**

On 6 February 1995 the Group acquired the entire issued share capital of Portals Group plc (Portals) for a consideration, including expenses, of £716.7m. The acquisition has been accounted for using the acquisition method.

On 7 March 1995 the Group announced its intention to dispose of all the Portals non-security papermaking businesses. These businesses are held as assets for disposal and their results are excluded from the operating profit of the Group. The book values of the assets and liabilities of the retained Portals businesses immediately prior to the acquisition and the fair value adjustments required in recognition of the change of ownership are as follows:

	Book value prior to acquisition £m	Revaluations £m	Accounting policy alignment £m	Assets for disposal £m	Fair value to the Group £m
Tangible fixed assets	**48.8**	**2.7a**	–	–	**51.5**
Stocks	**11.1**	–	**(0.8)b**	–	**10.3**
Debtors	**8.3**	**0.6c**	–	–	**8.9**
Assets held for disposal	–	–	–	**158.0d**	**158.0**
Cash at bank and in hand	**23,1**	–	–	–	**23.1**
Bank loans and overdrafts	**(6.9)**	–	–	–	**(6.9)**
Creditors due within one year	**(8.4)**	–	–	–	**(8.4)**
Taxation	**(2.1)**	–	–	–	**(2.1)**
Deferred taxation	**0.8**	**(0.8)c**	**(8.5)e**	–	**(8.5)**
Provisions for liabilities and charges*	**(5.1)**	**2.5c**	–	–	**(2.6)**
Net assets acquired	**69.6**	**5.0**	**(9.3)**	**158.0**	**223.3**
Consideration					
Cash					**402.8**
Shares issued (at market value)					**295.4**
Loan notes					**18.5**
Total consideration					**716.7**
Fair value of net assets acquired (as above)					**223.3**
Goodwill					**493.4**

Notes:

a The revaluations of plant and machinery employed in the security papermaking businesses are based upon depreciated replacement cost.

b The value of maintenance stocks has been adjusted as a result of applying De La Rue's accounting policies.

c The Portals pension scheme was revalued on acquisition. The assumptions upon which this revaluation is based are stated in note 24.

d The assets for disposal represent the anticipated net sale proceeds, as estimated by the Directors of De La Rue plc, discounted to their present value at the date of acquisition (see note 13).

e Deferred taxation has been provided for timing differences in accordance with the tax provisioning policy of De La Rue.

13 **Assets Held for Disposal**

Assets held for disposal represents the Group's investment in those companies listed as "Businesses held for resale" on page 62. These companies, all of which were subsidiaries of Portals Group plc when the Group acquired Portals Group plc, are held exclusively with a view to resale. They are held at the Directors' valuation of anticipated net sales proceeds discounted to their present value at 31 March 1995.

Included within other creditors is £3.3m owing to these businesses by the rest of the Group as at 31 March 1995, representing £2.6m of cash received and £0.7m of trading items. Apart from these transactions, during the period from acquisition to 31 March 1995 there were no material transactions between these businesses and the rest of the Group, and there were no dividends received or receivable from them.

* Note that, for years beginning on or after 1 January 2005, SI 2004/2947, 'The Companies Act 1985 (International Accounting Standards and other Amendments) Regulations 2004', changed the Companies Act line item to 'provisions for liabilities'.

25.336 Tucked away in the small print of the explanation is a sentence stating that the principles set out in the FRS for attributing expenses to the cost of an acquisition would also apply to the costs of disposals. [FRS 7 para 65].

25.337 Where fair value is based on net realised value, it is arrived at after deducting costs incurred in disposing of the business. The rules on acquisition costs restrict expenses that can be capitalised to fees and similar incremental costs that would not have been incurred had the acquisition not taken place (see para 25.426). They do not permit any allocation and capitalisation of internal costs that would have been incurred anyway. In the same way that the FRS takes a restrictive view on acquisition costs to avoid overstating the cost of acquisition, it takes a similarly restrictive view on disposal costs and prevents internal costs from being taken out of the profit and loss account and deducted from the disposal proceeds and, as a result, from increasing goodwill.

Fair valuing monetary assets and liabilities

25.338 The fair value of most short-term receivables and payables is usually not significantly different from their book values, because they reflect amounts expected to be received or paid in the short term. Fair value adjustments would usually be limited to those arising from the acquirer's different estimates of amounts recoverable or payable.

Example — Debtors

A significant debtor of an acquired company has gone into liquidation between the date of acquisition and the completion of the group accounts. No provision was made against the debtor in the acquired company's books. Is the provision now required as a fair value adjustment in the consolidated financial statements?

Any new evidence that comes to light before the fair value exercise is completed and that concerns the condition, as at the date of acquisition, of the acquired company's assets, would be taken into account in arriving at fair values. The adequacy of bad debt provisions is one area where a certain amount of hindsight is usually necessary.

FRS 21 cites the insolvency of a customer in the post balance sheet period as an example of an adjusting post balance sheet event. An adjusting event is an event that provides additional evidence relating to conditions existing at the balance sheet date. This principle is consistent with FRS 7's principle of reflecting conditions at the date of acquisition. Although the debtor was not in liquidation at the date of acquisition, it is likely that it was in financial difficulties, even if those only became apparent after the date of acquisition. On this basis we consider that the provision is a fair value adjustment.

25.339 For long-term monetary items, the time value of money also needs to be taken into account. The fair value of most long-term receivables and payables is represented by their face values where a market rate of interest is paid during the term the item is outstanding. However, fair values of long-term receivables and payables may be materially different from their book or face values where they either carry no interest or carry interest at rates significantly different from prevailing market rates at the date of acquisition. Long-term monetary items would include finance lease receivables and payables.

25.340 For example, the fair value today of £1 million receivable in one year's time is obviously less than £1 million. Similarly, the fair value today of a five year loan of £1 million carrying a fixed rate of interest of 12 per cent is greater than £1 million if the current rate for similar borrowings is 6 per cent.

25.341 In these circumstances, FRS 7 requires the items to be recognised at fair values, which are deemed to be one of the following:

- Market prices, where these are available.
- Current prices at which the business could acquire similar assets or enter into similar obligations.
- Discounted present values.

[FRS 7 para 14].

25.342 The effect of making such fair value adjustments is that the post-acquisition profit and loss account of the acquiring group shows finance charges or interest receivable that equate to market rates of interest at the date of acquisition.

25.343 The standard gives the following guidance on the choice of discount rate to be used for discounting items to their present values:

- Long-term borrowings: based on current lending rates for an equivalent term, the credit standing of the issuer and the nature of any security given.
- Long-term debtors: based on current lending rates, after any necessary bad debt provisions have been made.

[FRS 7 para 61].

25.344 The fair value of assets would be measured by their market value if an active market for them exists. For example, if an acquired company has invested in long-term debt issued by an entity that the market perceives to be at risk of default, there may be a secondary market in which the debt is traded at a discount to its face value. This discounted value may be the best available evidence of fair value.

25.345 Similarly, the fair value of any quoted debt securities issued by the acquired entity would usually be measured by their market values at the date of acquisition. However, an explanatory paragraph to the standard makes an exception where the acquired company is perceived to be at risk of defaulting on its debt obligations and the pre-acquisition market value of issued securities is reduced from its face value to reflect this risk. The standard states that such a reduction in the value of debt would not be recognised in the fair value allocation if the debt was expected to be repaid at its full amount after the acquisition. [FRS 7 para 63].

25.346 By making this exception to its general principles of fair valuing, the standard is recognising that, in such circumstances, the acquired company still has a liability to repay the gross amount of its debt. The acquired company is not absolved from its debt obligations where the market value of its debt is discounted to reflect market concerns. Accordingly, when attributing fair values to such debt in the financial statements of the acquiring group, the acquirer should recognise either the gross amount or, if the rates of interest on such debt are significantly different from current market rates, a present value that reflects current market rates, but not distress rates. If this were not done, recognising such debt in the fair value exercise at its (discounted) market value would mean a pre-acquisition gain would be attributed to the acquired company, followed by a post-acquisition loss attributed to the acquiring group, whereas, in fact, no such gain or loss has arisen.

25.347 It could also be inferred from the exception described above that a similar approach should be adopted where the debt issued by an acquired company that is in financial difficulty is not quoted, notwithstanding the reference to *"the credit standing of the issuer"* as mentioned in paragraph 25.343 above. To be consistent, and for the same reasons, we consider that it would be inappropriate to fair value the debt at a deep discount to its face or book value if the total payments (capital and interest) the acquired company is required to make under the terms of the debt are expected to be made.

25.348 The market interest rate applicable to a particular loan may alter because of a change in the perceived risk of the specific business, rather than because of a general change in market rates. An increase in business risk will increase the interest rate applicable to the entity, thus reducing the market value of its loans. This applies in particular to long-term fixed rate debt. In fair value accounting, we consider that fair values of unquoted debt obligations should not, in general, be reduced to reflect any deterioration in the creditworthiness of the acquired company since the debt was issued, if the debt is expected to be repaid at its full amount.

25.349 FRS 7 also requires the fair values of accruals and provisions to be determined by taking into account the amounts expected to be paid and their timing. [FRS 7 para 14]. It gives discounting to present value as one of the options for determining the fair values of monetary assets and liabilities generally. Accounting practices relating to the measurement of long-term provisions have previously varied according to the nature of the liability. However, FRS 12 introduced rules that apply to measuring all provisions — they should be measured at present values of expected expenditures where the effect of the time value of money is material. The discount rate should be a pre-tax rate that reflects current market assessments of the time value of money and the risks specific to the liability. Alternatively, the expected future cash outflows may be adjusted (that is, increased) for risk and discounted by using a risk-free rate (such as a government bond rate). Care should be taken to ensure the effect of risk is not double-counted — that is, risk should be taken into account either in estimating the (undiscounted) future expenditures or by adjusting (that is, reducing) the discount rate, but not both. The measurement basis required by FRS 12 should generally be consistent with the principles for determining fair values of provisions in FRS 7.

Fair valuing contingencies

25.350 The treatment of contingent purchase consideration is considered later in paragraph 25.410. The paragraphs that follow consider contingencies that affect the value of identifiable net assets.

Identification of contingencies

25.351 FRS 12 defines a contingent liability:

"(a) *a possible obligation that arises from past events and whose existence will be confirmed only by the occurrence of one or more uncertain future events not wholly within the entity's control; or*

(b) *a present obligation that arises from past events but is not recognised because:*

(i) *it is not probable that a transfer of economic benefits will be required to settle the obligation; or*

(ii) *the amount of the obligation cannot be measured with sufficient reliability*".

The standard defines a contingent asset as *"a possible asset that arises from past events and whose existence will be confirmed only by the occurrence of one or more uncertain future events not wholly within the entity's control"*. [FRS 12 para 2].

25.352 In acquisition accounting, a pre-acquisition contingency would be a contingent asset or liability of the acquired company that existed at the date of acquisition. For fair value exercises, the identifiable assets and liabilities of an acquired company must include certain contingent assets that existed before the date of acquisition (see below).

Measurement of contingencies

25.353 The normal rules in FRS 12 for recognising and measuring contingencies in financial statements are as follows:

- Contingent liabilities should not be recognised as provisions, but should be disclosed, unless the possibility of a transfer of economic benefits is remote. If it becomes probable that a transfer of economic benefits will be required for an item previously dealt with as a contingent liability, a provision should be recognised in the period in which the change in probability occurs. [FRS 12 paras 27 to 30].
- Contingent assets should not be recognised as assets, but should be disclosed where an inflow of economic benefits is probable. If it becomes virtually certain that an inflow of economic benefits will arise, the asset and the related profit should be recognised in the period in which the change occurs. [FRS 12 paras 31 to 35].

25.354 Under FRS 12, where an item is expected to result in a transfer of economic benefits, a provision should be recognised. Where a transfer of economic benefits is not probable, the item is a contingent liability and no provision should be recognised. In acquisition accounting, it is unlikely that a contingent liability (as defined in FRS 12) would result in the recognition of an identifiable liability, because by definition it is not probable that a transfer of economic benefits will be required – an exception would in rare cases be where the contingent liability had a fair value that could be determined from a market in such items.

25.355 In acquisition accounting, the identifiable assets to be included in the fair value exercise include contingent assets that are expected to result in an inflow of economic benefits, as assets, even though they are not normally included in financial statements as gains until their realisation becomes virtually certain. Recognition of contingent assets in a fair value exercise has no immediate profit and loss account effect; instead it means all assets that have value are recognised, with only the residual difference between the purchase price and the identified net assets being reported as goodwill. In contrast, omitting a pre-acquisition contingent asset in the fair value exercise would mean that a pre-acquisition asset may be recognised as a post-acquisition gain in succeeding financial statements. The recognition of such contingent assets should follow the same process as that of contingent liabilities. That is, contingent assets should be recognised in the fair value exercise where an inflow of economic benefits is probable.

25.356 FRS 7 requires all identifiable assets and liabilities to be recognised in the fair value exercise, provided they can be reliably valued. Fair values, representing the price at which such an item might be exchanged in an arm's length transaction, would rarely be ascertainable unless the contingent asset or liability were of a kind that is normally exchanged. Consequently, the standard allows reasonable estimates of the expected outcome to be used as the best approximation to fair value. [FRS 7 para 15].

25.357 For this purpose, the standard explains that the acquiring company's management's best estimate of the likely outcome should be used in place of any previous estimate, assuming that no post-acquisition events or other changes in circumstances are reflected in the valuation. [FRS 7 para 64].

25.358 Many contingencies, such as legal claims, require a considerable amount of time to be investigated in order to make reliable predictions of the outcome. Often it may not be possible to incorporate reliable figures in the first set of consolidated financial statements following the acquisition. In such circumstances, the fair values would be declared provisional and adjustments would be made in the second post-acquisition group accounts if new information becomes available within the permitted hindsight period that enables the resolution of the contingency to be reliably predicted. In practice, such items are sometimes covered by warranties given by vendors or by insurance (see para 25.425).

25.359 In accounting periods that follow the period in which the fair value exercise is completed, there may be changes in the amount of any contingent assets or liabilities that have been recognised. Such changes would be reflected in the profit and loss account for the period in which they are recognised in the same way as changes in estimates of other assets and liabilities are dealt with.

25.360 FRS 6 gives, as an example of a post-acquisition profit or loss that would require separate disclosure as an exceptional item in the financial statements of the acquiring group, the *"realisation of contingent assets or liabilities at amounts materially different from their attributed fair values"*. [FRS 6 para 85].

25.361 Where contingent assets are recognised on acquisition, but subsequently they do not materialise, there will be an adverse effect on the profit and loss account. In this respect, where a contingent asset is set up on acquisition, it will be necessary to consider in future periods whether there is a reduction in its value. Where there is, the asset should be written down, by providing an amount against post-acquisition profits. On the other hand, where a contingent asset is subsequently expected to be realised at an amount in excess of its attributed fair value on acquisition, the normal rules of FRS 12 would preclude the recognition of any gain in the profit and loss account of the acquiring group until its realisation becomes virtually certain.

25.362 Similarly, where contingent liabilities are recognised in the fair value exercise, they will have to be reconsidered in future periods to ascertain whether the provisions are adequate. Where they are not, an additional provision will have to be made and charged to the post-acquisition profit and loss account. On the other hand, where the amount accrued in the fair value exercise is subsequently found to be excessive, the excess provision would be written back in the post-acquisition profit and loss account.

25.363 If the amount of the expected inflow or outflow relating to a contingency in the acquired company cannot be reliably estimated from information available at the end of the period allowed for completing the fair value exercise, contingent assets or liabilities would not be recognised, but would be disclosed in the acquirer's consolidated financial statements as required by FRS 12.

25.364 When evaluating pre-acquisition contingencies, in practice it is not always clear whether adjustments to the acquired company's financial statements should be reported as fair value adjustments or as post-acquisition events. The following examples illustrate the difficulties.

Example 1

An acquired publishing company has a publishing subsidiary which has been sued for libel. The company's counsel has advised that, in his opinion, the case could be successfully defended. Accordingly, no provision has been included in the acquired company's financial statements, other than for estimated legal fees. The management of the acquiring company decide that the case should be settled out of court in order to avoid a protracted court case and the risk that the company could lose. The overall settlement cost exceeds the legal costs provision in the acquired company's financial statements.

It could be argued that the acquired company's financial statements reflected the best estimate of the likely outcome and that no further fair value adjustment is required. The financial effect of the acquirer's decision not to defend the case would then be reflected as a current, that is, post-acquisition, event.

However, a different view is that as the settlement related to a contingency that was already in existence and as there has been no new information or change in circumstances relating to the contingency, the cost of settlement is an event that confirms the outcome of the contingency. Therefore, the cost should be reflected as a fair value adjustment. This seems to be the more sensible interpretation and reflects the acquiring company's management's best estimate of the likely outcome as explained in paragraph 64 of FRS 7.

Example 2

An acquired company was pursuing a claim for negligence against a firm of accountants who had provided investigation services in respect of a previous acquisition that failed. The claim amounted to £10m. The accountants strenuously denied acting negligently. However, they had made an offer of settlement of £2m, which the company had rejected. The case was, therefore, scheduled for a court hearing. The management of the acquiring company subsequently negotiated, and accepted, an out of court settlement of £3m.

In this example, it is likely to be impossible to arrive at any meaningful fair value without the benefit of hindsight, that is, unless the actual outcome of the claim is reflected. If the claim was settled within the period for completing the fair value exercise, the credit of £3m should probably be accounted for as a fair value adjustment, because it relates to a contingency that was already in existence. However, it would be tempting for the management to argue that the settlement was due to their own efforts and skills, or that changes in the litigious environment had favoured a higher settlement and that, accordingly, some or all of the credit should be reflected in the post-acquisition profit and loss account.

If the settlement is not reached by the time the period for completing the fair value exercise has expired, the treatment would depend on the information available at the end of that period. If the outcome of the claim could be reliably predicted at that time, a best estimate of the settlement amount would be included as a contingent asset, that is, as a fair value adjustment. Later, when a settlement is reached, any income would be credited in the profit and loss account in the period it is received. Of course, it would be reported as an exceptional item, if material.

25.365 Table 25.18 gives an example where the receipt after the acquisition date of a pre-existing claim by the acquired company has been partly recognised as a fair value adjustment (increasing the fair value of debtors) and partly as an exceptional post-acquisition profit.

Table 25.18 — GKN plc — Report & Accounts — 31 December 1994

NOTES ON THE ACCOUNTS (extract)

23 ACQUISITIONS

Westland (extract from fair value table)

	BOOK VALUE PRIOR TO ACQUISITION £m	ACCOUNTING POLICY ALIGNMENT £m	REVALUATIONS £m	OTHER £m	FAIR VALUE TO THE GKN GROUP £m
Debtors — joint venture termination	–	–	–	112.0	112.0
— other	120.2	–	–	–	120.2

The fair value adjustments made include:

(c) a debtor for the net cash received in June 1994 amounting to £112 million arising from an arbitration award against the Arab Organisation for Industrialisation (AOI) following the termination of a joint venture between AOI and Westland Helicopters Limited to manufacture Lynx helicopters under licence. This receipt was secured as a result of actions initiated by Westland prior to acquisition and has accordingly been referred back to 31st March 1994. A further final net receipt of £51 million was negotiated in August 1994 and has been treated as a post acquisition exceptional profit (see note 4). These items, taken together with the net £15 million received by Westland in December 1993, give a total net receipt of £178 million from the award.

4 EXCEPTIONAL ITEMS (extract)

	1994 CONTINUING OPERATIONS £m	1994 DISCONTINUED OPERATIONS £m
Subsidiaries		
Profits (£83.7 million) less losses (£109.1 million) on sale or closure of businesses:		
Westland joint venture termination (note 23c)	**50.9**	–
Reduction in shareholding in Chep UK	**22.2**	–
Sale of US and Australian rental businesses	–	**(34.0)**
Provision for loss on sale of UES	**(59.6)**	–
Holdings		
Other	**(7.4)**	**2.5**
	6.1	**(31.5)**

Pensions and other post-retirement benefits

Identification of assets and liabilities

25.366 Where an acquisition involves the assumption of pension schemes or other post-retirement benefit plans, FRS 7 requires the following to be recognised as identifiable assets or liabilities in the fair value exercise:

- A surplus in a funded scheme, to the extent that it can be recovered through reduced contributions or through refunds from the scheme.
- A deficiency in a funded scheme.
- Accrued obligations in respect of an unfunded scheme.

[FRS 7 para 19 as amended by FRS 17 para 101(a)].

25.367 FRS 7 does not permit companies to recognise, as adjustments in the fair value exercise, changes in pension or other post-retirement arrangements following the acquisition. The cost of such changes should be dealt with in the post-acquisition profit and loss account under the normal rules for pension costs (see chapter 11). [FRS 7 para 20].

25.368 Defined contribution schemes do not pose any problems in acquisition accounting, because the employer's obligation at any point in time is restricted to the amount of contributions payable to date, including to the date of acquisition. A liability will exist in the acquired company's financial statements if all contributions due by it have not been paid to the scheme and an asset will exist where excess contributions have been paid.

25.369 Defined benefit schemes, however, pose greater problems because the employer's liability for future benefits payable is not, in the case of funded schemes, restricted to the amount of contributions paid to the scheme.

25.370 Arrangements for transferring pension obligations when a change of ownership takes place are many, varied and often complex. They may include: the acquisition of all schemes in the acquired group, in the case of the takeover of a listed group of companies; the acquisition of part of the vendor's pension schemes, in the case of the purchase of a subsidiary from a parent company; or simply the transfer of assets from the vendor's scheme to the purchaser's scheme reflecting transfer values of the accumulated pension rights of individual employees.

25.371 The value of the assets of a scheme acquired may exceed the estimated liability for the benefits that have accrued to members at the date of acquisition and, therefore, there may be a surplus. Equally, if the assets are insufficient to cover future liabilities for pensions there would be a deficiency. The surplus (with exceptions — see para 25.377 below) or deficiency should generally be recognised as an identifiable asset or liability in the fair value exercise.

Acquisition accounting

25.372 In the past, a problem faced by many companies, and particularly those that have acquired subsidiaries in the US, has been how to deal with post-retirement health care benefits, which were sometimes a substantial hidden liability of acquired subsidiaries. Both FAS 106 in the US and FRS 17 in the UK have introduced guidance for such schemes. Companies need to review acquisitions to ensure that any material post-retirement benefits are identified and appropriate liabilities recognised in the fair value exercise.

25.373 The appointed actuary, or an actuary acting for the acquirer in the due diligence exercise, will play a key role in determining the surplus or deficit position for pension schemes and in determining the liability for other post-retirement benefits.

Measurement of assets and liabilities

25.374 FRS 7 does not prescribe any rules for measuring the amount of surplus or deficiency to be recognised. The standard merely explains that the actuarial valuation depends on several assumptions about the future; and the *acquirer* would apply its own judgement in determining these assumptions. [FRS 7 para 73].

25.375 Generally, therefore, an actuarial valuation should be carried out as at the date of acquisition using actuarial methods and assumptions that are consistent with those the acquirer normally uses for the purpose of accounting for defined benefit schemes. These may differ from those previously used by the acquired company. FRS 17 requires use of the projected unit method for measuring scheme liabilities. [FRS 17 para 20].

25.376 However, the valuation should not take into account the cost of any retrospective changes in benefits and membership that are decided upon by the acquirer. Such costs should be written off in the acquirer's consolidated profit and loss account over the vesting period under the principles of FRS 17. The following are examples of items that should be treated as post-acquisition:

- Costs of benefit improvements following the acquisition.
- Pension effect of a significant reduction in the number of employees following a post-acquisition reorganisation.
- Cost of enhanced pensions initiated by the acquirer to induce early retirement.

25.377 FRS 7 notes that the fair value of the surplus or deficit should be measured in accordance with the rules of FRS 17.

25.378 Many defined benefit schemes are designed such that the employees pay a fixed rate of contribution and the employer has an obligation to fund the balance. If a scheme is in surplus, the employer may be able to suspend or reduce the normal level of contributions until the surplus is eliminated. Where a surplus in an acquired company's scheme is to be run off by a contribution holiday after the acquisition, the surplus at the date of acquisition should clearly be recognised as an asset in the fair value exercise. The same goes for amounts subsequently refunded to the employer.

25.379 Situations where it would be either inappropriate or imprudent to recognise the full amount of a surplus as an asset might include the following:

- It is a condition of the scheme that part of the surplus belongs to the employees.
- The employees share in a contribution holiday.
- The trust deed prevents a refund of surplus to the employer company, and the surplus is so large that even an extended employer contribution holiday would not recover the whole amount of the surplus in the foreseeable future. Accordingly, it may be prudent to recognise a smaller surplus in the fair value exercise, for example the present value of a contribution holiday.

25.380 One means of utilising a surplus is to allow it to finance benefit improvements to employees that would otherwise be funded by increased contributions. Because the standard is quite specific that the cost of changes in pension arrangements such as benefit improvements following an acquisition should be accounted for in the profit and loss account as post-acquisition variations, it appears that such costs should not be deducted from the amount of surplus recognised on acquisition. The treatment of the costs (and corresponding reduction in surplus) is dealt with in chapter 11.

Deferred taxation

25.381 Fair value adjustments made to the identifiable assets and liabilities of the acquired entity may give rise to timing differences. Deferred tax should be provided on those timing differences in the fair value exercise in the same way as they would be if they were timing differences arising in the acquired entity's own accounts. [FRS 7 para 74 as amended by FRS 19 para 71]. Such deferred tax should be provided in accordance with requirements of FRS 19. [FRS 7 para 21 as amended by FRS 19 para 71]. For example, if the acquired entity's property was fair valued on acquisition, this would be treated as a revaluation on which no deferred tax would be provided in the fair value exercise unless the acquired entity had entered into a binding agreement to sell the asset prior to its acquisition and no rollover relief was available.

25.382 It is also possible that the acquired entity may not have recognised deferred tax assets, including those arising in respect of tax losses, because it was unable to satisfy the recognition criteria for deferred tax assets as specified in FRS 19. As a result of the acquisition, such deferred tax assets may fall to be recognised because they now satisfy the recognition criteria. For example, a previously unrecognised tax loss may become recoverable because the acquiring group will have sufficient taxable profits to offset the tax losses acquired. In that situation, the unrecognised tax asset should be recognised in the fair value exercise. [FRS 7 para 22 as amended by FRS 19 para 71]. Deferred tax on fair value adjustments are considered further in chapter 13.

Fair valuing the purchase consideration

Cost of acquisition

25.383 The Companies Act 1985 and FRS 7 state that the acquisition cost of a subsidiary is made up of some or all of the following elements:

- Cash consideration.
- Fair value of other consideration.
- Expenses of acquisition.

[CA85 4A Sch 9(4); FRS 7 para 26].

25.384 Consequently, the objective of determining the fair value of the consideration given is to fix the acquisition cost of the investment. Where cash forms part of the consideration, the fair value will be the amount payable in respect of the item, unless settlement is deferred, where it may be necessary to discount it (see para 25.404 below).

25.385 Non-cash consideration may take the form of:

- The assumption of liabilities by the acquirer.
- Quoted securities issued.
- Unquoted securities issued.
- Consideration given in the form of non-monetary assets, including securities of another entity.

25.386 The assumption of liabilities by the acquirer may take the form of the repayment of borrowings in an acquired company owed to its former investors, including, in the case of the purchase of a subsidiary from its former parent, the repayment of an acquired company's intra-group debt.

25.387 The fair value would be the amount paid or payable, discounted to present value, if necessary, where settlement of the liabilities is due at a future date.

25.388 Securities issued by the acquirer may take the form of:

- Ordinary shares.
- Preference shares (convertible or non-convertible).
- Loan stock (convertible or non-convertible).

- Share warrants and other options relating to the securities of the acquiring company.

25.389 The various elements that make up the total consideration are considered further in the paragraphs that follow.

Quoted securities

25.390 The most common form of securities given as consideration is ordinary or equity shares. The standard states that the fair value would usually be taken to be the market price at the date of acquisition. For practical purposes, the mid-market price is normally used. There are two related issues:

- The point in time at which shares should be valued.
- The use of alternative valuations to a valuation based on the quoted market price.

25.391 Where control is transferred by a public offer, the fair value of securities given as consideration should be based on the market price of the security on the date on which the final successful offer becomes unconditional. This is in line with FRS 2 which defines this as the date on which an undertaking becomes a subsidiary. This price takes account of the market's reaction to a bid and movements in the share price of a bidder.

25.392 In order to avoid a major fluctuation in share price on a single day distorting the acquisition price, the standard states that market prices for a reasonable period before the date of acquisition, during which acceptances could be made, would need to be considered. It may then be appropriate to base the fair value on an average of market prices over a short period. Such method of valuation would, however, be the exception rather than the rule, because only in very unusual circumstances — for example, a market rumour causing a very temporary blip in the share price — would the actual market price on the date of acquisition fail to provide the most reliable measure of fair value.

25.393 Where the shares are quoted, but trade in them is infrequent, as in the case of some public companies with significant family shareholdings (close companies) and unprogressive dividend policies, market price could be an unreliable measure of fair value. In such circumstances, the approach applied for valuing unquoted securities, as set out below, may be more appropriate.

Unquoted securities

25.394 Where no market price is available for ordinary shares (or where the market price of quoted securities is inappropriate), the fair value should be estimated by traditional share valuation methods. For example, applying an appropriate capitalisation rate to earnings (P/E ratio), or discounting the cash flows of securities to their present value. The values of unquoted securities can sometimes be estimated by reference to securities with, and issued by enterprises with, similar characteristics.

25.395 In some cases it may not be possible to value the consideration given by any of the above methods. The cost of acquisition, in such circumstances, should be determined by valuing the business being acquired (that is, including its goodwill) rather than by valuing the securities issued.

Other securities

25.396 The general principles that apply to determining the fair value of ordinary shares can also be applied to other securities, such as preference shares, loan stock, share warrants and other options. Consequently, where there is a market price available, the market price on the date on which the successful offer finally becomes unconditional should be used. Where there is no market price, similar bases to those described above should be used. For convertible securities, such as convertible loan stock or preference shares, the fair value will include the value of the conversion rights and be related to the value of the security into which it can convert in the future.

Non-monetary consideration

25.397 FRS 7 states that where the purchase consideration takes the form of non-monetary assets, fair values would be determined by reference to market prices, estimated realisable values, independent valuations, or other available evidence. [FRS 7 para 80].

25.398 The purchase consideration may sometimes take the form of other assets, for example, where a company has an investment in a second company (which may be listed) and swaps that investment for a controlling interest in another company. In acquiring the holding in the new subsidiary, the consideration given will be the shares in the second company. Under FRS 7 it would be necessary to arrive at a current fair value of the holding in the second company and this would represent the cost of the holding in the new subsidiary.

25.399 If the fair value of the investment in the second company is greater than the carrying value, a difference will arise between the original carrying value of the second company and the cost of the investment in the new subsidiary. The question arises as to whether this difference represents a realised profit. The answer to this question would probably be that the profit should be treated as unrealised, because it will not be realised until the new subsidiary is disposed of.

Other consideration

25.400 There are certain forms of 'consideration' that for tax or other reasons are sometimes given. These include payments made for an agreement by a vendor not to compete with the acquirer for a number of years and bonus payments to vendors who continue to be directors of the acquired company after the acquisition. The standard mentions that in practice it will be necessary to look at the substance of the relevant transactions in order to determine the accounting treatment. If the payments represent compensation for post-acquisition services or profit sharing, they should be reported as post-acquisition revenue costs. If the payments are in substance consideration for the business acquired, they should be capitalised as part of the acquisition cost.

25.401 The accounting treatment should reflect the transaction's true commercial effect, both the initial purchase consideration and subsequent payments, in the eyes of the acquirer and vendor. UK GAAP does not give any detailed guidance on this point, however, factors that could indicate whether a contingent payment is in substance part of the purchase consideration or employee compensation are:

- Link between continuing employment and contingent consideration. If, for example, payments are conditional on the recipients remaining with, and providing continuing future services to, the acquired company, there would be a presumption that the post-acquisition payments should be charged as post-acquisition expenses in the acquiring group's profit and loss account. Arrangements that are not affected by employment ending may indicate that contingent payments are additional purchase consideration.

- Length of required employment period. If this coincides with, or is longer than, the contingent payment period, then this would suggest that the payment is compensation for post-acquisition services.

- Remuneration of vendors compared to other key employees. If the vendor's employee compensation, excluding the contingent payment, is comparable to other key employee's compensation then this would suggest that the contingent payment is consideration for the acquisition rather than a payment for employee services.

- Level of contingent payment for the vendors who stay on as employees compared to those who do not. If the vendors who stay on as employees are paid more than those who do not become employees then this would indicate that the additional amount received by the vendors who become employees is payment for post-acquisition services.

- Value of the business compared to the consideration paid upfront. If it can be clearly demonstrated that the purchase consideration has been reduced in anticipation of additional payments, and such payments are not conditional on the recipient providing future services to the company, the payments are likely in substance to be additional purchase consideration.

- Formula used to determine the amount of the contingent payment may help ascertain the arrangement's substance. Where the formula is based on a percentage of profit this may indicate a profit sharing arrangement, whereas if it is based on a multiple of EBITDA this suggests it is intended to verify the value of the business and, therefore, it is part of the acquisition cost.

- Other agreements between the vendor and acquirer should also be reviewed as they may provide some guidance to the arrangement's substance. If, for example, the vendor is also entering into an agreement to lease a property from the acquirer and they will be paying less than market rent, then this could be an indication that some or all of the contingent consideration is in substance lease payments.

The factors, listed above, should be considered in determining whether a contingent payment is part of the acquisition cost or compensation for post-acquisition employee services. The factors can be used to provide an indication of the substance of a payment. However, this is an area of judgement and the particular facts and circumstances should be considered in each case.

25.402 Purchase consideration can take the form of a special dividend paid by the acquirer after the date of acquisition. For example, as part of the offer a special dividend might be paid shortly after the acquisition to those members who became shareholders as a result of accepting the acquirer's offer for the shares of the acquired company, and the dividend may be equivalent to an interim or final dividend payable by the acquirer in respect of a period prior to the acquisition. This is not specifically mentioned in FRS 7, but in principle such dividends could be treated as part of the purchase consideration where it can be demonstrated that the payment was in substance part of the acquisition cost. An example of this treatment is shown in Table 25.19. Where a dividend is capitalised in this way, the acquirer would need to ensure that the cost of the dividend is not double-counted in arriving at the fair value of the total consideration. For example, the shares issued in consideration for the acquisition may need to be valued at an ex-div price.

Table 25.19 — Redland PLC — Report and Accounts — 31 December 1992

Notes to the accounts (extract)

6 Dividends	Year ended 31.12.92 £million	Year ended 31.12.91 £million
Ordinary shares:		
Interim paid: 8.25p per share net (1991: 8.25p)	39.5	27.9
Final proposed 1992: 16.75p per share net (1991: 16.75p)	80.3	57.0
Total dividends on Redland PLC ordinary shares: 25.0p per share net (1991: 25.0p)	119.8	84.9
Less: transfer to cost of investment to Steetley plc	(8.6)	—
	111.2	84.9

Scrip dividends to the value of £5.1 million in respect of the 1991 final dividend and £1.9 million in respect of the 1992 interim dividend were taken instead of a cash payment.

25.403 For tax reasons, payments that are in substance a form of purchase consideration are sometimes made by the acquired company itself (subject to financial assistance considerations), rather than by the acquirer. If the acquired company's financial statements include a provision in respect of such payments, on consolidation this provision should be regarded as part of the cost of acquisition rather than as a pre-acquisition liability of the acquired company. Accordingly, the obligation to make such payments should be treated in the fair value table as an element of the purchase consideration and not as a reduction in the net assets of the acquired company.

Deferred consideration

25.404 Part of the consideration for an acquisition may become payable at a date after the acquisition has been completed. Such deferred consideration could take the form of cash, shares or other consideration where the amounts are known with certainty. FRS 7 requires the fair value of all forms of consideration to be reflected in the cost of acquisition.

Deferred cash consideration

25.405 The fair value of deferred consideration payable in cash should be taken to be the amount of cash payable discounted to its present value. In addition, the present value of deferred cash consideration would be provided in the acquirer's financial statements as a liability. The standard states that the appropriate discount rate is the rate at which the acquirer could obtain a similar borrowing, taking into account its credit standing and any security given. [FRS 7 para 77].

25.406 The measurement of deferred consideration in FRS 7 is consistent with the treatment of the various forms of debt finance in FRS 4 (or for those entities applying FRS 26, the amortised cost valuation methodology of that standard). The difference between the amount (fair value) at which the liability is stated at the acquisition date and the total amounts payable at future dates is a finance cost, analogous to the finance costs of debt where a liability is carried at amortised cost, and should be charged as an interest expense in the acquirer's post-acquisition profit and loss account over the period the liability is outstanding. The 1994 financial statements of Verson International Group plc disclose deferred cash consideration that has been discounted to present value. The relevant extract is reproduced in Table 25.20.

Table 25.20 – Verson International Group plc – Annual Report – 31 January 1994
Notes to the accounts (extract)
16. Creditors — amounts falling due after more than one year (extract)

		Group	
		1994	1993
		£000	£000
Bank loans	— U.K. (secured)	**2,250**	2,750
	— overseas (secured)	**10,529**	10,204
Other loans		**2,023**	2,483
Deferred consideration		**6,554**	6,454
Hire purchase and finance lease creditors		**646**	1,306
Other long term creditors		**2,122**	1,923
		24,124	25,120

Deferred consideration includes an amount of £5,334,000 (1993 — £5.024,000) relating to the agreement to repurchase, on or before 8 September 1996, 42,094 non-voting preference shares in Clearing-Niagara Inc. (formerly Niagara Machine and Tools Works) held by the former owners, for a total amount of $9,500,000. The balance reflects amounts outstanding on the acquisition of a freehold property in the USA also acquired during 1993.

The deferred consideration in respect of the acquisition of Clearing-Niagara Inc. has been discounted from the anticipated settlement date at a rate of 6.875%. The difference between this present value and the mandatory purchase amount has been accrued through a charge to interest payable of £343,000 (1993 — £128,000) during the year.

Deferred share consideration

25.407 Where the deferred consideration is in the form of shares, the classification in the balance sheet is governed by FRS 25, 'Financial instruments: Disclosure and presentation'. If the deferred consideration meets the definition of an equity instrument then the fair value should be credited directly to shareholders' funds. The most appropriate treatment is to disclose such deferred consideration under share capital as a separate caption with a heading such as 'shares to be issued'. The shares would qualify as an equity instrument if, for example, the number of shares to be issued is fixed and, as a consequence, the acquiree's shareholders bear the risk of falls in the value of the shares and the rewards if the shares rise in value.

25.408 However, often with shares, the amount of deferred consideration payable is fixed at the acquisition date and the number of shares issued to satisfy that consideration varies according to the market price of the shares at the date the consideration is issued. A contractual obligation is a financial liability if it is required to be settled by a variable number of the entity's own shares equal in value to the amount of the contractual obligation. [FRS 25 para 21]. Where this situation applies, the shares to be issued are shown, not as equity, but as a financial liability. Debt/equity classification is dealt with further in chapter 6.

25.409 FRS 7 makes no reference to the question of discounting deferred share consideration classified as an equity instrument. The ASB's discussion paper that preceded FRED 7 explained that deferred share consideration is analogous to the issue of warrants, and that theoretically its fair value at the date of acquisition is the value of the right conferred upon the vendor to receive shares at a future date.

Contingent consideration

25.410 FRS 7 deals specifically with the treatment of deferred consideration where the amount payable is uncertain because it is contingent on the outcome of future events. The most common form of contingent consideration arises where the acquirer agrees to pay additional consideration if the acquired company achieves a certain level of performance.

25.411 The standard requires *"a reasonable estimate of the fair value of amounts expected to be payable in the future"* to be included in the cost of acquisition when the fair value exercise is undertaken. [FRS 7 para 27].

25.412 This amount will have to be adjusted, if necessary, when the final amount payable is determined, or when revised estimates are made. Such adjustments should continue to be made to the cost of acquisition and, therefore, to goodwill, until the consideration is finally determined. In contrast to fair valuing assets and liabilities acquired, there is no limit on the period in which this aspect of the fair value exercise must be determined.

25.413 Once a reasonable estimate has been made of the future consideration payable, the same principles of valuing the components of the consideration (including discounting estimated amounts to their present values) that are discussed in the above section on deferred consideration would be applicable in order to record the initial cost of acquisition at its estimated fair value.

25.414 In practice, the acquirer may need to look at profit forecasts for the acquired company on expected, best case and worst case scenarios. Provision for future consideration would normally be made on the basis of the expected outcome.

25.415 A practical problem is that it may be very difficult to make reliable estimates of the future consideration in some cases. For example, such consideration might depend on an average of profits of the acquired company for three years into the future and might not be payable at all unless the average exceeded a certain amount. The acquired company may be in a development phase where any forecasts are extremely subjective and unreliable. When the acquirer's first post-acquisition financial statements are prepared it could be very difficult to assess the probable amount, or indeed whether any amount will be payable. In those circumstances, the standard explains that at least those amounts that are reasonably expected to be payable would be recognised. [FRS 7 para 81].

25.416 If, for example, a minimum sum is guaranteed to be paid as part of contingent consideration, at least this minimum must be provided initially. Any further sums must be provided as soon as reasonable estimates can be made. It cannot be assumed that contingent consideration can adequately be dealt with by giving details of the contingency in a note to the financial statements, together with a range of possibilities. An example of a company that provided for contingent consideration is given in Table 25.21.

Table 25.21— Logica plc — Annual Report — 30 June 1994

Notes to the accounts (extract)

12 Acquisitions
On 2 May 1994 Logica North American Inc, acquired the business of Precision Software Corporation for an initial consideration of £2,340,000. The balance sheet of Precision Software Corporation on acquisition was as follows.

	Book value at 2 May	Fair value adjustments	Fair value at acquisition
	£000	£000	£000
Intangible assets	1,381	(1,381)	0
Tangible assets	296	68	364
Work in progress	66	0	66
Trade debtors	87	(45)	42
Creditors — amount falling due within one year	(217)	(198)	(415)
Net assets acquired	1,613	(1,556)	57
Goodwill			3,582
Consideration			3,639
Satisfied by:			
Cash			2,200
Related costs of acquisition			140
Deferred consideration			1,299
			3,639

The fair value adjustments relate to the revaluation of a freehold property, a debtor provision, and the alignment of accounting policies with those of the Group.

The deferred consideration is payable upon the achievement of certain minimum targets. This represents the minimum amount that is reasonably expected to be payable. Further performance related payments up to a maximum of £4,545,000 may become payable between the date of acquisition and June 1998.

Initial estimates of the deferred consideration will be revised as further and more certain information becomes available with corresponding adjustments to goodwill.

Discounting contingent cash consideration

25.417 Following the principle in paragraph 77 of FRS 7 (see para 25.405 above), the fair value of contingent consideration payable in cash should be taken to be the estimated amount of cash payable discounted to its present value.

25.418 A practical problem arises, because when the contingent consideration becomes more certain as the time gets nearer to its payment, the previously estimated amount may prove to be incorrect. Where this is so, the amount provided should be revised as the outcome becomes more certain until the ultimate amount is known. These amendments will also affect the amount of goodwill recognised on the acquisition and similar adjustments should be made to the goodwill figure until the consideration is finally determined. The problem is how to account for the interest effect in each accounting period if the estimate (undiscounted) of the future consideration is continually revised — in effect, how to discount a moving target. Consider the following example.

Example

An acquisition is made on 1 January 20X1. Part of the consideration for the acquisition, payable in cash on 1 January 20X4, is subject to the achievement of specified performance levels in the acquired company over the next three years. The maximum consideration payable is £20m, and the directors of the acquirer have estimated that the final figure will be £10m. This figure of £10m, subject to discounting, is to be added to the cost of acquisition and included as a provision in the acquirer's consolidated financial statements. A discount rate of 10%, reflecting the acquirer's cost of debt, is to be used.

The fair value (that is, net present value) at 1 January 20X1 of the estimated deferred liability of £10m is £7,513,000. This figure is included in the cost of acquisition and the calculation of goodwill. An interest cost of 10% should be charged on the deferred liability, giving an interest charge of £751,000 for 20X1, which is added to the deferred liability. At 31 December 20X1 the deferred liability will stand at £8,264,000.

During the year ending 31 December 20X2, interest of £826,000 is charged and added to the deferred liability, which then stands at £9,090,000 in the acquirer's books.

The acquired company performs better than expected during 20X2. When preparing the financial statements for the year ending 31 December 20X2, the directors revise their estimate of contingent consideration upwards to £12m.

The present value as at 31 December 20X2 of the revised estimate of £12m is £10,908,000; hence the provision in the acquirer's books needs to be increased from £9,090,000 to £10,908,000 (that is, by £1,818,000). The question arises as to what to debit. How much should be debited to cost of investment/goodwill and how much should be written off as additional interest? This is illustrated in the table below.

	Original estimate	Revised estimate	Difference
	£'000	£'000	£'000
Present value 1.1.X.1	7,513	9,015	1,502
Interest 20X1	751	901	150
Present value 31.12.X1	8,264	9,916	1,652
Interest 20X2	826	992	166
Present value 31.12.X2	9,090	10,908	1,818
Interest 20X3		1,092	
Present value 31.12.X3		12,000	

The most appropriate method is to recalculate the cost of investment and goodwill as at the date of acquisition, based on the present value of the revised estimate. The restated amounts are then the amounts that would have been recorded if the revised estimate had been available at the date of acquisition. The following adjustments would be necessary to restate the provision and goodwill as at 31 December 20X2.

	£'000	£'000
Dr Goodwill	1,502	
Dr P&L; backlog interest for 20X1	150	
Dr P&L; backlog interest for 20X2	166	
Cr Provision for deferred consideration		1,818
	1,818	1,818

As these adjustments arise from a change of estimate, the whole of the additional interest charge (including the backlog charge for 20X1 resulting from the increased estimate of the liability) would be recorded in the current year's profit and loss account. Thus the interest charge amounts to £1,142,000 (comprising £992,000 relating to 20X2 based on the increased estimate and £150,000 backlog adjustment relating to 20X1).

Interest would then be charged in 20X3 on the revised liability of £10,908,000, taking the book value of the liability to its nominal value of £12m at 31 December 20X3, assuming no further revisions of the consideration payable are made.

An alternative method is to account prospectively for the change in estimate, that is to discount the revised estimate back only to 31 December 20X1, and add the increase in the provision of £1,652,000 calculated as at 31 December 20X1 to cost of investment and goodwill. Under this method, the interest charged in 20X2 reflects the interest cost of £992,000 attributable to that year only (based on the revised estimate of the liability). The problem with this method is that, if the adjustment is material, the historical cost of investment and goodwill will be overstated.

A further question arises as to what effect the adjustment to goodwill has on the amortisation profile of the goodwill asset. This question is addressed in section III, paragraph 25.500.

Consideration involving settlement options

25.419 Whilst contingent consideration is notionally scoped out of FRS 25 by paragraph 4(c), FRS 7 paragraph 82 makes it clear that FRS 25 should be consulted for situations in which contingent consideration is to be settled by the issue of shares. As in paragraph 25.407, the classification will depend on whether the definition of 'equity instrument' is met. Where contingent consideration is payable by a pre-defined number of shares if certain conditions are met, then this will meet the definition of equity. For example, an agreement may state that if post acquisition profit in the first year is £40 million then 400 shares will be issued and if profit is £30 million then 300 shares will be issued. Where the contingent consideration is based on a variable amount of shares this will not meet the definition of equity, because the amount fluctuates in response to changes in a variable (for example, profits) rather than to the market value of the shares and, hence, will be a financial liability. [FRS 25 para 21]. The practical application of this is that previously under FRS 7 such consideration would have been classified within equity or shares to be issued, whereas under FRS 25 such consideration will be classified as a liability. An example of contingent share consideration meeting the definition of a liability would be when the earn-out agreement states that shares to the equivalent value of 10 per cent of profit in the first year post-acquisition will be issued. This is not a fixed number of shares and, therefore, will be shown as a liability.

25.420 Paragraph 26 of FRS 25 notes that where settlement options exist, the consideration will be treated as an equity instrument only if all of the settlement options would result in an equity instrument. Hence, if there is a cash option, for instance, the instrument will be a liability.

25.421 However presented, the amounts earmarked for settlement of consideration (and held, as appropriate, within liabilities or shareholders' funds) will be adjusted during the period the consideration is outstanding, such that the settlement will be recorded at the amount of cash payable or the market value of the shares to be issued. The balance sheet treatment required by the standard also has a profit and loss effect over the period the consideration is outstanding. Whilst changes in estimates of the final value of contingent consideration will result in changes to the cost of acquisition and goodwill, the time value of the deferral of monetary consideration (not deferred share consideration) will also result in an interest cost in the profit and loss account.

25.422 If the vendor has the option to demand shares or cash, and subsequently elects to receive shares rather than cash, the acquirer will, therefore, suffer an interest cost during the period the consideration was outstanding, because the deferred consideration would have been reported as a liability.

Disclosure of contingent consideration

25.423 FRS 6 requires the following to be disclosed in respect of deferred or contingent purchase consideration:

- The nature of the consideration.
- The range of possible outcomes.
- The principal factors that affect the outcome.

[FRS 6 para 24].

25.424 This disclosure is required individually for each material acquisition, and in aggregate for other acquisitions. [FRS 6 para 23]. The example in Table 25.21 covers these requirements.

Consideration contingent on net assets

25.425 In some cases the amount of contingent consideration depends not on the future performance of the acquired company, but on the outcome of an uncertainty in the valuation of the net assets acquired, for example, the settlement of a contingent liability. Purchase price contingencies not only relate to additional payments by the acquirer, but also to refunds by the vendor. Often in business combinations the acquired company may have various contingent liabilities (for example, tax risks, environmental problems or court cases) for which the acquirer may seek some form of indemnity or warranty from the vendor. By their nature these indemnities can be considered as negative contingent consideration as they are often repayments / reimbursements made by the vendor to the acquirer. Often the substance is that both the purchaser and vendor wish to 'set aside' these contingent obligations so that they do not have any economic impact on the acquisition.

25.425.1 Examples of compensation payments that may become payable by a vendor include:

- Redundancy costs.
- Reorganisation costs.
- Incentive payments to key employees.
- Contingent liabilities (for example, tax risks, environmental, legal, fines).
- General indemnity or warranty clauses.
- Contractual obligations in the event of a change of ownership.
- Accounting irregularities.

25.425.2 The outcome of the contingency may not be determined until after the hindsight period allowed for finalising the fair values of assets and liabilities has expired. FRS 7 does not deal with this situation. Although FRS 7 requires the cost of acquisition to be revised without time limit where any part of the purchase consideration is contingent, it does not normally permit any further fair value adjustments to the acquired subsidiary's assets and liabilities after the specified investigation period.

25.425.3 The consequences of FRS 7's requirements in relation to vendor compensation payments are that:

- Where the related cost that is being compensated is not an identifiable liability at the acquisition date, the cost is taken to the post acquisition profit and loss account, whereas the compensation from the vendor (that is, a reimbursement of the consideration) is taken to goodwill.
- Where the related cost that is being compensated is either an identifiable liability or contingent liability at the acquisition date and adjustments to the measurement of these liabilities occur after the hindsight period, those adjustments are taken to the post acquisition profit and loss account, whereas the compensation payment is taken to goodwill.

Therefore, asymmetric accounting results.

25.425.4 The accounting described in the second bullet point in paragraph 25.425.3 above may not reflect the underlying economics of the transaction, particularly when all of the following circumstances are present:

- There is an identifiable liability or contingent liability at the acquisition date that is not conditional on the entity being acquired.
- There is no burden of proof that the risk existed at the acquisition date and it is the explicit wish of both parties that the acquirer be compensated for these risks should they materialise.
- The vendor agrees to specifically indemnify the acquirer for all or a specified proportion of the costs to be incurred.
- The acquirer may have to provide evidence to substantiate the amount being claimed, but on delivery of that evidence there is no doubt that the amount will be reimbursed.
- There are no further negotiations to take place between the acquirer and vendor in relation to the subject matter of the claim or attached conditions. There are no clauses that allow for arbitration.
- The acquirer has not, in substance, economically assumed the liability as part of the business combination transaction. The liability has been 'set aside' in undertaking the purchase price negotiations.

In these circumstances, it might be possible to argue symmetrical accounting.

Fees and other expenses of acquisition

25.426 Costs incurred in carrying out an acquisition need to be analysed into two elements.

- Costs of raising capital for the acquisition and of issuing capital instruments in consideration for the acquisition. Where these fall within the restrictive definition of 'issue costs' contained in FRS 4 (or 'transaction costs' in FRS 26 for entities applying that standard), they should be accounted for as a deduction from the proceeds of those capital instruments.
- Fees and similar incremental costs, excluding costs of raising capital, incurred directly in making an acquisition. These should be added to the cost of acquisition.

25.427 Costs of raising capital that do not qualify to be treated as either of the above, and other expenses that cannot be treated as part of the cost of acquisition under FRS 7 (see para 25.430 below), should be written off to profit and loss account as incurred.

25.428 First, it is necessary to allocate the expenses between those that relate to issuing capital instruments and those that relate to other aspects of negotiating and transacting the acquisition. The treatment of issue/transaction costs required by FRS 4 (or FRS 26 for entities applying that standard – see further chapter 6) applies whether capital is raised to finance acquisitions or for any other purpose. Such costs might include underwriting, legal and other fees in connection with share issues, and arrangement fees payable to banks for providing loan finance. This will result in any issue costs associated with an acquisition being accounted for as follows:

- Issue costs relating to bank loans and other forms of debt (including shares classified as liabilities under FRS 25) should be initially deducted from the liability and subsequently written off in the profit and loss account over the term of the debt.

- Costs of issuing shares classed as equity instruments should be debited against reserves. The share premium account would be available for the write-off of such issue costs.

25.429 Secondly, it is necessary to consider which of those expenses that do not qualify for the above treatment should be capitalised by adding them to the cost of acquisition as required by FRS 7. By treating expenses as part of the cost of acquisition, they are included in the calculation of goodwill

25.430 FRS 7 also provides a narrow definition of costs that may be capitalised. They include *"fees and similar incremental costs incurred directly in making an acquisition"*, but must not include *"internal costs, and other expenses that cannot be directly attributed to the acquisition"*. [FRS 7 para 28].

25.431 The UITF took the view (Information Sheet No 35, issued in February 2000) that incidental financing costs that do not qualify to be treated as issue costs (such arrangement fees for bridging finance facilities, participation fees and costs of researching alternative financing arrangements) are not to be regarded as incremental costs incurred directly in making an acquisition. Consequently, such costs should not be included as part of the cost of acquisition, but should be written off immediately.

25.432 Therefore, costs eligible for capitalisation might include fees payable to merchant banks, lawyers, accountants and other advisors for:

- Investigating and valuing the target.

- Auditing the completion accounts.

- Negotiating the price and completing the transaction.
- Undertaking due diligence work.

25.433 The treatment of fees in respect of searching for and identifying the business that was subsequently acquired is marginal. A finders' fee resulting from work commissioned to identify a suitable target might qualify to be capitalised where it relates to the business that was acquired; however, in general, other search and investigation fees incurred before a specific target has been identified would need to be written off.

25.434 Moreover, where such services are provided by in-house departments of the acquirer rather than by external advisors, FRS 7 does not allow the costs to be capitalised. Previously there was sometimes argument over whether allocations of costs such as time spent by a company's management on researching and negotiating an acquisition, or specific overtime payments related to work on the acquisition, could be capitalised. FRS 7 precludes capitalisation of *any* internal costs.

25.435 The ASB had exposed an alternative view in FRED 7 that would also have allowed costs to have been capitalised where they were incurred in respect of equivalent services provided by in-house departments, such as legal advice or acquisition search and investigation services. The ASB decided that the difficulty of satisfactorily defining eligible internal costs, and the consequent risk of allowing excessive costs to be capitalised, outweighed the anomalies in the restrictive approach taken in FRS 7.

25.436 In practice, the work carried out by advisors in respect of transacting the acquisition will overlap the work on raising capital. It may then be necessary to make reasonable allocations of advisors' expenses to determine which accounting treatment is appropriate.

Section III — Goodwill

Introduction

25.437 Goodwill has been one of the most hotly debated subjects in accounting. The most fundamental issue was whether purchased goodwill arising from acquisitions should or should not be treated as an asset in the balance sheet. During one of the longest running of accounting debates, deeply entrenched views were held on both sides. The publication of FRS 10 in December 1997 was a major event that would change the shape of the financial statements of acquisitive companies. For financial years from December 1998, purchased goodwill has had to be accounted for as an asset.

[The next paragraph is 25.440.]

The move from immediate write-off to capitalisation

25.440 The immediate write-off of goodwill against reserves (which was allowed prior to FRS 10 under SSAP 22) reduces net assets, but has the perceived advantage that the profit and loss account does not have to bear any charge for goodwill, except on disposal. In contrast, capitalising and amortising goodwill has a positive balance sheet effect – increasing shareholders' funds and reducing gearing. But it has a negative effect on performance measures shown in the financial statements – reducing the rate of return on investments in new businesses and reducing earnings per share.

25.441 The ASB settled on capitalisation of purchased goodwill, rather than elimination, for a number of reasons:

- Management accountability for the cost of goodwill on acquisitions is maintained (rather than lost) in the accounting treatment.
- Purchased goodwill and intangibles that are similar to goodwill are accounted for consistently.
- Capitalisation had become the accepted treatment internationally.

25.442 One of the key issues for the ASB was to develop an acceptable method of dealing with the amortisation problem. Just as there is a conceptual divide between treating the amount spent on goodwill as an asset and treating it as a reduction in shareholders' equity, so there is a divide between treating capitalised goodwill as a depreciable asset and treating it as an investment with continuing value. One view is that the original purchased goodwill is depleted over time and replaced by internally generated goodwill which cannot be recognised. Another view is that the cost of goodwill to the group should be treated consistently with the cost of investment by the parent, which is only written down if its carrying value is impaired, that is, not supported by the value of the future cash flows of the acquired business.

25.443 The ASB has been sympathetic to the investment argument and to the principle that goodwill should be written off in the profit and loss account only if, and when, its value is impaired and not gradually over an arbitrary period. But an important constraint is that the Act requires purchased goodwill to be fully amortised over a finite period if it is treated as an asset. It does not allow goodwill to be carried permanently as an asset. FRS 10's method of accounting for goodwill is, however, something of a hybrid between the automatic amortisation and impairment approaches. The constraints of law and practicality led the ASB to develop a method that would allow goodwill to be amortised quickly, slowly or not at all according to the circumstances. But the final standard steers companies firmly towards automatic amortisation over a maximum 20-year period, which is the same approach that had previously met such strong opposition from the corporate sector.

25.444 International standard-setters are not constrained by the UK's legal requirements. The IASB considers that the useful life of acquired goodwill and the pattern in which it diminishes are, generally, not possible to predict. Consequently, the amount of goodwill amortised in any given period is an arbitrary estimate of the consumption of acquired goodwill during that period. The IASB's view is that the amortisation of goodwill over an arbitrary period fails to provide useful information. Therefore, in March 2004, the IASB issued IFRS 3, 'Business combinations', which brings IFRS into line with US GAAP by requiring that goodwill is no longer amortised, but instead is subject to an annual impairment test. IFRS 3 represented the completion of the first phase of the IASB's larger project on business combinations. In July 2005 the ASB issued an exposure draft proposing convergence of UK GAAP with IFRS in this area.

Scope of FRS 10

25.445 FRS 10 is really two standards rolled into one. It covers all goodwill (arising from business acquisitions and from acquisitions of equity accounted interests in associates and joint ventures) and, with a few exceptions, all intangible assets (including those identified in a business acquisition, those purchased separately and those developed internally). The ASB found it convenient to deal with both goodwill and intangibles in a single standard because they are closely related and the ASB decided the same accounting rules should apply to both.

25.446 Many intangibles and goodwill share similar characteristics. Accounting for intangibles is an important issue in acquisition accounting because any values ascribed to separate intangibles reduce the residual amount of goodwill. It is less of an issue, however, under FRS 10 than it was under SSAP 22 when, on the one hand, goodwill could be written off to reserves immediately on acquisition whilst, on the other hand, intangibles could be recognised as assets.

25.447 The rules relating to identifying intangible assets in acquisition accounting are discussed in section II, paragraph 25.178. The recognition and measurement rules that apply to purchased and internally developed intangible assets are discussed in chapter 15. The discussion in this chapter primarily considers purchased goodwill arising from business combinations. FRS 10's application to associates and joint ventures is discussed in chapter 27.

Definition of purchased goodwill

25.448 Purchased goodwill is simply an accounting difference. It is the amount by which the cost of a business entity as a whole exceeds the aggregate fair values of its identifiable assets and liabilities at the date of acquisition. Those fair values are determined by applying the rules in FRS 7 and they are used as the carrying amounts (a proxy for cost) for the newly acquired assets and liabilities in the acquirer's financial statements. If the aggregate fair values of the acquired business' identifiable assets and liabilities exceed the cost of acquisition, the difference is referred to as negative goodwill.

25.449 Purchased goodwill may arise in the acquirer's consolidated financial statements only (where a parent company acquires a new subsidiary), or in the acquiring entity's individual financial statements (where it purchases an unincorporated undertaking or a business and assets of another company).

Accounting for goodwill — summary

Internally generated goodwill

25.450 Internally generated goodwill may be viewed as the difference between the market value of a business entity and the aggregate fair value of its net assets. Neither the Act nor FRS 10 allows internally generated goodwill to be recognised on the balance sheet. The Act states that goodwill may be shown as an asset only if it was acquired for valuable consideration. [Note 3 on the balance sheet formats; FRS 10 para 8].

Purchased goodwill

25.451 FRS 10 requires purchased goodwill to be treated as an asset on the balance sheet. Its objective, in relation to capitalised goodwill, is:

- To ensure that goodwill is charged in the profit and loss account in the periods in which it is depleted.
- To ensure that disclosure is sufficient to enable users to determine the goodwill's impact on financial position and performance.

[FRS 10 para 1]

25.452 Goodwill should be amortised quickly, slowly or not at all according to the circumstances:

- Where goodwill has a limited useful economic life, it should be amortised systematically over that life.
- There is a rebuttable presumption that the useful economic life does not exceed 20 years.
- A longer life than 20 years, or an indefinite life, may be chosen where the value can be demonstrated to be more durable.
- Non-amortisation of goodwill is a 'true and fair override' of company law (which requires goodwill to be amortised down to zero) and so can only be adopted in special circumstances when following the basic rule of amortisation would not give a true and fair view.

25.453 If a company either amortises goodwill over more than 20 years or does not amortise goodwill at all, it has to carry out an annual impairment test. This is a thorough exercise which is aimed at demonstrating whether the present value of the future cash flows that the acquisition will earn are, or are not, enough to justify the carrying value of the goodwill. If they are not, an impairment write-down should be made.

25.454 If a company amortises goodwill over no more than 20 years, a recoverable amount check is required at the end of the first full financial year following the acquisition. This 'first year review' is intended to capture any overpayment for the acquisition or failure of the acquired business to meet expectations at the time of the acquisition. If the impairment review confirms that the carrying value of the goodwill is not recoverable, it should be written down. In other years an impairment test is required only if adverse events indicate that the amortised carrying value of the goodwill may not be recoverable, and an impairment write-down should be made if the test confirms this.

25.455 The details of the impairment tests are found in FRS 11, 'Impairment of fixed assets and goodwill'. The tests are complex and subjective. This is particularly so for the not infrequent case where a group acquires a new subsidiary and integrates it into the group. In these situations it is not possible to isolate and track the cash flows attributable to the acquisition and to perform the impairment test requires a complicated review procedure, set out in some detail in chapter 18.

25.456 Goodwill cannot be revalued above original cost.

25.457 Amortisation or impairment charged in previous periods cannot be reversed in subsequent periods except in limited circumstances with respect to impairment.

Useful economic life

25.458 For each acquisition the useful economic life of the residual amount of purchased goodwill must be estimated.

Definition

25.459 The useful economic life of purchased goodwill is defined as *"the period over which the value of the underlying business acquired is expected to exceed the values of its identifiable net assets"*. [FRS 10 para 2].

25.460 Purchased goodwill is in effect treated as an element of the investment in the acquired business, that is, the premium over its net asset value. In theory, the useful economic life can be indefinite if management continue to invest in the acquired business so as to maintain the premium; furthermore, the above definition allows for goodwill to be continuously regenerated after the acquisition.

25.461 The definition of useful economic life was a contentious issue during the development of FRS 10. The ASB has described its approach to amortisation as one which seeks to charge goodwill to the profit and loss account only to the extent that the carrying value of the goodwill is not supported by the *current* value of the goodwill within the acquired business. This allows for purchased goodwill to be carried permanently without amortisation in some circumstances.

25.462 Prior to FRS 10, SSAP 22 required capitalised goodwill (that is, the original purchased goodwill) to be amortised in all circumstances. The reason was that subsequent expenditure or other circumstances affecting the acquired business would have the effect of replacing the original purchased goodwill with internally generated goodwill, which cannot be recognised as an asset. The argument was that the benefits of purchased goodwill that existed (and was paid for) at the time of the acquisition are always consumed over a relatively short period; the continuing (or enhanced) premium over net asset value is eventually transformed into internally generated goodwill.

Rebuttable presumption of 20 years or less

25.463 Despite the opportunity given by FRS 10's definition to regard goodwill as having a very long or indefinite useful economic life, the practical emphasis in the standard is rather different. The standard explains that *"the transient nature of many business opportunities makes it appropriate for there to be a presumption that the 'premium' that an acquired business has over its net asset value cannot be maintained indefinitely"*. [FRS 10 para 20]. The framework for determining goodwill's useful economic life is as follows:

- There is a rebuttable presumption that the useful economic life does not exceed 20 years.
- A useful economic life exceeding 20 years, or an indefinite life, may be chosen *only* if:
  - the durability of the acquired business for the longer (or indefinite) period can be demonstrated; and
  - the goodwill is capable of continued measurement (so that annual impairment reviews will be feasible).

[FRS 10 para 19].

25.464 One reason for having a presumed arbitrary upper limit on the useful economic life is that it would otherwise frequently be difficult to estimate it. A period of 20 years is a benchmark that has had some significance internationally. However, the uncertainty involved in estimating useful lives does not allow 20 years to be automatically used by default, nor does it allow goodwill to be written off over an unrealistically short period. A company could not, for example, simply expense all goodwill as a one-off hit to earnings in the year of acquisition in order to avoid future amortisation charges. [FRS 10 paras 21, 22].

25.465 On the other hand, the FRS states that the 20-year upper limit may be rebutted if the conditions (that is, evidence of durability and continued measurability) are met. Furthermore, the standard's interpretation of those conditions make it improbable that a company could be forced to adopt a useful economic life of more than 20 years if it chose not to, even if the value of the goodwill was expected to be more durable. The assumptions used in forecasting become more vulnerable the longer the estimated life is. For example, in many industries the pace of developments means that consumer patterns cannot be predicted with much certainty over very long periods. Clearly the emphasis is on being prudent, without being unrealistically prudent.

25.466 The second condition for rebutting the 20-year upper limit, that the goodwill is capable of continued measurement, is important. The annual impairment reviews specified by FRS 11 have to be feasible and be expected to remain so for the foreseeable future. FRS 10 states that goodwill will not be capable of continued measurement if the cost of such measurement is viewed as being unjustifiably high. This clearly invites directors to opt not to rebut the presumption of a 20-year life if they judge that the cost of carrying out annual impairment reviews outweighs the benefits. The standard gives as an example the situation where businesses are integrated after acquisition so that the goodwill relating to the acquired business can no longer be readily tracked. Even if there are no such integration plans, the directors may not wish to rule out future reorganisations that could lose the separate identity of the acquired business. Other examples given are where the company's management information systems are not compatible with the detail of the impairment reviews required by the standard, and where the amounts of goodwill involved are not sufficiently material to justify the cost of carrying out the impairment reviews. [FRS 10 para 23].

Factors determining useful economic life

25.467 Apart from explaining the conditions for rebutting the 20-year threshold, FRS 10 gives little guidance on how to estimate the useful economic life. It gives examples of factors that contribute to the durability of goodwill and, since these will limit useful economic lives, they are also relevant for estimating lives that are considered to be 20 years or less. These factors refer to the nature of the business, the stability of the industry, the effects of future competition, the typical life-spans of the products of the acquired business and the extent to which the acquisition overcomes market entry barriers that will continue to exist. [FRS 10 para 20].

25.468 These factors often combine to present an overall picture of durability. A long life (20 years plus) will generally require a business, industry and products to have a long past track record of stability and achievement and to have high barriers to market entry. Added to this, of course, is the commitment of the new management to continue to invest in the acquired business for the long-term to maintain and enhance its value. Other businesses, industries and products may be relatively new, potentially much more volatile and possibly requiring a payback for the acquirer over a much shorter period. An amortisation period much shorter than 20 years may then be appropriate. This may be so for products with expected short life cycles or where there are few barriers to prevent new competitors from entering the market. An example of a business acquisition with an estimated useful life substantially below 20 years is shown in Table 25.22.

Table 25.22 – 3i plc – Annual Report and Accounts – 31 March 2000

Notes to the accounts (extract)

Goodwill in the year arose on the acquisition of TH Technologieholding GmbH (see note 22). This purchased goodwill relates to TH Technologieholding GmbH's market position and the experience in early stage technology investment of its staff. It is being amortised over its estimated useful economic life of five years, the period over which the Group expects to benefit from TH Technologieholding GmbH's reputation, contacts and skills, using the straight line method.

25.469 A group should assess the factors at the time it makes an acquisition. Examples of issues to consider are:

- Expected changes in products, markets or technology. A high technology company that only has one main product might have considerable goodwill while that product is leading the market, but if a competitor produces a better product, then the company's goodwill can diminish rapidly.
- Expected future demand, competition or other economic factors that may affect current advantages.
- The expected period of future service of certain employees or the retention period of key clients. An advertising agency's goodwill may be very dependent on key employees/clients and the agency's goodwill may depend significantly on their retention period.
- The extent to which goodwill is linked to the economic lives of intangible assets.

25.470 The last of the above is an important factor that is attached to the definition of useful economic life itself. Where intangible assets have been subsumed into the residual amount of goodwill, because they cannot be measured reliably, the useful economic life of the goodwill is linked to the lives of those intangibles. [FRS 10 para 2]. For example, an acquired company may have a licence to carry on a particular business for a finite period. If the licence were recognised as a separate intangible, it would be amortised over the licence period, unless the licence rights were renewable and renewal were assured. If the value of the licence were subsumed within purchased goodwill, the amortisation period should be the same, that is, aligned with the life of the underlying rights.

25.471 This factor could also work to demonstrate a long or indefinite useful economic life. For example, much of the value of goodwill on an acquisition may be in a brand name that does not meet the recognition criteria for a separate intangible asset. Nevertheless, the brand may have been well established for decades and an indefinite future life may be justifiable by linking the goodwill to the brand that is fundamental to maintaining the current value of the premium in the acquired business.

Accounting implications of life above or below 20 years

25.472 The accounting implications of choosing a useful economic life above or below 20 years are summarised below:

20 years or less	More than 20 years
Amortisation charge against earnings 5% or more	Amortisation charge against earnings less than 5%
	Nil amortisation requires true and fair override
Impairment review at end of first full year, thereafter only on exception basis	Detailed annual impairment reviews
Less exposure to future (unpredictable) impairment losses	Greater exposure to future (unpredictable) impairment losses
	Additional disclosure

25.473 FRS 10 requires disclosure of the amortisation periods and the reasons for choosing those periods. [FRS 10 para 55].

25.474 The additional disclosures required where the useful economic life is more than 20 years are as follows:

- the grounds for rebutting the 20-year presumption; including
- a reasoned explanation based on the specific factors contributing to the durability of the acquired business.

[FRS 10 para 58].

25.475 In addition, where goodwill is not amortised, additional disclosures are required to support the true and fair override required by the standard in such circumstances to comply with the Companies Act 1985 (see para 25.480). [FRS 10 para 59].

25.476 In May 2004, the FRRP issued a general warning on the need to provide adequate disclosures when the presumption of a 20 year useful economic life for an intangible asset or goodwill is rebutted. The FRRP points out that, however well known a brand or other asset is, the directors must provide a 'reasoned explanation' for their decision, sufficient to satisfy paragraphs 58 and 59 of FRS 10 so that users of the financial statements can understand the rationale for the chosen accounting treatment.

Indefinite life — true and fair override

25.477 The Companies Act 1985 states that where goodwill is treated as an asset, it should be reduced by provisions for depreciation calculated to write it off in full (that is, to nil) systematically over a period chosen by the company's directors, which must not exceed its useful economic life. [CA85 4 Sch 21(2)(3)]. Therefore, whilst the Companies Act 1985 permits goodwill to be amortised over a shorter period than its useful economic life, it does not allow either an indefinite useful economic life or any residual value to be assumed. The Companies Act 1985 in effect reflects the traditional view of the useful economic life where the value of purchased goodwill is depleted over time and replaced by non-purchased goodwill generated by the new owners.

25.478 So, non-amortisation can be adopted only by invoking the 'true and fair override' of the Act's requirement for amortisation. Moreover, the Act's true and fair override provisions can only be invoked in 'special circumstances' when following the basic rule of amortisation would not give a true and fair view. [CA85 Sec 227A(5)(6); CA06 Sec 404(5)].

25.479 In the appendix to FRS 10 that explains its development, the ASB states that it believes there may be circumstances where a true and fair view will be given only if goodwill or an intangible asset is not amortised, but is instead subject to annual reviews for impairment. [FRS 10, Appendix III para 35]. But FRS 10 in effect restricts non-amortisation to exceptional circumstances in order to avoid being in conflict with the Act, since the 'true and fair override' cannot be applied indiscriminately. Restricting non-amortisation of goodwill to such 'special circumstances' means that it raises a number of policy issues for companies making acquisitions:

- Non-amortisation must be considered on an acquisition-by-acquisition basis — it cannot be adopted as a general accounting policy.
- The circumstances specified in FRS 10 regarding the indefinite durability of the acquired business place a clear onus on a company's directors to demonstrate that they can maintain (or enhance) the value of the premium paid for the acquisition indefinitely.
- Non-amortisation would be restricted to material acquisitions where amortisation charges would not give a true and fair view.
- The directors must be confident that they will always in the future be able to measure the current value of such goodwill with sufficient reliability to carry out the annual impairment reviews; future business reorganisations may have an impact on this.
- The reaction of analysts and other users needs to be considered if a company claims it has demonstrated no need for amortisation, but other companies in similar sectors chose to amortise their goodwill (and *vice versa*). In this regard, the Society of Investment Professionals (formerly the Institute of Investment Management and Research) (IIMR) at present excludes goodwill amortisation from its definition of 'headline earnings'.

25.480 The required disclosures, which must also comply with FRS 18, give considerable prominence to the 'true and fair override'. The disclosures, which are intended to convey to users the circumstances justifying its use, are:

- A statement that the financial statements depart from the specific requirement of the Act to amortise goodwill over a finite period.

- Particulars of the departure from the Act. This means a statement that the Act would normally require amortisation and a description of the treatment actually adopted.

- The reasons for the departure from the Act, which should include an explanation of the specific factors contributing to the durability of the acquired business. Also there should be a statement as to why amortisation would not give a true and fair view.

- The effect of the departure from the Act — however, this will not normally be possible to quantify, because where goodwill arising from a particular acquisition is assigned an indefinite life, there is no benchmark for calculating an amortisation charge required by the Act. The circumstances should, therefore, be explained.

- The disclosure above should either be included, or cross-referenced, in the note required by paragraph 36A of Schedule 4 (regarding compliance with accounting standards).

[FRS 10 para 59; FRS 18 para 62].

25.481 An illustration of the disclosures required where the true and fair override has been invoked in shown in Table 25.23.

Table 25.23 – Kelda Group plc – Annual Report & Accounts – 31 March 2001

10 Intangible assets (extract)

The goodwill arising on the acquisition of Aquarion Company, which amounted to £164.3m, has, in the opinion of the directors, an indefinite life and, therefore, is not being amortised. The company operates in the stable US market of clean water supply in which barriers to entry are high due to significant infrastructure requirements. In addition, Aquarion Company has the rights to operate in its current territory in perpetuity. Consequently, the goodwill is demonstrated to be 'durable' and since it is not the Group's intention to merge the business with its existing businesses, is capable of 'continued measurement' as defined by FRS 10 'Goodwill and Intangible Assets' . In accordance with FRS 10 an impairment review was carried out on 31 March 2001, which showed that the company value of goodwill was not more than its recoverable amount. The accounting treatment is a departure from the requirements of Paragraph 21 of Schedule 4 to the Companies Act 1985 and is adopted in order to present a true and fair view of the Group's results. If the goodwill had been amortised over 20 years, the amortisation charge for the period ended 31 March 2001 would have been £8.2m and the net book amount of goodwill at 31 March 2001 would have been £154.0m (2000: £162.2m). Goodwill capitalised in respect of the Group's other acquisitions since 1 April 1998 has been assigned a useful economic life of 20 years.

Goodwill with more than one useful economic life

25.482 An acquisition of a group of companies may comprise two or more lines of business whose activities differ significantly from one another. The question arises whether the goodwill that arises overall on the acquisition should be allocated to the separate lines of business and, if applicable, those components attributed different useful economic lives. If that is done, the amortisation charge would reflect the different economic lives of the different components.

25.483 Some would argue that, since there is only one acquisition, there is only one composite goodwill amount and one life.

25.484 Allocation of purchased goodwill to different businesses is, however, necessary in order to properly account for future business disposals and to perform the impairment reviews which are specified by FRS 11, 'Impairment of fixed assets and goodwill'. FRS 11 requires capitalised goodwill to be allocated to income-generating units along with other assets and liabilities for the purpose of impairment reviews. It also requires goodwill on an acquisition comprising two dissimilar businesses to be reviewed separately for impairment. [FRS 11 para 34]. Therefore, an impairment loss is one business segment could not be offset against an increase in value of the other.

25.485 Although FRS 10 is silent as to whether goodwill can be divided into one or more elements for calculating amortisation periods, it would be consistent with FRS 11's impairment rules for goodwill attributable to dissimilar businesses to be amortised separately if they demonstrably have different useful economic lives. The resulting annual amortisation charge would also better reflect the estimated rate of depletion of the purchased goodwill than using, say, an average of the useful lives of different components.

Example

An acquisition comprises two different business segments. The total goodwill is £1m which is allocated £600,000 to segment A and £400,000 to segment B. The goodwill attaching to segment A is considered to have a useful life of 40 years, whereas the goodwill attaching to segment B has a useful life of 10 years.

One approach might be to estimate a weighted average of the useful economic life in aggregate, that is, 28 years. This may be shortened to 20 years if FRS 10's presumption of a maximum life of 20 years is not rebutted. A 20-year life would give an annual amortisation charge of £50,000; a 28-year life would give an annual amortisation charge of £35,714. However, this approach appears to be flawed, because averaging the short-life goodwill over a longer period means the amounts charged to the profit and loss account in the first 10 years (that is, the short life of segment B's goodwill) understates the amount by which the goodwill is in aggregate expected to be depleted. Therefore, this method may fail FRS 10's objective that goodwill is charged in the profit and loss account in the periods in which it is depleted. A preferable approach is to amortise the goodwill attributable to the two segments separately. This in turn could lead to two different amortisation patterns.

The first is to amortise £600,000 in segment A over 40 years (£15,000 per annum) and £400,000 in segment B over 10 years (£40,000 per annum). This produces an annual amortisation charge of £55,000 for 10 years and £15,000 for the subsequent 30 years. This pattern matches the actual expected rate of depletion of the goodwill. However, the goodwill in segment A would be subject to annual impairment reviews.

The second is to amortise £600,000 in segment A over 20 years (£30,000 per annum) and £400,000 in segment B over 10 years (£40,000 per annum), if the company decides not to rebut FRS 10's presumption of a maximum life of 20 years. This produces an annual amortisation charge of £70,000 for 10 years and £30,000 for the subsequent 10 years.

25.486 It should be noted that allocating goodwill to different segments could not result in negative goodwill being attributed to one segment and positive goodwill being attributed to another, because neither FRS 10 nor the Act permit purchased goodwill (positive or negative) arising on a single acquisition to be divided into positive and negative components.

Revisions of useful economic lives

25.487 Estimating useful economic lives of goodwill is very judgemental. FRS 10 requires that the useful economic lives should be reviewed at the end of each reporting period and revised if necessary. [FRS 10 para 33].

25.488 Useful lives may need to be revised to reflect previously unexpected events or changes in circumstances, such as a major technological change or a market being opened up to greater competition. Adverse factors that might lead to a write-off of goodwill (via the impairment review procedures) might similarly indicate that the remaining useful life of the balance has been shortened.

25.489 Where it is considered that previous estimates of useful economic lives need to be revised, the net book values at the date of revision should be amortised prospectively over the revised remaining useful economic lives. [FRS 10 para 33].

25.490 The requirement in paragraph 33 of FRS 10 means that if, for example, a company decided that the goodwill on an acquisition made in previous periods now had an indefinite life, whilst there would be no amortisation going forward, the goodwill amortisation already charged could not be written back.

25.491 UITF Abstract 27, 'Revision to estimates of the useful economic life of goodwill and intangible assets', confirmed that, other than on the initial implementation of FRS 10, a change from non-amortisation over a period should be dealt with prospectively by amortising the carrying value over the revised remaining economic life (that is, it should not be dealt with as a prior year adjustment). This applies even if the change results from a decision to no longer rebut the 20 year life presumption.

25.492 An estimated useful economic life may be shortened or increased. However, if it is increased from 20 years or less to more than 20 years from the date of acquisition, annual impairment reviews would be required thereafter in accordance with the normal rules for goodwill that is amortised over more than 20 years or not at all. Therefore, a 20-year life in effect remains a ceiling for those companies that are unable or unwilling to carry out annual impairment reviews.

25.493 Where a useful economic life is revised, the reason and the effect, if material, should be disclosed in the year of change. [FRS 10 para 56]. The effect of a change is the difference between the amortisation charge that results from applying the previous and the revised estimated useful lives (that is, how much more or less profit a company records as a result of changing useful economic lives).

Methods of amortising goodwill

25.494 Where goodwill is amortised, it must be amortised down to zero over its estimated useful economic life. No residual value is allowed to enter the calculation. [FRS 10 para 28; CA85 4 Sch para 21(2)].

25.495 For example, it would not be permitted to identify a useful economic life of 20 years and yet charge little or no amortisation because a significant residual value was expected at the end of 20 years. In that situation, the goodwill is in effect expected to be more durable than 20 years. A low or nil annual amortisation charge can only be arrived at if the presumption of a maximum 20-year life is rebutted and a longer or indefinite life is chosen. Of course, the goodwill would then be subject to annual impairment reviews. If the 20-year presumption is not rebutted, the goodwill must be amortised to zero over 20 years.

25.496 FRS 10 states that the method of amortising goodwill should reflect the expected pattern of its depletion. However, a straight-line method should be chosen, unless another method can be demonstrated to be more appropriate. [FRS 10 para 30]. Although arbitrary, specifying a benchmark method is a practical means of dealing with the difficulty of measuring depletion and it does promote comparability.

25.497 The FRS also explains that it is unlikely that methods that are less conservative that the straight-line method could be justified with sufficient evidence. It also states that interest methods, such as the 'reverse sum of digits' methods, which have the effect of backloading the amortisation charge to later periods, are not appropriate methods of amortising goodwill because they are not related to its depletion. [FRS 10 paras 31, 32].

25.498 FRS 10 requires the methods of amortising goodwill to be disclosed. [FRS 10 para 55].

25.499 A company may conceivably wish to change its method of amortising goodwill, say, to revert to the straight-line method from some other method. Where this occurs, FRS 10 requires the reason and the effect, if material, to be disclosed in the year of change. The effect of a change is the difference between the amortisation charge that results from applying the previous and the revised amortisation methods (that is, how much more or less profit a company records as a result of changing amortisation methods).

Acquisition with contingent consideration

25.500 An important practical effect of the goodwill amortisation requirements arises where the consideration for an acquisition is payable in the future and contingent on the acquired company achieving a specified level of performance in future years. FRS 7 requires a reasonable estimate of the fair value of amounts expected to be payable in the future to be included in the cost of acquisition when the fair value exercise is undertaken. Any such amounts recognised increase the purchased goodwill that is recognised when the acquisition is first accounted for.

25.501 Amortising the whole amount of the estimated purchased goodwill on a straight-line basis from the date of acquisition results in full charges against earnings in the immediate post-acquisition periods, before the future contingent payments have fallen due or been finally determined and possibly before the specified levels of post-acquisition earnings have been achieved. This situation can only be avoided if an amortisation pattern can be justified that increases in line with the actual consideration payments. But, although FRS 10 does not rule this out, as mentioned above, the standard suggests that it is unlikely that there will be circumstances justifying an amortisation pattern that is less conservative than straight-line.

25.502 When contingent consideration is finally determined any adjustments to the amounts estimated at the time of the acquisition would feed through as adjustments to purchased goodwill. The adjustments would have the effect of increasing or decreasing the annual amortisation charges over the goodwill's remaining useful economic life.

25.503 Where material adjustments are made to estimates of contingent consideration, a question arises as to what effect this has on the amortisation of goodwill. There are two possible ways of dealing with this:

- Amortise the revised carrying value prospectively.
- Restore the excess amortisation previously charged (crediting profit and loss account with the excess amount).

25.504 These methods are illustrated in the following example.

Example

An acquisition was made at the beginning of year 1. Consideration of £40m was paid on completion and further consideration was payable based on an earn-out formula relating to the performance of the acquired business over the next three years. £60m of further consideration was provided for in the acquirer's first post-acquisition accounts, giving an estimated cost of acquisition of £100m. Net assets were fair valued at £20m, leaving purchased goodwill of £80m. The goodwill is being amortised over five years (straight-line basis) – an amortisation charge of £16m was recognised in year 1, leaving a carrying value of £64m at the end of year 1.

The acquisition does not perform as well as expected. At the end of year 2, the estimate of further consideration payable is revised downwards from £60m to £20m, resulting in an adjustment reducing the carrying value of goodwill by £40m.

The two methods are illustrated in the following tables (a zero discount rate is assumed).

Method (a) — prospective amortisation

Year	1	2	3	4	5
Goodwill b/f	80	64	18	12	6
Adjustment		(40)			
		24			
Amortisation	(16)	(6)	(6)	(6)	(6)
Goodwill c/f	64	18	12	6	–

Method (b) — reversal of excess amortisation charged in previous year

Year	1	2	3	4	5
Goodwill b/f	80	64	24	16	8
Adjustment		(40)			
Amortisation reversal (credit P&L)		8			
		32			
Amortisation	(16)	(8)	(8)	(8)	(8)
Goodwill c/f	64	24	16	8	–

FRS 10 does not deal with a situation where the amount of goodwill relating to an acquisition is adjusted as a result of a revision of the estimated cost of acquisition. Apart from the reversal (in limited circumstances) of some impairment losses, FRS 10 states *"goodwill. . .should not be revalued, either to increase the carrying value above original cost or to reverse prior period losses arising from impairment of amortisation"*. [FRS 10 para 45]. Thus, for example, where the useful economic life is revised, the carrying value at the date of revision should be amortised (prospectively) over the revised remaining useful economic life. [FRS 10 para 33]. This corresponds with method (a) above.

However, the issue described above is not a revaluation in the sense of paragraph 45. The carrying value of goodwill has to be adjusted downwards as a result of the revised estimate of the cost of acquisition. The question in the example above is whether the carrying value at the beginning of year 2 should be adjusted to 24 (method (a)) or to 32 (method (b)).

One of the objectives of FRS 10 is *"to ensure that. . .capitalised goodwill and intangible assets are charged in the profit and loss account in the periods in which they are depleted. . ."*. Neither method properly achieves this.

Method (a) overstates the cumulative depletion of goodwill, because an amount has previously been charged in the profit and loss account which, with hindsight, will not be paid for. It also arguably understates the cost of goodwill consumed over the remaining estimated useful economic life.

Method (b) better reflects the cumulative depletion of goodwill, but the current year's amortisation charge does not properly reflect the goodwill consumed in that year, because it is credited with the excess charge of the previous year.

It should also be noted that if the purchased goodwill was being accounted for in the accounts of an individual company, the reversal or non-reversal of past amortisation would directly affect the company's distributable profits.

Our view is that either method is acceptable. Whilst we would normally expect the prospective treatment in method (a) to be adopted where estimates are revised, method (b) could be used where the effect of the adjustment to the cost of acquisition is material to the pattern of goodwill amortisation. Whichever method is chosen, material debits should be treated consistently with material credits in respect of different acquisitions.

Presentation of amortisation and impairment charges

25.505 FRS 11 requires impairment losses recognised in the profit and loss account to be included within operating profit under the appropriate statutory heading, and disclosed as an exceptional item if appropriate. [FRS 11 para 67].

25.506 FRS 10's note on legal requirements states that the formats in Schedule 4 to the Act prescribe the headings under which depreciation and other amounts written off tangible and intangible fixed assets are to be included in the profit and loss account. [FRS 10 appendix 1 para 16]. Amortisation and other amounts written off goodwill fall within those headings. Under Format 1, where expenses are classified by function, goodwill would normally be treated as an administrative expense. Under Format 2, where expenses are classified by type, there is a separate heading 'depreciation and amounts written off tangible and intangible fixed assets', which is an operating expense. Both amortisation and impairment losses in respect of goodwill should, therefore, be charged in arriving at operating profit. The FRRP confirmed in a statement (published in January 2000) regarding the financial statements of PWS Holdings PLC that regular goodwill amortisation charges are not exceptional items.

25.507 In the financial year in which an acquisition is made, FRS 3 requires the operating results of the acquired business to be disclosed separately in the acquiring entity's profit and loss account. The amortisation or impairment of any goodwill related to the acquisition for that period should be attributed to the results of the acquisition rather than included with other goodwill amortisation charges that are attributable to the results of continuing operations excluding the acquisition.

25.508 Although goodwill write-offs should generally be included in arriving at operating profit or loss, companies that report earnings per share figures may wish to exclude goodwill write-offs in any additional EPS calculated on another level of earnings. The 'headline' earnings figure defined by the Society of Investment Professionals (formerly the Institute of Investment Management and Research) (IIMR) in its Statement of Investment Practice No 1, which seeks to produce a standardised measure of trading performance, states that *"goodwill should not* *affect earnings in any way"*. Consequently, the 'headline' earnings figure excludes any charges in respect of goodwill in its reconciliation of FRS 3 earnings to IIMR 'headline' earnings.

Reversals of past goodwill write-offs

25.509 The carrying value of purchased goodwill cannot be increased by revaluation or by reversing past amortisation charges. If goodwill is considered to have been amortised too quickly in the past, its useful economic life may be increased, but the carrying value should be amortised prospectively over the remaining revised useful life.

25.510 Impairment losses in respect of goodwill may be reversed (that is, credited back in the profit and loss account), but only in limited circumstances. These are where (a) an external event caused the original impairment loss, and (b) subsequent external events clearly and demonstrably reverse the effects of that event in a way that was not foreseen in the original impairment calculations. [FRS 10 para 44; FRS 11 para 60].

25.511 An impairment loss in FRS terminology is similar to provision for permanent diminution in value in the Act. Where there is a permanent diminution in the value of any goodwill held as an asset which is expected to be permanent, a provision should be made in the profit and loss account. [CA85 4 Sch 19(2)]. If the reasons for such a provision no longer apply, then the provision should be written back to the extent that it is no longer necessary. [CA85 4 Sch 19(3)]. For all practical intents and purposes the reversal criteria in FRS 10 and the Companies Act 1985 are deemed to be the same.

25.512 The objective of restricting reversals of impairment losses is to prevent a goodwill write-off from being credited back to the profit and loss account if the credit is in effect attributable to the generation of new non-purchased goodwill. Consequently, situations that justify reversals are likely to be rare and in most cases amounts written off goodwill will stay written off. In this respect, the reversal criteria for goodwill (and most intangible assets) are stricter than those for tangible fixed assets, where impairment losses should be reversed in a much wider range of circumstances provided that subsequent increases in recoverable amount can be attributed to changed economic conditions. The reason given for the different approaches is that tangible fixed assets can in any case be revalued, whereas goodwill and most intangible assets cannot be.

25.513 One example of originating and reversing external events that would meet the reversal criteria for goodwill is the introduction of a new law that damages profitability (resulting in a goodwill write-off) and that is subsequently repealed by a new government. Another example is the confiscation of assets in an overseas territory (resulting in a goodwill write-off) that are subsequently released to allow the business to continue its operations. In both of these examples the original goodwill has been reclaimed.

25.514 The recoverable amount of an acquired business may increase in subsequent years after an impairment loss has been recognised, but the improvement will often be unrelated to the circumstances that gave rise to the original impairment. One example is where goodwill has been written off because a competitor has introduced a better product to the market; some years later, the company launches a new product of its own and regains its lost market share. Another example is where a business has been reorganised to curtail underperforming operations, resulting in a write-off of goodwill; in later years, the business may expand again as new market opportunities arise. In neither of these examples would the turnaround justify reversing the impairment loss relating to the goodwill if the recoverable amount of the business has increased above the balance sheet value of its net assets and goodwill, because the higher value of goodwill that now exists includes goodwill that has been generated internally since the original impairment.

25.515 The amount that can be written back to reverse an impairment loss is restricted to an amount that increases the carrying value of the goodwill to the carrying value that would have been recognised had the original impairment not occurred. [FRS 11 para 61]. Accounting for reversals of impairment losses is discussed in more detail in chapter 18.

25.516 The following disclosures relate to reversals of past impairment losses:

- The Companies Act 1985 requires provisions for permanent diminutions in value that are written back because they are no longer necessary to be disclosed in the profit and loss account or in a note to the financial statements. [CA85 4 Sch 19(3)].
- FRS 10 requires reversals of past impairment losses to be disclosed separately in the note that reconciles the movements between the opening and closing goodwill balances. [FRS 10 para 53].
- FRS 11 requires that the reason for the reversal of impairment losses in respect of fixed assets or goodwill should be disclosed, together with any changes in the assumptions upon which the calculation of recoverable amount is based. [FRS 11 para 70].

Allocation of purchased goodwill

25.517 Groups need to keep detailed records of the composition of the aggregate amount of purchased goodwill, that is, to which parts of the group it relates. Allocation of goodwill to business units is necessary in order to:

- Account for subsequent disposals.
- Carry out impairment reviews.
- Keep track of elements of goodwill with different useful economic lives.

Disposals

25.518 Where businesses are disposed of, the net book value of any related goodwill has to be eliminated from the balance sheet and written off as part of the profit or loss on disposal.

25.519 Even where pre-FRS 10 goodwill was written off to reserves, profits or losses on disposals of businesses had to include any related goodwill that had not previously been written off in the profit and loss account. This continues to be a requirement in respect of pre-FRS 10 goodwill that remains written off to reserves under FRS 10's transitional arrangements.

25.520 It has always been recognised that there are practical difficulties with attributing goodwill to businesses disposed of. Traceability of purchased goodwill is an issue in complex group structures, particularly where an acquired business quickly loses its separate identity or when businesses undergo change and restructuring. The requirement in UITF 3 (since superseded by FRS 10) was that records should normally be sufficient to enable *"an appropriate estimate or apportionment"* of goodwill to be made. This implied that the amount of goodwill attributed to disposals is often likely to be a 'soft' number which is the product of a judgmental allocation exercise. Nevertheless, groups have generally managed to make reasonable allocations of goodwill to disposals.

Impairment reviews

25.521 Some allocation of purchased goodwill to separate businesses may also be necessary for carrying out the impairment reviews required by FRS 10. For example, impairment tests on goodwill relating to dissimilar businesses have to be performed separately on each dissimilar business.

25.522 Any goodwill that is amortised over more than 20 years (or not amortised at all) must be formally reviewed for impairment each year. Even where goodwill is amortised over 20 years or less and, as a result, no annual impairment reviews are required, there is still a possibility that an impairment review will be required in the future. This will be the case if evidence emerges that the net book value may not be recoverable.

25.523 Principles of allocating purchased goodwill to different business units are discussed in chapter 18.

Positive and negative goodwill

25.524 The acquisition of a group may give rise to positive goodwill overall. Where the acquisition includes a loss-making or marginally profitable business, the issue is whether negative goodwill can be attributed to that business, leaving a larger amount of positive goodwill attributable to the others. This could have a significant impact on disposal profits and losses.

25.525 Allowing both positive and negative goodwill to be recognised in respect of a single acquisition would introduce far more subjectivity into the allocation process than already exists. The ASB specifically prohibited such an approach in FRS 10, following the principle that goodwill (positive or negative) is a residual difference that arises from fair valuing the acquisition as a whole.

25.526 Businesses would, therefore, receive a zero allocation of goodwill where it is believed to be negative or nil at the date of acquisition. The overall goodwill on the acquisition would be allocated to those businesses where it is believed goodwill does exist.

25.527 Similarly, where an acquisition gave rise to negative goodwill overall, the negative goodwill would be allocated to those businesses where it is believed negative goodwill existed. No positive goodwill would be attributed to other businesses.

Integrated acquisitions

25.528 Tracing goodwill is more difficult, and allocations may become more arbitrary, where acquired businesses lose their separate identity as a result of post-acquisition integration with pre-existing operations and reorganisation.

25.529 However, it is usually possible to make such allocations on a reasonable basis, for example by tracking products, markets and key assets introduced by acquisitions. Subsequent business reorganisations would require a reallocation of goodwill balances.

25.530 Allocations can normally be readily achieved where branded activities were acquired, since these may be easily identifiable in current business units, especially if the products have not changed significantly over time. In other cases, more judgement is required. For example, where an established brand has been re-branded since its acquisition, the original purchased goodwill would (assuming the acquired operation is still continuing in some form) be attributed to the operation where the re-branded activity resides.

25.531 It should be noted that if a subsidiary is acquired and the business is subsequently transferred to another part of the group, leaving the subsidiary to be liquidated, no goodwill is transferred to the consolidated profit and loss account (as would happen if the business were sold), because the goodwill attaches to the retained business, not to the legal entity.

Impairment reviews

Purpose of impairment reviews

25.532 The impairment review is a recoverable amount check. It follows the long-established principle that an asset's balance sheet carrying value should not exceed its recoverable amount, which is measured by reference to the future cash flows that can be generated from its continued use or disposal. Impairment is defined in FRS 10 as *"a reduction in the recoverable amount of a fixed asset or goodwill below its carrying value"*.

25.533 Measuring the recoverable amount of purchased goodwill is complicated, because goodwill is by definition not a separable asset — it attaches to a business as a whole. The details of impairment reviews for fixed assets and goodwill are quite prescriptive and are contained in FRS 11, 'Impairment of fixed assets and goodwill'.

When impairment reviews are required

25.534 The requirements for impairment reviews differ according to whether goodwill is amortised over more or less than 20 years, as illustrated below.

Impairment reviews

Useful life 20 years or less	**Useful life more than 20 years**
End of first full year (simplified review)	Every year (detailed review)
Other years — high level check for impairment indicators with a detailed review only if impairment indicators are present	

25.535 Where goodwill is carried permanently as an asset or amortised over a very long period, there is a greater risk of impairment in the future. Where goodwill is written off over a shorter period, there is less risk of impairment, because its net book value in any case diminishes more quickly. A threshold of 20 years has been chosen, below which the impairment reviews are less onerous than for longer periods.

Useful life 20 years or less

First year review

25.536 A first year impairment review is required on all acquisitions where goodwill arises. This should be carried out at the end of the first full financial year following the acquisition. The timing of this review corresponds with the end of the investigation period in FRS 7, when the fair value exercise on the assets and liabilities of the acquired business should be completed and the final goodwill figure established. This review is intended to identify factors such as:

- Overpayment.
- Under performance compared with expectations.
- Material adverse changes to the acquired business in the immediate post-acquisition period.

25.537 The first year review has two stages. The first stage in effect requires management formally to consider whether the acquisition has lived up to expectations. This is done by comparing post-acquisition performance with the forecasts used in the acquisition appraisal and by considering whether there have been any other unexpected adverse events or changes in circumstances that throw doubt on the recoverability of the capitalised goodwill. If the acquisition passes this test, there is no need to go on to the second stage.

25.538 The second stage, which is a full impairment review (as described from para 25.540 below), is only necessary if the first stage indicates that there may be an impairment problem. [FRS 10 para 40].

Reviews in other years

25.539 After the first full year, management has to consider whether events or changes in circumstances indicate that the amortised carrying value of goodwill may not be recoverable. If there are no such indicators, no further work is required. In many situations it would be immediately apparent that there is no impairment. The goodwill will in any case be fully written off over 20 years at most. If there are factors that indicate that the carrying value of goodwill may not be recoverable, a full impairment review has to be carried out and, if impairment is confirmed, the carrying value should be written down to the recoverable amount. Impairment reviews are considered in detail in chapter 18.

Detailed impairment review

25.540 A detailed impairment review is required in the following situations:

- Where goodwill is amortised over more than 20 years or carried permanently as an asset, an impairment review is automatically required at each year end (including the end of the year in which the acquisition took place).
- Where goodwill is amortised over 20 years or less:
  - At the end of the first full year following the acquisition, an impairment review is required *only* if there is an indicator of impairment or if the first year review indicates that the post-acquisition performance has failed to meet pre-acquisition expectations.
  - In other years, *only* if there is an indicator of impairment.

The requirements are considered in detail in chapter 18.

Negative goodwill

25.541 In some acquisitions, the fair value of the identifiable assets less liabilities may exceed the cost of acquisition, giving rise to negative goodwill.

25.542 Negative goodwill is the mirror image of positive goodwill and is an even more difficult accounting conundrum. FRS 10 requires negative goodwill to be shown as a separate (negative) item on the asset side of the balance sheet immediately below positive goodwill, followed by a net sub-total, as illustrated below. [FRS 10 para 48]. If the amount of negative goodwill exceeds the amount of positive goodwill, there would be a net credit figure on the assets side. An example of the disclosure of positive and negative goodwill is shown in the extract from the Babcock International Group plc accounts below in Table 25.24.

Table 25.24 – Babcock International Group PLC – Annual Report & Accounts – 31 March 2001

Group balance sheet (Extract)
at 31 March 2001

	Notes	**2001 £'000**	**2001 £'000**	2000 £'000	2000 £'000
Fixed assets					
Intangible assets	12				
Development costs			**1,507**		1,771
Goodwill					
- Goodwill		**88,279**		27,801	
- Negative goodwill		**(14,916)**		(18,703)	
			73,363		9,098

Goodwill

When the fair value of the consideration for an acquired undertaking exceeds the fair value of its separable net assets the difference is treated as purchased goodwill and is capitalised and amortised through the profit and loss account over its estimated economic life. The estimated economic life of goodwill is between ten and twenty years.

Where the fair value of the separable net assets exceeds the fair value of the consideration for an acquired undertaking the difference is treated as negative goodwill and is capitalised and amortised through the profit and loss account in the period in which the non-monetary assets acquired are recovered. In the case of fixed assets this is the period over which they are depreciated, and in the case of current assets, the period over which they are sold or otherwise realised.

25.543 Negative goodwill is generally attributed to one of two causes:

- The first is where the acquirer has made a genuine bargain purchase. This might occur as a result of a distress sale, for example, where the vendor is forced to sell the business quickly and cheaply to relieve cash flow problems.

- The second is where the purchase price is reduced to take account of future costs or losses, for example, where it is recognised that the acquirer will have to incur significant reorganisation costs to turn the business around. Such costs or losses are not identifiable liabilities of the acquired business at the date of acquisition.

25.544 FRS 10 seeks to restrict situations where negative goodwill is recognised. The first requirement where a fair value exercise appears to give rise to negative goodwill is that the fair values of the identifiable assets should be tested for impairment and the fair values of the identifiable liabilities should be checked carefully to ensure none has been omitted or understated. [FRS 10 para 48]. Any further reductions to the acquired net assets that need to be made as fair value adjustments as a result of this exercise will reduce or eliminate the negative goodwill.

25.545 The recoverable amount of the assets should be considered particularly carefully in the second of the situations mentioned in paragraph 25.543 above. Where the acquired business is loss-making or under-performing and in need of reorganisation, it must be questionable whether the fair values of the net assets in aggregate, which (as required by FRS 7) should be measured to reflect the conditions at the date of acquisition, are actually worth more than the price paid for the business as a whole. It should be noted that FRS 7 requires a valuation at recoverable amount to reflect the condition of the asset on acquisition (reflecting, for example, lack of profitability, under-utilisation or obsolescence). [FRS 7 para 47]. The ASB considers that much of any negative goodwill that would otherwise be attributed to future costs or losses would be eliminated by reducing the fair value of the assets in this way. [FRS 10 Appendix III para 57]. It follows that negative goodwill will most commonly arise in genuine bargain purchase situations.

25.546 A further restriction is that FRS 10 does not allow both negative goodwill and intangible assets to be recognised in respect of a single acquisition. It does this by capping the fair values attributable to any identifiable intangibles at an amount that does not give rise to negative goodwill overall, as illustrated below. [FRS 10 para 10].

	Valuation	**Restricted fair value**
	£m	**£m**
Tangible net assets	200	200
Intangibles	400	300
	600	500
Cost of acquisition	500	500

25.547 The ASB's reason for this treatment is that valuations of intangibles are very subjective. Also, many intangibles are similar to goodwill and FRS 10 does not allow both positive and negative goodwill to be recognised on the same acquisition. This requirement was reinforced by the FRRP decision in relation to Equator Group plc published in July 2002, which held that the directors should not have created negative goodwill on the acquisition of a company whose principal asset was film libraries, an intangible asset without a readily ascertainable market value. The same ruling welcomed the director's decision to revise the indefinite life attributed to the film libraries down to 20 years, with a nil residual value.

25.548 Negative goodwill that remains after the fair values of the acquired assets and liabilities have been re-checked should be accounted for as follows.

- Negative goodwill up to the fair values of the non-monetary assets acquired should be amortised to the profit and loss account in the periods in which the non-monetary assets are recovered, whether through depreciation or sale. [FRS 10 para 49]. Non-monetary assets include stocks as well as fixed assets.
- Any negative goodwill in excess of the fair values of the non-monetary assets acquired should be recognised in the profit and loss account in the periods expected to be benefited. [FRS 10 para 50].

25.549 The standard does not specify where in the profit and loss account amounts of negative goodwill credited should be shown. It would be consistent with the treatment of positive goodwill to include negative goodwill as a negative component of goodwill amortisation charges that are treated as operating costs in arriving at operating profit or loss.

25.550 By matching the release of negative goodwill into the profit and loss account with the depreciation or cost of sales of the non-monetary assets acquired, a wide range of amortisation patterns is possible. No guidance on this is given in FRS 10. If the release of negative goodwill is matched first with the depreciation of the fixed assets, it will be credited, say, over the average useful life of the fixed assets acquired. Intuitively, this would seem to be a sensible treatment in most circumstances. It is also prudent, considering that fair valuing tangible fixed assets acquired can sometimes be as subjective as fair valuing intangible assets. If the release of negative goodwill is matched first with the cost of sales relating to the sale of the stocks acquired, it will be credited much more quickly. But, relative to fixed assets, stock is less likely to be subject to measurement uncertainty.

25.551 Situations where negative goodwill exceeds the fair values of the non-monetary assets acquired should be very rare indeed. If, for example, the only non-monetary assets were debtors, it would be logical to credit the excess negative goodwill in the profit and loss account over the period the debtors were collected.

25.552 The following disclosures are required in respect of negative goodwill:

- The aggregate movements on negative goodwill should be disclosed separately from those on positive goodwill, detailing additions, disposals and amounts written back to profit and loss account in the period. [FRS 10 para 53].
- The period(s) in which negative goodwill is being written back in the profit and loss account. [FRS 10 para 63].
- Where negative goodwill exceeds the fair values of the non-monetary assets (which should be very rare), details of its amount and source and the period(s) in which it is being written back. [FRS 10 para 64].

Pre-FRS 10 goodwill that remains in reserves

25.553 SSAP 22's preferred method of accounting for goodwill was immediate elimination against reserves. FRS 10's transitional arrangements permitted, but did not require, previously eliminated goodwill to be reinstated on the balance sheet (see paragraph 25.598). Under the transitional options, unless all goodwill relating to pre-FRS 10 acquisitions is reinstated, one of the following amounts will remain eliminated against reserves:

- All goodwill written off before the adoption of FRS 10.
- All goodwill written off before the adoption of FRS 7 (which became effective in 1995).
- All goodwill written off before 23 December 1989 where its composition is not known.

Separate goodwill write-off reserve prohibited

25.554 Under the elimination method preferred by SSAP 22, there had been an increasing trend for groups to have a policy of writing goodwill off against a special reserve set up for the purpose. The reserve initially had a nil balance and so the reserve created would be negative and would equal the figure of goodwill written off. This was similar to a (prohibited) treatment known as a 'dangling debit' where goodwill would be carried on the balance sheet as a permanent debit deducted from shareholders' funds. One of the perceived advantages of this method was that the accounting treatment maintained some accountability for goodwill through its visibility in the financial statements, in contrast to writing goodwill off to, say, the profit and loss account reserve where it was 'lost'. The 'dissenting view' of one ASB member published with FRS 10 advocated an alternative approach to goodwill that was based on a separate goodwill reserve.

25.555 FRS 10 does not allow previously eliminated goodwill that is not reinstated on the balance sheet under the transitional arrangements to be carried forward in a separate goodwill write-off reserve. It requires such goodwill to be offset against the profit and loss account or another appropriate reserve. Furthermore, it does not allow such goodwill to be shown separately on the face of the balance sheet in any way, such as a separate component of the reserve to which it has been written off. [FRS 10 para 71(b)].

25.556 The ASB's justification for the decision to outlaw the goodwill write-off reserve is that, in the context of a new standard based on specific capitalisation, amortisation and impairment requirements, it could be misleading and confusing to have goodwill appearing in two different places on the balance sheet. Otherwise, some balance sheets would contain a permanent reminder of the transition. If continued accountability for the cost of past acquisitions is considered to be of overriding importance by companies, recapitalisation is the only method allowed to achieve this.

Reserves used for write-offs

25.557 The following reserves are the principal candidates for carrying goodwill that remains written off under FRS 10's transitional arrangements:

- Profit and loss account reserve.
- Merger reserve.
- Other non-distributable reserves (except those noted below).

25.558 The following reserves *cannot* be used to carry goodwill write-offs:

- Share premium account.
- Capital redemption reserve.
- Revaluation reserve.

Profit and loss account

25.559 Where more than one reserve is available to absorb the goodwill that is not recapitalised, no order of write-off is specified. Therefore, the profit and loss account can be used as a first choice or as a last choice to bear the goodwill write-off. In the latter case, the profit and loss account would absorb any balance of goodwill that cannot be offset against other reserves.

Merger reserve

25.560 A merger reserve arises on consolidation where a company issues shares as part of the consideration to acquire another company and it takes merger relief on the issue of those shares. The provisions of merger relief are explained fully in chapter 23. Where merger relief is available, the amount by which the fair value of the shares issued exceeds their nominal value results in a merger reserve on consolidation (rather than a share premium). Under the old rules for goodwill, a merger reserve could be used to write off goodwill that arose on the acquisition that gave rise to the reserve and it could also be used to write off any other goodwill. This was one of the key advantages of obtaining merger relief on the issue of shares to acquire another undertaking.

25.561 Where purchased goodwill is capitalised under FRS 10, the merger reserve can, of course, no longer be used to absorb goodwill write-offs on acquisition. But any old goodwill that is not recapitalised can continue to be offset against any existing merger reserve.

25.562 If a group wishes to use the merger reserve first to absorb any such goodwill, but the reserve is insufficient to offset all of the goodwill, the balance of goodwill would have to be offset against another reserve (that is, the profit and loss account reserve, if no other reserve is available). However, if the merger reserve subsequently increases as a result of a new share for share acquisition, there is nothing to prevent that balance of goodwill offset from being transferred from the other reserve to the increased merger reserve.

Other non-distributable reserves

25.563 Apart from the capital reserves that are governed by the Act (see below), neither the Act nor SSAP 22 restricted groups from writing off goodwill arising on consolidation against any other non-distributable reserves. Such reserves might include a special reserve created on a court-approved reduction of share premium which was carried out in the past specifically to enable goodwill to be written off against it on consolidation (see para 25.565 below).

Share premium account

25.564 The use of the share premium account is governed by the Companies Act 1985 and so it can only be used for specific purposes, namely to:

- Pay up fully paid bonus shares.
- Write off preliminary expenses.
- Write off expenses of any issue of shares or debentures.
- Write off commission paid or discount allowed on any issue of shares or debentures.
- Provide for the premium payable on any redemption of debentures.

[CA85 Sec 130(2)].

25.564.1 The Companies Act 2006 amends the specific purposes for which the share premium arising on the issue of shares can be used, namely to:

- Pay up fully paid bonus shares.
- Write off expenses of the issue of those shares.
- Write off commission paid on the issue of those shares.

[CA06 Sec 610(2)(3)].

25.565 However, although the share premium account can only be used for specific purposes, and writing off goodwill is not one of them, it does form part of a company's capital and, as such, can be reduced under section 135 of the Companies Act 1985 (CA06 Sec 641) by application to the court. Where groups fund acquisitions in part or in full by issuing shares then the parent, unless it is eligible for merger relief, has to credit the difference between the fair value of the shares issued and their nominal value to its share premium account. A share premium account may also exist from previous share issues. The parent company may take steps to reduce its share premium account by a specified amount and that amount would, in the consolidated financial statements, be redesignated as another reserve to be used specifically to write off consolidation goodwill that remains written off in reserves. The steps involved are determined by company law. Initially, a special resolution for the reduction is required and all of the relevant facts about the proposal must be set out in the documentation sent to shareholders.

25.566 Once the shareholders have passed the necessary special resolution, an application has to be made to the court to obtain its confirmation. Such confirmation is required by the Act and the court will be concerned in particular to ensure that the parent company's creditors are not prejudiced.

25.567 Share premium reductions of this nature were common when goodwill was eliminated against reserves. This route remains an option for groups that wish to write off all pre-FRS 10 goodwill against a reserve created by reducing share premium rather than against the profit and loss account reserve.

25.568 It should be remembered that the share premium account in such situations is that of the parent company. The reserve that is created from the share premium account is in most cases initially not available for distribution by the parent. It remains undistributable until certain conditions specified by the court have been satisfied, for instance, that the creditors that exist at the date of the reduction have been paid. Once these conditions have been fulfilled, the reserve becomes distributable. However, whether the reserve arising on the reduction is distributable is not relevant for consolidation purposes. Consolidation goodwill can be written off to the reserve created out of the parent's share premium account whether or not it is distributable by the parent.

Capital redemption reserve

25.569 Capital redemption reserves are set up for a specific purpose and will be utilised at some future date for that purpose. Therefore, their use is restricted. Furthermore, the normal provisions that apply to the reduction of share capital also apply to the capital redemption reserve. [CA85 Sec 170(4); CA06 Sec 733(5)(6)]. Consequently, except where there has been a reduction confirmed by the court, this reserve is not available to write off goodwill arising on consolidation.

Revaluation reserve

25.570 The use of the revaluation reserve is restricted by the Companies Act 1985 which states:

> *"An amount may be transferred a) from the revaluation reserve- (i) to the profit and loss account, if the amount was previously charged to that account or represents a realised profit, or (ii) on capitalisation; b) to or from the revaluation reserve in respect of the taxation relating to any profit or loss credited or debited to the reserve; and the revaluation reserve shall be reduced to the extent that the amounts transferred to it are no longer necessary for the purposes of the valuation method used.*

In sub-paragraph (a)(ii) 'capitalisation', in relation to an amount standing to the credit of the revaluation reserve, means applying it in wholly or partly paying up unissued shares in the company to be allotted to members of the company as fully or partly paid shares.

The revaluation reserve shall not be reduced except as mentioned in this paragraph."

[CA85 4 Sch 34(3)(3A)(3B)].

25.571 The wording of paragraph 34 was changed by the Companies Act 1989 specifically to ensure that goodwill arising on consolidation could no longer be written off against the consolidated revaluation reserve. Before that, the Act (by reference to the EC 4th Directive) prohibited goodwill arising in a company's individual financial statements from being written off against the company's revaluation reserve. However, this restriction did not extend to goodwill arising on consolidation.

25.572 The commencement order introducing part I of the Companies Act 1989 into the UK's legislation, however, included certain transitional provisions. One of these provisions concerned those groups that had in the past written off consolidation goodwill to their consolidated revaluation reserve. Where a group had previously written consolidation goodwill off against the revaluation reserve, it did not have to reverse this treatment. However, for any acquisitions that a group made following the change brought about by the Companies Act 1989 the treatment was no longer possible.

Effect on distributable profits — groups

25.573 Where, under the old rules, a group wrote off consolidation goodwill arising on the acquisition of subsidiaries immediately to reserves, the write-off did not affect the distributable profits of the parent or any individual group company. Since it is individual companies, not groups, that make distributions, the write-off of goodwill did not affect the amount of the total potential distributable profits of the group.

25.574 Consequently, whether pre-FRS 10 goodwill remains eliminated against the profit and loss account reserve or against unrealised reserves such as a merger reserve has no effect on distributable profits. Furthermore, a group does not need to transfer any amounts from unrealised reserves to realised reserves over the estimated useful economic life of such goodwill.

25.575 Although it is individual companies, not groups, that make distributions, users of consolidated financial statements may wish to know how much the parent could distribute if all the subsidiaries in the group were to pay up their realised profits by way of dividends to the parent. Some groups specifically disclose this amount. In the absence of such disclosure, users of the consolidated financial statements might mistakenly interpret the group's profit and loss account reserve as representing realised reserves.

Effect on distributable profits — companies

25.576 Where goodwill arises in a *company* as opposed to a group, questions arise as to whether, or how, any write-off affects realised and distributable profits. This situation would arise where a company purchased the trade and assets (including goodwill) of an unincorporated business. SSAP 22 provided guidance on this issue which is reproduced in Appendix V to FRS 10, because it is still relevant for pre-FRS 10 goodwill that remains eliminated against a company's reserves under the transitional options.

25.577 The appendix states that to the extent that goodwill is considered to have suffered an actual diminution in value, the write-off should be charged against realised reserves; but realised reserves should not be reduced immediately where goodwill is written off as a matter of accounting policy and there is no actual diminution in value. It goes on to explain that immediate depletion of realised reserves can be avoided by eliminating goodwill initially to a suitable unrealised reserve. The amount eliminated against the unrealised reserve should then be transferred to realised reserves over the goodwill's useful economic life so as to reduce realised reserves on a systematic basis in the same way as if the company had amortised goodwill. [FRS 10 appendix V para 2]. A transfer to realised reserves would also have to be made if the carrying value of goodwill deducted from the unrealised reserve was found to have been impaired because, for example, an adverse event damaged the profitability of the acquired business.

25.578 The availability of suitable unrealised reserves is, however, limited. Merger relief reserves (if recognised by the company), negative goodwill and other capital reserves (except for share premium, capital redemption and revaluation reserves) can be used. However, FRS 10's prohibition of carrying goodwill in a separate (negative) goodwill write-off reserve applies to companies as well as groups. The profit and loss account reserve can, therefore, no longer be protected from goodwill write-offs by carrying a separate negative reserve. If pre-FRS 10 goodwill remains eliminated against reserves, it has to be eliminated against the profit and loss account reserve to the extent that no other reserves are available. The appendix does not specifically address the question whether goodwill that is actually eliminated against the profit and loss account reserve has the effect of reducing a company's realised reserves.

25.579 We consider that the elimination of goodwill does not become a realised loss just because it is offset against the profit and loss account reserve. This is primarily a matter of presentation. The principle remains that goodwill only becomes a realised loss to the extent that it is amortised or considered to have suffered an actual diminution in value. Therefore, FRS 10's prohibition of a separate goodwill write-off reserve should make no difference to the basis on which a company had previously been allocating such goodwill from unrealised to realised reserves, that is, over its estimated useful economic life as determined under SSAP 22. It should be noted that SSAP 22 defined useful economic life differently from FRS 10 and did not allow goodwill to be carried in the balance sheet as a permanent item.

25.580 Where purchased goodwill has been offset against a company's profit and loss account reserve, it would be important to disclose in the notes the amount of goodwill offset that is an unrealised loss in order to give a clear picture of the company's distributable profits.

Goodwill on disposals

25.581 FRS 10 retains the rules previously set out in UITF Abstract 3. Where goodwill attributable to a past acquisition remains eliminated against reserves (and, hence, has not been previously charged in the profit and loss account) it must be transferred to the profit and loss account when the business is subsequently disposed of, by treating it as part of the profit or loss on disposal. The attributable goodwill is credited in reserves and debited in the profit and loss account. The amount of goodwill included as a component of the profit or loss on disposal should be separately disclosed. [FRS 10 para 71(c)]. The disclosure could be either on the face of the profit and loss account or in the notes.

25.582 An exemption from this treatment is given if the business disposed of was acquired before 1 January 1989 and it is impracticable or impossible to ascertain the attributable goodwill that was originally written off. In this situation the facts and the reasons should be stated. This exemption coincides with the transitional provisions of the Companies Act 1989, before which there was no necessity to keep detailed records of goodwill eliminated against reserves.

Impairment of goodwill

25.583 Where goodwill is capitalised, timely recognition of impairment losses is a key feature of FRS 10's rules. However, neither FRS 10 nor its predecessors have dealt with the issue of whether goodwill that is eliminated against reserves and has lost its value should be charged in the profit and loss account earlier than on disposal of the acquired business. FRS 11's rules for measuring and recognising impairments of capitalised goodwill specifically do not apply to old goodwill that remains written off to reserves. [FRS 11 para 7]. In some situations, either as a matter of accounting policy or as part of the accounting for an impending disposal, goodwill may be written off in the profit and loss account earlier to recognise an impairment. This issue is discussed in chapter 8. Any impairment that has been written off in the profit and loss account does not pass through the profit and loss account again on disposal of the business.

Disclosures

25.584 FRS 10's transitional provisions contain some specific disclosure requirements that relate to goodwill that remains eliminated against reserves.

Accounting policy

25.585 The accounting policy relating to that goodwill should be separately disclosed. [FRS 10 para 71(a)(i)]. It would be useful for companies to indicate what the balance eliminated against reserves comprises by reference to the transitional option they adopted: all goodwill eliminated before FRS 10 was adopted, or all goodwill eliminated before FRS 7 was adopted, or goodwill relating to acquisitions made before 23 December 1989.

25.586 Another policy issue that might be considered for disclosure is the basis on which such goodwill is charged in the profit and loss account, that is, on disposal or (if applicable) when an impairment is identified.

Cumulative amounts written off

25.587 The notes to the financial statements should disclose the cumulative amount of positive goodwill eliminated against reserves, net of any goodwill attributable to businesses disposed of before the balance sheet date. If both positive and negative goodwill have been taken to reserves, the cumulative amounts of each should be disclosed separately. [FRS 10 para 71(a)(ii)].

25.588 The notes should also state that this goodwill has been eliminated as a matter of accounting policy and would be charged or credited in the profit and loss account when the businesses to which it relates are subsequently disposed of. [FRS 10 para 71(a)(iii)]. Not all of the disclosable cumulative amount of goodwill may in fact be chargeable in the profit and loss account on disposal. For example, some of this goodwill may already have been written off in the profit and loss account, because the company has a policy of recognising impaired goodwill earlier. Another example is where the identity of goodwill relating to acquisitions made before 1 January 1989 is unknown and, hence, by virtue of the exemption in FRS 10, may never pass through the profit and loss account.

25.589 The Companies Act also requires the cumulative amount of goodwill written off that results from acquisitions in the current year and in earlier years to be disclosed. [CA85 4A Sch 14(1) as amended by SI 1996/189]. The amount disclosed should also be stated net of any goodwill attributed to an undertaking that has subsequently been sold. [CA85 4A Sch 14(2)]. This requires disclosure of the aggregate of amounts written off directly to reserves, but not the amounts amortised through the profit and loss account.

25.590 The FRRP published a statement in December 1995 in connection with the financial statements of Ferguson International Holdings PLC confirming that, where advantage is taken of the merger relief provisions of the Act, the figures disclosed for goodwill arising on acquisitions in the year and the cumulative amount of goodwill written off should be the gross amounts before deducting merger relief.

25.591 The Companies Act 1985, however, does not require the gross amount of *goodwill written off* to be disclosed in certain circumstances where an undertaking that is established outside the UK or that carries on its business outside the UK has obtained the permission of the Secretary of State. [CA85 4A Sch 16]. Similarly the transitional provisions on the introduction of the Companies Act 1989 do not require the amount to be disclosed in certain situations where it is not possible to ascertain the figure for goodwill written off that has arisen on acquisitions made prior to the introduction of the Companies Act 1989 and to do so would cause unreasonable expense or delay. In these situations the financial statements must state that the gross figure disclosed does not include an amount on these grounds.

Pre-FRS 10 negative goodwill that remains in reserves

25.592 SSAP 22 required negative goodwill to be credited directly to reserves. Under FRS 10's transitional arrangements, some or all negative goodwill attributable to pre-FRS 10 acquisitions may remain credited to reserves.

25.593 SSAP 22 did not require a group to set up a separate reserve for negative goodwill, but some companies and groups did so. FRS 10 does not allow the amount by which any reserve has been increased by the addition of negative goodwill to be shown separately on the face of the balance sheet. [FRS 10 para 71(b)]. To be consistent with positive goodwill, this implies that negative goodwill should also not be carried as a separate reserve if it can be credited to another appropriate reserve. Therefore, negative goodwill arising on consolidation may either be credited to a capital reserve, if any is available (excluding the statutory share premium, capital redemption and revaluation reserves), or to the consolidated profit and loss account reserve. In the former case, it would normally be included under 'other reserves' in the balance sheet format.

25.594 Such negative goodwill as remains credited to reserves should be transferred to the profit and loss account when the business to which it relates is sold or closed, by inclusion in the calculation of the profit or loss on disposal. The amount of negative goodwill transferred should be separately disclosed as a component of the profit or loss on disposal.

25.595 The cumulative amount of negative goodwill added to reserves, net of any attributable to businesses disposed of before the balance sheet date, should be disclosed in the notes, together with the fact that this would be credited in the profit and loss account on subsequent disposal of the business to which it related. If both positive and negative goodwill have been taken to reserves, the cumulative amounts of each should be disclosed separately. [FRS 10 para 71(a)].

Effect on distributable profits — companies

25.596 Where negative goodwill arises in a company, it should credit it initially to an unrealised reserve. The company may then transfer the negative goodwill from that unrealised reserve to realised reserves. This transfer should be in line with the depreciation or the realisation of the assets acquired in the business combination that gave rise to the goodwill in question. [FRS 10 App V para 3].

25.597 Unlike negative goodwill arising on consolidation, negative goodwill in an individual company should not be credited immediately to the profit and loss account reserve, because it is not a realised profit. It would have to be shown under the heading 'other reserves' in the company's balance sheet.

Implementing FRS 10 — transitional arrangements

Options for reinstating goodwill eliminated against reserves

25.598 FRS 10 had to be applied to goodwill relating to acquisitions first accounted for in financial years ending on or after 23 December 1998. Where goodwill relating to earlier acquisitions had been eliminated against reserves, the standard permitted, but did not require, the goodwill to be recapitalised as an asset on the balance sheet. There were effectively four options for dealing with old goodwill eliminated against reserves:

- Leave all goodwill eliminated against reserves.
- Reinstate all goodwill previously written off to reserves.
- Reinstate all goodwill relating to post-23 December 1989 acquisitions (where the information on earlier acquisitions cannot be obtained without unreasonable expense or delay), leaving the balance eliminated against reserves.
- Reinstate all goodwill eliminated since the adoption of FRS 7, leaving the balance eliminated against reserves.

[FRS 10 para 69].

25.599 Each of the reinstatement options required a prior period adjustment for a change of accounting policy from immediate write-off to capitalisation. The transitional arrangements were a once-only opportunity to establish the goodwill accounting going forward and hence there should be no change to the policy previously adopted without providing compelling reasons for such a change. Any goodwill reinstated is subject to the normal requirements of FRS 10 and FRS 11 outlined earlier in the chapter, notably the requirement to review useful economic lives at the end of each accounting period and the need to monitor the carrying value of the goodwill for impairment.

Additions to goodwill in existing subsidiaries

Increases in stake

25.600 If a parent company increases its stake in an existing subsidiary by purchasing additional shares from the minority, goodwill may arise on the purchase. The new goodwill must be capitalised if the purchase is accounted for when FRS 10 is effective. The old goodwill (pre-dating FRS 10) may or may not be capitalised, depending on whether or not it was reinstated under the transitional options. Therefore, it is possible that goodwill relating to one subsidiary may appear in two different places. The more recent purchase will appear on the balance sheet and be subject to the amortisation and impairment rules, whereas the older purchase will remain eliminated against reserves.

Earnout consideration

25.601 Sometimes an acquirer agrees to pay additional consideration for an acquisition that depends on its future performance. The additional consideration may give rise to more goodwill. In this situation, however, the additional goodwill does not relate to a new acquisition or to the acquisition of a further tranche of shares. It is an adjustment to the goodwill on the previous acquisition. FRS 7 in fact requires estimates of future performance-related consideration to be provided for when the acquisition is first accounted for. Therefore, any additional goodwill should always be treated in the same way as the goodwill that was accounted for when the acquisition was made.

Chapter 26

Disposals of subsidiaries

	Page
Introduction	26001
The accounting rules	26002
Rules in FRS 2	26002
FRS 10	26003
Implications of FRS 3	26005
Discontinued operations	26005
Date of sale	26007
Impact of FRS 1	26008
Accounting for the sale of a subsidiary	26008
Full disposal	26008
Sale of a subsidiary for shares	26010
In exchange for an interest in a subsidiary	26012
In exchange for an interest in a joint venture or associate	26015
Ceasing to be a subsidiary other than by sale or exchange of shares	26018
Partial disposals	26018
Remaining a subsidiary	26019
Becoming an associate	26020
Becoming an investment	26021
Deemed disposals	26022
Disclosure requirements	26027

Chapter 26

Disposals of subsidiaries

Introduction

26.1 Typically, an undertaking will cease to be a subsidiary of another when the group sells it or reduces its percentage interest in the undertaking. Equally a parent may lose control over an undertaking because of changes in the rights it holds or in those held by another party in that undertaking or because there is a change in some other arrangement that gave the parent its control (see further chapter 24).

26.2 A reduction in percentage interest may arise from a direct disposal (for example, the sale of shares in a company) or from a deemed disposal (for example, the exercise of share options by another party). A gain or loss will normally arise on both a disposal and a deemed disposal (for example, see Table 26.1).

Table 26.1 — Forte Plc — Report and Accounts — 31 January 1994

Notes to the Accounts (extract)

7 Profit on disposal of discontinued operation
The profit on disposal of discontinued operations, amounting to £122m, relates to the flotation of the Group's interest in its Airport Services Division (now called ALPHA Airports Group Plc — "ALPHA") on 25 January 1994 and the sale of the Group's interest in Kentucky Fried Chicken (Great Britain) Ltd on 2 December 1993. Proceeds amounting to £155m from the ALPHA disposal were outstanding at the year end and were received on 10 February 1994. The Group has retained a 25% interest in ALPHA.

14 Fixed assets — investments (extract)
ALPHA
Following the flotation of the Group's Airport Services Division in January 1994, the Group retained 25% of the ordinary shares of the new holding company, ALPHA Airports Group Plc. In addition the Group holds 46,000 6.5% cumulative redeemable preference shares of £1 each. The Group's share of the net assets of ALPHA as at 31 January 1994, calculated using Forte's accounting policies, amounted to £12m. ALPHA shares were listed on 10 February 1994 at a price valuing this interest at £53m.

26.3 Where a parent loses control because of changes in its rights or the rights of other parties, or because of changes in some other arrangement, neither a gain nor a loss will arise in the consolidated profit and loss account, unless there is a payment for the transfer of the control. This is because there will be no change in the net assets attributable to the group's holding in the former subsidiary. [FRS 2 para 86]. See further paragraph 26.24. However, a gain or loss (albeit normally unrealised) can arise where, for example, a company (company P) disposes of shares it holds in its subsidiary (company S) in exchange for shares in another company (company A). The subsidiary (company S) will often then become a subsidiary of the acquiring company (company A). The acquiring company will also often become a subsidiary of the original parent (company P). An example of this type of arrangement is given in paragraph 26.23.8.

26.4 The disposal of a business has to be accounted for in much the same way as a disposal of a subsidiary. Therefore, many of the principles explained in this chapter apply equally to the disposals of businesses as they do to disposals of subsidiaries. Furthermore, the disclosures that have to be given are also similar. Disposals of businesses are not dealt with in the Companies Act, but the provisions in FRS 2, FRS 3 and FRS 10 are the same for disposals of businesses and subsidiaries.

The accounting rules

Rules in FRS 2

26.5 Accounting for an undertaking that ceases to be a subsidiary is often as complex as accounting for the acquisition of a subsidiary. The matters that need to be considered when an undertaking ceases to be a subsidiary include both how to account for trading in the period after the implementation of the decision to dispose of the subsidiary and how to account for the cessation itself.

26.6 Where an undertaking ceases to be a subsidiary during a period, the consolidated profit and loss account for that period should include, to the extent that they have not already been provided for in the consolidated financial statements:

- The results of the subsidiary up to the date it ceases to be a subsidiary.
- The gain or loss arising on the cessation.

[FRS 2 para 46].

26.7 The calculation of the gain or loss arising on cessation (whether it is the result of a direct disposal, a deemed disposal or another event) is the difference between the following two amounts:

- The carrying amount of the net assets of the subsidiary attributable to the group's interest before the cessation (including any attributable goodwill — see para 26.10).
- Any remaining carrying amount attributable to the group's interest after the cessation (including any attributable goodwill), together with any proceeds received.

[FRS 2 para 47].

26.8 In many sales an element of contingent performance-related consideration is included as part of the proceeds. This element would normally be treated as a contingent asset under FRS 12; consequently it would not be recognised in the profit and loss account until it became receivable and, until then, it would merely be disclosed in the notes to the financial statements. Where consideration is simply deferred (and, hence, not contingent on future performance), the amount receivable may need to be discounted to its present value at the disposal date depending on the length of time over which it has been deferred and whether or not it bears interest.

26.8.1 Any contribution by the vendor to the purchaser's costs should be treated as a reduction in the proceeds received and, therefore, should be taken into account in determining the profit or loss on disposal.

26.8.2 Such a contribution may be dependent on future profits of the business being sold, for example, an agreement to reimburse the acquirer for a percentage of management bonuses granted by the acquirer depending on performance. The reduction in proceeds should be recognised when it is more likely than not that the reimbursement will be required.

26.8.3 If as part of the disposal arrangements the group continues to provide services to the business being disposed of for a specified period, for example providing IT support for twelve months at nil cost, the appropriate treatment is to defer part of the sales proceeds and release the deferred income to profit and loss over the twelve month period.

26.9 There may be other losses or gains that arise as a result of an undertaking ceasing to be a subsidiary that need to be recognised (for example, provisions for guarantees). Such gains or losses are not directly part of the profit or loss on the disposal, but where they need to be provided for, if they are quantifiable, they should normally be included as part of the profit or loss on disposal. If for some reason they are not provided for, they might need to be disclosed to show the full effect of the cessation. [FRS 2 para 87].

26.9.1 If the group has adopted FRS 23, the cumulative exchange differences previously taken to equity on the translation of the net investment in that subsidiary should also be included in the gain or loss on disposal. [FRS 23 para 48]. The practical impact of this requirement is that groups will need to keep detailed records in order to analyse the exchange reserve by entity.

26.9.2 The group may use the proceeds of the sale to redeem existing debt used to finance the business being sold. Any loss on the redemption of this debt is not part of the profit on disposal of the business. It should be shown as an exceptional finance cost (if material) and included within the interest line, but separately disclosed.

FRS 10

26.10 The value of net assets used to calculate the profit or loss on disposal (see para 26.7) should include any related goodwill (including any negative goodwill) not previously written off through the profit and loss account. [FRS 2 para 47]. The effect of this requirement in practice is that goodwill (or negative goodwill), arising before the introduction of FRS 10, which has remained written off (or credited) directly to reserves on acquisition following FRS 10's transitional provisions (FRS 10 para 71(c)), and any goodwill that has been capitalised but not yet amortised, must be charged (or credited) to the profit and loss account on disposal. This treatment is considered necessary to ensure that purchased goodwill (or negative goodwill) having been written off (or credited) to reserves prior to the implementation of FRS 10 does not bypass the profit and loss account completely. The requirement applies whether the disposal is a direct disposal, a deemed disposal or another event. In contrast, the treatment of such goodwill will differ under IFRS as both IFRS 3, 'Business combinations', and IFRS 1, 'First-time adoption of international financial reporting standards', prohibit the transfer of goodwill previously written off to reserves to the income statement on disposal of the subsidiary.

26.11 The practical impact of the provisions of both FRS 2 and FRS 10 means that groups have to keep detailed records of how the aggregate amount of goodwill written off direct to reserves prior to the implementation of FRS 10 is made up and to which parts of the group it relates. Because of the difficulties this can cause, particularly where the acquisition took place many years ago, there is some relief given, but this is subject to disclosure. In such a situation, it is necessary to state that goodwill has not been included in the calculation of the profit or loss arising on the sale and to explain the reason why this is so (see also para 26.41). [FRS 10 para 71(c)]. The requirement to include the attributable goodwill when calculating the profit or loss on sale of a subsidiary does pose particular problems. Consider the following examples.

Example

A group acquired another group of companies some years ago before the introduction of FRS 10. The consideration was £100m and the fair value of the net assets acquired was £40m. The resultant goodwill of £60m was written off to reserves on acquisition. The acquired group consists of five companies and the goodwill was allocated between them on the basis of a price earnings formula. The allocation was positive goodwill of £70m relating to four of the companies and negative goodwill of £10m relating to the fifth. The group is now disposing of the company in respect of which the negative goodwill arose.

Prior to FRS 10, companies could apportion the goodwill arising on acquisition in this way and, therefore, on the sale of the part of the group that gave rise to the negative goodwill, the negative goodwill would have been taken into the calculation of the profit or loss on the sale. However, for acquisitions arising following FRS 10's introduction purchased goodwill on a single transaction should not be divided into positive and negative components. In this situation, using the same facts as in the example, the £60m of goodwill should still be allocated over the five companies. However, because of the new rules in FRS 10 the original allocation would need to be changed. This would mean allocating a figure of nil to the first company and £60m of goodwill over the other four companies. As a result, goodwill of nil would be attributed to the company being disposed of.

26.12 As explained in chapter 25, prior to the introduction of FRS 10 it was acceptable to write goodwill off against the merger reserve and this continues to be acceptable practice for goodwill arising prior to FRS 10's implementation. On the sale of a subsidiary, as explained above, it is necessary to include in the calculation of any profit or loss on sale any goodwill written off direct to reserves on the original acquisition. Where an amount was credited to a merger reserve on the acquisition, that reserve would at the time be unrealised. On disposal the merger reserve arising on the acquisition becomes realised. The question then arises as to whether it is acceptable to take that part of the merger reserve to the profit and loss account on the sale of the subsidiary to mitigate the goodwill charged there. This is not, however, an acceptable treatment, because the intention of FRS 2 and FRS 10 is to measure the profit or loss on the sale by reference to its cost. The original cost for this purpose is represented by the fair value of the consideration, that is the nominal value of the shares issued plus the merger reserve. To take the release of the merger reserve to the profit and loss account would mean that the loss on sale of the subsidiary was not calculated by reference to this amount. Therefore, any merger reserve that is realised should instead be transferred to the profit and loss account reserve as a reserve movement.

Implications of FRS 3

26.13 FRS 3 requires the profit or loss on the sale of an asset to be calculated by reference to the carrying value of that asset. [FRS 3 para 21]. This requirement might seem to conflict with the FRS 2 calculation explained in paragraph 26.10 above, which requires goodwill written off to reserves in the past prior to FRS 10's implementation to be brought back into the calculation of the profit or loss on the sale of a subsidiary. The explanation of this apparent inconsistency is that the write-off of goodwill direct to reserves was not regarded as a recognised loss and, therefore, when the write-off was initially made it did not appear in the statement of total recognised gains and losses. Because it has not been 'recognised' in the past it follows that it must be recognised on disposal of the subsidiary by inclusion in the profit or loss recognised in the profit and loss account.

26.14 The treatment of profits and losses on disposals of operations, including the rules concerning loss provisions, is considered in detail in chapter 8.

Discontinued operations

26.15 Where an operation is sold, its results up to the date of sale should be disclosed as part of operating profit under either the heading 'discontinued operations' or, if it does not qualify as a discontinued operation (see para 26.16), as 'continuing operations'. The profit or loss on sale should be shown as an exceptional item after operating profit and before interest and should also be disclosed as relating to 'discontinued operations' or, if it does not qualify, it should be disclosed as relating to 'continuing operations'. [FRS 3 para 20]. It is quite possible for a business or a subsidiary that is being sold not to qualify as a discontinued operation under FRS 3 (see for example Table 26.2).

Table 26.2 — Grand Metropolitan Public Limited Company — Annual Report — 30 September 1996

Consolidated profit and loss account (extract)

for the year ended 30th September 1996

		1996			1995		
	Notes	Before exceptional items £m	Exceptional items £m	Total £m	Before exceptional items £m	Exceptional items £m	Total £m
Turnover							
Continuing operations		8,727		8,727	7,733		7,733
Discontinued operations		247		247	292		292
Total turnover	3	8,974		8,974	8,025		8,025
Operating costs	4	(7,866)		(7,866)	(6,993)	(122)	(7,115)
Operating profit							
Continuing operations		1,096		1,096	1,009	(122)	887
Discontinued operations		12		12	23	–	23
Total operating profit		1,108		1,108	1,032	(122)	910
Share of profits of associates	5	47	(24)	23	48	(15)	33
		1,155	(24)	1,131	1,080	(137)	943
Continuing operations							
Disposal of fixed assets			(3)	(3)		(9)	(9)
Sale of businesses	6		27	27		(44)	(44)
Provisions for losses on sale of businesses	6		(250)	(250)		–	–
Discontinued operations							
Sale of businesses	6		(327)	(327)		198	198
			(553)	(553)		145	145
Interest payable (net)	7	(190)	–	(190)	(168)	–	(168)
Profit on ordinary activities before taxation		965	(577)	388	912	8	920

Notes (extract)

6 Sale of businesses

	1996 Profit/(loss) on sale of businesses £m	1996 Provisions set up for businesses to be sold £m	1995 Profit/(loss) on sale of businesses £m
Continuing operations			
National food businesses in Europe (note (a))	35	(250)	–
Green Giant processing	–	–	(42)
Other	(8)	–	(2)
	27	(250)	(44)
Discontinued operations			
Pearle (note (b))	(291)	–	–
Betting and gaming (note (c))	(36)	–	–
Alpo Petfoods	–	–	198
	(327)	–	198

(a) The sale of the German food business, Erasco, was completed on 30th September for a consideration of £134m; provisions of £250m have been set up in respect of the remaining national food businesses in Europe. The profit on sale and the provisions are after charging goodwill previously written off attributable to the businesses of £222m.
(b) The sale of Pearle for a consideration of £138m was agreed on 25th September 1996 and was completed on 15th November 1996. The loss on sale was after charging goodwill previously written off attributable to Pearle of £270m.
(c) The £36m in respect of betting and gaming relates to a £118m downward adjustment to the consideration for the group's former retail betting operation, which was sold in December 1989 for £685m, offset by £82m which remained outstanding from The William Hill Group Ltd in relation to the sale. This disposes of the major aspect of a dispute with the purchaser, but there are other ongoing claims arising from the sale which have yet to be resolved.

26.16 FRS 3 defines discontinued operations as those operations that satisfy all of the following conditions:

- The sale or termination is completed either in the period or before the earlier of three months after the commencement of the subsequent period and the date on which the financial statements are approved.
- If a termination, the former activities have ceased permanently.
- The sale or termination has a material effect on the nature and focus of the reporting entity's operations and represents a material reduction in its operating facilities resulting either from its withdrawal from a particular market (whether class of business or geographical) or from a material reduction in turnover in the reporting entity's continuing markets.
- The assets, liabilities, results of operations and activities are clearly distinguishable, physically, operationally and for financial reporting purposes.

[FRS 3 para 4].

26.17 The very strict definition of 'discontinued operations' and the detailed disclosure requirements of both continuing and discontinued operations are considered in detail in chapter 8. Any reorganisation or restructuring of continuing operations resulting from a sale should be treated as part of the continuing operations. [FRS 3 para 17].

Date of sale

26.18 The date of sale is the date on which a binding legal agreement for the sale of an operation is entered into (see further chapter 8). The date on which an undertaking ceases to be another undertaking's subsidiary is the date on which control passes. [FRS 2 para 45]. Where control is transferred by public offer the relevant date is usually when an offer becomes unconditional. Where it is transferred by private treaty the date is usually where an unconditional offer is accepted. The signing of a binding legal agreement for the sale of an operation would, therefore, appear to be the date on which an offer becomes unconditional and is accepted and, therefore, should be the date from which the disposal is accounted for as having occurred. [FRS 2 para 85]. The effective date for accounting for changes in group membership is discussed in detail in chapter 25.

Impact of FRS 1

26.19 The provisions of FRS 1, 'Cash flow statements', require that where a group disposes of a subsidiary, the amounts of cash and overdrafts transferred as part of the disposal should be shown separately from the gross consideration received for the disposal. [FRS 1 para 23(a)]. Where a subsidiary is disposed of during the year, the cash flows of the group should include the cash flows of the subsidiary up to the date of sale. [FRS 1 para 43]. The provisions of FRS 1 are explained in detail in chapter 30 and the disclosure requirements relating to disposals are summarised in paragraph 26.39.

Accounting for the sale of a subsidiary

Full disposal

26.20 The most common transaction that results in an undertaking ceasing to be a subsidiary is a straight disposal. The consolidated profit and loss account should include the trading results of the undertaking up to the date of its ceasing to be a subsidiary, disclosed, where appropriate, as discontinued operations as explained above. Any gain or loss arising on disposal would be included in the profit and loss account on the basis explained above.

26.21 In effect, the profit or loss on disposal of all or part of a subsidiary will be the difference at the date of sale between the following amounts:

- The proceeds of the sale.
- The group's share of the subsidiary undertaking's net assets disposed of, together with any premium or discount on acquisition (apportioned if necessary to that element of the net assets sold) that has not been written off through the profit and loss account.

26.22 The calculation of the profit or loss on sale is illustrated by the following examples. The example below looks at the calculation of the gain on disposal of a subsidiary where the group capitalised goodwill arising on the initial acquisition and amortises that goodwill over its useful life.

Example

A parent purchased an 80% interest in a subsidiary for £80,000 during 19X1 when the fair value of the subsidiary's net assets was £87,500. Goodwill on consolidation that arose on the acquisition is being amortised over its estimated useful life of ten years and a full year's charge for amortisation was made in the consolidated financial statements to 31 December 19X1. The parent sold its investment in the subsidiary on 31 December 19X4 for £100,000.

The book value of the subsidiary's net assets in the consolidated financial statements on the date of the sale was £112,500.

The parent's profit and loss account for 19X4 would show a gain on the sale of the investment of £20,000 calculated as follows:

	£'000
Sale proceeds	100
Less: cost of investment in subsidiary	(80)
Gain on sale in the parent's accounts	20

However, the group's profit and loss account for 19X4 would show a gain on the sale of the subsidiary of £4,000 calculated as follows:

	£'000	£'000
Sale proceeds		100
Less: share of net assets at date of disposal (£112,500 × 80%)	(90)	
goodwill on consolidation unamortised at date of sale*	(6)	(96)
Gain on sale in the group's accounts		4

*The unamortised goodwill on consolidation is calculated as follows:

	£'000
Fair value of consideration at date of acquisition	80
Less: fair value of net assets of subsidiary at date of acquisition (£87,500 × 80%)	70
Goodwill arising on consolidation	10
Amortisation (4 years × £1,000)	4
Unamortised goodwill at 31 December 19X4	6

The difference between the gain in the holding company's profit and loss account and the gain reported in the group's consolidated profit and loss account is £16,000 (that is, £20,000 – £4,000). This difference represents the share of post-acquisition profits retained in the subsidiary of £20,000 (that is, (£112,500 – £87,500) × 80%) that have been reported in the group's profit and loss account up to the date of sale, less goodwill of £4,000 that has been written off in the group's profit and loss account.

26.23 The next example looks at the calculation of the gain or loss on disposal where the group on acquisition, prior to the implementation of FRS 10, wrote off the goodwill arising on purchasing the subsidiary direct to reserves.

Example

The facts are identical to those in the example in paragraph 26.22 except that the goodwill that arose on consolidation was written off direct to reserves in the year of acquisition.

As before, the parent's profit and loss account for 19X4 would show a gain on the sale of the investment of £20,000. The group's profit and loss account for 19X4 would show no gain or loss on the sale of the subsidiary calculated as follows:

	£'000	£'000
Sale proceeds		100
Less: share of net assets at date of disposal (£112,500 × 80%)	(90)	
goodwill written off directly to reserves*	(10)	(100)
		–

*The goodwill on consolidation is calculated as follows:

	£'000
Fair value of consideration at date of acquisition	80
Less: fair value of net assets of subsidiary at date of acquisition (£87,500 × 80%)	70
Goodwill arising on consolidation	10

The difference between the gain in the parent's profit and loss account and the gain reported in the group's consolidated profit and loss account is £20,000. This difference represents the share of post-acquisition profits retained in the subsidiary of £20,000 (that is, (£112,500 – £87,500) × 80%) that have been reported in the group's profit and loss account up to the date of sale. The goodwill is required by FRS 2 and FRS 10 to be written back to reserves on sale of the subsidiary and charged as part of the overall profit or loss on the disposal (see further para 26.10).

Sale of a subsidiary for shares

26.23.1 Disposals often arise where a parent sells a subsidiary for shares in another undertaking, which results in that other undertaking becoming an associate, joint venture or subsidiary of the vendor. Therefore, at the same time as the disposal there is an acquisition. UITF Abstract 31 sets out the approach to be adopted.

[The next paragraph is 26.23.3.]

26.23.3 The abstract requires that where an entity (A) exchanges a business or other non-monetary asset for an interest in another entity (B), which thereby becomes A's subsidiary or which becomes A's joint venture or associate, the following accounting treatment is required in A's consolidated financial statements.

- To the extent that A retains an ownership interest, that retained interest, including any related goodwill, should be included at its pre-transaction carrying amount (that is, it should not be fair valued).
- A's share of net assets acquired through its new interest in B should be accounted for at fair value, with the difference between these fair values and the fair value of the consideration given being accounted for as goodwill.
- To the extent that the fair value of the consideration received by A exceeds the book value of the part of the business or non-monetary assets no longer owned by A (and any related goodwill) together with any cash given up, A should recognise a gain. Any gain arising on the exchange that is not realised should be reported in the STRGL.

- Where the fair value of the consideration received by A is less than the book value of the part of the business or non-monetary assets no longer owned by A (and any related goodwill) together with any cash given up, A should recognise a loss, either as an impairment in accordance with FRS 11 or, for any loss remaining after an impairment review of the relevant assets, in A's profit and loss account.

26.23.4 The abstract states that no gain or loss should be recognised where the artificiality or lack of substance of the transaction is such that any gain or loss on the exchange could not be justified. In such cases the circumstances should be disclosed.

26.23.5 The method required for calculating the gain or loss and goodwill under UITF 31 is as follows:

- The book value of assets and liabilities effectively disposed of plus attributable goodwill is compared to the fair value of the consideration received, that is the fair value of the part of the business that is acquired (this is not necessarily the same as the fair value of the net assets acquired as the fair value of the business includes the goodwill of that element of the business that is acquired). The result is either a gain or a loss arising on the exchange.
- The fair value of the consideration given, which is the fair value of the part of the business disposed of (which again may be different from the fair values of the assets and liabilities given up as it will include a value for the unrecognised goodwill of the business) is compared with the fair values of the assets and liabilities acquired, with the result being recognised as goodwill (either positive or negative).
- The above calculations will be affected if cash settlements are made as part of the exchange.

26.23.6 To illustrate the first bullet above, if the book value of the net assets disposed of is £50 and the fair value of the net assets acquired is £60, but the fair value of the business acquired (which contains the net assets acquired) is £70, the comparison is between the £50 and the £70, not between the £50 and the £60.

26.23.7 Similarly to illustrate the second bullet point, if the book value of the net assets disposed of is £50 and their fair value is £55, but the fair value of the business given up is £70, it is £70 that is compared with the fair value of the net assets acquired in order to determine the goodwill arising.

26.23.8 The method prescribed by UITF 31 calculates the gain or loss only on the element that has been disposed of to a third party. Therefore, no intra-group profit or loss arises, which would otherwise need to be eliminated on consolidation.

In exchange for an interest in a subsidiary

Example

Company A has a wholly-owned subsidiary company B. Company A sells its subsidiary company B to company C, a listed company, for shares in company C and ends up owning 75% of company C's shares (as illustrated in the diagram).

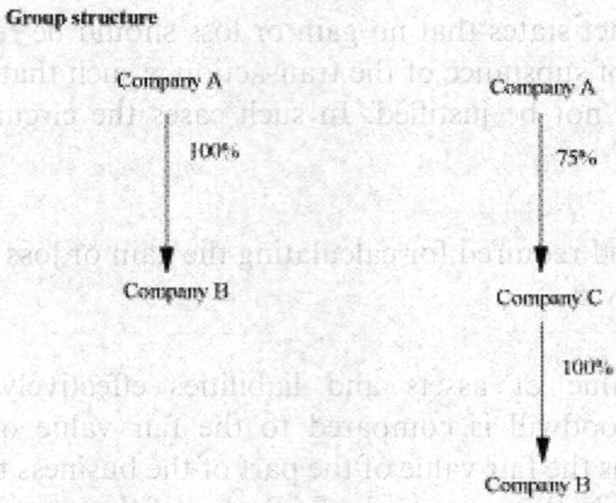

The net assets of company B prior to the disposal are £1 million (fair value £1.3 million) and goodwill previously capitalised is £600,000 (for simplicity, goodwill has not been amortised in this example); the carrying value of company B in company A's books is £1.5 million. At the date of its acquisition by company A, company B's profit and loss account reserve was £400,000 and B has since made £100,000 post acquisition profits. The position prior to the transaction was, therefore, as follows:

Consolidation of companies A and B before transaction	Co A	Co B	Consol
	£'000	£'000	£'000
Goodwill	–	–	600
Investment in subsidiary	1,500	–	–
Net assets	10,000	1,000	11,000
	11,500	1,000	11,600
Equity share capital	2,000	500	2,000
Profit and loss account reserve	9,500	100	9,600
- pre acquisition reserves	-	400	-
Equity shareholders' funds	11,500	1,000	11,600

The goodwill arising on the acquisition by company A of company B is calculated as follows:

Cost of control account/goodwill

	£000		£000
Investment	1,500	Equity share capital	500
		P&L reserve	400
			900
		Goodwill	600
	1,500		1,500

The net assets of company C prior to its acquisition of company B are £380,000 (fair value £500,000). Company C then issues shares worth £1.75 million (which is the fair value of the consideration given for the acquisition of 100% of B), being £600,000 nominal value and £1.15 million premium. The balance sheets of the three companies directly after the issue of shares by company C are as follows:

Summarised balance sheets	Co A £'000	Co B £'000	Co C £'000
Investment in subsidiary	1,500	–	1,750
Net assets	10,000	1,000	380
	11,500	1,000	2,130
Equity share capital	2,000	500	800
Merger reserve	–	–	1,150
Profit and loss account reserve	9,500	500	180
Equity shareholders' funds	11,500	1,000	2,130

The parent, company A, had an interest in company B that cost £1.5 million, and has in effect swapped this for an interest in company C's group. The cost to company A remains £1.5 million, although this investment has a market value of £1.75 million.

With regard to company A's consolidated financial statements, it is necessary to calculate the gain or loss and the goodwill arising in accordance with UITF 31.

Gain or loss on disposal of 25% of B	£'000
Book value of assets and liabilities given up plus attributable goodwill ((£1m + £600,000) x 25%)	400.0
Fair value of business received in consideration (£1.75m x 25%) (note 1)	437.5
Gain on disposal (note 2)	37.5
Goodwill on acquisition of 75% of C	
Fair value of business given in consideration (note 3)	437.5
Fair value of assets and liabilities acquired (£500,000 x 75%)	375.0
Goodwill	62.5

Note 1: A receives consideration (that is, shares in C) with a fair value of £1.75 million. However, the amount included in the UITF 31 calculation is the amount attributable to the interest in B that has been disposed of, that is 25% of £1.75 million.

Note 2: The gain is regarded by A as unrealised because it is received in the form of shares which, though listed, are in a company which is treated as a subsidiary and, accordingly, the gain is credited to the STRGL.

Note 3: The fair value of the part of the subsidiary B that is effectively disposed of is derived from the price paid by C for the whole of B, that is £1.75m.

Consolidation of A, B and C after the transaction (note: Company C's net assets are adjusted to fair value for the purpose of the consolidation as C has been acquired by A).

Consolidation of companies A, B and C after the transaction	Co A £'000	Co B £'000	Co C £'000	Consol £'000	Notes
Goodwill	–	–	–	512.5	1
Investment in subsidiary	1,500.0	–	1,750.0	–	
Net assets	10,000.0	1,000.0	380.0	11,500.0	2
	11,500.0	1,000.0	2,130.0	12,012.5	
Equity share capital	2,000.0	500.0	800.0	2,000.0	3
Merger reserve	–	–	1,150.0	–	4
Other reserve	–	–	–	37.5	5
Profit and loss account reserve	9,500.0	500.0	180.0	9,600.0	
Minority interest	–	–	–	375.0	
	11,500.0	1,000.0	2,130.0	12,012.5	

Note 1: The goodwill balance of £512,500 represents the balance (75%) of the goodwill of £600,000 arising on the acquisition of B, being £450,000 plus the goodwill of £62,500 arising on the acquisition of C.

Note 2: On consolidation the net assets of C are increased from £380,000 to their fair value of £500,000.

Note 3: The other reserve represents the unrealised gain arising on disposal of 25% of B.

Note 4: The consolidated profit and loss account represents the profit and loss account of A (£9,500,000) plus the post-acquisition profits of B of £100,000.

Note 5: The minority interest represents 25% of C's net assets of £500,000 at fair value being £125,000 plus 25% of B's net assets of £1,000,000, being £250,000, making £375,000 in total.

One complication that could arise in this situation is if C were required to prepare consolidated financial statements. In that case C would have to acquisition account for B, which would involve fair valuing B's net assets and not fair valuing its own. This is precisely the opposite of what happens where A accounts for the acquisition of C. The accounting by C for its acquisition of B in the consolidated financial statements of C is not dealt with further here.

In exchange for an interest in a joint venture or associate

26.23.9 In recent times there has been a large number of transactions through which companies have formed joint ventures or associates, to which each party has contributed businesses.

26.23.10 The following examples illustrate the accounting where the resulting interest is a joint venture or associate. Also illustrated is a case where there is a cash element in the transaction.

Example 1

Company A owns 100% of company B. The book value of company B's net assets is £400,000 and their fair value is £600,000. Goodwill on the acquisition of company B was £150,000 which has been amortised and stands at a book value of £100,000. The fair value of company B's business is estimated at £800,000 for the purpose of the transaction. Company C owns 100% of company D. The book value of company D's assets is £300,000 and their fair value is £400,000. The value of company D's business is £800,000.

A new joint venture company, Newco, is formed into which companies A and C contribute the businesses of companies B and D respectively and each of company A and company C receives shares in Newco giving each a 50% share.

The balance sheet of Newco immediately after the transaction is as follows:

	£'000
Net assets (at fair value) (600 + 400)	1,000
Goodwill	600
	1,600
Shareholders' funds	1,600

Shareholders' funds represents the fair value of the consideration given, which in this case is based on the fair values of the businesses acquired (800 + 800)

Under UITF 31, company A accounts for the gain or loss arising and the goodwill arising on acquisition of its 50% share in Newco as follows:

	£'000
Calculation of gain/(loss) on disposal of 50% of B	
Share of net assets disposed of at book value (50% x £400,000)	200
Share of goodwill disposed of (50% x £100,000)	50
	250
Share of value of D received as consideration (fair value of consideration being half of fair value of D's business)	400
Gain on disposal	150
Calculation of goodwill on acquisition of 50% of D	
Value of half of business of B given up	400
Fair value of net assets acquired (50% x£400,000)	200
Goodwill arising	200

Under UITF 31, company C accounts for the gain or loss arising and the goodwill arising on the acquisition of a 50% share in Newco as follows:

	£'000
Calculation of gain/(loss) on disposal of 50% of D	
Share of net assets disposed of at book value (50% x £300,000, assuming no goodwill in books of C)	150
Share of value of B business received as consideration (fair value of consideration being half of fair value of B business)	400
Gain on sale	250
Calculation of goodwill on acquisition of 50% of B	
Value of half of business of D given up	400
Fair value of net assets acquired (50% x £600,000)	300
Goodwill	100

Example 2

The facts are the same as in the above example except that the value of D is not £800,000 but £500,000. In order to make up the difference, company C pays £300,000 in cash into the joint venture.

The balance sheet of Newco immediately after the transaction is as follows:

	£'000
Net assets at fair value (excluding cash) (600 + 400)	1,000
Cash	300
Goodwill	300
	1,600
Shareholders' funds	1,600

The calculations for company A are as follows:

	£'000
Calculation of gain/(loss) on disposal of 50% of B	
Share of net assets and goodwill disposed of (at book value)	250
Share of value of D received as consideration	250
Cash (50%)	150
Gain on disposal	150
Calculation of goodwill on acquisition of 50% of D	
Share of businesses given up (half of B)	400
Fair value of net assets acquired (50% x £400,000)	200
Share of cash	150
	350
Goodwill	50

The calculations for company C are as follows:

	£'000
Calculation of gain/(loss) on disposal of 50% of D	
Share of net assets disposed of (50% x £300,000)	150
Cash (50%)	150
	300
Share of value of B received as consideration	400
Gain on disposal	100
Calculation of goodwill on acquisition of 50% of B	
Value of businesses and cash contributed ((500 + 300) x 50%)	400
Fair value of assets acquired (50% x £600,000)	300
Goodwill	100

A simple proof of the calculations can be done. For example, company A starts with net assets of £400,000 and goodwill of £100,000 in company B at book value. In example 2 it finishes with a share of assets of Newco of half of the book value of assets contributed by itself (50% x £400,000), half of the fair value of the assets contributed by company C (50% x £400,000) and half of the cash contributed by company C (50% x £300,000) making £550,000 in all. The difference (£550,000 less £500,000) is a net gain of £50,000, which when added to the £50,000 of goodwill which company A retains relating to company B, makes a net gain of £100,000. This is the same as the difference between the gain calculated as above of £150,000 and the goodwill of £50,000.

In company C's case it starts with net assets in company D at book value of £300,000 and cash of £300,000. It finishes with half of the original net assets at book value (£150,000), half of the cash (£150,000) and half of the fair value of the assets of company B contributed by company A (50% x £600,000). This gives £600,000 less £600,000, that is neither gain nor loss on a net basis. This is the same as the difference between the gain calculated as above on a UITF 31 basis of £100,000 and the goodwill of £100,000.

Ceasing to be a subsidiary other than by sale or exchange of shares

26.24 An undertaking may cease to be a subsidiary undertaking as a result of loss of control. Such loss of control could occur, for example, because of: changes in voting rights attaching to shares held; changes in the power to appoint or remove directors or their voting rights; or the parent no longer actually exercising or having the power to exercise dominant influence or control (see further chapter 24). In these situations no profit or loss will arise in the consolidated financial statements, unless there is a payment for loss of control, because there is no change in the net assets attributable to the group's holding in the former subsidiary undertaking.

26.25 Where loss of control arises in this way, the former subsidiary undertaking should not be consolidated, but should be shown instead at its net asset value as an associated undertaking (see chapter 27) or as an investment depending on the degree of influence retained. In addition, the circumstances that resulted in the undertaking ceasing to be a subsidiary should be explained in a note to the consolidated financial statements. [FRS 2 para 49].

[The next paragraph is 26.27].

Partial disposals

26.27 Partial disposals arise where a parent disposes of part of its interest in a subsidiary (for example see Table 26.4). The remaining interest of the parent in the undertaking might result in the undertaking continuing to be a subsidiary or it might become an associate or an investment.

Table 26.4 — Cable and Wireless plc — Report and Accounts — 31 March 1993

Notes to the Accounts (extract)

Exceptional items: profit on partial sale of subsidiaries		1993	1992
	£m	£m	£m
Consolidation adjustment arising as a result of the sale of 20% of Mercury Communications Limited to BCE Inc.	166.0		
Less: Goodwill previously written off to reserves (Note 25)	48.3		
		117.7	–
Profit arising on the sale of shares in Hong Kong Telecommunications Limited as a result of the exercise of warrants	63.6		
Less: Goodwill previously written off to reserves (Note 25)	3.5		
		60.1	–
		177.8	–

There was no taxation or minority interest charge or credit applicable to the exceptional items shown above.

26.28 The basic principles that apply to disposals also apply to partial disposals. Therefore, where a group reduces its stake in an undertaking any profit or loss should be calculated as the difference between the following:

- The carrying amount of the net assets of that subsidiary attributable to the group's interest before the reduction.
- The carrying amount attributable to the group's interest after the reduction together with any proceeds received.

The net assets compared should include any related goodwill not previously written off through the profit and loss account.

26.29 Where the undertaking continues to be a subsidiary after the disposal, the minority interests in that subsidiary should be increased by the carrying amount of the net identifiable assets that are now attributable to the minority interests because of the decrease in the group's interest. However, as explained in chapter 24, no amount for goodwill that arose on the acquisition of the group's interest in that subsidiary should be attributed to the minority interests.

26.30 Three examples follow that illustrate the consequences of a partial sale where the subsidiary undertaking after the sale:

- Remains a subsidiary, but with a reduced interest (see para 26.31).
- Becomes an associate (see para 26.32).
- Retains a small shareholders' interest (see para 26.33).

Remaining a subsidiary

26.31 The example that follows illustrates the calculation of the gain or loss arising on a partial disposal, where the undertaking remains a subsidiary.

Example

A parent purchased a 100% subsidiary for £500,000 during 19X1 when the fair value of the subsidiary's net assets was £400,000. Goodwill arising on the acquisition prior to the implementation of FRS 10 was written off direct to reserves in the year of acquisition. The parent sold 40% of its investment in the subsidiary in December 19X4 for £450,000. The book value of the subsidiary's net assets included in the consolidated balance sheet on the date of the sale was £800,000. The parent's profit and loss account for 19X4 would show a gain on the sale of the investment of £250,000 calculated as follows:

	£'000
Sale proceeds	450
Less: cost of investment in subsidiary (£500,000 × 40%)	(200)
Gain on sale in the parent's accounts	250

However, the group's profit and loss account for 19X4 would only show a gain on the sale of the subsidiary of £90,000 calculated as follows:

	£'000	£'000
Net assets and proceeds after disposal:		
Share of net assets (£800,000 × 60%)	480	
Goodwill written off directly to reserves (£100,000 × 60%)	60	
Sale proceeds	450	990
Less: net assets before disposal		
Net assets	800	
Goodwill written off directly to reserves*	100	900
Gain on sale to the group		90

*The goodwill on consolidation is calculated as follows:

	£'000
Fair value of consideration at date of acquisition	500
Less: fair value of net assets of subsidiary at date of acquisition	400
Goodwill arising on consolidation	100

The difference between the gain in the parent's profit and loss account and the gain reported in the group's consolidated profit and loss account is £160,000. This difference represents the share of post-acquisition profits retained in the subsidiary of £160,000 (that is, (£800,000 – £400,000) × 40%) that have been reported in the group's profit and loss account up to the date of sale.

The minority interests immediately after the disposal will be 40% of the net carrying value of the subsidiary included in the consolidated balance sheet of £800,000, that is, £320,000.

Becoming an associate

26.32 The next example illustrates the calculation of the gain or loss on a partial disposal where the subsidiary becomes an associate.

Example

The facts of this example are the same as the example in paragraph 26.31 except the group disposes of a 60% interest for £675,000, leaving the parent with 40% and significant influence. The parent's profit and loss account for 19X4 would show a gain on the sale of the investment of £375,000 calculated as follows:

	£'000
Sale proceeds	675
Less: cost of investment in subsidiary (£500,000 × 60%)	(300)
Gain on sale in the parent's accounts	375

However, the group's profit and loss account for 19X4 would only show a gain on the sale of the subsidiary of £135,000 calculated as follows:

	£'000	£'000
Net assets and proceeds after disposal:		
Share of net assets (£800,000 × 40%)	320	
Goodwill written off directly to reserves (£100,000 × 40%)	40	
Sale proceeds	675	1,035
Less: net assets before disposal		
Net assets	800	
Goodwill written off directly to reserves	100	900
Gain on sale to the group		135

In this situation, after the sale the undertaking will no longer be treated as a subsidiary, but rather as an associate and equity accounted. It will be included in the consolidated balance sheet as an investment in an associated undertaking of £320,000 (40% × £800,000) using the equity method of accounting. Goodwill relating to the associate of £40,000 has already been written off to reserves and will remain there.

Becoming an investment

26.33 The example below considers the situation where a parent disposes of part of its interest in a subsidiary such that it merely has a small remaining investment in the undertaking.

Example

The facts of this example are the same as the previous two examples above, except that the group disposes of a 90% interest for £855,000, leaving the parent with a 10% investment.

The parent's profit and loss account for 19X4 would show a gain on the sale of the investment of £405,000 calculated as follows:

	£'000
Sale proceeds	885
Less: cost of investment in subsidiary (£500,000 × 90%)	(450)
Gain on sale in the parent's accounts	405

However, the group's profit and loss account for 19X4 would only show a gain on the sale of the subsidiary of £45,000 calculated as follows:

	£'000	£'000
Net assets and proceeds after disposal:		
Share of net assets (£800,000 × 10%)	80	
Goodwill written off directly to reserves (£100,000 × 10%)	10	
Sale proceeds	855	945
Less: net assets before disposal		
Net assets	800	
Goodwill written off directly to reserves	100	900
Gain on sale to the group		45

In this situation the undertaking will no longer be treated as a subsidiary, but rather as an investment. Unless the entity has adopted FRS 26, 'Financial instruments: Recognition and measurement', the undertaking will be included in the consolidated balance sheet at 'cost' determined on an equity basis as £80,000 (£800,000 × 10%). The investment, however, is only recorded in the parent at £50,000 (that is, £500,000 × 10%). The double entry needed to ensure that the consolidation reserves reconcile on consolidation would be as follows:

	£'000	£'000
Dr Investment	40	
Cr Reserves		40
To recognise the group's share of post-acquisition reserves previously recognised in the consolidated financial statements which relates to the 10% investment retained.		
Dr Reserves	10	
Cr Investment		10
To recognise the group's share of the goodwill arising on the acquisition of the original investment which relates to the 10% investment retained.		

The reserves of £40,000 have already been recognised in the consolidated reserves as they represent the share retained of the post-acquisition reserves that have arisen from the subsidiary's original acquisition up to the date of sale. It can be argued that this is the only adjustment required and that the investment should be recorded at £90,000 in the consolidated financial statements. However, it is more prudent to show the goodwill investment value reduced by the amount of goodwill that has previously been written off to reserves.

The parent could in this circumstance revalue the investment from its cost of £50,000 to £80,000 to show the same figure as that shown in the group. It is necessary, of course, to consider whether the £80,000 is substantiated by the group's remaining share of the underlying value of the undertaking. If it is not, a provision would be required to write it down to the investment's underlying value.

If the entity has adopted FRS 26, the investment should be classified and measured in accordance with that standard (see chapter 6).

Deemed disposals

26.34 An undertaking may also cease to be a subsidiary, or the group may reduce its percentage interest, as a result of a deemed disposal. A deemed disposal may arise, *inter alia*, where:

- The group does not take up its full allocation of rights in a rights issue.
- The group does not take up its full share of a scrip dividend.
- Another party exercises its options or warrants.
- The subsidiary issues shares to other non-group parties (for example, see Table 26.5).

[FRS 2 para 87].

Table 26.5 — Capital and Regional Properties plc — Report and Accounts — 25 December 1993

Notes to the Accounts (extract)

27. Deemed disposal on flotation of CenterPoint

The flotation of CenterPoint on the American Stock Exchange reduced the Group's effective interest in its operations (excluding the additional shares acquired directly by the Group at the flotation) from approximately 60% to 18.8%. The reduction in the Group's effective interest is a deemed disposal within the meaning of Financial Reporting Standard No. 2 and resulted in a loss of £90,000, which has been dealt with as an exceptional item in the profit and loss account:

	£000
Group share of CenterPoint net assets at the date of deemed disposal	12,360
Loss arising on deemed disposal	(90)
Market valuation of shares retained in CenterPoint following flotation (see note 15)	12,270

No goodwill has been dealt with previously in reserves. US operations contributed £652,000 to the Group profit before taxation up to the date of the deemed disposal. The reduction in value of £6,582,000 arising on the US properties up to the deemed disposal is explained in note 13.

26.35 Deemed disposals have the same effect as changes in ownership by disposal and should be accounted for in the same way. Such disposals fall into three categories for accounting purposes:

- Another party subscribes for shares in an undertaking and the parent does not increase its investment (see Table 26.6 and example below).

  This might arise, for example, where another party exercises options or warrants, or it subscribes for rights in a rights issue, but the parent does not. It may also arise where another party subscribes for new shares in the subsidiary.

- Another party subscribes for shares in an undertaking and a proportionally smaller number of shares are subscribed for by the parent (see example in para 26.37).

- Another party subscribes for shares in an undertaking and the parent sells its right to subscribe to a third party (see example in para 26.38).

Table 26.6 — Daily Mail and General Trust plc — Annual Report — 2 October 1994

Notes to the Accounts (extract)

7 Surplus on the Reduction of Interest in Subsidiary

	1994	1993
	£m	£m
	15.9	–

In May 1994, Euromoney Publications raised cash of £23.1 million through a market placing of shares in which the Group could not participate for technical reasons. The Group has reported its share of the increase arising in its net assets as exceptional profit, as required by FRS 2.

Example

In January 19X4 a group had a 60% interest in a subsidiary with share capital of 100,000 £1 ordinary shares. The goodwill arising on the acquisition of £40,000 was written off directly to reserves in the year of acquisition prior to FRS 10's introduction. On 31 December 19X4 the 40% minority shareholder exercised an option to subscribe for a further 50,000 £1 ordinary shares in the subsidiary at £12 per share, raising £600,000. The net assets of the subsidiary in the consolidated balance sheet prior to the exercise of the option were £900,000.

Shareholdings	Before		After	
	No	%	No	%
Group	60,000	60	60,000	40
Other party	40,000	40	90,000	60
	100,000	100	150,000	100
Net assets	£'000	%	£'000	%
Group's share	540	60	600	40
Other party's share	360	40	900	60
	900	100	1,500	100

Calculation of group loss on deemed disposal	£'000	£'000
Net assets and proceeds after deemed disposal		
Net assets	600	
Goodwill written off directly to reserves*	27	
Proceeds	–	627
Less: net assets before deemed disposal		
Net assets	540	
Goodwill written off directly to reserves*	40	580
Profit on deemed disposal		47

* A loss of goodwill has been attributed to the deemed disposal, because the minority has in effect bought part of the goodwill in the price it has paid for its increased stake in the company. The group's interest is now 40% and, provided that the parent exercises significant influence over its former subsidiary, it will be treated as an associate and equity accounted. The goodwill attributable to the interest in the subsidiary was previously written off to reserves when the entity was originally acquired and consolidated. Part of this goodwill, £13,333 (that is £40,000 ÷ 60 × 20) is attributable to the deemed disposal and must be taken to the profit and loss account as part of the profit on sale of £47,000. The remaining goodwill of £26,667 is now attributable to the interest in the entity after the deemed disposal and under equity accounting the remaining goodwill would continue to be written off against reserves.

26.36 An illustration of such a deemed disposal is given in Table 26.1. In that situation, although the group's interest is diluted, a profit arises on the deemed disposal as the dilution took place by a public offer of shares.

26.37 The next example considers a deemed disposal that arises from the parent subscribing for proportionally fewer rights in a rights issue.

Example

At the beginning of the year a group had a 55% interest in a subsidiary company. The goodwill arising on the acquisition of £450,000 was written off directly to reserves in the year of acquisition, which was prior to the implementation of FRS 10. The subsidiary's share capital was £2 million (ordinary £1 shares) and its net assets were £10 million immediately prior to the rights issue. During the year the subsidiary made a 1 for 2 rights issue priced at £6 per share. The group exercised its rights to 100,000 shares and neither exercised nor sold its remaining rights. All the minority shareholders exercised their rights.

The group owned 55% of the share capital prior to the rights issue, that is, 1,100,000 shares. As it exercised rights to 100,000 shares it owns 1,200,000 shares after the rights issue.

Shareholdings

The number of shares of the subsidiary in issue following the rights issue was:

2,000,000 + 100,000 + (2,000,000 × 0.45 × ½) = 2,550,000 shares

	Before		After	
	No	%	No	%
Group	1,100,000	55	1,200,000	47
Other party	900,000	45	1,350,000	53
	2,000,000	100	2,550,000	100

Net assets

The net assets of the company post rights issue were:

£10,000,000 + (550,000 × £6) = £13,300,000

	£'000	%	£'000	%
Group's share	5,500	55	6,251	47
Other party's share	4,500	45	7,049	53
	10,000	100	13,300	100

Calculation of group profit on deemed disposal	£'000	£'000
Net assets and proceeds after deemed disposal		
Net assets	6,251	
Goodwill written off directly to reserves*	385	
Cost of subscribing for rights	(600)	6,036
Less: net assets before deemed disposal		
Net assets	5,500	
Goodwill written off directly to reserves*	450	5,950
Profit on deemed disposal		86

* A loss of goodwill has been attributed to the deemed disposal as the minority have subscribed for their rights issue at full market price. Assuming the voting rights follow the share capital the company would no longer be a subsidiary of the group and would be treated as an associated company and, therefore, equity accounted. The goodwill attributable to the interest in the subsidiary was £450,000 and was previously written off to reserves when the entity was originally acquired and consolidated. Therefore, an

adjustment needs to be made for that goodwill figure as a result of the deemed disposal. The group has disposed of an interest of 8% and this equates to goodwill of £65,455 (that is, £450,000 ÷ 55 × 8). This amount is written off to the profit and loss account and included in the net profit on disposal of £86,000. The residual £384,545 of goodwill will remain written off against reserves on equity accounting the retained associate interest of 47%.

26.38 The next example considers the situation where a deemed disposal arises from the sale by the parent of its rights in a rights issue.

Example

At the beginning of the year a group had a 55% interest in a subsidiary company. The goodwill arising on the acquisition of £450,000 was written off directly to reserves in the year of acquisition, which was prior to the implementation of FRS 10. During the year the subsidiary made a 1 for 2 rights issue priced at £6 per ordinary £1 share. The group did not exercise its rights, but sold them to a third party for £200,000. The third party then exercised those rights as did other minority shareholders owning 40% of the remaining 45% of the company's share capital. The rights issue was, therefore, taken up by 95% of the shareholders. The subsidiary's share capital was £2 million (ordinary £1 shares) and its net assets were £10 million immediately prior to the rights issue.

The group owned 55% of the share capital prior to the rights issue, that is, 1,100,000 shares. As it exercised no rights it also owned 1,100,000 shares following the issue.

Shareholdings

The number of shares of the subsidiary in issue following the rights issue was:

2,000,000 + (2,000,000 × 0.95 × ½) = 2,950,000 shares

	Before		After	
	No	%	No	%
Group	1,100,000	55	1,100,000	37
Other party	900,000	45	1,850,000	63
	2,000,000	100	2,950,000	100

Net assets

The net assets of the company post rights issue were:

£10,000,000 + (950,000 × £6) = £15,700,000

	£'000	%	£'000	%
Group's share	5,500	55	5,809	37
Other party's share	4,500	45	9,891	63
	10,000	100	15,700	100

Calculation of group profit on deemed disposal	£'000	£'000
Net assets and proceeds after deemed disposal		
Net assets	5,809	
Goodwill written off directly to reserves*	303	
Proceeds from sale of rights	200	6,312
Less: net assets before deemed disposal		
Net assets	5,500	
Goodwill written off directly to reserves*	450	5,950
Profit on deemed disposal		362

* A loss of goodwill has been attributed to the deemed disposal as the parent's percentage interest has reduced. As with the previous two examples, assuming the voting rights follow the share capital the company would no longer be a subsidiary of the group and would be treated as an associated company and, therefore, equity accounted. The goodwill attributable to the interest in the subsidiary previously written off to reserves was £450,000 when the entity was originally acquired and consolidated. Therefore, an adjustment needs to be made for that goodwill figure as a result of the deemed disposal and the group has in effect disposed of an 18% interest, which equates to goodwill of £147,272 (that is, £450,000 ÷ 55 × 18). This goodwill write off is charged to the profit and loss account as part of the net profit on the deemed disposal of £362,000. The balance of the goodwill will remain written off to reserves on equity accounting the associated interest.

Disclosure requirements

26.39 Where, during the period, an undertaking has ceased to be a subsidiary and this significantly affects the figures shown in the consolidated financial statements, the following should be disclosed in the notes to the financial statements:

- The name of the undertaking that has ceased to be a subsidiary. In the case of a group of undertakings ceasing to be subsidiaries, the name of the parent of that group. [4A Sch 15(a); FRS 2 para 48].
- The Act requires disclosure of the extent to which the profit or loss shown in the consolidated profit or loss account is attributable to the undertaking or group that has been disposed of. [4A Sch 15(b)]. In addition, FRS 3 requires that the results up to the date of sale should be disclosed as a discontinued operation assuming that the criteria are met. [FRS 3 para 14]. Therefore, if there is only one sale of an undertaking or group of undertakings during a period, the Act's requirement would be fulfilled by the FRS 3 disclosure of discontinued operations. However, if there is more than one undertaking or group disposed of during the year then the profit or loss attributable to each undertaking or group of undertakings disposed of would appear to require to be separately disclosed, as the Act refers to the profit or loss attributable to "*that undertaking or group*".
- The profit or loss on disposal shown as a non-operating item below operating profit and described as 'Profit or loss on sale of an operation' (see, for example, para 26.15). [FRS 3 para 20].
- The amount of purchased goodwill (or negative goodwill) attributable to the business disposed of included in the profit or loss on disposal, separately disclosed as a component of the profit or loss on disposal. [FRS 10 para 71(c)(ii)]. Where the item is presented as two components there should be, in addition, a single subtotal showing the total profit or loss on disposal. This disclosure can either be given on the face of the profit and loss account or in a note to the financial statements.
- The amount of any ownership interest retained in any material undertaking that has ceased to be a subsidiary in the period. [FRS 2 para 48].

- Where any material undertaking has ceased to be a subsidiary other than by the disposal of at least part of the interest held by the group, the circumstances should be explained. [FRS 2 paras 48, 49].
- 'Acquisitions and disposals' in the cash flow statement should include receipts from sales of investments in subsidiary undertakings and any balances of cash and overdrafts transferred as part of the sale (shown separately), but this can be in a note. [FRS 1 para 23].
- A note to the cash flow statement should show a summary of the effects of disposals indicating how much of the consideration was made up of cash. [FRS 1 para 45].
- Where the disposal has had a material effect on the amounts reported under each of the standard headings in the cash flow statements (such as operating, capital expenditure and financial investments, financing, etc.), the effect should be disclosed as a note to the cash flow statement. This information can be given by segregating cash flows between continuing and discontinued operations. [FRS 1 para 45]. However, the information need only be given in the period the disposal is made. [FRS 1 para 48].
- Where part of the consideration for the disposal is other than cash (such as, shares), it should be disclosed in the notes to the cash flow statement where this is necessary to fully understand the transaction. [FRS 1 para 46].
- The profit or loss on each material disposal of a previously acquired business or business segment. [FRS 10 para 54].

26.40 The Act provides that where the directors consider that the disclosure required by paragraph 15 of Schedule 4A to the Act (bullet points one and two above) would be seriously prejudicial to the business of any undertaking in the group and the subsidiary being sold is established, or carries on business, outside the UK, the information is not required to be given. However, the Secretary of State's permission is required. [4A Sch 16]. The Secretary of State's permission would only be given in certain extreme circumstances. For example, his permission might be given not to disclose the name of the subsidiary disposed of where it operates in a politically sensitive country. Although FRS 2 does not appear to extend this exemption to apply to its disclosure requirements, it would seem that it was not the ASB's intention to restrict this exemption and it should, therefore, be assumed that the exemption, if agreed by the Secretary of State for the Companies Act disclosures, also applies to the disclosures required by paragraph 48 of FRS 2 outlined above. It is probably best if the company's letter to the Secretary of State also covers the FRS 2 disclosures that the company proposes not to give.

26.41 In order to give the disclosure required in the third bullet point of paragraph 26.39 and to calculate the total profit or loss arising on a disposal, companies need to maintain detailed records of the cumulative amount of goodwill written off to reserves (net of disposals) and records of the parts of the group to which it relates. In practice, it may be necessary to estimate or apportion goodwill written off to the part of the business being disposed of. However, it is recognised in the Act and FRS 10 that there may be situations where it is not practicable to make a reasonable estimate of the purchased goodwill attributable to the business being disposed of. This situation might arise, for example, where the part of the group being disposed of was acquired many years ago prior to the implementation of FRS 10. In such a situation where it is not possible to ascertain the goodwill that was acquired before 1 January 1989 attributable to the disposal, or to make a reasonable apportionment of the goodwill arising on the acquisition of that part of the business, this fact and the reason should be explained in the financial statements. [FRS 10 para 71(c)].

Chapter 27

Associates, joint ventures and joint undertakings

	Page
Introduction	27001
Scope	27002
Investment funds	27003
Classification as associates and joint ventures	27004
Definition of associate	27004
Treatment of voting rights	27010
Definition of joint venture entities	27011
Equity method of accounting	27014
Introduction	27014
Profit and loss account	27015
Turnover	27015
Operating results	27016
Super-exceptional items	27016
Other line items	27017
How the Act's requirements are satisfied	27017
Ability to aggregate and relegate to the notes	27017
Illustrative example	27019
Segmental reporting	27020
Statement of total recognised gains and losses	27020
Balance sheet	27021
Goodwill	27022
Gross equity method	27024
Illustrative example	27024
Investor's individual financial statements	27026
Cash flow statement	27026
Additional disclosure	27026
General requirements	27026
15 and 25 per cent threshold information	27029
Optional disclosure for joint ventures	27031
Equity accounting principles	27034
Introduction	27034
Share	27034
Options, convertible shares and convertible debt	27036
Convertible shares	27040
Convertible debt	27040
Crossholdings	27042
Financial statements used	27043
Consolidation adjustments	27043
Consistent accounting policies	27044
Goodwill and fair values	27044

Abnormal transactions between year ends 27045
Elimination of intra-group trading 27046
Profits and losses included in assets 27046
Transfers of assets to a joint venture 27047
Intra-company trading transactions 27048
Partnerships that are joint venture entities 27051
Where the associate itself is a group 27051
Interests in losses and net liabilities 27052
Joint and several liability 27053
Minority interests 27054
Acquisitions and disposals 27054
Effective date of acquisition or disposal 27054
Acquisition rules 27055
Disposal rules 27058
A joint venture becomes an associate 27062
A subsidiary becomes an associate 27062
Equity accounting in a single company 27065
Joint arrangements 27065
Joint arrangement that is not an entity 27066
Joint venture with the substance of a joint arrangement 27069
Accounting for joint arrangements 27070
Joint agreements between participants 27071
Joint arrangements in unincorporated undertakings including partnerships 27074
Joint arrangements in limited companies 27075
Joint arrangements versus quasi-subsidiaries 27075

Chapter 27

Associates, joint ventures and joint undertakings

Introduction

27.1 Equity accounting for associates has stood the test of time with only minor amendments over the years and it was further endorsed by its incorporation into international accounting in November 1988 by the issue of International Accounting Standard (IAS) 28, 'Accounting for investments in associates' (and the improved version issued in December 2003, IAS 28, 'Investments in associates'). This basis of accounting recognises that through the investor's long-term significant influence over its associate it has a measure of direct responsibility for the return on its investment. Furthermore, that basis also recognises that the investor has an interest in its share of the reserves of its associate and is not merely interested in a dividend stream.

27.2 The Companies Act 1989, which incorporated the EU's 7th Directive into UK company law, brought with it the statutory requirement to equity account associated undertakings and most joint ventures. The term 'participating interest' was introduced by the Act and has become integral in determining whether or not an investment is an associated undertaking. A participating interest in an undertaking is necessary before it could be judged to be an associate, however, the legislation still envisages that there could be situations where a participating interest may be held in an undertaking that is not an associated undertaking, although in practice this is rare. Furthermore, it is presumed under the Act, unless otherwise shown, that a participating interest exists where the investing company holds more than 20 per cent of the voting rights in another undertaking.

27.3 FRS 9 was published by the ASB on 27 November 1997. The standard's objective is to reflect the effect on an investor's financial position and performance of its interests in two special kinds of investments – associates and joint ventures – for whose activities it is partly accountable, because of the closeness of its involvement:

- In associates, as a result of its participating interest and significant influence.
- In joint ventures, as a result of its long-term interest and joint control.

[FRS 9 para 1].

The FRS also deals with joint arrangements that do not qualify as associates or joint ventures, because they are not entities.

27.4 Under FRS 9 all associates and joint venture entities are required to be equity accounted. But the distinction between associates and joint ventures is now important, because the standard requires a different type of presentation for joint ventures called the 'gross equity method' and separate disclosure for associates and joint ventures. Proportional consolidation does not feature at all in the standard even for shared facilities; instead a new category of investment – a joint arrangement that is not an entity – is introduced. Consequently, it is also necessary to identify these joint arrangements separately from associates and joint ventures, as a new set of accounting requirements apply to them.

27.5 The 'gross equity' method was a new requirement in the standard. Under this method, the investor's share of joint ventures' turnover must be disclosed (equivalent disclosure for associates is optional). In addition, under the gross equity method the investor's share of joint ventures' gross assets and gross liabilities must be shown on the face of the balance sheet before the investor's share of associates' net assets. Other than these two additional disclosures, the gross equity accounting requirements are identical to those for associates using the normal equity accounting method.

27.6 The investor's share of investees' operating results is now required to be included immediately after the group operating result. In addition, the investor's share of super-exceptionals, interest and tax must be separately disclosed.

27.7 Additional disclosures arise where the investor's share in its associates in aggregate (or in its joint ventures in aggregate) exceeds 15 per cent, or individually 25 per cent, of the group's: gross assets; gross liabilities; turnover; or operating results (on a three-year average).

27.8 A new category of investment – joint arrangement that is not an entity – was introduced in FRS 9. An investor in such an entity should account for its own transactions in accordance with the terms of the agreement. Similarly, a participant in a joint venture structure used as a framework within which each participant carries on its own business should also account for its own transactions in accordance with the terms of the agreement.

27.9 This chapter considers in detail the distinction between associates and joint ventures and then from paragraph 27.68 looks at how to account for them. Other joint arrangements and their accounting requirements are considered from paragraph 27.177.

27.10 This chapter does not focus on the disclosure requirements required for these investments. Full details of the disclosure requirements for investments are found at the end of section I of chapter 24.

[The next paragraph is 27.25.]

Scope

27.25 FRS 9's requirements apply to all financial statements that are intended to give a true and fair view of the reporting entity's financial position and profit or loss (or income and expenditure) for the period. [FRS 9 para 2]. The standard became effective for accounting periods ending on or after 23 June 1998. [FRS 9 para 59].

27.26 The FRS states that entities entitled to report under the Financial Reporting Standard for Smaller Entities (FRSSE) are exempt from the standard's requirements, unless they prepare consolidated financial statements. It then goes on to state that, where the entity does prepare consolidated financial statements, it should apply the accounting standard that is required to be used by the FRSSE currently in issue. [FRS 9 para 3].

Investment funds

27.27 For a number of years prior to FRS 9's introduction, problems had arisen in the venture capital industry, where companies often invest in high risk start-up ventures and look for capital growth rather than an income return. As a consequence, the industry views valuation information as relevant and equity accounting as irrelevant. This issue led to a number of companies in that sector adopting the Act's true and fair override in order not to equity account such investments, which was a requirement of both the Act and SSAP 1. Following consultation with the Association of Investment Trust Companies (AITC) and others, the ASB now accepts that in such entities, whilst the interests held by the investor and the rights attaching to those interests vary according to particular circumstances, the investor's relationship to its investment tends to be that of a portfolio investor. [FRS 9 para 50]. The standard now requires that, in these circumstances, the stake is properly accounted for as an investment using the same accounting policy as that applied to other investments in the entity's investment portfolio, rather than accounting for the interests as associates or joint ventures. This applies even where the investor has significant influence or joint control. [FRS 9 paras 49, 50].

27.28 The standard explains that:

> *"Investments are held as part of an investment portfolio if their value to the investor is through their marketable value as part of a basket of investments rather than as media through which the investor carries out its business".* [FRS 9 para 49].

Consequently, investments of this nature are specifically exempted from FRS 9's requirements to equity account associates and joint ventures. However, it does appear that such investments might still fall to be treated as associates under the Act. This will depend on whether or not the investor has significant influence. Significant influence is defined in FRS 9 and this definition applies also to associated undertakings under the Act. The investor will exercise significant influence if it is actively involved and influential in the direction of its investee. In those situations where a company adopts FRS 9's relaxation in respect of its associates and joint ventures included in its investment portfolio, if the investor still exercises significant influence over those undertakings, it should recognise a departure from the Act by giving the particulars, reasons and effect as required by the Act and FRS 18, 'Accounting policies'. The reason should include the fact that FRS 9 specifies the accounting treatment to be adopted.

27.29 Investment companies might also have investments that should be treated as joint ventures and associates that are held outside their investment portfolio. Such joint ventures and associates often carry on businesses which are similar or complementary to those of the investor. In these circumstances, the provisions of FRS 9 should be applied and such joint ventures and associates should be equity accounted in accordance with the normal rules as explained below.

Classification as associates and joint ventures

27.30 As mentioned above, equity accounting applies to both associates and joint venture entities. However, under FRS 9 joint venture entities must give slightly more information using the 'gross equity method' of accounting than associates. Therefore, the distinctions between the two types of arrangement are important and the paragraphs below explain the definitions that apply in determining whether an investment is an associate or a joint venture entity.

Definition of associate

27.31 The term associate is defined in both the Companies Act and in FRS 9. The Act's definition hinges on the investing company having a participating interest and exercising significant influence. Under the legislation a participating interest is presumed to exist where the investing company holds more than 20 per cent of the voting rights in the other undertaking. This presumption is rebutted under FRS 9, which sets out a more stringent test to determine whether there is a participating interest. But where the Act's presumptions are rebutted the investor should explain the facts in the financial statements (see para 27.106 below).

27.32 An 'associated undertaking' is defined in the Act in the following terms:

> *"... an undertaking in which an undertaking included in the consolidation has a participating interest and over whose operating and financial policy it exercises a significant influence, and which is not—*
>
> *(a) a subsidiary undertaking of the parent company, or*
>
> *(b) a joint venture dealt with in accordance with paragraph 19."*

[CA85 4A Sch 20(1)].

27.33 'Participating interest' is defined in section 260(1) of the Act to mean "... *an interest held by an undertaking in the shares of another undertaking which it holds on a long-term basis for the purpose of securing a contribution to its activities by the exercise of control or influence arising from or related to that interest*".

27.34 The meaning of 'shares' in the definition is explained in section 259(2) of the Act. For this purpose, references to shares in relation to:

- An undertaking with a share capital, are to allotted shares.
- An undertaking with capital in a form other than share capital, are to rights to share in the capital of the undertaking.
- An undertaking without capital, are to interests:
  - conferring any right to share in the profits or the liability to contribute to the losses of the undertaking; or
  - giving rise to an obligation to contribute to the debts or expenses of the undertaking in the event of a winding up.

[CA85 sec 259(2), CA06 Sec 1161(2)].

27.35 In addition, it is quite clear under the Act that a participating interest includes an option to acquire shares or any interest that is convertible into shares. [CA85 sec 260(3)]. For this purpose, it does not matter whether the options can be exercised now or in the future, their mere existence is taken into account whether or not they are currently exercisable. An interest or option in shares falls within this definition even if the share to which it relates, until conversion or the exercise of the option, is unissued. [CA85 sec 260(3)]. In addition, interests held on behalf of an undertaking should be treated as held by it. [CA85 sec 260(4)].

[The next paragraph is 27.37.]

27.37 The definition of 'associated undertakings' in the Act is consistent with that given in FRS 9 for an associate. The definition in FRS 9 is also expressed making reference to the need for both a participating interest and the exercise of significant influence as follows:

> *"An entity (other than a subsidiary) in which another entity (the investor) has a participating interest and over whose operating and financial policies the investor exercises a significant influence."* [FRS 9 para 4].

27.38 Therefore, it is essential to have both a participating interest and be able to exercise significant influence and these two terms are also defined in the standard. A participating interest is:

> *"An interest held in the shares of another entity on a long-term basis for the purpose of securing a contribution to the investor's activities by the exercise of control or influence arising from or related to that interest. The investor's interest must, therefore, be a beneficial one and the benefits expected to arise must be linked to the exercise of its significant influence over the investee's operating and financial policies. An interest in the shares of another entity includes an interest convertible into an interest in shares or an option to acquire shares."* [FRS 9 para 4].

The term 'shares' in the definition has the same meaning as explained in paragraph 27.34 above.

27.39 As mentioned above, the Act presumes there is a participating interest where the investor holds 20 per cent or more of the shares in the undertaking. However, whilst both the Act and FRS 9 require the interest to be for the long term, FRS 9 introduces a very restrictive interpretation of the meaning of 'long-term'. Under FRS 9, an interest held on a long-term basis is one that is *not* 'held exclusively with a view to subsequent resale' and the latter term is defined in the standard as: *"... (a) an interest for which a purchaser has been identified or is being sought, and which is reasonably expected to be disposed of within approximately one year of its date of acquisition; or (b) an interest that was acquired as a result of the enforcement of a security, unless the interest has become part of the continuing activities of the group or the holder acts as if it intends the interest to become so".* [FRS 9 para 4]. Table 27.1 includes an example of an associate which is held for resale. The standard comments that 'enforcement of a security' should be interpreted to include other arrangements that, in substance, have the same effect.

Table 27.1— Granada Group PLC — Annual Report & Accounts — 27 September 1997

Notes to the Accounts (extract)

12 Investments

The investment in Savoy comprises 69.7% of the 'A' shares and 12.6% of the 'B' shares, representing 68.4% of the equity of Savoy and 42.1% of the voting rights. During the period Savoy was accounted for as an investment as it is not the Group's intention to hold this investment for the long term. As at 31 December 1996, Savoy had share capital and reserves amounting to £372.1 million and the loss for the financial year then ended amounted to £26.8 million.

27.40 The effect of the requirement for the investment to be for the long term on short-term property development investments, which might run for (say) up to 18 months, is considered in paragraph 27.185.

27.41 The 20 per cent presumption in the Act is also rebutted where the interest is a non-beneficial one. In judging whether an interest is, or is not, a beneficial one, dividends are not the only way that a beneficial interest might be enjoyed. There may be other ways of extracting benefits, for example, through a management contract with a fee that is based on performance, which would make the receiver of the fee more than just a manager.

27.42 The other essential element to the definition of an associate is that the investor must exercise a 'significant influence' over the entity's financial and operating policies for there to be an associate relationship. The Act similarly presumes that the investor will have significant influence where the investor holds more than 20 per cent of the voting rights in the undertaking. [CA85 4A Sch 20(2)]. Whilst the Act does not define 'significant influence' FRS 9 does. The definition of 'significant influence' in FRS 9 is as follows:

> *"The investor is actively involved and is influential in the direction of its investee through its participation in policy decisions covering aspects of*

policy relevant to the investor, including decisions on strategic issues such as:

(a) the expansion or contraction of the business, participation in other entities or changes in products, markets and activities of its investee; and

(b) determining the balance between dividend and reinvestment."

[FRS 9 para 4].

27.43 It is often difficult in practice to determine whether there is an associate relationship with an undertaking. FRS 9 indicates that significant influence over a company essentially involves participation in the financial and operating policy decisions of that company. It mentions that for significant influence to exist it must generally have a substantial basis of voting power and a holding of 20 per cent of more of the voting rights does not in itself ensure this level of influence. [FRS 9 para 16]. That is, even where the investing group holds more than 20 per cent of the voting rights it might not have significant influence. This situation could also arise where one or more other large shareholders could prevent the group exercising 'significant influence'. This might arise, for example, where the investor holds 25 per cent of the shares, but another entity holds the remaining 75 per cent (see for example Table 27.2). On the other hand, FRS 9 also confirms that it is not necessary to control those policies for an associate relationship to exist (otherwise the investment would be a subsidiary). In order to gain the level of influence necessary, representation on the board of directors (or its equivalent for unincorporated entities) is essential in most circumstances, unless it is clear that there are other arrangements in place that would allow the investor to participate effectively in policy-making decisions. [FRS 9 para 16].

Table 27.2 – Delancey Estates plc – Annual Report & Accounts – 31 March 1999

Notes to the Accounts (extract)

Participating interests

In accordance with the Companies Act 1985, Centrols Properties Limited (CPL) (a company in which Delancey Estates plc has a 37.5% interest) is described as a participating interest. As Delancey Estates plc does not participate in the commercial or financial policy decisions, and has no board representation, CPL is not regarded as an associated undertaking and is therefore included within the group balance sheet at cost and not equity value. The latest reported profit before tax of CPL was £219,721 and the net liabilities were £83,348. CPL is registered in England, which is also the main country of operation.

27.44 In order to obtain significant influence, the investor needs an agreement or understanding, formal or informal, with its associate to provide the basis for its significant influence. The investor must be actively involved in the operating and financial policy decisions – a passive role is clearly not sufficient. The type of relationship that is necessary is one whereby the investor uses its associate as a medium through which it conducts a part of its activities, although it is not envisaged that the associate need be in the same business as the investor. The associate's policies over time should accord with (and not be contrary to) the investor's strategy. Consequently, if an investee persistently implements policies that are inconsistent with its investor's strategy, no associate relationship exists. [FRS 9 para 14].

27.45 Significant influence means that the investor must be involved in strategic decisions, for example, determining the balance between dividend and reinvestment. Furthermore, the investor should not only be interested in maximising the payment of dividends, but should also be concerned that the entity's future cash flows are compatible with the investor's objective of reinvestment. The investor's participation in policy decisions should be with a view to gaining economic benefits from the entity's activities, but this involvement should also expose the investor to the risk that those activities might be loss-making. [FRS 9 para 15].

Example

A group has a 30% investment in a company at the beginning of the year. It has previously been treated as an associated company in the group's financial statements. Another shareholder increases his shareholding in the company during the year from 40% to 60%. The group no longer wishes to treat its investment in the undertaking as an associate.

As explained above, where the investment in another undertaking is greater than 20%, it will not be presumed that the undertaking is an associate. In this situation, if the group can demonstrate that it no longer has a significant influence over the undertaking then it may be necessary to treat the investment as a trade investment rather than as an associate.

27.46 A practical problem arises in judging the amount of influence the investor has over its investment where the investment has only just been made. In these circumstances the actual relationship usually becomes clear fairly soon after an investment is acquired. In the intervening period the number of board members the investor may nominate and the proposed decision-taking process may be used to evaluate the relationship before its record is established. [FRS 9 para 17]. If the actual relationship were to develop differently from that assumed from the arrangements on acquisition, it would be necessary subsequently to change the way in which the investment is accounted. For example, if it looked at the outset as if the entity were an associate, then it would have been equity accounted in the first financial statements produced post acquisition. If subsequently it was judged that this analysis did not prove to be correct in practice, then it would be necessary to treat the interest in the entity as an investment. This might, therefore, indicate that there was a fundamental error in accounting for the investment as an associate in the previous year and require a prior year adjustment. However, in practice, this is only likely to arise when the investment is made close to the investor's year end, in which case the profits brought in in error would be small.

27.47 Where an investing group ceases to exercise significant influence over an investment treated as an associate, it will be necessary to change the accounting treatment. In the case of British Telecommunications plc, a 20 per cent investment in MCI was treated as an associate from the date of acquisition in 1994. The subsequent proposed merger of MCI with WorldCom led British Telecommunications plc to change the treatment and to account for its interest in MCI as an investment (see Table 27.3 below).

Table 27.3 – British Telecommunications plc – Annual Report and Accounts – 31 March 1998

Notes to the accounts

Fixed asset investment (extract)

(b) MCI Communications Corporation

In September 1994, the company completed the acquisition of a 20% equity interest in MCI (the second largest carrier of long distance telecommunications services in the USA) represented by a holding of 136 million Class A common shares, whereupon MCI became the group's most significant associated undertaking. On 3 November 1996, the company entered into a merger agreement with MCI whereby the group would acquire the entire share capital of MCI, not already owned. On 21 August 1997, the terms of the merger agreement were modified. On 1 October 1997, WorldCom announced its intention to offer shares in its company to MCI shareholders as an alternative to the proposed merger and, following an improved offer from WorldCom on 9 November 1997, the company agreed that it would support the proposed merger with WorldCom to which the MCI board had agreed on the same day. On 11 March 1998, both MCI's and WorldCom's shareholders approved their merger.

The company has agreed with WorldCom and MCI to sell the group's holding of 136 million unlisted Class A common shares in MCI to WorldCom for US$51 per share in cash at the time the MCI/WorldCom merger is completed. The potential consideration of US$6,936m was equivalent to £4,137m, at the exchange rate ruling on 31 March 1998. The completion of the merger is subject to regulatory clearance. The group also holds 0.7 million listed common shares in MCI, most of which were purchased in November 1995. These shares will be exchanged for WorldCom common shares on completion of the merger. If fully listed, the market value of the MCI shares held by the group at 31 March 1998 would have been £4,048m.

As a consequence of the termination of the company's merger agreement with MCI and the company's agreement with WorldCom and MCI, the group ceased treating MCI as an associate from 1 November 1997. The group's share of its associates' results includes a loss before tax of £27m for its share of MCI's results up to that date (1997 — £175m profit, 1996 — £101m profit).

At 31 March 1998, the group's investment in MCI is stated at £813m (1997 — £834m). Goodwill amounting to £2,214m has been written off to group reserves in prior years in respect of this investment and this goodwill will be accounted for at the completion of the MCI/WorldCom merger in determining the profit on the sale of the shares which the group will recognise.

In the period 1 April 1997 to 31 October 1997, the group's turnover with MCI amounted to £108m (1997 — £134m, 1996 — £92m) and the group purchased £56m in the same period (1997 — £87m, 1996 — £77m) in services and products from MCI.

27.48 Furthermore, where an investing group treats an undertaking as an associate where it controls less than 20 per cent of the votes, it is important to ensure that it can clearly demonstrate that it has significant influence. But it is undoubtedly possible under FRS 9's definitions for significant influence to exist where the investing group controls less than 20 per cent of the voting shares.

27.49 An associate relationship can also arise where a company was initially legally a subsidiary of its investor, but the investor no longer controls or has the power to exercise dominant influence or control over the operating and financial policies of the undertaking. This could occur, for example, where the investor's interest is 40 per cent, but it previously had call options over a further 20 per cent that could be exercised at any time. The existence of the options gave the company the power to exercise control but, when the options lapsed, this power fell away and the company was no longer a subsidiary of the investor. Although there is no change in the shareholding, the investor's influence has reduced and it now exerts only significant influence and the investment is, therefore, an associate.

Treatment of voting rights

27.50 The Act gives a significant amount of guidance on when to take into account voting rights in order to determine whether an associate relationship exists between two undertakings. The paragraphs that follow summarise the guidance given in the Act.

27.51 For the purposes of the definition of an associated undertaking, 'voting rights in the undertaking' means the rights conferred on the shareholders in respect of their shares to vote at general meetings of the undertaking on all, or substantially all, matters. It can also mean, in a situation where the undertaking has no share capital, any other rights conferred on members to vote at the undertaking's general meetings on all, or substantially all, matters. [CA85 4A Sch 20(3)].

27.52 Voting rights should not be treated as held by a person (which includes an undertaking) if they are held in a fiduciary capacity. [CA85 4A Sch 20(4), 10A Sch 6]. Similarly, voting rights held by a person as nominee should not be treated as held by him. Such voting rights will be considered held 'as nominee' if they can only be exercised on the instructions or with the consent of another person. [CA85 4A Sch 20(4), 10A Sch 7(2)]. It is not possible to treat voting rights held by a parent undertaking as held by a subsidiary by using nominee holdings. [CA85 4A Sch 20(4), 10A Sch 9(2)].

27.53 Voting rights that are attached to shares held as security shall be treated as held by the person providing the security where those voting rights (excluding any right to exercise them to preserve the value of the security, or to realise it) are only exercisable in accordance with his instructions. This rule applies where the shares are held in connection with granting loans in the normal course of business and the rights are exercised only in the interest of the person providing the security. [CA85 4A Sch 20(4), 10A Sch 8]. This provision cannot be used to require voting rights held by a parent to be treated as held by any of its subsidiaries. [CA85 4A Sch 20(4), 10A Sch 9(2)]. Furthermore, voting rights should be treated as being exercisable in accordance with the instructions of, or in the interests of, an undertaking if they are exercisable in accordance with the instructions of, or in the interests of, any group undertaking. [CA85 4A Sch 20(4), 10A Sch 9(3)].

27.54 The voting rights in an undertaking have also to be reduced by any voting rights held by the undertaking itself. [CA85 4A Sch 20(4), 10A Sch 10].

Definition of joint venture entities

27.55 Although joint ventures are required under FRS 9 to be equity accounted, the level of detail that investors in joint ventures are required to give in their consolidated financial statements is greater than for investments in associates. Therefore, it is important that investors categorise their investments correctly between those in associates and those in joint ventures. FRS 9 makes a distinction between joint venture entities and joint arrangements that are not entities. Joint arrangements that are not entities are not equity accounted and their accounting requirements and how to distinguish them from other forms of joint venture are considered from paragraph 27.177.

27.56 Particular care needs to be taken in assessing whether an undertaking is a joint venture entity or a joint arrangement (under FRS 9), or a subsidiary undertaking (under FRS 2), or a quasi-subsidiary (under FRS 5). An FRRP ruling in February 1995 concerned joint ventures which were determined to be quasi-subsidiaries. The implications of this case for joint ventures and joint arrangements are considered from paragraph 27.205. The paragraphs that follow look at the definitions found within both the Act and FRS 9 concerning joint ventures.

27.57 Under the Act, paragraph 19(1) of Schedule 4A refers to a joint venture arising in a situation where an *undertaking* manages another undertaking jointly with one or more other undertakings that are not included in the consolidation. Consequently, the Act places emphasis on the undertaking's *joint management*. But the Act's provisions concerning joint ventures do not apply if the joint venture undertaking is a limited company, as proportional consolidation for joint ventures is only allowed for unincorporated undertakings under the Act. Also, the Act's provisions concerning joint ventures do not apply where the undertaking is a subsidiary for consolidation purposes under the definitions in the Act (see further chapter 24). [CA85 4A Sch 19(1)].

27.58 FRS 9 defines a joint venture in the following terms:

> *"An entity in which the reporting entity holds an interest on a long-term basis and is jointly controlled by the reporting entity and one or more other venturers under a contractual arrangement."* [FRS 9 para 4].

27.59 As can be seen from the definition, the interest must be held on a long-term basis and this is to be judged in the same way as for associates (see para 27.39 above). The definition also hinges on the term 'joint control' which is defined in FRS 9 as follows:

> *"A reporting entity jointly controls a venture with one or more other entities if none of the entities alone can control that entity but all together can do so*

and decisions on financial and operating policy essential to the activities, economic performance and financial position of that venture require each venturer's consent." [FRS 9 para 4].

27.60 This definition can be contrasted with 'control', which was originally defined in FRS 2 and is repeated in FRS 9 as:

"The ability of an entity to direct the operating and financial policies of another entity with a view to gaining economic benefits from its activities." [FRS 9 para 4].

27.61 Although to be treated as a joint venture partner the investor must have joint control with its other investors, the standard envisages the situation whereby *one* of the parties to a joint venture might not share control with the other joint venturers. In this type of situation, the investor that does not share control would account for its interest as an investment. [FRS 9 para 10]. The other venturers would gross equity account for their interests in accordance with the standard.

27.62 The standard explains that in a true joint venture the venturers exercise their joint control for their mutual benefit, each conducting its part of the contractual arrangement with a view to its own benefit. The venturers must play an active role in setting the operating and financial policies of the joint venture. However, their involvement can be at quite a high level, for example, setting the general strategy of the venture. [FRS 9 para 11]. But their interest should not necessarily only occur at the outset of a venture, for example, in setting the general policies to be included within a partnership agreement. If this were to be the case, then the financial and operating policies might be predetermined, in which case the entity could be a joint arrangement or a quasi-subsidiary (see further para 27.205).

27.63 It seems clear from the definition that it is quite possible to have a joint venture between investors where the venturers do not have equal shares in the entity, as long as they control the entity jointly together. For example, it would be possible to have an arrangement whereby the investors' interests were 30:35:35 or 25:35:40. But there must be joint control including the ability for one party to veto the wishes of the other parties. For example, the 25 per cent shareholder would have to have the ability to veto the financial and operating policies being advocated by the other two venturers owning 75 per cent of the shares. In this type of situation, one of the parties might manage the venture under a management agreement and, in this circumstance, it is important to establish clearly that the veto can be applied in practice.

27.63.1 An example of a joint venture where shareholdings are not equal is shown in Table 27.4.

Table 27.4 – Galliford Try plc – Annual Report & Accounts – 30 June 2003

Notes to the accounts (extract)

12 Investments (extract)

During the year the Group invested £120,000 in shares and loans in Oak Fire Protection Limited representing a 70% investment. Under the terms of the shareholders' agreement, the investment has been treated as a joint venture.

27.64 The standard also does not preclude a venturer from managing the joint venture provided that the venture's principal operating and financial policies are collectively agreed by the venturers and the venturers have the power to ensure that those policies are followed. [FRS 9 para 11]. This is often the case in the venture capital industry, where it is common for the venture capitalist investor to have an interest in the joint venture, but also to manage the venture *via* a separate management agreement.

27.65 The standard also points out that in some cases an investor may qualify as the parent of an entity under the definition of a subsidiary in the Act and FRS 2, but contractual arrangements with the other shareholder mean that in practice the shareholders have joint control over their investee. [FRS 9 para 11]. For example, a company might control over 50 per cent of the entity's voting rights, but the joint venture agreement might significantly restrict this control. It could, for example, require unanimous agreement between the venturers before it could: pay a dividend; change direction of the company's business; incur capital expenditure over a specified level; pay its directors and other employees; change other major operating and financial policies, etc. In this type of situation, the interests of the minority shareholder (the other joint venture partner) would amount to 'severe long-term restrictions' that would substantially hinder the exercise of the parent's rights over the assets or management of its legal subsidiary. In such cases, following from the requirements in FRS 2, the standard requires that the subsidiary should not be consolidated, but should instead be treated as a joint venture and be gross equity accounted. [FRS 9 para 11]. However, this type of situation is unlikely to arise frequently in practice, because even where there is such a shareholders' agreement, unless it does impose a significant restriction (which it will not if the agreement means the subsidiary follows the parent's wishes) it will remain a subsidiary.

27.66 Joint control of high-level strategic decisions will entail each venturer having a veto on those decisions. Such a veto distinguishes a joint venturer from a minority shareholder in a company, because the latter has no veto and, consequently, is subject to majority rule. [FRS 9 para 12]. It is the practical application of this which is important and, hence, it is not necessary that the consent to strategic decisions is set out in the joint venture agreement, although in many instances this will be the case in practice. One indication that the arrangement might be a joint venture is where the joint venture agreement sets out arbitration procedures in the event the parties to the venture cannot agree.

27.67 IAS 31, 'Interests in joint ventures', defines a joint venture in similar terms to those used in FRS 9: *"a contractual arrangement whereby two or more parties undertake an economic activity that is subject to joint control"*. Joint control is *"the contractually agreed sharing of control over an economic activity, and exists only when the strategic financial and operating decisions relating to the activity require the unanimous consent of the parties sharing control (the venturers)"*. [IAS 31 para 3]. IAS 31 comments that it is this contractual arrangement that distinguishes a joint venture from an associate and without a contractual arrangement to establish joint control a joint venture does not exist. Such a contractual arrangement can be evidenced in a number of ways, for example, by: contract; minutes of discussions between the venturers; or incorporation in the joint venture's articles or other by-laws. The matters that such an agreement might deal with are:

- The joint venture's activity, duration and reporting obligations.
- The appointment of the joint venture's board of directors or equivalent governing body and the voting rights of the venturers.
- Capital contributions by the venturers.
- The sharing by the venturers of the joint venture's output, income, expenses and results.

[IAS 31 para 10].

Equity method of accounting

Introduction

27.68 FRS 9 specifies that equity accounting is the method that should be used to reflect investors' interests in both associates and joint ventures. The form of presentation under this method has been extended for joint ventures and this is referred to in FRS 9 as the 'gross equity method'. The requirements for equity accounting differ from the form of equity accounting required by IAS 28, 'Investments in associates'. The Act also stipulates that associated undertakings should be accounted for by the 'equity method' of accounting, but leaves it to the accounting standard to specify what this method entails. [CA85 4A Sch 22(1)].

27.69 There is now an extensive definition in FRS 9 which explains what the equity method of accounting involves. It describes the equity method as:

> *"A method of accounting that brings an investment into its investor's financial statements initially at its cost, identifying any goodwill arising. The carrying amount of the investment is adjusted in each period by the investor's share of the results of its investee less any amortisation or write-off for goodwill, the investor's share of any relevant gains or losses, and any other changes in the investee's net assets including distributions to its owners, for example by dividend. The investor's share of its investee's*

results is recognised in its profit and loss account. The investor's cash flow statement includes the cash flows between the investor and its investee, for example relating to dividends and loans." [FRS 9 para 4].

27.70 The 'gross equity method' is identical in most respects with the normal equity method, but it requires in addition that the investor's share of the aggregate gross assets and liabilities underlying the net equity investment be shown on the face of the balance sheet [FRS 9 para 4]. Consequently, it is not adequate to disclose this information in the notes to the consolidated financial statements. In addition, in the profit and loss account, the investor's share of the investee's turnover has to be given. [FRS 9 para 4].

27.71 The disclosures required for both the equity method and the gross equity method have to be given separately. The information relating to the investor's share in its joint ventures must be given separately and before that relating to its share in its associates.

Profit and loss account

27.72 Under FRS 9's requirements, there are a number of line items in the profit and loss account for which the investor's share of its joint ventures' and its associates' results have to be included and disclosed. The requirements cover primarily:

- Turnover (but optional disclosure for associates).
- Operating profit.
- Super-exceptional items as specified in paragraph 20 of FRS 3.
- Interest.
- Taxation.

Turnover

27.73 As explained above, the gross equity method requires that the investor's share of turnover for joint ventures must be shown. [FRS 9 para 21]. Equivalent disclosure for associates is not required, but may be given where it is helpful to give an indication of the size of the business as a whole. [FRS 9 para 27]. The standard specifically states that joint ventures' and associates' turnover cannot be shown as part of group turnover, because the Act requires turnover to be disclosed excluding amounts attributable to associates and joint ventures. [CA85 sec 262(1), CA06 Sec 539]. So it is important that the turnover is shown in such a way that the group turnover excluding joint ventures and associates is clearly disclosed. Table 27.5 shows how this can be done.

Table 27.5 — Tate & Lyle Public Limited Company — Annual Report — 25 March 2000

GROUP PROFIT AND LOSS ACCOUNT **(extract)**

For the 78 weeks to 25 March 2000

Profit and Loss Account (extract)	2000 £ million	1999 £ million
Sales	**6183**	4467
Less share of sales of		
— joint ventures	**(491)**	(310)
— associates	**(46)**	(40)
Group sales	**5646**	4117

27.74 In addition, in the segmental analysis required by SSAP 25, the joint ventures' turnover (and associates' turnover where disclosed voluntarily) should be distinguished clearly from that of the group. [FRS 9 para 21, 27]. Segmental reporting is dealt with in chapter 10.

Operating results

27.75 The share of operating results of joint ventures and associates must be included *immediately* after the group's operating result. [FRS 9 paras 21, 27].

27.76 Unlike goodwill arising on an acquisition of a subsidiary, there is nothing in the Companies Act that specifies where goodwill arising on the acquisition of an interest in a joint venture or an associate should be amortised in the profit and loss account. As a consequence, the ASB has determined in FRS 9 that any amortisation or write-down of goodwill (that arose on the acquisition of a joint venture or an associate) should be charged at the same point as the share of operating results of associates and joint ventures. [FRS 9 para 21, 27]. This would seem to allow any amortisation or write-down of goodwill to be aggregated with the share of operating results on the face of the profit and loss account as a single item. But where this is done, the goodwill amortised or written off must be separately disclosed in the notes to the financial statements.

Super-exceptional items

27.77 The investor's share of joint ventures' and associates' super-exceptional items appearing after operating profit must be shown with the group's super-exceptionals, but separately from them. [FRS 9 paras 21, 27]. The super-exceptional items specified in FRS 3 are known as 'paragraph 20 items' and cover:

- Profits or losses on the sale or termination of an operation.
- Costs of a fundamental reorganisation or restructuring having a material effect on the nature and focus of the reporting entity's operations.
- Profits or losses on the disposal of fixed assets.

Other line items

27.78 The standard also specifies that the investor's share of joint ventures' and associates' interest must be shown separately from the amounts of the group. [FRS 9 para 21, 27]. In addition, for the line items that appear in the Act's formats at and below the level of profit before tax, the standard specifies that the investor's share of its joint ventures' and associates' equivalent line items must be included within the amounts for the group. This would include, for example, the investor's share of its joint ventures' and associates' taxation. Although the standard says that these amounts should be included with those of the group, it still requires separate disclosure of the investor's share of each such item for its joint ventures and its associates.

How the Act's requirements are satisfied

27.79 In addition to FRS 9's requirements, the Act indicates the position in the profit and loss account formats where associated undertakings (which includes joint venture entities) should be dealt with. In the profit and loss account formats shown in Schedule 4 to the Act, for the purposes of consolidated financial statements, the item 'income from shares in related companies' is replaced by 'income from interests in associated undertakings' and 'income from other participating interests'. [CA85 4A Sch 21(3)]. Although the position is specified in the formats, companies can draw their operating profit line before 'income from interests in associated undertakings'. This is because the formats do not contain a line item for operating profit. However, as can be seen from the explanation above, FRS 9 requires the line item in the Act to be split between share of: operating result (which must be shown immediately after the group's operating profit or loss); three super-exceptional items; interest; taxation and any further line items below profit before tax. There is nothing in the standard that explains how this anomaly is overcome, but appendix IV example 1 explains that the amounts shown for associates and joint ventures are subdivisions of the item for which the statutory prescribed heading is 'Income from interests in associated undertakings'. Paragraph 3(1) of Schedule 4 to the Act allows format line items to be shown in greater detail than required by the profit and loss account format adopted and there is nothing in the legislation that specifies that such additional analysis needs to be summed to show the total for the particular line item required by the formats.

Ability to aggregate and relegate to the notes

27.80 It is not at all clear from the standard which elements of the disclosures considered above have to be shown on the face of the profit and loss account and which can be relegated to the notes. The only help on this issue is again given in appendix IV example 1 which notes that subdivisions for which the statutory prescribed heading is 'Income from interests in associated undertakings' may be shown in a note rather than on the face of the profit and loss account. This seems to imply that all the disclosures specified above can be relegated to the notes and yet the example in FRS 9 that directly follows the note shows each of the required disclosures with the exception of taxation on the face of the profit and loss account (albeit the example does not include any super-exceptional items). In addition, all of these disclosures show the share of joint ventures' and associates' results separately on the face of the profit and loss account, which for many groups would be impracticable because of printing space constraints. To further compound the issue, the Act requires that 'Income from interests in associated undertakings' in the formats should be treated as if it is preceded by an Arabic numeral. Under the format rules, which are discussed in chapter 4, items preceded by an Arabic numeral can be relegated to the notes.

27.81 We, therefore, suggest the following practical solution to the issues raised above:

- The share of joint ventures' turnover should be shown separately from that of the group on the face of the profit and loss account in order to comply with the Act's requirements (as explained in para 27.73 above). It is also possible, however, to show a total figure for turnover including joint ventures, as long as joint ventures' turnover and the group's turnover excluding that of its joint ventures is clearly shown.
- Where the share of associates' turnover is disclosed voluntarily, it should be shown on the face of the profit and loss account, but may be combined with that of joint ventures, but must be separately analysed in the notes. It is also possible to give a total for the group's turnover including both joint ventures and associates as long as the group's turnover excluding that of its associates and joint ventures is clearly shown.
- Share of operating results of joint ventures and associates should be shown on the face of the profit and loss account, but may be combined in a single line item 'share of joint ventures and associates operating profit' as long as they are shown separately in the notes, with the share of joint ventures' operating results shown first.
- Amortisation or the write-down of goodwill arising on the acquisition of joint ventures or associates should be included within 'share of joint ventures and associates operating profit'. There should be separate disclosure of this item in the notes.
- Share of each super-exceptional item of joint ventures and associates should be shown separately on the face of the profit and loss account below any super-exceptional items of the group. (Immaterial amounts should be aggregated with the share of their operating results.) For each super-exceptional item, the investor's share of joint ventures' and associates' figures may be combined in a single line item suitably styled on the face of the profit and loss account, but should be shown separately in the notes, with the joint ventures' share shown first.
- Share of interest and format line items below the level of profit before tax should be included within the amounts shown on the face of the profit and

loss account for the group. The share should then be separately disclosed in the notes, with the share of joint ventures' items shown first.

- In addition, the share of results of associates and joint ventures has to be analysed between continuing activities (including acquisitions) and discontinued activities as required by FRS 3 (see further chapter 8).

Illustrative example

27.82 An illustration of this type of disclosure is given below:

Consolidated profit and loss account

	Notes	Continuing operations £m	Acquisitions £m	Total £m	Discontinued operations £m	Total £m
Turnover including share of joint ventures and associates		250	50	300	20	320
Less: Share of joint ventures and associates turnover	1	105	10	115	5	120
Group turnover		145	40	185	15	200
Cost of sales		89	23	112	8	120
Gross profit		56	17	73	7	80
Administrative expenses		28	4	32	8	40
Group operating profit (loss)		28	13	41	(1)	40
Share of operating profit of joint ventures and associates	2	52	3	55	(1)	54
Operating profit including joint ventures and associates		80	16	96	(2)	94
Sale of operations:						
Group					20	20
Joint ventures and associates	3				(15)	(15)
		–	–	–	5	5
Profit on ordinary activities before interest		80	16	96	3	99
Interest						(42)
Profit on ordinary activities before tax	5					57
Tax on profit on ordinary activities						12
Profit on ordinary activities after tax						45
Minority interests						6
Profit for the financial year						39
Equity dividends						10
Retained profit for the year						29

The notes to the financial statements would analyse the line items above to give the disclosures required by the standard as follows:

	Continuing operations	Acquisitions	Total	Discontinued operations	Total
1 Turnover (extract)	£m	£m	£m	£m	£m
Share of joint ventures' turnover	30	10	40		40
Share of associates' turnover	75	–	75	5	80
	105	10	115	5	120
2 Operating profit (extract)					
Share of joint ventures' operating profit	27	3	30	–	30
Share of associates' operating profit	25	–	25	(1)	24
	52	3	55	(1)	54
3 Profit/loss on sale of operations (extract)					
Share of joint ventures' profit on sale of operations				21	21
Share of associates' loss on sale of operations				(36)	(36)
				(15)	(15)
4 Interest (extract)				£m	£m
Interest receivable (group)					6
Interest payable:					
Group				(26)	
Joint ventures				(10)	
Associates				(12)	(48)
					(42)
5 Taxation (extract)		3			£m
Group					(5)
Joint ventures					(5)
Associates					(2)
					(12)

Segmental reporting

27.83 SSAP 25 and FRS 9 set out the segmental information to be disclosed in respect of associates and joint ventures and these are considered further in chapter 10.

Statement of total recognised gains and losses

27.84 The investors' share of its joint ventures' and associates' other gains and losses included in the statement of total recognised gains and losses (STRGL) must also be disclosed where they are material. The requirement would apply, for example, to the investor's share of any revaluation surpluses of its joint ventures and associates reported in their STRGLs. Here the standard is more helpful in that it states specifically that such amounts should be: *"shown separately under each heading, if the amounts are material, either in the statement or in a note that is referred to in the statement"*. [FRS 9 paras 21, 28]. The requirement is still to disclose separately the investor's share of joint ventures' relevant amounts from those of its associates and in that order, but this detail can be given in the notes to the financial statements.

Statement of total recognised gains and losses

	Notes	£m
Profit for the financial year		39
Unrealised surplus on revaluation of properties	6	25
Currency translation differences on foreign net investment		(8)
Other recognised gains and losses relating to the year		17
Total recognised gains and losses for the year		56

Notes to the financial statements

6 Fixed assets (extract)

The revaluation gains arising in the year are analysed as follows:

	£m
Group	19
Joint ventures	(8)
Associates	14
	25

Balance sheet

27.85 Unless it is shown at a valuation, the amount at which the investing company's interest in its joint ventures or its associates should be shown in the investing company's own financial statements is the cost of the investment less any amounts written off, as explained in chapter 6. [FRS 9 paras 20, 26].

27.86 The amount at which the investing group's interests in joint ventures and associates should be shown in the group's consolidated balance sheet is the value under the 'equity method' of accounting, being the total of:

- The investing group's share of the net assets (other than goodwill) of the joint ventures and associates, stated after attributing fair values to the net assets at the time the interests in the joint ventures and associates were acquired.
- The goodwill (or negative goodwill) arising on the acquisition of the interests in the joint ventures and associates, insofar as it has not already been written off or amortised.

[FRS 9 paras 21, 29].

27.87 It is not appropriate, once the balance sheet interest has been ascertained using the equity method of accounting as explained above, to then revalue the investment in the associate or joint venture to its market value, even where the entity is listed. This method was adopted by Foreign and Colonial Investment

Trust plc before the introduction of FRS 9. The FRRP issued a press notice in April 1996 in respect of the company's December 1994 financial statements. At issue was the adequacy of the *explanation* given for a departure from equity method of accounting in the balance sheet treatment of an associate, which was carried at a directors' valuation. Following discussions with the FRRP, the directors gave a fuller explanation of the departure and its effect in their 1995 financial statements. The departure from SSAP 1 was explained in the 1995 group accounts as follows:

> *"Hypo Foreign and Colonial Management (Holdings) Limited ('HFCM'), the group's associated undertaking, is accounted for in the revenue account using the equity method prescribed in SSAP 1. The carrying value is restated in the consolidated balance sheet at directors' or market valuation, to be consistent with the group's accounting policy for investments.*
>
> *As the investment in HFCM forms part of the group's investment portfolio, the directors believe adoption of the equity method in the balance sheet would not show a true and fair view. The effect of this departure from SSAP 1 is set out in note 12 on the accounts."*

We considered at the time that this was an odd ruling, because whilst criticising the disclosure the FRRP appeared to be condoning adoption of a policy for the balance sheet (that is, valuation) that was inconsistent with the policy adopted for the revenue account (that is, equity accounting). We consider that such a treatment would be an unacceptable departure from FRS 9. In addition, FRS 9 has special rules that apply to investment funds. Investments included within their investment portfolio should be accounted for using the same policy that applies to other investments included in the portfolio, namely cost or market value and not equity accounted (see further para 27.27).

Goodwill

27.88 Any goodwill carried in the balance sheet of the joint venture or associate on acquisition is excluded from the calculation of goodwill arising on the acquisition and is, therefore, not recognised separately on consolidation. [FRS 9 para 31]. It is acceptable to aggregate the two disclosures in paragraph 27.86 on the face of the balance sheet, but where this is done the standard requires that the balance of goodwill after amortisation and any write-downs should be disclosed separately. [FRS 9 para 29]. Furthermore, it is necessary to show a reconciliation of movements in the year on the goodwill arising on joint ventures and associates in a table in order to accord with FRS 10, 'Goodwill and intangible assets'. [FRS 10 para 53]. Although it is necessary to disclose this reconciliation separately from the reconciliation relating to goodwill arising on the consolidation of the group's subsidiaries, it does not seem necessary to analyse the movements between goodwill attributable to joint ventures and goodwill attributable to associates. It is only necessary to analyse the closing balance of goodwill between joint ventures and associates.

27.89 Where a parent company acquires a subsidiary which has an investment in an associate or joint venture, it will be necessary to apportion the goodwill arising on acquisition between the subsidiary undertaking and the associate or joint venture. Although allocation of goodwill is not specifically dealt with in FRS 7, it would appear to be required by FRS 11. This is because under FRS 11, capitalised goodwill should be allocated to income generating units along with other assets and liabilities for the purpose of impairment reviews.

27.90 Paragraph 34 of FRS 11 requires goodwill on an acquisition comprising two dissimilar businesses to be reviewed separately for impairment so that any impairment loss arising, say, in the subsidiary undertaking does not fall to be offset against an increase in value of the joint venture.

27.91 If the acquired subsidiary has an investment in an associate, the element of the goodwill arising on the parent's acquisition of the subsidiary which relates to the associate should be included in the associate's carrying amount under the equity method and disclosed separately.

27.92 Paragraph 21 of FRS 9 requires that, under the gross equity method, a joint venture should receive the same treatment as set out for associates, except that in the consolidated balance sheet the parent company's share of the gross assets and liabilities underlying the net equity amount for the joint venture should be shown in 'amplification of that net amount'. It follows, therefore, that it is appropriate to include the element of the goodwill arising on the acquisition of the subsidiary which relates to the joint venture as part of the gross asset disclosure on the face of the balance sheet, and to show it as a separate item either there or in the notes. Alternatively, it could be included in the net amount by disclosing it as a separate item on the face of the balance sheet, after the sub-total comprising the share of gross assets less the share of gross liabilities.

27.93 In addition, the Act requires that any goodwill arising on the acquisition of the associated undertaking (including joint venture entities) should be dealt with in accordance with the rules in Schedule 4, which require amortisation of capitalised goodwill to nil on a systematic basis over a period chosen by the directors. [CA85 4A Sch 22(1); 4 Sch 21(2)]. The rules in FRS 10 also apply to goodwill that arises on the acquisition of an associate. Under FRS 10 the required treatment is to capitalise goodwill and amortise it over its useful life, which would normally not exceed 20 years. There are special rules that apply where the goodwill life exceeds 20 years or is indeterminate. In certain special circumstances it is possible not to amortise goodwill, but this requires use of the true and fair override and specific impairment tests then apply. The rules in FRS 10 are considered in detail in chapter 25 and apply equally to goodwill arising on the acquisition of a joint venture or an associate. FRS 10 also included transitional provisions that allowed companies either to capitalise goodwill previously written off directly to reserves prior to the standard's introduction, or allowed it to remain written off against reserves. Where goodwill remains written off against reserves, the financial statements must state:

- The accounting policy followed in respect of that goodwill.
- The cumulative amounts of positive goodwill eliminated against reserves and negative goodwill added to reserves, net of any goodwill attributable to businesses disposed of before the balance sheet date.
- The fact that this goodwill had been eliminated as a matter of accounting policy and would be charged or credited in the profit and loss account on subsequent disposal of the business to which it related.

[FRS 10 para 71(a)].

Gross equity method

27.94 Investors have also to supplement the disclosure in paragraph 27.86 where they have interests in joint ventures. To accord with the gross equity method of accounting, the investor's share of both the aggregate gross assets and liabilities underlying the net amount included for the investment must be shown on the face of the balance sheet. [FRS 9 paras 4, 21]. In this situation, the standard is clear that this disclosure cannot be relegated to the notes to the financial statements and must appear on the face of the balance sheet.

Illustrative example

27.95 An illustration of the required disclosure is given below:

Consolidated balance sheet (extract)	Group £'000
Fixed assets	
Goodwill	130
Intangible assets	898
Tangible assets	31,082
Investments:	
Investments in joint ventures:	
Share of gross assets	1,273
Share of gross liabilities	(1,014)
	259
Investments in associates	148
Other investments	617
	1,024
	33,134

27.96 The share of gross liabilities of £1,014,000 shown in the example above includes the group's share of a loan from the group to the joint venture of £80,000 which is included in other investments (see following example). When there are intra-group transactions, it will normally be appropriate to eliminate a proportion of those transactions (see from para 27.145). In this case, however, the loan to the joint venture should not be eliminated with the element of that loan included in the share of joint ventures' gross liabilities, because the Companies Act formats require that loans to participating interests should be shown separately. This also applies to loans to and from associates.

27.97 The balance sheet formats in the Act require participating interests and loans to participating interests to be shown as separate line items. Separate disclosure of the loans to associates and the loans to joint ventures should, therefore, be given. In addition, paragraph 55 of FRS 9 requires disclosure of amounts owing and owed between an investor and its associates *or* joint ventures, that is, it distinguishes between the two. This is consistent with the general requirement for separate disclosure in respect of joint ventures and associates. One way of complying with this disclosure is to give a columnar presentation in the notes to the financial statements, where the column headings are the line items found in the formats, as illustrated in the example below:

Fixed asset investments (extract)

Group

	Joint ventures	Associates	Subsidiary excluded from consolidation	Loans to joint ventures	Loans to associates	Other investments	Total
	£'000	£'000	£'000	£'000	£'000	£'000	£'000
Cost or valuation							
At 31 March 20X6							
Goodwill	66	43	—	—	—	—	109
Other	172	121	654	80	40	352	1,419
	238	164	654	80	40	352	1,528
Additions	—	—	—	—	—	151	151
Share of retained profit	33	7	—	—	—	—	40
At 31 March 20X7							
Goodwill	66	43	—	—	—	—	109
Other	205	128	654	80	40	503	1,610
	271	171	654	80	40	503	1,719
Amounts written off							
At 31 March 20X6							
Goodwill	10	15	—	—	—	—	25
Other	—	—	654	—	—	6	660
	10	15	654	—	—	6	685
Amortisation of goodwill	2	3	—	—	—	—	5
Impairment of goodwill	—	5	—	—	—	—	5
At 31 March 20X7							
Goodwill	12	23	—	—	—	—	35
Other	—	—	654	—	—	6	660
	12	23	654	—	—	6	695

Net book value							
At 31 March 20X7							
Goodwill	54	20	—	—	—	—	74
Other	205	128	—	80	40	497	950
	259	148	—	80	40	497	1,024
Net book value							
At 31 March 20X6							
Goodwill	56	28	—	—	—	—	84
Other	172	121	—	80	40	346	759
	228	149	—	80	40	346	843

Investor's individual financial statements

27.98 For investments in both joint ventures and associates, in the investor's individual financial statements, the investments should be treated as fixed asset investments and shown either at cost, less amounts written off, or at valuation. [FRS 9 paras 20, 26].

Cash flow statement

27.99 FRS 9 also details how the results of associates and joint ventures should be dealt with in the cash flow statement and the standard makes a number of amendments to FRS 1, 'Cash flow statements'. The revised requirements are considered in chapter 30. Prior to FRS 9, dividends received from equity accounted entities were reported either within operating cash flows where their results were included as part of group operating profit or under returns of investments and servicing of finance where their results were reported outside group operating profit. Under FRS 9, the investor's share of the results of its equity accounted entities is included immediately *after* group operating profit rather than in group operating profit. Consistent with this treatment, the option of including dividends within operating cash flows is no longer available. The ASB also rejected the alternative of including dividends from equity accounted entities under returns on investments and servicing of finance, because it felt that such dividends have a different significance from the normal returns on investments. As a result, the cash flows relating to dividends received from joint ventures and associates are reported under a new heading 'Dividends from joint ventures and associates' between operating activities and returns on investment and servicing of finance. [FRS 1 para 12A].

Additional disclosure

General requirements

27.100 Schedule 5 to the Act includes certain additional information that has to be disclosed in the consolidated financial statements about an undertaking's investments in its joint ventures and associates. Some of this information is also required to be given by FRS 9. Investors have to give the following information:

- The name of the principal joint ventures and associates.
- If the joint venture or associate is incorporated outside Great Britain, the country of its incorporation.
- Where the joint venture or associate is unincorporated, the address of its principal place of business.
- In respect of shares held by the parent company or by other members of the group:
  - The identity of each class of shares.
  - The proportion held of the nominal value of each class.
  - Any special rights or constraints attaching to each class.

The disclosures in the first two bullet points have to be split between those held by the parent and those held by the group.

- The accounting period or date of the joint venture's or the associate's financial statements used if they differ from those of the investing group.
- An indication of the nature of the joint venture's or the associate's business.

[CA85 5 Sch 22; FRS 9 para 52].

This type of information is illustrated in Table 27.6.

Table 27.6 — Cable and Wireless plc — Annual report and accounts — 31 March 2000

Principal subsidiary undertakings, associates and joint ventures and trade investments at 31 March 2000 (extract)

Associates		Issued share capital m	Ownership Direct	Via subsidiaries	Class of shares	Country of incorporation	Area of operation
Bahrain Telecommunications Company B.S.C.*	Dinar	1,000	20%	–	Ordinary	Bahrain	Bahrain
Eastern Telecommunications Philippines, Inc.†*	P.Peso	200	40%	–	Ordinary	Philippines	Philippines
Joint ventures							
Gemini Submarine Cable System Limited†	US$	–	50%	–	Ordinary	Bermuda	Worldwide
Telecommunication Services of Trinidad and Tobago Limited†	T$	283	–	49%	Ordinary	Trinidad and Tobago	Trinidad and Tobago
MobileOne (Asia) Pte Ltd	Singapore $	140	–	30%	Ordinary	Singapore	Singapore

Notes
Full details of all subsidiary undertakings, associates and joint ventures and trade investments will be attached to the Company's Annual Return, to be filed with the Registrar of Companies.
* These companies had a financial year end of 31 December 1999 due to the requirements of the shareholders' agreements.
† These companies are audited by firms other than KPMG International member firms.

27.101 The information required by Schedule 5 above need not be disclosed where the joint venture or associate is established under the law of a country, or carries on a business, outside the UK, if in the directors' opinion the disclosure would be seriously prejudicial to the business of the joint venture or associate, or to the investor's business or any of its subsidiaries. But this information may only be withheld in this type of situation where the Secretary of State agrees that it need not be disclosed and this fact must be stated in the notes to the financial statements. [CA85 sec 231(3), CA06 Sec 409(3) and (4) (changed)].

27.102 Where the company's directors are of the opinion that the number of undertakings in respect of which the company is required to disclose the above information required by Schedule 5 would result in excessive disclosure being given, the information need only be given in respect of joint ventures and of associates whose results or financial position, in the opinion of the directors, principally affected the figures shown in the financial statements. Where advantage is taken of this provision the notes to the financial statements should state that the information is given only with respect to principal joint ventures and associates and should state that the full information (both that disclosed in the notes and that which is not) will be annexed to the company's next annual return. [CA85 sec 231(5)(6), CA06 Sec 410(1), (2) and (3)].

27.103 In addition, information is required to be disclosed concerning the trading balances with joint ventures and associates. The amount of loans owing and owed between an investor and its joint ventures or its associates must be disclosed (for example, see the illustration in para 27.97). [FRS 9 para 55]. Also, balances that arise from unsettled normal trading between joint ventures or associates and other group members should be included under current assets and current liabilities and disclosed separately if material. [FRS 9 para 55].

27.104 Furthermore, the standard requires other matters to be disclosed that are material in understanding the effect on the investor of its investments in its joint ventures and its associates. [FRS 9 para 53]. For example, this covers any notes of particular significance included in the joint venture's or associate's own financial statements. It also covers explanations of matters that should have been noted had the investor's accounting policies been applied. In addition, the investor's share in contingent liabilities incurred jointly with other venturers or investors should be given and its share of joint venture's, or associate's, capital commitments should be disclosed. It would seem to follow from the disclosure requirements given earlier in the standard that this information should be shown separately for joint ventures and associates.

27.105 If there are any significant statutory, contractual or exchange control restrictions on a joint venture's or an associate's ability to distribute its distributable reserves, the extent of the restrictions should be disclosed. [FRS 9 para 54]. This type of situation could arise where, for example, the associate is situated in a country where there are exchange control restrictions, which restrict the associate's ability to pay dividends out of that country.

27.106 A note of explanation is required in two situations where the Companies Act's presumptions concerning the definition of associates (including joint ventures) are rebutted. The first situation is where the presumption is rebutted that an investor holding 20 per cent or more of the voting rights of another entity exercises significant influence over its operating and financial policies. The second is where the presumption is rebutted that an investor holding 20 per cent or more of the shares of another entity has a participating interest. [FRS 9 para 56].

15 and 25 per cent threshold information

27.107 Additional disclosures arise where the investor's share in its associates in aggregate, or in its joint ventures in aggregate, exceeds 15 per cent of certain thresholds. In addition, where the investor's share in any of its individual joint ventures and associates exceeds 25 per cent of certain thresholds individually, then additional disclosures have to be given for that entity. The thresholds should be applied by comparing the investor's share for either its associates in aggregate or its joint ventures in aggregate (or its individual associates or joint ventures) of the following:

- gross assets;
- gross liabilities;
- turnover; or
- operating results (on a three-year average),

with the corresponding amounts for the group (excluding joint ventures and associates). If any of the thresholds are breached the additional disclosures detailed below have to be given. [FRS 9 para 57].

27.108 The intention is that additional disclosures should be given where associates or joint ventures have a significant impact on the group. It is possible for an associate or joint venture to make an insignificant profit over a three year period while still having a material impact on the group in each of the three years. Suppose an associate makes a profit of £300,000 in each of two years, but a loss of £600,000 in the third year. The total profit/loss for the three year period is £nil, but the group's share of the profit or loss in each of the three years may exceed the 15 per cent threshold. For this reason, we believe the operating results should, in calculating the three-year average, be included in absolute terms. In this case, the three year average would be (£300,000 + £300,000 + £600,000)/3 + £400,000. The investor's share of this average should then be compared with the average group's results (excluding results of associates and joint ventures) calculated on the same basis.

27.109 Where the 15 per cent threshold is exceeded for all associates the aggregate of the investor's share in its associates of the following must be given:

- Turnover (unless it is already included as a memorandum item).
- Fixed assets.
- Current assets.
- Liabilities due within one year.
- Liabilities due after one year or more.

[FRS 9 para 58(a)].

27.110 Similar information is required for joint ventures in aggregate where the 15 per cent threshold is exceeded for all joint ventures. But, in this case, the turnover will already have been given as one of the requirements of gross equity accounting. [FRS 9 para 58(b)].

27.111 Where the 25 per cent threshold is exceeded for an individual associate or joint venture, the associate or joint venture should be named and the investor's share of the following should be disclosed for that entity:

- Turnover.
- Profit before tax.
- Taxation.
- Profit after tax.
- Fixed assets.
- Current assets.
- Liabilities due within one year.
- Liabilities due after one year or more.

[FRS 9 para 58(c)].

27.112 However, where the individual joint venture or associate accounts for nearly all of the amounts included for that class of investment, only the aggregate, not the individual, information in paragraph 27.111 need be given, provided that this is explained and the associate or joint venture identified. [FRS 9 para 58(c)].

27.113 In addition to the disclosure requirements outlined above, the standard requires further analysis to be given where this is necessary to understand the nature of the amounts disclosed. The headings to be given under the disclosure requirements detailed above will not conform with those used by some joint ventures and associates. This might be because they are, for example, banks, insurance companies or investment companies. In this situation it is necessary to consider the nature of the joint venture's or associate's business in deciding the most relevant and descriptive balance sheet amounts to be disclosed. Furthermore, the standard says that it may be important to give an indication of the size and maturity profile of the liabilities held. [FRS 9 para 58].

Optional disclosure for joint ventures

27.114 For joint ventures, the ASB adopted equity accounting (albeit a slightly expanded version, the 'gross equity method') as it did not consider that proportional consolidation should be used for joint ventures. Its main reason for rejecting proportional consolidation was that it believed that it would be misleading to represent each venturer's joint control of a joint venture as being in substance equivalent to it having sole control of its share of each of that entity's assets, liabilities and cash flows. This becomes particularly apparent when considering the impact of proportional consolidation in the cash flow statement, which would lead to the venturer's share of the joint venture's cash flows being treated as direct cash flows of the investor.

27.115 However, the ASB believes that it is important to encourage experimentation concerning how best to report the results and operations of joint ventures, particularly where they are a significant part of a group's activities. The ASB is happy for groups to give additional information concerning their joint ventures provided that it is in a form that is consistent with the gross equity method of accounting. To this end, the ASB includes an illustration of an optional presentation in appendix IV to the standard. Two illustrative presentations are given below of the profit and loss account and the balance sheet showing memorandum information, which is based on the previous examples. One of the major constraints on this type of disclosure is purely a practical one and concerns how much information it is possible to get onto a printed page. Another issue concerns whether or not users will fully understand the implications of the additional information, which amounts to proportional consolidation.

The *pro forma* information given in the two right hand columns is of a memorandum nature only and is presented to give an indication of the effect of the group's share of the trading of its joint ventures on the results of the group.

Consolidated profit and loss account

	Continuing operations	Acquisitions	Total	Discontinued operations	Group	*Pro forma information* Joint ventures	*Pro forma information* Total
	£m	£m	£m	£m	£m	£m	£m
Turnover including share of joint ventures and associates	250	50	300	20	320		
Less: Share of joint ventures and associates	105	10	115	5	120		
Group turnover	145	40	185	15	200	40	240
Cost of sales	89	23	112	8	120	8	128
Gross profit	56	17	73	7	80	32	112
Administrative expenses	28	4	32	8	40	2	42
Group operating profit (loss)	28	13	41	(1)	40	30	70
Share of operating profit of:							
Joint ventures	27	3	30	–	30		
Associates	25	–	25	(1)	24		24
Operating profit including joint ventures and associates	80	16	96	(2)	94		94
Sale of operations:							
Group	–	–	–	20	20		
Joint ventures and associates	–	–	–	(15)	(15)		
	–	–	–	5	5		
Profit on ordinary activities before interest	80	16	96	3	99		
Interest					(42)		
Profit on ordinary activities before tax					57		
Tax on profit on ordinary activities					12		
Profit on ordinary activities after tax					45		
Minority interests					6		
Profit for the financial year					39		
Equity dividends					10		
Retained profit for the year					29		

Consolidated balance sheet

	Group	*Pro forma information* Joint ventures	Total
	£'000	£'000	£'000
Fixed assets			
Goodwill	130	–	130
Intangible assets	898		898
Tangible assets	31,082	835	31,917
Investments:			
Investments in joint ventures	259	(259)	–
Investments in associates	148	–	148
Other investments	617	23	640
	1,024		788
	33,134		33,733
Current assets			
Stocks	7,821	230	8,051
Debtors: amounts falling due after one year	510	22	532
Debtors: amounts falling due within one year	9,029	127	9,156
Investments	166	–	166
Cash at bank and in hand	843	36	879
	18,369	415	18,784
Creditors: amounts falling due within one year	8,520	530	9,050
Net current assets (liabilities)	9,849	(115)	9,734
Total assets less current liabilities	42,983	743	43,467
Creditors: amounts falling due after more than one year			
Borrowings and other creditors	7,851	380	8,231
Provisions for liabilities and charges	10,035	104	10,139
	17,886	484	18,370
Net assets	25,097		25,097
Capital and reserves			
Called up share capital	11,161		
Share premium account	1,512		
Revaluation reserve	5,426		
Profit and loss account	5,503		
Total shareholders' funds	23,602		
Minority interests	1,495		
	25,097		

The *pro forma* information shows the group's share of the gross assets and liabilities of its joint ventures and the effect on the group's assets and liabilities if it were to be proportionally consolidated. The figure of £259,000 represents the elimination of the group's share of its joint ventures' net assets included within the group column.

Equity accounting principles

Introduction

27.116 The principles concerning how to equity account for joint ventures and associates mainly follow those that apply to the consolidation of subsidiaries. These principles concern, for example, the date from which to equity account an interest in a joint venture or associate, how to determine goodwill and the types of consolidation adjustments that are necessary. The primary difference between an associate interest, or a joint venture interest, and an interest in a subsidiary is the level of the investor's control. An investor controls its subsidiaries, and therefore has access to the information necessary for carrying out certain consolidation procedures, but it exercises only significant influence over its associates or jointly controls its joint ventures. Consequently, this might mean that access to information necessary to make the required consolidation adjustments is limited. Where this is so, the standard states that estimates may be used. But such a limitation in itself might call into question the investor's relationship with its associate or joint venture. Where the information available is extremely limited, the investor will need to reassess whether or not it actually has significant influence over, or whether or not it jointly controls, its investment. [FRS 9 para 35].

27.117 Furthermore, the standard mentions that regulations on the dissemination of information could possibly restrict the extent to which the financial statements of an investor might contain information about its joint ventures and its associates, unless such information is available to other interested parties at the same time. [FRS 9 para 37]. This is of particular importance where the associate is itself listed (as explained in para 27.137 below). Investors should, therefore, consider how to satisfy any regulations that apply concerning publishing price sensitive information about its joint ventures and its associates.

27.118 The paragraphs that follow consider the consolidation rules that apply to equity accounting both associates and joint ventures, starting with examining how the share to be equity accounted is ascertained.

Share

27.119 Before it is possible to equity account for joint ventures and associates, it is necessary to establish what share the group owns. There are a number of matters that need to be considered in determining what is the appropriate share, as in many situations the percentage will not be easily ascertained. Paragraphs 27.33 to 27.35 above explain how to determine whether or not the investor has a participating interest in the joint venture or the associate and paragraphs 27.50 to 27.54 consider what voting rights should be taken into account. These rules also apply in determining what percentage share the group has in the joint venture or associate.

27.120 Where the investor is a group, its share of its associate or joint venture is the aggregate of the parent's interest and the interest of its subsidiaries in that entity. [FRS 9 para 32]. Therefore, it is the group's aggregate interest in the joint venture or associate which needs to be ascertained and this is the appropriate percentage which should be applied in equity accounting. But the holdings of any of the group's other associates or joint ventures should be ignored for this purpose. [FRS 9 para 32].

27.121 In a simple situation where the investor only has an interest in the equity share capital of the associate or joint venture it is easy to ascertain the share to be equity accounted: it will normally be the number of shares held divided by the total number of equity shares in issue. This amount will equate to the investor's entitlement to dividends and other distributions. Complications arise where the investee has different classes of shares or where the entitlement to dividends, or capital on winding up, vary. For example, the investor might have an interest in the non-equity capital as well as the equity capital. Clearly in this type of situation, the rights attaching to each class of share need to be considered carefully to determine the appropriate percentage to be brought into the equity interest calculation. It is a matter of looking at the substance of the respective rights to establish the appropriate accounting treatment.

Example

A group has an interest in the equity shares of its associate and owns all of the other class of the company's shares in issue, which are cumulative preference shares. The group owns 45% of the equity shares and 500,000 6% cumulative preference shares with a nominal value of £1 each. There were no issue costs relating to the preference shares. The preference shares are classified as debt of the associate (in accordance with FRS 25) and are accounted for in accordance with FRS 4 or FRS 26 (depending on which standard is being applied – see further chapter 6). The net assets of the associate are £1m, but it does not have sufficient distributable reserves in order to enable it to pay the cumulative dividend.

The liabilities of the associate include unpaid finance costs (dividends) of £60,000 which is solely attributable to the investor's interest in the cumulative preference shares. The investor's share of net assets is determined by adding together its entitlement to cumulative dividends and its interest in the preference shares before calculating its share of the remaining net assets. Ignoring fair values and goodwill, the investor's share of net assets would be £758,000 (that is, £60,000 + £500,000 + 45% (£1,000,000 – £500,000 – £60,000)).

27.122 In many situations the share to be taken into account will be derived from the percentage holding in shares, but in other situations the economic interest might differ from the shareholding, but will be the appropriate interest to take into account. For example, although the shareholding in a joint venture might be 50:50, the venturers might share profits in the ratio 40:60. Therefore, in this circumstance it will be appropriate to equity account for the economic share rather than the equity participation. Consequently, considerable care needs to be taken in establishing the appropriate share to be equity accounted.

27.122.1 A further complication arises when the group's interest is in a joint venture rather than an associate. This is because FRS 9 requires the investor to disclose, in addition to the amounts that would be included under the equity method if the investment was an associate, the investor's share of the gross assets and liabilities of its joint venture.

Example

Facts as in the example above except that the group's interest is in a joint venture, not an associate. The joint venture's balance sheet is as follows:

	£000
Gross assets	1,250
Gross liabilities (excluding preference shares)	(250)
	1,000
Preference shares (£500,000 capital plus £60,000 finance costs)	(560)
Net assets	440
Ordinary share capital	500
Profit and loss reserve	(60)
Share capital and reserves	440

The share of net assets of a joint venture is calculated in the same way as for associates and, accordingly, in this case, is £758,000 as per the previous example. That is, the group's share of net assets is 75.8% of the joint venture's net assets excluding preference shares. It follows, therefore, that the group's share of gross assets is 75.8% of the joint venture's gross assets, £947,500 (75.8% × £1,250,000), and similarly that its share of gross liabilities excluding preference shares is £189,500 (75.8% × £250,000).

It might be expected that the share of gross assets and liabilities would reflect the preferential treatment accorded to preference shareholders in the event of a winding up. Before the ordinary shareholders could be paid, the preference shareholders would be entitled to receive both the nominal value of their preference shares and any arrears of dividend. In this case, those two components amount to £560,000. If this approach was taken, the group's share of gross assets would be £870,500 (£560,000 + 45% × (£1,250,000-£560,000)) and its share of gross liabilities excluding preference shares would be £112,500 (45% × £250,000). However, this approach is conceptually flawed. In the event of a winding up, preference shareholders are, like ordinary shareholders, paid out of the proceeds of net assets, not gross assets. To allocate the share of gross assets by applying them first to the preference shareholder's interest, is to imply that the preference shareholders are paid out in advance, not just of the ordinary shareholders, but also of creditors.

Options, convertible shares and convertible debt

27.123 Where the investor holds options, convertibles or non-equity shares in its joint venture or its associate, the standard says that these should be taken into account in determining the investor's share where the conditions attaching to such holdings indicate that this is appropriate. The standard goes on to say that, in such cases, the costs of exercising the options or converting the convertibles, or future payments in relation to the non-equity shares, should also be taken into account. It also states that the necessary calculation depends on the relevant circumstances in any particular case, but notes that care should be taken not to count any interest twice. For example, such double counting would occur where an investor included a greater share of its associate under the equity method than that which would arise on the basis of the investor's existing equity holding, while simultaneously writing up the value of options held in the associate to reflect an increase in market value. [FRS 9 para 33]. It is not easy to see what these requirements mean in practice and these issues are explored in the paragraphs that follow.

27.124 The standard's section 'The development of the FRS' says that the basis of paragraph 33 outlined above is the requirement in FRS 5 that the substance of transactions should be reported. In particular, paragraph 14 of FRS 5 specifies that *"in determining the substance of a transaction, all its aspects and implications should be identified and greater weight should be given to those more likely to have a commercial effect in practice"*. FRS 9 goes on to say that the investor should, therefore, account for the substance of its interests in its joint ventures or its associates in cases where this is affected by its holdings of options, convertibles or non-equity shares. It gives one example where the existence of such a holding might affect the share. This is where the price of exercising or converting options or convertibles is so low that there is commercially near certainty that they will be exercised or converted. It is, therefore, quite clear from this explanation that the ASB considers that the share to be equity accounted should in certain special circumstances be adjusted to take account of the existence of options and convertibles.

27.125 As mentioned earlier, it is clear under the Act that a participating interest, which is defined in section 260, includes an option to acquire shares or any interest that is convertible into shares. [CA85 sec 260(3)]. For this purpose, it does not matter whether the options or other interests can be exercised now or in the future; their mere existence is taken into account whether or not they are currently exercisable. An interest or option in shares falls within this definition even if the shares to which it relates, until conversion or the exercise of the option, are unissued. [CA85 sec 260(3)]. In addition, interests held on behalf of an undertaking should be treated as held by it. [CA85 sec 260(4)].

27.126 These rules apply in determining whether or not an investor has a participating interest in an entity and, as a consequence, are important in establishing whether or not the entity is a joint venture or an associate. But the question arises as to whether such interests should be taken into account in determining the share to be equity accounted. Clearly for this purpose, having an option interest or a convertible interest is very different from holding the shares to which they relate. For example, it seems clear that if the options or convertible interests are not within their exercise or conversion period, it is unlikely that they should be brought into account in determining the investor's interest in the associate, unless they are exercisable at a purely nominal figure and it appears in the circumstances that it would be in the investor's interest to exercise them. However, where they are within their option period and exercisable at a fair market price and the holder can exercise them at any time unconditionally then whether or not they fall to be treated as part of the investor's interest will depend on a number of factors. It would be highly unusual to take options and convertible interests into account in determining the share before they have been exercised, so the circumstances would have to be considered very carefully before adjusting the share to be equity accounted for such interests. One issue to consider is the distribution policy of the associate. If, for example, the associate was planning to pay an enhanced dividend this would need to be taken into account. The example that follows illustrates some of these issues.

Example

A group has a 25% interest in its associate's equity share capital of £100,000. It also has options which it has held for a number of years to acquire a further 5,000 shares of £1 each from the company at £14 per share. The options, which cost £1 per share, are traded and have been valued in the group's financial statements at £2 per share. The net assets of the associate at the year end are £1m.

Ignoring fair values, the investor's equity interest in its associate's net assets is worth £250,000 which would normally be consolidated in the group's balance sheet. In addition, the group has shown the interest in the options at a value of £10,000. If the group had exercised its options at the year end and paid the £14 per share, the associate's net assets would increase by £70,000 (that is, 5,000 × £14) to £1,070,000 and the investor's interest would increase from 25% to 28.57% (that is, 30,000 ÷ 105,000 × 100). Therefore, the investor's share of the net assets and goodwill on the increase in stake would be £325,000. This is made up of the share of net assets of £305,700 (that is, £1,070,000 × 28.57%) and goodwill arising on the increase in stake of £19,300. The goodwill is the difference between the consideration of £75,000 (that is, the cost of the additional shares of £70,000 plus the initial cost of the options of £5,000) and the additional share of net assets of £55,700. Clearly, if this increased interest is booked in the consolidated balance sheet, then it would be necessary to eliminate the revaluation of the options of £5,000 in order to avoid double counting. In addition, it would be necessary to make a provision for the purchase of the additional shares, which would cost £70,000.

Consequently, in this example the net assets relating to the associate without taking into account the exercise of the options are £260,000 (that is, £250,000 + £10,000), but after taking into account the exercise of the options, the share of net assets of £325,000 (that is, share of net assets of £305,700 plus goodwill of £19,300) less a provision for consideration of £70,000 gives a total of £255,000; a net decrease of £5,000.

Following the introduction of FRS 10, because goodwill is capitalised the amount paid for an acquisition always equates to the increase in net assets plus goodwill recognised on consolidation (the fair value exercise only determining how the consideration figure is split between assets and goodwill). Consequently, anticipating an acquisition by providing for the consideration to be paid has a nil effect on the share of net assets plus goodwill shown on consolidation. In this example, the decrease in net assets of £5,000 is merely due to the reversal of the revaluation of £5,000 relating to the options recognised in the balance sheet.

27.127 Whether or not the investor would take into account an interest in options in ascertaining its share of its joint ventures and associates will depend on the facts of each case. The investor's intentions are, therefore, important. For example, if the options were exercisable at market value, the investor might intend to wait until the share price falls before it exercises its options or might intend to exercise them for other strategic business reasons. Where the investor does intend to exercise the options (say, shortly after the year end) then FRS 9 implies in paragraph 33 that it should take this into account in reflecting its interest in its joint venture or associate. But, as mentioned above, the circumstances that would justify adjusting the company's share for such options are not likely to arise very often in practice.

27.128 In certain situations the investor's intentions might be more obvious. This will be the case, in particular, where a fixed price put and call option exists. In this situation, either the investor or the investee is assured to exercise the option, as it will be in one of their economic interests to do so. However, care needs to be taken, because the effect of exercising options might not be obvious even where they are exercisable at below their market value. Consider the following example.

Example

If in the previous example the investor's options were exercisable at £2 per share as opposed to £14 per share, then the effect on the group's net assets would be as follows.

The investor's share of the net assets and goodwill on the increase in stake would be £265,000. This is made up of the share of net assets of £288,557 (that is, £1,010,000 × 28.57%) less negative goodwill arising on the increase in stake of £23,557. The goodwill is the difference between the consideration of £15,000 (that is, the cost of the additional shares of £10,000 plus the initial cost of the options of £5,000) and the additional share of net assets of £38,557. Consequently, if the exercise of the options is taken into account, the share of net assets of £265,000 (that is, share of net assets of £288,557 less negative goodwill of £23,557) less a provision for consideration of £10,000 gives a total of £255,000; a net decrease of £5,000.

The net assets recognised is the same as in the previous example. This is no coincidence and is the effect of having to recognise purchased goodwill or negative goodwill on the balance sheet. As mentioned in the previous example, the increase in net assets recognised on consolidation always equates to the amount paid for the acquisition. Similarly in this example, anticipating an acquisition by providing for the consideration to be paid has a nil effect on the net assets on consolidation. Again in this example the decrease in net assets of £5,000 is due to the reversal of the revaluation of £5,000 relating to the options recognised in the balance sheet.

27.129 As can be seen from the previous two examples, the exercise price has no impact on the net assets recognised before or after acquisition, the net assets will remain the same. However, there would be an impact on the gross assets and liabilities recognised.

27.130 Another situation which arises in practice is where the investor has options over shares in the joint venture or associate which are held by third parties. Again the facts of the situation will have to be considered carefully. The intention of the investor might be influenced by the purchase price compared to the increased interest and possibly by the additional influence this gives the investor.

27.131 Problems can also arise at the margins, because the existence of options might tip the balance at the opposite extremes of the associate/joint venture spectrum. At one end an investment might become an associate by taking into account options (as discussed in para 27.125 above). At the other end of the spectrum the existence of options might turn a joint venture or an associate into a subsidiary. The issues concerning when such an interest becomes a subsidiary are considered in detail in chapter 25.

Convertible shares

27.132 The standard applies the same rules to convertible shares as it specifies for options as explained in paragraph 27.123 above. Therefore, it is necessary to establish whether or not the convertible shares are within their conversion period. If they are, the next step is to consider whether this gives the investor the power to exercise dominant influence or control. If the investor does not have such power, only if it is clear that the investor intends to convert and no significant distributions will be made before it does so should the conversion be taken into account in determining the share to be equity accounted. Also it will be necessary to take into account any costs of conversion to ensure that there is no double counting.

Example

A group has a 25% interest in its associate's equity share capital of £100,000. It also holds 100,000 convertible redeemable preference shares of 25p. These are convertible into 10,000 £1 equity shares. The net assets of the associate at the year end are £1m. There is no cost of conversion, but if there was, then it would have to be provided for.

Ignoring fair values and goodwill, the investor's equity interest in its associate's net assets before conversion is £268,750 (that is, (£1,000,000 — £25,000) × 25% + £25,000), which would be consolidated in the group's balance sheet. If the group had exercised its options to convert at the year end, the investor's interest would increase from 25% to 31.82% (that is, 35,000 ÷ 110,000 × 100). Therefore, the investor's share of the net assets will increase to £318,200 (that is, £1,000,000 × 31.82%).

Convertible debt

27.133 Similar issues arise if the investor has invested in convertible debt of its joint venture or associate. It is necessary to consider the implications and substance of the transaction to determine whether the potential voting rights represent a present ownership interest. Also, anticipating conversion would have no impact on the net assets of the group as illustrated in the following example.

Example

A group has a 25% interest in its associate's equity share capital of £100,000. It also holds £100,000 of debt, convertible into a variable number of equity shares valued at £110,000. The net assets of the associate at the year end are £1m. There is no cost of conversion, but if there was, then it would have to be provided for.

Ignoring fair values, the investor's equity interest in its associate's net assets before conversion is £250,000 (that is, £1,000,000 × 25%) and it also has a loan to the associate of £100,000. Therefore, its total interest before conversion is £350,000. The share price is £10. If the group had converted its debt at the year end, the investor's interest would increase from 25% to 32.43% (that is, 36,000 ÷ 111,000 × 100). The associate's net assets increase by the £100,000 of debt which would be transferred to share capital and to share premium on conversion. Therefore, the investor's share of the net assets and goodwill after the conversion also comes to £350,000. This is made up of the share of net assets of £356,730 (that is, £1,100,000 × 32.43%) less negative goodwill arising on the increase in stake of £6,730. The negative goodwill is the difference between the consideration of £100,000 (that is, the value of the loan given up) and the additional share of net assets of £106,730.

As mentioned in the previous examples, the increase in net assets recognised on consolidation always equates to the amount paid for the acquisition. In this example, the group's net assets have remained the same, because the loan of £100,000 has been replaced by an increased share of net assets offset by negative goodwill.

27.134 Problems can also arise where other investors in the associate hold converting interests, which might have the effect of diluting the share of the associate to be equity accounted. Again it is necessary to consider carefully the implications and the substance of the transaction to determine whether or not the equity share should be adjusted.

Example

A group has a 38% interest in its associate's equity share capital. The associate has convertible debt in issue which is held by third parties. This debt will convert into equity shares of the associate in two years' time and it is almost certain that the debt-holders will opt for conversion. Once converted the investor's interest will decrease to 35%.

In this case, although it is almost certain that the debt will convert and conversion is not within the control of the investor, the investor should still equity account for its 38% interest until the conversion takes place. Only after conversion has taken place should the investor account using the 35%, because this is the actual date of the deemed disposal (see further para 27.170). However, because conversion is likely, the investor should provide for any losses (but not profits) in relation to the change in interest from 38% to 35%. It is, therefore, necessary to calculate the loss or gain on the deemed disposal. The gain or loss is calculated by comparing the share of net assets before the deemed disposal with the share of net assets after the deemed disposal (adjusted for any proceeds on the conversion of the debt). This calculation would also have to take into account a share of the goodwill given up on the deemed disposal, which would reduce any profit or increase any loss. If there is a resulting loss this would have to be provided for in the consolidated profit and loss account.

Crossholdings

27.135 One complicated issue that arises with equity accounting is how to deal with crossholdings of shares between the investor and its investee. This situation can arise whereby one company (the investor) issues shares to another company in exchange for shares in that other company. Obviously, without some adjustment there will be an element of double counting if the investor equity accounts for its share of the investee's net assets, which includes the holding of shares in the investor company. Therefore, this crossholding needs to be eliminated as explained in the following example.

Example

Company H takes a 25% stake in company A, which has net assets of £1m. The market value of the associate's shares is £1.5m. For simplicity, the net asset value and the fair value of the net assets is the same, that is, £1m. Company H issues shares with a value of £375,000 to acquire its interest.

In the simple situation where the investor issues its shares to the owners of the associate in exchange for the 25% interest, company H's share capital and share premium would increase by £375,000, being its investment in company A. On consolidation, the investment in company A of £375,000 is simply allocated between the group's share of the fair value of its net assets (that is, £250,000) and goodwill arising on the acquisition of £125,000 (that is, £375,000 — £250,000).

But now assume there is an equity swap, such that the investor issues shares worth £375,000 to the associate in consideration for the associate issuing the investor new shares. The associate's net assets increase by £375,000, the cost to it of the shares it holds in company H. Consequently, company A's worth has increased to £1,875,000 and it has net assets of £1,375,000. Company H's share of company A's increased net assets is £343,750 (that is, £1,375,000 × 25%), but this includes the value of the interest in its own shares of £93,750 (that is, 25% × £375,000). Company A's goodwill is still worth £500,000, of which company H's share is still £125,000. So it might appear that on consolidation the value of company H's interest in its associate should be £468,750 (that is, £1,875,000 × 25%), but company H's consolidated net assets (including goodwill) should not exceed £375,000, the value of the shares it has issued. If the group had recognised its share as £468,750 instead, it would have inflated its consolidated balance sheet by recognising some value for its own internally generated goodwill.

Therefore, to avoid double counting for the self-investment it is then necessary to split the interest in the associate of £375,000 between the share of the fair value of the net assets acquired and goodwill. It seems appropriate to reduce the value of company H's investment in company A's net assets by £93,750 to £250,000 and state goodwill at £125,000. The rationale is that the net assets are reduced to eliminate the crossholding and this also ensures that purchased goodwill in company A is recorded at the appropriate value. A problem arises if company A subsequently sells its interest in company H – an adjustment is required to bring company H's investment in its consolidated financial statements back up to the increased share of net assets of company A (that is, to £468,750). The double entry would be to credit the group's revaluation reserve with the increase in value of the associate interest.

In the consolidated profit and loss account, company H's share of company A's results should be included excluding any portion of those results attributable to company A's investment in company H. However, it should include a share of any dividends paid by company H to company A.

Financial statements used

27.136 The financial statements used for the purpose of including the results of joint ventures and associates should be either coterminous with those of the group (which for an associate with a different year end would involve preparing special financial statements to the same date as the investor's year end) or, where this is not practicable, made up to a date that is not more than three months before the investing group's period end. [FRS 9 para 31(d)].

27.137 If a joint venture or an associate is listed on a recognised stock exchange, only published information should be disclosed in the group's consolidated financial statements. This can cause particular problems in practice where, for example, there is more than six months between the year end of the associate and that of the group. In the situation where the use of financial statements drawn up for a period ending not more than three months before the investor's period end would release price-sensitive information, FRS 9 allows instead financial statements prepared for a period that ends not more than six months before the group's period end to be used. [FRS 9 para 31(d)]. Any changes after the period end of the associate or joint venture and before that of the investor that are material, should be taken into account by adjustment.

Example

A group draws up its consolidated financial statements to 31 December 20X2. It has an investment in a listed associate, which it equity accounts on consolidation. The associate's last year end was 31 January 20X2.

It is not possible for the group to consolidate results of its associate made up to coincide with its period end 31 December 20X2, because this would entail publishing information concerning its associate that has not been made available to the public. It is also not possible to equity account for the associate's results to 31 January 20X3, the period ending shortly after that of the group as this is not allowed under FRS 9. In addition, it is not possible to equity account for the previous year to 31 January 20X2, as this is also precluded by FRS 9. The associate will have to prepare interim accounts. Assuming it reported at the half year, the accounts that should be equity accounted in this case are those for the year to 31 July 20X2, the interim period end of the associate. This will entail taking into account the results for the second half of the associate's previous year and the first half of its current year, which together constitute the year to 31 July 20X2.

Consolidation adjustments

27.138 Adjustments similar to those required for the purposes of including subsidiaries in the consolidated financial statements should be made when the associates or joint ventures are incorporated into the group's consolidated financial statements. The type of adjustments that may be necessary cover the following matters:

- To achieve consistency of accounting policies.
- To set up goodwill arising on the associate's or joint venture's acquisition and to deal with fair value adjustments.
- To deal with abnormal transactions that arise between an associate's or joint venture's year end and its parent's year end.
- To eliminate the effects of intra-group trading.
- To translate the results of overseas associates or joint ventures.

27.139 These types of adjustments are similar to those made generally on the consolidation of subsidiaries. Some specific issues are considered in the paragraphs that follow.

Consistent accounting policies

27.140 The standard states that in arriving at the amounts to be included by the equity method of accounting, the same accounting policies as those of the investor should be applied. [FRS 9 para 31(c)]. This will entail making adjustments to the joint venture's or associate's results to harmonise accounting policies. However, in practice, such adjustments will not always be possible, because the information necessary to make them may not necessarily be available. Where this situation arises, the standard offers no guidance. However, this is also another area where the investor's relationship with its associate (that is, significant influence), or with its joint venture (that is, joint control), would be called into question, if the appropriate information is not available.

Goodwill and fair values

27.141 The standard requires that when an entity acquires a joint venture or an associate, fair values should be attributed to the investee's underlying assets and liabilities. [FRS 9 para 31(a)]. These fair values should be ascertained in accordance with the principles of FRS 7, 'Fair values in acquisition accounting', and adjustments should be made to conform with the investor's accounting policies. Again, as explained in the previous paragraph, where it is not possible to ascertain fair values on acquisition of a joint venture or an associate interest, this would call into question whether or not the entity fulfils the definitions of joint venture or associate, because it could suggest that the appropriate level of control or interest has not been achieved in practice.

27.142 For joint ventures and associates, it is unlikely that any necessary fair values adjustment would be booked in the joint venture's or associate's books of account, but nevertheless the fair value of assets should provide the basis for subsequent depreciation that is reflected in the investor's share of the results. The standard requires that both the consideration paid in the acquisition and the goodwill arising should be calculated in the same way as on the acquisition of a subsidiary. These issues are considered in detail in chapter 25. As explained in paragraph 27.88 above, the investee's assets used in calculating the goodwill arising on acquisition should not include any goodwill carried in the balance sheet of the joint venture or associate. Goodwill arising on the acquisition of joint ventures or associates has now to be accounted for in accordance with the provisions of FRS 10, 'Goodwill and intangible assets'. These requirements are fully explained in chapter 25.

27.143 Paragraph 31(a) in FRS 9, which specifies the above rules, deals with the measurement issues that arise when the equity accounting method is used, but it does not specify what disclosure requirements apply on acquisition. Therefore, for acquisitions of joint ventures and associates we do not consider that the disclosure requirements specified in FRS 6, 'Acquisitions and mergers', for acquisitions of subsidiaries apply. Consequently, there is no need to give the fair value table information required by that standard, although some companies do give this type of information — see Table 27.7. The disclosures required for joint ventures and associates are considered from paragraph 27.100 above.

Table 27.7 — British Telecommunications plc — Report & Accounts — 31 March 1998

Notes to the financial statements (extract)

15 Fixed asset investments (extract)

(c) Cegetel

On 24 September 1997, the group completed its acquisition of a 26% interest in Cegetel, a leading French telecommunications company. Of the cost of the investment in the associated undertaking of £1,029m, goodwill arising of £862m has been written off against reserves.

The acquisition of the interest in Cegetel comprised:

	£m
Group share of original book value of net assets	483
Fair value adjustment to achieve consistency of accounting policies	(316)
Fair value to the group	167
Goodwill	862
Total cost	1,029

Abnormal transactions between year ends

27.144 Care should be taken where the joint venture's or associate's year end does not coincide with that of the investing undertaking to ensure that there are no material events that have occurred since the joint venture's or associate's year end. Where such events have taken place, then if the effect is material it will be necessary to make adjustments to the results and net assets of the associate before they are consolidated with the group's financial statements. [FRS 9 para 31(d)]. For example, the associate might sell fixed assets to the group (or *vice versa*) during this period. Another example is where the group increases loans made to the joint venture or associate after the joint venture's or associate's year end.

Elimination of intra-group trading

Profits and losses included in assets

27.145 The method used to eliminate intra-group trading with joint ventures and associates may be different from that adopted for subsidiaries. The normal method of adjustment for a subsidiary company would be to eliminate profits and losses fully. However, the Act specifies that the elimination of profits and losses resulting from transactions between group undertakings, which have been included in the value of assets, may be eliminated in proportion to the group's interest in the shares of the undertaking. [CA85 4A Sch 6(3)]. The implication of this method of elimination as it applies to subsidiaries is restricted by FRS 2 and is considered further in chapter 24. Although only brought into the legislation by the introduction of the Companies Act 1989, this method of eliminating profits had been used for joint ventures and associates being equity accounted for some time before that date. This treatment is confirmed in FRS 9, which states that where profits and losses resulting from transactions between an investor and its associate, or its joint venture, are included in the carrying amount of assets in either entity, the part relating to the investor's share should be eliminated. [FRS 9 para 31(b)]. In addition, the standard notes that where the transaction provides evidence of the impairment of those assets or any similar assets, this should be taken into account. Blue Circle Industries PLC eliminates profits in this way as explained by their accounting policy (see Table 27.8).

Table 27.8 — Blue Circle Industries PLC — Annual Report & Accounts — 31 December 2000

1 Accounting Policies (extract)

13 Property (extract)

Sales of properties are recognised when a legally binding and unconditional contract for sale has been exchanged. Where properties are sold to joint ventures or associates, profits are only recognised in proportion to third parties' interests in these entities. The remaining profits are recognised when the properties are sold by joint venture or associate to unrelated parties.

27.146 The following example explains how the adjustment should be made.

Example

Company H prepares its consolidated financial statements to 31 December 20X7. It has a 25% investment in an associate. During the year company H purchased an investment from the associate for £120,000. The associate made £50,000 profit on the sale. On consolidation, using the equity method of accounting, that element of the associate's profit should be reduced to the extent of the group's investment in it (that is, reduced by 25%). Consequently, the share of the associate's profit consolidated with the group would be reduced by £12,500 (that is, 25% × £50,000), thereby, eliminating the group's share of that profit. In addition, to complete the double entry, the value of the investment shown in the group's consolidated balance sheet should be reduced by £12,500 to £107,500.

27.147 This type of adjustment is logical for joint ventures and associates, because the consolidated financial statements only include the group's share of the profits and losses of joint ventures and associates and, consequently, it would be wrong to eliminate a greater proportion of the profit. Furthermore, in the situation where a group member makes a sale to a joint venture or an associate, then a profit will arise in the group to the extent of the outside interest in the joint venture or associate. Similarly, the joint venture's or associate's assets will also, in this situation, be overstated by the profit element. Consequently, a similar adjustment will be required on consolidation to reduce the group's share of the joint venture's or associate's assets by the same amount.

Transfers of assets to a joint venture

27.148 The requirement to eliminate such profits applies equally to transfers of assets or liabilities to set up a joint venture or to acquire an initial stake in an associate as well as to all other transactions during the life of the associate or joint venture. [FRS 9 para 36].

Example

A group enters into a 50/50 joint venture with a third party. The joint venture is to be set up in a limited company and the group is to contribute assets worth £1,000,000 to the joint venture. The other party is to contribute cash for its 200,000 £1 shares. In consideration for the assets the group receives 200,000 £1 shares, long-term loan stock of £600,000 and cash of £200,000 (which the joint venture has received from its other shareholder).

The amount of the profit on the disposal of the group's property to the joint venture to be eliminated on consolidation depends upon the proportion of capital invested by the group and the other party to the venture. The proportions are as follows:

	Group	Other JV partner	Total capital
	£'000	£'000	£'000
Shares	200	200	400
Loan stock	600	—	600
	800	200	1,000
	80%	20%	100%

If the group made a gain on the disposal of the property to the joint venture, it should eliminate 80% of that gain, being the proportion of its interest it still retains in the asset (that is, share capital and long-term loan stock). Only 20% of the gain can be recognised in the consolidated financial statements. The elimination entry would be to debit the group's profit and loss account with the proportion of the gain being eliminated and credit the group's interest in the joint venture's assets shown on the face of the balance sheet following the gross equity method of accounting. Alternatively, the credit could be treated as deferred income, particularly where the assets will be realised subsequently. If the loan stock is subsequently repaid, the proportion to be eliminated would change to 50%.

In the individual entity making the disposal, the amount of the profit and any revaluation reserve being treated as realised will not depend on the capital invested in the joint venture, but will depend on the qualifying consideration (for instance, cash) received under the transaction.

	Proceeds £'000	Asset value £'000	Proportion
Cash received	200		20%
Loan Stock	600		60%
	800		80%
Shares	200		20%
Total	1,000	1,000	100%

Under Tech 7/03, 'Guidance on the determination of realised profits and losses in the context of distributions under the Companies Act 1985', where an asset is sold partly for qualifying consideration and partly for other consideration, any profit arising will be realised to the extent of the fair value of the qualifying consideration. Therefore, in this case the amount of the profit that can be recognised in the profit and loss account is £200,000 (that is, the amount received in cash). Any remaining unrealised gain would be recognised in the STRGL.

Intra-company trading transactions

27.149 The standard also makes the point that because associates and joint ventures are not part of the group, balances between the investor and its associates or joint ventures should not be eliminated and, therefore, unsettled normal trading transactions should be included as current assets or liabilities. [FRS 9 para 36]. Similarly, with the exception of turnover, normal trading transactions between the group and its joint ventures or its associates do not require elimination. These principles are illustrated in the three examples that follow:

Example 1

A group sells goods to a distribution joint venture (owned 50/50) which in turn sells on to third parties at a margin. In the period the group makes sales of £10m to the joint venture which cost £5m to produce. The joint venture in turn sells the goods to third parties for £12m and it cost of sales is £10m.

The turnover required to be disclosed under the Companies Act is that of the group excluding its joint venture (that is, £10m) and the standard requires the group's share of its joint ventures' turnover to be shown. It would clearly be misleading to show a total group turnover including joint ventures of £16m. Hence it is necessary to eliminate £5m relating to intra-group trading. The question then arises as to which figure of turnover to eliminate the £5m against. The £5m represents the group's share of the joint venture's cost of sales and it would be logical to eliminate this against the group's turnover reducing it to £5m and to show as share of joint venture's turnover £6m. This gives the correct total of, £11m, but does not comply with the Act's requirements, as the group's turnover, which must be disclosed under the Act, is £10m. Therefore, we suggest that the elimination is made against the share of the joint venture's turnover. This would result in the following presentation:

Consolidated profit and loss account (extract)	£m
Turnover including share of joint venture	11
Less: Share of joint venture	1
Group turnover	10
Cost of sales	5
Group operating profit	5
Share of operating profit of joint venture	1
Operating profit including share of joint venture	6

Depending on how material the group's share of its joint venture turnover is, it may be necessary to indicate that the reported share of joint venture turnover is stated after eliminating intra-group turnover of £5m.

An alternative presentation is to show the share of joint venture turnover before elimination of the £5m intra-group trading, with the intra-group element of the sales of the joint venture being shown separately. This would result in the following presentation.

Consolidated profit and loss account (extract)	£m
Turnover including share of joint venture	11
Less: Share of joint venture	(6)
Add: Sales to joint venture	5
Group turnover	10
Cost of sales	5
Group operating profit	5
Share of operating profit of joint venture	1
Operating profit including share of joint venture	6

This is the presentation adopted by Arcadia Group plc (see Table 27.9).

Table 27.9 — Arcadia Group plc — Report & Accounts — 25 August 2001

Consolidated profit and loss account (extract)

	2001	2000
For the financial year ended 25th August 2001	£m	£m
Turnover		
Total retail and joint ventures	1,896.8	1,955.3
Less: share of joint ventures	(21.6)	(30.3)
Add: sales to joint venture	14.6	20.0
Group	1,889.8	1,945.0

Example 2

The facts are the same as in example 1, except that the joint venture has sales of £9m and cost of sales of £7.5m, that is, a quarter of the goods purchased from the group by the joint venture remain unsold at the year end. The joint venture, therefore, has stock of £2.5m which was sold to it by the group at a profit of £1.25m. Since the joint venture is owned 50/50, 50% of that profit, £0.625m, should be treated as unrealised in the group's financial statements.

This would result in the following presentation.

Consolidated profit and loss account (extract)	£m
Turnover including share of joint venture (10 + 4.5 — 3.75)	10.750
Less: share of joint venture (4.5 — 3.75)	(0.750)
Group turnover	10.000
Cost of sales	5.625
Group operating profit	4.375
Share of operating profit of joint venture (50% × (9 — 7.5))	0.750
Operating profit including share of joint venture	5.125

The difference of £0.875m between the profit of £5.125m in this example and the profit of £6m in example 1 consists of two elements. First, in example 1 the group's results include its share of a profit on the additional £3m sales amounting to £0.25m. Secondly, in this example cost of sales has been increased by the reversal of the unrealised profit of £0.625m.

The group's share of the sales of the joint venture (50% × £9m = £4.5m), reduced by the group's share of the cost of sales of the joint venture (50% × £7.5m), reflects the group's share of incremental sales made by the joint venture to third parties. The turnover section of the profit and loss account now fairly represents the sales activity of the group and the group's share of joint venture combined. Similarly, the share of operating profit of the joint venture fairly reflects the profitability of the joint venture.

Consequently, the adjustment required to eliminate the unrealised profit in stock is best treated as an adjustment to cost of sales of the group.

The group's share of stock of the joint venture will be included in the share of gross assets shown on the face of the group balance sheet. This share of stock is £1.25m (50% × £2.5m) but since this includes the unrealised profit of £0.625m which requires elimination, the group's share of stock will be reduced to £0.625m. The double entry being – debit cost of sales and credit stock with £0.625m.

Example 3

A group has a 50% interest in a joint venture. The group charges the joint venture interest of £10,000 on a loan it has made to the joint venture. Therefore, the group has interest income in its profit and loss account of £10,000 and the joint venture has an interest expense of £10,000.

On consolidation the group would show for these items interest income of £10,000 and share of joint venture's interest payable of £5,000. Overall, therefore, the group has only recognised net income of £5,000, which represents the interest charged by the group to the other investor.

27.150 It can be seen from the examples that, with the exception of turnover, under equity accounting it is not necessary to eliminate inter-company trading on a line-by-line basis. Therefore, generally for trading transactions no consolidation adjustments are necessary as the group's share of the transaction is taken up in the share of its joint venture's or its associate's results. Consolidation adjustments are only necessary, as explained above, where profits and losses resulting from transactions between the investor and its joint venture, or its associate, are included in the carrying value of assets in either the group or the joint venture or associate and also to eliminate intra-group turnover.

Partnerships that are joint venture entities

27.151 Under the standard's provisions, a partnership may be either a joint venture entity or a joint arrangement that is not an entity. How to determine which type of joint arrangement an undertaking is, is considered from paragraph 27.177 below.

27.152 An issue arises with the accounting requirements for partnerships that are joint venture entities. In the group's consolidated financial statements, such partnerships should be equity accounted using the gross equity method. However, the question arises how the partnership should be accounted for in the investor's individual financial statements. The standard is silent as regards the treatment in the investor's own profit and loss account, but requires that, in the investor's own balance sheet, its interests in joint ventures should be treated as fixed asset investments and shown either at cost, less any amounts written off, or at valuation. It follows from this that in the company's profit and loss account only the investment income should be accounted for. Before the introduction of FRS 9, some partnerships of this nature were accounted for using proportional consolidation, or were equity accounted, in the investor's individual financial statements. Proportional consolidation is no longer possible following FRS 9's introduction. However, where there are no restrictions on the distribution of profits from the partnership, it may still be appropriate to record the investor's share of the results of its partnership. It could do this by showing its share of the results on one line representing its investment income rather than merely the distributions received from the partnership. In the balance sheet, the investment would be valued on the basis of the investor's share of the partnership's net assets. The accounting requirements that apply to partnerships that are joint arrangements are considered from paragraph 27.199 below.

Where the associate itself is a group

27.153 Where the associated undertaking (including joint ventures) is a group of undertakings, the Act requires that the net assets and the profits or losses that should be taken into account on equity accounting the associate should be those of the associate consolidated with its subsidiary undertakings. [CA85 4A Sch 22(2)]. This requirement is added to by FRS 9, which requires that the net assets and profits or losses to be dealt with should include the joint venture's or associate's share of the net assets and profits or losses of investments it may itself have in its own joint ventures or associates. [FRS 9 para 32].

Interests in losses and net liabilities

27.154 A problem may arise where a joint venture or an associate starts to make losses, particularly where those losses are such that the undertaking has net liabilities. Where this is so, the investing group should normally continue to record changes in carrying amounts of its joint ventures or associates in its consolidated balance sheet even where this results in recognising its share of any deficiency in a joint venture or an associate. [FRS 9 para 44]. This would apply, for example, where the investment is still regarded by the group as long-term (an essential condition of the definition of a joint venture or an associate).

27.155 The standard states that the only exception to equity accounting for such deficits is where there is sufficient evidence that an event has irrevocably changed the relationship between the investor and its investee, marking its irreversible withdrawal from its joint venture or associate. [FRS 9 para 44]. Consequently, where, for example, there is no intention to support the undertaking, then only the liabilities that the group will incur if the undertaking should cease to trade would need to be provided for in full in the consolidated financial statements. However, mere intention alone will not be adequate and the standard is looking for a demonstrable commitment to the withdrawal including a public statement to that effect. In particular, such a commitment will arise where the direction of the joint venture's or the associate's operating and financial policies has become the responsibility of its creditors (including bankers), for example where the joint venture or associate is in liquidation. Where the interest in a joint venture or an associate is in net liabilities, the amount recorded should be shown as a provision or a liability. [FRS 9 para 45].

Example

A company has an interest of 25% in an associate. The associate has net liabilities at the year end of £3.5m. The net liabilities include a loan of £2.5m from the investor. In the investor's individual financial statements a provision of £1.5m has been made against the loan.

In the group's consolidated financial statements, the investment in the associate is made up of its share of net liabilities together with any loan made to the associate. The group's share of the associate's net liabilities is £875,000 (that is, £3.5m × 25%). But of the net liabilities of £3.5m, the group has already made a provision of £1.5m against its loan. Consequently, it has, in effect, already made a provision against its share of net liabilities of £375,000 (that is, £1.5m × 25%) Therefore, the group only needs to provide for a further £500,000 on consolidation. This provision would also be made against the loan, giving a net investment in the associate of £500,000.

27.156 Often where a joint venture or an associate is making losses, there may be a significant diminution in the joint venture's or associate's value. Where there is any permanent diminution in value of any goodwill attributable to an investment in a joint venture or an associate, a provision should be made to write down that goodwill. [FRS 9 para 38]. A provision for any further impairment in the associate's net assets would not normally be required in the group's consolidated financial statements, because such an impairment in value would generally be reflected in the associate's net asset value. Where there is an impairment in goodwill, FRS 9 requires that the amount written off in the period should be separately disclosed. [CA85 4 Sch 19(2); FRS 9 para 38].

27.157 Where a group has an investment in an associate that has net liabilities, it is necessary to decide how to show the group's share of this deficit in the consolidated financial statements. It would not be appropriate to net the negative interest against other positive interests in associates. Positive interests should be shown within assets while negative interests should be shown within liabilities. The most appropriate caption in the balance sheet within which to show a negative interest is 'other provisions', although the standard states it can be shown as a provision or a liability. [FRS 9 para 45].

27.158 Table 27.10 shows a group that has treated its interest in negative net assets of an associate in a similar way to that described above.

Table 27.10 — Cordiant Communications Group plc — Annual report and accounts — 31 December 2000

Notes to the financial statements (extract)

21. Provisions (extract)

Provision for joint venture deficit

The Group share of net liabilities is as shown below:	**2000**	**1999**
	£m	**£m**
Fixed assets	**2.1**	1.7
Current assets	**128.5**	84.4
Share of gross assets	**130.6**	86.1
Liabilities due within one year	**(142.6)**	(99.9)
Liabilities due after one year	**(0.1)**	(0.6)
Share of gross liabilities	**(142.7)**	(100.5)
Share of joint venture net liabilities	**(12.1)**	(14.4)

Joint and several liability

27.159 FRS 9 makes the important point that, where unincorporated undertakings are treated as joint ventures or associates, a liability could arise in excess of that taken into account when accounting for the group's share of the joint venture or associate. In this case it is important that all such liabilities with respect to that entity are reflected appropriately in the financial statements. [FRS 9 para 46] The example given in the standard is that of joint and several liability in a partnership. [FRS 9 para 47]. Where such a potential liability exists (or a similar type of support agreement exists) it is necessary to consider whether a provision should be made for the possibility that the other party to the agreement may be unable to meet its obligations under that agreement.

27.160 In circumstances where it is clear that the other party is able to honour such an agreement, it is still necessary under the Act, FRS 9 and FRS 12 for the group to disclose the existence of its potential commitment as a contingent liability and clearly explain the circumstances in which the liability might crystallise. [FRS 9 para 47, FRS 12 para 29]. Table 27.11 shows the extent of guarantees given in respect of bank borrowings and funding of associates.

Table 27.11 — Associated British Ports Holdings PLC — Annual report and accounts — 31 December 1998

Notes to the accounts (extract)

28 Contingent liabilities (extract)

	Group		Company	
Contingent liabilities under claims, indemnities and bank guarantees are as follows:	**1998** **£m**	1997 £m	**1998** **£m**	1997 £m
Bank guarantees in respect of:				
— subsidiaries	—	—	**19.3**	22.7
— associated companies	—	0.1	—	0.1
Other guarantees and contingencies	**4.9**	0.6	—	—

The company has given guarantees of performance of contracts of work by one of its associated companies (Universal Pipe Coaters Limited) which totalled £18.5 million at 31 December 1998 (1997: £18.5 million). No claims had been notified under these guarantees at the year-end

Minority interests

27.161 Where the associate is held by a subsidiary that is partly held by a minority, the minority's share of the associate's results should be shown as part of minority interests in the consolidated financial statements.

Acquisitions and disposals

Effective date of acquisition or disposal

27.162 The effective date of acquisition of an associate is the date on which the investor begins to fulfil the two essential elements of the definition of an associate, that is, holding a participating interest and exercising significant influence. Similarly, the effective date for the acquisition of a joint venture interest is the date on which the investor begins to control that entity jointly with the other venturers. [FRS 9 para 40]. These requirements are equivalent to those in FRS 2, which states that for subsidiaries, the date on which an undertaking becomes a subsidiary is the date on which control passes to the parent. [FRS 2 para 45]. In addition, the investment must be a long-term interest, that is, it is not held for subsequent resale.

27.163 It follows, therefore, that the date on which an investment ceases to be an associate is the date on which it ceases to fulfil either element of the definition mentioned above. Similarly, the date on which an investment ceases to be a joint venture is the date on which the investor ceases to have joint control. [FRS 9 para 40].

27.164 Once the investment has qualified as a joint venture or an associate, minor temporary changes in the relationship between the investor and its joint venture or associate should not affect its status. In a similar way to the rules that apply to interests in subsidiaries, once the investor has accounted for its investments as associates or joint ventures, it should continue to equity account for them whether or not the investor intends to keep its interest or dispose of it. [FRS 9 paras 7, 43]. The investor should only stop equity accounting when the investment ceases to be a joint venture or an associate.

Acquisition rules

27.165 Often an investment in a joint venture or an associate is acquired in stages. Where this happens, FRS 9 states that the rules specified in paragraphs 50 to 52 of FRS 2 should be applied. [FRS 9 para 41]. These provisions require that where a group increases its interest in an undertaking that is already an associate or a joint venture, the identifiable assets and liabilities of that entity should be revalued to fair values and goodwill should be calculated only on the increase in interest by reference to those fair values. Consequently, a new fair value exercise will need to be carried out for each tranche of shares acquired, unless the difference between the fair values and the carrying amounts of the net assets attributable to the increase in stake is immaterial. For piecemeal acquisitions of subsidiaries, complying with FRS 2's requirements can conflict with the Act, because the Act requires the identifiable assets and liabilities of subsidiaries to be included in the consolidation at their fair value at the date of acquisition. This means that under the Act's provisions goodwill is calculated at the time the entity becomes a subsidiary, ignoring the effect of acquiring previous tranches. However, the conflict with the Act does not arise in accounting for piecemeal acquisitions of associates or joint ventures, because the Act does not deal with how to account for the acquisition of associates or joint ventures. Consequently, the rules in FRS 2 should be followed.

27.166 An undertaking might become an associate in a number of ways (whereas joint ventures tend to be set up as such from the outset), for example:

- The investing group acquires an additional investment in the undertaking to bring its voting rights to over 20 per cent.
- The investing group has an investment of over 20 per cent, but previously did not have board representation or significant influence over the financial

or operating policy decisions of the undertaking. It has now gained significant influence.

27.166.1 Acquisitions of associates or joint ventures can also arise where a parent sells a subsidiary for shares in another undertaking, which results in that other undertaking becoming an associate or joint venture of the vendor. Therefore, at the same time as the acquisition there is a disposal. The accounting for such transactions is considered in UITF Abstract 31, 'Exchanges of businesses or other non-monetary assets for an interest in a subsidiary, joint venture or associate', which is dealt with in chapter 26.

27.167 The treatment of an investment becoming an associate is illustrated in the example that follows.

Example

A group made an investment of 10% in a company a few years ago. The investment cost £25,000 and has subsequently been revalued to £50,000. It makes a further investment of 15% to bring its total investment to 25%. The fair value of the consideration given for the additional investment is £250,000. The net assets of the investee stand in its own books at the date of the second acquisition at £800,000. A fair value exercise has been undertaken at the date of acquisition which shows a fair value of net assets of £1.1m (including capitalised goodwill in the associate of £100,000). The adjusted capital and reserves of the associate are, as a consequence, £200,000 share capital and £900,000 reserves (which includes a £200,000 revaluation reserve). The associate has goodwill recognised in its balance sheet of £100,000. The goodwill arising on acquisition and the balance sheet treatment in the group would be as follows:

Cost of acquisition	£'000
Original investment	25
Fair value of consideration given	250
Total consideration	275
Consolidation goodwill	£'000
Total consideration	275
Adjusted capital and reserves excluding capitalised goodwill of £100,000 (being, 25% × (£1.1m – £100,000 goodwill))	250
Goodwill	25
Balance sheet (extract)	£'000
Interest in associated undertakings	
Share of net assets excluding goodwill (being, 25% × £1m)	250
Goodwill on acquisition	25
	275

The only adjustments that would be required in this example are to reduce the value of the original investment from its market value to cost and to eliminate the goodwill recognised in the associate. Consequently, the entries on consolidation would be to debit the revaluation reserve of the investor with £25,000 and credit the investment £25,000 and in the associate to credit goodwill £100,000 and debit reserves with £100,000. The goodwill arising on acquisition of £25,000 would be dealt with in accordance with FRS 10 (see chapter 25).

Alternatively, the goodwill arising on the acquisition of the additional 15% interest can also be calculated separately.

Goodwill arising on acquisition of the additional 15% interest	£'000
Fair value of consideration	250
Adjusted capital and reserves after elimination of goodwill arising in the associate (15% × (£1.1m – £100,000))	150
Goodwill	100

If goodwill of £100,000 is recognised, the difference between this amount and the goodwill of £25,000, being a credit of £75,000, calculated above represents a revaluation of the 10% interest and should be credited to the revaluation reserve. This calculation gives a fairer presentation of the goodwill arising on the increase in stake. At present, either method is acceptable.

27.168 In the example above, where an investment becomes an associate interest, it is possible to account for the increase in the investment in two ways. There are no specific rules in this area, so either method can be used. The technically correct method would be to calculate the goodwill arising on the acquisition of each tranche of the investment. However, this would generally not be practicable, because fair values would not necessarily be available at the time the original investment was made. The second method described above treats the increase in stake as a separate acquisition and gives a fairer result that the first method.

27.169 Although the second method described above is not required where an investment becomes an associate, it is necessary to consider each tranche separately where there is an increase in stake in an associate. FRS 2 requires that such a method is used for piecemeal acquisitions for subsidiaries and these same rules are applied *via* FRS 9 to increases in stake for associates. Consider the following example:

Example

A group made an investment in an associate of 20% in 20X2. The investment cost £12m and the book value (also fair value) of the associate's net assets at that date was £50m. In 20X8 it makes a further investment in the company of 20% to bring its total investment to 40%. Goodwill on the original acquisition of the associate was written off directly against reserves in the year of acquisition (following the rules that applied before the introduction of FRS 10). The net assets of the associate stand in its books at £68m on the date of the increase in stake. The associate would be treated as follows up to the date of the original acquisition:

Acquisition of associate	£m
Original investment in company	12.0
Fair value of net assets acquired (20% × £50m)	10.0
Goodwill arising	2.0

The fair value of the consideration given for the additional 20% is £16m. The fair value exercise shows that the company's net assets are worth £75m, which is also the adjusted capital and reserves. The goodwill on acquisition of the increase in stake would be calculated as follows:

Increase in stake in associate		
Cost of acquisition as shown in the investor's books	£m	£m
Original investment in company		12
Fair value of consideration given for new investment		16
Total investment in associate		28
Consolidation goodwill		
Total consideration		28
Adjusted capital and reserves		
being 20% × £50m	10	
being 20% × £75m	15	25
Goodwill		3
Goodwill previously written off		2
New goodwill arising on the increase in stake		1

The goodwill figure that emerges is instinctively correct as it reflects the fact that a premium of £1m arises on the acquisition of the additional 20% (that is, £16m – (£75m × 20%)). The results since the date of acquisition of the associate are attributable to the group and as such are correctly treated as post-acquisition. The alternative calculation of considering the total investment of £28m compared to the total share of net assets of £30m (that is, £75m × 40%) gives a total figure of negative goodwill of £2m and, as a consequence, negative goodwill of £4m arising on the increase in stake. This method understates the goodwill arising on the increase in stake and is not the method specified in FRS 2, but nevertheless may be used where the difference between the net fair values and the carrying amounts of the assets and liabilities attributable to the increase in stake is not material.

Disposal rules

27.170 The standard states that where an interest in a joint venture or an associate is disposed of, the profit or loss arising on disposal should be calculated after taking into account any related goodwill that has not previously been written off through the profit and loss account. [FRS 9 para 40]. For example, there may be a balance of unamortised goodwill that relates to the joint venture or associate which is capitalised as part of the interest in the investment. Alternatively, under FRS 10's transitional provisions, goodwill arising on the acquisition of joint ventures or associates that arose before the introduction of that standard may still be written off directly against reserves. Where this is so, the goodwill that applies to the proportion of the investment disposed of should be brought into account in calculating the profit or loss arising on the disposal.

27.171 When an entity ceases to be either a joint venture or an associate, the investor may retain all or some of its interest in that entity simply as an investment. In this circumstance, it is necessary to determine the carrying value of any remaining interest in the undertaking. This should be based on the percentage retained of the final carrying amount for the joint venture or associate at the date the entity ceased to qualify as a subsidiary or an associate. The remaining interest should also include any related goodwill. [FRS 9 para 42]. For example, if goodwill arising on the original acquisition of a 24 per cent interest in an associate was £50,000, then if the investment decreases to 12 per cent and the entity is no longer an associate, the carrying value of the investment should include 50 per cent of the goodwill arising on the original investment, that is, £25,000. The new carrying amount of the investment is a surrogate cost (not based on any consideration paid) and should be reviewed and written down, if necessary, to its recoverable amount. [FRS 9 para 42].

Example

A group has had an investment of 40% in an associate for a number of years. At the beginning of the accounting period, the balance sheets of the group excluding the associate and the group including the associate are as follows:

Summarised balance sheets

	Group excluding associate £'000	Associate £'000	Group including associate £'000
Fixed assets	500	230	500
Investment in associate:			
Cost	110	—	—
Equity accounting	—	—	125
Current assets	300	150	300
Current liabilities	(250)	(80)	(250)
	660	300	675
Share capital	300	100	300
Share premium	220	50	220
Profit and loss reserve	40	100	55
Other reserves	100	50	100
	660	300	675

The net assets of the associate at the date of acquisition of the 40% interest were £250,000. The goodwill that arose on the original acquisition of the associate is £10,000 (that is, £110,000 – (£250,000 × 40%)). The goodwill was capitalised on the acquisition of the associate to accord with FRS 10's requirements and £5,000 has been amortised to the profit and loss account since acquisition. Consequently, the group's investment in the associate of £125,000 is made up of its share of net assets of £120,000 (that is, £300,000 × 40%) plus the balance of goodwill unamortised of £5,000.

The group's profit and loss reserve of £55,000 is made up of £40,000 less goodwill amortisation of £5,000 plus the share of the associate's post-acquisition reserves of £20,000 (that is, £50,000 × 40%).

During the year the group disposes of 50% of its investment in the associate and no longer has board representation. Consequently, the remaining interest of 20% is no longer considered to be that of an associate, but represents a simple investment. The proceeds received on the sale are £70,000 and the net asset value of the associate at the date of sale is £320,000. Consequently, up to the date of sale of part of the group's investment in the associate, it made a profit of £20,000. The associate, therefore, becomes an investment part way through the year. The profit and loss accounts of the group excluding the former associate, the former associate and the group adjusted to include the revised carrying amount of the investment in the former associate are given below:

Summarised profit and loss accounts

	Group excluding interest	Former associate	Group including interest
	£'000	£'000	£'000
Operating profit	40	30	40.0
Share of operating profit of associate (note (a))	–	–	8.0
Operating profit including associate	40	30	48.0
Profit on sale of interest in associate (note (b))	15	–	3.5
Profit for the financial year	55	30	51.5
Reserve brought forward	40	100	55.0
Reserve carried forward	95	130	106.5

(a) The income from interest in the associated undertaking of £8,000 is the group's share of the results of the undertaking before the disposal (that is, 40% × £20,000).

(b) The profit on the sale of the share of the associate in the company selling the interest is £15,000, which is calculated by deducting from the sale proceeds of £70,000 the cost of the investment of £55,000 (that is, £110,000 × 50%). The profit on sale to the group is £3,500, which is calculated by deducting from the sale proceeds of £70,000 a 20% share of the associate's net assets consolidated up to the date of sale of £64,000 (that is, £320,000 × 20%) and half of the balance of unamortised goodwill of £2,500 that arose on the original acquisition.

At the group's year end, the balance sheets of the group and the former associate, which is now an investment, are set out below:

Summarised balance sheets

	Group excluding interest £'000	Former associate £'000	Group including interest £'000
Fixed assets	530	250	530.0
Investment (cost)	55	–	66.5
Current assets	390	170	390.0
Current liabilities	(260)	(90)	(260.0)
	715	330	726.5
Share capital	300	100	300.0
Share premium	220	50	220.0
Profit and loss reserve	95	130	106.5
Other reserves	100	50	100.0
	715	330	726.5

The investment in the former associate of £66,500 represents the share of net assets and goodwill retained by the group at the date of disposal (that is, (£320,000 × 20%) + (£5,000 × 50%)). The share of goodwill remaining is shown as part of the investment. The result is curious, because the investment in the company holding the interest is shown at a cost to that company of £55,000, but the group shows a cost to the group for the investment of £66,500. The difference of £11,500 represents the results of the associate recorded by the group which include retained reserves of £14,000 (that is, (£320,000 – £250,000) × 20%) less goodwill amortisation of £2,500. It is necessary to ensure that the carrying value of the investment in the group is not impaired, but as long as this is not the case, it would be possible in the company to revalue the investment to £66,500 the same value as shown in the group and credit to the revaluation reserve with the difference of £11,500.

27.172 An example of a disposal of a part interest in an associate is given in Table 27.12.

Table 27.12 – Lonmin Plc – Annual Report – 30 September 2004

Notes to the accounts (extract)

11 Associate (extract)

The investment in associate of $4 million shown above in 2003 represented an investment of 44% in the ordinary share capital of Platinum Australia Limited, a company incorporated in Australia. This investment was reduced to 38% during the year and on 30 September 2004 it was transferred to fixed asset investments following the resignation of Lonmin representatives from the board of Platinum Australia. The Group no longer exercises significant influence over the operating and financial policies of Platinum Australia and it is the Group's intention to realise this investment. These factors rebut the presumption that a holding of 20% or more should be presumed to exercise a significant influence and consequently this holding is now included as a fixed asset investment.

A joint venture becomes an associate

27.173 An interest in an entity that ceases to be a joint venture may still qualify as an associate. In this case, a profit or loss will arise on disposal, but the same rules, that is, equity accounting, will apply to the remaining interest, albeit disclosure is no longer required of the share of the associate's gross turnover or gross assets and gross liabilities on the face of the balance sheet. In addition, a joint venture can become an associate where the investor does not dispose of any interest in the entity. This would arise where the degree of influence the investor has over its investee changes from joint control to mere significant influence. In this situation, there will be no change to the share to be equity accounted only the level of disclosure will decrease from the 'gross equity' requirements to the less detailed normal equity accounting disclosures.

A subsidiary becomes an associate

27.174 Acquisitions of associates are considered from paragraph 27.165 above, but an associate can also arise from the disposal of an interest in a subsidiary, for example:

- The investing group sells a share of a subsidiary company, which has reduced the group's shareholding to below 50 per cent of the undertaking's voting rights although the group has retained significant influence and, accordingly, it is now an associate.
- A subsidiary issues shares to a third party such that the investing group's shareholding reduces below 50 per cent of the undertaking's voting rights, although significant influence is retained.
- The investing group ceases to exercise or have the power to exercise dominant influence at, for example, the 40 per cent level, but continues to have significant influence.

27.175 The treatment of a subsidiary becoming an associate is illustrated in the example that follows.

Example

A group has had an investment of 80% in a subsidiary for a number of years. At the beginning of the accounting period, the balance sheets of the group excluding the subsidiary and the group including the subsidiary are as follows:

Summarised balance sheets

	Group excluding sub £'000	Sub £'000	Group including sub £'000
Goodwill	–	–	10
Fixed assets	500	230	730
Investment in subsidiary	220	–	–
Current assets	300	150	450
Current liabilities	(250)	(80)	(330)
	770	300	860
Share capital	300	100	300
Share premium	220	50	220
Profit and loss reserve	150	100	180
Other reserves	100	50	100
Minority interests	–	–	60
	770	300	860

The goodwill that arose on the original acquisition of the subsidiary is £20,000 and is calculated as set out below. The goodwill was capitalised on the acquisition of the subsidiary to accord with the requirements of FRS 10 and £10,000 has been amortised to the profit and loss account since acquisition.

Cost of control account/goodwill

Investment	220,000	Share capital (80% × 100,000)	80,000
		Share premium (80% × 50,000)	40,000
		Pre-acq profit and loss reserve (80% × 50,000)	40,000
		Other reserves (80% × 50,000)	40,000
		Balance, *viz* goodwill	20,000
	220,000		220,000

The minority interests at the beginning of the year are calculated as follows:

Minority interests account

Minority interests	60,000	Share capital (20% × 100,000)	20,000
		Share premium (20% × 50,000)	10,000
		Profit and loss reserve (20% × 100,000)	20,000
		Other reserves (20% × 50,000)	10,000
	60,000		60,000

The group's profit and loss reserve of £180,000 is made up of £150,000 less goodwill amortisation of £10,000 plus the subsidiary's post-acquisition reserves of £40,000 (that is, £50,000 × 80%).

During the year the group disposes of 50% of its investment in the subsidiary. The proceeds received on the sale are £140,000 and the net asset value of the subsidiary at the date of sale is £320,000. Consequently, up to the date of sale of part of the group's investment in the subsidiary, it made a profit of £20,000. The subsidiary, therefore, becomes an associate part way through the year. The profit and loss accounts of the group excluding the associate, the associate, and the group including the associate using the equity method of accounting are given below:

Summarised profit and loss accounts

	Group excluding assoc £'000	Assoc £'000	Group including assoc £'000
Operating profit (note (a))	40	30	60
Share of operating profit of associate (note (b))	–	–	4
Operating profit including associate	40	30	64
Profit on sale of interest in subsidiary (note (c))	30	–	7
Operating profit	70	30	71
Minority interests (note (d))	–	–	(4)
Profit for the year	70	30	67
Reserve brought forward	150	100	180
Reserve carried forward	220	130	247

(a) The operating profit for the group of £60,000 represents the profit of the group of £40,000 (excluding the associate's profit), plus the profit of the subsidiary up to the date of sale of the 40% interest (which is £20,000).

(b) The income from interests in associated undertakings of £4,000 is the group's share of the results of the undertaking after it became an associate (that is, 40% × £10,000).

(c) The profit on the sale of the subsidiary in the company selling the interest is £30,000, which is calculated by deducting from the sale proceeds of £140,000 the cost of the investment of £110,000 (that is, £220,000 × 50%). The profit on sale to the group is £7,000, which is calculated by deducting from the sale proceeds of £140,000 a 40% share of the subsidiary's net assets consolidated up to the date of sale of £128,000 and half of the balance of unamortised goodwill that arose on the original acquisition of £5,000. The net assets of the subsidiary are made up of the net assets at the last balance sheet date of £300,000 plus the profit on ordinary activities to date of sale of £20,000. The group's share of those assets is £128,000 (that is, £320,000 × 40%).

(d) The minority interest figure of £4,000 is the minority's share of the profits of the subsidiary up to the date of sale of the 40% interest and is calculated by applying the minority's share of 20% to the profits recognised by the subsidiary in the period (that is, £20,000).

At the group's year end, the balance sheets of the group and the former subsidiary, which is now an associate, are set out below:

Summarised balance sheets

	Group excluding assoc £'000	Assoc £'000	Group including assoc £'000
Fixed assets	530	250	530
Investment in associate:			
Cost	110	–	–
Equity accounting	–	–	137
Current assets	460	170	460
Current liabilities	(260)	(90)	(260)
	840	330	867
Share capital	300	100	300
Share premium	220	50	220
Profit and loss reserve	220	130	247
Other reserves	100	50	100
Minority interest	–	–	–
	840	330	867

The investment in the associate of £137,000 represents the share of net assets and goodwill retained by the group at the date of sale (that is, (£320,000 × 40%) + (£10,000 × 50%)), together with the share of the associate's results that arose after the sale (that is, £10,000 × 40%). The goodwill is shown as part of the investment in the associate, but should also be separately disclosed in the notes to accord with FRS 9.

Equity accounting in a single company

27.176 How to account for investments in associates and joint ventures made by a single company is considered in chapter 6.

Joint arrangements

27.177 A 'joint arrangement' is a term which encompasses the following types of undertakings:

- A joint arrangement that has its own trade or business. This is a joint venture and should be gross equity accounted in accordance with the provisions of FRS 9, as explained earlier in this chapter.
- A 'joint arrangement that is not an entity'. This is a joint activity undertaken by two or more participants, whereby the activity does not amount to the carrying on of its own trade or business.
- A structure with the form, but not the substance, of a joint venture.

27.178 This section deals with the last two types of arrangement, which are referred to below as 'joint arrangements'. Joint arrangements of this type are required to be accounted for in a different way from associates and joint ventures; that is, interests in such arrangements should not be equity accounted. Both of these types of arrangement are somewhat similar in nature to joint ventures in that they will be formed by two or more participants and there will be an agreement covering the arrangement. But they differ from joint ventures in other respects.

Joint arrangement that is not an entity

27.179 A 'joint arrangement that is not an entity' is defined as:

> *"A contractual arrangement under which the participants engage in joint activities that do not create an entity because it would not be carrying on a trade or business of its own. A contractual arrangement where all significant matters of operating and financial policy are predetermined does not create an entity because the policies are those of its participants, not of a separate entity."* [FRS 9 para 4].

27.180 For this purpose, the term 'entity' is defined in FRS 9 to mean:

> *"A body corporate, partnership or unincorporated association carrying on a trade or business with or without a view to profit. The reference to carrying on a trade or business means a trade or business of its own and not just part of the trades or businesses of entities that have interests in it."* [FRS 9 para 4].

27.181 The term 'undertaking' in the Act uses identical wording to that in the first sentence of the definition of 'entity', but does not include the second qualifying sentence. Consequently, an undertaking can be a 'joint arrangement that is not an entity'. Appendix I to the standard, which includes a note on the legal requirements, says clearly that a joint arrangement may qualify as an undertaking under the Act, even where it does not carry on its own trade. It goes on to say that in such cases the undertaking acts merely as an agent for the venturers. [FRS 9 Appendix I para 6]. Therefore, a 'joint arrangement that is not an entity' can be an undertaking such as a limited company or a partnership or an unincorporated undertaking or may be a simple arrangement between the parties where a separate legal entity is not established, as it is the nature of its trading relationship that determines whether or not it will fall within the standard's definition, not how it is constituted. The term 'entity' is used to describe the substance rather than the legal form.

27.182 In contrast, for a joint arrangement to be a separate entity, that is, a joint venture, it must carry on a trade or business of its own and not just be part of its participants' trades or businesses. Such an entity will have some independence from its participants to pursue its own commercial strategy in buying and selling and will have access to the market in its own right for its main inputs and outputs.

[FRS 9 para 8]. This independence must be allowed within the objectives set by the agreement governing the entity, for example, in the joint venture agreement. If, on the other hand, the objectives are predetermined in that agreement and in effect the business unwinds exactly as specified within that agreement, the undertaking is likely to be a joint arrangement.

27.183 As stated above, to be a joint arrangement the undertaking must not carry on a trade or business of its own. For this reason, cost-sharing or risk-sharing arrangements are likely to be classified as joint arrangements and the standard gives as examples the following types of arrangements:

- Joint marketing.
- Joint distribution.
- Shared production facilities.

For example, a joint marketing arrangement established by two parties whereby the participants fund a joint marketing campaign is likely to be a joint arrangement. In such a case, the joint arrangement does not have access to the market in its own right, but is merely an extension of each participant's trade.

27.184 It follows that a company will normally *only* be a joint arrangement where it acts as an agent for its joint venturers. In this circumstance, it will not have access to the market in its own right as it is merely acting on its principals' behalf. Consequently, in the example of the joint marketing arrangement mentioned above, if the joint marketing is conducted within a limited company, it would only amount to a joint arrangement where the company is acting as an agent for its principals, otherwise it will be a joint venture or an associate.

27.185 Repetition of buying and selling is indicative of an arrangement carrying on a trade or business. Conversely, where an arrangement carries out a single project, such as a single property joint development, the undertaking will not carry on a separate trade or business where it acts as an agent for its principals' businesses. The undertaking would fall to be treated as a joint arrangement. [FRS 9 para 9]. This would apply, for example, to a short-term property development undertaken as a partnership. However, it appears that where a short-term property development is undertaken in a limited company, then it will not be a joint arrangement, unless the company is acting as an agent for its principals. Where an agency arrangement does not exist, such a company would fall within the definitions of an associate or a joint venture even where, for example, it only runs for 18 months. This is because in this situation the investment would be deemed to be held for the long term. Long term is defined in the standard by reference to whether or not the investment is held with a view to subsequent resale and not in relation to the length of time the undertaking will exist to fulfil its purpose. [FRS 9 para 4].

27.186 The standard mentions two further examples of joint arrangements that are not entities. The first is where the participants derive their benefit from products or services taken in kind, rather than by receiving a share in the results of trading. [FRS 9 para 8(a)]. This could, for example, be a joint research arrangement, whereby each of the participants benefits from the research, but are not billed a royalty specifically by the research company for using that patented research. The participants would fund the research through some other means. In addition, the standard states that joint arrangements can cover situations where the participants take their share of the joint product in cash where that commodity is actively traded. [FRS 9 para 8(a)]. This might arise, for example, in the oil and gas industry where two or more producers form a joint distribution arrangement.

27.187 The second situation described in the standard is where each participant's share of the output or result of the joint activity is determined by its supply of key inputs to the process producing that output or result. [FRS 9 para 8(b)]. An example might be where it is possible to segregate the activities of the entity so that each of the participants' results can be separately seen. This is very similar to the standard's description of a joint arrangement that has the form, but not the substance, of a joint venture (see further para 27.191).

27.188 The nature of a joint arrangement might change over time. For example, it might start out as such an arrangement whereby it is just an extension of its participants' trades, such as with the development and use of an oil or gas pipeline. But if the joint arrangement starts to trade with third parties that are not participants in the joint arrangement, then it may well take on the form of a joint venture entity and require to be gross equity accounted. [FRS 9 para 9].

27.189 In practice, it will often be difficult to judge whether or not an undertaking is a joint arrangement or a joint venture. The following examples illustrate two different structures.

Example 1

Three venturers form a company to supply IT services to a customer. The parties to the arrangement each own 33% of the company's shares. The venturers supply different IT products, with one supplying the software, another the hardware and the third supplying the systems expertise. The sole purpose for the company is to allow the parties to invoice the customer in one name. The supplier of the systems expertise manages the provision of the hardware and software supply and gives a performance guarantee to the customer. The hardware supply represents 50% of the company's turnover, the software accounts for 20% and the system development 30%. The operation of the company is governed by a shareholder agreement with the company and sub-contract agreements with the venturers. The company makes no margin on the on-billing of the hardware, software and systems development, any administrative expenses being recharged to the participants.

In this situation, it is clear that the financial and operating policies of the company are predetermined by the shareholder agreement and the other agreements surrounding the arrangement. In addition, the undertaking does not have access to the market in its own right as it is merely a facility through which the participants' businesses are conducted and, as a consequence, is acting as their agent. Therefore, the undertaking would be judged to be a joint arrangement rather than a joint venture under FRS 9's provisions.

Example 2

Three venturers form a company to bid for the provision of healthcare services to a Health Trust under the Private Finance Initiative (PFI). The parties to the venture are a construction company, a service provider and an equity investment fund. Each of the venturers owns 33% of the company's shares. The company constructs a hospital, which is financed in part by the equity venturers and also by bank funding secured on the payments to be made by the Health Trust (that is, the unitary payment). In substance the construction and the service provision are sub-contracted to two of the venturers. The unitary payment made by the Health Trust varies depending upon the delivery performance under the terms of the PFI contract. The property has been judged to be on balance sheet of the company. There is a shareholder agreement with the company and sub-contract agreements with the venturers. Under the shareholder agreement, profits or losses of the company are shared equally between the venturers and all decisions have to have full agreement of the venturers (there are also arbitration procedures specified in the agreement). The amount the service provider receives is dependent upon its performance and this is detailed in its sub-contract agreement.

For the service provider, the arrangement could be either a joint venture or a joint arrangement. At first sight, the structure has many of the features of a joint arrangement. For example, most of the financial and operating policies are predetermined in the agreements (these include, the PFI agreement, the shareholder agreement, the loan agreement with the bank and the sub-contract agreements with the venturers). Also, it could be argued that the company does not have access to the market in its own right, because it only has one customer under the PFI agreement and its relationship with the Health Trust was established in the agreements. But this argument ignores the fact that the company is carrying on a business of its own, which is the provision of an *integrated* service to the Health Trust, and is not acting as an agent in this respect. In addition, the company could provide a similar service for other customers in the future and, as a consequence, has access to the market in its own right. Therefore, the facts of this case indicate that the undertaking falls within the definition of a joint venture, which should be accounted for under the gross equity accounting method by its venturers rather than falling to be treated as a joint arrangement.

27.190 Joint arrangements will often be agency type arrangements, where it is clear that the undertaking's business is just an extension of the separate businesses of its venturers and where it does not have access to the market in its own right.

Joint venture with the substance of a joint arrangement

27.191 Another type of joint arrangement identified in the standard is an undertaking that has the form of a joint venture, but not the substance of one. Such an arrangement would arise where the joint venture undertaking is used only as a means for each participant to carry on its own business. [FRS 9 para 24]. In this type of situation the venturers would operate their own businesses separately within the structure. The framework entity would act merely as an agent for each of the venturers, who are able to identify their own share of the assets, liabilities and cash flows within the framework. [FRS 9 para 25]. Where such an arrangement exists and is conducted through a limited company, the undertaking will only be a joint arrangement if it acts as an agent for its principals. [FRS 9 App I para 5].

27.192 Some securitisation special purpose vehicles work in this way. Each of the originators/participants in the special purpose vehicle will be able to identify the assets (such as, mortgage receivables) that it has contributed to the venture and its benefits and risks arise directly from those assets and their related finance.

Accounting for joint arrangements

27.193 FRS 9 requires the same accounting treatment for both the types of joint arrangements identified above. The only requirement specified in the standard is that the participants in such a joint arrangement should account for their own assets, liabilities and cash flows, measured according to the terms of the agreement governing the arrangement (for example see Table 27.13). [FRS 9 paras 18, 24].

Table 27.13 — Lonrho Plc — Annual Report and Accounts — 30 September 1998

Notes to the Accounts (extract)

Statement on accounting policies (extract)

Joint arrangements
The Group has certain contractual agreements with other participants to engage in joint activities that do not create an entity carrying on a trade or business of its own. The Group includes its share of assets, liabilities and cashflows in such joint arrangements, measured in accordance with the terms of each arrangement, which is usually pro-rata to the Group's interest in the joint arrangement.

27.194 In practice this requirement gives rise to a number of interpretation problems. First, the requirement does not specifically state that the participants must account also for the trading impact of those transactions, but this is implied because this will be the effect of accounting for the changes in assets and liabilities. In addition, appendix III to the standard says the accounting should be for the investor's *"own share of the assets, liabilities and cash flows"* as compared to the standard itself which makes no mention of the word 'share'. [FRS 9 App III para 8]. Consequently, how to account for the transactions might not be obvious. In most situations the amounts to be accounted for will not be governed by the participant's equity share, but will be dependent upon the economic sharing arrangements under the arrangement. For example, a joint billing arrangement might be conducted through an undertaking where the equity share is 50/50, but where one of the participants generates 80 per cent of the transactions, in which case it should recognise its own transactions undertaken by the joint arrangement. In this type of situation it will be necessary to consider carefully how any residual profit or loss in the joint arrangement is dealt with. In other situations, it might be more appropriate to account for the underlying transactions that specifically relate to the particular investor, rather than a share of the joint arrangement's transactions.

27.195 The paragraphs that follow consider how participants in different types of joint arrangement should account for their underlying transactions.

Joint agreements between participants

27.196 Joint arrangements that are merely agreements between the participants where there is no undertaking involved are easily dealt with under the standard's provisions. It is relatively simple for the participants to account for their share of the assets and liabilities and cash flows under the arrangement in their individual financial statements. Indeed, this is how transactions of this nature were accounted for before FRS 9 became standard practice.

27.197 Joint arrangements of this nature encompass jointly controlled operations and jointly controlled assets. These are dealt with in IAS 31, 'Interests in joint ventures', and FRS 9 follows the same path. Because IAS 31 has more detailed guidance than FRS 9, the explanation that follows draws heavily on IAS 31's provisions. In these types of arrangements, the venturers use their own assets and resources rather than establishing a company, partnership or other entity. Examples given in IAS 31 of jointly controlled operations include the manufacture, marketing and distribution jointly of a particular product, such as an aircraft. Different parts of the manufacturing process are carried out by the venturers, which bear their own costs and take a share of the revenues of the aircraft in accordance with the joint agreement. The accounting for jointly controlled operations under FRS 9 is the same as under IAS 31, with each of the venturers recognising in its individual financial statements and in its consolidated financial statements:

- The assets that it controls and the liabilities that it incurs.
- The expenses that it incurs and its share of the income that it earns from the sale of goods or services by the joint venture.

No consolidation adjustments or other consolidation procedures are necessary, because the assets, liabilities, income and expenses are already recognised in each of the joint venturers' financial statements. [IAS 31 para 16].

Example

Two companies decide to undertake a joint road construction project. They agree to supply different assets and staff to the joint arrangement. The joint arrangement has a separate bank account. The participants charge rental for their plant used in the project to the bank account and also have an agreed staff cost per hour, which is also charged to that account. The participants fund the account and invoice the customer in their joint names. Any surplus is shared 50/50.

The joint arrangement transactions that need to be reflected in each participant's accounts are unlikely to be a straight share of those transactions, but will depend on the costs that the participants have borne themselves. Therefore, although a participant is charging a rental to the joint arrangement for the use of its plant, that plant is already accounted for as a fixed asset in that participant's balance sheet and its profit and loss account will already bear a normal depreciation charge for the asset's use. The rental to the joint arrangement should be eliminated and in its place the share of the joint arrangement's income should be recognised. Similarly, the participant will have charged its actual staff costs in its profit and loss account, so it will need to eliminate any charge made to the joint arrangement on a different basis. The joint arrangement will bill its customers for the work undertaken by the venture and it would be appropriate for the participant to recognise its share (50% in this case) in its turnover. In order to arrive at the correct profit share in the participant's profit and loss account, it will be necessary to book an equalisation charge or credit in order to take into account that the actual costs incurred by the participant might be different from its share of the joint arrangement's costs. Consequently, the participant may in part be funding the costs of its joint arrangement partner (or *vice versa*).

Example 2

Company A and company B have entered into a joint arrangement to develop products for sale. The strategy of the joint arrangement is agreed jointly. The day to day management of the production is provided by company A who builds the product. Company A makes a 10% margin on the products it sells to the joint arrangement. Company B identified the opportunity and provided £40,000 investment capital. Company A provided £10,000 investment capital. Profits are shared 50/50.

The joint arrangement took out a loan of £100,000 and the interest charge for the year on this loan is £8,000. During the joint arrangement's first year, company A incurred costs of £70,000 in respect of work in progress, of which £50,000 was charged to the joint arrangement at £55,000. The joint arrangement made property sales to third parties of £40,000 and the cost of those sales in the joint arrangement was £30,000. There are no third party debtors or creditors at the year end as all transactions have been settled.

	Company A	JA	50% JA	Adjustments	Company A adjustments
	£'000	£'000	£'000	£'000	£'000
Balance sheet					
Investment	10.0	—	—	(10.0) (c)	—
Stock and work in progress					
Costs	70.0	55.0	27.5	(27.5)(a)	70.0
Tfr to cost of sales	(50.0)	(30.0)	(15.0)	25.0(b)	(40.0)
	20.0	25.0	12.5	(2.5)	30.0
Cash	(25.0)	127.0	63.5		38.5
	5.0	152.0	76.0	(12.5)	68.5
Loan	—	100.0	50.0		50.0
	5.0	52.0	26.0	(12.5)	18.5
Liability to company B	—	50.0	25.0	(10.0)(c)	15.0
Profit and loss account	5.0	2.0	1.0	(2.5)	3.5
	5.0	52.0	26.0	(12.5)	18.5
Profit and loss account					
Sales	55.0	400	20.0	(27.5)(a)	47.5
Cost of sales	(50.0)	(30.0)	(15.0)	25.0(b)	(40.0)
Gross profit	5.0	10.0	5.0	(2.5)	7.5
Interest	—	(8.0)	(4.0)		(4.0)
Net profit	5.0	2.0	1.0	(2.5)	3.5

(a) Half of company A's sales have in effect been made to company B and these can continue to be recognised by company A. But £27,500 of company A's sales need to be eliminated and replaced by its share of the sales made by the joint arrangement (that is, £20,000).

(b) Similarly, half of company A's cost of sales relates to sales made in effect to company B, the other half relate (that is, £25,000) to the goods sold to the joint arrangement at a profit margin of 10% and these need to be eliminated. The balance of stock of £30,000 is made up of company A's stock and work in progress together with the share outstanding in the joint arrangement of £12,500, less the profit element included in this stock of £2,500, which has been eliminated.

(c) There is a disparity in the amount of capital contributed by both of the parties to the joint arrangement. In effect this means that company A has an obligation under the arrangement to fund part of the repayment of company B's contribution out of its share of the resources of the joint arrangement. This obligation is likely to be settled eventually out of company A's share of the cash resources of the joint arrangement.

27.198 Many activities in the oil, gas and mineral extraction industries involve the use of jointly controlled assets. An often cited example is where a number of venturers jointly control and operate an oil pipeline. Typically in such arrangements, each venturer uses the pipeline to transport its own product, in return for which it bears an agreed proportion of the expenses of operating the pipeline. Again the accounting under FRS 9 for such ventures is the same as required under IAS 31. Each venturer shows in its individual financial statements and in its consolidated financial statements:

- Its share of the jointly controlled assets, classified according to the nature of the assets rather than as an investment. For example, a share of a jointly controlled oil pipeline is classified as property, plant and equipment.
- Any liabilities that it has incurred, for example, those incurred to finance its share of the asset.
- Its share of any liabilities incurred jointly with other venturers.
- Any income from the sale or use of its share of the output, together with its share of any expenses incurred.
- Any expenses which it has incurred in respect of its interest in the venture, for example those related to financing the venturer's interest in the assets and selling its share of the output.

As with joint operations, no consolidation adjustments or other consolidation procedures are necessary, because the assets, liabilities, income and expenses are already recognised in each of the joint venturers' financial statements. [IAS 31 para 22].

Joint arrangements in unincorporated undertakings including partnerships

27.199 FRS 9 goes further than IAS 31 and identifies that joint arrangements can arise in unincorporated undertakings, such as partnerships. FRS 9 requires that participants who enter into joint arrangements that are carried out in unincorporated undertakings and in partnerships should similarly account for their share of the assets, liabilities and cash flows under the arrangement in their individual financial statements and, as a consequence, these transactions will find their way into the group's consolidated financial statements.

27.200 Two legal issues arise from this accounting treatment. First, whether on consolidation the Companies Act allows a company to account for its joint arrangement entity's results in this way. Before the introduction of FRS 9, it was quite acceptable in the group's consolidated financial statements to proportionately consolidate the results of unincorporated joint ventures such as partnerships, as this is an option under the legislation (equity accounting also being permissible under the Act). The Act's rules remain unchanged following the introduction of FRS 9, so it would appear possible to continue to adopt proportional consolidation for such entities under the Act. To all intents and purposes in the group's consolidated financial statements, proportional consolidation gives the same result as FRS 9's requirement to account for the participant's share of the assets and liabilities and cash flows under the arrangements.

27.201 The second issue arises in the participant's individual financial statements. The issue is whether or not it is legal to include the appropriate share of the joint arrangement's transactions, which arise in a separate legal entity, in the financial statements of the participant, which will generally be a limited company. Where the joint venture entity is a partnership, it will be possible for the partners to record their share of the partnership's transactions in their individual financial statements. It is generally appropriate to do this, however, only where there is no restriction on the distribution of the partnership's profits and reserves. This basis of accounting is the same as that used prior to the introduction of FRS 9 for many partnership arrangements of this nature.

27.202 Furthermore, where the joint arrangement is acting as an agent of each of the participants (which might arise, for example, where the joint arrangement entity is on-billing goods for each participant), the share of the transactions should rightly be included in each principal's (that is, each participant's) books. Whether the transactions will be recorded in the agent's (that is, the joint arrangement entity's) books, or will be recorded at nil value, depends upon whether or not the entity is acting as a disclosed or an undisclosed agent (see chapter 9).

Joint arrangements in limited companies

27.203 Because of the definition of a joint arrangement, it is quite possible under FRS 9 for a limited company to be a joint arrangement. As for other joint arrangements FRS 9 requires that participants who invest in limited companies that are joint arrangements should account for their share of the assets and liabilities and cash flows under the arrangement in their individual financial statements and, as a consequence, in their group's consolidated financial statements.

27.204 As explained in paragraph 27.184 above, joint arrangements will not normally arise in a company, unless the undertaking acts as an agent of its participants. Consequently, where the joint arrangement company acts as either a disclosed agent or an undisclosed agent, the appropriate share of transactions undertaken by the agent should rightly be included in each principal's (that is, each participant's) books. Consequently, the participant's share of the joint arrangement's transactions would appear in its individual financial statements and, as a result, in its consolidated financial statements. This accounting treatment complies with FRS 9 and also with the Act. Furthermore, whether or not the transactions are also recorded in the agent's (that is, the joint arrangement undertaking's) books will depend on whether the joint arrangement is a disclosed agent or an undisclosed agent (see further chapter 9).

Joint arrangements versus quasi-subsidiaries

27.205 Following the FRRP ruling made against Associated Nursing Services plc there has been confusion concerning the distinction between a joint venture and a quasi-subsidiary and, therefore, concerning the entities that need to be consolidated in full or accounted for in some other way in the group's consolidated financial statements. The ruling was made in February 1997, before FRS 9's publication and that confusion has now been compounded by the advent of joint arrangements. The FRRP ruling noted that Associated Nursing Services had entered into joint ventures with two partners and it had treated the joint ventures as associated undertakings in its 1995 and 1996 financial statements under the rules in SSAP 1 prior to FRS 9's publication.

27.206 In one case, which involved a joint venture with a bank, the board of the joint venture company in question was 'deadlocked'. It was the FRRP's view that the financial and operating policies of that company were substantially predetermined by underlying agreements; and through its interest in the joint venture Associated Nursing Services gained benefits arising from the net assets of the company, such that it had control. In the other case a venture capital arrangement with five venture capital funds had been set up through an intermediary. In the FRRP's view the financial and operating policies of that company were again substantially predetermined by underlying agreements. Even though in that case Associated Nursing Services held only a minority of the ordinary share capital, the investor's interests were effectively limited and the FRRP took the view that Associated Nursing Services gained benefits arising from the company's net assets, such that it had control.

27.207 In the FRRP's view, therefore, the substance of the arrangements was that the joint venture companies were in fact quasi-subsidiaries as defined by FRS 5. Consequently, they should not have been accounted for by the equity method, but should have been treated, as FRS 5 requires, as if they were subsidiaries. The ruling hinges on paragraph 34 of FRS 5 which states that: *"where the financial and operating policies of a vehicle are in substance pre-determined, contractually or otherwise, the party possessing control will be the one that gains the benefits arising from the net assets of the vehicle"*.

27.208 The wording in paragraph 34 of FRS 5 uses similar terminology to that used in the definition of a 'joint arrangement that is not an entity' in paragraph 4 of FRS 9. Part of the joint arrangement definition says that:

> *"A contractual arrangement where all significant matters of operating and financial policy are predetermined does not create an entity because the policies are those of its participants not of a separate entity."*

The feature which distinguishes a joint arrangement from a quasi-subsidiary seems to be that although in both a joint arrangement and a quasi-subsidiary the financial and operating policies may be predetermined, in a quasi-subsidiary the investor must gain the benefits arising from the net assets of the vehicle. This is because for an investment to meet the definition of a quasi-subsidiary the investment must give substantially the same benefits and risks to the investor as if it were an actual subsidiary.

Example

An entity is established to undertake a property development. There are two parties to the arrangement each providing 50% of the equity. The property development activities of the venture are all predetermined in the agreements with the venturers setting up the undertaking and with the providers of finance, including the profit-sharing arrangements. Where the profit-sharing arrangements are 50/50 between the parties, this type of venture would seem to fall within the joint arrangement category of investment under FRS 9. The investor would then account for its share of the arrangement, as considered in the paragraphs above. However, where the profit-sharing arrangements are not in line with the venturers' equity investment and, for example, one of the parties is given (say) 90% of the profits generated by the business, then this would indicate that that party gains the benefits arising from the net assets of the vehicle. If this is the case, then the venture is a quasi-subsidiary of that investor and should be consolidated in its financial statements. Where the profit sharing arrangements are (say) 60:40, judgment will be needed to decide whether to account for the arrangement as a joint arrangement or as a quasi-subsidiary.

27078

Chapter 28

Merger accounting

	Page
Introduction	28001
Merger accounting conditions	28002
Offer to shareholders test	28003
Ninety per cent holding test	28004
Immaterial cash or non-equity consideration test	28005
Disposal of peripheral part of business	28008
Vendor placings and vendor rights	28009
No identifiable acquirer or acquiree test	28010
Joint participation in management test	28012
Relative size test	28013
Full participation in future performance test	28014
Merger accounting principles	28016
Applicability to business combinations achieved by using a new parent company	28019
Applicability to group reconstructions	28020
Applicability to other forms of business combination	28024
Accounting treatment of the investment in an acquired company	28024
Difference on consolidation	28025
Merger expenses	28028
Accounting periods	28031
Comparison of acquisition accounting with merger accounting	28034
Disclosure for merger accounting	28039
Consolidated financial statements	28039

Chapter 28

Merger accounting

Introduction

28.1 Chapter 25 considers various matters concerning acquisition accounting. This chapter looks at the other accounting method a company must use in certain circumstances when preparing consolidated financial statements, namely merger accounting.

28.2 Although there are rare exceptions, a prerequisite for merger accounting is normally that shares issued as consideration for the combination must be eligible for merger relief or for group reconstruction relief. The legal provisions relating to these reliefs are described in chapter 23 and this chapter assumes knowledge of those provisions. Merger or group reconstruction relief may also be obtained where acquisition accounting rather than merger accounting is required for a combination. This is because the conditions for merger accounting are more restrictive than the conditions for obtaining merger or group reconstruction relief.

28.3 Schedule 4A to the Companies Act 1985 includes certain conditions that must apply to an acquisition before it can be accounted for as a merger in consolidated financial statements. Furthermore, Schedule 4A to the Act includes certain additional disclosure requirements that apply where an acquisition is accounted for as a merger.

28.4 In September 1994 the ASB issued FRS 6, 'Acquisitions and mergers', which introduced much more stringent criteria than those in the previous accounting standard (SSAP 23) and which required merger accounting to be adopted in consolidated financial statements in those situations where the criteria were met. The provisions of both the Act and FRS 6 are considered in detail in the paragraphs that follow.

28.5 Although the criteria for merger accounting in FRS 6 are stringent, international standard-setters do not consider that they are sufficient to enable 'true mergers' to be distinguished from business combinations in which one entity obtains control of another entity (or entities). Therefore, in March 2004, the IASB issued IFRS 3, 'Business combinations', which brings IFRS into line with US GAAP by prohibiting merger accounting. It requires the use of acquisition accounting ('the purchase method') for all business combinations within its scope. IFRS 3 represents the completion of the first phase of the IASB's larger project on business combinations. As part of its programme of converging UK GAAP with IFRS, in July 2005 the ASB issued FRED 36, 'Business Combinations', proposing the introduction of IFRS 3 into UK GAAP to replace FRS 6 and FRS 7.

[The next paragraph is 28.9.]

Merger accounting conditions

28.9 The objectives of FRS 6 are:

- To ensure that merger accounting is used only for those business combinations that are not, in substance, the acquisition of one entity by another, but the formation of a new reporting entity as a substantially equal partnership where no party is dominant.
- To ensure the use of acquisition accounting for all other business combinations.
- To ensure that in either case the financial statements provide relevant information concerning the effect of the combination.

28.10 To this end the FRS defines a merger as:

> *"A business combination that results in the creation of a new reporting entity formed from the combining parties, in which the shareholders of the combining entities come together in a partnership for the mutual sharing of the risks and benefits of the combined entity, and in which no party to the combination in substance obtains control over any other, or is otherwise seen to be dominant, whether by virtue of the proportion of its shareholders' rights in the combined entity, the influence of its directors or otherwise."* [FRS 6 para 2].

28.11 If a business combination satisfies the conditions for merger accounting outlined in the Act and the combination meets the definition of a merger under FRS 6 then the group must use merger accounting to account for it. To meet the definition of a merger in FRS 6 the combination *must* satisfy certain conditions which are described below. If the business combination fails to satisfy the conditions for merger accounting, then the group *must* use acquisition accounting for the business combination. [CA85 4A Sch 8]. Situations may arise where the Act's conditions are satisfied, but those of FRS 6 are not. Where this arises, merger accounting should not be used. This is because the Act says the adoption of the merger method of accounting must accord with generally accepted accounting principles or practice (which currently means the conditions contained in FRS 6). [CA85 4A Sch 10(1)(d)]. Similarly, if FRS 6's conditions are satisfied, but those of the Act are not, merger accounting should not be used.

28.12 The conditions contained in the Act and FRS 6 require certain tests to be satisfied as follows:

- Offer to shareholders test.
- 90 per cent holding test.
- Immaterial cash or non-equity consideration test.
- No identifiable acquirer or acquiree test.

- Joint participation in management test.
- Relative size test.
- Full participation in future performance test.

28.13 Each of these tests is considered in the paragraphs that follow and the provisions of the Act and FRS 6 are contrasted.

Offer to shareholders test

28.14 The Act requires that the shares acquired as a result of the acquisition must be obtained by an arrangement providing for the issue of equity shares by the parent or any of its subsidiaries. [CA85 4A Sch 10(1)(b)]. Furthermore, FRS 6 requires that all but an immaterial proportion of the consideration must be in the form of equity shares. (See 'Immaterial cash or non-equity consideration test' below.) The definition of equity in FRS 6 is much more restrictive than the Act's definition. [FRS 6 para 2]. The reason for adopting the more restrictive definition in FRS 6 is to prevent the Act's condition, that the offer is satisfied by the issue of equity shares, being met by the use of shares that, although within the legal definition of equity, have nonetheless characteristics that are closer to non-equity shares. The difference between equity as defined in the Act and as defined in FRS 6 is described below.

28.15 Equity shares are defined in the Act as the issued share capital of a company excluding any part which, neither as respects dividends nor as respects capital, carries any right to participate beyond a specified amount in a distribution. [CA85 Sec 744; CA06 Sec 548]. Equity shares represent the residual interests in a company and as such confer on their holders the right to share in the net assets of the company (after settling any prior claims). Such shares are normally termed ordinary shares, but it is quite possible for a preference share to be constructed in such a way that it meets the Act's definition of equity. Non-equity shares as defined in the Act, by contrast, are shares which fall outside this definition.

28.16 FRS 6 provides its own definitions of equity and non-equity shares rather than adopting the Act's definitions. These are framed by reference to FRS 25, the result of which is that shares are classified as equity or non-equity based on their substance. [FRS 6 para 2].

28.17 It follows that under FRS 6 non-equity is a broader category than under the Act. The definition of non-equity shares in FRS 6 has been deliberately widely drawn so that, for instance, a right to a dividend or to a redemption payment that is for a limited amount will require the share to be treated as non-equity. Consequently, it is quite possible for a company to issue (say) a preference share which is classified as equity share capital under the Act, but the preference share would be non-equity under FRS 6, for example, for the purposes of determining whether all but an immaterial proportion of the consideration given in a business combination is in the form of equity shares.

28.18 This situation could arise for instance where a company issued as consideration for a business combination preference shares which had a fixed dividend and unrestricted rights to distributions on winding up. The shares might, for instance, have a right on liquidation to share in a fixed percentage of the balance on the company's share premium account. Whereas these shares would qualify under the Act as equity because the limitations on distributions apply only to dividends and not to capital, they would not qualify as equity under FRS 6, because limitation on either dividends or capital means they are most likely non-equity under FRS 25. Therefore, although they qualify as equity for the purpose of obtaining merger relief under the Act, they do not count as equity under FRS 6 for the purpose of determining whether all but an immaterial proportion of the consideration is in the form of equity shares. (See 'Immaterial cash or non-equity consideration test' below.)

[The next paragraph is 28.21.]

Ninety per cent holding test

28.21 The Act requires that at least 90 per cent of the nominal value of the 'relevant shares' in an undertaking acquired (excluding any shares in the undertaking held as treasury shares) as a result of an arrangement must be held by or on behalf of the parent and its subsidiaries. [CA85 4A Sch 10(1)(a)]. In this context, 'relevant shares' means those shares in the acquired company that carry unrestricted rights to participate both in its distributions and in its assets upon liquidation. [CA85 4A Sch 10(2)]. This is in effect 'super-equity', and would include most ordinary share capital, but would exclude most other forms of participating preference shares (although these shares are often equity shares as defined in the Act). In this sense, therefore, the Act's definition of 'relevant shares' is similar to FRS 6's definition of equity.

28.22 The Act also states that the proportion referred to in paragraph 28.21, that is 90 per cent of the nominal value of the relevant shares, must be attained pursuant to an arrangement providing for the issue of equity shares. [CA85 4A Sch 10(b)]. However, this does not mean that, in order to merger account, the parent and its subsidiaries cannot hold more than 10 per cent of the nominal value of the relevant shares before the acquisition. It merely means that as a result of the offer the company must have reached at least a 90 per cent holding in the relevant shares (taking into account any prior holdings). For this purpose, 'relevant shares' has the same meaning as explained in paragraph 28.21 above.

28.23 Similarly under FRS 6 there is no limit on prior holdings, although the nature of the consideration given for the prior holding *is* relevant. As an example a company might hold 25 per cent of the relevant equity shares in another company that it acquired over two years before (see para 28.26 below) and might then obtain a further 65 per cent of the relevant shares of that other company as a result of an offer. In such a situation, and provided that all the other conditions for merger accounting were met, the existence of a prior holding of 25 per cent would not prevent merger accounting being adopted. This contrasts with

SSAP 23, which prohibited merger accounting where there was a prior holding of 20 per cent or more that had been acquired at any time in the past.

Immaterial cash or non-equity consideration test

28.24 Where merger accounting is adopted, the consideration given for the relevant shares can include other consideration such as debentures and cash. However, the provisions of the Act restrict significantly the other consideration that can be given where the merger accounting method is to be used. The fair value of such other consideration given by the parent and its subsidiaries cannot exceed more than 10 per cent of the *nominal value* of the equity shares issued as part of the consideration pursuant to the arrangement. [CA85 4A Sch 10(c)].

28.25 The provisions of the Act contrast with the requirement included in FRS 6 where the following conditions must apply:

- Under the terms of the combination or related arrangements the consideration received by equity shareholders of each party to the combination, in relation to their equity shareholding, comprises primarily equity shares in the combined entity; and any non-equity consideration, or equity shares carrying substantially reduced voting or distribution rights, represents an immaterial proportion of the fair value of the consideration received by the shareholders.
- Where one of the combining entities has, within the period of two years before the combination, acquired equity shares in another of the combining entities, the consideration for this acquisition should be taken into account in determining whether this criterion (that is, the immaterial cash or non-equity consideration test) has been met.
- For the purposes of the above provisions, the consideration should not be taken to include the distribution to shareholders of:
  - an interest in a peripheral part of the business of the entity in which they were shareholders and that does not form part of the combined entity; or
  - the proceeds of the sale of such a business, or loan stock representing such proceeds.

A 'peripheral part of the business' is one which can be disposed of without having a material effect on the nature and focus of the entity's operations. [FRS 6 paras 9, 10].

28.26 Under these requirements in FRS 6, the fair value of the total consideration that the offeror gives should include also the fair value of the consideration that the offeror gave for shares that it acquired within two years before the offer. [FRS 6 para 9]. (In contrast, it is not necessary to take prior holdings into account in calculating the Act's limit mentioned in paragraph 28.21.)

28.27 It should be noted that the non-equity restriction in the Act relates to ten per cent of the *nominal* value of equity shares issued, whereas the restriction in FRS 6 relates to an immaterial proportion of the *fair* value of the consideration.

28.28 In some circumstances this may mean that the conditions of the Act are more restrictive than those of the standard as the following example demonstrates.

Example

A company issues equity shares in connection with a business combination, which have a nominal value of £100,000 together with £15,000 in cash. The fair value of the shares issued is £1,485,000. In this situation the business combination does not qualify for merger accounting under the Act, because the cash element is greater than 10% of the nominal value of the equity shares issued. The combination would however satisfy the condition in FRS 6, that not more than immaterial proportion of the fair value of the consideration is in the form of non-equity consideration, because in this case it represents only 1% of the fair value. Because the Act's requirement also has to be satisfied, however, merger accounting would not be possible in this case.

If in the above example the consideration had been £100,000 nominal value of equity shares and £10,000 cash, the conditions of the Act would have been satisfied and merger accounting would be permitted under both the Act and FRS 6. This might be so even if the fair value of the consideration had been only £110,000, that is if the shares had been issued at par (the lowest possible amount for which they could be issued) because even then the cash element of the total fair value would have been less than 10% of the total fair value. This conclusion is based on the assumption that 'immaterial' in FRS 6 may be interpreted as less than 10%. However, interpretations may vary as discussed in paragraph 28.32 below.

28.29 Although the ten per cent condition in the Act appears more restrictive than the condition of FRS 6, the Act does not require holdings acquired before the offer, and which are not part of the arrangement through which the 90 per cent holding is acquired, to be taken into account in determining the cash or non-equity element of the consideration. In contrast, FRS 6 requires that any acquisition by one of the combining parties of equity shares in the other within two years before the combination should be taken into account in determining whether or not non-equity consideration represents more than an immaterial proportion of the total consideration. Where such acquisitions have taken place the conditions of FRS 6 may be more restrictive than those of the Act, as the following example demonstrates.

Example

Company B has share capital of 1,000 £1 equity shares. Company A has previously acquired 100 shares in company B for £5,000 (that is, £50 per share). These shares were acquired entirely for cash 18 months ago and were not acquired as part of an arrangement to acquire over 90% of company B. Company A now wishes to acquire the remaining 900 shares in company B. The value of company B has decreased since company A acquired its previous holding and the 900 shares are valued at £45 per share. The consideration for these 900 shares is to be given entirely by an issue of company A's equity shares. A's equity shares to be issued have a nominal value of £20,000 and fair value of £40,500.

The fair value of the total consideration that company A will have given is:

	£
Cash	5,000
Fair value of shares (namely, 900 × £45)	40,500
Total consideration	45,500

Company A makes its offer for 90% of the relevant shares of company B and because this offer is wholly for shares, the Act's provisions on the cash limit explained above do not apply. It, therefore, does not matter that the £5,000 cash exceeds 10% of the £20,000 nominal value of the A shares that are issued. However, because the previous acquisition was made within two years of the current offer and the non-equity element represents 10.9% of the fair value of the total consideration given in the acquisition, the non-equity element is material. The limit set out in FRS 6 is, therefore, exceeded and merger accounting cannot be used.

28.30 As explained in paragraph 28.15 above the definitions of equity in FRS 6 and the Act are different. When FRS 6 was issued, the ASB deliberately chose to adopt the meaning of 'equity' that was contained in FRS 4 to ensure that this test could not be avoided by the use of shares that are 'equity' under the Act, but are not so in substance. In 2004, the ASB issued FRS 25 such that, for years beginning on or after 1 January 2005, this definition was superseded. The principle remains, however, that for FRS 6 purposes the definition of 'equity' is based on substance rather than legal from. This difference between the definition included in FRS 6 and that in the Act may also affect the determination of whether the limitations placed on the proportion of non-equity consideration by the Act and FRS 6 have been exceeded. The following example illustrates how this might occur.

Example

Company A issues 100,000 ordinary shares and 250,000 participating preference shares as consideration for acquiring 100% of the equity shares of company B. The nominal values of the ordinary shares and the participating preference shares are £100,000 and £250,000 respectively and their fair values are £1,000,000 and £250,000 respectively. The participating preference shares have the right to a fixed dividend of 5% and, in addition, they receive a proportion of the dividends paid on the ordinary shares. They qualify as equity under the Act, because they carry a right to participate beyond a specified amount in a distribution, but they do not qualify as equity under FRS 6. This is because one of the rights of the participating preference shares is to a fixed dividend of 5% and, hence, is likely to be treated as a liability under FRS 25 and, therefore, as non-equity shares under FRS 6.

28.31 Under the Act, the whole of the consideration in this example qualifies as equity and, therefore, the ten per cent limitation for non-equity is not breached.

Under FRS 6, however, the participating preference shares are non-equity and as they amount to 20 per cent of the total fair value of the consideration the limit in FRS 6 that requires not more than an immaterial amount of the consideration to be in the form of non-equity, is breached.

28.32 In the above examples it has been suggested that the FRS 6 reference to immaterial might be interpreted as meaning less than ten per cent. No numerical figure is placed on the term 'immaterial' in FRS 6, but in practice it is often assumed that amounts representing less than five per cent are not material, between five and ten per cent may or may not be material and over ten per cent are material. As the Act uses a ten per cent limit for non-equity consideration compared to the nominal value of equity shares, it seems reasonable to assume that in the context of the FRS 6 condition, a non-equity element that represents over ten per cent of the total fair value of the consideration should be regarded as material.

Disposal of peripheral part of business

28.33 The consideration for a business combination should not include the distribution to shareholders of an interest in a peripheral part of a business of an entity in which they were shareholders and that does not form part of the combined entity. Nor should it include the distribution of the proceeds of sale of such a business or loan stock representing such proceeds. The implication of this is that where such a distribution or sale is not peripheral, then it should be counted as part of the consideration.

28.34 This situation might occur where two entities decide to merge, but there are certain businesses which do not fit in and that the two parties decide should be disposed of prior to the merger taking place. FRS 6 makes it clear that the disposal of such businesses must not materially affect the nature and focus of the disposing entity's operations. This seems rather a harsh condition as a group might well wish to merge certain of its operations only with another entity whilst allowing its shareholders to receive shares in the remainder of the group by, for instance, a distribution in kind. Provided that the operations to be merged with the other entity have a proper track record and are independent of the rest of the group there seems to be no good reason why the combination of that part of the group with another entity should not be eligible for merger accounting. However, FRS 6 would prohibit merger accounting in such a case, if the operations retained by the shareholders of the group and, therefore, excluded from the merger, materially affected the nature and focus of the original group's operations.

28.35 There is a similar prohibition in the Explanation section of FRS 6 which states that merger accounting is not appropriate for a combination where one entity divests itself of part of its business, which is then combined with another entity. The reason given in that section is that the divested business will not have been independent for a sufficient period to establish itself as being a party separate from its previous owner. The section continues that only once the divested business has established a track record of its own can it be considered as a party to a merger.

28.36 This condition is rather strange and appears over-restrictive. Many large groups have businesses that are run by their own management as quasi-independent entities under the group 'umbrella'. It is relatively straightforward to establish a trading record for such businesses. Evidence that this is so is the number of stock market flotations of businesses in recent years, which were hived off or demerged from larger groups.

Vendor placings and vendor rights

28.37 Prior to FRS 6, under the rules laid down by SSAP 23, it was possible to merger account for a business combination even where a vendor placing or a vendor rights was made to effect the combination.

28.38 The use of vendor rights or vendor placings enabled the target company's shareholders to receive cash whilst the acquiring company, because technically it had issued its own shares in exchange for shares in the target, was able not only to obtain merger relief, but also to merger account, provided all the other conditions of SSAP 23 were satisfied. Vendor placings and vendor rights are described briefly below.

28.39 A vendor placing normally works as follows. The acquiring company will offer its shares to the target company's shareholders in exchange for their shares in that company. If there are any shareholders of the target company who do not wish to retain the consideration shares of the acquiring company, then the acquiring company will arrange for its financial adviser (for example, a merchant bank) to place those consideration shares. The financial adviser will put together a placing list (that will normally include institutions such as pension funds and insurance companies) so that the target company shareholders may dispose of their consideration shares in the acquiring company for cash.

28.40 So after the vendor placing has occurred, cash has been transferred from the institutions, *via* the financial adviser (acting in his capacity as a broker) to some or all of the target company's shareholders. In return, the institutions now own shares in the acquiring company and the acquiring company now owns the target company. The acquiring company has issued shares, rather than paying cash, for the target company and, therefore, prior to FRS 6, as long as the offer complied with both the Act's and SSAP 23's merger conditions, the acquiring company could use merger accounting on consolidation.

28.41 The vendor rights normally work as follows. The acquiring company will offer its shares to the target company's shareholders in exchange for their shares in that company. If any shareholders of the target company do not wish to retain their consideration shares of the acquiring company, then the acquiring company will arrange for its financial adviser to place those consideration shares. Up to this point, the vendor rights method is the same as a vendor placing. However, as part of the placing agreement the acquiring company's shareholders will have an option to buy ('claw back') some of the consideration shares from the placees. They will be entitled to buy back at the placing price a certain proportion of the placed shares on a *pro rata* basis.

28.42 Therefore, after the vendor rights method is completed, cash has been transferred from the acquiring company's shareholders, *via* the financial adviser, to some or all of the target company's shareholders. In return, the acquiring company's shareholders now have a stake in a larger group, because the acquiring company now owns the target company. The acquiring company has issued shares, rather than paying cash, for the target company, and so, prior to FRS 6, it could use merger accounting on consolidation.

28.43 Even under SSAP 23, however, there were many who argued that vendor placings and vendor rights did not meet the spirit of SSAP 23, which stated in its Explanatory Note that "*Merger accounting is considered to be an appropriate method of accounting when two groups of shareholders continue, or are in a position to continue, their shareholdings as before but on a combined basis*". Although in a vendor rights at least the acquiree's shareholders are technically in a position to continue as shareholders, many people felt that the very structure of the consideration as a vendor rights or vendor placing indicated that many of the shareholders did not intend to continue investing in the combined entity.

28.44 FRS 6 resolves the possible contradiction between the offer of vendor placing or rights and the spirit of merger accounting by saying that equity shareholders would be considered to have disposed of their shareholdings for cash where any arrangement is made in connection with the combination that enables them to exchange or redeem the shares they receive for cash or other non-equity consideration. Such arrangements will include a vendor placing or a vendor rights. All arrangements made in conjunction with the combination must be taken into account, but a normal market transaction or a privately arranged sale by a shareholder is not deemed to be made in conjunction with the combination and does not prevent the immaterial cash or non-equity consideration criterion being met. [FRS 6 para 71].

28.45 Any convertible shares or loan stock that are outstanding at the time of the offer should not normally be regarded as equity for the purposes of satisfying the merger conditions. The only exception to this is where the convertible stock is converted into equity as a result of the business combination. [FRS 6 para 12].

No identifiable acquirer or acquiree test

28.46 In order to qualify for merger accounting, a business combination must represent a genuine partnership between the combining entities in which none of the parties dominates the other party or parties. No party to the combination should be portrayed as either acquirer or acquiree either by its own board or management or by that of another party to the combination. [FRS 6 para 6]. This is the principle that underlies the definition of a merger in the standard (see para 28.10 above).

28.47 The standard sets out a number of factors that may be evident in a business combination and which could indicate that one or other party is dominant. It makes clear that for merger accounting to be possible all of these factors must be absent.

28.48 The most straightforward of these factors is if one or other party is portrayed either by itself or by another party to the acquisition as the acquirer, or as having the subservient role of being acquired. One party's portrayal as acquirer or as acquiree is particularly likely to be a factor present in a contested bid, where one party attempts to gain control against the wishes of the other party's management.

28.49 As mentioned in paragraph 28.11 above, where all the conditions for merger accounting are satisfied the business combination must be accounted for as a merger. It is not an optional treatment. However, it is pointed out in paragraph 9 of the 'Development' section of FRS 6 that it would be relatively easy for merging parties to ensure that one of the conditions was not met, without fundamentally altering the commercial substance of the transaction, if they did not want to use merger accounting. This condition, that no party should be portrayed as an acquirer or as being acquired, seems to be probably the most susceptible to such manipulation.

28.50 FRS 6 lists a number of other aspects of a transaction that could indicate whether or not one party was dominant. These include:

- The form by which the combination was achieved.
- The plans for the combined entity's future operations (for instance whether any closures or disposals relate more to one party than to another).
- The proposed corporate image (such as name, logo, and location of headquarters and principal operations).
- In a publicly quoted company, the content of its communications with shareholders.

[FRS 6 para 62].

28.51 If any of these indicates that one party to the combination dominates the other or has the subservient role of being acquired, merger accounting is not permitted.

28.52 The standard indicates that where one party is seen to be paying a premium over the market value of the shares acquired, this is evidence that that party has assumed the role of acquirer, unless there is a clear explanation for the premium, other than its being a premium to acquire control. [FRS 6 para 61].

28.53 This condition is not always easy to put into operation. It appears to apply to cases where offers are made for listed companies which at the date of the announcement of the offer represent a substantial premium to the market price of the recipient of the offer at that date. During the course of the offer the target company's share price will often rise to the offer price level or even above. However, we consider that the comparison with the market price of the recipient should be made as at the date the offer is announced rather than at the later date when it goes unconditional in order to determine whether or not it is a premium to market price and, if so, whether it is a premium to acquire control. If there is a substantial premium it may be difficult to rebut the presumption that the premium is for control. As noted above, the standard requires that if that presumption is to be rebutted there must be a clear explanation for the premium other than it being a premium for control.

Joint participation in management test

28.54 The FRS requires that the boards of all the combining parties or their appointees should participate in setting up the management structure for the combined entity and in selecting the management personnel. They should set up this structure and select the management personnel on the basis of consensus decisions between the combining parties rather than purely by exercise of voting rights. [FRS 6 para 7].

28.55 This does not mean that the management structure and personnel have to be equally divided between the combining parties. Indeed it could be that one party provides most of the management. This would not contravene the joint participation rule provided that it reflected the wishes of all the parties to the merger.

28.56 In determining whether the condition of joint participation is satisfied consideration has to be given not just to the structure, but also to the identity of all persons involved in the main financial and operating decisions and the way in which the decision making process operates in practice. For instance, if all financial and operating decisions had to be approved by the managing director and only one of the parties to the combination could appoint the managing director, that party might be presumed to exert undue dominance over the management. As explained above, however, if that was in accordance with the wishes of all the parties it would not breach the 'joint participation' condition.

28.57 Sometimes there may be arrangements made at the date of combination whereby there is joint participation in management for a limited period only, with other arrangements being made thereafter. If at the outset there is such an agreement for short-term joint participation, but it is agreed that at the expiry of that period, one party may assume control of management whether or not the other party agrees, then that arrangement would probably breach the joint participation rule and merger accounting would not be permitted. Where, however, arrangements for the period that followed a short period of joint participation provided that management should be selected on the basis of merit only, such arrangements would not breach the joint participation rule, provided that all parties agreed to the policy at the outset.

28.58 The standard makes clear that only decisions made about management structure and personnel at the outset of the merger need be considered in determining whether there is joint participation, but as illustrated above both the short-term and long-term consequences of those decisions need to be evaluated.

Relative size test

28.59 The standard requires that the relative sizes of the combining entities are not so disparate that one party dominates the combined entity by virtue of its relative size. [FRS 6 para 8].

28.60 As to what constitutes dominance in terms of size the standard says that one party should be presumed to dominate if it is more than 50 per cent larger than each of the other parties to the combination. The test of size should be made by reference to the proportion of the equity of the combined entity attributable to each of the combining parties.

28.61 However the presumption of dominance, where one party is more than 50 per cent larger than each of the other parties, may be rebutted if it can be clearly shown that there is no such dominance. In some circumstances, for instance, there may be agreements between the parties that determine voting rights or other matters, such as powers of veto, which mean that the apparent dominance due to size is not effective in practice. Any such circumstances should be disclosed and explained.

Example 1

Company A is listed and has 100 million equity shares of £1 in issue which have a market value of £1,000 million. Company B is also listed and has 100 million 5p equity shares in issue with a market value of £600 million. Company A makes an agreed offer for company B and the offer is valued at £750 million, that is company A will issue 75m shares.

In this situation if the relative sizes pre-merger are considered company A is more than 50% larger than company B. However, this is not relevant for determining whether or not the relative size test is satisfied. It is the relative proportions of equity of the combined entity that are relevant. Comparison of A's share of the combined equity of £1,750 million with B's share, shows that the company A shareholders own 100 million shares (that is, 57% of the combined entity), which is not more than 50% larger than that of company B shareholders' interest of 75 million shares (that is 43% of the combined entity). By reference to the size test alone, therefore, the combination would be entitled to be merger accounted. However, consideration would then have to be given as to whether the substantial premium of £150 million paid by company A was a premium to acquire control (see paras 28.52 and 28.53 above).

Example 2

Company A is unlisted and has 15,000 equity shares in issue. There is no quoted market value available, but the company has net assets of £150,000. Company B is also unlisted and has 3,000 equity shares in issue. Its net assets are £50,000. Company A issues 5,000 equity shares to the shareholders of company B in consideration for their equity shares in that company.

A comparison of the respective holdings of the former shareholders of company A (15,000 shares) and the former shareholders of company B (5,000 shares) shows that the former shareholders of company A have a holding of 75% in the combined entity that is more than 50% larger than that of the former shareholders of company B who own 25%. Therefore, it is presumed that company A is dominant and merger accounting is not permitted (unless the presumption can be rebutted in some way).

Example 3

Company A has 10,000 equity shares in issue that have a market value of £500,000. Company B has 1,000 equity shares in issue having a market value of £200,000. Company A is in a period of low profitability and its markets are mature and declining. The shares in company B are owned by a dynamic individual Mr X who also manages that company and has built its business up rapidly. Company A wishes to retain the services of that individual to run the combined business. In turn he wishes to retain an effective say in the running of the business whilst enjoying the benefits of a larger organisation. Company A issues 4,000 shares to acquire company B. At the same time it enters into an agreement with Mr X as a shareholder in the combined entity. The agreement specifies that decisions on all major operational and financial matters must be agreed by shareholders representing at least 75% of the equity. In this way control is effectively shared between the shareholders in the old company A and Mr X, the shareholder of the former company B.

In this situation, although the former shareholders of company A hold over 50% (71%) more of the enlarged equity than the former shareholder of company B (29%) the shareholders' agreement means that control is effectively divided equally between the two. In such a situation, the presumption that company A is dominant can be rebutted and if all the other conditions for merger accounting are satisfied merger accounting would be required. The financial statements would have to disclose the reasons why company A was not considered to be dominant.

Full participation in future performance test

28.62 The FRS requires that no equity shareholders of any of the combining entities retain any material interest in the future performance of only part of the combined entity. [FRS 6 para 11].

28.63 A situation where different shareholders might retain material interests in different parts of a combined entity might be as follows:

Example 1

Company A and company B combine by means of a new holding company, company C, issuing shares to the former shareholders of companies A and B. The shares issued to the former shareholders of company A (A shares) are entitled to 80% of the profits of the former company A businesses and the shares issued to the former shareholders of company B (B shares) are entitled to 80% of the profits of the former company B businesses. All other profits are shared equally between the two sets of shareholders. Assuming that there are an equal number of A and B shares and that the company A businesses make £100,000 in the first year and the company B businesses make £50,000 the A shares would be entitled to £80,000 of the profits from the company A businesses while the B shares would be entitled to £40,000 from the company B businesses. The balance of £30,000 of the total profits would be shared equally.

Because, in this example, certain of the equity shareholders retain a material interest in only part of the future performance of the combined entity the condition of full participation in future performance would not be satisfied and merger accounting would not be permitted for the combination.

Similarly, where there is an earn out or similar performance related arrangement the condition would not be met.

Example 2

Company A and company B combine by means of shares issued by company A to company B shareholders. Part of the consideration (to be settled in shares) is deferred and is contingent on the performance of the company B businesses over the next three years. The potential amount of the contingent consideration is material.

Because the shareholders of company B have a material interest in only one part of the combined business, the issue of further equity shares to them depends solely on the performance of the company B businesses.

It might be argued that once the earn out is completed, then all shareholders will participate fully, but the standard appears to be concerned to ensure that the condition of full participation is satisfied based on conditions existing at the date of the combination.

An exception is where at the date of the combination there is uncertainty about the value of a specific asset or liability contributed by one of the parties, such as the eventual outcome of a legal action against one of the parties, or the eventual sales value of an asset owned by one of the parties. An agreement for the allocation of the consideration between the combining parties that depend on the eventual outcome of the uncertainty would not invalidate the full participation rule.

Example 3

At the date of a business combination between company A and company B, company A has not resolved a claim made by it against various former customers who have failed to take delivery of goods manufactured for them under contract. No account of any potential gain has been taken in determining the consideration to be allocated to company A shareholders at the date of the combination, but it has been agreed that those shareholders will be entitled to 80% of any subsequent gain arising from the claim.

In these circumstances, the participation of the company A shareholders in any future gain arising from the claim would not infringe the condition of full participation, because the outcome does not depend on the future performance of the combined business, but rather on the outcome of an uncertainty existing at the date of the combination.

28.64 The full participation in future performance test is not met where there is a material minority, that is ten per cent or more, of shareholders of one of the combining parties that has not accepted the offer. This is because if there is such a minority then it retains an interest in only part of the combined entity and the condition that no equity shareholders of the combining entities should retain a material interest in the future performance of only part of the combined entity, is not met. It is also unlikely that, if there was such a large minority, the other conditions for merger accounting could be met.

Merger accounting principles

28.65 The principles of acquisition accounting are explained in chapter 25 and the principles of merger accounting are considered in greater detail below.

28.66 When a group uses merger accounting to account for a business combination, the group does not need to incorporate into its consolidated financial statements the fair values of the subsidiary's assets and liabilities. [FRS 6 para 16]. Therefore, no goodwill arises in a merger and the group should incorporate into its consolidated financial statements the assets and liabilities at the amounts at which the subsidiary recorded them in its books before the combination. [CA85 4A Sch 11(2)].

28.67 One exception to this principle is that a group should adopt uniform group accounting policies for consolidation purposes in accordance with the Act and FRS 2. Consequently, if the acquired company's accounting policies are not the same as the acquiring company's, then adjustments should be made to achieve uniformity. One way of doing this might be for the subsidiary to make these adjustments in its own records. It could restate the amount of its assets and liabilities in its books to reflect the change in accounting policy. Alternatively, if it is not practicable for the acquired company to change its accounting policies, adjustments may be made on consolidation to the values of the acquired company's assets and liabilities that are stated in its books.

28.67.1 An example of disclosure of adjustments to conform accounting policies is Table 28.1. It is worth noting that changes to the policies of either party to the merger may be made depending on which of the combining parties' policies the enlarged entity chooses to adopt.

Table 28.1 — Royal & Sun Alliance Insurance Group plc — Directors' Report and Accounts — 31 December 1996

Accounting policies (extract)

Effects of merger on Group financial statements
On 19th July 1996, Sun Alliance Group plc (Sun Alliance) was renamed Royal & Sun Alliance Insurance Group plc and became the Parent Company of the new Group formed by the merger of Royal Insurance Holdings plc (Royal Insurance) and Sun Alliance.
Merger accounting principles have been used and the results have been presented as if the new Group had been established throughout the current and prior years.

Alignment of accounting policies and presentation
The new Group's accounting policies are set out on pages 17 to 19. The process of aligning policies and presentation across the new Group has resulted in the following principal changes:

a) General business is accounted for on an annual basis. Previously Sun Alliance used a fund basis of accounting for London market marine and aviation business.
b) Overseas revenue transactions are translated at rates ruling at the year end. Previously Royal Insurance used average rates of exchange during the year to translate revenue transactions.
c) The reinsurers' share of technical provisions is presented on the assets side of the balance sheet. Previously Royal Insurance presented these amounts on the liabilities side of the balance sheet in arriving at net technical provisions.
d) Balances arising from insurance broking transactions are presented gross. Previously Sun Alliance took advantage of the transitional provision within Financial Reporting Standard 5 permitting the offset of balances between insurance brokers and the Group.
e) The value of long term business, being the value of the shareholders' interest in the long term funds in excess of that recognised under the modified statutory solvency basis of reporting long term business, is included within investments in the consolidated balance sheet. Previously Sun Alliance did not include this value in the financial statements but disclosed it in the Group Chief Executive's review.
f) British Aviation Insurance Company Ltd is accounted for as a subsidiary of the Group. Previously this company was an associated undertaking of both Royal Insurance and Sun Alliance.
g) Sun Alliance and Royal Insurance Australia Holdings Ltd is accounted for as a subsidiary of the Group. This company was previously an associated undertaking of Royal Insurance and a subsidiary of Sun Alliance.
h) Scrip acceptances received under the scrip dividend alternative are subsequently added back to reserves. Previously Sun Alliance made no adjustment to reserves for scrip dividend acceptances which were accounted as shares issued at a premium.
i) Goodwill arising on acquisitions is written off to other reserves in the consolidated balance sheet along with the merger reserve arising on consolidation of Royal Insurance and Sun Alliance. Previously Sun Alliance wrote goodwill off against the consolidated profit and loss account reserve.

[The next paragraph is 28.68.]

28.68 The group's consolidated financial statements for the period in which the business combination takes place should include the subsidiary's income and expenditure and cash flows for the entire period. [CA85 4A Sch 11(3); FRS 6 para 17]. That is to say, they should include the subsidiary's results for the part of the period before the business combination, as well as the results of the subsidiary for the part of the period after the business combination. These results should be consolidated on a line by line basis in the profit and loss account and the cash flow statement as if the subsidiary had always been part of the group. In addition, the corresponding amounts in the consolidated financial statements should reflect the position that would have arisen if the companies had been combined throughout the previous period and also at the previous balance sheet date. [CA85 4A Sch 11(4)].

28.69 The aim of the consolidated financial statements in merger accounting is to show the combined companies' results and financial positions as if they had always been combined. Consequently, even the share capital issued during the year for the purposes of the merger has to be shown as if it had always been issued.

Example

In 20X1 company A and company B combine and the combination is eligible for merger accounting. The share capital of company A (which has remained unchanged since the beginning of 20X0) is 100,000 equity shares of £1 each prior to the merger and that of company B is 200,000 shares of 50p each. Company A issues 100,000 equity shares in consideration for the acquisition of company B the fair value of which is £1 million and incurs merger expenses of £10,000. Profits of company A for the year 20X0 were £150,000 and for 20X1 they were £200,000. Profits of company B for 20X0 were £190,000 and for 20X1 they were £100,000 to the date of merger and £75,000 for the post-merger period. There were no adjustments required to achieve uniformity of accounting policies.

The profits of the combined group would be presented as if company A and company B had always been combined. Thus the group profit and loss account would show profits for 20X0 of £340,000 (£150,000 + £190,000) and for 20X1 the profits would be £375,000 (£200,000 + £100,000 + £75,000), before merger expenses.

The share capital of company A would be adjusted so as to show the shares issued in respect of the merger as if they had been in existence at the start of 20X0. Therefore, company A's share capital at the beginning of 20X0 would be shown at £200,000. There would be no difference arising on consolidation as the nominal value of shares issued as consideration is equal to the nominal value of shares acquired. The merger expenses of £10,000 would be written off to the group profit and loss account for 20X1. (Although there might seem to be an argument for charging these expenses in 20X0 the standard specifically requires them to be charged at the date of the merger as reorganisation or restructuring expenses in accordance with paragraph 20 of FRS 3, that is as a post-operating profit exceptional item.)

28.70 The examples that follow illustrate some of the problems that can arise with the principles of merger accounting.

Example 1

Company A combines with company B during the year and merger accounts for the combination. Company A has large tax losses and has never had a tax charge. Company B paid tax last year and it is proposed that the two companies' results should be combined and the tax charge of company B excluded from the comparatives on the basis that if the companies had always been combined, this tax charge would never have arisen.

In this type of situation, it would be carrying the principles of merger accounting too far to eliminate the tax charge. The tax has been paid and cannot be recovered now that company B has joined the group. Consequently, the tax charge should be shown as a comparative in the merged profit and loss account. Company A could of course add a note to explain why the tax charge has arisen.

Example 2

A company combines with another and will use merger accounting. The company's year end is 31 December and the subsidiary's year end is 30 June. The company wishes to know how to deal with the difference in year ends.

The company should consolidate the results of the subsidiary for the 12 months ended 31 December. It should take the second six months from the year to 30 June and add the following six months of trading. This treatment is necessary to comply with the Act's requirements concerning the accounting period of the subsidiary that must be consolidated.

Example 3

A listed company with a December year end combines with a company with a June year end. Merger accounting is to be used. The second company had a subsidiary that made losses to June, but it disposes of its loss-making subsidiary before the date of merger which is in November.

The results of the loss-making subsidiaries should be included in the consolidation, because, although technically they never become subsidiaries of the listed company, the spirit of FRS 6 requires that the merged companies should incorporate the unaltered results of the two companies for the full year. The results of the subsidiaries that are sold should, if material, be shown separately and disclosed as discontinued operations, but they should still be included in the consolidated profit and loss account of the merged companies.

Applicability to business combinations achieved by using a new parent company

28.71 Often business combinations are effected by incorporating a new company which then issues shares to two or more combining companies. The accounting treatment in such cases will depend on the substance of the arrangement. This often means that the new parent should be ignored and the tests for merger accounting should be applied to the combining entities other than the new parent, (except insofar as it is necessary to bring in the new parent as, for instance, in satisfying the 'offer to shareholders', '90 per cent holding' and 'immaterial cash or non-equity consideration' tests).

28.72 If the substance is that a combination of the entities would have been a merger, merger accounting should be used. However, if the substance is that an acquirer can be identified, acquisition accounting should be used. In the latter case the new parent company and the acquirer should be accounted for by using merger accounting and then the other parties to the combination should be acquisition accounted. [FRS 6 para 14].

28.73 Where a new parent is used to effect a business combination and merger accounting is to be used it is advisable to ensure that the accounting period of the new parent company is the same as that of the combining companies and that the new parent has been in existence for the whole of the combining companies' current accounting periods (see para 28.106 below).

Applicability to group reconstructions

28.74 Merger accounting may be used for group reconstructions, even where there is no business combination that meets the definition of a merger. However, this is conditional on:

- The use of merger accounting not being prohibited by companies legislation.
- The ultimate shareholders remaining the same and the rights of each such shareholder, relative to other shareholders, being unchanged.
- No minority's interest in the net assets of the group being altered by the combination.

[FRS 6 para 13].

28.74.1 The conditions for merger accounting under the Companies Act and FRS 6 have been discussed above from paragraph 28.12. In the case of a group reconstruction only the Act's requirements need to be met. The additional conditions imposed by FRS 6 for merger accounting are not required to be met. The Act's conditions which are explained in more detail from paragraph 28.12 above, are:

- At least 90 per cent of the nominal value of the relevant shares in the undertaking acquired (excluding any shares in the undertaking held as treasury shares) is held by or on behalf of the parent company and its subsidiary undertakings.
- The proportion referred to above was attained pursuant to an arrangement providing for the issue of equity shares by the parent company or one or more of its subsidiary undertakings.
- The fair value of any consideration other than the issue of equity shares given pursuant to the arrangement by the parent company and its subsidiary undertakings did not exceed ten per cent of the nominal value of the equity shares issued.
- Adoption of the merger method of accounting accords with generally accepted accounting principles or practice.

[CA85 4A Sch 10(1)].

[The next paragraph is 28.75.]

28.75 The definition of a group reconstruction in FRS 6 extends the meaning of the term to include several types of business combination which would not have been considered to be group reconstructions in the past. Indeed it includes several types of combination which would be eligible for merger relief rather than group reconstruction relief under the Act. The definition is:

"Group reconstruction:-

Any of the following arrangements:

(a) the transfer of a shareholding in a subsidiary undertaking from one group company to another;

(b) the addition of a new parent company to a group;

(c) the transfer of shares in one or more subsidiary undertakings of a group to a new company that is not a group company but whose shareholders are the same as those of the group's parent;

(d) the combination into a group of two or more companies that before the combination had the same shareholders."

[FRS 6 para 2].

28.76 Where any of the above forms of combination is planned it will be necessary to determine whether group reconstruction relief or merger relief is applicable. These reliefs are explained in chapter 23.

Example 1

Company A is the parent company of a group. It is proposed to form a new parent company, company B. Company B is formed as an independent company, not as a subsidiary of company A. Company B issues shares in exchange for all the shares in company A.

In this situation company B does not qualify for group reconstruction relief, because it is not the wholly-owned subsidiary of company A, but it does qualify for merger relief.

Example 2

Company A is the US parent company of a group which has a number of UK subsidiaries. It is proposed to form a new UK parent company for the UK subsidiaries. Company B is formed as a wholly-owned subsidiary of the US parent. It issues shares to the US parent in exchange for the US parent's holdings in the UK subsidiaries.

In this situation, company B is eligible for group reconstruction relief, because it is the wholly-owned subsidiary of the US parent and issues shares to that parent in exchange for the transfer to company B of the parent's holdings in the UK subsidiaries.

28.77 In both of the above situations merger accounting is permitted by law, the ultimate shareholders remain the same as do their rights and there is no minority interest affected by the combination. Accordingly, merger accounting is permitted.

28.78 It is noticeable that FRS 6 does not make merger accounting compulsory in the case of group reconstructions, in contrast to other business combinations. However it is likely that, in most cases where there is a group reconstruction and the conditions set out above for merger accounting are satisfied, companies will wish to use merger accounting.

28.79 Example (d) in the definition of group reconstructions covers a situation where there is a so called 'horizontal' group. This is a group where the companies involved are not part of a legal group for Companies Act purposes, but are under the common ownership of an individual or individuals. Where this situation exists it would clearly be somewhat severe if the combination had to satisfy all the stringent tests for merger accounting that apply to combinations other than group reconstructions. For instance, the 'relative size test' and the 'no identifiable acquirer or acquiree tests' are not really relevant in this situation.

Example

Mr X and his family interests own the whole of the share capital of three companies — company A, company B and company C — which have net assets of 10, 100 and 1,000 respectively. It is decided that the three companies should be combined and company C issues shares to Mr X and his family interests in exchange for their shares in company A and company B. In this case, group reconstruction relief is not applicable, but company C is able to take merger relief. In addition, the combination is treated as a group reconstruction for the purposes of FRS 6 and the standard's conditions for merger accounting in the case of group reconstructions are satisfied. The conditions that FRS 6 sets out for business combinations that are not group reconstructions are not relevant. Thus it does not matter if company C is portrayed as the acquirer or that company C is much larger than the other two parties to the combination.

28.80 One of the conditions for merger accounting for a group reconstruction is that no minority's interest in the net assets of the group is altered by the transfer. A minority's interest may be unaffected, for instance, where a subsidiary undertaking is transferred within a subgroup that has a minority shareholder, but is likely to be affected if a subsidiary is transferred into or out of such a group.

Example

Company B is the intermediate parent company of subsidiary companies C, D and E. There is a minority interest of 10% in company B the remainder of whose shares are owned by the ultimate parent company, company A. Company A has a further direct subsidiary company X. Company B enters into two transactions, first it transfers ownership of company C to company E in exchange for shares in company E (which are issued to company B). Second, it transfers company E, (which now owns company C), to company X for shares. Both company E and company X prepare consolidated financial statements.

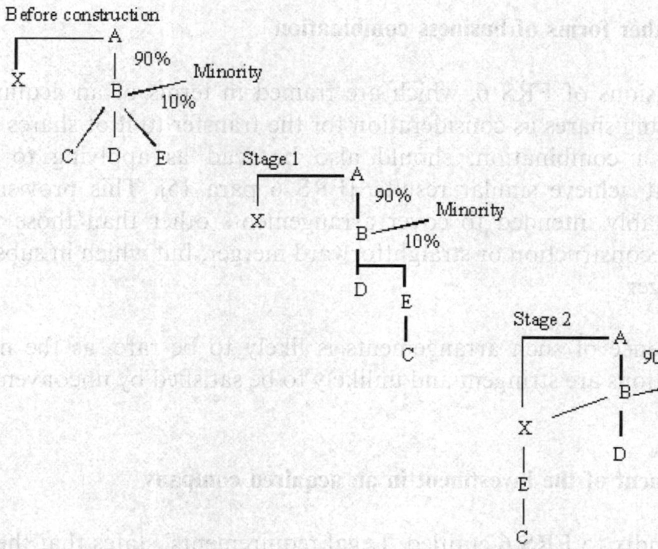

After stage 2, B holds an investment in X (which is not an associate or a subsidiary).

In the first transaction, the transfer of company C to company E, the minority interest is not affected because the composition of the subgroup headed by company B remains unchanged. In company E's consolidated financial statements, therefore, the combination with company C could be merger accounted.

In the second transaction company E and its subsidiary company C move out of the company B subgroup and company B's investment in company E (and its subsidiary company C) is replaced by an investment in company X (but company X does not thereby become a subsidiary of company B).

If the investment in company X is recorded in company B's consolidated financial statements at the same value as it had previously recorded the net assets of company E and company C (ignoring goodwill), the minority's share of net assets will be unchanged. In terms of the carrying values, this transaction might seem to satisfy the condition that the minority's interest in the net assets is not altered. However, the explanation section of the standard says:

> "*If a minority has effectively acquired, or disposed of, rights to part of the net assets of the group, the FRS requires the transfer to be accounted for by using acquisition accounting rather than merger accounting*." [FRS 6 para 79].

As the minority has indeed disposed of part of the company B group in this situation it appears that company X must acquisition account for the combination with company E and company C. This would appear to be so because the 'group' referred to in quotation above must be the company B sub-group. This interpretation is reinforced by a further quotation from the explanation section of the standard:

> *"Thus the transfer of a subsidiary undertaking within a subgroup that has a minority shareholder may qualify for merger accounting; but acquisition accounting must be used for the transfer of a subsidiary undertaking out of, or into, such a subgroup."* [FRS 6 para 79].

Applicability to other forms of business combination

28.81 The provisions of FRS 6, which are framed in terms of an acquirer or issuing entity issuing shares as consideration for the transfer to it of shares in the other parties to a combination, should also be read as applying to other arrangements that achieve similar results. [FRS 6 para 15]. This provision of FRS 6 is presumably intended to cover arrangements other than those which involve a group reconstruction or straightforward merger, but which in substance amount to a merger.

28.82 The incidence of such arrangements is likely to be rare, as the merger accounting conditions are stringent and unlikely to be satisfied by unconventional arrangements.

Accounting treatment of the investment in an acquired company

28.83 The appendix to FRS 6 entitled 'Legal requirements' states that the FRS does not deal with the form of accounting to be used in the acquiring or issuing company's own financial statements. However, the Companies Act 1985 clarifies the accounting treatment of an investment in an acquired company that should be used in an issuing company's balance sheet where there is:

- Merger relief under section 131.
- Group reconstruction relief under section 132.

28.84 In these circumstances, the amount at which the issuing company carries its investment in the acquired company does not need to include an amount corresponding to the premium (or the part of the premium) that the issuing company has not credited to its share premium account. [CA85 Sec 133(1); CA06 Sec 615]. That is, the issuing company has a choice. Disregarding other considerations such as cash, the issuing company can record both the shares it issues and the investment in the new subsidiary at either:

- the nominal value of the shares issued and any section 132 minimum premium; or
- the fair value of the shares issued, with the premium in excess of any section 132 minimum premium credited to a merger reserve instead of to a share premium account.

28.85 The accounting treatment of the investment in an acquired company is considered further in chapter 23 which deals in detail with merger relief and group reconstruction relief.

28.86 Where merger accounting is adopted on consolidation and the investment shown in the holding company's balance sheet does not include the premium it is debatable whether the investment should be described as being at cost, because the amount shown in the balance sheet may be quite different from the actual cost.

It could be argued that the 'true' cost of the shares issued is their fair value and not their nominal value. Consequently, the company may need to choose some appropriate wording other than 'cost' to describe the investment (for example, 'at nominal value of shares issued').

[The next paragraph is 28.92.]

Difference on consolidation

28.92 In merger accounting under the Act the parent's balance sheet will generally show its investment in the subsidiary at the nominal value of the shares that it issued as consideration plus the fair value of any additional consideration.

28.93 A difference may then arise on consolidation between the value at which the parent carries its investment in the subsidiary and the aggregate of the nominal value of the subsidiary's shares that the parent acquires together with any share premium account and capital redemption reserve of the subsidiary (these being the parts of the subsidiary's shareholders' funds that need to be eliminated on consolidation, that is the subsidiary's distributable reserves flow through into the consolidated reserves). The value of the investment will represent the aggregate of the following:

- The nominal value of the 'qualifying shares' issued by the parent in consideration for the acquisition of the shares in the subsidiary. [CA85 4A Sch 11(5)(a)]. 'Qualifying shares' means those shares where merger relief is obtained and, consequently, no share premium has to be recorded on them or those shares where group reconstruction relief applies and where, consequently, the appropriate amount is the nominal value together with any minimum premium value as defined in section 132 of the Act. [CA85 4A Sch 11(7)].
- The fair value of any other consideration given for the acquisition determined at the date of acquisition. [CA85 4A Sch 11(5)(b)].

28.93.1 In the extract from the Movement in Shareholders' Funds statement given in Table 28.2 below, the difference arising on consolidation is shown as £494 million. This has been calculated as the difference between the nominal value of 706 million 25p shares issued by Sun Alliance, that is £176 million, and the share capital and share premium account of the subsidiary Royal Insurance amounting to £670 million.

Table 28.2 — Royal & Sun Alliance Insurance Group plc — Directors' Report and Accounts — 31 December 1996

Movement in Shareholders' Funds (extract)

	Notes	Share capital premium £m	Revaluation reserve £m	Other reserves (see below) £m	Profit and loss account £m	1996 £m	1995 £m
Shareholders' funds at 1st January as previously reported by							
Royal Insurance		670	991	(381)	1,396	**2,676**	1,882
Sun Alliance		377	1,752	–	511	**2,640**	1,768
Merger reserve adjustment		(494)	–	494	–	–	–
Accounting policy alignment	*1d*	–	869	(286)	287	**870**	702
Merged shareholders' funds at 1st January		553	3,612	(173)	2,194	**6,186**	4,352

Other reserves as restated at 1st January represent the cumulative amount of goodwill written off (adjusted for disposals) of £667m and the merger reserve of £494m arising as a result of the merger of Royal Insurance and Sun Alliance on 19th July 1996. As at 31st December 1996 the cumulative amount of goodwill written off (adjusted for disposals) is **£675m.**

Note 31 (extract)
On 14th June 1996 the authorised share capital was increased by the creation of 1,00,000,000 ordinary shares of 25p each. Pursuant to a scheme of arrangement, 706,252,430 shares were issued on 19th July 1996 to former shareholders of Royal Insurance on the basis of 1,067 ordinary shares of 25p each in the Company for every 1,000 Royal Insurance shares of 25p each held.

[The next paragraph is 28.94.]

28.94 On consolidation, the inclusion of the subsidiary's share premium account and capital redemption reserve in the set off reflects the fact that these accounts are effectively part of the capital of the subsidiary. Because these amounts are included in the set off, the effect is that the share premium and capital redemption reserve in the consolidated balance sheet will comprise only the amounts from the parent's balance sheet.

28.95 The group should adjust the differences arising on consolidation against other reserves on consolidation and should show the movement in reserves in the reconciliation of movements in shareholders' funds. [CA85 4A Sch 11(6); FRS 6 para 18].

28.96 Where the investment's carrying value is less than the nominal value of the shares (plus any share premium and capital redemption reserve of the subsidiary) that the parent company has acquired, the group should treat the difference as an 'other reserve' that arises on consolidation. Where the investment's carrying value is greater than the nominal value of the shares (again plus any share premium and capital redemption reserve) acquired, the difference represents the extent to which the group has effectively capitalised its reserves as a result of the merger.

Consequently, the group should reduce its 'other reserves' by the amount of the difference.

28.97 The two examples that follow show how these consolidation differences arise and how they should be treated:

Example 1: Where the carrying value is less than nominal value

Company A acquires all of company B's £200,000 nominal share capital. The purchase consideration consists of new shares that company A issues and these have a nominal value of £190,000. The business combination satisfies all the merger conditions and the group uses merger accounting. The respective balance sheets, after the merger, of the individual companies and the group are as follows:

	Co A	Co B	Group
	£'000	£'000	£'000
Net tangible assets	1,500	1,400	2,900
Investment in subsidiary	190	–	–
	1,690	1,400	2,900
Share capital	400	200	400
Profit and loss account	1,290	1,200	2,490
Difference on consolidation	–	–	10
	1,690	1,400	2,900

The difference on consolidation of £10,000 is calculated as follows:

	£'000
Nominal value of shares acquired	200
Parent company's carrying value of investment	190
Difference on consolidation	10

The group should treat the difference on consolidation as a reserve that arises on consolidation, because the investment's carrying value is less than the nominal value of the shares acquired.

Example 2: Where the carrying value is greater than nominal value

The facts in this example are the same as those in example 1 above, except that the purchase consideration consists of new shares with a nominal value of £250,000. In this example, the respective balance sheets, after the merger, of the individual companies and the group are as follows:

	Co A	Co B	Group
	£'000	£'000	£'000
Net tangible assets	1,500	1,400	2,900
Investment in subsidiary	250	–	–
	1,750	1,400	2,900
Share capital	460	200	460
Profit and loss account	1,290	1,200	2,490
Other reserves	–	–	(50)
	1,750	1,400	2,900

The difference on consolidation of £50,000 is calculated as follows:

	£'000
Nominal value of shares acquired	200
Parent company's carrying value of investment	250
Difference on consolidation	(50)

The investment's carrying value is greater than the nominal value of the shares acquired, and so the group should reduce its reserves by the amount of the difference.

Merger expenses

28.98 Expenses of the merger must not be included in the calculation of the difference arising on consolidation. Merger expenses should instead be charged in the profit and loss account of the combined entity as reorganisation or restructuring expenses in accordance with paragraph 20 of FRS 3. [FRS 6 para 19]. This means that such expenses should be charged as a non-operating exceptional item, if material. An example of this is Table 28.3 which also shows exceptional operating costs arising from reorganisation as a pre-operating profit item.

Table 28.3 — United News & Media plc — Annual Report and Accounts — 31 December 1996
Group profit and loss account (extract)

	Notes	Before exceptional items 1996 £m	Exceptional items (note 4) 1996 £m	Total 1996 £m
Turnover	1			
Continuing operations		**1,917.5**		**1,917.5**
Acquisitions		**21.0**		**21.0**
		1,938.5		**1,938.5**
Discontinued operations		**52.2**		**52.2**
		1,990.7		**1,990.7**
Operating costs	2	**(1,710.0)**	**(112.5)**	**(1,822.5)**
Operating profit				
Continuing operations		**268.9**	**(94.4)**	**174.5**
Acquisitions		**0.7**	**(18.1)**	**(17.4)**
		269.6	**(112.5)**	**157.1**
Discontinued operations		**11.1**	–	**11.1**
		280.7	**(112.5)**	**168.2**
Income from interests in associated undertakings		**21.2**	**(62.5)**	**(41.3)**
Income from other fixed asset investments	3	**2.2**	–	**2.2**
Total operating profit	1	**304.1**	**(175.0)**	**129.1**
Continuing operations				
Merger expenses			**(31.0)**	**(31.0)**
Profit on the disposal of fixed asset investments			**11.6**	**11.6**
Discontinued operations				
Profit (loss) on sales and closure of businesses			**138.0**	**138.0**
Profit on ordinary activities before interest		**304.1**	**(56.4)**	**247.7**
Net interest expense	5	**(13.9)**	–	**(13.9)**
Profit on ordinary activities before tax		**290.2**	**(56.4)**	**233.8**
Tax on profit on ordinary activities	6	**(88.6)**	**12.7**	**(75.9)**
Profit on ordinary activities after tax		**201.6**	**(43.7)**	**157.9**
Minority interests		**(5.5)**	–	**(5.5)**
Profit for the year	7	**196.1**	**(43.7)**	**152.4**
Dividends	8			**(115.3)**
Retained profit for the year	23			**37.1**
Earnings per share after exceptional items	9			**31.1p**
Earnings per share before exceptional items	9			**40.0p**

28.99 The standard does not prohibit such expenses from being subsequently charged to share premium account by means of a reserve transfer from profit and loss account reserve to the share premium account provided the expenses are eligible to be charged to share premium account under section 130 of the Act. The relevant expenses that could be charged subsequently to the share premium account include, for example: the expenses of the issue of shares by the acquiring company; the preliminary expenses of any new parent company formed to effect the merger; and any commission paid on the issue of the shares.

28.100 The question of how merger expenses should be accounted for in the financial statements of the parent company that effects the combination is not dealt with in the standard. If the parent company has a share premium account and wishes to set eligible expenses against that account, it would seem reasonable that it should mirror the treatment on consolidation, by passing the expenses through its own profit and loss account and then making a transfer from the profit and loss account reserve to the share premium account.

28.101 However, where there is no share premium account or the parent does not wish to write the eligible costs off against that account, there would appear to be a further alternative to writing these and other costs relating to the merger off to the profit and loss account. Because the parent has acquired an asset, the shares in the other party to the combination, it should record that asset at its purchase price and to the purchase price should be added any expenses incidental to its acquisition. [CA85 4 Sch 17 and 26(1)].

28.102 The carrying value of the investment in the acquired entity may, therefore, be included in the parent company's balance sheet at the nominal value of shares issued plus the fair value of any other consideration given (where group reconstruction relief is obtained there may be some premium included) plus the expenses that are incidental to the merger. These expenses will of course have to be disregarded when comparing the carrying value of the investment with the nominal value of shares issued in order to determine the difference arising on consolidation that is discussed above. Also in the consolidated financial statements the costs will be charged to the group profit and loss account.

28.103 Any difference between the treatment of merger expenses in the parent's financial statements and those of the group will need to be disclosed in a note to the financial statements together with the reasons for the difference. [CA85 4A Sch 4]. An example of such a note where such expenses have been capitalised in the parent is shown below.

Example

Merger expenses of £5m have been included in the parent company's financial statements as part of the carrying value of the investment in X plc. On consolidation in accordance with the requirements of FRS 6, 'Acquisitions and mergers', these expenses have been charged to the consolidated profit and loss account. The difference in accounting treatment arises because such expenses may be included in the carrying value of the investment under the provisions of the Companies Act 1985, but must be written off to the profit and loss account on consolidation under the provisions of FRS 6.

28.104 Where relevant merger expenses are added to the carrying amount of investment in the parent's balance sheet care will need to be taken to ensure that the resultant carrying amount does not exceed the investment's recoverable amount. If it did, a provision would be needed against the investment. This might occur if the expenses were very large in relation to the value of the entity with which the parent is combining. However, the fact that the shares issued are recorded at their nominal value, rather than at their fair value, should usually mean that the carrying value including expenses is well below the recoverable amount of the investment and thus no provision will normally be needed.

28.105 The alternative treatment described above of costs that are eligible to be written off against share premium account, that is adding such costs to the carrying value of the investment, differs from the treatment of such costs prescribed by FRS 7 where acquisition accounting and fair valuing are required (see chapter 25). However, as the treatment of expenses on consolidation also differs between merger and acquisition accounting this difference is considered acceptable.

Accounting periods

28.106 Where a new parent company is formed to effect a merger between two companies or to effect a group reconstruction whereby it becomes the parent company of an existing group, problems can arise if the accounting period of the new parent differs from that of the other combining entities. Three examples are given below and two other examples are given above in paragraph 28.70.

Example 1

A new parent company is formed 1 July 20X1 and issues equity shares in exchange for the equity shares of company A. Company A's accounting reference period is the 12 months to December 20X1. The first reference period of the new parent company is fixed as the six months to 31 December 20X1. The combination satisfies the conditions for merger accounting.

The question arises as to what figures for company A should be included in the consolidated financial statements, which themselves must cover the period from 1 July to 31 December 20X1.

One argument would be that the consolidated financial statements should include the results of company A for the period from 1 July to 31 December 20X1 with comparatives for the period 1 July to 31 December 20X0. This treatment is the most obvious and is quite acceptable. However, this would mean that the group financial statements would omit the six months trading of company A from 1 January 20X1 to 30 June 20X1. It can also cause difficulties in obtaining figures for the 'stub period' of the combining entity. An alternative is that the consolidated financial statements would include the results of the new parent for the six months to 31 December 20X1 and the results of company A for the 12 months to December 20X1. The basis for this treatment is as follows:

Paragraph 2 of Schedule 4A of the Act requires that the consolidated balance sheet and profit and loss account shall incorporate in full the information contained in the individual financial statements of the undertakings included in the consolidation, subject to the adjustments authorised or required by the Schedule and to such other adjustments as may be appropriate in accordance with generally accepted accounting principles or practice.

Based on this provision of the Act, and because there do not appear to be any adjustments that would be required by the Schedule or generally accepted accounting principles or practice, we consider that in the situation described above the results of company A may be included in the consolidated financial statements for the full accounting reference period of company A. Thus the consolidated financial statements for the 6 months to 31 December 20X1 would include the results of the new parent for 6 months and the results of company A for 12 months. The comparative figures for the consolidated financial statements under merger accounting would comprise the profit and loss account, cash flow statement and balance sheet of the new subsidiary for the year to 31 December 20X0. An example of where a company has adopted the second approach is in Table 28.3A.

Table 28.3A — Allied Domecq PLC — Annual Report and Accounts — 31 August 1999

Accounting policies (extract)

Consolidation The group accounts consolidate the accounts of the company and its interests in subsidiaries. Interests in associates and joint ventures are equity accounted. During the year there was a capital reorganisation that required a new parent company for the group (refer to note 21). This has been accounted for using merger accounting principles.

Note 21 (extract)

Changes in authorised, allotted and issued ordinary share capital (extract)

Allied Domecq PLC was incorporated on 11 May 1999 as a public limited company with the name Allied Domecq 1999 PLC, which was changed to new Allied Domecq PLC ('the company') on 28 May 1999.

On 2 August 1999, the company acquired Allied Domecq PLC as part of the Scheme. Shares in Allied Domecq PLC were cancelled and in consideration shareholders received shares in the company, in the ratio of one share in the company for each share in Allied Domecq PLC. Allied Domecq PLC was renamed Allied Domecq (Holdings) PLC and new Allied Domecq PLC was renamed Allied Domecq PLC.

Group Profit and Loss Account (extract)
Year to 31 August 1999

		Year to 31 August 1999			Year to 31 August 1998		
		Before exceptional items	**Exceptional items**	**Total**	Before exceptional items	Exceptional items	Total
	Note	**£m**	**£m**	**£m**	£m	£m	£m
Continuing operations		**2,408**	**–**	**2,408**	2,398	–	2,398
Discontinued operations		**1,695**	**–**	**1,695**	1,910	–	1,910
Group turnover and share of turnover of joint venture undertaking	1	**4,103**	**–**	**4,103**	4,308	–	4,308
Less: share of turnover of joint venture – discontinued operation		**(624)**	**–**	**(624)**	–	–	–
Turnover		**3,479**	**–**	**3,479**	4,308	–	4,308
Operating costs	3	**(2,838)**	**(235)**	**(3,073)**	(3,609)	(87)	(3,696)
Continuing operations		**420**	**(220)**	**200**	415	(12)	403
Discontinued operations		**221**	**(15)**	**206**	284	(75)	209
Operating profit		**641**	**(235)**	**406**	699	(87)	612

Example 2

A similar approach may be adopted if the new parent company were formed on 1 October 20X0 and had its first year end on 31 December 20X1, a 15 month accounting period.

In this case the consolidated financial statements for the 15 months to 31 December 20X1 would include the new parent for 15 months from 1 October 20X0 and company A's results for its accounting reference period of one year from 1 January 20X1 to 31 December 20X1. Comparative figures would most sensibly be for the year to December 20X0 as this would give a continuous record for the combined group. (There would be no duplication of the new parent company's results on the reasonable assumption that it will not have traded in the period to 31 December 20X0.)

28.107 As the above two examples demonstrate, the apparent problems that arise, where the accounting periods of the new parent and the other combining entity are different, can be overcome. It is obviously much simpler, however, to arrange that where a new parent company is to be formed and merger accounting is to be adopted it should have the same accounting period as the company that it combines with. Where a new top company is used to implement a merger, the forward planning should always seek to avoid the problems that can arise through having different accounting periods for the new parent and the other combining entity.

28.108 Where no new parent company is involved, but the year ends of the combining companies differ, again problems may arise.

Example

Company A, which has a year end of 31 December, combines with company B which has a year end of 30 September. Company A is preparing consolidated financial statements for the year ended 31 December 19X5, the year in which the merger took place. There are three apparent possibilities at first sight in respect of inclusion of company B's results.

(i) Include the results of company B for the year ended 31 December 19X5 based on interim accounts prepared by company B for the 12 months to that date. This is permitted by Schedule 4A paragraph 2(2) to the Companies Act 1985 which states:

"*If the financial year of a subsidiary undertaking included in the consolidation does not end with that of the parent company, the consolidated accounts shall be made up —*

(a) from the accounts of the subsidiary undertaking for its financial year last ending before the end of the parent company's financial year provided that year ended no more than three months before that of the parent company, or

(b) from interim accounts prepared by the subsidiary undertaking as at the end of the parent company's financial year."

The comparatives for the year ended 31 December 19X4 would similarly include the results of company B for the year ended on that date based on interim accounts for 12 months.

(ii) Include the results of company B for the 15 months ended 31 December 19X5 with the comparative figures for the year ended 31 December 19X4 including company B for the 15 months ended on that date again based on interim accounts. This approach is not appropriate as it would involve double counting of company B's results for the period from September 19X4 to December 19X4.

(iii) Include the results of company B for the 12 months to September 19X5 with the comparatives similarly including the results of company B for the 12 months to September 19X4. Although permitted by the Act (because the year end of company B is not more than three months before that of the parent) it should be noted that FRS 2 requires that interim accounts should be prepared to 31 December, the parent's year end, unless it is impracticable to do so. Therefore, this approach should only be adopted in the rare circumstances where it is impracticable to prepare interim accounts.

Of the three possibilities, therefore, (i) is the appropriate treatment in all cases except where it is impracticable in which case (iii) would be adopted. The treatment in (ii) should not be adopted.

Comparison of acquisition accounting with merger accounting

28.109 FRS 6 highlights the following three main differences between acquisition accounting and merger accounting:

- In acquisition accounting, the consolidated financial statements reflect the acquired company's results from the date of acquisition only. However, in merger accounting, the consolidated financial statements incorporate the combined companies' results and cash flows as if the companies had always been combined. Consequently, under merger accounting, the consolidated financial statements reflect both companies' full year's results, even though the business combination may have occurred part of the way though the year. Under merger accounting, the corresponding amounts in the consolidated financial statements for the previous year should reflect the results of the combined companies, even though the business combination did not occur until the current year.

- In acquisition accounting, the acquiring group should account for the assets it acquired at the cost to the acquiring group. The acquiring group determines that cost by attributing a fair value to the assets and liabilities that it acquires. However, in merger accounting, the group does not restate any assets and liabilities at their fair values. Instead, the group incorporates the assets and liabilities at the amounts recorded in the books of the combining companies. As in the profit and loss account presentation, merger accounting shows the position of the combining companies as if the companies had always been combined.

- Acquisition accounting may give rise to goodwill on consolidation. However, goodwill does not arise in merger accounting. Merger accounting may lead to differences on consolidation. For example, in merger accounting, there may be a difference between the nominal value of the shares issued together with the fair value of any additional consideration given, and the nominal value of the other company's shares that have been acquired (see paras 28.92 to 28.97). However, such differences are not goodwill as defined in FRS 10, because they are not based on the fair values of both the consideration given and the identifiable assets and liabilities acquired.

28.110 The following example illustrates the difference between acquisition accounting and merger accounting. The example is somewhat artificial in that it shows both methods applying to the same situation whereas in practice under FRS 6 there is no choice between the methods of accounting. The combination will either have to be acquisition accounted or it will have to be merger accounted. The method will depend on whether or not all the conditions for merger accounting in FRS 6 are met.

Example

Company H (the issuing company) acquires the whole of company A's equity share capital. The effect of the acquisition will be to merge the interests of company H and company A.

Company A's shareholders accept an offer from company H of 400,000 shares in company H for the 410,000 issued shares in company A as at 31 December 20X0. The value at 31 December of the 400,000 of company H's £1 shares that are offered to company A's shareholders is £6.4 million, (that is, £16 per share). The fair value of company A's net assets is £6.1 million (that is, £90,000 above their net book value). The difference of £300,000 is attributable to goodwill. On 31 December 20X0, before the acquisition, the summarised balance sheets of the two companies are as follows:

	Co H	Co A
	£'000	£'000
Net assets	5,000	6,010
Share capital (shares of £1 each)	500	410
Reserves	4,500	5,600
	5,000	6,010

The summarised consolidated balance sheets of the issuing company and its subsidiary under the two methods of accounting are as follows:

	Notes	Acquisition accounting £'000	Merger accounting £'000
Goodwill on consolidation	(a)	300	–
Net assets	(b)	11,100	11,010
		11,400	11,010
Share capital	(c)	900	900
Distributable reserves	(e)	4,500	10,100
Merger reserve	(d)	6,000	
Other reserves	(f)		10
		11,400	11,010

Notes to the example above:

(a) Goodwill on consolidation is the amount by which the purchase consideration (that is, 400,000 shares at £16, or £6.4 million) exceeds the fair value of the underlying net assets acquired (that is, £6.1 million).

(b) Net assets are the two companies' total net assets. In acquisition accounting, the assets acquired are included at their fair value, as required by the Act and FRS 2. In merger accounting the assets of the combining companies are not fair valued.

(c) The share capital consists of the 500,000 shares originally in issue, together with the 400,000 shares allotted when company H combined with company A.

(d) The amount credited to the merger reserve taking merger relief under section 131 of the Act is £6 million (that is, 400,000 shares issued at a premium of £15 per share).

(e) Under merger accounting there is no requirement to transfer to a merger reserve the premium on the shares allotted to the acquired company's shareholders. Consequently, both companies' distributable reserves are pooled. In accordance with the Act and paragraph 16 of FRS 6 the excess of the fair value of company A's net assets over their book value (that is, £90,000) need not be incorporated into the consolidated financial statements.

(f) Under merger accounting the difference between the nominal value of shares issued (that is, £400,000) and the nominal value of shares received as consideration (that is £410,000) is credited to other reserves. Had the carrying value of the investment exceeded the nominal value of the shares received as consideration the difference would be debited to reserves.

28.111 The example that follows illustrates the differences between using acquisition accounting and using merger accounting in a group reconstruction where the group reconstruction qualifies for relief under section 132.

Example

In 19X1, company A acquired all of company C's issued share capital (100,000 £1 shares) for £390,000. Company C had no reserves at that time. On 31 December 19X5, another wholly-owned subsidiary (company B) allots 100,000 £1 shares to company A. In return for the allotment, company A transfers to company B the shares in company C that it owns. Subsequently, company A is to be liquidated, and its shareholders will receive shares in company B. At the time of the reconstruction, company B's shares that are issued to company A are worth £400,000 (that is, £4 per share) and the fair value of company C's recorded net assets is £360,000 (the difference of £40,000 being attributed to goodwill). The fair value of company A's and company B's net assets is equal to their book value.

Diagrammatically, the reconstruction is as follows:

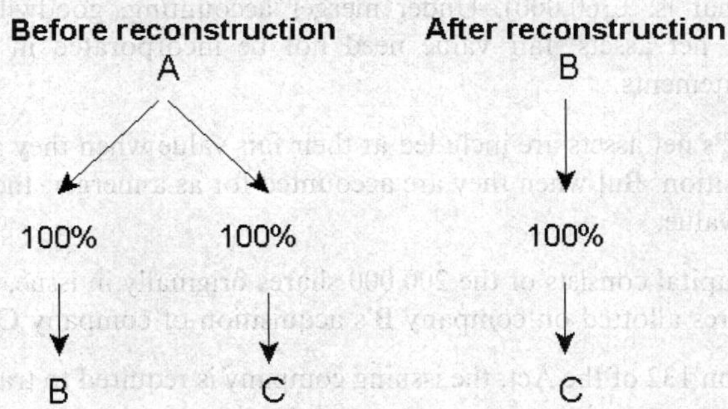

The individual balance sheets of the three companies as at 31 December 19X5 before the reconstruction are as follows:

	Co A	Co B	Co C
	£'000	£'000	£'000
Investment in B*	210	–	–
Investment in C*	320	–	–
Net assets	–	700	350
	530	700	350
Share capital (shares of 1 each)	150	200	100
Reserves	380	500	250
	530	700	350

*The investments are stated at the cost of shares to company A, reduced for company A's investment in company C by a write-down of £70,000 made in 19X2.

After the reconstruction, the summarised consolidated balance sheet of company B and its subsidiary company C is as follows:

	Notes	Acquisition accounting £'000	Merger accounting £'000
Goodwill on consolidation	(a)	40	–
Net assets	(b)	1,060	1,050
		1,100	1,050
Share capital	(c)	300	300
Share premium account	(d)	220	220
Merger reserve	(e)	80	–
Reserves	(f)	500	530
		1,100	1,050

Notes to the example above:

(a) Goodwill on consolidation is the amount by which the purchase consideration (that is, 100,000 shares at £4, or £400,000) exceeds the fair value of the underlying assets acquired (that is, £360,000). Under merger accounting, goodwill does not arise, because the net assets' fair value need not be incorporated in the consolidated financial statements.

(b) Company C's net assets are included at their fair value when they are accounted for as an acquisition. But when they are accounted for as a merger, they are included at their book value.

(c) The share capital consists of the 200,000 shares originally in issue, together with the 100,000 shares allotted on company B's acquisition of company C.

(d) Under section 132 of the Act, the issuing company is required to transfer to the share premium account only an amount equal to the minimum premium value. The minimum premium value is calculated as the amount by which the base value of the shares in company C, that are transferred from company A to company B, exceeds the aggregate nominal value of the shares that company B allots in consideration for the transfer. The amount of the transfer to the share premium account is calculated as follows:

	£'000	£'000
The base value of shares in company C is the lower of:		
The cost of the shares to company A	390	
The amount at which those shares are stated in company A's accounting records immediately before the transfer	320	
		320
	Less:	
Nominal value of the shares company B allotted in respect of the transfer		100
Transfer to the share premium account		220

(e) The amount credited to the merger reserve under acquisition accounting is the amount of the premium that is not required to be taken to the share premium account because of section 132 relief (that is, 100,000 shares issued at a premium of £3, or £300,000 less £220,000 required to be taken to share premium under section 132).

(f) Under acquisition accounting, the amount to be included in other reserves is the amount of company B's reserves (that is, £500,000). Under section 132 of the Act (which gives the relief in respect of group reconstructions) other reserves are made up as follows:

	£'000
Reserves of company B	500
Reserves of company C less minimum premium value (that is, £250,000 — £220,000)	30
	530

Disclosure for merger accounting

Consolidated financial statements

28.112 The issuing company should disclose certain information in respect of all material mergers. The parent must disclose in the consolidated financial statements that deal with the period in which the merger occurs:

- The names of the merging companies (other than the reporting entity). [CA85 4A Sch 13(2)(a); FRS 6 para 21 (a)]. The Act goes on to add that where the issuing company has merged with a group of companies, only the name of the group's parent needs to be disclosed.

- That the company adopted merger accounting for the combination. [CA85 4A Sch 13(2)(b); FRS 6 para 21(b)].

- The effective date of the merger. [FRS 6 para 21(c)].

28.113 In addition, further information is required to be disclosed for mergers. The FRS 6 disclosures listed below do not apply to group reconstructions (but the

Act's disclosure requirements *do* apply even where they are the same as in FRS 6). [FRS 6 para 82]. These requirements are as follows:

- The composition and the fair value of the consideration given by the parent and its subsidiaries. [CA85 4A Sch 13(3); FRS 6 para 22(c)].
- An explanation of any significant adjustments made to the assets and liabilities of the undertaking or group acquired. This should include a statement of any resulting adjustment to the consolidated reserves (including a restatement of opening consolidated reserves). [CA85 4A Sch 13(6); FRS 6 para 22(f)]. The figures above should be disclosed after taking into account the consolidation adjustments required by the Act. [CA85 4A Sch 13(7)]. This would include for example adjustments to achieve uniform accounting policies.
- The nature and the amount of significant accounting adjustments made to the net assets of any party to the merger to achieve consistent accounting policies and an explanation of any other significant adjustments made to the net assets of any party to the merger as a consequence of the merger. [FRS 6 para 22(e)].
- The aggregate book value of the net assets of each party to the merger at the effective date of the merger. [FRS 6 para 22(d)].

28.114 If in the directors' opinion the disclosure of any of the information above that is required by the Act (relating to an undertaking established under the law of a country, or one that carries on a business, outside the UK) would be seriously prejudicial to the business of the undertaking, its parent or its fellow subsidiaries, it need not be given if the Secretary of State's permission is obtained. [CA85 4A Sch 16].

28.115 In addition in respect of a material merger, other than a group reconstruction, the issuing company should disclose the following information in its financial statements that deal with a year in which a merger occurs:

- An analysis of the principal components of the current year's profit and loss account and statement of total recognised gains and losses into:
  - amounts relating to the merged entity for the period after the date of the merger; and
  - for each party to the merger, amounts relating to that party for the period up to the date of the merger.
- An analysis between the parties to the merger of the principal components of the profit and loss account and statement of total recognised gains and losses for the previous financial year.

[FRS 6 paras 22(a)(b)].

28.116 The standard specifies the headings that comprise the principal components of the profit and loss account and statement of total recognised gains and losses for the purposes of the disclosure requirements. These are:

- Turnover analysed between continuing operations (with acquisitions disclosed separately) and discontinued operations.
- Operating profit analysed in the same way as turnover.
- Exceptional items analysed in the same way as turnover.
- Profit before taxation.
- Taxation and minority interests.
- Extraordinary items (highly unlikely under FRS 3).

[FRS 6 para 22].

28.117 The principal components of the statement of total recognised gains and losses, whilst not specified in the FRS, would usually be:

- Profit for the financial year.
- Exchange gains or losses taken direct to reserves.
- Revaluation surpluses or deficits.
- Total recognised gains or losses.

28.118 In relation to the category of revaluation surpluses or deficits, the standard makes it clear that the requirement for disclosure does not mean that revaluations carried out at the end of a financial year would need to be repeated at the effective date of merger.

Example

An example of the extensive disclosure that might result from compliance with the requirements of the FRS and the Act is as follows:

XYZ plc merged with ABC plc on 30 June 20X1 and has accounted for the combination using merger accounting. The consideration was satisfied by the issue of £400,000 equity shares with a nominal value of £1 each. The fair value of the consideration was £5m based on the market price of XYZ plc shares at 30 June 20X1. No significant adjustments were made to the assets and liabilities of ABC plc which have been recorded at their book values immediately prior to the merger and no adjustments were made to the net assets of XYZ plc. The book value of net assets of XYZ plc and ABC plc at the date of the combination were £1.2m and £1m respectively. The difference of £50,000 arising on consolidation between the nominal value of XYZ plc shares issued (£400,000) and the nominal value of ABC plc shares acquired (£450,000) has been credited to reserves. ABC's financial year began on 1 January 20X1.

The analysis of the principal components of the profit and loss accounts and statements of total recognised gains and losses is as follows:

20X1	Combined post merger £m	XYZ plc pre merger £m	ABC plc pre merger £m	Total for the year £m
Profit and loss account				
Turnover				
Continuing	27	12	13	52
Acquisitions	4	–	1	5
Total continuing	31	12	14	57
Discontinued	1	1	–	2
	32	13	14	59
Operating profit				
Continuing	4	2	1	7
Acquisitions	1			1
Total continuing	5	2	1	8
Discontinued	(1)	–	–	(1)
	4	2	1	7
Exceptional items				
Discontinued operations				
Loss on sale of subsidiaries	(1)	–	–	(1)
Profit before taxation	3	2	1	6
Taxation	1	1	–	2
Profit after taxation and for the financial period	2	1	1	4
Total recognised gains and losses				
Profit after taxation and for the financial period	2	1	1	4
Exchange (losses)/gains	1	(1)	–	–
Revaluation surplus	3	–	–	3
Total recognised gains	6	–	1	7

The equivalent analysis for the previous year is as follows:

20X0	XYZ plc	ABC plc
	£m	£m
Profit and loss account		
Turnover		
Continuing	20	23
Discontinued	3	–
	23	23
(There were no acquisitions in 20X0)		
Operating profit		
Continuing	3	4
Discontinued	(1)	–
	2	4
(there were no post operating profit exceptional items in 20X0)		
Profit before taxation	2	4
Taxation	–	1
Profit after tax and for the financial year	2	3
Total recognised gains and losses		
Profit after tax and for the financial year	2	3
Exchange (losses)/gains	(1)	1
Revaluation surpluses	3	4
Total recognised gains	4	8

[The next paragraph is 28.121.]

28.121 Interest has been ignored in the above example. Also the totals for 20X1 are not required as they appear in the profit and loss itself, but have been given above to enable the figures for the pre-acquisition and post-acquisition periods to be reconciled.

28.122 A further example of the disclosures described above is Table 28.4.

Table 28.4 — United News & Media plc — Annual Report and Accounts — 31 December 1996

Accounting policies (extract)

Merger with MAI plc On 8 February 1996, United News & Media plc (United) and MAI plc (MAI) announced plans for the merging of their respective businesses. The merger was to be effected by way of offers made by United for the whole of the issued share capital of MAI. These offers became unconditional on 2 April 1996. The merger has been accounted for using the merger accounting principles set out in Financial Reporting Standard 6. Accordingly, the financial information for the current period has been presented, and that for the prior year restated, as if MAI had been owned by United throughout the current and comparative accounting periods.

Note 24

24. Merger adjustments The merger adjustments reflect the alignment of accounting policies following the merger:

(a) Intangible assets—in previous periods publishing rights and titles had been stated at directors' valuation*. These are now stated at fair value on acquisition and are not revalued. The effect of this restatement is a debit adjustment to the revaluation reserve of £73 million. The comparative figures for 1995 have been restated.

(b) Consolidation—on acquisition of subsidiary undertakings, business or associated undertakings the purchase consideration is allocated between underlying assets on a fair value basis. Any goodwill arising is written off direct to reserves*. Previously in MAI the goodwill relating to certain associates was amortised over its expected economic life. The effect of this restatement is a debit adjustment to goodwill of £27.7 million. The comparative figures for 1995 have been restated.

Note 29

29. Business merger As explained in the accounting policies, on 8 February 1996, United and MAI announced plans for the merging of their respective businesses. The merger was to be effected by way of offers made by United for the whole of the issued share capital of MAI, being 332,718,123 ordinary shares of 5 pence each and 120,956,330 preference shares of 5 pence each, for a consideration of 242,090,550 ordinary shares of 25 pence each, the fair value of which amounted to £1,560.3 million. These offers became unconditional on 2 April 1996. The merger has been accounted for using the merger accounting principles set out in Financial Reporting Standard 6. Accordingly the financial information for the current period has been presented, and that for the prior periods restated, as if MAI had been owned by United throughout the current and prior accounting periods.

The book value of net assets at the time of the merger together with adjustments arising from the alignment of accounting policies were:

	£m
United	
Book value of net assets at time of merger	238.0
Merger adjustment (note 24)	(73.0)
Restated net assets at time of merger	165.0
MAI	
Book value of net assets at time of merger	224.6
Merger adjustment (note 24)	(27.7)
Restated net assets at time of merger	196.9

29. *Business merger* continued

An analysis of contribution to the profit attributable to shareholders made by the combining groups in the period prior to the merger date on 2 April 1996, the principal components of the profit and loss accounts and statements of total recognised gains and losses is as follows:

Profit and loss account	United pre merger £m	MAI pre merger £m	Combined post merger £m	Total £m
Turnover				
Continuing operations	268.8	196.9	1,451.8	1,917.5
Acquisitions	2.7	–	18.3	21.0
Discontinued operations	6.8	14.6	30.8	52.2
	278.3	211.5	1,500.9	1,990.7
Operating profit				
Continuing operations	21.4	23.5	129.6	174.5
Acquisitions	0.7	–	(18.1)	(17.4)
Discontinued operations	0.2	4.0	6.9	11.1
	22.3	27.5	118.4	168.2
Income from interests in associated undertakings	1.9	3.9	(47.1)	(41.3)
Income from other fixed asset investments	0.6	–	1.6	2.2
Total operating profit	24.8	31.4	72.9	129.1
Merger expenses	–	–	(31.0)	(31.0)
Profit on the disposal of fixed asset investments	–	11.6	–	11.6
Profit on sales and closure of businesses	–	–	138.0	138.0
Profit on ordinary activities before interest	24.8	43.0	179.9	247.7
Net interest expense	(4.0)	(1.0)	(8.9)	(13.9)
Profit before tax	20.8	42.0	171.0	233.8
Tax	(6.8)	(14.0)	(55.1)	(75.9)
Profit after tax	14.0	28.0	115.9	157.9
Minority interest	–	(0.2)	(5.3)	(5.5)
Profit for the year	14.0	27.8	110.6	152.4
Total recognised gains and losses				
Profit for the year	14.0	27.8	110.6	152.4
Exchange gains	–	–	1.4	1.4
	14.0	27.8	112.0	153.8

The equivalent analysis for the year ended 31 December 1995 is as follows:

Profit and loss account	United £m	MAI £m	Total £m
Turnover			
Continuing operations	1,032.9	768.2	1,801.1
Discontinued operations	37.7	52.6	90.3
	1,070.6	820.8	1,891.4
Operating profit			
Continuing operations	111.2	89.1	200.3
Discontinued operations	3.9	12.8	16.7
	115.1	101.9	217.0
Income from interests in associated undertakings	0.9	12.9	13.8
Income from other fixed asset investments	3.3	–	3.3
Total operating profit	119.3	114.8	234.1
Loss on sales and closures of businesses	(2.9)	–	(2.9)

Profit on ordinary activities before interest	116.4	114.8	231.2
Net interest expense	(11.9)	(4.0)	(15.9)
Profit before tax	104.5	110.8	215.3
Tax	(34.3)	(36.0)	(70.3)
Profit after tax	70.2	74.8	145.0
Minority interest	(1.5)	1.4	(0.1)
Profit for the year	68.7	76.2	144.9
Total recognised gains and losses			
Profit for the year	68.7	76.2	144.9
Exchange losses	(0.5)	–	(0.5)
	68.2	76.2	144.4

* Note that since the publication of FRS 10, carrying intangible assets at directors' valuation and writing goodwill off to reserves are not permitted.

Chapter 29

Related party disclosures

	Page
Introduction	29001
Related parties	29002
The reporting entity	29002
Criteria for related party relationships	29003
Control	29003
Common control	29004
Influence	29005
Common influence	29005
Establishing influence and common influence	29005
Examples of control or influence from same source	29007
Effect of the group being the reporting entity	29008
Related parties which are specified by FRS 8	29009
Parties deemed to be related	29009
Parent, subsidiary and fellow subsidiary undertakings	29010
Associates and joint ventures	29010
Investors and venturers	29011
Directors	29012
Pension funds	29012
Pension funds and their investment manager	29013
Parties presumed to be related	29014
Key management	29014
Persons acting in concert	29015
Management contracts	29016
Persons connected to a related party	29018
Close family	29018
Partnerships, companies, trusts or other entities	29019
Identification of related parties	29020
Related parties for only part of the year	29021
Related party transactions	29021
Agency arrangements	29023
Materiality	29023
General purpose financial statements	29025
Comparison with 'materiality' under the Companies Act 1985	29025
Disclosure requirements	29026
Summary	29026
Disclosure of control	29026
Source of control or ownership	29028
Shared control	29028
Control by trusts	29029
Limited partnerships	29031

Disclosure of transactions and balances 29032
Material transactions 29032
Balances between related parties 29033
Aggregation of transactions 29034
Transactions with directors 29037
Comparatives 29038
Practical application 29038
Transactions between companies under common control 29038
Transactions entered into by group companies 29039
Subsidiaries acquired and disposed of during the year 29040
Quasi-subsidiary undertakings 29043
Associates and joint ventures 29044
Pension funds 29046
Shareholders 29047
Directors 29048
Close family 29051
Key management 29052
Exemptions from disclosure 29052
Introduction 29052
Intra-group transactions or balances eliminated on consolidation 29052
Parent's own financial statements 29054
Ninety per cent subsidiaries 29054
Pension contributions 29058
Emoluments for services 29058
Duty of confidentiality 29059
Additional relaxation of disclosure requirements 29059
Overriding requirement to give a true and fair view 29061
Interaction with disclosures required by the Companies Act 1985 29062
Loans and other similar transactions with directors 29062
Loans and other similar transactions with officers 29063
Transactions in which a director has a material interest 29063
Interaction with disclosures required by the Companies Act 2006 29064
Annex — Main disclosure requirements of the Companies Acts 1985 and 2006 29066

Chapter 29

Related party disclosures

Introduction

29.1 Related party transactions can take a variety of forms. Many of them include transactions in the normal course of business, for example, purchases or sales of goods at market values. However, others can include significant one-off transactions that may be at a fair value on an arm's length basis or which may be at book value or some other amount that differs from market prices. The stated objective of FRS 8, 'Related party disclosures', is to ensure that financial statements contain the disclosures necessary to draw attention to the possibility that the reported financial position and results may have been affected by the existence of related parties and by material transactions with them.

29.2 The ASB has given an indication of its reasoning for requiring disclosure of all material related party transactions (rather than just abnormal ones) by explaining the effect on a reporting entity of the existence of related party relationships. This may be summarised as follows:

- In the absence of contrary information, it is assumed that a reporting entity has power over its resources and transactions and acts independently of the interests of its owners, managers and others. Transactions are presumed to have been undertaken on an arm's length basis.

- These assumptions may not be justified where related party relationships exist, because free market dealings may not occur. Sometimes disclosure of the relationship alone may be sufficient to make users of the financial statements aware of the possible implications of related party relationships. This is why transactions between 90 per cent subsidiary undertakings and other group members need not be disclosed under FRS 8 in the subsidiary's financial statements (see further para 29.149).

- The reporting of material arm's length transactions between related parties is useful information, because such transactions are more susceptible to alteration. Although related party relationships sometimes preclude arm's length transactions, non-independent parties can deal at arm's length; for instance, where a parent places no restrictions on two subsidiaries, giving them complete freedom in their dealings with each other. However, financial statements should not imply that related party transactions were entered into on arm's length terms unless the parties have conducted the transactions in an independent manner.

[FRS 8 paras 8-10].

29.3 The disclosures required by FRS 8 complement the UK statutory disclosure requirements for related parties. These rules are considered from paragraph UK.29.174 onwards. FRS 8's perspective is somewhat broader in that it concentrates on the relevance of the information to the users of financial statements. It extends the amount of disclosure that has to be given in some instances and also requires disclosure of additional transactions and relationships.

29.4 FRS 8 applies to all financial statements that are intended to give a true and fair view of the reporting entity's financial position and profit or loss (or income and expenditure) for a period (subject to certain exemptions). In summary, the standard requires the following information to be disclosed in a reporting entity's financial statements about its related parties:

- The name of the party that controls the reporting entity and, if different, the name of the ultimate controlling party (whether or not any transactions have taken place with those parties).
- Details of material transactions between the reporting entity and any related parties.
- Details of balances due to, or from, related parties at the balance sheet date.

29.5 Under the standard, two or more parties are related parties when:

- one party has direct or indirect control of the other party;
- the parties are subject to common control from the same source;
- one party has influence over the other party; or
- the parties are subject to influence from the same source.

29.6 The international accounting rules are to be found in IAS 24, 'Related party disclosures'. This contains similar requirements and definitions to FRS 8, but it does not include most of the exemptions available under FRS 8.

[The next paragraph is 29.14.]

Related parties

The reporting entity

29.14 FRS 8 requires material transactions between the reporting entity and its related parties to be disclosed in its financial statements. The reporting entity will be the company, where it is preparing its individual financial statements. However, if the company is a parent company and is preparing consolidated financial statements, the reporting entity will be the group headed by the parent company. A parent company must under section 227 of the Companies Act 1985 (and section 399 of the Companies Act 2006) prepare group accounts, that is, consolidated financial statements comprising itself and its subsidiaries. 'Group' is defined in section 262 of the 1985 Act (and section 474 of the 2006 Act) as *"a parent undertaking and its subsidiary undertakings*". The criteria to establish related party relationships between a company and its related parties and the group and its related parties should, therefore, be applied at individual company level and, in the case of consolidated financial statements, at group level.

Criteria for related party relationships

29.15 A related party can be an individual or an entity, such as a company or unincorporated business. Where a group of individuals or entities act in concert to divert a reporting entity from pursuing its own separate interests, each individual or entity in the group will be a related party.

29.16 A related party is a party that has a relationship with the reporting entity which affects the pursuit of separate interests of either the reporting entity or the related party itself. This related party relationship arises because transactions between the parties could have a significant effect on the financial position and operating results of the reporting entity. The reporting entity can be any of the parties that are involved in the transaction or the group of which they are a member.

29.17 The FRS sets out four criteria for establishing whether certain parties are related parties as follows.

"Two or more parties are related parties when at any time during the financial period:

(i) One party has direct or indirect control of the other party; or

(ii) The parties are subject to common control from the same source; or

(iii) One party has influence over the financial and operating policies of the other party to an extent that that other party might be inhibited from pursuing at all times its own separate interests; or

(iv) The parties, in entering a transaction, are subject to influence from the same source to such an extent that one of the parties to the transaction has subordinated its own separate interests."

[FRS 8 para 2.5(a)].

29.18 These criteria, which give rise to a related party relationship, may be summarised as: control; common control; influence; and common influence. These terms are discussed below from paragraph 29.19. There are, in addition, certain relationships that the standard automatically regards as related party relationships. These are described from paragraph 29.33.

Control

29.19 FRS 8's definition of 'control' as used in paragraph 29.17 above is similar to the definition of control found in paragraph 6 of FRS 2, 'Subsidiary undertakings'. The accounting concept of control is explained in FRS 2 in connection with identifying parent and subsidiary undertakings in the context of consolidation. [FRS 2 paras 62-67]. The definition in FRS 8 (given below) differs in that the ability to control can be held by an individual as well as an 'undertaking'. 'Control' is defined as:

> *"The ability to direct the financial and operating policies of an entity with a view to gaining economic benefits from its activities."*

[FRS 8 para 2.2].

29.20 The definition of control encompasses control by individuals and, for example, partnerships, as well as parent companies. An example of control by a partnership would be where a limited partnership controls over 50 per cent of the voting rights in a reporting entity. This is discussed further in paragraph 29.110. The question of control in relation to a trust is discussed from paragraph 29.102.

29.21 Another issue that arises in practice is whether several shareholders acting together (a concert party) to control an entity should be viewed as one controlling party or whether they should be considered separately, despite the fact that they act together. This is discussed from paragraph 29.55.

29.22 Where control exists, even though no transactions have taken place, the disclosure required by FRS 8 goes further than that required by the Companies Act 1985. Schedule 5 to the Companies Act 1985 requires disclosure of the ultimate parent company (in addition to disclosure in respect of the parent undertaking of the largest group of undertakings for which group accounts are drawn up and the smallest such group of undertakings). Therefore, FRS 8 requires more disclosure than the Companies Act where the ultimate controlling party is not an entity.

29.23 Bearer shares cannot be issued to avoid disclosure of the controlling party. In addition to creating an auditing problem, it is difficult to see how this would be effective where the directors in practice know for whom they are working and to whom dividends are paid.

Common control

29.24 Entities subject to common control from the same source are included in the definition of a related party, because of the potential effect on transactions between them and on their financial position. Common control arises, for example, when two entities are subject to common control by an individual. Common control is also deemed to exist when both parties are subject to control from boards having a controlling nucleus of directors in common (for an example see para 29.29).

Influence

29.25 'Influence' as used in the definition of related party in paragraph 29.17 is where one party has influence over the financial and operating policies of another party to the extent that the other party *might* be inhibited from pursuing at all times its own separate interests.

Common influence

29.26 Where the parties that enter into a transaction are subject to influence from the same source (that is, common influence) to the extent that one of the parties to the transaction has put its own separate interests after those of the other party (that is, has subordinated them), they are deemed to be related parties. The requirement for one of the parties to have subordinated its separate interests was considered necessary by the ASB otherwise a subsidiary in a large group, not qualifying for exemption, might not be aware that it had had transactions with a related party which was an associate of the group. Thus, in the absence of common control, two related parties of a third entity are not necessarily related parties of each other. Examples of arrangements that do *not* necessarily create related party relationships are given below:

- Where one party, B, is subject to control from A, and the other party, C, is subject only to influence from the same source, A, the two parties, B and C, are not necessarily related parties of each other. Since C is subject only to influence rather than control, the relationship between B and C would not normally justify being treated as related parties of each other (see diagram in para 29.29 below).
- Entities are not related parties of each other if their only connection is by being associated companies of the same investor. The parties are subject only to influence (rather than common control) and that relationship is normally too tenuous to justify them being treated as related parties of each other.
- Two entities are not related parties simply because they have a director in common (see diagram in para 29.29 below).

However, FRS 8 states that in all circumstances it will be appropriate to consider whether one or both transacting parties, subject to control and influence from the same source or to common influence, has put its own interests after those of the other parties in entering into that transaction. If either has, they will be related parties for the financial year and disclosure will be required of that transaction and all other transactions undertaken in the year.

Establishing influence and common influence

29.27 FRS 8 requires disclosure of transactions between parties where the relationship results from *influence* (as defined in para 2.5(a)(iii) of FRS 8). It is sometimes not clear whether one party influences another party to the extent that it might be inhibited from pursuing at all times its own separate interests. Our view is that the fact that one party has the right or power to inhibit the other is sufficient. It does not have to use this power or to prevent the other at all times from pursuing its own interests. Where one party has the ability to influence the other at any time during the financial period, transactions between them for the whole year become disclosable.

29.28 Where, on the other hand, two parties are subject to *common influence* (as defined in para 2.5(a)(iv) of FRS 8), transactions between those two parties become disclosable only where influence is actually exerted. It must have been exerted so that one or both transacting parties have subordinated their own separate interests in entering into a transaction. It is necessary to look at the facts of each transaction to assess whether there has been subordination of a party's own separate interests (that is, placing its own interests after those of others). Transactions where the price is above or below the commercial rate would generally mean a subordination; but it also might arise if one party is obliged to contract with a particular party or for a particular purpose, as that party would not have bargained knowledgeably and freely, unaffected by any relationship between the parties. Where two associated companies are directed to transact business with each other, this could mean a subordination of their separate interests.

29.29 Illustrations of these related party relationships, for instance, where A and B, and A and C, are related parties and B sells goods to C, can be shown diagrammatically as follows:

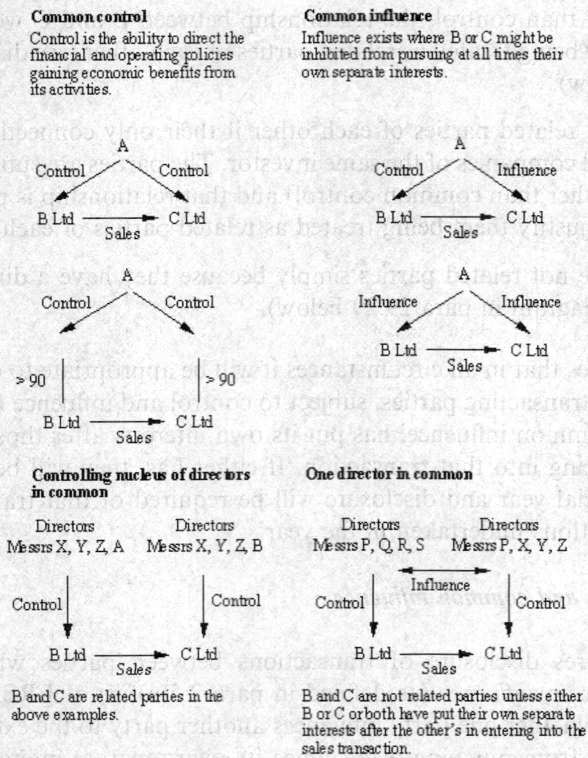

29.29.1 The last diagram above illustrates that entities that merely have a director (or other member of key management) in common are not necessarily related parties. This is considered further in the following example.

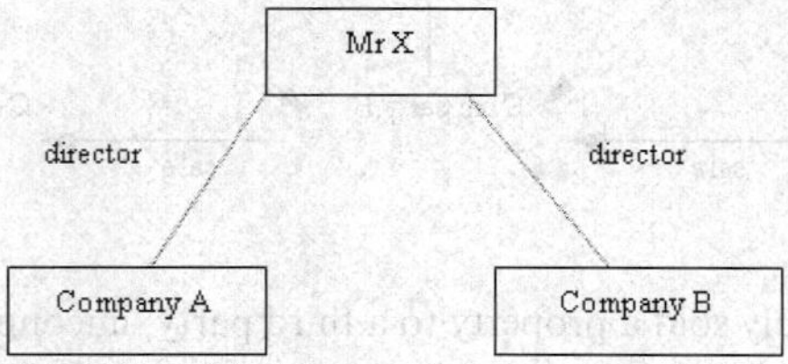

Example

A director (Mr X) of company A is also a director of company B. He does not control either company. There are no other directors in common. Company A has a trading relationship with company B. Are company A and company B related parties?

FRS 8 states that two companies are not related parties simply because they have a director in common. Although the director is able to influence both companies, that relationship would not normally justify treating the companies as related parties, since each company would be expected to pursue its separate interests for the benefit of its members.

There is an exception, though. If company A has entered into any transaction with company B where either or both companies have put their own separate interests after the other's (that is, subordinated its interest), FRS 8 deems them to be related parties for the whole of the financial year in question. A potential example of such a situation is where one company provides security in respect of the other company's borrowings, although companies would need to consider carefully the legal implications of such arrangements.

The answer would be different if companies A and B had a controlling nucleus of directors in common, for example, if each company had four directors, three of whom were common to both companies. FRS 8 explains that companies A and B would then be related parties, because they would be deemed to be subject to common control.

Examples of control or influence from same source

29.30 Transactions between parties subject to control or influence from the same source will be caught by the standard's disclosure requirements (see below).

Example

Company A is owned by Mr X and Mr Y who are its only directors and the company is in financial difficulties. Company A sells a property with a book value of £100,000 to company B, which is owned by Mr Z who is also B's sole director, for £50,000. Company B then sells the property to company C which is also owned by Mr X and Mr Y, who are its directors. Consider the disclosure in (i) company A and (ii) company C.

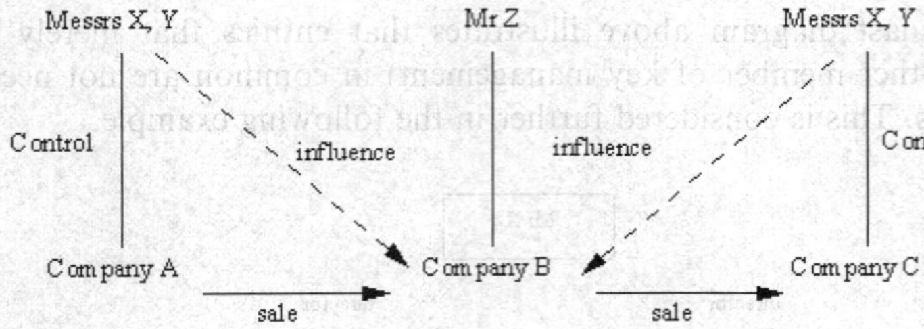

Company A has ostensibly sold a property to a third party, unconnected to its directors, at an undervalue. On the basis that the company is in financial difficulties it might be understandable that the sale is at an undervalue as it might be a forced sale. However, as company B makes neither profit or loss on the deal and appears to be an agent or intermediary for the transfer from A to C, it is very probable that Mr Z and company B are related parties of both A and C. This is because company B and Mr Z are unlikely to have agreed to participate in the transaction unless they were controlled or influenced by Mr X and Mr Y. It is clear that company A and company C are controlled by Mr X and Mr Y and that company B and Mr Z must have at least been influenced by them to such an extent that company B has subordinated its own separate interests in entering into the transaction. Company B is, therefore, a related party of both company A and company C.

In the financial statements of both company A and company C details of the transaction with company B should be disclosed. In addition, in company's A's financial statements details of the onward sale by company B to company C should be disclosed with details of the fact that company C has the same shareholders and directors as company A. Similarly, in company C's financial statements, additional details of the sale by company A to company B should be disclosed, with disclosure also of the fact that company A is under common control with company C. This would be because the standard requires disclosure of *"any other elements of the transactions necessary for an understanding of the financial statements"*. [FRS 8 para 6(e)].

Effect of the group being the reporting entity

29.31 Group undertakings will all be presumed to be related to each other (see para 29.35), but their inter-group transactions are not required to be disclosed under FRS 8 at group level as they will be eliminated on consolidation (see para 29.146). They will also be exempt from disclosure in the parent's own financial statements if those financial statements are presented together with its consolidated financial statements (see para 29.148), and at subsidiary company level if the exemption for 90 per cent subsidiaries applies (see para 29.149).

29.32 On the other hand, transactions between a subsidiary undertaking and its related parties outside the group may be disclosable at group level if material even if not disclosable in the subsidiary's financial statements. For instance, an associate of a subsidiary undertaking will also be an associate of the group and transactions between the associate and the group will be disclosable at group level if material to the group. However, if FRS 8 paragraph 3(c) applies, any transactions between the subsidiary and the associate will be exempt from disclosure in the subsidiary's financial statements (see para 29.135). In addition, a director of a subsidiary would be a related party of the group if he came within the definition of key management of the group. Material transactions between him and the subsidiary would be disclosable at both company and group level.

Related parties which are specified by FRS 8

29.33 The criteria referred to above are amplified in the FRS by two lists giving examples of related parties of the reporting entity. As has been mentioned, the reporting entity will either be the individual entity or the group in the case of consolidated financial statements. The related parties of a company may also be the related parties of the group.

29.34 The first list gives examples of parties that *are* related parties (because control or influence is deemed to exist) and the other list gives examples of parties that are *presumed* to be related parties because influence is presumed to exist in certain circumstances. Additionally, parties 'connected' to individual related parties may also be related parties of the reporting entity. However, the examples in the two lists and their connected parties are *not* intended to be exhaustive. These listings are considered in the paragraphs that follow.

Parties deemed to be related

29.35 The first list of related parties set out in FRS 8 includes parties that control or are controlled by the reporting entity or that are under control from the same source as it. The term 'reporting entity' should be read as referring to the individual undertaking where individual financial statements are being prepared and to the group where consolidated financial statements are being prepared. FRS 8 states that, for the avoidance of doubt, the following *are* related parties of the reporting entity:

- Its ultimate and intermediate parent undertakings, subsidiary undertakings, and fellow subsidiary undertakings.
- Its associates and joint ventures.
- The investor or venturer in respect of which the reporting entity is an associate or a joint venture.
- Directors of the reporting entity and the directors of its ultimate and intermediate parent undertakings.
- Pension funds for the benefit of employees of the reporting entity or of any entity that is a related party of the reporting entity.

Each of these related parties is discussed in turn in the paragraphs below.

Parent, subsidiary and fellow subsidiary undertakings

29.36 The ultimate and intermediate parent undertakings, subsidiary undertakings and fellow subsidiary undertakings of the reporting entity are its related parties.

29.37 There is no definition of parent undertaking and subsidiary undertaking in the FRS, but it is reasonable to assume that the terms have the same meaning as in paragraph 14 of FRS 2, which in turn is based on section 258 of the Companies Act 1985 (and section 1162 of the Companies Act 2006). See further chapter 24. It should be noted that the definition refers to undertakings, not just companies. Entities in a group, whether unincorporated or incorporated, will be related parties.

Associates and joint ventures

29.38 A reporting entity's associates and joint ventures are its related parties. [FRS 8 para 2.5(a)]. Again, it is reasonable to assume, that the definitions in FRS 9 and paragraph 20 of Schedule 4A to the Companies Act 1985 regarding associated undertakings would apply. Broadly, an associate is an undertaking (which is not a subsidiary undertaking or a joint venture) in which the investing company has 20 per cent or more of its voting rights and exercises a significant influence over its operating and financial policy. For an example of disclosure see Table 29.7. FRS 9, however, states that the 20 per cent holding must be held on a long-term basis and be a beneficial interest. The Act presumes that where an investor holds more than 20 per cent of the shares in an undertaking that this is a participating interest and, as a consequence, an associate relationship exists. However, under FRS 9's definition of an associate, the Act's presumption can be rebutted when the investor does not in practice have significant influence over the undertaking. See further chapter 27.

29.39 A joint venture, on the other hand, is an undertaking that the investing company manages jointly with other investors. [CA85 4A Sch 19]. Under FRS 9 a joint venture is defined as:

> *"An entity in which the reporting entity holds an interest on a long-term basis and is jointly controlled by the reporting entity and one or more other venturers under a contractual arrangement."* [FRS 9 para 4].

29.39.1 FRS 8 is clear that a reporting entity's associates and joint ventures are its related parties. However, the question arises as to whether a reporting entity's transactions with the related parties of its associate or joint venture should be disclosed as related party transactions. This is considered in the example below.

Example

Entity A owns 30% of the share capital of entity B and has the ability to exercise significant influence over it.

Entity B holds the following investments:
70% of the share capital of its subsidiary entity C;
50% of the share capital of the jointly controlled entity D; and
30% of the share capital of entity E, with the ability to exercise significant influence.

The structure is illustrated as follows:

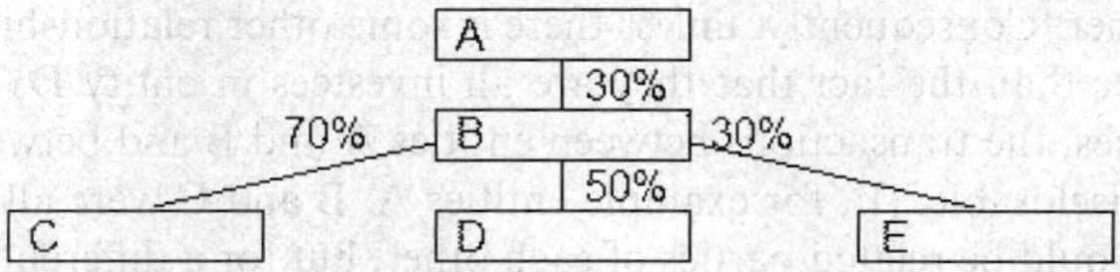

Entity A transacts with entities C, D and E. Should entity A disclose these transactions as related party transactions?

Entity A's management should disclose entity A's transactions with entity C in entity A's financial statements. Entity C is a related party of entity A, because entity A has significant influence over entity B, which controls entity C.

Entity A's management should disclose entity A's transactions with entity D in entity A's financial statements. Entity D is a related party of entity A, because entity A has significant influence over entity B, which jointly controls entity D.

Entity A's management is not required to disclose entity A's transactions with entity E in its financial statements. Entity E is not a related party of entity A, because entity A has no ability to exercise control or significant influence over entity E.

Consistent with the above, entities C and D are required to disclose their transactions with entity A in their respective financial statements, because, as explained above, entity A is a related party. Entity E is not required to disclose transactions with entity A, because they are not related parties.

Investors and venturers

29.40 An investor or venturer in respect of which the reporting entity is an associate or a joint venture is a related party of that reporting entity. For an example of disclosure of joint venture arrangements see Table 29.5 and Table 29.7.

29.41 There is nothing in the FRS to suggest that the venturers or investors in the same undertaking are themselves related parties by reason of their joint venture or investment.

Example

This situation may be illustrated by the following example in which entity D is a related party of each of entities A, B and C as it is an associate of those entities. Entity A sells goods to entity B, and entity C provides services to entity B.

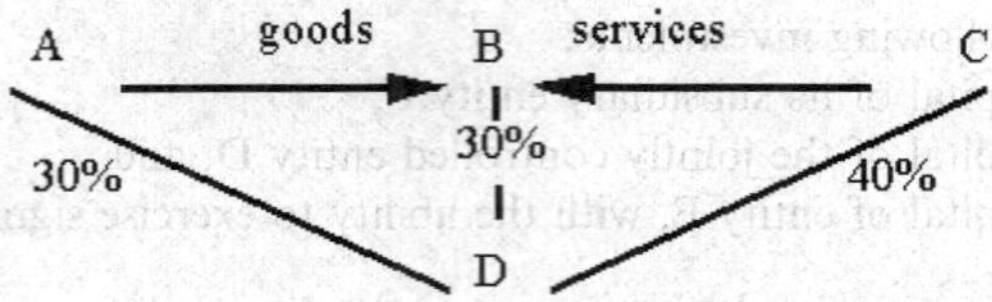

Entities A, B and C are also each related parties of entity D, but not necessarily related parties of each other. Consequently, unless there is some other relationship between entities A, B and C (other than the fact that they are all investees in entity D) that would make them related parties, the transactions between entities A and B and between entities C and B would not be disclosable. (If, for example entities A, B and C were all controlled by the same party they would be related parties of each other, but for a different reason than their investment in entity D).

29.41.1 An example dealing with the related party disclosure implications when a subsidiary transacts with a minority investor is considered in paragraph 29.129.

Directors

29.42 Directors of the reporting entity and the directors of its ultimate and intermediate parent undertakings are its related parties.

29.43 The FRS states that directors include 'shadow directors'. 'Shadow directors' are defined in section 741 of the Companies Act 1985 (and section 251 of the Companies Act 2006) as *"a person in accordance with whose directions or instructions the directors of the company are accustomed to act"*. It should be noted, however, that directors of subsidiary undertakings as such are not related parties by virtue of that appointment. Under FRS 8, such directors may, however, be related parties through control or influence, for instance through shareholdings, or, possibly, by being key management either of the individual reporting entity or the group, but not because they are merely directors of the subsidiary.

29.43.1 Disclosure of transactions with directors is dealt with from paragraph 29.138.

Pension funds

29.44 Pension funds for the benefit of employees of the reporting entity or of any entity that is a related party of the reporting entity are related parties of the reporting entity.

29.45 As well as applying to funds for the benefit of all such employees, this would appear to include pension funds whose membership is open to some, but not all, employees, for instance, those open to directors and senior managers only. On the other hand, it is understood that industry-wide pension schemes would not be regarded as related parties of a reporting entity under this definition. The fact that pension funds are related parties is not intended to call into question the independence of the trustees of the scheme. Transactions between the reporting entity and the pension fund may be in the interest of members but nevertheless need to be reported in the reporting entity's financial statements. [FRS 8 para 15].

29.46 'Pension fund' may need to be interpreted widely to include funds maintained by employers to pay pensions to employees disabled at work.

29.46.1 Related party disclosures in respect of pension funds are dealt with from paragraph 29.136.

Pension funds and their investment manager

29.47 The investment manager for a pension fund is a related party of the pension fund. Paragraph 2.125 of the SORP for pension scheme accounts states that:

> *"Entities engaged by the trustees to manage the pension scheme or its assets, including any scheme administrator or investment managers, should be presumed to be related parties…."*

29.48 However, the employer would not be a related party of the fund's investment managers by reason only of the investment managers acting for the fund. But if the company paid the investment managers' fees, this would, if material, be disclosable by the company as a related party transaction on behalf of the fund (because the fund is a related party of the company under FRS 8). See Table 29.1 below, and Table 29.7.

Table 29.1 — The Rank Group Plc — Annual Report and Accounts — 31 December 2000

Notes to the Accounts (extract)

34 Related party transactions (extract)

The Group recharges the Rank Group UK Pension Schemes with the costs of administration and independent pension advisers borne by the Group. The total amount recharged in the year ended 31 December 2000 was £1.8m (1999 £1.7m).

29.48.1 Furthermore, the situation is more complicated where the investment manager is a member of the group, as illustrated in the following example.

Example

A company's pension fund has investments that are managed by an investment manager that is a subsidiary of the company. Does the company, in its consolidated financial statements, have to disclose payments made by the pension fund to the investment manager?

Pension funds for the benefit of employees of the company are specifically identified as related parties under FRS 8. The investment manager would also be a related party of the pension fund and the management fees should be disclosed as related party transactions in the company's consolidated financial statements. If the manager purchases investments in its own name and transfers them to the scheme, acting as a principal, details of investments bought from and sold to the scheme would also be disclosable transactions (probably aggregated) in the consolidated financial statements. If the manager acts as a disclosed agent for the fund, however, the purchases and sales would not be disclosable in the consolidated financial statements, although commission paid to the manager would.

Parties presumed to be related

29.49 The second list of parties related because of the existence of influence is reproduced below and comprises parties that *are presumed* to be related parties unless it can be demonstrated that neither party has influenced the financial and operating policies of the other in such a way as to inhibit the pursuit of separate interests:

- The key management of the reporting entity and key management of its parent undertaking or undertakings (see para 29.52).
- A person owning or able to exercise control over 20 per cent or more of the reporting entity's voting rights, whether directly or through nominees.
- Each person acting in concert in such a way as to be able to exercise control or influence over the reporting entity (see para 29.55).
- An entity managing or managed by the reporting entity under a management contract.

[FRS 8 para 2.5(c)].

- Persons connected to an individual related party (see para 29.60). [FRS 8 para 2.5(d)].

29.50 The presumption that such parties are related will, therefore, apply unless it can be demonstrated otherwise. The reporting entity will have to produce the necessary evidence to rebut the presumption and may need evidence from the other party if its own evidence is inadequate.

29.51 As an example, the rebuttable presumption acknowledges that, whilst, in general, shareholders holding 20 per cent of the voting rights would have the required level of influence to make them related parties, this is not necessarily the case. For instance, a shareholder may live abroad and, as a result, not be actively associated with the company. However, that shareholder would be presumed to be a related party unless it could be demonstrated that he or she had not influenced the company's financial and operating policies so as to inhibit the pursuit of separate interests.

Key management

29.52 The key management of the reporting entity and key management of its parent undertaking or undertakings are related parties of the reporting entity. The term 'key management' is defined in the standard as follows:

> *"Those persons in senior positions having authority or responsibility for directing or controlling the major activities and resources of the reporting entity."* [FRS 8 para 2.3].

29.53 Key management includes directors of an entity's ultimate and intermediate parents, because those directors are, indirectly, responsible for directing the affairs of the entity. The term does not include directors of the entity's subsidiaries or fellow subsidiaries, unless those directors have a role in directing the entity's affairs.

29.53.1 Apart from directors, the term 'key management' would include people who are not appointed directors, but whose activities encompass duties normally carried out by directors. The following examples illustrate situations where the individuals who are key managers for the purpose of FRS 8 may include individuals who are not directors of the entity.

Example 1

An entity has two equal-sized operating divisions. Each of the operating divisions is headed up by a 'divisional manager'. Neither divisional manager is a director of the entity: rather each is responsible for an operating division and reports to the board of directors on its performance.

Although the divisional managers are not directors of the entity, they would fall within the definition of 'key management' in FRS 8, because they have authority and responsibility for directing and controlling approximately half of the entity's activities.

Example 2

A financial services entity has a board of directors that makes high level decisions about the markets in which the entity operates. It delegates decisions about the products that should be offered within those markets and the customers to whom those products should be marketed, to a management committee.

Because the management committee has authority for directing and controlling the entity's activities, its members, together with the board of directors, are key management.

29.53.2 The term 'key management' will also include people who have responsibilities for the administration or direction of reporting entities, such as trusts, which are not incorporated.

29.54 As a reporting entity can be a group as well as an individual entity, key management must also be considered in relation to directing or controlling the group's resources. Whilst the term 'key management' could include a divisional director or the director of a subsidiary, such a person would need to direct or control a major part of the activities and resources of the group or the company.

Persons acting in concert

29.55 The term 'persons acting in concert' used in paragraph 29.49 above is defined in the standard to mean:

"Persons who, pursuant to an agreement or understanding (whether formal or informal), actively co-operate, whether by the ownership by any of them

of shares in an undertaking or otherwise, to exercise control or influence over that undertaking." [FRS 8 para 2.4].

29.56 The FRS states that 'influence' means influence over the financial and operating policies of the other party to an extent that that other party *might* be inhibited from pursuing at all times its own separate interests. Each person acting in concert will be a related party.

29.57 The question arises whether a small group of shareholders constitutes a concert party and, therefore, potentially a controlling party. For example, the shares in a company might be held by a husband and wife or by two (or three or four etc) brothers, or by two or more parties in a normal joint venture. In the absence of one party influencing the other(s) in a 'close family' context (for instance, they are husband and wife) the fact that they co-operate or vote the same way would not make them concert parties. They would just be shareholders working in the normal way for their collective benefit. We consider that acting in concert must mean more than this, that is, it must relate to a subgroup of the total shareholder base who, for example, meet and agree a common line before meetings of the board or shareholders. However, from an auditing perspective it might be presumed that, for example, members of the same household act in concert unless it can be demonstrated they do not.

Management contracts

29.58 Entities managing or managed by the reporting entity under a management contract are presumed to be related parties unless it can be shown that neither influenced the financial and operating policies of the other in such a way as to inhibit the pursuit of separate interests. Investment managers that manage a fund can be related parties to the fund. For instance, a unit trust is managed under a management contract. The managers are likely to have the required influence, because the unit trust has no separate voice and they effectively decide upon and manage all its investment activities. Consequently, the manager will be a related party. See Table 29.2 below for an example of disclosure by a unit trust.

29.59 By contrast, a listed investment trust, although generally managed under a management contract, has a board of directors that will need to be able to demonstrate that it will act independently of the managers. Whilst in these circumstances the manager is responsible for day to day management of the investment trust's affairs, overall policy and strategy matters are determined by the board. The presumption under paragraph 2.5(c) of FRS 8, mentioned at the beginning of the previous paragraph, is that managers under a management contract will be a related party of the managed entity unless the presumption can be rebutted. In the case of a listed investment trust, the investment managers will be a related party of the trust, unless it can be demonstrated that neither party has influenced the financial and operating policies of the other in such a way as to inhibit the pursuit of separate interests. Typically, it is thought that the presumption will be rebutted in the case of most managers of listed investment trusts so that they will not be related parties.

Table 29.2 — M&G European Fund Managers' Final Investment Report & Financial Statements — 18 June 1999

Notes to the financial statements (extract)

8. Related parties

M&G Securities Limited, together with Lloyds TSB Bank plc are regarded as controlling parties by virtue of having the ability to act in concert in respect of the operations of the Fund.

M&G Securities Limited, a related party, acts as principal on all the transactions of units in the Fund. The aggregate monies received through creations and liquidations are disclosed in the statement of movements in unitholders' funds; amounts due to/from M&G Securities Limited in respect of unit transactions at the period end are disclosed in the balance sheet.

Amounts paid to M&G Securities Limited in respect of Managers' periodic charges are disclosed in note 6. No balances were due at the period end.

Amounts paid to Lloyds TSB Bank plc in respect of trustee services, safe custody charges and overdraft interest are disclosed in note 6. No balances were due at the period end.

Cash balances on deposit with Lloyds TSB Bank plc are disclosed in the balance sheet together with interest due. Interest receivable is disclosed in note 5.

Neither M&G Securities Limited nor Lloyds TSB Bank plc entered into any other transactions with the Fund during the period.

	1999	1998
5. Gross income		
Stock dividends	641	150
Unfranked income		
Overseas dividends	7,896	6,229
Interest on debt securities	0	10
Bank deposit interest	510	238
	9,047	6,627
6. Expenses		
Payable to the Managers or associate		
Managers' periodic charge	4,276	3,598
Registrar's fee (including VAT)	402	338
	4,678	3,936
Payable to the Trustee or associate		
Trustee's fee (including VAT)	43	39
Safe custody charges	250	214
Bank overdraft interest	49	17
	342	270
Other expenses		
FSA fee	1	1
Audit fee (including VAT)	8	6
	9	7
Total expenses	5,029	4,213

Persons connected to a related party

29.60 In addition, FRS 8 also includes within the definition of 'related parties' persons (including individuals, companies and other entities) who are connected to a related party. Because of their relationship with certain parties that are, or are presumed to be, related parties of a reporting entity, the following are also *presumed* to be related parties of the reporting entity:

- Members of the close family of any individual who is, or is presumed to be, a related party.
- Partnerships, companies, trusts or other entities in which any individual, or member of the close family of any individual who is or is presumed to be a related party, has a controlling interest.

[FRS 8 para 2.5(d)].

29.61 A party falling into one of the categories in paragraph 29.60 will be presumed to be a related party of the reporting entity. For instance, a company controlled by a director of the reporting entity would be its related party. See Table 29.3 below for an example of disclosure.

Table 29.3 — Fine Art Developments PLC — Annual Report and Accounts — 31 March 1999

Notes to the Accounts (extract)

30 RELATED PARTY TRANSACTIONS

The companies demerged to form the Creative Publishing group were classed as related parties during the year ended 31 March 1998 and transactions and balances with those companies fall to be disclosed. During the year 31 March 1998 the Creative Publishing group supplied product to the Fine Art Developments group on normal commercial terms. The amount charged by the Creative Publishing group was £9.5m. During the year ended 31 March 1998 the continuing Fine Art Developments group provided the Creative Publishing group with product and services. The amount charged to Creative Publishing during the year was £3.3m for product and £2.2m for services. At 31 March 1998 the amount owed to the Creative Publishing group was £4.8m and the amount owed by the Creative Publishing group was £3.7m.

The group has a trading relationship with Herbert Walker & Son (Printers) Limited, a commercial printing company which is controlled by Mr K Chapman, a director. During the year to 31 March 1999 group purchases from Herbert Walker on normal commercial terms amounted to £2.56m (£2.97m) and in the same period the group supplied goods and services to Herbert Walker of £0.19m (£0.17m). At 31 March 1999 the group indebtedness to Herbert Walker was £0.17m (£0.20m) and that of Herbert Walker to the group was £0.01m (£0.01m).

Close family

29.62 The term 'close family' used in paragraph 29.60 above is defined in the standard as follows:

> *"Close members of the family of an individual are those family members, or members of the same household, who may be expected to influence, or be influenced by, that person in their dealings with the reporting entity."* [FRS 8 para 2.1].

29.63 This definition will apply to make close family of directors, key managers and other individual related parties, themselves related parties of the reporting entity, but only where influence can be expected to exist.

29.64 'Close family' under the FRS, not being limited to spouses and minor children, includes a wider range of family members. Such family could include, for example, brother, adult child, parent and mother-in-law. In addition, the definition extends to members of the same household as the related party (for example, a co-habitee).

Partnerships, companies, trusts or other entities

29.65 Related parties are presumed to include partnerships, companies, trusts or other entities in which any individual, or member of the close family of any individual who is or is presumed to be a related party, has a controlling interest. [FRS 8 para 2.5(d)]. The words 'controlling interest' are not themselves defined, but can be interpreted to mean an interest that gives, or results from, 'control', as defined. Consequently, it seems that to have a 'controlling interest' the individual related party must have an interest enabling him to direct the financial and operating policies of an undertaking and obtain economic benefits as a result of that direction.

29.66 The following is an example of a situation where a trust may be a related party because of the existence of a controlling interest and the influence that brings.

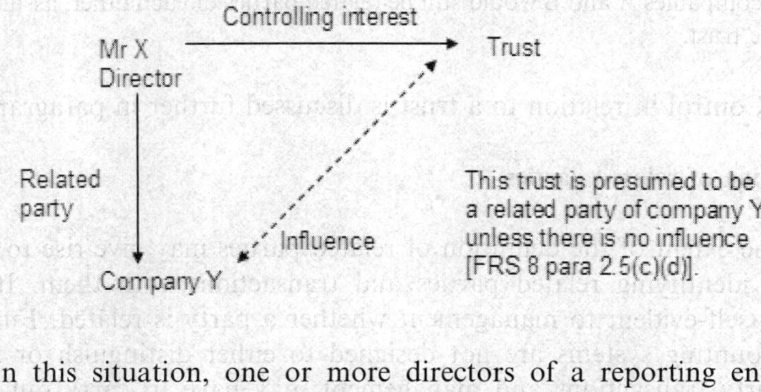

29.66.1 In this situation, one or more directors of a reporting entity has a controlling interest in a trust. The trust would, it seems, be presumed to be a related party of the reporting entity by virtue of its relationship with the directors.

29.66.2 The following example considers the implications for related party disclosures of a director's relationship with a trust.

Example

A director (Mr X) owns 95% of company A. He is also beneficiary of a trust that owns 100% of company B, of which he is also a director.

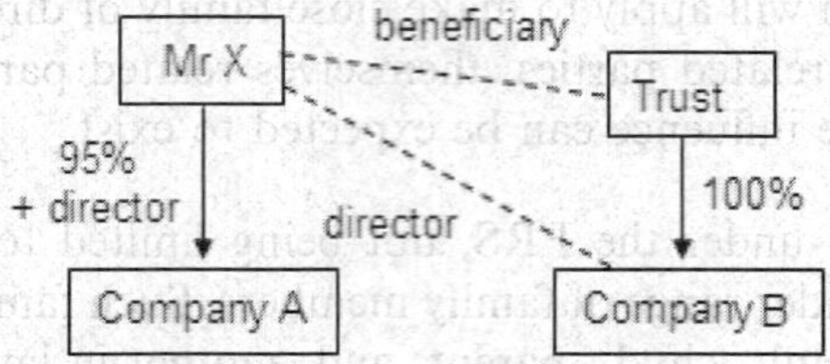

Companies A and B will be related parties if the director controls the trust that owns company B. Would the situation be any different if:

(a) He transferred his 95% of company A to the trust, but remained a director of company A?

In this situation, if he controls the trust, the two companies will still be related under FRS 8 by being under common control.

(b) He resigned as a director of company A, but retained his 95% holding?

In this situation he is likely to be a shadow director. In addition as he still controls company A through his 95% holding, companies A and B will still be related parties by being under common control.

(c) He resigned as a director of companies A and B and transferred the 95% holding in company A to the trust?

If the director is a shadow director, that is, a person in accordance with whose instructions the directors of the companies were accustomed to act, he would still be caught as a related party, and companies A and B would still be related parties of each other, assuming that he controls the trust.

29.66.3 Control in relation to a trust is discussed further in paragraph 29.102.

Identification of related parties

29.67 The extent of the definition of related parties may give rise to difficulties regarding identifying related parties and transactions with them. It may not always be self-evident to management whether a party is related. Furthermore, many accounting systems are not designed to either distinguish or summarise related party transactions and management may have to carry out additional analysis of the accounting records to identify related party transactions. It will be necessary for entities to implement adequate accounting and internal control systems to ensure that related parties and related party transactions are adequately disclosed in the financial statements.

29.67.1 These systems may include formal policies and codes of conduct dealing with relationships with related parties that cover the approval, recording and reporting of related party transactions entered into, on behalf of the entity, by directors and employees.

Related parties for only part of the year

29.68 Questions arise as to what transactions are disclosable where the parties are related for only part of the year. Under paragraph 2.5 of FRS 8, if parties are related at any time in the year they are deemed to be related for the whole year. Therefore, under FRS 8, disclosure is given in respect of transactions for the whole year, even if the parties were only related for part of the year. This is considered in the following example.

Example

Entity A became an associate of the group in February 20X5 and was sold in November 20X5. Entity A is a regular supplier to the group and during 20X5 it continued to supply goods to the group.

How should the group disclose transactions with entity A in its financial statements for the year ended 31 December 20X5, given that it was a related party for only part of the year?

Under FRS 8, if parties are related at any time in the year they are deemed related for the whole year. Therefore, management should disclose in the consolidated financial statements details of the transactions between entity A and the rest of the group for the entire year (that is, 1 January 20X5 to 31 December 20X5). This includes the transactions between entity A and the rest of the group in the months of January and December 20X5.

29.68.1 The disclosure requirements in consolidated and separate financial statements where a group has acquired or disposed of a subsidiary during the year are dealt with in paragraph 29.131.

29.68.2 Note that the definition of a related party in IAS 24 under IFRS differs from that in FRS 8. A consequence of this is that, under IAS 24, disclosure is only required in respect of transactions during the period for which the entities are related and so it is necessary to consider separately the period when the parties were related in the year and the period when they were not. This contrasts with FRS 8, where if parties are related at any time in the year they are deemed related for the whole year.

Related party transactions

29.69 A 'related party transaction' is defined in FRS 8 as follows:

> "*The transfer of assets or liabilities or the performance of services by, to or for a related party irrespective of whether a price is charged.*" [FRS 8 para 2.6].

29.69.1 In addition to direct transfers between related parties, our view is that arrangements that involve transfers to third parties, undertaken because of the exercise of control, joint control or significant influence by a related party, are also disclosable as transactions with that related party. The reason is that in entering into such a transaction with the third party the entity is performing a service for the related party or, alternatively, fulfilling an obligation to the related party.

29.70 The following are examples of related party transactions that require disclosure by a reporting entity in the period in which they occur:

- Purchases or sales of goods (finished or unfinished).
- Purchases or sales of property and other assets.
- Rendering or receiving of services.
- Agency arrangements (see para 29.72).
- Leasing arrangements.
- Transfer of research and development.
- Licence agreements.
- Provision of finance (including loans and equity contributions in cash or in kind).
- Guarantees and the provision of collateral security.
- Management contracts (see para 29.58).

[FRS 8 para 19].

It is clear that the definition of related party transaction is very wide ranging and that these are just examples, not a definitive list.

29.71 The definition envisages that some related party transactions might not be entered into a company's accounting records or might not involve any consideration passing. Examples of such transactions are:

- Management services provided by one company to another free of charge.
- Goods manufactured under a patent owned by a fellow subsidiary which makes no charge.
- Guarantees given by directors (see para 29.140).
- Rent free accommodation or the loan of vehicles or other assets at no charge.

Reporting entities' information systems must, therefore, be able to capture data that may not be in the accounting records for disclosure as related party transactions.

Agency arrangements

29.72 The standard specifically states that agency arrangements are disclosable. So, where a related party performs services as agent for the reporting entity, or the reporting entity performs services as agent for a related party, there is a related party transaction to disclose even where no commission is charged. For instance, if a company controlled by a director of the reporting entity paid the reporting entity's suppliers on its behalf and was reimbursed by it, these payments are likely to constitute agency arrangements which should be disclosed if material. If the reporting entity made the payment to the agency company before it settled the invoices, the arrangement could constitute a loan to a director.

29.73 Furthermore, section 234 ZZA(1) of the Companies Act 1985 (and section 416(1)(b) of the Companies Act 2006) requires the directors' report to state the principal activities of a company during the year. Consequently, disclosure of the fact that the reporting entity acts as agent will be required if this is one of the principal activities of the agency company.

29.74 Transactions entered into by the agents on behalf of their principals during the year under the agency arrangements and any balances with the principal are, therefore, disclosable. However, certain transactions and balances entered into by an agent with its principal may come within the exemptions from disclosure. For instance, the standard does not require disclosure of transactions and balances in the agent's financial statements if the agent is a subsidiary of its principal and comes within the exemption for 90 per cent subsidiaries (see para 29.149).

29.75 A parent company preparing consolidated financial statements does not have to show in those financial statements transactions or balances with its agent that have been eliminated on consolidation (see para 29.146). If the third parties with whom the principal has contracted, via the agency, are themselves its related parties (for instance, the third parties and the principal are under common control), these transactions will also fall to be disclosed in the principal's financial statements as related party transactions, unless they are themselves exempted.

[The next paragraph is 29.77.]

Materiality

29.77 FRS 8 requires disclosure of *all* transactions with related parties provided that they are *material*. Because potentially all related party transactions are disclosable, the interpretation of what is material in this context is particularly important.

29.78 The FRS defines 'material' in the following way:

> "*Transactions are material when their disclosure might reasonably be expected to influence decisions made by the users of general purpose financial statements.*" [FRS 8 para 20].

Whilst this does not explicitly say *"only disclose transactions that are abnormal"*, it does appear to exempt from disclosure those transactions that would be of no interest to users of financial statements. For example, a director buying a chocolate bar in the staff canteen is not of interest, but the director or his close family buying a six-bedroom house from the company at a price other than fair value certainly would be. Where the director bought a house from the company at its market value, the situation, interpreted by reference only to the above, requires further consideration.

29.79 The FRS, however, goes on to provide that:

> "*The materiality of related party transactions is to be judged, not only in terms of their significance to the reporting entity, but also in relation to their significance to the other related party when that party is:*
>
> *(a) a director, key manager or other individual in a position to influence, or accountable for stewardship of, the reporting entity; or*
>
> *(b) a member of the close family of any individual mentioned in (a) above; or*
>
> *(c) an entity controlled by any individual mentioned in (a) or (b) above.*" [FRS 8 para 20].

29.80 The FRS explains that these words address the perspective that needs to be considered when a related party transaction has been undertaken directly or indirectly with an individual who is in a position to influence, or accountable for stewardship of, the reporting entity. [FRS 8 app IV para 19]. Consequently, in the examples given above, not only the significance to the company, but the transaction's significance to the director would need to be considered in order to form a judgement as to whether the transaction involving the purchase of the house was material. The transaction could be small to the company, but a major investment for the director. We believe the intention of the FRS is that transactions of the type and size shown in the example in paragraph 29.78, that is, the purchase of a house at market value, would be regarded as material to the director and, therefore, disclosable.

29.81 Although it is clear that the purchase of a house is material from the director's point of view and that the purchase of a chocolate bar is not, there will in practice be a number of transactions in between these two extremes whose materiality is borderline. It is not possible to be definitive about how materiality should be established, as much will depend on the facts of each case. However, at the margin, a transaction being at arm's length and on normal commercial terms would contribute to its being regarded as immaterial. Equally, a transaction that is on terms advantageous to the director would contribute to its being regarded as material and, therefore, disclosable. See also paragraph 29.141.3.

29.81.1 In addition, if a director enters into several small transactions in a financial year, they will need to be aggregated. If these transactions are material when aggregated, then they will need to be disclosed in accordance with FRS 8.

General purpose financial statements

29.82 The definition of 'materiality' refers to users of general purpose financial statements. Chapter one of the ASB's Statement of principles lists users as including present and potential investors, employees, lenders, suppliers and other trade creditors, customers, governments and their agencies and the public, and sets out some of their different needs.

29.83 The statement acknowledges that financial statements cannot meet the information needs of all types of users mentioned above, but that there are needs that are common to all users. All users have some interest in the financial position, performance and financial adaptability of the reporting entity as a whole. Hence, when considering whether disclosure of a particular related party transaction is 'material', the interest of a wide range of users in information on such matters should be considered. The statement notes that there should be a rebuttable assumption that focussing on investors' interests will, in effect, focus on the common interest of all users.

Comparison with 'materiality' under the Companies Act 1985

29.84 Under Part II of Schedule 6 to the Act, disclosure must be made of transactions in which a director has a material interest. In this context, an interest will not be material if the board of directors has honestly and reasonably concluded that it is not material. Two tests for deciding what is material have been suggested, which are discussed in paragraph 29.178.

29.85 The criterion in the FRS for determining materiality of transactions with related parties is expressed not only in terms of their significance to the reporting entity, but also in relation to their significance to the director or other individual related party.

29.86 However, the FRS contains no specific exemption similar to the exemption in paragraph 20 of Schedule 6 (see para 29.179) for material transactions with directors that are in the ordinary course of the company's business and at arm's length. As a result, it is likely to result in greater disclosure of transactions with directors as it is fair to assume that even relatively small transactions between directors (or their close family) and the company might be regarded as material, as described above.

Disclosure requirements

Summary

29.92 Where a reporting entity's financial statements are intended to give a true and fair view the standard requires the following information to be disclosed in a reporting entity's financial statements about its related parties:

- The name of the party controlling the reporting entity and, if different, the name of the ultimate controlling party (whether or not any transactions have taken place).
- Details of material transactions between the reporting entity and any related parties.
- Details of balances due to, or from, related parties at the balance sheet date.

29.92.1 There is no requirement in FRS 8 to disclose information about related party transactions in any specific note. However, it is likely to be more helpful to users to present the information in one comprehensive note, instead of including different aspects of related party disclosures in several notes to the financial statements. Where information is also required by other standards, then cross-references can be used, in order to avoid duplicated information.

Disclosure of control

29.93 Where the reporting entity is controlled by another party, disclosure should be made of:

- the name of the controlling party; and
- if different, the name of the ultimate controlling party.

In both instances, the related party relationship should also be disclosed. [FRS 8 para 5].

29.94 These disclosures have to be made whether or not there have been any transactions between the parties. If the controlling party or ultimate controlling party of the reporting entity is not known, that fact should be disclosed. [FRS 8 para 5]. Disclosure is only required where there is control, as defined, and the above information is not required to be given where there is merely influence.

29.95 The explanation given in FRS 8 for requiring the disclosure of control is as follows. Where the reporting entity is controlled by another party, whether or not transactions have taken place with that party, the control relationship prevents the reporting entity from being independent, in the sense of being able to pursue its activities independently of the interests of its individual owners and others. The FRS sees identification of the controlling party as being important because it may establish the entity's standing in the business community, with consequent effects upon sources and types of products, and may affect the allegiance of the reporting entity's management. [FRS 8 para 18].

29.96 The controlling party could be an individual, partnership or other entity. Alternatively, it could be a group of individuals or entities acting in concert (see from para 29.55) if the individuals or entities, although each with small shareholdings, were able to control the entity by active co-operation.

29.97 The disclosure of the existence of control by a parent company is called for even if the reporting entity is a wholly-owned subsidiary. The exemption for 90 per cent subsidiaries that applies to the disclosure of transactions and balances with other group companies does not apply to disclosure of controlling relationships. However, in practice, this requirement is partially satisfied by the disclosure, required by Schedule 5 to the Act, which requires a company to give the name of the company regarded by its directors as its ultimate parent company. An example of these disclosures is given in Table 29.4.

Table 29.4 — Midland Bank plc – Annual Report and Accounts – 31 December 1998

Notes to the Accounts (extract)

39 Ultimate parent company

The ultimate parent company of Midland Bank plc is HSBC Holdings plc, which is incorporated and registered in England.

HSBC Holdings plc is the only undertaking for which consolidated accounts which include the consolidated accounts of Midland are drawn up.

HSBC Holdings plc is Midland's direct and ultimate controlling party as defined under Financial Reporting Standard 8 'Related Party Disclosures'.

Copies of HSBC Holdings plc's 1998 Annual Report and Accounts can be obtained from its registered office at 10 Lower Thames Street, London EC3R 6AE.

29.98 If the party disclosed under Schedule 5 to the Companies Act 1985 as the ultimate parent company is also the ultimate controlling party, the disclosure will need to make clear, for the purposes of the standard, that that company is also the ultimate controlling party and give the related party relationship.

29.99 However, where the ultimate parent company is itself controlled by, say, an individual or a trust, the ultimate controlling party would be that individual or trust. In this case, a higher level of control will fall for disclosure under FRS 8 than merely the Companies Act's requirement to disclose the ultimate parent company. As a result, where a reporting entity is owned by, say, a US private company, the name of any controlling shareholder of the US private company will need to be given, even if not disclosed in the US company's financial statements, if this information is known to the reporting entity or its directors.

Source of control or ownership

29.100 Where no ultimate parent company has been disclosed, because the company is directly controlled by, say, an individual or a trust (rather than a parent company), disclosure of the identity of the controlling party and the nature of the relationship is required by the standard. Where the controlling party is a trust, it will be necessary to consider whether the trust itself is controlled by a person or persons who will, therefore, need to be disclosed as the ultimate controlling party (see also para 29.102). Where the controlling party or the ultimate controlling party is not known, this fact must be stated.

29.100.1 In special circumstances, section 231 of the Companies Act 1985 permits a company to claim an exemption from disclosing information required by Schedule 5, including the identification of the ultimate parent company. Where a subsidiary carries on business outside the UK and, in the opinion of the directors, disclosure of the ultimate parent company would be seriously prejudicial to its business, the company can, with the consent of the Secretary of State, avoid the disclosure in its financial statements. It would seem unlikely that FRS 8 intends to require disclosure of the controlling party where specific permission for non-disclosure has been given by the Secretary of State. However, these situations are likely to be rare in practice.

Shared control

29.101 As noted in paragraph 29.96 above, the term 'ultimate controlling party' could relate to a group of individuals or entities acting in concert if the individuals or entities, actively co-operated to control the entity. Concert parties are discussed from para 29.55.

29.101.1 Where control is shared in the form of a joint venture, the question arises as to whether the venturers should be disclosed as a controlling party under FRS 8. This is considered in the following example.

Example

A company is owned as to 50% by one company and 50% by another. It is a joint venture under the definition in FRS 9. Should the two venturers be treated as the controlling party, thus requiring them to be disclosed as such under FRS 8?

In principle if two or more parties act in concert to control a company they would be disclosable collectively as the ultimate controlling party under FRS 8. However, acting in concert to control a company would seem to require more than a normal joint venture agreement. A joint venture agreement is normally an agreement to work together, but not necessarily to agree on everything.

This reflects the view that even if two or more shareholders, for example a family, owned a majority of the shares, they would not be deemed to be acting in concert, unless there was an agreement between them to vote in a particular way so as jointly to exercise control.

Therefore, unless there is an agreement or understanding that the investors in a joint venture will act in concert, they would not be regarded as acting in concert simply as a result of the joint venture agreement and would not be disclosed as the controlling party under FRS 8.

29.101.2 Where investors in a joint venture act as intermediaries for an ultimate controlling party, then that party will be required to be disclosed, as shown in the following example.

Example

Who should be disclosed as the ultimate controlling party when there is a joint venture whose investors act as intermediaries?

Mr. A owns shares that entitle him to 100% of the voting rights in entity B and entity C.

Entity B and entity C jointly control entity P, which controls entity S.

The following diagram shows the structure of the group:

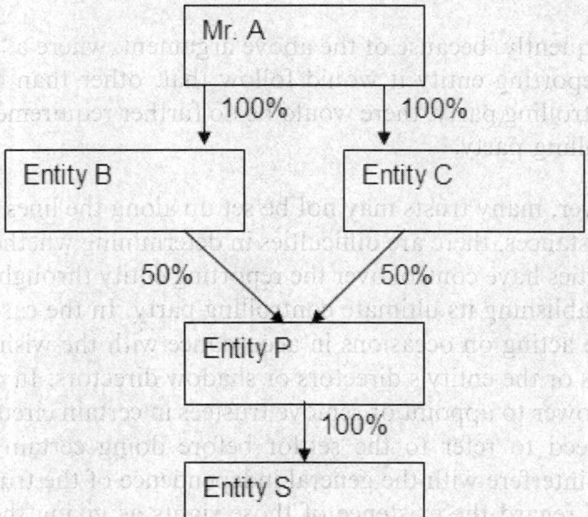

Entity S's management should disclose Mr A as the ultimate controlling party of entity S, irrespective of whether there were transactions between them during the year. [FRS 8 para 5].

Mr A controls entities B and C, which jointly control entities P and S. Entities B and C form a group which will vote according to Mr A's instruction.

Control by trusts

29.102 As has been mentioned previously, the definition of control in FRS 8 comprises two elements:

- the ability to direct the financial and operating policies; and

- the ability to benefit from their direction.

Consequently, the question of establishing whether control exists is particularly difficult in relation to trusts. Trusteeship may be viewed as an example of where the two aspects of control are divided between two parties. The trustee has the power to deploy the trust assets: the beneficiary benefits from their deployment. In what may be called a pure trust, neither the trustee nor the beneficiary controls the trust. Not all vehicles created in the legal form of a trust will fall into the category of a pure trust and the rights and duties of the trustees and beneficiaries may be divided differently where the trust is not a pure trust. In fact, UITF Abstract 38 and UITF Abstract 32 rule that many employee share trusts and other employee benefit trusts are controlled by the sponsoring company, and FRS 5, 'Reporting the substance of transactions', also identifies trusts among the categories of entity that may qualify as quasi-subsidiaries, where they are in substance controlled by one party. In a pure trust, however, it is possible to argue that there is no controlling party of the trust, because neither the trustees nor the beneficiary have both elements of control. The question of whether or not control exists over a trust is one that will need particular care and scrutiny of the facts of each individual case.

29.103 Consequently, because of the above argument, where a 'pure trust' holds shares in the reporting entity it would follow that, other than disclosure of the trust as the controlling party, there would be no further requirement to disclose an ultimate controlling party.

29.104 However, many trusts may not be set up along the lines of a 'pure trust'. In these circumstances, there are difficulties in determining whether the trustees or any outside parties have control over the reporting entity through the trust for the purposes of establishing its ultimate controlling party. In the case of some trusts, trustees may be acting on occasions in accordance with the wishes of the settlor, the beneficiaries or the entity's directors or shadow directors. In others the settlor may have the power to appoint or remove trustees in certain circumstances, or the trustees may need to refer to the settlor before doing certain things. If these matters do not interfere with the general independence of the trustees, it may not be necessary to regard the existence of those rights as giving the settlor (or any other party, as the case may be) control over the trustees, or the trust, in the sense that control (as opposed to influence) is used in the standard. Alternatively, there may be no evidence of the trustees having given independent consideration to matters relevant to the reporting entity in the light of independent advice. These circumstances may point to trustees allowing outside parties, such as settlors or beneficiaries, in a position to do so, to exercise unfettered control. If they do exercise control, such parties would then need to be disclosed as the ultimate controlling party of the reporting entity.

29.105 As mentioned in paragraph 29.102, an ESOP trust is an example of a trust which a party other than the trustees will be deemed to control under FRS 5, 'Reporting the substance of transactions'. UITF Abstract 38, 'Accounting for ESOP trusts', states:

"*Although the trustees of the ESOP trust must act at all times in accordance with the interests of the beneficiaries under the trust, most ESOP trusts (particularly those established as a means of remunerating employees) are specifically designed so as to serve the purposes of the sponsoring company, and to ensure that there will be minimal risk of any conflict arising between the duties of the trustees and the interest of the company. Where this is so, the sponsoring company has de facto control and there will be nothing to encumber implementation of its wishes in practice.*" [UITF 38 para 6(d)].

29.106 It would seem that similar reasoning can be applied to ascertaining the party, if any, to be disclosed as the controlling party of a trust for the purposes of FRS 8. That is, the controlling party is likely to be the party that both:

- has the ability to direct the trust, or ensure the implementation of its wishes concerning the trust's financial and operating policies; and
- derives the principal economic benefit, whether or not that party is a named beneficiary under the trust.

29.107 Where a party controls a trust that holds shares in the reporting entity, that party will need to be disclosed as the ultimate controlling party. The purpose for which a trust is established may, therefore, often indicate who the ultimate controlling party is, or whether there is one at all. For instance, where the reporting entity is a special purpose vehicle and a trust is established as a parent undertaking of the reporting entity as part of a securitisation, this will indicate that the trust and the reporting entity are probably controlled by one or other party to the securitisation.

29.108 Another complex situation would be where a director or other related party is a trustee of a trust that holds shares in the company (and the director or related party controls the trust), the shares held by the trust should be added to those held directly by the director for the purpose of establishing where control lies. Where a director or other related party — such as an adult or a minor child — is a beneficiary, but not a trustee, under a trust it would appear to be a question of establishing, on the facts of each case, whether the trustees administer the trust independently or whether the director or other related party control it.

[The next paragraph is 29.110.]

Limited partnerships

29.110 Where a limited partnership in the form of a managed fund controls over 50 per cent of the shares with voting rights in a reporting entity, the question arises as to who controls the reporting entity. The limited partnership holds the majority of the voting rights in the reporting entity and would control it. As the general partner has control of a limited partnership the general partner of the investing partnership would, it seems, be the reporting entity's controlling party. However, the general partner may, itself, have a parent undertaking or ultimate controlling party which it discloses in its financial statements. This would mean that the reporting entity would have to disclose that party as its ultimate controlling party.

Disclosure of transactions and balances

Material transactions

29.111 The FRS states that financial statements should disclose material transactions undertaken by the reporting entity with a related party. [FRS 8 para 6]. What is meant by material in this context is considered from paragraph 29.77. All *material* transactions, not just abnormal ones, must be disclosed. This is because the ASB considers that when transactions with related parties are material in aggregate, they are of interest whatever their nature. [FRS 8 App IV para 18]. This disclosure should be made irrespective of whether a price is charged. The information to be disclosed should include all the following:

- The names of the transacting related parties.
- A description of the relationship between the parties.
- A description of the transactions.
- The amounts involved.
- Any other elements of the transactions necessary for an understanding of the financial statements.

[FRS 8 para 6(a) to (e)].

29.112 FRS 8 gives an example of an appropriate disclosure of "*any other elements*" (required by the last bullet point above) as the need to give an indication that the transfer of a major asset has taken place at an amount materially different from that obtainable on normal commercial terms. [FRS 8 para 22]. The ASB believes that the absence of this information could reasonably be expected to influence decisions made by users of the financial statements. [FRS 8 App IV para 20]. The reference to a 'major asset' and 'materially different' in the example gives rise to the possible interpretation that such disclosure would be required only in respect of an unusual transaction or of a large number of transactions where the price difference could be of significance. A statement giving an indication that such sales or purchases or other transfers have taken place at amounts materially different from that obtainable on normal commercial terms may then be necessary for an understanding of the financial statements.

29.113 Disclosure of 'other elements' could also be necessary, for example, to give an indication that premises owned by the reporting entity are occupied by an associate company at a rent that is considerably lower than the market rent.

29.114 There is no requirement to disclose the actual difference between the fair value and the transacted amount. On the other hand, it should not be implied that the transactions were effected at arm's length, unless the related parties concerned acted in an independent manner. [FRS 8 para 10]. The FRS states that transactions are presumed to have been undertaken on an arm's length basis when they have been undertaken on terms such as could have been obtained in a transaction with an external party, in which each side bargained knowledgeably and freely, unaffected by any relationship between them. [FRS 8 para 8].

29.115 *"Any other elements of the transaction"* might also include disclosure of the profit made on a transaction if this was necessary for an understanding of the financial statements. However, in normal circumstances the requirement to disclose the *"amounts involved"* would be met by disclosure of the turnover or invoiced amount and would not seem to extend to separate disclosure of the profit made.

Example

A property is being transferred (for cash) from a company to an associate at market value. Is the profit that will be made on the transaction an amount that needs to be disclosed under FRS 8?

Paragraph 2.5(b)(ii) and (iii) of FRS 8 includes associates and their investors within the scope of related party relationships.

Paragraph 19 of FRS 8 states that the types of transaction that may lead to disclosures include *"purchases or sales of property and other assets"*.

Paragraph 6 of FRS 8 requires a description of the transaction and the amounts involved to be given. In normal circumstances the 'amount involved' would be the transfer price. The profit to be made from a transaction would not seem to be an 'amount involved' – rather it is a figure that results from the transaction. However, it may need to be given as 'any other element of the transaction' if this is necessary for an understanding of the financial statements. Therefore, it is a matter of judgement in each case.

Balances between related parties

29.116 In addition to the information described above concerning transactions, the standard also requires the following information regarding *balances* to be disclosed:

- The amounts due to or from related parties at the balance sheet date and provisions for doubtful debts due from such parties at that date.
- Amounts written off in the period in respect of debts due to or from related parties.

[FRS 8 para 6(f)(g)].

29.117 The need to give the balances referred to arises independently of the requirement to disclose details of specific transactions undertaken during the year. For example, a balance may arise from a prior year transaction. If, after what may be an unusually long credit period, a balance due from a related party is written off, that information could be significant for users and is, presumably, an example of what the disclosure requirement is directed at. The disclosure of balances due to and from fellow subsidiaries is considered in paragraph 29.121.

29.117.1 Where a company has fully provided against a balance owed to it by a related party, disclosure of the gross balance and the amount written off should be given, as illustrated in the following example.

Example

A company has outstanding balances with joint ventures. It has fully provided against these balances in the past, although the financial statements of the joint ventures still show them as owing to the company. Do the balances and the amounts written off have to be disclosed under FRS 8?

FRS 8 specifically identifies joint ventures as related parties. [FRS 8 para 2.5(b)(ii)].

FRS 8 requires disclosure of balances with related parties and any provisions made. In our view this means that the gross balances and the amounts written off should be disclosed as we do not think there is intended to be a different meaning ascribed to 'written off' as opposed to 'provided'. If the balances had been legally forgiven and were, therefore, no longer shown by the joint ventures we would agree that the net amounts could be disclosed.

Aggregation of transactions

29.118 To reduce the volume of disclosures of transactions with related parties, the FRS allows disclosure of details of transactions and details of balances to be made on an aggregated basis unless disclosure of an individual transaction or connected transactions (or balances) is either:

- necessary for an understanding of the impact of the transactions on the financial statements of the reporting entity; or
- required by law.

[FRS 8 para 6].

29.119 As a consequence, similar transactions and similar balances may be aggregated by type of related party. However, aggregation should not result in either of the following:

- Aggregation should not be done in such a way as to obscure the importance of significant transactions.
- Material related party transactions should not be concealed in an aggregated disclosure.

[FRS 8 para 21].

29.120 An example of aggregation given in the FRS is that purchases or sales with other group companies may be aggregated and described as such in the individual financial statements of a group company. Purchases or sales of goods should not, however, be aggregated with purchases or sales of fixed assets as this would obscure the importance of significant transactions. [FRS 8 para 21]. It seems clear from these examples that sales cannot be aggregated with purchases and that, therefore, the netting of transactions is not permitted. In addition, a material related party transaction with an individual should not be concealed in an aggregated disclosure. [FRS 8 para 21].

29.121 If intra-group transactions comprise different categories of transactions, for instance, purchases or sales of stock, or purchases or sales of fixed assets, individual balances for such categories of transactions will need to be separately disclosed. This is because, under the requirements of FRS 8, dissimilar transactions and balances cannot be aggregated. Generally, the Act requires the disclosure of balances with other group entities in the balance sheet formats. This will satisfy the standard's requirements for the disclosure of balances only if the amounts contain transactions which are similar.

29.122 Where permitted, aggregation may be made by type of related party. It does not necessarily require the individual names of the related parties to be disclosed. The extent of detail to be disclosed will depend on materiality. For example, when sales to all other group companies (that is, including parents, fellow subsidiaries and subsidiaries) are material but do not dominate the company's trading, then one total would suffice. But if such sales do constitute the majority of the trading, then analysis into (say) (i) ultimate and intermediate parent; (ii) fellow subsidiaries; and (iii) subsidiaries would be appropriate. In addition, transactions with associates and joint ventures would normally be separately disclosed. An example of separate disclosure of transactions with joint ventures is given in Table 29.5 below.

Table 29.5 — BAE SYSTEMS plc — Annual Report and accounts — 31 December 2001

Notes to the Accounts (extract)
31 Related party transactions

The Group has an interest in a number of joint ventures the principal ones of which are disclosed in note 12.
Transactions occur with these joint ventures in the normal course of business. The more significant transactions are disclosed below:

Related party	Sales to related party £m	Purchases from related party £m	Amounts owed by related party £m	Amounts owed to related party £m
Airbus SAS	207	47	16	214
Eurofighter Jagdflugzeug GmbH	505	–	179	–
MBDA SAS	69	4	111	415
Panavia Aircraft GmbH	80	35	15	–
AMS NV	16	83	13	56

29.122.1 The following examples consider further the aggregation of related party disclosures.

Example 1

An entity has six associates and makes sales of goods to those associates. 50% of those sales are to two of the associates. If the amount of the sales is not material to the entity as a whole it may aggregate the sales to associates because they are similar in nature. However, it may be necessary to identify the two associates to which 50% of the sales are made and to disclose the extent of the sales (50%) to those associates. If, on the other hand, the sales to associates are a material proportion of the entity's sales as a whole, it may be necessary to disclose separately details of the transactions with the two associates to which the 50% of sales is made and the amounts of the sales transactions and debtor balances for each of those associates. If the sales to the remaining four associates are not material to the entity as a whole disclosure for those may continue to be given in aggregate.

Example 2

Entity A enters into transactions with the following related parties:

Entity	**Type of sale**	**Number of transactions**	**Value**
Entity B	Security equipment	1	10,000
Entity C	Security services	10	5,000
Entity D	Security services	12	6,000
Entity D	Security equipment	1	10,000
Entity E	Security services	8	4,500

Entity C is an associate of entity A. Entities B, D and E are subsidiaries of entity G, a fellow subsidiary of entity A. The group structure is as follows:

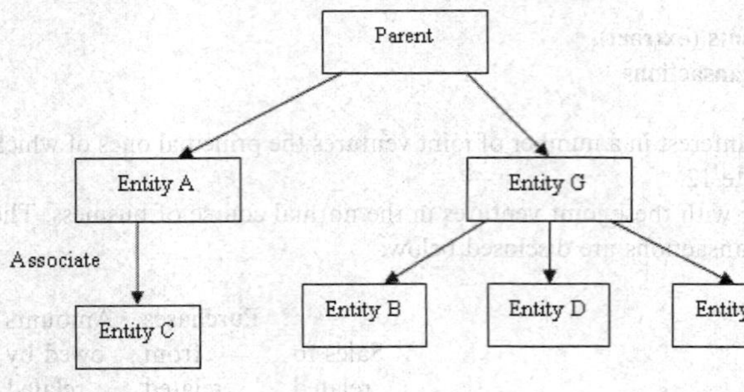

There have been no transactions between entity G and entity A. Other than the types of sale, all terms and conditions of the transactions are similar. How should management aggregate sales to related parties?

Like sales to a common related party may be aggregated. The following is a suggested aggregate disclosure:

Sales of security equipment	
G group	20,000
Sales of security services	
Entity C	5,000
G group	10,500
	15,500

29.122.2 Related party disclosures in respect of associates and joint ventures are considered further from paragraph 29.135 below.

Transactions with directors

29.123 Special considerations arise in connection with directors' transactions. In general, it seems that the standard does not permit the aggregation of material transactions with directors. This is certainly the case when directors' transactions are unusual or unique. For example, separate disclosure is needed where a director of a company buys a property from the company.

29.124 However, aggregation may be an acceptable approach in cases such as the following:

- A situation sometimes arises where all directors have material transactions with the company. For example, where the company is an association or co-operative serving all its members, the members may put all or most of their turnover or purchases through the company. Some of the members are elected directors for certain periods and they enter into similar transactions to all other members and on the same terms. Here it is thought acceptable to aggregate the transactions for disclosure purposes. However, this approach cannot be used to conceal unusual transactions.
- In other circumstances, some or all directors may enter into transactions with the company that are or may be material, but less material than the transactions described in the previous bullet point. An example would be insurance policies taken out by directors of insurance companies on normal or staff terms. Here again it seems reasonable to aggregate the transactions for disclosure purposes. However, this approach would not apply to unusual contracts or heavily discounted policies. See Table 29.6 below.

Table 29.6— Royal & Sun Alliance Group plc — Annual Report and Accounts — 31 December 2000

NOTES ON THE ACCOUNTS (extract)

43. TRANSACTIONS WITH RELATED PARTIES

A number of the directors, other key managers, their close families and entities under their control have general and/or long term insurance policies with subsidiary companies of the Group. Such policies are on normal commercial terms except that executive directors and key managers are entitled to special rates which are also available to other members of staff. The Board has considered the financial effect of such insurance policies and other transactions with Group companies and has concluded that they are not material to the Group or the individuals concerned and, if disclosed, would not influence decisions made by users of these financial statements.

The Board has also concluded that there are no transactions with other directors or key managers that are material to their own financial affairs.

29.125 In contrast to these two cases, consider the following example. Some directors of a house-building company may, over a period of a few years, buy houses from that company for their own or family use. However, given the nature of house purchases, they are likely to be less frequent than is the case with the insurance policy example. Moreover, they would be more clearly material to the directors. Hence, in this example we do *not* believe that aggregation is an appropriate approach, even where house-building is the company's normal business and the transactions are on normal commercial terms.

Comparatives

29.126 The standard is silent on comparatives. FRS 28, 'Corresponding amounts', however, requires comparatives information to be disclosed for each item in the notes to the financial statements, which will include related party disclosures.

29.126.1 It may be necessary to disclose narrative information from the previous period that continues to be relevant in the current period. For instance, if the parent or ultimate controlling party has changed in the current period, users may benefit from knowing that at the previous year end the entity was controlled by one party (comparative information about the name of the controlling party last year) and that during the year the controlling party has changed (current year information about the change and the name of the controlling party at the current year end).

Practical application

Transactions between companies under common control

29.127 FRS 8 requires disclosure of transactions between entities under common control. The standard's requirements extend to the disclosure of transactions even where these might subsequently have been reversed due to the accounting implications of FRS 5, because the transactions have still taken place. For instance, even though a transaction may have been reversed, the fact that the initiation and reversal of a transaction span a year end could be highly significant.

Example

Company A, which is owned by Mr X, has slow-moving stock and a large overdraft from its bank. Prior to the year end it sells some of the stock to company B at a price that is below its market value. Company B pays for the goods before company A's year end and company A pays the proceeds into its bank account with its bank. Company A thus shows a lower overdraft in its year end financial statements. After the year end the transaction is reversed. No fee is payable to company B as it has agreed that company A will do a similar favour for company B at its (different) year end. Does FRS 8 affect the transaction?

The transaction should not be shown as a sale of stocks in company A's financial statements as under FRS 5 it is not a proper sale and the cash received from company B should be treated as a short-term loan. Thus, although the overdraft will still show a reduced balance, stocks will remain as before and there will be an additional creditor for the amount owed to company B.

Whilst FRS 5 also requires that disclosure of the transactions should be sufficient to enable a user to understand its commercial effect, FRS 8 may require further disclosures if company B is a related party of company A.

If, for instance, company A and company B are under common control, or if the owner of company B is a member of the close family of the owner of company A, disclosure would be required of the names and relationship of the related parties, details of the transaction, amounts, balances at the year end and the implications for the financial statements.

This might be as follows for company A with a 31 December year end:

> *"On 30 December 20X6 the company sold goods with a book value of £100,000 to company B limited, a company controlled by Mr Smith, the brother-in-law of the company's principal shareholder Mr Jones, for £80,000. This amount was received as cash and has been shown in the financial statements as a reduction in bank overdrafts which without the benefit of the transaction would be shown at £263,000 which is in excess of the company's present overdraft limit of £250,000. Subsequent to the year end, the goods were repurchased by the company for the original sale price of £80,000. In these financial statements, in accordance with FRS 5, the transaction has been recorded as a secured loan rather than as a sale and, accordingly, the financial effects of the transactions have been to decrease the overdrafts by £80,000 as described above and to increase creditors by the same amount, which is separately disclosed as 'amounts due to company B limited' in the balance sheet. There were no such transactions in 20X5."*

Transactions entered into by group companies

29.128 An example of a transaction entered into by a group company is where a subsidiary of a group enters into a transaction with an associate of a group. This is discussed in paragraph 29.135 below.

29.129 Where a group of companies includes a partially-owned subsidiary, the question arises as to whether transactions between the subsidiary and its minority investor are related party transactions from the group's perspective. This may depend on the significance of the subsidiary to the whole group. This is considered in the following example.

Example

Company A, which is a large trading company, owns 70% of the shares in a smaller company B, which it consolidates. Company X owns the remaining 30% of the shares in company B. Company B sells a property to company X at its market value established by outside valuation. Company X, being an investor with more than 20% of the voting rights in company B, is presumed to be a related party of company B. [FRS 8 para 2.5(c)(ii)]. Company B will, therefore, have to disclose details of the transaction in its financial statements, including any other elements of the transaction necessary for an understanding of the financial statements.

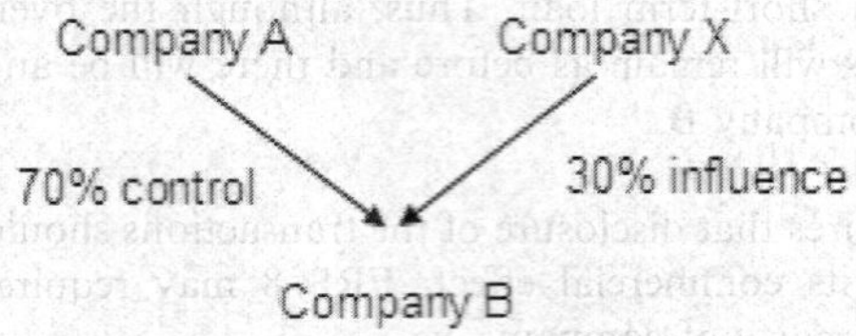

The question also arises whether company X is a related party of company A's group for the purpose of disclosing the transaction in the group's consolidated financial statements. However, the fact that company A and company X have an investment in the same company, company B, does not by itself make company A and company X related parties of each other as there would appear to be no related party relationship between them. [FRS 8 para 12]. Company A's *group* and company X will be related parties of each other only if they fall within the definition of related parties in FRS 8 paragraph 2.5(a), that is, if there is the necessary control or influence.

For instance, if company A's group was influenced by company X such that company X persuaded company A's group to dispose of the property to company X at below its market value (that is, company X exerted influence over company A), they would be related parties because company A subordinated its interests in entering into the transaction. This is a question of fact, but as the transaction was at market value, the question of one party having subordinated its interests is unlikely. Consequently, in this situation company A and company X would not be related parties and no disclosure would be necessary under FRS 8.

29.130 The implications where the minority investor is a director of the subsidiary (and possibly a key manager of the group) are considered in paragraph 29.141.1.

Subsidiaries acquired and disposed of during the year

29.131 The situation where parties are related for only part of the year is dealt with in paragraph 29.68 onwards. In practice, questions arise as to what transactions are disclosable in consolidated and individual financial statements where a group has acquired or disposed of a subsidiary during the year. It is considered that disclosure should be made on the following basis.

Consolidated financial statements

- Where a group has acquired a subsidiary, transactions between the members of the acquiring group and the acquired subsidiary prior to the date of acquisition are disclosable in the consolidated financial statements. This is because an acquired subsidiary is deemed to be a related party of the group for the entire period, but only transactions prior to acquisition are disclosable as post-acquisition transactions are eliminated on consolidation. Under this rationale, comparatives for the prior year would be required.
- Where a group has disposed of a subsidiary during the year, only post-disposal transactions between the members of the group and the subsidiary disposed of are disclosable in the consolidated financial statements as pre-disposal transactions are eliminated on consolidation. Under this rationale, comparatives for the prior year would not be required.

Parent entity financial statements

- No related party disclosure is necessary in a parent's own financial statements when those statements are presented together with its consolidated financial statements – see paragraph 29.148.

Subsidiary financial statements

- If the company disposed of was a 90 per cent subsidiary of a group at its previous year end, but is no longer a 90 per cent subsidiary of that group at its current year end, all transactions for the whole period with the group of which the company was formerly a subsidiary are disclosable in the company's financial statements. This is because the company is unable to use the exemption in paragraph 3(c) of FRS 8 as it is no longer a subsidiary of the former group at its year end. Under this rationale, comparatives for the prior year would be required.
- Where a company is acquired during the year, all transactions for the whole period with the other companies in the new group are disclosable in the financial statements of the acquired company, unless the company is 90 per cent owned at the year end, in which case transactions with group companies are exempt from disclosure. Under this rationale, comparatives for the prior year would not be required.

29.131.1 The example below considers the related party disclosures in the financial statements of a subsidiary in the situation where a fellow subsidiary is disposed of by the group.

Example

Company A had two wholly-owned subsidiaries, subsidiary B and subsidiary C. During the year subsidiary C was sold outside the group. In the financial statements of subsidiary B, it did not disclose transactions with subsidiary C last year, because it took advantage of the exemption in paragraph 3(c) of FRS 8, for subsidiaries, 90 per cent or more of whose voting rights are controlled within the group, from disclosing transactions with entities that are part of the group or investees of the group qualifying as related parties, provided that the consolidated financial statements in which the subsidiaries are included are publicly available. However, what should subsidiary B disclose this year, in respect of transactions with subsidiary C in the periods before and after subsidiary C left the group?

Paragraph 2.5 of FRS 8 states that two parties are related parties when *at any time* during the financial period they are subject to common control from the same source. As subsidiary B and subsidiary C were wholly-owned by company A for part of the year they are related parties for the whole year, including the period following the disposal of subsidiary C.

However, transactions between companies B and C whilst company C was a wholly-owned subsidiary remain exempt from disclosure as company C is still a member of the group until that point and company B can, therefore, still use the exemption from disclosure under paragraph 3(c) of FRS 8.

However, once company C is disposed of and ceases to be a member of the group, company B can no longer use the exemption in paragraph 3(c) and, therefore, company B must disclose transactions with company C that occur in the period following the disposal of company C by company A.

In the next year, company C will not be a related party of company B by virtue of common control during the year and, therefore, no disclosure of transactions between companies B and C will be required in company B's financial statements.

29.131.2 Similar principles apply where there has been a change in stake in a subsidiary – see the following example.

Example

A subsidiary was 85% owned at the start of the year and 100% owned at the end of the year by a parent company that prepares publicly available consolidated financial statements. In the year of the change in stake, how is the exemption in FRS 8 from disclosing transactions with other group companies applied in the subsidiary's financial statements:

(a) No disclosure required as the subsidiary is exempt at year end?

(b) Disclosure required for period up to when the subsidiary became exempt?

(c) Full disclosure required as the subsidiary was not exempt for part of the year?

This is similar to the situation where subsidiaries are acquired in the year (see para 29.131 above). Our view is that if the subsidiary is more than 90% owned at the year end then it is entitled to the exemption for transactions with group companies during the year – that is, the year end view.

Therefore, transactions that occurred before the company was 90% owned are not required to be disclosed as the exemption is applied to the entire period, that is (a) above. Also, under this rationale, comparatives for the prior year would not be required.

The company would have to state that it has taken advantage of the exemption in paragraph 3(c) of FRS 8.

29.132 An example of disclosure of transactions with a company after disposal (in this case by demerger) can be found in Table 29.3 above.

Quasi-subsidiary undertakings

29.133 FRS 5 defines 'quasi-subsidiary' as *"a company, trust, partnership or other vehicle that, though not fulfilling the definition of a subsidiary, is directly or indirectly controlled by the reporting entity and gives rise to benefits for that entity that are in substance no different from those that would arise were the vehicle a subsidiary".*

29.133.1 Although FRS 8 does not specifically mention quasi-subsidiaries, a quasi-subsidiary must by definition be a related party of its 'quasi-parent'. FRS 8 states that parties are related where one has direct or indirect control over the other; and direct or indirect control is part of the definition of a quasi-subsidiary in FRS 5. Therefore, transactions are disclosable in each entity's financial statements, unless one of FRS 8's exemptions applies.

29.134 Where a company qualifies as a quasi-subsidiary and has transactions with its group, FRS 8 applies as follows:

- In consolidated financial statements no disclosure is necessary for transactions between group companies and quasi-subsidiaries, because the latter are treated as group entities and the transactions are eliminated on consolidation. [FRS 8 para 3(a)]. However, FRS 5 does require other disclosures in the consolidated financial statements in respect of quasi-subsidiaries, including summaries of their balance sheet, profit and loss account and cash flow statement.
- In the parent's financial statements no disclosure is required if they are presented with the parent's consolidated financial statements. [FRS 8 para 3(b)].
- In the quasi-subsidiaries' financial statements the exemption in FRS 8 paragraph 3(c) for 90 per cent subsidiaries does not apply, because quasi-subsidiaries are not legally subsidiary undertakings. Therefore, they need to disclose details of transactions and balances with the group, although sensible aggregation is permitted. In addition, quasi-subsidiaries need to disclose their 'quasi-parent' as a controlling party, irrespective of who legally owns their shares.

Associates and joint ventures

29.135 In general, any material transactions between the investing company and the associate or joint venture are disclosable by both parties. The situation can become more complicated in a group where the transaction may be between a subsidiary of the investing company and the associate of the investing company. The implications for disclosure are illustrated in the example below:

Example

Company H has a subsidiary, company S, and an associate, company A.

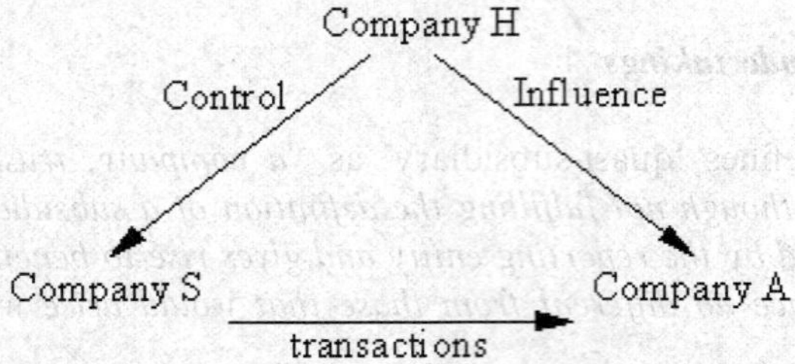

If company H transacts with company A and assuming that the transaction is material, then the disclosure in the relevant financial statements will be as follows:

Company A's financial statements – company H is a related party of company A and so company A will be required to disclose details of the transaction.

Company H's consolidated financial statements – company A is a related party of company H and H's group, being an associate of both; so company H will be required to disclose details of the transaction.

If the transaction is between company S and company A, then the position is more complicated. Company H controls company S, but exercises influence over company A. Both company S and company A are related parties of company H, but are not necessarily related parties of each other. During the financial year they transact business. The questions arise whether those transactions are related party transactions that should be disclosed: in the individual financial statements of company S; in the consolidated financial statements of company H; and in the individual financial statements of company A.

Company S and company A would be related parties if either or both of them had put their own separate interests below those of the other parties (that is, subordinated their separate interests) in entering into those transactions. The following table considers the situations where they are and where they are not related parties for the purposes of disclosure of the transactions undertaken during the financial year.

Financial statements	Transactions where S and A are *not* related parties.	Transactions where S and A *are* related parties.
Company S	No disclosure	No disclosure as company S takes exemption for 90% subsidiaries for transactions with subsidiaries and associates of the group. [FRS 8 para 3(c)].
H's group	Disclosure as company A is related party of H's group. (see note below)	Disclosure as A is not a group entity and balances are not eliminated on consolidation. [FRS 8 para 3(a)].
Company A	No disclosure	Disclosure as A is not a 90% subsidiary and so not entitled to exemption.

Company H's consolidated financial statements – Although in this instance company A may not be a related party of company S, as it is an associate of company H it is by definition a related party of the reporting entity (that is, company H's group). So company H will be required to disclose details of transactions between the members of the group and company A in the consolidated financial statements.

29.135.1 Disclosure in respect of associates and joint ventures in considered in the examples below.

Example 1

A company shows in its balance sheet a combined figure for amounts owed to equity-accounted joint ventures and to associates. Should these amounts be split between amounts owed to joint ventures and amounts owed to associates?

Yes, separate disclosure should be given because paragraph 55 of FRS 9, 'Associates and joint ventures', refers to amounts owed between an investor and its associates **or** joint ventures, that is, it distinguishes between the two. This is consistent with the general requirement in FRS 9 for separate disclosure in respect of associates and joint ventures. The split of the amounts owed can be given in the notes to the financial statements.

Example 2

Should a joint venture's trading balances with its two investors be disclosed as amounts owed to group undertakings?

No. In accordance with section 259(5) of the Companies Act 1985 (and section 1161(5) of the Companies Act 2006), a group undertaking in relation to an entity is either a parent or subsidiary undertaking of that entity or a fellow subsidiary. Therefore, a joint venture is not part of the same group as either of its investors.

But the investors are both related parties of the joint venture and so FRS 8's disclosure requirements must be followed in both the joint venture's and its investors' financial statements. This will include disclosure of the amounts due to or from the related parties at the balance sheet date, as well as a description of the transactions.

The joint venture's investors are also required to analyse the amounts owing to and owed from the joint venture between amounts relating to loans and amounts relating to trading balances, under paragraph 55 of FRS 9, 'Associates and joint ventures'. However, this information should already be given as part of the FRS 8 disclosures.

Pension funds

29.136 Transactions with pension funds for the benefit of the reporting entity's employees or any related party (other than contributions paid – see para 29.158) will be related party transactions. Table 29.7 below illustrates this type of disclosure.

Table 29.7 — Kingfisher plc — Annual Report and Accounts — 2 February 2002

38 Related party transactions

During the year, the Company and its subsidiaries carried out a number of transactions with related parties in the normal course of business and on an arm's length basis. The names of the related parties, the nature of these transactions and their total value is shown below:

£ thousands	2002 Value of transactions	2002 Receivable/(Payable) at year end	2001 Value of transactions	2001 Receivable/(Payable) at year end
Transactions with B&Q International Co. in which the Group holds a 50% interest:				
Provision of employee services	623	–	305	–
Sale of store fixtures	977	598	686	438
Transactions with Cinema Club Ltd in which the Group held a 50% interest, until the demerger				
Provision of administration and distribution services	779	–	1,609	685
Turnover payable less royalties	(7,136)	–	(12,111)	(6,465)
Transactions with Woolworths Group plc, following the demerger:				
Redemption of Kingfisher gift vouchers, issued pre-demerger	(1,372)	(695)	n/a	n/a
Rent charged	12,208	159	n/a	n/a
Charges in respect of services provided by Kingfisher plc and its subsidiaries	3,159	2,509	n/a	n/a
Contributions by Woolworths Group plc to the Kingfisher plc pension plan	8,249	(94)	n/a	n/a
Transactions with Flogistics Ltd, since 28 August 2001, in which the Group holds a 50% interest:				
Administration charge	(96)	–	n/a	n/a
Sale of Kingfisher gift vouchers, net of discount	22,047	7,237	n/a	n/a

Transactions with Superdrug Stores plc, following the disposal:				
Purchase of goods for resale				
Redemption charge received in respect of				
Kingfisher gift vouchers				
Redemption of Kingfisher gift vouchers issued				
pre-disposal	(1,997)	–	n/a	n/a
Rent charged	365	–	n/a	n/a
Charges in respect of services provided by	(5,284)	(2,645)	n/a	n/a
Kingfisher plc and its subsidiaries	1,695	–	n/a	n/a
Contributions by Superdrug Stores plc to the	300	(327)	n/a	n/a
Kingfisher plc pension plan	2,797	(45)	n/a	n/a
Sale of property by Castorama Dubois Investissements S.C.A. to AGSR, a company owned by A. Gariaud the chairman of BUT S.A.:				
Proceeds	1,528	–	n/a	n/a
The Company provides administrative services to the Group's pension schemes. The amounts charged to the schemes and the balances outstanding at the year end were:				
Kingfisher Pension Scheme	1,605	82	1,354	376
Kingfisher Retirement Trust	41	24	26	(4)

Shareholders

29.137 Transactions with shareholders will be disclosable under FRS 8 if the shareholders meet the definition of a related party under FRS 8 (see further para 29.17).

29.137.1 The example below considers whether transactions in shares are related party transactions.

Example

FRS 8 paragraph 2.6 defines a related party transaction as the transfer of assets or liabilities or the performance of services by, to or for a related party irrespective of whether a price is charged. Is disclosure required by FRS 8 in respect of the following transactions in shares by a related party (for example, a director)?

(a) The purchase or sale of shares in the market.

The transactions are between the related party and the market. We consider that purchases and sales of shares by a related party in a market transaction that does not involve the company are not disclosable in a company's financial statements as related party transactions under FRS 8.

(b) Subscribing for shares in a rights issue.

Where a related party subscribes for shares in the company under a rights issue, there is a transaction between the company and the related party that meets the definition of a related party transaction. Therefore, disclosure would be required under FRS 8 if the transaction is material (see para 29.77 onwards).

(c) Underwriting a rights issue and, as a result, subscribing for additional shares in respect of rights not taken up.

The underwriting of the rights issue is a separate arrangement from the rights issue. By underwriting the issue, the related party is performing a service for the company. The underwriting arrangement and the subscription for additional shares would be disclosable related party transactions under FRS 8 (and would be presumed to be material, if they are unusual transactions).

(d) Subscribing for shares on exercise of share options granted under a senior executive long-term incentive scheme.

Under paragraph 3(e) of FRS 8, emoluments in respect of services as an employee of the reporting entity are exempt from disclosure. Therefore, shares acquired under long-term incentive schemes that a director is entitled to participate in under his contract of employment are outside the scope of FRS 8. Disclosure of directors' remuneration is, however, required by the Companies Act 1985 (and the Companies Act 2006) and the Listing Rules.

Directors

29.138 This section considers the disclosure of transactions with directors (other than emoluments in respect of services as an employee, for which there is an exemption – see para 29.159).

29.139 Subscriptions for shares in an entity by a director will be related party transactions and disclosable if the transactions are material. However, purchases and sales of an entity's shares in the market by a director that do not involve the entity as a party to the transaction are not disclosable as related party transactions. See further paragraph 29.137.1 above.

29.139.1 An example of disclosure under FRS 8 of a subscription for shares as a result of the exercise of a share option by a director is given in Table 29.8 below.

Table 29.8 — Wolseley plc — Annual Report and Accounts — 31 July 1996

Notes to the Accounts (extract)

28. RELATED PARTY TRANSACTIONS

Pursuant to an arrangement in place on the acquisition of Brossette in 1992, Mr G Pinault, who was appointed a director on 1 August 1994, held call and put options in relation to 7,000 shares in Brossette BTI. Having exercised the call option in early 1994, and paid the appropriate price, Mr Pinault exercised the put option during the year. Due to certain changed circumstances occurring during the period from the grant of the option to exercise, amendments to the original put option were agreed. Mr Pinault subsequently sold his entire share holding in Brossette BTI to an intermediary holding company at an agreed price of £508.40 per share. The company's auditors, Price Waterhouse, have reported to the directors that the terms of the amendment of the original put option were fair and reasonable as far as the members of Wolseley plc are concerned.

There are no other related party transactions requiring disclosure in this year's accounts in accordance with FRS8 (Related Party Disclosures).

29.140 Guarantees are given as one of the examples of related party transactions in paragraph 19 of the standard. Personal guarantees by directors of the borrowings of the reporting entity would, therefore, be disclosable. It is probable that a director's personal guarantee is a material item both to him and to the company.

Example

A company director has given a bank a personal guarantee as security for his company's overdraft facility. Does this have to be disclosed in the company's financial statements?

FRS 8 defines a related party transaction as *"the transfer of assets or liabilities or the performance of services by, to or for a related party irrespective of whether a price is charged"*. The explanatory section of the standard gives a number of examples of types of transactions and other arrangements that come within the definition, including guarantees and the provision of collateral security. Therefore, any guarantees given by, to or for a related party are disclosable if they are material. A director is by definition a related party. The standard requires materiality to be judged from the perspective of both the users of the company's financial statements and the director. It is probable that a director's personal guarantee of a company's borrowings is a material item, in which case it would be disclosable as a related party transaction under FRS 8.

29.141 Dividends paid to directors are related party transactions. Paragraph 4 of FRS 8 has an exemption for providers of finance, but this is *"... in the course of their business in that regard"* and directors are more than mere providers of finance. Therefore, dividends due to directors (or their close family) should be disclosed under FRS 8. See Table 29.9 for an example of disclosure of dividends paid to directors.

29.141.1 Paragraph 29.129 above considers the situation where a group of companies includes a partially-owned subsidiary that enters into transactions with the minority investor. Where the minority investor is also a director of the subsidiary, it will be necessary to consider if he or she is a key manager of the group. This is illustrated in the example below.

Example

Entity X owns 70% of the share capital of its subsidiary, entity Y. Mr B, a director of entity Y, owns the remaining 30% of the shares. Entity Y has sold a property to Mr B for C300,000. Mr B is not a director of entity X.

How should management disclose a subsidiary's sale of property to one of its directors:

(a) in the subsidiary's financial statements; and
(b) in the group's financial statements?

(a) Subsidiary – entity Y's financial statements

Mr B is a director and also a shareholder of entity Y, and has significant influence over it. He, therefore, qualifies as a related party of entity Y. Management should, therefore, disclose details of the property sale in entity Y's financial statements.

(b) Group – entity X's consolidated financial statements

Entity X's management should disclose the property sale to Mr B in the consolidated financial statements if management considers that Mr B, in his role as a director of entity Y, is a related party of X's group, unless it can be demonstrated that neither party has influenced the financial and operating policies of the other in such a way as to inhibit the pursuit of separate interests.

Mr B and entity X are not related parties simply because they both have an investment in entity Y. Entity X's management should assess whether Mr B is key management of X's group by considering whether entity Y constitutes a major activity or resource of X's group and whether, as a director of entity Y, Mr B occupies a senior position with the necessary authority and responsibility in X's group.

29.141.2 As noted in paragraph 29.60, an entity's related parties include entities in which a director (or a member of close family) has a controlling interest. This will have implications where an entity enters into trading transactions with another entity in which a director has an interest, as illustrated in the following example.

Example

A parent has a wholly-owned subsidiary. One of the subsidiary's directors is the majority shareholder of an otherwise independent third party entity that sells goods on normal commercial terms to the subsidiary.

How should transactions with the supplier be presented in:

(a) the subsidiary's financial statements; and
(b) the consolidated financial statements?

(a) The subsidiary's financial statements

An entity's related parties are presumed to include entities in which a director has a controlling interest. [FRS 8 para 2.5(d)(ii)]. Management should disclose in the subsidiary's financial statements information related to the purchases of goods from this supplier, as well as the nature of the relationship between the subsidiary and the supplier.

(b) The consolidated financial statements

The parent's management should disclose this information in the consolidated financial statements if it is determined that the director of the subsidiary is a member of the key management of the group, unless it can be demonstrated that neither party has influenced the financial and operating policies of the other in such a way as to inhibit the pursuit of separate interests.

29.141.3 Transactions with directors are required to be disclosed if they are material. This is discussed in more detail in paragraph 29.77 onwards. In addition to considering the significance to the entity, the transaction's significance to the director would also need to be considered in order to form a judgement as to whether the transaction is material. For instance, under FRS 8, transactions that are material to the director (such as the purchase of a house), whether at market value or not, would be regarded as material and, therefore, disclosable.

Example

A company is a house builder. From time to time key managers (including directors) buy houses for their own use from the company. Of 20 to 30 senior employees about three to four buy houses per year. The transactions are in the normal course of business and on an arm's length basis. Do they have to be disclosed under FRS 8?

This raises the question of what, if any, disclosure should be made under FRS 8 where directors or key managers buy their company's products, for instance suits from a retailer, cars from a vehicle distributor, etc. Normally it can be argued that if a transaction is immaterial to a director no disclosure need be made. If a transaction is material or untypical then disclosure must be made. If there is something of a half-way house for example:

(a) material to the director, but just the same as other directors (for example, farming co-ops); or
(b) material but less so and like transactions that all directors enter into, (for example, insurance policies);

then aggregated disclosure may be possible (see para 29.123 onwards). However, buying a house from the company, which is clearly material to the related party, does not seem to fall into this category as it is not something most of the senior people do, nor do they do it each year. Therefore, in this case we consider that disclosure should be made of each transaction.

Close family

29.142 Transactions with adult children and other 'close family' (as defined) of a director or a shareholder holding at least 20 per cent of the voting rights, and persons connected with them, will be disclosable, as illustrated below.

Example 1

Mr Y's father owns 100% of the shares in company A Ltd. Mr and Mrs Y own 100% of the shares and are the only directors of company B. Mrs Y's sister provides book-keeping services from time to time to company B, but is not an employee. Company A has increased its loan of £150,000 to company B to £200,000 during the year, for which company A charges an advantageous rate of interest.

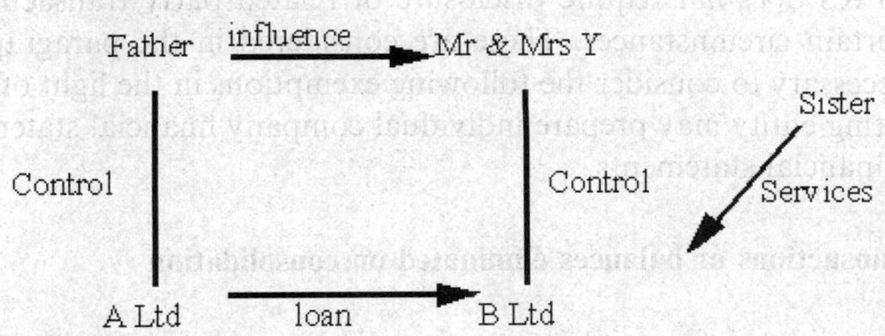

Under FRS 8, Mr Y's father and Mrs Y's sister will be related parties of company B if either may be expected to influence or be influenced by Mr or Mrs Y in dealings with company B. It seems that Mr Y's father could be expected to exert some influence over Mr and Mrs Y. It is, however, unlikely that Mrs Y's sister influences or is influenced by Mr or Mrs Y in dealings with company B. It can, therefore, be assumed for this example that Mr Y's father is a related party of company B and that Mrs Y's sister is not. Mr Y's father has a controlling interest in company A. It follows, therefore, that company A will be a related party of company B.

Both companies will need to disclose the necessary details regarding the increase in the loan to £200,000 in their financial statements. In addition, if any part of the existing loan of £150,000 and the additional loan of £50,000 is outstanding at the balance sheet date, company A will need to disclose the amounts due to it from company B on that date, together with any provisions and amounts written off. Company B will need to disclose the amount it owes to company A at the balance sheet date.

Example 2

A company sells a property to the brother of a director. The brother is regarded as 'close family' as defined in FRS 8. The sale is at an arm's length price of £100,000. Disclosure of this is required in the company's financial statements and may read as follows:

> *"In April 20X6, the company sold a property for £100,000 to Mr X, the brother of Mr Y, a director of the company. Half of the price was payable in July 20X6 and the other half was paid after the year end in January 20X7. No interest was charged on this transaction. The balance owing to the company by Mr X was £50,000 at the year end (20X6: no transactions or balances)."*

[The next paragraph is 29.144.]

Key management

29.144 The examples given from paragraph 29.139 of transactions with directors would also apply to key management.

Exemptions from disclosure

Introduction

29.145 The FRS does *not* require disclosure of related party transactions and balances in certain circumstances. These are considered in the paragraphs that follow. It is necessary to consider the following exemptions in the light of the fact that the reporting entity may prepare individual company financial statements or consolidated financial statements.

Intra-group transactions or balances eliminated on consolidation

29.146 In consolidated financial statements, disclosure is not required of any transactions or balances between group entities that have been eliminated on consolidation. [FRS 8 para 3(a)]. The following points should be considered in relation to this exemption.

- Groups that take advantage of available exemptions in the Companies Act 1985 (and Companies Act 2006) not to prepare consolidated financial statements are not able to use this FRS 8 exemption.
- Disclosure of control is not exempted.

29.147 Transactions with entities in the wider group (for example, fellow subsidiaries) will be required to be disclosed, as these are not eliminated on consolidation. For an example of disclosure where transactions presumably are not eliminated see Table 29.9 below and Table 29.7 above.

Table 29.9 — Associated British Foods plc — Report and Accounts — 15 September 2001

Notes forming part of the financial statements (extract)

31. Related party transactions

The group's related parties, as defined by Financial Reporting Standard 8, the nature of the relationship and the extent of the transactions with them, are summarised below:

	Sub note	**2001** **£'000**	2000 £'000
Management charge from Wittington Investments Limited, principally in respect of directors and secretarial staff of ABF paid by Wittington	1	**186**	450
Charges to Wittington Investments Limited in respect of services provided by the company and its subsidiary undertakings	1	**(59)**	(57)
Dividends paid by ABF and received in a beneficial capacity by:			
(i) Trustees of The Garfield Weston Foundation	2	**3,214**	3,118
(ii) Directors of Wittington Investments Limited who are not Trustees of The Foundation		**589**	563
(iii) Directors of the company who are not Trustees of the Foundation and are not directors of Wittington Investments Limited	3	**4**	9
(iv) a member of the Weston family employed within the ABF group	4	**328**	313
Sales to fellow subsidiary undertakings on normal trading terms	5	**7**	5
Amounts due from fellow subsidiary undertakings	5	**2**	–
Sales to joint ventures and associates on normal trading terms	6	**55**	46
Purchases from joint ventures and associated on normal trading terms	6	**9**	7
Amounts due from joint ventures and associates	6	**6**	6
Amounts due to joint ventures and associates	6	**3**	3

Sub notes

1. At 15 September 2001 Wittington Investments Limited together with its subsidiary undertaking, Howard Investments, held 431,515,108 ordinary shares (2000 — 431,515,108)

representing in aggregate 54.5% (2000 — 54.5%) of the total issued ordinary share capital of the company.

2. The Garfield Weston Foundation ("the Foundation") is an English charitable trust, established in 1958 by the late W Garfield Weston. The Foundation has no direct interest in the company, but as at 15 September 2001 held 683,073 shares in Wittington Investments Limited representing 79.2% of that company's issued share capital and is, therefore, the company's ultimate controlling party. At 15 September 2001, Trustees of the Foundation comprised four of the late W Garfield Weston's children and five of Garry H Weston's children.

3. Details of the directors are given on page 33. Their beneficial interests, including family interests, in the company and its subsidiary undertakings are given on page 39. Directors' remuneration, including share options, is disclosed on pages 36 to 38.

4. A member of the Weston family who is employed by the group and is not a director of the company or Wittington Investments Limited and is not a Trustee of the Foundation.

5. The fellow subsidiary undertaking is Fortnum & Mason PLC.

6. Details of the group's principal joint ventures and associates are set out on page 70.

Parent's own financial statements

29.148 No disclosure is necessary in a parent's own financial statements when those statements are presented together with its consolidated financial statements. [FRS 8 para 3(b)]. Thus, in these circumstances, under the FRS, disclosure of who controls the entity or of transactions or balances need not be given by the parent as a separate entity.

Ninety per cent subsidiaries

29.149 In the financial statements of subsidiary undertakings, 90 per cent or more of whose voting rights are controlled within the group, no disclosure is required by the standard of transactions or balances with entities that are part of the group or investees of the group qualifying as related parties, provided that the consolidated financial statements in which that subsidiary is included are publicly available. [FRS 8 para 3(c)]. However, certain information regarding subsidiaries has to be given as the balance sheet formats under the Companies Act 1985 require the disclosure of amounts owed by group undertakings and amounts owed to group undertakings. The disclosure of control is still required.

29.150 For this purpose, investees of the group qualifying as related parties include associates and joint ventures of group companies with whom the reporting subsidiary has transacted in circumstances where they are subject to influence from the same source to such an extent that one of the parties has put its own interest after those of the other party. For an example see paragraph 29.135.

29.151 This exemption permits 90 per cent subsidiary undertakings with, for instance, a small external holding in the equity or with third-party non-voting preference shareholders to take advantage of it.

29.152 No definition is given in the FRS of the phrase 'publicly available', but it seems clear that it means available to the public in general and not, for instance, just to shareholders. Section 240 of the Companies Act 1985 refers to the publication of accounts and states:

> *"For the purposes of this section a company shall be regarded as publishing a document if it publishes, issues or circulates it or otherwise makes it available for public inspection in a manner calculated to invite members of the public generally, or any class of members of the public, to read it."*

29.152.1 Similarly, section 436 of the Companies Act 2006 refers to the publication of accounts and states:

> *"For the purposes of those sections a company is regarded as publishing a document if it publishes, issues or circulates it or otherwise makes it available for public inspection in a manner calculated to invite members of the public generally, or any class of members of the public, to read it."*

29.153 We consider that 'publicly available' may be interpreted in this way. However, the test should in practice be judged by reference to whether a copy of the consolidated financial statements can be acquired relatively easily. The financial statements may be on a public register, for example, but if the financial statements themselves cannot be easily obtained, they would not be regarded as publicly available. Where there is no public register but the address from which they may be obtained is given, the financial statements would be regarded as publicly available. See also the example below.

Example

A company is a 100% UK subsidiary of a US company. The company derives 80% of its income from the US company. The company is aware of the exemption in FRS 8 for over 90% owned subsidiaries, but notes that this is dependent on the parent's consolidated financial statements being publicly available. At present the US company's consolidated financial statements are not publicly available. However, the US company is proposing to prepare non-statutory consolidated financial statements that it would make available to the public on request. If they stated in the UK company's financial statements that these consolidated financial statements of the US parent could be obtained from a particular address, could the UK company take the exemption?

The term 'publicly available' does not, we believe, mean that the US parent has to be SEC-listed and publish its financial statements widely. It does mean that the UK company should include in its financial statements wording to the effect that copies of the consolidated financial statements of the US parent are available from a stated address and that if someone writes to that address they will be sent those financial statements. As to what 'consolidated financial statements' means for the purpose of the FRS 8 exemption, in our view it does not need to be a full set of financial statements under US GAAP or UK

GAAP. But what is provided must be reasonable, that is, at least a balance sheet and profit and loss account with reasonable detail, for example, at least the Companies Act format headings plus accounting policies etc. The consolidated financial statements do not need to be audited.

29.154 The Act requires a company that is a subsidiary undertaking to give the name of the largest group and the smallest group of undertakings of which the company is a member and for which consolidated financial statements are drawn up. In addition, if copies of those financial statements are available to the public, the addresses from which they can be obtained must be stated in the notes to its financial statements. If no such address is given in its financial statements, it will be difficult for a subsidiary company to argue that consolidated financial statements in which it is included are publicly available. [CA 85 5 Sch 11, 30]. These provisions are illustrated in the examples that follow.

Example 1

A UK company is 100% owned by a private US group. The US parent also has a subsidiary in Canada. The UK company sells finished goods to the Canadian company at prices that are not typically arm's length. Do these transactions have to be disclosed?

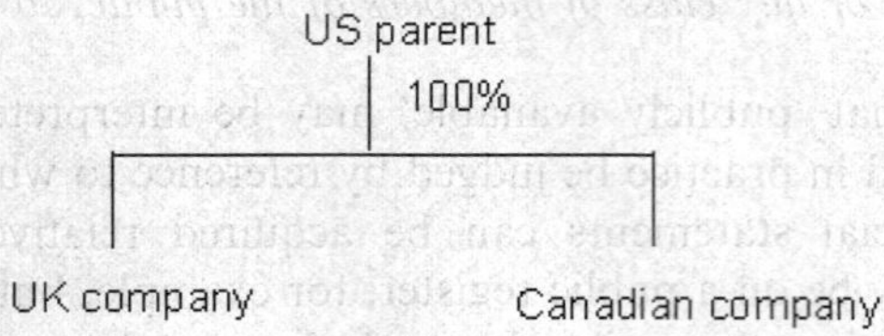

In this example, it is clear from paragraph 3(c) of the standard that the transactions between the UK company and the Canadian company would be disclosable. This is because the US parent, being privately owned, would not publish its financial statements. If the US parent made its consolidated financial statements publicly available, for example, by filing them with the SEC or publishing the address from which they can be obtained, the position would be different: the intra-group transactions in the UK company would not then need to be disclosed.

Example 2

This example is similar to Example 1, except that there is a UK sub-group, as shown in the next diagram. Here, the UK *subsidiary* sells finished goods to the Canadian company at prices that are not typically arm's length. Do these transactions have to be disclosed?

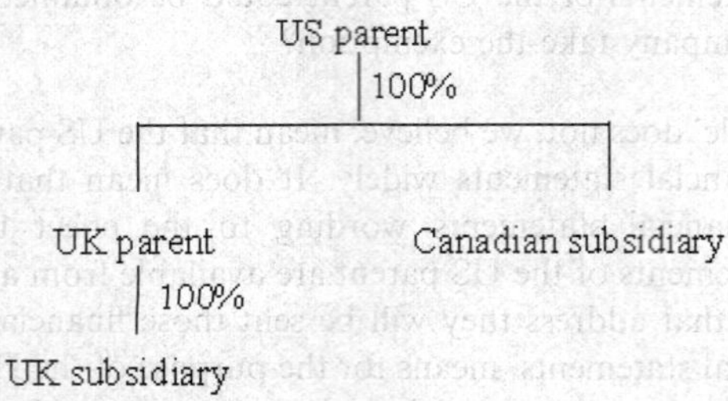

The wording of paragraph 3(c) of the standard indicates that in the financial statements of the UK subsidiary, transactions with entities that are part of the group (for example, the Canadian company) need not be disclosed provided the consolidated financial statements in which the UK subsidiary is included are publicly available. The financial statements of the US group are *not* publicly available, as it is privately owned. However, the UK parent has to prepare a UK consolidation in which the financial statements of the UK subsidiary are included. Because of this, the transactions with the Canadian company need not be disclosed in the financial statements of the UK subsidiary (and this is so, even though the Canadian company is outside the UK group). This, however, is not the full picture, because the disclosure question also arises in the context of the consolidated financial statements of the UK parent, and in that context, the exemption is not available. Hence the transactions and any balances with the Canadian company *would* be disclosable in the UK consolidated financial statements.

Example 3

A sub-group, headed by H company, is less than 90% owned by UH company plc, a company registered in England. Some subsidiaries in the sub-group, S1 and S2, enter into transactions with UH company. UH company and H company prepare consolidated financial statements. Do these transactions have to be disclosed in S1 and S2's and H company's financial statements?

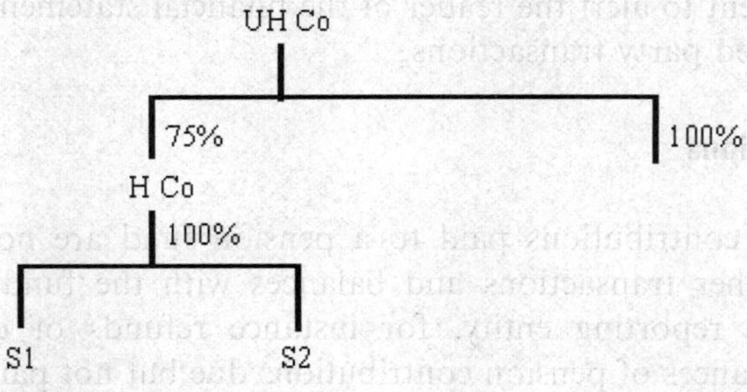

This situation can be distinguished from the situation in Example 2. There the UK group and the Canadian company are 100% owned by the US parent. In this example, S1 and S2 are not 90% owned within the group headed by UH company and they are transacting with that group. Therefore, they do not meet the 90% criterion, whether or not they are included in consolidated financial statements that are publicly available (for example, those of H company). Consequently, S1 and S2 cannot take the exemption in paragraph 3(c) of FRS 8 in respect of their transactions with UH company. As H company prepares consolidated financial statements, the transactions between S1 and S2 and UH company will also be disclosable in these financial statements as they will not be eliminated on consolidation.

If S1 and S2 had transacted with X, a 100% subsidiary of UH company which is outside the sub-group headed by H company, the disclosures in S1, S2 and the H company consolidated financial statements would be the same, for the same reasons.

An alternative view is that 90% or more of the voting rights in S1 and S2 are controlled within the UH group. This is because H company controls 100% (that is, over 90%) of the voting rights of S1 and S2 and H company is itself controlled by UH company through its majority holding. Therefore, there is a view that S1 and S2 can take the exemption for 90% subsidiaries relying on being included in UH company's publicly available consolidated financial statements. However, it can be argued that this view is not within the spirit of the exemption. Also, as H company prepares consolidated financial statements it will still need to disclose the transactions because they will not be eliminated on consolidation and H company is not more than 90% controlled.

29.155 A company that is part of a group where the parent company takes advantage of available exemptions in the Companies Act 1985 (and Companies Act 2006) and does not prepare consolidated financial statements, will not be able to take advantage of the exemption in paragraph 3(c) of FRS 8 and will have to disclose intra-group transactions and balances in its own financial statements.

29.156 It is only transactions and balances between 90 per cent subsidiary undertakings and group related parties (including associates and joint ventures) that are exempted by the standard. Disclosure would, therefore, be required of transactions and balances with related parties of the reporting subsidiary other than those that are excluded by the exemption. [FRS 8 para 17]. In addition, disclosure of the party controlling the subsidiary undertaking is still required.

29.157 Reporting entities that take advantage of the exemption for 90 per cent subsidiaries not to disclose intra-group transactions, are required to state that fact. The ASB considers disclosure of the fact that the exemption has been invoked is sufficient to alert the reader of the financial statements to the possible existence of related party transactions.

Pension contributions

29.158 Pension contributions paid to a pension fund are not required to be disclosed, but other transactions and balances with the fund still need to be disclosed by the reporting entity, for instance refunds of contributions. In addition, any balances of pension contributions due but not paid at the year end are disclosable, as effectively they would constitute a loan from the pension fund.

Emoluments for services

29.159 No disclosure is required of emoluments in respect of services as an employee of the reporting entity. This exemption covers payments 'in respect of services' and it, therefore, does not cover any *ex gratia* payment or other payment not in respect of services as an employee. For instance, payments under consultancy arrangements are not covered by the exemption.

29.160 Although it is not clear from the standard, it appears that the intention is to exclude from disclosure payments made or costs incurred in respect of persons employed under contracts of service, which are included in staff costs and disclosed in the profit and loss account or the notes. What constitutes staff costs is set out in section 231A of the Companies Act 1985 (and section 411 of the Companies Act 2006) and is considered in chapter 5.

29.161 Executive directors, who perform management functions, will usually have contracts of service; non-executive directors will usually have contracts for services. In each case it is a question of fact as to which type of contract they have. Amounts paid to directors under contracts for services should not be included in staff costs and, therefore, would seem to fall within the scope of FRS 8. However, extensive disclosure of directors' emoluments and their emoluments for services in connection with the management of the affairs of the company is already required, primarily, by Part I of Schedule 6 to the 1985 Act. These disclosures are likely to satisfy the disclosures which would be required by FRS 8 in respect of any directors' remuneration that is not covered by this exclusion.

Duty of confidentiality

29.162 Related party disclosure will also not be required by the FRS if disclosure would conflict with the reporting entity's duties of confidentiality arising by operation of law (but not from contractual provisions relating to confidentiality). Thus, banks that, by law, have to observe a strict duty of confidentiality about their customers' affairs will not have to disclose details concerning related parties which would be in conflict with that duty. [FRS 8 para 16].

[The next paragraph is 29.166.]

Additional relaxation of disclosure requirements

29.166 The FRS does not require disclosure of the relationship and transactions and balances between the reporting entity and the parties listed below simply as a result of their role as:

- Providers of finance in the course of their business in that regard.
- Utility companies.
- Government departments and their sponsored bodies.
- A customer, supplier, franchiser, distributor or general agent with whom an entity transacts a significant volume of business.

[FRS 8 para 4].

29.167 Disclosure is not required of the relationship and details of transactions and balances between the reporting entity and the parties in the first three bullet points above, even though the parties may circumscribe the freedom of action of an entity or participate in its decision-making process. This provision has the effect that the parties listed above do not become related parties of a reporting entity just as a result of the four relationships specified.

29.168 The paragraph 4 exemptions are transaction based, which means that, for example, a bank providing a loan would not be treated as a related party merely because it could exert its influence by calling in the loan or charging a higher than normal rate of interest. However, the position is different where one of these parties is a related party for some other reason. For example, a venture capitalist, as a provider of finance, may provide debt finance to the reporting entity and also have an equity stake which exceeds 20 per cent and thereby be a related party – see example 2 in paragraph 29.169 below.

29.169 Where one of the parties listed in paragraph 29.166 qualifies as a related party for some other reason, we consider that all transactions with that related party are disclosable by the reporting entity, including any transactions that arise out of the related party's role as, for example, a supplier or a provider of finance. This is illustrated in the following examples.

Example 1

A reporting company might be heavily dependent on a supply of gas from a gas company. But that does not, by itself, result in the gas company becoming a related party of the reporting company.

However, there may already be a related party relationship between a utility and another company. For example, a gas utility may have a 30% interest in a consulting company which it treats as an associated company. The two companies are, therefore, related parties, and, in the financial statements of the consulting company, transactions with the gas utility would be disclosable; they would not, for example, be eliminated on consolidation and would not, therefore, be exempted under paragraph 3(a) of the standard. The paragraph 4 exemption does not apply in this context, because the two are already related and the normal rules apply. However, bills for gas supply would not need to be disclosed if the transactions were immaterial (see para 29.78). It will presumably be easier for the gas company to argue immateriality in relation to disclosure in its financial statements of its transactions with the purchasing company.

Example 2

A venture capitalist has helped to finance a management buyout. In addition to providing loan finance, it has taken a 30% equity stake in the MBO company and placed a director on its board. The venture capitalist receives various payments from the company, including management fees, interest and dividends. Can the company avoid disclosing these transactions by using the exemption in paragraph 4 of FRS 8 in respect of transactions with providers of finance?

Paragraph 4 of FRS 8 says that the standard does not require disclosure of the relationship and transactions between a company and other parties simply as a result of their role as providers of finance in the course of their business in that regard, even though they may be able to influence the company's decision-making. The same applies to transactions with utility companies, government departments and their sponsored bodies and some other parties such as major customers and suppliers.

This means that, for example, a major customer would not be treated as a related party merely because the importance of retaining its business had a significant effect on the company's decision-making, nor would a lending bank be treated as a related party merely because the terms of the loan enabled the bank to restrict the company's borrowing or investing activities. However, the position is different where such parties are related for some other reason. In such circumstances all material transactions with those related parties would be disclosable, including those relating to the provision of finance.

It is, therefore, necessary to consider whether the venture capitalist is a related party as a result of its 30% equity interest. The relevant part of FRS 8's definition is that parties are related if *"one party has influence over the financial and operating policies of the other party to an extent that that other party might he inhibited from pursuing at all times its own separate interests"*.

Where a company is an associate of an investor (as would often be the case where it has an equity interest greater than 20%), FRS 8 states that, for the avoidance of doubt, they are related parties. But many venture capitalists do not regard companies in which they have invested as associates. This is acknowledged in FRS 9, 'Associates and joint ventures', which refers to investors whose business is to provide capital, often accompanied by advice and guidance. It says that in such circumstances, the stake is properly accounted for as an investment rather than an associate.

FRS 8 goes on to presume a person owning or able to exercise control over 20% or more of a company's voting rights is a related party. In many circumstances, an investor with a 30% stake and a director on the board would be expected to have the level of influence over the company's financial and operating policies that would make it a related party. If this were the case, the company would have to disclose all material transactions with the venture capitalist. Disclosable transactions may include the management fees paid, interest charged, and the amount and terms of the loan due to the venture capitalist. Only if it could be demonstrated that the venture capitalist does not have such an influence over the MBO company would FRS 8 not require disclosure.

29.170 The reporting entity and major suppliers or customers are not related parties by virtue of that connection alone, because the reporting entity is still able to make decisions in its own interests. It is clear that this would not be so where the relationship between them affects the pursuit of their separate interests. For instance, this might arise where a director of the reporting entity is also the controlling shareholder of the supplier.

Overriding requirement to give a true and fair view

29.171 Sections 226 and 227 of the Companies Act 1985 (and sections 396 and 404 of the Companies Act 2006) oblige the directors of a company that prepares Companies Act accounts to prepare individual and consolidated financial statements that give a true and fair view. The view expressed by the ASB in its Foreword to accounting standards is that the requirement to give a true and fair view may in special circumstances require a departure from accounting standards. However, it envisages that only in exceptional circumstances will such a departure be necessary in order for the financial statements to give a true and fair view. [ASB Foreword para 18].

29.172 There may be circumstances, however, where, in order to give a true and fair view, it is necessary to give certain disclosures that would be exempt from disclosure under FRS 8. Such additional disclosure would not be a departure from the standard, because even though the standard may not specifically require the particular disclosure, it does not prohibit such disclosure being made.

29.173 Such a situation might arise where, in a group of companies suffering from financial difficulties, cheques are passed from one group company to another through a series of different banks (that is, by cheque kiting), in order to give the bankers the impression of high liquidity and of trading activities that do not actually exist. Because the subsidiaries are wholly-owned and the transactions are eliminated on consolidation, the exemption in respect of 90 per cent subsidiaries whose parents' consolidated financial statements are publicly available, would apply. However, in order to give a true and fair view, it may, in our view, be necessary for the extent and nature of the artificial payments and receipts to be disclosed both in the subsidiaries and the group's consolidated financial statements.

Interaction with disclosures required by the Companies Act 1985

29.174 The Companies Act 1985 does not use the term 'related party'. The provisions in Part II of Schedule 6 to the Act require disclosure of certain transactions with directors and persons connected with directors. A person connected with a director falls broadly into the following categories:

- A director's spouse or minor children.
- A body corporate in which a director owns at least 20 per cent of the shares (excluding any shares held as treasury shares) or which is controlled by a director or the persons connected with him.
- A trustee of a trust of which the director or any persons connected with him are beneficiaries.
- A partner of the director (or a person connected with the director) in his capacity as partner.

[CA85 Sec 346].

29.175 The disclosures that the Act requires to be made concerning related party transactions are considered briefly in the paragraphs that follow. The annex to this chapter summarises the Act's sections that require such disclosures and makes reference to where the provisions are considered in more detail in chapter 6 of the Manual of Accounting – Management reports and governance.

Loans and other similar transactions with directors

29.176 Details of directors' loans, quasi-loans, credit transactions, guarantees and security given for such transactions and other related assignments and arrangements are disclosable under Part II of Schedule 6. Disclosure extends to transactions entered into by the reporting company or any subsidiary with a director of the company or its holding company or with persons connected with such directors. The information required in connection with the above disclosure is usually consistent with the disclosure of such transactions with directors under FRS 8, (although under FRS 8, the scope of related parties also includes other members of key management). For example, neither the Act nor FRS 8 specifically requires disclosure of the rate of interest on a loan. Disclosure of that information, however, seems implicit in the Act's phrase *"the principal terms of the transactions"* and the words of the FRS *"description of the transactions"* or *"the amounts involved"*. [CA85 6 Sch 22(1); FRS 8 para 6].

Loans and other similar transactions with officers

29.177 A statement must be given of the aggregate amounts outstanding at the end of the financial year in relation to the types of transactions mentioned in paragraph 29.176 with officers of the company who are not directors. This does not apply to transactions that do not exceed £2,500. [CA85 6 Sch 28-30].

Transactions in which a director has a material interest

29.178 In addition to loans and similar transactions, paragraphs 15(c) and 16(c) of Schedule 6 to the Companies Act 1985 require disclosure of certain transactions entered into by the reporting company or a subsidiary in which the director of the company or its holding company (or a person connected with him) has a material interest. This would include substantial property transactions under section 320. The Act says that an interest in a transaction is not material if in the opinion of the board of directors it is not so. However, they must consider the matter honestly and reasonably and come to a reasonable conclusion. Although 'material interest' is not defined by the Act, two tests have been suggested to interpret it. The first test of materiality is whether disclosure of the transaction is likely to be of relevance to shareholders or creditors. The second test is whether the director's interest in the transaction is substantial. The guidance given by FRS 8 on establishing materiality is broadly similar to the two tests mentioned above (see from para 29.78).

29.179 The main exception from disclosure under the Act is for transactions in the normal course of business and at arm's length. Although the wording of this exemption has caused confusion, it is normally interpreted as exempting transactions that the reporting company or a subsidiary company:

- Enters into in the ordinary course of its business.
- On terms that are not less favourable to the reporting entity or its subsidiary company than it would be reasonable to expect if the person with the material interest had not been a director of the company or its holding company.

[CA85 6 Sch 20].

29.180 Details of the disclosures required in the financial statements for transactions in which a director has a material interest are given in chapter 6 of the Manual of Accounting – Management Reports and Governance. If disclosure is required by the Companies Act 1985, the information it requires to be disclosed, which includes the transaction's principal terms, will in general give sufficient information for the purposes of FRS 8 for such transactions (and will also apply to other members of key management under the wider scope of FRS 8). As discussed in paragraph 29.179, the Companies Act 1985 gives exemption for transactions with directors in the normal course of business and at arm's length. However, these are disclosable under FRS 8, even though they may be exempted from disclosure under the Act.

29.181 There is one further aspect where the disclosure of information required by FRS 8 for related party transactions may go further than the existing disclosures required by the Act. Paragraph 6(e) of FRS 8 requires disclosure of *"any other elements of the transactions necessary for an understanding of the financial statements"*. The FRS gives as an example of this: the need to given an indication that the transfer of a major asset has taken place at an amount materially different from that obtainable on normal commercial terms. However, the disclosure required in each instance will depend on the facts.

Interaction with disclosures required by the Companies Act 2006

29.182 The disclosures that the Companies Act 2006 requires to be made concerning related party transactions are considered briefly in the paragraphs that follow. The annex to this chapter summarises the Act's sections that require such disclosures and makes reference to where the provisions are considered in more detail in chapter 6 of the Manual of Accounting – Management reports and governance.

29.183 The disclosure requirements in respect of advances, credit and guarantees entered into with directors are contained in section 413 of the Companies Act 2006. Where a company does not prepare consolidated financial statements, it is required to disclose details of advances and credits granted by the company to its directors and guarantees entered into by the company on behalf of its directors. Where a parent company prepares consolidated financial statements, it is required to disclose details of advances and credits granted to the directors of the parent company, by that company or by any of its subsidiary undertakings and guarantees entered into on behalf of the directors of the parent company, by that company or by any of its subsidiary undertakings. [CA06 Sec 413(1),(2)].

29.184 The details required to be disclosed in respect of an advance or credit are its amount, an indication of the interest rate, its main conditions and any amounts repaid. The details required in respect of a guarantee are its main terms, the amount of the maximum liability that may be incurred by the company (or its subsidiary) and any amount paid and any liability incurred by the company (or its subsidiary) for the purpose of fulfilling the guarantee (including any loss incurred by reason of enforcement of the guarantee). [CA06 Sec 413(3),(4)].

29.185 In respect of advances and credits to directors, the Companies Act 2006 also requires disclosure of the totals of amounts of advances and credits and the amounts repaid. In respect of guarantees entered into with directors, the Companies Act 2006 also requires disclosure of amounts of the maximum liability that may be incurred and of amounts paid and any liability incurred for the purpose of fulfilling the guarantee. [CA06 Sec 413(5)].

Annex — Main disclosure requirements of the Companies Acts 1985 and 2006

Disclosures regarding the related parties shown below include the following.

Related party	Disclosures	Manual chapter No
Directors and officers		
Section 232	**Notes to financial statements to contain details of:**	
Schedule 6 — Part I	Directors' emoluments, pensions and compensation.	MRG 5
Part II	Loans by company or subsidiary to directors, and other transactions directly or indirectly for directors' benefit.	MRG 6
Part III	Aggregate loans by company or subsidiary to and credit transactions with officers	MRG 6
2006 Act		
Section 412	Notes to financial statements to contain details of directors' remuneration.	MRG 5
	[Schedule to be published]	
Section 413	Details of advances and credits granted by the company (or its subsidiaries) to its directors.	MRG 6
Section 413	Details of guarantees entered into by the company (or its subsidiaries) on behalf of its directors.	MRG 6
	Directors' remuneration report to contain details of:	
1985 Act Schedule 7A	The company's remuneration policy and details of individual directors' remuneration packages.	MRG 5
2006 Act Schedule	[Schedule to be published]	
	Directors' report to state:	
1985 Act Section 234ZZA	Name of directors	MRG 3
2006 Act Section 416	Name of directors	MRG 3
Substantial shareholders		
1985 Act 5 Sch 12, 31	Notes of subsidiary to disclose ultimate parent company.	24
2006 Act	[Schedule to be published]	

Related party	**Disclosures**	**Manual chapter No**
Group companies and investees		
Section 231	**Notes to financial statements to contain:**	
5 Sch 12, 31	Disclosure by subsidiary of ultimate *parent company*	24
5 Sch 1-6 and 15-20	Disclosure by parent of name and financial information for each *subsidiary undertaking*.	6,24
5 Sch 22	Disclosure details of investment of consolidated undertakings in and name of *associated undertakings* (20% plus of voting rights).	6,27
5 Sch 21	Name and information on *joint ventures*.	6,27
5 Sch 7-9, 23-28	Name of and information on *significant holdings* of company or group in investees.	6,24
5 Sch 9A, 28A	Details of membership of company or group in and name of unlimited company or partnership.	24
4 Sch 59	**Formats** require separate disclosure of intra-group balances.	4
4 Sch — notes 15,16 to the formats, 4A Sch 21	Notes to profit and loss account require separate disclosure of group income/interest.	4
2006 Act		
Section 409	Notes to the financial statements to contain information about related undertakings.	24
	[Schedule to be published]	
Section 410	Alternative disclosure where compliance with section 409 would result in information of excessive length.	24

References to chapter numbers prefixed 'MRG' (for example 'MRG 5') are reference to chapters in the Manual of Accounting – Management Reports and Governance.

Chapter 30

Cash flow statements

	Page
Objectives and scope of FRS 1	30001
Objectives	30001
Scope	30002
Available exemptions	30002
Subsidiary undertakings	30002
Mutual life assurance companies	30003
Pension schemes	30003
Open-ended investment funds	30003
Small companies and groups	30004
Medium-sized companies and groups	30005
Small unincorporated entities	30006
Other entities	30006
Listed subsidiary companies	30006
Preparation of cash flow statements	30008
Definition of cash	30008
Meaning of 'repayable on demand'	30008
Definition of liquid resources	30009
Treatment of borrowings	30011
Format of cash flow statements	30011
Classification of cash flows	30014
Gross or net cash flows	30015
Additional classification	30016
Departure from the standard presentation	30017
Classification of cash flows by standard headings	30017
Cash flow from operating activities	30017
Reconciliation of operating profit to net cash flow from operating activities	30018
Dividends from joint ventures and associates	30019
Returns on investments and servicing of finance	30020
Taxation	30021
Capital expenditure and financial investment	30022
Acquisitions and disposals	30024
Equity dividends paid	30025
Management of liquid resources	30025
Financing	30026
Exceptional and extraordinary cash flows	30028
Reconciliation with balance sheet figures	30029
Reconciliation to net debt	30029
Analysis of changes in net debt	30031
Consolidated cash flow statements	30033

Minority interests. 30033
Investments accounted on the equity method 30034
Investments in joint arrangements. 30034
Acquisitions and disposals of subsidiaries 30034
Changes in stake 30038
Foreign currency 30038
Individual companies. 30039
Settled transactions 30039
Unsettled transactions. 30040
Borrowings used for hedging equity investments 30044
Group companies. 30044
Temporal method 30044
Closing rate method 30045
Intra-group transactions 30051
Hedging transactions. 30053
Notes to the cash flow statements. 30054
Specific disclosures. 30054
Supplementary disclosures 30055
Reporting of gross operating cash flows. 30055
Cash flows from discontinued operations. 30055
Commentary on cash flows in operating and financial review. 30056
Restrictions on remittability. 30058
Comparative figures. 30059
Practical application of FRS 1. 30060
Balance sheet cash versus FRS 1 cash 30060
Discounts and premiums 30060
Gains and losses. 30062
Reorganisation costs following an acquisition. 30063
Refinancing of borrowings 30063
Cash subject to restriction 30064
Proceeds of a rights issue by subsidiary 30065
Proceeds from sale and leaseback 30066

Chapter 30

Cash flow statements

Objectives and scope of FRS 1

Objectives

30.1 The success, growth and survival of every reporting entity depends on its ability to generate or otherwise obtain cash. Cash flow is a concept that everyone understands and with which they can identify. Reported profit is important to users of financial statements, but so too is the cash flow generating potential of an enterprise. What enables an entity to survive is the tangible resource of cash not profit, which is merely one indicator of financial performance. Thus, owners look for dividends, suppliers and lenders expect payments and repayments, employees receive wages for their services, and the tax authorities are legally entitled to tax revenues due.

30.2 The principal objective of FRS 1 is to require reporting entities falling within its scope to:

- Report their cash generation and cash absorption for a period by highlighting the significant components of cash flow in a way that facilitates comparison of the cash flow performances of different businesses.
- Provide information that assists in the assessment of their liquidity, solvency and financial adaptability.

[FRS 1 para 1].

30.3 The form of cash flow reporting required under FRS 1 provides useful information on liquidity, solvency and financial adaptability that is additional to that provided by the profit and loss account and balance sheet. A combination of profitability and liquidity data enables users of financial statements to view both perspectives when assessing corporate viability over time (business survival depends on both profits from operations and sound cash management). Reporting historical cash flows also helps management to discharge its stewardship function by showing an enterprise's past cash flows, solvency and liquidity performance. Although historical cash flow is not necessarily a good indicator of future cash flows, it may nevertheless help users to review the accuracy of their previous predictions and, therefore, act as a base for assessing future cash flow performance and liquidity.

30.4 The standard also sets out how cash flow information should be presented and how extensive it should be. A standard format results in uniform presentation of cash flow information and makes such information much more comparable among companies. This comparability should make the information useful to investors, creditors and other users of financial statements.

[The next paragraph is 30.22.]

Scope

30.22 There is no statutory requirement for companies to prepare a cash flow statement. However, FRS 1 requires all reporting entities that prepare financial statements intended to give a true and fair view of their financial position and profit or loss (or income and expenditure) to include a cash flow statement as a *primary* statement within their financial statements, unless specifically exempted. [FRS 1 paras 4, 5].

Available exemptions

30.23 The following entities are exempt from preparing a cash flow statement.

Subsidiary undertakings

30.24 A subsidiary undertaking, 90 per cent or more of whose voting rights are controlled within a group, is exempt from producing a cash flow statement, provided the consolidated financial statements in which the subsidiary undertaking is included are publicly available. There is no requirement for the parent undertaking's consolidated financial statements to be prepared under the same GAAP as that of the subsidiary or for the parent to prepare and make publicly available a consolidated cash flow statement that includes the cash flows of the subsidiary undertaking. [FRS 1 para 5(a)]. This exemption is similar to the 90 per cent or more exemption included in FRS 8, 'Related party disclosures', (see chapter 29). The meaning of 'publicly available' is considered further in chapter 29.

Example 1

A subsidiary company was 100% owned by a US listed company at the balance sheet date of 31 December 20X6. Because of this it states in its financial statements that it has taken advantage of the exemption in FRS 1 not to prepare a cash flow statement.

The US company is selling the subsidiary to an individual and this is going to occur prior to the financial statements being signed, resulting in the subsidiary no longer qualifying as a 90% owned subsidiary on the date of signing. Does this mean that the subsidiary will have to prepare and disclose a cash flow statement and also disclose its transactions with the US company in the financial statements as at 31 December 20X6? That is, do the rules apply to the situation at the balance sheet date or at the date of signing?

A company that is wholly-owned at its year end (31 December 20X6) and consolidated into the parent's publicly available consolidated financial statements at that date is entitled to the exemptions in FRS 1. The fact that the company is subsequently sold by the parent does not affect the entitlement to the exemption in the company's financial statements for the year ended 31 December 20X6, that is, the exemption applies to the situation at the balance sheet date.

Example 2

Company A was not a subsidiary at its last year end, 31 December 20X5, and under FRS 1, prepared a cash flow statement. In April 20X6 it was acquired by another company, company B, which is producing financial statements to 31 December 20X6. The financial statements of company B will be consolidated and will include company A from the date of acquisition in April 20X6. Does company A have to produce a cash flow statement for the year to 31 December 20X6 in its individual financial statements?

FRS 1 exempts subsidiaries, 90% or more of whose voting rights are controlled with in the group, from the requirement to present a cash flow statement provided that consolidated financial statements in which the company is included are publicly available. [FRS 1 para 5]. Although not specifically stated in the standard, the year end position is the one we take and, therefore, if company A has 90% or more of its voting rights owned by company B at the year end and company B makes its consolidated financial statements publicly available, then company A can take the exemption and is not required to present a cash flow statement.

[The next paragraph is 30.26.]

Mutual life assurance companies

30.26 Mutual life assurance societies that are owned by policy holders and friendly societies that carry on mutual life assurance business are exempt from producing a cash flow statement. [FRS 1 para 5(b)].

Pension schemes

30.27 Pension schemes are exempt from producing a cash flow statement. [FRS 1 para 5(c)]. The SORP, 'Financial reports of pension schemes', does not require pension schemes to produce a cash flow statement. This is because information about the cash flows of the scheme is normally provided by the fund account and net asset statement. Although the fund account adopts an accruals basis of accounting rather than a strict cash flow basis, re-presenting the information in the format of a cash flow statement would generally not provide any significant additional information for the readers of pension scheme financial statements.

Open-ended investment funds

30.28 The standard exempts open-ended investment funds from producing a cash flow statement provided certain conditions are satisfied. For this purpose, the standard defines an investment fund by using three of the four conditions for qualifying as an investment company as set out in section 266(2) of the Companies Act 1985 (CA06 Sec 833(2)). [FRS 1 para 2]. The fourth condition, which prohibits capital profits from being distributed, is intentionally left out of the standard's definition so as to allow unauthorised unit trust type vehicles (often used for unquoted or venture capital investments) and certain investment entities whose trust deeds or articles do not prohibit distribution of capital profits to claim the exemption from preparing a cash flow statement.

30.29 Clearly, the exemption is broad and means that a wide range of authorised and unauthorised investment vehicles will not have to prepare cash flow statements. However, the exemption is conditional on meeting all of the following criteria:

- Substantially all of the entity's investments are highly liquid.
- Substantially all of the entity's investments are carried at market value.
- The entity provides a statement of changes in net assets.

[FRS 1 para 5(d)].

Most investment vehicles should have little difficulty in meeting the above conditions.

[The next paragraph is 30.31.]

Small companies and groups

30.31 Small (but not medium-sized) companies entitled to file abbreviated financial statements with the Registrar under section 246 of the Companies Act 1985 (section 444 of the Companies Act 2006) need not prepare a cash flow statement. [FRS 1 para 5(f)]. Generally, a company qualifies as small if it meets the relevant conditions and the size criteria specified in the Act (see further chapter 32). A small company is not actually required to file abbreviated financial statements, but merely has to be entitled to do so in order to claim the exemption from preparing a cash flow statement. However, the exemption is not available where the small company is any one of the following:

- A public company.
- An authorised insurance company, banking company, e-money issuer, ISD investment firm or UCITS management company (as defined by the Financial Services and Markets Act 2000).
- A person who carries on insurance market activity.
- A member of a group containing one or more of the above mentioned entities.

30.32 The FRSSE encourages, but does not require, smaller entities to prepare a cash flow statement. Where a smaller entity voluntarily produces a cash flow statement, the statement should be prepared using the indirect method as discussed in paragraph 30.71. This is because the indirect method is helpful in

30.39.3 For periods beginning prior to 20 January 2007, the un-amended listing rules will apply. Paragraph 9.8.2R(4) of these rules requires that if the report and accounts of a listed company do not give a true and fair view of the state of affairs, profit or loss and *cash flows* of the group, more detailed information must be provided. In respect of cash flows, this would appear to require a cash flow statement.

30.39.4 Whether the subsidiary company must present a cash flow will depend on whether the company has listed equity shares, listed preference shares, listed securities convertible to equity shares or listed debt (non-convertible) and specialist securities. The continuing obligation requirements in chapter 9 apply to companies with listed equity shares, listed preference shares and listed securities convertible to equity shares. However, they do not apply to companies with listed debt (non-convertible) and specialist securities, as the requirements of chapter 17 of the listing rules apply.

30.39.5 For companies with listed preference shares or securities convertible into equity shares there are no exemptions from the requirements of LR 9.8.2R(4). Therefore, our view is that in this situation a cash flow statement is required (and this applies whether or not the reporting entity concerned is itself a single company or a group).

30.39.6 However, for companies with listed debt (non-convertible) and specialist securities, the requirements of chapter 17 of the listing rules apply. Paragraph 17.3.5G(2) requires that if the annual accounts do not give a true and fair view of the assets and liabilities, financial position and profits and losses of the issuer or group, additional information must be provided. Therefore, there is no similar requirement for the annual accounts to give a true and fair view of cash flows and, as a consequence, a cash flow statement is not required.

30.39.7 For periods beginning on or after 20 January 2007, the amended listing rules apply. Paragraph 9.8.2R of chapter 9, relating to continuing obligations, has been deleted. Reference is made instead to paragraph 4.1 of the Disclosure and Transparency Rules, which contains the continuing obligation requirements for listed companies.

30.39.8 The Disclosure and Transparency Rules require companies to include audited financial statements in their annual report. For individual company financial statements, these audited financial statements must be prepared in accordance with national law (in this case under UK GAAP). [DTR para 4.1.6]. Paragraph 4.1 does not contain an overriding requirement to include information on cash flows in the financial statements. On this basis, there does not appear to be any requirement that precludes listed subsidiaries from taking the FRS 1 exemption and not producing a cash flow statement. Although there is no requirement to do so, companies may wish to include a cash flow statement in their annual report as this provides useful and relevant information to the users of the financial statements.

Preparation of cash flow statements

30.40 It is consistent with the objective stated in paragraph 30.5 above that a cash flow statement should focus on identifying the cash effects of transactions with parties that are external to the reporting entity and their impact on its cash position. Only those transactions that involve a *cash flow* should be reported in the cash flow statement [FRS 1 para 6]. *Cash flow* is defined as an increase or decrease in an amount of cash. [FRS 1 para 2].

Definition of cash

30.41 As the cash flow statement only reflects movements in cash, the definition of cash is central to its proper preparation. The standard does not define cash as used in common parlance, but extends the definition to include overdrafts that are repayable on demand. Overdrafts are included in the definition because they are generally viewed as negative cash balances and effectively repayable on demand. Thus cash includes:

- Cash in hand, and also deposits, including those denominated in foreign currencies, *repayable on demand* with any bank or other qualifying financial institutions.

- Overdrafts from any bank or qualifying financial institutions repayable on demand.

[FRS 1 para 2].

For this purpose, a qualifying financial institution is an entity that as part of its business receives deposits or other repayable funds and grants credits for its own account. [FRS 1 para 2].

30.42 One impact of the definition of cash is that monies transferred between deposits that qualify as cash do not result in cash inflows and outflows, but are merely movements within the overall cash balance. For instance, a transfer from a deposit account to reduce the company's overdraft would not be reflected in cash flows as it is an intra cash movement. However, all charges and credits on accounts qualifying as cash, such as bank interest, bank fees, deposits or withdrawals other than movements wholly within them, represent cash inflows and outflows of the reporting entity.

Meaning of 'repayable on demand'

30.43 In order to qualify as cash, deposits must be *'repayable on demand'*, which they are if they meet one of the following criteria:

- They can be withdrawn at any time or demanded without notice and without penalty.

- A period of notice of no more than 24 hours or one working day has been agreed.

[FRS 1 para 2].

Without notice implies that the instrument would be readily convertible into known amounts of cash on demand, that is, not subject to any time restriction. Therefore, monies deposited in a bank account for an unspecified period, but which can only be withdrawn by giving notice of more than 24 hours or one working day would not fall to be treated as cash under the definition. However, such funds often can be withdrawn early by paying a penalty. In some situations, this penalty payment may not be significant enough to cause any appreciable change in the capital amount withdrawn. Nevertheless, the standard makes it clear that cash is repayable on demand if it is in practice available within 24 hours *without penalty*. Therefore, repayable on demand implies both withdrawal without penalty and without notice, or if a notice period has been agreed it must not exceed 24 hours or one working day. If the deposits can be withdrawn immediately (that is, with no notice or, for example, with 24 hours notice) but with loss of interest earned then this is a penalty and so the deposits do not fall within the definition of cash. We interpret penalty to be wider than simply the loss of original capital invested, that is, it includes loss of interest.

Definition of liquid resources

30.44 The definition of cash is sufficiently narrow to exclude investments, however liquid or near maturity. Nevertheless, companies normally use a range of such investments like term deposits, gilts, money market instruments, listed equity securities and Euronotes, not for their investment potential, but for managing their overall cash or net debt position. If the focus of the cash flow statement is to report movements in pure cash, the question arises as to where in the cash flow statement movements in such investments, which do not qualify as cash, but which are nevertheless used increasingly in cash management and treasury operations, should be reported.

30.45 The heading 'management of liquid resources' differentiates investments that are effectively used in managing the entity's net debt or net funds position from those that are held for their investment potential. However, to qualify as a liquid resource, the investment must be held as a readily disposable store of value. To be held as a readily disposable store of value, the investment must be held as a current asset investment. Fixed asset investments do not qualify, because by definition these are held for use on a continuing basis and so are not readily disposable. For this purpose, a readily disposable investment is one that is not only disposable by the entity without curtailing or disrupting its business, but also satisfies either of the following criteria:

- It is readily convertible into known amounts of cash at or close to its carrying amount.

- It is traded in an active market.

[FRS 1 para 2].

30.46 The first criterion is particularly relevant for classifying investments in short-term deposits. Although a measure of liquidity, or a maturity period, is not specifically mentioned in the definition, the standard explains that the criterion that the deposit should be readily converted into cash at or near its carrying amount would tend to exclude any that are more than one year from maturity on acquisition. [FRS 1 para 52]. A period of one year would also be consistent with the investment's classification in the balance sheet as a current asset investment, a condition that is necessary for the investment to qualify as a liquid resource.

30.47 Liquid resources meeting the first condition are likely to encompass investments held with qualifying financial institutions that are short-dated and on which there are very little price fluctuation between the time the deposit was made and its ultimate conversion into cash. Therefore, it does not matter whether a term-deposit can be withdrawn by giving notice of more than 24 hours or whether the deposit can be withdrawn prior to its maturity by payment of a penalty, provided the penalty is not significant to cause any appreciable change in capital value. It does not also matter whether the maturity period is of a short duration (say three months) or medium duration (say six months to a year). As long as the deposit is readily convertible into a known amount of cash at or near its carrying amount and there are no restrictions as to the investor's ability to dispose of the investment without curtailing the business, it will qualify as a liquid resource. Deposits intended to be held for a long term, say between one and two years, are unlikely to qualify, even though they may be used by the entity in managing its overall cash or debt position. This is because, according to the definition, they are not sufficiently liquid. Therefore, any movements in them would fall to be reported under capital expenditure and financial investments.

30.48 The second condition allows current asset investments such as government securities, equity and debt instruments in other entities and derivative instruments to be treated as liquid resources, provided they are traded in an active market. Where an active market exists, the inference is that the instruments are easily exchangeable into known amount of cash and, hence, will represent readily disposable stores of value. Therefore, unlisted investments held as current assets are unlikely to qualify as liquid resources.

30.49 Provided they represent readily disposable stores of value, and meet either of the conditions set out in paragraph 30.45, a wide range of current asset investments will qualify as liquid resources. The emphasis is on a wider measure of liquidity rather than the type of the investment. The standard does not *require* all readily disposable investments to be classified as liquid resources. An entity can *choose* which of its current asset investments will be treated as liquid resources. However, it would need to explain its policy and any changes to its policy (see further para 30.106).

Treatment of borrowings

30.50 Borrowings, whether short or long-term, do not qualify as liquid resources, although bank overdrafts repayable on demand are included in cash (see para 30.41). It follows that, except for bank overdrafts, cash flows arising from all forms of borrowings, including commercial paper, should be included within the financing section of the cash flow statement.

30.50.1 A company may have an invoice discounting facility with a lending institution that is not a registered bank. Paragraph 2 of FRS 1 defines an overdraft as *"a borrowing facility repayable on demand that is used by drawing on a current account with a qualifying financial institution"*. To the extent that the lender meets the definition of a qualifying financial institution (that is, it was an entity that as part of its business receives deposits or other repayable funds and grants credit for its own account) and the discounting facility is repayable on demand, the discounting facility would meet the definition of an overdraft. It would thus be classified as cash under FRS 1. The operating cash flow would occur when the debtors repay.

30.50.2 If the balance shown in the cash flow statement as 'cash' includes items that are otherwise classified in the balance sheet, a note should be presented reconciling the cash per the cash flow statement with the two or more relevant headings on the balance sheet.

Format of cash flow statements

30.51 The standard requires cash flows to be classified under the following standard headings:

- Operating activities.
- Dividends from joint ventures and associates.
- Returns on investments and servicing of finance.
- Taxation.
- Capital expenditure and financial investments.
- Acquisitions and disposals.
- Equity dividends paid.
- Management of liquid resources.
- Financing.

30.52 The cash flows for each of the headings should be listed in the order set out above. However, the last two headings may be combined under a single heading relating to the management of liquid resources and financing provided the cash flows relating to each are shown separately and separate subtotals are given. [FRS 1 para 7]. Some companies that manage their liquid investments and borrowings as an integrated treasury operation, making investments when rates are good and drawing down on borrowings when rates are low, and matching investments with borrowings, may find this ability to combine the two headings particularly useful (see Table 30.0.2).

30.53 Presenting a subtotal after any of the above headings is neither required nor prohibited. Therefore, it is possible to present a subtotal, for instance, after capital expenditure and before acquisitions and disposals. Indeed, some entities may consider it appropriate to highlight this figure as it indicates a measure of 'free cash flow' that their businesses have generated and over which they have discretionary spending ability. An example is given in Table 30.0.1 below. Although this measure does not necessarily distinguish between discretionary capital expenditure for expansion from that incurred for routine replacement and presumes that acquisitions and, more importantly, disposals are discretionary it may nevertheless be useful. Some may find it preferable to present a subtotal after equity dividends paid as indicated in Table 30.0.2 below. Others may find it useful to draw a sub-total before financing as shown in Table 30.0.3 below. The ability to present a subtotal at any level enables entities to highlight cash flows that they consider appropriate to their particular circumstances as illustrated in the examples below.

Table 30.0.1 — Coats Viyella Plc — Annual Report and Accounts — 31 December 1998

Analysis of free cash flow

For the year ended 31 December 1998	1998 £m	1997 £m
Net cash inflow from operating activities	187.1	177.3
Returns on investments and servicing of finance	(43.5)	(54.9)
Tax paid	(25.2)	(45.9)
Capital expenditure and financial investment	(57.2)	(85.3)
Free cash flow	61.2	(8.8)

Table 30.0.2 — Bass PLC — Annual Report and Financial Statements — 30 September 1996

GROUP CASH FLOW STATEMENT

For the year ended 30 September 1996	Note	**1996 £m**	**1996 £m**	1995 £m	1995 £m
Operating activities	25		**992**		885
Interest paid		**(127)**		(128)	
Dividends paid to minority shareholders		**(5)**		(4)	
Interest received		**51**		57	
Returns on investments and servicing of finance			**(81)**		(75)
UK corporation tax paid		**(92)**		(112)	
Overseas corporate tax paid		**(19)**		(39)	
Taxation			**(111)**		(151)
Tangible fixed assets		**(547)**		(372)	
Trade loans		**(60)**		(65)	
Other fixed asset investments		**(56)**		(68)	

Paid		**(663)**	(505)
Tangible fixed assets		**24**	97
Trade loans		**85**	96
Other fixed asset investments		**45**	28
Received		**154**	221
Capital expenditure and financial investment		**(509)**	(284)
Consideration for acquisitions	24	**(246)**	(306)
Cash for overdrafts acquired		**12**	–
Acquisitions		**(234)**	(306)
Equity dividends		**(205)**	(189)
Net cash flow	25	**(148)**	(120)
Management of liquid resources and financing	26	**154**	123
Movement in cash and overdrafts		**6**	3

Table 30.0.3 — TI Group plc — Annual Report — 31 December 1997

CASH FLOW STATEMENT (extract)
FOR THE YEAR ENDED 31ST DECEMBER 1997
(extract)

	Notes	1997 £m	1996 £m
Net cash inflow from operating activities	**23**	**241.4**	218.1
Dividends received from joint ventures and associates	**23**	**10.6**	11.6
Returns on investments and servicing of finance	**24**	**(13.3)**	(4.7)
Taxation	**25**	**(73.5)**	(61.5)
Capital expenditure and financial investment	**26**	**(59.6)**	(50.0)
Acquisitions and disposals	**27**	**(13.7)**	(175.4)
Equity dividends paid		**(69.6)**	(55.2)
Management of liquid resources	**28**	**(94.0)**	60.8
Cash flow before financing		**(71.7)**	(56.3)
Issue of shares		**5.8**	12.8
Capital element of finance leases		**(0.4)**	(0.7)
Increase/(decrease) in loans		**26.7**	64.2
Financing		**32.1**	76.3
(Decrease)/increase in cash		**(39.6)**	20.0

30.54 There is also a degree of flexibility allowed in the reporting of the individual elements of cash inflows or outflows that make up each of the standard headings. Although the individual cash inflows or outflows should not be netted against each other, except in certain circumstances as explained in paragraph 30.59 below, they could either be reported gross on the face of the cash flow statement under the appropriate standard headings or shown in the notes. This means that it is acceptable to present the (net) totals for each of the above headings on the face of the cash flow statement. This may avoid clutter on the face of the cash flow statement and possibly make it easier to understand.

Classification of cash flows

30.55 A cash flow statement must classify cash receipts and cash payments under each of the nine standard headings. The classification of cash flows into reasonably distinct groups provides useful analysis about the relative importance of each of these groups and the inter-relationship between them. It should also provide useful information for comparison purposes across reporting entities.

30.56 The standard provides specific guidance for classifying cash flows. It sets out each individual element of cash inflows and outflows that should be included under a particular standard heading. Entities are required to disclose separately, where material, the individual categories of cash flows within each standard headings, either in the cash flow statement or in a note. [FRS 1 para 8]. The way in which elements of cash flow are attributed to each standard heading is considered from paragraphs 30.67 below.

30.57 There are other elements of cash flows, not considered in the standard headings, that may cause classification difficulties. Clearly, it is not possible for the standard to provide an exhaustive list of all types of different cash flows. Consequently, the standard stipulates that where a cash flow is not specified in the categories set out in the standard headings, it should be shown under the most appropriate standard heading in accordance with the transaction's substance. [FRS 1 para 10]. Since the transaction's substance also determines the way in which it is normally reported in the profit and loss account and the balance sheet, it follows that there should be consistency of treatment in the cash flow statement and in the other primary statements. This requirement for consistency eliminates subjectivity in classifying cash flows not identified as specific items under the standard headings. [FRS 1 para 57]. Therefore, following this general principle, cash outflows relating to development expenditure that are capitalised in the balance sheet would fall to be shown under capital expenditure in the cash flow statement. Similarly, where the expenditure is written off as part of operating profit in the profit and loss account, the cash outflows would fall to be included in operating cash flows. Another example is the receipt of a government grant. To the extent that the grant is made as a contribution towards fixed assets, the substance argument would require the cash receipt to be shown under capital expenditure in the cash flow statement, irrespective of whether it is reported in the balance sheet as a deduction from the cost of the specific asset or included as deferred income and amortised over the expected useful economic life of the asset. Similarly grants given as a contribution towards revenue expenditure should be included in operating cash flows to match their treatment in the profit and loss account.

30.58 There is one situation where the general rule of classifying cash flows according to the transaction's substance is not considered appropriate. This applies to interest paid that is capitalised, for instance, as part of the construction cost of an asset in the balance sheet. Following the general rule would require reporting the interest paid under capital expenditure in the cash flow statement. However, all interest paid is specifically required to be shown under 'returns on investments and servicing of finance' heading, regardless of whether or not it is capitalised in the balance sheet. [FRS 1 para 10].

Gross or net cash flows

30.59 Generally cash inflows and outflows under each of the standard headings should be reported gross, whether on the face of the cash flow statement or in a note to it. However, there are some exceptions. These are as follows:

- The reporting of gross cash flows does not apply to operating activities where the indirect method is followed (see para 30.71).
- Cash inflows and outflows relating to the management of liquid resources or financing may be netted against each other provided the inflows and outflows meet either of the following conditions:
  - They relate in substance to a single financing transaction.
  - They are due to short maturities and high turnover occurring from rollover or reissue (for example, a commercial paper programme or short-term deposits).

[FRS 1 para 9].

30.60 The ability to net cash inflows and outflows relating to the management of liquid resources or financing allows a more reasonable presentation of transactions in many cases. Many large industrial and commercial companies raise funds by issuing commercial paper in the form of unsecured promissory notes with fixed maturity between seven and 364 days. Normally these are issued at a discount to the face value and provide a cheaper source of finance than other means of borrowing. A commercial paper programme may involve issues and redemptions throughout the financial year and often these are backed up by committed bank facilities. The reporting of these transactions as net may be considered to give a fairer representation of the transactions' substance.

[The next paragraph is 30.62.]

30.62 Similarly, short-term funds that are continuously rolled over by successive deposits and withdrawals will fall to be reported net under the second condition. A question arises as to whether netting is permissible in circumstances where withdrawals from short-term deposits and payments into short-term deposits are effected with different parties. The standard is silent on this point, but in practice, treasurers often withdraw funds from one party and place them on deposits with another party to increase the overall returns on those funds. Therefore, as long as the short-term deposit is constantly renewed or rolled over, whether with the same party or with a different party, it is acceptable to report the cash inflows and outflows on a net basis.

30.63 The ability to report net cash flows in relation to rollover and reissue transactions is consistent with the International standard IAS 7. The alternative of showing the gross amounts for raising and repaying money under a commercial paper programme or constantly renewable short-term deposits would not add very much to users' understanding of a company's treasury activities.

30.63.1 A further question can be raised with regards to the presentation of cash flows for a transaction where linked presentation is used in other primary statements.

Example

An entity may adopt linked presentation for a debt factoring arrangement when the requirements of FRS 5, 'Reporting the substance of transactions', are met. Should the cash flows be reported gross, with the proceeds from factoring as a source of financing, or net, with the movement in net debtors treated as an operating cash flow?

FRS 5 says that a scheme that qualifies for linked presentation is, in substance, a financing arrangement, but the non-returnable proceeds are not a liability, nor is the gross amount of the debtor an asset. These two statements may seem contradictory, but since the net amount is regarded as the asset, it is logical to show the non-returnable proceeds as operating cash flows. On this basis, the non-returnable proceeds should be treated as a partial collection of the debtors.

Additional classification

30.64 The individual items of cash inflows and outflows set out under each of the standard headings in FRS 1, other than operating activities, should not be regarded as depicting a rigid set of classification rules. The analysis under each heading merely refers to those items that would normally fall to be included under that heading and, hence, prescribe a minimum acceptable level of disaggregation of cash flow information. The individual items may be further sub-divided or new items added, if appropriate, to give a full description of the activities of the business or to provide segmental information. [FRS 1 para 8]. Indeed, the standard encourages entities to disclose additional information relevant to their particular circumstances. [FRS 1 para 56]. For example, repayments of amounts borrowed may be sub-divided further to show payments made on the redemption of debentures and other repayments of long-term borrowings. Another example would be to divide the cash flows from operating activities into those relating to continuing activities and those relating to discontinued operations (see further para 30.168).

30.65 Whatever level of detail is disclosed, it must be sufficient and relevant so that the user is able to understand the relationship between the entity's different activities and the way in which they generate and expend cash. On the other hand, too much information can cloud or obscure key issues. The problem is one of striking a balance between what the entity needs to report and how much explanation is required by the users. The amount of detail to be presented will be an area of judgement based upon the reporting entity's circumstances.

Departure from the standard presentation

30.66 Entities can add new items within each of the standard headings, but are not permitted to use a different heading, or depart from the format headings.

Classification of cash flows by standard headings

Cash flow from operating activities

30.67 Cash flows from operating activities generally include the cash effects of transactions and other events relating to the operating or trading activities of the enterprise. The net cash flow from operating activities, therefore, represents the movements in cash resulting from the operations shown in the profit and loss account in arriving at operating profit. In addition, cash flows relating to any provision in respect of operating items, whether or not the provision was included in operating profit, should also be included as part of operating cash flows. For example, cash flows in respect of redundancy payments provided as part of the cost of a fundamental reorganisation or closure of operations that is reported outside operating profit in accordance with FRS 3, 'Reporting financial performance', will fall to be included in operating cash flows (see para 30.114). Similarly, operating cash flows will also include cash flows in respect of provision for integration costs following an acquisition. [FRS 1 para 11].

[The next paragraph is 30.69.]

30.69 Operating cash flows may be reported on the gross or net basis (also known as the direct method and the indirect method respectively). [FRS 1 para 7]. Under the direct method, the major classes of gross operating cash receipts (for example, cash collected from customers) and gross operating cash payments (for example, cash paid to suppliers and employees) are reported on the face of the cash flow statement under operating activities. An example of the direct method of presentation for net operating cash flow is illustrated in Table 30.2.

Table 30.2 — Marks and Spencer p.l.c. — Annual Report and Financial Statements — 31 March 1996

Consolidated cash flow statement (extract)

FOR THE YEAR ENDED 31 MARCH 1996

	Notes	**1996 £m**	*1995 £m*
OPERATING ACTIVITIES			
Received from customers		**7,046.0**	*6,665.0*
Payments to suppliers		**(4,741.9)**	*(4,426.3)*
Payments to and on behalf of employees		**(928.4)**	*(782.8)*
Other payments		**(566.9)**	*(547.1)*
Net cash inflow from operating activities	**24**	**808.8**	*908.8*

Notes to the financial statements (extract)

24 RECONCILIATION OF OPERATING PROFIT TO NET CASH INFLOW FROM OPERATING ACTIVITIES

	THE GROUP	
	1996	*1995*
	£m	*£m*
Operating profit	**940.2**	*896.5*
Depreciation	**160.4**	*150.7*
Increase in stocks	**(45.8)**	*(22.4)*
Increase in customer balances	**(190.2)**	*(144.5)*
Increase in other debtors	**(109.6)**	*(22.7)*
Increase in creditors	**53.8**	*51.2*
Net cash inflow from operating activities	**808.8**	*908.8*

Operating profit has increased by £43.7m whereas the net cash inflow from operating activities of £808.8m is £100.0m lower than last year. This reflects the £90.0m payment in respect of the pension scheme deficit (see note 10A) together with an increase of £45.7m in the movement of customer balances within Financial Services.

30.70 The standard allows, but does not require, reporting entities to provide information on gross operating cash flows. [FRS 1 para 58]. However, the standard makes it mandatory to provide a reconciliation between operating profit and net cash flow from operating activities as discussed in paragraph 30.72 below, *even where the direct method is adopted* as indicated in Table 30.2 above. For this reason and because of the additional burden of producing gross cash flow information, the direct method has not been commonly used in the UK.

30.71 Under the indirect method, the same operating cash flows as under the direct method are reported except that the net figure is produced by adjusting operating profit for non-cash items (such as depreciation), changes in working capital (such as accruals and prepayments) and bringing in cash flows relating to any provision in respect of operating items, whether or not the provision was included in operating profit. However, in keeping with the objective that a cash flow statement should only include items of pure cash flows, the standard requires that under the indirect method the cash flow statement should start with the net cash flow from operating activities.

Reconciliation of operating profit to net cash flow from operating activities

30.72 The reconciliation of operating profit to net cash flow from operating activities is not part of the cash flow statement. However, companies may choose whether to present the reconciliation as a supplementary note to the cash flow statement, or adjoining the cash flow statement. If the latter approach is adopted, the reconciliation statement should be separately identified and clearly labelled to maintain the distinction that it is not part of the primary cash flow statement. [FRS 1 para 12]. This is because the reconciling items are not themselves cash flows and to report them as part of the cash flow statement itself would be inappropriate.

30.72.1 The first example in Appendix 1 of FRS 1 presents the reconciliation statement immediately under the general heading 'Cash flow statement'. In this way, the reconciliation appears to be part of the cash flow statement itself, which is clearly not the intention. It may also be confusing to have two headings for cash flow statement on the same page. A way of dealing with this is to entitle the page something along the lines of 'Information on cash flows'. The term 'Cash flow statement' could then be used to describe the statement itself. A way of avoiding the problem is to position the reconciliation either under the cash flow statement or in a note.

30.73 The reconciliation should disclose separately the movements in stock, debtors and creditors related to operating activities and other differences (for example, depreciation or impairment of fixed assets included within operating profit, provisions, etc) between cash flow and operating results.

30.74 For the reconciliation to be properly carried out, it will be necessary to analyse the movements in opening and closing debtors and creditors in order to eliminate those movements that relate to items reported in the standard headings other than operating activities. For example, a company may purchase a fixed asset prior to the year end on credit. In this situation, the closing creditor balance would need to be adjusted to eliminate the amount owing for the fixed asset purchase before working out the balance sheet movements for operating creditors. It follows that movements in working capital included in the reconciliation would not be the same as the difference between the opening and the closing balance sheet amounts. Indeed, under FRS 1 this is rarely the case except in very simple situations. This is because the balance sheet movements in stock, debtors, and creditors may be affected by such items as acquisitions and disposals of subsidiaries during the year (see para 30.134), exchange differences on working capital of foreign subsidiaries (see example para 30.156) and other non-cash adjustments for opening and closing accruals of non-operating items.

30.75 A question arises as to whether the eliminated items within each balance sheet movement of working capital need to be reported separately so that the overall movement between the opening and closing balance sheet amounts is readily understandable. For example, a company could identify the total balance sheet movement in creditors and then separately itemise the operating element and the other movements. The standard is silent on this point and, in practice, this is rarely done, in the majority of cases only the operating movements are reported.

Dividends from joint ventures and associates

30.75.1 FRS 9 requires that the investor's share of the results of its equity accounted entities is included immediately *after* group operating profit rather than in group operating profit. Consistent with this treatment the cash flows relating to dividends received from joint ventures and associates are reported under a specific heading, between operating activities and returns on investment and servicing of finance. [FRS 1 para 12A].

Returns on investments and servicing of finance

30.76 'Returns on investments and servicing of finance' are receipts resulting from the ownership of an investment and payments to providers of finance, non-equity shareholders and minority interests, excluding those items that are specifically required by the standard to be classified under another heading. [FRS 1 para 13].

[The next paragraph is 30.78.]

30.78 Cash inflows in respect of returns on investments include the following items that should be separately disclosed:

- Interest received, including any related tax recovered.
- Dividends received net of any tax credits (except dividends from equity accounted entities).

[FRS 1 para 14].

30.79 Similarly, cash outflows from servicing of finance include:

- Interest paid (even if capitalised), including any tax deducted and paid to the relevant tax authority.
- Cash flows that are treated as finance costs (this will include issue costs on debt and non-equity share capital).
- The interest element of finance lease rental payments.
- Dividends paid on non-equity shares of the entity.
- Dividends paid by subsidiaries to equity and non-equity minority interests.

[FRS 1 para 15].

This is consistent with FRS 25, which requires financial instruments that have the substance of debt, such as certain non-equity shares, to be classified as such on the balance sheet and the dividends paid on those shares to be recognised as interest in the profit and loss account.

30.80 Investment income included under this heading will include income from current asset investments, irrespective of whether they are regarded as liquid resources, and on fixed asset investments other than equity accounted entities whose results are included as part of operating profit.

30.81 The standard requires that the cash flow effect of any tax relating to interest should be shown as part of the interest. [FRS 1 para 15(a)]. This applies to tax deducted at source on interest received as well as to tax withheld on interest paid. This means that the actual cash received (or paid) in respect of interest must be shown, but where tax has been deducted at source (or withheld) and is subsequently recovered (or paid), it should also be included under this heading as part of interest received (or paid) at the time of receipt (payment). For example, where there is a timing difference between the actual interest received (or paid) and the settlement of the tax, the net interest received (or paid) would fall to be shown in the period in which the cash is received (or paid), whereas the cash flow effect of any tax deducted at source (or withheld) would fall to be shown in the period in which the tax is recovered (or paid).

30.82 Interest paid should be the actual amount of interest paid during the period, irrespective of whether it is charged to the profit and loss account or capitalised in the balance sheet. Similarly, the interest paid on finance lease obligations should be reported under this heading.

[The next paragraph is 30.84.]

30.84 The cash flows relating to finance costs for debt (including shares classified as debt under FRS 25) should be reported under this heading. Therefore, in addition to reporting finance costs such as dividends paid on shares classified as liabilities and interest paid on debt instruments, this heading would also include any payments made for the issue of those shares and debt instruments. Furthermore, the cash flow effects of items such as discounts and premiums on such shares and debt instruments, which are treated as finance costs, would also fall to be included under this heading (see para 30.180).

30.85 The segregation of interest and dividends received and interest paid under the heading 'returns on investments and servicing of finance' is relevant particularly to non-financial companies, as these items are normally shown after operating profit. However, many investment companies and financial institutions show interest received and dividends received in their profit and loss account prior to arriving at their operating profit. Banks and insurance companies also include interest paid in operating profit. Where the special nature of the business requires the inclusion of items relating to interest and dividend in operating profit, the cash flows relating to these items should remain as part of the operating cash flows. If any interest paid clearly relates to financing, then it should be included under 'returns on investments and servicing of finance'. [FRS 1 para 60].

[The next paragraph is 30.87.]

Taxation

30.87 Reporting entities need to include under this heading the following items in respect of taxation relating to revenue and capital profits:

- Cash receipts from the relevant tax authority of tax rebates, claims or returns of overpayments.
- Cash payments for corporation tax.

For a subsidiary undertaking, payments received from or made to other members of the group for group relief should be included under this heading. [FRS 1 paras 17, 18].

30.88 It should be noted that cash flows relating to VAT or other sales taxes, employees income taxes, property taxes and any other taxes not assessed on revenue and capital profits should not be shown under the heading of 'taxation'. [FRS 1 para 16].

30.89 Generally, payments or receipts of VAT or other sales taxes should be netted against the cash flows that gave rise to them. For example, payments for fixed assets should be shown net of VAT under capital expenditure. However, where the VAT falls to be irrecoverable, because the entity carries on an exempt or partially exempt business, or incurs VAT on items that are disallowed (for example, VAT on purchase of motor vehicles), the cash flows should be shown gross of the irrecoverable tax. If this is not practicable for any reason, the irrecoverable tax should be included under the most appropriate standard heading. [FRS 1 para 39].

30.90 The net movement on the VAT payable, or receivable should be allocated to cash flows from operating activities unless it is more appropriate to allocate it to another heading. [FRS 1 para 39]. Generally, the majority of the VAT transactions would be relevant to operating activities, but where a significant proportion of the VAT payments (or receipts) relate to other cash flow headings, such as 'capital expenditure and financial investments' or 'acquisitions and disposals', it may be appropriate to include the net payment (or receipt) under that heading. The effect of including the net movement on the VAT account in operating cash flows means that there will be no need to eliminate the amount of VAT included in opening and closing debtors or creditors when carrying out the reconciliation between operating profit and net cash flow from operating activities.

30.91 Taxation cash flows excluding those in respect of tax on revenue and capital profits, VAT or other sales taxes should be included in the cash flow statement under the same standard headings as the cash flow that gave rise to the taxation cash flows. [FRS 1 para 40]. For example, employers' national insurance contributions and amounts paid in respect of PAYE to the tax authorities should be included in operating activities. Where the direct method is followed, they will be included in the amounts shown as paid to or on behalf of employees.

Capital expenditure and financial investment

30.92 The cash flows included in 'capital expenditure and financial investment' include the cash effects of transactions relating to the acquisition and disposal of any fixed asset (including investments) and current asset investments not regarded by the entity as liquid resources. For this purpose, fixed asset investments exclude a trade or business, or investment in an entity that is an associate, joint venture or a subsidiary undertaking. The cash flows relating to the acquisitions and disposals of these fixed asset investments are reported under 'acquisitions and disposals'. Therefore, cash flows relating to acquisitions and disposals of certain financial investments, for example long-term investments in gilts or other financial investments that are held purely for investment purposes and not for the management of liquid resources, would be reported under this heading, but returns on them would be reported under 'returns on investments and servicing of finance'. If no cash flows relating to financial investments fall to be included under this heading, the caption may be reduced to 'capital expenditure'. [FRS 1 para 19].

30.93 Cash inflows in respect of 'capital expenditure and financial investments' include the following items that should be separately disclosed:

- Receipts from sales or disposals of property, plant or equipment.
- Receipts from the repayment of the reporting entity's loans made to other entities or sale of other entities' debt instruments other than receipts forming part of an acquisition or disposal or a movement in liquid resources.

[FRS 1 para 20].

30.94 Cash outflows in respect of 'capital expenditure and financial investments' include the following items that should be separately disclosed:

- Payments to acquire property, plant or equipment.
- Loans made by the reporting entity and payments to acquire debt instruments of other entities other than payments forming part of an acquisition or disposal or a movement in liquid resources.

[FRS 1 para 21].

30.95 The amount paid in respect of tangible fixed assets during the year may not be the same as the amount of additions shown in the tangible fixed asset note. The difference may be due to a number of reasons. For example, tangible fixed assets may be purchased on credit, in which case the amounts for additions shown in the fixed asset note would need to be adjusted for the outstanding credit to arrive at the cash paid. Furthermore, the change in fixed asset creditors should be eliminated from the total change in creditors, to arrive at the movement in operating creditors, a figure needed for the reconciliation of operating profit to net cash flow from operating activities. Another example is where fixed assets have been acquired in foreign currencies. In this situation, the sterling equivalent of the foreign currency amount paid that is reported in the cash flow statement is not necessarily the same as the sterling equivalent of the cost recorded at the date of the transaction and included in the balance sheet, because of changes in exchange rates. In addition, where interest has been capitalised during the period, the figure for interest would need to be deducted to arrive at the correct amount of cash paid for the acquisition or construction of a fixed asset. The amount of interest capitalised and paid during the period would be shown under 'returns on investments and servicing of finance'.

30.96 A further example arises where assets have been acquired during the year under finance leases. Most companies do not show assets acquired under finance leases separately, but include them in the total additions figure for the year in their fixed assets movements note. Since assets acquired under finance leases do not involve any cash outlay at the inception of the lease, it will be necessary to eliminate the fair value of the leased assets that is included in the figure for fixed assets additions so that the true cash outflow for fixed assets actually purchased can be reflected in the cash flow statements. The finance lease rental payments should be analysed between interest and capital, with the interest element shown under 'returns on investments and servicing of finance' and the capital element shown under 'financing'.

[The next paragraph is 30.98.]

Acquisitions and disposals

30.98 As already discussed in paragraph 30.92 above cash flows included in, 'acquisitions and disposals' are those related to the acquisition or disposal of any trade, business or an entity that is an associate, joint venture or a subsidiary undertaking. [FRS 1 para 22].

30.99 Cash inflows from 'acquisitions and disposals' include:

- Receipts from sales of investments in subsidiary undertakings, showing separately any balances of cash and overdrafts transferred as part of the sale (see further para 30.133).
- Receipts from sales of investments in associates or joint ventures.
- Receipts from sales of trades or businesses.

[FRS 1 para 23].

30.100 Similarly, cash outflows from 'acquisitions and disposals' include:

- Payments to acquire investments in subsidiary undertakings, showing separately any balances of cash and overdrafts acquired (see further para 30.133).
- Payments to acquire investments in associates and joint ventures.
- Payments to acquire trades or businesses.

[FRS 1 para 24].

Cash flows arising under this standard heading are discussed from paragraph 30.132 onwards.

Equity dividends paid

30.101 Equity dividends paid by the reporting entity should be disclosed separately. These are dividends paid on the reporting entity's, or, in a group, the parent's equity shares. For this purpose, equity shares are those that fall to be treated as equity under FRS 25. The dividends paid should be the cash dividend paid. [FRS 1 para 25]. Dividends paid by subsidiaries to shareholders outside the group, both in respect of equity and non-equity interests must be reported under 'returns on investments and servicing of finance'. Therefore, equity dividends paid to minority interests should not be shown under this heading.

Management of liquid resources

30.102 The heading 'management of liquid resources' includes cash flows relating to items that the reporting entity used to manage its liquidity (as opposed to earning returns from investments), but which fall outside the FRS 1 definition of cash. The type of liquid resources that should be reported under this heading are considered from paragraph 30.44.

30.103 Cash inflows in management of liquid resources include:

- Withdrawals from short-term deposits not qualifying as cash — to the extent that they do not relate to deposits that qualify for net reporting under a rollover or reissue transaction as explained in paragraph 30.59.
- Inflows from disposal or redemption of any other investments held as liquid resources.

[FRS 1 para 27].

30.104 Cash outflows in management of liquid resources include:

- Payments into short-term deposits not qualifying as cash to the extent that they do not relate to deposits that qualify for net reporting under a rollover or reissue transaction as explained in paragraph 30.59.
- Outflows to acquire any other investments held as liquid resources.

[FRS 1 para 28].

30.105 Only cash flows relating to short-term deposits that are not repayable on demand and, therefore, do not meet the definition of cash would fall to be included under this heading. Generally, the gross cash inflows and outflows should be reported, unless the deposit is one that is continuously rolled over, in which case the net cash flows may be shown as explained further in paragraph 30.59.

30.106 Cash outflows and inflows relating to a wide range of other non-cash current investments would also fall to be reported under this heading provided they are easily and promptly convertible into cash through an active market without curtailing or disrupting the entities business as explained in paragraph 30.48. Although many such current asset investments may qualify as liquid resources, not all of them may be used in the entity's treasury activities. Some current asset investments may be held purely for investment purposes. Others may be held for trading purposes, although this would generally apply to banks and investment companies. Given that there is a choice as to which current asset investment can be used for managing the net funds or net debt position, the standard requires entities to explain what it includes as liquid resources and any changes in its policy. [FRS 1 para 26]. This is a sensible requirement as an investment initially acquired for investment purposes in one year could be designated as a liquid resource in the following year depending on the company's circumstances. A change in policy regarding the use of a particular investment would not give rise to any cash flows in the year of change, but would need to be reported as a non-cash movement in the reconciliation and analysis of net debt (see para 30.119). An example of a company that explains what it includes as liquid resources is given in Table 30.4.1 below.

Table 30.4.1 — Unilever Group — Annual Accounts — 31 December 1996

Notes to the consolidated accounts (extract)

	£ million	
	1996	1995
23 Analysis of cash flows for headings netted in the cash flow statement (extract)		
Management of liquid resources		
Purchase of current investments	**(409)**	(383)
Sale of current investments	**342**	547
(Increase)/decrease in cash on deposit	**(226)**	94
	(293)	258
Financing		
Issue of ordinary share capital (employee share schemes)	–	3
Issue of shares by group companies to minority shareholders	**14**	14
Debt due within one year:		
Increases	**1 381**	1 529
Repayments	**(1 473)**	(1 790)
Debt due after one year:		
Increases	**507**	315
Repayments	**(135)**	(148)
	294	(77)

Included as liquid resources are term deposits of less than one year, government securities and AI/PI rated corporate commercial paper.

[The next paragraph is 30.108.]

Financing

30.108 Financing cash flows comprise receipts from or repayments to external providers of finance. [FRS 1 para 29]. They will generally include the cash effects of transactions relating to the manner in which the operating and investing activities of the enterprise have been financed. However, only cash flows that relate to the principal amounts of finance are dealt with under this heading, since the cash flows relating to the servicing of finance (that is, dividends and interest) are dealt with under returns on investments and servicing of finance heading and equity dividends paid.

30.109 Cash inflows in respect of financing include the following items:

- Receipts from issuing shares or other equity instruments.
- Receipts from issuing debentures, loans, notes and bonds, and from other long and short-term borrowings (other than bank overdrafts).

[FRS 1 para 30].

30.110 Cash outflows in respect of financing include the following items:

- Repayments of amounts borrowed (other than overdrafts). The treatment of discounts and premiums on debt instruments is considered in paragraph 30.180 below.
- The capital element of finance lease rental payments.
- Payments to re-acquire or redeem the entity's shares.
- Payments of expenses or commissions on any issue of equity shares.

[FRS 1 para 31].

Table 30.5 shown below provides an illustration of the items that are normally included under this heading.

Table 30.5 — Coats Viyella Plc — Annual Report and Accounts — 31 December 1998

32 Notes to the cash flow statement (extract)

		1998	1997
b Analysis of financing cash flows		£m	£m
Issue of ordinary share capital		0.3	0.1
Issue of shares to minorities		0.6	12.9
		0.9	13.0
(Decrease)/increase in borrowings:	— new long-term loans	0.4	–
	— new short-term loans	161.5	175.0
	— repayment of amounts borrowed	(212.7)	(162.8)
	— redemption of convertible debt	2.5	–
	— capital element of finance lease rental payments	(4.9)	(5.6)
		(58.2)	6.6
Net cash (outflow)/inflow from financing		(57.3)	19.6

30.111 The cash flows under financing can be shown in a single section with those under 'management of liquid resources', provided that separate subtotals for each are given. [FRS 1 para 29]. The flexibility to report cash flows relating to liquid resources and financing under a combined heading may appeal to a number of companies that manage their borrowings and liquid investments as an integrated treasury operation (See Table 30.0.2).

Exceptional and extraordinary cash flows

30.112 Where cash flows relate to items that are classed as exceptional, these exceptional cash flows should be shown under the appropriate standard heading, according to the nature of each item. The exceptional cash flows should be separately identified in the cash flow statement or a note to it and the relationship between the cash flows and the exceptional item should be explained. [FRS 1 para 37].

30.113 FRS 3 requires three exceptional items to be reported after operating profit:

- Profits or losses on the sale or termination of an operation.
- Profits or losses on sale of fixed assets.
- Costs of a fundamental reorganisation or restructuring.

The first two items are not themselves cash flows, but the net cash proceeds from the sale of operations will fall to be included under 'acquisitions and disposals', and those arising from the sale of fixed assets under 'capital expenditure and financial investment', irrespective of where the gain or loss is charged in the profit and loss account (see further para 30.182).

30.114 The disclosure of cash flows relating to costs of a fundamental reorganisation or restructuring that is reported outside operating profit is not so clear. In general, the cash outflows are likely to include an amalgam of items, such as:

- Redundancy costs.
- Costs associated with the elimination and reduction of product lines.
- Costs to consolidate or relocate plant facilities.
- Costs for new systems developments or acquisition.
- Costs to retrain employees to use newly deployed systems.
- Losses on asset impairments and disposal of assets.

However, as stated in paragraph 30.67 above, the standard makes it clear that the cash flows relating to any operating items should be reported in operating cash flow, whether or not the costs are included in operating profit. This means that the nature of each item included within the total reorganisation costs needs to be analysed, with the result that some cash flows fall to be reported under operating activities, some under capital expenditure and some under acquisitions and disposals. The cash flow effect of reorganisation provisions arising on an acquisition of a subsidiary is considered in paragraph 30.186 below.

[The next paragraph is 30.116.]

30.116 There may be instances where the cash flows are exceptional because of their size or incidence, but are not related to items that are treated as exceptional in the profit and loss account. These exceptional cash flows should also be disclosed and sufficient explanation given to explain their cause and nature. [FRS 1 para 38]. An example cited in the explanatory paragraph of the standard is that of a large prepayment against a pension liability which is not reported as part of an exceptional item in the profit and loss account. [FRS 1 para 63]. Disclosure of exceptional cash flows where there is no corresponding exceptional item in the profit and loss account is likely to arise where the provision to which the cash flows relates was reported as an exceptional item in a previous period.

30.117 Sufficient disclosure of the nature of the exceptional item and the related cash flows should also be given in a note to the cash flow statement so that users may gain an understanding of how these transactions have affected the reporting entity's cash flows.

30.118 Cash flows from extraordinary items would be reported in a similar manner. [FRS 1 paras 37]. In practice, however, such cash flows will rarely arise, if at all, following the virtual abolition of extraordinary items under FRS 3 (see further chapter 8).

Reconciliation with balance sheet figures

Reconciliation to net debt

30.119 One of the objectives of the cash flow statement is to provide information that is useful in assessing the liquidity, solvency and financial adaptability of an enterprise.

30.120 The standard requires a note that reconciles the movement of cash in the period with the movement in *net debt* for the period. The changes in net debt should be analysed from the opening to the closing component amounts as shown in the opening and closing balance sheets. The reconciliation is not part of the cash flow statement and, if adjoining the cash flow statement (for example, presented at the foot of the statement), it should be clearly labelled and kept separate. [FRS 1 para 33]. For this purpose, net debt is defined to include the borrowings of the reporting entity (comprising debt as defined in FRS 25, together with related derivatives and obligations under finance leases), less cash (including overdrafts) and liquid resources. Where cash and liquid resources exceed the borrowings of the entity, reference should be made to 'net funds' rather than to 'net debt'. [FRS 1 para 2].

30.121 The reconciliation should begin with the increase or decrease in cash for the period as shown at the bottom of the cash flow statement. Because this movement in cash includes cash flows relating to management of liquid resources and cash flows relating to borrowings included in financing, these cash flows should be added back to give the total change in net debt resulting from cash flows during the period. These separate components of cash flows should be separately disclosed in the reconciliation where material. There may be other changes in net debt for the period that do not arise from cash flows. Typically these non-cash movements may relate to items such as exchange differences, acquisition of assets under finance leases, loans and finance leases acquired as part of an acquisition and other movements that have an effect on the closing figure for net debt. These non-cash changes in net debt should also be disclosed in the reconciliation, if material. [FRS 1 para 33].

30.122 The total change in net debt arising from both cash flows and non cash items should then be reconciled with the opening and closing net debt amounts. In particular, the standard requires the following reconciling items to be disclosed, where material:

- The cash flows relating to the separate component of net debt as explained above.

- The acquisition or disposal of subsidiary undertakings. These relate to borrowings acquired or transferred as part of the acquisition or disposal of a subsidiary undertaking because these are not reflected in the financing section of the cash flow statement, but have an effect on the closing amount of net debt.

- Other non-cash changes — an example being the acquisition of fixed assets under finance leases.

- The recognition of changes in market value and exchange rate movements. For example, changes in market values relating to current asset investments that are treated as liquid resources do not have any cash flow impact during the period, but may affect the carrying value of those investments at the balance sheet date (for example, if the company has a policy of carrying those investments at fair value). Similarly, exchange rate adjustments arising from the retranslation of opening foreign currency cash and borrowings and those arising from translating the cash flows of subsidiaries at rates other than the year end rate, do not give rise to any cash flows, but form part of the carrying values of cash and borrowings at the period end.

[FRS 1 para 33].

30.122.1 An example of a reconciliation required by the standard is given in Table 30.8 below.

Table 30.8 — Airtours plc — Annual Report and Accounts — 30 September 1996

Notes to the financial statements

25) **Reconciliation of net cash flow to movement in net funds**

	1996 £000	Restated 1995 £000
(Decrease)/increase in cash in the year	(26,310)	53,544
Cash outflow/(inflow) from decrease/(increase) in debt and lease financing	15,142	(83,459)
Cash outflow/(inflow) from increase/(decrease) in liquid resources	156,928	(41,801)
Changes in net debt resulting from cash flows	145,760	(71,716)
Loans and finance leases acquired with subsidiary undertakings	(15,040)	(1,606)
Transfer to accruals	–	29,641
New unsecured loan notes	–	(9,000)
Provisions	–	(38)
Exchange differences	(5,142)	2,074
Movement in net funds in the year	125,578	(50,645)
Net funds at 1st October	223,005	273,650
Net funds at 30th September	**348,583**	223,005

Analysis of changes in net debt

30.123 Where the opening and closing amounts of net debt shown in the above reconciliation are not readily apparent, because they are included under different balance sheet headings, sufficient details should be shown to enable the cash and other components of net debt to be respectively traced back to the amounts shown under the equivalent caption in the balance sheet. [FRS 1 para 33]. For example, bank loans and overdrafts included as a single figure within current liabilities would need to be identified separately because overdrafts, unlike other borrowings, are included within the cash component of net debt. Another example where separate identification may be necessary relates to the situation where some current asset investments are used for managing liquid resources, but others are not. This additional note is also necessary to enable the movements in net debt for the period to be readily understood. For example, the reclassification of an amount of debt from long-term to current categories in the balance sheet would not appear in the reconciliation to net debt, because it is a movement within the same component of net debt, but would need to be separately identified in the analysis of the changes in net debt for the closing amount of current and non-current debt to be readily identified with balance sheet figures. The ways in which an analysis of net funds or net debt can be presented are shown in Table 30.8.1 and Table 30.8.2 below.

Table 30.8.1 — Airtours plc — Annual Report and Accounts — 30 September 1996

Notes to the financial statements
26) Analysis of net funds

	At 1st October 1995 £000	Cash flow £000	Acquisitions £000	Other non-cash changes £000	Exchange movements £000	30th September 1996 £000
Cash at bank and in hand	142,416	(26,378)	–	–	(4,491)	**111,547**
Term deposits	162,088	151,953	–	–	–	**314,041**
Overdrafts	(65)	68	–	–	(3)	–
Debt due within one year	(35,216)	130	–	(185)	44	**(35,227)**
Debt due after one year	(43,958)	–	–	185	13	**(43,760)**
Finance leases	(7,012)	15,012	(15,040)	–	(705)	**(7,745)**
Current asset investments	4,752	4,975	–	–	–	**9,727**
	223,005	145,760	(15,040)	–	(5,142)	**348,583**

Table 30.8.2 — Bass PLC — Annual Report and Financial Statements —30 September 1996

NOTES TO THE FINANCIAL STATEMENTS (extract)

	Cash and overdrafts			Other borrowings			
29 Net debt 30 September 1996	**Cash at bank and in hand £m**	**Overdrafts £m**	**Total £m**	**Current asset investments £m**	**Due within one year £m**	**Due after one year £m**	**Total £m**
At 30 September 1995	69	(47)	22	684	(392)	(1,177)	(863)
Net cash flow (note 25)	(151)	3	(148)	–	–	–	(148)
Financing and liquid resources movement	154	–	154	(202)	69	7	28
Other borrowings acquired	–	–	–	–	(36)	(7)	(43)
Exchange adjustments	–	–	–	(1)	(4)	(4)	(9)
At 30 September 1996	**72**	**(44)**	**28**	**481**	**(363)**	**(1,181)**	**(1,035)**

30.124 The reconciliation to net debt and the corresponding analysis note is relevant only to non-financial companies. Banks and insurance companies are not required to give a reconciliation of net debt because the concept of net debt is not *really applicable to them.* Banks should, therefore, continue to give the notes reconciling the movements in cash and changes in financing with the related items in the opening and closing balance sheet. It should be noted that this requirement for banks is not explicitly stated in the standard, but is illustrated in example 3 in appendix I to FRS 1. Insurance companies, on the other hand, are required to give an equivalent note that analyses the movement in portfolio investments less financing, either adjoining the cash flow statement or in a note. [FRS 1 para 35]. A note linking the movements to the related balance sheet amounts for portfolio investments and financing is also required. [FRS 1 para 36].

Consolidated cash flow statements

30.125 The form and content of cash flow statements discussed above apply equally to any group of entities where consolidated financial statements are prepared. Therefore, a parent company of a group that is required to prepare a consolidated balance sheet and a consolidated profit and loss account should also prepare a consolidated cash flow statement reflecting the cash flows of the group. In preparing consolidated cash flow statements, adjustments should be made to eliminate those cash flows that are internal to the group. Only those cash receipts and payments that flow to and from the group as a whole should be included. [FRS 1 para 43].

Minority interests

30.126 Where there are minority interests in any subsidiary that is consolidated as part of a group, the treatment of the minority interest in the consolidated cash flow statement should be consistent with the overall approach followed in preparing the group's financial statements. Companies are required by law and FRS 2 to eliminate intra-group balances and intra-group transactions in the consolidated financial statements. Therefore, they should do the same in preparing a consolidated cash flow statement even where minority interests, which may be substantial, are involved. Intra-group transactions should be eliminated because the group, including partly owned subsidiaries, is a single entity for financial reporting purposes. Therefore, in this situation, only cash flows that are external to the group, which includes those with minorities, should be reflected in the cash flow statements. In particular, the standard requires dividends to minorities to be shown under the heading 'returns on investments and servicing of finance'.

30.127 FRS 25 requires minority interests to be shown as liabilities where the parent or any fellow subsidiary undertaking has guaranteed their dividends or redemption, or undertaken to purchase the minority shares if the subsidiary fails to make the expected payments. If minority interests are classified as liabilities, the dividends paid on those shares should be shown as part of the interest charge in the consolidated profit and loss account. It follows that, in the consolidated cash flow statement, the dividends paid should similarly be shown as interest paid and not as dividends to minorities; but they would still be included under the heading 'returns on investments and servicing of finance'.

Investments accounted on the equity method

30.128 Where a group has investments in associated undertakings or joint ventures that are included in the consolidation under the equity method, the consolidated cash flow statement should include only the cash flows between the group and those entities, but not the cash flows of those entities. [FRS 1 para 44]. This means that only the following cash flows should be included:

- Cash flows from investments in, and dividends from, the associated undertakings or joint ventures.
- Cash flows from sales or purchases between the group and the associated undertakings or joint ventures.

The same treatment will apply to any non-consolidated subsidiaries that are included in the consolidation using the equity method.

30.129 Specifically, the following information should be disclosed separately for equity accounted entities:

- Dividends received from these entities should be shown under their own heading. [FRS 1 para 12A].
- Cash flows relating to acquisitions and divestments should be shown under acquisitions and disposals. [FRS 1 paras 23, 24].
- Financing cash flows received from or paid to equity accounted entities should be shown under financing. [FRS 1 para 32].

Investments in joint arrangements

30.130 As stated in chapter 27, a company may have an investment in a joint arrangement, which does not carry on a trade or business in its own right and is merely an extension of its participants' trades or businesses. In that situation, the participants in the joint arrangement should account for their own assets, liabilities and cash flows, measured according to the terms of the agreement governing the arrangement, that is, the investor's share of the relevant cash flows of the joint arrangement will be included in the related line items for the investing company. Adjustments may have to be made to eliminate cash transactions between the investor and the joint arrangement.

[The next paragraph is 30.132.]

Acquisitions and disposals of subsidiaries

30.132 When a parent undertaking acquires or disposes of a subsidiary undertaking during a financial year, the cash flows relating to the consideration should be reported under 'acquisitions and disposals' in the consolidated cash flow statement.

30.133 The standard specifies the treatment of cash and overdrafts acquired or transferred on acquisition, or disposal, of a subsidiary. It requires that the amounts of cash and overdrafts acquired or transferred to be shown separately along with the gross consideration paid or received for the acquisition or disposal. [FRS 1 paras 23(a), 24(a)]. An example is given in Table 30.8.3 below.

Table 30.8.3 — Airtours plc — Annual Report and Accounts — 30 September 1996

Group cash flow statement (extract)

Year ended 30th September 1996	Notes	1996 £000	1996 £000	Restated 1995 £000
Acquisitions				
Purchase of subsidiary undertakings		**(18,350)**		(41,384)
Acquisition expenses		**(2,337)**		(786)
Cash at bank and in hand acquired with subsidiaries		**8,509**		5,931
Net cash outflow from acquisitions			**(12,178)**	(36,239)

30.134 Recording the gross consideration separately along with the cash and overdraft balances transferred means that any fixed assets, working capital excluding cash and overdrafts, and borrowings of the subsidiary at the date of acquisition or disposal would need to be eliminated so as to avoid double counting. For example, stock, debtors and creditors acquired or disposed of would need to be eliminated from the total balance sheet changes in stock, debtors and creditors in the reconciliation of operating profit to operating cash flows. Similarly, borrowings including finance lease obligations taken over or transferred would need to reflected in the reconciliation to net debt and the note that analyses the changes in net debt during the period.

30.135 Where the consideration for the acquisition or disposal has been discharged partly in *cash* and partly by the issue of *shares*, the cash flow statement would show only the cash element of the consideration paid or received. This would be shown as a single item (along with any cash and overdrafts of the subsidiary acquired or disposed of) under the heading 'acquisitions and disposals'. The shares that are issued as part of the consideration in exchange for net assets acquired do not give rise to any cash flows and, consequently, they should not be shown in the cash flow statement, but disclosed as a major non-cash transaction in a note to the cash flow statement (see para 30.165 below).

Example 1

A parent company pays £20,000 in cash and issues shares with a fair value of £40,000 and £50,000 in loan notes to acquire a subsidiary with cash balances of £30,000, borrowings of £60,000 and other net assets including goodwill of £70,000.

In this situation, the cash flow statement would show a cash outflow of £20,000 and a cash inflow of £30,000 under acquisitions and disposals, despite it being an acquisition. The loan notes of £50,000 issued and the borrowings of £60,000 acquired would be reported in the reconciliation statement that analyses the changes in the balance sheet amounts making up net debt. The shares and loan notes would be disclosed in the note giving details of material non-cash transactions (see para 30.165). A note summarising the effects of the acquisition indicating how much of the consideration comprised cash is also required (see para 30.137).

Example 2

A group acquired a subsidiary that had loans in its balance sheet. As part of the acquisition agreement, the acquiring group immediately repaid the loans. How is this treated in the cash flow statement?

If the repayment of loans is included as a financing outflow then 'loans acquired' would have to be shown as a non-cash movement in net debt. However, where the acquisition agreement requires the repayment of the loans as part of the overall consideration for the acquisition of the subsidiary (which would be referred to in the acquisitions note), then the repayment of the loans would be shown as an outflow in 'acquisitions' (with separate disclosure). In that case the loan obligations acquired would not be shown as a movement in net debt as they have not been considered to be part of the group's financing.

Example 3

Company A acquired subsidiary B. As part of the purchase agreement subsidiary B's shareholders authorised a dividend, pre-acquisition, that is payable to the former shareholders (the vendors). The purchase consideration payable by company A was reduced to take account of this. This dividend was paid to the vendor after the date of acquisition. Where should the cash flow resulting from the payment of the dividend be shown in the post-acquisition consolidated cash flow statement? Should it be under 'Acquisitions and disposals'?

Where there is a payment by the acquired company to the vendors which is, in substance, part of the vendor's proceeds and the purchaser's cost of acquisition, this should be accounted for as part of the fair value of the consideration paid for the acquisition. Because the payment in this case falls into this category and would be treated as part of the consideration in the fair value table, it should be shown under the acquisitions and disposals heading in the cash flow statement.

If, however, an acquired company had a normal dividend authorised prior to its acquisition, which was payable to the former shareholders, and this was not part of any arrangement with the purchaser, that dividend would be shown as a creditor in the fair value table in the normal way. It would not form part of the consideration paid. When the dividend was paid it would be included in the post-acquisition consolidated cash flow statement as part of cash inflow/outflow from operating activities as it would represent the settlement of a normal creditor (brought in on acquisition).

30.136 Where acquisitions and disposals take place during a financial year the cash flows of the group should include the cash flows of the subsidiary for the same period as the group profit and loss account includes the subsidiary's results (see further chapter 25). [FRS 1 para 43]. Care should be taken to eliminate all cash flows between the group and the subsidiary acquired or disposed of for the period that the subsidiary is included within the consolidated figures.

30.137 The standard also requires significant amounts of other disclosures to be made in respect of the cash flow effects of a subsidiary acquired or disposed of during the financial year. First, a note to the cash flow statement should show a summary of the effects of acquisitions and disposals indicating how much of the consideration comprised cash. [FRS 1 para 45]. In order to show the effects of the acquisition and disposal fully, it is necessary to disclose separately the assets and liabilities of the subsidiary acquired or disposed of. In practice, the summary of the effects of acquisitions and disposals required by the standard can be combined with that required by the relevant Companies Act and FRS 6. An example of the relevant disclosures is given in Table 30.9.

30.138 Secondly, reporting entities are required to disclose, as far as practicable and where material, the extent to which the amounts reported under each of the standard headings have been affected by the cash flows of a subsidiary acquired or disposed of during the year. This information can be given by segregating cash flows between continuing and discontinued operations and acquisitions. [FRS 1 para 45]. Consequently, users of financial statements will be able to ascertain the amount of the contribution to the group's cash flows that has been made by acquired subsidiaries and how much the group's cash flows have been depleted as a result of a disposal. This information need only be given in the financial statements for the period in which the acquisition or disposal occurs. [FRS 1 para 48]. In practice, it may be difficult, if not impossible, to give this information, particularly where the business of the acquired subsidiary has been integrated with the group. Many companies, therefore, omit this disclosure on the basis that it is not practicable. An example where a company has been able to disclose the material effects of an acquisition on the amounts reported under each standard heading is shown in Tables 30.9 and 30.10.

Table 30.9 — Bowater PLC — Annual Report — 31 December 1993

NOTES TO THE CASH FLOW STATEMENT (extract)

	Acquisitions		Disposals	
IV EFFECTS OF ACQUISITION AND DISPOSALS OF SUBSIDIARY UNDERTAKINGS AND BUSINESSES	**1993**	1992	**1993**	1992
	£m	£m	**£m**	£m
Tangible assets	**162.7**	144.6	**10.9**	11.2
Business for resale	**13.5**		**13.5**	
Associates	**1.3**	1.5	**0.1**	0.1
Associates goodwill eliminated		(0.7)		
Equity holding in associate	**(16.6)**			
Surplus properties	**0.2**			
Working capital	**44.2**	50.3	**(1.5)**	3.9
Current and deferred taxation	**8.5**	10.2		
Provisions	**(49.5)**	(65.2)	**1.1**	1.5
Cash and cash equivalents	**14.5**	(48.6)	**(2.3)**	(0.1)
Loan capital	**(89.6)**	(176.9)	**(3.0)**	
Finance leases	**(0.3)**	(3.6)		(0.8)
Minority interests	**(1.0)**	(0.3)		
Goodwill	**239.8**	326.0	**47.4**	16.9
Surplus/(deficiency) on disposal			**10.3**	(0.6)
	327.7	237.3	**76.5**	32.1

Consideration: cash	**312.3**	226.0	**76.5**	32.1
deferred	**26.7**	11.3		
Taxation relief	**(11.3)**			
	327.7	237.3	**76.5**	32.1

VANALYSIS OF MOVEMENTS OF CASH AND CASH EQUIVALENTS IN RESPECT OF ACQUISITIONS AND DISPOSALS OF SUBSIDIARY UNDERTAKINGS AND BUSINESSES

	1993	1992	**1993**	1992
	£m	£m	**£m**	£m
Cash consideration	**312.3**	226.0	**76.5**	32.1
Cash and cash equivalents	**(14.5)**	48.6	**2.3**	0.1
	297.8	274.6	**78.8**	32.2

Table 30.10 — Bowater PLC — Annual Report — 31 December 1993

NOTES TO THE CASH FLOW STATEMENT (extract)

III CASH FLOW MOVEMENTS ARISING FROM BUSINESSES ACQUIRED AND DISPOSED DURING THE YEAR

	1993	1992
Acquisitions:	**£m**	£m
Net cash inflow from operating activities	**56.4**	53.7
Returns on investments and servicing of finance	**(4.9)**	(3.2)
Taxation paid	**(1.4)**	(2.3)
Investing activities	**(20.2)**	(39.2)
Net cash inflow before financing	**29.9**	9.0

Disposals have not had a material impact.

Changes in stake

30.138.1 Paragraph 22 of FRS 1 says:

> *"The cash flows included in 'acquisitions and disposals' are those related to the acquisition or disposal of any trade or business, or of an investment in an entity that is, or, as a result of the transaction, becomes or ceases to be either an associate, a joint venture, or a subsidiary undertaking."*

This means that cash flows associated with changes in stake, even where there is no change in classification (say from associate to subsidiary) should be classified as 'acquisitions and disposals' in the cash flow statement.

Foreign currency

30.139 A company may engage in foreign currency operations in two main ways:

- First, it may enter directly into business transactions that are denominated in foreign currencies.
- Secondly, it may conduct its foreign operations through a subsidiary, associated company or branch whose operations are based in a country other than that of the investing company or whose assets and liabilities are denominated in a currency other than that of the investing company (a 'foreign entity').

30.140 The results of foreign currency transactions and the financial statements of the foreign entity will need to be translated into the currency in which the company reports. This translation process should produce results that are compatible with the effect of exchange rate changes on a company's cash flows and its equity. The accounting treatment of foreign currency operations in cash flow statements can be complex and there is little guidance on the subject. The guidance that follow deals with the treatment of exchange differences in individual companies first, followed by their treatment in consolidated financial statements.

Individual companies

30.141 Where an individual company has cash receipts or makes cash payments in a foreign currency, it is consistent with the objectives of cash flow statements that those receipts and payments should be translated into the reporting currency at the rate ruling at the date on which the receipt or payment is received or paid.

30.142 Exchange differences may, therefore, arise because of a rate change between the transaction date (the date at which the transaction is recorded) and the settlement date. Exchange differences also arise where a transaction remains unsettled (that is, not realised in cash) at the balance sheet date and is required to be retranslated at that date. Such differences relate to the retranslation of monetary assets and liabilities.

Settled transactions

30.143 Where a transaction is *settled* at an exchange rate which differs from that used when the transaction was initially recorded, the exchange difference will be recognised in the profit and loss account of the period in which the settlement takes place. To the extent that the settled transaction relates to operations, the gain or loss would be included in arriving at operating profit. This exchange gain or loss would also have the effect of increasing or decreasing the reporting currency equivalent of amounts paid or received in cash settlement. Consequently, no adjustment for the exchange gain or loss is necessary in the reconciliation of operating profit to operating cash flow. Consider the following example:

Example

A UK company was set up in January 20X5 and raised £200,000 by issuing shares. It purchased goods for resale from overseas in February 20X5 for CU992,500 when the exchange rate was £1 = CU7.94. It entered the purchase in its stock records as: CU992,500

@ 7.94 = £125,000. Under the terms of the contract, the company settled the debt in October 20X5 when the exchange rate was £1 = CU8.58. The amount paid in settlement was: CU992,500 @ 8.58 = £115,676. The company would, therefore, record an exchange gain of £125,000 — £115,676 = £9,324 in arriving at its operating profit for the year.

Assuming that there are no other transactions during the year and the stock remained unsold at the balance sheet date at 31 December 20X5, a simplified cash flow statement is given below:

Cash flow statement		
	£	£
Net cash flow from operating activities		(115,676)
Financing		
Issue of shares		200,000
Increase in cash		84,324
Workings		
Proceeds of share issue	200,000	
Less: payment for stocks	(115,676)	
Increase in cash		84,324
Reconciliation of operating profit to net cash flow from operating activities		
Net operating profit		9,324
Increase in stocks		(125,000)
Net cash flow from operating activities		(115,676)

It is obvious that the net cash flow from operating activities comprises the payment of £115,676 for the stock. Because the outstanding creditor for £125,000 was settled during the year for £115,676, the exchange gain of £9,324 is already reflected in the payment and, therefore, no adjustment for the exchange gain is necessary in the reconciliation of operating profit to operating cash flow as illustrated above. Therefore, as a general rule, exchange differences on settled transactions relating to operations will not appear as a reconciling item in the reconciliation of operating profit to net cash flow from operating activities.

30.144 Where a settled transaction does not relate to operations and the exchange gain or loss is included in the profit and loss account, but not within operating profit, the exchange gain or loss will be included as part of the cash flows arising from the settlement. An example would be income receivable from a foreign investment. In this situation, the sterling equivalent of foreign cash actually received would be shown under 'returns on investments and servicing of finance', and would include any exchange gain or loss that arises at the time of receipt reported in the profit and loss account below operating profit.

Unsettled transactions

30.145 Where the transaction remains *outstanding* at the balance sheet date, an exchange difference arises as a consequence of recording the foreign currency transaction at the rate ruling at the date of the transaction (or when it was translated at a previous balance sheet date) and the subsequent retranslation to the rate ruling at the balance sheet date. This exchange difference will generally be included in the profit and loss account. Normally such exchange differences arise on monetary items (for example, foreign currency loans, debtors and creditors). In the context of an individual company's operations, these exchange gains or losses will ultimately be reflected in cash flows. However, the way in which they affect the cash flow statement will depend upon the nature of the monetary assets or liabilities, that is, whether they are short-term or long-term.

30.146 Where they relate to short-term monetary items such as debtors and creditors, no adjustment for the exchange difference arising on their retranslation at the balance sheet date is necessary in the reconciliation of operating profit to net cash flow from operating activities, even though they do not involve any cash flows. This is because increases or decreases in the debtor or creditor balances will include exchange differences on their retranslation at the balance sheet date, and the total movement in debtors and creditors would form an adjusting item in the reconciliation of operating profit to operating cash flows. The effect is that the net cash flow from operating activities will not be distorted by such retranslation differences as illustrated in the following example.

Example

The facts are the same as in the previous example except that at the company's year end 31 December 20X5 the account had not been settled. At 31 December 20X5 the exchange rate was £1 = CU8.25 so that the original creditor for £125,000 would be retranslated at CU992,500 @ 8.25 = £120,303. The gain on exchange of £125,000 — £120,303 = £4,697 would be reported as part of operating profit for the year. The cash flow statement would be as follows:

Cash flow statement	£
Net cash flow from operating activities	Nil
Financing	
Issue of shares	200,000
Increase in cash	200,000
*Represented by closing cash balances	200,000

Reconciliation of operating profit to net cash flow from operating activities:

Net operating profit	4,697
Increase in stocks	(125,000)
Increase in creditors	120,303
Net cash flow from operating activities	Nil

It is clear that the exchange difference included in operating profit and in the year end creditor balance cancels each other with the result that operating cash flows are not affected. Therefore, as a general rule balance sheet movements in foreign currency trade debtors and creditors, except where they relate to foreign subsidiaries (see example below), will include the impact of exchange differences reported in operating profit and no adjustments for such exchange differences are necessary in the reconciliation.

30.147 Exchange differences on long-term monetary items such as long-term loans would normally be reported as part of the profit or loss for the financial year. To the extent that such differences are included in operating profit, they need to be eliminated in arriving at the net cash flows from operating activities. This is because the actual movement on long-term monetary items which includes the relevant exchange difference is not reported in the reconciliation of operating profit to operating cash flow. Whether or not the exchange differences are reported within operating profit, they should, nevertheless, fall to be included in the reconciliation to net debt and the note that analyses the changes in the balance sheet amounts making up net debt. Consider the following example:

Example

The opening balance sheet at 1 October 20X5 of a company consists of cash of £100,000 and share capital of £100,000. The company takes out a long-term loan on 31 March 20X6 of US$270,000 when the rate of exchange is £1 = US$1.8. The proceeds are immediately converted to sterling, that is, £150,000. There are no other transactions during the year. The exchange rate at the balance sheet date 30 September 20X6 is £1 = US$1.5.

The summarised balance sheet at 30 September 20X6	
	£'000
Cash	250
Long-term loan ($270,000 @ 1.5)	(180)
Net assets	70
Share capital	100
P&L account	(30)
	70

The foreign currency loan having been translated at the rate ruling at the date of receipt to £150,000 (US$270,000 @ 1.8), is retranslated at the balance sheet date to £180,000 (US$270,000 @ 1.5). The exchange loss of £30,000 is recognised in operating profit for the year. The cash is made up of £100,000 received from the share issue and £150,000 received on converting the currency loan immediately to sterling.

Simplified cash flow statement

	£'000
Net cash flow from operating activities	–
Financing	
Receipt of foreign currency loan	150
Increase in cash	150

Notes to the cash flow statement

Reconciliation of operating profit to net cash flow from operating activities

Operating loss	(30)
Adjustment for exchange loss	30
Net cash flow from operating profit	–

Reconciliation on net cash flow to movement in net funds

Increase in cash in the period	150
Cash inflow from increase in debt	(150)
Change in net funds resulting from cash flows	–
Net funds at 1 October 20X5	100
Exchange difference on loan	(30)
Net funds at 30 September 20X6	70

Analysis of net funds

	At 1 Oct 20X5 £'000	Cash Flows £'000	Exchange movement £'000	At 30 Sept 20X6 £'000
Cash	100	150	–	250
Loans	–	(150)	(30)	(180)
Total	100	–	(30)	70

It is apparent from the above illustration that the exchange loss of £30,000 does not have any cash flow effect and, therefore, needs to be eliminated from operating profit. A similar adjustment would be necessary if the loan remains outstanding at 30 September 20X7. However, if the exchange loss of £30,000 is included outside operating profit, for example in 'other interest receivable/payable and similar income/expense', the exchange difference would only fall to be reported in the reconciliation and the analysis of net funds during the year.

30.148 Similarly, where exchange differences arise on the retranslation of foreign currency cash balances, they will not appear in the cash flow statement. This is because they are non-cash movements within the cash balances and will not form part of the increase or decrease in cash for the financial year. They do, however, form part of the reconciliation of opening to closing balances and will, therefore, appear in the reconciliation to net debt and the note that analyses the changes in net debt during the year.

Borrowings used for hedging equity investments

30.149 Where a company has used foreign currency borrowings either to finance, or to provide a hedge against, its foreign equity investments, exchange differences on the borrowings may have been taken directly to reserves in accordance with paragraph 51 of SSAP 20 or paragraph 102 of FRS 26 (for companies applying that standard – see further chapter 6). These exchange differences will have no cash flow impact and will not be included in the cash flow statement or in the reconciliation of operating profit to net cash flow from operating activities. They must, however, be included in the reconciliation to changes in net debt and the note that analyses the changes in net debt during the year (as illustrated in the example above). Similarly, the exchange difference on retranslating the hedged equity investment (taken to reserve) has no cash flow effect.

30.149.1 To the extent that exchange movements on the foreign borrowings are not subject to hedge accounting, their impact will be seen in the profit and loss account. Should this be the case, the exchange movements are treated as discussed in paragraphs 30.147 and 30.148 above.

Group companies

30.150 Where a group conducts part of its business through a foreign entity, different considerations arise from those for individual transactions discussed above. This is because the cash flows of the foreign entity are considered as a whole rather than as a series of single transactions. There are two commonly accepted methods of translation, the temporal method and the closing rate/net investment method. The latter method is generally used for translation purposes, unless the foreign entity's operations are regarded as being more dependent on the economic environment of the investing company's currency, when, under SSAP 20, the temporal method is used. Where a company is reporting in accordance with FRS 23 (see further chapter 6), it is likely that such a foreign operation would have the same functional currency as the parent company and no retranslation gains or losses will occur. Foreign currency is considered further in chapter 7.

Temporal method

30.151 Under the temporal method, all non-monetary items and profit and loss account items of the foreign subsidiary or branch are translated at the rate ruling on the transaction date or at an average rate for a period if this is not materially different. Where the reporting entity uses the temporal method to translate the financial statements of the foreign enterprise, then the only exchange differences that arise will be those relating to monetary items and these will be reported as part of operating profit.

30.152 By using the temporal method, the consolidated financial statements reflect the transactions of the foreign enterprise as if they had been entered into by the reporting entity itself. Accordingly, the treatment of exchange differences in the consolidated cash flow statement will be similar to that explained above for exchange differences arising in individual companies.

Closing rate method

30.153 Under the closing rate/net investment method, the profit and loss account of the foreign entity is translated at the rate ruling at the date of each transaction (which may, under certain circumstances, be approximated to an average rate) for companies reporting under FRS 23 and at either the closing rate or at an average rate for the period for companies reporting under SSAP 20. [SSAP 20 para 54; FRS 23 para 23]. FRS 1 requires that the rate that is used for translating the results of activities in the profit and loss account of the foreign subsidiary should also be used for translating the cash flows of those activities for inclusion in the consolidated cash flow statement. [FRS 1 para 41]. This means that *all* the cash flows of the foreign subsidiary (not just those arising from its operating activities) must be included in the consolidated cash flow statement using the same exchange rates as were used for translating the results of its activities in the consolidated profit and loss account.

30.154 Where the group uses the closing rate method of translating the financial statements of a foreign entity, then all exchange differences relating to the retranslation of the opening net assets of the foreign enterprise to the closing rate will have been taken directly to reserves. As such exchange differences have no actual or prospective cash flow effect, they will not be included in the consolidated cash flow statement. However, where the opening net assets include foreign currency cash, overdrafts and loan balances then, to that extent, the exchange difference arising on their retranslation at the closing rate for the current period will have been reflected in the closing balances. Such translation differences should not be reported in the cash flow statement itself, but should be included in the effect of exchange rate movements shown as part of the reconciliation to net debt. [FRS 1 para 33(d)].

30.155 Where the group translates the foreign entity's profit and loss account at either the transaction date rate or an average rate, a further translation difference between the result as translated at the average rate and the result translated at the closing rate will have been taken to reserves. This difference will include the exchange rate effect of the movement in foreign currency cash and overdrafts from the transaction date or average rate to the closing rate. Under FRS 1, this exchange difference will be included with the exchange differences arising on the retranslation of the opening foreign currency cash, overdrafts and loan balances (as stated in the preceding paragraph) in the note that provides a reconciliation between the movements of cash to net debt. [FRS 1 para 33(d)].

30.156 In summary, the treatment specified in the standard has the effect of removing all exchange differences from the cash flow statement that do not have any cash flow impact in the reporting period. The treatment of foreign currency exchange differences in the consolidated cash flow statement can be fairly complex.

30.156.1 In practice, a reporting entity will find it simpler to require each of its foreign subsidiaries to prepare a cash flow statement with supporting notes. Where the subsidiary's profit and loss account is translated using either the closing rate or the average rate, that cash flow statement could be prepared in the subsidiary's domestic currency and translated into the reporting entity's relevant local or functional currency at the rate used for translating the profit and loss account. Where, however, a transaction date rate is used (or, say, monthly average rates are used as a proxy for the transaction date rates), this will not be possible and the task is more complex. In such cases, it will be necessary for a cash flow statement in the reporting entity's relevant local or functional currency to be produced from the subsidiary's accounting records. The subsidiary's cash flow statement in that currency can then be consolidated with the reporting entity's cash flow statement after eliminating intra-group items such as dividends and inter-group loans.

30.157 Some companies will apply the closing rate method discussed in paragraphs 30.153 and 30.154 above. The following example illustrates the application of those principles.

Example

Company A, a UK company, whose accounting period ended on 30 September 20X5, has a wholly-owned US subsidiary, S Corporation, that was acquired for US$600,000 on 30 September 20X4. The fair value of the net assets at the date of acquisition was US$500,000. The exchange rate at 30 September 20X4 and 20X5 was £1 = US$2.0 and £1 = US$1.5 respectively. The average rate for the year ended 30 September 20X5 (which company A considers to be a good approximation for the transaction date rate) was £1 = US$1.65.

The summarised balance sheet at 30 September 20X4 and 20X5 and an analysis of the retained profit for the year ended 30 September 20X5 of S Corporation, extracted from the consolidation returns, in dollars and sterling equivalents, are as follows:

Balance sheets of S Corporation	**20X5**	20X4	**20X5**	**20X5**	20X4
	$'000	$'000	**£'000**	**£'000**	£'000
			P&L closing	**P&L average**	
Exchange rate £1 =			**$1.50**	**$1.65**	$2.00
Fixed assets:					
Cost (20X5 additions: $30)	255	225	170.0	170.0	112.5
Depreciation (20X5 charge: $53)	98	45	65.3	65.3	22.5
Net book value	157	180	104.7	104.7	90.0
Current assets:					
Investments	250	100	166.6	166.6	50.0
Stocks	174	126	116.0	116.0	63.0
Debtors	210	145	140.0	140.0	72.5
Cash at bank	240	210	160.0	160.0	105.0
	874	581	582.6	582.6	290.5

Current liabilities:					
Bank overdraft	150	–	100.0	100.0	–
Trade creditors	125	113	83.3	83.3	56.5
Taxation	30	18	20.0	20.0	9.0
	305	131	203.3	203.3	65.5
Net current assets	569	450	379.3	379.3	225.0
Loan stock	150	130	100.0	100.0	65.0
Net assets	576	500	384.0	384.0	250.0
Share capital	300	300	150.0	150.0	150.0
Reserves:					
Pre acquisition	200	200	100.0	100.0	100.0
Post acquisition	76	–	50.7	46.1	–
Exchange difference					
Net assets ($500/1.5 — $500/2.0)	–	–	83.3	83.3	–
Increase ($76/1.5 — $76/1.65)	–	–	–	4.6	–
	576	500	384.0	384.0	250.0

Analysis of retained profit for year ended 30 September 20X5

		Closing rate	Average rate
	$'000	£'000	£'000
Operating profit	135	90.0	81.8
Interest paid	(15)	(10.0)	(9.0)
Taxation	(30)	(20.0)	(18.2)
Dividends paid in the year	(14)	(9.3)	(8.5)
Retained profit	76	50.7	46.1

It is further assumed that company A does not trade on its own and its only income is dividends received from S Corporation. The summarised balance sheet of company A at 30 September 20X4 and 20X5 is as follows:

Company A — Balance sheets	**20X5**	**20X4**
	£'000	**£'000**
Investments in subsidiary ($600,000 @ 2.0)	300	300
Cash	208	200
Net assets	508	500
Share capital	500	500
P&L account (dividend received: $14,000 @ 1.75*)	8	–
	458	500

* actual rate on date dividend received.

Where company A applies SSAP 20 and uses the closing rate/net investment method, it may use either the closing rate or the average rate for translating the results of S Corporation. The summarised consolidated profit and loss account for the year ended 30 September 20X5 drawn up on the two basis and the summarised consolidated balance sheet at that date are as follows:

Consolidated profit and loss account for the year ended 30 September 20X5	**£'000 Closing rate**	**£'000 Average rate**
Operating profit of S corporation	90.0	81.8
Operating profit of Company A	8.0	8.0
	98.0	89.8
Adjustment — inter company dividend	(9.3)	(8.5)
Retranslation of goodwill	16.7	16.7
Net operating profit	105.4	98.0
Interest paid	(10.0)	(9.0)
Taxation	(20.0)	(18.2)
Retained profit	75.5	70.8
Consolidated balance sheet as at 30 September 20X5		
Fixed assets	104.7	104.7
Goodwill ($100,000 @ 1.5)	66.7	66.7
	171.4	171.4
Current assets:		
Investments	166.6	166.6
Stocks	116.0	116.0
Debtors	140.0	140.0
Cash (S Corporation: £160; Company A £208)	368.0	368.0
	790.6	790.6
Current liabilities:		
Bank overdraft	100.0	100.0
Trade creditors	83.3	83.3
Taxation	20.0	20.0
	203.3	203.3
Net current assets	587.3	587.3
Loan stocks	100.0	100.0
Net assets	658.7	658.7
Share capital	500.0	500.0
Reserves:		
Retained profit	75.5	70.8
Exchange difference on opening net assets	83.3	83.3
Exchange difference on P&L account	—	4.7
	658.8	658.8

In the above illustration, goodwill has been regarded as a currency asset which is retranslated at the closing rate. This is a treatment permitted by SSAP 20 and required by FRS 23. An alternative treatment that is permitted by SSAP 20 is to translate goodwill at the rate ruling on the date of acquisition on the grounds that it arises only on consolidation and is not part of the net assets of the foreign enterprise.

Given the above information, the consolidated cash flow statement drawn up in accordance with the exchange rate used in the profit and loss account and the related notes to the cash flow statement are as follows:

Consolidated cash flow statement for the year ended 30 September 20X5	**£'000**	**£'000**
	Closing	**Average**
Net cash flow from operating activities	56.7	52.2
Returns on investments and servicing of finance		
Interest paid ($15,000 @ 1.5 and 1.65)	(10.0)	(9.1)
Taxation		
Overseas tax paid ($18,000* @ 1.5 and 1.65)	(12.0)	(10.9)
Capital expenditure		
Purchase of fixed assets ($30,000 @ 1.5 and 1.65)	(20.0)	(18.1)
Management of liquid resources		
Purchase of current asset investments ($150,000 @ 1.5 and 1.65)	(100.0)	(90.9)
Financing		
Issue of loan stock ($20,000 @ 1.5 and 1.65)	13.3	12.1
Decrease in cash	(72.0)	(64.7)

* Overseas tax paid relates to settlement of previous year's liability.

Reconciliation of net cash flow to movement in net funds	**£'000**	**£'000**
	Closing	**Average**
Decrease in cash for the period	(72.0)	(64.7)
Cash flow from increase in liquid resources	100.0	90.9
Cash flow from increase in debt	(13.3)	(12.1)
Change in net fund resulting from cash flows	14.7	14.1
Translation difference (see note 2)	29.9	30.5
Movement in net funds in the period	44.6	44.6
Net funds at 1 October 20X4	290.0	290.0
Net funds at 30 September 20X5	334.6	334.6

Notes to the cash flow statement

1 Reconciliation of operating profit to net cash inflow from operating activities	**Closing rate**	**Average rate**
	£'000	**£'000**
Operating profit	88.7	81.3
Depreciation ($53,000 @ 1.5 and 1.65)	35.3	32.1
Increase in stocks ($48,000 @ 1.5 and 1.65)	(32.0)	(29.1)
Increase in debtors ($65,000 @ 1.5 and 1.65)	(43.3)	(39.4)
Increase in creditors ($12,000 @ 1.5 and 1.65)	8.0	7.3
Net cash flow from operating activities	56.7	52.2

The movement in working capital in note 1 above could also be obtained by taking the difference between the closing and the opening balance sheet figures and adjusting the result to eliminate the non-cash effects of exchange rate adjustments. But this method is rather cumbersome as illustrated below for stocks:

	Closing rate	**Average rate**
	£'000	**£'000**
Stocks at 30 September 20X5 ($174 @ 1.5)	116.0	116.0
Stocks at 30 September 20X4 ($126 @ 2.0)	63.0	63.0
Increase in stocks ($48)	53.0	53.0
Exchange difference:		
On opening balance ($126 @ 1.5 — $126 @ 2.0)	(21.0)	(21.0)
On movement ($48 @ 1.5 — $48 @ 1.65)		(2.9)
Increase in stocks included in reconciliation above	32.0	29.1

The effect of foreign exchange rate changes on net funds may be reconciled as follows:

2 Analysis of net funds — Closing rate method

	1 Oct 20X4	**Cash flow**	**Exchange difference**	**30 Sep 20X5**
	£'000	£'000	£'000	£'000
Cash				
Cash at bank	305.0	28.0	35.0	368.0
Bank overdraft	–	(100.0)	–	(100.0)
	305.0	(72.0)	35.0	268.0
Liquid resources				
Current asset investments	50.0	100.0	16.6	166.6
Debt				
Loan stock	(65.0)	(13.3)	(21.7)	(100.0)
Net funds	290.0	14.7	29.9	334.6

Analysis of net funds — Average rate method

	1 Oct 20X4	**Cash flow**	**Exchange difference**	**30 Sep 20X5**
	£'000	£'000	£'000	£'000
Cash				
Cash at bank	305.0	26.2	36.8	368.0
Bank overdraft		(90.9)	(9.1)	(100.0)
	305.0	(64.7)*	27.7	268.0
Liquid resources				
Current asset investments	50.0	90.9	25.7	166.6
Debt				
Loan stock	(65.0)	(12.1)	(22.9)	(100.0)
Net funds	290.0	14.1	30.5	334.6

*Note:

Movements in cash — (S Corp $30 @ 1.65 = £18.2 + A Ltd £8)	£26.2
Movement in overdraft (S corp $150 @ 1.65)	£90.9

See workings below for calculation of exchange differences

	Closing rate £'000	Average rate £'000
Cash at bank		
Opening balance ($210 @ 1.5 — $210 @ 2.0)	35.0	35.0
Increase in the period ($30 @ 1.5 — $30 @ 1.65)	–	1.8
	35.0	36.8
Bank overdraft:		
Opening balance	–	–
Increase in the period ($150 @ 1.5 — $150 @ 1.65)	–	(9.1)
	–	(9.1)
Liquid resources — current asset investment		
Opening balance ($100 @ 1.5 — $100 @ 2.0)	16.6	16.6
Increase in the period ($150 @ 1.5 — $150 @ 1.65)	–	9.1
	16.6	25.7
Debt — loan stock		
Opening balance ($130 @ 1.5 — $130 @ 2.0)	(21.7)	(21.7)
Increase in the period ($20 @ 1.5 — $20 @ 1.65)	–	(1.2)
	21.7	(22.9)

[The next paragraph is 30.158.]

Intra-group transactions

30.158 Transactions between members of a group located in different countries may not cancel out on consolidation because of exchange differences. As explained in chapter 7, these exchange differences are usually reported in the consolidated profit and loss account, particularly if they relate to intra-group trading transactions and dividends. Such exchange differences may have an effect on group cash flows. For consolidated cash flow statements, these intra-group cash flows may not cancel out unless the actual rate at the date of transfer is used for translation. In the previous example, the only intra-group transaction that took place between the parent and the subsidiary was in respect of a dividend payment. The consolidated operating profit after cancellation of the inter-company dividend is shown below for the two situations where the subsidiary's profit and loss account has been translated at the closing rate and the average rate.

Consolidated profit and loss account for the year ended 30 September 20X5	**£'000 Closing rate**	**£'000 Average rate**
Operating profit of S corporation	90.0	81.8
Operating profit of Company A	8.0	8.0
	98.0	89.8
Adjustment — inter company dividend	(9.3)	(8.5)
Net operating profit	88.7	81.3

30.159 As can be seen the amount of £9,300 and £8,500 is used to cancel the dividend paid by the subsidiary and not the £8,000 received by the parent. It would, therefore, appear that an exchange difference has been left in operating profit, which would need to be eliminated in the reconciliation of operating profit to operating cash flow. However, this is not the case. Deducting the amount for the dividend paid by the subsidiary in the consolidated profit and loss account at the same amount included in the subsidiary's profit and loss account translated at closing rate or average rate, cancels the dividend paid, and so ensures that the consolidated profit and loss account reflects the dividends received by the parent at the sterling amount received. In the consolidated cash flow statement, the same approach is adopted. In effect, the subsidiary's cash flows are reported at the closing rate or average rate, except that the dividend payment is reversed at that same rate and included at the sterling amount actually received by the parent. As a result, no further adjustment for the exchange difference is necessary in the reconciliation of operating profit to operating cash flow, or in the reconciliation to net debt. Indeed, this is to be expected as the transaction was settled during the year, any exchange difference already being reflected in cash flows. The standard, therefore, permits the use of an actual rate, or an approximation thereto, to translate intra-group cash flows in order to ensure that they cancel out in the preparation of the consolidated cash flow statement. [FRS 1 para 41].

30.160 If, on the other hand, the amount of £8,000 received by the parent had been used to cancel the intra-group dividend, the consolidated operating profit would have increased as shown below.

Consolidated profit and loss account for the year ended 30 September 20X5	**£'000 Closing rate**	**£'000 Average rate**
Operating profit of S corporation	90.0	81.8
Operating profit of Company A	8.0	8.0
	98.0	89.8
Adjustment — inter company dividend	(8.0)	(8.0)
Net operating profit	90.0	89.8

30.161 Using identical amounts to cancel the intra-group dividend in the consolidated profit and loss account does not mean that the exchange difference has been eliminated in the cash flow statement. The effect of using the actual amount received in the cancellation process means that the profits remitted by the subsidiary are being translated at the closing rate or the average rate. As a result the intra-group dividend paid and received does not cancel out in the consolidated cash flow statement. The difference of £1,300 for the closing rate or £500 for the average rate then needs to be eliminated. The standard states that if the rate used to translate intra-group cash flows is not the actual rate, any exchange rate differences should be included in the effect of the exchange rate movements shown as part of the reconciliation to net debt. [FRS 1 para 41]. It could be argued that it makes more sense to report this exchange rate difference in the reconciliation of operating profit to operating cash flows. This is because the subsidiary's cash has gone down by £9,300 and the holding company's cash has gone up by £8,000, resulting in a real economic loss to the group which normally falls to be recognised in the consolidated profit and loss account as explained in chapter 6. However, the treatment required by the standard ensures that the profit and loss account and the cash flow statement are treated in a consistent way. Because, in the above example, operating profit does not include any exchange difference on the intra-group dividend, it follows that no adjustment for the exchange difference is necessary in the reconciliation of operating profit to operating cash flows. The only other place to report this exchange difference is in the reconciliation to net debt.

Hedging transactions

30.162 Hedging transactions are normally undertaken by entities to protect themselves from financial loss, especially loss that would occur if prices or exchange rates were to vary. For example, an entity may purchase or sell a hedging instrument, such as a futures contract or a forward contract, in order to protect itself from price fluctuations that may arise in connection with the sale or purchase of stocks. The question arises as to how cash flows that result from the purchase or sale of the hedging instrument should be classified in the cash flow statement. Should these be shown under capital expenditure and financial investments or classified in the same category as the cash flows of the items being hedged, for example, under operating activities?

30.163 The standard provides that cash flows that result from transactions undertaken to hedge another transaction should be reported under the same standard heading as the transactions which are the subject of the hedge. [FRS 1 para 42]. The treatment required by the standard for hedging transactions applies only to futures contracts, forward contracts, options and swaps that are taken out as hedges of identifiable transactions or events. For example, the reporting entity may purchase a futures contract in order to reduce its exposure to increases in the price of a planned stock purchase and, therefore, any cash flows arising on the futures contract should be reported in operating cash flows.

30.164 The treatment required by the standard for hedged transactions cannot apply to situations where the reporting entity hedges a net investment in a foreign subsidiary with a borrowing that is denominated in the same currency as the net investment being hedged. Accounting for the borrowing as a hedge is incidental; it cannot change the basic fact that it is still a borrowing. Furthermore, the foreign subsidiary may have contributed to group cash flows reported under each of the standard headings. Since the cash flows from the borrowings cannot be identified with any specific cash flows from that subsidiary, it follows that the cash flows from the borrowing can only be classified in the cash flow statement under financing in the consolidated financial statements.

Notes to the cash flow statements

Specific disclosures

30.165 In addition to the cash flow statement itself, the standard requires a number of explanatory notes to the cash flow statements. The positioning of these notes within the financial statements varies from company to company, but in general they are either presented immediately after the cash flow statement itself or are included in the notes to the financial statements with appropriate cross-references to the cash flow statement. Many of the specific disclosures that are necessary to supplement the information presented in the cash flow statement have already been discussed and illustrated by practical examples, but are restated below for completeness.

- A note showing the reconciliation between operating profit and net cash flow from operating activities should be provided. This reconciliation should disclose all differences between operating cash flows and operating profits (see para 30.72). This reconciliation should be presented either adjoining the cash flow statement or in a note to the statement.
- A reconciliation of the movement in cash to the movement in net debt should be provided showing the changes in net debt during the year and the way in which such changes are related to the opening and closing balance sheet figures. This reconciliation, like the previous one, may be presented either adjoining the cash flow statement or in a note to the statement. Where several balance sheet items or parts thereof have to be combined to permit a reconciliation, sufficient detail should be shown to enable the movements to be understood. This detail should be given in a note to the statement (see para 30.123).
- Where a group acquires or disposes of a subsidiary undertaking, the notes to the cash flow statements should show a summary of the effects of the acquisition or disposal. Disclosure should also be made of the extent to which the amounts reported under each of the standard headings have been affected by the cash flows of the subsidiary acquired or disposed of during the year (see paras 30.137 and 30.138).
- Major non-cash transactions should also be disclosed. Such transactions do not involve any cash flow, but have the same effect as if several cash transactions were made together. For example, conversion of debt to equity can be viewed as the equivalent of repaying debt in cash and then receiving cash on the issue of new shares. Because there are no actual cash flows, the transaction would not feature in the cash flow statement. But important

information would thereby remain undisclosed merely because, in effect, a notional cash outflow has been cancelled by an equal and opposite notional cash inflow. Therefore, in order to report the activities of an enterprise in full, material non-cash transactions should be disclosed in a note to the cash flow statement if disclosure is necessary for an understanding of the underlying transactions.

Supplementary disclosures

30.166 In addition to the specific disclosures identified above, the standard *encourages* reporting entities to provide additional information relevant to their particular circumstances. [FRS 1 para 56]. The additional information that may be presented is considered below.

Reporting of gross operating cash flows

30.167 Entities are allowed to provide information on gross operating cash receipts and gross operating cash payments. [FRS 1 para 7]. Clearly, presentation of such information produces a cash flow statement in its purest form with new information that is not otherwise available from the profit and loss account or the balance sheet. The way in which such information should be presented is illustrated in Table 30.2.

Cash flows from discontinued operations

30.168 Entities are encouraged to distinguish between net cash flows from continuing operating activities and those arising from discontinued operations. [FRS 1 para 56]. Although not specifically required in the standard section of FRS 1, the analysis is given in example 2 of the illustrative examples included in the FRS. This disclosure is consistent with the separate disclosure in the profit and loss account of the results of continuing activities from those relating to discontinued operations required by FRS 3. Many companies have not given this analysis, but an example of a company that has separately analysed its net cash flows from operating activities between continuing and discontinued operations is shown in Table 30.11 below.

Table 30.11 — Pearson plc — Directors' Report and Accounts — 31 December 1996
Notes to the Accounts (extract)

25 Notes to consolidated statement of cash flows

a) Reconciliation of operating profit to net cash inflow from operating activities	**Continuing 1996 £m**	**Discontinued 1996 £m**	**Total 1996 £m**	Continuing 1995 £m	Discontinued 1995 £m	Total 1995 £m
Operating profit	**146.0**	**35.3**	**181.3**	237.6	22.0	259.6
Depreciation charges	**56.8**	**6.4**	**63.2**	54.7	6.8	61.5
Share of profit of partnerships and associated undertakings	**(53.1)**	–	**(53.1)**	(43.3)	–	(43.3)
Dividends from partnerships and associated undertakings	**33.5**	–	**33.5**	30.7	–	30.7
Decrease/(increase) in stocks	**4.6**	**1.9**	**6.5**	(34.6)	(1.9)	(36.5)
Decrease/(increase) in debtors	**21.8**	**(1.0)**	**20.8**	(80.3)	(0.2)	(80.5)
Increase/(decrease) in creditors	**59.9**	**1.0**	**60.9**	20.2	(2.0)	18.2
(Decrease)/increase in operating provisions	**1.6**	**(3.5)**	**(1.9)**	29.2	(0.2)	29.0
Exchange adjustments	**(7.7)**	–	**(7.7)**	2.8	–	2.8
Other	**(10.6)**	**(1.7)**	**(12.3)**	(5.1)	–	(5.1)
Net cash inflow from operating activities*	**252.8**	**38.4**	**291.2**	211.9	24.5	236.4
Purchase of fixed assets and finance leases	**(85.9)**	**(5.0)**	**(90.9)**	(97.6)	(4.3)	(101.9)
Sale of operating tangible fixed assets	**6.5**	**0.4**	**6.9**	31.6	0.5	32.1
Other	**10.0**	**1.8**	**11.8**	(20.1)	–	(20.1)
Operating cash flow	**183.4**	**35.6**	**219.0**	125.8	20.7	146.5

* Cash inflow for 1996 includes a £20.9m outflow relating to exceptional items charged in 1996 and £12.5m outflow relating to exceptional items charged in prior years.

Commentary on cash flows in operating and financial review

30.169 It is acknowledged that the assessment of liquidity, viability and financial adaptability of an entity requires more information than just a statement of cash flows. The Business Review or Operating and Financial Review (OFR), which are discussed further in chapters 2 and 3 of the Manual of Accounting – Management Reports and Governance, give opportunities for companies to provide a commentary on their cash flows. The ASB's 'Reporting statement: Operating and financial review', recommends discussion in the 'financial position' section of the statement concerning 'cash flows' and 'liquidity'. [RS (OFR) paras 68, 71]. Many companies use this opportunity to provide further information on their cash generating potential and liquidity position that goes beyond that required by FRS 1.

30.170 In discussing the cash generated from operations and other cash inflows during the period, the reporting statement encourages companies to disclose and discuss segmental cash flows where they are significantly out of line with segmental profits, because of the impact of capital expenditure. [RS (OFR) para 70]. In fact, FRS 1 also encourages enterprises to give a segmental breakdown of their cash flows, but does not specify how this information should be given. [FRS 1 para 8]. Many companies, following SSAP 25, 'Segmental reporting', already give segmental information about their operations in terms of turnover, profits, capital employed, etc. The extension of segmental information to cash flows enables users to understand the relationship between the cash flows of the business as a whole and those of its component parts.

30.171 The type of segmental cash flow information that should be reported is not specifically identified by FRS 1, or the reporting statement, but we consider that, as a minimum, an entity should give an analysis of the most important elements of operating cash flows between the major reportable segments. Clearly, there may be problems of allocation, such as common costs and interest, but they could be allocated between segments in the same way as other segmental information. Guidance on the allocation of common costs and interest is given in SSAP 25 and discussed in chapter 10. An example of a company that has given a segmental analysis of operating cash flows is shown in Table 35.13 below.

Table 30.13 — Bass PLC — Annual Report and Financial Statements — 30 September 1996

NOTES TO THE FINANCIAL STATEMENTS (extract)

28 Operating cash flow		**1996 £m**	1995 £m
Hotels:	Holiday Inn Worldwide	**184**	115
Leisure retailing:	Bass Taverns	**114**	204
	Bass Leisure	**(22)**	19
Branded drinks:	Bass Brewers*	**139**	160
	Britvic Soft Drinks	**43**	41
Other activities*		**(9)**	24
		449	563

*Figures for 1995 have been restated to include in Bass Brewers operating cash flow related to its overseas brewing operations which was previously included in other activities; this restatement amounts to £28m outflow.

30.172 Some companies also disclose 'cash flow per share'. There is, in principle, nothing wrong with disclosing this information provided that it is clear that it is not a substitute for earnings per share. Indeed, there is no such prohibition in FRS 1 or the reporting statement. Cash flow per share information presented over time would reveal the trend of cash flows and, when compared to earnings per share, would demonstrate the quality of profits earned.

30.173 In discussing current liquidity, the reporting statement calls for disclosure and comments on the level of borrowings including seasonality, peak borrowing levels and maturity profile of both borrowings and committed borrowing facilities. [RS (OFR) para 71]. At present, financial statement disclosure about actual borrowings at the year end is provided by analysing bank and other borrowings by maturity period of up to one year, one to two years, two to five years and beyond five years. However, there is no requirement to disclose the amount of undrawn borrowing facilities (both committed and uncommitted). Disclosure of an entity's borrowing facilities together with its ability to access further resources will, no doubt, go a long way in providing useful information about the entity's viability and financial adaptability. However, the level of disclosure is left to the company for obvious reasons. For example, companies could resist such disclosure on the grounds that it provides too much competitive information. Also the company's main bankers could object because disclosure may provide competitors with valuable information on their lending policies.

30.174 The discussion on borrowings suggested by the reporting statement should also refer to any restrictions on the ability of the group to transfer funds from one part of the group to another and restrictions and breaches of borrowing covenants. [RS (OFR) paras 71, 73, 74]. The disclosure of the amounts of cash that are not freely remittable to the parent company coupled with sufficient information on the restrictions (for example, exchange controls) provides useful information for users of financial statements to make an assessment of the probable future effect of the restriction on the company's cash flows. As discussed in paragraph 30.175, FRS 1 requires disclosures on the treatment of cash that is subject to restriction. Similarly, information on assets and liabilities denominated in foreign currencies, which incidentally is not directly relevant for supplementing information reported in the cash flow statement, may be useful for making assessments of a company's liquidity and financial viability. Information on any restrictive financial covenants on current borrowing agreements and breaches or likely breaches of covenants is equally important in assessing its viability and financial adaptability.

Restrictions on remittability

30.175 Sometimes cash may be held in a separate blocked account or an escrow account to be used only for a specific purpose, or held by subsidiaries operating in countries where exchange control restrictions are in force such that cash is not freely transferable around the group. The standard requires that where restrictions prevent the transfer of cash from one part of the business or group to another, a note to the cash flow statement should disclose the amount and explain the nature of the restriction. [FRS 1 para 47]. However, disclosure is required only in circumstances where the restriction is imposed by external factors outside the company's control. Restrictions arising from a specific purpose designated by the reporting entity need not be disclosed. A typical example of disclosure is where a foreign subsidiary is prevented from remitting funds to its overseas parent, because of local exchange control regulations. [FRS 1 para 68]. Other examples given in the standard where disclosure may be relevant, depending on the regulatory environment, relate to cash balances in escrow, deposited with a regulator or held within an employee share ownership trust. The treatment of cash subject to restriction is considered from paragraph 30.190.

Comparative figures

30.176 Comparative figures should be given for all items reported in the cash flow statements and in the supplementary notes. Comparative figures are required for the reconciliation of the movement of cash to the movement in net debt, but not for the note that analyses the changes in the balance sheet amounts making up net debt. Nor are comparative figures required for the amounts included under each of the standard headings in respect of the cash flows of subsidiaries acquired or disposed of during the year. [FRS 1 para 48].

Example

A company was a wholly-owned subsidiary of another company at the previous year end and took the exemption in FRS 1 from preparing a cash flow statement, which is available to 90% controlled subsidiaries. However, during the year the parent sold 20% of the company, so that it is less than 90% controlled at this year end and, therefore, has to produce a cash flow statement. Can the company just do a cash flow for the current year and not give comparatives, on the grounds that it was exempt last year?

No. Paragraph 48 of FRS 1 clearly states that comparatives are required for a cash flow statement and this applies even if the company was exempt in the prior year.

30.177 Normally, it is a relatively simple matter to provide comparative figures for all items reported in the cash flow statement itself. However, disclosure of comparative amounts for all items reported in the notes to the cash flow statement may cause some practical difficulties in interpreting this requirement. For example, the illustrative example in the standard provides a detailed breakdown of the assets and liabilities of subsidiaries acquired or disposed of during the year, together with an analysis of the net consideration paid or received in the transfer. Normally, such disclosures are also required by the Act and FRS 6, but only in the year of acquisition or disposal. If the strict wording of the standard is to be followed, then comparative figures would be required. Many companies do not provide such comparative information, although it is arguable that where an acquisition or disposal has taken place both in the current and the preceding year, the analysis of the net consideration should be given for both years in the notes as illustrated in Table 30.9.

Practical application of FRS 1

30.178 This section attempts to clarify some of the practical problems that may arise in interpreting and applying the standard.

Balance sheet cash versus FRS 1 cash

30.179 The strict definition of cash used for the purposes of cash flow reporting explained in paragraph 30.41 above is unlikely to accord with the interpretation of cash used in the balance sheet classification 'cash at bank and in hand'. Although some companies follow a narrow interpretation of cash by including only cash held in current accounts and short-term deposits repayable on demand under the balance sheet heading, others follow a wider interpretation by including the total amount of money on deposit with a bank or financial institution without regard to whether the deposit was short or long-term. If the wider interpretation is followed, the movements in cash as reported in the cash flow statement are unlikely to agree with the movements in cash as disclosed in the balance sheet caption. The differences are likely to be for those short-term deposits that are regarded as liquid resources and whose movements are reported under 'management of liquid resources' and for other long-term deposits that are not regarded as liquid resources whose movements are reported under 'capital expenditure and financial investment'.

Discounts and premiums

30.180 Where a deep discounted bond is redeemed or a premium is paid on the redemption of a debt security, the question sometimes arises as to where in the cash flow statement the premium should be reported. An intuitive response may be to include it within financing together with the other principal amount repaid on the instrument. However, under FRS 4 (or FRS 26, for companies applying that standard – see further chapter 6) the discount on issue and the redemption premium form part of the finance cost of the instruments, which is reported in the profit and loss account as interest expense over the life of the instruments. FRS 1 takes a similar approach. It requires that the cash flow effects of these items should be reported within 'returns on investments and servicing of finance' when the instruments are redeemed in order to provide a link between the profit and loss account and the cash flow statement as illustrated in the following example.

Example

A company issues a ten year zero coupon bond with a face value of £100,000 at a discount of £61,446. Its issue price is, therefore, £38,554 and the effective yield is 10%. How should the transaction be reflected in the cash flow statement?

At the issue date, the proceeds of £38,554 would be shown as a cash inflow in financing. The discount of £61,446 represents a rolled-up interest charge which would be amortised to the profit and loss account as an interest expense over the life of the bond while the bond remains outstanding. However, there would be no cash flow in these periods, because no cash has been paid.

On maturity, the discount of £61,446, which is part of the finance cost under FRS 4 (and FRS 26), should be shown under 'returns on investments and servicing of finance' separately classified, if material, as premium paid on redemption of bond in accordance with paragraph 15(a) of the standard. The balance of £38,554 should be shown under financing as repayment of the bond. The result is that a decrease in cash of £100,000 would be reported at the end of the cash flow statement. It should be noted that although the discount has been accrued over the years when the bond was in issue, the repayment of the discount on redemption means that the accrual should be adjusted as a non-cash change in the reconciliation to net debt as shown below:

Reconciliation to net debt	£'000
Decrease in cash in the period	(100,000)
Cash flow from decrease in debt financing	38,554
Change in net debt from cash flows	(61,446)
Other non cash changes — reversal of accrual for discount	61,446
Movement in net debt for the period	–
Opening net funds (say cash of £150,000 less bond of £100,000)	50,000
Closing net funds (cash of £50,000)	50,000

It is clear from the above example that accruals for finance costs would need to be reported as other non-cash changes in the reconciliation to net debt. This adjustment should be made both in the year(s) in which the accrual arises (as an increase in net debt) and in the year in which it reverses, otherwise the movement in net debt for the period cannot be reconciled with the opening and closing component of net debt.

A similar treatment would apply to the investor. The investor should record the payment for the bond of £38,554 as part of cash outflow in financial investment. On maturity, the receipt of £100,000 should be split and shown as to £38,554 under financial investment and £61,446 under 'returns on investments and servicing of finance'.

30.181 Where debt instruments (including shares that are classified as liabilities) are redeemed at a premium, it will also be necessary to separate the principal and the interest element of the amounts paid on redemption. For example, where supplemental interest is paid on convertible bonds that are redeemed rather than converted, the whole amount of the supplemental interest accrued over the life of the bond and paid at redemption should be reported under 'returns on investments and servicing of finance'. See further chapter 6.

30.181.1 Note, issue costs of equity instruments (which are not amortised to the profit and loss account) are shown in the financing section of the cash flow statement and are separately disclosed (see para 30.110).

Gains and losses

30.182 It is consistent with the objective of cash flow reporting that gains and losses that do not give rise to any cash flows should be excluded from the cash flow statement. Gains and losses are reported in the profit and loss account or in the statement of total recognised gains and losses of the reporting entity. To the extent that these are included in arriving at operating profit, they should be adjusted (gains should be deducted and losses added) in the reconciliation to arrive at the net cash flow from operating activities. For example, a gain on the sale of plant and machinery that has been included in operating profit (as a depreciation adjustment) should be excluded from cash flow from operating activities. The gain is not a cash flow as such, but forms part of the proceeds from the sale that are disclosed under capital expenditure in the cash flow statement.

30.183 A similar treatment would apply to gains and losses on investments. However, where investments are used for trading activities (typically by a bank or a financial institution), any gain or loss arising on their disposal during the year would be included in operating profit. In this situation, operating profit need only be adjusted for the movement in investments and not for the gain or loss arising (which is realised) to arrive at the net cash flow from operating activities.

30.184 Gains and losses on current asset investments that are regarded as liquid resources, would need to be eliminated from operating profit, if the gain or loss is also reported as part of operating profit, to give the correct cash flow from operating activities. Irrespective of whether or not the gain or loss is reported within operating profit, the gain or loss would need to be reported as a non-cash item in the reconciliation to net debt.

30.185 In relation to debt securities, a further question arises as to whether a gain or loss that arises on the early settlement of a debt security issued by a reporting entity should be reported as part of the finance cost under 'returns on investments and servicing of finance' or as part of the capital repayment under 'financing'. Consider the following example.

Example

The facts are the same as in the previous example except that the company has decided to redeem the bond early at the beginning of year 4 for £55,000.

The carrying value of the bond in the balance sheet at the end of year 3 is calculated as follows:

	£'000	£'000
Proceeds at beginning of year 1		38,554
Interest accrued in year 1 — 10% on £38,554	3,854	
Interest accrued in year 2 — 10% on £42,408	4,241	
Interest accrued in year 3 — 10% on £46,649	4,665	12,760
Carrying value (capital value of bond £100,000 less unamortised discount of £61,446 — £12,760 = £48,686)		51,314
Loss on redemption:		
Redemption payment		55,000
Less carrying value		51,314
		3,686

The loss should be allocated to interest paid, giving £16,446 (£12,760 + £3,686) to be reported under returns on investments and servicing of finance and £38,554 to be reported as capital repayment under financing. This treatment is appropriate because the total cash cost of the finance is reflected in the cash flow statement. Under FRS 4 (and FRS 26, for companies applying that standard), the difference between the net proceeds of an instrument (in this example, £38,554) and the total amount of the payments made (£55,000) is finance cost (£16,446). As explained before, FRS 1 also requires the cash flow effect to be treated in a similar way. The alternative of reporting the loss incurred as part of the capital repayment, giving £42,240 (£38,554 + £3,686) to be reported under financing and £12,760 to be reported as interest paid under returns on investments and servicing of finance, is not considered acceptable.

Reorganisation costs following an acquisition

30.186 Where a company undertakes to reorganise the business of a recently acquired subsidiary, it may incur costs that are provided for in periods prior to the actual disbursement of cash. The question arises as to whether the subsequent cash outflow in respect of the amount provided should be disclosed as part of operating activities or 'acquisitions and disposals'.

30.187 FRS 7 requires such costs to be reported in the post acquisition profit and loss account of the acquiring group. The cash outflows should, therefore, be reported under operating activities if such costs are also reported in the post acquisition profit and loss account in arriving at operating profit. Where the costs are reported as a non-operating exceptional item in accordance with FRS 3 and FRS 6, 'Acquisition and mergers', (that is, if the reorganisation is fundamental to the enlarged group), the exceptional cash flows would also fall to be reported separately under operating activities as discussed in paragraph 30.114 above.

Refinancing of borrowings

30.188 Companies may renegotiate their existing borrowings on terms that are different from those that were in place prior to the renegotiation. For example, as part of the renegotiation, a significant part of the company's current overdraft balance may be converted into a long-term loan. The question arises as to how such a reclassification should be dealt with in the cash flow statement.

30.189 The answer depends on whether the renegotiation gives rise to any cash flows. If the renegotiation is undertaken with the same bankers, it is likely that no cash flows are involved. In that situation, the proper treatment would be to reclassify the relevant portion of the overdraft balance from cash to financing in the notes that analyse the changes in net debt during the year. On the other hand, if the refinancing is carried out with a different bank, such that the proceeds of the new loan are utilised to settle all or part of the old overdraft balance, a cash inflow and outflow have taken place. Consequently, the new loan would be shown in financing with the result that the net movement in the overdraft balance will automatically be reflected in the increase or decrease in cash for the period.

30.189.1 Even if the refinancing is carried out with the same bank, it is possible that cash flows have occurred. This may be the case if the old facilities have been extinguished and new facilities put in place. The factors to be considered by both FRS 4 and FRS 26 users when determining whether a refinancing is a modification/replacement of pre-existing debt or the extinguishment of an old facility and inception of a new facility are considered separately in the relevant sections of chapter 6. If the old facility has been extinguished, it would be consistent with the treatment in the balance sheet to show the repayment of this old facility as a financing outflow and the cash receipt from the new facility would be shown as an inflow.

Cash subject to restriction

30.190 The treatment of cash subject to restriction (sometimes called 'ring-fenced' cash) in the cash flow statement is not specifically covered by the standard, although disclosure is required, where access is severely restricted (see para 30.175). Nevertheless, the question arises as to how they should be dealt with in the cash flow statement itself. Consider the following example.

Example

A property company has secured development finance of £10m from its bankers during the year ended 31 December 20X5. The funds are held in a special blocked account to be used only for a specific development. Development on the property commenced during the year and by the end of its financial year the company had expended £2m. At 31 December 20X5, there was a balance of £8m in the blocked account.

The balance of £8m in the blocked account should not be included in cash, because to do so would create a distorted impression of the company's liquidity position. In that situation, the company would show the net cash outflow of £2m from operating activities, a cash inflow of £10m in financing with the balance of £8m as fixed deposits under capital expenditure and financial investment. Adequate disclosure on the restrictions should also be given in a note if funds can only be drawn down with the banker's permission.

It would not be appropriate to show the £8m balance as part of cash, as cash held in a special blocked deposit account does not meet the narrow definition of cash as set out in the standard (see para 30.41).

30.191 In general, the treatment of cash subject to restriction should depend on the nature of the item and the restriction in force. For example, client money is not generally available for business's own use and falls outside the definition of cash, even though it may be reported in the balance sheet along with the related liability. Another situation is where a company is required to give a bond or a guarantee to a third party, for example, a bond may be held by HM Revenue and Customs for the clearance of imported merchandise. In that situation, the payment to Customs would form part of operating cash flows. Where there are restrictions on the transfer of cash from a foreign subsidiary to the parent in the UK because of exchange control restrictions, the cash balances held in the foreign subsidiary would be treated as part of group cash in the cash flow statement, provided they meet the definition of cash in the foreign subsidiary that owns them. Furthermore, this restriction would need to be disclosed as stated in paragraph 30.175.

Proceeds of a rights issue by subsidiary

30.191.1 When a subsidiary company undertakes a rights issue, some of the cash flows generated will be internal to the group and, if there are minorities, some external cash flows may be generated. Only the external cash flows would be presented in the consolidated cash flow statement.

Example

A partly-owned subsidiary has made a rights issue of new equity shares *pro rata* to its parent and minority shareholders. How should the proceeds be shown in the group's cash flow statement? Does it make any difference if the new share issue is made to the minority shareholders only, assuming the subsidiary remains a subsidiary after the share issue?

In the subsidiary's own cash flow statement, the whole of the proceeds from the rights issue should be shown under the 'financing' section, which includes receipts from issuing shares. In the group's cash flow statement, the cash received from issuing shares to the parent will be eliminated on consolidation, leaving the receipt from the minority shareholders as a cash inflow to the group. Since there is no change in the group's interest in the subsidiary, this cash inflow should also be shown as financing.

In the second case, where the subsidiary issues new shares to the minority shareholders only, the receipts will again be shown as financing in the subsidiary's own cash flow statement. However, as far as the group is concerned, although the minority shareholders have injected new funds, the issue of shares outside the group gives rise to a reduction in the group's interest in the subsidiary. FRS 2, 'Accounting for subsidiary undertakings', refers to this as a deemed disposal. Deemed disposals are accounted for in consolidated financial statements in the same way as direct disposals of interests in subsidiaries. They may give rise to profits or losses on disposal in the consolidated profit and loss account.

FRS 1 encourages cash flows to be classified on a basis that is consistent with the treatment of the related items elsewhere in the financial statements. Receipts from sales of investments in subsidiaries are required to be shown under the 'acquisitions and disposals' section of the cash flow statement. It would be consistent for receipts relating to deemed disposals to be similarly classified.

Proceeds from sale and leaseback

30.192 FRS 1 has an overriding principle that each cash flow should be classified according to the substance of the transaction that gave rise to it. Where the treatment of a particular source of cash flow is not specified in the standard, the substance should prevail.

Example

How should the sale and leaseback of fixed assets be dealt with in the cash flow statement?

If the sale and leaseback results in an operating lease, the proceeds would simply be shown as receipts from the sale of fixed assets, under the cash flow statement heading 'capital expenditure and financial investment'. Thereafter, the operating lease rentals would be included in operating cash flows.

If the leaseback is a finance lease, then under FRS 5, 'Reporting the substance of transactions', the transaction is in substance analogous to raising loan finance secured on the asset, and the asset has in substance never been disposed of. The guidance notes in SSAP 21, 'Accounting for leases and hire purchase contracts', discuss the substance in these terms and suggest leaving the asset unchanged on the balance sheet, setting up a creditor for the amount received on sale, and treating the lease payments partly as principal and partly as a finance charge. Application of FRS 5's principles would also result in this treatment. From a cash flow perspective, this means that the proceeds received would be treated as a financing inflow. The future cash payments (lease payments) would be allocated between repayment of that principal and interest payments as consistent with the treatment in the balance sheet and profit and loss account.

Chapter 31

Small and medium-sized companies and groups

Page

Introduction 31001
Categorisation of small and medium-sized companies and groups 31001
  Excluded companies and groups 31001
  Small and medium-sized companies 31002
    Basic size tests 31002
    Further qualification criteria 31004
  Small and medium-sized groups 31006
    Basic size tests 31006
    Further qualification criteria 31007
Small and medium-sized company financial statements 31007
  Accounting standards 31010
    Small companies and groups 31010
    Medium-sized companies and groups 31011
    Summary 31012
  Form and content of shorter-form financial statements 31012
  The balance sheet 31013
    Formats 31013
  The profit and loss account 31015
    Formats 31015
  Notes to the financial statements 31015
    Notes to the balance sheet 31015
    Notes to the profit and loss account 31016
    Other disclosure exemptions 31017
    Additional statement required by company law and the FRSSE 31018
  Directors' report 31018
  Audit requirements 31020
    Auditors' report 31020
  Abbreviated financial statements for filing 31021
    Directors' responsibilities 31023
    Auditors' responsibilities 31023
  Full financial statements for filing 31023
Medium-sized companies 31025
  Accounting exemptions for medium-sized companies 31025
  Abbreviated financial statements 31026
    Statements to be made where advantage is taken of the exemptions 31027
  Directors' report 31027
  Auditors' reports 31027
Small and medium-sized parent companies 31028
Small and medium-sized groups 31029
  Exemptions from consolidation 31029

Abbreviated financial statements 31031
Consolidated shorter-form financial statements 31032
Agency companies 31033
Agent acting for an undisclosed principal 31033
Agent acting for a disclosed principal 31034
Transactions that need to be recorded by agency companies 31034
Disclosure in the financial statements 31035
Financial Reporting Standard for Smaller Entities 31036
Tangible fixed assets and depreciation 31037
Start-up costs and pre-contract costs 31039
Leases 31039
Investments 31040
Investment properties 31040
Government grants 31041
Intangible fixed assets 31041
Write-downs to recoverable amount 31042
Stocks and long-term contracts 31042
Consignment stock 31042
Debt factoring 31042
Provisions, contingencies and post balance sheet events 31043
Financial instruments 31043
The effect of FRS 3 31044
Revenue recognition 31045
Taxation 31045
Retirement benefits 31046
Share-based payments 31047
Foreign currencies 31047
Accounting policies and estimation techniques 31047
Related party disclosures 31049
True and fair override disclosures 31050
Annex — Decision tables 31051
Decision table 1 — Company without subsidiaries 31051
Decision table 2 — Company with subsidiaries 31052
Decision table 3 — Eligibility 31053

Chapter 31

Small and medium-sized companies and groups

Introduction

31.1 In the UK, company law defines what is meant by 'small' and 'medium-sized' companies and groups. Subject to meeting certain criteria small and medium-sized companies and groups may be able to use specific exemptions in their accounting and reporting. This chapter sets out the criteria required to meet the definition of small or medium-sized in company law, explains the exemptions permitted and discusses the accounting framework options for small companies as set out in the Financial Reporting Standard for Smaller Entities (FRSSE).

Categorisation of small and medium-sized companies and groups

Excluded companies and groups

31.2 The concessions that allow small companies to prepare shorter-form financial statements for members and small and medium-sized companies to file abbreviated financial statements exclude certain companies. These concessions are not available to any company, regardless of its size, that is, or was at any time during a financial year ending on or after 31 December 2006, any one of the following:

- A public company.
- A small company that is an authorised insurance company, a banking company, an e-money issuer, an ISD investment firm or a UCITS management company (as defined by the Financial Services and Markets Act 2000).
- A company, other than a small company, that has permission under Part 4 of the Financial Services and Markets Act 2000 to carry on a regulated activity.
- A company that carries on insurance market activity.
- A member of an ineligible group. An ineligible group is, broadly, a group in which any of its members is one of the types of companies stated in the above bullet points. In addition, an ineligible group includes a body corporate (other than a company) that is able lawfully to issue shares or debentures to the public. This includes a foreign company with the legal authority and power under its constitution to offer its shares to the public.

[CA85 Sec 247A(1) (amended by SI 2006/2782); CA06 Sec 384(1)(2), Sec 467(1)(2)].

31.3 The restrictions on the ability of certain small companies that are regulated by the Financial Services and Markets Act 2000 to take advantage of these concessions were relaxed by SI 2006/2782, 'The Companies Act 1985 (Small Companies' Accounts and Audit) Regulations 2006'. This relaxation applies only to companies preparing financial statements for years ending on or after 31 December 2006.

31.4 For years beginning on or after 1 January 2005 and ending on or after 1 October 2005, SI 2005/1011, 'The Companies Act 1985 (Operating and financial review and directors' report etc.) Regulations 2005', introduced a concession for small companies that are members of ineligible groups. They are not required to file a directors' report with Companies House. [CA85 Sec 247A(1A)]. However, they are still required to prepare a directors' report, although it need not include those items set out in paragraph 31.61.

31.5 Further information about the directors' report is contained in chapter 3 of the Manual of Accounting – Management Reports and Governance.

31.6 The Companies Act 1985 (the 1985 Act) has similar exclusions in relation to small and medium-sized groups. Consequently, a parent company cannot take advantage of the exemptions from preparing consolidated financial statements in section 248 if the group headed by it is an ineligible group. In this respect, an ineligible group is one that has among its members any of the entities mentioned in paragraph 31.2 above. [CA85 Sec 248(2)].

31.6.1 The Companies Act 2006 (the 2006 Act) has a different approach to the requirement to prepare consolidated financial statements. It allows companies subject to the small company regime to opt into preparing consolidated financial statements. It then imposes a duty on the directors of all other parent companies to prepare consolidated financial statements. [CA06 Sec 398, 399(1)(2)].

31.7 However, a company that is a subsidiary of a large *private* company and satisfies all the other qualification criteria set out in paragraph 31.2 will not be excluded from qualifying as small if all the other criteria are met.

Small and medium-sized companies

Basic size tests

31.8 A company may qualify as small or medium-sized for a financial year if it satisfies *any two* of the three conditions under the applicable heading in the following table during that year:

	Small	**Medium-sized**
■ Annual turnover not exceeding	£5,600,000	£22,800,000
■ Balance sheet total not exceeding	£2,800,000	£11,400,000
■ Average number of employees not exceeding	50	250

[CA85 Sec 247(3); CA06 Sec 382(3), 465(3)].

31.9 The basic size parameters are subject to periodic amendment and are derived from limits laid down by the EU. The latest such amendment occurred in January 2004 when SI 2004/16 doubled the annual turnover and balance sheet totals for small companies and more than doubled the turnover and balance sheet total criteria for medium-sized companies. It is important to ensure, therefore, that reference is made to the latest set of thresholds, and that advantage is taken of any transitional provisions that may apply.

31.10 In March 2007 a consultation paper was published by the DTI on proposals to increase the above thresholds. The revised limits are given in the following table. There is currently no timetable as to when such increases may be enacted, nor any indication as to what transitional rules will apply.

	Small	Medium-sized
■ *Proposed* annual turnover not exceeding	£6,500,000	£25,900,000
■ *Proposed* balance sheet total not exceeding	£3,260,000	£12,900,000
■ Average number of employees not exceeding	50	250

31.11 Where a company has not prepared its financial statements in respect of a 12 month period, the turnover thresholds must be proportionately adjusted in order to establish whether the appropriate conditions have been satisfied. [CA85 Sec 247(4); CA06 Sec 382(4), 465(4)]. For example, in the case of a company that prepares financial statements for a nine-month period, the turnover threshold will be £4,200,000 (that is, 9/12 × £5,600,000) for a small company, and £17,100,000 (that is, 9/12 × £22,800,000) for a medium-sized company. Neither the balance sheet threshold, nor the employee number threshold, is affected by shorter or longer accounting periods.

31.12 Where a company adopts the Companies Act 1985 Format 1 for its balance sheet, the 'balance sheet total' is the aggregate of the amounts shown under the headings that are preceded by the letters A to D inclusive in the formats shown in either Part 1 of Schedule 4 or Part 1 of Schedule 8. [CA85 Sec 247(5)(a)]. Where a company adopts Format 2 for its balance sheet, the 'balance sheet total' is the aggregate of the amounts shown under the general heading *Assets*. [CA85 Sec 247(5)(a)]. In either case, the effect is to equate 'balance sheet total' to gross assets.

31.12.1 The approach in the Companies Act 2006 is different. All balance sheet sizes are given in terms of the aggregate amounts shown as assets and not by reference to formats. [CA06 Sec 382(5), 465(5)]. The effect, though, is still to equate 'balance sheet total' to gross assets.

31.13 The number of employees means the average number of persons employed by the company in the year, determined on a monthly basis. The method prescribed by the relevant Act (CA85 Sec 231A(2)(3); CA06 Sec 411(3)(4)) should be adopted for the calculation; that is, adding up those defined as employed for each month and dividing the total thereby derived by the number of months in the period. [CA85 Sec 247(6); CA06 Sec 382(6), 465(6)].

Further qualification criteria

31.14 The application of the criteria for small and medium-sized companies can prove complex, because, in addition to satisfying the basic size tests referred to above, companies must also satisfy other qualification criteria that may be more difficult to interpret.

31.15 The Act sets out the following additional criteria that must be applied in determining whether a company qualifies as small or medium-sized in relation to a financial year, for the purposes of filing abbreviated financial statements (small and medium-sized companies) or preparing shorter-form financial statements (small companies only):

- In respect of a company's first financial year, it will qualify as small or medium-sized, provided that it satisfies the appropriate size conditions under section 247(3) of the 1985 Act or section 382(3) of the 2006 Act in that year. [CA85 Sec 247(1)(a); CA06 382(1), 465(1)].
- In subsequent years, a company will qualify as small or medium-sized, provided that it satisfies the appropriate size conditions under section 247(3) of the 1985 Act or section 382(3) of the 2006 Act in both the year in question and the preceding year. [CA85 Sec 247(1)(b); CA06 382(2), 465(2)].
- A company that qualifies as small or medium-sized under section 247(3) of the 1985 Act or section 382(3) of the 2006 Act in one year will be treated as qualifying in the following year, even if it fails to satisfy the size conditions in that following year. However, if it does not satisfy the qualifying conditions in the year after that, then, for that third year, it must produce its financial statements in a format appropriate to its size. On the other hand, if the company reverts to satisfying the qualifying conditions in this third year, then it may continue to take advantage of available accounting exemptions. This test is required in every situation and not just in the initial years of incorporation as explained above. The aim of this legislation is to permit an occasional variation in the company's trading without requiring the company to be classified as a different sized entity. Therefore, a company will be required to trade at the same level for two consecutive years before any change in size classification is required. [CA85 Sec 247(2)(a)(b); CA06 382(2), 465(2)]

31.16 The application of these qualification criteria is best illustrated by way of an example:

Example

Consider the following details relating to two companies, S and M. While company S is incorporated on the first day of year 2, company M is a long-established entity that fulfilled the size conditions of a medium-sized company in the year immediately before year 1.

Company S	**Small criteria memo**	**Year 1**	**Year 2**	**Year 3**	**Year 4**
Turnover	£5.6m	—	£5.2m	£6.0m	£5.2m
Gross assets	£2.8m	—	£2.6m	£3.0m	£2.4m
Average number of employees	50	—	55	60	55

In year 2, its year of incorporation, company S fulfils the size criteria for qualification as a small company. This is because it fulfils the criteria both for turnover and gross assets, although not for average number of employees. As year 2 is its first financial year, company S qualifies as a small company by virtue of section 247(1)(a) of the 1985 Act or section 382(1) of the 2006 Act. As such, it can file abbreviated financial statements and prepare shorter-form financial statements for its members.

In year 3, company S has exceeded all three size criteria for small company qualification. However, by virtue of section 247(2)(a) of the 1985 Act or section 382(2) of the 2006 Act, it still qualifies as a small company, because it fulfilled the size conditions in the preceding year, which was its first financial year. It can, therefore, file abbreviated financial statements and prepare shorter-form financial statements for this year.

In year 4, company S satisfies the size criteria for qualification as a small company. Despite the fact that it did not satisfy the size conditions in year 3, it still qualifies as a small company by virtue of section 247(2)(b) of the 1985 Act or section 382(2) of the 2006 Act, because it was treated as so qualifying in year 3 and currently meets the qualifying criteria. It can, similarly, file abbreviated financial statements and prepare shorter-form financial statements for this year.

Company M	**Medium criteria memo**	**Year 1**	**Year 2**	**Year 3**	**Year 4**
Turnover	£22.8m	£20.4m	£23.2m	£24.6m	£22.0m
Gross assets	£11.4m	£10.8m	£11.0m	£12.0m	£10.0m
Average number of employees	250	250	255	255	250

In year 1, company M fulfils all the size criteria that qualify it to be treated as a medium-sized company. Since it has fulfilled the size-conditions its first year, it can take advantage of the exemptions allowed to it to file abbreviated financial statements. As a medium-sized company it cannot prepare shorter-form financial statements as these are only available to small companies.

In year 2, company M ceases to fulfil the size conditions for a medium-sized company because both its turnover and its average number of employees exceed the specified thresholds. However, it still qualifies as a medium-sized company for abbreviated financial statements purposes by virtue of section 247(2)(a) of the 1985 Act or section 465(2) of the 2006 Act, in that it fulfilled the size criteria for qualification in the previous year.

In year 3, company M fails to meet the size criteria for a medium-sized company for a second consecutive year. Consequently, it no longer qualifies as a medium-sized company and cannot, therefore, file abbreviated financial statements for year 3.

In year 4, company M reverts to fulfilling the size conditions of a medium-sized company. However, it does not qualify as a medium-sized company for abbreviated financial statements purposes, because it has not fulfilled the size criteria for qualification for two consecutive years. Should it meet these criteria in year 5, it would then be able to revert to filing abbreviated financial statements.

31.17 For parent companies, there is a further condition that they must satisfy before filing abbreviated financial statements. A parent company should not be treated as qualifying as a small or medium-sized company in relation to a financial year, unless the group headed by it qualifies also as a small or medium-sized group. [CA85 Sec 247A(3); CA06 Sec 383(1), 466(1)]. Consequently, if the parent is a small company, it can only file abbreviated financial statements applicable to small companies if it is also the parent of a 'small group'. If it were the parent of a 'medium-sized group', it could only file abbreviated financial statements applicable to a medium-sized company. Similarly a medium-sized parent can only file abbreviated financial statements if it is the parent of a 'medium-sized group'. These rules are explained further from paragraph 31.101.

Small and medium-sized groups

Basic size tests

31.18 A group may qualify as small or medium-sized for a financial year (and, therefore, be exempted from the requirement to prepare consolidated financial statements) if it satisfies *any two* of the three conditions under the applicable heading in the following table during that year:

	Small	Medium-sized
■ Aggregate net turnover not exceeding	£5,600,000	£22,800,000
or		
Aggregate gross turnover not exceeding	£6,720,000	£27,360,000
■ Aggregate net balance sheet total not exceeding	£2,800,000	£11,400,000
or		
Aggregate gross balance sheet total not exceeding	£3,360,000	£13,680,000
■ Average number of employees not exceeding	50	250
[CA85 Sec 249(3); CA06 Sec 383(4), 466(4)].		

31.19 For groups, the figures for turnover, balance sheet total and average number of employees are arrived at by adding together the relevant figures for each group company. The net figures refer to the relevant amounts after making consolidation adjustments for set-offs and other matters. As an alternative the gross figures can be applied to the relevant amounts before making such adjustments. [CA85 Sec 249(4); CA06 Sec 383(5)(6), 466(5)(6)]. A company may satisfy the qualifying criteria on the basis of gross or net figures and in any year it is permissible to mix the use of gross and net figures. Rather than having to eliminate group transactions, the gross size criteria should be checked first, and the net size criteria checked only if required.

31.20 If the financial year of a subsidiary company is not coterminous with that of the parent company, then the subsidiary's latest financial statements, for a year which immediately predates the financial year of the parent, should be used. [CA85 Sec 249(5)(b); CA06 Sec 383(7), 466(7)]. However, if the subsidiary's figures cannot be ascertained without disproportionate expense or undue delay, the latest available figures should be used. [CA85 Sec 249(6); CA06 Sec 383(7), 466(7)].

Further qualification criteria

31.21 The other qualification criteria outlined in paragraph 31.15 of this chapter relating to small and medium-sized companies, are mirrored by similar criteria affecting small and medium-sized groups. [CA85 Sec 249(1)(2); CA06 Sec 383(2)(3), 466(2)(3)]. Thus, both Acts state that a group qualifies as small or medium-sized in relation to a financial year, where:

- The size test conditions set out in section 249(3) of the 1985 Act or section 383(4) (small companies) or section 466(4) (medium-sized companies) of the 2006 Act are met and it is the parent company's first financial year. [CA85 Sec 249(1)(a); CA06 Sec 383(2), 466(2)].
- In any subsequent financial year the size test conditions are met and were met in the year immediately preceding. [CA85 Sec 249(1)(b); CA06 Sec 383(3), 466(3)].
- The size test conditions were met in the preceding year, but are not met in the current year. [CA85 Sec 249(2)(a); CA06 Sec 383(3), 466(3)].
- The size test conditions are met in the current year but were not met in the previous year, yet the group still qualified on that occasion. [CA85 Sec 249(2)(b); CA06 Sec 383(3), 466(3)].

31.22 The application of the qualification criteria is complicated and is illustrated in the example in paragraph 31.16. Furthermore, if a group qualifies as small or medium-sized on, say, a net basis in a particular year, it is not required to apply the same basis in the following year. In each year, it may apply the net basis, the gross basis or a mixture of the two (see para 31.18).

[The next paragraph is 31.24.]

Small and medium-sized company financial statements

31.24 It was the 1981 Act that first distinguished 'small and medium-sized companies' from the body of companies as a whole, in terms of the form and content of their statutory financial statements. As set out from paragraph 31.8 onwards these criteria evaluate companies by reference to annual turnover levels, the amount of the company's assets and the size of its workforce.

31.24.1 The Companies Act 2006 has made some changes, which are mentioned within this chapter, where relevant. At the time of writing, the schedules that will replace Schedules 4 to 8 of the Companies Act 1985 have not been published in final form. Where references appear to these schedules of the 1985 Act, there are no corresponding references given to the 2006 Act.

31.25 Other changes to company law have resulted in:

- Revised thresholds regarding the annual turnover and balance sheet total for small and medium-sized companies and groups, while the employee numbers criterion remained unchanged.
- *'Special accounting exemptions'* allowing companies qualifying as *small* to prepare financial statements for members in a less extensive format than that required for other reporting entities. These exemptions also enable qualifying companies to omit certain of the disclosures required in full financial statements from the directors' report. For small companies these exemptions are set out in Schedule 8A regarding the financial statements for members and in Schedule 8A regarding abbreviated financial statements for filing at Companies House. The exemptions available to medium-sized companies are set out in section 246A. The equivalent exemptions are expected to be included in regulations not finalised at the time of writing.
- Exemptions from certain disclosures in the directors' report. Also the directors' statements and the rules governing audit reports have been simplified.

31.26 A small company has the following options in preparing and filing its statutory financial statements.

- It may prepare and file full financial statements without taking any concessions, following full accounting standards and the Act's reporting rules and Schedule 4 formats discussed in the main body of this Manual.
- It may prepare its annual financial statements in accordance with the FRSSE and the special provisions available to small companies under Schedule 8, or add additional Schedule 4 requirements to the Schedule 8 minimum, and file them.
- It may prepare either of the above financial statements for members, but file abbreviated financial statements prepared in accordance with Schedule 8A.
- There are further concessions regarding disclosures in the directors' report, which may be taken independently of the above points. These are discussed at 31.60 and 31.95 below.

31.27 Note that the financial statements prepared under Schedule 8 are those that a company prepares for its members. If the company also prepares abbreviated financial statements under Schedule 8A this does not remove the requirement for the company to prepare financial statements for its members. Therefore, if a small company wishes to file abbreviated financial statements, then it must prepare financial statements under the first and third bullet points above, or the second and third bullet points. In summary, where a small company delivers abbreviated financial statements to the Registrar of Companies, it must still prepare full financial statements (Schedule 4) or shorter-form financial statements (Schedule 8) for its members.

31.28 Financial statements prepared under the provisions of Schedule 8 refer to the individual or group financial statements that small companies are permitted to prepare for members by virtue of section 246(2)-(4) of the 1985 Act or the small company regime of the 2006 Act. In this chapter, such financial statements are referred to as 'shorter-form financial statements' (Schedule 8). However, it should be noted that this term is not used in company law, but is used in this chapter purely for convenience, to avoid confusion with the term 'abbreviated financial statements'.

31.28.1 There is a fundamental difference between the 1985 and 2006 Acts in the way that they give relief from accounting rules and disclosures of small companies. The 1985 Act started from the premise that all companies would prepare full financial statements and a complex web of exemptions evolved that gave some relief from the rules. As a result, many of the sections dealing with small companies in the 1985 Act have become difficult to understand. The 2006 Act creates a 'small company regime' to which all eligible companies will belong, unless they choose to opt out of it. At the time of writing, there are still gaps in the Regulations that will govern how the regime will work. Where there are no details, or the details are incomplete, the following paragraphs are silent.

31.29 'Abbreviated financial statements' means the individual financial statements that small and medium-sized companies are permitted to file by virtue of sections 246(5) or (6) or 246A(3) of the 1985 Act. For small companies the provisions required by 1985 Act are set out in Schedule 8A.

31.30 There are major differences between the form and content of shorter-form financial statements (Schedule 8) and abbreviated financial statements (Schedule 8A). Shorter-form financial statements (Schedule 8) are prepared for members and are required to give a true and fair view. In contrast, abbreviated financial statements (Schedule 8A) do not purport to give a true and fair view and on commercial or confidentiality grounds they exclude financial information that is integral to the true and fair view. Hence, the disclosure exemptions available in Schedule 8 are much less extensive than those available in respect of abbreviated financial statements in Schedule 8A.

31.31 For shorter-form financial statements, the concessions from the detailed disclosure requirements of Schedule 4 concerning the items to be disclosed in the formats and in the notes appear extensive. However, small companies may not have many of the items allowed to be aggregated under the rules and, hence, the concessions have less impact in practice. For example, under the heading of intangible assets, development costs, concessions and patents and payments on account are allowed to be aggregated under the single item 'other intangible assets'. Many small companies will not have such assets and, as a consequence, this concession has little impact.

Accounting standards

Small companies and groups

31.32 The ASB issued a Financial Reporting Standard for Smaller Entities (FRSSE) in November 1997, which has been revised regularly in the intervening years. The FRSSE contains relevant sections of the Companies Act in order to provide small companies with a 'one-stop-shop' standard incorporating accounting standards and legal requirements. The most recent version relates to accounting periods beginning on or after 1 January 2007, FRSSE (2007). It is designed to provide small companies with a single reporting standard that is focussed on their particular circumstances. The FRSSE is not compulsory, but where a small company chooses to adopt the FRSSE, the financial statements should state that they have been prepared in accordance with it. [FRSSE para 2.6]. This additional statement may be combined with the note of accounting policies, or for those companies taking advantage of the exemptions for small companies in company legislation, it may be included in the statement required by company legislation to be given on the balance sheet. An example of such a combined statement giving the disclosure required by the Act and the FRSSE is set out in paragraph 31.59. A company adopting the FRSSE is exempt from other accounting standards and UITF Abstracts, unless preparing consolidated financial statements, in which case certain other accounting standards apply, as set out in paragraph 31.109 below. Should a small company not adopt the FRSSE it will still be exempt from certain accounting standards and UITF Abstracts, such as FRS 1, 'Cash flow statements', (see chapter 30) and those standards listed in paragraph 31.37. A summary of the accounting requirements of the FRSSE is set out from 31.127 onwards.

31.33 The FRSSE imports disclosure rules from existing standards that are considered to be relevant to small companies. Section C of the FRSSE contains definitions of terms that apply to the accounting practices set out in the FRSSE. These terms have been imported from existing accounting standards suitably modified in certain cases.

31.34 Previously the FRSSE, in table format, contained an analysis of each paragraph of the FRSSE and explains the source and whether that source has been adopted in its entirety, or with minor amendments, or with major changes. In the current version this derivation table has been excluded. However, the derivation table is freely available from the ASB web site (see derivation tables at www.frc.org.uk/asb/technical/frsse.cfm).

31.35 There may be circumstances where a small company enters into transactions on which accounting guidance is not provided in the FRSSE. It may be that guidance on such transactions is provided in the accounting standards applying to larger entities. In that situation, where a practice that has been clearly established and accepted, unless there are good reasons, a small company would normally follow it. Indeed, the FRSSE takes the view that for transactions and events not dealt with in the FRSSE, small companies should have regard to other accounting standards and UITF Abstracts, not as mandatory documents, but as a means of establishing current practice. [FRSSE App IV para 33]. In that situation, adequate disclosure should be made in the notes to the financial statements of the transaction or arrangement concerned and the treatment adopted. This requirement is implicit in paragraph 2.5 of the FRSSE. It follows that for transactions and events not dealt with in the FRSSE, but dealt with in other accounting standards and UITF Abstracts, a small company should have regard not only to the measurement rules, but also to any disclosure requirements relevant to those transactions.

31.36 The FRSSE is revised and updated periodically to reflect developments in financial reporting. The ASB has established a Committee on Accounting for Smaller Entities that recommends to the ASB how new standards or revisions to existing standards apply to smaller entities. The Committee is also responsible for reviewing the operation of the FRSSE. Any proposed changes to the FRSSE are subject to public consultation. Revisions of the FRSSE are formally approved and issued by the ASB.

Medium-sized companies and groups

31.37 There are no special accounting standards for medium-sized companies and groups. Therefore, all accounting standards and UITF Abstracts apply to them except for the following:

- SSAP 13, 'Accounting for research and development', excludes from profit and loss account disclosures private companies less than ten times the financial criteria defining a medium-sized company (see chapter 15).
- SSAP 25, 'Segmental reporting', excludes private companies as in SSAP 13 above from some of the more detailed segmental disclosures (see chapter 10).
- FRS 2, 'Accounting for subsidiary undertakings', mirrors the Act in allowing parents of small and medium-sized groups an exemption from preparing consolidated financial statements in most circumstances. Indeed, because of this exemption, such groups are also effectively exempt from complying with FRS 6, FRS 7 and FRS 10. (see chapter 24). Note, though, that the Companies Act 2006 removes this exemption from medium-sized companies.
- FRS 13, 'Derivatives and other financial instruments: Disclosures', is applicable primarily to listed companies and banks (see chapter 6).
- FRS 22, 'Earnings per share', is applicable to listed companies only (see chapter 14).

- FRS 23, 'The effects of changes in foreign exchange rates', FRS 26, 'Financial instruments: Measurement' and the disclosure requirements of FRS 25, 'Financial instruments: Disclosure and presentation', and FRS 29, 'Financial instruments: Disclosures', all of which are mandatory primarily for listed companies and banks.

31.38 As can be seen from the above, while the exemptions in FRS 2 apply to small and medium-sized companies as defined in the Act, the exemptions allowed in SSAP 13 and SSAP 25 are based on size criteria, which serve to exempt far larger companies from compliance.

Summary

31.39 The options that are available to small and medium-sized companies in company law for the preparation and audit of financial statements for filing and for members are complex and are summarised in the annex to this chapter.

Form and content of shorter-form financial statements

31.40 The general provisions that relate to the form and content of small company financial statements are detailed in Schedule 8 to the Act. These provisions are supplemented by specific requirements of the FRSSE that provide a link with the Schedule 8 provisions. In preparing financial statements, a small company is permitted to comply with the provisions of Schedule 8, or it may comply instead with one or more of the corresponding provisions of Schedule 4. Any reference in section 226A in the 1985 Act or section 396 of the 2006 Act (Companies Act individual accounts) to compliance with the provisions of Schedule 4 is then construed accordingly. [CA85 Sec 246(2)].

31.41 Section 246(3) gives further exemptions from the disclosure requirements of other schedules to the Act while section 246(4) gives exemptions from certain of the disclosures generally required for the directors' report. These exemptions are explained in paragraphs 31.61 and 31.95 respectively.

31.42 Three primary statements included within a small company's financial statements are:

- Profit and loss account.
- Statement of total recognised gains and losses.
- Balance sheet.

31.43 Schedule 8 sets out two alternative formats for the balance sheet, which are a simplification of those set out in Schedule 4 and four alternative formats for the profit and loss account, which are identical to those set out in Schedule 4. It also lays down certain general guidelines to be followed. In addition, the Schedule requires small companies to give in the notes to the balance sheet and in the notes to the profit and loss account many of the disclosures that apply to the generality of companies.

31.44 The Act does not require companies to include in their financial statements a statement of total recognised gains and losses. This primary statement is required by the FRSSE for all small companies' financial statements that are intended to give a true and fair view. However, where the only recognised gains and losses are the results included in the profit and loss account no separate statement to this effect is required. [FRSSE para 5.1].

31.45 There is no requirement in the Act for companies to prepare a cash flow statement. The FRSSE, like FRS 1, encourages, but does not require, small entities to prepare a cash flow statement. Section D of the FRSSE sets out the voluntary disclosures relating to cash flow information.

The balance sheet

Formats

31.46 The balance sheet formats set out in Schedule 8 are simplifications of those set out in Schedule 4. The table below considers Format 1 of the balance sheet and indicates how the Schedule 8 formats take those in Schedule 4 and combine certain of the headings preceded by Arabic numerals. Format 2 allows identical combination of headings.

Items in italic in column 1 are combined under the item in italic shown opposite in column 2. The items with Roman numerals remain unchanged.

	Schedule 4, Format 1		**Schedule 8, Format 1**
A	Called up share capital not paid	A	Called up share capital not paid
B	Fixed assets	B	Fixed assets
B I	Intangible assets	B I	Intangible assets
	3. Goodwill		1. Goodwill
	1. Development costs		*2. Other intangible assets*
	2. Concessions...		
	4. Payments on account		
B II	Tangible assets	B II	Tangible assets
	1. Land and buildings		1. Land and buildings
	2. Plant and machinery		*2. Plant and machinery, etc*
	3. Fixtures, fittings...		
	4. Payments on account...		
B III	Investments	B III	Investments
	1. Shares in group undertakings		*1. Shares in group undertakings and participating interests*
	3. Participating interests		
	2. Loans to group undertakings		*2. Loans to group undertakings and undertakings in which the company has a participating interest*
	4. Loans to undertakings, etc		
	5. Other investments other than loans		3. Other investments other than loans
	6. Other loans		*4. Other investments*
	7. Own shares		
C	Current assets	C	Current assets
C I	Stocks	C I	Stocks
	1. Raw materials, etc.		*1. Stocks*

	2. Work in progress		
	3. Finished goods/goods for resale		
	4. Payments on account		2. Payments on account
C II	Debtors	C II	Debtors
	1. Trade debtors		1. Trade debtors
	2. Amounts owed by group undertakings		*2. Amounts owed by group undertakings and undertakings in which the company has a participating interest*
	3. Amounts owed by undertakings in which the company has a participating interest		
	4. Other debtors		*3. Other debtors*
	5. Called up share capital not paid		
	6. Prepayments and accrued income		
C III	Investments	C III	Investments
	1. Shares in group undertakings		1. Shares in group undertakings
	2. Own shares		*2. Other investments*
	3. Other investments		
C IV	Cash at bank and in hand	C IV	Cash at bank and in hand
D	Prepayments and accrued income	D	Prepayments and accrued income
E	Creditors: amounts. . .within one year	E	Creditors: amounts. . .within one year
	2. Bank loans and overdrafts		1. Bank loans and overdrafts
	4. Trade creditors		2. Trade creditors
	6. Amounts owed to group undertakings		*3. Amounts owed to group undertakings and undertakings in which the company has a participating interest*
	7.Amounts owed to undertakings in which the company has a participating interest		
	1. Debenture loans		*4. Other creditors*
	3. Payments received on account		
	5. Bills of exchange payable		
	8. Other creditors including taxation and social security		
	9. Accruals and deferred income		
F	Net current assets (liabilities)	F	Net current assets (liabilities)
G	Total assets less current liabilities	G	Total assets less current liabilities
H	Creditors amounts. . .after one year	H	Creditors: amounts. . .after one year
	2. Bank loans and overdrafts		1. Bank loans and overdrafts
	4. Trade creditors		2. Trade creditors
	6. Amounts owed to group undertakings		*3. Amounts owed to group undertakings and undertakings in which the company has a participating interest*
	7. Amounts owed to undertakings in which the company has a participating interest		
	1. Debenture loans		*4. Other creditors*
	3. Payments received on account		
	5. Bills of exchange payable		
	8. Other creditors including taxation and social security		
	9. Accruals and deferred income		
I	Provision for liabilities	I	Provisions for liabilities
	1. Pensions and similar obligations		*(Items 1-3 need not be shown)*
	2. Taxation, etc		
	3. Other provisions		
J	Accruals and deferred income	J	Accruals and deferred income
K	Capital and reserves	K	Capital and reserves
KI	Called up share capital	KI	Called up share capital
KII	Share premium account	KII	Share premium account
KIII	Revaluation reserve	KIII	Revaluation reserve
KIV	Other reserves	KIV	Other reserves

	1. Capital redemption reserve		*(Items 1-4 need not be shown)*
	2. Reserve for own shares		
	3. Reserves provided for by articles		
	4. Other reserves		
KV	Profit and loss account	KV	Profit and loss account

31.47 The following additional exemptions are available:

- In the case of both Formats 1 and 2, a small company need not show amounts falling due after more than one year separately for each item included under debtors if it discloses the aggregate amount of debtors falling due after more than one year in the notes. [CA85 8 Sch 8(5)]. However, following UITF Abstract 4, in some instances where the amount of long-term debtors is so material the split might need to be given on the face of the balance sheet.
- In the case of Format 2, a small company need not show separately the amounts falling due within one year and after one year for each of the items included under creditors if it discloses the aggregate amount of creditors falling due within one year and the aggregate amount falling due after more than one year in the notes. [CA85 8 Sch 8(10)].
- Although the balance sheet formats do not include a separate line for creditors in respect of taxation and social security, this amount should be shown separately. [CA85 8 Sch 8(7)].

The profit and loss account

Formats

31.48 The Act permits small companies to use any one of the four alternative formats of the profit and loss account set out in Schedule 8 and it leaves the choice between these formats to the company's directors. In addition, the Act attaches to the formats certain notes and comments on specific profit and loss account items. Since the formats and the related notes set out in Schedule 8 are the same as those set out in Schedule 4, the discussions in chapter 4 relating to formats are relevant.

Notes to the financial statements

Notes to the balance sheet

31.49 Schedule 8 to the Act requires small companies to disclose information which either supplements the information given with respect to any particular item shown in the balance sheet and the profit and loss account or is otherwise relevant to assessing the company's state of affairs in the light of the information so given. In order to provide a link between this chapter and the other chapters of this manual that deal with all the disclosure requirements of Schedules 4, 5 and 6 of the Act, the paragraphs that follow specify the relevant paragraphs of the three schedules with which a small company need not comply and hence which are not included in Schedule 8.

31.50 A small company need *not* give any of the information supplementing the balance sheet required by the following paragraphs of Schedule 4:

- Paragraph 40 — particulars of any contingent right to the allotment of shares in the company.
- Paragraph 41 — information regarding issues of debentures.
- Paragraph 44 — details of the company's freehold and leasehold properties.
- Paragraph 45B — the fair value of derivatives not included in the balance sheet at fair value.
- Paragraph 47 — separate disclosure of the amount of any provision for deferred taxation (however, paras 9.10 and 9.11 of the FRSSE require this disclosure).
- Paragraph 48(2) — the terms of repayment and interest rates for debts.
- Paragraph 48(4)(b) — the nature of securities given for debts.
- Paragraph 51(2) — the aggregate amount of loans provided by way of permitted financial assistance for the purchase of own shares, such as under an employees' share scheme.

31.51 Further exemptions and modifications that are permitted in respect of balance sheet information are as follows:

- Where the carrying value of stocks and fungible assets included in the financial statements is calculated by a permitted approximation methodology, such as FIFO, and that value differs materially from their relevant alternative amount, in effect replacement cost, the amount of the difference need not be disclosed.
- Disclosure of debts repayable in more than five years need not be made for each item included in 'creditors', if the required information is given in aggregate for all items.

Notes to the profit and loss account

31.52 A qualifying small company also receives disclosure exemptions in respect of certain supplementary information to the profit and loss account normally required by Schedule 4 to the Act. Accordingly, it need *not* make separate disclosure of:

- Paragraph 53(2) — details of interest payable or similar charges.
- Paragraph 54 — particulars of tax, including details of corporation and income tax charges, and special circumstances affecting the tax charge

(however, paragraph 9.2 of the FRSSE requires disclosure of the material components of the current and deferred tax charge).

- Paragraph 55 — segmental particulars of turnover. If, however, the company has supplied geographical markets outside the UK, the notes must state the percentage of turnover attributable to those markets. In giving this information, the directors must consider the manner in which the company's activities are organised.
- Section 231A – disclosure required in notes to annual accounts: particulars of staff.

Other disclosure exemptions

31.53 Section 246(3) gives further exemptions from the disclosure requirements of other schedules to the Act. In particular, the following information from Schedule 6 regarding directors' emoluments need *not* be given:

- Paragraph 1(2)(b) — The numbers of directors exercising share options and receiving shares under long-term incentive schemes.
- Paragraph 2 — Details of the highest paid director's emoluments.
- Paragraph 7 — Details of directors' and past directors' excess retirement benefits.

[CA85 Sec 246(3)(b)].

31.54 In summary, therefore, the information which *must still be given* in respect of directors' emoluments is as follows:

- The aggregate amount of directors' emoluments, amounts receivable under long-term incentive schemes and contributions paid or treated as paid to a money purchase pension scheme. A small company may disclose a single figure, being the aggregate of these three items, rather than disclose the items separately. [CA85 Sec 246(3)(a)].
- Number of directors to whom retirement benefits are accruing under each of money purchase and defined benefit schemes respectively.
- Aggregate compensation to directors for loss of office.
- Sums paid to third parties for making available the services of directors.

31.55 Small companies are also entitled to omit the information required by paragraph 4 of Schedule 5 concerning financial years of subsidiary undertakings. [CA85 Sec 246(3)(b)(i)].

31.56 There is no exemption from disclosure in the notes in respect of audit fee disclosures required by Regulation 3 of Statutory Instrument 2005/2417, 'The Companies (Disclosure of Auditor Remuneration) Regulations 2005'. However, qualifying small and medium-sized companies are not required to disclose the amounts paid to auditors for non-audit services. Abbreviated financial statements filed with the Registrar may, on the other hand, omit disclosure of both audit and non-audit fees.

Additional statement required by company law and the FRSSE

31.57 Where the directors of a small company prepare shorter-form financial statements, those financial statements must contain a statement in a prominent position on the balance sheet, above the signature required by section 233 of the Act, that they are prepared in accordance with the special provisions of Part VII of the Act relating to small companies. [CA85 Sec 246(8)(a); CA06 Sec 414(3), 419(2), 444(5), 450(3)].

31.58 There is also a similar requirement in the FRSSE for a statement that the financial statements have been prepared in accordance with the FRSSE. [FRSSE para 2.6].

31.59 A suitable wording that combines both the above statements is included by way of a foot note to paragraph 2.6 of the FRSSE. A similar example is given below.

Example

The financial statements have been prepared in accordance with [the special provisions relating to small companies within Part VII of the Companies Act 1985/the small companies regime of the Companies Act 2006] and with the Financial Reporting Standard for Smaller Entities (effective January 2007).

Directors' report

31.60 Where a small company prepares either full accounts in accordance with Schedule 4 or shorter-form financial statements for members in accordance with Schedule 8, it is also allowed to omit certain disclosures required in full financial statements from its directors' report. Even if a small company is a member of an ineligible group it is still able to take the following exemptions in relation to the directors' report and in addition they are not required to file the directors' report (para 31.4). As with the balance sheet and profit and loss account exemptions, these exemptions are not compulsory, so the company may give fuller disclosure requires if it so wishes.

31.61 Where advantage is taken of these exemptions, the directors' report need *not* disclose any of the information that is required by the following provisions:

- A fair review of the development of the business of the company and a description of the principal risks and uncertainties facing it. [CA85 Sec 234ZZB; CA06 Sec 417].
- The dividends recommended by the directors. [CA85 Sec 234ZZA(1)(c); CA06 Sec 416(3)].

- Disclosures relating to the use of financial instruments. [CA85 7 Sch 5A].
- Particulars of important events that have occurred between the end of the financial year and the date of approval of the financial statements. [CA85 7 Sch 6(i)(a)].
- An indication of likely future developments in the business. [CA85 7 Sch 6(i)(b)].
- An indication of the activities, if any, in the field of research and development. [CA85 7 Sch 6(i)(c)].
- An indication of the existence of branches, as defined in section 698(2), of the company outside the UK. [CA85 7 Sch 6(d)].
- Any information in respect of employee involvement in the company where the average weekly number of employees during the year exceeded 250. [CA85 7 Sch 11].

[CA85 Sec 246(4)].

31.62 The usefulness of the above exemptions will depend on the specific circumstances of the company concerned. Thus, a company that has little trading activity, no dividend payments, and only a few employees, will benefit little from these exemptions. Indeed, many of the concessions given relate to disclosures that a small company might not have to comply with anyway, because its trading activities and business will be far simpler than that of larger companies. This contrasts with the situation of abbreviated financial statements, which are much shorter than either full financial statements or shorter-form financial statements and are, therefore, filed by many small companies to maintain business confidentiality.

31.63 Where the directors also take advantage any of the exemptions in respect of the preparation of the directors' report, they must make a statement in a prominent position above the signature on the directors' report that the report has been prepared in accordance either with the special provisions of Part VII of the Act relating to small companies (1985 Act) or with the small companies regime (2006 Act). [CA85 Sec 246(8)(b); CA06 Sec 414(3), 419(2), 444(5), 450(3)].

31.64 Suitable wording for such a statement is as follows:

Example

This report has been prepared in accordance with the [special provisions of Part VII of the Companies Act 1985 relating to small companies/small companies regime of the Companies Act 2006].

Audit requirements

31.65 As a further complication, some (but not all) small companies and groups are exempt from the requirement for any external audit. This exemption is dealt with in chapter 8 of the Manual of Accounting – Management Reports and Governance. The following paragraphs discuss the requirements in the auditors' report when an audit is carried out on small and medium-sized companies.

Auditors' report

31.66 In general, shorter-form financial statements (Schedule 8) prepared in accordance with section 246 are capable of giving a true and fair view. However, there may be instances where the use of the exemptions means that the financial statements do not give a true and fair view. For example, a particular item may be of such significance that the auditors consider that it should be disclosed separately, but instead it is combined with other items using the available exemptions.

31.67 Where the shorter-form financial statements of a small company fail to give a true and fair view for any reason, including the use of the exemptions, the auditors will need to qualify their opinion in the same way as for a larger company.

31.68 The question also arises as to whether permitted non-compliance by small companies with the provisions of certain accounting standards affects the true and fair view. The following general guidance can be given:

- Where a matter of disclosure required by an accounting standard is specifically referred to in company law, and the law also allows exemption from that disclosure, it need not be given when preparing shorter-form financial statements for members.
- Where an accounting standard requires sub-analysis of an item which is exempted from disclosure under the law, that sub-analysis need not be given when preparing shorter-form financial statements for members.

31.69 Except for the above categories of item, all other disclosures required by accounting standards should be included when preparing shorter-form financial statements for the members of small companies.

31.70 As discussed in chapter 3 of the Manual of Accounting – Management Reports and Governance, the directors are not required to comment on the re-appointment of the auditor, but it is customary to do so. If, when preparing the current year's audited financial statements, the directors become aware that the company will be eligible for audit exemption in the following year, the directors may wish to make an appropriate comment in the directors' report. Such a situation may arise when a company reduces in size and qualifies as a small company for the first time. In such a case suitable wording for such a statement may be:

> *"The directors do not propose to appoint an auditor at the AGM as the company will be eligible for audit exemption as permitted by [section*

249A(1) of the Companies Act 1985/ section 477(1) of the Companies Act 2006] in the following year."

31.71 However, note that audit exemption will not be available if members holding more than ten per cent of the company's nominal share capital deposit a notice at the registered office of the company demanding an audit.

31.72 Conversely, where a company had previously been exempt from audit but now finds it no longer satisfies the audit exemption thresholds, the in-coming auditor will be required to consider the reliability of the opening balances and may need to refer to this in the auditors' report. If the auditor is satisfied with the opening balances and the disclosure that the corresponding figures are unaudited, a suitable disclosure in the auditors' report may be:

> *"The financial statements of the company for the [year/period] ended XX/XX/20X6, forming the corresponding figures in the financial statements for the period ended XX/XX/20X7, are unaudited."*

In addition, some explanation should be included as to why the prior years figures were unaudited (presumably because they were previously entitled to an audit exemption), in which case, the paragraph above could start with "*As explained in [note xx/the directors' report]…..*".

Abbreviated financial statements for filing

31.73 Abbreviated financial statements (Schedule 8A) for small companies contain much less extensive financial information than shorter-form financial statements (Schedule 8). (For a medium-sized company's abbreviated financial statements see para 31.89.) A *small* company may file abbreviated financial statements with the Registrar of Companies taking advantage of the following exemptions:

- It is not required to file a profit and loss account.
- It is not required to file a directors' report.
- It is permitted to file either an abbreviated (Schedule 8A) or a shorter-form balance sheet (Schedule 8) and notes thereto. (See para 31.77.)

[CA85 Sec 246(5); CA06 Sec 444(1)(3)].

31.74 It is also permitted to omit certain other information normally required to be given in the notes to financial statements, including any information relating to emoluments, pensions and compensation for loss of office paid or payable to the directors (see further para 31.78). [CA85 Sec 246(6)].

31.75 The formats for an abbreviated balance sheet are set out in Schedule 8A. They adopt a similar layout to those in Schedule 4 (both Format 1 and Format 2), but disclose only those items preceded by either a letter or a Roman numeral. However, the aggregate amount of debtors and creditors falling due after more than one year must be shown separately from those falling due within one year, unless this information is given in the notes. [CA85 8A Sch 2].

31.76 A Format 1 balance sheet from Schedule 8A is shown in the table below.

Balance sheet – Format 1	
A	Called up share capital not paid
B	Fixed assets
	I Intangible assets
	II Tangible assets
	III Investments
C	Current assets
	I Stocks
	II Debtors
	III Investments
	IV Cash at bank and in hand
D	Prepayments and accrued income
E	Creditors: amounts falling due within one year
F	Net current assets (liabilities)
G	Total assets less current liabilities
H	Creditors: amounts falling due after more than one year
I	Provisions for liabilities
J	Accruals and deferred income
K	Capital and reserves
	I Called up share capital
	II Share premium account
	III Revaluation reserve
	IV Other reserves
	V Profit and loss account

31.77 A small company need only include the following information by way of notes to its abbreviated financial statements:

- Accounting policies. [CA85 8A Sch 4].
- Details of share capital. [CA85 8A Sch 5].
- Particulars of allotments of shares. [CA85 8A Sch 6].
- A fixed assets table, so far as it relates to items to which a letter or Roman number is assigned in the adopted balance sheet format. [CA85 8A Sch 7].
- Details of financial fixed assets. [CA85 8A Sch 7A inserted by SI 2004/2947].
- Details of indebtedness. [CA85 8A Sch 8].
- The basis used in translating foreign currency amounts into sterling. [CA85 8A Sch 9(1)].
- Corresponding amounts in respect of each of the above, with the exception of fixed assets. [CA85 8A Sch 9(2)].

31.78 Although the above information must be disclosed, the notes to the financial statements, whether abbreviated or not, need not include the following information normally required by other Schedules and sections of the Act (see further para 31.87):

- Paragraph 4 of Schedule 5 (financial years of subsidiary undertakings).
- Paragraph 6 of Schedule 5 (shares of company held by subsidiary undertakings).
- Part I of Schedule 6 (directors' and chairman's emoluments, pensions and compensation for loss of office).

[CA85 Sec 246(6)].

31.79 It is worth noting that a *small* company's abbreviated financial statements will not disclose the amount of its profit or loss for the year. As the company's profit and loss account will not be filed with the Registrar of Companies, it will not be available to the company's competitors. In fact, the best estimate available to a reader will be the difference between the profit and loss reserve in the balance sheet at both the beginning and the end of the period that the financial statements cover.

31.80 In view of the extensive range of exemptions allowed in abbreviated financial statements, they cannot give a true and fair view. Since they are not intended to present a true and fair view, there is no requirement for them to comply with the disclosure provisions contained in accounting and financial reporting standards. However, because abbreviated financial statements are based on full financial statements prepared for members, the measurement methods adopted will generally be consistent with those set out in accounting standards.

Directors' responsibilities

31.81 The provisions of company law regarding the signing of the copy of the full balance sheet delivered to the Registrar apply equally to abbreviated financial statements filed in their place. [CA85 Sec 233; CA06 Sec 414]. Therefore, where abbreviated financial statements are filed, the balance sheet must be signed on behalf of the board by a director. [CA85 Sec 246(7); CA06 Sec 444(6), 450(1)(2)].

31.82 Abbreviated financial statements filed by a small company must also contain a statement in a prominent position on the balance sheet, above the signature required by company law, that they are prepared in accordance with the special provisions of Part VII of the 1985 Act relating to small companies or in accordance with the small companies regime of the 2006 Act. [CA85 Sec 246(8)(c); CA06 Sec 414(3), 419(2), 444(5), 450(3)].

31.83 A suitable wording for such a statement is as follows:

Example

The abbreviated financial statements have been prepared in accordance with the [special provisions of Part VII of the Companies Act 1985 relating to small companies/small companies regime of the Companies Act 2006].

Auditors' responsibilities

31.84 Abbreviated financial statements prepared under the 1985 Act and delivered to the Registrar by a small company must be accompanied by a *special auditors' report*, unless the company is exempt from the requirement for an audit by virtue of sections 249A(1) or (2) or 249AA. This report must state that, in the auditors' opinion:

- The company is entitled to deliver abbreviated financial statements.
- The abbreviated financial statements are properly prepared in accordance with sections 246(5) and/or (6).

[CA85 Sec 247B(2)].

31.84.1 Abbreviated financial statements prepared under the 2006 Act and delivered to the Registrar by a small company must be accompanied by a *special auditors' report*, unless the company is exempt from the requirement for an audit by virtue of sections of section 477(1) or section 480(1). This report must state that, in the auditors' opinion:

- The company is entitled to deliver abbreviated financial statements in accordance with the section in question.
- The abbreviated financial statements are properly prepared in accordance with regulations made under that section.

[CA06 Sec 444(4), 445(4), 449(2)].

31.85 The above report assumes that the exemptions in respect of both directors' report and financial statements are taken (see para 31.73 and 31.74). If the exemptions in only one of the sections are taken the references in the report should be amended accordingly.

31.86 The full audit report required by section 235 of the 1985 Act or section 475 of the 2006 Act need not be delivered with abbreviated financial statements. However, if the full audit report report was qualified, then the special report must include the full text of that report, together with any further material necessary to understand the qualification. [CA85 Sec 247B(3)(a); CA06 Sec 449(3) to (5)]. If that audit report contained a statement under section 237(2) of the 1985 Act or section 498(2) of the 2006 Act (accounts, records or returns inadequate or accounts not agreeing with records and returns) or section 237(3) of the 1985 Act or section 498(3) of the 2006 Act (failure to obtain necessary information and explanations) then that statement should be reproduced in full. [CA85 Sec

247B(3)(b); CA06 Sec 449(3)(5)]. Section 236 of the 1985 Act or section 503 of the 2006 Act (signature of auditors' report) apply to a special report as it applies to a full report under relevant section. [CA85 Sec 247B(4); CA06 Sec 449(3)(5)].

Full financial statements for filing

31.87 Under the 1985 Act, a small company is not required to take advantage of any of the exemptions available under section 246. It may, if it wishes, prepare and file full financial statements. Alternatively, it may prepare full financial statements in accordance with Schedule 4, but omit the information specified in section 246(6) from the copy of the financial statements filed with the Registrar (see para 31.78). If advantage is taken of this exemption, the financial statements are considered to be abbreviated and must include the statements and special audit report discussed from paragraph 31.81. [CA85 Sec 247B(1)(a); CA06 Sec 449(1)].

31.87.1 Under the 2006 Act, a small company follows the small company regime. It may, if it wishes, prepare and file full financial statements. Further details will be in regulations to be made under the Act. If a company follows the small company regime, the financial statements must include the statements and special audit report discussed from paragraph 31.81. [CA85 Sec 247(B)(1)(a); CA06 Sec 449(1)].

Medium-sized companies

Accounting exemptions for medium-sized companies

31.88 The exemptions available to medium-sized companies are considerably less than those available to small companies. The exemptions are given differently under the 1985 Act and the 2006 Act. In the case of the latter, some of the details will be included in regulations not published in final form at the time of writing. Where details are available about the 2006 Act they are included. Concessions available to medium-sized companies are:

- The individual financial statements of a medium-sized company need not comply with the requirements of paragraph 36A of Schedule 4 (disclosure with respect to compliance with accounting standards). [CA85 Sec 246A(2)]. The equivalent rule in the Companies Act 2006 has still to be published in final form at the time of writing.
- The directors' report for the year need not comply with the requirements of section 234ZZ(B)(3) of the 1985 Act and section 417(6) of the 2006 Act (business review to include analysis using key performance indicators) so far as they relate to *non-financial* information. [CA85 Sec 246A(2A); CA06 Sec 417(7)].
- Medium-sized companies are entitled to file financial statements with the Registrar of Companies in an abbreviated format. However, this format

differs from that available to small companies, since medium-sized companies are permitted very few disclosure exemptions. [CA85 Sec 246A(3)]. The equivalent rule in the Companies Act 2006 has still to be published in final form at the time of writing.

- Unlike small companies, medium-sized companies are not entitled to prepare shorter-form financial statements (Schedule 8) for members. Other than the exemption from paragraph 36A noted above, the financial statements prepared for the members must comply in full with Schedule 4.

Abbreviated financial statements

31.89 The modifications that the Act permits in respect of the abbreviated financial statements that a medium-sized company may deliver to the Registrar of Companies relate principally to the profit and loss account. Consequently, the normal requirements for full directors' report, balance sheet and notes to the financial statements are generally unaffected.

31.90 The limited exemptions available to medium-sized companies allow the following profit and loss account items to be combined and shown as one item under the heading 'Gross profit or loss':

- In Formats 1 and 3: turnover, the cost of sales, gross profit or loss and other operating income.
- In Formats 2 and 4: turnover, the change in stocks of finished goods and in work in progress, own work capitalised, other operating income, raw materials and consumables, and other external charges.

[CA85 Sec 246A(3)(a)].

31.91 In addition, the notes to the financial statements may omit the segmental analysis of turnover that would otherwise be required by paragraph 55 of Schedule 4. [CA85 Sec 246A(3)(b)].

31.92 Since the concessions permitted to medium-sized companies by the Act are so limited, with the requirements for the balance sheet, related notes and the directors' report fundamentally the same as those for large companies, the additional cost of preparing abbreviated financial statements for medium-sized companies will tend to exceed the potential confidentiality benefits that might derive from them. It is clear that the abbreviated accounts of small companies prepared for filing and in accordance with Schedule 8A contain insufficient information to enable them to give a true and fair view. It then follows that they do not need to include disclosures required only by accounting standards to those abbreviated accounts. It is less clear whether the same position applies to the abbreviated accounts of medium-sized companies. The concessions that a medium-sized company can take are restricted to those listed in section 246A, which allow omission of the disclosure of whether or not the accounts have been prepared in accordance with applicable accounting standards and allows some merging of items in the profit and loss account.

Statements to be made where advantage is taken of the exemptions

31.93 Where the directors of a medium-sized company file abbreviated financial statements, those financial statements must contain a statement in a prominent position on the balance sheet, above the signature required by company law, that they are prepared in accordance with the special provisions of the 1985 Act or 2006 Act (as appropriate) relating to medium-sized companies. [CA85 Sec 246A(4); CA06 Sec 450(3)].

31.94 An example of such a statement would be:

> *"The abbreviated financial statements have been prepared in accordance with the special provisions of [Part VII of the Companies Act 1985/ the Companies Act 2006] relating to medium-sized companies."*

Directors' report

31.95 Where the directors take advantage, in the directors' report, of the exemption in respect of non-disclosure of non-financial information from the business review, they must make a statement in a prominent position above the signature on the directors' report that the report has been prepared in accordance with the special provisions of Part VII of the 1985 Act or the special provisions of the 2006 Act relating to medium-sized companies. [CA85 Sec 246A(2A); CA06 Sec 417(7)].

Suitable wording for such a statement is as follows:

> *"This report has been prepared in accordance with the special provisions of [Part VII of the Companies Act 1985/the Companies Act 2006] relating to medium-sized companies."*

Auditors' reports

31.96 The abbreviated financial statements filed by a medium-sized company must be accompanied by a special auditors' report. This report must state that, in the auditors' opinion:

- The company is entitled to deliver abbreviated financial statements.
- The abbreviated financial statements are properly prepared in accordance with section 246A(3) of the 1985 Act or with regulations made under section 445(3) of the 2006 Act.

[CA85 Sec 247B(2); CA06 Sec 445(4), 449(2)].

The matters discussed in paragraph 31.86 above, concerning qualification of the auditors' report on a small company's full financial statements, apply equally to medium-sized companies.

Small and medium-sized parent companies

31.97 The fact that a company qualifies as a small or a medium-sized company does not preclude it from also being the parent company of a group. Consequently, some consideration needs to be given to this category of entity and how it is affected by the shorter-form and the abbreviated financial statement exemptions. One of the main advantages of the small and medium-sized company regime is that if the group headed by the company qualifies as small or medium-sized, it is exempt from the requirement to prepare consolidated financial statements. However, the Companies Act 2006 will remove this exemption for medium-sized groups. The expected implementation date for this change is for years beginning on or after 6 April 2008.

31.98 The Act provides specific guidance in this area by stating that:

- A parent company shall not be treated as qualifying as a small company in relation to a financial year, unless the group headed by it qualifies as a small group.
- A parent company shall not be treated as qualifying as a medium-sized company in relation to a financial year, unless the group headed by it qualifies as a medium-sized group.

[CA85 Sec 247A(3); CA06 Sec 383(1), 466(1)].

31.99 The criteria for determining small and medium-sized groups are considered from paragraph 31.18 and the exclusions thereto from paragraph 31.2. What they imply, however, is that parent companies that meet the general criteria for qualification as either small or medium-sized companies will need to undertake some form of partial group consolidation exercise in order to establish whether they meet the additional conditions set out in paragraph 31.98 above.

31.100 When considering the reporting position at an individual entity level, some guidance on interpretation may be of value:

- Where the group headed by a small parent company also qualifies as a small group, the parent may utilise the concessions generally available to small companies. Thus, it may opt to file abbreviated financial statements (Schedule 8A) and prepare shorter-form financial statements (Schedule 8) for members.
- Where the group headed by a small parent company does not qualify as a small group, but does qualify as a medium-sized group, the parent cannot take advantage of the concessions generally available to small companies.

However, it will be entitled to utilise the concessions generally available to medium-sized companies in terms of filing abbreviated accounts. It is emphasised in this regard that the exemptions allowed therein are much less extensive than those allowed in small company abbreviated financial statements.

- Where the group headed by a small parent company fails to meet the criteria for determining small or medium-sized groups, the parent will not be allowed to avail itself of the exemptions generally available to small or medium-sized companies respectively. Thus, it cannot prepare shorter-form financial statements, nor can it file any form of abbreviated financial statements, or take the exemption not to prepare consolidated financial statements (see below).
- Where the group headed by a medium-sized parent company meets the criteria for determining a medium-sized group, the parent may take advantage of the reporting concessions generally available to medium-sized companies. Thus, it may opt to file abbreviated financial statements in the permitted format.
- Where the group headed by a medium-sized parent fails to meet the criteria for determining small and medium-sized groups, the parent will not be allowed to avail itself of any of the concessions generally available to small or medium-sized companies, in terms of preparing shorter-form financial statements for members or filing abbreviated financial statements. Nor will it be able to take the exemption not to prepare consolidated financial statements (see below).

Small and medium-sized groups

31.101 In general terms, the 1985 Act requires parent companies to prepare consolidated financial statements and specifies the form which those financial statements should take. [CA85 Sec 227]. However, the 2006 Act assumes that the directors of parent companies within the small companies regime will not prepare consolidated financial statements, although section 398 allows them to opt to prepare them if they so desire. For all other parent companies there is a duty to prepare consolidated financial statements imposed in section 399 of the 2006 Act. In addition, FRS 2, 'Accounting for subsidiary undertakings', requires parent companies preparing financial statements intended to give a true and fair view of the financial position and profit or loss of the group, to prepare them in the form of consolidated financial statements. [FRS 2 para 18]. Furthermore, the standard (but not the Act) applies to *"all parent undertakings"* (FRS 2 para 18), a term designated to include not just corporate parents, but also partnerships and unincorporated associations.

Exemptions from consolidation

31.102 Both the Act and the standard allow specific exemptions from the general requirement to prepare consolidated financial statements. Included in these exemptions is the exemption allowed to a parent company not to prepare consolidated financial statements, if the group of which it is parent is a small or medium-sized group as defined in section 249 of the 1985 Act and section 466 of the 2006 Act. Additionally, it must not be an ineligible group. [CA85 Sec 248(1); CA06 Sec 398; FRS 2 para 21(a)]. The definitions of small and medium-sized groups and ineligible groups are covered from paragraph 31.2. Note, though, that once the 2006 Act is fully effective, the exemption for medium-sized parent companies will be lost.

31.103 There is a subtle difference in the application of the exemptions. A small or medium-sized company is not entitled to the exemptions with respect to abbreviated or shorter-form financial statements if it is, or was at any time during the financial year, a *member* of an ineligible group. A similar company is not entitled to the exemption from preparing consolidated financial statements if, at the year end, it is a *parent* of an ineligible group. This is shown in the example below.

Example

Companies A to D are manufacturing companies. Company A is incorporated in the USA and company D is a public company. Company B is small in size, as is the sub-group of which it is parent.

Company B will not be entitled to file abbreviated financial statements as it is a member of an ineligible group (company D being a public company). It will, however, be entitled to exemption from the preparation of consolidated financial statements as the sub-group headed by it is not ineligible.

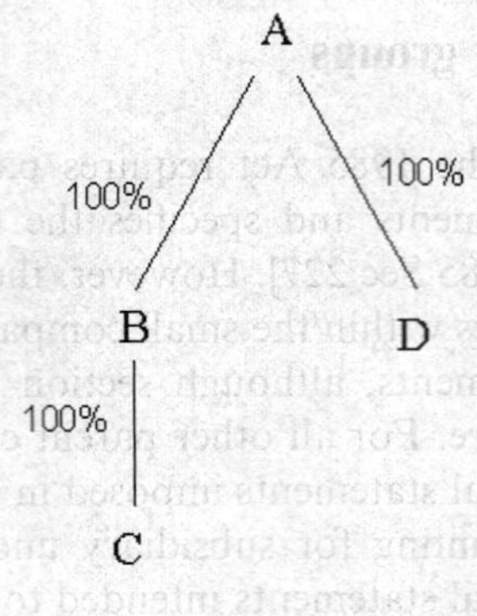

31.104 Company law requires the auditors to make a statement in their audit report only where they consider the company's directors are not entitled to take advantage of the exemption. [CA85 Sec 237(4A); CA06 Sec 498(5)].

31.105 Where a parent company makes use of the exemption from consolidation, it is required to:

- Comply with the disclosure requirements of Part 1 of Schedule 5 to the Act in respect of parent companies not required to prepare consolidated financial statements. [CA85 Sec 231(2)].

- State that its financial statements present information about it as an individual undertaking and not about its group. [FRS 2 para 22]. The statement should include or refer to the note giving the grounds on which the parent undertaking is exempt from preparing consolidated financial statements, as required by Schedule 5 paragraph 1(4).

31.106 Set out below are two examples of an appropriate wording to be included in the accounting policies of a parent company or undertaking that uses the exemption from preparing consolidated financial statements for small and medium-sized groups:

Example 1 — parent company of a small group

The financial statements contain information about GAAP UK Limited as an individual company and do not contain consolidated financial information as the parent of a group. The company is exempt under section 248 of the Companies Act 1985 from the requirement to prepare consolidated financial statements as the group it heads qualifies as a small group. Under section 398 of the Companies Act 2006, the fact that it is a small group means that there is no requirement for it to prepare consolidated financial statements.

Example 2 — unincorporated parent undertaking of small-sized group

The financial statements contain information about GAAP UK Co as an individual undertaking and do not contain consolidated financial information as the parent of a group. The partnership is exempt under paragraph 21(a) of Financial Reporting Standard No 2 from the requirement to prepare consolidated financial statements as the group it heads qualifies as a small-sized group.

31.107 While the exemption offers potential cost savings, particularly to complex groups where consolidation might be time consuming, directors may choose not to take advantage of it, on the grounds that the parent company's members require information about the activities of the group as a whole.

Abbreviated financial statements

31.108 As was discussed in paragraph 31.100 above, a parent company qualifying as small or medium-sized may file abbreviated financial statements if the group headed by it qualifies as a small or medium-sized group and is not ineligible. [CA85 Sec 247A; CA06 Sec 384, 467]. However, any abbreviated financial statements filed with the Registrar of Companies must be abbreviated individual company financial statements, because abbreviated consolidated financial statements are not permitted. In such instances, therefore, it is implicit that the parent company must take advantage of the exemption from consolidation which is available to small or medium-sized groups in respect of those abbreviated financial statements. Non-statutory consolidated financial statements may still be prepared for the members, but these must be accompanied by the appropriate statements set out in chapter 8 of the Manual of Accounting – Management Reports and Governance.

Consolidated shorter-form financial statements

31.109 Where the small parent company of a small group has prepared individual shorter-form financial statements and is exempt from preparing consolidated financial statements under section 248, it may nevertheless choose to prepare and file such consolidated financial statements. If it does, it may adopt the shorter-format that is available to small companies in preparing their individual financial statements and directors' report, as suitably modified for consolidated financial statements. [FRSSE para 16.2, 16.3].

31.110 Therefore, where a small parent company voluntarily prepares small group consolidated financial statements, it will have available to it the standard exemptions available to small companies, as explained from paragraphs 31.46. However, greater detail than that required by Schedule 8 must be given in respect of investments and this is reflected in the FRSSE's requirements with respect to consolidated financial statements. Item B III (investments) in the balance sheet formats should be broken down as follows:

- Shares in group undertakings.
- Interests in associated undertakings.
- Other participating interests.
- Loans to group undertakings and undertakings in which a participating interest is held.
- Other investments other than loans.
- Others.

[FRSSE para 16.4; CA85 Sec 248A(3)].

31.111 Small companies voluntarily preparing consolidated financial statements are also entitled to take advantage of the FRSSE's provisions as discussed above. In addition, consolidated financial statements prepared under the FRSSE should be prepared in accordance with the accounting practices and disclosure requirements set out in FRSs 2, 6, 7 and, as they apply in respect of consolidated financial statements, FRSs 5, 9, 10, 11 and 28. Where the reporting entity is part of a group that prepares publicly available consolidated financial statements, it is entitled to the exemptions given in FRS 8 paragraph 3(a)-(c). [FRSSE para 16.1].

31.112 As for individual company financial statements, the consolidated financial statements must include a statement in a prominent position above the signature on the balance sheet that they are prepared in accordance with the special provisions of Part VII of the 1985 Act relating to small companies or in accordance with the small companies regime of the 2006 Act (see paras 31.57 and 31.64) and (if applicable) in accordance with the FRSSE. [FRSSE para 16.5].

31.113 As medium-sized companies are not permitted to prepare shorter-form financial statements, it follows that medium-sized groups cannot prepare shorter-form consolidated financial statements.

Agency companies

31.114 Chapter 9 deals with the presentation of turnover as principal or as agent and the requirements of FRS 5 Application note G on revenue recognition. The application note states that where a seller has not disclosed that it is acting as agent, there is a rebuttable presumption that it is acting as principal. [FRS 5 App G para G64]. The question often arises as to whether a company that acts as an agent for either a disclosed principal or, where the above presumption is successfully rebutted, an undisclosed principal is dormant and, therefore, entitled to take advantage of the audit exemption available to dormant companies. From a practical point of view, many groups have reverted to operating on a divisional basis, rather than through a network of active subsidiaries. In such instances, divisionalisation tends to be achieved through transferring the trade of subsidiary companies to their parent company. Where this occurs, however, it is common for agency agreements to be drawn up, to the effect that the subsidiary continues to carry on trading in its own name and acts exclusively as an agent for its parent. This is often a preferred route post-acquisition, where the acquired subsidiary has an established reputation in a particular market-place or region, or where the subsidiary's name is synonymous with a branded product that it produces.

31.115 The over-riding principle is that a company may only be treated as dormant if it is not required to record any transaction in its accounting records during the reporting period in question. This is sometimes a difficult matter and several factors need to be considered. [CA85 Sec 249AA(4); CA06 Sec 1169(1)].

31.116 An agency company that enters into transactions outside the agency arrangements will have to record these transactions in the usual way. In addition, if it has incurred rights against its principal it is likely to have an accounting transaction to record, for instance, where it has bought goods under the agency for the principal and has the right to repayment of the price from its principal. Alternatively, the agent may have incurred a liability towards its principal, for instance, to account for money it receives. These points are dealt with in more detail later.

Agent acting for an undisclosed principal

31.117 The situation regarding a subsidiary acting as an agent for an undisclosed principal is as follows. In legal terms, where an agent acts for an undisclosed principal without disclosing the existence of the principal, the agent is deemed to contract on its own behalf and is personally liable on the contract to the other party. As a consequence, if an agent acquires rights and assumes liabilities under such contracts it will have accounting transactions to record in its accounting records. The agent cannot then be a dormant company. This is also the presumption made in FRS 5 Application note G and noted above in paragraph 31.114, that where a seller does not disclose that it is acting as agent it is presumed to be acting as principal.

Agent acting for a disclosed principal

31.118 Where, however, the agent contracts on behalf of a disclosed principal (that is, it discloses the existence or identity of its principal), it is generally the principal who, by virtue of the agency, becomes a party to the contract. The transactions effected under the agency can, therefore, be shown in the principal's accounts. In this instance, to ensure that the agent avoids direct liability under the contract, all contractual documents must make it clear no later than the time the contract is entered into that the agent is contracting as agent only. If the agent does not carry on any business other than under the agency, earns no commission and incurs no rights to liabilities towards its principal, it may not have any accounting transactions to record in its own accounting records.

Transactions that need to be recorded by agency companies

31.119 Even where a company is acting as agent the precise terms of the agency agreement are important in determining whether the company may qualify as dormant. Since an agency company may be treated as dormant only if it is not required to record any transaction in its accounting records, it may not qualify as a dormant company if it is involved in any one or more of the following types of activity:

- Receiving and expending monies.
- Disposing or acquiring of assets.
- Dealing in goods or stocks that it holds.

31.120 With any of the above activities, it will be a matter of fact as to whether a particular agency company performs any such activity. In the first instance, it is necessary to look to the agency agreement for guidance. This agreement defines the relationship between the principal company and the agency company and it sets out the tasks the respective companies are to perform. As mentioned in paragraph 31.114 above guidance on establishing the way in which an entity is functioning in the context of an agency arrangement is given in chapter 9.

31.121 When considering the agreement, the following points may assist in determining whether the agency company is in fact dormant:

- Receiving and expending monies

  An agency company that is merely required to account to its principal for the amount (or the net amount) of the monies it has received for its principal in the course of the agency, is the owner of the monies it receives when acting as agent. The agency company should enter such receipts in its own accounting records. Where, however, the agency company is obliged to hand over to its principal the very monies it receives as agent, it will receive those monies as a trustee for its principal. It will then not be obliged to record those receipts in its own accounting records. Where the agent is a trustee, the agency company must pay the monies it receives on behalf of the principal into a separate bank account belonging to the principal.

As regards expenditure, it is not sufficient that the principal indemnifies the agency company against any liabilities the company incurs in the course of acting as agent. The agency company must contract with third parties solely in its capacity as agent and without assuming any liability on the resultant contract. It does not so contract if it does not disclose the existence or identity of its principal. If the agency company does assume a liability on the contract, it would have a significant accounting transaction and it would not qualify as dormant.

- Disposing or acquiring of assets

  An agency company might not, in fact, own any assets. However, care should be taken in situations where the agency company remains the legal owner of property. Provided that the agency agreement passed all the beneficial interests in freehold or leasehold property to the principal and has left only the legal title to that property in the name of the agency company, the subsequent transfer of that title would not constitute a transfer of assets. This is because a bare legal title that is held to the order of the principal cannot be said to be an asset of the agent.

- Dealing in goods or stocks that the agency company holds

  If the agent's sole business is that of trading for and on behalf of the principal, the agent is unlikely to 'hold' any stocks of its own.

31.122 It would, therefore, appear that there is no reason in principle why agency companies, in certain types of agency arrangements, should not qualify to be treated as dormant companies, although it seems that many agency companies are unlikely to be eligible on the above principles. In general, the agency arrangements should be evidenced by a formal agreement entered into before the company acts as agent, setting out the terms of the agency appointment. It should be noted that where the principal is undisclosed it cannot ratify transactions entered into before the agency appointment.

Disclosure in the financial statements

31.123 As has been mentioned in paragraph 31.118 above, where the existence or identity of the principal is disclosed, the transactions the agency company carries out as agent will generally not be required to be recorded in its accounting records and, therefore, these would not constitute transactions to be shown in its financial statements. If the agency company has no other transactions that it needs to enter in its accounting records, it may be in a position to prepare dormant financial statements and take advantage of audit exemption.

31.124 Where the principal is undisclosed and the presumption that it is, therefore, acting as principal cannot be rebutted (see para 31.114 above), the agent will have to account as if it were the principal for all transactions entered into as agent and constituting accounting transactions in its books of account. This then leads to the question of what should be shown in its statutory financial statements for these transactions. Clearly, as it is contracting in its own name, it is likely to have, at the balance sheet date, debtor and creditor balances with the third parties (that is, parties other than the principal) with which it has contracted. These balances should be reported in the agent's balance sheet.

31.125 What is reported in the profit and loss account might depend on the trading relationship between the principal and the agent. If the principal invoices the agent for goods that the agent sells on, and the agent in turn invoices the customer, then, because it is presumed to be acting as principal, the gross trading should be recorded in the profit and loss account. However, in many divisionalisations the principal does not invoice the agent in this way and sometimes transactions with the subsidiary that is acting as agent are dealt with through the inter-company account. Where this is the case, the exact terms of the agency agreement between the parent and its subsidiary need to be carefully examined to determine the appropriate accounting for the inter-company transactions in the parent and the subsidiary and for the sales to third parties, in accordance with the principles and guidance in Application note G of FRS 5 and the legal requirements described above. In many cases specific legal advice on interpreting the agency agreement may be required.

31.126 Clearly it is desirable to avoid the uncertainty and expense that may be involved in interpreting agency arrangements in situations where there is non-disclosure by the agent that it is acting as such. Therefore, in setting up agency arrangements it is always best to ensure that the agency is disclosed, where practicable.

Financial Reporting Standard for Smaller Entities

31.127 The following sections summarise the accounting requirements of the FRSSE (effective 2007). Throughout this section mention of 'FRSSE' is to be understood to mean the 2007 version of the FRSSE. As discussed from paragraph 31.66, shorter-form financial statements will be capable of giving a true and fair view by complying fully with all relevant requirements of the FRSSE. There is generally no need to refer to other accounting standards, UITF abstracts or legislation to satisfy this requirement.

Tangible fixed assets and depreciation

31.128 In the revised FRSSE, published in January 2007 and effective for accounting periods commencing on or after 1 January 2007, tangible fixed assets and depreciation are dealt with from paragraph 6.1 of the FRSSE.

31.129 The valuation bases and the depreciation rules discussed in chapter 16 are equally applicable to small companies, except for some simplifications, which are discussed below. Certain accounting treatments for tangible fixed assets have been simplified from the FRS 15 requirements:

- As is evident from the balance sheet formats at paragraph 31.46 above, small companies are permitted to sub-analyse tangible fixed assets into two categories of land and buildings and of other tangible fixed assets in aggregate. [CA85 Sch 8].
- Where a small company adopts an accounting policy of revaluation in respect of tangible fixed assets, the basis for revaluation is market value or the best estimate thereof, unless judged inappropriate by the directors, in which case current value (lower of replacement cost and recoverable amount) can be used instead. [FRSSE para 6.23]
- The FRSSE allows the valuation to be performed by an experienced valuer, who does not necessarily need to be a qualified valuer as FRS 15 requires. [FRSSE para 6.24].
- Revaluation losses are taken to the profit and loss account irrespective of recoverable amounts, except when losses are caused only by a change in market value, where the losses are taken to the STRGL until the carrying amount reaches depreciated historical cost. [FRSSE para 6.25].
- Revaluation gains are recognised in the STRGL except to the extent (after adjusting for subsequent depreciation) that they reverse revaluation losses on the same asset that was previously recognised in the profit and loss account. To that extent they should be recognised in the profit and loss account. [FRSSE para 6.26].

31.130 The FRSSE does not provide any guidance for dealing with:

- Start-up or commissioning periods.
- When capitalisation of finance costs should begin.
- Construction of a tangible fixed asset being completed in parts.
- Major inspections or overhauls.
- Cases where it is impossible to obtain a reliable valuation.
- Insurance companies.

In these situations the accounting treatment in FRS 15 should be followed as current best practice. There is further discussion of this in paragraph 31.35 above. Start-up costs are dealt with in paragraph 31.137 below.

31.131 The Act's disclosure requirements for fixed assets are dealt with in paragraphs 40 and 41 of Schedule 8. These disclosure requirements are a replica of the equivalent Schedule 4 disclosure requirements, which are discussed in chapter 16. In addition, the FRSSE also requires the following information to be disclosed in respect of depreciation for each of the two categories of fixed assets mentioned in the first bullet point of paragraph 31.129 above:

- The depreciation methods used.
- The useful economic lives or the depreciation rates used.
- The financial effect, where material, of a change during the period in either the estimate of useful economic lives or the estimate of residual values.

[FRSSE para 6.42].

31.132 Any change in the depreciation method used and the effect, if material, should be disclosed in the period of change. The reason for the change should also be disclosed. [FRSSE para 6.43].

31.133 Certain accounting treatments in relation to depreciation and impairment have been simplified from the FRS 15 requirements:

- Residual values and useful economic lives for tangible fixed assets should be reviewed regularly rather than annually and revised when necessary rather than when expectations are significantly different from previous estimates.
- Disclosure of depreciation to be given for the two categories of land and buildings and of other fixed assets in aggregate.
- There is no specific requirement for an annual impairment review where an asset's life exceeds 50 years or where depreciation is not charged as it is immaterial.
- The statement in FRS 15 that subsequent expenditure does not negate the need for depreciation is omitted.

31.134 The FRSSE does not provide any guidance for dealing with:

- Impairment and the basis on which residual values are priced.
- Renewals accounting.

In these cases the accounting treatment in FRS 15 should be followed as current best practice.

31.135 There is no requirement for small companies to disclose the investment revaluation reserve relating to investment properties on the face of the balance sheet as required by paragraph 15 of SSAP 19. The information can be given by way of a note to the balance sheet. However, the revaluation reserve is a separate line item in the balance sheet formats in Schedule 8 and has to be shown on the face of the balance sheet.

31.136 In respect of government grants, the FRSSE does not provide any guidance for dealing with financial support grants. If a small company receives such a grant, it should follow the accounting treatment specified in paragraph 23 of SSAP 4 as current best practice.

Start-up costs and pre-contract costs

31.137 Paragraph 8.15 of the FRSSE repeats the accounting requirement of the UITF Abstract 24, 'Accounting for start-up costs' for such costs to be accounted for on a basis consistent with similar costs incurred as part of an entity's on-going activities. Where there are no such similar costs, start-up costs that do not meet the criteria for recognition as assets under another specific requirement of the FRSSE should be written-off as incurred. They should not be carried forward as an asset. The FRSSE does not include any reference to the disclosures detailed in UITF Abstract 24.

31.138 The FRSSE also provides guidance in respect of pre-contract costs within paragraph 8.16 based on the requirements of UITF Abstract 34, 'Pre-contract costs'. Such costs should be written-off with the exception of directly attributable costs, which should only be recognised as an asset where it is virtually certain that a contract will be obtained and the present value of expected future net cash inflows expected to arise from the contract are not less than all amounts to be recognised as an asset. Costs incurred before the asset recognition criteria are met should not be recognised as an asset.

Leases

31.139 The FRSSE modifies the recognition rules for finance leases in SSAP 21 for small companies. Where a small company leases an asset on a finance lease, both the asset and the corresponding lease obligations should normally be recorded at the asset's fair value, rather than the present value of the minimum lease payments. [FRSSE para 7.2]. However, where the asset's fair value does not give a realistic estimate of the asset's cost to the lessee, because, for example, the lessee has benefited from grants and capital allowances that had the effect of reducing the aggregate minimum lease payments to below the fair value of the asset, the asset and the obligation should be recorded at the present value of the minimum lease payments. A negative finance charge should not be shown. [FRSSE para 7.3].

31.140 Where a small company is a lessor of assets under finance leases, the total gross earnings should be recognised on a systematic and rational basis. In most cases, this would be achieved by allocating gross earnings so as to give a constant periodic rate of return on the lessor's net investment. [FRSSE para 7.9].

31.141 The information to be disclosed by lessees and lessors is dealt with in paragraphs 7.16 to 7.18 of the FRSSE. They do not cover all the disclosure requirements given in SSAP 21 and discussed in chapter 19. In particular, small companies need *not* give the following information:

- For finance leased assets, the total depreciation for the period by major class of asset. This is because small companies are only required to analyse tangible fixed assets into land and buildings and other tangible fixed assets, rather than by major class of asset.
- Analysis of obligations under finance leases between amounts payable in the next year, amounts payable in the second to fifth year inclusive from the balance sheet date, and the aggregate amounts payable thereafter.
- Finance charges and operating lease rentals charged for the period.
- Analysis of operating lease commitments between land and buildings and other operating leases.
- Aggregate rentals receivable by lessors in the accounting period in relation to both finance and operating leases.

31.142 Paragraph 7.6 of the FRSSE deals with operating lease incentives, from both the lessee's and the lessor's perspective. It repeats the main principle from UITF Abstract 28, 'Operating lease incentives', that incentives should be spread on a straight-line basis over the lease term, or if shorter, over the period to the first review to market rental.

Investments

31.143 Paragraphs 6.30 to 6.33 of the FRSSE set out the requirements of CA85 in respect of disclosures required for fixed asset investments. Fixed asset investments should initially be carried at cost or market value as determined at the date of their last valuation or on any other basis as determined by the directors. Paragraphs 6.34 to 6.36 explain the accounting and disclosure requirements on the revaluation reserve of all fixed assets including investments.

31.144 Paragraphs 8.13 to 8.14 of the FRSSE consider the accounting and disclosure requirements for current asset investments. Such investments may be carried at the lower of cost or net realisable value or measured at their current cost.

Investment properties

31.145 The accounting requirements of investment properties are in line with SSAP 19. Such properties should be carried in the balance sheet at market value. Paragraphs 6.50 to 6.53 of the FRSSE set out these requirements and explains that the following points need to be disclosed:

- The name of the persons making the valuation, or particulars of their qualifications.
- The bases of the valuation used.
- If the person making the valuation is an employee or officer of the company or group that owns the property this fact need be disclosed.

Government grants

31.146 The requirements of SSAP 4 are included in the FRSSE in paragraphs 6.54 to 6.57.

Intangible fixed assets

31.147 Small companies need only classify intangible assets into goodwill and other intangible assets. Other intangible assets may include development expenditure. Paragraphs 6.3 to 6.10 of the FRSSE deal with the accounting and disclosure requirements for research and development expenditure, which are imported from SSAP 13 and discussed in detail in chapter 15.

31.148 Small companies are *not* required to disclose:

- The total amount of research and development expenditure charged to the profit and loss account.
- Movements on deferred development expenditure.

31.149 On goodwill, the FRSSE reflects the provisions of FRS 10. Paragraphs 6.11 to 6.17 of the FRSSE deal with other intangible assets and goodwill. The FRSSE imports none of the disclosure requirements of FRS 10, but does import most of the recognition and measurement rules with a number of exceptions, the key ones being:

- There is a requirement, rather than a presumption that useful economic lives are limited to 20 years.
- The exceptions in FRS 10 allowing recognition of internally generated intangible assets with a 'readily ascertainable' market value and revaluation of intangible assets with a 'readily ascertainable' market value are omitted in the FRSSE.
- Old goodwill previously eliminated against reserves should either be wholly reinstated or wholly left in reserves.

31.150 It is important to note that these exceptions only apply to goodwill and intangible assets arising in the financial statements of an individual entity. Consolidated financial statements should be based on FRS 10 in its entirety.

Write-downs to recoverable amount

31.151 The FRSSE reflects the principles of FRS 11, 'Impairment of fixed assets and goodwill'. However, the FRSSE only includes the key principle that assets held at above recoverable amount should be written down to recoverable amount and the conditions for recognising the reversal of write-downs. The rules are set out in paragraphs 6.44 to 6.49 of the FRSSE.

Stocks and long-term contracts

31.152 Many of the problems that small companies face in valuing stocks and long-term contracts are usually of a practical nature rather than matters of principle. The FRSSE recognises this and incorporates the whole of appendix I of SSAP 9 dealing with further practical considerations in appendix III. The valuation principles and the recognition rules relating to stocks and long-term contracts, which are dealt with in paragraphs 8.1 to 8.8 of the FRSSE, are consistent with SSAP 9 and are discussed in chapter 20. Consistent with the balance sheet formats, small companies are not required to sub-analyse the amount of stock stated in the balance sheet.

Consignment stock

31.153 Small companies are likely to enter into arrangements where goods are supplied to them on a consignment basis. Therefore, the FRSSE provides a table in appendix III, illustrating the factors that should be considered in deciding whether or not consignment stock is an asset. This table is a replica of the one contained in Application note A in FRS 5 and is reproduced in chapter 20 of this manual.

31.154 Where consignment stock is in substance an asset, a small company should recognise it in the balance sheet and show the amount due to the supplier, after deducting any deposits, as trade creditors. Where consignment stock is not in substance an asset, it should not be recognised. Any deposits paid should be shown in 'other debtors'. [FRSSE para 8.9].

Debt factoring

31.155 Debt factoring and invoice discounting arrangements provide an important source of finance for small companies. A small company will need to analyse whether or not it should continue to show factored debts as an asset in its balance sheet. Therefore, like consignment stocks, the FRSSE imports the table illustrating the considerations affecting the treatment of debt factoring from Application note C of FRS 5 into appendix III. This table is reproduced in chapter 3.

31.156 Paragraphs 8.10 to 8.12 of the FRSSE provide guidance on the three accounting treatments, *viz*, derecognition, linked presentation and separate presentation, that might apply to debt factoring arrangements. These issues are also considered in detail in chapter 3.

Provisions, contingencies and post balance sheet events

31.157 Requirements relating to provisions and contingencies are dealt with in paragraphs 11.1 to 11.11, and those relating to post balance sheet events are dealt with in paragraphs 14.1 to 14.4 of the FRSSE.

31.158 The rules for provisions and contingencies are a simplification of the rules in FRS 12, 'Provisions, contingent liabilities and contingent assets', which are considered in chapter 21. The rules for post balance sheet events reflect those found in FRS 21, 'Events after the balance sheet date', although there is no requirement to disclose owners' or others' power to amend the financial statements after issue. FRS 21 is considered in detail in chapter 22.

31.159 Disclosure for provisions and contingencies has been simplified from FRS 12 with only the nature and financial effect of contingent liabilities (unless remote) and probable contingent assets being required.

31.160 In particular, the FRSSE does not provide guidance on and makes no reference to:

- Financial instruments, executory contracts, long-term contracts or insurance entities.
- Rare cases where it is not clear whether there is a present obligation.
- Risks, uncertainties and future events being taken into account in measuring a provision.
- Detailed rules relating to discount rates.
- Provisions and capitalising assets.
- Future operating losses, onerous contracts, restructuring or the sale of an operation.
- Restriction on the amounts recognised as reimbursements not exceeding the related provision.

31.161 However, where the FRSSE is silent, small companies should refer to FRS 12 as a means of establishing current best practice.

Financial instruments

31.162 Financial instruments, other than shares, bank loans and overdrafts and leasing obligations, are unlikely to form a major source of finance for small companies. Accordingly, paragraphs 12.1 to 12.12 of the FRSSE deal with only the basic principles of FRS 4 and FRS 25 relating to debt, the treatment of dividends under FRS 21 and disclosure requirements relating to the company's share capital. The term 'debt' has been replaced in the FRSSE by borrowings, which are defined in the FRSSE to include all capital instruments that are classified as liabilities. [FRSSE Section C].

31.163 The FRSSE has included in appendix III new guidance on the FRS 25 requirement for the classification of capital instruments as debt or equity.

31.164 It is common for banks providing loans to small companies to charge arrangement fees. The accounting treatment of arrangement fees is not explicitly covered in FRS 4, so the FRSSE provides the following guidance:

- Where an arrangement fee is such as to represent a significant additional cost of finance when compared to the interest payable over the instrument's life, it should be allocated to periods over the term of the instrument at a constant rate on the carrying amount of the instrument.

- Where this is not the case, it should be charged immediately to the profit and loss account.

[FRSSE para 12.4].

31.165 In light of FRS 21 and FRS 25, the FRSSE mirrors the guidance with respect to dividends contained within these standards. As such, dividends relating to financial instruments or a component that is a financial liability should be recognised as an expense in the profit and loss account. Dividends relating to equity instruments should be debited to equity net of any related income tax benefit and any dividends declared after the balance sheet date should not be recognised as a liability at the balance sheet date. [FRSSE para 12.6]. The FRSSE also provides guidance with respect to fixed cumulative dividends on the company's shares. Where such dividends are in arrears, the amount of the arrears and the period for which each class of dividends is in arrears should be disclosed. [FRSSE para 12.8].

The effect of FRS 3

31.166 FRS 3 contains supplementary provisions relating to the format of the profit and loss account, but its effect on the profit and loss account formats for small companies is not significant. This is because the FRSSE does not include the FRS 3 requirements for small companies to analyse turnover, costs, results and exceptional items into continuing operations, acquisitions and discontinued operations. There is also no requirement for small companies to produce a note of historical cost profits and losses or a reconciliation of movements in shareholders' funds.

31.167 The FRSSE, nevertheless, requires small companies to show all exceptional items, other than the three items imported from paragraph 20 of FRS 3 and included in paragraph 3.6 of the FRSSE, under the statutory format headings to which they relate, either in the notes or on the face of the profit and loss account if this is necessary in order to give a true and fair view. [FRSSE para 3.5]. The FRS 3 paragraph 20 items are shown separately on the face of the profit and loss account after operating profit and before interest.

Revenue recognition

31.168 The FRSSE incorporates in full the requirements of FRS 5 Application note G with respect to revenue recognition so that small companies have definitive guidance in this area. These requirements are considered further in chapter 9.

31.169 Additional guidance, in line with UITF 40, 'Revenue recognition and service contracts', has been included in FRSSE 2007 from paragraphs 4.10 to 4.15.

Taxation

31.170 Paragraphs 9.1 to 9.15 of the FRSSE deal with the measurement and disclosure relating to taxation. These paragraphs cover most of the measurement provisions of FRS 16 and FRS 19 dealt with in chapter 13 of this manual, but omit many of the disclosures required by those standards.

31.171 In particular, the FRSSE:

- Does not include the FRS 16 prohibition on adjustments to income and expenses to reflect notional tax.
- Makes no reference to tax rates (to be used for measuring current tax).
- Omits the detailed disclosure requirements of FRS 16 relating to the major components of the current tax charge.
- Omits the requirement in FRS 19 to provide deferred tax when assets are 'marked to market'.
- Omits the requirements of FRS 19 relating to unremitted earnings of subsidiaries, associates or joint ventures.
- States that discounting of deferred tax is not required (but if done, it should be done consistently) and makes no further reference to discounting except to say that the unwinding of the discount should be shown as a component of the tax charge and disclosed separately.
- Omits the presentational requirements of FRS 19.
- Omits the detailed disclosure requirements of FRS 19, except for the requirement relating to the unwinding of discount referred to above and those relating to revalued assets (disclosure of tax that would be payable or recoverable if the assets were sold at the values shown).

31.172 Although small companies are required to disclose any special circumstances that affect the overall tax charge or credit in accordance with paragraph 9.3 of the FRSSE, there is no specific reference in the FRSSE to disclose special circumstances affecting the tax attributable to the three non-operating exceptional items included in paragraph 3.6 of the FRSSE. In practice, however, it is likely that the explanation of the special circumstances affecting the overall tax charge or credit will include the tax effects of the three non-operating items.

31.173 Paragraph 9.15 of the FRSSE deals with disclosure of turnover and repeats the requirement of SSAP 5, 'Accounting for value added tax', that turnover should exclude VAT on taxable outputs. Irrecoverable VAT that can be allocated to fixed assets and to other items disclosed separately in the financial statements should be included in their cost where practicable and material.

Retirement benefits

31.174 Paragraphs 10.1 and 10.3 of the FRSSE deal with defined contribution schemes and repeat the requirements of FRS 17. Paragraph 10.2 deals with the Companies Act requirements with respect to disclosure of pension commitments. Appendix II of the FRSSE deals with defined benefit schemes.

31.175 Paragraph 1 of appendix II contains the accounting requirements for periods ending on or after 22 June 2006. These may also be adopted early and such early adoption is encouraged in the FRSSE.

31.176 The requirements in paragraph 1 are based on FRS 17, but with many of the disclosure requirements omitted. The accounting treatment is largely the same as FRS 17, but again has been simplified. The main simplifications are:

- No reference to multi-employer schemes.
- Omission of the requirement to attribute benefits according to the schemes benefit formula.
- Omission of the requirement to reflect expected future events in the actuarial assumptions.
- Omission of detailed requirements relating to the treatment of a scheme surplus.
- Omission of detailed requirements relating to the treatment of gains and losses.
- Omission of requirement relating to recognition of current tax relief on contributions.
- Omission of requirement relating to death-in-service and incapacity benefits.
- Omission of many of the detailed disclosure requirements including financial assumptions, analysis of fair value of assets by class and expected rates of return, analysis of amounts charged to profit and loss account and of amounts included in the STRGL and analysis of amounts included in reserves in respect of defined benefit assets or liabilities.

Share-based payments

31.177 The requirements of FRS 20 had not been included in previous versions of the FRSSE until the FRSSE 2007 edition. [FRSSE paras 12.13 to 12.15]. For cash-settled share-based payment transactions the company should recognise the goods or services when it obtains them. The amount of the goods or services and the corresponding liability should be the best estimate of the expenditure required to settle the liability at the balance sheet date. The liability should be re-measured at each balance sheet date and at the date of settlement. [FRSSE para 12.13]. Note that this is similar to FRS 20, but uses best estimate rather than fair value.

31.178 For equity-settled share-based payment transactions only disclosure and no measurement or recognition is required. [FRSSE para 12.13]. This is a significant difference to FRS 20.

Foreign currencies

31.179 Paragraphs 13.1 to 13.12 of the FRSSE cover most of the provisions relating to measurement, but none of the disclosure requirements of SSAP 20. Foreign currencies are dealt with in chapter 7.

Accounting policies and estimation techniques

31.180 Although there is no requirement for small companies to state whether the financial statements have been prepared in accordance with applicable accounting standards, both the Act and FRS 18 require disclosure of each material accounting policy and these requirements are incorporated into the FRSSE. [FRSSE paras 2.7, 2.8]. In addition, the FRSSE requires that the financial statements should state that they have been prepared in accordance with the FRSSE (effective January 2007).

31.181 The FRSSE incorporates the principal requirements of FRS 18, 'Accounting policies'. In addition to requiring disclosure of each material accounting policy it requires details to be given of any change in policy and a brief explanation of why each new policy is thought more appropriate. Prior period adjustments should be accounted for by restating comparatives and disclosing the cumulative effect at the foot of the STRGL. The effect of the change in the current and preceding period should be given, where practicable. [FRSSE para 2.15].

31.182 The FRSSE repeats the requirements of FRS 18 for accounting policies and estimation techniques to be the most appropriate for the purpose of giving a true and fair view, taking account of the objectives of relevance, reliability, comparability and understandability. It requires that the policies and techniques should be consistent with company legislation and the FRSSE's requirements. [FRSSE para 2.9].

31.183 Accounting policies should be reviewed regularly to ensure that they remain the most appropriate. Policies should be applied consistently within the same financial statements and from one financial year to the next. In judging whether a new policy is more appropriate due weight should be given to the impact on consistency and comparability. Changes in policy should be accounted for by a prior year adjustment. [FRSSE para 2.10].

31.184 Changes in estimation techniques are not accounted for as a prior year adjustment, but where the effect of such a change is material a description of the change and, where practicable, the effect on the results for the current period, should be given. [FRSSE para 2.7(c)].

31.185 A company is presumed to be carrying on business as a going concern. The financial statements should be prepared on this basis unless the directors determine after the balance sheet date either that they intend to liquidate the entity or to cease trading, or that they have no realistic alternative but to do so. When preparing financial statements directors should assess whether there are any significant doubts about the entity's ability to continue as a going concern. If there are material uncertainties they should be disclosed. Where the period considered by the directors in making this assessment is less than one year from the date of approval of the financial statements, that fact should be stated. [FRSSE para 2.12]. Companies will need to ensure that they have projections covering a sufficient period into the future for directors to give reasonable consideration to their assessment of going concern, if this disclosure is to be avoided.

31.186 The requirements relating to accounting policies, estimation techniques and prior year adjustments are contained in paragraphs 2.6 to 2.15 of the FRSSE and definitions are included in section C of the FRSSE. The FRSSE omits the following features and requirements of FRS 18:

- Reference to departures in exceptional circumstances from accounting standards or UITF Abstracts.
- Reference to preparation of financial statements on a going concern basis (but see para 31.185 above).
- Reference to preparation of financial statements on the accruals basis.
- Reference to selection of estimation techniques that enable the financial statements to give a true and fair view.
- Reference to constraints to be taken into account in judging the appropriateness of accounting policies.
- Requirement relating to accounting for changes in an estimation technique.
- Disclosure requirement relating to significant estimation techniques.
- Reference to SORPs.
- Reference to disclosures required when financial statements are not prepared on a going concern basis.
- Requirement to cross-refer disclosure of departures to disclosures required by companies legislation.

31.187 In addition to the above matters, paragraph 2.2 of the FRSSE requires that financial statements should give a true and fair view and that to achieve this, regard should be given to the substance of any arrangement or transaction that the entity has entered into.

Related party disclosures

31.188 Related party transactions are generally prevalent in small businesses. As a result, the FRSSE, recognising that the full requirements of FRS 8 would be unduly onerous for smaller entities, only requires disclosure of those related party transactions that are considered to be material to the small reporting entity. Without this concession, small companies would have been required to disclose related party transactions that were material in relation to the other related party, even when that related party was an individual. Such disclosures would have been unnecessarily burdensome for small companies. Since the FRSSE revises the requirements of FRS 8, the provisions of the FRSSE are considered in the paragraphs that follow.

31.189 Where a small reporting entity purchases, sells or transfers goods and other assets or liabilities; or renders or receives services; or provides or receives finance or financial support (irrespective of whether a price is charged) to, from or on behalf of a related party, then any such material transactions (materiality to be judged in terms of its significance to the reporting entity) should be disclosed, including:

- The names of the transacting related parties.
- A description of the relationship between the parties.
- A description of the transactions.
- The amounts involved.
- Any other elements of the transactions necessary to understand the financial statements.
- The amounts due to or from related parties at the balance sheet date and provisions for doubtful debts due from such parties at that date.
- Amounts written off in the period in respect of debts due to or from related parties.

[FRSSE para 15.1].

31.190 In addition, the FRSSE clarifies that personal guarantees given by directors in respect of borrowings by the reporting entity should be disclosed. [FRSSE para 15.2]. Transactions can be disclosed on an aggregated basis (aggregation of similar transactions by type of related party), unless disclosure of individual transactions or connected transactions is necessary to understand the impact of the transactions on the financial statements or is required by law. [FRSSE para 15.6]. FRS 8 does not require disclosure of related party transactions in certain circumstances which are considered in chapter 29. These circumstances are also listed in paragraph 15.7 of the FRSSE.

31.191 The FRSSE also incorporates the requirements of Schedule 8 to the Companies Act with respect to related party transactions. As such, where investment income, interest received or receivable, interest paid or payable and other similar income or charges relates to a group undertaking, they are required to be disclosed separately. [FRSSE para 15.3, 15.4]. Separate disclosure is also required of commitments that are undertaken on behalf of, or for the benefit of, any group undertaking. [FRSSE para 15.5].

31.192 Where the reporting entity is controlled by another party, disclosure should be made of:

- The name of the controlling party.
- If different, the name of the ultimate controlling party.

In both instances, the related party relationship should also be disclosed. These disclosures should also be made whether or not there have been any transactions between the parties. If the reporting party's controlling party or ultimate controlling party is not known, that fact should be disclosed. [FRSSE para 15.8]. The Companies Act 1985 requirements incorporated into the FRSSE also require disclosure of the ultimate parent company's country of incorporation. [FRSSE para 15.9].

31.193 The FRSSE also incorporates the Companies Act 1985 Schedule 6 requirements to disclose transactions with directors. These requirements are discussed in chapter 29. In addition, the Companies Act 1985 Schedule 5 requirements in relation to disclosure of holdings in subsidiary undertakings and related financial information as well as membership of qualifying undertakings are also incorporated within the FRSSE in full. These requirements are discussed further in chapter 6 (for individual financial statements) and chapter 24 (for consolidated financial statements).

True and fair override disclosures

31.194 The directors of a small company may depart from any of the Act's accounting provisions in order to give a true and fair view. In that situation, particulars of the departure, the reasons for it and its effect should be given in a note to the financial statements. The FRSSE uses the principles of FRS 18 in providing guidance on how the statutory disclosure requirements should be interpreted. [FRSSE para 2.2]. Where a departure continues in subsequent financial statements the disclosures should continue to be made and should include corresponding amounts. [FRSSE para 2.4].

Annex — Decision tables

Decision table 1 — Company without subsidiaries

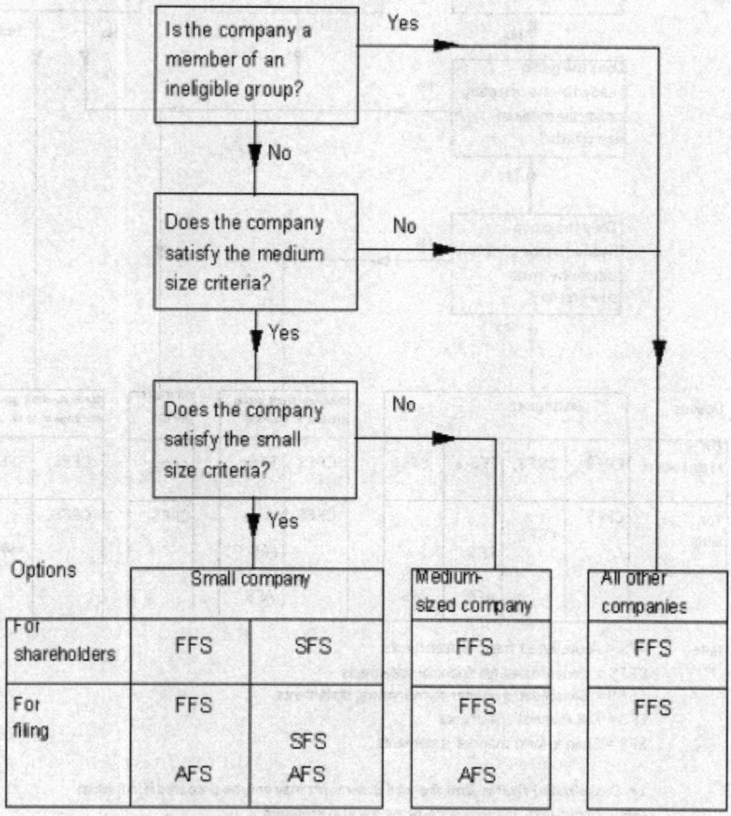

Note: AFS = Abbreviated financial statements
FFS = Full financial statements
SFS = Shorter-form financial statements

Decision table 2 — Company with subsidiaries

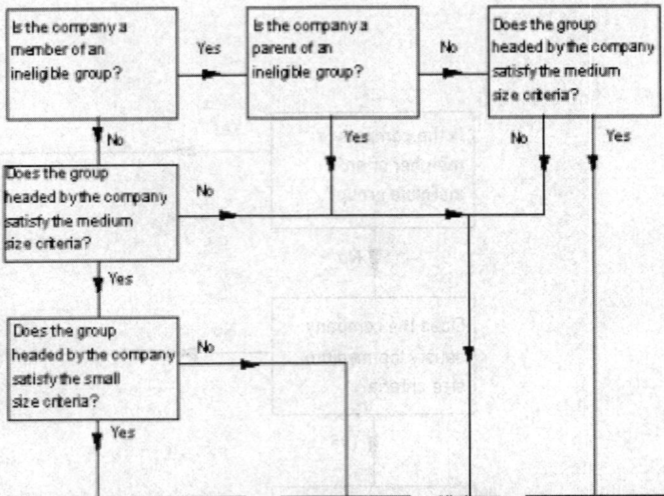

Options	Small group				Medium-sized group eligible to file AFS		All other groups	Medium-sized group not eligible to file AFS	
For shareholders	CFFS	CSFS$_1$	FFS$_{1,2}$	SFS$_2$	CFFS	FFS$_2$	CFFS$_3$	CFFS$_3$	FFS$_2$
For filing	CFFS	CSFS$_1$	FFS AFS	SFS AFS	CFFS	FFS AFS	CFFS$_3$	CFFS$_3$	FFS

Note: AFS = Abbreviated financial statements
CFFS = Consolidated full financial statements
CSFS = Consolidated shorter-form financial statements
FFS = Full financial statements
SFS = Shorter-form financial statements

1 = Consolidated shorter-form financial statements may only be prepared if individual entity shorter-form financial statements are also prepared.

2 = If entity financial statements are filed, non-statutory consolidated financial statements may be prepared for the shareholders.

3 = Exemption from consolidation may also be available under section 228 if the company itself is a subsidiary.

Decision table 3 — Eligibility

Size criteria

Not more than:	Small Company	Small Group Gross	Small Group Net	Medium Company	Medium Group Gross	Medium Group Net
Turnover – £ million	5.6	6.72	5.6	22.8	27.36	22.8
Gross assets – £ million	2.8	3.36	2.8	11.4	13.68	11.4
Average number of employees	50	50	50	250	250	250

Client figures (Note: a minimum of three periods must be reviewed, unless the company meets size criteria in current and previous periods)

	(a) Current 200X	v/X	(b) Previous 200X	v/X	(c) 2nd Previous 200X	v/X	(d) 3rd Previous 200X	v/X
Turnover – £ million								
Gross assets as balance sheet date – £ million								
Average number of employees								

Two of three must be satisfied to meet size criteria.

Notes:

- If the company heads a group the appropriate figures are the consolidated (net basis) or aggregated (gross basis) figures irrespective of whether consolidated accounts have been prepared.
- Gross assets = fixed assets plus current assets without deduction for current or long term liabilities.
- There is a *pro rata* adjustment to turnover if the period is not 12 months.

Consideration of eligibility

Ensure that the company is not an ineligible company nor a member of a group that contains an ineligible company. Answering 'yes' to any to these items will make the reporting entity ineligible, without the need to look further at size:

	Circle which
■ Is the company a public company?	Yes/No
■ Does the company that have permission under Part 4 of the Financial Services and Markets Act 2000 to carry on a regulated activity?	Yes/No
■ Does the company that carry on an insurance market activity?	Yes/No
■ Does the group contain a body corporate that has power under its constitution to offer shares or debentures to the public and may lawfully exercise that power?	Yes/No
■ Does the company or group meet the size criteria in the current period?	Yes/No
■ Does the company or group meet the size criteria in the previous accounting period?	Yes/No
■ Does the company or group meet the size criteria in the 2nd previous accounting period?	Yes/No
■ Does the company or group meet the size criteria in the 3rd previous accounting period?	Yes/No
■ In the case of the company's first financial period does it qualify in that period?	Yes/No

Evaluations	**Tick which**
If Yes to (a) and (b) the company is eligible.	
If No to (a), but Yes to (b) and (c) the company is eligible.	
If No to (a), Yes to (b) and No to (c) the company is ineligible unless the 2 previous periods were Yes.	
If Yes to (a), No to (b) and No to (c) the company is ineligible.	
If Yes to (a), No to (b), Yes to (c) and Yes to (d) the company is eligible.	
If Yes to (a), No to (b), Yes to (c) and No to (d) the company is ineligible unless the 2 previous periods were Yes.	

Chapter 32

Oversea companies

	Page
Introduction	32001
Companies Act 2006	32003
Definitions	32003
Oversea company	32003
Place of business	32004
Branch	32005
Registration of oversea companies	32006
Place of business registration	32006
Branch registration	32007
Change in registration regime	32007
Particulars to be registered	32008
Place of business regime	32008
Branch registration regime	32008
Accounting records	32008
Accounting reference period	32009
Place of business regime	32009
Branch registration regime	32009
Preparation of financial statements	32009
Place of business regime	32009
Branch registration regime	32012
Filing of financial statements with the Registrar	32013
Place of business regime	32013
Branch registration regime	32013
Disclosure required in state of incorporation	32014
Disclosure not required in state of incorporation	32015
Listed overseas companies	32015
Oversea companies traded on AIM	32018
Audit requirements	32018
Practical issue	32018

Chapter 32

Oversea companies

Introduction

32.1 Companies incorporated outside Great Britain (meaning England, Wales and Scotland) frequently establish branches to trade in Great Britain. It is, therefore, necessary for the protection of the public that such companies are brought, to some extent, within the regulatory framework applicable to companies incorporated in Great Britain. This is done by requiring the registration of oversea companies with the Registrar of Companies, but extending wide exemptions to them so as not to discourage them from operating in Great Britain.

32.2 Oversea companies (defined in para 32.8) are regulated currently in accordance with Part XXIII of the Companies Act 1985 (the Act) which will be replaced by Part 34 of the Companies Act 2006 (the 2006 Act) from October 2008 (see para 32.7.1 below). The 1985 Act provides for:

- Registration of oversea companies, including the regulation of names used by oversea companies.
- Preparation and filing of financial statements.
- Registration of charges. The provisions inserted into the 1985 Act by the Companies Act 1989 have never been brought into effect. Sections 409 and 424 of the 1985 Act still apply.
- Particulars to be delivered to the Registrar of Companies on winding up of a limited company incorporated outside the UK (meaning Great Britain and Northern Ireland) and Gibraltar with a branch in Great Britain.

32.3 The 1985 Act contains two regimes requiring an oversea company operating in Great Britain to register with the Registrar of Companies – the *place of business regime* and the *branch registration regime*. An oversea company must register under one or other of these regimes. There is a fundamental difference between a place of business and a branch and the distinction between the two terms is considered in paragraphs 32.9 to 32.13 below.

32.4 Prior to 1 January 1993, an oversea company that had established a branch was regulated in the same way as an oversea company that had established a place of business in Great Britain. From 1 January 1993, however, new rules in relation to the registration and filing of financial statements and other corporate information were introduced for foreign companies (that is, companies incorporated outside the UK and Gibraltar) that conduct business in Great Britain through a branch. The need to introduce new rules for oversea companies that have a branch in Great Britain stems from the EU 11th Company Law Directive on Branch Accounts (89/666/EEC) ('EU 11th Directive').

32.5 The EU 11th Directive deals with disclosures to be made in respect of a branch established in a particular member state where the limited company that controls it is established in another member state or a non-EU country. The EU Bank Branches Directive (89/117/EC) complements this by establishing special rules for filing of financial statements and reports and other corporate information of branches of credit or financial institutions in a member state whose head office is outside that state. Both directives were implemented in the UK by The Oversea Companies and Credit and Financial Institutions (Branch Disclosure) Regulations (SI 1992/3179). These provisions are incorporated into Part XXIII of the 1985 Act.

32.6 The branch registration regime created by the regulations complemented the existing place of business registration scheme set out in Part XXIII of the Act. However, the regulations made a number of amendments to Part XXIII, including the addition of four schedules as follows:

- Regulation 2 and Schedule 1 of SI 1992/3179 implemented the EU Bank Branches Directive and introduced Schedule 21C, which sets out the requirements for delivering reports and financial statements of oversea companies that are credit or financial institutions to which the EU Bank Branches Directive applies. For this purpose, a credit or financial institution is an entity that is incorporated or otherwise formed outside the UK and Gibraltar, has its head office outside the UK and Gibraltar, and has a branch in Great Britain. [CA85 Sec 699A; CA06 Sec 1173].
- Regulation 3 and Schedule 2 of SI 1992/3179 implemented the EU 11th Directive. It inserts three schedules into the 1985 Act as follows:
    - Schedule 21A, which sets out the particulars to be disclosed under the branch registration regime by a limited company incorporated outside the UK and Gibraltar and which has a branch in Great Britain.
    - Schedule 21B, which provides for certain transitional arrangements where an oversea company moves from the place of business registration regime to the branch registration regime and *vice versa.*
    - Schedule 21D, which sets out the requirements for the reports and financial statements to be delivered by a limited company that is incorporated outside the UK and Gibraltar, has a branch in Great Britain and which is not an institution to which section 699A applies.

32.7 This chapter primarily deals with the accounting and the disclosure requirements for oversea companies that are not credit institutions engaged in deposit taking or lending, or financial institutions. As stated in paragraph 32.6 above, there are additional rules in Schedule 21C to the 1985 Act relating to the reports and financial statements to be delivered by credit and financial institutions as defined in section 699A of the 1985 Act. These rules are outside the scope of this chapter. All references in this chapter to an oversea company are to a company other than a credit or financial institution, unless it is stated otherwise.

Companies Act 2006

32.7.1 Part 34 of the Companies Act 2006 (the 2006 Act) will replace the current legislation on oversea companies and will apply to 'overseas companies', a wider definition than the 1985 Act's 'oversea companies' (see para 32.8). The commencement date for Part 34 of the 2006 Act is October 2008, but Part 34 contains little detail of the provisions that will apply to overseas companies, instead giving the power to the Secretary of State to make regulations to set out the specific requirements. These regulations have, at the time of writing, not been created. However, the government has indicated that it wishes to create a single regulatory regime to replace the current place of business and branch registration regimes.

32.7.2 In creating the single regime, the Department for Business, Enterprise and Regulatory Reform (BERR (formerly the DTI)) wishes to establish the single regime on the wider concept of 'place of business'. In order to comply with the EU 11th Directive, the registration and reporting requirements of the new regime will match those currently required for an EU branch and apply to all UK registered places of business of overseas companies, regardless of their country of incorporation. In its current thinking, BERR wishes to dispense with the section 700 of the 1985 Act form of accounts (see from 32.27) and instead allow overseas companies to file financial statements that they prepare and have audited for their own jurisdiction's purposes. If an overseas company is not subject to any local requirements for such financial statements, the regulations would require something akin to the current 'section 700 accounts'(see para 32.28). Any local financial statements would be balanced by a requirement for greater transparency about the information filed. This may involve greater clarity as to the legislation and other principles that have been followed in preparing, making disclosures in and auditing those financial statements or where they have not followed principles to say so.

32.7.3 As at the beginning of October 2007, the detail of the new regime for overseas companies under the 2006 Act has yet to be published by the government, the following parts of this chapter are confined to the current place of business and branch registration regimes under the 1985 Act, unless the text indicates otherwise.

Definitions

Oversea company

32.8 An 'oversea company' is defined in the 1985 Act as any 'company' incorporated outside Great Britain (that is, England, Wales and Scotland) which has established a 'place of business' in Great Britain. [CA85 Sec 744]. It includes unlimited as well as limited companies. The 2006 Act refers to 'overseas companies', which are defined as companies incorporated outside the UK (that is, Great Britain and Northern Ireland). [CA06 Sec 1044]. There are special rules under the 1985 Act for dealing with Northern Ireland, Channel Islands, Isle of Man and Gibraltar companies operating in Great Britain (see paras 32.16 and 17). When Part 34 of the 2006 Act comes into operation it will apply to the whole of the UK including Northern Ireland and thus Northern Ireland companies will be no different from their counterparts in Great Britain. Channel Island, Isle of Man and Gibraltar companies will continue to be subject to special rules.

Place of business

32.9 There is no comprehensive statutory definition in English law of what constitutes a 'place of business'. The 1985 Act merely states that the term includes a share transfer or share registration office. [CA85 Sec 744]. Those companies that have a place of business in the form of a branch are subject to the branch registration scheme; those that do not have a branch are subject to the place of business regime. In general, if an oversea company performs functions in Great Britain that are only ancillary or incidental to the company's business as a whole (for example, warehouse facilities, administrative offices, internal data processing facilities), then the company has established a place of business in Great Britain but not a branch. It follows that it is not necessary for the oversea company to carry out its main activities at the locality in Great Britain, but merely to restrict its activities there to matters incidental to its main business for it to have established a place of business. If this crucial test is met, the oversea company will be subject to the registration requirements under the place of business regime.

32.10 Whether a place of business has been established must be a question of fact in each particular circumstance. Guidance can be found by reference to decided cases that illustrate the following principles:

- A local habitation of its own.

  The company must have a "local habitation of its own". Accordingly, a company will not be regarded as having established a place of business if it carries on its activities through an agent. [*Lord Advocate v Huron & Erie Loan and Savings Co*. [1911] SC 612].

- Level of corporate activity required.

  It is sufficient that the company carries on some business activity at its representative office. It does not matter if that business is incidental and does not form a substantial part of its main activities. [*South India Shipping Corporation Limited v Export-Import Bank of Korea*. [1985] 1 WLR 585]. A share transfer or share negotiation office is a 'place of business'. [CA85 Sec 744].

- Corporate presence of company officers.

A hotel that a director frequently stays in when in Great Britain and from which he transacts the company's business is sufficient to denote an 'established place of business'. [*Re. Tovarishestvo Manufactur Liudvig-Rabenek*. [1944] Ch 404]. However, the mere presence of the directors in their private residence will not make the residence a place of business. [*Re. Oriel Ltd*. [1986] 1 WLR 180].

Branch

32.11 The concept of a 'branch' is one of EU law and has no ready counterpart in English law. Whilst the term 'branch' is defined in section 699A of the 1985 Act (section 1050(2) of the 2006 Act), for the purposes of establishing whether a credit or financial institution is one to which section 699A of the 1985 Act (section 1050(2) of the 2006 Act) applies, as 'a place of business which forms a legally dependent part of the institution and which conducts directly all or some of the operations inherent in its business', there is no definition of the term for the purposes of the branch registration regime in the 1985 Act. All that section 1046(3) of the 2006 Act says is that a *"'branch' means a branch within the meaning of the Eleventh Company Law Directive (89/666/EEC)"*. As the term is not defined in the EU 11th Directive, it will ultimately be a question for the European Court of Justice to decide. Some guidance may, however, be found in the decisions of the Court. The Court considered the meaning of 'branch or agency' in *Somafer SA v Saar-Ferngas Ag*. Case 33/78 [1979] 1 CMLR 490 and said that the concept of a branch or agency implies a place of business:

- Which has the appearance of permanency, such as the extension of a parent body.
- Has a management.
- Is materially equipped to negotiate business with third parties so that the latter, although knowing that there will if necessary be a legal link with the parent body, the head office of which is abroad, do not have to deal directly with such parent body, but may transact business at the place of business constituting the extension.

Companies House has issued a Guidance Note (GB01) dated February 2005 entitled 'Oversea companies', which contains guidelines on its view on the definition of a branch: *"A 'branch' is part of an oversea limited company organised to conduct business through local representatives in Great Britain rather than referring it abroad"*, and how it differs from a place of business: *"'A place of business' is a premises where there is a physical or visible indication that the company may be contacted there"*.

32.12 In general, if the functions performed in Great Britain are not ancillary or incidental to the oversea company's business, but are conducted on behalf of the company, then the oversea company has established a branch. It should be noted, however, that the term 'branch' is not used in the commonly understood sense of a local bank branch or an office branch at a single locality. It is closer in meaning to a subsidiary, although it will not be a separate body corporate.

32.13 Further, a single oversea company may set up more than one branch in Great Britain, if each branch has a separate management structure. This is important, since each 'branch' has to be separately registered (see para 32.22 below).

Registration of oversea companies

32.14 There is no obligation upon a company incorporated outside Great Britain to register in Great Britain unless it has established a place of business or a branch here. That is, the oversea company has no physical location in Great Britain. Companies House February 2005 Guidance Note GB01, illustrates this with the example of an independent agent who conducts business on behalf of the company, would not represent a place of business of an oversea company. Neither would an occasional location such as a hotel where a director may conduct business during periodic visits to Great Britain. However, where an oversea company has established a place of business or a branch, it must register in Great Britain either under the current place of business registration regime or under the current branch registration regime. An oversea company cannot have both a branch registration and a place of business registration in the UK at the same time. This is because every branch may comprise one or more places of business, but not every place of business is necessarily a branch.

32.15 It is, therefore, important for every oversea company wishing to establish a business activity in Great Britain to consider whether they should be registered under the branch or place of business regime and what sort of accounting disclosures should be made (see paras 32.38 to 32.50 below). Legal advice should be sought where there is doubt concerning the regime under which the oversea operations in Great Britain should be registered.

32.15.1 According to the Companies House February 2005 Guidance Note GB01 other types of commercial enterprises such as partnerships, limited partnerships, unincorporated bodies or government agencies cannot register in Great Britain as an oversea company.

Place of business registration

32.16 As stated in paragraph 32.5 above, the scope of the EU 11th Directive is confined to disclosures to be made in respect of a branch established in a particular member state where the limited company that controls it is established in another member state or a non-EU country. The Directive does not deal with any disclosure member states may require from a foreign company with any lesser presence, such as a place of business, in their territory. Consequently, some companies continue to be subject to the place of business registration regime if they have established a place of business in Great Britain. [CA85 Sec 691]. These companies, which cannot register under the branch regime and remain subject to the place of business regime however large their operations, are as follows:

- *Unlimited* companies incorporated outside Great Britain (the EU 11th Directive applies only to limited companies incorporated outside the UK).
- Limited companies incorporated in Northern Ireland or Gibraltar. As Northern Ireland and Gibraltar are treated as being within the United Kingdom, the EU 11th Directive does not apply to companies incorporated in these regions if they open a branch in Great Britain. However, if such companies establish a place of business in Great Britain, they will be treated as oversea companies in Great Britain and, accordingly, become subject to the place of business regime.
- Limited companies incorporated outside Great Britain that do not have a branch in Northern Ireland and whose activities in Great Britain are not sufficient to fall under the branch registration regime but is sufficient to fall within the place of business regime. Such activities might include internal computer processing, warehousing, or simply a representative office

32.16.1 Channel Island and Isle of Man companies are also treated as oversea companies, however, a special regime applies to them under section 699 of the 1985 Act unless they establish a branch, in which case they are treated as third countries (that is, not within the UK reflecting their position as UK dependencies, but not part of the EU).

Branch registration

32.17 Every *limited* company, incorporated outside the UK and Gibraltar, which opens or has a branch in Great Britain is required to register under the branch registration regime. [CA85 Sec 690A]. All other oversea companies (see para 32.16 above) that do not qualify to be registered under the branch registration regime must register under the place of business regime. Channel Island and Isle of Man companies that establish branches in Great Britain are treated for the purposes of the branch regime as third countries.

Change in registration regime

32.18 When an oversea company changes the nature of the business it conducts within Great Britain so that it moves from the place of business regime to the branch regime, or *vice versa*, it must re-register accordingly. [CA85 Sec 692A]. There are transitional provisions in relation to the change from one registration regime to the other. These are set out in Schedule 21B to the 1985 Act.

Particulars to be registered

Place of business regime

32.19 An oversea company that has established a place of business in Great Britain must, *within one month* of doing so, deliver to the appropriate Registrar of Companies (England & Wales, Companies House, Cardiff; Scotland, Companies House, Edinburgh), a return in the prescribed form (Form 691). In general, Form 691 requires details of the company's constitution and related documents and information on the company's directors and secretary. The detailed information and the particular documents to be filed are set out in section 691 of the 1985 Act.

32.20 Oversea companies incorporated in the Channel Islands or the Isle of Man that have a place of business in Great Britain are additionally treated, for the purpose of the provisions of the Act relating to documents to be forwarded, delivered or filed with the Registrar of Companies, as if they were registered in England and Wales or Scotland, subject to certain exceptions. [CA85 Sec 699].

Branch registration regime

32.21 An oversea company that has opened a branch in Great Britain must, *within one month* of doing so, deliver to the appropriate Registrar of Companies, a return in the prescribed form (Form BRA) containing particulars about the company and the branch. The detailed information and the particular documents to be filed are set out in Schedule 21A to the 1985 Act.

32.22 The branch registration requires certain information to be filed in respect of *each branch*. As a branch can operate from more than one place in Great Britain, it is necessary to consider whether each location constitutes a branch in its own right. The test is to establish whether each location has its own management structure, with distinct reporting lines back to the parent company. If that is the case, then each of these locations must be registered in its own right as a branch. If, however, the locations of the company in Great Britain are linked within a uniform management structure, through which reports are made to the parent company, then all the locations, no matter how numerous, count as one branch and require only one registration. The registration must be made with the Registrar of Companies for the appropriate jurisdiction (England & Wales or Scotland) according to the branch's principal place of business (for example, its head office or main office).

Accounting records

32.23 There are no provisions in the 1985 Act requiring an oversea company registered in Great Britain to keep adequate, or even any, accounting records. This is despite the detailed requirements to prepare and file financial statements considered in the paragraphs below. In practice, however, such records as are necessary for conducting the affairs of the oversea company in Great Britain are often kept.

Accounting reference period

Place of business regime

32.24 The accounting reference period of an oversea company subject to the place of business registration regime is determined in the same way as for a company incorporated under the 1985 Act, except that the equivalent of the date of incorporation of a company registered under the 1985 Act is the date on which an oversea company establishes a place of business in Great Britain. [CA85 Sec 701]. Accounting reference periods are considered further in chapter 8 of the Manual of Accounting – Management Reports and Governance.

32.25 Furthermore, such an oversea company, unlike a company incorporated in Great Britain, is permitted to extend its accounting reference period even though more than five years have not elapsed since an earlier accounting period was extended by virtue of section 225 of the 1985 Act. [CA85 Sec 701(3)].

Branch registration regime

32.26 The accounting reference period of an oversea company subject to the branch registration regime is the period for which the company is required or permitted by the law of the country in which it is incorporated to prepare financial statements. Consequently, section 701 of the 1985 Act does not apply to such companies.

Preparation of financial statements

32.27 The form of the reports and financial statements required to be prepared and delivered by an oversea company to the Registrar of Companies depends upon whether the company in question has established a place of business or a branch in Great Britain.

Place of business regime

32.28 Every oversea company that is subject to the place of business regime must prepare individual and (if appropriate) consolidated financial statements in respect of each accounting reference period. The basic rule is that these must be made up by reference to such dates and contain the same information as if the company had been formed and registered under the 1985 Act. [CA85 Sec 700(1)]. The Secretary of State, however, has taken advantage of the power contained in section 700(2) and (3) of the 1985 Act to modify these requirements or exempt oversea companies from some of them. The current statutory instrument giving effect to the exemption is The Oversea Companies (Accounts) (Modifications and Exemptions) Order 1990 (SI 1990/440). Such accounts drawn up under section

700 of the 1985 Act (as amended by SI 1990/440) are known as 'section 700 accounts' and must relate to the company and not solely to the place of business.

32.29 The financial statements, subject to the available exemptions set out in paragraph 32.33 below, have to comply with the requirements of sections 258 and 259 of, and Schedule 9 to, the original Companies Act 1985 *before it was amended by the Companies Act 1989 and all later amendments* as if the oversea companies were, what in 1985 were regarded as special category companies insofar as those requirements applied. [SI 1990/440 para 2(1)(b)]. There is no requirement, however, to refer to the fact that the financial statements have been drawn up in compliance with section 258 or section 259 of, and Schedule 9 to, the original unamended Companies Act 1985. [SI 1990/440 Sch 5]. The original Schedule 9 applied to shipping, banking and insurance companies, but in the context of the place of business regime for oversea companies, it applies to companies in all industry sectors. The original Schedule 9 is very minimalist in its requirements and contains neither the specialised content that the 1985 Act has today for banking and insurance companies nor even the level of detail required for non-banking and insurance companies required by Schedule 4 to the 1985 Act or IAS 1. A set of 'section 700 accounts' consists of a profit and loss account, a balance sheet and supporting notes, which must include details of a company's share capital.

32.29.1 Sections 258 and 259 of, and Schedule 9 to, the original unamended 1985 Act make no reference to any accounting framework. It might be inferred 'section 700 accounts' should be drawn up using UK GAAP, as that was the only GAAP used by GB companies preparing their financial statements in 1985. The requirement for GB companies to use UK accounting standards introduced by the 1989 Act is not relevant nor is the 2004 amendment to the 1985 Act (SI 2004/2947, 'The Companies Act 1985 (International Accounting Standards and Other Accounting Amendments) Regulations 2004', to permit companies to use either UK GAAP (Companies Act accounts) or EU-adopted IFRS (IAS accounts). Consequently, we consider that 'section 700 accounts' can be prepared using any GAAP.

32.30 Oversea companies are, of course, permitted to give additional information, including that required by Schedule 4 to the 1985 Act or IAS 1 or even to prepare full Companies Act or IAS accounts. Any information that an oversea company wants to include in its financial statements may alternatively be disclosed in a statement annexed to the financial statements.

32.31 Oversea companies may not take advantage of the exemptions available to small, medium-sized or dormant companies. [SI 1990/440 para 2(1)(c)].

32.32 An unlimited oversea company that, if it were a company registered in Great Britain, would be exempt from the requirement to deliver financial statements to the Registrar of Companies in respect of a particular accounting period under section 241(4) of the 1985 Act, is also exempt from the requirement to prepare (and hence deliver) such annual financial statements. [SI 1990/440 para 2(3)].

32.33 The exemptions in SI 1990/440 referred to above allow oversea companies to omit the following information from their financial statements:

- An audit report (see also para 32.53).
- A directors' report.
- Taxation information:
  - The basis of computation and amount of any provision, or charge to revenue for UK corporation tax (ignoring double tax relief) and UK income tax.
  - The amount of any charge for taxation imposed outside the UK on profits, income and capital gains (to the extent that capital gains are credited to revenue).
- The amount of turnover and the method by which it is arrived at.
- Details in the parent company's financial statements of the identities of, the place of incorporation of, and particulars of the company's shareholdings in subsidiaries.
- Details of investments that exceed one-tenth of the nominal value of any class of the issued equity share capital of another body corporate and details of any investment that exceeds one-tenth of the company's own assets.
- Details of the name and place of incorporation of the company's ultimate parent company.
- Particulars of the chairman's and the highest-paid director's emoluments and the banding of all directors' emoluments (although this is no longer a requirement of the 1985 Act).
- Details of any emoluments that directors have waived.
- Details of the bandings of higher-paid employees' emoluments (although this is no longer a requirement of the 1985 Act).
- Particulars of loans and other transactions with directors and officers.

[SI 1990/440 Sch 2-6].

32.34 Where an oversea company avails itself of the above exemptions, the contents of its financial statements will be substantially different from those of a company incorporated in Great Britain. Consequently, it is recommended that any oversea company that takes advantage of the provisions of the regulation should disclose this fact in the notes to its financial statements. This recommendation applies whether or not those financial statements are audited. A suitable wording for inclusion in the basis of preparation note is:

Example

The financial statements have been prepared in accordance with the Companies Act 1985 applicable to oversea companies. The company has taken advantage of the modifications and exemptions from disclosure that are set out in the Oversea Companies (Accounts) (Modifications and Exemptions) Order 1990.

32.35 It should be noted that the 'section 700 accounts' (see para 32.28 above) must be the financial statements not of the UK operation, but of the legal entity incorporated overseas (containing the transactions of the UK operation as appropriate). Consequently, an oversea company with a place of business in Great Britain may have to disclose more information concerning its financial statements than is required by the laws of the country in which it is incorporated. In practice, however, the effect of the exemptions outlined above will generally mean that the oversea company can file its own 'parent law' financial statements if they comply with the original, unamended 1985 Act's provisions or amend them as necessary to comply with that Act's provisions. 'Parent law' in this connection means the law of the country in which the company is incorporated.

Branch registration regime

32.36 One of the principal purposes of the EU 11th Directive is to protect companies operating in other EU countries from having to meet disclosure requirements in their financial statements that are more onerous than those required in their home state. This relaxation in reporting rules, which was incorporated into the 1985 Act when the EU 11th Directive was implemented in the UK by SI 1992/3179, allows an oversea company that is a foreign limited company (see para 32.6) to file the financial statements that have been prepared, audited and disclosed under its 'parent law' together with a certified English translation. 'Parent law' in this connection means the law of the country in which the company is incorporated.

32.36.1 Where an oversea company, with a branch in Great Britain, is not required to prepare, have audited and make public disclosure of its financial statements under its 'parent law', it is required to prepare and file its financial statements in the same manner as an oversea company subject to the place of business regime as described above. That is 'section 700 accounts' (see 32.28 above). This situation may apply, for example, to a private company incorporated in the US with a branch in Great Britain.

32.37 The rules relating to the delivery of reports and financial statements by a foreign limited company that has established a branch in Great Britain are set out in Schedule 21D to the 1985 Act and are considered further in paragraphs 32.43 to 32.50 below.

Filing of financial statements with the Registrar

32.38 All oversea companies must deliver (file) a copy of the required financial statements (as discussed in paras 32.28 to 32.37) for each accounting reference period to the Registrar of Companies irrespective of whether they have established a place of business or a branch in Great Britain. However, the form of the financial statements to be delivered and the period allowed for delivery to the Registrar are different for the two regimes.

Place of business regime

32.39 As discussed in paragraph 32.28 above, an oversea company that is subject to the place of business registration regime must file its 'section 700 accounts' with the Registrar of Companies together with a certified translation thereof where they are not written in the English. There is no requirement that such financial statements must be circulated to shareholders. [CA85 Sec 702(1)].

32.40 The period allowed for delivery to the Registrar is 13 months from the accounting reference date. [CA85 Sec 702(2)]. This is longer than the current time limits for companies incorporated in Great Britain, which are allowed ten months for a private company, and seven months for a public company. Under the 2006 Act, the time limits for UK companies are shortened to nine and six months respectively.

32.41 If the oversea company's first accounting reference period exceeds 12 months, the period allowed is 13 months from the first anniversary of the company establishing a place of business in Great Britain. [CA85 Sec 702(3)].

32.42 If the oversea company shortens its accounting reference period by giving notice under section 225 (alteration of accounting reference date), the period allowed for filing will be 13 months after the date on which the new accounting reference date ends or three months from the date of notice under that section, whichever expires last. [CA85 Sec 702(4)].

Branch registration regime

32.43 As stated in paragraph 32.37 above, an oversea company that is a foreign limited company that has established a branch in Great Britain is required to file its 'parent law' reports and financial statements or its 'section 700 accounts', as the case may be, with the Registrar of Companies in accordance with Schedule 21D to the 1985 Act. These requirements are in some respects different from those applicable to companies merely establishing places of business in Great Britain. Furthermore, the form of the reports and the financial statements required to be delivered under Schedule 21D differ depending on whether the company in question is required to prepare, have audited and disclose its reports and financial statements under its parent law, or whether no such disclosure is required.

Disclosure required in state of incorporation

32.44 If the law of the state in which the oversea company is incorporated requires it to prepare, have audited and publicly disclose its financial statements it must, within one month of opening a branch, deliver to the Registrar of Companies with the return (Form BRA) for registration copies of its latest accounting documents prepared and disclosed in accordance with that law. [CA85 21D Sch 2(2)]. Publicly disclose means disclosure in a registry or by publication in a register, gazette or equivalent provision. Laws requiring disclosure to shareholders alone are not laws requiring public disclosure.

32.45 In the subsequent years after first registration, accounting documents prepared in relation to a financial period of the company must be delivered within three months of the date when they are first disclosed in accordance with the parent law. [CA85 21D Sch 4]. As a general rule the documents must be filed in respect of each branch. However, it is possible for a principal branch to file financial statements in respect of other branches provided this is specified in those branch returns. [CA85 21D Sch 3].

32.46 The accounting documents in relation to the financial period of the company referred to in the preceding paragraph consist of:

- The individual financial statements of the company.
- Its consolidated financial statements where it has subsidiaries.
- The directors' report for the period if any.
- The auditors' report on the financial statements.
- The auditors' report, if applicable, on the directors' report.

[CA85 21D Sch 6(2)].

A duly certified translation must also be provided of any document that is not in English. [CA85 21D Sch 2(4)].

32.47 If the parent law permits the company to disclose its accounting documents in a modified or abbreviated form, the oversea company may file these with the Registrar of Companies. [CA85 21D Sch 2(3)]. This is in contrast to an oversea company with a place of business in Great Britain that cannot take advantage of the modified financial statements provisions relating to small or medium-sized GB companies (see para 32.31 above).

32.48 A company incorporated outside the EU and required to file home country financial statements must notify the Registrar of Companies on registration of its accounting reference period and the date by which it is required to file its financial statements under its parent law. [CA85 21A Sch 2(2)].

Disclosure not required in state of incorporation

32.49 Where an oversea company with a branch is not required to prepare, have audited and make public disclosure of its financial statements under its parent law, it is required to prepare and file 'section 700 accounts' (see para 32.36.1).

32.50 It follows that in order for financial statements prepared under a non-EC country's laws to be acceptable for filing in the UK, its parent law must *require* audited and publicly disclosed financial statements. It would not be sufficient, for example, if an oversea limited company with a branch in Great Britain whose country of incorporation did *not* require such financial statements, voluntarily drew up, had audited and disclosed financial statements in a form other than that required by the place of business regime. Such a company would still have to prepare 'section 700 accounts' in order to comply with the UK filing requirements.

Listed overseas companies

32.51 Regardless of any of the exemptions or modifications referred to above, any oversea company that has obtained a listing on the Main Market of the London Stock Exchange or the Plus-listed market is bound by the requirements of the UK Listing Authority's (UKLA) Listing Rules and Disclosure and Transparency Rules (LR and DTR). For accounting periods that commenced prior to 1 January 2007, a listed oversea company is still subject to Listing Rule 14.4 to circulate annual audited financial statements to all holders of its listed securities whose addresses are in the UK. [LR 14.4.4(4)]. For accounting periods that commenced after 1 January 2007, a listed oversea company should consider its obligations under DTR 4 (Periodic financial reporting), DTR 5 (Vote holder and issuer notification rules) and DTR 6 (Access to information). [LR.14.3.22].

32.52 Specifically, a foreign company with a listing on the Main Market of the London Stock Exchange, whose accounting period commenced prior to 1 January 2007, must publish financial statements that comply with the following requirements:

- They must be prepared in accordance with the oversea company's national law and, in all material respects, with its national accounting standards or International Accounting Standards.
- They must have been independently audited and reported on in accordance with the auditing standards applicable in an EEA State or an equivalent auditing standard and the audit report must be attached to the financial statements.
- They must be in consolidated form (if the oversea company has subsidiary undertakings).

- If they do not give a true and fair view of the state of affairs, profit or loss and cash flows of the group, they must provide more detailed and additional information.
- The company's own financial statements must be published in addition to the consolidated financial statements where these contain significant additional information.
- Disclosure must be made of the particulars of the interest of each director and major shareholder in the company's share capital.
- Disclosure must be made of any information necessary for the holders of the company's securities resident in the United Kingdom to obtain any tax relief to which they are entitled.

[LR 14.4.2-14.4.4].

32.52.1 An oversea company with a listing on the Main Market of the London Stock Exchange or on the Plus-listed market, whose accounting period commences on or after 1 January 2007, must publish annual financial statements and half yearly interim reports that comply with the requirements of DTR 4.16 and 4.2.4 (essentially, the annual financial statements must be prepared using IFRS and the condensed interim financial statements must comply with IAS 34 respectively). The annual financial statements must be audited. However, oversea companies are exempt from the requirement to prepare their annual consolidated financial statements and half yearly reports in accordance with IFRS and IAS 34 respectively prior to accounting periods starting on or after 1 January 2009 and provided certain conditions are met (see para 32.52.2). [UKLA DTR TP 1(3A)]. Furthermore, an oversea company whose registered office is in a non-European Economic Area (EEA) State whose relevant laws are considered equivalent by the FSA is exempted from the rules on annual financial reports (DTR 4.1), half-yearly financial reports (DTR 4.2) and interim management statements (DTR 4.3) [DTR 4.4.8]. The FSA maintains a list of non-EEA States that are judged to have laws that lay down requirements equivalent to those imposed on issuers by DTR 4. [DTR 4.4.9].

32.52.2 The exemption in the period from 1 January 2007 to 31 December 2008 is a transitional relief to allow certain overseas companies (third country) issuers that have their securities admitted to trading in the EU to use their own local accounting standards rather than EU-adopted IFRS. [European Commission (EC) Regulation 1787/2006]. During the transitional period third country issuers can continue to publish financial statements using GAAPs that meet one of the following criteria:

- A GAAP that enables the issuer to make a declaration that it complies with the requirements of IAS (an 'IAS 1 declaration'); or
- A GAAP where a national standard setter has publicly stated an intention to converge with IFRS; has established a work programme that demonstrates the intention to progress towards that convergence before

31 December 2008 and where the issuer has provided to the competent authority (the UKLA in the UK) satisfactory evidence of these two conditions being satisfied.

32.52.3 In this transitional period, oversea companies can also provide financial statements that comply fully with IFRS (even if it does not comply with IFRS as adopted in the EU).

32.52.4 In addition, the transitional relief specifically allows issuers to use Canadian, Japanese and US GAAP on the basis that they already satisfy the second criterion above. For other GAAPs to satisfy this criterion, however, the local standards setter's declaration needs to be made before the start of the financial year to which the financial statements relate. Although alternative GAAPs to EU-adopted IFRS are permitted in this transitional period, it does not necessarily indicate that the use of that GAAP will be permissible once the transitional period ends and the EC finally has determined which other GAAPs are equivalent to EU-adopted IFRS. The Committee of European Securities Regulators (CESR) has issued a list of countries at 5 April 2007 that it believes satisfies the transitional criteria. The countries on that list include those countries:

- Able to satisfy the IAS 1 declaration provision: Australia, Hong Kong, New Zealand, South Africa and Singapore.
- With convergence programmes already identified: Brazil, China and Taiwan.

32.52.5 In addition to these countries, the transitional provisions specifically allows users of Canadian, Japanese or US GAAPs to continue using these standards irrespective of the countries of incorporation. CESR has identified the following countries from which issuers likely to satisfy the transitional measures are expected to come: Canada, Japan, USA, Cayman Islands, Bermuda, Netherlands Antilles, Jersey, Guernsey and the British Virgin Islands.

32.52.6 The list of countries above is not intended by CESR to be exhaustive. The UKLA has advised that it is important that issuers proposing to submit financial statements containing financial information, other than as indicated above, not only allow time in their submission process for a GAAP assessment to be made but also to provide at the outset any evidence required by the transitional measures, as it is not the UKLA's responsibility to gather such information. An early approach to the UKLA is therefore recommended.

32.52.7 A LSE publication, 'Main Market Continuing Obligations', can be downloaded from its web site and this document sets out in summary-checklist form the key continuing obligations for companies that have either a primary listing of equity or a secondary listing of equity or depositary receipts.

32.52.8 Consequently, depending on the requirements that the UKLA imposes, a listed oversea company may be unable to take advantage of many of the exemptions available to unlisted oversea companies outlined above.

Oversea companies traded on AIM

32.52.9 The LSE requires EEA companies traded on its second market, AIM to publish annual and half yearly financial statements using IFRS. Where, at the end of the relevant financial period, such a company is not a parent company, it may prepare and present such financial information either in accordance with IAS or in accordance with the accounting and company legislation and regulations that are applicable to that company due to its country of incorporation. [AIM Rule 18 and 19].

32.52.10 An AIM company incorporated in a non-EEA country must present these financial statements using either IFRS, US, Canadian or Australian GAAP.

[The next paragraph is 32.53.]

Audit requirements

32.53 No requirement for an audit is imposed by the 1985 Act on oversea companies with a place of business in Great Britain, although the law of the oversea company's country of incorporation may still do so. This is subject to the obligations on oversea companies which are listed on the Main Market of the London Stock Exchange or on the Plus-listed market as discussed in paragraphs 32.51 to 32.52.7 above.

Practical issue

32.54 Given that the financial reporting responsibilities of an unlisted limited company incorporated outside the UK under the place of business registration regime are fundamentally different from the branch registration regime, the question arises as to which of the current two regimes provides the more effective environment for such a company to operate in Great Britain.

32.55 The answer depends firstly on the extent of the operations to be carried out by the oversea company in Great Britain. If the operations to be carried out in Great Britain are more than merely incidental to its main activities outside the UK, then the established operations would qualify as a branch rather than a place of business. Secondly, it is necessary to consider whether the oversea company is required to prepare, have audited and make public disclosure of its financial statements under its parent law. In that situation, it can meet the 1985 Act's filing requirements by simply filing its financial statements prepared under its parent law (including the transactions of the Great Britain branch) without any further modifications. On the other hand, if parent law does not require financial statements to be prepared, filed and audited then from the disclosure of financial statements point of view, it does not matter whether its operations in Great Britain are registered under the place of business registration regime or the branch registration regime. This is because, in either situation, the oversea company currently has to file its 'section 700 accounts' although these financial statements need not be audited.

32.56 However, in both situations, there is the disadvantage that the financial statements filed under the 1985 Act contain the transactions of the oversea operations as well as those of the Great Britain operations. It may be that the oversea company would prefer to file financial statements that deal only with its Great Britain operations, without divulging its identity or nature of its business carried on outside the UK. In that situation, the only route is to conduct the local operations through a UK incorporated subsidiary. Although there is a requirement to disclose in the financial statements of the UK subsidiary the identity and the country of incorporation of the ultimate parent, the subsidiary undertaking can take the exemption under section 231(3)(b) of the 1985 Act (section 409(3) and (4) of the 2006 Act) not to disclose such information, if it would, in the opinion of the directors, be seriously prejudicial to the business of its parent undertaking, or to its own or any of its subsidiaries, and the Secretary of State agrees that the information need not be disclosed. Indeed, some companies have taken advantage of this concession where its directors are of the opinion that disclosure of the ultimate or the immediate parent company's nationality would be unacceptable or offensive to its own customers.

32.57 As indicated in paragraph 32.7.1, when implementing the 2006 Act, the government has indicated that it wishes to replace the two current regimes with one single regulatory regime and to simplify the 'section 700 accounts' in the process. This, hopefully, reduces the dilemma discussed in paragraph 32.55, but not the disadvantage referred to in paragraph 32.56.

Index

Locators are:
paragraph numbers: 11.149, for Chapter 11, paragraph 149

Entries are in word-by-word alphabetical order, where a group of letters followed by a space is filed before the same group of letters followed by a letter, eg 'capital structure and treasury policy' will appear before 'capitalisation'. In determining alphabetical arrangement, initial articles, conjunctions and small prepositions are ignored.

Abandonment costs
provisions, and, 21.249—21.257
Abbreviated financial statements
medium-sized companies, and, 32.134—32.139
medium-sized groups, and, 32.154
small companies, and
auditors' responsibilities, 32.128—32.131
directors' responsibilities, 32.125—32.127
introduction, 32.117—32.124
small groups, and, 32.154
Abnormal transactions between year ends
associates and joint ventures, and, 27.144
Accelerated capital allowances
deferred tax, and, 13.104—13.106
Accounting for subsidiary undertakings
and see **Consolidated financial statements**
consolidation rules, 24.296—24.343
executive summary, 24.1—24.1.15
exemptions to requirement to prepare, 24.56—24.75
form, 24.41—24.50
introduction, 24.2—24.40
minority interests, and, 24.344—24.388
purpose, 24.27
requirement to prepare, 24.32—24.39
true and fair view, 24.51—24.55
Accounting policies
alteration
generally, 2.135—2.138
overview, 2.93.10—2.93.12
consistency, 2.138.1—2.138.7
generally, 2.121—2.127
overview
changes, 2.93.10—2.93.12
generally, 2.93.4
selection, 2.93.5—2.93.9
review, 2.135—2.138
selection
generally, 2.128—2.134
overview, 2.93.5—2.93.9
small companies, and, 32.98—32.99.6
taxation, and, 13.235
Accounting principles and rules
capital maintenance concepts, 2.145—2.146
Companies Act
compliance with accounting standards, 2.35—2.36
introduction, 2.21
requirement to prepare financial statements, 2.22—2.22.8
true and fair requirement, 2.23—2.34
compliance with accounting standards, 2.35—2.36
conventions
capital maintenance concepts, 2.145—2.146
current cost, 2.154
current purchasing power, 2.152—2.153

Accounting principles and rules—*cont*.
fair value, 2.151.1—2.151.4
generally, 2.149
historical cost, 2.150
introduction, 2.144
modified historical cost, 2.151
units of measurement, 2.148
valuation bases, 2.147
current cost convention, 2.154
current purchasing power convention, 2.152—2.153
fair value convention, 2.151.1—2.151.4
financial reporting structure
ASB Ltd, 2.54—2.64
Companies Act requirements, 2.48—2.50
Dearing Report proposals, 2.45—2.47
Financial Reporting Review Panel, 2.85—2.87
FRC Ltd, 2.51—2.53.7
FRSs, 2.65—2.73
SORPs, 2.74—2.77
SSAPs, 2.65—2.73
true and fair requirement, 2.78—2.80
Urgent Issues Task Force, 2.81—2.84
financial statements, 2.22—2.22.8
FRS18
accruals. 2.108—2.111
disclosures, 2.102—2.107
estimation techniques, 2.139—2.143
generally, 2.88—2.93
going concern, 2.94—2.101
policies, 2.121—2.138.7
prudence, 2.112
realisation, 2.112—2.115
separate valuation, 2.116—2.120
GAAP
Companies Act, 2.21—2.44
composition, 2.5—2.9
development, 2.10—2.20.4
historical cost convention, 2.150
modified historical cost convention, 2.151
introduction, 2.1—2.4
preparation of financial statements, 2.22—2.22.8
setting accounting standards
ASB Statement of principles, 2.191—2.215
background, 2.155—2.163
true and fair requirement, 2.23—2.34
units of measurement, 2.148
valuation bases, 2.147
Accounting records
oversea companies, and, 33.23
Accounting Regulatory Committee (ARC)
introduction, 1.5
Accounting Standards Board (ASB)
financial reporting structure, and, 2.54—2.64
introduction, 1.2

Index

Accounting Standards Board (ASB)—*cont.*
Statement of principles, 2.191—2.215
Accounting standards, compliance with
generally, 2.35—2.40
notes to balance sheet and profit and loss account, 4.132
Accruals
accounting principles, and
generally, 2.108—2.111
overview, 2.93.15
balance sheet, and, 4.92—4.94
Accrued income
balance sheet, and, 4.46—4.54
Accumulated depreciation
tangible fixed assets, and, 16.226—16.230
Acquisition accounting (FRS 6 and FRS 7)
accounting method, 25.1.1—25.1.2
adjusted capital, 25.39
adjustments to fair values, 25.42
associates, and
effective date, 27.162—27.164
generally, 27.165—27.169
business combinations, 25.2—25.3.1
cash flow statements, and
consolidated statements, and, 30.132—30.138
generally, 30.98—30.99
introduction, 25.125—25.127
comparison with IFRS, and, 25.3—25.7
comparison with merger accounting
generally, 28.109—28.111
introduction, 25.3—25.7
consolidation of new subsidiary
adjusted capital, 25.39
adjustments to fair values, 25.42
cost of acquisition, 25.31—25.34
date for recognising trading, 25.39—25.48
fees and expenses of acquisition, 25.35—25.38
goodwill, 25.43
identifiable assets and liabilities, 25.40—25.41
introduction, 25.29—25.30
reserves acquired, 25.39
cost of acquisition
generally, 25.31—25.34
summary, 25.1.12—25.1.15
date of changes in group membership
background, 25.18
definition, 25.19—25.27
effective date post balance sheet, 25.28
disclosure requirements
cash flow statement, 25.125—25.127
fair values of identifiable assets and liabilities, 25.96
general, 25.91—25.93
introduction, 25.88—25.90
post-acquisition activities, 25.114—25.124
pre-acquisition activities, 25.103—25.113
purchase consideration, 25.94—25.95
summary, 25.1.23—25.1.26
table of acquired assets and liabilities, 25.97—25.102
executive summary
cost of acquisition, 25.1.12—25.1.15
disclosures, 25.1.23—25.1.26
fair values of assets and liabilities, 25.1.3—25.1.9
goodwill, 25.1.16—25.1.20
method of accounting, 25.1.1—25.1.2
negative goodwill, 25.1.21—25.1.22
provisional fair values, 25.1.10—25.1.11
scope of standard, 25.1
fair values of assets and liabilities
generally, 25.96
summary, 25.1.3—25.1.9

Acquisition accounting (FRS 6 and FRS 7)—*cont.*
fair values of net assets
background, 25.96
contingent consideration, 25.410—25.425
deferred consideration, 25.404—25.409
deferred taxation, 25.381—25.382
fees and expenses of acquisition, 25.426—25.4
identifying assets and liabilities, 25.158—25.177
intangible assets, 25.178—25.231
introduction, 25.144—25.148
measuring fair values of assets and liabilities, 25.232—25.380
non-monetary consideration, 25.397—25.399
objective, 25.154—25.156
other consideration, 25.400—25.403
other securities, 25.396
overriding principles, 25.157
purchase consideration, 25.383—25.425
purchase of business or assets, 25.151—25.153
quoted securities, 25.390—25.393
scope, 25.149—25.150
summary, 25.1.3—25.1.9
unquoted securities, 25.394—25.395
fees and expenses of acquisition, 25.35—25.38
goodwill
accounting policy, 25.585—25.586
additions in existing subsidiaries, 25.600
allocation of purchased goodwill, 25.517
amortising goodwill, 25.494—25.499
capital redemption reserve, 25.569
capitalisation, and, 25.439—25.444
contingent consideration, 25.500—25.504
cumulative amounts written off, 25.587—25.591
disclosures, 25.584
disposals, 25.518—25.520, 25.581—25.582
earnout consideration, 25.601
effect on distributable profits, 25.573—25.580
impairment, 25.583—25.5
impairment reviews, 25.521—25.523, 25.532—25.552
implementing FRS 10, 25.598—25.599
indefinite life, 25.477—25.481
integrated acquisitions, 25.528—25.531
internally generated goodwill, 25.450
introduction, 25.437—25.438
merger reserve, 25.560—25..561
multiple useful economic lives, 25.482—25.493
non-distributable reserves, 25.563
positive and negative goodwill, 25.524—25.527
pre-FRS 10 goodwill remaining in reserves, 25.553
pre-FRS 10 negative goodwill remaining in reserves, 25.592—25.597
presentation of amortisation and impairment charges, 25.505—25.508
profit and loss account, 25.559
prohibition of separate write-off reserve, 25.554—25.555
purchased goodwill, 25.448—25.476
reserves used for write-offs, 25.557—25.558
revaluation reserve, 25.570—25.572
reversal of write-offs, 25.509—25.516
scope of FRS 10, 25.445—25.447
share premium account, 25.564—25.568
summary, 25.1.16—25.1.20
true and fair override, 25.477—25.481
useful economic life, 25.458—25.476
group reconstruction relief, 25.14
increases in stake
accounting principles, 25.68—25.73
agreement with shareholder, 25.86—25.87
associate becomes subsidiary, 25.81—25.83

Acquisition accounting (FRS 6 and FRS 7)—*cont.*
introduction, 25.64—25.67
investment becomes subsidiary, 25.75—25.80
parent acquires part of minority, 25.84—25.85
practical examples, 25.74—25.86
intangible fixed assets, and
generally, 15.41—15.45
IFRS, and, 15.134
introduction
business combinations, 25.2—25.2.3.1
comparison with merger accounting, 25.4—25.9
generally, 25.8—25.10
joint ventures, and
effective date, 27.162—27.164
generally, 27.165—27.169
merger accounting, and
generally, 28.109—28.111
introduction, 25.3—25.7
merger relief, 25.13
method of accounting, 25.1.1—25.1.2
negative goodwill, 25.1.21—25.1.22
parent company's financial statements
carrying value of investment, 25.41.6—25.41.43
pre-acquisition reserves, 25.62—25.63
post-acquisition activities
exceptional items, 25.118—25.120
layered formats, 25.114—25.117
provisions, 25.123—25.124
reorganisation and integration, 25.121—25.122
pre-acquisition activities
material acquisitions, of, 25.103—25.105
substantial acquisitions, of, 25.106—25.113
provisional fair values, 25.1.10—25.1.11
purchase consideration, 25.94—25.95
reporting financial performance, and
introduction, 8.70—8.76
mergers, 8.77—8.78
reserves acquired, 25.39
retirement benefits, and, 11.135—11.138
reverse acquisitions
cash alternatives, 25.143
generally, 25.128—25.142
scope of standard, 25.1
segmental reporting, and, 10.127—10.135
summary rules, 25.15—25.17
Actuarial gains and losses
retirement benefits, and
generally, 11.109—11.114
summary, 11.1.19
Adjusted capital
acquisition accounting, and, 25.39
Adjustments
consolidation rules, and
generally, 24.309
other, 24.317—24.318
uniform accounting policies, 24.310—24.316
fair values, and, 25.42
Administrative expenses
profit and loss account, and, 5.7—5.12
Admission fees
revenue recognition, and, 9.141—9.142
Advance corporation tax (ACT)
current tax, and, 13.50.1—13.50.9
Advance payments
revenue recognition, and, 9.73—9.74
Advertising agency commission
revenue recognition, and, 9.172
Agency arrangements
related party transactions, and, 29.72—29.75
revenue recognition, and, 9.161—9.171
Agency companies
disclosed principals, and, 32.179
disclosure requirements, 32.184—32.187
IFRS, and, 32.188
introduction, 32.176—32.177.1
recordable transactions, 32.180—32.183
undisclosed principals, and, 32.178
Agency fees
revenue recognition, and, 9.286—9.288
Aggregation
related party transactions, and
directors, with, 29.123—29.125
generally, 29.118—29.122
All employee share ownership plan (AESOP)
and see now **Share incentive plans**
generally, 12.86
Allocation of costs
segmental reporting, and, 10.62—10.66
Allocation of interest and taxation
reporting financial performance, and, 8.20—8.21
Allotment of shares during year
share capital, and, 23.35—23.37
Amortisation
intangible fixed assets, and
IFRS, and, 15.139
introduction, 15.66—15.69
methods, 15.84—15.85
residual values, 15.82—15.83
useful economic life, 15.71—15.81
PFI and PPP, and, 3.179.5
research and development, and, 15.125
Amounts received on account
balance sheet, and, 4.82
Amounts unpaid on debentures and shares
share capital, and, 23.233
Analysing complex transactions
conditions, 3.56
introduction, 3.52
linkage with other transactions, 3.54
options, 3.55—3.58
severance of legal title, 3.53
Annuity method
depreciation, and, 16.264—16.267
Application notes
consignment stock, 3.122
debt factoring, 3.136—3.136.16
introduction, 3.120—3.121
loan transfers, 3.168—3.179
PFI and PPP, 3.179.1—3.179.56
sale and repurchase agreements, 3.123—3.135
securitised assets, 3.137—3.167
summary, 3.1.20—3.1.21
Articles of association
share capital, and, 23.236—23.237
ASB Ltd
financial reporting structure, and, 2.54—2.64
Statement of principles, 2.191—2.215
ASB Statement of principles
elements, 2.205—2.209
group structure, and, 24.16—24.17
interests in other entities, 2.215
introduction, 2.191—2.192
materiality, 2.198—2.204
measurement, 2.212
objective, 2.193
presentation, 2.213—2.214
provisions, and, 21.7—21.8
qualitative characteristics, 2.195—2.197
recognition, 2.210—2.211
reporting entity, 2.194

Index

Asset recognition
provisions, and, 21.133—21.134
Assets
identification and recognition, and, 3.59—3.62
provisions, and, 21.25
Assets carried at historical cost
impairment, and, 18.250—18.251
Assets held for disposal
disclosure requirements, 18.263—18.269
generally, 18.214—18.220
Assets recognised by operator
accounting by operator, 3.179.50—3.179.53
accounting by purchaser, 3.179.54
Assets recognised by purchaser
accounting by operator, 3.179.55—3.179.55.2
accounting by purchaser, 3.179.55.3—3.17955.5
Assets surplus to requirements
tangible fixed assets, and, 16.189
Assets under construction
tangible fixed assets, and, 16.43—16.46
Assets used in business
tangible fixed assets, and, 16.185—16.188
Associates (FRS 9)
abnormal transactions between year ends, 27.144
accounting principles
acquisitions, 27.162—27.169
associate as group, 27.153
consolidation adjustments, 27.138—27.150
disposals, 27.170—27.1 72
extent of share, 27.119—27.122.1
financial statements, 27.136—27.137
interests in losses, 27.154—27.158
introduction, 27.116—27.118
joint and several liability, 27.159—27.160
joint venture becomes associate, 27.173
minority interests, 27.161
partnerships, 27.151—27.152
subsidiary becomes associate, 27.174—27.175
accounting requirements, 27.1.6—27.1.7
acquisitions
effective date, 27.162—27.164
generally, 27.165—27.169
additional disclosure
15% threshold information, 27.107—27.113
generally, 27.100—27.106
25% threshold information, 27.107—27.113
balance sheet
example, 27.95—27.97
goodwill, 27.88—27.93
gross equity method, 27.94
introduction, 27.85—27.87
cash flow statements, and
consolidated statements, and, 30.128—30.129
generally, 27.99
classification, 27.1.2—27.1.5
consolidation adjustments
abnormal transactions between year ends, 27.144
consistent accounting policies, 27.140
elimination of intra-group trading, 27.145—27.147
fair values, 27.141—27.143
goodwill, 27.141—27.143
intra-group trading transactions, 27.149—27.150
introduction, 27.138—27.139
transfer of assets to joint venture, 27.148
contractual arrangements, 27.1.19
convertible debt, 27.133—27.134
convertible shares, 27.132
cross-holdings, 27.135
definition, 27.55—27.67
disclosures, 27.1.23—27.1.29
disposals

Associates (FRS 9)—*cont.*
effective date, 27.162—27.164
generally, 27.170—27.172
equity accounting
additional disclosure, 27.100—27.113
balance sheet, 27.85—27.97
cash flow statement, 27.99
individual financial statements, 27.98
introduction, 27.68—27.71
optional disclosure, 27.114—27.115
principles, 27.116—27.175
profit and loss account, 27.72—27.82
segmental reporting, 27.83
statement of total recognised gains and losses, 27.84
summary, 27.1.15—27.1.18
executive summary
accounting requirements, 27.1.6—27.1.7
classification, 27.1.2—27.1.5
contractual arrangements not joint ventures, 27.1.19
disclosures, 27.1.23—27.1.29
equity accounting, 27.1.15—27.1.18
individual financial statements, 27.1.21—27.1.22
introduction, 27.1
joint arrangements not entities, 27.1.20
presentation, 27.1.8—27.1.14
scope of standard, 27.1.1
voluntary disclosures, 27.1.30
extent of share
convertible debt, 27.133—27.134
convertible shares, 27.132
cross-holdings, 27.135
introduction, 27.119—27.122.1
options, 27.123—27.131
fair values, 27.141—27.143
financial instruments, and, 6.116—6.121
financial statements, 27.136—27.137
goodwill
balance sheet, 27.88—27.93
principles, 27.141—27.143
gross equity method
generally, 27.94
introduction, 27.4—27.5
individual financial statements
generally, 27.98
summary, 27.1.21—27.1.22
interests in losses, 27.154—27.158
intra-group trading transactions, 27.149—27.150
introduction, 27.2—27.11
investment funds, 27.27—27.29.1
investments by single company, 27.176
joint and several liability, 27.159—27.160
joint arrangements not entities, 27.1.20
minority interests, 27.161
options, 27.123—27.131
participating interest, 27.2—27.3
presentation, 27.1.8—27.1.14
profit and loss account
example, 27.82
introduction, 27.72
notes, 27.80—27.81
operating results, 27.75—27.76
other line items, 27.78
satisfying requirements, 27.79
super-exceptional items, 27.77
turnover, 27.73—27.74
related parties, and, 29.38—29.39
related party transactions, and, 29.135
scope of standard
generally, 27.25—27.26
investment funds, 27.27—27.29.1

Associates (FRS 9)—*cont.*
summary, 27.1.1
segmental reporting, and
generally, 10.100—10.106
introduction, 27.83
statement of total recognised gains and losses, 27.84
transfer of assets, 27.148
venture capital funds, 27.27—27.29.1
voluntary disclosures, 27.1.30
voting rights, 27.50—27.54
Audit of small companies
introduction, 32.30
summary, 32.34
Audit requirements
oversea companies, and, 33.53
Auditors' remuneration
appointment after year end, 5.81
audit of company's associates, 5.65
audit work
audit-assist, 5.57
consolidated financial statements, 5.56—5.56.1
disclosure in which year, 5.58
individual financial statements, 5.55
auditor's associates, 5.69—5.69.1
change of auditor, 5.80
company's associated pension schemes, 5.71—5.73
company's associates, 5.70—5.70.3
exemptions from disclosure
audit fees, 5.74—5.74.1
other services' fees, 5.75—5.75.6
introduction, 5.53—5.54.6
joint auditors, 5.79
more than one auditor
appointment after year end, 5.81
change of auditor, 5.80
joint auditors, 5.79
other services
all other services, 5.68
audit of company's associates, 5.65
categories, 5.64—5.
fees for services supplied pursuant to legislation, 5.66
format of disclosure, 5.59—5.62
sub-totals, 5.63
taxation services, 5.67
services supplied pursuant to legislation, 5.66
single audit fees for group, 5.76—5.76.2
sub-totals, 5.63
taxation services, 5.67
third party payments, 5.77—5.78
Auditors' report
medium-sized companies, and, 32.140—32.142
small companies, and, 32.113—32.114
Average rate determination
consolidated financial statements, 7.53—7.55
individual company financial statements, 7.16—7.18
Avoir fiscal
income and expenses subject to non-standard rates, 13.38—13.43
introduction 13.37.1—13.37.1
measurement of current tax charge, 13.44—13.50

Back-to-back leases
introduction, 19.111—19.112
head lessor, 19.113
intermediate party, 19.114—19.119
Balance sheet
accruals, 4.92—4.94
accrued income, 4.46—4.54
amounts received on account, 4.82
associates, and

Balance sheet—*cont.*
example, 27.95—27.97
goodwill, 27.88—27.93
gross equity method, 27.94
introduction, 27.85—27.87
cash flow statements, and, 30.179
cash of bank and in hand
definition of cash, 4.55—4.57
restricted cash balances, 4.71
set-off on bank balances, 4.62—4.66
consolidated formats
amounts due to and from group undertakings, 4.103—4.106
generally, 4.97—4.99
interests in group undertakings, 4.103—4.106
particular items, rules for, 4.100—4.102
debentures, 4.81
deferred income, 4.92—4.94
deferred tax, and
analysis of deferred tax balance, 13.267—13.270
Companies Act requirements, 13.253
deferred tax asset, 13.272—13.273
material balances, 13.263—13.266
offset of assets and liabilities, 13.258—13.262
standards requirements, 13.254—13.257
summary, 13.1.8—13.1.15
dividends, 4.139
financial instruments, and
generally, 6.170—6.171
introduction, 4.137
historical summaries, 4.90
individual company formats
accruals, 4.92—4.94
accrued income, 4.46—4.54
amounts received on account, 4.82
cash of bank and in hand, 4.55—4.71
debentures, 4.81
deferred income, 4.92—4.94
generally, 4.27—4.29
net current assets and liabilities, 4.72—4.80
other liabilities, 4.95—4.96
own shares, 4.40
participating interests, 4.39
payments on account, 4.41
prepayments,. 4.46—4.54
presentation of debtors, 4.42—4.45
trade creditors, 4.83
trade loans, 4.85—4.92
transfers from current to fixed assets, 4.30—4.38
investment properties, and, 17.13—17.14
joint ventures, and
example, 27.95—27.97
goodwill, 27.88—27.93
gross equity method, 27.94
introduction, 27.85—27.87
minority interests, and, 24.357—24.359
net current assets and liabilities
classification as long or short-term, 4.77—4.80
disclosure, 4.73—4.76
generally, 4.72
notes to
accounting policies, 4.134—4.136
additional statements required by FRS3, 4.131
compliance with accounting standards, 4.132
financial instruments, 4.137
general requirements, 4.125—4.130
reserves and dividends, 4.139
true and fair override disclosures, 4.133
own shares, 4.40
participating interests, 4.39
payments on account, 4.41

Balance sheet—*cont.*
prepayments,. 4.46—4.54
presentation of debtors, 4.42—4.45
reserves and dividends, 4.139
retirement benefits, and
generally, 11.55—11.61.1
summary, 11.1.9—11.1.12
small companies, and
capital instruments, 32.80—32.82
consignment stock, 32.75—32.76
contingencies, 32.79—32.79.4
debt factors, 32.77—32.78
depreciation, 32.64—32.67
formats, 32.62—32.63
intangible fixed assets, 32.71—32.73.1
leases, 32.68—32.70.1
long-term contracts, 32.74
notes, 32.90—32.92
post balance sheets events, 32.79—32.79.4
pre-contract costs, 32.67.1—32.67.2
provisions, 32.79—32.79.4
start-up costs, 32.67.1—32.67.2
stocks, 32.74
tangible fixed assets, 32.64—32.67
write-downs to recoverable amount, 32.73.2
taxation, and
analysis of deferred tax balance, 13.267—13.270
Companies Act requirements, 13.253
deferred tax asset, 13.272—13.273
material balances, 13.263—13.266
offset of assets and liabilities, 13.258—13.262
standards requirements, 13.254—13.257
summary, 13.1.8—13.1.15
trade creditors, 4.83
trade loans, 4.85—4.92
Balance sheet cash
cash flow statements, and, 30.179
Bank branches
impairment, and, 18.80
Bank deposits
financial instruments, and, 6.147
Barter transactions
revenue recognition, and, 9.187—9.199
Bases of valuation of tangible fixed assets
assets surplus to requirements, 16.189
assets used in business, 16.185—16.188
depreciated replacement cost, 16.197—16.200
existing use value, 16.193—16.196
introduction, 16.177—16.184
open market value, 16.190—16.192
plant and machinery value, 16.201—16.203
Bed and breakfasting
reporting the substance of transactions, and, 3.243—3.249
Benefit to employees
employee share ownership plans, and, 12.24
Best estimate
estimation techniques, 21.117
introduction, 21.110—21.116
large population of similar claims, 21.118
Bill and hold sales
revenue recognition, and, 9.65—9.72
Bills of exchange
reporting the substance of transactions, and, 3.197
Binding sale agreement
restructuring, and, 21.168—21.170
Board decision
restructuring, and, 21.157—21.158
Bonus issues
share capital, and, 23.230—23.232
Book value
fair value disclosures, and, 6.107—6.112
Borrowing costs
tangible fixed assets, and, 16.345
Borrowings
cash flow statements, and, 30.50
Branches
filing of financial statements, 33.43—33.50
financial statements, 33.36—33.37
generally, 33.11—33.13
particulars to be registered, 33.21—33.22
reference period, 33.26
registration, 33.17
Brands
and see **Intangible fixed assets**
generally, 15.1
impairment, and, 18.86.1—18.86.2
Building society branches
impairment, and, 18.80
Business combinations
acquisition accounting, and, 25.1—25.2.1
reverse acquisitions, and, 25.1321
Buyback guarantee
employee share schemes, and, 12.59
Called up share capital
generally, 23.18—23.19
Cancellation of shares
treasury shares, and, 23.56—23.59
Capacity transactions
revenue recognition, and
exchange and reciprocal transactions, 9.214—9.218
generally, 9.201—9.205
presentation, 9.208—9.213
sale of asset or service, 9.206—9.207
Capital expenditure
cash flow statements, and, 30.92—30.96
generally, 10.148
Capital grants (SSAP 4)
disclosure requirements, 16.339—16.340
IFRS, and, 16.346
introduction, 16.329
non-depreciable fixed assets, 16.341—16.343
revision of standard, 16.331—16.338
scope of standard, 16.330
Capital instruments (FRS 4)
application under UK GAAP, 6.33—6.34
background, 6.288—6.290
Companies Act requirements, 6.375—6.381
contingent payments, 6.352—6.355
definition of capital instrument, 6.296—6.298
disclosure, 6.372—6.374
dividends, 6.306
facility fees, 6.323—6.325
finance costs
dividends, 6.306
elements, 6.305
interest, 6.306
introduction, 6.299—6.300
issue and redemption premiums, 6.307
issue costs, 6.308—6.322
initial recognition, 6.345
interest, 6.306
issue and redemption premiums, 6.307
issue costs, 6.308—6.322
measurement
contingent payments, 6.352—6.355
initial recognition, 6.345
renegotiation of debt, 6.362—6.371
repurchase of debt, 6.356—6.361
subsequent recognition, 6.351

Capital instruments (FRS 4)—*cont.*
treatment of finance costs, 6.346—6.350
objectives, 6.291—6.292
options, 6.329—6.340
renegotiation of debt, 6.362—6.371
repurchase of debt, 6.356—6.361
scope, 6.293—6.295
small companies, and, 32.80—32.82
subsequent recognition, 6.351
term
definition of term, 6.238
extended, 6.340—6.341
generally, 6.326—6.327
indeterminate, 6.344
options, 6.329—6.339
shortened, 6.342—6.343
treatment of finance costs, 6.346—6.350
Capital losses
deferred tax, and, 13.165—13.166
Capital redemption reserve
share capital, and, 23.119
Capitalisation of development costs
distributable profits, and, 23.190—23.191
Capitalisation of earnings
intangible fixed assets, and, 15.59—15.60
Capitalisation of finance costs
accounting treatment, 16.106—16.110
definition of 'finance costs', 16.102—16.105
disclosure requirements, 16.126—16.129
general borrowings, 16.121
group situations, 16.122—16.124
IFRS, and, 16.344
introduction, 16.100—16.101
period of, 16.111—16.117
specific borrowings, 16.118—16.120
taxation, 16.125
Capitalisation of interest
tangible fixed assets, and, 16.24—16.25
Cash flow forecasts
central overheads, 18.125—18.126
constraints, 18.128—18.159
future capital expenditure, 18.148—18.155
future reorganisations, 18.147
generally, 18.115—18.122
growth rates, 18.129—18.135
inflation, 18.127
'look-back' tests, 18.136—18.140
reorganisation expenditure, 18.141—18.155
transfer pricing between IGUs, 18.123—18.124
Cash flow statements (FRS 1)
acquisitions
consolidated statements, and, 30.132—30.138
generally, 30.98—30.99
introduction, 25.125—25.127
associates
consolidated statements, and, 30.128—30.129
generally, 27.99
balance sheet cash, 30.179
borrowings, 30.50
capital expenditure, 30.92—30.96
cash subject to restriction, 30.190—30.191
classification of cash flow
acquisitions, 30.98—30.99
additional, 30.64—30.65
capital expenditure, 30.92—30.96
disposals, 30.98—30.99
dividends from joint ventures and associates, 30.75.1
equity dividends paid, 30.101
financial investment, 30.92—30.96
financing, 30.108—30.111
Cash flow statements (FRS 1)—*cont.*
generally, 30.55—30.58
liquid resource management, 30.102—30.106
operating activities, from, 30.67—30.75
returns on investments, 30.76—30.85
servicing of finance, 30.76—30.85
taxation, 30.86—30.91
comparative figures, 30.176—30.177
consolidated statements
acquisition of subsidiaries, 30.132—30.138
associates investments, 30.128—30.129
disposal of subsidiaries, 30.132—30.138
introduction, 30.125
joint arrangement investments, 30.130
joint venture investments, 30.128—30.129
minority interests, 30.126—30.127
definitions
'cash', 30.41—30.42
'liquid resources', 30.44—30.49
'repayable on demand', 30.43
discounts and premiums, 30.180—30.181
disposals
consolidated statements, and, 30.132—30.138
generally, 30.98—30.99
dividends from joint ventures and associates, 30.75.1
equity dividends paid, 30.101
exceptional cash flows, 30.112—30.118
executive summary, 30.1—30.1.12
exempt entities
introduction, 30.23
medium-sized companies, 30.35—30.37
mutual life assurance companies, 30.26
open-ended investment funds, 30.28—30.29
other entities, 30.39
pension schemes, 30.27
small companies, 30.31—30.34
small unincorporated entities, 30.38
subsidiary undertakings, 30.24—30.25
extraordinary cash flows, 30.112—30.118
financing, 30.108—30.111
foreign currency
group companies, 30.150—30.161
hedging transactions, 30.162—30.164
individual companies, 30.141—30.149
introduction, 30.139—30.140
foreign currency (group companies)
introduction, 30.150
intra-group transactions, 30.158—30.161
net investment method, 30.153—30.157
temporal method, 30.151—30.152
foreign currency (individual companies)
borrowings for hedging equity investments, 30.149
generally, 30.141—30.142
introduction, 30.139—30.140
settled transactions, 30.143—30.144
unsettled transactions, 30.145—30.148
format
classification of cash flows, 30.55—30.65
departure from standard, 30.66
gross cash flows, 30.59—30.63
introduction, 30.51—30.54
net cash flows, 30.59—30.63
gross cash flows, 30.59—30.63
hedging transactions, 30.162—30.164
intra-group transactions, 30.158—30.161
introduction, 30.2
joint arrangements, 30.130
joint ventures
consolidated statements, and, 30.128—30.129
generally, 27.99
linked presentation, and, 3.251

Cash flow statements (FRS 1)—*cont.*
liquid resources
definition, 30.44—30.49
management, 30.102—30.106
medium-sized companies, 30.35—30.37
minority interests, 30.126—30.127
mutual life assurance companies, 30.26
net cash flows, 30.59—30.63
net debt reconciliation
analysis of changes, 30.123—30.124
generally, 30.119—30.122.1
notes
comparative figures, 30.176—30.177
specific disclosures, 30.165
supplementary disclosures, 30.166—30.175
objectives of standard, 30.5—30.21
open-ended investment funds, 30.28—30.29
operating activities, 30.67—30.75
pension schemes, 30.27
practical application of standard
balance sheet cash, 30.179
cash subject to restriction, 30.190—30.191
discounts and premiums, 30.180—30.181
gains and losses, 30.182—30.185
introduction, 30.178
refinancing of borrowings, 30.188—30.189
reorganisation costs, 30.186—30.87
premiums, 30.180—30.181
preparation
borrowings, 30.50
definition of 'cash', 30.41—30.42
definition of 'liquid resources', 30.44—30.49
introduction, 30.40
meaning of 'repayable on demand', 30.43
reconciliation with balance sheet figures
net debt, 30.119—30.124
refinancing of borrowings, 30.188—30.189
reorganisation costs, 30.186—30.87
repayable on demand, 30.43
returns on investments, 30.76—30.85
scope of standard
exempt entities, 30.23—30.39
generally, 30.22
segmental reporting, and, 10.117—10.120
servicing of finance, 30.76—30.85
small companies, 30.31—30.34
small unincorporated entities, 30.38
subsidiary undertakings, 30.24—30.25
summary, 30.1—30.1.12
taxation, 30.86—30.91
worked example, 30.192
Cash of bank and in hand
balance sheet, and
definition of cash, 4.55—4.57
restricted cash balances, 4.71
set-off on bank balances, 4.62—4.66
Cash-settled commodity contracts
financial instruments, and, 6.176—6.180
Cash-settled share-based payment transactions
and see **Share-based payment transactions**
generally, 12.2
introduction, 12.14—12.15
Cash subject to restriction
cash flow statements, and, 30.190—30.191
Ceasing to be subsidiary
disposal of subsidiaries, and, 26.24—26.25
Central assets
allocation of impairment losses, 18.196—18.200
generally, 18.91—18.97
Central overheads
impairment, and, 18.125—18.126
Changes in accounting policies
disclosures, 8.195—8.202
generally, 8.190—8.194
IFRS, and, 8.208
Changes in discount rates
provisions, and, 21.139—21.142.1
Changes in estimates
employee share schemes, and, 12.47—12.48
provisions, and, 21.135—21.138.1
tangible fixed assets, and
decommissioning costs, of, 16.83
residual life, of, 16.306—16.307
useful economic life, of, 16.302—16.305
Changes in method
tangible fixed assets, and, 16.307—16.308
Changes in relevant costs
PFI and PPP, and, 3.179.41—3.179.43
Changes in technology
PFI and PPP, and, 3.179.44
Changes to estimation techniques
generally, 8.205
IFRS, and, 8.208
Characteristics of financial instruments (IFRS)
conditional rights and obligations, A6.4.13—A6.4.15
contingent rights and obligations, A6.4.13—A6.4.15
contractual basis, A6.4.8—A6.4.12
definitions
equity instrument, A6.4.6
financial asset, A6.4.4
financial instrument, A6.4.3
financial liability, A6.4.5
introduction, A6.4.2
key features, A6.4.7
derivatives
accounting, A6.4.42
contracts to buy or sell non-financial items, A6.4.39
definition, A6.4.25
examples, A6.4.38
initial net investment, A6.4.33—A6.4.34
introduction, A6.4.23—A6.4.24
key features, A6.4.26—A6.4.37
notional amounts, A6.4.31—A6.4.32
payment provisions, A6.4.31—A6.4.32
regular way contracts, A6.4.41
settlement at future date, A6.4.35—A6.4.37
'underlying', A6.4.27—A6.4.30
exchange under potentially favourable or unfavourable terms, A6.4.16
identification, A6.4.22
introduction, A6.4.1
non-derivative transactions, A6.4.40
non-financial assets and liabilities, and, A6.4.17—A6.4.21
overview, A6.1.8—A6.1.13
'Cherry-picking'
tangible fixed assets, and, 16.16—16.20
Claims
long-term contracts, and, 20.94—20.95
Classification of financial instruments (IFRS)
disclosure of financial instruments, and, A6.11.39—A6.11.41
financial assets
available-for-sale financial assets, A6.6.66—A6.6.68
fair value through profit or loss, A6.6.3—A6.6.25
held-to-maturity investments, A6.6.26—A6.6.57
introduction, A6.6.2
loans and receivables, A6.6.58—A6.6.65
reclassification between categories, A6.6.69—A6.6.74
financial liabilities

Classification of financial instruments (IFRS)—*cont.*
fair value through profit or loss, A6.6.77—A6.6.81
introduction, A6.6.75—A6.6.76
other liabilities, A6.6.82
reclassification between categories, A6.6.83
introduction, A6.6.1
Close family members
related parties, and, 29.62—29.64
related party transactions, and, 29.142—29.143
Closing rate/net investment method
foreign currency translation, and, 7.35—7.41
Commission
revenue recognition, and, 9.286—9.288
Commitments
and see **FRS 12**
introduction, 21.2—21.3
Common control, companies under
related parties, and, 29.24
related party transactions, and, 29.130
Common influence
establishing, 29.27—29.29
introduction, 29.26
Companies Act requirements
capital instruments, and, 6.375—6.381
compliance with accounting standards, 2.35—2.40
consolidation rules, and, 24.297—24.299
financial instruments, and
application under UK GAAP, 6.31—6.32
companies adopting fair value accounting, 6.101.8
companies not adopting fair value accounting, 6.101.9—6.101.11
comparatives, 6.101.14
directors' report, 6.101.12—6.101.13
disclosures, 6.91—6.147
introduction, 6.12
financial reporting structure, and, 2.48—2.50
impairment, and
disclosure, 18.281—18.282
identification of impaired assets, 18.41—18.44
intangible fixed assets, and, 15.3—15.8
investment properties, and
market value measurement, 17.14.1—17.14.2
true and fair override, 17.15—17.16
override disclosures, 2.41—2.44
principles and rules
compliance with accounting standards, 2.35—2.40
introduction, 2.21
override disclosures, 2.41—2.44
requirement to prepare financial statements, 2.22—2.22.8
true and fair requirement, 2.23—2.34
UITF abstracts, compliance with, 2.35—2.40
requirement to prepare financial statements, 2.22—2.22.8
segmental reporting, and
disclosure, 10.68—10.73
introduction, 10.6—10.9
small companies, and, 32.11—32.22
taxation, and
balance sheet, 13.253
profit and loss account, 13.236
true and fair override
disclosures, 2.41—2.44
investment properties, 17.15—17.16
requirement, 2.23—2.34
UITF abstracts, compliance with, 2.35—2.40
Comparison with market transactions
intangible fixed assets, and, 15.61—15.62
Comparative figures
cash flow statements, and, 30.176—30.177
generally, 10.110
related party transactions, and, 29.126
Compensation
provisions, and, 21.266—21.267
Component depreciation
background, 16.26—16.27
generally, 16.276—16.278
implementation of standard, and, 16.339
Component replacement
tangible fixed assets, and, 16.143—16.149
Compulsory redundancies
restructuring, and, 21.183—21.189
Computer software
intangible fixed assets, and, 15.135—15.138
Concert parties
related parties, and, 29.55—29.57
Conditions
analysing complex transactions, and, 3.56
Confidentiality, duty of
related party transactions, and, 29.162
Connected persons
related party transactions, and
close family, 29.62—29.64
companies, 29.65—29.67
introduction, 29.60—29.61
partnerships, 29.65—29.67
trusts, 29.65—29.67
Consignment stock
accounting treatment, 20.57—20.60
conclusion, 20.66
example of required analysis, 20.61—20.63
introduction, 20.48
manufacturer's position, 20.64—20.65
reporting the substance of transactions, and, 3.122
objective, 20.49—20.51
small companies, and, 32.75—32.76
sources of benefits and risks, 20.52—20.56
Consistency
accounting policies, and, 2.138.1—2.138.7
Consolidated cash flow statements
acquisition of subsidiaries, 30.132—30.138
associates investments, 30.128—30.129
disposal of subsidiaries, 30.132—30.138
introduction, 30.125
joint arrangement investments, 30.130
joint venture investments, 30.128—30.129
minority interests, 30.126—30.127
Consolidated financial statements (FRS 2)
acquisitions, 24.1.6—24.1.7
ASB Statement of principles, 24.16—24.17
balance sheet, and
amounts due to and from group undertakings, 4.103—4.106
generally, 4.97—4.99
interests in group undertakings, 4.103—4.106
particular items, rules for, 4.100—4.102
consolidation rules
and see **Consolidation rules**
summary, 24.1.9—24.1.12
deferred tax, and
effects of adjustment, 13.206—13.208
fair value adjustments, 13.209—13.213
foreign exchange differences, 13.216
general principles, 13.203—13.205
goodwill, 13.213.1—13.213.3
unremitted earnings, 13.214—13.215
disposals, 24.1.8
entity concept, 24.13—24.14
exclusions, 24.1.4—24.1.5
executive summary
acquisitions, 24.1.6—24.1.7
consolidation rules, 24.1.9—24.1.12
disposals, 24.1.8

Consolidated financial statements (FRS 2)—*cont.*
exclusions, 24.1.4—24.1.5
exemptions, 24.1.3
introduction, 24.1—24.1.2
minority interests, 24.1.13—24.1.15
exemptions to requirement to prepare
accounting treatment, 24.71
all subsidiaries excluded, 24.70
disclosure, 24.72—24.74
intermediate parent exemption, 24.56.1—24.66
introduction, 24.56
suggested wording, 24.75
summary, 24.1.3
foreign currency translation, and
average rate determination, 7.53—7.55
change between methods, 7.59—7.61
closing rate/net investment method, 7.35—7.41
deferred trading balances, 7.70—7.75
dual rates, 7.56
goodwill, 7.76—7.78
intercompany dividends, 7.62—7.66
intra-group companies transactions, 7.67
intra-group long-term loans, 7.70—7.75
introduction, 7.33—7.34
local currency, 7.57—7.58
other matters, 7.52
summary, 7.11.8—7.11.15
suspension of rates, 7.56
temporal method, 7.42—7.51
unrealised profit on stocks, 7.68—7.69
foreign equity investments financed by foreign borrowings, and, 7.105—7.112
form, 24.41—24.50
'group' concept
entity concept, 24.13—24.14
introduction, 24.6
parent company concept, 24.11—24.12
proprietary concept, 24.7—24.10
group structure
and see **Group structure**
accounting for investments, 24.18—24.19
definition of 'group', 24.6—24.14
distributable reserves, and, 24.252—24.255
limited partnerships, 24.212.1—24.212.16
membership of qualified undertaking, 24.247—24.251
parent undertakings, 24.26—24.31
profit and loss account, 24.47—24.50
realised reserves, and, 24.252—24.255
scope of provisions, 24.21—24.25
Statement of principles, 24.16—24.17
subsidiaries excluded from consolidation, 24.176—24.212
true and fair view, 24.51—24.55
intermediate parent exemption
application in practice, 24.66
certified translations, 24.64—24.65
conditions, 24.62
EEA companies, 24.57—24.62.1
generally, 24.56.1—24.56.2
non-EEA group, 24.62.1.1—24.62.10
relevant date, 24.63
introduction, 24.2—24.4
medium-sized companies, by
exemptions, 32.148—32.153
introduction, 24.35—24.36
shorter-form, 32.155—32.159
merger accounting, and, 28.112—28.122
minority interests, and
acquisition of direct subsidiary, 24.377
acquisition of indirect subsidiary, 24.378

Consolidated financial statements (FRS 2)—*cont.*
auction market preferred shares, 24.366—24.367
balance sheets, 24.357—24.359
basis of recognition, 24.353—24.354
compulsory acquisition, 24.379
definition, 24.346—24.350
director's interests, 24.369—24.370
equity, 24.356
fair value, and, 24.381—24.382
indirect holdings, 24.375—24.376
introduction, 24.344—24.345
loss making subsidiaries, 24.383—24.388
measurement, 24.355, 24.371—34.374
minority or majority interests, 24.351—24.352
presentation in financial statements, 24.357—24.365
profit and loss account, 24.360—24.365
stapled shares, 24.368
summary, 24.1.13—24.1.15
treatment on acquisition, 24.377—24.382
parent companies, by, 24.33—24.34
parent company concept, 24.11—24.12
profit and loss account, and
effect of FRS3, 4.120—4.121
generally, 4.111
particular items, rules for, 4.112—4.119
proprietary concept, 24.7—24.10
purpose, 24.27
requirement to prepare
exemptions, 24.56—24.75
generally, 24.32
medium-sized companies, 24.35—24.36
other parent undertakings, 24.37—24.39
parent companies, 24.33—24.34
small companies, 24.35—24.36
small companies, by
exemptions, 32.148—32.153
introduction, 24.35—24.36
shorter-form, 32.155—32.159
subsidiary undertakings
and see **Subsidiary undertakings**
board majority, 24.96—24.104
company law, and, 24.78—24.79
control, 24.155—24.159
definition, 24.26—24.31
dominant influence, 24.121—24.150
European law, 24.79
example, 24.175
expressions and interpretations, 24.160—24.174
introduction, 24.76—24.77
majority of voting rights, 24.89—24.95
meaning, 24.80—24.85
participating interest, 24.152—24.154
terminology, 24.86—24.88
summary
acquisitions, 24.1.6—24.1.7
consolidation rules, 24.1.9—24.1.12
disposals, 24.1.8
exclusions, 24.1.4—24.1.5
exemptions, 24.1.3
introduction, 24.1—24.1.2
minority interests, 24.1.13—24.1.15
true and fair view, 24.51—24.55
Consolidation adjustments
associates and joint ventures, and
abnormal transactions between year ends, 27.144
consistent accounting policies, 27.140
elimination of intra-group trading, 27.145—27.147
fair values, 27.141—27.143
goodwill, 27.141—27.143
intra-group trading transactions, 27.149—27.150

Consolidation adjustments—*cont.*
introduction, 27.138—27.139
transfer of assets to joint venture, 27.148
Consolidation balances
related party transactions, and, 29.146—29.147
Consolidation of new subsidiary
adjusted capital, 25.39
adjustments to fair values , 25.42
cost of acquisition, 25.31—25.34
date for recognising trading, 25.44—25.48
fees and expenses of acquisition, 25.35—25.38
goodwill, 25.43
identifiable assets and liabilities, 25.40—25.41
introduction, 25.29—25.30
reserves acquired, 25.39
Consolidation rules
see also **Consolidated financial statements**
adjustments
generally, 24.309
other, 24.317—24.318
uniform accounting policies, 24.310—24.316
Companies Act 1985 requirements, and, 24.297—24.299
excluded subsidiaries, 24.330—24.343
FRS 2, and, 24.300
GAAP, 24.303—24.304
interim financial statements, 24.321—24.325
intra-group transactions
elimination calculations, 24.337
generally, 24.332—24.336
introduction, 24.296—24.302
losses, 24.339
parent year end differs, 24.328—24.331
procedure, 24.305—24.308
profit from fixed assets, 24.138
subsidiary year end differs
disclosure, 24.326
generally, 24.319—24.320
interim financial statements, 24.321—24.325
practical problems, 24.327
subsidiary year ends, 24.319—24.320
summary, 24.1.9—24.1.12
true and fair view, and, 24.296
uniform accounting policies, 24.310—24.316
Construction contracts
long term contracts, and, 20.120
Construction periods
leases, and, 19.104
Constructive obligations
provisions, and, 21.52—21.53
Contingencies (FRS 12)
disclosure requirements
contingent assets, 21.308—21.309
contingent liabilities, 21.306—21.307
exemptions, 21.314—21.318
guarantees, 21.310—21.313
introduction, 21.2—21.3
objective of standard, 21.20
recognition
contingent assets, 21.97—21.102
contingent liabilities, 21.92—21.96
introduction, 21.91
scope of standard, 21.21—21.24
small companies, and, 32.79—32.37.4
Contingent assets
disclosure requirements, 21.308—21.309
recognition, 21.97—21.102
Contingent liabilities
disclosure requirements, 21.306—21.307
provisions, and, 21.37—21.39
recognition, 21.92—21.96
Contingent payments
capital instruments, ands, 6.352—6.355
Contract purchase arrangements
reporting the substance of transactions, and, 3.228—3.231
Contract separability
PFI and PPP, and, 3.179.8—3.179.16
Contractual rights
financial instruments, and, 6.20—6.23
Contributions
accounting by operator, 3.179.55.15
accounting by purchaser, 3.179.55.16—3.179.55.17
Control
intangible fixed assets, and, 15.23—15.25
related parties, and
examples, 29.30
introduction, 29.19—29.23
Conventions
capital maintenance concepts, and, 2.145—2.146
current cost, 2.154
current purchasing power, 2.152—2.153
fair value, 2.151.1—2.151.4
generally, 2.149
historical cost, 2.150
introduction, 2.144
modified historical cost, 2.151
units of measurement, and, 2.148
valuation bases, and, 2.147
Convertible debt
associates and joint ventures, and, 27.133—27.134
Convertible shares
associates and joint ventures, and, 27.132
Copyrights
intangible fixed assets, and, 15.101—15.103
Corporation tax
and see **Taxation**
general principles, 13.7—13.8
imputation system, 13.9—13.17
share incentive plans, and, 12.89
Cost of acquisition
generally, 25.31—25.34
summary, 25.1.12—25.1.15
Cost of sales
long-term contracts, and, 20.99—20.102
profit and loss account, and, 5.4—5.12
Cost of stocks
definition, 20.8—20.14
determination, 20.15—20.27
Cost of tangible fixed assets
decommissioning costs
arising later in asset's life, 16.79—16.82
changes in estimate, 16.83
generally, 16.75—16.78
directly attributable costs
generally, 16.61—16.65
period of capitalisation, 16.84
generally, 16.55—16.60
incremental costs, 16.68—16.71
IFRS, and, 16.344
labour costs, 16.66—16.67
software development costs, 16.72—16.74.10
Coupons
free products, 9.239
loyalty programmes, 9.240—9.245
options granted as part of sales transaction, 9.223—9.236
options granted for consideration, 9.219—9.222
options granted without consideration, 9.237—9.238
other benefit schemes, 9.246—9.250
point schemes, 9.240—9.245

Credit enhancement
quasi-subsidiaries, and, 3.115—3.116
Credit entry
employee share schemes, and, 12.45—12.46.1
Creditors
balance sheet, and, 4.83
provisions, and, 21.80
Cross-currency swap
hedging, and, , 6.133—6.137
Cross-holdings
associates and joint ventures, and, 27.135
Currency risk
financial instruments, and, 6.230—6.240
Current asset investments
alternative accounting rules, 6.76
historical cost accounting rules, 6.77—6.78
Current assets and liabilities
hedging, and, 6.127—6.129
Current cost convention
accounting principles, and, 2.154
Current purchasing power convention
accounting principles, and, 2.152—2.153
fair value, 2.151.1—2.151.4
historical cost, 2.150
modified historical cost, 2.151
Current service cost
generally, 11.81—11.84
Current tax (FRS 16)
accounting policies, 13.235
ACT, and, 13.50.1—13.50.9
avoir fiscal
income and expenses subject to non-standard rates, 13.38—13.43
introduction 13.37.1—13.37.3
measurement of current tax charge, 13.44—13.50
balance sheet
analysis of deferred tax balance, 13.267—13.270
Companies Act requirements, 13.253
deferred tax asset, 13.272—13.273
material balances, 13.263—13.266
offset of assets and liabilities, 13.258—13.262
standards requirements, 13.254—13.257
circumstances affecting tax charges, 13.274—13.290
disclosure requirements
accounting policies, 13.235
balance sheet, 13.253—13.273
circumstances affecting tax charges, 13.274—13.290
generally, 13.234
profit and loss account, 13.236—13.248
statement of total recognised gains and losses, 13.249—13.252
summary, 13.1.7
dividends
incoming, 13.31—13.33
outgoing, 13.28—13.30
executive summary
disclosure, 13.1.7
introduction, 13.1—13.1.1
measurement, 13.1.6
recognition, 13.1.2—13.1.5
general principles, 13.8—13.9
generally, 13.18—13.20
imputation tax system, 13.10—13.16
incoming dividends, 13.31—13.33
interest
payable, 13.28—13.30
receivable, 13.31—13.33
introduction, 13.2—13.7
measurement
generally, 13.44—13.50
summary, 13.1.6
Current tax (FRS 16)—*cont.*
non-operating exceptional items, 13.245—13.248
outgoing dividends, 13.28—13.30
presentation
accounting policies, 13.235
balance sheet, 13.253—13.273
circumstances affecting tax charges, 13.274—13.290
generally, 13.234
profit and loss account, 13.236—13.248
statement of total recognised gains and losses, 13.249—13.252
profit and loss account
analysis of current tax, 13.239
analysis of deferred tax, 13.240—13.244
Companies Act requirements, 13.236
non-operating exceptional items, 13.245—13.248
notes, 13.238
standards requirements, 13.237
recognition
generally, 13.21—13.23
summary, 13.1.2—13.1.5
recoverability of ACT, 13.50.1—13.50.9
statement of total recognised gains and losses
generally, 13.249—13.250
notes, 13.251—13.252
tax credits
incoming dividends, 13.31—13.33
interest payable, 13.28—13.30
interest receivable, 13.31—13.33
introduction, 13.24
outgoing dividends, 13.28—13.30
underlying tax, 13.35—13.37
withholding tax
incoming dividends, 13.31—13.33
interest payable, 13.28—13.30
interest receivable, 13.31—13.33
introduction, 13.25—13.27
outgoing dividends, 13.28—13.30
Curtailments
generally, 11.100—11.108

Date of changes in group membership
background, 25.18
definition, 25.19—25.27
effective date post balance sheet, 25.28
Dearing Report proposals
financial reporting structure, and, 2.45—2.47
Debentures
balance sheet, and, 4.81
share capital, and, 23.233
Debt factoring
accounting treatment
derecognition, 3.136.10
examples of required analysis, 3.136.15—3.136.16
linked presentation, 3.136.11—3.136.12
separate presentation, 3.136.13—3.136.14
benefits and risks, 3.136.5—3.136.9
introduction, 3.136—3.136.4
small companies, and, 32.77—32.78
Debtors, presentation of
balance sheet, and, 4.42—4.45
Decommissioning costs
provisions, and, 21.249—21.257
tangible fixed asserts, and
arising later in asset's life, 16.79—16.82
changes in estimate, 16.83
generally, 16.75—16.78
Deemed disposals
disposal of subsidiaries, and, 26.34—26.38
Deemed related, parties who are
associates, 29.38—29.39

Deemed related, parties who are—*cont.*
directors, 29.42—29.43
introduction, 29.35
investors, 29.40—29.41
joint ventures, 29.38—29.39
parent companies, 29.36—29.37
pension funds
generally, 29.44—29.46
investment manager, 29.47—29.48
subsidiary undertakings, 29.36—29.37
venture capitalists, 29.40—29.41
Deferral method
deferred tax, and, 13.55—13.56
Deferred income
balance sheet, and, 4.92—4.94
provisions, and, 21.88—21.90
Deferred revenue expenditure
deferred tax, and, 13.116—13.117
Deferred tax (FRS 19)
accelerated capital allowances, 13.104—13.106
accounting policies, 13.235
background, 13.4
balance sheet
analysis of deferred tax balance, 13.267—13.270
Companies Act requirements, 13.253
deferred tax asset, 13.272—13.273
material balances, 13.263—13.266
offset of assets and liabilities, 13.258—13.262
standards requirements, 13.254—13.257
summary, 13.1.8—13.1.15
balance sheet liability method, 13.73—13.78
capital losses, 13.165—13.166
circumstances affecting tax charges, 13.274—13.290
computation
balance sheet liability method, 13.73—13.78
deferral method, 13.55—13.56
income statement liability method, 13.63—13.72
introduction, 13.54
liability method, 13.57—13.59
liability method with full provisioning, 13.62
liability method with partial provisioning, 13.60—13.61
consolidated financial statements, treatment in
effects of adjustment, 13.206—13.208
fair value adjustments, 13.209—13.213
foreign exchange differences, 13.216
general principles, 13.203—13.205
goodwill, 13.213.1—13.213.3
unremitted earnings, 13.214—13.215
deferral method, 13.55—13.56
deferred revenue expenditure, 13.116—13.117
deferred tax assets
capital losses, 13.165—13.166
general rule, 13.142—13.146
going concern uncertainty, 13.167—13.168
recovery against deferred tax liabilities, 13.156
recovery against future taxable profits, 13.157
review of recoverability, 13.169—13.170
suitable taxable profits, 13.147—13.148
tax planning opportunities, 13.149—13.155
trading losses, 13.158—13.164
disclosure requirements
accounting policies, 13.235
balance sheet, 13.253—13.273
circumstances affecting tax charges, 13.274—13.290
generally, 13.234
profit and loss account, 13.236—13.248
statement of total recognised gains and losses, 13.249—13.252
summary, 13.1.26
discounting

Deferred tax (FRS 19)—*cont.*
calculation, 13.185—13.188
introduction, 13.176—13.184
rates, 13.192—13.195
scheduling cash flows, 13.189—13.190
scheduling timing differences, 13.191
summary, 13.1.19—13.1.22
worked examples, 13.196—13.202
executive summary
balance sheet, 13.1.8—13.1.15
disclosure, 13.1.26
discounting, 13.1.19—13.1.22
introduction, 13.1—13.1.1
measurement, 13.1.18
performance statement, 13.1.16—13.1.17
presentation, 13.1.23—13.1.25
recognition, 13.1.8—13.1.17
fair value adjustments, 13.209—13.213
foreign exchange differences, 13.216
general principles, 13.97—13.98
going concern uncertainty, 13.167—13.168
goodwill, 13.213.1—13.213.3
government grants, 13.118—13.121
holdover relief, 13.136—13.141
impairment, and, 18.19—18.20
imputation tax system, 13.10—13.16
income statement liability method, 13.63—13.72
industrial building allowances, 13.107—13.110
infrastructure assets, 13.111—13.113
introduction, 13.51—13.53
leases, 13.122—13.125.1
liability method
balance sheet, 13.73—13.78
generally, 13.57—13.59
income statement, 13.63—13.72
with full provisioning, 13.62
with partial provisioning, 13.60—13.61
marked to market assets, 13.131—13.135.1
measurement
average rates, 13.173—13.175
introduction, 13.171—13.172
summary, 13.1.18
non-operating exceptional items, 13.245—13.248
objectives of standard, 13.90—13.96
performance statement, 13.1.16—13.1.17
post-retirement benefits, 13.126—13.126.10
presentation
accounting policies, 13.235
balance sheet, 13.253—13.273
circumstances affecting tax charges, 13.274—13.290
generally, 13.234
profit and loss account, 13.236—13.248
statement of total recognised gains and losses, 13.249—13.252
summary, 13.1.23—13.1.25
profit and loss account
analysis of current tax, 13.239
analysis of deferred tax, 13.240—13.244
Companies Act requirements, 13.236
non-operating exceptional items, 13.245—13.248
notes, 13.238
standards requirements, 13.237
provisions, 13.114
recognition, 13.1.8—13.1.17
retirement benefits, 13.126—13.126.10
revaluation of non-monetary assets
general rule, 13.128—13.130
holdover relief, 13.136—13.141
marked to market assets, 13.131—13.135.1
rollover relief, 13.136—13.141
rollover relief, 13.136—13.141

Deferred tax (FRS 19)—*cont.*
share-based payment transactions
cash-settled transactions, 13.127.8
equity-settled transactions, 13.127—13.127.7
standardisation of accounting, 13.80—13.88
statement of total recognised gains and losses
generally, 13.249—13.250
notes, 13.251—13.252
timing differences
accelerated capital allowances, 13.104—13.106
deferred revenue expenditure, 13.116—13.117
discounting, and, 13.191
generally, 13.99—13.103
government grants, 13.118—13.121
industrial building allowances, 13.107—13.110
infrastructure assets, 13.111—13.113
leases, 13.122—13.125.1
provisions, 13.114
retirement benefits, 13.126—13.126.10
trading losses, 13.158—13.164
unremitted earnings, 13.214—13.215
Deferred tax assets
capital losses, 13.165—13.166
general rule, 13.142—13.146
going concern uncertainty, 13.167—13.168
recovery against deferred tax liabilities, 13.156
recovery against future taxable profits, 13.157
review of recoverability, 13.169—13.170
suitable taxable profits, 13.147—13.148
tax planning opportunities, 13.149—13.155
trading losses, 13.158—13.164
Deferred trading balances
foreign currency translation, and, 7.70—7.75
Defined benefit schemes
acquisitions, 11.135—11.138
actuarial gains and losses, 11.1.19
balance sheet entries
generally, 11.55—11.61.1
summary, 11.1.9—11.1.12
disclosure requirements
generally, 11.139—11.148
summary, 11.1.21—1.1.24
frequency of valuations, 11.74—11.77
future developments, 11.148.1—11.148.14
introduction, 11.19
limit on pension asset, 11.115—11.126
measurement
assets, 11.62—11.67
liabilities, 11.68—11.73
summary, 11.1.4—11.1.8
reporting performance
generally, 11.78—11.114
summary, 11.1.13
profit and loss account, 11.1.14—11.1.18
reserves, 11.149—11.164
scheme assets, 11.43—11.148
scheme liabilities, 11.46—11.54
summary
actuarial gains and losses, 11.1.19
balance sheet recognition, 11.1.9—11.1.12
disclosures, 11.1.21—1.1.24
measurement, 11.1.4—11.1.8
performance components, 11.1.13
profit and loss account, 11.1.14—11.1.18
STRGL, 11.1.19—11.1.24
tax, 11.1.20—11.1.21
taxation
generally, 11.127—11.129
summary, 11.1.20—11.1.21
Defined contribution schemes
accounting treatment, 11.35
definition, 11.31—11.34
disclosure, 11.36
introduction, 11.18
summary, 11.1.3
Delivery of returns
treasury shares, and, 23.60—23.62
Demand risk
PFI and PPP, and, 3.179.25—3.179.28
Depreciated replacement cost
tangible fixed assets, and, 16.197—16.200
Depreciation
change in estimate, 16.302—16.307
change in method, 16.307—16.308
components, of, 16.276—16.278
definition, 16.249—16.251
determination of useful economic life and residual life, 16.252—16.256
disclosure requirements, 16.309—16.314
impairment, and, 18.212—18.213
IFRS, and, 16.344
introduction, 16.247—16.248
methods
annuity, 16.264—16.267
introduction, 16.257—16.258
reducing balance, 16.260—16.261
'rule of 78', 16.262
straight line method, 16.259
sum of the digits, 16.262
unit-of-production, 16.263
non-depreciation, 16.279—16.291
profit and loss account, and, 5.29—5.31
renewals accounting, 16.293—16.300
revalued assets, of, 16.268—16.275
segmental reporting, and, 10.150
small companies, and, 32.64—32.67
summary, 16.1.14—16.1.17
Derecognition
debt factoring, and, 3.136.10
reporting the substance of transactions, and, 3.258
tangible fixed assets, and, 16.344
transactions in previously recognised assets, and
full, 3.73
partial, 3.74—3.81
Derecognition of financial instruments (IFRS)
accounting treatment
collateral, for, A6.8.141
continuing involvement in transferred assets, A6.8.127—A6.8.140
introduction, A6.8.99
non-qualifying transfers, A6.8.119—A6.8.126
qualifying transfers, A6.8.100—A6.8.118
transferee, by, A6.8.142
application of criteria
factoring arrangements, A6.8.87—A6.8.89
generally, A6.8.74
loan transfers, A6.8.96—A6.8.98
repurchase agreements, A6.8.75—A6.8.86
securitisations, A6.8.90—A6.8.95
stock lending, A6.8.75—A6.8.86
balance sheet disclosures, and, A6.11.55
bed and breakfast transactions, A6.8.84
collateral
accounting treatment, A6.8.141
repurchase agreements, A6.8.85—A6.8.86
consolidation of subsidiaries, A6.8.31—A6.8.32
continuing involvement in transferred assets
associated liability, A6.8.129—A6.8.130
general, A6.8.127—A6.8.128
guarantees, through, A6.8.133

Derecognition of financial instruments (IFRS)—*cont.*
measured at amortised cost, A6.8.136
measured at fair value, A6.8.137—A6.8.138
options, through, A6.8.134—A6.8.135
part of financial asset, A6.8.139—A6.8.140
subsequent measurement, A6.8.131—A6.8.132
control analysis
continuing involvement in transferred asset, A6.8.73
practical ability to sell transferred asset, A6.8.68—A6.8.72
retention of control of asset, A6.8.66—A6.8.67
credit guarantees, A6.8.123
deep out-of-the-money put options, A6.8.113—A6.8.114
derivatives
non-qualifying transfers, A6.8.124
qualifying transfers, A6.8.110—A6.8.118
exchange of debt instrument
cost and fees on debt restructuring, A6.8.157—A6.8.158
generally, A6.8.152—A6.8.156
expiry of rights to cash flow from assets, A6.8.37
extinguishment of financial liabilities
gain or loss arising, A6.8.150—A6.8.151
general principles, A6.8.144—A6.8.145
in-substance defeasance, A6.8.148
legal release by creditor, A6.8.146—A6.8.147
transfer of assets that fails derecognition, A6.8.149
factoring arrangements
generally, A6.8.87
with recourse, A6.8.89
without recourse, A6.8.88
fair value put or call option, A6.8.117
financial liabilities, of
exchange of debt instrument, A6.8.152—A6.8.158
extinguishment, A6.8.144—A6.8.151
introduction, A6.8.143
flow chart
application, A6.8.33—A6.8.36
generally, A6.8.30
forward repurchase agreement, A6.8.117
generally, A6.8.24—A6.8.25
interest rate swaps, A6.8.118
introduction, A6.8.3—A6.8.4
loan syndications, A6.8.97—A6.8.98
loan transfers, A6.8.96—A6.8.98
mixed approach, A6.8.26—A6.8.29
modification of debt instrument
cost and fees on debt restructuring, A6.8.157—A6.8.158
generally, A6.8.152—A6.8.156
non-qualifying transfers
credit guarantees, A6.8.123
derivatives, A6.8.124
introduction, A6.8.119—A6.8.120
sale and repurchase agreements, A6.8.121—A6.8.122
subordinated retained interests, A6.8.123
total return swaps, A6.8.126
overview, A6.1.26—A6.1.30
pass-through arrangements, A6.8.43—A6.8.54
pledge, A6.8.83
qualifying transfers
deep out-of-the-money put options, A6.8.113—A6.8.114
derivatives, A6.8.110—A6.8.118
fair value put or call option, A6.8.117
forward repurchase agreement, A6.8.117
interest rate swaps, A6.8.118
introduction, A6.8.100—A6.8.102

Derecognition of financial instruments (IFRS)—*cont.*
readily obtainable assets subject to at-the-money call option, A6.8.115—A6.8.116
servicing assets and liabilities, A6.8.106—A6.8.109
transferred asset part of larger asset, A6.8.103—A6.8.105
repurchase agreements
bed and breakfast transactions, A6.8.84
collateral, A6.8.85—A6.8.86
generally, A6.8.75—A6.8.78
price, A6.8.79
return of substantially the same asset, A6.8.80
right of first refusal to repurchase at fair value, A6.8.82
right to pledge, A6.8.83
security, A6.8.85—A6.8.86
substitution of similar asset with equal fair value, A6.8.81
wash sales, A6.8.84
risk and rewards analysis
generally, A6.8.55—A6.8.56
retention of substantially all risk and rewards of ownership, A6.8.63—A6.8.65
transfer of substantially all risk and rewards of ownership, A6.8.57—A6.8.62
sale and repurchase agreements, A6.8.121—A6.8.122
securitisations
credit guarantees, A6.8.92—A6.8.93
generally, A6.8.90—A6.8.91
removal of accounts provisions, A6.8.94—A6.8.95
subordinated retained interests, A6.8.92—A6.8.93
security, A6.8.85—A6.8.86
servicing assets and liabilities, A6.8.106—A6.8.109
special purpose entities, A6.8.31—A6.8.32
stock lending, A6.8.75—A6.8.86
subordinated retained interests, A6.8.123
total return swaps, A6.8.126
transfer by entity of cash flows from assets
assumption of obligations to pay to others, A6.8.43—A6.8.54
contractual rights to receive cash flows, A6.8.39—A6.8.42
generally, A6.8.38
transferred asset part of larger asset, A6.8.103—A6.8.105
wash sales, A6.8.84

Derivatives
generally, 6.172—6.175

Detailed numerical disclosures
currency risk, 6.230—6.240
details of financial assets, 6.224—6.229
fair value
book value, and, 6.251—6.256
category, by, 6.247—6.250
determination of fair value, 6.243—6.246
introduction, 6.241—6.242
hedges
current assets and liabilities, 6.269—6.270
forward purchase of stock, 6.273—6.274
gains and losses, 6.269—6.270
gross gains and losses, 6.268
information table, 6.261—6.263
introduction, 6.260
item being hedged, 6.264—6.266
net investment using cross-currency swap, 6.276—6.180
non-derivative hedging, 6.267
non-equity shares, 6.127—6.129
purchase of fixed asset using option, 6.275
interest rate risk, 6.209—6.215
introduction, 6.207—6.208

Detailed numerical disclosures—*cont.*
market price risk, 6.281—6.287
maturity analyses, 6216—6.223
trading assets and liabilities, 6.257—6.259
Details of financial assets
financial instruments, and, 6.224—6.229
Determining segments
generally, 10.32—10.37
Development costs
capitalisation
distributable profits, and, 23.190—23.191
generally, 15.121—15.123
generally, 15.120
Dilapidations
provisions, and, 21.234
Diminution in value
investment properties, and
generally, 17.20
permanent diminution in value, 17.24—17.31
temporary diminution in value, 17.21—17.23
research and development, and, 15.131—15.133
Direct costs
leases, and, 19.90—19.95
Directly attributable costs
generally, 16.61—16.65
period of capitalisation, 16.84
Directors
minority interests, and, 24.369—24.370
profit and loss account, and, 5.25—5.26
related parties, and, 29.42—29.43
related party transactions, and
Companies Act, under, 29.174—29.180
dividends, 29.141
guarantees, 29.140
introduction, 29.138
loans, 29.176
material interest transactions, 29.179—29.180
share interests, 29.181
share transactions, 29.139
remuneration
employee share schemes, and, 12.61
Directors' reports
financial instruments, and, 6.151—6.152
Disclosure
accounting principles, and
generally, 2.102—2.107
overview, 2.93.18
acquisition accounting, and
cash flow statement, 25.125—25.127
fair values of identifiable assets and liabilities, 25.96
general, 25.91—25.93
introduction, 25.88—25.90
post-acquisition activities, 25.114—25.124
pre-acquisition activities, 25.103—25.113
purchase consideration, 25.94—25.95
summary, 25.1.23—25.1.26
table of acquired assets and liabilities, 25.97—25.102
agency companies, and, 32.184—32.187
associates and joint venture entities, and, 27.1.23—27.1.29
capital instruments, and, 6.372—6.374
contingencies, and
contingent assets, 21.308—21.309
contingent liabilities, 21.306—21.307
exemptions, 21.314—21.318
guarantees, 21.310—21.313
current tax, and
accounting policies, 13.235
balance sheet, 13.253—13.273
circumstances affecting tax charges, 13.274—13.290

Disclosure—*cont.*
generally, 13.234
profit and loss account, 13.236—13.248
statement of total recognised gains and losses, 13.249—13.252
summary, 13.1.7
deferred tax, and
accounting policies, 13.235
balance sheet, 13.253—13.273
circumstances affecting tax charges, 13.274—13.290
generally, 13.234
profit and loss account, 13.236—13.248
statement of total recognised gains and losses, 13.249—13.252
summary, 13.1.26
disposal of subsidiaries, and, 26.39—26.41
employee share ownership plans, and, 12.20—12.21
financial instruments, and
accounting policies, of, 6.58—6.62
detailed numbers, of, 6.63—6.143
examples, 6.Annex 1
generally, 6.42—6.45
objectives, policies and strategies, of, 6.46—6.57
financial instruments (Companies Act 1985), and
all investments, 6.94—6.101
associates, 6.116—6.121
bank deposits, 5.147
building society deposits, 6.147
exemptions, 6.108—6.111
introduction, 6.91—6.93
joint ventures, 6.116—6.121
loan for acquisition of own shares, 6.145
other investments, 6.146—6.147
own shares, 6.137—6.142
parent company information, 6.131
participating interests, 6.112—6.115
qualifying undertakings, 6.132—6.136
shares in own parent, 6.137—6.144
significant holdings greater than 20%, 6.102—6.107
subsidiary undertakings, 6.122—6.130
financial instruments (FRS 13), and
accounting policies, of, 6.201—6.206
detailed numbers, of, 6.207—6.208
examples, 6.Annex 1
generally, 6.185—6.188
objectives, policies and strategies, of, 6.189—6.200
financial instruments (IFRS), and
and see **Disclosure of financial instruments (IFRS)**
introduction, A6.11.27—A6.11.29
foreign currency translations, and
requirements of Companies Act, 7.143
requirements of standard, 7.144—7.148.2
impairment, and
assets carried at historical cost, 18.250—18.251
assets held for disposal, 18.263—18.269
Companies Act requirements, 18.281—18.282
fixed asset movements, 18.270—18.271
revalued assets, 18.252—18.262
revalued assets held at depreciated replacement cost, 18.274
revalued assets held at market value, 18.272—18.273
reversal, 18.280
value in use, 18.275—18.279
intangible fixed assets, and
generally, 15.96—15.98
IFRS, 15.139
other information, 15.100
summary, 15.1.19—15.1.20
investment properties, and
generally, 17.35—17.39

Disclosure—*cont.*
IFRS, and, 17.40
summary, 17.1.8—17.1.9
leases, and
accounting by lessees, 19.50—19.53
accounting by lessors, 19.78—19.89
IFRS, and, 19.134
loan transfers, and, 3.178—3.179
long-term contracts, and
generally, 20.106—20.114
provision for foreseeable losses, 20.115—20.118
merger accounting, and
generally, 28.112—28.122
summary, 27.1.9—27.1.10
parent companies, and, 24.238—24.246
provisions, and
acquisitions, 21.305
categorisation by class, 21.289—21.292
exemptions, 21.314—21.318
introduction, 21.288
narrative information, 21.297—21.298
pensions, 21.300—21.302
summary, 21.1.16
tabular information, 21.293—21.296
taxation, 21.303
unwinding of discount, 21.299—21.299.1
quasi-subsidiaries, and, 3.119
related party transactions, and
additional relaxations, 29.166—29.170
aggregation of transactions, 29.118—29.125
balances, 29.116—29.117
comparatives, 29.126
control, 29.93—29.110
exemptions, 29.145—29.165
interaction with Companies Act, 29.127—29.129
IFRS, and, 29.195
introduction, 29.92
transactions and balances, 29.111—29.115.1
true and fair view, and, 29.171—29.173
reporting financial performance, and, 8.208
reporting substance of transactions, and, 3.1.19
research and development, and
exemptions, 15.129—15.130
generally, 15.126—15.128
reserves, and, 23.125—23.133
retirement benefits, and
aggregation of schemes, 11.146—11.148
comparatives, 11.144—11.145
defined benefit schemes, 11.139—11.148
defined contribution schemes, 11.36
future developments, 11.148.1—11.148.14
summary, 11.1.21—11.1.24
revenue recognition, and
agency fees, 9.286—9.288
commissions, 9.286—9.288
government grants, 9.293—9.298
introduction, 9.283
other operating activity, 9.289—9.292
trading activities, 9.285
turnover, 9.284
securitisation of assets, and
group's financial statements, 3.154—3.155
originator's financial statements, 3.148—3.150
segmental reporting, and
acquisitions, 10.127—10.135
associates, 10.100—10.106
cash flow statements, 10.117—10.120
Companies Act requirements, 10.68—10.73
comparative figures, 10.110
discontinued operations, 10.127—10.135
exceptional items, 10.136—10.142

Disclosure—*cont.*
inter-segment sales, 10.81—10.85
introduction, 10.67
joint arrangements, 10.107
joint ventures, 10.100—10.106
reconciliation of figures, 10.108
segment net assets, 10.91—10.99
segment result, 10.86—10.90
SSAP 25, 10.74—10.80
subsidiary undertakings, 10.122—10.126
summary, 10.1.4—10.1.11
turnover sales, 10.81—10.85
share-based payments, and
ESOP trusts, 12.73—12.74
generally, 12.22
share capital, and
allotment of shares during year, 23.35—23.37
Companies Act requirements, 23.30—23.34
stocks, and
generally, 20.34—20.36
replacement value, 20.37—20.41
subsidiaries excluded from consolidation, and
aggregation, 24.204—24.208
Companies Act requirements, 24.202—24.202.2
exemptions, 24.209—24.212
FRS requirements, 24.203
introduction, 24.200—24.201
subsidiary undertakings, and
company shares, 24.221—24.226
excessive information, 24.236—24.237
financial years, 24.219
holdings in subsidiaries, 24.217.1—24.218
introduction, 24.213
place of origin, 24.214—24.217
'seriously prejudicial', 24.233—24.235
'shares held by group', 24.232
significant investment holdings, 24.227—24.231
tangible fixed assets, and
capital grants, 16.339—16.340
capitalisation of finance costs, 16.126—16.129
depreciation, 16.309—16.314
revaluation, 16.204—16.212
taxation, and
accounting policies, 13.235
balance sheet, 13.253—13.273
circumstances affecting tax charges, 13.274—13.290
generally, 13.234
profit and loss account, 13.236—13.248
statement of total recognised gains and losses, 13.249—13.252
treasury shares, and, 23.74—23.79
Disclosure of financial instruments (IFRS)
accounting policies, A6.11.66—A6.11.67
aggregation, A6.11.43
balance sheet disclosures
allowance amount for credit losses, A6.11.59
collateral, A6.11.56—A6.11.58
compound instruments with multiple embedded derivatives, A6.11.60
defaults and breaches, A6.11.61—A6.11.63
derecognition, A6.11.55
fair value through profit or loss, A6.11.47—A6.11.53
introduction, A6.11.45—A6.11.46
multiple embedded derivatives, A6.11.60
re-classification, A6.11.54
classes of financial instruments, A6.11.39—A6.11.41
credit risk
collateral enhancements, A6.11.93—A6.11.94
financial assets either past due or impaired, A6.11.95—A6.11.96

Disclosure of financial instruments (IFRS)—*cont.*
generally, A6.11.90—A6.11.92
expenditure, A6.11.64—A6.11.65
fair value, A6.11.72—A6.11.78
financial instrument risk disclosures
credit risk, A6.11.90—A6.11.96
introduction, A6.11.79—A6.11.82
liquidity risk, A6.11.97—A6.11.105
market risk, A6.11.106—A6.11.120
qualitative disclosures, A6.11.83—A6.11.84
quantitative disclosures, A6.11.85—A6.11.89
gains and losses, A6.11.64—A6.11.65
general matters
aggregation, A6.11.43
classes of financial instruments, A6.11.39—A6.11.41
level of disclosure, A6.11.42—A6.11.43
location of disclosure, A6.11.42—A6.11.43
risks arising from financial instruments, A6.11.44
hedge accounting, A6.11.68—A6.11.71
income statement, A6.11.64—A6.11.65
introduction, A6.11.27—A6.11.29
level of disclosure, A6.11.42—A6.11.43
liquidity risk, A6.11.97—A6.11.105
location of disclosure, A6.11.42—A6.11.43
market risk
other disclosures, A6.11.116—A6.11.120
sensitivity analysis, A6.11.106—A6.11.117
objectives of IFRS 7, A6.11.32—A6.11.35
overview, A6.1.52—A6.1.54
qualitative disclosures, A6.11.83—A6.11.84
quantitative disclosures, A6.11.85—A6.11.89
risks arising from financial instruments, A6.11.44
scope of IFRS 7, A6.11.30—A6.11.31
transition to IFRS 7, A6.11.36—A6.11.38
Discontinued operations
and see **Disposals**
definition, 8.24—8.26
goodwill on disposals, 8.54—8.57
IFRS, and, 8.208
materiality, 8.28
meaning of 'ceased permanently', 8.27
operations discontinued by closure
generally, 8.58—8.59
provisions for losses, 8.60—8.69
operations discontinued by sale
generally, 8.37—8.38
goodwill, 8.54—8.57
profits and losses, 8.39—8.53
profits and losses on sales
exceptional items, 8.90—8.93
generally, 8.39—8.40
provisions for losses, 8.41—8.53
retention of interest in disposed of subsidiary, 8.34—8.36
segmental reporting, and, 10.127—10.135
separability of activities, 8.29—8.33
Discount rate
generally, 18.160—18.167
pre-tax rate, 18.168—18.178
Discounting
deferred tax, and
calculation, 13.185—13.188
introduction, 13.176—13.184
rates, 13.192—13.195
scheduling cash flows, 13.189—13.190
scheduling timing differences, 13.191
summary, 13.1.19—13.1.22
worked examples, 13.196—13.202
provisions, and
effects of taxation, 21.130
Discounting—*cont.*
inflation adjustments, 21.121—21.123
introduction, 21.119—21.120
risk adjustment, 21.124—21.129
selection of appropriate discount rate, 21.131
unwinding the discount, 21.132
revenue recognition, and
generally, 9.185—9.186
introduction, 9.45
Discounts and premiums
cash flow statements, and, 30.180—30.181
Disposal of associates
effective date, 27.162—27.164
generally, 27.170—27.172
Disposal of goodwill
generally, 8.54—8.57
Disposal of joint ventures
effective date, 27.162—27.164
generally, 27.170—27.172
Disposal of subsidiaries
and see **Discontinued operations**
accounting rules
FRS 1, 26.19
FRS 2, 26.5—26.12
FRS 3, 26.13—26.18
IFRS, 26.42—26.45
cash flow statements, and
consolidated statements, and, 30.132—30.138
generally, 30.98—30.99
ceasing to be subsidiary, 26.34—26.25
comparison with IFRS, and, 26.42—26.45
deemed disposals, 26.34—26.38
disclosure requirements, 26.39—26.41
FRS 1, 26.19
FRS 2, 26.5—26.12
FRS 3
date of sale, 26.18
discontinued operations, 26.15—26.17
introduction, 26.13—26.14
full disposal, 26.20—26.23
IFRS, and, 26.42—26.45
introduction, 26.1—26.4
partial disposals
becoming an associate, 26.32
becoming an associate, 26.33
generally, 26.27—26.30
remaining a subsidiary, 26.31
sale for shares
exchange for interest in joint venture, 26.23.9—26.23.10
exchange for interest in subsidiary, 26.23.8
generally, 26.23.1—26.23.7
types
ceasing to be subsidiary, 26.34—26.25
deemed disposals, 26.34—26.38
full disposal, 26.20—26.23
partial disposals, 26.27—26.33
sale for shares, 26.23.1—26.23.10
Disposal of tangible fixed assets
intended, 16.325—16.328
introduction, 16.315
reporting gains and losses, 16.316—16.318
revalued assets, 16.319—16.324
Disproportionate expense
subsidiaries excluded from consolidation, and, 24.181
Dissimilar activities
generally, 24.203
Distributable profits
capitalisation of development costs, 23.190—23.191
conditions
companies, 23.162—23.164

Distributable profits—*cont.*
investment companies, 23.172—23.176
public companies, 23.165—23.171
definition of 'distribution', 23.161
development costs, 23.190—23.191
effect of revaluations
depreciation of revalued assets, 23.178—23.180
diminution in value of assets, 23.185
introduction, 23.177
subsequent sale of revalued assets, 23.181—23.184
employee share ownership plans, and
generally, 12.23—12.23.7
public companies, 12.23.8—12.23.12
foreign currency translations
generally, 23.186—23.189
introduction, 7.149—7.160
goodwill, and, 23.192—23.195
other transactions, 23.202
pre-acquisition profits, 23.201
relevant accounts
interpretation of statutory provisions, 23.221
introduction, 23.203—23.213
qualified audit reports, 23.223—23.229
summary of action, 23.222
treatment of revalued assets, 23.214—23.220
share-based payments, and, 12.56—12.62
transactions within the group, 23.196—23.198
treasury shares, and, 23.80—23.83
Distributable reserves
disclosure requirements, 23.127—23.130
group structure, and, 24.252—24.255
Distribution costs
profit and loss account, and, 5.6—5.12
Distributions in kind
share capital, and, 23.238—23.243
Dividend shares
accounting implications, 12.103—12.105
introduction, 12.88
Dividends
capital instruments, and, 6.306
current tax, and
incoming, 13.31—13.33
outgoing, 13.28—13.30
realised profits, and, 23.156.1—23.156.2
related party transactions, and, 9.251—9.253
share capital, and, 23.134—23.138
Dividends from joint ventures and associates
cash flow statements, and, 30.75.1
Dividends paid to directors
related party transactions, and, 29.141
Dominant influence
cessation of, 24.147—24.149
commercial relationships, 24.143—24.145
definition, 24.132—24.136
disclosure requirements, 24.151
financial policies, 24.137—24.139
generally, 24.121—24.124
method of exercise, 24.144—24.148
operating policies, 24.137—24.139
power to exercise or exercises influence, 24.130—24.131
practical effect, 24.140
reserve powers, 24.141—24.142
right to exercise, 24.125—24.129
special purpose entities, 24.149.1—24.149.3
summary, 24.150
two parents, 24.146
veto power, 24.141—24.142
Donated assets
tangible fixed assets, and, 16.90—16.93
Dormant companies
cessation of qualification, 32.174
definition, 32.159.6
introduction, 32.159.1
significant accounting transactions, 32.159.7—32.159.9
Dual rates
consolidated financial statements, 7.56
individual company financial statements, 7.19—7.20

Earnings per share (FRS 14)
generally, 14.1—14.12
IFRS, and, A14.1—A14.207
Earnout consideration
goodwill, and, 25.601
Electrical and electronic equipment
provisions, and, 21.248.1—21.248.6
Elements of financial statements
ASB Statement of principles, and, 2.205—2.209
Embedded derivatives
accounting, A6.5.94—A6.5.99
application of closely related criteria
debt host contracts, A6.5.23—A6.5.56
equity host contracts, A6.5.57—A6.5.61
executory contracts, A6.5.74—A6.5.91
insurance contracts, A6.5.92—A6.5.93
introduction, A6.5.22
lease host contracts, A6.5.62—A6.5.73
assessment of closely related criteria, A6.5.19—A6.5.21
balance sheet disclosures, and, A6.11.60
base state, A6.5.4
call option linked to equity index, A6.5.36
call options
debt host contracts, A6.5.43—A6.5.45
equity host contracts, A6.5.58—A6.5.61
callable convertible bond, A6.5.106
caps, floors and collars, A6.5.83
'closely related'
application of criteria to hosts, A6.5.22—A6.5.107
assessment of criteria, A6.5.19—A6.5.21
generally, A6.5.11—A6.5.12
leverage embedded features in host contracts, A6.5.13—A6.5.14
commodity linked bond, A6.5.36
conditions for separation, A6.5.6—A6.5.10
contingent rentals
based on related sales, A6.5.66
based on variable interest rate, A6.5.67
convertible preference shares, A6.5.61
credit derivatives, A6.5.49—A6.5.51
credit sensitive payments, A6.5.49—A6.5.51
debt host contracts
call option linked to equity index, A6.5.36
call options, A6.5.43—A6.5.45
commodity linked bond, A6.5.36
credit derivatives, A6.5.49—A6.5.51
credit sensitive payments, A6.5.49—A6.5.51
debt subject to interest rate collar, A6.5.42
dual currency bond, A6.5.55
equity conversion features, A6.5.52—5-54
equity kicker, A6.5.54
equity linked interest and principal payments, A6.5.36—A6.5.37
floating rate debt, A6.5.30
foreign currency features, A6.5.55—A6.5.56
forward starting interest rate swap, A6.5.30
index linked interest payments, A6.5.26—A6.5.30
inflation-linked bond, A6.5.35
inflation-linked interest and principal payments, A6.5.31—A6.5.35

Embedded derivatives—*cont.*
interest rate caps, floors and collars, A6.5.38—A6.5.42
introduction, A6.5.23—5-25
leveraged inverse floater, A6.5.30
loan with currency option, A6.5.56
payments linked to share price of UK plc, A6.5.36
pre-payment options, A6.5.43—A6.5.45
put options, A6.5.43—A6.5.45
term-extending options, A6.5.46—A6.5.48
debt subject to interest rate collar, A6.5.42
definition, A6.5.4—A6.5.5
dual currency bond, A6.5.55
equity conversion features, A6.5.52—5-54
equity host contracts
call options, A6.5.58—A6.5.61
convertible preference shares, A6.5.61
introduction, A6.5.57
put options, A6.5.58—A6.5.61
puttable preference shares, A6.5.61
equity kicker, A6.5.54
equity linked interest and principal payments, A6.5.36—A6.5.37
executory contracts
caps, floors and collars, A6.5.83
flow chart, A6.5.91
foreign currency features, A6.5.84—A6.5.90
inflation related features, A6.5.82
introduction, A6.5.74—A6.5.75
price adjustment features, A6.5.76—A6.5.77
purchase contract linked to inflation, A6.5.82
volume adjustment features, A6.5.78—A6.5.81
floating rate debt, A6.5.30
foreign currency features
debt host contracts, A6.5.55—A6.5.56
executory contracts, A6.5.84—A6.5.90
forward starting interest rate swap, A6.5.30
hedging instruments, as, A6.5.107
identifying terms, A6.5.15—A6.5.18
index linked interest payments, A6.5.26—A6.5.30
inflation-linked bond, A6.5.35
inflation-linked interest and principal payments, A6.5.31—A6.5.35
inflation related features, A6.5.82
inflation indexed rentals, A6.5.63—A6.5.65
insurance contracts
generally, A6.5.92—A6.5.93
scope of standards, A6.3.19
interest rate caps, floors and collars, A6.5.38—A6.5.42
introduction, A6.5.1—A6.5.3
key characteristics, A6.5.4—A6.5.5
lease host contracts
contingent rentals based on related sales, A6.5.66
contingent rentals based on variable interest rate, A6.5.67
inflation indexed rentals, A6.5.63—A6.5.65
introduction, A6.5.62
payment in foreign currency, A6.5.72—A6.5.73
purchase options in lease agreements, A6.5.68
renewal options, A6.5.69
residual value guarantee, A6.5.70
term extension, A6.5.69
termination clause, A6.5.71
leverage embedded features, A6.5.13—A6.5.14
leveraged inverse floater, A6.5.30
loan with currency option, A6.5.56
multiple embedded derivatives
callable convertible bond, A6.5.106
generally, A6.5.105—A6.5.106
overview, A6.1.14—A6.1.15

Embedded derivatives—*cont.*
payments linked to share price of UK plc, A6.5.36
pre-payment options, A6.5.43—A6.5.45
price adjustment features, A6.5.76—A6.5.77
purchase contract linked to inflation, A6.5.82
purchase options in lease agreements, A6.5.68
put options
debt host contracts, A6.5.43—A6.5.45
equity host contracts, A6.5.58—A6.5.61
puttable preference shares, A6.5.61
renewal options, A6.5.69
residual value guarantee, A6.5.70
separation
non-option-based derivative, 5-100
option-based derivative, A6.5.101—A6.5.104
term-extending options, A6.5.46—A6.5.48
volume adjustment features, A6.5.78—A6.5.81
Emissions obligations
provisions, and, 21.248.7—21.248.13
Employee costs
directors, 5.25—5.26
disclosure by groups, 5.26.1—5.26.2
generally, 5.15—5.20
numbers of employees, 5.21—5.24
practical issues, 5.27—5.28
Employee numbers
profit and loss account, and, 5.21—5.24
segmental reporting, and, 10.145—10.147
Employee share ownership plans (FRS 20)
and see **Employee share ownership plans (UITF 38)**
accounting, 12.46—12.54
background, 12.42—12.45
disclosure, 12.73—12.74
distributable profits, 12.56—12.62
gains, 12.71—12.72
generally, 12.40—12.41
introduction, 12.19—12.21
legal issues, 12.55
public companies, and, 12.63—12.70
trustee company, 12.72
Employee share ownership plans (UITF 13)
and see below
introduction, 12.2
replacement, 12.3.1
Employee share ownership plans (UITF 38)
analysing risks and rewards, 12.9—12.12
background, 12.1—12.3.3
benefit to employees, 12.24
comparison with IFRS, and, 12.134
disclosure requirements, 12.20—12.21
distributable profits, and
generally, 12.23—12.23.7
public companies, 12.23.8—12.23.12
examples, 12.25—12.26
gains, 12.28
IFRS, and
generally, 12.134
introduction, 12.3.3
introduction, 12.4—12.8
legal considerations, 12.22
practical implications
examples, 12.25
gains, 12.28
requirements of abstract, 12.13—12.17
trustee company, 12.29
Employee share schemes (UITF 17)
and see **Employee share ownership plans**
background, 12.1—12.3.3
buyback guarantee from parent company, 12.59
cash payment to employee trusts, 12.81—12.85
changes in estimates, 12.47—12.48

Employee share schemes (UITF 17)—*cont.*
comparison with IFRS, and, 12.134
credit entry, 12.45—12.46.1
date of grant of award, 12.55—12.56.5
directors' emoluments, 12.61
flotations, 12.54—12.54.3
group situations
buyback guarantee from parent company, 12.59
introduction, 12.58—12.60
recharge from parent company, 12.58
IFRS, and
generally, 12.134
introduction, 12.3.3
introduction, 12.1—12.3.3
national insurance contributions on gains
background, 12.62—12.64
practical application, 12.78—12.80
reimbursement of liability, 12.74—12.77
requirements of abstract, 12.65—12.72
transfer of liability, 12.74—12.77
practical implications
changes in estimates, 12.47—12.48
credit entry, 12.45—12.46.1
date of grant of award, 12.55—12.56.5
flotations, 12.54—12.54.3
group situations, 12.58—12.60
variation of awards, 12.57
quantification of charge, 12.40—12.44
recharge from parent company, 12.58
roll-over of options, 12.57
scope of abstract, 12.30—12.34
timing of charge, 12.37—12.39
variation of awards, 12.57
vesting period, 12.57
Employee trusts
cash payments, and, 12.81—12.85
Environmental liabilities
provisions, and, 21.245—21.248
Equity (IFRS)
accounting, A6.7.1
classification principles
contingent settlement, A6.7.30—A6.7.34
contractual obligations to deliver cash, etc, A6.7.13—A6.7.23
equity instruments, A6.7.35—A6.7.44
introduction, A6.7.6—A6.7.12
obligations that can be settled using own shares, A6.7.24—A6.7.29
compound financial instruments
conversion at or before maturity, A6.7.51—A6.7.52
convertible bond denominated in foreign currency, A6.7.59—A6.7.60
early redemption or repurchase, A6.7.54—A6.7.55
introduction, A6.7.45
mandatorily convertible instruments, A6.7.53—A6.7.53.1
modification of terms to induce early conversion, A6.7.56
separation of instrument containing non-equity derivatives, A6.7.50
separation on initial recognition, A6.7.46—A6.7.49
settlement options, A6.7.57—A6.7.58
contingent settlement
generally, A6.7.30—A6.7.31
liquidations, and, A6.7.34
non-genuine terms, A6.7.32—A6.7.33
contractual obligations to deliver cash, etc
absence of explicit obligations, A6.7.21—A6.7.23
introduction, A6.7.13—A6.7.23
puttable instruments, A6.7.16—A6.7.20
restriction on ability to satisfy, A6.7.15

Equity (IFRS)—*cont.*
debt to equity conversions, A6.7.64—A6.7.66.1
decision tree, A6.7.42
derivatives over own equity instruments
accounting as derivative assets or liabilities, A6.7.73—A6.7.774
accounting as equity instruments, A6.7.68—A6.7.70
accounting as financial liabilities, A6.7.71—A6.7.72
holder's settlement options, A6.7.75—A6.7.76
introduction, A6.7.67
issuer's settlement options, A6.7.75—A6.7.76
derivatives with settlement options, A6.7.43—A6.7.44
dividends, A6.7.77—A6.7.81
'economic substance', A6.7.4
'equity instrument', A6.7.8
equity instruments
discretionary payments, A6.7.36
introduction, A6.7.35
payment at option of issuer, A6.7.36—A6.7.38
shares issued by subsidiaries, A6.7.39—A6.7.41
'financial liability', A6.7.7
gains and losses, A6.7.77—A6.7.81
generally, A6.7.1—A6.7.5
interest, A6.7.77—A6.7.81
non-redeemable preference shares, A6.7.14
overview, A6.1.20—A6.1.25
perpetual debt, A6.7.14
preference shares with rights, A6.7.61—A6.7.63
redeemable preference shares, A6.7.14
settlement using own shares, A6.7.24—A6.7.29
transaction costs of equity instruments, A6.7.82—A6.7.86
Treasury shares, A6.7.87—A6.7.88
zero coupon bond, A6.7.14
Equity accounting
additional disclosure, 27.100—27.113
balance sheet, 27.85—27.97
cash flow statement, 27.99
individual financial statements, 27.98
introduction, 27.68—27.71
optional disclosure, 27.114—27.115
principles, 27.116—27.175
profit and loss account, 27.72—27.82
segmental reporting, 27.83
statement of total recognised gains and losses, 27.84
summary, 27.1.15—27.1.18
Equity dividends paid
cash flow statements, and, 30.101
Equity investments financed by foreign borrowings
consolidated financial statements
generally, 7.105—7.110
goodwill, 7.111—7.112
individual company financial statements
borrowing restriction, 7.87—7.88
borrowing taken out before or after investment, 7.93—7.94
carrying value of foreign equity investment, 7.95—7.98
consistent accounting treatment, 7.89
intermediate holding companies, 7.103—7.104
introduction, 7.79—7.82
offset restriction, 7.83—7.86
partial hedges, 7.99—7.102
termination of hedging during year, 7.91—7.92
upstream loans, 7.90
summary, 7.11.16—7.11.20
Equity-settled share-based payment transactions
and see **Share-based payment transactions**
generally, 12.16—12.18
introduction, 12.2
measurement, 12.5—12.7

ESOPs (FRS 20)
and see **ESOPs (UITF 38)**
accounting, 12.46—12.54
background, 12.42—12.45
disclosure, 12.73—12.74
distributable profits, 12.56—12.62
gains, 12.71—12.72
generally, 12.40—12.41
introduction, 12.19—12.21
legal issues, 12.55
public companies, and, 12.63—12.70
trustee company, 12.72
ESOPs (UITF 13)
and see below
introduction, 12.2
replacement, 12.3.1
ESOPs (UITF 38)
analysing risks and rewards, 12.9—12.12
background, 12.1—12.3.3
benefit to employees, 12.24
comparison with IFRS, and, 12.134
disclosure requirements, 12.20—12.21
distributable profits, and
generally, 12.23—12.23.7
public companies, 12.23.8—12.23.12
examples, 12.25—12.26
gains, 12.28
IFRS, and
generally, 12.134
introduction, 12.3.3
introduction, 12.4—12.8
legal considerations, 12.22
practical implications
examples, 12.25
gains, 12.28
requirements of abstract, 12.13—12.17
trustee company, 12.29
Estimation techniques
accounting principles, and
generally, 2.139—2.143
overview, 2.93.16—2.93.17
changes to
generally, 8.205
IFRS, 8.208
small companies, and, 32.98—32.99.6
Euro translations
associated costs, 7.180—7.183
cumulative differences, 7.184—7.185
introduction, 7.178—7.179
European Financial Reporting Advisory Group (EFRAG)
introduction, 1.5
Exceptional cash flows
cash flow statements, and, 30.112—30.118
Exceptional items
definition, 8.79—8.83
fundamental reorganisation or restructuring, 8.94—8.99
introduction, 8.22—8.23
non-operating exceptional items, 8.84—8.87
other, 8.121—8.136
profits and losses on disposals of fixed assets
generally, 8.103—8.112
impairments, 8.114—8.117
profits and losses on sale or termination, 8.90—8.93
segmental reporting, and, 10.136—10.142
summary, 8.1.4—8.1.6
tax attributable, 8.137—8.143
Exchange gains and losses
foreign currency translation, and, 7.25—7.31
revenue recognition, and, 9.214—9.218
Exchanges
investment properties, and, 17.40
Executory contracts
onerous contracts, and, 21.197
Existing use value
tangible fixed assets, and, 16.193—16.196
Expected return on assets
generally, 11.87—11.89.2
Expenses
merger accounting, and, 28.98—28.105
Experience surpluses and deficiencies
discounting, 11.59—11.60
introduction, 11.45—11.51
level percentage method, 11.52—11.53
mortgage method, 11.57—11.58
straight line method, 11.54—11.56
Extended warranties
revenue recognition, and, 9.92—9.93
External charges
profit and loss account, and, 5.32—5.34
Extraordinary cash flows
cash flow statements, and, 30.112—30.118
Extraordinary items
reporting financial performance, and, 8.144

Facility fees
capital instruments, and, 6.323—6.325
Fair value
and see **Fair value (acquisition accounting)**
and see **Fair value disclosures**
accounting principles, and, 2.151.1—2.151.4
deferred tax, and, 13.209—13.213
financial instruments, and
changes, 6.85
generally, 6.81—6.84
marking to market, 6.86—6.88
new rules, 6.48—6.51
Fair value (acquisition accounting)
background, 25.96
contingent consideration, 25.410—25.425
deferred consideration, 25.404—25.409
deferred taxation, 25.381—25.382
fees and expenses of acquisition, 25.426—25.4
identifying assets and liabilities
adjustments for differing accounting policies, 25.175—25.176
definitions of assets and liabilities, 25.158—25.163
examples, 25.177
exclusion of assets and liabilities, 25.173—25.174
inclusion of assets and liabilities, 25.164—25.172
intangible assets
anti-avoidance measures, 25.198—25.207
background, 25.190—25.192
disclosure of acquisition provisions, 25.230—25.231
disclosure of post-acquisition reorganisation costs, 25.208—25.217
fundamental reorganisation, 25.218—25.222
generally, 25.178—25.189
nature of reorganisation costs, 25.223—25.229
post-acquisition activities, 25.193—25.197
introduction, 25.144—25.148
investment properties, and, 17.40
measuring fair values of assets and liabilities
contingencies, 25.350—25.365
depreciated replacement cost, 25.271—25.279
disposals of business segments, 25.322—25.337
fixed assets, 25.259
long-term contracts, 25.313—25.321
market value, 25.260—25.270
meaning of fair value, 25.232—25.242.1
monetary assets and liabilities, 25.338—25.349

Fair value (acquisition accounting)—*cont.*
pensions, 25.366—25.380
period for completing fair value exercise, 25.243—25.247
recoverable amount, 25.280—25.294
retirement benefits, 25.366—25.380
stocks, 25.295—25.312
subsequent amendments to fair values, 25.248—25.258
minority interests, and, 24.381—24.382
non-monetary consideration, 25.397—25.399
objective, 25.154—25.156
other consideration, 25.400—25.403
other securities, 25.396
overriding principles, 25.157
purchase consideration, 25.383—25.425
purchase of business or assets, 25.151—25.153
quoted securities, 25.390—25.393
reserves, and, 23.124.1
scope, 25.149—25.150
unquoted securities, 25.394—25.395
Fair value adjustments
deferred tax, and, 13.209—13.213
Fair value disclosures
acquisition accounting, and
generally, 25.96
summary, 25.1.3—25.1.9
associates, and, 27.141—27.143
book value, and, 6.107—6.112
category, by, 6.103—6.106
determination of fair value, 6.99—6.102
financial instruments, and
book value, and, 6.251—6.256
category, by, 6.247—6.250
determination of fair value, 6.243—6.246
introduction, 6.241—6.242
introduction, 6.97—6.98
joint ventures, and, 27.141—27.143
Fair value reserve
reserves, and, 23.124.1
Fees and expenses
acquisition accounting, and, 25.35—25.38
15% threshold information
associates and joint ventures, and, 27.107—27.113
Finance and Lease Association SORP
leases, and, 19.67.1—19.67.4
Finance costs
dividends, 6.306
elements, 6.305
interest, 6.306
introduction, 6.299—6.300
issue and redemption premiums, 6.307
issue costs, 6.308—6.322
Finance leasebacks
leases, and, 19.55—19.59
Finance leases
accounting by lessees
disclosure requirements, 19.50—19.53
generally, 19.39—19.42
residual values, 19.126
accounting by lessors
disclosure requirements, 19.78—19.89
actuarial after-tax method, 19.75
generally, 19.68—19.74
IFRS, and, 19.134
introduction, 19.1.2
provisions, and, 21.272
Financial assets (IFRS)
carried at amortised cost
absence of observable data, A6.9.144—A6.9.145
appropriate discount rate, A6.9.132—A6.9.135
Financial assets (IFRS)—*cont.*
bad and doubtful debts, A6.9.146—A6.9.147
evaluation of impairment on portfolio bias, A6.9.136—A6.9.143
general requirements, A6.9.126—A6.9.131
interest on impaired assets, A6.9.147—A6.9.149
reversal of impairment losses, A6.9.150
classification of financial instruments, and
available-for-sale financial assets, A6.6.66—A6.6.68
fair value through profit or loss, A6.6.3—A6.6.25
held-to-maturity investments, A6.6.26—A6.6.57
introduction, A6.6.2
loans and receivables, A6.6.58—A6.6.65
reclassification between categories, A6.6.69—A6.6.74
definition, A6.4.4
overview, A6.1.9
subsequent measurement
available-for-sale assets, A6.9.29—A6.9.35
fair value through profit or loss, at, A6.9.23—A6.9.25
general, A6.9.21
hedged items, A6.9.36
held-to-maturity investments, A6.9.28
loans and receivables, A6.9.26—A6.9.27
negative fair values, A6.9.42
reclassifications between categories, A6.9.37—A6.9.39
settlement date accounting for regular way transactions, A6.9.40—A6.9.41
Financial instruments (FRS 13)
and see **Financial instruments (IFRS)**
application under UK GAAP
all entities, and, 6.55—6.153
banks, 6.52—6.53
Companies Act requirements, 6.31—6.32
companies not applying FRS 26, 6.154—6.287
FRS 4, 6.33—6.34
FRS 13, 6.35
FRS 25, 6.36—6.38.1
FRS 26, 6.39—6.41
FRS 29, 6.41.1—6.41.2
insurance companies, 6.52—6.53
introduction, 6.26—6.30.1
listed companies, 6.41—6.47
new fair value accounting rules, 6.48—6.51
practical examples, 6.54
associates, 6.116—6.121
balance sheet instruments, 6.170—6.171
bank deposits, 5.147
building society deposits, 6.147
cash-settled commodity contracts, 6.176—6.180
Companies Act 1985 requirements, and
application under UK GAAP, 6.31—6.32
companies adopting fair value accounting, 6.101.8
companies not adopting fair value accounting, 6.101.9—6.101.11
comparatives, 6.101.14
directors' report, 6.101.12—6.101.13
disclosures, 6.91—6.147
introduction, 6.12
comparative information
Companies Act 1985 requirements, 6.153
FRS 25 and FRS 26, 6.396—6.400
currency risk, 6.230—6.240
current asset investments
alternative accounting rules, 6.76
historical cost accounting rules, 6.77—6.78
derivatives, 6.172—6.175
details of financial assets, 6.224—6.229

Financial instruments (FRS 13)—*cont.*
directors' report, 6.151—6.152
disclosures (Companies Act 1985)
all investments, 6.94—6.101
associates, 6.116—6.121
bank deposits, 5.147
building society deposits, 6.147
exemptions, 6.108—6.111
introduction, 6.91—6.93
joint ventures, 6.116—6.121
loan for acquisition of own shares, 6.145
other investments, 6.146—6.147
own shares, 6.137—6.142
parent company information, 6.131
participating interests, 6.112—6.115
qualifying undertakings, 6.132—6.136
shares in own parent, 6.137—6.144
significant holdings greater than 20%, 6.102—6.107
subsidiary undertakings, 6.122—6.130
disclosures (FRS 13)
accounting policies, of, 6.201—6.206
detailed numbers, of, 6.207—6.208
examples, 6.Annex 1
generally, 6.185—6.188
objectives, policies and strategies, of, 6.189—6.200
detailed numerical disclosures
currency risk, 6.230—6.240
details of financial assets, 6.224—6.229
fair value, 6.241—6.256
hedges, 6.260—6.280
interest rate risk, 6.209—6.215
introduction, 6.207—6.208
market price risk, 6.281—6.287
maturity analyses, 6216—6.223
trading assets and liabilities, 6.257—6.259
excluded financial instruments
balance sheet instruments, 6.170—6.171
cash-settled commodity contracts, 6.176—6.180
derivatives, 6.172—6.175
generally, 6.25
introduction, 6.163—6.165
non-equity minority interests, 6.181—6.184
non-equity shares, 6.181—6.184
short-term debtors and creditors, 6.166—6.169
facility fees, 6.323—6.325
fair value accounting
changes, 6.85
generally, 6.81—6.84
marking to market, 6.86—6.88
new rules, 6.48—6.51
fair value disclosures
book value, and, 6.251—6.256
category, by, 6.247—6.250
determination of fair value, 6.243—6.246
introduction, 6.241—6.242
finance costs
dividends, 6.306
elements, 6.305
interest, 6.306
introduction, 6.299—6.300
issue and redemption premiums, 6.307
issue costs, 6.308—6.322
financial liabilities
currency analysis, 6.209—6.215
maturity analysis, 6.216—6.220
fixed asset investments
alternative accounting rules, 6.69—6.75
historical cost accounting rules, 6.66—6.68
FRS 4 (capital instruments)
application under UK GAAP, 6.33—6.34
background, 6.288—6.290

Financial instruments (FRS 13)—*cont.*
Companies Act requirements, 6.375—6.381
definition of capital instrument, 6.296—6.298
disclosure, 6.372—6.374
dividends, 6.306
facility fees, 6.323—6.325
finance costs, 6.299—6.322
interest, 6.306
issue and redemption premiums, 6.307
issue costs, 6.308—6.322
measurement, 6.345—6.371
objectives, 6.291—6.292
options, 6.329—6.340
scope, 6.293—6.295
term, 6.326—6.344
FRS 25 (disclosure and presentation)
application under UK GAAP, 6.36—6.38.1
comparative information, 6.396—6.400
derecognition, 6.387
EU carve-out of IAS 39, 6.388—6.390
fair value option, 6.390.1—6.390.5
flowchart, 6.Annex 2
generally, 6.383—6.383.1
hedge accounting, 6.403—6.410
introduction, 6.9—6.13.1
other differences, 6.390.6
recognition, 6.386—6.387.5
scope exclusion, 6.384—6.384.1
transitional guidance, 6.391—6.395
FRS 26 (recognition and measurement)
amendments, 6.406.1—6.406.4
application under UK GAAP, 6.39—6.41
comparative information, 6.396—6.400
derecognition, 6.387
EU carve-out of IAS 39, 6.388—6.390
fair value option, 6.390.1—6.390.5
flowchart, 6.Annex 2
generally, 6.383—6.383.1
hedge accounting, 6.403—6.410
introduction, 6.9—6.13.1
recognition, 6.386—6.387.5
transitional guidance, 6.391—6.395
FRS 29 (disclosures)
application under UK GAAP, 6.41.1—6.41.2
generally, 6.406.5—6.406.7
introduction, 6.9.1
hedges
current assets and liabilities, 6.269—6.270
forward purchase of stock, 6.273—6.274
gains and losses, 6.269—6.270
gross gains and losses, 6.268
information table, 6.261—6.263
introduction, 6.260
item being hedged, 6.264—6.266
net investment using cross-currency swap, 6.276—6.180
non-derivative hedging, 6.267
non-equity shares, 6.127—6.129
purchase of fixed asset using option, 6.275
historical cost accounting rules
current asset investments, 6.77—6.78
fixed asset investments, 6.66—6.68
holdings of assets and liabilities for trading, 6.257—6.259
IFRS, and
and see **Financial instruments (IFRS)**
generally, 6.Annex 3
insurance companies, 6.52—6.53
interest rate risk, 6.209—6.215
introduction, 6.1—6.15
joint ventures, 6.116—6.121

Financial instruments (FRS 13)—*cont.*
listed companies, 6.41—6.47
loan for acquisition of own shares, 6.145
market price risk, 6.281—6.287
marking to market, 6.86—6.88
maturity analyses
financial liabilities, of, 6.216—6.220
undrawn committed borrowing facilities, of, 6.221—6.223
measurement rules
current asset investments, 6.76—6.78
fair value accounting, 6.79—6.88
fixed asset investments, 6.66—6.75
generally, 6.64—6.65
minority interests, 6.20
non-equity minority interests, 6.181—6.184
non-equity shares, 6.181—6.184
onerous contracts, and, 21.198
own shares, 6.137—6.142
parent company information, 6.131
participating interests, 6.112—6.115
presentation rules, 6.89—6.90
qualifying undertakings, 6.132—6.136
relevant financial instruments
contracts and contractual rights, 6.21—6.24
examples, 6.19
introduction, 6.16—6.20
requirements applicable to all entities
classification, 6.61—6.63
definition of investments, 6.57—6.60
generally, 6.55—6.56
measurement rules, 6.64—6.88
presentation rules, 6.89—6.90
scope, 6.155—6.162
shares in own parent, 6.137—6.144
short-term debtors and creditors, 6.166—6.169
significant holdings greater than 20%, 6.102—6.107
subsidiary undertakings, 6.122—6.130
trading, assets and liabilities held for, 6.257—6.259
Financial instruments (IFRS)
and see under individual headings
accounting, A6.2.1—A6.2.2
characteristics
generally, A6.4.1—A6.4.42
overview, A6.1.8—A6.1.13
classification
financial assets, A6.6.2—A6.6.74
financial liabilities, A6.6.75—A6.6.83
introduction, A6.1.16—A6.1.19
Companies Act 1985 requirements, A6.12.1—A6.12.3
definition, A6.4.3
derecognition
generally, A6.8.24—A6.8.158
introduction, A6.8.3—A6.8.4
overview, A6.1.26—A6.1.30
derivatives, A6.1.12
disclosure
generally, A6.11.27—A6.11.120
overview, A6.1.52—A6.1.54
embedded derivatives
generally, A6.5.1—A6.5.107
overview, A6.1.14—A6.1.15
equity, and
generally, A6.7.1—A6.7.88
overview, A6.1.20—A6.1.25
equity instruments, A6.1.11
financial assets
carried at amortised cost, A6.9.126—A6.9.150
definition, A6.4.4
overview, A6.1.9
subsequent measurement, A6.9.21—A6.9.41
Financial instruments (IFRS)—*cont.*
financial liabilities
equity, and, A6.1.20—A6.1.25
generally, A6.1.10
first-time adoption of IFRS, and, A6.13.1—A6.13.7
hedge accounting
criteria, A6.1.42—A6.1.43
discontinuance, A6.1.48—A6.1.51
generally, A6.10.1—A6.10.203
hedging instruments, A6.1.40—A6.1.41
introduction, A6.1.37—A6.1.39
rules, A6.1.44—A6.1.47
measurement
generally, A6.9.1—A6.9.168
overview, A6.1.31—A6.1.36
nature
generally, A6.4.1—A6.4.42
overview, A6.1.8—A6.1.13
presentation
generally, A6.11.1—A6.11.26
overview, A6.1.52—A6.1.54
recognition
generally, A6.8.5—A6.8.23
introduction, A6.8.1—A6.8.2
overview, A6.1.26—A6.1.30
regulatory framework, A6.1.1—A6.1.7
Financial liabilities
currency analysis, 6.209—6.215
maturity analysis, 6.216—6.220
Financial liabilities (IFRS)
classification of financial instruments, and
fair value through profit or loss, A6.6.77—A6.6.81
introduction, A6.6.75—A6.6.76
other liabilities, A6.6.82
reclassification between categories, A6.6.83
definition, A6.4.5
derecognition of financial instruments, and
exchange of debt instrument, A6.8.152—A6.8.158
extinguishment, A6.8.144—A6.8.151
introduction, A6.8.143
equity, and
and see **Equity**
generally, A6.7.1—A6.7.88
overview, A6.1.20—A6.1.25
overview, A6.1.10
subsequent measurement
fair value through profit or loss, at, A6.9.45—A6.9.46
financial guarantee contracts, A6.9.48
hedged items, A6.9.50
introduction, A6.9.43—A6.9.44
off-market loans, A6.9.49
transfer of assets, on, A6.9.47
Financial Reporting Council
financial reporting structure, and, 2.51—2.53.7
Financial Reporting Review Panel
financial reporting structure, and, 2.85—2.87
Financial reporting standards (FRSs)
financial reporting structure, and, 2.65—2.73
Financial reporting structure
ASB Ltd, 2.54—2.64
Companies Act requirements, 2.48—2.50
Dearing Report proposals, 2.45—2.47
Financial Reporting Review Panel, 2.85—2.87
FRC Ltd, 2.51—2.53.7
FRSs, 2.65—2.73
SORPs, 2.74—2.77
SSAPs, 2.65—2.73
true and fair requirement, 2.78—2.80
Urgent Issues Task Force, 2.81—2.84

Financial services fees
revenue recognition, and
earned as result of providing services, 9.281
earned on execution of significant act, 9.282
integral part of effective interest rate, 9.279—9.280
Financial statements
accounting principles and policies, and, 2.22—2.22.8
associates, and, 27.136—27.137
balance sheet
consolidated formats, 4.40—4.106
historical summaries, 4.90
individual company formats, 4.27—4.96
notes to, 4.125—4.139
consolidated formats (balance sheet)
amounts due to and from group undertakings, 4.103—4.106
generally, 4.97—4.99
interests in group undertakings, 4.103—4.106
particular items, rules for, 4.100—4.102
consolidated formats (profit and loss account)
effect of FRS3, 4.120—4.121
generally, 4.111
particular items, rules for, 4.112—4.119
corresponding amounts, 4.19.1—4.24
general rules
choice of formats, 4.7—4.9
corresponding amounts, 4.19.1—4.24
headings, 4.10—4.19
offsetting, 4.25—4.26
sub-headings, 4.10—4.19
half-yearly reports, 4.142
headings, 4.10—4.19
historical summaries, 4.143—4.146
IFRS, and, 4.151
individual company formats (balance sheet)
accruals, 4.92—4.94
accrued income, 4.46—4.54
amounts received on account, 4.82
cash of bank and in hand, 4.55—4.71
debentures, 4.81
deferred income, 4.92—4.94
generally, 4.27—4.29
net current assets and liabilities, 4.72—4.80
other liabilities, 4.95—4.96
own shares, 4.40
participating interests, 4.39
payments on account, 4.41
prepayments,. 4.46—4.54
presentation of debtors, 4.42—4.45
trade creditors, 4.83
trade loans, 4.85—4.92
transfers from current to fixed assets, 4.30—4.38
individual company formats (profit and loss account)
classification of expenses by function, 4.109
classification of expenses by type, 4.110
effect of FRS3, 4.120—4.121
generally, 4.107—4.108
particular items, rules for, 4.112—4.119
interests in group undertakings, 4.103—4.106
introduction, 4.1—4.6
joint ventures, and, 27.136—27.137
listed companies' historical summaries, 4.143—4.146
notes to balance sheet and profit and loss account
accounting policies, 4.134—4.136
additional statements required by FRS3, 4.131
compliance with accounting standards, 4.132
general requirements, 4.125—4.130
true and fair override disclosures, 4.133
offsetting, 4.25—4.26
preliminary results statements, 4.142
preparation requirement, 2.22—2.22.8

Financial statements—*cont*.
profit and loss account
consolidated formats, 4.111—4.119
effect of FRS3, 4.120—4.121
historical summaries, 4.90
individual company formats, 4.107—4.110
notes to, 4.125—4.139
parent company, 4.122—4.124
pro forma financial statements, 4.147—4.150
small companies, 4.141
sub-headings, 4.10—4.19
summary financial statements, 4.140
true and fair override , 4.133
Financial statements in foreign currencies
generally, 7.172—7.176
Financial statements, preparation of
Companies Act principles, and, 2.22—2.22.8
Financing
cash flow statements, and, 30.108—30.111
Fixed asset using option, purchase of
hedging, and, 6.131—6.132
Fixed assets
and see **Impairment of fixed assets**
and see **Intangible fixed assets**
and see **Tangible fixed assets**
categories, 16.10—16.11
consolidation rules, and, 24.138
definition, 16.9
excluded items, 16.12—16.13
generally, 16.3—16.8
segmental reporting, and, 10.148
Fixed asset investments
alternative accounting rules, 6.69—6.75
historical cost accounting rules, 6.66—6.68
Fixed asset movements
impairment, and, 18.270—18.271
Flotations
employee share schemes, and, 12.54—12.54.3
Foreign currency (cash flow statements)
group companies
introduction, 30.150
intra-group transactions, 30.158—30.161
net investment method, 30.153—30.157
temporal method, 30.151—30.152
hedging transactions, 30.162—30.164
individual companies
borrowings for hedging equity investments, 30.149
generally, 30.141—30.142
introduction, 30.139—30.140
settled transactions, 30.143—30.144
unsettled transactions, 30.145—30.148
introduction, 30.139—30.140
Foreign currency commitment
foreign currency hedging, and, 7.132
Foreign currency options
foreign currency hedging, and, 7.139—7.142
Foreign currency translation (SSAP 20)
average rate determination
consolidated financial statements, 7.53—7.55
individual company financial statements, 7.16—7.18
change between methods, 7.59—7.61
closing rate/net investment method, 7.35—7.41
closing rate/net investment method, 7.35—7.41
consolidated financial statements, and
average rate determination, 7.53—7.55
change between methods, 7.59—7.61
closing rate/net investment method, 7.35—7.41
deferred trading balances, 7.70—7.75
dual rates, 7.56
goodwill, 7.76—7.78

Foreign currency translation (SSAP 20)—*cont.*
intercompany dividends, 7.62—7.66
intra-group companies transactions, 7.67
intra-group long-term loans, 7.70—7.75
introduction, 7.33—7.34
local currency, 7.57—7.58
other matters, 7.52
summary, 7.11.8—7.11.15
suspension of rates, 7.56
temporal method, 7.42—7.51
unrealised profit on stocks, 7.68—7.69
date of transaction, 7.15
deferred trading balances, 7.70—7.75
disclosures
requirements of Companies Act, 7.143
requirements of standard, 7.144—7.148.2
distributable profits, and, 7.149—7.160
dual rates
consolidated financial statements, 7.56
individual company financial statements, 7.19—7.20
euro, and
associated costs, 7.180—7.183
cumulative differences, 7.184—7.185
introduction, 7.178—7.179
exchange gains and losses, 7.25—7.31
executive summary
consolidated financial statements, 7.11.8—7.11.15
equity investments financed by foreign borrowing, 7.11.16—7.11.20
individual company financial statements, 7.11.1—7.11.7
introduction, 7.11
financial statements in foreign currencies, 7.172—7.176
foreign currency commitment, 7.132
foreign currency options, 7.139—7.142
foreign equity investments financed by foreign borrowings
consolidated financial statements, 7.105—7.112
individual company financial statements, 7.79—7.104
summary, 7.11.16—7.11.20
forward exchange contracts
existing assets or liabilities, 7.131
generally, 7.125—7.128
taken out at transaction date, 7.129—7.130
FRS 23, and
disclosure, A7.117—A7.122.2
first time adoption of IFRS, A7.130—A7.132
foreign currency transactions, A7.48—A7.114
functional currency approach, A7.27—A7.47
introduction, A7.1—A7.7
objectives, A7.23
other matters, A7.126—A7.127
overview, 7.188—7.189
presentation, A7.115—A7.116
scope, A7.24—A7.26
future results of foreign investments, 7.135—7.137
goodwill, 7.76—7.78
hedging transactions
foreign currency commitment, 7.132
foreign currency options, 7.139—7.142
forward exchange contracts, 7.125—7.131
future results of foreign investments, 7.135—7.137
introduction, 7.120—7.124
net investment, 7.133—7.134
speculative forward contracts, 7.138
hyper-inflationary economies, 7.161—7.169
IAS 21 (foreign exchange rates), and
disclosure, A7.117—A7.122.2

Foreign currency translation (SSAP 20)—*cont.*
first time adoption of IFRS, A7.130—A7.132
foreign currency transactions, A7.48—A7.114
functional currency approach, A7.27—A7.47
introduction, A7.1—A7.7
objectives, A7.23
other matters, A7.126—A7.127
overview, 7.188—7.189
presentation, A7.115—A7.116
scope, A7.24—A7.26
IAS 29 (hyperinflationary economies), and
generally, A7.109—A7.114
overview, 7.188—7.189
individual company financial statements, and
average rate determination, 7.16—7.18
date of transaction, 7.15
dual rates, 7.19—7.20
exchange gains and losses, 7.25—7.31
general rules, 7.14
intra-group companies transactions, 7.32
monetary items, 7.23—7.24
non-monetary items, 7.21—7.22
settled transactions, 7.26
summary, 7.11.1—7.11.7
suspension of rates, 7.19—7.20
unsettled transactions, 7.27—7.31
intercompany dividends, 7.62—7.66
intra-group companies transactions
consolidated financial statements, 7.67
individual company financial statements, 7.32
intra-group long-term loans, 7.70—7.75
introduction, 7.1—7.10.1
local currency, 7.57—7.58
monetary items, 7.23—7.24
multi-currency share capital, 7.170—7.171
net investment in foreign operation, 7.133—7.134
non-monetary items, 7.21—7.22
objectives, 7.12
procedures, 7.13
reserves, and, 23.124.3
scope of standard, 7.11
settled transactions, 7.26
speculative forward contracts, 7.138
suspension of rates
consolidated financial statements, 7.56
individual company financial statements, 7.19—7.20
temporal method, 7.42—7.51
UITF abstract
19, 7.113—7.119
21, 7.178—7.185
unrealised profit on stocks, 7.68—7.69
unsettled transactions, 7.27—7.31

Foreign currency translation reserve
reserves, and, 23.124.3

Foreign equity investments financed by foreign borrowings
consolidated financial statements
generally, 7.105—7.110
goodwill, 7.111—7.112
individual company financial statements
borrowing restriction, 7.87—7.88
borrowing taken out before or after investment, 7.93—7.94
carrying value of foreign equity investment, 7.95—7.98
consistent accounting treatment, 7.89
intermediate holding companies, 7.103—7.104
introduction, 7.79—7.82
offset restriction, 7.83—7.86
partial hedges, 7.99—7.102
termination of hedging during year, 7.91—7.92

Foreign equity investments financed by foreign borrowings—*cont*.
upstream loans, 7.90
summary, 7.11.16—7.11.20
Foreign exchange differences
deferred tax, and, 13.216
Forward exchange contracts
existing assets or liabilities, 7.131
generally, 7.125—7.128
taken out at transaction date, 7.129—7.130
Forward purchase of stock
hedging, and, 6.130—6.131
Franchise fees
revenue recognition, and, 9.259—9.262
FRC Ltd
financial reporting structure, and, 2.51—2.53.7
Free product
revenue recognition, and, 9.239
Free shares
accounting implications, 12.94—12.95
introduction, 12.88
Frequency of valuations
retirement benefits, and, 11.74—11.77
FRS 1 (cash flow statements)
acquisitions
consolidated statements, and, 30.132—30.138
generally, 30.98—30.99
introduction, 25.125—25.127
associates
consolidated statements, and, 30.128—30.129
generally, 27.99
balance sheet cash, 30.179
borrowings, 30.50
capital expenditure, 30.92—30.96
cash subject to restriction, 30.190—30.191
classification of cash flow
acquisitions, 30.98—30.99
additional, 30.64—30.65
capital expenditure, 30.92—30.96
disposals, 30.98—30.99
dividends from joint ventures and associates, 30.75.1
equity dividends paid, 30.101
financial investment, 30.92—30.96
financing, 30.108—30.111
generally, 30.55—30.58
liquid resource management, 30.102—30.106
operating activities, from, 30.67—30.75
returns on investments, 30.76—30.85
servicing of finance, 30.76—30.85
taxation, 30.86—30.91
comparative figures, 30.176—30.177
consolidated statements
acquisition of subsidiaries, 30.132—30.138
associates investments, 30.128—30.129
disposal of subsidiaries, 30.132—30.138
introduction, 30.125
joint arrangement investments, 30.130
joint venture investments, 30.128—30.129
minority interests, 30.126—30.127
definitions
'cash', 30.41—30.42
'liquid resources', 30.44—30.49
'repayable on demand', 30.43
discounts and premiums, 30.180—30.181
disposals
consolidated statements, and, 30.132—30.138
generally, 30.98—30.99
dividends from joint ventures and associates, 30.7.1
equity dividends paid, 30.101
exceptional cash flows, 30.112—30.118

FRS 1 (cash flow statements)—*cont*.
executive summary, 30.1—30.1.12
exempt entities
introduction, 30.23
medium-sized companies, 30.35—30.37
mutual life assurance companies, 30.26
open-ended investment funds, 30.28—30.29
other entities, 30.39
pension schemes, 30.27
small companies, 30.31—30.34
small unincorporated entities, 30.38
subsidiary undertakings, 30.24—30.25
extraordinary cash flows, 30.112—30.118
financing, 30.108—30.111
foreign currency
group companies, 30.150—30.161
hedging transactions, 30.162—30.164
individual companies, 30.141—30.149
introduction, 30.139—30.140
foreign currency (group companies)
introduction, 30.150
intra-group transactions, 30.158—30.161
net investment method, 30.153—30.157
temporal method, 30.151—30.152
foreign currency (individual companies)
borrowings for hedging equity investments, 30.149
generally, 30.141—30.142
introduction, 30.139—30.140
settled transactions, 30.143—30.144
unsettled transactions, 30.145—30.148
format
classification of cash flows, 30.55—30.65
departure from standard, 30.66
gross cash flows, 30.59—30.63
introduction, 30.51—30.54
net cash flows, 30.59—30.63
gross cash flows, 30.59—30.63
hedging transactions, 30.162—30.164
intra-group transactions, 30.158—30.161
introduction, 30.2
joint arrangements, 30.130
joint ventures
consolidated statements, and, 30.128—30.129
generally, 27.99
linked presentation, and, 3.251
liquid resources
definition, 30.44—30.49
management, 30.102—30.106
medium-sized companies, 30.35—30.37
minority interests, 30.126—30.127
mutual life assurance companies, 30.26
net cash flows, 30.59—30.63
net debt reconciliation
analysis of changes, 30.123—30.124
generally, 30.119—30.122.1
notes
comparative figures, 30.176—30.177
specific disclosures, 30.165
supplementary disclosures, 30.166—30.175
objectives of standard, 30.5—30.21
open-ended investment funds, 30.28—30.29
operating activities, 30.67—30.75
pension schemes, 30.27
practical application of standard
balance sheet cash, 30.179
cash subject to restriction, 30.190—30.191
discounts and premiums, 30.180—30.181
gains and losses, 30.182—30.185
introduction, 30.178
refinancing of borrowings, 30.188—30.189
reorganisation costs, 30.186—30.87

FRS 1 (cash flow statements)—*cont.*
premiums, 30.180—30.181
preparation
borrowings, 30.50
definition of 'cash', 30.41—30.42
definition of 'liquid resources', 30.44—30.49
introduction, 30.40
meaning of 'repayable on demand', 30.43
reconciliation with balance sheet figures
net debt, 30.119—30.124
refinancing of borrowings, 30.188—30.189
reorganisation costs, 30.186—30.87
repayable on demand, 30.43
returns on investments, 30.76—30.85
scope of standard
exempt entities, 30.23—30.39
generally, 30.22
segmental reporting, and, 10.117—10.120
servicing of finance, 30.76—30.85
small companies, 30.31—30.34
small unincorporated entities, 30.38
subsidiary undertakings, 30.24—30.25
taxation, 30.86—30.91
worked example, 30.192
FRS 2 (subsidiary undertakings)
see also **Consolidation rules**
balance sheet, and
amounts due to and from group undertakings, 4.103—4.106
generally, 4.97—4.99
interests in group undertakings, 4.103—4.106
particular items, rules for, 4.100—4.102
deferred tax, and
effects of adjustment, 13.206—13.208
fair value adjustments, 13.209—13.213
foreign exchange differences, 13.216
general principles, 13.203—13.205
goodwill, 13.213.1—13.213.3
unremitted earnings, 13.214—13.215
exemptions to requirement to prepare
accounting treatment, 24.71
all subsidiaries excluded, 24.70
disclosure, 24.72—24.74
intermediate parent exemption, 24.56.1—24.66
introduction, 24.56
suggested wording, 24.75
foreign currency translation, and
average rate determination, 7.53—7.55
change between methods, 7.59—7.61
closing rate/net investment method, 7.35—7.41
deferred trading balances, 7.70—7.75
dual rates, 7.56
goodwill, 7.76—7.78
intercompany dividends, 7.62—7.66
intra-group companies transactions, 7.67
intra-group long-term loans, 7.70—7.75
introduction, 7.33—7.34
local currency, 7.57—7.58
other matters, 7.52
summary, 7.11.8—7.11.15
suspension of rates, 7.56
temporal method, 7.42—7.51
unrealised profit on stocks, 7.68—7.69
foreign equity investments financed by foreign borrowings, and, 7.105—7.112
form, 24.41—24.50
intermediate parent exemption
application in practice, 24.66
certified translations, 24.64—24.65
conditions, 24.62
EEA companies, 24.57—24.62.1

FRS 2 (subsidiary undertakings)—*cont.*
generally, 24.56.1—24.56.2
non-EEA group, 24.62.1.1—24.62.10
relevant date, 24.63
medium-sized companies, by
exemptions, 32.148—32.153
introduction, 24.35—24.36
shorter-form, 32.155—32.159
merger accounting, and, 28.112—28.122
minority interests, and
acquisition of direct subsidiary, 24.377
acquisition of indirect subsidiary, 24.378
auction market preferred shares, 24.366—24.367
balance sheets, 24.357—24.359
basis of recognition, 24.353—24.354
compulsory acquisition, 24.379
definition, 24.346—24.350
director's interests, 24.369—24.370
equity, 24.356
fair value, and, 24.381—24.382
indirect holdings, 24.375—24.376
introduction, 24.344—24.345
loss making subsidiaries, 24.383—24.388
measurement, 24.355, 24.371—34.374
minority or majority interests, 24.351—24.352
presentation in financial statements, 24.357—24.365
profit and loss account, 24.360—24.365
stapled shares, 24.368
treatment on acquisition, 24.377—24.382
parent companies, by, 24.33—24.34
profit and loss account, and
effect of FRS3, 4.120—4.121
generally, 4.111
particular items, rules for, 4.112—4.119
purpose, 24.27
requirement to prepare
exemptions, 24.56—24.75
generally, 24.32
medium-sized companies, 24.35—24.36
other parent undertakings, 24.37—24.39
parent companies, 24.33—24.34
small companies, 24.35—24.36
small companies, by
exemptions, 32.148—32.153
introduction, 24.35—24.36
shorter-form, 32.155—32.159
true and fair view, 24.51—24.55
FRS 3 (reporting financial performance)
acquisitions
introduction, 8.70—8.76
mergers, 8.77—8.78
allocation of interest and taxation, 8.20—8.21
changes in accounting policies
disclosures, 8.195—8.202
generally, 8.190—8.194
IFRS, and, 8.208
changes to estimation techniques
generally, 8.205
IFRS, and, 8.208
comparison with IAS, and, 8.209
disclosures, 8.208
discontinued operations
definition, 8.24—8.26
goodwill on disposals, 8.54—8.57
IFRS, and, 8.208
materiality, 8.28
meaning of 'ceased permanently', 8.27
operations discontinued by closure, 8.58—8.69
operations discontinued by sale, 8.37—8.57
profits and losses on sales, 8.39—8.53

FRS 3 (reporting financial performance)—*cont.*
retention of interest in disposed of subsidiary, 8.34—8.36
separability of activities, 8.29—8.33
disposal groups to be abandoned, 8.208
exceptional items
definition, 8.79—8.83
fundamental reorganisation or restructuring, 8.94—8.99
introduction, 8.22—8.23
non-operating exceptional items, 8.84—8.87
other, 8.121—8.136
profits or losses on disposals of fixed assets, 8.103—8.112
profits and losses on sale or termination, 8.90—8.93
summary, 8.1.4—8.1.6
tax attributable, 8.137—8.143
executive summary
exceptional items, 8.1.4—8.1.6
introduction, 8.1
other items, 8.1.7—8.1.9
other statements, 8.1.10—8.1.12
prior period adjustments, 8.1.13
profit and loss account, 8.1.1—8.1.3
extraordinary items, 8.144
IAS, and, 8.209
fundamental errors
generally, 8.203—8.204
IFRS, and, 8.208
fundamental reorganisation or restructuring, 8.94—8.99
goodwill
disposals, 8.54—8.57
statement of total recognised gains and losses, 8.155—8.159
IFRS, and
changes in accounting policies, 8.208
changes to estimation techniques, 8.208
convergence, 8.208
disclosures, 8.208
discontinued operations, 8.208
disposal groups to be abandoned, 8.208
fundamental errors, 8.208
introduction, 8.206—8.209
non-current assets to be abandoned, 8.208
presentation of non-current assets, 8.208
related pronouncements, 8.208
scope, 8.208
subsidiaries acquired exclusively with view to resale, 8.208
impairments, 8.114—8.117
introduction, 8.1—8.8
mergers, 8.77—8.78
movements in reserves, 8.160—8.164
non-current assets to be abandoned, 8.208
non-operating exceptional items, 8.84—8.87
note of historical cost profits and losses, 8.169—8.182
operating profit, 8.13—8.19.1
operations discontinued by closure
generally, 8.58—8.59
provisions for losses, 8.60—8.69
operations discontinued by sale
generally, 8.37—8.38
goodwill, 8.54—8.57
profits and losses, 8.39—8.53
presentation of non-current assets, 8.208
prior period adjustments
changes in accounting policies, 8.190—8.202
changes to estimation techniques, 8.205
fundamental errors, 8.203—8.204
introduction, 8.188—8.189

FRS 3 (reporting financial performance)—*cont.*
summary, 8.1.13
profit and loss accounts
allocation of interest and taxation, 8.20—8.21
exceptional items, 8.22—8.23
introduction, 8.9
layered format, 8.10—8.12
operating profit, 8.13—8.19.1
summary, 8.1.1—8.1.3
profits and losses on disposals of fixed assets
generally, 8.103—8.112
impairments, 8.114—8.117
profits and losses on sales
exceptional items, 8.90—8.93
generally, 8.39—8.40
provisions for losses, 8.41—8.53
purchased goodwill, 8.155—8.159
reconciliation of movements in shareholders' funds, 8.183—8.187
retention of interest in disposed of subsidiary, 8.34—8.36
statement of total recognised gains and losses
generally, 8.145—8.154.1
movements in reserves, 8.160—8.164
purchased goodwill, 8.155—8.159
subsidiaries acquired exclusively with view to resale, 8.208
tax attributable to exceptional items, 8.137—8.143
FRS 4 (capital instruments)
application under UK GAAP, 6.33—6.34
background, 6.288—6.290
Companies Act requirements, 6.375—6.381
contingent payments, 6.352—6.355
definition of capital instrument, 6.296—6.298
disclosure, 6.372—6.374
dividends, 6.306
facility fees, 6.323—6.325
finance costs
dividends, 6.306
elements, 6.305
interest, 6.306
introduction, 6.299—6.300
issue and redemption premiums, 6.307
issue costs, 6.308—6.322
initial recognition, 6.345
interest, 6.306
issue and redemption premiums, 6.307
issue costs, 6.308—6.322
measurement
contingent payments, 6.352—6.355
initial recognition, 6.345
renegotiation of debt, 6.362—6.371
repurchase of debt, 6.356—6.361
subsequent recognition, 6.351
treatment of finance costs, 6.346—6.350
objectives, 6.291—6.292
options, 6.329—6.340
renegotiation of debt, 6.362—6.371
repurchase of debt, 6.356—6.361
scope, 6.293—6.295
small companies, and, 32.80—32.82
subsequent recognition, 6.351
term
definition of term, 6.238
extended, 6.340—6.341
generally, 6.326—6.327
indeterminate, 6.344
options, 6.329—6.339
shortened, 6.342—6.343
treatment of finance costs, 6.346—6.350

FRS 5 (reporting the substance of transactions)
application notes
consignment stock, 3.122
debt factoring, 3.136—3.136.16
introduction, 3.120—3.121
loan transfers, 3.168—3.179
PFI and PPP, 3.179.1—3.179.56
revenue recognition, 9.3—9.7
sale and repurchase agreements, 3.123—3.135
securitised assets, 3.137—3.167
summary, 3.1.20—3.1.21
background, 3.2—3.5
bed and breakfasting, 3.243—3.249
bills of exchange, 3.197
cash flow statement, 3.251
comparison with IFRS, and, 3.257—3.261
consignment stock, 3.122
contract purchase arrangements, 3.228—3.231
debt factoring
benefits and risks, 3.136.5—3.136.9
derecognition, 3.136.10
examples of required analysis, 3.136.15—3.136.16
introduction, 3.136—3.136.4
linked presentation, 3.136.11—3.136.12
separate presentation, 3.136.13—3.136.14
derecognition, 3.258
disclosure, 3.1.19
executive summary
application notes, 3.1.20—3.1.21
disclosure, 3.1.19
introduction, 3.1
linked presentation, 3.1.8—3.1.13
offset, 3.1.18
principles, 3.1.1—3.1.7
quasi-subsidiaries, 3.1.14—3.1.17
scope, 3.1.21.1
identification of assets and liabilities
analysing complex transactions, 3.52—3.58
assets, 3.59—3.62
introduction, 3.51
liabilities, 3.63—3.64
IFRS, and
derecognition, 3.258
quasi-subsidiaries, 3.259
'substance over form', 3.257
insubstance debt defeasance, 3.184—3.185
interaction with Companies Act and accounting standards, 3.42.1—3.46
linked presentation
cash flow statement, 3.251
detailed conditions, 3.88—3.90
general rules, 3.83—3.87
linking part of finance, 3.91—3.92
profit recognition, 3.93—3.96
summary, 3.1.8—3.1.13
loan transfers
disclosure requirements, 3.178—3.179
generally, 3.168—3.177
objective, 3.47—3.50
offsetting
generally, 3.97—3.99
summary, 3.1.18
partial derecognition
generally, 3.181—3.182
IFRS, and, 3.258
PFI and PPP
accounting treatment, 3.179.50—3.179.55.23
application of FRS 5, 3.179.17—3.179.24
contract separability, 3.179.8—3.179.16
example of quantitative analysis, 3.179.56
introduction, 3.179.1—3.177.7

FRS 5 (reporting the substance of transactions)—*cont.*
property factors, 3.179.25—3.179.48
summary of risks, 3.179.49
practical issues
purchase commitments, 3.250
repurchase agreements, 3.219—3.224
stock lending, 3.232—3.242.1
take-or-pay contracts, 3.252—3.256.1
trade loans, 3.183
principles
identifying and recognising assets and liabilities, 3.51—3.65
introduction, 3.47—3.50
linked presentation, 3.83—3.96
offset rules, 3.97—3.99
quasi-subsidiaries, 3.100—3.119
summary, 3.1.1—3.1.7
transactions in previously recognised assets, 3.66—3.822
purchase commitments, 3.250
quasi-subsidiaries, accounting for
accounting treatment, 3.108—3.112
credit enhancement, 3.115—3.116
disclosure, 3.119
IFRS, and, 3.259
introduction, 3.100—3.106
linked presentation, 3.113—3.114
parent's financial statements, and, 3.118
securitisation, 3.117
subordinated debt, 3.115—3.116
summary, 3.1.14—3.1.17
true and fair overriding disclosures, and, 3.107
recognition of assets and liabilities
generally, 3.65
introduction, 3.51
repurchase agreements, 3.219—3.224
revenue recognition
and see **Revenue recognition**
generally, 9.3—9.7
sale and repurchase agreements
accounting treatment, 3.130—3.132
examples of required analysis, 3.133—3.135
introduction, 3.123
sources of benefits and risks, 3.124—3.129
scope of standard
generally, 3.37—3.42
summary, 3.1.21.1
securitisation of assets
example of required analysis, 3.167
group's financial statements, 3.151—3.155
interest rate swaps, 3.156—3.158
introduction, 3.137—3.143
multi-originator programmes, 3.166
originator's financial statements, 3.144—3.150
revolving assets, 3.159—3.165
stock lending, 3.232—3.242.1
'substance over form', 3.257
take-or-pay contracts, 3.252—3.256.1
trade loans, 3.183
transactions in previously recognised assets
continued recognition, 3.71—3.72
full derecognition, 3.73
generally, 3.66—3.70
insurance, 3.82
partial derecognition, 3.74—3.81
FRS 6 (acquisitions and mergers)
accounting periods, 28.106—28.108
acquisition accounting, and
and see **Acquisition accounting**
comparison, 28.109—28.111
generally, 25.1

FRS 6 (acquisitions and mergers)—*cont.*
conditions
full participation in future performance test, 28.62—28.64
immaterial cash test, 28.24—28.36
introduction, 28.9—28.13
joint participation in management test, 28.54—28.58
90% per cent holding test, 28.21—28.23
no identifiable acquirer test, 28.46—28.53
non-equity consideration test, 28.24—28.36
offer to shareholders test, 28.14—28.18
relative size test, 28.59—28.61
vendor placings, 28.37—28.45
consolidated financial statements, 28.112—28.122
criteria, 28.1—28.1.4
disclosure requirements
generally, 28.112—28.122
summary, 27.1.9—27.1.10
executive summary
criteria, 28.1—28.1.4
disclosure, 27.1.9—27.1.10
group reconstructions, 28.1.5—28.1.6
principles, 28.1.7—28.1.8
expenses, 28.98—28.105
full participation in future performance test, 28.62—28.64
group reconstructions
generally, 28.74—28.80
summary, 28.1.5—28.1.6
immaterial cash test
disposal of peripheral part of business, 28.33—28.36
generally, 28.24—28.32
IFRS, and, 28.123—28.124
introduction, 28.2—28.6
joint participation in management test, 28.54—28.58
90% per cent holding test, 28.21—28.23
no identifiable acquirer test, 28.46—28.53
non-equity consideration test
disposal of peripheral part of business, 28.33—28.36
generally, 28.24—28.32
offer to shareholders test, 28.14—28.18
principles
difference on consolidation, 28.92—28.97
group reconstructions, 28.74—28.80
introduction, 28.65—28.70
investment in acquired company, 28.83—28.86
other forms of business combinations, 28.81—28.82
summary, 28.1.7—28.1.8
use of new parent company, 28.71—28.73
relative size test, 28.59—28.61
vendor placings, 28.37—28.45
FRS 7 (fair values in acquisition accounting)
adjusted capital, 25.39
adjustments to fair values, 25.42
associates, and
effective date, 27.162—27.164
generally, 27.165—27.169
business combinations, 25.2—25.3.1
cash flow statements, and
consolidated statements, and, 30.132—30.138
generally, 30.98—30.99
introduction, 25.125—25.127
comparison with IFRS, and, 25.3—25.7
comparison with merger accounting
generally, 28.109—28.111
introduction, 25.3—25.7
consolidation of new subsidiary
adjusted capital, 25.39

FRS 7 (fair values in acquisition accounting)—*cont.*
adjustments to fair values, 25.42
cost of acquisition, 25.31—25.34
date for recognising trading, 25.39—25.48
fees and expenses of acquisition, 25.35—25.38
goodwill, 25.43
identifiable assets and liabilities, 25.40—25.41
introduction, 25.29—25.30
reserves acquired, 25.39
cost of acquisition
generally, 25.31—25.34
summary, 25.1.12—25.1.15
date of changes in group membership
background, 25.18
definition, 25.19—25.27
effective date post balance sheet, 25.28
disclosure requirements
cash flow statement, 25.125—25.127
fair values of identifiable assets and liabilities, 25.96
general, 25.91—25.93
introduction, 25.88—25.90
post-acquisition activities, 25.114—25.124
pre-acquisition activities, 25.103—25.113
purchase consideration, 25.94—25.95
summary, 25.1.23—25.1.26
table of acquired assets and liabilities, 25.97—25.102
executive summary
cost of acquisition, 25.1.12—25.1.15
disclosures, 25.1.23—25.1.26
fair values of assets and liabilities, 25.1.3—25.1.9
goodwill, 25.1.16—25.1.20
method of accounting, 25.1.1—25.1.2
negative goodwill, 25.1.21—25.1.22
provisional fair values, 25.1.10—25.1.11
scope of standard, 25.1
fair values of assets and liabilities
generally, 25.96
summary, 25.1.3—25.1.9
fair values of net assets
background, 25.96
contingent consideration, 25.410—25.425
deferred consideration, 25.404—25.409
deferred taxation, 25.381—25.382
fees and expenses of acquisition, 25.426—25.4
identifying assets and liabilities, 25.158—25.177
intangible assets, 25.178—25.231
introduction, 25.144—25.148
measuring fair values of assets and liabilities, 25.232—25.380
non-monetary consideration, 25.397—25.399
objective, 25.154—25.156
other consideration, 25.400—25.403
other securities, 25.396
overriding principles, 25.157
purchase consideration, 25.383—25.425
purchase of business or assets, 25.151—25.153
quoted securities, 25.390—25.393
scope, 25.149—25.150
summary, 25.1.3—25.1.9
unquoted securities, 25.394—25.395
fees and expenses of acquisition, 25.35—25.38
goodwill
accounting policy, 25.585—25.586
additions in existing subsidiaries, 25.600
allocation of purchased goodwill, 25.517
amortising goodwill, 25.494—25.499
capital redemption reserve, 25.569
capitalisation, and, 25.439—25.444
contingent consideration, 25.500—25.504
cumulative amounts written off, 25.587—25.591

FRS 7 (fair values in acquisition accounting)—*cont.*
disclosures, 25.584
disposals, 25.518—25.520, 25.581—25.582
earnout consideration, 25.601
effect on distributable profits, 25.573—25.580
impairment, 25.583—25.5
impairment reviews, 25.521—25.523, 25.532—25.552
implementing FRS 10, 25.598—25.599
indefinite life, 25.477—25.481
integrated acquisitions, 25.528—25.531
internally generated goodwill, 25.450
introduction, 25.437—25.438
merger reserve, 25.560—25..561
multiple useful economic lives, 25.482—25.493
non-distributable reserves, 25.563
positive and negative goodwill, 25.524—25.527
pre-FRS 10 goodwill remaining in reserves, 25.553
pre-FRS 10 negative goodwill remaining in reserves, 25.592—25.597
presentation of amortisation and impairment charges, 25.505—25.508
profit and loss account, 25.559
prohibition of separate write-off reserve, 25.554—25.555
purchased goodwill, 25.448—25.476
reserves used for write-offs, 25.557—25.558
revaluation reserve, 25.570—25.572
reversal of write-offs, 25.509—25.516
scope of FRS 10, 25.445—25.447
share premium account, 25.564—25.568
summary, 25.1.16—25.1.20
true and fair override, 25.477—25.481
useful economic life, 25.458—25.476
group reconstruction relief, 25.14
increases in stake
accounting principles, 25.68—25.73
agreement with shareholder, 25.86—25.87
associate becomes subsidiary, 25.81—25.83
introduction, 25.64—25.67
investment becomes subsidiary, 25.75—25.80
parent acquires part of minority, 25.84—25.85
practical examples, 25.74—25.86
intangible fixed assets, and
generally, 15.41—15.45
IFRS, and, 15.134
introduction
business combinations, 25.2—25.2.3.1
comparison with merger accounting, 25.4—25.9
generally, 25.8—25.10
joint ventures, and
effective date, 27.162—27.164
generally, 27.165—27.169
merger accounting, and
generally, 28.109—28.111
introduction, 25.3—25.7
merger relief, 25.13
method of accounting, 25.1.1—25.1.2
negative goodwill, 25.1.21—25.1.22
parent company's financial statements
carrying value of investment, 25.41.6—25.41.43
pre-acquisition reserves, 25.62—25.63
post-acquisition activities
exceptional items, 25.118—25.120
layered formats, 25.114—25.117
provisions, 25.123—25.124
reorganisation and integration, 25.121—25.122
pre-acquisition activities
material acquisitions, of, 25.103—25.105
substantial acquisitions, of, 25.106—25.113
provisional fair values, 25.1.10—25.1.11

FRS 7 (fair values in acquisition accounting)—*cont.*
purchase consideration, 25.94—25.95
reporting financial performance, and
introduction, 8.70—8.76
mergers, 8.77—8.78
reserves acquired, 25.39
retirement benefits, and, 11.135—11.138
reverse acquisitions
cash alternatives, 25.143
generally, 25.128—25.142
scope of standard, 25.1
segmental reporting, and, 10.127—10.135
summary rules, 25.15—25.17
FRS 8 (related parties)
and see **Related party transactions**
associates, 29.38—29.39
background, 29.2—29.8
close family, 29.62—29.64
common control, 29.24
common influence
establishing, 29.27—29.29
introduction, 29.26
concert parties, 29.55—29.57
connected persons
close family, 29.62—29.64
companies, 29.65—29.
introduction, 29.60—29.61
partnerships, 29.65—29.67
trusts, 29.65—29.67
control
examples, 29.30
introduction, 29.19—29.23
criteria for related party relationships
common control, 29.24
control, 29.19—29.23
influence, 29.25—29.29
introduction, 29.15—29.18
deemed related, parties who are
associates, 29.38—29.39
directors, 29.42—29.43
introduction, 29.35
investors, 29.40—29.41
joint ventures, 29.38—29.39
parent companies, 29.36—29.37
pension funds, 29.44—29.48
subsidiary undertakings, 29.36—29.37
venture capitalists, 29.40—29.41
directors, 29.42—29.43
executive summary
disclosure requirements, 29.1.7—29.1.9
exemptions from disclosure, 29.1.6
generally, 29.1.1—29.1.3
introduction, 29.1
influence
establishing, 29.27—29.29
examples, 29.30
introduction, 29.25
IFRS, and
convergence, 29.195
disclosure, 29.195
exemptions, 29.195
first time adoption of IFRS, 29.195
introduction, 29.195
overview, 29.195
related parties, 29.195
related party transactions, 29.195
related pronouncements, 29.195
scope, 29.195
investment manager, 29.47—29.48
investors, 29.40—29.41
joint ventures, 29.38—29.39

FRS 8 (related parties)—*cont.*
key management, 29.52—29.54
management contracts, 29.58—29.59
objectives of standard, 29.12—29.13
parent companies, 29.36—29.37
partnerships, 29.65—29.67
pension funds
generally, 29.44—29.46
investment manager, 29.47—29.48
presumed related, parties who are
connected persons, 29.60—29.67
introduction, 29.49—29.51
key management, 29.52—29.54
management contracts, 29.58—29.59
persons acting in concert, 29.55—29.57
related parties, 29.195
related party transactions, 29.195
reporting entity
generally, 29.14
group as, 29.30.1—29.31
specified related parties
identification, 29.68
IFRS, and, 29.195
introduction, 29.33—29.34
parties deemed related, 29.35—29.48
parties presumed related, 29.49—29.50
subsidiary undertakings, 29.36—29.37
trusts, 29.65—29.67
venture capitalists, 29.40—29.41
FRS 8 (related party transactions)
and see above
agency arrangements, 29.72—29.75
aggregation of transactions
directors, with, 29.123—29.125
generally, 29.118—29.122
associates, with, 29.135
background, 29.2—29.8
close family, with, 29.142—29.143
common control, between companies under, 29.130
Companies Act, under
introduction, 29.174—29.175
loans to directors, 29.176
material interest transactions, 29.179—29.180
comparatives, 29.126
confidentiality, duty of, 29.162
consolidation balances, 29.146—29.147
definition, 29.69
directors, with
Companies Act, under, 29.174—29.180
dividends, 29.141
guarantees, 29.140
introduction, 29.138
share interests, 29.181
share transactions, 29.139
directors under Companies Act, with
introduction, 29.174—29.175
loans, 29.176
material interest transactions, 29.179—29.180
disclosure of control
introduction, 29.93—29.97.1
limited partnerships, 29.110
source of control, 29.100—29.101
trusts, 29.102—29.108
ultimate controlling party, 29.98—29.99
unit trusts, 29.109
disclosure of balances, 29.116—29.117
disclosure of transactions, 29.111—29.115.1
disclosure requirements
additional relaxations, 29.166—29.170
aggregation of transactions, 29.118—29.125
balances, 29.116—29.117

FRS 8 (related party transactions)—*cont.*
comparatives, 29.126
control, 29.93—29.110
exemptions, 29.145—29.165
interaction with Companies Act, 29.127—29.129
IFRS, and, 29.195
introduction, 29.92
transactions and balances, 29.111—29.115.1
true and fair view, and, 29.171—29.173
dividends paid to directors, 29.141
executive summary
disclosure requirements, 29.1.7—29.1.9
exemptions from disclosure, 29.1.6
generally, 29.1.4—29.1.5
introduction, 29.1
exemptions from disclosure
consolidation balances, 29.146—29.147
duty of confidentiality, 29.162
emoluments for services, 29.159—29.161
introduction, 29.145
intra-group transactions, 29.146—29.147
medium-sized companies, 29.163—29.165
90% subsidiaries, 29.149—29.157.1
parent company's financial statements, 29.148
pension contributions, 29.158
small companies, 29.163—29.165
guarantees by directors, 29.140
implications for directors
auditors' role, 29.91
generally, 29.87—29.90
IFRS, and
convergence, 29.195
disclosure, 29.195
exemptions, 29.195
first time adoption of IFRS, 29.195
introduction, 29.195
overview, 29.195
related parties, 29.195
related party transactions, 29.195
related pronouncements, 29.195
scope, 29.195
intra-group transactions, 29.146—29.147
joint ventures, with, 29.135
key management, with, 29.144
loans
directors, to, 29.176
officers, to, 29.177
material interest transactions, 29.179—29.180
materiality
Companies Act, and, 29.84—29.86
general purpose financial statements, 29.82—29.83
generally, 29.77—29.81
medium-sized companies, 29.163—29.165
90% subsidiaries, 29.149—29.157.1
pension contributions, 29.158
pension funds, with, 29.136
quasi-subsidiary undertakings, with, 29.133—29.134
related parties, 29.195
services, emoluments for, 29.159—29.161
share interests of directors, 29.181
share transactions by directors, 29.139
small companies, 29.163—29.165
specified transactions, 29.70—29.72
subsidiaries acquired and disposed of during year, with, 29.131—29.132
true and fair view, and, 29.171—29.173
FRS 9 (associates and joint venture entities)
abnormal transactions between year ends, 27.144
accounting principles
acquisitions, 27.162—27.169
associate as group, 27.153

FRS 9 (associates and joint venture entities)—*cont.*
consolidation adjustments, 27.138—27.150
disposals, 27.170—27.1 72
extent of share, 27.119—27.122.1
financial statements, 27.136—27.137
interests in losses, 27.154—27.158
introduction, 27.116—27.118
joint and several liability, 27.159—27.160
joint venture becomes associate, 27.173
minority interests, 27.161
partnerships, 27.151—27.152
subsidiary becomes associate, 27.174—27.175
accounting requirements, 27.1.6—27.1.7
acquisitions
effective date, 27.162—27.164
generally, 27.165—27.169
additional disclosure
15% threshold information, 27.107—27.113
generally, 27.100—27.106
25% threshold information, 27.107—27.113
balance sheet
example, 27.95—27.97
goodwill, 27.88—27.93
gross equity method, 27.94
introduction, 27.85—27.87
cash flow statements, and
consolidated statements, and, 30.128—30.129
generally, 27.99
classification, 27.1.2—27.1.5
consolidation adjustments
abnormal transactions between year ends, 27.144
consistent accounting policies, 27.140
elimination of intra-group trading, 27.145—27.147
fair values, 27.141—27.143
goodwill, 27.141—27.143
intra-group trading transactions, 27.149—27.150
introduction, 27.138—27.139
transfer of assets to joint venture, 27.148
contractual arrangements, 27.1.19
convertible debt, 27.133—27.134
convertible shares, 27.132
cross-holdings, 27.135
definition, 27.55—27.67
disclosures, 27.1.23—27.1.29
disposals
effective date, 27.162—27.164
generally, 27.170—27.172
equity accounting
additional disclosure, 27.100—27.113
balance sheet, 27.85—27.97
cash flow statement, 27.99
individual financial statements, 27.98
introduction, 27.68—27.71
optional disclosure, 27.114—27.115
principles, 27.116—27.175
profit and loss account, 27.72—27.82
segmental reporting, 27.83
statement of total recognised gains and losses, 27.84
summary, 27.1.15—27.1.18
executive summary
accounting requirements, 27.1.6—27.1.7
classification, 27.1.2—27.1.5
contractual arrangements not joint ventures, 27.1.19
disclosures, 27.1.23—27.1.29
equity accounting, 27.1.15—27.1.18
individual financial statements, 27.1.21—27.1.22
introduction, 27.1
joint arrangements not entities, 27.1.20
presentation, 27.1.8—27.1.14
scope of standard, 27.1.1

FRS 9 (associates and joint venture entities)—*cont.*
voluntary disclosures, 27.1.30
extent of share
convertible debt, 27.133—27.134
convertible shares, 27.132
cross-holdings, 27.135
introduction, 27.119—27.122.1
options, 27.123—27.131
fair values, 27.141—27.143
financial instruments, and, 6.116—6.121
financial statements, 27.136—27.137
goodwill
balance sheet, 27.88—27.93
principles, 27.141—27.143
gross equity method
generally, 27.94
introduction, 27.4—27.5
individual financial statements
generally, 27.98
summary, 27.1.21—27.1.22
interests in losses, 27.154—27.158
intra-group trading transactions, 27.149—27.150
introduction, 27.2—27.11
investment funds, 27.27—27.29.1
investments by single company, 27.176
joint and several liability, 27.159—27.160
joint arrangements not entities, 27.1.20
minority interests, 27.161
options, 27.123—27.131
participating interest, 27.2—27.3
presentation, 27.1.8—27.1.14
profit and loss account
example, 27.82
introduction, 27.72
notes, 27.80—27.81
operating results, 27.75—27.76
other line items, 27.78
satisfying requirements, 27.79
super-exceptional items, 27.77
turnover, 27.73—27.74
related parties, and, 29.38—29.39
related party transactions, and, 29.135
scope of standard
generally, 27.25—27.26
investment funds, 27.27—27.29.1
summary, 27.1.1
segmental reporting, and
generally, 10.100—10.106
introduction, 27.83
statement of total recognised gains and losses, 27.84
transfer of assets, 27.148
venture capital funds, 27.27—27.29.1
voluntary disclosures, 27.1.30
voting rights, 27.50—27.54

FRS 10 (intangible fixed assets)
acquisition accounting
generally, 15.41—15.45
IFRS, and, 15.139
amortisation
IFRS, and, 15.139
introduction, 15.66—15.69
methods, 15.84—15.85
residual values, 15.82—15.83
useful economic life, 15.71—15.81
capitalisation of earnings, 15.59—15.60
comparison with market transactions, 15.61—15.62
Companies Act requirements, 15.3—15.8
computer software, and, 15.135—15.138
control, 15.139
copyrights, and, 15.101—15.103
definition

FRS 10 (intangible fixed assets)—*cont.*
control, 15.23—15.25
generally, 15.12—15.15
IFRS, and, 15.139
separability, 15.16—15.22
disclosure requirements
generally, 15.96—15.98
IFRS, 15.139
other information, 15.100
summary, 15.1.19—15.1.20
executive summary
disclosures, 15.1.19—15.1.20
impairment reviews, 15.1.12—15.1.13
'intangible assets', 15.1.1—15.1.2
measurement, 15.1.7—15.1.11
recognition, 15.1.3—15.1.6
research and development costs, 15.1.14—15.1.18
identifiability, 15.139
IFRS, and
acquisition accounting, 15.139
amortisation, 15.139
control, 15.139
convergence, 15.139
definition, 15.139
disclosures, 15.139
identifiability, 15.139
impairment, 15.139
internally generated assets, 15.139
overview, 15.139
part of business acquisition, 15.139
purchased assets, 15.139
recognition criteria, 15.139
related pronouncements, 15.139
retirements, 15.139
scope, 15.139
separability, 15.139
separate acquisition, 15.139
subsequent expenditure on acquired project, 15.139
useful life, 15.139
impairment
IFRS, and, 15.139
introduction, 15.66—15.69
methods, 15.84—15.85
residual values, 15.82—15.83
reviews, 15.86—15.95
useful economic life, 15.71—15.81
impairment reviews
detailed procedure, 15.94—15.95
first year review, 15.88—15.90
introduction, 15.86—15.87
other year reviews, 15.91—15.92
summary, 15.1.12—15.1.13
'intangible assets', 15.1.1—15.1.2
internally generated assets
generally, 15.31—15.33
IFRS, and, 15.139
introduction, 15.2—15.2.1
know-how, and, 15.104—15.106
licences, and, 15.107—15.109
measurement, 15.1.7—15.1.11
part of business acquisition, 15.139
patents, and, 15.110—15.111
premium profits, 15.54—15.58
purchased assets
generally, 15.37—15.40
IFRS, and, 15.139
readily ascertainable market value, 15.27—15.30
recognition
criteria, 15.139
summary, 15.1.3—15.1.6
relief from royalties, 15.51—15.53

FRS 10 (intangible fixed assets)—*cont.*
research and development (SSAP 13), and
amortisation, 15.125
development costs, 15.120—15.123
diminution in value provisions, 15.131—15.133
disclosure, 15.126—15.130
effect on realised reserves, 15.134
generally, 15.113—15.119
introduction, 15.112
summary, 15.1.14—15.1.18
retirements, 15.139
revaluation of assets, 15.63—15.64
scope of standard
generally, 15.9—15.11
IFRS, and, 15.139
separability
generally, 15.16—15.22
IFRS, and, 15.139
separate acquisition, 15.139
software, and, 15.135—15.138
subsequent expenditure on acquired project, 15.139
trade marks, and, 15.110—15.111
useful economic life
generally, 15.71—15.81
IFRS, and, 15.139
impairment reviews, 15.88—15.92
valuation methods
capitalisation of earnings, 15.59—15.60
comparison with market transactions, 15.61—15.62
introduction, 15.48—15.50
premium profits, 15.54—15.58
relief from royalties, 15.51—15.53
FRS 11 (impairment of fixed assets)
allocation of impairment losses to assets of IGUs
central assets, 18.196—18.200
generally, 18.184—18.189
goodwill previously written off to reserves, 18.210—18.211
integration of acquired business, 18.201—18.209
methods of treating goodwill, 18.190—18.195
assets carried at historical cost, 18.250—18.251
assets held for disposal
disclosure requirements, 18.263—18.269
generally, 18.214—18.220
bank branches, 18.80
brands, 18.86.1—18.86.2
building society branches, 18.80
cash flow forecasts
central overheads, 18.125—18.126
constraints, 18.128—18.159
future capital expenditure, 18.148—18.155
future reorganisations, 18.147
generally, 18.115—18.122
growth rates, 18.129—18.135
inflation, 18.127
'look-back' tests, 18.136—18.140
reorganisation expenditure, 18.141—18.155
transfer pricing between IGUs, 18.123—18.124
central assets
allocation of impairment losses, 18.196—18.200
generally, 18.91—18.97
central overheads, 18.125—18.126
Companies Act requirements
disclosure, 18.281—18.282
identification of impaired assets, 18.41—18.44
deferred tax, and, 18.19—18.20
definition of 'impairment', 18.14—18.18
depreciation, 18.212—18.213
disclosure requirements
assets carried at historical cost, 18.250—18.251
assets held for disposal, 18.263—18.269

FRS 11 (impairment of fixed assets)—*cont.*
Companies Act requirements, 18.281—18.282
fixed asset movements, 18.270—18.271
revalued assets, 18.252—18.262
revalued assets held at depreciated replacement cost, 18.274
revalued assets held at market value, 18.272—18.273
reversal, 18.280
value in use, 18.275—18.279
discount rate
generally, 18.160—18.167
pre-tax rate, 18.168—18.178
executive summary
measurement, 18.1.6—18.1.10
objective of standard, 18.1—18.1.3
presentation of losses, 18.1.11—18.1.13
recognition of losses, 18.1.11—18.1.13
reversal of past losses, 18.1.14
scope of standard, 18.1—18.1.3
when reviews required, 18.1.4—18.1.5
fixed asset movements, 18.270—18.271
future capital expenditure, 18.148—18.155
future reorganisations, 18.147
goodwill, and
first year review, 18.38—18.40
generally, 18.33—18.37
purchased goodwill, 18.98—18.114
reversal of impairment losses, 18.242—18.249
growth rates, 18.129—18.135
hotels, 18.82
identification of impaired assets
Companies Act requirements, 18.41—18.44
deferred tax, and, 18.19—18.20
goodwill, 18.33—18.40
intangible assets, 18.33—18.40
introduction, 18.14—18.18
review, 18.22—18.32
income-generating units
allocation of assets and liabilities, 18.87—18.114
bank branches, 18.80
brands, 18.86.1—18.86.2
building society branches, 18.80
central assets, 18.91—18.97
hotels, 18.82
identification, 18.64—18.86.2
indefinite-lived assets, 18.86.1—18.86.2
petrol stations, 18.83
public houses, 18.81
purchased goodwill, 18.98—18.114
retail establishments, 18.76—18.148.2
vertically integrated operations, 18.84—18.86
indefinite-lived assets, 18.86.1—18.86.2
intangible fixed assets, and
and see below
generally, 15.66—15.95
identification of impairment, 18.33—18.40
reversal of impairment losses, 18.242—18.249
integration of acquired business, 18.201—18.209
introduction, 18.2—18.7
'look-back' tests, 18.136—18.140
measurement of recoverable amount
general matters, 18.45—18.49
net realisable value, 18.50—18.56
summary, 18.1.6—18.1.10
value in use, 18.57—18.63
net realisable value, 18.50—18.56
objective of standard
generally, 18.11—18.13
summary, 18.1—18.1.3
petrol stations, 18.83

FRS 11 (impairment of fixed assets)—*cont.*
presentation and disclosures
assets carried at historical cost, 18.250—18.251
assets held for disposal, 18.263—18.269
Companies Act requirements, 18.281—18.282
fixed asset movements, 18.270—18.271
revalued assets, 18.252—18.262
revalued assets held at depreciated replacement cost, 18.274
revalued assets held at market value, 18.272—18.273
reversal, 18.280
summary, 18.1.11—18.1.13
value in use, 18.275—18.279
public houses, 18.81
purchased goodwill
generally, 18.98—18.103
guidelines, 18.104—18.114
recognition of impairment losses
allocation to assets of IGUs, 18.184—18.211
assets held for disposal, 18.214—18.220
depreciation, 18.212—18.213
parent company issues, 18.221—18.229
summary, 18.1.11—18.1.13
reorganisation expenditure
future capital expenditure, 18.148—18.155
future reorganisations, 18.147
generally, 18.141—18.146
retail establishments, 18.76—18.148.2
revalued assets
generally, 18.252—18.262
held at depreciated replacement cost, 18.274
held at market value, 18.272—18.273
reversal of impairment losses
disclosure requirements, 18.280
general rules, 18.230—18.241
goodwill, and, 18.242—18.249
intangible assets, and, 18.242—18.249
summary, 18.1.14
review of impairment
generally, 18.22—18.24
indicators, 18.25—18.32
scope of standard
generally, 18.9—18.10
summary, 18.1—18.1.3
tangible fixed assets, and, 16.97—16.99
transfer pricing, 18.123—18.124
value in use
cash flow forecasts, 18.115—18.159
disclosure requirements, 18.275—18.279
discount rate, 18.160—18.178
introduction, 18.57—18.63
vertically integrated operations, 18.84—18.86
FRS 12 (provisions, contingencies and commitments)
abandonment costs, 21.249—21.257
ASB Statement of principles, 21.7—21.8
assets, against, 21.25
best estimate
estimation techniques, 21.117
introduction, 21.110—21.116
large population of similar claims, 21.118
changes in discount rates, 21.139—21.142.1
changes in estimate, 21.135—21.138.1
compensation, 21.266—21.267
constructive obligations, 21.52—21.53
contingent liabilities, 21.37—21.39
creditors, as, 21.80
decommissioning costs, 21.249—21.257
deferred income, 21.88—21.90
deferred tax, and, 13.114
definition, 21.40—21.46

FRS 12 (provisions, contingencies and commitments)— *cont.*
dilapidations, 21.234
disclosure requirements
acquisitions, 21.305
categorisation by class, 21.289—21.292
exemptions, 21.314—21.318
introduction, 21.288
narrative information, 21.297—21.298
pensions, 21.300—21.302
summary, 21.1.16
tabular information, 21.293—21.296
taxation, 21.303
unwinding of discount, 21.299—21.299.1
discounting
effects of taxation, 21.130
inflation adjustments, 21.121—21.123
introduction, 21.119—21.120
risk adjustment, 21.124—21.129
selection of appropriate discount rate, 21.131
unwinding the discount, 21.132
electrical and electronic equipment, 21.248.1—21.248.6
emissions obligations, 21.248.7—21.248.13
environmental liabilities, 21.245—21.248
executive summary
disclosure, 21.1.16
measurement, 21.1.8—21.1.11
other rules, 21.1.12—21.1.15
recognition, 21.1.2—21.1.7
scope of standard, 21.1—21.1.1
specific applications, 21.1.17—21.1.20
finance leases, 21.272
future events
changes in provisions, 21.81—21.82
generally, 21.79
measurement, and, 21.143—21.146
provision becomes creditor, 21.80
infrastructure renewals, 21.273—21.274
introduction, 21.2—21.3
legal obligations, 21.50—21.51
litigation, 21.258—21.265
maintenance, 21.268
measurement
application of rules, 21.142.2—21.142.6
asset recognition, 21.133—21.134
best estimate, 21.110—21.118
changes in discount rates, 21.139—21.142.1
changes in estimate, 21.135—21.138.1
changes in estimate of provisions, 21.142.2—21.142.6
discounting, 21.119—21.132
future events, 21.143—21.146
introduction, 21.109
related asset, 21.133—21.134
summary, 21.1.8—21.1.11
narrative information, 21.297—21.298
objective of standard, 21.20
onerous contracts
and see **Onerous contracts**
executory contracts, 21.197
financial instruments including derivatives, 21.198
general rules, 21.199—21.201
illustrative examples, 21.210—21.213
interpretation, 21.202—21.209
introduction, 21.193
leasehold properties, 21.194—21.196
measurement, 21.214—21.218
operating leasehold improvements, 21.235—21.236
operating leases, 21.271
other liabilities, 21.31—21.36

FRS 12 (provisions, contingencies and commitments)— *cont.*
past event
introduction, 21.54—21.56
legal enforcement, 21.57—21.60
third party expectation, 21.61—21.64
pensions, 21.300—21.302
practical application of rules
abandonment costs, 21.249—21.257
compensation, 21.266—21.267
decommissioning costs, 21.249—21.257
dilapidations, 21.234
environmental liabilities, 21.245—21.248
finance leases, 21.272
infrastructure renewals, 21.273—21.274
introduction, 21.222—21.224
litigation, 21.258—21.265
maintenance, 21.268
operating leasehold improvements, 21.235—21.236
operating leases, 21.271
refunds, 21.228—21.229
regulatory fines, 21.266—21.267
repairs, 21.268
self-insurance, 21.238—21.244
systems rectification, 21.266—21.267
tariff over-recoveries, 21.275—21.278
warranties, 21.225—21.227
present obligation
constructive obligations, 21.52—21.53
introduction, 21.49
legal obligations, 21.50—21.51
recognition test, and, 21.70—21.73
recognition
deferred income, 21.88—21.90
future events, 21.79—21.82
future operating costs, 21.65
introduction, 21.26—21.39
no reliable estimate, 21.77—21.78
past event, 21.54—21.64
placement of double entry, 21.83—21.87
present obligation, 21.49—21.53
reimbursement, 21.104—21.107
rules, 21.47—21.48
summary, 21.1.2—21.1.7
two stage test, 21.69—21.76
recognition test
groups of similar obligations, 21.76
introduction, 21.69
probability of present obligation, 21.70—21.73
transfer of economic benefits, 21.74—21.75
redundancies
compulsory redundancies, 21.183—21.189
introduction, 21.182
voluntary redundancies, 21.190—21.192
refunds, 21.228—21.229
regulatory fines, 21.266—21.267
reimbursement, 21.104—21.107
related assets, 21.133—21.134
repairs, 21.268
restructuring
and see **Restructuring**
application of recognition criteria, 21.155—21.170
definition, 21.153—21.154
introduction, 21.148—21.151
post balance sheet events, 21.174—21.175
redundancy provisions, 21.182—21.192
restructuring costs, 21.177—21.181
rules, 21.152
termination of operations, 21.171—21.172
scope of standard
generally, 21.21—21.24

FRS 12 (provisions, contingencies and commitments)— *cont.*
summary, 21.1—21.1.1
self-insurance, 21.238—21.244
small companies, and, 32.79—32.79.4
specific applications, 21.1.17—21.1.20
Statement of principles, 21.7—21.8
systems rectification, 21.266—21.267
tabular information, 21.293—21.296
tariff over-recoveries, 21.275—21.278
taxation
disclosure requirements, 21.303
third party expectation, 21.61—21.64
transfer of economic benefits, 21.74—21.75
test
groups of similar obligations, 21.76
introduction, 21.69
probability of present obligation, 21.70—21.73
transfer of economic benefits, 21.74—21.75
unwinding of discount, 21.299—21.299.1
warranties, 21.225—21.227
waste electrical and electronic equipment, 21.248.1—21.248.6
FRS 13 (financial instruments)
application under UK GAAP
all entities, and, 6.55—6.153
banks, 6.52—6.53
Companies Act requirements, 6.31—6.32
companies not applying FRS 26, 6.154—6.287
FRS 4, 6.33—6.34
FRS 13, 6.35
FRS 25, 6.36—6.38.1
FRS 26, 6.39—6.41
FRS 29, 6.41.1—6.41.2
insurance companies, 6.52—6.53
introduction, 6.26—6.30.1
listed companies, 6.41—6.47
new fair value accounting rules, 6.48—6.51
practical examples, 6.54
associates, 6.116—6.121
balance sheet instruments, 6.170—6.171
bank deposits, 5.147
building society deposits, 6.147
cash-settled commodity contracts, 6.176—6.180
Companies Act 1985 requirements, and
application under UK GAAP, 6.31—6.32
companies adopting fair value accounting, 6.101.8
companies not adopting fair value accounting, 6.101.9—6.101.11
comparatives, 6.101.14
directors' report, 6.101.12—6.101.13
disclosures, 6.91—6.147
introduction, 6.12
comparison with IFRS, and
and see **Financial instruments (IFRS)**
generally, 6.Annex 3
comparative information
Companies Act 1985 requirements, 6.153
FRS 25 and FRS 26, 6.396—6.400
currency risk, 6.230—6.240
current asset investments
alternative accounting rules, 6.76
historical cost accounting rules, 6.77—6.78
derivatives, 6.172—6.175
details of financial assets, 6.224—6.229
directors' report, 6.151—6.152
disclosures (Companies Act 1985)
all investments, 6.94—6.101
associates, 6.116—6.121
bank deposits, 5.147
building society deposits, 6.147
FRS 13 (financial instruments)—*cont.*
exemptions, 6.108—6.111
introduction, 6.91—6.93
joint ventures, 6.116—6.121
loan for acquisition of own shares, 6.145
other investments, 6.146—6.147
own shares, 6.137—6.142
parent company information, 6.131
participating interests, 6.112—6.115
qualifying undertakings, 6.132—6.136
shares in own parent, 6.137—6.144
significant holdings greater than 20%, 6.102—6.107
subsidiary undertakings, 6.122—6.130
disclosures (FRS 13)
accounting policies, of, 6.201—6.206
detailed numbers, of, 6.207—6.208
examples, 6.Annex 1
generally, 6.185—6.188
objectives, policies and strategies, of, 6.189—6.200
detailed numerical disclosures
currency risk, 6.230—6.240
details of financial assets, 6.224—6.229
fair value, 6.241—6.256
hedges, 6.260—6.280
interest rate risk, 6.209—6.215
introduction, 6.207—6.208
market price risk, 6.281—6.287
maturity analyses, 6216—6.223
trading assets and liabilities, 6.257—6.259
excluded financial instruments
balance sheet instruments, 6.170—6.171
cash-settled commodity contracts, 6.176—6.180
derivatives, 6.172—6.175
generally, 6.25
introduction, 6.163—6.165
non-equity minority interests, 6.181—6.184
non-equity shares, 6.181—6.184
short-term debtors and creditors, 6.166—6.169
facility fees, 6.323—6.325
fair value accounting
changes, 6.85
generally, 6.81—6.84
marking to market, 6.86—6.88
new rules, 6.48—6.51
fair value disclosures
book value, and, 6.251—6.256
category, by, 6.247—6.250
determination of fair value, 6.243—6.246
introduction, 6.241—6.242
finance costs
dividends, 6.306
elements, 6.305
interest, 6.306
introduction, 6.299—6.300
issue and redemption premiums, 6.307
issue costs, 6.308—6.322
financial liabilities
currency analysis, 6.209—6.215
maturity analysis, 6.216—6.220
fixed asset investments
alternative accounting rules, 6.69—6.75
historical cost accounting rules, 6.66—6.68
FRS 4 (capital instruments)
application under UK GAAP, 6.33—6.34
background, 6.288—6.290
Companies Act requirements, 6.375—6.381
definition of capital instrument, 6.296—6.298
disclosure, 6.372—6.374
dividends, 6.306
facility fees, 6.323—6.325
finance costs, 6.299—6.322

FRS 13 (financial instruments)—*cont.*
interest, 6.306
issue and redemption premiums, 6.307
issue costs, 6.308—6.322
measurement, 6.345—6.371
objectives, 6.291—6.292
options, 6.329—6.340
scope, 6.293—6.295
term, 6.326—6.344
FRS 25 (disclosure and presentation)
application under UK GAAP, 6.36—6.38.1
comparative information, 6.396—6.400
derecognition, 6.387
EU carve-out of IAS 39, 6.388—6.390
flowchart, 6.Annex 2
generally, 6.383—6.383.1
hedge accounting, 6.403—6.410
introduction, 6.9—6.13.1
other differences, 6.390.6
recognition, 6.386—6.387.5
scope exclusion, 6.384—6.384.1
transitional guidance, 6.391—6.395
FRS 26 (recognition and measurement)
application under UK GAAP, 6.39—6.41
comparative information, 6.396—6.400
derecognition, 6.387
EU carve-out of IAS 39, 6.388—6.390
flowchart, 6.Annex 2
generally, 6.383—6.383.1
hedge accounting, 6.403—6.410
introduction, 6.9—6.13.1
recognition, 6.386—6.387.5
transitional guidance, 6.391—6.395
FRS 29 (disclosures)
application under UK GAAP, 6.41.1—6.41.2
introduction, 6.9.1
hedges
current assets and liabilities, 6.269—6.270
forward purchase of stock, 6.273—6.274
gains and losses, 6.269—6.270
gross gains and losses, 6.268
information table, 6.261—6.263
introduction, 6.260
item being hedged, 6.264—6.266
net investment using cross-currency swap, 6.276—6.180
non-derivative hedging, 6.267
non-equity shares, 6.127—6.129
purchase of fixed asset using option, 6.275
historical cost accounting rules
current asset investments, 6.77—6.78
fixed asset investments, 6.66—6.68
holdings of assets and liabilities for trading, 6.257—6.259
IFRS, and
and see **Financial instruments (IFRS)**
generally, 6.Annex 3
insurance companies, 6.52—6.53
interest rate risk, 6.209—6.215
introduction, 6.1—6.15
joint ventures, 6.116—6.121
listed companies, 6.41—6.47
loan for acquisition of own shares, 6.145
market price risk, 6.281—6.287
marking to market, 6.86—6.88
maturity analyses
financial liabilities, of, 6.216—6.220
undrawn committed borrowing facilities, of, 6.221—6.223
measurement rules
current asset investments, 6.76—6.78

FRS 13 (financial instruments)—*cont.*
fair value accounting, 6.79—6.88
fixed asset investments, 6.66—6.75
generally, 6.64—6.65
minority interests, 6.20
non-equity minority interests, 6.181—6.184
non-equity shares, 6.181—6.184
onerous contracts, and, 21.198
own shares, 6.137—6.142
parent company information, 6.131
participating interests, 6.112—6.115
presentation rules, 6.89—6.90
qualifying undertakings, 6.132—6.136
relevant financial instruments
contracts and contractual rights, 6.21—6.24
examples, 6.19
introduction, 6.16—6.20
requirements applicable to all entities
classification, 6.61—6.63
definition of investments, 6.57—6.60
generally, 6.55—6.56
measurement rules, 6.64—6.88
presentation rules, 6.89—6.90
scope, 6.155—6.162
shares in own parent, 6.137—6.144
short-term debtors and creditors, 6.166—6.169
significant holdings greater than 20%, 6.102—6.107
subsidiary undertakings, 6.122—6.130
trading, assets and liabilities held for, 6.257—6.259
FRS 14 (earnings per share)
generally, 14.1—14.12
IFRS, and, A14.1—A14.207
FRS 15 (tangible fixed assets)
accumulated depreciation, 16.226—16.230
assets surplus to requirements, 16.189
assets under construction, 16.43—16.46
assets used in business, 16.185—16.188
background, 16.3—16.8
bases of valuation
assets surplus to requirements, 16.189
assets used in business, 16.185—16.188
depreciated replacement cost, 16.197—16.200
existing use value, 16.193—16.196
introduction, 16.177—16.184
open market value, 16.190—16.192
plant and machinery value, 16.201—16.203
borrowing costs, and, 16.345
capital grants (SSAP 4), and
disclosure requirements, 16.339—16.340
IFRS, and, 16.346
introduction, 16.329
non-depreciable fixed assets, 16.341—16.343
revision of standard, 16.331—16.338
scope of standard, 16.330
capitalisation of finance costs
accounting treatment, 16.106—16.110
definition of 'finance costs', 16.102—16.105
disclosure requirements, 16.126—16.129
general borrowings, 16.121
group situations, 16.122—16.124
IFRS, and, 16.344
introduction, 16.100—16.101
period of, 16.111—16.117
specific borrowings, 16.118—16.120
taxation, 16.125
capitalisation of interest, 16.24—16.25
changes in estimate
decommissioning costs, of, 16.83
residual life, of, 16.306—16.307
useful economic life, of, 16.302—16.305
changes in method, 16.307—16.308

FRS 15 (tangible fixed assets)—*cont.*
'cherry-picking', 16.16—16.20
classification
assets under construction, 16.43—16.46
introduction, 16.38—16.42
payments on account, 16.43—16.46
component depreciation
background, 16.26—16.27
generally, 16.276—16.278
implementation of standard, and, 16.339
component replacement, 16.143—16.149
cost
decommissioning costs, 16.75—16.83
directly attributable costs, 16.61—16.65
generally, 16.55—16.60
incremental costs, 16.68—16.71
IFRS, and, 16.344
labour costs, 16.66—16.67
software development costs, 16.72—16.74.10
decommissioning costs
arising later in asset's life, 16.79—16.82
changes in estimate, 16.83
generally, 16.75—16.78
definition, 16.35—16.37
depreciated replacement cost, 16.197—16.200
depreciation
change in estimate, 16.302—16.307
change in method, 16.307—16.308
components, of, 16.276—16.278
definition, 16.249—16.251
determination of useful economic life and residual life, 16.252—16.256
disclosure requirements, 16.309—16.314
IFRS, and, 16.344
introduction, 16.247—16.248
methods, 16.257—16.267
non-depreciation, 16.279—16.291
renewals accounting, 16.293—16.300
revalued assets, of, 16.268—16.275
summary, 16.1.14—16.1.17
depreciation methods
annuity, 16.264—16.267
introduction, 16.257—16.258
reducing balance, 16.260—16.261
'rule of 78', 16.262
straight line method, 16.259
sum of the digits, 16.262
unit-of-production, 16.263
directly attributable costs
generally, 16.61—16.65
period of capitalisation, 16.84
disclosure requirements
capital grants, 16.339—16.340
capitalisation of finance costs, 16.126—16.129
depreciation, 16.309—16.314
revaluation, 16.204—16.212
disposal of
intended, 16.325—16.328
introduction, 16.315
reporting gains and losses, 16.316—16.318
revalued assets, 16.319—16.324
donated assets, 16.90—16.93
executive summary
depreciation, 16.1.14—16.1.17
initial measurements, 16.1.1—16.1.4
scope of standard, 16.1
subsequent expenditure, 16.1.5—16.1.6
transfer of assets, 16.1.18
valuation, 16.1.8—16.1.13
web site costs, 16.1.7
existing use value, 16.193—16.196

FRS 15 (tangible fixed assets)—*cont.*
'fixed assets'
categories, 16.10—16.11
definition, 16.9
excluded items, 16.12—16.13
generally, 16.3—16.8
IFRS, and
borrowing costs, 16.344
capital grants, 16.346
capitalisation of finance costs, 16.344
convergence, 16.344
cost model, 16.344
current value, 16.344
definitions, 16.344
depreciation, 16.344
derecognition, 16.344
disclosures, 16.344
exchanges of assets, 16.344
finance lease costs, 16.344
first time adoption of IFRS, 16.344
government grants, 16.346
initial measurement, 16.344
introduction, 16.344—16.344
investment properties, 16.344
market value, 16.344
overview, 16.344
recognition, 16.344
related pronouncements, 16.344
revaluation model, 16.344
scope, 16.344
subsequent costs, 16.344
subsequent measurement, 16.344
impairment
generally, 16.97—16.99
IFRS, and, 16.344
implementation of standard
change in measurement, 16.331—16.332
component depreciation, 16.339
introduction, 16.329—16.330
non-depreciation, 16.340—16.345
options for previously revalued assets, 16.333—16.337
revisions to estimates, 16.338
incremental costs, 16.68—16.71
initial measurement, 16.1.1—16.1.4
intended disposal of, 16.325—16.328
interest capitalisation, 16.24—16.25
introduction, 16.2
labour costs, 16.66—16.67
major inspections and overhauls, 16.150—16.153
measurement
cost, 16.55—16.
implementation of standard, and, 16.331—16.332
introduction, 16.51—16.54
summary, 16.1.1—16.1.4
non-depreciation
background, 16.28—16.30
generally, 16.284—16.290.1
implementation of standard, and, 16.340—16.345
introduction, 16.279—16.283
non-depreciable land, 16.291
objectives of standard, 16.31
open market value, 16.190—16.192
payments on account, 16.43—16.46
plant and machinery value, 16.201—16.203
pre-FRS 15, and, 16.14—16.15
previously assessed standard of performance, 16.135—16.142
recoverable amount, 16.97—16.99
replacing components, 16.143—16.149
residual life

FRS 15 (tangible fixed assets)—*cont.*
change in estimate, 16.306
determination, 16.252—16.256
implementation of standard, and, 16.338
revalued assets
depreciation, 16.268—16.275
disposal of fixed assets, 16.319—16.324
revaluation
bases, 16.177—16.203
class of assets, 16.158—16.163
disclosure requirements, 16.204—16.212
frequency, 16.164
IFRS, and, 16.344
introduction, 16.154—16.157
material changes in value, 16.175—16.176
other assets, 16.173—16.174
properties, 16.169—16.172
qualified valuers, 16.165—16.168
revaluation of gains and losses
accumulated depreciation, 16.226—16.230
gains, 16.216
introduction, 16.213—16.215
losses, 16.217—16.225
reserve, 16.231—16.241
taxation, 16.242—16.246
scope of standard
generally, 16.32—16.34
summary, 16.1
small companies, and, 32.64—32.67
software development costs, 16.72—16.74.10
start-up costs
generally, 16.85—16.89.5
introduction, 16.21—16.23
subsequent expenditure
accounting treatment, 16.133—16.134
IFRS, and, 16.344
introduction, 16.130—16.132
major inspections and overhauls, 16.150—16.153
previously assessed standard of performance, 16.135—16.142
replacing components, 16.143—16.149
summary, 16.1.5—16.1.6
taxation
revaluation of gains and losses, 16.242—16.246
transfer to and from assets
generally, 16.47—16.49
summary, 16.1.18
unknown purchase price or production cost, 16.94—16.96
useful economic life
change in estimate, 16.302—16.305
determination, 16.252—16.256
implementation of standard, and, 16.338
valuation, 16.1.8—16.1.13
web site costs, 16.1.7
FRS 16 (current tax)
accounting policies, 13.235
ACT, and, 13.50.1—13.50.9
avoir fiscal
income and expenses subject to non-standard rates, 13.38—13.43
introduction 13.37.1—13.37.3
measurement of current tax charge, 13.44—13.50
balance sheet
analysis of deferred tax balance, 13.267—13.270
Companies Act requirements, 13.253
deferred tax asset, *13.272—13.273*
material balances, 13.263—13.266
offset of assets and liabilities, 13.258—13.262
standards requirements, 13.254—13.257
circumstances affecting tax charges, 13.274—13.290
FRS 16 (current tax)—*cont.*
disclosure requirements
accounting policies, 13.235
balance sheet, 13.253—13.273
circumstances affecting tax charges, 13.274—13.290
generally, 13.234
profit and loss account, 13.236—13.248
statement of total recognised gains and losses, 13.249—13.252
summary, 13.1.7
dividends
incoming, 13.31—13.33
outgoing, 13.28—13.30
executive summary
disclosure, 13.1.7
introduction, 13.1—13.1.1
measurement, 13.1.6
recognition, 13.1.2—13.1.5
general principles, 13.8—13.9
generally, 13.18—13.20
imputation tax system, 13.10—13.16
incoming dividends, 13.31—13.33
interest
payable, 13.28—13.30
receivable, 13.31—13.33
introduction, 13.2—13.7
measurement
generally, 13.44—13.50
summary, 13.1.6
non-operating exceptional items, 13.245—13.248
outgoing dividends, 13.28—13.30
presentation
accounting policies, 13.235
balance sheet, 13.253—13.273
circumstances affecting tax charges, 13.274—13.290
generally, 13.234
profit and loss account, 13.236—13.248
statement of total recognised gains and losses, 13.249—13.252
profit and loss account
analysis of current tax, 13.239
analysis of deferred tax, 13.240—13.244
Companies Act requirements, 13.236
non-operating exceptional items, 13.245—13.248
notes, 13.238
standards requirements, 13.237
recognition
generally, 13.21—13.23
summary, 13.1.2—13.1.5
recoverability of ACT, 13.50.1—13.50.9
statement of total recognised gains and losses
generally, 13.249—13.250
notes, 13.251—13.252
tax credits
incoming dividends, 13.31—13.33
interest payable, 13.28—13.30
interest receivable, 13.31—13.33
introduction, 13.24
outgoing dividends, 13.28—13.30
underlying tax, 13.35—13.37
withholding tax
incoming dividends, 13.31—13.33
interest payable, 13.28—13.30
interest receivable, 13.31—13.33
introduction, 13.25—13.27
outgoing dividends, 13.28—13.30
FRS 17 (retirement benefits)
acquisitions, 11.135—11.138
actuarial gains and losses, 11.109—11.114
balance sheet entries
generally, 11.55—11.61.1

FRS 17 (retirement benefits)—*cont.*
summary, 11.1.9—11.1.12
comparison with SSAP 24, 11.212
components of performance, 11.1.13
current service cost, 11.81—11.84
curtailments, 11.100—11.108
defined benefit schemes, and
acquisitions, 11.135—11.138
balance sheet entries, 11.55—11.61.1
disclosure requirements, 11.139—11.148
frequency of valuations, 11.74—11.77
future developments, 11.148.1—11.148.14
limit on pension asset, 11.115—11.126
measurement of assets, 11.62—11.67
measurement of liabilities, 11.68—11.73
reporting performance, 11.78—11.114
reserves, 11.149—11.164
scheme assets, 11.43—11.148
scheme liabilities, 11.46—11.54
taxation, 11.127—11.129
defined contribution schemes, and
accounting treatment, 11.35
definition, 11.31—11.34
disclosure, 11.36
disclosure requirements
aggregation of schemes, 11.146—11.148
comparatives, 11.144—11.145
defined benefit schemes, 11.139—11.148
defined contribution schemes, 11.36
summary, 11.1.21—11.1.24
executive summary
balance sheet recognition, 11.1.9—11.1.12
components of performance, 11.1.13
disclosures, 11.1.21—11.1.24
introduction, 11.1
measurement, 11.1.4—11.1.8
profit and loss account, 11.1.14—11.1.18
scope of standard, 11.1.1—11.1.3
STRGL, 11.1.19
tax, 11.1.20—11.1.21
expected return on assets, 11.87—11.89.2
first time adoption, and, 11.157
frequency of valuations, 11.74—11.77
future developments, 11.148.1—11.148.14
group schemes
disclosure, 11.41—11.42.2
generally, 11.37—11.41.8
summary, 11.1.2
interest cost, 11.85—11.86
introduction, 11.2—11.7
limit on pension asset
benefit improvements, 11.118—11.120
introduction, 11.115—11.117
required accounting, 11.121—11.126
measurement of assets
generally, 11.62—11.67
summary, 11.1.4—11.1.8
measurement of liabilities
generally, 11.68—11.73
summary, 11.1.4—11.1.8
multi-employer schemes
disclosure, 11.41—11.42.2
generally, 11.37—11.41.8
summary, 11.1.2
objective of standard, 11.28—11.30
past service costs, 11.93—11.99
Pensions Act 2004, and
introduction, 11.170—11.172
minimum funding objective, 11.179—11.182
moral hazard precisions, 11.177—11.178
Pensions Protection Fund, 11.173—11.175

FRS 17 (retirement benefits)—*cont.*
Pensions Regulator, 11.176
statutory funding objective, 11.179—11.182
profit and loss account
generally, 11.90—11.92
summary, 11.1.14—11.1.18
reporting performance
actuarial gains and losses, 11.109—11.114
current service cost, 11.81—11.84
curtailments, 11.100—11.108
expected return on assets, 11.87—11.89.2
interest cost, 11.85—11.86
introduction, 11.78—11.80
past service costs, 11.93—11.99
profit and loss account, 11.90—11.92
settlements, 11.100—11.108
reserves
composition of reserves, 11.162—11.164
distributable reserves, 11.150—11.156
introduction, 11.149
scheme assets
generally, 11.43—11.148
measurement, 11.62—11.67
scheme liabilities
generally, 11.46—11.54
measurement, 11.68—11.73
scope of standard
generally, 11.24—11.27
summary, 11.1.1—11.1.3
settlements, 11.100—11.108
STRGL, 11.1.19
taxation
generally, 11.127—11.129
summary, 11.1.20—11.1.21
FRS 18 (accounting principles)
accounting policies
alteration, 2.135—2.138
consistency, 2.138.1—2.138.7
generally, 2.121—2.127
overview, 2.93.4—2.93.12
review, 2.135—2.138
selection, 2.128—2.134
accruals
generally, 2.108—2.111
overview, 2.93.15
disclosures
generally, 2.102—2.107
overview, 2.93.18
estimation techniques
generally, 2.139—2.143
overview, 2.93.16—2.93.17
going concern
generally, 2.94—2.101
overview, 2.93.13—2.93.14
introduction, 2.88—2.93.1
overview
accounting policies, 2.93.4—2.93.12
accruals, 2.93.15
changes in accounting policy, 2.93.10—2.93.12
disclosures, 2.93.18
estimation techniques, 2.93.16—2.93.17
going concern, 2.93.13—2.93.14
introduction, 2.93.2—2.93.3
selection of accounting policies, 2.93.5—2.93.9
prudence, 2.112
realisation, 2.112—2.115
separate valuation, 2.116—2.120
FRS 19 (deferred tax)
accelerated capital allowances, 13.104—13.106
accounting policies, 13.235
background, 13.4

FRS 19 (deferred tax)—*cont.*
balance sheet
analysis of deferred tax balance, 13.267—13.270
Companies Act requirements, 13.253
deferred tax asset, 13.272—13.273
material balances, 13.263—13.266
offset of assets and liabilities, 13.258—13.262
standards requirements, 13.254—13.257
summary, 13.1.8—13.1.15
capital losses, 13.165—13.166
circumstances affecting tax charges, 13.274—13.290
computation
deferral method, 13.55—13.56
introduction, 13.54
liability method, 13.57—13.59
liability method with full provisioning, 13.62—13.71
liability method with partial provisioning, 13.60—13.61
consolidated financial statements, treatment in
effects of adjustment, 13.206—13.208
fair value adjustments, 13.209—13.213
foreign exchange differences, 13.216
general principles, 13.203—13.205
goodwill, 13.213.1—13.213.3
unremitted earnings, 13.214—13.215
deferral method, 13.55—13.56
deferred revenue expenditure, 13.116—13.117
deferred tax assets
capital losses, 13.165—13.166
general rule, 13.142—13.146
going concern uncertainty, 13.167—13.168
recovery against deferred tax liabilities, 13.156
recovery against future taxable profits, 13.157
review of recoverability, 13.169—13.170
suitable taxable profits, 13.147—13.148
tax planning opportunities, 13.149—13.155
trading losses, 13.158—13.164
disclosure requirements
accounting policies, 13.235
balance sheet, 13.253—13.273
circumstances affecting tax charges, 13.274—13.290
generally, 13.234
profit and loss account, 13.236—13.248
statement of total recognised gains and losses, 13.249—13.252
summary, 13.1.26
discounting
calculation, 13.185—13.188
introduction, 13.176—13.184
rates, 13.192—13.195
scheduling cash flows, 13.189—13.190
scheduling timing differences, 13.191
summary, 13.1.19—13.1.22
worked examples, 13.196—13.202
executive summary
balance sheet, 13.1.8—13.1.15
disclosure, 13.1.26
discounting, 13.1.19—13.1.22
introduction, 13.1—13.1.1
measurement, 13.1.18
performance statement, 13.1.16—13.1.17
presentation, 13.1.23—13.1.25
recognition, 13.1.8—13.1.17
fair value adjustments, 13.209—13.213
foreign exchange differences, 13.216
general principles, 13.97—13.98
going concern uncertainty, 13.167—13.168
goodwill, 13.213.1—13.213.3
government grants, 13.118—13.121
holdover relief, 13.136—13.141

FRS 19 (deferred tax)—*cont.*
impairment, and, 18.19—18.20
imputation tax system, 13.10—13.16
industrial building allowances, 13.107—13.110
infrastructure assets, 13.111—13.113
introduction, 13.51—13.53
leases, 13.122—13.125.1
liability method
general, 13.57—13.59
with full provisioning, 13.62—13.71
with partial provisioning, 13.60—13.61
marked to market assets, 13.131—13.135.1
measurement
average rates, 13.173—13.175
introduction, 13.171—13.172
summary, 13.1.18
non-operating exceptional items, 13.245—13.248
objectives of standard, 13.90—13.96
performance statement, 13.1.16—13.1.17
post-retirement benefits, 13.126—13.126.10
presentation
accounting policies, 13.235
balance sheet, 13.253—13.273
circumstances affecting tax charges, 13.274—13.290
generally, 13.234
profit and loss account, 13.236—13.248
statement of total recognised gains and losses, 13.249—13.252
summary, 13.1.23—13.1.25
profit and loss account
analysis of current tax, 13.239
analysis of deferred tax, 13.240—13.244
Companies Act requirements, 13.236
non-operating exceptional items, 13.245—13.248
notes, 13.238
standards requirements, 13.237
provisions, 13.114
recognition, 13.1.8—13.1.17
retirement benefits, 13.126—13.126.10
revaluation of non-monetary assets
general rule, 13.128—13.130
holdover relief, 13.136—13.141
marked to market assets, 13.131—13.135.1
rollover relief, 13.136—13.141
rollover relief, 13.136—13.141
share-based payment transactions
cash-settled transactions, 13.127.8
equity-settled transactions, 13.127—13.127.7
standardisation of accounting, 13.80—13.88
statement of total recognised gains and losses
generally, 13.249—13.250
notes, 13.251—13.252
timing differences
accelerated capital allowances, 13.104—13.106
deferred revenue expenditure, 13.116—13.117
discounting, and, 13.191
generally, 13.99—13.103
government grants, 13.118—13.121
industrial building allowances, 13.107—13.110
infrastructure assets, 13.111—13.113
leases, 13.122—13.125.1
post-retirement benefits, 13.126—13.126.10
provisions, 13.114
trading losses, 13.158—13.164
unremitted earnings, 13.214—13.215
FRS 20 (share-based payment)
alternative share-based payment transactions, 12.2
cancellations, 12.13
cash payments to employee trusts, 12.94—12.102
cash-settled share-based payment transactions
generally, 12.2

FRS 20 (share-based payment)—*cont.*
introduction, 12.14—12.15
comparison with IFRS, 12.113
deferred tax, and
cash-settled transactions, 13.127.8
equity-settled transactions, 13.127—13.127.7
disclosures
ESOP trusts, 12.73—12.74
generally, 12.22
employee share ownership plans
accounting, 12.46—12.54
background, 12.42—12.45
disclosure, 12.73—12.74
distributable profits, 12.56—12.62
gains, 12.71—12.72
generally, 12.40—12.41
introduction, 12.19—12.21
legal issues, 12.55
public companies, and, 12.63—12.70
trustee company, 12.72
equity-settled share-based payment transactions
generally, 12.16—12.18
introduction, 12.2
measurement, 12.5—12.7
examples, 12.103
excluded grants of instruments, 12.110—12.112
exclusions from scope, 12.3
first time adoption, and, 12.23
GAAP, and, 12.24
grants to which not apply, 12.110—12.112
IFRS, and
generally, 12.25—12.26
text, A12.1—A12.245
introduction, 12.1
modifications and cancellations, 12.13
NICs on option gains
background, 12.27—12.34
introduction, 12.11—12.12
reimbursement of liability, 12.36—12.39
transfer of liability, 12.36—12.39
objective, 12.6—12.11
practical implications
employee share ownership plans, 12.42—12.72
QUESTs, 12.75—12.93
share symmetry arrangements, 12.75
QUESTs
introduction, 12.75—12.84
pre-funding by parent company, 12.90—12.91
pre-funding by subsidiary company, 12.92—12.93
simultaneous funding by parent company, 12.85—12.88
simultaneous funding by subsidiary company, 12.89
recognition of transactions
generally, 12.4
measurement, 12.5—12.7
vesting conditions, 12.8—12.10
scope, 12.6—12.11
share-based payments transactions, 12.16—12.18
share symmetry arrangements, 12.75
transitional provisions, 12.104—12.109
types of transactions, 12.2
vesting conditions, 12.8—12.10
FRS 21 (post balance sheet events)
and see **IAS 10 (post balance sheet events)**
introduction, 22.1—22.3
small companies, and, 32.79—32.79.4
FRS 23 (foreign exchange rates)
and see **Foreign currency translation**
disclosure, A7.117—A7.122.2
first time adoption of IFRS, A7.130—A7.132
foreign currency transactions, A7.48—A7.114
FRS 23 (foreign exchange rates)—*cont.*
functional currency approach, A7.27—A7.47
introduction, A7.1—A7.7
objectives, A7.23
other matters, A7.126—A7.127
overview, 7.188—7.189
presentation, A7.115—A7.116
scope, A7.24—A7.26
FRS 24 (hyperinflationary economies)
and see **Foreign currency translation**
generally, A7.109—A7.114
overview, 7.188—7.189
FRS 25 (financial instruments – disclosure and presentation)
application under UK GAAP, 6.36—6.38.1
comparative information, 6.396—6.400
derecognition, 6.387
EU carve-out of IAS 39, 6.388—6.390
fair value option, 6.390.1—6.390.5
flowchart, 6.Annex 2
generally, 6.383—6.383.1
hedge accounting
documentation, 6.404—6.406
introduction, 6.403
introduction, 6.9—6.13.1
other differences, 6.390.6
recognition, 6.386—6.387.5
scope exclusion, 6.384—6.384.1
transitional guidance, 6.391—6.395
FRS 26 (financial instruments – recognition and measurement)
amendments, 6.406.1—6.406.4
application under UK GAAP, 6.39—6.41
comparative information, 6.396—6.400
derecognition, 6.387
EU carve-out of IAS 39, 6.388—6.390
fair value option, 6.390.1—6.390.5
flowchart, 6.Annex 2
generally, 6.383—6.383.1
hedge accounting
documentation, 6.404—6.406
introduction, 6.403
introduction, 6.9—6.13.1
other differences, 6.390.6
recognition, 6.386—6.387.5
scope exclusion, 6.384—6.384.1
transitional guidance, 6.391—6.395
FRS 29 (financial instruments – disclosures)
application under UK GAAP, 6.41.1—6.41.2
generally, 6.406.5—6.406.7
introduction, 6.9.1
FRSs
financial reporting structure, and, 2.65—2.73
Full participation in future performance test
merger accounting, and, 28.62—28.64
Fundamental errors
generally, 8.203—8.204
IFRS, and, 8.208
Fundamental reorganisation or restructuring
reporting financial performance, and, 8.94—8.99
Funded schemes
pension costs, and, 11.20—11.22
Future capital expenditure
impairment, and, 18.148—18.155
Future costs
long-term contracts, and, 20.89—20.91
Future events
changes in provisions, 21.81—21.82
generally, 21.79
measurement, and, 21.143—21.146
provision becomes creditor, 21.80

Future reorganisations
impairment, and, 18.147
Future results of foreign investments
foreign currency hedging, and, 7.135—7.137

Gains and losses
employee share ownership plans, and, 12.28
hedging, and, 6.126 0
Generally accepted accounting principles (GAAP)
Companies Act, and
compliance with accounting standards, 2.35—2.36
introduction, 2.21
requirement to prepare financial statements, 2.22—2.22.8
true and fair requirement, 2.23—2.34
composition, 2.5—2.9
consolidation rules, and, 24.303—24.304
development, 2.10—2.20.4
Geographical segments
segmental reporting, and, 10.47—10.57
Going concern
generally, 2.94—2.101
overview, 2.93.13—2.93.14
Going concern uncertainty
deferred tax, and, 13.167—13.168
Goodwill (FRS 10)
see also **Negative goodwill**
accounting policy, 25.585—25.586
acquisition accounting, and, 25.1.16—25.1.20
additions in existing subsidiaries, 25.600
allocation of purchased goodwill, 25.517
amortising goodwill, 25.494—25.499
associates, and
balance sheet, 27.88—27.93
principles, 27.141—27.143
capital redemption reserve, 25.569
capitalisation, and, 25.439—25.444
contingent consideration, 25.500—25.504
cumulative amounts written off, 25.587—25.591
deferred tax, and, 13.213.1—13.213.3
disclosures, 25.584
disposals, 8.54—8.57, 25.518—25.520, 25.581—25.582
distributable profits, 23.192—23.195
earnout consideration, 25.601
effect on distributable profits, 25.573—25.580
foreign currency translation, and, 7.76—7.78
impairment, 25.583—25.5
impairment of fixed assets, and
and see **Impairment of fixed assets**
first year review, 18.38—18.40
generally, 18.33—18.37
purchased goodwill, 18.98—18.114
reversal of impairment losses, 18.242—18.249
impairment reviews, 25.521—25.523, 25.532—25.552
implementing FRS 10, 25.598—25.599
indefinite life, 25.477—25.481
intangible fixed assets, and
and see **Intangible fixed assets**
introduction, 15.1—15.2
integrated acquisitions, 25.528—25.531
internally generated goodwill, 25.450
introduction, 25.437—25.438
joint ventures, and
balance sheet, 27.88—27.93
principles, 27.141—27.143
merger reserve, 25.560—25..561
multiple useful economic lives, 25.482—25.493
non-distributable reserves, 25.563
positive and negative goodwill, 25.524—25.527
pre-FRS 10 goodwill remaining in reserves, 25.553

Goodwill (FRS 10)—*cont.*
pre-FRS 10 negative goodwill remaining in reserves, 25.592—25.597
presentation of amortisation and impairment charges, 25.505—25.508
profit and loss account, 25.559
prohibition of separate write-off reserve, 25.554—25.555
purchased goodwill
generally, 25.448—25.476
impairment of fixed assets, 18.98—18.114
reserves used for write-offs, 25.557—25.558
revaluation reserve, 25.570—25.572
reversal of write-offs, 25.509—25.516
scope of FRS 10, 25.445—25.447
share premium account, 25.564—25.568
statement of total recognised gains and losses, and, 8.155—8.159
true and fair override, 25.477—25.481
useful economic life, 25.458—25.476
Government grants
deferred tax, and, 13.118—13.121
revenue recognition, and, 9.293—9.298
Grants
revenue recognition, and, 9.263—9.270
Gross equity method
generally, 27.94
introduction, 27.4—27.5
Gross cash flows
cash flow statements, and, 30.59—30.63
Gross gains and losses
hedging, and, 6.125
Gross profit
profit and loss account, and, 5.13
'Group', definition of
entity concept, 24.13—24.14
introduction, 24.6
parent company concept, 24.11—24.12
proprietary concept, 24.7—24.10
Group's financial statements
disclosure requirements, 3.154—3.155
generally, 3.151—3.153
Group reconstruction relief
acquisition accounting, and, 25.14
merger relief, and, 23.105—23.112
Group reconstructions
merger accounting, and
generally, 28.74—28.80
summary, 28.1.5—28.1.6
Group relief
introduction, 13.291—13.294
no payments made for, 13.295—13.297
payment is less than amount of tax saving, 13.301
payment is less than gross amount of loss surrendered, 13.302
payment represents amount of tax saving, 13.299—13.300
payment represents gross amount of loss surrendered, 13.303—13.305
payments made for, 13.298
Group schemes
retirement benefits, and
disclosure, 11.41—11.42.2
generally, 11.37—11.41.8
summary, 11.1.2
Group structure
accounting for investments, 24.18—24.19
consolidated financial statements
and see **Consolidated financial statements**
exemptions, 24.56—24.75
form, 24.41—24.50

Group structure—*cont.*
purpose, 24.20
requirement to prepare, 24.32—24.39
true and fair view, 24.51—24.55
definition of 'group'
entity concept, 24.13—24.14
introduction, 24.6
parent company concept, 24.11—24.12
proprietary concept, 24.7—24.10
distributable reserves, and, 24.252—24.255
employee costs, 5.26.1—5.26.2
introduction, 24.1—24.3
limited partnerships
accounting for as part of portfolio, 24.212.12
accounting for interests in subsidiaries, 24.212.13—24.212.15
associated undertakings, 24.212.9
consolidation by general partner, 24.212.2—24.212.4
implications of financial statements, 24.212.16
interest more than 50%, 24.212.10
introduction, 24.212.1—24.212.2
joint ventures, 24.212.9
long-term restrictions do not apply, 24.212.11
long-term restrictions on general partner's control, 24.212.5—24.212.8
membership of qualified undertaking, 24.247—24.251
parent undertakings, 24.26—24.31
profit and loss account, 24.47—24.50
realised reserves, and, 24.252—24.255
scope of provisions, 24.21—24.25
Statement of principles, 24.16—24.17
subsidiaries excluded from consolidation
disclosure requirements, 24.200—24.212
disproportionate expense, 24.181
dissimilar activities, 24.203
interest held exclusively with view to subsequent resale, 24.193—24.198
introduction, 24.176—24.180
severe long-term restrictions, 24.182—24.192
undue delay, 24.181
subsidiary undertakings
and see **Subsidiary undertakings**
board majority, 24.96—24.104
company law, and, 24.78—24.79
control, 24.155—24.159
definition, 24.26—24.31
dominant influence, 24.121—24.150
European law, 24.79
example, 24.175
expressions and interpretations, 24.160—24.174
introduction, 24.76—24.77
majority of voting rights, 24.89—24.95
meaning, 24.80—24.85
participating interest, 24.152—24.154
terminology, 24.86—24.88
true and fair view, 24.51—24.55
Growth rates
impairment, and, 18.129—18.135
Guarantees by directors
related party transactions, and, 29.140

Half-yearly reports
content, 4.142
Handling charges
revenue recognition, and, 9.97—9.99
Hedge accounting (IFRS)
all-in-one hedges, A6.10.77—A6.10.78
cash flow hedges
accounting, A6.10.115—A6.10.117
definition, A6.10.106

Hedge accounting (IFRS)—*cont.*
discontinuing accounting, A6.10.121—A6.10.123
examples, A6.10.107
forecast transactions, A6.10.108—A6.10.114
reclassifying equity gains and losses, A6.10.118—A6.10.120
combination of derivative instruments, A6.10.65—A6.10.68
consolidated subsidiaries investment, A6.10.46—A6.10.48
criteria for obtaining
designation, A6.10.138—A6.10.139
documentation, A6.10.138—A6.10.144
effectiveness of hedge, A6.10.145—A6.10.182
ineffectiveness of hedge, A6.10.183—A6.10.195
introduction, A6.10.136—A6.10.137
derivative financial instruments
all-in-one hedges, A6.10.77—A6.10.78
combination of instruments, A6.10.65—A6.10.68
dynamic hedging strategies, A6.10.74—A6.10.75
internal hedging instruments, A6.10.79—A6.10.82
introduction, A6.10.54—A6.10.55
more than one risk with single instrument, A6.10.62—A6.10.64
options, A6.10.69—A6.10.73
portions and proportions, A6.10.56—A6.10.61
derivative instruments, A6.10.50
designation, A6.10.138—A6.10.139
disclosure of financial instruments, and, A6.11.68—A6.11.71
documentation
forecast transactions, A6.10.140—A6.10.144
generally, A6.10.138—A6.10.139
dynamic hedging strategies, A6.10.74—A6.10.75
effectiveness
assessment methods, A6.10.159—A6.10.182
benchmark rate method, A6.10.171
counterparty credit risk, A6.10.156
critical terms comparison, A6.10.160—A6.10.163
cumulative assessment basis, A6.10.154—A6.10.155
dollar offset method, A6.10.164—A6.10.167
hypothetical derivative method, A6.10.168—A6.10.170
introduction, A6.10.145
period-by-period assessment basis, A6.10.154—A6.10.155
pre-payment risk, A6.10.157—A6.10.158
regression analysis, A6.10.173—A6.10.182
requirements for assessment, A6.10.146—A6.10.153
sensitivity analysis method, A6.10.172
equity method investment, A6.10.46—A6.10.48
examples, A6.10.201—A6.10.203
fair value hedges
accounting, A6.10.93—A6.10.97
adjustments to hedged items, A6.10.98—A6.10.100
definition, A6.10.91
discontinuing accounting, A6.10.103—A6.10.105
examples, A6.10.92
firm commitments, A6.10.101—A6.10.102
financial items
introduction, A6.10.22
loans and receivables, A6.10.30
partial term hedging, A6.10.29
portions and proportions, A6.10.23
risk component of financial instrument, A6.10.24—A6.10.28
firm commitments
fair value hedges, A6.10.101—A6.10.102
generally, A6.10.34

Hedge accounting (IFRS)—*cont.*
forecast transactions
documentation, A6.10.140—A6.10.144
generally, A6.10.35
intra-group/entity transactions, A6.10.38—A6.10.40
future earnings, A6.10.49
general business risk, A6.10.51
groups of items, A6.10.15—A6.10.18
hedge effectiveness
assessment methods, A6.10.159—A6.10.182
benchmark rate method, A6.10.171
counterparty credit risk, A6.10.156
critical terms comparison, A6.10.160—A6.10.163
cumulative assessment basis, A6.10.154—A6.10.155
dollar offset method, A6.10.164—A6.10.167
hypothetical derivative method, A6.10.168—A6.10.170
introduction, A6.10.145
period-by-period assessment basis, A6.10.154—A6.10.155
pre-payment risk, A6.10.157—A6.10.158
regression analysis, A6.10.173—A6.10.182
requirements for assessment, A6.10.146—A6.10.153
sensitivity analysis method, A6.10.172
hedge ineffectiveness
change in fair value method, A6.10.193
change in variable cash flow method, A6.10.194—A6.10.195
measurement, A6.10.188—A6.10.195
minimisation, A6.10.184—A6.10.187
hedged items
adjustments to, A6.10.98—A6.10.100
definition, A6.10.10—A6.10.14
financial items, A6.10.22—A6.10.28
firm commitments, A6.10.34
forecast transactions, A6.10.35
groups of items, A6.10.15—A6.10.18
intra-group transactions, A6.10.36—A6.10.40
introduction, A6.10.9
non-financial items, A6.10.31—A6.10.33
non-qualifying items, A6.10.41—A6.10.51
overall net position, A6.10.19—A6.10.21
subsequent measurement of assets, A6.9.36
subsequent measurement of liabilities, A6.9.50
hedging instruments
definition, A6.10.52—A6.10.53
derivative financial instruments, A6.10.54—A6.10.84
embedded derivatives in host contracts, and, A6.5.107
non-derivative financial instruments, A6.10.85—A6.10.86
non-qualifying instruments, A6.10.87—A6.10.88
overview, A6.1.40—A6.1.41
hedging overall net position, A6.10.19—A6.10.21
held-to-maturity investments, A6.10.43—A6.10.45
IAS 39, and, A6.10.5—A6.10.8
ineffectiveness
change in fair value method, A6.10.193
change in variable cash flow method, A6.10.194—A6.10.195
measurement, A6.10.188—A6.10.195
minimisation, A6.10.184—A6.10.187
sources, A6.10.183
internal hedging instruments
generally, A6.10.79—A6.10.82
offsetting, A6.10.83—A6.10.84
intra-group/entity transactions

Hedge accounting (IFRS)—*cont.*
forecast transactions, A6.10.38—A6.10.40
generally, A6.10.36—A6.10.37
introduction, A6.10.1—A6.10.2
loans and receivables, A6.10.30
macro hedging, A6.10.196—A6.10.200
meaning, A6.10.3—A6.10.4
models
cash flow hedges, A6.10.106—A6.10.123
fair value hedges, A6.10.91—A6.10.105
introduction, A6.10.89
net investment hedges, A6.10.124—A6.10.135
risk reduction, A6.10.90
more than one risk with single instrument, A6.10.62—A6.10.64
net investment hedges
accounting, A6.10.125—A6.10.128
criteria for accounting, A6.10.129
definition, A6.10.124
derivatives, A6.10.132—A6.10.133
individual financial statements, A6.10.134—A6.10.135
non-derivative financial instruments, A6.10.130—A6.10.131
separate financial statements, A6.10.134—A6.10.135
non-derivative financial instruments, A6.10.85—A6.10.86
non-qualifying hedged items
consolidated subsidiaries investment, A6.10.46—A6.10.48
derivative instruments, A6.10.50
equity method investment, A6.10.46—A6.10.48
future earnings, A6.10.49
general business risk, A6.10.51
held-to-maturity investments, A6.10.43—A6.10.45
introduction, A6.10.41
own equity instruments, A6.10.42
non-qualifying hedging instruments, A6.10.87—A6.10.88
options, A6.10.69—A6.10.73
overall net position, A6.10.19—A6.10.21
overview
criteria, A6.1.42—A6.1.43
discontinuance, A6.1.48—A6.1.51
hedging instruments, A6.1.40—A6.1.41
introduction, A6.1.37—A6.1.39
rules, A6.1.44—A6.1.47
own equity instruments, A6.10.42
partial term hedging, A6.10.29
portfolio hedging, A6.10.196—A6.10.200
portions and proportions
hedged items, A6.10.23
hedging instruments, A6.10.56—A6.10.61
risk component of financial instrument, A6.10.24—A6.10.28
risk reduction, A6.10.90

Hedging
cash flow statements, and, 30.162—30.164
current assets and liabilities, 6.269—6.270
foreign currency translations, and
foreign currency commitment, 7.132
foreign currency options, 7.139—7.142
forward exchange contracts, 7.125—7.131
future results of foreign investments, 7.135—7.137
introduction, 7.120—7.124
net investment, 7.133—7.134
speculative forward contracts, 7.138
forward purchase of stock, 6.273—6.274
gains and losses, 6.269—6.270
gross gains and losses, 6.268

Hedging—*cont.*
information table, 6.261—6.263
introduction, 6.260
item being hedged, 6.264—6.266
net investment using cross-currency swap, 6.276—6.180
non-derivative hedging, 6.267
non-equity shares, 6.127—6.129
purchase of fixed asset using option, 6.275
reserves, and, 23.124.2
Hire of plant and machinery
profit and loss account, and, 5.82—5.83
Hire purchase contracts
and see **Leases (SSAP 21)**
accounting by lessees, 19.39—19.67
accounting by lessors, 19.67.1—19.133
classification, 19.7—19.38
executive summary, 19.1—19.1.20
IFRS, and, 19.134
introduction, 19.2—19.6.1
Historical cost accounting
accounting principles, and, 2.150
current asset investments, and, 6.77—6.78
fixed asset investments, and, 6.66—6.68
Historical summaries
content of financial statements, and, 4.143—4.146
Holdings of assets and liabilities for trading
financial instruments, 6.257—6.259
Holdover relief
deferred tax, and, 13.136—13.141
Hotels
impairment, and, 18.82
Hyper-inflationary economies
FRS 24, and, 7.188—7.189
generally, 7.161—7.169

IAS 10 (Post-balance sheet events)
and see **FRS 21 (post balance sheet events)**
acquisitions and disposals, A22.43
adjusting events
assets sold or purchased before year end, A22.24—A22.25
examples, A22.20
fraud, error and irregularities, A22.30
generally, A22.18—A22.20
impairment, A22.26—A22.29
net realisable value, A22.26—A22.29
settlement of court case, A22.21—A22.23
summary, A22.4—A22.5
agriculture, and, A22.67
assets sold or purchased before year end, A22.24—A22.25
background, 22.1—22.3
breach of banking covenants, A22.48—A22.51
business combinations and, 25.355—25.356
capital commitments, A22.67
changes in asset prices, A22.46
changes in foreign exchange rates, A22.46
changes in tax rates, A22.47
Companies Act 1985, and, A22.76
comparison with GAAP, and, A22.77
date of approval of financial statements for issue
generally, A22.55—A22.58
preliminary announcements, A22.59—A22.61
definitions, A22.2—A22.3
disclosures
Listing Rules, and, A22.61.1—A22.61.3
summary, A22.8—A22.12
updating, A22.36
dividends
generally, A22.52—A22.54.6
summary, A22.6

IAS 10 (Post-balance sheet events)—*cont.*
"events after the balance sheet date", A22.2
executive summary
definitions, A22.2—A22.3
disclosures, A22.8—A22.12
going concern, A22.7
introduction, A22.1
recognition, A22.4—A22.6
financial instruments, and, A22.69
first time adoption of IFRS, and, A22.74
fraud, error and irregularities, A22.30
going concern
generally, A22.31—A22.35
summary, A22.7
impairment, A22.26—A22.29
intangible assets, and, A22.67
interests in joint ventures, and, A22.70
interim financial reporting, and, A22.71
introduction, A22.13
leases, and, A22.68
Listing Rules, and, A22.61.1—A22.61.3
net realisable value, A22.26—A22.29
non-adjusting events
acquisitions and disposals, A22.43
changes in asset prices, A22.46
changes in foreign exchange rates, A22.46
changes in tax rates, A22.47
examples, A22.39
generally, A22.37—A22.42
restructuring, A22.44—A22.45
summary, A22.10—A22.11
objectives
generally, A22.16
summary, A22.1
preliminary announcements, A22.59—A22.61
presentation of financial statements, and, A22.31
property, plant and equipment, and, A22.67
recognition, A22.4—A22.6
restructuring
generally, 21.196—21.198
introduction, A22.44—A22.45
scope
generally, A22.16—A22.17
summary, A22.1
settlement of court case, A22.21—A22.23
IAS 14 (segment reporting)
and see **Segmental reporting**
generally, 10.153
IAS 21 (foreign exchange rates)
and see **Foreign currency translation**
disclosure, A7.117—A7.122.2
first time adoption of IFRS, A7.130—A7.132
foreign currency transactions, A7.48—A7.114
functional currency approach, A7.27—A7.47
introduction, A7.1—A7.7
objectives, A7.23
other matters, A7.126—A7.127
overview, 7.188—7.189
presentation, A7.115—A7.116
scope, A7.24—A7.26
IAS 29 (hyperinflationary economies)
and see **Foreign currency translation**
generally, A7.109—A7.114
overview, 7.188—7.189
IAS 33 (earnings per share)
generally, 14.1—14.12
IFRS, and, A14.1—A14.207
IASB
and see **IFRS**
introduction, 1.4—1.6
setting IFRS standards, and, 2.217—2.222

Identification of assets and liabilities
analysing complex transactions
conditions, 3.56
introduction, 3.52
linkage with other transactions, 3.54
options, 3.55—3.58
severance of legal title, 3.53
assets, 3.59—3.62
introduction, 3.51
liabilities, 3.63—3.64
IFRIC
IASB, and, 2.219
IFRS
agency companies, and, 32.188
changes in accounting policies, and, 8.208
changes to estimation techniques, and, 8.208
discontinued operations, and, 8.208
disposal of subsidiaries, and, 26.42—26.45
dividends, and, 5.72
employee information, and, 5.71
employee share ownership schemes, and, 12.134
employee share schemes, and, 12.134
foreign currency translations, and, 7.Annex
format of financial statements, and, 4.151
fundamental errors, and, 8.208
intangible fixed assets, and
acquisition accounting, 15.139
amortisation, 15.139
control, 15.139
convergence, 15.139
definition, 15.139
disclosures, 15.139
identifiability, 15.139
impairment, 15.139
internally generated assets, 15.139
overview, 15.139
part of business acquisition, 15.139
purchased assets, 15.139
recognition criteria, 15.139
related pronouncements, 15.139
retirements, 15.139
scope, 15.139
separability, 15.139
separate acquisition, 15.139
subsequent expenditure on acquired project, 15.139
useful life, 15.139
introduction, 1.3
leases, and
classification of lease, 19.134
convergence, 19.134
disclosures, 19.134
financial lease, 19.134
introduction, 19.134
lessees, 19.134
lessors, 19.134
manufacturer/dealer lessors, 19.134
operating lease, 19.134
overview, 19.134
related pronouncements, 19.134
sale and leaseback transactions, 19.134
summary, 19.134
long-term contracts, and, 20.120
medium-sized companies, and, 32.188
merger accounting, and, 28.123—28.124
oversea companies, and, 33.57
related party transactions, and
convergence, 29.195
disclosure, 29.195
exemptions, 29.195
first time adoption of IFRS, 29.195
introduction, 29.195

IFRS—*cont.*
overview, 29.195
related parties, 29.195
related party transactions, 29.195
related pronouncements, 29.195
scope, 29.195
reporting financial performance, and
changes in accounting policies, 8.208
changes to estimation techniques, 8.208
convergence, 8.208
disclosures, 8.208
discontinued operations, 8.208
disposal groups to be abandoned, 8.208
fundamental errors, 8.208
introduction, 8.206—8.209
non-current assets to be abandoned, 8.208
presentation of non-current assets, 8.208
related pronouncements, 8.208
scope, 8.208
subsidiaries acquired exclusively with view to resale, 8.208
reporting substance of transactions, and
derecognition, 3.258
quasi-subsidiaries, 3.259
'substance over form', 3.257
segmental reporting, and, 10.153
setting IFRS standards, and, 2.217—2.222
share-based payment, and
generally, 12.25—12.26
text, A12.1—A12.245
small companies, and, 32.188
stocks, and, 20.119—20-120
substance of transactions, and
derecognition, 3.258
quasi-subsidiaries, 3.259
'substance over form', 3.257
tangible fixed assets, and
borrowing costs, 16.344
capital grants, 16.346
capitalisation of finance costs, 16.344
convergence, 16.344
cost model, 16.344
current value, 16.344
definitions, 16.344
depreciation, 16.344
derecognition, 16.344
disclosures, 16.344
exchanges of assets, 16.344
finance lease costs, 16.344
first time adoption of IFRS, 16.344
government grants, 16.346
initial measurement, 16.344
introduction, 16.344—16.344
investment properties, 16.344
market value, 16.344
overview, 16.344
recognition, 16.344
related pronouncements, 16.344
revaluation model, 16.344
scope, 16.344
subsequent costs, 16.344
subsequent measurement, 16.344
Immaterial cash test
disposal of peripheral part of business, 28.33—28.36
generally, 28.24—28.32
Impairment of fixed assets (FRS 11)
allocation of impairment losses to assets of IGUs
central assets, 18.196—18.200
generally, 18.184—18.189
goodwill previously written off to reserves, 18.210—18.211

Impairment of fixed assets (FRS 11)—*cont.*
integration of acquired business, 18.201—18.209
methods of treating goodwill, 18.190—18.195
assets carried at historical cost, 18.250—18.251
assets held for disposal
disclosure requirements, 18.263—18.269
generally, 18.214—18.220
bank branches, 18.80
brands, 18.86.1—18.86.2
building society branches, 18.80
cash flow forecasts
central overheads, 18.125—18.126
constraints, 18.128—18.159
future capital expenditure, 18.148—18.155
future reorganisations, 18.147
generally, 18.115—18.122
growth rates, 18.129—18.135
inflation, 18.127
'look-back' tests, 18.136—18.140
reorganisation expenditure, 18.141—18.155
transfer pricing between IGUs, 18.123—18.124
central assets
allocation of impairment losses, 18.196—18.200
generally, 18.91—18.97
central overheads, 18.125—18.126
Companies Act requirements
disclosure, 18.281—18.282
identification of impaired assets, 18.41—18.44
deferred tax, and, 18.19—18.20
definition of 'impairment', 18.14—18.18
depreciation, 18.212—18.213
disclosure requirements
assets carried at historical cost, 18.250—18.251
assets held for disposal, 18.263—18.269
Companies Act requirements, 18.281—18.282
fixed asset movements, 18.270—18.271
revalued assets, 18.252—18.262
revalued assets held at depreciated replacement cost, 18.274
revalued assets held at market value, 18.272—18.273
reversal, 18.280
value in use, 18.275—18.279
discount rate
generally, 18.160—18.167
pre-tax rate, 18.168—18.178
executive summary
measurement, 18.1.6—18.1.10
objective of standard, 18.1—18.1.3
presentation of losses, 18.1.11—18.1.13
recognition of losses, 18.1.11—18.1.13
reversal of past losses, 18.1.14
scope of standard, 18.1—18.1.3
when reviews required, 18.1.4—18.1.5
fixed asset movements, 18.270—18.271
future capital expenditure, 18.148—18.155
future reorganisations, 18.147
goodwill, and
first year review, 18.38—18.40
generally, 18.33—18.37
purchased goodwill, 18.98—18.114
reversal of impairment losses, 18.242—18.249
growth rates, 18.129—18.135
hotels, 18.82
identification of impaired assets
Companies Act requirements, 18.41—18.44
deferred tax, and, 18.19—18.20
goodwill, 18.33—18.40
intangible assets, 18.33—18.40
introduction, 18.14—18.18
review, 18.22—18.32

Impairment of fixed assets (FRS 11)—*cont.*
income-generating units
allocation of assets and liabilities, 18.87—18.114
bank branches, 18.80
brands, 18.86.1—18.86.2
building society branches, 18.80
central assets, 18.91—18.97
hotels, 18.82
identification, 18.64—18.86.2
indefinite-lived assets, 18.86.1—18.86.2
petrol stations, 18.83
public houses, 18.81
purchased goodwill, 18.98—18.114
retail establishments, 18.76—18.148.2
vertically integrated operations, 18.84—18.86
indefinite-lived assets, 18.86.1—18.86.2
intangible fixed assets, and
and see below
generally, 15.66—15.95
identification of impairment, 18.33—18.40
reversal of impairment losses, 18.242—18.249
integration of acquired business, 18.201—18.209
introduction, 18.2—18.7
'look-back' tests, 18.136—18.140
measurement of recoverable amount
general matters, 18.45—18.49
net realisable value, 18.50—18.56
summary, 18.1.6—18.1.10
value in use, 18.57—18.63
net realisable value, 18.50—18.56
objective of standard
generally, 18.11—18.13
summary, 18.1—18.1.3
petrol stations, 18.83
presentation and disclosures
assets carried at historical cost, 18.250—18.251
assets held for disposal, 18.263—18.269
Companies Act requirements, 18.281—18.282
fixed asset movements, 18.270—18.271
revalued assets, 18.252—18.262
revalued assets held at depreciated replacement cost, 18.274
revalued assets held at market value, 18.272—18.273
reversal, 18.280
summary, 18.1.11—18.1.13
value in use, 18.275—18.279
public houses, 18.81
purchased goodwill
generally, 18.98—18.103
guidelines, 18.104—18.114
recognition of impairment losses
allocation to assets of IGUs, 18.184—18.211
assets held for disposal, 18.214—18.220
depreciation, 18.212—18.213
parent company issues, 18.221—18.229
summary, 18.1.11—18.1.13
reorganisation expenditure
future capital expenditure, 18.148—18.155
future reorganisations, 18.147
generally, 18.141—18.146
retail establishments, 18.76—18.148.2
revalued assets
generally, 18.252—18.262
held at depreciated replacement cost, 18.274
held at market value, 18.272—18.273
reversal of impairment losses
disclosure requirements, 18.280
general rules, 18.230—18.241
goodwill, and, 18.242—18.249
intangible assets, and, 18.242—18.249

Impairment of fixed assets (FRS 11)—*cont.*
summary, 18.1.14
review of impairment
generally, 18.22—18.24
indicators, 18.25—18.32
scope of standard
generally, 18.9—18.10
summary, 18.1—18.1.3
tangible fixed assets, and, 16.97—16.99
transfer pricing, 18.123—18.124
value in use
cash flow forecasts, 18.115—18.159
disclosure requirements, 18.275—18.279
discount rate, 18.160—18.178
introduction, 18.57—18.63
vertically integrated operations, 18.84—18.86
Impairment of intangible fixed assets
identification, 18.33—18.40
IFRS, and, 15.139
introduction, 15.66—15.69
methods, 15.84—15.85
residual values, 15.82—15.83
reversal of impairment losses, and, 18.242—18.249
reviews
detailed procedure, 15.94—15.95
first year review, 15.88—15.90
introduction, 15.86—15.87
other year reviews, 15.91—15.92
useful economic life, 15.71—15.81
Impairment reviews
fixed assets, and
generally, 18.22—18.24
indicators, 18.25—18.32
intangible fixed assets, and
detailed procedure, 15.94—15.95
first year review, 15.88—15.90
introduction, 15.86—15.87
other year reviews, 15.91—15.92
summary, 15.1.12—15.1.13
Imputation system of tax
and see **Taxation**
generally, 13.9—13.17
Incentives for operating leases
accounting by lessees, 19.44—19.49
accounting by lessors, 19.77.7—19.77.10
IFRS, and, 19.134
Inception fees
revenue recognition, and, 9.136—9.139
Income-generating units (IGUs)
allocation of assets and liabilities, 18.87—18.114
bank branches, 18.80
brands, 18.86.1—18.86.2
building society branches, 18.80
central assets, 18.91—18.97
hotels, 18.82
identification, 18.64—18.86
indefinite-lived assets, 18.86.1—18.86.2
petrol stations, 18.83
public houses, 18.81
purchased goodwill, 18.98—18.114
retail establishments, 18.76—18.148.2
vertically integrated operations, 18.84—18.86
Incoming dividends
current tax, and, 13.31—13.33
Incomplete contractual programme
revenue recognition, and, 9.116—9.126
Increases in stake of business
accounting principles, 25.68—25.73
agreement with shareholder, 25.86—25.87
associate becomes subsidiary, 25.81—25.83
introduction, 25.64—25.67
Increases in stake of business—*cont.*
investment becomes subsidiary, 25.75—25.80
parent acquires part of minority, 25.84—25.85
practical examples, 25.74—25.86
Incremental costs
tangible fixed assets, and, 16.68—16.71
Indefinite-lived assets
impairment, and, 18.86.1—18.86.2
Individual financial statements
associates, and
generally, 27.98
summary, 27.1.21—27.1.22
balance sheet
accruals, 4.92—4.94
accrued income, 4.46—4.54
amounts received on account, 4.82
cash of bank and in hand, 4.55—4.71
debentures, 4.81
deferred income, 4.92—4.94
generally, 4.27—4.29
net current assets and liabilities, 4.72—4.80
other liabilities, 4.95—4.96
own shares, 4.40
participating interests, 4.39
payments on account, 4.41
prepayments,. 4.46—4.54
presentation of debtors, 4.42—4.45
trade creditors, 4.83
trade loans, 4.85—4.92
transfers from current to fixed assets, 4.30—4.38
foreign currency translations, and
average rate determination, 7.16—7.18
date of transaction, 7.15
dual rates, 7.19—7.20
exchange gains and losses, 7.25—7.31
general rules, 7.14
intra-group companies transactions, 7.32
monetary items, 7.23—7.24
non-monetary items, 7.21—7.22
settled transactions, 7.26
summary, 7.11.1—7.11.7
suspension of rates, 7.19—7.20
unsettled transactions, 7.27—7.31
foreign equity investments financed by foreign borrowings, and
generally, 7.79—7.104
summary, 7.11.16—7.11.20
joint ventures, and
generally, 27.98
summary, 27.1.21—27.1.22
profit and loss account
classification of expenses by function, 4.109
classification of expenses by type, 4.110
effect of FRS3, 4.120—4.121
generally, 4.107—4.108
particular items, rules for, 4.112—4.119
Industrial building allowances
deferred tax, and, 13.107—13.110
Influence
establishing, 29.27—29.29
examples, 29.30
introduction, 29.25
Infrastructure assets
deferred tax, and, 13.111—13.113
Infrastructure renewals
provisions, and, 21.273—21.274
Installation fees
revenue recognition, and, 9.94—9.96
Insubstance debt defeasance
reporting the substance of transactions, and, 3.184—3.185

Insurance companies
financial instruments, and, 6.52—6.53
Insurance recoveries
revenue recognition, and, 9.271—9.274
Intangible fixed assets (FRS 10)
acquisition accounting
generally, 15.41—15.45
IFRS, and, 15.139
amortisation
IFRS, and, 15.139
introduction, 15.66—15.69
methods, 15.84—15.85
residual values, 15.82—15.83
useful economic life, 15.71—15.81
capitalisation of earnings, 15.59—15.60
comparison with market transactions, 15.61—15.62
Companies Act requirements, 15.3—15.8
computer software, and, 15.135—15.138
control, 15.139
copyrights, and, 15.101—15.103
definition
control, 15.23—15.25
generally, 15.12—15.15
IFRS, and, 15.139
separability, 15.16—15.22
disclosure requirements
generally, 15.96—15.98
IFRS, 15.139
other information, 15.100
summary, 15.1.19—15.1.20
executive summary
disclosures, 15.1.19—15.1.20
impairment reviews, 15.1.12—15.1.13
'intangible assets', 15.1.1—15.1.2
measurement, 15.1.7—15.1.11
recognition, 15.1.3—15.1.6
research and development costs, 15.1.14—15.1.18
identifiability, 15.139
IFRS, and
acquisition accounting, 15.139
amortisation, 15.139
control, 15.139
convergence, 15.139
definition, 15.139
disclosures, 15.139
identifiability, 15.139
impairment, 15.139
internally generated assets, 15.139
overview, 15.139
part of business acquisition, 15.139
purchased assets, 15.139
recognition criteria, 15.139
related pronouncements, 15.139
retirements, 15.139
scope, 15.139
separability, 15.139
separate acquisition, 15.139
subsequent expenditure on acquired project, 15.139
useful life, 15.139
impairment
IFRS, and, 15.139
introduction, 15.66—15.69
methods, 15.84—15.85
residual values, 15.82—15.83
reviews, 15.86—15.95
useful economic life, 15.71—15.81
impairment reviews
detailed procedure, 15.94—15.95
first year review, 15.88—15.90
introduction, 15.86—15.87
other year reviews, 15.91—15.92

Intangible fixed assets (FRS 10)—*cont.*
summary, 15.1.12—15.1.13
'intangible assets', 15.1.1—15.1.2
internally generated assets
generally, 15.31—15.33
IFRS, and, 15.139
introduction, 15.2—15.2.1
know-how, and, 15.104—15.106
licences, and, 15.107—15.109
measurement, 15.1.7—15.1.11
part of business acquisition, 15.139
patents, and, 15.110—15.111
premium profits, 15.54—15.58
purchased assets
generally, 15.37—15.40
IFRS, and, 15.139
readily ascertainable market value, 15.27—15.30
recognition
criteria, 15.139
summary, 15.1.3—15.1.6
relief from royalties, 15.51—15.53
research and development (SSAP 13), and
amortisation, 15.125
development costs, 15.120—15.123
diminution in value provisions, 15.131—15.133
disclosure, 15.126—15.130
effect on realised reserves, 15.134
generally, 15.113—15.119
introduction, 15.112
summary, 15.1.14—15.1.18
retirements, 15.139
revaluation of assets, 15.63—15.64
scope of standard
generally, 15.9—15.11
IFRS, and, 15.139
separability
generally, 15.16—15.22
IFRS, and, 15.139
separate acquisition, 15.139
software, and, 15.135—15.138
subsequent expenditure on acquired project, 15.139
trade marks, and, 15.110—15.111
useful economic life
generally, 15.71—15.81
IFRS, and, 15.139
impairment reviews, 15.88—15.92
valuation methods
capitalisation of earnings, 15.59—15.60
comparison with market transactions, 15.61—15.62
introduction, 15.48—15.50
premium profits, 15.54—15.58
relief from royalties, 15.51—15.53
Integration of acquired business
impairment, and, 18.201—18.209
Intended disposal
tangible fixed assets, and, 16.325—16.328
Intercompany dividends
foreign currency translation, and, 7.62—7.66
Interest
capital instruments, and, 6.306
current tax, and
payable, 13.28—13.30
receivable, 13.31—13.33
Interest capitalisation
tangible fixed assets, and, 16.24—16.25
Interest cost
retirement benefits, and, 11.85—11.86
Interest held exclusively with view to subsequent resale
accounting treatment, 24.198
generally, 24.193—24.197

Interest payable
profit and loss account, and, 5.42—5.44
Interest rate risk
financial instruments, 6.209—6.215
Interest rate swaps
securitisation of assets, and, 3.156—3.158
Interest rate variations
leases, and, 19.101—19.103
Interests in losses
associates and joint ventures, and, 27.154—27.158
Interests in other entities
ASB Statement of principles, and, 2.215
Interim financial statements
consolidation rules, and, 24.321—24.325
Intermediate parent exemption
application in practice, 24.66
certified translations, 24.64—24.65
conditions, 24.62
EEA companies, 24.57—24.62.1
generally, 24.56.1—24.56.2
non-EEA group, 24.62.1.1—24.62.10
relevant date, 24.63
Internally developed assets
generally, 15.31—15.33
IFRS, and, 15.139
International Accounting Standards Board (IASB)
and see **IFRS**
introduction, 1.4—1.6
setting IFRS standards, and, 2.217—2.222
International Financial Reporting Issues Committee
IASB, and, 2.219
Inter-segment sales
segmental reporting, and, 10.81—10.85
Intra-group company transactions
cash flow statements, and, 30.158—30.161
consolidated financial statements, 7.67
individual company financial statements, 7.32
realised profits, and, 23.157—23.157.3
related party transactions, and, 29.146—29.147
Intra-group long-term loans
foreign currency translation, and, 7.70—7.75
Intra-group trading transactions
associates and joint ventures, and, 27.149—27.150
consolidation rules, and
elimination calculations, 24.337
generally, 24.332—24.336
realised profits, and, 23.157—23.157.3
Investment funds
associates and joint ventures, and, 27.27—27.29
Investment income
profit and loss account, and, 5.35—5.41
Investment manager
pension funds, and, 29.47—29.48
Investment properties (SSAP 19)
accounting requirements
generally, 17.6—17.12
summary, 17.1.1—17.1.6
balance sheet presentation, 17.13—17.14
Companies Act 1985 requirements, and
market value measurement, 17.14.1—17.14.2
true and fair override, 17.15—17.16
comparison with IFRS, and
convergence, 17.40
cost model, 17.40
definitions, 17.40
disclosure, 17.40
disposals, 17.40
exchanges, 17.40
fair value, 17.40
first-time adoption, 17.40
initial measurement, 17.40
Investment properties (SSAP 19)—*cont.*
introduction, 17.40
overview, 17.40
recognition, 17.40
related pronouncements, 17.40
scope, 17.40
subsequent expenditure, 17.40
subsequent measurement, 17.40
transfers, 17.40
cost model, 17.40
definition
generally, 17.3
summary, 17.1
diminution in value
generally, 17.20
permanent diminution in value, 17.24—17.31
temporary diminution in value, 17.21—17.23
disclosures
generally, 17.35—17.39
IFRS, and, 17.40
summary, 17.1.8—17.1.9
disposals, 17.40
exchanges, 17.40
excluded properties, 17.4
executive summary
accounting, 17.1.1—17.1.6
definition, 17.1
disclosure, 17.1.8—17.1.9
valuations, 17.1.7
fair value, 17.40
first-time adoption, 17.40
IFRS, and, 17.40
initial measurement, 17.40
introduction, 17.2—17.2.1
investment revaluation reserve
diminution in value, 17.20
generally, 17.17—17.19
negative revaluation reserves, 17.32—17.33
permanent diminution in value, 17.24—17.31
temporary diminution in value, 17.21—17.23
market value measurement, 17.14.1—17.14.2
negative revaluation reserves, 17.32—17.33
owner-occupied properties, 17.34
recognition, 17.40
SSAP 12, and, 17.1—17.2
subsequent expenditure, 17.40
subsequent measurement, 17.40
transfers, 17.40
true and fair override, 17.15—17.16
valuations, 17.1.7
Investment revaluation reserve
diminution in value, 17.20
generally, 17.17—17.19
negative revaluation reserves, 17.32—17.33
permanent diminution in value, 17.24—17.31
temporary diminution in value, 17.21—17.23
Investments
associates, and, 27.176
joint ventures, 27.176
Investors
related parties, and, 29.40—29.41
Issue and redemption premiums
capital instruments, and, 6.307
Issue costs
capital instruments, and, 6.308—6.322
Issue of shares, expenses of
fixed assets, and, 16.12

Joint and several liability
associates and joint ventures, and,
27.159—27.160

Joint arrangements (FRS 9)
accounting treatment
agreements between participants, 27.196—27.198
introduction, 27.193—27.195
limited companies, 27.203—27.204
partnerships, 27.199—27.202
unincorporated undertakings, 27.199—27.202
cash flow statements, and, 30.130
financial instruments, and, 6.116—6.121
generally, 27.177—27.178
introduction, 27.8—27.10
'joint venture with substance of', 27.191—27.192
'not an entity', 27.179—27.190
partnerships, and, 27.199—27.202
quasi-subsidiaries, and, 27.205—27.208
segmental reporting, and, 10.107
unincorporated undertakings, and, 27.199—27.202
Joint participation in management test
merger accounting, and, 28.54—28.58
Joint venture entities (FRS 9)
abnormal transactions between year ends, 27.144
accounting principles
acquisitions, 27.162—27.169
associate as group, 27.153
consolidation adjustments, 27.138—27.150
disposals, 27.170—27.1 72
extent of share, 27.119—27.122.1
financial statements, 27.136—27.137
interests in losses, 27.154—27.158
introduction, 27.116—27.118
joint and several liability, 27.159—27.160
joint venture becomes associate, 27.173
minority interests, 27.161
partnerships, 27.151—27.152
subsidiary becomes associate, 27.174—27.175
accounting requirements, 27.1.6—27.1.7
acquisitions
effective date, 27.162—27.164
generally, 27.165—27.169
additional disclosure
15% threshold information, 27.107—27.113
generally, 27.100—27.106
25% threshold information, 27.107—27.113
balance sheet
example, 27.95—27.97
goodwill, 27.88—27.93
gross equity method, 27.94
introduction, 27.85—27.87
cash flow statements, and
consolidated statements, and, 30.128—30.129
generally, 27.99
classification, 27.1.2—27.1.5
consolidation adjustments
abnormal transactions between year ends, 27.144
consistent accounting policies, 27.140
elimination of intra-group trading, 27.145—27.147
fair values, 27.141—27.143
goodwill, 27.141—27.143
intra-group trading transactions, 27.149—27.150
introduction, 27.138—27.139
transfer of assets to joint venture, 27.148
contractual arrangements, 27.1.19
convertible debt, 27.133—27.134
convertible shares, 27.132
cross-holdings, 27.135
definition, 27.55—27.67
disclosures, 27.1.23—27.1.29
disposals
effective date, 27.162—27.164
generally, 27.170—27.172
equity accounting

Joint venture entities (FRS 9)—*cont*.
additional disclosure, 27.100—27.113
balance sheet, 27.85—27.97
cash flow statement, 27.99
individual financial statements, 27.98
introduction, 27.68—27.71
optional disclosure, 27.114—27.115
principles, 27.116—27.175
profit and loss account, 27.72—27.82
segmental reporting, 27.83
statement of total recognised gains and losses, 27.84
summary, 27.1.15—27.1.18
executive summary
accounting requirements, 27.1.6—27.1.7
classification, 27.1.2—27.1.5
contractual arrangements not joint ventures, 27.1.19
disclosures, 27.1.23—27.1.29
equity accounting, 27.1.15—27.1.18
individual financial statements, 27.1.21—27.1.22
introduction, 27.1
joint arrangements not entities, 27.1.20
presentation, 27.1.8—27.1.14
scope of standard, 27.1.1
voluntary disclosures, 27.1.30
extent of share
convertible debt, 27.133—27.134
convertible shares, 27.132
cross-holdings, 27.135
introduction, 27.119—27.122.1
options, 27.123—27.131
fair values, 27.141—27.143
financial instruments, and, 6.116—6.121
financial statements, 27.136—27.137
goodwill
balance sheet, 27.88—27.93
principles, 27.141—27.143
gross equity method
generally, 27.94
introduction, 27.4—27.5
individual financial statements
generally, 27.98
summary, 27.1.21—27.1.22
interests in losses, 27.154—27.158
intra-group trading transactions, 27.149—27.150
introduction, 27.2—27.11
investment funds, 27.27—27.29.1
investments by single company, 27.176
joint and several liability, 27.159—27.160
joint arrangements not entities, 27.1.20
minority interests, 27.161
options, 27.123—27.131
participating interest, 27.2—27.3
presentation, 27.1.8—27.1.14
profit and loss account
example, 27.82
introduction, 27.72
notes, 27.80—27.81
operating results, 27.75—27.76
other line items, 27.78
satisfying requirements, 27.79
super-exceptional items, 27.77
turnover, 27.73—27.74
related parties, and, 29.38—29.39
related party transactions, and, 29.135
scope of standard
generally, 27.25—27.26
investment funds, 27.27—27.29.1
summary, 27.1.1
segmental reporting, and
generally, 10.100—10.106

Joint venture entities (FRS 9)—*cont*.
introduction, 27.83
statement of total recognised gains and losses, 27.84
transfer of assets, 27.148
venture capital funds, 27.27—27.29.1
voluntary disclosures, 27.1.30
voting rights, 27.50—27.54

Key management
related parties, and, 29.52—29.54
related party transactions, and, 29.144
Know-how
intangible fixed assets, and, 15.104—15.106

Labour costs
tangible fixed assets, and, 16.66—16.67
Leasehold properties
onerous contracts, and, 21.194—21.196
Leases (SSAP 21)
accounting by lessees
disclosure requirements, 19.50—19.53
finance leases, 19.39—19.42
operating leases, 19.43—19.49
sale and leaseback transactions, 19.54—19.67
summary, 19.1.7—19.1.13
accounting by lessors
back-to-back leases, 19.111—19.119
direct costs, 19.90—19.95
disclosure requirements, 19.78—19.89
finance leases, 19.68—19.75
FLA SORP, 19.67.1—19.67.4
manufacturer/dealer lessors, 19.105—19.110
operating leases, 19.76—19.77.10
rental variation, 19.96—19.104
residual values, 19.120—19.133
summary, 19.1.14—19.1.18
back-to-back leases
introduction, 19.111—19.112
head lessor, 19.113
intermediate party, 19.114—19.119
classification
generally, 19.7—19.14
IFRS, and, 19.134
implicit interest rate, 19.29—19.31
minimum payments, 19.21—19.28
present value calculation, 19.32—19.33
property leases, 19.34—19.38
summary, 19.1.1—19.1.6
term, 19.14.2—19.20
comparison with IFRS, and, 19.134
construction periods, 19.104
deferred tax, and, 13.122—13.125.1
direct costs, 19.90—19.95
disclosure requirements
accounting by lessees, 19.50—19.53
accounting by lessors, 19.78—19.89
executive summary
classification of leases, 19.1.1—19.1.6
introduction, 19.1
lessee accounting, 19.1.7—19.1.13
lessor accounting, 19.1.14—19.1.18
sale and leaseback, 19.1.19—19.1.20
finance leasebacks, 19.55—19.59
finance leases (accounting by lessees)
disclosure requirements, 19.50—19.53
generally, 19.39—19.42
IFRS, and, 19.134
residual values, 19.126
finance leases (accounting by lessors)
disclosure requirements, 19.78—19.89
actuarial after-tax method, 19.75

Leases (SSAP 21)—*cont*.
generally, 19.68—19.74
IFRS, and, 19.134
FLA SORP, 19.67.1—19.67.4
IFRS, and, 19.134
incentives for operating leases
accounting by lessees, 19.44—19.49
accounting by lessors, 19.77.7—19.77.10
IFRS, and, 19.134
interest rate variations, 19.101—19.103
introduction, 19.2—19.6.1
lessee accounting
disclosure requirements, 19.50—19.53
finance leases, 19.39—19.42
operating leases, 19.43—19.49
sale and leaseback transactions, 19.54—19.67
summary, 19.1.7—19.1.13
lessor accounting
back-to-back leases, 19.111—19.119
direct costs, 19.90—19.95
disclosure requirements, 19.78—19.89
finance leases, 19.68—19.75
FLA SORP, 19.67.1—19.67.4
manufacturer/dealer lessors, 19.105—19.110
operating leases, 19.76—19.77.10
rental variation, 19.96—19.104
residual values, 19.120—19.133
summary, 19.1.14—19.1.18
manufacturer/dealer lessors
generally, 19.105—19.110
IFRS, and, 19.134
operating leasebacks, 19.60—19.63
operating leases (accounting by lessees)
disclosure requirements, 19.52—19.53
generally, 19.43
IFRS, and, 19.134
incentives, 19.44—19.49
residual values, 19.123—19.125
operating leases (accounting by lessors)
disclosure requirements, 19.80—19.89
generally, 19.76—19.77.6
IFRS, and, 19.134
incentives, 19.77.7—19.77.10
rental variation
construction periods, 19.104
interest rate variations, 19.101—19.103
tax variation clauses, 19.96—19.97
repurchase options, 19.64—19.67
residual values
finance leases, under, 19.126
fluctuations in anticipated residual values, 19.127—19.131
introduction, 19.120—19.121
operating leases, under, 19.123—19.125
tax-free grants, 19.132—19.133
sale and leaseback transactions
finance leasebacks, 19.55—19.59
IFRS, and, 19.134
introduction, 19.54
operating leasebacks, 19.60—19.63
repurchase options, 19.64—19.67
summary, 19.1.19—19.1.20
sub leases
introduction, 19.111—19.112
head lessor, 19.113
intermediate party, 19.114—19.119
tax-free grants, 19.132—19.133
tax variation clauses, 19.96—19.97
Lessee accounting
disclosure requirements, 19.50—19.53
finance leasebacks, 19.55—19.59

Lessee accounting—*cont*.
finance leases
disclosure requirements, 19.50—19.53
generally, 19.39—19.42
IFRS, and, 19.134
residual values, 19.126
operating leasebacks, 19.60—19.63
operating leases
disclosure requirements, 19.52—19.53
generally, 19.43
IFRS, and, 19.134
incentives, 19.44—19.49
repurchase options, 19.64—19.67
sale and leaseback transactions
finance leasebacks, 19.55—19.59
IFRS, and, 19.134
introduction, 19.54
operating leasebacks, 19.60—19.63
repurchase options, 19.64—19.67
summary, 19.1.19—19.1.20
summary, 19.1.7—19.1.13
Lessor accounting
back-to-back leases
introduction, 19.111—19.112
head lessor, 19.113
intermediate party, 19.114—19.119
comparison with IFRS, and, 19.134
construction periods, 19.104
direct costs, 19.90—19.95
disclosure requirements, 19.78—19.89
finance leases
disclosure requirements, 19.78—19.89
actuarial after-tax method, 19.75
generally, 19.68—19.74
IFRS, and, 19.134
FLA SORP, 19.67.1—19.67.4
IFRS, and, 19.134
incentives for operating leases
generally, 19.77.7—19.77.10
IFRS, and, 19.134
interest rate variations, 19.101—19.103
manufacturer/dealer lessors
generally, 19.105—19.110
IFRS, and, 19.134
operating leases
disclosure requirements, 19.80—19.89
generally, 19.76—19.77.6
incentives, 19.77.7—19.77.10
IFRS, and, 19.134
rental variation
construction periods, 19.104
interest rate variations, 19.101—19.103
tax variation clauses, 19.96—19.97
residual values
finance leases, under, 19.126
fluctuations in anticipated residual values, 19.127—19.131
introduction, 19.120—19.121
operating leases, under, 19.123—19.125
tax-free grants, 19.132—19.133
sale and leaseback transactions
finance leasebacks, 19.55—19.59
IFRS, and, 19.134
introduction, 19.54
operating leasebacks, 19.60—19.63
repurchase options, 19.64—19.67
summary, 19.1.19—19.1.20
sub leases
introduction, 19.111—19.112
head lessor, 19.113
intermediate party, 19.114—19.119
Lessor accounting—*cont*.
summary, 19.1.14—19.1.18
tax-free grants, 19.132—19.133
tax variation clauses, 19.96—19.97
Liabilities
identification and recognition, and, 3.63—3.64
Liability method
balance sheet, 13.73—13.78
general, 13.57—13.59
income statement, 13.63—13.72
with full provisioning, 13.62—13.71
with partial provisioning, 13.60—13.61
License income
revenue recognition, and, 9.256—9.258
Licences
intangible fixed assets, and, 15.107—15.109
Limited partnerships
accounting for as part of portfolio, 24.212.12
accounting for interests in subsidiaries, 24.212.13—24.212.15
associated undertakings, 24.212.9
consolidation by general partner, 24.212.2—24.212.4
implications of financial statements, 24.212.16
interest more than 50%, 24.212.10
introduction, 24.212.1—24.212.2
joint ventures, 24.212.9
long-term restrictions do not apply, 24.212.11
long-term restrictions on general partner's control, 24.212.5—24.212.8
Linked presentation
cash flow statement, 3.251
debt factoring, 3.136.11—3.136.12
detailed conditions, 3.88—3.90
general rules, 3.83—3.87
linking part of finance, 3.91—3.92
profit recognition, 3.93—3.96
quasi-subsidiaries, and, 3.113—3.114
summary, 3.1.8—3.1.13
Linked transactions
revenue recognition, and, 9.158—9.160
Liquid resources
definition, 30.44—30.49
management, 30.102—30.106
Listed companies
content of financial statements, and, 4.143—4.146
financial instruments, and, 6.41—6.47
Litigation
provisions, and, 21.258—21.265
Loan for acquisition of own shares
financial instruments, and, 6.145
Loan to directors
related party transactions, and, 29.176
Loan to officers
related party transactions, and, 29.177
Loan transfers
disclosure requirements, 3.178—3.179
generally, 3.168—3.177
Local currency
foreign currency translation, and, 7.57—7.58
Long-term contracts (SSAP 9)
accounting treatment, 20.74—20.75
claims, 20.94—20.95
comparison with IFRS, and, 20.120
construction contracts, 20.120
cost of sales, 20.99—20.102
definition, 20.72—20.73.1
disclosure requirements
generally, 20.106—20.114
provision for foreseeable losses, 20.115—20.118
summary, 20.1.16—20.1.18
executive summary

Long-term contracts (SSAP 9)—*cont.*
disclosure, 20.1.16—20.1.18
generally, 20.1.9—20.1.15
future costs, 20.89—20.91
generally, 20.1.9—20.1.15
IFRS, and, 20.120
introduction, 20.71
losses, 20.96—20.98
onerous contracts, and, 21.211
profit recognition
amounts recoverable on contracts, 20.103—20.105
claims, 20.94—20.95
cost of sales, 20.99—20.102
determination of future costs, 20.89—20.91
generally, 20.78—20.88
losses on contracts, 20.96—20.98
variations, 20.92—20.93
recoverable amounts, 20.103—20.105
small companies, and, 32.74
summary, 20.1.9—20.1.15
turnover, 20.76—20.77
variations, 20.92—20.93
Long-term purchase contracts
onerous contracts, and, 21.211
'Look-back' tests
impairment, and, 18.136—18.140
Losses
consolidation rules, and, 24.339
long-term contracts, and, 20.96—20.98
Loyalty schemes
revenue recognition, and, 9.240—9.245

Maintenance
provisions, and, 21.268
Major inspections and overhauls
tangible fixed assets, and, 16.150—16.153
Management contracts
related parties, and, 29.58—29.59
Manufacturer/dealer lessors
generally, 19.105—19.110
IFRS, and, 19.134
Marked to market
deferred tax, and, 13.131—13.135.1
financial instruments, and, 6.86—6.88
Market price risk
financial instruments, and, 6.281—6.287
Market value measurement
investment properties, and, 17.14.1—17.14.2
Matching shares
accounting implications, 12.100—12.102
introduction, 12.88
Material balances
taxation, and, 13.263—13.266
Material interest transactions
related party transactions, and, 29.179—29.180
Materiality
ASB Statement of principles, and, 2.198—2.204
related party transactions, and
Companies Act, and, 29.84—29.86
general purpose financial statements, 29.82—29.83
generally, 29.77—29.81
Maturity analyses
financial liabilities, of, 6.216—6.220
undrawn committed borrowing facilities, of, 6.221—6.223
Measurement
ASB Statement of principles, and, 2.212
capital instruments, and
contingent payments, 6.352—6.355
initial recognition, 6.345
renegotiation of debt, 6.362—6.371

Measurement—*cont.*
repurchase of debt, 6.356—6.361
subsequent recognition, 6.351
treatment of finance costs, 6.346—6.350
current tax, and
generally, 13.44—13.50
summary, 13.1.6
deferred tax, and
average rates, 13.173—13.175
introduction, 13.171—13.172
summary, 13.1.18
financial instruments, and
current asset investments, 6.76—6.78
fair value accounting, 6.79—6.88
fixed asset investments, 6.66—6.75
generally, 6.64—6.65
financial instruments (IFRS), and
and see **Measurement of financial instruments (IFRS)**
introduction, A6.9.1—A6.9.3
impairment, and
general matters, 18.45—18.49
net realisable value, 18.50—18.56
summary, 18.1.6—18.1.10
value in use, 18.57—18.63
intangible fixed assets, 15.1.7—15.1.11
onerous contracts, and, 21.214—21.218
provisions, and
application of rules, 21.142.2—21.142.6
best estimate, 21.110—21.118
changes in discount rates, 21.139—21.142.1
changes in estimate, 21.135—21.138.1
changes in estimate of provisions, 21.142.2—21.142.6
discounting, 21.119—21.132
future events, 21.143—21.146
introduction, 21.109
related asset, 21.133—21.134
summary, 21.1.8—21.1.11
retirement benefits, and
scheme assets, 11.62—11.67
scheme liabilities, 11.68—11.73
summary, 11.1.4—11.1.8
revenue recognition, and
advertising agency commissions, 9.172
agency arrangements, 9.161—9.171
barter transactions, 9.187—9.199
capacity transactions, 9.201—9.2
generally, 9.42—9.55
settlement discounting, 9.185—9.186
two-way trading arrangements, 9.176—9.184
volume discounting, 9.185—9.186
share capital, and, 23.11—23.17
tangible fixed assets, and
cost, 16.55—16.
implementation of standard, and, 16.331—16.332
introduction, 16.51—16.54
summary, 16.1.1—16.1.4
Measurement of financial instruments (IFRS)
amortised cost (effective interest method)
amortisation period, A6.9.60—A6.9.61
changes in estimated cash flows, A6.9.63—A6.9.64
estimation of cash flows, A6.9.54—A6.9.58
examples, A6.9.62
fixed interest instruments, A6.9.62
floating rate instruments, A6.9.66—A6.9.69
general, A6.9.51—A6.9.53
issuer call option in debt instruments, A6.9.65
perpetual debt instruments, A6.9.70—A6.9.71
transaction costs and fees, A6.9.59
available-for-sale assets, A6.9.29—A6.9.35

Measurement of financial instruments (IFRS)—*cont*.
commitment fees, A6.9.15
direct loan origination fees, A6.9.16
effective interest method
amortisation period, A6.9.60—A6.9.61
changes in estimated cash flows, A6.9.63—A6.9.64
estimation of cash flows, A6.9.54—A6.9.58
examples, A6.9.62
fixed interest instruments, A6.9.62
floating rate instruments, A6.9.66—A6.9.69
general, A6.9.51—A6.9.53
issuer call option in debt instruments, A6.9.65
perpetual debt instruments, A6.9.70—A6.9.71
transaction costs and fees, A6.9.59
fair value measurement
credit risk of liabilities, A6.9.112—A6.9.113
day '1' gain or loss, A6.9.107—A6.9.109
demand deposit liabilities, A6.9.110—A6.9.111
general, A6.9.72—A6.9.76
initial measurement, A6.9.4—A6.9.9
quoted prices in active markets, A6.9.77—A6.9.103
unquoted equity instruments and related derivatives, A6.9.104—A6.9.106
fair value through profit or loss, at
subsequent measurement of assets, A6.9.23—A6.9.25
subsequent measurement of liabilities, A6.9.45—A6.9.46
financial assets carried at amortised cost
absence of observable data, A6.9.144—A6.9.145
appropriate discount rate, A6.9.132—A6.9.135
bad and doubtful debts, A6.9.146—A6.9.147
evaluation of impairment on portfolio bias, A6.9.136—A6.9.143
general requirements, A6.9.126—A6.9.131
interest on impaired assets, A6.9.147—A6.9.149
reversal of impairment losses, A6.9.150
financial guarantee contracts, A6.9.48
foreign currency financial instruments
assets held in foreign operations, A6.9.168
general, A6.9.158—A6.9.160
impairment of assets, A6.9.165—A6.9.167
monetary financial assets, A6.9.162—A6.9.163
non-monetary financial assets, A6.9.164
subsequent measurement, A6.9.161—A6.9.168
general rule, A6.9.1
hedged items
subsequent measurement of assets, A6.9.36
subsequent measurement of liabilities, A6.9.50
held-to-maturity investments, A6.9.28
impairment of financial assets
available-for-sale assets, A6.9.152—A6.9.153
carried at amortised cost, A6.9.126—A6.9.150
carried at cost, A6.9.151
equity instruments, for, A6.9.123—A6.9.125
foreign currency instruments, A6.9.158—A6.9.
generally, A6.9.114—A6.9.116
incurred vs expected losses, A6.9.117—A6.9.119
objective evidence, A6.9.120—A6.9.122
reversal of losses, A6.9.154—A6.9.157
initial measurement
commitment fees, A6.9.15
direct loan origination fees, A6.9.16
general rule, A6.9.1
initial fair value, A6.9.4—A6.9.9
loan origination fees, A6.9.14
settlement date accounting for regular way transactions, A6.9.20
transaction costs, A6.9.10—A6.9.19
introduction, A6.9.1—A6.9.3
loan origination fees, A6.9.14

Measurement of financial instruments (IFRS)—*cont*.
loans and receivables, A6.9.26—A6.9.27
negative fair values, A6.9.42
off-market loans, A6.9.49
overview, A6.1.31—A6.1.36
quoted prices in active markets
ask prices, A6.9.82—A6.9.85
bid prices, A6.9.82—A6.9.85
inputs to valuation techniques, A6.9.94
introduction, A6.9.77—A6.9.81
large blocks of instruments, A6.9.88
other valuation techniques, A6.9.100—A6.9.103
price information about similar instruments, A6.9.98—A6.9.99
recent transaction prices, A6.9.95—A6.9.97
unavailability of published prices, A6.9.86—A6.9.87
valuation in absence of active market, A6.9.89—A6.9.93
reclassifications between categories, A6.9.37—A6.9.39
regular way transactions
initial measurement, A6.9.20
subsequent measurement, A6.9.40—A6.9.41
settlement date accounting for regular way transactions
initial measurement, A6.9.20
subsequent measurement, A6.9.40—A6.9.41
subsequent measurement of assets
available-for-sale assets, A6.9.29—A6.9.35
fair value through profit or loss, at, A6.9.23—A6.9.25
general, A6.9.21
hedged items, A6.9.36
held-to-maturity investments, A6.9.28
loans and receivables, A6.9.26—A6.9.27
negative fair values, A6.9.42
reclassifications between categories, A6.9.37—A6.9.39
settlement date accounting for regular way transactions, A6.9.40—A6.9.41
subsequent measurement of liabilities
fair value through profit or loss, at, A6.9.45—A6.9.46
financial guarantee contracts, A6.9.48
hedged items, A6.9.50
introduction, A6.9.43—A6.9.44
off-market loans, A6.9.49
transfer of assets, on, A6.9.47
transaction costs, A6.9.10—A6.9.19
transfer of assets, A6.9.47

Medium-sized companies
abbreviated financial statements, 32.134—32.139
accounting standards, 32.28—32.29
audit requirements
introduction, 32.30
summary, 32.34
auditors' reports, 32.140—32.142
cash flow statements, and, 30.35—30.37
categorisation
other criteria, 32.40—32.42
size criteria, 32.35—32.39
Companies Act requirements, 32.11—32.22
consolidated financial statements, and, 24.35—24.36
excluded companies, 32.50—32.52
financial statements
abbreviated financial statements, 32.134—32.139
auditors' reports, 32.140—32.142
introduction, 32.133
IFRS, and, 32.188
introduction, 32.1—32.10
regulatory framework

Medium-sized companies—*cont.*
accounting standards, 32.28—32.29
audit requirements, 32.30
Companies Act requirements, 32.11—32.22
related party transactions, and, 29.163—29.165
Medium-sized groups
and see **Medium-sized companies**
abbreviated financial statements, 32.154
categorisation
other criteria, 32.47—32.49
size criteria, 32.44—32.46
consolidated financial statements
exemptions, 32.148—32.153
shorter-form, 32.155—32.159
excluded groups, 32.50—32.52
introduction, 32.147
Medium-sized parent companies
generally, 32.143—32.146
Membership of qualifying undertaking
group structure, and, 24.247—24.251
share capital, and, 23.236—23.237
Merger accounting
accounting periods, 28.106—28.108
acquisition accounting comparison, 28.109—28.111
conditions
full participation in future performance test, 28.62—28.64
immaterial cash test, 28.24—28.36
introduction, 28.9—28.13
joint participation in management test, 28.54—28.58
90% per cent holding test, 28.21—28.23
no identifiable acquirer test, 28.46—28.53
non-equity consideration test, 28.24—28.36
offer to shareholders test, 28.14—28.18
relative size test, 28.59—28.61
vendor placings, 28.37—28.45
consolidated financial statements, 28.112—28.122
criteria, 28.1—28.1.4
disclosure requirements
generally, 28.112—28.122
summary, 27.1.9—27.1.10
executive summary
criteria, 28.1—28.1.4
disclosure, 27.1.9—27.1.10
group reconstructions, 28.1.5—28.1.6
principles, 28.1.7—28.1.8
expenses, 28.98—28.105
full participation in future performance test, 28.62—28.64
group reconstructions
generally, 28.74—28.80
summary, 28.1.5—28.1.6
immaterial cash test
disposal of peripheral part of business, 28.33—28.36
generally, 28.24—28.32
IFRS, and, 28.123—28.124
introduction, 28.2—28.6
joint participation in management test, 28.54—28.58
90% per cent holding test, 28.21—28.23
no identifiable acquirer test, 28.46—28.53
non-equity consideration test
disposal of peripheral part of business, 28.33—28.36
generally, 28.24—28.32
offer to shareholders test, 28.14—28.18
principles
difference on consolidation, 28.92—28.97
group reconstructions, 28.74—28.80
introduction, 28.65—28.70
Merger accounting—*cont.*
investment in acquired company, 28.83—28.86
other forms of business combinations, 28.81—28.82
summary, 28.1.7—28.1.8
use of new parent company, 28.71—28.73
relative size test, 28.59—28.61
vendor placings, 28.37—28.45
Merger relief
acquisition accounting, and, 25.13
application of, 23.100—23.104
generally, 23.96—23.99
group reconstructions, 23.105—23.112
Mergers
reporting financial performance, and, 8.77—8.78
Milestone payments
revenue recognition, and, 9.134—9.135
Minority interests
associates, and, 27.161
cash flow statements, and, 30.126—30.127
consolidated financial statements, and
acquisition of direct subsidiary, 24.377
acquisition of indirect subsidiary, 24.378
auction market preferred shares, 24.366—24.367
balance sheets, 24.357—24.359
basis of recognition, 24.353—24.354
compulsory acquisition, 24.379
definition, 24.346—24.350
director's interests, 24.369—24.370
equity, 24.356
fair value, and, 24.381—24.382
indirect holdings, 24.375—24.376
introduction, 24.344—24.345
loss making subsidiaries, 24.383—24.388
measurement, 24.355, 24.371—34.374
minority or majority interests, 24.351—24.352
presentation in financial statements, 24.357—24.365
profit and loss account, 24.360—24.365
stapled shares, 24.368
summary, 24.1.13—24.1.15
treatment on acquisition, 24.377—24.382
financial instruments, and, 6.20
joint ventures, and, 27.161
Mixed contracts
revenue recognition, and
allocation of consideration, 9.148—9.156
linked transactions, 9.158—9.160
separation of components, 9.145—9.147
Modified historical cost convention
accounting principles, and, 2.151
Movements in reserves
reporting financial performance, and, 8.160—8.164
Multi-currency share capital
foreign currency translations, and, 7.170—7.171
generally, 23.42—23.45
Multi-employer schemes
retirement benefits, and
disclosure, 11.41—11.42.2
generally, 11.37—11.41.8
summary, 11.1.2
Multi-originator programmes
securitisation of assets, and, 3.166
Mutual life assurance companies
cash flow statements, and, 30.26

Narrative statements
provisions, and, 21.297—21.298
National insurance contributions on gains
background, 12.27—12.34
introduction, 12.11—12.12
practical application, 12.78—12.80

National insurance contributions on gains—*cont.*
reimbursement of liability, 12.36—12.39
requirements of abstract, 12.65—12.72
transfer of liability, 12.36—12.39
Nature of financial instruments (IFRS)
conditional rights and obligations, A6.4.13—A6.4.15
contingent rights and obligations, A6.4.13—A6.4.15
contractual basis, A6.4.8—A6.4.12
definitions
equity instrument, A6.4.6
financial asset, A6.4.4
financial instrument, A6.4.3
financial liability, A6.4.5
introduction, A6.4.2
key features, A6.4.7
derivatives
accounting, A6.4.42
contracts to buy or sell non-financial items, A6.4.39
definition, A6.4.25
examples, A6.4.38
initial net investment, A6.4.33—A6.4.34
introduction, A6.4.23—A6.4.24
key features, A6.4.26—A6.4.37
notional amounts, A6.4.31—A6.4.32
payment provisions, A6.4.31—A6.4.32
regular way contracts, A6.4.41
settlement at future date, A6.4.35—A6.4.37
'underlying', A6.4.27—A6.4.30
exchange under potentially favourable or unfavourable terms, A6.4.16
identification, A6.4.22
introduction, A6.4.1
non-derivative transactions, A6.4.40
non-financial assets and liabilities, and, A6.4.17—A6.4.21
overview, A6.1.8—A6.1.13
Negative goodwill
acquisition accounting, and, 25.1.21—25.1.22
Negative revaluation reserves
investment properties, and, 17.32—17.33
Net cash flows
cash flow statements, and, 30.59—30.63
Net current assets and liabilities
balance sheet, and
classification as long or short-term, 4.77—4.80
disclosure, 4.73—4.76
generally, 4.72
Net debt reconciliation
analysis of changes, 30.123—30.124
generally, 30.119—30.122.1
Net investment
foreign currency hedging, and, 7.133—7.134
Net investment using cross-currency swap
hedging, and, 6.133—6.137
Net realisable value
impairment, and, 18.50—18.56
stocks, and, 20.28—20.33
90% per cent holding test
merger accounting, and, 28.21—28.23
90% subsidiaries
related party transactions, and, 29.149—29.157.1
No identifiable acquirer test
merger accounting, and, 28.46—28.53
Non-audit work
auditor's remuneration, and, 5.55—5.63
Non-availability penalties
PFI and PPP, and, 3.179.38—3.179.40
Non-depreciation of tangible fixed assets
background, 16.28—16.30
generally, 16.284—16.290.1
implementation of standard, and, 16.340—16.345
Non-depreciation of tangible fixed assets—*cont.*
introduction, 16.279—16.283
non-depreciable land, 16.291
Non-derivative hedging
hedging, and, 6.124
Non-equity consideration test
disposal of peripheral part of business, 28.33—28.36
generally, 28.24—28.32
Non-equity minority interests
financial instruments, and, 6.181—6.184
Non-equity shares
financial instruments, and, 6.181—6.184
Non-operating exceptional items
reporting financial performance, and, 8.84—8.87
taxation, and, 13.245—13.248
Non-pension post-retirement benefits
accounting treatment, 11.199—11.204
disclosure requirements, 11.206—11.207
introduction, 11.195—11.198
Norwalk Agreement
generally, 1.4
Note of historical cost profits and losses
generally, 8.169—8.182
Notes to financial statements
accounting policies, 4.134—4.136
additional statements required by FRS3, 4.131
compliance with accounting standards, 4.132
current tax, and, 13.238
dividends, 4.139
financial instruments, 4.137
general requirements, 4.125—4.130
joint ventures, and, 27.80—27.81
reserves and dividends, 4.139
small companies, and
balance sheet, 32.90—32.92
profit and loss account, 32.93—32.97
true and fair override disclosures, 4.133
Notes to cash flow statements
comparative figures, 30.176—30.177
specific disclosures, 30.165
supplementary disclosures, 30.166—30.175

Obsolescence
PFI and PPP, and, 3.179.44
Offer to shareholders test
merger accounting, and, 28.14—28.18
Offsetting
format of financial statement, and, 4.25—4.26
individual company financial statements, and, 7.83—7.86
reporting the substance of transactions, and
generally, 3.97—3.99
summary, 3.1.18
taxation, and, 13.258—13.262
Onerous contracts
executory contracts, 21.197
financial instruments including derivatives, 21.198
general rules, 21.199—21.201
illustrative examples
generally, 21.210
long-term purchase contracts, 21.211
operating leases on property, 21.212—21.213
interpretation
asserts dedicated to the contract, 21.206—21.209
expected economic benefits, 21.202—21.205
introduction, 21.193
leasehold properties, 21.194—21.196
measurement, 21.214—21.218
Open-ended investment funds
cash flow statements, and, 30.28—30.29

Index

Open market value
tangible fixed assets, and, 16.190—16.192
Operating activities
cash flow statements, and, 30.67—30.75
Operating leasebacks
leases, and, 19.60—19.63
Operating leases
accounting by lessees
disclosure requirements, 19.52—19.53
generally, 19.43
incentives, 19.44—19.49
residual values, 19.123—19.125
accounting by lessors
disclosure requirements, 19.80—19.89
generally, 19.76—19.77.6
incentives, 19.77.7—19.77.10
IFRS, and, 19.134
introduction, 19.1.3
onerous contracts, and, 21.212—21.213
profit and loss account, and, 5.82—5.83
provisions, and, 21.271
Operating leases on property
onerous contracts, and, 21.212—21.213
provisions, and, 21.235—21.236
Operating profit
reporting financial performance, and, 8.13—8.19.1
Operating results
associates and joint ventures, and, 27.75—27.76
Operations discontinued by closure
generally, 8.58—8.59
provisions for losses, 8.60—8.69
Operations discontinued by sale
generally, 8.37—8.38
goodwill, 8.54—8.57
profits and losses, 8.39—8.53
Option, purchase of fixed asset using
hedging, and, 6.131—6.132
Options
as part of sales transaction, 9.223—9.236
associates and joint ventures, and, 27.123—27.131
capital instruments, and, 6.329—6.340
for consideration, 9.219—9.222
without consideration, 9.237—9.238
Originator's financial statements
disclosure requirements, 3.148—3.150
generally, 3.144—3.147
Outgoing dividends
taxation, and, 13.28—13.30
Override disclosures
generally, 2.41—2.44
investment properties, 17.15—17.16
notes to balance sheet and profit and loss account, 4.133
quasi-subsidiaries, 3.107
Oversea companies
accounting records, 33.23
audit requirements, 33.53
branches
filing of financial statements, 33.43—33.50
financial statements, 33.36—33.37
generally, 33.11—33.13
particulars to be registered, 33.21—33.22
reference period, 33.26
registration, 33.17
definition, 33.8
filing of financial statements
branches, 33.43—33.50
introduction, 33.38
place of business, 33.39—33.42
financial statements
branches, 33.36—33.37

Oversea companies—*cont.*
introduction, 33.27
place of business, 33.28—33.35
IFRS, and, 33.57
introduction, 33.1—33.7
listed, 33.51—33.52
particulars to be registered
branches, 33.21—33.22
place of business, 33.19—33.20
place of business
filing of financial statements, 33.39—33.42
financial statements, 33.28—33.35
generally, 33.9—33.10
particulars to be registered, 33.19—33.20
registration, 33.16
practical issues, 33.54—33.56
reference period
branches, 33.26
place of business, 33.24—33.25
registration
branches, 33.17
generally, 33.14—33.15
place of business, 33.16
reference period, 33.24—33.25
Overseas branches
filing of financial statements, 33.43—33.50
financial statements, 33.36—33.37
generally, 33.11—33.13
particulars to be registered, 33.21—33.22
reference period, 33.26
registration, 33.17
Own shares
balance sheet, and, 4.40
financial instruments, and, 6.137—6.142
Own work capitalised
profit and loss account, and, 5.14
Owner-occupation
investment properties, and, 17.34

Parent companies
and see **Group structure**
consolidated financial statements, and, 24.33—24.34
disclosure requirements, 24.238—24.246
financial instruments, and, 6.131
financial statements
carrying value of investment, 25.49—25.58
pre-acquisition reserves, 25.62—25.63
membership of qualified undertaking, 24.247—24.251
related parties, and, 29.36—29.37
Parent undertakings
group structure, and, 24.26—24.31
Partial derecognition
generally, 3.181—3.182
transactions in previously recognised assets, 3.74—3.81
Partial disposal of subsidiaries
becoming an associate, 26.32
becoming an associate, 26.33
generally, 26.27—26.30
remaining a subsidiary, 26.31
Participating interests
associates and joint ventures, and, 27.2—27.3
balance sheet, and, 4.39
financial instruments, and, 6.112—6.115
Partnership shares
accounting implications, 12.96—12.99
introduction, 12.88
Partnerships
joint arrangements, and, 27.199—27.202
joint venture entities, and, 27.151—27.152
related parties, and, 29.65—29.67

Past event
introduction, 21.54—21.56
legal enforcement, 21.57—21.60
third party expectation, 21.61—21.64
Past service costs
retirement benefits, and, 11.93—11.99
Patents
intangible fixed assets, and, 15.110—15.111
Payments in advance
revenue recognition, and, 9.73—9.74
Payments on account
balance sheet, and, 4.41
tangible fixed assets, and, 16.43—16.46
Pension contributions
related party transactions, and, 29.158
Pension costs
deferred tax, and
generally, 13.126—13.126.10
SSAP 24, 11.184—11.194
FRS 17, and
and see **Retirement benefits**
defined benefit schemes, 11.43—11.164
defined contribution schemes, 11.31—11.36
executive summary, 11.1—11.1.24
introduction, 11.2—11.30
multi-employer schemes, 11.37—11.42.2
introduction, 11.1
Pensions Act 2004, and
introduction, 11.170—11.172
minimum funding objective, 11.179—11.182
moral hazard precisions, 11.177—11.178
Pensions Protection Fund, 11.173—11.175
Pensions Regulator, 11.176
statutory funding objective, 11.179—11.182
provisions, and, 21.300—21.302
SSAP 24, and, 11.2—11.3
types of pension scheme
defined benefit schemes, 11.19
defined contribution schemes, 11.18
funded schemes, 11.20—11.22.1
introduction, 11.12—11.17
unfounded schemes, 11.23
Pension funds
related parties, and
generally, 29.44—29.46
investment manager, 29.47—29.48
related party transactions, and, 29.136
Pension schemes
cash flow statements, and, 30.27
defined benefit schemes, 11.19
defined contribution schemes, 11.18
funded schemes, 11.20—11.22.1
introduction, 11.12—11.17
Pensions Act 2004, and
introduction, 11.170—11.172
minimum funding objective, 11.179—11.182
moral hazard precisions, 11.177—11.178
Pensions Protection Fund, 11.173—11.175
Pensions Regulator, 11.176
statutory funding objective, 11.179—11.182
unfounded schemes, 11.23
Performance
revenue recognition, and, 9.27—9.41
retirement benefits, and, 11.1.13
Performance over time
incomplete contractual performance, 9.116—9.126
stage of completion, 9.127—9.132
Petrol stations
impairment, and, 18.83
Place of business
oversea companies, and

Place of business—*cont.*
filing of financial statements, 33.39—33.42
financial statements, 33.28—33.35
generally, 33.9—33.10
particulars to be registered, 33.19—33.20
registration, 33.16
Plant and machinery hire
profit and loss account, and, 5.82—5.83
Plant and machinery, value of
tangible fixed assets, and, 16.201—16.203
Points schemes
revenue recognition, and, 9.240—9.245
Post-acquisition activities
exceptional items, 25.118—25.120
layered formats, 25.114—25.117
provisions, 25.123—25.124
reorganisation and integration, 25.121—25.122
Post balance sheet events (FRS 21)
and see below
introduction, 22.1—22.3
small companies, and, 32.79—32.79.4
Post-balance sheet events (IAS 10)
acquisitions and disposals, A22.43
adjusting events
assets sold or purchased before year end, A22.24—A22.25
examples, A22.20
fraud, error and irregularities, A22.30
generally, A22.18—A22.20
impairment, A22.26—A22.29
net realisable value, A22.26—A22.29
settlement of court case, A22.21—A22.23
summary, A22.4—A22.5
agriculture, and, A22.67
assets sold or purchased before year end, A22.24—A22.25
breach of banking covenants, A22.48—A22.51
business combinations and, 25.355—25.356
capital commitments, A22.67
changes in asset prices, A22.46
changes in foreign exchange rates, A22.46
changes in tax rates, A22.47
Companies Act 1985, and, A22.76
comparison with GAAP, and, A22.77
date of approval of financial statements for issue
generally, A22.55—A22.58
preliminary announcements, A22.59—A22.61
definitions, A22.2—A22.3
disclosures
Listing Rules, and, A22.61.1—A22.61.3
summary, A22.8—A22.12
updating, A22.36
dividends
generally, A22.52—A22.54.6
summary, A22.6
"events after the balance sheet date", A22.2
executive summary
definitions, A22.2—A22.3
disclosures, A22.8—A22.12
going concern, A22.7
introduction, A22.1
recognition, A22.4—A22.6
financial instruments, and, A22.69
first time adoption of IFRS, and, A22.74
fraud, error and irregularities, A22.30
going concern
generally, A22.31—A22.35
summary, A22.7
impairment, A22.26—A22.29
intangible assets, and, A22.67
interests in joint ventures, and, A22.70

Post-balance sheet events (IAS 10)—*cont.*
interim financial reporting, and, A22.71
introduction, A22.13
leases, and, A22.68
Listing Rules, and, A22.61.1—A22.61.3
net realisable value, A22.26—A22.29
non-adjusting events
acquisitions and disposals, A22.43
changes in asset prices, A22.46
changes in foreign exchange rates, A22.46
changes in tax rates, A22.47
examples, A22.39
generally, A22.37—A22.42
restructuring, A22.44—A22.45
summary, A22.10—A22.11
objectives
generally, A22.16
summary, A22.1
preliminary announcements, A22.59—A22.61
presentation of financial statements, and, A22.31
property, plant and equipment, and, A22.67
recognition, A22.4—A22.6
restructuring
generally, 21.196—21.198
introduction, A22.44—A22.45
scope
generally, A22.16—A22.17
summary, A22.1
settlement of court case, A22.21—A22.23
Pre-acquisition activities
material acquisitions, of, 25.103—25.105
substantial acquisitions, of, 25.106—25.113
Pre-combination profits
distributable profits, and, 23.201
Pre-contract costs
PFI and PPP, and, 3.179.55.12—3.179.55.14
small companies, and, 32.67.1—32.67.2
Pre-corporation tax profits and losses
share capital, and, 23.234—23.235
Pre-funded QUEST
generally, 12.121—12.124
pre-funding by parent company, 12.125—12.126
pre-funding by subsidiary company, 12.127—12.129
Preliminary expenses
fixed assets, and, 16.12
Preliminary results statements
content of financial statements, and, 4.142
Premium profits
intangible fixed assets, and, 15.54—15.58
Premiums
cash flow statements, and, 30.180—30.181
Preparation of financial statements
Companies Act principles, and, 2.22—2.22.8
Prepayments
balance sheet, and, 4.46—4.54
Present obligation
constructive obligations, 21.52—21.53
introduction, 21.49
legal obligations, 21.50—21.51
recognition test, and, 21.70—21.73
Presentation of debtors
balance sheet, and, 4.42—4.45
Presentation of financial instruments (IFRS)
bank facilities, A6.11.8
current or non-current assets, as, A6.11.3—A6.11.5
current or non-current liabilities, as, A6.11.6—A6.11.14
introduction, A6.11.1—A6.11.2
offsetting financial assets and liabilities
general principle, A6.11.15—A6.11.17
inappropriate situations, A6.11.23
Presentation of financial instruments (IFRS)—*cont.*
intention to settle on net basis, A6.11.20—A6.11.21
legal right, A6.11.18—A6.11.19
master netting agreements, A6.11.24—A6.11.26
simultaneous settlement, A6.11.22
overview, A6.1.52—A6.1.54
Presentation of financial statements
ASB Statement of principles, and, 2.213—2.214
associates and joint venture entities, and, 27.1.8—27.1.14
financial instruments, and, 6.89—6.90
IASB framework, and, 2.190
impairment, and
assets carried at historical cost, 18.250—18.251
assets held for disposal, 18.263—18.269
Companies Act requirements, 18.281—18.282
fixed asset movements, 18.270—18.271
revalued assets, 18.252—18.262
revalued assets held at depreciated replacement cost, 18.274
revalued assets held at market value, 18.272—18.273
reversal, 18.280
summary, 18.1.11—18.1.13
value in use, 18.275—18.279
minority interests, and, 24.357—24.365
revenue recognition, and
agency fees, 9.286—9.288
commissions, 9.286—9.288
government grants, 9.293—9.298
introduction, 9.283
other operating activity, 9.289—9.292
trading activities, 9.285
turnover, 9.284
taxation, and
accounting policies, 13.235
balance sheet, 13.253—13.273
circumstances affecting tax charges, 13.274—13.290
generally, 13.234
profit and loss account, 13.236—13.248
statement of total recognised gains and losses, 13.249—13.250
summary, 13.1.23—13.1.25
Presumed related, parties who are
connected persons, 29.60—29.67
introduction, 29.49—29.51
key management, 29.52—29.54
management contracts, 29.58—29.59
persons acting in concert, 29.55—29.57
Previously assessed standard of performance
tangible fixed assets, and, 16.135—16.142
Previously recognised assets, transactions in
continued recognition, 3.71—3.72
full derecognition, 3.73
generally, 3.66—3.70
insurance, 3.82
partial derecognition, 3.74—3.81
Prior period adjustments
changes in accounting policies
disclosures, 8.195—8.202
generally, 8.190—8.194
IFRS, and, 8.208
changes to estimation techniques
generally, 8.205
IFRS, and, 8.208
fundamental errors
generally, 8.203—8.204
IFRS, and, 8.208
IFRS, and
changes in accounting policies, 8.208
changes to estimation techniques, 8.208

Prior period adjustments—*cont.*
fundamental errors, 8.208
introduction, 8.188—8.189
summary, 8.1.13
Private finance initiative (PFI)
accounting treatment
amortisation of financial asset, 3.179.55.23
assets recognised by operator, 3.179.50—3.179.54
assets recognised by purchaser, 3.179.55—3.179.55.5
contributions, 3.179.55.15—3.179.55.17
pre-contract costs, 3.179.55.12—3.179.55.14
residuals, 3.179.55.18—3.179.55.22
use of SSAP 9, 3.179.55.6—3.179.55.9
amortisation of financial asset, 3.179.55.23
application of FRS 5, 3.179.17—3.179.24
assets recognised by operator
accounting by operator, 3.179.50—3.179.53
accounting by purchaser, 3.179.54
assets recognised by purchaser
accounting by operator, 3.179.55—3.179.55.2
accounting by purchaser, 3.179.55.3—3.179.55.5
changes in relevant costs, 3.179.41—3.179.43
changes in technology, 3.179.44
contract separability, 3.179.8—3.179.16
contributions
accounting by operator, 3.179.55.15
accounting by purchaser, 3.179.55.16—3.179.55.17
demand risk, 3.179.25—3.179.28
example of quantitative analysis, 3.179.56
introduction, 3.179.1—3.177.7
non-availability penalties, 3.179.38—3.179.40
obsolescence, 3.179.44
pre-contract costs, 3.179.55.12—3.179.55.14
property factors
changes in relevant costs, 3.179.41—3.179.43
changes in technology, 3.179.44
demand risk, 3.179.25—3.179.28
non-availability penalties, 3.179.38—3.179.40
obsolescence, 3.179.44
person determining nature of property, 3.179.31—3.179.37
residual value risk, 3.179.45—3.179.48
technology changes, 3.179.4
third party revenues, 3.179.29—3.179.30
under-performance penalties, 3.179.38—3.179.40
summary of risks, 3.179.49
residual value risk, 3.179.45—3.179.48
residuals
asset on operator's balance sheet, 3.179.55.18—3.179.55.20
asset on purchaser's balance sheet, 3.179.55.21—3.179.55.22
technology changes, 3.179.4
third party revenues, 3.179.29—3.179.30
under-performance penalties, 3.179.38—3.179.40
use of SSAP 9, 3.179.55.6—3.179.55.9
Profit and loss account
administrative expenses, 5.7—5.12
allocation of interest and taxation, and, 8.20—8.21
associates, and
example, 27.82
introduction, 27.72
notes, 27.80—27.81
operating results, 27.75—27.76
other line items, 27.78
satisfying requirements, 27.79
super-exceptional items, 27.77
turnover, 27.73—27.74
auditors' remuneration
audit work, 5.55—5.58
Profit and loss account—*cont.*
auditor's associates, 5.69—5.69.1
company's associated pension schemes, 5.71—5.73
company's associates, 5.70—5.70.
exemptions from disclosure, 5.74—5.75.6
more than one auditor, 5.79—5.81
other services, 5.59—5.68
single audit fees for group, 5.76—5.76.2
third party payments, 5.77—5.78
consolidated formats
effect of FRS3, 4.120—4.121
generally, 4.111
particular items, rules for, 4.112—4.119
cost of sales, 5.4—5.12
depreciation, 5.29—5.31
directors, 5.25—5.26
distribution costs, 5.6—5.12
dividends paid and payable
reserves, and, 4.139
effect of FRS3, 4.120—4.121
employee costs
directors, 5.25—5.26
disclosure by groups, 5.26.1—5.26.2
generally, 5.15—5.20
numbers of employees, 5.21—5.24
practical issues, 5.27—5.28
employee numbers, 5.21—5.24
exceptional items, and, 8.22—8.23
external charges, 5.32—5.34
financial instruments, 4.137
gross profit, 5.13
group structure, and, 24.47—24.50
hire of plant and machinery, 5.82—5.83
historical summaries, 4.90
individual company formats
classification of expenses by function, 4.109
classification of expenses by type, 4.110
effect of FRS3, 4.120—4.121
generally, 4.107—4.108
particular items, rules for, 4.112—4.119
interest payable, 5.42—5.44
introduction, 5.1—5.3
investment income, 5.35—5.41
joint ventures, and
example, 27.82
introduction, 27.72
notes, 27.80—27.81
operating results, 27.75—27.76
other line items, 27.78
satisfying requirements, 27.79
super-exceptional items, 27.77
turnover, 27.73—27.74
minority interests, and, 24.360—24.365
notes to
accounting policies, 4.134—4.136
additional statements required by FRS3, 4.131
compliance with accounting standards, 4.132
financial instruments, 4.137
general requirements, 4.125—4.130
reserves and dividends, 4.139
true and fair override disclosures, 4.133
operating lease rentals, 5.82—5.83
operating profit, and, 8.13—8.19.1
other disclosures, 5.52
own work capitalised, 5.14
parent company, 4.122—4.124
plant and machinery hire, 5.82—5.83
reporting financial performance, and
allocation of interest and taxation, 8.20—8.21
exceptional items, 8.22—8.23
introduction, 8.9

Profit and loss account—*cont.*
layered format, 8.10—8.12
operating profit, 8.13—8.20.1
summary, 8.1.1—8.1.3
research and development, 5.84—5.85
reserves, and
dividends, 4.139
generally, 23.86
retirement benefits, and
generally, 11.90—11.92
summary, 11.1.14—11.1.18
self-review threat, 5.80—5.81.7
small companies, and
effect of FRS 3, 32.84—32.85
foreign currencies, 32.89
formats, 32.83
notes, 32.93—32.97
retirement benefits, 32.88—32.88.4
taxation, 32.86—32.87.1
staff costs
directors, 5.25—5.26
disclosure by groups, 5.26.1—5.26.2
generally, 5.15—5.20
numbers of employees, 5.21—5.24
practical issues, 5.27—5.28
staff numbers, 5.21—5.24
taxation, and
analysis of current tax, 13.239
analysis of deferred tax, 13.240—13.244
Companies Act requirements, 13.236
non-operating exceptional items, 13.245—13.248
notes, 13.238
standards requirements, 13.237
Profit recognition
linked presentation, and, 3.93—3.96
long-term contracts, and
amounts recoverable on contracts, 20.103—20.105
claims, 20.94—20.95
cost of sales, 20.99—20.102
determination of future costs, 20.89—20.91
generally, 20.78—20.88
losses on contracts, 20.96—20.98
variations, 20.92—20.93
Profits and losses on disposals of fixed assets
generally, 8.103—8.112
impairments, 8.114—8.117
Profits and losses on sales
exceptional items, 8.90—8.93
generally, 8.39—8.40
provisions for losses, 8.41—8.53
Proforma financial statements
content of financial statements, and, 4.147—4.150
Property sales
revenue recognition, and, 9.100—9.105
Provisional fair values
acquisition accounting, and, 25.1.10—25.1.11
Provisions, contingencies and commitments (FRS 12)
abandonment costs, 21.249—21.257
ASB Statement of principles, 21.7—21.8
assets, against, 21.25
best estimate
estimation techniques, 21.117
introduction, 21.110—21.116
large population of similar claims, 21.118
changes in discount rates, 21.139—21.142.1
changes in estimate, 21.135—21.138.1
compensation, 21.266—21.267
constructive obligations, 21.52—21.53
contingent liabilities, 21.37—21.39
creditors, as, 21.80
decommissioning costs, 21.249—21.257

Provisions, contingencies and commitments (FRS 12)—*cont.*
deferred income, 21.88—21.90
deferred tax, and, 13.114
definition, 21.40—21.46
dilapidations, 21.234
disclosure requirements
acquisitions, 21.305
categorisation by class, 21.289—21.292
exemptions, 21.314—21.318
introduction, 21.288
narrative information, 21.297—21.298
pensions, 21.300—21.302
summary, 21.1.16
tabular information, 21.293—21.296
taxation, 21.303
unwinding of discount, 21.299—21.299.1
discounting
effects of taxation, 21.130
inflation adjustments, 21.121—21.123
introduction, 21.119—21.120
risk adjustment, 21.124—21.129
selection of appropriate discount rate, 21.131
unwinding the discount, 21.132
electrical and electronic equipment, 21.248.1—21.248.6
emissions obligations, 21.248.7—21.248.13
environmental liabilities, 21.245—21.248
executive summary
disclosure, 21.1.16
measurement, 21.1.8—21.1.11
other rules, 21.1.12—21.1.15
recognition, 21.1.2—21.1.7
scope of standard, 21.1—21.1.1
specific applications, 21.1.17—21.1.20
finance leases, 21.272
future events
changes in provisions, 21.81—21.82
generally, 21.79
measurement, and, 21.143—21.146
provision becomes creditor, 21.80
infrastructure renewals, 21.273—21.274
introduction, 21.2—21.3
legal obligations, 21.50—21.51
litigation, 21.258—21.265
maintenance, 21.268
measurement
application of rules, 21.142.2—21.142.6
asset recognition, 21.133—21.134
best estimate, 21.110—21.118
changes in discount rates, 21.139—21.142.1
changes in estimate, 21.135—21.138.1
changes in estimate of provisions, 21.142.2—21.142.6
discounting, 21.119—21.132
future events, 21.143—21.146
introduction, 21.109
related asset, 21.133—21.134
summary, 21.1.8—21.1.11
narrative information, 21.297—21.298
objective of standard, 21.20
onerous contracts
and see **Onerous contracts**
executory contracts, 21.197
financial instruments including derivatives, 21.198
general rules, 21.199—21.201
illustrative examples, 21.210—21.213
interpretation, 21.202—21.209
introduction, 21.193
leasehold properties, 21.194—21.196
measurement, 21.214—21.218

Provisions, contingencies and commitments (FRS 12)— *cont.*
operating leasehold improvements, 21.235—21.236
operating leases, 21.271
other liabilities, 21.31—21.36
past event
introduction, 21.54—21.56
legal enforcement, 21.57—21.60
third party expectation, 21.61—21.64
pensions, 21.300—21.302
practical application of rules
abandonment costs, 21.249—21.257
compensation, 21.266—21.267
decommissioning costs, 21.249—21.257
dilapidations, 21.234
environmental liabilities, 21.245—21.248
finance leases, 21.272
infrastructure renewals, 21.273—21.274
introduction, 21.222—21.224
litigation, 21.258—21.265
maintenance, 21.268
operating leasehold improvements, 21.235—21.236
operating leases, 21.271
refunds, 21.228—21.229
regulatory fines, 21.266—21.267
repairs, 21.268
self-insurance, 21.238—21.244
systems rectification, 21.266—21.267
tariff over-recoveries, 21.275—21.278
warranties, 21.225—21.227
present obligation
constructive obligations, 21.52—21.53
introduction, 21.49
legal obligations, 21.50—21.51
recognition test, and, 21.70—21.73
recognition
deferred income, 21.88—21.90
future events, 21.79—21.82
future operating costs, 21.65
introduction, 21.26—21.39
no reliable estimate, 21.77—21.78
past event, 21.54—21.64
placement of double entry, 21.83—21.87
present obligation, 21.49—21.53
reimbursement, 21.104—21.107
rules, 21.47—21.48
summary, 21.1.2—21.1.7
two stage test, 21.69—21.76
recognition test
groups of similar obligations, 21.76
introduction, 21.69
probability of present obligation, 21.70—21.73
transfer of economic benefits, 21.74—21.75
redundancies
compulsory redundancies, 21.183—21.189
introduction, 21.182
voluntary redundancies, 21.190—21.192
refunds, 21.228—21.229
regulatory fines, 21.266—21.267
reimbursement, 21.104—21.107
related assets, 21.133—21.134
repairs, 21.268
restructuring
and see **Restructuring**
application of recognition criteria, 21.155—21.170
definition, 21.153—21.154
introduction, 21.148—21.151
post balance sheet events, 21.174—21.175
redundancy provisions, 21.182—21.192
restructuring costs, 21.177—21.181
rules, 21.152

Provisions, contingencies and commitments (FRS 12)— *cont.*
termination of operations, 21.171—21.172
scope of standard
generally, 21.21—21.24
summary, 21.1—21.1.1
self-insurance, 21.238—21.244
small companies, and, 32.79—32.79.4
specific applications, 21.1.17—21.1.20
Statement of principles, 21.7—21.8
systems rectification, 21.266—21.267
tabular information, 21.293—21.296
tariff over-recoveries, 21.275—21.278
taxation
disclosure requirements, 21.303
third party expectation, 21.61—21.64
transfer of economic benefits, 21.74—21.75
test
groups of similar obligations, 21.76
introduction, 21.69
probability of present obligation, 21.70—21.73
transfer of economic benefits, 21.74—21.75
unwinding of discount, 21.299—21.299.1
warranties, 21.225—21.227
waste electrical and electronic equipment, 21.248.1—21.248.6

Prudence
accounting principles, and, 2.112

Public houses
impairment, and, 18.81

Public private partnership (PPP)
accounting treatment
amortisation of financial asset, 3.179.55.23
assets recognised by operator, 3.179.50—3.179.54
assets recognised by purchaser, 3.179.55—3.179.55.5
contributions, 3.179.55.15—3.179.55.17
pre-contract costs, 3.179.55.12—3.179.55.14
residuals, 3.179.55.18—3.179.55.22
use of SSAP 9, 3.179.55.6—3.179.55.9
amortisation of financial asset, 3.179.55.23
application of FRS 5, 3.179.17—3.179.24
assets recognised by operator
accounting by operator, 3.179.50—3.179.53
accounting by purchaser, 3.179.54
assets recognised by purchaser
accounting by operator, 3.179.55—3.179.55.2
accounting by purchaser, 3.179.55.3—3.179.55.5
changes in relevant costs, 3.179.41—3.179.43
changes in technology, 3.179.44
contract separability, 3.179.8—3.179.16
contributions
accounting by operator, 3.179.55.15
accounting by purchaser, 3.179.55.16—3.179.55.17
demand risk, 3.179.25—3.179.28
example of quantitative analysis, 3.179.56
introduction, 3.179.1—3.177.7
non-availability penalties, 3.179.38—3.179.40
obsolescence, 3.179.44
pre-contract costs, 3.179.55.12—3.179.55.14
property factors
changes in relevant costs, 3.179.41—3.179.43
changes in technology, 3.179.44
demand risk, 3.179.25—3.179.28
non-availability penalties, 3.179.38—3.179.40
obsolescence, 3.179.44
person determining nature of property, 3.179.31—3.179.37
residual value risk, 3.179.45—3.179.48
technology changes, 3.179.4
third party revenues, 3.179.29—3.179.30

Public private partnership (PPP)—*cont.*
under-performance penalties, 3.179.38—3.179.40
summary of risks, 3.179.49
residual value risk, 3.179.45—3.179.48
residuals
asset on operator's balance sheet, 3.179.55.18—3.179.55.20
asset on purchaser's balance sheet, 3.179.55.21—3.179.55.22
technology changes, 3.179.4
third party revenues, 3.179.29—3.179.30
under-performance penalties, 3.179.38—3.179.40
use of SSAP 9, 3.179.55.6—3.179.55.9
Purchase commitments
reporting the substance of transactions, and, 3.250
Purchase consideration
acquisition accounting, and, 25.94—25.95
Purchase of fixed asset using option
hedging, and, 6.131—6.132
Purchased assets
goodwill, and
generally, 18.98—18.103
guidelines, 18.104—18.114
intangible fixed assets, and
generally, 15.37—15.40
IFRS, and, 15.139

Qualified audit reports
distributable profits, and, 23.223—23.229
Qualifying employee share ownership trust (QUEST)
introduction, 12.106—12.108
pre-funded QUEST
generally, 12.121—12.124
pre-funding by parent company, 12.125—12.126
pre-funding by subsidiary company, 12.127—12.129
share-based payments, and
introduction, 12.75—12.84
pre-funding by parent company, 12.90—12.91
pre-funding by subsidiary company, 12.92—12.93
simultaneous funding by parent company, 12.85—12.88
simultaneous funding by subsidiary company, 12.89
share symmetry arrangements, and, 12.130
simultaneous QUEST
funding by parent company, 12.111—12.117
funding by subsidiary company, 12.118—12.120
generally, 12.109—12.110
Qualitative characteristics
ASB Statement of principles, and, 2.195—2.197
Quasi-subsidiaries, accounting for
accounting treatment, 3.108—3.112
credit enhancement, 3.115—3.116
disclosure, 3.119
IFRS, and, 3.259
introduction, 3.100—3.106
joint arrangements, and, 27.205—27.208
linked presentation, 3.113—3.114
parent's financial statements, and, 3.118
related party transactions, and, 29.133—29.134
securitisation, 3.117
subordinated debt, 3.115—3.116
summary, 3.1.14—3.1.17
true and fair overriding disclosures, and, 3.107
Quoted companies
auditor's remuneration, and, 5.64—5.79

Readily ascertainable market value
intangible fixed assets, and, 15.27—15.30
Realised losses
fair value accounting, 23.152—23.156
Realised losses—*cont.*
generally, 23.150—23.151
intra-group transactions, 23.157—23.157.3
other matters, 23.158—23.160
principles, 23.139—23.144
Realised profits
accounting principles, and, 2.112—2.115
fair value accounting, 23.152—23.156
generally, 23.146—23.149
intra-group transactions, 23.157—23.157.3
other matters, 23.158—23.160
principles, 23.139—23.144
proposed dividends, 23.156.1—23.156.2
Realised reserves
disclosure requirements, 23.127—23.130
group structure, and, 24.252—24.255
research and development, and, 15.134
Recharge from parent company
employee share schemes, and, 12.58
Reciprocal transactions
revenue recognition, and, 9.214—9.218
Recognition
ASB Statement of principles, and, 2.210—2.211
assets and liabilities, of
generally, 3.65
introduction, 3.51
current tax, and
generally, 13.21—13.23
summary, 13.1.2—13.1.5
financial instruments (IFRS), and
and see **Recognition of financial instruments (IFRS)**
introduction, A6.8.1—A6.8.2
impairment of fixed assets, and, 18.1.11—18.1.13
intangible fixed assets, and, 15.1.3—15.1.6
investment properties, and, 17.40
provisions, and
deferred income, 21.88—21.90
future events, 21.79—21.82
future operating costs, 21.65
introduction, 21.26—21.39
no reliable estimate, 21.77—21.78
past event, 21.54—21.64
placement of double entry, 21.83—21.87
present obligation, 21.49—21.53
reimbursement, 21.104—21.107
rules, 21.47—21.48
summary, 21.1.2—21.1.7
two stage test, 21.69—21.76
revenue recognition, and
generally, 9.16—9.19
performance, 9.27—9.41
timing, 9.20—9.26
share-based transactions, and
generally, 12.4
measurement, 12.5—12.7
vesting conditions, 12.8—12.10
Statement of principles, and, 2.210—2.211
Recognition of financial instruments (IFRS)
commitments to buy or sell non-financial assets, A6.8.10—A6.8.12
exchange of non-cash assets, A6.8.23
forward contracts, A6.8.8
general principles
application, A6.8.6—A6.8.13
introduction, A6.8.5
regular way transactions, A6.8.14—A6.8.23
introduction, A6.8.1—A6.8.2
options, A6.8.9
overview, A6.1.26—A6.1.30
planned future transactions, A6.8.13
regular way transactions

Recognition of financial instruments (IFRS)—*cont.*
exchange of non-cash assets, A6.8.23
generally, A6.8.14—A6.8.17
trade date versus settlement date accounting, A6.8.18—A6.8.22
unconditional receivables and payables, A6.8.7
Reconciliation of figures
generally, 10.108
net debt, 30.119—30.124
Reconciliation of movements in shareholders' funds
reporting financial performance, and, 8.183—8.187
Reducing balance method
depreciation, and, 16.260—16.261
Redundancy, provisions for
compulsory redundancies, 21.183—21.189
introduction, 21.182
voluntary redundancies, 21.190—21.192
Reference period
oversea companies, and
branches, 33.26
place of business, 33.24—33.25
Refinancing of borrowings
cash flow statements, and, 30.188—30.189
Refunds
provisions, and, 21.228—21.229
Registration of oversea companies
branches, 33.17
generally, 33.14—33.15
place of business, 33.16
reference period, 33.24—33.25
Regular cost
generally, 11.40—11.43
variations, 11.44—11.108
Regulatory fines
provisions, and, 21.266—21.267
Reimbursements
provisions, and, 21.104—21.107
Reinvestment period
securitisation of revolving assets, and, 3.162
Related parties (FRS 8)
and see **Related party transactions**
associates, 29.38—29.39
background, 29.2—29.8
close family
generally, 29.62—29.64
introduction, 29.1.3
common control, 29.24
common influence
establishing, 29.27—29.29
introduction, 29.26
concert parties, 29.55—29.57
connected persons
close family, 29.62—29.64
companies, 29.65—29.
introduction, 29.60—29.61
partnerships, 29.65—29.67
trusts, 29.65—29.67
control
examples, 29.30
introduction, 29.19—29.23
criteria for related party relationships
common control, 29.24
control, 29.19—29.23
influence, 29.25—29.29
introduction, 29.15—29.18
deemed related, parties who are
associates, 29.38—29.39
directors, 29.42—29.43
introduction, 29.35
investors, 29.40—29.41
joint ventures, 29.38—29.39

Related parties (FRS 8)—*cont.*
parent companies, 29.36—29.37
pension funds, 29.44—29.48
subsidiary undertakings, 29.36—29.37
venture capitalists, 29.40—29.41
definition, 29.1.1
directors, 29.42—29.43
executive summary
disclosure requirements, 29.1.7—29.1.9
exemptions from disclosure, 29.1.6
generally, 29.1.1—29.1.3
introduction, 29.1
influence
establishing, 29.27—29.29
examples, 29.30
introduction, 29.25
IFRS, and
convergence, 29.195
disclosure, 29.195
exemptions, 29.195
first time adoption of IFRS, 29.195
introduction, 29.195
overview, 29.195
related parties, 29.195
related party transactions, 29.195
related pronouncements, 29.195
scope, 29.195
investors, 29.40—29.41
joint ventures, 29.38—29.39
key management, 29.52—29.54
management contracts, 29.58—29.59
objectives of standard, 29.12—29.13
parent companies, 29.36—29.37
partnerships, 29.65—29.67
pension funds, 29.44—29.48
presumed related, parties who are
connected persons, 29.60—29.67
introduction, 29.49—29.51
key management, 29.52—29.54
management contracts, 29.58—29.59
persons acting in concert, 29.55—29.57
related parties, 29.195
related party transactions, 29.195
reporting entity
generally, 29.14
group as, 29.30.1—29.31
specified related parties
identification, 29.68
IFRS, and, 29.195
introduction, 29.33—29.34
parties deemed related, 29.35—29.48
parties presumed related, 29.49—29.50
subsidiary undertakings, 29.36—29.37
trusts, 29.65—29.67
venture capitalists, 29.40—29.41
Related party transactions (FRS 8)
and see **Related parties**
agency arrangements, 29.72—29.75
aggregation of transactions
directors, with, 29.123—29.125
generally, 29.118—29.122
associates, with, 29.135
background, 29.2—29.8
close family, with, 29.142—29.143
common control, between companies under, 29.130
Companies Act, under
introduction, 29.174—29.175
loans to directors, 29.176
material interest transactions, 29.179—29.180
comparatives, 29.126
confidentiality, duty of, 29.162

Related party transactions (FRS 8)—*cont.*
consolidation balances, 29.146—29.147
definition, 29.69
directors, with
Companies Act, under, 29.174—29.180
dividends, 29.141
guarantees, 29.140
introduction, 29.138
share interests, 29.181
share transactions, 29.139
directors under Companies Act, with
introduction, 29.174—29.175
loans, 29.176
material interest transactions, 29.179—29.180
disclosure of control
introduction, 29.93—29.97.1
limited partnerships, 29.110
source of control, 29.100—29.101
trusts, 29.102—29.108
ultimate controlling party, 29.98—29.99
unit trusts, 29.109
disclosure of balances, 29.116—29.117
disclosure of transactions, 29.111—29.115.1
disclosure requirements
additional relaxations, 29.166—29.170
aggregation of transactions, 29.118—29.125
balances, 29.116—29.117
comparatives, 29.126
control, 29.93—29.110
exemptions, 29.145—29.165
interaction with Companies Act, 29.127—29.129
IFRS, and, 29.195
introduction, 29.92
transactions and balances, 29.111—29.115.1
true and fair view, and, 29.171—29.173
dividends paid to directors, 29.141
executive summary
disclosure requirements, 29.1.7—29.1.9
exemptions from disclosure, 29.1.6
generally, 29.1.1—29.1.3
introduction, 29.1
exemptions from disclosure
consolidation balances, 29.146—29.147
duty of confidentiality, 29.162
emoluments for services, 29.159—29.161
introduction, 29.145
intra-group transactions, 29.146—29.147
medium-sized companies, 29.163—29.165
90% subsidiaries, 29.149—29.157.1
parent company's financial statements, 29.148
pension contributions, 29.158
small companies, 29.163—29.165
guarantees by directors, 29.140
implications for directors
auditors' role, 29.91
generally, 29.87—29.90
IFRS, and
convergence, 29.195
disclosure, 29.195
exemptions, 29.195
first time adoption of IFRS, 29.195
introduction, 29.195
overview, 29.195
related parties, 29.195
related party transactions, 29.195
related pronouncements, 29.195
scope, 29.195
intra-group transactions, 29.146—29.147
joint ventures, with, 29.135
key management, with, 29.144
limited partnerships, 29.110

Related party transactions (FRS 8)—*cont.*
loans
directors, to, 29.176
officers, to, 29.177
material interest transactions, 29.179—29.180
materiality
Companies Act, and, 29.84—29.86
general purpose financial statements, 29.82—29.83
generally, 29.77—29.81
medium-sized companies, 29.163—29.165
90% subsidiaries, 29.149—29.157.1
pension contributions, 29.158
pension funds, with, 29.136
quasi-subsidiary undertakings, with, 29.133—29.134
related parties, 29.195
services, emoluments for, 29.159—29.161
share interests of directors, 29.181
share transactions by directors, 29.139
small companies
disclosures, 32.100—32.103.1
generally, 29.163—29.165
specified transactions, 29.70—29.72
subsidiaries acquired and disposed of during year, with, 29.131—29.132
true and fair view, and, 29.171—29.173
trusts, 29.102—29.108
ultimate controlling party, 29.98—29.99
unit trusts, 29.109

Relative size test
merger accounting, and, 28.59—28.61

Relief from royalties
intangible fixed assets, and, 15.51—15.53

Remuneration of auditors
appointment after year end, 5.81
audit of company's associates, 5.65
audit work
audit-assist, 5.57
consolidated financial statements, 5.56—5.56.1
disclosure in which year, 5.58
individual financial statements, 5.55
auditor's associates, 5.69—5.69.1
change of auditor, 5.80
company's associated pension schemes, 5.71—5.73
company's associates, 5.70—5.70.3
exemptions from disclosure
audit fees, 5.74—5.74.1
other services' fees, 5.75—5.75.6
introduction, 5.53—5.54.6
joint auditors, 5.79
more than one auditor
appointment after year end, 5.81
change of auditor, 5.80
joint auditors, 5.79
other services
all other services, 5.68
audit of company's associates, 5.65
categories, 5.64—5.
fees for services supplied pursuant to legislation, 5.66
format of disclosure, 5.59—5.62
sub-totals, 5.63
taxation services, 5.67
services supplied pursuant to legislation, 5.66
single audit fees for group, 5.76—5.76.2
sub-totals, 5.63
taxation services, 5.67
third party payments, 5.77—5.78

Remuneration of directors
employee share schemes, and, 12.61

Renegotiation of debt
capital instruments, and, 6.362—6.371

Rental variation
construction periods, 19.104
interest rate variations, 19.101—19.103
tax variation clauses, 19.96—19.97
Reorganisation expenditure
future capital expenditure, 18.148—18.155
future reorganisations, 18.147
generally, 18.141—18.146
Reorganisation and integration costs
cash flow statements, and, 30.186—30.87
Repairs
provisions, and, 21.268
Repayable on demand
cash flow statements, and, 30.43
Repayment period
securitisation of revolving assets, and, 3.163—3.165
Replacement value
stocks, and, 20.37—20.41
Replacing components
tangible fixed assets, and, 16.143—16.149
Reporting entity
ASB Statement of principles, and, 2.194
related parties, and
generally, 29.14
group as, 29.30.1—29.31
Reporting financial performance (FRS 3)
acquisitions
introduction, 8.70—8.76
mergers, 8.77—8.78
allocation of interest and taxation, 8.20—8.21
changes in accounting policies
disclosures, 8.195—8.202
generally, 8.190—8.194
IFRS, and, 8.208
changes to estimation techniques
generally, 8.205
IFRS, and, 8.208
comparison with IAS, and, 8.209
disclosures, 8.208
discontinued operations
definition, 8.24—8.26
goodwill on disposals, 8.54—8.57
IFRS, and, 8.208
materiality, 8.28
meaning of 'ceased permanently', 8.27
operations discontinued by closure, 8.58—8.69
operations discontinued by sale, 8.37—8.57
profits and losses on sales, 8.39—8.53
retention of interest in disposed of subsidiary, 8.34—8.36
separability of activities, 8.29—8.33
disposal groups to be abandoned, 8.208
exceptional items
definition, 8.79—8.83
fundamental reorganisation or restructuring, 8.94—8.99
introduction, 8.22—8.23
non-operating exceptional items, 8.84—8.87
other, 8.121—8.136
profits or losses on disposals of fixed assets, 8.103—8.112
profits and losses on sale or termination, 8.90—8.93
summary, 8.1.4—8.1.6
tax attributable, 8.137—8.143
executive summary
exceptional items, 8.1.4—8.1.6
introduction, 8.1
other items, 8.1.7—8.1.9
other statements, 8.1.10—8.1.12
prior period adjustments, 8.1.13
profit and loss account, 8.1.1—8.1.3

Reporting financial performance (FRS 3)—*cont.*
extraordinary items, 8.144
fundamental errors
generally, 8.203—8.204
IFRS, and, 8.208
fundamental reorganisation or restructuring, 8.94—8.99
goodwill
disposals, 8.54—8.57
statement of total recognised gains and losses, 8.155—8.159
IAS, and, 8.209
IFRS, and
changes in accounting policies, 8.208
changes to estimation techniques, 8.208
convergence, 8.208
disclosures, 8.208
discontinued operations, 8.208
disposal groups to be abandoned, 8.208
fundamental errors, 8.208
introduction, 8.206—8.209
non-current assets to be abandoned, 8.208
presentation of non-current assets, 8.208
related pronouncements, 8.208
scope, 8.208
subsidiaries acquired exclusively with view to resale, 8.208
impairments, 8.114—8.117
introduction, 8.1—8.8
mergers, 8.77—8.78
movements in reserves, 8.160—8.164
non-current assets to be abandoned, 8.208
non-operating exceptional items, 8.84—8.87
note of historical cost profits and losses, 8.169—8.182
operating profit, 8.13—8.19.1
operations discontinued by closure
generally, 8.58—8.59
provisions for losses, 8.60—8.69
operations discontinued by sale
generally, 8.37—8.38
goodwill, 8.54—8.57
profits and losses, 8.39—8.53
presentation of non-current assets, 8.208
prior period adjustments
changes in accounting policies, 8.190—8.202
changes to estimation techniques, 8.205
fundamental errors, 8.203—8.204
introduction, 8.188—8.189
summary, 8.1.13
profit and loss accounts
allocation of interest and taxation, 8.20—8.21
exceptional items, 8.22—8.23
introduction, 8.9
layered format, 8.10—8.12
operating profit, 8.13—8.19.1
summary, 8.1.1—8.1.3
profits and losses on disposals of fixed assets
generally, 8.103—8.112
impairments, 8.114—8.117
profits and losses on sales
exceptional items, 8.90—8.93
generally, 8.39—8.40
provisions for losses, 8.41—8.53
purchased goodwill, 8.155—8.159
reconciliation of movements in shareholders' funds, 8.183—8.187
retention of interest in disposed of subsidiary, 8.34—8.36
statement of total recognised gains and losses
generally, 8.145—8.154.1
movements in reserves, 8.160—8.164

Reporting financial performance (FRS 3)—*cont.*
purchased goodwill, 8.155—8.159
subsidiaries acquired exclusively with view to resale, 8.208
tax attributable to exceptional items, 8.137—8.143
Reporting the substance of transactions (FRS 5)
application notes
consignment stock, 3.122
debt factoring, 3.136—3.136.16
introduction, 3.120—3.121
loan transfers, 3.168—3.179
PFI and PPP, 3.179.1—3.179.56
sale and repurchase agreements, 3.123—3.135
securitised assets, 3.137—3.167
summary, 3.1.20—3.1.21
background, 3.2—3.5
bed and breakfasting, 3.243—3.249
bills of exchange, 3.197
cash flow statement, 3.251
comparison with IFRS, and, 3.257—3.261
consignment stock, 3.122
contract purchase arrangements, 3.228—3.231
debt factoring
benefits and risks, 3.136.5—3.136.9
derecognition, 3.136.10
examples of required analysis, 3.136.15—3.136.16
introduction, 3.136—3.136.4
linked presentation, 3.136.11—3.136.12
separate presentation, 3.136.13—3.136.14
derecognition, 3.258
disclosure, 3.1.19
executive summary
application notes, 3.1.20—3.1.21
disclosure, 3.1.19
introduction, 3.1
linked presentation, 3.1.8—3.1.13
offset, 3.1.18
principles, 3.1.1—3.1.7
quasi-subsidiaries, 3.1.14—3.1.17
scope, 3.1.21.1
identification of assets and liabilities
analysing complex transactions, 3.52—3.58
assets, 3.59—3.62
introduction, 3.51
liabilities, 3.63—3.64
IFRS, and
derecognition, 3.258
quasi-subsidiaries, 3.259
'substance over form', 3.257
insubstance debt defeasance, 3.184—3.185
interaction with Companies Act and accounting standards, 3.42.1—3.46
linked presentation
cash flow statement, 3.251
detailed conditions, 3.88—3.90
general rules, 3.83—3.87
linking part of finance, 3.91—3.92
profit recognition, 3.93—3.96
summary, 3.1.8—3.1.13
loan transfers
disclosure requirements, 3.178—3.179
generally, 3.168—3.177
objective, 3.47—3.50
offsetting
generally, 3.97—3.99
summary, 3.1.18
partial derecognition
generally, 3.181—3.182
IFRS, and, 3.258
PFI and PPP
accounting treatment, 3.179.50—3.179.55.23

Reporting the substance of transactions (FRS 5)—*cont.*
application of FRS 5, 3.179.17—3.179.24
contract separability, 3.179.8—3.179.16
example of quantitative analysis, 3.179.56
introduction, 3.179.1—3.177.7
property factors, 3.179.25—3.179.48
summary of risks, 3.179.49
practical issues
purchase commitments, 3.250
repurchase agreements, 3.219—3.224
stock lending, 3.232—3.242.1
take-or-pay contracts, 3.252—3.256.1
trade loans, 3.183
principles
identifying and recognising assets and liabilities, 3.51—3.65
introduction, 3.47—3.50
linked presentation, 3.83—3.96
offset rules, 3.97—3.99
quasi-subsidiaries, 3.100—3.119
summary, 3.1.1—3.1.7
transactions in previously recognised assets, 3.66—3.822
purchase commitments, 3.250
quasi-subsidiaries, accounting for
accounting treatment, 3.108—3.112
credit enhancement, 3.115—3.116
disclosure, 3.119
IFRS, and, 3.259
introduction, 3.100—3.106
linked presentation, 3.113—3.114
parent's financial statements, and, 3.118
securitisation, 3.117
subordinated debt, 3.115—3.116
summary, 3.1.14—3.1.17
true and fair overriding disclosures, and, 3.107
recognition of assets and liabilities
generally, 3.65
introduction, 3.51
repurchase agreements, 3.219—3.224
sale and repurchase agreements
accounting treatment, 3.130—3.132
examples of required analysis, 3.133—3.135
introduction, 3.123
sources of benefits and risks, 3.124—3.129
scope of standard
generally, 3.37—3.42
summary, 3.1.21.1
securitisation of assets
example of required analysis, 3.167
group's financial statements, 3.151—3.155
interest rate swaps, 3.156—3.158
introduction, 3.137—3.143
multi-originator programmes, 3.166
originator's financial statements, 3.144—3.150
revolving assets, 3.159—3.165
stock lending, 3.232—3.242.1
'substance over form', 3.257
take-or-pay contracts, 3.252—3.256.1
trade loans, 3.183
transactions in previously recognised assets
continued recognition, 3.71—3.72
full derecognition, 3.73
generally, 3.66—3.70
insurance, 3.82
partial derecognition, 3.74—3.81
Repurchase agreements (repos)
reporting the substance of transactions, and, 3.219—3.224
Repurchase of debt
capital instruments, and, 6.356—6.361

Repurchase options
leases, and, 19.64—19.67
Requirement to prepare financial statements
Companies Act principles, and, 2.22—2.22.8
Research and development (SSAP 13)
amortisation, 15.125
development costs
capitalisation, 15.121—15.123
generally, 15.120
diminution in value provisions, 15.131—15.133
disclosure
exemptions, 15.129—15.130
generally, 15.126—15.128
effect on realised reserves, 15.134
fixed assets, and, 16.12
generally, 15.113—15.119
introduction, 15.112
profit and loss account, and, 5.84—5.85
segmental reporting, and, 10.152
summary, 15.1.14—15.1.18
Research costs
fixed assets, and, 16.12
Reservation of title, goods with
stocks, and, 20.67—20.70
Reserves
capital redemption reserve, 23.119
disclosure requirements, 23.125—23.133
fair value reserve, 23.124.1
foreign currency translation reserve, 23.124.3
group reconstructions, 23.105—23.112
hedging reserve, 23.124.2
introduction, 23.84—23.85
merger relief
application of, 23.100—23.104
generally, 23.96—23.99
group reconstructions, 23.105—23.112
profit and loss account, 23.86
retirement benefits, and
composition of reserves, 11.162—11.164
distributable reserves, 11.150—11.156
introduction, 11.149
measurement, 11.68—11.73
revaluation reserve, 23.120—23.124
share premium account
generally, 23.87—23.93
implications of *Shearer v Bercain*, 23.94—23.95
merger relief, 23.96—23.112
reduction, 23.113—23.118
tangible fixed assets, and, 16.231—16.241
Reserves acquired
acquisition accounting, and, 25.39
Residual life
change in estimate, 16.306
determination, 16.252—16.256
implementation of standard, and, 16.338
Residual value risk
PFI and PPP, and, 3.179.45—3.179.48
Residuals
leases, and
finance leases, under, 19.126
fluctuations in anticipated residual values, 19.127—19.131
introduction, 19.120—19.121
operating leases, under, 19.123—19.125
tax-free grants, 19.132—19.133
PFI and PPP, and
asset on operator's balance sheet, 3.179.55.18—3.179.55.20
asset on purchaser's balance sheet, 3.179.55.21—3.179.55.22
Restructuring
application of recognition criteria
binding sale agreement, 21.168—21.170
board decision, 21.157—21.158
introduction, 21.155—21.156
re-structuring time-frame, 21.163—21.167
third party expectation, 21.159—21.162
definition, 21.153—21.154
introduction, 21.148—21.151
redundancy provisions
compulsory redundancies, 21.183—21.189
introduction, 21.182
voluntary redundancies, 21.190—21.192
restructuring costs, 21.177—21.181
rules, 21.152
termination of operations, 21.171—21.172
Retail establishments
impairment, and, 18.76—18.148.2
Retention of interest in disposed of subsidiary
reporting financial performance, and, 8.34—8.36
Retirement benefits (FRS 17)
acquisitions, 11.135—11.138
actuarial gains and losses, 11.109—11.114
balance sheet entries
generally, 11.55—11.61.1
summary, 11.1.9—11.1.12
comparison with SSAP 24, 11.212
components of performance, 11.1.13
current service cost, 11.81—11.84
curtailments, 11.100—11.108
deferred tax, and
generally, 13.126—13.126.10
SSAP 24, 11.184—11.194
defined benefit schemes, and
acquisitions, 11.135—11.138
balance sheet entries, 11.55—11.61.1
disclosure requirements, 11.139—11.148
frequency of valuations, 11.74—11.77
future developments, 11.148.1—11.148.14
limit on pension asset, 11.115—11.126
measurement of assets, 11.62—11.67
measurement of liabilities, 11.68—11.73
reporting performance, 11.78—11.114
reserves, 11.149—11.164
scheme assets, 11.43—11.148
scheme liabilities, 11.46—11.54
taxation, 11.127—11.129
defined contribution schemes, and
accounting treatment, 11.35
definition, 11.31—11.34
disclosure, 11.36
summary, 11.1.3
disclosure requirements
aggregation of schemes, 11.146—11.148
comparatives, 11.144—11.145
defined benefit schemes, 11.139—11.148
defined contribution schemes, 11.36
future developments, 11.148.1—11.148.14
summary, 11.1.21—11.1.24
executive summary
balance sheet recognition, 11.1.9—11.1.12
components of performance, 11.1.13
disclosures, 11.1.21—11.1.24
introduction, 11.1
measurement, 11.1.4—11.1.8
profit and loss account, 11.1.14—11.1.18
scope of standard, 11.1.1—11.1.3
STRGL, 11.1.19
tax, 11.1.20—11.1.21
expected return on assets, 11.87—11.89.2
first time adoption, and, 11.157

Retirement benefits (FRS 17)—*cont.*
frequency of valuations, 11.74—11.77
group schemes
disclosure, 11.41—11.42.2
generally, 11.37—11.41.8
summary, 11.1.2
interest cost, 11.85—11.86
introduction, 11.2—11.7
limit on pension asset
benefit improvements, 11.118—11.120
introduction, 11.115—11.117
required accounting, 11.121—11.126
measurement of assets
generally, 11.62—11.67
summary, 11.1.4—11.1.8
measurement of liabilities
generally, 11.68—11.73
summary, 11.1.4—11.1.8
multi-employer schemes
disclosure, 11.41—11.42.2
generally, 11.37—11.41.8
summary, 11.1.2
objective of standard, 11.28—11.30
past service costs, 11.93—11.99
Pensions Act 2004, and
introduction, 11.170—11.172
minimum funding objective, 11.179—11.182
moral hazard precisions, 11.177—11.178
Pensions Protection Fund, 11.173—11.175
Pensions Regulator, 11.176
statutory funding objective, 11.179—11.182
profit and loss account
generally, 11.90—11.92
summary, 11.1.14—11.1.18
reporting performance
actuarial gains and losses, 11.109—11.114
current service cost, 11.81—11.84
curtailments, 11.100—11.108
expected return on assets, 11.87—11.89.2
interest cost, 11.85—11.86
introduction, 11.78—11.80
past service costs, 11.93—11.99
profit and loss account, 11.90—11.92
settlements, 11.100—11.108
reserves
composition of reserves, 11.162—11.164
distributable reserves, 11.150—11.156
introduction, 11.149
scheme assets
generally, 11.43—11.148
measurement, 11.62—11.67
scheme liabilities
generally, 11.46—11.54
measurement, 11.68—11.73
scope of standard
generally, 11.24—11.27
summary, 11.1.1—11.1.2
settlements, 11.100—11.108
STRGL, 11.1.19
taxation
generally, 11.127—11.129
summary, 11.1.20—11.1.21
Retirement of assets
intangible fixed assets, and, 15.139
Return of goods
revenue recognition, and, 9.75—9.85
Returns on investments
cash flow statements, and, 30.76—30.85
Revaluation
gains and losses, and
accumulated depreciation, 16.226—16.230
Revaluation—*cont.*
gains, 16.216
introduction, 16.213—16.215
losses, 16.217—16.225
reserve, 16.231—16.241
taxation, 16.242—16.246
intangible fixed assets, and, 15.63—15.64
non-monetary assets, and
general rule, 13.128—13.130
holdover relief, 13.136—13.141
marked to market assets, 13.131—13.135.1
rollover relief, 13.136—13.141
Revaluation of tangible fixed assets
bases
assets surplus to requirements, 16.189
assets used in business, 16.185—16.188
depreciated replacement cost, 16.197—16.200
existing use value, 16.193—16.196
introduction, 16.177—16.184
open market value, 16.190—16.192
plant and machinery value, 16.201—16.203
class of assets, 16.158—16.163
disclosure requirements, 16.204—16.212
frequency, 16.164
IFRS, and, 16.344
introduction, 16.154—16.157
material changes in value, 16.175—16.176
other assets, 16.173—16.174
properties, 16.169—16.172
qualified valuers, 16.165—16.168
Revaluation reserve
generally, 23.120—23.124
tangible fixed assets, and, 16.231—16.241
Revalued assets
distributable profits, and
depreciation of revalued assets, 23.178—23.180
diminution in value of assets, 23.185
introduction, 23.177
subsequent sale of revalued assets, 23.181—23.184
impairment, and
generally, 18.252—18.262
held at depreciated replacement cost, 18.274
held at market value, 18.272—18.273
tangible fixed assets, and
depreciation, 16.268—16.275
disposal of fixed assets, 16.319—16.324
Revenue recognition
admission fees, 9.141—9.142
advertising agency commissions, 9.172
agency arrangements, 9.161—9.171
agency fees, 9.286—9.288
allocation of consideration, 9.148—9.156
barter transactions, 9.187—9.199
bill and hold sale, 9.65—9.72
capacity transactions
exchange and reciprocal transactions, 9.214—9.218
generally, 9.201—9.205
presentation, 9.208—9.213
sale of asset or service, 9.206—9.207
capital/revenue distinction, 9.275—9.278
commissions, 9.286—9.288
continuing managerial involvement, 9.86—9.89
contracts containing significant acts, 9.133
disclosure
agency fees, 9.286—9.288
commissions, 9.286—9.288
government grants, 9.293—9.298
introduction, 9.283
other operating activity, 9.289—9.292
trading activities, 9.285
turnover, 9.284

Revenue recognition—*cont.*
discounting
generally, 9.185—9.186
introduction, 9.45
dividends, 9.251—9.253
exchange transactions, 9.214—9.218
extended warranty, 9.92—9.93
financial services fees
earned as result of providing services, 9.281
earned on execution of significant act, 9.282
integral part of effective interest rate, 9.279—9.280
franchise fees, 9.259—9.262
free products, 9.239
FRS 5, and, 9.3
goods shipped subject to conditions, 9.75—9.85
government grants, 9.293—9.298
grants, 9.263—9.270
handling charges, 9.97—9.99
inception fees, 9.136—9.139
installation fees, 9.94—9.96
insurance recoveries, 9.271—9.274
introduction, 9.1—9.9
license income, 9.256—9.258
linked transactions, 9.158—9.160
loyalty programmes, 9.240—9.245
measurement
advertising agency commissions, 9.172
agency arrangements, 9.161—9.171
barter transactions, 9.187—9.199
capacity transactions, 9.201—9.2
generally, 9.42—9.55
settlement discounting, 9.185—9.186
two-way trading arrangements, 9.176—9.184
volume discounting, 9.185—9.186
milestone payments, 9.134—9.135
mixed contracts
allocation of consideration, 9.148—9.156
linked transactions, 9.158—9.160
separation of components, 9.145—9.147
options granted
as part of sales transaction, 9.223—9.236
for consideration, 9.219—9.222
without consideration, 9.237—9.238
payments in advance, 9.73—9.74
performance of transactions, 9.27—9.41
performance over time
incomplete contractual performance, 9.116—9.126
stage of completion, 9.127—9.132
point schemes, 9.240—9.245
presentation
agency fees, 9.286—9.288
commissions, 9.286—9.288
government grants, 9.293—9.298
introduction, 9.283
other operating activity, 9.289—9.292
trading activities, 9.285
turnover, 9.284
property sales, 9.100—9.105
reciprocal transactions, 9.214—9.218
recognition of transactions
generally, 9.16—9.19
performance, 9.27—9.41
timing, 9.20—9.26
"revenue", 9.10—9.15
royalties, 9.255
sale of goods
handling charges, 9.97—9.99
installation fees, 9.94—9.96
introduction, 9.64
shipping charges, 9.97—9.99
transfer of significant risks and rewards, 9.65—9.89

Revenue recognition—*cont.*
warranties, 9.90—9.93
sale of property, 9.100—9.105
sale of services
admission fees, 9.141—9.142
contracts containing significant acts, 9.133
inception fees, 9.136—9.139
milestone payments, 9.134—9.135
performance over time, 9.116—9.132
subscriptions, 9.140
tuition fees, 9.143—9.144
up-front fees, 9.136—9.139
sale of software, 9.106—9.115
sale or return, 9.75—9.85
separation of components, 9.145—9.147
settlement discounting, 9.185—9.186
shares for services, 9.254
shipping charges, 9.97—9.99
software sales, 9.106—9.115
subscriptions, 9.140
trading activities, 9.285
transfer of significant risks and rewards
bill and hold sale, 9.65—9.72
continuing managerial involvement, 9.86—9.89
goods shipped subject to conditions, 9.75—9.85
payments in advance, 9.73—9.74
sale or return, 9.75—9.85
tuition fees, 9.143—9.144
turnover, 9.284
two-way trading arrangements, 9.176—9.184
up-front fees, 9.136—9.139
variable consideration
customer's control, within, 9.57
introduction, 9.56
neither party's control, within, 9.61—9.63
seller's control, within, 9.58—9.60
volume discounting, 9.185—9.186
vouchers
free products, 9.239
loyalty programmes, 9.240—9.245
options granted as part of sales transaction, 9.223—9.236
options granted for consideration, 9.219—9.222
options granted without consideration, 9.237—9.238
other benefit schemes, 9.246—9.250
point schemes, 9.240—9.245
warranties
extended warranty, 9.92—9.93
initial warranty, 9.90—9.91
Reversal of past losses
impairment of fixed assets, and, 18.1.14
Reverse acquisitions
cash alternatives, 25.143
generally, 25.128—25.142
Review of impairment
generally, 18.22—18.24
indicators, 18.25—18.32
Revolving assets
introduction, 3.159—3.161
reinvestment period, 3.162
repayment period, 3.163—3.165
Risks and rewards analysis
employee share ownership plans, and, 12.9—12.12
Rollover relief
deferred tax, and, 13.136—13.141
Royalties
intangible fixed assets, and, 15.51—15.53
revenue recognition, and, 9.255
'Rule of 78' method
depreciation, and, 16.262

Sale and leaseback transactions
finance leasebacks, 19.55—19.59
IFRS, and, 19.134
introduction, 19.54
operating leasebacks, 19.60—19.63
repurchase options, 19.64—19.67
summary, 19.1.19—19.1.20
Sale and repurchase
stocks, and, 20.42—20.47
Sale and repurchase agreements
accounting treatment, 3.130—3.132
examples of required analysis, 3.133—3.135
introduction, 3.123
sources of benefits and risks, 3.124—3.129
Sale of goods
handling charges, 9.97—9.99
installation fees, 9.94—9.96
introduction, 9.64
shipping charges, 9.97—9.99
transfer of significant risks and rewards, 9.65—9.89
warranties, 9.90—9.93
Sale of property
revenue recognition, and, 9.100—9.105
Sale of services
admission fees, 9.141—9.142
contracts containing significant acts, 9.133
inception fees, 9.136—9.139
milestone payments, 9.134—9.135
performance over time, 9.116—9.132
subscriptions, 9.140
tuition fees, 9.143—9.144
up-front fees, 9.136—9.139
Sale of shares
treasury shares, and, 23.56—23.59
Sale of software
revenue recognition, and, 9.106—9.115
Sale of subsidiary for shares
exchange for interest in joint venture, 26.23.9—26.23.10
exchange for interest in subsidiary, 26.23.8
generally, 26.23.1—26.237
Sale or return
revenue recognition, and, 9.75—9.85
Securitisation of assets
example of required analysis, 3.167
group's financial statements
disclosure requirements, 3.154—3.155
generally, 3.151—3.153
interest rate swaps, 3.156—3.158
introduction, 3.137—3.143
multi-originator programmes, 3.166
originator's financial statements
disclosure requirements, 3.148—3.150
generally, 3.144—3.147
quasi-subsidiaries, and, 3.117
revolving assets
introduction, 3.159—3.161
reinvestment period, 3.162
repayment period, 3.163—3.165
Segment net assets
segmental reporting, and, 10.91—10.99
Segment result
segmental reporting, and, 10.86—10.90
Segmental reporting (SSAP 25)
acquisitions, 10.127—10.135
allocation of costs, 10.62—10.66
associates
generally, 10.100—10.106
introduction, 27.83
capital expenditure, 10.148
cash flow statements, 10.117—10.120
Segmental reporting (SSAP 25)—*cont.*
changes to segments, 10.1.12
classes of business, 10.42—10.46
Companies Act requirements
disclosure, 10.68—10.73
introduction, 10.6—10.9
comparison with IFRS, and, 10.153
comparative figures, 10.110
depreciation, 10.150
determining segments
generally, 10.32—10.37
summary, 10.1.1—10.1.3
disclosure requirements
acquisitions, 10.127—10.135
associates, 10.100—10.106
cash flow statements, 10.117—10.120
Companies Act requirements, 10.68—10.73
comparative figures, 10.110
discontinued operations, 10.127—10.135
exceptional items, 10.136—10.142
inter-segment sales, 10.81—10.85
introduction, 10.67
joint arrangements, 10.107
joint ventures, 10.100—10.106
reconciliation of figures, 10.108
segment net assets, 10.91—10.99
segment result, 10.86—10.90
SSAP 25, 10.74—10.80
subsidiary undertakings, 10.122—10.126
summary, 10.1.4—10.1.11
turnover sales, 10.81—10.85
discontinued operations, 10.127—10.135
employee numbers, 10.145—10.147
exceptional items, 10.136—10.142
executive summary
changes to segments, 10.1.12
determining segments, 10.1.1—10.1.3
disclosures, 10.1.4—10.1.11
introduction, 10.1
fixed assets, 10.148
general guidance
allocation of costs, 10.62—10.66
classes of business, 10.42—10.46
determining segments, 10.32—10.41
geographical segments, 10.47—10.57
significant business segments, 10.58—10.61
geographical segments, 10.47—10.57
inter-segment sales, 10.81—10.85
introduction, 10.2—10.3.1
joint arrangements, 10.107
joint ventures
generally, 10.100—10.106
introduction, 27.83
reconciliation of figures, 10.108
regulatory framework
Companies Act requirements, 10.6—10.9
other standards, 10.31
SSAP 25, 10.13—10.30
research and development, 10.152
segment net assets, 10.91—10.99
segment result, 10.86—10.90
significant business segments, 10.58—10.60
SSAP 25
disclosure, 10.74—10.79
introduction, 10.13
scope, 10.14—10.22
truth and fairness, 10.24—10.30
subsidiary undertakings, 10.122—10.126
truth and fairness, 10.24—10.30
turnover sales, 10.81—10.85
voluntary disclosures

Segmental reporting (SSAP 25)—*cont.*
capital expenditure, 10.148
depreciation, 10.150
employee numbers, 10.145—10.147
fixed assets, 10.148
introduction, 10.144
research and development, 10.152
Self-insurance
provisions, and, 21.238—21.244
Separability
intangible fixed assets, and
generally, 15.16—15.22
IFRS, and, 15.139
Separable components of contract
revenue recognition, and, 9.145—9.147
Separate presentation
debt factoring, and, 3.136.13—3.136.14
Separate valuation
accounting principles, and, 2.116—2.120
Serious loss of capital
share capital, and, 23.38—23.41
Services, emoluments for
related party transactions, and, 29.159—29.161
Servicing of finance
cash flow statements, and, 30.76—30.85
Setting accounting standards
ASB Statement of principles
elements, 2.205—2.209
interests in other entities, 2.215
introduction, 2.191—2.192
materiality, 2.198—2.204
measurement, 2.212
objective, 2.193
presentation, 2.213—2.214
qualitative characteristics, 2.195—2.197
recognition, 2.210—2.211
reporting entity, 2.194
background, 2.155—2.163
Settlement discounting
revenue recognition, and, 9.185—9.186
Settlements
retirement benefits, and, 11.100—11.108
Severe long-term restrictions
accounting treatment, 24.188—24.192
generally, 24.182—24.187
Share-based payment transactions (FRS 20)
alternative share-based payment transactions, 12.2
cancellations, 12.13
cash payments to employee trusts, 12.94—12.102
cash-settled share-based payment transactions
deferred tax, 13.127.8
generally, 12.2
introduction, 12.14—12.15
comparison with IFRS, 12.113
deferred tax, and
cash-settled transactions, 13.127.8
equity-settled transactions, 13.127—13.127.7
disclosures
ESOP trusts, 12.73—12.74
generally, 12.22
employee share ownership plans
accounting, 12.46—12.54
background, 12.42—12.45
disclosure, 12.73—12.74
distributable profits, 12.56—12.62
gains, 12.71—12.72
generally, 12.40—12.41
introduction, 12.19—12.21
legal issues, 12.55
public companies, and, 12.63—12.70
trustee company, 12.72

Share-based payment transactions (FRS 20)—*cont.*
equity-settled share-based payment transactions
deferred tax, 13.127—13.127.7
generally, 12.16—12.18
measurement, 12.5—12.7
summary, 12.2
examples, 12.103
excluded grants of instruments, 12.110—12.112
exclusions from scope, 12.3
first time adoption, and, 12.23
GAAP, and, 12.24
grants to which not apply, 12.110—12.112
IFRS, and
generally, 12.25—12.26
text, A12.1—A12.245
introduction, 12.1
measurement, 12.5—12.7
modifications and cancellations, 12.13
NICs on option gains
background, 12.27—12.34
introduction, 12.11—12.12
reimbursement of liability, 12.36—12.39
transfer of liability, 12.36—12.39
objective, 12.6—12.11
practical implications
employee share ownership plans, 12.42—12.72
QUESTs, 12.75—12.93
share symmetry arrangements, 12.75
QUESTs
introduction, 12.75—12.84
pre-funding by parent company, 12.90—12.91
pre-funding by subsidiary company, 12.92—12.93
simultaneous funding by parent company, 12.85—12.88
simultaneous funding by subsidiary company, 12.89
recognition
generally, 12.4
measurement, 12.5—12.7
vesting conditions, 12.8—12.10
scope, 12.6—12.11
share-based payments transactions
generally, 12.16—12.18
summary, 12.2
share symmetry arrangements, 12.75
transitional provisions, 12.104—12.109
types, 12.2
vesting conditions, 12.8—12.10
Share capital
accounting treatment, 23.20—23.29
allotment of shares during year, 23.35—23.37
amounts unpaid on debentures and shares, 23.233
articles of association, 23.236—23.237
Aveling Barford decision, 23.244—23.253
bonus issues, 23.230—23.232
called up share capital, 23.18—23.19
debentures, and, 23.233
disclosure requirements
allotment of shares during year, 23.35—23.37
Companies Act requirements, 23.30—23.34
distributable profits
and see **Distributable profits**
capitalisation of development costs, 23.190—23.191
conditions, 23.162—23.176
definition of 'distribution', 23.161
foreign currency translation, 23.186—23.189
goodwill, 23.192—23.195
other transactions, 23.202
pre-acquisition profits, 23.201
relevant accounts, 23.203—23.229
revaluations, and, 23.177—23.185
transactions within the group, 23.196—23.198

Share capital—*cont.*
distributions in kind, 23.238—23.243
dividends, 23.134—23.138
"equity share capital", 23.6
introduction, 23.1—23.4
measurement, 23.11—23.17
memorandum of association, 23.236—23.237
multi-currency capital, 23.42—23.45
"ordinary share capital", 23.7
pre-ACT profits and losses, 23.234—23.235
purchase of own shares, 23.9
realised losses
fair value accounting, 23.152—23.156
generally, 23.150—23.151
intra-group transactions, 23.157—23.157.3
other matters, 23.158—23.160
principles, 23.139—23.144
realised profits
fair value accounting, 23.152—23.156
generally, 23.146—23.149
intra-group transactions, 23.157—23.157.3
other matters, 23.158—23.160
principles, 23.139—23.144
proposed dividends, 23.156.1—23.156.2
reserves, and
and see **Reserves**
capital redemption reserve, 23.119
disclosure requirements, 23.125—23.133
fair value reserve, 23.124.1
foreign currency translation reserve, 23.124.3
hedging reserve, 23.124.2
introduction, 23.84—23.85
profit and loss account, 23.86
revaluation reserve, 23.120—23.124
share premium account, 23.87—23.118
serious loss of capital, 23.38—23.41
treasury shares
accounting treatment, 23.63—23.73
cancellation, 23.56—23.59
conditions, 23.51—23.55
delivery of returns, 23.60—23.62
disclosure, 23.74—23.79
effect on distributable profits, 23.80—23.83
general rules, 23.46—23.50
sale, 23.56—23.59
types of shares, 23.5—23.10
unrealised profits, and, 23.63—23.65
Share incentive plans (SIPs)
accounting implications
dividend shares, 12.103—12.105
free shares, 12.94—12.95
matching shares, 12.100—12.102
overview, 12.90—12.93
partnership shares, 12.96—12.99
corporate tax, and, 12.89
dividends shares
accounting implications, 12.103—12.105
introduction, 12.88
free shares
accounting implications, 12.94—12.95
introduction, 12.88
introduction, 12.86—12.87
matching shares
accounting implications, 12.100—12.102
introduction, 12.88
partnership shares
accounting implications, 12.96—12.99
introduction, 12.88
principal features, 12.88
tax-free reinvestment of dividends, 12.88
Share interests of directors
related party transactions, and, 29.181
Share premium account
generally, 23.87—23.93
implications of *Shearer v Bercain*, 23.94—23.95
merger relief
application of, 23.100—23.104
generally, 23.96—23.99
group reconstructions, 23.105—23.112
reduction, 23.113—23.118
Share symmetry arrangements
generally, 12.130
share-based payments, and, 12.75
Share transactions by directors
related party transactions, and, 29.139
Shares issued for services
revenue recognition, and, 9.254
Shipping charges
revenue recognition, and, 9.97—9.99
Short-term debtors and creditors
financial instruments, and, 6.166—6.169
Significant accounting transactions
dormant companies, and, 32.159.7—32.159.9
Significant business segments
generally, 10.58—10.60
Significant holdings greater than 20%
financial instruments, and, 6.102—6.107
Simultaneous QUEST
funding by parent company, 12.111—12.117
funding by subsidiary company, 12.118—12.120
generally, 12.109—12.110
Small companies (FRSSE)
abbreviated financial statements
auditors' responsibilities, 32.128—32.131
directors' responsibilities, 32.125—32.127
introduction, 32.117—32.124
accounting policies, 32.98—32.99.6
accounting standards, 32.23—32.27.1
audit requirements
introduction, 32.30
summary, 32.34
auditors' report, 32.113—32.116.2
balance sheet
capital instruments, 32.80—32.82
consignment stock, 32.75—32.76
contingencies, 32.79—32.79.4
debt factors, 32.77—32.78
depreciation, 32.64—32.67
formats, 32.62—32.63
intangible fixed assets, 32.71—32.73.1
leases, 32.68—32.70.1
long-term contracts, 32.74
notes, 32.90—32.92
post balance sheets events, 32.79—32.79.4
pre-contract costs, 32.67.1—32.67.2
provisions, 32.79—32.79.4
start-up costs, 32.67.1—32.67.2
stocks, 32.74
tangible fixed assets, 32.64—32.67
write-downs to recoverable amount, 32.73.2
capital instruments, 32.80—32.82
cash flow statements, and, 30.31—30.34
categorisation
other criteria, 32.40—32.42
size criteria, 32.35—32.39
Companies Act requirements, 32.11—32.22
consignment stock, 32.75—32.76
consolidated financial statements, and, 24.35—24.36
content of financial statements, and, 4.141
contingencies, 32.79—32.79.4
debt factors, 32.77—32.78

Small companies (FRSSE)—*cont.*
depreciation, 32.64—32.67
directors' report, and, 32.108—32.112
estimation techniques, 32.98—32.99.6
excluded companies, 32.50—32.52
financial statements
abbreviated statements, 32.117—32.131
auditors' report, 32.113—32.116.2
balance sheet, 32.62—32.82
directors' report, 32.108—32.112
form and content, 32.56—32.61
full statements, 32.132
introduction, 32.53—32.55
notes, 32.90—32.107
profit and loss account, 32.83—32.89
foreign currencies, 32.89
intangible fixed assets, 32.71—32.73.1
IFRS, and, 32.188
introduction, 32.1—32.10
leases, 32.68—32.70.1
long-term contracts, 32.74
post balance sheets events, 32.79—32.79.4
pre-contract costs, 32.67.1—32.67.2
profit and loss account
effect of FRS 3, 32.84—32.85
foreign currencies, 32.89
formats, 32.83
notes, 32.93—32.97
retirement benefits, 32.88—32.88.4
taxation, 32.86—32.87.1
provisions, 32.79—32.79.4
regulatory framework
accounting standards, 32.23—32.27.1
audit requirements, 32.30—32.34
Companies Act requirements, 32.11—32.22
related party transactions
disclosures, 32.100—32.103.1
generally, 29.163—29.165
retirement benefits, 32.88—32.88.4
start-up costs, 32.67.1—32.67.2
stocks, 32.74
tangible fixed assets, 32.64—32.67
taxation, 32.86—32.87.1
true and fair overrides, 32.104
write-downs to recoverable amount, 32.73.2
Small groups
and see **Small companies**
abbreviated financial statements, 32.154
categorisation
other criteria, 32.47—32.49
size criteria, 32.44—32.46
consolidated financial statements
exemptions, 32.148—32.153
shorter-form, 32.155—32.159
excluded groups, 32.50—32.52
introduction, 32.147
Small parent companies
generally, 32.143—32.146
Small unincorporated entities
cash flow statements, and, 30.38 6
Software
intangible fixed assets, and, 15.135—15.138
Software development costs
tangible fixed assets, and, 16.72—16.74.10
Software sales
revenue recognition, and, 9.106—9.115
SORPs
financial reporting structure, and, 2.74—2.77
Speculative forward contracts
foreign currency hedging, and, 7.138
Spreading variations, principle of
examples, 11.63—11.68
exceptions, 11.69—11.88
introduction, 11.59—11.62
SSAP 4 (capital grants)
disclosure requirements, 16.339—16.340
IFRS, and, 16.344
introduction, 16.329
non-depreciable fixed assets, 16.341—16.343
revision of standard, 16.331—16.338
scope of standard, 16.330
SSAP 9 (long-term contracts)
accounting treatment, 20.74—20.75
claims, 20.94—20.95
comparison with IFRS, and, 20.119—20-120
construction contracts, and, 20.120
cost of sales, 20.99—20.102
definition, 20.72—20.73.1
disclosure requirements
generally, 20.106—20.114
provision for foreseeable losses, 20.115—20.118
summary, 20.1.16—20.1.18
executive summary
disclosure, 20.1.16—20.1.18
generally, 20.1.9—20.1.15
introduction, 20.1—20.1.2
future costs, 20.89—20.91
generally, 20.1.9—20.1.15
IFRS, and, 20.120
introduction, 20.71
inventories, and, 20.120
losses, 20.96—20.98
profit recognition
amounts recoverable on contracts, 20.103—20.105
claims, 20.94—20.95
cost of sales, 20.99—20.102
determination of future costs, 20.89—20.91
generally, 20.78—20.88
losses on contracts, 20.96—20.98
variations, 20.92—20.93
recoverable amounts, 20.103—20.105
turnover, 20.76—20.77
variations, 20.92—20.93
SSAP 9 (stocks)
consignment stock
accounting treatment, 20.57—20.60
conclusion, 20.66
example of required analysis, 20.61—20.63
introduction, 20.48
manufacturer's position, 20.64—20.65
objective, 20.49—20.51
sources of benefits and risks, 20.52—20.56
cost of stocks
definition, 20.8—20.14
determination, 20.15—20.27
summary, 20.1.3—20.1.8
disclosure requirements
generally, 20.34—20.36
replacement value, 20.37—20.41
summary, 20.1.16—20.1.18
executive summary
determining cost, 20.1.3—20.1.8
disclosure, 20.1.16—20.1.18
introduction, 20.1—20.1.2
IFRS, and, 20.119—20-120
introduction, 20.2—20.4
net realisable value, 20.28—20.33
replacement value, 20.37—20.41
reservation of title, goods with, 20.67—20.70
sale and repurchase, 20.42—20.47

SSAP 12 (depreciation)
investment properties, and, 17.1—17.2
SSAP 19 (investment properties)
accounting requirements
generally, 17.6—17.12
summary, 17.1.1—17.1.6
balance sheet presentation, 17.13—17.14
Companies Act 1985 requirements, and
market value measurement, 17.14.1—17.14.2
true and fair override, 17.15—17.16
comparison with IFRS, and
convergence, 17.40
cost model, 17.40
definitions, 17.40
disclosure, 17.40
disposals, 17.40
exchanges, 17.40
fair value, 17.40
first-time adoption, 17.40
initial measurement, 17.40
introduction, 17.40
overview, 17.40
recognition, 17.40
related pronouncements, 17.40
scope, 17.40
subsequent expenditure, 17.40
subsequent measurement, 17.40
transfers, 17.40
cost model, 17.40
definition
generally, 17.3
summary, 17.1
diminution in value
generally, 17.20
permanent diminution in value, 17.24—17.31
temporary diminution in value, 17.21—17.23
disclosures
generally, 17.35—17.39
IFRS, and, 17.40
summary, 17.1.8—17.1.9
disposals, 17.40
exchanges, 17.40
excluded properties, 17.4
executive summary
accounting, 17.1.1—17.1.6
definition, 17.1
disclosure, 17.1.8—17.1.9
valuations, 17.1.7
fair value, 17.40
first-time adoption, 17.40
IFRS, and, 17.40
initial measurement, 17.40
introduction, 17.2—17.2.1
investment revaluation reserve
diminution in value, 17.20
generally, 17.17—17.19
negative revaluation reserves, 17.32—17.33
permanent diminution in value, 17.24—17.31
temporary diminution in value, 17.21—17.23
market value measurement, 17.14.1—17.14.2
negative revaluation reserves, 17.32—17.33
owner-occupied properties, 17.34
recognition, 17.40
SSAP 12, and, 17.1—17.2
subsequent expenditure, 17.40
subsequent measurement, 17.40
transfers, 17.40
true and fair override, 17.15—17.16
valuations, 17.1.7

SSAP 20 (foreign currency translation)
average rate determination
consolidated financial statements, 7.53—7.55
individual company financial statements, 7.16—7.18
change between methods, 7.59—7.61
closing rate/net investment method, 7.35—7.41
closing rate/net investment method, 7.35—7.41
consolidated financial statements, and
average rate determination, 7.53—7.55
change between methods, 7.59—7.61
closing rate/net investment method, 7.35—7.41
deferred trading balances, 7.70—7.75
dual rates, 7.56
goodwill, 7.76—7.78
intercompany dividends, 7.62—7.66
intra-group companies transactions, 7.67
intra-group long-term loans, 7.70—7.75
introduction, 7.33—7.34
local currency, 7.57—7.58
other matters, 7.52
summary, 7.11.8—7.11.15
suspension of rates, 7.56
temporal method, 7.42—7.51
unrealised profit on stocks, 7.68—7.69
date of transaction, 7.15
deferred trading balances, 7.70—7.75
disclosures
requirements of Companies Act, 7.143
requirements of standard, 7.144—7.148.2
distributable profits, and, 7.149—7.160
dual rates
consolidated financial statements, 7.56
individual company financial statements, 7.19—7.20
euro, and
associated costs, 7.180—7.183
cumulative differences, 7.184—7.185
introduction, 7.178—7.179
exchange gains and losses, 7.25—7.31
executive summary
consolidated financial statements, 7.11.8—7.11.15
equity investments financed by foreign borrowing, 7.11.16—7.11.20
individual company financial statements, 7.11.1—7.11.7
introduction, 7.11
financial statements in foreign currencies, 7.172—7.176
foreign currency commitment, 7.132
foreign currency options, 7.139—7.142
foreign equity investments financed by foreign borrowings
consolidated financial statements, 7.105—7.112
individual company financial statements, 7.79—7.104
summary, 7.11.16—7.11.20
forward exchange contracts
existing assets or liabilities, 7.131
generally, 7.125—7.128
taken out at transaction date, 7.129—7.130
FRS 23, and
disclosure, A7.117—A7.122.2
first time adoption of IFRS, A7.130—A7.132
foreign currency transactions, A7.48—A7.114
functional currency approach, A7.27—A7.47
introduction, A7.1—A7.7
objectives, A7.23
other matters, A7.126—A7.127
overview, 7.188—7.189
presentation, A7.115—A7.116

SSAP 20 (foreign currency translation)—*cont.*
scope, A7.24—A7.26
future results of foreign investments, 7.135—7.137
goodwill, 7.76—7.78
hedging transactions
foreign currency commitment, 7.132
foreign currency options, 7.139—7.142
forward exchange contracts, 7.125—7.131
future results of foreign investments, 7.135—7.137
introduction, 7.120—7.124
net investment, 7.133—7.134
speculative forward contracts, 7.138
hyper-inflationary economies, 7.161—7.169
IAS 21 (foreign exchange rates), and
disclosure, A7.117—A7.122.2
first time adoption of IFRS, A7.130—A7.132
foreign currency transactions, A7.48—A7.114
functional currency approach, A7.27—A7.47
introduction, A7.1—A7.7
objectives, A7.23
other matters, A7.126—A7.127
overview, 7.188—7.189
presentation, A7.115—A7.116
scope, A7.24—A7.26
IAS 29 (hyperinflationary economies), and
generally, A7.109—A7.114
overview, 7.188—7.189
individual company financial statements, and
average rate determination, 7.16—7.18
date of transaction, 7.15
dual rates, 7.19—7.20
exchange gains and losses, 7.25—7.31
general rules, 7.14
intra-group companies transactions, 7.32
monetary items, 7.23—7.24
non-monetary items, 7.21—7.22
settled transactions, 7.26
summary, 7.11.1—7.11.7
suspension of rates, 7.19—7.20
unsettled transactions, 7.27—7.31
intercompany dividends, 7.62—7.66
intra-group companies transactions
consolidated financial statements, 7.67
individual company financial statements, 7.32
intra-group long-term loans, 7.70—7.75
introduction, 7.2—7.10.1
local currency, 7.57—7.58
monetary items, 7.23—7.24
multi-currency share capital, 7.170—7.171
net investment in foreign operation, 7.133—7.134
non-monetary items, 7.21—7.22
objectives, 7.12
procedures, 7.13
scope of standard, 7.11
settled transactions, 7.26
speculative forward contracts, 7.138
suspension of rates
consolidated financial statements, 7.56
individual company financial statements, 7.19—7.20
temporal method, 7.42—7.51
UITF abstract
19, 7.113—7.119
21, 7.178—7.185
unrealised profit on stocks, 7.68—7.69
unsettled transactions, 7.27—7.31
SSAP 21 (leases and HP contracts)
accounting by lessees
disclosure requirements, 19.50—19.53
finance leases, 19.39—19.42
operating leases, 19.43—19.49

SSAP 21 (leases and HP contracts)—*cont.*
sale and leaseback transactions, 19.54—19.67
summary, 19.1.7—19.1.13
accounting by lessors
back-to-back leases, 19.111—19.119
direct costs, 19.90—19.95
disclosure requirements, 19.78—19.89
finance leases, 19.68—19.75
FLA SORP, 19.67.1—19.67.4
manufacturer/dealer lessors, 19.105—19.110
operating leases, 19.76—19.77.10
rental variation, 19.96—19.104
residual values, 19.120—19.133
summary, 19.1.14—19.1.18
back-to-back leases
introduction, 19.111—19.112
head lessor, 19.113
intermediate party, 19.114—19.119
classification
generally, 19.7—19.14
IFRS, and, 19.134
implicit interest rate, 19.29—19.31
minimum payments, 19.21—19.28
present value calculation, 19.32—19.33
property leases, 19.34—19.38
summary, 19.1.1—19.1.6
term, 19.14.2—19.20
comparison with IFRS, and, 19.134
construction periods, 19.104
deferred tax, and, 13.122—13.125.1
direct costs, 19.90—19.95
disclosure requirements
accounting by lessees, 19.50—19.53
accounting by lessors, 19.78—19.89
executive summary
classification of leases, 19.1.1—19.1.6
introduction, 19.1
lessee accounting, 19.1.7—19.1.13
lessor accounting, 19.1.14—19.1.18
sale and leaseback, 19.1.19—19.1.20
finance leasebacks, 19.55—19.59
finance leases (accounting by lessees)
disclosure requirements, 19.50—19.53
generally, 19.39—19.42
IFRS, and, 19.134
residual values, 19.126
finance leases (accounting by lessors)
disclosure requirements, 19.78—19.89
actuarial after-tax method, 19.75
generally, 19.68—19.74
IFRS, and, 19.134
FLA SORP, 19.67.1—19.67.4
IFRS, and, 19.134
incentives for operating leases
accounting by lessees, 19.44—19.49
accounting by lessors, 19.77.7—19.77.10
IFRS, and, 19.134
interest rate variations, 19.101—19.103
introduction, 19.2—19.6.1
lessee accounting
disclosure requirements, 19.50—19.53
finance leases, 19.39—19.42
operating leases, 19.43—19.49
sale and leaseback transactions, 19.54—19.67
summary, 19.1.7—19.1.13
lessor accounting
back-to-back leases, 19.111—19.119
direct costs, 19.90—19.95
disclosure requirements, 19.78—19.89
finance leases, 19.68—19.75
FLA SORP, 19.67.1—19.67.4

SSAP 21 (leases and HP contracts)—*cont.*
manufacturer/dealer lessors, 19.105—19.110
operating leases, 19.76—19.77.10
rental variation, 19.96—19.104
residual values, 19.120—19.133
summary, 19.1.14—19.1.18
manufacturer/dealer lessors
generally, 19.105—19.110
IFRS, and, 19.134
operating leasebacks, 19.60—19.63
operating leases (accounting by lessees)
disclosure requirements, 19.52—19.53
generally, 19.43
IFRS, and, 19.134
incentives, 19.44—19.49
residual values, 19.123—19.125
operating leases (accounting by lessors)
disclosure requirements, 19.80—19.89
generally, 19.76—19.77.6
IFRS, and, 19.134
incentives, 19.77.7—19.77.10
rental variation
construction periods, 19.104
interest rate variations, 19.101—19.103
tax variation clauses, 19.96—19.97
repurchase options, 19.64—19.67
residual values
finance leases, under, 19.126
fluctuations in anticipated residual values, 19.127—19.131
introduction, 19.120—19.121
operating leases, under, 19.123—19.125
tax-free grants, 19.132—19.133
sale and leaseback transactions
finance leasebacks, 19.55—19.59
IFRS, and, 19.134
introduction, 19.54
operating leasebacks, 19.60—19.63
repurchase options, 19.64—19.67
summary, 19.1.19—19.1.20
sub leases
introduction, 19.111—19.112
head lessor, 19.113
intermediate party, 19.114—19.119
tax-free grants, 19.132—19.133
tax variation clauses, 19.96—19.97
SSAP 24 (pension costs)
and see **Pension costs**
introduction, 11.2—11.3
SSAP 25 (segmental reporting)
acquisitions, 10.127—10.135
allocation of costs, 10.62—10.66
associates
generally, 10.100—10.106
introduction, 27.83
capital expenditure, 10.148
cash flow statements, 10.117—10.120
changes to segments, 10.1.12
classes of business, 10.42—10.46
Companies Act requirements
disclosure, 10.68—10.73
introduction, 10.6—10.9
comparative figures, 10.110
depreciation, 10.150
determining segments
generally, 10.32—10.37
summary, 10.1.1—10.1.3
disclosure requirements
acquisitions, 10.127—10.135
associates, 10.100—10.106
cash flow statements, 10.117—10.120
SSAP 25 (segmental reporting)
Companies Act requirements, 10.68—10.73
comparative figures, 10.110
discontinued operations, 10.127—10.135
exceptional items, 10.136—10.142
inter-segment sales, 10.81—10.85
introduction, 10.67
joint arrangements, 10.107
joint ventures, 10.100—10.106
reconciliation of figures, 10.108
segment net assets, 10.91—10.99
segment result, 10.86—10.90
SSAP 25, 10.74—10.80
subsidiary undertakings, 10.122—10.126
summary, 10.1.4—10.1.11
turnover sales, 10.81—10.85
discontinued operations, 10.127—10.135
employee numbers, 10.145—10.147
exceptional items, 10.136—10.142
executive summary
changes to segments, 10.1.12
determining segments, 10.1.1—10.1.3
disclosures, 10.1.4—10.1.11
introduction, 10.1
fixed assets, 10.148
general guidance
allocation of costs, 10.62—10.66
classes of business, 10.42—10.46
determining segments, 10.32—10.41
geographical segments, 10.47—10.57
significant business segments, 10.58—10.61
geographical segments, 10.47—10.57
inter-segment sales, 10.81—10.85
introduction, 10.2—10.3.1
joint arrangements, 10.107
joint ventures
generally, 10.100—10.106
introduction, 27.83
reconciliation of figures, 10.108
regulatory framework
Companies Act requirements, 10.6—10.9
other standards, 10.31
SSAP 25, 10.13—10.30
research and development, 10.152
segment net assets, 10.91—10.99
segment result, 10.86—10.90
significant business segments, 10.58—10.60
SSAP 25
disclosure, 10.74—10.79
introduction, 10.13
scope, 10.14—10.22
truth and fairness, 10.24—10.30
subsidiary undertakings, 10.122—10.126
truth and fairness, 10.24—10.30
turnover sales, 10.81—10.85
voluntary disclosures
capital expenditure, 10.148
depreciation, 10.150
employee numbers, 10.145—10.147
fixed assets, 10.148
introduction, 10.144
research and development, 10.152
SSAPs
financial reporting structure, and, 2.65—2.73
Staff costs
directors, 5.25—5.26
disclosure by groups, 5.26.1—5.26.2
generally, 5.15—5.20
numbers of employees, 5.21—5.24
practical issues, 5.27—5.28

Staff numbers
profit and loss account, and, 5.21—5.24
segmental reporting, and, 10.145—10.147
Stage of completion of performance
revenue recognition, and, 9.127—9.132
Standards Advisory Council
IASB, and, 2.218
Standing Interpretations Committee
IASB, and, 2.219
Stapled shares
minority interests, and, 24.368
Start-up costs
generally, 16.85—16.89.5
introduction, 16.21—16.23
small companies, and, 32.67.1—32.67.2
Statement of movement of reserves
disclosure requirements, 23.131—23.133
Statement of principles
elements, 2.205—2.209
group structure, and, 24.16—24.17
interests in other entities, 2.215
introduction, 2.191—2.192
materiality, 2.198—2.204
measurement, 2.212
objective, 2.193
presentation, 2.213—2.214
provisions, and, 21.7—21.8
qualitative characteristics, 2.195—2.197
recognition, 2.210—2.211
reporting entity, 2.194
Statement of total recognised gains and losses (STRGL)
associates, and, 27.84
generally, 8.145—8.154.1
joint ventures, and, 27.84
movements in reserves, 8.160—8.164
purchased goodwill, 8.155—8.159
retirement benefits, and, 11.1.19, 11.1.19—11.1.24
taxation, and
generally, 13.249—13.250
notes, 13.251—13.252
Stock, forward purchase of
hedging, and, 6.130—6.131
Stock lending
reporting the substance of transactions, and, 3.232—3.242.1
Stocks (SSAP 9)
consignment stock
accounting treatment, 20.57—20.60
conclusion, 20.66
example of required analysis, 20.61—20.63
introduction, 20.48
manufacturer's position, 20.64—20.65
objective, 20.49—20.51
sources of benefits and risks, 20.52—20.56
cost of stocks
definition, 20.8—20.14
determination, 20.15—20.27
summary, 20.1.3—20.1.8
disclosure requirements
generally, 20.34—20.36
replacement value, 20.37—20.41
summary, 20.1.16—20.1.18
executive summary
determining cost, 20.1.3—20.1.8
disclosure, 20.1.16—20.1.18
introduction, 20.1—20.1.2
IFRS, and, 20.119—20-120
introduction, 20.2—20.4
net realisable value, 20.28—20.33
replacement value, 20.37—20.41
reservation of title, 20.67—20.70
Stocks (SSAP 9)—*cont.*
sale and repurchase, 20.42—20.47
summary, 20.1—20.1.2
Straight line method
depreciation, and, 16.259
STRGL
associates, and, 27.84
generally, 8.145—8.154.1
joint ventures, and, 27.84
movements in reserves, 8.160—8.164
purchased goodwill, 8.155—8.159
retirement benefits, and, 11.1.19, 11.1.19—11.1.24
taxation, and
generally, 13.249—13.250
notes, 13.251—13.252
Sub leases
introduction, 19.111—19.112
head lessor, 19.113
intermediate party, 19.114—19.119
Subordinated debt
quasi-subsidiaries, and, 3.115—3.116
Subscriptions
revenue recognition, and, 9.140
Subsequent expenditure on tangible fixed assets
accounting treatment, 16.133—16.134
IFRS, and, 16.344
introduction, 16.130—16.132
major inspections and overhauls, 16.150—16.153
previously assessed standard of performance, 16.135—16.142
replacing components, 16.143—16.149
summary, 16.1.5—16.1.6
Subsidiaries excluded from consolidation
consolidation rules, and, 24.330—24.343
disclosure requirements
aggregation, 24.204—24.208
Companies Act requirements, 24.202—24.202.2
exemptions, 24.209—24.212
FRS requirements, 24.203
introduction, 24.200—24.201
dissimilar activities, 24.203
interest held exclusively with view to subsequent resale
accounting treatment, 24.198
generally, 24.193—24.197
introduction, 24.176—24.180
severe long-term restrictions
accounting treatment, 24.188—24.192
generally, 24.182—24.187
undue delay, 24.181
Subsidiaries acquired and disposed of during year
related party transactions, and, 29.131—29.132
Subsidiary undertakings
actual exercise of dominant influence
cessation of, 24.150—24.152
commercial relationships, 24.141—24.143
definition, 24.131—24.134
disclosure requirements, 24.151
financial policies, 24.135—24.137
method of exercise, 24.144—24.148
operating policies, 24.135—24.137
practical effect, 24.138
reserve powers, 24.139—24.140
summary, 24.153
two parents, 24.149
veto power, 24.139—24.140
appointment of board majority, 24.96—24.104
cash flow statements, and, 30.24—30.25
company law, and, 24.78—24.79
control
contrast with shared control, 24.159

Subsidiary undertakings—*cont.*
governed by agreement, 24.155—24.156
definition, 24.26—24.31
disclosure requirements
company shares, 24.221—24.226
excessive information, 24.236—24.237
financial years, 24.219
holdings in subsidiaries, 24.217.1—24.218
introduction, 24.213
place of origin, 24.214—24.217
'seriously prejudicial', 24.233—24.235
'shares held by group', 24.232
significant investment holdings, 24.227—24.231
disposal of
and see **Disposal of subsidiaries**
accounting rules, 26.5—26.19
disclosure requirements, 26.39—26.41
IFRS, and, 26.42—26.45
introduction, 26.1—26.4
types of disposal, 26.20—26.38
dominant influence
cessation of, 24.147—24.149
commercial relationships, 24.143—24.145
definition, 24.132—24.136
disclosure requirements, 24.151
financial policies, 24.137—24.139
generally, 24.121—24.124
method of exercise, 24.144—24.148
operating policies, 24.137—24.139
power to exercise or exercises influence, 24.130—24.131
practical effect, 24.140
reserve powers, 24.141—24.142
right to exercise, 24.125—24.129
special purpose entities, 24.149.1—24.149.3
summary, 24.150
two parents, 24.146
veto power, 24.141—24.142
European law, 24.79
expressions and interpretations
capital provisions, 24.171
introduction, 24.160
parent undertakings, 24.161—24.164
rights provisions, 24.165—24.170
subsidiary undertakings, 24.161—24.164
financial instruments, and, 6.122—6.130
introduction, 24.76—24.77
majority of voting rights, 24.89—24.95
meaning, 24.80—24.85
participating interest, 24.152—24.154
practical situations, 24.175
related parties, and, 29.36—29.37
removal of board majority, 24.96—24.104
segmental reporting, and, 10.122—10.126
terminology, 24.86—24.88
Substance of transactions, reporting the (FRS 5)
application notes
consignment stock, 3.122
debt factoring, 3.136—3.136.16
introduction, 3.120—3.121
loan transfers, 3.168—3.179
PFI and PPP, 3.179.1—3.179.56
sale and repurchase agreements, 3.123—3.135
securitised assets, 3.137—3.167
background, 3.1—3.4
bed and breakfasting, 3.243—3.249
bills of exchange, 3.197
cash flow statement, 3.251
consignment stock, 3.122
contract purchase arrangements, 3.228—3.231
debt factoring

Substance of transactions, reporting the (FRS 5)—*cont.*
benefits and risks, 3.136.5—3.136.9
derecognition, 3.136.10
examples of required analysis, 3.136.15—3.136.16
introduction, 3.136—3.136.4
linked presentation, 3.136.11—3.136.12
separate presentation, 3.136.13—3.136.14
identification of assets and liabilities
analysing complex transactions, 3.52—3.58
assets, 3.59—3.62
introduction, 3.51
liabilities, 3.63—3.64
insubstance debt defeasance, 3.184—3.185
interaction with Companies Act and accounting standards, 3.42.1—3.46
linked presentation
cash flow statement, 3.251
detailed conditions, 3.88—3.90
general rules, 3.83—3.87
linking part of finance, 3.91—3.92
profit recognition, 3.93—3.96
loan transfers
disclosure requirements, 3.178—3.179
generally, 3.168—3.177
objective, 3.47—3.50
offsetting, 3.97—3.99
partial derecognition, 3.181—3.182
PFI and PPP
accounting treatment, 3.179.50—3.179.55.23
application of FRS 5, 3.179.17—3.179.24
contract separability, 3.179.8—3.179.16
example of quantitative analysis, 3.179.56
introduction, 3.179.1—3.177.7
property factors, 3.179.25—3.179.48
summary of risks, 3.179.49
practical issues
purchase commitments, 3.250
repurchase agreements, 3.219—3.224
stock lending, 3.232—3.242.1
take-or-pay contracts, 3.252—3.256.1
trade loans, 3.183
principles
identifying and recognising assets and liabilities, 3.51—3.65
introduction, 3.47—3.50
linked presentation, 3.83—3.96
offset rules, 3.97—3.99
quasi-subsidiaries, 3.100—3.119
transactions in previously recognised assets, 3.66—3.822
purchase commitments, 3.250
quasi-subsidiaries, accounting for
accounting treatment, 3.108—3.112
credit enhancement, 3.115—3.116
disclosure, 3.119
introduction, 3.100—3.106
linked presentation, 3.113—3.114
parent's financial statements, and, 3.118
securitisation, 3.117
subordinated debt, 3.115—3.116
true and fair overriding disclosures, and, 3.107
recognition of assets and liabilities
generally, 3.65
introduction, 3.51
repurchase agreements, 3.219—3.224
sale and repurchase agreements
accounting treatment, 3.130—3.132
examples of required analysis, 3.133—3.135
introduction, 3.123
sources of benefits and risks, 3.124—3.129
scope of standard, 3.37—3.42

Substance of transactions, reporting the (FRS 5)—*cont.*
securitisation of assets
example of required analysis, 3.167
group's financial statements, 3.151—3.155
interest rate swaps, 3.156—3.158
introduction, 3.137—3.143
multi-originator programmes, 3.166
originator's financial statements, 3.144—3.150
revolving assets, 3.159—3.165
stock lending, 3.232—3.242.1
take-or-pay contracts, 3.252—3.256.1
trade loans, 3.183
transactions in previously recognised assets
continued recognition, 3.71—3.72
full derecognition, 3.73
generally, 3.66—3.70
insurance, 3.82
partial derecognition, 3.74—3.81
'Substance over form'
reporting the substance of transactions, and, 3.257
Sum of the digits method
depreciation, and, 16.262
Super-exceptional items
associates and joint ventures, and, 27.77
Suspension of rates
consolidated financial statements, 7.56
individual company financial statements, 7.19—7.20
Systems rectification
provisions, and, 21.266—21.267

Tabular information
provisions, and, 21.293—21.296
Take-or-pay contracts
reporting the substance of transactions, and, 3.252—3.256.1
Tangible fixed assets (FRS 15)
accumulated depreciation, 16.226—16.230
assets surplus to requirements, 16.189
assets under construction, 16.43—16.46
assets used in business, 16.185—16.188
background, 16.3—16.8
bases of valuation
assets surplus to requirements, 16.189
assets used in business, 16.185—16.188
depreciated replacement cost, 16.197—16.200
existing use value, 16.193—16.196
introduction, 16.177—16.184
open market value, 16.190—16.192
plant and machinery value, 16.201—16.203
borrowing costs, and, 16.345
capital grants (SSAP 4), and
disclosure requirements, 16.339—16.340
IFRS, and, 16.346
introduction, 16.329
non-depreciable fixed assets, 16.341—16.343
revision of standard, 16.331—16.338
scope of standard, 16.330
capitalisation of finance costs
accounting treatment, 16.106—16.110
definition of 'finance costs', 16.102—16.105
disclosure requirements, 16.126—16.129
general borrowings, 16.121
group situations, 16.122—16.124
IFRS, and, 16.344
introduction, 16.100—16.101
period of, 16.111—16.117
specific borrowings, 16.118—16.120
taxation, 16.125
capitalisation of interest, 16.24—16.25
changes in estimate
decommissioning costs, of, 16.83

Tangible fixed assets (FRS 15)—*cont.*
residual life, of, 16.306—16.307
useful economic life, of, 16.302—16.305
changes in method, 16.307—16.308
'cherry-picking', 16.16—16.20
classification
assets under construction, 16.43—16.46
introduction, 16.38—16.42
payments on account, 16.43—16.46
component depreciation
background, 16.26—16.27
generally, 16.276—16.278
implementation of standard, and, 16.339
component replacement, 16.143—16.149
cost
decommissioning costs, 16.75—16.83
directly attributable costs, 16.61—16.65
generally, 16.55—16.60
incremental costs, 16.68—16.71
IFRS, and, 16.344
labour costs, 16.66—16.67
software development costs, 16.72—16.74.10
decommissioning costs
arising later in asset's life, 16.79—16.82
changes in estimate, 16.83
generally, 16.75—16.78
definition, 16.35—16.37
depreciated replacement cost, 16.197—16.200
depreciation
change in estimate, 16.302—16.307
change in method, 16.307—16.308
components, of, 16.276—16.278
definition, 16.249—16.251
determination of useful economic life and residual life, 16.252—16.256
disclosure requirements, 16.309—16.314
IFRS, and, 16.344
introduction, 16.247—16.248
methods, 16.257—16.267
non-depreciation, 16.279—16.291
renewals accounting, 16.293—16.300
revalued assets, of, 16.268—16.275
summary, 16.1.14—16.1.17
depreciation methods
annuity, 16.264—16.267
introduction, 16.257—16.258
reducing balance, 16.260—16.261
'rule of 78', 16.262
straight line method, 16.259
sum of the digits, 16.262
unit-of-production, 16.263
directly attributable costs
generally, 16.61—16.65
period of capitalisation, 16.84
disclosure requirements
capital grants, 16.339—16.340
capitalisation of finance costs, 16.126—16.129
depreciation, 16.309—16.314
revaluation, 16.204—16.212
disposal of
intended, 16.325—16.328
introduction, 16.315
reporting gains and losses, 16.316—16.318
revalued assets, 16.319—16.324
donated assets, 16.90—16.93
executive summary
depreciation, 16.1.14—16.1.17
initial measurements, 16.1.1—16.1.4
scope of standard, 16.1
subsequent expenditure, 16.1.5—16.1.6
transfer of assets, 16.1.18

Tangible fixed assets (FRS 15)—*cont.*
valuation, 16.1.8—16.1.13
web site costs, 16.1.7
existing use value, 16.193—16.196
'fixed assets'
categories, 16.10—16.11
definition, 16.9
excluded items, 16.12—16.13
generally, 16.3—16.8
IFRS, and
borrowing costs, 16.344
capital grants, 16.346
capitalisation of finance costs, 16.344
convergence, 16.344
cost model, 16.344
current value, 16.344
definitions, 16.344
depreciation, 16.344
derecognition, 16.344
disclosures, 16.344
exchanges of assets, 16.344
finance lease costs, 16.344
first time adoption of IFRS, 16.344
government grants, 16.346
initial measurement, 16.344
introduction, 16.344—16.344
investment properties, 16.344
market value, 16.344
overview, 16.344
recognition, 16.344
related pronouncements, 16.344
revaluation model, 16.344
scope, 16.344
subsequent costs, 16.344
subsequent measurement, 16.344
impairment
generally, 16.97—16.99
IFRS, and, 16.344
implementation of standard
change in measurement, 16.331—16.332
component depreciation, 16.339
introduction, 16.329—16.330
non-depreciation, 16.340—16.345
options for previously revalued assets, 16.333—16.337
revisions to estimates, 16.338
incremental costs, 16.68—16.71
initial measurement, 16.1.1—16.1.4
intended disposal of, 16.325—16.328
interest capitalisation, 16.24—16.25
introduction, 16.2
labour costs, 16.66—16.67
major inspections and overhauls, 16.150—16.153
measurement
cost, 16.55—16.
implementation of standard, and, 16.331—16.332
introduction, 16.51—16.54
summary, 16.1.1—16.1.4
non-depreciation
background, 16.28—16.30
generally, 16.284—16.290.1
implementation of standard, and, 16.340—16.345
introduction, 16.279—16.283
non-depreciable land, 16.291
objectives of standard, 16.31
open market value, 16.190—16.192
payments on account, 16.43—16.46
plant and machinery value, 16.201—16.203
pre-FRS 15, and, 16.14—16.15
previously assessed standard of performance, 16.135—16.142

Tangible fixed assets (FRS 15)—*cont.*
recoverable amount, 16.97—16.99
replacing components, 16.143—16.149
residual life
change in estimate, 16.306
determination, 16.252—16.256
implementation of standard, and, 16.338
revalued assets
depreciation, 16.268—16.275
disposal of fixed assets, 16.319—16.324
revaluation
bases, 16.177—16.203
class of assets, 16.158—16.163
disclosure requirements, 16.204—16.212
frequency, 16.164
IFRS, and, 16.344
introduction, 16.154—16.157
material changes in value, 16.175—16.176
other assets, 16.173—16.174
properties, 16.169—16.172
qualified valuers, 16.165—16.168
revaluation of gains and losses
accumulated depreciation, 16.226—16.230
gains, 16.216
introduction, 16.213—16.215
losses, 16.217—16.225
reserve, 16.231—16.241
taxation, 16.242—16.246
scope of standard
generally, 16.32—16.34
summary, 16.1
small companies, and, 32.64—32.67
software development costs, 16.72—16.74.10
start-up costs
generally, 16.85—16.89.5
introduction, 16.21—16.23
subsequent expenditure
accounting treatment, 16.133—16.134
IFRS, and, 16.344
introduction, 16.130—16.132
major inspections and overhauls, 16.150—16.153
previously assessed standard of performance, 16.135—16.142
replacing components, 16.143—16.149
summary, 16.1.5—16.1.6
taxation
revaluation of gains and losses, 16.242—16.246
transfer to and from assets
generally, 16.47—16.49
summary, 16.1.18
unknown purchase price or production cost, 16.94—16.96
useful economic life
change in estimate, 16.302—16.305
determination, 16.252—16.256
implementation of standard, and, 16.338
valuation, 16.1.8—16.1.13
web site costs, 16.1.7

Tariff over-recoveries
provisions, and, 21.275—21.278

Tax attributable to exceptional items
reporting financial performance, and, 8.137—8.143

Tax credits
incoming dividends, 13.31—13.33
interest payable, 13.28—13.30
interest receivable, 13.31—13.33
introduction, 13.24
outgoing dividends, 13.28—13.30

Tax-free grants
leases, and, 19.132—19.133

Tax-free reinvestment of dividends
accounting implications, 12.103—12.105
introduction, 12.88
Tax variation clauses
leases, and, 19.96—19.97
Taxation
accounting policies, 13.235
balance sheet
analysis of deferred tax balance, 13.267—13.270
Companies Act requirements, 13.253
deferred tax asset, 13.272—13.273
material balances, 13.263—13.266
offset of assets and liabilities, 13.258—13.262
standards requirements, 13.254—13.257
cash flow statements, and, 30.86—30.91
circumstances affecting tax charges, 13.274—13.290
corporation tax, and
general principles, 13.7—13.8
imputation system, 13.9—13.17
current tax (FRS 16), and
and see **Current tax**
avoir fiscal, 13.37.1—13.43
dividends, 13.28—13.33
executive summary, 13.1.2—13.1.7
generally, 13.18—13.20
introduction, 13.2—13.16
measurement of charge, 13.44—13.50
recognition, 13.21—13.23
tax credits, 13.28—13.33
underlying tax, 13.35—13.37
withholding tax, 13.25—13.33
deferred tax (FRS 19), and
and see **Deferred tax**
background, 13.4
computation methods, 13.54—13.79
consolidated financial statements, 13.203—13.216
deferred tax assets, 13.142—13.170
discounting, 13.176—13.202
executive summary, 13.1.8—13.1.26
general principles, 13.97—13.98
generally, 13.51—13.53
introduction, 13.2—13.16
measurement issues, 13.171—13.175
objectives of standard, 13.90—13.96
revaluation of non-monetary assets, 13.128—13.141
share-based payment transactions, 13.127—13.127.8
standardisation of accounting, 13.80—13.88
timing differences, 13.99—13.126
disclosure requirements
accounting policies, 13.235
balance sheet, 13.253—13.273
circumstances affecting tax charges, 13.274—13.290
generally, 13.234
profit and loss account, 13.236—13.248
statement of total recognised gains and losses, 13.249—13.252
summary, 13.1.7
group relief
introduction, 13.291—13.294
no payments made for, 13.295—13.297
payment is less than amount of tax saving, 13.301
payment is less than gross amount of loss surrendered, 13.302
payment represents amount of tax saving, 13.299—13.300
payment represents gross amount of loss surrendered, 13.303—13.305
payments made for, 13.298
introduction, 13.1—13.6

Taxation—*cont.*
non-operating exceptional items, 13.245—13.248
presentation
accounting policies, 13.235
balance sheet, 13.253—13.273
circumstances affecting tax charges, 13.274—13.290
generally, 13.234
profit and loss account, 13.236—13.248
statement of total recognised gains and losses, 13.249—13.252
profit and loss account
analysis of current tax, 13.239
analysis of deferred tax, 13.240—13.244
Companies Act requirements, 13.236
non-operating exceptional items, 13.245—13.248
notes, 13.238
standards requirements, 13.237
provisions, and
disclosure requirements, 21.303
retirement benefits, and
generally, 11.127—11.129
summary, 11.1.20—11.1.21
small companies, and, 32.86—32.87.1
statement of total recognised gains and losses
generally, 13.249—13.250
notes, 13.251—13.252
tangible fixed assets, and, 16.242—16.246
Technology changes
PFI and PPP, and, 3.179.4
Temporal method
foreign currency translation, and, 7.42—7.51
Termination of operations
restructuring, and, 21.171—21.172
Third party expectation
provisions, and, 21.61—21.64
restructuring, and, 21.159—21.162
Third party revenues
PFI and PPP, and, 3.179.29—3.179.30
Timing differences
accelerated capital allowances, 13.104—13.106
deferred revenue expenditure, 13.116—13.117
discounting, and, 13.191
generally, 13.99—13.103
government grants, 13.118—13.121
industrial building allowances, 13.107—13.110
infrastructure assets, 13.111—13.113
leases, 13.122—13.125.1
post-retirement benefits, 13.126—13.126.10
provisions, 13.114
Trade creditors
balance sheet, and, 4.83
Trade loans
balance sheet, and, 4.85—4.92
reporting the substance of transactions, and, 3.183
Trade marks
intangible fixed assets, and, 15.110—15.111
Trading, assets and liabilities held for
financial instruments, and, 6.257—6.259
Trading losses
deferred tax, and, 13.158—13.164
Transactions in previously recognised assets
continued recognition, 3.71—3.72
full derecognition, 3.73
generally, 3.66—3.70
insurance, 3.82
partial derecognition, 3.74—3.81
Transfer from current to fixed assets
balance sheet, and, 4.30—4.38
Transfer of assets
associates and joint ventures, and, 27.148
tangible fixed assets, and

Transfer of assets—*cont.*
generally, 16.47—16.49
summary, 16.1.18
Transfer of economic benefits
provisions, and, 21.74—21.75
Transfer pricing
impairment, and, 18.123—18.124
Treasury shares
accounting treatment, 23.63—23.73
cancellation, 23.56—23.59
conditions, 23.51—23.55
delivery of returns, 23.60—23.62
disclosure, 23.74—23.79
effect on distributable profits, 23.80—23.83
general rules, 23.46—23.50
sale, 23.56—23.59
True and fair requirement
accounting standards, compliance with
generally, 2.35—2.40
notes to balance sheet and profit and loss account, 4.132
consolidated financial statements, and, 24.51—24.55
consolidation rules, and, 24.296
financial reporting structure, and, 2.78—2.80
generally, 2.23—2.34
investment properties, and, 17.15—17.16
override disclosures
generally, 2.41—2.44
investment properties, 17.15—17.16
notes to balance sheet and profit and loss account, 4.133
quasi-subsidiaries, 3.107
related party transactions, and, 29.171—29.173
segmental reporting, and, 10.24—10.30
small companies, and, 32.104
UITF abstracts, compliance with, 2.35—2.40
Trustee company
employee share ownership plans, and, 12.29
Trusts
related parties, and, 29.65—29.67
Truth and fairness
segmental reporting, and, 10.24—10.30
Tuition fees
revenue recognition, and, 9.143—9.144
Turnover
associates and joint ventures, and, 27.73—27.74
long-term contracts, and, 20.76—20.77
revenue recognition, and, 9.284
Turnover sales
segmental reporting, and, 10.81—10.85
25% threshold information
associates and joint ventures, and, 27.107—27.113
Two-way trading arrangements
revenue recognition, and, 9.176—9.184

UITF abstracts
and see below
foreign currency translations, and
19, 7.113—7.119
21, 7.178—7.185
true and fair requirement, and, 2.35—2.40
UITF 13 (employee share ownership plans)
and see **UITF 38**
introduction, 12.2
replacement, 12.3.1
UITF 17 (employee share schemes)
and see **Employee share ownership plans**
background, 12.1—12.3.3
buyback guarantee from parent company, 12.59
cash payment to employee trusts, 12.81—12.85
changes in estimates, 12.47—12.48
UITF 17 (employee share schemes)—*cont.*
comparison with IFRS, and, 12.134
credit entry, 12.45—12.46.1
date of grant of award, 12.55—12.56.5
directors' emoluments, 12.61
flotations, 12.54—12.54.3
group situations
buyback guarantee from parent company, 12.59
introduction, 12.58—12.60
recharge from parent company, 12.58
IFRS, and
generally, 12.134
introduction, 12.3.3
introduction, 12.1—12.3.3
national insurance contributions on gains
background, 12.62—12.64
practical application, 12.78—12.80
reimbursement of liability, 12.74—12.77
requirements of abstract, 12.65—12.72
transfer of liability, 12.74—12.77
practical implications
changes in estimates, 12.47—12.48
credit entry, 12.45—12.46.1
date of grant of award, 12.55—12.56.5
flotations, 12.54—12.54.3
group situations, 12.58—12.60
variation of awards, 12.57
quantification of charge, 12.40—12.44
recharge from parent company, 12.58
roll-over of options, 12.57
scope of abstract, 12.30—12.34
timing of charge, 12.37—12.39
variation of awards, 12.57
vesting period, 12.57
UITF 18 (pension costs)
and see **Pension costs**
retirement benefits, and, 11.3
UITF 38 (employee share ownership plans)
analysing risks and rewards, 12.9—12.12
background, 12.1—12.3.3
benefit to employees, 12.24
comparison with IFRS, and, 12.134
disclosure requirements, 12.20—12.21
distributable profits, and
generally, 12.23—12.23.7
public companies, 12.23.8—12.23.12
examples, 12.25—12.26
gains, 12.28
IFRS, and, 12.134
introduction, 12.4—12.8
legal considerations, 12.22
practical implications
examples, 12.25
gains, 12.28
requirements of abstract, 12.13—12.17
trustee company, 12.29
Underlying tax
current tax, and, 13.35—13.37
Under-performance penalties
PFI and PPP, and, 3.179.38—3.179.40
Undisclosed principals
agency companies, and, 32.178
Undrawn committed borrowing facilities
maturity analysIs, and, 6.77—6.79
Undue delay
subsidiaries excluded from consolidation, and, 24.181
Unfunded schemes
retirement benefits, and, 11.23
Unincorporated undertakings
joint arrangements, and, 27.199—27.202

Unit-of-production method
depreciation, and, 16.263
Unknown purchase price or production cost
tangible fixed assets, and, 16.94—16.96
Unrealised profit on stocks
foreign currency translation, and, 7.68—7.69
Unrealised profits
share capital, and, 23.63—23.65
Unremitted earnings
deferred tax, and, 13.214—13.215
Unwinding of discount
provisions, and, 21.299—21.299.1
Up-front fees
revenue recognition, and, 9.136—9.139
Urgent Issues Task Force (UITF)
financial reporting structure, and, 2.81—2.84
Useful economic life
intangible fixed assets, and
generally, 15.71—15.81
IFRS, and, 15.139
impairment reviews, 15.88—15.92
tangible fixed assets, and
change in estimate, 16.302—16.305
determination, 16.252—16.256
implementation of standard, and, 16.338

Valuation methods
intangible fixed assets, and
capitalisation of earnings, 15.59—15.60
comparison with market transactions, 15.61—15.62
introduction, 15.48—15.50
premium profits, 15.54—15.58
relief from royalties, 15.51—15.53
investment properties, and, 17.1.7
tangible fixed assets, and, 16.1.8—16.1.13
Value in use
cash flow forecasts, 18.115—18.159
disclosure requirements, 18.275—18.279
discount rate, 18.160—18.178
introduction, 18.57—18.63
Variable consideration
customer's control, within, 9.57
introduction, 9.56
neither party's control, within, 9.61—9.63
seller's control, within, 9.58—9.60
Variations
long-term contracts, and, 20.92—20.93
Variations from regular cost
changes in actuarial assumptions, 11.96—11.101
experience surpluses and deficiencies, 11.45—11.88
improvements in benefits, 11.102—11.108
increases in payment, 11.90—11.95
introduction, 11.44
Vendor placings
merger accounting, and, 28.37—28.45
Venture capital funds
associates and joint ventures, and, 27.27—27.29.1
Venture capitalists
related parties, and, 29.40—29.41
Vertically integrated operations
impairment, and, 18.84—18.86
Volume discounting
revenue recognition, and, 9.185—9.186
Voluntary disclosures
associates and joint venture entities, and, 27.1.30
Voluntary redundancies
restructuring, and, 21.190—21.192
Voting rights
associates and joint ventures, and, 27.50—27.54
Vouchers
free products, 9.239
loyalty programmes, 9.240—9.245
options granted as part of sales transaction, 9.223—9.236
options granted for consideration, 9.219—9.222
options granted without consideration, 9.237—9.238
other benefit schemes, 9.246—9.250
point schemes, 9.240—9.245

Warranties
provisions, and, 21.225—21.227
revenue recognition, and
extended warranty, 9.92—9.93
initial warranty, 9.90—9.91
Waste electrical and electronic equipment
provisions, and, 21.248.1—21.248.6
Web site costs
tangible fixed assets, and, 16.1.7
Withholding tax
incoming dividends, 13.31—13.33
interest payable, 13.28—13.30
interest receivable, 13.31—13.33
introduction, 13.25—13.27
outgoing dividends, 13.28—13.30
Write-downs to recoverable amount
small companies, and, 32.73.2